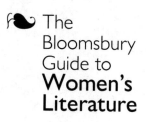

The
Bloomsbury
Guide to
**Women's
Literature**

The Bloomsbury Guide to Women's Literature

EDITED BY
CLAIRE BUCK

Prentice Hall General Reference

New York · London · Toronto · Sydney · Tokyo · Singapore

In memory of
Angela Carter
(1940–1992)

A good writer can make you believe time stands still.
(*Expletives Deleted: Selected Writings*, 1992)

Prentice Hall General Reference
15 Columbus Circle
New York, New York 10023

Simultaneously published in Great Britain by Bloomsbury Publishing Ltd.

PRENTICE HALL and colophon are registered trademarks
of Simon & Schuster Inc.

Library of Congress Cataloging-in-Publication Data

The Bloomsbury guide to women's literature / edited by Claire Buck.
p.   cm.
Includes bibliographical references.
ISBN 0-13-689621-9 : ISBN 0-13-089665-9 (pbk)
1. Women authors—Dictionaries.   2. Women authors.   3. Women in
literature—Dictionaries.   4. Women in literature.   I. Buck, Claire.
PN471.B57 1992   92–10415
809'.89287'03—dc20   CIP

Designed by Geoff Green
Typeset by Florencetype Ltd, Kewstoke, Avon

Manufactured in the United States of America
10 9 8 7 6 5 4 3 2 1

First Edition

Contents

Acknowledgements

Editor
Claire Buck

Contributors
Greek and Roman antiquity: Richard Hawley (Royal Holloway and Bedford New College, London University)
Medieval Britain: Gopa Roy (Queen Mary and Westfield College, London University)
Britain 1500–1800: Sue Wiseman (University of Kent), Theresa Kemp (Indiana University)
Nineteenth-century Britain: Kathryn Burlinson (University of Southampton)
Twentieth-century Britain: Laura Marcus (Birkbeck College, University of London), Lynnette Turner (Cheltenham and Gloucester College of Higher Education)
Ireland: Ailbhe Smyth (Women's Education, Research and Resource Centre, University College, Dublin)
France: the Middle Ages to 1700: Elizabeth Woodrough (University of Exeter)
Eighteenth- and nineteenth-century France: Jennifer Birkett, Alex Hughes (both University of Birmingham), Louise Robbins (King's College, London)
Twentieth-century France: Lyn Thomas, Nicki Hitchcott, Denise Ganderton (all Polytechnic of North London), Trista Selous, Mary Evans (University of Kent at Canterbury)
Germany: Agnès Cardinal (University of Kent at Canterbury)
Spain: Stephen M. Hart (University of Kentucky)
Italy: Ursula Fanning (University College Dublin)
Portugal: Darlene J. Sadlier (Indiana University)
Modern Greece: Maria Moore
The Netherlands and Flanders: Olga van Marion (University of Leiden)
Scandinavia: Karen Klitgaard (Aarhus University)
Eastern Europe: Joanna Labon, Dagmar Krocanova (University of Bratislava), Robert Pynsent, Celia Hawkesworth (both School of Slavonic and East European Studies, University of London)
Russia: Charlotte Rosenthal (University of Southern Maine), Mary Zirin
Early North America: Sharon Harris (University of Nebraska-Lincoln)
Nineteenth-century US: Carol Klimick Cyganowski (De Paul University, Illinois)
Twentieth-century US: Mara McFadden (State University of New York, Brockport), Nicola Bown (University of Sussex), Lyndsey Stonebridge (Queen Mary and Westfield College, University of London), Claire Buck (Polytechnic of North London)
Canada: Aritha van Herk (University of Calgary)
Latin America: Luiza Lobo (University of Rio de Janiero)
Australia: Shirley Walker (University of New England, New South Wales)
New Zealand and Oceania: Lydia Wevers (Victoria University of Wellington), Celia Dunlop
Israel: Risa Domb (University of Cambridge), Tsila Ratner
North Africa and the Middle East: Laïla Ibnlfassi (City of London Polytechnic), Amel Benhassine-Miller (Polytechnic of North London), Fatma Moussa-Mahmoud
East Africa: Phyllis Pollard (Humberside Polytechnic)

Southern Africa: Carli Coetzee, Dorothy Driver, Jenny McDonogh, assisted by Aurelia Driver, Marion Walton, Ingrid Webster, Fiona Zerbst (all University of Cape Town)

West Africa: Jane Bryce (University of the West Indies)

Indian Subcontinent: Sangeeta Ahuja, Maya Jaggi, Kathy Prior

South-East Asia: Koh Tai Ann (National University of Singapore), Thelma Kitanar (University of the Philippines)

English-speaking Caribbean: Susheila Nasta (Institute of Commonwealth Studies, Polytechnic of North London), Elizabeth Obi (Polytechnic of North London)

French Antilles: Vivienne Liley (Queen Mary and Westfield College, London)

China: Zhu Hong (Chinese Academy of Social Sciences)

Japan: Noriyo Hayakawa (Iwaki Meisei University, Japan), Akiko Ogata (Tokyo Jogakukan Junior College)

Critical approaches: Catherine Belsey, Jane Moore (both Centre for Critical and Cultural Theory, University of Wales, Cardiff)

Advisors

Dima Abjulrahim, Catherine Batt (Queen Mary and Westfield College, University of London), Elleke Boehmer (University of Leeds), Catherine Boyle (Kings College, University of London), Shirley Chew (University of Leeds), Charles Davis (Queen Mary and Westfield College, University of London), Alan Deyermond (Queen Mary and Westfield College, University of London), Claire Duchen (University of Bath), Rod Edmond (University of Kent), Evi Fishburn (Polytechnic of North London), Barbara Garvin (University College, University of London), Nicki Hitchcott (Polytechnic of North London), Lyn Innes (University of Kent), Paula M. Krebs (Wheaton College), Jo Labanyi (Birkbeck College, University of London), Marina Ledkovsky (Barnard College, Columbia University), Jan Montefiore (University of Kent), Hilary Owen (Queen's University, Belfast), Wendy Perkins (University of Birmingham), Agnes Sneller (University of Leiden), Judith Still (University of Nottingham), John Thieme (University of Hull), Jan Whetnall (Queen Mary and Westfield College, University of London), Margaret Williamson, Briar Wood (Polytechnic of North London), Frances Wood (British Library), Mio Uraguchi (School of Oriental and African Studies), Anna Zarenko

Additional contributors

Mary Brennan, Sheila Field (Institute of Education), Tricia Lootens (University of Georgia at Athens), Jan Montefiore (University of Kent), Takako Okada (Tokyo Jogakukan Junior College), Lyndsey Stonebridge (Queen Mary and Westfield College, University of London), Maida Tilchen, Takako Ubukata, Ruth Wallsgrove, Wendy Wheeler (Polytechnic of North London), Briar Wood (Polytechnic of North London)

Editorial

Editorial Director Kathy Rooney
Project Editor Kate Newman
Picture Researcher Charlotte Cox

With thanks to: Richard Aczel, Kate Bell, Louise Bostock, Jane Bryce, Trish Burgess, Judy Collins, Norma Depledge, Elizabeth Dozois, Catherine Ellis, Susan Faircloth, Sheila Field, Forest Books, Anna Girling, Alison Grace, Carey Hendron, William Humphreys Jones, Mike Hirst, Huw Jones, Robyn Karney, Michael March, James Naughton, Rosemary Nixon, Jenny Parrott, Linden Stafford, Nicky Thompson, Belin Tonchev

The Netherlands and Flanders contribution was supported financially by the State University of Leiden and by the Department of Welfare, Public Health and Culture of the Ministry of the Flemish Community in Brussels.

Introduction

No literary guide with the scope of the *Bloomsbury Guide to Women's Literature* has appeared before now. In this guide we have aimed to introduce the reader to the true global and historical dimensions of that 'horde of scribbling women' by which the 19th-century US writer Nathaniel Hawthorne felt so threatened. It covers the huge range of cultural groups from across the world and throughout all ages, from the earliest recorded women writers in ancient Greece and China to the spectrum of contemporary writing. The reader will find here the pre-Sapphic poets Helena, Manto and Phantasia, of whom Homer, according to tradition, was an imitator; the legendary Chinese warrior poet Mu Lan; Su Hui of the Jin dynasty who embroidered an 841-character poem which could be read in any direction; and contemporary writers as varied as Janet Frame, Keri Hulme, Christa Wolf, Clarice Lispector, Adrienne Rich, Alice Walker, Gloria Anzaldúa, Ama Ata Aidoo, Ooderoo Noonuccal, Dale Spender, Leah Goldberg, Jeanette Winterson, Jackie Collins, Judith Krantz, Margaret Atwood and Nawal Sa'dawi.

Not surprisingly then, the question that I was most often asked by contributors while I was editing the *Bloomsbury Guide to Women's Literature* began with the words: 'Is it all right to include . . .?' Virtually everything that needs saying to the reader about the *Guide* stems from this question and the challenge of answering it. None of us wanted to leave out anything. My intention in the book was to bring together for the first time information about writing by women from all periods and from the whole world in a form that was accessible and affordable for as many readers as possible. English-speaking countries know far too little about the wealth of writing by women of their own nationality because of the long history of the marginalization of women's writing. The problem has been exacerbated in the case of writing in foreign languages. The relative paucity of work available in translation is matched by ignorance about the histories and contexts which give the reader more than superficial access to the text, and which encourage an understanding of the important differences between women as well as what they have in common. The short introductory essays with which the *Guide* begins are designed to give the reader such an understanding, by introducing the culturally specific contexts and histories of the women writers represented in the A-Z section.

The general perception of the history of women's writing similarly rests upon serious misconceptions. Until quite recently, feminist criticism in the West, following a trend set by Virginia Woolf in *A Room of One's Own* (1929), was engaged in explaining the historical absence of women writers. However, their research has now shown that the project was itself misconceived because women have been writing in considerable numbers for as long as men. That we don't know about their writing is one important focus of inquiry: how women wrote and under what circumstances is another. The historical as well as international scope of the *Guide* is intended to display the sheer volume and range of this writing, while the essays, in particular Catherine Belsey's section on feminist criticism and theory, explore these questions.

Sadly, the selective nature of this book and the richness of the field meant leaving out many women writers whom we would have liked to include. Contributors agonized with me over this process, and well after the deadlines had passed and manuscripts been delivered they would send me 'just one more entry' on a writer 'who couldn't possibly be left out'. Our aim has been to ensure that the writers included represent as many different kinds of literary production as possible. My particular concern was that while we met the requirement that the better-known figures of women's literature be covered, there should be a full representation of writers and kinds of writing that have hitherto been marginalized. Women have excelled in most kinds of popular fiction genres, and the *Guide* therefore treats as literature genres such as science fiction and detective fiction which are often refused the same kind of critical attention as 'serious' literature. In particular, the women's romance and children's literature have been important categories for women writers who have historically been encouraged to adopt genres suitable to conventional ideas about women's social role.

Decisions about inclusions and exclusions were not always clear cut, however. We chose the word 'literature' rather than 'writing' in the title to indicate the *Guide*'s limits. Women's writing would have suggested the huge range of writing by women across all the disciplines from politics, history, sociology, and psychoanalysis to medicine and law. The *Guide* could not of course represent this range without becoming an encyclopaedia and losing its focus on the literary. However, 'literature' is not a term that means the same thing across different periods or cultures. Moreover, the historical circumscription of women's lives means that the kinds of writing which they could produce do not always fit well into mainstream categories of literature. The traditional categories of English literary criticism suffer from cultural as well as gender bias. Letters and diaries are a good example of a literary genre, often treated as peripheral or secondary, which assumes major importance for women where they are excluded from the 'public' domain. But they are also crucial to the history of white women's involvement in colonization and pioneer cultures such as those of Africa, North America, Australia, New Zealand and Canada. The Early American contribution would have been very brief indeed had we decided to exclude the diaries and letters of ordinary and unknown women. For many colonized peoples oral traditions predate the literary culture represented here, and although the *Guide* cannot include them, the reader will find the influence of oral culture constantly discussed in the essays. Similarly, certain key examples of writing on education or politics, although not conventionally candidates for inclusion in a literary guide, could not be left out without seriously distorting the reader's understanding of the long traditions of women's political consciousness and resistance which provide a context for women's literature.

Another unexpectedly tricky question is whether women's literature has to be by women. One definition of women's literature includes works by male authors, if they are directed at women readers and concerned about issues which are conventionally understood to be the proper concern of women. The need to give space to women writers made this category easy to exclude. It turns out, however, that men have on occasions been known to adopt female pseudonyms and personae, for example in the case of the *trobairitz* (women troubadours) who wrote love lyrics in medieval France. Since we don't always know which of these texts were written by men we can only assume that some of the works in this *Guide* are here under false pretences. Authorship and gender are also slippery with regard to the category of women's deathbed speeches, an established Renaissance English genre. Are these to count as women's literature or not?

The real pleasures and interests of my editorial role, as well as the headaches, have been in negotiating these kinds of questions. There is an inevitable tension in this kind of work between the demand towards homogeneity and consistency and the fact that the writing represented here is marked more by its differences than its similarities. Perhaps the only consistent point about women's writing is its refusal to fit the categories or to stay in place. But this is the result of the inevitable inadequacies of systems of classification and a sign of the need to challenge them, rather than a problem with women's writing. As a result, my advice to contributors has always been to foreground the moments at which the categories do not fit because these are the points at which the significant differences of gender, race and class emerge.

Because women's literature isn't a consistent category, either historically or culturally, the amount of research which has been done on writing by women in different countries and periods is uneven. For example, in the countries of middle and Eastern Europe, with the exception of what was East Germany, women's literature has not operated as a significant category for writers and historians. Joanna Labon wrote to me at one point in her researches saying that 'even in the original languages I have not seen a single book on the subject of women writers. To see the lay of the land, I spent hours among dusty tomes at SEES [School of Slavonic and East European Studies] and elsewhere, where I found paltry, desultory references to them in guides to the literature of each country which, if they mention one at all, typically fall back on stereotyping her style as delicate and emotional and her identity as the wife or lover of a man. I felt rather like Virginia Woolf in the British Museum in search of Shakespeare's sister'. She found, of course, that women were indeed writing in the countries of Eastern Europe and they are represented here. The fact that there seem to be fewer early women writers than others should therefore only be seen as a statement about the kind of research that has been done to date. We have done our utmost to cover all ages, cultures and language groupings, but the coverage of some areas is less full than we would wish because of the difficulties of Western access to information. It is also important to note that one of our criteria for the selection of texts and writers was availability in translation, in order that a reader could follow up writers as easily as possible. Carried to an extreme this would have left us with a sadly small *Guide* which was entirely misrepresentative of the literature of the world. Many of the writers included in the *Guide* have never been translated into English. The simple truth is that very little work by women has been translated, and one of the purposes of the *Guide*, by showing readers what they are missing, is to challenge translators and publishers to remedy the situation.

If women's literature is an unstable category, nation and nationality are even more so. Political changes dramatically affect national borders and even as we worked on the *Guide*, Eastern Europe, the Soviet Union and East and West Germany disappeared while Yugoslavia plunged into racial conflict. Additionally, peoples and individuals have, for a variety of reasons, moved from country to country. The instability of national boundaries combines with migrancy, so that both languages and people cross borders. For example, the history of colonialism and slavery mean that the Caribbean is composed of a variety of language groups, including Creole, indigeneous languages, Spanish, English, Dutch and French. As a result, our decision to use regional divisions for the introductory essays hasn't always sat easily with the linguistic diversity of a region. The essays often address, too, the tensions generated by the internal political and historical relationships between different language users. Spain is another good example, Spanish competing with the Basque and Catalan languages. Migrancy presented us with other problems since nationality is not always commensurate with geographical boundaries. Anglophone Caribbean writers, for example, have often grown up with British passports, and a number of Caribbean-born writers now live and work in Britain where they have had a decisive impact on the literature. They therefore belong in both essays. Maghrebian writers from North Africa live out an equivalent relationship to France. Latina writers in the US today write texts which combine Spanish, English and even Tex-Mex to mark their own linguistic migrancy. The system of cross-reference in both essays and entries is designed to help the reader map these inter-relationships. Completely adequate coverage of this complexity in the space available seems to me to be virtually impossible. The extent to which we have succeeded is entirely owing to the inspired work of the contributors whose expertise and labour made the *Guide* possible. Their dedication to the project comes from a commitment to the work of the women writers represented here.

After the contributors, the people who deserve the most recognition and probably receive the least must be that largely invisible workforce from Bloomsbury. Particular thanks go to the editors, Kathy Rooney and Kate Newman, who have lived this project with me and without whom it would definitely never have reached publication. I would also like to thank Trevor Griffiths for introducing me to the task originally, to Sheila Field who worked on the project as a research student, and to my student Charlotte Cox whose work placement at Bloomsbury embroiled her in the *Guide* for far longer than she deserved. Many others have been unstintingly generous with their time. In particular my gratitude goes to Paula M. Krebs for her intelligent responses to my many dilemmas and her persistent belief that I could do the job. A project as wide-reaching as this in scale was inevitably demanding on the patience of all those numerous people to whom I turned for advice and encouragement and to whom I offer my sincere thanks. I also wish to thank the Polytechnic of North London for their financial support in the form of a research grant, and my colleagues and students for their tolerance of my often distracted state and for their consistent interest and support throughout.

Without the collaboration of so many different and able people this *Guide*, with its historical and geographical breadth, would not have been possible. In that respect it is very much like women's writing itself. In her novel *The Woman Warrior*, Maxine Hong Kingston uses the stories passed on by her mother to express the inter-relationships which have sustained women's writing: 'Here is a story my mother told me, not when I was young, but recently, when I told her I also am a story-talker. The beginning is hers, the ending mine.' We have sought to do justice in this *Guide* to this vital and open-ended process by which women's stories have been passed on, retold and reworked. The vast number of women writers, from all ages and cultures, whose work has too often been hidden from us represent the beginning. The ending belongs with the reader who picks up the book and begins to read, and in turn becomes part of the same enriching collaborative process.

Claire Buck
March 1992

Editor's note

Cross references
A liberal use of cross references has been made. In both the essays and the reference entries, names, titles and topics are frequently marked with an arrow (▷) to guide the reader to the appropriate entry in the reference section for a more detailed explanation. Cross-reference arrows appear both in the text and at the end of entries.

Translations
Titles of works appear in their original language except where these use an alphabet other than Roman. Works originally published in Arabic, Chinese, Greek, Japanese and Russian etc appear only in English.

Where an English translation of a work has not been published, an 'informal' translation of the title has been provided to assist the reader. If the translation of a title is not preceded by a cross-reference arrow (referring the reader to the entry on the English translation), or followed by a publication date, this indicates an informal translation.

Essay section

Greek and Roman antiquity

General background

In the classical world, women's writing is intimately affected by the role of women within society. The first of many factors is that almost all classical literature was written by and for men. Women writers were always unusual. Our equation is further complicated by the variables of time, place, social status and textual transmission.

Firstly, time. Women's economic and cultural freedom developed during this period at different rates – and not always in a forward direction. The women of 5th-century BC Athens, for instance, were much more restricted socially than their counterparts a century earlier.

Our second variable is place. Most of the evidence for classical Greek society concerns Athens, because it was so dominant politically in the 5th century BC, and therefore the generalization 'Greece' must be avoided. But, ironically, most Greek women writers were not Athenian. This is because Athenian society had complex systems for controlling women, through ideology, convention and law.

Social status is our third variable. The women writers mentioned here were, like most classical male writers, from the upper strata of society. Women of low status rarely speak to us. Their literature is unfortunately only that of graffiti or inscriptions. But inscriptions conform to genre conventions that restrict literary individuality and can be affected by intermediaries (stonemasons, etc.). Dedicators of inscriptions are therefore not included in this guide as 'women writers'.

Fourthly, textual transmission. The preservation of classical texts is very selective, almost accidental. ▷Sappho wrote much, but very little is extant today. Some of her best fragments only survive as examples of linguistic curiosities in late antiquarian texts. Much so-called biography is unreliable, often late, anecdote.

Women and culture

Much early Greek literature served a public function. Epics were recited at feasts or civic competitions; drama was performed before a predominantly male audience, by male actors and in plays written by male writers. Women's cultural expression was restricted. ▷Religion was almost the only area where she was allowed to play a dominant, public role. Lyric verse was often choral and religious in nature. It was thus easiest for women to adopt lyric poetry.

A woman's freedom of cultural expression begs the question of her access to culture, which in turn introduces the further complication of women's education. This seems to vary widely across the period, in both extent and focus. It is hard to gauge the extent of women's education because our sources seldom touch on it. It was never institutionalized like that of boys'. Texts concerning ▷household management in the 5th–4th centuries BC, for example, seem to assume that women in charge of a household will command basic numeracy and perhaps literacy. But by the time of the Roman period, the women of the classes with whom literature concerns itself were educated more widely. They read, inspired and participated in the creation of literature to a much greater extent.

Education was also closely connected with social status in the city and period most discussed by modern scholars, Athens in the 5th–4th century BC. Proscriptive ideological texts, such as those on household management or women and philosophy, limited a respectable woman's education to the requirements of domesticity. Perhaps some more 'literary' reading was acceptable, but one had always to be modest. Modesty was the hallmark of a good woman. Thus a woman's public display of education signified her less-than-reputable status, such as that of the courtesans who were the only women allowed to attend the all-male drinking-parties which formed such a central part of the leisured Athenian male's recreation and even education. Several women writers, especially philos-ophers, were said to belong to this social group.

Also problematic is the extent of literacy, for men as for women. But in general it seems that, contrary to the often gloomy picture offered by some modern discussions, women were not much less literate than men. However, again, social status would be important for access to education and culture. In the Roman period, the sources assume a high degree of female literacy in the cultured classes.

Historical survey

Greece: pre-5th century BC

Extant Greek literature begins with the epic hexameter poems of Homer, the *Iliad* and the *Odyssey*. But the Greek mythical imagination found no difficulty in accommodating stories of women poets who wrote epic poems before Homer on the same subjects (the Trojan War and the Wanderings of Odysseus respectively) (▷Helena, ▷Manto, ▷Phantasia). Myth explained Homer's creativity in terms of his reading and imitating texts of the women's poems. However, such stories presuppose written texts, and Homer's epics are in fact the end result of a long tradition of oral poetry. The stories might also seem unusual because women writers are so small in number. But they draw upon a subcons-cious association of women and language, most clearly expressed in the figures of the divine ▷Muses and the semi-divine prophetess.

We have few records or literary remains of women writers from this period, apart from those of Sappho, who is the exception that proves the rule. We do know that in Sparta there was the woman poet ▷Megalostrata, reputed lover of the Spartan male poet Alcman, but nothing is known about her. As is the case with so many women in classical antiquity, her name alone survives because of its link with her male counterpart.

Greece: 5th century BC

Despite the Athenocentric bias of our male literary sources, the women poets of 5th-century BC Greece came from outside Athens. In Athens, the stress on a woman's modesty and respectability severely hampered opportunities for cultural, and thus public, ex-pression. But the societies in which the women poets worked offered a freer environment for women's active cultural achievement. ▷Myrtis came from Boeotia, ▷Corinna from Tanagra, ▷Praxilla from Sicyon and ▷Telesilla from Argos.

That they wrote lyric poetry is important. Since the context of lyric poetry actively included women – as singers, dancers or otherwise religious participants – it was but a small and respectable step from singer to writer. The women's poetry centres upon myth, just as much as that written by men. But they highlight their own contribution to myth's protean character by telling new versions of old stories, as for example did Praxilla. If it were not for these innovations, recorded by later antiquarian writers, fragments of their work would not survive. Creative biographical tradition confirms Corinna's importance in this sphere by employing the motif of poetic rivalry with the most famous male poet of the genre, Pindar, who lived in nearby Thebes. Indeed Corinna's use of a readily understand-able local dialect apparently made her more popular than the self-consciously allusive and complex Pindar.

Notices of the works of these women were preserved and discussed by ancient writers without any explicit reference to their sex. There was no interest, as there is today, in 'women's writing' as such. But while there was no explicit theoretical distinction, practice implies an underlying nexus of regulating assumptions that associated gender and genre.

The first of these is that it was not felt unnatural for a woman from outside Athens to express herself in lyric poetry.

The qualification 'outside Athens' is important because, as noted above, in 5th-century BC Athens creative, public cultural expression was severely restricted for women. Women could excel in dance, music or song: achievements aimed to please men, performed often by courtesans and slaves at entertainments to which only men were admitted. 'Respectable' women (mothers, wives, daughters) would distance themselves and be distanced by their menfolk from such environments.

The Greek world: 4th–2nd centuries BC

Poetry

Lyric was a socially acceptable vehicle for female expression in women outside Athens. From the 4th century BC onwards, women began to attempt other genres. They wrote Greek ▷epigram, a genre also growing in popularity among male poets. Here too the most famous women epigrammatists came from outside Athens: ▷Anyte from Tegèa, ▷Nossis from southern Italy, ▷Moero from Byzantium and ▷Erinna from a Greek island. But, once again, the range is restricted. Pointed, witty, with great potential for artistic expression, epigrams have one obvious and significant feature: the poems are short. Women's productions could thus be accepted and even highly praised, but the scope never threatened the genres that were felt to be exclusively masculine – drama and philosophy. Neither did the content.

The content of the women's extant epigrams confirms conventional areas of 'woman's interest': dedications to deities exemplifying piety, the pathetic care of the dead, especially pet animals or young girls and women cut off in or before their prime. Although once serving a practical purpose, on tombstones, for example, epigrams were becoming more of a self-conscious art form, divorced from actual occasions. As they became less 'public', it became easier to accept that women might write them. None the less, the art form continued to retain themes associated with women. Erinna's ▷'Distaff', although longer than an epigram, still evokes the pathos of the dead girl, Baucis, with a series of images, each of which could easily have been encapsulated in epigrammatic form: children's games or pathetic lamentation for the dead. Its evocation of marriage also recalls the other 'acceptable' genre of lyric poetry.

Thus we can see that the women poets of the period were implicitly directed to certain genres and themes. Their work can therefore be praised genuinely, without explicit reference to their sex, because the themes themselves are commonly associated with women. It seems natural.

Philosophy

What is less natural is prose, especially philosophy. While ancient sources accept women poets in certain genres without surprise, we know about women ▷philosophers precisely because they were considered such an unusual phenomenon. Sometimes a male philosopher's teaching encouraged women to study. Popular tradition recorded that the woman Axiothea read Plato's *Republic*, which explores the utopian theory of relative sexual equality, donned male dress and then went to study under Plato. The names of Axiothea and another woman pupil, Lasthenia, with no other details, serve simply as concrete examples of Plato's theory of sexual equality in education. He practised what he preached.

The school of Epicurus openly favoured relatively more freedom for women. But the examples of women philosophers in this school bear courtesan names. The interest of the sources often lies in exposing the comic and hypocritical sexual relationships between the detached male philosophers and their lovers. These women philosophers are not discussed as respectable women; often they become weapons of invective against their male consorts. It is thus difficult to assess the women's importance or their contributions to philosophy. According to the sources, first and foremost the women illuminate, and indeed owe their very preservation to, the men in their lives.

The Cynic philosopher ▷Hipparchia is a classic case. She is the only woman to receive a *Life* of her own in Diogenes Laertius's *Lives of the Philosophers* (2nd century AD). But the *Life* does not discuss her philosophy. Instead it tells of her infatuation with her teacher and later husband, Crates, and of her unconventional adoption of male philosophical dress. Other sources focus upon the couple's unusual sexual habits. Hipparchia is thus merely a sidelight on a great man; her *Life* depicted in Diogenes almost an Appendix to the *Life* of Crates.

The sources paint Hipparchia as a woman who defied convention. Anecdotes about ▷Theano (I) the Pythagorean emphasize her role as ideal mother and wife. She is the appropriate mouthpiece for Pythagorean doctrine when women are the target audience. Her works focus upon 'women's matters': moderation in dress, sexual chastity, household management and child rearing. Her 'philosophy', therefore, is also firmly restricted to acceptable themes. This is why it is hard to say for certain that she, or any of the other ▷Pythagorean women, actually wrote these works. So, although Theano is a woman philosopher, her works are still gender-defined.

The Roman world: 1st century BC–5th century AD

Although the period covers five centuries, women's social position in the Roman world was strong even from the start. They could control property and have a voice of their own. Economic controls over women and their goods, which lay in the hands of male relatives, became less and less powerful in practice. Their status in society increased, using as a role model the influential wife of a powerful man. Initially the wives of senators provided this model, later to be replaced by those of the imperial family.

But, despite their greater social freedom, the women writers of the Roman period merely consolidated the restrictive associations of gender and genre. Superficially, they appear to embrace new genres. But, on closer inspection, we see otherwise.

The woman ▷Sulpicia (I) was a poet. But her genre is elegiac, pathetic love poetry: not that different in tone or theme from lyric or epigram. It was appropriate that a Roman woman poet wrote elegy. After all, a popular image of woman was that of a creature enslaved to her emotions, her nature, her passions. No Roman women wrote in the harsher, more masculine genres of satire, drama or epic. There *were* some women orators at Rome. But, looking at the testimonials, one sees they are described and praised in connection with men. Both ▷Hortensia and ▷Laelia remind their audiences of their orator fathers.

Letters are attributed to ▷Cornelia. But they are preserved partly because they express the Roman ideal of motherhood: devotion to male children, dissuasion from violence, and encouragement of respect for the Roman state. Her culture is elsewhere remarked upon favourably. But her writing survives for reasons less to do with her personally.

Even when Roman women are admired by men for their pure Latin style, this still implies a gender characteristic. Women were often thought to be more traditional in language, a link to the past. It is significant that male writers make such admiring remarks of both Cornelia and Laelia (cf. Hortensia).

What of history? Memoirs are credited to the Roman Empress ▷Agrippina the Younger; ▷Pamphila wrote a *Miscellaneous History* that was highly respected and used as a source by several later anthologists. Here too gender defines genre. Agrippina's memoirs (if written by her) were probably full of scandal and gossip. But because it would have been appropriate for a notorious woman to recount her infamy, some doubt their authenticity. A similar problem concerns the works of erotica (▷Pornography, Ancient Greece) that are ascribed to women writers in the 3rd century BC.

Pamphila's preface explicitly describes her source acquisition as the quiet assimilation of the wisdom offered her by her husband, his male visitors, and books (probably written by men). Pamphila's creative achievement is thus also limited to passive accumulation and arrangement. Where are the women writers of more political prose histories such as Tacitus's *Annals* or Suetonius's *Lives of the Caesars*?

In the later Roman period women could attain great influence, both politically and economically. But, once again, the social and literary worlds remain separated. Women writers of the later Roman period continued to keep to expected areas of interest: cosmetics (▷Timoxena) or religious matters (▷Egeria, ▷Proba, ▷Perpetua, ▷Eudocia Augusta). ▷Hypatia's forays into mathematics and science were rewarded with extinction.

Conclusion

There are many classical women writers who have been forgotten or ignored, by ancient and even modern authors. It is a difficult task to gather assorted anecdotes, fragments, secondary comments often written centuries after the fact, and then to assemble them into any kind of biography. It is not surprising that scholars sometimes doubt whether the works attributed to women writers were indeed written by women (▷Philaenis, ▷Erinna, ▷Pythagorean women, ▷Agrippina the Younger). But if the effort is made, and if one focuses upon their work as a group, its analysis reveals patterns of subtle cultural controls. Their works and the genres in which women write are firmly associated with conventional male images of woman. They are thus a literary extension of contemporary or traditional societal regulation.

Bib: Snyder, Jane McIntosh, *The Woman and the Lyre*; Pomeroy, Sarah B., *Goddesses, Whores, Wives and Slaves*; Lefkowitz, Mary R. and Fant, Maureen B., *Women's Life in Greece and Rome*.

▷Philosophers, Ancient Greek and Roman women; Diaries, Ancient Greek and Roman; Religion, Ancient Greek and Roman.

GOPA ROY

Medieval Britain 2

The background

The conversion of the English to Christianity, which began in AD 597, instituted a new era of literacy. The first language of education was Latin, and a knowledge of Latin continued to be identified with literacy throughout most of the Middle Ages. The vernacular language used alongside Latin by the Anglo-Saxons was ▷Old English. After the Norman Conquest of 1066 ▷Anglo-Norman joined Latin and English (which developed into 'early Middle English'). English ('Middle English') only came to predominate as a literary language at the end of the 14th century (in Chaucer's lifetime). By the 15th century English was used in all levels of society, and literacy had become much more widespread.

During most of the medieval period, literacy was associated with the Church. Until the 15th century it was the cloister which most often provided both the education and the freedom from marriage and children that enabled women to write if they were inclined to do so.

The Anglo-Saxon period

From the advent of Christianity, men and women were equal partners in both the acceptance and cultivation of the new faith, and the learning that came with it. It is often easier, however, to establish the influence of women on the development of writing than it is to name women writers. ▷Hilda's abbey at Whitby was a centre of learning, and she is credited with having nurtured the gift of the first Christian poet known to compose in Old English (c 657–680). Letters in Latin passed between men and women in religious houses. The abbess and nuns in the abbey of ▷Barking received works written for them by the monk Aldhelm in difficult and ornate Latin. Of the letters connected with the 8th-century missionary ▷Boniface, those written by ▷Berthgyth are perhaps the most 'literary'. A more extensive (and curious) work is the saint's life written by the nun ▷Hygeburg.

In the 9th century Alfred the Great circulated instructions for the education of children – apparently both boys and girls, since his biographer, Asser, says that Alfred's own daughters could read books in both Latin and English. It is worth remembering that Asser's mother, Osburh, had been the first to instil in him a love of English poetry, and encourage him to learn to read.

There is no literature in Old English that we can ascribe with any certainty to a woman; but there do survive two moving and atmospheric poems, ▷'The Wife's Lament' and ▷'Wulf and Eadwacer', in which the speakers are women. These poems provide us with rare expressions of female perceptions in secular literature from the Anglo-Saxon period. The poems may be compared with the ▷Old Irish poems, ▷'The Old Woman of Beare', ▷'Creidhe's Lament', and ▷'Deirdre's Farewell to Scotland', and with continental women's songs known as *Frauenlieder*.

There is evidence of women's literacy outside religious houses in the 10th century. In her will (of c 950), Wynflæd bequeathed books to her daughter Æthelflæd, and two queens of the late Anglo-Saxon period, ▷Emma and ▷Edith, commissioned works in Latin. References to a poet named ▷Muriel give some indication of what may have been lost in the way of writing by women at the close of the Anglo-Saxon period.

The post-Conquest period

After the Norman Conquest opportunities for women to obtain a good education declined: religious houses for women after the Conquest were much poorer than those of men; their libraries were less well-stocked; and there was strict segregation between men and women, which would further restrict women's access to learning. However, this situation had interesting and important repercussions for the development of literature in the vernacular languages.

Early Middle English

By the early 13th century, books of instruction for anchoresses (women who chose to live religious lives in seclusion), which had in the 11th and 12th centuries been written in Latin, had to be produced in one of the vernaculars. The *Ancrene Wisse* was written in early Middle English. Its recipients appear to have been able to read and write English and French – although they had to obtain the permission of their confessor before they could write. The group of saints' lives known as the 'Katherine Group', closely associated in date, dialect and manuscript tradition with the *Ancrene Wisse*, was also written for a female audience. It has been suggested that some of the lyrical devotional pieces known as ▷'The Wooing Group' may have been written by a woman. It has also been argued that the early 13th-century debate poem *The Owl and the Nightingale* may have been written for and by the nuns at the wealthy and aristocratic Benedictine abbey of Shaftesbury. However, it is not until the 14th century that we can identify for certain any works written by women in the English vernacular (see below).

Anglo-Norman

A large number of saints' lives were written in Anglo-Norman in the 12th and 13th centuries, presumably to cater for both the tastes and the abilities of contemporary audiences not proficient in Latin. ▷Clemence of Barking, an ▷anonymous nun of Barking, and ▷Marie, who may have been a nun of Chatteris, had sufficient learning and ability to be able to produce versions in Anglo-Norman verse of Latin prose lives. Among writers on secular themes was ▷Marie de France, the most celebrated woman writer of the 12th century in England.

Patronage

The most important way in which women influenced the development of literature in the vernacular, however, was through their patronage. Courts and country houses became centres where books were in demand: for entertainment (reading aloud), devotions, and for teaching children. ▷Maud (1079–1118) and ▷Adelaide of Louvain (died 1151), the first and second queens of Henry I, were recognised across Europe as important patrons. Literary and artistic patronage grew and flourished in the reign of Henry II and ▷Eleanor of Aquitaine (1122–1204). Patrons among the provincial nobility of the 12th century were ▷Constance FitzGilbert, ▷Adelaide de Condet and ▷Dionysia.

The loss of Normandy in 1204 and the break-up of the Angevin empire led to the recognition of some degree of separateness for England. But French, either in its continental or insular form (Anglo-Norman) continued to predominate, and literary production continued to respond to the requirements and tastes of female patrons such as ▷Eleanor of Provence (1223–1291), ▷Aline, ▷Matilda, Countess of Winchester, ▷Isabel of Warenne, and ▷Dionyse de Munchensy.

In the 14th and 15th centuries women were prominent among lay owners of devotional and other religious works in French and, later, English. Most common were Books of Hours; but women also owned psalters, gospels, lives of saints, and works by the mystical writers Richard Rolle (?1290–1349) and Walter Hilton (died 1396). ▷Margaret, Duchess of Burgundy and ▷Margaret Beaufort were patrons of the translator and printer William Caxton (born between 1415 and 1424, died 1492), and of the printer Wynkyn de Worde (died ?1534). An influential work by Nicholas Trevet was written for ▷Mary, a nun of Amesbury who had close connections with the court.

Latin

We have a rare example of a woman composing in Latin in the second half of the 14th century, ▷Katherine of Sutton, the religious dramatist. Katherine's work shows that the cloisters, like the courts and castles, were open to French influences. It is worth noting that Katherine was Abbess of Barking, which had produced writers in earlier centuries. Katherine was in the English tradition of learned abbesses including, for example, Hilda of Whitby and ▷Beatrice of Kent.

Middle English religious prose

Among the large amount of religious prose written in English in the 14th and 15th centuries, the works of two women stand out, those of ▷Julian of Norwich and ▷Margery Kempe. The anchoress Julian describes herself as 'a symple creature unlet-tyrde', who wrote because she must: 'I am a woman, ignorant, weak and frail. But I know very well that what I am saying I have received by the revelation of him who is the sovereign teacher. But because I am a woman, ought I therefore to believe that I should not tell you of the goodness of God when I saw at the same time that it is his will that it be known?' Julian writes for all Christians, not just for those who have chosen the religious life; and one of her distinctive themes is the aspect of the feminine in the divine (compare ▷Birgitta av Vadstena, also known as Bridget of Sweden).

Religious experience also moved Margery Kempe to dictate her *Book*, although in other respects she could scarcely have been more different from the enclosed and celibate Julian. Her story demonstrates the difficulties faced by a woman who feels compelled to lead a religious life while remaining 'in the world', particularly if the character of her devotion is found unacceptable by many around her. Responses to her were often ambivalent: 'The said creature was . . . desired by many people to be with them at their dying and to pray for them, for although they had no love for her weeping or her crying during their lifetimes, they desired that she should both weep and cry when they were dying, and she did.' Margery's inability to write caused difficulties, and it took more than one attempt for her to have her *Book* written down satisfactorily. Both Julian and Margery were influenced by Bridget of Sweden. But while Julian fits easily into the tradition of English mysticism, Margery may rather be compared with women in continental religious traditions: ▷Angela da Foligno; Dorothea of Montau; the ▷Beguines of Belgium; the Dominican nuns of Germany. The survival of ▷'A Revelation Respecting Purgatory' suggests there may well have been other women who would have composed religious prose.

Other contributions by women to religious prose took the form of translations. Those of Margaret Beaufort were published and popular; ▷Eleanor Hull's were more a pious exercise. 15th-century English audiences were given access to the works of continental saints and mystics through translations: ▷Mechthild of Hackeborn, ▷Marguerite Porete, ▷Bridget of Sweden, ▷Catherine of Siena.

Middle English secular prose
Two secular prose works of the 15th century, those of ▷Julyans Bernes, and the English ▷'Trotula' texts, indicate the increasingly varied use women were making of their literacy.

Middle English poetry
Among the great variety and number of anonymous lyrics, both religious and secular, which survive in Middle English, some are likely to have been composed by women. These poems were usually intended for performance, accompanied by music; and since we know that there were female performers (for example, a woman minstrel is referred to in Stratford-on-Avon in the 15th century), this perhaps increases the likelihood of female composition. The evidence of the ▷*Findern Anthology* suggests that it may not have been unusual for women to compose verse in English by the 15th century, when literacy had become much more widespread than before (and compare, in Scotland, the anonymous ▷'Lay of Sorrow' and the poems by ▷Isobel, Countess of Argyll). More than this, however, it is scarcely possible to say. A 15th-century poem to the Virgin is attributed to a ▷Holy Anchoress of Mansfield, but we lack names. There are many secular lyrics spoken in a woman's voice, such as cradle songs, love songs, and complaints of betrayed maidens, which may have been written by women. These poems provide a female perspective to many situations, and often also act as antidotes to the popular anti-feminist literature. We must be cautious, however, since some of the poems in which the speaker is female are known to have been written by men. The 14th-century poem ▷'The Good Wife Taught Her Daughter', of anonymous authorship, gives a practical, relatively unprejudiced view of women. There are two longer 15th-century 'Chaucerian' poems which are written as if by women: the elegant courtly allegory ▷'The Floure and the Leafe'; and the dream vision entitled ▷'The Assembly of Ladies'. The theme of the latter poem is the faithfulness and loyalty of women; as is that of ▷Christine de Pisan's 'Letter of Cupid', which the poet Hoccleve (c 1368–1426) translated in 1402 for an English audience.

Letters
The letters written by women in the earlier post-Conquest period were probably (like letters sent by men) dictated to professional scribes, and until about 1400 they were

generally written in Latin (particularly on ecclesiastical matters) or Anglo-Norman (or French). Among the interesting letters which survive are some from Maud (Edith), ▷Mary, Countess of Boulogne, ▷Empress Matilda and ▷Christine Dunbar. Private letters were unusual before the 15th century, when the growth in general literacy and the use of English at all levels led to an increased use of letters as a means of communication. It was still frequently the practice, however, for both women and men to use clerks to write their letters. The letters to and from women among the ▷Paston Letters, the ▷Stonor Letters, the ▷Plumpton Correspondence, and the papers of the ▷Cely family deal with an interesting variety of subjects, and cover business and personal matters. Amongst the Plumpton letters, for instance, we find that Mawd Rose has to write to Sir Robert Plumpton asking for the payment of a debt he owes her and her husband; and Dorothy Plumpton is able to write to her father, Sir Robert, asking to be brought home from the household of Lady Darcy.

Conclusion

The two main difficulties in assessing the literary contribution of women during this period are the scarcity of surviving material and the anonymity of much that remains. If more writing had survived (particularly from the Anglo-Saxon period), we would, perhaps, be able to confirm the impression that women were often active in the production as well as influential in the development of literature, from the coming of Christianity to the close of the 15th century.

Bib: Barratt, Alexandra, *Women's Writing in Middle English*; Bell, Susan Groag, 'Medieval Women Book Owners', in *Women and Power in the Middle Ages*, ed. Mary Erler and Maryanne Kowaleski; Dronke, Peter, *Women Writers of the Middle Ages*; Fell, Christine, *Women in Anglo-Saxon England*; Meale, Carol (ed.), *Women and Literature in Britain, c.1150–1503*; Wilson, Katharina M., *Medieval Women Writers*.

SUE WISEMAN

Britain 1500–1800   3

The period 1500–1800 is characterized by a gradual (though uneven and by no means progressive) change in attitudes to women writing. In the England of the 16th century, it was unthinkable that a woman might earn her keep by writing, and any writing undertaken by women was bound up with their differential position in relation to material and ideological determinants such as money, education, status, genre and conduct. In contrast, by the end of the period, it was openly thinkable that women should participate in the literary pursuits that were part of both the post-feudal ▷patronage economy and the capitalist trade in words and print.

1500–1660

In 1578 ▷Margaret Tyler justified her translation of a Spanish secular tale of masculine deeds of chivalry with both bravado and self-effacing humility:

> So if the question now ariseth of my choice, not of my labour, wherefore I preferred this story before matter of more importance. For answere wherein gentle reader, the truth is, that as the first notion to this kind of labour came not from my selfe, so was this peece of work put upon me by others . . . yet because refusall was within my power, I must stand to answer for my easie yeelding . . . (Margaret Tyler quoted in *First Feminists: British Women Writers 1587–1799*, ed. M. Ferguson, 1986)

This evidently selfconscious statement about women's authorship uses two potentially contradictory arguments to defend her choice of subject. She claims that in obeying the requests of others she was passive and feminine, but she accepts responsibility for agreeing to translate a work that was both secular and about the deeds of men – and therefore inappropriate for a woman. Thus she manipulates the accepted codes of femininity in order to present her activity as, at least in part, properly feminine because (paradoxically) it indicates her obedience.

As suggested by Tyler's careful 'placing' of her text for a reader, 16th and 17th-century women in England found themselves in a very ambivalent and highly-charged relation to the written and printed word. And they were in a very different position from male writers with regard to the means of production and circulation of written material.

Men were free to use the economy of favour and patronage whereby poetry, translation and digests of political or educational material dedicated to patrons would often serve as a means to a political career or a position as a tutor to the sons of aristocracy, even at court. These paths were closed to women, though if women interested in letters happened to find themselves at the top of the social hierarchy they could certainly be influential. Thus there were rich aristocratic women patrons such as Lucy Russell, Countess of Bedford and ▷Mary Sidney Herbert, Countess of Pembroke. Newer routes to money were open to male writers: by the end of the 16th century men from a range of social backgrounds produced writings for the growing quasi-capitalist economy of the London theatre and print culture, but the printing of works, as Margaret Tyler's equivocation indicates, was also more problematic for women. And authorship among the literate upper classes continued to consist mainly in the circulation of manuscripts. Thus, as ▷Virginia Woolf points out in her famous example of Shakespeare's sister (▷*A Room of One's Own*), writing careers leading to economic independence were barred to women, and very few achieved economic independence even by the end of the 18th century (▷Hannah More is one exception).

The strictures against women's writing, contradicted by the possibility of doing it, combine to produce a particular selfconsciousness in women's texts about their status as gendered texts. They are particularly aware of their specific relation to the contexts governing their writing – especially the gradually changing relationships to the production of texts, money, education and the literary market. Despite the severe obstacles, hundreds of women did write, their writings circulated in manuscript and in print, and they gradually became aware of each other as authors.

Education

The extent of literacy was a crucial determinant of women's literary production, and it is notoriously hard to estimate. Female literacy was probably higher among the aristocracy, where girls might be allowed their own tutor or allowed some access to the leftovers of their brothers' education. Queens and aristocratic women were literate, and queens were leaders in taste, so their writings make up a substantial part of what has been transmitted to us from the early part of the period, including the work of ▷Catherine of Aragon, ▷Mary Stuart, ▷Anne Boleyn and, of course, Elizabeth I (▷Elizabeth Tudor). Indeed, Elizabeth I was an important figurehead for the achievements of women (as the poem of praise by ▷Diana Primrose suggests), and so too was the Protestant heroine, Elizabeth of Bohemia. Later queens and consorts, such as the masque-loving Henrietta Maria and the pious Mary of Modena, affected expectations governing aristocratic women's accomplishments at court, but in the latter part of the period there were leaders in learning and literary achievement both within and outside court circles. Despite the differences in education enforced by both gender and status, during the 17th century an increasing number of women seem to have gained reading and writing skills. At the beginning of the 17th century, female literacy is estimated at only eleven per cent, but in literacy overall there was a steady rise during the century (see David Cressy, *Literacy and the Social Order: Reading and Writing in Tudor and Stuart England*, 1980). However, the whole question of whether girls learned writing and languages was bound up with the criteria governing what was felt to be appropriate for women, and often educational programmes placed little emphasis on reading and writing.

In the pre-Reformation period (before Henry VIII broke with Rome to establish himself as head of the Protestant Church of England) there was a ▷humanist influence on the education of aristocratic women, emphasizing classical and pious texts. This was mediated through the circle of Henry VIII's wife, Catherine of Aragon. The central figures in the humanist wave of education for women were Sir Thomas More, whose wife was educated, and whose daughter ▷Margaret (More) Roper was a translator and letter-writer, the Dutch humanist scholar Desiderius Erasmus (?1469–1536), Sir Thomas Elyot (c 1490–1546) and Juan Luis Vives (1492–1540). Vives was employed by Catherine of Aragon to educate ▷Mary Tudor, and in his influential ▷*Instruction of a Christian Woman* (1523, translated by Richard Hyrde 1529) he argues that the 'brynyng up of a Christen woman' had hitherto been treated by writers merely as a matter of exhortation, whereas Vives proposed to 'compyle rules of lyvyng' which by offering women classical and religious learning would make them pious and disinclined to frivolity, 'daunces and suche other wanton . . . plaies'.

Much of the humanist debate centred on the European culture in which Latin was a common language. Notably, the skills of which women felt themselves to be deprived throughout the period 1500–1800, and which if obtained warranted comment, were skills in the élite ancient languages (for example, the one published piece to which the novelist ▷Sarah Fielding actually put her name was her translation from the classics, *Xenophon's Memoirs of Socrates*, 1762). Humanist educators argued that classical learning enabled women to form a more sound basis for their religious faith; they were in favour of educating women for spiritual ends, conceiving of it as an aid to piety, and women were actively encouraged to turn their learning to pious literary ends in the production of ▷translations, ▷prayers and meditations on spiritual topics – as did the women of the More family. However, humanists did not conceive of education as taking women outside their domestic sphere.

The Reformation brought another impulse in the education of women, in which educators such as Thomas Becon and Miles Coverdale (and later Richard Mulcaster) used biblical examples of 'good' women to support and justify women's education – a line of argument taken up by women themselves during the Civil War (1648–1651) when women sectaries such as the ▷Quakers, ▷Anna Trapnel and others used biblical precedent to justify their own participation in theological and political debate. Protestant emphasis on education was connected with the reading of religious treatises in the vernacular, but also with suitable skills for the running of a household – from needlework to the making of preserves, even brewing. A number of schools for women were established during the 17th century, such as the Red Maids School, founded by a Bristol merchant in 1627, and there were dame schools, but all women's education placed little emphasis on writing. Indeed, the education of pious women was inseparable from the education and training of women to fulfil the social functions becoming to their station, and much educational literature for women overlaps with instruction on the behaviour or 'conduct' of maids, wives and widows to form a growing body of literature on the socially appropriate conduct of women.

Conduct and status

A woman's sphere was bounded by religious and legal interdictions which debarred her from official status within the family, made inheritance by women problematic (see ▷Lady Ann Clifford) and forbade her participation in the public arena. But, although confined to the household, women in the 16th century and the first part of the 17th century were often actively involved in making and marketing goods: They were not sequestered from the economic sphere, because the household was often a unit of economic production, and women (especially widows) did participate in trades, including brewing and printing, service industries, such as cooking and serving, and the professions that 'modesty' reserved as a predominantly feminine preserve – such as that of midwife.

▷Conduct books circulated very widely, addressing women on how to carry out their roles in society, and the most famous was probably William Gouge's *Of Domesticall Duties*, translated by Miles Coverdale in 1541. These books confirmed Biblical interdictions and prescriptions. However, the area of conduct became one of the fields in which women wrote, either in private or public ▷letters to sons and daughters (as in the case of ▷Lady Brilliana Harley) or in manuscript or, later, printed books of ▷advice to sons and daughters. Particularly poignant is ▷Elizabeth Joceline's *The Mothers Legacie* – advice to her child, during whose birth she died, published after her death. She writes, 'Therefore, deare childe, read here my love, and if God take me from thee, bee obedient to these instructions as thou oughtest to be unto me' (Elizabeth Joceline, *The Mothers Legacie*, 1624, extracts in Betty Travitsky, ed., *The Paradise of Women Writing By Englishwomen in the Renaissance*, 1981, pp. 60–63). Conduct literature assumed that women's main concern was virtue, principally chastity, which one writer advised her daughter was 'the Seale of Grace, the staffe of devotion, the mark of the Just, the crowne of virginity, the glory of life, and a comfort of Martyrdome' (MR., *The Mother's Counsell*, extracts in Travitsky, pp. 66–8.). This was not an extreme view.

While women's writing on conduct did not challenge the predetermined nature of feminine virtue, the Bible, and the basis of conduct on biblical example, led to women writing about the pretext of their subordination, Eve, and women's commentary on female conduct and morality began to use the question of Eve's culpability to intervene in debate on the nature of women. They asked why, if Eve was indeed the 'weaker vessel', Adam was not tempted instead, and suggested that Adam and Eve were originally created equal, or argued that Eve was tempted by Satan himself, whereas Adam fell at the suggestion of a mere woman. In ▷*Salve Deus Rex Judaeorum*, ▷Aemilia Lanyer turned Eve's predicament to a hint on women's education: Eve's 'undiscerning ignorance perceived / No guile', ▷Rachel Speght's analysis makes Adam and Eve equal sinners: 'And Sathan thinking this their good too great, / Suggests the woman, she the man, they eate. / Thus eating both, they both did joyntly sinne.' (Rachel Speght, *Mortalities Memorandum*, 1621)

Both Speght and Lanyer were women of a lower rank, neither royalty nor great ladies, and therefore subject to slightly different regulations (obviously, the religious, social, material and legal conditions which determined women's conduct were not uniform across all social classes). The rules were also potentially internally contradictory. For example, piety would encourage a woman to wear simple dress, and in the 16th and early 17th centuries the sumptuary laws, which governed the relations between clothes and status, would restrict the kinds of materials she could use, yet a well-dressed woman would indicate a prosperous business.

Some women writers begin to question the rules that governed their conduct, and in 1617 a controversy blew up in print indicating both the importance of the new print culture for debate, and the fact that women of middle social status – such as ▷Isabella Whitney, Lanyer, Speght and the later religious controversists – had some access to it. In this ▷woman controversy, the misogynist Joseph Swetnam's printed attacks on women, which provoked replies from Rachel Speght, the pseudonymous Esther Sowernam and Constantia Munda. Not all these replies were necessarily by women, but they provide evidence of a developing response to anti-feminist writings. For instance, Esther Sowernam exposes Swetnam's false logic in his charge that 'Woman was made of a crooked rib so she is crooked of conditions, *Joseph Swetnam* was made as from *Adam* of clay and dust, so he is of a durty and muddy disposition.' (See Esther Sowernam, *Esther Hath Hanged Haman*, 1617, and Travitsky, pp. 107–9)

Thus in the area of conduct women both acceded to their given place *and* began to turn their knowledge of the Bible to their own ends, and to question traditional interpretations and uses of key biblical texts such as the Fall. One of the products of the interdiction on women's activity in the secular public sphere is that the writing they produced which addressed such questions was highly self-reflexive about the act of writing itself, and the genres within which they wrote, or which they turned to their own ends. Indeed, women writing in the Early Modern period accordingly produce ingenious justifications for their literary activity, and manipulate the codes which forbade them to write in a way that actually encourages women's writing as a pious excercise. In short, they manipulate genres of writing in order to find a place in them.

Genre

Genres were morally loaded, particularly when used by women, and the modern division into 'private' feminine versus 'public' masculine genres does not provide an adequate explanation of women's relationship to the written word in the 16th and 17th centuries. The genres acceptable for women's use were those that were 'private' in the sense of being contained within and addressed to the domestic sphere. However, these were themselves highly codified and explicitly religious genres – meditations, ▷prayers, ▷translations of pious works were all encouraged by humanist and later Protestant educators. Such genres found sophisticated employers in Renaissance women. For instance, Mary Sidney Herbert, the Countess of Pembroke, was able to combine poetic innovation and piety in her famous metrical translation of the psalms. Women produced prayers, meditations, religious dialogues and domestic advice, and these might be circulated in manuscript. Even when printed, such genres were acceptable because they indicated a pious attitude to a woman's sphere. Thus the domestic sphere cannot, precisely, be equated with 'private' writing, in that such writing could become 'public', and this is true also of the secular genres we might think of as private – ▷letters and diaries.

Letter-writing gave women both the opportunity to construct a relatively informal persona and to elicit a response, and women used them to negotiate their terms, from Ann Boleyn with Henry VIII to ▷Dorothy Osborne writing to her future husband, Sir William Temple, or Elizabeth I making tricky political negotiations with her family before she came to the throne. But the fragile 'privacy' of letters is obvious, and letter-writing could be construed as an unfeminine attempt to influence the world outside the domestic sphere. Thus we find ▷Brilliana Harley writing in semi-secrecy to her son at Oxford – 'Your father dous not knowe I send. Thearefore take no notis of it, to him, nor to any.' (Brilliana Harley, *Letters*, ed. T.T. Lewis, 1854, in Travitsky, pp. 82–3). Moreover, in the formation of the 20th-century canon of 'English literature' letters have been classified as of minor importance, except where the writer produced more overtly 'literary' genres, and this has reinforced the invisibility of women operating in this field. On the other hand, letters both offer an insight into the construction of a persona on paper – demonstrate the self-presentation of women in the period – and, in the later 17th century particularly, blend with other genres which often present themselves as the private 'revealed' – such as diaries, memoirs and novels.

As women's restricted and unequally distributed access to education implies, status and learning also affected the genre a woman might write in. Two early secular writers were the aristocratic ▷Joanna Lumley, who executed a manuscript translation of Euripedes's ▷*Iphigenia at Aulis*, and ▷Isabella Whitney, who seems to have been a woman of the middle class – her poems, published in 1572 and 1573 suggest that she worked as a servant in the City of London. It is to be noted that the aristocratic Lumley translated a secular classical text, whereas Whitney, conscious of her own lack of classical learning, wrote poetry in popular ballad metre, and used at least some of the genres of emerging popular print culture. Status and learning affected a woman's choice of genre, but so did the ideological nature of particular genres themselves.

Secular poetic genres presented complex choices for women. Elegies for children overlapped with the pious exercises prescribed for women, and were acceptable. On the other hand Petrarchan discourse, in which a lover addressed his mistress, presented a difficult negotiation of poetic persona because the object of the poem was, traditionally, the (implicitly female, or feminized) beloved of the masculine poetic persona. Despite the particularly explicit situating of women as objects of desire rather than producers of discourse, courtly love poetry was adapted by ▷Katherine Philips in the 1650s. She reworked the customary tropes of love poetry in poems celebrating friendship between women.

Secular prose genres that might be printed included romance (often stories of knights, ladies, chivalry) and the work of ▷Lady Mary Wroth indicates an emerging sense of interrelationship between women as writers when she emphasizes her connection with the Sidney family in her long prose romance, *The Countess of Montgomeries Urania* (1621). The *Urania* reinterpreted the prose romance used by Sir Philip Sidney's *Arcadia* (1590), but it also changed the significance of the genre because she was understood by contemporaries to have used the form to evaluate contemporary scandals – often from a point of view that involved analysis of the complex psychological states of women in erotic and affective relationships to unsatisfactory male lovers. Contemporaries held romance to be a less than edifying staple of women's entertainment, and Mary Wroth was only the first of many women in the period to begin to write in and comment on the genre. In the 18th century it was used by ▷Delarivier Manley, and ▷Clara Reeve's *The Progress of Romance* (1785) addressed its specific connection to women readers. Women wrote in other prose genres, including advice books, cookery and household books (as in the case of ▷Hannah Wolley), and utopias, as in ▷Margaret Cavendish's *The Blazing World*.

The Civil War brought new genres within the reach of women, as female sectaries and radicals began to preach and make religio-political prophesies and texts. This period and the later 17th century saw a sequence of prose relations of their travels, ▷conversion narratives, justifications of conduct, warnings of God's wrath – see, for example, ▷Mary Cary, ▷Anna Trapnel (who wrote radical visions of the millenium), and ▷Katherine Evans and ▷Sarah Cheevers (Quakers who set out to replicate the voyages of St Paul). Women's opinions and conversions were published by themselves and by men, especially those of Quaker women, such as ▷Margaret Fell and ▷Barbara Blaugdone. Other women wrote spiritual autobiographies and conversion narratives. The Civil War changed the lives of many women, whether radicals, Cromwellians or Royalists, and many recorded in memoirs, either for publication or for their own families, their part in the proceedings – not only Margaret Cavendish, ▷Lady Ann Halkett, ▷Ann Fanshawe (all Royalists), but also ▷Lucy Hutchinson, who, like Brilliana Harley, ran a siege.

These memoirs and records might be seen as 'private', or at least manuscript docu-ments, but women also began to write politico-religious works during the 17th century. These included ▷Lady Eleanor Douglas's obscure acrostic prophesies, ▷Elizabeth Poole (protesting at the beheading of Charles I in 1649) and ▷Elinor Channel's protests – all published, as were the works of religious radical women. Although the political sphere was officially forbidden to women, they were inevitably implicated in it – from ▷Lady Arabella Stuart, who was held prisoner in the Tower of London, to the Tory polemicist ▷Mary Astell. The Civil War saw women taking an active part in political and military activities, and political activists included women who demonstrated outside Parliament in 1642 and 1643, and presented petitions, carrying on their activity as petitioners throughout the 1640s. Women's petitions and demonstrations in favour of the

Leveller John Lilburne may have been led by ▷Katherine Chidley. However, despite this political activity, women remained excluded from Parliament and the franchise.

In drama, after Joanna Lumley's translation, ▷Elizabeth Cary, Lady Falkland, both wrote and published ▷*The Tragedie of Mariam, Faire Queene of Jewry* (1613). Women danced in court masques, and in the 1620s and 1630s Queen Henrietta Maria sponsored a court culture in which women took part. They also danced and performed in entertainments at great houses, and possibly in plays of the 1630s staged at Oxford, but they took no part in the commercial theatre before the Civil War. A woman appreared on stage in William Davenant's opera *The Siege of Rhodes*, staged under the Protectorate of Oliver Cromwell in 1656. Margaret Cavendish fled the country with her husband, the Duke of Newcastle, after the defeat of the Royalists at the battle of Marston Moor in Yorkshire (1644), and during her exile she wrote a large volume of probably unperformed plays (as well as volumes of letters and orations and scientific speculations), which she published herself and sent to the universities of Oxford and Cambridge.

The final defeat of the English Republic in 1659 has been seen by some as precipitating a return of women to the domestic sphere. However, although the activities and writings of women sectaries were curtailed after the Restoration, and although the next 150 years did witness an actual shrinking of the number of professions open to women, they participated in different and new ways in a burgeoning literary public sphere. That is not to say that women were accepted in print: the Restoration discourse of the place of women echoed that of earlier periods, and Milton (1608–1674) was by no means alone in thinking of men as primary, as his contrast of Adam and Eve suggests – 'He for God only, she for God in him'.

1660–1800

A poet of the early 18th century, ▷Anne Finch, Countess of Winchelsea, wrote:

> Did I my lines intend for public view,
> How many censures would their faults pursue
>
> . . .
>
> True judges might condemn their want of wit,
> And all might say, they're by a woman writ.
> Alas a woman that attempts the pen,
> Such an intruder on the rights of men,
> Such a presumptuous creature is esteemed,
> The fault can by no virtue be redeemed.
>
> (*Selected Poems*, ed. Denys Thompson, 1987, p. 26)

Compared to the introduction to Margaret Tyler's translation quoted earlier, Finch's poem is firmer about being her own work, and defends itself against criticism by anticipating the form it might take. Although self-deprecating, the poem simultaneously implies the unfairness of condemning writing merely on the basis of its author's sex. It differs from Tyler in being an original production rather than a translation, and it is in the rhymed couplet so popular with poets from Dryden (1631–1700) onwards. These lines also demonstrate that the issue of women's agency as poets continued to be associated with transgression of the boundaries of the home, and, implicitly, transgression of a sexual norm. Indeed, it was claimed that 'punk [prostitute] and poetess agree . . . pat' – suggesting that the terms were synonymous.

Two important female writers of the mid-to-late 17th century became the figures around whom this debate about the sexual morality of women's writing was played out. ▷Aphra Behn, known as Astrea, the brilliant dramatist, novelist and poet, had led an irregular life by late 17th-century standards, and was unafraid to write about the erotic subjects of courtly love – she even mocked impotence. The poet, dramatist and correspondent ▷Katherine Philips on the other hand, though also a Royalist (or Tory, as they came to be known) was dubbed 'the chaste Orinda', and held to be a suitable model for a women poet, especially as standards of morality changed during the 18th century. Another division with simultaneous political and aesthetic implications was the difference between Dissenters and those who agreed with the established Church of England after the Restoration. It is possible to detect a rather different aesthetic in the emerging trradition of dissenting writings, from Quakers to the dissenting poet ▷Elizabeth (Singer) Rowe and and the brilliant Whig historian ▷Catherine Macaulay (see Neil Keeble, *The Literary Culture of Nonconformity*, 1987). This might be contrasted with the emerging Tory women writers of political and scandalous narrative, such as Delarivier Manley.

The Restoration of Charles II (greeted with poems by Katherine Philips, among others) saw a changed relationship between women and literary production. In part through the expansion of print and the active part played by women in the Civil War, their participation in the literary public sphere was permanently enlarged as both readers and writers. As readers, women formed a new market for the burgeoning periodical literature which had been growing since 1640 (see Kathryn Shevelow, *Women and Print Culture*, 1989). The late 17th-century periodicals, such as John Dunton's *Athenian Mercury* which began in 1691, avoided using Latin, and set about inventing their feminine readership as in need of guidance. Women also contributed to these periodicals, as correspondents, and as editors and writers (Delarivier Manley took over the editorship of *The Examiner* in 1711). As readers of periodicals, women were taken into account, and many of the questions answered in John Dunton's *The Athenian Oracle* address specifically the conduct of affairs between the sexes. For instance: '*Q. What Behaviour and Carriage in the Progress of an Amour will be most Winning and Acceptable to a Lady of Ingenuity and Fortune?*' – the answer to which is designed to be both pleasing and mildly prescriptive for any woman reader: '*Faithfulness, Assiduity, Liberality, and good Sense, will at last carry her, if she is not pre-ingaged or wholly impregnable.*' Thus, women were addressed as readers, their conduct was discussed seriously, and their roles reinforced. But – as in the case of conduct literature – women themselves began to participate in a discourse which could be seen as specifically for women, and by the 1740s ▷Eliza Haywood was running *The Female Spectator*. More than this, the diversely talented ▷Lady Mary Wortley Montagu set up a Whig political journal, *The Nonsense of Common Sense*.

Schooling and the debate on the education of daughters

By the end of the 17th century a fairly wide range of high- and low-quality educational establishments existed, from increasingly élite grammar scools and the two universities for boys, to tutors and dame schools. Girls were barred from most educational institutions, and a classical education including Greek and Latin was still very rare – something which was also a handicap for middle-class and poorer literate men.

Education for women had been disrupted by the Civil War, and seems to have changed thereafter, as is suggested by the career of ▷Bathsua Makin. She had been tutor to Charles I's daughter, Princess Elizabeth, and after the war, in 1673, seems to have been planning to run a school, and wrote an advertisement for it, *An Essay to Revive the Antient Education of Gentlewomen*. Like ▷Mary Astell in her ▷*A Serious Proposal to the Ladies* (1697), Makin saw education as a necessary and neglected accomplishment of the upper classes. An influential treatise on education was Françoise de Salignac de la Mothe-Fenelon's *Treatise on the Education of Daughters* (1687, translated 1707). Where the humanists had argued that the education of women rendered them wise and pious, Fenelon noted, 'if women do great good to the community when well educated, they are capable of infinite mischief when viciously instructed.' A literature grew up advocating the education of women, emphasizing on the one hand women's equal rationality with men, and on the other their heightened sensibility. However, like Fenelon, much of this literature saw women as to be educated for the benefit of men and children, rather than for themselves, and as Alice Brown explains 'distinctively feminist arguments in favour of improving women's education are often hard to disentangle from instrumental ones' (Alice Brown, *The Eighteenth Century Feminist Mind*, 1987, p. 109).

Women participated in this discourse, producing increasingly serious demands for equal education. Examples include ▷Hester Chapone's *Letters on the Improvement of the Mind Addressed to a Young Lady* (1773) and Catherine Macaulay's *Letters on Education* (1790). ▷Hannah More emphasized the class dimension of the debate. By the end of the 18th century it had come to be accepted that at least upper-class women should be educated. Emphasis on the way education fitted women to social roles continued, and as Catherine Macaulay argued, the 'social duties . . . of daughter, wife and mother will be but ill-performed by ignorance and levity.' In ▷*Thoughts on the Education of Daughters* (1787) ▷Mary Wollstonecraft did examine the way education influenced a woman's own experience of the world, noting particularly the fact that by the late 18th century very few professions remained open to women, and that 'Few are the modes of earning a subsistence, and these very humiliating . . . A teacher in a school is only a kind of upper servant, who has more work than the menial ones.' She also argued that women should be given a chance to perfect their understandings (see Alice Brown, p. 109).

Wollstonecraft's emphasis on the necessity for women to adapt themselves to circumstances, and on education as a resource for an oppressed mind, did not mean that her texts were entirely depoliticized, and it was to a large extent her doing that the discourse of rights, so important to the French Revolution and the idea of the citizen, began to permeate thinking about women and the public sphere. The very title ▷*Vindication of the Rights of Women* implies a discourse that 20th-century feminists have recognized as fundamental to that aspect of the 20th-century women's movement that envisaged a more egalitarian society based on a recognition of basic legal rights. Although women's legal status changed little during the 18th century, there was a change in attitude to women's rights, particularly in relation to marriage and property.

Women and the literary market

If women were both producers and readers of ▷periodicals, and a market-target of many of them, they were also producers and consumers of the ▷romance and, by the end of the period, of novels. Throughout the 17th century women were characterized as the main readers of 'romances', but the meaning of this word gradually changed during the 17th and 18th centuries, and the genre, considered to be read by women, became also an area in which women's writing was influential. By the 18th century, women were writing and selling romance. However, the flexibility of what was considered to be romance has to some extent been obscured by critical obsession with the 'rise' of the novel (Ian Watt, *The Rise of the Novel*, 1963), and a more fruitful way to think about 18th-century prose is as a discursive field inhabited by periodicals, romance, and what Lennard Davies has called 'factual fictions' – fictions which re-present to the reader the world around her (Lennard Davies, *Factual Fictions: the Origins of the English Novel*, 1983; Michael McKeon, *The Origins of the English Novel 1600–1740*, 1987). In her *Progress of Romance*, Clara Reeve praises Aphra Behn's ▷*Oroonoko* (1688) as a romance – indicating the extendable boundaries of the genre. And *Oroonoko*'s introduction shows how fact, fiction and romance were interwoven, when it describes itself as a story full of 'natural intrigues' in 'a world where [the reader] finds diversions for every minute, new and strange'. Needless to say, the world which can so exotically combine fact and fantasy is that of colonial conquest, including heavily eroticized power relations. It is not until towards the end of the 18th century that the campaign against slavery began, let alone the publication of narratives by slaves and ex-slaves (▷Slave narratives).

Thus, women wrote romances as well as reading them – Delarivier Manley used them to explore power relations in political and sexual issues, and in some ways, ▷Gothic tales, such as ▷Ann Radcliffe's ▷*The Mysteries of Udolpho* (1744), with its emphatic insistence on feminine passivity, were connected to this genre. Women were able to make money by publishing fictions of various sorts – particularly scandalous memoirs. ▷Mary Carleton used a literary genre to tell the story of her own financial and marital disaster, and ▷Anna Maria Bennet's *Anna, or Memoirs of a Welch Heiress* (1785) and Mary Robinson's memoirs (published in 1801) of being an actress and the mistress of the Prince of Wales, show how closely overlapping fictional and factual writing was, and the extent to which the dominant narrative of virtue, resisting or conquered, dominated nominally distinct discourses.

The scenario of virtue in peril found its most famous adumbration in Samuel Richardson's *Clarissa* (1747–48) (▷Richardson, Samuel, influence of), in which the heroine is raped. The novel sparked much controversy, and women novelists reworked the plot, as well as that of Jean Jacques Rousseau's *Julie, ou, la Nouvelle Heloïse* (1761) which also uses the perilous theme of forbidden love. *Julie* fostered the emergent sense that women might not be wholly 'bad', despite sexual misconduct. A new attention to feeling gave women a slightly greater scope to redeem their name, but, simultaneously, the Marriage Act (1753) made it more difficult for women to enforce promises of marriage (see Alice Brown, pp. 145–6). Moreover, novels of feeling were considered damaging to the very audience they were intended for, and women were assumed to get locked into erotic fantasy lives. However, as in Richardson's *Pamela* (1740–41) and ▷Fanny Burney's very different ▷*Evelina* (1778), the sexual peril of the heroine and her feelings about the hero are inseparable from issues of morality.

Theatre allowed women to enter the cash economy when Charles II limited the number of London theatres to two, and women began to play women's parts. For the rest of the period there were either one or two London theatres (as well as provincial venues), and the theatre became a way for women to support themselves after 1660. Indeed, one critic suggests that more plays by women were staged in the period 1660–1720 than in the period 1920–1980 (Fidelis Morgan, *The Female Wits*, 1981, p. xi). The theatre was a precarious living for both actresses and writers, but there are signs of collaboration between women writers and actresses – for example, Aphra Behn wrote prologues and epilogues for the great comic actress Nell Gwyn. In the first wave of Restoration works came plays written by women – Katherine Philips, ▷Elizabeth Polwhele and Aphra Behn (who wrote almost twenty plays). After Behn's death a new generation of women dramatists emerged, characteristically writing for money. These later dramatists included ▷Mary Pix, ▷Susanna Centlivre, ▷Catherine Trotter Cockburn, Delarivier Manley and ▷Jane Wiseman. Trotter, Pix and Manley all began writing for the stage in 1695, a season in which many of the plays were by women. When John Dryden died in 1700 the emergence of a selfconsciously interrelated circle of women writers (sometimes referred to as 'the Daughters of Behn') is clearly indicated by the fact that one of the volumes of elegies for him, ▷*The Nine Muses* (1700) was a volume of poetry by women, edited by Delarivier Manley. Indeed, the prefatory poems to plays by women very often contain praise of contemporary women's efforts. During the 18th century, women went on writing for the stage, and the Irishwoman ▷Mary Davys had a great success with *The Northern Heiress, or the Humours of York* (staged 1716). However, standards of morality changed, and this is perhaps suggested by the career of Hannah More, who began as a dramatist in the 1770s, but moved increasingly towards Christian and moral writing, ending her career campaigning against ▷slavery, and publishing the *Cheap Repository Tracts* (1795–1798), designed for the education of the lower classes.

Differences: women intellectuals and labouring women

The theatre and fiction provided income for women, but, increasingly, the ideology of femininity prescribed domestic inactivity. Daniel Defoe (1661–1731) suggested that men attempted to turn their wives into mere decorations, preventing them from working so 'that they may not value themselves upon it, and make themselves, as it were, the equals of their husbands' (Daniel Defoe, quoted in Robert Alfrey Utter and Gwendolen Bridges Needham, *Pamela's Daughters*, 1937. Also, Shervelow, p. 55). In the 18th century the

▷Bluestockings, as they were known, were a circle of women who, while broadly conforming to the notion that the feminine sphere is domestic, yet found a way to establish a social role which came close to that of the woman intellectual.

In the mid-18th century, ▷Elizabeth Montagu, her sister ▷Sarah Scott, ▷Elizabeth Vesey, the Anglo-Saxon scholar ▷Elizabeth Elstob, Hester Chapone, ▷Elizabeth Carter, and ▷Hester Thrale Piozzi, who invited Fanny Burney (see also ▷the Ladies of Llangollen) formed a loosely-knit circle of women who corresponded with one another, translated, and were to an extent arbiters of taste and morality. It is significant that the best-known of Elizabeth Montagu's works is her literary critical essay on Shakespeare – a kind of writing that brought together literature and morality. Burney made fun of these women, but, although Elizabeth Vesey's attempts to hold salons at which men and women discussed intellectual matters rather than playing cards seems strange to us, this was a serious attempt to claim a semi-official place for women in the contemporary literary élite, and one which was not mediated through discourses of social control to quite the same extent as low- and middle-brow periodicals. However, the position of the woman intellectual was open to ridicule (as the later use of 'Bluestocking' suggests), and it was predicated on the preservation of a relatively rigid morality – one which could withstand Sarah Scott leaving her husband, but not Hester Thrale marrying a second time to a man of inferior status, – Piozzi, the singer and singing teacher.

If the position of women intellectuals was threatened by women's sexuality (the Ladies of Langollen were shocked to be thought lesbians), then women writers of low status or holding different values, were perhaps even more disturbing to society. During the 17th and 18th centuries, against the odds, women of low social status from urban and country backgrounds found their way into manuscript and into print, from Isabella Whitney to Anna Trapnel. The 18th century saw a range of such women – such as ▷Ann Yearsley, ▷Janet Little and ▷Mary Leapor. Some patronage relations between women worked well, for instance, that between ▷Elizabeth Cobbold and the transported convict ▷Margaret Catchpole. However, the case of Ann Yearsley 'the Bristol milkwoman' and her relationship with Hannah More points to some of the ways in which conservative assumptions about social status influenced relationships between women of different classes. Yearsley's family were destitute when her poems were first shown to More, and More arranged for their publication by subscription, raising a large sum thereby. But afterwards she was reluctant to give Yearsley control of the money raised – fearing what she took to be labouring-class improvidence. Yearsley protested against this and, incidentally (as her success in running a ▷circulating library indicates), was a capable business-woman. The story illuminates clearly that, although women writers made alliances on the basis of gender, ideological and material questions – such as money, staus and expectations based on conceptions of class – formed a crucial and problematic context for such alliances.

Another labouring-class poet, ▷Mary Collier, was, among other things, a field labourer. She wrote her first poem in response to Stephen Duck's *The Thresher's Labour*, which she felt ignored the hardships of women. Duck was a field labourer who was taken up by society as a curiosity; and despite criticism of Duck, Collier seems to have identified and sympathized with his position. The writings of labouring-class poets, such as Collier, Mary Leapor and the Scots poet, Janet Little suggest, as do the political prophecies of the mid-17th century, the interrelated placing of women in social status and gender. The poetry of Janet Little, who was very aware of writing in the shadow of Burns (1756–1796), alerts us to the increasing marginalization of other languages, or non-standard English, during the 17th and 18th centuries. Little selfconsciously uses a Scots dialect, indicating the possibility of a different intellectual and poetic tradition, where Scottish poetry is often categorized as (implicitly naïve) 'dialect poetry', Irish poetry is found in translations – such as those of ▷Charlotte Brooke. It is notable also that ▷Maria Edgeworth both wrote about class and colonial relations in Ireland, and took an active interest in the French

Revolution. The pull of the metropolis in the 18th century and the present may blind us to the significant intellectual traditions and developments outside the self-imposed centre.

Although there were few legal measures for women in the 18th century, and as yet no coherent campaign for equal rights in the public sphere, attitudes to women of upper-middle-class status and above had changed, and a significant part of this change was that their access to the literary sphere was – more or less – accepted, if not acknowledged by 1800.

▷ Scotland

KATHRYN BURLINSON

4 Nineteenth-century Britain

Robert Southey's famous statement to ▷ Charlotte Brontë, that literature 'cannot be the business of a woman's life, and it ought not to be', did not represent an isolated, eccentric opinion. It was an attitude that lay deeply embedded in the sexual ideology of a society where women and men were seen to have separate and distinct roles to fulfil in life. Woman's supreme duty was to be a devoted wife and mother, an ▷ 'Angel in the House' who reigned as queen within the private domestic realm, while men were kings of the public domain of work, enterprise and competition. Beneath the social division of labour lay a profound belief in sexual difference, according to which men were seen as naturally dominant, active and strong, while women were naturally subordinate, passive and weak. If woman had a part to play in any creative process, it was as a figure of inspiration, a muse rather than a maker.

In spite of the opposition to their creativity, however, many women did make literature their business. By the middle of the 19th century women's writing was vying with that of men's in the literary marketplace, generating a feeling of insecurity in the male literary establishment. 'It's a melancholy fact', wrote George Henry Lewes in 1850, 'that the group of female authors is becoming every year more multitudinous and more successful. Women write the best novels, the best travels, the best reviews, the best leaders, and the best cookery books . . . Wherever we carry our skilful pens, we find the place preoccupied by a woman.'

Despite their strength in numbers, however, literary women were not unaffected by the ideology that constructed them as transgressive. Many did not wish to deviate from their allotted position as homemakers, and writers such as ▷ Elizabeth Gaskell, ▷ Rosa Nouchette Carey and ▷ Mrs Humphry Ward supported the view that writing must take place only after familial responsibilities had been entirely fulfilled. Such women were at pains to stress that their creativity neither hindered their housekeeping nor threatened their femininity. Yet the difficulty of reconciling the practical needs of a writer with those of a housekeeper was frequently acknowledged. The situation in which ▷ Margaret Oliphant found herself was by no means uncommon: 'I had no table to myself, much less a room to work in . . . I don't think I ever had two hours undisturbed (except at night, when everybody is in bed) in my whole literary life. Miss Austen, I believe, wrote in the same way.'

The critical double standard

If women managed to overcome the practical obstacles to their creativity, they had then to endure the notorious critical double standard that was brought to bear once a work had been written, accepted by a ▷publisher, and marketed. Contemporary reviewers read fiction and poetry according to their own gender stereotypes. Women's writing was praised when it conformed to feminine ideals and expressed delicate sentiments, tender emotions and domestic affections. However, as many women were aware, such praise was back-handed, for the very qualities which were deemed admirable in women's writing also signified its limitations. Women might be able to write well about love, but they were seen as incapable of producing the 'universal' truth to which male writers were deemed to have access. ▷Essentialist theories of the difference between male and female writing were widely supported; even ▷George Eliot maintained that women writers' special skill lay in representing maternal feeling.

The critical double standard and the emphasis on sexual difference ran contiguously throughout the 19th century. Yet enormous social changes also occurred between 1800 and 1900, and these changes inevitably affected, and were reflected in, the writing produced.

Romance and Romanticism: the pre-Victorian period

At the turn of the 19th century, Britain was increasing its wealth and world influence through colonial expansion overseas and rapid industrialization at home. Many writers and intellectuals were recoiling from the violent aftermath of the French Revolution, while the ruling classes were nervous about the possibility of uprisings in Britain. ▷Romanticism is today seen as the most significant literary movement of the late 18th and early 19th centuries, yet the majority of women writers of the day were not working in the mainstream of this tradition. ▷Jane Austen's novels, for example, share the preoccupations of the mid-18th century rather than those of the early 19th. Austen reacted against the revolutionary fervour of the romantic movement; in a period when shared moral values were supplanted by an individual responsibility for ethical judgement, Austen reverted to an ▷Augustan faith in the community. The poetry of ▷Felicia Hemans, ▷Jane and Ann Taylor and ▷Letitia Landon may be affiliated with Romanticism, but their work does not venture so far into the exploration of subjectivity, nor embrace so wholeheartedly the philosophy of individualism that fired the imaginations of Wordsworth, Coleridge and Shelley.

It is not difficult to understand this measured reserve. Women were constructed not as independent but as *relational* beings, therefore the individualist ethos was problematic. As mothers, daughters or wives they had few, if any, legal rights. ▷Conduct books stressed woman's role as helpmeet, and lambasted her intellectual aspirations. Women's ▷education consisted in acquiring feminine 'accomplishments' designed to attract husbands, and there was no access to university education. The woman poet, therefore, was neither as well-educated as her male counterpart (although Hemans and Landon *were* well-read), nor did her social conditioning encourage her to think of herself and her own perceptions as a territory for poetic exploration. This is not to imply that Hemans and Landon do not investigate feminine subjectivity, but rather to suggest that such explorations occur in the interstices of their predominantly ▷sentimental, domestic and religious verse.

If women's relation to Romanticism is problematic, their relation to ▷romance is arguably more straightforward. With the exception of ▷Mary Shelley, whose ▷*Frankenstein* was greatly influenced by contemporary philosophical, aesthetic and scientific thought and may be seen to offer a critique of the Promethean impulses of Romanticism, women's writing of the early 19th century is characterized by its focus on love and marriage. The novel, traditionally affiliated to romance, was an appealing and accessible genre for women writers to work within, and a form which reached an eager audience in the steadily increasing number of women readers. ▷Anna Eliza Bray, ▷Susan Ferrier and ▷Amelia Opie were popular novelists of the period, as was ▷Catherine Gore, who wrote within a sub-genre of the romantic novel, the ▷'fashionable' novel or 'silver-fork' school. 'Silver-fork' fiction not only portrayed glamorous heroes and heroines, but lured its readers into the indulgent world of the wealthy and elite, offering advice on contemporary fashion and tips on where to shop. With the advent of the Victorian age, such fiction was superseded by writing that engaged to a greater extent with the realities of society and the position of women within it.

A changing society

The material benefits of colonial expansion and indigenous industrialization were inherited by the Victorian middle classes, by then the most powerful group in society. The English perceived themselves to be culturally and morally superior to the rest of the world. Although national confidence was high, there was yet a considerable anxiety about the pace at which the country seemed to be changing. The developments in science and technology brought 'progress', but society appeared to be unstable, threatened by the potential power of a newly industrialized working class. In the decade known as the 'hungry forties', the condition of the poor was acknowledged by middle-class philanthropists and reformers (many of whom were women). The middle class salved its conscience through gestures towards the alleviation of suffering, but reforms were intended to placate, rather than to liberate working men and women from their economic and class position. The strict social divisions of Victorian society also affected middle-class women seeking employment. The only respectable options open to them were the poorly paid jobs of ▷governess and school teacher. Since these were unattractive, many middle-class women who needed money to support their families turned to writing, a profession that required no expensive materials and could be pursued within the home.

Tension and triumph: the early Victorians

Charlotte Brontë's ▷*Jane Eyre* and ▷Emily Brontë's ▷*Wuthering Heights* are perhaps the most famous women's novels of the 1840s. *Jane Eyre* in particular made a huge impact on its contemporary audience and spawned numerous imitations. Elizabeth Gaskell's ▷*Mary Barton*, a 'social problem' novel calling for reconciliation between workers and employers, was also popular and influential. Many other women, including ▷Geraldine Jewsbury, ▷Catherine Crowe, ▷Frances Trollope, ▷Elizabeth Sewell and ▷Julia Kavanagh were also producing highly successful works and ensuring that women's literary efforts could not be brushed aside as the work of one or two 'exceptional' females. Women's achievements in poetry in this period were not equal to their fictional productions, but the emergence of ▷Elizabeth Barrett Browning was highly significant. Here was a woman poet who was both extremely knowledgable about poetic tradition and well-schooled in classical thought. She became the most respected and critically acclaimed 'poetess' of the Victorian age, and an inescapable influence on succeeding women writers.

Women's literary production found a corresponding increase in their exploration of gendered social relations. Much writing of the early Victorian period illustrates the growing frustration women were experiencing, and the contradictions that they recurrently confronted. The anger of Jane Eyre and the unruly energy of Catherine Earnshaw in *Wuthering Heights* are powerful examples, but by no means unsingular representations of dissent from the prevailing ideology of womanhood. The contradictions of a society which promulgated a belief in individualism and self-help while denying half its population the legal or social right to pursue any such autonomy were becoming apparent. Social 'problems' such as the burgeoning number of unmarried women, the lowly treatment of governesses and the status of the ▷'fallen woman' generated much debate. In the 1850s the ▷'Woman Question', as the Victorians themselves called it, became a pressing concern, and fiction in the mid-century intervened in all areas of this debate. Gaskell's ▷*Ruth* exposed the sexual double standard of Victorian society and called for sympathy for the fallen woman. ▷Grace Aguilar's ▷*Woman's Friendship* exhorted solidarity between women; Charlotte Brontë's ▷*Villette* explored the internal labyrinth of female identity. But perhaps the fullest treatment of the 'Woman Question' occurred in Barrett Browning's epic poem ▷*Aurora Leigh*, which articulated a powerful protest against the restrictions and prejudices that thwarted female endeavour. The early Victorian period also witnessed the emergence of ▷feminists such as ▷Anna Jameson, ▷Harriet Martineau and ▷Barbara Bodichon, all of whom published influential works arguing the case for legal reform and wider vocational opportunities for women.

Yet, for many women, the 'strong-minded' female represented an unacceptable challenge to deeply held religious and cultural beliefs. ▷Charlotte Yonge, for example, a High Anglican influenced by the ▷Oxford Movement, was a highly successful novelist, but one who permitted her conservatism and strict morality to overshadow her fiction. There was, then, no general consensus on the 'Woman Question', but rather a multivocal debate representing many contrasting shades of opinion. The presence of so many women writers on the literary scene, not only as novelists and poets but as journalists and, occasionally, editors, helped to fuel the fire of the debate and ensure that the exploration of issues affecting women continued into the 1860s and beyond.

Sensation and realism: the middle Victorian period

The literary marketplace expanded considerably in the 1860s, partly as a result of cheaper methods of book production, and partly because the network of railways that now covered the country enabled more efficient distribution of written material. If 'three-decker' novels were still too expensive to purchase, they could be borrowed from one of the ▷circulating libraries which allowed Britain's increasingly literate population access to its stock of perfectly proper fiction.

One of the most commercially successful genres of the 1860s was the novel of ▷sensation, the form chosen by writers such as ▷Rhoda Broughton, ▷'Ouida', ▷Mrs Henry Wood and ▷Mary Braddon. Braddon's ▷*Lady Audley's Secret* became a bestseller and was later adapted into a popular stage melodrama, while Mrs Wood's ▷*East Lynne* sold over two-and-half million copies and was translated into several languages. The novel of sensation, characteristically packed with intrigue, passion and melodrama, represented an alternative to ▷realism, the pervasive Victorian genre. In the 1860s and '70s, Mary Anne Evans, writing under the ▷pseudonym George Eliot, produced a series of novels that are generally acknowledged as the paradigm of Victorian high realism. Eliot is greatly admired for her scientific and philosophical knowledge, her precocious grasp of the function of history in shaping human destiny, and for her acuity in viewing the development of character as a function of environment. Eliot distanced herself from the emerging women's movement and articulated her distaste for much women's writing in ▷'Silly Novels by Lady Novelists', an essay that attacked fanciful romantic fiction. Her own work depicted strong heroines such as Maggie Tulliver in ▷*The Mill on the Floss* and Dinah Morris in ▷*Adam Bede*, yet Eliot's insistence on the need to repress individual desires in the face of social duty finally eliminates the efficacy of her characters' independence of spirit.

Poetry and politics: the later Victorian period

The latter half of the 19th century produced a larger number of respected poets than the first. ▷Christina Rossetti, ▷Jean Ingelow and ▷Dora Greenwell had established reputations in the 1860s; they were succeeded in the final decades of the 19th century by ▷Mary Coleridge, ▷Alice Meynell and ▷Michael Field. Rossetti currently has the highest standing, based on poems such as ▷*Goblin Market*, the 'Monna Innominata' sonnets, and many haunting and melancholy lyrics which speak repeatedly of loss, death and the deferral of hope. If Victorian women's poetry often articulated mourning, however, it was also increasingly channelled to political ends. Rossetti, ▷Augusta

Webster, ▷Adelaide Procter, ▷Amy Levy, ▷Emily Pfeiffer, and ▷Elizabeth Wolstenholme-Elmy directly addressed contemporary sexual political issues in their verse. Most of these writers were also active campaigners in real life.

The fight for women's ▷suffrage began in the 1860s, and despite numerous defeats, maintained its momentum throughout the rest of the century. Other campaigns, including the struggle for improved vocational opportunities and legal ▷reform for women all gained pace in the 1870s and 1880s. There was, of course, enormous conservative opposition to these movements from women as well as men. Mrs Humphry Ward succeeded in collecting the signatures of many notable women writers for her 'Appeal Against Female Suffrage' in 1889, and Eliza Linton harshly criticized activists in her fiction. However, there was also a proliferation of overtly feminist writing, and the ▷'New Woman' was born in the 1890s in the work of ▷Sarah Grand, ▷George Egerton, ▷Mona Caird, ▷Mary Cholmondeley and others. Many late-19th-century feminists believed that women were the spiritual guardians of the race and that female values could transform gender relations in the new century. Such a perception grew directly out of the previous construction of the middle-class woman as the white light of moral purity, and did little to undermine essentialist perceptions or to engage with issues affecting working-class women. Yet this feminist movement nevertheless articulated resistance to patriarchal control of women, and produced writing that was bold in expression and Utopian in its expectations. How far this was effective or influential in the history of British women's writing can be decided only in the light of the ongoing debates of our own troubled century.

▷Ghost stories (19th-century Britain)

LAURA MARCUS

5 Twentieth-century Britain

Literary periodization by centuries is in many ways an arbitrary device. The ▷suffrage novels of the first years of the 20th century, for example, grew out of the feminist protest literature of the 1890s. The development of literary ▷modernism, with its war-cry 'Make it New', has been seen, rightly or wrongly, as the more significant point of transition. 'Modernism' is, however, a contested term, a retrospective construction of a period (1910–1940 are the dates most commonly given) which has usually been defined by the features of a few 'major' authors and works. Until recently, ▷Virginia Woolf was the only British woman writer to be included in this canon. A number of feminist studies, however, have now substantially redrawn the map of modernism, both to include the work of more women writers and to redefine the nature of the 'movement' itself. Such studies have tended to focus on the *institutions* of literary modernism – for example literary coteries, small journals and presses – and the substantial role played by women writers and patrons in these. (One interesting example is that of the periodical edited by Dora Marsden in the 1910s in three manifestations, the *Freewoman*, the *New Freewoman*, and the *Egoist*, which took up an oppositional stance to the suffrage movement and endorsed, among other issues, more sexual freedom for women.) Another central topic is the way modernism gave a voice to previously marginal or outlawed female identities, including, in Kate Fulbrook's words, 'the expatriate woman, the lesbian or bisexual woman, the politically or socially rebellious woman, the self-directing woman'.

Feminist and cultural theorists are also beginning to explore the relationship between 'modernism' as a literary and artistic movement and 'modernity' as a state of human history and social relations, whose beginning is variously dated but usually taken to precede modernism. These debates are complex but important ones, not least because they allow us to broaden our accounts of literary modernism out of a primarily aesthetic framework.

The novel before 1945

The work of a number of early 20th-century women novelists is of particular significance here. In Virginia Woolf's and ▷Dorothy Richardson's fiction we find those features associated with literary modernism (the use of ▷stream-of-consciousness techniques, fluid characterizations and explorations of subjectivity, and experiments with temporality) in conjunction with the depiction of aspects of modernity (the centrality of the city as metropolis, and an uneasy awareness of 'historicity'). The modern city is of particular significance for a number of reasons. Its new forms of transport and communication systems and the chance encounters it sustains provided powerful metaphors for human relationships, as Woolf showed in ▷Mrs Dalloway. For women, specifically, entry into the public spaces of the city was used to mark a liberation from their enclosure in the private, domestic sphere. Richardson's extraordinary novel sequence ▷Pilgrimage is in part a celebration of her protagonist, Miriam's, journeying in and around London, finding opportunities, despite economic hardship, for self-creation and relationships denied to the heroine of the 19th-century novel. Lily Briscoe, in Woolf's ▷To the Lighthouse, finds that her 'vision' (artistic and conceptual) comes to her from encounters in railway carriages and omnibuses, and that it must be 'perpetually remade'. Female identity, in Woolf's and Richardson's writing, is also not a fixed and single essence, but fluid and changing. In their work we see the self as a process.

Alongside those writers celebrating modernity, there were also those, such as ▷May Sinclair, who used modernist explorations of consciouness and the new findings of ▷psychoanalysis to depict the continuation of Victorian constraints upon women's lives. Modernity can also have conservative aspects, including the desire to construct an imaginary past to serve present needs and to resolve present anxieties. As Alison Light, in *Forever England*, her outstanding study of women's fiction between the wars, notes of ▷Ivy Compton-Burnett, 'she belonged to that regiment of modernisers between the wars who found their future in making anew the past.'

This remaking of the present and future in the image of the past was one response to the trauma of World War I, which had an enormous impact on women's lives. The question of the 'benefits' of the war for women, as in ▷Sandra Gilbert and ▷Susan Gubar's claim that it precipitated the shattering of 'patrimony' and provided women for the first time with 'first class jobs – and first-class pay', is highly contentious. It is not, understandably, the issue at the forefront of women's novels written during or immediately after the war. Of these, one might single out ▷Rebecca West's fine novel *The Return of the Soldier* (1918), with its depiction of the psychic damage caused by war, ▷Cicely Hamilton's *William – An Englishman* (1919) and May Sinclair's *The Tree of Heaven* (1917). Sinclair's novel contains the telling lines from one of its women characters, 'All those years like a fool – over that silly suffrage'. Sinclair suggests here that feminism fades into insignificance in comparison to the 'larger' cause, a view with which, in various forms, women have become very familiar throughout the century.

Militant feminism certainly declined in the 1920s, although the reasons for this are complex. Olive Banks, in her *Faces of Feminism*, argues that it was replaced by 'welfare feminism', concerned with economic and social issues; the novels of ▷Vera Brittain and ▷Winifred Holtby, in particular, reflect these concerns. A number of women writers, including ▷Sylvia Townsend Warner and ▷Storm Jameson, played an important part in the culture of the British left in the 1930s and 1940s. They used their writing – novels, poetry and autobiography – to explore women's roles in society and the tensions between social expectations and women's desires. Warner is particularly interesting in this context, because the diversity of her writing and her experiments with different forms are a part of her concern with the relationship between art and politics, including the question of whether modernist or realist writing is the more appropriate vehicle for political literature.

If World War I had created an ambivalent attitude in many women writers towards a war whose destructiveness they deplored but whose conduct they felt inhibited from criticizing, World War II saw a strengthening of feminist pacifism. Woolf's ▷*Three Guineas* (1938) was a central work in this context, with its argument that peace depends upon an end to the oppression of women. Woolf appeals for a recognition of the links between the private and public spheres of life, along with an end to the system that links the private with the feminine and the public with the masculine. By contrast, ▷Stevie Smith's novel *Over the Frontier* (1938) contains more fantasy and dream material than polemic, and at times seems to celebrate the idea of a woman empowered by fighting a just war. Smith also explores the link between war and the 'battle' between the sexes. Her narrator, Pompey, suggests that a more androgynous society will emerge in post-war Britain: 'Never again in England I think shall we breed exclusively masculine and exclusively feminine types at any high level of intelligence, but there will always be much of one in the other.'

The image of the androgynous self, much debated in recent feminist criticism and theory, takes us back to perhaps the most influential text of 20th-century 'literary' feminism, Woolf's ▷*A Room of One's Own* (1929), with its claim that 'it is fatal for anyone who writes to think of their sex. It is fatal to be a man or woman pure and simple; one must be woman-manly or man-womanly'. However one interprets this – as an idealist rejection of a gendered and political literature and language, or as a 'postfeminist' appeal for a move beyond the constraints and conventions of gender difference – it co-exists with Woolf's more grounded social and material analysis of the impediments, external and psychological, faced by women writers throughout the centuries. The conflict between women's creativity and the conventional roles women are required to play is also a theme in a number of women's novels of the early 20th century. ▷Elaine Showalter has referred to the female *Künstlerroman* (the ▷*Bildungsroman* of the artist) of this period as 'a saga of defeat . . . there is indeed a new interest in the creative psychology of women, but it is full of self-recrimination'.

Central to 20th-century women's writing of the 1920s and 1930s, and often sharing the ambivalence to which Showalter points, are explorations of female sexuality, from Sinclair and ▷F.M. Mayor's depictions of emotionally starved or 'repressed' heroines (or, in some cases, anti-heroines) to Woolf's play with the transgression of gender boundaries in ▷*Orlando* (1928) and ▷Radclyffe Hall's representation of lesbianism in ▷*The Well of Loneliness* (1928). The theories of Freud and Havelock Ellis were a significant influence, and their accounts of femininity and female development provide complex links with the women novelists' use of the *Bildungsroman*, which, in novels by Sinclair and ▷Rosamond Lehmann, at times registers the destructive aspects of childhood experience or of young women's entry into the adult sexual/social world.

The emphasis on 'female experience' in women's fiction of the early and mid-20th century is at times critical of, at others confirmatory of, traditional roles for women. In either case, the focus is strongly directed towards middle- and upper-class women's experiences. Nicola Beauman, in her study of women writers between the wars, *A Very Great Profession*, defines the 'woman's novel' as 'written by middle-class women for middle-class women', suggesting that the role of these novels (she includes Sinclair,

Lehmann, West and ▷E.M. Delafield, among others) was to confirm a settled world-view rather than to disrupt it. The issues raised by the category of the 'woman's novel' are complex ones, bearing on definitions of 'female experience', on the tensions between feminist radicalism and class conservatism, and on the ways we choose to draw the literary map to link or to distinguish between disparate woman writers. There is only sufficient space here to suggest that such questions deserve further investigation.

The post-war novel

Elizabeth Wilson writes that 'the decade after the war was marked in British fiction by a general sense of retreat and nostalgia for a pre-war world that had been lost.' ▷Elizabeth Bowen, in her short stories of the 1940s and in ▷*The Heat of the Day*, both exposes the limitation of conventional morality and mourns the dissolution of traditional values. Other women writers give us an indication of the ways in which women's uncertainties about their roles were an aspect of the general instabilities of post-war Britain. ▷Rose Macaulay, in *The World My Wilderness*, depicts her heroine, painfully but more positively, as a survivor in a bombed-out London, her independence defined by her patriarchal father as 'something rather new . . . come on since the war, I think'. Lehmann, ▷Elizabeth Taylor and ▷Antonia White dramatize the difficulties middle-class women faced in adjusting to a new order and, as Wilson suggests, to the prevailing ideology of female emancipation as an achieved state which so often conflicted with women's actual experiences and self-images.

These writers were, of course, part of an earlier generation, a fact that was to become particularly apparent with the upsurge of the cult of youth in the 1950s and 1960s. The various new literary movements heralded, and perhaps in part created, by the press were in fact largely composed of male writers. Working-class experience, now more widely represented in literature, was seen as largely a male preserve. Women characters were often depicted, as in that central play of the 'angry young men', John Osborne's *Look Back in Anger* (1956), as part of the conservative, middle-class, deadening consensus against which Osborne's hero reacts so violently. ▷Iris Murdoch was one of the few women writers to be situated as a part of the new 1950s writing, with *Under the Net* (1954) and *The Flight from the Enchanter* (1956), novels strongly influenced by Existentialist philosophy in their emphases on contingency and human choice. An analysis of women novelists beginning their careers in the 1950s should also include the innovative and unsettling work of ▷Brigid Brophy and the selfconscious fictions or 'fabulations' of ▷Muriel Spark.

In her essay 'Against Dryness' (1961), Murdoch stated 'we have been left with far too shallow and flimsy an idea of human personality . . . what we require is a renewed sense of the difficulty and complexity of the moral life and the opacity of persons.' Murdoch raises a number of themes: ethics and the novel, the need for a literature of commitment, a renewed concern with character rather than literary form, and a revaluation of 19th-century ▷realism and naturalism. These concerns are shared by a number of post-war women novelists, including ▷Margaret Drabble, ▷Pat Barker, ▷A.S. Byatt, ▷Anita Brookner and, though from a more critical perspective, ▷Doris Lessing. Drabble's fiction, for example, has become progressively more 'naturalistic' over the last two decades (although its depictions of inner-city decay and of human cruelty and violence also belong to a tradition of literary dystopia), attempting to revitalize the 'condition of England' novel. Barker, one of the very few writers to focus on working-class women's experience, uses the form of the 19th-century realist novel in *The Century's Daughter*. Byatt, from her intensively 'literary' and aesthetic perspective, is writing a 'history' of post-war Britain, combining realism and allegory; the first two books, *The Virgin in the Garden* (1979) and *Still Life* (1985), of her projected quartet have appeared to date. Lessing's ▷*The Golden Notebook* (1962), now read as the 'originator' of second-wave (post-1960s) feminist fiction, focuses on crises in ethical and political commitment, interwoven with an interrogation of social and psychological identities and women's experiences, as well as inquiry into whether the novel form can reflect or represent external reality. In her more recent writing, Lessing has turned to ▷science fiction as a way of exploring multiple realities and 'realisms'.

Murdoch's agenda was not one which gave a particular place to 'female experience' or to women's specific predicaments, although these were becoming increasingly central in the work of a number of women novelists in the 1960s, including Drabble, ▷Penelope Mortimer, ▷Nell Dunn, ▷Lynne Reid Banks and ▷Edna O'Brien. Their novels dealt primarily with sexuality, love, marriage and motherhood – including the experience of childbirth – and with the burdens placed on women's emotional and sexual lives. These themes are also central to ▷Fay Weldon's fiction of the late 1960s and 1970s, although she has always used satire and exaggeration to depict the tragicomedy of sexual relations. Women novelists' focus on women and the family must be seen in relation to the intense concern with family life in conservative thought, as well as the politics of the family in left-wing and newly emergent feminist theory. Feminist texts from the 1960s, such as ▷Betty Friedan's ▷ *The Feminine Mystique* (1963), Hannah Gavron's *The Captive Wife* and Juliet Mitchell's 'Women: The Longest Revolution' (1966) are of particular importance here.

Women's fiction writing of the last two decades has followed a number of different paths. Although hard and fast distinctions between 'women's' and 'feminist' novels should be treated with some caution, a number of prominent women writers were profoundly influenced by the upsurge of the women's movement in the late 1960s. ▷Angela Carter, for example, wrote that, 'I can date to that time and to some of those debates and to that sense of heightened awareness of the society around me in the summer of 1968 my own questioning of the nature of my reality as a *woman*.' The members of the Feminist Writers Group – ▷Sara Maitland, ▷Michelene Wandor, Valerie Miner ▷Michèle Roberts and ▷Zöe Fairbairns – who published their early work in the collectively produced ▷ *Tales I Tell My Mother* (1978) – continue to write and to reaffirm their commitments to a socialist feminist politics. The diversity of their ways of writing, however, provides a strong argument against the existence of any single 'feminist aesthetic'. Fairbairns, like Miner, uses the conventions of literary realism, but adopts the genres of popular fiction – the historical saga, the power saga, the literary dystopia – to feminist ends. Maitland is much less interested in ▷social realism, and tends to work with the materials of myth, legend and religion, exploring, in particular, Christianity from a feminist perspective. Both she and Roberts are involved in using, and transforming, the dominant archetypes of women in myth and religion. Their writing has parallels in that of the Indian writer ▷Suniti Namjoshi, who, in her *Feminist Fables*, retells legends and fairytales from a lesbian feminist perspective, and, in ▷ *The Conversations of Cow*, combines images from Hindu mythology with contemporary feminist ideas. The work of ▷Emma Tennant who, in ▷ *The Bad Sister* and *Queen of Stones*, both rewrites classic male narratives and exploits the idea of the unreliability of all narration, is also of relevance in this context.

The feminist strategy of 'revising' traditional stories was both used and questioned by Angela Carter. She wrote in the 1980s of the advantages for oppressed or marginalized groups of rewriting traditional myths, 'myth being more malleable than history'. On the other hand, she also spoke of the need to create new forms and to transform rather than to revise. Even when Carter uses the materials of fairytale, in fact, as in the stories in *The Bloody Chamber* (1979), the rewritings and narrative layerings are so complex that we move beyond the idea of a single 'original' story and its retelling. And, as Elaine Jordan notes of Carter's ▷ *Nights at the Circus* (1984), it 'writes out, erases, a number of myths, including ones by which Angela Carter was once enthralled'. With its multiple narrative voices and levels and its temporal shifts, *Nights at the Circus* has become a classic of ▷postmodernist fiction. ▷Jeanette Winterson shares some of Carter's themes, most notably the transgression of gender boundaries, and a preoccupation with temporal and spatial dislocations and with re-imaginings of the historical past. The postmodern challenge to traditional stories and 'grand narratives' should also be understood in relation to the challenge to traditional race and gender inscriptions in black, Asian and lesbian writing. ▷Barbara Burford, in *The Threshing Floor* (1986), explores attitudes to race and sexuality in her depiction of an English country town. Caribbean-born writers ▷Grace Nichols, ▷Merle Collins and ▷Joan Riley, and Asian-born writers ▷Leena Dhingra and ▷Ravinder Randhawa depict the difficulties of cultural migrations and the painful imagining of generational histories.

The growth of writing by women in the last two decades is inextricably linked to the development of feminist presses from the 1970s onwards, which have 'recovered' earlier women writers, published much new and original fiction, and developed lists in increasingly popular genre fiction, such as feminist ▷detective fiction and science fiction. Some critics and writers have seen the move to genre fiction as something of a retreat from innovative and radical new forms, although, as we have seen, genres can be transformed. The more fundamental issue is that the future of feminist fiction, and developments in women's writing more generally, cannot be thought about in isolation from feminist politics and feminist publishing. The novel has traditionally been the genre most hospitable to women, but it is important that it should not become merely a safe haven.

Poetry

> It is a good time to be a woman poet, perhaps never better. . . . Not yet equal, never to be equal in innumerable things, nevertheless now and lately women in the western world have found an audience readier than ever before to listen to their testimony. Poetry, always more specialized and professionalized (and therefore male) than prose, has slowly followed this trend (Marion Shaw, in *Poetry Review*, vol. 74, no. 3, Sept. 1984, p. 67)

Marion Shaw's comments refer to Virago Press's opening of their lists to women's poetry in the mid-1980s. The relative lateness of this move indicates the secondary role that poetry has played to the novel in feminist publishing, which contrasts with the important place of poetry in the women's movement itself. Women poets' exclusion from mainstream poetry publishing and general anthologies has been very marked; to this day authoritative anthologies and critical surveys appear in which they have little more than token presence. Much work remains to be done, then, in reconstructing and interpreting the history of 20th-century women's poetry.

Like other literary forms, poetry played its part in the early 20th-century women's movement. The suffragette (▷Suffrage) Sylvia Pankhurst's poems about her experiences in prison were published in her *Writ on Cold Slate* (1922). ▷Anna Wickham's relationship to the women's movement is less direct, but her mocking accounts of marriage and of the limitations placed on women's lives express a powerful feminist consciousness. Her near contemporary, ▷Charlotte Mew, often used the mediated form of dramatic monologue to explore the difficulties of relationships between men and women and the conflictual nature of women's duties and desires.

Mew's poetic responses to World War I were included in a recent anthology of World War I women's poetry, which took its title, *Scars upon My Heart* (1981), from a poem by Vera Brittain. The anthology reveals the extent to which standard literary histories have excluded women writers, World War I having been previously seen as an exclusively male affair. Critic Jan Montefiore, in her *Feminism and Poetry* (1987), has pointed out that the entrapment of women 'war poets' in history is at times paralleled by their use of traditional Victorian and Georgian poetic forms, and a 'masculinist' symbolic language and imagery of war. Nevertheless, a number of women poets of this period escaped such literary and ideological traps, or at least worked well within their confines, among them Rose Macaulay, ▷Alice Meynell and ▷Elizabeth Daryush. More devastating, and formally experimental, critiques of war were produced by Mary Borden, whose 1914–1918 poems and sketches were first collected in *The Forbidden Zone* (1929), and Sylvia Townsend Warner, in the later ▷*Opus 7* (1931).

The label 'war poet' is in some ways a misleading one, not only because of the diversity of women poets' experiences of the war, but because many of these poets were writing before and after the war years. The question of labels raises a separate and difficult issue – that of identifying significant 'groupings' for early to mid-20th-century women poets. Of the best-known of these, ▷Frances Cornford, Sylvia Townsend Warner and Stevie Smith wrote poetry that does not obviously fit within a modernist aesthetic as conventionally defined, although their work is often striking and original. ▷Mina Loy was one of the very few British women poets to engage with the European ▷avant-garde; sadly, her work is rarely read today.

▷Edith Sitwell's modernist poetics have always met with a mixed reception. *Façade* (1922), her best-known work, is a verse-sequence set to music by William Walton and described by Sitwell as 'the poetry of childhood overtaken by the technician'. Sitwell, whose aristocratic attitudes often jar, has not been substantially claimed for women's writing as such, although her uses of fantasy, myth and images of childhood, particularly in her early poetry, merit renewed attention. Myth, legend and fantasy are also the stock-in-trade of the less patrician Stevie Smith, whose poetic voice, unlike Sitwell's, is remarkable for its simplicity of diction. Smith's witty and poignant adoptions of improbable perspectives and personae coexist with an insistent focus on the disturbing themes of death and loneliness. Although Smith is a very different poet from Mew, they share a poetic practice of role and gender transformations that is as central to women's writing as more direct and confessional forms.

Sylvia Townsend Warner's poetry of the 1930s and 1940s is a combination of this poetry of projection and displacement into other places and persons; a more direct and passionate love poetry, typically in the form of a dialogue between two (female?) lovers; and political poetry. Warner was one of a number of women writers, inluding ▷Naomi Mitchison, Storm Jameson, Winifred Holtby and ▷Nancy Cunard, to contribute to the newly-formed anti-fascist journal *Left Review* (1934). She drew on her experiences in Spain during the Spanish Civil War in political writings, in her novel *After the Death of Don Juan* (1938), and in a number of poems. Even more strikingly than in the case of World War I writing, the important role played by women in the political and literary life of the 1930s has been belittled or overlooked, and the task of rewriting this history remains to be performed.

World War II returned Edith Sitwell to the poetic scene after a silence of ten years, with a poetry now centred on moral absolutes and human suffering in a framework of religious imagery, as in 'Still Falls the Rain' and the apocalyptic 'Three Poems of the Atomic Bomb'. A spiritual perspective has been a central element in mid-20th-century poetry generally; indeed, with some exceptions (for example, the fine poetry of E.J. Scovell), British women poets of this period tended to turn away from contemporary realities, including the experiences of the war years. ▷Ruth Pitter, ▷Anne Ridler and ▷Kathleen Raine, writing from the 1920s and 1930s, share a love of the natural world, a visionary mysticism and a use of lyrical, traditional poetic forms. ▷Elizabeth Jennings's religious vision is present throughout her poetry. Some of her most powerful poems also explore the realities of mental breakdown, and in *The Mind Has Mountains* (1966), she movingly presented her experiences in a mental hospital. Although neither Raine nor Jennings views the difficulties of the poetic 'vocation', about which both have written, as a gender issue, their experiences, and those of other 20th-century women poets, must raise questions about the particular problems women poets face. Some of these may well result from the isolation of the writer, perceived (rightly or wrongly) to be even greater in the case of poets, and seen to conflict with the demands of family and relationships – often more pressing for women. Another problem for the woman poet must surely be the striking domination of the poetry scene by male poets and critics.

▷Anne Stevenson wrote, in her influential essay 'Writing As a Woman', that 'one way out of the dilemma of the woman/writer is to write about the dilemma itself'. Stevenson, like ▷Sylvia Plath, was a young woman in the 1950s, a period in which there was much at stake for society in defining and redefining 'proper' femininity, after the relative freedom and independence gained by many British and North American women during the war years. Stevenson's poetry sequence ▷*Correspondences* (1974) is her most 'feminist' text, but her relationship to the women's movement is an ambivalent one, and she has indicated her unease with the title of feminist poet.

The label may indeed be one to be wary of, if it suggests a sameness of voice, themes and structures, or an unproblematic unity of women. The black, Scottish-born writer ▷Maud Sulter has written that 'black women have to consider how much a part of the feminist movement they are', and has pointed to the racism of many white feminists. The history of British colonialism in the Caribbean, Asia and Africa means, too, that women of colour write about and within the tensions of both race and gender. Poets such as ▷Grace Nichols in *The Fat Black Woman Poems* and ▷*i is a long memoried woman*, and ▷Amryl Johnson in *Long Road to Nowhere* establish a black woman's perspective on sexism, racism and the history of emigration from the Caribbean. That history makes Nichols, Johnson and many other significant migrant writers including ▷Merle Collins, ▷Meiling Jin, ▷Valerie Bloom and Debjani Chatterjee difficult to locate, and for a fuller treatment the reader should see the essays on English-speaking Caribbean and on the Indian subcontinent. Nonetheless, these poets, with other British born writers such as Barbara Burford, ▷Jackie Kay and ▷Maud Sulter, are centrally involved in challenging and redefining notions of Englishness, literary ▷canon and poetic form.

From a different perspective, Michèle Roberts has written that 'many crass generalisations about feminist poetry still fly about, whereas I find it hard to generalize about a movement which has produced so many, and such varied, poets.' A very partial list of these poets should include ▷Judith Kazantsis, Michelene Wandor, ▷Liz Lochhead, ▷Wendy Mulford, ▷Denise Riley, ▷Carol Ann Duffy and ▷Alison Fell – poets whose work is enormously varied, despite their shared concern with class and gender politics. Wandor, for example, emphasizes that feminist poetry should arise out of women's experiences, while Mulford's and Riley's more experimental work subverts the very notion of stable identities and 'expressive' language. Kazantsis's *The Wicked Queen* (1980) and Lochhead's *The Grimm Sisters* (1981) retell myths, legends and fairy tales as allegories of female experience, in a recasting of traditional stories similar to those to be found in such prose works as Angela Carter's *The Bloody Chamber* (1979) and ▷Sara Maitland's *Telling Tales* (1983).

The poet Fiona Pitt-Kethley has recently gained popularity with her iconoclastic jibes at men, their sexualities and their bodies, with which Pitt-Kethley's poetic persona has much to do on a fairly fleeting basis. Sometimes criticized for her sensationalism, Pitt-Kethley has at least introduced a (to some) welcome note of vulgarity into the poetic scene. Until quite recently, 20th-century women poets were predominantly white, middle-class and Oxbridge-educated, and their tones were muted ones.

The increase in poetic volume (in both senses of the word) attributed to feminism by ▷Carol Rumens, among others, is criticized in her anthology *Making for the Open; The Chatto Book of Post-Feminist Poetry 1964–1984* (1985). Rumens uses a distinction between 'post-feminist' and 'feminist' to separate 'those writers concerned with the "stern art of poetry"' from 'the noisy amateurs proclaiming that women, too, have a voice'. Rumens includes ▷U.A. Fanthorpe, Anne Stevenson, ▷Patricia Beer and Wendy Cope, best-known for her parodies of the literary canon, in her anthology of 'authentic' poets. The inclusion or exclusion of particular names, however, is not necessarily the most important issue. A number of recent feminist anthologies, including ▷*One Foot on the Mountain* (1979), *Bread and Roses* (1982), *A Dangerous Knowing: Four Black Women Poets* (1985), *In the Pink* and ▷*Right of Way*, clearly present the poetic project as a shared and collective one, a way out of the often destructive (for the person, if not for the 'stern art') isolation of an earlier generation of women writers.

The development of small presses, the opening up of feminist presses to poetry, the challenge to the British poetry scene by women of colour and non-British writing in English, and the popularity of poetry in performance, are all aspects of, and crucial elements in, the revitalization of the poetic field.

Drama before 1968

With some exceptions, 20th-century women's drama has been closely linked to feminism as a cultural and political movement. In the early part of the century, a number of women dramatists were at the centre of the suffrage movement, and plays and theatre were used as vehicles and platforms for feminist views. The relationship of women's drama to 'second wave' feminism is more complex, but it is certainly the case that, as Michelene Wandor has argued, 'the arrival of the new feminism in the late 1960s fortuitously combined with a liberalization of theatre practice to pave the way for challenge and experiment' (*Feminist Review*, 18, Nov. 1984, p. 76). As with all theatre, it is never simply a question of the individual dramatist and the textual play, but in recent theatre the collective emphasis is very strong. An adequate history of late 20th-century theatre, in particular, would need to go beyond individual dramatists to embrace women's theatre companies, as well as those involved in transforming the play as text into the play as performance. Unfortunately the scope of this essay does not allow for this analysis.

Early 20th-century women dramatists include Cicely Hamilton, Elizabeth Baker and the US-born ▷Elizabeth Robins. These, and other women actresses and dramatists of the period, were closely involved with such organizations as the Women Writers' Suffrage League (1908), the Actresses' Franchise League (1908) and the Pioneer Players (1911), all of which grew out of more specifically social and political organisations, such as the Pankhursts' Women's Social and Political Union. As in the present-day women's movement, cultural and literary production had a central place; Elizabeth Robins asserted that 'one of the most important, indispensable services to Social Reform would have to be undertaken by the writers.' Drama played an important role here because of its immediacy and its suitability as 'agit-prop'; and short plays were often performed at suffrage meetings.

Women's drama in this period shares a number of themes and preoccupations. Cicely Hamilton's *Diana of Dobson's* (1908) depicts the drudgery endured by overworked shop-girls, and explores, as in her *Marriage as a Trade* (1909), the economic basis of marriage. Elizabeth Baker's *Chains* (1909) dramatizes the 'choice' for women between low-paid and unrewarding work and the ties of matrimony. In these and other plays of the period, the popular image of the ▷New Woman as a sexually and economically free agent is tempered by the women dramatists' presentation of the constraints of lower- and middle-class women's lives. Hamilton's satire *How the Vote Was Won* (1909), co-written with Christopher St John, explores the financial and domestic chaos (for men) that would ensue if women really did act upon the law's assertion that women are dependent upon men.

The period of suffrage drama obviously ended with the winning of the vote. Women's drama between the wars was more conservative, and few women dramatists had any prominence. ▷Clemence Dane (Winifred Ashton) and Gordon Daviot (▷Josephine Tey) wrote plays based on historical characters; for example Daviot's *Richard of Bordeaux* (1933) and Dane's *Will Shakespeare* (1921). ▷Dodie Smith, with *Dear Octopus* (1938) and ▷Enid Bagnold, with *The Chalk Garden* (1955), were among the few women dramatists to achieve success in West End theatre, working within the conventions of naturalistic, domestic drama and the 'well-made' middle-class play.

The work of ▷Shelagh Delaney and ▷Ann Jellicoe in the 1950s brought new class-images and more experimental dramatic forms into the mainstream of theatre production. Delaney's *A Taste of Honey* (1958; first produced by Joan Littlewood's Theatre Workshop) was a landmark in post-war theatre; its setting – Northern and working-class – and its socially marginal characters, were new departures, answering calls for a 'vital theatre'. Ann Jellicoe's work is more experimental than Delaney's, although their themes are linked. Jellicoe's ▷ *The Sport of My Mad Mother* (1956), also first performed in 1958, uses fantasy and myth and, in Wandor's phrase, 'choric violence', to explore male images and fears of the mother archetype. *The Knack* (1962) uses the conventions of absurdist theatre to explore the violence attendant upon male attitudes towards women and the use and abuse of power in sexual relationships. Doris Lessing's *Play with a Tiger* (1962) was also a central play of this period, a dramatization of the preoccupations of her novel *The Golden Notebook*.

Post-1968 theatre

1968 is seen as the watershed year in women's theatre, as in many other areas of cultural and political life. The late 1960s in Britain saw a number of legal reforms relating to sexuality, divorce, abortion and equal pay for women, and a new sense of the political nature of everyday life. A reform of specific import to the theatre was the abolition of the role of the Lord Chancellor as theatre censor. The theatre's (partial) liberation from censorship coincided, or, more accurately, was a part of liberalization in other cultural spheres.

▷Maureen Duffy's *Rites* (1969) was a powerful lead into post-1968 theatre, Set in a women's lavatory, it explores gender roles and the creation of scapegoats (the figure of the lesbian), even within an all-female community. The play also alternates everyday life with mythic narratives. Since the 1970s, women's theatre has grown in strength and prominence. Of the generation of women dramatists beginning their writing careers in the 1970s, ▷Caryl Churchill and ▷Pam Gems are among the best-known. Like other recent feminist drama, Churchill's work has explored the arbitrariness of gender and role definitions, notably in *Light Shining in Buckinghamshire* (1976) and ▷*Cloud Nine* (1978), and the need to reclaim women 'hidden from history', as in her ▷*Top Girls* (1982). *Vinegar Tom* (1976), which Churchill wrote for and with the feminist theatre company Monstrous Regiment, is a play about the demonization of women labelled as witches in the 17th century, the period in which *Light Shining in Buckinghamshire* is also set. By contrast, her recent work *Serious Money* (1987) is a satire on 1980s materialism and 'yuppie' culture.

Pam Gems's *Dusa, Fish, Stas and Vi*, (1975) like Duffy's *Rites*, presents an all-female cast, and explores, through dramatic juxtaposition, women's attempts and failures to find viable ways of living as personal and political beings. In other plays Gems has dramatized the lives of famous women, past and present, as in her *Queen Christina* (1977) and *Piaf* (1973). Gems's career, like Churchill's, has provided important links between mainstream and feminist, alternative theatre, both writers having worked extensively with feminist theatre companies in the 1970s.

Poet, dramatist and critic Michelene Wandor was prominent in 1970s feminist theatre, but since then has been less successful in writing for the stage. She is well-known, however, for her excellent radio plays and dramatizations, and has made a major contribution to theatre criticism, particularly to the knowledge and understanding of gay and women's theatre. Other recent women dramatists who have worked extensively with fringe theatre companies and have also contributed substantially to the development of lesbian theatre in the 1980s include Bryony Lavery, Sarah Daniels, and black dramatists Jacqueline Rudet and Jackie Kay, both of whom have had plays performed by the Theatre of Black Women and the Black Theatre Cooperative, founded in the 1980s.

It would be a misrepresentation of the current state of the theatre, however, to suggest that fringe and feminist theatre is thriving. Much of the influential critical material on women's drama and theatre was based on the situation in the 1970s when, as Wandor records, the Arts Council subsidy to fringe theatre rose from around £7,000 in 1971 to £1,500,000 in 1978. The 1980s, by contrast, saw a series of cuts in public funding for the arts, hitting both metropolitan and regional theatre. This steady impoverishment, coupled with the fragmentation of the women's movement, and hence of a politics of 'collective' work, has made the future of feminist theatre uncertain. Fringe theatre provided a space for women dramatists, actresses and theatre workers of all kinds, and it is now under threat. At the same time, mainstream theatre (which has also suffered substantial cuts) has not proved much more open to women than in a pre-feminist era. The scene is not entirely gloomy – in addition to the dramatists already mentioned, there is some new and exciting work by women dramatists, including that of the increasingly acclaimed Liz Lochhead, Ayshe Raif and ▷Timberlake Wertenbaker.

Theatre is perhaps the most directly political of all the arts, and has provided a crucial forum for feminist ideas. It is also the literary form in which women writers have had to struggle hardest for recognition, and there have been long periods this century in which women dramatists have been almost completely absent from the literary map. It is unlikely that such a situation will recur, but any real growth in women's theatre is dependent upon changes in the political and economic climate. This is not to suggest that creative drama will not be written, but it will not necessarily be performed. Whether 'alternative'/ 'counter-cultural' or 'mainstream' theatre is the more appropriate site for women's drama, and the related issue of a shift from 'feminist' to 'post-feminist' theatre, are questions which continue to demand our attention.

AILBHE SMYTH

6 Ireland

> There was only one small part left to tell: the *terra incognita* of herself, as she knew herself to be, not as men liked to imagine her.
>
> ▷George Egerton, 'Ten Contemporaries'

Irish women have been striving to tell themselves, making stories, songs and poems about their experiences, their realities, their hopes and dreams for a long time. But their work has suffered the same fate as that of women in so many other cultures: lost, abandoned, dismissed, allowed to fall out of print and out of mind, it is still largely unrecorded by literary history. Barely and grudgingly acknowledged in Ireland, Irish women's writing is almost totally unknown abroad – a doubly disturbing irony in a country which prides itself on its literary exports. If Ireland is famous for its writers – the poet and dramatist, W.B. Yeats (1865–1939), the novelist, James Joyce (1882–1941), the dramatist and novelist, Samuel Beckett (1906–1990) and others – it is, or should be, equally infamous for its ferocious denial of political, sexual and cultural selfhood to Irish women.

What has survived and what feminist literary scholars are now discovering in those seemingly empty spaces, is richer and more complicated, less narrowly bounded by male imaginings than we were led to believe. For we were led to believe something of a contradiction: (a) that women had written nothing at all, and (b) that women had written nothing worthy of note. That contradiction, just to confuse matters, is not absolutely false. It is a fact that Irish women (like women elsewhere) have written less than men, but male accounts of their silence omit to mention the strategies used to limit if not to stifle their creative expression, the social, cultural and educational constraints which have largely denied women a public role. When rare women did succeed in breaking the patriarchally imposed vow of silent isolation, their work was – and still is – subjected to contemptuous relegation to the margins of literary life. Just one example: the prolific and intrepid ▷Sydney Owenson's (Lady Morgan) third novel, *The Wild Irish Girl* (1809), was dismissed in a recent survey of Irish literature as 'a work deficient in almost everything a novel should have, except success' (Seamus Deane, *A Short History of Irish Literature*, 1986). The latest and without doubt the most disgracefully damaging insult to the history of Irish women's writing is the scant attention paid to earlier women, and the almost total omission of contemporary women writers from the three-volume *Field Day Anthology of Irish Writing* (1991, edited by Seamus Deane and Andrew Carpenter). The work of feminist publishers (Attic Press is now the only women's press in Ireland) and of women scholars and critics is vital in counteracting the contempt of the 'mainstream' literary establishment, but the literary élite in Ireland remains a powerful and almost wholly male bastion. There is still evidence of considerable resistance to publishing work by women writers, and a tangible reluctance to treat it seriously when it does appear.

Irish women writers, and all Irish women, urgently need a literary history which will restore to them the story of their creative expression. They need to understand why that story has not been told, or told only in fragments. They need to explore the place of women in the literature of Gaelic Ireland, in both aristocratic poetry and the oral tradition. They need to see the connections between late 18th- and 19th-century novelists, such as ▷Maria Edgeworth, Sydney Owenson and ▷Emily Lawless, and modern writers, such as ▷Kate O'Brien, ▷Elizabeth Bowen and ▷Mary Lavin, and how their work in turn has nurtured that of contemporary novelists. Irish women's writing has an honourable history which does not deserve to remain a *terra incognita* (unknown territory).

What Irish women are writing now is increasingly bold and challenging, questioning the myths and metaphors of self-sacrifice and martyrdom, the 'unending domestic urgencies' (as ▷Eithne Strong puts it), which have been used to keep women in submission and silence. Because we know so little of women's resistance to the strategies of dismissal and erasure, present rebellions surge up, unsuspected, as if from nowhere:

> Then it happened. The revolutionary thought made her gasp. It was all a swindle. It was a man's church for a man's world. The clarity of the revelation was astounding. A terrible oppressive sense of betrayal settled on her. She stared at the tabernacle, the flowers, the candles, at the priest in his lace and John Thompson in his best suit. And she knew nothing mattered, nothing mattered. The words began to sing dizzily in her mind, It made her feel weak and a little faint. 'Are you alright?' Mrs Rogers whispered. 'Yes,' she mumbled back. 'You're not that way again?' Mrs Rogers said accusingly. 'No. Not anymore. Once a month. Is it time, little mother?'
>
> Maeve Kelly, *A Life of Her Own* (1976)

As the critic Marie Kane ('Maeve Kelly and New Irish Women's Writing', *Women's Studies International Forum*, Vol. 5, No. 5, 1982) has pointed out, the title of ▷Maeve Kelly's collection of short stories is significant: it is 'a potent formula in Ireland where both Church and State preach to women the stony path of self denial. *A Life of Her Own*, says Maeve Kelly, and her words have all the full resonance of a battle cry.'

It is not, and never has been, easy for any woman to write outside the areas permitted to women, by her writing to break from the traditions and institutions which have limited their freedoms and muted their voices. Irish women have been seduced by the promise of sanctity for those who fulfil their womanly duties, tempted into resignation and compromise by promises of protection and security, and they have not always resisted the comforting ease of sentimentalism and nostalgia. ▷Katharine Tynan's poem, 'Any Woman', assumes with depressing willingness the role women have been trained to play, without question, for so long:

I am the pillars of the house;
The keystone of the arch am I.
Take me away, and roof and wall
Would fall to ruin utterly . . .

There is a whole world of difference between the self-abnegation of a Katharine Tynan (herself, ironically, an extremely successful poet and journalist) and the new-found anger of contemporary Irish women, such as the poet ▷Medbh McGuckian, who refuse the old strictures and exhausted images. But the old weariness is hard to root out; it competes with their rage, creating confusion and uncertainty – although these are necessary foundations of the way forward:

> *Caprice*
> Hand me a hammer
> or an axe
> That I may break and
> that I may wreck
> this house,
> that I may reduce the
> lintel to a doorstep
> and the walls to floors,
> that scraws
> and roof and
> chimney
> may come crashing down
> as a result of my labours . . .
> Pass me the boards and the nails now
> that I may build this other house . . .
>
> But, dear God, I'm tired!
> ▷Caitlín Maude, 'Treall' (trans. P. Riggs)

Sometimes, simply, there is a failure of nerve, fear of their own courage, the legacy of centuries of 'disproportionate silence', as ▷Eavan Boland writes. Hilary, the mother in ▷Mary Beckett's story, 'Heaven', dreams of a life beyond life, where she will have perfect peace to be at one with herself:

> Now and again, though, she did catch a distant glimpse of calm corridors and vaulted roofs all soundless and it gave her a feeling of great sweetness in anticipation.

The challenge, which Hilary, too worn out and worn down, does not – cannot – take up, is to move beyond anticipation into a new terrain of the imagination. The dream is good, but the territory must be named and explored. Hilary needs the daughters of the next generation to know of her exhaustion and sense of entrapment. She needs them to move her beyond acceptance of the realities of this (woman's) life and vague dreams of something more. She depends upon them to create real spaces where women can redefine their relation to society, to culture and to history.

Irish women still undoubtedly suffer material, economic and physical disadvantages they can do little to control: approximately one-third of the population of Ireland today are living in poverty – more than half of them women. Over two-thirds of married women in Ireland do not work outside the home. Divorce is constitutionally prohibited. Contraception was legalized in the 1980s, but is still difficult to obtain in many parts of rural Ireland. Abortion is a criminal offence, and, as a consequence of a referendum in 1983, women are effectively denied access to any information about abortion.

'Women', 'choice' and 'freedom' are still diametrically opposite terms in a society which remains heavily dominated by the puritanical ideology and misogynistic values of the

Catholic Church. It is still extraordinarily difficult for Irish women to write about their bodies, about physical pleasure, and about sexuality especially. There appears to be no readily available language – or what there is has been used against them, used to construct them into passively malleable objects. It is hard to trust feelings they have never been allowed to name, difficult to name desires they have never been allowed to have. There is so much that is still secret.

> Alone in the room
> with the statue of Venus
> I couldn't resist
> cupping her breast
>
> It was cool
> and heavy in my hand
> like an apple.
>
> ▷Paula Meehan, 'Fruit'

Irish women do reach out to find the words, the new syntax that will enable them to become subjects for themselves. 'An Ungrammatical Poem' by ▷Mary Dorcey, one of the very few Irish writers to write openly of lesbian sexuality, maps out a hitherto forbidden space:

> And you,
> the rain on our skin,
> the sun beating,
> you – sweet, guileful sister
> of pleasure,
> you said in my ear
>
> my mind turning
> my body in your hands
> turning,
> you said,
> say my name
> when you come
>
> and I did . . .

Censorship remains a live issue in Ireland in the 1990s: censorship of information, censorship of sexuality, inexorable censorship of women themselves. ▷Edna O'Brien, whose novels were consistently banned in the 1960s on grounds of sexual immorality and, more vaguely but no doubt as significantly, on the basis that they were a betrayal of 'Irish womanhood', believes that censorship is a continuing threat: 'Not as many books are now banned, but we have to take into account the prevailing social climate. Banning is only the tip of the iceberg. Keeping our psyches closed is the main bogey' (Edna O'Brien, quoted in Julia Carlson, *Banned in Ireland: Censorship and the Irish Writer*, 1990). The task of going against the grain, of rowing against the prevailing tide to open up their own psyches requires great clarity of vision and the ability to withstand considerable pain. Perhaps it is the tenacity in Ireland of what Mary Dorcey has called 'the finger-wagging patriarchy' (Mary Dorcey, quoted in Nicci Gerrard, *Into the Mainstream: How Feminism has Changed Women's Writing*, 1989) that is most striking and most difficult for Irish women writers. There is much history to be rewritten before women can celebrate their freedoms.

For in Ireland, history is inescapable and women's writing continues to be burdened with the remnants of their bitter colonial past. 'Irishness' remains an overwhelming question for Irish women and men, obsessively explored. What does it mean? What path can they negotiate between two cultures, two languages, two traditions? How are they marked by nationality? Are those marks the same for all of them, born on the same soil but of differing descent? Catholic and Protestant, North and South, 'Gaelic Irish', 'Anglo-Irish': immeasurable complexities – unanswerable questions.

> It is impossible to draw Ireland as she now is in a book of fiction – realities are too strong, party passions too violent to bear to see or care to look at their faces in the looking-glass.
>
> Maria Edgeworth (quoted in J.M. Calahan, *The Irish Novel*, 1988, p. 24)

The pioneering Anglo-Irish novelist Maria Edgeworth wrote these words in 1817, but they could just as well be written today. The passions run as strongly and the problems appear as insoluble now as they did then. But they are not to be evaded, and Maria Edgeworth confronted the impossibility of 'Ireland' as directly as she knew how, which was more than many.

The idea of Ireland is especially complicated for women because colonized Ireland has conventionally been represented as a woman – a weak, vanquished victim. When a woman looks in the glass of Ireland she sees inextricably reflected there her own image and that of her poor, sorry country. She symbolizes 'Ireland' – and Ireland stands for 'Woman'. That is how 'men like to imagine her' and she has no space, no voice, no right to imagine herself differently – or even to imagine at all. As symbol, 'woman' is allowed no history, no story, no capacity for change – she is a given. Her particularity is overwhelmed by the primary demands of the nation. To be free, therefore, Irish women must find some way of extricating themselves from the double burden of patriarchy and colonization, whether consciously identified or not. But how can this be done? There is no one, easy answer. An important part of what Irish women writers are doing now is bound up with finding new ways of being a woman without denying 'Irishness', however they (variously) decide to define it. As Moya Roddy, an Irish woman living in England, puts it:

> Twenty two years in Ireland, eleven in England. Two languages. Irish English and English English. Both with completely different sets of assumptions, historical realities, attitudes, touchstones. When I was growing up they used to say 'The best English is spoken in Dublin.' I never knew what they meant. I was always warned by my parents 'not to speak like Dublin kids'. Coming from the country they had an inbuilt suspicion of everything the city offered. Coming to London I had the same. Now I look for the gaps between the two languages in order to escape. (Moya Roddy, quoted in Gail Chester, and Sigrid Nielsen (eds), *In Other Words: Writing as a Feminist*, 1987)

For ▷Nuala Ní Dhomhnaill, Irish is the 'language of the Mothers' (Nuala Ní Dhomhnaill, in conversation with Michael Cronin, *Graph: Irish Literary Review*, No. 1, 1986) because it was deprived of status after the collapse of Gaelic Ireland at the end of the 17th century. Paradoxically, perhaps, it provides a freer, less occupied space for women to confront their fears and reinvent themselves:

> I thought I saw the hills were moving
> like a giantess with swaying breasts
> and that she was about to arise and gobble me up.
>
> Nuala Ní Dhomhnaill, 'Cailleach' ('The Hag')
> (trans. N. Ní Dhomhnaill)

Perhaps it is easier for Irish women to tell themselves to themselves in 'forms and material which appear to offer a way out of . . . history', as critic Gerardine Meaney suggests, which may explain why poetry is an unusually strong force in contemporary Irish women's writing. It is true that centuries of colonization have left their marks of diffidence and fear, and the sense of bleak dispossession is often unbearably strong in Irish women's writing. The question of identity and its intricate historical complexities is a constant theme: for some an undertow, for others a source of anguish or a dilemma which must be resolved. One way and another, contemporary Irish women writers are gradually making new meanings through their insistent exploration of areas of experience denied significance by history and culture, freeing Irish women from the stranglehold of symbols and secrecy, discovering the *terra incognita* of themselves.

▷Gregory, Lady Augusta

Bib: Boland, Eavan, *A Kind of Scar: The Woman Poet in a National Tradition*; Bourke, Angela, 'The Irish Traditional Lament and the Grieving Process', *Women's Studies International Forum*, Vol. 11, No. 4 (1988); Bourke, Angela, 'Performing – Not Writing', *Graph* 11 (1991); Calahan, James M., *The Irish Novel: A Critical History*; Deane, Seamus, *A Short History of Irish Literature*; Donognue, Emma, 'Finding Yourself in a Bookshop (Irish Lesbian Fiction)', *Graph* 10 (1991); Kane, Marie, 'Maeve Kelly and New Irish Women's Writing', *Women's Studies International Forum*, Vol. 5, No. 5 (1982); Kelly, A.A. (ed.), *Pillars of the House: An Anthology of Verse by Irish Women from 1690 to the Present*; Madden Simpson, Janet, *Woman's Part: An Anthology of Short Fiction By and About Irish Women 1890–1960*; Meaney, Gerardine, *Sex and Nation: Women in Irish Culture and Politics*, and 'History Gasps: Myth in the Poetry of Eilean Ni Chuilleanain and Sara Berkeley', *Studies in Contemporary Irish Literature*, Vol. 2 (1991); Meehan, Paula, *The Man Who Was Marked by Winter*; Ní Chuilleanain, Eilean (ed.), *Irish Women: Image and Achievement*; O'Brien Johnson, Toni and Cairns, David (eds), *Gender in Irish Writing*; Smyth, Ailbhe, 'The Contemporary Irish Women's Movement', *Women's Studies International Forum*, Vol. 11, No. 4 (1988), and (ed.), *Wildish Things: An Anthology of New Irish Women's Writing*; Ward, Margaret, *The Missing Sex: Putting Women into Irish History*; Weekes, Ann Owens, *Irish Women Writers: An Uncharted Tradition*.

ELIZABETH WOODROUGH

France: the Middle Ages to 1700   7

A question of identity

Compiling an account of the earliest women to write in French is rather like trying to judge the size of an iceberg from the tip that lies above the surface. The deliberate selection of writers by gender merely exaggerates the difficulties usually associated with locating new research data for the period before the printing press was introduced in France in 1470, some six years earlier than in England. Under the Capetians and the Valois, as under the first of the Bourbon kings, the majority of French women did not and could not write, and very few of the remarkable minority who did showed an open commitment. Even during the Renaissance and the 17th century, women hardly dared to admit to having written anything other than letters, let alone to record their dealings with publishers, sign their work, or allow their names to be printed on the title-page of books. In response to a dual prejudice against their sex and the very process of creative and professional writing, the first French women poets, novelists and memoir-writers, many of whom were either of aristocratic birth or otherwise connected to court circles, developed a highly deliberate form of obscurity. Where public approval and princely praise led the principal poets of the ▷*Pléiade* and the great poet-dramatists of the Age of Richelieu and the reign of Louis XIV to wish to rival the ancients in their search for fame and immortality, most women writers remained in a private world. The defensive mechanisms of anonymity and restricted circulation, instinctive to any writer under attack, remained central to the French woman writer's code of practice from the Middle Ages to the end of the 17th century.

This secretive sisterhood has therefore succeeded in maintaining a greater distance between themselves and the written text than almost any other group of early writers. Vital elements of information will probably never now be brought to light concerning the names, dates, personal circumstances, education, influences, associations and affinities of many of the early French women writers included in this volume. Since they were much underestimated at the time, the impact and influence of the first generations of women's writing are not easy to assess after so many centuries of critical neglect or deliberate repression.

As a result of the continuing need for secrecy, not even the sex of the women who managed to write during the period 1100 to 1700 against all the odds can always be taken for granted. Scholars are even now questioning how many of the twenty or so early poets with a female voice or name of whom we have trace in southern France in the 12th and 13th centuries actually were women. Now referred to as ▷ *trobairitz*, they include in their number the names of three ladies of the highest aristocracy: the ▷Comtesse de Die, the ▷Comtesse de Proensa and ▷Maria de Ventadorn. Yet it cannot be ruled out that some of the others engaged in a form of debate (poetic 'jousting matches' called *tensos*) with other real or fictitious male and female poets were perhaps only male troubadours experimenting with playful linguistic disguise.

In other cases, too, biographical information proves more difficult to ascertain where the poet has a woman's name. We do not yet know, and may never know, the exact identity or identities of the poet who became known as ▷Marie de France, who wrote lays and fables in French at the English court of Henry II (1133–1189) around the time of the earliest *trobairitz*. The first woman to write in a European vernacular, she was clearly preoccupied with her own poetic identity, but she chose to call herself by the most revered and least distinctive of French Christian names: '*Marie ai num, si sui de France*' ('Marie is my name and I come from France'). Her verses reveal few other clues. Scholars continue to debate the question of which of the many celebrated Maries associated with both England and France in the late 12th century she may have been. Dismissing Marie de Champagne, daughter of Eleanor of Aquitaine (1122–1204) and patroness of the poet Chrétien de Troyes (c 1135–c 1190); ▷Mary, Countess of Boulogne (?1154–?); Marie, Abbess of Shaftesbury in Dorset (fl 1181–1215); and Marie, Abbess of Reading, for one reason or another, Glyn Burgess, for instance, regards Marie (1140/50–?), daughter of Waleran de Meulan, who held lands in Normandy and southern England, as one of the more likely candidates (*The Lais of Marie de France*, 1986). It seems that we may rule out the theory that the real Marie de France was an anonymous male scribe at court, an interesting reflection of the poet's own fear that, with all the secrecy surrounding her work, some clerk might well come along after her and lay claim to it.

We can deduce more about the life of the late medieval poet and moralist ▷Christine de Pisan than about many later writers of her sex, from the semi-autobiographical *Avision-Christine* (1405) and other sources, though again the information is relatively thin. After centuries of neglect and repeated public 'discoveries', Pisan's work has in the past few years finally joined the pantheon, though much of her vast corpus of works remains unedited. Symbol of the struggle and the achievement of an entire sex, she is still perhaps better-known and respected elsewhere in Europe and the USA than in France.

The persistent air of mystery and deliberate mystification surrounding anything written by women also complicates the compilation of biographical entries for the later period. It has been suggested, for instance, that the name of ▷Jeanne Flore, under which two collections of passionate and erotic tales were published in Lyon between 1530 and 1540, is just another example of the use of a female name as a cover by a male writer who did not wish to be directly associated with libidinous accounts. However, other factors within the two surviving texts which bear this name seem not to support this argument. Their fragmentary form serves as yet another tantalizing reminder of all the other female-authored texts written in French that have been repressed or destroyed down the ages, whether through misplaced modesty, male censorship or sheer carelessness.

▷Louise Labé, the most celebrated of all the society of 16th-century Lyon women poets, was among the most exceptional in her attitude to every aspect of the writing process, signing and even publishing her own brief poetic *Euvres* (*Works*) in the mid-1550s. Yet even *la belle cordière* ('the beautiful ropemaker') remains something of an enigma. The author of one of the latest studies, *Louise Labé: Renaissance Poet and Feminist* (1990), Keith Cameron, candidly admits:

> Almost as much factual mystery as legendary fantasy surrounds the life of Louise Labé. We know she existed; her published work bears witness to her activity as a poet; legal documents record her marriage; the poet who loved her inscribed the fact in his poems; contemporary and later references in books and papers demonstrate her 'celebrity' during and after her life. Uncertainty, however, enshrouds the actual date of her birth, the nature of her education and her actual life style. Since her death, would-be biographers and scholars have argued frequently about the evidence and have often enhanced what little there is.

Conjecture and ignorance were fertile ground for scandalous gossip and slander, particularly where a woman who dared to write for a public audience was concerned. The ropemaker-poet, renowned for her beauty, and described as chaste, virtuous and erudite, was soon the subject of scurrilous songs, denounced by the religious reformer Jean Calvin (1509–1564) as a *plebeia meretrix* (common prostitute), and by many others as a courtesan. For consorting openly with men other than her old husband, dressing on occasion as a man, and notably for writing as one, Captain Labé (as she was also known) had to pay the full price of public attention by gratifying the general expectation that women's reading and writing of love poetry and was a sign of sexual misbehaviour.

When we progress to the 17th century, access to biographical facts and details of publication becomes much easier, but areas of uncertainty persist. We know almost all there is to know, for instance, about the private life of the *Pucelle du Marais* (the Virgin of the Marais), ▷Madeleine de Scudéry, the most prolific novelist of the period and among the least physically attractive, who was said to 'sweat ink through every pore' ('*suer l'encre par tous ses pores*'). It has never been established with certainty, however, what proportion of the early novels with which she is associated she wrote herself. Right up to the death of her jealous and cantankerous brother Georges, she continued to allow his name to stand for her own on the title-pages of each of the volumes of the enormous novels that they had begun together but finished apart. Neither has the division of labour been satisfactorily resolved in the case of ▷*La Princesse de Clèves* (*The Princess of Cleves*), the most important early woman's text to be published in French. ▷Madame de Lafayette always denied authorship. References in contemporary correspondence suggest that much of this novel – which freely adapts and abridges passages taken from contemporary and near-contemporary histories, memoirs and books of ceremonial – should be more accurately attributed to the distinguished editorial board of male friends and admirers to whom she submitted parts of all her works for correction and approval.

The 'Querelle des Femmes'

Early modern France may be regarded as one of the nations of Europe where women were kept most subordinate. The inferiority of woman, described as the 'mutilated and imperfect male' ('*masle mutilé et imparfaict*'), was established by law and reinforced by countless anti-feminist tracts, theological teachings and medical treatises, abounding in unflattering epithets like 'divine sinner' ('*divine pécheresse*') and 'domestic devil' ('*diable domestique*'). Apart from a '*parenthèse dorée*' or 'golden interlude' in Provence between 1180 and 1230 when the *trobairitz* were most productive, women were singularly oppressed in every domain right up to the end of the 17th century. Throughout the early period, women were branded by men as socially and sexually inferior, and positively pernicious. It was the '*Querelle de la Rose*' ('The Quarrel of the Rose'), arising from Christine de Pisan's letters (*Le Dit de la Rose, A Commentary on the Rose*) attacking the misogyny of Jean de Meung's 13th-century continuation of the *Roman de la Rose (Romance of the Rose)*, immensely popular among male readers, which opened up the 'The Women's Question' or '*Querelle des Femmes*' and turned it into a real debate. To counter her arguments, hundreds of male authors joined the other side. François Rabelais (c 1483–1553) was a principal figure in the development of the male view: his *Tiers Livre* (1546) (*Third Book*) aired most of the arguments against women, though the intention, as often with 16th-century anti-feminism, was humorous, and seems to have been to satirize women's detractors as much as women themselves.

Very few men wrote anything in direct defence of women before the 17th century, and even the most ardent of the original Gallic champions of the woman's cause never seemed to think to make reference to their literary potential or achievement. In a rare Renaissance treatise written on behalf of 'the monstrous regiment of women' and of the occasional male secretary generous enough to take up his pen to portray the 'Singular qualities of the rather imperfectly known feminine sex' ('*Singulieres Qualitez de l'assez mal connue Condition femenine*'), the bizarre François de Billon saw fit to remind his reader of the basic grammatical point that the word for pen in French (*plume*) is feminine in gender, 'even if it is not of the same sex'. This obscure pen-pusher, whose treatise attacked Rabelais for his satire on women, suspected no direct connection between that sex and writing. On the subject of Billon's own talents as a writer, the princesses of France, whose patronage he had sought for his work, seem to have been more than content to observe the ancient sexist adage, *mulieres maxime decet silentium et taciturnas* (absolute silence is most becoming in women).

A number of aristocratic women in Renaissance France had already assumed for themselves what Billon called 'the voice of the pen' ('*la voix de la plume*'), recognizing it as the key to their emancipation. The hours which such women were used to spending in leisure pursuits, or devoted to tapestry and to the art of conversation – through which women were gradually becoming recognized as a civilizing force – were increasingly otherwise occupied by the great Renaissance women of letters. The decorous virtue of silence, lauded by men to deprive women of the power that comes from speech, ironically also offered the *fragilior sexus* or 'weaker sex' an ideal opportunity to develop their natural talent for a less ephemeral form of communication, provided that they kept as quiet as possible about their role in the end product.

Making their mark in a man's world

The dialectical opposition in early women's writing in France between fear of identification and desire for liberation through a literature of their own is closely related to what we may now call 'the sexual textual politics' of the era, which made women the subject of intense debate and placed all other avenues to power totally beyond their reach. Women were only marginally more emancipated during the so-called 'heroic age' of Marie de Medici (1573–1642), Louis XIII (1601–1643) and Anne of Austria (1601–1666), when they momentarily and accidentally took centre stage in politics and society following the untimely deaths of successive kings. Rigid observance of the ancient Salic law excluding females from the the inheritance of land and property, associated with the denial in France of their right of succession to the throne – an embodiment of the male fear of sharing any of their exclusive privileges on equal terms with the opposite sex – held women back throughout the *Ancien Régime*. One of the first French women to have enjoyed a degree of autonomous political power, '*la très illustre Princesse, Madame Marguerite de France, soeur unique du Roy François Ier*' ('the very illustrious Princess, Madame Marguerite of France, only sister of King François I'), otherwise known as ▷Marguerite de Navarre and often portrayed as a modern Pallas Athene, might have enjoyed a great deal more authority, as her mother, ▷Louise de Savoie, is supposed to have observed on occasion. In his anecdotal *Dames illustres* (*Illustrious Ladies*), Brantôme (c 1540–1614) recounts how the Queen Mother was wont to muse on what might have been '*si par abolition de la loy salique, le royaume venoit à ma fille par son juste droict, comme aussy d'autres royaumes tumbent en quenouille*' ('had the kingdom come to my daughter as by right through the abolition of the Salic law, as other kingdoms pass to the female line'). Special legislation had to be enacted on each of the three occasions between the reigns of Henri II (1519–1559) and Louis XIV (1638–1715) when the king's widow was called upon to become regent to rescue France from a constitutional crisis. Whatever power ▷Catherine de Medici and the two subsequent queens of France may have wielded at different points in their careers as wives, mothers and regents, and however much other women of the period may have indirectly influenced the course of history, most women at the French court – among the most patriarchal in all Europe – were held in suspended animation. The silent majority of their sex were kept in a state of subservience in both the public domain and the private household.

This almost universal powerlessness could again be said, ironically, to have increased the time and energy which the socially and intellectually privileged minority of females were able to devote to one of the few independent activities that could never be totally denied them by men, however virulently it was condemned by those who claimed it did not become their sex. Writing, with a high degree of secrecy or protection, allowed women to respond to their detractors and to rewrite the history of women's experience in love and marriage. Feminism *avant la lettre* was certainly a factor in most works by women, but its social and political dimensions should not be exaggerated. The priority of women writers was to claim their right to write, not to challenge the divine right of kings. Most women writers were associated with male-dominated courts, and many were related to men of power and influence or to male writers, and directly inspired by them. Very few might be said to have written with what the critic ▷Hélène Cixous has called the 'white ink' of their mothers. The main subject of their works was their relationship with men. It should also be noted here that many of the brief entries on early French women writers relate to women who never married, were widowed early, were unhappily married or otherwise found themselves in an irregular marital situation.

It has recently been argued by eminent medieval scholars that women's motivation for writing was emotional rather than literary or didactic. Yet, already at the time of transition from oral to literary cultures, women seem to have been concerned with playing the game of verbal power for its own sake rather than simply trying to exorcize their emotions by writing about them. Several *trobairitz* already display a preoccupation with speech and the act of poetic composition. Caught in a vicious circle of unrequited love, they hope at least to gain a degree of mastery over the unfaithful men who have made them suffer to the point of making written supplication in verse. The *trobairitz* imitated and undermined the male rhetoric of courtly love, where the poet venerates his lady. The early economic development of southern France, the absence of husbands at the Crusades, and the temporary restoration of the woman's right to inherit are among the recognized factors encouraging women to compose poetry themselves in the early Middle Ages. Béatrice de Die, the boldest and most 'volcanic' of the abandoned women who erupted into verse, often accompanied by music, sought a never-ending audience for her trials:

> Estat ai en conssirer
> per un cavallier qu'ai agut
> E voill sia totz temps saubut
> Cum eu l'ai amat a sobrier
> Ara vei qu'ieu sui traida
> Quar eu no li donei m'amor

(I have been extremely troubled / By a knight who once was mine / And I want it to be known for all time / That I had an excess of love for him. / Now I find myself betrayed / Was it because I did not love him enough?')

The 13th-century *trobairitz*, ▷Na Castelloza, was both conscious of the unconventionality of her position as woman composer and prepared to defend it. In one of four extant poems, she accused herself:

Mout aurei mes mal usatge
A las autras amairitz
C'hom sol trametre mesatge,
E motz triaz et chauzitz

(Many times shall I have set a very bad example / To other women in love / It is the man who usually transmits the message / And carefully selected words.)

In another, Castelloza stated her intention to plead her own cause with her knight, 'though everyone says that it is improper for a lady to do so, and make him so long a sermon all the time', simply because it pleases her.

It is difficult not to be impressed, too, by the highly developed literary vocation of the mysterious Marie de France. The lays and fables, probably written at the English court around the time of the first *trobairitz*, reveal that she was fully conscious of her duty to her profession to make public display of her knowledge and talent, if not her precise identity. The prologue to her twelve brief *Lais* (*Lays*) begins:

Ki deus a duné escience
e de parler bon'eloquence
ne s'en deit taisir
ainz se deit voluntiers mustrer

(Those to whom God has given knowledge / and great eloquence in speech / owe it to themselves not to keep quiet / They should make it public of their own free will).

Marie de France acknowledged the importance of retelling these lays (oral tales in the Celtic tradition) and the fables (based on Latin and English translations of the Greek fables of Aesop from the 6th century BC) in written French 'according to the letter' ('*selonc la letre et l'escriture*'). To accomplish this feat, she never shirked the labour of working late into the night, a time which has always particularly favoured the writer's desire for secrecy. We are told that Marie de France's rhymes were loved everywhere, and therefore they were often retold, but we know little enough about their circulation in manuscript form. They gave a new feminine perspective to musical lays already popular at the English court, and have been described as a biography of the 'unhappily married woman' ('*la mal mariée*'), but marriage remains an ideal. Marie de France's view of love inside and outside marriage can best be summarized by the formula, '*Amur n'est pruz se n'est egals*', ('Love is only honourable between equals'), which again challenges the ideal of courtly love. It is through telling their tale in this way that women can rise above their situation and represent a different social order. Conscious of her role as writer, Marie notes at the beginning or end of each lay, and sometimes in both places, that it is she who is responsible for giving form to the experiences related therein. With one exception, all the *Lais* are narrated by female characters, and several of her heroines also mirror Marie's attempt to transform unhappy experience into narrative by writing down their experiences.

Women were among the first to realize the potential of the invention of the printing press. The intensely personal and committed late medieval lyric poet and prose writer, Christine de Pisan, exhibited a new kind of professionalism, which was an example to both men and women writers. Faced with destitution, following the untimely death of the husband she adored, she needed the financial reward which writing at court could bring to provide for herself and her three children. She described herself in one of her most famous poems, a ballade entitled 'Solitude', where every line except the one which she addresses to her prince, Charles V (1337–1380), begins with the words '*Seulette sui*' ('A woman alone I am'), thus: '*Seulette sui de tout deuil menaciée*' ('A woman alone I am and under the shadow of mourning'). We know that she often wrote for money, and have records of occasional payments by Jean Sans Peur (Duke of Burgundy, died 1419), the king and others. She went further than most writers of either sex, acting virtually as her own editor, supervising the copying and illustration of her manuscripts and dedicating them to a range of wealthy patrons.

Such details are extremely valuable for the history of the book, but they are more precious still for the history of her sex. Here at the dawn of the modern age is a professional woman writer of irreproachable conduct, producing erudite poetry and prose for the élite, who makes women central to social, cultural and literary history. An 'anti-anti-feminist', rather than a feminist in the modern sense, Pisan anticipates the development of French feminism up to the present day in many exciting ways. Almost 700 years before the present volume, Pisan made an initial attempt at a universal history of virtuous women, to support her argument. In her thick-walled *Cité des Dames* (*City of Ladies*), she brought all her own erudition to bear to undermine the major masculine myths and demonstrate the intellectual capacity of her sex. She argues, for instance:

CONTRE CEUX QUI DISENT QU'IL N'EST PAS BON QUE FEMMES
APPRENNENT LETTRES
Je me merveille trop fort de l'opinion d'aucuns hommes, qui disent qu'ils ne voudraient point que leurs filles ou femmes ou parentes apprissent sciences et que leurs moeurs en empireraient. Par ce peux-tu bien voir que toutes opinions d'hommes ne sont pas fondées sur raison, et que ceux ont tort: car il ne doit mie estre présumé que de savoir les sciences morales, et qui enseignent les vertus, les moeurs en doivent empirer, ains n'est point de doutes qu'elles s'en amendent et anoblissent.

(AGAINST THOSE WHO SAY THAT IT IS NOT RIGHT FOR WOMEN TO STUDY
I am particularly amazed at the view which some men hold who would prevent their daughters, wives or female relations from learning because they would be corrupted by it. This certainly shows you that not all views held by men are rational, and that these men are wrong: for there is not the least reason for presuming that knowledge of the moral sciences which teach virtue necessarily corrupts, as there is no doubt that they in fact correct and ennoble a person's behaviour.)

Pisan's work offers some of the first tangible proof of her personal belief that '*se femmes eussent les livres fait / Je sçay de vray qu'autrement fut de faire / Car bien sceuvent qu'a tort sont encoulpées*' ('if women had written the books / I know for a fact that it would have been done quite differently, / for they are very often wrongly accused in them').

The Renaissance marks the transition in women's writing from poetic regional myths to the emergent novel forms where women would take an early advantage. Extant examples of the light verse of the 15th-century women court poets of northern France are rarer even than the *cansos* (verses) of the *trobairitz*. Many names of 16th-century women court poets are known to us, but the biographical information is incomplete more often than not. The principal texts of this period are four prose narratives relating women's experience in love: ▷Hélisenne de Crenne's *Les Angoisses douloureuses qui procedent d'amours* (1538) (*The Painful Anxieties Which Proceed from Love*) Jeanne Flore's *Les Comptes amoureux* (*Tales of Love*) and *Pugnition de l'Amour contempné* (1530–1540) (*Punishment of Despised Love*) and ▷Marguerite de Navarre's ▷*Heptaméron* (1558–9), all written in the middle of the 16th century. Hélisenne de Crenne's *Angoisses* is one of the first examples in French of an epistolary novel and an autobiographical journal. It also prefigures, among many other novels, *La Princesse de Clèves* (*The Princess of Cleves*) with its dilemma of a young married woman's repression of illicit passion. In her novel, Hélisenne de Crenne champions the rights of an entire sex as both writers and readers (*'lisantes'*), and of battered wives everywhere. Encarcerated in a tower by her violent husband, the heroine decides 'to gather up her strength' (*'reprendre [ses] forces'*) and write out her 'anxieties' (*angoisses*), just as the author had herself rewritten her text in captivity after her husband had burned the first draft.

The other narratives in this group are to a large extent feminine versions of the 'hundred short stories by Boccaccio, recently translated from the Italian into French' (*'[les] cent nouvelles de Jan Bocace, nouvellement traduites d'italian en françoys'*). The seven extant tales of Jeanne Flore and the 72 which Marguerite de Navarre completed before her death have been accused in the past of being mediocre adaptations, on occasion quite shocking in their immorality. Such deprecatory judgements underestimate the true originality of the *Heptaméron*, which owes more to the form of the *Decameron* (1352) by the Italian writer Boccaccio (1313–1375), and in particular the Boccaccian *société conteuse*, or narrative frame of tale-tellers, than to the content of individual tales. Marguerite de Navarre's adoption and adaptation so early in the history of French literature of a formal structure, fundamental to the evolution of almost all fiction up to 1700, makes this a singularly important work. Dominated by the figure of Parlemente, who represents the author, the *société conteuse* could henceforth be used by women in their own name. Among so many diverse examples of lovers' adventures inside and outside marriage in the *Heptaméron*, showing that men are usually as much, if not more, to blame than women, one isolated case must here suffice to illustrate the persistence of the motif of reading and writing as a form of defence, the woman writer's self-reflexive emphasis which links almost all the texts under consideration in this chapter. Towards the end of the *Heptaméron*, 'very great praise' (*'bien grande louange'*) is accorded to Robertval's unnamed wife, who, like Marguerite de Navarre herself, 'spent her time reading, and in meditation, praying and preaching' (*'passoit son tems en lectures, contemplations, prieres et oraisons'*). She also chose to devote herself to teaching others of her sex 'to read and write, determining to devote the rest of her life to this honest profession' (*'à lire et à escrire [détermina] à cet honneste metier là gagner le surplus de sa vie'*).

Brantôme offers a valuable and engaging record of the king's elder sister, so erudite that she burned to learn as much grammar as it was possible to know. He relates how she would write down the tales of the *Heptaméron* in the privacy of her litter, as his own grandmother held her writing tablet steady:

> *Elle composa toutes ses Nouvelles, la pluspart dans sa litière en allant par pays, car elle avoit de plus graves occupations estant retirée. Je l'ay ouy ainsi conter à ma grand-mère qui alloit toujours avecques elle dans la lictière . . . et luy tenoit l'escritoire dont elle escripvoit, et les mettoit par escrit aussy habilement ou plus que si on luy eust dicté.*

> (She composed all her own stories, for the most part in her litter as she travelled through the country, for she had more serious occupations when she retired. I have heard my grandmother tell how she always accompanied her everywhere in her litter . . . and held her writing-tablet for her, and how the queen wrote them down as easily as if they had been dictated to her.)

He tells us too that the Queen Mother and others at the court of François I (1494–1547) tried to do likewise, but, recognizing the inferiority of their efforts, threw them on the fire 'and refused to let them see the light of day any more'. This can be taken as further anecdotal evidence that more women wrote than we know, and that they wrote more than we know. All publications of the tremendously popular *Heptaméron* were posthumous, as so often with women's writing. The notorious first edition concealed the author's name and almost completely changed the form, but the true order and spirit of Marguerite's original manuscript was promptly restored the following year at the request of her indignant daughter, ▷Jeanne III d'Albret.

The new Muses of Lyon (Muses Lionnoizes)

Women's traditional role in poetry was to inspire by physical beauty and metaphysical charm. The ancient ▷Muses symbolized the ability of the 'weaker sex' to empower the male poet with the gift of composition. Their feminity was so exciting for the poet because allusion to his Muse allowed him to embrace, in this one word, love, the loved one, all the classical tradition of poetry and his own poetic genius, with no trace of immodesty; but could their mythical beauty equally inspire female poets, without arousing suspicions of lesbian love? The question has been shown to have preoccupied the 'Ladies of Lyon' ('*Dames Lionnoizes*'), who took advantage of the status of their native city in the mid-16th century as the centre of printing in France and the confluence of rivers and routes bringing Italian ▷humanism, neoplatonism and respect for women and their developing intellect to France. ▷Pernette du Guillet, supposedly the inspiration for Maurice Scève's (1501–c 1560) famous poem in 440 ten-syllable lines (*dizains*) entitled '*Délie, objet de plus haute vertu*' (1544) ('Delia, Object of the Highest Virtue'), is a particularly interesting example of the paradoxical duality of the Muse who also writes poetry. There is a certain strain in the *Rymes* and *Elegies* in which she was forced to reinterpret the ▷Petrarchan conventions. Du Guillet's poetry, interrupted by her death at the age of twenty-five and rewritten by Scève, has generally been considered inferior to that of her contemporary, Louise Labé. Labé, who associated her poetic glory with the civic pride of Lyon, has left us a collection of only twenty-four sonnets and three elegies, but this tiny tip of published work has aroused extraordinary passions.

The supposed lover of the poet Olivier de Magny (1529–1561), to whom the erudite sonnets were probably addressed as a way of winning back his love, Labé also invaded masculine territory in her provocative exploration of the folly of love. Her new grammar of love, hesitating between the different genders of the word *l'amour*, which in the 16th century was feminine in the singular and masculine in the plural, has recently been intriguingly re-examined. One of the most interesting cases of an apparent error, which may relate to the problems of self-expression from a female point of view, occurs in the second elegy, where she writes:

Ami. Ami, ton absence lointeine
Depuis deus mois me tient en cette peine,
Ne vivant pas, mais mourant d'une Amour,
Lequel m'occit dix mille fois le jour.

(Friend. Friend, your absence far away / these past two months continues to trouble me. / I am not living any more, but dying from a love / which kills me ten thousand times a day.)

The principal originality of this poet, though, lies less with form and versification than with the politicization of woman's plight, again expressed most strikingly in her defence of her profession. A male lover, or lovers, and male readers were her primary audience, but her solidarity with her sex is given pride of place in the preface of the sonnets, addressed in code to 'Mademoiselle Clémence de Bourges Lionnoize', where she writes:

Estant le tems venu, Mademoiselle, que les severes Loix des hommes n'empeschent plus les
femmes de s'appliquer aus sciences et disciplines, il me semble que celles qui ont la commodité
doivent employer cette honneste liberté que nostre sexe ha autre fois tant desirée, à icelles
aprendre: & montrer aus hommes le tort qu'ils nous faisoient en nous privant du bien & de
l'honneur qui nous en pouvoit venir & si quelcune parvient en tel degré que de pouvoir mettre
ses concepcions par escrit, le faire soigneusement & non dedaigner la gloire, & s'en parer
plustot que de chaines, anneaus, & somptueus habis.

(The time has come, Mademoiselle, for the harsh laws of men to stop preventing women from applying themselves to all branches of Knowledge. It seems to me that those who can should use the honest freedom that our sex once so desired and show men the wrong that they did us by depriving us of the good and the honour which could come to us from learning and, if some woman manages to reach the point of writing down her ideas, she should do it carefully and far from refusing fame should wear it more proudly than jewels and rich clothes.)

The 17th century

Nothing less than a separate book could possibly do justice to the quality and quantity of the literature produced by women in the 17th century. It has been decided here to sacrifice the colourful detail of the anecdotal evidence recorded by contemporary historians and to concentrate on the main trends in the genres where women dominated. Virtually forsaking verse, and with only the most occasional foray into the theatre, most 17th-century women writers gravitated towards the minor literary forms of fiction, fairytales and personal memoirs, scarcely recognized as genres at all at the time, leaving the higher ground of history and verse drama, or *poèmes dramatiques*, to men. Personal correspondence was also an increasingly important area of self-expression for women, since letter-writing was an essentially private occupation. In the notable cases of the ▷Marquise de Sévigné and Madame de Villedieu (▷Marie-Catherine Hortense Desjardins), it was their male correspondents and publishers who pushed for the publications that would bring them fame, whether they wanted it or not. ▷Marie le Jars de Gournay stands apart in the first half of the century for her defence of the rights and virtues of women. The adopted daughter of the philosopher Montaigne (1533–1592), she was known mainly for her editing work on the *Essays*, but went on to write a number of challenging 'feminist' texts such as the *Egalité des hommes et des femmes (Equality of Men and Women)*, *Le Grief des dames (The Ladies' Grievance)* and *Apologie pour celle qui escrit (Defence of She Who Writes)*.

From 1650 onwards the number of women writers increased exponentially. When so many examples of broadly feminist statements from the same generation could be cited, it seems invidious to single out one or two quotations as though they were more important than the rest. This was a vital stage of what may already be called, in the literary context at least, a women's liberation movement. It would again be a mistake to exaggerate the politicization and exclusivity of women's writing in the 17th century. Male writers, often also close relations, were still a major influence, and there was clearly a high degree of escapism in women's exploration of the female–male relationship through prose fiction and memoirs.

Yet the sudden and dramatic proliferation of women writers during the second half of the 17th century can be directly attributed to the role of those of their sex who, without necessarily leaving any writing in their own hand, founded a new republic of letters in the salons of the great Paris *hôtels* (mansions) which soon became an alternative focus for French cultural and intellectual life. Salons in the Italian tradition first manifested themselves in France in the 16th century in the entourages of Monsieur and Madame de Villeroy, otherwise known as ▷Madeleine de l'Aubespine, in Paris, the ▷Dames des Roches in Poitiers and Monsieur and Madame de Retz (Claude-Catherine de Clermont-Dampierre, ?1545–1603) in Lyon. The most famous of all, however, was the *Chambre bleue* (Blue Chamber) of the Marquise de Rambouillet (1588–1665), whose salon in the rue Saint-Thomas-du-Louvre in Paris was for almost forty years the meeting-place for the most cultivated courtiers and men and women of letters. Such Parisian salons devised a highly eccentric social code in their attempt to refine the relationship between the sexes by making men acknowledge that women were precious objects. The dominant concept was *honnêteté*, an ideal of civilized social conduct, achieved by cultivating social graces and good manners, combined in the case of women with chastity and piety. In the Hôtel de Rambouillet, male *habitués*, or guests, came regularly to pay homage to the hostess, who reclined like a queen on her bed raised on a dais, and to the other female *habituées*, seated beside her on the other side of a symbolic balustrade dividing the sexes. Such gatherings were a live *société conteuse* (tale-telling society), where conversation was the main, and sometimes the only, pleasure. Conditions were far from ideal in the winter months, since the 'incomparable Arthénice', as she was known in her salon, was allergic to the heat. While she lay wrapped in furs in the winter months, the rest were left to suffer the cold as they endeavoured to entertain her. Light literature was the mainstay of such circles. Without group readings and discussion of the latest woman-centred texts, the dialogue between the sexes would soon have lost its inspiration.

At first, women were considered merely the natural arbiters of oral language. Without formal training, they were obliged to make judgements according to what they were used to saying or hearing. They were thus best placed to decide whether a word was generally used in spoken language. The turning-point came in the 1650s, the decade of *préciosité* (▷ Precious Women), the new feminism so easily ridiculed for its affectations in speech, manners and literature, but so vital for adding value to women as writers, readers and lovers. It was during this period that a significant number of women changed from the passive to the active mode and began writing their own texts in celebration of their sex. The *Samedis* (the Saturday salons) hosted by the socially inferior popular novelist Madeleine de Scudéry, which for a few short years replaced the salons at the Hôtel de Rambouillet after the marquise's death, made up in creativity much of what they lacked in refinement. These weekly meetings were born out of, and sustained by, the incredibly successful multi-volume novels which their affable hostess developed into a cult form with *Le Grand Cyrus* (▷*Artamenes, or The Grand Cyrus*) and *Clélie, histoire romaine* (1645–1660) (▷ *Clelia: An excellent new romance*, 1661). A prime example of what the feminist writer ▷ Germaine Greer has called 'the transience of female fame', Madeleine de Scudéry's influence on the development of the novel into a genre which women wanted to write for themselves is not to be underestimated. What could be more ridiculous than the idea of a work of fiction based in Persia in the 6th century BC, where an entire empire is unwittingly conquered by Cyrus the Great in pursuit of the heroine, abducted by a jealous rival at least once a tome, until a marriage ceremony closes the proceedings in the final pages of volume 10? The answer has to be Mademoiselle de Scudéry's next novel. Set in Rome during the First Republic, *Clélie* begins with a wedding procession, divided down the middle by an earthquake. The bride-to-be is then kidnapped by one Horatius Cocles, on the first of three occasions, unaware why he loves her so much until it is suddenly revealed in the final pages of the narrative, nine tomes later, that she is his half-sister, enabling him to rejoice with everyone else as the novel comes full circle back to the wedding ceremony of volume 1 after so many perilous adventures.

With its ancient Roman foot-soldiers dashing between the defence of the last bridge against the Tarquins one minute and the heroine's salon the next, so that they might not miss the opportunity to muse with the ladies on the ▷ *Carte de Tendre* (an allegorical map of love) and exchange endless love-stories, *Clélie* is undoubtedly the most tedious of Madeleine de Scudéry's novels. Even she never wrote another quite like it, changing to the ▷*nouvelle* (short fiction) form that she was developing within it the moment that *préciosité* and its excrescences began to bring her more blame than praise. Yet in terms of the complexity of their reflection of contemporary social relations, their analyses of the infinite diversity of the emotions, and their influence on the early development of historical fiction, Madeleine de Scudéry's long novels are 'precious' in the positive sense of a term which French women originally embraced so that they might be esteemed by men for their brilliance and rarity, like precious gems.

At the beginning of Louis XIV's personal reign in 1661, the court once more became the focus of literature, as of all else, and women were among the first and the best of those who chose to reflect the new forces of centralization in novels and memoirs, while maintaining the cover of secrecy and disguise so essential to their freedom as writers. The

Comtesse de Lafayette was one of the very first novelists to view the French court from close quarters, introducing a 16th-century perspective to give her readers the illusion that this was history and to protect herself from the consequences of direct criticism of the court of her day. The early *nouvelle*, *La Princesse de Montpensier* (*The Princess of Montpensier*), which was taken as a history by the most eminent of 17th-century historical theorists, is as much of a landmark in the new historical realism in which female novelists excelled as *La Princesse de Clèves* itself. This *petite histoire* (short story) outlines the theme of the fatality of love and marriage during the Wars of Religion (1562–1598), which *La Princesse de Clèves* develops in greater detail against the backdrop of Valois court society during the preceding brief interlude of peace that was punctuated by Henri II's death in a tournament at the Château des Tournelles, omen of the troubles to come.

In a letter to a friend, Madame de Lafayette paid this great novel – which she always insisted that she had not written – the highest compliment when she described it as not a *novel* at all, but a collection of memoirs which offered '*une parfaite imitation du monde de la cour et de la manière dont on y vit*' ('a perfect imitation of the world of the court and life there'). It is noticeable that the novelist here felt no need to distinguish between the 16th-century court and that of her own day. For Madame de Lafayette, the court was a timeless institution. She presents court society as a form of *société conteuse* (tale-telling society), but for the first time makes this standard convention of early fiction central to the dynamics of the plot. Madame de Lafayette's court characters do not simply tell a series of detached tales for the amusement of an assembled group, as in earlier fiction. Gossip is the principal danger of the court, and the principal threat to the lover. The unwritten law of court society is that confidences are only made in order to be broken. At court, love always proves a fatal passion, death the inevitable conclusion of every affair. There are no exceptions. Total secrecy is the lover's one hope, but can only be maintained by the exceptional few, like Chabannes in *La Princesse de Montpensier*, or *La Princesse de Clèves*, prepared to take their secret to the grave. In a bitter-sweet posthumous *nouvelle*, *La Comtesse de Tende* (*The Countess of Tende*), the most pessimistic of all Madame de Lafayette's court literature, the heroine finds her last solace before her own death agony in the death of the lovechild to whom she has just given birth, knowing that she has thus doubly fulfilled her husband's cold and heartless '*désir d'empêcher l'éclat de [sa] honte*' ('the desire to keep her shame secret').

Although Madame de Lafayette's most celebrated heroine ends her days in a convent, like so many heroines of early fiction, novels, whether written by men or women, were long regarded as having no religious dimension. In recent decades, however, study of the links between writers such as Madame de Lafayette and the centre of Jansenist thinking at Port-Royal (▷Jansenism) has led to a richer understanding of the Augustinianism in a work like *La Princesse de Clèves*. In the second half of the century, Port-Royal-des-Champs, where the French tragic poet Jean Racine (1639–1699) received his education, became the spiritual home of many aristocratic women tired of both the court and the salon, who were in search of deeper meaning to life. Most continued to correspond with the outside world, though only those who wrote extensively receive separate entries in this *Guide*. Some, like Marquise d'Aumont (c 1618–1658), Mademoiselle de Vertus (1617–1692) or Marie-Louise de Gonzague-Clèves (1611–1667), sought simply to devote themselves to God. Others, like the Duchesse de Longueville (1619–1679) and Mademoiselle de Joncoux (1668–1715), were more militant in their defence of the monastery against persecution by the Church establishment – as were the Solitaires who took refuge there, such as ▷Gilberte Pascal and ▷Jacqueline Pascal, sisters of the French philosopher, mathematician and scientist Blaise Pascal (1623–1662), and ▷Mère Agnès Arnauld and ▷Mère Jacqueline Arnauld, the two most celebrated Mothers Superior from the Jansenist Arnauld family, who were the principal figures at Port-Royal during the crisis years. For their sincerely held belief in this austere faith, all were the subject of terrible persecution throughout the second half of the 17th century. Jansenism was regarded as a threat to the unity of the Church in France and had to be eradicated. Still others, like the ▷Marquise de Sablé, were merely looking for a more intellectually stimulating environment. Two other *Précieuses*, Mademoiselle de Scudéry and the ▷Marquise de Sévigné, were supporters of Port-Royal. A great admirer of Pascal's *Lettres provinciales* (*Provincial Letters*), Madeleine de Scudéry described the Jansenist 'desert' in flattering terms in *Clélie*. The Marquise de Sévigné's letters are testimony to her inner struggle between love for her daughter and love for God. As the years passed and death approached, her admiration for the Arnauld family, the Jansenist Pierre Nicole (1625–1695) and Pascal was increasingly manifest.

Conversions, particularly in later life, transform our perspective of many 17th-century women writers, including the most notorious libertine, Madame de Villedieu (Marie-Catherine Desjardins), who saw the error of her ways after she had finally found someone to marry her. In terms of the scope and impact of her fiction, if not its quality, Madame de Villedieu deserves as much attention as her more distinguished contemporary, Madame de Lafayette, but its diversity inevitably dissipates the worthy attempts in recent years of such scholars as Micheline Cuénin to present it to new generations of readers. Scorned by the man whose name she assumed by having it printed on the title-pages of her books after a bogus marriage ceremony, Madame de Villedieu became one of the very first writers of either sex to make her living by her poetry, fiction and drama. Surviving in circumstances more difficult than those faced by her most daring heroines, this woman writer is a figure of at least equal stature with the English novelist and dramatist, ▷Aphra Behn, who was her almost exact contemporary. Her wide-ranging short fiction (*nouvelles*) and novels about a succession of court *galanteries* (love-affairs) have one distinguishing feature which may be usefully abstracted where their diversity cannot be studied in any detail. Like *La Princesse de Clèves*, they fuse two genres which the male literary establishment were desperate to keep apart: history and fiction. As her name was prominently displayed on the frontispiece, Madame de Villedieu was held personally responsible for the new fashion for making fiction look like history. As the writer Pierre Bayle (1647–1706) remarked, this was a technique which women novelists had refined to the point where they had almost completely undermined the work of the official historians, who were vainly trying to write a perfect history of France according to the classical ideal.

Since French women were clearly very good at writing as well as reading novels, the general misconception that early novels were written by men to be devoured by empty-headed women needs correction. Although over 90 per cent of 17th-century French novelists were men, all the main novelists after Honoré d'Urfé (1567–1625) were women. There is also substantial evidence of men reading their novels. The Prince de Condé (1621–1686) considered *Le Grand Cyrus* essential reading while on campaign in his bivouac, and the writer Bussy-Rabutin (1618–1693) was far keener to lay his hands on a copy of *La Princesse de Clèves* than was his cousin Madame de Sévigné. The fashion for French novels in England was at its height in the 17th century, and most of the examples of popular fiction mentioned here were rapidly translated for the English audience.

Women were not allowed, and never dared, to write official history. Unofficial ▷*mémoires*, a self-justificatory genre largely developed in France by disaffected members of the court, offered a suitable compromise, helping to blur still further the distinction between history and fiction. The number of distinguished women who recorded their disappointments in life and love in this way towards the end of the 17th century has made the use of a feminine gender with the word *mémorialiste* (memoir-writer) in French indispensable. Written in disgrace or exile, or at least in private apartments at the Louvre or Versailles, intended for posterity rather than publication, and with little apparent concern for formal considerations, this was the aristocratic genre *par excellence*. Originally notes for history, which would be written up by professional historians, *mémoires* overcame many of the principal prejudices against professional writing, considered akin to manual labour in the 17th century, and likely to result in *dérogation*, or loss of status. Published in many cases only in the 18th century or much later, *mémoires* represent the secret triumph of women writers. By writing the authentic *mémoires* of her tragic friend Henriette d'Angleterre (1644–1670) and of the court of France as well as memoir-novels like *La Princesse de Clèves*, Madame de Lafayette placed herself in the same category of writer as the king, his niece, ▷Mademoiselle de Montpensier, and, if we are to believe the publishers, ▷Marie de Mancini, the woman who might have found herself Queen of France had not the rules of love at court been as cruel in reality as in any novel. By date of publication, most of the important *mémoires* written by women were the legacy of future generations and take us beyond the boundary of 1700. Their circulation in manuscript form among a closed circle of initiates at court ensured that they were already a vital element in the continuity and growing sophistication of women's writing before the majority dared or deigned to go public.

Bib: Albistur, M. and Armogathe, D., *Histoire du féminisme français*; Angenot, M., *Les Champions des femmes*; Baron, D., *Grammar and Gender*; Cameron, K., *Louise Labé: Renaissance Poet and Feminist*; Dronke, P., *Women Writers of the Middle Ages: a critical study of texts from Perpetua to Marguerete Porete*; Dulong, C., *La Vie quotidienne des femmes au grand siècle*; Ferguson, M.W., Quilligan, M. and Vickers, N.J. (eds), *Rewriting the Renaissance: the discourses of sexual difference in early modern Europe*; Feugère, L., *Les Femmes poètes au XVIe siècle: French Literary Studies*, Vol. XVI (1989); Gibson, W., *Women in Seventeenth-Century France*; Guggenheim, M., *Women in French Literature*; Lougee, C.C., *Le Paradis des femmes*; Maclean, I., *Woman Triumphant*; Moi, T., *Sexual/Textual Politics*; Paden, W.D. (ed.), *The Voice of the Trobairitz: perspectives on the women troubadours*; Wilson, K.M., *Medieval Women Writers*; Wilwerth, E., *Visages de la littérature féminine*; Woodrough, E., 'Le Concept de l'honnêteté dans *Le Fort inexpugnable de l'honneur du sexe féminin* de François de Billon' in *Renaissance, Humanisme, Réforme*, 1985.

A. HUGHES & J. BIRKETT

8 Eighteenth- and nineteenth-century France

1690–1890: the historical context
In political and economic terms, the 200 years reviewed in the following pages cover the revolutionary making of the modern French state: the transformation of absolute monarchy to liberal bourgeois Republic, which fostered the growth of industry and finance capital, followed by the emergence of mass society and the mass market. The process could be described in various ways: the rise of democracy, the centralization of political power, the consolidation of capital, the rise of the nation, and so on. But however

it is described, the question of women's place has always been central to it. In 1808, Charles Fourier wrote that:

> As a general thesis: *Social progress and change from one era to the next are brought about in proportion to the progress of women toward freedom, and social decline is brought about in proportion to the decrease in women's freedom.* (Charles Fourier, *Théories des quatre mouvements et des destinées générales: prospectus et annonce de la découverte*, 1808, rpt 1967, p. 147; cit. Claire Goldberg Moses, *French Feminism in the Nineteenth Century*, 1984, p. 92.)

The link between women's emancipation and social change is not one of simple cause and effect. But the female body is a keystone in the socio-economic structures of any period, and the right to dispose of it is an issue with public as well as private implications. Women fulfil the function of reproducing the established order, however defined. They act as stewards of men's property, and as mediators of their property relationships. They are the instruments by which wealth and property are transmitted or redistributed according to law, and they disseminate the political and moral values associated with that law. Much of the writing produced by women during this period assumes this conservative role. As the period advances, women's writing, like women's action, becomes more contestatory, but the shift from books of manners to militant journalism is by no means absolute. Writers like the ▷Comtesse de Ségur are ever-present, providing conservative publishers with cautionary tales to limit the ambitions of the next female generation.

The beginning of emancipation was, as always, women's education, discussed incessantly by the 18th-century *philosophes* (philosphers) and their opponents, and in the literary, philosophical and, later, political salons presided over by their female counterparts from ▷Louise d'Epinay to ▷Madame de Staël. The intellectual independence of the salons was for the aristocratic few, but the need was acknowledged for better provision for the many, to enable them to play an effective supporting role in the economy of the new France. ▷Stephanie de Genlis aimed her educational writings at all classes and both sexes, though she reserved her most important work for the sisters of the progressive aristocracy: *Adèle et Théodore ou Lettres sur l'éducation* (1782) (▷*Adelaide and Théodore or Letters about Education*). The extension of education for strictly vocational purposes had unwanted side-effects. As the libertine novelist Choderlos de Laclos (1741–1803) pointed out in his prize essay on women's education, *Discours sur la question proposée par l'Académie de Chalons-sur-Marne: Quels seraient les meilleurs moyens de perfectionner l'éducation des femmes* (1783) (*Discourse on the Question Proposed by the Chalons-sur-Marne Academy: What are the best ways of improving Women's Education*), education can encourage a woman to recognise a potential which society is not constituted to allow her to realize. Women's education leads inevitably to questions of women's place. There was general agreement that this was not the public sphere. (See Joan B. Landes, *Women and the Public Sphere in the Age of the French Revolution*, 1988.)

The women who marched on Versailles in 1789 performed an important service for the Revolution, but civil rights were still for men only. When the Revolution transformed questions of human rights and freedoms from academic argument into political practice, women's participation in the state was set aside. Only Condorcet, of all the *philosophes*, raised his voice in favour of female suffrage in his discourse *Sur l'admission des femmes au droit de cité* (1790) (*On Giving Women Citizenship*). The Constitutions of 1791 and 1793 both explicitly barred women from citizenship: they had to remain passive, the blank page on which the redistributed property rights of the new order could be inscribed. In the 1790s the legislation on marriage, separation and divorce and associated property rights was crucial to the direction of constitutional change, and the struggles in the legislature over its drafting mirror the factional struggles for possession of the Revolution. Napoleon's intervention in the drafting of the *Code civil* of 1804, to abolish the divorce legislation set up in September 1792 and to insist on the retention of the husband's position as head of household, in control of the property and person of his wife, stabilized the new social edifice at the price of women's civil rights. (For an extended account of this connection, see Jennifer Birkett, ' "A Mere Matter of Business" ': Marriage, Divorce and the French Revolution' in Elizabeth M. Craik (ed.), *Marriage and Property*, 1984. See also Lynn Hunt (ed.), *Eroticism and the Body Politic*, 1991; Dorinda Dutram, *The Body and the French Revolution: Sex, Class, and Political Culture*, 1989.)

The 19th century began with more conservative reformulations of women's function, in which counter-revolutionary women writers took a major part. Madame de Genlis's historical novels, almost as popular as those of Sir Walter Scott in the circulating libraries of Europe, helped make the enterprising and independent woman the scapegoat for the disorder provoked by revolution; they popularized the sentimental representation of woman as, by nature, victim and martyr, who should voluntarily subordinate herself to the male in private and public domains. Recuperation came slowly, and within an agenda set by the debates of the men of the left. Clair Goldberg Moses, in *French Feminism in the Ninetheenth Century* (1984) and James E. McMillan in *Housewife or Harlot: The Place of Women in French Society 1870–1940*, (1984) carefully trace the history of the period. In the first part of the century, Saint-Simonist and Fourierist doctrines gave a special place to the promotion of women's equality which, in the case of ▷ Saint-Simonism, acquired a religious dimension. Renascent feminist organizations soon split with the mystics, but the combination was a potent influence on a whole generation. It contributed to that romantic idealization of feminine power exploited by writers such as ▷ George Sand, and prepared the ground for the work of a new generation of writers and activists such as ▷ Suzanne Voilquin and ▷ Flora Tristan. The provisional government of 1848, however, though extending voting rights to all men, disregarded feminist calls for the same privilege. The conservative Constituent Assembly voted down a proposal on women's suffrage by 899 votes to one. By 1852, women's political clubs were closed and their leaders scattered. ▷ Proudhonist anti-feminism set the tone for the left. The Republican Jules Michelet, at first sight more sympathetic, was equally convinced of women's inferiority and of the need to confine them to the domestic sphere – see *L'Amour* (1858) (*Love*), *La Femme* (1859/60) (*Woman*), *La Sorcière* (1862) (*The Witch*).

Feminist energies gathered again in the closing years of the Second Empire. The talents of activists such as ▷ Louise Michel came to the fore in the defence of the Commune; the *pétroleuses* (female fire-raisers during the Commune) terrified the right-wing press of the 1870s; and the repression was proportionate. But the more sympathetic Republican governments of the next two decades, passing new laws on freedom of assembly and freedom of the press, made new advances possible. In 1878, Paris saw the first Congrès international du droit des femmes (International Congress on the Rights of Women) discuss women's education and economic situation – though ▷ Hubertine Auclert was not allowed to speak for the right to vote. In 1879 the government approved the establishment of the Société pour l'amélioration du sort des femmes (Society for the Improvement of the Situation of Women). Women were needed in the workforce, in the service sector of a mass market to staff the growing number of shops and offices, and as teachers, to satisfy employers' need for more trained workers. The Camille Sée law of 1880 set up secondary schools for girls, including *lycées*. The separate curriculum made it impossible for girls to take the *baccalauréat*, the qualifying examination for entry to university and to the major professions, but even so, 842 women were enrolled in universities in 1895. (Debora Silverman's essay, 'The "New Woman" in Fin-de-siècle France', in the collection by Lynn Hunt cited earlier, spells out the details.) In 1884, the Naquet Law re-established divorce (though man's legal status as head of the household remained protected until 1970). In 1900, three separate feminist Congresses would be held simultaneously in Paris: one Catholic, one moderate and one militant. The ▷ New Woman of the 1890s wanted education and a career, not marriage and domesticity.

The New Woman, economically necessary, was nevertheless, as Debora Silverman describes, pilloried in the Paris press. Learned and pseudo-learned treatises on gender and physiology argued for women's natural inferiority. The writing and painting of the whole Decadent movement was profoundly anti-feminist as well as anti-socialist in its inspiration, carrying in its sado-masochistic representations of the feminine the sense of impotence experienced by a generation of middle-class men before a history that no longer seemed theirs. (See Jennifer Birkett, *The Sins of the Fathers: Decadence in France 1870–1914*, 1986.) Yet despite opposition, women's ambition, and especially women's literary ambition, continued to thrive. Octave Uzanne's biographical study published in 1894, *Nos Contemporaines* (*Women Today*), reports that by the 1890s there were some 1,200 female members of the Société de gens de lettres, while the Société des auteurs dramatiques counted thirty-two women adherents.

The canonical perspective

The polemical attack by the ageing dandy Barbey d'Aurevilly on the new generation of 19th-century women writers, ▷*Les Bas-bleus* (*Bluestockings*), is part of a critical tradition. Readers of literary histories from La Harpe to the present day will find a minimum of space allocated to the women writers of the 18th and 19th centuries. Nancy K. Miller has pointed out particularly the exclusion of women novelists from Etiemble's two-volume anthology published in 1966, *Romanciers du XVIIe siècle* (*Novelists of the 17th Century*). (See Nancy K. Miller, 'Men's Reading, Women's Writing: Gender and the Rise of the Novel' in Joan DeJean and Nancy K. Miller (eds), *Displacements: Women, Tradition, Literatures in French*, 1991.) Women's novels, Miller argues, have traditionally been pigeonholed into categories which present their interests as narrow ones: they are, for example, discussed for their sentimental interest, not as realistic fictions of social life. Or, again, an exclusively male critical fraternity has looked narcissistically in a novel for its own flattering self-image (hence its foregrounding of libertine fiction), and failed to identify with female representations of the subject. Naomi Schor has pointed out that political prejudice is as blinkering as simple misogyny. Schor links the decline in George Sand's reputation in the second half of the century to a switch of critical interest to Balzacian realism, for which Hippolyte Taine is said to be chiefly responsible. Sand's idealism, she argues, is marginalized because it brings together a double demand for an end to exploitation based on gender and class. (See Naomi Schor, 'Idealism in the Novel: Recanonizing Sand' in the collection edited by DeJean and Miller cited earlier.) Information on women writers of the 18th and 19th centuries in standard dictionaries and encyclopaedias always begins by defining them in relation to fathers, husbands and lovers. In truncated form, the present entries still register this practice, but for different reasons: that women were writing in and against a patriarchal context is a factor that criticism must always take into account.

Gender and genre: the forms of women's writing

Common prejudice in the 18th century allowed men to produce works of both intellect and feeling, while women's creativity was deemed to be limited to the latter. There were a few exceptions. Education was a legitimate sphere of feminine activity: Madame de Genlis's innovatory pedagogical treatises had a cross-Channel following. Translations by women (from Latin, German and English) contributed to the widening horizons of the Enlightenment. ▷Madame du Châtelet published scientific work; ▷Madame de la Briche reported on her travels. Some imaginative genres were less accessible to women because of the nature of their production. Theatre required public, collective effort and substantial budgets, which few companies would entrust to women dramatists. (See Elaine Showalter, Jr, 'Writing Off the Stage: Women Authors and Eighteenth-Century Theater' in the collection edited by DeJean and Miller cited earlier.) It was easier to publish poetry, and personal memoirs were numerous, especially towards the end of the century. But the most popular genre with women writers was that of prose fiction. ▷Madame de Graffigny's *Lettres d'une Péruvienne* (1747) (*Letters of a Peruvian Princess*) made a major contribution to the development of epistolary narrative; ▷Madame Riccoboni, to the novel of sensibility; Madame de Genlis introduced the historical novel into France. While love intrigues were the primary focus of interest, 'love' took very different forms, from the cut and thrust of ▷Madame de Tencin's salon skirmishes, to the Gothic melodrama and sentimentality of Madame de Genlis, and the pre-romantic anguish of Madame de Staël's ▷*Corinne ou l'Italie* (1807) (▷*Corinne, or Italy*, 1987).

A glance at the A–Z entries for both centuries shows that women's writing really 'took off' in France – or at least, became more visible – during the 19th century, when its class base expanded. Before 1800, women authors were almost exclusively aristocrats, with wealth, culture and time enough to indulge their passion for writing. In the 19th century, while ▷Marie de Flavigny, George Sand and ▷Gyp all belonged to noble families, their ranks were swelled by bourgeois and, more importantly, working-class women, such as the poets ▷Marceline Desbordes-Valmore and ▷Elisa Mercoeur. The proliferation of female-authored texts mirrors the quest for social and sexual emancipation on which women now embarked. A large number of these texts still fall into the categories traditionally considered as 'feminine': the novel, educational writing for young ladies and gentlemen and, to a lesser extent, poetry. Autobiography remained a popular genre, as Jean Larnac commented in his *Histoire de la littérature féminine* (1929) (*History of Women's Literature*), reiterating the time-honoured contention that women authors are incapable of writing about anything but themselves. Opting to employ a conventional 'female' textual form is not, however, necessarily unadventurous or intellectually limited. The memoirs of women like ▷Suzanne Voilquin, ▷Louise Michel, Marie de Flavigny and ▷Madame d'Abrantès include much historical, social and political comment, and are far from representing the kind of introspective ramblings which critics like Larnac commonly associate with feminine discourse. The novels of Sand, ▷Marguerite Audoux and ▷Marie-Louise Gagneur illuminate and denounce the inequalities and injustices that characterized 19th-century French society.

The *écrivaines* (women writers) of 19th-century France did not, however, restrict themselves to their allotted genres. A number of them, including ▷Marguerite Ancelot, ▷Alexandrine de Bawr, ▷Delphine de Girardin and ▷Anaïs Ségalas, were successful dramatists; de Bawr and ▷Arvède Barine also produced volumes of literary criticism. The hitherto closed world of newspaper journalism increasingly attracted women (women had contributed to earlier periodicals, including ▷*Journal des Dames, Ladies' journal*). Two of the best-known columnists of the period were Delphine de Girardin, whose humorous *Lettres Parisiennes* (*Parisian Letters*) delighted the public for twelve years, and ▷Séverine, who wrote for *Le Cri du peuple* (*The Cry of the People*) and other socialist journals. Political, polemical and historical treatises came from the pens of, for example, ▷Hortense Allart and Louise Michel. Flora Tristan, the most famous female political writer of the period, wrote *Promenades dans Londres* (1840) (*London Walks*), a critique of urban deprivation in Britain, and *L'Union ouvrière* (1843) (*Workers' Union*), a work which, for the sophistication and scope of its analysis, has been compared to Marx's *Das Kapital*.

Most significantly, throughout the 19th century, from the Saint-Simonians of the 1830s to *fin de siècle* suffragists like Hubertine Auclert, women of the bourgeoisie and proletariat were producing both fictional and non-fictional feminist discourses which denounced the sexual and socio-economic oppression to which they were subject: ▷Claire Démar, ▷Hortense Allart, ▷Juliette Adam and ▷Jenny d'Héricourt. Béatrice Slama contends that analytical, non-fictional works by 19th-century Frenchwomen were frequently more original and courageous than the quantities of female-authored novels and poems produced in the period. (See Béatrice Slama, 'Femmes écrivains' in Jean-Paul Aron (ed.), *Misérable et glorieuse: la femme du XIXe siècle*, 1980.)

Themes

Writing to the agenda set by the society of the period, male and female authors alike home in on the same key areas of argument: politics, religion and sexuality. To conclude this introductory essay, we focus briefly on one area for each of the two centuries.

The political dimension in women's writing is that which is generally most neglected. This is particularly so for the 18th century. In much women's fiction, centred usually on the personal life, it appears at several levels of remove, much-mediated (the work of Madame Riccoboni, for example), and can be difficult to recognize without prior knowledge of the historical context in which a text was produced. Analyses of sexual intrigue – sexual politics – raise questions which automatically extend from the private to the public sphere because of the function of marriage, divorce, and women's property rights in the socio-economic system. Some novelists are politically explicit: ▷Madame de Charrière's novel *Lettres trouvées dans des portefeuilles d'émigrés* (1793) (*Letters from an Émigré's Wallet*) considers the causes of the Revolution; Madame de Genlis's *Les Chevaliers du cygne* (1795) (*The Knights of the Swan*), star-crossed lovers at the court of Charlemagne, is an apology for constitutional monarchy; while her *Les Parvenus* (1824) (*The New Era*) is both an attack on the Revolution and an exculpation of the Constitutional aristocracy.

Non-fictional political writings from the period have until very recently been out of sight and out of mind. Their writers had no status, and thus no authority, in the public sphere, and they raised issues which were either irrelevant or actively damaging to the interests of a patriarchal state. The exception traditionally recognized is Madame de Staël, whose sharp and eloquent political analyses several times provoked her exile from Revolutionary or Napoleonic Paris, and who was responsible for the first study of the interaction of politics and literature. The feminist debate produced political interventions throughout the century from individuals such as the ▷Marquise de Lambert, writing on women's right to education, or ▷Dame Suzanne Necker, who wrote *Réflexions sur le divorce* (*Reflections on Divorce*). And recent research on the pamphlets and petitions produced by groups of women in the Revolution has emphasized the strength of the collective work, relying not only on emotive eloquence, but also rigorous rational argument. The work of ▷Olympe de Gouges, now emerging from undeserved obscurity, is the tip of an iceberg. (See Béatrice Didier, *Ecrire la Révolution: 1789–99*, 1989.)

Bridging the gap between history and fiction, autobiography provided a form in which women could write themselves into the historical record. Madame de Caylus's memoirs (1770) give an account of the court of Louis XV from 1709 to 1715; ▷Madame de Chastenay's, of the upheavals of 1771–1815. ▷Madame Roland took her leave of history in the memoirs written in prison in 1793; Madame de Staël, whose *Considérations sur les principant événements de la Révolution francaise* (*Considerations on the Main Events of The French Revolution*) was written in 1818 and published posthumously, was conscious of political battles still to fight. Béatrice Didier, in the book reference to earlier, has described how, for women in particular, writing in the revolutionary moment brought together the private and the public domains (sensibility and politics), and forged a new awareness of feminine identity as historical product.

Not unsurprisingly, a considerable proportion of the novels, plays and poems written by women in 19th-century France deal with the subject of love. From ▷Sophie Cottin and ▷Claire de Duras to ▷Jeanne Marni and ▷Marcelle Tinayre, Frenchwomen did what was expected of them, and produced 'love stories'. This is not to say that they wrote mere sentimental pap, or aimed exclusively at a feminine readership hungry for bittersweet tales of connubial bliss, lovers' tiffs or tortuous emotional entanglements. While there *were* women writers who produced what can best be described as 'popular romance' – ▷Camille Pert, ▷Dash, ▷Jean Bertheroy – many others used the form to condemn, tacitly or explicitly, sexual inequality and exploitation, particularly within the institution of marriage. George Sand is the best-known, but the same tendency is apparent in ▷André Léo's *Un mariage scandaleux* (1862) (*A Scandalous Marriage*) and *Un Divorce* (1866) (*A divorce*), Suzanne Voilquin's ▷*Souvenirs d'une fille du peuple* (1866) (*Memories of a Daughter of the People*), ▷Daniel Stern's *Valentia* (1883) and ▷Marcelle Tinayre's *L'Ennemi intime* (1931) (*The Intimate Enemy*). 19th-century French heroines are frequently shown to be superior to the male consorts to whom they are devoted, and who cause them pain or distress. Sex emerges in Stern's *Valentia* (1883) and Sand's ▷*Lélia* (1833) as that which men impose upon women, rather than as a source of pleasure. The vast majority of women writers of the period were reticent about inscribing their sexuality in their texts. Since for much of the period bigotry, prudery and censorship held sway, this is hardly surprising. Claudine Brécourt-Villars argues that the limitations placed upon the expression of erotic desire and pleasure in 19th-century France are especially apparent in women's writing, which is characterized by an 'overestimation of cerebral, desexualized love'. (See Béatrice Didier, '*Femmes écrivains*' cited earlier.) She suggests that even when censorship became less fierce, those women who wrote erotic texts – ▷Céleste Mogador, for example – produced works which were rather 'tame'. Despite these reservations, it is worth noting that, setting aside the handful of texts produced in the 18th century by ▷Marie-Antoinette Fagnan, ▷Madame Morency and the equivocal ▷Chevalier d'Eon, the 19th century saw the first major erotic novels by women. The fact that a number of female authors were prepared to publish erotic works, even if anonymously, or pseudonymously, and 'borrowed' from male-authored models, indicates the extent of women's revolt against the restrictions on their creative autonomy. By the end of the period, as the example of ▷Rachilde indicates, women writers were no longer afraid to address frankly and openly the complexities of human sexuality.

As Béatrice Slama observes, 19th-century French female authors are often criticized for aping their male counterparts or mentors, and failing to evolve literary models of their own. Even if this is so – and the contention is not totally justified – the achievements of these writers are not to be underestimated. Unlike their British sisters, the vast majority of Frenchwomen at the end of the 18th century had no reason to believe that the literary sphere might one day be open to them. That it became so is due to the persistence of those middle- and working-class women who were brave enough to offer their works for publication, even though they did not belong to the privileged aristocratic sub-section of French womanhood which had already achieved a '*venue à l'écriture*' (*a place in literature*). Literary innovation can only come into being once a firm hold has been established within the literary space. The French women writers of the 19th century paved the way for the more radical and experimental textual productions of their 20th-century successors.

Twentieth-century France

9

The place of women writers in contemporary French culture can perhaps best be introduced by considering the terms used to designate them in a language where gender is marked grammatically. A word meaning female author – *autrice* – existed briefly in France in the eighteenth century, but it did not survive, so that the two current words for writer in French – *auteur* and *écrivain* – are masculine. Recent feminist neologisms such as *écrivaine*, *auteuse*, or the reclaimed *autrice* have not become common usage, and *femme auteur*, which is similar to the English 'woman writer', though slightly more acceptable than the neologisms, is also not generalized; in the *Dictionnaire Bordas* (*Bordas Dictionary*), a guide to French literature published in 1985, for example, ▷Hélène Cixous, who has attempted to explore and reclaim feminine identity, is ironically referred to by the masculine *un écrivain*. The feminine form of *poète* – *poétesse* – remains pejorative, denoting the writer of frivolous rhymes. While it is therefore linguistically difficult for women to aspire to the heights of real literary status as authors or poets, it is significant that there is a feminine form for novelist, *romancière*, a comment perhaps on the low status of certain genres of the novel, or permissible because of the connection with 'romance'.

Women writers and the French language

As this introduction would suggest, the French language poses particular problems to women writers, in that the grammatical structure expresses and reinforces gender inequality to a greater extent than is the case in less inflected languages, such as English. It is only possible here to provide a few examples which indicate the nature of these problems. Feminine forms are described by most grammars as deviations from the masculine norm, and feminine endings sometimes have pejorative connotations (as in *poétesse* above). Where the pronouns 'we' or 'they' refer to a mixed group, masculine forms are used wherever possible. The quandary over the term *femme auteur* described above is replicated in relation to many other professions: terms for high-status professions often exist only in the masculine form, the feminine form sometimes denoting the wife of the high-status male, as in *la générale* or *la présidente*. It is also significant that the gender of a word can change, regardless of the sex of the post-holder, when it is used to denote more or less prestigious roles: thus the president of a parent-teacher association can be feminine – *la présidente*, whereas the managing director of a firm is masculine – *le président directeur général*.

The nature of the French language itself can therefore be seen as a factor contributing to the preoccupation with language which can be observed in a range of contemporary French women writers. This is, however, a relatively recent phenomenon, and in the early years of the century the language issue was not perceived as a problem; the lesbian poet ▷Renée Vivien, for example, could be said to have exploited the inflected nature of the language subversively by emphasizing the grammatically obvious femininity of the object of desire addressed by her poems, collected and published posthumously in 1923. Many years before feminism in France became publicly aware of language issues, the ▷*Négritude* movement of African francophone writers, which began in the 1930s, had already begun to reclaim the French language. (The word *Négritude* itself is claiming a positive meaning for *nègre* – 'negro' or 'nigger'.) However, this movement was dominated by male writers, and it is only very recently that women from francophone African countries, such as the Franco-Senegalese writer ▷Marie Ndiaye and the Camerounian novelist

▷Calixthe Beyala have published texts which experiment with linguistic register and conventions.

In the 1980s the question of language was politicized both by feminist sociolinguists, such as Marina Yaguello, and by socialist reformers: Yvette Roudy, as Minister for Women's Rights, set up a commission for the feminization of professional titles in 1984. In the realm of fiction the issues were already being addressed in the 1960s and 1970s by writers who, nevertheless, adhere to conventional realist narrative forms. Their challenge to patriarchal language, in some ways similar to that of socialist reform, consists of reclaiming words, questioning the inequalities of gender inscribed in language, and perhaps most importantly, bringing women's repressed experience to the surface. These writers can thus be seen to have more common ground with Anglo-American feminist writing of the period than the more radical exponents of ▷*écriture féminine* (*feminine writing*) discussed below. In *Les Stances à Sophie* (1963) (*Cats Don't Care for Money*, 1965), ▷Christiane Rochefort juxtaposes the narrator's satirical and colloquial language with the formulas and received ideas of male middle-class speech, while ▷Claire Etcherelli was perhaps the first French woman writer to examine the interconnected relationship of language to gender, race and class in her first novel ▷*Élise ou la vraie vie* (1967) (*Élise or the Real Life* 1970). In her autobiographical novel, *Les Armoires vides* (1974) (*The Empty Cupboards*), ▷Annie Ernaux carries out a more personal exploration of the links between gender, sexuality and social class. These are encoded in the differences between the polite, middle-class formulas she is learning at school, and the language used in her working-class home, which is characterized by its more direct, closer relationship to physical experience. In the mid-1970s, even the title of ▷Marie Cardinal's most well-known novel, ▷*Les Mots pour le dire* (1975) (*The Words to Say It*, 1983), is revelatory of its main theme: the narrator's struggle to name her specifically feminine experience, and thus to heal herself.

The more radical concept and practice of *écriture féminine*, developed in the 1970s and 1980s, can partly be linked to the avant-garde tradition in French literary production of the 20th century; in this sense, writers such as ▷Nathalie Sarraute and ▷Marguerite Duras who, as early as the 1950s, produced plays and novels which questioned linguistic and narrative conventions, can be seen as its precursors. Although in 1980 Duras rejected her earlier solidarity with the exponents of *écriture féminine*, the silences of her women characters, and her experimentation with narrative forms, for example through unusual juxtapositions of image and sound in films such as *Nathalie Granger* (1972) and *Hiroshima, mon amour* (1960) (*Hiroshima, My Love*), are expressive of alienation and resistance to patriarchal linguistic norms. French philosophical traditions, and particularly the work of a range of contemporary theorists such as Derrida (▷deconstruction) and Lacan (▷psychoanalysis), are at least equally influential in the development of feminine writing by writers such as Hélène Cixous and ▷Luce Irigaray. Despite their differences, these writers share the desire to question dominant and monolithic systems of meaning by using non-traditional narrative structures, and emphasizing linguistic ambiguity and the gaps in patriarchal discourse. Irigaray, for example, makes positive use of the lexical limitations of French, compared, for instance, with English, by emphasizing double meanings, or the potential presence of other meanings within a word: for example, from *dépenser*, meaning 'to spend', and *penser*, 'to think', Irigaray creates *dé-penser* – 'to unthink'. ▷Annie Leclerc also rejects traditional narrative, and both the title of her essay ▷'*Parole de femme*' (1974) ('Woman's Word') and her experimental style, are indicative of the author's attempt to find a new language to express women's experience. It is, however, in the novels of the lesbian feminist writer ▷Monique Wittig that we find one of the most direct and fundamental attacks on the patriarchal structures inherent in the French language in contemporary writing. Basic grammatical conventions, such as the dominance of the masculine pronoun *ils* they are, for instance, questioned by Wittig's consistent use of the feminine form in texts such as ▷*Les Guérillères* (1969), where the lists of female names and circles which interrupt the narrative render its radical departure from the traditions of the novelistic form immediately visible.

Conditions of production: the publishing industry
The question of who publishes women writers in France could usefully become the subject of research, given its primordial importance in determining the fate of women's writing; here it is only possible to indicate some of the most immediately obvious characteristics of the relationship between the publishing industry and French women writers. Early in the century it seems likely that the mainly upper-class women who published, such as Renée Vivien, ▷Lucie Delarue-Mardrus or ▷Louise de Vilmorin, did so at their own expense, or, in the case of the materially less secure, such as ▷Colette, as a result, initially at least, of male patronage. The improvement in the social position, particularly of middle-class women, in the post-war period was accompanied by an increase in the number of women writers being published. This improvement, combined with the academic status she acquired through her achievement of second place in the national competitive examination, the *agrégation* in philosophy, were perhaps factors which facilitated ▷Simone de Beauvoir's acceptance as a young writer by a major publishing house, Gallimard, in the 1940s.

Throughout the century, and particularly since World War II, women writers of romantic fiction have been published in relatively large numbers by mainstream publishers, though the field of romantic fiction, or *littérature rose* as it is known in France, has become increasingly dominated by translations of English and US writers in recent years. The multinational ▷Harlequin took over Duo, the romantic fiction branch of the paperback publishers J'ai Lu in 1986. Although Hachette somewhat reluctantly became a major shareholder in the Paris branch of Harlequin, the US management recently made the decision to close down Harlequin's French writers' collection, apparently on the grounds that their work was too literary. This would seem to lend some support to the notion that the work of many French women writers belongs to a category which French culture has created specially for them, somewhere between romantic pulp fiction and literature. Their novels are clearly more complex than the formulaic products of Harlequin, but their focus on relationships and personal rather than public life has rendered them not quite respectable; even de Beauvoir laments the narrow viewpoint of women writers in ▷*The Second Sex*. The novels of ▷Françoise Sagan are typical of this category, and one can see the extent of the cultural prejudice against popular women writers in the phrase used by one critic to describe Claire Etcherelli's complex study of class, race and gender, *Élise or the Real Life*, as 'Zola re-written by Sagan'.

The women's movement has had less impact on the publishing scene in France than in the anglophone world, and although certain publishers such as Denoël-Gonthier have a women's collection, there is no equivalent of Britain's Virago or The Women's Press; it therefore seems likely that access to publishing for women writers has increased less than in England or the USA. The ▷*Psych et Po* group has dominated the feminist publishing scene through their ownership of ▷Éditions des femmes: as a result, the only feminist publisher in France tends to concentrate on texts which combine feminism with psychoanalytical interests and/or ▷*avant-garde* forms, such as the work of Hélène Cixous. Éditions des femmes has nonetheless reprinted some little-known early writers such as ▷Liane de Pougy, and translations of writings by women's collectives from Chile, Italy, Japan and Latin America. Avant-garde texts by women such as Monique Wittig or the Franco-Senegalese writer; Marie Ndiaye have also been published by Les Éditions de Minuit. Although Les Éditions Persona seems to specialise in work by gay writers, their list is dominated by male writers. Lesbian and gay writing is rather better represented in the field of journals, for example by the fairly successful cultural review *Masques* (*Masks*).

Two of the publishing houses in Paris specializing in African work since the 1950s, Présence Africaine and Silex, have recently gone into receivership, and this may have serious implications for African francophone writers seeking to publish in France. For North African women writers critical of the régimes in their own countries, publication in Paris has provided a useful escape from censorship, and Algerian writers such as ▷Assia Djebar and ▷Leila Sebbar have been well-known in France for some time. Although several African and Caribbean francophone women writers have penetrated the literary establishment in France, particularly recently, they have not gained a cultural presence as groups of writers equivalent to that acquired by black women writers in Britain, where anthologies and individual works have been published by the feminist press.

It seems to be the case that theoretical or avant-garde writers such as Cixous, ▷Kristeva, Irigaray and Wittig have been translated despite their difficulty, and have received more attention abroad than feminist writers of ▷realist novels, such as ▷Michèle Perrein, Rochefort or Cardinal. French feminism is frequently considered in anglophone contexts, to consist entirely of high theory, perhaps as a result of perceptions, of French intellectualism both in France and abroad. As a result of these perceptions and of the role of publishing houses such as Minuit, whose publications are by definition serious and avant-garde, feminism in France does not seem to have resulted in the questioning of the categories of high and low culture, or of the association of radical politics with high culture, which to some extent has taken place in Britain, for example through the publication by the Women's Press of lesbian crime fiction. The categories dividing and defining women's writing in France remain rigid.

The cultural and social context

The early years
The early years of the century are characterized by the relative absence of women writers from the literary scene, one significant exception being the group of women writers working in Paris which included Renée Vivien, Liane de Pougy and Lucie Delarue-Mardrus, as well as US expatriates such as ▷Natalie Barney. Colette knew, and was involved with, this group during her years as a music-hall artist, but she is the only francophone member of the group to have achieved celebrity. The group was dominantly lesbian and upper-class, and writers such as Vivien were clearly both celebrating and struggling with lesbian identity in their work. The presence of these writers perhaps indicates the greater tolerance of 'perversion' which existed in Paris at this time, compared with post-Victorian England, but their disappearance from the literary scene may in part be attributed to their sexuality, and to the fact that most of them lived in an exclusively female world. The *Dictionnaire Bordas* of 1985, for example, does mention Vivien, but the emphasis is at least as much on the scandal of her 'disordered life' as on her poetry, which is described as a pale reflection of Baudelairian sensuality. The class background of the members of this group, as well as the necessity of recourse to male patrons or pseudonyms, are indicative of the difficulties experienced by women writers in the early part of the 20th century in France. It is significant that despite this, and perhaps partly as a result of her years in a lesbian social milieu, Colette constantly questions conventional gender identity and roles; her heroines' struggle to retain their independence, their awareness of a possible conflict between heterosexuality and creativity, and the strength of the bonds between women in her novels make it possible to see her as a precursor of more recent feminist writing, and it is not surprising that The Women's Press reprinted the translation of *La Naissance du Jour* (1928), ▷*Break of Day*, in 1979.

The influence of de Beauvoir
Major landmarks in 20th-century French women's writing are the publication of *La Deuxième Sexe* in 1949, and the figure of de Beauvoir herself, the first woman writer simultaneously to be accepted by the male literary establishment and to create a scandal

because of her critique of patriarchy and her own unconventional life. De Beauvoir can perhaps be said to have set a precedent which has been followed by Cixous, Irigaray and Kristeva, in that they have all become writers on the basis of a firmly established academic reputation. Given the high value attributed to intellectualism by French culture, it was perhaps inevitable that French feminism should develop in this way, but in her descriptions of 'the independent woman', de Beauvoir may have helped to create a socially acceptable role, at least for some middle-class women intellectuals. The influence of de Beauvoir's analysis of the social construction of femininity on the women's movement, and therefore on a wide range of women's writing, has been seminal, and de Beauvoir's work can be said to have substantially altered the ideological climate in which women in France are writing. Marie Cardinal and Annie Leclerc, for example, in *Autrement Dit* (1977) (*In Other Words*) are to some extent pursuing one of the main themes of *The Second Sex* in their exploration of female social conditioning and of the feelings of alienation resulting from the experience of oneself as cultural 'other'. It is impossible here to provide more than a few examples of de Beauvoir's influence on recent feminist theory; it is, however, interesting to note that the tension between social construction theories of gender and an apparent tendency towards biological essentialism which has been seen as characteristic of exponents of feminine writing such as Cixous and Irigaray is already present in *The Second Sex*, perhaps indicating the difficulty, in a Catholic culture, of escaping from a sense of female biology as destiny, whether negative, as in the case of de Beauvoir, or positive, as in the case of writers such as Irigaray. ▷Evelyne Le Garrec's work on the heterosexual couple could be seen as a development of de Beauvoir's critique of bourgeois marriage, while for Monique Wittig, de Beauvoir's assertion that 'one is not born a woman' provides not only a title for one of her articles but also a basis for her contention that lesbians by definition do not conform to this process of socialization, and are therefore not 'women'. Irigaray's use of terms such as 'disguise' in connection with femininity, or her discussion of the market forces which determine the lives of women perceived as 'goods' under a patriarchal system, are not inimical to de Beauvoir's analysis of the various forms of slavery – married woman, woman in love or narcissist – which society deems acceptable roles for women.

The ▷MLF: new genres and new contents

De Beauvoir's influence came to fruition mainly after ▷May 1968, and in conjunction with the development of the women's movement, which itself has clearly had a formative impact on women's writing internationally. As a result of the movement's emphasis on the importance of women's experience and on consciousness-raising, women writers in the 1970s began to produce confessional novels; for francophone writers such as ▷Mariama Bâ from Senegal and the Camerounian ▷Lydie Dooh-Bunya the confessional has provided a suitable vehicle for the exploration of the experience of women in post-colonial Africa. Although France has contributed one of the most well-known examples of the genre – Marie Cardinal's *The Words to Say It* – the confessional novel was not widely adopted by French feminist writers, with the exception of a particular type of confessional – the 'intimate journal' of an adolescent girl. Colette's 'Claudine' (▷*Claudine Married*) novels are perhaps the first example of this phenomenon in the 20th century, but writers such as Sagan, ▷Françoise Mallet-Joris and Perrein returned to the theme in the 1950s, and they have had some feminist successors. Sagan's ▷*Bonjour Tristesse* (1954) and *Le Rempart des Béguines* (1951) (*The Illusionist*) by Mallet-Joris provoked a scandal in the 1950s because of their depiction of female sexuality, and the heroines' combination of *naïveté* and amorality, but these novels are certainly pre-feminist, in that there is no political critique of, for example, the ideology of romantic love. Nevertheless, their heroines' independence and fundamental solitude create the possibility of linking them with later feminist texts such as Rochefort's ▷*Children of Heaven* or Annie Ernaux's *Les Armoires vides*, where the confessions of the adolescent heroine show a critical awareness of her social situation, and where, unlike the 1950s texts, the issue of class background is raised.

It is clearly in this politicization of women's writing that the impact of the MLF (*Mouvement de Libération des Femmes*, French Women's Liberation Movement) is most profoundly felt. It is, however, important to note that for francophone writers the MLF has been a less formative influence politically than the experience of racism and colonialism, and that these writers were often politicized at a much earlier stage as a result of participation in liberation struggles. Assia Djebar, for example, was a member of the FLN (Algerian Liberation Front), and her writing focuses on the disillusionment which has resulted from the fact that, although Algerian women participated equally in the revolutionary struggle, independence has not fulfilled the promise of equality. For writers such as ▷ Maryse Condé from Guadeloupe, the legacy of colonialism and the question of black identity are fundamental.

In France from 1968 onwards the critique of patriarchy becomes a dominant theme for writers such as ▷ Elizabeth Badinter, ▷ Catherine Clément, Perrein, Le Garrec, Irigaray, Wittig and many others. Politically motivated texts such as ▷ Gisèle Halimi's *La Cause des femmes* (1972) (▷ *The Right to Choose*, 1977), an account of the struggle to legalize abortion in France, interspersed with autobiographical material and general discussion of women's oppression, are as much part of the MLF as political tracts such as the *Manifeste des 343* (*The Manifesto of the 343*), the petition signed by famous French women, including de Beauvoir, stating that they had all aborted.

In the realm of fiction, the formal innovations of feminine writing or of writers such as Wittig, are based on post-1968 questioning of patriarchal narrative and linguistic structures (see 'Women writers and the French language' earlier in this essay, and the essay 'Critical approaches'). In terms of content, the increased importance and politicization of issues of gender and sexuality in novels by women in the 1970s and 1980s in France, and the prevalence of texts dealing with motherhood, the mother–daughter relationship, or abortion are inextricably linked to the MLF's struggles in these areas, and reflect the preoccupations of the women's movement in a Catholic country where abortion was only legalized in 1974. In *Les Armoires vides*, for example, the narrative is framed by descriptions of the effects of a back-street abortion. The ideological pressure on women to become wives and mothers, particularly in provincial areas, has to some extent been institutionalized in post-war France by government policies which reward large families, and by discrimination against single people, for example, in the teaching profession. Writers such as Rochefort, Wittig and Ernaux have produced fictional critiques of this ideology using a variety of narrative techniques.

The influence of the MLF does not, however, confine itself to overtly feminist writing or to 'serious' literature: in the 1980s romantic fiction by writers such as ▷ Jacqueline Dana juxtaposed feminist ideologies of independence and self-sufficiency with the dominant view that normality is marriage and motherhood, and in the 1990s even here there is no certainty of a happy end.

▷ Lesbian feminist criticism

Germany, Austria and Switzerland

10

To this day, we have only a fragmentary history of women's writing in the German-speaking countries. Sporadic and often arbitrary highlights intersperse enormous areas that are still awaiting research. Countless women's texts have been lost through a simple lack of interest on the part of those who, in the course of time, created and determined the literary ▷canon.

As in other parts of the world, women writers in German-speaking Europe have been subject to a twofold set of determining circumstances. Like men's, their writing has been shaped by the historical and cultural particularities of their lifetime. Yet, unlike their male counterparts, female artists have also always had to contend with the specific cultural implications and limitations arising out of the simple fact of their having been born women.

German women's literature first emerges in the Middle Ages, especially during the 12th and 13th centuries, when Europe had begun to enjoy an unprecedented economic and cultural boom. It was a time when high-born men had gained enough wealth and enlightenment to have their daughters educated, to grant them access to books, and thus to make them aware of themselves and their cultural heritage; at last women could begin to write. Moreover, in the convents and the courts existed two main venues which offered women that further commodity, 'a room of one's own', in which to concentrate and have the solitude essential to all creative activity.

The literature of holy women

From the 10th century onwards, mystical texts composed in Latin by German-speaking women began to make an impact on the contemporary world. The writers, invariably nuns living in the seclusion of a convent, were on the whole well-educated, fluent in Latin, and familiar with classical culture. Many were teachers: the 10th-century Saxon nun ▷Hrotsvith von Gandersheim and the 12th-century Alsatian abbess ▷Herrad von Landsberg wrote first and foremost for the instruction of the sisters under their care, while the writings of the Dutch mystic and poet ▷Hadewijch became influential amongst the ▷Béguines, or lay sisters, of Nijvel in 13th-century Brabant. Other authors such as ▷Frau Ava, of Melk in Austria, the first woman known to have written in the German language, began their literary careers in old age, after retiring to a convent.

This period saw the rise of the literary genre known as ▷*Visionsliteratur*: writings by nuns who, often from early childhood onwards, had had intense religious experiences and visions. The most important author of such mystic texts was the 11th-century abbess ▷Hildegard von Bingen. Her prolific work, which comprises not only visionary writing but also scholarly treatises, poetry, musical compositions and much more, became known throughout Europe, and gained her a unique position of influence as a spiritual guide of her time.

By far the most famous and influential of 12th-century mystical texts was ▷Mechthild von Magdeburg's *Das fließende Licht der Gottheit* (1250–1260) (▷*The Revelations of Mechthild*, 1953). Written in a Swabian dialect, it was accessible to women who knew little Latin, and inspired a host of younger mystics, such as ▷Mechthild von Hackeborn, ▷Gertrud von Helfta, ▷Christine Ebner and ▷Margarethe Ebner.

In time, a new genre of chronicles recounting the spiritual lives of holy sisters began to emerge, especially in the Benedictine and Dominican convents of Alsace, southern

Germany, Hesse, Saxony, Switzerland and Austria. The writings of ▷Anna von Munzingen, ▷Katharina von Gebweiler, ▷Elsbeth Stagel and ▷Adelheid Langmann achieved wide circulation and became the focus of intense social and political interest, remaining influential for generations of German women. Indeed, the next two centuries saw a proliferation of unstructured, spontaneous texts written by nuns. These are records of all manner of personal religious experiences, frequently not dissimilar to modern psychological case-histories. They speak of real and imaginary illnesses, hysterical pregnancies, identifications with the Virgin Mary, and many similar phenomena. Such confessions remained an important strand of women's writing throughout the following centuries, and have been subject to interpretations as varied as expressions of Christian mysticism, and outbreaks of heresy and witchcraft.

The last medieval nun to achieve fame through her writing was ▷Caritas Pirckheimer, abbess of the Convent of St Klara in Nuremberg. A remarkable ▷humanist scholar and tolerant intellectual, she commanded widespread respect. From 1524 to 1528 she drew up a meticulous account of the raging arguments for and against the Lutheran Reformation, in an effort to ward off the mounting polarization of viewpoints. She sought in vain to protect her Catholic establishment against all kinds of fanaticism and the tide of change.

Court literature
Medieval European aristocracy was essentially cosmopolitan. Through intermarriage and a shared culture, the ruling families of the courts of Germany were in constant contact with the rest of the Holy Roman Empire and beyond. Hence, when during the 15th century noblewomen began to write in German, they saw their mission as being, above all, to translate and edit those texts that were already well known in the Florentine, Venetian and French courts, and in comparison with which Germany was something of a cultural backwater. ▷Elisabeth von Nassau-Saarbrücken belonged to a highly sophisticated and well-educated family. It had its political and cultural roots in France, where a tradition of courtly arts had long been flourishing. Elisabeth's family had been keen to spread French cultural refinement to German territory. Of the many *chansons de geste* which her mother, Margarete von Vaudemont, had collected, Elisabeth translated four into German: *Sibille*, *Herpin, Loher und Maller* and, must popular of all, ▷*Huge Scheppel* (c 1450). (The later reprinting of these works aroused new interest at the beginning of the 19th century, when ▷Dorothea Schlegel undertook a reappraisal of Elisabeth's work.) In the same way, ▷Eleonore von Österreich's novel ▷*Pontus und Sidonia* (c 1450) is a transcription from the French *Pontius et la belle Sidonie*, a tale of adventure and chivalry which went on to enjoy great popularity, especially in the 17th century.

It was in the 17th century that the quest for courtly refinement in Germany began to gather momentum, finding its great exponent in ▷Sophie Elisabeth von Braunschweig-Lüneburg. A composer and poet herself, she was a vigorous promoter of the arts, which she understood to be an essential instrument for the education and refinement of her children and her courtiers. She too based her only novel on a French model, hoping to make French sophistication accessible to her readers. Her step-daughter, ▷Sibylle Ursula von Braunschweig-Lüneburg, initially continued in this tradition by translating a number of French plays and novels; moreover, together with her brothers and sisters, she produced a completely original piece of German fiction, the fragment *Aramena* (c 1660).

The Reformation
During the Reformation the rise of the German middle-class to economic power, self-awareness and self-esteem accelerated the shift in cultural emphasis from Latin and Romance languages to the vernacular. Since literature was no longer confined to the clergy and the aristocracy, middle-class women too could now occasionally have access to education. Interestingly, the women who began to make an impact with their writing were almost all Protestant. ▷Katharina Zell, who married a Catholic priest, the indefatigable

▷Argula von Grumbach and the combative ▷Anna Ovena Hoyers all devoted their creative energies and personal happiness to the Protestant cause, while an ordinary lay-person and woman teacher, ▷Magdalena Heymair, made a name for herself in homes and classrooms throughout southern Germany with her handy books aimed at teaching children Christian behaviour and Bible stories. Among the aristocracy, the poet ▷Elisabeth von Braunschweig-Lüneburg distinguished herself as a fervent, if unsuccessful, promoter of Protestantism, with her religious polemic *Christlicher Sendebrieff (Christian Epistle)* of 1545, with which she attempted to convert her subjects.

The 17th century

The era of the German Baroque saw the rise of *Sprachgesellschaften*, societies which aimed to improve and purify the German language and to enhance poetic endeavour. Although a small number of women, the precocious ▷Sybilla Schwarz among them, were beginning to make names for themselves as poets, they were usually excluded from these literary societies. However, one progressive literary society, the *Pegnesischer Blumenorden* in Nuremberg, began to accept membership of both men and women writers. When ▷Maria Catharina Stockfleth and the Austrian poet ▷Catharina Regina von Greiffenberg became associated with this literary group, they were amongst the first German women able, in some measure, to develop their literary talent within a protective circle of like-minded colleagues.

This was also a time when exceptionally gifted women could, very occasionally, begin to publicize their talents. The German-Dutch Renaissance genius ▷Anna Maria van Schurmann, for example, who knew twelve languages, achieved international fame because of her erudition in the sciences and the arts. As a rare privilege she was permitted to follow lectures from within a screened cage in a lecture theatre at the University of Utrecht. However, very few of her published works remain, apart from a Latin treatise from 1638 on the subject of whether women were capable of scientific argument. However, within a few decades, two other notable female scientists were able to publish works, in Silesia and in Frankfurt. The first of these, by ▷Maria Cunitz, was an introduction to Kepler's mathematical calculations, *Urania propitia* (1650) (*Propitious Urania*); the second, by ▷Maria Sibylla Merian, was a detailed study in two volumes of the ecology and development of the caterpillar, *Der Raupen wunderbare Verwandelung und sonderbare Blumen-nahrung* (1679 and 1683) (*The Marvellous Metamorphosis, and Especial Sustenance from Flowers, of Caterpillars*). Both works contributed greatly to the advancement of science in Germany.

The 18th century

The 18th century was a period of unprecedented cultural and artistic achievement in Germany. The Age of the ▷Enlightenment saw the upsurge of male writers and literary theorists, such as Gottsched, Bodmer and Breitinger, who scoured the classics for new models appropriate to the 18th-century German artistic sensibility. The tiny court of Weimar became the unrivalled cultural centre of the German-speaking world, and Goethe (1749–1832) and Schiller (1759–1805) extended the influence of German literature far beyond the borders of the Holy Roman Empire. This was also a period when education for women became more widespread. Indeed men increasingly considered the company of refined and educated women as a desirable status symbol, a sign of their own cultural sophistication. In such a climate, the poets ▷Christiana Mariana von Ziegler and ▷Sidonia Hedwigh Zäunemann developed their poetic work, and even aspired to the rare honour of becoming poet laureates at German universities.

On the whole, however, women's literary achievement was still considered to be an exception, if not an aberration. Popular opinion held that a respectable woman would never wish to expose herself to the limelight of publicity by publishing a book. Invariably those women who did write did so anonymously, or else published their work under their husband's name, or, failing that, under an invented ▷pseudonym. More often than not, their literary achievement remained unattributable, while their literary discourse continued to be peripheral to the great German intellectual currents of the Enlightenment and 18th-century classicism.

Respite the limitations imposed upon women's literature, a number of distinct genres of women's writing did, none the less, begin to emerge and develop in the 18th century.

Letters and memoirs

Letter-writing became a mode of expression in which women could excel. Letters addressed to family and friends about domestic issues, personal experiences and private thoughts and emotions were a means of self-expression for educated women. Among the earliest German letter writers were Elisabeth Charlotte (Liselotte) von der Pfalz, ▷Luise Gottsched and ▷Sophie La Roche, whose elegant and sophisticated correspondence reveals their complex intellects. Of particular value and interest today are the letters written by ▷Henriette Herz and ▷Rahel Varnhagen, who were active participants in Berlin ▷salon culture at the beginning of the 19th century. Above all, the great women letter-writers were those figures associated with the German romantic movement, ▷Sophie Mereau, ▷Caroline Schlegel-Schelling, ▷Dorothea Schlegel, and especially ▷Bettina von Arnim. Their wide-ranging correspondence with friends and public figures brought new heights of achievement to the art of women's letter-writing.

Letter-writing as a literary genre is closely related to the writing of diaries, confessions, memoirs and autobiographies, all of which have been central to women's writing in many languages from the earliest times. Indeed, throughout the course of German literary history we find sporadic examples of such writing. The confessional and visionary texts of medieval nuns can certainly be seen in this light. We also have the remarkable memoirs of ▷Helene Kottaner, recounting the political intrigue at the 15th-century Viennese court, and the Yiddish autobiography of the housewife ▷Glückel von Hameln, which offers a rare account of Jewish life in 17th-century Hamburg. Even more extraordinary is the account of a woman's life on the Napoleonic battlefields related by the Swiss writer ▷Regula Engel, the wife of a French officer, and mother of twenty-one children.

Diaries and memoirs such as these began to proliferate towards the end of the 18th century. The journals of ▷Elisabeth von der Recke, for example, and the recollections of Goethe's Weimar by ▷Johanna Schopenhauer, offer valuable insights into aspects of women's lives in those times.

Early women's fiction

From real diaries, memoirs and letters it was but a small step to the fictional genre of the novel in letter form. In 1771 appeared, anonymously, the first German woman's novel: ▷*Geschichte des Fräuleins von Sternheim* (*The Story of Fräulein von Sternheim*). Once it became public knowledge that the author was Sophie La Roche, the respectable mother of five, the book created a sensation and became the touchstone for further German women's novels: ▷*Die Familie Seldorf* (1795) (*The Seldorf Family*) and *Ellen Percy, oder die Erziehung durch Schicksale* (1822) (*Ellen Percy, or Education Through Fate*) by ▷Therese Huber, *Agnes von Lilien* (1796) by ▷Friederike Wolzogen, *Gabriele* (1819) by ▷Johanna Schopenhauer and *Elisa, oder das Weib wie es sein sollte* (1802) (*Elisa, or Woman as She Should Be*) by ▷Wilhelmine Wobeser, all, in one way or another, emulate Sophie La Roche's seminal example. Henceforth the novel became the paramount medium for women seeking to give a literary form to their own experiences. The ▷*Bildungsroman* (novel of early life) was already a well-established genre in German literature, and early women novelists such as ▷Ida von Hahn-Hahn, ▷Fanny Lewald, ▷Luise Mühlbach and ▷Wilhelmine von Hillern firmly established the heroine as the subject in this kind of German fiction. Their books enjoyed a large and enthusiastic readership throughout the 19th century.

Periodicals

Journals and periodicals were a further medium through which German women began to find literary expression. In 18th-century Germany, journals edited by established male writers such as Wieland or Schiller were extremely fashionable. There were also a number of periodicals issued by women and directed at a specifically female readership. One of the most successful was Sophie La Roche's *Pomona*. It became an acknowledged model and encouraged a number of younger women, including the Swiss writer ▷Marianne Ehrmann and the German ▷Sophie Mereau, to edit magazines of their own. Indeed, women's periodicals were to become an increasingly important factor in the education and consciousness-raising of German women in the revolutionary years of the early 19th century. The *Frauen-Zeitung* (1849–1852) (*Women's Journal*), for example, issued by the progressive thinkers ▷Mathilde Franziska Anneke and ▷Louise Otto-Peters, was a sophisticated and innovative cultural and political organ. Although closed down by the Saxon authorities after only four years, it created an important precedent for later journals such as *Die Frau* (*Woman*). Edited for a time by the important early feminists Helene Lange and ▷Gertrud Bäumer, it became a leading voice within the German women's movement.

The stirrings of revolution

No one in Europe remained untouched by the cataclysm of the revolution which shook France in 1789. The ferment of radical thinking had already been growing for some time in Germany, even among women. Flickers of an awareness of social injustice can, for example, be traced back as far as the poems of ▷Anna Rupertina Fuchs towards the end of the 17th century. Interestingly, it was always the most successful woman writers of the early 18th century, such as ▷Christiana Mariana von Ziegler, ▷Sidonia Hedwig Zäunemann, ▷Anna Louisa Karsch and ▷Johanne Charlotte Unzer, who complained loudest about the restricted role women were forced to play in German society. Indeed, the women who dared to challenge received notions of womanhood had often gained the courage and self-confidence to do so from the fact that they could earn a living from their writing.

The romantics

Of the handful of women prominently associated with the romantic movement in Germany, most were caught up in the cross-currents of progressive and regressive thinking so typical of German romanticism. Dorothea Schlegel, Caroline Schlegel-Schelling, Sophie Mereau, Bettina von Arnim and her friend, ▷Karoline von Günderode, were all women of exceptional literary talent and progressive, even revolutionary, ideas. With their unconventional lifestyles, they were ready to confront public opinion and challenge received notions about the role of women. Yet in their personal relationships with their male associates and lovers, these women seemed to be subject to the dictates of a patriarchal society, just like generations of women before them. Dorothea Schlegel, and especially her sister-in-law, Caroline Schlegel-Schelling, were utterly dependent on the support of the influential Schlegel brothers, who also became their respective husbands. For years these two women worked for and with their husbands without acknowledgement, often publishing their own work under their husbands' names. Similarly, Sophie Mereau, one of the first professional women writers in Germany, published her first novel anonymously. Once she had married the poet Clemens von Brentano (1778–1842), having divorced Friedrich Mereau, who had been supportive of her literary ambitions, she completely gave up publishing and died in childbirth three years later. Karoline von Günderode sought in vain for an utopian alternative to social reality and committed suicide at the age of twenty-six. Of all the women linked with the romantic movement, only Bettina von Arnim seems to have managed to approach her full creative potential.

Fairytales, stories of village life and the novella
An important aspect of German romanticism was its interest in German history and cultural heritage. This interest led to a revival of traditional forms of story-telling. Indeed, the collections of folk stories, *Kinder- und Hausmärchen* (*Tales of Children and the House*), which the brothers Grimm began publishing in 1812 were to inspire countless other writers to regenerate and modify this oral tradition of folk tales, told for centuries by old women around the hearths of German cottages. What is not generally known, however, is that almost two decades before the brothers Grimm, between 1789 and 1793, ▷Christiane Naubert had published a collection of folk stories in *Die neuen Volksmärchen der Deutschen* (*The New German Folktales*). This work remains unaccountably neglected to this day, though the Grimms and other contemporaries certainly knew of it. Equally, Naubert's own superb 'art-tales' have not been republished since 1826.

Fairytales and stories of the supernatural seem to have been the favourite medium of countless women writers in 19th-century Germany. Scores of unsigned tales were published by authors such as ▷Karoline de la Motte Fouqué, ▷Sophie Bernhardi and ▷Adele Schopenhauer. Many of these stories were set in a specific German locality.

Stories of village life were a particularly popular genre in 19th-century German literature generally, and women writers were as attracted to it as their male counterparts. ▷Ottilie Wildermuth, ▷Hermine Villinger, ▷Ida Boy-Ed, ▷Margarethe von Bülow, ▷Helene Christaller, ▷Helene Voigt-Diederichs and ▷Lena Christ all wrote evocative stories set in the closely-knit, even claustrophobic, rural communities of 19th- and early 20th-century Germany. As a more ambitious medium for the same kind of subject matter, the novella also became extremely popular among women writers. One of the best-known and most accomplished of these is ▷Annette von Droste-Hülshoff's *Die Judenbuche* (1841) (▷ *The Jew's Beech*). Other prominent writers of novellas were ▷Isolde Kurz, and, above all, the Austrian ▷Marie von Ebner-Eschenbach. Her ▷*Krambambuli* (1875) is to this day considered the greatest example of this genre.

Travelogues
The late 19th century was also a time when women began to travel and note down their experiences in travelogues. The genre began with ▷Emilie von Berlepsch, whose journeys in Scotland gave rise to the book *Caledonia* (1802–1804). Johanna Schopenhauer also published an account of her travels in England in 1818, *Reise durch England und Schottland* (1818) (*Journey through England and Scotland*). The outstanding exponent of such writing is the Austrian ▷Ida Pfeiffer, who wrote a remarkable account of her travels around the world. The works of ▷Therese von Bacheracht and ▷Claire von Glümer, and especially ▷Frieda von Bülow's descriptions of East Africa, were also to open up the world for generations of German women readers at home. In fact women's travel writing became so popular that by the beginning of the 20th century even quite ordinary working women from remote Swiss villages, such as ▷Lina Bögli or ▷Annelise Rüegg, could envisage travelling the world and publishing their impressions.

Women who dared: the advent of feminine dissent
Women's intellectual emancipation, so tentatively initiated in the Age of the Enlightenment, began to gather momentum in the 19th century. In the aftermath of the French Revolution (1789) and the Napoleonic Wars, the Congress of Vienna in 1815 ushered in a period of extreme ideological and cultural repression in German-speaking Europe. With ruthless authoritarianism and censorship, the German and Austrian authorities tried to stem the tide of progressive thinking. It was also a time when women writers began to divide into distinct factions. One of the foremost writers and poets of 19th-century Germany, Annette von Droste-Hülshoff belongs to the traditionalist, bourgeois group, along with Austrian poet ▷Betty Paoli and Wilhelmine von Hillern, as well as the prolific and hugely popular novelists, ▷Eugenie Marlitt and Helene Christaller, who

supplied the conservative majority of ordinary housewives with innumerable escapist romances. In the opposing camp were ▷Fanny Lewald and Ida von Hahn-Hahn, whose novels were early analyses of women's bondage in marriage.

One of the first women to brave controversy with her political writing was Bettina von Arnim, who took up the general cause of the dispossessed in ▷*Dies Buch gehört dem König!* (1843) (*This Book belongs to the King!*), and in an unpublishable book about the poor, *Das Armenbuch* (*The Book of the Poor*). ▷Louise Aston, on the other hand, espoused the more specific issue of women's emancipation; her autobiographical *Meine Emanzipation* (*My Emancipation*) of 1846 eloquently portrays the repressive authoritarian system and the misogynistic attitudes with which a radical woman had to contend in 19th-century Berlin. Against the background of growing German nationalism, the Franco–Prussian War (1871) and the unification of the German states under Bismarck, the women's movement began to sharpen its focus.

Pamphlets and essays that discussed the position of women in a new world appeared in increasing numbers. They range from the fairly liberal arguments of early writers like ▷Luise Büchner and Elisabeth von der Recke to Louise Otto-Peters's more pronounced demands for equal rights. Many of these early feminists, such as the Germans Fanny Lewald, ▷Hedwig Dohm, ▷Elisabethm Dauthenday, ▷Lily Braun; the Austrians ▷Minna Kautsky, ▷Irma von Troll-Borostyani, ▷Rosa Mayreder, ▷Maria Janitschek and the Swiss ▷Meta Salis-Marschlins, came from wealthy bourgeois or aristocratic families. Moreover, the most popular novels of the time, although progressive in thought, invariably depict the struggle of wealthy, middle-class heroines to achieve personal emancipation. Typical of this kind of novel are ▷Gabriele Reuter's ▷*Aus guter Familie* (1895) (*Of Good Family*) and ▷Helene Böhlau's ▷*Halbtier!* (1899) (*Half-animal!*). It was not until 1909, with the autobiography of the ▷factory worker ▷Adelheid Popp, that a working-class woman made any impact at all upon women's literature in German.

The 20th century: new departures
In the broader political struggle for universal social justice, three German-speaking women made an impact which extended far beyond the confines of their own countries. The Austrian pacifist ▷Bertha von Suttner, the socialist orator ▷Clara Zetkin, and above all the revolutionary ▷Rosa Luxemburg, reached positions of political and ideological influence unprecedented in the history of German women.

The end of the 19th century had brought a surge of female intellectual emancipation. The University of Zurich was the first to open its doors to women in the 1860s, and soon attracted outstanding students including ▷Ilse Frapan, ▷Käthe Schirmacher, ▷Lou Andreas-Salomé, ▷Ricarda Huch and Rosa Luxemburg herself. Women's writing took on a new professionalism, exemplified in Huch's work on the Thirty Years War (1618–1648), and Andreas-Salomé's writings on Freud and female sexuality. Interestingly, these non-fictional works exhibit an independence of thought which neither author could match in her fiction.

World War I
The advent of war galvanized a number of women writers into taking a conscious stance on the events overtaking Europe. In 1915 the octogenarian feminist Hedwig Dohm came out of retirement to publish a blistering attack on the new barbarism committed in the name of European culture. On the whole, however, women writers of the older generation, such as Käthe Schirmacher, Ricarda Huch and ▷Ina Seidel, betray a certain ambivalence about the war, tending to vacillate uneasily between describing the glories of death on the battlefield and their anguish at the destruction of Germany's youth. It was the younger and more radical writers, like ▷Berta Lask, ▷Annette Kolb and ▷Claire Goll, who were ready to challenge public opinion with powerful anti-war poems, stories and polemics. Ten years after the German defeat, ▷Ilse Langner's ▷*Frau Emma kämpft im Hinterland* (*Emma Fights on the Home Front*) was performed in Berlin, the first anti-war

play by a woman, and, in 1930 ▷Adrienne Thomas briefly became famous for her bestselling anti-war novel, *Die Katrin wird Soldat* (*Katrin becomes a Soldier*).

After the war, women's fiction also began to focus increasingly on aspects of everyday life. Austrian writer ▷Hermynia Zur Mühlen, and the Germans ▷Gabriele Tergit, ▷Christa Anita Brueck, ▷Marieluise Fleißer, ▷Hedda Zinner and ▷Irmgard Keun (*Das kunstseidene Mädchen*, 1932, ▷*The Artificial Silk Girl*, 1933) wrote pithily about the stifling hypocrisies of the German petite-bourgeoisie.

The early decades of the 20th century also saw an unprecedented blossoming of women's poetry. Young women such as Berta Lask and ▷Ruth Schaumann responded clearly to the challenge of Expressionism. Claire Goll, ▷Elisabeth Langgässer, ▷Paula Ludwig, and especially ▷Else Lasker-Schüler and ▷Gertrud Kolmar, began to write about womanhood, sexuality and religious feeling in arresting new mythic images.

The advent of the Third Reich under Adolf Hitler brought all this progressive activity to an end. Women were once again relegated to the task of producing children; the women's movement went underground. Jewish writers such as Else Lasker-Schüler, ▷Nelly Sachs, ▷Anna Seghers and ▷Hilde Domin were forced into exile. Those Jewish writers who stayed, ▷Rose Ausländer and Gertrud Kolmar, faced persecution and even death. Many novelists writing during the 1930s turned inwards and expressed their anguish in strangely-coded and repressed form. Langgässer's *Das unauslöschliche Siegel* (*The Indelible Seal*) (written in the 1930s and published in 1946), ▷Marie Luise Kaschnitz's *Elissa* (1937) or ▷Luise Rinser's *Die gläsernen Ringe* (1941) (*The Glass Rings*) are all typical of this response to fascism. There were, of course, also women writers whose work wittingly or unwittingly gained the approval of the Nazis. They included ▷Agnes Miegel, Ina Seidel and ▷Josefa Berens-Totenohl.

Women writers in East Germany

After the German defeat in World War II, the German nation split into two: the Federal Republic of Germany (FRG) in the west and the socialist German Democratic Republic (GDR) in the east. From the outset, women writers in East Germany, just like male authors, were called upon to help build up the new communist state. Berta Lask, ▷Anna Seghers and ▷Elfriede Brüning responded to this challenge, dedicating their creative efforts to the socialist cause. Young writers adopted the idiom of ▷socialist realism, ▷Brigitte Reimann with her *Ankunft im Alltag* (1961) (*Arrival in Everyday Life*) and ▷Christa Wolf with the novel *Der geteilte Himmel* (1963) (*The Divided Heaven*, 1965).

In the 1970s new themes began to appear. In 1974 ▷Irmtraud Morgner achieved acclaim in the West with her artful and extravagant critique of universal patriarchy, ▷*Leben und Abenteuer der Trobadora Beatriz nach Zeugnissen ihrer Spielfrau Laura* (1974) (*Life and Adventures of the Troubadour Beatriz According to the Testimony of her Minstrel Laura*). Two years later came the publication of *Kindheitsmuster* (1976) (▷*Patterns of Childhood*, 1984), ▷Christa Wolf's highly-acclaimed examination of recent German history from a woman's point of view, and, with the publication of *Kassandra* (1983) (▷*Cassandra*, 1984), a complex analysis of male militarism, Wolf firmly established herself as a powerful voice in the international women's movement.

Despite censorship and oppressive authoritarianism, women's literature thrived in East Germany during the 1970s and 1980s. Writers included ▷Gerti Tetzner, ▷Helga Schütz, ▷Helga Königsdorf, ▷Monika Maron and ▷Helga Schubert – as well as ▷Maxie Wander, who in 1958 had moved to East Germany from Vienna. Some East German women writers did move (or were expelled) to the West. Yet these authors too, ▷Christa Reinig, ▷Helga Novak and ▷Sarah Kirsch, had all first developed as artists within the formative force-field of socialist optimism.

Coming to terms with the past in the Federal Republic

In 1945 Germany had reached the nadir of its social and cultural existence. In the east, Germans strove to build a state following a new, communist model, but in the west too, everything had to be rethought, reinvented and rebuilt. Women writers now played an important part in the revival of German literature. ▷Marie Luise Kaschnitz's poems of 1947 about the destruction of Frankfurt, the novel *Die größere Hoffnung* (1948) (*The Greater Hope*) by Austrian ▷Ilse Aichinger, Luise Rinser's novella ▷*Jan Lobel aus Warschau* (1948) (*Jan Lobel from Warsaw*) and ▷Ingeborg Drewitz's play about concentration camps, *Alle Tore waren bewacht* (1951) (*All Gates Were Guarded*), are early examples of women writers seeking to confront the moral repercussions of the Third Reich. It is a subject which, to this day, remains central to German literature by men and women alike, in both east and west. Among the novels which tackle the subject from a woman's point of view are Austrian ▷Ingeborg Bachmann's *Jugend in einer österreichischen Stadt* (1961) (*Growing up in an Austrian Town*), ▷Geno Hartlaub's *Lokaltermin Feenreich* (1972) (*Fairyland in Local Terms*), ▷Christa Wolf's *Kindheitsmuster*, ▷Helga Novak's ▷*Die Eisheiligen* (1979) (*Saints of Ice*), ▷Karin Reschke's *Memoiren eines Kindes* (*Memoirs of a Child*) (1980) and ▷Eva Zeller's *Solange ich denken kann* (1981) (*As Long as I can Think*).

With the advent of the German economic miracle in the 1960s, women writers began to deal with the theme of women's alienation in a modern consumer society. ▷Marlen Haushofer, ▷Renate Rasp, ▷Hannelies Taschau, ▷Gisela Elsner and ▷Angelika Mechtel, and especially ▷Ingeborg Bachmann and ▷Gabriele Wohmann, have been steady chroniclers of women's lives in post-war West Germany and Austria. They have written about rampant materialism, women's anguish in the face of moral and cultural bankruptcy, and the absurdities of modern existence. A poignant example of a novel in this vein is ▷Barbara Frischmuth's ▷*Über die Verhältnisse* (1987) (*Beyond One's Means*).

Another strand to women's writing in German is the radical feminism that emerged out of the student unrest of 1968. Most sensationally the Swiss writer ▷Verena Stefan broke new ground with ▷*Häutungen* (1975) (▷*Shedding*, 1978), an innovative and experimental piece of feminist writing which became the touchstone for the radical women's movement. *Klassenliebe* (1973) (*Love of Class*) by ▷Karin Struck and ▷Svende Merian's *Der Tod des Märchenprinzen* (1980) (*The Death of the Fairy Prince*) also enjoyed great popularity with increasing numbers of angry young women in the 1980s.

A growing interest in psychoanalysis and its patriarchal roots underlies recent novels on the father–daughter relationship, such as *Mitteilung an den Adel* (1976) (*Message to the Noble*) by German ▷Elisabeth Plessen, *Das Kartenhaus* (1978) (*House of Cards*) by Swiss ▷Margrit Schriber and *Lange Abwesenheit* (1980) (*Prolonged Absence*) by Austrian ▷Brigitte Schwaiger. Mother-daughter relationships are examined in the novels *Die Mutter* (1975) (*The Mother*) by Karin Struck, *Ausflug mit der Mutter* (1976) (*Outing with the Mother*)by ▷Gabriele Wohmann, and especially in *Die Eisheiligen* by Helga Novak and *Über die Verhältnisse* by Austrian Barbara Frischmuth.

In a world where the 'macho' values of technological progress, material wealth and public success are seen to count for everything, women's literature begins to speak, increasingly, of women as victims. Indeed, the premature deaths of two most accomplished Austrian novelists, ▷Marlen Haushofer and Ingeborg Bachmann, have often been interpreted in this light. ▷Maria Erlenberger's *Hunger nach Wahnsinn* (1977) (*Hunger for Madness*) led the way for a series of novels in which illness becomes a metaphor for feminine alienation. These include the Swiss writers ▷Claudia Storz's *Jessica mit Konstruktionsfehlern* (1977) (*Jessica with Construction Faults*) and ▷Maja Beutler's *Fuß fassen* (1980) (*Gaining a Foothold*) and German Gabriele Wohmann's ▷*Ach wie gut, daß niemand weiß* (1980) (*Oh How Lucky No One Knows*).

At the same time, women are also writing socially-committed novels which focus on specific public issues. ▷Monika Maron was one of the first authors to tackle the subject of industrial pollution in East Germany, with *Flugasche* (1981) (*Flying Ash*), though Ilse Langner, Christa Wolf and ▷Gertrud Wilker have also addressed the various dangers of pollution and nuclear technology.

Another strand of women's writing in the 1970s and 1980s has been the surge of experimental literature which seeks to express the female sensibility through new styles and forms. The prime example of this trend is Verena Stefan's *Häutungen*, but less polemical texts by ▷Erica Pedretti, ▷Hanna Johansen, Barbara Frischmuth and particularly ▷Brigitte Kronauer and ▷Gertrud Leutenegger have also succeeded in finding fresh ways of expressing the modern woman's experience.

▷German-speaking Swiss writers

Bib: Arnold, Heinz Ludwig (ed.) *Kritisches Lexikon zur deutschsprachigen Gegenwartsliteratur*; Brinker-Gabler, Gisela (ed.), *Deutsche Literatur von Frauen*, Vols. 1 & 2 and *Deutsche Dichterinnen*; Brinker-Gabler, Gisela, Ludwig, Karola and Wöffen, Angela (eds.), *Lexikon deutschsprachiger Schriftstellerinnen 1800–1945*; Frederiksen, Elke (ed.), *Women Writers of Germany, Austria and Switzerland*; Gnüg, Hiltrud and Möhrmann, Renate (eds.), *Frauen Literatur Geschichte*.

STEPHEN M. HART

11 Spain

The earliest surviving literary text in Spanish, probably written some time during the 9th century, expresses a woman's love, and may have been written by a woman:

> *Tant' amare, tant' amare,*
> *habib, tant' amare;*
> *enfermiron welyos nidios*
> *e dolen tan male.*

(So much loving, so much loving, / my lover, so much loving; / my eyes have fallen ill / they grieve me so.)

Despite such a promising start, however, it is not until the 15th century that a definite tradition of women writers in Spain emerges, and even then the tradition is Sappho-like and fragmentary. The first work known to be written by a woman published in the Iberian peninsular is the ▷*Memorias* (*Memoirs*) of ▷Leonor López de Córdoba. Other important writers of the time are ▷Teresa de Cartagena and ▷Florencia Pinar. One female writer of this period who deserves special mention is ▷Isabel de Villena, whose major work ▷*Vita Christi* was published posthumously in 1497. Written towards the end of her life, it describes the life of Christ, paying special attention to the episodes relating to women. Arguing against the misogyny prevalent in the Middle Ages, Villena's work points to woman's fundamental role in the redemption of the human race and in the life of Jesus Christ.

The Golden Age

The year 1492 saw three major events in Spain's history – the 'discovery' of the Americas by Columbus, the expulsion of the Jews from the Iberian Peninsular and the publication of Nebrija's *Gramática castellana*. These events ushered in the Golden Age (or *Siglo de Oro*) of Spanish culture.

The *Siglo de Oro* is dominated by two female literary figures. The first of these was

▷Santa Teresa de Ávila. Her masterpiece, ▷*El libro de la vida* (*The Book of Her Life*), is written in a plain, direct style which echoes the rhythms of everyday speech, and the metaphors she uses to describe her mystic experience are drawn from everyday life. By any standards, Santa Teresa's works are classics. Another important figure during this period was ▷María de Zayas y Sotomayor, whose witty portraitures of love in the 17th century, particularly her ▷*Novelas amorosas y exemplares* (*Exemplary Love Stories*) and *Desengaños amorosos* (*Disillusionment in Love*), were widely acclaimed.

Women writers and patriarchy – 18th to 20th century

The 18th century in Spain is a relatively barren field for the study of women's writing, but the picture soon changes when we reach the 19th century. Like ▷George Eliot in England and ▷George Sand in France, many Spanish female writers in the 19th century felt constrained to adopt a male pseudonym for the furtherance of their professional career. ▷Cecilia Böhl von Faber was Spain's most acclaimed writer from the mid-19th century to the revolution of 1868 and the advent of realism, yet still she felt the need to adopt a male pseudonym – Fernán Caballero, '*caballero*' meaning 'gentleman'. Her masterpiece, ▷*La gaviota* (*The Seagull*), tells a tale of love in a rural setting, and true to her adoptive name, reveals an uncritical acceptance of patriarchal views concerning the role expected of women by society. A young German surgeon, Stein, falls in love with, transforms and marries a beautiful peasant girl, Marisalada. When her husband eventually dies, she returns to her native village and marries the barber.

The need to retain a veil of gender secrecy continued well into the 20th century, as witnessed by ▷Caterina Albert, who used the pseudonym Victor Català throughout her writing career. Her best work, ▷*Solitud* (*Solitude*), is a savage fishing tale. It tells the story of how Mila accompanies her ineffectual husband to a remote hermitage where he has taken a keeper's job. When her husband eventually has a nervous breakdown, Mila is left at the end of the novel, alone but liberated. When Albert's identity became known she was attacked by her contemporaries, who considered it improper for a woman to write such 'crude' works.

Another type of gender secrecy, more implicit than explicit, which has also tended to keep women writers of this period in the shade, is dominance by their more famous literary husbands. Examples are ▷Josefina R. Aldecoa, the wife of Ignacio Aldecoa; ▷Clementina Arderiu, wife of Carles Riba; ▷María Teresa de León, wife of Rafael Alberti; and ▷María de la O Martínez Sierra, wife of Gregorio Martínez Sierra. While being married to an established writer might be thought to provide greater opportunity in the sense of introductions to potential publishers through literary coteries, in some cases it proved to have a negative effect. It is now clear, for example, that many of the novels which Gregorio Martínez Sierra originally passed off as his own were in fact penned by his wife. Marriage to a famous writer has also occasionally led to a wife's work being seen as an accompaniment in a minor key to the major work of the husband (as in the case of Clementina Arderiu with Carles Riba).

Perhaps understandably, much of the literature written by women in Spain in the 19th century conforms to patriarchal assumptions. In works such as *Cantares gallegos* (*Galician Songs*) and ▷*Follas novas* (*New Leaves*), ▷Rosalía de Castro combined a sensitive use of traditional metre with a peculiarly ▷Galician structure of feeling, epitomized by *saudade* (longing, nostalgia), a term which covers both longing for an absent loved one and nostalgia for one's homeland. In its recourse to melancholy and its plangent tone, however, Castro's poetry became an easy target for masculinist critics eager to dismiss her work in terms of the 'weaker sex'.

Some 19th-century female writers, however, definitely did not languish in the shade of their male contemporaries. ▷Gertrudis Gómez de Avellaneda, for example, who wrote romantic poetry, novels and dramas, did not shy away from forcefully expressing the fact that women were victims of the society in which they lived; she also attacked the institution of marriage. A similar stridency of tone is evident in the work of the Galician countess, ▷Emilia Pardo Bazán, indisputably one of the giants of 19th-century naturalism. Her novels are on a par with the best of her male contemporaries, such as Pérez Galdós, Leopoldo Alas and Valera. In her Catholic-naturalist novel, ▷*Los pazos de Ulloa* (1886) (*The House of Ulloa*), Pardo Bazán unmasks the decadence of the upper classes: a marquis who has no right to the title; a steward, Primitivo, who exploits the estates, and the outwitting of a responsible priest by a lie. The novel is a feminist exposure of patriarchy and the physical maltreatment of women. The sequel to this novel, *La madre naturaleza* (*Mother Nature*), involves an 'innocent' incest theme set against a lush natural backdrop.

Post-war Spain

In the various 'generations' which dominated the literary map of Spain during the first few decades of the 20th century – such as the Generation of 1898, the Generation of 1927 (or 1925, as it is sometimes called), the Generations of 1936 and of 1950 – women writers were conspicuously absent: Ernesta de Champourcin and ▷Rosa Chacel were the exceptions who proved the rule. It was only in the post-war period that some of the promise held out by such writers as Gómez de Avellaneda and Pardo Bazán bore fruit. The victors of the Spanish Civil War (1936–1939) were a right-wing coalition of Army, Church, capitalists and wealthy landowners, and the propaganda machine set up by General Franco after the war alienated sections of the Spanish population, such as the communists, the working class, writers and, of course, women. Franco forbade the use of any language in Spanish territory other than Castilian, and this had dire consequences for literature written in ▷Catalan, Galician and ▷Basque. Women writers who wished to write in one of these minority languages found themselves, therefore, doubly disenfranchised, 'the proletariat of the proletariat' as it were.

Despite the resistance of officialdom, however, some women writers continued to publish in their native vernacular, especially in Catalan. Of the Spanish women writers included in this book, almost a quarter have published in Catalan, which gives an indication of how important the contribution of the literature of the minority languages is to Spain's cultural heritage. (The actual percentages for the period from the 14th century to the present day are: Castilian 73 per cent; Catalan 22 per cent; Galician 3 per cent; Basque 1 per cent; and Latin 1 per cent.) Two Catalan post-war novelists, ▷Mercè Rodoreda and ▷Montserrat Roig, are among the finest contemporary writers in Spain. Castilian has not, after all, always been the pre-eminent literary language; we may recall that, in terms of quality, the work of the 19th-century Galician poet Rosalía de Castro compares favourably with anything written at that time in Castilian.

Even without linguistic and political opposition, it was difficult for women writers of the post-war generation. They were unique in that they were the first women writers to embark on the painful process of discovering the gender-specificness of their own identity through their writing; they also began actively subverting male or patriarchal models of experience. ▷Carmen Laforet and Mercè Rodoreda, for example, rewrote the masculinist premises of the *Bildungsroman* in order to give a sense of what it meant to be a woman growing up in Franco's Spain. Laforet's masterpiece, ▷*Nada* (*Nothing*), recounts the life of an adolescent, Andrea, who arrives in war-ravaged Barcelona to study at the university. While clearly operating on the level of a socio-historical document, the slice of life depicted in the novel is simultaneously an allegory of Spain, cut off economically and diplomatically from the rest of the world and thrown back on its own resources.

Rodoreda's rather morbid novel, ▷*La plaça del Diamant*, which has been translated into several languages, including twice into English (▷*The Pigeon Girl*, 1967 and ▷*The Time of the Doves*, 1983), is the sombre narration of a working-class woman, Natàlia, during the 1930s and 1940s. It focuses on her marriage, the loss of her husband during the civil war, her remarriage and subsequent lapse into insanity. Natàlia's story is symbolic of many in Spain whose lives were destroyed by the historical calamity of the civil war, but it is intrinsically feminine in that it unmasks the patriarchal structures which (mis)govern her life, especially in matters of love.

Later writers were able to build on the *Bildungsroman* technique mastered by Laforet and Rodoreda. Three such writers, ▷Ana María Matute, ▷Dolores Medio and ▷Elena Quiroga, for example, used the ▷realist mode in order to focus on female experience during the Franco years (1939–1975). Some novelists, however, cheerfully adopted the idiom of ▷postmodernism. One important transition writer was ▷Carmen Martín Gaite, best known for ▷*El cuarto de atrás* (*The Back Room*), which skilfully manages to weave together the author's reminiscences of her childhood, the literature of the fantastic, and sentimental romance.

The New Wave
When the era of Franco's dictatorship finally came to an end, Spanish society changed drastically. Franco's death in 1975 and the gradual advent of democracy gave rise to an unprecedented boom in women's writing, in the 1980s especially. This New Wave of female writing centred on the novel, and included novelists such as ▷Adelaida García Morales, ▷Concha Alós, ▷Carme Riera, ▷Marina Mayoral, and ▷Carmen Gómez Ojea.

Though it is perhaps invidious to put writers in order of rank, the single most important New Wave novelist is ▷Esther Tusquets, who is best-known for her trilogy of novels: ▷*El mismo mar de todos los veranos* (*The Same Sea as Every Summer*); ▷*El amor es un juego solitario* (*Love is a Solitary Game*); and *Varada tras el último naufragio* (1980) (*Beached After the Last Shipwreck*), which shocked the reading public with their frank treatment of female and ▷lesbian sexuality.

Other important New Wave female novelists are Montserrat Roig and ▷Rosa Montero. Roig's best-known works, *El temps de les cireres* (1977) (*The Time of the Cherries*) and ▷*L'hora violeta* (1980) (*The Violet Hour*), consist of dialogues between two female protagonists who attempt to transform an alienating patriarchal history into 'herstory'. Rosa Montero's fiction, such as ▷*Crónica del desamor* (*Chronicle of Falling Out of Love*), concentrates on feminist issues such as contraception, abortion and the single mother, many of which were taboo during the Franco regime. Her most recent novel ▷*Temblor* (*Trembling*) is set in a world in which women have control over men. By reversing sexual laws, Montero persuades the reader to question the supposed immutability of patriarchy.

While the novel has been the main breeding-ground for experimental women's writing in the post-war period, other genres have had their moments as well. An important female poet of the post-war era is ▷Gloria Fuertes; typical of her work is ▷*Cuando amas aprendes geografía* (*When You Love You Learn Geography*), which is introspective and rooted in an exploration of the female body. Fuertes's poetry also has a postmodernist edge to it since she employs word-play in order to subvert the limitations of language. Also significant is the poetry of ▷Clara Janés, whose ▷*Lapidario* (*Lapidary*) depicts a feminine identity created through a fusion with 'other' identities; of ▷María Victoria Atencia, which focuses on the ontological and social limitations imposed on women, and that of ▷Ana Rossetti, whose work, and in particular her ▷*Devocionario* (*Prayerbook*), expresses a specifically feminine sexuality. Important contributions have been made in the dramatic field by ▷Ana Diosdado, ▷Maribel Lázaro and ▷Pilar Pombo. Some works by dramatists have deliberately used shock tactics for publicity purposes. Lázaro's play, ▷*Humo de Beleño* (*Henbane Smoke*), for example, which describes the struggle between the Inquisition and a group of women accused of witchcraft in the 17th century, contains a scene in which the witches enact a sexual ritual which parodies Church ritual, lubricating their genitalia with holy oil.

Whether writing novels, poetry or drama, the New Wave of women writers have made their mark on the Spanish literary canon. Ignoring Sophocles's advice in *Ajax* that 'silence gives the proper grace to women', the New Wave of women writers have spoken out. In emperor's-new-clothes mode they have have pointed to the artificiality of the patriarchal system which rules our lives; patriarchy, it seems, is the obstacle getting in the way of paradise.

Further reading

For reasons of space it has not been possible to include all Spanish women writers in this volume, especially those from the contemporary period. The reader is referred to an excellent, definitive anthology which contains biographical and bibliographical information: *Litoral femenino: literatura escrita por mujeres en la España contemporánea (Litoral femenino: Women's Writing in Contemporary Spain)*, edited by Lorenzo Saval and J. Garcia Gallego (1986).

Bib: Brown, Joan L. (ed.), *Women Writers of Contemporary Spain*; Calvo de Aguilar, Isabel, *Antología biográfica de escritoras españolas*; Conde, Carmen (ed.), *Poesía femenina española (1939–1950), Poesía femenina española (1950–1960)*; Condé, Lisa and Hart, Stephen (eds), *Feminist Readings in Spanish and Latin-American Literature*; Deyermond, Alan, 'Spain's First Woman Writers' in Miller, Beth (ed.), *Women in Hispanic Literature: Icons and Fallen Idols*; *Estreno, X:2* (1984) (devoted to Spain's women dramatists); Fox-Lockett, Lucia, *Women Novelists in Spain and Spanish America*; Galerstein, Carolyn (ed.), *Women Writers of Spain: An Annotated Bio-Bibliographical Guide*; Martín Gaite, Carmen, *Desde la ventana: enfoque femenino de la literatura española*; O'Connor, Patricia, '*Glorias y miserias de la dramaturgia femenina española*', in Paolini, G. (ed.), *La Chispa '87: Selected Proceedings*, pp. 195–99; O'Connor, Patricia, *Dramaturgas españolas de hoy: una introducción*; Pérez, Janet, *Contemporary Women Writers of Spain*; *Revista Canadiense de Estudios Hispánicos*, XIV: 3 (1990); Serrano y Sanz, *Apuntes para una biblioteca de escritoras españolas desde el año 1401 al 1833* (reprinted in *Biblioteca de Autores Españoles*, Vols 268–71); Saval, Lorenzo and García Gallego, G., *Litoral femenino: literatura escrita por mujeres en la España contemporánea*; Wilson, Katharin M., *An Encyclopedia of Continental Women Writers* (2 vols), and *Women Writers in Translation: An Annotated Bibliography, 1945–1962*.

URSULA FANNING

12 Italy

Drawing the map

Per una donna che scrive è importante sapere se e quali altre l'hanno preceduta . . . È importante pensare alle proprie pagine come a un dono da trasmettere a chi verrà, a un'eredità da madre a figlia

(For the woman writer it's important to know if she has had female predecessors, and who they are . . . it's important to think of one's own pages as a gift to pass on to those who follow, as an inheritance from mother to daughter) (Rosa Maria Colombo)

The contours of the map of Italian women's writing are, as yet, blurred. It is, indeed, only relatively recently that any interest has been shown, in either Italy or the English-speaking world, in making an attempt to trace the faded outlines which make up the history of

Italian women's writing. Critics involved in this enterprise perform the work, alternately, of archaeologists and cartographers: first comes the excavation, and then the process of mapping.

Anthologies of the works of women writers have, of course, been compiled in Italy. In the 1500s and in the 1600s there was considerable interest in this type of enterprise in the context of the debate on women (▷16th-century treatises on women). Texts with intriguing titles, such as *Collected Poetry of Some Most Noble and Virtuous Women* (1559), edited by Ludovico Domenichi, began to appear. The first large-scale anthology, presenting the works of 248 women writers and entitled *Componimenti poetici delle più illustri rimatrici d'ogni secolo (Poetic Extracts from the Most Illustrious Female Poets of Each Century)* (1726) was produced by ▷Luisa Bergalli Gozzi, herself a poet and dramatist. Such collections appeared sporadically through the 19th century, with works of both prose and poetry anthologized. The most useful of recent anthologies (for literature of the 19th and early 20th centuries at least) is that by ▷Giuliana Morandini, *La voce che è in lei: Antologia della narrativa femminile italiana tra '800 e '900 (The Voice Within Her: An Anthology of Italian Women's Narratives between 1800 and 1900)*. Within an Italian context, then, such anthologies have been available at various stages, though they tended to go out of print remarkably quickly and, in general, are now only available through libraries to those engaged in research. None of these anthologies has been translated into English.

Within the last five years Italian women's writing has received some degree of critical attention in the English-speaking world. In 1987 the English journal *The Italianist* produced an issue entitled 'Women and Italy' which was reworked for publication in book form as *Women and Italy: Essays on Gender, Culture and History* (eds. Z.G. Barański and S.W. Vinall). As the title implies, however, the focus of this work is broader than that of women's writing. Its concerns are the position of women in Italian society both past and present and the textual representation of gender in texts by male and female authors. In 1989 another work was produced, in the University of Toronto Italian Series, which had a more specifically literary focus, again on the representation of gender in works by women and men, *Donna: Women in Italian Culture*. Also in 1989 *Annali d'Italianistica*, a North American journal produced by the University of North Carolina, written partly in English and partly in Italian, produced an issue devoted to 'Women's Voices in Italian Literature' on the same topic, dealing once more with the writings of both men and women. Rebecca West, in her introduction to this last work, highlighted the need for this new focus in Italian studies. In her words, 'although there is no dearth broadly speaking of published studies regarding women and literature, there have been many fewer publications entirely dedicated to women in *Italian* literature and culture'. Barański and Vinall, in their introduction to *Women and Italy*, also state: 'given the variety and strength of women's studies in the English-speaking world, it might come as a surprise that so little and belated attention has been paid to Italy'. What is equally surprising is the continuing lack of attention, even within the context of this new interest in Italian women as cultural subjects, to *their writing*. The map has begun to be drawn, but there remains much to do.

Canon fodder

> *Scorsi il profilo del babbo addormentato . . . il viso materno non si distingueva fra i cuscini e le coltri*
> (I could see my father's sleeping profile . . . the maternal face was not visible between the pillows and the covers) (Sibilla Aleramo, *Una donna*)

On consideration of the canon of Italian literature, and certainly the canon as institutionalized and taught in Italian University departments worldwide, it becomes obvious that the names which comprise it are monolithically male. As we scan the centuries, we encounter Dante, Petrarch, Boccaccio, Machiavelli, Ariosto, Tasso, Goldoni, Alfieri, Manzoni, Verga, D'Annunzio, Pirandello, Svevo, Vittorini, Pavese, Moravia, Sciascia, Calvino and

Eco. Some of these names are more familiar to the English-speaking reader than others, but most have been translated into English at some stage. The list of names would, in itself, provoke some debate about inclusion and exclusion, but most of these authors would be, to a greater or lesser extent, acceptable (perhaps alongside others) as sufficiently 'great names' to form the basis of various courses on Italian literature.

This institutionalized bias is reflected in reference works on Italian literature, histories of which generally devote very little space to women writers; indeed, these often allot a paragraph at the end of a section in which all women writers of the period/genre are unproblematically linked together. Women sometimes attain prominence in sections/collections entitled '*I minori*' ('Minor Writers', ironically of masculine gender in Italian).

Such gaps may be 'explained away' by various strategies, the most popular being that of the relative 'inferiority' of the (paradoxically largely unknown) body of women's writing. Natalia Costa-Zalessow, in her useful anthology *Scrittrici italiane dal xiii al xx secolo (Italian Women Writers From the 13th to the 20th Century)* of 1982, makes the apparently valid point that in the medieval period, at least, it is no wonder that there appear to have been few Italian women writers, given that the skills of reading and writing were restricted to a select group (▷Education). And yet there *were* women writing in Italy in this period: their work has been well buried beneath that of their male contemporaries, and it is undeniable that Italian women's writing, even to the present to some extent, remains submerged.

Part of the task of the feminist critic approaching Italian women's writing is truly that of excavation. It is difficult, firstly, to find and, secondly, to evaluate the work of Italian women writers for a guide such as this, especially in the earlier centuries. Even now, we feel as though the excavation has not been sufficiently deep, as though we have merely scratched the surface. In some respects, this work is inevitably incomplete; in other areas, the selections made will, no doubt, be considered by some to be misguided. We have tried, following the principle of this guide, to concentrate, where possible, on those writers whose work has been translated into English, but this applies to such a pitifully small number that we have cast our net wider, selecting and evaluating according to inevitably personal criteria.

The function of the Italian contribution to this guide is primarily to record and to provide signposts towards the work of women writers. Our criteria, moving on from this starting-point, have involved highlighting the work of women writers who seem most conscious of themselves as such. We are most interested in those women who seek to articulate the notion of *differenza* (difference) in their writings, who take on the conventions of male genres and seek to subvert them, who are concerned with women's plots in narrative and drama, and with the first-person female *io* (I) in their poetry. As Franco Cassano says in *Approssimazione (Approximation)* of 1989 (quoted in the journal *Passaggi* 1.1990.iv, devoted to '*donne scrittura differenza*'/'Women Writing Difference'): '*La cultura femminile non è una prigione . . . essa non è un handicap dal quale liberarsi per muovere verso una competizione asessuata in una società ad una solo dimensione, ma una ricchezza da valorizzare*' (Women's culture is not a prison . . . it is not a handicap from which one must free oneself in order to move towards asexual competition in a one-dimensional society, it is a richness to be exploited).

Beginnings: 1200–1400

La bocca sua non diceva se non Gesù e Caterina, e così dicendo ricevetti el capo nelle mani mie, fermando l'occhio nella divina bontà: dicendo – io voglio!
(His mouth spoke only the words Jesus and Catherine, and as he spoke, I took his head in my hands, his eyes closed in God's blessed will and he said: 'I want it!') (Saint Catherine of Siena)

Many, though not all, of the texts (poetry, letters, writings) of this period are religious in tone and inspiration (▷Religious writings). Writing of Latin, and even of the vulgar Italian, was restricted to the religious and the wealthy educated class. So, both ▷Angela da Foligno and ▷ Santa Caterina da Siena are unusual in the context of this guide in that neither was actually able to write. Both dictated their thoughts, visions and letters to scribes. Their work, less well known today, perhaps, than that of Saint Francis (▷ Franciscan literature) is interesting both as a record of the life of the religious woman in this period, and in its mystical dimension (▷ Mystical writings).

A common feature of the writings of both Angela da Foligno and Caterina da Siena is the placing of themselves, and their personal experiences, at the centre of their texts. The mystical experience for Angela da Foligno involves a renunciation of all earthly attachments and affections; unsurprisingly, perhaps, as her spiritual crisis coincided with the deaths of the other members of her family. In this extract, she places herself at the centre of her third-person narrative: '*volendo seguitare la via della croce, che l'era bisogno ch'ella si spogliasse . . . e ignuda andasse alla croce. Ciò è che prima perdonasse a tutti coloro che l'avessero offesa; appresso si spogliasse di tutte le cose terrene e dell'amore di tutti gli uomini e di tutte le femmine*' ('as she wanted to follow the way of the cross, it was necessary that she should strip . . . and go naked to the cross. That is, that she should first pardon all those who had offended her; and then she should divest herself of all earthly things and of the love of all men and all women') (from *La via della croce*, *The Way of the Cross*).

The mystical, and indeed sensuous tone of Angela da Foligno's writing is evident in this passage. For her, in the same way as for Caterina da Siena, her relationship with Christ is intimate and personal. She wishes to be his 'companion on the cross' in order ultimately to share in his glory. Mortification of the flesh and sensual ecstasy mingle in her writings.

As can be seen from the quotation which introduces this section, Caterina da Siena also couples herself with Christ. This quotation is taken from a letter of Saint Catherine to Fra Raimondo da Capua, in which she describes the death of Niccolò Toldo, a nobleman of Perugia, condemned to death by the Republic of Siena. Caterina, drawing together the religious and political aspects of her life, as was her wont, persuaded him to confess his sins and to accept his death as a form of union with Christ and, obviously, as a form of union with her, too. Again we find the conjunction of the mystical and the sensual, as Caterina comforts him with the promise that they will soon be together in heaven: '*Crescendo el desiderio nell'anima mia e sentendo el timore suo, dissi: "Confòrtati, fratello mio dolce, che tosto giogneremo alle nozze"*' (As the desire grew in my soul and I could feel his fear, I said to him: "Be consoled, my sweet brother, soon the marriage will take place" '). The whole account reads more like a tale of sensual love than the narrative of the journey of a soul to God.

The writings of this period, as exemplified in the works of these two women, record the daily events of the lives of religious women, tell of the political dimensions of the role (in the case of Caterina), and state their religious beliefs and experiences. Their significance, however, resides in their narration, from a female point of view, of the mystical and unabashedly sensuous dimension of these experiences. The metaphors they use are strikingly consistent.

Some of the work of the marginally earlier ▷ Compiuta Donzella, about whom very little is known, stands in sharp contrast. Her poetry claims independence and self-determination for women. She reacts, in her first sonnet, against the force of paternal authority: '*lo mio padre donar mi vole a mia forza segnore, ed io di ciò non ho disio né voglia*' ('my father wishes to give to me a lord against my will, and I have no desire nor wish for this'). Her second sonnet, interestingly, sets up the alternative of a religious life in opposition to the future mapped out for her by her father: '*Lasciar vorria lo mondo, e Dio servire . . . ond'io marito non vorria né sire*' ('I wish to leave the world to serve God . . . for I want neither lord nor husband'). Her third sonnet is, however, a love poem, paradoxically far less sensuous than the work of the two women writers dealt with above. It is restrained in tone. In it, she appropriates the traditional position of the male poet of the Provençal school (▷ Poetry), that of love's servant: '*d'Amor sono e vogliolo ubbidire*' ('I am of Love, and wish to obey him').

The poetry of the Compiuta Donzella, her declarations of independence, and her appropriation of the male 'I'/'io', seem to have served as inspiration for later generations of women poets, as did the expression of female sensuality in the works of Angela da Foligno and Caterina da Siena.

The Renaissance for women, and its aftermath: 1400–1800

Venite a confunder tutto il regno d'amore . . . e in somma mettete ogni cosa in scompiglio
(You confuse the entire realm of love . . . and, in fact, you turn everything upside down)
(Moderata Fonte)

This period includes the time of the ▷Renaissance, of ▷humanism, of ▷Petrarchism; that 'great flowering of art, architecture, politics and the study of literature', as it is described in *The Oxford Companion to English Literature,* a culturally rich age, a time of rediscovery. But what did the Renaissance mean for women writers, and what came after it?

There was certainly a flowering of women's writing in the period from 1400–1700, with its greatest concentration in the 1500s and 1600s. This was hardly a rebirth for women writers, however, nor a rediscovery of their culture. They were, rather, consolidating the work of their predecessors, while still working within a predominantly male culture. The importance attached to education in this period, however, worked in favour of some women, in that daughters of noble families were frequently encouraged to study and to come to grips with certain aspects of the classical and humanist education extended to their brothers.

Relatively little survives of the works of 15th-century women writers in Italy and, in some respects, the women writing in this period are less interesting than their immediate predecessors. The value, for example, of the letters of ▷Alessandra Macinghi Strozzi resides in their lively portrayal of the lifestyle of a reasonably wealthy Florentine woman in the mid-1400s. We also have access to similar writings by Lucrezia Tornabuoni de Medici (1425–1482), letters based on her family life in Florence in the same period, as well as some interesting religious poetry. Antonia Giannotti Pulci (c1452–?) is one of the first women writers of religious plays of whom we have any record, but perhaps the most interesting woman writer of the later part of this period, and of the early 16th century, is ▷Maria Savorgnan. A Venetian poet, many of whose letters are also still extant, Savorgnan claims passion as subject matter for women poets in a manner not achieved previously. She does not trouble to cloak it with mystical overtones: *'io mi consumo in fiame ardente'* ('I am consumed by burning flames'). Her work is also interesting for the tension it betrays between literary creativity and love. The physical presence of her love impinges on her ability to write: *'Io non poso scrivere, perchè B. non si parte mai'* ('I cannot write, because B. is still here').

In the 16th century women produced more work of value than in any previous century. The writings of ▷Veronica Gambara, ▷Vittoria Colonna, ▷Gaspara Stampa, ▷Tullia D'Aragona, ▷Veronica Franco and ▷Moderata Fonte all date from this time. Women were more highly visible as both producers and subjects of Italian culture than ever before. The ▷16th-century treatises on women, a body of writings to which many of these women contributed, drew attention to the nature, culture and place of women in society in a new way. Many of these women poets openly claimed and exercised their right to write, and their right to sexual freedom (▷*cortegiane oneste*). Veronica Gambara, who defined herself as a *'cortegiana onesta'*, wrote love poetry in the Petrarchan style, in common with many of her female and male contemporaries. Like Vittoria Colonna, Gambara claims for the female poet the right to write of love, and of politics and war, too. Gaspara Stampa, like both Gambara and Colonna, writes largely in the Petrarchan tradition. The aspect of physical celebration in her poetry is remarkable. In one sonnet she addresses the night as bearer of joy, for it is she who *'tutti gli amori de la mia vita hai fatto dolci e cari, resomi in braccio lui*' ('has made all the bitterness of my life sweet and dear, having given him into my arms'). Tullia D'Aragona and Veronica Franco both celebrate their relatively free lifestyles in their poetry. Both also compile collections of their poetry, along with poems by male 'authorities' in praise of them. Apparently self-deprecating, they orchestrate eulogies to themselves. Stampa, D'Aragona, and Franco struggle to name themselves in their poetry, as Flora Bassanese points out in her article 'What's in a Name? Self-Naming and Renaissance Women Poets' in *Women's Voices in Italian Literature* (1989). In doing so, they raise, in Bassanese's words, issues of 'gender identity, social subordination, and intellectual mastery'.

Moderata Fonte, in her turn-of-the-century contribution to the debate on women, confronts the same issues. In the quotation which introduces this section, we see Fonte playing with established conventions, with established discourses on love, and inverting all. Her work, like that of ▷Lucrezia Marinelli Vacca, celebrates women and takes men to task for their very use of the rhetoric of love and the manner in which they traditionally represent women in their writings. Marinelli Vacca, on the same theme, refers to men's *'emple e disoneste parole'* ('impious and dishonest words').

The principle of inversion is profitably used, too, by ▷Suor Annalena Odaldi in her convent farce (▷Carnival drama). In these plays, men appear in a far from favourable light, while her female characters are given possibilities of acting in various socially unacceptable ways in order to resolve their dilemmas. Odaldi's manipulation of dramatic conventions mirrors the inversion techniques used by Fonte and Vacca in their poetry and is related, in turn, to the structural manipulations of the text practised by D'Aragona and Franco.

Two poets writing in the 17th and into the 18th century were ▷Faustina Maratti and ▷Petronilla Paolini Massimi, both writers in the ▷Arcadian mould, whose work is remarkable for its celebration of female fortitude. In Paolini Massimi's words: *'Mente capace d'ogni nobil cura ha il nostro sesso'* ('Our sex has a mind fit for any noble task'). In her female universe, the only tyrant is man! The work of ▷Luisa Bergalli Gozzi is also worthy of consideration, both for her creative writing and her interest in earlier women writers.

A new selfconsciousness appeared in this period, both during and after the Renaissance, in the works of women writers. They are conscious of their roles as women writers, and they are aware of the gradual formation of a new and distinctively female tradition.

Politics and poetics: the 19th century

Stanca, abbattuta, senza un centesimo in tasca, dopo una giornata di lavoro, ella tornava a invidiare sua madre che era morta
(Tired, downcast, without a penny in her pocket, after a day of work, she began to think enviously of her mother, who was dead) (Matilde Serao)

The 19th century was a time of political and social upheaval for Italy as a whole. This upheaval often had specific consequences for women, to which women writers responded in various ways. The experience of the ▷*Risorgimento* was, for instance, reflected in women's writing. But perhaps more important for women was the change in attitude towards women's education in the post-*Risorgimento* period of the 1870s. A subtle identification between the terms *donna*/woman and *patria*/country was set up by theorists and moralists. Woman was deemed to be the most appropriate educator of her children in the home, and thus it became desirable that she herself should acquire a reasonable standard of education. The task of creating a new, morally upright nation was to rest squarely on the shoulders of Italian women. Writers, such as ▷Anna Vertua Gentile, contributed to the flood of moral pamphlets addressed to young women and girls of the period. Ultimately, this drive to educate women of all classes, born of conservative politics, was to have far-reaching effects because it enabled women other than those of the fortunate aristocracy and upper-middle classes to gain access to the skills of reading and, most significantly, writing.

Another significant development of the 1870s was the entry of women of both the lower and middle classes into the workforce in large numbers, particularly in the more industrialized north of Italy. Lower-class women found employment in the agricultural sector, in industry, and as domestic servants. Their pay was roughly half of that earned by men in comparable work and, like their male counterparts, they worked long hours in appalling conditions.

For the first time, the experiences of women of this class find representation in Italian literature, with the advent of ▷realism. ▷Bruno Sperani, in *la fabbrica* (*The Factory*) deals with the poverty and exploitation of factory work. ▷La Marchesa Colombi's *In risaia* (*The Rice Field*) describes '*nove ore e mezza colla zappa in mano*', '*una vita d'inferno!*' ('nine and a half hours with the hoe', 'a hellish life!'), centred as it is on women agricultural workers. ▷Matilde Serao, in the quotation which introduces this section, describes the life of a woman factory worker, Carmela, in her novel ▷*The Land of Cockayne*. Indeed, in her novels, Serao covers a whole range of work done by women – domestic service, factory work, casual labour – and effectively portrays the harsh nature of it all.

The economic hardships which led working-class women into prostitution are also represented in women's writing of this period. ▷Emma, in ▷*Una fra tante* (*One Among Many*), stresses that many young women earned such an inadequate wage that they were forced into prostitution, a fact supported by historical studies of the period (J.W. Scott and L.A. Tilly, 'Women's Work and the Family in 19th-Century Europe' in *The Family in History*, 1975). Serao, in *Storia di due anime* (*A Tale of Two Souls*) makes the same point in a similar narrative.

The experiences of middle-class women, employed largely as office workers and teachers, are also reflected in novels of this period. The conditions of these workers are only marginally less appalling. Experiences of deprivation and hunger are accurately recorded in this fiction. Bruno Sperani's ▷*Nell'ingranaggio* (*Caught in the Wheel*) tells this tale from a northern point of view, while Serao's ▷'*Telegrafi dello stato*' ('State Telegraphs') and ▷*Scuola normale femminile* (*A Girls' School*) recount it from a southern perspective. The last work is particularly striking for Serao's interweaving of fact and fiction, in her account of the suicide of an impoverished and sexually hounded young woman teacher, in a mirroring of the notorious Italia Donati case (detailed in several histories of women's lives in 19th-century Italy).

This kind of exploitation led, particularly in the case of middle-class women, to an increasing interest in organized ▷feminism, especially in northern Italy. Women in the south were even more exploited, but less politically aware. In the literary field, however, they were spoken for, and to, by writers such as Serao and ▷Maria Giuseppa Guacci Nobile.

Among the demands made by feminist groups in this period, and into the 20th century, was that for women's suffrage. Interestingly, this demand was not universally supported by women writers, even those such as ▷Neera and Serao who wrote repeatedly of women's problems. Suffrage seemed an irrelevance to Serao, for instance, as in 1900 only six per cent of the Neapolitan population was eligible to vote. These writers were aware that suffrage is only one index of the status of women in society.

Women writers expressed their political opinions largely through the medium of ▷journalism. These opinions were, in the case of some of these writers, often far more guarded and conservative than might be inferred from their fictional works, suggesting that, through the medium of fiction (and often fantastical fiction) they were less wary of expressing their views and aspirations on women's role in society. They were also conscious, no doubt, of writing with a different audience in mind. The novels of most of these women writers are specifically addressed to, and mindful of, a female readership.

Such a concentration on the representation of the realities of the lives of lower and middle-class women might well lead to the supposition that many of the women writers mentioned formed part of the ▷realist school or, in its specifically Italian form, ▷*verismo*. It is certainly the case that writers such as ▷Caterina Percoto, Matilde Serao and ▷Grazia Deledda produced much work classifiable as realist, often with a particular slant in favour of representing the experiences of women. Women had also written in the earlier style of ▷romanticism. Women poets also continued to produce prolifically: ▷Maria Giuseppa Guacci Nobile investigating women's role through poetry, ▷Vittoria Aganoor Pompilj writing erudite love poetry, ▷Annie Vivanti producing both poetry and fiction.

Other genres, such as the ▷*romanzo d'appendice* and the ▷Gothic novel were predominantly written by women. Serao, ▷Carolina Invernizio and ▷Regina di Luanto appear to delight in presenting a predominantly female reading public with narratives of adventure, danger and transgression of social norms. The other side of the socially responsible realist coin appears to be the dark fantastical world of the melodramatic cliff-hanger and the Gothic. The Gothic, in particular, allows the woman writer to try out different notions of identity (▷Dualities/Doubles), and continues to be popular into the 20th century, in the writings of women writers whose lives and works spanned these two centuries.

Work in progress: the 20th century

Si dice uomo per dire uomo e donna, . . . si dice omicidio per indicar l'assassinio di un uomo e di una donna

(One says man, meaning man and woman . . . one says homicide for the murder of a man or of a woman) (Oriana Fallaci, *Letter to a Child Never Born*)

The richness and diversity of Italian women's writing in this century is striking. There are literally hundreds of women writers in different genres, influenced by different political and cultural currents which have left an imprint on their writings. We have sought, in the individual entries on them and their works, to give some idea of the breadth of this creativity.

Women writers have trafficked with ▷decadentism in the early part of the century, with the ▷fantastical, the ▷surreal, and with ▷science fiction narratives in the latter part. Formal experimentation has, in many cases, coincided with forms of experimentation in the roles open to their female characters. The title of ▷Gilda Musa's 1979 novel *Esperimento donna (Woman Experiment)*, for instance, highlights its genre, and its experimental nature on more than one level. The fantastical, women writers of this century have discovered, can be liberating.

The presence of women writers has been highly visible within the confines of other literary movements this century, most notably, perhaps, those of ▷neo-realism and ▷futurism. Writers such as ▷Anna Franchi, ▷Nalia Ginzburg, ▷Joyce Lussu, ▷Anna Maria Ortese, ▷Rinata Viganò and ▷Giovanna Zangrandi have, at least, set their narratives in the period of the ▷Resistance, and dealt with the political and social impinging on, or forming a background to, the private world of the individual; at most, they have joined in the formal, stylistic experimentation typical of the genre. Most interestingly, all of these writers have provided this literature with an overtly female perspective, in sharp contrast to the male writer's representation of the male intellectual.

The same cannot be said of the involvement of women writers in the futurist movement, and their literary output. There is great divergence here between individual writers in their degree of adherence to the futurist doctrine in terms of its perspective on women. The writings of ▷Benedetta, ▷Enif Robert-Angelini, ▷Rosa Rosà, Maria Goretti and ▷Maria Ginanni provide us with a comprehensive debate on the nature of woman, and the 'biology-as-destiny' conflict.

Women writers have, perhaps, produced most of their best works this century in the form of narrative fiction. There are hundreds of well-written novels and short story collections by Italian women, many of which have a specific focus on women in 20th-century society. An abbreviated list of the most significant names would include ▷Aleramo, ▷Banti, ▷Bellonci, ▷Bonanni, ▷Cialente, ▷Corti, ▷de Cespedes, ▷de Stefani, ▷di Falco, ▷Duranti, ▷Fallaci, ▷Garufi, ▷Ginzburg, ▷Guidacci, ▷Guiducci, ▷Lagorio, ▷Loy, ▷Manzini, ▷Maraini, ▷Milani, ▷Morante, ▷Negri, Ortese, ▷Percoto, ▷Prosperi, ▷Ramondino, ▷Romano, ▷Sanvitale, and Zangrandi.

Many women have also produced much poetry of value. The three greatest names in this field are, perhaps, those of ▷Frabotta, Guidacci and Musa, but the works of ▷Borgese Freschi, de Stefani, ▷Guglielminetti, ▷Rosselli, ▷Spaziani and ▷Tosatti should also be highlighted.

In theatre, the works of Ginzburg, Maraini and ▷Rame are both critically and publically acclaimed. All three dramatists concentrate specifically on representations of women and thus provide, incidentally, some challenging roles for the Italian interpreters of their work.

In the fields of journalism and literary criticism, women continue to write prolifically. ▷Cederna, de Cespedes, Fallaci, and ▷Quaretti are among the most famous Italian journalists of this century. From Corti's writings on philology to those of Elisabetta Rasy, Nadia Fusini and ▷Frabotta on women writers and writing in general, Italian women academics (often creative writers themselves) have begun to make their voices heard.

Such is the diversity of style and content in the works of all of these writers that it is not possible to generalize about their work. Surely that is in itself a good thing. Women's writing in Italy is extending itself, testing boundaries, adding new routes to the Italian literary map.

Certain themes do recur in this writing, however, and are identifiable as of significance to these writers. A frequent preoccupation is the investigation of the role of the mother from the perspectives of both daughter and mother. It is central to much of the work of Serao, Aleramo, Ginzburg, Guiducci, Fallaci, Maraini, Ramondino and Sanvitale. Linked with this is the investigation of the notion of self in the works of these and other writers. Women writers seek to define themselves; in Rebecca West's words (introduction to *Annali d'Italianistica*, vol. 7): 'To "speak themselves", to be subjects as well as objects of discourse and experience'. This concern is identifiable in the works of women writers in all genres. Investigating themselves as writers, they investigate their relationship to language, to literary discourse itself, as the Fallaci quotation introducing this section indicates.

Any kind of conclusion to this section would be both inappropriate and impossible. Italian women continue to write their stories, and critics have only begun to map this literary terrain. As Rosa Maria Colombo says in *Passaggi* (1.1990.iv): '*costruirsi entro l'area della tradizione letteraria più accreditata una nostra mappa di territori, di stanze, di nomi, è . . . veramente una necessità primaria*' ('to construct for ourselves within the field of recognized literary tradition our own map of territories, rooms, names, is . . . really a primary necessity'). We would hope that this work represents a step in that direction, an outline for that map.

Portugal

Medieval and renaissance Portugal

Some of the earliest writing by Portuguese women appeared in the ▷*Cancioneiro Geral* (1516) (*General Songbook*), a collection of mid-15th- and early 16th-century verse compiled by the poet Garcia de Resende. Of the nearly 300 poets represented in this work, seventeen are women of the court, the most prominent being ▷Dona Filipa de Almada. But according to ▷Carolina Michaëlis de Vasconcelos (1851–1925), women were composing lyrics long before the 15th century. Songs sung by *cantadeiras* (women singers) during *romarias* (pilgrimages) and festivals probably inspired numerous compositions in earlier ▷*cancioneiros* – especially the ▷*cantigas de amigo*, in which the speaker is always a woman.

The 15th and 16th centuries saw other manifestations of a literary activity among women. For example, ▷Queen Leonor of Portugal (1458–1525), who was instrumental in introducing the printing press to her country, ordered the publication of ▷*Espelho de Cristina* (1518) (*Christine's Mirror*), the Portuguese version of ▷Christine de Pisan's celebrated *Livre des Trois Vertues* (*Book of Three Virtues*). Interestingly, a predecessor of Leonor, ▷Queen Isabel of Portugal (died 1455), had originally commissioned the translation of this work.

The ▷Infanta Dona Maria (1521–1577), daughter of Queen Leonor, was also an enthusiastic supporter of literature and the arts. Her court was renowned for its important women scholars, most notably ▷Luisa Sigea (c 1531–1560), whose long poem in Latin, 'Sintra', is thought to have inspired two 19th-century poets, the Portuguese Almeida Garrett and the English Lord Byron. Another important figure of this period was ▷Públia Hortênsia de Castro, an impressive scholar and woman of letters, who received a university doctorate in 1565, at the age of seventeen.

The 15th and 16th centuries in Portugal were renowned for the voyages that enabled the monarchy to lay claim to territories in Africa, Asia and South America. While some Portuguese women accompanied men, the vast majority were left behind to care for their families, and most were confined to the home. Education for women outside the nobility and the extremely wealthy merchant class was virtually nonexistent, and few professions did not belong exclusively to men. In fact, all Portuguese citizens were subject to legislation known as *Ordenações* (Ordinances), an extension of early Roman law, which codified the privileged status of men and described women as mentally weak and innately inferior.

Until the mid-18th century, convents were amongst a few establishments to provide women with an education. Not suprisingly, the most prominent women writers in the ▷Baroque period were nuns – among them ▷Sóror Violante do Céu, ▷Sóror Maria do Céu and ▷Sóror Madalena da Glória. Another nun, ▷Sóror Mariana Alcoforado, was erroneously regarded for centuries as having authored the celebrated *Lettres Portugaises* (1669) (▷*The Letters of a Portuguese Nun*).

Neo-classicism and romanticism

The Enlightenment in Portugal challenged stereotypical notions about women, particularly regarding their limited mental capabilities. In 1715 a little-known writer, Paula da Graça, satirized a popular publication entitled *Malícia das Mulheres* (*Maliciousness of Women*) in a long poem entitled 'Bondade das Mulheres Vindicada e Malícia dos Homens Manifesta' ('The Goodness of Women Vindicated and the Maliciousness of Men Revealed'). Three decades later, Luís António Verney's ▷*Verdadeiro Método de Estudar*

(1746) (*True Method of Study*) called for a massive reform of Portugal's archaic instructional system. Verney urged that women be given access to education, and he even suggested that, if granted such access, women would probably surpass men in intellectual achievements.

Throughout the Age of Reason, long-held general assumptions regarding the inferior or 'weaker' sex were challenged, and a few treatises on this topic were actually composed by women. For example, in 1752 the Brazilian-born ▷Teresa Margarida da Silva e Orta, who had resided in Portugal since childhood, authored an impressive feminist and didactic work entitled ▷*Aventuras de Diófanes* (*Adventures of Diófanes*), which is widely regarded as the first Brazilian novel. And in 1761 Gertrudes Margarida de Jesus published the feminist tract *Primeira Carta Apologética em Favor e Defesa das Mulheres* (*First Apologetic Letter in Favour and Defence of Women*). Of course, not every text published during this period was progressive. In 1747, just one year after the publication of Verney's call for the reform of Portuguese education, a new edition of Dom Francisco Manuel de Melo's *Carta de Guia de Casados* (1651) (*Letter-Guide to Married Couples*) was released, claiming that women were incapable of logical thought; and a 1761 study, *Espelho Crítico no Qual Claramente Se Vêem Alguns Defeitos das Mulheres* (*Critical Mirror in Which Some Defects of Women Are Clearly Seen*), was overtly misogynous.

The 1700s were also marked by a return to classical forms and themes in Portuguese literature. Poets of this period (often referred to as *arcadistas*) adopted pastoral names derived from classical verse, and in their writings they cultivated a 'noble simplicity'. A major figure of the period was the ▷Marquesa de Alorna, who used the pen-name Alcipe. During her nineteen years of enforced seclusion in a convent (1758–1777), she wrote a number of poetic works, including odes, eclogues, sonnets and verse epistles, as well as translations of Horace and Pope. Despite her preference for classical forms, however, Alorna prefigures the ▷romantic movement, which is usually described as beginning in 1825 in Portugal, with the publication of Almeida Garrett's *Camões*. In many of her poems she is drawn to Gothic, funereal themes, and to the strange beauty of the night.

One of the centres where the new romantic literature flourished was Oporto, in northern Portugal, and the most important literary salon in that city was presided over by the poet ▷Maria da Felicidade do Couto Browne. For years historians ignored Browne's contribution to the literature of the period, preferring instead to focus on her romantic relationship with the writer Camilo Castelo Branco. Not until the 1940s, when the critic Jacinto Prado Coelho raised her to canonical status in his study of Portugal's ▷'ultra-romantics', was serious attention paid to her work. Even today several other women writing during the romantic period remain virtually unknown, among them ▷Henriqueta Elisa and ▷Amélia Janny.

Early feminism

In 1867, during a constitutional monarchy instituted by the bourgeoisie, a Civil Code was introduced into Portugal that made life especially difficult for married women. Divorce was not permitted, and the only way a woman could legally separate from her husband was if he physically abused her or committed adultery in their home with his mistress. A man also had the right to force his wife back to the home if she left him. Ultimately the Civil Code became a catalyst for political activism, leading many women of the middle and upper classes into organized forms of protest.

Among the most prominent activists in the mid-19th century were ▷Guiomar Torrezão and ▷Antónia Gertrudes Pusich, who were also prolific writers of poetry, novels and drama. In addition to working in the political sphere, these two also founded and edited important publications – an unprecedented act for women. In 1871, Torrezão began publishing the *Almanaque das Senhoras* (*Ladies' Almanac*), a highly successful women's review that featured poetry, essays and fiction, as well as lists of new books written by women. Pusich oversaw three publications: *A Cruzada* (*The Crusade*); *A Beneficiária* (*The Beneficiary*); and ▷*A Assembléia Literária* (*The Literary Assembly*) which was dedicated exclusively to women's instruction.

Educational reform was a prominent theme in women's journalism and fiction in the late 19th century. In her bestselling novels ▷Maria Amália Vaz de Carvalho (1847–1921) encouraged women to continue their education after marriage and childbirth – if only to provide their husbands with stimulating conversation. Carvalho might be described as the ▷Mrs Humphrey Ward of Portugal – a woman whose conservative attitudes towards women helped to construct a new female subject, in keeping with industrial modernity. A more radical proponent of women's rights was the writer ▷Caiel (1860–1929), whose essays called for better instruction for women, as well as improved maternity and health care. In an important study entitled *O Que Deve Ser a Instrução Secundária da Mulher?* (1892) (*What Should Women's Secondary Education Be?*), Caiel called attention to the alarmingly high percentage of illiterates in the country, and denounced the educational system in Portugal as antiquated and discriminatory. The university professor ▷Carolina Michaëlis de Vasconcelos (1851–1925) was also active in the struggle for women's rights, and, like Caiel, wrote passionately about educational reform for women.

Other important women of this period were ▷Ana de Castro Osório, who wrote the country's first feminist manifesto, *Às Mulheres Portuguesas* (1905) (*To the Portuguese Women*); and ▷Adelaide Cabete, a physician and author of works on women and children's health. Together they founded the Republican League of Portuguese Women (1909); a branch of the Republican party, the League immediately demanded that divorce be legalized, that women be given the vote, and that the 1867 Civil Code be revised. With the fall of the monarchy and the establishment of the Republic in 1910, the League saw many of its demands realized. For example, divorce was permitted for the first time in Portugal, and legislation called 'Family Laws' was instituted. Nevertheless, the new government refused to give women the vote. Throughout the next several decades activists struggled to secure this basic right, which they finally achieved in 1969.

Modernism, the Estado Novo and censorship

Histories and anthologies have generally ignored the substantial literary output by women in the early 20th century, much of which appeared in small reviews and journals such as *Sociedade Futura* (*Future Society*), ▷*Alma Feminina* (*Woman's Soul*), *Modas e Bordados* (*Fashions and Embroideries*) and *Portugal Feminino* (*Female Portugal*). Only two women writers are regularly mentioned in scholarly references to the modernist period (1915–1940): ▷Florbela Espanca, whose anguished, self-reflexive poems often bordered on the erotic; and ▷Irene Lisboa, author of numerous books that portrayed in various ways the isolation of middle-class women. Other figures working in the same period were ▷Virgínia Vitorino, a poet and dramatist; ▷Fernanda de Castro, a poet who was married to the writer António Ferro, a prominent official in the Salazar government; ▷Maria Lamas (1893–1983), who later authored two important feminist studies: *Mulheres do Meu País* (1948) (*Women of My Country*) and *A Mulher no Mundo* (1952) (*Woman in the World*); the law scholar ▷Elina Guimarães, who wrote on the legal status of women; and ▷Teresa Leitão de Barros, who, in 1924, published ▷*Escritoras de Portugal*, the first history of women writers in Portugal. Unfortunately the works of these and other authors, such as ▷Branca de Gonta Colaço, ▷Olga Alves Guerra and ▷Emília de Sousa Costa, have largely been neglected.

Politically unstable throughout its sixteen-year existence, the Republic fell in 1926 and a dictatorship was established. The regime of António de Oliveira Salazar, also known as the *Estado Novo* (New State), was in place for over forty years, and effectively crushed many of the advances gained by women during the Republic. In 1946 Salazar abolished the National Council of Portuguese Women, the largest and longest-sustained women's organization in the country. Four years later, in 1950, a law was enacted to prevent married women from obtaining a passport or leaving the country without the notarized permission of their husbands – even if they were legally separated. Feminist activism was held in check during the regime; nevertheless a number of women made important contributions to literature in the post-World War II period, and several are prominent writers in the country today. These include the poets ▷Sophia de Mello Breyner Andresen and ▷Ana Hatherly, and the novelists ▷Agustina Bessa-Luís and ▷Fernanda Botelho. Other impressive writers to appear in the 1940s and later were ▷Maria Judite de Carvalho, ▷Isabel da Nóbrega, ▷Maria Natália Nunes, ▷Maria Alberta Meneres, ▷Maria Ondina Braga, ▷Salette Tavares and ▷Y.K. Centeno.

Throughout the dictatorship books were scrutinized by government censors, and several women were officially reprimanded. The novelist ▷Maria Archer (1905–?) had two of her books banned because of their attitude towards the Salazar dictatorship. The novelist, poet and dramatist ▷Natália Correia (born 1923) repeatedly defied the regime by publishing books that dealt with topics considered indecent or subversive; among her most controversial projects was an anthology of erotic and satirical medieval verse, *Antologia da Poesia Portuguesa Erótica e Satírica* (1965). Maria Lamas and the poet ▷Fiama Hasse Pais Brandão (born 1938) were also victims of the censor. So great was the persecution against Lamas that she finally went into exile in Paris in the 1960s.

The 'Three Marias' and the post-revolutionary generation
The most famous instance of censorship in Portugal occurred just prior to the revolution. In 1972 three radical women writers collaborated on an unusual volume consisting of letters, poems and essays. Entitled *Novas Cartas Portuguesas* (▷*The Three Marias: New Portuguese Letters*), this mixture of fiction and non-fiction was unified by feminist themes. Shortly after publication it was banned, and the authors, ▷Maria Isabel Barreno, ▷Maria Teresa Horta, and ▷Maria Velho da Costa, were arrested and put on trial for having written an 'obscene' book. Reported internationally, their trial was a *cause célèbre*, and the women became known world-wide as the ▷'Three Marias'. In April 1974, shortly before their sentencing, the military overthrew the dictatorship, and a pre-democratic form of government was instituted. The case against the writers was dismissed, and their book remains one of the most important literary manifestations of feminism in Portugal.

Much of the literature of post-revolutionary Portugal was indirectly inspired by the 'Three Marias', whose radical work challenged not only the politics of the Salazar regime but also the conventions of literary realism. In different ways, many of Portugal's new authors are critical of Portuguese society, and their writing is formally unorthodox. Some of the most impressive works to appear since 1974 have been written by women, among them ▷Lídia Jorge, ▷Teolinda Gersão, ▷Hélia Correia, Clara Pinto Correia (born 1960), ▷Olga Gonçalves and Maria Gabriela Llansol (born 1931). Among the controversial topics addressed by these writers are the colonial wars in Africa, the problems of emigration, and the goals of the Portuguese revolution. With regard to more specifically feminist issues, the new generation has been equally concerned with the silence of women under patriarchy, and with the possibility of developing a 'female' discourse. In recent years Portuguese women have also produced a large amount of fantasy literature and science fiction, as evidenced by the anthology ▷*Fantástico no Feminino* (1985) (*Fantastic in the Feminine*), which contains stories by fourteen leading writers. Although the struggle for sexual equality continues, this literature is symptomatic of the fact that Portugal's culture has been profoundly affected by feminism. Women authors are now in the vanguard of every literary development.

The first modern Greek women writers appeared during the second half of the 19th century, when Greece started to emerge as an independent country after four centuries of Turkish rule. Long occupation by a foreign power had stunted cultural and artistic life, severing all intellectual connections with the ancient Greek and the Byzantine past. The European powers who had helped the Greeks during the Greek War of Independence (1821–1829) also assumed the role of organizing the new Greek state, under a new monarchy, and of developing within it a new middle-class society based on Western forms of life and thought. Women always supported men, but at the same time were eager to help themselves and their fellow women. ▷Evanthia Kairi, from the island of Andros, was the first woman who combined her educational assets with a will to struggle against the Turks. She managed to win the financial help of famous European women in favour of Greek fighters. ▷Elisavet Moutza-Martinengou, from the island of Zante, was the first Greek woman who, although isolated and reclusive, wrote about her own oppressive upbringing in order to highlight the situation of women in Greece.

It was education that precipitated the first real exodus of Greek women from their homes into the public sphere. Middle-class women in the few flourishing towns of Greece lived a more or less secluded life. They were without education and had no real public power or role. But in 1834 a royal decree declared education compulsory for both sexes. Women from economically privileged backgrounds started to receive education in private schools run by foreign teachers. Before long, many women were continuing their education abroad in order to qualify as teachers in girls' schools. Proficient in teaching skills, they returned to Greece full of confidence and eager to help women improve their lot. These teachers published books on the importance of women's education as well as studies of children's education. Sappho Leontias, Kalliopi Kehagia and Eleni Laskaridou were the first women teachers who wrote about education for women, which they saw as a necessary means of entry into the public sphere. Not surprisingly there was considerable male opposition, and much criticism was directed at what were thought to be the adverse effects of women's education.

Undeterred, women started to produce their own journals, *Thaleia* (1867), published weekly for a year, and *Evridice* (1870–1873), issued every week for a short time, and later every fifteen days, which were run exclusively by women. These journals were vigorous, both in argument in favour of women having a more active role in society and in criticism of the misguided ideas held about them by men. They contained commentaries on the current situation of women in Greek society, and ideas about how to improve it, as well as articles on education, poetry and other topics. It was out of this kind of journalism that there gradually grew a women's literature with specifically Greek themes.

It was through poetry that women first appeared in the world of modern Greek literature. They wrote mainly love poems, full of expressions of unfulfilled yearnings and of surrenderings to imaginary lovers. Love was the only thing they could expect in their lives, the only thing that would take them out of the oppressive suroundings of their homes into what they imagined would be the relative freedom of a husband's household. These poems were intensely personal, with a strong confessional character and much implicit eroticism. Yet women were reluctant to admit to this activity, and hid their poems rather than daring to publish them.

As women began to make more of an appearance in public life, their writings began to be published. They wrote books about women from the ancient Greek and Byzantine past, as well as about their predecessors who, earlier in the century, had fought against the

Turks. Women also collected folk songs and recorded details about rural customs. They wrote children's literature, and they published translations of English and French novels.

It is worth emphasizing that Greek women at this time were not writing novels. It was not until the end of the 19th century that Arsinoi Papadopoulou wrote short stories and ▷Alexandra Papadopoulou the first Greek novel, *Miss Lesviou's Diary* (1894). Both women came from Constantinople (Istanbul), were teachers and took part in the literary circles of Athens. Women in Greece were deprived of the conditions that in other European countries positively encouraged this form of literature. There was no tradition of education, nor any class of leisured people with the opportunity to observe and analyze the society around them. Yet many women travelled abroad to enrich their education, made contact with Western women and brought back feminist ideas.

Feminism gave Greek women the vocabulary with which to express the unease they had felt for so long, and the ideas with which to construct arguments in favour of a new social role for women. ▷Kallirroi Parren, a journalist and novelist, published the weekly ▷*The Ladies' Newspaper* for thirty years (1887–1917). It became the first publication to raise the banner of feminism by addressing a whole range of social and cultural issues affecting women and by generally exposing the discrimination against women as a group. Parren also voiced her feminist ideas through novels whose heroines, by freeing themselves from society's narrow imperatives, led their lives independently of men. In 1890 the first woman entered a Greek university, hitherto a strictly male preserve, an event achieved in the face of great scorn and hostility.

At the beginning of the 20th century socialism and Marxism had been embraced by a number of women intellectuals as systems which could help solve society's ills. This new inspiration now guided women as they became more active and outspoken in their demands for equal rights. Poets and novelists felt freer now to express their personal, emotional and critical stance in life. ▷Galateia Kazantzaki, ▷Elli Alexiou, ▷Lilika Nakou and others wrote socially realistic novels exposing the inequalities suffered by women and the public hyprocrisies concerning women both in domestic and public spheres. In the past, women's poetry, like the work of ▷Maria Polidouri, had evoked little more than sentimentality, but now it transcended its sentimental content to address more social and objective themes, projecting a sense of optimism and change. Such was ▷Melissanthi's poetry: she started as a religious poet, but later moved to more intellectual themes and is better known for her Existentialist work. Women also began writing new kinds of children's literature with the aim of handing on to children an understanding of the past and a knowledge of the present. ▷Penelope Delta's books are still read with great enthusiasm and affection for their historical subject by both children and grown-ups.

Through all the upheavals of recent history – the Metaxas dictatorship (1936–1941), World War II and the German occupation – a new generation of women writers appeared, called ▷'The Thirties Generation'. Elli Alexiou wrote short stories about the hardships witnessed by the people during the German occupation between 1940 and 1944. ▷Melpo Axioti impressed her critics with her poetic monologues, and ▷Theony Dracopoulou wrote poems about children's hunger in Athens and later about the liberated city. ▷Athena Tarsouli and Angeliki Hatzimihali are two of the women of this era who collected much folklore material and preserved an enormous variety of peasant culture. Melissanthi's poetry is characterized by 'personal agony' and ▷Zoe Karelli's work, highly individual in style, contains elements of the surreal and metaphysical.

During the civil war between the communists and monarchists (1944–1949), the dictatorship of the 'Colonels' (1963–1974) and the restoration of democracy, women writers were actively establishing themselves within Greek culture as more than the equals of their male counterparts, contributing a distinctive female voice to a literature engaged with contemporary historical events and social change. ▷Eva Vlami, ▷Alki Zei, ▷Tatiana Gritsi-Milliex and ▷Dido Soteriou wrote very successful novels characterized by sensitivity and high emotional tension. Many of the women writers in the latter half of the 20th century belonged to a generation of Greeks who returned to Greece after being expelled from Asia Minor. They wrote of the hard times they survived and the dreams and ideas cherished about the land they lost. Dido Soteriou's and ▷Maria Iordanidou's writings are widely read.

Nowadays Greek women writers are prolific in all fields of literature and manifest a liberated consciousness fully in touch with contemporary literary tendencies in the West. Their novels, poetry, plays, children's literature, art criticism, journalism and translations dominate the Greek market. Poets ▷Nana Isaia, ▷Katerina Anghelaki-Rooke, ▷Maria Laina and ▷Jenny Mastoraki express themselves in a mixture of styles beyond the traditional strict forms of poetry. ▷Maro Douka, ▷Katerina Plassara, ▷Maro Vamvounaki and ▷Lili Zographou may follow traditional forms of writing, but the feminist core of their subject matter always represents a critique of their society without aggressiveness. They write about alienation in human relationships, and the fragmented lives of individuals in modern society. Their female characters are often solitary figures, standing aloof from the stories they tell, yet maintaining their integrity and dignity without animosity. They react against the now subtler forms of male oppression and prejudice they experience without actually making war against it. ▷Galateia Saranti's protagonists identify dissatisfactions in human relationships and try to achieve what they desire in life, realizing it is not easy: there is hope and optimism in the present and for the future.

Some Greek women writers have been translated into other languages, and a few have achieved international recognition, but their work as a whole is not well-known in the West, perhaps because Greece is still considered a country on the edge of the European cultural map.

OLGA VAN MARION

The Netherlands and Flanders   15

The heritage of Anna Bijns and Hadewych

'My head is full of ▷Anna Bijns,' says ▷Elly de Waard in the November 1985 issue of the feminist magazine *Opzij*, listing that year's main events: the first (Dutch-Belgian) 'Week of the Women's Book', the start of the *Amazone* festival of women poets, and the creation of a major award for the female voice in literature. The Anna Bijns prize is awarded biennially, alternately for prose and poetry (in 1985 to ▷Josepha Mendels, in 1987 to ▷Ellen Warmond, in 1989 to ▷Inez van Dullemen and in 1991 to ▷Christine D'haen.

Events like these, concerning women and literature, reflect the recent changes in Dutch and Belgian study of language, literature and texts. Where the emphasis in women's studies initially lay on women's growing awareness of their position in society, it has shifted towards studying the repressed female element in texts, and analysing how the symbolic and linguistic order was disturbed by a specifically female style of writing. A struggle began to re-evaluate important women writers and bring forgotten writers back into the limelight. As a result, the question has arisen: what implicit and explicit values lie at the basis of the production and critical appraisal of literary texts?

The earliest women writers in the northern and southern Netherlands

'Who was Anna Bijns?' asks De Waard in her column in *Opzij*. Anna Bijns is one of only nine female writers whose work is discussed in Reinder P. Meijer's *Literature of the Low Countries* (together with that of hundreds of male authors). De Waard, a poet herself, calls Bijns 'the first independent woman in our literature'. At her own expense she founded a school in Antwerp, teaching there until she was eighty. She wrote refrains in praise of Jesus and Mary, but was also a prolific and lively composer of invective poems, campaigning – with the most forceful verbal means available – against Lutheran Reformists, as well as against marriage, even urging her (female) readers to remain single:

> Heed my advice: take care
> For I divine, often having perceived,
> That when a woman marries, even though she be of noble blood
> And well off, her feet will be
> In fetters. But should she remain single,
> And keep herself pure and clean,
> She is lord and mistress, none ever lived better.

Equally influential was the 13th-century ▷Hadewych from Antwerp, considered to be one of Europe's most impressive mystics. With her *Strophic Poems* she created a new genre of mystic love poetry, written in the vernacular. There is a sample of her poetry, 'On love', in *A Selection of Early Dutch Poetry*:

> Whoever is lacking aught of tenderness
> Is not yet fully grown in love.
> When all their deeds from flawless love shall spring,
> Then is their love enough.

The interest in women writers from the past, including the 'forgotten' women poets, is steadily growing, exemplified by the articles of Hanneke van Buuren and Hannemieke Stamperius (▷Hannes Meinkema) in *Chrysallis* 6 and 7 (1980–1981), and by recent research carried out at the University of Leiden into a large group of women poets from the northern and southern Netherlands between 1550 and 1750. These authors were mostly nuns or patrician women, publishing independently or in books by men, writing and translating poems and plays in Dutch, as well as other languages. Their subjects included faith, love, the native soil, family matters and matters of social importance.

Barbara Ogier (1648–1670), for instance, was a dramatist for a chamber of rhetoric, and Katharina Questiers (1631–1669), an artist from Amsterdam (where she owned a gallery), translated plays from Spanish. Anna Roemers Visscher (1584–1651) wrote verse for an emblem book, and translated emblematic verses from French. Her sister, Maria Tesselschade (1594–1649), known for her correspondence with poets like P.C. Hooft, translated poetry from Italian. The extraordinarily learned ▷Anna Maria van Schuurman (1607–1678) published poetry in French and Italian, and her Latin treatise on the question of whether women were capable of pursuing science was translated from Latin into French, German, Italian and Swedish. Research into these Renaissance writers is still in its infancy, and though a considerable amount of material has been gathered, there is as yet no reference work available comparable with *A Biographical Dictionary of English Women Writers 1580–1720* or *A Dictionary of British and American Women Writers 1660–1800*.

The 18th and 19th centuries

The 18th and 19th centuries brought many changes. The first 'modern' novel, ▷*Sara Burgerhart* (1782), an epistolary work dealing with the education of a young girl who is meant to be an example of moral independence and responsibility, was written by two established writers, ▷Betje Wolff and ▷Aagje Deken (1741–1804). It inspired baroness Belle van Zuylen (1740–1805) to write a comparable novel, the *Lettres Neuchâteloises* (1784). In the 18th century a modest cultural movement emerged, of learned women, mutually supportive of each other.

Two famous authors of those days, 'enlightened' women admired by Betje Wolff, were ▷Lucretia Wilhelmina van Merken, writer of epic poetry, a didactic poem on the benefit of adversity, and French classicist drama, and Petronella Johanna de Timmerman (1724–1786), a poet whose interest in mathematics and philosophy surpassed her interest in poetry. Others included the edifying poet and novelist Petronella Moens (1762–1843), the more sentimental Elisabeth Maria Post (1755–1812), whose subjects included pastoral life and friendship, and the poet and dramatist Juliana de Lannoy (1738–1782), a champion of woman's equality to man. While some writers turned against woman's traditional place in society, most of them, especially Betje Wolff and Elisabeth Maria Post, conformed with traditional thinking on women's erudition: the purpose of educating a woman is to make her into a 'pleasant housewife'.

The 20th century
The late 19th and early 20th centuries, when socialism and women's emancipation were prominent in literature, saw some remarkable women authors; among them Truitje Bosboom-Toussaint (1812–1886), author of the very popular romantic novel of manners *Majoor Frans* (1875) (*Major Frans*), Hélène Swarth (1859–1941), who changed her nationality from French to Dutch, and wrote poetry ranked with the best of that from the otherwise male *Tachtigers* (writers from the 1880s), and the socialist-turned-communist ▷Henriëtte Roland Holst. The Flemish ▷Virginie Loveling and her sister, Rosalie (1834–1875), first produced poetry in a ▷realist style with a sentimental overtone. Loveling's later novels are naturalistic. Bestselling writers were Ina Boudier-Bakker (1875–1966) and Top Naeff (1878–1953). Women in literature became the subject for Annie Salomons's (1885–1980) *De vrouw in de Nederlandse letterkunde* (1912) (*The Woman in Dutch Literature*), and ▷Annie Romein-Verschoor's *De Nederlandse romanschrijfster na 1880* (or *Vrouwenspiegel*) (*The Dutch Woman Novelist After 1880*), her thesis from 1935, and *Slib en wolken* (1947) (*Silt and Sky*, 1969).

Literary and cultural contacts between the English-speaking world (especially the United States) and the Dutch-speaking world received a major impetus from the activities of ▷Dola de Jong, who, while working as a literary agent, brought hitherto unknown writers and publishers from both sides of the Atlantic into contact with each other. She also translated and published in English as well as Dutch, and was among the first to write explicitly against anti-Semitism and other forms of racism, her famous war novel *The Field* (1946) (the English edition of which was reprinted many times) being a prime example. Earlier, ▷Carry van Bruggen had published *Het huisje aan de sloot* (1921) (*The Little house Beside the Ditch*), stories about her youth in a poor Jewish community.

During World War II, writers could apply for a subsidy from the National Socialist government, but the majority refrained from doing so. Several Jewish writers have since given vivid descriptions of their experiences. The stark language and sober style of ▷Marga Minco effectively evokes the realities and emotions of war, for example in *Het bittere kruid* (1957) (Bitter Herbs, 1960). Anne Frank's (1929–1945) diary and the letters and diaries of ▷Etty Hillesum have become world-famous. The suffering of Jewish children is described in *Star Children* (1946) (English edition 1986) by Clara Asscher-Pinkhof.

The 1950s: an emerging female style
The 1950s was a period of reconstruction and restoration, not only of bombed cities, but also of the family and the traditional role of women. Motherhood was strongly promoted,

and few women took up jobs. Women played only a marginal role in cultural life. What was left of feminism had gone underground. For many writers, such as ▷Ida Gerhardt, ▷M. Vasalis, ▷Hanny Michaelis, Ellen Warmond and Mischa de Vreede (born 1936), the 1950s was a turning point. In her thesis *Lust for Letters: Dutch Women-poets and the Literary System* (1988) Maaike Meijer compares the work of these poets with that of women poets in the 1930s and 1940s, like Henriëtte Roland Holst, and with that of male poets. Meijer establishes that there is to some degree an evolution in their poetry that is specific to women. Classical forms and rhyme were rejected, though grammatical structures were left intact. Women poets appeared to have more faith in the expressive powers of language than men, and they did not try to use language to distance and defamiliarize familiar meanings. Religion gradually lost its importance as a subject and a point of reference. Erotic poetry was more explicit, and allusions to lesbianism became possible; everyday life and colloquial language gained a place, and a growing political awareness became apparent.

The two new themes that emerged in this poetry play an important role in literature to this day: a strong sense of doom and depression, and life is depicted as death-like, without purpose and worth (this is what Meijer refers to as 'the great melancholy'). Secondly, a pre-feministic conciousness emerges in the form of dissatisfaction with traditional gender patterns; feelings and thoughts which were to be brought out collectively at the start of the present-day feminist movement.

> Involuntarily, almost
> without noticing it
> I have incorporated you
> in the music which doesn't move you,
> in the language which you don't speak
> and don't understand, in me
> whom you don't love.

(Hanny Michaelis, *The Shape of Houses: Women's Voices from Holland and Flanders*, 1974)

▷Anna Blaman's themes of loneliness, fear of life, and the inadequacies of love created a sensation when her four novels were published. *Eenzaam avontuur* (1948) (*Lonely Adventure*), about eroticism and lesbian love, was one of the most famous and controversial books from the post-war period. It was followed by *Op leven en dood* (1954) (*A Matter of Life and Death*, 1974).

We can find the 'great melancholy', political awareness, sexual openness and a feminine point of view in the prose of the most important women writers from the 1950s up to the present: Josepha Mendels, ▷Andreas Burnier, Hannes Meinkema, ▷Doeschka Meijsing, ▷Mensje van Keulen, ▷Anja Meulenbelt, ▷Ethel Portnoy, ▷Renate Rubinstein and the Flemish ▷Mireille Cottenjé,

In this brief outline, ▷historical novelists, such as Hella Haasse (born 1918), Hélène Nolthenius (born 1920) and Nelleke Noordervliet (born 1945) cannot receive the attention they deserve. Neither can important Flemish women poets, such as Christine D'haen, ▷Clara Haesaert and ▷Patricia Lasoen, the Dutch poet M. Vasalis, poet, dramatist and prose writer ▷Judith Herzberg, and the most famous Dutch writer of ▷children's literature, Annie M.G. Schmidt (born 1911).

Excellence from the 1980s

A number of excellent female authors have emerged from the 1980s. Marijke Höweler (born 1938), though she had published before, established herself in 1982 with *Van geluk gesproken* (*Speaking About Happiness*), followed by *Bij ons schijnt de zon* (1983) (*The Sun Shine on Us*), *Ernesto* (1984), *Mooi was Maria* (1985) (*Beautiful Was Maria*) as well as other titles, ridiculing trends such as emancipation and psychotherapy. In her first novel *De meisjes van de suikerwerkfabriek* (1983) (*The Girls from the Candy Factory*), Tessa de Loo (born 1946) focuses on the problems of young women growing up, as does Hermine de Graaf (born 1951) in her collections of stories featuring headstrong young women as her main characters: *Een kaart, niet het gebied* (1984) (*A Map, Not the Area*), *De zeevlam* (1985) (*The Seaflame*) and *Aanklacht tegen onbekend* (1987) (*Complaint Against Unknown*). *Havinck* (1984), *De feniks* (1985) (*The Phoenix*) and *De lichtjager* (1990) (*The Lighthunter*) are compelling psychological novels by Marja Brouwers (born 1948) (*Usurpatian*), dealing respectively with a lawyer unable to identify himself with the emotional life of those dear to him, the decline of a family, and, finally, a frustrated art historian. A kind of Dutch realism is to be found in *Onttroning* (1984) (*Usurpation*), the first novel of Nelly Heykamp (born 1944), in which the writer looks back on a strongly Calvinist youth. The emotional life of women struggling for freedom and independence is the central theme in *Spoorloos* (1985) (*Without a Trace*), about poor women in Chile and Argentina, and in *De terugkeer* (1986) (*The Return*) and *Wat het water gaf* (1989) (*What the Water Gave*) by Fleur Bourgonje (born 1946). The main characters in the books of Margriet de Moor (born 1942) often feel alien in their environment, and retreat into their imagination (*Op de rug gezien*, 1988, *Seen from Behind*; and *Dubbelportret*, 1989, *Double Portrait*).

Recent Flemish contributions to Dutch literature
In the 1970s ▷Monika van Paemel wrote three books that are to some extent related to the experimental novel. In 1985 she published *De vermaledijde vaders* (*The Cursed Feathers*), the sad story of a Belgian woman, that is also a socio-political novel about post-war Belgium. The year 1987 saw the publication of *Een zuil van zout* (*A Pillar of Salt*) by Kristien Hemmerechts (born 1954), the story of a girl student's return to the Flemish countryside, where her isolation and fear of abandonment become ever more apparent. Following several collections of stories, Hemmerechts's novel *Brede heupen* (*Broad Hips*) appeared in 1989, the description of relationships within a family progressively falling apart.

Dutch literature abroad
Dutch literature was written not only in the Netherlands and Flanders, but also in Dutch-speaking communities overseas. The former Dutch East Indies, with their own specific literature, produced important women writers, such as ▷Maria Dermoût (1888–1962), whose novels *Nog pas gisteren* (1951) (*Yesterday*, 1957, *Days before Yesterday*, 1960) and *De tiendiuzend dingen* (1955) (*The Ten Thousand Things*, 1983) are published in several English editions, and Beb Vuyk. In her work, Vuyk consistently aligned herself on the side of repressed people, a political choice that made her and her books controversial, as in *Het laatste huis van de wereld* (1939) (*The Last House in the World*, 1983). Women writers who are strongly influenced by the former Dutch East Indies are Augusta de Wit (1864–1939), Marion Bloem (born 1952) and Margaretha Ferguson (born 1920). Other women writers were, or still are, at work in Suriname and the Dutch Antilles. In South Africa, numerous writers publish in Afrikaans, a language closely related to Dutch. The poet ▷Elisabeth Eybers , living in the Netherlands but writing in her native Afrikaans, received several Dutch literary prizes for her work.

The Dutch-language literary world is a blooming one, with female authors extending their own tradition and playing a distinct part; they deserve wider attention because of their quality, as well as their diversity.

Bib Brouns, Margo, *The Development of Women's Studies: a report from the Netherlands*; *The Defiant Muse. Dutch feminist poems from the Middle Ages to the present: a bilingual anthology*; Holmes, J.S. and Smith, W.J. (eds), *Dutch interior: postwar poetry of the Netherlands and Flanders*; Hopkins, Konrad and van Roekel, Ronald (eds), *Quartet: an anthology of Dutch and Flemish poetry*; Jacobs, Maria (ed.), *With Other Words: a bilingual anthology* *of contemporary Dutch poetry by women*; Meijer, Maaike, *De lust tot lezen: Nederlandse dichteressen en het literaire systeem*; Meijer, Reinder P., *Literature of the Low Countries: a short history of Dutch literature in the Netherlands and Belgium*; *Post-war Dutch and Flemish Poetry*; Morris, Peter, *A selection of Early Dutch Poetry*; Rollin, Scott and Ferlinghetti, Lawrence (eds), *Nine Dutch Poets*; Snoek, Paul and Roggerson, William (eds), *A Quarter Century of Poetry from Belgium 1945–1970*; Wolf, Manfred, *Change of Scene: Contemporary Dutch and Flemish poems in English translation*; (trans.), *The shape of houses: women's voices from Holland and Flanders*; 'Exploring the world of women', *Writing in Holland and Flanders*, No. 36, Spring 1979.

KAREN KLITGAARD

16 Scandinavia

The following literatures are dealt with under the Scandinavian heading: Danish, Norwegian, Swedish, Fenno-Swedish, Finnish and ▷Icelandic. Other literatures in Scandinavia, for example, literature from Greenland (▷Inuit literature), the ▷Faroe Islands and that of the ▷Samian culture, are dealt with in the A–Z entries. The Scandinavian countries do not have a common language. Danish and Norwegian are closely related and may be read in both countries, but ▷New-Norwegian and the county-dialects are nearly impossible to read for others than Norwegians. Danish and Swedish may be read by others with some difficulty, whereas Icelandic is quite different and Finnish, as a Uralian language, has nothing in common with the other Scandinavian languages.

The Scandinavian countries do have a common history in so far as Denmark, for many years, governed Norway, parts of Sweden, Greenland and the Faroe Islands, but, until recently, Finnish literature has had its own developments, much more in common with Russian. Of course, the literature written in Swedish in Finland, ▷Fenno-Swedish literature, has a closer connection to Scandinavian trends. During many periods, Danish literature was ideologically in the lead because of its nearness to German and other European influences. This is very clear in the ▷modern breakthrough in the 1880s, where the leading Scandinavian figure was the Danish literary critic Georg Brandes (1842–1927). This movement was very influential in relation to modern women's literature as we know it.

Until the 1970s, Scandinavian literary history was a male history, with a few exceptions, such as ▷Sigrid Undset and ▷Selma Lagerlöf. At best, women's literature was treated in a separate chapter or at the end of each chapter, always defined by the writer's sex. During the last twenty years, sustained research has been taking place in the Nordic countries, especially in Denmark, Norway and Sweden. In Finland, this research has only begun fairly recently. It has been carried out by new generations of women researchers who have not only rediscovered many neglected women writers, but who have also set new theoretical standards for literary research. The ▷canon of literary history has undergone a radical change. The following pages owe a deep debt to the pioneering researchers in the field of women's writing in Scandinavia.

Women in Scandinavia have been writing literature long before the modern break-through. Already around the year 1000, women in Iceland were producing ▷scaldic poetry and some women writers were mentioned in the ▷sagas. The new Christian culture, the monks and clerks, wrote down the heathen, Nordic mythology, but within a Christian, patriarchal understanding that concealed women's active role as storytellers and producers. From around 1200, women had a high status influenced by the trends of central Europe, where so many men had died in the crusades. We hear about independent and wilful women in the sagas and in the ballads, too, for example, the self-possessed Gudrun.

Religious literature became important for women writers after Christianity came to Scandinavia. Some convents were famous for their women writers, for example, Vadstena in Sweden, where ▷Birgitta av Vadstena (1303–1373) lived as the most important writer in Scandinavia in the 14th century. Many ▷prayer books and ▷legends about holy women are preserved. Vadstena became a centre in Scandinavia for ▷learned women's writing. Well-known are Margareta Clausdotter (or Nikolausdotter, ?1420–1486) and Anna Fikkesdotter Bülow (1412–1519). The former wrote in Swedish, the latter in Latin.

During the Renaissance, as well as during the period of the Reformation and after, this tradition continued as a religious and learned literature written by women. First and foremost aristocratic women, but also women from the lower classes, began to write psalms and religious poetry. In Sweden, Queen Christina (1626–1689) wrote in connection with the *précieuses* (▷Precious Women) in France, and Sophia Elisabeth Brenner (1659–1730) made a living out of writing. In Norway, Dorothe Engelbretsdatter (1634–1716) wrote psalms; in Denmark, the king's daughter, ▷Leonora Christine Ufelt (1621–1698), wrote her autobiography and memoirs. It was difficult, however, to exist as a woman writer. The lives and works of Birgitta Lange (1714–1752), Magdalena Sophie Buchholm (1758–1825), and not least the famous ▷Charlotta Dorothea Biehl (1731–1788), who was a very productive writer, tell of poverty and stultification, not only during their lifetime but also later in literary histories. These women did not alter the literary traditions, but they were the first signs of a new relation between women and fiction, which became dominant over the next 100 years. Women became the most important readers, and many more women than ever before began to write.

In the second half of the 17th century and during the 18th century, women writers' lives were dominated by the literary ▷salons and the discussions taking place there. In Sweden and in Denmark, bourgeois and aristocratic women led salons and were dominant in the development of new aesthetic tastes, for example, Hedvig Charlotta Nordenflycht (1718–1763) and Anna Maria Lenngren (1754–1817). Many of the women did not write much, and rarely large works, but their influence on literature in general was great. Norway had no salons, but dramatic societies played a similar role there. Drama was an important part of salon life in general. The literary salons in Europe formed a sort of cultural club. The members visited each other, and read and discussed the same works of art and music. The Danish Frederike Brun (1765–1835) travelled for fifteen years, and lived in Geneva, at ▷Madame de Staël's Coppet, and in Rome; the Swedish Malla Silverstolpe (1782–1861) visited salons, in Germany. Many of the trends in modern cultural life were born in the salons and were formed by the leading women there as the most important audience at the time.

During the romantic era, many women writers in Scandinavia chose to be realistic, epic writers. They wrote about everyday life, and about the new individualist psychology, often idealizing femininity and motherhood. Women writers began to contribute with their special insights, already practised as writers of letters and diaries. For some women writers, writing now became a way of making a living, for example, if their husband died and they had to support themselves. Many of the women writing in the 19th century led very unusual lives, and the connection between their art and their personal destinies has been stressed in literary histories. Some of them are exceptional writers even by today's standards – not because of their outstanding lives, but because of their ability to describe new topics in a new way.

In Sweden, ▷Fredrika Bremer (1801–1865) was the first realist author, the first to write novels in the modern sense of the word. She chose to work as a writer, and she wrote much about the women's question. In this sense, she was a forerunner of the 'modern breakthrough', where the most important topics were sexuality and the woman's question (▷woman question). Other women writers in Sweden were the aristocratic Sophie von Knorring (1797–1848) who wrote in continuation of Scandinavian salon life, and ▷Emilie Flygare-Carlén (1807–1892) who became a very successful writer and made a small fortune from writing novels about country life in a region of Sweden. The new bourgeois audience found her works fascinating.

In Finland, ▷Fredrika Runeberg (1807–1879) was the first woman writer. She wrote more romantically than most of the other Scandinavian women writers.

In Denmark, ▷Thomasine Gyllembourg (1773–1856) founded the psychological and realist short story. She and her daughter-in-law, Johanne Luise Heiberg (1802–1890), held a literary salon and were admired, not only as writers, but also as creators of themselves – a new, bourgeois femininity, in the style of Rousseau, very self-conscious and formed as an image of ideal nature. In recent years, much research has been done on both them and the period, and biographies have been written.

In Norway, the first realist woman writer is ▷Camilla Collett (1813–1872) who criticized conventional marriage, and became a well-known advocate of women's liberation.

As is shown, the modern breakthrough in Scandinavia did not occur as a sudden earthquake brought about by Georg Brandes, an impression one easily gains when reading traditional literary histories. One of the central themes of the modern breakthrough was how to live one's sexual life, and for the first time this consideration included both sexes. This also meant that the discussions of woman's place, of her education, marriage and status, became a very important topic, not only for women writers but for men, too. The modern breakthrough in Scandinavian literature not only became the breakthrough of new, modern ideas and a modern, naturalistic way, of describing them; it was also a breakthrough for women writers because they already had a realistic tradition, and a tradition for discussing the central themes: sexuality, woman's place in society, and marriage and social problems. After 1850, many more women had the time and knowledge to read and write. That is why so many more women writers wrote and were published during and after the 1870s.

A forerunner was the Danish Mathilde Fibiger (1830–1872), who wrote the first Danish novel that demanded equal rights for women (*Clara Raphael*, 1850). Adda Ravnkilde (1862–1883) demanded more equal rights in her descriptions of women's passions and sufferings, but her works also show a typical fascination for masochist women. She committed suicide. Many Danish women began to write during the modern breakthrough. For many years a great number of them were forgotten, but during the 1980s new research has been carried out.

In Finland, the leading figure of the modern breakthrough was a woman who was, at the same time, the first great woman writer in Finland, namely ▷Minna Canth (1844–1897). She introduced the ideas of the British philosopher John Stuart Mill (1806–1873) and Georg Brandes, and was a productive writer and dramatist. She was the first realist Finnish writer, describing the lives of women and the poor. Another famous woman writer of the modern breakthrough was the Danish-Norwegian ▷Amalie Skram (1846–1905), who experienced a personal breakthrough during her own lifetime. Her novels are about women who fail in conventional marriage and life, but who are at the same time unable to live another life. The parallel themes of the modern breakthrough – woman's longing for another life, and her entrapment in traditional sexuality – are very convincingly described in her works.

The Swedish writer ▷Victoria Benedictsson (1850–1888) is now considered a very important woman writer of the modern breakthrough. During the last ten years she has been republished, and much research has been done on her life and her work. Another important woman writer of the modern breakthrough in Sweden was ▷Anne Charlotte Leffler (1849–1892). She was a very prominent figure of literary life in Stockholm of the 1880s, where she had a literary salon until she divorced her husband and married an Italian duke. She is the only Scandinavian woman writer who wrote about happy love and sexuality. Some Scandinavian women writers were involved in the great debate of the 1880s in which all leading writers participated. The theme was chastity, and the question was whether men should be as chaste as women when entering marriage. A few men, among them Georg Brandes, thought that women had a right to a free sexual life before marriage, but most women writers were to be found on the other side, along with Bjørnstjerne Bjørnson (1832–1910). The radical men were not realistic. They did not realize what poor contraception and the many dangerous venereal diseases meant to women. As may be apparent from many of the lives of the women writers, sexual freedom could be a question of life or death, and many died very young.

With the modern breakthrough, ▷modernism had made its appearance in Scandinavian women's literature. In the following century, women writers can be found among the advocates as well as the opponents of modernism. Modernism also meant that a new mass literature of entertainment was produced, and many women writers found a living for themselves as journalists or as writers of literature for children and young girls. A new situation had arisen. It might still have been difficult to be a woman writer and to be acknowledged as such, but it became easier as time went by. And maybe it was a little easier in Scandinavia than in other places in the world. Two of the first women to receive the Nobel Prize were Scandinavians.

Selma Lagerlöf (1858–1940) was awarded the Nobel Prize in 1909. Her literature and development may be read as a symbol of the new and different status of women's literature in the 20th century. She wrote outside the literary tradition of her own time. She looked back, and wrote in the epic naïve tradition of the sagas, but this meant a modernist turn that was very new; she was not only in literary fashion, she was creating fashion, and she had an audience. She was widely translated and read, and was very much appreciated in her own time; she was the first woman to receive an honorary doctorate, to receive the Nobel Prize and to be a member of the Swedish Academy, but for a time she was not much acknowledged. She was regarded as a rather naïve storyteller, but now she is re-read and appreciated by new feminist literary research. She has meant much to women's writing in Sweden. Her biographer ▷Elin Wägner (1882–1949) was the leading Swedish feminist author for many years, and she and ▷Ellen Key (1849–1926) were the founders of a tradition of outstanding Scandinavian women debaters and intellectual writers.

In Denmark, a new breakthrough of women writers became apparent around 1900, with authors like ▷Thit Jensen (1876–1957), ▷Agnes Henningsen (1868–1962), ▷Karin Michaëlis (1872–1950) and Edith Rode (1879–1956). They were cultural radicals, their themes were female sexuality and psychology, but their writings were heterogeneous. While Jensen found her genre in the ▷historical novel, as did the less radical Norwegian Sigrid Undset, Henningsen wrote controversial memoirs, and Michaëlis experimented with language without ever slipping out of realism. Today, all four are being republished after new readings by feminist critics. For many years they were seen as propagandists. Indeed, all of them *were* propagandists, but, first and foremost, writers with an immense audience, because their themes were central to their time. All of them were realists, but some of Karin Michaëlis's works show a new experimental interest, pointing to modernist literature.

Sigrid Undset was also a realist, but, like Thit Jensen, she found in the historical novel a means of writing about important conflicts in her own time in the metaphor of former times. Undset was as famous as Lagerlöf in her time, and has also experienced a revival during the 1980s. She wrote about woman's sexuality and female identity, in the tradition dating back to the modern breakthrough but she created a hierarchical world with clear positions for God, men and women. Women had to take their place below God and men, but if they did so, their chances of a life with love and religious fulfilment were better than men's. The problems for women writers had changed: it seemed as if it had become possible to live and to write from within a female sexuality. But this created many conflicts and much ambivalence and pessimism, as, for example, in Undset's contemporary novels. Some very pessimistic voices were heard, for example, the Norwegian ▷Cora Sandel (1880–1974) wrote about women who did not succeed in their love affairs, but eventually *did* succeed in their work, or art, after many conflicts and battles, but Sandel was an innovator in theme rather than form, who introduced the impressionistic light to Scandinavian women's prose. The Swedish ▷Agnes von Krusenstjerna (1894–1940) was a more pessimistic voice. She described the poverty, social and cultural, within aristocratic families, the victims of which were the younger, unmarried women. For many years, the most important conflict in writing women's prose was the one between love and work, or art. This may still be true today, but what has definitely changed is the religious tone. God has been dethroned, the conflict has been secularized and made easier to overcome, but the specific relation between religious and feminist observation has been more difficult to establish, and today it is only found in a radical eco-feminism and in mystical modernism, where religion is something other than Christianity.

The Danish writer ▷Karen Blixen (1885–1962), or Isak Dinesen as she called herself in English-speaking countries, was outside this tradition. She was the first of many Scandinavian women writers who travelled, looked back, and then saw something that nobody else had seen. She came from the same aristocratic circles as von Krusenstjerna, and experienced the same social decline. She also found her solution in writing and making a living from it, but she wrote in another tradition – a very male-oriented symbolism – already old-fashioned, but much more in accordance with her themes than Krusenstjerna's realism in relation to her experiences of a divided self. Blixen succeeded in creating myths, not only in her literature but also about and around herself. She stood alone surrounded by men. Only recently have young women writers begun to take up her aristocratic, intellectual tradition, for example, in Denmark ▷Suzanne Brøgger (born 1944). She has combined it with a radical ▷post-modernism where all values are set adrift – at least for a time.

Women from the working class wrote about their specific problems. They often wrote a simpler, realist prose, connected to the oral traditions in Scandinavia, but much of their work has been underestimated as serious literature, for example, Moa Martinson (1890–1964). This simple realist literature was important to the new feminist literature of the 1970s. It was an act of the feminist movement to republish many forgotten proletarian women writers, and a new proletarian feminist literature evolved in all the Scandinavian countries during the 1970s. Today, most of it has been forgotten again, for example, Maja Ekelöf (born 1918), Grethe Stenbæk Jensen (born 1932) and many others.

It is difficult to describe the Scandinavian women's literature of the 20th century. It is not *one* literature, but consists of many styles and themes, and each generation has had its own currents and directions. But the fundamental change in this century is the birth of modernist writing. In Scandinavia, modernist poetry was introduced by two Fenno-Swedish women writers ▷Edith Södergran (1892–1923) and ▷Hagar Olsson (1893–1978). Södergran drew her inspiration from German Expressionism, and Olsson argued theoretically. ▷Katri Vala (1901–1944) is also usually seen as part of this tradition, and has in recently been followed by ▷Eeva-Liisa Manner (born 1921) and ▷Helvi Juvonen (1919–1959), the two most important Finnish modernists of the 1950s, and by ▷Marja-Liisa Vartio's (1924–1966) ironic prose writings. The influence from radical modernism is still to be found in Finnish women writers' works, for example, ▷Rosa Liksom (born 1958).

The modernist influence from Finland and Germany soon gained followers in the other Scandinavian countries. In Sweden, ▷Karin Boye (1900–1941) was radical in her experiments with poetry and science fiction, and today, ▷Birgitta Trotzig (born 1929) is an interesting example of spiritual and religious modernism. ▷Sonja Åkeson (1926–1977) formed the link to the neo-realist confessional women's prose of the 1970s. In Denmark, ▷Hulda Lütken (1896–1947) and today, ▷Inger Christensen (born 1935) have written very influental poetry while ▷Tove Ditlevsen (1918–1976) and ▷Kirsten Thorup (born 1942) linked modernism to the neo-realism of the 1970s. In the 1980s, a neo-modernism came to light, for example in the writings of ▷Pia Tafdrup (born 1952) and many others. Norway also had its modernist literature, with authors like ▷Aslaug Vaa (1889–1967), who was writing modernistic poems before modernism came to Norway, and ▷Gunvor Hofmo (born 1921), who has written beautiful modernist poems.

Today, it is evident that many different modernisms exist. The first generation of women modernists were followed by the generation of women writing between World Wars I and II. They often have religious themes and a mystical tone, combined with very depressing descriptions of modern life, especially for women. They write about alienation, and experiment with new techniques for bringing that alienation into the text and into the language itself. We see a modernism of the 1950s, still heavy with the aftermaths of the previous generation and that experience of World War II, and we see the modernism of the 1960s, a new minimalist and rationalistic prose and poetry, for example, ▷Inger Christensen (born 1935).

In the 1970s, a neo-realist confessional prose and poetry, with feminist emancipation as an important perspective, was written by authors like the Norwegian ▷Liv Køltzow (born 1945) and the Danish Vita Andersen (born 1949). This trend was seen all over the Western world, and it points to the tradition of political realism, a genre also used by women writers from the working class, who were rediscovered in the 1970s, only to be forgotten again in the neo-modernism or postmodernism of the 1980s. This movement was very closely connected to feminism and socialism. It was the most definitive clash with the domination of modernism in the fine arts. This development meant that women writers again attained a very wide audience – realism was easier to read for most women – but in the long run it meant that many more women readers discovered modernism. It is evident when discussing the new modernist trend of the 1980s, post-modernism or neo-modernism, that women writing in this tradition have more readers than ever before.

Today, the distinction between realism and modernism can be very difficult to define. Some women writers began with modernism, and developed a more realistic writing – others began with realism and have developed a more modernist writing. The fluctuation between these two main poles has never been greater. We see this as one of the most important consequences of the new women's literature of the 1970s. These recent developments also mean that it has become more difficult than ever before to speak of a women's literature in opposition to something else, for example, men's literature. It seems that the discrepancies are now more social than artistic. It still seems to be more difficult for a woman writer to decide to become a professional writer and to be acknowledged as such. But today, no one can seriously claim that women's writing plays a minor role in literature.

One genre remains to be mentioned: ▷children's literature. Scandinavian women writers have a long and fine tradition of writing books for children without much moralizing. Elsa Beskow (1874–1953) was an early example. Today, ▷Astrid Lindgren (born 1914) ▷Anne-Cath Vestly (born 1920), Cecil Bødker (born 1927) and ▷Tove Jansson (born 1914) are known all over the world. But many others write in this enlightened tradition, where children are accepted as human beings. This brief description does not indicate that this is a minor literature but that it is a vast literature, with so many important names to mention that it is impossible to do justice to it in this context.

Women's writing in Scandinavia can no longer be seen as a homogeneous tradition. Women writers are to be found in all new literary movements and genres. They want to be read for their writings, not because of their gender. But, of course, their gender, even in emancipated Scandinavia, remains just as crucial, especially to their writing.

17 Eastern Europe

The countries we call eastern Europe include, for the purposes of this essay, present-day Albania, Bulgaria, Czechoslovakia, Hungary, Poland, Romania, and the countries that made up the Yugoslav federation. In these countries there have been many women writers – and yet, not as many as men. The reasons one might consider for this, such as free time, available money, privacy, longevity, health, education and self-esteem, only partly explain the disparity. But while the experience of women writers in the area has undoubtedly been affected by the accident of being born women, the fact that they have left behind so few works of literature is still mysterious (even if the prejudice of men who might have published them, but didn't, is taken into account). The impulse to creativity, the need to write, the fact that women write or that women do not write: these are phenomena at once related to, and divorced from, political, social and economic conditions. Paper and pencil are, after all, usually cheap.

Researching east European women writers can be a thankless task. The index of many a literary history book may yield fewer than three female names. And more often than not, when the page reference is sought, one name may be that of a famous mistress, another of a beauty who inspired (male) poets, the third a writer whose work will probably, at best, be lasciviously described as delicate, feminine and sensitive, or, worse, florid, gushing and effeminate. For what is here, therefore, we owe a great debt of thanks to the scholars, expert in each particular country's literature, who have written many of the entries in this guide or advised more generally.

Throughout history, the countries which comprise present-day eastern Europe have been characterized by shifting boundaries, rule by various foreign powers (interspersed with brief periods of autonomy), and mixed and changing populations, religions and languages. The different empires they fell under are described by the Slovakian writer ▷Margita Figuli in ▷*Babylon* (1946). Few writers could be unaware of the remarkable mix of cultures which characterizes the area and is, of course, one of the main reasons for its unique cultural richness and diversity. Empires which have claimed these territories at one time or another include the Roman, the Byzantine, the Ottoman, the Habsburg and the Russian. Each of these left its mark on culture and language. Languages spoken or written have included German, Polish, Hungarian, Latin, Russian, Romanian, Yiddish, Hebrew, Turkish, Bulgarian, Croatian, Serbian and Slovenian. Religions vary although, broadly, central Europe is Catholic and south-east Europe Orthodox. Until the decimation of eastern European Jewry under Nazism, Judaism had a strong following.

The southern lands of present-day Bulgaria and Romania hardly had a native literature until as late as the mid-19th century, while other parts of the area, such as Prague, produced the early centres of literature and learning.

The first women writers we find, then, came, not surprisingly, from the aristocracy or, like ▷Zuzana Černínová z Harasova and ▷Cvijeta Zuzović, the clergy. The 18th century brought ▷Konstancja Benisławska, ▷Princess Izabela Czrtoryska and ▷Teofila Glinska. The 19th century brought a new breed of educated women, such as ▷Maria Konopnicka, and ▷Karolina Světlá, who took 1848, a year of revolutions, as the theme of her later works.

Several writers whose names have survived in history have been social commentarists and pioneers for education, such as ▷Eva Takács, ▷Marija Jambrišak and ▷Blanka Teleki. Others, like ▷Margit Kaffka, have been brilliant social observers. Writers who campaigned for women's rights include ▷Elena Maróthy-Soltesová, ▷Draga Dejanović and ▷Zagorka (Maria Jurić), especially in ▷*Kujeginja iz Petrinjske ulice* (1910) (*The*

Princess from Petrinskja Street). ▷Maria Dąbrowska's epic ▷*Noce i Dnie* (1932–1934) (*Nights and Days*) is one of the greatest family sagas ever, but many others have used the family as the setting for their work, such as ▷Magda Szabó, ▷Masa Halamová and ▷Lydia Vadkerti-Gavorniková. Maróthy-Soltesorá integrated the theme of family with questions of nationhood. Nationalism was also a focus for ▷Terézia Vansová.

The idea of women being central to humanity arises in the work of Slovak poet Mila Havgova, with her feminine principle of love, and in that of ▷Viera Handzová. On the other hand, the Serbian poet ▷Milica Stojadinović-Srpkinja aped a masculine style to conceal her gender. The effects on individuals of war and occupation have been examined in fiction by ▷Alaine Polcz in *Woman on the Battlefront* (1991), by ▷Timrava in ▷*Hirdinovia* (1918) (*The Heroes*) and Svetlana Velmar-Janković in ▷*Lagum* (1991) (*The Cavern*). The 1945 era was described by Eda Kriseová in ▷*Křížová cesta kočárového kočího* (*The Coachman's Coach Crusade*), and by ▷Katarina Lazarová.

In an area of shifting power, the influence of outside cultures is inevitable: Italian on ▷Anica Bošković, German on ▷Teréza Nováková and ▷Desanka Maksimović, French on Ružena Sesenska in ▷*Rudé západy* (1904) (*Crimson Sunsets*) and on ▷Franciszka Radziwiłł, Scandinavian on ▷Hana Zelinová and Russian on ▷Daniela Hodrová. There have been urban writers like Ana Maria Tolschova, who wrote ▷*Stará rodina* (1916) (*The Old Family*), Margit Kaffka, ▷Sophié Török and ▷Hortensia Papadat-Bengescu. Milka Zicina, in ▷*Devojka za sve* (1960) (*Jill of All Trades*), has shown the divide between country and city, while, from far-flung provinces and small towns, come ▷Jiřina Hauková, ▷Eliza Orzeskowa and ▷Maria Konopnicka. Others write about rural life, such as Božena Němcová in ▷*Babička* (1855) (*Grandmother*), Karolina Světlá, Timrava and ▷Zuska Zguriska. Ethical and moral debates have been the focuses of writing for ▷Maria Dąbrowska and Margita Figuli. Figuli also wrote about religion, as did ▷Gabriela Preissová.

If we speak of eastern Europe, we mean the countries which fell inside a political boundary agreed at Yalta in 1945. These include the countries noted above, but also the German Democratic Republic. The multitude of languages, cultures and aural and literary traditions to be found in these countries at that point defied generalization. Their literary histories and linguistic identities were multifarious; 'Yugoslavian literature' encompasses Slovene, Croatian and Serbian literatures, for example. Until the end of World War II there was nothing to connect the literatures of the eastern part of Europe more closely to one another than to, say, the German tradition or the French, or that of any other neighbouring or pan-European influence.

How did the communist era affect women? After World War II women became equal economic citizens with men. The post-war labour shortage saw them drafted into all forms of manual and professional labour, as in the West. But during the 1950s, when women here were tempted back to housewifery, in eastern Europe they stayed at work – and did the 'double shift' of paid work outside the home, followed by unpaid domestic labour and child care. Although the state and its ideologues had embraced theoretical notions of sexual equality, socially, children and cooking were still women's work. Rights that the Western women's movement was fighting for as late as the 1960s – equal pay for equal work, child care, free abortion and maternity leave – had been bestowed on women in eastern Europe and enshrined in law since 1945. There, women grew up with equal, mixed education and sexually integrated trades, professions and social lives. Yet still they wrote less than their brothers (with the notable exception of eastern Germany, where many of the best writers were women).

The state institution of sexual equality had several ramifications. Firstly, women did not define themselves as an interest group. In the West the women's movement of the 1960s was born of a sexual apartheid. At school and at work women and men were segregated, and gender difference was deemed important to character. Western feminists extended this, and orchestrated their resistance from a position of segregation and exclusion. Many cherish their separateness, making it political, and gaining strength from it for the 'battle of the sexes'. Meanwhile, women in eastern Europe blamed dissatisfaction not on gender division but on the totalitarian regime. Men and women were almost equal in their oppression, but even if women were disadvantaged, to admit it was dissent (oppression, in communist rhetoric, was a word applicable to the past or to non-communist countries, not the here and now). The underground opposition movements – involving men and women alike – saw sexual inequality as a minor problem compared to the monolithic state oppression of the Soviet Empire, and any mention of women's own struggle was dismissed as special pleading.

Since there was no such thing as an eastern European women's movement, the academic sphere has produced little by way of a feminist historical re-evaluation of women's roles in art, literature or music. Departments for women's studies are unheard of in most universities in the area. The field of eastern European studies in the West also tends to be conservative, and one of the last to really take sexual politics into its sphere of debate. A question such as, 'Who were the greatest Romanian women writers?' can, even now, produce merely a swift dismissal. The deconstruction of ▷patriarchal history that has burgeoned over the last twenty years in the fields of, say, English literature, history or art history has not happened with regard to eastern Europe – either here or there.

Artists and theorists in Russia in the 1920s defined the role of the artist in a communist state thus: to raise the socialist consciousness of the people through art, a people's art. When Soviet-style communism took root in eastern Europe in the late 1940s, writers were prescribed a similar role, and by the 1950s ▷socialist realism became the dominant style. Writers joined writers' unions – parallels to their brothers in industry – which at once affirmed writing as a profession, and also created a structure through which censorship was easy to impose. It was important to gain and retain membership of a writers' union in order to publish, and, providing one was adaptable, one could have a comfortable life supported by the state. Ironically, literary life under communism became a pastiche of 19th-century Paris. Its members were not arty young men of the *haute bourgeoisie*, but people of talent – the poorer their background the better – who could tailor their art to fit the regime. The salons (writers' union meetings), the country house weekends (at Socialist Party hotels), the literary debates (in official, censored newspapers) made for a literary life with an atmosphere of a gentleman's club. Women were not barred from any of these institutions, although they formed a minority of the writers themselves. If women wrote, they wrote as equals. To this day, few would accept the label 'woman writer' because 'women's literature' is a term of derision, calling to mind second-rate romantic novels and tear-jerking family sagas.

As individuals, as writers, women wrote about what concerned them, and their experience was naturally shaped by being female. Women have written, and continue to write, but as for eastern European women's writing – there is no such genre.

In the era when eastern Europe gained its current definition, socialist realism as a style influenced many writers, both male and female. Whereas ▷Marie Majerová embraced communism, Jane Červenkova, in ▷*Semestr Života* (1982) (*A Term of Life*), wrote of her disillusion with it, and ▷Nina Cassian's poetry shifts from an idealistic embrace of communism to a rejection of its 20th-century practice. The show trials of the 1950s (during which dedicated communists would publicly confess to false charges of anti-communist activities, believing that their imprisonment or execution would ultimately help the communist cause) were described by Jarmira Kolarova in ▷*Jen o rodinných záležitos-tech (1965) (Only Family Matters)*, and by ▷Erzsébet Galgóczi. ▷Eva Kantůrková wrote about events in Prague in 1968. Many suffered censorship or harsh criticism by the communist regime – Alexandra Berková, who wrote ▷*Knížka s červeným obalem*, (1986) (*The Little Book with a Red Cover*), and ▷Vesna Parun included – while Bara Basikova, in ▷*Rozhovory sútěkem* (1990) (*Conversations with Escape*), chronicles its decline.

The revolutions of 1989 brought to an end the era of the Eastern Bloc. But while these countries share the fact that they are in a post-communist and post-revolutionary era, each one is moving into the 21st century in quite a different way. The Yugoslavian women's movement was set up and has its own literary champions, such as ▷Slavenka Drakulić. Elsewhere the contemporary scene shows writers like ▷Jana Pohanková, ▷Elena Kadaré, Taťjana Lehenová (▷*Pre vybranú spoločnosť*, 1989, *For Select Society*), Svatava Antošová (▷*Ta Ženská musí být opila!*, 1990, *That Woman Must Be Drunk!*) and Gabriela Rothmayerová (▷*Šťastie je drina*, 1989, *Happiness Is Hard Work*) coming into their own. These include: the 'Angry Young Women' who emerged in Czechoslovakia in the 1980s. Women writers from eastern Europe whose works are available in English now include: ▷Elisaveta Bagryana, ▷Blaga Dimitrova, ▷Wisława Szymborska, ▷Ana Blandiana, Nina Cassian, Slavenka Drakulić and ▷Dubravka Ugrešić. Meanwhile, major writers such as ▷Ágnes Nemes Nagy, ▷Isidora Sekulić and Maria Dąbrowska have yet to gain, in the West, the recognition they deserve. The cultural integration of the two Europes should alter this. Current political changes have brought with them a new spirit of individual liberty: new freedoms of thought, of movement, and of sexuality. How women will define themselves within these new orders – and how they will write in them – is an exciting prospect.

C. ROSENTHAL & M. ZIRIN

Russia 18

Eighteenth-century Russia under Western-oriented rulers, from Peter I (1672–1725) to ▷Catherine II, saw reforms leading to the creation of a Russian literature which combined native values with the European cultural inheritance. The combination made for a rich synthesis that nurtured the genius of Aleksandr Pushkin (1799–1837), Leo Tolstoy (1828–1910), and Fyodor Dostoevsky (1821–1881). The active role that women writers played in this transformation has largely been ignored by literary historians; an accurate picture of their participation in the development of Russian literature has just begun to emerge as feminist scholars delve into a welter of forgotten books and journals.

The role of women writers *per se* in the medieval period is still a subject barely touched by specialists. There was a relatively high level of female literacy in medieval Russia, and some aristocratic women were well-educated. In the early 13th century Evfrosin'ia of Suzdal' was known as a scholar of classical Greek literature, and her sister, Mariia of Rostov, participated in writing the *Life* of their father, Mikhail of Chernigov, and in compiling the Rostov chronicles (cf N.L. Pushkarëva, *Women of Ancient Rus'*). Mariia Odóevskaia, who lived in 16th-century Novgorod, left an autobiography. The earliest Russian women writers in the modern period came from court circles. In the late 17th century Peter the Great's sisters wrote and staged plays; his daughter, Empress Elizabeth (1709–1761), left a few poems. Catherine II produced comedies, satires, philosopical essays, and over 10,000 letters. As head of the Russian Academy, ▷Ekaterina Dáshkova directed publication of the first major Russian dictionary and wrote memoirs. Well into the 19th century the nobility tended to regard writing by women as a graceful accomplishment, best confined to the domestic circle and family archives, but from the 1750s gentry women – Ekaterina Kniazhniná, Elizaveta Kheráskova (died 1809), and Aleksandra

Rzhévskaia (1740–1769) – were moving in literary circles and publishing works in neo-classical genres in magazines edited by male relatives. However, their writings, like those of many other women well into the next century, were either printed anonymously or subjected to unceremonious editing. With the aid of royal patronage and grants from the Russian Academy, the poet ▷Anna Búnina became the first Russian woman to live, albeit frugally, by her pen.

Changes in social mobility are seen in the growing ranks of women who took up literature as a profession, hoping at least to supplement their income by writing. Women writers came from non-gentry classes as early as the late 18th century, although their participation in literature remained sporadic throughout the 19th century (for example, ▷Elizaveta Kúl'man, ▷Nadezhda Teplóva, ▷Aleksandra Kobiakóva, ▷Anna Kirpíshchikova). A surprising number came from non-Russian families or had parents of different nationalities (for example, ▷Karolina Pávlova, ▷Anastasiia Márchenko, ▷Elena Apréleva, ▷Ol'ga Shapír). From the 1840s, debate around the ▷'woman question' encouraged greater female independence, but even the relatively accessible profession of letters held formidable obstacles for women. Men, with greater educational opportunities and mobility, also had to struggle to make a living as writers; few women had the financial means and independent position (as well-off spinster or widow) to make a career, as their male peers did, in the capitals and literary centres of ▷Moscow and ▷St Petersburg. ▷Nadezhda Khvoshchínskaia was exceptional in making a living for herself and her family by her pen from the provincial city of Riazan'. Nevertheless, despite the handicaps of provincial isolation, lack of formal education, and the constraints of ▷patriarchy, women were determined to write, and their literary output, especially in fiction, rose dramatically during the latter half of the 19th century. At the same time a few women editors and critics (▷Evgeniia Tur and ▷Mariia Tsébrikova) were playing a role in introducing Western culture into Russia and moulding public opinion.

The first generation of women to come of age entirely, after the emancipation of the serfs and other social reforms of the 1860s, turned to writing for complex reasons. The gradual breakdown of the gentry family structure, which could no longer provide for its unmarried young women, forced them to seek employment. Greater educational opportunities, including admission to university-level courses, gradually became open to women. Late in the century, as in Western countries, a women's liberation movement arose in Russia that encouraged women to take on new roles. While many professions remained closed to them, the advent of ▷modernism in the ▷Silver Age (1892/3–c 1925) attracted many women into literature despite the social opprobrium that still accompanied transgression of traditional roles as wife and mother. In the late 19th century most women writers were the daughters of professional families. (Few were of peasant or proletarian origins; exceptions were ▷Valentina Dmítrieva and ▷Elizaveta Milítsyna.) The 'world of art' was often part of the family heritage, or acquired through marriage. A large fraction of women writers was born in, or eventually moved to, one of the two capital cities. Most had secondary-school education, a minority attended universities, while another fraction attended art and music schools. In the Silver Age women gained prominence as literary historians and critics (▷Varvara Komaróva, ▷Zinaida Vengérova, Elena Koltonóvskaia, ▷Zinaida Gíppius) and editors of influential ▷'thick journals' (▷Liubov' Gurévich). As the scholar E.W. Clowes put it in *The Revolution of Moral Consciousness*, by the early 20th century 'a large number of women were gaining greater stature in the literary world as well as elsewhere . . . They were helping to create taste and consciousness.'

This flourishing community of women writers was broken up by the upheavals of World War I, the October Revolution, and the Civil War (1918–21). Much of it was gradually reconstituted in the centres of exile (Berlin, Paris and Prague), and in diaspora outposts from Belgrade to Shanghai. The Soviet Union, which imposed Communist Party control over literature in the 1930s, became an increasingly hostile environment for female creativity. An interesting generation of women writers emerged during and immediately after the Khrushchev 'thaw' of the 1960s (for example, ▷Bella Akhmadúlina, ▷Inna Varlámova, ▷Natal'ia Baránskaia, and ▷I. Grékova). In the 'stagnation' years from the late 1960s to the early 1980s, so-called dissident writers increasingly resorted to publication abroad (▷*tamizdat*) or private circulation of typescripts (▷*samizdat*). The end of the censorship that enforced the norms of socialist realism in literature produced a stronger resurgence of women writers in the 1980s, as well as intensive publication of supressed and *émigré* writings.

Throughout the history of modern Russian literature, use of ▷pseudonyms has been a sensitive indication of women's awareness of a distinct and separate set of expectations for them as writers. Russian critics for the most part held (and continue to hold) rigid ideas of what constitutes 'masculine' and 'feminine' writing. In the ▷Golden Age of the early 19th century, when the dominant genres were the 'feminine' ones of lyric poetry and sentimental/romantic prose, women felt free to use female pseudonyms or even publish under their own names. During the period of Russian realism (roughly 1850 to 1890), women who chafed at being confined to the 'domestic' subject matter that society considered their natural sphere increasingly resorted to masculine or neuter-gendered pseudonyms in order to get a fair hearing for their portrayals of contemporary society. Among those best known under male pseudonyms are: N. Stanitskii (▷Avdot'ia Panáeva), ▷Marko Vovchók (Mariia Markovich), V. Krestovskii (Nadezhda Khvoshchínskaia), Iv. Vesen'ev (▷Sof'ia Khvoshchínskaia), E. Ardov (Elena Apréleva), and V. Mikulich (▷Lidiia Veselítskaia). The end of the century saw a return to the use of real names and female pseudonyms. A number of Silver Age poets adopted pseudonyms that enhanced the 'poetic' resonance of their authorial personae: Anna Gorenko became ▷Anna Akhmátova; Elizaveta Dmítrieva, ▷Cherubina de Gabriak; Glafira Èinerling, ▷G. Gálina; Iraida Geinike, ▷Irina Odóevtseva; and Elizaveta Movshenzon, E.G. Polónskaia. A few women like ▷Tèffi (Nadezhda Buchinskaia) and ▷Ol'nem (Varvara Tsekhovskaia), whose prose seems consciously written against expectations of what 'ladies' would produce, still took masculine or neuter pseudonyms.

Genres in writings by Russian women developed in a different pattern to that of English literature. Drama generally follows the English-language continuum: women began writing plays very early, the genre languished until a resurgence in the late 19th century, and there has been a new burst of creativity in the ▷*glásnost* era. Recording their own lives and those of their families has always had a strong attraction for Russian women, and autobiography and memoirs have flourished since the late 1700s, at first for domestic archives and, from the mid-19th century, for publication. Women were also recognized as poets from the late 18th century; the genre developed steadily into the glories of the Silver Age, and remained alive in emigration and in the works of some Soviet poets. Prose fiction has been a much-practised mode of expression since the 1830s, and in the late 20th century seems to have become the major genre for women writers.

Drama

Drama, along with song one of the first genres women were known to practise (in court theatres), is the most difficult to reconstruct. Plays by Catherine the Great and Ekaterina Dáshkova have survived from the 18th century. In the first decade of the 19th a few derivative sentimental plays by Elizaveta Titóva (1780–?) were performed in St Petersburg, but her example does not seem to have made it possible for other women to see their plays produced. By mid-century women were writing plays that received at most a few performances before being forgotten, or were published in ephemeral journals. The concept of writing plays as a profession for women received an impetus in the 1880s, when 'well-made' popular plays on topical themes (undoubtedly influenced by the French '*boulevard*' theatre) by fiction writers like ▷Kapitolina Nazár'eva and Ol'ga Shapír were staged.

In the Silver Age more women were writing dramas, but not in sufficient numbers to create continuity and form a tradition of women dramatists. Most successful plays were written by women better known as poets or fiction writers, including Zinaida Gíppius, ▷Izabella Grinévskaia, ▷Lidiia Zinóv'eva-Annibál, Tèffi, ▷Liubov' Stólitsa, ▷Ol'ga Forsh, and ▷Mariètta Shaginián. Many of their plays were light farces or brief comic scenes. Several women wrote for the new film industry, either scenarios based on their own literary works (▷Anastasiia Verbítskaia's adaptation of ▷*The Keys to Happiness*) or original scripts (▷Evdokiia Nagródskaia and Forsh). While *émigrés* like Tèffi and ▷Nina Berbérova, and Soviet writers like Shaginián, ▷Vera Panóva, and ▷Vera Inber tried their talents at plays and film scripts, the absence of a tradition of play-writing as a genre for women, combined with inhospitable conditions both in the USSR and abroad, made the post-revolutionary period a relatively barren one for women dramatists. There were Russian theatres in Paris and Prague but, overall, the scattered *émigré* groups could not provide the permanent audience and complex material elements that theatrical productions require. In the USSR, the lighter fare that women dramatists had written earlier became unacceptable to the demands of the new state under construction. Inadmissible, too, were the religious themes, often combined with a strong, rebellious heroine who questions social values, which were features of pre-revolutionary plays by ▷Anna Barkóva, ▷Nina Ánnenkova-Bernár, ▷Izabella Grinévskaia, and ▷Mirra Lókhvitskaia. The stage adaptation of ▷Lidiia Seifúllina's novella ▷*Virineia*, with its combination of attractive heroine and pro-Soviet moral, was a major hit of the 1920s. One of the most striking developments in Russian drama of the 1970s and 1980s is the appearance and acceptance of works by exciting women dramatists (Zoia Boguslávskaia, Nina Sadúr, Mariia Arbátova, Liudmila Razumóvskaia, Elena Grimena and Tamara Vasilénko). Several of ▷Liudmila Petrushévskaia's humorous and pathetic plays have been performed in England and the USA. One factor that made production of these women's works possible was the breakdown of artificial socialist realist norms that mandated optimistic portrayals of society. Audiences obviously appreciate their depictions of the unadorned daily grind (Russian *byt*) in a milieu marked by cynicism and self-interest.

Autobiography and memoirs
Feminist scholars have demonstrated the importance of autobiography as a women's genre – one in which nobody can deny them the right to their own plot (B. Heldt, *Terrible Perfection*, pp. 64–102). Russian women began writing reminiscences in the 18th century for the edification of family and friends (Dáshkova). ▷Natal'ia Dolgorúkaia's memoir of her journey into exile in the 1730s was the first to appear in print (1810). Catherine the Great's autobiography, written in French and circulated widely in St Petersburg, was published only in 1859 in England. With rising interest in the recovery of private experience, memoirs were dug out of family archives and published in popular history journals in the second half of the 19th century and early 20th century. Reminiscences of wives who followed husbands condemned to Siberia after the Decembrist revolution of 1825 (Pauline Annenkova's 'Notes of a Decembrist Wife', dictated in French; Mariia Volkonskaia's *Notes*) were published in the late imperial period. Relatively unlettered and provincial women sometimes produced autobiographies marked by a naive authenticity and power that escaped their more worldly sisters (▷Nadezhda Dúrova's ▷*The Cavalry Maiden*, 1836; ▷Nadezhda Sokhánskaia's *Autobiography*, 1848). Along with those two works, ▷Avdot'ia Panáeva's bleak autobiographical novella (▷*The Tal'nikov Family*) is an early depiction of childhood. Girls' education in state-run boarding schools ('institutes') became an obsessive topic of memoirs, perhaps because the schools (to which until 1864 the students were confined without home visits for six to nine years) were emblematic of the restrictions of female lives (S. Khvoshchínskaia, Sokhánskaia) and, by analogy, state paternalism. In the Soviet epoch, depictions of women's experience in pre-revolutionary underground movements appeared, most notably Vera Figner's famous *Memoirs of a Revolutionist* (English translation 1927) and Valentina Dmítrieva's *The Way It Was* (1930).

Figner's account of twenty years of imprisonment foreshadowed the literature of Stalinist repression.

Autobiography exerted a great influence on women's prose fiction. Some of the most widely-read and discussed books of the Silver Age were autobiographical works, including those by ▷Marie Bashkirtseff (excerpts published in Russian in 1887), the famous mathematician ▷Sof'ia Kovalévskaia, and ▷Elizaveta D'iákonova. Bashkirtseff's diary, written in French, delineated the quintessential female Decadent: ambitious, whimsical, and egocentric, seeking a vocation worthy of her talents and intelligence, and testing the bounds of conventional behaviour.

The emigration kept its memories of pre-revolutionary Russia and the *émigré* experience alive in extensive memoir literature; major examples include Odóevtseva's *On the Banks of the Neva* (1967), Berbérova's ▷ *The Italics Are Mine* (1969), and works by Gíppius, ▷Galina Kuznetsóva, Sofiia Dubnóva, and Alexandra Tolstoy. In the Soviet Union, Vera Inber's ▷*Leningrad Diary* (1971) and ▷Lidiia Gínzburg's ▷ *The Siege of Leningrad: Notes of a Survivor* documented the day-to-day experience of the 900-day siege of the city during World War II. From the late 1960s autobiographical works, some of them already classic works of *samizdat*, were smuggled abroad (*tamizdat*) to pay witness to the horrors of Stalinism, either directly (▷Evgeniia Gínzburg, ▷Nadezhda Mandel'shtám) or obliquely in autobiographical fiction and poetry (▷Lidiia Chukóvskaia's ▷*Going Under*, Anna Akhmátova's ▷'Requiem'). Most of these works have now been printed in the Soviet Union, and the impulse to witness so characteristic of Russian culture continues: for example, Berbérova's memoirs of pre-revolutionary Russia and *émigré* life, *The Italics Are Mine*, were published in the US in 1969 and have recently appeared in the USSR. ▷Irina Ratushínskaia's *Grey Is the Color of Hope*, a memoir of imprisonment in a labour camp from 1983 to 1986 came out in the West in 1988.

Poetry

The Pushkin era, known as the Golden Age of Russian poetry (roughly 1820–1840), was the first to have an active coterie of women poets. In her jocular poem, 'A Conversation Between Me and Women' (c 1810), ▷Anna Búnina defended her right to address a wide variety of themes, including the exploits of men – not without irony: as she pointed out, 'an author's fame is in their hands.' Golden Age poets like Nadezhda Teplóva, however, generally confined their works to the 'feminine' lyric that society deemed more appropriate to their sex. As one male commentator dismissively noted, women's poetry, unlike men's, 'cannot be powerful, cannot affect the soul, stir it from the depths.' Women were expected to adhere to 'intimate' themes, and their tone was to be light or melancholy. Nicholas I ostracized ▷Evdokiia Rostopchiná for her 1846 allegorical ballad, ▷'The Forced Marriage.' Karolina Pávlova, one of the most distinguished poets of the 19th century, was denied even the grudging acceptance given her properly 'feminine' peers because she failed to observe the recognized conventions. Her philosophical cast of mind, innovations in form, and ambition to be taken seriously led to derision and neglect. Education for women from the 18th century to the Soviet period emphasized fluency in modern foreign languages, and many women poets were also accomplished translators, whose work played an important role in introducing Russians to Western poets. For some of them (for example, Elizaveta Kúl'man, Karolina Pávlova, ▷Anna Barýkova, ▷Ol'ga Chiuminá) translations and adaptations are an integral part of their poetic profile. Along with more famous male poets like Fet and Tiutchev, a few talented women kept the tradition of lyric poetry alive through the middle and late decades of the 19th century when prose was the dominant mode. Their close observations of their surroundings often carried an implicit protest against the broader inequities of their society (▷Iuliia Zhádovskaia, Nadezhda Khvoshchínskaia, Anna Barkóva).

The Silver Age, commencing in the 1890s, once again brought poetry to the fore as the most important and innovative mode. Women poets became a prominent part of the literary scene, gained widespread critical recognition, introduced major innovations in form, and greatly expanded the thematic range available to women poets. The 'feminine' tradition was well represented by Lókhvitskaia – who, however, extended the terms that women poets could use in speaking of love to include overt sensuality and self-gratification. In the early 20th century, her work was both popular and esteemed and became a standard against which other women's poetry was measured. In contrast, Gíppius used masculine and androgynous personae in her abstract and intellectual poetry. By the early 1890s, it was clear that she was an innovator in both form and themes. Her poetry was highly regarded by her male peers, including Briusov and Blok.

With the recovery of major poetic talents from the past (especially Pávlova), the expanded range of possible approaches to poetry developed by Lókhvitskaia and Gíppius, and their critical recognition and success, women poets now had fertile ground in which to flourish. As a result the Silver Age produced an astonishing body of fine poetry by women. The renowned Anna Akhmátova and ▷Marina Tsvetáeva must be seen against the background of a milieu that also produced outstanding work by contemporaries (▷Adelaida Gértsyk, Cherubina de Gabriak, ▷Elena Guró, ▷Sofiia Parnók, Vera Merkúr'eva, Tat'iana Efiménko, Izabella Grinévskaia, Liubov' Stólitsa, ▷Nataliia Krandiévskaia, ▷Mariia Shkápskaia, Irina Odóevtseva, Anna Barkóva, and ▷Mariia Petrovýkh).

Women continued as important poets in the years immediately after the Revolution, but by the mid-1920s poetry, especially the lyric that had been the cornerstone of their achievement, ceased to be valued in the new Soviet state. A number of the best poets emigrated, fell victim to political persecution and critical inattention, or were simply denied the right to publish. Inber, ▷Ol'ga Berggól'ts, and ▷Margarita Aligér managed to tailor their verse to the 'social command' without too great sacrifice of personal integrity. Akhmátova was a living avatar of the Silver Age who, although unpublished from 1925 to 1940 and 1946 to 1958, wrote some of her best work in those years. Historical circumstances prompted her to bear witness to the collective ordeal in long poetic narratives, 'Requiem' (1935–43, published in 1989 in the USSR) and ▷'Poem Without a Hero' (1940–1962). Other poets with personal and aesthetic ties to the Silver Age include Bella Dizhúr, Mariia Petrovýkh, and ▷Inna Lisniánskaia. The Silver Age has also influenced younger poets: while the more 'intimate' verse of Bella Akhmadúlina bears Akhmátova's stamp, the intense poetry of ▷Natal'ia Gorbanévskaia reflects that of Tsvetáeva. These younger poets and others – Elena Shvarts, ▷Novella Matvéeva, ▷Iunna Mórits, Ol'ga Sedakóva (born 1949), and Maia Borísova came of age in the relatively relaxed post-Stalin period.

In emigration, Russian poets were faced with the need to earn a living as members of a community too small to support publication on a sufficiently profitable scale. Women like ▷Mother Mariia, Gíppius, and Tèffi who were well-known before the Revolution fared best. Tsvetáeva wrote some of her finest poetry while living abroad, and expanded into the long poem and verse drama, as well as prose. The ranks of *émigré* writers increased with poets of the 'first' (pre-World War II), 'second' (post-World War II), and 'third' (since the 1960s) waves of emigration: among them were ▷Lidiia Chervínskaia, Galina Kuznetsóva, ▷Vera Búlich, ▷Lidiia Alekséeva, Anna Prísmanova, ▷Zinaida Shakhovskáia, ▷Ol'ga Anstei, Irina Búshman, and ▷Tamara Velichkóvskaia. Despite hardships, deprivation, and separation from Russia, these poets kept alive the modernist heritage, both in formal range and in the recurrent religious and philosophical themes one finds in their works.

The last wave of Soviet repression struck the poets ▷Iuliia Voznesénskaia, who was forced into emigration in 1980, and ▷Irina Ratushínskaia, imprisoned three years later. *Glásnost* made possible the publication in the Soviet Union of a wide range of poetry by women, from that of Olesia Nikoláeva, which is deeply imbued with Russian Orthodox traditions, to several poets who write primarily 'free verse' (for example, Marina Andriánova, Tat'iana Shcherbína, and Elena Skúl'skaia). With the return to the USSR of Irina Odóevtseva in 1987, the Soviet Union gained a living representative of the Silver

Age. Much poetry from that period and from emigration is also being published, so that Russians now have access to a far more complete picture of their own cultural heritage.

Pre-revolutionary prose

Women had carved out a niche in poetry that critics saw as appropriately 'feminine.' In contrast, in men's view, it took male intelligence and experience to produce fiction relating to anything beyond the domestic sphere; possession of a 'masculine' talent was the highest compliment that could be paid a female prose writer. In the latter half of the 19th century, fiction became a weapon in the political struggle, a way of discussing the social agenda obliquely enough to evade censorship. Russian women struggled to write in an atmosphere impatient of depictions of their own lives and concerns; at the same time they were discouraged in attempts to write directly about the larger social agenda from what critics (including the radical Mariia Tsébrikova) saw as their hopelessly limited perspective. The demand that literature address 'big' themes led to a persistent retrospective downgrading of women's fiction. In retrospect they fared no better: women were largely written out of the history of Russian realism (roughly 1850–1890), and their interactions with and reactions against their male peers forgotten. Their success with the contemporary audience is easily demonstrated by the huge amount of fiction, mainly novels and novellas (sometimes self-deprecatingly described as 'sketches' or 'jottings'), which they published in the major 'thick journals' of the time and in separate editions.

The scant legacy of early 19th-century sentimental novels and tales by women seems to have no ironic subtext; in that period there was apparently no sharp-eyed contemporary of ▷Jane Austen to portray her society with gently acerbic wit (Y. Harussi, 'Women's Social Roles as Depicted in Early Nineteenth-Century Russian Fiction' in *Issues in Russian Literature before 1917*). By the late 1830s, however, writers like ▷Elena Gan, ▷Mariia Zhúkova, and Nadezhda Dúrova in their individual ways began producing fiction that expressed strong female egos and portrayed contemporary society in a harsh light. Their works made the ▷'society tale' the first important prose genre for women.

As in women's poetry, critics often seemed blind to irony in women's prose and failed to realize that the closure of possibilities, restriction to confined spaces, and denial of basic rights that women portrayed within their own domestic milieu (▷Sofia Èngel'gárdt, Elena Apréleva, Ol'ga Shapír) related by implication to the larger society as well. Women made a virtue of necessity, writing works that reflected a strong sense of place (the country estate, the provincial town) and the variety of people they knew best: peasants (Marko Vovchók, Valentina Dmítrieva), merchants (Aleksandra Kobiakóva), factory folk (Anna Kirpíshchikova). Ukrainian culture stimulated the talents of several Russian writers. Vovchók, ▷Aleksandra Montvid, and Stefaniia Karaskévich portrayed the hard lot of Ukrainian peasants, especially women. Nadezhda Sokhánskaia wrote exuberant tales of the past and present life of merchants and landowners on the east Ukrainian-Russian borderlands.

Women's prose shows the fascination with 'liberating' women exemplified in Nikolai Chernyshevsky's famous prescriptive novel ▷*What Is to Be Done?* In the late 1830s, well before the 'Woman Question' entered the social agenda, Gan had protested the plight of talented women in a philistine society; and, in a gentler vein, Zhúkova portrayed attractive young women struggling for financial and moral independence. Along with Anastasiia Márchenko and Evgeniia Tur, she led the trend to realism in women's writings. Their novellas featured heroines who were neither beautiful nor emotionally exalted, and denouements that were closer to observed life. Panáeva published stories which express a bitter view of male exploitation of women's drive for emancipation. Her 'A Girl of the Steppes' (1855), Zhádovskaia's ▷*Apart from the Great World* (1857) and Sofia Khvoshchínskaia's 'City Folk and Country Folk' (1863) all feature provincial heroines who easily detect the falsity behind urban men's seductive idealism. Orphaned young gentry women who lead an independent, rational life and evade the traps set by courting males have no counterparts in contemporary fiction by men (Anastasiia Márchenko's 'Hills', 1856, and Zhadóvskaia's 'Woman's Story', 1861). In many stories by women, men are mere stock characters – desirable or conniving suitors, domineering or understanding fathers, spendthrift brothers. They come and go, a chance factor in a daily life governed by domestic routine. The hegemony of a widow, who dominates a female household of unmarried relatives, poor dependents and servants, and revels in her power to determine the inheritance of male and female family members, is a frequent topic (N. Khvoshchínskaia's ▷*In Hope of Better Days*, Èngel'gardt's 'Dream of a Grandaunt and Grandniece'). From the late 1850s Nadezhda Khvoshchínskaia and her sister, Sof'ia, used male voices and characters in stories and sketches that portrayed the struggles of a society in transition. By the 1870s and 1880s women writers, like their male counterparts, were carving out a larger spectrum of topics, including ever franker discussion of women's sexual nature and needs (Elena Apréleva) and increasingly bitter depictions of Russian society. From 1879 to the revolution Ol'ga Shapír both worked for the emancipation of women – which, as she saw it, meant not only civil and political rights, but spiritual independence and parity with men in creative vocation – and portrayed women's struggles toward that end in well-crafted fiction. Sof'ia Smirnóva and Kapitolina Nazár'eva wrote popular novels and stories with believable male heroes, and broad social interactions.

By the end of the 19th century, critics commented on the 'flood' of women's fiction or, at least, the growing visibility of women prose writers. Their numbers and popularity grew with the opening up of a market for popular fiction in the early 20th century. This fiction, aimed at a wide audience, was influenced by the themes, character types, and forms of 'serious' literature, so that the boundary between the two is at times obscured. Like their male counterparts, women now favoured shorter prose narratives: the short story, the novella, and, to a lesser extent, the sketch. With occasional exceptions, novels became the province of women like ▷Lidiia Chárskaia, ▷Nadezhda Láppo-Danilévskaia, ▷Nadezhda Lukhmánova, ▷Evdokiia Nagródskaia, ▷J.W. Rochester, and Anastasiia Verbítskaia who wrote for a mass readership.

Women's prose in the Silver Age, like men's, bifurcated into realist and modernist camps, although, as with men's prose, the boundary was not always clear. Realists continued to favour 'objective' narration, the depiction of character within a recognizable social setting and, often, against a background of contemporary history and ideas. Modernists tended to experiment with prose forms, departing from realism in areas such as point of view and narrative system, trying various forms of 'impressionistic' and subjective narration, character depiction, and imagery. A common form of experiment was the mixing of genres – prose and poetry, autobiography and fiction, autobiography and essay. Both groups turned inward and became more concerned with self-exploration. Whereas the realists approached the psyche in terms of motivational causality, the modernists tended to depict it as the 'soul', the internal battleground of metaphysical forces. However, there are works that aim to do both. Realists and modernists deal with some of the same subject matter: concerns about women's self-definition and what might be called 'protest fiction', in which the female experience of powerlessness, subordination, frustration and anger was transposed onto others: children, the unemployed, the poor, social outcasts, and outsiders (▷Lidiia Avílova, Mariia Kiselëva, Elena Guró, Zinaida Gíppius, Nina Ánnenkova-Bernár, ▷Tat'iana Shchépkina-Kupérnik, Anastasiia Krandiévskaia, Ol'nem). Character types that Silver Age women were fascinated by included the 'new woman,' the 'infernal' woman (the *fin de siècle*'s *femme fatale*), and the female counterpart of the already stereotypical ▷superfluous man. What is strikingly rare in their fiction is the 'terribly perfect' (Heldt, *Terrible Perfection*) heroine of much 19th-century fiction by men: attractive, cultured, moral, and content with her traditional role as helpmate.

Much of women's fiction can be regarded as attempts to define woman's role and what she needed to make her happy. Anastasiia Verbítskaia set out the terms in the novella

▷*Discord* (1887), and over the next three decades she and other writers debated whether happiness for women was constituted relationally – through marriage, motherhood, family, and friendship – or individually – through work, be it a vocation or an avocation, and such developmental modes as education and sexual exploration. A recurrent theme in women's exploration of happiness is the mother–daughter relationship and female friendship. Repeatedly, strong ties between women form the emotional core of many women's fictions. Sometimes female attachments, as in ▷*Jane Eyre*, are cemented in educational institutions (Nadezhda Lukhmánova, ▷Mariia Krestóvskaia, Ol'nem). They are usually, but not always, positively portrayed. Mother–daughter relationships can also be links between a surrogate mother and a 'daughter' looking for a mentor in works like Tat'iana Shchépkina-Kupérnik's ▷*Happiness* (1897), Mariia Krestóvskaia's 'Howl' (1900), and Ol'nem's 'Without Illusions' (1903). Families in conflict are portrayed sporadically in women's works from the 1860s (N. Khvoshchínskaia's *In Hope of Better Days*; Kobiaková's *The Podoshvin Household*), but the family chronicle *per se* becomes a major genre for women only in the Silver Age. In fiction of this type, women writers who were interested in supra-personal themes used the family as a unit emblematic of larger social and historical forces. Examples include Ol'nem's 'Dynasty' (1910), ▷Veselkóva-Kil'shtét's ▷*The Kolychevs' Patrimony* (1911) and *On Native Soil* (1914), Anastasiia Krandiévskaia's *The Secret of Joy* (1916), Mariètta Shaginián's *One's Own Fate* (1923), and Láppo-Danilévskaia's popular variant *A Russian Gentleman* (1914) (▷*Michail or The Heart of a Russian*, 1917)).

The Soviet period

After the revolution, some women prose writers – among them, Tèffi, Evdokiia Nagródskaia, Nadezhda Láppo-Danilévskaia, and Ol'ga Bébutova – emigrated, while a number, including Shaginián, stayed. Shaginián became the subject of much negative criticism; her interest in psychology and religion, which was shared by many women writers, was declared too inward-looking and passive for the new revolutionary literature. In a series of novels – ▷*Mess Mend: Yankees in Petrograd* (1923), *Kik* (1929), and *Hydrocentral* (1931) – we see her moving toward socially oriented narratives for a broad audience. To avoid repression and preserve their integrity, both women and men sought refuge in writing about the past – in memoirs and historical fiction – and in relatively 'safe,' accepted fields such as journalism, children's literature, and translation. The imposition of socialist realism, with its demand for characters depicted primarily as social and political actors, thwarted women's interest in private lives and relationships. In the article 'Four Women', written in 1927 for the tenth anniversary of the 1917 Revolution, Vera Inber discussed the switch to journalism of four women writers: Shaginián, Mariia Shkápskaia, ▷Larisa Réisner, and Zinaida Rikhter. Inber demonstrates the degree to which women writers accepted the dominant views of what was 'good' and 'relevant' writing in the new Soviet state. For her, poetry had been women's forte because it dealt with 'warm, specific items', while criticism (and by implication, journalism) required 'cold, abstract generalizations' and clarity of thought. The domestic world which women knew best is denigrated as the world of 'petty hearths', destroyed by the 1917 Revolution. Now men and women were on equal footing in the exploration of a wider world, and even such maternal woman as the poet Shkápskaia had become a social activist. Inber did not realize that by propagating these views, she was frustrating women's creative impulse rather than nurturing it: Shkápskaia never wrote poetry again.

Popular prose of the type written by Láppo-Danilévskaia, Lukhmánova, and Bébutova was suppressed. In the 1920s writers like Lidiia Seifúllina and ▷Aleksandra Kollontái could deal with some of the themes of women's Silver Age prose – questioning of gender roles, liberated sexuality, happiness through self-contained identity versus love for a man – provided their heroines sympathized with the Communist Party. Prose remained the dominant mode, and by the 1930s, as in the earlier period of realism, the panoramic novel, now straitjacketed by socialist realism, was once again the dominant form. Russian women contributed extensively to the genre, but the socialist realist novel seems hardly likely to have any lasting interest outside the now-defunct government that decreed its constricted style and subject matter. From the 1930s to the 1960s there was a return to the 19th-century prose stereotype of women as beings who sacrifice personal happiness to larger social ideals. Sturdy peasant activists and austere builders of socialism yielded to the 'amazons' of World War II and resilient postwar abandoned or widowed women devoted to the welfare of family and country (Vera Panóva's *Fellow-Travellers*, 1945, and *Evdokiia*, 1944–58; Galina Nikoláeva's *The Harvest*, 1950; and I. Grékova's ▷*The Hotel Manager* and ▷*The Ship of Widows*, 1981. As in the past, some of women's best writing focused on children (Inber and Panóva). With the mid-1960s the image of woman as the touchstone of 'true values' gradually evolved into more human outlines. The modern urban professional, faced with the daily round of problems and questioning her position in family and society, appeared more and more often in Soviet fiction (for example, Baránskaia's 'A Week Like Any Other'). Portraits of a truly emancipated woman seeking self-fulfilment can be found in Grékova's 'The Ladies' Hairdresser' (1963) and more recently in ▷Maia Gánina's prose. ▷Viktoriia Tókareva addresses the dilemmas of women's lives in a lighter, more optimistic vein.

In emigration between the wars, established prose writers like Tèffi and Evdokiia Nagródskaia continued to publish, although their audience was a small one. Since the 18th century foreign languages, and French in particular, had been in common usage among the upper classes, and many pre-revolutionary women wrote in French (▷Bashkirtseff, Varvara Komaróva, ▷Anna Aníchkova). Some younger *émigrés* felt the pull of their newly adopted cultures and switched languages: Elsa Triolet, who had published several novels in the USSR, and the Russian poet Zinaida Shakhovskáia) both began writing French fiction. Others, like Berbérova, Georgi Peskov (real name: Elena Déisha, 1885–1977), Nadezhda Gorodétskaia (born 1903), and ▷Irina Sabúrova, continued to write prose in Russian. ▷Iuliia Voznesénskaia rapidly adapted the Western standards of sexual frankness in her ▷*The Women's Decameron*. Even before *glásnost'* proper began, a more relaxed attitude toward experimentation in subject matter, language, stylistics, and genre had led to the appearance of innovative prose by younger writers (▷Elena Makárova, ▷Tat'iana Tolstáia, ▷Liudmila Petrushévskaia). Ongoing interchange between Russian women writers in the Soviet Union and their *émigré* counterparts today offers promise of a broader role for women in Russian literature, built on the newly recovered heritage of the past.

Early North America 19

Although early North American women are typically regarded as those European women who settled in the New World before 1800, there were, of course, numerous Native American women present in North America before the Spanish began exploring the southern and western regions of the continent and before English settlements in Massachusetts Bay Colony were established. In one of the earliest known ▷Native American legends, 'The First Ship', it is a woman who sights a ship carrying the first Spanish explorers and who runs to warn her people of a seemingly monstrous creature about to land on shore.

Since Native American women were part of an oral culture, we have no written documents by them, but later explorers and anthropologists began to record their oral histories, legends and myths. While these transcriptions of Native American legends offer us certain insights into women's roles in the community and the customs that controlled and encouraged them, we must always realize that most of the transcribers were men, who often did not value women's everyday contributions to the society and who often edited out material that they did not deem valuable or, as in the customs of birthing and sexuality, found embarrassing to their 'civilized' sensibilities. Still, early Native American women's lives are more accessible to us today because of these histories and legends, and their contributions to the development of North American culture should not be underestimated.

In the early Virginia settlements it was soon discovered that social order and prosperity required the presence of women; thus, in the early 17th century, women began arriving in the colony, either as spouses of settlers or as single women sent as prospective spouses. In Plymouth Plantation and Massachusetts Bay Colony, women were integral members of the first communities, and their early writings constitute not only significant historical documents but often valuable literary texts as well. The poet ▷Anne Dudley Bradstreet (1612–1672), for instance, came with the first ships to Massachusetts Bay Colony, and her renowned poetry and spiritual meditations remain classic texts in North American literary history. While a few Puritan women, such as ▷Jane Dunlap (fl 1771) and ▷Margaretta V. Bleecker Faugeres (1771–1801), followed in Bradstreet's poetic footsteps, most New England women's writings were in less traditional forms, such as the diary of ▷Esther Edwards Burr (1732–1758) or the 'death-bed' declaration of ▷Rebekah Chamblit (died 1733).

But the continent was not a vast expanse of uninhabited land between Virginia and Massachusetts. In historical and literary circles emphasis has always been placed on the development of New England; but in expanding early North American studies we discover numerous settlements in other areas that emerged during the 17th century: in New Netherland (later New York), Dutch immigrants established colonies that are of particular interest to scholars of early North American women's lives, since Dutch women's roles in society were much different from those of the more repressive English societies. Both ▷Maria van Cortlandt van Rensselaer (1645–1689) and ▷Alida Schuyler van Rensselaer Livingston (1656–1727), members of the aristocratic Dutch founding families, were active businesswomen, and Livingston established a decidedly egalitarian marriage relationship. In the mid-Atlantic states, early Swedish and Quaker settlers developed the region into a sound economic venture. Here, too, many women had opportunities to develop their talents and participate in the religious and civic formation of their communities. ▷Hannah Callowhill Penn (1671–1726) arrived in the proprietorship of Pennsylvania in 1700; through her business acumen she became an instrumental figure in the maintenance of the Penn family's control over the region until the American Revolution (or War for Independence).

For many women, however, life was very different. Africans were kidnapped and transported to North America in ever-increasing numbers during the 17th and 18th centuries. Only when North Americans sought independence did the issue of slavery arise as a topic for general debate; but, if the new republic's concept of 'liberty' excluded white women, it was even more pervasive in its exclusion of African-Americans as a race. Yet a few African-American women did rise above their enslavement to produce literary records of their lives. The first known poem by an African-American woman was written by ▷Lucy Terry (c 1730–1821); and the renowned slave-poet, ▷Phillis Wheatley (c 1753–1784), gained international fame – while she was a slave. Racial prejudice in early North America is nowhere so evident as in the denial of Wheatley's talents once she was freed. For Wheatley, life in this world was something to be endured; her Christian training offered her only the next world as a place in which 'fetters' and 'iron bands' would be removed and her body – like her imagination – would be freed.

Religion played a dominant role in shaping most women's experiences during this period. In New England, Puritan Calvinism and subsequent offshoot sects acted both to oppress and to liberate women in the region. A highly hierarchical theology (God–man–woman/child), Calvinism determined the domestic lives to which most women were confined, either as mistresses of a household or as servants. The correspondence of women such as ▷Margaret Tyndal Winthrop (c 1591–1647) and her sister-in-law, ▷Lucy Winthrop Downing (1600/1601–1679), offers important avenues into understanding the daily lives of women; even well-to-do and socially prominent women like Winthrop and Downing had to confront the day-to-day hardships of establishing a new colony.

But Calvinism also deemed salvation a personal experience, and thus women who might have been limited to correspondence as their only mode of writing found a means of written expression in spiritual autobiographies or diaries, genres that allowed them to record the joys and sorrows of their individual journeys toward salvation. With the advent of the Great Awakening and subsequent evangelical revivals, however, women gained much greater access to the public ear. ▷Sarah Parsons Moorhead (fl 1741–1742) published poetry addressed to James Davenport and Gilbert Tennent, ministers and leaders of the Great Awakening; in the fervour of Expressionism that was the touchstone of the revivals, she had the freedom to offer advice and counsel to the leaders in a way that had heretofore been deemed 'unwomanly'. So, too, did a few women use the opportunities of the Great Awakenings to take on even larger roles in their religion. Most notable was ▷Sarah Haggar Wheaten Osborn (1714–1796), who was the leader of a revival in Newport, Rhode Island, in the 1760s. Other notable Puritan religious writers include ▷Sarah Pierpont Edwards (1710–1758), ▷Sarah Prince Gill (1728–1771) and ▷Jenny Fenno (fl 1791).

In Quaker communities, however, women's roles had always been much more public. Although meetings typically separated men and women physically, women were free to express their opinions and experiences. Education for women was highly valued by this faith as well, and, through that social tenet, we see the rise of women writers as commonplace rather than an exception much earlier than in other communities. As early as 1660 ▷Mary Traske and Margaret Smith challenged the patriarchal order in their Boston community; and in Philadelphia, where Quakers were not persecuted but, in fact, controlled large portions of the economy and government, women's writings flourished. Because of the emphasis upon New England literature in early North American studies,

▷Quaker women's writings have rarely gained their deserved attention. Throughout the 17th and 18th centuries, Quaker women published their writings, and, although they often included the 'apologia' that was almost requisite in all women's writings of this period, the writings of women such as ▷Bathsheba Bowers (c 1672–1718), ▷Jane Fenn Hoskens (1694–?), ▷Hannah Griffitts (1727–1817) and ▷Hannah Callender (1737–1801) were much more outspoken and confrontational in style than those of their Puritan counterparts.

No aspect of early North American life opened the door more widely for women's entry into the realms of literature and publishing, however, than did the American Revolution. Women's roles in the American Revolution had been virtually ignored until recent feminist historians' rediscovery of the multifaceted ways in which women contributed to the war efforts and to the establishment of a new nation: while men (and a few women) participated in the battles, women often maintained the family estates and the local economies, raised money for the war, nursed the wounded and provided life-saving supplies to the troops. The American Revolution also acted as the impetus for the development of politically active ▷women's organizations in colonial North America. In private journals and letters, as well as in published broadsides, poems and political tracts, women expressed their opinions on the war and entered into the philosophical debates about the proper political order for the new nation. Among the numerous notable writers in these traditions were ▷Elizabeth Sandwith Drinker (1734–1807), ▷Eliza Farmar (fl 1774–1783), ▷Dorothy Dudley (fl 1775–1776), ▷Mary Bartlett (fl 1775–1778), ▷Grace Growden Galloway (died 1782) and ▷Mary Willing Byrd (1740–1814).

With the inroads gained during the American Revolution, and in spite of the fact that the 'Founding Fathers' preferred women to return to the role of mother and wife after its conclusion, women forged ahead in developing their literary talents. The majority of women continued to write in 'private' genres such as diaries and correspondence; some of the records of North American women's lives in the early federal period suggest the continuing oppression and occasional horrors of their lives, such as the account of domestic violence recorded by ▷Abigail Abbott Bailey (1746–1815). Significant numbers of women, however, began to record privately, and among members of a corresponding circle of friends, their changing attitudes; for instance, ▷Hannah Apthorp Bulfinch (1768–1809), ▷Julia Cowles (1785–1803), ▷Eliza Southgate Bowne (1783–1809) and ▷Mary Coburn Dewees (fl 1787–1788).

In the early federal period, many women also began to move into the field of writing as a profession: ▷Mercy Otis Warren (1728–1814) became one of North America's major dramatists; ▷Susanna Haswell Rowson (1762–1824), was North America's first bestselling novelist, as well as an actress, dramatist and educator; and ▷Judith Sargent Murray (1751–1820) a prolific author of essays, poetry and dramas, became North America's first major feminist author. If the monetary success remained out of reach for most of these women (as it did for most male authors), their voices were being heard and their challenge to the patriarchal order would be continued by their counterparts in the 19th century who carried on even more public demands for women's rights. When ▷Abigail Smith Adams (1744–1818) demanded that her husband and other authors of the new political order 'remember the Ladies', she told her friend, Mercy Otis Warren, that she had made great strides in presenting a list of 'Female Grievances' and advancing woman's cause. While Adams's husband scoffed, Warren, like other women of her generation, listened, and learned, and began, as Adams had prophesied, to 'foment a rebellion' for equality.

▷Captivity narratives; Early American letters; Early American narratives of witchcraft cases; *Correspondence of Maria van Rensselaer*; *Diaries of Julia Cowles, The*; 'Diary and Letters of Elizabeth Murray Inman, The'; *Diary of Grace Growden Galloway*; *Letters of Mrs Lucy Downing*; *Journals of Madam Knight, The*; *Memoir of Miss Hannah Adams*.

Bib: Davidson, Cathy, *Revolution and the Word: The Rise of the Novel in America*; Caldwell, Patricia, *The Puritan Conversion Narrative*; Wright, Luella, *The Literary Life of the Early Friends, 1650–1725*; Kerber, Linda, *Women of the Republic: Intellect and Ideology in Revolutionary America*; Ulrich, Laurel Thatcher, *Good Wives: Image and Reality in the Lives of Women in New England, 1650–1750*.

C. KLIMICK CYGANOWSKI

20 Nineteenth-century US

Nineteenth-century North American literature is the domain of women writers. Despite the traditional focus of the North American canon on 19th-century New England white male writers, for most of the century American authorship and the audience for it were dominated by women. Successful literary careers, the development of distinctive forms, the introduction of new subjects, and national and international attention to diverse voices firmly establish 19th-century North American literary history as a history of women readers, women writers and women's writing.

The century's turn and early decades of traditional forms to 1820
At the end of the 18th century, the literary world's sense of North American women writers was directed to a few early and notable 18th-century poets, ▷Anne Bradstreet and the African-American slave poet ▷Phillis Wheatley, to dramatist ▷Mercy Otis Warren, to religious historian ▷Hannah Adams and to British-American novelists writing in the 18th-century tradition: ▷Susanna Haswell Rowson, ▷Sarah Keating Wood, and ▷Helena Wells. North American women would later develop unique fictional techniques and genres, but the first decades of the 19th century saw fairly conventional novels with variations on standard seduction plots. Rowson's early 19th-century novels show women's sexuality at risk because of traditional economic dependency. Sarah Keating Wood's novels centre on women characters who face adversity with virtue and strength. As Wood moved to North American characters and settings, her novels anticipate a North American women's tradition of realistic fiction with regional subjects, focused on women overcoming family and economic hardship.

While the ▷'woman question' would come to highest prominence in the 1840s, the early decades were rife with non-fiction debate on reform and the proper rights and roles of women, including ▷Hannah Mather Crocker's traditional, religious answer to those who were questioning 'the Real Rights of Women'. The novel itself was still under dispute as a proper form of entertainment and instruction. For those who took the negative view, numerous tomes combined religious, domestic and spiritual issues – often with a historical bent. Hannah Adams, usually considered the first professional North American woman writer, continued her 18th-century career of religious writing with *The Truth and Excellence of the Christian Religion Exhibited* (1804) and *The History of the Jews* (1812). Warren followed her 18th-century plays on the politics of the American Revolution with the first North American history written by a woman, ▷*History of the Rise, Progress and Termination of the American Revolution*.

Most of the works of these decades are identifiably North American in their use of scene or incident. The most distinctly native women's genre of the century's turn, the ▷captivity narrative, got little attention as literature – but made its mark raising cultural and women's issues before the reading public.

Looking only at *belles-lettres*, however, discards a major portion of North American women's writing: diaries; personal narratives; and ▷letters – both private letters, only later collected and published, and public letters, published as articles or columns in literary newspapers or as calls to social and gender action and justice. Both 'private' writing and journalism shaped women's knowledge of themselves and presaged the importance of periodical publication for 19th-century North American literature and North American women writers and readers.

Periodical publication and woman's fiction to 1850

After 1820 women writers are at the centre of North American popular literature, both in the development of new genres and in the public discourse on issues of social, racial and gender justice. While early 19th-century histories, novels and treatises appeared in volume publication from a number of publishers, the development of popular, periodical anthology formats – ▷miscellanies, ▷souvenirs, ▷gift books and other annuals – marked a new stage of women's publishing, bringing a larger number and diversity of writers to public attention. Most women writers found their first, lasting and most remunerative publication in periodicals. A spectrum of regional and special-interest magazines – like ▷Lydia Maria Child's pioneering work for children, the *Juvenile Miscellany*, and William Lloyd Garrison's (1805–1879) anti-slavery journal, *The Liberator* – provided a market, and thus an impetus, for women to be writers. Because periodicals were particularly receptive to shorter works such as poetry, essays, stories and sketches, women writers developed these forms. The periodical market for new subjects encouraged writers to deal with regional topics and current social issues. Some of the earliest published African-American women's poetry appeared in magazines such as *The Liberator*, notably the anti-slavery poems which appeared under the pseudonym 'Ada' and the poems of ▷Charlotte L. Forten Grimké.

In volume publication in the 1820s, North American women writers developed a distinctive and enormously popular novel form that critic Nina Baym terms ▷'woman's fiction' in her 1978 book, *Woman's Fiction: A Guide to Novels by and about Women in America, 1820–1870*, and dates from ▷Catharine Sedgwick's *New-England Tale* (1822). The woman's fiction formula brought singular native settings and characters to the national literature, while transforming the 18th-century novel tradition of imperilled women.

The woman's novel focused on a heroine outside the promises and protections of the patriarchal family, who overcomes misfortune and adversity by virtue of her own strength and talent. Wronged or abandoned by family, left without support, these heroines often succeed by taking on professional roles competently – modelling the acts of their creators: women writers who themselves often overcame adversity and took on roles as professional authors to support themselves and their families. What is unique to the woman's novel is that the heroines survive and succeed, to be rewarded not with continuing independence but with marriage and domesticity – albeit a domesticity more fulfilled, more equal than the traditional wife and mother's role in patriarchal society.

Woman's novels by Sedgwick, ▷Mrs E.D.E.N. Southworth, ▷Susan Warner, ▷Maria Cummins, ▷Augusta Evans and others were so popular that they dominated the US book market from 1820 to 1870, an effect which seriously disturbed male writers and critics, who decried the popular audience's rejection of 'higher' literature. Because of their domestic endings and their success, women's novels were labelled ▷domestic or ▷sentimental fiction by critics reacting to the gender of the writers rather than to the texts. While some of these mid-century novels contain sentimentality (especially about mother–child relations) and purple prose (especially around issues of spirituality and temperance), most of the popular women's writing advanced a new, realistic agenda and style – while simultaneously engaging social issues of regional, national and international prominence.

Crucial to the careers of North American women writers, however, is not critics' reaction to these novels but the 19th-century response of audiences and publishers. Since the 19th-century reading audience was predominantly composed of women, and women's writing was what the audience wanted, these novels were outstanding sellers.

Along with the formula woman's fiction, the 1820s saw the continuation of earlier novel traditions. Rowson's ▷*Lucy Temple* was a next-generation sequel to her famous ▷*Charlotte Temple*. Child pursued historical subjects with *The Rebels* and valorized Native Americans in ▷*Hobomok*, a variant on earlier captivity narratives. Perhaps most telling for the future directions of North American fiction was Wood's *Tales of the Night*, which used a distinctively native Maine setting and, in its regional focus, was a precursor to the development of North American ▷local color fiction.

Non-fiction prose also remained important. The continuing dialogue on domesticity and women's roles began to show itself in manuals for a new domesticity, including Child's *The Frugal Housewife*. As well as redefining domesticity, women in the 1830s devoted increased attention to the anti-slavery cause, to education and to writing for other women. Writing on and for schools proliferated – as did the number of regional and women's magazines. ▷*Godey's Lady's Book* made its début in 1830, and for more than half a century it remained a standard of fashion and household advice and a proponent of women's education, but also a conservative nay-sayer on women's suffrage and women's rights. New women's magazines developed for other contributors and audiences. The non-commercial periodical ▷*The Lily* dedicated its pages to women's suffrage; the commercial ▷*Peterson's Magazine* developed as a less expensive competitor to *Godey's*.

As *Godey's* and its writers promoted women's dominion in a separate moral and domestic sphere of influence, women increasingly entered the public sphere as writers, and especially as writers for the anti-slavery cause. Periodicals like *The Genius of Universal Emancipation* and the *National Anti-Slavery Standard* welcomed women contributors, and writers like ▷Elizabeth Margaret Chandler made careers from describing the horrors of slavery. Stalwart anti-slavery women like Child formed the public discussion through both novels and prose non-fiction. In the 1840s anti-slavery writing in poetry, fiction and non-fiction continued unabated, but the first women's rights conventions also brought position pieces on women's issues and social justice.

Traditional women's subjects, devotional writing and poetry also remained important avenues of publication, with an increasing number and variety of women writers being published and self-published. In 1841 ▷Ann Plato's volume, *Essays; Including Biographies and Miscellaneus Pieces in Prose and Poetry*, appeared as the first book of essays published by an African-American.

Amid rapid redefinitions of public roles and domesticity, even conservatives like ▷Catharine Beecher reoriented their concepts of the domestic sphere with her ▷*Treatise on Domestic Economy* (1841) establishing a new scientific conception of the home. Young rural women left the home for industrial work in textile mills, and, with their non-domestic working roles, found new cultural roles. Workers' self-improvement societies brought another wave of working women to literature. ▷*The Lowell Offering* (1840–5), a publication by and for ▷mill girls, attracted national and international attention, demonstrating the capacity of women writers as well as women workers. Along with the focus on new writers and social issues, women moved into established native forms, for example ▷Ann Sophia Stephens in the formerly male preserve of Yankee humour.

Bestsellers, national magazines and the Civil War to 1870

The 1850s and 1860s saw the rise of the runaway bestseller, not only in woman's fiction but also with Fanny Fern's (▷Sara Parton) autobiographical novel, ▷*Ruth Hall*, and her collection of periodical prose, ▷*Fern Leaves from Fanny's Portfolio* (1853), and ▷Harriet Beecher Stowe's novels of life under slavery. Like the country as a whole, the North American literary world was agitated by movement toward Civil War. Abolition of slavery dominated periodicals and both fiction and prose non-fiction.

As women had continuously been at the forefront of the abolition movement (and had forgone pushing suffrage issues to centre energy on the anti-slavery cause), so women's issues and anti-slavery issues retained mixed prominence throughout the decade. The personal prominence of the African-American speaker and activist ▷Sojourner Truth grew with the 1850 publication of the *Narrative of Sojourner Truth*. Her increasing association with the women's rights movement in the 1850s strongly bound together questions of racial and gender justice, as she asked 'Ain't I A Woman?', and as her speeches were reprinted in abolitionist journals. New periodicals provided markets and audiences for literature focused on both anti-slavery and women's issues. Harper, the primary national publishing house, developed the first broad-audience national magazine, ▷*Harper's Monthly Magazine*, dedicated to both politics and literature.

Harriet Beecher Stowe's ▷*Uncle Tom's Cabin* (1852), first serially published in an anti-slavery periodical, became the bestselling vehicle for national and international responses to slavery. In scores of pirated editions and stage plays, Stowe's characters, Uncle Tom and ▷Little Eva, became personifications for the anti-slavery movement. Harriet E. Wilson's ▷*Our Nig* (1859), the first published novel by an African-American, added a powerful voice to the literary dialogue on slavery.

Despite Stowe's increasingly public role and forum, her sister, Catharine Beecher, maintained her conservative position on women's influence within the domestic sphere with *The True Remedies for the Wrongs of Women* (1851). But, both within and outside the still-popular genre of woman's fiction, most prominent women writers of the 1850s denied Beecher's belief in the protection of domestic life. ▷Elizabeth Stuart Phelps's ▷*The Angel over the Right Shoulder* (1852) showed the daily trials of mothers; Stephens, in *Fashion and Famine* (1854), opposed the ideal with the true; ▷Alice Cary, in ▷*Clovernook* (1852), showed the hardship of women's reality on the romantic western frontier.

The California ▷gold rush opened a new area of the country and new native topics to literature. Again, first with periodical publication, new women's voices and perspectives deepened North Americans' understanding of their changing country and character. Women satirists developed personae who were objects of humour as well as ironic commentators on the doings of male society. ▷Louise Clappe's humorous 'Dame Shirley' letters provided a woman's view of the gold rush and its boom towns. ▷Frances Whitcher continued Yankee humour with the persona of 'Widow Bedott'.

With woman's novels and women novelists controlling the market in volume publication, critics and publishers decried the taste of the popular audience. Publishers, looking for means to cultivate audiences and to promote the developing ranks of male prose writers and poets, established more national literary magazines dedicated to North American writing. ▷*The Atlantic Monthly, Scribner's Monthly* and, later, ▷*The Century Illustrated Monthly Magazine* joined the growing ranks of Harper magazines (▷ *Harper's Bazar*). While these magazines sustained interest and renewed subscriptions on the basis of serialized novels and non-fiction on contemporary events (for example, the US Civil War), they published significant amounts of poetry.

Many women writers who considered themselves primarily poets answered public interest in the Civil War. Poems like ▷Julia Ward Howe's ▷'Battle Hymn of the Republic' and ▷Ethel Beers's 'Picket Guard' were published in the new national literary magazines that developed in the 1860s. Magazine editors dedicated to guiding audiences' political positions and literary tastes were not particularly supportive of these popular women poets, but magazines were glad enough to publish poetry which caught fire with the popular imagination (and sold magazines). Women's poems on the Civil War were set to music and, quite literally, inspired a nation – much as Stowe's novels had in the decade before.

Along with specifically topical poems and popular poets, the magazines drew diverse contributions and women contributors. Typical among them was the nature poet ▷Celia Thaxter. The magazines' publication of poetry and seeming openness to women also drew even the most untypical of poets. In 1862, in response to Thomas Wentworth Higginson's (1823–1911) *Atlantic Monthly* advice to the 'young contributor', ▷Emily Dickinson sent poems to Higginson. Higginson and the *Atlantic* editors hardly knew what to make of Dickinson's innovative prosody, and Dickinson found conformity too high a price to pay for magazine publication. As Howe and other more conventional poets had found before, magazine editors were more willing to experiment with public issues as subject matter than with personal poetic form.

In poetry, fiction and prose non-fiction, racial issues specifically and social injustice generally continued as the subjects of the time. ▷Harriet Jacobs's ▷*Incidents in the Life of a Slave Girl*, (1861) first published by a Child, transformed the traditional ▷slave narrative form into a powerful African-American personal narrative. In 1861 the *Atlantic* published ▷Rebecca Harding Davis's ground-breaking ▷'Life in the Iron Mills'. Winning instant fame, it brought industrialism's natural and human costs to centre stage. Harding Davis continued to develop the themes of race, and economic and gender restrictions and injustices, in ▷*Margaret Howth* (1862) and *Waiting for the Verdict* (1868). Davis's focus on stunted lives and the criminalization of socially marginal people added energy to the literature, as social justice became plot as well as theme.

Issues of justice of various kinds characterized the literature of the Civil War period – ranging from ▷Sarah Helen Power Whitman's literary defence of Poe to ▷Caroline Wells Healey Dall's *Woman's Right to Labor; or, Low Wages and Hard Work*. Other women's writing begun during this period would have a lasting effect on popular attitudes and popular literature: ▷Mary Chesnut was writing her Civil War diary of a southern woman, and Ann Stephens found a new form and publishing format in ▷*Malaeska*, the first ▷dime novel.

Realism and regional fiction to 1890

The 1870s were boom times in the North American economy, and also for American publishers, magazines and fiction writers. Though the popularity of the woman's novel was waning after a half-century of dominating the North American book market, realistic local color (or regional) writing by women was moving toward its zenith, in both popular reception and critical acclaim. William Dean Howells became editor of *The Atlantic Monthly* in 1871 and edited the magazine for a decade – providing publishing and critical support for realist writers from all parts of the country and of both sexes. Almost alone among editors, Howells not only successfully promoted new North American writers (he even got audiences to read his friend Henry James, Jr, 1843–1916), but also acknowledged that women were significant contributors in both subject matter and technique.

Pivotal new work offered realistic treatment of regional subjects. Novels like ▷Elizabeth Stuart Phelps (Ward)'s ▷*The Silent Partner* (1871) and Davis's *John Andross* continued women's critique of capitalism. Women's education and the failings of traditional marriage remained central topics, addressed with increasing particularity, in works like Caroline Dall's *Sex and Education* and ▷Jane Croly's *For Better or Worse*. Biography and fictionalized biography became increasingly popular women's forms, perhaps an indicator of US women's increasing sense of their own accomplishments and models. The most literary of these is ▷Helen Maria Hunt Jackson's fictionalized biography of Emily Dickinson, ▷*Mercy Philbrick's Choice*.

With ▷*The Leavenworth Case* (1878), ▷Anna Katharine Green opened the modern popular genre of the detective story. ▷Nellie Bly transformed the personal narrative of oppression in first-person investigative journalism. As with Stephens and the dime novel, women writers continuously developed popular genres later associated with male writers and writing. As with most particularly North American approaches and techniques, women writers were first – and large national audiences followed in close order.

Nineteenth-century North American women's writing reached its climax and established its most distinctive forms and themes in the 1880s and 1890s. Decades of attention to women characters, to social issues, to reform, to distinctly American topics, to regionalism and to ▷realism fed a new generation of lasting achievement.

Established and new writers transformed local color fiction into realistic fictional treatment of pressing social topics and new aspects of American life. Short stories and sketches were the primary forms in a phenomenal volume and quality of fiction on regional subjects. ▷Sarah Orne Jewett and ▷Mary E. Wilkins Freeman, both New Englanders, were among the finest, most popular and most critically acclaimed of these regionalists. Helen Maria Hunt Jackson's ▷*A Century of Dishonor* (1881) and ▷*Ramona* (1884) were among the first works of fiction to deal with prejudicial mistreatment of Native Americans (▷Sarah Winnemucca Hopkins), and ▷Mary Hallock Foote's *Led-Horse Claim* (1883) was one of the first to deal with the life of western mining towns. In poetry as well, these decades gave the North American west increasing prominence, as ▷Ina Coolbrith and other western poets gained recognition and magazine publication.

The entire conception of North American women's poetry was transformed when Emily Dickinson's work was collected and published. Almost thirty years before, when Dickinson had sent selected poems to Thomas Wentworth Higginson, he had acknowledged her genius, though he failed to interpret her to magazine editors. With publication of the first posthumous collection of her *Poems* in 1890, Higginson and others promoted her singular voice in criticism and reviews, highlighting her unique qualities and establishing Dickinson as one of the few women writers to endure in the 20th century's canon of 19th-century North American literature.

While Dickinson eschewed publication and audience in her lifetime and received lasting critical acclaim after her death, most 19th-century North American women writers benefited from both publication and audience in their lifetimes – and lost critical ground in the 20th century. In their own time, 19th-century women writers knew their record of establishment, accomplishment and diversity. Strong in their sense of self and sure in their interpretations – unaware of how early 20th-century critics would rewrite their own literary histories – many women turned to rewriting and to theorizing the nation's and women's history. ▷Amelia Barr's *Remember the Alamo* (1888) and ▷Mary Catherwood's ▷*The Romance of Dollard* (1889) focused on the national past. More importantly, perhaps, women moved to writing feminist histories and theory. ▷Susan B. Anthony and others began the multi-volume history of the women's suffrage movement. ▷Anna Julia Cooper, in *A Voice from the South by a Black Woman of the South* (1892), established the feminist voice in African-American critique. ▷Jeanette Gilder began her own periodical, ▷*The Critic.*

The century's end, economic bust and the cult of personality

In the 1890s the North American economy, and therefore American publishing, faced difficult times. The firm of Harper underwent reorganization; national literary magazines lost audience; publishers' lists were cut; many American writers found themselves with long delays for publication – and new voices were trying to be heard. In this climate, women writers – especially with works seen as regionalism or local color – did surprisingly well. Publishers and audiences welcomed ▷Mary E. Wilkins Freeman and ▷Alice Brown writing on New England, ▷Gertrude Atherton and Mary Hallock Foote on the American west, ▷Kate Chopin on Creole society in Louisiana, and ▷Alice Dunbar Nelson on African-American life in New Orleans – the first nationally known short fiction collections by an African-American woman.

More than regional subjects, however, this work focused on women's conditions, and their conflicts with socially prescribed roles. Kate Chopin achieved fame (and infamy) with ▷*The Awakening*, a novel of a woman's growing awareness of sensuality and self. Dunbar Nelson, in lyric and fiction, joined Anna Julia Cooper's feminist critique of the voicelessness and circumscribed roles of African-American women. ▷Charlotte Perkins Gilman, in non-fiction and fiction (most notably in her short story, ▷'The Yellow

Wallpaper'), showed the damage done by traditional marriage and by societal and family constraints on women's lives.

▷Frances E.W. Harper's novel ▷*Iola Leroy* in 1892, along with the work of Alice Dunbar Nelson and Anna Julia Cooper, marked a new wealth of African-American women's writing and publication. In his preface to ▷*The Schomburg Library of 19th Century Black Women Writers*, Henry Louis Gates, Jr has suggested that the period 1890–1910 could be called 'The Black Woman's Era', as the century's turn brought substantial increases in African-American women's publishing – in the new magazine *Woman's Era*, and with a variety of novels in serial and volume publication.

Overview of 19th-century North American women writers and writing

Women writers commanded the popular audience of 19th-century North American literature, in numbers disproportionate to their education and opportunity, and in influence disproportionate to their numbers. In a century when national, regional and special-interest periodicals established authorship as a profession and built audiences hungry for new subjects and new voices, North American women writers developed new forms, distinctive native topics, and a national literature focused on social analysis and change.

Woman's fiction, local color, dime novels, ▷detective novels, short stories and sketches, the African-American literary tradition, anti-slavery narratives, popular poetry, Dickinson's unique poetic form, discussions of women's rights, historical narratives, biography, first-person investigative reporting, the development of literary regionalism and literary realism, fiction about the conditions of Native Americans, labour, the disenfranchised – these are the legacies of 19th-century North American women writers. While women writers' popularity inspired 19th-century critics to denigrate women's literary achievements, many women were acknowledged and established in the 19th-century canon of North American writers. The early 20th-century canon-makers and arbiters wiped much of this achievement from the literary map, recasting North American literary history as the province of eastern seaboard literature and teaching generations of readers 19th-century North American literature that was largely unread in its time. Women's studies and women's literature scholarship of the last decades has rediscovered and reclaimed the North American women's literary tradition.

▷Genteel tradition

MARA McFADDEN

21 Twentieth-century US

In 'From an Old House in America' (1975), a poem about the poet's relationship to the obscure history of the North American women who preceded her, ▷Adrienne Rich writes, 'I place my hand on the hand / of the dead, invisible palm-print / on the doorframe.' It turns out that her scrutiny of the past is an imaginative act of identification; it is also an interpretation of the past, a fictional creation rather than a straightforward retrieval of something waiting to be uncovered – the matching palm-print is invisible after all. It would not be true to say that the history of women's writing in the 20th-century US has been consistently invisible, as often the ways in which writing by women has been judged and defined is a more significant issue than its invisibility, although a statement of this kind quickly loses its validity when applied to African-American, ▷Native American, ▷Latina and ▷Asian-American writing.

However, the interpretive and identificatory processes which Rich describes are inherent to writing a history of women's writing in the 20th-century US. There is no single history to this writing and no homogeneous version of the woman who writes. For example, while modernist writers such as ▷Gertrude Stein, ▷Djuna Barnes and ▷H.D. were able to achieve an important measure of autonomy by emigrating to Europe, Native American women were trapped by a history of colonialism into cultural and linguistic dispossession, economic and educational disadvantage, making it hard to find more than a handful of these writers until the post-World War II period. Differences of race and class imply very different histories, and feminist criticism in the US and Britain since the 1970s has been engaged with the problem of the dominance of an account which operates on the assumption of a white middle-class norm. The act of imaginative identification which Rich proposes carries with it the risk of creating the history of other women in that image. Rich also writes, 'I do not want to simplify / Or: I would simplify / by naming the complexity.'

1900–1920

The emergence of the ▷New Woman ushered in the 20th century. Women from the mid-19th century onwards had been campaigning for rights and equality in all spheres. They sought the vote but they also demanded access to higher education and the professions, as well as fairer employment conditions, property rights, equal legal rights within marriage, access to birth control, and control over their sexuality. From the 1890s the image of the New Woman encapsulated the actual changes in women's position and the desire for progress. But for some writers resistant to change she also embodied the evils of female emancipation.

The New Woman refused to stay in her traditional place in the home. Her entry into the educational, professional and business spheres in increasingly dramatic numbers was linked to the economic and social transformations of the US entering a new technological era, dominated by corporate capital, and with an emerging confidence in itself as an imperial world power. This period encompasses World War I, which temporarily opened up jobs in munitions factories, mines, transport and agricultural work, raising women's expectations and eventually obtaining them the vote in 1920. For many women this social revolution provided an avenue of escape from the domestic sphere. One beneficiary was the novelist ▷Willa Cather, who studied at the University of Nebraska and then worked as a journalist, joining *McClure's Magazine* in New York in 1906. ▷Edith Wharton, at the height of her career, became the highest-paid novelist in the US. The poet ▷Sara Teasdale was the first recipient of a Pulitzer Prize for poetry, and the dramatist ▷Rachel Crothers became a commercial success on Broadway; her play *The Three of Us* (1906) introduced the New Woman to the US stage.

The work of many women writers during these decades reflects the New Woman's struggle to determine her own destiny, featuring heroines who struggle between their desire for romantic love and their need for fulfilment through work or art, and who fight to overcome the pull towards the biological destiny of motherhood. Greeted as a truly feminine love poet, Sara Teasdale reveals the emotional suffering of a woman unable to achieve her own autonomy. Novelists such as ▷Mary Austin, a South western regionalist, Willa Cather, and ▷Ellen Glasgow, a Southerner, emphasize the self-destructiveness of romantic love for women. Glasgow's novel ▷*Virginia* (1913) explores the fantasy ideal of romantic love exposing its costs. Characters often reject romantic love, like the frontier woman and Swedish immigrant, Alexandra Bergson, in Cather's ▷*O Pioneers!* (1913), who as a farmer obtains independence and power by denying herself romantic or sexual fulfilment. Novelist ▷Edna Ferber shows her characters fabricating identities for themselves through their work. Both Cather and Glasgow show women deriving their strength from an agrarian culture where women's work is economically central, and creativity for women is expressed in these novels through their farm work, although Cather's *The Song of the Lark* (1915) uses a successful woman artist to mediate between the role of women in the rural and frontier West and the urban, sophisticated world of the East.

Novelists such as the New-York-born Edith Wharton and the Southerner ▷Mary Johnston expose how capitalism, manifesting itself for women in the institution of marriage, deprives them of their sense of self. Johnston, in her bestselling historical romance ▷*To Have and To Hold* (1900), highlights the effects of the rigid Southern social hierarchy on women. Wharton, a pioneer like Cather and Henry James in the development of the novel towards ▷modernism, explores marriage as an economic transaction which promises women power and autonomy, but which actually commodifies them. In ▷*The House of Mirth* and ▷*The Custom of the Country* she uses the position of women to satirize the emerging commodity culture of the 'gilded age'. In the theatre Crother's work was matched by ▷Susan Glaspell, one of the founders of the experimental Provincetown Players in 1915, who dramatized women's rebellion, albeit sometimes covert, against oppressive social norms, in plays such as ▷*Trifles* (1916) and *The Verge* (1921).

In the sphere of poetry, four imagist poetry anthologies heralding Anglo-American modernism appeared between 1914 and 1917, including work by H.D. and ▷Amy Lowell, while the periodicals *Poetry* and the *Egoist* were also beginning to publish their work along with that of ▷Marianne Moore. H.D. and Lowell used the experimental verse forms of imagism to explore female desire and sexuality, as in the poems of H.D.'s *Sea Garden* (1916) and Lowell's love poems to her lifelong companion Ada Russell, such as 'Madonna of the Evening Flowers'. Similar emphases can also be discerned in African-American poet ▷Angelina Weld Grimké, whose work the critic Sandi Russell, in *Render Me My Song* (1990), daringly inserts into the Anglo-American tradition of imagism and modernism.

It was during this period that leading African-American intellectuals were debating new strategies for the advancement of their race. While Booker T. Washington was promoting assimilation, W.E.B. Du Bois was arguing in 'The Talented Tenth' (1903) for an educated élite to lead their race. Issues such as colonialism and the relationship of African-Americans to African cultural traditions were also on the agenda, and from the 1890s women had been prominent in these debates. The critic Hazel Carby, in *Reconstructing Womanhood* (1987), has shown the significance of the works of writers and political activists such as ▷Ida B. Well's *Southern Horrors: Lynch Law in all its Phases* (1892), ▷Anna Julia Cooper's collection of essays about black women's oppression, *A Voice from the South* (1892), Emma Dunham Kelley's novel *Megda* (1891), ▷Frances Ellen Watkins Harper's ▷*Iola Leroy* (1892), ▷Alice Dunbar-Nelson's short stories and poems *St. Rocque and Other Stories* (1890), and Pauline Hopkins's *Contending Forces* (1900). As well as writers, blues singers emerged, such as Bessie Smith and 'Ma' Rainey, who had an important formal influence on 20th-century African-American writers. Between 1900 and 1920, Dunbar Nelson, a prominent activist for African-American rights as well as a poet, Angelina Weld Grimké, Anne Spencer and ▷Georgia Douglas Johnson were all writing and publishing in magazines. However, they faced considerably more difficulty in publishing their work in book form than white American women writers of the period, and until recently have been obliterated from literary histories. Hum-Ishu-Ma (▷Mourning Dove), one of the first Native American novelists, also confronted the racism of the white American literary world. Her novel ▷*Cogewea, the Half-Blood* was finished in 1916, but Hum-Ishu-Ma was asked to contribute to the publication costs; she 'worked long hours thinning apples' to earn the money, and the novel eventually appeared eleven years later.

The inter-war years

Although World War I did not bring the same experience of devastation in the US that it did in Europe, in its aftermath North Americans experienced social and cultural transformation. The increased emancipation of women, represented by the extension of the franchise to women in 1920, was a locus for anxieties about change. In popular imagination the New Woman was replaced by the jazz-age flapper, who linked fears of a consumer society based on the commodification of art to a threatening, voracious feminine sexuality. This figure is represented in the works of F. Scott Fitzgerald, but it is his wife ▷Zelda Fitzgerald who became the spokeswoman for the flapper, reworking the figure as a morally courageous, liberated playgirl, who links female emancipation to modernity. By the Depression and the 1930s, however, the flapper had come to seem an unjustifiably frivolous figure whom novelist ▷Nancy Hale depicted as self-indulgent.

The 1920s are usually seen as the high point of two cultural movements: modernism and the ▷Harlem Renaissance. In both cases recent feminist literary criticism has had the task of redrawing the conventional gender mappings which marginalized the women writers who are central to these movements, and this has demanded an analysis of the inter-relationship of aesthetic criteria with models of sexual difference. For women, modernism has been seen as a series of crossings or traversals of conventional boundaries: national, sexual and artistic. Many of the major figures such as Gertrude Stein, H.D., Djuna Barnes, ▷Natalie Barney, ▷Anaïs Nin and ▷Janet Flanner, like their male counterparts Ezra Pound and T.S. Eliot, literally crossed national boundaries by emigrating to Europe. As such, they were seen by writers such as William Carlos Williams, as representatives of a destructive US tendency to invest in European cultural models instead of developing a native, indigenous culture. The result, Williams argued, was an alienated and deracinated art as commodity. Nevertheless, as expatriates these writers were able to achieve a degree of artistic and personal freedom in Europe, and in the work of H.D. and Stein a European / US divide was always central.

Natalie Barney is famous for her literary salon in Paris during the 1920s, which provided the centre for a network of women writers and artists, and promoted a self-defined lesbian culture. Different though their work is, Djuna Barnes, H.D. and Gertrude Stein are all linked by a radical experimentation with language in order to explore the interrelation of sexuality and subjectivity. Stein eschews representation, following the example of impressionist and post-impressionist artists such as Cezanne, Braque, Matisse and Picasso. Even ▷*Three Lives* (1909), one of her most accessible works, offers only a deceptive surface naturalism (▷realism) as a lure to the reader. In ▷*Tender Buttons* (1914), which has a certain cult status as a lesbian erotic prose poem, Stein writes, 'A table means does it not my dear it means a whole steadiness,' indicating the disconcerting disjunction between being and meaning. H.D., psychoanalyzed by Freud in the early 1930s and influenced by the discourse of psychoanalysis, investigates the category of bisexuality in works such as *Her* (written 1927), *Kora and Ka* (1934) and *Nights* (1935). Her poems of this period begin the investigation of the inscription of femininity by cultural tradition and myths which mark her later mature works, as in ▷*Trilogy* (written 1942–1946), ▷*Helen in Egypt* (written 1952–1955) and *Hermetic Definition* (written 1960–1961). Barnes, in ▷*Nightwood* (1936), uses the world of Paris and Vienna prior to World War II to explore the uncertain ground of racial and sexual identity.

It is not only modernist authors who were investigating and undermining ▷patriarchal values in their writing during the 1920s. Writers such as the poet ▷Louise Bogan, ▷Dorothy Parker, ▷Agnes Smedley, ▷Anzia Yezierska, ▷Helen Hull, ▷Edith Summers Kelley and ▷Elinor Wylie all expose the damage inflicted on women when they define themselves in conformity with traditional social expectations. Smedley and Wylie focus on women's powerlessness in marriage, and examine how marriage leaves women emotionally, spiritually and intellectually dissatisfied. Wylie's 'Portrait in Black Paint, with a Very Sparing Use of Whitewash' takes an ironic look at feminine self-sacrifice and self-abnegation, while 'Epitaph' (1923) satirizes the regimens that feminine beauty imposes. Novelist Anzia Yezierska, a representative of the influx of East European Jewish immigrants to the US in the 19th and 20th centuries, adds a new dimension to this depiction of women's entrapment in marriage and traditional ideals of femininity by exploring the conflicts of women caught between Jewish tradition and the New World of the US. Yezierska begins a line of Jewish-American women writers which runs through to contemporary figures such as ▷Grace Paley and ▷Cynthia Ozick, both of whom are distinctive for their interest in tradition, narrative and interpretation in relation to the women writer's authority.

Bogan, Smedley and Wylie also emphasize the potential psychological disintegration and damage inflicted on women by social pressures. In 'Cassandra' Bogan uses the mythological figure of the Cassandra who was doomed to prophesy without being believed to represent the social and psychic tensions of the woman poet: 'Song, like a wing, tears through my breast, my side, / and madness chooses out my voice again, / again.' Hull, in ▷*Islanders* (1927), the story of an unmarried woman dependent on an exploitative middle-class family, and Kelley in ▷*Weeds* (1923), a novel about a woman who marries a tenant tobacco farmer, expose the dependence of the white American family on the victimization of women. However, not all women present such a critical view. Whereas Kelley's novels suggests that farming saps a woman's vitality, ▷Bess Streeter Aldrich, in *A Lantern in Her Hand* (1928), and ▷Elizabeth Madox Roberts, in ▷*The Time of Man* (1926), celebrate the endurance and inner strength of pioneer women who laboured to settle the North American frontier.

The Harlem Renaissance movement of the 1920s cannot be entirely divorced from modernism, connected as it is to various icons of urban modernity: New York, bar life and jazz. Moreover, the movement had to negotiate a difficult relationship between the development of a distinctive African-American culture and the modernist fascination with primitivism. The experience of rural poverty, discrimination and violence in the South led to a large-scale migration of Southern blacks to the industrial North, and in particular to Harlem. The combination of this urban concentration of African-Americans with greater economic prosperity, the presence of publishing and communication networks, and the influence of political ideas, from Garveyism to the ideas of Du Bois, contributed to a cultural flowering in the areas of fiction, poetry, art and music. The movement, although centred on Harlem, extended well beyond, to other centres such as Washington DC, and abroad to Paris.

The famous names of the Harlem Renaissance, such as Langston Hughes, Claude Mckay and Countee Cullen, tend to be male. ▷Zora Neale Hurston, whose short stories and plays were appearing in the 1920s, is the only female member who has acquired an equivalent reputation, although women were central to the movement, both as writers and in fostering the cultural and intellectual work of the Renaissance. ▷Jessie Redmon Fauset, herself an important novelist, was influential in her role as literary editor for the African-American journal, *Crisis*, the poet Ethel Ray Nance was secretary for another journal, *Opportunity*, and Regina Anderson worked as a public librarian in Harlem to promote these new writers. Nance and Anderson also operated as literary hostesses, as did Georgia Douglas Johnson in Washington and Anne Spencer in Lynchburg, Virginia, where she also set up a local chapter of the NAACP (National Association for the Advancement of Colored People). These support roles, often an extension of women's traditional roles, were crucial to the success of the movement.

As writers these women played an even more important role. Dunbar-Nelson, Grimké, Spencer and Johnson continued to publish stories, poetry and plays. Johnson's major works, such as her collection of protest poetry, *Bronze* (1922), and her love poetry, *An Autumn Love Cycle* (1928), appeared in the 1920s, and from 1927 she was also writing plays confronting the racism of the South, such as *Blue Blood* (1927), which is about the sexual exploitation of black women by white men. Other significant writers emerged in the context of the movement, such as Jessie Redmon Fauset, whose novels concentrate on the effects of racial discrimination on middle-class African-Americans, and ▷Nella Larsen, whose novels *Quicksand* (1928) and ▷*Passing* (1929) use the figure of the mixed-race woman to explore the difficulty of racial identity and the sexual stereotyping of black women. *Passing* also provides a complex exploration of the sexual attraction between its protagonists Clare and Irene. Poets include ▷Gwendolyn Bennett and Helene Johnson, whose work was appearing in *Opportunity* at the time, and Effie Lee Newsome.

Despite the productivity of women writers, they faced greater barriers than their male counterparts as the patronage system which was crucial to African-American writers at the time benefited male writers more than female because the codes of respectable femininity restricted the women writers' access to the bar culture around which much of the movement focused. But the most important point, perhaps, is the critic Gloria Hull's view in *Color, Sex and Poetry: Three Women Poets of the Harlem Renaissance* (1987) that the pressure to 'toe the racial line' as a result of the black political consciousness which defined the period presented women with difficulties. Hull writes, 'Unfortunately, these post-Victorian black women authors could not always effectively reconcile their color, sex and poetry, poetry here encompassing also their poetics (concepts of literature) and their imaginative writing in general.' Nevertheless, their writing began to work out the inter-relationship of race, gender and poetics which is central to the work of contemporary African-American women writers.

Although the Harlem Renaissance is usually considered to be over by the 1930s, stifled by the disastrous economic and social effects of the Depression, Hurston's novels and folklore collections did not appear until after 1930. Her writing provides a good example of the contradictory position of writers at this period, whether African-American or Native American, as a result of the Anglo-American interest in primitivism. Her folklore research into African-American communities in the South, which appeared as *Mules and Men* (1935), was encouraged and funded by white patrons such as Mrs R. Osgood Mason, whose interests were fuelled by a fascination with the 'primitive' and 'exotic'. A similar interest in ethnography motivated research in the 1920s and 1930s into Native American language and culture, resulting in Lucullus V. McWhorter's encouragement of Mourning Dove to collect the materials for her story cycle *Coyote Stories* (1933). For Hurston, however, her use of Southern black idioms and folk culture material in ▷*Their Eyes Were Watching God* (1937) was met by criticism from African-Americans: for example, Richard Wright described her novel as stereotypically 'minstrel'.

The Depression years of financial, industrial and agricultural collapse, and high unemployment, produced writers critical of the capitalist system and politically active on the left. The climate created by labour protest, race riots and the programme of federal government intervention under the New Deal was sympathetic to communist and socialist ideals. Writers, either proletarian themselves or with proletarian sympathies, such as ▷Tillie Olsen, ▷Meridel Le Sueur, ▷Muriel Rukeyser and ▷Josephine Herbst wrote in protest against the destructiveness of the capitalist economic system and its victimiza-tion of the worker. Olsen, who combined political activism in the labour movement with motherhood and writing, writes in 'Silences' (1962) about the gag on women's creativity as a result of class and gender restrictions. Olsen's own life is emblematic of her argument: she published a chapter of a novel in the left-wing journal *Partisan* in 1935, but the restraints of her life forced her to abandon the novel form in favour of the short stories which finally appeared as *Yonnondio: From the Thirties* in 1974. During the 1930s Le Sueur wrote about the lives of women in the agrarian Midwest as well as immigrant farm and factory workers, while Rukeyser wrote poetry concerned with economic and political repression, as in *Theory of Flight* (1935). Popular novelists of the period like ▷Pearl S. Buck and ▷Fannie Hurst were offering a considerably more conservative view of both women's role and the values of the American Dream. In Hurst's ▷*Imitation of Life* (1933) a woman achieves economic success by running a chain of restaurants, but without romantic love her success is seen as incomplete.

The critical view of US society and the effects of capitalism were given a distinctive slant by some Southern women writers. ▷Lillian Hellman, one of the leading dramatists of the period, explores the industrialization of the South in her social melodrama ▷*The Little Foxes* (1939), satirizing the nuclear family, Southern gentility and the competitive greed of capitalism. In her immensely popular historical romance ▷*Gone With the Wind* (1936), ▷Margaret Mitchell represents industrialism as a destructive masculine power in the agrarian South. ▷Caroline Gordon likewise defends Southern agrarianism against the intrusion of industrialism, but in so doing, maintains the need for a hierarchical social order to control man's will to dominate. Against this tendency, ▷Katherine Anne Porter, another Southern writer, exposes the South's mythologizing of its agrarian past as a self-protective idealization against which women struggle to define themselves.

Children's writers of the period like ▷Rachel Field, ▷Marjorie Kinnan Rawlings and ▷Laura Ingalls Wilder also reflect the dominant preoccupations of the 1930s. Field writes historical fiction, while Wilder and Rawlings depict the hardships of farm and pioneering life in works such as ▷*Little House on the Prairie* (1935) and ▷*The Yearling* (1938), a novel in which a child's initiation into manhood involves the sacrifice of his pet to protect his family from starvation. These writers reflect the age also in their focus on the individual's struggle against external forces which propel the child into adulthood, and they all celebrate the spirit of the individual in its confrontation with hardship.

Some women writers of the 1930s, including Hellman and the social satirist Dorothy Parker, both of Jewish origin, were active against the growing threat of fascism. In *Watch on the Rhine* (1941) Hellman represents fascism as an internal threat and not simply a danger in Europe. Both these writers also represent the new significance of Hollywood and the growing media industry for 20th-century writers. Hellman worked as a scenario reader for Hollywood, while Parker collaborated on the film script of the 1937 version of *A Star is Born*. In the late 1940s their political activities led Joseph McCarthy's House Un-American Activities Committee to blacklist them when Hellman told the committee, 'I cannot and will not cut my conscience to fit this year's fashions.'

1945–1960

The late 1940s and 1950s are popularly regarded as an era of ideological conformism, with the McCarthy witch-hunt of communists and 'subversives' as its emblem. At the end of World War II the US entered an era of economic prosperity and considerable confidence, believing itself to be the world power that could provide a bastion against the threat of communism. Writers and intellectuals evacuated the left in response to Stalinism and the Cold War fears of totalitarianism, and the philosophy of Existentialism seemed the most apt response to the horror of the Jewish Holocaust and the atomic devastation of Hiroshima and Nagasaki. A series of books in the 1950s, such as David Riesman's *The Lonely Crowd* (1950) and Sloan Wilson's *The Man in the Gray Flannel Suit* (1955), testify to the fears of an increasingly bureaucratized society. This period saw also the growth of suburban middle-class culture at the expense of the inner cities, which were left to African-Americans and more recent immigrant groups such as the Chicanos and Puerto Ricans. Women who had entered the workforce as part of the war effort were replaced by the returning soldiers, and forced back into domesticity and that emblem of conformity, the nuclear family.

Politically, liberalism and a renewed commitment to the values of North American democracy in the face of totalitarianism dominated. Lionel Trilling, a major advocate of liberal values, published *The Liberal Imagination* in 1950. ▷Mary McCarthy's novels in the 1940s, such as *The Groves of Academe* (1952), similarly explore the viability of liberalism. The Agrarians and New Critics, Alan Tate and John Crowe Ransom wrote about poetry and art as a bastion against the commodified culture of the newer mass media. Writers such as Norman Mailer expressed similar snobbish anxieties about a conformist middle-brow culture. The poet ▷Elizabeth Bishop finds a place in this context with her cautious affirmation of the poetic imagination, although she is sceptical about the power of the human ego. By contrast two popular writers, ▷Taylor Caldwell, in her historical romances, and ▷Ayn Rand, in novels such as ▷*Atlas Shrugged* (1957), espouse the values of individualism and the entrepreneur.

However, the writing of women in the 1940s and 1950s rarely testifies to the image of a quiescent and self-satisfied society, focusing instead on the disastrous consequences of women's conformity and the conflicts behind the surface harmony of the family and suburbia. The popular novelist ▷Shirley Jackson, also a writer for women's magazines, exploits the genres of the Gothic and psychological thrillers to demonstrate the dangers of ideals of femininity such as passivity and self-sacrifice, and represents social conformity as a placid surface concealing savagery and madness.

The 1950s saw also the rise in popularity of mass-produced popular ▷romance fiction for women, often in the gothic mode, suggesting a tension between the emphasis on romantic fulfilment and women's fears, anxieties and more unruly desires. The lesbian novelist ▷Ann Bannon began in 1957 her 'Beebo Brinker' series, which was about a lesbian's search for romance.

The fiction of ▷Elizabeth Hardwick, Mary McCarthy, ▷Grace Metalious and ▷Jean Stafford considers the struggle of women to maintain their moral integrity in a culture hostile to them. McCarthy's *A Charmed Life* (1955) represents the restrictions faced by educated middle-class women because of their gender. Like McCarthy, Metalious and some of the writers of what is often termed ▷lesbian pulp fiction, focus on women who struggle to define themselves outside the constraints of their prescribed social roles. Hardwick's women, characters struggle to reinvent their lives, but in Stafford's work the social pressures are so great that women, divided between conformity to a prescribed role and an authentic inner self, opt for the latter; even in Stafford's novel ▷*The Mountain Lion*, when the heroine resists it is at the cost of her death.

White American Southern women writers, such as ▷Carson McCullers, ▷Flannery O'Connor and ▷Eudora Welty, portray women who either rebel against the ideal of the ▷Southern lady or who appear as misfits beside her. McCullers and O'Connor investigate the destructive and vindictive power of sexuality. In works such as ▷*The Heart is a Lonely Hunter* (1940), ▷*The Ballad of the Sad Café* (1951) and *Member of the Wedding* (1946), McCullers features young women whose independence renders them freaks, and she establishes a conflict between their artistic aspirations and their sexual experiences, which will potentially entrap them in romance, marriage and motherhood. Welty, on the other hand, celebrates a matriarchal power which she sees hidden behind Southern patriarchy, and in novels such as ▷*The Optimist's Daughter* (1972) she depicts this power as deriving from women's traditional domestic sphere. O'Connor's novel *The Violent Bear it Away* (1960), by contrast, explores the impossible patriarchal inheritance the South offers to the boy Francis Marion Tarwater in the form of his great-uncle's gift of prophesy; ultimately, it is only the black farmers, the dispossessed, who can inherit anything from the past. Other Anglo-American Southern women writers – ▷Shirley Ann Grau, Harper Lee (▷*To Kill a Mockingbird*) and ▷Lillian Smith – protest against the racism of Southern patriarchy, which is institutionalized through segregation laws, and maintained by violence. Grau, in ▷*The Keepers of the House* (1964), depicts an interracial sexual relationship to emphasize that racism is socially constructed, while Smith, in ▷*Strange Fruit* (1944), uses the theme of miscegenation to explore the disturbing psychological investments by white men in black women. As Lillian Smith implies, racial segregation entails a psychic disintegration for white Southerners.

With the flight of the white American middle class to the suburbs, the inner cities became predominantly inhabited by the socially and economically disadvantaged ethnic

North American groups. African-American women writers centre on the plight of the urban poor and the evils of racism that keep their community oppressed. The impact of the Depression years on the lives of urban African-Americans is charted in novels such as ▷Ann Petry's bestseller, ▷*The Street* (1946), which describes a woman's unsuccessful struggle for survival and dignity in a nightmare version of Harlem. ▷Gwendolyn Brooks, ▷Alice Childress, ▷Lorraine Hansberry and ▷Margaret Walker express disillusionment with the American Dream in their depiction of the realities of racism. Hansberry, winner of the New York Drama Critics Circle Award in 1959 for *A Raisin in the Sun*, investigates the issue of assimilation as a route to a better life. ▷Dorothy West, author of *The Living is Easy* (1948), also depicts the process of assimilation to white middle-class values, but with the focus on its dehumanizing effects. White liberal racism is Alice Childress's chief target, using the perspective of ordinary black working people. The work of Brooks shows the absurdity of characterizing the era as one of conformity; her first two collections of poems ▷*A Street in Bronzeville* (1945) and ▷*Annie Allen* (1949) explore the contrast between the dreams and the oppressed lives of African-Americans, but by 1960 ▷*The Bean Eaters* is fully engaged with the political events of the 1950s civil rights movement in poems such as 'The Last Quatrain of the Ballad of Emmett Till' and 'The Chicago Defender Sends a Man to Little Rock'.

Asian-American writers are also finding a voice at this period. ▷Diana Chang and ▷Jade Snow Wong examine the cultural divisions that they experience as second-generation immigrant women in the US. Wong, writing in 1945 at a period when Asian-American immigrants' experience of the war had revealed hostility and distrust from white Americans, depicts a painful process of assimilation as a response to her childhood experience of racism, poverty and the family demands on her to conform to traditional gender stereotypes of the Asian woman. Chang, like ▷Jo Sinclair, a Jewish writer, envisions the possibility of social reconciliation through female bonding across ethnic and racial lines.

The 1960s to the present
'The America of 1968, with its assassinations, torched ghettos, campus wars, crime waves, alienations, deposed kings and crazed pretenders, almost seems too much for a single book. Offered as a novel, it might be rejected even by the lowliest of publishing house readers.' This description by Larry L. King in the *New Republic* in 1969 captures the 1960s' image as a backlash against the previous decades, an era of radical politics and change, and most of all an era of mythologies, explored also in the journalism of ▷Joan Didion. Unlike the 1950s the dominant emphasis was now on cultural diversity. The civil rights movement, already strong in the 1950s, gathered momentum, achieving a much higher media profile, drawing new support from white North American youth. The militant Black Power movement appeared as a challenge to the strategies of civil rights supporters. The 1960s saw too also the growth of a counter-culture movement – rock and roll. The protest movement against the Vietnam War and later US imperialism provided a focus for poets such as Rukeyser, ▷Diane Di Prima and ▷Denise Levertov, as well as the younger generation of writers such as Carolyn Forché. Out of the 1960s emerged gay liberation and the contemporary women's movement, which was to have the single biggest impact on women's writing of the period.

The 1960s and 1970s are marked by the white American woman's rebellion against the values of the suburban middle class. 'In 1960,' wrote ▷Betty Friedan in her groundbreaking text *The Feminine Mystique* (1963), 'the problem that has no name burst like a boil through the image of the happy American housewife.' The poetry of ▷Sylvia Plath provides a bridge between the 'quiet desperation' of the 1950s, and Friedan's naming of women's misery and frustration in 1963, the year Plath killed herself. Plath and ▷Anne Sexton investigate the psychic terrorism of the nuclear family, and the difficulties of 'proper' femininity and motherhood. They emphasize the conflict between the social roles of housewife and mother, and women's creative aspirations. Their work does not frame these issues within a feminist context, unlike ▷Adrienne Rich in her third collection of poems, *Snapshots of a Daughter-in-Law* (1963). These poems are described by Rich as the first where she 'was able to write . . . directly about experiencing myself as a woman', about the 'secret emptinesses' and the isolation of middle-class women's 'careers of domestic perfection'. The novel which marked this trend most forcefully was ▷Marilyn French's hugely successful, *The Woman's Room* (1977), which charts the transformation of a bored and depressed housewife into an autonomous woman. French's novel belongs to a spate of women's movement ▷*Bildungsromans* by writers such as ▷Marge Piercy, whose novels shift the perspective to that of working-class women. The work of ▷Louise Fitzhugh extends the idea of female rebellion into children's literature through her novels directed at adolescent girls, ▷*Harriet, The Spy* (1964) and *Nobody's Family is Going to Change* (1974).

The influence of feminism has been pervasive in women's writing since the 1960s, given ironic treatment in ▷Wendy Wasserstein's *Uncommon Women and Others* (1977) and ▷Alison Lurie's *The War Between the Tates* (1974). The poetry of ▷Louise Gluck and ▷Maxine Kumin explore the domestic sphere still central to the majority of women's lives, as does Marilynne Robinson's novel *Housekeeping* (1980), albeit in order to deconstruct that sphere. For Southern writers, such as ▷Gail Godwin, Beth Henley (▷*Crimes of the Heart*), ▷Ann Tyler and ▷Marsha Norman, feminism has fuelled the longer tradition of fiction and drama which critiques both the social structures of the South and the ideals of family and southern feminine gentility. Writers such as ▷Bobbie Ann Mason and ▷Jayne Ann Phillips have brought together the strategies and concerns of the dirty realist school with a gender focus to write about working-class middle-America.

Women's sexuality has been another prominent issue for women writers. The 1960s emphasized sexual liberation as a form of social and political revolution, while the women's movement soon pointed out the contradictions of free love for women. Writers such as ▷Joyce Carol Oates, ▷Erica Jong, ▷Doris Grumbach, Marge Piercy and ▷Judy Blume explore the relationship of womens' identities to their bodies and desires. Characterized by its violence, which is often associated with male sexual aggression, Oates's fiction depicts women's sexual anxieties as tied to a loss of identity. Jong in ▷*Fear of Flying* (1973), Lisa Alther, and ▷Rita Mae Brown celebrate women's sexual liberation. Brown, Alther, Grumbach and ▷May Sarton each consider women in lesbian relationships and who derive their identity from loving other women.

In the late 1970s and 1980s Rich began a systematic exploration of the significance of 'women-identified' relationships in her poetry and literary criticism. In her important essay ▷'Compulsory Heterosexuality and Lesbian Existence' (1980) she argued that all primary relationships between women needed to be defined as lesbian because of the challenge they represented to the patriarchal institution of heterosexuality as an instrument of oppression. Rich, ▷Audre Lorde, ▷Cherríe Moraga, ▷Olga Broumas and ▷Judy Grahn celebrate women's sexuality as a source of female power and the basis of a lesbian-feminist poetics.

Moraga, a poet who has pioneered a feminist literary consciousness for Latino women, writes too about the potential conflicts between her race and her sexuality, as does Lorde in her autobiography ▷*Zami* (1982). Other Latino writers, such as ▷Gloria Anzaldúa, ▷Ana Castillo, ▷Sandra Cisneros and ▷Helen Viramontes, challenge the mores of their communities through their struggle to appropriate their own sexuality. They show how control of a woman's own sexuality, whether lesbian or heterosexual, is seen as a betrayal of their race and class, placing them in a double-bind which most Anglo-American women never have to confront. Moraga counters these accusations by arguing that she reclaims her mother's race by affirming her sexuality as a lesbian and loving other women.

In the 1970s and 1980s a group of women poets emerged who also addressed issues about gender, sexuality and the body, although their work has received little mainstream attention. Writers such as ▷Susan Howe, Lyn Hejinian, Beverley Dahlen, ▷Fanny Howe, Leslie Scalapino, Rae Armantraut and Rachel Blau Du Plessis have ventured beyond what the British poet ▷Wendy Mulford has described as 'familiar poetics, in which language is not seen to be problematic,' to explore the interrelationships of sexual difference, subjectivity and language which have been given a theoretical frame by ▷post-structuralism and ▷psychoanalysis. French theorists such as ▷Hélène Cixous and ▷Luce Irigaray, as well as ▷Lacan and ▷Derrida, have influenced this poetry, arguing that writing does not lend itself to reading as an act of interpretation in search of stable meanings; instead their work questions the ways in which meanings are constructed, and in particular how language puts in place, but also disrupts, gendered identity.

Susan Howe's poetry, such as in *A Secret History of the Dividing Line* (1978) and *Singularities* (1990), investigates the colonization and invention of North America. Author of *My Emily Dickinson* (1986), Howe is engaged in 'a widening and roving sceptical scrutiny of the sources of North American tradition and culture and her place as woman poet in it' (Wendy Mulford, 'Curved, Odd . . . Irregular' in *Women, a cultural review* 1.3. Winter, 1990). Hejinian sums up her own language play, which repudiates meaning in any simple sense, by saying that 'one is so familiar with one's own language that its rigidities, its laws pass unnoticed. It is fluid, and in it one is lost, experiencing.' The postmodernist work of ▷Kathy Acker, a textual assault on social, political and literary histories which have marginalized women, is in many ways a parallel fictional development.

Popular fiction genres, such as ▷romance, ▷science fiction and ▷detective fiction have become increasingly important for women writers since the end of World War II, challenging the traditional literary divide between 'good' serious literature and popular entertainment and escapism. In the field of horror, ▷Anne Rice, author of *Interview with the Vampire* (1976), *The Vampire Lesat* (1985) and *Queen of the Damned* (1988), exploits the erotic potential of the vampire myths to explore issues of marginality. Romance fiction has always been significant for women as both readers and writers. Since the rise in the 1950s of the mass-market paperback romance, women writers such as ▷Jacqueline Susann, ▷Judith Krantz and ▷Danielle Steel have dominated the field. Recently, in response to the gains of feminism, some of the main romance writers, such as Krantz, have developed plots which centre on women who make it in business, becoming financially powerful. Generational sagas also allow these women to pass on their success to daughters and granddaughters. The influence of film and television is also apparent in the glamourous, jet-set world, reminiscent of television's *Dynasty* and *Dallas*, which figures in contemporary romances. Another influence of both the 1960s and the women's liberation movement can be seen in the explicit sex scenes where the passive heroine is gone in favour of women like Jackie Collins's sexually confident Lucky Santangelo of *Chances* (1981), *Lucky* (1985) and *Lady Boss* (1989).

▷Science fiction is another popular genre into which contemporary women have moved, although ▷Mary Shelley and ▷Charlotte Perkins Gilman offer earlier models. ▷Octavia Butler, ▷C.J. Cherryh, ▷Zenna Henderson, ▷Madeleine L'Engle, ▷Ursula Le Guin, ▷Anne McCaffrey, ▷Marion Zimmer Bradley, Marge Piercy, and ▷Joanna Russ are all writers prominent in the field. The genre offers obvious opportunities for women to explore alternative worlds as a way of envisioning political and social change, although by no means all women writers of science fiction are feminists. Butler exploits the genre as one of the first African-American woman to publish science fiction. Le Guin in *The Left Hand of Darkness* (1969), Piercy in ▷*Woman on the Edge of Time* (1976), and Russ in ▷*The Female Man* (1975), each explore the possibility of worlds where gender differences and sexuality are fluid. Le Guin's strategy is to propose a respect for differences which will undermine oppression, while Piercy and Russ advocate a radical militancy in overthrowing patriarchy. Le Guin and Piercy, however, share a concern for environmental issues. L'Engle's space and time travel trilogy for children, ▷*A Wrinkle in Time* (1962), *A Wind in the Door* (1973) and *A Swiftly Tilting Planet* (1978), although using a female heroine, is mainly concerned with promoting the value of the individual. This is also the case with Henderson, whose books explore prejudice based on difference and otherness.

In the area of detective fiction, a distinct sub-genre of feminist and lesbian-feminist detective novels emerged in the 1980s. This genre has had considerable appeal for feminist writers in that it enabled them to subvert a form which at least in its North American hard-boiled version has always distinctly masculine. ▷Sara Paretsky, with her tough, independent private eye V.I. Warshawksi, has led the field and uses a female private eye to challenge stereotypes of women. Although sometimes criticized for merely inverting the terms Paretsky's novels are interesting because of their setting in large corporations and their representation of the diverse ethnic population of Chicago. ▷Sue Grafton is another writer who has ventured into the hard-boiled genre. ▷Carolyn Heilbrun's books, written under the pseudonym Amanda Cross, reworks the campus novel as murder mystery, as do Valerie Miner, Victoria Silver and Susan Kenney. Lesbian detective novels are written by ▷Katherine V. Forrest, ▷Barbara Wilson, Sarah Dreher, Mary Wings and Vivienne McConnell. Forrest, whose books feature a lesbian police detective, represents those writers who use the term to explore women's, and more particularly, the lesbian's relationship to the law, while women's sexuality is the main subject of Wilson's novels, which are set in a Seattle printing collective.

A self-confident generation of African-American women writers have set a new agenda for the civil rights and black power movements, that have invigorated the women's movement. ▷Maya Angelou and Anne Moody, drawing on the tradition of the slave narrative, wrote autobiographies chronicling their experience of racial oppression and of their sexual abuse at the hands of African-American men, and writers such as ▷Adrienne Kennedy, ▷Gayle Jones, ▷Gloria Naylor and ▷Toni Morrison explore the psychic damage inflicted on African-American women by racism; their work often represents women who are destroyed by their internalization of racial hatred. Morrison emphasizes the African-American women's role as scapegoat within her own community, but also the possibilities of resistance available at the margins of society.

These are writers who have developed new forms. As a dramatist, Kennedy makes use of Surrealist and expressionist techniques in ▷*Funnyhouse of a Negro* (1962), while Jones explored the idea of a blues novel in *Corregidora* (1975) and *Eva's Man* (1987). Morrison, who with two other inspired writers, ▷Alice Walker and ▷Toni Cade Bambara, has often acted as a spokeswoman for African-American women writers, and has said in interview that she is attempting to develop a specifically black aesthetic. The poets ▷Nikki Giovanni and ▷Sonia Sanchez, both activists in the 1960s, have developed a militant poetry based on popular black musical forms and street talk, advocating revolution against white American oppression. Their work also confronts the dilemmas created by the sexism that pervades black politics as much as white, and celebrates African-American women for their beauty and power.

Bambara, ▷Lucille Clifton, ▷Virginia Hamilton, ▷June Jordan, Lorde, ▷Louise Meriwether and ▷Ntozake Shange depict the experiences of urban African-American women who have been ghettoized. Meriwether sets her novel ▷*Daddy Was a Number Runner* (1970) in Harlem during the Depression years. Shange's choric verse drama *for colored girls who have considered suicide / when the rainbow is enuf* (1976) is representative of a general concern with the writer's political responsibilities in its concern with giving voice to those who have been silenced. Many writers, including Jordan and Alice Walker, have talked about the need for a collective voice as a way of drawing power from and defining community. In her essays about poetry and politics, *Civil Wars* (1981), Jordan also discusses the dangers of appropriating the voices of those others who cannot speak for themselves. Their writing often bears out the argument of the critic Mae Gwendolyn Henderson in 'Speaking in Tongues: Dialogues, Dialectics, and the Black Woman Writer's Literary Tradition' where she argues that black women 'weave into their work competing and complementary discourses – discourses that seek both to adjudicate competing claims and witness common concerns'.

Mothers have also been a central preoccupation of many African-American women writers. Bambara, Clifton, Jordan and, in particular, Alice Walker emphasize the maternal nurturing that sustains the African-American community. Walker's influential essay 'In Search of Our Mothers' Gardens' (▷*In Search of Our Mothers' Gardens: Womanist Prose*, 1983) constructs a genealogy of black women's creativity which redefines 'art', to include the sphere of women's domestic work, from quilting to flower-gardening. However, Walker's civil rights novel, ▷*Meridian* (1976), like ▷Paule Marshall's earlier work, ▷*Brown Girl, Brownstones* (1959), explores some of the more conflictual aspects of motherhood for black women, as does Audre Lorde in her autobiography, *Zami* (1982). Motherhood is potentially entrapping for black women as much as white, and the mother is as likely to be a figure insisting on conformity to conventional models of femininity as she is a source of empowerment against patriarchy. The particular history of African-American women as the legal property of white men, dispossessed of maternal rights to keep or name their children, is at the centre of Toni Morrison's prize-winning novel ▷*Beloved* (1987).

The relationship between cultural and maternal origins for women has also preoccupied a number of Latina, Asian-American and Native American writers. In the Creek (Muscogee) poet ▷Joy Harjo's writing, the spirituality with which she invests the female body is associated with her mother's ethnicity. Other writers like ▷Maxine Hong Kingston, ▷Amy Tan, ▷Ruthanne Lim McCunn and ▷Lucha Corpi are concerned with a maternal ancestral history which has been erased. ▷Shirley Geok-lim Lin, ▷Cathy Song, Tan and Kingston give equal attention to the tensions between Asian mothers and Asian-American daughters, seeking a reconciliation which will allow the daughters an identity.

Ethnic writers of the 1960s and 1970s were often concerned with issues of identity and assimilation. Writers like ▷Jessica Hagedorn, ▷Nicholasa Mohr, ▷Bharati Mukherjee and ▷Mitsuye Yamada portray the conflict between the dominant white American culture and their own specific cultural heritage, as they struggle to define themselves; their work explores the transformation of ethnic peoples as they become victims of white American exploitation. Yamada, an Asian-American, uses her experience of internment as an 'enemy alien' during World War II to examine the alienation felt by immigrants attempting to construct an identity which encompasses both nationalities. The poetry and fiction of Hagedorn, a Filipino immigrant, criticizes the racism and materialism of US culture by portraying the assimilation as a process of loss; while the fiction of Nicholasa Mohr, daughter of Puerto Rican immigrants, represents the contradiction between the demand to fit into society and the entrapment in the poverty of the *barrio*. ▷Angelo de Hoyos, ▷Carol Lee Sanchez, ▷Leslie Silko and ▷Nellie Wong attempt to recuperate the dignity of ethnic peoples by challenging dominant stereotypes, envisioning their collective cultural inheritance, often a specifically maternal inheritance, as a source of resistance and power. The Latina poet de Hoyos, in *Chicano Poems for the Barrio* (1975), and Silko, a Laguna Pueblo of mixed descent, also interrogate history as an essential part of reconstructing cultural identities.

The act of writing itself is for many of these writers an important sign of commitment to their communities. This is expressed by writers such as de Hoyos and ▷Gloria Anzaldúa in the mixture of languages they use, ranging from Spanish and English to Mexican dialects, Tex-Mex and Náhuatl. This linguistic diversity or 'code switching' refuses cultural assimilation, and reflects what Anzaldua calls the experience of 'living on borders and in margins, keeping intact one's shifting and multiple identity and integrity'. ▷Paula

Gunn Allen, ▷Lorna Dee Cervantes and ▷Evangelina Vigil dedicate their work to the perpetuation of their cultural traditions. Native American writers, such as Allen, Silko, Erdrich and ▷Linda Hogan, use the traditional story cycles of their nations to interweave the past with present-day exploitation, political resistance and regeneration. ▷Denise Chavez and Cisneros additionally shape their work according to a commitment to give meaning to the lives of the ordinary women of their community.

The 1980s and 1990s have been marked by an increasing political confidence in a politics of difference on the part of Latina, Native American and Asian-American writers. The anthology ▷*This Bridge Called My Back: Writings by Radical Women of Color* (1981), bringing together writing by American women of color, marked an important assertion of political connection and a decisive challenge to the biases of a largely white women's movement. In it the Asian-American writers Yamada and ▷Hisaye Yamamoto make the bonding of members from different ethnic groups a crucial source of empowerment, although this has to rest on a recognition of differences and potentially competing interests. Lorde best sums up the utopianism, the necessity and the fragility of such a project at the end of 'On My Way Out I Passed Over You and the Verrazano Bridge', a reworking of Walt Whitman's ideal of a democratic North America in 'Crossing Brooklyn Ferry':

> And I dream of our coming together
> encircled driven
> not only by love
> but by lust for a working tomorrow
> the flights of this journey
> mapless uncertain
> and necessary as water.

ARITHA VAN HERK

Canada   22

The tradition
It is curious that, although almost every landmark text in Canadian literature has been authored by a woman, Canadian women writers, with the exception of contemporary figures like ▷Margaret Atwood and ▷Alice Munro, remain to a large extent ignored and undervalued. The literary canon, enshrined and revised by the male critical establishment, has been willing to acknowledge isolated instances of women important to the development of a Canadian tradition, but recalcitrantly refuses to recognize the extent to which women have shaped the long-disputed territory, if it can be called that, of Canadian literature. Perhaps the steerage towards an historical and Eurocentric model of national literatures has been responsible: after all, the notion of a coherent Canadian literature as such is both preposterous and sublime, and a good deal of critical energy has been directed toward the argument that there *is* an explicable Canadian literature, or at least a literature of Canada. This, unfortunately still urgent, dispute over Canadian literature –

what is it? what characterizes it? – has perhaps been the culprit in the deflection of critics' attention towards national concerns (witness the many attempts to define Canadian literature, including Margaret Atwood's *Survival*, 1972, Frank Davey's *Surviving the Paraphrase*, 1983, Northrop Frye's *The Bush Garden: Essays on the Canadian Imagination*, 1971, D.G. Jones's *Butterfly on Rock*, 1970 and Carl Klink's *Literary History of Canada*, 1976), and away from texts and authors themselves; and it may, also be responsible for the extent to which individual women writers and their works have been overshadowed by local, historical and political moments.

This attempt to read nationally could also result from the shaping of Canada as a colonial territory: the belief that such wilderness must necessarily be represented by virility in a male guise, rather than any feminine tracing. There is current recognition that Canadian culture is not hegemonic, but diverse, and it is accepted that the literature of Canada 'is not bounded by citizenship' and is not restricted to Canadian content or setting (see W.H. New, *A History of Canadian Literature*, 1989, p. 2). ▷Canon formation is now appropriately subject to intense interrogation (see especially Robert Lecker's 'The Canonization of Canadian Literature: An Inquiry into Value', Frank Davey's 'Critical Response' and Robert Lecker's 'Critical Response' in *Critical Inquiry*, Vol. 16, No. 3, Spring 1990; while this may seem a semantically boyish war zone, it is interesting that the best critics cited are feminist critics), but there is still a strong masculine bias to literary analysis that has effectively shadowed, if not shrouded, many of Canada's germinal voices. Recovering literary women's initiative and effect is now an active concern of feminist criticism(s), and the magnitude of work still to be done speaks to a richness of influence and production that is worthy of celebration. Whatever theories emerge about the literature of Canada, it has always been a site for women's words; and despite continuing apprehensions of this country as *tabula rasa* ('a blank slate'), an opportunity for outdoor activity and not penpersonship, there is a long, traceable tradition of women's writing inscribing the terrain.

Canada as colony: beginnings

Perhaps its daunting nordicity made northern North America one of the last areas of the world to be 'discovered,' or 'explored', both concepts now recognized for the imperialistic notions that they are. Certainly, the great northern land mass endured a collision of mythologies when its indigenous people and Europeans met. The connection between Indian and ▷Inuit culture and the invading European culture was difference: their readings of one another were conceptual disjunctions. The imposition of European languages inevitably served as more than signage; naming made the place seem to be what it was called, whether wilderness, Eden or unknown territory. The first inscriptions of Canada are coincidental with those 'explorers' who made maps; cartography was the principle inscription, and the journals and records that the mapmakers kept, secondary. Joan of Arc may have been martyred in 1431, but the list of early French, English and Spanish explorers (Cabot, Cartier, Fox, Frobisher, de Champlain, Hudson), contains no women's names. But exploration was a indication of economic exploitation, and the first European settlements were essentially trading posts, along with religious missions established to convert the natives. Aside from general references to native women, virtually nothing is recorded about women until the Ursulines arrived in Quebec in 1639 (see Jean Johnston, *Wilderness Women: Canada's Forgotten History*, 1973). Jeanne Mance, who came with Governor de Maisonneuve and the first settlers to Montreal in 1641, began the Hôtel Dieu hospital there; Marguerite Bourgeoys founded a school, and chaperoned girls sent from France as brides for settlers. Thus, the first writings by women were the spiritual and autobiographical records of Catholic and secular nuns: Mère Marie Morin (1649–1730), Margeurite Bourgeoys (1620–1700), and Marie de l'Incarnation (1599–1672). The zeal for conversion can be measured by the penitent life of the first Native American saint (beatified in 1980), Kateri (Catherine) Tekakwitha, a Mohawk baptized in 1676, who made a private vow of chastity in 1679, and died in 1680 at the St Francis Xavier Mission, Caughnawaga, Quebec.

North American colonies were always at the mercy of political and military conflicts elsewhere. The Peace of Utrecht in 1713 (see Alice Munro's story by that title in *Dance of the Happy Shades*) won England Acadia (Nova Scotia); the expulsion of the French Acadians in 1755 (and their return from Louisiana) has been the subject of much Canadian writing. Although Canada was originally French territory, the defeat of the French General Montcalm by the English General Wolfe in the Battle of the Plains of Abraham at Quebec (1759) forever changed the position of New France; the Treaty of Paris in 1763 ceded all of New France to England. However, settlement did not necessarily imply loyalty to one or the other colonial power, and there was persistent tension between the colonies and Europe and between the colonies themselves. But the insistence of settlement brought with it the presence, if not the written words, of women.

It is significant that the first Canadian novel, ▷ *The History of Emily Montague* (1769), was written by a woman, ▷Frances Brooke. Brooke had already edited, translated and published work when she joined her husband in Quebec; obviously the five years that she spent in British North America (1763–1768) did not curtail her interest in, or acute observations of, literary and political affairs. *The History of Emily Montague* is debunked by some as a typical arcadian romance of garrison life, espousing merely 'conventional responses to Canada' (W.H. New, p. 60), but others praise 'Brooke's sophisticated use of Canadian dichotomies' (see John Moss, *A Reader's Guide to the Canadian Novel*, 1987, p. 36). Clearly, there is discomfort that the first identifiably Canadian text must be attributed to a woman, one who did not hesitate to transgress her role in matter and manner (see Lorraine McMullen, *An Odd Attempt in a Woman: The Literary Life of Frances Brooke*, 1983).

It is sometimes contended that Canada as nation and literature has not come into its own because the country did not undergo the necessary catharsis of revolution (as did the United States in 1776). But British North America evolved in a different direction; on this alternate territory, both United Empire Loyalists and French *Canadiens* tried to find some mutual ground. The Quebec Act of 1774 enshrined French language and civil law in Quebec, and allowed for what would develop as Canadian diversity, which might be read as a feminized political system. Upper and Lower Canada were ultimately linked, and Canada successfully repulsed the US invasion of 1812. Exploration continued, much of it in search of a Northwest Passage that would presumably permit travel through the continent by water. Mackenzie, Hearne, Vancouver, and Thompson mapped land and water. Again, this mythic search, that looms so large in the Canadian imagination, is without reference to women as participants or recorders.

Travel and 19th-century writing

From 1791 to 1796 Elizabeth Simcoe, the wife of the first Lieutenant-Governor of Upper Canada, kept a frontier diary of sketches, notes, and narrative (*Mrs. Simcoe's Diary*, edited by Mary Quayle Innes, 1965). Privileged by her education, like Frances Brooke, Simcoe was the first of many women diarists who made an effort to apprehend in writing this world so different from the one they were familiar with, although they necessarily brought to their writing their social biases and their gendered positioning. But ▷Anna Bronwell Jameson, in her journal-form travel book, ▷ *Winter Studies and Summer Rambles in Canada* (1838), succeeds in recording both the physical setting around Toronto in Upper Canada and the distinctiveness of a woman's observations. 'Jameson's writing was marked by her awareness of the subversive nature her activity assumed in a society which regarded femininity and serious artistic and intellectual pursuits as mutually exclusive' (Bina Friewald, '"Femininely speaking": Anna Jameson's *Winter Studies and Summer Rambles in Canada*' in ▷ *A Mazing Space*, edited by S. Neuman and S. Kamboureli, 1986, p. 62). The woman's point of view which she calls 'femininely speaking' enables and articulates the difference of female voice and narrative, a difference that continues to reverberate through writing by Canadian women to this day. Although Jameson stayed only a short time before returning to England, her very independence is a reminder that the position of a woman, who had no intrinsic rights, was dictated by the position of her husband. And as settlement proceeded, class and education became greater sources of social tension.

In the early 1800s various newspapers were established and universities founded: the colony was showing the expected signs of paternal cultural development. But again, the first novel published in British North America by a writer born there was the work of a woman, ▷Julia Catherine Hart's *St Ursula's Convent: or The Nun of Canada* (1824). Criticism derides the melodrama and colonial conditioning of the novel's plot, but despite the obvious moral romance and the characters' inevitable restoration to European rank and privilege, Hart permits herself to use Quebec as a site of discovery. That in itself is important; writers were beginning to reflect their indigenous landscape and history.

The 1837 rebellion against the Family Compact (the name given to the small group of powerful and conservative men who controlled the social and political world of upper Canada) was largely incited by the issue of land being unjustly set aside for a privileged few. But that reform movement was quickly squashed, and Canada did not enjoy a revolution. Instead, Upper and Lower Canada were united (1840). Despite their linguistic and cultural differences, differences which continue to divide them, both French and English Canada collaborated long enough to lay the groundwork for Confederation in 1867. During this period of pioneer settlement, Canadian letters were enriched by the work of the two Strickland sisters who emigrated to Canada, ▷Susanna Moodie and ▷Catherine Parr Traill. Catherine Parr Traill's writings are pragmatic: a botanist and splendidly adaptable pioneer, she not only described her settler's world, but also how to survive it. Susanna Moodie displays more obviously the conventions of her time, and the restraints of current literary expectation. Moodie approved of the novels of her contemporary, Irish-Catholic Montrealer ▷Rosanna Leprohon, which she felt upheld moral values; still, despite their inevitable ties to European paradigms, Moodie and Leprohon sought to articulate their adjustment to a changing milieu, caught as they were between their backgrounds and the rapidly transforming colony they lived in. Moodie's ▷*Roughing It In the Bush* (1852) and Traill's ▷*The Backwoods of Canada* (1836) are now classics that have become the subject of much critical discussion and resurrection (see Margaret Atwood's *The Journals of Susanna Moodie*, 1970; ▷Margaret Laurence's *The Diviners*, 1974, and Eva-Marie Kröller, 'Resurrections: Susanna Moodie, Catherine Parr Traill and Emily Carr', *Journal of Popular Culture*, 15, 3, Winter 1981). For all their restraining decorum, the Strickland sisters signal a continuing legacy of Canadian literature enriched by the writing of women.

Confederation: 1867
The mid-1860s tried to assert the possibility of national coherence despite Canada's colonial status and diversity. The 1864 Charlottetown Conference laid the groundwork for the British North America Act of 1867, when Ontario, Quebec, Nova Scotia, and New Brunswick were united as the Dominion of Canada. The Fathers of Confederation were generically that: fathers. But while the political profile of Canada underwent enormous changes in the next ten years (the establishment of the Northwest Territories and the North West Mounted Police; Manitoba, British Columbia, and Prince Edward Island joining Confederation), and many male writers were airing their versions of nationalism and historical portentousness, women quietly continued to make their presence known. ▷Juliana Ewing's letters home describe Fredericton, New Brunswick between 1867 and 1869 (published as *Canada Home*, 1983); ▷May Agnes Fleming published successful popular fiction in the US and England; Mount Allison University in New Brunswick awarded Grace Anne Lockhart a Bachelor's Degree in Science and English Literature (the first baccalaureate to be conferred on a woman in the British Empire, 1875); Dr

Emily Howard Stowe graduated from the New York Medical College for Women, and began to practise in Toronto (1867), organized the Women's Medical College in Toronto (1883), and founded the Toronto Women's Literary Club (1876), Canada's first suffrage group. These women were enmeshed in an uncompromisingly ▷patriarchal Victorian world, and their successes are larger than they might seem.

But changes in social expectations and hierarchies occurred with enormous rapidity; libraries were established as the railroad was being built. In 1884 ▷Laure Conan's ▷epistolary novel about a woman's lack of choice, *Angéline de Montbrun*, appeared and ▷Isabella Valancy Crawford published her volume of extraordinary narrative verse, *Old Spookses' Pass, Malcolm's Katie, and Other Poems*. One of the most interesting and under-rated of Canada's women poets, Crawford is considered only marginally part of the powerful, otherwise male Confederation group (its members were all born in the 1860s) of poets. There is much work to be done on her life and writing.

The intensely bipartisan tension between English Protestant and French Catholic cultures exploded through the Riel Rebellion and Riel's subsequent execution (1885). When the Canadian Pacific Railroad (intended to unite the country 'from sea to sea') was completed (1885), the adventurous ▷Sarah Jeanette Duncan was writing for the *Washington Post*, and ▷Susie Francis Harrison was determined to convey a particularly Canadian sensibility in *Crowded Out! and Other Sketches* (1886). ▷Sarah Anne Curzon's dramatic celebration of *The Story of Laura Secord, the Heroine of 1812* (1887) signals emerging interest in both patriotism and suffrage for women. ▷Jean McIlwraith wrote popular historical novels, but ▷Agnes Maule Machar, ▷Lily Dougall and Alice Jones all created strong female characters.

Transformation, suffrage, and the 'Persons case'

▷Sarah Jeanette Duncan continues to occupy a central position as 'the foremost pioneer-ing woman in Canadian journalism in the 1880s' (*New Women: Short Stories by Canadian Women, 1900–1920*, edited by Sandra Campbell and Lorraine McMullen, 1991, p. 79). Her novel ▷*The Imperialist* (1904) embodies Canada's uneasy political position between the United States and England at the turn of the century. Most important, Duncan's work reflects the changing situation of women in Canada, asserting their right to independence and recognition. Issues of suffrage and temperance were brought to the forefront with the Women's Press Club, the Women's Christian Temperance Union, and the Women's Political Equality League, all vigorous organizations dedicated to advancing the cause of women. Canadian women won the right to vote federally in 1918, and most provinces had granted suffrage to women by 1925. Quebec, where women did not receive the vote until 1940, was the exception. If any one writer represents the fight for women's rights in both her life and her writing, that writer is ▷Nellie McClung. Vehemently political, she campaigned actively for suffrage, and was elected to the Alberta provincial legislature in 1921. Her first novel, *Sowing Seeds in Danny* (1908), sold 100,000 copies, appearing in the same year as the even more famous ▷*Anne of Green Gables*, by ▷L.M. Montgomery. Montgomery's books have been criticized for their moral and sentimental content, and McClung's work dismissed as overtly didactic, facile judgments that appear to be coloured by male standards of matter, opinions now being revised by feminist criticism. With ▷Emily Murphy, who in 1916 became the first female magistrate in the British Empire, McClung was instrumental in fighting the 'Persons Case'. In 1928 the court ruled that, under the British North America Act, women were not 'persons'. On appeal, the British Privy Council reversed that ruling in 1929.

But rights for women did not necessarily imply rights for everyone. Canada was deliberately racist in its immigration and settlement policies, particularly with regard to peoples of Asian extraction (the *Komagata Maru* incident, dramatized in ▷Sharon Pollock's 1976 play, occurred in 1914). And the Mohawk poet ▷Emily Pauline Johnson or (Tekahionwake) (*Legends of Vancouver*, 1911; *Flint and Feather*, 1912) enjoyed fame mostly for her dramatic exoticism, and because her audience forced her to tailor her work to appeal to Eurocentric tastes (see Betty Keller, *Pauline*, 1981).

The wars

World War I gave Canadian women an opportunity to step past their traditional roles, and for the furtherance of the pacifist movement and the suffrage cause. McClung's *In Times Like These* (1915) is 'a wartime attack on female parasitism' (Veronica Strong-Boag, 'Introduction', Nellie McClung, *In Times Like These*, 1972, p. xiv). L.M. Montgomery continued to publish fiction; she was not afraid to write about the futility of war. Georgina Sime's *Sister Woman* (1919) describes how World War I changed the accepted position of women. Poet ▷Marjorie Pickthall had returned to England from Canada in 1912; determined to contribute to the war effort, and despite ill health, she trained to be an ambulance driver (see Janice Williamson, 'Framed by History: Marjorie Pickthall's Devices and Desire' in *A Mazing Space*). Her verse collection, *The Lamp of Poor Souls*, appeared in 1916. The conscription crisis of 1917 again split the country along French/ Anglo lines. Although it might be contended that the war was very much a male enterprise, Canada's role seemed to symbolize the changing position of women: the country entered the war on the coat-tails of Britain, but it signed the armistice as a separate nation.

Between the wars came a blossoming of literary and intellectual life and women's increasing public visibility. The Canadian Authors Association and various periodicals were established; universities grew; a number of literary histories and anthologies appeared (W.H. New, p. 138). Needless to say, women were not well represented in the anthologies. Memoirs and romances proliferated. But both the Depression and social unrest followed, resulting in a more political art and literature. Actively publishing in the 1920s and 1930s were ▷Lily Adams Beck, L.M. Montgomery, ▷Martha Ostenso, ▷Laura Goodman Salverson, ▷Dorothy Livesay and ▷Mazo de la Roche, whose popular Loyalist ▷*Jalna* series sold in massive numbers. But against the larger reputation of male writers like Thomas Raddall, E.J. Pratt, A.J.M. Smith, Frank Scott, Morley Callaghan, and F.P. Grove, these excellent women writers had to struggle to be heard.

One outcome of social upheaval was a relentless shift toward realism, a paradoxical presence that continues to haunt Canadian writing. ▷Martha Ostenso's novel ▷*Wild Geese* (1925) is one of the best examples of ▷prairie realism, although it also succeeds as a parable endorsing women's rebellion against overbearing male authority. In the 1930s, influenced by US writers, many Canadian writers joined the literary exodus to Paris, among them Dorothy Livesay, who was a student at the Sorbonne in 1932. Writing was for Livesay an act of responsibility; *Right Hand Left Hand* (1977) recounts how she was politically educated through communism and social work in the 1930s. In her powerfully erotic poetry, the political and the personal merge.

In 1936 the English Canadian Broadcasting Corporation (CBC) (along with French Radio-Canada) was established to prevent the broadcasting industry from being swallowed by the giant maw of the United States. The CBC became, and continues to be, an important outlet for literary material (W.H. New, pp. 181–4). In 1937 the Governor General's Awards were first presented to works published in English (there were no parallel French-language awards until 1959). From their inception, these most prestigious Canadian awards were received by many women writers, an indication that women's work was of such quality that it could not be ignored.

World War II further altered the position of women. That this world upheaval continues to exert its presence in writing is not surprising: poets and fiction writers feel compelled to re-examine its horror. Canada was heavily involved, as if its contribution measured its nationhood. Again, the spectre of conscription created tension; a 1942 plebiscite resulted in the repeated Quebec (against)–Anglo (for) split. And shamefully,

Canada interned its citizens of Japanese origin as enemy aliens, a political atrocity later to become the subject of ▷Joy Kogawa's novel ▷*Obasan* (1981).

The new nationalism

There followed a period when writing by Canadian women began to develop in diverse directions, almost separate from the governance of male history. ▷Elizabeth Smart was living in England; her ▷*By Grand Central Station I Sat Down and Wept* was published in 1945, but not distributed in Canada until 1966. The extraordinary painter ▷Emily Carr began to write and publish fictional sketches in 1941. Quebec writers ▷Anne Hébert and ▷Gabrielle Roy published their first works in the mid-1940s. And ▷P.K. Page and Dorothy Livesay were developing as poets. Social realism appeared to be a powerful force, unless one were to notice ▷Sheila Watson's ▷*The Double Hook* (1959), an enigmatic departure from its contemporaneous novels.

In 1947 Canadian citizenship became available; proud of its performance in the war, Canada began to think of itself more particularly as a country, and less as a member of the Commonwealth. Newfoundland entered confederation in 1949. Social services were in place, and immigration was rising. In the 1950s the National Ballet and the National Library of Canada were founded; and in 1957 the Canada Council, that important instrument of state encouragement for the arts, was established. Canadian literature courses developed, a prelude to the inevitable process of canon formation. Canada enjoyed relative prosperity, as if preparing for the powerful new nationalism that would soon evidence itself. The conservative and centrist 1950s seem, in retrospect, an over-whelmingly male literary decade, celebrating heroism, with the few women's names bright shards of difference. ▷Ethel Wilson, ▷Mavis Gallant, ▷Jay Macpherson, ▷Marie-Claire Blais, and Sheila Watson made their appearance, but did not come into their own until the 1960s.

The upsurge of cultural nationalism evidenced when Canada celebrated its 100th birthday in 1967 intensified public awareness of writers and writing. The Canada Council sponsored public readings by writers, and writer-in-residence programmes. Creative writing courses became an accepted part of post-secondary education and, for the first time, Canadians began to take their literary figures seriously enough to look critically at their literary representations. Literary presses, magazines and critical periodicals sprang up, as if Canadian literature were growing out of its own clothes. Most literary evaluations and directions were still determined by male writers (especially because the academy was primarily male), but slowly the work of ▷Margaret Avison and ▷Phyllis Webb, of Margaret Laurence and ▷Gwendolyn MacEwan, of Margaret Atwood and ▷Audrey Thomas, of Mavis Gallant and Alice Munro, of ▷Jane Rule and ▷Miriam Waddington was recognized. An unusual configuration of Canadian literature was the overwhelming presence of women, and one of the current sources of scholarly interest is the extent to which this is now a literature so much represented by the writing of women.

Canada's proximity to the US means that it is perennially affected by US cultural movements, and during the Vietnam war many US citizens of pacifist conscience emi-grated to Canada. Although they did not have to evade the draft, a number of women writers decided that Canada offered a less combative political environment. The 'October Crisis' of 1970, when FLQ actions resulted in the imposition of the War Measures Act, and a loss of civil liberties for many Quebec citizens, contradicted that assumption. Canada too began to experience a resistance to centricity, marked by the rise of political and post-colonial frictions surrounding region, gender, and ethnicity. Not surprisingly, language became the arena for re-definition of what had always been accepted as given, as 'normal', as 'universal'. Nationalism and nationhood began to undergo the questioning that has reached its head now, with the 1992 Canadian constitutional crisis.

Regionalism

Geographically, Canada is a sublime impossibility, so it is not surprising that different areas of the country follow different agendas. Given the country's enormous size, literary criticism designates most writers in terms of where they locate themselves, whether that be the maritimes, the west, or Toronto. The concept of region comes out of the notion of the effect of a particular place, but for women writers, region has become much more, as articulated by ▷Marian Engel in 1978: 'if you think that gender is not a region, try writing a novel from the other gender's point of view. I'm conditioned also by my species, by my race, by what they call the ethnic origin of that race. And I'm conditioned by the rootedness of my particular family in the nation in which I grew up. Now at various points in my career, I have had to choose various poisons from among these various elements that have predominated in the work that I have done' (Engel in response to Eli Mandel, 'The Regional Novel: Borderline Art' in *Taking Stock*, edited by Charles Steele, 1982, p. 122). Aside from the women writing in Quebec, who identify with their region through a culture and language different from the Anglophonic, most Canadian women writers do not define their work primarily by the region where they live and that they write about. Still, there is persistent tendency in the critical community to place a writer according to where she writes from, whether that be the ▷prairies or the maritimes. And, almost automatically, more credence is given to the dominant and centralist region of Toronto.

Quebec writing

The powerful writing of Quebec women (beginning with those early nuns) has contributed immeasurably to the articulate energy of French-Canadian literature. If Gabrielle Roy and Anne Hébert emphasized their cultural difference from the Anglophone mainstream without hesitation, they did so willing to expose their own tradition's social and religious dogmas. The early writings of ▷Claire Martin and Marie-Claire Blais attempted to exorcise a constraining religious ideology. French-Canadian writers have always been more politically driven than their English-Canadian counterparts; writing in a disenfranchised language added an edge to their quiet revolt (it is useful to note the extent to which language embodied Anglo racism, evident in Michèle Lalonde's poem, 'Speak White'). But the rise of Quebec nationalism in the 1960s and 1970s, and the exciting possibility of cultural independence, energized literature, especially for women writers eager to embrace the literary theories of the French feminists. These concomitant politicizations had a powerful effect on francophone women: they gained a language with which to articulate their oppression and alienation (see ▷Nicole Brossard, 'Poetic Politics' in *The Politics of Poetic Form*, edited by C. Bernstein, 1990, p. 77). Nicole Brossard, ▷France Théoret, and ▷Louky Bersianik celebrate the body of language, the effacement of genre, and the guerrilla action of semiotics. Language is the ultimate arena of subversion. As ▷Denise Boucher has said, 'I write in French and in the feminine because I know the two languages' (see Shirley Neuman, 'Importing Difference: Feminist Theory and Canadian Women Writers' in *Future Indicative: Literary Theory and Canadian Literature*, edited by J.Moss, 1987). Because many of these writers are translated into English, the influence of Quebec women's writing on Anglo-Canadian literature has been strong.

Feminism

Political feminism and its social criticism reverberates for most women currently writing in Canada. The 1970 *Report on the Status of Women in Canada* challenged commonly-held perceptions about women; they became aware of their marginality. Feminist consciousness-raising and feminist literary theory posed questions about power, patriarchy, the body as a site for occupation, and the extent to which language disenfranchises women. ▷Daphne Marlatt, ▷Gail Scott, and ▷Lola Lemire Tostevin responded to French feminist theory through their contacts with Quebec writers, but the far-reaching influence of feminism as a world movement has reached writers, their work, and their audience. The burgeoning popular and academic interest in women's writing can be attributed to feminism's effect on the media and systems of knowledge. Although there is currently a reactive tendency to view 'feminism' as a pejorative term, Margaret Laurence, Sharon Pollock, Alice Munro, ▷Leona Gom, ▷Sharon Riis and ▷Carol Shields can all, different as they are in genre, in age, and in politics, be considered feminist writers, and have been read as such, whether or not they choose to identify themselves using the term.

Lesbian writing

Jane Rule's ▷*Lesbian Images* (1975) is the obvious point at which the lesbian writer enters Canadian literary history, even though Rule was then not known as a Canadian writer. Her writing continues to concern itself with gender politics in the broadest sense; and many of Canada's most powerful poets and fiction writers explore lesbian experience. Nicole Brossard remembers her sexual development in relation to her writing in terms of paradox: 'In 1974, I became a mother and about the same time fell in love with another woman. Suddenly, I was living the most common experience in a woman's life which is motherhood and at the same time I was living the most marginal experience in a woman's life which is lesbianism. Motherhood made life absolutely concrete . . . and lesbianism made my life absolute fiction in a patriarchal heterosexual world. Motherhood shaped my solidarity with women and gave me a feminist consciousness as lesbianism opened new mental space to explore' (Brossard, 'Poetic Politics', pp. 77–8) The space of the body in a different incarnation gives the writer ideas and, as in Daphne Marlatt's beautiful poetic essay, 'Musing with Mothertongue', the desire of the body and the body of language articulate together (▷*Touch to My Tongue*, 1984).

'Ethnic' writing

The much-vaunted plurality or diversity of multicultural Canadian society has recently given rise to the development of a literature and criticism that is termed 'ethnic' writing. The danger of both the concept and its application is implicit in its designation: in Canada, 'ethnic' relates to one who is an immigrant, one who is a member of a marginal group, whose mother tongue is neither English nor French. That ethnicity can provide a token and provisional ghetto to effectively ▷'other' – or indeed, to discount or silence writing not considered mainstream – is not remote. At the same time, Canadian criticism has always looked for ways to define writing by such women as ▷Laura Goodman Salverson, ▷Vera Lysenko, ▷Dionne Brand, ▷Kristjana Gunnars, ▷Adele Wiseman, Joy Kogawa, ▷Myrna Kostash and ▷Claire Harris. The safety of categorization does not ease the discomfort of the critic anxious to locate this writing; unfortunately, this designatory preoccupation revives the patriarchal focus on identity within Canadian literature, and doubly colonizes these writers, for their gender and for their ethnicity. The possibility of these separated writings taking their place within the larger body of Canadian literature, of 'tensional totality' (Francesco Loriggio, 'The Question of the Corpus: Ethnicity and Canadian Literature' in *Future Indicative: Literary Theory and Canadian Literature*, p. 63) is an attractive alternative.

Native Canadian writing

Even more discomfiting is the ambiguous placement of any writer who is one of Canada's first peoples. Try as they might, Europeans could not erase completely the imprint of the indigenous. Although these civilizations were subject to literal and figurative genocide during the course of Canada's European settlement, their tales and iconography permeate the cultural weft of the country, and continue to weave an imaginative thread. But the step from the oral to the written has taken place: native women have shifted from being subject and object of white writing and history to actively inscribing the page themselves. ▷Maria Campbell's ▷*Halfbreed* (1973) broke the surface as the first contemporary book by a Native Canadian woman. Since then, especially in reaction to white writers appropriating their material, women have begun to tell their own stories and to write their own dramas and poems. Pauline Johnson's life and writing adhered to a romantic stereotype, but Native Canadian writers now are refusing to be co-opted by any patronizing expectation of either content or form. ▷Lenore Keeshing-Tobias, ▷Lee Maracle, ▷Ruby Slipperjack, and ▷Beatrice Culleton are active writers whose work resonates strongly in terms of current questions about Native Canadian languages and mythologies. ▷Jeannette Armstrong directs the ▷En'owkin School of International Writing, which has been important in encouraging the development of Native Canadian women writers.

Contemporary writing
Women are now firmly located in any consideration of Canadian literature. The conjunction of postmodernism with the pluralities of feminism has certainly permitted women writers to invade the hallowed space of academic criticism, but more important than theoretical endorsement or canonization is a pure and simple physical fact: Canadian women are writing, about the world and about themselves; Canadian women are reading, about the world and about themselves. Literature's space in this over-informed technological moment is to hold up an elusive mirror, a silvery invitation to observe ourselves. Canadian women writers, through their fiction and drama, poetry and prose, are doing this. ▷Susan Swan shows us the giant women we are; Phyllis Webb estimates the plenitude of nakedness; Sharon Pollock suggests the most useful way to hold an axe; ▷Janice Kulyk Keefer expresses the elegance of travel; ▷Erin Mouré insists that we should stay furious. Their writing promises that they will not lose faith or energy, humour or anger. And their readers, the audience who complete the process of creation, turn a page, respond, and read on.

LUIZA LOBO

23 Latin America

The development of women's writing in Latin America has been hindered and greatly influenced by the social context in which women have found themselves, and the languages, culture and political circumstances of the countries which comprise the region. The pace at which their literature has evolved has been quite different from that of their fellow countrymen and their literary contemporaries in Europe. Writing by women from this part of the world does not fit comfortably into the established male canon because, until very recently, cultural activities and initiatives were dominated by men, and often lacked any female participation.

Women's writing in Latin America consists almost entirely of poetry, memoirs, novels and short stories with a strong autobiographical slant and personal viewpoint. Only as women have become more independent has their writing become less restricted, and in this essay the development of literature by women in Latin America is best examined as independent from the output of their male counterparts and those abroad.

The linguistic and historical background

The dominant languages throughout the American continent have naturally affected the emerging literature. While Spanish, Portuguese and the South American Indian languages are spoken in Central and South America, English dominates the wide linguistic diversity of North America, and in the Guyennes and Caribbean islands, French, Dutch, Spanish and English are spoken, in addition to the Indian languages and the ▷Creoles which make up ▷Nation language (▷essays on English-speaking Caribbean and French Antilles). Alhough the colonial term 'Latin America' was coined by the French in the 19th century, in fact Latin American culture and language as a whole began in 1492 with the Spanish colonization of South and Central America, followed by the colonization of Brazil by the Portuguese in 1500. Although the Spanish and Portuguese colonists can be regarded as geographically united (both belonging to the Iberian peninsula), they had conflicting historical interests, and a great opposition to each other. An example of this antagonism was the Tordesillas Treaty, an imaginary line drawn in 1492 which split Latin America in two – the east for the Portuguese and the west for the Spanish. A political and cultural rivalry persisted in the colonies; in Brazil only Portuguese and the South American Indian languages were employed; Spanish, English, Indian and other languages were spoken elsewhere. Only recently have the Spanish-speaking countries and Brazil slowly begun to unite their economic outlook and to defend their common Iberian identity in culture and language.

The Indian and negro tradition

It is not surprising that the most notable literary figures to emerge in Latin America wrote in either Spanish or Portuguese, but other cultures and languages have made a significant impression on the development of writing by both men and women. The Indian tradition on the continent, particularly in Peru, Paraguay, Bolivia and Mexico, and the negro tradition in the Caribbean and Mexico, have yielded few authors. Both cultures had an oral tradition, and poems and songs, centring on myths and folklore, were frequently anonymous. There are no traces of any early female Indian writing, though women have often adopted the cause of the Indian, the negro and similar oppressed minority groups. For instance, at the beginning of the 19th century the Brazilian mulatto poet and novelist ▷Maria Firmina dos Reis wrote a romantic novel, *Ursula* (1859), which was the first to condemn slavery in Brazil. Similarly, the Puerto Rican poet ▷Julia de Burgos, a North American exile, and the Cuban ▷Lydia Cabrera both published stories in the 1940s based on the plight of the negro, and on negro anthropology and culture, collected from oral narratives.

The enormous cultural diversity in Latin America has naturally contributed to the literary themes and style of writing by women and men. Negro culture had been present in Brazil since early colonial times, from the 16th to 18th centuries, when slaves were employed on the sugar-cane plantations and in the gold mines, while in the Spanish colonies on the western coast, Indians were worked in silver mines. The immigrant population increased in the 19th century when Africans were brought to the continent as workers on the coffee and sugar-cane plantations. Then, after the abolition of slavery in 1888, with the consequent reduction in available manpower, the cultural diversity increased further with the introduction of yet more immigrants, mainly Spanish, Italian, German and Polish, who provided essential agricultural labour, and, about thirty years later, Japanese, when a Japanese workforce arrived to work on the rubber plantations. Gradually the immigrants in Brazil have become integrated, and the population has become more urban than rural.

The role of women

During the whole process of the formation of the nations which make up Latin America today, the public role of women has been negligible, since this was a period when women were confined to domestic activities and reproduction, a situation inherited from the Arabs, who invaded the Iberian peninsula in the 8th century. Women were expected to run the house, work alongside slaves in the kitchen, were frequently dressed inadequately, sometimes physically abused, and often banished from sight if guests came to visit. A country's literary tradition cannot be separated from its social and economic life and so, while women were oppressed in a social context, while their education was ignored, and while they were denied the opportunities afforded to male writers, their literary potential remained restricted. The first notable women writers to emerge were therefore those who managed to escape the confines of the role expected of women.

The influence of the Church
The cultural gap between the Portuguese and Spanish cultures imposed on Latin America was perpetrated by the striking difference between the Spanish-American Church in Mexico and the Church in Brazil. Convents in Spanish America became powerful because nuns from wealthy families used to take a fortune with them when they left home. Religion also caused an imbalance in the development of education. For example, while the Spanish Catholics founded the University of San Marco in Lima in 1554, Jesuit schools in Brazil were way behind in terms of academic achievement. A direct result of this disparity was that, whereas no prestigious women writers appeared on the literary scene in Brazil until the middle of the 19th century (▷Ana Eurídice de Barandas published a novel in 1845), women began to start writing much earlier in the Spanish-speaking world.

A 17th-century Mexican nun, Sor Juana Inés de la Cruz (▷Juana de Asbaje y Ramirez de Santillana), produced some of the first and most important women's literature in Spanish America. She was an intelligent woman who, since universities were then only open to men, rejected the option of a suppressed existence at court, and adopted instead a religious life which enabled her to devote time to study, writing, research and intellectual pursuits. She became embroiled in an ecclesiatical debate with the Bishop of Puebla, but is remembered in particular for her poems, which she wrote in the style of Gongora y Argote (1561–1627), a celebrated Spaniard known for his florid, inverted and pedantic poetry. Another woman who benefited from the education and freedom afforded by the Church was the Colombian religious poet and prose writer ▷Madre María Francisca Josefa del Castillo y Guevara, who had a considerable number of poems and an autobio-graphy published posthumously. Both she and Sor Juana were able to lead independent lives from the privacy of their cells, which at the time was the equivalent of having 'a room of one's own' (▷*A Room of One's Own*), and which would not have been possible outside the Church. They were responsible for developing in Latin America the genre that most frequently occurs among early women writers: subjectivism portrayed through lyric poetry and autobiography.

The emergence of women writers
During the first half of the 19th century, the dominant flourishing literary movement was ▷romanticism, which in Latin America involved freedom of expression, emphasis on the individual, and a general spirit of nationalism. Social practice did not encourage women writers, but a few emerged, some with distinction. The most outstanding was perhaps the Cuban ▷Gertrudis Gómez de Avallaneda, whose plays, poetry and novels made a significant impact in Spain and Spanish America. Her most remarkable works were an anti-slavery novel, ▷*Sab* (1839), and ▷*Guatimozín* (1846), which gives a historical account of the South American Indian and the conquest of Mexico.

Like many of her fellow authors, Avallaneda adopted a pen-name – women writers frequently hid their identity. The reason was sometimes political: the Chilean poet ▷Mercedes Marín del Solar anonymously published a poem in praise of the hero of the Chilean Republic, and the Brazilian ▷Patrícia Galvão was forced to use a ▷pseudonym

(Mara Lobo) by the Communist Party, which did not want her to attract adverse publicity on their behalf. Other writers simply chose men's names because men were socially accepted and women were not. For instance, the Argentinian novelists ▷Ema de la Barra de Llanos and ▷Eduarda Mansilla de García, and the prolific Brazilian writer ▷Júlia Lopes de Almeida all wrote behind masculine names, sometimes pretending to be their own husband or sons.

Prejudice against women writers then was such that when a woman did use her own name, or revealed her identity after publication of a work under a pen-name, contemporary male critics often expressed doubt at their true authorship. This happened to the Brazilian poets ▷Auta de Sousa and ▷Gilka Machado, and the novelist ▷Francisca Júlia. However, although some men also used pen-names (as protection against literary failure), women during this period gradually formed a strong body, producing work, frequently written in the first person, that could never have been written by men, since it was too strongly based on the personal experiences of women and on their observations.

Writing in the 20th century

As in so many parts of the world, from the turn of the century women began to participate in the intellectual life of their cities, contributing in particular to the press. But while for European writers it was the time of the *belle epoque*, in Latin America the women's literary movement was only just beginning to be recognized. Following on from romanticism, the mood of women was rebellious and determined. Among the forerunners of writers with a new voice, the Uruguayan poet ▷Delmira Agustini was one of the most daring. Influenced by the German philosopher Nietzsche (1844–1900) and Decadentism, she developed an erotic, poetic style in an attempt to free the female body from repression. The Argentinian ▷Alfonsina Storni, the Uruguayan ▷Juana de Ibarbourou, and the Brazilian Gilka Machado were other major Latin American poets who adopted this erotic form of expression.

In the early 1920s new trends appeared in literature in the form of didactic novels on everyday subjects – morals, hygiene, politics and education – for instance, in the work of the Brazilian feminist ▷Nísia Floresta, and in *Correio da roça* by her fellow Brazilian Júlia Lopes de Almeida. This was the early stage of the ▷modernist movement in Brazil.

Subjectivism and self-discovery

From the 19th century onwards, women writers had begun cautiously to exert more self-expression, almost as if taking a step back and assessing themselves in a mirror. The Argentinian novelist ▷Victoria Ocampo, founder of the influential magazine ▷*Sur* in the 1930s, was one such writer. In a number of volumes she describes her memories, providing valuable insight into the life of contemporary women, based on her own experience. Journals, memoirs and autobiographies almost constitute a specific literary genre typical of women writers in Latin America, who were at ease when they could write in the first person.

The poetry of the Paraguayan ▷Dora Acuña was a natural development following the uninhibited poems by Gilka Machado, de Ibarbourou and Agustini. Acuña took as her poetic theme the body in relation to the earth, expressing the sensations of life and nature in an erotic way. Some critics, including Suarez Calimano and Rosenbaum, have pointed out how Spanish American women writers have a tendency towards Sapphism, hedonism and self-reference, which can be interpreted as a general reaction against repression. By writing about their feelings and bodies, women were able to acknowledge the differences between men and women, and to assert their individuality.

The influence of mysticism

In their pursuit of self-discovery, women writers were also inspired by mysticism, the belief, often based on intuition, in realities existing beyond everyday perception. Among women, the leader of this subliminal trend was the Chilean poet, teacher and Nobel Prize-winner ▷Gabriela Mistral, whose initiation to literature began with ▷*Desolacíon* (1922) (*Solace*). She was influenced by a number of Europeans, including the Italian writer and political leader Gabriele D'Annunzio (1863–1938) (▷*D'Annunzianesimo*), and she drew inspiration from religion, with love, death and spiritual matters her central themes. Another Chilean, the novelist ▷María Luisa Bombal, wrote in a similar traditional vein. These mystic writers were in direct opposition to contemporary ▷*avant-garde* modernists, who were followers of the Surrealism associated with the French poet André Breton (1896–1966) and the Futurism founded by Italian writer Emilio Marinetti (1876–1944), and who are known for their innovative language. In Brazil, however, the poet ▷Cecília Meireles adopted her own form of *avant-garde* colloquialism, revealing in her poems a withdrawn, secluded vision, while maintaining a mystical appraisal of life. Similarly, ▷Adélia Prado is a Brazilian mystic poet who explores the spiritual aspects of women's everyday life.

Regionalism and politics

From about 1930 to 1945, though the trend began a little earlier, ▷regionalism in Latin America became an important focus for realistic literature, and a forum for political issues and social problems, particularly the tense situation in the rural areas of north-east Brazil. In these ▷1930s' novels, sometimes referred to as the north-eastern series or cycle, writers tried to describe the living conditions in Brazil's different regions. This style of writing corresponds to ▷*costumbrismo* in Spanish American literature. *O Quinze* (1930) (▷*The Fifteenth*) by the Brazilian novelist ▷Raquel de Queirós and ▷*Ifigenia* (1924) by the Venezuelan novelist ▷Teresa de la Parra respectively describe life in rural and urban areas, often portraying through their female protagonists the characteristics of a woman's existence in their own countries.

Towards the end of this period, the ▷1945 Generation continued to write, either following the mysticism developed by Mistral, or else, like the ▷*Viernes* Group from Venezuela, they pursued the regionalist trend. However, women on the whole rarely produced political texts before the 1970s. ▷Josefina Pla, writing political comedies in the Paraguay of the 1940s and 1950s, de Queirós and Galvão are rare exceptions. After the 1970s, women writers became more concerned with social problems, and some were involved with guerrilla warfare, either directly (as were a few younger Brazilians) or indirectly, through their family or friends, as was ▷Isabel Allende, a Chilean exile living in Peru, whose work is centrally within the genre of ▷magic realism.

Writing since the 1950s

The most notable trend in literature by women in contemporary times has been the development of writing in the first person from the female point of view, as in Allende's novels, for instance. Particularly noticeable has been how women have recently become more confident in their expression, expecially in intellectual fields. Journals, memoirs and autobiographical writing have always been an obvious option for women in Latin America, but they have made it a genre of their own, even while writing from a difficult position in society and while experiencing social repression. ▷Clarice Lispector, an outstanding exponent in the long line of women who have written about life from a woman's perspective, skilfully uses the ▷stream-of-consciousness technique, and writes from an intimate, sometimes philosophical view.

As the intellectual capabilities of women in Latin America have become recognized, so it has become easier for their writing to be accepted, and many women have combined their academic and literary talents. The Brazilian ▷Ana Cristina César, for example, was a literary critic and translator, while also being a poet. Today, the majority of better-known women authors have an academic background, many of them having studied, and often taught, at university at home and abroad. The situation is changing, but the past exploitation and repression of women has resulted in a lack of recognition for much of their work, and there is a distinct literary vacuum in relation to women from the lower classes, and those in deprived circumstances.

Bib: Bassnett, Susan (ed.), *Knives and Angels: Women Writers in Latin America*; Fox-Lockert, Lucia, *Women Novelists in Spain and Spanish America*; Pinto, Magdelena Garcia, *Women Writers of Latin America: Intimate Histories*; Rosenbaum, S.C., *Modern Women of Spanish America*.

SUSHEILA NASTA

The English-speaking Caribbean   24

A recent bibliography compiled by ▷Brenda Berrian of the University of Pittsburgh contains entries for 558 published women writers in the section dealing with the English Caribbean and Guyana. This covers the islands of ▷Jamaica, ▷Trinidad and Tobago, ▷Barbados, ▷St Lucia, ▷Dominica, ▷Grenada, ▷Antigua, ▷Guyana and many of the smaller islands that were colonized by the British. In many ways the linguistic division of the Caribbean, which has its roots in the area's colonial past, is an arbitrary one, as the whole of the Caribbean, whether supposedly English-speaking, Francophone (▷Essay on French Antilles), Dutch- or Spanish-speaking, can be linked by less rigid and more homogenous cultural factors.

The cultural heritage of many of the islands draws on a variety of common factors, whatever the official *lingua franca*, which pre-date a particular area's individual colonial history. These include the Native American heritage, a history of slavery, the incorporation of a number of West African languages, the ▷indentured labour system from India at the end of the 19th century, and the contemporary and popular usage of a number of indigenous Creoles which span the entire ▷language continuum. Frequently referred to as ▷nation language, and influenced strongly by oral traditions prior to the emancipation of the slaves, these language systems derive from a far more complex background than the previous imperial history might suggest.

Caribbean women writers have been central from the outset in exploring and subverting both the limitations and the potentialities of these inherited languages, and much of their writing has been shaped and stimulated by the nature of the socio-political realities of the region. Among these are some names with which people will be familiar – ▷Jean Rhys, ▷Phyllis Allfrey, ▷Louise Bennett or (pseudonym Miss Lou), ▷Una Marson, ▷Paule Marshall and ▷Rosa Guy – but the majority of writers have remained unknown, their voices unheard until the latter part of the 20th century. And it remains a sad fact of Caribbean literary history that a large number of writers failed to gain the recognition they deserved, either regionally or internationally. Clearly, publishing opportunities have been limited. Many of the problems which faced the early generations of male writers, many of whom migrated to the metropolis or 'mother-country' in the 1950s to find publishers for their work, still operate today. Furthermore, enormous socio-political and cultural factors contributed to this ▷silence. Economic poverty, and a high rate of illiteracy among large sectors of the rural population, restricted educational opportunities for women (in the pre-independence period), a migrant male labour force, and many other factors, have limited the development of a sustained literary output from Caribbean women. Perhaps most important is the fact that, as ▷ Olive Senior of Jamaica has pointed out, over two-thirds of Caribbean households are headed by women, whose responsibilities for child-rearing within an extended family context are enormous. Not paradoxically, but ironically perhaps, given the central importance of the ▷matrifocal base to Caribbean society and culture, the men have tended to hold the political power and, until recently, have been solely responsible for articulating the nature, boundaries, concerns and innovations of the Caribbean literary tradition. This predominance has clearly been challenged since the mid-1970s, and a number of important critical works on the history of Caribbean women's writing have appeared over the past three or four years which are beginning the process of retrieving women's writing from its obscurity (see Elaine Fido and Carol Boyce Davis (eds.) *Out of the Kumbla: Caribbean Women and Literature*, 1990, and S. Cudjoe (ed.), ▷ *Caribbean Women Writers*, 1990).

This is not an unfamiliar or uncommon problem for women writers in previously colonized countries. Frequently the issue of women's 'independence' or 'liberation' (we won't use the term feminism) is seen as subordinate to and often a betrayal of, traditional codes of practice and belief, a betrayal of the broader struggle for decolonization, nationhood and independence.

In addition, the imported notion of Western feminist models and arguments within what are predominantly rural communities has been regarded with suspicion by both women and men, and seen as another form of cultural imperialism. Women writers, who are often torn between traditional culture and the city, the oral and ▷creolized tradition of the community and language forms imposed by what is still in many cases a patriarchal, colonial education system, therefore have an ambivalent and ambiguous role. Indeed, the subjects of ▷education, ▷bonding between women, ▷identity, ▷mother–daughter relationships, the decolonization of ▷patriarchal forms, and the significance of ▷childhood and ▷autobiography are concerns common to many early and contemporary Caribbean women writers who are struggling not only to gain appropriate recognition but also to write the unwritten ▷oral history of the community in a form that is both liberating and innovative.

Early writing: the 19th century

The significance of the oral tradition has already been mentioned; its background has been well documented by scholars such as Roger Abrahams, Daniel Crowley, J.D. Elder (see bibliography) and the poet Edward Brathwaite's research on the *Folk Culture of Jamaican Slaves* (1969), yet apart from Maureen Warner-Lewis's study of women in ▷Kumina, these works make little mention of the central importance of women in Caribbean oral literature. It has frequently been shown that not only did women suffer the same conditions as the male slaves, they were often the catalysts for rebellious activity – composing songs, dances and other modes of satiric communication to unite the various groups. Thus they were the instigators of movements of resistance, and developed for this purpose an ironic mode of communication, or an alternative language, a ▷'double-talk', which, like the ▷*picong* tradition of present-day ▷calypsonians, could effect to mean one thing, but in fact suggest quite the opposite. The need to subvert the power of the dominant language (whether of ex-slave-master or imperial power) has always been central in Caribbean women's writing.

During the period of resistance to the ideologies of slavery, a number of stories by slaves who had escaped were published in the ▷*Anti-Slavery Reporter*. One of the most significant accounts was ▷ *The History of Mary Prince, A West Indian Slave, Related by Herself* (1831). ▷Mary Prince, originally from ▷Bermuda, is the earliest known woman writer from the English-speaking Caribbean. Her account is illuminating, not only for its depiction of the harsh conditions of slavery, but also for the strength and independence with which this first black woman writer resisted what Ziggi Alexander has called her 'physical and psychological degradation' (Ziggi Alexander in *The History of May Prince, a West Indian Slave, Related by Herself*, ed., Moira Ferguson, 1987, p. vii). As one of the few surviving slave accounts from the British Caribbean, Mary Prince's autobiographical narrative is an important milestone in the literary history of the region, as well as a potent symbol for those women writers who followed her.

Succeeding women writers to be published came mainly from Jamaica, namely ▷Mary Seacole, ▷Pamela C. Smith, ▷Clarine Stephenson and ▷Mary F. Lockett. The most revealing of these works is Mary Seacole's ▷*The Wonderful Adventures of Mrs Seacole in Many Lands*, an autobiographical travelogue that appeared in London in 1857. Seacole was the daughter of a free black mother and a Scottish soldier father. Her life as a doctor, her extensive travels, and her enthusiasm for the army which led to her eventually working in Crimea (where she met Florence Nightingale), combined with her entrepreneurship, were remarkable for a woman of her colour and time. The travelogue portrays the unconventionality and independence of Seacole's observations in a colonial world largely dominated by white men; it also acts as a 'counterdiscourse to the nineteenth century bourgeois ideology of what a woman's place and behaviour ought to have been in her society' (*Caribbean Women Writers*, p. 15).

Pamela Smith's pioneering collection of folklore, ▷*Anancy Stories* (1899), has important roots in the West African ▷oral tradition and goes some way to providing early information on what still remains a 'virtually untapped . . . cultural/critical source'. (*Out of the Kumbla*, p. 167.)

The early 20th century

As Rhonda Cobham has shown in ▷'Women in Jamaican Literature 1900–1950', there was a great deal of interest in women during this period, both in the writings of men and in the literary output of two major Jamaican poets, Una Marson and Louise Bennett. From an early point in Jamaican modern history the strength of the black Jamaican woman had been a subject of controversy. Some observers regarded her independence and the continuing practice of ▷obeah as obstructive to the 'civilizing' of the former slaves. In fact the social patterns of slavery had heightened the free, working black woman's desire to be economically, financially and sexually independent; it was a lifestyle which contrasted dramatically with the position of women in post-Victorian England, and which threatened the values of the dominant colonial culture. Two opposing images of women therefore began to be popular, and appeared in the fiction of the period: the powerful lower-class woman of doubtful sexual behaviour and, later, the idealized black Virgin Madonna, who would maintain the social values of the new black bourgeoisie in the years after World War II. These images were, of course, largely defined by men. However, Una Marson, without pretension, questioned the status of Jamaican women during this period. Described by Lloyd Brown in ▷*West Indian Poetry* (1984) as 'the earliest poet of significance to appear in West Indian literature' (Lloyd Brown, *West Indian Poetry*, 1978, p. 32). Marson was active in the movements which led to the political independence of former British colonies, as well as with the Women's International League for Peace and Freedom. She lived in Britain for several years, and helped to launch the influential BBC World Service 'Caribbean Voices' programme, as well as establishing a number of literary journals in Jamaica.

Marson was a major poet as well as a dramatist. Her published collections of poetry include *Tropic Reveries* (1930), *Heights and Depths* (1932), ▷*The Moth and the Star* (1937) and *Towards the Stars* (1945). Other women were published during this period, such as ▷Constance Hollar and ▷Stephanie Ormsby, but Marson was one of the first women to support feminist and nationalist issues in a period when black women poets were not recognized. *The Moth and the Star* is perhaps her most confident work; in this she deals with the theme of blackness and imported Eurocentric concepts of beauty which negated the self-confidence of black identity. In 'Cinema Eyes' and 'Kinky Hair Blues' she attempts to break down the images which degrade and psychologically diminish her speakers:

> I like me black face
> And me kinky hair . . .
> But nobody does loves dem,
> I jes don't tink it's fair.
> (Una Marson, 'Kinky Hair Blues', *The Moth and the Star*, 1937, p. 91).

Her writing is innovative, and many poems in this collection reflect a successful attempt to fuse creative uses of language typical of the ▷Harlem Renaissance with the vernacular usage in Jamaica.

The use of the vernacular, or 'dialect' as it was then called, was developed in the writings of Louise Bennett, commonly known as Miss Lou. Her poetry was fundamental to the establishment of the Caribbean oral tradition, and authenticated a unique culture which subverted and transformed the realities of the dominant white discourse. Moreover, Miss Lou expressed the sentiments of the ordinary Jamaican people. Her first collection, *Dialect Verses*, was published in 1942, and was followed swiftly by several others, the best-known being ▷*Jamaica Labrish* (1966), which reveals both her subtle irony and her use of Jamaican folk-tale and mythology to portray the actual conditions of women's lives. Bennett was criticized by those who could not accept that the language of the people could be described as 'poetry' but, in the words of Rhonda Cobham, she 'initiated a tradition of popular verse' in the tradition of the African ▷*griot* to which the 'entire region is indebted' (*Out of the Kumbla*, p. 217).

There were many other women writing during this period in Jamaica and the other islands, such as ▷Vera Bell, the Ormsby sisters (▷Stephanie Ormsby), ▷Julia Warner Michael and ▷Barbara Ferland. But it was the work of Una Marson and Louise Bennett that paved the way for the women poets writing today, such as ▷Velma Pollard, ▷Lorna Goodison, ▷Grace Nichols, ▷Jean Binta Breeze, ▷Elean Thomas, ▷Dionne Brand, ▷Marlene Nourbese Philip, and many others.

Jean Rhys

Jean Rhys has always been something of an enigma in the Caribbean literary tradition, and in relation to other Caribbean women writers. She was born in Dominica in 1890. Her writing pre-dates that of the Jamaican group described above but also covers the later 20th century. Rhys was a white ▷Creole, and the great-granddaughter of a slave-owner; her position as a white West Indian, growing up in a period of enormous social and political change when the power of the white community was diminishing, was always an ambivalent one. In fact, Rhys's childhood in Dominica made a very significant impact on her later development as a writer; Teresa O'Connor explores this at length in her study *Jean Rhys: The West Indian Novels* (1986), and illustrates the extent to which the conflicts of the island community in terms of race, colour, sex and religion were to appear again and again throughout her literary career; frequently the heroines of her novels are torn between a lost childhood on a lush tropical island and the alienation of existence in a northern clime; similarly, many of her protagonists exist on the edges of communities, black or white, not belonging to either. Carole Angier's recent biography, *Jean Rhys* (1990), gives extensive information on these early formative years.

Rhys's first collection of short stories was published in 1927 – ▷*The Left Bank and Other Stories*. It was prefaced by Ford Madox Ford, who had done a good deal to get Rhys's work accepted within literary circles. Her novels followed: ▷*Quartet* (or *Postures* as it was originally known) in 1928; *After Leaving Mr Mackenzie* (1931), ▷*Voyage in the Dark* (1934), ▷*Good Morning Midnight* (1939) and ▷*Wide Sargasso Sea* (1966). Her later works include a further collection of short stories, *Sleep It Off Lady* (1976), and an autobiography published after her death, ▷ *Smile Please: An Unfinished Autobiography* (1979). In fact *Voyage in the Dark* was her first written piece, and was based on her unpublished diary entries for 1910.

In *Voyage in the Dark* many of the central concerns of Rhys's later work are already clear. Unable ever to reconcile the world of her Dominican childhood with the harshness of her experiences as a Creole woman in Europe, Rhys constantly navigated a world in which it was 'not just the difference between heat, cold; light, darkness; purple, grey. But a difference in the way I was frightened and the way I was happy' (p. 4). This attempt to portray different ways of feeling and perception, and to move beyond the essentially limited and limiting labels cast upon her by her gender, race and colonial background, are recurrent themes. They come to a mature realization in *Wide Sargasso Sea*, in which she locates her heroine, Antoinette Cosway, within the slave history of the Caribbean, and re-examines the causes for the ultimate destination of Bertha Mason in ▷ Charlotte Brontë's ▷ *Jane Eyre*.

It is not possible to do justice here to the breadth of Rhys's work or her literary reception, but there are several critical studies as well as E.W. Mellown's full, descriptive and annotated bibliography. Also useful is ▷ Jean D'Costa's 'Jean Rhys' in ▷ *Fifty Caribbean Writers* (1986). Since the publication of *Wide Sargasso Sea*, which earned international acclaim, Rhys has been of particular interest to Caribbean and Western feminist scholars. A wealth of research has explored questions such as: how far she is a Caribbean writer; the role of woman as victim; fiction and autobiography; absent mothers and cultural roots, and her challenge in her writing to the literary and ideological traditions of Britain and Europe. Sadly, it has mainly been after her death that Rhys has become a central figure in Caribbean women's literature. She is without doubt a literary mother to many contemporary writers from the region such as ▷ Jamaica Kincaid. Her role as such is discussed in, ▷ *Motherlands: Black Women's Writing From Africa, the Caribbean and South Asia* (1991).

The mid-20th century and nationalism

It was in the 1950s that Caribbean literature first began to be recognized internationally. With the publication of a number of nationalist novels by male writers which won international acclaim, critics began to refer to a West Indian literary Renaissance. Little attention was given, however, to a number of significant works by women writers who, also affected by the social and political changes in the region, attempted to define their roles within the context of political independence from colonial rule.

▷ *The Orchid House* (1953) by Phyllis Allfrey has been described as a 'feminist classic' (Elaine Campbell, 'Phyllis Shand Allfrey', *Fifty Caribbean Writers*, p.15), and was one of the first novels to illustrate the shift in power relations between the white and the black communities. Like Rhys, Allfrey was a white West Indian from Dominica, and concerned with the breakdown of the old white planter society. Lally, the black woman narrator, represents the strength of the black ▷ matriarchal figure who supports the white Creole family as their position in society is threatened. Allfrey portrays the strength of all the women, whether black or white, and it is the women who sustain and effect the family's survival and the island's growth.

Allfrey was also a major poet. Her first volume, *Palm and Oak*, appeared in 1950, being followed by *Contrasts* (1955) and *Palm and Oak II* (1974). As Elaine Campbell has recently demonstrated, she was also the author of a great number of unpublished short stories. (*Caribbean Women Writers*, p. 42) Many of these are to be included in an anthology of West Indian women writers, *The Whistling Bird* (forthcoming from Three Continents Press, USA).

Amid talk of a ▷ West Indies Federation and the growth of important literary magazines such as ▷ *BIM* from Barbados and ▷ *Kyk-over Al* in Guyana, women writers at this time began to be concerned with their own perspective on nationhood, and the possibility of a more collective cultural identity. An extract from ▷Lucille Iremonger's first novel, *Creole* (1951), was published in the *Jamaican Independence Anthology* (1965), and the period saw the arrival of several talented young writers, including the Trinidadian ▷Clara Rosa de Lima, Rosa Guy and ▷Sylvia Wynter.

Clara Rosa De Lima's two novels ▷*Tomorrow Will Always Come* (1965) and *Not Bad; Just a Little Mad* (1975) have been discussed in the context of the rise of nationalism by Selwyn Cudjoe in his introduction to ▷*Caribbean Women Writers* (1990). *Tomorrow Will Always Come* is set in Brazil, and examines the corrupt political situation in Brazil, as well as the sufferings of women within that society. Openly exploited as objects of sexual pleasure, women to some extent enact a political process themselves as a part of a culture of poverty.

Similarly Rosa Guy's ▷*Bird At My Window* (1966) was set, not in Trinidad where she was born, but in the black community of Harlem in the USA. Rosa Guy's novel pre-dates the work of African-American women writers such as ▷Toni Morrison, ▷Maya Angelou, and ▷Louise Merriwater. She explores the West Indian immigrant's experience in New York, although she was profoundly affected by her early years in the West Indies: 'the ▷calypso, the ▷carnival, the religion that permeated our life . . . superstitions, ▷voodoo, the ▷zombies . . . all of these frightening aspects of life that combine the lack of reality with the myth coming from Africa, had a genuine effect on me.' (Jennie Norris, *Presenting Rosa Guy*, 1988, p. 13). Guy went on to write several books for children, including a trilogy entitled *The Friends* (1973), *Ruby* (1976) and *Edith Jackson* (1978). A West Indian voice and consciousness pervades all of her fiction and, like later women writers who emigrated to North and South America, such as Paule Marshall, ▷Michelle Cliff and ▷Audre Lorde, Guy's attempts to explore her dual heritage and the background to the Afro-Caribbean and North and South American ▷diasporas is a powerful and persistent theme.

Finally, ▷Sylvia Wynter's work, both as literary critic and novelist, was crucial during this phase of Caribbean women's writing. ▷*The Hills of Hebron* (1966) examines the occurrence of religious revivalism in Jamaica by an exploration of folk culture and the history of 'three centuries of placelessness' (*Caribbean Women Writers*, p. 42). The novel is symbolic in its vision of a new black prophet, Moses who breaks away from oppression to found a new colony in Hebron. The dawnings of a political consciousness among the ordinary people portrayed in the novel reflected Sylvia Wynter's own critical interests, which appeared in essays such as 'We Must Learn to Sit Down Together and Talk About a Little Culture: Reflections on West Indian Writing and Criticism' (1968). In this essay and other critical writings, Wynter stressed her belief that folk culture was the source all creative traditions in the Caribbean. Even though *The Hills of Hebron* gained little notice when first published, it still stands as a bridge between the early writings of the first woman writer, Mary Prince, who suffered the realities of slavery, and the concerns of women writers today whose work draws on a similar heritage (*Caribbean Women Writers*, p. 42).

The later 20th century

Since the publication of ▷Merle Hodge's ▷*Crick Crack Monkey* in 1970, there has been a flowering of a whole range of literary works by women writers from the various islands, as well as those now living abroad in the USA, Canada and Britain. Clearly the writing from individual islands differs according to particular cultural histories, such as the greater focus on the Asian experience in Trinidad and Guyana, where indentured Indians worked on the plantations in the 19th century, but certain identifiable preoccupations among many of these writers have emerged. These have been examined at length in two recent books, ▷*Out of the Kumbla: Caribbean Women and Literature* (1990) and *Caribbean Women Writers*. The latter is a collection of essays from the first international conference on

Caribbean women's writing held in 1988. In addition, several anthologies of creative works have been published: a milestone in poetry was ▷*Jamaica Woman: An Anthology of Poems* (1980), edited by ▷Pamela Mordecai and Mervyn Morris. This brought together several writers, including ▷Christine Craig, Lorna Goodison, ▷Gloria Escoffery, Olive Senior, Jean D'Costa and several others. Both Lorna Goodison and Olive Senior later became winners of the Commonwealth Writers' Prize: Goodison for her collection of poetry ▷*I am Becoming My Mother* (1986) and Senior for an anthology of short stories, ▷*Summer Lightning* (1986). In Guyana ▷Shana Yardan was one of the six main contributors to *Guyana Drums* (1972), another anthology of women's poetry. This has been followed by the work of ▷Meiling Jin and ▷Mahadai Das who deal specifically with the Indo-Guyanan experience. In addition there are several well-established women poets writing abroad: Marlene Nourbese Philip's *She Tries Her Tongue Her Silence Softly Breaks* (1989) explores the whole theme of motherlands and mother tongues by experimenting with poetic modes that differ from the dominant form. Dionne Brand, like Marlene Nourbese Philip, lives in Canada, and fuses the experience of being black, Trinidadian and immigrant within a Canadian context. Similarly, Grace Nichols, Jean Binta Breeze, Elean Thomas, ▷Merle Collins and ▷Valerie Bloom live outside the region – in Britain. All of these writers draw on the strengths of the oral tradition, and Grace Nichols's long poem ▷*i is a long memoried woman* (1983) is epic in its re-creation of the story of the ▷Middle Passage from a woman's perspective. It provides an alternative vision to that of E.K. Brathwaite in *The Arrivants* (1973). The current range of women's poetry is vast, and is represented in ▷Rambabai Espinet's recent book ▷*Creation Fire* (1990), which brings together over 250 Caribbean poets and was initiated by the formation of ▷CAFRA (the Caribbean for Association Feminist Research and Action).

The publication of prose works such as ▷*Her True True Name: An Anthology of Women's Writing from the Caribbean* (1989) has also been extremely impressive, and several dominant themes have begun to emerge (Pamela Mordecai and Betty Wilson, eds., *Her True True Name*, 1989). The significance of the relationship between childhood and identity is explored in several novels which take the name of the main character as their title: ▷Zee Edgell's ▷*Beka Lamb* (1982) won the Fawcett Society Book Prize, and concerns the making of Belize, as well as being a powerful ▷*Bildungsroman* (novel of early development) on the coming to consciousness of a young girl growing up in the 1950s, a turbulent period in the history of Belize. Similarly, Jamaica Kincaid of Antigua has focused on pubescence and the disorientating effects of the expectations produced by a colonial education system in ▷*Annie John* (1985) and her stories in ▷*At the Bottom of the River* (1983); her most recent novel, ▷*Lucy* (1991), is set in the USA, but is again preoccupied with the process of 'becoming' for a young girl away from home for the first time. And in Merle Collin's ▷*Angel* (1987) and ▷Janice Shinebourne's *Timepiece* (1986) the investigation of childhood is presented from an intimate autobiographical viewpoint, but is closely accompanied by overt socio-political elements, as is also the case in ▷Maryse Condé's ▷*A Season in Rihata* (1988) and ▷Michelle Cliff's *No Telephone to Heaven* (1987). Frequently the young heroines in these novels either experience a period of mental instability themselves, or are closely associated with witnessing the effects of 'madness'. Madness, or an alternative state of consciousness, lends a Surrealistic quality to some of the writing, while at the same time enabling the writer to transform reality by using language and style unconventionally. Beginning with Rhys (*Wide Sargasso Sea*) and Marion Patrick Jones (*J'Ouvert Morning*, 1976), women writers have persistently addressed this issue. Evelyn O'Callaghan's recent essay 'Interior Schisms Dramatised: The Treatment of the "Mad" Woman in the Work of Some Female Caribbean Novelists' investigates this question with reference to some of the works mentioned above and the writing of ▷Erna Brodber's novel, ▷*Jane and Louisa Will Soon Come Home* (1980), as well as Paule Marshall's ▷*Praisesong For the Widow* (1983). Interestingly, Erna Brodber's sister, Velma Pollard, is a Jamaican poet.

Many of the writers have attempted to create new ways of metaphorical and symbolic expression. *Jane and Louisa Will Soon Come Home* is an example of this type of innovation, and is perhaps indicative of the resources available to contemporary women writers: it contains a vast kaleidoscope of modes and styles, ranging from autobiography to lyric poetry to historical narrative, psychoanalytic explanation, and so on. It also draws extensively on oral history and the central importance of relationships between women.

Through mother–daughter relationships and bonding between women, important stories and values are passed down to younger generations, stories that represent women's collective experience. Olive Senior's collection of short stories, ▷*Summer Lightning* (1986), is a particularly fine example of this, as is ▷Opal Palmer Adisa's *Bake-Face and Other Guava Stories* (1976). Similarly ▷*Lionheart Gal: Life Stories of Jamaican Women* (1986), written by the ▷Sistren Collective of Jamaica, is a major volume in nation language and the life histories of Jamaican working-class women.

The question of new languages deriving from the positive effects of the cross-fertilization and creolization of languages is central to the remarkable energy emanating from women's writing in the Caribbean today. This theme and its broader ramifications in relation to mother tongues and mother cultures is explored at length in *Motherlands: Black Women's Writing From Africa, the Caribbean and South Asia*.

It is not possible iin this essay to mention all the issues which contemporary writers from this region have raised, but it is worth noting two further trends. First, the relationships between men and women often threaten and damage – as is evident in ▷Joan Riley's works *The Unbelonging* (1985) and *Waiting in the Twilight* (1987); indeed men are often absent from these works, as they are in ▷Beryl Gilroy's more positive work, *Frangipani House* (1986).

Second, several of the works are concerned with the theme of journeying, whether in the literal sense of departure and exile, or in the spiritual/psychic sense of seeking a cultural homeland. As was mentioned earlier, many contemporary Caribbean women writers live abroad. These women bring different perceptions to their writing, created by their new contexts. Thus a number of women writers who live in Britain, for instance, such as Joan Riley, ▷Amryl Johnson, Merle Collins, ▷Lakhshmi Persaud, ▷Pauline Melville, ▷Janice Shinebourne and Grace Nichols, are able to reflect aspects of the 'Black-British' experience in their art; a similar process is going on in the USA and Canada. But where the writers actually live is not as important as the themes of survival and resistance that emerge again and again; it is, as Merle Collins once wrote, a 'struggle which places the liberation of women within the context of the anti-imperialist and anti-colonial struggle' being waged throughout the world (Merle Collins, 'Women Writers From the Caribbean', *Spare Rib*, No. 124, 1988, pp. 18–22).

Bib: Abrahams, Roger, *The Man-of-Words in the West Indies: Performance and the Emergence of Creole Culture* and *Talking Black*: Braithwaite, Edward K., *The Folk Culture of Jamaican Slaves, The Development of Creole Society in Jamaica 1770–1820* and *The History of the Voice*; Crowley, Daniel, 'The Traditional Masques of Carnival and 'The Midnight Robbers', *Caribbean Quarterly*, Vol. 4, pp. 194–223 and 263–74, and 'Towards a Definition of Calypso', *Ethnomusicology*, Vol. 3, pp. 57–66 and 117–24; Elder, J.D., 'The Male/Female Conflict in Calypso', *Caribbean Quarterly*, Vol. 14, No. 3 (September 1968), *Ma Rose Point: An Anthology of Rare and Strange Legends and Myths from Trinidad and Tobago*; Nasta, Susheila, 'Motherlands, Mothercultures, Mothertongues: Women's Writing in the Caribbean', *Aspects of Common Literature*, Vol. 1, No. 39, Institute of Commonwealth Studies (1990), pp. 28–37.

French Antilles

As elsewhere in the Caribbean, the European imperial enterprise in Guadeloupe and Martinique, the two islands of the French-speaking Antilles still under French hegemony, ensured that the worst features of colonialism would be combined in the region. The native Carib and Arawak population had virtually been exterminated within a century of the European invasion; the deracination and atrocities of the slave trade and plantation slavery, the subsequent systems of indenture which 'stranded' Chinese and Indians in the Caribbean when the return clauses of indenture contracts were dishonoured, and the harm wrought by colonial policies of ▷education and language suppression have inevitably left their mark. Yet much of the early literature of the post-abolition period has chosen to portray these 'far-flung parts of France' as resembling Eden.

The year 1992 is the 500th anniversary of the beginning of the appropriation of the New World by the Europeans. It is also the year in which some of the nations of Europe (including France) will move towards a closer degree of economic and political co-operation and the French 'motherland' will drag her Guadeloupean and Martiniquan 'children' into the confines of the European family. It is thus an appropriate moment to consider this specific area of French post-colonial writing.

In the general field of writing in French from the Caribbean, little attention has been paid to women writers. ▷Berrian includes a comprehensive list and bibliography of women writers from the French Antilles, Haiti and ▷Guyana in her *Bibliography of Women Writers from the Caribbean* and ▷Mordecai and Wilson include in ▷*Her True True Name* extracts by the limited number of writers whose works are available in translation. Marie-Denise Shelton provides an overview of women writers from the French-speaking Caribbean in ▷*Caribbean Women Writers*. ▷Maryse Condé has broached the issue of women's writing from the Antilles in *La Parole des Femmes* (1979) (*Women's Words*), while France Alibar and Pierrette Lembeye-Boy use their research to examine the social position of women in the Antilles in *Le Couteau Seul . . .: la condition féminine aux Antilles* (1982) (*Only the Knife . . . the Condition of Women in the French Antilles*). Jack Corzani's six-volume *La Littérature des Antilles Guyane Françaises* (1978) (*The Literature of the French Antilles and of French Guyana*) remains the most comprehensive study of Antillean literature in general.

Literature from Guadeloupe and Martinique is frequently considered *en bloc*. Although some would like to present a united front to the common (neo-)colonial enemy, and the metropolitan government makes little distinction between Guadeloupe and Martinique, differences do exist which may be directly attributed to history. The two islands are called sisters, and share the same status (made into a *département d'outre mer* of France in 1946 in return for services rendered after the World War II, during which Guadeloupe and Martinique resisted the Vichy government). On both islands the present-day population consists of a variety of racial groups. Although officially no longer colonies, both are still subject to pressure from the European 'owner', France, and the evolution of their populations, language and culture is similar. But the Guadeloupean novelist and dramatist, Max Jeanne, draws our attention to one cultural difference with his claim that the well-known French Antillean writers tend to be men from Martinique (Aimé Césaire, Glissant and Chamoiseau, for example), whereas in Guadeloupe the better-known writers tend to be women in whose works, he suggests, an *intimiste* point of view prevails (using first person narrative, psychological analysis and depicting conflicting relationships with the West Indian male) (Max Jeanne, 'French West Indian Literature', *Présence Africaine*, 121/122, 1982, p. 137).

Early writing

Much of the early writing in these colonies was produced by those who represented France there, and, despite their detailed reportage of landscape, customs and language, they inevitably have a Eurocentric focus, emphasizing the 'home' over the 'native', the 'metropolitan' over the 'provincial' or 'colonial'. At a deeper level, their claim to objectivity simply serves to hide the imperial discourse within which they were created. Direct or unpaid slavery was abolished in Guadeloupe and Martinique by the post-Revolution Convention in 1794, only to be reinstated in 1802 by Bonaparte and reintroduced by Richepance following the successful quashing of such revolts as those led in Guadeloupe by the celebrated hero, Delgres, and the legendary woman, Solitude. It was finally abolished in 1848 (see André Schwarz-Bart, *A Woman Named Solitude*). After abolition, a new *petite bourgeoisie* of colour emerged which was generally conservative and pro-France. Many of the works of this period praise the local beauty but ignore the social and economic reality of the Antilles. In *Cristlline bois-Noir ou les dangers du Bal Doudou* (1929), for example, Thérèse Herpin insists upon the charm and seduction of the islands, the warm welcome of the people.

One of the early published studies of a ▷Creole woman is *Yvette, histoire d'une jeune créole* (1888) (*Yvette, the Story of a Young Creole Woman*) by the Martiniquan, Thérèse de Betzon (also known as Mlle de Solms and Mme Thérèse Blanc). Suzanne Lacascade's novel, ▷*Claire-Solange, âme africaine* (1924) (*Claire-Solange, African Soul*), stands out from those of many of her contemporaries for the emphasis it gives to the black struggle for emancipation, and the pride the heroine takes in being a woman of colour. Other women writing at the beginning of the century include the Martiniquan novelists and poets, Drasta Houël, Hélène Lémery, Simone Yoyotte and Marie Berté (also known as Emmbé).

The mid-20th century

Little effect of the waves created by the ▷*négritude* and ▷Harlem Renaissance movements is reflected in the creative writing of Antillean women of this time. As Clarisse Zimra observes, 'Liberation was started by men and the *négritude* prophets who stood in its vanguard were all men. The liberation of one sex was subsumed under that of one race and thereby deferred' (Clarisse Zimra, 'Patterns of Liberation in Contemporary Women Writers', *L'Esprit Créateur*, Vol. XVII, No. 2, Summer 1977, p. 103).

Assimilationist policies, reflected in education policies in the two islands, have meant that the local has been ignored in favour of the metropolitan. Exotic descriptions provide introductions to readers unfamiliar with Guadeloupe and Martinique. *Sonson de la Martinique* (1932) by the Martiniquan, Irmine Romanette (pseudonym: Yves Miramant) provides an encyclopaedic initiation for the European reader to a captivating island. In a similarly exotic vein, Maryse Elot wrote her novels and poems, and the Martiniquan Alice Joyau-Dormoy, collaborated with her husband, Auguste Joyau, to write the sentimental novel *Guiablesse Martinique* (1958). Many of the poems by the Guadeloupean, Jeanne de Kermadec, are melancholic, concerned with the landscape of the Antilles rather than the people and customs, or the cultural and racial originality of her country (*Feux du soir*, 1966, *Evening Lights*, for example). The Martiniquan Kiki Marie-Sainte has written one novel, *L'Antillaise à l'amour double* (1966) (*The Antillean Woman Twice in Love*), which, set in Toulon, Paris and Martinique, and on board a transatlantic liner, examines the ambiguous relationship of colonized and colonizer, contrasting 'islanders' to the French. An exception to this 'exotic' literature is to be found in *La Fille du Caraïbe* (1960) (*The Daughter of the Carib Indian*), the semi-historical novel by ▷Emma Monplaisir.

Like Marie-Thérèse Julien-Lung Fou (co-founder of the journal *Dialogue* in 1956, and collector and writer of *Fables créoles, transposées et illustrées*, 1958, *Creole Fables*), Monplaisir was also interested in Antillean folklore. The Guadeloupean Florette Morand-Capasso was a poet, short story writer and novelist, perhaps best-known for the 'simple' verse of her poems (*Mon coeur est un oiseau des îles*, 1955, *My Heart is Like a Bird of the Islands*).

In the folktales of Emma Monplaisir, the tales in creole of Marie-Thérèse Lung-Fou, and the poems of Claude and Marie-Magdeleine Carbet, it is possible to observe a slight change in Antillean consciousness. These writers appear to seek to affirm themselves without jeopardizing the politics of the metropolis. Later creative writers such as ▷Michèle Lacrosil, ▷Françoise Ega and ▷Mayotte Capécia continue to reflect a belief in French humanism.

The later 20th century

Many of the novels by contemporary Antillean women writers are presented as (women's) ▷autobiographies. The protagonists are frequently suffering from a sense of fragmentation, 'madness' or ▷folie Antillaise. Apparently aware of a condition of racial and cultural amnesia, they must undergo a confessional process in order to gain the authenticity or understanding necessary to be able to confront a future. Their literal or figurative 'journey' is not merely to be a quest for 'roots', a quest in a white world for an autonomous self, or a mission to exorcize some vision of a woman's predicament of being of colour and female in a social world defined by white males, and a political system based on colonialism and imperialism. It is a quest for fulfilment or a sense of wholeness for both woman and island.

One recurring theme in the work of these women novelists is that of the quest of the woman of colour, brought to the test by a man. This includes the prerequisite affair and eventual abandonment (see ▷Mon Examen de Blanc, ▷L'Autre qui danse). Constant father figures and male partners are noticeable for their absence in ▷Simone Schwarz-Bart's ▷The Bridge of Beyond and ▷Dany Bebel-Gisler's ▷Léonora (1985), and the important role played by grandmothers as nurturers in Caribbean households is reflected in Schwarz-Bart's novels. (As ▷Olive Senior of Jamaica has pointed out, over two-thirds of Caribbean households are headed by women; see Joycelin Massiah, *Women as heads of households in the Caribbean: family structure and feminine status*, 1983, and France Alibar and Pierrette Lembeye-Boy, *Le Couteau Seul*, 1982, and Beverley Ormerod, 'L'aïeule: figure dominante chez S. Schwarz-Bart', *Présence Francophone*, No. 20, Spring 1980.) Schwarz-Bart's Télumée and Bebel-Gisler's Léonora are strong, resilient women, as is Délia in Ega's *Les Temps de Madras*. Schwarz-Bart depicts bonding between women as a source of Télumée's strength, portraying her ability to resist adversity as having been learnt and inherited from her female ancestors, the four generations of Lougandor women, and in particular her grandmother (see Ronnie Scharfman, 'Mirroring and Mothering in Simone Schwarz-Bart's *Pluie et Vent sur Télumée Miracle* and Jean Rhys's *Wide Sargasso Sea*' in *Yale French Studies*, No. 62, 1981, pp. 88–106). This concern with ancestry is also reflected in Schwarz-Bart's second novel, ▷Between Two Worlds, in which the hero, Ti-Jean, a character from the Antillean folktale (who is also used by ▷Ina Césaire), embarks upon a quest for his ancestor.

Ti-Jean's quest brings him to the edge of the chasm of madness, or the *folie Antillaise*, which hovers threateningly throughout *Bridge of Beyond*. Madness also threatens Zétou in ▷As the Sorcerer Said and ▷Juletane. As Clarisse Zimra reflects, 'madness has . . . been the constant temptation in the Caribbean universe, both as theme (an object of discourse) and as textual strategy (subject of discourse)' (Clarisse Zimra, '*Négritude* in the Feminine Mode', *Journal of Ethnic Studies* Vol. 121, No. 11, 1984, p. 71). In the case of Zétou and Juletane (and also Lacrosil's ▷Sapotille and ▷Cajou, Schwarz-Bart's Mariotte, ▷Manicom's Madévie, and Fanny in ▷Au Peril de ta joie), confession or journal-writing emerges as an attempt to control and correct personal history and to explain and investigate the past. The journal form of Warner-Vieyra's two novels describes the alienation of Antillean women in Africa and France, and their betrayal by mother, lover or husband, factors which thus provide an explanation for apparent madness.

Silence surrounding the brutal pattern of conquest and control, the importation and the psychological and physical annihilation of peoples has led to a situation termed 'rootlessness' or 'historylessness', described by the Guadeloupean writer, Simone Schwarz-Bart, as being that of '*une branche coupée*' ('a sawn-off branch'). The silence which surrounds the past can become a 'theme' so that the literature is 'about' a void, a psychological abyss between cultures. A double-edged attitude to the past has emerged, whereby the writer is viewed as having the didactic role of teaching about the past, and also the psychologically healing role of removing a sense of shame associated with the past. Alternatively, this concern with the past may appear as a loss of some form of Eden. The harsh experience of slavery, of dispossession and uprooting which deprived part of a race of its rightful inheritance, freedom, culture, religion and language is felt to be an expulsion from a state of harmonious existence (Beverly Ormerod, *Introduction to the French Caribbean Novel*, 1985).

Filling or rewriting this silence may be seen in the works of Schwarz-Bart, Condé and Ega, among others. Schwarz-Bart and ▷Jeanne Hyvrard seek to comprehend a collective Caribbean history in their novels, while Condé's novel *La Vie scélérate* (1987) (*Life is Wicked*) attempts to encompass fragments of the black experience from many areas of North and Central America outside the Guadeloupe in which much of the saga is set. In her novels ▷*Segu* and *Moi, Tituba. . .* (1986), Condé rewrites history, creating in Tituba the black woman who has been omitted from the chronicles concerning the witches of Salem. Lacrosil turns to a mythical version of the past to motivate her novel, ▷*Demain Jab-Herma*, and Schwarz-Bart celebrates the achievements and history of black women in her *Homage à la Femme Noire* (1989) (*In Praise of Women of Colour*). A concern with the more immediate past is reflected in Schwarz-Bart's *Bridge of Beyond*, which, according to the author, was written to preserve the passing of the way of life of a generation of women who have greatly influenced her, and who have taught her what it means to be an Antillean woman (see Hélène and Roger Toumson. 'Interview avec Simone et André Schwarz-Bart: sur les pas de Fanotte', R. Toumson, ed., *Textes et Etudes Documents* No. 2., 1979, pp. 13–23). Similarly, Bebel-Gisler declares that her novel *Léonora* is the transcribed autobiography of an elderly creolophone woman, and Ina Césaire's first play, *Mémoires d'Isles* (1988) (*Memories of the Islands*), uses research material, the collected life-histories of elderly women of Guadeloupe and Martinique. In contrast to many of their predecessors, all three of these writers turn to the ▷oral histories of peasant women of colour, depicting with sensitivity the dignity with which they confront a harsh existence.

The theme of the past forms a pervasive link with the organizing elements of exile and alienation, a journey into the past or quest for identity (especially to Africa and/or France) and the importance of naming, and thus forms a structural and formal pattern. The journeying is linked to a sense of displacement or not-at-homeness which motivates the reconstruction of a social and imaginary world (see ▷*Hérémakhonon* and *Sapotille* for examples). The journey to France, like the journeys in the novels of Condé, Myriam Warner-Vieyra and Lacrosil, is both a physical and a psychological voyage, the journey of an alienated, homeless individual in search of a motherland, and of a people deprived of their identity who have a triple heritage, African, European and Antillean. The recourse to the imperial centre of power to find an identity conveys a perception that being is located at the centre, and thus there is an implication that nothingness is the only possibility in the margins.

The concepts of *Antillanité* and, more recently, of *Créolité*, attempt to counter the allegedly alienating effects of *négritude* and, of course, of the idea of assimilation, of which it is the apparent rival but actual ally (see Edouard Glissant, *Le discours antillais*, 1981, and Jean Bernabé, Patrick Chamoiseau, and Raphaël Confiant, *Eloge de la Créolité*, 1989). These two movements call for a focus on the heterogeneous human and cultural heritage of the Antillean or Creole islands themselves. The prolific and versatile writer Maryse Condé adopts an anti-colonialist approach in her work and is critical of *négritude* (see Maryse Condé, 'Pourquoi la négritude? Négritude ou révolution?', *Les Littératures d'expression française: négritude africaine, Négritude caraïbe*, 1973). Along with other women from

Guadeloupe and Martinique, she has been prominent in presenting the multifarious nature of the Antillean heritage. A celebration of the heterogeneity of the Antillean and of the Antilles is reflected in the importance given to heredity and syncretism in Monplaisir's novel, *La Fille du Caraïbe* (1960) (*The Daughter of the Carib Indian*). Schwarz-Bart and Césaire have used the oral culture of the Antilles, the traditional *conte* (folktale) in their work. In particular, the new form created by Schwarz-Bart in *Bridge of Beyond* and *Between Two Worlds* celebrates the heritage of Guadeloupe, presenting a sense of completeness and presence which contrasts with the sense of absence and fragmentation in the novels of many of her contemporaries. The island is retrieved as a site of self-discovery; family and island history are recovered as a source of nourishment and strength; and a creolized language is used to convey a creole world-view, which incorporates the magical realm that lies beyond empirical reality.

Thus, women writers from Martinique and especially Guadeloupe have been in the vanguard of those experimenting with language, style and form, demonstrating that it is not enough to abolish an institution like slavery to erase its traces. Their works reveal that it is not sufficient to name Guadeloupe and Martinique a *département d'outre mer* to halt their colonial status, and neither is it enough for Antilleans to be issued with French or European passports to conceal the cultural, historical and socio-political realities of the Antilles.

Haiti

Literature from Haiti has frequently been subsumed under 'Francophone Caribbean Writing', and sometimes under 'French Afro-Caribbean Literature'. The first black republic in the world, Haiti, has experienced a destiny radically different from that of her sister Caribbean islands. The only Caribbean land where the aspiration to independence was born of the struggle against slavery, Haiti is also the only Caribbean land where both emancipation and nationhood were achieved at the same time, and were not granted but wrested from European hands.

Ceded to France by Spain in 1697, the western third of Hispaniola became known as Saint-Domingue, and was organized in a similar manner to other New World 'sugar colonies'. But unlike other West Indian islands, Haiti made an early bid to break free from European hegemony. The general slave uprising which broke out in 1791, inspired by the French Revolution (1789), was followed by twelve years of intermittent violence. After the defeat by the Haitians (and by yellow fever) of an expeditionary corps sent by Napoleon in 1802, Jean-Jaques Dessalines proclaimed the independence of Haiti on 1 January 1804. Political independence has never guaranteed a genuine autonomy, and Haitian history has continued to be characterized by dependence upon, and exploitation by, imperial powers – Germany and England, as well as France and the USA – and by periods of political instability. For nearly two centuries Haiti has been suffering all the problems of a violent and prolonged process of decolonization.

Perhaps more than other creative writers in French from the Caribbean, Haitian writers have been concerned with the possibility of expressing the specific originality of Haitian literature (see Maximilien Laroche, 'La quête de l'identité culturelle dans la littérature haïtienne', *Notre librairie*, No. 48, April–June 1979, pp. 55–67; Jean-B. Cinéas, 'Y-a-t-il une littérature haïtienne?', *Le Temps*, 26 June 1940; or Anne Marty, 'La Littérature haïtienne en quête d'identité', *L'Afrique littéraire et artistique*, Vol. 28, No. 4, 1975, pp. 2–9). The language situation in Haiti is unlike that of her French-controlled Caribbean 'sisters', Guadeloupe and Martinique. Creole is thought to have reached Haiti in 1690. Today the linguistic situation in Haiti is unique: all citizens are fluent in Creole, but no more than 10 per cent have a working knowledge of French. In 1979 Creole became the language used to teach younger children at primary level, with French being taught as a foreign language. The problems of publishing and distribution are perhaps greater in Haiti than elsewhere in the Caribbean as a consequence. With so few of the population literate in French, and very few Haitian printing houses, many writers find they have to turn to Québecois or Parisian publishers. The controversial situation of aiming at a double public (home and abroad), which affects most Caribbean writers, is thus arguably more troubled in Haiti.

Of the thirty–eight woman novelists from Guadeloupe, Martinique and Haiti listed by Berrian as writing between 1831 and 1986, only eleven are Haitian. Little critical attention has been devoted to Haitian literature in general and virtually none to the creative work of Haitian women (see Léon-François Hoffmann, *Essays on Haitian Literature*, 1984; *Le Roman Haïtien: Idéologie et Structure*, 1982; see also Marie-Denise Shelton, *L'image de la société dans le roman haïtien*, 1979, and Gérard Etienne, 'La Femme noire dans le discours littéraire haïtien', *Présence Francophone*, No. 18, Spring 1979, pp. 109–126). Very little of the creative writing by Haitian woman is available in translation (exceptions include translations of two of Marie Chauvet's novels into English: *Dance on the Volcano*, 1959, a translation by S. Attanasio of *La Danse sur le volcan*, 1957, and Joyce Marie Codgell-Travis, 'A Translation of *Amour*, the first Book of the Trilogy Novel *Amour, colère et folie* by Marie Vieux Chauvet with a Critical Introduction – Haiti from a Woman's Point of View', Ph.D. Dissertation, Brown University, June 1980). A little more attention paid to this neglected area reveals that Haitian women writers, like many of their male counterparts, are concerned with the issues of language (French and Creole), cultural ▷identity (the choice between African, French or 'home-grown' models), racial identity, the very particular religious issue, the place and value of *vaudou* (▷voodoo), and, more recently, the exile of many writers due to the political situation (in 1986, out of a Haitian population of five million, one million were living abroad). Their work, unlike that of many of their male counterparts, also reflects a concern with the Haitian woman, and the contradictions and injustices she has to negotiate. (See M. Dash, 'Haitian Literature – A Search for Identity', *Savacou*, 5, June 1971, pp. 81–94; Asselin Charles, 'Voodoo Myths in Haitian Literature', *Comparative Literature Studies* 17, 4, December 1980, pp. 391–398; Pradel Pompilus, 'Le vodou dans la littérature haïtienne', *Rond Point* 8, June–July 1963; J. Joubert, J. Lecarme *et al*, *Les Littératures francophones depuis 1945*, 1986).

Early writing

As in many former colonies, early creative writing in Haiti was largely mimetic, turning to French models for reference. The poet Madame Frantz Colbert St-Cyr (born 1889) is one of the better-known early women writers. She moved from Haiti to New York, and in 1949 published a volume of poetry, *Gerbe de fleurs* (*Spray of Flowers*). A strong supporter of the feminist movement, she was in the forefront of those campaigning for better conditions for women. Many novels written before 1915 recount the heroic times of the struggle for independence, and few indicate the existence of a particularly Haitian consciousness. The explanations provided by Madame Virgile Valcin in her two novels *La Blanche Négresse* (1934) (*The White Negress*) and *Cruelle destinée* (1929) (*Cruel Destiny*) suggest that she was aiming at a non-Haitian readership. She presents a soothing picture of a nourishing land for those who possess nothing.

The contemporary Haitian novel was born of the US occupation of Haiti (US marines were based there from 1915 to 1934; see J. Joubert *et al.* eds, *Les Littératures francophones depuis 1945* (1986); see also Léon-François Hoffmann, *Essays on Haitian Literature*, 1984). Together with the spread of Marxist ideas, the occupation spawned an indigenist school, which contested the use of foreign models in creative writing. Celebrating Haiti's African heritage and cultural originality, this school generated a period of national renewal. Peasant life was exalted, and *vaudou* celebrated as a manifestation of *haïtianité*, symbolizing autocthonous resistance to foreign influences. The influence of such a shift in literary focus may be detected in the observation and responsible analysis of Haitian society shown by Katherine Dunham in her *The Dances of Haiti* (1947). One reaction to the

American occupation is reflected in Annie Desroy's *Le Joug* (1934) (*The Yoke*), in which she evokes the shame and discouragement experienced by Haitians at that time.

Recent writing

Many more recent novels written by women turn to an analysis of a woman's condition in Haiti. Jan Dominique presents, in *Memoires d'une amnesique* (1986) (*An Amnesiac's Memories*), the disorientation of a woman who tries to break the silence into which amnesia has forced her. ▷Marie Chauvet presents female characters whose psychological fragmentation can only be understood within the context of Haiti's repressive social and political institutions. In two of her novels, ▷*Fille d'Haïti* (1954) (*Daughter of Haiti*) and ▷*Amour* (1968) (*Love*), Chauvet depicts women who suffer from a sense of fragmentation, threatened from the inside by a sense of worthlessness, and from the outside by the violent social and political climate of Haiti. In *Fonds des Nègres* (1961) Chauvet portrays Marie-Ange as formed and deformed by Haitian society.

Set against a background of political terror, Chauvet's trilogy, *Amour, colère et folie* (1968) (*Love, Anger, Madness*) is concerned with a frustrated woman. The publication of the trilogy, which contains a virulent denunciation of Haiti's tyrannical regimes, forced its author, like many other Haitians, to go into exile. Marie-Thérèse Colimon also deals with emigration, exposing the contradictions of the exodus of Haitians to foreign lands in search of economic or personal salvation in her six short stories, *Le Chant des sirènes* (1979) (*The Song of the Sirens*). Seen at times as a last resort, emigration is more often an ardently pursued ideal. Colimon portrays the attraction of the USA, land of refrigerators and supermarkets, and, slipping English expressions into the speech of those who have left long ago, shows the popularity of English, part of the dream of settling in New York or Boston. But she also condemns a society which forces its members to seek fulfilment abroad. Combining humour and gravity, she depicts the attraction of 'over-there' (*là-bas*) as delusive and maddening, like the song of the sirens heard by disorientated sailors.

In the manner of the 19th-century French social novelists, *Fils du misère* (1973) (*Son of Misfortune*) by Marie-Thérèse Colimon depicts the conditions of the masses, showing them to be the powerless victims of an indifferent or brutal social structure. Liliane Devieux-Dehoux also shows inequality to be rampant in her *L'Amour, oui, la mort, non* (1976) (*Love, Yes! Death, No!*).

More didactic and strident in tone than either Chauvet or Colimon, Nadine Magloire has been very committed to the improvement of conditions for women in Haiti. Her novel *Le Mal de Vivre* (1968) (*The Pain of Living*) is the interior monologue of an upper-class woman who has dared to seek intellectual and erotic freedom despite the strait-laced puritanism of the élite. In this novel, Magloire testifies to the persistence of the preference (also found in several Guadeloupean and Martiniquan novels) for white husbands, by having her heroine enumerate the financial, social and racial advantages of marrying a white man. This concern with colour prejudices is reflected also in Palette Poujol-Oriol's *Le Creuset* (1980) (*The Crucible*), which depicts the relationship of the student Pierre Tervil and a blonde typist from Boston. Magloire's provocative tone also characterizes her novel *Le Sexe Mythique* (1975) (*Mythical Sex*) where, once more, her intention to denounce the conditions in Haiti is to the fore. Her novels become a pretext for reflecting on the issues of language, readership and cultural support which have been problematic in Haiti.

An overview of works by women from Haiti shows the diversity of the responses and preoccupations. It shows their various ideological perspectives, but also reveals a thematic current which permeates many of the works; a concern with a female protagonist whose psychological fragmentation should be viewed within the context of Haiti's repressive social and political institutions, and against a background of political upheaval.

26 Australia

The Aboriginal tradition

As white settlement took place only 200 years ago, in 1788, the Australian literary tradition is fairly new. Preceding it, however, was an oral tradition among the Aboriginal inhabitants of the continent. Part of this, but as yet comparatively unknown, is a tradition of women's song, performance and ritual, often of a sacred nature, which does not translate easily into the written word. Versions by well-meaning whites such as ▷Catherine Langloh Parker and ▷Daisy Bates invariably distort and Europeanize the original. (▷The Aborigine in non-Aboriginal Australian women's writing.) However, Aboriginal women's songs from the 'Wudal-Maimai Song Sequence' and from the North Eastern Arnhem Land region, published in both the original language and in English translation in ▷ *The Penguin Book of Australian Women Poets* (1986), edited by Susan Hampton and Kate Llewellyn, give some sense of the spirit and power of the tradition. ▷Aboriginal women writers in English, such as ▷Oodgeroo Noonuccal, ▷Sally Morgan, ▷Aileen Corpus and the dramatist Eva Johnson, while maintaining their separate identity and the authenticity of their cultural voice, are now taking their rightful place in the Australian literary tradition.

Women's writing and the national tradition

The distinctive feature of women's writing in Australia is its energy, its resilience, and its determination to tell the truth, even when this contradicts the comfortable complacencies of Australian belief. The popular perception of Australian life has been that of a society governed by caring, sharing and 'mateship', and characterized by a rugged independence and a strong national pride. The egalitarianism and fairness upon which Australians pride themselves were supposedly born and nurtured in the bush, and were to be found in their purest form among the bush workers. (The most persistent exponent of this view has been Russel Ward in his *The Australian Legend* (1958).) The national male type, according to this view, was the hard-working pioneer, a self-sufficient individualist with a love for the bush and a concern for his (invariably male) 'mates'. The female heroic type was that of mother and martyr who, patiently and usually alone, as in Henry Lawson's 'The Drover's Wife', endured the endless privations of bush life. From the very beginning the women's literary tradition challenged these assumptions at every point. The female tradition has provided the voice of the ▷'other', a voice from the periphery sometimes harmonizing with, but more often challenging the insistent, optimistic, centralist version of Australian life.

Letters and diaries – the autobiographical tradition

The first literature written by white women is made up of the ▷letters, diaries and ▷journals (some still in manuscript form in Australian libraries) in which they insistently record their psychic disorientation, the hardships of female life in the bush, including lonely and dangerous childbirths, and their efforts to construct a life there. Letters, journals and memoirs give a strong sense of the individuality and resourcefulness of their writers and are an invaluable literary, historical and social resource. They are supported by ▷feminist accounts of Australian experience, such as Anne Summers's *Damned Whores and God's Police* (1975) and Miriam Dixson's ▷*The Real Matilda* (1976), and collections of documents such as Beverley Kingston's *The World Moves Slowly* (1977), Ruth Teale's *Colonial Eve* (1978) and Kay Daniels's and Mary Murnane's *Uphill All the Way* (1980).

In women's personal histories we hear the multiple voices of the female colonist, whether convict, like ▷Margaret Catchpole, middle-class, like Louisa Clifton, ▷Eliza

Brown, Georgiana Molloy and ▷Rachel Henning, or more privileged, like the energetic Elizabeth Macarthur, who pioneered the wool industry in the colony during the frequent absences of her more famous husband. Many writers found the landscape arid and featureless; the society – a volatile mixture of ex-convicts, bushrangers, gold-seekers, well-off pastoralists and free emigrants – degrading. Others, such as Ellen Clacy (▷*A Lady's Visit to the Gold Diggings of Australia in 1852–1853*), sensationalized their experience, cashing in on the prevailing interest, in England, in travel literature and tales from dangerous and exotic places.

Among the most interesting of the letters are those of Margaret Catchpole, who was twice sentenced to death for horse-stealing and escaping from Ipswich jail yet, after transportation to Botany Bay, made a successful and prosperous life on a farm near Sydney. Others were not so fortunate, and extracts from the journals of ▷Annie Baxter and Sarah Davenport, included in Lucy Frost's ▷*No Place for a Nervous Lady: Voices from the Australian Bush*, convey not only the perils of the voyage out (Davenport lost two children on board ship and almost died herself) but also the uncertain position of women married to shiftless (Davenport) or hostile (Baxter) husbands.

Others provide valuable historical as well as psychological insights. ▷Louisa Meredith's ▷*My Home in Tasmania During a Residence of Nine Years* (1852), for instance, recounts colonial life from the point of view of the white ruling class and, at the same time, provides a chilling contemporary approval of the massacre of the Tasmanian Aborigines. A number of the writers, including Louisa Meredith, Georgiana Molloy and ▷Louisa Atkinson, were accomplished botanists and artists, and helped to record and classify the Australian flora and fauna. Molloy and Atkinson died tragically at an early age, a consequence of childbirth, victims of the dangerous conditions for women in a frontier society. Women's personal histories, either letters, ▷autobiographies, or fictionalized autobiographies such as ▷Miles Franklin's ▷*My Brilliant Career* and ▷Henry Handel Richardson's ▷*The Getting of Wisdom* also form an important part of 20th-century Australian literature. Joy Hooton's *Stories of Herself When Young* (1990) provides an excellent discussion of Australian women's personal histories and a comprehensive bibliography.

The 19th-century romance tradition

The tradition in Australian women's fiction in the 19th century, in both short stories and novels, is that of romance and melodrama, with its emphasis upon love, marriage and happy endings. The authors of these romances tend to distort reality, creating tales with contrived plots and the over-use of coincidence. At the same time – and this is the distinctive feature of Australian women's writing over two centuries – the early fiction almost invariably provides a clear-eyed and satiric analysis of social injustice. Satiric targets range from the colonial Church, the penal system, the massacre of the Tasmanian Aborigines, to the political situation in Melbourne, where Elizabeth Murray, in her ▷*Ella Norman, or a Woman's Perils* (1864), saw the weak English governor to be at the mercy of a Parliament composed of upstart Irish and ignorant backwoodsmen who wore their blucher boots into the chamber. Of particular concern to women writers was the plight of emigrant women, often despatched by do-gooder societies in England, such as the Female Middle-Class Emigration Society of 1862, in order to find husbands. These young women were pitifully ill-equipped to deal with colonial society and all too often ended up either as governesses (a common euphemism for household drudge) or as prostitutes. The tradition, then, is that of romance, but romance which is leavened by shrewd and often cutting social satire. Moreover the early colonial writers not only discern social evils, but prescribe the remedy, which is, with variations, that of the moral regeneration of society through the rehabilitation of the individual.

It is not surprising then that early fiction such as ▷Mary Vidal's *Tales for the Bush* (1845), Louisa Atkinson's ▷*Gertrude the Emigrant* (1857) and ▷Caroline Leakey's ▷*The*

Broad Arrow (1859) were heavily didactic, warning of the dangers of strong drink and the punishment for moral rectitude. *The Broad Arrow* is the first example of the convict novel, a genre that was to become increasingly important in the male tradition. Its beautiful, high-born and wilful heroine, Maida Gwynnham, is a tragic figure of considerable stature. She is seduced by a scoundrel, bears his child, takes the blame for a crime which he, not she, committed, is transported to Van Dieman's Land, yet must pay with her life to satisfy the author's high-minded notion of justice. In Elizabeth Murray's *Ella Norman, or a Woman's Perils* (1864) another genteel Englishwoman, Mary Hawley, who has been seduced and brutalized by a drunken shanty keeper, is rescued and rehabilitated by her English friends, yet marriage to her former fiancé, who still loves her, is unthinkable.

These works, together with ▷Anna Maria Bunn's *The Guardian* (1838) (the first novel to be written and published by a woman in Australia) and ▷Catherine Spence's ▷*Clara Morison* (1854), mark the true beginning of female fiction in Australia, and from them we can clearly discern the distinctive features of a romance tradition which is also concerned with feminine independence, with politics and social justice. Australian ▷short story writers in the 19th century also favoured romance but, as is demonstrated in Fiona Giles's collection, ▷*From the Verandah: Stories of Love and Landscape by Nineteenth Century Australian Women* (1987), there is a tremendous range of interest and competence within a tradition which includes the work of ▷Mary Fortune ('Waif Wander'), the first Australian writer of detective fiction.

'Tasma', Ada Cambridge and Rosa Praed

More famous romance writers of the latter decades of the 19th century – 'Tasma', whose real name was ▷Jessie Couvreur, ▷Ada Cambridge and ▷Rosa Praed – have been accused of writing vapid romance (in contrast to the tough and realistic male tradition), and also of the over-use of colonial stereotypes, for instance that of the handsome and aristocratic Englishman who carries off a local girl and takes her 'home' to England. Such stereotypes were seen, particularly in the context of the rise of nationalism in the 1880s and 1890s, as an aberration from the dominant (male) literary tradition with its concern for national identity. Couvreur, Cambridge and Praed were excellent writers, cosmopolitan in outlook, who exploited the genre of colonial romance, yet transcended it in order to express their own, often subversive, concerns.

'Tasma', who eventually became the Brussels correspondent for the London *Times*, is mainly concerned with urban experience and satirizes not only the patriarchal family structure, but also the social and financial pretentions of 'marvellous Melbourne'.

Ada Cambridge emigrated to Australia with her clergyman husband, carried out her parish duties in dusty outback towns, bore five children (of whom two died in infancy), and wrote thirty novels, as well as short stories, autobiography and poems. The extent of her disaffection is shown by the satire of marriage and sexuality in her novels, but more especially in her poems. Cambridge's volume of poems ▷*Unspoken Thoughts* (1875) was published anonymously and almost immediately withdrawn from sale. Here Cambridge expresses her indignation with social inequality, with the irrelevance of organized religion, and with the sexual horrors of loveless marriages.

Rosa Praed's interest in the corruption of colonial politics, in the occult and in female relationships (her novel *Affinities*, 1885, has been read as a lesbian text) certainly subverts not only the romance tradition, but also the preoccupation, in the male literary tradition of Henry Lawson, A.B. ('Banjo') Paterson and Joseph Furphy, with 'mateship' and the bush.

Miles Franklin and Barbara Baynton

Two works which were published at the turn of the century – Miles Franklin's *My Brilliant Career* (1901) and ▷Barbara Baynton's ▷*Bush Studies* (1902) – mark a turning point in women's writing. Both utilize the literary modes of the dominant male tradition –

the supposedly realistic yarn and the short story – yet each, in its own way, savagely demolishes the dominant value system.

My Brilliant Career was seen by reviewers as the first truly Australian novel, and was ranked with the works of ▷Olive Schreiner and ▷Emily Brontë. It recounts the efforts of the young and defiant Sybylla Melvyn to come to terms with her life on a struggling dairy farm at Goulburn, and later as governess to an ignorant and filthy bush family. Although it is unequivocal in its love of the Australian landscape, it totally rejects bush life for any woman, let alone a sensitive, aspiring young writer. Most of the women in the bush are, like Sybylla's mother, pathetic drudges. Suitors from among the Australian bushmen are rejected by Sybylla – one of them savagely with a whip.

Barbara Baynton's *Bush Studies*, a series of short stories, is even more savage in its condemnation of conditions for women and children in the Australian bush. One woman is scorned because she is part-Chinese, another abandoned to a miserable existence after her back has been broken by a falling limb, and another raped and murdered by a passing swagman. Grim as these stories are, they are skilfully written and mark a new realism in the Australian women's literary tradition.

Women's fiction in the first half of the 20th century
The tradition of realism persists with the women writers of the first half of the 20th century who are discussed in ▷Drusilla Modjeska's *Exiles at Home: Australian Women Writers 1925–1945* (1981). These writers – Miles Franklin, ▷Marjorie Barnard and ▷Flora Eldershaw (who collaborated on a number of works under the pseudonym of M. Barnard Eldershaw), ▷Eleanor Dark, ▷Katharine Susannah Prichard, ▷Jean Devanny, and the writer and critic ▷Nettie Palmer – were committed both to socialist politics and to the realist tradition. Prichard and Devanny were members of the Communist Party of Australia, and Prichard visited the Soviet Union in 1933.

Prichard's writings, despite certain romantic elements which have excited critical attention (for example in John Hay's essay, 'Betrayed Romantics and Compromised Stoics in Shirley Walker (ed.), *Who Is She? Images of Woman in Australian Fiction*, 1983), exemplify the realist tradition in Australian women's fiction. Her carefully researched novels deal with the life of the timber cutters in the jarrah forests of Western Australia, on the big stations in the north and the mines of Kalgoorlie, with the opal miners and with a travelling circus. The most striking and controversial is ▷*Coonardoo: The Well in the Shadows* (1929), a novel which deals with the relationship between a white station-owner and an Aboriginal girl who bears his son. The implication is that Coonardoo was a wholly appropriate wife for Hugh Watt and that, in rejecting her, he has rejected the land itself.

Jean Devanny also wrote works of social realism, her most striking being ▷*The Butcher Shop* (1926), written in New Zealand and banned in many countries because of its brutal depiction of New Zealand country life. ▷*Sugar Heaven* (1936) deals with the shocking working conditions of the cane-cutters on the North Queensland canefields and the political and sexual activism of its heroine, Dulcie.

Other novels of this period such as ▷Kylie Tennant's ▷*Ride on Stranger* (1943) and ▷Dymphna Cusack's ▷*Come in Spinner* (1951), are more concerned with life in the Australian cities during the Depression and World War II. The most famous Australian writer of this period is undoubtedly ▷Henry Handel Richardson, nominated for the Nobel prize for her services to literature, and author of the great realistic epic of Australian literature ▷*The Fortunes of Richard Mahony* (1930). Most of these writers also attempted the ▷short story form, usually with a great deal of success. The best two short stories of this period are probably Katharine Susannah Prichard's 'The Cooboo' and Marjorie Barnard's 'The Persimmon Tree'.

Poetry
The leading literary figure for the first half of the 20th century, however, was the poet, essayist and autobiographist ▷Mary Gilmore. A nationalist and a radical in politics,

Gilmore managed for over fifty years to both challenge and express the feelings of the Australian people. Her poem ▷'No Foe Shall Gather Our Harvest' provided a rallying point for the Australian nation during the worst times of the Pacific war. Many women poets emerged in 19th-century Australia, such as ▷Eliza Dunlop, ▷Caroline Leakey, Ada Cambridge and ▷Marie Pitt and, after the turn of the century, ▷Zora Cross, but Gilmore was the first woman poet of distinction.

▷Judith Wright, probably Australia's best poet, began to publish during the war. Her first two volumes, ▷*The Moving Image* (1946) and ▷*Woman to Man* (1949), mark the beginning of a more sophisticated, less naively national poetic movement. Many of the early poems, such as 'Bullocky' and 'South of My Days', express the pioneer ethic and transcend it, while the poem 'Woman to Man' is justly celebrated as a moving expression of female sexuality. Wright's poetic career has spanned the period from the 1940s to the present (her latest volume, *Phantom Dwelling*, was published in 1985), and, while still retaining her interest in the Australian landscape, she has moved beyond the Australian poetic tradition into realms of Eastern thought and verse-forms. At the same time she has been politically active, spending much of her energy on conservation issues and in the cause of justice for the Aborigines. ▷Rosemary Dobson, ▷Gwen Harwood and ▷Dorothy Hewett are also major poets of the post-war period.

There has been a dramatic upsurge in the writing and publishing of women's poetry in the last thirty years, and ▷*The Penguin Book of Australian Women Poets* (1986), edited by Susan Hampton and Kate Llewellyn, provides an excellent indication of the diversity and skill of more modern poets such as J.S. Harry, ▷Antigone Kefala, Rhyll McMaster, Jennifer Maiden, Chris Mansell, Jennifer Rankin, ▷Judith Rodriguez, ▷Jennifer Strauss, ▷Vicki Viidikas and ▷Fay Zwicky.

Writing for children

The first children's book written in Australia was Charlotte Barton's *A Mother's Offering to her Children*, by 'A Lady Long Resident in New South Wales' (1841). (Charlotte Barton was the mother of ▷Louisa Atkinson.) In fact, writing for children has always been a popular and acceptable occupation for Australian women. Classics of children's fiction in Australia are ▷*Seven Little Australians* (1894) by ▷Ethel Turner, the ▷*Billabong Series* (1910–1942) by ▷Mary Grant Bruce, *The Little Black Princess* (1905) by ▷Jeannie Gunn and, for smaller children, the ▷*Snugglepot and Cuddlepie Series* (1916–1940) by ▷May Gibbs and the ▷*Blinky Bill Series* (1933–1936) by Dorothy Wall. The last two are notable for their personifications of uniquely Australian flora and fauna, and have formed part of the process of coming to terms with the Australian bush in which children's illustrators such as Ida Rentoul Outhwaite and Pixie O'Harris have also played a leading part.

Ethel Pedley's ▷*Dot and the Kangaroo* (1899) marks a significant turning-point in the relationship between Australian children and the bush. Literature of the 19th century is replete with accounts of lost children perishing in the bush, reflecting an all too common tragedy of bush life. *Dot and the Kangaroo* indicates an increasing fondness for the bush and its creatures. The bush is no longer a feared and alien place, for Dot is rescued, nurtured and returned to her home by the bush creatures.

Modern writers of children's work, such as ▷Hesba Brinsmead, ▷Nan Chauncy and ▷Patricia Wrightson, have continued the tradition of an indigenous literature for children, combining Aboriginal and white, urban and bush themes. The annual Children's Book of the Year Award has fostered an indigenous literature for children (▷Children's literature), much of which reflects the social issues of the time, such as racial injustice.

Writing for theatre, radio and television

Australian women dramatists and scriptwriters have been active in the theatre, radio and television. (▷Dramatists (Australia) and ▷Writers for film and television (Australia).) The ▷New Theatre movement has provided a venue for ideologically committed writers such as ▷Mona Brand, ▷Oriel Gray, ▷Betty Roland and ▷Katharine Susannah Prichard, while others, such as ▷Gwen Meredith, have been highly successful writers for radio.

▷Alma de Groen and ▷Jill Shearer are among the best-known of contemporary dramatists, but Australia's most famous is undoubtedly Dorothy Hewett. Hewett is an energetic and provocative writer who was for a time an active member of the Communist Party of Australia. Her plays, the most successful of which are ▷*The Chapel Perilous* (1972) and ▷*The Man from Muckinupin* (1979), are vital and surrealistic in their melding of myth and romance with social satire, vaudeville and popular song. Hewett has published one novel, *Bobbin Up* (1959), which deals with her experiences as a worker in a spinning mill, an autobiography, ▷*Wild Card* (1990), and a number of volumes of lyric poetry. Hewett is a larger-than-life figure whose considerable literary and dramatic virtuosity enlivens the contemporary Australian scene.

Women's fiction since 1960

The last thirty years have seen a tremendous upsurge in women's fiction in Australia to the extent that publishers, granting bodies and reviewers have been accused (quite wrongly) of a feminist bias. Established writers such as ▷Shirley Hazzard, ▷Elizabeth Harrower, ▷Jessica Anderson, ▷Thea Astley and ▷Christina Stead have continued to publish, each in her own individual style. Hazzard is a cosmopolitan and polished writer who sets much of her work in Italy in order to convey the urbane and timeless values of the classical world. However, her most important novel, ▷*The Transit of Venus* (1980), moves easily between Australia, North America and Europe to demonstrate the workings of love and destiny in the lives of individual women. Elizabeth Harrower is concerned with power relationships within the family, which she sees as a dangerous place for unprotected females. At the same time she does not necessarily favour her female characters, for women such as Lilian in *The Long Prospect* (1958) are among her most skilful tormentors of the young.

Jessica Anderson is a writer with an international reputation whose novels, in particular ▷*Tirra Lirra by the River* (1978), have been compared with those of ▷Jane Austen in their poise and understanding of social and interpersonal dynamics. Thea Astley is a social satirist whose enduring themes are those of the persecution of the vulnerable individual, and the prevalence of colonialism and racism in Australian and Pacific Island countries. Her satire is cutting, her narrative technique experimental, and her linguistic virtuosity often overwhelming.

Of this group of established novelists, the most important is undoubtedly Christina Stead who died in 1983. Her most powerful novels, ▷*The Man Who Loved Children* (1940) and ▷*For Love Alone* (1944), are concerned with the dynamics of struggle, the exercise of the will, and the search for love and artistic integrity.

Novelists of the 1970s and 1980s include ▷Barbara Hanrahan, a South Australian writer and print-maker whose novels are an extraordinary melding of nostalgia, realism, fantasy and the grotesque, with a strong visual element which undoubtedly stems from her artistic training and inclination. A number of modern writers such as ▷Elizabeth Jolley, ▷Glenda Adams and ▷Marion Campbell, writing in a literary climate which is permeated with ▷post-modernist theory, are selfconsciously experimental. The most important of these is undoubtedly Elizabeth Jolley, whose novels are textually complex, often containing reflective fictions within fictions which question the basis of reality. Jolley is concerned with sexual freedom for the individual, with the freedom for women to express themselves without inhibition or shame within lesbian or other relationships, and with the sexual needs of the old, the fat and the ugly. At the same time she is fascinated with the power-play and exploitation which is possible within her unconventional relationships.

Other powerful modern writers are ▷Kate Grenville and ▷Helen Garner. Grenville's most important work, ▷*Lilian's Story* (1986), recounts the life of the fat and eccentric

Lilian Singer (based on a well-known Sydney personality, Bea Miles) who is raped by her father, victimized by society, and whose bizarre behaviour becomes an affront to the genteel and polite. Garner's first novel, ▷*Monkey Grip* (1977), set in the inner-Melbourne suburb of Carlton, deals with communal living, drug-culture, and the exploitation of the heroine by a personable addict. Her other works are also concerned with the *Angst* of the urban scene. All three – Jolley, Grenville and Garner – are skilful and powerful writers who have each also published volumes of short stories.

Short story writing
One of the most striking features of Australian literature has been the tradition, in women's writing, of powerful and realistic short stories which challenge comfortable presumptions about Australian life. This tradition has intensified during the last thirty years with a dramatic upsurge in the quantity and quality of women's short story writing. All of the writers mentioned above have published challenging stories within the realist tradition, but the most striking have been those of ▷Jean Bedford and ▷Olga Masters. Bedford's ▷*Country Girl Again and Other Stories* (1985) is in the tradition of Barbara Baynton's ▷*Bush Studies* in its exposure of the conditions for women and children in both the bush and the city. Olga Masters did not publish fiction until her early 60s, but the volumes she published before her death in 1986 contain some of the most powerful of Australian short stories. Usually set on farms and in the small towns of the Depression years, they are concerned with the lives of women and children caught up in hopeless cycles of poverty, cruelty and geographic isolation.

Migrant writing since World War II
Since World War II Australia has, through successive waves of immigration, entered a new phase as a multicultural society, and the writings of non-Aboriginal women for whom English is a second language (▷Migrant women's writing (Australia).) have added to the vitality and diversity of the literary scene. The work of migrant writers such as ▷Rosa Cappiello, Antigone Kefala and Ania Walwicz is contributing to the rich diversity of women's writing. Critical commentary, notably that of Dr Sneja Gunew, and the bibliographical work of Lolo Houbein, is ensuring that their contribution is recognized.

The critical climate
The 1980s saw not only an upsurge in women's writing in Australia, but also the publication of a great number of commentaries and research guides which have fostered an awareness of a female cultural heritage which had all too often been forgotten. *The Oxford Companion to Australian Literature* (1985), edited by William H. Wilde, Joy Hooton and Barry Andrews, and *Australian Women Writers: A Bibliographic Guide* (1988) by Debra Adelaide (▷Bibliography (Australia).) have both provided invaluable source material for this essay and for the compilation of the alphabetical listing for Australian women's writing. ▷Dale Spender's *Writing a New World: Two Centuries of Australian Women Writers* (1988), the accompanying ▷*Penguin Anthology of Australian Women's Writing* (1988), ▷*The Penguin Book of Australian Women Poets* (1986), edited by Susan Hampton and Kate Llewellyn, Pam Gilbert's ▷*Coming Out from Under: Contemporary Australian Women Writers* (1988), and books of essays such as my own *Who Is She? Images of Woman in Australian Fiction* (1983), Carole Ferrier's ▷*Gender, Politics and Fiction* (1985), and ▷*Poetry and Gender* (1989), edited by David Brooks and Brenda Walker, have all added to a climate where contemporary women's writing flourishes, and where the works of the past, such as women's colonial romances, are being reprinted by presses such as Virago, Pandora and Penguin.

New Zealand and Oceania

Writing by women in New Zealand has, until recently, been viewed as a literature of exceptions within a general field of generic stereotypes. Women's writing is largely seen as outside or irrelevant to the serious concern of mainstream male-authored New Zealand literature. Romantic novels, women's writing, or kitchen-sink realism, the work of women has been categorized in a way that has allowed it to remain largely invisible, with the occasional writer of interest (▷Katherine Mansfield, ▷Janet Frame) appearing isolated, monolithic and as having escaped from the gendered preoccupations of her contemporaries.

However, recent research has shown how a combination of cultural and practical questions has resulted in what ▷Joanna Russ has called the suppression of women's writing. (See Joanna Russ, *How to Suppress Women's Writing*, 1984, also see Heather Roberts, *Where Did She Come From?*, 1989, for a discussion of women writers in New Zealand literary history.) But it is not so much a suppression of writing by women that is evident in New Zealand literary history, as a generic categorization of their work, which relegates women writers to certain fields of writing considered less significant or valuable. The work of ▷Jessie Mackay, for instance, an immensely popular 19th-century poet whose work, though characterized by sentimentality and inappropriate idioms, was hardly less readable than that of her male contemporaries. Her writing was dismissed by E.H. McCormick in his highly influential history *New Zealand Literature: A Survey* (1959) as 'mellifluous, quaint but sterile'. However, McCormick points out that there *is* an area of literary history where the 'feminine and domestic' have pride of place, and that is the 'novels and memoirs which have as their background the farming industry'. (*New Zealand Literature*, p. 42.) Chief among these writers of the 'feminine and domestic' is of course ▷Lady Barker, whose charming and elegant descriptions of her life on a South Island station are regularly reprinted, and who said of the 'lady's influence' in the colony that 'she represents refinement and culture . . . and her footsteps on a new soil such as this should be marked by a trail of light'. (Lady Mary Anne Barker, *Station Life in New Zealand*, 1870, p. 105.)

'Refinement and culture' are the typifying marks of some of the earliest novelists, such as Mrs Aylmer, who wrote *Distant Homes*, which was published in England in 1862, without ever having been to New Zealand. The novelist Mrs Evans (1842–1882), (*Over the Hills and Far Away*, 1874, and *A Strange Friendship*, 1874) wrote for an English readership about English gentry who happen to be in a New Zealand landscape, but one which bears little relation to the scene of privation and difficulty recorded in the journals of early missionaries' wives. (See Alison Drummond ed., *Married and Gone to New Zealand*, 1960, which features extracts from the writings of women pioneers, mostly the wives of missionaries.) One tell-tale remark is that of the Rev Vicesimus Lush who, when asked in the 1850s what aspect of the colony he admired most, replied: 'The workworn hands of the women'.

While letters, journals and memoirs such as ▷Charlotte Godley's *Letters from Early New Zealand* (1930) or Sarah Courage's *Lights and Shadows of Colonial Life* (1897) focused on recording experience of a new country, poets and fiction writers tended to stick to the familiar models of popular English writing – Victorian lyric and ▷romance narrative, stressing a romantic, pre-domestic version of the female. Numbers of short stories by women published in journals such as *The New Zealand Annual* or *The New Zealand*

Illustrated Magazine follow the predictable narratives of courtship romance, and even those writers who focused on masculine activity such as G.B. Lancaster (▷Edith Lyttleton), who wrote stories from a male point of view about surveyors, engineers and stockmen, usually incorporated some romance elements.

By the 1890s the idealization of motherhood and the family propagated by publications like *White Ribbon*, a monthly established by the Women's Christian Temperance Movement, reflected a shift in focus – particularly evident in novels by women – away from courtship romance to the social questions contained in marriage. A number of novelists such as ▷Ellen Ellis, ▷Kathleen Inglewood and ▷Susie Mactier advocate temperance and prohibition as a means of improving the lot of women and families (see *Where Did She Come From?*, pp. 9–36), while more radical writers, like ▷Edith Searle Grossmann and ▷Jean Devanny, related alcohol to much larger questions of equity and gender roles. Even the romantic novelists, like ▷Louisa Baker who published large numbers of novels under the pseudonym 'Alien', and ▷Constance Clyde, raised questions about the status of women in marriage and stressed the role of women in maintaining social values.

The political implications of writing by women became clearer in the work of Jean Devanny, a communist writing in the 1920s and 1930s, Edith Searle Grossmann, writing in the 1890s and ▷Jane Mander, who is the best known of the early-20th-century women novelists. Their fiction represents domesticity and the family as the primary location of gender politics and social/sexual revolution. A clear line of political/polemical fiction using some of the conventions of romance narrative can be traced, running from the Temperance movement through to Devanny and Mander, and reflecting the issues and conflicts which are central to female experience, widening in Devanny's case into class ideologies.

Few women writers tackled questions of race, and those who did in the early 20th century, such as ▷B.E. Baughan, in her stories *Brown Bread from a Colonial Oven* (1912) did so from a colonial point of view, paternalistically and sentimentally. Later writers have been more outspoken. ▷Robin Hyde (Iris Wilkinson), for example, wrote about the dispossessions of Maori, particularly in her journalism.

The focus of most of Hyde's fictional work was gender-related, especially on the question of the freedom of women to act independently of conventional social roles. She was the natural successor to Devanny and Mander and became well known for her unconventional attitudes. Hyde thought of herself initially as a poet, but never became part of the main tradition of New Zealand poetry, unlike her near contemporary ▷Mary Ursula Bethell, whose gardening and religious poetry seemed to her male audience to correspond to a nationalist mythography of cultural identity. Poet and writer D'Arcy Cresswell (1896–1960) said of Bethell's work that New Zealand was not really discovered until Bethell, 'earnestly digging', raised her head to look at the mountains. Along with the later poet ▷Eileen Duggan, whose work reflects both her Catholicism and her sense of a regional landscape, Bethell has been frequently represented in important anthologies.

However, the work of many women poets did not conform to dominant ideas of what was significant in poetry, as is amply illustrated by ▷Riemke Ensing's anthology ▷*Private Gardens* (1977). Often poetry concentrated on the domestic and personal as a primary location of meaning, which, combined with the longstanding association of women writers with 'refinement and culture', has been to the detriment of their literary reputations. Moreover, it has been used as a judgement on their personal lives. Perhaps New Zealand's most famous example of a writer who resisted refinement and culture in her life and work is Katherine Mansfield, who established herself as a European modernist and whose life has attracted as much international attention as her work. Mansfield has never fitted comfortably into New Zealand literary history, but she can stand as an extreme example of the lengths a woman writer would go to escape from the conventional expectations of a family-based small society. But in literary terms Mansfield cannot be said to represent anything about New Zealand as a place of literary production; for example, the kinds of connections made by critic Heather Roberts between social movements such as Temperance and the work of women novelists do not have any relevance to Mansfield's work. Like ▷Greville Texidor, who came to New Zealand as a refugee in the 1940s, Mansfield retained in the country of her birth the status of itinerant (though acute) observer writing for an audience constructed elsewhere.

By the time Janet Frame appeared on the scene in the 1950s, writing by women in New Zealand literary journals was represented by a few well-known names who appeared fairly regularly, and a larger quantity of writers who contributed occasionally. Popular writers like ▷Ngaio Marsh, ▷Mary Scott and ▷Essie Summers, who published large numbers of novels and were read by a local as well as international readership, have only recently made it into the house of literature. The numbers of women who wrote for children, from ▷Edith Howes in the 1920s to well-known ▷Margaret Mahy in the 1980s, have similarly been invisible to 'serious' literary commentators until recently.

New Zealand's major 20th-century novelist Janet Frame made her appearance in 1951 with the publication of her short story collection, *The Lagoon*, but it has taken many years and wide international recognition for Frame to become a household name in New Zealand. Frame's novels, stories and poems are notable for their resistance to the comfortable certainties that might seem to construct 'refinement and culture' in writing by women. Not only has Frame never withdrawn from a conventionally taboo subject (female sexuality, and particularly the bodily existence of women, has always been a focus of her writing), she has questioned all forms of certainty and structure in her fiction; from the procedures of institutions such as mental hospitals (*Faces in the Water*, 1961) to language, subjectivity and gender. Recently the three volumes of her autobiography have elaborated connections between her life and her work and thrown particular emphasis on the way in which her experience as a female and as a member of an impoverished working class family contributed to the radical unconventionality of her work. Although Frame cannot be said to have had direct successors in fictional writing, her work effectively broke down preconceptions about writing generally, and particularly about writing by women. Much of her fiction constructs domestic 'life' and the family as the place in which there is least certainty of meaning, and also most danger (as well as reward). Frame's later novels are set as much in the States as they are in New Zealand and so help to put the kinds of questions she characteristically explores into a wider context, moving her fiction away from the kind of regional experience – including the classic voyage to Britain – of New Zealand and particularly Otago, in the 1950s. Later writers have, in a sense, caught up with Frame, in their focus on the way in which femaleness is constructed in language. But where Frame was always formally innovative in her fictional structures, women writers of the 1970s tended to stick to social and expressive realism as their preferred medium.

Like most other Western countries, New Zealand experienced a great increase in the numbers of published women writers in the 1970s, a phenomenon that appears to have been generated by the women's movement and its determined efforts to rewrite literary history. Many of these writers in New Zealand – ▷Lauris Edmond, ▷Fiona Kidman, ▷Sue McCauley, ▷Rachel McAlpine, ▷Cilla McQueen, ▷Elizabeth Smither – explicitly addressed their work to a feminist readership and explored gender-based social and political questions, as well as simply making work by women visible in a way it hadn't been previously. Sue McCauley has said of her youth in the 1950s:

> When I was young there was a terrible dearth of books about women – or about New Zealand for that matter. Most of the stuff I read wasn't relevant to me. It wasn't about New Zealand; it wasn't written by women and the men that were writing it weren't covering territory that related to my ordinary, everyday experiences. (Interview with Sue Kedgley in *Our Own Country*, 1989, p. 41.)

A number of ▷Maori women writers, most notably ▷Patricia Grace and ▷Keri Hulme, also became well known at this time, undoubtedly also benefiting from the greater openness towards and access to published work by women, though in fact Maori women writers had been publishing continuously through the late 1950s and 1960s. Although ▷J. C. Sturm's collection *The House of the Talking Cat* was not published until 1983, her stories appeared in the 'Maori Magazine' *Te Ao Hou* during the 1950s and 1960s along with those of Arapera Blank (▷Arapera Hineira), Rora Pahi, and other Maori writers.

When Grace and Hulme published in the 1970s they were acclaimed as the first Maori women writers, but in fact were the first whose work appeared in book form to a wider readership. Since then Grace's work and Hulme's famous novel ▷*the bone people* have made writing by Maori women visible on an international scale, and many other writers have begun to appear in what is the most important diversification of New Zealand literature since it had its origins in the work of European men. A recent collection *Tahuri* (1989) by ▷Ngahuia Te Awekotoku takes the double marginality of being Maori and lesbian for its focus, commenting historically on both kinds of invisibility. ▷Lesbian fiction, futurist feminist fiction, ▷magic realism and ▷postmodern fiction have all been part of the diversification of women writers away from 'refinement and culture', as has work in non-fictional fields such as oral history. Poetry, traditionally perhaps the most restricted area for women writers, has now become, with the advent of feminism, a genre in which the outspokenness of women like Rachel McAlpine, Cilla McQueen or ▷Dinah Hawken is matched by the technical sophistication of ▷Michele Leggott, ▷Jenny Bornholdt or ▷Elizabeth Nannestad. Since the gendered connection has been made between the bookbuying public and the work of women writers, publishing opportunities for women have appeared everywhere, and the result is a large quantity of highly accomplished writing from women of increasing race and class diversity. While women writers in New Zealand may have abandoned their role as bringers of some kind of refinement, their activity in representing culture in a trail of light has never been so blazing.

Oceania

The literature of the Pacific region – which includes Papua New Guinea, Vanuatu, Solomon Islands, Tuvalu, Tokelau, Kiribati, Western Samoa, Fiji, Nuie, Cook Islands and Tonga – is generally referred to as Oceanian. It is a region which has more than 1200 indigenous languages, and for whom written literatures are a relatively recent phenomenon after centuries of oral tradition in which women played a central part. Albert Wendt, the major novelist of Oceania, has described his Samoan childhood as typical of most in that he spent every evening listening to the 'good yarns' told by his grandmother: 'She was steeped in Samoan culture and the Bible, and she spoke fairly fluent English. Every night she would reward us with *Fagogo*.' (Albert Wendt interviewed by Marjorie Crocombe in *The Mana Annual of Creative Writing*, p. 45.)

A few texts by women writers appeared earlier in the 20th century, for example Florence (Johnny) Frisbie's *The Frisbies of the South Seas* (1916), and *Miss Ulysses from Puka-puka* (1948), both autobiographical, and Tom and Lydia Davis's *Doctor to the Islands* (1955). But writing by Pacific women, like that of Pacific men, began to appear in the late 1960s and early 1970s, in association with writing groups set up initially at the University of Papua New Guinea and then the various branches of the University of the South Pacific. ▷Vanessa Griffen and others set up the University of the South Pacific Arts Centre (UNISPAC) with the aim of promoting creative writing, and in 1973 ▷Marjorie Crocombe set up the South Pacific Creative Arts Society to encourage writers and artists. Members of SPCAS published in the *Pacific Islands Monthly* and eventually in the group's own journal *Mana*, founded in 1976.

Oceanian written literature has its origins in the colonial activity of missionaries who transcribed local languages and introduced printing, but took its more recent impetus from the independence movement within the region. (See Subramani, *South Pacific*

Literature: from Myth to Fabulation, 1985.) The experience of colonialism (French, German, British, American, Australian and New Zealand) is an insistent subject in Oceanian writing as well as providing the medium for a different kind of independence. As Marjorie Crocombe has said:

> Denigrated, inhibited and withdrawn during the colonial era, the Pacific people are again beginning to take confidence and express themselves in traditional forms . . . that remain part of a valued heritage, as well as in new forms and styles reflecting the changes within the continuity of the unique world of our island cultures . . . (Marjorie Crocombe, quoted in introduction to *Lali: a Pacific Anthology*, 1980, ed. Albert Wendt, p. xiii.)

The new Oceanian literature, as Wendt has pointed out, both 'examines (and laments) often angrily, the effects of colonialism. It argues for the speeding up of decolonisation; the development of cultural and national and individual identity . . .' (*Lali.*, p. xvi.)

For women writers such as Vanessa Griffen, ▷Marjorie Crocombe, ▷Konai Helu Thaman, ▷Jully Sipolo, ▷Momoe von Reiche and ▷ Tili Peseta the questions of identity associated with postcolonialism involve gender as well as national issues. These writers, and the other women who publish occasionally in Oceanian journals, typically focus on family structures, cultural and social contexts and the place and role of women within them. Thaman's long poem 'You, the Choice of My Parents', described by Subramani in *South Pacific Literature* as among the 'best dozen or so poems in the new literature', engages with the double oppression of race-colonialism and gender. In her poem 'My Blood' Thaman writes:

> No brother . . .
> My problem is not 'exploitation'
> Or unequal pay, or unawareness;
> My problem is that I
> have been betrayed and tramped on
> By my own blood.

Thaman's poetry represents the place of women in traditional culture as one that is no longer unchallenged. The work of Momoe von Reiche raises similar questions within the context of cultural conflict and loss of tradition. In the work of women writers, Oceanian literature is a literature governed by the connections between identity, culture, politics and gender. As in the work of male writers, the oral literatures of the region form part of the textual strategies of women writers, creating a rich mix of traditional and contemporary reference, juxtaposing Polynesian legend and matriarchal tale-telling with the story of female life in the alien cultures of New Zealand, the US or Australia. The political context of colonialism is explicit in the work of women writers such as ▷Loujaya M. Kouza, but coexists with the transference of oral tradition into written texts, as in the work of a number of writers featured in local collections such as the *Mana* issue devoted to the Solomon Islands. (*Mana*, Vol. 4, No. 1.) It is this mix of postcolonial and traditional literatures that characterizes Oceanian literature.

▷Children's literature, New Zealand; Maori literature; Romance writing, New Zealand; Anthologies, New Zealand.

28 East Africa

The title of ▷Muthoni Likimani's poem ▷*What Does A Man Want?* (1974), a series of monologues by women speakers who have failed to integrate the conflicting demands of family and work, is a reminder of the sexual polarization of the world of the East African woman writer. (For the purposes of this report East Africa comprises Kenya, Uganda and Tanzania, a broad geo-political territory, in which considerable differences of ethnicity, language and colonial and national history pertain. The ethnic origins and country of birth of each writer mentioned will be found in the author entries.) In a recent interview the Kenyan novelist and playwright ▷Asenath Odaga observed that 'the male has always been dominant in Africa; this is their world, the society is theirs.' (Adeola James (ed.), *In Their Own Voices, African Women Writers Talk*, 1990, p. 129.) That this remark was apparently made without rancour, simply in pragmatic recognition of the status quo, reinforces this sense of polarization.

The world of the woman writer in Africa is defined by gender for historical reasons. It is a matter of debate whether patriarchal culture came over with the white colonialists or is inherent in African society, but it is evident that, in addition to the female roles prescribed within traditional culture, contacts with Islam and the West brought new sets of relationships that affected the condition of women. European colonization and traditional African attitudes combined to exclude women from those educational processes that prepare for the craft of writing. The routine of African women's lives as childbearers and rearers, agricultural workers and water carriers impedes literary creativity. The requirements, described by ▷Virginia Woolf for the woman writer, of leisure and solitude, have no place in the lives of the majority of African women. Whether trying to liberate herself from negative aspects of traditional culture or caught between the conflicting worlds of Africa and the West, the African woman meets conditions which inhibit and repress. And since literature does not passively reflect but transmutes and searches for new realities, what is striking about much writing by East African women is its failure to project new roles.

From this gender polarization much else follows. Like their 19th-century counterparts in Europe, East African women in the 20th century have had slower access to education than men. ▷Pamela Kola says of the Kenyan situation, 'Education was given to men first. If you don't have the basic education you are not exposed to other people in different spheres of life, how can you write?' (*In Their Own Voices*, p. 49.) And the Tanzanian ▷Penina Muhando makes the same point that 'women have suffered historically, being left behind even when they are very capable, because of the structure of society.' (See Carol Boyce Davies's attempt to define what she calls 'an African feminist consciousness' in *Ngambika: Studies of Women in African Literature*, 1986.)

Statements like these illustrate the different priorities of Western and African feminism. Feminism is by definition an individualistic ideology, in contrast to the communal nature of African society. As a Western discourse it continues to be debated and qualified by African and African-American women writers and critics like ▷Alice Walker, ▷Ama Ata Aidoo and ▷Buchi Emecheta. The use of concepts from Western critical theories as an aspect of cultural appropriation is central to this debate. (*Ngambika*, p. 86.) The term 'pragmatic feminism' used later in this report is an attempt to recognize this debate and the problems of cultural production faced by African women writers.

Creative writing in English by men in East Africa emerged at a later date than in many other parts of the continent because of the relatively recent establishment of colonialism in comparison with West and Southern Africa. It was only in the middle decade of the 20th century, with the establishment of Makerere College in Uganda, that literary activity took off. In these early days Makerere had a cosmopolitan and international character reflecting the inter-territorial outlook that was central to British colonial policy in East Africa. It rapidly became the centre of an East African intellectual élite, out of which was to grow the University of East Africa with its constituent colleges at Nairobi and Dar es Salaam as well as Makerere. The English department at Makerere ran a student literary magazine, *Penpoint*, established in 1958 by the English lecturer David Cook. The contributors to *Penpoint*, one of whose early editors was Jonathan Kariara, included the Malawian poet David Rubadiri, the Kenyan novelist James Ngugi (later Ngugi wa Thiong'o) and two women, ▷Rebeka Njau and ▷Grace Ogot, both among the first graduates of Makerere, and now East Africa's best-known women writers.

It is misleading, of course, to suggest that the only creative writing in East Africa was that produced in English. Alongside the oral art of the region, written Swahili poetry had been in existence for several centuries. However, the Makerere Conference of African Writers of English in June 1962 acted as an important catalyst for budding East African authors, and the publication of Ngugi's *Weep Not Child* (1964) and the Ugandan poet Okot p'Bitek's *Song of Lawino* (1966) led to a burst of creativity in English in East Africa. In 1965 the East African Publishing House was established, issuing its first novels in 1966.

Although the 'white settler' writing of Elspeth Huxley and ▷Karen Blixen has contributed powerfully to the mythologizing of East Africa by the white imagination, it is a product of a relatively brief set of historical circumstances. If this white settler writing is discounted as belonging to the European tradition, the first woman novelist in East Africa is Grace Ogot, whose novel ▷*The Promised Land* (1966) was one of the earliest to come from the East African Publishing House, and the first piece of imaginative writing in English by a member of the Luo tribe. The novel centres on the clash between personal ambition and domestic ties, while recounting the move of Luo pioneers to Tanzania in search of a better life. Typical of its period, it reveals Ogot's interest in collecting traditional folk tales and re-creating the African past. The novel is subtitled 'a true fantasy', indicating the blending of romance or 'gothic' situations with contemporary settings and issues, which is the formula for Ogot's two collections of short stories, ▷*Land Without Thunder* (1968) and *The Other Woman* (1976). In *The Form of the African Novel* (1979), critic Kole Omotoso suggests that traditions of orature provide the basis for what Western critics have called ▷magic realism. Ogot uses aspects of traditional culture, like magic and witchcraft, in such a way that the reader is free to choose between a 'rational' or a 'magical' explanation.

Reclaiming the African past was a predictable theme for African writers in the 1960s. Destroying the colonial myth that Africa, before the arrival of the Europeans, was without a history, and recording African traditions at a time when they seemed to be rapidly disappearing, was an urgent task for writers like the Nigerian Chinua Achebe and Ngugi wa Thiong'o in Kenya. In the same way in which writers like Buchi Emecheta in Nigeria and Ama Ata Aidoo in Ghana have shown that the past looks different from a woman's perspective, East African women writers have demystified traditional life as well as celebrating its diversity and richness. The urge to celebrate the past and defend its threatened traditions is evident in ▷Barbara Kimenye's two collections of Ganda village tales, ▷*Kalasanda* (1965) and *Kalasanda Revisited* (1966). During the colonial period the Ganda region of Uganda had experienced relatively little disruption of its traditional political system, and this and the fact that Kimenye is writing for a Western audience, as her introduction to the second collection makes clear, explains the absence of social tension, the prevailing comic tone and the peaceful resolutions of her short stories.

The wave of terror that followed Idi Amin's coup of 1971 radically affected the intellectual life of Uganda. ▷Elvania Namukwaya Zirimu's poem 'Fighting in the Village', first published in a student journal at Leeds in the mid-1960s and republished in the journal *Dhana* after Amin's coup, explores the political and social problems that led to the rise of Amin. Best known as a dramatist, Zirimu mourns the loss of traditional values, overwhelmed by European materialism, in her short play *Keeping up with the Mukasas* (1965). ▷*Family Spear*, one of the runners-up in the BBC's African Theatre Competition of 1971, looks at the conflict between old and new from the woman's point of view. Muweesi defies tradition when he refuses to allow his father to 'break the ground' with his young bride, Birungi. In this struggle Zirimu suggests that there are no easy answers. The play ends tragically with the departure of the younger generation and the death of the father.

As *Family Spear* indicates, celebrating the African past as part of the process of liberation is by no means simple for the African woman writer when it is precisely such aspects of traditional life which are the source of the problem. The Nigerian critic Omalara Ogundipe-Leslie has remarked that it is easier to eliminate the colonial influences that were imposed from outside than to eliminate generations of tradition from within African society. Consequently, one of the tasks of the African woman writer has been to highlight those customs that operate as institutionalized forms of male oppression of women. Central to these is the institution of slavery. The dominant archetype for African women's experience in the novels of Buchi Emecheta is the figure of the futilely defiant slave girl, ordered to be buried alive by her male master. Grace Ogot's short story 'The Rain Came' (1964) is an ironic social comment on the same theme of female sacrifice. In Ogot's tale, Oganda, a chief's daughter, is to be sacrificed to the water-god to bring rain. In the event she survives and the rains nevertheless come. Another way women are oppressed is through polygamy, the focus of ▷Miriam Were's novel ▷*The Eighth Wife* (1972), which explores the feelings of Murugi, lonely and frustrated as a result of her position in a polygamous household. In Ogot's short story 'The Wayward Father' the central character stays with her husband, though he has destroyed her love for him by getting a young girl pregnant and then taking her as his second wife.

The circumcision of women is the issue that most divides opinion between Africa and the West. A barbaric custom from the point of view of missionary Christianity, a means of social control from the point of view of Western feminism, circumcision is much more problematic for the African woman, who may condemn the practice in theory but may be emotionally reluctant to abandon so entrenched an aspect of her heritage. Mariana in Rebeka Njau's *The Scar* (1965) is committed to freeing the young women of her village from oppressive aspects of Kikuyu custom, particularly circumcision. A strong and progressive character, her childless and husbandless lifestyle and radical statements pose a threat to the status quo:

> I want them to free themselves from slavery,
> I want them to respect their bodies and minds
> I want them to break away the chains
> That have so long
> Bound them. (Rebeka Njau, *The Scar*, 1965, pp. 13–14.)

Mariana's struggle fails when the local pastor reveals that he is the father of a child she bore when she was sixteen. She admits defeat and leaves the village.

Njau is clearly making a feminist statement in *The Scar*, but more ambivalent in its attitude to circumcision and therefore more typical is ▷Muthoni Likimani's novel ▷ *They Shall Be Chastised* (1974). Likimani is the daughter of one of the first Anglican ministers in Kenya and it is not surprising that her novel is a literary attempt at reconciling Christianity and traditional cultural practices. *They Shall Be Chastised* shows that women are forced to fight against both the narrow confines of traditional custom and the equally narrow standards of Christian culture. Like Ngugi wa Thiong'o in *The River Between* (1965) Likimani recognizes the female bonding of circumcision, 'You associate yourself with those in your circumcision age group. You work as a team . . . You are all one, helping one another.' (Muthoni Likimani, *They Shall Be Chastised*, 1974, p. 109.) Reconciliation is again evident in ▷Charity Waciuma's ▷*Daughter of Mumbi* (1969), one of the best works produced by the Emergency in Kenya (1952–6), when the Mau Mau, members of the Kikuyu tribe, revolted against British rule. It is a moving record of those tragic years, seen through the eyes of a young Kikuyu girl, and is set against a background of culture clash. Waciuma makes evident the strain on both circumcised and uncircumcised girls caught up in this clash of cultures.

The turbulent years of the Emergency inevitably formed a major theme for Kenyan writers. As Jacqueline Bardolph has written, it seems to have a lasting appeal beyond immediate political relevance, 'it is in literature a permanent source for probing, for examining, the nature of national identity, for the problem of divided loyalties, the actual meaning of all suffering.' (Jacqueline Bardolph, 'The Literature of Kenya', in *The Writing of East and Central Africa*, ed. G. D. Killam, 1984, p. 39.) For Ngugi wa Thiong'o, Mau Mau was central to the struggle against colonialism and neo-colonialism in Africa and he has frequently commented on the heroic role played by Kenyan women 'in the fighting in the forests and mountains, and in prisons and detention camps, and in the homes'. (Ngugi wa Thiong'o, *Barrel of a Pen, Resistance to Repression in Neo-Colonial Kenya*, 1983, p. 41.) In *The Trial of Dedan Kimathi* (1976), co-authored with Ngugi, ▷Micere Githae Mugo deliberately shifts the focus from the great heroic figure of Kimathi, the Mau Mau freedom fighter, to the strength of the women and their contribution to the liberation struggle, because 'whereas the part that the men played in the struggle has been recorded by historians and biographers, the women on the whole have simply been forgotten.' (*In Their Own Voices*, p. 99.) Muthoni Likimani's latest work of fiction, *Passbook Number F47927: Women and Mau Mau in Kenya* (the title a reference to Likimani's identity number during the Mau Mau struggle) also offers heroic images of Kenyan women:

> We read about men in detention, but nobody said there was also a gang of women guerrillas fighting, carrying guns, hiding and feeding the Mau Mau. Even the prostitutes incited the white soldiers and got their guns after getting their men to beat them. These women made their own contribution, and they were reliable spies. Yet nobody talks about them. (*In Their Own Voices*, p. 60.)

The most revealing and symptomatic novel to have been written so far by an East African woman writer is Rebeka Njau's *Ripples in the Pool* (1975), a strikingly powerful symbolic work, interweaving psychological 'gothic' elements with social analysis. *Ripples in the Pool* contains one of the most disturbing representations of madness in African fiction in its portrayal of Selina, the deracinated urban woman, victim of the combined forces of tradition – her barrenness a punishment for her evil ways according to traditional norms – and of the new freedom of choice for women. Njau is too intelligent and complex a writer to suggest that Selina's fate is the result of her rejection of tradition: Selina is the victim of all the contradictions and confusions of an unstable society, and her creator has the true novelist's gift of translating the moment of history into resonant archetypes:

> I broke away completely from my childhood. I changed my name even. It helped me to forget I was an outcast, an illegitimate child. Life was good in the city. I made friends. Men waved to me from their cars. They gave me rides in their Mercedes. They bought me clothes and perfumes. I began walking in the streets like a woman of fashion. Everyone knew me in Pumwani, Majengo, and Eastleigh. I became a queen in the narrow streets of the city after dark. Men fought over me in bars and money came to me in plenty. Man after man came, and I played with them like we play with a pack of cards. Success came. I moved up to the highest rung on the ladder. White men used my body and paid highly for it. I tell you these things so that you may understand my sickness. (Njau, *Ripples in the Pool*, 1975, p. 65.)

Suffering herself, she inflicts suffering on others, coercing the unwilling Gaciru into a lesbian relationship – a depiction rare in African literature – and eventually killing her in a fit of destructive rage. Selina's madness is preceded by that of one of the other characters,

Karuga's mother, driven mad because of her failure to integrate her African identity with that offered to her by the missionaries: 'She preached the "new faith" to the whole village. But she found herself unwelcome in every house she entered. The villagers talked about her and her "new faith". She began to feel haunted. She dreamt of devils pursuing her. Fear followed her everywhere.' (*Ripples in the Pool*, p. 58.)

Ripples in the Pool anticipates the depiction of neo-colonialism in James Ngugi's *Petals of Blood* (1977) and contains the same quest to find the healing sources within traditional society which will renew the troubled present. But it is a much bleaker novel, especially in what it suggests about the future for women in Kenya. Adeola James has referred to 'the environment of failure' in Njau's writing (*In Their Own Voices*, p. 105.); and as a parable of social change in a violent and disrupted period *Ripples in the Pool* shows female aspiration defeated (in spite of the images of renewal and rebirth with which the novel ends), and in its depiction of Selina's psychic stress offers a moving portrayal of the deadlocked position of the African woman.

Appropriately, since the end of the Decade of Women was celebrated in Kenya in 1985 new voices have emerged reflecting the diversity of writing by East African women. East African writing has never been homogeneous; as the critic Chris Wanjala has remarked, 'the different cultural policies of East African government have escalated conflicting theories in the East African Community.' ('Imaginative Writing Since African Independence: the East African Experience', in *The East African Experience: Essays in English and Swahili Literature*, ed. Ulla Schild, 1980, p. 24.) Nevertheless, there are shared themes and aspirations, the most urgent being the need to reconcile the traditional identities of women with the demands of the modern world. Although the young woman narrator in Miriam Were's ▷ *Your Heart Is My Altar* (1980) comments bleakly, 'What was there in this world for a youngster that happened to be a woman? Someday there must be an answer', women's writing in East Africa is becoming more assertive and less prone to project images of suffering and defeat. There is a general consensus that women write under severe constraints, chief of which is still the sexual divisions in society. The East African women writers interviewed by Adeola James for *In Their Own Voices*, 1990, share a well articulated awareness that, as ▷ Asenath Odaga puts it, 'to be black and female means that you are at a disadvantage in this world and in our society today.' (*In Their Own Voices*, p. 123.) In general the feminism of East African women writers is a pragmatic one. Muthoni Likimani is typical in combining her writing with the demands of work and family; she is a broadcaster and producer and owns a company that publishes the *Kenya Food Directory* and *Fashion and Beauty*. Similarly Penina Muhando argues that the woman issue cannot be separated from the overall problems 'since women cannot be separated from the rest of society. I believe that the liberation of women has to be part of the liberation of the society itself.' (*In Their Own Voices*, p. 82.) Rebeka Njau suggests that women are not courageous enough to come out and unite on social and political issues and that they are overburdened with work, 'Time is not there; they have too many children and they are busy looking after the family in the evening and working during the day.' (*In Their Own Voices*, p. 107.) Asenath Odaga emphasizes the 'traditional beliefs and practices which put you down and make it difficult for you to be as free as if you were not married and not an African'. (*In Their Own Voices*, p. 124.) She adds that she could not write if she did not have a husband to support her, 'In Africa it is only Achebe and probably Ngugi and Soyinka who can live on their writings. I . . . don't think there is an African woman who can live solely on her writing.' (*In Their Own Voices*, p. 127.)

On the same point Penina Muhando says that writing in Tanzania is unprofitable because of a limited readership, a common constraint of African writers: 'Generally speaking, Africans have not cultivated the habit of reading, we are an oral people.' (*In Their Own Voices*, p. 89.) And Muthoni Likimani reiterates this: 'I rarely publish novels, they are difficult to sell.' (*In Their Own Voices*, p. 61.) It follows from this that the preferred aesthetic is a functional one: Likimani likes literature to be about 'issues' and Muhando says that art for art's sake has no place in Tanzania. Her play *Harakati za Ukombozi* (*Liberation Struggles*) is a critical assessment of the history of struggle in Tanzania from the pre-colonial period to the development of *Ujaama* (socialist) politics. She is committed to writing plays that are directly concerned with social problems, as a title such as *Talaka si mke wangu* (*Woman, I Divorce You*) indicates.

Micere Mugo is an exception to the general sense of a pragmatic feminism. Exiled from her homeland, Kenya, since 1982 for political reasons and now living in Zimbabwe, she does not consider herself an exile, as the struggle there is part of the same one that embraces the whole of Africa. Mugo's writing is consciously ideological: 'A writer has to develop a special sensibility and a specified ideological position in order to show people in which direction the imagination is going.' (*In Their Own Voices*, p. 95.) As a committed Marxist she considers that the role of the progressive writer who aligns herself with the suffering majority is to create a consciousness by the kind of poems, novels and drama she writes. She sees African women doubly oppressed by class and by patriarchy, and her call to African women writers is to find ways of reaching the mass of African women and speaking for them.

Another dominant note, and one which links contemporary East African literary production with earlier writing, is a continuing interest in the oral tradition and in the question of language. Although the male writers came first in all parts of Africa, in the oral tradition women have always been prominent. Several writers are conscious of themselves as inheritors of an oral culture. A unique insight into the persistence of traditional ways of looking at the world in the contemporary situation is given by ▷Jane Tapsubei Creider in *Two Lives: My Spirit and I* (1986), two autobiographies in one, the life of the author, a Nandi woman now resident in Canada, and the life of the first Tapsubei, one of Creider's ancestors, of whom she believes herself to be a reincarnation. Pamela Kola writes traditional folk tales which she produces first in her native tongue Dho-Luo, the language in which the tales were first told to her by her mother, then translates them herself into English. Asenath Odago writes in both English and Luo. Clearly it is audience, ideology and national culture that determine choice of language. Njau writes in English for an African audience but wishes she could write in her own Kikuyu language, 'but then I know that I have a bigger audience if I write in English'. (*In Their Own Voices*, p. 107.) In contrast, Muhando, Professor of Theatre Arts at the University of Dar es Salaam, writes in Kiswahili because of her desire to communicate first and foremost with her Tanzanian and East African audience.

Representations of women in the formula fictions of popular literature are a valuable source of ideological signification. There is evidence of Western-style romance fiction, of the Mills and Boon type, produced for the recently literate urban reader, illustrating, as the critic Elizabeth Knight has pointed out, a kind of cultural imperialism. (A. S. Gérard (ed.), *European-Language Writing in Sub-Saharan Africa*, 1986.) The ethos of such fiction is urban, individualistic and materialistic, with the pursuit of happiness as the overriding theme. Typical here is ▷Pat Wambui Ngurukie, whose writing is a fascinating attempt to grapple with the problems besetting women in modern Kenyan society from an ideological perspective that is both progressive and conservative. Ngurukie's heroines have invariably internalized the values of their society, their aspirations reveal the roles offered to women and their achievements reinforce the strongly family-centred frame within which the author is operating. *I Will Be Your Substitute* (1984) revolves around Nyokabi, a wealthy orphan who, after various misadventures, is happily married to the Asian, Sanjay, and at the end of the novel is the proud mother of two children. Nyokabi is the child of 'civilised Christian parents' (Pat Wambui Ngurukie, *I Will Be Your Substitute*, 1984, p. 2.), takes her vacations at the Europeanized resort, Nyali beach, and, notwithstanding the sexual warfare of the romance genre, is happy to take her place in society as wife and mother. Ngurukie's intention is to reconcile Asian and African and to reject those aspects of tradition which inhibit integration – Nyokabi's family do not request a dowry for her. In

Soldier's Wife (1989) the same author deals bravely with the theme of male infidelity and second marriage.

▷Marjorie Olhude Macgoye, a poet, but better known as a novelist, writes for a very different audience. Her *Murder in Majengo* (1972) is an acclaimed thriller written for the Oxford University Press New Fiction from Africa series. Her first novel to be published in Britain, ▷ *Coming to Birth*, won the Sinclair Prize for Fiction in 1986. Set in Nairobi in 1956 against the background of the politics of independence, this novel explores the theme of a failed marriage, childlessness and the central character's subsequent success as an independent woman.

The continued development of women's writing in East Africa, like that in other parts of Africa, is in the hands of writers like Asenath Odaga who is setting up her own publishing company to encourage young writers. 'The publishers we have here', she says, 'are foreigners, multinationals. They are here not to develop local writers but to make money. They only accept what they think will sell internationally.' (*In Their Own Voices*, p. 130.) She wants to publish books in the various local languages and, in so doing, to encourage women's literacy: 'I won't make lots of money, but I hope I will make a lot of literature.' (*In Their Own Voices*, p. 131.) If, as Ama Ata Aidoo has suggested, the revolutionizing of Africa hinges on the woman question, East African women writers have added their voices to the liberation of the continent.

DOROTHY DRIVER

29 Southern Africa

Southern African culture is multilingual, multicultural, and patriarchal. Male domination has existed, and still exists, in different ways across different groups, complicated, of course, by race and class oppression. However, women have played a central part in cultural life, although one not necessarily antagonistic to hierarchies of gender, race or class.

Most Southern Africans speak two, and often three or more languages, sometimes as part of daily life. But for literary purposes, English generally operates as a *lingua franca*, although literature is published in Afrikaans and African languages as well. While most Southern Africans who read and write in English are doing so in a second language, they have made this language their own: Southern African English is a language much modified by local usage. Moreover, the boundaries between one language and another are continually being transgressed. In Zimbabwe, for instance, many poets write bilingually, incorporating oral idiom from Shona or Ndebele into their English-language writing. Contemporary South Africa offers a comparable trend, with its many different languages.

Southern African literature includes oral as well as written forms, with an aboriginal literary heritage dating from pre-colonial times and extending into the present. Writing itself, in English and Dutch, was originally imported into South Africa in the 17th century, spreading later to its neighbouring regions. An English-language literature gradually established itself, as did Dutch literature in South Africa and German literature in South-West Africa, initially in the form of diaries and journals. Local English-language fiction, drama and poetry dates from the early to mid-19th century, establishing itself slowly. ▷Afrikaans literature started in the early part of the 20th century, its language primarily derived from Dutch, but also incorporating words from languages indigenous to Africa. ▷African-language literature started being published in the late 19th century, in newspapers, and in the early 20th century in book form.

Southern Africa refers, here, to South Africa, Botswana (formerly Bechuanaland), Lesotho (formerly Basutoland), Namibia (formerly South-West Africa), Swaziland and Zimbabwe (formerly Rhodesia). (Mozambique is excluded, since it is taken to be part of Lusophone (Portuguese-speaking) Africa). Given the racial divisions which developed in the colonial period, and which were codified in South Africa under the system of apartheid, Southern African literature is generally spoken of in terms of two categories: literature written by those of European or 'white' origin (largely Dutch and English in South Africa, South African and English in Rhodesia, and German in South-West Africa); and literature by those of African or Asian origin, people who have been classified under various categories of 'non-white' and who generally group themselves in the political category 'black'. Without in any way wishing to perpetuate a state-directed system of classification that has done inestimable damage to the spiritual and material existence of generations of people, or wishing to simplify other categories created by the state, but also recognizing the way in which 'black' has become an important category of resistance to white domination, this essay uses the terms 'white' and 'black' (the latter including those officially classified as being of racially mixed parentage, or of Asian origin) in order to point to the cultural or political affiliations of the writers concerned.

Race and class differences, which are often, but not always, conflated in Southern African life, interrupt, with particular visibility and force, the category 'women' with which this *Guide* is concerned. Moreover, racial, ethnic and geographical differences disrupt any potential homogeneity among the group 'Southern African'. Yet it is the task of this essay to try to gather together a disparate mass of writers, to group them in certain ways, and to highlight some as more significant or interesting than others. Choosing which writers and texts to refer to in the essay, which deserve entries in the A–Z section, and which should be ignored has been difficult. Selection has tended to favour writers whose work has appeared in English: no hierarchization is intended, and the decisions should be seen in the context of the readership envisaged by this *Guide*. It has obviously been necessary to focus on women writers to the exclusion of men, although gender cannot really be discussed in such isolation.

Women performers and writers, and the oral tradition
In the ▷oral tradition of the pre-colonial Southern African world, the oral tale is performed at the homestead, mostly by women, while epic and praise poetry is performed by men, at public and ceremonial gatherings. As bearers of culture, associated with imagined worlds, rather than factual and historical ones, women reproduce and creatively adapt stories handed down by their mothers' and grandmothers' generations, thus taking care of an important part of the education of boys and girls. Especially skilful performers sometimes attract a wider audience.

Oral forms, kept alive in rural areas, are sometimes transcribed and translated by missionaries and scholars. Violet Dube's *Wozanazo izindaba zika Phoshozwayo* (1935) (*Tell Us the Stories of Phoshozwayo*) stands as the first example of a collection by a woman. Even in the cities, for various reasons, cultural work sometimes originates in, and remains in, oral form: only about half the population is literate in any language, few have the leisure time to write, and what remains oral can be more easily hidden from hostile authorities. Since the 1970s, orature has been revalued as a consequence of ▷Black Consciousness's interest in the cultural past. At least three genres exist: ▷popular theatre, which does not always issue in script, let alone print, ▷performance poetry, which enlivens political meetings, and storytelling, currently being revived on stage as an oral art-form, most notably by ▷Gcina Mhlophe. Moreover, increasing numbers of ▷children's books are based on African tales. In a different way, orature enters writing as part of literary technique, as in some of ▷Bessie Head's and ▷Miriam Tlali's stories. The political intent is distinct from that of Alan Paton in *Cry the Beloved Country* (1948), for instance.

Of course, an oral tradition is not practised simply by African women. Storytelling is an everyday act, and has been used to transmit the culture and shape the identity of various groups. ▷Pauline Smith's stories, for instance, are indebted to tales told her by rural Afrikaner women in the first decades of the 20th century, and often strive to preserve an atmosphere of orality. More recently, ▷Nadine Gordimer has used a Zulu oral tradition to inform her novel ▷*The Conservationist*, and Afrikaans poet ▷Antjie Krog has based some of her verse on Sotho oral praise poems. In this way, Gordimer and Krog, empowered by an indigenous tradition, strive to transcend the racial difference of apartheid, and to turn, finally, from the heritage of colonialism, which denied them identity as Africans.

Writing by women in colonial Southern Africa

In the 18th and 19th centuries, given the literacy and middle-class status of at least some of the European travellers and settlers, along with the interest of British publishers in colonial fiction, white women began establishing themselves as Southern Africa's major prose writers. ▷Diaries and journals, as well as ▷letters, were written by settlers and travellers to the country, largely from England, Scotland, and the Netherlands. The earliest preserved writing is a set of letters written by Johanna Maria van Riebeeck, between 1709 and 1711, in Dutch. ▷Lady Anne Barnard's letters and her travel journal, ▷*Journal of a Tour into the Interior*, the latter written in 1798 and published in part in 1849, are particularly interesting examples of this early genre.

By the late 19th century, with the discovery of diamonds (1867) and gold (1886), public attention was more and more focused on South Africa. Encouraged by a British readership hungry for tales of 'exotic' life or for information on immigration, colonial women began publishing memoirs and settler romances, engaged in one way or another with 'frontier' experience. Some designed their writing specifically for potential immigrants, like ▷Harriet Ward, whose *Jasper Lyle: A Tale of Kafirland* (1851) is the first Southern African colonial novel. Others, like Mary Ann Carey-Hobson, who published seven novels and collections of stories, claimed to be recording their remarkable adventures for future generations, taking care to keep the tall-tale tradition at bay by insisting that these adventures came from firsthand knowledge.

Although few texts of the colonial period may be remembered, they are generally notable for the part they play in the reproduction – and occasional interrogation – of the social divisions of race, gender and class. brought by Europeans, as well as in the representation of what colonists called 'the frontier'. The perspective of women often provides a particularly interesting angle on what was otherwise represented as an essentially masculine pioneering enterprise. Frontier life loses some of its macho glamour, as in ▷Anna de Brémont's fiction, for example. Yet most English-language texts by women writers chauvinistically reproduced a reassuring image of 'Britishness'. To this end, the Southern African landscape is generally reduced to a set of spaces – most notably, the diamond fields and the bushveld – where 'character' is formed. Similarly, the people of Southern Africa are reduced to a set of social groupings, British, Boer, and 'Kaffir', along with 'Bushman' and 'Hottentot' in the Cape. Barbarism being displaced onto black Southern Africans or (more rarely) onto Dutch (Boer) settlers, the British remain righteous and pure in their self-representation, apart from some expatriate ruffians.

Colonial Southern African writing by women still awaits rigorous critical reading, but what seems clear is that textual engagement with the Victorian ideals of masculinity and femininity required some re-negotiation on the part of women writers. Given conditions on the frontier, where women generally lived more independent lives than their British counterparts, conventional divisions between the so-called 'masculine' and 'feminine' spheres were often transgressed by virtue of the privileges of race and class afforded these colonial women. The aristocratic Lady Anne Barnard, for example, writing well before the Victorian era, experiences relative freedom. Yet, equally, she chafes at the limitations imposed by the feminine ideal, envious of her contemporary, John Barrow (1764–1848), who could penetrate further into Africa than she, and did not need to write in secret. Barrow became famous as an explorer; she did not.

The homestead represents 'feminine' space: distinct from the outdoor spaces where 'character' is formed, and opposed to the brutality apparently demanded by pioneering activity, its (white) women signify the continuing presence of maternal care: infinite kindness, to the point of self-abnegation. Yet, however much women were encouraged to soften, through charity and compassion, the harshness of pioneer life, the role of white women was to preserve the white race from 'taint'. A literature of 'miscegenation' flourished in the late 19th and early 20th centuries. Anna Howarth (c 1854–1943), who produced four sentimental romances during her sojourn in South Africa, was one of those bent on revealing the moral flaws consequent on racial mixing.

Still, colonial texts written by women often tell stories of unusual enterprise. *Adventures in Mashonaland, by two hospital nurses* (1893) recounts the establishment of the first nursing facilities there, including a walk of 140 miles undertaken by the nursing sisters. Although colonial writers were often blind to the social reality around them – Ethel Jollie's *The Real Rhodesia* (1924), with its unconsciously ironic title, is a case in point – they wrote with a sense of taking part in a history in the making. Melina Rorke (1875–?), in her racy and extravagant autobiography, *Melina Rorke . . . Told by Herself* (1939), which casts back to the colonial period, exults in her meetings with famous and notorious frontier men, and at having lived through battles, wars, and national epidemics. Writing by women involved in the ▷Anglo–Boer War (1899–1902) offered more seriously considered views, often pacifist, often outraged at the brutal treatment by the British of Boer prisoners of war. Emily Hobhouse (1860–1926), a crucial figure here, published an English translation of a Boer woman's diary as part of her campaign against the war.

Particularly popular novelists of the Rhodesian colonial period were ▷Gertrude Page and ▷Cynthia Stockley, prolific writers in the first decades of the 20th century, whose Rhodesia offered freedom from the claustrophobic constraints of drawing-room England. Alongside books by popular writers such as Rider Haggard (1856–1925), there was a plethora of colonial romances written by women: *Ingram Place* (1874), *Power's Partner* (1876), *Miss Molly* (1876), *Tales Written in Ladybrand* (1885), *Keith Deramore* (1893), *Maria de la Rey* (1903); these are a few of the titles. They are scarcely remembered: most writers strove only through the most superficial verbal overlay to transfer a literary style conceived in Britain to Southern African conditions, so that their work has become dated. Reprint series of women writers have not been generated in Southern Africa as they have elsewhere. There was, however, a brief nostalgic trend among whites in the 1970s in Rhodesia, in the last years before black majority rule: in 1970 the Heritage series reprinted Alice Blanche Balfour's *Twelve Hundred Miles in a Waggon* (1895), for example.

In the context of colonial settler romance, ▷Olive Schreiner's writing stands out for the way it explicitly rejects adventure story and melodrama. Schreiner had dipped her brush, she said, 'into the grey pigments of the Karoo life', rather than adopting the method of exoticist writers, with their interest in fabricating 'local colour'. She also rejected the artificial plots of colonial adventure novels, to include instead 'a strange coming and going of feet', a metonym for the variety of South Africans brought to the country under colonialism, as well as its native inhabitants. Given the extraordinary energy and intelligence of her writing, she stands as one of Southern Africa's finest novelists, to whom generations of later writers, both men and women, have been indebted. Her pioneering interest in gender, in particular, has given her international status as a writer: *Woman and Labour* (1911) was called 'the bible of the women's movement'. Yet even she, so alert to forms of oppression, was caught up in contradictions around gender and race, as ▷*From Man to Man* (1926), in particular, shows.

Early 20th-century writing by black women

Despite the vibrancy and cultural importance of the female-associated oral tradition, the missionaries who arrived in the 18th and 19th centuries encouraged African men to translate the parables and write the didactic tales needed to help spread the Christian message: African women's literary voices were thus to a large extent displaced by print. Yet among the novels published in the early part of the 20th century, there were some by black Southern African women. The earliest work in ▷African-language literature written by women was in Xhosa, given the location of one of the major mission presses, extending later to other languages. The earliest surviving extant work is Victoria Swartbooi's novel *UMandisa* (1934), whose title, like most, is the name of a young woman, in this case 'bringer of joy'. Publication in genres other than prose fiction was scant. A rare example of a published poem written in English by a black South African woman is Mrs A.C. Dube's lyrical 'Africa: My Native Land'. Published in 1913, the year of the Natives' Land Act which forced thousands of black South Africans off their land into reserves, the poem celebrates Africa and laments its lost freedom. Nontsizi Mgqwetho, writing in Xhosa, published numerous poems in newspapers in the 1920s.

The earliest written vernacular prose was modelled on allegories and biblical parables. Even into the 1940s and 1950s, and to a lesser extent the 1960s, the allegorical tendency remained, fanned both by missionary influence and the didactic interest of traditional African narrative. Novels accepted for publication tended to reproduce a Christian perspective, measuring their distance from such things as witchcraft and polygyny (▷polygamy). But as allegory gave way to social ▷realism, female characterization became more complex. There is no critical evidence as yet that early writing by women interrogated stereotypes of femininity, except to the extent that writing itself was an act of transgression: women's novels tended to be conduct books, showing in minute detail the socialization of young girls, and the rewards and dangers that awaited obedient and disobedient girls. African patriarchy, Christian ▷patriarchy and racism combined to subordinate women, as shown in a set of early letters written by a young Xhosa schoolgirl to a prominent white woman in the hopes of furthering her education, and evading the marriage being arranged for her. These letters appear in *Not Either an Experimental Doll* (1987).

What seems to be a moralistic and essentially conservative literature needs to be read for its negotiation, by black women, of the extremely rapid and disturbing social changes to which they were subject. With the dependence of the mining industry on migrant labour, along with the control of the number of women who might live with their husbands in the cities, family life was being massively disrupted. And in the cities, extreme poverty was the norm.

1910–1948: writing by white women

In South Africa the colonial period ended, at least technically, in 1910, whereas it continued through the first half of the century in Southern Africa generally. Virtually all published writing was in English; Afrikaans developed as a literary language from as late as 1875, so Afrikaans literature therefore has a short history. Although the Afrikaans cultural tradition is Calvinist and patriarchal, there are a number of important women writers. The first substantial women writers were the novelist Hettie Smit (1908–1973), and the poet ▷Elisabeth Eybers, whose work continues up to the present.

In English, still in the first half of the 20th century, a good deal of poetry was published, publication costs often being met by the poets themselves. English-language poetry in the early decades was largely an exercise in belated Victorian romanticism, as is clearly illustrated in the verse produced by the Veldsingers' Club. Formed in 1908, it included poets such as Gertrude Vallance (1873–1941) and Mary Byron (1870–1935), who was also a short story writer, as well as Olive Schreiner, who was president for a time. Poetic voices were directed towards England, and English poetic precedents were dutifully followed. ▷Mary Morison Webster, writing in the 1930s, stands out during this period, among several fairly prolific poets: Dorothea Botha, later Spears (1901–1991), Mary Boyd (1880–1960), Olive Bridgman (1880–1971) and Edith King (1871–1962), for example. Webster quietly and skilfully establishes an individual voice, despite constraining traditional influences.

In fiction, the novel of adventure gave way to the social problem novel. The period is dominated by ▷Sarah Gertrude Millin and ▷Pauline Smith. Although Millin gave detailed literary representation to a social grouping of poorer South Africans hitherto unexplored in South African fiction, her writing is contaminated by racist attitudes, inherited from a pseudo-scientific belief in blood 'purity' and 'taint'. She represents contemporary attitudes, yet it is worth noting that some other novels of the time took a different line. ▷Ethelreda Lewis's *The Harp* (1925) and ▷Frances Charlotte Slater's *The Sure Years* (1931) present a vision of a South Africa in which the question of racial supremacy is settled by love and intermarriage, rather than persisting, as in Millin, to plague later generations. British writer ▷Winifred Holtby, a friend of Millin's, also recognized the evils of white–black racism in a way Millin did not. These writers tend to focus, sometimes sentimentally, on individual acts of love and compassion as antidotes to the pervasive and deep-rooted racism in the white South African heritage.

Pauline Smith's work, like Schreiner's and Millin's, is marked by an intellectually serious attitude to writing, a desire to evade melodramatic romance, and an interest in the relation between character and environment (the influence of late 19th-century European realism). She avoids black–white politics, turning instead to the relations between English and Afrikaans, and between rich and poor. Her representation of rural Afrikaners at the turn of the century offers a critique of Afrikaner religious and patriarchal thinking, although her writing is careful to show them sympathetically, too, dissociating itself from colonial writers' patronizing attitudes to the Boer peasantry. Her stories are echoed in a number of less interesting writers, Madeleine Masson, for instance, with her *The Slave Bell and Other Stories* (1946), and Sampie de Wet (1906–1984), with her *Nine Stories* (1956). ▷Bertha Goudvis deals unsentimentally with village communities of roughly the same historical period as Smith's.

As in the colonial period, there were numerous writers no longer remarked by critics, although they sometimes wrote prolifically and had success in their lifetimes. Daphne Muir (1896–?), who wrote poetry, short stories and five novels, won the Chatto and Windus historical novel competition for her second novel, *The Lost Crusade* (1930), published in the USA as *Pied Piper*. The suffragist climate had helped open up the world for white Southern African women. Besides the short stories, Masson wrote much: two novels, *Icara* (1936) and *The Narrowing Lust* (1949), two children's books, three works of non-fiction, including *Lady Anne Barnard* (1948), and five plays. With Goudvis, who also wrote five plays, she is the only woman dramatist to speak of in this early period. Dorothea Fairbridge (1862–1931) wrote and edited a variety of fiction and non-fiction, among which is *Piet of Italy* (1913), which tries to deal sympathetically with the Cape's Moslem community which had so interested Lady Lucie Duff Gordon (1821–1869), whose letters Fairbridge edited. Ethelreda Lewis's work, especially *Four Handsome Negresses* (1931), also develops out of this feminist period, as does that of Elizabeth Charlotte Webster (1905–1934), Mary Morison Webster's sister, with her daring, quirky, social satire, *The Expiring Frog* (1946), published abroad as *Ceremony of Innocence* (1949). Jessica Grove and Olga Racster (died 1955) co-authored *Dr James Barry: Her Secret Story* (1932), about a woman who spent her life masquerading as a man in order to practise as a doctor. Barry was also the topic of a novel, *The Tavern* (1920), by René Juta (1887–1940). Many of these writers, and others such as Thelma Gutsche (1915–1984) and Vera Buchanan-Gould, one of Olive Schreiner's early biographers, formed a literary circle that had some influence over cultural life.

Much of the writing of this period casts back to colonialism, both historically – in terms of its content – and ideologically. During the 1950s, however, after the National Party came to power in 1948, racism assumed a considerably more brutal face, and writers gradually began to address the question of race in a more urgent and less sentimental manner.

1948–1990: writing by white women

Fifty years after Schreiner's ▷ *The Story of an African Farm* was published, the protagonist in Nadine Gordimer's *The Lying Days* says: 'I had never read a book in which I myself was recognizable; in which there was a "girl" like Anna who did the housework and the cooking and called the mother and father Missus and Baas.' ▷Doris Lessing, speaking from colonial Rhodesia, might have said the same.

Even in their early work, Gordimer and Lessing stand out for their interest in female sexuality and their critical attitudes towards racism. These attitudes were rooted in different political beliefs, Lessing being a member of the Communist Party and Gordimer committed to reformist Liberal politics. Gordimer's later texts developed an increasingly critical attitude toward South African liberalism, which offered so fainthearted an opposition to apartheid that it was felt to inhibit political change. Lessing's early writing is Rhodesian, but her later work, after she emigrated to Britain, takes on a wider reference. The work of both writers marks an important stage in Southern African writing's progress from a colonial to an indigenous movement, in the sense that they attend without sentimentality to the complex relations between black and white.

Although their work is concerned to engage with an Africa that breaks free of its European version, they both saw themselves as part of world literature, being deeply influenced by a range of European writing. Gordimer's early novels and short stories were deeply indebted to the tradition of British realism – E.M. Forster (1879–1970), and ▷George Eliot, who interwove personal and political life, as well as the New Zealander ▷Katherine Mansfield, with her oblique irony. While Lessing turned to embrace ▷modernism, Gordimer's fiction, reaching out for political truth-telling, combines realist with modernist strategies.

Gordimer is one of South Africa's most acclaimed writers (she won the Nobel Prize for Literature in 1991), whose writing career is not yet over. In her fiction, non-fiction and public speeches she has made a number of imaginative and courageous political statements. Her work has been path-breaking for younger South African writers.

Among contemporary white women novelists writing in English are ▷Jillian Becker, who produced three South African novels in the 1960s and 1970s, one of which has been recently reprinted, and also ▷Yvonne Burgess, ▷Sheila Roberts, and ▷Rose Zwi, who are still writing. All of them belong to a realist tradition, and examine the limitations of white South African life, satirically, in the case of Burgess and Roberts. Zwi's fiction stands out for its scrutiny of South African Jewish life, her series of novels covering early immigration from Eastern Europe in the late 19th century to the more recent exodus to Israel. Also worth noting here is the fiction of Rhona Stern (born 1918), better known as a sculptor, who published *The Cactus Land* (1964), *The Bird Flies Blind* (1965) and *Stop Half-Way and Look at the View* (1969).

Alongside this writing, a lighter, popular tradition has been maintained. Starting in the 1940s and continuing into the 1970s, ▷Joy Packer wrote a number of melodramatic romances and personalized travel books. Fiction by ▷Daphne Rooke, from the 1950s into the 1970s, also looked back to a tradition of melodrama, but informed it with a somewhat more enlightened attitude towards race. Her interest in the relations between young black and white women, and in sexuality as it intersects with race, gives her work a certain current appeal. ▷Mary Renault also falls into this period, but her fiction focuses on classical Greece. There are a few popular writers whose books are widely read but who are unremarked in the literary critical world. June Drummond (born 1923), for instance, has published nearly twenty novels, some translated into several languages.

Also notable during this period is the gradual shift in children's writing, which shows a good deal more cross-cultural perviousness than in the past. In both South Africa and Rhodesia, efforts to reinstate cultural traditions eroded by colonialism meant an increase in the use of oral tradition to enliven children's literature. Julia Boyd Harvey and Marjorie Bereza's *Tutti and the Magic Bird*, published first in South Africa in 1980 and reprinted in Zimbabwe the following year, was chosen as favourite by a panel of Zimbabwean children. It recounts Tutti's journey back in time to claim an African heritage.

For poetry written in English, 1965 was a watershed year. The poetry journal *New Coin* was established, providing a vehicle for serious poets, and two important volumes were produced by a local publishing house: ▷Adèle Naudé's *Only a Setting Forth* (1965) and ▷Ruth Miller's *Floating Island* (1965). Miller, above all, makes a break with colonial sentiments and poetic precedents, shifting into modernism with 'metaphysical' wit, self-deprecating irony, and, sometimes, an odd combination of rhetorical difficulty and elaborately casual technique. Less well-established, but also interesting, poets of this period were Tania van Zyl (born 1908), Anne Welsh (born 1922), and Helen Segal (1929–1988). Phyllis Haring (born 1919), Lola Dunston (born 1922), and Ruth Keech (born 1928) all started publishing relatively late in life, as did ▷Jean Lipkin, who stands out among this group. Among a later generation, which includes such poets as Eva Royston (1942–1976), Lynn Bryer (born 1946) and Sally Bryer (born 1947), ▷Jeni Couzyn's work is the best established. Her work is interesting for its technical achievement and its relation to Africa. ▷Geraldine Aron has emerged as a significant dramatist.

Among the serious contemporary Afrikaans novelists, only ▷Wilma Stockenström and ▷Elsa Joubert are well-known in the English-speaking world, although there are others whose work is available in English: Elisabeth Eybers, ▷Ingrid Jonker, and ▷Sheila Cussons. Dalene Matthee (born 1938) has written two highly successful books about Knysna forest and village life, subsequently translated into English by the author: *Circles in a Forest* (1984) and *Fiela's Child* (1986). Both have been made into films. Other important well-established writers are ▷Henriette Grové, ▷Antjie Krog, ▷Anna M. Louw, and ▷Lettie Viljoen.

Contemporary writing by Afrikaans women is important for the way it interrogates patriarchy as well as the Calvinist cultural tradition whereby Afrikaners are placed as God's 'chosen people', a myth which has had disastrous consequences in South African history. Particularly crucial in this regard is Louw's writing, across different generic categories, Viljoen's fiction, and poetry by Jonker, Stockenström and Krog.

Perhaps the most exciting English-language work of this period, bar Gordimer's, has been in the set of novels and political ▷autobiographies written by women whose activism in anti-apartheid politics led to ▷exile; Ruth First, for example, as well as ▷Mary Benson and ▷Hilda Bernstein. For these women, as for others, the Defiance Campaign of 1952 provided a key turning point: politics took on a new seriousness for them as activists were imprisoned, and many saw that their political goals could only be achieved by the revolutionary transfer of political power. Ruth First was the first white woman to be detained under the 90-day Detention Clause instituted by the Nationalist Government in 1964. She was assassinated by agents of the South African government on 17 August 1982. Her prison autobiography (▷Prison writing, South Africa), *117 Days* (1965), is an account of this period. Her other non-fiction is equally impressive: *Olive Schreiner: A Biography* (1980, co-written with Ann Scott), and *South West Africa* (1963). Helen Joseph (born 1905), who has spent some of her life in South Africa in prison, and some under house arrest, stands as a comparable figure, although she did not go into exile. Her non-fiction, which includes *If This Be Treason* (1963) and *Side by Side* (1986), testifies to the transformation of white Southern African women who open their eyes to the political reality around them.

A bridge, of a kind, is formed between white and black writing during this period by means of sociological writing. Hilda Kuper's play, *A Witch in My Heart* (1970), which emanates from her work as a sociologist, and offers a sensitive portrayal of Swazi people, appears to be the only creative writing published by a woman in Swaziland, black or white. In Rhodesia, Nan Partridge's *Not Alone: A Story for the Future* (1972), which won her the Joost de Blank annual award for 'furthering racial understanding', combines fiction with a set of sociological research reports. Developing out of this sociology is a set of what may best be grouped as autobiographical texts in an ethnological mode, whose intention is to give voice to women who might, in a different dispensation, be writing themselves. Elsa Joubert's *The Long Journey of Poppie Nongena*, written first in Afrikaans and then translated into English, is the best-known work of this kind.

State repression was increasingly severe after the pass campaign at Sharpeville, and the attendant massacre, in 1960. But the repeated States of Emergency during the 1980s could not fully repress or obscure the increasingly courageous dissidence and massive popular discontent. In English and Afrikaans writing alike, stock was being taken: Southern African identities were being forged within a newly emerging cultural context, with important work emerging from a younger generation of Southern African writers. Like some of the better-established writers, English and Afrikaans – Gordimer, Krog, Viljoen, and others – they consciously, even aggressively, turn to a new Southern African order. Most notable among these are ▷Ingrid de Kok, ▷Welma Odendaal and ▷Menán du Plessis. Jeanne Goosen (born 1940) is also emerging as a notable talent. Elleke Boehmer's *Screens Against the Sky* (1989) describes the personal and political transformation that leads up to such writing. In the novel, a young woman constructs a new place in the world, partly through her own stories and diary, and partly through her job as a volunteer in a local hospital, where – following on from Gordimer's ▷*Burger's Daughter* – she can see her own needs for personal fulfilment in the context of political (and human) commitment.

1953–1990: writing by black women
Bantu Education had been entrenched in South Africa in 1953, changing the medium of education (primary education, plus the first year of high school) from English to whatever African language dominated in any one region. Vernacular writing became closely geared to educational publishing, and was thus firmly controlled, black education being largely in the hands of the state. In Rhodesia, from the 1950s to 1980, political inquiry was taboo, and Shona and Ndebele writing, published largely by the white government's Literature Bureau, was limited to stories about love and crime. Very few titles were written by women. In Botswana and Lesotho, even after independence in the mid-1960s, little was published. But Caroline Khaketla, a Sotho writer, stands out: a novel called *Mosali eo u'neileng eena* (1956) (*The Woman You Gave Me*), a play, *Pelo eo Monna* (1976) (*The Heart of a Man*), and a volume of poetry, *Mantsopa* (1963), some of which reappears in anthologies. There is no record of vernacular writing by women from Swaziland and Namibia having been published in book form.

In South Africa, since schools' anthologies and prescribed texts still provide the only medium for African-language writers, there is virtually no African-language adult fiction in the real sense of the term, and so it is largely through writing in English that a literary tradition starts to present itself. While some poems and stories had been published in magazines and newspapers by the 1960s, ▷Noni Jabavu emerged as the first South African black woman writer to publish a book in English. Jabavu, a Xhosa speaker born into a family fluent in English, incorporates Xhosa terms into her writing and skilfully describes linguistic moments whose complexity would not be adequately reproduced by translation, thus recreating for readers illiterate in Xhosa a sense of the richness of the

Xhosa language. Later, ▷Fatima Dike, one of Southern Africa's most important drama-tist, composed ▷*The Sacrifice of Kreli* (1978) by first writing it out in Xhosa, and then translating it into English, in order to preserve indigenous idiom. Gcina Mhlophe's play *Have You Seen Zandile?* (first staged in 1986, and published in 1988), continually moves between English, Xhosa and Zulu. ▷Miriam Tlali's most recent writing includes Sotho.

A sense of national identity – across language and other barriers – was gradually being created among black writers, and was even extending, with exiles and freedom fighters moving across borders, to cover Southern Africa as a whole. ▷Bessie Head, among Southern Africa's finest writers, embodies a sign of this border crossing. South African by birth and upbringing, Botswanan by geographical circumstance though not by affiliation, Head draws together the two countries in a way that has been enriching to both. Written just after she arrived in Botswana, ▷*When Rain Clouds Gather* (1967) celebrates the possibilities which Botswana, signifying black Africa, offers the south, made arid and heartless by apartheid. Head produced an extremely rich and varied *oeuvre* during the 1970s and 1980s. Her work is remarkable for its energetic and challenging explorations of an African heritage, and its penetrating insight into the psychic consequences of racial, sexual and imperialist oppression.

In the 1970s and into the 1980s, ▷Black Consciousness was an important force for political and cultural change. As a philosophy, it asserted African communality, and encouraged a literature of optimism rather than despair, which yet testifies to the abuses and deprivations suffered under apartheid. Black Consciousness informs the early writing of Miriam Tlali in particular. Social critique is directed against white domination, the major form of physical and psychological violence launched against black women. In the terms set by Black Consciousness, African womanhood is celebrated as a powerful and enduring force. During the 1970s and early 1980s there was virtually no investigation of the relation between women and patriarchy: feminism was regarded with suspicion, for white South African women's 'liberation' has often depended on the subordination of black women. This political emphasis squares with Black Consciousness's desire to restore rather than question an African tradition.

Besides Tlali's two novels, stories and essays, only one other novel in English by an African woman was published in South Africa during the 1980s: ▷Lauretta Ngcobo's significant novel, *Cross of Gold* (1981). This deals with events around Sharpeville, and the ensuing political struggle. The period also produced various important ▷autobiographies; ▷Ellen Kuzwayo's *Call Me Woman* (1985) is the best-known of these. Joyce Sikakane's superb *A Window on Soweto* (1977) was, like much writing in this period – by Tlali, Ngcobo and others – immediately banned. A number of ethnological autobiographies appeared, such as Carol Hermer's *The Diary of Maria Tholo* (1980). Township drama developed out of the new trend in ▷popular theatre.

In poetry – some published in individual volumes, but most in anthologies – protest, exhortation to resistance, and threats of retribution dominate the voices of black women, as in the case of men. Ilva Mackay, in the anthology *Black Voices Shout* (1974), calls upon the youth not to let their ideas be smothered by their parents, in a gesture that foreshadows the ▷Soweto children's revolt. The anthology, which also contains poems by Christine Douts, was banned, as was Gladys Thomas's *Cry Rage* (1972), a volume shared with poet James Matthews. Zindzi Mandela's volume, *Black As I Am* (1978), deals with the angers and frustrations of being black, in poems with religious overtones whose dynamic is sometimes occasioned by personal quest. In a few cases, then, more personal, lyrical forms and themes enter the verse, as in Cikizwe Mokoena's and Portia Rankoane's recent volumes, too, which formulate experience in Christian philosophical terms. More suc-cessfully, in poems which have been appearing in magazines since 1966, and are collected in *Searching for Words* (1974), Jennifer Davids alludes to her life as factory worker and teacher, and gives a sense of what is happening in the mind of a young woman perched as precariously as she is, 'at the tip of a continent', and at the point where silence turns into 'a possibility of speaking'. Among anthologized poets, ▷Gcina Mhlophe, ▷Nise Malange and Mavis Smallberg particularly stand out. The poetry of all three, and Malange's most markedly, fits into a tradition of ▷performance poetry, occasion for which is found at concerts, funerals, political meetings and private parties.

In the latter half of the 1980s there was a marked increase in writing by women. ▷Zoë Wicomb's *You Can't Get Lost in Cape Town* (1987) comes out of a Griqua community in the north-western Cape, whose members have, until now, only been the object of other people's writing: Millin's, for instance. Women of East Indian ancestry (classified by the State as one of the four 'races' in South Africa) have recently begun publishing in English. In 1970 Fatima Meer published a sociological study, *Portrait of Indian South Africans*. The late 1980s saw the emergence of fiction by ▷Farida Karodia, with *Daughters of the Twilight* (1986) and *Coming Home and Other Stories* (1988); Jayapraga Reddy, with *On the Fringe of Dreamtime* (1987); Beverley Naidoo, with *Chain of Fire* (1989), and Agnes Sam, with *Jesus is Indian* (1989). The writing workshops initiated in the late 1970s by Tlali, Gordimer and others sometimes attracted women, though many could not steal time from days taken up by their dual role as working mothers. Among publishing companies oriented to women, Seriti sa Sechaba stands as a first, for it is entirely run by black South African women. Women were further encouraged by the increasing number of ▷anthologies, many of them women-oriented. Several were published by the Congress of South African Writers, an organization committed to democratization. In 1990 the Cultural Desk of the African National Congress, headed by poet Barbara Masekela, started a literary magazine, *Rixaka*, the first issue largely devoted to women. Along with Masekela, other writers hitherto in exile have started returning to South Africa, preparing for a new dispensation. Among prominent or politically active women, many began to establish themselves as writers while in exile: Lindiwe Mabuza, Rebecca Matlou and Baleka Kgositsile, for example. Moreover, the ANC's women's league has introduced gender into the current political discussion.

Important here is not just the increase in writing by women, nor its new range, but also the depth of inquiry and the interest in literary experimentation. Zoë Wicomb's writing makes, unusually for Southern African fiction, a shift out of a realist mode, and is also interested in the complex intersections of race, class and gender. This interest emerges, too, in Mhlophe's short stories, few though they are, which stand as the work of an extremely interesting new writer: her story 'The Toilet', is a haunting account of a writer's genesis. Emma Mashinini's *Strikes Have Followed Me All My Life* (1989) articulates with poignancy and skill the feelings of self-annihilation she experienced in prison after being detained for trade union work, marking a new (after Head), introspective stage in black South African autobiography. She also defines a voice for working-class women.

The most remarkable evidence of literary renaissance lies in recent Zimbabwean writing. Since independence in 1980, two cultural trends in particular ushered in this new era. Firstly, adult education and other programmes started encouraging and utilizing popular theatre to reach a wide, often not literate, audience. The Women's Action Group, established in the early 1980s, helped create communication between rural and urban women. Secondly, in the wake of the war of liberation, anthologies have been compiled, with interviews encouraging women to relate their wartime experiences, as well as creative work. Barbara Makhalisa's *The Underdog and Other Stories* (1987) marks a more general shift from vernacular to English, for she had already established herself as an Ndebele writer. Three volumes of poetry have appeared – Kristina Rungano's *A Storm is Brewing* (1984), Freedom Nyamubaya's *On the Road Again* (1986) and Isabella Pupurai Matshikidze's *Zimbabwean Collectibles* (1990), the first two dealing particularly with the war of liberation and its attendant problems for women, and the last dealing largely with rural women, as well as economic exploitation by the 'First World': 'selling / English tea when Britannia doesn't have tea plantations'. Rungano's poetry is particularly important for its explicitly anti-war stance. Her poetry sometimes adopts the persona of a disillusioned male guerrilla, and sometimes the voice of a feminist speaker contemptuous of the atrocities perpetrated in the name of freedom. Given the martial tradition in Southern African verse, with its many heroic portrayals of war and male comradeship (women being accorded a stereotyped symbolic position on the sidelines), this is an important moment in literary history.

In drama, besides a play by Bertha Msora called *I Will Wait* (1986), notable work comes from Hope Dube, originally from Zimbabwe, though she has lived in South Africa and Botswana as well, who has published three plays: *Curse God and Die*, *The Great Flood*, and *Breaking Free*, collected under the title *Junior Play Anthology* (1987), as well as four short, skilful political thrillers, for young people or for adults starting to read fiction. Undoubtedly the most exciting work comes from ▷Tsitsi Dangarembga, with her first and, to date, only novel, *Nervous Conditions* (1989). Its sustained interest in neo-colonialism introduces a new spirit of inquiry in Southern African writing.

The cultural revival taking place among Zimbabwean and South African women comes at a time of massive political change. The South African state, under internal and international pressure, is gradually dismantling apartheid, at least into its overt legal and economic manifestations, and has publicly ceased its strategy of economic and military destabilization of neighbouring countries. Geographical, linguistic and racial boundaries are places of constant border-crossings rather than limits (though there are tragic exceptions), and so is the boundary between writing and orality. More clearly than ever, literature cannot refer only to writing. The recent increase in writing by women, and the new turn to gender as a literary topic, is a symptom of a more general surge in literary energy and experiment, although severe patriarchal constraints still remain. Given the range and depth of the new writing by women, it appears that a literary renaissance has come into being, one that harks back to the vision offered, variously, by Southern Africa's most challenging writers: Olive Schreiner, Nadine Gordimer and Bessie Head, for example, and also looks forward to a world more hospitable to difference and multiplicity. Still, it is essential to recall that black South Africans have no vote in central government, that five per cent of the population owns eighty-eight per cent of the wealth, that only half of South Africa's population is literate, and that the estimated number of rapes each year (320,000) is just one particularly violent indication of the region's abuse of women.

Bib: General: Adey, David, *et al*, *Companion to South African English Literature*; Alvarez-Perèyre, Jacques, *The Poetry of Commitment in South Africa*; Barnett, Ursula A., *A Vision of Order: A Study of Black South African Literature in English (1914–1980)*; Brink, André, *Mapmakers: Writing in a State of Siege*; Chennells, A. J., *Settler Myths and the Southern Rhodesian Novel* (D Phil thesis, University of Zimbabwe); Coetzee, J. M., *White Writing: On the Culture of Letters in South Africa*; Cope, Jack, *The Adversary Within: Dissident Writers in Afrikaans*; Coplan, David B., *In Township Tonight!; South Africa's Black City Music and Theatre*; Daymond, M. J., *et al* (eds.), *Momentum: On Recent South African Writing*; Gerard, Albert S. (ed.), *European-Language Writing in Sub-Saharan Africa*; Gray, Stephen, *Southern African Literature: An Introduction*; Kavanagh, Robert Mshengu, *Theatre and Cultural Struggle in South Africa: A Study in Cultural Hegemony and Social Conflict*; Parker, Kenneth (ed.), *The South African Novel in English: Essays in Criticism and Society*; Shava, Piniel Viriri, *A People's Voice: Black South African Writing in the Twentieth Century*; Smith, Malvern van Wyk, *Grounds of Contest: A Survey of South African English Literature*; Trump, Martin (ed.), *Rendering Things Visible: Essays on South African Literary Culture*; Watts, Jane, *Black Writers from South Africa: Towards a Discourse of Liberation*; White, Landeg and Couzens, Tim (eds), *Literature and Society in South Africa*.

On Women: Berrian, Brenda, *Bibliography of African Women Writers and Journalists (Ancient Egypt–1984)*; Clayton, Cherry (ed.), *Women and Writing in South Africa*; Congress of South African Writers (ed.), *Buang Basadi: Khulumani Makhozikazi: Women Speak*; Gaidzanwa, Rudo B., *Images of Women in Zimbabwean Literature*; Mtuze, Peter, *Xhosa*

Women Writers: A Feminist Analysis (PhD thesis, Rhodes University, Grahamstown).

Anthologies of writing by Southern African women: Bond-Stewart, K. and Mudimu, L. C. (eds), *Young Women in the Liberation Struggle: Stories and Poems from Zimbabwe*; Brown, Susan *et al.* (eds), *LIP from Southern African Women*; Lockett, Cecily (ed.), *Breaking the Silence: A Century of South African Women's Poetry*; Mabuza, Lindiwe (ed.), *One Never Knows: An Anthology of Black South African Women Writers in Exile*; Moerat, Nohra (ed.), *Siren Songs: An Anthology of Poetry Written by Women*; Oosthuizen, Ann (ed.), *Sometimes When It Rains: Writings by South African Women*; Seriti sa Sechaba (ed.), *Women in South Africa: From the Heart*; Van Niekerk, Annemarié (ed.), *Raising the Blinds: A Century of South African Women's Stories*.

See also Bibliographies on Southern Africa and South Africa in *Journal of Commonwealth Literature*, published in December each year.

JANE BRYCE

30 West Africa

The existence of contemporary African literature in European languages is a direct result of Western education, introduced to Africa by missionaries and later promoted by the colonial authorities as a way of producing an elite for government and administration. In the francophone countries the purpose was ▷assimilation, and the pinnacle of individual achievement was to go on to further education in France. The final product was the 'black Frenchman'. British colonialism never allowed such a possibility, preferring to stress separateness and thereby providing some space for indigenous African culture.

One effect of colonialism has been to impose a false homogeneity on a region which is, in fact, extraordinarily diverse in its ethnic groupings or nationalities, its languages, religious beliefs and practices. To define a literature as 'West African' is as useful and accurate as speaking of 'west European' or 'North American' literature. It is a shorthand, no more. To understand the cultural production of West Africa it is essential to appreciate that it is far older than colonialism, and that both francophone and anglophone authors write from within a dual tradition. Whether or not they speak a West African language, they are informed by an awareness of the techniques of orature, overlaid by Western education and a European language.

Orature, or oral literature (▷oral tradition, West Africa), has traditionally been overlooked by Western commentators or relegated to the category of folklore. The same is true of West African history. Because it was not written down (with a few exceptions such as the *Hausa Chronicle* of Northern Nigeria, which documents a culture that flourished in the Middle Ages) people from literate cultures tend to assume that Africa has no history. Yet archaeology, bronze and gold artefacts, and oral poetry like the epic poem 'Sundiata', which survives in an Arabic manuscript, point to the existence of great kingdoms and ancient civilizations: the empires of Mali and Benin, and the kingdom of Ashanti.

The displacement of African languages was an intrinsic part of the colonial incursion, with its aim of bringing colonized peoples under both the moral and legal sway of the 'mother country'. This was accomplished by educating members of the elite to perform the tasks of the colonial administration, thereby dividing them from the unschooled majority. The decolonization movement, which began as early as the 1920s, consciously turned to the culture of that majority for inspiration and self-definition. Today, this cultural self-assertion exists in tension with the neocolonial mentality of the ruling elite, whose position is reinforced by the economics of dependency. The literature of West Africa is marked by this contradiction, since it is written mainly in European languages and is therefore inaccessible to 80 per cent or more of the population.

Language

Of all the debates surrounding African literature, the language debate is the most vexed. Commentators and practitioners alike are split. Some hold that writing in indigenous languages is the only way truly to express one's culture and identity as an African. Others, while possibly agreeing in principle, take the pragmatic view: that the colonial intervention in their history is an irrefutable fact which has inscribed itself, above all, in language, in that many educated Africans are simply more fluent in French or English than in an African language. Moreover, the market dictates that only works in these languages will be recognized by the wider literary community, and the multinational publishers, with their bases in the metropolitan centres, are only interested in promoting such works. However, many women do recognize the importance of addressing a specifically local readership and of maintaining culture by writing in indigenous languages. This is especially true in the area of ▷children's literature and education. For example, ▷Grace Ake Yamusa, a worker with the Jukun Language Development Project in Wukari, Northern Nigeria, has written a novel in Jukun which she then translated into English as *Clock of Justice*.

A century or more of use of the adopted language, however, means that the French and English spoken in the former colonies have inevitably taken on a local flavour which makes them, essentially, also African languages. But the local inflection may not conform to a critic's notion of 'literary' language. The Nigerian writer ▷Flora Nwapa is often criticized for her stilted use of English, whereas in her earlier novels she deliberately writes in a way which evokes the actual language of her Igbo-speaking characters.

Besides formal English and French, the languages of education and administration, there is also in West Africa a variation known as pidgin, or creole. This originated as a trading dialect, consisting of elements of an indigenous language and English or French. It may be universally spoken, as with Krio in Sierra Leone, or it may exist in parallel with the official lingua franca and indigenous languages, as in Nigeria, where it operates as a leveller and a bridge between different classes and ethnic groups. The Sierra Leonean poet ▷Gladys Casely-Hayford, the Nigerian novelist ▷Adaora Lily Ulasi and dramatist ▷Tess Onwueme have all experimented with pidgin.

Lastly, even when formal English or French is used, in many cases they bear the traces of an older, oral tradition. This is very obvious in the theatre of ▷Werewere Liking, which combines dialogue, dance, music and masks. But it is also true of writers like Flora Nwapa, ▷Ama Ata Aidoo, ▷Zaynab Alkali, ▷Catherine Acholonu, ▷Mariama Bâ and others. Their narratives are interwoven with oral elements of dramatic dialogue, storytelling, direct address to the audience, repetition and semiotic references to specific myths and traditions, in the form of poetic motifs and archetypes.

Publishing

An important part of the colonial legacy in West Africa is the predominance of the multinational publishers, whose values and criteria for selection of manuscripts have, over the years, done much to influence the direction of African literature. In Britain, no publisher has been more instrumental in determining the canon – what constitutes a 'classic' – than Heinemann. The African Writers Series (HAWS), begun in 1958 with the publication of Chinua Achebe's *Things Fall Apart*, still to a large extent determines what is seen as 'good' literature. Next to Heinemann, the other two multinational companies most active in anglophone African publishing are Longman, with its more popular Drumbeat series, and Macmillan, with the very successful, mass-market Pacesetters. Interestingly, women are best represented in the Macmillan series, perhaps because it is the least self-consciously 'literary'.

Women in the West have combated the 'canon' and a male definition of excellence by setting up women-only publishing houses. In West Africa, as indeed Africa as a whole, where problems of production and distribution are enormous, this has not so far been a viable option. Those who have established their own presses, like Flora Nwapa with Tana and ▷Buchi Emecheta with Ogugwu Afor, have done so mainly to publish themselves. ▷Aminata Sow Fall is different, in that her organization, CAEC (Centre d'Animations et des Échanges Culturelles), which includes a publishing house, aims to encourage other writers.

Indigenous publishing, in spite of the physical problems of cost and scarcity of materials, has grown steadily in West Africa. Women have benefited both from easier access and from the widening of what is considered acceptable. The economic and cultural ties between France and its ex-colonies mean that the situation there is somewhat different, in that books produced by Africa-based publishers are also distributed in France, with the attendant benefits to writers.

Of the francophone publishers, Nouvelles Editions Africaines (NEA), based in Dakar and Abidjan, was founded by the Senegalese president, Leopold Sédar Senghor, in 1972 (▷Négritude); Les Editions CLE was founded in Yaoundé in 1963. Both exist specifically to publish books appropriate and desirable to an African readership. In terms of canon formation, NEA fulfils a similar role to that of HAWS.

The question of selection, of determining what is acceptable to a perceived reader or market, remains. The other major francophone African publisher, Présence Africaine, was started by Alioune Diop in 1947 as a vehicle for the combative philosophy of *Négritude*. It consists of a cultural journal as well as a publishing house and bookshop, all based in Paris. But the decision whether to publish with a multinational publisher and be read internationally, and perhaps not at all at home, or to publish at home and remain unknown abroad, remains an agonizing one. This is particularly true in the case of women, whose works suffer doubly from an alien definition – imposed by a foreign culture and by men – of what constitutes 'good' writing.

Women's movements

Though separate women's organizations have always existed in West Africa, very few women would define themselves as 'feminist' in the Western sense. Feminism is indeed a vexed issue, being by and large identified with the more extreme aspects of 'women's lib' and perceived as inappropriate in an African cultural milieu. As with African-American 'womanism', the key difference between black and white feminist ideologies is the refusal of the former to repudiate men and the family. It is very common to read highly-placed women being interviewed in the press, who preface their remarks with 'I am not a women's libber'. Many of the writers share this antipathy for the 'feminist' label, even those who, like Buchi Emecheta or Ama Ata Aidoo, are most readily identifiable as feminists.

The traditional separation of spheres, by which men and women had their own organizations and took separate decisions, meant that women had a voice and were listened to. This recognized space for women and the status it afforded them were undermined by colonial assumptions about the place of women. Women's organizations may not have carried the same weight as men's, but they were an integral part of the social structure. This is one reason why West African women have often felt alienated from the demands of the Western women's movement – for a voice, or for the right to work, for example. In West Africa, women have always worked. Under a ▷polygamous system, each woman is responsible for her own children, and gains status from her success in trade, business or a profession. Economic independence is not therefore an aspiration so much as a necessity.

Naturally, there are cultural and regional variations to this pattern, but even women living in seclusion in Islamic societies have money-making activities available to them. In general, West African women are famous as traders, and often have enormous influence over the domestic economy through the price and availability of goods. Powerful market-women's associations in West Africa can bring a country to a standstill if they feel the need to protest, or can swing an election. In Ghana in 1982, Accra market-women went on strike until their control over pricing was reinstated. They were scapegoated by the revolutionary Rawlings regime as symbols of wealth, and Accra's largest market was burned down.

West Africa has a plethora of women's professional organizations representing doctors, lawyers, accountants, academics, journalists, and so on, and women's religious, philanthropic and social groups. National organizations, under the title of 'National Congress' or 'Council', emerged in the independence era, and were given a boost in 1975 by the passing of a resolution in International Women's Year to set up national organizations in every country. While these tend to reflect the interests of the middle-class elites, the December Third Women's Movement in Ghana, though a government organization, does address grass-roots issues like literacy. The small but articulate and radical group, Women in Nigeria (WIN), based in Zaria in the north, is the most explicitly feminist and grass-roots-oriented.

Such organizations are all the more important in the light of women's secondary relationship to political power in post-colonial African states. This is in spite of women's mass involvement in anti-colonial movements, often in dramatic and decisive ways. Notable examples are the Women's War of 1929 in eastern Nigeria, as documented by ▷Nina Mba and Judith Van Allen; the Abeokuta women's uprising of 1945 in western Nigeria; the Guinean market-women's support for the railway strike of 1947–1948, described by the Senegalese writer Ousmane Sembène (born 1923) in *Les bouts de bois de dieu* (1960, English translation *God's Bits of Wood*, 1962); and the Ivorian women's march on the jail at Bassam in 1949 to demand the release of their menfolk, imprisoned by the colonial authorities. The relative indifference of a majority of West African women today towards politics is therefore more an indication of the way the political machinery is controlled by a small elite than of women's passivity. Of the many forms of women's indirect resistance to oppression, writing is emerging as one of the most powerful and enduring.

Women and the means of expression

Within the oral tradition, women played a very important part, as storytellers and educators, sometimes as poets and historians, and universally as participants in the significant rituals of their communities – those accompanying birth, initiation, marriage and death. With colonization came missionary education, through the vehicle of European languages. In West Africa these were English – in Nigeria, Ghana, the Gambia and Sierra Leone – and French – in Senegal, Côte d'Ivoire (Ivory Coast), Mali, Niger, Guinea, Benin, Upper Volta (Burkina Faso), Chad, Cameroon and Togo. Because these were the languages of government and adminstration, they were also the languages of power.

From the start, girls were at a disadvantage in gaining access to the new education, as traditionally they were trained for the home, and the colonizers failed to recognize the importance of women's traditional roles. If it was a choice for a family of educating a boy or a girl, it was naturally the boy who would be picked to go to school. This has meant that women have been slower to acquire literacy and a level of proficiency in the colonial language that would enable them to write. When they did come under the influence of the missionaries, they received often confusing messages about traditional culture and accepted practices like polygamy.

This experience is described by the Nigerian novelist Flora Nwapa in her autobiographical novel ▷ *Women are Different*. Her account of the school attended by the group of three friends whose lives she documents is based on her own attendance at the Archdeacon Crowther Memorial Girls' School, Elelenwa, in eastern Nigeria, from 1945 till 1948. As a first-hand account by one of the very few women who had access to missionary education at this time, the novel is instructive. It reflects a sense of pride and responsibility at being hand-picked to be among the country's leaders, rather than trained in domestic skills to become wives and mothers. But it is also clear that part of the purpose of this elitist education is to counteract the influence of the nationalist, anti-colonial movement gaining ground in Nigeria at this time. Another aspect of it is the inculcation of values and aspirations which turn out to be quite inappropriate to life in post-colonial Nigeria. The girls acquire idealistic concepts of romantic love and monogamous marriage, and of work as service to the community, which lead to disillusion in their adult lives. In the end, it is the pragmatism of the younger generation – as when one of their daughters becomes the second wife of a rich older man – that is endorsed, rather than the missionary school ideals of faithfulness and monogamy:

> Chinwe had done the right thing. Her generation was doing better than her mother's own. Her generation was telling the men that there are different ways of living one's life fully and fruitfully . . . Marriage is not THE only way. (Women are Different p. 119)

This statement by Flora Nwapa, and her emphasis on pragmatism and self-sufficiency, is not, however, unequivocal. The dominant strain in the fiction of West African women writers is the struggle to reconcile the contradictions in their lives: between a traditional perception of their roles and the new demands of professional work, or the opportunities for making money; between the high premium placed on motherhood and the increasing desire for personal fulfilment. Nor should it be forgotten that, of 156 million illiterate people in Africa, two-thirds are women. So, though women may be vocal and visible in their traditional occupations of trade and farming, educated women are still a tiny minority. This creates a problem in terms of audience – who is going to read what women write? Consequently, there has been tremendous flourishing of popular fiction on the continent, despised by the university-educated elite, but voraciously consumed by people with minimal Western education and a lower level of literacy.

The pioneers

West African women writers, though there have always been fewer than their male counterparts, are nothing new. ▷ Adelaide Casely-Hayford, born in Sierra Leone in the mid-19th century, and married into a distinguished Ghanaian family, was probably the earliest. She exemplifies many of the dilemmas which contemporary West African women are still wrestling with, in particular the search for an identity in the welter of Western influences and a changing African society. Her memoirs and some literary pieces were published in the *West African Review* in the 1950s. Her daughter, Gladys Casely-Hayford, was the well-known poet, whose best work was in Krio, the Sierra Leonean pidgin, or creole. Adelaide's husband, and Gladys's father, Joseph Casely-Hayford, was the author of the first novel in English by an African, *Ethiopia Unbound*, published in 1911.

However, the real flowering of West African literature has occurred since the 1960s, the decade of independence. The first novel by a West African woman, published in 1966, was Flora Nwapa's ▷ *Efuru*, a story of a woman in a traditional village in eastern Nigeria. The novel is remarkable in two ways. First, despite the obligatory nature of motherhood, Efuru is childless. The author presents her heroine as a strong, respected, independent woman, who is chosen by the town's goddess, the Woman of the Lake, who is herself childless, to be her acolyte. Second, the novel is remarkable in its narrative technique. Flora Nwapa says that *Efuru* is the story of many women whom she heard talking in her mother's sewing shop. It is told in a form of English as close as possible to Igbo, with the use of Igbo expressions like 'Let the day break' and 'It is only hunger', and Igbo proverbs, which are an intrinsic part of oral culture, and the repository of traditional wisdom. In other words, the writer gives us, not an individual heroine, but a collective consciousness, which is refracted through the oral storytelling elements of her prose.

It is interesting to compare *Efuru* with the work that has been called the Archetypal African Novel, *Things Fall Apart* by Chinua Achebe, published in 1958. Achebe is also Igbo, and his novel also has a traditional village setting, and uses oral elements. However, where Achebe shows the conflict between the old world of tradition and the new values brought by colonialism, Flora Nwapa focuses exclusively on the village, with barely a reference to the white man. Achebe creates in Okonkwo a tragic hero who is destroyed by his inability to change, but Flora Nwapa suggests that, for her heroine, the conflicts are already present in her own community.

Nwapa's emphasis on community and the collective voice brings to mind the emphasis of African-American and Caribbean women writers on 'foremothers' as a source of inspiration. By this they mean the older women whose stories they heard as children, the women talking in the kitchen, as described by ▷Paule Marshall. If there is one factor binding West African women's writing in all its diversity, it is very likely this sense of kinship with the oral tradition, and of a collective experience.

The personal voice

There is a strong strain of autobiographical writing, often fictionalized but nevertheless personal, in West African women's writing. In Nigeria, Buchi Emecheta's three novels, ▷*The Slave Girl*, ▷*The Bride Price* and *Joys of Motherhood* (1979) draw on her grand-mother's and mother's stories, while her own autobiography, *Head Above Water* (1986), relates her experiences as an immigrant to Britain in the 1960s. The most recent publication in this genre is ▷Simi Bedford's ▷*Yoruba Girl Dancing* (1991), an account of the author's childhood in Lagos in the 1940s, and of her being sent to an English boarding school at the age of seven. ▷Mabel Segun's ▷*My Father's Daughter* recalls her childhood in a village parsonage in Nigeria in the colonial era, while in *Ping Pong* (1989) she recounts her exploits as Nigeria's first woman table tennis champion. Ama Ata Aidoo's ▷*Our Sister Killjoy* and the novels of Flora Nwapa similarly contain autobiographical elements.

Of the younger generation, Zaynab Alkali, in her two novels ▷*The Stillborn* and *A Virtuous Woman* (1987), draws on her own childhood in her portrayal of growing up in the Middle Belt of Nigeria, where Christianity, Islam and traditional religion coexisted peacefully. These, and *Destiny* (1988) and *Victory* (1989) by ▷Hauwa Ali, are especially interesting as the only published works in English by northern Nigerian, Moslem women.

Among the francophone women writers the Senegalese ▷Ken Bugul (a pseudonym meaning 'nobody wants it' in Wolof) published a remarkably outspoken book in 1982, entitled ▷*Le Baobab fou (The Mad Baobab)*. In it, she describes, as in Aidoo's *Our Sister Killjoy*, an African woman's first encounter with Europe. The frankness of her account, which includes how she survived as a prostitute in Brussels, is unusual enough in the context of African women's writing, but especially an Islamic society like Senegal. Sexuality is generally treated with a decorous silence in the writing of most West African women. *Our Sister Killjoy* is also unusual in this respect, with its depiction of a quasi-lesbian relationship between Sisi, the heroine, and a young German woman. But Ken Bugul is unique in her explicit treatment of sexuality as a metaphor for oppression.

▷Nafissatou Diallo, another Senegalese writer, prefaces her autobiography, ▷*A Dakar Childhood*, with the statement: 'I am not the heroine of a novel, but an ordinary woman of this country, Senegal: a mother and a working woman . . . What would a woman write about who has no claim to any exceptional imagination or outstanding literary talent? She could only write about herself, of course.' This deceptively simple assertion masks the extent of the stereotyping, misrepresentation and idealization of women that African women writers are seeking to combat. The very act of writing is subversive of received notions of what women are and what they ought to be – hence, perhaps, the need for a disclaimer.

West African women, despite their high profile in prestige professions such as law, accountancy and journalism, still have to contend with the abiding prejudice that discourse is not the woman's realm, that it is somehow inappropriate or immoral. To be critical, therefore, of the status quo is an an act of courage, which some women writers have paid for with personal suffering in the form of divorce, imprisonment, or even having their manuscripts destroyed by their husbands (as described by Buchi Emecheta in *Head Above Water*, 1986).

In the face of such repressive influences, the Senegalese feminist writer ▷Awa Thiam has asked, 'what use will it be to write of the black woman if by her writing we do not learn who she really is? It is the task of black women to re-establish the truth' (*La Parole aux négresses*, 1978, ▷ *Speak Out, Black Sisters*). Works which draw, directly or in a fictionalized form, on the writer's own experience are, therefore, important documents of an often-repressed social reality. Included here are the novels ▷ *Pélandrova* by the Madagascan writer Pélandrova Dreo, and ▷ *La Brise du jour* (*The Dawn Breeze*) by the Cameroonian Lydie Dooh-Bunya.

Writing as dialogue

Beyond social realism, West African women's writing has a definable aesthetics which distinguishes it both from Western feminist writing and from writing by male counterparts. It is an aesthetics which privileges communication, setting up a dialogue into which the reader is invited to enter, rather than alienating the reader by the use of mystifying literary techniques or imagery. The Senegalese writer ▷Mariama Bâ's first novel, *So Long a Letter* (1979), exemplifies this tendency. Written in the form of an intimate letter from one friend to another, it is a dialogue between two women who represent the choices available to Moslem women faced with the prospect of polygamy. Ramatoulaye, the letter-writer, expresses her anguish, not only at her widowhood, but at the pain and humiliation she felt when displaced by a younger second wife. Aissatou, the letter's recipient, is an independent woman living and working in the USA. Her response to the same situation was to take her children and go abroad. Both, in their different ways, have paid the price of exile and alienation. Though Mariama Bâ was herself divorced, she is not arguing against marriage. Like Ama Ata Aidoo and many of the romantic fiction writers, she seeks rather to redefine love and relationships in a less materialistic, less conventional way, and to show women's dissatisfaction with the limited choices available to them.

The question of male infidelity in a society rooted in a polygamous tradition is central to much of West African women's writing. Men may defend polygamy as part of 'our' culture, but women have a different story to tell. This is the theme of ▷Funmilayo Fakunle's realistic portraits of Yoruba family life in her novels *Chasing the Shadow* (1980), *The Sacrificial Child* (1978) and *Chance or Destiny?* (1983), and of the Ivorian ▷Anne-Marie Adiaffi's *La Ligne brisée* (1989) (*The Broken Line*).

Another central concern is ▷infertility, and the suffering imposed on a woman by childlessness. In the Nigerian ▷Ifeoma Okoye's novel *Behind the Clouds* (1982), it is assumed by everyone, as is usual, that the couple's failure to have a child is the woman's fault. The marriage breaks under the strain, and it is only when the problem is diagnosed as being the husband's that the couple are restored to each other. The element of romantic fantasy in the conventional happy ending is not just an easy way out. It expresses a very real desire on the part of many women for something other than what they have. This desire finds expression in the creation of a fantasy of ideal love, as defined by the woman. It represents a yearning for social, as well as personal, transformation. The enormous popularity of ▷romantic fiction, imported and indigenous, testifies to the desire, not simply for escape, but for change. Unlike the Western romantic tradition, the heroines of romantic fiction writers like the Nigerians ▷Helen Ovbiagele, Rosina Umelo,

Hauwa Ali, Funmilayo Fakunle and Gracy Osifo, the Sierra Leonean Yemi Lucilda Hunter, Ami Gad from Togo and Thérèse Kuoh-Moukouri from Cameroon, are women in the process of forging their own identities. They accomplish this through their own efforts, after a struggle which may involve recourse to all sorts of means of survival, including prostitution to pay for an education. The happy ending, involving the perfect man, the white wedding and material success, is therefore the heroine's reward for daring to stand by her principles.

Drama

West African women have always participated in traditional performing arts, including dance, song and recitation. The fact that few women have written or published plays testifies to two important factors. The first is that the written play script is a product of an elite, Westernized concept of theatre, which privileges dialogue and sets up an artificial division between the different elements of performance. The second is the suspicion with which a woman's close involvement with the theatre is regarded, since it requires long hours away from home, attending rehearsals and working with men.

However, a handful of West African women have made names for themselves in the theatre. Prominent among these is ▷Efua Sutherland, a key figure in the growth of a modern theatre culture in Ghana. She was an active participant in the cultural ferment which accompanied Ghana's transition to being the first independent African country in March 1957. In September of that year she established the Ghana Drama Studio as a centre for cultural experimentation and a testing ground for new writers. Both in her theatre work and in her writing (the plays *Foriwa*, 1967, ▷*Edufa* and ▷*The Marriage of Anansewa*), she has consciously drawn on indigenous traditions of performance and oral storytelling, in an attempt to create a contemporary theatre rooted in the Ghanaian artistic heritage. Sutherland's younger contemporary, Ama Ata Aidoo, worked with her in the Drama Studio in the early 1960s. Aidoo's first published work was a play, *Dilemma of a Ghost* (1965), dramatizing the conflict between traditional and contemporary values, while ▷*Anowa* (1968) is a subversive play which makes connections between slavery, gender domination and the corruption of power.

The Cameroonian writer Werewere Liking is perhaps the most radical in her assertion of traditional theatrical forms in a contemporary setting. Her Ki-yi Mbock Theatre, founded in 1984 and based in the Ivorian capital, Abidjan, is part of a remarkable cultural project celebrating African indigenous art forms in all their guises. Calling her dramatic practice 'ritual theatre', she uses traditional elements, including giant puppets, masks, drumming and storytelling. The vibrant and spectacular performance which results makes imaginative use of the traditional relationship between the genres of visual art, music, poetry and movement.

In Nigeria, the Yoruba tradition of travelling theatre consists of large hierarchical companies under the leadership of a male figure such as the late Hubert Ogunde or Duro Ladipo. In these, women play an active part as performers and are often the wives and daughters of the patriarchal figurehead. The English-language theatre is very much a product of the universities, and it is here that women have emerged as dramatists. The best-known and most prolific is ▷Zulu Sofola, whose plays, such as ▷*King Emene* and ▷*The Sweet Trap*, assert the centrality and importance of the traditional status quo, and women's place within it. In form, they follow a conventional western pattern of dialogue within a linear narrative. This is broadly true of all the Nigerian women dramatists, even where they use oral performance elements. ▷Tess Onwueme's play ▷*The Desert Encroaches*, in which the characters are portrayed as animals, draws on the festival masking tradition. She consciously repudiates the Western theatre tradition, emphasizing rapport and interaction with the audience, as well as traditional motifs. Like Zulu Sofola, Tess Onwueme, ▷Catherine Acholonu and ▷Julie Omoifo-Okoh are university-based, giving them access to student companies to perform their works.

Poetry

Here again, women have traditionally participated in the creation and performance of oral poetry, and are also writing in European and African languages. There is, for instance, a long tradition of Hausa women's poetry in northern Nigeria, largely disregarded due to the invisibility of women in seclusion, and the scandal attaching to public utterance. Women praisesingers (traditional singers of praises to royalty, heroes etc.) and composers tend to be atypical, while writers are even fewer. The researcher Beverly Mack has documented two Hausa women publishing poetry in the conservative Islamic tradition, Hauwa Gwaram and Hajiya 'Yar Shehu.

Among the francophone poets, the most prominent are Jeanne Ngo-Mai (Cameroon), Tanella Boni, Pascale Quao-Gaudens and ▷Véronique Tadjo (Côte d'Ivoire), and a number from Senegal: ▷Kiné Kirama Fall, Ndaye Coumba Mbengwe Diakhate and Annette M'Baye. The critic Kembe Milolo has pointed out that the elite education provided as part of the French project of assimilation was available mainly to boys. Until very recently, the main priority for girls was marriage, and for women the care of children and their husbands. When the poetry of Kiné Kirama Fall was published as *Chants de la rivière fraîche* in 1976, it was partly due to the encouragement and patronage of President Leopold Sédar Senghor, himself a poet. In his preface, he draws attention to the fact that Fall left school at fourteen to get married, and her writing is limited above all by lack of confidence in handling language. '*Ses livres*,' says Senghor, '*ce sont les rues de Dakar*' ('her books are the Dakar streets').

This is not, of course, true of the younger, cosmopolitan, university-educated writers like Véronique Tadjo, whose facility with language is striking. Yet the intensity of observation and emotion Fall brings to bear, the imagery drawn primarily from nature and familiar places, renders her poetry memorable. Nor is she unaware of the musical potential of language, the devices of incantation, apostrophe and echo. Annette M'Baye's volume *Kaddu* (1966) displays a similar sensitivity to nuances of sound, counterpoising rhythms evocative of blues, drums and popular music in the expression of a specifically feminine African perspective.

The published anglophone women poets, from Gladys Casely-Hayford to Tess Onwueme and Catherine Acholonu, all fall within the category of elite, Western-educated women. In Nigeria, ▷Mabel Segun has been writing and publishing poems and stories since the 1950s. Her *Conflict and Other Poems* (1989) contains a selection of forty poems, which bear witness to a cool, ironic, appraising eye levelled at all aspects of Nigerian society over four decades.

The most explicitly feminist anglophone poet is ▷Molara Ogundipe-Leslie, whose volume *Sew the Old Days* (1985) includes poems of protest and satire unique in their outspokenness. This collection, and Ama Ata Aidoo's *Someone Talking to Sometime* (1985) represents an *oeuvre* stretching back to the 1960s. The latter is characterized by pain: of witnessing a dream destroyed, of watching corruption and coercion replace idealism and equality in the aspirations of Ghana's leaders, and the pain of loss – of friends, of loves, of home. The prevailing tone of all these poets is disillusionment. There is little of the lyrical, celebratory quality of the francophone poets, and a far sharper, more explicit expression of bitterness and criticism than is generally to be found in the prose. However, the celebration of traditional forms, through the use of Igbo motifs and the oral tradition, emerges in the poetry of ▷Ifi Amadiume and Catherine Acholonu.

Disguises and departures

Some women prose writers have stepped outside the world of specifically women's issues to treat subjects traditionally defined as masculine. Notable here is the Nigerian Adaora Lily Ulasi, whose novels are an unconventional amalgam of genres: detection and suspense, anticolonial satire and the supernatural, using standard English and badly-realized pidgin. One of the older generation of writers, she, like Mabel Segun, arguably tries to conceal her femininity beneath a 'masculine' style and content. The likelihood of not being taken seriously in a world where the academy and the publishing industry tend to be male-dominated is not confined to West African women writers, but they have the added anxiety of social censure if they speak too openly or expose too much. It is interesting to note that though Marietou Mbaye (▷Ken Bugul) was prepared to publish under her own name, her publishers insisted on a pseudonym. The younger writer, ▷Ifeoma Okoye, also uses a male protagonist in her novel ▷*Men Without Ears*, satirizing the rampant materialism and corruption of oil-boom Nigeria. The Senegalese Khadi Fall's novel *Mademba* (1989) similarly has a male protagonist, while Aminata Sow Fall's novel ▷*The Beggars' Strike* satirizes the hypocrisy of those who pretend to live by Islamic precepts but only really care about themselves. She exposes the complicity of the rich in a system which depends on the poverty of the majority, whether gaining religious credit by giving alms to beggars on the streets of Dakar, or in the relationship of dependency by which the developing world receives aid from the developed world.

With certain notable exceptions, West African women's writing tends to opt for linguistic clarity and simplicity, and a fairly linear narrative. This is no doubt due in part to the priority that oral storytelling places on communication. Some of the younger writers are, however, experimenting with form, notably the Cameroonian Werewere Liking and her compatriot ▷Calixte Beyala. Whereas many of the writers discussed here remain within a tradition which can broadly be classified as classic realism, Liking evolves an innovative new form using poetic techniques and drawing on myth and the subconscious, as in her novel, ▷*Elle sera de jaspe et de corail: journal d'un misovire* (*She will be of jasper and coral: diary of a manhater*).

Another young writer, Véronique Tadjo of the Côte d'Ivoire, has shown that she is equally adept at poetry, the novel and children's fiction. Her children's story *Lord of the Dance* (1988), illustrated by her, fuses a medieval English church song and Ivorian mythology in a wholly original retelling of the creation myth. Perhaps, as the body of women's writing grows, providing a context and a language for women to write in, women will experiment further with form and with new ways of telling women's story.

Writing today

The title of Ama Ata Aidoo's second novel, ▷*Changes*, published more than a decade after *Our Sister Killjoy*, is emblematic of the current state of West African women's writing. In other respects it also points to a new confidence and maturity emerging in women's writing as a specific category. This has long been the case with African-American writers like ▷Toni Morrison, ▷Alice Walker and ▷Ntozake Shange, or the Caribbean writers Paule Marshall, ▷Jamaica Kincaid and ▷Olive Senior. Enforced displacement and deracination, though agonizing, have enabled certain very positive factors to emerge. The imposition of a foreign language on the diaspora has led, in time, to a form of English of far greater poetic resonance, thanks to its African inflexions. A communal experience of suffering, loss and contemporary economic and racial inequality has similarly given rise to a deep-seated notion of survival through community. The reverence of African-American women writers for the culture of their slave grandmothers is one source of literary richness.

For writers in Africa, the fact that English and French, no matter the level of proficiency, are second languages, is of some significance. However, women's writing as a recognizable body of work within a coherent framework of shared experience and aesthetics is more elusive because of the cultural and historical diversity of the region. Yet it is beginning to take shape, as the audience for women's writing grows with increasing literacy and self-awareness. The contours of a definable aesthetics are perceptible in the universal references, implicit and explicit, to oral tradition. An increasingly important element of West African women's writing is a sophistication in their meshing of oral and literary techniques, and in their humour and subtlety. Aidoo's ironic, self-deprecatory 'confession' at the start of *Changes*, that she once said she could never write about lovers in Accra because there were too many more important issues, demonstrates confidence and autonomy both as a woman and as a writer. For a writer, known for her critical relationship to power politics in Africa, to encase a serious and subversive message in so despised a feminine form as the romance is itself subversive. In form and content the novel deals with struggle, the process of change, the taking of risks, and is close in spirit to the works of Mariama Bâ, Ken Bugul, Lydie Dooh-Bunya, Flora Nwapa and others less well-knqwn, such as ▷Aminata Maiga-Ka and Funmilayo Fakunle. Collectively, these writers are rewriting the script of social and intellectual possibilities for women in West Africa.

▷Bride price (West Africa); Clitoridectomy/Infibulation (West Africa); Journalism (West Africa); Prostitution (West Africa); Religion: Christianity, Islam and traditional Beliefs in West Africa; Slavery (West Africa); Witchcraft (West Africa)

FATMA MOUSSA-MAHMOUD

31 Turkey and the Arab Middle East

The area covered in this essay formed one colossal political and cultural unit for some 400 years (1516–1919). The dismantling of the Ottoman Empire at the end of World War I, and the tide of nationalism that swept over the Middle East, first set Arabic and Turkish cultures apart. The process of 'modernization' – imitating western European models by adopting European science and technology – started slowly in the 19th century in reaction to Napoleon's ▷French Expedition to Egypt (1798–1801). This was the first serious European incursion into the vast Oriental Islamic empire that had survived almost intact from the Middle Ages. Among the results of this incursion was the beginning of the study of European languages, particularly English and French. The translation of European literature, and therefore the introduction óf new literary forms (drama, the novel and the short story) into both Turkish and Arabic, proceeded along parallel lines, with Turkish a decade or two ahead.

Classical Arabic poetry
Poetry is the most prized art among the Arabs; a skill in versification was and still is a highly regarded accomplishment for both men and women. 'Abbas Aqqad (1889–1964) whose Friday salon pronouncenents are as widely circulated in the Arab world as Dr. Johnson's *bons mots* are in the West, affirmed that women could not excel in poetry, which, to him, was a full and free expression of emotion. Singling out ▷al-Khansa as the only great woman poet in classical Arabic, he attributes her power to the fact that 'she appears before us weeping tears of lamentation'.

al-Khansa set the model for *marathi* (elegies) in Arabic poetry. Her laments for the death of her two brothers in tribal wars are the best poems in her *diwan* (collection of poetry). The best-known of these elegies is responsible for many images (and clichés) that have passed into common usage in Arabic. It also set the model for the attributes ascribed to the lost one: from savage courage in war to great compassion and generosity in times of drought. The same virtues are celebrated in the elegies of ▷Layla al-'Akhyaliyya lamenting the death of her lover, murdered by her own people.

An anthology of *Sha'irat al-'Arab* (Arab female poets) published in 1967 gives specimens of verse by 242 women, from al-Khansa and her pre-Islamic contemporaries to the 11th-century Andalusian princess, ▷Wallada bint al-Mustakfi. The editor admits that their verse covers a variety of subjects, but, with the puritanical self-censorship of latter-day Moslems, he notes that he has eliminated all erotic verse and anecdotes of exchanges of *mujun* (open sexual repartee) by ▷*jawari* (slave women), reported freely in the great medieval anthologies of Arabic literature and history. The same sources were ransacked to better purpose by an Iraqi woman academic in 1981, Wadja al-Atraqji, who gives a fascinating account of forty-four women poets in the first hundred years of the Abbasid reign (754–1258) in *Women in Abbasid Literature*.

Many were ▷*hara'ir* (free women) but a larger number were *jawari*; of the former, 'Ulaya bint al-Mahdi (died 825), Harun al-Rashid's sister, is said to have attended his *majlis* (court) behind a ▷*hijab* or curtain. Of the *jawari*, two names particularly stand out because of the excellence of their compositions, both in verse and prose: ▷'Uraib and ▷'Anan, who was whipped by her master when she protested she was too tired to join his guests in a poetic contest.

One woman stands almost alone in a poetic tradition new to Islam, *Sufi* (or Islamic mystic poetry). She is ▷Rabi'a al-'Adawiyya, who composed fervently erotic poetry addressed to the all-enveloping Divine Lover.

Modern times

An accomplished man of letters in the 18th and 19th centuries was one who could compose verse in Arabic, Persian and Turkish. One of the last poets to write verse in all three languages was a woman, the Egyptian ▷'Aisha al-Taymuriyya. Only her Arabic poetry and prose are now discussed as specimens of early feminist writing. As a member of the Turkish aristocracy in Egypt she grew up and was educated within the ▷*harem*, in the women's quarters, where she was taught entirely by women. She managed, however, through the offices of a sympathetic, learned father, to study languages and *'arud* (versification), rather than music and embroidery.

Education for women has now spread over the whole of the Arab world, and women's place in work and public life has changed drastically since the publication of Qasim Amin's (1863–1908) ▷*The Liberation of Women* (1899) and *The New Woman* (1900). Still many Arab poets, from the reserved ▷Fadwa Tuqan to the 'rebellious' ▷Zabiya Khamis, celebrate the memory of a supportive poet in the family – a brother or a father. ▷Nazik al-Mala'ika's father was a poet, and so were her mother and sister. A comparison of the verse of ▷Umm Nizar, her mother, traditional in form and content, with the poetry and criticism of Nazik al-Mala'ika, one of the great modern innovators, reveals the progress of Arabic poetry in the 20th century. With her compatriot, Badr Shakir al-Sayyab (1926–1964), Nazik al-Mala'ika is credited with initiating the ▷New Movement in Arabic poetry.

Politics and poetry

Most Arabic literature in the 20th century has been influenced by politics, poetry no less than other literary forms. The course of the century is punctuated by uprisings against occupation by the British in Iraq, Egypt and Palestine, and by the French in Syria and Lebanon. In the second half of the century the three Maghreb states, Tunis, Morocco and Algeria, waged a war of independence against the French. The tragedy of Palestine, the plight of the Palestinian people and the repeated defeats of the Arabs, both military and political, dominate Arabic poetry to this day. The ▷*naksa* (1967) and the *nakba* (▷*naksa*) (1947–8) are lamented in some of the most daring and innovative poetry by women as well as men. The tone of disillusionment and alienation in these writings is unusual in Arabic poetry and is evocative of some of the western European literary movements. Many Arab writers, however, including Arab women poets, who have consistently contributed to the mainstream of Arabic poetry, see no contradiction in asserting an independent national identity while acknowledging Western influence.

This mainstream has carried a strong current of reflective poetry on nature and love, to which we have notable contributions by women. From the romanticism of ▷May Ziyadah, influenced by ▷*Mahjar* poets, to the 'whispered verse' of ▷Malak 'Abdel-'Aziz, we have evidence of the development in Arabic poetry of a new idiom and a new sensibility. Ali Mahmoud Taha (1902–1949), one of the last romantic poets of the Apollo group, seems to have deeply influenced Fadwa Tuqan, Nazik al-Mala'ika and scores of their generation, though the magic of his poetry was rendered inappropriate by the mid-century traumas of war, defeat and displacement. It is now the caustic, explicit, rebellious poetry of ▷Nizar Qabbani that is most widely read. Signs of his influence can easily be seen in the verse of the Kuwaiti poet ▷Su'ad al-Sabah.

Much of the best poetry written in Arabic today is accused of being 'modernist' (a pejorative term in Arab countries). Such poetry, particularly that written by women, has raised alarm among conservative critics, and opposition in the state-funded publishing establishments in many Arab countries. Only in ▷Beirut, with its more or less free press and its thriving commercial publishing firms, has the voice of feminist protest continued to be heard, alongside dissent from all over the Arab world.

Arabic fiction

Classical Arabic literature is rich in *qasas* (narrative fiction) of all kinds. Tales, anecdotes and quasi-historical narratives are included in the medieval anthologies mentioned above. Traditional literature in Arabic includes ▷*The Arabian Nights*. These stories are narrated by a woman, Shahrazad, who spins tales of wonder for a thousand and one nights to save her life. Though testifying to the creativity of Arab traditional storytellers, this old tradition had little to do with the introduction of the novel and the short story in Arabic literature early in this century; these were modern literary forms borrowed entirely from the West. The first practitioners of these new arts were men; the women mainly produced poetry, essays and journalism.

It is only in the second half of this century that we get any significant fiction written by Arab women. With the exception of Beirut, publishing as a trade in the Arab world has little place for fiction, and women have few opportunities with publishers who are interested only in big names. They have better chances with state-funded publishing, but as newcomers they are still a minority.

Many Arab readers (and critics) dismiss fiction by women as simply autobiographical, and focused on the relationship between the sexes. If the writer was ready to dare family and social disapproval by going beyond these boundaries, she secured a wide readership and ready publishers. ▷Colette Khuri's *Days With Him* (1959) was the first novel by an Arab woman to go into five editions within a few years.

The outspoken voice of ▷Ghada al-Samman is the most widely heard in Arabic fiction today. Her work is voluminous, and includes journalism, travel writing, memoirs, interviews, poetry and fiction, with little difference in the language used in the different forms. Her message is one of the necessity of freedom and of speaking the truth.

The Egyptian writer ▷Nawal El Sa'dawi has also taken advantage of the lack of censorship in Beirut to publish some outspoken feminist works on the sexual and social oppression of women in a patriarchal Arab society. Originally trained as a physician, she has had the courage to discuss problems of 'female anatomy'. She introduced for the first time into fiction characters of sexually repressed women, whose neurosis and depression may be attributed to the childhood traumas of ▷*khitan* (clitoridectomy) or male sexual abuse. The same subjects are also treated in fiction by ▷Alifa Rif'at in her short stories.

Heroines of significance

Many Arab (male) novelists' heroines are symbolic of nationalist values. Perceptive women readers have complained that such heroines are simply signs, invested with the writers' romantic, diffident or openly aggressive attitudes. The female characters in the fiction of ▷Nagib Mahfuz are often cited as examples. For many years women writers modelled their characters on the prototypes set by the men, with an added measure of sentimentality. *The Open Door* (1960) by ▷Latifa al-Zayyat marked the birth of a new kind of heroine. The novel combines conscious painstaking skill with a partisan feminist plea, tracing the growth and liberation of Layla, a middle-class schoolgirl, whose growth to maturity and self-fulfilment parallel the development of the national struggle for independence in Egypt.

▷Emily Nasralla's *Birds of September* (1962) gives us a heroine, Muna, whose career is representative of the plight of her home village in the south of Lebanon. The streams are dry and the land is unploughed through a shortage of strong arms; though Muna loves her village, she cannot feel part of it, or accept the elderly North American immigrant who has come home to buy himself a wife. She leaves for the city, where she ends up in a stifling office, her fingertips glued to a typewriter.

Zahra in ▷Hanan al-Shaykh's *Story of Zahra* (1980) is another Lebanese woman, a neurotic victim of violence and fear. Raped and morally degraded, the ugliness of her experience erupts in spots and sores on her skin.

The nightmare of Beirut is not just the experience of middle-class Syrian or Lebanese writers; it was part of the daily routine of thousands of Palestinian refugees in their shanty towns and congested camps. ▷Liana Badr recreates for the reader the seething life of the women in those camps. In her *View Over Fakahani* (1983), a short novel, there are four voices: three women's and one man's. The women's discourse is low-keyed, dealing with the day-to-day chores of living, fetching water, cooking, sheltering from the bombs and trying to cure a child's wound with 'black ointment' because they cannot get to the first aid centre. Men are killed and called martyrs, but the women have to go on living and bringing up children as best as they can.

The city in female consciousness

The decay of other Arab cities apart from Beirut is seen through the eyes of women writers whose characters are alienated by the ugliness and wanton destruction of the cities. The Palestinian women in Liana Badr's story grow potted plants in a narrow balcony high above the busy street. In ▷Salwa Bakr's Cairo a woman can be driven crazy by the *tufan* (deluge) of high-rise buildings, uprooted trees and broken pavements which has taken over the street of her childhood, once notable for its 'thirty-one beautiful green trees'.

Damascus is often presented in literature as a woman, always associated with the fragrance of jasmine. The history of the city in its struggle against French rule is told in the memoirs of a woman, *Damascus Smile of Sorrow* (1980) by ▷'Ulfah al-Idlibi. Sabriya, a variant of *sabr* (patience), is in the end crushed by male despotism in the family, by the weight of social customs.

Lena, a heroine of a later generation, gets away. ▷Samar 'Attar's *Lena: Portrait of a Girl of Damascus* (1982) ends with the heroine leaving her home town: 'I refuse to serve what I have ceased to believe in, whether you call it family, friends or motherland.' The novel is clearly modelled on James Joyce's *Portrait of the Artist as A Young Man* (1916), but the decay of Damascus is drawn from life.

New feminist discourse

The work of younger women writers is marked by a new feminist discourse. They have come to realize that the male revolutionary discourse, which tied women's liberation to national liberation and the growth of democracy, has failed to produce any concrete results. Liana Badr said on Woman's Day, March 1990, that after twenty years of active participation in the Palestinian Resistance, women's subordinate status has hardly changed. ▷Sahar Khalifa's educated professional journalist, Rafif, in *Sunflowers* (1980) comes to the bitter conclusion that 'gender is class.' The 'democratic' discussions of her male colleagues on the editorial board get her nowhere. The magic words 'majority vote' only make her sad: 'The majority defeated the women of Iran; the majority defeated the women of Algeria . . . Ataturk did it on his own, decades ago, without socialism, without slogans.' Not only the educated, politicized Rafif, but the simple women of Nablus, the poor workers and mothers, also speak in a language which contrasts starkly with the discussions of the 'comrades', and the clipped, suspicious words of the masked partisans on the run.

The new feminist discourse works mainly by writing the female body – or rather bodies. The heat and steam of the decaying Turkish bath, with its wet walls, slippery floors and crowds of naked women with their squealing babies, provides Sahar Khalifa with an *inferno* for her working-class heroine. For Aliya Mamduh, it is the 'female continent' in the heart of Baghdad; Huda the inquisitive tomboyish girl of nine in ▷*Mothballs* (1986), is there confronted with the truth of female flesh without ornament, without clothing.

'Women in their apartments', women going about their business: in the kitchen, with their shopping baskets in the market, at the hairdresser's, or supervising the arrangements for an elegant wedding, are carefully recreated in the novels of ▷Radwa 'Ashur. A scene in her novel *A Warm Stone* (1985) could be used as a manual on how to prepare the traditional Egyptian dish of *mulukhia* and rice.

Women at their lowest, in the trash-bin of society – the women's jail – are the subject of a recently published novel, *The Golden Chariot Does Not Go Up To Heaven* (1991), by Salwa Bakr. The feminine discourse here breaks away completely from accepted rules of narrative or good taste. It is the closest we get to the archetypal female narrator, Shahrazad, of the traditional tales.

Drama and short stories

There have up to now been very few Arab women dramatists, but there are now some writing television dramas and film scripts. The short story, on the other hand, has from the start been women writers' favoured medium. Varying in length, quality and literary affiliation, short stories by Arab women can hardly be classified: from the committed Moroccan ▷Khanatta Binnuna to the romantic Kuwaiti ▷Layla al-'Uthman to the 'modernist' Egyptian ▷I'tidal 'Uthman, their output reflects the whole range of modern literary techniques or influences. The few women's stories which have appeared in English translation hardly represent the sheer quantity of stories which have been produced over a period of more than fifty years.

Arab women writing in French or English

Because they originally went to a foreign language school, or lived in Europe for many years, a number of Arab women writers have written verse, novels and stories in French, and some in English. Only a few have made any impression on European readers. Among these, ▷Nadia Tueni was awarded the Prize of the French Academy in 1973; ▷Andrée Chedid, poet, novelist and dramatist, has won many literary prizes and also the approval of Arab critics, who claim her as an Arab poet. The serene clarity of her French style shows no signs of tension between an Egyptian identity and her French medium of expression.

The Algerian ▷Assia Djebar is the most talented woman among francophone writers in North Africa. She writes of the life of Algerian women in French, her 'father tongue', not Arabic, her 'mother tongue'. The tension between subject matter and medium of expression at one time led Assia Djebar to stop writing altogether and turn to film-making. The same tension informs the writings of ▷Ahdaf Soueif, whose English is modulated to interpret material for which standard English would be inadequate. Soraya Antonius also writes in English: her novel, ▷*The Lord* (1986), depicts the troubles in

Palestine. ▷Etel 'Adnan is a poet whose subjects are mainly Lebanon and Palestine, though she writes in French and English. It distresses her not to have mastered Arabic enough to write poetry in that language. She has found a solution for her Arab soul; she *paints* in Arabic, she says.

Turkish women's writing

Turkish literature has a shorter history than Arabic or Persian literature. In the centuries of conquest and expansion the polite language of the Ottoman Empire was Persian, while the language of religion was Arabic. Turkish was the language of the common people: the Turan nomadic tribes and the peasants of Anatolia. Turkish poetry started with the *Sufi* tradition; when Maulana Jalal-udin al-Rumi (1207–1273) settled in Konya, he composed verses in Turkish to instruct his poor Turkish disciples.

The earliest record of a woman composing Turkish poetry was ▷Mihri Khatun. She composed a number of love poems in the tradition of Persian poetry, of which only twenty-eight survive in manuscript.

Another 15th-century poet was Zeinab, whose father had instructed her because he had noticed 'sparks' of talent. She was a friend of Mihri and exchanged verse correspondence with her. She stopped writing after her marriage, but some fragments of her *diwan* (collection) have survived and are printed in E.J.W. Gibb's *History of Ottoman Poetry*, II (1902). In the 16th century, we have the name of one female poet connected with court circles, Hubba Kadin (died 1589). She was the only woman to write a romantic *masnavi* (a verse form in Persian and Turkish of 3,000 couplets), 'Jamshid and Hurshid'. She also composed a number of *ghazels* (odes in the Persian tradition) and *qasidas* (odes in the Arabic tradition). Another woman who received tutoring because she showed special talent was Sitke Umetullah (died c 1704). She left a *diwan* of poetry, and so did Fatima Khanim (died c 1710).

The 18th century produced the first Turkish woman with a recognized, collected *diwan*, ▷Fitnat-Khanim (c 1725–1780). She was treated gallantly by famous poets of the period, apparently at the expense of her husband, who was satirized in lively exchanges between the poets. Another liberated poet was ▷Leyla Khanim (died ?1847–8) who broke away early from her marriage bonds. Sheref Khanim (1809–?) composed a large *diwan* of religious poetry. She wrote some of the finest elegies in Turkish on the death of al-Hussain and the Martyrs of Karbela.

One of the first products of the early hesitant steps of 'modernization', ▷Nigâr, is described as a poet-memoirist; she held a weekly salon, made famous by French novelist Pierre Loti (1850–1923), where she received Turkish and foreign literary figures. Another daughter of the aristocracy who was tutored at home and was influenced by French literature was ▷Fatima Aliye.

Modern Turkish writers

The name of ▷Halidé Edib is associated with all the changes that have transformed Turkey since the opening decades of the 20th century. Her literary output was enormous, covering two distinctive periods of Turkish literature. The thorough 'modernization' of Turkey with the establishment of the Turkish Republic (1923), and the forcible break with the old traditions of the Islamic Ottoman Empire, officially revolutionized the position of Turkish women. Secular education for women and equal opportunities in university education boosted their numbers in professional careers, notably in journalism and the media. Women writers had to cope with the problems caused by the new ethic, by the new social forces, and – professionally – with problems of the new language: the modern Turkish advocated by the poet-philosopher for the republic, Ziya Gokalp (1876–1925). Modern Turkish, based on the language of Istanbul, aimed at discarding all lexical and grammatical borrowings from Arabic and Persian. Gokalp's linguistic recommendations were taken further by Kemalist legislation (1928): the modern Turks were to look to Europe and to write from left to right in a new Latin script, not the traditional Arabic 'incomprehensible signs'.

Of the women who exemplify these changes, ▷Süküfa Nihal Başar is an obvious writer to cite, while ▷Halidé Nusret Zorlutuna was affected all her life by the political upheavals in Turkey. Others are ▷Suat Dervis, who studied literature in Berlin, worked as a journalist and ended with a long list of novels to her name, and ▷Güner Ener, who taught English and wrote short stories before devoting her time to design.

The secularization imposed by Mustafa Kemal (1881–1938) on Turkish culture did not always go very deep, and many writers, including women, stuck to the old traditions. Some examples are ▷Samiha Ayverdi, who wrote of Turkish life as being dominated by the ideals of Islamic *Jihad*, and ▷Nezihe Araz, who wrote for conservative pro-Islamic newspapers and composed *Sufi* poetry. Many women, however, took advantage the opportunities offered by the abolition of *hijab* and Kemal's invitation to them to participate fully in public and political life. A few deserve particular mention as representative of a great current in modern Turkish literature.

▷Sevgi Soysal studied in Ankara and Göttingen, and worked for Turkish radio and television. ▷'Adalet Agoglu was for many years Director of Ankara Radio Theatre. ▷Füruzan is an actress and short story writer who shows deep sympathy for the weak and the poor. The work of Güner Ener and ▷Gülten Akin shows the influence of foreign travel and foreign literature. ▷Leyla Erbil and Sevim Burak (born 1931) had unconventional experiences of work and education, and both wrote interesting fiction. ▷Tomris Uyar is a recognized critic of contemporary literature who started her career by translating English literature.

Turkish women's writing today is rich with revelations of a society in turmoil, where 'modernization' imposed from above is only skin-deep. The position of women in this contradictory situation is particularly precarious, as is brilliantly illustrated in Aysel Özakin's novel ▷*The Prize Giving* (1980).

▷French-speaking North Africa

Bib: Andrews, Walter G., *An Introduction to Ottoman Poetry*; Evin, Ahmet, *Origins and Development of the Turkish Novel*; Garnet, Lucy, *The Women of Turkey and their Folklore*; Gibb, E.J.W., *A History of Ottoman Poetry*; Hofman, H.F., *Turkish Literature: A Bibliographical, Survey*; Iz, Fahir (ed.), *An Anthology of Modern Turkish Short Stories*; Mittler, Louis, *Ottoman Turkish Writers: A Bibliographical Dictionary of Significant Figures in Pre-Republican Turkish Literature*, and *Contemporary Turkish Writers: A Critical Bio-Bibliography of Leading Turkish Writers up to 1980; The Penguin Book of Turkish Verse*; Sonmez, Emel, *Turkish Women in Turkish Literature of the Nineteenth Century*.

Israel

Israeli literature is part of a continuous literary corpus, called 'Modern Hebrew literature', which extends beyond fixed geographical boundaries. Modern Hebrew literature emerged not in Israel but in Europe over two hundred years ago, at the time when Jewish life began to come out of its seclusion and reach out for Western culture. Along with European Humanism, it was then that Modern Hebrew literature shifted its vision from God to man and became secular, giving rise to the movement of ▷Jewish Enlightenment (1781–1881). T. Carmi noted in his introduction to ▷ *The Penguin Book of Hebrew Verse*, that this movement began in Prussia as a rationalist movement. By the middle of the 19th century, it had assumed a romantic-nationalistic aspect, as the major Jewish cultural centres shifted from western to eastern Europe. The wave of pogroms that struck Russian Jewry in the 1880s undermined the possibility of the ideal of Jewish emancipation in Europe and indirectly initiated the Zionist movement. This brought about yet another geographical shift. The different waves of Jewish immigration finally moved the Hebrew cultural centre from Europe to the Holy Land, or Palestine as it was then called. It is only since 1948, with the establishment of the state of Israel, that 'Israeli literature' came into being. Because of this unique history, any discussion of women's writing has to take into consideration the centres in Europe, Palestine and Israel.

In these centres, women writers were scarce. During the whole period of Jewish Enlightenment, Rachel Morpurgo (1970–1881) published one volume of mediocre poems, and was the exception in the male-dominated world of Modern Hebrew literature, as noted by E. Silberschlag in his book *From Renaissance to Renaissance II* (1977). Jewish tradition was partly responsible for this situation, since it had opposed the education of women. Hebrew was only taught to young men, because it was used for religious and ritual purposes in which women had no part. R. Alter pointed out in his anthology, ▷*Modern Hebrew Literature* (1975), that Hebrew, which has been used by Jews ever since biblical times, over a period of some 3,000 years, was adopted as the means of creating the new Enlightened Jewish culture. Thus Jews established a new relationship between modern culture and the Jewish past. Women, however, could not participate in the new literary activity. They could give vent to their poetic talents either in Yiddish, their spoken language, or in Russian, but not in Hebrew. In the early 1920s, Fradel Stock and Zilla Drapkin wrote erotic poems in Yiddish. But when it came to writing in Hebrew there was a poetic as well as a linguistic obstacle for women writers. Whilst Yiddish writing did not insist on a national element as a required poetic norm, Hebrew poetry did. D. Miron convincingly claimed (in '*Imahot meyasdot, 'ahayot horgot, 'al shtey hathalot bashira ha'erets-yisrelit hamodernit*, 1991) that because of this prevailing poetic norm at the turn of the century, women's Hebrew writing, and women's poetry in particular, could not be accommodated. There were no women writing poetry during this period. The leading male poets of the time, H.N. Bialik (1873–1934) and S. Tchernichovsky (1875–1943), set the ideological dictum which insisted on the association of the collective experience with the private, of the nation with the individual. Since women did not take part in public life or in the initial stages of the Hebrew revival, they could not respond to these poetic demands. Only when the poetic ideals of Bialik's generation were challenged by the new generation of writers of the 1920s did women's poetry come into its own.

The development of women's prose writing was different from that of poetry for several reasons. At the turn of the century, Hebrew prose was more open to autobiographical and confessional writing than poetry was. Women were able to contribute to this genre, as they could incorporate the full range of their experience. In addition, their horizons and experiences were further extended as they began to assume a full role in the Hebrew revival in Palestine. Significantly, the women writers of the time were married to public figures and were exposed to people and events which shaped the new society. They all received secular education in Europe, and were as ideologically committed as their male counterparts. They were just as eager to describe the new pioneering life and to encourage further immigration to the Jewish homeland. A further reason which might have facilitated women's participation in prose writing was put forward by Y. Berlowitz (in *Sipoorey nashim bnot ha'aliya harishona*, 1984). She suggested that, to a certain extent, it was due to the efforts of Eliezer Ben-Yehuda (Ben-Yehuda, 1858–1922, is the compiler of the first Hebrew dictionary and is regarded as the initiator of the use of Hebrew as a spoken language) who attempted to transform what he regarded to be a cold, rational literature of the Diaspora into a more sensuous and emotional literature in Palestine. Believing that women are more emotional than men, he appealed to them for their help, and opened the leading literary magazines, of which he was the influential editor, to their work. He encouraged women writers, including his wife ▷Hemda Ben-Yehuda, whose sentimental stories describe with great pathos the important role of women in raising the future generation in the homeland. Unlike Ben-Yehuda's optimistic stories, Nehama Puhachevsky's (1869–1934) works portrayed the disillusionment of the pioneers and described their hardships, especially those of the oriental and Yemenite communities in the new settlements. Yita Yelin (1868–1943) gave a detailed picture of the everyday life of a Jewish family in Jerusalem and, like other contemporary women writers, focused on her immediate surroundings. The writing of these women was not revolutionary, but rather followed contemporary male writing. They shared a common feature with their male counterparts in their aim to express love of their country.

A similar theme dominated most of women's poetry written in the period following World War I, when the prevailing literary norms of Bialik's generation were challenged. As a result, personal, lyrical poetry was allowed to flourish. This was one reason why, at that time, women Hebrew writers could participate in literary life and, unlike their European counterparts, found their niche in poetry rather than prose. The outstanding woman poet of the period was ▷Rachel, whose poetry is an uninterrupted hymn to the Holy Land. It has been suggested by Miron that Rachel's poems deal with 'feminine' subjects such as bareness or unfulfilled love, and that they are typically 'feminine: they are lyrical, short, emotional, intellectually unpretentious and they deal with highly personal subjects such as loneliness, illness and death'. In her poetry, Rachel paved the way for many other women writers. ▷Elisheva who, like Rachel, started her literary career in Russian, wrote romantic, sentimental poetry in Hebrew, and in her prose dwelt mainly on the themes of alienation and love.

By contrast to the conservative poetic themes of Rachel and Elisheva, the poetry of ▷Esther Raab, the only woman poet native to Palestine at that time, was radical. In her poetry she expressed unrestrained desires, and used the cruel landscape of Palestine as a suitable background for expressing her social rebelliousness and the anarchy of her emotional state. This was especially reflected in her uncontrolled, unrhymed verse, and in her deliberately 'incorrect' syntax. ▷Yocheved Bat-Miriam, was just as radical. Whilst the themes of her poetry were traditional (yearning for childhood innocence, love for a person or a landscape, fear of death, and alienation) she managed to assimilate the techniques of contemporary Russian poets, first of the symbolists and then of the futurists. This created a tension between her idiom and her Jewish piety, which made her verse difficult. As Arnold Band pointed out in ▷*The Modern Hebrew Poem Itself*, it often defies the critic. ▷Lea Goldberg, as well as Anda Pinkerfeld-Amir (born 1902), wrote verse for children, but she is best-known for her ▷modernist poetry. She worked on literary criticism and translation, especially from the Russian, and, in search of revolutionary techniques, she experimented with drama. Her play *Ba'alat Ha'armon* (1974) (*The Castle Owner*) introduced the difficult theme of the Holocaust to women's writing. Modern Hebrew drama was slow to develop, partly because traditional Judaism was opposed to the performing arts, but mainly because in its early stages there were few Hebrew-speakers who could participate as an audience.

None of these women poets spoke in the first person plural, as some of their male counterparts did; they wrote out of personal experience without attempting to represent it as the collective experience. They paved the way for the future generation of women poets, such as ▷Dalia Ravikovitch, whose first book of poems established her as one of Israel's leading younger poets when it appeared in 1959. In ungrammatical language and unfinished sentences, she produced a new kind of poetry. Her verse conveys a strong feeling of disorientation and loss, and a complaint about the injustice that the poet finds in existence itself. Her rebelliousness against reality stands in contrast with the traditional and religious world of ▷Zelda. She was the only woman poet of her generation who was an orthodox Jew, and who possessed the inner security of a religious person. Her poetry oscillates between the 'visible', which is everybody's, and the 'invisible', which is her own.

These two poets, different though they are, were not provocative in their writing, and cannot be defined as 'feminist' writers. They did not strive to differentiate themselves from male writing, but rather to complement it. This stance has changed during the late 1970s and 1980s, with the appearance of poets such as Leah Ayalon, Hamutal Bar-Yosef, ▷Maya Bejerano, Sigalit Davidowitz, Rachel Halfi, Hedva Harkabi, Dalia Hertz and Agi Mishol. Although they do not overtly call for sexual equality, these writers expose erotic feelings and emotions which are exclusively feminine, and which their predecessors were inhibited in expressing. The revolutionary poet who paved the way for the poets of the 1980s was ▷Yonah Wallach. She dared to portray a provocative woman with blatant sexuality. She expressed a wounded and rejected female soul which turned towards madness and mystery.

As shown above, women poets have enjoyed a fairly uninterrupted span of creativity ever since the lyrical and personal poetry became acceptable. However, due to cultural and historical circumstances, the development of women prose writers was intermittent. ▷Devorah Baron stands out as an exception. She is the link between the beginning of women's writing at the turn of the century and its subsequent development. Although some of her stories are set in Palestine, she mostly wrote about the small Jewish towns of eastern Europe. In her book *The Thorny Path and Other Stories* (1969), she portrays the difficult burden of orthodox Jewish womanhood in a restrained, realistic style. It should be noted that her preoccupation with recapturing a vanished Jewish world was not entirely out of line with mainstream Hebrew fiction.

The experience of war was naturally the main theme which occupied the literature of the first generation of Hebrew writers in the newly-established Israel, the writers of the War of Independence generation of the 1940s and early 1950s. Still feeling the responsibility to help shape their society, they glorified heroism and comradeship. It has been suggested that women could not reflect any of this in their writing, as it was outside their personal experience. Be this as it may, their writing was peripheral to the central experience of the country. It was only with the next generation of writers in the 1960s and 1970s, the 'new wave' as it was termed by the leading Israeli scholar Gershon Shaked, that women's prose writing found its niche. These writers reacted against their predecessors and moved away from regionality towards universalism, from reflecting the problems of the community to reflecting those of the individual. Once the Zionist dream had started to take shape, the hitherto shared communal values began to shake. Instead of the native Israeli hero fighting for freedom, marginal and displaced characters began to occupy Israeli fiction. ▷Amalia Kahana-Carmon, whose first book was published in 1966, is the most prominent female fiction writer of that generation as well as of this one. She is a prose poet whose work concerns ordinary human beings, who seek and find a mystic moment of revelation in their everyday life, only to lose it again. As Rochelle Furstenberg said in the periodical *Modern Hebrew Literature* (Spring/Summer 1991, published by the

Institute for the Translation of Hebrew Literature, Tel-Aviv), Kahana-Carmon mythologized her strong feminist theories, the underlying myth being that of man and woman as 'other' to each other, coming together in a moment of epiphany (or manifestation), which is often the sexual moment. In more recent stories, such as those in the book *Lema'alah be'Montifer* (1984) (*Up in Montifer*), she portrays man as the doer, or hunter, who is close to the inarticulate beast. Women, subjugated and dependent on him, accept their role. The pluralistic expansion of Hebrew literature enabled the novelist ▷Naomi Fraenkel to incorporate new immigrants as characters in her prose. These survivors of the Holocaust are the complete antithesis of the native Israeli hero who occupied Israeli fiction for over a decade. The eccentric, lonely, Jerusalemite characters of S. Har-Even (born 1931) join the new literary scene of anti-heroes. Her collection of essays on social, cultural and political issues in her book *Tismonet Dulcinea* (1981) (*Dulcinea Syndrome*) are an important contribution to this declining literary genre. ▷Yehudit Hendel, in her novel *Rehov Ha'Madregot* (1956) (*The Street of Steps*), wrote about the clashes, tensions and misunderstandings arising when Eastern and Western Jews meet in the homeland. This uncomfortable facet of Israeli society was not much reflected in earlier fiction. In her more recent book of short stories, *Kesef Katan* (1988) (*Small Change*), Hendel reveals hostility to men. ▷Shulamit Lapid took an even more blatant feminist stance in her short stories and novels. Most of ▷Ruth Almog's characters are passive women who, like the seven women in her book *Nashim* (1988) (*Women*), cannot find an expression for their intense femininity and eroticism. The protagonist in her novel *Shorshey Avir* (1987) (*Dangling Roots*), who does have the courage to search for it, fails even in finding an alternative.

The shift of marginal characters to centre-stage in Israeli fiction today, as well as the departure from the male-orientated national concerns, opened the doors to an influx of women writers. ▷Hannah Bat-Shachar, Orly Kastel-Bloom (born 1960), ▷Yehudit Kazir, and ▷Savyon Liebrecht are of the new generation of women novelists that has emerged during the 1980s. ▷Batya Gur introduced the popular detective novel, making a conscious break from the seriousness which has dominated Modern Hebrew literature since its inception. The change in the mainstream Israeli experience meant greater openness in literature, and a pluralism of voices emerged, including those of women writers. As a result they could, at last, abandon their traditional place in Hebrew literature and assume their rightful role in its development.

▷*Anthology of Modern Hebrew Poetry; Hebrew Short Stories; Modern Hebrew Poem Itself, The; New Writing From Israel; Voices Within the Ark, the Modern Jewish Poets*

MAYA JAGGI

33 The Indian Subcontinent

South Asia, or the Indian subcontinent, encompasses India, Pakistan (a separate state since 1947), Bangladesh (East Pakistan until 1971), Sri Lanka, Nepal and Bhutan, and is culturally and linguistically diverse. (India alone has fourteen major languages and innumerable dialects.)

Three waves of conquest brought lasting influences to bear on its literature. The Aryan invasions from the north-west in c 2000 BC established the Indo-Aryan language of Sanskrit, from which Hindi and the languages of northern India derive. The Islamic conquests from the 8th century AD onwards added Perso-Arabic and Muslim elements to the Hindu and Sanskritic tradition in the north, giving rise to the language of Urdu. British influence, beginning with trade in the 17th century and lasting till the end of the Raj (colonial rule) in 1947, bequeathed the legacy of English, which some would argue has become an Indian language in the subcontinent.

Classical and medieval literatures: the forerunners

Women have traditionally been storytellers in the subcontinent, the chief upholders of and contributors to a powerful oral tradition which embraces myths, legends, fables, folklore and songs stretching back millennia. The area's ancient literature began by gathering and transcribing much of the accumulated, though anonymous, wisdom of orature (oral literature).

While the earliest Sanskrit literature dates back to the Vedas, or sacred hymns, of 1500 BC, the most influential ancient texts are the Hindu epic poems, the ▷*Mahabharata* (400 BC–AD 400) and the ▷*Ramayana* (200 BC–AD 200). Compendia of myths, beliefs and folklore, they demonstrated Hindu concepts, such as ▷*puja* (worship), *dharma* (religious duty or role) and the hierarchical system of ▷caste, while creating, alongside their respective heroes – Krishna and Rama – archetypal heroines who embodied putative ideals of motherhood (▷Devi, ▷Shakti, ▷Ganga) or wifehood (▷*Pati vrata dharm*, ▷Sita, ▷Savitri, ▷Draupadi, ▷Radha, ▷Lakshmi, ▷Sati/Parvati). These ideals of womanhood were reinforced by the *Code of Manu* (c AD 1–200), which defined women, not as individuals with independent destinies, but in terms of their roles as daughters, wives and mothers. The epics were spread through local versions (including one by a woman, the *Molla Ramayana* by Mollati, in the 16th century). Together with the animal fables of the *Panchatantra*, they remain a pervasive and rich source for modern tales, not least for feminist writers who challenge and subvert their models.

The *bhakti* movement, which swept first the south of India then the north in the medieval period, gave rise to a literature of lyrical, devotional poetry in vernacular languages. Partly a reaction against the Sanskritic, Brahminical tradition, with its omnipotent priestly caste, *bhakti* aimed to inspire people to worship a personal Hindu deity without an intermediary. There were many women among the *bhakti* poets, or saint-poets. Of the four Dravidian languages in the south of India, Tamil is the oldest (the others are Kannada, Telugu and Malayalam), and has its own classical tradition. (One of the earliest recorded woman poets was the Tamil, Uwaiyyar, of the 2nd century AD.) The earliest Tamil *bhakti* poet was also a woman, Karaikkal Ammaiyyar, in the 7th century AD, whose poetry was devoted to the god Shiva.

Similarly, in Kashmir in the north, the most famous medieval poets are women: Lalla Didi (1335–?), Hubb Khatun (16th century) and Arani-mal (18th century), famed for hauntingly beautiful love lyrics. Most legendary of all saint-poets is ▷Mirabai, a saint and princess who lived in Rajasthan in the 16th century, and whose poetry celebrates her relationship with the god Krishna, whom she deemed her true husband and lover. While the many women *bhakti* poets frequently used sexual love and longing as a metaphor for divine love and spiritual yearning, as was the medieval convention, they are now being 'rediscovered' as precursors of female rebellion and liberation. (See ▷*Manushi*, 10th anniversary issue, 1989.)

The dynastic Mughal emperors who ruled India from the 16th to 18th centuries used Persian as a court language until Urdu (a form of Hindi using Persian and Arabic loan words and script) emerged as a literary language in the 17th century. As with other literatures of the subcontinent, the Mughal tradition was largely a poetic one until the beginnings of fiction in the 19th century, and there were women poets, such as ▷Zeb-un-

Nissar, the daughter of Emperor Aurangzeb and a Sufi poet of the late 17th century. But, following in a tradition of historical prose, ▷Begam Gulbadam, daughter of Emperor Babur, and the first female historian and memoirist, chronicled in Persian the lives of three Mughal emperors. Among her works is the *Humayun Nama* (1587), the chronicle of the times of Emperor Humayun.

The birth of the women's movement and the growth of women's writing

Although rare access to education for the daughters of privilege produced some outstanding works, the rise of women's writing in general can be linked to the inception of the women's movement, and the spread of women's education.

Moves to reform the position of women began in the 19th century, initially led by men seeking general political change. The Bengali reformer Raja Rammohan Roy, who founded the Brahmo movement in 1828, campaigned for equal rights for men and women, while others agitated against ▷child marriage and the sanctions deterring widow re-marriage. In 1829 ▷*sati* (suttee: a widow's self-immolation on her husband's funeral pyre) was outlawed – though the practice persisted. As access to women's education improved (the first women's college was established in Madras in 1914), autonomous women's organizations burgeoned. In the 1910s and 1920s women campaigned for legal reforms over property and inheritance rights, marriage, ▷dowry, and dowry deaths, the status of widowhood, polygamy and other issues.

The period also saw the spread of English among the Indian middle classes. In 1835 the British decreed that English would be the medium of Indian higher education. The result was Indo-Anglian literature: writing by Indians in English (the term Indo-Anglian distinguishes it from Anglo-Indian writing, meaning writing either by people of mixed Indian and English descent, or by English writers about India). While Indians began to write in English in the late-18th century, and the first Indo-Anglian novel was generally taken to be *Rajmohan's Wife* (1864) by the Bengali writer, Bankim Chandra Chatterjee, women were among the first Indo-Anglian writers.

▷Toru Dutt, a precocious and gifted Bengali woman who died aged twenty-one, wrote in both English and French. She translated French poetry into English, as well as rendering Hindu myth and tales into English, published in *Ancient Ballads and Legends of Hindustan* (1882). She left, in addition to a novel in French, a fragment of an Indo-Anglian romantic novel, *Bianca; or the Young Spanish Maiden* (1878).

The tone of most women's fiction of the time was didactic and reformist, much of it thinly-veiled autobiography criticizing repressive practices against women. Raj Lakshmi Debi's *The Hindu Wife* (1876), Ramabai Saraswati's *The High-caste Hindu Woman* (1886), ▷Krupabai Sattianathan's *Kamala* (1894) and *Saguna* (1895), ▷Shevantibai Nikambe's *Ratnabai: A Sketch of a Bombay High-caste Hindu Wife* (1895), or the early 20th-century stories of Cornelia Sorabji, told of individual women's struggles against repressive orthodoxies at a time when society was changing rapidly, and women's traditional status was being questioned.

Meanwhile, fiction was developing in regional languages, notably in Bengali and Urdu. ▷Begum Rokeya Sakhawat Hossain, a campaigner against *purdah* (the veil) among Bengali Muslim women, wrote in both Bengali and English, while the first women writers of Urdu fiction included Akbari Begum (who published the first major Urdu novel by a woman, *The Ruby in the Pauper's Quilt*, in 1907) and Nazar Sajjad Haider, writing in the 1910s. Like their Indo-Anglian counterparts, their intention was chiefly didactic and meliorative.

Nationalism, realism and the progressive writers

The women's movement was from the outset linked to the anti-colonial struggle against British rule. Demands for political reform embraced calls for women's education and emancipation. The Freedom, or 'Quit India', Movement which culminated in Indian independence in 1947 and the creation of Pakistan as a separate Moslem state, gathered pace in the 1920s and 1930s under the leadership of Mahatma Gandhi (1869–1948). His strategy of *satyagraha* (non-violent resistance) explicitly called on both men and women of all social classes. Active participation in the freedom struggle helped bring women out of their traditional seclusion, eroding the distinction between the 'male' public and 'female' domestic domains. Nationalism also acted as a spur to literature. ▷Sarojini Naidu, among the most celebrated Gandhiite leaders, and a pioneer of the women's movement, is also known for her romantic verse in English, such as her collection, ▷*The Sceptred Flute* (1928).

The 1930s were a period of literary progressivism, marked by moves to enlist literature in the cause of social revolution. The ▷Progressive Writers' Association was formed by the Urdu and Hindi writer Premchand in 1936. Its leftist manifesto argued against obscurantism in religion and tradition, identifying the repression of women as an obstacle to progress, while its writers tended towards realism and social comment in their work.

Among the radical women in the group were the highly accomplished and innovative fiction writers ▷Ismat Chughtai and ▷Attia Hosain. Both were Moslems writing out of a rich Urdu storytelling tradition (Hosain in English), their stories depicting the restrictions on women in a male-dominated society – whether at its apex of privilege, as in their own class, or among the servant class and peasantry. They also articulated the bonds between Hindus and Moslems, ruptured by ▷Partition in 1947, (see Hosain's collection, ▷*Phoenix Fled*, 1951, and a translation of Chughtai's stories, ▷*The Quilt and Other Stories*, 1990). Chughtai's as yet untranslated novel, *The Crooked Line* (1944) and Hosain's novel, ▷*Sunlight on a Broken Column* (1961), explore their respective female narrators' quests for personal independence and a degree of sexual freedom during the nationalist struggles of the 1930s and 1940s.

Among many other women writing fiction by the 1930s and 1940s were Hijab Imtiaz Ali, whose Urdu novella, *My Unfulfilled Love* (1933), explored female sexuality and women's dilemmas in breaking free from ▷arranged marriage and repressive practices; ▷Lalitambika Antarjanam, writing in Malayalam, and ▷Ashapurna Devi, in Bengali. Unlike their instrusively didactic predecessors, they depicted women's lives in a realist vein, with a strong anti-colonial undercurrent, while making advances in language and subject matter, pushing to new limits the areas of women's experience that could be publicly expressed.

Post-independence women's writing
Despite the strength of nationalism, English continued as a literary language after independence. It remains an official language in India (together with Hindi), and although its use is mainly confined to the middle classes, it can cross regional boundaries to address a national – albeit élite – audience. (Partly owing to its limited usage, there has been very little drama in English in the subcontinent.) Yet, many argue that English has effectively been 'Indianized' or 'nativized' through the incorporation of vocabulary, idiom, and even syntax, from the regional languages – most Indo-Anglian writers being bilingual or trilingual. (▷Kamala Das chose Malayalam for her stories and English for her poetry, though she has described her innovative poetic language as 'half-English, half-Indian'.)

Indo-Anglian literature draws on regional literary traditions, as well as regional languages, and there is now a salutary tendency to view it alongside translations from the regional languages, rather than treating Indo-Anglian writing as an isolated category. (This treatment was probably encouraged by its international accessibility, and by its incorporation into the body of writing known as Commonwealth Literature, without the regional literatures which cross-fertilize it.) Recent English-language anthologies of women's writing which demonstrate the newer trend by including translations from writing in the vernacular languages are ▷*Truth Tales* (1986) and *The Slate of Life* (1990), edited by ▷Kali for Women, and ▷*The Inner Courtyard* (1990), edited by Lakshmi Holmstrom.

The period after independence saw a growing number of distinguished women writers in all languages, alongside those already publishing in the 1930s and 1940s. In Indo-Anglian fiction came ▷Santha Rama Rau, author of travel books and autobiography, as well as the novel *Remember the House* (1955); ▷Kamala Markandaya's many novels, including ▷*A Handful of Rice* (1966) and ▷*The Golden Honeycomb* (1977); ▷Anita Desai, whose finest novels are widely acknowledged to be *The Clear Light of Day* (1980) and ▷*In Custody* (1984); ▷Nayantara Sahgal, novelist and author of two volumes of autobiography, ▷*Prison and Chocolate Cake* (1954) and *From Fear Set Free* (1962); and ▷Shashi Deshpande. ▷Ruth Prawer Jhabvala, born in Germany of Polish parents, who married an Indian and lived in India for twenty years, is often included among Indo-Anglian writers, with books such as ▷*The Householder* (1960) and ▷*Heat and Dust* (1975).

While their subjects are infinitely varied, many Indo-Anglian writers return to a theme inherited from the English writer E.M. Forster's paradigmatic novel, *A Passage to India* (1924): that of a conflict between 'East' and 'West'. The theme may be the tensions within English-educated, middle-class Indians torn between tradition and Western ideas, as in Rau's work, or the friction between Indians and the British, during and after the Raj, as in novels by Markandaya and Jhabvala.

History often provides the setting, particularly in Sahgal's novels, where her female, upper-class protagonists are involved both in personal struggles for autonomy and in movements for political change. ▷*Rich Like Us* (1985) examines the erosion of democracy thirty years after independence, during the Indian Emergency of 1975–1977, when the Prime Minister, Indira Gandhi, suspended the Constitution and ruled by decree.

Deshpande approaches feminist themes more directly than the others, her best-known novel, ▷*That Long Silence* (1988), depicting a woman's growing awareness of the self she has repressed since marriage. Yet its feminism has been interpreted as reconciling contemporary women's needs with Indian values, inviting comparisons with Desai's *The Clear Light of Day* in which the heroine, an unmarried and economically independent university lecturer, balances personal ambition with more traditional reponsibilities towards the family. In the final resolution in *The Clear Light of Day* the main character reaffirms the importance of family – despite its constraints.

Perhaps the best-known Indo-Anglian woman poet is Kamala Das, whose confessional poetry in the 1960s challenged still further the taboos surrounding female sexuality and self-revelation. Younger Indo-Anglian poets include ▷Eunice De Souza, Melanie Silgardo and ▷Meena Alexander.

Arguably the most radical Indian writing is to be found in the regional languages. ▷Qurratulain Hyder, one of the leading Urdu writers of this century, whose novels include *River of Fire* (1959) and *A Woman's Life* (1979), is known for an uncompromising feminism, as are the Hindu novelists ▷Krishna Sobti, author of ▷*Blossoms in Darkness* (1979), ▷Mannu Bhandari, ▷Mrinal Pande and ▷Mridula Garg. ▷Mahasveta Devi's writing in Bengali often mirrors her concerns as a journalist, and campaigner on behalf of peasant labourers and tribal people, while ▷Maitreyi Devi is both a Bengali writer and a social worker. Writers of the south include the Tamils ▷Lakshmi Kannan and C.M. Lakshmi (▷Ambia), and ▷Vaidehi, who writes in Kannada.

Amrita Pritam, one of the most famous Punjabi poets, expressed a rebellious desire for sexual freedom in her poetry, which also describes the horrors inflicted by ▷Partition – particularly on women.

Pakistani novelists writing in Urdu include Khatija Mastoor, Jamila Hashmi, Razia Fasih Ahmed, Altaf Fatima and Bano Qudsia. Notable works by Pakistani women in English are the novels of ▷Bapsi Sidhwa, including ▷*The Crow Eaters* (1978), and the autobiographies ▷*From Purdah to Parliament* (1963), by ▷Shaista Ikramullah, and ▷*Meatless Days* (1989), by Sara Suleri.

Recent Pakistani women writers have been outspoken in their criticisms of martial law and the Islamicizing campaign and introduction of ▷*Shariat* that accompanied it. Many feel they have reversed the gains made for women in Pakistan. ▷*We Sinful Women* (1991), translated and edited by Rukhsana Ahmad, collects and introduces the work of radical Urdu poets such as ▷Kishwar Naheed, ▷Fahmada Riaz and ▷Zehra Nigah. Among Sri Lankan writers are ▷Wijenaike Punyakanthi and ▷Chitra Fernando.

Myth, identity and the woman writer

Anita Desai, perhaps the best-known Indian woman writer internationally, has commented on how the deification of women in Indian religion and mythology acts as a form of imprisonment:

> Around [the ideal woman] exists a huge body of mythology. She is called by several names – Sita, Draupadi, Parvati, Lakshmi, and so on. In each myth, she plays the role of the loyal wife, unswerving in her devotion to her lord. She is meek, docile, trusting, faithful and forgiving.
>
> 'A Secret Connivance', *The Times Literary Supplement*, 14–20 September 1990.

These myths, Desai continues, 'the cornerstone on which the Indian family and therefore Indian society are built', keep women 'bemused, bound hand and foot'.

This case can be overstated. In a modern society of India's complexity, the degree to which such traditions still hold sway varies enormously. Since at least nominal equal rights for men and women were constitutionally guaranteed after independence, and after the legislative reforms that followed, there has been a rapid growth in women's education and in the number of women in all forms of work. Yet it seems possible to generalize that women's writing this century – diverse and multilingual as it is – has tended to share a preoccupation with interrogating and challenging the traditional roles assigned to women, dismantling the mythology to make space for other identities, within the family or wider society.

The diaspora

The ▷diaspora from the Indian subcontinent extends from the Caribbean, and South and East Africa, through Britain, the USA and Canada, to South-east Asia, Fiji and Australia. Writers of the diaspora – some migrants in their own lifetime, others with only an ancestral link with the subcontinent – may return to southern Asia as a setting, or add to their concerns the themes of migration, displacement, alienation and assimilation.

Among such writers are ▷Santha Rama Ran, ▷Bharati Mukherjee (initially based in Canada, and who styles herself a North American writer, rather than an Indian-American one), ▷Gita Mehta, ▷Padma Perera, ▷Gayatri Spivak and ▷Anjana Appachana in the USA; ▷Attia Hosain, ▷Kamala Markandaya, ▷Suniti Namjoshi, ▷Leena Dhingra, Debjani Chatterjee, ▷Ravinder Randhawa, Rukhsana Ahmad and women of the Asian Women Writers'. Collective in Britain; Agnes Sam, an Indian South African now living in Britain; ▷Meira Chand in Japan; and the poet Sujata Bhatt in Germany.

34 South-east Asia

The emergence of women's writing in Thailand, the Philippines, Malaysia, Singapore and Burma (Myanmar) is inextricably linked to influence from abroad, together with political, historical and social developments in the countries concerned, and, in particular, the relatively recent changes in the status, recognition of, and attitude towards women throughout the region.

Thailand

Women began to write at about the same time as the birth of Thai modern fiction, the novel and short story being literary by-products of the opening up to Western influence entailed by Thai modernization in the late 19th century. The concomitant development of the print media, especially magazines (which have a circulation of between 50,000–750,000 copies and multiple readership of each copy), has been crucial to the growth of Thai realist and women's fiction. This is because a characteristic feature of Thai magazines is to feature serialized novels (usually about four, but sometimes as many as fifteen per issue). The more popular novels are concerned with ▷romance and family matters, and for this reason have been considered below standard by Thai society. There are, however, many women writers who have produced valuable novels, poems, short stories and plays.

The earliest of these writers to become established in the Thai literary canon were, not unexpectedly, Thai women of royal and high-ranking families, who had long received education privately. With modernization, they enrolled in Western-run mission schools, studied abroad or in the country's first university, Chulalongkorn, founded in 1916. Meanwhile the Compulsory Education Act of 1921 gave most Thai women a basic education, increasing the reading public and pool of potential writers.

But the writings of this first generation and succeeding women authors (like Thai literature in general) have often been responses to major developments in national life and are influenced thematically by them, especially their impact on women. The most significant was modernization and Western influence, culminating in the 1932 coup, or 'democratic revolution', which brought about a constitutional monarchy. Awareness of socio-economic injustice at home was to bring about the call, 'literature for social justice' in the 1950s and subsequently, the student-led uprising of 1973 against the military leaders' attempts to perpetuate their rule. In its wake came protests against rural and urban poverty with leftist demands for *wannakam pua chivit* (literature for life's sake) which turned against the older generation's alleged perpetuation of class values.

Of the earliest writers, two of the most influential were half-sisters who wrote under the pen-names ▷Dok Mai Sod and ▷Boonlua. Throughout their work they tackle the problems of the conflict between traditional Thai culture and modern Western influence, especially with regard to suppressed women. Their contemporary, ▷K. Surangkhanang, who used a number of ▷pseudonyms, was a prolific novelist who shared their views and wrote on a similar theme.

Some years after the 1932 coup, ▷Krisan Asokesin and ▷Botan emerged as the most significant Thai writers, both concentrating on aspects of the new social class, and women's role in society. ▷Si Dao Ruang, one of the better-known members of the 1970s' 'literature for life's sake' movement, expanded this topic in her short stories, exploring social realist (▷social realism) ideas in depth.

Other Thai women writers of note are Suwanee Sukontha, known as the 'Thai ▷Françoise Sagan', and winner of the 1970 SEATO (South-East Asia Treaty

Organization) literary award for her novel, *Kha Chue Karn* (*His Name is Karn*), which depicts a dedicated doctor's work among rural folk and his tragic end; Si Pha, who won the annual Book Fair Award for 1973, and whose novel *Kao Nok Na* (*Outside the Field*) is about the children of US servicemen fathers and Thai mothers who become social problems; and Duong Chai, whose novel *Buang Kam* (1974) (*The Snare of Karma*) is set on a university campus, enabling her to explore the conflict between traditional practices, such as polygamy and monogamous marriages based on love, in a context of relationships between the lecturers and their students. Two novels which are among the few Thai women's writings available in English are *Prisna* (the name of the heroine who returns to Thailand after an upbringing and education in the USA) by V. na Pramuanmarg, pen-name of Vibhavadi Rangsit, translated by Chulachandra (1961), and an autobiographical work, *Little Things* (1971), by Prajuab Thirabutana. A brief introduction to the Thai short story, the writers, and English translations of stories by Pensri Kiengsiri (the novelist Narawadee), Suwanee Sukontha and Thanom Mahapaurya may be found in the anthology *Taw and Other Thai Stories* by Jennifer Draskau (1975).

The Philippines
The Philippines' unique experience of having been colonized, first by Spain, and then by the USA in 1899, led to the creation of a Filipino literature, first in Spanish and then in English. With the introduction of printing technology, literatures in the Philippines' own eight major languages also developed, especially in Tagalog, on which Filipino, the national language, is based. Moreover, a colloquial language, Taglish, has evolved and is widely used in popular as well as serious literature by, for instance, ▷Lualhati Bautista.

To describe the women writers and their work is also to describe the Filipino historical and cultural experience expressed through a rich variety of languages, but seen from a woman's perspective. As in Thailand, the early women writers tended to be from the elite class, and much of the subsequent literature is a product of the urban middle class. The literature also reveals an emergent radicalization of women's consciousness in response to socio-political developments in their society, the earliest being nationalism, which culminated in the Philippine Revolution of 1896 and, more recently, the overthrow of the Marcos regime by 'people power'.

Having been longer exposed to Western education and modernization, which introduced democratic and secular values to their society, Filipino women writers are among the region's earliest feminists and the most prolific writers. ▷Leona Florentino was probably the first woman writer from South-east Asia to be read in the West, and whose work was recognized there.

In 1955, feminist writers in both Filipino and English formed the only known women writers' group in South-east Asia, WICCA (Women Involved in Creating Cultural Alternatives). It aims to raise the consciousness of women writers, create publication opportunities for them, and promote the use of non-sexist language. Among its activities are poetry readings, training workshops, and book publishing. It has a large membership, among whose most active members are the poets Mabanglo, Evasco, Lanot, Monte de Ramos, Aguilar, the poet and short story writer, Santiago, and the poet and dramatist, Barrios. Together, these women writers confront what Evasco has called 'the most difficult task women face: recreating the world. Seeing in new alternative ways, they redefine [in their writing] significant relationships and realities in their own terms.'

There are numerous Filipino writers, but the following have established a presence in Philippine women's literary history in a significant way: ▷Magdalena Jalandoni (prolific novelist, short story writer and poet), ▷Estrella Alfon (short story writer), ▷Liwayway Arceo (feminist novelist and short story writer in Tagalog), ▷Edith L. Tiempo (fiction writer and poet), ▷Virginia R. Moreno (poet and dramatist), ▷Gilda Cordero Fernando (who writes stories and non-fiction), ▷Linda Ty Casper and ▷Ninotchka Rosca (who both write short stories and novels), Lualhati Bautista (feminist novelist) and ▷Kerima Polotan (who specializes in fiction and essays).

Malaysia and Singapore

Almost two centuries of British rule, accompanied by Chinese and Indian immigration, have resulted in co-existent literatures in English, Chinese, Tamil and the indigenous Malay language in peninsular Malaysia and the island of Singapore. In 1957 the Federation of Malaya achieved independence, and in 1963 economics and a shared history led to Singapore joining Malaya and the British Borneo territories to form the new, independent state of Malaysia. Singapore left Malaysia in 1965 and the two countries have since pursued different language policies. In Malaysia, Malay is the national language and the literature in Malay the national literature, with consequent full-scale official funding and support. However, in Singapore, although Malay remains the national language, and English is virtually the lingua franca, literatures in the four official languages, including Chinese and Tamil, are accorded equal status, publication activity being left to market forces.

According to a study of Malay women writers by Rosnah bt. Baharuddin (see bibliography), 'the initial breakthrough of [Malay] women's involvement in literary writing was the women's magazine, *Bulan Melayu (The Malay Moon)*', published in 1930 by a Malay Women Teachers Association founded by Hajjah Zainon Sulaiman (Ibu Zain). But, in practice, its significance was less its publication and direct encouragement of women's literary efforts than its emphasis on its precondition – the education (and hence literacy) of women, stressing education as the major means of bettering their and their children's lot. That education was seen as the key to the emancipation of Malay women (and backward Malay society generally) is evident from its being a recurrent theme in mainstream women's fiction. The other, not unrelated, recurrent theme is the condition of women trapped by traditional cultural values, and customs such as arranged marriages, unquestioning obedience to fathers, and sexual inequality, which put the woman at a gross disadvantage during marriage, and even more so when divorced. There is thus a strongly missionary and didactic character to much of the women's prose fiction, the modern form that most South-east Asian women writers adopt, partly because magazines and newspapers facilitated the publication of short stories and partly because female education in South-east Asian societies tended, like the short story and the novel (and the mass media), to come in the wake of modernization and Westernization.

With Malayan Independence in 1957, mainly the result of Malay nationalism and the desire to better the socio-economic position of the Malay community, more Malay women acquired more years of education, including tertiary education locally and abroad. Consequently their writings, like Malay literature in general, rapidly increased in confidence and quantity, and so did publication opportunities.

Until the 1960s there was little published writing of note by women of all races in Malaya and Singapore (and, to date, none by women in Tamil), partly because, as in most poor and traditional Asian societies, they tended to be married off young and be given little or no education, and partly because, in the late colonial and early post-colonial period, any noted writing that was published was socio-political and nationalistic in its concerns. It was thus dominated by activist male writers. English, meanwhile, remained a foreign language until a generation had graduated from the University of Malaya (established in 1947) and felt confident enough in the language to originate a local literature in English.

Since Independence, and after the separation of the two countries, the literature in Malay, in Malaysia has grown tremendously, and with it, women's writing in Malay, so that a women's literary tradition with distinctive preoccupations is now discernible. Meanwhile, in post-Independence Singapore, the output of writing in English is outstripping that in the other languages. Writing in Chinese is declining in local readership in both Malaysia and Singapore but recently Singapore writers are being published more often in China, finding a growing readership there and in Taiwan and Hong Kong, the most popular being ▷ You Jin.

This internationalizing trend is mirrored in the situation of several women writers in English, such as ▷ Shirley Lim and ▷ Wong May, who have both emigrated to the USA, and ▷ Minfong Ho, who also lives abroad. Not surprisingly, as they use different languages the women writing in Malay, Chinese and English reach separate audiences nationally and internationally, and the various language communities are barely aware of each others' writings. There has been very little translation of women's writing from one language into another; the little that exists consists mostly of translations into English of works contributed to regional journals or featured in bilingual anthologies of contemporary Malaysian literature.

The earliest volume to be published by a woman writer was Janet Lim's autobiography *Sold for Silver*, about her rise from *mui-tsai* (bond-maid) to hospital matron in Singapore. Although frequently ignored as literature, the biographical writing of South-east Asia is uniquely revealing. Non-fictional, and by women with no literary pretensions, such writing turns out to represent a cross-section of women's lives in an immigrant, formerly colonial and Westernized society. In contrast to Lim's work, Yeap Joo-kim's *The Patriarch* (1975) and Queeny Chang's *Memories of a Nonya* (1981) focus on female lives in the fabulously wealthy households of famous Chinese South-east Asian entrepreneurs, while Ruth Ho's *Rainbow Over My Shoulder* (1975), Joan Hon's *Relatively Speaking* (1984) and Aisha Akbar's *Aisha Bee at War* (1990) are women's fond records of comfortable lives as daughters of successful English-educated professionals of the class produced by British colonial rule in Malaya and Singapore. The most recent is the bestselling autobiography, *Excuse Me, Are You a Model?* (1990) by Bonnie Hicks, a young fashion model and illegitimate daughter of a British soldier and a Chinese domestic servant. A well-written first book, it challenges various stereotypes, and, for the first time in local women's writing, touches on lesbian love and is open about female sexuality.

No Malayan, and, to date, no Malaysian woman novelist has written in English. Indeed, it was not until the mid-1970s that women novelists and short story writers were published and noticed in this part of the world. The first novel in English to be published by a Singaporean woman was *Sing to the Dawn* by Minfong Ho. As in Ho's fiction, a number of writers, particularly those of Chinese origin, tend to describe memories of an immigrant past, or focus on questions of cultural and personal identity – how women cope with traditional expectations while meeting contemporary challenges in a period of transition. The fiction of ▷ Catherine Lim, Singapore's best-known and most successful short story writer, covers the entire range of such preoccupations.

Other Singaporean women short story writers are represented in *The Sun in Her Eyes: Stories by Singapore Women* (1976) compiled by Geraldine Heng. *Her World*, a popular English-language women's magazine, has a collection of its prize-winning stories, *How to Hook a Husband and Other Stories* (1982), mostly by women, with an introduction by the Malaysian woman academic, Fadzilah Amin.

The first women poets were not published until the mid-1960s. Unlike the dominant poetry of male writers, who tend to dwell on social and political issues, women's poetry – although socially conscious – ranges from the more private and introspective work of ▷ Lee Tzu Pheng to poems about marginalization by Shirley Lim, the most consciously feminist and accomplished of the women poets.

Other women poets include Geraldine Heng (*Whitedreams*, 1976); Angeline Yap (*Collected Poems*, 1986); Hilary Tham (*No Gods Today*, 1969; *Paper Boats*, 1987), and Leong Liew Geok (*Love is Not Enough*, 1991).

In the 1980s, women dramatists such as Li Lien-fung (mother of the novelist Minfong Ho), S. Kon, Ovidia Yu and Eng Wee Ling also came into their own with the surge in interest in Singaporean drama in English. S. Kon's one-woman drama about a vulnerable yet domineering Straits-born Chinese matriarch, *Emily of Emerald Hill*, for instance, has been enormously successful, and has also been staged in Malaysia, Hawaii and Edinburgh, Scotland.

The first novels by Malay women appeared in 1941, some fifteen years after the publication of the first Malay novel. These were *Cinta Budiman* (*Wise Love*) by Rafiah Yusuf and *Dua Pengembara* (*Two Adventures*) by Kamariah Saadon, who followed it with *Panggilan Ibunda* (1984) (*The Call of the Motherland*). That same year, Jah Lelawati, a well-known singer, essayist and short story contributor to popular women's magazines, published *Cincin Kahwin* (*The Wedding Ring*). The conservative cast of these novels is evident in that the female heroines of the last two novels, for instance, like those of the early Thai women's novels, are typical in behaving according to traditional notions of virtuous women – submissive, patient and uncomplaining despite unjust treatment by fathers and husbands – and being rewarded at the end (in both these instances, with happy marriages the second time).

Other Malay writers of distinction include the novelists ▷Khalida Adibah binti Haji Amin, ▷Salmi Manja, ▷Fatima Busu, ▷Khalida Hashim, and the poets ▷Zurinah Hassan and ▷Siti Zainon Ismail. Zahrah Nawawi (born 1940) and Salmah Mohsin (born 1944) have also built up a substantial body of work.

Many new writers have emerged, encouraged by the numerous publication opportunities, literary awards and competitions that have been created, and it is too soon to note significant preoccupations – except one. Since the 1980s, women writers have been influenced by a trend towards Islamic novels and short stories, reinforced by government-sponsored Islamic novel writing contests. But as one critic has noted, 'these "Islamic novels" are inferior as they tend to idealize the religion rather than observe reality itself; they seem conservative in form, stereotyped in plot and less creative linguistically.'

Burma (Myanmar)

As throughout the rest of South-east Asia, writing by women has been restricted by cultural attitudes, tradition and female oppression. However, women in the 20th century have begun to make a literary presence, particularly the following (some writing in Burmese, others in English): ▷Daw Khin Myo Chit, ▷Daw Mi Mi Khaing, ▷Moe Moe (Inya), ▷Daong Khin Khin Lay and ▷Journalgyaw Ma Ma Lay.

Bib: Supa Sirisingh, 'Women and Books in Thailand', *Asian/Pacific Book Development Quarterly*, XXI: 3, 1990; The National Identity Board of Thailand, *Treasury of Thai Literature: the Modern Period*; Phillips, Herbert P., *Modern Thai Literature: With an Ethnographic Interpretation*; Anderson, B. and Mendiones, R. (eds. and trans.), *In the Mirror: Literature and Politics in Siam in the American Era*; Wibha Senanan, *The Genesis of the Novel in Thailand*; Casper, Linda Ty, 'Philippine Women Writers: a Room Shared', *Pilipinas* 9: Fall, 1987; Mella, Cesar Jr. T., *Directory of Filipino Writers Past and Present*; Polotan, Kerima, 'The Woman As Writer', *Focus Philippines*, 25 November 1975; Valeros, Florentino B. and Valeros Luxemberg, Estrellita, *Filipino Writers in English: a Biographical and Bibliographical Directory*; Koh Tai Ann, 'Biographical, Literary Writings and Plays in English by Women from Malaysia and Singapore', *Commentary: Journal of the National University of Singapore Society*, December 1987; Rosnah bt. Baharuddin, 'Women Writers in Malaysian Literature', *Sari: Journal of Malay Language, Literature and Culture*, July 1989; Mohd, Taib Osman, *An Introduction to the Development of Modern Malay Language and Literature*; Majid and Rice (eds), *Modern Malay Verse*; Newman, Barclay (trans.), *Modern Malaysian Poetry*.

China   35

In a society where women were expected to be neither seen nor heard, and lack of learning was considered a feminine virtue, it is surprising that Chinese women managed to produce some outstanding literature. ▷Ban Zhao (1st century AD) of the East Han dynasty (202 BC–AD 220) completed the historical record for the early years of the dynasty, the *Han Shu*, continuing the work of her Brother, Ban Gu. The 1st century BC poet ▷Wang Zhaojun is famous for her role as patriot and peacemaker between China and the tribes of its western borders. The legendary Mulan (5th century AD) took up arms in her father's stead and spent ten years on the battlefield in male disguise. The *Poem of Mulan*, describing the whole episode, is attributed to her. These were the women of action.

Writing also provided some outlet for repressed emotions. ▷Su Hui of the Jin dynasty, (4th century AD) wrote a 841-character palindromic poem on her banishment by her husband and embroidered it on cloth in an intricate pattern which could be read in any order – a feat unparalleled in Chinese writing. A close study of women's writing in ancient China would unearth many unhappy women who gave vent to their emotions in verse. The above-mentioned Su Hui and Hou Furen (fl AD 600), concubine to the Emperor of the Sui Dynasty (6th century AD), who hanged herself with her verses hidden in her bosom, were but two examples.

But Chinese women writers are not just marginal figures on the literary scene. ▷Xue Tao was an outstanding poet of the Tang dynasty (AD 618–907), when Chinese poetry was at its pinnacle of development. And under the pen of ▷Li Qingzhao, the *ci* form of poetry (irregular poetry intended to be sung to a musical accompaniment) which flourished in the Song dynasty (AD 960–1279), achieved its most exquisite blend of form and diction. Both are firmly positioned in the Chinese literary canon. There were no significant women writers in the *zaju* dramatic form, the dominant literary form in the Yuan dynasty (1260–1368) following Song, though there were courtesans who were literary. Nor were there outstanding women writers in the Ming dynasty (1368–1644). The next significant appearance of women writers occurred in the Qing dynasty (1644–1911) in the vernacular short story form and the *pintan* narrative in verse sung to accompaniment. With a young heroine as the centre of interest, these narratives could run to prodigious lengths, such as ▷Chen Duansheng's *Tale of the After-Life* in twenty volumes.

The May Fourth Movement of 1919, a turning point in Chinese history, also heralded a new age for writing by and about women. The movement itself was first sparked by protests against the government, which had caved in to excessive territorial demands by foreign powers at the end of World War I. It quickly developed into a widespread anti-imperialist and anti-feudal movement, with sweeping attacks on traditional institutions. Science and democracy were the catchwords.

The dawn of this national awakening was heralded by sweeping literary reform. In literary writing the vernacular took over from the classical style, and translations of Ibsen's *Nora, or A Doll's House* (1879), Walt Whitman's *Leaves of Grass* (1855) and myriad Western and Russian writers brought fresh inspiration. A new age in Chinese literature had arrived, and with it an unprecedented flowering of women's writing. The staging of Ibsen's *Nora* in Chinese translation became a focus for rethinking women's role by society as a whole. The new liberalism produced a constellation of women writers. Many expressed a sense of assertiveness and rebelliousness, often through themes of love and marriage. Others, with no role models, searched painfully for new identities on a journey without maps. ▷Bai Wei, ▷Bing Xin, ▷Ding Ling, ▷Feng Yuanjun, ▷Lu Yin and ▷Luo Shu are among the most outstanding. Often under attack for their unorthodox ideas and independent lifestyles, these writers made a spectacular contribution to modern Chinese literature and to the world body of women's writing.

One of the most significant figures to emerge from the May Fourth Movement is Ding Ling. Ding Ling's career spans 60 years, in which her writing underwent many changes, from private rebellion to radical politics, all the way to adapting to socialist realism. But her unique genius sustained her, and throughout her prolific output she explored in depth the problems of being a woman in China.

The establishment of communist rule over mainland China in 1949 (known as the Liberation) ushered in a new literature regulated by a ruling ideology. The late Chairman Mao Zedong's (1893–1976) personal admonitions to writers on how to and how not to write – 'Talks at the Yenan Forum on Literature and Art' – upheld 'eulogizing the new society' as the legitimate end of literary writing. Images of women figured prominently on stage and in the written word to typify the oppressed slave liberated by the Party. But there was no conscious effort to encourage writing on women's issues, nor were there any special measures to promote women writers. Yet even during the 1930s and 1940s, before the Liberation, many women wrote and published at the communist base in Yenan, drawing inspiration from the revolutionary struggle. ▷Yuan Jing, co-author of *Sons and Daughters*, tells a gripping story of the peasants' guerrilla war against Japanese invasion. In Ding Ling's *Sun Over Sanggan River* (1948), the newly implemented land reform provided the background.

The literary scene in 1950s post-Liberation China was studded with many campaigns against 'deviations' of one kind or another. Many women writers' careers were cut short by the 'anti-rightist' campaign of 1957. It was a diabolic twist to the 'Hundred Flowers' campaign of the preceding year, when Chairman Mao personally called on the nation to offer criticism and comment on the Party. Those who took him at his word were labelled 'rightists' and became the 'enemy' overnight. Ding Ling, ▷Chen Ruiqing and ▷Ge Cuilin were just a few among the half a million people implicated. Others, like ▷Chen Zufen, ▷Wen Jieruo, ▷Ye Wenling and ▷Yu Luojin were implicated through parents and relatives, and their careers were either inhibited or marred.

As far as women's writing in the 1950s is concerned, a planned attack against ▷Zong Pu's short story 'The Red Beans' (1957) is significant. The story, describing the internal conflict of a young woman torn between the young man she loves and the call of the revolution was attacked as a 'poisonous weed' and 'petty bourgeois sentimentalism'.

The destructive decade of the 'cultural revolution' (1966–1976) is remembered on the cultural side by the 'eight model operas' personally supervised by Jiang Qing, Mao's wife. Here again, images of women are used to drive home the extremist revolutionary message. They stand out sharply as 'super' Party-women, making supreme sacrifices, and forging ahead unflinchingly.

The death of Mao in 1976 and the Chinese Communist Party's 'reform' and 'opening up' policy of the 1980s were matched by a relaxation of control in literary affairs. Comparatively speaking, writers had more freedom to write and publishers more auton-omy to publish. Although still clouded now and again by ideological and literary cam-paigns, this decade of liberalization saw an unprecedented flowering of creative writing. This 'literature of the new era', as it is called, is innovative in both form and content, and women's contributions are outstanding.

A group of middle-aged writers, including ▷Shen Rong, ▷Zhang Jie and ▷Dai Qing, brought special flavour and insight to the so-called 'literature of reform' which flourished in the early 1980s. These writers abandoned stereotypes in exposing the abuses of the pre-reform period. In moving works, such as Shen Rong's ▷*At Middle Age*, and Dai Qing's 'No' and 'Anticipation', they conveyed the psychological depths of the sufferings of those subjected to political injustice or bureaucratic harassment. The social evils they expose are not just seen as a conflict between good and bad communists, but in terms of basically human and inhuman attitudes. Zhang Jie's novel *Leaden Wings* (1981) also flouted convention in going behind and inside the perverted mentalities of Party hard-liners, making clear that it is not just a set of working rules but a whole way of thinking that is at the root of China's problems. One measure of the impact of these works is that they have all been attacked as 'anti-Party'.

Women writers brought a totally new dimension to Chinese literature by consciously raising for the first time the issue of sexual inequality in a society where everyone is declared liberated and equal. Familiar themes of love and marriage were given an unfamiliar twist. Exploding the myth of love and happiness founded on dedication to 'the common cause', these writers reveal how women are victims of male chauvinism in the home and in the workplace. Zhang Jie's ▷ *The Ark* (1982), the first consciously feminist novella in contemporary China, exposes current sexist attitudes through the frustrations of three single women.

In recent years a wealth of stories and plays have appeared which reveal the manifold problems confronting women: the pressure to marry, the pressure against widows' remarriage, the pressure to keep a marriage together even when it is unhappy, the pressure for women to carry the double burden of housework and job, the obstacles to a woman's career, the hypocritical and tyrannical double standard in matters of sex, psychological and sexual repression . . . namely, the pressure for women to conform to so-called 'socialist' male standards, and their punishment if they do not. The fact that a trilogy of plays by ▷ Bai Fengxi on the theme of women has been successfully staged and shown on television may indicate the extent of the new interest in women's issues. On another level, a writer of the younger generation, ▷ Lu Xin'er, shows a rare irony in exploring the myth of the 'liberated' woman and overthrows many easy assumptions about women's liberation. ▷ Wang Anyi, another talented young writer who emerged in the 1980s, shocked critics with her *Trilogy of Sexual Love* (1988). She boldly portrayed the sexual drive as natural – thus above morality; and irrational – thus beyond the control of the individual.

Journalist-writers like ▷ Huang Zongying and Dai Qing also deserve special mention. Huang was the first to write about women professionals who are kept down by their male competitors using political means – the basest form of sexual discrimination. Dai Qing is, among other things, also the first to venture into the field of investigative journalism on women's lives today. She has interviewed victims of rape, prostitutes, political prisoners and entrepreneurs.

Women writers were also among the earliest to experiment with new techniques. The successful use of the stream-of-consciousness in Shen Rong's *At Middle Age* is just one example. Zong Pu pioneered a blend of Kafkaesque elements with moral allegories of evil, fear, and irrationality. ▷ Zhang Xinxin put her dramatic training to good use in stories like 'Orchid Mania' (1985), in which the absurd takes over when men are consumed by greed. And surprisingly, it is a self-employed young woman from Hunan province, ▷ Can Xue, who has attained distinction and provoked controversy in consciously absorbing the influences of the new Latin-American writers. Poets in China have a more limited following, yet one of the foremost recent schools of poetry, the 'misty' school, is represented by a young woman, ▷ Shu Ting, known at home and abroad for her work's striking imagery and emotional intensity. The 'misty' school is a group of young poets who came into prominence in the early 1980s: their terse language and striking imagery express a spirit of free inquiry, but elude pinning down by ideological clichés, for all of which they have been attacked as being politically incorrect.

The way in which images of women are manipulated during periods of rigid politiciza-tion, and the way women writers break out creatively in liberal intervals, seem to form a pattern. Half a century after Ding Ling's ▷ *Miss Sophie's Diary* (1928), mainland Chinese women writers have seized the moment and made themselves heard, not only in China, but in translations around the world.

While mainland writers struggle to uphold the integrity of their version of reality, other writers outside the mainland reflect its changes, detached by geographical distance and different social systems. ▷Zhang Ailing (Eileen Chang), in works like *Rice Sprout Song* (1954), comments on the nature of repression through the story of a peasant family. ▷Chen Ruoxi had spent part of the 'cultural revolution' years in China, and her stories carry the ring of authenticity, sometimes with a touch of sardonic humour thrown in.

N. HAYAKAWA & A. OGATA

36 Japan

The earliest writing

Japan has a long history of literature written by women. The oldest collection of *Tanka* (a 31-syllable Japanese poem) is *The Manyoshu*, which appeared c AD 806–9. It contains 4,462 poems, the oldest one composed in the 4th century, by 480 people, including a few ordinary women as well as empresses.

Later, in the early 11th century, Lady Murasaki Shikibu wrote the 54-volume story *The Tales of Genji*. In her work Murasaki depicted the aristocratic society – centring on Prince Genji Hikaru's love of many noble women – and expressed the sensitive aspects of human nature. During the same period *The Sketch Book of the Lady Sei Shonagon* appeared. The author makes sharp, witty observations on nature, human interaction and life at court based on the time she herself spent there. A noble woman, known only as the mother of Fujiwara Michitsuna, a high official at court, left a diary entitled *Kagero Nikki* in the 10th century. It is the first known diary kept by a woman in the history of Japan, although there were a few other diaries and stories written by women. All these early works are written in *Hiragana* (Japanese cursive *Kana* character).

The early modern period

It has been generally said that the 17–19th centuries of the Edo era was a dark time for women and that there were no eminent women or women's writing worthy of note. Recent research on women's history, however, has shown that women in the Edo era were not only active agents, but also respectable writers. For example, women such as Ema Saiko and Hara Saihin produced *Kanshi* (poems written in the style of Chinese characters), an area which previously had been occupied only by male poets. Tadano Makuzu is a rare woman thinker. Her essay *My Own Idea* expresses her original view that men and women should be regarded as equal because both are capable of strength and weakness, it is a characteristic shared by both sexes that the weak becomes the victim of the strong.

The modern period

In Japan the modern era began with the Meiji Restoration in 1867, and a profusion of writing by women has appeared since then.

With warm sympathy, Higuchi Ichiyo (1872–1896) described the harsh experiences of poor women within the *ie* system, which forced women to live only as wives and mothers without any political or social rights. Her main works are *The Thirteenth Night (Jusanya)*, *The Last Day of the Year* and *Love Between a Boy and a Girl* (*Takekurabe*), written in a particularly beautiful style. Yosano Akiko (1878–1942) was not only a poet in the field of

Tanka – she published twenty-four volumes – but also a powerful feminist. She openly expressed her desire for her lover, Tekkan, in her first collection of *Tanka*, *Midaregami*. She fought for women's emancipation, demanding equal rights in education, employment and politics. Her essays are included in fifteen anthologies, and while writing she managed to raise eleven children.

Seito (The Bluestockings, 1911–1916), the first women's literary journal, was published in 1911, and its chief editor was Hiratsuka Raicho (1886–1972). *Seito* quickly became a magnet for women seeking emancipation through self-expression. Tamura Toshiko (1884–1945), Okamoto Kanoko (1889–1939) and ▷Nogami Yaeko were among the contributors to *Seito*. Tamura was not only the first woman novelist in Japan to voice women's right to free sexual expression; she also depicted the struggle of a wife wanting to be independent from her husband in such works as *Red Coloured Lipstick of the Dead* and *Her Life*.

Okamoto had a deep knowledge of Buddism and was a novelist and *Tanka* poet. She compared a woman's life to a river, and described the life of a mature woman in *Aged Geisha, An Ample Body*, which suggests a nihilism inherent in women, and other works. Nogami described everyday people trying to establish their identity as citizens in modern society. Also active from around 1920 was ▷Uno Chiyo, who developed a unique narrative style and succeeded in capturing the complex relationship between the sexes, based on her own experience of loving many men.

The emergence of women's writing

An upsurge in writing by professional women occurred around the beginning of the Showa era (1926–1989) when women seemed to come into their own. In the field of proletarian literature a number women writers dominated this period.

Miyamoto Yuriko (1899–1951) depicted the life of a woman trying to be her own master in works such as *Nobuko, Two Gardens* and *Guidepost*. Hirabayashi Taiko (1905–1702), ▷Sata Ineko and Tsuboi Sakae (1899–1967) are other proletarian writers. *The Magazine for Proletarian Literary Women* was published in 1931.

Feminine Art (1928–1932) encouraged other eminent writers, including Hayashi Fumiko (1905–1951) and ▷Enchi Fumiko. Hayashi, who was illegitimate and led a vagabond life as girl, portrayed a woman living an indomitable life, repeatedly divorcing, in *The Vagrant*. She described the lives of old and young women during World War II and the post-war period.

After 1910, new magazines for women were issued, such as *Fujin Koron* and *Shufu no Tomo* and newspapers began to include a women's column. *Fujin Koron* carried many articles on women's emancipation, and there were generally more places for a woman's voice to be heard. From the 1920s to the early 1930s more women's magazines were established, the chief editors of which were women. One of these publications was *Women's Liberation Front* (*Fujin Sensen* – a women's anarchist group) published in 1931, whose chief editor was ▷Takamure Itsue.

Writing after World War II

In the post-war period, the writers mentioned above were inspired to produce remarkable works. Both the new constitution and the new civil code, which provided political and social rights for women, made women feel totally liberated, and stimulated women writers. In addition, new women writers began to emerge, such as ▷Shibaki Yoshiko ▷Ohara Tomie, ▷Setouchi Harumi and ▷Tanabe Seiko. As a group they fall between writers who have been active since the pre-war period and those who were brought up in the post-war democracy. Women writers of the latter generation, such as ▷Ariyoshi Sawako and ▷Sono Ayako, had a shining talent, with a keen eye for communication in the mass media as well as an understanding of economic progress. All these writers describe women trying to find their independence in a male-dominated society. They have exposed a myth about women, and described a new relationship between the sexes. Their down-to-earth literary style is reminiscent of the realism that was popular in the 19th century.

In contrast, writing in a non-realist mode, ▷Kurahashi Yumiko dealt with the relationship between political parties and individuals in *Partei* (1960). Kurahashi's literary style, influenced by the Austrian novelist Franz Kafka (1883–1924) and the French philosopher and novelist Jean-Paul Sartre (1905–1980) had in turn great influence on women writers such as ▷Kono Taeko, Saegusa Kazuko (born 1929), ▷Oba Minako, ▷Takahashi Takako, ▷Tomioka Taeko and others. They denounced the traditional, stereotyped view of women by describing sadism, masochism, illusion, violence, incest, spouse-swapping and murder. They are trying to establish a new relationship between the sexes and want recognition that women are individuals just like men – the major difference being their child-bearing capacity. Although their efforts have so far failed, they have begun a new wave of feminist literature in Japan.

More recent developments
Subsequent writers such as Mori Yoko (born 1940), ▷Tsushima Yuko, Masuda Mizuko (born 1948), Hikari Agata (born 1943) and ▷Yamada Eimi are pursuing the same theme. Both Masuda, who bases her work on the recognition that women and men are both isolated, and Yamada, who tries to find real human interaction beyond sex, show one possible future trend of feminist literature. In contrast, Yoshimoto Banana (born 1964) and Tawara Machi (born 1962), a writer of *Tanka*, express the emotion of a private world without insisting on individual identity. The younger generation in Japan has shown a great sympathy with their work.

Other important women writers who have emerged since the 1950s include Nagai Michiko (born 1925) and ▷Sugimoto Sonoko, writing historical novels. There are also women writers who have continued to describe their personal war experiences such as Ota Yoko (1903–1963), ▷Go Shizuko and ▷Sawachi Hisae. In addition, ▷Ariyoshi Sawako and Ishimure Michiko (born 1927) have continued to focus on social issues such as pollution. In the field of poetry, including *Tanka* and *Haiku* (a seventeen-syllable Japanese poem), there are many eminent women writers, and a journal, *Contemporary Poems for Women – La Mer*, started in 1983, edited by Yoshiwara Sachiko (born 1932) and Shinkawa Kazue (born 1929).

There are two additional characteristics about women's writing in Japan today. An increasing number of biographies and autobiographies of women have been published since 1970, about two-thirds of them in the 1980s, and, increasingly, a number of women have started their own publishing businesses and are publishing outstanding books on women. Ochiai Keiko (born 1945) a feminist writer herself, established a women's bookshop in Tokyo in 1989, for example. More important, there is now a strong readership among women in Japan, supporting their many talented women writers.

Critical Approaches

How should feminists read? That is the question all feminist literary and critical theory sets out to answer, whether implicitly or explicitly. And this question in turn necessarily prompts a whole series of further questions. Are some literary texts more appropriate than others for feminists to read? What does it mean to read politically? Is feminist criticism committed to a critique of ▷patriarchal representations of women? Or should we be more concerned with the positive interpretation and revaluation of works by women writers excluded by a ▷patriarchal tradition? And if so, what are the standards by which we revalue? Are traditional critical values themselves patriarchal? How do we want feminists to write? And how, as feminist critics, should we ourselves write about what we read?

It is a tribute to the vitality of feminist criticism that these questions continue to elicit differing answers and to generate new debates. From a polemical and peripheral position on the margins of literary criticism, feminist critical theory has grown into an activity that is recognised as central to literary education as well as feminist politics. The change has not taken place without a struggle against a literary institution which identified male authors as the norm, the generalized reader as 'he', and 'man' as the inevitable theme of great literature. In the course of the struggle new ways have emerged of specifying the questions and identifying the possible answers. Nor are feminists satisfied with our achievements so far. Until women's interests are taken as seriously as men's, until patriarchal social relations are radically transformed, feminist criticism will continue to develop new areas of exploration and new strategies. These developments, and the debates they produce, are the primary concern of feminist literary and critical theory.

Representations of women

In the late 1960s, Europe and North America seemed everywhere preoccupied by the politics of emancipation. ▷Kate Millett's *Sexual Politics* and ▷Germaine Greer's *The Female Eunuch*, both published in 1970, fluently and wittily addressed the issues raised by the emergent ▷Women's Liberation Movement, and in the process inaugurated a new phase of feminist literary criticism. Their common concern was the stereotype of femininity that consistently reappeared in the work of male writers. Millett offered close readings of passages from the work of Henry Miller to show how the sexual episodes repeatedly celebrated male power and female submission to it. And she and Greer between them rendered D.H. Lawrence's phallic fictions virtually unreadable for a whole generation of feminists.

Sexual Politics and *The Female Eunuch* were both bestsellers in paperback. Neither was offered as a work of academic literary criticism. Neither, indeed, confined itself to literary criticism: both saw the stereotypes they identified as symptomatic of a whole patriarchal culture. But both took it for granted that fiction mattered to feminists. Feminist criticism can claim much of the credit for our current willingness to take imaginative writing seriously. In a culture which paid lip-service to fiction as art, but in practice privileged hard fact, and in an academy where F.R. Leavis felt compelled to mount a vehement defence of literature, but only by denouncing what he called ▷'mass culture', feminist criticism implicitly recognized the crucial importance of fiction of all kinds in reproducing or challenging existing meanings and values.

Women, according to ▷Dale Spender in *Mothers of the Novel*, were the first writers of novels. Women were predominantly their first readers. And one of the motives for reading fictions which construct an illusory reality is curiosity about the world they depict. ('How does it feel to have *that* kind of experience? How do the people relate to each other? What does it mean to be a woman or a man?') Many of us encounter major events like love and death more commonly in fiction than we should in a normal life, and to that extent fiction influences, perhaps unconsciously, our understanding of these events themselves and our experience of them. If fiction is often the unconscious source of our images of ourselves and the world, it follows that fiction can make an important contribution to the process of reaffirming or reconstituting cultural norms. Feminist writers, at least since ▷Virginia Woolf, and perhaps since ▷Mary Wollstonecraft, have always known this. A good many of the political propositions recently put forward by feminists have been formulated in fiction, and to an only slightly lesser degree in film and drama. Correspondingly, when feminists like ▷Rosalind Coward, ▷Tania Modleski and ▷Janice Radway write about current popular fiction addressed to women, they take it seriously as the location of both patriarchy and possible pressure points for change.

Feminists, it began to appear, read differently. Where traditional criticism read in quest of truth, feminists discovered evidence of patriarchal values and assumptions. Where traditional criticism distinguished certain texts as great art, feminists found writing that bore the characteristic marks of a whole society, and a society, moreover, that was badly in need of change. And where traditional criticism identified the triviality of mass culture, feminism located an affirmation of cultural values in all their contradictory complexity.

▷Female traditions

Feminist criticism characteristically breaks limits. Millett and Greer crossed the boundary between canonical and popular fiction, and between literature and the culture of which it was a part. A second strand of feminist criticism saw all this attention to writing by men as yet another kind of limit – and set out to break it. The new imperative was to establish a tradition of writing by women which would demonstrate that the ▷canon of great literature, the list of books traditionally thought to be worthy of serious critical attention, was itself a patriarchal construct. ▷Elaine Showalter's title, *A Literature of Their Own*, gives an indication of the project, and her witty coinage of the term ▷'gynocritics' implies the method. This was to be a ▷'woman-centred' criticism which would establish the existence of a female subculture, in which fiction by women is understood to constitute a record of their own experience. Even when women imitate masculine structures, Showalter argues, their interests are distinctively feminine. The history of the novel in the 19th and 20th centuries is one of increasing differentiation, as women's writing becomes more confident about its own independent identity.

Showalter's book was published in 1977. If her Victorian women were relatively calm about their differential destiny, the 19th-century female writers portrayed by ▷Sandra Gilbert and ▷Susan Gubar were enraged. Here too the title is indicative of a project. *The Madwoman in the Attic*, which appeared in 1979, is an account of women struggling to resist the enclosure and the invisibility to which a patriarchal literary tradition confined them. Gilbert and Gubar share some of the anger and the intensity they attribute to the ▷Brontës, ▷George Eliot, ▷Emily Dickinson and others, and they offer fundamental reinterpretations of canonical works. *The Madwoman in the Attic* is wide-ranging, scholarly, fluent, confident and committed. In conjunction with Showalter, Gilbert and Gubar identified an entirely new direction for academic feminist criticism.

But if white, Western, heterosexual women were entitled to a literature of their own, what about non-Western women, Afro-American women and lesbians? Suddenly the traditional literary canon and the practices of traditional literary criticism began to seem very limited indeed. Black women and lesbians are subject to a double displacement from the centres of power in white, Western culture. Where patriarchy joins forces with racism and ▷heterosexism, such women are marginalized twice over. The 'democratic' societies of the West secure a degree of conformity by reproducing powerful images of what is 'normal', and these norms, often barely visible to those who share them, can be experienced as deeply coercive by those who do not. Feminists who are products of these societies are no less liable than anyone else to generalize their own position as representative. In her essay ▷'Compulsory Heterosexuality and Lesbian Existence', first published in 1980, ▷Adrienne Rich takes to task four influential feminist works which simply assume that women's sexual relationships are with men: 'In none of them is the question ever raised, whether in a different context, or other things being equal, women would *choose* heterosexual coupling and marriage.'

One of the radical effects of the project of constructing a lesbian tradition is that the process calls into question the universality of a system of differences taken for granted in the 20th century. There is now mounting evidence that other cultures and other historical periods have acknowledged the possibility of a wider range of affective and sexual relationships, and corresponding forms of subjectivity. It is not inevitable that emotional or, indeed, erotic activity should be seen as the outcome of sexual identity, or sexual identity in turn as the key to the individual. When Rich cites instances of what she calls ▷'the lesbian continuum' in women's writing, she includes ▷Toni Morrison's *Sula*, which is about a female friendship deeper and more lasting than the heterosexual relationships the two women experience. Alternative forms of subjectivity are explored most evidently in fiction, particularly by ▷Jeanette Winterson, but in the mean time literary criticism has been interested in historical difference. As early as 1975 ▷Caroll Smith-Rosenberg published an article in the feminist journal *Signs* recording a strong tradition of close, affectionate and often romantic relationships between women in the deeply sexually divided society of 18th- and 19th-century North America. ▷Lilian Faderman's *Surpassing the Love of Men: Romantic Friendship and Love between Women from the Renaissance to the Present* was first published in 1981. In relation to the modern period, of course, it is possible to be more decisive about the meaning of lesbianism, as work by ▷Sue Ellen Case, ▷Terry Castle and ▷Teresa de Lauretis indicates.

If Gayatri Spivak has done much in her book *In Other Worlds: Essays in Cultural Politics*, published in 1987, to bring the writing of non-Western women to the attention of the Anglo-American literary and critical establishment, Afro-American feminist criticism has a well-established identity there already. ▷Barbara Christian published *Black Women Novelists* in 1980 and *Black Feminist Criticism* in 1985. Together these books constituted a plea for recognition of a strong tradition of Afro-American women's writing to match the existing male black tradition. The case was hard to resist in a period of extremely powerful fictional writing by Afro-American feminists, two of whom also reinforced the critical argument with passionate eloquence. ▷Alice Walker's *In Search of Our Mothers' Gardens* was published in 1983, and ▷Audre Lord's *Sister Outsider* in 1984. ▷Hazel Carby's *Reconstructing Womanhood: The Emergence of the Black Woman Novelist* invoked both history and cultural theory in an analysis of the reciprocal relationship between earlier fictional texts and contemporary debates about race and gender.

▷French feminism

Meanwhile in France a different cultural heritage pushed different questions to the fore. ▷Psychoanalysis had a stronger purchase there. Showalter and Gilbert and Gubar had taken for granted that it was possible to use Freud as a key to the interpretation of texts, but in France Freud was admired not merely as a guide to the meaning of textual images, but as the theorist who reversed Cartesian dualism by deriving the mind from the body. Meanwhile ▷structuralism, with its quest for the universal structures of language and culture, was beginning to give way to what we now call ▷poststructuralism, which emphasized ▷difference. Woman's bodily and psychic difference was the primary concern of ▷Luce Irigaray and ▷Hélène Cixous, though this difference was not understood to be a universal fact of nature, but on the contrary the preoccupation of a patriarchal culture.

French feminism of the 1970s owed much to ▷Simone de Beauvoir's monumental work ▷*The Second Sex*, first published in 1949. *The Second Sex* shows woman in patriarchy as consistently ▷'other', all that is not masculine, while man stands supreme as the real protagonist of human history. Woman, de Beauvoir argues, has always been necessary to man, as the means by which he recognizes his identity, fulfils his destiny and creates dynasties. But she has never been accorded an equal respect or an equal centrality. Whether as enchantress or slave, woman is always other than the thing itself, ex-centric, different.

The next generation of French feminists was to reverse the patriarchal privilege and celebrate woman's otherness, often figured in images of anatomical difference. In place of reason, with its rules and prohibitions and exclusions, they offered spontaneity, rhapsody, poetry. In place of the plodding masculine mind, French feminism endorsed the ecstatic, transported female body. Whatever the male tradition ignored – intuition, imagination, lyricism – and whatever it condemned – wild festivity, witchcraft – French feminism promoted.

If patriarchy allocated these values to the feminine, then women, we were to understand, should embrace them joyfully. And yet the process of allocation is precisely patriarchal, that is to say cultural, not a fact of nature. It is not anatomy but history which divides men and women. 'The problem,' Cixous insists, 'is not with men: one finds a great deal of femininity in men.' And this includes the men whose literary work she reads with pleasure: James Joyce, Jean Genet, Shakespeare . . . Inventiveness, play, creativity depend on the inclusion of otherness in either men or women.

Then why 'feminine'? Because, Cixous replies, of the old story. The story in question is in this instance the Bible, which allotted pleasure to Eve and the law to Adam. French feminist reading practices are themselves creative, poetic. When Cixous reads, she mythologizes, makes of the text not a mere interpretation but a new text, a myth. In her reading of the creation story Cixous proposes that there are two possibilities. On the one hand stands the law of God that sin brings death into the world. This law is abstract, absolute and, to Eve, who knows nothing of the threatened 'death', meaningless. And on the other hand there is the apple, a physical presence, vital, pleasurable. Eve chooses pleasure in preference to the arbitrary, empty prohibition. But we should not forget that 'it is the Book which has written this story. The Book wrote that the person who had to deal with the question of pleasure was a woman, was woman.' The Book, books, not nature but culture, define the feminine.

If Cixous's reading practices are creative, so too is the process of writing. She herself has written fiction as well as criticism, and her mode of writing calls into question the conventional distinction between the two. ▷*Écriture féminine* (female/feminine writing: French does not distinguish between the two adjectives) is written by and from the female body. It repudiates all the classic patriarchal prescriptions for 'good style' (more rigorous in France than in Britain or North America). It is lyrical, breathless, surprising, disruptive. Its project is to enact feminist subversion in the practice of writing itself.

Julia Kristeva

▷Julia Kristeva, while working in Paris, has always distanced herself slightly from the more ecstatic French celebrations of the feminine. Indeed, she displays a certain ambivalence towards feminism itself. And yet her work has been important for feminists because it addresses some of the theoretical concerns of a politics committed to change. Kristeva's analyses have done much to legitimate feminist confidence in the possibility of transforming patriarchal relations, and in the importance of literature in the social process.

'Women's Time', first published in 1979, addresses the question of feminism directly. The essay insists on the limitations of a feminism that simply seeks rights for women within the existing order, and leaves that order otherwise unchanged. Kristeva goes on to take more detailed issue with what she calls the 'religious' representation of ▷essential, universal Woman. In place of either of these forms of feminism, and on the basis of the poststructuralist stress on difference, the essay proposes the internalization within identity of difference itself. Beyond ▷bisexuality, beyond androgyny, this third utopian project imagines for each individual a multiplicity of possible sexual identities, eliminating for ever the patriarchal rivalry between men and women.

Meanwhile, ▷*Revolution in Poetic Language*, published in 1974, defined a radical role for literature. The book, Kristeva's doctoral thesis, still only partly available in English translation, considers the theoretical and practical implications of the distinction she makes between the *semiotic* and the *thetic*. The thetic (derived from *thesis*) is what we understand by ordinary rational language. It puts forward meaningful propositions which lay claim to truth and arguments founded in reason. But in Kristeva's analysis the child's acquisition of the thetic is preceded by the semiotic, the rhythmic, pulsing beginning of difference, which does not yet fully aspire to meaning. Literary language, especially modern poetry, invokes and enlists the semiotic within the thetic, and the release of this other form of difference, this proto-meaning, has the effect of undermining the pretensions of the thetic to mastery. The thetic remains, but in literature the semiotic 'constantly tears it open' and effects in the process a protest against its 'posturing'.

Kristeva's analysis offers a way of beginning to think through one of feminism's recurring concerns. In historical practice, at least, rational argument seems generally to have operated in the interests of patriarchy. Conversely, feminists have constantly had recourse to literature, fiction or poetry, to define a critique of or an alternative to the patriarchal world in which they find themselves. Patriarchy blandly ignores the challenge: real men don't read literature. But to many feminists the challenge has seemed substantial, in ways that existing literary theory did not wholly seem to account for. Kristeva's account of the possibility of a disruption *within* writing might serve a double purpose. On the one hand it might help to explain the attractions of literature for feminists, and on the other it might suggest a way in which feminists could effectively write their resistance.

Kristeva has more to say about writing in ▷*Tales of Love*, published in 1983. The book includes discussions of *The Song of Songs*, the troubadours, *Romeo and Juliet*, Baudelaire and Stendhal. Its theme is love and writing in Western culture, and it reaches what is in many ways a surprising conclusion. 'Love,' it affirms, 'is something spoken, and it is only that: poets have always known it.' The place of this speech is above all poetic writing. Love is the remedy for our modern emptiness, and creativity (literature) is its manifestation.

Feminism and poststructuralism

Kristeva's work takes for granted recent developments in the poststructuralist theory of language and culture. Feminist politics needs an analysis of the present in order to be able to identify the pressure points for change. The more incisive the analysis, the more effective the political practice is likely to be. Many feminists are ambivalent towards poststructuralism, partly on the grounds that theory in general has tended to support patriarchy, and partly because poststructuralism in particular calls into question the category Woman. But in *Feminist Practice and Poststructuralist Theory* ▷Chris Weedon puts forward a strong case for taking this theory seriously.

Poststructuralism proposes that language precedes identity. Children are born into a world in which language already exists, and in learning their 'native' language, they learn the range of meanings and values which are taken for granted in their culture. Language is a system of differences. In learning these differences – in being taught to distinguish, for instance, between 'man' and 'woman' – we learn the meanings of those terms at a specific moment in a changing culture.

This explains how patriarchal values are transmitted from one generation to another. And it also explains their tenacity. Because we learn to understand words at such an early age, they seem to be transparent, to tell us real truths about the world. But although at a given moment 'masculine' means muscular, rational and authoritative, while 'feminine' means soft and submissive, there is not necessarily anything in the world to guarantee the truth of these meanings, except the degree to which little girls and little boys have grown up to *live* the meanings they have internalized.

If there is nothing in the world outside language to hold meaning in place, it follows that meaning is plural, dispersed, even contradictory. 'Woman' might mean soft and submissive and at the same time 'able to be prime minister'. It has for a long time meant 'human', and in the free West this category generally brings with it certain entitlements. As early as 1700 ▷Mary Astell drew attention with some asperity to one of the contradictions confronting women in a world where the word 'men' was supposed to include both sexes: 'If all men are born free, how is it that all women are born slaves?'

These contradictions are evidence of the precariousness of patriarchy's hold on us. Mary Astell was angered by a culture which offered equal opportunities with one hand and took them away with the other. At the same time, if meaning is not held in place by the world outside language, we could in due course remake the system of differences in line with a new politics. It is on this basis that Kristeva is able to imagine a future sexual identity which refuses the existing opposition between masculine and feminine, and internalizes difference itself, in order to bring out 'the multiplicity', as she puts it, 'of every person's possible identifications'.

The poststructuralist theory of language releases the critical process from the obligation to reproduce the 'obvious' meaning of the text. ▷Shoshana Felman and ▷Barbara Johnson, for example, ▷deconstruct works of literature in order to reveal the blindnesses, the uncertainties and the anxieties within the texts they analyze.

Of course, it would be naive to suppose that by identifying patriarchy's blindnesses, or changing the meanings inscribed in the utterances and images of our culture, we should do away with patriarchal relations. On the contrary, masculine privilege prevails in institutions, in education, in the economy. But the poststructuralist theory of language helps to indicate why literature and literary criticism matter politically to feminists.

Feminism and ▷postmodernism

If instead of merely naming things which already exist in the world, language is constitutive of our understanding of those things, then feminism is instantly released from the Great Truths of our culture, and is free to make its own histories, construct its own traditions. There is no longer a single, true (masculine, white, heterosexual) knowledge, but a range of knowledges which we make in our own interests. This does not mean that we simply invent them. On the contrary, these knowledges are as rigorous and scholarly as any. But they no longer compete with each other for possession of the single truth. Black feminism does not exist at the expense of white feminism, except in instances where the one practises a political exclusion or oppression of the other.

The postmodern condition, plural, sceptical towards truth, is able to base its politics on political interests rather than 'facts'. In *Gynesis* (1985) ▷Alice Jardine argues that postmodernism is incompatible with feminism to the degree that feminism is the single story of Woman. But she also urges that in so far as woman has meant in patriarchal writing the unknown, the dark continent, all that is unintelligible within the limits of Western philosophy, this meaning itself defines a space from which to turn and endanger the very tradition which produced it.

Feminism and cultural histories

Released from the grand narratives of the ▷Enlightenment, feminists have begun the construction of more modest stories which prize culture away from nature. These are accounts of gender relations in all their particularity, histories of sexuality (Julia Kristeva), of cultural difference and cultural imperialism (Gayatri Spivak), or even of department stores (▷Rachel Bowlby in *Just Looking*). The project is to demonstrate that masculine privilege is not always the same at all times and in all places, and indeed that it can be shaken.

In this context literature is important as the location of (other) meanings. Feminist cultural histories look to fiction and poetry as the location of changing understandings of what it is to be a gendered human being. These histories tell stories of difference from a present which is denaturalized in the process.

Feminism and writing

How, then, should we write these stories? Other-wise, of course. With a difference. In 1979 ▷Mary Jacobus argued that feminists should deconstruct the opposition between reason and madness, the plain style and poetry, allowing the one to invade the other. The political challenge of feminism requires a style which withholds the comfort of easy familiarity, but which does not risk sliding into pure ineffability. The proposal bears some relation to Kristeva's account of poetic language, where the rational is in evidence, but is sporadically disrupted by an unexpected change of tone or by the kind of lyrical passage that literary criticism values.

Thus defined, feminist writing, like feminism itself, is perpetually full of surprises.

Reference section

'Abdel 'Aziz, Malak (born 1923)
Egyptian poet and editor, graduated from the
Department of Arabic, Cairo University, with a
sound training in classical Arabic; her poetry
shows the new sensibility introduced by the
▷*mahjar* (*émigré*) poets and the Apollo school, a
home-grown offshoot of *mahjar*. The new, almost
pantheistic relationship with nature, the yearning
and questioning of a soul in search of answers,
which might come in a vision or a whisper, are a
mark of the new romanticism in Arabic poetry.
Her verse is new but not revolutionary, highly
dramatic and musical. She has four collections of
poetry, written and published over some thirty
years, from the late 1950s to the 1970s: *Songs of
Youth, The Evening Said, Sea of Silence* and *To
Touch the Heart of Things*.

Aboriginal women's poetry in Australia
The Aboriginal tradition has been an oral one,
and therefore difficult to define, especially by
white critics. However, in the last thirty years, a
strong group of modern Aboriginal women poets
writing in English has emerged. The first was
▷Oodgeroo Noonuccal (Kath Walker) with her
collections *We Are Going* (1964), *The Dawn is at
Hand* (1966) and *My People* (1970). The second
was ▷Bobbi Sykes with her *Love Poems and Other
Revolutionary Actions* (1979). A more recent group
of Aboriginal poets, mainly published in
anthologies, literary magazines and the journal
Identity includes Vicky Davey, Mary Duroux,
Karen Nangala Foster, Hyllus Maris, Ngitji Ngitji
(Mona Tur), Nyra Rankin, Valda Naburula
Shannon, Daisy Utemorrah, Pansy Rose
Napaljarri, Maureen Watson, and ▷Aileen
Corpus, who stands out, not only for the quality of
her work, but because it deals with urban
experience.

Aboriginal women writers in Australia
Significant Aboriginal literature written in English
is listed in the bibliographies of Adam
Shoemaker's *Black Words, White Page: Aboriginal
Literature 1929 to 1988* (1989), and *Paperbark: a
collection of Black Australian writings* (1990), edited
by Jack Davis, Stephen Muecke, Mudrooroo
Narogin and Adam Shoemaker. The Aboriginal
tradition is an oral one, and women who have
collected and published the legends of their
people include Sylvia Cairns (*Uncle Willie
Mackenzie's Legends of the Goundins*, 1967), Elsie
Jones (*Kilampa Wura Kaani: The Galah and the
Frill Neck Lizard*, 1978), Ursula McConnel (*Myths
of the Munkan*, 1957), Daisy Utemorrah (*Visions of
Mowanjum – Aboriginal Writings from the Kimberley*,
1980) and ▷Oodgeroo Noonuccal (Kath Walker)
(*Stradbroke Dreamtime*, 1972). Autobiographies
include those of Theresa Clements (*From Old
Maloga! The Memoirs of an Aboriginal Woman*),
Evonne Goolagong (*Evonne! On the Move*, 1975),
Ella Simon (*Through My Eyes*, 1978), Cheryl
Buchanan (*We Have Bugger All! The Kulaluk Story*,
1974); Margaret Tucker (*My People's Life: An
Aboriginal's Own Story*, 1976); Shirley C. Smith,

(*MumShirl: An Autobiography*, 1981, written with
the assistance of ▷Bobbi Sykes); to which must
be added the more recent Marnie Kennedy's *Born
a Half-Caste* (1985); and ▷Sally Morgan's ▷*My
Place* (1987); Glenyse Ward's *Wandering Girl*
(1988) and Ruby Langford's *Don't Take your Love
to Town* (1989).

Novels include ▷Faith Bandler's *Wacvie*
(1977), and Monica Clare's *Karobran* (1978), both
of which have a significant autobiographical
content. Autobiographical and representational
fiction are often chosen as the most effective way
to communicate the traumatic experiences of
Aboriginal women. Short story writers include
Hyllus Maris, Ngitji Ngitji (Mona Turl), Maureen
Watson, Louise West and Oodgeroo Noonuccal
(Kath Walker). Short stories appear either in
anthologies such as *Paperbark* or in the journal
Identity. Aboriginal women dramatists include
Daisy Utemorrah (*Mugugu*, 1975), Hyllus Maris
and Sonia Borg (*Women of the Sun*, 1983,
subsequently republished in novel form) and Eva
Johnson (*Murras: Plays from Black Australia*, 1989).

**Aborigine in non-Aboriginal Australian
women's writing, The**
Non-Aboriginal Australian women writers have
displayed considerable interest in Aboriginal
culture and, although some have reflected the
prejudices of the general community, there have
been notable exceptions. ▷Eliza Dunlop's poem
'The Aboriginal Mother' (1838) is an early
expression of sympathy prompted by the Myall
Creek Massacre; ▷Louisa Meredith, affected by
Aboriginal raids on white homesteads in
Tasmania, demonstrated her prejudice in her
▷*My Home in Tasmania* (1852), while ▷Rosa
Praed, who had mixed freely with Aboriginal
children, yet had also lived near the scene of the
Hornet Bank massacre of whites by Aborigines,
oscillated between fear of their supposed savagery
and admiration of their myths and ceremonies.

An early and sympathetic treatment is
▷Catherine Martin's ▷*The Incredible Journey*
(1923), while ▷*Coonardoo* (1929), by ▷Katharine
Susannah Prichard, treats the relationship
between a white man and an Aboriginal girl
sensitively. Mary Durack's *Keep Him my Country*
(1955) deals with the oppression experienced by
both white women and black women and men;
▷Thea Astley's *A Kindness Cup* (1974) with white
reactions to a massacre of Aborigines; and
▷Nene Gare's ▷*The Fringe Dwellers* (1961) with
the difficulty, for an Aboriginal girl, of
transcending her familial and cultural
circumstances. ▷Catherine Langloh Parker and
▷Daisy Bates have written valuable
anthropological studies of the Aborigines, while
the poets ▷Mary Gilmore and ▷Judith Wright
have dealt sympathetically with the scandal of the
white treatment of the Aboriginal race. 'Bora
Ring', 'Nigger's Leap, New England' and 'At
Cooloola' are impressive Wright poems on the
massacre of the Aboriginal tribes, a subject which
is also treated in her two books, *The Cry for the*

Dead (1981) and *We Call for a Treaty* (1985).
These two books, together with Lyndall Ryan's
The Aboriginal Tasmanians (1981), constitute a
formidable indictment of white Australian society.

Abrantès, Laure d' (1785–1838)
French novelist. Born in Montpellier of a
Corsican mother, she was a close friend of the
Bonaparte family. After the suicide of her mad,
alcoholic husband, General Junot, she found
herself facing severe financial difficulties.
Fortunately, she became friendly with the novelist
Honoré de Balzac (1799–1850) and began, with
his encouragement, to write her own novels.
These were of limited literary merit and have
fallen into oblivion, but her eighteen-volume
*Mémoires sur Napoléon, la Révolution, le Directoire et
la Restauration* (1831–1834) (*Recollections of
Napoleon, the Revolution, the Directory and the
Restoration*), which were hugely popular, provide a
lively and picturesque, albeit inaccurate, account
of life in early 19th-century France. The 70,000
francs these memoirs earned her did not,
however, prevent her from dying in extreme
poverty, with only a servant for company.
▷Aubert, Constance
Bib: Crosland, M., *Women of Iron and Velvet.*

Abridgement of the History of New England for the Use of Young People (1807)
▷*Summary History of New England, A*

Aburgavennie, Frances ▷*Prayers made by the Right Honorable Lady Frances Aburgavennie* (1582)

Abyss, The (1976)
Translation of *L'Oeuvre au noir* (1968), novel by
French writer ▷Marguerite Yourcenar. The
intellectual history of Europe in the first half of
the 16th century, torn between a medieval society
in the hands of religious zealots and the first signs
of modernity, is expressed through the central
character of Zenon, medical genius, alchemist and
philosopher.

Académie Française
The esteemed controlling body of the French
literary establishment, the Académie Française
was created in 1635 by Cardinal Richelieu (1585–
1642), Prime Minister to Louis XIII. Its main
function was – and still is – to monitor changes in
French language usage, in the form of a
periodically updated dictionary; however, this task
is approached with a rigorous dedication to
perfecting and regulating the language, in line
with rules and literary models considered sacred.
The Academicians form a committee of forty
members, elected from the ranks of prominent
intellectuals. When an Academician dies, new
candidates must be nominated by existing
members. The successful candidate, elected by
majority vote, must be approved by the President,
and must give an address in praise of the
Academician he is replacing. To be elected to the
Académie has always been regarded as the highest

accolade of intellectual or literary merit, but one
that was denied to women during the 18th and
19th centuries. Women writers of the period were,
however, eligible to receive the Académie's
literary prizes and awards (eg ▷Louise Colet).
With the election of the novelist ▷Marguerite
Yourcenar in 1980, the Académie Française
ceased to be an exclusively male preserve.
▷Bentzon, Thérèse; Roy de Clotte le Barillier,
Berthe; Blanchecotte, Auguste; Descard, Maria;
Dieulafoy, Jane; Girardin, Delphine de; Lapauze,
Jeanne; Noailles, Anna de

Account of Charles Town in 1725, An (1960)
Personal writings by North American writer
▷Margaret Brett Kennett. Like so many private
writings by early Euro-American women,
Kennett's account of her years in Charleston,
South Carolina, was not published until more
than two centuries later. Yet her careful, detailed
assessments of the consequences of the rapid
commercial growth in the region (in which she
participated by starting a business with her
husband) and the consequent religious
factionalism, is an important contribution to our
understanding of early 18th-century South
Carolina and of women's contributions to the
growth of that region.

Account of Some Spiritual Experiences and Raptures, An (1736)
The spiritual autobiography of ▷Elizabeth Mixer,
a resident of Ashford, Massachusetts. *An Account*
describes Mixer's three visions of Christ
appearing to her, and her desire thereafter to
become a full member of the Puritan congregation
in Ashford. It captures the flavour of early North
Americans' rapturous experiences during the
Great Awakening. Although formulaic and
impersonal, the text is significant as one woman's
record of these years of evangelical revival.

Acevedo, Doña Angela de (died 1644)
Spanish dramatist. Born in Lisbon, Acevedo was
the daughter of a nobleman, a favourite of Isabel
de Borbón, and the first wife of Philip IV. Her
main works are plays, including: *El muerto
disimilado* (*The Hidden Corpse*); *La Margarita del
Tajo* (*The Pearl of the Tagus*); *Dicha y desdicha del
juego* (*The Joys and Sorrows of Gambling*); and
Devoción de la Virgen (*Devotion to Our Lady*). All
four of these were performed ▷ in the 17th century.

Achilles' Fiancée (1987)
Novel by Greek writer ▷Alki Zei. It is the story
of a young woman from the years of the Greek
civil war (1944) up until the Colonels' dictatorship
in 1974. The story is told in flashbacks by the
heroine, who lives and works in Paris as an
actress. Certain incidents from her life trigger
recollections which are recounted with warmth
and tenderness, as if she does not want to disturb
those years or her memories of the men who kept
her around them while working against the
Germans during the occupation of Greece, or

who pursued their political purposes from Russia after the war. Greek feminists recognized in the book the lives of women marginalized by the purposes of men.

Acholonu, Catherine Obianuju
Nigerian dramatist and poet. Based in Owerri in eastern Nigeria, Acholonu is one of the younger generation of women writers. She has published the plays *Trial of the Beautiful Ones* (1985), which draws on the mythical Igbo figure of the 'mammy water', and *The Deal and Who is the Head of State* (1986), as well as volumes of poetry.
Bib: Otokunefor, H. and Nwodo, O., *Nigerian Female Writers: A Critical Perspective.*

Ach wie gut, daß niemand weiß (1980) (Oh How Lucky No one Knows)
A novel by the German writer ▷Gabriele Wohmann. The title alludes to the Grimm fairytale of the voracious Rumpelstiltskin who keeps his true name a secret. The novel itself revolves around the question of the real identity of the heroine, Marlene Ziegler, a successful German psychologist who suddenly leaves her glib partner and her male colleagues to begin a new life in Switzerland. Her flight from a structured existence turns into a disaster, however. She begins to steal, is victimized by others, and eventually turns to alcohol and barbiturates.

This is one of the most acerbic in a series of recent critiques of the nature of women's bondage, largely self-induced, within the supposedly emancipated West German middle class.

Acker, Kathy (born 1948)
US novelist. Born in the United States, Acker lived and worked in London, England during the 1980s. Her early work was developed in ▷avant-garde New York circles and was much influenced by the language work of the Black Mountain School of poets. Linguistically adventurous and often sexually explicit, Acker's writing engages the reader in a textual assault on social, political and literary histories that have marginalized women. Appropriating titles, real names and phrases from male-authored texts, her work challenges the idea of author-ity as ownership and explores the relationship between sexuality and power. In *Blood and Guts in High School* (1984) the pervasiveness of monopoly capitalism is linked to hierarchical ideological constructs that oppress and marginalize both women, and communities or individuals considered racially or sexually deviant. Acker's writing can be read as having a strong satirical vein and frequently tips into black humour – a feature common to the work of William Burroughs, who is also a strong influence. The writing is highly inventive in its combination of a wide variety of discourses, from autobiography to film script to 'dream maps'.

Other works include: *The Childlike Life of the Black Tarantula, by the Black Tarantula* (1973), *I Dreamt I Became a Nymphomaniac: Imagining* (1974), *The Adult Life of Toulouse Lautrec, by Henri Toulouse Lautrec* (1975–76), *Kathy Goes to Haiti* (1978), *Great Expectations* (1983), *Don Quixote* (1986), *Empire of the Senseless* (1988) and *In Memoriam to Identity* (1990).

Ackermann, Louise (1813–1890)
French poet. Born Victorine Choquet, brought up in the Oise, and educated by a Voltairean, atheist father, her childhood was a lonely one. She began to write poetry at the age of nine, and by fourteen was a keen admirer of Victor Hugo (1802–1885). A period of study in Berlin resulted in marriage to the pastor and teacher Paul Ackermann; she was widowed after three years, however, and retired to Nice, where she divided her time between farming and writing. The influence of German philosophy and of French positivist thought is apparent in her poetry, which has been likened to that of the Parnassian poets, and which offers a largely bleak vision of the human condition. In particular, her *Poésies philosophiques* (1871) (*Philosophical Poems*) bear witness to the emotional and intellectual pessimism which the solitude of her early years, her premature widowhood, and her extensive reading instilled in her. An 1885 edition of Ackermann's work contains her *Premières poésies*, (*First Poems*), her *Poésies philosophiques* and *Ma Vie* (*My Life*). This last is an autobiographical text, in which she declares that women poets are always more or less ridiculous, and confesses that her husband, who would not have tolerated such 'immodesty', never knew that she wrote – remarks which reveal just how problematic an activity literary production could be for 19th-century French women.
Bib: Citoleux, M., *La Poésie philosophique au XIXe siècle.*

Ackland, Valentine (1906–1968)
English poet and short story writer. An extrovert and unorthodox figure in London 'society' circles of the 1920s, Ackland became a friend of ▷Nancy Cunard and, later, the lover of ▷Sylvia Townsend Warner. Warner and Ackland lived together in Dorset, and in 1934 published a joint collection of their individual poetry, *Whether a Dove or Seagull* (1934). Her other collections of poetry, *The Nature of the Moment* (1973) and *Further Poems* (1978), were published posthumously. Her temporary estrangement from Warner is described in *For Sylvia: An Honest Account* (1985).
Bib: Harman, Claire, *Sylvia Townsend Warner: a Biography.*

Acosta de Samper, Soledad (1833–1903)
Colombian novelist, short story writer and dramatist. A historian, educator and journalist, who founded and directed several magazines in Bogotá, she wrote under the pen-names Aldebarán, Bertilda and Olga, among others. Her best novel is *Los piratas en Cartagena* (1885) (*The Pirates in Cartagena*). An extremely cultivated and productive author, she perhaps endangered

recognition of the quality of her novels and comedies by the very quantity of her work. She belonged to the second generation of romantic historical novelists, following the tradition of the Mexican O'Reilly, the Chilean Manuel Bilbao and the Guatemalan Salomé (Jil José Milla). She wrote many biographies and more than forty-five novels, including *El corazón de la mujer, Dolores* (*Dolores, The Story of a Leper*).

Across the Acheron (1987)

Translation of *Virgile, Non* (1985), fourth novel of French writer ▷ Monique Wittig. Wittig combines the structure of Dante's *Divine Comedy* with a critique of heterosexual femininity, which is depicted as mindless acceptance of slavery and torture. Hell is heterosexuality, limbo is sipping tequila in a San Francisco gay bar, paradise is a community of female angels breaking through the limitations of patriarchal language and delighting in nature's abundance. The narrator/lesbian writer 'Wittig' is catapulted between hell, where she fights the demons, and limbo, or lesbian subculture, which is seen as a momentary respite, however limited, from the horrors of ▷ patriarchy. Finally, her struggle with words is rewarded by the sweet air and dulcet tones of paradise.

Actors (17th- and 18th-century Britain)

Women began to act on the public stage during the Interregnum (1649–1660), when Mrs Coleman appeared in *The Siege of Rhodes* (1656), an opera or entertainment by William D'Avenant (1606–1668) – her entrance was signalled by the stage direction 'Enter Ianthe veiled'. Women had participated in court masques (Henrietta Maria would even dance in them on Sundays), and in home performances, but the Restoration brought the change of theatre regulations to emulate the French stage – and women began to act. Famous actresses included Eleanor Gwyn, ▷ Charlotte Charke and ▷ Elizabeth Inchbald.

Acuña, Dora

Paraguayan poet, precursor, with Julio Correa (1900–1953) during the 1930s, of the 1940s poetry. She is a master of erotic poetry, following the ▷ postmodernist poetry of the Uruguayan ▷ Delmira Agustini. She proclaims a love of nature without prejudice, and writes simple, uncultivated verses, with occasional flashes of true poetry. Her lyrical, exotic personal voice, echoes ▷ modernism in style, and her poetry has appeared in magazines and newspapers. Her works include *Flor de caña* (1940) (*Reed flower*), *Barro celeste* (1943) (*Heavenly Mud*) and *Luz en el abismo* (1954) (*Light in the Abyss*).

Adam, Juliette (1836–1936)

French novelist. The daughter of a public official from Verberie in the Oise, she was married first, and unhappily, to a Soissons lawyer, Alexis de la Messine, and then to the free-thinker and senator, Edmond Adam. After her second marriage, she established a salon which became one of the best-known in Paris, and which was frequented by the leading intellectuals and Republicans of the period. A devoted Republican herself, she founded the journal *La Nouvelle Revue* (*The New Review*) after the death of her husband in 1877, and used it as a forum in which to campaign in favour of the Republican cause. She began her writing career with the philosophical text ▷ *Idées antiproudhoniennes sur l'amour, la femme et le mariage* (1858) (*Anti-Proudhonist Ideas on Love, Women and Marriage*), in which she attacked the anti-feminist beliefs of the socialist thinker Pierre-Joseph Proudhon (1809–1865). She subsequently produced a great many novels, including *Grecque* (1879) (*The Greek Woman*), which illuminates her enthusiasm for the civilization of Ancient Greece, and *Païenne* (1883) (*The Pagan Woman*), an exchange of letters between two lovers that celebrates sensual passion. Towards the end of her life she became less attached to the egalitarian, anti-clerical ideals of her youth and became more and more narrowly nationalistic. During this period she wrote her memoirs and the novel *Chrétienne* (1913) (*The Christian Woman*), a work that marks her return to Catholicism.

▷ Proudhonism; Héricourt, Jenny d'

Bib: Carton, H., *Histoire des femmes écrivains de la France*; Cormier, M., *Mme Juliette Adam: l'aurore de la III République*; Moses, C., *French Feminism in the Nineteenth Century*; Sullerot, E., *Women on Love*.

Adam Bede (1859)

A novel by ▷ George Eliot, set in a village in the English Midlands at the turn of the 19th century. The narrative is principally concerned with three characters: Adam Bede, the village carpenter, Hetty Sorrel, with whom he is in love, and Arthur Donnithorne, the local squire. Hetty is seduced by Arthur, who thereafter leaves her to face life as a ▷ 'fallen woman'. Discovering that she is pregnant, Hetty flees the village to search for Arthur, abandons her newborn child, and is arrested and convicted for its murder. Sentenced to death, she is saved by Arthur's intervention and the sentence is commuted to transportation. Hetty is visited in prison by another central female figure in the novel, Dinah Morris, a Methodist preacher whose strength of mind and nurturing capacities have a calming influence on Hetty in her confusion and distress. Towards the end of the novel Adam discovers that Dinah is in love with him, and finally they marry. The novel has always been acclaimed for its characterization and its realistic depiction of rural life. Recently, feminists have focused on Eliot's treatment of Hetty, with some critics arguing that the author's attitude towards female sensuality is severe. Another strand of feminist criticism has emphasized the novel's foregrounding of the importance of caring and sympathy, epitomized in the character of Dinah.

▷ Realism (19th-century Britain)

Adams, Abigail Smith (1744–1818)

North American letter-writer. She was born on 11 November 1744, in Weymouth, Massachusetts, to Elizabeth Quincy and William Smith. Her excellent if informal home education prepared her for the role in North American revolutionary history – and in women's history – that she would embark upon as an adult. Through her marriage to the North American statesman and president, John Adams (1735–1826), she was at the forefront of the origins of revolution; but it was her own interests in 'women's concerns' that led to her famous call for her husband to 'Remember the Ladies' when the laws of the new nation were being formed. If her husband ignored her admonition, others listened attentively. It is for her prolific and humane correspondence that she remains a notable chronicler of 18th-century North American culture. In letters to Thomas Jefferson (1743–1826), her sister Mary Cranch and her friend ▷Mercy Otis Warren, she debated the most complex political issues of the day and continued her argument for women's rights. Although her writings (collected in the ▷*Adams Family Papers*, and excerpted in works such as ▷*The Adams–Jefferson Letters*, ▷*The Book of Abigail and John* and ▷*New Letters of Abigail Adams 1788–1801*) were not published in her lifetime, their influence remained constant. Her call to 'Remember the Ladies' became a byword of the next century's women's rights movement. She died in Quincy, Massachusetts, on 28 October 1818.

▷Cranch, Elizabeth; Early North American letters

Adams, Glenda (born 1939)

Australian novelist. Adams was born in Sydney and taught Indonesian language and literature there before moving to New York in 1964 and returning to Sydney in 1990. She has published two collections of short stories, *Lies and Stories* (1976) and *The Hottest Night of the Year* (1979), and three novels *Games of the Strong* (1982), the prize-winning ▷*Dancing on Coral* (1987), and *Longleg* (1990). Her work is lively, complex, ambitious and often experimental.

Adams, Hannah (1755–1831)

North American historian and memoirist. Born on 2 October 1755 in Medfield, Massachusetts, to Eleanor Clark and Thomas Adams, she became one of the first North American women to pursue writing as a career. Her modesty and quiet manner belied her intellectual aggressiveness; she pursued interests in political and religious history throughout her life. Her studies of religious history, which were remarkably objective for the fractious period in which she lived, focused not only on Christianity, in the ▷*Alphabetical Compendium* (1784) and *The Truth and Excellence of the Christian Religion Exhibited* (1804), but also on Judaism (*The History of the Jews*, 1812). One of her most enduring areas of interest, however, was her ▷*Summary History of New England*, first

published in 1799 and abridged in 1807. She observed in her ▷*Memoir*, published the year after her death, that at an early age she learned the 'love of literature'; although it never proved highly profitable for her, it was the career to which she dedicated her life. She never married; she died in Brookline, Massachusetts, on 15 December 1831.

Adams, Sarah Flower (1805–1848)

English poet and writer of ▷hymns. She was born in Great Harlow, Essex, the daughter of Eliza Flower and of journalist Benjamin Flower, who educated her at home. In 1829, after the death of her parents, she went to live with the family of William Johnson Fox, a Unitarian minister, until she married William Bridges Adams in 1834. She published poems, essays and stories in the *Monthly Repository* from 1832–6, and contributed to the *Westminster Review*, for which she wrote a review of ▷Elizabeth Barrett Browning's ▷*Poems* (1844). Thirteen of her lyrics appear in *Hymns and Anthems* (1841), including her most famous hymn, 'Nearer, My God, to Thee.' The same year also saw the publication of her blank verse ▷drama, *Vivia Perpetua*, based on the life of a Christian woman martyr. Adams's writings express religious faith, together with a belief in the enlightening powers of art.

Bib: Stephenson, H.W., *The Author of Nearer, My God, to Thee.*

Adams Family Papers (1963–1973)

The correspondence of ▷Abigail Smith Adams, collected in the papers of one of North America's most renowned political families. Abigail Adams's exchanges with her husband John, her son and other family members depict the everyday concerns and occurrences in 18th-century aristocratic life. Perhaps most important, however, is the epistolary exchange between Adams and her sister, Mary Quincy; Abigail's trust in Mary allowed her to express freely her concerns over women's rights and health issues, as well as the frustrations and excitements of running the household as the nation's first family to occupy the White House. Her compassion, political astuteness and federalist proclivities pervade her letters, giving us a very personal sense of her life and of the nation's early development.

▷*Adams–Jefferson Letters, The*; *Book of Abigail and John, The*; *New Letters of Abigail Adams 1788–1801*; Early North American letters

Adams–Jefferson Letters, The (1959)

Although this collection is devoted to the correspondence of the American statesmen John Adams (1735–1826) and Thomas Jefferson (1743–1826), it includes almost thirty letters from ▷Abigail Smith Adams to Jefferson, covering the years 1785 to 1817. Her forthright political exchanges with Jefferson offer a keen sense of Adams's astuteness and of her concern for the human consequences of political actions. These letters also include a poignant rendering of

Adams's sense of loss after the death of her daughter. Perhaps in no other exchange of letters do we find the political and personal lives of Abigail Adams so openly exposed.
▷*Adams Family Papers; Book of Abigail and John, The; New Letters of Abigail Adams 1788–1801;* Early North American letters

Adam-Smith, Patsy (born 1924)

Prolific Australian writer of factual and historical works, born in Melbourne. Her most famous is the autobiographical *Hear the Train Blow* (1964). Other works include *Moonbird People* (1965), which is concerned with the people of the Furneaux Islands in Bass Strait, *The Anzacs* (1978), a powerful account of the participation of Australians in World War I, and *The Shearers* (1982). She has been awarded an OBE.

Adcock, Karen Fleur (born 1934)

Fleur Adcock

New Zealand poet. Fleur Adcock was born in Auckland but spent her childhood in Britain during World War II. She returned to New Zealand as a teenager and studied Classics at Victoria University, Wellington. Married for a time to the poet Alistair Campbell, Adcock was associated with a number of New Zealand writers in the 1950s before leaving for Britain, where she has spent the bulk of her adult life. She has published nine volumes of poetry and is a prominent literary figure both in New Zealand and the UK. Her early work was heavily influenced by classical writers, especially the satiric Roman writers, and the forms of classical poetry. The longer she has been resident outside New Zealand the less her work belongs to 'New Zealand' literature. Characterized by irony and its attention to form, Adcock's work has been praised for its 'principles of orderliness and good clear

sense' ('Fleur Adcock, New Zealand's Expatriate Poet', *More*, July 1989).
Other works include: *The Eye of the Hurricane* (1964); *Tigers* (1967); *High Tide in the Garden* (1971); *The Scenic Route* (1974); ▷*The Inner Harbour* (1979); *Below Loughrigg* (1979); *Selected Poems* (1983); *The Virgin and the Nightingale: Mediaeval Latin Poems* (1983); *The Incident Book* (1986).

Addio, Amore! (1890) ▷*Farewell, Love!*

Address to Young People (1733)

An early example of North American religious advice literature. This ten-page 'Warning' from the youthful ▷Mercy Wheeler, who had been confined to her bed by an extended illness, is formulaic in style and content. Its interest lies in the youthfulness of its author and her special condition.

Adelaide and Theodore, or Letters on Education (1783)

Translation of *Adèle et Théodore ou lettres sur l'éducation* (1782), ▷epistolary novel by French writer ▷Stéphanie-Félicité Ducrest, Comtesse de Genlis. The book was written while Genlis was governess to the children of the duc de Chartres – the future duc d'Orléans, Philippe Egalité, whose political ambitions for a reformed Constitutional monarchy she energetically seconded, and whose faction she was held to direct. The book secured her a European reputation as an educationalist. It was much admired by court circles in both France and England. ▷Maria Edgeworth's father gave it to her to read as a model, and it is mentioned in ▷Jane Austen's ▷*Emma* (1816). One of its few detractors, ▷Mary Wollstonecraft, produced a pertinent critique of its fundamental philosophy, attacking: '[Genlis's] absurd manner of making the parental authority supplant reason. For everywhere does she inculcate not only *blind* submission to parents, but to the opinion of the world . . . Is it possible to have much respect for a system of education that thus insults reason and nature?' ('Animadversions on Some of the Writers who have rendered Women Objects of Pity, Bordering on Contempt', in ▷*Vindication of the Rights of Women*, 1792).
De Genlis's educational philosophy is based on wordly wisdom, and the assumption that compliance with established order is the way to success. Lip-service is paid to the need to realize individual potential; but that potential must always be expressed within the existing social hierarchy, and involves no more than the better performance of an allotted role. Adèle enjoys an unusually extensive curriculum of physical training, household management, history and modern languages, which stretches her undoubted intellectual and practical talents. At the same time, she is trained to subordinate these to the career of a male partner. The first independent creative task set her by her mother-tutor is to write her half of a correspondence with an imagined older

brother, to induce him back from the fleshpots of Paris to the family fold. Women, in de Genlis's book, carry the responsibility for sustaining the morality of men and, in consequence, the social order men have established.

Ellen Moers (see bibliography) praises de Genlis for the 'rigorous' quality of educational treatises, which show that 'in the history of pedagogy [she] has a distinct place as an innovating follower as well as an opponent of Rousseau'. The praise is misplaced. Genlis is not so much 'rigorous' as an authoritarian stickler for detail and control. She follows Rousseau Jean-Jacques in (1712–1778) extending women's education to make them more useful to men, while opposing all Rousseau's arguments for individual freedom and autonomy and the need for social change.

Bib: Moers, E., *Literary Women*.

Adelaide (Alice) de Condet (12th century)
Patron in England. Adelaide was lady of Thorngate Castle, on the outskirts of Lincoln. She was married to Robert, a Lincoln landowner. In about 1150 Sanson de Nanteuil translated for her, at her request, the *Proverbs of Solomon*, a moral treatise, into elegant ▷ Anglo-Norman verse, perhaps for the instruction of her son, Roger.

Adelaide (Adeliza) of Louvain (died 1151)
Patron. Adelaide, second wife of Henry I, was one of several queens in England of the early medieval period who were important patrons of literature in ▷ Anglo-Norman. The *Bestiaire* of Philippe de Thaon, an Anglo-Norman metrical version of the Latin *Physiologus*, and the oldest bestiary in the French language (written probably between 1121 and 1135) was dedicated to Adelaide. A certain David wrote a *Life of Henry I* for her in verse, probably in Anglo-Norman, but which has not survived. The *Voyage of St Brendan* by Benedeit was rededicated to Adelaide after the death of ▷ Maud (Edith), the first wife of Henry I. She also took Gaimar, the chronicler and historian, under her patronage.

Bib: Legge, M. Dominica, *Anglo-Norman Literature and its Background*

Adèle et Theodore ou lettres sur l'éducation
(1782) ▷ *Adelaide and Theodore, or Letters on education* (1783)

Adeline Mowbray (1804)
A novel by ▷ Amelia Opie. It is based on the life of ▷ Mary Wollstonecraft Shelley, although it is not strictly biographical. Adeline has been influenced by the radical ideas and free-thinkers of the late 18th century, and defies social convention by cohabiting with her lover, Glenmurray. The portrait of Adeline is sympathetic, but the author demonstrates her resistance to radical ideas as, after the death of her lover, Adeline is persuaded to turn back to social conformity and religion by a Quaker. She dies a religious woman, having seen the error of her ways.

Adiaffi, Anne-Marie (born 1951)
Novelist from the Côte d'Ivoire. Adiaffi is the author of two novels: *Une vie hypothequée* (1984) (*A Hypothetical Life*) and *La Ligne brisée* (1989) (*The Broken Line*), published in Abidjan. She studied in the Côte d'Ivoire, France and Senegal, and qualified as a bilingual secretary. Married to a diplomat, she has lived in Morocco, Tunisia and Algeria.

Adisa, Opal Palmer (born 1954)
Carribbean writer, teacher, storyteller and community organizer, born in ▷ Jamaica, she is studying for her doctorate at the University of California at Berkeley. Her published works include *Pina, The Many-Eyed Fruit* (1985), *Bake-Face and Other Guava Stories* (1976) and *Travelling Women* (1989). Her poems have been included in several anthologies in both the USA and Jamaica.

Admiración operum Dey (Wonder at the Works of God)
The second book by the 15th-century Spanish writer ▷ Teresa de Cartagena. It expands on themes already touched upon in Cartagena's earlier work, such as the lessons to be drawn from meditating on nature and humanity, but there are also the reflections of a writer on the creative process, which is unusual for this early period of literature. It also contains hints that Cartagena may have been questioning the authority of her male peers.

▷ *Arboleda de los enfermos*

'Adnan, Etel (born 1925)
Lebanese poet and painter. Daughter of a Syrian father and a Greek mother, she grew up in Beirut at the time of the French Mandate and went to a French convent school. The impact of World War II on the Arab world changed her life; she went out to work in the French Information Bureau in Beirut, and was encouraged by its administrator to sit for the French *baccalauréat*. After her father's death in 1947, she left for Paris with a scholarship for the Sorbonne. Later, she studied at Berkeley and Harvard, and taught philosophy from 1959–1972 at the Dominican College in San Rafael, California. In 1972 she went back to Beirut to work as literary editor for a French Lebanese paper. After the outbreak of the civil war in Lebanon, Etel 'Adnan lived in France and the USA. She writes poetry in both French and English, but is recognized as an Arab poet; many extracts from her work are translated into Arabic with her collaboration, and published in Arabic poetry magazines.

Her political poetry covers both Palestine and Vietnam; at the time when she was active in the movement against the Vietnam War, she composed *Five Senses for One Death* (1971) in English, and *Jebu et l'Express Beyrouth–Enfer* (1973) (*Jebu and the Beirut–Hell Express*) on Palestine, in

French. Other collections of her English verse are: *Moonshots* (1966), *Pablo Neruda is a Banana Tree* (1982) and *The Indian Never Had a Horse* (1985). Her French volume *Apocalypse Arabe* (1980) (*Arab Apocalypse*) is an intermingling of verse and visual signs, for it is illustrated by the poet herself. Her only novel, *Sitt Marie Rose* (1978), was written in French and translated into English (1982). Etel 'Adnan paints, illustrates books and designs carpets.

Bib: Boullata, Kamal (ed.), ▷*Women of the Fertile Crescent*; Kilpatrick, Hilary, 'Interview with Etel 'Adnan,' in Schipper, Mineke (ed.), *Unheard Words*; 'Adnan, Etel, 'Growing Up to be a Woman Writer in Lebanon'; Badran, Margot and Cooke, Miriam (eds), ▷*Opening the Gates.*

adultera, L' (1964) (The Adulteress)

This novel, by Italian writer ▷Laudomia Bonanni, begins in Milan, and moves to Naples through the actions of its central character, a married woman who is ostensibly travelling in connection with her work, but who is actually en route to her lover. The story of her relationship with her husband is told in a series of flashbacks which indicate a relationship at once affectionate and bitter. The war has been the dividing force in their lives and, again through flashbacks, we witness a succession of the protagonist's sexual encounters with various men during the war years. The novel ends in a manner at once tragic and absurd, with the woman's accidental death in her lover's flat as the result of a gas leak. This work is significant for its apparent use of its protagonist as an exemplum of female destiny (she weeps bitter tears on the birth of her *daughter*), and it is typical of Bonanni's work in its focus on the female character.

Advice literature (18th-century Britain)

Debates about the status and nature of women altered advice literature in the 18th century. Women were still addressed as maids, wives or widows, but the debate about friendship in marriage inevitably brought up the question of the education of women, and this fed into debates on conduct. The changes in advice on conduct are subtle, and the literature continued to advise the woman to adapt herself to circumstances, and particularly to her husband. For example, a relatively conservative advice book, *The Lady's New-Year's Gift: or, Advice to a Daughter* by George Savile, Marquis of Halifax, concentrates on the need for a woman to adapt her feelings. He recommends 'wise use of everything [one] may dislike in a husband' to transform that which might breed 'aversion' to be 'very supportable'. But he hopes that his daughter gets 'a Wise Husband, one that by knowing how to be Master . . . will not let you feel the weight of it'. In *Letters Moral and Entertaining* (1729–33), ▷Elizabeth (Singer) Rowe has a character note the relationship between feelings and conduct when she says, 'I was sensible of the delusion and how easily vice betrays an unguarded mind.' ▷Mary

Wollstonecraft's (early) ▷*Thoughts on the Education of Daughters* (1787) adds this perception, that feelings and conduct are linked, to the argument for education. She writes, 'in a comfortable situation a cultivated mind is necessary to render a woman contented; and in a miserable one it is her only consolation.'

Bib: Jones, Vivian, *Women in the Eighteenth Century.*

Aedelers, Etta Palm d' (1743–?)

Dutch activist in the French Revolution. Born in Holland, she lived in Paris from 1774 to 1793 where she founded the *Société des amis de la vérité*. The text of her founding speech in 1791, and others she made during the revolutionary period, including *Pétition de femmes à l'Assemblée legislative* (*Women's Petition to the Legislative Assembly*) which argues in favour of the principle of equality between the sexes being enshrined in law, have been published in recent collections of women's revolutionary documents (▷French Revolution: pamphlets, register of grievances, petitions and speeches). Her plans to set up women's patriotic societies in each section of Paris are detailed in *Lettre à une amie de la vérité* (1791) (*Letter to a Friend of Truth*). Following her return to Holland, she was arrested in 1795 on suspicion of being an Orangewoman.

Her work appears in: P. Duhet, (ed.), *Cahiers de Doléances des femmes et autres textes* (*Register of Women's Grievances and Other Texts*). English trans. in Levy, Applewhite and Johnson, *Women in Revolutionary Paris.*

Bib: Villiers, M., de, *Histoire des clubs de femmes et des légions d'Amazones.*

Ælflæd, Abbess of Whitby (8th century)

English abbess. A letter from Ælflæd (in Latin) is preserved in the ▷Boniface Correspondence. Written in Latin, it is addressed to Adola, Abbess of Pfalzel, near Trier, and recommends a woman on pilgrimage to Rome to the care of the community at Pfalzel. It is the only letter in the collection from a woman to a woman, but there must have been many such letters written from English religious houses.

Aesara (4th century BC)

Philosopher from Lucania, Italy. Iamblichus (3rd century AD), biographer of the Greek philosopher Pythagoras, notes that she was one of the leading theorists of the school after Pythagoras's death. She is credited with a Greek treatise *On Human Nature*, which discusses the three divisions of the human soul into reason, passion and appetite, in terms similar to those of Plato (4th Century BC). Like Plato, she sees justice as the harmony of the soul's component parts.

▷Philosophers, ancient Greek and Roman women

African-language literature (Southern Africa)

Black Southern African women started publishing fiction at the beginning of the 20th century. The earliest work, published mostly at the Lovedale mission, was in Xhosa. Lovedale had imported a Ruthven printing press in 1823, primarily for biblical translations, parables and dictionaries. Publication gradually extended to other languages: Ndebele, Shona, Sotho, Tsonga, Tswana, Venda, Xhosa and Zulu, and perhaps others. The focus here is on Xhosa prose writing by women, given current research. A detailed literary history remains to be constructed. Nontsizi Mgqwetho's poetry, for instance, published in a Johannesburg newspaper in the 1920s, is only now being translated and reprinted: intensely political, often celebratory of women, with a fine sense of literary tradition, it deserves to be widely known.

Early mission literature modelled itself on allegories and biblical parables, and was, above all, didactic. Characters represented specific virtues and vices, usually arranged in terms of a conflict between urban/modern and rural/traditional life. 'Good' and 'evil' were readily represented by 'chaste' and 'unchaste' women, the latter associated with the corruptions of city life. Thus, while African and Christian values sometimes jostled uneasily against each other, they concurred as regards patriarchy. In the words of an early Xhosa writer, 'Children should obey their mothers; the mothers should obey the fathers; the fathers should obey the chiefs; the chiefs should obey God.' Within this doubly justified ▷patriarchal structure, women's lives were charted as a passage from father to husband, and were fulfilled by motherhood rather than by career. The allegorical cum patriarchal tendency gave rise to stereotypes such as scheming, untrustworthy women and hen-pecked men.

While two very early novels written by Xhosa-speaking women are referred to in bibliographies: Laetitia Kakaza's *Intyatyambo yomzi* (1913) (*The Flower in the Home*), and *UThandiwe wakwaGcaleka* (1914) (*Thandiwe of the Gcaleka People*), along with one play, Mary Waters's *UNongqawuse* (1924), the earliest surviving extant work is Victoria Swartbooi's novel *UMandisa* (1934). This novel presents in great detail the socialization of a young girl, Mandisa, by her grandmother, and continues to show how diligently Mandisa performs her household chores even when she becomes a teacher. Through the rest of the 1930s and into the 1940s, 1950s and 1960s, novels written by women tend to reproduce a Christian perspective, measuring their distance from such things as witchcraft and polygyny. An example here is *UJujuju* (1938) (*Magic*), by Zorah Futshane, who also wrote *Mhla ngenqaba* (1960) (*Mhla in Trouble*).

As allegory gave way to social realism, female characterization became more complex. Rose Silinga's *UNonzuzo* (1965) presents women as the major force of the household, while Elishia Mda's second novel, *Ntengu Ntengu Macetyana* (1972) (*Fork-tailed Drongo*), looks at a young woman compelled to find work in the city, thus standing as an early example of fiction interested in the changing economic position of women. While her brother disappears in the city, the daughter can be relied on to return. In this world of poverty and deprivation, *lobola* (bride-wealth) is commercialized, with women becoming something that men can or cannot 'afford', rather than a contract between kinship groups. Yet women continue to be the bearers of specific virtues.

With writing being subjected to as strenuous a screening by education authorities as it had been under missionary direction, and with the protective attitudes towards the family that were developed in an age of migrant labour and urban influx control, feminist inquiry has been scant. In the introduction to *UNongxaki nezakhe* (1976) (*UNongxaki and Her Troubles*), Gertrude Belebesi says that she is responding to the claim that woman's place is in the kitchen. The novel explores women's equal access to the land, in a context of male migrant labour. Siphokazi Angelina Dazela's *Owu ndanele* (1977) (*O! I'm Finished*) presents a female character who has grown up performing both indoor (feminine) and outdoor (masculine) chores. Her heroine manages to outwit the man who tries to abduct her in forced marriage (*ukuthwalwa*), and fulfils herself by qualifying as a nurse and marrying a doctor. A poem entitled 'Ubufazi' ('Womanhood'), in which the Xhosa-speaker Nobantu Ndlazulwana sees womanhood in terms of subordination rather than idealization, stands as a rare example of feminist interrogation.

Just as the South African government was using indigenous languages to divide the country's African population and return them to 'ethnicity', the interest in Rhodesia (now Zimbabwe) in vernacular literature was not an innocent one. In the 1950s, the Rhodesian colonial government started educating the black inhabitants, and set up a Literature Bureau to promote vernacular literature, which then became strictly controlled. This situation continued into the 1970s. While adult writing seems not to have been encouraged at all in South Africa, given the market projected, in Rhodesia there were adult novels in Shona and Ndebele, but limited to 'popular' rather than political themes. There were few titles by women: *Qaphele Ingane* (1962) (*Take Care of the Boy*), by Lassie Ndondo; *Ngano Dzepasi Chigare* (1964) (*Tales of Old*), by Jane Chifamba; *Ndochema Naani* (1974) (*It's All My Fault*), by Stella Mandebvu; and *Vatete Vachabvepi* (1977) (*Where Will the Aunt Come From*), by Tendai Makura. It appears that women were not encouraged to publish a second time.

In Botswana and Lesotho, which became independent in the mid-1960s, little has been published, due to the poor economic situation and, hence, scanty formal education. However, Caroline Khaketla (Lesotho) has been relatively prolific: a novel called *Mosali eo u'neileng eena* (1956) (*The Woman You Gave Me*), a play, *Pelo eo Monna* (1976) (*The Heart of a Man*), and a volume of poetry, *Mantsopa* (1963), some of which reappears in anthologies. Other Sotho publications were Emely Selemeng Mokorosi's set of poems entitled *Bolebali* (1951) (*Forgetfulness*), and a novel and play from Maggie Rammala (born 1924). There is no record of vernacular writing by women from Swaziland and Namibia.

Critics have claimed that, since publication is at present geared to school prescription, there is little possibility of a tradition of adult African-language fiction developing. Because of the variety of African languages, the south has not seen the kind of movement associated with post-colonialism in Africa more generally, where writers and publishers turn back to the mother tongue. At the moment, writers prefer to publish in English. However, a number of African English-language writers incorporate African languages into their texts, sometimes without translation, reminding monolingual readers, both in Southern Africa and abroad, of the rich multilinguism that properly characterizes Southern African culture. Examples here are ▷Noni Jabavu, ▷Gcina Mhlophe, and ▷Miriam Tlali. ▷Popular theatre and ▷performance poetry are often in the vernacular, or in a variety of vernacular languages. In Soweto, for instance, people speak Ndebele, Northern Sotho, Shangaan, Tswana, Venda, Xhosa and Zulu, as well as the official languages, English and Afrikaans. Not all Southern Africans speak English, or are literate in it (over half the overall population is not literate in any language). With the changing dispensation in South Africa, as the country moves from white minority to black majority rule, it is likely that more publication will take place in the indigenous African languages. The African National Congress has recently been engaged in discussions on precisely that issue.
Bib: Mtuze, Peter, *Xhosa Women Writers: A Feminist Analysis* (Ph.D Thesis, Rhodes University, Grahamstown).

Afrikaans women writers

Since the Afrikaans language, as a medium for literature, has a very short history, an Afrikaans literature can be said to have come into being only in the late 19th century. Although Afrikaner culture is Calvinist and patriarchal, Afrikaans literature includes a number of women writers who have played an important part in its development. The novelist Hettie Smit (1908–1973) is one of the first two women who may be regarded as substantial Afrikaans literary figures. The other is the poet ▷Elisabeth Eybers, who is still writing today. There are also a number of important contemporary writers, only some of whom are known in the English-speaking world.

The Afrikaner cultural tradition foregrounds the ideal of the *volksmoeder* (the mother of the nation), an ideal continually recollected in the mythologized *Voortrekker* tradition of strong and independent women. Correspondingly, much of the writing by Afrikaans women reproduces a traditionally feminine role. ▷M.E.R.'s regional writing conveys this role in rural, even feudal, terms. A proletarian reading of the *volksmoeder* is given by members of the Garment Workers'

Union, writing between the two World Wars, in poetry, prose and plays published in their union magazine. This literary impulse came to an end as white women workers were gradually replaced in the factories by women of colour.

In the 1940s and 1950s a number of journalists, influenced by the work of M.E.R., wrote essays, short stories and narratives. The collection *Die Dammetjie en Ander Sketse en Essays* (1960) (*The Little Dam and Other Sketches and Essays*) contains work by the most significant of these: besides M.E.R., Audrey Blignaut (born 1916), Alba Bouwer (born 1920), Freda Linde (born 1915), Elise Muller (born 1919), and Rykie van Reenen (born 1923). In children's fiction Linde is the most important, often writing sensitively about nature. Other essayists of note are Hymne Weiss (born 1910), Sannie Uys (1866–1976) and M.I. Murray (born 1899).

It is perhaps for their contribution to South African poetry that Afrikaans women writers are most remarkable. Elisabeth Eybers, whose work continues up to the present, is notable for the way in which she incorporates European neoclassicism of the 1920s and 1930s, and draws deeply on religion and mythology. As a woman writer she is significant, too, for the way in which her work traces changes in attitudes to femininity. She was preceded by two interesting figures: Olga Kirsch (born 1924) and Ina Rousseau (born 1926). Kirsch's poetry reflects on Jewish identity, often in the tradition of the Old Testament songs of lamentation. After Eybers, the most significant poets are ▷Sheila Cussons, ▷Ingrid Jonker, ▷Antjie Krog, and ▷Wilma Stockenström.

Among contemporary writers, the best-established in fiction are ▷Elsa Joubert, ▷Henriette Grové, and ▷Anna M. Louw, who also writes drama, as well as Stockenström, fiction writer as well as poet. Louw and Stockenström, in particular, interrogate the premises of the Afrikaner cultural tradition, and especially the myth whereby Afrikaners are God's 'chosen people'. This myth has played itself out in exclusivist, racist terms in the country's history. These writers specifically interrogate the ▷patriarchal tradition, too, which continues to be propagated in radio and television programmes. Louw's influential critique, in fiction and drama, is followed by ▷Lettie Viljoen, in fiction, and ▷Reza de Wet, in drama, who has recently emerged as a significant dramatist. In poetry, Jonker established an important oppositional voice, which is recalled in the new wave of feminist, politicized writing by Jeanne Goosen (born 1940), who is emerging as a substantial fiction writer and poet, as well as by Krog. The personal career of ▷Welma Odendaal in the national broadcasting system attests to the punishments meted out to critics of Afrikanerdom. In some of her short stories Odendaal explores lesbian themes, as do Marlise Joubert, in her epistolary novel, *Klipkus* (1978) (*Rocky Coast*), Jeanne Goosen in her novel, *Om 'n mens na to boots* (1975) (*To Mimic a Human Being*), and the prolific Joan Hambidge, in, for example, *Bitterlemoene* (1986) (*Bitter Oranges*).

Besides Joubert, who is well-known in the English-speaking world for her *The Long Journey of Poppie Nongena*, later published as *Poppie Nongena*, the work of only a few Afrikaans women writers is available in English. Some of Jonker's poetry in the 1960s and some of Cussons's early poems have been translated. More recently, Cussons has written in both English and Afrikaans. Several of Eybers's poems have been translated and anthologized, though she does not, as Jonker does, have a volume to herself. Dalene Matthee's recent novels about the Knysna forest in the Cape have been translated, and have been extremely successful. One of a number of popular writers in Afrikaans, including Audrey Blignaut, Matthee is the only one to have been translated.

Afrikaans is not spoken only by white South Africans: in the Cape, it is the first language of many so-called 'coloured' people. M.C. Mackier has published some of her Afrikaans poems in the anthology *Aankoms uit die skemer* (1988) (*Arrival out of the Dusk*).
Bib: Brink, André, *Mapmakers: Writing in a State of Siege*; Cope, Jack, *The Adversary Within: Dissident Writers in Afrikaans*.

Aganoor Pompilj, Vittoria (1855–1910)
Italian poet. Of Armenian origin, she was born in Padua and moved to Naples, where she studied European poetry. In 1901, she married Guido Pompilj, who committed suicide hours after her death. Her poetry is mainly love poetry, and in her writing she questions the meaning of life, while in her later writings she expresses the sadness of growing older. *Leggenda eterna* (*Eternal Legend*) of 1908 is perhaps her best known volume of love poetry, rich in literary allusions. She wrote *Nuove liriche* (*New Lyrics*) in 1908, while much of her work was published posthumously: *Opere complete* (1912 and 1927) (*Complete Works*), *Lettere di Vittoria Aganoor a Giacomo Zanella* (1924) (*Letters of Vittoria Aganoor to Giacomo Zanella*), and *Lettere a D. Gnoli* (1927) (*Letters to D. Gnoli*).

Age of Innocence, The (1920)
US novel. ▷Edith Wharton's Pulitzer Prize-winning work examines the ramifications of innocence. Newland Archer is innocent in his belief that love can transcend social constraints; he must discover how sexual relationships function as social and economic exchanges. He marries his fiancée, May Welland, instead of the woman he loves, Ellen Olenska. May's innocence shows both the damage her culture does to her and how she damages others. Lacking imagination, May pursues only what she has been raised to pursue – marriage – and she denies Newland happiness by separating him from Ellen. As an expatriate, Ellen views her country's culture with a moral clarity and, as an autonomous woman, Ellen represents Wharton's vision of an alternative to woman's commodification.

Age of Suspicion: Essays on the Novel, The (1963)
Translation of *L'Ere du soupçon: essais sur le roman* (1953), four essays by French writer ▷Nathalie Sarraute, considered as a landmark of ▷*nouveau roman* criticism. Sarraute reviews the evolution of the novel and the necessity of doing away with description, characterization and ▷realism; major references are made to Kafka, Dostoevsky, Camus, ▷Virginia Woolf and ▷Ivy Compton-Burnett. In 'Conversation and Sub-conversation' she defines her own technique of 'tropism' as the more adequate tool of psychological realism for the modern novel.

Agnes, Prioress (12th century)
Agnes was the second prioress of the English Benedictine Priory of Castle Hedingham, Essex. This nunnery had been founded in the late 12th century by Lucy, Countess of Oxford, who became the first prioress, and her husband, Aubrey de Vere, first Earl of Oxford. A letter from Agnes (in Latin) in the form of a roll (a 'bede-roll') was circulated to various monasteries to request prayers for Lucy after her death in 1198. The answers of more than a hundred monasteries are recorded on the roll.
Bib: Knowles, David and Hadcock, R. Neville, *Medieval Religious Houses in England and Wales*; Moriarty, Catherine, *The Voice of the Middle Ages in Personal Letters 1100–1500*.

Agnese va a morire, L' (1949) (Agnes Goes Off to Die)
This novel, by Italian writer ▷Renata Viganò, is autobiographical insofar as it arises from Viganò's experience as a partisan in the ▷resistance movement. It tells the story of a country woman who is instantly politicized when her husband is murdered by the Germans, and ultimately she finds that she, too, is capable of murder. She joins the partisans when she kills a German soldier. As the title indicates, she is finally captured and executed. It is unusual as a ▷resistance novel in that it centres on an active female partisan. The novel also addresses issues of class as much as those of gender, and is strikingly humorous in parts.

Agnes Grey (1847)
A semi-autobiographical novel by ▷Anne Brontë which first appeared under the ▷pseudonym Acton Bell. Agnes is a rector's daughter who joins the household of the Bloomfield family to work as a ▷governess. The vivid portrayal of the spoilt children owes much to Brontë's experience with the Ingham family, for whom she worked in 1839. Similarly, the portrait of Rosalie, the flirtatious daughter of the Murray family draws on Brontë's experience working for the Robinsons (1841–45). The novel departs from autobiography in its later chapters, as the gentle and modest Agnes is united with the kind curate, Mr Weston, by whom she has three children.

Agoglu, 'Adalet (born 1929)

Turkish dramatist, novelist and short story writer.
She graduated from the French Department of
the University of Ankara, and worked mainly for
Turkish radio. She was director of Ankara Radio
Theatre for which she wrote her play *Yaşamak*
(1955). It was also broadcast on French and
German radio in 1955. She wrote a number of
other plays for both radio and stage, and her short
stories were collected and published in 1973.

Agosin, Marjorie (Marjorie Stela Agosin Halpern) (born 1955)

Chilean fiction writer and poet. Born in the
United States of Chilean parents, she spent her
childhood and adolescence in Chile, but returned
to the US to finish high school. She studied
philosophy as an undergraduate, then completed
an MA in Spanish literature. At present she
lectures in Latin American literature at Wellesley
College. In her writings she contrasts the United
States with Latin America. In the prologue to
Chile: gemidos y cantares (1977) (*Chile: Groans and
Songs*), ▷María Luisa Bombal notes that Agosin
writes a 'love song' for Chile. *Conchalí* (1980), a
collection of thirty poems, was her first work to be
published in the US. These poems juxtapose
North and South America, especially in regard to
women's roles, in a playful yet lyrical manner. She
has also published four books of literary criticism,
and *Scraps of Life* (1988) on the Chilean women's
arpilleras.

Ágreda, Sor María de (Coronel de Jesús) (1602–1665)

A Spanish writer. Agreda was a correspondent of
Philip IV. Her main works are: *Mística ciudad de
Dios* (*Mystic City of God*); *Escala espiritual* (*Spiritual
Ladder of the Soul*) and *Leyes de la esposa* (*The
Spouse's Laws*).

Agrippina the Younger (1st century AD)

Roman diarist. Born c AD 13–17, died AD 60.
Daughter of Germanicus Caesar, she was accused
of incest with her brother Gaius, later the
emperor Caligula, and banished to an island in AD
39. Returning to Rome in AD 41, she married the
emperor Claudius, whom she later allegedly
poisoned to ensure the succession as emperor of
her son, Nero. The Roman historian Tacitus (2nd
century AD) mentions that he used as a source
some memoirs written by Agrippina. Renowned in
antiquity for her intrigue and ambition, the
memoirs, which we do not possess, were probably
full of scandal and thus may not have been
genuine.
▷Diaries, ancient Greek and Roman

Aguilar, Grace (1816–1847)

British author. She was born in Hackney,
London, the eldest child of Spanish-Jewish
parents. Aguilar is chiefly remembered today as a
▷sentimental novelist and prose writer, although
she was also a poet. She never married, and after
her father's death she wrote for a profession,

Agrippina

publishing several works on Judaism. *The Spirit of
Judaism* (1842) was a controversial attack on the
formalities of institutionalized religion, while
Women of Israel (1845) and *The Jewish Faith*
(1846) express a concern with the position of
women within the faith. Her first novel, *Home
Influence* (1847), was the only one to be published
in her lifetime. Posthumously published novels
include *The Mother's Recompense* (1851) and
▷*Woman's Friendship* (1853).

Aguirre, Mirta (born 1912)

Cuban poet, novelist and essayist. Although not
well-known outside Cuba, Aguirre was a strong
presence in Cuban politics, who reacted against
Stalinist practices. Influenced by Nicolás Guillen
she employs ▷*criollismo* as a means for social and
political denunciation in her poetry, while also
profiting from a study of his rhythms. A second
influence has been García Lorca (1899–1936),
from whom she adopted the idea of the *Romancero
gitano* (Gypsy ballad), using it as a basis for tales
of revolutionary accomplishments. Her work
attempts to unite literary forms with popular ones,
such as those performed in a *romancero*, or set of
ballads. In 1932 she published ten poems that
later formed part of *Ayer de hoy* (1980) (*Yesterday
Today*). Poem VIII refers to the 'mother-Latin
American,' with its 'heroic legacy' from the
conquistadors Francisco Pizarro (c 1476–1541)
and Hernán Cortés (1485–1547). In poem II she
condemns Stalinism, and contrasts power in Cuba
with the poverty amongst its people. In a poem of
1933 she sings of the '*Hermano negro*', and praises
in a later poem the 'Indian of America', from

'Alaska, Ecuador or from Chile', fighting prejudice. She identifies these races as the foundation stones of the American continent. Her work includes *Juegos y otros poemas* (1974) (*Games and Other Poems*) and four books of essays.

Agustini, Delmira (1886–1914)

Uruguayan poet. After an over-protected childhood in a bourgeois milieu, she married a horse dealer, Enrique Reyes, who, during their divorce after one year of marriage, murdered her and killed himself violently. There is evidence of a more profound love for the seductive Argentinian writer Manuel Ugarte (1878–1951). Her best book, *Los cálices vacíos* (1913) (*The Empty Cups*), combined her first one, *El libro blanco* (1907) (*The White Book*), and *Cantos de la mañana* (1910) (*Morning Songs*), along with newer poems. She belonged to the outstanding male-dominated ▷Rio de la Plata group of poets (1910–1920) and was part of the ▷1900 Generation, which included Julio Herrera y Reissig, Leopoldo Lugones, and the much-admired poet, Rubén Dario (1867–1946). However, her main influences were the French symbolists and Nietzsche (1844–1900). Delmira Agustini wrote erotic poems, showing the anxious, spiritual and erotic expectation for the beloved in biological images and daring confessions, as in 'Visión', 'Otra estirpe' and 'El Arroyo'. Her 'hyperaesthetic' moments are transformed into voluptuous images of incredible imagination, with similies, metaphors, allegorical forms and a freedom approaching the fantastic. Her correspondence has been edited and published (1969).

Ahlefeld, Charlotte Elisabeth Sophie Louise Wilhelmine von (1781–1849)

German writer. From a wealthy military family, she grew up in the cultured atmosphere of late 18th-century Weimar. At sixteen she published her first novel, *Liebe und Trennung* (1797) (*Love and Separation*). Two years later she married a landowner, whom she divorced in 1807 because of his violent temper. Thereafter she earned a comfortable living by writing popular novels. Her plots revolve around family dramas, often with a chivalrous medieval setting. They bear the mark of Weimar classicism, in which conflict is resolved by the victory of reason over emotion, and by the noble comportment of all concerned.

Aïcha la rebelle (1982) (Aïcha the Rebel)

Novel by Moroccan writer ▷Halima Ben Haddou. Set in the time when Morocco was under both French and Spanish occupation (1912–1956), the novel is a combination of fact and fiction. Adopted by a Spanish farmer who later tries to rape her, Aïcha is rejected by the people of the neighbouring village who contemptuously refer to her as '*l'Espagnole*' (the Spaniard). Unlike her creator, who was paralysed, Aïcha is a lively character who spends her days running and riding her horse. Being brought up in a Spanish environment, Aïcha enjoys the freedom of moving outside home which is unavailable to the rest of the Moslem women of the village. She uses her freedom in an attempt to show the villagers her involvement in the fight against colonialism, by helping the rebels who hide in the mountains.

Aïcha rebels in two ways: against the adoptive Spanish culture which she finds alienating, and against the Moslem one, which does not accept her as a free woman. Her story ends on a nihilistic note, where only death can liberate.

Aichinger, Ilse (born 1921)

Austrian novelist and poet. Born in Vienna of a Jewish mother and an 'Aryan' father, Aichinger's parents divorced when she was five. Yet it was thanks to the protection of her father that her family was saved from deportation under Hitler. Her only novel, *Die größere Hoffnung* (1948) (*The Greater Hope*) is one of the earliest to portray Germany's recent past. Intensely poetic and allusive in language and imagery, it nevertheless succeeds in dealing effectively with urgent issues, such as persecution and aspects of private resistance.

After the war, Aichinger became involved albeit somewhat sceptically with the *Gruppe 47* (Group of '47), which sought to define a 'denazified' voice for a new German literature. In 1952 she was awarded its prize for her novella, *Rede unter dem Galgen* (*Speech Beneath the Gallows*). Her poems, collected in *Verschenkter Rat* (*Advice Freely Given*) (1978), often take the form of a challenge to the reader to consider paradoxical aspects of moral issues. Her sensitivity to the difficulties of achieving poetic authenticity remains a key issue throughout her work. In her short prose, collected in *Eliza, Eliza* (1965), *Meine Sprache und ich* (1968) (*My Language and I*) and *Schlechte Wörter* (1976) (*Bad Words*), she sets out to rediscover and explore words, and thus to distance herself from language, in a bid to remain vigilant against its abuse.

Aidoo, Ama Ata (born 1942)

Ghanaian dramatist, short story writer, poet and novelist. A writer for over thirty years in several different genres, Aidoo, like many other African women writers, is still little-recognized by the mainstream. Her play ▷*Anowa*, published in 1970, was produced in Britain in 1991, the year of publication of her novel ▷*Changes*. Moreover, her feminist publishers have since decided not to publish any more black women's writing 'because it doesn't sell'. Aidoo's experiences are an object lesson in the kind of difficulties faced even by established African women writers.

Aidoo, who attended the University of Ghana at Legon, worked with ▷Efua Sutherland in the Drama Studio in the early 1960s. She has written two plays, *The Dilemma of a Ghost* (1965) and *Anowa*. Her book of short stories, *No Sweetness Here* was published in 1970. One of a group of political activists who saw the potential of the

Ama Ata Aidoo

socialist revolution led by Flight-Lieutenant Jerry Rawlings in 1981, she became for a short time Ghana's Secretary for Education. Since 1983 she has lived in Harare, Zimbabwe, where she has worked for the Curriculum Development Unit of the Ministry of Education. Her collection of poems, *Someone Talking to Sometime*, was published in Zimbabwe in 1985, and she is active in the Zimbabwe Women Writers Group, of which she currently holds the chair.

Aidoo's first novel, ▷ *Our Sister Killjoy*, was published in 1981. It explores the experience of racism by Africans in Europe, and is an indictment of those who criticize their countries from a distance rather than going back and involving themselves. Her second and only other novel, *Changes*, was published ten years later. Both novels are remarkable for the way Aidoo incorporates elements of oral techniques, like addressing the reader/audience directly, the use of dramatic dialogue, narrative meditations within the text and a style that veers between prose and poetry.

▷ Children's literature (West Africa); Polygam, (West Africa); Oral Tradition (West Africa)
Bib: Adams Graves, A. and Boyce-Davies, C. (eds), *Ngambika: Studies of Women in African Literature;* James, A., *In Their Own Voices: Interviews with African Women Writers;* Taiwo, O., *Female Writers of Tropical Africa.*

Aiken, Joan (born 1924)
English novelist, short story writer, poet and dramatist. Aiken is best-known as a prolific writer for children, and her novels are, typically, historical fantasies. *The Wolves of Willoughby Chase* (1962) creates a fictional James III in a 19th-century Yorkshire setting. Other works for children include the 'Mortimer Cross' stories, and *Tales of Arabel's Raven* (1974). She has also written

The Way to Write for Children. Aiken's books for adults include psychological suspense novels, such as *Died on Rainy Sunday* and *Hate Begins at Home*, and thrillers including *Last Movement* (1979), *The Butterfly Picnic* and *A Cluster of Separate Sparks.* Her other works include: *The Fortune Hunters, The Ribs of Death, The Embroidered Sunset* and *Trouble with Product X.*

Aikin, Lucy (1781–1864)
British poet, critic and historian. She was born in Warrington, the daughter of John Aikin, writer and physician, who educated her at home. She became fluent in French, Italian and Latin and was well-read in history and biography. She was also acquainted with the writings of her aunt, ▷ Anna Letitia Barbauld. In 1801 she edited an anthology, *Poetry for Children*, which was several times reprinted. *Epistles on Women*, a moral and didactic work, appeared in 1810, and *Lorimer*, a novel of sensibility, in 1814. Three historical works followed: *Memoirs of the Court of Queen Elizabeth* (1818); *Memoirs of the Court of James I* (1822); *Memoirs of the Court of Charles I* (1833). Her ventures into biography include a *Life of Addison* (1843), and memoirs of her father and aunt. She was well-known in literary circles and respected for her scholarship. A staunch Unitarian, she was also a ▷ feminist who protested against the dominant perception of woman's role in society.
Bib: Le Breton, P.H. (ed.), *Memoirs, Miscellanies and Letters of the Late Lucy Aikin.*

Aimuc de Castelnou (early 13th century)
French ▷ *trobairitz* of the third period, who has been identified as Almodis, the wife of Guigue de Châteauneuf de Randon. Author of one extant *cobla*, answering Iseut de Capio, in manuscript form.
Bib: Paden, W.D. (ed.), *The Voice of the Trobairitz: perspectives on the women troubadours.*

Ainsi soit-elle (1975) (*So be it*)
Essay by French writer ▷ Benoîte Groult which discusses feminism and 'femininity' in an international frame. In a study which ranges from women's magazines to female genital mutilation, Groult examines the various traditions which contribute to women's oppression throughout the world. As its title suggests ('elle' is used in an attempt to combat the dominance of masculine forms in French grammar), the text challenges the myths which condition a woman's sexual identity, and combines scholarly documentation with irony and colloquial French.

Aisha (1983)
Collection of short stories written in English by Egyptian writer ▷ Ahdaf Soueif. The collection is described as a 'cycle' because most of the stories selected are narrated through the consciousness of Aisha, though she may not be a protagonist in the story. The stories bring to life scenes from modern Cairo or Alexandria, as well as glimpses of

London seen through the eyes of this young Egyptian girl. 'Knowing' describes her arrival in London as a child, and '1964' recalls an adolescence in the 1960s.

'Returning', the first story in the collection, describes the impact of Cairo on Aisha, returning home after an absence of six years. The last and longest of the stories stands out. This story, 'The Nativity' ends with the death of Aisha in childbirth. Aisha has been lured to an unfamiliar part of town by a supernatural presence, a 'familiar' who hopes to become her master. Among the crowds celebrating a saint's nativity she is raped, impregnated with the child whose birth kills her. The story ends as it starts, with the words of the familiar; he will wait.

Aïsha (born 1942)

French/Algerian novelist. ▷Pseudonym of Aïsha Bernier, the daughter of a Polish Jewish mother and an Algerian father, who met in France after her mother was forced to leave Poland during the Nazi occupation. Aïsha's troubled childhood, after the death of her parents in a concentration camp, and her later involvement in the Algerian Liberation Movement, are two important elements in her struggle for justice and recognition. Her novel *Décharge publique, Les Emmurés de l'assistance* (1980) is strongly autobiographical. Aïsha writes about her adolescent years in an orphanage and gives an account of other children in care.

Aïssé, Charlotte-Elisabeth Aïcha (?1694–1733)

Letter-writer, French by adoption. Thought to be of Circassian origin, Aïssé (originally Haïdé) was purchased at the age of five by the Baron Ferriol at the slave market in Constantinople. She was raised, amid the intrigues of the court in Paris, by his sister-in-law, Madame de Ferriol, sister of the novelist ▷Madame de Tencin. Her literary reputation is founded on her letters (1726–1733), addressed to her intimate friend, Madame Calandrini in Geneva, first published by Calandrini's daughter in 1787. The correspondence, which contains some extraordinary anecdotes of Parisian life under the Regency (later annotated by Voltaire) also records Aïssé's reactions to Jonathan Swift's *Gulliver's Travels* (1726) and the novels of Prévost (1697–1763) and Destouches. The text is chiefly renowned for the melancholic and guilt-ridden evocation of her relationship with the Chevalier d'Aydie. As a literary work, the letters have been regarded as prefiguring the ▷epistolary novels of ▷Mme Riccoboni.
Bib: Arland, M., *Le Promeneur*; Praed, *The Romance of Mlle Aïssé*; Gosse, E., *Selected Essays*; Ferval, C., *Mlle Aïssé et son chevalier*; Ivray, J., *L'Etrange Destinée de Mlle Aïssé*, Henriot, E., *D'Héloïse à Marie Bashkirtseff*).

Akello, Grace

Ugandan poet. In ▷*My Barren Song* (1980) Akello writes of the disruption of Ugandan society under Idi Amin and of the effect of traditional male-centred values on women. Her protagonist in the title poem is exploited from an early age, experiences the stigma of barrenness and is cast out as a mad woman.

Åkeson, Sonja Berta Maria Hammarberg (1926–1977)

Swedish lyric poet and prose writer. Sonja Åkeson grew up on the island of Gotland, in an illiterate community. In 1951 she moved to Stockholm, and soon after she began to write about her childhood and people outside of the literary culture.

In 1957 she published her first collection of poems, *Situationer* (*Situations*), in 1961, *Leva livet* (*Living Life*), and in 1963, *Husfrid* (*Domestic Peace*). She was soon applauded by the critics, and she became a very influential figure for younger women writers. She experimented with lyrical poetry, prose (*Pris*, 1968) (*Prize*), collages and music, and wrote bitter critiques of society, eg the famous poem 'Be White Man's Slave' (1963) that criticized the role of a modern housewife. In *Sagan om Siv* (1974) (*The Saga of Siv*), she wrote haiku poems, and together with her husband she wrote plays for the radio. She is considered an important literary figure of the 1960s in Sweden.

Akhmadúlina, Izabella Akhatovna (born 1937)

Russian poet. Bella Akhmadúlina, whose career began in the Khrushchev ▷thaw, has made her works and life an expression of faith in the power and probity of poetry. Despite periods of suppression – temporary expulsion from the ▷Writers' Union in the 1960s; a few years of silence after she participated in the unauthorized literary almanac *Metropol* in the late 1970s – she has remained a free spirit. Her poems inventively combine modern diction and vocabulary with classical standards of metre and rhyme. She celebrates the interrelation of nature and art in poems like 'The Garden,' and at the other extreme of her range, 'St Bartholomew's Night' is a sombre meditation on human cruelty. Akhmadúlina pays repeated homage to great predecessors from Pushkin to ▷Akhmátova, ▷Tsvetáeva, Pasternak, and ▷Mandel'shtám. 'Biographical Information' traces Tsvetáeva's career, and 'I Swear,' turns the name of the town where Tsvetaeva committed suicide – Elabuga – into a monstrous symbol for the personal and societal forces lying in wait to destroy poets. Among infrequent prose works Akhmadúlina has written a charming impressionistic reminiscence, 'Grandmother' and, for *Metropol*, 'The Many Dogs and the Dog', the story of a man recovering from a stroke at a Black Sea resort who perceives the life around him – from rutting dogs to human lovers – through a surreal haze.
Bib: Reeve, F.D. (ed. and trans.) *The Garden*; Wilson, K. (ed.), *Encyclopedia of Continental Women Writers* 1.

Akhmátova, Anna (1889–1966)

Born Anna Andreevna Gorenko, Akhmatova is one of the major Russian poets of the 20th century, and left an impressive legacy, both as a poet and as a human being. Her work is generally divided into two major periods: the so-called 'intimate' Akhmátova whose major theme was love (1909–1922) and the later Akhmátova of more 'public' themes (1935–1966). There was a lengthy silence between the two periods, as Akhmátova found herself out of favour with the new communist regime and unable to publish. In the earlier period, Akhmátova wrote almost exclusively short lyrics, while in the later period she devoted herself increasingly to larger forms such as the epic poem.

Her first book of poetry, *Evening*, of which 300 copies were published in 1912, immediately sold out. In it she treated the love theme in a new, highly psychological way: as condensed mini-dramas, usually between a 'she' and a 'he'. Precise external details, gestures, and snippets of dialogue or monologue are used to portray an inner world of feeling. Love is usually tragic. From early on, Akhmátova excelled at an almost aphoristic style. This was combined with a mastery of word placement. The lines often have the appearance of conversational Russian because of their syntax and colloquial vocabulary.

Akhmátova's second collection, *Rosary* (1914), went through nine editions. In this collection she continued to develop her love lyric, and added the theme of Russian culture represented by place, history, the orthodox religion, and folklore. Both the public and the critical establishment were delighted. Akhmátova had avoided the pitfalls – formal weakness and lack of 'femininity' – for which other women poets had been criticized. Akhmátova was a moderate innovator: as she wrote in a review, women's strength is not in form, but 'in the ability to express fully the most intimate things and the marvellously simple things found within themselves and the surrounding world' (*Russian Thought* 1, 1914).

After the publication of *Evening*, Akhmátova was at the height of her popularity. Another young poet, ▷Nina Berbérova, described the combination of poetic achievement and personal charisma that made Akhmátova so popular: 'slender, beautiful, dark-haired, elegant . . . this was the heyday of her glory, the glory of her new prosody her bangs, her profile, her charm' (▷ *The Italics Are Mine*, p. 70).

Between 1917 and 1922, Akhmátova brought out three more books of poetry, and in the early 1920s serious studies of her poetry were published by leading critics. But at the same time, she experienced a series of tragic events brought on by the repressive Soviet regime: between 1921 and 1953 many of the people closest to her emigrated or were killed or imprisoned. Publication of her work was banned between 1925 and 1952, with only a brief respite during World War II.

Akhmátova did not live to see the full publication of her great long poems ▷'Requiem' and ▷'Poem Without a Hero'. In these and other works from the second part of her career, she linked the tragedy of her own personal life with that of Russia. Because of her poetry and her integrity, personal courage, and deeply felt love for her native land, in the second part of her career Akhmátova once more garnered enormous popularity. She had become, as she once wrote ('To the Many', 1922) the 'voice' of all Russians.

▷Aligér, Margarita; Berggól'ts, Ol'ga; Leningrad; Lisniánskaia, Inna; Lóknvitskaia, Mirra; Petrovýkh, Mariia; *tamizdat*
Bib: Reeder, R. (ed.) and Hemschemeyer, J. (trans.), *The Complete Poems of Anna Akhmátova* (2 vols.); Thomas, D. (trans.), *You Will Hear Thunder* and *Requiem* and *A Poem Without a Hero*; Arndt, W., Kemball, R. and Proffer, C. (trans.), *Selected Poems*; Driver, B., *Anna Akhmátova*; Haight, A., *Anna Akhmátova: A Poetic Pilgrimage*; Ketchian, S., *The Poetry of Anna Akhmátova*; Mandelstam, N., *Hope Against Hope* and *Hope Abandoned*; Rosslyn, Wendy, *The Prince, the Fool and the Nunnery*; Chukóvskaya, L. *Conversations with Akhmátova*, Vol. 1.

Akimoto Matsuyo (born 1911)

Japanese scriptwriter. Akimoto was born in Yokohama, the younger sister of the anti-war *Haiku* poet Akimoto Fujio. Her first work *Light Dust* was published in *Drama* in 1947. Her later works frequently portrayed the lives of contemporary commoners and folklore. Some of her writing appears in *The Collected Works of Akimoto Matsuyo* (1976)

Akin, Gülten (born 1933)

Turkish poet. She grew up in the new capital, Ankara, and graduated from the Ankara Law School in 1955. An avid reader of modern European authors, her poetry shows the influence of Lorca and Brecht. Married to a district governor, she worked as a teacher in different places where he was stationed, and got to know village people closely. On their return to Ankara she resumed her career in law, though she was also writing poetry all the time. Her early work shows romantic agony and discontent; her later work captures the speech of common people and expresses sympathy for their suffering. Her publications include: *The Hour of the Wind* (1956), *My Black Hair I Cut* (1960), *On the Shoals* (1964), *Red Carnation* (1971), *The Legend of Marash and Okkesh* (1972) and *Dirges and Ballads* (1976).

al-'Adawiyya, Rabi'a (died c 802)

Sufi poet of Basra. A beautiful woman, born into a poor family, she was reported to have lived 'a life of low pleasures and indulgence', before she turned to religion and severe mortification of the body. She acquired a high rank in *Sufi* discipline and composed a volume of *Sufi* love poetry which is still popular in Arabic reading and singing to this day. The erotic strain is an accepted

attraction in such poetry. She is described as the Martyr of Divine *'Ishq* (passion).
Bib: Smith, Margaret, *Rabi'a the Mystic and Her Fellow Saints.*

al-'Akhyaliyya, Layla (died c 700)
An Arab poet of the early Islamic period, famous for her independent character: riding to the seat of the governor or the king to recite her poetry, engaging other poets in contests and demanding her prize in the form of camels or land. She first composed poetry lamenting the murder of her lover, whose noble qualities she glorified to a degree that made the *Khalifa* (Islamic leader) himself jealous. Tawba, a young man of a neighbouring tribe, had loved Layla and written love poetry, confessing the name of his beloved. Arab custom was adamantly against citing the names of women in the verse, which travelled with telegraphic speed over the desert. Layla's father refused Tawba, and married her into another tribe. The lover could not stay away and repeatedly visited her in her new tents. Their love was chaste, but the husband and his people were enraged and planned to kill the obstinate lover on his next visit. To alert him, Layla met him without her *burqu'* (bedouin woman's veil covering the lower part of the face). Tawba, who had never before seen her unveiled, escaped. He was later killed by another tribe after a raid. Layla mourned him, 'discarding female ornament to the end of her life'. Her poetry was collected by later anthologists.

Åland Island literature
The Åland Islands are situated in the Gulf of Bothnia, between Sweden and Finland. The language is ▷Fenno-Swedish, and the culture Swedish. The Åland Islands have a high degree of self-rule, and possess a local culture.
   Anni Blomqvist (born 1909) has become a symbol of the local (and past) culture of the Åland Islands. Uneducated, she began to write in the 1960s after her husband and eldest son had drowned at sea. In *I stormens spår* (1966) (*In the Track of the Storm*), she described the life of a seaman's wife. Since then she has been writing a vast epic about the Åland archipelago, part of which has been made into a film and has been shown on television. Her epic takes place in the 19th century, and is written in simple and familiar language. Anni Blomqvist's own story, together with those of her heroines Janne and Maja, and the romantic cult around the Åland Islands, tells us about strong women with strong feelings in a local and past culture. Today, Anni Blomqvist is one of the most widely-read authors in Finland.

Alarm Sounded to Prepare the Inhabitants of the World to Meet the Lord in the Way of His Judgment, An (1709)
Beginning with an assertion of her right as a woman to publish her own spiritual autobiography, the North American writer ▷Bathsheba Bowers details her conversion to

Quakerism. In counselling her readers to accept the Lord, Bowers uses her own experiences as evidence of the possibilities of conversion: from youthful 'keeping of wild Company', she details how her brother's death from smallpox and her own near death from the disease led her to 'the Contemplation of Matters Philosophical and Divine' and eventually to public professions of her beliefs.

Albert, Caterina (1869–1966)
Spanish novelist. Born into a family of rural Catalan gentry, Albert spent most of her life in the small Mediterranean fishing village of L'escala on the Costa Brava. Her early works were mostly poetry and drama, and in 1901 she published *Quatre monologs* (*Four Monologues*), intended for the stage. But Albert is better known for her novels, especially ▷*Solitud* (1905) (*Solitude*), and *Caires vius* (1907) (*Living Aspects*). *Solitud* is her masterpiece.
   Like many other 19th century female writers, Albert wrote under a male pseudonym: Victor Catala. When her identity became known, however, she was attacked by her contemporaries, who considered it improper for a woman to write such 'crude' works.

Albert, Marie-Madeleine Bonafous d' (18th century)
French writer of prose fiction. Little is known of her early life, except that she was educated at the prestigious Abbaye de Pentemont. Her first work, the allegorical *Tanastès* (1745), contained her observations of court and Parisian life, too thinly veiled, and led to a brief period of imprisonment at the Bastille. She later went into retreat, first at the convent of the Bernadines de Moulins (1746–1759), and subsequently at the convent of the Petit Saint-Chaumont. Her only novel from this period, the *Confidences d'une jolie femme* (1775) (*Secrets of a Pretty Woman*), relates the complicated amorous adventures of a young coquette, Mademoiselle de Tournemont, analysing her reactions to the inconstancy of her multiple male suitors.

Alberte
The heroine of ▷Cora Sandel's Norwegian trilogy *Alberte og Jakob* (1926) (*Alberte and Jacob*), *Alberte og friheten* (1931) (*Alberte and Freedom*), and *Bare Alberte* (1939) (*Alberte Alone*). The trilogy was a very big success, and has been printed in remarkably large numbers. It was written in Norwegian, but was soon translated into Swedish and Danish.
   The character of Alberte has many autobiographical traits, but the trilogy is also a work of high aestheticism. In form as well as in content, it is the novel of a woman who starts to write, and becomes the subject of her own life. But first she tries to paint, falls in love, is married to an artist who leaves no room for his wife's paintings, and has a son. Alberte is a woman with masochistic traits; she is unable to write while

living with a man. Her art expresses a constant longing for love and tenderness.

Albrecht, Sophie (1757–1840)
German writer and actress. Born in Erfurt, the daughter of a professor of medicine, she was barely fifteen when her father died. She at once married a doctor with a taste for adventure who became a writer and theatre manager. She went on many tours with him, and became a successful actress. In Frankfurt she met the dramatist Friedrich von Schiller (1759–1805) who remained her friend until his death. In the 1780s she published three volumes of fiction, drama and verse. Her poems are characterized by a fashionable sombre melancholy, and her stories revolve around Gothic stereotypes.

Albret, Jeanne III d' (1528–1572)
French author of letters, poems and memoirs. Queen of Navarre from 1552 to 1572, she was the daughter of ▷Marguerite de Navarre and Henri II d'Albret, and was educated by Nicolas Bourbon. After the annulment of her first marriage, she married Antoine de Bourbon (1518–1562) in 1548. She preserved the independence of her kingdom and imposed Calvinism upon it, corresponding with the religious reformer Jean Calvin (1509–1564) about the dissolute behaviour of her husband, whom she soon abandoned. She left for Paris, where she founded 'a school for the study of the Reformed religion' in her house in the rue de Grenelle with her brother-in-law Louis, the Prince de Condé (1530–1569). A leading Huguenot, she also helped to defend the Protestants at La Rochelle in 1568. She died shortly before the marriage of her son, Henri IV (1553–1610), to ▷Marguerite de Valois, sister of Charles IX (1550–1574). She wrote four sonnets in response to the fourteen which Joachim Du Bellay (1522–1560) had addressed to her. Instrumental in the publication of an accurate edition of her mother's ▷*L'Heptaméron*, she also left poems in *langue d'oc* (the medieval French spoken south of the Loire) and memoirs in manuscript form. Agrippa d'Aubigné (1552–1630), the Protestant poet, wrote of her: '*Cette reine n'avait de femme que le sexe, l'âme entière [était adonnée] aux choses viriles*' ('This queen was womanly only by her sex, her entire soul was devoted to things male').

Alcayaga, Lucila Godoy ▷Mistral, Gabriela

Alcipe
The pastoral pen-name of the Portuguese poet ▷Marquesa de Alorna, which was suggested to her by the *arcadista* Padre Francisco Manuel do Nascimento – better known as Filinto Elísio (1734–1819).
▷*Arcadismo*

Alcoforado, Mariana, Sóror (1640–1723)
Portuguese nun in the convent of Conceição in the town of Beja. For centuries she was regarded as the author of ▷*Lettres Portugaises*, which documents the love affair between a French officer and a nun. She remains an important symbol of the oppression women suffered as a result of being confined to the cloister. Her story, as told in *Lettres Portugaises*, inspired the ▷'Three Marias', in their feminist book ▷*Novas Cartas Portuguesas*.

Alcorta, Gloria (born 1915)
Argentinian poet, novelist, dramatist and sculptor. Her father was a diplomat in Paris, and French became her second language. After studying dramatic art (1932–1938) and sculpture in Paris, she won several sculpture prizes in both Paris and Buenos Aires. Her grandmother is the writer ▷Eduarda Mansilla de García. Her first work was a book of poetry in French, *La prison de l'enfant* (1935), (*The Child's Prison*), with an introduction by Jorge Luis Borges and drawings by Héctor Basaldúa. Both her dramas *Visages* (1952) (*Faces*) and *Le Seigneur de Saint Gor* (1954) (*The Lord of Saint Gor*) staged in Paris won prizes there. *El hotel de la luna* (1958) (*The Moon Hotel*), winner of several prizes in Argentina and Paris, is her most representative book. The narratives in it recall the haunted past of the huge mansion of Dardo Rocha, in Lavalle Street, Buenos Aires, and show the splendour of a decadent oligarchy of the *belle époque*. She was a correspondent for *La Prensa* (*The Press*) and collaborated in the magazine *Ficción* (*Fiction*). Her style is fantastic, and focuses on a trivial and decadent upper middle class. She is 'able to transform the most ordinary events of everyday life into a miracle. . . . Verisimilitude sometimes approaches the oneiric', state Borges, ▷Ocampo and Casares in their *Antología poética argentina* (1940) (*Anthology of Argentinian Poetry*).

Other works: *Noches de nadie* (1962) (*Nights of No One*); *En la casa muerta* (1966) (*In the Dead House*); *Sophie où le bout du monde* (1958) (*Sophie or The End of the World*); *La almohada negra* (1980) (*The Black Pillow*), and *Le crime de Doña Clara* (1988) (*The Crime of Doña Clara*).

Alcott, Louisa May (1832–1888)
US fiction and non-fiction writer, and occasional poet. The daughter of Bronson Alcott (1799–1888), she was a member of the transcendentalist circle in Concord, Massachusetts (▷transcendentalism). Alcott began writing to relieve the poverty in which her visionary father left his family. After miserable experiences working as a domestic servant (recorded in ▷*Work: A Story of Experience*, 1873), in 1851 she began writing and publishing in periodicals. A poem and tale in ▷*Peterson's Magazine* began a varied career in almost all genres. She published essays on the transcendentalist group under her own name, melodramatic thrillers under 'A. Barnard', poetry and short fiction under 'Flora Fairfield'.

Alcott's first volume, *Flower Fables* (1855), was addressed to children, an audience with whom she would become firmly identified with ▷*Little*

Frontispiece from an 1868 edition of Little Women *by Louisa May Alcott*

Women (1868) and its many successors which followed the fortunes of the March family girls: Meg, Beth, Amy and Jo. The success and popularity of *Little Women*, *Little Men* (1871) and *Jo's Boys* (1886) were immediate, international and lasting. Alcott's work remains enormously popular with children and adults to this day. Her pseudonymous work continues to be discovered, to the delight of readers and critics who first knew her through *Little Women*.

Aldecoa, Josefina R. (born 1926)

Spanish writer of articles, short stories and novels. Born in La Robla (León), Aldecoa wrote her doctoral thesis for the Faculty of Philosophy and Letters at the University of Madrid. From the 1940s onwards, together with her husband, the novelist Ignacio Aldecoa, she moved in literary circles associated with the reviews *Espadaña* and *Revista española*, in which she published articles, stories and translations. *El arte del niño* (1960) (*The Art of the Child*) is a pedagogical study; *A ninguna parte* (1961) (*Going Nowhere*) is a collection of short stories; and *Los niños de la guerra* (1983) (*Children of Wartime*) is a personal memoir. Her first novel, *La enredadera* (1984) (*The Clinging Vine*), narrates the lives of two women united by their struggle against second-class citizenship, and their desire for self-affirmation. *Porque éramos jóvenes* (1986) (*Because We Were Young*) uses different but converging time planes to chronicle the life of her generation. Her most recent work is *El vergel* (1988) (*The Orchard*).

Aldrich, Bess Streeter (1881–1954)

US novelist and short story writer. Born of a pioneer family, Aldrich graduated from Iowa State Teacher's College in 1901, and when her husband died in 1925 she supported her children by writing. She was also book editor of the *Christian Herald*. Her novels, set in the Midwest, offer a realistic presentation of the back-breaking labour performed by women settling the frontier. In her bestselling novel, *A Lantern in Her Hand* (1928), the sacrifice of artistic dreams is rewarded. Set in the 1850s, the novel depicts the life of Abbie Deal who devotes her life to marriage, motherhood and farming in Nebraska. Aldrich shows how pioneer women played a vital part in North American civilization by lighting the way for their children to prosper.

Other works include: *Mother Mason* (1924), *Rim of the Prairie* (1925), *The Cutters* (1926), *A White Bird is Flying* (1931), *Miss Bishop* (1933), *Spring Came On Forever* (1935), *Man Who Caught the Weather and Other Stories* (1936), *Song of Years* (1937), *The Drum Goes Dead* (1941), *The Lieutenant's Lady* (1942), *Journey into Christmas and Other Stories* (1949), *The Bess Streeter Aldrich Reader* (1950) and *A Bess Streeter Aldrich Treasury* (1959).

Alegría, Claribel (born 1924)

El Salvadorean poet and prose writer, who has been living in Nicaragua. She is married to Darwin J. Flakoll, with whom she has translated some of the work Robert Graves into Spanish. The couple met Graves in Mallorca, where they own a house. The island itself was a source of inspiration for Alegría's second book of poems, *Pueblo de Dios y de mandinga* (*People of God and the Devil*). Claribel Alegría is a symbol of both the El Salvadorean and the Nicaraguan fight for freedom, and her presence in the First Meeting of Intellectuals for the Independence of the Peoples of '*Nuestra América*', in La Habana, in 1981, where she made a speech on the revolution in both countries, was a motive for many important presences. Among them the famous poet and Minister of Culture, Ernesto Cardenal, the writer Garcia Márquez and the critic Mario Benedetti. Her third book, entitled *Luisa in Realityland* (1987), is an autobiography, based on her grandparent's house in Santa Ana, back in El Salvador. She has also written a notebook as a journal in poetry, *La mujer del río Sumpul* (*The Woman from the Sumpul River*). The bilingual anthology *Flowers from the Volcano* is a useful means to reading her poems. Her poetical biography has been written by the founder of the literary 'Vanguard Movement' in Guatemala, José Coronel Urtecho, dated 14 February 1988, when he was very old, and published in 1989. She dedicated her poem 'Escribir' ('Writing') to him.

Family Album, published in English in 1992, incorporates three novellas, *The Talisman* (1977), *Family Album* (1982) and *Village of God and the Devil* (1985).

Alekséeva, Lidiia Alekseevna (born 1909)
Poet and short story writer Alekséeva emigrated
from Russia in 1920, first living in Yugoslavia,
then Austria, and finally in the United States in
1949. She began publishing poetry in the 1930s in
émigré journals. Several collections of poetry
appeared between 1954 and 1980. Alekséeva is a
lyric poet, building many of her short poems on
an extended metaphor. Sometimes, like
▷Akhmátova, she can be a careful observer of
places, objects, and people which suggest
psychological and emotional states of mind.
Themes of loneliness, human cruelty and
destructiveness alternate with those of resignation
and a sense of acceptance in the midst of the
natural, spiritualized world.
Bib: Morrison, R. (trans.), *America's Russian Poets*;
Wilson, K. (ed.), *Encyclopedia of Continental Women
Writers*, Vol. 1.

Aleramo, Sibilla (1876–1960)
Italian novelist, poet and political essayist, real
name Rina Faccio. She was raped when very
young by an employee of her father and, as was
expected following an event of this nature at that
time, married him at the age of sixteen. The
marriage was a horrendous experience, the story
of which is told in fictional form in her most
famous work, *Una donna* (▷*A Woman*) of 1906.
She had a son and, because of him, stayed in the
marriage for nine years until she could bear it no
longer. Leaving her husband meant leaving her
son, as she had no legal right to him. She later
travelled widely in Europe. As well as writing for
socialist and feminist periodicals, she was involved
in the organization of an adult literacy scheme,
along with Giovanni Cena. Much of her work
centred on representations of woman's role in
society, and on the obstacles, legal and otherwise,
faced by women. *Amo dunque sono* (*I Love Therefore
I Am*) of 1927 is a novel which is at once erotic
and poetic. She also translated the love letters of
▷George Sand and Alfred de Musset, while her
own letters, especially those to Dino Campana,
provide us with a portrait of the writer, her society
and her work.
Her other works include: (poetry): *Momenti*
(1921) (*Moments*); *Poesie* (1929) (*Poems*); *Sì alla
terra* (1934) (*Yes to the Earth*); *Selva d'amore*
(1947) (*Forest of Love*); *Aiutatemi a dire*
(1951)(*Help Me to Speak*) ; *Luci della mia sera*
(1956) (*Light of My Evenings*); (prose): *Il passaggio*
(1919) (*The Crossing*); *Andando e stando* (1921)
(*Moving and Being*); *Trasfigurazione* (1922)
(*Transfiguration*); *Gioie d'occasione* (1930)
(*Occasional Pleasures*); *Il frustino* (1932) (*The
Whip*); *Orsa minore* (1938) (*Ursa Minor*) ; ▷*Diario
e lettere: dal mio diario* (1945) (*Diary of a Woman*);
Gioie d'occasione e altre ancora (1954) (*More
Occasional Pleasures*); (theatre): *Endimione* (1923)
(*Endymion*); (letters): *Lettere* (1958) (*Letters*).

Alexander, Meena (born 1951)
Indian poet. She was born in Allahabad, and
educated at the Universities of Khartoum and

Nottingham. She has taught English literature at
the University of Delhi, Jawaharlal Nehru
University, New Delhi, and the Central Institute
of English in Hyderabad. She now lives in the
USA. She has published several volumes of
poetry, including *The Bird's Bright Ring* (1976),
Without Place (1977), *Stone Roots* (1980) and *House
of a Thousand Doors* (1988). Many of these poems
share a search for roots or a tangible point of
origin, some touchstone to the past in a world of
disturbance and change.
She has also published a one-act play, *In the
Middle Earth* (1977), and two works on
romanticism, *The Poetic Self* (1979) and *Women in
Romanticism:* ▷*Mary Wollstonecraft,* ▷*Dorothy
Wordsworth and* ▷*Mary Shelley* (1989).

Alexiou, Elli (1898–?)
Greek novelist. Alexiou was born in Herakleion,
Crete, the daughter of an intellectual journalist
whose entire family followed the path of literature.
She became a teacher when very young, working
in girls' schools in Crete and Athens. Her
experience with the socially deprived inspired her
first collection of short stories, *Hard Struggles for a
Short Life* (1931). This is a moving account of life
in the uneventful but anxious world of a poor
peasant community – a world Alexiou wanted to
change just as it had changed her. ▷*The Third
Christian School for Girls* (1934) is a moving novel
based on her educational work in Athens. Full of
affection and sympathy, it incorporates a number
of progressive ideas for improving the hard lives
of young girls. While a teacher in Athens, Alexiou
had studied French and German, and this led to
her working for nineteen years as a secondary
school teacher. In 1928 she joined the Greek
Communist Party, of which she was to remain a
staunch lifelong member. Her strong communist
convictions were to bring her many difficulties.
During the German occupation she worked for
the communist Resistance. In 1945 she went to
Paris as a teacher of the Greek community, at the
same time studying at the Sorbonne. From 1949
she taught the children of Greek communities
living in various East European communist
countries. On her return to Greece in 1962 she
was arrested on false charges, and when released
was refused a passport. Earlier in her life she had
taken part in many international conferences,
meeting intellectuals from other European
countries. In Greece she kept company with the
leading artists and writers of the day.
Alexiou's novel *Louben*, published in 1940,
combines descriptions of provincial customs with
observations of female psychology. It recounts the
domestic life of the submissive wife of a tyrannical
husband. The book was received as a strongly
feminist work exposing the oppressed lives of
women in the Greek provinces. ▷*Spondi* (1963) is
a collection of writings in honour of her sister,
▷Galateia Kazantzaki. *That He May Become Great*
(1966) is a biography of Nikos Kazantzakis, who
was Galateia's husband, and whose work Alexiou
greatly admired. *The Reigning One* (1972)

expresses her socialist ideals through stories of the lives of a group of people in Athens. *Demolished Mansions* (1977) is a collection of stories about six elderly women, abandoned and lonely, reviewing their past lives. Alexiou's work is deeply humane rather than pessimistic, showing how people can transcend the harsh conditions of the world they live in.

Alf Layla wa Layla ▷*Arabian Nights, The*

Alfon, Estrella (1917–1982)
Filipino writer in English – the first to come from a non-elite background. Her father was a grocer on Ezpeleta Street in Cebu City (in Central Visayas), a street immortalized as the locale of her many short stories. Her writing career began with a literary prize won when she was twelve, and she became one of the few women members of several important writing circles when she attended the University of the Philippines. Her short story *Fairy Tale in the City* (*This Week* Sunday Magazine, 21 April 1955) caused an obscenity suit to be filed against her, but it seems it was more her unconventional lifestyle that was at issue than the story, which was neither sexually explicit nor written in bawdy language.

Alfon wrote mainly about women, children and other minority groups. Her best-known story, *Magnificence*, is about mother–daughter bonding, when a mother acts with magnificent rage to protect her daughter from a sexual pervert. Another story, *English*, depicts a labourer painstakingly trying to learn English, the language of the rich and powerful, to better his life and that of his family.

Alfonsina ▷Storni, Alfonsina

Alford, Edna (born 1947)
Western Canadian writer of short stories chronicling people who live on the edge of time, both in age and infirmity, with especially powerful renditions of old women in relation to young women. *A Sleep Full of Dreams* (1981) won the Gerald Lampert Memorial Award. *The Garden of Eloise Loon* (1986) also received critical acclaim. Comically grotesque, Alford's stories examine the physical images of women. She was born, and lives, in Saskatchewan.

Ali, Hauwa
Nigerian novelist. A native of Sokoto, the northernmost state in Nigeria, she, along with ▷Zaynab Alkali, is one of the few northern Nigerian women to have published in English. Her first novel, *Destiny* (1988), is a romance which dramatizes the culture clash between conservative Islam and the aspirations of a contemporary woman to choose a husband for herself. Her second, *Victory* (1989), also a romance, depicts the experience of a young woman from the south of Nigeria who comes to Kano, a northern city, to work. Hauwa is concerned to show the differing cultural practices, both ethnic and in terms of traditional versus contemporary values, with which women have to contend in Nigeria.
▷Romantic fiction (West Africa)

al-Idlibi, 'Ulfah (born 1921)
Syrian teacher, novelist and short story writer, born and educated in Damascus. A teacher by profession, she is a committed writer who believes in the social function of literature and in the moral mission of writers. She believes that 'a man of letters carries a difficult responsibility; he is responsible before God, his own conscience, his readers – and before history too for every word he publishes. It is an unforgivable sin that he should mislead his readers or knowingly deceive them.'

'Ulfah al-Idlibi published more than 100 short stories, all inspired by the life of Damascus. Her first collection of short stories was *Shamian Stories* (1954); Damascus is known to Syrians as al-Sham. Her next was *Farewell Damascus* (1963). Her major novel is *Damascus, Smile of Sorrow* (1980) depicting the modern history of Syria at the end of Turkish rule, under the French Mandate and during the national uprising for independence which ended with the bombardment of Damascus. It is all narrated through the life of a Damascene family, portrayed by two women of different generations. The older woman, who leaves her memoirs for her niece after committing suicide, is the real protagonist. Her attempts at making a new life for herself were as violently and as treacherously frustrated as was the city's uprising. The writer's skill is not very impressive and much of the material of her fiction borders on the mediocre because of her matter-of-fact realism. ▷Realism and an obvious moral stand go down well with many Arab readers, and this writer occupies a very high position in the world of letters in Syria.

'Alien' ▷Baker, Louisa

Aligér, Margarita Iosifovna (born 1915)
Russian poet, journalist, and translator. Aligér's early childhood in an assimilated Jewish family in Odessa was marked by the rigours of the Civil War (1918–21), and her adult life was scarred by the deaths of her husband and children. In 1931, determined to be a poet, she moved to Moscow, and her first volume of poems, *Year of Birth* (1938), revealed talent. Her pre-war journalism, wartime poetry (including *Zoia*, an epic poem about a young martyred partisan), and her postwar hymn to the construction of the new Moscow University, 'Lenin Hills,' proved her a Soviet patriot. After the war she was permitted to travel extensively in Europe, South America, and Japan and, like ▷Inber and ▷Shaginián, often transmitted her impressions in the peculiar Soviet genre of travel diaries in verse. In the 1970s Elaine Feinstein described her as preoccupied by 'the question of guilt' and alienated from the generation too young to remember the 1930s ('Poetry and Conscience: Russian Women Poets

of the Twentieth Century', *Women Writing and Writing about Women*). Aligér's guilt is revealed in lyrics, like 'The House in Meudon', about ▷ Tsvetáeva in *Quarter of a Century* (1976). *Path Through the Rye* (1980) is a collection of her self-effacing, affectionate portraits of contemporary writers, including a perceptive memoir of ▷ Akhmátova. Aligér's lyrics, which she characterized as 'my soul, myself as I am', reflect Akhmátova's influence.

Bib: Wilson, K. (ed.), *Encyclopedia of Continental Women Writers* 1.

Aline (12th century)

Patron in England. A considerable number of high-born women (apart from royalty) were known to have been patrons of literature in ▷ Anglo-Norman. Aline was possibly a member of the Montfort family. Her chaplain, Robert of Greatham, wrote for her a collection of verse sermons in Anglo-Norman, the *Miroir*.

Alison's House (1930)

US play. ▷ Susan Glaspell's Pulitzer Prize-winning play borrows from the life of ▷ Emily Dickinson. It takes place on the last day of the 19th century and focuses on a reporter's search for a famous poet's dark secret. Alison's secret resides in poems that her family refuses to publish; these poems allude to Alison's affair with a married man. Like the reporter, Glaspell revises the conventional notion of the woman poet. Alison's family is convinced finally of the value of bequeathing her poems to the future. Glaspell recovers a 19th-century precursor to the 20th century's ▷ New Woman.

Aliye, Fatima (1862–1936)

Turkish writer and educator. She was the daughter of the famous statesman and historian, Ahmad Cevdet Pasha. She was educated at home and read and translated French. She married an army officer in 1879 and accompanied him on his various postings, where she continued to read and translate. An aristocratic lady of the governing class, she had great impact on the call for education for all. Her translations from French covered both literature and science, and influenced education in Turkey.

Her novels in the French tradition were very popular: *Muhadarat* (1892), *Mercy* (1898) and *Udi, the Lute Player* (1899) are some of the best-known. She wrote a *History of Women of Islam* (1892) and compiled the *Biographies of Philosophers* (1900), as well as a history of her father and his times.

She lived for many years under the new republic but, with the fall of the Ottoman regime in 1919, she ceased to play any part as a literary figure.

Alkali, Zaynab

Nigerian novelist. Despite a long-standing tradition of Hausa women's poetry in northern Nigeria, Alkali was the first northern Nigerian Moslem woman to publish fiction in English, as recently as 1984. This fact is probably due to the conventional sanctions on Moslem women for speaking out in public or even being visible. That Alkali is a lecturer at the northern university of Maiduguri already makes her somewhat unconventional in this context. Her origins in Nigeria's Middle Belt, in a village setting where Moslem, Christian and traditional practices co-existed, are reflected in both her published novels. Her writing to date has explored the process of growing up under conflicting social and personal pressures. ▷ *The Stillborn* (1984) traces the intertwined but very different lives of three childhood friends, and the repercussions of their different choices as women. *A Virtuous Woman* (1987) is a rite-of-passage story about three girls on a journey to school, from the village to the city. Alkali is interesting, not only because she writes about and is from the Moslem north, but also for her narrative technique, which goes beyond the tendency of the anglophone writers to adhere to the linear narrative of the classical realist tradition.

▷ Religion: Christianity, Islam and traditional beliefs in West Africa

Bib: James, A., *In Their Own Voices: Interviews with African Women Writers*; Otokunefor, H. and Nwodo, O., *Nigerian Female Writers: A Critical Perspective*.

al-Khansa (died 646)

Arab pre-Islamic poet, famous for her elegies in the age of oral composition. She was born in Najd, the central plateau in the heart of Arabia. Her poetry reflects the life of the warring tribes before the mission of the prophet Muhammad put an end to the feuds of the *Jahiliya* (the Age of Ignorance). al-Khansa lost two brothers in these wars, Sakhr and Mu'awiya, and she composed a number of famous elegies lamenting their 'heroic' deaths. Her *ra'iyya* (poem rhyming with r) is the greatest elegy in classical Arabic poetry. Sakhr was the subject; he seems to have been dearer or more important to her than Mu'awiya. She was said to have worn a hair shirt in mourning for him for years. When she embraced Islam she became a favourite poet of the Prophet. She gave up the passions of *Jahiliya*; she lost four sons in the Islamic battle of Qadisiya, but did not shed a tear for them, simply saying: 'I thank the Lord for honouring me with their martyrdom.'

All About Love (1985)

Short story collection by Russian writer ▷ Tèffi. There is some disagreement over the original date of publication (thought to be 1930) since it was published in Paris without a date. The title is somewhat misleading: although many stories revolve around relationships between men and women, the emphasis is not on romantic entanglements *per se*.

The book consists of stories that Tèffi wrote while living in Paris, and has many of the hallmarks of her humorous stories. First of all there is the tendency to structure the stories around oppositions: in 'Time' it is the contrast between youth and old age; in 'Two Diaries', 'Don Quixote and the Turgenevan Girl', and 'Points of View' it is two seemingly opposite views of the same issue, and in 'Two Affairs with Foreigners', it is opposite reactions to the aftermath of a failed love affair. Tèffi uses a narrator whose judgement is often not to be trusted, whose narrative clearly contradicts the narrator's own pronouncement, and whose logic is often questionable. The narrator and characters often spin a lot of verbiage out of non-existent events and actions, as in stories that include phrases like: 'If such and such were the case, then . . .', or project their fantasies into an unlikely future. She usually uses few characters, but opens up the text by using interpolated anecdotes.

Tèffi's work shares a lot in common with the great 19th century humorist, Nikolai Gogol' (1809–1852). The world of both writers is absurd and ultimately tragic. As in Gogol', Tèffi's text is littered with outrageous similes, wordplay, preposterous names (Mr Chicken in 'Two Affairs'), incongruous lists, and details about food. Other influences include Chekhov (1861–1904), with his brevity, and an emphasis on the failure of communication.

Allart, Hortense (1801–1879)

French novelist and essayist, whose romantic liaisons (including an affair with the writer Chateaubriand, 1768–1898) have proved of greater interest to critics than her literary and historical writings. Her best-known work is the largely autobiographical *Les Enchantements de Prudence* (1872) (*The Delights of Prudence*), whose heroine cocks a snook at 19th-century social and sexual convention, and leads a much more independent life than the majority of her female contemporaries. Despite her aristocratic background, and the wariness of radical socialist women she shared with her friend ▷Marie de Flavigny, Allart was influenced by ▷Saint-Simonian feminism. She subscribed to the feminist *Gazette des femmes* (*Women's Gazette*), attended editorial meetings of the journal, and argued, in *La Femme et la démocratie de notre temps* (1836) (*Women and Democracy Today*), in favour of free love and an improvement in the status of women. Her other works include: *Lettres sur les ouvrages de Mme de Staël* (1824) (*Letters on the Work of Mme de Staël*); *Settimie* (1826); *Gertrude* (1827); *L'Indienne* (1832) (*The Indian Girl*); *La Vie rose* (1833); *Histoire de la République de Florence* (1837) (*History of the Florentine Republic*) and *Essai sur l'histoire politique depuis l'invasion des barbares jusqu'en 1848* (1857) (*Essay on Political History from the Barbarian invasion to 1848*).

▷Feminine/feminist journalism (France)
Bib: Billy, A., *Hortense et ses amants*; Moses, C., *French Feminism in the 19th Century*; Rabine, L., 'Feminist Writers in French Romanticism', *Studies in Romanticism*, Vol. 16; Sullerot, E., *Women on Love*.

All Cretans Are Liars (1987)

Poems by New Zealand writer ▷Anne French. Although Anne French had published occasional poems for some years *All Cretans Are Liars* was her first collection, and it received an enthusiastic response when it appeared. French's carefully structured personal lyrics, addressed to friends and lovers and focusing on personal events (the birth of a child, a trip abroad) are characterized by their ironic tone, and the way they satirize and criticize stereotypes and conventional assumptions. French's very precise use of language allows nothing to be taken for granted in these poems; the self is continually reconstructed as experience is analyzed and reconsidered. French has since published two more collections.

Allegro con disperazione (1965) (Allegro, Despairingly)

A novel, by Italian writer ▷Gianna Manzini, of psychological analysis, in which superficial veneers of civilization are stripped away. It tells the story of Marcello and Angela, who fall in love and marry. Their past lives (Marcello's orphan status, his upbringing by a Jewish family and Angela's petty bourgeois life, marred by sexual abuse as a child) become important with the entry of the disturbing character, Candutti. He leads them both into an amoral world in which their trust in each other is destroyed. This is a fable about the corruption of innocence in which innocence is not ascribed a particularly positive value. It is a novel with elements both ▷naturalistic and ▷surreal, which is particularly interesting for its movement away from the more clearly autobiographical frame of much of Manzini's work, as well as for its temporal experimentation.

Allen, Charlotte Vale (born 1941)

Fiction writer, born in Toronto, Canada. she spent more than ten years as a singer, actress, and cabaret performer before turning to writing. *Love Life* (1976), her first novel, has been followed by twenty-five works of popular fiction, including *Painted Lives* (1990). Her most important book is an autobiographical account of incest, *Daddy's Girl* (1980). She now lives in Connecticut, USA.

Allen, Hannah (Archer)

English religious memoirist who published a ▷conversion narrative, *Satan's Methods and Malice Baffled* (1683), which tells the story of her recovery from melancholy and temptations to suicide. At one point, 'the Devil found me out a place on the top of the house, a hole where some boards were laid, and there I crowded in myself and laid a long, black scarf upon me and put the boards as well as I could to hide me from being found, and there intended to lie till I should starve to death.'

▷Davy, Sarah; Trapnel, Anna
Bib: Graham, Elspeth *et al.* (ed.) *Her Own Life*.

Allen, Pamela Kay (born 1934)

New Zealand picture book artist and author. From the late 1960s, and with two small children, Allen became active in pre-school groups, and between 1975 and 1977 illustrated *Mummy, Do*

Monsters Clean Their Teeth? and other booklets written by a playcentre friend, Jan Farr. After her first book *Mr Archimedes' Bath* (1980), she won several awards: in 1983 the Children's Book Council of Australia Picture Book of the Year Award for *Who Sank the Boat* (1982); the same award in 1984 for *Bertie and the Bear* (1983); the New Zealand Library Association's Russell Clark Award in 1986 for illustrating *A Lion in the Night* (1985). Allen writes her books to be read aloud with children and to include the 'creative possibilities' that arise between adult and child. *Fancy That* (1988), for example, illustrates Allen's contention that a picture book is akin to the theatre, with the pages like scenes in a play. She says a picture book must be designed to control pace and drama because it is not merely 'a story written down', but 'drama unfolding'.

▷ Children's literature, New Zealand

Allen, Paula Gunn (born 1939)

US poet and novelist. A Laguna/Sioux ▷ Native American, Allen was born in New Mexico, and she teaches Native American studies at the University of California at Berkeley. Her poetry reflects her political activism in the anti-war, anti-nuclear and feminist movements.

Her novel, *The Woman Who Owned the Shadows* (1983), explores the relationships of woman-lore to an individual woman's life. Abandoned by her husband, Ephanie Ataencio suffers a mental breakdown. She undertakes a journey toward psychic balance and discovers that her life parallels the tribal narratives of god-women. She learns to accept her place in her tribe's ritual tradition and her responsibility to continue that tradition. Allen argues that tradition empowers the self and gives life shape and direction. The *Sacred Hoop* (1986) emphasizes women's centrality and power in Native American culture.

Other works include: *The Blind Lion* (1975), *Coyote's Daylight Trip* (1978), *Star Child* (1981), *A Cannon Between My Knees* (1981), *Shadow Country* (1982), *Studies in American Indian Literature* (1983) and *Spider Woman's Granddaughters*.

Allende, Isabel (born 1942)

Isabel Allende

Chilean novelist, short story writer and journalist. A journalist in Chile at seventeen, shortly after the fall of her uncle's government she moved to Caracas with her family. Her first novel, *La casa de los espíritus* (1982) (▷ *The House of the Spirits*, 1985), gave her worldwide fame. This novel is a saga of Estebán Trueba's family, contrasting his patriarchy to the imaginative spiritual life of his wife, Clara. Their grandchild, Alba, quotes from Clara's 'notebooks of life', mixing these family memories with the facts of her own life. Even though Allende's style is criticized for its similarity with Marquez's ▷ magic realism in *One Hundred Years of Solitude*, it can be seen that she uses the same devices for different ends: her novel is about women's roles in society. Isabel Allende's own mother was a model for Clara, and many of her relatives served as other models. The book touches not only on the violence done to women but also on political violence within society. Although Chile is her primary topic, Allende's works have gained an international readership, as can be seen with the popularity of her novel *De amor y de sombra* (1984) (*Of Love and Shadows*, 1987). *The Tales of Eva Luna* (1987) is a book of short stories.

Allfrey, Phyllis Shand (1915–1986)

Caribbean poet, novelist, journalist and politician. Allfrey was born in Dominica of ▷ Creole ancestry, her father being Crown Attorney of Dominica. She began writing at an early age, and sold her first short story at the age of 13. She married Robert Allfrey. She became politically active as a young woman, and lived in both the USA and Britain. Co-founder of the Dominica Labour Party, she was elected to federal government in 1958 and served as a federal minister. With the failure of federal government in 1962 she became active as a journalist, and founded and edited *The Dominica Star* (1965–1982). She was one of the first women to contribute to the growth of Caribbean literature and is best known for her novel ▷ *The Orchid House*, published in 1953.

She has written four collections of poetry: *In Circles* (1940); *Palm and Oak I;* (1950) *Contrasts* (1955), and *Palm and Oak II* (1974). Several of her numerous short stories are included in the forthcoming anthology, *Whistling Bird*. Most of her published material is in the field of journalism. Her second novel, *In the Cabinet*, remained unfinished at the time of her death.

For biographical background see Donald Herdeck's *Caribbean Writers* (1979) and Elaine Campbell's introduction to the ▷ *The Orchid House*, ▷ *Fifty Caribbean Writers* and ▷ *Caribbean Women Writers*.

Allingham, Margery Louise (1904–1966)

English ▷ detective fiction writer. Many of Allingham's novels feature the aristocratic sleuth Albert Campion, a character who develops through the course of the novels from his initial somewhat caricatured portrayal. Her novels frequently feature strong, resourceful women characters, and her later novels probe the psychology of the criminal mind. Her novels include: *The Crime at Black Dudley* (1929), *Look to the Lady* (1931), *Mr Campion Criminologist* (1937) and *The Allingham Case-Book* (1969).

Allison, Gay (born 1943)

Canadian poet, editor and teacher, born in Saskatchewan, whose poetry resonates with precision, humour and intimacy. Active in feminist circles in Toronto, she was a co-founder of the Women's Writing Salon there, a founding editor of ▷*Fireweed*, and an initial member of the Women's Writing Collective. Her books of poetry include *Life: Still* (1981) and *The Unravelling* (1987). Her poetry is lyrical but angry in its reconstruction of women's experience. She lives in Stratford, Ontario.

All Our Yesterdays (1956)

Translation of a novel, *Tutti, nostri ieri*, written in 1952 in Italian by ▷Natalia Ginzburg, and dealing with the war and the ▷Resistance in Italy. Set in the world of a middle-class northern family, the tale begins in the pre-war period. The father is typical of a Ginzburg father, an imposing, authoritative figure. He witnesses the tragic effects which the war has on his family: Ippolito, his son, commits suicide, his unmarried daughter Anna is pregnant. The family is, in effect, splintered by the war. Through the characters of Giuma, the father of Anna's child, who leaves her, and Cenzo Rena, whom she marries, Ginzburg explores issues of freedom and commitment. All are altered by the experience of war. The novel analyses the nature of the family, and of society, in crisis.

All Said and Done (1974)

Translation of *Tout compte fait* (1972), final volume of French writer ▷Simone de Beauvoir's autobiography. De Beauvoir writes of her life in the 1970s and of particular importance among the various themes discussed are her growing involvement in French feminism and the establishment of her friendship with Sylvie le Bon, whom she was eventually to adopt. The relationship between de Beauvoir and philosopher Jean-Paul Sartre (1905–1980) receives relatively little attention; as Deirdre Bair's biography makes clear, it was in this period – the final decade of Sartre's life – that relations between one of the most famous couples of the 20th century became strained.

All That Swagger (1936)

Australian novel by ▷Miles Franklin. It is loosely modelled on the lives of four generations of the Franklin family (the Delacy family in the novel) on the land around the headwaters of the Murrumbidgee River. In this episodic and discursive account, the family's fortunes span the years from 1833 to 1933 and are set against the backdrop of significant historical events such as the gold rushes, free selection (a system of land tenure), self-government and the Boer War. Next to ▷*My Brilliant Career*, this is Franklin's most important work.

All the Rivers Run (1978)

Australian novel by ▷Nancy Cato. This bestselling novel, a composite of three earlier novels, *All the Rivers Run* (1958), *Time, Flow Softly* (1959) and *But Still the Stream* (1962), was published simultaneously in Australia, England and the USA in 1978. It was chosen by the Literary Guild as its first choice for its members, and later formed the basis for an extremely successful television series. Set in Echuca on the River Murray, the saga of the life of its heroine, Philadelphia (Delie) Gordon, spans the years 1899–1956. The orphaned Delie buys a part-share in a riverboat, marries and survives her husband, takes over his role on the riverboat *Philadelphia*, raises six children, takes lovers, and finally lives out her days by the river at Goolwa. It is a rich evocation of life on the riverboats and in the riverside towns of Australia's mightiest river, the Murray.

All This and Heaven Too (1938)

US novel. In this book ▷Rachel Field fictionalizes her great-aunt Henriette's biography. Before moving to the US in 1849, Henriette had worked in Paris as a governess, and her life there culminated in a notorious murder and a king's overthrow. Through Henriette, Field provides a personal reaction to the day's historical events. She also introduces contemporary issues – like the abolition of slavery – which Henriette discusses with various literary figures. Field presents a strong, vital heroine with an intensity for life.

Almada, Filipa de, Dona

A 15th-century Portuguese noblewoman and poet. One of the learned women in the Avis dynasty during the reigns of King Afonso V (1448–1481) and King João II (1481–1495). She is one of the women featured in Garcia de Resende's (c 1470–1536) ▷*Cancioneiro Geral* (1516).

Alma Feminina (Woman's Soul)

The principal publication of the National Council of Portuguese Women. Two special numbers were dedicated to the First and Second Portuguese Feminist Congresses, held in 1924 and 1928. Among the topics discussed in the magazine were women's suffrage and educational reform. The magazine also featured short biographies of important women leaders and news of international feminist activities.
▷Osório, Ana de Castro; Cabete, Adelaide

al-Mala'ika, Nazik (1923–1992)

Leading Iraqi poet and critic. Born to a family of poets, she graduated from the Department of Arabic at the Higher Teachers' College in Baghdad, read French and English, and was particularly influenced by the English romantics in her earlier work. Her first volume of poetry contained a translation of Gray's 'Elegy', and of excerpts from Byron's *Childe Harold* turned into Arabic rhyming quatrains (1945–6). A serious professional poet, by 1978 she had published seven volumes of verse and three volumes of criticism of Arabic poetry. Her poem 'Cholera', published in 1947, on the cholera epidemic raging in Egypt at the time, signalled an important break with classical verse forms and initiated the ▷New Movement in modern Arabic poetry. Her critical work *Issues of Contemporary Arabic Poetry* (1962) discusses the necessity of a new prosody for Arabic, for which she tries to formulate a set of new rules. Nazik al-Mala'ika taught Arabic literature in the University of Mosul in Iraq and in the University of Kuwait. A critical study of the poetry of Ali Mahmoud Taha (1902–1948), published 1965, shows how well-versed she was in the poetry of the 20th century. Taha's seminal *diwans* (collections of poetry), *The Lost Sailor* (1934) and *Nights of the Lost Sailor* (1940), are carefully explicated in relation the poetry of his contemporaries and to the poetry of one of her own generation: ▷Nizar Qabbani. Nazik al-Mala'ika's poetry covers all possible subjects, touching a highly cultured Arab sensibility in an age of change, revolutions, world disasters and national defeats, with the added alienation of being a well-read woman. Some of her feminist writings published in a collection of her social criticism, *Fragmentation in Arab Society* (1974), dissect the inherent contradiction of men calling for freedom while wishing to keep women in chains. She criticizes women for swallowing the rhetoric of the fashion and cosmetics trades, but concludes that men are finally responsible: they are as backward as the women for they prefer their females with weak intellects and heavy make-up. Her poem on Jamila, an Algerian woman who fought with the FLN (Algerian Liberation Movement) and was imprisoned and tortured by the French, was written in 1958; it is even more apt today with the knowledge that Jamila had no place in the state of Algeria after independence:

We said they have given her blood and flames to drink.
We said: they have nailed her to a cross and sung her glory.
We said: we will save her, we shall, and drowned in our
drunken words and sang
Long live Jamila! Long live Jamila!
Shame on us for the wounds of Jamila!

▷Umm Nizar

Bib: Boullata, Kamal (ed.), ▷*Women of the Fertile Crescent: An Anthology of Modern Poetry by Arab Women*; al-Udhari, Abdullah (ed. and trans.), *Modern Poetry of the Arab World*.

Almeida, Júlia Lopes de (1862–1934)

Brazilian novelist, short story and chronicle writer and dramatist, who also wrote under the pseudonyms A. Jalinto, Filinto de Almeida, and

Eila Worns. She is the most important and prolific Brazilian writer of the pre-modernist period, publishing more than forty books in forty years and contributing to several newspapers. In 1922 she did not follow the move to ▷modernism. For the critic José Veríssimo, she and Coelho Neto were the two novelists of national recognition after the deaths of Machado de Assis and Aluísio Azevedo. Her novels deal with everyday problems, employ a simple plot, and convey a female perspective, as in *A família Medeiros* (1919) (*The Family Medeiros*), *A viúva Simões* (1897) (*The Widow Simões*), *Ansia eterna* (1903) (*Eternal Desire*) and *A Intrusa* (1908) (*The Intruder*). Her style is straightforward and sometimes didactic, as in *Correio da roça* (1913), in which a widow moves to her inherited property and through letters tries to instruct her urban women friends how to live and support themselves on a farm. *A Falência* (1901) (*The Bankrupt*) describes bankrupcy due to inflation in the last decades of the 19th century. *A família Medeiros* centres on the abolition of slavery (enacted in 1888) and the life of a family from São Paulo. Some of her short stories, such as those in *Ansia eterna*, make use of horror. She wrote *A casa verde* (1898) (*The Green House*) with her husband, the Portuguese writer Filinto de Almeida (1847–1945); her sister and her three sons were also writers.

Almog, Ruth (born 1936)

Israeli novelist and journalist. Almog studied at Tel-Aviv University and then worked as teacher for many years. She currently writes for a leading Israeli daily newspaper. At the centre of her novels are individuals struggling with what seems to be their fate. The protagonists are usually women caught between their expectations and their desire for personal freedom. Through these conflicts, Almog portrays Israeli society itself. Her novels include ▷*Mavet Ba'geshem* (1982) (*Death in the Rain*), *Shorshey Avir* (1987) (*Dangling Roots*) and *Nashim* (1988) (*Women*).

Almy, Mary Gould (1735–1808)

North American diarist. Little is known about her early years, but in July 1778, when Patriot and French troops brought the American Revolution to her doorstep in Newport, Rhode Island, she recorded her defiant and heartfelt disdain for the Patriot cause. A dedicated Loyalist who was married to a Patriot soldier, she captured in ▷*Mrs Almy's Journal* the hardships of a war she abhorred.

Alonso, Carmen de (born 1909)

Chilean novelist and short story writer, whose pen-name was Margarita Carrasco. She is a *criollista* (▷*criollismo*), but she brings variations to the treatment of this topic. Critics have noted the precision of her writing. She often makes subjective observations about her characters and employs a narrative focus and solutions akin to ▷María Luisa Bombal's, although she deals with more concrete themes and presents a stronger novelesque structure. Her works include *Provena* 1935); *Gleba* (1936) (*Clod*); *Anclas en la ciudad* 1941) (*Anchors in the City*); *Y había luz de estrellas* 1950) (*And There Was Starlight*); *Medallones de una* (1956) (*Moon Medallions*), and *La Cita* (1962) *The Rendezvous*).

Alonso, Dora (born 1910)

Cuban novelist, short story writer, journalist and poet, who wrote under the pen-names Nora Lin and D. Polimita. She belonged to an Antillan group, linked by land, race and sex, along with the Cuban Rosa Hilda Zell (born 1910) and others. She was an influential member of the Communist Party, and won several literary prizes.

She travelled throughout Mexico, Spain, Switzerland, France and the Soviet Union. Her short stories have been included in several publications of Central and South America, and she has written many children's books. Her works have been translated into foreign languages and have appeared in several Cuban and foreign anthologies.

Works: *Tierra inerme* (1961) (*Defenceless Land*), *Panolani* (1966) and *Once caballos* (1970) (*Eleven Horses*).

Alorna, Marquesa de (Leonor de Almeida Portugal de Lorena e Lencastre) (1750–?1839)

Portuguese poet, who used the pen-name ▷Alcipe. At the age of eight, she and her mother and sister were interred in the Convent of Chelas while her father, a nobleman, served a prison sentence for conspiracy against King José. In 1777, after nineteen years of forced seclusion, and upon the death of the king, she and her family were released. Two years later she married a diplomat, the Count of Oeynhausen, and moved to Vienna, where Oeynhausen was stationed. There Alorna gave birth to two children; she also came into contact with the new romantic literature and with writers such as ▷Madame de Staël. Upon the death of her husband in 1793, she moved to England for political reasons; finally, in 1814, she returned to Portugal, where she reclaimed the title and properties that had been stripped of her family years earlier.

Imbued with the liberalism spreading throughout Europe, she had a decided impact on Portuguese literary circles through her salon, to which the country's most prominent writers were invited. Many of her poems sing the virtues of progress and scientific reasoning. There is also a melancholic side to her poetry, as exemplified by her sonnets, and she is frequently considered a precursor of romanticism. Her poems, comprising six volumes, were published posthumously in 1844.

▷*Arcadismo*; Romanticism (Portugal)

Alós, Concha (born 1922)

Spanish novelist, born in Valencia of a working-class family. During the Spanish Civil War (1936–9) Alós's family fled to Murcia, where they suffered from hunger and the imprisonment of her father. After training in Palma in Majorca, she worked as a school teacher for ten years. Then in 1969 she moved to Barcelona, where she began to write.

Alós's fiction has roots in social ▷realism, and is concerned with exposing and denouncing inequalities, most particularly as they affect women. Her first novel, *Los enanos* (1963) (*The Dwarfs*), is set in a large Spanish city, and depicts life as a jungle in which the strongest survive; most human beings are dwarfs while society is the giant. Her second novel, *Los cien pájaros* (1963) (*A Hundred Birds*), describes the sexual and social awakening of Christina, a working-class girl in a provincial city. *Las hogueras* (1964) (*Bonfires*), which won the Planeta Prize, is set in Majorca and shows a cross-section of a society which is suffocated by passion or frustration. *El caballo rojo* (1966) (*The Red Horse Inn*) is based on the refugee experience of Alós and her parents as they fled the approaching Franco forces during the civil war, a theme also treated in *La Madama* (1970) (*The Madam*). *El rey de gatos* (*Narraciones antrópagas*) (1972) (*King of Cats, Cannibalistic Tales*) contains nine short stories. Generally seen as her best work is ▷*Os habla Electra* (1975) (*Electra Speaking*), in which Alós transcends the social realist style of her earlier novels. A similar mythical atmosphere pervades her more recent novels: *Argeos ha muerto, supongo* (1983) (*Argeo's Dead, I Suppose*) and *El asesino de los sueños* (1986) (*The Assassin of Dreams*).

Alphabetical Compendium of the Various Sections Which Have Appeared from the Beginning of the Christian Era to the Present Day (1784)

The North American writer ▷Hannah Adams's *Alphabetical Compendium* is a meticulously researched and (although Adams referred in her memoirs to the text as 'my View of Religions') objectively written history of Christianity. Written during the volatile post-revolutionary years of dissent among numerous religious sects, the *Compendium* seeks to present the history and basic tenets of all sects with justice and accuracy.

al-Sabah, Su'ad (born 1942)

Kuwaiti poet. Born in Kuwait, she grew up in Iraq and studied in Egypt and Britain. She is active on the boards of human rights and development organizations in the Arab world. She funds numerous literary projects in different Arab capitals: the Su'ad al-Sabah Prize for young poets, dramatists and short story writers is now a regular feature of the annual International Cairo Book Fair. She has published several volumes of poetry with a growing sensitivity to the plight of the Arabs in general, and the Arab woman in particular. Her early verse in *A Wish* (1972) and *To You My Son* (1982) is conservative and traditional in many ways, but the dedication to the lost child and the poetry of bereavement in the second collection introduce a distinctive personal note into her work. Her third collection, *In the*

Beginning Was Woman (1988), marks a great change in her verse, a liberated celebration of love in new, terse short lines: 'After every one of your visits / I sit – like a victim of the earthquake / on the edge of my seat counting my dead / gathering my fragments.' Her fourth collection, *Fragments of a Woman* (1989), is her best. The voice of Arab protest is combined with the voice of feminist challenge: 'I am the daughter of Kuwait inhabiting the sun / I number the morning among my surnames.'

al-Samman, Ghada (born 1942)

Syrian novelist, poet, short story writer and journalist, she is probably the best-known woman writer in Arabic today. She graduated from Damascus University and worked in broadcasting, translation and journalism. She has written some twenty-seven books, of which five were published in 1977. She is her own publisher (Ghada al-Samman Publications), showing business acumen in view of the popularity of her work. ▷ *The Incomplete Works of Ghada al-Samman* (1978) shows the depth of her involvement and the independence of her stance.

Al-Samman insists that she will not subscribe to any of the self-deception rampant in Arab discourse today. Her heroines are depressed or alienated, or may even become alcoholic, not just because they have been abandoned by a lover, though that may happen in the course of the narrative, but because of the great shocks that have been dealt to the Arab consciousness: war, defeat, and the savage self-destruction of Lebanon. Her *Beirut Nightmares* (1976) is an imaginative record of life in ▷Beirut at the start of the civil war. The narrator lives near a pet shop. Because of the sniping and the random bombing, the animals are hungry – and so are the narrator and her brother. When the shop owner returns after three days, bringing his animals some food – they are, after all, his livelihood – he is torn to pieces by his hungry dogs – set free by the narrator who has imagined them to be fellow-prisoners. Her earlier work, ▷*Beirut, 75* (1975) was her first novel.

When Ghada al-Samman was asked in 1983 what women writers had given to Arab women, she replied 'a spark of rebellion'. Her verse is written in the same direct, personal style as her prose works; its simplicity betrays the daring explicitness of the emotions described. *I Declare Love on You!* (seven editions, 1976–1983) is the provocative title of her favourite collection (between 'love' and 'war' there is the difference of only one letter in Arabic). *Love In The Veins* (1980), or rather 'cut-throat love', has many simple statements: 'I took you for a knight / from past ages of faith / you took me for a *ghaniya* come from the secret corridors of deceit, to trifle with you / we were both wrong'; a later collection of equally frank confessional verse, ▷*I Testify Against the Wind*, was published in 1987. After the experience of Beirut, she now lives in Paris,

contributing a regular column to an Arabic newspaper in Beirut.
▷*Naksa*

al-Shaykh, Hanan (born 1945)

Lebanese journalist, novelist and short story writer. She grew up in ▷Beirut and went to college in Cairo, where she wrote her first novel, *Suicide of a Dead Man*. On her return to Beirut she had a successful career in journalism, working for *al-Nahar*, an important Lebanese daily newspaper. She published her short stories in various periodicals, and in 1980 brought out her first major novel, ▷*The Story of Zahra* (1980, trans. 1986). It is a daring picture of the life of a girl who is neither attractive nor romantic, and whose experience in Lebanon, in Damascus, in Africa, and later in the civil war in Beirut, is representative of the degradation and near-destruction of her family and her country. The novel was banned in some Arab countries, which led to a wider readership for smuggled copies. The author uses other voices besides Zahra's to tell her story from various angles. Her next novel, *Women of Sand and Myrrh* (trans. 1988) is a daring exploration of female consciousness in an alien and oppressive environment. It is set in a Persian Gulf desert state, where the fundamentalist ethic keeps the women segregated and suffocatingly close to each other. The narrative is taken up by four women: two outsiders and two indigenous characters. Suha, the Lebanese 'modern' woman used to living in Beirut and Europe, has no outlet for her tremendous energy in the rich, highly technologized, but socially cramped Gulf state. The discoveries she makes about herself and about the other women, their sexuality and their destructive energy, send her flying back to Beirut, preferring the war-torn country to the land of sand and myrrh.

Bib: 'The Persian Carpet' in *Arabic Short Stories*.

al-Taymuriyya, 'Aisha 'Esmat (1840–1902)

Egyptian poet. Born in Cairo to a family of the Turkish aristocracy, she showed early interest in the readings and discussions going on in her father's *salamlek* (male quarters), rather than the female talk and embroidery classes in her mother's ▷*harem*. 'Aisha was nine when she finished the course set for girls of her class fortunate enough to be educated at home, learning the *Qu'ran* by heart, reading and writing Turkish and Arabic. Al-Taymuriyya later described how her father took pity on her tears, and undertook to read with her and instruct her himself, relieving her of her mother's regimen. She could not attend the meetings of men of letters in the salamlek because of her ▷*hijab* (seclusion), but listened breathlessly behind the door. She was married at fourteen, and accompanied her husband to Istanbul. She later wrote that marriage and the care of her young children gave her no time for writing, but she continued to read and recite poetry. On the death of her husband in 1885, she settled in Cairo, employed two female instructors in prosody, and composed verse in Turkish, Persian and Arabic. Her Turkish and Persian verses are hardly remembered, except that in the introduction to the Persian volume she gave a detailed account of her upbringing and readings.

Her Arabic verse covered conventional subjects, and was composed in the traditional forms of the last century. Her most anthologized poem was a lament upon the death of her daughter, whom she mourned for seven years. Another poem, recited by every Arab schoolgirl in the first half of this century, is ostensibly a defence of the veil, but develops into *fakhr* (boasting) that a woman can achieve greatness if she is noble and sets her mind to it: it is not the veil that guards her honour, but her own modesty.

Her prose was typical of the highly ornamented 'decadent' style of the 19th century. She was no innovator in terms of the style or subject matter of Arabic writing in her age, but broke new ground by the act of writing and publishing in 19th-century Cairo. ▷May Ziyadah was responsible for bringing her work to the attention of early 20th-century feminists by lecturing on her life and work, and publishing her biography in 1924.
Bib: Badran, Margot and Cooke, Miriam, ▷*Opening the Gates: A Century of Arab Feminist Writing*.

al-'Uthman, Layla (born 1945)
Kuwaiti journalist, poet and short story writer. She grew up in Kuwait in a literary family; her father was a poet, and she started working early in broadcasting and journalism. She had a regular column in a national daily newspaper and a weekly magazine. Her first published book was a collection of verse, *Whispers* (1972), but she later devoted herself to fiction. She published her short stories in periodicals all over the Arab world. Her collections include *Two Women in A Vessel* (1976), *Leaving* (1979), *Eyes Come In The Night* (1980), *Forms of Love* (1985) and *A Case of Love Madness* (1989). Hers is the most outspoken voice among Gulf women prose writers; the stuff of her stories is the web of interactions between the self and external reality. She explores areas of human experience generally regarded as taboo in traditional societies: adultery, incest and the cruel insensitivity of adults towards children. Above all, she speaks of love and its over-powering force that can drive men to madness or crime.

It is not only love that is stifled in a patriarchal household, but all yearning for colour and beauty. In one of her later stories, 'The Accusation', a little girl is falsely accused by her stepmother, and the father ties her to a post in the courtyard for a whole day. The figure of the scheming, cruel stepmother is real enough in an environment where polygamy is a fact of life, but the author does not leave it at that. Growing up, the girl is accused of 'possessing brightly coloured paper and pens daring and throbbing that stimulate the senses and prick at stagnant thoughts'.

The sympathies of this writer are with the poor and the weak; the plight of the Palestinians is a recurrent theme in her stories from the start. Her attempts at tying in the particular sufferings of characters with a universal theme can be rather naïve; mottos from Nazim Hikmat and quotations from Pablo Neruda (1904–1973) sit awkwardly in the narrative. On the other hand, she excels in imaginatively recreating Gulf scenery in pre-oil times. The little villages of seafaring fishermen and pearl fisheries against the background of desert sands and a few palm trees are the scene of age-old romances and tragedies of love and death. Her novel *Wasmiya Comes Out of the Sea* (1986) is exemplary, a tragedy of star-crossed lovers against a background of desert and sea.

Alvar ▷Mansilla de García, Eduarda

Alvarez de Toledo, Luisa Isabel (Duchess of Medina Sidonia) (born 1936)
Contemporary Spanish novelist whose work focuses on social and humanitarian issues. She was jailed for political activism in 1969, and her subsequent writing reveals an anti-capitalist stance. Set in Andalusia, *La huelga* (1967) (*The Strike*) is a *roman à thèse* that seeks to demonstrate injustice and brutality in the treatment of workers by landowners and capitalists, who are presented as being in collusion with the authorities and the Church. Alvarez's later novels, *La base* (1971) (*The Base*) and *La cacería* (1977) (*The Hunt*), are highly critical of the moneyed classes in Spain.

Álvarez Rios, María (born 1919)
Cuban poet and dramatist. A professor in music, she has contributed to various Cuban publications and has won prizes for her dramatic plays. She has travelled in England, France, Spain, Belgium, Holland and Portugal.
Works: *Cosecha* (1948) (*Harvest*), *Poemario* (1948) (*Book of Poems*); *Martí 9* (1952) (*Tuesday 9th*), *Según el color* (1955) (*According to Colour*); *Funeral* (1958) and *La Víctima* (1959) (*The Victim*).

al-Zayyat, Latifa (born 1923)
Egyptian critic, novelist, short story writer and university teacher. She graduated from the Department of English, Cairo University, in 1946 and obtained an MA and PhD from the same university. She is now Emeritus Professor of English at the Women's College of Ain Shams University in Cairo, where she has taught and chaired the department for many years. Active in national and class politics since student days, she is now a veteran member of a number of associations and committees set up by national, leftist and feminist groups in resistance to the growing drift towards the right in Egyptian politics.

Her novel *The Open Door* (1960) shows that she learned her craft from Flaubert (1821–1880) and Henry James (1843–1916), as well as ▷George

Eliot. The novel is one of the first to use what is now a popular device, which one might call the 'Maggie Tulliver syndrome' (▷*Mill on the Floss, The*) for plot and characters. The brother is a sympathetic character, but it is the difference of treatment and expectations of the boy and the girl that carry the message to the reader. The parents cannot stop their only son from taking part in student demonstrations calling for independence in 1946. They cannot stop him from joining the *fidaiyeen* (partisans) in the Canal Zone. When Layla demonstrates along with the other girls in her school, her father gives her a sound beating with a slipper, the instrument intensifying the indignity of her situation. She is shut up at home and not allowed to go to school for some time.

Al-Zayyat has continued to write literary criticism, to write and lecture on political and social causes, and to write shorter fiction. A collection, *Old Age and Other Stories* (1986), is a clever exploration of the consciousness of a number of women, or perhaps the same woman, through various cycles of introspection and illumination. There is no illusion here that the open door will lead to freedom and self-fulfilment, for in many cases it has led to frustration, defeat or sheer self deception: 'She nurtured the anger as a pregnant woman nurtures her foetus, realizing that calling for help is of no use. The woman has, when all is said and done, to stand on her own feet.'

Amadiume, Ifi

Nigerian poet. A resident in Britain, she is author of *Passion Waves* (1985), a volume of poetry combining Sufi philosophy and Igbo transliterations and oral usages, and of *Male Daughters, Female Husbands* (1987), an anthropological study of the place of women in traditional Igbo society.

Amália, Narcisa (1852–1924)

Brazilian poet, essayist, and translator. At eleven she moved from São João da Barra, where she was born, to the town of Resende, and later to Rio. Her first book of poetry, *Nebulosas* (1872) (*Starry Skies*), was a success, and was followed in 1874 by *Flores do Campo* (*Flowers of the Field*).

Amandla (1980)

A novel of political resistance by South African writer ▷Miriam Tlali, whose title is a popular freedom cry meaning 'Power'. The book was banned in South Africa shortly after publication. Set during the year following the schoolchildren's rebellion in ▷Soweto in 1976, the novel structures itself around the experiences and conversations of an extended family living in the Rockville area of Soweto. The story focuses on Pholoso, a high-school student who becomes the leader of the Soweto Student Representative Council after he sees one of his friends shot in a political demonstration; he is imprisoned and

tortured before finally leaving the country so that he can continue the struggle from outside. Felleng, his lover and the mother of his child, represents both the sacrifice of personal happiness for the struggle, and the resilience of women who tend the garden while the men fight for change.

Several other stories are interwoven with this one, giving a panoramic view of black township life in political ferment: meetings, demonstrations, strikes, funerals, retributive violence against traitors to the people as well as against whites. In one strand of action, the obsessive sexual passion of the corrupt policeman, Nicodemus, towards a woman who is married to his senior officer, is used to symbolize the world of 'the private' which has been discarded in this time of political exigency.

Several South African novels deal with Soweto in 1976: Tlali's has been called the best of these, in the quality of its art, by writer and critic Njabulo Ndebele.

Amant, L' (1984) ▷*Lover, The* (1985)

Amarilis (17th century)

Anonymous poet of Peru. She wrote *Epístola a Belardo* (1621) (*Letter to Belardo*), a letter to the Spanish poet Lope de Vega (1562–1635), which he published at the end of his collection of prose and verse *Filomena* (1621). It is thought that Amarilis was Doña María de Alvarado, a descendant of Alvarado, a conqueror who founded the city of Léon de Huanaco, in Peru. Her poems have been attributed to several authors, including Lope de Vega himself.

A Mazing Space: Writing Canadian Women Writing (1986)

Edited by Shirley Neuman and Smaro Kamboureli, *A Mazing Space* is an anthology of critical essays on Canadian women writers, the first of its kind in scope and breadth. It set out to question the established critical reading of women's work, and determined to reach beyond those authors (such as ▷Margaret Atwood and ▷Margaret Laurence) usually treated in academic criticism. A superb dislocation and extension of the canon, the anthology contains some thirty-six essays on as diverse figures as ▷Nicole Brossard and ▷Betty Lambert. Its 'recuperation of a female tradition and of feminist theory' apprehended an important moment in Canadian literary criticism, and has served as a measurement for subsequent anthologies.

Ambai

Indian short story writer. Ambai is the pseudonym adopted by C.M. Lakshmi for her works composed in the south Indian language Tamil. She has published two collections of short stories, and individual pieces have appeared in various Tamil journals and ▷*Manushi*. A short story, 'Yellow Fish', translated from the Tamil, is included in ▷*The Inner Courtyard*. A work of criticism written in English, *The Face Behind the Mask*, was published in 1984.

Ambler, Mary Cary (fl 1770)

North American diarist. It was the discovery that physicians in Baltimore were offering to inoculate people against smallpox that led her to make her arduous journey from her home in Jamestown, Virginia, to Maryland. Her ▷*Diary of M. Ambler, 1770* details the three-month journey, undertaken for the benefit of her children, and is a precise account of the early medical procedures of inoculation as well as the hardships of such travel in the pre-revolutionary South.

América, Juana de ▷Ibarbourou, Juana de

American Ladies' Magazine (1828–1836)

US women's magazine, founded by ▷Sarah Josepha Hale, who later edited ▷*Godey's Lady's Book*. The first US women's magazine to last more than a few years, *American Ladies' Magazine* directly reflected Hale's values; it was conservative, didactic, moralistic and sentimental – favouring education for women, but not suffrage or public roles.

  ▷Whitman, Sarah Helen Power

American Women Writers Series

US reprint series publishing 19th-century women writers in edited editions, with critical and/or biographical introductions as well as bibliographies. Along with the ▷Feminist Press, AWWS of Rutgers University Press is a principal source of rediscovered women's writing that has been 'lost' for generations.

Amin, Adibah ▷Amin, Khalida Adibah binti Haji

Amin, Khalida Adibah binti Haji (born 1936)

Malay novelist, journalist, radio dramatist and actress, who is a former teacher, school principal and lecturer. She is the elder daughter of Ibu Zain, who in 1930 published an influential women's magazine, *Bulan Melayu* (*The Malay Moon*). She is better known as Adibah Amin, and in the 1950s was one of the rare English-educated Malay woman graduates. Her prize-winning radio plays appear in *Pulang Gadisku Pulang* (1977), a joint publication with Habsah Hassan. As a journalist she wrote a highly literate and popular column, 'As I Was Passing' (collected under the same title, 1976), in an English-language paper, under the pen-name, Sri Delima, and was named Malaysian Journalist of the Year in 1979. In 1983 she was honoured by the Sultan of Johor, her native state, and also won the SEA (South-East Asia) WRITE Award.

  Amin has translated into English the modern Malay classic, Shanon Ahmad's *Ranjau Sepanjang Jalan* (*No Harvest But a Thorn*), and into Malay Johnny Ong's novel *Garam Gula Duka Bahagia* (1980) (*Sugar and Salt*). Two early novels written while still at school were adaptations of English

children's works: *Puteri Asli* (1949) (*The True Princess*) and *Gadis Sipu* (1949) (*Shy Maiden*). *Bangsawan Tulen* (1950) (*Genuine Aristocrat*), critical of the arrogance of some Malay royalty, was her third children's novel and her own. She also made a name for herself as a short story contributor to the women's magazine *Ibu* (*Mother*), and her work appears in the anthology of Malay women's short stories, *Wanita* (1964) (*Woman*) with that of six other well-known women writers. Her later work is generally regarded among her best: ▷*Seroja Masih di Kolam* (1968) (*The Lily is Still in the Pond*) and the autobiographical *Tempat Latuh Lagi Dikenang* (1983) (*Remembrances*).

Amor, Guadalupe (born 1920)

Mexican poet. Her poetry captured a large and faithful readership. She is an agonic and metaphysical writer. She reveals in the prologue of *Antologia poética* (1956) (*Poetry Anthology*) that she was interested in the theatre, the cinema and material goods, but with her failure on the stage, the death of her mother and the loss of her house she looked back to childhood to find something of a more lasting nature. As a result she published the books *Yo soy mi casa* (1946) (*I Am My House*), *Círculo de angustia*) (1948) (*Circle of Anguish*) and *Polvo* (1949) (*Dust*), among others. In the prologue of *Décimas a Dios* (1953) (*Stanzas to God*) she confesses that '*Diós fué mi máxima inquietud. Lo busqué primero como quien busca a un ser humano, me hubiese gustado hablar con él, como jamás pude hacerlo con mis padres, con mis hermanos ni con mis amigos. Más tarde busqué su cielo, olvidándome de su presencia. Después, fué su ausencia lo que me inquietó.*' ('God was my greatest worry. At first I looked for him as one looks for a human being, I might have wanted to talk to him, as I never could talk to my parents, my brothers or my friends. Later I looked for his heaven, forgetting his presence. After that, it was his absence which worried me.') She respected the purest Castillian form in her poems, as in 'Décima XVI' ('Stanza XVI'). In a prose version of *Yo soy mi casa* and in *Galería de títeres* (1959) (*Puppet Gallery*), she combines biography and imagination, revealing her unmasked self, along with an impressive gallery of characters described with mystery, sarcasm and tenderness. Other works include: *Como reina de barajas* (1966) (*As Queen of Cards*); *El zoológico* (1975) (*The Zoo*); *Las amargas lágrimas de Beatriz Sheridan* (1981) (*The Bitter Tears of Beatriz Sheridan*); *A mí me ha dado en escribir sonetos* (1981) (*I Have Taken to Writing Sonnets*); *Pita y otros monstruos* (1983) (*Agave and Other Monsters*), and *Soy dueña del universo* (1984) (*I Am the Mistress of the Universe*). She has a great number of poems included in anthologies and magazines, and narratives and prologues in a number of books and periodicals.

Amor es un juego solitario, El (1979) (*Love is a Solitary Game*)

Second novel in the trilogy by ▷Esther Tusquets, arguably the most significant female novelist now writing in Spain. It describes a *ménage à trois* involving Elia, Clara and Ricardo. The focus, as in the first novel, ▷*El mismo mar de todos los veranos* (*The Same Sea as Every Summer*), is a middle-aged protagonist who desperately attempts to reverse the ageing process through eroticism; the attempt is unsuccessful.

Amortajada, La ▷*Shrouded Woman, The*

Amory, Katherine (1731–1777)
North American diarist. A resident of Boston, Massachusetts, she rejected the notion of national independence that was circulating in North America in 1775. To avoid the consequences for a Loyalist in revolutionary North America, she sought passage to London, where she remained until her death some time after March 1777. Her diary, ▷*The Journal of Mrs John Amory 1775–1777*, includes observations on her journey and her final years in London.

Amour (1968) (*Love*)
The first narrative in the trilogy *Amour, Colère, Folie* (*Love, Anger, Madness*), by the Haitian writer ▷Marie Chauvet, *Amour* focuses upon a frustrated woman against a background of political terror and violence. Chauvet portrays Claire as a complex, intelligent and sensitive woman, who is resentful because of her black skin and unmarried state. In love with her brother-in-law, Claire dreams of becoming as elusive as a shadow, and she fears the gaze of others. She chooses madness as a form of liberation, recording in her diary her revolt against society (see also Warner-Vieyra's ▷*Juletane* and ▷*As the Sorcerer Said*). Fascinated by the sadistic military commander, Calédu, the object for her of irrepressible attraction and violent repulsion, Claire kills him. The publication of the trilogy, with its virulent denunciation of Haiti's tyrannical regimes, forced Chauvet to go into exile.
▷*Fille d'Haïti*

Amour en plus, L' (1980) ▷*Myth of Motherhood, The* (1981)

Amrane, Djamila (born 1941)
Algerian novelist. Works as an historian and senior lecturer at the University of Algiers. During the Algerian war against the French occupation, she was, alongside the very well-known Djamila Bouhired and ▷Zohra Drif, one of the *poseuses de bombes* (bomb-carriers), with the pseudonym Danielle Minne. She was arrested and imprisoned for many years in France. Her novel ▷*Les Femmes algériennes dans la guerre* (1991) (*Algerian Women in the War*) is an account of the participation of Algerian women in the liberation struggle.

Amritvela (1988)
First novel by Indian writer ▷Leena Dhingra, strongly autobiographical. It is the story of Meera, a British-based Indian woman's trip back to her aunts in India, and her attempts to narrow the gap between the two identities that she feels she carries inside her. Sometimes amused and sometimes despairing, Meera chronicles herself shuttling between her Western habits and thoughts and her Indian ones.

Amrouche, Fadhma Ait Mansur (1882–1967)
Algerian novelist from the Kabylie (the Berber region of Algeria). An illegitimate child who went to a convent school, she was christened Marguerite at the age of sixteen and married at the same age. Her autobiographical novel, *Histoire de ma vie* (1968) (*The Story of My Life*), was published after her death. Amrouche explores her acculturation and expresses her attachment to her Kabylie. Unable to feel at home either with French or Arab people, she said: 'I am still the eternal exile, who never will feel at home anywhere.'

Amrouche, Marie-Louise (Taos) (1913–1976)
Algerian novelist. Born in Tunis into a Kabyle (Berber) family who converted to Christianity and took French nationality. Marie-Louise is her Christian name, Taos her Berber name. Has also published under the name of Marguerite, her mother's Christian name (▷Amrouche, Fadhma Ait Mansur). She took a special interest in translating and performing popular Berber songs, which brought her acclaim around 1937. She was awarded the La Casa Velasquez Scholarship, which enabled her to study in Madrid, and collaborated on radio programmes in Tunis and Algiers. She lived in France from 1945 until her death. Her major novel, *Jacinthe noire* (1947) (*Black Hyacinth*), was the first to be published by an Algerian woman. Her subsequent novels ▷*Rue des Tambourins* (1960) and *L'Amant imaginaire* (1975) (*The Imaginary Lover*) are strongly autobiographical. In them she examines and explores exile and marginality, based on her own experiences as an expatriate. Her French translations of Berber stories and poems are published as *Le Grain Magique* (1966) (*The Magic Seed*).

Anagnostaki, Loula (born 1940)
Greek dramatist. She was born in Thessaloniki. She is considered one of those modern Greek dramatists whose work is situated outside Greek tradition, her characters being universal human types rather than specifically Greek individuals. These characters move through complex plots which remain unresolved or end in unexpected ways. There is an irrational element in her plays, where often the passage of time is irrelevant. Yet her characters seem motivated by a desire to relate to one another more closely. Her one-act plays *Overnight Stay*, *The City*, and *Parade*, published under the title *The City* (1974), peopled with unconnected and emotionally confused characters, demonstrate a desire for communication which is never fulfilled. The same theme informs her many other plays – for instance, the 1978 play *Victory*, which features

expatriate Greeks searching for an identity of their own. Outside Greece, her plays have been staged in Cyprus, Italy, England, and Poland.

'Anan (died c 846)

First of a line of famous *jawari* (slave-women) Arabic poets. Her master, al-Natifi, set her up in Baghdad at the time of Harun al-Rashid, and invited poets and men of wit to meet her. Her poetry includes famous *ijazas* (compositions on measures similar to great classical poems), considered a tough test of a poet's talents. There are also many verses of *mujun* (explicit sexual repartee) exchanged with the great cynic of the age, the poet Abu Nuwas, and some touching love lyrics to the 'chaste' poet, Abbas ibn al-Ahnaf, who loved her.

There are various reports in medieval sources about her relationship with Harun al-Rashid: that she sent him a messenger inviting him to buy her, that he sent someone to 'view' her and test her talent, that he paid the price, but sent her back when he realized how many poets had abused her in their verse, and that her master gave away the money to the poor (a hundred thousand dirhams). On his death she was sold for double the sum, it is not clear to whom.

Anancy Stories (1899)

Tales recounted by the Caribbean writer ▷Pamela Smith, relating the exploits of 'Anancy, the Spider Man' (also known as Brer Anancy), a legendary being originating from African folklore whose chief characteristic is trickery. Predominantly West African in origin, he is also found in variations throughout Africa. He has the metaphoric shape of a spider. These stories form part of the folk traditions of Caribbean oral literature.

Ancelot, Marguerite (1792–1875)

French novelist and dramatist. Born in Dijon, in 1830 she began to write dramatic works in collaboration with her husband, Jacques. She made her real literary début with *Un mariage raisonnable* (1835) (*A Sensible Marriage*), even though this play was still published under her husband's name, and her most successful theatrical work was *Marie ou les trois époques* (1836) (*Marie or The Three Eras*). She presided over one of the more fashionable salons of the July Monarchy (1831–48), and left behind two fascinating chronicles of salon life: *Les Salons de Paris, foyers éteints* (1858) (*The Paris Salons: Dead Flames*) and *Un salon de Paris 1824–64* (1866) (*A Paris Salon 1824–64*). Her novels, which are thematically melodramatic and stylistically precious, were extremely popular with 19th-century French readers (particularly those who were fond of sentimental and moralistic tales), and include *Georgine* (1855); *Une route sans issue* (1857) (*A Road to Nowhere*) and *Un noeud de ruban* (1858) (*A Ribbon Bow*).

Anderson, Barbara (born 1926)

New Zealand writer. Born and brought up in Hawkes Bay, Anderson completed a science degree at the University of Otago and spent most of her life working as a teacher and laboratory technician. Thirty years later she completed an arts degree at Victoria University of Wellington and began to publish prize-winning stories. Her story collection, *I Think We Should Go Into the Jungle*, was published in 1989, and a novel, *Girls High*, in 1990. Anderson uses ▷postmodern strategies within a context of ▷realist and often historically specific narrative. A deeply ironic writer, Anderson destabilizes convention and satirizes social orthodoxies in her work.

Anderson, Doris (born 1921)

Writer and journalist, born in Calgary, Alberta, in the west of Canada, she was for eighteen years (from 1958) editor of *Chatelaine*, a women's magazine of fashion and popular issues. After leaving *Chatelaine*, she became for a time President of the Canadian Advisory Council on the Status of Women. Her novels include *Two Women* (1978) and *Rough Layout* (1981); she incorporates her experiences as a journalist and editor in her fiction. *The Unfinished Revolution: the Status of Women in Twelve Countries* (1991) traces the personal, social, and professional progress of women in twelve Western nations.

Anderson, Jessica

Australian writer. Anderson writes with consummate skill and subtlety, and has won the Miles Franklin Award twice, for ▷*Tirra Lirra by the River* (1978), and *The Impersonators* (1980), as well as other prestigious Australian awards. She has attracted considerable international attention, particularly in the USA. Her novels are in the tradition of ▷Jane Austen and Henry James, of sophisticated irony and the study of subtle interpersonal relationships. Her best is undoubtedly *Tirra Lirra by the River*. Other novels are *An Ordinary Lunacy* (1963), *The Last Man's Head* (1970), *The Commandant* (1975), and *Taking Shelter* (1990). Her short story collection, *Stories from the Warm Zone and Sydney Stories* (1987), won a number of literary awards.

▷Writers for film and television (Australia); Short story (Australia); *Coming Out from Under*; *Eight Voices of the Eighties*

Anderson, Linda (born 1949)

Irish writer. Anderson she was born in Belfast into a Protestant working-class family. After taking her degree at Queen's University in Belfast, she went to London, where she now lives. Her stories and poetry have appeared in a number of collections, and *Charmed Lives* (1988), her first play, obtained an award in the London Writers' Competition in 1988. She has published two novels, *To Stay Alive* (1984) and *Cuckoo* (1986). The exploration of the impact of violence and conflict on people's lives is a particular focus of her work. At once passionate and laconic, her writing is often boldly experimental and subversive.

Anderson, Margaret ▷ *Little Review, The*

Andreas-Salomé, Lou (1861–1937)
German novelist, biographer, literary critic, Freudian ▷psychoanalyst and feminist. She was born in St Petersburg of a German mother and a Russian army officer. A spirited young girl with a keen intelligence, she became one of the first female students to be accepted by the University of Zurich. From 1880 to 1881 she studied philosophy and religion, and then began an itinerant life through Europe, nurturing intense relationships with people of genius. Prominent writers everywhere, including the dramatists Hauptmann (1862–1946) in Berlin, Gerhard Frank Wedekind (1864–1918) in Paris and Arthur Schnitzler (1862–1931) in Vienna, fell under the spell of her exceptional beauty and intellect, and her women friends included ▷Malvida von Meysenbug and ▷Frieda von Bülow. In 1881 she met Friedrich Nietzsche (1844–1900), who fell in love with her while she was living with the philosopher Paul Ree (1850–?). The poet Rilke (1875–1926) also fell in love with her after her marriage to the orientalist F.C. Andreas. Her two Russian journeys with Rilke in 1899 and 1901 were crucial to his artistic development. She composed biographies of both Nietzsche and Rilke, as well as countless essays of literary criticism.

Andreas-Salomé's fiction explores aspects of female psycho-sexuality, and argues for the free expression of femininity outside marriage. Having intuitively established her own notions of emotional and erotic emancipation, she spent the year 1912–1913 studying psychoanalysis, first with Alfred Adler (1870–1937) and then with Sigmund Freud (1856–1939), whereupon she herself became a practising analyst.

Her works include: the stories, *Ruth* (1896), *Fenitschka* (1896) and *Eine Ausschweifung* (1898) (*Wandering from the Path*); *Friedrich Nietzsche in seinen Werken* (1894) (*Friedrich Nietzsche in his works*); *Die Erotik* (1910) (*Eroticism*); *Mein Dank an Freud* (1931) (*My Gratitude to Freud*), and *Grundriß einiger Lebenserinnerungen* (1933) (*Sketches for a Memoir*).

Andresen, Sophia de Mello Breyner (born 1919)
Portuguese poet, short story writer and author of children's books. One of the country's major poets, she has written over a dozen volumes since 1944, when her first book of verses, *Poesia*, appeared. Most of her poetry is concerned with the natural world – especially the sea, as evidenced by the titles of her collections, *Dia do Mar* (1947) (*Day of the Sea*), *Coral* (1950) and *Mar Novo* (1958) (*New Sea*). Myths and classical motifs are also important in her works. Introspective and frequently hermetic, her poetry is often classified as symbolist. But this classification ignores the existential quality of her poetry as well as her more recent interest in historical and social themes. In addition to poetry she has also written children's books and two collections of short fiction: *Contos Exemplares* (1962) (*Exemplary Stories*) and *Histórias da Terra e do Mar* (1984) (*Stories of the Earth and the Sea*).
Bib: *Longman Anthology of World Literature by Women*, pp. 604–5.

Andreu, Blanca
Contemporary Spanish poet. Andreu was born in La Coruña, and studied at Madrid University. Her poetic career blossomed in the 1980s; her first work, *De una niña de provincias* (1980) (*From a Provincial Girl*) won the *Premio Adonais*. Others, such as *Báculo de Babel* (1982) (*Babel's Wand*) and *Elphistone* (1988), have also been widely acclaimed.

Andrezel, Pierre ▷Blixen, Karen

And They Didn't Die (1990)
Second novel by South African writer ▷Lauretta Ngcobo. Written, in part, for a readership which needs to be instructed as regards the South African political situation, this novel is also a celebration of the endurance of rural people, and particularly women, in apartheid South Africa. As the title so starkly suggests, the context in which they live seems to demand their death, so that survival itself is an act of rebellion. The women rebel in other ways, too, as shown, for example, by the text's portrayal of the Natal pass law campaigns of the late 1950s and 1960s.

The story focuses on Jezile, who functions as an everywoman figure for this collective group. At first she ekes out an existence from barren land and starved cattle, alongside her thriving white neighbours, whose agricultural projects are assisted by state subsidies, irrigation schemes and cheap labour. Her husband, Siyalo, is a migrant worker, so that their married life is compressed into one month each year. Jezile goes to the city to take up domestic work: she is raped by her employer, bears the child, and watches her marriage disintegrate. As the mother of three children in all, she experiences their suffering, too, as they grow up: her firstborn maimed by a soldier's bullet in a schoolchildren's rebellion; one of her daughters raped by a white soldier. Jezile kills the rapist, and suffers the consequences.

Angel (1987)
This work by the Caribbean writer ▷Merle Collins was described as 'an outstanding first novel'. It centres on the lives of three generations of Grenadian women, provides a strong picture of ▷Grenada and the people, and an impassioned statement about the problems in the society. The central character, Angel, represents the generation growing up in the post-nationalist, post-revolutionary era in Grenada, who witness the arrival of the new North American colonialism. Exploring the themes of ▷education, language

and power, Merle Collins uses both French *patois* (the language of her mother and grandmother) and English creole as part of the integral structure of this novel.

See Janice Shinebourne, 'Second Coming' in *Artrage*, No. 18, Autumn 1987, pp. 36–7, for an interview with Merle Collins discussing *Angel*.

'Angel in the House, The'

A term which has come to exemplify the Victorian middle-class ideal of submissive womanhood, used originally by Coventry Patmore in his domestic epic *The Angel in the House* (1854–62). The Victorian feminine ideal embodied purity and selflessness, strong moral and religious principles, coupled with a willingness to submit to the will of men. Woman's realm was the home, viewed as a sanctuary from the harsh public world of capitalist competition. The 'Angel in the House' stereotypically provided spiritual succour as well as domestic comforts for the entrepreneurial middle-class male, and cherished her maternal role as a God-given duty. In Victorian literature, characters such as Dickens's Agnes Wickfield in *David Copperfield* represent such an ideal, but as the 19th century progressed a number of writers challenged the stereotype. Well-known texts such as ▷Charlotte Brontë's ▷*Jane Eyre*, ▷Elizabeth Barrett Browning's ▷*Aurora Leigh* and ▷George Eliot's ▷*Middlemarch* and ▷*The Mill on the Floss* all present anti-angelic heroines straining to be released from conventional domestic roles. The Angel in the House was nevertheless an extremely powerful idea, and the emphasis on English women's moral and spiritual superiority was crucial in the construction of national identity. In her famous work on women writers, ▷*A Room of One's Own* (1929), ▷Virginia Woolf cites the import of the Angel in the House as a central impediment to early 20th-century women's attempts to write professionally.

▷Feminism (19th-century Britain); 'Woman Question, The'; Imperialism; Sentiment and Sentimental; Taylor, Jane and Ann
Bib: Poovey, Mary, *Uneven Developments: The Ideological Work of Gender in Mid-Victorian Britain*.

Angelou, Maya (born 1928)

US autobiographer, poet, screenwriter and editor. Angelou was born in St Louis, Missouri, but moved with her brother, Bailey, to Stamps, Arkansas after her parents' divorce. In ▷*I Know Why the Caged Bird Sings* (1970), the first of an immensely popular five-volume autobiography, Angelou describes her upbringing by her grandmother and the effects of the racism of the Anglo-American community in Arkansas. Angelou also recounts the devastating experience of rape by her mother's boyfriend when she was eight, and her ensuing five-year silence. The role of literature is central to Angelou's portrayal of her life in this book. The second and third volumes, *Gather Together in My Name* (1974) and *Singin' and Swingin' and Gettin' Merry Like Christmas* (1976), record the years where she moved to San

Maya Angelou

Francisco, California with her mother, a professional gambler, working as waitress, the city's first African-American woman streetcar conductor, and training as a dancer and singer. She went on to tour Europe and North Africa as a feature dancer with *Porgy and Bess*. Her work with performance arts, film and theatre have been important ever since, and Angelou has worked as screenwriter, composer and director.

Her years in the Harlem Writer's Guild, meeting writers such as ▷Paule Marshall and James Baldwin (born 1924), and becoming active within the Civil Rights Movement are charted in *The Heart of a Woman* (1981). *All God's Children Need Travelling Shoes* was published in 1986, and breaks new ground with its exploration of the relationship of African-Americans to Africa, and the difficulties of cultural division experienced by the migrant. Angelou's autobiography has been located in a tradition of African-American autobiography extending back to the slave narratives of ▷Harriet Jacobs and Frederick Douglass (1817–1895).

Angelou is also a prominent poet, whose work displays an astute and diverse technical range, encompassing both formal and performance elements, as well as a thematic commitment to the politics of race and gender. Angelou is currently at Wake Forest University in Winston-Salem, North Carolina holding the Reynolds Chair.

Her other works include: *Just Give Me a Cool Drink of Water 'fore I Diiie* (1971), *Oh Pray My Wings Are Gonna Fit Me Well* (1975), *And Still I Rise* (1978), *Shaker, Why Don't You Sing?* (1983), *Now Sheba Sings the Song* (illustrated by Tom Feelings), and *I Shall Not Be Moved* (1990).
Bib: Russell, Sandi, *Render Me My Song*.

Angel Over the Right Shoulder, The (1852)

US autobiographical fiction by ▷Elizabeth Stuart Phelps (pseudonym: H. Trusta). The narrative powerfully presents, with grinding verisimilitude, a mother's domestic duties and struggles. Belying the stereotypical judgement that Phelps/Trusta wrote religious pap which begged realistic concerns with regard to women's lives, *Angel* shows its mother character torn between maternal/domestic duty and her compelling need to develop her own self and talent.

Anger, Jane ▷ *Jane Anger, her Protection for Women* (1589)

Anghelaki-Rooke, Katerina (born 1939)
Greek poet. She was born in Athens, where she studied Greek literature and foreign languages. She later studied in Nice, and also in Geneva, where she received a poetry prize. She has taught poetry in the United States. She now lives in Athens and on the island of Aegina. The striking erotic elements in her poetry extend beyond simple images of human sexuality to a concern with all the main problems of life. Through the medium of ancient Greek myths and legends she presents female characters who ruminate on the sadness and ugliness of life but also find new energies for living. *Wolves and Clouds* (1963) was the first of her many collections of poems. Another collection, *The Suitors* (1984), won her the second State Prize for Poetry. Since then she has published many other collections of poetry. Her work has been translated into English, French, Russian, Italian and Bulgarian. She herself has published Greek translations of English, North American, French and Russian writers.

Anglada, Maria Angels (born 1930)
Spanish novelist. Anglada was born in Vich, and studied Classics. She won the Josep Plà prize with her first novel, *Les Closes* (1979) (*The Enclosed*), which is a historical novel set against the background of 19th-century Catalan society. It recreates the personal history of Dolors Canals in the difficult years immediately prior to the Liberal Revolution of 1868 which ushered in the First Republic. *No em dic Laura* (1981) (*My Name Isn't Laura*) is a collection of stories, characterized by emphasis on things Greek. *Viola d'amore* (1983) (*Viola of Love*) differs from Anglada's earlier fiction by no longer depending on historical reconstruction. The main theme and structure is provided by music.
▷ Catalan women's writing

Anglo–Boer War writing
The Anglo–Boer War (1899–1902), the first war to be fought by literate common soldiers, inspired a vast amount of writing – verse, sketches, short stories and reminiscences – which is most often by men. However, there is significant work by women writers. Johanna Brandt (née van Warmelo) (1876–1964) returned to South Africa with her Dutch husband at the start of the war, undertaking voluntary nursing at the concentration camp in Irene, Transvaal, as well as underground liaison work with the Transvaal burghers. Her two

major works, published in English as well as Dutch, *The Irene Concentration Camp* (1904) and *The Petticoat Commando, or Boer Women in Secret Service* (1913), are exposés of British treatment of Boer prisoners. Early drafts, smuggled out of South Africa, were published in *Review of Reviews*.

Emily Hobhouse (1860–1926), who also came to South Africa at the start of war, kept records of the appalling conditions in the British prisoner-of-war camps, the first of which appeared as *The Brunt of War and Where it Fell* (1902). She also published *War Without Glamour; or, Women's War Experiences Written by Themselves, 1899–1902* (1924), and wrote numerous polemical letters, collected in *Emily Hobhouse: Boer War Letters* (1984). An important part of her liberal pacifist programme was the translation of the diary of a Boer woman, Alie Badenhorst, published as *Tant Alie of the Transvaal: Her Diary, 1880–1902* (1923), annotated and introduced by Hobhouse, with a paean to British politician Lloyd George. Badenhorst's diary is an emotional, personal record, refracted through an intense evangelical Christianity, which documents the nightmarish use of lyddite shells by the British, the wholesale destruction of farms, and the internment of families in concentration camps.

The Anglo–Boer War also enters a number of the popular romances of the early 20th century, Anna Howarth's *Nora Lester* (1902) and ▷ Frances Charlotte Slater's *The Veldt Dwellers* (1912), for example. It functions as a fictional device whereby family and friends are divided from one another, and provides occasion for heroic deaths.

Two British women, Alice Buckton (1867–1944) and Clothilde Graves (1863–1932, the latter publishing under the pseudonym Richard Dehan), also wrote about the war. Though Buckton never visited South Africa, British anxiety about the war was such that she felt able to represent sympathetically the point of view of a Boer woman. Graves's *The Dop Doctor* (1910, published as *One Braver Thing* in the USA), was a bestseller. It was reprinted by Heinemann in 1964.

The treatment of Boers by the British continued to haunt Afrikaners. Sampie de Wet (1906–1984), an Afrikaner who wrote in English, published a fine story called 'The Concentration Camp', part of her *Nine Stories* (1956).

Anglo–Norman
A dialect of French, Anglo-Norman was one of the three languages current in England in the period following the Norman Conquest of 1066 (the others were English and Latin). It was used at court, for administrative matters, and for much literature, especially that associated with courtly and aristocratic circles. Anglo-Norman literature influenced developments in literary taste on the continent. Women played a major role in the production of Anglo-Norman literature through their patronage, and some also wrote in it.
▷ Barking, Anonymous Nun of; Clemence of Barking

Bib: Legge M. Dominica, *Anglo-Norman Literature and its Background* and *Anglo-Norman Letters and Petitions*; Short, I, 'On Bilingualism in Anglo-Norman England', *Romance Philology* 33 (1979–80) pp. 467–79.

Angria

An imaginary kingdom created by British writers Branwell and ▷Charlotte Brontë in 1834, matched by ▷Emily and ▷Anne Brontë's imaginary world, ▷Gondal. The inspiration for Angria and Gondal came from a box of wooden soldiers given to Branwell by his father in 1826. All four children took part in the creation of a narrative that became known as the 'Glass Town Confederacy'. Charlotte and Branwell went on to develop their Angrian tales, while Emily and Anne broke away to create Gondal. Charlotte's Angrian stories of 1837–1839, 'Mina Laury', 'Henry Hastings' and 'Caroline Vernon', anticipate the themes of her mature novels.
Bib: Ratchford, F., *The Brontës' Web of Childhood*.

Aníchkova, Anna Mitrofanovna (1868–1935)

Russian prose writer and critic. After Aníchkova married, she and her husband, the literary critic E.V. Aníchkov, settled in Paris in the late 1890s and early 1900s, where her literary salon was visited by such major French and Russian writers as Anatole France and Viacheslav Ivanov. From 1901 to 1906 she published several novels in French, including *L'ombre de la maison* (1904) (*The Shadow of the House*), which has been translated into English. She was also on the staff of the French periodicals *Revue de Paris*, *Revue Bleu*, and *Figaro*. In 1903 she published *La pensée russe contemporain* (*Contemporary Russian Thought*), a collection of articles on contemporary Russian thinkers.

The Aníchkovs returned to Russia in 1909. In 1910 Aníchkova began publishing short stories and novellas in Russian ▷'thick journals'. She deals primarily with the themes of love and marriage as depicted in terms of psychological and mystical experience. Her fiction received very positive reviews. After the 1917 revolution Aníchkova devoted herself to translation work.
Bib: *The Shadows of the House*, trans. E. Clinton; Polinanov, K., *Russkie pisateli*, Vol. 1.

Anker, Nini Roll (1873–1942)

Norwegian prose writer. ▷Pseudonyms: Jo Nein, Kaare P. Nini Roll Anker was born at Molde into a bourgeois family. Her father was a judge. When she was eighteen, she married the wealthy owner of a large manor. In 1907, the marriage was dissolved, but in 1910, she married a cousin of her previous husband, also a wealthy man.

All her life she lived in very comfortable circumstances while campaigning for the weak and oppressed working-class men and women. She broke through the barriers of class and sex, perhaps as a result of her own security.

Her début, *I blinde* (1898) (*Blindly*) presented a modern, rebellious individual, but she had the first of many successes with the diary-novel *Benedicte Stendal* (1909). Her work – twenty-nine books and many articles and essays – is uneven. The best novels are *Det svake kjøn* (1915) (*The Weaker Sex*), the trilogy *Huset i Søgatan* (1923) (*The House in Lake Street*), *I amtmandsgaarden* (1925) (*In the House of the Prefect*), *Under skraataget* (1927) (*Under the Pitched Roof*) and, especially, *Den som hænger i en Traad* (1935) (*Those Hanging by a Thread*) and the posthumously published *Kvinnan og den svarte fuglen* (1945) (*The Woman and the Blackbird*), also a diary-novel.

Anker was a neo-realist and a pacifist. Under the pseudonym Kaare P. she wrote sparklingly light books for the young. For many years the critics believed that these books were written by a male writer.

Annabella, Queen of Robert III of Scotland (late 14th century)

Scottish queen. Annabella wrote a letter in 1394 (in French), to King Richard II of England, concerning the intended marriage negotiations between the royal families of England and Scotland, and announcing the birth of a son (who was to become James I of England in 1406).
Bib: Moriarty, Catherine, *The Voice of the Middle Ages in Personal Letters 1100–1500*.

Annales galantes de Grèce, Les (1687) (*The Gallant Annals of Greece*) ▷Desjardins, Marie-Catherine Hortense de

Anna von Munzingen (? – after 1327)

South German chronicler. The highborn abbess of the Dominican Convent of Adelhausen, she composed the *Chronik der Mystikerinnen zu Adelshausen* (*Chronicle of the Adelshausen Mystics*) in Latin, of which only a German translation survived. The first chronicle of its kind, it comprises the biographies of thirty-four visionary nuns, and offers a fascinating insight into medieval female mystic experience.
▷*Visionsliteratur*

'Anne' (1892)

US short story by ▷Rebecca Harding Davis. The title character is a middle-aged woman, a widow and mother noted for her social graces and business abilities. Falling asleep, Anne dreams that she is again a beautiful young girl, in love with a promising artist, whom she had in fact rejected as an impractical match. Upon awakening, Anne finds her family uninterested in her dream or her former self, and she leaves on a train journey to a vision of a more cultured life. On the train she encounters and is disgusted by her former artist lover, 'a mere shopman of literature', who saves himself when the train crashes.
Bib: 'Anne', in Davis, Rebecca Harding, *Life in the Iron Mills and Other Stories*, ed. and with a Biographical Interpretation by ▷Tillie Olsen (1985).

Anneke, Mathilde Franziska (1817–1884)

German writer. A feminist, Social Democrat, and member of the anti-slavery campaign, she was also editor of the liberal newspaper, *Neue Kölnische Zeitung* (*New Cologne Times*), which she renamed *Frauen-Zeitung* (*Women's Journal*) to sidestep censorship. After her husband had been arrested during the 1848 Revolution, she fled with her family to the USA, where she met ▷Susan B. Anthony and ▷Elizabeth C. Stanton, and joined the North American women's movement. She had an early literary success with the play, *Oithono* (1842), but is now largely known for her poems and stories published in German and US newspapers. She is particularly noted for the novellas, *Die Sclaven-Auction* (1862) (*The Slave Auction*) and *Gebrochene Ketten* (1864) (*Broken Chains*), which attack slavery, and especially the double yoke borne by women slaves.

Ánnenkova-Bernár, Nina Pavlovna (1859/64–1933)

Pen-name of the Russian actress, prose writer, and dramatists Anna Pavlovna Bernard. She acted in the provinces, Moscow and St Petersburg from 1880 to 1893. Thereafter she devoted most of her time to writing prose fiction and plays. Her writing is marked by social protest and by a concern for defenceless and marginalized characters: children, the poor, elderly women. Her most outstanding work is the play ▷*Daughter of the People* (1903) about Joan of Arc. After 1917 she lived in Orenberg, where she headed a theatre studio.

▷Bashkirtseff, Marie

Anne of Bohemia (1366–1394)

First queen of Richard II of England, and patron. Anne was the eldest daughter of Emperor Charles IV (who founded the University of Prague) and his fourth wife, Elizabeth of Pomerania. Anne was highly educated and we know that she could read the Gospels in three languages: Bohemian (Czech), German and Latin. She married Richard in 1382. On her arrival in England she commissioned a translation of the Gospels into English for her own use, perhaps to help her learn the language. This appears to have been the translation with glosses (explanations from patristic commentaries) by the Wycliffite (follower of John Wycliffe, c 1328–1384, who was branded a heretic when he attacked orthodox Church doctrine) John Purvey (who was Archbishop of York in 1394). The translation of the Scriptures into the vernacular was the subject of controversy at this time; but it appears that permission to possess such translations was often granted to individuals – royalty or members of the nobility. Anne was instrumental, at least indirectly, through her marriage, in the transmission of Wycliffite ideas to Prague and to the reformer John Huss (?1372–1415). Chaucer (c 1340–1400) may have written his *Legend of Good Women* at Anne's request, in order to counteract his depiction of female infidelity in *Troilus and Criseyde*.

Bib: Bell, Susan Groag, 'Medieval Women Book Owners' in Erler, Mary and Kowaleski, Maryanne (eds.), *Women and Power in the Middle Ages*.

Anne of Green Gables (1908)

▷Lucy Maud Montgomery's children's classic about a red-headed orphan who is mistakenly adopted by an elderly brother and sister. Anne ('with an e') Shirley's spirit and feistiness are connected to her red hair, the bane of her existence. Anne's inadvertant scrapes, despite her desire to be good, inform the humour and drama of a story that chronicles not only turn-of-the-century Prince Edward Island, but a small community's pride and prejudice. L.M. Montgomery wrote *Anne of Green Gables* in 1904–1905, but it was rejected five times before it was finally published in Boston in 1908. Since then, it has sold millions of copies in numerous languages, and continues to speak to girls and women about the choices they must make between freedom and acceptance. A girl's version of a ▷*Bildungsroman*, Anne's development focuses on the conflict between imagination and propriety, and concludes with the ascendancy of decorum and practicality, a theme which its seven sequels – in chronological order of Anne's life, *Anne of Avonlea* (1909), *Anne of the Island* (1915), *Anne of Windy Poplars* (1936), *Anne's House of Dreams* (1918), *Anne of Ingleside* (1939), *Rainbow Valley* (1919), and *Rilla of Ingleside* (1921) – continue to develop. Nevertheless, Anne Shirley's flaming hair and rebellious energy have made her an enduring heroine; she is perhaps the best known Canadian literary character of all time. There have been several film, television, and dramatic versions of the novel, and tours of the stage musical across Canada and to New York, London, and Japan.

Annie Allen (1949)

US poetry. ▷Gwendolyn Brooks was awarded a Pulitzer Prize for this collection of poems, in which she examines the intersection of race and gender. It traces an African-American woman's development from childhood to adulthood, and her growing sense of self. Annie matures by adjusting her romantic dreams and aspirations of heroic action to reality, when her socio-economic position as a dark-skinned African-American woman limits her actions and restrains her from fulfilling her dreams; she adjusts her dream to accommodate the reality of marriage and children. Brooks shows how the aspirations of African-American women are limited by an oppressive society and she examines the plight of the African-American urban poor.

Annie John (1985)

The first novel by Caribbean writer ▷Jamaica Kincaid, this developed from a collection of short stories published in the *New Yorker*. It is a semi-▷autobiographical work rooted in her own ▷childhood in St John's, ▷Antigua. Three aspects of West Indian culture form the central construction of this book: the storytelling tradition, the tradition of the ▷*obeah* woman and matrilinear bonding. Drawing upon the storytelling tradition of her family, Kincaid relates the life of the central character, Annie, from the age of ten to the age of seventeen, and uses her experience of growing up to explore questions of autonomy and independence for women.

See Donna Perry's article in ▷*Caribbean Women Writers*.

Another Way (1986)

Translation of the Hungarian novella *Egymásra nézve* (1980), by ▷Erzsébet Galgóczi, who also wrote the screenplay for the film of that title made by Karoly Makk in 1986. The story is set in the aftermath of the events of 1956, among those thinking people who chose not to leave the country after the revolution. It traces the history of a young peasant girl, Eva, who goes from an extremely poor background to become a journalist in Budapest. Her high principles and political integrity have kept her from an official post for years. Eva and her new colleague, Livia, fall in love, but Livia is shot by her jealous husband. Eva then tries to break across the border, knowing that she too will be shot. The book – and the film – begin when a soldier finds her body, realizes he knew her at school and, to satisfy his own curiosity, goes back to trace out her life. The structure of the whole novel is thus rather like a detective story. *Another Way* is a slim novel, but undoubtedly a lesbian classic. However, Galgóczi, who detested gay liberation movements and demanded recognition as a *writer* (not a woman writer or a lesbian writer), would probably have despised such a description.

Anowa (1970)

A play by Ghanaian writer ▷Ama Ata Aidoo, based on the legend of a girl who defied her parents in the choice of a husband, and the price she paid for disobedience. Aidoo uses the legend to comment on the nature of patriarchy and the distorting effects of power, as these affect both women and others who are powerless. Anowa is portrayed as a woman with a marked destiny – an inability to conform, ultimately an inability to bear a child. As she and her husband grow rich through trade, he announces his intention to acquire some 'helpers', that is, slaves. Anowa is resolutely opposed to this, her free spirit being unable to tolerate any form of servitude. She and her husband become increasingly estranged, until he attempts to send her back to her parents. In a frenzy of despair, she accuses him of wanting to get rid of her because he has sold his manhood for wealth and slaves. The tragic outcome is an implicit comment on the price exacted from women for nonconformity.

▷Slavery (West Africa)

Anstei, Ol'ga Nikolaevna (1912–1985)

Russian religious poet. Anstei was born in Kiev. Although she began writing poetry while still a child, she started to publish poetry and prose only after emigrating from the USSR in 1943. Since 1950 Anstei has lived in New York and has published poems, articles, reviews, and stories in the *émigré* press. Separate books of poetry appeared in 1949 and 1976. She has also translated Western poets into Russian.
Bib: Morrison, R.H. (trans.), *America's Russian Poets*.

Antarjanam, Lalitambika (born 1909)

Indian poet and novelist. She was born in the south Indian state of Kerala. She had little formal education, but her family was a literary one, both her parents being poets. She was politically active during the struggle for independence, first with the Indian National Congress and later with the Marxist Party of Kerala. Her political views and commitment to social reform are prominent in her fiction, most of which she writes in her mother tongue, of Malayalam. She has published nine collections of short stories, six volumes of poetry, several books for children and a novel. Her novel, *Agnisaksi* (1976) (*Testimony of Fire*), won the Kerala Sahitya Akademi Award for the best literary work of the year. A short story, 'Revenge Herself', translated from the Malayalam, appears in ▷*The Inner Courtyard*.

Anthologies

Australia: The first anthology of Australian women's writing was *Coo-ee: Tales of Australian Life by Australian Ladies* (1871), edited by Harriette Anne Martin. There have been few, if any, others until their proliferation in the 1970s as a corrective to the perceived marginalization of women's writing, particularly that of the 19th century, in the Australian literary canon. They include *Mother I'm Rooted* (1975), edited by Kate Jennings; *Stories of Her Life* (1979), edited by Sandra Zurbo; *Hecate's Daughter* (1978), edited by Carole Ferrier; *The True Life Story of . . .* (1981) and *Frictions* (1982), both edited by Anna Gibbs and Alison Tilson; *The Half-Open Door* (1982), edited by Patricia Grimshaw and Lynne Strahan; *Her Selection: Writings by Nineteenth-Century Australian Women* (1988) edited by Lynne Spender; ▷*From the Verandah: Stories of Love and Landscape by Nineteenth-Century Australian Women* (1987), edited by Fiona Giles; ▷*The Penguin Anthology of Australian Women's Writing* (1988) edited by ▷Dale Spender; ▷*Eclipsed: Two Centuries of Australian Women's Fiction* (1988), edited by Connie Burns and Margai McNamara; ▷*Eight Voices of the Eighties* (1989), edited by Gillian Whitlock; ▷*The Penguin Book of Australian Women Poets* (1986), edited by Susan Hampton and Kate Llewellyn; *Beyond the Echo: Multicultural Women's Writings* (1988), edited by Sneja Gunew and Jan Mahyuddin; *Moments of Desire: Sex and Sensuality by Australian Feminist Writers* (1989), edited by Susan Hawthorne and Jenny Pausacker; and *Angry Women: An Anthology of Australian Women's Writing* (1989), edited by Di Brown, Heather Ellyard and Barbara Polkinghorn.
New Zealand: Since the huge growth in demand

for writing by women that took place in the 1970s, large numbers of collections or anthologies representing poetry or short fictions by women have appeared, beginning with ▷*Private Gardens* edited by ▷Riemke Ensing in 1977. Short fiction by women appeared in *Women's Work* (1985) edited by Marion McLeod and Lydia Wevers, which was republished as *One Whale Singing Stories from New Zealand* in 1986. This collection was followed by number of others, including a series, *New Women's Fiction*, published annually by the New Women's Press; two collections of Australian and New Zealand writers (*Happy Endings*, 1987 and *Goodbye to Romance*, 1989, both edited by Elizabeth Webby and Lydia Wevers); a historical anthology, *In Deadly Earnest* (1989), edited by Trudie McNaughton; a poetry anthology *Yellow Pencils* (1988) edited by Lydia Wevers, and a new series of story collections based on the British annual anthology of writing by women, *Storia*, called *Speaking with the Sun* (1991), edited by Stephanie Dowrick and Jane Parkin.

Southern Africa: Since the late 19th century, there have been a number of anthologies of South and Southern African poetry. The proportion of women to men ranges from between ten per cent and forty per cent of the total. ▷Ruth Miller stands out as the woman poet to be given most space in these various constructions of literary history. A recent anthology, *Breaking the Silence: A Century of South African Women's Poetry* (1990), edited by Cecily Lockett, strives to repair this imbalance: it includes just over 140 poets. The editor calls them 'the kinds of poems most often overlooked by male anthologists', and takes care to include what she sees as specifically feminine poetry, celebrations of 'their biological motherhood', for instance. The general impression given by other anthologies of South African poetry is that women poets were rare before the 1960s, and neither as interesting nor as distinguished as their male counterparts. To an extent this impression has been dispelled by Lockett's anthology, for it offers nearly fifty poets from the period 1820 to 1960. There are twice as many contemporary poets represented.

In prose fiction, on the other hand, women writers have generally dominated the literary scene. In the companion volume to the poetry anthology, called *Raising the Blinds: A Century of South African Women's Stories* (1990), edited by Annemarié van Niekerk, the orientation is towards redressing racial and class imbalances. The editor also introduces currently emergent voices.

In a variety of other publications the process of feminist historical reconstruction is continuing, especially in the area of black women's writing. The 1980s, in particular, brought a significant number of anthologies of life-histories and interviews, as well as more orthodox genres: *LIP from Southern African Women* (1983); *A Talent For Tomorrow: Life Stories of South African Servants* (1984); *We Make Freedom* (1984); *Vukani Makhosikazi: South African Women Speak* (1985);

Sometimes When It Rains (1987); *Siren Songs* (1989); *One Never Knows: Women Writers in Exile* (1989); *Lives of Courage* (1989); *Women in South Africa: From the Heart* (1988).

In Zimbabwe, after independence in 1980, some important anthologies of interviews were compiled in the wake of the war of liberation: *Black Women in Zimbabwe* (1980), *Zimbabwean Women in Chimurenga* (1981), and *Mothers of the Revolution: The War Experiences of Thirty Zimbabwean Women* (1990). A collection of stories and poems has also appeared: *Young Women in the Liberation Struggle* (1984).

Anthology of Modern Hebrew Poetry (1966) and *Hebrew Short Stories* (1965)

These two anthologies present translated works by the major Hebrew poets and writers, from the turn of the century to the 1950s. Both anthologies follow a chronological order and each writer is introduced by biographical notes, a survey of their writing and a short bibliography. Women writers included are ▷Rachel, ▷Esther Raab, ▷Yocheved Bat-Miriam, ▷Lea Goldberg and ▷Devorah Baron.

Anthony, C.L. ▷Smith, Dorothy Gladys (Dodie)

Anthony, Susan Brownell (1820–1906)
US leader of women's suffrage movement, lecturer and co-editor with ▷Elizabeth Cady Stanton of the multi-volume *History of Woman's Suffrage* (1881–1922). The personification of the struggle for women's rights in the USA, Susan B. Anthony was also active at mid-century in the abolition and temperance movements.

Antigua
This geographical region of the Caribbean is French- and English-speaking. It is the birthplace of ▷Jamaica Kincaid.

Anti-Slavery Reporter
This journal, established by the Anti-Slavery Society to publicize its work and concerns, was first published in 1840. The journal now deals with contemporary forms of slavery, ie bonded labour. The journal originally published ▷*The History of Mary Prince*.

Amtmanders Døtre (1855) (*The Governor's Daughter*)
Regarded as the principal work of the Norwegian prose writer ▷Camilla Collet, the novel, her earliest extensive narrative, was printed anonymously, and started a great public discussion because of its new views on marriage and women's position in Norwegian society. The novel is ▷realistic, socially as well as psychologically. It offers the first picture of Norwegian country life among the official class of prefects and ministers, where women's only hope is to get married. The novel was originally read as propaganda, but today it is read for its minute portrayal of women's

everyday life and love. It is regarded as the first social novel in Norway, and is a forerunner of the central themes of the Norwegian ▷modern breakthrough. In this respect, Collett's ally is the Danish ▷Thomasine Gyllembourg, who also wrote realist prose about the new everyday life, with women at the centre. But where Gyllembourg was moderate in her criticism, and idealized woman as wife and mother, Collett was, in her own time, read as a radical critic of marriage as the only possibility for women from the patrician families in Scandinavia.

Antremont, Marie-Henriette-Anne Payan Delestang, Marquise d' (1746–1802)

French poet. Born in Dresden, Antremont was the niece of the scholar ▷Madame Dacier. She was a contributor to the ▷*Journal des Dames* (*The Women's Journal*), where some of her poetry, later collected in *Poésies de Mme la marquise d'Antremont* (1770) (*Poems of Mme la Marquise d'Antremont*), was first published.

Anyte (4th century BC)

Poet, from Tegèa in southern Greece. The contemporary poet Meleager includes her in his list of famous women poets, with ▷Praxilla, ▷Moero and ▷Sappho. He styled her the 'female Homer'. Twenty-four poems survive in the *Greek Anthology* of ▷epigrams, of which some twenty-one or twenty-two are probably genuine. The extent of her literary remains is thus second only to that of Sappho. Twelve poems are pseudo-epic epitaphs for pet animals. They were probably not composed to commemorate, but as a literary genre, of which some see her as the origin. Her pastoral epigrams were written before the time of the famous Greek pastoral poet Theocritus, whom she may have influenced. Seven epigrams are literary pieces, in the style of tombstone inscriptions. Four concern the deaths of young girls or women. Three other epitaph epigrams discuss male heroism and the commonplace that 'death is for all' regardless of social status.

Her poems are marked by a neat variety of tone and theme. The pathos of dead pet animals is sometimes increased by a focus upon the owner. In one, a young girl, Myro, mourns her dead pet grasshopper and cicada. The poem is technically subtle, as it uses epic language to describe such un-epic material. Two male imitators' works on similar themes are less skilful. Such imitation of her work confirms her importance. The epigrammatists Callimachus and Nicias may have used as one of their models a poem of Anyte's celebrating the dedication of a spear to the gods.

Her influence on later pastoral poetry is perhaps her most important contribution to literary history. Anyte's poems evoke the landscape of shadows, fountains and goatherds later developed by Theocritus and Virgil.
▷Muses; Parthenis
Bib: (text & trans.) Paton, W.R., *Greek Anthology*.

Anzaldúa, Gloria E.

US poet and fiction writer. A Chicano and lesbian-feminist, Anzaldúa writes about the history, politics, myth and experience of the fragmented and devalued identities forced on Chicano immigrants by US racism. 'This is my home / this thin edge of barbwire' she says in *Borderlands / La Frontera*, which uses the national border and the barriers, crossings and refusals it imposes to explore issues of migrancy, cultural and sexual identity. The book mixes poetry, autobiography and history. To achieve this, Anzaldúa interleaves Castillian Spanish, North Mexican dialect, Tex-Mex and Nahuatl with English to make the point that: 'Until I am free to write bilingually and to switch codes without having always to translate . . . and so long as I have to accommodate the English speakers rather than having them accommodate me, my tongue will be illegitimate.'

Anzaldúa is politically active on a number of fronts: as a writer, a university teacher in Chicano and feminist studies, within the migrant farm workers' movement, and as an editor. She was co-editor of the influential anthology ▷*This Bridge Called My Back: Writings by Radical Women of Color* (1981) in which she wrote a powerful essay about the relationship of writing and her body for a woman of color. Since 1984 she has been contributing editor for the feminist journal *Sinister Wisdom*.

Her work has appeared in *Third Woman*, *Cuentos: Stories by Latinas*, *Labyris*, *IKON*, *Bilingual Review* and *Conditions*.

Aoki Yayohi (born 1927)

Japanese critic. An ecologist and feminist, she takes the view, after cross-cultural research on women, gender and sexuality, that the problems of contemporary women's issues have been caused by modern civilization, and that women and their reproductive role will only regain respect in society when men and women are living together on an equal basis. Her main books are *Woman, Gender and Mythology* and *A Culture of Sexual Difference*.

Aouchal, Leila (born 1937)

French-Algerian novelist. She comes originally from Caen in France, but became an Algerian citizen following her marriage to an Algerian immigrant. Her novel ▷*Une autre vie* (1978) (*Another Life*) is an autobiography in three parts.

Apart from the Great World (1857)

Novel by Russian poet ▷Iuliia Zhádovskaia. Zhádovskaia's leisurely novel is an episodic ▷*Bildungsroman* in which many aspects of her own life can be recognized. Genichka, a quick-witted, self-possessed girl, recounts her years from twelve to seventeen, during which she moves back and forth between the small estate of the strict but good-hearted aunt who has raised her and the rigidly managed home of a rich aunt in the nearest city. Three men contribute to her education: a neighbour's likeable young tutor; the demonic Tarkhanov who tutors her in Russian and French – and would like to include sex in the curriculum; and Daurov, whose contribution to her sentimental education ends disastrously. Zhádovskaia creates effective genre scenes – a fair; a monastery; the rollicking family of Genichka's cousins. The rhythm of the seasons and the moods of nature inform Genichka's narrative, as they did her creator's poetry.

Aphra Behn (1849)
A novel by the 19th–century German novelist ▷Luise Mühlbach. Written in the idiom of the German ▷*Bildungsroman*, it is a rather fanciful, fictionalized account of the life of the eponymous 17th–century British dramatist (▷Aphra Behn). The young Aphra is abducted to Surinam, where she falls in love with the black slave Oronooko. Once back in London, she leaves her husband and embarks on a successful literary career. Although the novel is over-dramatic and lacks structure and control, it is none the less interesting on two counts: as an early example of a German novel about a white woman in love with a black man, and for its exploration of a woman's total emancipation.

Apologia pro Ecclesia Anglicanae (1589)
▷*Apologie or answeare in defence of the Churche of England concerning the state of religion used in the same*

Apologie or answeare in defence of the Churche of England concerning the state of religion used in the same (1564)
▷Anne Cooke Bacon's translation of Bishop John Jewell's *Apologia pro Ecclesia Anglicanae* (1562). Jewell's *Apologia* was a key document in the establishment and justification of a unified English Church. As such, its rendition into English was an important task. One inaccurate and poorly translated edition had already appeared before Bacon sought to publish hers. In 1564 Jewell and the Archbishop of Canterbury approved Bacon's version, granting her permission to publish her work. A fine example of the art of Renaissance translation, Bacon's *Apologie* is concise, accurate, and fluent. Jewell's use of her translation in his continuing debate with anti-Anglican parties attests to the significance of Bacon's work to the Protestant Reformation in England.
Bib: Booty, J.E., *An Apology of the Church of England*.

Appachana, Anjana
Indian short story writer. She was educated in Delhi, and now lives in the USA where, with her husband, she teaches at Arizona State University. Several of her short stories, which first appeared in journals in India and the USA, have been published together in *Incantations* (1991). This collection includes 'Her Mother' which won the O. Henry Festival Prize. Her stories, which often have a gentle irony about them, commonly focus on the choices besetting young middle-class Indian women, who may have been educated in the aspirations of the West but are not always free to take up its challenges. In 1991 Appachana was working on her first novel.

Appel des arènes L' (1982) (Call of the Ring)
The third novel by Senegalese writer ▷Aminata Sow Fall. Nalla, the twelve-year-old son of parents who have forsaken traditional culture for the false lures of modernity and the nuclear family, announces that he want to become a wrestler. Professional wrestling, with its accompaniment of drumming and its popular appeal, symbolizes traditional culture in Senegal. It represents the boy's rejection of his parents' sterile Westernized middle-class aspirations, in favour of the vitality of poetry and myth and the mutual interdependence of a community with shared beliefs.

Appleton's Journal (1869–1881)
US New York weekly periodical to 1876, monthly thereafter. It published topical non-fiction and illustrated fiction by US writers including ▷Constance Fenimore Woolson and ▷Rebecca Harding Davis.

Apréleva, Elena Ivanovna (1846–1923)
A Russian writer of prose fiction and ethnic sketches, Apréleva (pseudonym: E. Ardov) was the child of a Greek mother and a French father, a geodesist in the Russian army, and grew up in a cultivated St Petersburg home. She began writing works for children in the early 1870s and then, with Turgenev's encouragement, turned to adult fiction. Her first story, 'Apollon Markovich' (1877), portrayed a Dostoevskian 'eternal husband' willing to undergo any humiliation to be near the woman he loves. The novel *Guilty But Guiltless* (1877) dealt with what Apréleva described as a 'new topic in Russian literature': rape as the extreme manifestation of a husband's violations of his wife's personal integrity. Her typically aphoristic short stories, most of which also feature mismatched couples and unhappy liaisons, were reprinted under the title *Quick Sketches* in 1893. In *Rufina Kazdoeva* (1884) her heroine is disillusioned by life in a short-lived commune like those that sprang up in the 1860s. Critics were impatient with her tendency to let extraneous description interrupt her plots; her eye for detail informs her sketches of life in Ukraine and the Crimea, and in Central Asia where she lived with her husband from 1890. She died in Belgrade.
▷*What Is To Be Done?*

Arabian Nights, The or A Thousand and One Nights (Alf Layla wa Layla)
Famous collection of Arabic oral tales, originally narrated in coffee houses and gatherings of every kind all over the Arab world. The tales were first brought to the West by a French diplomat at the beginning of the 18th century, when Antoine

Galland, Secretary to the French Embassy in Constantinople, first heard them in Aleppo. He obtained a handwritten copy and translated it in Paris with the help of a Maronite interpreter called Hanna. The French translation (1704) was immediately translated into English and other European languages, and started the whole movement of 'orientalism' in European literature. Galland had taken great liberties with the Arabic text, modifying his material to suit European taste, which was probably the reason for its popularity. Later, more scholarly and literal translations do not make such fascinating reading for the layperson. The frame tale of *The Arabian Nights* particularly struck European readers; of ancient Indian and Persian origin, it is embroidered with strange details from the Arab oral tradition.

Two brother kings, shocked at the adultery of their respective wives, leave home to wander in disgust and despair. Before long, they meet with a sobering adventure: a giant comes out of the water carrying his human wife in a locked box, which he keeps under the sea. He brings her out and has a little nap; she soon manages to cuckold him with both kings, whom she sees hiding up a tree, and shows them a hundred rings she acquired during previous adventures. The two brothers return home, and the older, more powerful king, Shahriar, wreaks vengeance on womankind by taking a virgin bride every evening and putting her to the sword in the morning. When there are no more virgins left in the city, because those who have escaped the king's sword have been whisked away by their families, the *wazir's* (minister's) daughter, Shahrazad, volunteers to be the king's bride. She takes her younger sister with her, who waits in the bridal chamber and asks Shahrazad to tell them all a story. Shahrazad tells stories for a thousand and one nights, taking care to start on a new one before dawn breaks. She holds the king spellbound with her stories, and so escapes execution.

The tales told by Shahrazad were tales of wonder, magic and adventure but also of homely everyday life in Arab Moslem countries in the Middle Ages. The figure of Harun Al-Rashid, with his rich capital Baghdad and its port of Basra, his *wazir* Ja'far al-Barmaki (the Barmicide), his wife Zubeida and his profligate poet, Abu Nuwas, figure prominently in many of the stories. The stories of *The Arabian Nights*, from 'Aladdin' to 'Sinbad' and 'Ali Baba', have become part of the consciousness of readers and listeners everywhere in the world. Arabic printed editions, based on the Egyptian version of the *Nights*, were first issued in the 19th century. *The Arabian Nights* was frowned upon by classical scholars and religious people, because of its sexual explicitness and lack of inhibition, typical of oral tradition. The book was kept away from 'young persons'. According to Taha Hussain (1889–1973), the Dean of Arabic Literature, if a copy was found in a house it was considered an omen of *kharab* (disaster). The loose structure and the vulgar colloquial language of the narrative, which once

disqualified it as literature, have now been adopted by women writers trying to find a new discourse, and other writers experimenting with methods of narration in Arabic.

The character of Shahrazad has long intrigued male writers, who have interpreted her as a symbol representing freedom or art, or as an enigma of mysterious womanhood. Feminists have reclaimed her as a female archetype, constantly having to employ her wits in her dealings with the patriarchal/childish figure of her king/husband. In the original frame tale of *The Arabian Nights*, Shahrazad presents Shahriar with three sons she has borne him in the thousand and one days: one just walking, one crawling and one still at the breast! She begs the king to spare her life that she might bring up his children, and he 'pardons' her, declaring that he had intended to do so even before seeing the babies. She accomplishes this reprieve through her virtue and chastity, but above all, her skill as a storyteller.

Aracoeli (1982)

The protagonist-narrator of this novel by Italian writer ▷Elsa Morante is Emanuele, who goes to Andalusia (his mother's birthplace) in an attempt to recreate his past. This is a piece which, like much of Morante's work, highlights the importance of memory. It operates a shifting time scale, full of vivid flashbacks to the narrator's childhood, in which his relationship with his mother is of central importance. The tragic tale of the mother's loss of her baby daughter, her ultimate descent into prostitution, and the gap in Emanuele's relationship with both mother and father all appear to contribute to his homosexuality, which is judged negatively. This is, above all, a novel which draws attention to how each of us is isolated and to the virtual impossibility of making real connections with others.

Aragona, D'Tullia (1510–1556)

Italian poet. In many ways, she was a typical ▷'*cortegiana onesta*' of the period. As an educated and talented courtesan, she appears to have been admired, as well as loved, by many writers of her time. She travelled considerably as a young woman, spending time in Rome, Siena, Florence and Ferrara as well as Venice. In 1543 she married, thus protecting herself from the rigorous laws against courtesans. Her ▷Petrarchan *Rime* (*Rhymes*) of 1547 is her most famous work. In this she presents herself in a feminine, self-deprecating and virtuous guise. Interestingly, she functions as both poet (subject) and lady (object) of discourse in her writing. She fights against the stereotype of the courtesan, and is an anti-establishment figure in her sonnet addressed to Bernardino Ochino (a strict friar) whom she rebukes for banning dancing and music on the grounds that it constitutes an infringement of free will. Her lively and humorous *Dialogo dell'infinità di amore* (*Dialogue on the Infinity of Love*) was published in 1552. Her *Meschino altramente detto il*

Guerrino (*Meschino,Otherwise Known as Guerrino*) was published posthumously in 1560.

Araz, Nezihe (born 1922)

Turkish educationalist, editor, and writer of children's books and religious poetry. She graduated from the University of Ankara in 1946 with a degree in psychology and philosophy, and started writing for conservative pro-Islamic newspapers. Her poetry advocates a philosophic tolerance and piety derived from the teachings of Jalal-al-Din al-Rumi (known as '*Mawlana*' to his disciples): 'The way of Mevlana is the way of love, the way of humanity, the way of affection. Mevlana perceived Islam as a ray of morality and love . . .', she wrote.

Her poems were collected as *My World* (1950) and *Wretched Treadmill* (1961). She also wrote a play: *Ode to the Steppes* (1974), and religious historical works, starting with *The Spiritual History of Sultan Muhammed the Conqueror* (conqueror of Constantinople) (1953); *Muhummed, Prophet of Prophets* (1960); *The Tale of Jelaleddin Rumi* (1962) and *Grandchildren of the Prophet* (1969). She was one of the chief editors of the Turkish language edition of *Larousse Encyclopaedia* and of several volumes of the Turkish *Turkiye* (1923–1973).

Arboleda de los enfermos (c 1450) (*The Grove of the Sick*)

An allegorical work by the medieval Spanish writer ▷Teresa de Cartagena. It is typical of the late medieval period, both in its allegorical use of an ideal landscape, and in its theme, which is the spiritual benefits of illness. The imagery used in this work is rich and varied.

Arcadian poetry (Italy)

The academy (*accademia*) of Arcadia was founded in Rome in 1690 by a group of writers, some of whom had formed part of the Roman 'court-in-exile' of Queen Christina of Sweden. Features of Arcadian poetry included an attempt to achieve a pastoral simplicity, the use of pseudonyms which emphasized this pastoral inspiration, and a reaction to what was seen by the Arcadians as the affectations of earlier poetry. Women poets contributed a considerable body of poetry in this genre. ▷Petronilla Paolini Massimi and ▷Faustina Maratti Zappi are perhaps its best-known women exponents.

Arcadismo

Literary movement introduced into Portugal in 1756, with the founding of the *Arcádia Lusitana*. Reacting against the excesses of the Baroque, *arcadistas* looked to the classics for inspiration. Primarily a poetic movement, *arcadismo* is associated with the theme of *locus amoenus*, whereby nature is seen as a pastoral and serene emblem of civilized values.

▷Alcipe; Alorna, Marquesa de

Arceo, Liwayway (born 1924)

Filipino novelist and short story writer. She was a pioneer of modernism in Tagalog literature, and an early feminist writer, who started writing in her teens and is still productive. To date she has written some fifty novels and 900 short stories, most of them published in the popular Tagalog weekly, *Liwayway*. As its literary editor for many years, she was a major influence in the training and development of many young writers in Tagalog. She also wrote a long-running serial drama for radio, *Ilaw ng Tahanan* (*Light of the Home*), which highlighted the woman's role in holding a home together. She has been described recently as 'a feminist long before the word became fashionable. She wrote of women who worked, women who took care of their families when their husbands left them – or when they left their husbands – and women who stayed married not because of security, but always . . . out of love.'

Archambault, Mademoiselle (c1724–?)

French essayist. Born in Laval, where her father was a collector of taxes. Well-known as a feminist, she published an essay in support of '*la cause des dames*' (*the cause of women*): *Dissertation sur la question*: *lequel de l'homme ou de la femme est plus capable de constance?*' (1750) ('Essay on the Question: Are Men or Women More Loyal?). A second essay', '*La femme peut-elle aller de pair avec l'homme tant par la force que par la solidité d'esprit?*' ('Can Women be as equal to Men in Strength and Intellectual Ability?'), remains in manuscript form in the Bibliothèque de Laval.

Archer, Maria (1905–?)

Portuguese novelist, short story writer, essayist and dramatist. Archer is rarely mentioned in literary histories and anthologies despite her impressive output, which included novels, short fiction, essays and plays. Several of her books were openly critical of the Salazar regime; her novel *Casa Sem Pão* (1946) (*House Without Bread*) was banned by the censors, as was her study *Os Últimos Dias do Fascismo Português* (1961) (*The Last Days of Portuguese Fascism*), which was published in Brazil. Among her best works are the short stories in *Ida e Volta duma Caixa de Cigarros* (1938) (Round Trip of a Cigarette Box); *Há de Haver uma Lei* (1949) (*There Ought to be a Law*) and *Filosofia duma Mulher Moderna* (*Philosophy of a Modern Woman*). An important theme in these and other works by Archer is the difficulties women face in an authoritarian society.

Arderiu, Clementina (born 1899)

A Spanish poet. Born in Barcelona, Arderiu studied languages. Her main works are: *Cançons i elegies* (1916) (*Songs and Elegies*); *L'Alta llibertat* (1920) (*Lofty Liberty*); *Cant i paraules* (1936) (*Song and Words*); *Sempre i ara* (1946) (*Always and Now*); and *Es a dir* (1958) (*That is to Say*). Her work often echoes popular verse schemes, themes and imagery. She married the famous Catalan poet, Carles Riba, in 1916.

Ardov, E. ▷Apéleva, Elena

Arendt, Hannah (1906–1975)
German political philosopher. Born in Hanover into an old Jewish family from Königsberg, she studied philosophy, theology and Greek in Marburg, Freiburg and Heidelberg, met the existentialist philosopher Karl Jaspers (1883–1969) and had an affair with Martin Heidegger (1889–1976), whose ideas were a lasting influence. In 1929 she published her doctoral thesis on St Augustine's concept of love. Briefly arrested by the Nazis in 1933, she moved to Paris, where she worked with Jewish refugees. In 1940 she married the art historian Heinrich Blücher and also completed her first book, *Lebensgeschichte einer deutschen Jüdin aus der Romantik* (1958) (*The Life of a German Jewish Woman in the Romantic Period*), a biography of ▷Rahel Varnhagen. After the Occupation, Arendt and Blücher escaped to New York, where she wrote on *Aufbau* (*Construction*), the German emigré paper. She established herself as an important political thinker with *The Origins of Totalitarianism* (1951) and *The Human Condition* (1958), penetrating analyses of the historical roots of 20th-century fascist ideology. In 1959 she became the first woman professor at Princeton University. After attending the Eichmann trial in 1961 she published *Eichmann in Jerusalem. A Report on the Banality of Evil* (1963), arguing that Adolf Eichmann was but one banal cog in a mechanism of culpability in which even Jews were implicated. The book was violently criticized and lost her many friends. Ever ready to apply philosophical thought to current events, she first welcomed, then deplored the revolutions of the 1960s, voicing her ideas in *On Revolution* (1963) and *On Violence* (1970). Her last, most personal and reflective book, *The Life of the Mind*, was published posthumously in 1978.

Arete (5th–4th century BC)
Athenian philosopher. Educated by her father, the Greek philosopher Aristippus, she herself educated her own son, also called Aristippus. As a result the younger Aristippus was nicknamed 'Mother-Taught'. There survives one letter to Arete from her father, commending her general moderation. This extant fragment may be spurious, but the letter is mentioned by the philosophical biographer Diogenes Laertius (2nd century AD) in the list of Aristippus's works.
▷Philosophers, ancient Greek and Roman women

Are You There God? It's Me, Margaret (1970)
US novel. Considered sexually offensive and amoral by some, ▷Judy Blume's novel focuses on a girl becoming a woman. Margaret begins to menstruate and to worry about boys, and she questions her sense of identity, wondering if anyone knows the real her. She grapples also with her feelings about religion. Blume articulates a cultural concern with feelings about the self and the body.

Ariel (1965)
Poems by US writer ▷Sylvia Plath. *Ariel* brings together Plath's later poems written before her suicide in 1963. Edited and selected by her husband, the poet Ted Hughes (born 1930) after Plath's death, as critic Jacqueline Rose points out in *The Haunting of Sylvia Plath*, these poems unavoidably present a partial picture of Plath's last work. Indeed, the poems themselves stitch together partial pieces of female subjectivity with fragments from history. Poems such as 'Tulips' and 'Death & Co.' tell of the 'hooks' that snare the narrator to her life as wife and mother from the position of her invalid's bed, revealing a tension between the trappings of femininity and a deathly psychic subtext. Other poems connect personal suffering to wider political and historical themes. The 'dissolving selves' of 'Fever 103°', for example, insert the question of identity into the historical text of Hiroshima. Most famously, the poems 'Lady Lazarus' and 'Daddy' ('Every woman adores a fascist . . .') explore the links between suicide and paternity with Nazi ideology and the victims of the Holocaust, thereby rendering the link between the 'personal and the political' uncompromisingly inescapable.

Aristodama
Poet, from Smyrna. No work survives, but there remains an inscription honouring her with citizenship of Lamia in Thessaly because she praised their ancestors in her poetry.

Aritzeta, Margarida (born 1953)
Spanish novelist. Aritzeta was born in Vals, and read history and philology at university. She has participated in a radio arts programme and taught at the Escola Universitaria in Tarragona. Her first novel, *Quan la pedra es torna fang a les mans* (1981) (*When Stone Turns to Mud in One's Hand*), was awarded the Victor Català Prize. *Un febrer a la pell* (1983) (*February Under the Skin*), which won the San Jordi prize, portrays a man's unexplained disappearance, set against the background of the attempted coup in the Cortes on 23 February 1981. *Vermell de cadmi* (1984) (*Cadmium Red*) blends fantasy with ▷realism and reflects the politics of the day, complete with misinformation, blunders and cover-ups.
▷Catalan women's writing

Ariyoshi Sawako (1931–1984)
Japanese novelist. She started her career as a writer when she was a university student, and in 1956 she won the Bungaku Prize for a New Writer for *Ballad*, which depicts people performing classical arts such as *shamisen*. Afterwards she published such works as *River Ki* in which she describes the lives of women from

her birthplace, Kishu. Towards the end of her life, she took social problems as her subject. She deals with racism in ▷*Coloured People*, environmental problems in *Complex Pollution* and the problem of ageing in *The Twilight Years*. Her works also involve dramas: for instance, in *Doctor's Wife* she describes the rivalry between a doctor, his wife and his mother in the 19th century.

Ark, The (1982)

Novella by ▷Zhang Jie, generally considered the first genuinely feminist piece of writing of contemporary China.

Instead of a linear narrative, *The Ark* describes the lives of three women, all in their early forties, in a series of illuminating scenes which revolves around the central theme of 'how hard it is to be a woman.' Cao Jinghua, divorced for having an abortion, is an intellectual now under attack for 'overstepping the bounds' in her writing. She eventually gets off without a penalty, thanks to the kindly intervention of the elderly Party secretary. The price – rumours about their special 'relationship'.

Liang, a film director, is the daughter of a party VIP. She is estranged from her husband, who refuses to give her a divorce as he needs to exploit her family prestige. Her film, on which she has worked for years, fails the censor's test – the breasts of the leading actress are 'too prominent'. Her husband, too, contributes to her failure, by spreading rumours about her.

Liu Quan, a hardworking divorcee with an excellent command of English, slaves away at a menial office job because of her family background. Every day she has to go through humiliating scenes with her boss, who talks to her lewdly, with his fly open. Liu finally lands a job at the foreign affairs department where her skills can be put to use. Her victory is only achieved through Liang's influence.

At the end the three women drink to a better generation of men, personified in Liu Quan's little son, Monmon.
Bib: Hallet, Stephen (trans.), *The Ark* in Zhang Jie, *Love Must Not Be Forgotten*.

Arky Types (1987)

Novel by ▷Sara Maitland and ▷Michelene Wandor. Epistolary in form, the novel plays with the tradition of this genre, coventionally regarded as a 'feminine' form. *Arky Types* consists of letters, fictional or actual, written by and about women, letters about Maitland, Wandor, feminism, writing, publishing and creative identity.
Concerned with the process of writing fiction and with shifting and changing textualized identities, the novel makes these issues explicit in details of contributors, where the authors provide several entries on themselves and others, with differing information.

Armários Vazios, Os (1966) (The Empty Cupboards)

A novel written by the Portuguese ▷Maria Judite de Carvalho (born 1921), *Os Armários Vazios* is about a Portuguese widow, Dora, who works in an antiques shop to provide for herself and her daughter. The book portrays Dora's conflicts with her domineering mother-in-law; her troubled relationship with her rebellious teenage daughter; her painful memories of her husband, who was unfaithful; and her unsuccessful romance with an untrustworthy man who ultimately marries her daughter. The book is told from two points of view: an unidentified speaker begins the story in the first person, but her account is mingled with that of a third-person narrator. Like ▷Fernanda Botelho's (born 1926) ▷*Xerazade e os Outros* (1964), *Os Armários Vazios* is an implicit indictment of the Salazar regime, whose policies towards married women were particularly repressive.

Armentières, Péronnelle d' (c 1340–?)

French poet. She fell in love with the poet Guillaume de Machaut (c 1300–1377) in his old age. *Voir dit* (*Seeing Said*) is a collection of their letters and poems, but Péronnelle's are not particularly distinctive.
Bib: Wilwerth, E., *Visages de la littérature féminine.*

Armour, Rebecca Agatha (1846–1891)

Canadian novelist, born at Fredericton, New Brunswick. She wrote many local sketches of area 'landmarks'. Her four novels are primarily of historical interest. Fredericton society as it was between 1824 and 1829 is depicted in *Lady Rosamund's Secret* (1878), and *Marguerite Verne; or, Scenes from Canadian Life* (1886) describes St John, New Brunswick.

Armstrong, Jeannette

Canadian children's writer and novelist, grand-niece of Hum-Ishu-Ma (▷Mourning Dove, 1888–1936), considered the first Native American woman novelist. Armstrong grew up near Penticton, British Columbia, and was educated at Okanagan College and the University of Victoria. Her children's books are *Enwhisteetkwa: Walk on Water* (1982) and *Neekna and Chemai* (1984). *Slash* (1985) is a novel about a young native man involved in the struggle for aboriginal rights. In 1989 she became director of ▷En'owkin School of International Writing in the Okanagan, British Columbia.
Bib: Godard, B. in ▷*A Mazing Space*; Lutz, H., *Contemporary Challenges: Conversations with Canadian Native Authors.*

Arnaud, Angélique (1799–1884)

French novelist. Arnaud went to Paris from the provinces in 1830 because she was attracted by ▷Saint-Simonian feminism, devoted herself to campaigning for sexual equality, wrote articles and polemical pamphlets, and published the novels *La Comtesse de Sergy* (1838) (*The Countess of Sergy*) and *Clémence* (1841). Two others, *Une tendre dévote* (1874) (*A Pious Lady in Love*) and *La Cousine Adèle* (1879) (*Cousin Adèle*) eventually followed, as did a critical study of Del Sarte.

Arnauld, Mère Agnès (1593–1671)

French author of numerous letters. She was a prominent member of the leading ▷Jansenist family, which was inextricably linked with the abbey of Port-Royal and the struggles of this austere and persecuted Catholic sect. The sister of Arnauld d'Andilly (1588–1674) the lawyer who restored the abbey, and Antoine, 'le Grand Arnauld' (1612–1694), and a close friend of the philosopher Blaise Pascal (1623–1662), she remained in many ways in the shadow of her elder sister ▷Mère Jacqueline Marie Angélique Arnauld. Mère Agnès was abbess of Port-Royal from 1636 to 1642 and again from 1658 to 1661. She refused to sign an official condemnation of Jansenism in 1661 and was imprisoned in the Convent of the Visitation from 1663 to 1665. She continued the correspondence with Marie-Louise de Gonzague-Clèves (1611–1667), later Queen of Poland, which Mère Angélique had begun, but her letters were not thought important enough for every one to be kept and copied before being sent. Although her writing has a fine sense of irony, much of the interest of her letters comes from the people to whom they are addressed: ▷Jacqueline Pascal, ▷Madame de Sablé and the Chevalier de Sévigné, ▷Madame de Sévigné's uncle.

Arnauld, Mère Jacqueline Marie Angélique (1591–1661)

French writer of letters, known as Mère Angélique, and elder sister of ▷Mère Agnès Arnauld. A member of the great ▷Jansenist family, whose history is interwoven with the abbey of Port-Royal, she was abbess of Port-Royal from 1602, reformed the abbey in 1609 and founded the institute of Saint-Sacrement. She introduced Jansenism to Port-Royal by appointing the Abbé de Saint-Cyran (1581–1643) as the nuns' spiritual director. She corresponded, among others, with the Queen of Poland. A *dossier de sainte* (hagiology) was prepared during her lifetime, and, apparently without her knowledge, everything she wrote and said was eagerly copied down and kept.

Arnim, Bettina von (1785–1859)

German romantic writer, granddaughter of ▷Sophie La Roche, and sister of the poet Clemens Brentano (1778–1842). After her marriage in 1811 to the poet Achim von Arnim (1781–1831), with whom she had seven children, she continued to live her independent lifestyle, often leaving their country estate to spend time in Berlin, where she thrived on meeting famous writers and artists. After Arnim's death in 1831 she moved permanently to Berlin, took up writing, and vigorously argued the case for democracy and the rights of women.

In her forties, von Arnim began to develop her own semi-fictional, narrative mode. Drawing on authentic letters she composed epistolary novels around her relationships with important people. These included: *Goethes Briefwechsel mit einem Kinde* (1835) (▷*Goethe's Correspondence with a Child*); *Die Günderrode* (1840), based on her friendship with ▷Karoline von Günderrode, and *Clemens Brentanos Frühlingskranz* (1844) (*Clemens Brentano's Springtime Garland*). At the same time she became increasingly socially and politically active. She gathered documentary material for a book about the poor (*Das Armenbuch, The Book of the Poor*, which was not published until 1969) and composed a public text, addressed to the Prussian king, ▷*Dies Buch gehört dem König!* (1843) (*This Book belongs to the King!*). It exhorted him to become 'the people's king' by helping the poor. When her pleas remained unheeded she expressed her disappointment in the sequel, *Gespräche mit Dämonen* (1852) (*Conversations with Demons*).

▷Salon culture

Arnothy, Christine (born 1930)

French novelist. Born in Budapest, Hungary, Arnothy moved to Paris, where she published two very successful autobiographical novels describing her experiences during World War II: *J'ai quinze ans et je ne veux pas mourir* (1954) (translated as *I am Fifteen and I Don't Want to Die*, 1956) and *Il n'est pas si facile de vivre* (1957) (translated as *It is Not so Easy to Live*, 1958). Since then she has produced a bestseller almost annually, usually conforming to the conventions of romance or melodrama.

Arnow, Harriette Simpson (1908–1986)

US novelist and prose writer. Arnow was born into a strict religious family in rural Kentucky and she graduated with a Bachelor of Science degree from the University of Louisville in 1930. Following family tradition, she taught school. In 1934 she scandalized her family by moving to Cincinnati to write stories. She worked for Roosevelt's Federal Writers' Project. Upon marrying in 1939 she farmed in rural Kentucky. In 1944 she moved to Detroit, Michigan. *Mountain Path* (1936), *Hunter's Horn* (1949) and ▷*The Dollmaker* (1954) focus on the confrontation between the individual conscience and socio-economic forces. Arnow's characters struggle to make choices based on their deepest instincts and values, and her work rescues Kentuckians from their literary stereotype as lazy, ignorant and violent.

Other works include: *Seedtime on the Cumberland* (1960), *Flowering of the Cumberland* (1963), *Old Burnside* (1977) and *The Weed Killer's Daughter* (1970).

Bib: Eckley, Wilton, *Harriette Arnow*.

Aron, Geraldine (born 1941)

South African dramatist and short story writer. Born in Galway, Ireland, she came to South Africa in 1965 and lived in Cape Town. Her works have recently been collected in *Seven Plays and Four Monologues* (1985), the first of which, *Bar and Ger* (1975), traces the relationship between a sister and her younger brother as it develops from their childhood to the brother's premature death. In some of her later plays Aron shifts to marriage, focusing on issues of gender and class. Her work has been widely performed in South Africa, with much of it also travelling abroad: *Bar and Ger*, for instance, won *Variety*'s 'Ten Best' award at the Edinburgh Festival in 1979. *Seven Plays and Four Monologues* also contains (in order of their first performance) *Mr McConkey's Suitcase* (1977), *Mickey Kannis Caught My Eye* (1978), *A Galway Girl* (1979), *Joggers* (1979), *The Spare Room* (1981), and *Spider* (1985); the monologues are: 'The Shrinking of Alby Chapman', and three entitled 'On the Blue Train', with different narrators: Kathy, Constantia Gable, and Joe Harris. Her other plays are: *Same Old Moon, The Guest Room, Why Strelitzias Cannot Fly* (1982) (for children), and *Zombie*, along with *The Final Sting of the Dying Wasp* (1979), which she co-authored.

Arquimbau, Rosa Maria (born 1910)

Spanish novelist. Born in Barcelona, Arquimbau has also written under the pseudonym ▷Rosa de Sant Jordi. As a journalist she collaborated on several leftist periodicals during the Second Republic. Exiled after the war, she experienced difficulty publishing her work in Catalan.

The protagonists in her novels are usually women, seen outside the family or domestic setting. *Historia d'una noia i vint braçalets* (1934) (*Story of a Girl and Twenty Bracelets*) is a novel about a girl sent to study in Barcelona. *Home i dona* (1936) (*Man and Woman*) retraces a woman's efforts to live her own life following separation from her husband. An example of her more recent fiction is *40 anys perduts* (1971) (*Forty Years Lost*), a novel about a dressmaker suddenly catapulted to fame.

▷Catalan women's writing

Arranged marriage

A practice common in southern Asia, whereby a person's parents arrange his or her marriage with a view to ensuring religious, economic, educational and physical compatability between the couple to be wed and between their families.

Artamène, ou le Grand Cyrus (1649–1653)

▷*Artamenes, or The Grand Cyrus*

Artamenes, or The Grand Cyrus (1653–1655)

Translation in five volumes of the French novel in ten volumes, *Artamène, ou le Grand Cyrus* (1649–1653), by ▷Madeleine de Scudéry. One of the most successful *romans à clé* to be published in early modern France, this epic novel has, like its sister novel *Clélie* (▷*Clelia*), been much maligned by critics ever since. In recent years, its importance in the evolution of the historical novel has become increasingly appreciated, as it was a major influence on the work of such novelists as ▷Madame de Lafayette. In a misguided attempt to imitate the epic in order to raise the status of fiction, mid-17th-century salon society is transposed to Persia in the 6th century BC, with scant regard for the resultant anachronisms. The novel begins in the middle of the action, with the abduction of the heroine, Mandane, during the destruction of Sinope. The hero, who at first tries to pass incognito under the pseudonym Artamène, has then to pursue his mistress from country to country across Asia Minor as she is kept beyond his reach by a succession of jealous rivals. In retrieving his bride at the end of the novel, Cyrus discovers that he has also unwittingly conquered an empire. By far the most extensive part of the narrative is, however, devoted to secondary stories loosely intercalated into the main plot, as Cyrus and Mandane continue on their travels, meeting innumerable lovesick characters, whose servants or friends proceed to tell of their past adventures. The novel thus gives ample illustration of every kind of passion, providing endless material for group analysis of the psychology of love, both within the narrative and among 17th-century readers. Another of the attractions of this novel for a contemporary audience was its portrayal of recognisable figures in pseudo-historical disguise. Cyrus represents the Prince de Condé (1621–1686) and the first volumes reflect and seem even to anticipate the events of the civil wars known as the *Frondes* (1648–1653). Later volumes include, among other society portraits, a flattering image of the Marquise de Rambouillet (1588–1665).

Artemisia (1947)

A biographical novel by Italian writer ▷Anna Banti, based on the life of Artemisia Gentileschi (1597–1651), the painter, in which the author has an ongoing dialogue with her heroine. Banti declares herself attracted to the figure of Gentileschi because of the latter's desire for creative, constructive work, and because she recognises the ability of this painter who also happened to be a woman. For Banti, Gentileschi appears to function as a mythical female figure who embodies the dilemma of the woman artist.

Artificial Silk Girl, The (1933)

Translation of *Das kunstseidene Mädchen* (1932), a novel by the German writer ▷Irmgard Keun. Set in Berlin during the Depression of the 1930s, it is the story of a young office worker from a lower middle-class family who dreams of becoming a star. At first she seems to be achieving what she wants, until her impulsive theft of a fur coat forces her to go underground, and she has to face the realities of life as an outlaw in the metropolis. Written in the form of an interior monologue, the book accurately captures the idiom and atmosphere of its time, and offers a penetrating analysis of the pernicious influence of cinematic glamour on ordinary young women.

Arturo's Island (1959)

Translation of *L'isola di Arturo* (1957), a novel by Italian writer ▷Elsa Morante, which tells the story of Arturo through his memories of the past. The island referred to in the title is Procida, near Naples. Arturo's mother died when he was born, and he was brought up largely by a friend of his father. Arturo adored his father, whom he saw relatively infrequently, because of his long trips away from the island. His apparently idyllic childhood is shattered when his father, Wilhelm, marries another woman, Nunziata, and brings her to the island. Arturo feels driven to make sexual advances towards her (perhaps because of his sense of betrayal by his father, perhaps in an attempt to relate to a 'mother' figure), which she rebuffs. Ultimately, Arturo leaves the island, disillusioned about life in general, as well as about his adored father, whom he now knows is homosexual. Homosexuality carries negative connotations here, as is the case in ▷*Aracoeli*. Memory, and its constructions, are important in this novel, as in much of Morante's writing, and the child-parent relationship, another favourite theme, is also scrutinized.

Arvelo Larriva, Enriqueta (1886–1963)

Venezuelan poet. She was a sister of the poet Alfredo Arvelo Larriva. A self-taught woman, she lived most of her life in her native village, which inspired deeply lyrical poetry. She was one of the most representative figures of the 1918 Generation, and later belonged to both the 1938 'transit poetry' group and the 1940s ▷*Viernes* Group. In *El cristal nervioso* (1931) (*The Narrow Mirror*) and *Poemas perseverantes* (1963) (*Persistent Poems*) she was concerned with the liberation of women, but the elegiac poems of *Mandato del canto* (1957) (*Mandate of the Song*) were intended to be more universal, rather than specifically feminine.

Asbaje y Ramirez de Santillana, Juana de

▷Juana de Asbaje y Ramirez de Santillana

Ascham, Margaret Howe (?1535–1590)

English letter-writer. After the death of her husband, Roger, in 1568, she took upon her the task of having his educational tract, *The Scholemaster* published in 1570. She composed the brief letter which prefaced the 1570 edition, dedicating her husband's work to William Cecil. *The Scholemaster* became a key text in the development of humanist education in England.
▷Letters (English Renaissance); Humanism (England)

Ashbridge, Elizabeth (1713–1755)

North American spiritual autobiographer. She was born in England in 1713 and came to North America some time before 1752, when she settled in Pennsylvania. Her remarkable text, ▷*Some Account of the Fore Part of the Life of Elizabeth Ashbridge*, is an outstanding example of a Quaker woman's spiritual autobiographical narrative. It follows the details of her early life, her decision to come to North America, her period as an indentured servant, and her integration into the Quaker community in Pennsylvania, where she gained recognition among the leaders of the Society of Friends. Her pursuit of 'Truth's service' took her around the world. She died in Ireland on 16 May 1755.

▷Early North American Quaker women's writings

Ashford, 'Daisy' (Margaret Mary Julia) (1881–1972)

British writer. Born in Petersham, Surrey, and educated primarily at home, Ashford is known today for her comic tale *The Young Visiters, or, Mister Salteena's Plan*, which she wrote at the age of nine. The manuscript was unearthed in 1919 and sent to Chatto and Windus, who published it with an introduction by J.M. Barrie in the same year. It became a great success, enjoyed for its erratic spelling and its humorous observations of social mores.

Ashton, Winifred ▷Dane, Clemence

Ashton-Warner, Sylvia Constance (1908–1984)

New Zealand novelist. One of eight children, Sylvia Ashton-Warner spent her childhood at a number of small country schools where her mother, Margaret, taught. Ashton-Warner's father, Francis, was an invalid and the family, whose poverty Ashton-Warner described in her autobiography, was dependent on the mother's income. Ashton-Warner also trained as a teacher in Auckland 1928–9, and with her husband, Keith Henderson, taught in several country schools with largely Maori populations, an experience she records in her first book ▷*Spinster* (1958). Ashton-Warner was an innovative teacher who became famous for her unorthodox method of teaching Maori children to read by using a 'key' vocabulary. She also wrote a number of Maori primer books but received little recognition within New Zealand for her work.

It was Ashton-Warner's experiences in the Native School Service that began her writing career. She submitted stories to the New Zealand *Listener* from the late 1940s on and published *Spinster* in 1958, a book hailed at the time as the best ever written in New Zealand. *Spinster* focuses on the questions of educational theory and racial understanding which preoccupied Ashton-Warner's teaching, and became a bestseller in the US. Three novels and two autobiographical books followed *Spinster*, and Ashton-Warner became an internationally-known writer. She spent time living and working overseas, especially in North America, partly as a result of the hostile reception she felt both her writing and educational work received in New Zealand, which she described in *Spinster* and *Teacher*. Ashton-Warner had a complex personality, and her self-representation in her novels and autobiography has generated great interest in her, both personally and as a writer and teacher, and her work has come to suggest some of the gender difficulties experienced by women of her generation.

Other works include: *Incense to Idols* (1960); *Teacher* (autobiography) (1963); *Bell Call* (1964); *Greenstone* (1966); *Myself* (autobiography) (1967); *Three* (1970); *Spearpoint* (1972); *O Children of the*

World (1974); *I Passed This Way* (autobiography) (1979); *Stories from the River* (1986).
Bib: Lynley Hood, *Sylvia! A Biography of Sylvia Ashton-Warner.*

'Ashur, Radwa (born 1946)

Egyptian novelist, critic and university teacher, trained at the University of Cairo and in the USA. Her first full-length work was a study of the novels of the Palestinian Ghasan Kanafani (1977), followed by a study of the West African novel (1980). Having published short stories in Arabic periodicals since her student days, in 1985 she published her first novel, *A Warm Stone*. The stone of the title is the pedestal of the statue 'Egypt Awakening', which stands at one end of University Avenue, which depicts an Egyptian *fallaha* (peasant woman) standing looking out over the Nile, her hand resting on the head of the Sphinx. It is still warm in the evening with the stored heat from the sun when Bushra, one of the major characters of the novel, sits and leans her back against it and falls asleep. She is one of the 'new women' in the novel: daughter, mother, loving wife, breadwinner, graduate student and almost a single parent. Her husband is in and out of prison all the time, accused of being a communist and a troublemaker. She, with the help of her mother, brings up their child, holds a job as a teacher and occasionally makes the long journey to his village in Upper Egypt to comfort *his* mother.

Radwa 'Ashur's recent novel *Khadiga and Sawsan* (1989) is more condensed, though it is narrated in two voices. The voice of the mother, Khadiga, is more convincing than that of the daughter, Sawsan, trying to break away from the mother's authority and run her life along lines never included in Khadiga's plans for her children. A woman of exceptional talent herself, she had wanted to become a doctor, but was made to leave school and marry a man much older than herself. She devotes her tremendous energy to running his home and bringing up three children, and later to organizing and running his private hospital. Her strong character and arrogant obstinancy run to destruction when it comes to her children's lives. In 1983 Radwa 'Ashur published *al-Rihla (The Voyage: Days of an Egyptian Female Student in America)*, an interesting contribution to the 'passage-to-the-West' tradition in Arabic literature, to which women's contributions are rare. A collection of her short stories was published as *I Saw the Palm Trees* (1990). A translation of two of the stories is published in Marilyn Booth's ▷*My Grandmother's Cactus: Stories by Egyptian Women* (1991).

Asian-American writing

Asian-American is a term encompassing those who have emigrated to the US from East and South Asia, and their descendants.

The two largest groups are the Japanese and the Chinese. Asian-Americans have lived in the US since 1785, although substantial immigration did not begin until the mid-19th century. Chinese men came to the West coast to work on the Central Pacific Railroad. Japanese immigrants followed from 1869, with the largest influx between 1890 and 1924; many settled in Hawaii where there were fewer restrictions on immigration. Japanese women frequently came over as 'picture-brides', as a result of arranged marriages. After the completion of the railroad the Chinese worked as miners, laundrymen, cooks and servants, while the Japanese were primarily farm labourers. Since World War II the communist revolution in China and the role of the US in South-East Asia and the Korean and Vietnam wars, has generated further immigration and an increasing diversity of peoples.

The immigrants met with a hostile reception as far back as the 1880s, partly as a result of fears about the effect of their cheap labour on Anglo-American employment. The conditions at Angel Island, the West coast reception point for immigrants, were inhuman; articles and cartoons appeared in US newspapers of the period promoting racist stereotypes such as Fu Manchu, and restrictive laws were passed making it impossible for immigrants to become US citizens or to own land. An Exclusion Act, which was only repealed in 1943, made it impossible for Chinese women to join their husbands legally.

During World War II Asian-Americans were shocked by the government response to the Japanese bombing of Pearl Harbour. Thousands of Japanese-Americans, *Nikkei*, were interned, highlighting their true status in many Anglo-American eyes as 'enemy aliens': ▷Mitsuye Yamada's writing addresses this experience. Another Japanese woman, Monica Sone, wrote about her feelings in *Nisei Daughter* (1953) as a 'despised, pathetic, two-headed freak, a Japanese and an American, neither of which seemed to do me any good'. This sense of alienation from both Japanese and American cultural identities is typical of much post-war writing from all Asian-American groups. For women this alienation was intensified by the clash between the greater range of opportunities open to them in US society, and the constraining expectations of their families, communities and traditions. The Chinese-American writer, ▷Jade Snow Wong, in ▷*Fifth Chinese Daughter*, published at the end of World War II, is representative in emphasizing the divisions between herself and her first-generation immigrant parents in a society which had promised incorporation and fulfilment.

Recent women writers such as ▷Maxine Hong Kinston, ▷Amy Tan and ▷Nellie Wong shatter the myths and stereotypes of Asian women as submissive, sexually available and domestic. This generation rejects the status of victim, and affirms itself through the figure of the woman warrior. Their engagement with the issues of cultural identity, tradition and assimilation addresses the potential loss of heritage, and also the sexism and abuse of women in their mother culture.

Philippino writer ▷Jessica Hagedorn criticizes the materialist values of US society, while ▷Shirley Geok-Lim's work attacks female infanticide and the sexual exploitation of Asian women. The mapping of an Asian-American history now being erased by the dominant Anglo-American culture is an important aspect of this work, as in ▷Cathy Song's poetry. This rewriting of history includes attention to the role of the mother-daughter relationship in the transmission of their cultural heritage; and the mother becomes part of a feminist myth of origins. Kingston, Tan and Geok-Lim, among others, explore the conflicts of this relationship, but also depict their mothers as courageous fighters who empower their daughters to tell their own stories.

Other writers include: ▷Diana Chang, ▷Ruthanne lum McCunn, ▷Hisaye Yamamoto, ▷Bharati Mukherjee and the critic ▷Gayatri Chakravorty Spivak.

Askew (Kyme), Anne (1521–1546)
English autobiographer and poet. She received a good education, was particularly well-read in scriptures, and often discussed religious doctrine with priests. Askew was forced to marry Thomas Kyme when her older sister, who had been betrothed to him, died before the marriage could take place. Her marriage to Kyme, an uneducated and staunchly Catholic landowner, proved an ill match. As Askew's conversion to Protestantism became decisive, her readiness to argue interpretive points with clergy increased. At some time before 1544, Kyme threw her out of their home because she 'offended the priests'. In 1544 she unsuccessfully petitioned for divorce on the basis of I Corinthians 7:15. She also seems to have been living in London, and was connected with ▷Catherine Parr's court during this time.

In 1545 Askew was first examined for heresy concerning the sacrament; because of inadequate evidence she was released. The following year she was arrested, examined, and then released once again, only to be arrested for a third and final time. During her final imprisonment Askew was brought to the Tower of London and severely tortured. This was extremely unusual because gentlewomen and those already condemned to die were rarely tortured during this period. Askew's torture and the number of questions she was asked regarding Protestant women at court suggest that her ordeal was part of a larger plot to obtain evidence against more powerful Reformist women at court, possibly including the queen, Catherine Parr.

While in prison, Askew managed to write an account of the final years of her life. In 1546 she was burned to death along with three other Protestants. Her body had been so badly crippled by torture that she had to be carried to the place of execution and then chained upright to the stake.

Her autobiography was printed in two parts: ▷*The First Examynacyon of Anne Askewe* (1546) and ▷*The Lattre Examynacyon of Anne Askewe*

(1547) along with ▷'The Balade whych Anne Askewe Made and Sange whan she was in Newgate'.

▷Companionate Marriage; Confession of faith; *Monument of Matrones, The*; Protestant Reformation.
Bib: Beilin, E.V., *Redeeming Eve: Women Writers of the English Renaissance*; Travitsky, B., *The Paradise of Women: Writings by Englishwomen of the Renaissance*.

Aspasia (5th century BC)
Philosopher, born in Miletus, who later lived in Athens. Biographical anecdotes abound concerning her life as a courtesan before she lived with the great Athenian statesman Pericles, to whom she bore a son. Contemporary Athenian comic drama satirized her in the guise of various mythical tyrannical women. Plato (4th century BC) in his *Menexenus* claims that she in fact wrote the Funeral Speech, read at the ceremony for some war dead, for which Pericles was most famous. This is highly unlikely. Many sources paint her unsympathetically because of political hostility to Pericles. In several references, writers say she offered advice to women on marriage and ▷household management. Although we have no evidence she wrote anything, she nevertheless inspired later writers to see her as a rare female intellectual at Athens.

▷Philosophers, ancient Greek and Roman women

Assembléia Literária, A (1849–1851) (The Literary Assembly)
The Literary Assembly was the first magazine written primarily by women about women's issues. A progressive publication, founded and edited by the Portugese writer ▷Antónia Gertrudes Pusich, it was especially concerned with education and social reform. *A Assembléia Literária* also contained articles on literature, the arts and religion, and it published three novels in serial form.

'Assembly of Ladies, The' (15th century)
The sex of the author of this English 'Chaucerian' poem has been debated; the author presents herself as a woman (see also ▷'The Floure and the Leafe'). The poem is a vindication, cast in the form of a dream vision – that most popular poetic form of the Middle Ages – of the truth and loyalty of women. It thus forms part of the late medieval debate about women:

▷Christine de Pisan
Bib: Pearsall, Derek, (ed.), *The Floure and the Leafe and The Assembly of Ladies*; Barratt, Alexandra, *Philological Quarterly* (1987) pp. 1–24.

Assimilation (West Africa)
The French imperial project, unlike the British, was characterized by the philosophy of *la mission civilatrice*, with its roots in the French 18th-century philosophy of civilization. The essence of French civilization was thought to reside in

language, and the speaking of French has always been of primary importance in French relations with its vassal states. It offered colonized people one advantage: if you were educated in the French system and spoke perfect French, you *were* French – you became a black French person. This achievement was attainable, however, only by a carefully selected elite. The price they were expected to pay was the sloughing off of African identity, to be born anew as something else. The policy of assimilation has permitted France to maintain a relationship of almost symbiotic closeness with its ex-colonies since independence, to the extent that a cheque written today in Dakar can be cashed tomorrow in Paris.

Assing, Ottilie (1819–1884)

German writer and feminist. She emigrated to the United States at the age of thirty-three, and worked in New York as a reporter for the German newspaper *Morgenblatt* (*Morning Paper*). She wrote vivid descriptions of the US way of life, argued against slavery, and took a keen interest in the US women's suffrage movement. Some of her essays were republished in 1885 as part of an anthology, *Was die Deutschen aus Amerika berichten, 1828–1865* (*What Germans Report Back from America, 1828–1865*).

Association pour le droit des femmes

The most enduring of the women's rights groups formed in the 1860s and 1870s in France. Involved in it were, among others, the socialist feminist writers ▷Maria Deraismes, ▷André Léo and ▷Louise Michel. The group was linked with the feminist weekly *Le Droit des femmes* (*The Rights of Women*), launched in 1869 by a man, Léon Richer. Other groups which came into being in the later decades of the 19th century were the Ligue francaise pour le droit des femmes (French League for the Rights of Women) (also founded by Richer, in 1882), the Union universelle des femmes (1889) (Universal Union of Women) and the Fédération française des sociétés féministes (1891) (French Federation of Feminist Societies). During this period, in contrast to the 1830s, French women's rights organizations were run by bourgeois feminists. A number of feminist conferences and congresses also took place in the 1880s and 1890s, including the Congrès français et international du droit des femmes (June 1889) (French and International Congress of Women's Rights), which was organized by Deraismes.

Astell, Mary (1666–1731)

English polemicist, poet, social theorist and defender of women. An Anglican and Tory, Astell was born in Newcastle upon Tyne, but came to London in her twenties, and lived for much of the time in Chelsea. In 1693 she began a correspondence with the Cambridge Platonist, John Norris, and these letters were published in 1695, dedicated to Lady Catherine Jones, who became her friend. But her first publication was ▷*A Serious Proposal to the Ladies* (1697), in which she advocates 'Religious Retirement': the setting up of religious (Anglican) and educational communities of women, who could stay as long as they wanted, and within which they would be engaged in religious observance, and learning languages and other skills. Her vision seems to have incorporated furnishing the minds of the well-to-do residents with 'a stock of solid and useful Knowledge', *Some Reflections Upon Marriage, Occasion'd by the Duke and Duchess of Magazine's Case* (1700) was published anonymously, addressing the miseries of marriage to 'an absolute Lord and Master, whose follies all her Prudence cannot hide, and whose Commands she cannot but despise', Astell produces a searing critique of the powerlessness of women within marriage, and her contemporaries found her a trenchant defender of women. She later wrote against the toleration of Dissenters (writing against novelist Daniel Defoe, 1660–1731, and others), and wrote vindicating the conduct of Charles I. She was a friend of ▷Lady Mary Wortley Montagu.

Other publications: *Letters Concerning the Love of God* (1695); *Moderation Truly Stated* (1704); *A Fair way with the Dissenters* (1704); *An Impartial Enquiry into the Causes of Rebellion and Civil War in this Kingdom* (1704), and *Bartlemy Fair or an Enquiry after Wit* (1709).

▷Ladies of Llangollen, The; Makin, Bathsua; *Millenium Hall*; Scott, Sarah; Macaulay, Catherine
Bib: Hill, Bridget (ed.), *The First English Feminist*; Perry, Ruth, *The Celebrated Mary Astell*.

As the Sorcerer Said (1982)

Translation by Dorothy Blair of the novel by the Caribbean writer Myriam Warner-Vieyra, *Le Quimboiseur l'avait dit* (1980). Written while in hospital, Zétou's confession recalls her mother's return visit to the village of Cocotier six years after having left with Roger, a white man. Drawn by the attraction of Paris and eager to pursue her schooling, Zétou returns with her mother and Roger to France, but is first taken by her grandmother to the *quimboiseur* (sorcerer). In France, she becomes the servant of her mother and Roger, who plan to marry Zétou to an elderly business acquaintance. To force Zétou's co-operation, Roger seduces her. Zétou's attack on her mother on discovering her conspiracy is interpreted as madness by the police and judge; Zétou is sent to hospital. Like Warner-Vieyra's second novel, ▷*Juletane*, this confession describes the social pressures and personal betrayals which induce in a fictional woman a state described as madness or hysteria (▷*folie Antillaise*).

Astley, Thea (born 1925)

Australian novelist. Astley is a social satirist of subtlety and power, with a considerable international following. Her finely-tuned novels and short stories focus upon the darker side of Australian society – small-town prejudice, institutionalized violence, racism and sexism. Her favourite setting is tropical Queensland or, in *A*

Boatload of Home Folk (1968) and ▷*Beachmasters* (1985), a tropical island. Other novels are *Girl with a Monkey* (1958), *A Descant for Gossips* (1960), *The Well Dressed Explorer* (1962), *The Slow Natives* (1965), *The Acolyte* (1972), *A Kindness Cup* (1974), *An Item from the Late News* (1982), *It's Raining in Mango* (1987) and *Reaching Tin River* (1990). ▷*Hunting the Wild Pineapple* (1979) is a collection of short stories. Astley's plots usually place a vulnerable individual in an enclosed environment where human weakness, cruelty and hypocrisy can develop without hindrance and where Astley can demonstrate her fine perception of social and political power-play. Her novels are usually experimental in form and structure and her language is striking and original. She has won the Miles Franklin Award three times as well as other prestigious Australian literary awards.
▷The Aborigine in Australian women's writing; Short story (Autralia); *Coming out from Under; Eight Voices of the Eighties*

Aston, Louise (1814–1871)
German writer, revolutionary and feminist. Twice she married and divorced the English industrialist Samuel Aston, twenty-three years her senior. Her first novel, *Aus dem Leben einer Frau* (1847) (*From a Woman's Life*) is an account of this relationship. An active feminist, she modelled herself on ▷George Sand, and in 1846 expounded her views in the pamphlet, *Meine Emanzipation* (*My Emancipation*). Her novel, *Revolution und Conter-Revolution* (1849) (*Revolution and Counter-revolution*), describes the events of 1848 from the point of view of a revolutionary woman. In 1850 she married a doctor who, five years later, lost his job because of his wife's continued political activies.

Astraea ▷Behn, Aphra

Astragal (1967)
Translation of *L'Astragale* (1965), novel by French writer ▷Albertine Sarrazin. Sarrazin's story of a young woman learning independence and love during a period of escape from prison is set against the seedy background of the 'alternative' society seen from the inside, and is a near-autobiography.

Atencia, María Victoria (born 1931)
Spanish poet. Her works rail against the limitations imposed on female identity, and use images drawn from domesticity to express that spiritual entrapment. One of her aims is to find a new language to express female experience. Her works include: *Los sueños* (1976) (*Dreams*); *Marta y María* (1976); *El mundo de MV* (1976) (*MV's World*); *Paseo de la Farola* (1978) (*Lighthouse Walk*); *Venezia Serenissima* (1978); *El coleccionista* (1979) (*The Collector*); *Paulina. El libro de las aguas* (1984) (*Pauline. The Book of Waters*), and *De la llama que arde* (1988) (*The Burning Flame*).

Atherton, Gertrude (1857–1948)
US novelist. She was especially notable for novels focused on California and the American west. Atherton began writing as a widow, after a twelve-year marriage, and never stopped writing until she died. She developed the concept and character of a distinctive western American heroine, who represents a re-vision not only of the roles of women and the relations between the sexes but also of civilization itself and the roles of nature and nurture.
Since she was fond of shaking up literary, social and regional conventions – and published dozens of books over a fifty-year career – Atherton's work is difficult to place in the traditional US literary categories of romanticism, realism, etc. Definitely centred on regional effects by her interests in nature and culture, she was as likely to focus on psychological realism as romantic plot. Among her 19th-century publications are: *Los Cerritos, A Romance of the Modern Time* (1890); *The Doomswoman* (1893); *Before the Gringo Came* (1894); *Patience Sparhawk and Her Times* (1897); *American Wives and English Husbands* (1898); *The Californians* (1898).

Atkinson, Louisa (1834–1872)
Australian novelist. Atkinson was the first Australian-born woman novelist. She was also a naturalist and botanist who illustrated her own work. She married at the age of thirty-six and died two years later, three weeks after the birth of her daughter. Four serials were published in the *Sydney Mail* and the *Sydney Morning Herald* between 1861 and 1872. Her three published novels ▷*Gertrude the Emigrant: A Tale of Colonial Life* (1857), *Cowanda, the Veteran's Grant* (1859) and *Tom Hellicar's Children* (first published in book form in 1983) deal with life in the Australian bush and on the Turon goldfields.
▷*On Her Selection; Peaceful Army, The*

Atlantic Monthly, The (1857–present)
US Boston-based magazine devoted to North American literature, culture and politics. Founded by the period's establishment literary figures to promote the anti-slavery cause and the fortunes of US authors, it was edited by James Russell Lowell (1857–1861), James T. Fields (1861–1871), William Dean Howells (1871–1881) and Thomas Bailey Aldrich (1881–1890). In the early years the *Atlantic* was often accused of a New England provincialism and upper-class bias, but it was recognized as the most prestigious US literary journal. Under Lowell and Fields, relatively few innovative women writers were published, but ▷Harriet Beecher Stowe and ▷Julia Ward Howe were represented. Under Howells, the *Atlantic* welcomed, promoted and fairly reviewed writing from all regions, realism, and a range of the best women writers of the era.
▷Davis, Rebecca Harding; *Authors and Friends;* Chesebro', Caroline; Spofford, Harriet Elizabeth Prescott; *Galaxy, The*; Murfree, Mary Noailles; Thaxter, Celia Laighton

Atlantis: A Women's Studies Journal (1975–present)

Canadian feminist journal for different aspects of women's studies, although it has contributed a great deal to literary studies. Its focus is broad, covering not only literature but art, social patterns, history, and cultural configurations. Published in Halifax, Nova Scotia, its original co-ordinating editor was ▷Donna Smyth.

Atlas Shrugged (1957)

US novel. This book established ▷Ayn Rand's reputation as an intellectual cult figure. It depicts the US government as becoming increasingly socialist, and one which will violate individual rights and human reason in protecting the public good. The male protagonist claims that it is irrational to sacrifice the self for the good of society. He creates a capitalist utopia – Galt's Gulch – which promotes free enterprise without government controls. Rand's novel argues for the virtue of rational selfishness.

At Middle Age (1980)

Novella by Chinese writer of short fiction, ▷Shen Rong. *At Middle Age* was published in Chinese in 1980, and won a national prize. It has been made into a popular film. Told in a series of flashbacks as the heroine drifts in and out of a coma after a heart attack, *At Middle Age* recounts the ordeal of an ophthalmologist, Dr Lu Wenting, representative of the hard-driven professional classes of contemporary China.

Dr Lu must perform three operations in a single morning. First, on a child who is frightened and must be reassured. Second, on an old peasant who has been waiting for a cornea transplant and cannot afford another delay. Last, but not least, on a vice-minister of the government whose cataract operation has to be interrupted for an imaginary cough. Pressure has been building up for the doctor ever since the vice-minister appeared with his wife Qin Bo, who asked impertinent questions to check the doctor's qualifications. Added to the family burdens of a sick baby daughter and a son clamouring for attention, it is more than the doctor can bear and she collapses after the operation. As she rises painfully from her sickbed to work again, her best friend – an old classmate and long-time colleague – leaves for Canada.

One of the most important works of the post-Mao era, *At Middle Age* describes the pitiable situation of the intellectuals in China through the plight of a woman, thus combining a call for the restoration of human values with a deep concern for women's issues. The introduction of the ▷stream-of-consciousness technique, innovative at the time, opened a way to portray a woman's inner being.

Bib: Decker, Margaret (trans.), *At Middle Age*; Link, Perry (ed.), *Roses and Thorns*.

Atossa (6th century BC)

Letter collector. Queen of Persia, daughter of King Cyrus, wife of Kings Cambyses and Darius, and mother of King Xerxes, Atossa was perhaps the most famous Persian woman for classical Athenians. The historian Hellanicus (6th century BC), whose works are preserved in the Christian writer Tatian (2nd century AD), records that she was the first to make a collection of letters.

'Attar, Samar (born 1940)

Syrian poet, novelist and university teacher. She was born in Damascus, where she graduated from the university, and later obtained a PhD from the University of New York at Binghamton. During her student days in Damascus she worked for radio, and was a regular contributor to Syrian and Beirut periodicals. She has taught Arabic and English at universities in Algeria, Germany and the USA, and now lives and teaches in Sydney, Australia. Living in two worlds, Samar 'Attar writes poetry in Arabic, which she often translates into English, and it translates well. It can be easily related to English poetry and to the ▷New Movement in modern Arabic poetry. Her novels are about Damascus, now seen through the consciousness of someone steeped in western European culture. *Lena, Portrait of a Girl of Damascus* (1982) is modelled on James Joyce's *Portrait of the Artist as a Young Man* (1916). The flight of the heroine from a decaying city torn by internal strife to the freedom of the alien is presented in almost the same words as the flight of Stephen Dedalus. In 1988 the author went back to Damascus for ▷*The House on Arnus Square*.

Bib: (trans.) Yates, J. Michael (ed.), *Volvox: Poetry from the Unofficial Languages of Canada*; MacEwan, Gwendolyn, *The Armies of the Moon*; Boullata, Kamal (ed.), *Women of the Fertile Crescent*; Cosmah, Carol, Keefe, Joan and Weaver, Kathleen (eds), *The Penguin Book of Women Poets*; Badran, Margot and Cooke, Miriam (eds), *Opening the Gates: A Century of Arab Feminist Writing* contains a translation of chapters from *The House on Arnus Square*.

At the Bottom of the River (1983)

This is a collection of ten short stories and sketches by the Caribbean writer ▷Jamaica Kincaid, originally published in the *New Yorker* and the *Paris Review*. Densely poetic, they provide a collage of images and impressions of her island experience. The sequence culminates in the key stories 'My Mother' and 'At the Bottom of the River', which explore the experience of growing up in ▷Antigua, and are concerned with intense▷ mother–daughter relationships. They form the basis for her novel ▷*Annie John*.

See Louis James's article in *Wasifiri*, No. 9, Winter 1988/1989, and Helen P. Timothy's article in ▷*Caribbean Women Writers*.

Atwood, Margaret Eleanor (born 1939)

Novelist, poet, short story writer, critic, and editor, Atwood is Canada's most important contemporary writer, without peer in range and international stature. She was born in Ottawa, the

Margaret Atwood

second of three children. Until the age of twelve she spent most of her summers in the Quebec and Ontario bush. In 1946 her family moved to Toronto, where Atwood attended high school (1952–1957), and studied Honours English (with Northrop Frye and ▷Jay Macpherson) at the University of Toronto (1957–1961). Her first collection of poetry, *Double Persephone*, a privately printed chapbook, won the E.J. Pratt medal in 1961. She won a Woodrow Wilson Fellowship, and became a graduate student at Radcliffe College, Harvard University, receiving her MA in 1962. She began to read for a Ph.D. at Harvard, but interrupted her studies to work for a market-research company in Toronto and to teach English at the University of British Columbia in Vancouver (1964–1965), where she wrote the first draft of ▷*The Edible Woman* (1969). In 1966 she published *The Circle Game*, which received the Governor General's Award for Poetry. *The Animals in that Country* appeared in 1968; with ▷*The Journals of Susanna Moodie* and *Procedures for Underground* (both 1970), and *Power Politics* (1971), Atwood established herself as a profoundly important poet. The publication in 1972 of both ▷*Surfacing* and ▷*Survival: A Thematic Guide to Canadian Literature* consolidated her significance as a novelist and critic.

She continued to publish prolifically. *You are Happy* (poetry) appeared in 1974, and ▷*Lady Oracle* and *Selected Poems* appeared in 1976, the same year that her daughter, Jess, was born. *Dancing Girls* (short stories) and *Days of the Rebels: 1815–1840* (history) were published in 1977, *Two-Headed Poems* (poetry) in 1978. The novels ▷*Life Before Man* (1979), ▷*Bodily Harm* (1981), ▷*The Handmaid's Tale* (1985) and ▷*Cat's Eye* (1988) brought Atwood international fame, but she nevertheless continued her diverse activities, publishing poetry – *True Stories* (1981), *Interlunar* (1984) and *Selected Poems II* (1986) – and short stories, *Bluebeard's Egg* (1983) and *Wilderness Tips* (1991), as well as the prose poems of *Murder in the Dark* (1983). She has published two children's books: *Up in a Tree* (1978), and *Anna's Pet* (1980).

Her work as an editor has been a major influence on Canadian literature. In 1982 she edited *The New Oxford Book of Canadian Verse in English*, and in 1986 *The Oxford Book of Canadian Short Stories in English*, but was criticized for including too many women in the former; Atwood is an unapologetic force in the re-evaluation of the Canadian ▷canon. She also edited *The CanLit Foodbook* (an alternative cookbook, 1987), and published her own critical writings in *Second Words: Selected Critical Prose* (1982). She is politically active in PEN and in Amnesty International; she works tirelessly as an activist and a speaker for social justice. *Surfacing* and *The Handmaid's Tale* have been made into films. The influence of Atwood's work on contemporary writing by women is indisputable. She articulates the various experiences of women and of girls in powerfully moving ways that function also as acerbic and telling social criticism. She has a deadly stylistic capacity for skewering the most essential point of language; at the same time, her writing can convey a haunting tenderness for which she is seldom given credit.

Atwood has won the Governor General's Award twice (1966 and 1986); the Welsh Arts Council International Writer's Prize (1982); the Los Angeles Times Prize for Fiction (1986), and has been several times short-listed for the Booker Prize. Her work is continually scrutinized, discussed, and taught as a barometer of feminist thought.

Bib: Brownstein, R.M., *Becoming a Heroine: Reading about Women in Novels*; Christ, C., *Diving Deep and Surfacing: Women Writers on Spiritual Quest*; Davey, F., *Margaret Atwood: A Feminist Poetics*; Davidson, A.E. and C.N. (eds), *The Art of Margaret Atwood: Essays in criticism*; Grace, S.,*Violent Duality: A study of Margaret Atwood*; Grace, S. and Weir, L. (eds.), *Margaret Atwood: Language, Text and System*; Howells, C., *Private and Fictional Words*; Rigney, B.H., in *Madness and Sexual Politics in the Feminist Novel: Studies in Brontë, Woolf, Lessing and Atwood*; Rosenberg, J., *Margaret Atwood*; Sandler, L. *The Malahat Review*, 41 (1977); Van Spanckeren, K. and Castro, J.G., *Margaret Atwood: Vision and Forms*; Waters, K.E., in *Mother was Not a Person*; Yalom, M., in *Maternity, Mortality and the Literature of Madness*.

Aubert, Constance (1803–?)
French journalist and novelist. The daughter of ▷Laure d'Abrantès, she collaborated with her mother on a number of novels, wrote the fashion column for *Le Temps*, and was the editor of a number of fashion and style journals, including *Les Abeilles parisiennes* (*The Bees of Paris*). She also contributed to the ▷*Journal des Dames* (*Ladies Journal*), and published a *Manuel d'économie élégante* (1859) (*Handbook of Economy and Style*).
▷Feminine/feminist journalism (France)

Aubespine (or Laubespine), Madeleine de l'Dame de Villeroy (1546–1596)
French poet. She was the daughter of Jean de Brabant, wife of Nicolas de Neufville, secretary of

state and lady-in-waiting to ▷Catherine de
Medici. In their house near the Louvre and their
country residence at Conflans, they held one of
the first salons. She was celebrated for her beauty
and intelligence as a poet by fellow poets Pierre
de Ronsard (1524–1585), who called her his
daughter, and Philippe Desportes (1546–1606),
who wrote of his love for her under the
pseudonym Callianthe. Her own sonnets, *La
Chanson de Callianthe* (*The Song of Callianthe*),
were first published in 1926. The question of
attribution seems to have been satisfactorily
resolved, and her verses allow us to appreciate her
role in the gatherings of poets who frequented
Conflans.
Bib: Aubespine, M. de l', *Les Chansons de
Callianthe*, ed. R. Sorg (1926); Grente, G.,
Dictionnaire des lettres françaises.

Auclert, Hubertine (1848–1914)
French polemical writer. One of the most
significant figures in the suffrage movement,
Auclert founded the group *Le Droit des femmes*
(The Rights of Women) in 1876. She also set up
the weekly newspaper *La Citoyenne* (1881–1891)
(*The Female Citizen*) in order to campaign for
political rights for women in 19th-century France.
Her most memorable publications are *Le Vote des
femmes* (1908) (*Women's Suffrage*) and the
posthumous *Les Femmes au gouvernail* (1923)
(*Women at the Helm*), which is a collection of
Auclert's articles and speeches on the suffrage
issue.
▷Feminine/feminist journalism (France)
Bib: Moses, C., *French Feminism in the 19th
Century*; Albistur, M. and Armogathe, D., *Histoire
du féminisme français*.

Audouard, Olympe (1830–1890)
French novelist, travel writer and journalist. Born
in Marseilles, she married a notary, from whom
she soon separated, but was unable to obtain a
divorce until 1885. An enthusiastic traveller, she
supported herself by writing about her journeys to
the Middle East, Russia and North America, and
founded the literary review *Le Papillon* (*The
Butterfly*). She attempted to set up a political
journal, *La Revue cosmopolite* (*Cosmopolitan Review*),
but was legally prevented from doing so because
of her sex. This setback, and her experience of
married life, led her to write *Guerre aux hommes*
(1866) (*War on Men*), a pamphlet which demands
equal rights for women, and contains a series of
hostile pen-portraits of different male types.
Audouard's fictional works have evocative titles,
such as: *Un Mari trompé* (1863) (*A Deceived
Husband*); *Il n'y a pas d'amour sans jalousie et de
jalousie sans amour* (1863) (*There is No Love without
Jealousy and No Jealousy without Love*) and
Singulière nuit de noces (1886) (*A Strange Wedding
Night*).
Bib: Moses, C., *French Feminism in the 19th
Century*; Albistur, M. and Armogathe, D., *Histoire
du féminisme français*.

Audoux, Marguerite (1863–1937)
French novelist. After her mother died and her
father abandoned her, Audoux was sent to an
orphanage, and later became a farm servant in the
Sologne. Having moved to Paris, she began to
work as a seamstress and, through her friendship
with the writer Charles-Louis Philippe, to move in
literary circles. Her first novel, *Marie-Claire*
(1910), was largely autobiographical, and was
extremely well-received. Its popularity owed much
to the acutely observed tableau of working-class
life it contains – Audoux's apparently naïve,
unanalytical narrator tells the reader a great deal
about the French proletariat of the *belle époque*
without seeming to do so. Her later novels were,
however, less successful, and were considered by
critics to be excessively emotional in their tone.
Bib: Lanoizelée, L., *Marguerite Audoux: sa vie, son
oeuvre*; Reyer, G., *Marguerite Audoux*.

Auel, Jean (born 1936)
US novelist. Auel was born in Chicago, Illinois,
and she earned a Master of Business
Administration degree from the University of
Portland in 1976. Auel's 'Earth Children' series
revises stereotypical notions of prehistoric life.
Clan of the Cave Bear (1980) focuses on a woman,
Ayla, who is raised by a people less evolved than
she. Innovative and creative, Ayla poses a threat
because she undermines conventional gender
roles. Nevertheless, her skills repeatedly save the
group. Auel examines how gender roles were
established to repress women's power.
   Other works include: *The Valley of Horses* (1982)
and *The Mammoth Hunters* (1985).

Aulnoy, Marie-Catherine Le Jumel de Barneville, Comtesse d' (1650/1–1705)
French author of fairytales and pseudo-historical
novels, ▷*mémoires*, and a Spanish travel book.
She used the pseudonyms of Dunnois and
Madame D. One of the most widely read and
popular authors of her day, Madame d'Aulnoy
was born near Honfleur in Normandy into a
family of the minor nobility. In 1666 she was
married to the Baron d'Aulnoy. Her five children,
not all by her husband, would have been the
natural audience for her charming and fashionable
fairytales (*contes de fées* or *fées à la mode*), which
include *L'Oiseau bleu* (*The Blue Bird*), *Gracieuse et
Percinet*, *La Chatte blanche* (*The White Cat*) and *La
Belle aux cheveux d'or* (*Goldilocks*), for which she is
best-known. Madame d'Aulnoy was said to be as
famous for her disorderly life as for her books, but
much of the scandal is conjecture. The story of
her life after the birth of her fourth child in 1669
is as overlaid with fantasy as her work. She was
accused of plotting with her mother to have her
dissolute husband committed for treason; and
there was even an extravagant rumour that she
helped her friend, Madame Ticquet, to try to
poison her husband. Partly because of these
alleged crimes, Madame d'Aulnoy travelled a
great deal in Europe, and her novels, *mémoires* and
travel books contain an autobiographical element.

Between 1690 and her death, she remained mostly in Paris and published ten books, making a total of twenty-seven volumes in all. Her first novel, the *Histoire d'Hypolite Comte du Duglas*, a romance of love and adventure set in England, was an instant success. It also contained her first published fairytale. Several of her *mémoires* would be more accurately classified as romantic novels, but the *Mémoires de la cour d'Espagne* (*Memoirs of the Court of Spain*), published later the same year, were closely based on authentic documents and ran to several editions. Her *Relation du voyage en Espagne* (1691) (*Account of Travels in Spain*), written in the form of fifteen precisely dated letters, which run from 20 February 1679 to 28 September 1680, is one of the most famous of all accounts of travels in Spain in the 17th century. She also wrote two religious works and a collection of *Nouvelles espagnolles* (1692) (*Spanish Stories*) – tales of thwarted love, duels and abductions, with little local colour other than the use of proper names. Her memoirs of the English court (published in 1695) contain a chapter offering twenty items of advice on letter-writing. Her last work, *Le Comte de Warwick* (1703) (*The Earl of Warwick*), was the only one of her books to bear her name in full upon the title-page. In 1698 she was admitted to the female Academy of the Ricovrati in Padua, and modestly assumed the identity of Clio, Muse of History. This honour reflected her not inconsiderable talent in the imaginative interpretation of historical fact and authentic memoirs, which allowed her to challenge the historians of her day.
Bib: Aulnoy, Madame d', *Travels into Spain*.

Au Péril de ta Joie (1972) (At the Peril of Your Joy)
First novel by Marie-Magdeleine Carbet, a writer from the French Antilles. Fanny, the protagonist, confesses to her current suitor the manner in which she had interpreted the absence of her white lover, Pierre, as an indication of his inability to plan a future with a woman of a different skin colour to himself. Believing he had given in to his family's disapproval of her, she had fled. It was only years later that she had learnt of Pierre's accidental death. The novel raises the question of racism through the well-worn plot of a woman protagonist's cathartic confession of her racially-mixed affair (see also ▷*Mon Examen de Blanc*).

Aurora Leigh (1857)
A poem by ▷Elizabeth Barrett Browning. Described by its author as a 'novel in verse', this 11,000-line poem concerns the making of a woman poet. The narrative charts the life-story of Aurora from childhood to literary success, and ultimately to marriage with her cousin, Romney Leigh. A subplot involves Marian Erle, a working-class woman whom Aurora befriends. The narrative is indebted to other 19th-century texts such as ▷Elizabeth Gaskell's ▷*Ruth* and ▷Charlotte Brontë's ▷*Jane Eyre*, as well as to ▷Madame de Staël's ▷*Corinne*. The story,

however, is less important than Barrett Browning's discussion of art, politics, poetic tradition and women's writing. Although it promotes an elitist political stance and demonstrates a fear of the working class, *Aurora Leigh* is the fullest exposition of issues surrounding female creativity in Victorian literature. It is considered Barrett Browning's major work, tracing her own development as a poet as well as recording the obstacles and assumptions placed in the path of aspiring women writers. It was a sensational success, although some Victorian parents refused to let their daughters read it, fearful of the model of female independence and autonomy that it presented.

Aus guter Familie (1895) (Of Good Family)
A novel by the German writer ▷Gabriele Reuter. A penetrating and uncompromising critique of German middle-class patriarchy, it traces the tragic 'career' of Agathe Haidling, daughter of wealthy, bourgeois parents, from dreamy young girl to impoverished and crazy old maid. Agathe grows up conditioned by sentimental fictions about her future role as wife and mother, and, barred access to any knowledge of the real world, falls victim to the rule of a father and brother who consider the self-sacrifice of their womenfolk as unquestionable. When her brother appropriates her dowry to pay off his gambling debts, her suitor promptly abandons her. All her subsequent attempts to break away from her oppressive circumstances fail, and Reuter allows her heroine no reprieve.

Ausländer, Rose (1901–1988)
Poet, born Rosalie Scherzer in Austro-Hungarian Czernowitz, now Chernovtsy in the Ukraine, of German-speaking Jewish parents. In 1921 she emigrated to the USA. Her marriage there to Ignaz Ausländer lasted only three years, and in 1931 she returned to her native town. After spending the war years hiding in the cellars of the Czernowitz ghetto, she left once more for the USA in 1946, but suffered a collapse upon her mother's death in 1947. For a while she tried to write in English, but returned to Europe in 1964 and began publishing poetry in German, with little initial acclaim. It was only in the 1970s that she began to attract attention with a number of collections of poems, notably *Blinder Sommer* (1965) (*Blind Summer*), *Inventar* (1972) (*Inventory*), *Doppelspiel* (1977) (*Double Game*), *Mutterland* (1978) (*Motherland*) and *Ein Stück weiter* (1979) (*A Little Further*). Exile, alienation, the Holocaust, and the loss of both mother and mother tongue, are her recurrent themes. She is now recognized as one of the foremost lyrical poets of post-war Germany and, together with ▷Getrud Kolmar and ▷Nelly Sachs, is regarded as a leading exponent of German-Jewish experience in this century.

Austen, Jane (1775–1817)
English novelist, the sixth child in a family of seven, born in the rectory at Steventon,

Hampshire. During her childhood she read widely, encouraged by her father, the Rev. George Austen. Her life was outwardly uneventful and she never married, although she had several suitors, one of whom she accepted only to turn him down the following morning. Her fiction is characterized by its focus on middle-class provincial life and by its subtle psychological analysis and caustic humour. '3 or 4 families in a Country Village is the very thing to work on', wrote Austen in 1814. In order of publication, her novels are as follows: ▷*Sense and Sensibility* (1811); ▷*Pride and Prejudice* (1813); ▷*Mansfield Park* (1814); ▷*Emma* (1816); ▷*Northanger Abbey* (1818) and ▷*Persuasion* (1818). The novels, however, were not written according to this chronology. *Sense and Sensibility* is a re-worked version of *Elinor and Marianne* (1795–6) and *Pride and Prejudice* was revised from *First Impressions* (1797). *Northanger Abbey* was the next to be composed, followed by an unfinished novel, *The Watsons*, which was abandoned after her father's death in 1805. Both *Northanger Abbey* and *Persuasion* were posthumously published, and at her death Austen was writing the unfinished ▷*Sanditon*. She occupies a unique place in English literary history, being viewed as the writer who brought the English novel to maturity and paved the way for its development in the 19th century.
Bib: Austen-Leigh, J.E., *A Memoir of Jane Austen*; Lascelles, M., *Jane Austen and Her Art*; Mudrick, M., *Jane Austen: Irony as Defence and Discovery*; Leavis, Q.D., *A Critical Theory of Jane Austen's Writings*; Butler, M., *Jane Austen and the War of Ideas*; Southam, B.C. (ed.), *Jane Austen: The Critical Heritage*; Cecil, D., *A Portrait of Jane Austen*.

Austin, Mary (1864–1934)

US novelist, dramatist and prose writer. Born in Carlinville, Illinois, Austin endured an antagonistic relationship with her mother. She studied maths and science at Blackburn College. In 1888 she and her mother moved to California where Austin married in 1891. On leaving her husband, she joined a bohemian community of artists. In 1911 she moved to New York, where she worked for social reforms for women in the areas of birth control and employment. After suffering a breakdown in 1923 she settled in Sante Fe, New Mexico.

With *The Land of Little Rain* (1903) Austin pioneered a new Southwestern regional literature. It celebrated the land and Native American Indian culture, and protested its exploitation. As in ▷*A Woman of Genius* (1912) and *Earth Horizons* (1932), Austin's autobiographical fiction focuses on an extraordinary woman who can transcend her vulnerabilities. Austin believed in an individual genius who thinks for all women.

Other works include: *The Arrowmaker* (1911), *The Ford* (1917), *The Young Woman* (1918), *No. 26 Jayne Street* (1920), *The American Rhythm* (1923),

Everyman's Genius (1925), *Experiences Facing Death* (1931) and *Starry Adventure* (1931).

Australian Girl, An (1894)

Novel by Australian writer ▷Catherine Martin. A particularly impressive and well-written colonial novel. Its heroine, Stella Courtland, is a girl of intellectual curiosity and independence who has a cynical attitude towards marriage. The novel explores complex philosophical and religious themes through the eyes of its heroine and examines the issues of class, education and worth which were of great concern in a colonial context. The novel was republished in 1988.

Authors and Friends (1896)

US literary reminiscences by ▷Annie Adams Fields. Fields's record of the Boston literary circle centred around ▷*The Atlantic Monthly* and her husband's publishing empire. *Authors and Friends* is one of the fullest sources for the discussions and relationships which underlie the publishing history of many 19th-century US women writers.

Autobiography

Australia: A comprehensive listing of Australian women's autobiographies is given in Joy Hooton's ▷*Stories of Herself When Young* (1990). As well as overt autobiographies, there are many fictionalized accounts of Australian women's experience, including ▷*The Getting of Wisdom* (1910) by ▷Henry Handel Richardson, ▷*My Brilliant Career* by ▷Miles Franklin, and ▷*The Man Who Loved Children* by ▷Christina Stead. For Aboriginal women's autobiographies see ▷Aboriginal women writers in Australia.
Caribbean: The first two published works by Caribbean women were both autobiographical: ▷Mary Prince's ▷*The History of Mary Prince* and ▷Mary Seacole's ▷*The Wonderful Adventures of Mrs Seacole in Many Lands*. Autobiography forms the central element in the writings of ▷Jean Rhys, ▷Merle Hodge, ▷Zee Edgell, ▷Erna Brodber and ▷Jamaica Kincaid.
Southern Africa: Besides the ▷diaries and journals, and the ▷letters written by 19th- and early 20th-century Southern African women, a number of memoirs were written by women such as Melina Rorke and Elsa Smithers, recounting pioneering or homesteading days. There have been some autobiographies by literary figures, ▷Sarah Gertrude Millin, for instance, as well as by less well-established writers, such as Sampie de Wet, Madeleine Masson, and Marjorie Juta, whose title *Boundless Privilege* (1974) offers telling comment on the latter days of the genre.

In a different kind of white writing, political autobiographies were written by South African women in ▷exile, most notable among them ▷Mary Benson, Ruth First and ▷Hilda Bernstein, all active in underground political activities during the 1950s and 1960s. Bernstein's *The World That Was Ours* (1967, revised 1989) tells the story of the period leading up to and during the Rivonia trial, where Nelson Mandela and others were sentenced to life imprisonment. First's *117 Days* (1965, reprinted 1982), as the title suggests, is an account of her time spent in solitary confinement in prison, in 1963.

In black writing, the autobiographical genre established itself among women writers from the 1960s into the 1980s, increasing, it seems, with the development of ▷Black Consciousness. Before this, however, a genre of mediated autobiographies – or what are best described as ethnological autobiographies, generally linked with sociological research – had developed. Here, others (most often white women) began to write the stories that black women told but did not write themselves. Rebecca Reyher's *Zulu Woman* (1948) is the first of such a tradition, recounting the story told her by Christina Sibiya, a Zulu woman born in 1900 who married Solomon, the King of the Zulus a little time after Shaka. It is both the personal record of a woman married to a polygynous husband and the story of profound national change. Other works which fall, if somewhat haphazardly, into this sub-genre are John Blacking's *Black Background* (1964), whose Venda informant, Dora Magidi, sometimes takes up a voice from the ▷oral tradition; ▷Elsa Joubert's ▷ *The Long Journey of Poppie Nongena* (1978), Carol Hermer's *The Diary of Maria Tholo* (1980); Marjorie Shostak's *Nisa: The Life and Words of a !Kung Woman* (1981) and *Paulina Dhlamini: Servant of Two Kings* (1986), compiled by H. Filter and edited and translated by H. Bourquin.

In their different ways, these form an important and fascinating part of South African literature. *Nisa* delves into a world that had hitherto not been represented in literature, but for tales from the oral tradition. *Paulina Dhlamini* presents the recorded memories and subsequent clarifications of a woman who had been a junior member of the Zulu King Cetshwayo's *isigodlo* (the young women given to the king as tribute). When the British troops advanced on the king in the Zulu War, she and others from the *isigodlo*, along with her parents, fled to King Zibhebhu for protection. When the king started to behave as if these women were his property, there was a further escape. After living in caves for nearly a year, Paulina and her parents and siblings became servants on a white-owned farm in Natal. Converted to Christianity, she became a lay-preacher, along with the white farmer, he preaching to whites, she to blacks.

The Diary of Maria Tholo was originally spoken into a tape-recorder. Maria Tholo (an assumed name, for her protection) was a schoolteacher in Cape Town, at the height of the schoolchildren's rebellion leading from events in ▷Soweto. It gives a complex view of the difficult choices to be made, by a teacher and mother, at a time when children were assuming authority.

Other autobiographical accounts which straddle the distinction between autobiography and ethnological autobiography are Winnie Mandela's *Part of My Soul Went With Him* (1985) and

Miriam Makeba's *My Story* (1988). The former, largely spoken rather than written, is edited by Ann Benjamin and adapted by ▷Mary Benson, compiled from tape-recorded interviews as well as letters and other documentation. The latter is compiled from a set of tape-recorded monologues in which Makeba tells of her rise to fame as a nightclub star in New York, as well as her political campaign against apartheid, and how in South Africa in the 1940s and 1950s, she was continually harassed by police, gangsters and managers.

These various works may claim to recapture the 'real' experiences of women whom a racist and sexist society has otherwise rendered silent, but it may also be argued that they represent the 'selves' blacks have been constrained to construct for whites, since the experience of the informants is, on an obvious level, mediated by those they specifically address. Nevertheless, these life-stories give insight into social situations not hitherto documented, and into belief systems under stress and change, as well as providing – at least in part – the 'other' side to histories already told.

▷Noni Jabavu's two autobiographies, which appeared in the early 1960s, both strive to make a secure return to her childhood world, which sometimes involves concealing the individual, adult, British-educated voice beneath the community voice. ▷Bessie Head's autobiographical novel ▷*A Question of Power* strains to make a comparable shift to the rural and communal existence of her historical past, stripped from her by white South Africa. Joyce Sikakane's autobiography, *A Window on Soweto* (1977), moves between social documentary and personal account in a detailed and poignant presentation of the lives of a subordinated people and of her own career as a journalist, her seventeen-month prison detention, and the banning order which prohibited her from working as a journalist and forced her into ▷exile.

An explicit proponent of ▷Black Consciousness, ▷Ellen Kuzwayo balances her individual story in *Call Me Woman* (1985) with the stories of other women. Unlike Jabavu, her express intention is not to obscure differences between herself and the community, but to register her own story as typical of many, as well as to show community aspirations rather than personal ambition. A community 'I' interweaves with and frames her personal account, in accordance with Black Consciousness, which rejects individualism as part of a more general rejection of white standards.

The development away from individualism, and from a self constructed in terms of white standards, forms part of the dynamic of Emma Mashinini's fascinating trade-union autobiography, *Strikes Have Followed Me All My Life* (1989), which also presents a moving account of the humiliations and terrors of prison detention. Focusing exclusively on her prison experience, Caesarina Kona Makhoere's *No*

Child's Play (1988) speaks from the position of one of the rebellious schoolchildren. She takes on more thoroughly than the earlier writers the voice of retribution associated with contemporary poetry by black South African women.

Two recent autobiographies are Sindiwe Magona's *To My Children's Children* (1990) which, like Jabavu's, Kuzwayo's and Mashinini's texts, is eager to speak across the generation gap, and Maggie Resha's *'Mangoana o Tsoare Thipa ka Bohaleng: My Life in the Struggle* (1992). Magona's book, addressed to the 'Child of the Child of My Child', presents itself as 'speaking' rather than 'writing', for it intends to compensate present-day children for their loss of ▷oral tradition. Inevitably political, since no black South African life-story can be otherwise, the focus is nevertheless on personal growth. Resha's book, whose title means 'The child's mother grabs the sharp end of the knife', recounts her career as a nurse in the late 1940s and 1950s, and her involvement in the African National Congress in the 1950s and 1960s. She was a founder member of the African National Congress's women's section, and of the Federation of South African Women (FEDSAW).

There are also a number of anthologies of life-stories and interviews which give voice to black South and Southern African women.

▷Anthologies (Southern Africa); ▷Exile writing (South Africa)

Autobiography of Alice B. Toklas, The (1932)

Work of non-fiction by US writer ▷Gertrude Stein. Less her lover, Alice Toklas's, autobiography than a record of Stein's own life and work *The Autobiography of Alice B. Toklas* is easily Stein's most popular and accessible book. Indeed, it was this fascinating chronicle of Parisian art, writing, friends and lovers which first won Stein the recognition that she craved from a North American audience, although Stein continued to be disappointed that it was this book, and not her more challenging experimental work, that assured her reputation. On one level 'Alice's' duplicitous narrative 'I' functions as a prism through which we can view Stein's 'genius' and her centrality to the artistic and literary ▷modernist movement. However, the narrative duplicity of *The Autobiography* also raises the fundamental question of how a woman writer can write herself into the history of an artistic movement. Failing 'official' sanction of her place in history, Stein's solution, in using the voice of her long-term lesbian lover, is to chronicle herself from the margins. Depicting her relationships with key figures of the period such as artists Picasso (1881–1973) and Matisse (1869–1984), Eugene and Maria Jolas, Hemingway (1899–1961), Sylvia Beach and T.S. Eliot (1888–1965), this was not a view of history that the 'movement' itself approved of. *The Autobiography* inspired an aggressive rejection of Stein's version of the artistic and intellectual scene and, indeed, her place in its history, in the form of *A Testimony*

Against Gertrude Stein (1935), which included criticisms from Henri Matisse, Georges Braque and Tristan Tzara.

Autobiography of Christopher Kirkland, The, (1885)

The autobiography of ▷Eliza Lynn Linton, anti-feminist journalist and author of the sensational essay ▷'The Girl of the Period' (1868). Although the book accurately and frankly records Linton's life, it is written from the perspective of a male. One reason for this may have been that a male persona enabled Linton to write more freely about her own close female companions without attracting speculation or scandal (especially since she had explicitly condemned lesbianism in *The Rebel of the Family*, 1880). The book was not a commercial success.

Autre qui danse, L' (1989) (*The Other who Dances*)

This novel by the Caribbean writer from the French Antilles, Suzanne Dracius-Pinalie, concentrates upon Rehvana, a mulatto from Martinique who lives in Paris. Caught between nostalgia for the island of her birth (Martinique) and adaptation to the country in which she lives (France), and between the conflicting images of herself she develops from her contact with others, Rehvana's quest for ▷identity takes her by way of three lovers. Through Abdoulaye she identifies with an African group in Paris; Jérémie, black, bourgeois and very French, wants marriage and children; through Eric, a macho mulatto, Rehavana returns to Martinique. The novel ends with the death of Rehvana and her unborn baby. The novel thus uses the paradigmatic fable of the coloured woman's quest, brought to the test by men, which is also used in other novels from the French Antilles, such as ▷*Heremakhonon* and ▷*Mon Examen de Blanc*.

Autre vie, Une (1978) (*Another Life*)

A novel by the French-Algerian writer ▷Leila Aouchal. The story of a French girl from the middle class who meets Hamid, an Algerian worker at the age of 19, and marries him, despite the disapproval of her father. Aouchal explores her thoughts, the events which contribute to her transformation, and her discovery of a new identity. Written in the first person, the narrative is divided into three parts. The first is set in Caen, where she meets Hamid, and becomes aware of the racism towards Algerians. In the second part, Leila and Hamid decide to go to live in Algeria, to the Kabylie, where Leila meets Hamid's family and is warmly accepted. She writes about the family and the social life. The third part focuses on Algiers, where Leila discovers the real nightmare of the battle of Algiers. She realizes that the oppression and racism, which she thought she had left behind her, is even worse in Algiers. She develops a political awareness and works for the liberation movment. The novel finishes with the departure of the *Pieds-Noirs* (French nationals born in the Maghref), and Algerian independence in 1962. In writing about oppressed people, Aouchal keeps her sentences short and uncomplicated, but the emotional intensity conveys her complete identification with the struggle of the Algerian people.

Ava, Frau (?–1127)
The first woman known to have written in German. According to her own manuscript she was a widow and mother of two, who spent her last years in total isolation in a convent cell in Melk, Austria. She wrote religious poetry and books based on the New Testament: *Das Leben Jesu* (*The Life of Jesus*); *Johannes* (*John*); *Die sieben Gaben des heiligen Geistes* (*The Seven Gifts of the Holy Spirit*); *Antichrist*; and *Das jüngste Gericht* (*The Last Judgement*).
▷ *Visionsliteratur*

Avant-garde
A much-used critical term applied to literature and the visual arts. The term is militaristic in origin ('advance guard'), and was initially associated with the magazine *L'Avant-garde*, founded by the Russian romantic and anarchist Mikhail Bakunin (1814–1876). By the end of the 19th century the meaning of the term was shifting towards a cultural and artistic usage and came to be associated with innovation, invention, with something 'advanced'. First applied to the French symbolist poets, *avant-garde* is frequently regarded as synonymous with artistic ▷modernism because of the modernist attack on established forms and traditions. It is arguable, given the context of postmodern debate, whether the forms associated with ▷postmodernism can be regarded as *avant-garde*.
▷Cunard, Nancy; Richardson, Dorothy; Jellicoe, Ann; *Sport of My Mad Mother, The*

Avellaneda, La ▷Gómez de Avellaneda, Gertrúdis

Aventuras de Diófanes (1752) (*Adventures of Diófanes*)
Written by ▷Teresa Margarida da Silva e Orta, this book is widely regarded as the first Brazilian novel. The plot involves a journey by Diófanes, the King of Thebes, who travels with his wife and daughter to Delos, where the daughter is to be wed. *En route*, a storm breaks out, and the royal family is taken captive by enemies. Separated from one another, the three endure hardships for over fifteen years. Despite their trials they maintain their virtuous characters, and are finally reunited. A didactic, moralist book, *Aventuras de Diófanes* exhibits a progressive interest in social reform and a liberal attitude towards women.
Bib: Sousa, Ronald W., 'The Divided Discourse of *Aventuras de Diófanes* and Its Socio-Historical Implications', in *Problems of Enlightenment in Portugal*.

Aves sin nido (1889) ▷*Birds without a Nest* (1968)

Avílova, Lidiia Alekseevna (1864/65–1943)
Russian short story writer and memoirist. Avílova was the most successful of several women 'tutored' in the art of short prose fiction by Anton Chekhov (1860–1904), who thought highly of her language and style, but criticized her for sentimentality, prolixity and vagueness.

Avílova published her first collection of stories in 1896, and by the end of the 1890s she had received praise from such notable figures as Leo Tolstoy (1828–1910) and Ivan Bunin (1870–1953). Tolstoy wrote, 'She selects old moral themes and writes . . . wisely and dryly.' She produced several novellas from 1898 to 1907 and then abandoned the genre. Additional story collections appeared in 1906, 1913 and 1914. In 1910 she wrote the first of several reminiscences about Chekhov. Her last new stories appeared in 1915. Avílova emigrated to Czechoslovakia with her daughter from 1922 to 1924, but then returned to the USSR. After the Revolution a few of her stories were republished as part of the 'Bargain Library' series, and she was published again in the 1980s. Her other works in the Soviet period consisted primarily of memoirs, including *Chekhov in My Life* (written 1939–1940, complete version published 1947). Avílova was in her 70s when she started writing these memoirs, and their accuracy has been questioned.

Avílova's stories are of varying quality. She took Chekhov's advice very seriously, usually making the changes he suggested to her, which often consisted of excision. But she was not a writer who developed over time, perhaps because of a strong ambivalence about traditional women's roles and a writing career. Avílova's stories have a wide variety of protagonists: children, peasants, migrant workers, and members of the upper class. Her most successful stories, such as 'On the Road' and 'First Borrow', are those about characters distanced from herself by age or class or both, where the point of view is not just that of the narrating voice, and where Chekhov's influence on mood and theme are least apparent. She is close to Chekhov, though, in her complex presentation of the peasants. Her stories contain a great deal of dialogue in which she is able to differentiate her characters by class. Plot does not play a large role in her stories; instead they often involve the psychological process of self-discovery and awakening.
Bib: De Maegd-Soep, C., *Chekhov and Women: Women in the Life and Work of Chekhov*; Heim, M.H., (trans.) and Karlinsky, S. (ed.), *Anton Chekhov's Life and Thought: Selected Letters and Commentary*.

Avison, Margaret (born 1918)
Canadian poet, born in Galt, Ontario, but lived as a child in western Canada, where the landscape and light shaped her sensibility. She studied creative writing in the USA at the Universities of

Indiana (1955) and Chicago (1956–1957). She began writing in 1939, but worked as a librarian, a lecturer at the University of Toronto, and a social worker. A modernist poet, Avison writes out of a densely textured metaphysical drive that is both demanding and stimulating. *Winter Sun* (1960) is intensely engaged with belief and understanding; it won a Governor General's Award. Following her conversion to Christianity in 1963, she published *The Dumbfounding* (1966), which addresses her religious vision. These two books have been re-issued together in *Winter Sun/The Dumbfounding: Poems 1940–1966* (1982). Her third collection, *Sunblue* (1978), continues to explore spiritual conviction. Finally, her poems have been gathered in *Collected Poems* (1990), for which she was awarded another Governor General's Award. Her intense and paradoxical writing is richly evocative.
Bib: Kent, D. (ed.), *'Lighting up the Terrain': the Poetry of Margaret Avison*; Redekop, E., *Margaret Avison*.

Awakening, The (1899)
US novel by ▷Kate Chopin. Path-breaking story of a middle-class woman's gradually awakening consciousness and sensuality. Trapped in an unhappy marriage in urban New Orleans, Edna Pontellier discovers a different self and sensibility in the seaside resort of Grand Isle, where she also finds a lover. Unable to live with the consequences of her consciousness and her love, Edna commits suicide by walking into the sea.
A celebration of awakening sensuality, the novel – and its author – suffered from public criticism which effectively ended Chopin's literary career. The devastating potency of the negative public response can be attributed in part to the US economic climate in the 1890s and its debilitating effects on US publishing. *The Awakening* has become a germinal work in US women's literature and women's studies and has entered the canon of classic works of US literature.

Axioti, Melpo (1906–1973)
Greek novelist and poet. Born in Athens and educated in a Roman Catholic school on the island of Tinos. She travelled widely in Europe. Her first novel, *Difficult Nights* (1938), elicited a mixed response from critics, because of the attractive but inconsequential character of her

writing. In 1939 she published *Coincidence*, a collection of poems charged with great sensitivity. Her novel *Would You Like to Dance, Maria?* (1940) is similar in style to her first. Later she published a number of chronicles, which combined accounts of personal experience with strong arguments for social reform.
▷*Contrabando*

Ayverdi, Samiha (born 1906)
Turkish novelist who grew up in a traditional family atmosphere in the old Istanbul. She left school at fifteen and continued reading and educating herself. She wrote of the life of religious Turks, inspired by ideas of the fundamentalist group, Islamic Jihad. She wrote many essays on politics, religion and the importance of the spiritual life. Her novels include *So This Is Love* (1939), *A Night In the Temple* (1940), *The Fire Tree* (1941), *Living Dead* (1942) and *The Chaplain* (1948).

Azalais D'Altier (13th century)
French ▷*trobairitz* of the fourth period, author of a letter in Occitan to Clara d'Anduza, probably the '*dompna d'Andutz*' mentioned in a *razo* to a poem by Uc de Saint-Circ.
Bib: Paden, W.D. (ed.), *The Voice of the Trobairitiz*.

Azevedo, Maria ▷Júlia, Francisca

Aziza (1955)
A novel by the Algerian writer, ▷Jamila Debeche. Aziza is a young woman who has been educated in French institutions, and has lived in Algiers with her governess since her parents' death, where she works in a French press agency. She marries Ali Kamal, an Arab politician and lawyer, but very quickly becomes disillusioned with his attitudes. Aziza is disappointed by the fact that Ali is not the liberated person he pretends to be, and expects his wife to be submissive and traditional. As she refuses to play this role, he rejects her. Through her experience, Aziza realizes that her biculturality puts her in a marginal position. Her French friends desert her for having married an Arab, and for the Algerians she is 'too French' to be one of them.

Bâ, Mariama (1929–1981)

Senegalese novelist. Brought up in the traditional manner by her grandparents, she was a brilliant scholar, and became a teacher in 1947. After twelve years, poor health forced her to resign and join the inspectorate. A divorcee, she was active in women's associations working for change in the social position of women, including the Soeurs Optimistes Internationales. Her first novel, *Une si longue lettre* (1979) (*So Long a Letter*, 1981), won the Noma Award for Publishing in Africa. Her second, *Un Chant écarlate* (▷*Scarlet Song*) was published posthumously in Dakar in 1981, just after her death.

▷Polygamy (West Africa)

Bib: Adams Graves, A. and Boyce-Davies, C. (eds), *Ngambika: Studies of Women in African Literature*; Blair, D, *A History of African Literature in French*; Milolo, K. (trans), *L'image de la femme chez les romancières de l'Afrique*.

Bab (1903)

Five-act verse play by Russian writer ▷Izabella Grinévskaia. *Bab* was described by the author as a philosophical, religious, and social drama. The basic metre of the play is iambic hexameter, with some shorter lines used very effectively in interpolated songs.

The title means 'The Door of Truth', a name which became attached to Ali Mukhamed, the hero of the play, and a leader of the Islamic reform movement called 'Babism' that arose in Persia in the 1840s.

In Grinévskaia's depiction the story of Bab has much in common with that of Christ: Bab's message of all people's equality before God; his humble origin; his betrayal by his own apostles; his moment of doubt before his death; the perception of his movement as a threat by the established Church; a virginal 'bride'; the preservation of his ideas in written form by an apostle; the literal interpretation of his metaphorical speeches (to his dismay). The one conspicuous difference is the strong message of equality between the sexes.

When the play was staged at the Literary-Artistic Society in ▷St Petersburg in 1904, it was a resounding success. But this production was closed down for two years by the censors, probably because it depicts a popularly-based rebellion and criticizes the Church's involvement in politics.

In its depiction of a social and religious rebellion, Grinévekaia's play resembles ▷Ánnenkova-Bernár's ▷*Daughter of the People* (also 1903) about Joan of Arc, and also has points in common with ▷Lókhvitskaia's *In nomine Domini* (*In the Name of the Lord*).

Bab al-Saha (1990)

Novel in Arabic by Palestinian writer ▷Sahar Khalifa. The title is the name of a central square in the old quarters of Nablus, a city on the West Bank. The subject is the place of women in the escalating resistance to Israeli occupation. It is mainly the story of three women: Zakiya, Samar and Nuzha. Zakiya, an elderly midwife deserted by her husband, has had to bring up her children almost single-handed. She is now called *Um al-Shabab* (the mother of the young men). She is a familiar figure to the Israeli soldiers, allowed to pass in the dark narrow alleys of the quarter to help with the delivery of babies, whose number is not affected by the violence enveloping the city.

Samar, a young student, is trying to conduct a piece of research. She tries to apply a questionnaire to Zakiya: 'How has the *intifada* changed the life of women here?' The 'innocent' student is shocked at the elderly woman's reply: 'Frankly, nothing. Their burden is heavier and their hearts are broken. God help the women! Their old chores and cares are the same and their new ones are innumerable . . . not least the young men scattered in the hills.'

The third woman is Nuzha, daughter of a brothel-keeper in the quarter, whose mother is found stabbed to death. Zakiya's nephew, Husam, a wounded young man on the run, has to hide in Nuzha's house. When a curfew is imposed on the quarter, Zakiya and Samar are also caught in Nuzha's house. The long hours of confinement bring many secrets into the open, as Nuzha cynically answers the items of Samar's questionnaire. Nuzha is bitter, cursing Palestine, as she waits for Ahmad, her younger brother, to come back, so that she can take him and escape to North America. But Ahmad is with the Resistance, and he too is 'martyred' in the end.

The military forces conduct house-to-house searches, dynamiting houses, erecting cement blocks at the entrances of narrow alleys. The men have to hide or they are rounded up. It is the women and children who face the soldiers, the women sending up their shrill *zagharid* (ululations) at the explosion of a house. Samar's questionnaire is answered in action; the men had intended to keep their women in their place at home while they went out to fight. The soldiers have forced their way into the houses, and the women have risen in confrontation in their houseclothes and night-dresses, their hair unkempt and their faces uncovered, with the only weapons they know: stones, pieces of wood, and loud voices.

Babička (1855) (Grandmother)

Novel by Czech writer Božena Němcová (1820–1862). It quickly became part of the Czech literary ▷canon. Němcová wrote verse, prose (particularly remarkable is her short story, 'Four Seasons', 1854, concerning feminine sensual desire), and adaptations of oral tradition tales. She wrote *Babička* after her favourite son died. The narrative framework, the bulk of the novel, describes a grandmother leading a perfect Bohemian village life, where her influence leads to the happiness of all classes – the nobility (the manor house is as influenced by her as the lowest peasant), the rural middle classes (particularly her own daughter's family) and the ordinary villagers. The grandmother's religion, a mixture of folk custom and Roman Catholicism, can potentially solve all human problems. The interpolated tales, particularly that of the character Viktorka, who had broken the rules by submitting, or being forced to submit to, passion, provide the action to a novel which essentially proposes custom and ritual as the only potential stabilizing force in life.

Babois, Marguerite-Victoire (1760–1839)
French poet. The daughter of a shopkeeper from Versailles, she married in 1780 and separated in 1788. The death of her own daughter in 1792 led her to express her grief in verse, and to publish the very successful *Elégie sur la mort de ma fille* (*Elegy on the Death of My Daugher*). Various other collections of elegies followed this work, and are contained in the 1810 edition of Babois's *Elégies et poésies diverses* (*Diverse Elegies and Poems*). A retiring woman, she was a friend of the neo-classical French poets Ducis and Marie-Joseph Chénier.

Babylon (1946)
Novel by Slovak writer ▷Margita Figuli. It is one of the last works to come out of the Slovak school of Lyrical Prose. The first part of an intended trilogy, it is based on the decay of Babylon under the attack of the Persians, and provides an analogy with the contemporaneous European situation. The substitution of one system, power and values by another one is shown through individual destinies. Figuli concentrates on the vacillation from tradition, law and intellect to justice, truth and emotions, between politics and morals. Her decorative, lyrical, exotic style, her colour and symbolism, portray sensual delight, sin and an atmosphere of inevitable decay. The publication of *Babylon* provoked debate about the problems of the literary interpretation of allegories, and about the limits of aestheticism and escapism.

Bacheracht, Therese von (1804–1852)
German travel-writer. The well-educated, glamorous daughter of a diplomat, she married a Russian consul, and later became the lover of the writer Karl Gutzkow, who encouraged her to publish her diaries and letters about her many journeys to places such as Russia and the Far East. Her main works are *Briefe aus dem Süden* (1841) (*Letters from the South*) and *Menschen und Gegenden* (1845) (*People and Places*).

Bachmann, Ingeborg (1926–1973)
Austrian poet and novelist. Born in Klagenfurt, the daughter of a teacher, she remembered the day Hitler's troops marched into town as the day her childhood ended. This childhood was evoked in her memoir, *Jugend in einer Österreichischen Stadt* (1961) (*Growing up in an Austrian Town*). She studied law and philosophy in Innsbruck, Graz and Vienna, and submitted a doctoral thesis on Heidegger's Existentialism. In 1953 she published her first collection of poems, *Die gestundete Zeit* (*Time by the Hour*) and was awarded the prize of the literary *Gruppe 47* (Group of '47).

Ingeborg Bachmann

Anrufung des großen Bären (*Call of the Great Bear*), her second, equally successful collection, followed in 1956.

Bachmann's poetry combines exceptional beauty of language with arresting images of a world destroyed, of guilt and death beyond redemption. In the way it lets private anguish weep amidst a collective sense of disarray, it appealed to many Germans seeking solace after the war. Her radio plays also helped to establish Bachmann as a leading voice in post-war German culture, and many of her short stories, notably *Undine* (1973) and *Simultan* (1973) (*Simultaneously*), anticipate the feminist debate of the 1980s. Her work is dominated by the themes of bondage and helplessness, and of individuals falling mute in the face of power. Her experimental novel *Malina* (1971) offers a poignant self-portrait of a woman, poet and failed lover, living within a hostile male world.
▷*Fall Franza, Der*

Backwoods of Canada, The (1836)
▷Catherine Parr Traill's most famous book; its complete title is *The Backwoods of Canada: Being Letters from the Wife of an Emigrant Officer, Illustrative of the Domestic Economy of British America*. It consists of a series of letters home describing the situation of the female settler in Canada; it follows the Traills' departure from Scotland in 1832 to the spring of 1835, when they were settled on their homestead, close to Lakefield, Ontario, where ▷Margaret Laurence later lived. Traill describes the landscape, the seasons, the flora and fauna, and her own situation. The book is pragmatic and good-humoured and contains excellent advice for potential emigrants.

Bacon, Anne Cooke (1528–1610)
English translator and letter-writer. The second of five well-educated daughters of Anthony and Anne Fitzwilliam Cooke, Bacon was fluent in several languages. She may have assisted her father in his duties as tutor to Edward VI. Bacon's most important works were her translations of Reformist religious works. In 1550 John Day published her translations of Barnadine Ochine's

Italian *Sermons* on election and predestination. For the second edition, published in 1564, she composed a dedicatory ▷preface to her mother. In 1556 Anne Cooke married Nicholas Bacon. Eight years later she finished ▷*An Apologie or answeare in defence of the Churche of England*, her ▷translation of John Jewell's Latin defence of the Anglican Church. Bacon also wrote numerous ▷letters, mostly to her two sons, Anthony and Sir Francis Bacon (1561–1626). Stylistically similar to the prose of her more famous son, Francis, Anne Bacon's letters include numerous Latin and Greek quotations. The letters to her sons are characterized by a deep concern for their well-being, and an emphasis on their morality.

▷Humanism (England); *Instruction of a Christian Woman*; Protestant Reformation; Russell, Elizabeth

Bib: Hogrefe, P., *Women of Action in Tudor England*; Spedding, J. (ed.), *The Works of Francis Bacon*, Vol. 8.

Badinter, Elisabeth (born 1944)
French historian, and lecturer at the Ecole Polytechnique and other institutions. The author of socio-historical studies, she is best known for her feminist approach to history. She examines critically the biological assumptions of gender-linked behaviour, discussing maternal instinct in *L'Amour en plus* (1980) (▷*The Myth of Motherhood*, 1981) and the relations between the sexes in *L'Un est l'Autre* (1986) (▷*Man/Woman: The One is the Other*, 1989). Her other works include biographies of a number of 18th-century political and literary figures: *Emilie, Emilie: l'ambition féminine au 18me siècle* (1983) (*Emilie, Emilie: Female ambition in the 18th century*) and *Condorcet: un intellectuel en politique* (1989) (*Condorcet: An Intellectual in Politics*) with Robert Badinter.

Badr, Liana (born 1952)
Palestinian novelist and short story writer. Born in Jerusalem, she left for Amman with her father in 1967. She studied at the University of Jordan, Amman, but had to leave after September 1970. In common with many Palestinians of the diaspora, she lived in ▷Beirut, then Damascus and now lives in Tunis. Apart from a number of stories for children, she has published one novel and three collections of short stories. She is conscious of the subordinate position of women, even in the Resistance movement, where they have been active for some twenty years. Her first novel, *A Compass for the Sunflower* (1979), contrasts the native common sense of Umm Mahmud, living in the Chateela refugee camp, with her daughters' confidence in their modern stance, even though their lives in the impoverished camp can only be peripheral to the modern city.

Liana Badr works for the PLO (Palestine Liberation Organization), but does not subscribe to the view that the national cause should have precedence over feminist problems. She has mercilessly analysed the setback in feminist

consciousness in the Arab world, and particularly in the Palestinian Resistance after the defeat of June 1967. She concludes that the subject of her work will always be women and war, women and exile, and the plight of women, facing not only the national enemy but a massed weight of inhuman traditions and a heritage of male oppression. Collections of her short stories are: *Stories of Love and Pursuit* (1983), *View Over Fakahani* (1983) and *I Want The Day* (1985).

Bib: Shaaban, Bouthaina, *Both Right and Left Handed: Arab Women Talk About Their Lives*; Cobham, Catherine (trans.), *A Compass for the Sunflower*.

Bad Sister, The (1978)
A novel by ▷Emma Tennant, based on James Hogg's Scottish ▷Gothic novel *The Private Memoirs and Confessions of a Justified Sinner* (1824), which explored the image of the divided self and the theme of demonic possession, through an unreliable narrator whose story is presented to the reader by a fictitious editor. In Tennant's modern-day version, the protagonist, Jane Wild, is a young woman 'possessed' by the mysterious Meg, leader of a militant feminist community, who encourages her to murder her father and her half-sister. As in Hogg's novel, Jane's narrative is framed by the accounts of her story given by an editor – raising the question of which version of reality is to be believed. Jane's imaginative world consists in large part of dreams and fantasies, and through her, Tennant interrogates the themes of madness, female identity and women's violence. Tennant's use of the Gothic has affinities with ▷Angela Carter's work.

Bagnold, Enid (1889–1981)
English novelist and dramatist. A prize-winning poet in her teens, Bagnold attained personal and financial independence at the age of nineteen. While living in Chelsea, she rapidly became friends with writers and artists, including ▷Vita Sackville-West and H.G. Wells (1866–1946). She also studied with the founder of the Camden town group of artists, Walter Sickert. Bagnold was a successful journalist, and her (1860–1942) wartime diaries were published as *A Diary Without Dates* (1917). Her post-war life in France forms the basis of the love story *The Happy Foreigner* (1920), whose female protagonist believes in relationships being founded on complete equality. *The Squire* (1938) achieved notoriety through its depiction of childbirth and breast-feeding. Bagnold's most famous novel is ▷*National Velvet* (1935), a story of a young woman's strong-willed independence. Other writings include: *The Sailing Ship and Other Poems* (1918), *The Door of Life* (1938), *Serena Blandish, or The Difficulty of Getting Married* (1924) and *Enid Bagnold's Autobiography* (1969).

Bagryana, Elisaveta (1893–1991)
Bulgarian poet. Bagryana was a leading poet of her day, and a lively, independent-minded

feminist. Her famous love affairs, her proclamation to have had 'a husband in every country' and the impassioned descriptions of love in her novels made her very popular among the bourgeoisie between the wars.

Her early poems soon established her as a poet with *Zlatorog* (*Golden Horn*), the most important literary magazine of the time (1922–1944), which promoted the ideas of perfection of form and simplicity of message. In 1927 she published *Vechnata i suyatata* (*The Eternal and the Saint*). She visited Paris and Venice 1928 to 1929, and this was the inspiration for her book *From Other Shores*. But although she travelled widely, she was always drawn back to Bulgaria, and wrote of the unceasing beauty of its natural landscape, especially the Black Sea and the Nesebăr coast. In 1932 she published *Zvezda ne moryaka* (*The Sailor's Star*).

Her style is direct and anti-symbolist. Although she embraced progress, she argued that increased sophistication of technology should be used to allow a fuller expression of human feeling, not to function in order to deaden it and to destroy nature. Her book *Choveshko sărtse* (1936) (*Seismograph of the Heart*), used this machine to express anti-humanism of the modern world. Two of her novels, *Pet zvezdi* (1953) (*Five Stars*) and *Ot bryag do bryag* (1963) (*From Shore to Shore*), are quite socialist in feel. During the 1950s she edited the literary monthly *Septemvri*.

Bai Fengxi (born 1934)

Chinese dramatist. Bai began work as an actress in the 1950s. Her concern for women influenced her decision to write on women's themes: 'I don't think that I can dry the tears of all the suffering women,' she said, 'but I want to make a plea with my pen and fight for their rights.' She gained widespread critical attention with her trilogy *First Bathed in Moonlight, Once Loved and in a Storm Returning* and *Say, Who Like Me Is Prey to Fond Regret?*, all dealing with different aspects of problems confronting women: love, marriage, mother–daughter relationships and careers. The trilogy was staged with great success and shown on national TV, eliciting widespread discussion of women's issues in the press.

Bailey, Abigail Abbott (1746–1815)

North American memoirist. Born on 2 February 1746 in Rumford, Connecticut, she was a devout Congregationalist when she married Asa Bailey in 1767. Little is known of her early life, but she bore seventeen children. The impetus for her memoirs was not the continual physical abuse and infidelity she suffered during her twenty-five years of marriage but the discovery that her husband had sexually abused one of their daughters. The ▷*Memoirs of Mrs Abigail Bailey* constitutes one of the few explicit early American accounts of domestic violence recorded by a woman. She details with honesty and openness her difficulty believing that her husband could commit incest, and how she found the courage to remove her

daughter from his influence and to seek a divorce for herself. Included in the memoir are several letters she wrote to her husband; she recognized that he could never be redeemed as a spouse, but she sought to compel him to understand the consequences of his actions so there might 'be excited in your heart some feeling sense of the miseries and tortures you have occasioned me'. Written for her Church and only published posthumously, her memoirs recount one woman's rise above Puritan passivity, and her refusal to remain a victim of spousal abuse.

Baillie, Joanna (1762–1851)

Scottish (▷Scotland) dramatist and poet. Born in Lanarkshire, the daughter of a Presbyterian minister. After her father's death in 1778, Baillie moved to London, settling in Hampstead in 1791. Her first work was *Fugitive Verses* (1790), followed by the highly successful *Plays on the Passions*, published in three volumes between 1798 and 1812. *Basil*, on the subject of love, and *De Montfort*, on hatred, were the most popular of these. Baillie also wrote *Miscellaneous Plays* (1804), and *The Family Legend* (1810), a drama based on a bitter Scottish feud. Sir Walter Scott greatly admired Baillie's work and they became lifelong friends. Her house in Hampstead became a regular meeting point for a lively literary circle. Another volume of poetry, *Metrical Legends*, appeared in 1821, and her verse and ▷drama was collected in a three-volume edition in 1836. She died at the age of 89, declaring herself tired of life.

Bib: Carhart, M., *The Life and Works of Baillie*; Badstuber, A., *Joanna Baillie's Plays on the Passions*.

Bainbridge, Beryl (born 1934)

English novelist and dramatist. Born in Liverpool, she worked as an actress until 1960, and as a publisher's clerk until 1973. Bainbridge's novels are black comedies: portraits of urban life that draw out the eccentric in the ordinary, and combine banality with violence and absurdity. She won the *Guardian* Fiction Prize with *The Bottle Factory Outing* (1974), which explores the friendship of two women on a works outing, and foregrounds the recurrent theme of misunderstanding and misapprehension culminating in death. *Injury Time* (1977) took the Whitbread Prize, and similarly deals with an irruption of violence in a seemingly ordered and innocuous setting, when a dinner party is disrupted by armed criminals who take the guests hostage. Earlier novels, such as *Harriet Said* (1972) and *The Dressmaker* (1973), explore adolescent self-awareness in relation to the residual provincialism of urban Liverpool. *Winter Garden* (1980) picks up the theme of confusion and alienation transposed to a cross-cultural Cold War setting where the protagonist, alone in the Soviet Union, suffers the breakdown of his sense of reality and perspective. The preoccupations of Bainbridge's writings attest to a period of English literary output, particularly television drama of the 1970s, which depicted the eccentricities of working-class and lower-middle-class life, and frequently highlighted themes of alienation and aggressiveness. Other exponents include dramatist Harold Pinter (born 1930) and Mike Leigh.

Other novels: *A Weekend With Claude* (1967), *Another Part of the Wood* (1968), *Sweet William* (1975), *A Quiet Life* (1976), *Young Adolf* (1978), *Watson's Apology* (1985). Television drama includes: *Tiptoe through the Tulips* (1976), *Blue Skies from Now On* (1977), *Words Fail Me* (1979), *The Journal of Bridget Hitler* (1981) and *Somewhere More Central* (1981).

Baird, Irene (1901–1981)
Novelist, born Irene Todd in England, she came to Canada with her parents at the age of eighteen. She worked as a reporter for the Vancouver *Sun* and the *Daily Province*, as well as for Canada's National Film Board and the federal civil service. Her novels mirror her life and various occupations. *John* (1937) is a character study that takes place on Vancouver Island. *Waste Heritage* (1939) is an important and neglected depiction of the Depression. It documents the historic trek to Victoria (the provincial capital) by the unemployed, who were expelled from their sit-down demonstration at the Vancouver Post Office in 1938, and its characters express the frustration and anger of people who have been robbed of their dignity. *He Rides the Sky* (1941) is a rather stilted ▷epistolary novel – the letters home of a young pilot training with the RAF, who is lost in battle in 1940. When Baird retired from the Canadian civil service, she was information chief for the Department of Indian Affairs and Northern Development. *The Climate of Power* (1971) is interesting for its depiction of how government bureaucracy, despite its attempted good will, destroys the ▷Inuit culture.

Bai Wei (born 1894)
Chinese dramatist. Bai had some schooling, but was forced into an arranged marriage at an early age. She escaped in male disguise and continued her education, performing brilliantly at her studies, and even made her way briefly to Japan. Her first piece of writing, *Tragic Life*, was autobiographical. Fired by Ibsen's *Nora, or A Doll's House* (1879) and the plays of Gerhart Hauptmann (1862–1946) and Maurice Maeterlinck (1862–1949), Bai Wei wrote plays on tragic love and patriotic themes, and personally starred in the performances. She was hailed as a rising star for her play *Lin Li* (1925), one of the earliest portrayals of sexual love. In *Patricide*, another play, a tyrannical head of household is killed by his natural daughter whom he, unaware of the relationship, had tried to violate. Before she dies herself, the young woman is reunited with her long-lost mother. The autobiographical *Tragic Life* is an anguished record of betrayed love. Her tragic life and the passionate intensity of her

emotions made Bai Wei one of the most pathetic figures in modern Chinese literature.

Bakaluba, Jane J.
Ugandan popular novelist. Her ▷*Honeymoon for Three* (1979) explores the theme of marital conflict in modern society.
Bib: Taiwo, Oladele, *Female Novelists in Modern Africa.*

Baker, Louisa Alice (1858–1926)
New Zealand novelist. Louisa Alice Dawson was born in the South Island in 1858. Before leaving for England and marriage in 1894, she wrote for some years for local newspapers, and continued publishing serials under a pseudonym, 'Alien', in New Zealand journals while living in Britain. Baker published a large number of romantic novels (sixteen between 1894 and 1913), most of which had heavily Europeanized New Zealand settings. Her emphasis was on New Zealand as a pastoral and exotic landscape and on marriage as the achievement of spiritual/sexual satisfaction for women, and the means for establishing a moral order implemented by women. Baker was unusual for her time in that she wrote about extra-marital relations as well as courtship, which caused local reviewers to describe her novels as evil and decadent. Baker's novels were widely serialized and read and she was celebrated in New Zealand as a successful, if ex-patriate, local.

Works include: *A Daughter of King* (1894); *In Golden Shackles* (1896); *The Majesty of Man* (1895); *Wheat in the Ear* (1898); *The Untold Half* (1899); *The Devil's Half Acre* (1900); *A Slum Heroine* (1904); *An Unanswered Question* (1906); *The Perfect Union* (1908); *A Double Blindness* (1910); *A Maid of Mettle* (1913).
▷Romance writing, New Zealand

Bakr, Salwa (born 1949)
Egyptian novelist and short story writer, graduated with a management degree from Cairo University, and then read for a degree in criticism at the Institute of Drama, Cairo. Salwa Bakr is a truly new voice in Arabic fiction. Most of her characters are women from the lower classes who speak the language of the marginalized, as described by ▷Assia Djebar. In her last novel, ▷*The Golden Chariot Does Not Go Up To Heaven* (1991), the discourse is very close to the colloquial narrative of ▷*The Arabian Nights*: anecdotal, involved, one story leading into another, finally recreating before the reader the life of the inmates of the women's jail. It is a descent into a hellish pit inhabited by women only, including the female gaolers. In an earlier novel, *Maqam 'Attiya* (1986), there are different narrators with different voices. The mystery of 'Attiya's grave, which has grown into a sacred *mazar* (in the Islamic world, a sacred place visited by those seeking miracles or spiritual comfort) in the imagination of the simple inhabitants of the quarter is not solved, but the figure of 'Attiya ('the giving'), representing the mother, the lover, or Isis Hathur, the goddess

with the full, hanging breasts, can bear even more interpretations than there are voices. Bakr's short stories are published in three small collections that mark her as a leading short story writer: *Zeenat in the Funeral of the President* (1986), *Maqam 'Attiya and Other Stories* (1986) and *The Stealing of the Soul, Gently* (1989).
Bib: Booth, Marilyn (trans.), ▷*My Grandmother's Cactus* (1991) contains two of her short stories.

'Balade Whych Anne Askewe Made and Sange whan she was in Newgate, The' (1547)
Poem by ▷Anne Askew appended to ▷*The Lattre Examynacyon*, published by John Bale. Taking the theme of the Christian soldier of Ephesians, Askew's 'Balade' begins with the image of a knight armed with faith. Her poem also serves as a kind of prayer. It echoes a number of concerns manifested in *The Lattre Examynacyon*, particularly her desire for strength in maintaining her convictions, and her desire for God's forgiveness of her wrongdoers.

Balbilla (2nd century AD)
Ancient Roman poet. A companion of the Empress Sabina, wife of Roman Emperor Hadrian, Julia Balbilla inscribed a lyric poem upon the Statue of Memnon in Egypt to celebrate the imperial visit.
Bib: (text & trans.) Edmonds, J.M., *Greek Elegy and Iambus.*

Ballad (19th-century Britain)
Associated with oral tradition and song, ballads were a popular form for women poets in the 19th century, and proved equally popular with readers. ▷Felicia Hemans, ▷Letitia Landon, ▷Elizabeth Barrett Browning, ▷Emily Brontë and ▷Christina Rossetti are among those women writers who practised the form. Victorian ballads often had a medieval setting, such as Barrett Browning's 'The Romaunt of the Page' (1839) and 'The Lay of the Brown Rosary' (1840).

Ballad of the Sad Café, The (1951)
US novel. Unlike ▷*The Heart is a Lonely Hunter* (1940) and ▷*Member of the Wedding* (1946), this book by ▷Carson McCullers focuses on a woman who remains a tomboy. Amelia Evans refuses to conform to a prescribed social role and she befriends a male dwarf who is sexually impotent and poses no threat. Her relationship with Cousin Lymon inverts traditional masculine and feminine roles. Nevertheless, Amelia fears male vengeance for denying her sex and dominating men. Her fears are realized when her former husband and Lymon join forces to destroy her. In this novel McCullers indulges the desire to appropriate masculine power and escape womanhood.

Ballard, Martha Moore (1735–1812)
North American diarist. Though she was born in Oxford, Massachusetts, the best-known years of her life were spent in Augusta, Maine, where she and her family settled in 1777. At the age of fifty, she began keeping a diary of her day-to-day experiences, ▷*The Diary of Mrs Martha Moore Ballard*. She had numerous careers, but most important was that of a midwife for her community, a service which she performed in addition to helping her husband Ephraim manage their farm, and raising eight children (three of whom died of diphtheria in 1769). In her twenty-seven-year diary, she records a life of amazingly hard work and personal stamina. 'A womans work is never Done', she observed with a hearty spirit, 'and happy shee whose strength holds out to the end of the rais'. She 'held out' for 77 years and her diary is a rare account of an older woman's lifelong labours.

Ballata levantina (1961) ▷*Levantines, The*

Ballesteros de Gaibrois, Mercedes (born 1913)
Spanish journalist and novelist. Born in Madrid of an aristocratic family. From the 1940s onwards, Ballesteros wrote newspaper articles; she soon established her reputation as a humorist. Her first major novel, *La cometa y el eco* (1956) (*The Kite and the Echo*), centres on the life of the orphaned protagonist, Augusta, and the family she lives with. The title figures, the kite and the echo, are symbols of time and communication with the dead. Her other novels are: *Eclipse de tierra* (1954) (*Eclipse of the Earth*); *Taller* (1960) (*The Workshop*); *Mi hermano y yo por esos mundos* (1962) (*My Brother and I On Our Travels*); *La sed* (1965) (*Thirst*); and *El chico* (1967) (*The Boy*).

ballo dei sapienti, Il (1966) (Dance of the Sages)
This Italian novel by ▷Maria Corti, set in Milan's University and schools in the 1960s, addresses the problems, hopes and experiences of intellectuals in this fraught and exciting period. It highlights many of the hypocrisies of university life, and mocks its conventions. It also considers the barriers between academia and the 'real world' through the dilemmas of three characters in particular: Foschina, a student who suddenly discovers the importance of the sensual life; Beretta, an unsuccessful academic who feels out of place and inadequate amongst his rather cruel colleagues, and Lanfranchi, a positive character, a generous intellectual toying with the idea of embarking on a love affair. The fast-paced narrative moves through different linguistic registers, as one might expect of the work of an eminent philologist such as Corti.

Balún Canán (1958) ▷*Nine Guardians, The* (1970)

Bambara, Toni Cade (born 1939)
US short story writer and novelist Bambara was raised by her working-class mother in New York's poorer neighbourhoods. In 1963 she earned a Master's degree at the City College of New York, and has been a social worker, a community

organizer and a college professor. In *The Black Woman* (1970) Bambara provides diverse African-American women's perspectives on the civil rights movement and the women's movement. Bambara's work describes the sense of caring for neighbours that sustains the African-American community. The stories in *Gorilla, My Love* (1972) undermine the stereotypes of African-American women; 'The Lesson' and 'My Man Bovanne' depict the struggles between different generations of African-Americans. Her novel *The Salt Eaters* (1980), a complex and experimental interweaving of multiple voices, emphasizes the significance of cultural traditions for spiritual renewal and envisions a joint coalition of Third World people. Like ▷Toni Morrison, Bambara situates her work as part of a process of constructing an African-American literary tradition and aesthetic, which in Bambara's case owes much to jazz, be-bop and urban African-American culture.

Other works include: *Tales and Stories for Black Folks* (1971), *The Sea Birds Are Still Alive: Collected Stories* (1977).
Bib: Bell, Roseann, Parker, Bettye and Guy-Sheftall, Beverly (eds), *Sturdy Black Bridges: Visions of Black Women in Literature*; Tate, Claudia (ed.), *Black Women Writers at Work*; Evans, Mari (ed.), *Black Women Writers (1950–1980)*.

Bancroft, Francis ▷Slater, Frances Charlotte

Bandler, Faith (born 1918)
Australian writer and Aboriginal rights activist. Bandler is the daughter of a Pacific Islander brought to Australia by slave traders in 1883 to work in the canefields, and was born in northern New South Wales. *Wacvie* (1977) and *The Time Was Ripe* (1980, with Len Fox) tell her father's story. Bandler has also published *Marani in Australia* (1980, with Len Fox) and *Welou, My Brother* (1984). She has also received the Order of Australia.
▷Aboriginal women writers in Australia

Ban Jieyu (c 48–c 6 BC)
Royal concubine to Emperor Cheng of the Chinese Han dynasty (202 BC–AD 220). Her name is lost, *jieyu* being her title as a royal concubine. Record has it that she refused the emperor's request to sit next to him on the imperial chariot, an exercise in feminine self-depreciation that won her the emperor's favour, although not for long. She was soon displaced and dispatched to serve the dowager empress. She relieved her wretchedness by writing poetry bemoaning her fate. Over a round fan – silk stretched over a bamboo frame – she inscribed a poem, 'Resentful Song', bemoaning that 'winter's chills' soon cool the 'ardours of summer'. Thus the phrase 'autumn fan' passed into the language to denote a deserted wife. Her poems were known in her time, and she is mentioned in *Admonitions to Women*, a book of moral advice to young women of ancient China.
▷Ban Zhao

Banks, Isabella (1821–1887)
English novelist, poet and journalist, born in Manchester, the daughter of a successful tradesman. She was sixteen years old when her poem 'A Dying Girl to Her Mother', was published in the *Manchester Guardian*. More of her work was published in *Bradshaw's Three* (1841–42), and her first collection of poems, *Ivy Leaves*, appeared in 1844. Banks then grew prolific, writing a series of novels set in the Manchester area, the best-known of which are *The Manchester Man* (1876), *Caleb Booth's Clerk* (1878) and *Wooers and Winners: A Yorkshire Story* (1880). Her novels were so rooted in her native environment that she was labelled the 'Lancashire Novelist'. They are mainly of historical interest today, seeming overloaded with detailed local description and lacking narrative pace.

Banks, Lynne Reid
English novelist and dramatist. She trained and worked as an actress, and then as a television news reporter and scriptwriter. Her first publications were plays, broadcast on radio and television. Her first novel, ▷*The L-Shaped Room* (1960), was also her most successful. Her portrayal of her unmarried, pregnant heroine's experiences in London bed-sitter land has been seen as a landmark in post-war British fiction. Its sequels, *The Backward Shadow* (1970) and *Two's Company* (1974) were far less successful.

At the beginning of the 1960s Banks went to Israel, married, and lived on a kibbutz for some years. A number of her novels are set in Israel, including *An End to Running* (1962) and *Children at the Gate* (1968), which uses Israeli–Arab relations as a background to its story of a Jewish woman whose emotionally impoverished life is redeemed when she takes on the care of her Arab friend's three children.

Banks returned to London after spending some eight years in Israel. Her other works include books for children and teenagers, and a two-part account of the life of the ▷Brontës.

Bannon, Ann (born c 1937)
US novelist. Bannon is unquestionably the most popular and highly-regarded writer of the lesbian paperback original novels, or 'pulps' (▷Lesbian pulp fiction), a genre involving thousands of books published from 1957 to 1963. Her six novels were *Odd Girl Out* (1957), *Women in the Shadows* (1959), *I Am a Woman* (1959), *Journey to a Woman* (1960), *The Marriage* (1960) and *Beebo Brinker* (1962), all of which were reissued in 1975 and again in the 1980s. Her first book was an enormous success and the publisher encouraged her to continue the stories of her characters. As a result, Bannon's six novels tell the ongoing stories of three lesbians in the 1950s, moving from a scandalous college affair to the bars of Greenwich Village to a troubled marriage. The most significant character is Beebo Brinker, who has come to personify the 1950s bar butch and her ongoing search for true love.

Bannon's books tell a throughly North American story of lesbians seeking their identity and community, as they are peopled with recognizable prototypes – 'All American Girl' co-eds, working-class New York women, suburban housewives, and even a glamorous movie star. The books are also notable for their depiction of the supportive relationship between a lesbian and a gay man: and for one of the few presentations of a lesbian of color in any lesbian novel before the 1970s.

Bannon is currently a professor at a California State University, and is working on a new novel that will take her unforgettable 'Beebo' into the contemporary lesbian world.

Banti, Anna (1895–1985)

Italian novelist, short story writer, essayist and translator; real name Lucia Longhi Lopresti. She was born in Florence, and took a degree in history of art there. This interest is reflected in her essays and in her prose fiction. She won many literary prizes for her work, and co-founded the magazine *Paragone* with her husband, Roberto Longhi. She translated some of the works of both Thackeray and ▷Virginia Woolf, and was also a respected literary critic. A recurrent theme in her work, exemplified in ▷*Artemisia* (1947), is woman's place in society. She sees modern women as particularly isolated, and regards society as negatively disposed to recognise women's abilities – and right – to work in fulfilling occupations. Women form the focal point of her work.

Her other works include: (criticism): *Lorenzo Lotto* (1953); *Opinioni* (1961) (*Opinions*); *Matilde Serao* (1965); *Giovanni da San Giovanni, pittore della contraddizione* (1978) (*GdSG, a Painter of Contradictions*); (prose fiction): *Itinerario di Paolina* (1937) (*Paolina's Itinerary*); *Il coraggio delle donne* (1940), (1988) (*Women's Courage*); *Sette lune* (1941) (*Seven Moons*); *Le monache cantano* (1942) (*The Nuns Are Singing*); ▷*Le donne muoiono* (1951) (*Women Are Dying*); *Il bastardo* (1953) (*The Bastard*); *Allarme sul lago* (1954) (*Alert on the Lake*); *La monaca di Sciangai* (1957) (*The Nun of Shanghai*); *La casa piccola* (1961) (*The Little House*); *Le mosche d'oro* (1962) (*The Golden Flies*); *Campi elisi* (1963) (*The Elysian Fields*); *Noi credevamo* (1967) (*We Used to Believe*) ; *Je vous écris d'un pays lointain* (1971) (*I Am Writing to You from a Far-away Land*); *La camicia bruciata* (1973) (*The Burned Shirt*); *Da un paese vicino* (1975) (*From Near at Hand*); *Un grido lacerante* (1981) (*A Rending Cry*); *Quando anche le donne si misero a dipingere* (1982) (*When Women Too Began to Paint*).

Ban Zhao (AD?52–125)

A learned woman of the East Han dynasty (202 BC–AD 220). Widowed when young, she was admitted to the court of the emperor and respected as a teacher. Ban Zhao completed the *Han Shu*, records of the Han dynasty for the years 206–23 BC, an undertaking which her brother, Ban Gu, left unfinished at his death. Ban Zhao also composed the *Admonitions to Women* in seven chapters of about 1600 characters. This is the earliest manual of education for women, and also the first piece of writing to systematically consolidate the concept of the natural inferiority of women.

Baobab fou, Le (1982) (The Mad Baobab)

A personalized account by Senegalese writer ▷Ken Bugul on the familiar theme in African literature of a traumatic encounter with white civilization. An ordinary village girl finds herself a student in Belgium, in a world for which she is entirely unprepared and which she describes with devastating honesty. She becomes pregnant, has an abortion, falls into the hands of a pimp and becomes a prostitute. On her father's death, she returns home, but realizing she can no longer adapt to her old environment, goes back a life of prostitution in Brussels. Eventually, after considering suicide, she makes the decisive break and returns home finally, recognizing it as her only hope of redemption.

Bao Chuan (born 1942)

Chinese short story writer. Bao graduated from a teachers' college in 1966 and worked as a clerk in her native Sichuan. She started writing in 1973. Much-anthologized short stories include 'Before the Wedding' (1979), 'Maternal Love', 'Toast to our Bicycles!' and 'The Loudspeaker', mostly on the day-to-day frustrations of the underprivileged in an ostensibly egalitarian society.
Bib: Zhu Hong (trans.), 'The Loudspeaker' in *The Serenity of Whiteness*.

Baptist, R. Hernekin ▷Lewis, Ethelreda

Barandas, Ana Eurídice de

Brazilian poet, short story and chronicle writer and novelist. She has been defined as the first Brazilian woman novelist for her book *O ramalhete ou flores escolhidas no jardim da imaginacão* (1845) (*A Bunch of Flowers Chosen in the Garden of Imagination*), in place of ▷Maria Firmina dos Reis or Teresa Margarida da Silva e Orta. She also wrote *A filosofia do amor* (1845) (*The Philosophy of Love*).

Baránskaia, Natal'ia Vladimirovna (1908–?)

Russian prose writer. Baránskaia began publishing fiction only in 1964, after retiring from a curatorial post at the Pushkin Museum in Moscow. Her most famous work is the novella ▷*A Week Like Any Other*, which is typical of her realistic chronicles of daily life in the Soviet Union. Her portraits of women – Shura, an unmarried mother and worker in a provincial factory ('The Spell', *Images of Women in Contemporary Fiction*, 1976); a troubled teenager ('Liubka', *A Week Like Any Other*, 1977); Laine, an Estonian who lives with a terrible secret ('Laine's House', *Soviet Women Writing*, 1981) – are affectionate and perceptive.

Barbados

This geographical region of the Caribbean is English-speaking. It is the birthplace of Undine Guiseppi, ▷Paule Marshall, Millicent Payne (born 1911) and Monica Skeete (born 1920).

Barbara is Singing (1989–1990)

Work by Japanese writer Ochiai Keiko (born 1945). Ayumi is illegitimate, and, although thirty-five, is living with her grandmother and her mother, who suffers from an obsessive compulsive nervous condition. The two older women go to Tokyo, leaving their home town. Ayumi does not have a good relationship with her lover because she refuses to have a child. Ayumi's aunt, however, married with two children, often sees the lover. This work describes the difficulties of female solidarity and the troubles of a professional working woman, encouraging women readers to free themselves from the conventional role they are expected to adopt.

Barbauld, Anna Laetitia (Aikin) (1743–1825)

English poet, essayist and writer for children. Her father ran a Dissenting academy in Warrington (of which she wrote 'Here callow chiefs and embryo statesmen lie'), and he taught her Latin and Greek. Her brother, John (a doctor), was proud that some of her first poems were written at his house. They published some pieces together (in *Miscellaneous Pieces in Prose*, 1773) but the first of her poems to be published was the 'Ode on Corsica' (1768). She was already a known poet when her *Poems* (1773) were published: they went through four editions in twelve months. When she married M. Rochemont Barbauld her father wrote that she was under 'the baleful influence of [J.J. Rousseau's (1712–1778)] *nouvelle Heloise*'. They ran a boys' school together before travelling in France and coming to London, where the marriage broke down. Rochemont Barbauld eventually committed suicide. Barbauld spent much of the rest of her life in Stoke Newington, London, writing for ▷periodicals, including *The Spectator*, *The Guardian* and the *Freeholder*. Her *Lessons for Children* (1778) and *Hymns in Prose for Children* (1781) were in the new genre of educational publications. She published the long narrative poem *Eighteen Hundred and Eleven* (1812), and edited the work of other writers including Mark Akenside, William, Collins and the correspondence of Samuel Richardson (▷Richardson, influence of). She knew ▷Hester Chapone, and met ▷Maria Edgeworth in 1799.
  Other publications: *Epistle to William Wilberforce* (1791).
Bib: Aikin , Lucy (ed.), *Works* (1825); Rogers, Betsy, *Georgian Chronicle: Mrs Barbauld and Her Family* Scott, W.S., *Letters of . . . Barbauld and Maria Edgeworth*.

Barbier, Marie-Anne (1670–1745)

French dramatist. Born in Orléans, Barbier was well-read in dramatic theory and French tragedy, and was one of the most successful female dramatists of her time. Her four full-length tragedies, performed at the Comédie-Française between 1700 and 1710, made up almost one-sixth of the total number staged in the period. She was also the most overtly feminist of the women then writing for the theatre. Her first three tragedies were all dedicated to women, and in her prefaces she attacks the tradition by which women's literary achievements are persistently denied by the attribution of their work to male collaborators. She defends female authorship by listing major female figures in the literary canon. In her staged plays – *Arrie et Pétrus* (1702), *Cornélie, mère des Graques* (1703) (*Cornélie, Mother of Graques*), *Tomyris* (1707, adapted from Madelaine de Scudéry's novel *Le Grand Cyrus* and *La mort de César* (1710) (*The Death of Caesar*) – the main focus is on the tragic heroine. Even in dealing with the death of Caesar, she emphasizes the role of Octavia. Intertwined in the histories of powerful male figures, and displacing them from centre stage, are the lives of the women caught in the conflicts between the political and the domestic, passions and principles. Barbier's feminist and populist ideas are reflected in the periodical she edited, *Saisons littéraires* (1714) (*Literary Seasons*). She also produced a comedy, three operas, a collection of prose fiction, literary criticism and occasional verse.
  Other works: *Brutus, tragédie* (1691) (*Brutus, a Tragedy*); *Le Théâtre de l'amour et de la fortune* (1713) (*The Theatre of Love and Fortune*); *Les fêtes de l'été, ballet* (1716) (*Summer Festivities, a Ballet*); *Le jugement de Paris, pastorale héroique* (1718) (*The Judgement of Paris, an Heroic Pastoral*); *La Faucon, comédie* (1719) (*The Falcon, a Comedy*); *Les plaisirs de la campagne, ballet* (1719) (*Country Delights, a Ballet*).
  ▷*Journal des Dames*
Bib: Lancaster, H. C., *Sunset: A History of Parisian Drama in the Last Years of Louis XIV 1701–1715*; Showalter, Jr, E., 'Writing off the stage: Women Authors and Eighteenth-Century Theater' in Dejean, J. and Miller, N. K. (eds), *Displacements*.

Bardwell, Leland (born 1928)

Irish novelist, poet and dramatist. Born in India, she grew up in County Kildare, then travelled widely, living in London and Paris during the 1940s and 1950s. Her plays have been produced on Irish radio and on stage, and she has published two collections of poetry: *The Mad Cyclist* (1970) and *The Fly and the Bed Bug* (1984). Her novels and short stories include: *Girl on a Bicycle* (1978), *That London Winter* (1981), *The House* (1984), *Different Kinds of Love* (1987) and *There We Have Been* (1989). Her work is marked by a subtle blend of poetic ▷realism and black humour.

Barfoot, Joan (born 1946)

Canadian novelist, and journalist with the *London Free Press* in London, Ontario. Joan Barfoot was born and raised in Owen Sound, and attended the University of Western Ontario. Her first novel,

Abra, won the *Books in Canada* First Novel Award in 1978. *Dancing in the Dark* (1982) is a strikingly intense novel about a woman in an insane asylum chronicling how and why she has murdered her unfaithful husband. It was made into an award-winning film. *Duet for Three* appeared in 1985, and *Family News* in 1989. Barfoot's fiction deals with family conflict and the betrayals of domesticity, charting the shoals of contemporary relationships in realistic and intense detail.

Barford, Chérie (born 1960)

New Zealand poet. Chérie Barford was born in Auckland and is now a relief teacher there. She has published one collection of poems, *A Plea to the Spanish Lady* (1985), which deals with travelling and cross-cultural, post-colonial experience, especially in Samoa.

Barine, Arvède (1840–1908)

French critic, historian and biographer. Barine began writing at the age of thirty-nine, after marriage, motherhood and a brief career as a translator. She produced prodigious quantities of literary, socio-political and philosophical articles for the major journals of the period, many of which reveal her fascination with foreign climes. However, her speciality was evocative, finely-drawn pen-portraits of famous women, and her *Portraits de femmes* (1887) (*Portraits of Women*) and *Princesses et grandes dames* (1890) (*Princesses and Great Ladies*) are probably her best-known works. Two other texts, a monograph on the poet Alfred de Musset (1810–1857) published in 1893, and *Poètes et névrosés* (1898) (*Poets and Neurotics*), indicate that she was also fascinated by the relationship between creative genius and mental abnormality, and suggest that she was a kind of psychological/psychoanalytical critic '*avant la lettre*'.
Bib: Tissot, E., *Princesses des lettres*.

Barker, Jane (1652–?1727)

English poet and writer of fiction, Barker may have followed James II to Paris in 1688 after becoming a Roman Catholic, returning to England by 1713. Many of her poems remain in manuscript in Oxford and London. Her poetry was first published in *Poetical Recreations: Consisting of Original Songs, Poems, Odes Etc.* (1688) by Barker with others. In 1713 she published *Love's Intrigues: or the History of the Amours of Bosvil and Galesia* (1713). There followed a collection of stories, *Exilus: or The Banished Roman* (1715), and *A Patch-Work Screen For the Ladies* (1723), a series of 'told' embedded narratives, as is its sequel, *The Lining for the Patch-Work Screen* (1726). She explains her use of tales as 'patch-work': 'I think I ought to say something in Favour of Patch-Work, the better to recommend it to my Female Readers, as well in their Discourse as in their Needle-Work . . . but in the little I have read, I do no remember any thing relating to Patch-Work, since the Patriarch Joseph (whose Garment was of sundry Colours).'

Bib: Spencer, Jane, *The Rise of the Woman Novelist*; small selection in Greer, Germaine, *et al.*, *Kissing the Rod*, and Ferguson, Moira, *First Feminists*.

Barker, Lady Mary Anne (1831–1911)

New Zealand writer. Born Mary Anne Stewart in Jamaica, Lady Barker came to New Zealand in 1865 with her second husband, Frederick Broome, a New Zealand sheep farmer. Lady Barker's account of the time spent on a sheep run in the South Island, ▷*Station Life in New Zealand*, was published in 1870 and is based on letters written to her sister. In 1868 the Broomes returned to England where Lady Barker spent the next decade writing books, stories and reviews, and working as the Lady Superintendent of the National School of Cookery. In 1875 Frederick Broome moved to Natal, then Mauritius and western Australia as a colonial administrator, accompanied by Lady Barker for most of the time: much of this travelling is recorded in her books.

Lady Barker's books were widely read during her lifetime and many are still in print. She is one of the most interesting commentators on colonial life in New Zealand.

Works include: *Station Life in New Zealand* (1870); *Station Amusements in New Zealand* (1873); *A Christmas Cake in Four Quarters* (1872); *Letters to Guy* (1885).

Barker, Pat (born 1943)

Pat Barker

English novelist. Barker was first encouraged by ▷Angela Carter to utilize her working-class background as source material, and this advice led to the prize-winning ▷*Union Street* (1982). *Blow Your House Down* (1984) focuses on a group of prostitutes haunted by the threat of a serial killer, and *The Man Who Wasn't There* (1989) forms an analysis of media representations of masculinity. Barker's novels are characterized by her frank and unadulterated portrayals of working-class deprivation.

Barking, Anonymous Nun of (fl after 1163)

Hagiographer in England. A deliberately anonymous nun of Barking Abbey was the author of the *Life of Edward the Confessor* (*La Vie d'Edouard le Confesseur*), an ▷Anglo-Norman verse adaptation of the prose life of Edward by the English Cistercian, Aelred of Rievaulx. It may have been written at the request of Adeliza Fitz-John (died 1173), who had been appointed abbess by Henry II of England, for the use of the women of the abbey or for presentation at court. The work was written in octosyllabic couplets, a popular verse form (it was used for romance, for example, and also by ▷Marie de France). The author employs the modesty topos, writing that she is not worthy that her name should be mentioned in a book where she has written the holy name of St Edward. She also apologizes for the poor quality of her French, and says that she produced the translation against her will. The *Life* is one of the two important verse saints' lives produced at Barking, an Anglo-Saxon foundation with a long tradition of scholarship.
  ▷Clemence of Barking
Bib: Södergård, Östen (ed.), *La Vie d'Edouard le Confesseur*.

Barking Abbey

This Benedictine Abbey in Barking, Essex, was founded as a double monastery for women and men in about AD 666, with an abbess in charge (as was customary for Anglo-Saxon double houses). It was a wealthy foundation with royal connections. During the Anglo-Saxon period the standard of education for women there was high. The tradition was evidently maintained to some degree after the Norman Conquest (1066), when religious houses for women were in general much poorer than those of men, and resources and opportunities for the education of women were much diminished in comparison with the pre-Conquest period.
  ▷Barking, Anonymous Nun of; Clemence of Barking
Bib: Knowles, David and Hadcock, R. Neville, *Medieval Religious Houses in England and Wales*.

Barkóva, Anna Aleksandrovna (1901–1976)

Russian poet. Barkóva was from a working-class family, and initially supported the Revolution fervently. Her poetry first appeared in 1919 in a newspaper in the town of Ivanovo under the pseudonym 'Wandering Cripple'. Her collection, *Woman*, was published in 1922, and a year later her only play, ▷*Nastas'ia Kostër*, was published. During the 1920s she worked at *Pravda*, and

St Aldehelm presenting his book to the nuns of Barking Abbey

individual poems and reviews appeared there and in leading ▷'thick journals' and anthologies.
  Barkóva chose to open *Woman* with 'Two Poets' in which the speaker addresses a woman poet of a 'Great Era' whose coming she foresees in a 'madly prophetic dream.' Many of the poems in the collection deal with themes of transition and prophesy that echo 'The Smithy', a contemporary group of proletarian writers. The female speaker boldly rejects the past and sees herself as a forerunner of future women, although not without inner conflict. Barkóva consciously takes up arms against the prevailing style, imagery, and form of 'feminine' poetry. If women wrote – and were expected to write – mellifluous and graceful verse, Barkóva's is deliberately cacophonous and awkward, and uses assonance instead of rhyme. *Woman* received generally positive notice, and one reviewer called her the 'Joan of Arc' of a new poetry. Late in life, Barkóva said that she would keep only fifteen of the poems in *Woman*.
  Between 1934 and 1965 the poet spent more than twenty years in prison camps. She never stopped writing poetry. In the 1930s Barkóva sets her lyrical persona in the midst of a demonic world. In the 1940s and 1950s the theme of suffering and powerlessness to change one's situation becomes more prominent. The folkloric language that she had used in *Nastas'ia Kostër* appears also in her late poetry. In the ▷*glásnost'*

period several articles appeared on Barkóva's work and her tragic fate, and the first collection of her poetry since 1922 was published in 1990.

Barnard, Lady Anne (1750–1825)
Scottish poet, diarist and letter-writer; eldest daughter of Anne Dalrymple and James Lindsay, fifth Earl of Balcarres. She achieved a minor reputation in Scotland for her ballad 'Auld Robin Gray', composed in the 1770s, but is more properly a figure in South African English literature. During time spent at the Cape from 1797 to 1802, she kept a journal, part of which has been published, along with extensive letters to Lord Dundas, Secretary for War and the Colonies and to Lord Macartney, sometime Governor of the Cape. Married to the Colonial Secretary of the Cape, and taking on the role of 'First Lady' in the absence of the Governor's wife, she offers a lively epistolary account of official life and local politics, of her excursions around the Cape, and of the various people she met. She gives frequent glimpses of herself, too: a woman whose interests and energies were continually thwarted by current definitions of femininity. In her ▷*Journal of a Tour into the Interior*, addressed to her sisters in England, Barnard negotiates the orthodoxies of local life, to do largely with class and decorum, but also with race: she found the views of the local Dutch narrow and unsympathetic. Her attitude to the Boers was patronizing (except where she found evidence of intelligence and pleasing manners) as was her attitude to the indigenous people. A sketcher and painter as well as a writer, Barnard's compositional approach to the landscape and its people is of particular interest. Her writing has been collected in two major publications: *Lady Anne Barnard at the Cape of Good Hope, 1797–1802* (1924), edited by Dorothea Fairbridge; and *The Letters of Lady Anne Barnard to Henry Dundas . . . together with her Journal of a Tour into the Interior . . .*(1973), edited by A. M. Lewin Robinson. More work is currently being edited.
▷Diaries and Journals (Southern Africa); Letters (Southern Africa)

Barnard, Marjorie (1897–1987)
Australian novelist and historian. Barnard graduated in 1920 with a first class honours degree from the University of Sydney but, feeling her duty to her parents prevented her taking up an Oxford graduate scholarship, became a librarian. Barnard collaborated with ▷Flora Eldershaw under the joint pseudonym of ▷M. Barnard Eldershaw in the writing of four novels: *A House is Built* (1929), *Green Memory* (1931), *The Glasshouse* (1936) and *Plaque with Laurel* (1937). *Tomorrow and Tomorrow* (1947), an ambitious and impressive futuristic novel, republished in an uncensored version as ▷*Tomorrow and Tomorrow and Tomorrow* (1983), is essentially Barnard's, as is ▷*The Persimmon Tree and Other Stories* (1943) and *The Ivory Gate* (1920), for children.
Barnard also wrote a number of historical

studies and some literary criticism, including a critical study of ▷Miles Franklin. In collaboration with Flora Eldershaw, as M. Barnard Eldershaw, she published *Essays in Australian Fiction* (1938). Barnard was awarded the Patrick White Award (1983), the New South Wales Premier's Special Award (1984) and an Honorary Doctorate of Letters from the University of Sydney in 1986. She has also received the Order of Australia.
▷Short story (Australia)

Barnes, Charlotte Mary Sanford (1818–1863)
US writer of historical drama, some in blank verse. Because she dramatized characters and plots already familiar to her audience, Barnes could focus on effect and language. Most notable and distinctively North American are her retelling of the Pocahontas story in *The Forest Princess* (1848) and her recasting of a famous 19th-century revenge murder in *Octavia Bradaldi* (1837, 1848).

Barnes, Djuna (1892–1982)

Djuna Barnes

US novelist, short story writer, dramatist and journalist. A crossing or transgression of conventional political, sexual and artistic boundaries marks both Djuna Barnes's life and work. Born into an unconventional, although rich, family at Cornwall-on-Hudson, New York, Barnes was educated at home by her 'visionary' father and writer grandmother. Beginning professional life as a journalist in New York, Barnes soon crossed into poetry, illustrated by her own striking artwork, novel writing and eventually dramatic work. In about 1919 she moved to Paris where she became a significant figure in the literary community of the 1920s, which was central to Anglo-American ▷modernism. Writers with whom she was associated include ▷Gertrude Stein, ▷Natalie Barney, ▷Mina Loy, T.S. Eliot (1888–1965), James Joyce (1882–1941), ▷Janet Flanner and ▷Kay Boyle. Barnes later returned to New York, and from 1941 until her death she lived in Patchin Place in Greenwich Village.

Her early experimental work with journalistic form, with its shrewd political observation of gendered mores and manners, anticipates both the stylistic daring of her later works and the exploration of female sexuality that is found both there and in her own life and loves. *Ladies' Almanack* (1928), for example, chronicles the mission of a lesbian saint and crusader, whilst the powerfully-charged eroticism and violence of ▷*Nightwood* (1936) focuses on a lesbian love affair.

Other works include: *The Book of Repulsive Women: Eight Rhythms and Five Drawings* (1915), *A Book* (1923), *Ryder* (1928), *A Night Among the Horses* (1929), *The Antiphon* (1958), *Spillway* (1962), *Selected Works of Djuna Barnes* (1962), *Vagaries Malicieux To Stories* (1974), *Creatures in an Alphabet* (1982) and *Smoke and Other Early Stories* (1982).
Bib: Scott, James B., *Djuna Barnes:* Kannestine, Louis B., *The Art of Djuna Barnes: Duality and Damnation*; Field, Andrew and Messerli, Douglas, *Djuna Barnes: A Bibliography*.

Barney, Natalie (1876–1972)

US poet, dramatist and novelist. Born in Dayton, Ohio, Barney became legendary as the centre of a lesbian coterie and international literary salon in Paris. Following her mother's example, she chose to live and express herself as she pleased, earning a reputation for the emancipated ideas by which she lived. She espoused the ideals of the classical Greek poet, ▷Sappho, and her views on lesbianism were distinctive. She rejected the adoption and imitation of masculine codes of dress and behaviour. Barney published her views on Sapphic love in *Pensees d'une Amazone* (1920) (*Thoughs of an Amazon*). Left independently wealthy Barney established her literary salon in rue Jacob. It was frequented by a wide group of women including ▷Gertrude Stein, ▷Renee Vivien, ▷Djuna Barnes ▷Radclyffe Hall, Una Troubridge, ▷Anna Wickham, ▷Janet Flanner and the painter Romaine Brooks. Both Barnes in *Ladies' Almanack* and Hall in ▷*The Well of Loneliness* offer portraits of Barney and her salon. Whilst Barney's salon is usually remembered for the 'exotic' sexuality of those who frequented it, the salon's true importance lies in the creation of a 'community of women committed to producing serious art'. Barney published three volumes of memoirs that provide an important literary history of her time and make an invaluable contribution to the history of lesbian culture.

Other works include: *Quelques portraits – sonnets de femmes* (1900), *Cinq petits dialogues grecs* (1901), *Actes et entr'actes* (1910), *Aventures de l'esprit* (1929), *Nouvelles pensees de l'amazone* (1939), *Souvenirs indiscrets* (1960), and *Traits et portraits* (1963).
Bib: Benstock, Shari, *Women of the Left Bank: Paris, 1900–1940*.

Baron, Devorah (1887–1956)

Israeli short story writer and translator. Born in Russia, the daughter of a rabbi, Baron was brought up in a traditional Jewish home. She was educated in Russia and emigrated to Palestine in 1911. With her husband, the editor of an influential magazine, she was part of the main literary circle of her day. Her realistic stories describe the struggles of individuals within the constraints of their surroundings. The fate of women in a traditional, restrictive society is a major concern, especially in the stories set in the small Jewish towns of eastern Europe. Baron published several collections of stories, including *Sipurim* (1927) (*Stories*), ▷*Parshiyot* (1968) (*Episodes*) and *The Thorny Path* (1969). Her main translation work was *Madam Bovary* by Flaubert.
▷*Anthology of Modern Hebrew Poetry*

Baroque (Portugal)

Literary and artistic movement dating from 1580 (the death of the epic poet Luís Vaz de Camões) to 1746 (the publication of Luís António Verney's ▷*Verdadeiro Método de Estudar*). For much of this period, from 1580 to 1640, Portugal was ruled by a Spanish king, and the Spanish writers Góngora and Quevedo were particularly influential. Stylistic and conceptual devices associated with their works (*cultismo* – an approach to poetic form which favoured elaborate forms of expression, utilizing hyperbole, antithesis and puns – and ▷*conceptismo*) were in evidence in Portuguese prose and verse in the 17th and 18th centuries. An important author of this period is ▷Sóror Violante do Céu. Her poetry as well as samples of other poets' writings from the period can be found in the collection ▷*Fênix Renascida*.

Barr, Amelia Edith Huddleston (1831–1919)

US writer of historical fiction, journalism and autobiography. British born, Barr lived in the USA after 1853, when she began her writing career. Along with a successful career as a journalist, Barr is most significant for her forty years' production of historical novels with North American subjects and settings, eg, *Remember the Alamo* (1888). Her autobiography is *All the Days of My Life* (1913).
▷*Frank Leslie's Popular Monthly*

Barra de Llanos, Ema de la (1861–1947)

Argentinian novelist, painter and classical singer, who wrote under the pseudonym César Duayen. She moved to Buenos Aires as a child. She married her uncle, Juan de la Barra, and lived in one of the first luxurious residences of Avenue Alvear. Widowed in 1904, she became a writer and painter, and sang in family concerts. Her novel ▷*Stella* (1905), published under her ▷pseudonym, caused much curiosity and brought her immediate fame, partly because she was a woman. She married Julio Llanos, who was at first thought to be the author of *Stella*, but this was soon denied. The novel was *costumbrista* (▷*costumbrismo*) and realistic in style, but with romantic traits. She received an advance for her novel *Mecha Iturbe* (1906) (*The Burning Wick*), which was exceptional then, but she did not achieve the same success as with *Stella*, nor did she with her novel *Eleonora*. She also published articles and short stories in magazines and newspapers.

Barrage contre le Pacifique, Un (1950) ▷*Sea Wall, The* (1986)

Barren Ground (1925)

US novel. ▷Ellen Glasgow's book portrays a woman who defies social conventions. Dorinda Oakley rejects the role of the ideal ▷Southern lady. She begins by yielding to her instincts, and starts a pre-marital sexual relationship; but, Glasgow emphasizes, those instincts are fatal to the self. Dorinda abdicates her will and becomes a victim because she has yielded to her biological destiny as a woman. After she is jilted, she experiences a rebirth, and finds her vein of iron, her will, and she channels her passion into the land, gaining revenge by making the barren land fertile. But Dorinda's own sexuality has been sacrificed. Glasgow exposes the realities concealed by such evasive ideals as romantic love. Her heroine forges her own identity and finds fulfilment in her work.

Barreno, Maria Isabel (born 1939)

Portuguese novelist, short story writer and essayist. In addition to collaborating on the bestselling ▷*Novas Cartas Portuguesas* (1972), she has written several volumes of fiction, including *A Morte da Mãe* (1979) (*The Death of the Mother*), a provocative account of the history of woman; and, most recently, *Crónica do Tempo* (1990) (*Chronicle of Time*), a saga about three generations of a Portuguese family. A feminist writer, Barreno's critiques of Portuguese society are often imbued with a subtle irony and wit. Her books *Célia e Celina* (1985) (*Célia and Celina*) and *O Mundo Sobre o Outro Desbotado* (1986) (*The World over the Other Faded One*) are experiments in fantasy and science fiction. Barreno has also written important studies of women and contemporary Portuguese society. Among her publications are *A Imagem da Mulher na Imprensa Nacional* (1976), which deals with the image of women in the Portuguese press, and *O Falso Neutro* (1985), an account of sex discrimination in schools. Currently she is editor of the magazine *Marie Claire* in Lisbon.
▷*Three Marias: New Portuguese Letters, The*; Costa, Maria Velho da; Horta, Marià Teresa

Barrett, Elizabeth ▷Browning, Elizabeth Barrett

Barros, Teresa Leitão de ▷*Escritoras de Portugal*

Barroso, Maria Alice (born 1926)

Brazilian novelist, chronicle and short story writer and journalist. Her first novel, linked to social

realism, *Os Posseiros* (1955) (*The Squatters*), showed the invasion of property by squatters, due to the lack of agrarian reform. She is best-known for *Um nome para matar* (1967) (*A Name to Kill*), a detective story about a family saga, whose plot is continued by the almost satyrical *Quem matou Pacífico?* (1969) (*Who Killed Pacífico?*). After the 1960s she began to write psychological novels.

'Bars Fight' (1855)

The only extant poem of North America's first African-American poet, ▷Lucy Terry. 'Bars Fight' was written in 1746 and became part of the oral tradition of Massachusetts for over a century before it was recorded and published. In couplets it graphically details the horrors of a Native American raid in Deerfield, Massachusetts, on 25 August 1746. Notable as the first known poetry by an African-American, it is also interesting for its complementary relationship to early North American ▷captivity narratives; it ends, however, where most captivity narratives begin: 'Young Samuel Allen, Oh lackaday! / Was taken and carried to Canada.'

Bartlett, Mary (died 1789)

North American correspondent. Born in Newton, New Hampshire, she was the daughter of Sarah Hoyt and Joseph Bartlett; in 1754 she married her cousin Josiah, and they settled in the agrarian community of Kingston. She gave birth to twelve children, eight of whom lived to adulthood. Her correspondence (▷'The Letters of Josiah and Mary Bartlett') during the years 1775 to 1778, when Josiah was attending the Continental Congresses in Philadelphia, reveals the efforts to maintain the local and national economies that constituted many women's most significant contributions to the war cause. She details the difficulties of planting, tending and harvesting crops as well as managing the hired workers, while raising a family and giving birth to her twelfth child. Her commonplace record becomes a representative text of women's endeavours during the revolutionary years. She died on 14 July 1789, in Kingston.
▷Early North American letters

Barýkova, Anna Pavlovna (1839–1893)

Barýkova, a Russian poet and translator, put her sharp pen to the service of her liberal convictions. She was born Kamenskaia into a family of writers and spent her childhood in the privileged St Petersburg circle of her maternal grandfather, the artist Fëdor Tolstoi. She graduated from a state boarding school in Moscow with, as she put it, 'a large silver medal and a very small stock of knowledge'. Modest and self-deprecating, Barýkova considered 'my children my best work', and her writing a sideline. She was active in the underground populist movement of the 1870s and early 1880s. Her anonymous 'Tale of How Tsar Akhreian Went to Complain to God' (1883), circulated illegally, delighted readers with its satirical portrait of Tsar Alexander III. In her last years she tirelessly adapted and translated popular works for Lev Tolstoy's publishing enterprise, Intermediary. Barýkova's polemic poem, 'A Votary of Aesthetics' (1884), condemned art-for-art's-sake poetry in her suffering land, and 'My Muse' (1878) depicted her inspiration as an old nanny telling tales of humble folk. With their carefully detailed portraits of the poor and dispossessed, her capable poems were printed in all the democratic ▷'thick journals' of her day, and attacked as low and 'dirty' by right-wing critics. In 'Favourite Dolls,' the narrator watches her daughter at play and wonders about her future in a society that treats women as toys: 'After all, children don't break all their dolls . . . / And aren't at least some women happy?'

▷Chiuminá, Ol'ga

Başar, Süküfe Nihal (1896–1973)
Turkish poet and novelist. She was the daughter of an army colonel, and travelled widely with him. She graduated from the University of Istanbul in 1919, and taught literature and geography. She was active in the movement for National Defence, and later in women's rights movements in Turkey. After her marriage she tried to create a French salon at her home. She wrote her poetry from an early age and her work testifies to the change in Turkish writing which came with the break with traditional Arabic-Persian 'arud (versification) to which her early poems conform. Her later poems follow the syllabic metres of modern Turkish poetry. Seven volumes of her poetry were published between 1919 and 1960, and six novels between 1928 and 1951, together with a travel book on Finland (1935).

Bas-bleus, Les (1878) (Bluestockings)
The title of a critical work by the novelist Barbey d'Aurevilly, in which he expressed dismay at the fact that increasing numbers of 19th-century French women were turning to writing, and dismissed the majority of these women as unregenerate pedants whose fundamental desire was to ape men. His conclusion was that female bluestockings, because they were so desperate to usurp masculine privilege and authority, represented a threat to the social and sexual status quo, and needed in consequence to be treated 'like uppity children who deserve a thorough whipping'.

▷Bluestocking; Deraismes, Maria; Flavigny, Marie de; Guérin, Eugénie de; Léo, André

Bashkirtseff, Marie (1858–1884)
French diarist. A Russian émigré who came to Paris as a child, Bashkírtseff began a promising career as a painter, only to succumb to the tuberculosis that eventually killed her at the age of twenty-six. After her death, a number of her written works were published posthumously, the most famous of which are her Journal (1887) and her Cahiers intimes (1925) (Intimate Notebooks). Both texts reveal the extent of her narcissism, and offer such remarkable insights into this aspect of

the feminine psyche that ▷Simone de Beauvoir chose to discuss Bashkirtseff's writing in some detail in her ▷The Second Sex. Bashkirtseff also attracted the interest of the French fin-de-siècle decadent writers, who discerned in her work echoes of their own passionate self-absorption.

Russia also received her diaries as a major event. In Russia in 1888 the young ▷Liubov' Gurévich wrote a sympathetic article about it, and ▷Ol'ga Chiuminá dedicated a poem to Bashkirtseff stressing that, because of the latter's 'Russianness', she would be best understood in her native land. Parts of the diaries were published in Russian translation at least nine times between 1889 and 1916, and her work permeated the culture of the ▷Silver Age. Echoes can be found both in other women's diaries, such as ▷Elizaveta D'iákonova's (published 1904–5), and in fiction: ▷Ánnenkova-Bernár's actress-heroine in the story 'Ona' (1901) calls Bashkirtseff's diary her 'gospel', and ▷Láppo-Danilévskaia's protagonist in the diary-like novella A Young Woman (1917), strongly resembles Bashkirtseff. The spoiled, beautiful, rebellious artist-heroine reappears later in novels like ▷Verbítskaia's ▷The Keys to Happiness and ▷Nagródskaia's The Wrath of Dionysus, the latter also in diary form. ▷Zinaida Vengérova, comparing her diary and ▷Annie Besant's Confession in 1895, found Bashkirtseff to be the very embodiment of aesthetic 'decadence.'

For Russian women, Bashkirtseff became the ideal of the dedicated female artist. In 1910 ▷Marina Tsvetáeva dedicated Evening Album to Bashkirtseff's memory, and planned to name her third book of poetry Mariia Bashkírtseva. Her Journal was reprinted in England in 1985, and by a Soviet publishing house in 1991.

▷Krestóvskaia, Mariia; Lukhmánova, Nadezhda

Bib: de Beauvoir, S., The Second Sex. Vol. II; Crosland, M., Women of Iron and Velvet; Marks, E., 'I am my own heroine', Female Studies: Teaching about Women in the Foreign Languages, Vol. 9; Sullerot, E., Women on Love.

Bashkírtseva, Mariia Konstantinovna
▷Bashkirtseff, Marie

Basque women's writing
The Basque language was one of Spain's three vernacular languages (the others being Catalan and Galician) that were prohibited from public use in Spain after the Spanish Civil War (1936–1939). This prohibition, which applied during Franco's regime (1939–1975) to published works as well as speech, has clearly hindered the evolution of a Basque literary tradition. The most significant contemporary Basque woman writer is ▷Arantza Urretavizkaia.

▷Catalan women's writing, Galician women's writing

Basset, Mary Roper (fl 1544–1572)
English translator. The daughter of William and ▷Margaret More Roper, she was born before

1544, and died in 1572. She was married first to Stephen Clarke, and then to James Basset. Although not as fine a scholar as her mother, Basset was well-educated, and capable in Latin and Greek. She rendered into English her mother's Latin version of Eusebius's Greek history of the church. Basset also translated Thomas More's (1478–1535) *Treatise on the Passion*. In the 1557 edition of her grandfather's works, her ▷translation was printed as *An Exposition of a part of the passion made in Latine*.
▷Humanism (England); *Instruction of a Christian Woman*

Bâtarde, La (1965)

Translation of, *La Bâtarde* (1964) first volume of French writer ▷Violette Leduc's autobiography. The book elaborates material already present in previous works. Her relationships are fatally warped due to her conflictual relationship with her mother, and show her gravitating towards the sexually deviant. She struggles for economic independence while remaining incapable of emotional autonomy.

Bates, Daisy (1863–1951)

Australian journalist, anthropologist and Aboriginal welfare worker. Bates was born in Tipperary, Ireland, and came to Australia at the age of twenty-one, married twice (the second marriage was probably bigamous), returned briefly to England to work as a journalist and, on her return to Western Australia in 1899, became involved in Aboriginal welfare and the compilation of an Aboriginal dictionary. Bates, or 'Kabbarli' as she was known to the Aborigines, lived from 1912 to 1945 with the Aborigines on the Nullarbor Plains. She has been awarded a CBE.
Her published works include *The Passing of the Aborigines, A Lifetime Spent Amongst the Natives of Australia* (1938), *Tales Told to Kabbarli: Aboriginal Legends Collected by Daisy Bates* (re-told by B. Ker Wilson, 1972) and *The Native Tribes of Western Australia* (edited by Isobel White, 1986).
▷Aborigine in Australian women's writing, The

Bat-Miriam, Yocheved (1901–1980)

Israeli poet. Born in Russia, Bat-Miriam studied at the universities of Odessa and Moscow. She started writing in 1923, while still in Russia. She emigrated to Palestine in 1928, and her first book of verse was published in 1929.
Her poetry is a challenge for both readers and critics. She adopted the techniques of the Russian futurist poets, thus creating tensions between her futurist idiom and her traditional, Hasidic background. Her forceful poems attempt to capture intense emotional experiences. Like others who began writing before emigrating to the Holy Land, in her work there is a deep sense of conflict between her two homelands.
Her collections include *Merahok* (1932) (*From Distances*), *Eretz Israel* (1937) (*Land of Israel*),
Shirim La'ghetto (1946) (*Poems to the ghetto*), and ▷*Shirim* (1963) (*Poems*).
▷*Anthology of Modern Hebrew Poetry; Modern Hebrew Poem Itself, The; Voices Within the Ark*

Bat-Shachar, Hannah (born 1944)

Israeli short story writer. Bat-Shachar was born in Jerusalem into an orthodox Jewish family. Her short stories portray deeply frustrated women, living in religious homes, who cannot break free from the prohibitions set by their society. With no other way out, they escape into fantasies. Her books include *Sipurey Ha'sefel* (1987) (*Stories of the Cup*) and *Kri'at Ha'atalefim* (1990) (*The Bat's Call*).

'Battle Hymn of the Republic, The' (1862)

US Civil War poem by ▷Julia Ward Howe. Inspired by a visit to the troops in 1861, Ward Howe claimed the poem came to her in the course of one night. The inspirational stanzas, marked by a series of refrains, eg 'His truth is marching on', and set to the tune of 'John Brown's Body', became one of the most popular songs/poems of the Civil War era – especially among the Union troops it described and inspired. The general public's response to the poem was testimony to its heartening message that God supported the progress of the war and the pursuit of liberty for slaves.
Initially published in ▷*The Atlantic Monthly* in 1862, 'Battle Hymn' brought Ward Howe only a $5.00 US fee from the *Atlantic* – far below the going rates for poetry. Ward Howe's compensation for the poem documents the differential pay rates for many women contributors to 19th-century US literary magazines as well as magazine editors' willingness simultaneously to exploit and denigrate popular women's poetry.

Baughan, Blanche Edith (1870–1958)

New Zealand poet and prose writer. Blanche Baughan arrived in New Zealand in 1900 and is said to have 'learned to sound more colonial than the colonials' (P. Evans, *The Penguin History of New Zealand Literature*, 1990). Her third volume of poetry, ▷*Shingle-Short and Other Verses* (1908), is characterized by its switch from sentimental Victorian ballads to a less decorated and more ▷realist style. Baughan's collection of stories, *Brown Bread from a Colonial Oven* (1912), is an attempt to record a way of life she felt to be passing, and comprises a documentary rather than romantic form of narrative. Baughan also wrote extensively of the New Zealand landscape in *Studies in New Zealand Scenery* (1916).

Baum, Vicki (1888–1960)

Austrian popular novelist. Born in Vienna, she began her career as a harp player. A first marriage to a journalist in 1914 was short-lived, but served to introduce her to the world of letters and the Viennese cultural scene. After a brief spell of nursing during World War I, she married the conductor Richard Lert in 1916. She began work as an editor for Ullstein and in 1920 published her first novel, *Der Eingang zur Bühne* (*The Stage Door*). Some stories for children followed, but it was with *Menschen im Hotel* (1929) (*People in a Hotel*) that she attained fame overnight. In 1931, this book was made into the Hollywood film *Grand Hotel*, starring Joan Crawford and Greta Garbo.

In the wake of her success, and given the political situation at home, Baum emigrated with her family to Hollywood and was granted US citizenship in 1939. She became a prolific writer of novels, short stories, drama and film scripts. Adept at inventing gripping stories, she often wrote about powerful, self-reliant women caught up in the social and economic turbulence of 20th-century Europe or the US. Her books were translated into several languages, making her one of the most widely-read authors of her time.

Baume, Madame de la (17th century)

French transcriber and circulator of a manuscript copy of the *Histoires amoureuse des Gaules* (1665) (*Amatory History of the Gauls*) by Roger de Bussy-Rabutin. This was a *roman-à-clé* satirizing the court of Louis XIV (1638–1715) under the guise of fictitious characters, and as a result its author was exiled. Thereafter, Bussy-Rabutin constantly accused Madame de la Baume of having rewritten parts of his novel, adding all the scandalous passages and producing the scurrilous portraits of the Prince de Condé (1621–1686), ▷Madame de Sévigné and others for which he had been condemned.
Bib: Woodrough, E., '*Bussy-Rabutin et la satire de cour*', *Rabutinages*, No. 7 (1988).

Bäumer, Gertrud (1873–1954)

German feminist, novelist and biographer. A descendant of Protestant theologians, she became a teacher, and later studied literature and philosophy in Berlin. In 1899 she met the radical thinker Helene Lange, and became intensely involved in left-wing politics until the Nazis came to power. Besides numerous articles on social, political and women's issues, she wrote popular biographies of Dante, the philosopher Fichte, Goethe and his mother, the poet Rilke, the actress Eleonora Duse, ▷Ricarda Huch and many others. Bäumer's novels include *Sonntag mit Silvia Monika* (1933) (*Sunday with Silvia Monika*) and *Adelheid, Mutter der Königreiche* (1936) (*Adelheid, Mother of Kingdoms*).

Baur, Margrit (born 1937)

German-speaking Swiss novelist. In gently poetic, often experimental prose, she writes about loneliness and emptiness in the life of an ordinary modern woman. Her works include: *Von Straßen, Plätzen und ferneren Umständen* (1971) (*Of Streets, Squares and Distant Circumstances*); *Zum Beispiel irgendwie* (1977) (*For Example Somehow*); *Überleben. Eine unsystematische Ermittlung gegen die Not aller Tage* (1981) (*Survival. An Unsystematic Inquiry into Everyday Misery*).

Bautista, Lualhati (born 1946)

Filipino feminist writer. Her novels have consistently won awards in major literary competitions. Two, *Dekada 70* (*Decade 70*) and *Bata, Bata, Paano Ka Ginawa?* (*Child, Child, How Were You Made?*), both published in the 1980s, portray the awakening or awakened consciousness of her women protagonists as they cope with the increasingly repressive political conditions under the martial law rule (1965–1986) of Ferdinand Marcos. Significantly, these women see the injustice and inequality suffered by women as part of a larger pattern of injustice in Philippine society. Writing in Tagalog, Bautista uses a style which reflects the use of that language by the Manila middle class, with much code-switching liberally interspersed with English words and phrases. Sometimes called Taglish, it is an entirely appropriate vehicle for rendering dialogue, as well as the conflicts and anguish of her characters.

Bautista also writes for the screen, and has been acclaimed for her filmscript of *Bulaklak ng City Jail* (*Flower of the City Jail*). The film depicts the oppression of Filipino women, and has won many awards.

Bawr, Alexandrine de (1773–1860)

French dramatist and novelist. The daughter of an actress and of an aristocratic father who brought her up, she married the Comte de Saint-Simon, was divorced from him because he wished to marry ▷Madame de Staël, and became the wife of a Russian officer, who was crushed to death by a cart several years later. After this tragic incident she turned to literature in order to support herself and wrote novels and twelve plays, some of which – *Le Rival obligeant* (1811) (*The Helpful Rival*) and *Le Double stratagème* (1811) (*The Double Stratagem*), for example – were very well received. Apart from a series of novels and collections of short stories, including *Auguste et Frédéric* (1817), *Cecilia* (1852) and *Histoires fausses et vraies* (1835) (*True and False Tales*), she also wrote a *Cours de littérature* (1821) (*Guide to Literature*) and an *Histoire de la musique* (1823) (*History of Music*), which show her to have been a critic of some perspicacity.

Baxter, Annie Maria (1816–1905)

Australian diarist. Baxter came to Australia from England in 1833 with her husband, a lieutenant with a regiment stationed in Van Diemen's Land (Tasmania). After her first husband's suicide, Baxter married Robert Dawbin. She recorded the many vicissitudes of her colonial life in the thirty-five volumes of her diary covering the years 1834–1865. ▷*Memories of the Past, by a Lady in Australia* (1873) is based upon these diaries.
▷Journals (Australia); *On Her Selection*

Bay Is Not Naples, The (1955)

A translation of *Il mare non bagna Napoli* (1953); this collection of short stories by Italian writer ▷Anna Maria Ortese, has been described as

▷neo-realist in both style and content. One story, '*Un paio di occhiali*' ('A Pair of Glasses'), won the Viareggio Prize in 1953. Yet, though there is much realism in the stories, and they do tell of the ordinary lives of ordinary people in a Neapolitan setting, they also contain ▷fantastical and lyrical elements. The language, though bare, is quite striking.

Bayly, Ada ▷Lyall, Edna

Baynton, Barbara (1857–1929)
Australian short story writer and novelist. Baynton was the daughter of a carpenter, born in Scone, New South Wales. She married Alexander Frater in 1880 and, while living in the bush, bore three children before he deserted her. In 1890, the day after her divorce, she married Dr Thomas Baynton, a wealthy, elderly Sydney surgeon. Baynton began to write and publish short stories in the 1890s. After her second husband's death, she became a well-known figure in London society as a literary hostess and collector of fine antiques. She married the fifth Lord Headley, President of the Moslem Society, in 1921 but separated almost immediately.

The stories in ▷*Bush Studies* (1902) depict the horrors of life in the bush, particularly for women and children, who are invariably seen as the victims of cruel and predatory males. Her only novel ▷*Human Toll* (1907), though possibly an artistic failure, deals with the plight of the unprotected heroine, Ursula, in the society of the bush. Baynton's grim realism and her confrontation of bush conditions provides an antidote to the often idealized versions of Australian country life.

▷Short story (Australia); *From the Verandah*

Bay of Noon, The (1970)
Novel by Australian author ▷Shirley Hazzard. The book deals with the experience of an English girl, Jenny, attached to the NATO establishment in Naples. This is a beautifully crafted novel which deals with varieties of love experience – Jenny's friendship with a beautiful and sensitive Italian girl, Giaconda, her brief but intense love affair with Giaconda's middle-aged lover, Gianni – and, finally, her departure for North America. Above all the novel is concerned with the effect upon Jenny of Italian culture and values.

Bayou Folk (1894)
US story collection by ▷Kate Chopin. It collects Chopin's earliest Louisiana sketches and stories, many dealing with the ambiguities of race and sexuality in Creole society. *Bayou Folk* contains what is perhaps her most famous, and certainly most reprinted, work: 'Desiree's Baby', the story of a woman disowned and evicted by her aristocratic husband when their baby shows black heritage, the husband learning only later that he, not she, is of African-American background.

Bazincourt, Mademoiselle Thomas de (18th century)
French poet. Bazincourt received a royal pension and resided at the Longchamp Convent just outside Paris. The *Abrégé historique et chronologique des figures de la Bible* (1768) (*Short History and Chronology of Biblical Figures*) was written in verse form, dedicated to the queen, and intended for use in the education of young women.

Beachmasters (1985)
Novel by Australian writer ▷Thea Astley. *Beachmasters* is set on a Pacific Island, perhaps Vanuatu, at a time of crisis when the natural aspirations of the natives are manipulated by colonial powers, both British and French, and by multinational corporations. Astley demonstrates her fine perception of political corruption as she sets her protagonist, Gavi Salway, a vulnerable thirteen-year-old, at the point where he has just discovered his mixed blood and is coerced into giving a hand with some gun-running. As a result, he is indirectly responsible for the death of a friend and the expulsion of his family from their tropical paradise. As is usual with Astley, the satire is finely-honed, the landscape lovingly recreated, the language rich and evocative, and the structure of the novel is complex.

Beacon Hill: A Local Poem, Historic and Descriptive (1790)
Poem by the North American poet, ▷Sarah Wentworth Apthorp Morton. First published on 4 December 1790 in the *Columbian Centinal*, this poem honours the battle at 'Beacon Hill' during the American Revolution. In 1797, it was expanded and published in book form, maintaining its style of neo-classical couplets but extending its scope to include colonial history. Decidedly nationalistic in tone but not unbalanced in its assessment of North American accomplishments, it includes a call for the abolishment of slavery in the south.

▷*Virtues of Society: A Tale Founded on Fact, The*

Beadle, The (1926)
A novel by South African writer, ▷Pauline Smith, set in the Little Karoo region of the Cape in the last decades of the 19th century. The story centres on Andrina, an innocent and generous young girl in service to the Van der Merwe family, who live on a farm called Harmonie in the Aangenaam valley. Into their benevolent, neo-feudal, patriarchal community comes the Englishman, Henry Nind, a selfish and irresponsible figure who seduces Andrina. Andrina falls pregnant and leaves Harmonie to search for her father, whom she believes to live in more northerly regions.

Behind this story lurks the beadle's story, and Andrina's mother's story, too. The beadle, now a gloomy, bitter man, is Andrina's secret father, having raped her mother. In the course of the novel, he makes himself known to the community by confessing his guilt. His intense hatred for

Nind functions in the novel both as the suspiciousness of the Afrikaner towards the English, and as the repressed recognition of identity between himself and this irresponsible interloper. The Englishman goes back to England, and, at the end of the novel, father and daughter are reconciled. Quite unashamed at giving 'illegitimate' birth, and at having been active in her own seduction, Andrina offers a 're-vision' (in ▷Adrienne Rich's terminology) of her mother's story. Her final representation in terms reminiscent of, yet different from, the Christian Madonna, poses a question regarding her difference from the conventional Western figure of maternity.

Although *The Beadle* offers an idealized representation of patriarchal social relations in its depiction of Harmonie, where food is plentiful and servants appear to adore their master, it also reveals the destructive potential of patriarchalism. The novel is about the perfectability of social relations, while at the same time recognizing the ways in which exploitation and oppression constantly threaten to enter the ideal world.

The novel is generally taken to be a classic of South African fiction, and gave its author a secure, if short-lived, literary reputation in Britain and the US. Critics of the time were responsive to the sympathetic treatment of the 'fallen woman', and the relatively daring representation of Andrina's sexual life.

Bean Eaters, The (1960)

US poetry. ▷Gwendolyn Brooks focuses on social and racial issues in this collection which was written during the years of the Civil Rights Movement. The African-American characters live in a ghetto in Chicago, Illinois. In 'My Little 'Bout-town Gal' they are aware of socio-economic limitations imposed upon them and, as the persona laments in 'The Chicago Defender Sends a Man to Little Rock', the tragedy is that racism exists everywhere. In 'A Bronzeville Mother Loiters in Mississippi. Meanwhile, a Mississippi Mother Burns Bacon' and 'Bronzeville Woman in a Red Hat' Brooks exposes the myths that serve to dehumanize African-Americans, showing how these myths bolster Anglo-American egotism. The youths in 'We Real Cool' respond by becoming self-destructive delinquents, although the poverty-stricken couple in 'The Bean Eaters' respond by savouring memories of their life together.

Bear (1976)

▷Marian Engel's notorious, unforgettable and much misunderstood Canadian novel about a woman who discovers herself through a bestial relationship with a bear. The main character, Lou, is an archivist who has long buried herself in the detritus of other people's lives. When she is given an assignment to catalogue the contents of a 19th-century library on a remote island in northern Ontario, it seems that she is entering a world of ▷Gothic possibility. The presence of a Byronic bear complicates the idyllic landscape,

and serves as a catalyst for Lou to discover her own losses and desires. The novel functions both literally and figuratively: with extraordinary brevity, it undermines and illuminates the dichotomies of male/female; human/animal; contemporary/19th century; desire/guilt.
Bib: Pratt, A., 'Affairs with Bears' in *Gynocritics*; ▷van Herk, A., 'Afterword' to 1990 edition of *Bear*.

Béatrice (Bieiris) de Romans (13th century)

French ▷*trobairitz*. She was the author of verses in Occitan to Marie, probably the only old Provençal poem addressed by one woman to another.

Beatrice of Kent, Abbess of Lacock (died after 1280)

Lacock (Wiltshire) was a house of Augustinian canonesses. It was founded (as a priory) by Ela, Countess of Salisbury, in 1230. Lacock became an abbey from 1239–40, and Ela became its first abbess. Beatrice was abbess from 1257 until after 1269. She was the author of works now lost, including a piece about Ela, who died in 1261. She is also said to have composed 'Epitaphs, and amusing lines of poetry'.
Bib: Russell, Josiah Cox, *Dictionary of Writers of Thirteenth-Century England*; Knowles, David and Hadcock, R. Neville, *Medieval Religious Houses in England and Wales*.

Beattie, Ann (born 1947)

US novelist and short story writer. Raised in Washington DC, Beattie earned a Master's degree at the University of Connecticut in 1970. Her fiction focuses on the despair of New England's Anglo-American upper-middle class. The world it describes is constantly in flux, including interpersonal relationships, and the characters are suspended in their lives, lacking direction. *Chilly Scenes of Winter* (1976) depicts the disillusionment of the 1960s' youthful idealists as they reach middle age. The stories in *The Burning House* (1982) feature women suffering from a sense of alienation as their interpersonal relationships disintegrate. Beattie suggests, however, that women survive by learning how to fall.

Other works include *Distortions* (1976), *Secrets and Surprises* (1978), *Falling in Place* (1981) *Jacklighting* (1981), *Love Always* (1985), *Alex Katz* (1987), *Where You'll Find Me* (1987), *Picturing Will: A Novel* (1989) and *What Was Mike and Other Stories* (1991).

Beaufort, Margaret, Countess of Richmond and Derby (1443–1509)

English translator, letter-writer and patron. She was the mother of Henry VII and grandmother of Henry VIII. She is best-known for her ▷patronage of the work of the first English printers, William Caxton (?1422–1491), Wynkyn de Worde (died 1534), and Richard Pynson. She commissioned a number of translations, having

Lady Margaret Beaufort

many of them printed at her own expense. She was also a patron of the universities, endowing readerships at Oxford and Cambridge, and establishing Christ's College and St John's College. Although fluent in French, she lamented her limited skills in Latin. Her ▷translation from French into English of *The Mirroure of Golde for the Sinfull Soule* (1522) was first printed by Richard Pynson, and then several times again later. Her translation of the fourth book of a French version of Thomas à Kempis's ▷*The Imitation of Christ* (1504) was printed by Wynkyn de Worde.

Bib: Cooper, Charles Henry, *Memoir of Margaret, Countess of Richmond and Derby*; Simon, Linda, *Of Virtue Rare: Margaret Beaufort, Matriarch of the House of Tudor*; Barratt, Alexandra (ed.), *Women's Writing in Middle English*.

Beauharnais, Marie-Anne-Françoise Mouchard, Comtesse de (1737–1813)

French writer of prose fiction and verse. Born in Paris, she married at sixteen but chose to live apart from her husband, and resided in her father's house in the rue de Montmartre. Here she held a literary salon, later transferred to the rue Tournon. The epistolary novel, *Sacrifices de l'amour* (1771) (*Sacrificed for Love*), attributed to her lover Dorat and on which she probably collaborated, is said to portray the tensions of her marriage. The essay *A tous les penseurs salut!* (1774) (*Greetings to all Thinkers!*) argues in favour of education and intellectual occupations for all women. Her feminist views are stated in her contributions to the periodical ▷*Journal des Dames* (*Ladies' Journal*). Apart from an historical novel, *Lettres de Stéphanie* (1778) (*Letters from Stéphanie*), and an unsuccessful play, *La Fausse*

Inconstance (1787) (*Falsely Fickle*), she wrote mostly fantastical, philosophical and humorous tales, as well as poetry. Beauharnais was aunt to Josephine Bonaparte, and in later years maintained her connections with the imperial family, receiving a pension from Napoleon. Her work has received scant positive attention from literary historians, but in her lifetime her reputation was acknowledged by membership of several minor academies in Rome, Toulouse, Villefranche, and also Lyon, where she and her friend, the poet ▷Dame Marianne du Bocage, were the only women admitted. The *Encyclopédie des dames* (*Women's Encyclopaedia*), a work intended for the education of women, was dedicated to her in 1806.

Other works: *Féeries en dialogues* (1776) (*Enchanted Dialogues*); *Mélanges de poésie fugitives et de prose sans conséquences* (1776) *Medley of Light Poetry and Slight Prose*); *Volsidor et Zulménie* (1776); *Zabbet* (1776); *L'Abaillard supposé* (1780); *L'aveugle par amour* (1781) (*Blinded by Love*); *Le Cabriolet* (1784) (*The Cabriolet*); *Le somnambule* (1786) (*The Sleepwalker*); *Les Amants d'autrefois* (1787) (*Past Lovers*); *La Fausse Inconstance* (1787); *L'Ile de la félicité* (1801) (*The Island of Happiness*); *Léandre et Héro de Musée* (1806); *La Cyn-Achantide* (1811); *La marmotte philosophe* (1811) (*The Philosophical Mouse*); *A la mémoire de Mme du Bocage* (1802) (*In Memory of Mme du Bocage*)

▷Montesson, Marquise de

Bib: Marquiset, A., *Les Bas-bleus du premier Empire*; Turgeon, F. K., 'Fanny de Beauharnais' in *Mod. Philol.*, XXX (1923–33) pp. 61–80.

Beaumer, Madame de (died 1766)

French journalist and prose writer. Little is known of Beaumer's origins, but it is thought that she was a Huguenot with connections in Holland, where she died. She is best-known for her assertive editorship of the ▷*Journal des Dames* (*Ladies' Journal*) between 1760 and 1765, a job for which she adopted a masculine style of dress, which she said was more practical and economical. When she took over the periodical it became overtly feminist, carrying politically sensitive material on a wide range of issues, and was condemned by the censor for its popular radicalism. Her one novel, *Lettres de Magdelon Friquet* (*The Letters of Magdelon Friquet*), which featured a lower-class heroine, was refused by the censors and no longer exists. A published collection of various writings, *Oeuvres mêlées* (1760, 1761), also contains radical material, disguised for the benefit of the censors by the use of myth and metaphor. The *Dialogue entre Charles XII roi de Suède et Mandarin* (1760) (*Conversation between Charles XII, King of Sweden, and Mandarin*) praises the insurrectional spirit of the bandit, Mandarin, later to become a mythical symbol of the Revolution and a banned topic. She was one of the first women to adopt the feminine forms of the words for author and editor calling herself both *éditrice* and *autrice*.

Bib: Gelbart, N., *Feminine and Oppositional*

Journalism in Old Régime France: Le Journal des Dames.

Beauvain d'Althenheim, Gabrielle (1814–1886)

French poet, novelist and dramatist. The daughter of the writer Alexandre Soumet, she was introduced at an early age into the rarefied atmosphere of her father's literary salon, met the leading lights of the French romantic movement, and by the age of nine had already composed a biblical epic in prose. In later life she wrote collections of short stories (*Les Filiales*, 1836, *The Affiliates*; *Nouvelles Filiales*, 1838, *New Affiliates*), novels (*Berthe Bertha*, 1843; *Les Deux Frères*, 1858, *The Two Brothers*), volumes of poetry (*La Croix et la lyre*, *The Cross and the Lyre*), historical studies, and literary criticism. She also wrote two plays in collaboration with her father, *Le Gladiateur* (1841) (*The Gladiator*) and *Jane Grey* (1844). Her works are quite forgotten today, but were immensely popular with her contemporaries, who particularly appreciated their moral and religious aspect.
Bib: Boilly, J., *Biographie des femmes auteurs contemporains*.

Beauvau, Princesse de (1729–?)

French memoir-writer. Widowed in 1749, she married the maréchal de Beauvau of the ▷Académie Française in 1764. Although the family were of the nobility, they made concessions to contemporary opinions, and lived quietly through the revolutionary period in their country home. Her *Souvenirs* (*Memoirs*), which record her life and the pain experienced over the loss of her second husband, were arranged and published by her grand daughter, Mme Standisch, in 1872.
  ▷*Mémoires*

Bebel-Gisler, Dany

A sociolinguist and ethnologist, from Guadeloupe in the French Antilles, Bebel-Gisler has concentrated her research upon the alienation of a Creole people by colonial civilization. Her mother was an agricultural worker on the property of Dany's father, and Dany recalls being caught between the bourgeois culture of her father's family, in which only French was spoken, and the Creole culture of her mother. Demonstrating in her research that a second language may only be properly learnt once a first, or mother language has been thoroughly acquired, she wrote *La langue créole, force jugulée* (1976) (*Creole, a Subjugated Force*), in which she describes the problematic relationship between forged language (Creole) and imposed language (French). In *Le défi culturel GuadeloupéenSouthern Africa* (1989) (*Guadeloupe's Cultural Challenge*), she calls for a rejection of colonial culture and an acceptance of Creole culture as a basis for future development. Bebel-Gisler's political and sociological ideology is expressed in her novel, ▷*Léonora* (1985), and also in her involvement with the Bwadoubout Centre Project, an educational centre in Guadeloupe in which all academic teaching and professional training is conducted in Creole.

Beccary, Madame (18th century)

French novelist. The four novels published by Beccary were all presented as supposed translations from English, and include: *Lettres de Milady Bedfort*, (1769) (*Letters of Lady Bedfort*); *Mémoires de Lucie d'Olbery* (1770) (*Memoirs of Lucie d'Olbery*); *Mémoires de Fanny Spingler* (1781) (*Memoirs of Fanny Spingler*) and *Milord d'Ambi* (1778) (*Lord d'Ambi*).
Bib: Streeter, H.W., *The 18th-century English Novel in Translation*.

Beck, Lily Adams (died 1931)

Canadian writer of religious, philosophical, and historical romance, who travelled extensively in Asia before settling in Victoria, British Columbia, in 1919. Born Lily Moresby, she wrote under several different pseudonyms. As Lily Adams Beck she authored numerous books about oriental culture: *The Ninth Vibration and 8 Other Stories* (1922), *Dreams and Delights* (1922), *The Key of Dreams* (1922), *The Perfume of the Rainbow* (1923), *The Treasure of Ho* (1925), *The Way of the Stars* (1925), *The Splendour of Asia* (1926), *The Way of Power* (1928), *The Story of Oriental Philosophy* (1928), *The Garden of Vision* (1929) and *The Joyous Story of Astrid* (1931). As E. Barrington she wrote popular historical romances: *The Ladies* (1922), *The Chaste Diana* (1923), *The Gallants* (1924), *Glorious Apollo* (1925), *The Exquisite Perdita* (1926), *The House of Fulfilment* (1927), *The Thunderer* (1927), *The Empress of Hearts* (1928), *The Laughing Queen* (1929), *The Duel of the Queens* (1930), *The Irish Beauties* (1931), *Anne Boleyn* (1932) and *The Great Romantic* (1933). As Louis Moresby she wrote oriental historical romances: *The Glory of Egypt* (1926), *Rubies* (1927) and *Captain Java* (1928). Astoundingly prolific, she died in Japan.

Becker, Jillian (born 1932)

South African novelist. Born in Johannesburg, she left South Africa for England in 1961, subsequently publishing three novels about contemporary South African life: *The Keep* (1967); *The Union* (1971), and *The Virgins* (1976). *The Virgins* satirizes the lives of wealthy whites in Johannesburg, and focuses sharply on the South African equivalent of the British public school for girls. The schoolgirl Annie Firman and her friend, Barb, are eager to experience adult life, and to this end Annie seduces Edward, doubly taboo since he is classified 'coloured' under apartheid law. The novel provides a poignant glimpse of adolescent yearnings and uncertainties, and also a refreshing presentation of inter-racial sex, so central a theme in South African fiction. More recently, Becker published *Hitler's Children: The Story of the Baader-Meinhof Terrorist Gang* (1978), and *The P.L.O.: The Rise and Fall of the Palestinian Liberation Organisation* (1984).

Beckett, Mary (born 1926)

Irish fiction writer. Beckett was born in Belfast, where she grew up and taught for several years. She has lived in Dublin since the mid-1950s. Although she started writing in her early twenties and had several stories published then, she stopped writing for twenty years while rearing her family of five children. *A Belfast Woman*, her first collection of short stories, appeared in 1980; *Give Them Stones*, a novel, in 1989, and *A Literary Woman*, more short stories, in 1990. Invariably set in Belfast, her writing provides wry and perceptive insights into the shape of women's lives in situations of great trouble and conflict.

Bedford, Jean (born 1946)

Australian novelist, journalist and short story writer. Bedford was literary editor of the *National Times* for three years, then a literary consultant to the same journal. She belongs to a contemporary group of realist women writers who paint a grim and deterministic picture of Australian life in both the city and the bush. Bedford's historical novel, *Sister Kate* (1982), is based on the life of the sister of the bushranger Ned Kelly, and her publications include *Country Girl Again* (1979), ▷*Country Girl Again and Other Stories* (1985), *Colouring-In, A Book of Ideologically Unsound Love Stories* (1986, with Rose Creswell) and *Love Child* (1986).

▷Short story (Australia); *Coming Out from Under*

Bedford, Simi (born 1942)

Nigerian novelist. The eldest of five children in an upper-class Nigerian family, she was brought up by her grandparents in a large household in Lagos. Her family was one of those known as *Saro*, meaning that her great-grandfather was the son of a freed slave brought back by the British to Sierra Leone. Her grandfather was a well-to-do businessman, in whose household six languages were spoken. *Saro* families, like those returned from Brazil, constitute an elite group in Lagos society. Bedford's family boasts five generations of lawyers. Her father was Lord Chief Justice of Nigeria, while her aunt was the first African woman to be called to the Bar. In those colonial days, doctors and lawyers automatically went to England to be trained, and upper-class families sent their children there to school. Bedford's book, ▷*Yoruba Girl Dancing* (1991) is based on her experiences and those of others like her, abandoned in English boarding schools at the age of seven. She has remained in England, where she works in television and film.

▷Slavery (West Africa)

Bedford, Sybille (born 1911)

Anglo-German novelist, travel writer and biographer, born in Brandenburg (Berlin), Germany, daughter of Elizabeth Bernard and Maximilian von Schoenebeck. She was educated privately and travelled with her mother to Italy, France and then to England. She wrote her first novel when she was nineteen, at a time when her mother was recovering from drug addiction, the period during which she made the acquaintance of novelist Aldous Huxley (1894–1963). As a law reporter, Bedford covered events such as the Auschwitz Trial in Frankfurt and the *Lady Chatterley* trial at the Old Bailey, London. Her first published novel, *A Legacy* (1956), is a semi-autobiographical historical novel detailing the marriages between two wealthy German families and looking at a Catholic-Jewish alliance against the background of events in Germany preceding World War I. As with her other historical novels, *Favourite of the Gods* (1963) and its sequel *A Compass Error* (1968), specific historical and political context functions primarily as a backdrop against which Bedford's portrayal of family intrigue and scandal is played out. These two novels focus on three generations of women: the New England wife of a licentious Italian count, the sexually active daughter whom she rejects and the granddaughter who also becomes involved in this close family web of sexual rivalries. Bedford's travel book, *A Sudden View* (1953), was reprinted in 1960 as *A Visit to Don Otavio* (1960), the new title highlighting the central position of this landowner within Bedford's travel narrative.

She has also written extensively on food and drink, and her law journalism includes *The Best We Can Do: An Account of the Trial of Dr Adams* (1959) and *The Faces of Justice: A Traveller's Report* (1961). Her two-volume biography of Aldous Huxley, commissioned by his family, was published in 1973–4, and an autobiographical novel, *Jigsaw: An Unsentimental Education*, appeared in 1989.

Bedott, Widow ▷Whitcher, Frances Miriam Berry

Bedregal, Yolanda (born 1916)

Bolivian poet and essayist. She has been a professor of aesthetics, and has collaborated on several journals. Her compatriots gave her the title of 'Yolanda de Bolivia'. Her work ranges from poetry to essays, from education to folklore, and, in her own words, aims at 'achieving a higher moral and aesthetic elevation'. She employs autobiographical traits in her subjective lyrical poems, using clear musical verses, from *Naufragio* (1936) (*Shipwreck*) to *Nadir* (1950). She is inspired by the same sense of mysticism as ▷Gabriela Mistral, as in 'Nocturno en Dios' ('Nocturne in God') from *Nadir*, and her poems have an eternal dimension. Other works include *Poemar* (1937) (*Poems*); *Ecos* (1940) (*Echoes*); *Almadía* (1942) (*Raft*), and *Del mar y la ceniza* (1957) (*From the Sea and Ashes*).

Bed Time (1985)

This work by Japanese novelist ▷Yamada Eimi is about, the love between a Japanese woman singer and a black deserter, from their first encounter to their parting. At first the couple lust only for sex, but before they realize it their desire turns to a deeper love. Yamada describes the purity of their love and also goes into vivid erotic detail – a new departure in Japanese literature.

Beecher, Catharine (1800–1878)

US non-fiction writer and educator. Member of the famous New England Protestant Beecher family, Catharine Beecher was sister to Henry Ward Beecher (1813–1887) and ▷Harriet Beecher Stowe, and the daughter of Lyman Beecher (1775–1863). As an educator, she founded schools for women, including the Hartford Female Seminary. An active advocate of women's education, she none the less saw domesticity as women's sphere. Beecher's non-fiction ranged from *The Evils Suffered by American Women and American Children: The Causes and the Remedy* (1848), which focused on the need for education, through the much-reprinted ▷*Treatise on Domestic Economy* (1841), the first US manual of scientific household management, to *The True Remedies for the Wrongs of Women* (1851) and *Common Sense Applied to Religion* (1857).

Beer, Patricia (born 1924)

English poet. The title poem of Beer's first collection, *The Loss of the Magyar* (1959), deals with a shipwreck that involved her great-grandfather. *The Survivors* (1963) similarly examines aspects of Beer's past experience and family history, and much of her poetry focuses on the landscapes and history of Devon. By the 1970s her poetry had become less narrative and more experimental, with a pronounced concentration on formal concerns. *Selected Poems* was published in 1979, followed by *The Lie of the Land* (1983). *Mrs Beer's House* (1968) is a prose sequel to the autobiographical *Just Like the Resurrection* (1967). Her critical studies include *Reader, I Married Him* (1974) on the women characters of 19th-century women novelists.

Beers, Ethel Lynn (1827–1879)

US poet and fiction writer. A regular contributor to the literary magazines, Beers was most noted in her own time, and is remembered now, for her Civil War poetry. Her 'The Picket Guard' (1861), like ▷Julia Ward Howe's later ▷'Battle Hymn of the Republic,' became a popular rallying point during the Civil War. 'The Picket Guard' appears in her collection, *All Quiet along the Potomac and Other Poems* (1879).

Beggars' Strike The (1981)

Translation of *La Grève des battu* (1979), the second novel by Senegalese writer, ▷Aminata Sow Fall. It plays on the Islamic precept of the blessedness of alms-giving, which is a requirement of the faithful, and the hypocrisy of the rich and powerful who seek to clear the city of beggars to make a good impression on foreign visitors. The politician, Mour Ndiaye, who is responsible for the move, then consults a *marabout* about the likelihood of his election as vice-president. He is told he must give alms generously; the beggars, aware of their power, refuse to accept.

There are many levels of irony in this novel: the clash of Western and traditional values in many aspects of Senegalese life, not least religion; the implications of a patriarchal power relationship, both for the poor and for women within a polygamous system, and the contradictions of an independent African state still bound by economic and cultural ties to its former colonial master. ▷Polygamy (West Africa)

Béguine

Medieval term relating to religious women in the Low Countries, France and England. The derivation of the word continues to puzzle etymologists, but is generally taken to mean a lay follower of the apostolic life who, in imitation of Christ, lived a life of poverty and abstinence.

Béguine Anonyme, La (13th century)

A northern French poet. In three *Dits de l'âme* (*Sayings of the Soul*), this unnamed ▷*béguine* proclaimed her passion for Christ in vigorous verses addressed to her fellow *béguines*.
Bib: Wilwerth, E., *Visages de la littérature féminine*.

Behn, Aphra (1640–1689)

English poet, dramatist and writer of fiction. Known as 'Astrea'. Little is known of her early life; the earliest record we have is the anonymous 'The Life and Memoirs of Mrs Behn Written by One of the Fair Sex' which prefaced the first collection of her writings. She may well have lived in Surinam and presented a feather costume for the play *The Indian Queen*. She also worked as a royal spy in Holland (at the instigation of Sir Thomas Killigrew, 1612–1683, the London theatrical impresario), but was not paid, despite repeated pleas for money on her return in 1667. She may well have been imprisoned for debt. She began to write for money, and has been singled out by critics since ▷Virginia Woolf (see ▷*A Room of One's Own*) as the first Englishwoman to earn her living by writing, though the precise meaning of this description is open to dispute. She wrote eighteen plays, of which *The Forc'd Marriage* was the first, produced at the Duke's Theatre in 1670. In the preface to *The Dutch Lover* (1673), she complains that 'the day 'twas acted first, there comes to me in the pit a long, lithe, phlegmatic, white, ill-favored, wretched fop . . . this thing, I tell you, opening that which serves it for a mouth, out issued such a noise as this to those that sat about it, that they were to expect a woeful play, God damn him, for it was a woman's.' Her best-known plays are currently *The Lucky Chance* and ▷*The Rover* (1679). *The Lucky Chance* (1686) details the plight of young women married to rich, foolish old city men. In *The Widow Ranter* she dramatizes colonial America. In prose fiction she wrote ▷*Love Letters Between a Nobleman and His Sister* and ▷*Oroonoko, or the Royal Slave* (c 1688), set in colonial Surinam. Her poems (famously) include 'The Disappointment', and she also wrote about desire in 'To the Fair Clarinda, Who Made Love to Me, imagin'd more than Woman': 'Fair lovely Maid, or if that Title be / Too weak, too Feminine for Nobler thee, / Permit a Name that more Approaches Truth: And let me call thee, Lovely Charming Youth. / This last will justify my soft complaint; / . . . And without Blushes I the Youth persue, / When so much beauteous Woman is in view.'

Her works are collected in: *The Histories and Novels of the Late Ingenious Mrs Behn* (1696).
Bib: Goreau, A., *Reconstructing Aphra*.

Behrens, Katia (born 1942)

German novelist and short story writer. She first worked as a translator of US novels, and in 1981 published an anthology of letters by women of the German romantic movement. Her first novel, *Die dreizehnte Fee* (1983) (*The Thirteenth Fairy*), explores the relationship between three generations of women in modern Germany. Her short stories, collected in *Die weiße Frau* (1978) (*The White Woman*) and *Jonas* (1981) (*Jonah*), are fable-like investigations into modern Existential themes such as role-playing, alienation and desire.

Beig, Maria (born 1920)

West German novelist. She grew up in a large family on a farm in Swabia, and draws upon childhood memories for her 'anti-idyllic' novels, *Rabenkrächzen* (1982) (*The Cawing of the Ravens*) and *Hochzeitsose* (1983) (*Out of Wedlock*). Her short stories, collected in *Urgroßelternzeit* (1985) (*Great-grandparent-time*), are further painstaking investigations into a rural past about which she feels ambivalent. Although it is described as coarse and cruel, the past is none the less evoked with a sense of magical fascination.

Beirut

Capital of Lebanon, for many years the haven of a free press and uncensored publishing for Arabic literature. In Beirut, publishing was big business, producing standard editions of Arab poets from all regions, books on politics, philosophy and religion that could not be published elsewhere, as well as pirating library editions of the classics expensively produced by state publishers in other capitals. Two literary monthlies, *al-Adib* and *al-Adab*, have published poems, criticism and short stories by writers from every part of the Arab world, their pages serving as a meeting-place for writers who may never see each other.

The civil war in Lebanon, which started in 1975, shattered the illusion of a haven of freedom in Beirut and destroyed any semblance of law and order. However, it remains one of the major publishing capitals of the Arab world. The trauma experienced by writers who tried to continue to live in Beirut under threat of kidnapping, sniping and shelling is well-represented in their work: ▷Ghada al-Samman's *Beirut Nightmares* (1976) does not just record the horror, but tries to present the indifference of those mainly responsible. ▷Emily Nasralla and other women

writers, known as 'the Beirut Decentrists', continued to live in Beirut and 'write the war'. ▷Andrée Chedid's contribution, *La Maison Sans Racines* (1985) (*The House without Roots*), tells of two girls who stage a 'meeting' across the line splitting the city in two and are shot. ▷Nizar Qabbani's great poem 'Balqis' was the product of a personal tragedy: his wife dying in an explosion at the Iraqi Embassy in 1981.
Bib: Chedid, Andrée, *The Return to Beirut*; Cooke, Miriam, 'Beirut . . . theatre of the absurd . . . theatre of dreams. The Lebanese Civil War in the Writings of Contemporary Arab Women', *Journal of Arabian Literature*, 13 (1982) pp. 124–41, 'Women Write War . . .', *British Society for Middle Eastern Studies Bulletin* 14 (1988) pp. 52–67, *War's Other Voices: Women Writers on the Lebanese Civil War*.

Beirut, 75 (1975)

Arabic novel by ▷Ghada al-Samman. This was her first attempt at writing a full-length novel, when she was already well-known as a journalist and short story writer. She captures the atmosphere and social conditions that led to the eruption of the civil war in ▷Beirut in 1975, almost simultaneously with the publication of this prophetic novel. The action is built on the conventional plot of the naïve country boy and girl arriving in the city, lured by the bright lights and promises of fame and wealth. In spite of the hackneyed plot, the novel is saved by the imaginative treatment of characters and atmosphere.

The two protagonists, a young man and a young woman, leave Damascus in the same taxi to Beirut, each seeking a career in the greatest capital of opportunity in the Arab world. The usual clichéd roles are reversed: it is the girl who is hoping to make her name in literature, and the boy who has the voice that will make him a great singer. They arrive in Beirut on Good Friday and they are both eventually 'crucified', but with no redemption. Images and sounds of forboding hang over the journey from the start; three women shrouded in black ▷hijab occupy the back seat of the taxi, murmuring lamentations among themselves, and disappear at the first stop.

The image of the city, developed in the course of the novel, is that of the merciless sea with the sharks in their air-conditioned offices in control of the small fry: shoals of working men eking out a miserable livelihood for their large families.

The girl becomes a prostitute, and is murdered by her brother, ostensibly for honour, but in fact in anger and disbelief at the drying-up of his source of income when she is discarded by her seducer.

Her fellow traveller, after plumbing the lowest depths of despair in the uncaring city, is finally taken up by a media tycoon. He is given much publicity, but is privately humiliated by the homosexual attentions of the great entrepreneur.

The only hopeful young survivor in the novel is Mustafa, a student and poet, who has to give up school to work with his father, an old fisherman who constantly dreams of one day finding a 'magic lantern' in his net and commanding the genie of the lamp to give him the house, the orchard and the treasure he needs for his family. It is Mustafa who has to wake up to the necessities of making a living from a merciless sea. At the end of the novel he is trying to organize the men into a fishermen's union, to ensure a measure of social security for his comrades and family.

Bejerano, Maya (born 1949)

Israeli poet, musician and photographer. Bejerano was born in Israel and studied at Tel-Aviv University. Sensations are the dominant theme in her poetry, and this is reflected in her use of language. The constantly changing boundaries of a person's perception are expressed in the free syntax and changing imagery. Bejerano examines the limits of her own sensations by constantly breaking and reconstructing the boundaries of language. Her works include: *Bat Ya'ana* (1978) (*Ostrich*); *Shir Shel Tziporim* (1985) (*Bird's Poem*); *Shirim Nivharim* (1987) (*Selected Poems*) and *Livyatan* (1990) (*Whale*).

Beka Lamb (1982)

This novel by Caribbean writer ▷Zee Edgell won the Fawcett Society Book Prize and was the first novel by a Belizian to reach an international audience. Set in the 1950s during a turbulent period of Belize's history, it is concerned with decolonization, nationalist movements in politics, and the growth of an independent consciousness. The story focuses on the central character, a young girl whose developing consciousness is an articulation of the country's social relations. The personal and historical are inter-related, as are the questions of gender and politics.

See Roger Bromley's article in *Wasifiri*, No. 2 (1985).

Belgrave, Valerie

Novelist and artist born in ▷Trinidad. She was educated in Trinidad, and at Sir George Williams University, Montreal, Canada. Her historical romance *Ti Marie* (1989) is an unusual novel in that it takes the popular genre of the romance and applies it to the period of slavery. The work is discussed by the author in 'Thoughts on the Choice of Theme and Approach to Writing *Ti Marie*' in ▷*Caribbean Women Writers*.

Belisarius: A Tragedy (1795)

Play by North American poet, essayist and dramatist ▷Margaretta V. Bleecker Faugeres. Faugeres's artistic expression of her political ideals culminated in the drama *Belisarius*. The play, classic in style and indebted to the ideals of liberty brought forth in the American and French Revolutions, advocates political policies developed for matters of 'peace, not to extend dominion'. The play was published by subscription in 1795. The title character represents the honourable man, perhaps humanity itself, who is destroyed by the corruption on both sides of any political battle that values power more than liberty.

▷*Posthumous Works of Ann Eliza Bleecker, The*

Bell, The (1954)

Novel by ▷Iris Murdoch which was later televised. The novel announces Murdoch's consistent interest in notions of 'love', 'truth' and 'reality' and is concerned, like ▷*A Severed Head* (1961), with love, betrayal and confession within an insular, tightly-knit community. *The Bell*, however, poses this discussion within an analysis of the explanatory capabilities of secular and Christian treatments of these themes. As in *A Severed Head*, love is the dynamic or motive force of the narrative, and is seen largely as an exercise of power. Set in an Anglican lay community in Oxfordshire, the novel presents a series of events which cohere around the replacement bell to be hung in an abbey tower. The manner in which the bell acquires symbolic weight is crucial to Murdoch's analysis of the structures, boundaries and meanings by which, or against which, her central characters define their identities and relationships.

Bell, Currer, Ellis, Acton ▷Brontë, Charlotte, Emily, Anne

Bell, Vera (born 1906)

This Caribbean poet, storywriter and editor was born in Jamaica. She was educated at Wolmer's Girls School, Columbia University's School of Library Service, New York, and London University. Before leaving Jamaica she was editor of the *Welfare Reporter*, and worked as an executive officer in the government's Welfare Commission. She has published poetry in a range of prestigious literary journals and contributed to *Jamaican Short Stories* (1950), *New Ships: An Anthology of West Indian Poems* (1972) and *You Better Believe It: Black Verse in English from Africa, the West Indies and the United States* (1973).

Belli, Gioconda (born 1948)

Nicaraguan poet. Belli began her career as a poet in 1970, and soon published her work in several magazines, among them *La Prensa Literaria* and *El Gallo Ilustrado*. In 1972 she was awarded the Mariano Fiallos Gil Prize for poetry. Her first book was *Sobre la grama* (1974) (*On the grass*), which revealed an extensive knowledge of the poetical art and insight into women's concerns. The poems are lyrical, but not overly sentimental, and express the feelings of motherhood and a love for her children. *Linea de fuego* (*Line of fire*), a book consisting of 55 poems, was published in 1978, winning the Casa de las Américas Prize for poetry the same year. It is divided into three sections: 'Country or death', 'Steel', and 'To Sergio'. These parts juxtapose love for one's country, a frustration with it, and personal love. The poems mix real and surreal, using powerful images and inventive metaphors, and play with a variety of forms, including the prose poem and a combination of prose and poetry together.

Bell Jar, The (1963)

US *künstlerroman* (a ▷*Bildungsroman* about an artist) by ▷Sylvia Plath, originally published under the ▷pseudonym Victoria Lucas. This sardonically comic, autobiographical novel has suffered from uncritical readings of it as solely confessional and a direct reflection of Plath's life, because the narrator, Esther Greenwood is an aspiring writer and attempts suicide after visiting her father's grave. *The Bell Jar* uses elements of Plath's life to examine the position of women in 1950s North America, and it asserts its precise historical location and its perspective on the 1950s from the opening sentence, in which Esther announces that it was 'the summer they electrocuted the Rosenbergs'. Plath exposes the way in which the stereotyping of women's roles limits the talented, ambitious woman's options through Esther's agonized experiments with different types of female identity.

Belloc, Louise (1796–1881)

French educational writer. Born Louise Swanton, the daughter of an Irish army officer, she married a French painter. Belloc translated literary and pedagogical texts from English, and published an educational journal, *La Ruche*, between 1836 and 1839. She wrote a biography of Byron in 1824, and, in old age, produced numerous books for children, including *Histoires et Contes de la grand-mère* (1871) (*Grandmother's Tales and Stories*) and *Le Fond du sac de la grand-mère* (1873) (*Tales from Grandmother's Bag*).
▷Feminine/feminist journalism (France)

Bellon, Loleh

French dramatist, who rapidly built on the success of *Changement à vue* (1979) (*Scene Change*). *De si tendres liens* (1984) (*Such Sweet Ties*) and *Les Dames du jeudi* (1986) (*Thursday's Ladies*), followed by *L'Eloignement* (1987) (*The estrangement*) and *Une Absence* (1988) (*An Absence*) prove that some feminist ideas have become acceptable to the theatre-going public.

Bellonci, Maria (1902–1986)

Italian journalist and novelist. Born in Rome, she married literary critic Goffredo Bellonci and organised the literary group *Amici della domenica*, which awards the Strega Prize. Bellonci contributed to many periodicals and newspapers, but is most famous for her historical biographies, such as those on Lucrezia Borgia and Isabella d'Este, which are well-researched and full of psychological insight. Her narratives are at once realistic and imaginative.

Her main works are: *Lucrezia Borgia, la sua vita e i suoi tempi* (1939) (*The Life and Times of Lucrezia Borgia*); *I segreti dei Gonzaga* (1947) (*Secrets of the Gonzaga*); *Pubblici segreti* (1965) (*Public Secrets*); ▷*Tu vipera gentile* (1972) (*You, Gentle Viper*); *Delitto di Stato* (1982) (*State Crime*); *Marco Polo*,

(1984); *Rinascimento privato* (1986) (*Private Renaissance*); *Io e il premio Strega* (1987) (*The Strega Prize and Me*); *Segni sul muro* (1988) (*Marks on the Wall*).

Belot, Madame (1719–1804)

French essayist and translator. The widow of a Parisian parliamentary lawyer, she later married the president Durey de Meinières. The first of her two published essays, *Réflexions d'une provinciale sur le discours de J.J. Rousseau* (1756) (*Reflections of a Provincial Lady on the Arguments of J.J. Rousseau*), is a criticism of Rousseau's discourse on equality, and his idealization of natural life. In her second essay, *Observations sur la noblesse et le tiers état* (1758) (*Remarks on the Nobility and the Third Estate*), she examines ways of reinforcing the system of military nobility. Her translations include two novels by Johnson (1709–1784): *The Prince of Abyssinia* and *The History of Ophelia*, and a history of the Plantagenets by Hume (1711–1776).

Beloved (1987)

US novel by ▷Toni Morrison which won the Pullitzer Prize for fiction in 1988. The book is set in Ohio in the aftermath of the Civil War and the abolition of slavery, and explores the relationship of African-Americans to the history of slavery. Morrison rewrites that history from an African-American perspective by drawing on the literary tradition of the slave narrative. The past haunts the present in Morrison's novel in a variety of ways, and Beloved, the daughter who Sethe has killed to save from slavery, becomes the emblem of that past, haunting the house where her mother lives, and then returning as a young woman insatiable for reparation in the form of love and stories.

The non-linear narrative based on storytelling, Morrison's other main aesthetic model, enables her to interweave past and present. Stories are told from more than one perspective and by different characters – for example, Sethe's other daughter, Denver, tells the story of her own birth – so that individual and collective identity are entwined. Maternity in the context of a history of radical dispossession, and the exploration of non-misogynist masculinity for black men, are key themes in *Beloved*, which links Morrison's work to other African-American women writers such as ▷Alice Walker, ▷Paule Marshall and ▷Ntozake Shange.

Ben (Haim), Myriem (born 1928)

Algerian novelist, born in Algiers. She taught in different Algerian villages. Between 1955 and 1962 she participated in the war of liberation, and was condemned by the military court of Algiers to twenty years' forced labour. Later she became involved in the organization of foreign-language teaching. She is also a painter. Her novels include *Ainsi naquit un homme* (1982) (*Thus a Man is Born*), *Sur le chemin de nos pas* (1984) (*In Our*

Footsteps) and ▷*Sabrina, ils t'ont volé ta vie* (1986) (*Sabrina, They've Stolen Your Life*).

Benedetta (Cappa Marinetti) (1899–1977)
Italian essayist, painter and writer of fiction, she married F.T. Marinetti, the 'father' of ▷futurism, and formed part of the futurist movement. Involved in polemics on futurism, Benedetta contributed to collections of futurist writings, including poetry, and exhibited her paintings with others of the avant-garde. She prescribes very specific roles for women, but her view of the ideal futurist woman is, in fact, very close to traditional prescriptions. For Benedetta, woman is ideally a source of inspiration for man. Her tone is religious in its call for female self-sacrifice. Motherhood, in her opinion, is the only true female vocation in the modern world. During the Ethiopian war, she spoke out strongly on the role of women in time of war, rejecting any idea of woman as rival to man, and calling on her sex to make the supreme sacrifice of leaving the heart of the family in order to temporarily fill the gaps left by men in the world of work. She advocated, above all, a new conformism. In her writings, she strove to achieve a sort of prose painting. She wrote three novels. *Le forze umane* (1924) (*Human Strength*) is an abstract autobiographical novel. *Viaggio di Gararà* (1931, 1942) (*Gararà's Journey*), described as a cosmic novel for the theatre, is an allegorical tale. *Astra e il sottomarino* (1935) (*Astra and the Submarine*), delves into the unconscious, and is somewhat surreal in tone.

Benedictsson, Victoria (1850–1888)
Swedish epic writer. Pseudonym: Ernst Ahlgren, She was born in Skåne, and wanted to be a painter. As her parents resisted this choice, she married a fifty-year-old postmaster, Christian Benedictsson, in 1871. He already had five children aged five to thirteen from a previous marriage. She herself gave birth to two daughters, the younger of which died as an infant.

From 1881 to 1883 she was seriously ill, and became disabled because of a bad leg. During her illness she began to write, and in 1884 she made her début, under the pseudonym of Ernst Ahlgren, with a collection of realist short stories, *Från Skåne* (*From Skåne*). The autobiographical novel *Pengar* (*Money*) with many was published in 1885, and *Fru Marianne* (*Mrs Marianne*) in 1887, as was the collection of short stories *Folklif och Småberättelser* (*Folklife and Little Tales*).

From 1886 she lived for long periods in Copenhagen, and made friends with the critic and writer Georg Brandes (1842–1927). When he did not want to develop the relationship, and did not give public acclaim to the novel *Fru Marianne*, she committed suicide. In the 1980s an unabridged version of her diaries, *Stora Boken* (*The Big Book*), was published.

Together with August Strindberg, Victoria Benedictsson continues to be recognized as the most talented writer of the 19th century. She was called the genius of the 1880s because of her realistic descriptions and clear style.

Today, *Stora Boken* is probably considered her finest work, a central document of the social history of the 1880s in Sweden, that examines the ambiguity of self-assertion and self-destruction in lively and deeply-felt prose.

Ben Haddou, Halima
Moroccan novelist, born in Nador in the Rif mountains. Paralysed from the age of nine, Halima Ben Haddou spent nearly a year writing ▷*Aïcha la rebelle* (1982) (*Aïcha the Rebel*) in school notebooks, then another year typing it with one finger. *Aïcha la rebelle* was a great success on publication, and for Halima Ben Haddou it represented a triumph over her paralysis.

Benisławska, Konstancja (1986) (1747–1806)
Polish religious poet. A noblewoman who lived in the remote province of Livonia, she turned to religious poetry at the 'advanced age' of twenty-eight, after bearing several children. She ranks among the better baroque poets, of whom she is a late descendant. In *Piesni sobie spiewanr* (1776) (*Songs Sung to Oneself*), for example, she bears resemblance to the baroque poets for the rusticism of some passages and for her scholastic subtlety.

Benjamin Franklin and Catharine Ray Greene: Their Correspondence 1755–1790 (1949)
▷Catharine Ray Greene was a lifelong friend and correspondent of the North American statesman, Benjamin Franklin (1706–1790), and his sister, ▷Jane Franklin Mecom (some of Mecom's letters are also included in this collection). An astute political analyst and pro-revolutionary activist, Greene's letters to her 'Dear Friend' are an important contribution to the literature of the American Revolution, especially in terms of the war's effect on her home state of Rhode Island.
   ▷*Letters of Benjamin Franklin and Jane Mecom, The*; Early North American letters

Bennett, Anna Maria (Evans) (c 1750–1808)
Welsh novelist and writer of scandalous memoirs. She came to London and married David Evans before becoming the mistress of Admiral Sir Thomas Pye. She published *Anna, or Memoirs of a Welch Heiress* anonymously in 1785, and wrote five more novels including *Agnes de Courci* (1789) which was influenced by Samuel Richardson (▷Richardson, influence of). She also became manageress of the Theatre Royal, Edinburgh.

Other publications: *Juvenile Indiscretions* (1786); *Ellen, or the Countess of Castle Howel* (1794), and *The Beggar Girl and her Benefactress* (1797).
   ▷Carleton, Mary; Charke, Charlotte
Bib: Fuller, J.F., *A Curious Genealogical Medley*; Doody, Margaret Ann and Sabor, Peter (eds), *Samuel Johnson*.

Bennett, Louise Simone (born 1919)

Caribbean poet, actress and folklorist, also known as Miss Lou, born in Jamaica. Acknowledged as one of the foremost writers of Jamaican oral culture (see ▷Nation language), she began writing poetry at an early age, initially using standard English, but she soon developed her use of Creole. She was awarded a scholarship to the Royal Academy of Dramatic Art in London in 1945. She wrote and performed for radio in both Britain and the USA. She returned to Jamaica in 1955, where she pursued her interest and research into ▷oral history and folklore. She has had a central influence on the development of Jamaican pantomime, and has written and performed extensively for both television and radio. Her honours include an MBE (1960), the Norman Manley Award for Excellence in the Arts (1972), and an honorary D.Litt. from the University of the West Indies (1983).

Her first collection of poetry was *Dialect Verse* (1942), which was followed by *Jamaican Humour in Dialect* (1943), *Anancy Stories and Poems in Dialect* (1944), *Miss Lou Sez* (1949), *Laugh With Louise* (1961), ▷*Jamaica Labrish* (1966), *Anancy and Miss Lou* (1979) and *Selected Poems* (1983).

Her recordings include *Jamaican Folk Songs* (1954) and *The Honourable Miss Lou* (1981).

For a full listing of critical essays and biographical details see Mervyn Morris's chapter in ▷*Fifty Caribbean Writers*.

Benoist, Françoise-Albine Puzin de la Martinière (1724–1809)

French novelist and dramatist. Born in Lyon, Benoist received no formal education, and does not appear to have frequented well-known literary circles. In her first work, *Journal en forme de lettres* (1757) (*Diary in Letter Form*), she defends the right of women to write, suggesting that if they are allowed to give citizens to the nation then they should also be permitted to provide 'children for the republic of letters'. Of her eleven novels published over a twenty-year period, including *Célianne* (1766), *Elisabeth* (1766), *Lettres du colonel Talbert* (1767) (*Letters of Colonel Talbert*), *L'Erreur des désirs* (1770) (*The Error of Desires*) and *Les Aveux d'une jolie femme* (1782) (*The Confessions of a Pretty Woman*), only *Les Erreurs d'une jolie femme ou la nouvelle Aspasie* (1781) (*The Mistakes of a Pretty Woman, or the new Aspasie*) has received recent critical attention. Here the reputedly conformist Benoist presents the memoirs of an astute libertine heroine of peasant origins who, in the course of her social ascension and career as a courtesan, shows herself to be morally superior to the society which condemns her. Benoist also published two plays, *La Superchérie réciproque* (1768) (*Reciprocal Trickery*) and *Le Triomphe de la probité* (1768) (*The Triumph of Integrity*), after the style of Italian dramatist Carlo Goldoni (1707–1793).

Other works: *Mes principes* (1759–60) (*My Principles*); *La Vertu persécutée 1767* (*Persecuted Virtue*); *Agathe et Isidore* (1768); *Les Aventures du beau cordonnier* (1769) (*Adventures of the Handsome Cobbler*); *Sophronie* (1769); *Folie de la prudence humaine* (1771) (*The Folly of Human Prudence*); *Lettres sur le désir de plaire* (1786) (*Letters on the Wish to Please*).

Bib: Girou-Swiderski, M., 'Comment peut-on être parvenue?', *Etudes Littéraires*, December 1979; Prudhomme, L. M., *Répertoire universel historique et biographique des femmes célèbres*.

Benson, Mary (born 1919)

South African novelist, dramatist, documentary writer, and autobiographer. Born in Pretoria, she has lived part of her life in England and North America, campaigning actively against apartheid, and part in South Africa, working as a political journalist and as secretary to political figures and organizations. She was banned in 1966 and forced into exile. Her documentary writing includes three biographies: *Tshekedi Khama* (1960), *Chief Albert Luthuli* (1963), and *Nelson Mandela* (1986); a history of the African National Congress, first published as *The African Patriots* (1963) and updated in 1985 under the title *South Africa: The Struggle for a Birthright*; and some political pamphlets, one of which was published by the United Nations Organization under the title *The Struggle in South Africa Has United All Races* (1984). She also edited *The Sun Will Rise: Statements from the Dock by South African Political Prisoners* (1974).

Benson has published one novel, *At the Still Point* (1969), and an autobiography, *A Far Cry* (1989), whose subtitle, *The Making of a South African*, expresses the major theme of both autobiography and novel. Drawing on South African political life in the 1950s and 1960s, a period marked by a set of harrowing and patently unjust political trials and the gradual decision by certain groups to offer armed resistance, both books strive to define a role and a place for a woman whose politically progressive ideals alienate her from most other white South Africans, yet whose pacifism distinguishes her in turn from radical political groupings, both black and white. Like her contemporary ▷Nadine Gordimer, Benson draws sharp attention to the politicization of personal life in a South Africa ruled by apartheid, but does not make the shift from liberalism to radicalism that Gordimer makes in her later work.

Besides a set of political plays and documentaries for the BBC, Benson has scripted various literary documentaries; she also edited Athol Fugard's *Notebooks: 1960–1977* (1983), and adapted Winnie Mandela's *Part Of My Soul* (1985), edited by Anne Benjamin.

▷Autobiography (Southern Africa); Exile writing (South Africa)

Benson, Stella (1892–1933)

English novelist, poet and travel writer. An active campaigner for women's rights, Benson focuses in her first novel, *I Pose* (1915), on the life of a suffragette, and subsequent novels maintain this strong autobiographical element. In 1918 Benson travelled to San Francisco, and her introduction to Californian 'society' forms the basis of the satirical *The Poor Man* (1922). In the 1920s, Benson married, settled in China, and pursued her concern for women's welfare, opposing the Hong Kong brothel systems. Her characteristic interest in cross-cultural analysis is central to *Tobit Transplanted* (1930), an allegory that looks at exiles in China. Travel writings include *The Little World* (1925) and *Worlds within Worlds* (1928).

Bentley, Catherine (fl 1635)
English translator, a nun of the Por Clares in Douai, who took the name Sister Magdalene Augustine. She translated Francis Hendriques's extracts from the life of St Clare, which she called 'the life of a Saint of *Feminine* Sexe, but *Masculine* Virtue'. It was published in 1635, and dedicated to the Catholic English queen, Henrietta Maria, because 'the manifold starres of virtue which render this saint most illustrious, we shall find also in your Majestie by a certain semblance.'

Bentzon, Thérèse (1840–1907)
French novelist and critic. Brought up in the country by her mother and an English governess, she was married at sixteen and divorced at nineteen. Her second husband introduced her to ▷George Sand, who in turn presented her to the editor of *La Revue des deux mondes*, the journal in which she published much of her writing. She was the author of translations, travelogues and literary criticism, and produced a novel a year, beginning with *Un divorce* (1872) (*A Divorce*). Her most popular fictional works were *Un remords* (1878) (*A Pang of Remorse*) and *Tony* (1884), which were awarded prizes by the ▷Académie Française, and her most successful non-fiction text was *Les Américaines chez elles* (1896) (*American Women at Home*). Although her critical writings were superficial, she was responsible for introducing US writers Mark Twain (1835–1910), Henry James (1843–1916) and Walt Whitman (1819–1892) to the French reading public.

Ben-Yehuda, Hemda (1873–1951)
Hebrew story writer. She was the wife of Eliezer Ben-Yehuda (1858–1922), the Hebrew writer and lexicographer, generally considered the father of Modern Hebrew. She helped her husband in his literary work and, after his death, helped publish the remaining volumes of his dictionary. She also published a book about his life, entitled *Yehuda, hayav umif'alo* (1940) (*Yehuda, his Life and his Work*). Her sentimental stories describe life in the Holy Land romantically, with a clear didactic aim of impressing her readers with its beauty.

Benzoni, Julie (born 1920)
French novelist. Benzoni writes traditional historical romance and has achieved considerable popularity. Both the 'Catherine' series, set in 15th-century France, and the 'Marianne' series, set in the Napoleonic period, have been translated into English. Typical titles are *Catherine, ma mie* (1967) (translated as *Catherine and Arnaud*) and *Marianne et l'inconnu de Toscane* (1971) (translated as *Marianne and the Masked Prince*).

Berbérova, Nina Nikolaevna (born 1901)
Russian prose writer, poet, historian, biographer, and autobiographer. Berbérova was born in St Petersburg, where she began writing poetry before the 1917 Revolution. She emigrated in 1922. Between 1925 and 1950 she lived in Paris, where she published three novels, biographies of the composers Chaikovskii (1936) and Borodin (1938) and of the poet Blok (1948, in French), and a collection of six novellas, *The Easing of Fate* (1948). In 1938 her play *Madame* was staged at the Russian theatre. In 1950 she moved to the United States, where she taught Russian literature at Yale and Princeton Universities. Active in preserving the work of her former husband, the poet Vladislav Khodasevich, she edited his *Literary Articles and Reminiscences* and *A Collection of Khodasevich's Poems* (1961). In 1969 she published her autobiography, ▷*The Italics Are Mine* in English, and in 1972 in Russian. Between 1980 and 1986, Berbérova published a novel, a collection of poetry from the years 1921–1983, a biography of the Baroness Mar'ia Budberg (Zakrevskaia-Benkendorf), and a study of Russian Freemasonry, a subject she first broached in her autobiography.

Berbérova's early novels were influenced by Dostoevskii. Her novella, *The Accompanist* (1935, English translation 1988), set in post-revolutionary Russia, is the story of a triangle: a young pianist, her employer – a beautiful soprano, and the latter's husband. In 1991 another collection of Berbérova's novellas, *The Tattered Cloak*, appeared in English to positive reviews.

▷Akhmátova, Anna

Bib: Radley, Philippe (trans.), *The Italics Are Mine* (1969); Schwartz, Marian (trans.), *The Accompanist* and *The Tattered Cloak* (1991); Glad, J. and Weissbort, D. (eds), *Russian Poetry: The Modern Period*; Weber, H. (ed.), *The Modern Encyclopedia of Russian and Soviet Literature*, Vol. 2.

Berenguer, Amanda (born 1912)
Uruguayan poet. She began her career with *A través de los tiempos que llevan a la gran calma* (1940) (*Through the Times Which Lead to Great Calmness*). *El río* (1952) (*The River*), and even more so *La invitación* (1957) (*The Invitation*) – eight poems with a melancholy interior force – made Berenguer well-known. *Contracanto* (1961) (*Countersong*) and *Quehaceres e invenciones* (1962) (*Chores and Inventions*) brought a change in her poetry and the achievement of her high goals, with some of the best moments of Uruguayan lyricism. *Declaración conjunta* (1964) (*Joint Declaration*) and *Materia prima* (1966) (*First Matter*) have been seen as daring and unexpected books, typical of the ▷1945 Generation. As her collected works, *Poesía* (1980) (*Poetry*) and *Composición de lugar* (1976) (*Composition of Place*), demonstrate, she has

become increasingly experimental, employing the voice, sound, and the visualized word in space. *Los signos sobre la mesa* (1986) (*The Signs on the Table*) won a prize from the Universidad de la República.

Berens-Totenohl, Josefa (1891–1969)
German poet and fiction writer. Of humble origin, she drew inspiration from the German oral tradition, its fairytales, legends and ballads. Her novels, *Der Femhof* (1934) (*The Femhof Estate*) and *Frau Magdlene* (1935) (*Mrs Magdlene*), are set in 14th-century Westphalia, and centre on heroic mother-figures. Her work was welcomed by the Nazis as exemplifying the values of German 'blood and soil'.

Beresford, Anne (born 1929)
English poet and radio dramatist. Beresford's poetry of the 1970s and 1980s is characterized by her interest in myth and folklore, and collections such as *The Curving Stone* (1975) and *The Songs of Almut from God's Country* (1980) combine contemporary, mythic and antiquarian references. Other volumes include: *Walking Without Moving* (1967), *The Lair* (1968), *Footsteps on Snow* (1972), *Unholy Giving* (1977).

Beresford-Howe, Constance (born 1922)
Canadian novelist, born in Montreal. She was educated at McGill University and Brown University, taught at McGill and, from 1971 until her retirement, at Ryerson Polytechnical Institute in Toronto. Her early novels are not well-known, but lay the groundwork for her later, more important, work. *The Unreasoning Heart* (1946) deals with a homeless adolescent; *Of This Day's Journey* (1947) follows a young college lecturer; *The Invisible Gate* (1949) is essentially about a failed romance. These are all contemporary novels, but her fourth, *My Lady Greensleeves* (1955), is a historical romance set in 16th-century England. After an eighteen-year hiatus, Beresford-Howe published three novels that form a trilogy questioning the accepted mythologies of domesticity and sexuality: ▷ *The Book of Eve* (1973), *A Population of One* (1977) and *The Marriage Bed* (1981). All of these novels deal with women characters challenging convention and coming to terms with versions of independence. Subsequently, *Night Studies* (1985) explores life at a night school, and *Prospero's Daughter* (1988) a conflict between father and daughter. *A Serious Widow* (1991) is an acerbic exploration of widowhood's unexpected treacheries. The latter are less clearly resolved than the preceding novels, and suggest darker shadows for women and independence.
Bib: Beresford-Howe, C., in *A Fair Stake: Autobiographical Essays by McGill Women*.

Bergalli Gozzi, Luisa (1703–1779)
Italian poet and dramatist based in Venice; real name Irminda Partenide. She married Gasparo Gozzi in 1738. Well educated, she also wrote

short stories and translated the works of other writers. When in serious financial difficulties, she and her husband took on the management of the Teatro Sant'Angelo, but this also proved financially disastrous. She was particularly interested in women poets, and compiled an anthology of her female predecessors. Her main works are: *Agide*, a musical play (1725); *L'Elensà*, a musical play (1730); *Le avventure del poeta* (1730) (*The Poet's Adventures*); *Teba*, a tragedy (1738).

Bergen, Veritas Leo ▷ Troll-Borostyani, Irma von

Berggól'ts (Bergholz), Ol'ga Fëdorovna (1910–1975)
Most famous as a Russian poet, Berggól'ts also wrote newspaper articles, prose, plays, and children's stories. Between 1934 and 1938 she published three books of lyric poetry, as well as fiction and poetry in the ▷ socialist realist mould. At the same time she apparently wrote rather defiant poetry 'for the drawer' which was published only in the 1950s. She was subjected to some of the worst horrors of the 1930s and 1940s: her first husband was shot in a purge and she herself was imprisoned for two years. After prison, she lived in Leningrad through the terrible Nazi blockade of the city, devoting herself to the war effort by working on the radio. During one broadcast, she helped ▷ Akhmátova deliver an appeal to the inhabitants of the besieged city. Akhmátova regarded her as a 'devoted friend' (R. Reeder, *The Complete Poems of Anna Akhmátova*). Though Berggól'ts survived the blockade, her second husband died from starvation. The war was the major theme of her poetry and plays well into the 1950s. In Berggól'ts' poetry, rhetorical devices and epithets dominate, along with simple but elaborated metaphors; at her best this creates an emotional pitch that conveys her passion. Some of her poetry shows ▷ socialist realist style: the use of the collective 'we', 'us', 'our', optimism about the future, and so on. Berggól'ts considered her major work to be the fictionalized autobiography *Diurnal Stars* (1959). She continued to publish books of poetry in the 1960s and 1970s, and a three-volume *Collected Works* appeared in 1972–73.
Bib: Glad, J. and Weissbort, D. (eds), *Russian Poetry: The Modern Period*; Markov, V. and Sparks, M. (eds), *Modern Russian Poetry*; Dobson, R. and Campbell, D. (trans.), *Seven Russian Poets*; Conquest, R. (ed.), *Back to Life: Poems from Behind the Iron Curtain*; Williams, A. and de Sola Pinto, V. (trans.), *The Road to the West: Sixty Soviet War Poems*; Wilson, K., *An Encyclopedia of Continental Women Writers*, Vol. 1.

Berkeley, Sara (born 1967)
Irish poet. Born in Dublin, she took a degree in English at Trinity College, Dublin. Her first collection, *Penn*, appeared in 1986, and was followed by *Home Movie Nights* in 1989, both acclaimed as evidence of a new generation of

younger, more outward-looking Irish poets, breaking free of the influence of W.B. Yeats (1865–1939) and the Irish Revival (a nationalist and cultural movement which flourished in the late 19th century and early 20th century).

Berlepsch, Emilie von (1755–1830)
German essayist and travel writer. The wife of a nobleman at the Hanover Court, she was principally known for *Caledonia* (1802–1804), an account of her travels in Scotland. She also published unsigned essays on marriage, misogyny and the status of women.

Bermuda
This geographica region of the Caribbean is not one island, but an archipelago of seven major and over 150 smaller islands and rocks. Turks Island lies 720 miles south, in the remote Caicos group. Bermuda lacked the natural resources to become a plantation colony. Bermuda was the birthplace of ▷Mary Prince.

Bernal, Emilia (1884–1964)
Cuban poet. Bernal, who spent her childhood in Nuevitas, was the daughter of a primary school teacher. She had no formal education. During the 1895 war, her house was set on fire, and her parents moved with her to Santo Domingo. However, they soon returned because they could not find a way to support themselves there. In 1910 she began to publish her first poems. Bernal followed the lead of poet Julián del Casal (1863–1893) in his use of ardent and intuitive themes, instead of being influenced by symbolism, or ▷*modernismo*. She published in newspapers, and travelled widely, spending most of her life out of Cuba.

Works: *Alma errante* (1916) (*Roving Spirit*); *¡Como los pájaros!* (1922) (*Like the Birds!*); *Poesías inéditas* (1922) (*Unpublished Poems*); *El romance de cuando yo era niña* (1925) (*The Ballad of When I Was a Girl*); *Los nuevos motivos* (1925) (*New Themes*); *Vida* (1928) (*Life*); *Negro* (1934) (*Black*); *América* (1937) (*America*); *Sentido* (1937) (*Meaning*); *Sonetos* (1937) (*Sonnets*), and *Mallorca* (1938).

Bernard, Catherine (1662–1712)
French novelist and author of fairytales. She left Rouen for Paris at the age of seventeen and quickly became accepted in literary and court society, publishing her first short narrative and recognizing writing as her career. A series of novellas (▷*nouvelles*) and novels followed, and she also had two plays performed. In 1687 she published *Les Malheurs de l'amour, première nouvelle, Eléonor d'Yvrée* (*The Misfortunes of Love, First Story, Eléonor d'Yvrée*). Bernard, who never married, wrote fiction in the concise analytical tradition of ▷Madame de Lafayette. Without passing moral judgement, she aims in her portrayal of a woman caught in a triangular relationship to present '*un Tableau des Malheurs de cette passion*' ('a picture of the misfortunes of this

passion'). *Inès de Cordoue, nouvelle espagnole* (1696) (*Ines of Cordoba, a Spanish Novella*) is a historical romance, which also presents two fairytales, much in fashion at the time: '*Le Prince rosier*' ('The Prince of the Rose') and a version of '*Riquet à la houppe*' ('Riquet with the Topknot'). In these tales, she resists both the temptation of the fantastic and the facile happy ending, concluding that '*le mariage, selon la coutume, finit tous les agréments de la vie*' ('marriage, according to custom, ends all of life's pleasures').
Bib: Wilwerth, E., *Visages de la littérature féminine*.

Bernes, Dame Julyans (15th century)
English writer. The authorship of part of *The Boke of St Albans*, a compilation of treatises on hawking, hunting and heraldry, is attributed to 'Dame Julyans Bernes' in the edition printed by Wynkyn de Worde (died ?1534) in 1496. Nothing is known about her beyond her name – she was also known as Julyans Barnes and Juliana Berners – and association with this work. She has traditionally been identified – on very tenuous grounds – as holding the position of prioress at Sopwell, Hertfordshire (near St Albans), some time after 1430; and it has been suggested that she may have spent her early years at court, where she might have engaged in hunting and hawking. The parts of the treatise attributed to her contain detailed entries connected with hawks and hawking (diseases, care of the birds, terminology); more general information on hunting (the beasts of the chase, the dogs, hunting terms), and some additional material relating to the social niceties surrounding these activities. The association of Dame Julyans with this popular work suggests that the literature (or theory) of these sports was not necessarily a male prerogative, any more than was the practice.
Bib: Hands, Rachel (ed.), *English Hawking and Hunting in 'The Boke of St Albans'*; Barratt, Alexandra (ed.), *Women's Writing in Middle English*.

Bernhardi, Sophie (1775–1833)
German writer. Sister of the romantic poet and writer Ludwig Tieck, she published a first collection of short stories, *Straußfedern* (1795) (*Ostrich Feathers*), anonymously at the age of twenty. She contributed to romantic journals, wrote two novels, fairytales and plays. Her '*Flore und Blancheflur*' (1822) was a highly-acclaimed reworking of a medieval poem.

Bernstein, Hilda (born 1915)
South African novelist, documentary writer and autobiographer. Born Hilda Watts in London, she moved to South Africa in 1933, where she became involved with radical political organizations campaigning for black and women's rights. She published a pamphlet about her visit to China in 1961 for *New Age*, the radical Cape Town magazine. In 1964 she left the country illegally, under threat of arrest, and now lives in London. Her political autobiography, *The World*

That Was Ours (1967, revised 1989), tells the story of the period leading up to and during the Rivonia trial, where Nelson Mandela and others were sentenced to life imprisonment. Her novel *Death Is Part of the Process* (1983), a political thriller set in the early 1960s, won the first Sinclair Prize for Fiction in Britain: a group of South Africans of all races commit themselves to sabotage in their fight against apartheid, and are gradually hemmed in by the police.

Her other works are: *South Africa: The Terrorism of Torture* (1972); *For Their Triumphs and for Their Tears: Women in Apartheid South Africa* (1978), and *No. 46 – Steve Biko* (1978).
▷Autobiography (Southern Africa); Exile writing (South Africa)

Berrian, Brenda F.
Her *Bibliography of Women Writers from the Caribbean (1831–1986)* 1989) provides a comprehensive index of women authors from the Caribbean, grouped by country. The index includes entries on Autobiography/Biography, Broadcast Literature, Children's Literature, Novels, Short Stories, Drama: Performed Plays, Drama: Published Plays, Folklore, Poetry, Other Writings by Authors, Criticism of Author's Works, Book Reviews and Interviews.

Bersianik, Louky (born 1930)
▷Pseudonym of Canadian Lucile Durand, one of the most significant of Quebec's feminist writers. She studied at the University of Montreal, at the Sorbonne, and at the CERT in lssy-les-Moulineaux, France. She has written for radio and television and published several books for children. Her important book, *L'Euguélionne*, was published in 1976, and translated into English in 1981. It has been described as 'a French-Canadian feminist anti-Bible'. A satiric picaresque novel with the quality of a manifesto, it seeks to describe women's experience in a new way. Bersianik's other works include: *La Page de garde* (1978) (*The Flyleaf*), *Le Pique-nique sur l'Acropole* (1979) (*Picnic on the Acropolis*), *Maternative: les Prè-Ancyl* (1980), *Les Agénésies du vieux monde* (1982) (*Beginnings of the Old World*), *Au beau milieu de moi* (1983) (*At the Very Heart of Me*), and *Axes et eau* (1984) (*Axis and Water*). All of her works confront the problem of language as power. Only *The Euguélionne* and *Noli Me Tangere* (▷*Room of One's Own*, No. 68–69, 1978) have been translated.
▷Marlatt, Daphne
Bib: Gould, K., *Writing in the Feminine: Feminism and Experimental Writing in Quebec*; Hadjukowski-Ahmed, M., in *Traditionalism, Nationalism and Feminism: Women Writers of Quebec*; Waelti-Walters, J., in ▷*A Mazing Space*.

Bertheroy, Jean ▷Roy de Clotte le Barillier, Berthe

Berthgyth (? late 8th century)
English nun and letter-writer. Some of Berthgyth's letters are included in the ▷Boniface Correspondence. Berthgyth was the daughter of Cynehild, aunt of Boniface's fellow missionary, Lull. Cynehild and her daughter were both educated women who went to teach in Thuringia, presumably at the request of Boniface. Three letters from Berthgyth (in Latin) survive. They are addressed to her brother, Balthard. They express her loneliness after the death of her mother, and beg her brother to visit her. They are literary compositions (which may be why they have been preserved), and have been compared with some of the Old English Elegies, including ▷'The Wife's Lament' and ▷'Wulf and Eadwacer'.
Bib: Dronke, Peter, *Women Writers of the Middle Ages*; Fell, Christine E., 'Some Implications of the Boniface Correspondence' in Damico, Helen and Hennessey Olsen, Alexandra (eds.), *New Readings on Women in Old English Literature*.

Bertrana, Aurora (1899–1974)
Spanish novelist. Aurora Bertrana was born in Gerona, the daughter of Prudenci Bertrana, a well-known Catalan writer. Two of her early novels reflect the experience of the Spanish Civil War (1936–9): *Tres presoners* (1957) (*Three Prisoners*) and *Entre dos silencis* (1958) (*Between Two Silences*). Her other novels are: *La nimfa d'argili* (1959) (*The Clay Nymph*); *Fracàs* (1966) (*Failure*), and *Vent de grop* (1967) (*Tailwind*). She has also published collections of short stories. Her prose is characterized by precise observation.
▷Catalan women's writing

Berwick, Mary ▷Procter, Adelaide

Bessa-Luís, Agustina (born 1923)
Portuguese novelist, dramatist and historian. One of Portugal's most distinguished authors, Bessa-Luís has written over thirty volumes. Her first two novels went unnoticed by the critics; however, in 1953 she gained widespread recognition with ▷*A Sibila* (*The Sibyl*), whose main character is believed to possess prophetic powers. The novel takes place in northern Portugal, the birthplace of the author and the setting for several of her novels.

Village communities, the rural aristocracy, conservative customs and mores are stock themes in many of Bessa-Luís' books. She is particularly fond of writing about matriarchal characters who preserve the traditions passed down to them from their mothers. Several of her novels are based on historical figures: for example, in *Adivinhas de Pedro e Inês* (1983) (*Riddles of Pedro and Inês*) she re-examines the legendary romance between the Portuguese prince Dom Pedro and Dona Inês de Castro, a noblewoman in the royal court; and her *Os Meninos de Ouro* (1983) (*The Golden Boys*), about the bid for power in early post-revolutionary Portugal, is a *roman à clef* about former prime minister Francisco Sá Carneiro.

In addition to novels, Bessa-Luís has written non-fictional works on such figures as Saint Anthony, the poet ▷Florbela Espanca, and the artist and writer Maria Helena Vieira da Silva.

Among her least-known works are her plays and travel literature.

Bib: *Longman Anthology of World Literature by Women*.

Best of Husbands, The (1952)

A novel by Italian writer ▷Alba de Cespedes, translated from *Dalla parte di lei* (1949), it is the story of a young woman, Alessandra, who murders her husband after just one year of marriage. The backdrop to the novel is Rome during the German occupation, and the novel touches on the issues of the ▷Resistance. It is possible to read Alessandra's resistance in the light of political symbolism but, in fact, her story seems somewhat remote from the political dimension of the novel. Above all, this work is a passionate defence of a woman's moral right to decide her own fate. The historical and social background to the main plot is realistically portrayed.

Betham-Edwards, Matilda (1836–1919)

English novelist, essayist and ▷travel writer, born on a farm in Suffolk. Her mother died when she was twelve, after which Betham-Edwards educated herself, developing early an interest in France and the French. She began her first novel, *The White House by the Sea*, while still a teenager. Eventually published in 1857, it became an immediate success, reprinting continuously for the next forty years. The author went on to write more than thirty novels, of which *Forestalled* (1880) and *Love and Marriage* (1884) were her favourites. Her travel writing includes *A Winter with the Swallows* (1866) and *Through Spain to the Sahara* (1867), which record her trips with the ▷feminist ▷Barbara Bodichon. Betham-Edwards was a believer in women's equality and signed the 1866 petition for female ▷suffrage. Her sympathy to socialist perspectives is evident in *The Sylvesters* (1871). In 1884, she published *Six Life Studies of Famous Women*, which included a biographical sketch of her aunt and godmother, Matilda Betham, who wrote poetry and diaries.

Beth Book, The, (1897)

A novel by ▷Sarah Grand. The narrative begins with Beth's childhood in Ireland and describes the suffering she experiences as the daughter of an alcholic father and depressive mother. She later marries a doctor who works in a Lock Hospital, where prostitutes were forcibly detained for medical treatment and examination. The oppressive marriage becomes unbearable when Beth's unfaithful and objectionable husband moves his mistress into the house. Beth liberates herself when she discovers a secret room, in which she disciplines herself to become a writer, finally triumphing when her anonymously published work is well-received by the male literary establishment.

▷'New Woman, The'

Bethell, Mary Ursula (1874–1945)

New Zealand poet. Ursula Bethell, who originally published under the pseudonym Evelyn Hayes, was born in England but moved to Canterbury, New Zealand as a child. She was educated largely in England and spent most of her young adult life in Europe studying painting and music before she chose, for social and religious reasons, to work amongst poor children in south London. In 1924 she decided to move permanently to Christchurch, New Zealand and with her lifelong friend Effie Pollen settled in the hills where she wrote poetry focused on gardening, landscape and religion. Bethell's friend, the poet D'Arcy Cresswell (1896–1960), said of her work that 'New Zealand wasn't truly discovered until Ursula Bethell, "very earnestly digging", raised her head to look at the mountains.'

Works include: ▷*From a Garden in the Antipodes* (1929); *Time and Place* (1936); *Day and Night: Poems 1924–35* (1939); *Collected Poems*, ed. Vincent O'Sullivan (1985).

Between Two Worlds (1981)

Translation by Barbara Bray of the novel by the Guadeloupean writer ▷Simone Schwarz-Bart, *Ti Jean l'horizon* (1979). Schwarz-Bart takes as the protagonist for her second novel Ti-Jean, the cunning hero of many of the tales of creolophone peoples who have links with Africa. The epic voyage on which Ti-Jean embarks starts when he walks into the mouth of the Beast who has swallowed the sun and Egée, his love, and killed his mother. The long journey takes him to the present and the past, the realms of reality and Surreality. Ti-Jean searches throughout his voyage in Africa, the kingdom of the dead and France for a way back to Guadeloupe and to his love. Narrated in the innovative creolized style developed in Schwarz-Bart's earlier novels, Ti-Jean's journey is not only a quest for mother and lover, for Guadeloupe and for light; it is also a search for the Father, the Heroic Ancestor, and for a History.

Beutler, Maja (born 1936)

German-speaking Swiss novelist. A native of Berne, she now works for Swiss radio. She achieved a first success with her semi-autobiographical novel, *Fuß fassen* (1980) (*Gaining a Foothold*), which describes a middle-aged woman's fight against cancer whilst also returning to work after raising a family. Isolation is a major theme in Beutler's work and she discusses the impossibility of communication – between man and woman in *Die Wortfalle* (1983) (*The Trap of Words*), and between individuals more generally in *Das Bildnis der Doña Quichotte* (1989) (*The Portrait of Dona Quixote*).

Beutler, Margarete (1876–1949)

German poet. Born in the rural province of Pomerania, she moved to Berlin to become a teacher. After the birth of a son 'conceived in free love' she worked as an editor in Munich, took part in the cabaret show, *Elf Scharfrichter* (*Eleven Executioners*), and translated plays by Molière (1622–1673). She also wrote her own stories, and the play *Das Lied des Todes* (1911) (*The Song of Death*). She then studied medicine and became a practising gynaecologist. The poems of her successful first collection, *Gedichte* (1902) (*Poems*), revolve around the problems of modern life. Later poems, such as '*Die Puppe*' ('The Doll') in *Leb' wohl, Boheme!* (1911) (*Farewell, Bohemia!*), tend to concentrate more specifically on the issue of women's position in society.

Bewitched Crossroad, A (1984)

Subtitled 'An African Saga', this is the last book published by Southern African writer ▷ Bessie Head during her lifetime, and significant also as the first historical reconstruction of the Southern African past by a black woman, following only her own earlier book, *Serowe: Village of the Rain Wind* (1981), which is smaller in scope. As in her other texts, Head reaches back into the past in order to shape the future: in this case, to restore the past as represented by the Sebina clan of the Bamangwato people in the 19th century, who fuse with the people of Khama the Great. Both Sebina and Khama are, for Head, great leaders who neither hanker for a tribal past nor are threatened by the new. They manage to withstand the colonial invasion and expropriation of land, which black South Africans had had to succumb to, even while embracing the book-learning offered by the missionaries. Khama, as Head sees him, was also a leader who restored dignity and voice to Botswanan women. The title refers to the magical possibilities opened up for Africa by Botswanan history: South Africa, as Head so often said in her interviews, was a place where people had lost the power to dream.

Beyala, Calixte

Cameroonian novelist. Author of two novels: *C'est le soleil qui m'a brulee* (1987) (*It's the Sun which has Burnt Me*) and *Seul le diable le sait* (1990) (*The Devil Only Knows*).

Beynon, Francis Marion (1884–1951)

Canadian novelist and activist, born in Ontario, but moved to a homestead near Hartney, Manitoba at the age of five. She attended school there, and trained to be a primary school teacher, a profession she never actually engaged in. She moved to Winnipeg in 1908, and was one of the first women to work in the advertising department of a large store. Her sister, Lillian Beynon Thomas, was elected first President of the Manitoba Political Equality League, an organization whose ideals of suffrage and more power for women were in direct conflict with the predominant Victorian ideology. Francis Beynon was active in the fight for suffrage, and worked as the first full-time women's editor for the populist *Grain Growers' Guide*, where she raised issues of essential importance to women. Her pacifism and opposition to conscription forced her resignation

from the *Guide* in 1917, and she moved to New York. *Aleta Dey* (1919), Beynon's only novel, contains much of her 'grief and anger over the militarism that had swept through Canadian society and politics'. Although *Aleta Dey* is essentially romantic, it speaks to the intellectual and social bankruptcy of late Victorianism and its reaction against a changing position for women.

Beyond the Limit (1987)

A selection in Russian and English translation of poems which ▷ Irina Ratushínskaia wrote under unimaginably harsh conditions while a Soviet political prisoner in the mid-1980s. The poems intermingle testimony to the immediate experience, memories of the texture of normal life, and meditations on the thread of cruelty running through human history. Ratushínskaia's poetry reflects the influence of ▷ Silver Age predecessors, including ▷ Tsvetáeva's proud diction and ▷ Akhmátova's gift for sensory nuance.

Bhandari, Mannu (born 1931)

Indian novelist and short story writer. She is one of India's leading writers in Hindi, and teaches Hindi at the University of Delhi. Her novel *Mahabhoj* (1979) was a great success on the stage, and its English adaptation, ▷ *The Great Feast* (1981), was broadcast by the BBC in London. Her other novels include *Apala Banti* (1974) (*Your Banti*), *Apane se Pare* (1981) (*Apart From Oneself*) and *Svami* (1982) (*My Lord*).

Bianchini, Angela (born 1921)

Italian essayist, literary critic and novelist. Of a Jewish family, she moved to North America following the introduction of the racial laws in Italy, and read her degree in French semantics at Johns Hopkins. She moved back to Rome, where she became director of the Sarah Lawrence College, in charge of American Studies. She has contributed to many Italian newspapers, as well as to radio and television programmes. Most of her work, including ▷ *Spiriti costretti* (1963) (*Driven Souls*), lies in the field of literary criticism.

Other main works: *Romanzi d'amore e d'avventura* (1957) (*Tales of Love and Adventure*); *Lungo equinoxio* (1962) (*Long Equinox*), three short stories set in New York which follow the gradual maturation of a young woman; *Le nostre distanze* (1965) (*The Distance*); *Il romanzo di appendice* (1969) (*Serial Novels*); *Cent'anni di romanzo spagnolo* (1971) (*One Hundred Years of Spanish Novels*); *Voce donna* (1979) (*Woman's Voice*).

Bibliography (Australia)

The most accurate and valuable bibliography is Debra Adelaide's *Australian Women Writers: A Bibliographic Guide* (1988). Also invaluable are Margaret C. Murphy's *Women Writers and Australia*, issued by the University of Melbourne Library in 1988 and Joy Hooton's *Stories of Herself When Young: Autobiographies of Childhood by Australian Women* (1990).

Bichfifa Achat (1966) (*Under One Roof*)
A collection of short stories by Israeli writer
▷Amalia Kahana-Carmon. It was her first
collection, and established her as one of the
leading writers in Israel. The lyrical stories are
similar to a ▷stream of consciousness in their
style. Using associations, images and metaphors,
the stories portray delicate movements in the lives
of the characters. The protagonists, mainly
women, are caught up in a lonely existence. They
try to make a meaningful contact with the 'other',
usually a man. When the contact is made, it is a
true mystical insight. However, this is only
momentary, and the characters immediately lapse
into their previous existence.

Biehl, Charlotta Dorothea (1731–1788)
Danish prose writer, dramatist and translator.
Biehl was the most famous author in Denmark
and Norway in the 18th century. She grew up in
the heart of the aristocratic society in Copenhagen
and Denmark. Her beloved grandfather was the
palace steward of Copenhagen Castle. Her father
became the inspector of Charlottenborg Castle,
where she lived from 1755 until his death in
1777. She never married.

Her father was a choleric man, who forbade his
daughter to learn languages or read books. In
spite of this, she described in her memoirs *Mit
ubetydelige Levnetsløb* (1787) (*My Insignificant Life*)
how she learnt Danish, German, French, Italian
and Spanish, the last in order to translate the
Spanish writer Cervantes into Danish. She also
described her bitterness at being born a woman.

She became most famous as a dramatist,
producing thirteen comedies from 1764, including
the anonymous *Den kierlige Mand* (1764) (*The
Affectionate Husband*). But she also wrote four
volumes of *Moralske Fortællinger* (1781–1782)
(*Moral Tales*) and an epistolary novel, *Brevveksling
mellem fortrolige Venner* (1783) (*Correspondence
Between Intimate Friends*).

She was a ▷sentimental author, and had a
great influence as a writer on the national theatre.
Her sentimental comedies are moral satires, in
which young women of the aristocracy choose
between The Old Order (the father), The New
Non-Order (the aristocratic court) and a New
Order of Morals – a more bourgeois order, where
women were allowed to have a soul and a feeling
heart.

**'Big House, The' (19th- and 20th-century
Ireland)**
The magnificent mansions of the Irish
Ascendancy (the Anglo-Irish aristocracy) provide
the setting for many Irish novels throughout the
19th century and well into the 20th century. First
introduced into fiction by ▷Maria Edgeworth, the
'Big House' – inhabited by the aristocracy and
serviced by the peasantry – was a symbol of the
omnipresent power of the colonizers. In the novels
of ▷Molly Keane, ▷Jennifer Johnston and
others, it was to become a metaphor for the moral
and material decline of a redundant class.

Bijns, Anna (1493–1575)
Poet from the southern Netherlands. From the
13th century onwards there was a tradition of
writing by nuns. In this sphere, women could use
their literary talents, despite a lack of formal
education, in their quest for unification with God
(for example ▷Hadewych; others include Beatrijs
van Nazareth and Sister Bertken). But women
who confronted the world individually and who
also wrote secular literature were unheard of in
Dutch literature before Anna Bijns appeared.
This schoolteacher from Antwerp lived with
relatives and then her brother, who was head of a
school; in her forties she founded her own school.
Bijns wrote poetry in the style of the rhetoricians;
her motto was 'Sour rather than sweet'. The
Antwerp Minorites, with whom she was in close
contact, urged her to publish three collections of
refrains with lamentations about the decline of the
Mother Church, fierce attacks on Luther (1528,
1548), poems in praise of Jesus and Mary, and
meditations (1567). Amorous and humorous
refrains from her early period (1522–1529) have
been handed down in manuscript.

Bildungsroman
German: Genre of German novel that charts a
central character's education and development.
The *Bildungsroman* evolved in 18th-century
Germany, with novels which follow the progress
of a hero or heroine from innocence to maturity,
through a series of formative experiences. The
prototype of the genre was Goethe's *Wilhelm
Meisters Lehrjahre* (1795–1796) (*The Apprenticeship
of Wilhelm Meister*).

One of the first *Bildungsromane* written by a
woman was ▷Therese Huber's *Ellen Percy, oder
die Erziehung durch Schicksale* (1822) (*Ellen Percy,
or Education through Fate*). During the 19th
century the genre was to become a central aspect
of German women's fiction; ▷Wilhelmine von
Hillern's *Ein Arzt der Seele* (1869) (*A Physician of
the Soul*), ▷Gabriele Reuter's ▷*Aus guter Familie*
(1895) (*Of Good Family*), ▷Maria Waser's *Die
Geschichte der Anna Waser* (1913) (*The Story of
Anna Waser*), ▷Isolde Kurz's *Vanadis* (1931),
▷Josefa Berens-Totenohl's *Frau Magdlene* (1935)
(*Mrs Magdlene*), ▷Luise Rinser's *Die gläsernen
Ringe* (1940) (*The Glass Rings*), ▷Brigitte
Reimann's *Franziska Linkerhand* (1974), to
mention but a few, are all novels which trace the
development of a girl into a woman against the
background of a specific cultural period in
Germany.

However, the German woman's *Bildungsroman*
has always had a tendency to turn into a
Schicksalsroman: a 'novel of destiny', in which the
heroine, fulfilling her social role as a woman,
progresses inexorably towards self-sacrifice. Such
novels are, in fact, almost always
Entsagungsromane: 'novels of renunciation' –
▷Wilhelmine Karoline Wobeser's *Elisa, oder das
Weib wie es sein sollte* (1795) (*Elisa, or Woman as
She Should Be*), ▷Johanna Henriette
Schopenhauer's *Gabriele* (1819–1820), ▷Helene

Böhlau's ▷*Halbtier!* (1899) (*Half-animal!*) and ▷Christa Wolf's *Der geteilte Himmel* (1963) (*The Divided Heaven*, 1965) must be seen in this light. One notable early exception to this trend is ▷Caroline Auguste Fischer's *Honigmonathe* (1802–1804) (*Honey-months*).

Feminist: The term *Bildungsroman* was originally used to describe a genre of the novel developed in 18th-century Germany (see above). It has since been appropriated by feminist critics to describe the feminist genre created by European and North American women writers, particularly in the 1970s: the novel of self-development in which the heroine typically moves from being a victim of patriarchy to independence or increased awareness. Examples would be ▷Margaret Atwood's ▷*Surfacing* and ▷Alice Walker's ▷*The Color Purple*.

　▷Cardinal, Marie; *Elise or the Real Life*; *Jane Eyre*; *Mill on the Floss, The*
Bib: Felski, Rita, *Beyond Feminist Aesthetics*.

Billabong Series, The

A series of fifteen Australian books for adolescents written by ▷Mary Grant Bruce. The series begins with *A Little Bush Maid* (1910) and concludes with *Billabong Riders* (1942). It deals with an idealized and privileged life on a pastoral station in northern Victoria. Billabong is the home of the widower, David Linton, his children, Jim and Norah, and their friend, Wally. The series traces the adventures of the three as they grow up, as Jim and Wally go to fight in World War I, and with the courtship and marriage of Wally and Norah after the war and the birth of their first child.

　The Billabong Series was immensely popular with both children and adults and, as a result, its values – those of the delights of rural life and the need for hard work, responsibility and 'mateship' (even between men and women) – became a part of the Australian ethos.

　▷Children's literature (Australia)

Billetdoux, Raphaële (born 1951)

French novelist. Billetdoux has worked in television and cinema, and in 1979 directed a film, *La Femme enfant* (*The Child Woman*), which was selected for the Cannes festival in 1980. Her most well-known novel, *Mes Nuits sont plus belles que vos jours* (1985) (*Night Without Day*) which won the *Prix Renaudot*, describes a brief encounter which ends in a sadistic *Liebestod* (death for the sake of love). Billetdoux is an example of a writer whose work is more complex than traditional romantic fiction, but nevertheless retains some of its characteristics. Her other novels are: *Jeune fille en silence* (1971) (*Silent Girl*), *L'Ouverture des bras de l'homme* (1973) (*The Man's Embrace*), *Prends garde à la douceur des choses* (1976) (*Beware the Sweetness of Things*) and *Lettre d'excuse* (1981) (*Letter of Apology*).

BIM

An important journal of West Indian writing, *BIM* was first published in Barbados in 1942, and edited by Frank Collymore. *BIM* was one of the first literary magazines to be published in the Caribbean, and provided a forum for the early works of E.K. Brathwaite, who has also worked as its editor, Lamming, Selvon, Naipaul, Walcott and others. It has played a major role in the development of West Indian literature.

Binary opposition/binarism/binary

An opposition comprising two terms which are ordered hierarchically, so that the second half of the opposition is subordinate to, and appears to be derived from, the first. For example, Man/Woman. ▷Deconstruction has drawn attention to the prevalence of binary oppositions in Western patriarchal thought.

Binchy, Maeve (born 1940)

Irish novelist and journalist, born in Dublin. She taught for several years before becoming a journalist with *The Irish Times* in 1968. 'The Saturday Column', which she continues to write for that paper, provided the basis for *My First Book* (1976) and *Maeve's Diary* (1980). In the 1970s she began to write fiction, beginning with short stories (*Central Line*, 1977, *Victoria Line*, 1980, *Dublin 4*, 1982) and several award-winning stage plays and television scripts. The huge popular success she has achieved with bestselling novels such as *Light a Penny Candle* (1982), *Echoes* (1985), *Circle of Friends* (1991) and others has meant that no serious attention has been paid to the shrewd social analysis which forms the basis of her writing, and especially her charting of the changes in Irish women's lives over the past two decades.

Bing Xin (born 1900)

Chinese writer. A native of Fujian, Bing Xin graduated from Wellesley College in the US in 1926. Influenced by the May Fourth Movement (1919), she began writing poetry and prose in the early 1920s. She was concerned with the problems of Chinese society in transition: the so-called 'modern marriage', the liberation of women and the inner world of the young generation.

　On her return to China, Bing Xin taught at Yenching University in Beijing while continuing to write. She is the author of many stories, essays and novellas which reflect her pacifist philosophy of universal love and her concern for human values. Among her works, the prose collection *For Young Readers* won national acclaim. *About Women*, a satire in the voice of a male narrator, was published under the pen-name 'A Gentleman'. Bing Xin spent the post-war years studying in Japan, and returned to China in 1951. *After the Return* and *We Have Woken up the Spring* are representative works of this period. After the 'cultural revolution' (1966–1976), Bing Xin published *For Young Readers: Third Batch of Letters*, a sequel to the earlier popular success. Bing Xin is widely translated and admired for her sensitive touch and sympathetic understanding, especially of the young. She has also translated the poetry of

the Nobel Prize-winning Indian poet and writer, Rabindranath Tagore (1861–1941), into Chinese.
▷ Lu Yin

Binnuna, Khanatta (born 1940)

Moroccan teacher, novelist and short story writer. One of the foremost Maghreb Arabs active in politics, in women's education and in the movement for women's right to work and to participate in the social and political life of Morocco. Her political involvement is closely tied up with her feminist beliefs: 'Chains tie both the oppressor and the oppressed; a diseased society produces only maimed individuals . . . if you break the shackles tying your hands and my feet, our relations would be healthy, so would the future.'

Her stories posed a challenge to male critics, which led ▷ Fatima Mernissi to accuse them of 'understanding nothing of women . . . not listen[ing] to her words'. In common with a number of Arab writers, the term 'silence' figures prominently in titles of her work. Her first collection of short stories was *Down With Silence* (1967), and twenty years later she published *Articulate Silence* (1987). Her novel *Fire and Choice* (1971) stresses the importance of work – and not just education – for Moroccan women. Her later works carry vociferous protest in their titles: *The Storm* (1979) and *Anger and Tomorrow* (1981). The title story of *Articulate Silence* is fairly representative of Binnuna's preoccupation with the consciousness of her protagonists, which extends beyond the personal and particular to the predicament of the whole Arab nation, with the wound of Palestine still throbbing with pain.
▷ *Naksa*

Bins, Patrícia (born 1930)

Brazilian novelist, short story writer and translator. She has been a teacher and plastic artist in the south of Brazil, and has worked for newspapers. Her best-known novel, *Jogo de fiar* (1983) (*The Weaving Game*), is on a woman's recollections, written with a feminine perception. *Antes que o amor acabe* (1984) (*Before Love Ends*) is a novel about a bourgeois woman living through an intense psychological crisis after she and her husband retire to the seaside.

Birch-Pfeiffer, Charlotte (1800–1868)

German dramatist. She was a successful actress who travelled the length and breadth of German-speaking Europe, and, from 1837–1843, held the position of director of a theatre in Zurich. She wrote over 100 plays in a variety of modes, ranging from classicism to realism. Her themes include historical and family drama, as well as astute explorations of the social questions raised by the ideas of the French Revolution (1789). Her plays were popular, but came under fierce attack from the critics, who claimed that she derived much of her material from the novels and short stories of other writers. Birch-Pfeiffer also wrote poetry and novellas, and maintained a lively correspondence with people from a wide variety of social backgrounds. Still largely unexplored, her works are collected in the 1863–1880 editions of her *Gesammelte Dramatische Werke* (23 vols) (*Collected Dramatic Works*) and *Gesammelte Novellen und Erzählungen* (3 vols) (*Collected Novellas and Short Stories*).

Bird At My Window (1966)

This novel by Caribbean writer ▷ Rosa Guy recounts the story of Wade Williams and his family, documenting the hardships they experience when forced to migrate from the southern USA because Wade's father refuses the advances of a white woman, and because the struggle for survival in Harlem. Guy provides a detailed examination of a destructive mother–son relationship as Wade Williams realizes, too late, that his devotion to his mother and her manipulation of his love has enslaved him to her and prevented him from achieving his dreams. His personality disorder and his eventual act of murder result from this maternal tie. Considered a 'magnificent achievement', this novel tackles some of the problems later writers would attempt to examine. Dedicated to Malcolm X, this is a complex novel in which Guy demonstrates her ability to treat the crippling effects of racism in the USA and its impact on the lives of African-Americans and West Indian immigrants.

See Jerrie Norris, *Presenting Rosa Guy* (1988) for a critical analysis.

Birdsell, Sandra (born 1942)

Novelist, short story writer, script writer and dramatist, born in Canada's rural Manitoba. She left school early, and, after marriage, children and divorce, now lives in Winnipeg. Her first two linked short story collections, *Night Travellers* (1982) and *Ladies of the House* (1984), are powerful evocations of small-town rivalry and hierarchy. Her novel, *The Missing Child* (1989), has a wider sweep, but continues to focus on the claustrophobia of an insular community. Her work is full of sexual energy but stylistically unembellished, deceptive in its simplicity and balance.

Birds Without a Nest; A Story of Indian Life and Priestly Oppression in Peru (1968)

Translation of a novel by the Peruvian romantic writer ▷ Clorinda Matto de Turner, *Aves sin nido*. Originally published in 1889, and Peru's first indigenous work, it relates the Indians' contemporary life. Because she wrote the book as a brave defence of the Indian, Matto de Turner is considered by some critics to be the Latin American ▷ Harriet Beecher Stowe.

Birgitta av Vadstena (St Bridget of Sweden) (1303–1373)

Swedish religious prose writer. Birgitta belonged to one of the most distinguished families in Sweden. Her mother was a member of the royal family, and as a knight and member of the king's council, her father was one of the leading men in Sweden. The family was also very pious; to Birgitta, the ideal woman was the learned nun. But Birgitta's father would not allow her to become a Bride of Christ. At the age of twelve she was married to Ulf Gudmarsson, a brave knight. Birgitta had borne eight children by the time of his death in 1344.

Now God began to talk to Birgitta. She wrote down her revelations and founded a new convent, the Bridgettine Order, at Vadstena Castle. In 1350 she went to Rome, where she lived for the rest of her life. She was declared a saint in 1391. Her work was printed in 1492 as the *Revelationes Celeste* (*Heavenly Revelations*): 1,400 folio sheets in Latin. It was later translated into Swedish (four volumes) and many other European languages.

In 1919 the Swedish writer Emilia Fogelklou (1878–1972) wrote the biography *Birgitta*.

What distinguishes the *Revelationes Celeste* is its realism, together with an imaginary symbolism, and its roots in this world's problems, joys and politics.

Birthday Deathday and Other Stories (1985)

A collection of short stories by Indian writer ▷Padma Perera. The stories, all set in the present, share an awareness and appreciation of the encircling, almost abstract nature of the Indian past. The title story tells of twin sisters, one who has accepted an orthodox marriage and life in India, and the other, the narrator, who has broken away from it to live and marry in the USA. The latter comes home to India every now and then to revive her love of India's cultural diversity and chaos, but it is only when she and her sister are faced with sudden death that she sees how far she has travelled from her roots. Having survived, her sister calmly begins living the next moment, shocking the narrator into a realization of her own dependence on linear time and chronology.

Bisexuality

Traditionally invoking a ▷binary couple, the 'bi' of bisexuality reproduces an oppositional structure of sexual difference. ▷Hélène Cixous, however, complicates bisexuality with her dual definition: on the one hand bisexuality 'melts together and effaces' sexual difference. On the other hand, Cixous proposes an 'other bisexuality', defined as 'the location within oneself of the presence of both sexes, evident and insistent in different ways according to the individual'. It is a version of bisexuality which does not ignore the trace of the ▷other in the selfsame. ▷Julia Kristeva also seeks to go beyond the binary logic of bisexuality in her reconceptualization of subjectivity as that which includes a multiplicity of possible identifications and is constantly in process.

Bishop, Elizabeth (1911–1979)

US poet and short story writer. Born in Worcester, Massachusetts, Bishop was raised by grandparents in Nova Scotia and New England. In 1934 she graduated from Vassar College.

While still at college she co-founded a literary magazine, *The Conspirito*, with friends, including ▷Mary McCarthy. She also began to publish her poetry and short stories in magazines and periodicals, including *The Partisan Review*. She was encouraged by ▷Marianne Moore to pursue her writing. Other friends and influences include Robert Lowell (1917–1977) and Pablo Neruda (1904–1973). Bishop travelled extensively, and settled in Brazil, living there off and on, from 1951 until the 1970s. Between 1966 and her retirement in 1977, she taught at the University of Washington, Seattle, New York University and at Harvard University.

Influenced by Surrealism, Bishop's poetry aims at the transcription of an inner reality, frequently through an extended, associative meditation on an external object or event. The interrelationship of subjective processes and the outside world are the terrain of her verse. Her Pulitzer Prize-winning *North & South: A Cold Spring* (1946) contains some of her best-known poems. 'The Man-Moth', stemming from a newspaper misprint of 'mammoth', juxtaposes a figure of night and imagination with 'man' who reduces the world to his uses. The poem explores the self's fragility and alienation in the modern world. 'Jeronimo's House' traces the self's efforts to establish order out of poverty. 'At the Fishhouses' is typical of Bishop's work in its presentation of the active, meditative and observant mind.

Other works include: *Questions of Travel* (1965), *Brazil* (1967), *Selected Poems* (1967), *The Ballad of the Burglar of Babylon* (1968), *The Complete Poems* (1969), *Geography III* (1946), *The Collected Poems of Elizabeth Bishop* (1984).
Bib: Stevenson, Anne, *Elizabeth Bishop*; Schwartz, Lloyd and Estess, Sibyl P., (eds), *Elizabeth Bishop and her Art*.

Bishop, Isabella Bird (1831–1904)

British ▷travel writer. She was born in Boroughbridge, one of two daughters of Edward Bird, curate, and Dora Lawson, Sunday-school teacher. She began travelling abroad in 1854 with a visit to the United States. *The Englishwoman in America* (1856) was an immediate success, launching her career as a writer. *Aspects of Religion in America* (1859) was written during her second trip to North America; this was followed by *The Hawaiian Archipelago: Six Months Among the Palm Groves, Coral Reefs and Volcanoes of the Sandwich Islands* (1874). In 1878 she left for Japan, returning in 1879 after travelling through Hong Kong, Saigon, Singapore and Malaysia. *Unbeaten Tracks in Japan* (1880) and *The Golden Cheronese* (1883) record these journeys. In 1889 she set out for the Middle East, continuing through India, Tibet, Central Asia and Persia. During this trip she organized the building of two hospitals in India, in memory of her father and sister. *Journeys in Persia and Kurdistan* was published in 1894, the year in which Bishop left Britain on a missionary trip to China. She sailed up the Yangtze River, rode 300 miles alone on a mule, and built three

hospitals and an orphanage. Returning to London in 1897, she prepared *Korea and Her Neighbours* (1898), *The Yangtze Valley and Beyond* (1899) and *Chinese Pictures* (1900). Her final missionary trip was to Morocco in 1900–1901. She was now severely weakened by the ill-health that had plagued her for many years, and she died of a tumour in 1904. She appears as a character in ▷Caryl Churchill's play, ▷*Top Girls*.
Bib: Stoddart, A., *The Life of Isabella Bird (Mrs Bishop)*.

Bittari, Zoubida (born 1937)
Algerian novelist, born in Algiers. Her real name is Louise Ali-Rachedi. She started school at the age of nine. After she was forced into marriage at the age of twelve, a French couple took her into their custody. She has been living in France since 1961, where she earns her living as a maid. *Ô mes soeurs musulmanes, Pleurez!* (1964) (*Cry, My Moslem Sisters!*) retraces her own dramatic experiences.

Bizarre Story of a Husband and Wife during Wartime (1990)
Japanese novelist ▷Kono Taeko prepared for a long time before writing this. On the first night after the wedding ceremony, a wife notices a masochistic tendency in her husband. He says that his ultimate hope is to be killed by her during the final stage of sexual intercourse. The wife gets to realize his hope. Facing death, they are living from day to day during the Pacific War (1941–1945). Kono describes a rare couple who intend to hold onto their individual life – even in wartime Japan – by pursuing their unusual sexual love.

Black Consciousness
A political philosophy whose origins lie both in African ▷*négritude* and in the North American Civil Rights Movement of the 1960s, as well as the anti-colonial and Pan-Africanist movements of the 1920s and 1930s. It has motivated much of the South African political activism from the 1970s, and has given rise to a specific body of writing distinct from the protest tradition of the 1950s and 1960s, in that it turns instead to black readers for an audience, to a black community for self-definition, and to African culture for its values. In its populist mode, Black Consciousness is an oppositional or reactive movement, involving a confrontation between oppressive whites and oppressed blacks. In this regard, it deploys a characteristic strategy of reversal: 'black' becomes the positive term, and 'white' the negative. While this strategy may persist in contemporary thinking, by the mid-1980s Black Consciousness had started giving way to class analysis instead.

Black Consciousness began to emerge as a coherent ideological, political and cultural perspective in the 1970s. Its tenets were laid out in the magazine *Black Review*, edited by Steve Biko and others, whose various essays continually position 'the black man' as the political subject, occasionally including 'his black sister' as a figure whose solidarity must be courted but who, in effect, does not speak. The manifesto of the Black Women's Federation, formed in 1975, states that black women bear responsibility for the survival and maintenance of their families and, largely, for the transmission of the black cultural heritage to the youth.

Moreover, Black Consciousness issues a plea to women, made explicit in Noel Chabani Manganyi's *Being-Black-in-the-World* (1973), not to participate in any process of dehumanization, discouragement and demasculinization, but to help men feel manly again. It is in this context that the writing of women such as ▷Ellen Kuzwayo. ▷Lauretta Ngcobo and ▷Miriam Tlali should be read, both for their elevation of the figure of the mother in black community life, and for the hesitancy with which they begin to offer a critique of black South African ▷patriarchy. Emma Mashini's *Strikes Have Followed Me All My Life* (1989), an important addition to ▷autobiography in South Africa, explicitly builds into her text the personal and political growth occasioned by Black Consciousness, but also redirects its racial focus into analysis of class and gender relations.

Black feminist criticism
Not single, but comprising many strands, black feminist criticism has been most influential in the USA, where critics have focused on African-American women's writing. Barbara Smith's essay 'Toward a Black Feminist Criticism' (1977) broke the silence surrounding the specific concerns of black feminists that it detects in existing ▷female traditions. Other black feminists, such as ▷Alice Walker, went on to write scholarly histories of black women's creativity in conjunction with publishing anthologies of their fiction and poetry, absent from the white mainstream feminist canon. An early example is ▷Toni Cade Bambara's anthology *The Black Woman* (1970).

During the 1980s critics further explored the historical and cultural specificity of black women's writing and critical theory. Developing the concerns of Barbara Smith's essay, Deborah McDowell's paper 'New Directions for Black Feminist Criticism' (1980) distinguishes between writing on black women and a black feminist theoretical approach. In Britain and North America, black feminists often use the term 'women of colour' or 'color'. In Britain this includes South Asian women and other recent migrant groups. The term in the USA includes women of Chinese, Japanese and Chicano origin among a wide range of migrant peoples, but also refers to the indigenous Native American peoples of North America. Recent examples of work by British black feminists include ▷Hazel Carby, *Reconstructing Womanhood: The Emergence of the Afro-American Woman Novelist* (1987); Shabnam Grewal et al. (eds), *Charting the Journey: Writings by Black and Third World Women* (1988).
Bib: McDowell, D., 'New Directions for Black Feminist Criticism'; Smith, B., 'Toward a Black Feminist Criticism'.

Black Night of Quiloa (1971)
Novel by Kenyan writer ▷Hazel Mugot. Mugot
depicts an inter-racial marriage which fails when
Cy takes Hima home to Britain. Mugot is clearly
suggesting that breaking social conventions and
giving way to romantic passions can lead
ultimately to tragedy.

Blais, Marie-Claire (born 1939)
Enigmatic novelist and dramatist, born in Quebec
City, Canada. She left school at fifteen, but
published her first novel (*La Belle bête*, 1959,
translated as *Mad Shadows*, 1960), a compulsive,
intense work of fantasy, to considerable acclaim
at the age of twenty. She claims that reading the
▷Brontë sisters started her as a writer. *Tête
Blanche* (1960), which appeared in English as
White Head in 1961, began for Blais a brillant
and prolific career chronicling a world full of
doubts and shadows, of madness and shifting
realities. *Le Jour est Noir* followed in 1962;
it was translated, along with *Les Voyageurs Sacrés*,
a collection of short stories, as *The Day is Dark
and Three Travelers* (1967). Then came *Une
Saison Dans La Vie d'Emmanuel* (1965, translated
as *A Season in the Life of Emmanuel*, 1966), a
child's-eye vision of the brutality of life in rural
Quebec, and considered one of her most
important works. Her trilogy, *Les manuscrits de
Pauline Archange* (1968), *Vivre! Vivre!* (1969) (the
two translated and published together as *The
Manuscripts of Pauline Archange*, 1970), and *Les
Apparences* (1970, translated as *Dürer's Angel*,
1976) is important for its depiction of a young
heroine's fierce struggle against distortion and
death. It consolidated the acclaim that Blais had
already garnered as one of the new voices
speaking from Quebec.

Blais explores the complexities of homosexuality
in *Le Loup* (1972, translated as *The Wolf*, 1974),
and lesbianism in *Les Nuits d'underground* (1978,
translated as *Nights in the Underground*, 1979). Her
novels are generally about characters thwarted by
a strictured and destructive society, as in
L'insoumise (1966, translated as *The Fugitive*,
1978), *David Sterne* (1967, translated with the
same title), and *Une Liaison Parisienne* (1975,
translated as *A Literary Affair*, 1979). Blais is
unafraid, too, of tackling the political aspects of
Quebec intellectualism, as in *Un Joualonais sa
Joualonie* (1973, translated as *St Lawrence Blues*,
1974); *Le Sourd dans La Ville* (1979, translated as
Deaf to the City, 1981); *Visions d'Anna* (1982,
translated as *Anna's World*, 1985), and *Pierre, ou la
Guerre du Printemps 81* (1984) (*Pierre, or the Spring
War*, 1991), all of which confront the struggle to
live in a brutal and indifferent world. Her writing
is characterized by a gritty texture and syntax that
is unapologetic in its obsessiveness, yet her style
can shift from stripped harshness to lyrical
intensity. Within the luminosity of her Surreal
worlds is portrayed a collision of monstrous evil
and sheer innocence, devouring both adults and
children. She is particularly powerful in her
depiction of children's powerlessness in relation to

a relentless adult world. Blais has published two
collections of poetry: *Pays Voilés*, (1963), *Existences*
(1967, translated as *Veiled Countries/Lives*, 1984).
She has also written a number of plays: *L'execution*
(1968, translated as *The Execution*, 1976), *Fièvre et
autres textes dramatiques* (1974) (*Fever and Other
Dramatic Works*), *L'Ocean, suivi de Murmures*
(1977, translated as *The Ocean* in the same year),
Sommeil d'hiver (1984) (*Sleep of Winter*) and *La Nef
des Sorcières* (1976, *Ship of Sorceresses*, with
▷Nicole Brossard and ▷France Théoret).
Translated into more than thirteen languages,
Blais has won the Prix Médicis of France, the Prix
France-Québec, two Governor General's Awards,
and in 1980 was made a Member of the Order of
Canada.
Bib: Green, M.J., in *Traditionalism, Nationalism
and Feminism: Women Writers of Quebec*; Howells,
C., *Private and Fictional Words*.

Blaman, Anna (1905–1960)
Dutch prosewriter. ▷Pseudonym of Johanna
Petronella Vrugt. Initially she was a French
teacher, but later devoted herself exclusively to
her literary work. The influence of French
Existentialism is undeniable, though she retains
her originality: she recognizes man's tragic
position, but wishes him to have the courage to
maintain his dignity. *Vrouw en vriend* (1941)
(*Woman and Friend*), a psychological analysis of
eroticism as man's most powerful urge, was a
pioneering novel. In her novels *Eenzaam avontuur*
(1948) (*Lonely Adventure*), *Op leven en dood* (1954);
(*A Matter of Life and Death*, 1974) and *De verliezers*
(1960) (*The Losers*), as well as in some of her short
stories, especially in the collection *Overdag en
andere verhalen* (1957) (*A Day and Other Stories*),
she describes the confusion of emotions, the
unavoidable human loneliness, and the primeval
fear of nothingness. *Eenzaam avontuur* was one of
the most famous and controversial books from the
post-war period. Critics found the explicit defence
of lesbian love, and the dominating power of
eroticism that urges the characters on, hard to
stomach. In 1957 Blaman received the P.C. Hooft
Prize for her complete *oeuvre*.

Blamire, Susanna (1747–1734)
English poet from Cumberland, near Carlisle,
from yeoman stock. Her aunt was her guardian.
Educated at the village school, she wrote poems
from an early age, and played the guitar, later
composing the songs in the Scots and
Cumberland dialects for which she is famous. Her
married sister moved to the Highlands; Susanna
visited her there, as well as well as in London and
Ireland. Her songs began to be printed in the
1780s, and her collected works began to be
assembled in 1836. Her poetry uses the natural
world to register mood, as in 'Written on a
Gloomy Day in Sickness', in which she writes 'No
emblem for myself I find, / Save what some dying
plant bestows.'
Bib: Lonsdale, Henry, *Worthies of Cumberland*.

Blanchecotte, Auguste Malvina (1830–1895)

French poet. A seamstress who was passionately enthusiastic about poetry. Her first collection of verse, *Rêves et Réalités* (*Dreams and Realities*), appeared in 1855. It was signed 'Mme B . . ., worker and poet', and was crowned by the ▷Académie Française. Her other works include: *Tablettes d'une femme pendant la Commune* (1872) (*Jottings by a Woman in the Commune*) and *Les Militantes* (1875) (*Militant Women*). Of greatest interest is her *Impressions d'une femme, pensées, sentiments et portraits* (1868) (*Impressions of a Woman: Ideas, Feelings and Portraits*). In this text she indicates that she herself began to write so that she might no longer seem worthless in the eyes of the world. She also advocates the demolition of the alienating, unnatural images of femininity prevalent in the society in which she lived – images that placed woman upon a pedestal or consigned her to the gutter. Blanchecotte was one of a number of 19th-century French working-class women who, like ▷Marceline Desbordes-Valmore, managed to write despite the twin handicaps of social 'inferiority' and poverty. French women writers of previous centuries had, on the whole, emerged from the aristocracy, so something of a social and literary revolution was clearly occurring in 19th-century France.

Bland, Fabian ▷Nesbit, Edith

Blandiana, Ana (born 1942)

Romanian poet. Blandiana was born in Timisoara. In 1967 she graduated in philology from Cluj University. After working as an editor on the literary journals *Viata Romanaesca* and *Amfitreatru*, she became a librarian at the Institute of Fine Arts in Bucharest.

Her first volume of verse appeared in 1964, and since then she has published, in Romanian, *Cincizeci De Poeme* (1970) (*Fifty Poems*), *Octombrie, Noiembre, Decembrie* (1972) (*October, November, December*), *Somnul Din Somn* (1977) (*Sleep Within Sleep*) and *Ora De Nisip* (1983) (*The Hour of Sand*, 1990). She has also written several children's books. In English, she has published *The Hour of Sand* (1990) and contributed poems to *Silent Voices: An Anthology of Contemporary Romanian Women Poets* (1986) and to *An Anthology of Contemporary Romanian Poetry* (1984), both edited by Andrea Deletant and Brenda Walker. She is now a freelance writer.

Blaugdone, Barbara (c 1609–1705)

English memoirist and Quaker minister, who published *Account of the Travels, Sufferings, and Persecutions of Barbara Blaugdone* (1691), which tells of her travelling and imprisonments for preaching in England and Ireland. Her conversion seems to have alienated her from most of her old acquaintances – she writes, 'People were so offended with it when I went into their Publick Places and Steeple-houses to speak, that they took away their children from me.' She later preached in the West Country, sleeping in sheds, and

vividly describes a shipwreck in which she nearly died on one of her crossings to Ireland.

▷Carey, Mary; Evans, Katherine; Fell, Margaret; Quaker women (England).

Blaze de Bury, Rose (died 1894)

French journalist, travel writer and novelist. Little is known about the youth of Blaze of Bury, who was believed to be the illegitimate daughter of an English lord. After her marriage she travelled widely in German-speaking countries, published a *Voyage en Autriche, en Hongrie et en Allemagne pendant les événements de 1848 et de 1849* (1851) (*A Journey through Austria, Hungary and Germany during the Events of 1848 and 1849*), and became involved in the financial and political negotiations that took place between England and Austria in the 1860s. A bilingual author, she wrote articles, novels and short stories in French, but also wrote on French life and letters for English journals, including the *Daily News*. Her *Voyage en Autriche* (*A Journey Through Austria*) is by far her best-known work.

Bleecker, Ann Eliza Schuyler (1752–1783)

North American poet and novelist. Born to aristocratic New Yorkers, Margareta Van Wyck and Brandt Schuyler, she was encouraged in her literary abilities from a young age. When, at age seventeen, she married John J. Bleecker, Esq, her life was dramatically changed by their move to the small rural community of Tomhanick. Her loneliness was soon coupled with the dangers of the American Revolution; at one point she was forced to flee her home with her two daughters, and the younger, Abella, died on the journey. She never fully recovered from the loss, but she found her artistic endeavours in poetry and novel-writing to be a means of expressing her grief. Even after the war, she suffered from chronic depression, and during this period destroyed some of her writings. She died on 23 November 1783, at the age of thirty-one. Her eldest daughter, ▷Margaretta Bleecker Faugeres, paid tribute to her mother by following in her footsteps as a poet and by collecting and publishing her mother's works in ▷*The Posthumous Works of Ann Eliza Bleecker* (1793). Additionally, her novel, ▷*The History of Maria Kittle*, which is indebted to the literary tradition of the early North American ▷captivity narrative, was published posthumously in 1791.

Blé en herbe, Le (1923) ▷Ripening Seed, The (1955)

Blind, Mathilde (1841–1896)

British poet, biographer, translator and editor, who also wrote under the ▷pseudonym Claude Lake. Born in Mannheim, Germany, she adopted the name of her stepfather, Karl Blind (a revolutionary who led the Baden revolt 1848–49). Educated by her mother and at schools in Belgium and England, she was politically committed from an early age. Her writings are eclectic: her first volume of *Poems* appeared in 1867, followed by *Shelley: A Lecture* in 1870. She edited a well-respected *Selection from the Poems of P.B. Shelley* (1872), translated Strauss's *The Old Faith and the New* (1873) and wrote a long poem based on a Scottish legend, *The Prophecy of St Oran* (1881). A biography of ▷George Eliot followed in 1883, then came a ▷romance, *Tarantella* (1884). *Heather on Fire* (1886) was a political protest against the clearances of the Scottish Highlands. Other works include the epic poem *The Ascent of Man* (1889), a translation of Marie Bashkirtseff's *Journal* (1890) and four further volumes of poetry. Always committed to raising the status of women and improving their educational opportunities, Blind left her estate to Newnham, the Cambridge women's college.

▷Education (19th-century Britain); Feminism (19th-century Britain)
Bib: Robertson, E.S., *English Poetesses*; Symons, A. (ed.), *The Poetical Works of Mathilde Blind.*

Blinky Bill Series, The

Australian books for children, written and illustrated by Dorothy Wall. They concern a mischievous, curious and engaging young koala bear, Blinky Bill, and have become perennial favourites with Australian children, rivalling ▷May Gibbs's ▷*Snugglepot and Cuddlepie series.*
▷Children's literature (Australia)

Blixen, Karen (1885–1962)

Karen Blixen

Danish prose writer who often wrote in English. Pseudonyms: Isak Dinesen and Pierre Andrezel

Blixen had a good bourgeois upbringing; she studied English at Oxford and painting in Paris and Rome, and was a talented painter.

She married her cousin, Baron Bror von Blixen-Finecke, who did not return her affection. They went to Kenya to grow coffee, and there the childless marriage was dissolved. Blixen was a farmer herself until 1931. She fell in love with Denys Finch Hatton who died in an aeroplane accident, and, after going bankrupt, she returned to Denmark and wrote *Seven Gothic Tales* (1934) under the pseudonym Isak Dinesen, an immediate success, which she herself translated into Danish. Other successes were *Out of Africa* (1937), *Winter's Tales* (1942) and *Angelic Avengers* (1944), written under the pseudonym Pierre Andrezel, and published in an English translation by her secretary Clara Selborn. She wrote in a symbolic style, old-fashioned for the 1890s, and yet modern.

In Denmark, Blixen lived at Rungstedlund in aristocratic style and with a circle of young admirers. She has had a great impact on modern Danish authors such as ▷Suzanne Brøgger.

Blixen's prose is Existentialist, as well as fantastic and artificial, the language being symbolic and simple. She believed in a synthesis between nature and culture, between humanity and its destiny. But she encountered difficulties in finding and creating her own place as a woman writer in Danish society.

As a storyteller she created myths – and she made herself into a myth, too.
Bib: Thurmann J., *Isak Dinesen: The Life of a Storyteller.*

Blondal, Patricia (1926–1959)

Novelist, born in Souris in the Canadian province of Manitoba. The daughter of a railroad engineer, she writes about the Canadian small town during the 1950s. After her family moved to Winnipeg, she studied at the University of Manitoba (1944–1947), where she wrote poetry, which she later abandoned for fiction. She married, had two children, travelled in Europe, and wrote obsessively. In 1959, *Chatelaine* serialized 'Strangers in Love', which would later be published posthumously as her second novel, *From Heaven With a Shout* (1963). Her first novel, *A Candle To Light the Sun* (1960) appeared after Blondal had died of cancer. Concerned with the tension between small-town and city life, the novel's candour aroused considerable controversy. Despite, or perhaps because of, the irony of her early death, Blondal is hailed as a writer of 'unfulfilled promise'.

Blooded Earth (1962)

Novel by Greek writer ▷Dido Soteriou. This is a fictional story of the destruction of Smyrna (Izmir), based on the reminiscences of real people who lived there, fought to survive and finally escaped to Greece, defeated by the Turks. The book is written objectively, revealing the cruelty of each side against the other. The book has been translated into Romanian, Russian and French.

Blood of Others, The (1948)
Translation of *Le Sang des autres* (1948), novel by French writer ▷Simone de Beauvoir. *The Blood of Others* is widely known as de Beauvoir's 'Resistance' novel. Written – and set – during the German occupation of Paris in World War II, it concerns the lives of a group of Resistance fighters, and in it de Beauvoir discusses the issue of the limits of personal freedom. As in ▷*She Came to Stay*, people have to resolve questions of individual responsibility in terms of the impact of their actions on others, but in this book the author accepts that people are both social beings and individuals. The hero, Jean Blomart, comes to recognize that other people have freedom as well as he; even if the consequences may be tragic (as they are in this case), the freedom to choose how to act nevertheless remains.

Bloom, Valerie (born 1956)
This Caribbean poet and performer, born in ▷Jamaica, was influenced by her family's tradition of storytelling and the work of ▷Louise Bennett. She worked briefly as a librarian before training as a teacher at Mico College, and teaching English, speech, drama and home economics from 1976 to 1979. Having already published some early poetry, she went to Britain in 1979 to study for a BA in English and African and Caribbean Studies at the University of Kent. She became a Multicultural Arts Officer involved in the teaching of dance, drama, poetry and song.

Her first collection of poems, *Touch Me, Tell Mi* (1982), reflects the range of her use of language which she calls 'dialect' or *patois* rather than ▷nation language. Her poetry draws on an oral folk tradition, and is satirical in tone. She has discussed her childhood in Lauretta Ngcobo (ed.), *Let It Be Told: Black Women Writers in Britain* (1988).

Bloomsbury
Never a self-defined group, 'Bloomsbury Group' is the label given retrospectively to a number of writers, intellectuals and artists who met together regularly from about 1905. Initially based at the Gordon Square residence of the two Stephen sisters ▷Virginia (Woolf) and Vanessa (Bell), these Thursday evening meetings were initiated by Thoby Stephen to introduce his sisters to his Cambridge friends. Early visitors included art critic Clive Bell (1881–1964), biographer Lytton Strachey (1880-1932) and publisher Leonard Woolf. Following the marriage of Vanessa and Clive Bell, Virginia Stephen moved to Brunswick Square, where she was in close contact with the economist Maynard Keynes (1883–1946) and Leonard Woolf. The consolidation of the group's belief in unifying epistemological and aesthetic concerns, initially influenced by the philosopher G.E. Moore (1873–1958), occurred after 1910, the year that Clive Bell met painter Roger Fry

(1866–1934) and the first exhibition of post-impressionist art was held. The influence of the group's ideas extended beyond literature and the visual arts into economics and political theory.

Blossoms in Darkness (1979)
Translation of the Hindi novel *Surajmukhi Andhere Ke* (1972) by Indian writer ▷Krishna Sobti. The novel, the Hindi title of which literally means 'the sunflowers of the darkness', tells of the painful climb of a woman to sexual fulfilment. Raped in childhood, and taunted at school for her 'badness', she is locked out of a conventional marriage. Ironically, therefore, she has a degree of sexual freedom unthinkable for most unmarried Indian women, but she can only drift from man to man, each rejecting her because of her frigidity.

Blue Flame (1987)
English translation of the letters of Lebanese poet Khalil Gibran (1883–1931) to ▷May Ziyadah, first collected and published in Arabic by Salma al-Haffar al-Kuzbery and Suhail Badi' Bushruy (1977). The two editors are responsible for the English translation, and also for the French translation published in Paris, *La Voix Ailée* (1984) (*The Winged Voice*).

The correspondence continued intermittently from 1914 to 1931, the year of Gibran's death. The letters are love-letters written by the only Arab ▷*mahjar* (*émigré*) poet and artist to make a name for himself in English as well as Arabic. They are dated from New York and Boston and often included drawings by Gibran, or postcards of drawings and sculptures in famous museums of the world, to communicate to May how he felt about them. He also sent her reviews of his books and invitations to his exhibitions. This strange love relationship between two poets, conducted by correspondence across thousands of miles, obviously had its ups and downs. They never met, and there are occasionally gaps of months and sometimes a year or two between letters. He addressed her as 'Marie', her original Christian name, and sometimes as 'Mariam', the name of the Blessed Mary in Arabic.

May Ziyadah had kept the letters in their envelopes, which the editors used to determine the dates. The Arabic edition provides a facsimile of all the letters in Gibran's beautiful, close Arabic handwriting. His last letter to her was a cablegram for Christmas 1930, and his last communication in March 1931 a beautiful drawing of a hand (he was a disciple of Rodin), carrying the 'Blue Flame that gives light and does not change', which he had set as a symbol of their love as early as 1919.

We learn a great deal about Gibran from these letters: his Christian transcendentalism, his experience of 'the woods, the sand and the sea', and his work. He wrote in his famous letter of 1919, the 'Blue Flame', 'As for the *Prophet*, it is a book I have thought of for a thousand years, but I did not write a single chapter of it before last year. What can I say about this Prophet? He is my second birth and first baptism. He is the only idea that entitles me to stand before the sun. He composed me before I thought of composing him and made me follow him over seven thousand miles, before he stopped to dictate to me his wishes.'

It was May Ziyadah who started the correspondence in 1912 with a review of his *Broken Wings*, and a letter challenging his conception of the heroine of that book. Some of Gibran's letters reciprocate with discussions of her work, in most cases expressing great admiration.

As far as we know, May's letters to Gibran have not been found, apart from one or two published among letters to other correspondents in 1951, probably from copies. We can sometimes guess the content of the letters from Gibran's replies, and he occasionally repeats her actual words, especially when he seems to be holding her down to a confession of love. One of May's letters, published in 1951, was a rare thing in Arabic, a love-letter in prose written by a woman. Gibran's reply (26 February 1924) to her passionate letter is a wonderful piece of evasion; after three pages on other matters, and a comic drawing of his beard he writes: 'You say you are afraid of love. Why are you afraid of it my little one? Are you afraid of the light of the sun? Are you afraid of the sea? of the dawn? of the coming of spring? Why, I wonder, are you afraid of love? . . . Listen Marie, I am today a prisoner of desires . . . born in me. I am tied to the shackles of an old thought, as old as the seasons. Can you stand by me in my prison till we come out to day light? Can you stand by me untill those shades are broken and we walk freely to the peak of our mountain?'

May stopped writing for some months. In a short note written in November of the same year, Gibran asks for her news, stating at the start that only *she* knows the reason for her silence; he does not, and it is not fair that his days and nights should be disturbed for something of which he is ignorant.

Bluest Eye, The (1970)

US novel by ▷Toni Morrison. Set in Ohio just before World War II it explores the destructive effects of racism on the lives of the African-American characters. In particular, the internalization of white norms of physical appearance and social success dominate the story. Narrated from a child's perspective, everything from the child star, Shirley Temple, and the 'blue-eyed, yellow-haired, pink-skinned doll' that arrives at Christmas, to the Mary Jane candy wrapped in an image of a blonde-haired, blue-eyed white girl, contribute to the acceptance of inferiority. The text repeatedly quotes to ironic effect, and fragments the words of a children's reading book about a stereotypical happy nuclear family.

Pecola, the victim of her own and her family's lack of self-esteem, ends up pregnant and mad after she is raped by her father; this incest theme

has proved controversial in the book's reception. The bleak picture of Pecola's family is counterbalanced by the narrator, Claudia, who refuses to accept the white norms, (she breaks up the white doll), and her positive experience of her mother's 'love, thick and dark as Alaga syrup', as compensation for the physical poverty which surrounds her.

Bluestocking

Name for an intellectual woman, in use by the 1770s. It originally referred to a group of educated, intellectual women (the Blue Stocking Circle), which met and flourished in London in the latter part of the 18th century. The name is drawn from blue stockings made from worsted rather than silk, and was probably originally taken from the day stockings of Benjamin Stillingfleet, who was too poor to afford evening wear. Women members of the group included ▷Elizabeth Montagu (known as their 'Queen of the Blues'), ▷Elizabeth Vesey, ▷Hannah More, ▷Frances Boscawen, ▷Elizabeth Carter, Mary Delaney, ▷Hester Chapone, ▷Fanny Burney and ▷Sarah (Robinson) Scott. Many men also attended, and these included Samuel Johnson (1709–1784), James Boswell (1740–1795), Horace Walpole (1717–1797) and Samuel Richardson (▷Richardson, influence of).
▷*Bas-Bleus, Les*

Blum, Klara (born 1904)

German-Jewish poet and fiction writer. Born in Romania, she moved to Vienna to gain independence from her family. In 1934 her anti-fascist poetry won a communist prize, and she went to live in Moscow until 1947, when she followed her Chinese husband to join the Revolution in China. Her later poems and the novellas, collected in *Das Lied von Hongkong* (1960) (*The Song of Hong Kong*), are distinctive and original in that they succeed in combining oriental settings and imagery with modern Western thought.

Blume, Judy (born 1938)

US novelist. Born in Elizabeth, New Jersey, Blume graduated from New York University in 1961 with a degree in early childhood education. Her children's and adolescent's fiction raises issues germane to young people without prescribing solutions or moralizing. *The One In the Middle Is the Green Kangaroo* (1969) explores the feelings of a middle child. *It's Not the End of the World* (1972) portrays the feelings of children faced with their parent's divorce. *Reenie* (1973) focuses on a child afflicted with scoliosis. Her fiction also exposes forms of discrimination: racism in *Iggie's House* (1970) and fat oppression in *Blubber* (1974). Subject to censorship, Blume's work portrays sexual feelings as normal, as in ▷*Are You There God? It's Me, Margaret* (1970).

Blume's adult novels, *Wifey* (1978) and *Smart Women* (1984), look at women trapped in a traditional marriage, and the alternative of divorce.

Other works include: *Then Again, Maybe I Won't* (1971), *Tales of a Fourth Grade Nothing* (1972), *Otherwise Known as Sheila the Great* (1972), *Forever . . .* (1975), *Superfudge* (1980), *Tiger Eyes* (1981), *Together* (1987) and *Just As Long As We're Fudge-A-Mania* (1990).

Bly, Nellie (1867–1922)

Pseudonym of Elizabeth Cochrane Seaman, US investigative journalist and travel writer. The first intrepid woman reporter, Seaman became a journalist when she responded indignantly to a Pittsburgh *Dispatch* newspaper article, 'What Girls Are Good For'. She reported for the *Dispatch*, then quickly moved to the New York *World*, where she made her career and created a new genre of feature writing.

Focusing on social issues, primarily exploitation and any mistreatment of the powerless, she researched not only by traditional means but also by putting herself literally into the situation. For example, she obtained employment in a box factory in order to write about the conditions of young women factory labourers; she had herself committed to the notorious asylum on Blackwell's Island in order to report conditions suffered by the mentally ill. Her investigative method and first-person reporting in ▷ *Ten Days in a Mad House* (1887), and her writing on the lives of factory and domestic workers, chorus girls and prisoners, anticipated by a half-century or more the 'new' journalism methods and forms of the late 20th century.

With her US reputation well established in the 1880s, in 1889 Bly contracted with the *World* to make a round-the-world tour to beat the current record. The publicity of her trip, her dispatches and ▷ *Nellie Bly's Book: Around the World in Seventy-Two Days* (1890) solidified international recognition.

Blyton, Enid (1897–1968)

English writer of children's fiction. While working as a teacher, and shortly before opening her own infants' school, Blyton was contributing to, and later editing, the journal *Sunny Stories*. After writing poetry and compiling a children's encyclopaedia, Blyton turned to children's fiction in the 1940s. She published over 400 books, which were hugely popular and frequently translated. Her most famous stories include the *Noddy* books, and the *Famous Five* and *Secret Seven* series. Blyton's fiction posits an idyllic vision of rural England and hearty Englishness. Her work has been at the centre of debate and controversy concerning values in children's literature, and in the 1960s librarians imposed sanctions on her writings owing to the books' limited vocabulary, and reproduction of race and gender stereotypes.

Boarding School; or, Lessons of a Preceptress to Her Pupils, The (1798)

The second novel published by the North American author ▷Hannah Webster Foster. The *Boarding School* centres on Mrs Williams, a pious widow, who supports herself by educating young women in the proprieties of courtship, marriage and motherhood. The precepts of *The Boarding School* are more conventional in focus than Foster's first novel, ▷ *The Coquette*, and it was dedicated to 'the Young Ladies of America' in the tradition of late 18th-century North American advice literature.

Boatman, The (1957)

▷Jay Macpherson's third collection of poetry, and one of the most important in Canadian literature, comprised of a sequence of poems that retell biblical and classical myths. Heavily influenced by and dedicated to Northop Frye, the poems utilize strict metre but playful language. The collection is divided into six parts, describing the different stages of fallen and redemptive man, and is important for its mythological imprimatur.

Bocage, Marie-Anne Le Page du (1710–1802)

French dramatist and poet. Born in Rouen of a bourgeois family, du Bocage married at seventeen, and moved to Paris in 1733. She held a literary salon from 1758 onwards, which continued throughout the Revolution (1789), even though she had by then lost her former wealth. Her play *Les Amazones* (*The Amazons*) performed in 1749, was the first work by a woman to be performed at the Comédie Française for some thirty years. It is not clear whether the play's potentially subversive feminist elements were recognized by contemporaries, but it does not appear to have caused any controversy. However, it was not well received, even by her friends. Abandoning the theatre, Madame du Bocage concentrated on poetry, for which she had received a prize from the Academy of Rouen in 1748. She published *La Colombiade* (1756) (*The Journey of Columbus*), an epic poem structured around Columbus's voyage to the New World. She also produced translations and imitations of other authors, including John Milton (1608–1674). Her poem, *Paradis terrestre* (1748) (*The Earthly Paradise*), led to the nickname '*Le Milton français*', which vied with that earned her by her play and her general reputation as a woman writer: '*l'illustre Amazone*' (the illustrious Amazon).

▷Beauharnais, Countesse de
Bib: Beauharnais, F., *A la mémoire de Mme du Bocage*; Chesse, J., 'Mme du Bocage' in *French Review*, XXX (1957); Gill-Mark, G., *Une femme de lettres au XVIIe siècle*.

Bodichon, Barbara Leigh Smith (1827–1891)

British ▷feminist and polemicist, born in London, the illegitimate daughter of a Unitarian minister and a milliner's apprentice. She enrolled in the Ladies' College in Bedford Square in 1849 and chose to study art. Later in life her drawings and paintings were widely exhibited and sold for substantial amounts. Bodichon is best-known today as an active campaigner in the fight for women's ▷suffrage and legal ▷reform. *A Brief*

Summary in Plain Language of the Most Important Laws Concerning Women (1854) was a highly influential pamphlet that brought attention to women's powerlessness and lack of legal rights. In *Women and Work* (1857), she argued that all professions should be available to women, and in her two pamphlets on suffrage, *Reasons for the Enfranchisement of Women* (1866) and *Objections to the Enfranchisement of Women Considered* (1866), she argued lucidly for female voting rights, substantiating her points with empirical evidence she had collected. Bodichon was also concerned with ▷education, setting up a radical school and assisting Emily Davies in establishing Girton College, Cambridge. She left £10,000 to Girton at her death. She was involved in the editing and production of *The Englishwoman's Journal* and published her *American Diary* in 1872. In this work she protested against the injustice she had seen in the American South during a trip there in 1857–8, and drew parallels between the position of slaves and the position of women.

▷Slavery; Travel writing (19th-century Britain)
Bib: Herstein, S.R., *A Mid-Victorian Feminist: Barbara Leigh Smith Bodichon*; Burton, H., *Life.*

Bodily Harm (1981)
▷Margaret Atwood's novel about a 'lifestyle' journalist, Rennie Wilford, who travels to the Caribbean to recuperate from a partial mastectomy. There she discovers that her private disfigurements are nothing compared to what physical abuses are possible. Inadvertantly caught in a political coup, Rennie comes to re-evaluate the concept of innocence. Through the terrifying time that she spends in a prison cell, she discovers the underbelly of power and control, and how she must push past her own victimization to compassion for others.
Bib: Irvine, L., *Sub/Version.*

Bogan, Louise (1897–1970)
US poet, translator and essayist. Bogan was born in Liermore Falls, Maine into a lower-middle-class family. In Boston, Massachusetts she attended the Boston Girls' Latin School. She claimed that her first marriage in 1916 was to escape her family: the marriage subsequently failed. From 1931 to 1951 Bogan was poetry critic at *The New Yorker*, but also wrote for *Nation, Poetry, Scribner's* and *Atlantic Monthly*. She corresponded with a number of writers including Edmund Wilson, (1895–1972), ▷May Sarton and Theodore Roethke (1908–1963). A highly respected poet and critic, she was Fellow in American Letters at the Library of Congress (1944) and then Chair of Poetry from 1944 to 1946. She also won the Bollingen Prize in 1955 and an Academy of American Poets Award in 1959.

Her poetry is distinguished by a fine use of traditional metrics and has frequently been compared to the work of the English metaphysical poets. Roethke commented that she worked in 'the severest lyrical tradition in English'. Despite

the subject matter which may be 'the wildest weeping, the fiercest delusion', mental breakdown, frustrated or repressed desire, as in 'Body of this Death' (1923), Bogan's poems have a condensed control which keeps them impersonal but powerful. This is also a consequence of her use of the natural world. 'Dark Summer' (1929) expresses a yearning to integrate with the natural world and to transcend time. The natural world provides moments of stasis that suggest psychic stillness and peace. Bogan's work is collected in *The Blue Estuaries: Poems 1923–1968* which represents her own choice of an *oeuvre*.

Other works include: *The Sleeping Fury* (1937), *Achievement in American Poetry, 1900–1950*, *Collected Poems, 1923–1952* (1954), *Selected Criticism* (1955) and *Journey Around My Room: The Autobiography of Louise Bogan* (1980). Among her translations are Ernst Juenger's *The Glass Bees* (1961), Goethe's *Elective Affinities* (1963), and his *The Sorrows of Young Werther* (1971).

Bögli, Lina (1858–1941)
German-speaking Swiss writer. Born into a poor family in a small village, she worked first as a maid in Italy and Poland, and then as a teacher in England, before returning once more to Poland. When a Polish officer seemed about to ruin his career by wanting to marry her, she embarked on a ten-year trip around the world, and subsequently published an account of her adventures, first in English, *Forward* (1905), and then in German, *Vorwärts* (1906) (*Forward*). This book became an international bestseller, and was translated into many other languages. In 1910 she embarked on a second voyage, wrote a sequel to her first book, *Immer Vorwärts* (1913) (*Always Forward*) and then retired to her native village.

Böhlau, Helene (1859–1940)
German fiction writer. The well-educated, much-travelled daughter of a Weimar publisher, she gained a wide reputation, largely because of her humorous stories about Goethe's Weimar, *Rathsmädelgeschichten* (1888) (*Stories of Councillors' Daughters*). However, her best novels – *Der Rangierbahnhof* (1896) (*The Railway Junction*), *Das Recht der Mutter* (1896) (*The Right of the Mother*) and ▷*Halbtier!* (1899) (*Half-animal!*) – are about the fate of contemporary heroines. Written in the naturalist idiom, they are serious explorations of women's condition and the problems of female creativity and emancipation.

Böhl von Faber, Cecilia (1796–1877)
Spanish novelist. From the mid-19th century to the revolution of 1868 and the advent of ▷realism, Böhl von Faber, who wrote under the pseudonym Fernán Caballero, was acknowledged as Spain's most prestigious novelist. Her masterpiece is ▷*La gaviota* (1849) (*The Seagull*). Her other works include: *Lágrimas* (1850) (*Tears*); *Clemencia* (1852), and *Un servilón y un liberalito* (1855) (*A Groveller and a Little Liberal*). Böhl von Faber's work is seen as the most significant link

between romanticism and the regional and realistic movements in the 19th-century Spanish novel. She also published collections of short stories, including: *Relaciones* (1857) (*Tales*); *Cuadros de costumbres* (1857) (*Tales of Customs*), and *Cuentos y poesías andaluces* (1859) (*Andalusian Tales and Poetry*).

Boio (? 4th century BC)

Ancient Greek poet. There is great confusion regarding the identification of the woman Boio and the male writer Boius, and about her date. Myth made Boio wife of the Athenian king Actaeus, and mother of the poet Palaephatus. She is said to have served as priestess of Apollo at Delphi, where she wrote in Greek hexameter verse a *Hymn to Apollo*, concerning the Athenian origin of the hexameter metre and the original builders of the oracle at Delphi. The historian Philochorus (4th century BC) quotes her work *On Divination* (which does not survive). The Christian writer Clement (2nd century AD) mentions her along with the mythical poetesses ▷Manto and Hippo. She is also credited with a poem on the metamorphoses of people into birds, *Ornithogonia*, used by later writers such as the Roman poet Ovid in his *Metamorphoses*. But this title could refer to a work by Boius, for Boio's title might, rather, have been *Ornithomanteia*, as she dealt with augury using birds. The similar subject matter and names create the confusion.

Boismortier, Suzanne Bodin de (18th century)

French novelist. The daughter of a composer from Perpignan, she published two novels: *Mémoires historiques de la comtesse de Marienberg (1751)* (*Historical Memoirs of the Countess of Marienberg*) and *Histoire de Jacques Féru et de la valeureuse demoiselle Agathe Mignard* (1766) (*The Tale of Jacques Féru and the Courageous Miss Agathe Mignard*). The last of her published works was a collection of short stories, *Histoires morales* (1768) (*Moral Tales*).

Boland, Eavan (born 1944)

Irish poet and essayist. Born in Dublin, she was educated in London and New York. She studied English at Trinity College, Dublin, where she lectured for a year. One of the most important poets writing in Ireland today, her work is both sensuous and cerebral, free and formally rigorous. Seeking to articulate the connections between the private themes and experiences of womanhood and the public sphere of history and nationhood, her writing has been a major force in shaping Irish women's sense of themselves. Her collections include: *The War Horse* (1975), *In Her Own Image* (1980), *Night Feed* (1982), *The Journey* (1987) and *Outside History* (1990). A regular reviewer for *The Irish Times*, she has written, in addition to her poetry, a number of important essays on the status of Irish writing and of Irish women writers. In *A Kind of Scar: The Woman Poet in a National Tradition* (1989), she reflects on the 'momentous' and 'disruptive' transit made by Irish women from being 'the subjects and objects of Irish poems to being the authors of them'.

Boleyn, Anne (c 1507–1536)

English poet and letter-writer. She was the daughter of Thomas Boleyn and Elizabeth Howard. From 1514 to 1522 she was educated at the French court. Upon her return she caught the attention of the English court and king. In 1533 Henry VIII replaced Catherine of Aragon as queen by marrying Boleyn. Her only surviving child, the future ▷Elizabeth I (▷Elizabeth Tudor), was born the same year. Over the next few years, however, Boleyn failed to produce the male heir so greatly desired by Henry. She was beheaded in 1536 after being declared guilty of adultery, and therefore treason. Her ▷letters attest to the greatness of her skillfully managed yet ultimately tragic ambition. She is also credited with two lyrics, said to have been written by her as she awaited her execution: 'Defiled is my Name Full Sore' and 'Rock me on Sleep' (sometimes attributed to her brother).

▷Lisle, Honor; Vivien, Renée
Bib: Green, M.A.E. (ed.), *Letters of Royal and Illustrious Ladies of Great Britain*.

Bolt, Carol (born 1941)

Canadian dramatist. Born Carol Johnson in Winnipeg, she grew up in Vancouver, and studied playwriting at the University of British Columbia gaining a BA in 1961. A prolific dramatist, she has also been a stage manager and director, and many of her scripts were developed through a collective creation process with Toronto Workshop Productions and Theatre Passe Muraille. Her first comedy, *Daganawida*, was produced in 1970. She is best-known for her political dramas *Buffalo Jump* (1972), about the prairie riots during the depression, *Gabe* (1973), about two descendants of Louis Riel and Gabriel Dumont (Metis leaders of the 1885 Northwest Rebellion on the prairies), and *Red Emma: Queen of the Anarchists* (1973). These plays theatrically explore historical events or characters without being documentaries. *Red Emma*, about New York anarchist Emma Goldman, 'the most dangerous woman in the world', signals Bolt's movement towards contemporary issues and a greater focus on character motivation in *Shelter* (1975) and in subsequent plays. *One Night Stand* (1977) is a psychological thriller that won three Canadian Film Awards for Bolt's adaptation of the play to a television film. *Escape Entertainment* (1981) continues Bolt's interest in the conflict between the imagination and reality, at the same time as it strips bare the Canadian film industry. *Love or Money* was produced in 1982. Bolt has also written a number of children's plays: *My Best Friend is Twelve Feet High* (1972), *Cyclone Jack* (1972), *Tangleflags* (1973), *Maurice* (1974), and *Finding Bumble* (1975). She lives in Toronto.

Bölte, Amely (1811–1891)
German novelist. The niece of ▷Fanny Tarnow, she yearned for a literary career, and took a job as a governess in a highly-cultured family so as to educate herself. With the money she earned she went to England, and made a scanty living by translating English novels. For her own fiction she modelled herself on ▷Charlotte Brontë, writing in the genre of the 'governess's novel', and describing English high society to a German public. Upon her return home she wrote biographies, including one on ▷Fanny Tarnow in 1865, as well as historical novels, and took up the cause of poor and unemployed women.

Bombal, María Luisa (1910–1980)
Chilean novelist and short story writer. In 1922 she moved to Paris, where she studied literature and philosophy at the Sorbonne, and acquired an extensive knowledge of avant-garde movements. In 1931 she returned to Santiago, where she collaborated with ▷Marta Brunet and Vera Zouroff in the experimental theatre of Pizarro Espoz. She was invited to Buenos Aires from 1933 to 1940 by Pablo Neruda (1904–1973), then Consul, and director of ▷Sur. There she published her most famous books: La última niebla (1935), which she rewrote and translated with her husband as The House of Mist (1947), and La amortajada (1938) (The Shrouded Woman, 1948). The latter is a first-person singular narrative told through flashbacks by the corpse of a woman, and is said by Jorge Luís Borges to be a 'book of sad magic . . . of occult efficient organization'. The House of Mist is a psychological analysis of characters observed by a woman dissatisfied in her marriage. Mist symbolizes for her the feelings of her past, those of love and family, which are now useless. Human and superhuman mingle in a poetic arena, in which the reader is allowed to see reality only through her eyes. Bombal also wrote film scripts and dialogues during the 1930s. Beginning with her first short novels written when she was twenty-one, she was successful, and later received the Chilean Academy Prize for her book La historia de María Griselda (1976) (The Story of María Griselda). In 1940 she moved back to Chile, and eventually to the United States.

Bonacci Brunamonti, Maria Alinda (1841–1903)
Italian poet. Her father, Gratiliano Bonacci, was also a writer, and she received a sound classical education. She was a friend and correspondent of many literary luminaries of the period. A keen student of history of art, particularly that of Umbria, she published a critical volume, Discorsi d'arte (1898). One of the recurrent themes of her work centres on the difficulty of writing.

Her main works are Canti (1856) (Lyrical Poems), her first work, published at the age of fifteen; Canti nazionali (National Poems), appropriately published in 1860, as the new Italy came into being; Versi (1875) (Verses); L'ultimo sonno – La seconda vita (1876) (The Last Sleep – The Second Life); Nuovi canti (1887) (New Songs); Flora (1898); Ricordi di viaggio (1907) (Memories of Travelling).

Bonanni, Laudomia (born 1908)
Italian novelist and short story writer. A teacher for most of her life, she was very involved with young people's problems in a legal capacity as well as in terms of her work. A regular contributor to many Italian newspapers and magazines, she has won many literary prizes for her fiction. Much of her work, including ▷Il fosso (1949) (The Trench), a collection of short stories, is concerned with the lives of the poor, particularly with women of the working class and the lack of choice in their lives. In the 1950s, she wrote of women's dilemmas: in Palma e sorelle (1955) (Palma and Sisters), she examined their tendency to self-sacrifice, and the repetitive nature of their stories because of this trait; ▷L'adultera (1964) (The Adulteress) is a sometimes unsympathetic portrayal of similar dilemmas in the life of a middle-class woman. Vietato ai minori (1974) (Off-limits to Children) is based on her experiences in the juvenile court, particularly her observations of the effects of violence on children. Il bambino di pietra: Una nevrosi femminile (Child of Stone: A Tale of Female Neurosis) of 1979 is another work which analyses the female psyche, this time through a first-person narrative in which a female character presents us with her journey through psychoanalysis. Stylistically, Bonanni's work combines ▷verismo with lyricism.

Her other main works include: Storie tragiche della montagna (1927) (Tragic Tales of the Mountains); Noterelle di cronaca scolastica (1932) (Notes from School); Le due penne del pappagallino Verzé (1948) (The Two Feathers of Verzé); L'imputata (1960) (The Accused); Città del tabacco (1977) (Tobacco City); Le droghe (1982) (Drugs).

Bonding between women (Caribbean)
This theme is explored in the works of the Caribbean writers ▷Jamaica Kincaid (▷Annie John and ▷At the Bottom of the River), and ▷Zee Edgell (▷Beka Lamb). ▷Jean Rhys, in ▷Wide Sargasso Sea, deals with the absence of bonding.

bone people, the (1984)
Novel by New Zealand writer ▷Keri Hulme. the bone people, Keri Hulme's first novel, won four awards in the year after publication, two national and two international, including the prestigious Booker McConnell Prize. the bone people began life as a story about a dream Hulme had when she was eighteen, and developed into a very long novel over the next ten years. Hulme had great difficulty finding a publisher and eventually the book was produced by a feminist publishing collective, Spiral, in an edition of 2000 copies. After the phenomenal success of the bone people the novel attracted a great deal of widely differing critical attention and is still one of the most controversial New Zealand books.

It is a narrative about an isolated woman

thinker/artist, Kerewin Holmes, and her relationship with a mute European child, Simon, and his Maori foster father, Joe. The first half of the novel is graphically realist, especially in the violent scenes between Joe and Simon, and the second half is mystical and visionary. Hulme's unorthodox writing style, grammar and punctuation have been much discussed, and many commentators think more editing was necessary, but it is also clear that Hulme's unconventional style and the novel's scope and length are part of its power. *the bone people* has had its greatest significance as a work of ▷Maori literature, highlighting particular cultural and racial issues and taking on the status of a cultural treasure.

Bonheur d'Occasion (1945) ▷ *Tin Flute, The* (1947)

Boniface Correspondence (8th century)
Collection of letters (in Latin) connected with the English missionary Boniface. Boniface was born c 675 near Exeter. He left England in 719, abandoning a promising career as a grammarian and scholar, to become a missionary to the unconverted Germanic peoples on the continent. He was martyred in Friesland in 754. A collection of his correspondence was assembled after his death, and this has been preserved. It includes, as well as letters to and from Boniface, letters from Lull (also a missionary, educated at Malmesbury in England, and Boniface's successor as Archbishop of Mainz). There are several women numbered among Boniface's circle of correspondents and fellow-missionaries. Letters to Boniface from ▷Ælflæd, ▷Cena, Eangyth (▷ Bucge), ▷Egburg, ▷Bucge and ▷Leoba are preserved, as is one from the heads of three religious communities, written by one of the abbesses, ▷Cneoburg. ▷Eadburg received four letters from Boniface and one from Lull, although no letter from her is extant. Lull wrote to ▷Switha and ▷Cyniburg, both abbesses in England, but no letter from either of these women survives. Three letters from ▷Berthgyth to her brother are preserved. The collection reflects the power and authority residing in English abbesses, and reveals the high degree of learning of the women: Leoba and Berthgyth both attempt Latin verse. It also expresses the mutual affection and respect shared by the correspondents, and indicates the high status of women in Anglo-Saxon times.
Bib: Emerton, E., *The Letters of St Boniface*; Talbot, C.H., *The Anglo-Saxon Missionaries in Germany*; Fell, Christine E., 'Some Implications of the Boniface Correspondence', in Damico, Helen and Hennessey Olsen, Alexandra (eds.), *New Readings on Women in Old English Literature*; Fell, Christine E., *Anglo-Saxon Letters and Letter-Writers*.

Bonjour Tristesse (1955)
Translation of *Bonjour Tristesse* (1954), novel by French writer ▷Françoise Sagan. Sagan wrote this, her first novel, at the age of eighteen, and achieved immediate notoriety. Although in the 1950s the adolescent heroine's amorality was found remarkable, perhaps the most striking feature of this novel today is the direct, classical, almost minimalist style. The novel is presented as the intimate journal of the heroine, Cécile, and depicts her reactions to her carefree father's proposed marriage to the beautiful and sober Anne, and to the physical pleasures offered by the equally beautiful Cyril.
Sagan effectively evokes a sense of the aimlessness and hedonism of the lives of Cécile and her father, which contrasts with Anne's purposeful and regulated existence, but the factual style avoids moral judgements and the sentimentality which is usually associated with Sagan. An interesting ambivalence results from the combination of first-person narration and the heroine's evident immaturity. The confessional style has caused this novel to be regarded as a precursor of the more recent upsurge in such writing by women.

Book of Abigail and John: Selected Letters of the Adams Family 1762–1784, The (1975)
In the exchange of letters maintained during their courtship years and throughout their marriage, the Americans ▷Abigail Smith Adams and John Adams balanced the extraordinary events of their lives by establishing with one another an intimate record of their feelings. In this collection of letters, Abigail's development of letter-writing into an art form is most evident. Whether discussing the stillbirth of a child or the political machinations in Massachusetts, Adams crafted her feelings into a remarkably poetic and dramatic life-record.
▷*Adams Family Papers*; *Adams–Jefferson Letters, The*; Early North American letters

Book of Eve, The (1973)
Canadian writer ▷Constance Beresford-Howe's most important novel, about a woman who, without warning, at the age of 65, leaves her cold and ungrateful husband of forty years. With only her inadequate pension to live on, Eva survives as a scavenger and a bag-lady, but derives real pride from her independence. Beresford-Howe's portrait of a woman trading middle-class respectability for chaotic poverty is both moving and humorous, but with subtlety and elegance posits many important questions about women and financial exigency, as well as the effacement of older women from societal recognition. The free play of eccentricity as territory forbidden to respectable women makes this a profoundly important novel: its social, sexual, and financial transgressions raise questions about the extent to which middle-class paradigms are embedded in literary explorations of the lives of women.

Book of the City of Ladies, The (1521)
Translation of *La Cité des Dames* (from 1405) by ▷Christine de Pisan.

Boonlua (1911–1982)

Pen-name of Thai writer Boonlua Kunjara Debyasuvan. Compared to her half-sister, ▷Dok Mai Sod, she is more sympathetic to the 'modern' woman, whom she portrays as a determined, intelligent and active individual, self-sufficient rather than dependent on men for her identity. A Chulalongkorn University graduate with a US MA, she was much celebrated in Thai society as an influential writer, essayist, and active intellectual. She supported the teaching of English in Thai schools, and translated not only Thai fiction into English, but also English fiction into Thai. The flavour and outlook of her writing are perhaps best conveyed by her novels ▷*Caak Nyng Chiiwid* (1964) (*Scenes from Life*) and ▷*Tutiyawises* (*Symbol of Merit*).

Boothby, Frances (fl 1669)

English Restoration dramatist, whose tragicomedy *Marcelia: or the Treacherous Friend* (1670) was performed before ▷Alpha Behn's plays – at the Theatre Royal, in 1669. It is her only known work. The plot concerns misapprehensions and deceits in love, initiated by the king's desire for a new lover, Opening, 'I'm hither come, but what d'ye think to say? / A Womans Pen presents you with a Play,' it goes on to make great play of leaving the stage, returning only to express great surprise that the audience is still there despite female authorship. The tragicomic denouement restores stability to the original relationships.
    ▷Polwhele, Elizabeth

Borgese Freschi, Maria (1881–1947)

Italian poet and novelist; occasionally used the pseudonym Erinni. Wrote reviews for and contributed to literary periodicals. Married, separated, with one son. Her first publication, a collection of poetry, was published under the pseudonym Erinni. This was *I canti dell'alba e della sera* (1909) (*Songs of the Dawn and of the Evening*), stylistically reminiscent of the *crepuscolari* (▷*crepuscolarismo*). Her narrative fiction was D'Annunzian (▷*D'Annunzianesimo*) in tone, set among the middle classes and revolving round the twin themes of duty and sacrifice. She also wrote historical fiction in which she displayed a predilection for similar narratives of passion versus duty, in a literary setting. These included: *La contessa Lara, una vita di passione e poesie nell'ottocento italiano* (1930) (*Countess Lara, A Life of Passion and Poetry in Nineteenth-century Italy*) ; *L'appassionata di Byron* (1949) (*Byron's Love*), a tale of Byron's relationship with Countess Guiccioli; *Corrispondenza fra Giovanni Verga e Felice Cameroni* (1935) (*Letters of Giovanni Verga and Felice Cameroni*); *Anime scompagnate* (1937) (*Lone Souls*), the story of the relationship between Verga and Gisella Foianesi, and *Costanza Perticari nei tempi di Vincenzo Monti*, a biography of the poet Costanza Perticari.

    Her other main works include: *Aurora la amata* (1930) (*Beloved Aurora*); *Dodici donne e due cani* (1935) (*Twelve Women and Two Dogs*); *Quelli che vennero prima* (1942) (*Those Who Came First*); *Benvenuto* (1945) (*Welcome*); *La pelle della volpe* (1946) (*The Fox Skin*).

Bormann, Maria Benedita Câmara de (1853–1895)

Brazilian novelist who used the ▷pseudonym Délia. She was married to a marshal of the Paraguay War, and moved in the best society of Rio de Janeiro. Her novel *Lésbia* (1890) has aroused curiosity because of its lesbian theme.
    Other works: *Aurélia* (1883); *Uma vítima* (1884) (*A Victim*); *Duas irmãs* (1884) (*Two Sisters*); *Madalena* (1881); *Celeste* (1893), and *Angelina* (1894).
Bib: Coutinho, Afrânio, Sousa, J. Galante de, *Enciclopédia de literatura brasileira*; Egert, Nanci, introduction to *Celeste*.

Bornholdt, Jenny (born 1960)

New Zealand poet. Jenny Bornholdt lives in Wellington and supports herself in various jobs while writing. Bornholdt is a recent arrival in New Zealand poetry, and her work is lyrical and personal but is given an ironic edge by her use of minimalist forms and reference to a ▷postmodern cultural context.
    Her work includes *This Big Face* (1988).

Borrero, Dulce María (1883–1945)

Cuban poet. The sister of ▷Juana Borrero, Dulce Borrero was also an artist. She was educated in a literary milieu. In 1895 her father, Esteban Borrero Echeverría, moved the family to Key West (Cayo Hueso). There Borrero published her first verses in *Revista de Cayo Hueso* (*The Key West Review*). Later she moved to Costa Rica with her father, then returned to Cuba in 1899, after the Independence War. She contributed to several magazines and lectured on art, literature and education, as well as fighting actively for feminism. Her works include *Horas de mi vida* (1912) (*Times of my Life*). She published several lectures and essays on art, education and feminism.

Borrero, Juana (1877–1896)

Cuban poet. She was the daughter of Esteban Borrero Echeverría and the sister of ▷Dulce María Borrero. In 1895, because of her father's involvement in a revolution, the family emigrated to Key West (Cayo Hueso), in Florida. As a girl Borrero attended drawing classes, and in 1886 she entered the Academy of Beaux Arts in San Alejandro. In 1892 she travelled with her father to New York, where she met Martí, who offered a literary evening party in her honour at Chickering Hall. In Washington, D.C., she studied painting, and in 1893 she returned to Cuba. She contributed to *La Habana Elegante*, *El Fígaro*, and *Gris y Azul*. She left an extensive body of letters and poems, pen-and-ink drawings and paintings.

Borson, Roo (born 1952)

Poet Ruth Elizabeth Borson, born in Berkeley, California, emigrated to Canada in 1974. She studied at Goddard College, Vermont, and at the University of British Columbia (briefly with ▷Pat Lowther); she has worked as a librarian and a lab technician. *Landfall* appeared in 1977, followed by *In the Smoky Light of the Fields* (1980), *Rain* (1980), *A Sad Device* (1981), *The Whole Night, Coming Home* (1984), *The Transparence of November / Snow* (1985, with Kim Maltman, her partner), and *Intent, or the Weight of the World* (1989). Her work focuses on physical description, and on the spiralled labyrinth of language. It has been noted that she is the youngest poet included in ▷Margaret Atwood's edition of the *New Oxford Book of Canadian Verse* (1982).
Bib: Harasym, S., in ▷*A Mazing Space.*

Boscawen, Frances (1719–1805)

▷Bluestocking, letter-writer, and friend of ▷Hannah More, married Edward Boscawen the MP. Her letters feature in collections of other Bluestockings.

Bosco, María Angélica (born 1917)

Argentinian novelist, short story writer, essayist and translator. Her first novel, *La muerte baja en el ascensor* (1954) (*Death Goes Down in the Lift*), is written somewhat like a detective story, with a lively and circumspect technique. This book, along with *La Trampa* (1960) (*The Trap*) and *Historia privada* (1972) (*Personal History*), won an award. Bosco states the novel is a reaction against the 'feminine rhetoric' that permeates novels 'in our women's literature, which usually "drowns in curtains"'. She has translated Kierkegaard from the French, along with Flaubert's *Madame Bovary*, one of her most outstanding translations, and works by Zola and Rimbaud. In the past she has been active in radio and television. Other works include: *La muerte soborna a Pandora* (1956) (*Pandora is Bribed by Death*); *El comedor de diario* (1963) (*The Day-to-day Dining Room*); *¿Donde está el cordero?* (1965) (*Where is the Lamb?*); *Borges y los otros* (1967) (*Borges and the Others*); *La Negra Vélez y su ángel* (1968); *Carta abierta a Judas* (1971) (*Open Letter to Judas*); *Cartas de mujeres* (1975) (*Letters from Women*); *Retorno a la 'ilusión'* (1976) (*Return to The 'Illusion'*); *En la estela de un secuestro* (1977) (*In the Wake of a Kidnapping*); *Muerte en la costa del río* (1978) (*Death on the Riverbank*); *En la piel del otro* (1981) (*In the Skin of the Other One*); *La noche dos mil* (*The Night Two Thousand*), and *La muerte vino de afuera* (1983) (*Death Came From Outside*).

Bosco, Monique (born 1927)

Born in Vienna, she emigrated to Canada in 1948. She studied at the University of Montreal, and worked as a freelance journalist before becoming a professor in the French department at the University of Montreal in 1963. Her novels include *Un Amour Maladroit* (1961) (*An Awkward Love*), *Les Infusoires* (1965) (*The Infusions*), *La*

femme de Loth (1970, translated as *Lot's Wife* 1975), *New Medea* (1974), *Charles Lévy M.D.* (1977), and focus to a large extent on women's impotent rage in the face of male sexual betrayal. Her poetic works, *Jéricho* (1971) and *Schabbat 70– 77* (1978), share the energy and physical intensity of her fictional style.

Bošković, Anica (1714–1804)

Croatian poet. Bošković was from a highly-educated Dubrovnik family; her brother was a scientist of international renown. She never married, and looked after her mother who lived to over a hundred years of age. In her spare time she wrote poetry. She knew Latin and Italian, and translated from both, but wrote her own poetry in Croatian. Very little of her work was published, and that which survives is mostly religious and in manuscript form. *Razgovor pastirski vrhu porodjenja Gospodinova jedne djevočice Dubrovkinje* (*A Pastoral Discourse on the Birth of Our Lord by a Maid of Dubrovnik*) was published anonymously in Venice in 1758, but the signature and dedication to her brother confirm Bošković's authorship.

Boston, Lucy (1892–1990)

English novelist and writer for children. Boston's best-known works are those about Green Knowe, and were written in her 60s. They were inspired by the 12th-century manor house near Cambridge where she had been resident since 1939. Beginning with *The Children of Green Knowe* (1954), the novels are transhistorical narratives concerned with endurance over time, and the series ends with *The Stones of Green Knowe* (1976). Novels for adults include: *Yew Hall* (1954) and *Persephone* (1969). Autobiographical writings include *Perverse and Foolish: A Memoir of Childhood and Youth* (1979).

Boswell, Annabella (1826–1916)

Australian writer. Annabella Boswell, formerly Innes, was one of the first Australian-born women to record her girlhood experience. Her journal details her life as a schoolgirl in Sydney, her journeys through the bush, and a period spent at Port Macquarie in the busy and sociable house of her uncle, Major Innes. Re-worked in adulthood, the journal became *Early Recollections and Gleanings from an Old Journal* (1908). This was followed by *Further Recollections of my Early Days in Australia* (1911) and reprinted, edited by Morton Herman, as *Annabella Boswell's Journal* (1965).
▷Journals (Australia)

Botan (born 1945)

Pen-name of Supa (Luesiri) Sirisingha, a Thai writer of Chinese ethnic origin. She was originally a teacher, but after obtaining an MA from Chulalongkorn University, worked for *Satrisarn* and *Chaiyapruek* magazines. She continues to write for popular magazines, and also runs with her husband, Biriya Sirisingha, the Chom-Rom Dek which specializes in publishing children's books. '*Ai Dam*', her first published story, appeared in the *Kwanjit Journal* when she was an undergraduate. She has since published thirty novels (some dozen of which have been made into films or television drama series), four children's books and translated over 100 children's books into Thai. Winner of eight annual national literary awards, she is best known for her three novels on Chinese immigrants to Thailand and their adjustment, one of which, *Chotmai Chak Muang Thai* (*Letters from Thailand*), based on her own family's experience, won the SEATO (South-East Asian Treaty Organization) literary award in 1969 and has been translated into English and six other languages.

Noted for her skill in rendering dialogue, the social concerns of Botan's writings are seen in her portrayal of women whose intelligence, diligence and patience are rewarded with hard-won success. In her novels, the ideal marriage is between equals, based on mutual respect, while traditionally-minded mothers generate tension by misjudging their more modern daughters. She is also critical of elements in Chinese culture which oppress women, as when, in *Letters from Thailand*, an already harassed daughter, appearing regularly to clean her elderly Chinese father's house, receives a typical response to the fact that her Thai husband helps with the housework before they all leave for work: 'Just because you work, you shouldn't expect him to get down on his knees with a scrubbing brush.'

Botelho, Fernanda (born 1926)
Portuguese poet and novelist. Born in Oporto, she was a student of classical philology at the universities of Coimbra and Lisbon, and like many young authors of the post-war period she began her literary career by collaborating on journals and reviews dedicated to experimental writing. More than two dozen of these small press publications circulated during the 1950s. Although most were short-lived, together they formed a distinctive voice which, in opposition to the entrenched ▷neo-realist movement, heralded the advent of Existentialism and a neo-metaphysical poetry in Portugal.

One of the most prominent journals of the group, ▷*Távola Redonda* (*Round Table*), published Botelho's book of poems, entitled *As Coordenadas Líricas* (1951) (*The Lyrical Coordinates*); her novella *O Engima de Sete Alíneas* (1956) (*The Enigma of the Seven Lines*) was featured in the first issue of *Graal* (*Grail*), another vanguard publication. In quick succession Botelho authored the novels *O Angulo Raso* (1957) (*The Level Angle*); *Calendário Privado* (1958) (*Private Calendar*), and *A Gata e a Fábula* (1960) (*The Cat and the Fable*), which was awarded the prestigious Camilo Castelo Branco Prize (1960) for best novel. These works, as well as her subsequent novels, ▷*Xerazade e os Outros* (1964) (*Scheherazade and the Others*), *Terra Sem Música* (1969) (*Land Without Music*) and *Lourenço é Nome de Jogral* (1971) (*Lourenço is a Minstrel's Name*) are some of the finest examples of Existentialist writing in Portugal. Botelho recently

published two novels after more than a decade of silence: *Esta Noite Sonhei com Brueghel* (1987) (*Tonight I Dreamed of Brueghel*) and *Festa em Casa de Flores* (1990) (*Party in the House of Flowers*). Her earlier novels, long out of print, are currently being reissued and are enjoying a new and wider readership.

▷*Armários Vazios, Os*; Nóbrega, Isabel da; Modernism (Portugal)

Boucher, Denise (born 1935)
Canadian dramatist and the author of the notorious *Les Fées ont Soif* (1978, *The Fairies Are Thirsty*, 1982), which was banned from a reputable Montreal theatre for its attack on the idealization of women and their role through its allegedly blasphemous representation of the Virgin Mary as prostitute. The play pointed towards the extent to which feminists consider that Quebec women are politically and socially repressed by the religious valorization of this icon. Boucher is also the author of *Cyprine: Essaicollage Pour Etre Une Femme* (1978) (*Cyprine: Essay-collage on Being a Woman*).
Bib: Cotnoir, L., in ▷*A Mazing Space*.

Boudalia, Nafissa (born 1948)
Algerian artist and poet. She has worked as a journalist since 1969 for Algerian newspapers like *El Moudjahid* and *Algérie Actualités*. In 1967 her poems won instant acclaim, culminating in the award of the Prix Saint Germain des Prés in Paris. Boudalia's collection of poems, ▷*Réflexions sur l'Algérie* (1989) (*Reflections on Algeria*) focuses on the political situation in Algeria, especially the position of women. Since 1972 she has lived in London with her English husband and her five children, whom she educates herself at home.

Bourdic-Viot, Marie-Henriette Payan de d'Estang de (1746–1802)
French poet and essayist, also known as Madame d'Antremont. Born in Dresden, she lived in France from the age of four. Well educated, she read Latin, German, English and Italian. From 1769 onwards she collaborated on the periodical *L'Almanach des Muses* (*The Muses' Almanac*), where the most well known of her poems, 'Ode au silence' (Ode to Silence), was published. In 1782 she was received as a member of the Académie de Nîmes, and her inaugural speech, *Éloge de Montaigne* (*In praise of Montaigne*), was published in 1800. Her other works include an opera, *La Forêt de Brama* (*The Forest of Brama*), which was never produced, and a romance written as a response to Choderlos de Laclos's *Les Liaisons dangereuses* (1782) (*Dangerous Liaisons*)
Bib: Séché, A., *Les Muses françaises*.

Bourette, Charlotte Rouyer (1714–1784)
French poet. Her father, and her first and second husbands, were all *limonadiers*, professional preparers of non-alcoholic beverages. Known as 'La Muse Limonadière', she ran the Café Allemand in the rue Croix-des-Petits-Champs, a meeting place for writers where dissertations were

read. Plays, some the work of the ▷Muse herself, were also performed in the café. She published a selection of her verse, *La Muse limonadière* (1755), addressed to a vast spectrum of figures, from her laundry woman to the King of Prussia and King Stanislas of Poland, and to literary figures such as Voltaire. Her one published play, *La Coquette punie* (*Punishment for a Flirt*), was performed at the Théâtre de Maestricht in 1779. She was also a contributor to the ▷*Journal des Dames* (*Ladies' Journal*). Her activities were surveyed by the police, who kept a file on her.
Bib: Lancey, C. Ver Heyden de, *Coup d'oeil sur deux figures curieuses de la vie parisienne au XVIIième siècle*; Prudhomme, M. L., *Répertoire universel historique et biographique de femmes célèbres*.

Bourgeois, Louise (1563–1636)
French author of three books on midwifery. She was midwife to the French queen, Marie de Medici (1573–1642), from 1601 to 1609 and also an independent practitioner with a flourishing business. She was at the centre of the medical world in the early decades of the 17th century. Her first treatise was published in three parts between 1609 and 1626 and entitled *Observations diverses sur la stérilité perte de fruict, foecondité, accouchements et maladies des femmes et enfants nouveaux naiz* (*Various Observations on Sterility, Miscarriage, Fecundity, Confinements and Illnesses of Women and Newborn Infants*). Her second, *Récit véritable de la naissance de Messeigneurs & Dames les Enfans de France* (*True Account of the Birth of the Ladies and Gentlemen, the Children of France*), appeared in the 1617 edition of the *Various Observations* with *Instructions à ma fille* (*Instructions to my Daughter*). The *Observations* along with *Instructions à ma fille* are an admixture of theory and case histories. They give detached advice about every aspect of childbirth and practice for the midwife in attendance. The author affirms '*la diversité du naturel des femmes*' ('the diversity of women's nature'), that every woman is an individual, with her own idiosyncratic constitution, conforming to the dominant medical theory of the age, based on humours. Louise Bourgeois wished to be perceived as equal to male physicians and capable of judgement of equal value. A *Recueil de Secrets de Louyse Bourgeois* (*Collection of the Secrets of Louise Bourgeois*) was published in 1635, offering 280 recipes for conditions ranging from the common cold to the plague.
Bib: Perkins, W., 'The Relationship between Midwife and Client in the Works of Louise Bourgeois', *Seventeenth-Century French Studies*, XI (1989); and 'Louise Bourgeois's *Recueil des Secrets*', *Seventeenth-Century French Studies*, XIII (1991).

Bourin, Jeanne
French, historian and novelist. Bourin is the author of historical novels set in the Middle Ages, such as *La Chambre des dames* (1979) (*The Ladies' Room*), its sequel, *Le Jeu de la tentation* (1981) (*The Temptation Game*) and *Le Grand Feu* (1985) (*The Great Fire*). These novels adhere to the generic conventions of historical romance, including lavish descriptions of the heroine's physique, and of the carnal pleasures to which she succumbs, but suitable punishments are provided to force the heroine to return to the path of virtue.

Bowen, Elizabeth (1899–1973)
Irish novelist of Anglo-Irish parentage. Born in Dublin and educated in England, Bowen maintained strong links with Ireland throughout her life, keeping up the family home in County Cork, which she inherited in 1930. Her early life in Ireland forms the basis for the autobiography *Seven Winters* (1942), and the family history *Bowen's Court* (1942). One of the few novels to draw directly on her experiences in Ireland is *The Last September* (1931), which focuses on a country house during the Irish uprisings of 1920. Bowen's first publication was a collection of short stories, *Encounters* (1923), followed by several other volumes of stories, including *Ann Lee's* (1926), *Joining Charles* (1929) and *Look at all the Roses* (1941). *Collected Stories* appeared in 1980. Her first novel, *The Hotel* (1927), is a comedy of manners, as is *Friends and Relations* (1931), and much of her fiction depicts, often satirically, the social life of the upper middle classes. Further characteristics of Bowen's fiction include her attention to setting and sense of place, and her interest in the destabilizing aspects of love.
In 1935 Bowen moved to Clarence Terrace, London, and became a prominent figure in London literary circles. She became a close friend of ▷Virginia Woolf and ▷Iris Murdoch, and the tone of her subsequent concern with women's psychology, as in ▷*The Death of the Heart* (1938), as well as the reflection of this concern in formal patterning and structure, shows the influence of Woolf. Themes of innocence and infatuation yoke together Bowen's novels of the 1930s, beginning with *To the North* (1932) and culminating in *The Death of the Heart*. ▷*The Heat of the Day* (1949) and many of Bowen's short stories have confirmed her reputation as one of the leading writers depicting World War II.
Bib: Blodgett, H., *Patterns of Reality: Elizabeth Bowen's Novels*, Kenney, E., *Elizabeth Bowen*.

Bowering, Marilyn (born 1949)
Canadian poet and novelist. Born in Winnipeg, she grew up in Victoria, British Columbia, where she attended university; she has lived and worked in various countries, and now teaches Creative Writing at the University of Victoria. Her books of poetry include *The Liberation of Newfoundland* (1973), *One Who Became Lost* (1976), *The Killing Room* (1977), *Sleeping with Lambs* (1980), *Giving Back Diamonds* (1982) *The Sunday Before Winter* (1984), *Grandfather was a Soldier* (1986), *Winter Harbour* (1987), and *Anyone Can See I Love You* (1987). Her poetry is notable for a subtle but earthy magnetism, and its utilization of Canadian west-coast, including Native American, content. With David Day, she edited *Many Voices:*

Contemporary Indian Poetry (1977). Her first work of fiction, *The Visitors Have All Returned* (1979), is not well-known, but she received a great deal of attention for *To All Appearances a Lady* (1989), which is a superb historiographical novel of Victoria. She lives in Sooke, British Columbia.

Bowers, Bathsheba (c 1672–1718)
North American spiritual autobiographer. The third of Elizabeth Dunster and Benanuel Bowers's twelve children, she was born around 1672 in Charlestown, Massachusetts. Persecuted by the Puritans, her Quaker parents remained in Massachusetts to confront their enemies but sent their daughters to the safety of Quaker Philadelphia. A devout woman who felt the calling to public preaching and authorship, she chose not to marry, but rather to live alone and to publish her writings. ▷*An Alarm Sounded* (1709) is her only extant publication, but it is notable for her challenge (even in the more tolerant society of Quakers) to personal and religious limitations on women, especially in terms of the publication of their writings. She makes a heartfelt and powerful argument for the necessity of women giving voice to their beliefs and experiences.
▷Early North American Quaker women's writings

Bowlby, Rachel (born 1957)
British poststructuralist feminist and literary theorist. Bowlby is senior lecturer in English at Sussex University. Her first book *Just Looking: Consumer Culture in Dreiser, Gissing and Zola* (1985) analyzes the role played by department stores in constructing women as desiring ▷subjects in the late 19th century. Her main thesis is that consumer culture in patriarchal society constitutes women as victims of an ideal image of femininity, whose fulfilment is endlessly deferred by the constantly changing requirements of fashion culture. Bowlby is author of *Virginia Woolf: Feminist Destinations* (1988) and co-translator with Geoff Bennington of Jacques Derrida's *Of Spirit: Heidegger and the Question* (1989) (▷Deconstruction).

Bowne, Eliza Southgate (1783–1809)
North American letter-writer. She belonged to one of the wealthiest families in Maine. Her parents, Mary King and Robert Southgate, emphasized education for their daughters as well as sons, and she attended ▷Susanna Haswell Rowson's boarding school. Married to Walter Bowne in 1803, she gave birth to two children before her health began to fail. In 1809 she sailed for South Carolina to seek a more healthful climate, but she died on 20 February from lingering complications after her second childbirth. She was a prolific correspondent, and her letters to family and friends detail the day-to-day existence of a North American upper-class young woman at the end of the 18th century. Independent in mind and spirit, she voiced her opinions on marriage, education and political

events of the day. Perhaps no topic so occupied her early years as the vital question of women and marriage: 'I may be censured', she wrote 'for declaring it as my opinion that no one woman in a hundred married for love'; but in her own case, she asserted, 'I do not esteem marriage absolutely essential to happiness', and she refused to marry until she discovered a match of 'equal affection'. Her letters are collected in ▷*A Girl's Life Eighty Years Ago* (1888), a remarkable record of a highly intelligent and opinionated woman's triumph over societal expectations.
▷Early North American letters

Boyd, Elizabeth (fl 1727–1745)
English bookseller and poet, whose poem *Variety* (1726) praises contemporary women writers. She also wrote a prose romance and published it by subscription – *The Happy-Unfortunate* (1732). It was reissued in 1737 using its subtitle, *The Female Page*, and the money raised from this enabled her to set up as a bookseller. She went on writing, and published her own work, including *The Humorous Miscellany* (1733), *Don Sandro, or the Student's Whim* (1739) and an ephemeral periodical – *The Snail, or the Lady's Lucubrations* (1745). In 'On the Death of an Infant of five Days old' she wrote, 'Oh! could the stern-souled sex but know the pain, / Or the soft mother's agonies sustain, / . . . [would] the shocked father tear for tear return'.

Boye, Karin (1900–1941)
Swedish lyric poet and prose writer. She was brought up in comfortable conditions, her father being an engineer. Even as a young girl and student, she began to write and participate in cultural debates, at first from a religious standpoint, later from a radical political view. She became a member of the radical left-wing student's cultural organization Clarté. She was very interested in ▷psychoanalysis, and from 1932–1933 she consulted a psychoanalyst in Berlin. She suffered from serious depression, and in 1941 she committed suicide.

In spite of her depression she was a very lively teacher, contributed to many journals and was, from her lyrical début in 1922 with *Moln* (*Clouds*), seen as an important writer. *Gömda Land* (1924) (*Hidden Lands*) and *Härdarne* (1927) (*The Hearths*) may now be considered youthful works, whereas in *För trädets skull* (1935) (*For the Sake of the Tree*) she breaks through with a new symbolic and tragic poetry, very much influenced by her interests in psychoanalysis.

She was also a prose writer. The novels *Astarte* (1931), *Merit vakner* (1933) (*The Awakening of Merit*) and *För lite* (1936) (*Too Little*) were all praised, but her most important works of fiction are the autobiographical novel *Kris* (1934) and the science fiction novel *Kallocain* (1940).

Karin Boye's works are written in a symbolic language, confessional in tone, and containing an underlying conflict between the spontaneous enjoyment of life and the restrictions of religious moral standards. Her poetry has a deep rhythm and musical beauty.

Boy-Ed, Ida (1852–1928)

German novelist and biographer. Well-educated and widely travelled, she married a Hanseatic businessman who initially disapproved of her literary activity. In rebellion against him, she spent a year on her own in Berlin, but then returned to her family and became a successful writer of village stories and family sagas. She also wrote biographies of famous women, such as ▷Germaine de Staël and Charlotte von Stein, the inspiration behind many of Goethe's works.

Boy in the Bush, The (1924)

Australian novel by ▷Mollie Skinner, written in collaboration with D.H. Lawrence. It concerns the adventures of a young English migrant, Jack Grant, in the outback of Western Australia in the 1880s. Written by Mollie Skinner under the title *The House of Ellis*, it was rewritten by Lawrence, who met Skinner in Australia in 1922. According to Lawrence, 'the only thing was to write it all out again, following your MS almost exactly, but giving a unity, a rhythm, and a little more psychic development than you have done'. Accounts of the collaboration are given in the autobiographies of Frieda Lawrence and Mollie Skinner, *Not I, but the Wind* (1935) and *The Fifth Sparrow* (1972) respectively. *The Boy in the Bush* was adapted for ABC Television in 1984.

Boylan, Clare (born 1948)

Irish short story writer and novelist. She was born and grew up in Dublin, and now lives in County Wicklow. Originally a journalist, she worked for some time on the *Irish Press*, and was later editor of *Image* magazine, but now devotes her time fully to her writing. *Nail on the Head*, a collection of short stories, appeared in 1983, and was followed by three novels, *Holy Pictures* (1983), *Last Resorts* (1984) and *Black Baby* (1986), and a further collection of short stories, *Concerning Virgins* (1989).

Boyle, Kay (born 1902)

US short story writer, novelist, essayist and poet. Boyle was born in St Paul, Minnesota, in a well-to-do family. From 1923 to 1941 she lived mostly in France. She has worked since as a political activist for civil rights and against the Vietnam War. As a writer Boyle assumes moral responsibility for every act of oppression: in ▷*Monday Night* (1938) she depicts the human spirit in conflict with oppressive forces.

She explores also the human need for love in distressing situations. *Gentlemen, I Address You Privately* (1933) shows how the perversion of love results in social maladjustment. The novels written during World War II emphasize the individual's commitment to humanity. In *Primer for Combat* (1942) and *Avalanche* (1944) the characters find love through their identification

with humanity. Boyle's characters demonstrate her commitment to democracy and liberalism.

Other works include: *Wedding Day and Other Stories* (1930), *Plagued by Nightingale* (1931), *Year Before Last* (1932), *My Next Bride* (1934), *Death of a Man* (1936), *A Frenchman Must Die* (1946), *1939, a Novel* (1948), *His Human Majesty* (1948), *The Seagull on the Step* (1955), *Generation Without Farewell* (1960), *The Long Walk at San Francisco State and Other Essays* (1970) and *The Underground Woman* (1975).

Brabant, Marie de (1530/1540–1600/1610)

French poet. The daughter of Jean de Brabant, she married Claude de Tourotte. Marie de Brabant translated 'Le Cantique des cantiques' ('The Song of Songs') in verse, which was published in 1602 together with her *Annonces de l'esprit de l'âme fidèle* (*Declaration of the Spirit of the Faithful Soul*). Worthy of particular note is the *Epître aux Bombancières* (*Letter to the Carousing Women*), a virulent condemnation of various types of women, such as *bourgeoises* and coquettes, which nevertheless has a sensuality all of its own.
Bib: Wilwerth, E., *Visages de la littérature féminine*.

Brachmann, Karoline Louise (1777–1822)

German poet. She was a friend of both the romantic poet Novalis (1772–1801) and the dramatist Friedrich Schiller (1759–1805), who published her first poems. A late exponent of German classicism, she explored mainly mythological themes, using traditional and sometimes Hellenic poetic forms. In spite of her prolific output, she struggled in vain to justify and support herself as a writer, and finally committed suicide.

Braddon, Mary Elizabeth (1835–1915)

British writer, the author of over 70 novels, twenty of which were written between 1861 and 1871. She was born in London and brought up by her mother, who left her husband when Mary was three. In 1856 Braddon began writing in order to support the family, the impulse also behind her taking to the stage in 1857 under the name Mary Seyton. She met the publisher John Maxwell whose wife was in an asylum, in 1860, and lived with him until they were able to marry in 1874. Her writing helped to support the five children of Maxwell's first marriage and the six from her own (one of whom died as a baby). Her fourth novel, ▷*Lady Audley's Secret* (1862), was a sensational bestseller, a melodramatic, lurid tale of criminality and sexual passion which shocked readers by representing its deviant heroine as an angelic-looking blonde. ▷Margaret Oliphant described Braddon as 'the inventor of the fair-haired demon of modern fiction'. Apart from prolific novel-writing, Braddon also wrote nine plays and edited several London magazines including *Belgravia* (1866) and *The Mistletoe Bough* (1878–92).

▷Drama (19th-century Britain); Ghost stories; Sensation and sensational
Bib: Wolff, R.L., *The Sensational Victorian: the Life*

and Fiction of Braddon*; Hughes, W., *The Maniac in the Cellar: Sensation Novels of the 1860's.*

Bradford, Barbara Taylor (born 1933)

British novelist. Born in Leeds, Bradford worked as a journalist in Yorkshire and London until she moved to New York with her husband. Bradford writes romantic fiction about apparently autonomous, successful heroines. She published her first hugely popular novel, *A Woman of Substance*, in 1979, a dynastic saga about a rich, powerful business woman, Emma Harte. Her other novels are *The Voice of the Heart* (1983), *Hold the Dream* (1986), *Act of Will* (1986), *To Be the Best* (1988) and *The Women in his Life* (1990), which marks a break with Bradford's usual formula by making a man the centre of the novel, and *Remember* (1991). Several of her works have been serialized for television.

Bradford, Mistress ▷'Praier that Maister Bradfords Mother Said'

Bradley, Katherine ▷Field, Michael

Bradley, Marion Zimmer (born 1930)

US novelist. Born in Albany, New York, Bradley graduated from Hardin-Simmons College in 1964. Her science fiction novels focus on the struggle between opposing forces. In the 'Darkover' series, a technological culture conflicts with an agrarian one; Bradley envisions survival through the complementary use of knowledge from both cultures. Similarly, in *Hunters of the Red Moon* (1973) the characters cannot survive alone, only by working together. In *The Shattered Chain* (1976) and *The Rains of Isis* (1978) Bradley emphasizes women's equality to men.

Her fantasy novels re-imagine classical legends from a woman's point of view. The bestselling *The Mists of Avalon* (1982) retells the story of King Arthur, recovering the role of the Celtic religion and the Great Mother in ancient Britain.

Other works include: *The Door Through Space* (1961), *The Sword of Aldones* (1962), *The Planet Savers* (1962), *Star of Danger* (1965), *Endless Voyage* (1975), *The Survivors* (1979), *The Colors of Space* (1983), *The Catchtrap* (1984), *City of Sorcery* (1984), *The Heritage Hasture* (1984), *House Between the Worlds* (1984), *The Inheritor* (1984), *The Bloody Sun* (1985), *Warrior Woman* (1985), *Night's Daughter* (1985), *Lythande* (1986), *Survey Ship* (1986), *The Fall of Atlantis* (1987), *The Firebrand* (1987), *The Other Side of the Mirror* (1987), *Dark Satanic* (1988), *Spells of Wonder* (1989), *Star of Danger* (1988) and *The World Wreckers* (1988).

Bradshaw, Máire (born 1943)

Irish poet. Born and educated in Limerick, she now lives in Cork. Founder of the Cork Women's Poetry Circle, she was instrumental in the publication in 1986 of the Circle's first collection, *The Box Under the Bed*, the title of one of her poems. She has since published two collections of her own, *Instinct* (1988) and *Eurydice* (1991), while continuing to work with the Circle.

▷Community writing (20th-century Ireland)

Bradstreet, Anne Dudley (1612–1672)

Bradstreet is 17th-century North America's most renowned woman poet. Born in Northampton, England, to Dorothy Yorke and Thomas Dudley, she arrived in the New World in 1630, two years after her marriage to Simon Bradstreet. When her poetry was taken without her permission by her brother-in-law and published in England under the title of ▷*The Tenth Muse Lately Sprung up in America*, she became the first colonist to have a volume of poetry published. Although she maintained an outer appearance of adhering to Puritan conventions, her poetry (most notably, 'Contemplations') both works within English and biblical traditions and extends those traditions in the direction of 19th-century romanticism. Her poems are equally notable for the manner in which she subverts traditional attitudes about women's capabilities and social roles. She also wrote a series of 'Meditations' that convey to her children her own religious struggles and convictions. Renowned in her own time but ever concerned with revising and improving her literary talents, she died on 16 September 1672 in Andover, Massachusetts.

Braga, Maria Ondina (born 1932)

Portuguese novelist and short story writer. Born in the northern town of Braga, she was educated in Paris and London. She taught for several years in Goa, Macao and Beijing, and many of her early stories, such as the ones in *A China Fica ao Lado* (1968) (*China Is at the Side*), are based on her experiences in the Far East. In addition to stories, she has written a fictional autobiography, *Estátua de Sal* (1969) (*Statue of Salt*), and *A Personagem* (1978) (*The Character*), which is in the form of a woman's diary. She also authored a collection of biographical accounts of canonical women writers, entitled *Mulheres Escritoras* (1980). Her novella *A Casa Suspensa* (1982) (*The Suspended House*) is written in the fantastic mode.

Brand, Dionne (born 1953)

Caribbean poet and activist who was born and educated in Trinidad and left to attend the University of Toronto in Canada; where she graduated with a BA in English and Philosophy in 1975. She worked briefly as an information/communications co-ordinator in Grenada during 1983 until the USA's invasion, when she returned to Canada. She has become well known as a community activist and a 'black socialist and feminist poet' in Canada.

Her poetry reveals a concern to document the history of both her personal and the collective experience of life in the Caribbean and Canada, exploring themes of alienation, domination, racism and sexism. Her published poetry includes *Fore Day Morning* (1978), *Earth Magic* (1980), *Primitive Offensive* (1982), *Winter Epigrams and Epigrams to*

Ernesto Cardenal in Defence of Claudia (1983) and *Chronicles of the Hostile Sun* (1984).

There is little critical study of her work, although a chapter in ▷*Fifty Caribbean Writers* examines her poetry in some detail.

Brand, Mona (born 1915)
Australian poet, dramatist and non-fiction writer. Brand travelled and worked in Europe from 1948 to 1954, and lived in Hanoi from 1956 to 1957. Her plays reflect her socialist politics, and from 1948 onwards were mainly presented by Sydney's left-wing ▷New Theatre. Brand has published four volumes of poetry: *Wheel and Bobbin* (1938), *Silver Singing* (1940), *Lass in Love* (1946) and *Daughters of Vietnam, Hanoi* (1958), as well as numerous plays (not all have been published) and a number of non-fiction works. She has won several awards, the most important being first prize in the New South Wales Arts Council Drama Festival 1968 for *Our 'Dear' Relation*.

Brandão, Fiama Hasse Pais (born 1938)
Portuguese poet and dramatist. At the University of Lisbon, she specialized in German philology. Her first volume of poems, *Em Cada Pedra um Vôo Imóvel* (*In Each Stone an Immobile Flight*), appeared in 1957, and she has published several collections since that time. Brandão was a member of *Poesia 61*, a movement of the 1960s opposed to the neo-realist tendency that had dominated Portuguese literature from the early 1940s. Unlike most of the authors in this group, however, Brandão wrote on political themes. Her volume of plays, entitled *A Campanha (The Campaign), O Golpe de Estado (The Coup d'Etat), Diálogo dos Pastores (Shepherds' Dialogue), Auto de Família (Play of the Family)* (1965), was banned by the Salazar government shortly after publication. Today Brandão is regarded as one of the country's major poets.

Brandt, Di
Diana Brandt was born in the Mennonite community of Winkler and now lives in Winnipeg, Manitoba. A startlingly talented young Canadian poet, her work is an articulate expression of struggle against the ▷patriarchal impositions of family, community and culture. Her first book of poetry, *questions I asked my mother* (1987) won the Gerald Lampert Memorial Award; her second book, *Agnes in the Sky*, was published in 1990.

Brannon, Carmen (1899–1974)
Salvadoran poet. The daughter of an Irish father and a *criollo* (▷*criollismo*), she used the pseudonym Claudia Lars. Along with writing, she worked as a diplomat. She is considered to be one of the most representative writers of Central America. Her first book, *Estrellas en el pozo* (1934) (*Stars in the Well*), one of her major works, shows anti-symbolist tendencies, as in the Mexican González Martínez's sonnet '*Tuércele el cuello al cisne de engañoso plumaje*' ('Wiring the neck of the swan with deceitful plumage'). In this book, and in her second, *Romances de norte y sur* (1946)

(*Ballads of North and South*), she was influenced by García Lorca (1899–1936), but she later found her own authentic style, as evidenced by *Donde llegan los pasos* (1953) (*Where The Steps Go To*), which has an atmosphere of music and magic.

Works: *Canción de vidrio* (1942) (*Glass Song*); *Sonetos* (1947) (*Sonnets*); *Escuela de pájaros* (1955) (*Bird School*); *Tierra de infancia* (1958) (*Land of Childhood*); *Fábula de una verdad* (1959) (*Tale of a Truth*); *Canciones* (1960) (*Songs*); *Girasol* (1962) (*Sunflower*); *Sobre el ángel y el hombre* (1962) (*On the Angel and the Man*), and *Poesía última* (1975) (*Recent Poetry*).

Brantenberg, Gerd (born 1941)
Norwegian prose writer. Brantenberg grew up in Frederiksstad, went to college, and taught history and English in secondary schools. She was an active member of the new women's movement from the early 1970s, and her literary work is chiefly concerned with the development of modern feminism, for example, the feminist science-fiction novel *Egalias døtre* (1977) (*Daughters of Egalia*). In the earlier novel *Opp alle jordens homofile* (1973) (*Arise all Gays of the World*) problems of and the emancipation of the gay community are discussed (see also *Sangen om St Croix*, 1979, *The Song of St Croix*). Brantenberg writes in *bokmål* and dialect. She is one of the few Scandinavian radical feminist writers.

Brasileira Augusta, Madame ▷Floresta, Nísia

Brasileira, Floresta Augusta ▷Floresta, Nísia

Brasileira, Uma ▷Reis, Maria Firmina dos

Braun, Lily (1865–1916)
German writer. The daughter of an itinerant military family, her literary career began when she moved to Berlin and published her grandmother's memoirs, *Aus Goethes Freundeskreis* (1892) (*From Goethe's Circle of Friends*). She was introduced to socialist thought and feminism by the philosopher Gizycki (died 1895), whom she married in 1893. After his death she married the left-wing politician Heinrich Braun (1854–1927). She continued to write widely on social and political issues, but remains best-known for her autobiography, *Memoiren einer Sozialistin* (1909–1911) (*Memoirs of a Socialist Woman*).

Braunschweig-Lüneburg, Elisabeth von (1519–1558)
German monarch, writer and poet. The daughter of Joachim I (1499–1535), the Catholic elector and prince of Brandenburg, she had been well-educated in true Renaissance fashion, and at the age of fifteen married Erich I of Braunschweig-Lüneburg, a man forty years her senior. After his death in 1540 she assumed power and, with her *Christliche Sendebrieff* (1545) (*Christian Epistle*), introduced her subjects to Protestantism. She wrote a guide to running the affairs of state for her son, instructions on marriage for her

daughter, and a book of consolation for widows. During the Wars of the Reformation she and her daughter were exiled by her Catholic son to Hanover, where, living in extreme poverty, she wrote religious poems and songs of consolation. When her son secretly married off his sister to a Catholic prince, Elisabeth von Braunschweig-Lüneburg began to lose her reason, and died soon afterwards.

Braunschweig-Lüneburg, Sibylle Ursula von (1629–1691)

German poet, novelist and translator. One of the most gifted of the children of Duke August the Younger of Braunschweig-Lüneburg, she had an excellent education due to the care of her stepmother, ▷Sophie Elisabeth von Braunschweig-Lüneburg. Avoiding marriage for as long as possible, Sibylle Ursula dedicated herself to her writing. A first, untitled, play of 1649 explores the ideas of feminine courtly virtue. Her *Geistliches Kleeblatt* (1655) (*Spiritual Clover-leaf*) is a statement of religious belief, while *Seuffzer* (*Sighs*) contains an inner autobiography spanning the years 1647–68. She was an accomplished translator of French plays and novels, but her most important work remains *Aramena* (5 vols., 1669–1673), the fragment of a baroque novel, later expanded by her brother, Anton Ulrich, together with her other sisters and brothers. She married at the age of thirty-four, and died during the birth of her fourth child.

Braunschweig-Lüneburg, Sophie Elisabeth von (1613–1676)

German composer, writer and promoter of courtly baroque art in Germany. Of aristocratic descent, at the age of twenty-two she married Duke August the Younger of Braunschweig-Lüneburg, a widower and father of four children. Because of her dedication to art and music she became known as the 'Juno' of Braunschweig-Lüneburg. She wrote educational songs for her stepchildren, and prayers and meditations on the Bible, as well as plays and librettos for the court theatre. She based her novel, *Die histori der Dorinde* (1641–1652) (*The Story of Dorinde*) on the French pastoral, *Astrée* (1607–1627) (*Astrea*) by Honoré D'Urfé (1567–1625), thus introducing her own compatriots to French courtly mores.

Bray, Anna Eliza (1790–1883)

English novelist. Born in Newington, Surrey, she married the artist Charles Alfred Stothard in 1818. Her first published work, *Letters Written During a Tour Through Normandy, Brittany and Other Parts of France* appeared in 1820. This volume recorded travels with her husband, who died in an accident in 1821. Anna married the Rev. Edward Bray in 1822, and from 1826 to 1874 published fourteen novels, as well as historical biographies and descriptive sketches. In fiction, she favoured historical ▷romances set in the English countryside. These were extremely popular in their day, though some literary critics

considered them out of date. She is best-known for her series of letters to Robert Southey, *A Description of that Part of Devonshire Bordering on the Tamar and the Tary* (1836). Subjects of her biographies include Handel (1857) and Joan of Arc (1874). She also wrote a non-fictional work for children, *A Peep at the Pixies, or, Legends of the West* (1854).

▷Children's literature (19th-century Britain)

Break of Day (1961)

Translation of *La Naissance du jour* (1928), novel by French writer ▷Colette. This novel is an example of the way Colette's writing occupies a border-zone between autobiography and fiction: the narrator is the writer 'Colette', who is spending the summer months on the Mediterranean coast, surrounded by a mixture of real and fictional characters, both animal and human. The climax of the novel is 'Colette's' renunciation of the passion of a much younger man, Vial, in favour of a new, more peaceful stage of existence. The mother figure, often associated with transcendence of heterosexual passion and closeness to nature in Colette's work, is present on two levels – firstly in the constant references to Colette's mother, Sido, and in the rewritten texts of her letters, and secondly, in the role 'Colette' herself plays in relation to Vial, and the young woman, Hélène, who is in love with him. The opening description of Sido's wrinkled face bent over the pink cactus which is about to flower is typical of the novel's poetic qualities, of the association of femininity with growth and regeneration, and more generally of Colette's use of nature images to describe human characters and relationships.

Breed of Women, A (1979)

Novel by New Zealand writer ▷Fiona Kidman. *A Breed of Women* has been described as the 'first New Zealand novel which set out quite consciously to say something specific about the lives and experiences of women of our generation' (S. Kedgeley, *Our Own Country*, 1989). The novel documents Harriet Wallace's life from puritanical and racist small-town New Zealand to women's liberation in late-1960s Wellington, a journey towards knowledge of various kinds and a political view of the position of women. Kidman said in an interview that *A Breed of Women* was the first consciously feminist New Zealand novel, 'the first one which consciously set out to right the wrongs, to address women's lives in the sense that there were problems which had to be worked through'. Although *A Breed of Women* became a bestseller it was attacked by critics and called a 'thinking woman's Mills and Boon'; however, as Kidman has pointed out recently, *A Breed of Women* has been credited with turning the tide for women writers in New Zealand, heralding the beginning of sustained interest in publishing writing by women.

Breeze, Jean Binta (born 1956)
Caribbean Dub poet and performer (Dub is a
form of rhythmic performance poetry, sometimes
accompanied by music). She was born into a rural
▷Jamaican community, and began writing poetry
at the age of ten. Educated in Jamaica, she
worked as a teacher from 1973 to 1977 and with
the Jamaica Cultural Development Commission.
In 1978 she entered the Jamaica School of
Drama, where she first met the Dub poets Oku
Onuora and Michael Smith. The first woman to
write and perform Dub poetry, she performed at
Reggae Sunsplash in 1983. In 1985 she moved to
London, where she now lives and works.

Her first published poetry, *Answers* (1982) was
followed a recording of 'Slip' (1982). Recordings
of her poems 'To Plant' and 'Aid travels with a
bomb' were included in the Dub poetry, album,
Word Soun' 'Ave Power. Reggae Poetry (1985).

See Christian Habekost *Dub Poetry: 19 Poets
from England and Jamaica* (1986) and Carolyn
Cooper, 'Words Unbroken By the Beat: The
Performance Poetry of Jean Binta Breeze and
Mikey Smith', Wasifiri, No. 11 (1990).

Bremer, Fredrika (1801–1865)
Swedish prose writer. She was born near Åbo in
Finland. Her father was wealthy and moved to
Stockholm in 1804. The children's upbringing
was very severe and disciplinary. Fredrika was
rebellious and clumsy. In 1821, the family
travelled in Europe, and Fredrika fell ill. For years
she was depressed and anxious. She longed for
some serious work.

In 1828, she anonymously published Part 1 of
Teckningar utur Hvardagslifvet (*Scenes from Everyday
Life*), which became a success. She wrote two
more parts, and in 1831 she received a Gold
Medal from the Swedish Academy. In the same
year she befriended a minister, but for three years
she hesitated, and he married another woman.
However, during those years she learned enough
from him to realize that she wanted to write, not
to be married. During the 1830s she wrote a
number of novels about family life and womens'
circumstances, eg *Presidentens Döttrar* (1834) (*The
President's Daughters*), *Grannarna* (1837) (*The
Neighbours*) and *Hemmet* (1839) (*The Home*).

In the 1840s she became even more engaged in
the women's question (▷woman question), eg *En
Dagbok* (1843) (*A Diary*). Her works were
translated into English, and she travelled to the
USA. In 1856, she wrote her most famous novel
▷*Hertha*, which expressed her attitude towards
the role of women in Sweden, and generated
much discussion that finally led to economic and
political reforms for women.

Stylistically, Bremer went from ▷romanticism
in her early works to ▷realism in her later novels.
She is considered the founder of the Swedish
novel.

Brent of Bin Bin ▷Franklin, Miles

Brésilienne, Une ▷Floresta, Nísia

Bretas, Ana Lins dos Guimarães Peixoto
▷Coralina, Cora

Brewster, Elizabeth (born 1922)
Canadian poet and fiction writer, born in
Chipman, New Brunswick. She attended the
University of New Brunswick, Radcliffe College,
and King's College, London, as well as the
University of Toronto Library School and Indiana
University. She worked as a librarian until 1972,
when she joined the English department at the
University of Saskatchewan. *East Coast*, her first
book of poetry, appeared in 1951; *Lillooet* (1954)
won the E.J. Pratt Medal. Her poetry speaks to
the pull between memory and detachment,
between nostalgia for a lost childhood and
acceptance of an uneventful and unvarnished
actuality. Her subsequent poetry books include:
Roads and Other Poems (1957), *Passage of Summer:
Selected Poems* (1969), *Sunrise North* (1972), *In
Search of Eros* (1974), *Sometimes I Think of Moving*
(1977), *The Way Home* (1982), *Selected Poems of
Elizabeth Brewster, 1944–1977* (1985), and
Entertaining Angels (1988). She is also the author
of three short story collections: *It's Easy to Fall on
the Ice* (1977), *A House Full of Women* (1983) and
Visitations (1987). Her novels, *The Sisters* (1974)
and *Junction* (1983), are structured, like her
stories, on the process of ordering and
reminiscence, with a tangy detail to every gesture
and character appraisal. Her work inscribes the
haunted grace and sly self-deprecation of
women's steadily uneventful but universal lives.
Bib: Pearce, J., in *Twelve Voices*.

Brewster, Martha Wadsworth (fl 1725–1757)
North American poet. In 1757 she published a
thirty-five-page collection of her poetry, ▷*Poems
on Divers Subjects*, which includes works written in
the 1740s and 1750s. Although few biographical
details are known about Brewster, her poetry
reveals that she and her husband Oliver had at
least one daughter, Ruby Brewster Bliss, to whom
she addressed several poems. A pious woman, she
wrote a number of poems on religious themes; but
she was also concerned with the political issues of
the day and with women's position in society.
Describing herself as 'a Female Bard', she
integrated her day-to-day life into many of her
poems.

Briche, Adélaïde-Edmée Prévost de la (1755–1844)
French memoir and travel writer. Born in Nancy
to a wealthy bourgeois family, she was married in
1780, and widowed at the age of thirty. She
maintained contacts with the world of the
philosophes, and her salon at the Hotel Saint-
Florent was popular throughout its fifty-year
existence. She travelled extensively in Switzerland,
northern Italy, England and Scotland. Her travel
memoirs, *Les Voyages en Suisse de Mme de la Briche
1785–1832* (*Swiss Travels of Mme de la Briche
1785–1832*), were edited by P. de Zurich in 1935.
Bib: De Zurich, P., *Une femme heureuse*.

Bride Price, The (1976)

A novel by Nigerian writer ▷Buchi Emecheta. On her father's death, Aku-nna's mother is inherited by her husband's brother, and the family go to live with him in the village. According to custom, Aku-nna will be married to someone of her uncle's choosing. Instead, she flouts tradition, not only by running away with the lover of her choice, but by choosing a man from a slave family. The title refers to the belief that failure to pay the ▷bride price will lead to the death of the woman in childbirth, and Aku-nna pays this penalty. Her fate demonstrates the ways in which women are restricted by tradition, and the price exacted for nonconformity.

▷Slavery (West Africa)

Bride price (West Africa)

In some West African societies, notably that of the Igbo of eastern Nigeria, bride price is an important part of the ritual of transition of a woman leaving her father's home to join another family group in marriage. Traditionally, it signified the value attached to the woman, and the right of the family to be compensated for her loss. However, it also suggests that a woman's worth can be computed in material terms, and is therefore open to abuse.

▷*Bride Price, The*

Bridge of Beyond, The (1974)

Translation by Barbara Bray of the novel by the Guadeloupean writer ▷Simone Schwarz-Bart, *Pluie et Vent sur Télumée Miracle* (1972). The author has declared that she wrote *Pluie et Vent* to preserve a certain way of life for future generations no longer in contact with the past of their island. The novel is the narrative of Télumée, an old woman who, after miraculously surviving with dignity the metaphorical winds and rains in the forsaken area around the 'Bridge of Beyond' where slavery has not yet disappeared, affirms her desire to relive her life in the same manner. Beginning with a presentation of Télumée's female lineage, Schwarz-Bart presents Télumée's life as a reflection of those of the Lougandor women, Télumée's clan, who accept their destiny but refuse to be bowed by it. In particular, she depicts Télumée's life as a mirror image and continuation of that of her grandmother. Even the best of the male characters in the novel seem vulnerable and inadequate in comparison to these women, symbols of strength and resistance. An immensely popular novel, which is remarkable for its style and poetry, *The Bridge of Beyond* has been misjudged as a 'folk' narrative. The innovative aesthetic practice which Schwarz-Bart develops here celebrates the Antilles, retrieving the island of Guadeloupe as a site of self-discovery, recovering family and island history as a source of nourishment and strength, and creating a creolized language to convey a Creole world-view which incorporates a magical realm that lies beyond empirical reality. The poetry of presence and completeness which she articulates here contrasts with the absence and state of fragmentation which characterize the novels of many of her contemporaries.

▷*Folie Antillaise*

Bridger, Bub (born 1924)

New Zealand poet and short story writer. Born in Napier, Bub Bridger (also known as Ngati Kahungunu) has lived most of her life in Wellington. Bridger began writing in her fifties while attending writers' workshops. Since then she has published occasional stories, appeared in a number of anthologies, and published a collection of poems, *Up Here on the Hill* (1989). Bridger's stories do not focus on political or race questions as do those of other ▷Maori writers, but explore unconventional female characters and satirize social customs.

Bridget of Sweden: English translations

Saint whose works were translated into English. St Bridget, her *Revelations*, and the *O's* (the fifteen meditations on the passion of Christ attributed to her), rapidly achieved popularity in England. There are seven manuscripts from 15th-century England containing English translations of the *Revelations*, and such translations are mentioned in several wills of the 15th century. There is also a mid-15th-century Welsh translation of the fifteen prayers.

▷Birgitta av Vadstena; Kempe, Margery.

Bib: Barratt, Alexandra, *Women's Writing in Middle English*; Cumming, William Patterson, *The Revelations of Saint Birgitta*; Ellis, Roger (ed.) *Revelations* (Early English text society 291); Evans, D. Simon, *Medieval Religious Literature: Writers of Wales*.

Bright and Fiery Troop: Australian Women Writers of the Nineteenth Century, A (1988)

This collection, edited by Debra Adelaide, contains essays on the following: 19th-century letters and diaries, ▷Annie Baxter and her journal, 19th-century women poets, ▷Anna Maria Bunn and ▷Mary Vidal, ▷Louisa Atkinson, ▷Caroline Woolmer Leakey, ▷Catherine Helen Spence, ▷Mary Fortune ('Waif Wander'), ▷Ada Cambridge, ▷Catherine Martin, ▷Jessie Couvreur ('Tasma'), ▷Mary Gaunt, ▷Rosa Praed, ▷Louisa Lawson, and ▷Marie Pitt.

Brinsmead, Hesba (born 1922)

Australian novelist. Brinsmead is a prolific writer, producing novels for adolescents. *Pastures of the Blue Crane* (1964) won the Mary Gilmore Award and the Children's Book of the Year Award for 1965, and was adapted for television in 1971. *Longtime Passing* also won the Children's Book of the Year Award in 1972. Her books have been translated into several other languages.

▷Children's literature (Australia)

Brise du jour, La (1977) (Dawn Breeze)

Novel by the Cameroonian journalist, Lydie Dooh-Bunya. It traces the emotional and psychological development of Zinnie, who at the age of ten falls in love with her cousin, Pat. Though her love is all-consuming, it is not reciprocated, and he marries someone else. The focus remains throughout on Zinnie's internal world, conveyed through monologues. In the end, she is forced to draw on her own strength to come to terms with reality.

▷Journalism (West Africa)

Brittain, Vera (1893–1970)

English novelist, biographer, journalist and poet. Born in Newcastle under Lyme into a prosperous paper-manufacturing family, she was educated at St Monica's School, Surrey, and, despite parental opposition, also at Somerville College, Oxford. Brittain left Somerville temporarily in 1915 to become a Voluntary Aid Detachment nurse following the death of her fiancé, Roland Leighton, killed in action during World War I. In 1925 Brittain married the political philosopher George Catlin, who spent a great amount of time in the United States while Brittain remained in England with her close friend ▷Winifred Holtby. She is the mother of Shirley Williams, who became a prominent politician.

Brittain's childhood years, her struggle for education, the early influence of ▷Olive Schreiner and in particular her wartime experiences are detailed in her most famous book, ▷Testament of Youth (1933), which became an instant bestseller. The second volume of her autobiographical trilogy, Testament of Friendship (1940), forms a tribute to Winifred Holtby, who died in 1935, and deals with a friendship founded on their shared commitment to feminist and pacifist concerns. The further development of these convictions is outlined in the final volume, Testament of Experience (1957), which focuses on the period 1925–1950. Other writings on women include: Lady into Woman: A History of Women from Victoria to Elizabeth II (1953), Radclyffe Hall: A Case of Obscenity? (1968) and Women's Work in Modern England (1928). Brittain's novels are also largely autobiographical. Her first novel, The Dark Tide (1923), is an account of life in Oxford following World War I, and Born 1925 (1948) is a family saga dealing with the responses of two generations to World War II. Poems of the War and After was published in 1934, and the Selected Letters of Winifred Holtby and Vera Brittain in 1960. Her diaries between 1913 and 1917 have been published as Chronicle of Youth (1981).

▷Hall, Radclyffe; West, Rebecca

Bib: Bailey, H., Vera Brittain: The Story of the Woman Who Wrote Testament of Youth.

Brlič-Mažuranić, Ivana (1874–1938)

Croatian children's writer. She was the first woman member of the Yugoslav Academy of Science and Arts. She married at the age of eighteen, ten years before her first work was published. The only library in the small town where she lived was that of her husband, and this was her sole intellectual stimulus. She wrote exclusively for children, and saw her role as stimulating the imaginations of future generations, who might then produce something worthwhile.

Three of her most important works are children's classics and are still read, including a historical novel, a collection of fairy tales and Čudnovate zgode šegrta Hlapića (1913) (The Strange Adventures of Apprentice Hlapić), a miniature picaresque novel about the development of a bright and hard-working boy who overcomes many obstacles on the way to growing up. She has been described as the 'Croatian Hans Andersen', and her stories were an important source of solace to many young people during World War I. They are still a formative influence on children today.

Broad Arrow: Being Passages from the History of Maida Gwynnham, a Lifer, The (1859)

Australian novel by ▷Caroline Woolmer Leakey (Oliné Keese). The Broad Arrow is the first Australian convict novel, and the precursor of a number of more famous novels written by men dealing with convict experience. Its heroine, Maida Gwynnham, is both beautiful and strong-minded. She is transported to Van Dieman's Land (Tasmania) for a crime she did not commit, and steadfastly endures her imprisonment until death. Though melodramatic and frequently didactic, The Broad Arrow is a powerful novel which was extremely popular in 19th-century Australia and England.

Brodber, Erna (born 1936)

This Caribbean novelist, poet and dramatist was born in a village in ▷Jamaica. She wrote and published stories from an early age. Having graduated with a BA (Hons) from the University of the West Indies in 1963, she was awarded a scholarship for postgraduate study, and in 1967 won a Ford Foundation scholarship for study in the USA. A historian and respected sociologist, her literary career developed out of her academic writing. Her first novel, ▷Jane and Louisa Will Soon Come Home was originally conceived as a case study in abnormal psychology. She was awarded a prize in the Jamaican Festival 1975 for her short story 'Rosa'. Brodber's work documents the social history of Jamaica through the oral traditions, cultural life and survival patterns of the people. A Rastafarian, she works as a freelance journalist. She is the sister of ▷Velma Pollard.

Her published works include: Abandonment of Children in Jamaica (1974); A Study of Yards in the City of Kingston (1975); Perceptions of Caribbean Women: Towards a Documentation of Stereotypes (1982); Oral Sources and the Creation of a Social History in the Caribbean (1983), and the novels Jane and Louisa Will Soon Come Home and Myal (1988).

For a detailed bibliography and critical references see ▷Fifty Caribbean Writers.

Brøgger, Suzanne (born 1944)
Danish novelist and essayist. Brøgger had a very
unusual childhood, during which she learned that
she had to be an extraordinary person. She has
written about her childhood and her mother, who
often threatened to commit suicide. Above all, she
has written about personal life as a political
statement, and has created a masterpiece from her
life.

In 1973 she made her début with *Fri os fra
kærligheden* (*Deliver us from Love*), and this,
together with *Crème Fraîche* (1978) (*Fresh Cream*)
made her a public person, always involved in
cultural debates, always radical and different,
speaking for free love, and against the nuclear
family, from an aristocratic point of view.

Since 1980 she has changed course. Now she
speaks in favour of marriage (she has a husband,
and a daughter, born in 1984), asceticism and
discipline, and is as outspoken in the cultural
debate now as ever) (see *Kvælstof*, 1990, *Nitrogen*).

But she is not merely a polemicist. Her works
are a mixture of genres, from philosophy to essays
to fiction, always seemingly autobiographical,
eliminating the border between private and public
spheres. Writing for her is a way of life – of being
dynamic and Existentially in motion. Stagnation
seems like death. She is deeply influenced by
▷postmodern philosophers like Baudrillard, but
also by oriental Taoism. Widely translated, she
has gained the status of a new ▷Karen Blixen.

Brohon, Jacqueline-Aimée (1731–1778)
French novelist and essayist. Unknown in her own
lifetime, she was famous between 1790 and 1793,
when her works were adopted by a group of
Jacobin thinkers. A religious convert, she wrote an
early novel *Les Amants philosophes* (1755)
(*Philosopherers in Love*). There followed a
conventional book of religious devotion,
Instructions édifiantes (*Moral Teaching*), and the
more unusual *Réflexions édifiantes* (*Moral
Reflections*) both published after her lifetime, in
1791. In the second text, which records her
visions and prophecies, Brohon virulently attacks
the established Church, and sees herself as head
of a new sect of male and female expiatory victims
who would replace the corrupt clergy. The
mysticism and sentimental philosophy of this work
suggests the influence of Jean-Jacques Rousseau
(1712–1778) and has also led to a comparison
with Emmanuel Swedenborg (1688–1772). As late
as 1811 ▷Julie de Krudener, visiting Strasbourg,
found a group of women avidly reading the
Réflexions édifiantes.
Bib: Viatte, A., 'Une visionnaire au siècle des
Lumières', *Revue des Questions Historique*, XCVIII
(1923) pp. 336–44.

Brontë, Anne (1820–1849)
British novelist and poet, sister of ▷Charlotte,
▷Emily and Branwell Brontë. Anne was the
youngest of the family, and was educated largely
at home, though she briefly attended school at
Roe Head in 1836–7. She had more experience as

The Brontë sisters by P.B. Brontë

a ▷governess than either Charlotte or Emily,
working for the Ingham family at Blake Hall in
1839 and from 1841–45 for the Robinsons of
Thorp Green Hall. Branwell joined her there in
1843, but he was dismissed as a result of his
obsession with Mrs Robinson, and Anne followed
him home. ▷*Agnes Grey* (1847) is a semi-
autobiographical novel based on her experiences
as a governess. It was published under the
▷pseudonym Acton Bell, as were Anne's poems
in the 1846 collection, ▷*Poems by Currer, Ellis and
Acton Bell*. Her second novel, ▷*The Tenant of
Wildfell Hall*, was published in 1848. Her work is
not generally considered on a par with that of
Emily or Charlotte, yet it often contains vivid and
powerful descriptions. She died on a visit to
Scarborough in May 1849.
Bib: Gerin, W., *Anne Brontë: A Biography*.

Brontë, Charlotte (1816–1855)
British novelist. The third of five daughters
including ▷Anne and ▷Emily Brontë. After the
death of their mother in 1821, the children
(including Branwell, the only son) were looked
after by Elizabeth Branwell, their aunt. Charlotte
attended school at Cowan Bridge and later at Roe
Head (1831–32), returning to the latter as a
teacher (1835–38). She was ▷governess to the
Sidgwick family in 1839 and to the White family
in 1841. In 1842 she went with Emily to Brussels
to study languages, but had to return at the end of
the year, recalled by their aunt's death. Charlotte
returned to Brussels alone in 1843 and remained
there a year, forming a deep attachment to her
tutor M. Héger, who was fictionalized in both
▷*The Professor* (1857) and ▷*Villette* (1853). She
wrote a great deal as a child, inventing with
Branwell the imaginary world of ▷Angria. In
1845, according to her own account, she
'discovered' Emily's poetry and in 1846 a volume
of verse was published: ▷*Poems by Currer, Ellis*

and Acton Bell (▷pseudonyms of Charlotte, Emily and Anne). It sold only two copies, but Charlotte was undeterred. Her first novel, *The Professor*, written in 1846 was not published until 1857, after her death, but her second, ▷*Jane Eyre* (1847) was immediately successful. In 1848, both Branwell and Emily died, followed by Anne in 1849. Charlotte continued to write during this traumatic period, ▷*Shirley* appearing in 1849 and ▷*Villette* in 1853. In 1850 she met ▷Elizabeth Gaskell who became a great friend and wrote her biography (1857). She married A.B. Nicholls, her father's curate, in 1854, but died a few months later, during pregnancy. She was recognized as an extraordinarily powerful and talented writer in her day, though some critics accused her of being a 'strong-minded' woman and of writing 'coarse' novels. Brontë's bold depiction of the social and psychological situation of 19th-century women has generated much recent feminist commentary. **Bib:** Gaskell, E., *Life*; Gerin, W., *Charlotte Brontë: The Evolution of Genius*; Ratchford, F., *The Brontës' Web of Childhood*; ▷Gilbert, S. and ▷Gubar, S., *The Madwoman in the Attic*; Boumelha, P., *Charlotte Brontë*.

Brontë, Emily (1818–1848)

British novelist and poet, sister of ▷Charlotte, ▷Anne and Branwell Brontë. Emily lived most of her life in Haworth, Yorkshire. She briefly attended Cowan Bridge school (1824–25) and went to Roe Head in 1835, returning after a few months, suffering from homesickness. A short period spent working as a ▷governess at Law Hill and a brief excursion to Brussels with Charlotte in 1842 were the only other occasions on which she left home. With Anne, Emily created the imaginary world of ▷Gondal, and in many of her poems she adopts the personae of Gondal characters. Charlotte 'discovered' Emily's poetry in 1845, and ▷*Poems by Currer, Ellis, and Acton Bell* appeared in 1846. Her poetry has been overshadowed by ▷*Wuthering Heights* (1847), but she wrote many complex and interesting lyrics exploring personal identity and the poet's relationship to language and to the natural landscape. 'Loud without the wind was roaring', 'Ah! why, because the dazzling sun' and 'I am the only being whose doom' are some of her finest poetic achievements. Other lyrics such as 'O Thy Bright Eyes Must Answer Now' and 'I'll come when thou art saddest' represent a masculine muse figure with whom the poet establishes a dynamic relation. Emily Brontë's originality and power were recognized when *Wuthering Heights* appeared, and she has been extensively discussed ever since, though her work has at times taken second place beside the 'myth' of the Brontës.

▷Ballad (19th-century Britain)
Bib: Davies, S., *Emily Brontë: The Artist as Free Woman*; Smith, A. (ed.), *The Art of Emily Brontë*; Pykett, L., *Emily Brontë*.

Brooke, Charlotte (died 1793)

Irish translator and poet. She nursed her father, a dramatist, until he died in 1783. She contributed an anonymous ▷translation to *Historical Memoirs of Irish Bards* (1786), and published *Reliques of Irish Poetry* (1788) by subscription. She also wrote a tragedy, *Belisaious*, which is lost. In her translation she is concerned over the difficulty of translating not only words and genre but cultural contexts. Introducing her translation of elegies she notes, 'in the original, they are simple and unlearned, but pathetic to a great degree, and this is a species of beauty in composition, extremely difficult to transcribe into any other language'. **Bib:** Gantz, K.F., *Studies in English*.

Brooke, Frances (1724–1789)

Important as the author of the first Canadian novel, she was born Francis Moore in Claypole, England, grew up in Lincolnshire and Peterborough, and was educated at home. By 1748, she had moved to London and established herself as a woman of no small literary importance, with friends like the critic Samuel Johnson (1709–1784), ▷Anna Seward and ▷Fanny Burney. She married the Reverend John Brooke in 1755, but enjoyed a measure of freedom to pursue her literary interests. Under the name 'Mary Singleton, Spinster,' she edited *The Old Maid*, a weekly periodical (1755–1756). She tried to persuade actor/manager David Garrick (1717–1779) to produce her blank verse tragedy, *Virginia*, but he was unwilling to do so, and it was finally published in 1756, with other poems and translations. She also translated, from the French, ▷Marie-Jeanne Riccoboni's *Letters from Juliet, Lady Catesby, to her Friend, Lady Henrietta Campley* in 1760. Meanwhile, her husband had left for Canada. After the appearance of her ▷epistolary novel, *The History of Lady Julia Mandeville* (1763), she went to join her husband, who was stationed in Quebec as military chaplain. This work, suitably concluded with the deaths of both central characters, enjoyed popular success. Frances Brooke's stay in Quebec (until 1768) informed ▷*The History of Emily Montague*, which is popularly considered the first 'Canadian' novel (1769). The book's major characters and correspondents, Edward Rivers and Arabella Fermor, describe in considerable detail political and social aspects of 18th-century Canada, with notable emphasis on the landscape, and on the relations between the English and the French.

After Frances Brooke's return to England, she translated Framéry's *Memoirs of the Marquis de St Forlaix* (published in 1770), and Millot's *Elements of the History of England, from the Invasion of the Romans to the Reign of George the Second* (published in 1771). There is critical debate about whether Frances Brooke is the author of the anonymous novel *All's Right at Last; or, The History of Miss West* (1774), although Lorraine McMullen's 1983 biography of Brooke supports the attribution. Brook's next novel, *The Excursion* (1777), is about a heroine in London seeking success as a writer; David Garrick comes under direct attack for not supporting new work. From 1773 to 1778,

Frances Brooke was involved, with actress Mary Ann Yates, in managing the Haymarket opera house. Three of her dramatic works were staged: *The Siege of Sinope: A Tragedy* in 1781; *Rosina* and *Marion*, both comic operas, in 1783 and 1788. Her last novel, *The History of Charles Mandeville* (1790), was not published until after her death. She is buried in Sleaford, Lincolnshire, England. **Bib:** McMullen, L., *An Odd Attempt in a Woman: The Literary Life of Frances Brooke.*

Brooke-Rose, Christine (born 1923)
Novelist, literary critic and translator, born in Switzerland and educated in England. She worked as a freelance journalist during the 1950s and 1960s, moving to France in 1969, where she took up an academic post as lecturer, and then Professor of American Literature at the University of Paris VIII (Vincennes). She retired in 1988.

Brooke-Rose's works of literary criticism and theory include *A Grammar of Metaphor* (1958), *A ZBC of Ezra Pound* (1971), *A Rhetoric of the Unreal* (1981) and *Stories, Theories and Things* (1991). She has made a major contribution to formalist and ▷structuralist literary approaches, particularly to the analysis of narrative, and to the diffusion outside France of work of this kind. The range of literature and theories she explores is very wide, although there is a core of preoccupations to which she returns. The relationship between ▷'realism' and 'anti-realism' is a central concern; Brooke-Rose argues strongly for closer analyses of the types of literature too often assimilated to the vague category of 'experimental' writing. She is also particularly interested in the responses modern literature has made to the 'reality crisis' of the 20th century; ▷science fiction, the literature of the 'fantastic', the *nouveau roman*, 'metafiction' and ▷postmodern narratives are among the genres she discusses. Her theoretical writings centre on the formal dimensions of writing, and in *Stories, Theories and Things* she expresses a concern that recent feminist criticism has often neglected formal innovation, tending to be directed towards feminist 'themes', 'whether or not these create new modes or structures'.

Brooke-Rose's novels were often grouped with the ▷*nouveau roman* of Alain Robbe-Grillet (born 1922) (whose work she has translated), ▷Nathalie Sarraute and others. Her early fiction includes *Out* (1964), *Such*, (1966) *Between* (1968) and *Thru'* (1975). *Between* explores the condition of bilingualism or multilingualism which Brooke-Rose has addressed in her theoretical work through the consciousness of a simultaneous interpreter 'whose mind is a whirl of topics and jargons and foreign languages'. Despite the novel's experimentalism – it was written, for example, without the verb 'to be' and subverts the novelistic conventions of representing time-shifts – it is, Brooke-Rose insists, a work of mimetic realism, in that it mirrors the interpreter's loss of identity. Her 'Intercom Quartet' comprises *Amalgamemnon* (1984), *Xorander* (1986), *Verbivore* (1990) and *Textermination*. In these novels

Brooke-Rose continues to play with the use of tenses and time-shifts, and with the interplay between natural and scientific/computer languages.

Brookner, Anita (born 1938)
English-born novelist of Polish parents. A lecturer in fine art and art history since 1964, Brookner has published a number of critical studies, and academic life figures greatly within her novels. *A Start in Life* (1981) explores a critic's ascetic devotion to the study of the French novelist Balzac, and *Providence* (1982) focuses on a woman split between domestic and academic lives. Brookner's fiction, like that of ▷A.S. Byatt, is erudite and full of allusions and intertextual references. Her novels generally concentrate on intelligent but isolated women characters, disappointed in love, as in *The Misalliance* (1986), or, in *Family and Friends* (1985), finding solace in the writings of Balzac. Brookner won the Booker Prize with ▷*Hotel du Lac* (1984).

Brooks, Gwendolyn (born 1917)
US poet. Brooks was born in Topeka, Kansas to the descendant of an escaped slave, and was raised in Chicago, Illinois. At school she was the victim of African-American intra-racial prejudice. She worked as a maid and as a spiritual adviser's secretary, and published her first poem at the age of thirteen. Her work chronicles a move from the personal to the political. Brooks writes poetry for the people, 'plain black folks', describing the everyday struggles of ordinary urban African-Americans in ▷*A Street in Bronzeville* (1945). In 1950 she became the first African-American to win the Pulitzer Prize, for ▷*Annie Allen* (1949), and has since been awarded a number of prestigious grants and fellowships, testifying to the recognition her work has achieved.

In her novel *Maud Martha* (1953) an African-American woman woman learns to accept and imaginatively transmute the confines of her life. ▷*The Bean Eaters* (1960) deals with issues of inter-racial and intra-racial prejudice. *In the Mecca* (1968) envisions black solidarity as the means to redemption. *Riot* (1969), *Family Pictures* (1970) and *Beckonings* (1975) focus on the sociopolitical struggles of African-Americans. Technically, Brooks has been important for her transformation and adaptation of traditional forms, such as the ballad, to her own ends, and for her development of a black North American poetics out of cultural forms, such as the spiritual. Active in promoting the work of others, Brooks also established the Illinois Poet Laureate Awards to encourage young talent.

Other works include: *Bronzeville Boys and Girls* (1956), *Aloneness* (1971), her autobiography *Report from Part One* (1972), *Young Poet's Primer* (1980), *to disembark* (1981), *Winnie* (1991) and *Blacks* (1991). **Bib:** Shaw, Harry B., *Gwendolyn Brooks.*

Brooks, Maria Gowen (c 1794–1845)
US poet. A poet of some distinction, Gowen Brooks both parallels the British romantics (Robert Southey, 1774–1843, admired her poetry and became a friend) and anticipates the themes and techniques of modern British and North American poetry. Her work is remarkable among US poetry of the period, but remains unreprinted and undiscovered in the late 20th-century revival of interest in women writers. Unlike her contemporaries in the USA, she acknowledged and celebrated women's sensuality and physicality, in highly symbolic and erudite poetry. Her principal works are *Judith, Esther, and Other Poems* (1820); *Zophiel; or, The Bride of Seven* (1833), and *Idomen* (1838 in serial publication, 1843 as volume). Brooks used the pseudonym 'Maria of the West', a name first suggested by Southey; when she lived in Cuba late in her life, she used the Spanish 'Maria del Occidente'.

Brophy, Brigid (born 1929)
English novelist. A prolific writer throughout the 1950s and 1960s, Brophy consistently articulates a libertarian treatment of sexual and social themes. Her non-fiction writings include an analysis of eroticism in the work of the artist Aubrey Beardsley (1872–1898) (*Black and White*, 1968), while *The Snow Ball* (1964), a companion novel to her study *Mozart the Dramatist* (1964), caused controversy through its description of female orgasm. *The Adventures of God in His Search for the Black Girl* (1973) is a collection of 'modernized' fairy-tales. Her first novel, *Hackenfeller's Ape* (1953), explores the human subject as zoological species and exhibit, using this scenario to interrogate contemporary debates in child and developmental psychology. Despite her thematic affinity with ▷Angela Carter, Brophy has remained sceptical of feminist orthodoxy, and her interest in sexuality is never glossed by an intentional allegiance with feminist politics.

Brossard, Nicole (born 1943)
Born in Montreal and educated at the University of Montreal, Canadian Nicole Brossard is one of the leading avant-garde writers to have emerged from the political tensions of the 1960s and the new writing in Quebec. An active feminist and lesbian, her work has had a profound influence on contemporary women's writing, both French and English, in Canada. Brossard insists on a stance that takes risks and severs with tradition. She was co-founder and editor of *La Barre du Jour* (1965) (*Bar of Day*), and its subsequent *La Nouvelle Barre du Jour* (1977) (*New Bar of Day*), an experimental journal reflecting the revolutionary nature of Quebec nationalistic literature. Her early poetry is 'resolutely modern', defiantly challenging convention. Her first book of poems, *Aube à la saison* (*Dawn of the Season*) appeared in 1965, followed by *Mordre en sa chair* (1966) (*To Die in the Flesh*), *L'echo bouge beau* (1968) (*Beautiful Echo Howl*) and *Suite logique* (1970) (*Logical Sequel*), all reprinted in *Le Centre blanc* (1970) (*The White*

Centre 1980), which collects her writing of this period. *Méchanique jongleuse suivi de masculin grammaticale* (1974, translated as *Daydream Mechanics*) and *La Partie pour le tout* (1975) (*A Part for All*) are collected in the reprint of *Le Centre Blanc* (1978). 'Brossard's notion of a *centre blanc* as a space of absolute nakedness, ecstasy, and concentrated meanings functions as a unifying concept in much of her early poetry' (Gould, 57). This focus on the mysterious origins of desire marks her powerful influence on the development of feminist 'body writing' (▷écriture féminine). With *Amantes* (1980, translated as *Lovhers*, 1987), Brossard merges the personal, the literary, and the political in what she calls 'writing in the feminine', and her subsequent books, including *Double Impression* (1984); *L'Aviva* (1985); *Domaine d'écriture* (1985) (*Domain of Writing*); *Mauve* (1985), with ▷Daphne Marlatt; *Character/Jeu de lettres* (1986), with Daphne Marlatt; *Sous la langue/Under Tongue* (bilingual) (1987); and *Dont j'oublie le titre* (1986) (*The Forgotten Title*), enunciate her activist lesbian stance. She has won two Governor General's Awards for poetry. Her first novel, *Un livre* (1970, translated as *A Book*, 1976), prefigures her continuing preoccupation with the body as a site for writing, the intimacy of words and page. Her 'theoretical fiction' includes: *Sold-Out* (1973, translated as *Turn of a Pang*, 1976), *French Kiss* (1974, translated as *French Kiss or: A Pang's Progress*, 1986), *L'Amèr ou Le Chapitre effrité* (1977, translated as *These Our Mothers or: The Disintegrating Chapter*, 1983), *Le Sens apparent* (1980, translated as *Surfaces of Sense*, 1989), *Picture Theory* (1982, translated under the same title, 1991), *Journal intime* (1984) (*Private Diary*), and *Le Désert Mauve* (1987, translated as *Mauve Desert*, 1990). Her essays are collected in *La lettre aérienne* (1985, translated as *The Aerial Letter*, 1988). Brossard was president of the Third International Feminist Book Fair in Montreal (1988). She continues to exert a profound and visionary influence on cultural and feminist thought and writing in Canada.
▷Théoret, France
Bib: Forsyth, L., in ▷*A Mazing Space*; Forsyth, L., in *Traditionalism, Nationalism and Feminism: Women Writers of Quebec*; Forsyth, L., in *Gynocritics/Gynocritiques*; Gould, K., *Writing in the Feminine*; Weir, L., *A Mazing Space*.

Broughton, Rhoda (1840–1920)
British novelist, the daughter of Jane Bennet and clergyman Delves Broughton, she began to write novels at the age of twenty-two. After moving to Headington, Oxford, in 1892, she became well-known in literary and academic circles. Her first work, *Not Wisely, But Well*, was published in 1867. Altogether she wrote twenty-four novels, mostly sensational ▷romances centring on 'strong-minded women', unhappy marriages and scandalous affairs. She was one of the best-selling novelists of the Victorian period, and was paid large amounts for copyright by her publisher, Bentley. Her works include ▷*Cometh Up as a*

Flower (1867), *Alas!* (1890) and *Scylla or Charybdis?: A Novel* (1895). Her last novel was *A Fool in Her Folly* (1920).

▷Ghost stories (19th-century Britain); Sensation and sensational

Broumas, Olga (born 1949)

US poet of Greek origin, Broumas was born in Syros, where she was brought up. She moved to the US to study architecture, followed by creative writing, which she teaches at Boston University, as well as working as a massage therapist. Broumas writes what she describes as 'a poetry of the *body*' which is explicitly erotic and lesbian defined. *Beginning with O* (1977) marries the lover's body to a language which 'defies / decoding, appears / to consist of vowels, beginning with O, the O- / mega, horse-shoe, cave or sound'. In poems such as 'Rapunzel', 'Circe' and 'Maenad', Broumas also revises stories and myths about women. Her Greek background is often evident in her poetry, either as landscape, a source of mythology, or in references to a Greek literary tradition, as in 'Between Two Seas' in *Perpetua* (1989), which begins, 'Tonight I think of Bouboulina, / the poetry she used against the Turks'. Her other poetry collections include *Soie Sauvage* (1980) and *Pastoral Jazz* (1983). Broumas has also collaborated with Jane Miller on a prose poem called *Black Holes, Black Stockings* (1985) and has translated works by the Greek poet Odysseas Elytis into English.

Brown, Alice (1857–1948)

US fiction and non-fiction writer, novelist, dramatist, poet, critic and biographer. Brown is primarily noted now for her New England ▷local color stories and for her play *Children of the Earth* (1915). The first of the second rank of New England regional writers (after ▷Rebecca Harding Davis, ▷Mary E. Wikins Freeman and ▷Sarah Orne Jewett), Brown was far more versatile than her contemporaries, who wrote mostly fiction.

Brown's considerable 19th-century reputation was established by New England stories and sketches, collected in *Meadow-Grass* (1895) and *Tiverton Tales* (1899). Her ironic humour, finely developed characterization and focus on distinctive regional types – primarily the New England spinster and the provincial farmer – presented a deft investigation rather than celebration of rural life. Her technique changed throughout her long career, resulting in some critics preferring the works of one period over those of another. Brown wrote a substantial number of novels over a period of more than forty years, including *Fools of Nature* (1887), *Margaret Warrener* (1901), *Rose MacLeod* (1908) and *Old Crow* (1922). Her strongest fiction and one-act plays are those which focus on the consciousness and experience of a single character, often a woman. In her extensive body of work in almost every conceivable genre, Brown's writing is substantive and usually original, though perhaps least so in poetry.

Brown, Anna (1747–1810)

Scottish collector, singer and transmitter of Scottish ballads. Poet.

Brown, Audrey Alexandra (born 1904)

Canadian poet, born and brought up in Nanaimo, British Columbia, whose work was influenced by the romantics. She has published five collections of verse: *A Dryad in Nanaimo* (1931), *The Tree of Resurrection and Other Poems* (1937), *Challenge to Time and Death* (1943), *V-E Day* (1946), and *All Fools' Day* (1948). Her work is considered to some extent derivative, but colour and pattern are strongly articulated. *The Log of a Lame Duck* (1938) is her diary memoir of a lengthy treatment for rheumatic illness at a solarium on Malahat Beach, British Columbia. *Poetry and Life* (1944), originally an address to the Canadian Authors' Association, defines her poetic position. She was awarded the Royal Society's Lorne Pierce Medal in 1944.

Brown, Eliza (died 1896)

Australian letter-writer, Brown arrived in Western Australia in 1841, and her letters to her father, William Bussey, in Oxfordshire provide a comprehensive account of life in the new colony. They have been collected in *A Faithful Picture: the Letters of Eliza and Thomas Brown at York in the Swan River Colony 1841–1852* (1977), edited by Eliza's descendant, Peter Cowan.

▷Letters (Australia)

Brown, Elizabeth Brown (1753–1812)

North American letter-writer. She was a resident of Concord, Massachusetts. Marriage had separated her and her two sisters, Rebecca Brown French and Anna Brown Spaulding, both of whom resided in Vermont. As a means of maintaining not only the sisterly but the spiritual bond that had developed among them, the three women, used epistolary exchanges (▷ *The Brown Family Letters*) in order to share their religious concerns with one another.

Brown, Margaret (1867–?)

Canadian novelist, born Margaret Porter in western Ontario. She was educated in Goderich and at Toronto Normal School, and wrote mostly journalism. She is best known for her romantic Ottawa novel, *My Lady of the Snows* (1908), about political salon society.

Brown, Rita Mae (born 1944)

US poet, novelist and essayist. Like her heroine in ▷*Rubyfruit Jungle* (1973), Brown was an orphan born out of wedlock. Adopted, she grew up in poverty in Pennsylvania and Florida. She was expelled from the University of Florida for her activism in the civil rights movement and her lesbianism. Brown subsequently earned a Bachelor of Arts degree in history at New York

Rita Mae Brown

University. A former member of lesbian separatist groups, she protests against ▷patriarchy's division of people into arbitrary, hierarchical categories.

Infused with humour, her novels revise history to include the experiences of women. *Six of One* (1978) recuperates an empowering Southern tradition of female moral influence. In *Southern Discomfort* (1982) a ▷Southern lady violates the taboo against miscegenation. *Sudden Death* (1983) exposes the politics of women's professional tennis. *High Hearts* (1986) revises Civil War history, and pays due to Southern women who disguised themselves as men and fought as soldiers.

Other works include: *The Hand That Cradles the Rock* (1971), *Songs to a Handsome Woman* (1973), *The Plain Brown Rapper* (1976), *In Her Day* (1976), *Bingo* (1988) and *Starting From Scratch* (1988).

Browne, Maria da Felicidade do Couto (?1797–1861)

Portuguese poet. Married to a wealthy merchant of Irish descent, she transformed her home into one of the most celebrated literary salons in Portugal. Among those in attendance was a young man called Camilo Castelo Branco, now regarded as one of the country's major novelists. A relationship developed between Browne and the young Castelo Branco; he dedicated his play *O Marquês de Torres Novas* to Browne and an exchange of poems between the two appeared in the newspapers. According to historians, Castelo Branco withdrew from the relationship and Browne never fully recovered. The themes of love and disillusionment are central in her poems, whose passionate, 'excessive' quality is regarded as ultra-romantic.

She published her poems under pen-names and these names served as the titles of her first two books. *A Coruja Trovadora* (*The Troubador Owl*)

was published without a date, and *Sóror Dolores* (*Sister Dolores*) appeared in 1849. In 1854 she published her third and final volume of poetry, entitled *Virações da Madrugada* (*Fresh Breezes of the Dawn*).

▷Ultra-romanticism; Romanticism (Portugal)

Brown Family Letters, 1792–1852, The (1977)

This collection of family letters centres on the correspondence of the North American ▷Elizabeth Brown Brown with her two sisters, Rebecca Brown French and Anna Brown Spaulding, who had settled in distant Vermont. Highly devout women, the sisters used the mail as a means of extending the support system they had established for one another, and of sharing their spiritual explorations.

▷Early North American letters

Brown Girl, Brownstones (1959)

Autobiographical novel by North American writer ▷Paule Marshall. *Brown Girl, Brownstones* depicts a brown girl's growth into womanhood, caught between the conflicting values of her hard-working, demanding mother, and her idealistic father whose pride lies in the plot of land he owns back in Barbados. The novel made a unique contribution to African-American literature by focusing on Selina's Barbadian-American community in Brooklyn, New York. This community had emerged as the result of immigration in search of employment and wealth during the first half of the 20th century. Set in 1939, Marshall's novel shows the Barbadian-American culture struggling to survive in the hostile materialistic culture of Anglo-Americans. In the hope of succeeding in the US, Barabadian-American women clean Anglo-American houses, aspiring to buy their own. Marshall shows how they keep alive their own cultural traditions and values while trying to assimilate. The novel also examines the ways in which culture defines sex roles.

▷Early North American letters

Browning, Elizabeth Barrett (1806–1861)

British poet, the eldest child of Edward and Mary Moulton Barrett. She was the most respected and successful woman poet of the Victorian period, considered seriously for the laureateship that eventually was awarded to Tennyson in 1850. An experimental writer, she wrote ballads, political odes, allegories, sonnets, poetic dramas and an epic, as well as publishing essays in literary criticism and translations of Greek poetry. She spent her childhood at Hope End in Herefordshire reading widely and schooling herself in the classics. Her juvenilia includes *The Battle of Marathon* (1820) and *An Essay on Mind* (1826), her first mature collection being *The Seraphim, and Other Poems* (1838). For six years between 1838 and 1844 Barrett was confined as an invalid, though during this period she wrote extensively, culminating in ▷*Poems* (1844). In 1845 Robert Browning began a correspondence with her, and a year later she ran away from her tyrannical father in order to marry Browning in secret. The couple left immediately for Italy and based themselves in Florence for the rest of Barrett's life. *Poems* (1850) includes the celebrated sequence of love-lyrics written during her courtship, ▷*Sonnets from the Portuguese*, and ▷'The Runaway Slave at Pilgrim's Point'.

▷*Aurora Leigh* (1857), an epic poem concerned with the making of a woman poet is now considered one of Barrett Browning's major achievements. Other works include *Casa Guidi Windows* (1851), *Poems Before Congress* (1860) and a posthumously published collection, *Last Poems* (1862).

▷Ballad (19th-century Britain)
Bib: Taplin, G., *The Life of Elizabeth Barrett Browning*; Hayter, A., *Mrs Browning: A Poet's Work and its Setting*; Leighton, A., *Elizabeth Barrett Browning*; Cooper, H., *Elizabeth Barrett Browning: Woman and Artist*; Mermin, D., *Elizabeth Barrett Browning*.

Bruce, Mary Grant (1878–1958)
Australian writer for children. Bruce went to England in 1913 to work for the *Daily Mail*, married there and lived at various times in Ireland (where one of her sons was accidently killed), at Bexhill in Sussex, and in Taralgon, Victoria. She is one of the most prolific and celebrated writers of adolescent fiction in early 20th-century Australia, and her work did much to shape an ideal vision of Australian pastoral life.

As 'Cinderella', Bruce edited the children's page of the *Leader*. She contributed articles, short stories and serials not only to the *Age* and the *Leader*, but also to many other periodicals. Her first novel, *A Little Bush Maid*, was serialized in the *Leader* from 1905 to 1907, published as a book in 1910, and was the first of fifteen books which became known as ▷*The Billabong Series*. Bruce published twenty-two other books for children, a book of Aboriginal legends, *The Stone Age of Burkamukk* (1922), a collection of radio talks, *The Power Within* (1940), as well as a great deal of short fiction, poetry and journalism. Sales of her work are said to have reached 2 million copies. *Seven Little Billabongs* (1979) by Brenda Niall compares the writings of Mary Grant Bruce with those of ▷Ethel Turner, and *Billabong's Author* (1979), by Alison Alexander, is a biography.

▷Children's literature (Australia)

Brückner, Christine (born 1921)
West German popular novelist. Spurned by critics as an author of trivial fiction, she has nevertheless been successful in alerting a wide readership to issues surrounding women's emancipation. Novels such as *Ehe die Spuren verwehen* (1954) (*Before all Trace Fades Away*), *Der Kokon* (1966) (*The Cocoon*) or *Jauche und Levkoyen* (1975) (*Gillyflower Kid*, 1982), which was made into a successful television series in 1978, are vividly recounted stories about women who learn to become tough and self-

reliant in difficult circumstances. More artistically ambitious is her recent collection of fictitious speeches by famous women: *Wenn du geredet hättest, Desdemona. Ungehaltene Reden ungehaltener Frauen* (1983) (*If Only You Had Spoken, Desdemona! Angry Words from Angry Women*).

Brueck, Christa Anita (born 1899)
German novelist. Her novels, *Schicksale hinter Schreibmaschinen* (1930) (*Destinies Behind Typewriters*), *Ein Mädchen mit Prokura* (1932) (*A Young Woman Executive*) and *Die Lawine* (1941) (*The Avalanche*), are evocative accounts of the difficulties encountered by women doing low-paid office work.

Bruggen, Carry van (1881–1932)
Dutch prose writer. Born Carolina Lea de Haan, daughter of a Jewish cantor, and sister of the writer and poet Jacob Israël de Haan. She was a teacher for some time, and lived in the Dutch East Indies for several years. She retained the name of her first husband, but also used the ▷pseudonym Justine Abbing. Her work is notable for her self-analysis, her experiences of a Jewish youth, and her restless character. Especially noteworthy are her novels, the autobiographical *Heleen* (1913) (*Helen*), *Het huisje aan de sloot* (1921) (*The Little House Beside the Ditch*), consisting of twenty-four scenes from the life of a small Jewish girl and her little brother in an Orthodox Jewish family, the philosophical *Hedendaagsch fetischisme* (1925) (*Contemporary Fetishism*), dealing with the abuse of language, and the autobiographical *Eva* (1927) (*Eve*), describing the evolution of a schoolgirl into a woman.

Brun, Friederike Sophie Christiane (1765–1835)
German poet. Born into a cultured clerical family and surrounded by many literary figures, (the poet Klopstock, 1724–1803, and the nationalist philosopher Herder, 1744–1803, among them) she began to write poetry at an early age. She married Konstantin Brun in 1783, and had ten children. In ill health and increasingly deaf, she spent much time seeking cures in Switzerland and southern Europe. In 1795 she published a collection of her poems, *Gedichte von Friederike Brun* (*Poems of Friederike Brun*). Besides some occasional poetry, the volume contains lyrical evocations of Alpine and Mediterranean landscapes which rank amongst the best of her time.

Brun, Marie-Marguerite de Maison-Forte (1713–1794)
French poet. Born in Coligny, she was well-educated, and her home in the Franche Comté was a meeting place for provincial literati. Her first work, *Essai d'un dictionnaire comtois-français*, (*Sketch for a Dictionary of the Franche Comté Tongue*) was published in 1753. Two of her poetic works were published: *L'Amour maternel* (1773) (*Motherly Love*), which was singled out in the

literary competition held in that year by the Académie Française, and *L'amour des Français pour leur roi* (*The Frenchman's Love for His King*).

Brunet, Marta (1897–1967)

Chilean short story writer and novelist. She was educated in a well-to-do home, and was a diplomat. Her first and most important novel, *Montaña adentro* (1923) (*Mountain Interior*), achieved immediate success. Part of ▷*criollismo*, it was filled with lyrical and tragical feeling in the ▷realist-naturalist style, which she later abandoned for the psychological. Women are the protagonists in her novels, and she has been considered to be Chile's instigator of women's literature. In the stories in *Aguas abajo* (1930) (*Waters Below*), she abandoned *criollismo* and adopted an international style, with an elaborate formal technique, to show a woman's conflicts and frustrations. Her novel *Humo hacia el sur* (1946) (*Smoke to the South*), thought to be influenced by North American literature, examines a conflict between progress and conservatism, in which the latter prevails. The novel *María Nadie* (1957) (*María Nobody*) tries to reconcile *criollismo* and the peasant theme, and the psychological and the cosmopolitan, as in ▷Virginia Woolf's characters. In *Amasijo* (1962) (*Mixture*), the solitary life of the homosexual Julián, who commits suicide, is analyzed in the light of cosmopolitanism and of an oppressive, demanding mother. Brunet received numerous literary prizes, and in particular, the National Prize for Literature (1961). Other important works are *Florisondo* (1921), short stories, and the novels *Bestia dañina* (1926) (*Harmful Beast*) and *María Rosa, flor del Quillén* (1929) (*María Rosa, Flower of The Quillén*).

Brüning, Elfriede (born 1910)

East German novelist. From a workers' family, she was imprisoned briefly in the 1930s for being a communist agitator. In novels such as *Und außerdem ist Sommer* (1934) (*And Moreover, It Is Summertime*), *Junges Herz muß wandern* (1936) (*Young Hearts Must Travel*) and *. . . damit du weiterlebst* (1949) (*. . . So You May Live On*), she analyzes human relationships, principally that between mother and child, but also between men and women who are trying to live their lives with a new socialist perspective. *Regine Haberkorn* (1955) is an early example of a socialist ▷*Bildungsroman*. Written in the idiom of ▷socialist realism at the time when East Germany was building up its economy, the novel portrays the development of a young woman from housewife to committed factory worker.

Bryher (Annie Winifred Ellerman) (1894–1983)

English novelist and poet. Bryher was a close friend of the poet ▷H.D., through whom she met the US writer Robert McAlmon. McAlmon and Bryher contracted a marriage of convenience in 1929. The couple moved to Paris, and Bryher became involved in Parisian *avant-garde* circles and started a long friendship with ▷Gertrude Stein. Better-known for her non-fiction and critical writings beginning with a study of ▷Amy Lowell (1918), she founded the film journal *Close-up*, and shortly after published *Film Problems of Soviet Russia* (1929). Bryher also helped establish the *Psychoanalytic Review* in England. Her fiction primarily consisted of historical novels, such as *The Coin of Carthage* (1963). *The Days of Mars, 1940–46* (1972) describes her relationship with H.D. Another volume of autobiography is *The Heart to Artemis* (1962).

Bucge (Bugga, Heaburg) (8th century)

English abbess. A letter to ▷Boniface from Bucge and her mother, Eangyth, survives, which reveals some of the administrative problems faced by communities such as theirs. Bucge was one of those to whom Boniface wrote requesting books, so it appears that manuscripts were copied in her scriptorium (manuscript workshop).

Buchan, Anna ▷Douglas, O.

Buchinskaia, Nadezhda Aleksandrovna ▷Tèffi

Büchner, Luise (1821–1877)

German writer and feminist. The sister of the writer Georg Büchner, she was actively involved in helping middle-class women who had fallen on hard times. In 1855 she published, anonymously, *Die Frau und ihr Beruf* (*Woman and Her Profession*), a book arguing for the right of women to acquire marketable skills. She also published poems and novels. Her fairytales for children were a great popular success at the time.

Buck, Heather (born 1926)

English poet. Buck began writing in 1966 during Jungian analysis. From the 1970s her work has appeared in magazines such as *Outposts*, *English* and *Agenda*. Her first collection of poems, *The Opposite Direction*, was published in 1972, and was followed by *At the Window* (1982) and *The Sign of the Water Bearer* (1987). She has also published *Elegy for a Nun* (1987). Buck's work combines the influence of a long tradition of religious and mystical writing with the insights of psychoanalytic theory and practice.

Buck, Pearl S. (1892–1973)

US novelist. Born in Hillsboro, West Virginia, Buck lived in China, where her parents were missionaries, until 1934. She graduated from Randolph-Macon Women's College in 1914. In 1917 she married John Buck, and divorced him in 1935. In 1926 she earned a Master of Arts degree in English from Cornell University. Buck was awarded the Nobel Prize for Literature in 1938.

Her novels, like Chinese sagas, emphasize plot. Her goal is to entertain and enlighten the masses. *East Wind: West Wind* (1930) raises the issue of Chinese women's bound feet. ▷*The Good Earth*

(1931) extols the virtues of Chinese farming life. *The Mother* (1934) affirms a maternal view of life that highlights the eternal and the universal. *Dragon Seed* (1942) and *The Promise* (1943) support China's struggle against Japanese imperialism. *The Hidden Flower* (1952) protests against anti-miscegenation laws, while *Command the Morning* (1952) protests against the use of atomic weapons.

Other works include: *Fighting Angel* (1936), *The Exile* (1936), *This Proud Heart* (1938), *The Patriot* (1939), *Pavilion of Women* (1946), *The Time Is Noon* (1967) and *The Goddess Abides* (1972).
Bib: Stirling, Nora, *Pearl Buck: A Woman in Conflict.*

Buffet, Marguerite (died 1680)

French grammarian. She was the author of *Nouvelles Observations sur la langue françoise* (1668) (*New Observations on the French Language*), '*faisant profession d'enseigner aux Dames l'art de bien parler & de bien écrire sur tous sujets, avec l'Orthographe Françoise par regles*' ('setting out to teach ladies the art of speaking and writing well on all subjects, with French Spelling according to the rules'). This work includes a *Traitté sur les Eloges des Illustres Sçavantes, Anciennes et Modernes* (*Treatise on the Praise of Famous Scholars, Ancient and Modern*). Little is known about either Buffet or her work, but she has left a rare and valuable document in this linguistic treatise written specifically for women, which seems also to refer to an earlier work giving her pupils rules for spelling French correctly. Buffet was thought to be simply a compiler of the French grammarian Claude de Vaugelas (1595–1650), who showed particular care in collecting decisions regarding '*la chasteté du langage*' ('the purity of language') but has recently been revalued. Her aim was to convince women that the study of good speech and writing was a serious subject that should not be left to '*les hommes de cabinet*' ('men in their studies'). She hoped to encourage women to '*mépriser la bagatelle pour s'attacher aux choses les plus belles & les plus nobles de la vie*' ('have contempt for unimportant trifles and fix their attention on the most noble and beautiful things of life'), by organizing their time more efficiently. Her purpose was '*d'inspirer aux femmes le desir des sciences & de la vertu*' ('to inspire in women the thirst for knowledge and virtue'). She did not want to force all women to devote themselves entirely to the study of speaking well, but believed in a kind of cultural élite: '*il y en a que leur condition appelle tous les jours dans les belles conversations, celles-là semblent être obligées à se cultiver un peu plus que les autres qui sont plus retirées du grand monde*' ('there are those who are drawn by their condition to become involved in beautiful conversations every day. It seems to be incumbent upon those women to cultivate themselves a little more than others who are more withdrawn from high society').
Bib: Ayres-Burnett, W., 'Women and Grammar in Seventeenth-Century France', *Seventeenth-Century French Studies*, XII (1990).

Bugul, Ken (born 1948)

Senegalese novelist. This pseudonym, meaning in Wolof 'nobody wants it', was imposed on Marietou Mbaye by her publishers, Les Nouvelles Editions Africaines. In writing ▷*Le Baobab fou* (1982) (*The Mad Baobab*) a fictionalized autobiography, she claims she had no intention of writing a book, and did not even know she had written one, until she gave it to a friend to read, who took it to NEA. For her, she said, the writing was a form of therapy which enabled her to come to terms with 'the difficulty of being a woman, of being a child without any idea of parents, of being black and colonized' (interview with Bernard Magnier in *Notre Librairie*, 79, 1985). She has since written a novel, *La Chute des nuages* (*Cloudfall*).
▷Prostitution (West Africa)

Bulfinch, Hannah Apthorp (1768–1841)

North American diarist and letter-writer. She was orphaned during the American Revolution and raised by her grandfather, Stephen Greenleaf, a noted Loyalist. On 20 November 1788 she married the architect Charles Bulfinch. At first their future held great promise, but economic problems left them nearly impoverished. She maintained a journal and a steady correspondence with close relatives that chronicle these difficult years. Her writing is lucid and heartfelt, revealing the consequences of war for people of all classes in 18th-century North America. It was several years before the Bulfinches re-established themselves, eventually becoming a leading family in Massachusetts. She died on 8 April 1841.
▷'Letters and Journal of Hannah Bulfinch, The'

Búlich, Vera Sergéevna (1898–1954)

Russian *émigré* poet. In 1920 Bulich's family fled from Russia to Finland, where she supported herself by working at the Helsinki University Library and began publishing poetry in *émigré* periodicals. She also wrote articles on both canonized and contemporary Russian poets and prose writers. Between 1934 and 1954, she published four volumes of poetry. Her short, musical verse has been compared to ▷Akhmátova's, particularly in her dominant themes and moods, and the restraint and straightforward syntax of her lyrics. But she is more formally innovative and more abstract and philosophical than Akhmátova. One of her favourite devices is the incomplete statement, in which the speaker lets her thought trail off. The movement of her lyrics is often from an abstract contemplation to the insertion of the persona with a concrete action. Her themes include the fleeting nature of happiness, the helplessness of the individual to affect fate, the unchanging nature of the human condition, immortality, the role of memory and poetry in erasing the passage of time, and the mystery of poetic inspiration.
Bib: Pachmuss, T. (trans.), *Russian Literature in the Baltic Between the World Wars*.

Bullrich, Silvina (1915–1989)

Argentinian novelist and short story writer, poet, journalist, translator and essayist. She taught French literature, wrote for the press, worked on television, and published prolifically. Her first book, of poetry, was *Vibraciónes* (1935) (*Vibrations*). She won many prizes in Argentina, and in 1982 also won the French Academic Award. In the first phase of her literary career, she expressed an intimate feminism, as in *Bodas de cristal* (1951) (*Glass Wedding*), and *Teléfono ocupado* (1955) (*Telephone Engaged*), which was developed further in *Mañana digo basta* (1968) (*Tomorrow I Talk Enough*). Her female characters, who often have been married for a long time, speak rebelliously, but are only half-emancipated women. The second phase of her career consists of *Los burgueses* (1964) (*The Bourgeoisie*), *Los salvadores de la patria* (1965) (*The Saviours of the Fatherland*) and *La creciente* (1970) (*The Crescent Moon*), which are mainly concerned with political issues. The first two of these works present the decadence of politicians and the life of rural workers in a light and ironical tone. Her most famous novel, *Los burgueses*, examines the plight of the landed gentry. There exists in Bullrich's novels the wish for social change, which is based on faith in the human spirit. She lectured abroad and narrated her travels in reports and chronicles for *La Nación*.

Bülow, Frieda Freiin von (1858–1909)

German novelist and travel writer. Daughter of a Prussian consul, and sister of ▷Margarethe Freiin von Bülow, she founded the Women's Guild for Nursing in the Colonies, and travelled widely to implement her ideas. A close friend of ▷Lou Andreas-Salomé, she wrote about German colonial life and about social issues concerning the women of her time. Her books include: *Reiseskizzen und Tagebuchblätter aus Deutsch-Ostafrika* (1889) (*Travel Sketches and Diaries from German East Africa*); *Am andern Ende der Welt* (1890) (*At the Other End of the World*); and *Allein ich will!* (1903) (*Because I Want To!*).

Bülow, Margarethe Freiin von (1860–1884)

German novelist and writer of novellas. Daughter of a Prussian consul, and sister of ▷Frieda Freiin von Bülow, her work was published posthumously, after she died when trying to save a child from drowning. Her novellas in particular offer evocative glimpses of 19th-century Berlin and the countryside of Thuringia. The novellas, *Der Oberlieutnant Percy* (*Chief Lieutenant Percy*), *Der Herr im Hause* (*Lord of the Manor*), *Gabriel* and *Tagesgespenster* (*Ghosts by Daylight*) appear in the collection *Novellen* (1885) (*Novellas*).

Bunge de Gálvez, Delfina (1881–1952)

Argentinian poet, short story writer, novelist and travel writer. Her first book, *Simplement* (1911) (*Simply*), was written in French, and was followed by *La nouvelle moisson* (1918) (*The New Harvest*), also in French. Many of her writings won prizes, and some of her poems were translated from the French by ▷Alfonsina Storni. She directed the magazine *Ichthys*, and was deeply religious. She contributed to periodicals, lectured and wrote children's stories and educational books.

Other works: *Nuestra Señora de Lourdes, Las mujeres y la vocación* (*Our Lady of Lourdes, Women and the Vocation*); *Las imágenes del infinito* (1922) (*Images of Infinity*); *El tesoro del mundo* (1923) (*The World's Treasure*); *Oro, incienso y mirra* (1924) (*Gold, Frankincense and Myrrh*); *Los malos tiempos de hoy* (1927) (*The Bad Times of Today*); *Tierras del mar azul* (1928) (*Lands of the Blue Sea*); *El reino de Dios* (*The Reign of God*); *La belleza en la vida cotidiana* (*The Beauty in Daily Life*); *Hogar y patria* (*Home and Country*); *Iniciación literaria, Viaje alrededor de mí infancia* (*Literary Initiation, Journey Around my Childhood*).

Búnina, Anna Petrovna (1774–1829)

Russia's first major woman poet, Búnina was the sixth child in an ancient gentry family of modest means. She began writing poetry young, but it was not until her father died in 1801 that she moved from the country to St Petersburg, spent her small inheritance on intensive self-education, and devoted herself to poetry and translation. Her first two volumes of poems, *An Inexperienced Muse* (1809, 1812), brought instant fame, and the Imperial Russian Academy issued her collected works in three volumes (1819–1821). In 1815 Búnina went to England to seek treatment for the breast cancer from which she may have suffered as early as 1812 (▷'A Sick Woman's Maytime Walk'). Unfortunately, her widely circulated letters with impressions of the journey have been lost. Incurably ill and in pain, she wrote little from 1817 on. Búnina's poetry plays on the genres typical of classicism and pre-romanticism, and reflects the clumsy syntax and vocabulary of the search for a modern Russian idiom (▷Golden Age). She defines her range of subjects from pastoral to heroic ode in 'A Conversation Between Me and Women'; the flighty tone of the women's complaint about calumnies of their sex by male poets is wicked and apt. Búnina wrote the obligatory occasional hymns to royal patrons and responded to the 1812 War with patriotic fervour. On the other hand, her clever fables and light verse were a gentle mode of social criticism. Death is a preoccupation of her lyrics: in 'From the Seashore' (1806), a description of an idyllic evening scene abruptly breaks off in a fit of violent despair, signalled in advance by the poem's short choppy lines and lack of rhyme; 'Song of Death' (1812, *Russian Literature Triquarterly*, 9) exalts that end to life's woes.

Bib: Heldt, Barbara, *Terrible Perfection*.

Bunn, Anna Maria (1808–1899)

Bunn was born in Ireland, came to Australia in 1827, married, and remained in Australia until her death. Her novel, *The Guardian* (1838), her only published work, for which she used the

pseudonym 'An Australian', was the first novel to be written and published by a woman in Australia.
▷ On Her Selection

Burford, Barbara (born c 1946)

British poet, fiction writer, editor and dramatist. Burford's definition of herself as 'Black woman, an active feminist and the mother of a ten-year-old daughter' also defines her work. Her poems are frequently celebratory in their energetic language, and reject the stereotypical definitions of black women as victims: 'We refuse your abyss, and your rope. / Cannot see your net. / Your cloudy reality, / We tread by our own heedless path.' They were published in *A Dangerous Knowing: Four Black Women Poets* (1985), which was the first anthology of British-based black women's poetry.

Burford's poems and her fiction bear out the US poet ▷ Audre Lorde's dictum, which is used as an epigraph for *A Dangerous Knowing*, that, 'the furthest horizons of our hopes and fears are cobbled by our poems, carved from the rock experiences of our daily lives.' Burford's short stories, *The Threshing Floor* (1986), are set in Canterbury, England, and explore women's creativity and lesbian relationships. She also writes science fiction, edited *Dancing the Tightrope: New Love Poems by Women* (1987), and her play, *Patterns*, was commissioned by Changing Women's Theatre and was performed in 1984.

Burger's Daughter (1979)

A novel by South African writer ▷ Nadine Gordimer which examines the dialectic between the personal and the political. Written during the aftermath of the ▷ Soweto uprising of 1976, it includes, as part of its text, various historical documents, notably, a leaflet written by the Soweto Students' Representative Council, and echoes a speech made by Bram Fischer, who died in prison towards the end of his life sentence for political activities called 'subversive' by the South African state. The novel is narrated by Rosa Burger, daughter of Lionel Burger, Fischer's fictional avatar. The book is, in part, Rosa's address to her father, whose political views she first shifts away from and then returns to: the ending presents a moving account of the daughter imprisoned in the same cell as her father, looking up to the light that once illuminated his face. Before this, her quest for freedom takes her to Europe, where her life as the mistress of an academic leads her to rethink her political position, as does her contact with her black childhood friend, Zwelinzima Vulindlela.

Burgess, Yvonne (born 1936)

South African novelist, born in Pretoria. She worked as reviewer, art critic and feature writer for the *Eastern Province Herald* in Port Elizabeth from 1960 to 1972, and since 1974 has lived in Nelspruit, Transvaal, writing full-time. Her first novel, *A Life to Live* (1973), is an ironic account of a 'poor-white' Afrikaner woman, whose life-story gives an interesting picture of the social and economic transformation of rural Afrikaners and those becoming urbanized in the first half of the 20th century. The moments of pathos and the feminist sympathy for the protagonist are not always entirely successfully integrated with the satire, and the ending is disconcertingly romanticized. Her next two novels retain the black humour and authorial distance of the first. *The Strike* (1975), a satirical vision of apocalypse, views the disparate experiences of various South Africans whose destinies are linked by a general strike which plunges the country into revolution. *Say a Little Mantra for Me* (1979) humorously studies three generations of white South African women. As in the earlier novel, feminism, religion and politics jostle slightly uncomfortably with Burgess' ever-present cynicism.

Burgos, Julia de (1914–1953)

Puerto Rican poet. She participated in the 'Feminist Parnassian of the 1930s', in the words of Josefina Rivera de Alvarez (1970). Her poetry is concerned with love, social problems, and justice and death, and *Rio grande de Loiza* (*Great River of Loiza*) is her main work. She is one of the best lyrical women poets of Puerto Rico, and describes love in sheer metaphysical flights. As a negro, she wrote strong poems in the defence of a negro's aesthetics. She participated in the ▷ négritude movement, and lived as an exile in New York.

Other works: *Poemas exactos a mí misma* (1937) (*Precise Poems to Myself*); *Poemas en veinte surcos* (1938) (*Poems in Twenty Grooves*); *Canción de la verdad sencilla* (1939) (*Song of the Simple Truth*), and *El mar y tú y otros poemas* (1954) (*The Sea and You and Other Poems*).

Burgos Seguí, Carmen de (c 1870–1932)

Spanish novelist, who often wrote under the pseudonym Colombine. Burgos Seguí was the daughter of the Consul of Portugal in the province of Almeria. She was an active suffragist and polemical columnist. The main influences in her novels range from the post-romantic adventure novel, evident in *El último contrabandista* (1920) (*The Last Smuggler*), to deterministic naturalism, seen in *Los inadaptados* (1909) (*The Misfits*). Her other novels include: *La rampa* (1917) (*The Ramp*), and *En la sima* (1915) (*On Top*).

Burkart, Erika (born 1922)

▷ German-speaking Swiss poet and novelist. Originally a teacher, she now lives as a recluse in an old abbey. Her poems, of which the best are collected in *Der dunkle Vogel* (1953) (*Dark Bird*), in *Augenzeuge* (1978) (*Eyewitness*) and in *Die Zärtlichkeit der Schatten* (1991) (*The Tenderness of Shadows*), are characterized by an intense feeling for an organic, natural world which she celebrates with incantatory words. Her novel *Moräne* (1970) (*Moraine*) explores Jungian (▷ psychoanalysis) notions of male and female while *Der Weg zu den*

Schafen (1979) (*The Path to the Sheep*) is a spiritual autobiography evocatively situated in the moorlands of her native Aargau.

Burkholder, Mabel (1881–1973)
Canadian journalist and historian, born and educated in Hamilton, Ontario. Her writing exemplifies social feminism; her novel, *The Course of Impatience Carningham* (1912), addresses labour and industrial issues. She also wrote a number of biographies, including one of the newspaperwoman, ▷Kathleen 'Kit' Coleman.
Bib: Campbell, S. and McMullen, L. (eds), *New Women.*

Burnett, Frances Eliza Hodgson (1849–1924)
British-born US novelist and writer of stories, children's fiction, drama and autobiography. Hodgson Burnett is most famous for her extremely popular children's novels, especially ▷*Little Lord Fauntleroy* (1886) and ▷*The Secret Garden* (1911), many still available in multiple paperback and hardcover editions. Her characters and plots have repeatedly been filmed, becoming so culturally integral that far more people know of the character types of little Lord Fauntleroy and the little princess than know that these originated in Hodgson Burnett's novels.

Like many 19th-century US women, Hodgson Burnett began writing to support her families, first publishing in the popular US women's magazines, and later in the national literary magazines. She found fame and success with international popular and critical audiences. In the 19th century many of her novels were dramatized by others, and she collaborated with the US actor and writer William Gillette (1857–1937) on the play *Esmeralda* (1881).

Like ▷Louisa May Alcott, she owed her fame to novels for children which were also read by adults; but unlike Alcott she incorporated fantasy, the supernatural, aristocracy and rags-to-riches and riches-to-rags plot-lines. In US publishing history and for her own critical reputation, Hodgson Burnett's most important novel is ▷*Through One Administration* (1883). She published more than fifty books; among her novels, for children and adults, are: *That Lass O'Lowries* (1877); *A Fair Barbarian* (1881); *Sara Crewe* (1888); *Editha's Burglar* (1888); *A Woman's Will* (1888); *The Making of a Marchioness* (1901), and *The Shuttle* (1902). Her autobiography is *The One I Knew the Best of All* (1893).
▷*Century Illustrated Monthly Magazine, The*; Children's literature
Bib: Thwaite, A., *Waiting for the Party: the life of Burnett.*

Burney, Fanny (Frances) (1752–1850)
English novelist, correspondent and writer of a journal. Fanny Burney was the daughter of Charles Burney, the musicologist. Her mother died when she was ten, and she had little rapport with her stepmother. She wrote ▷*Evelina* in secret and published it anonymously in 1778 – her siblings helped her to keep her identity a secret. *Evelina* features the awful Madam Duval – constantly threatening the heroine with social ruin. Through *Evelina* she got to know Samuel Johnson (1709–1784) and Hester Thrale (later ▷Piozzi Piozzi) and other ▷Bluestockings. When she was to meet ▷Elizabeth Montagu, Johnson rallied her: 'attack her, fight her and down with her at once'. Burney's attitude to Bluestockings was ironical. She published ▷*Cecilia* (1782) before taking up the position of Second Keeper of the Robes to Queen Charlotte – a post which provided yet more information for her journal. She left the position with a pension of £100, married Alexandre D'Arblay in 1793, and became involved in the upheavals in France, staying for a decade, and writing letters. She published *Camilla* in 1796, and her last novel, *The Wanderer*, in 1814. Burney wrote plays, but only *Edwy and Elgiva* was performed. She continued to write letters, journals and a memoir of her father, published in 1832.

Burney, Sarah Harriet (1772–1844)
English novelist and half-sister of ▷Fanny Burney. She published *Clarentine* (1798) anonymously, and it became a success. She went to live with her half-brother James, and worked as a governess and companion, as well as writing.

Other publications: *Geraldine Fauconberg* (1808); *Traits of Nature* (1812); *Tales of Fancy* (1816–1829), and *The Romance of Private Life* (1839).

Burnford, Sheila (1918–1984)
Children's writer, born Sheila Every in Scotland, and educated there and in France and Germany. In 1951 she emigrated to Canada with her husband and three children. Her best-known book, *The Incredible Journey* (1961), is about two dogs and a cat who undertake a 200-mile journey to get back to their home. *Bel Ria, Dog of War* (1977) is again about the adventures of animals in World War II. *Without Reserve* (1969) and *One Woman's Arctic* (1973) are autobiographical descriptions of Burnford's travels in northern Ontario and Baffin Island.

Burnier, Andreas (born 1931)
Dutch prose-writer, poet and essayist. ▷Pseudonym of Catharina Irma Dessaur. She studied philosophy, but obtained her doctor's degree with a social-criminological thesis, and was Professor of Criminology in Nijmegen. Her work is dominated by her opposition to discrimination against women and homosexuals, and anti-Semitism (she is of Jewish descent). Her novels stand out because of their unconventional, often fragmented structure. Her first novel, *Een tevreden lach* (1965) (*A Satisfied Laugh*), deals with lesbianism, transsexuality, and the fact that men have far more opportunities than women. These themes recur in *De verschrikkingen van het noorden* (stories, 1967) (*Terrors of the North*)and the novel *Het jongensuur* (1969) (*The Boys' Hour*). *De huilende libertijn* (1970) (*The Crying Libertine*) is a

description of a women's academy where feminists are trained to change the world. Subsequently she wrote novels of 'ideas'; in her later works, Buddhism, Hinduism and the theory of reincarnation are considered, subjects on which she wrote a study in 1982. *De achtste scheppingsdag* (1990) (*The Eighth Day of Creation*) contains her essays from 1987 to 1990. Although Burnier does not agree with all aspects of present-day feminism, she is one of the most important feminist writers of our time.

Burns, Carolyn
New Zealand dramatist. Carolyn Burns was born and grew up in Dunedin. An actor and journalist, she wrote her first plays for a small Auckland children's theatre group. Her well-known play *Objection Overruled* (1984) uses a courtroom structure to suggest the deficiencies of other social structures, particularly the family, with ironic feminist connections.

Burr, Esther Edwards (1732–1758)
North American diarist. Born on 13 February 1732 in Northampton, Massachusetts, she was the daughter of the renowned Puritans, ▷Sarah Pierpont Edwards and Jonathan Edwards. After her marriage to Aaron Burr in 1752, she lived in Newark and later Princeton, New Jersey. From 1754 to 1757, she maintained a journal; addressed to her Boston friend, Sarah Prince, ▷*The Journal of Esther Edwards Burr* recounts her exhausting daily activities, her devoutness, and also her frustrations with limited opportunities to engage in intellectual pursuits. As the spouse of the President of the College of New Jersey, she had an opportunity to meet the leading citizens of the region, but she often longed for female companionship. After inoculation against smallpox, she died on 7 April 1758 at the age of twenty-six.

Bush Studies (1902)
Australian short stories by ▷Barbara Baynton. Baynton's stark and realistic stories are concerned with the hardships of life in the Australian bush, particularly for women and children. 'The Chosen Vessel' is an account of the murder of a bushwoman by a passing tramp, and 'Squeaker's Mate' tells of an industrious bush woman whose back is broken by a branch of the tree she is felling. The neighbours ignore her, the shiftless and lazy Squeaker sells her sheep, drinks the proceeds, banishes her to an outbuilding, and brings home another woman. The cruelty in these stories is relentless and the bush is seen as a place of fear, inhabited by ignorant and predatory creatures, both male and female.
▷Short story (Australia)

Business Letters of Alida Schuyler Livingston, 1680–1726 (1982)
▷Alida Schuyler van Rensselaer Livingston and her husband Robert became two of the most prosperous landowners and merchants in the North American colony of New Netherland. The first decade of Livingston's letters to her husband (translated from her native Dutch) span the years in which they were establishing their holdings. In the following years she relates to Robert her progress in managing their estate while he was attending the Assembly in New York. Eventually Alida managed both their Albany properties and Livingston Manor. Though some letters to 'My Dearest Love' are of a personal nature, most of Livingston's epistles are dominated by her business dealings. Few documents of the early Dutch settlers in North America are as resplendent with details as Livingston's account of everyday life in the colony.
▷Early North American letters

Busta, Christine (1915–1987)
Austrian poet. Her early poetry, *Der Regenbaum* (1951) (*The Rain-tree*), belongs to an Austrian romantic tradition which celebrates the beauty of nature in small and humble things. It is a theme which, in her later work such as *Unterwegs zu älteren Feuern* (1965) (*On the Way to the Older Fires*), developed into a yearning for a harmonious world and which culminated in a collection of sensuous and sensitive love poems published two years before her death, *Immitten aller Vergänglichkeit* (1985) (*Among Transitory Things*).

Busu, Fatima (born 1948)
Malay novelist. Born in Penang, she is a university lecturer who has published several novels, among them *Ombak Bukan Biru* (1977) (*The Waves are Not Blue*) and *Kepulangan* (1980) (*Return*), and is considered a significant woman writer. She has won several literary prizes chiefly for her short stories, which are available in two collections, *Lambaian Tanah Hijau* (1980) (*The Waving of the Green Land*) and *Yang Abadi* (1980) (*The Eternal*). Her story 'Bunga-Bunga Palau' ('Island Flowers') dwells on Malay rural poverty, while *The Children from Kampung Pasir Pekan* (English translation in *Tenggara*, 1980) characteristically dwells on Malay roots in the countryside, a life which generates nostalgia but is also the cause of economic backwardness. Timah's life there is full and carefree, and she tearfully leaves it all when she departs for further education.

Butala, Sharon (born 1940)
Canadian short story writer and novelist. Born in Nipawin, Saskatchewan, Butala moved to Saskatoon after spending her early years in northern Saskatchewan. She put herself through university, worked as a special educator, married, had a son, and divorced in 1975, a year before remarrying and moving to a cattle ranch near Eastend, Saskatchewan. Her first novel, *Country of the Heart*, was published in 1984, followed by *The Gates of the Sun* (1986), *Luna* (1988) and *Upstream* (1991). A collection of short stories, *Queen of the Headaches*, appeared in 1985, and *Fever* in 1990. Her novels are overwhelmingly realistic, but the

intense writing of her short stories steps past its own location and cadence, and shines.

Butcher Shop, The (1926)

Novel by New Zealand writer ▷Jean Devanny. After six printings of the first edition, *The Butcher Shop* went out of print in 1931 and was not republished in New Zealand until 1981. After its first publication *The Butcher Shop* won Devanny instant notoriety and was banned in New Zealand, Boston, Australia and Germany, while selling 15,000 copies (see H. Roberts, introduction to *The Butcher Shop*, 1981). In New Zealand *The Butcher Shop* was believed to have been banned because its portrayal of farm conditions was considered 'detrimental' to immigration policy. The book is informed by Devanny's socialism and feminism. It describes the marriage of Margaret and Barry Messenger, whose 'pure', innocent and equal relationship is distorted by social pressure (society is compared to a slaughter house as the title suggests) into one of male dominance and female subservience in which the woman is economically dependent on the man. The novel provides a Marxist analysis of women as a class and also shows how, when civilized and rational behaviour is disrupted by passion, the butcher shop of human emotions, and especially sexuality, asserts itself. With the renewed late-20th-century feminist interest in early women writers, *The Butcher Shop* has emerged as a significant novel of the 1920s and an early feminist critique of social conditions and assumptions.

Butcher's Wife, The (1983)

Set in the little seacoast town of Lugang in Taiwan, this story – by the gifted Taiwanese writer ▷Li Ang – was based on the press report of a sensational case in Shanghai in the early 1930s. The most striking part of the case was that the woman murdered her husband, not for a lover as generally presumed, but because she had been driven to it by her husband's abuse.

After Chen Linshi's father dies and her mother is caught in adultery, Lin is taken away by her uncle and later married off to a butcher, Chen Jiangshui.

The butcher, reduced to a beast himself by daily repeated acts of killing, rapes her day and night, experiencing a thrill as her cries pierce the air like the squeal of dying pigs. Lin endures life with him from day to day, getting to know something of the viciously gossip neighbourhood, and partaking in the various sacrificial rites of a fishing community ruled by superstition. Finally she rebels. Her acts of resistance include a search for employment, and obstinate silence in the face of her husband's sexual violence. The butcher responds with brutality. Finally, he forces her to the slaughter house to witness a killing, and then wash the entrails. Something snaps in Lin's mind. That same night, with the confused memories of her mother being pinned down under a man, mixed up with nightmarish images of the slaughter house, she picks up the butcher's knife and does to him what she saw him do to the pigs.

After her arrest and execution, the neighbours call it 'divine retribution.'

Butler, Lady Eleanor ▷Ladies of Llangollen, The

Butler, Octavia (born 1947)

US novelist and short story writer. Born in Pasedena, California, Butler was raised by strict Baptist women. As in ▷*Kindred* (1979), her ▷science fiction novels feature black women struggling against racism and sexism. Butler's Patternist series centres on a society of telepaths linked through a mental 'pattern'. In *Patternmaster* (1976) those in power oppress those without power through mind control, but the heroine defeats the oppressor through her healing powers. In *Mind of My Mind* (1977) she learns to control her destructive power and, as leader, she substitutes maternal caring for patriarchal domination. In *Survivor* (1978) she accepts the social obstacles imposed on her but discovers her source of strength in learning to compromise and survive. In *Wild Seed* (1980) the heroine brings healing and loving to an oppressive ▷patriarchal world. Butler's women use their power to conquer the notion of tyranny through compassion.

Other works include: *Clay's Ark* (1984).

Butts, Mary (1890–1937)

English novelist and short story writer. She grew up in South Dorset, the setting for her novels *Ashe of Rings* (1925), *Armed with Madness* (1928) and *Death of Felicity Taverner* (1932), a number of short stories and her autobiography *The Crystal Cabinet: my childhood at Salterns* (1937). In these writings, Butts explores the relationship between the land and its dwellers, attacking urban development and the loss of the countryside. She does not sentimentalize nature, however, but presents it as alien and powerful. Throughout her life she was interested in the occult and the supernatural, a preoccupation which emerges strongly in her writing, and which was consolidated when she became a part of the occult group around satanist Aleister Crowley in the early 1920s.

During World War I, Butts became a part of London literary circles, befriending poet Ezra Pound (1885–1972), ▷H.D., ▷Bryher, ▷Rebecca West and ▷May Sinclair. Her marriage to the writer John Rodker over, she left for the Continent with the artist Cecil Maitland, living on the Left Bank in Paris during the 1920s as part of the group of British and US writers which included Sylvia Beach and ▷Djuna Barnes. Her poems and short stories were published in journals of ▷modernist writing, including *The Little Review*, *The Dial* and *Pagany*. In 1930 she married the artist Gabriel Aitken; they separated in 1934. She settled in Cornwall in

1932, and continued to write reviews and short stories, as well as historical fictions and monographs, including *Scenes from the Life of Cleopatra* (1935). Her short stories were collected in three volumes: *Speed the Plough* (1923), *Several Occasions* (1932) and *Last Stories* (1938), published posthumously at Bryher's instigation. Butts died in 1937 of a burst appendix.

Byatt, A.S. (born 1936)
English novelist, literary critic and scholar. Born in Sheffield, and sister of ▷Margaret Drabble. She read English at Newnham College, Cambridge, and worked as an English lecturer in England and in the United States. Byatt is recognized equally as a scholar and a novelist. This dual occupation is evident throughout her fiction, with its characteristic erudition and its combination of literary and literary critical concerns, preoccupations treated most successfully in the Booker Prize-winning novel ▷*Possession: A Romance* (1990). Her first novel, *Shadow of a Sun* (1964), is a ▷*Bildungsroman* dealing with the attempts made by a teenage daughter of a successful novelist to escape from his powerful and dominant personality. *The Game* (1967) explores the relationship of two sisters whose childhood conflicts and gaming based on shared imaginary worlds is reawakened with tragic consequences in later life. The imaginary and the real are unstable as discrete realms in *The Game*, as are the categories of art and life in Byatt's analysis. *Virgin in the Garden* (1979) and *Still Life* (1985) are the first volumes in a projected series of four. Set in the 1950s and around the coronation of Elizabeth II, the novels contrast events, through allegory and allusion, with the first Elizabethan (▷Elizabeth Tudor) reign. Her critical writings include two volumes on ▷Iris Murdoch (1976, 1988), a writer who has greatly influenced Byatt, and *Unruly Times* (1989), a study of 'Wordsworth and Coleridge: Poetry and Life'.

Byatt has also edited an edition of ▷George Eliot's *The Mill on the Floss* (1979).
▷Anita Brookner

By Grand Central Station I Sat Down and Wept (1945)
▷Elizabeth Smart's elegaic love story, written as an antiphonic chorus to 'The Song of Solomon'. A classic of Canadian literature (although not distributed in Canada until 1966), it is considered a masterpiece of poetic prose. The novel centres on the narcissistic narrator's overwhelming passion for a married man, but their flight from the world that would curtail their love is strangely suspended. Moored in futility, but haunting in its lament, the novel orchestrates the failure of romantic love with an intensity and passion echoed through its mythological references. ▷Brigid Brophy, who wrote the foreword, claims it is a 'masterpiece'.
Bib: Sullivan, R., *By Heart*.

Byrd, Mary Willing (1740–1814)
North American letter-writer. She was born in Philadelphia, but little is known of her early life. In 1761 she married Colonel William Byrd of the aristocratic Virginia Byrds. Upon his death, she discovered she was an impoverished widow with eight children to support. She redeveloped their plantation into a prosperous property, but during the American Revolution her loyalty to the Patriot cause was questioned, nearly destroying her livelihood once again. Byrd fought against those who questioned her loyalty, writing directly to Thomas Jefferson and enlisting his authority in her cause. No proof of her collaboration with the enemy was found and charges against her were dropped. Her letters, included in *The Papers of Thomas Jefferson*, are powerfully written and express one woman's outrage at challenges to her loyalty and contributions to the American Revolution.
▷'Letters of Mary Willing Byrd'; Early North American letters

Caak Nyng Chiiwid (1964) (Scenes from Life)
Novel by Thai writer ▷Boonlua. The heroine,
Phachongchid, is brought up to be *phu di* (genteel)
and *sri pharaya* (the 'perfect wife') – an ideal
homemaker, cook, lover, mother and hostess, who
places her husband's interests above all else – and
she is therefore not given higher education. Her
parents match her with Praphan, who having lived
and been educated abroad is, ironically, bored
with the very qualities which make her *phu di*.
Contradicting the Thai saying that 'an enchanting
cooking spoon can charm her man until the day
he dies', he devalues her home-making skills,
since a good cook may be hired, but not
intellectual compatibility. Sensing her husband's
undefined dissatisfaction with her, Phachongchid
decides to leave him, but when he accidentally
discovers her intention, he acquires a new respect
for her untypical initiative – and the marriage is
saved. The rendition of the narrative through
Phachongchid's rather than her husband's
consciousness subtly suggests the condition of the
Thai woman trapped into a sense of inadequacy
or self-blame, resulting from a customary
upbringing dissonant with modern notions of
equality between the sexes.

Caballero, Fernán ▷Böhl von Faber, Cecilia

Cabello de Carbonera, Mercedes (1845–1907)
Peruvian novelist. She participated in the evening
readings of ▷Juana Manuela Gorriti in Lima,
Peru, showing herself to be a writer of 'great
talent'. Her three initial novels, influenced by
romanticism, are uninteresting and sentimental,
but *Blanca Sol* (1889), written in a naturalistic
manner, is a keen analysis of the vices and
hypocrisies of society at the time, and shows the
decadence of the higher ranks of society. *El
Conspirador: autobiografía de un hombre público*
(1892) (*The Conspirator: Autobiography of a Public
Figure*), probably her best novel, is a fictitious
memoir of a party leader in prison, and is also
▷naturalistic in style. *Las Consecuencias* (1890)
(*Consequences*) criticizes gambling and switches to
a rural setting.
   Other works: *Los amores de Hortensia* (1888)
(*The Love Affairs of Hortensia*); *Sacrificio y
recompensa* (1886) (*Sacrifice and Reward*), and
Eledora (1887).

Cabete, Adelaide (1867–1935)
Portuguese physician, feminist activist and
essayist. Born into a working-class family, Cabete
was self-taught. When she was nineteen, she
married a sergeant in the Republican party, who
encouraged her to pursue her education. In 1900
she graduated with a medical degree, having
written a thesis on the predicament of working-
class mothers-to-be. In addition to co-founding
the Republican League of Portuguese Women
with ▷Ana de Castro Osório, she established the
National Council of Portuguese Women, an
umbrella organization for the different women's
groups in the country. As head of the Council,

she organized the First Feminist Congress, which
took place in Lisbon in 1924. She also
collaborated on the magazine ▷*Alma Feminina
(Woman's Soul)*, an official publication of the
Council, to which she contributed essays on
health care for women and children, with special
emphasis on the poor.
   In 1929 Cabete left Portugal for Angola, where
she continued to write on health issues. While in
Africa, she suffered an accident and never
regained her health. She returned to Lisbon in
1934, and died the following year.

Cabrera, Lydia (born 1899)
Cuban short story writer. She was educated in
Havana, where throughout her childhood she felt
attracted to the legends and magical faith of the
negroes. Fernando Ortiz was her mentor in the
Afro-Cuban folklore of the island. Beginning in
1913, under the pseudonym Nena, she wrote a
social chronicle for the magazine *Cuba y América*.
On her return from France to Cuba in the 1930s,
she became an anthropologist and a folklorist.
The oral narratives of old representatives of the
African culture were integrated into *Contes nègres
de Cuba* (1936) (*Negro Stories of Cuba*), which
appeared in Paris, in a French translation. Later
Porqué . . . cuentos negros de Cuba (1948) (*Why . . .
Negro Stories of Cuba*) appeared in French
translation in 1954. She participated in the avant-
garde movement of ▷magic realism, together with
Cuban novelist Alejo Carpentier (1904–1980) and
Guatemalan writer Miguel Angel Asturias (1899–
1974). Her works were published in the French
magazines *Cahiers du Sud*, *Revue de Paris* and *Les
Nouvelles Littéraires*, as well as in Cuban
magazines. Her compilation *Refranes de negros
viejos* (1955) (*Sayings of Old Negros*) was published
in Havana. She lived in Cuba until the 1960s,
then left because of the Castro revolution.
Other works include *Ayapá, cuentos de jicotea*
(1971) (*Ayapá, Wasp Stories*), and *Cuentos para
adultos, niños y retrasados mentales* (1983) (*Stories
for Adults, Children and the Mentally Retarded*).

Cáceres, Esther de (1903–1971)
Uruguayan poet and essayist. She graduated in
medicine, but also studied to be a teacher. She
was an attaché in the Uruguayan embassy in
Washington. Her poetic work began with *Las
ínsulas extrañas* (1929) and flowed with a constant
thematic unity until her death. It has been said
that in her book *Tiempo y abismo* (1965) (*Time and
Abyss*) the religious themes deepened. The tone is
of intense fervour and devotion, with a delicate
musicality, and a purity and transparency felt to be
rare in women's poetry. Her frequent
correspondence with important personalities of
both Uruguay and North America made her into
an active member of the cultural life of the
continent.
   Other works: *Canción de Esther Cáceres* (1931)
(*The Song of Esther de Cáceres*); *Libro de la soledad*
(1933) (*Book of Solitude*); *Los cielos* (1935) (*The
Heavens*); *Cruz y éxtasis de la Pasión* (1937) (*Cross

and *Ecstasy of the Passion*); *El alma y el ángel* (1938)
(*The Spirit and the Angel*); *Espejo sin muerte* (1941)
(*Mirror Without Death*); *Concierto de amor* (1944)
(*Love Concert*); *Antología de Esther de Cáceres
(1929–1945)* (1945) (*Anthology of the Works of
Esther de Cáceres, 1929–1945*); *Madrigales, trances,
saetas* (1947) (*Madrigals, Moments, Arrows*); *Paso de
la noche* (1957) (*Passage of the Night*); *Los cantos del
destierro* (1963) (*Songs from Exile*), and *Canto
desierto* (1969) (*Desert Song*).

Caddie, a Sydney Barmaid (1953)

Australian autobiographical work edited by
▷Dymphna Cusack. The harrowing story of
Caddie, who has left an adulterous husband, and
her efforts to support her two young children in
Sydney during the Depression of the 1930s. The
atmosphere of the slums in Sydney, and the
kindness of their inhabitants, is realistically evoked
as Caddie moves from one job to another, living
in squalid surroundings, with her children at
times minded by money-hungry 'baby farmers'.
Caddie has a brief experience of love and security,
but her lover is killed. She does, however, find the
strength to survive the Depression and rear her
children. The story of her struggle became the
immensely popular Australian film *Caddie* (1976).

Caesar, Mary (1677–1741)

Jacobite who wrote a manuscript 'book' or journal,
as well as corresponding with English poet
Alexander Pope (1688–1744). Her book reshapes
the (for her) depressing and disappointing history
of her times.
Bib: Rumbold, Valerie, in Grundy and Wiseman
(eds), *Women, Writing, History*.

CAFRA

The Caribbean Association for Feminist Research
and Action, founded in 1985 and based in
Trinidad, includes among its members individual
feminists, women activists and women's
organizations spanning the Dutch, English,
French and Spanish-speaking Caribbean and its
▷diaspora. CAFRA focuses on all the strategic
issues facing women in Caribbean societies –
social, economic, cultural, political and sexual.
See ▷*Creation Fire: A CAFRA Anthology of
Caribbean Women's Poetry*.

Caiel (Alice Pestana) (1860–1929)

Portuguese feminist activist, novelist and
dramatist. In her 1898 study, 'La Femme et la
Paix: Appel aux Mères Portugaises' ('Woman and
Peace: Appeal to Portuguese Mothers'), Caiel
denounced the inadequacies of the educational
system in Portugal – especially with regard to
women's instruction. Her commitment to
pedagogical matters and women's liberation was
untiring. She wrote a fascinating overview of
women's secondary education and offered specific
suggestions for reform in *O Que Deve Ser a
Educação Secundária da Mulher?* (1892) (*What
Should Women's Secondary Education Be?*), a project
subsidized by the government. The following year

she visited women's professional schools in other
west European countries, and published her
findings in newspapers in Lisbon. In addition to
her treatises and reports on the subject of
women's education, Caiel also wrote fiction,
adopting her pen-name in 1885. Much of this
work, such as the novel *Desgarrada* (1902) (*The
One Who Went Astray*), concerns middle-class
women who struggle for more liberated lives.
    In 1901 Caiel married and moved to Madrid
with her Spanish-born husband. She played an
important role in literary and cultural exchanges
between Spain and Portugal; for example, she
translated the work of several Spanish authors
into Portuguese, and she published numerous
▷*crônicas* about Spanish life in the Lisbon
newspaper *Diário de Notícias*. She continued to
pursue her interests in pedagogy, and she wrote
on the Spanish educational system. Towards the
end of her life, she became especially interested in
the education of delinquent children.

Caird, Mona (1858–1932)

English novelist, born on the Isle of Wight. She
married J.A. Henryson in 1877 and lived in
Hampstead from then until the end of her life.
From 1883 to 1915 she wrote seven novels, as
well as a non-fictional work, *The Morality of
Marriage and Other Essays* (1897). She argued,
both in this work and in her fiction, for marriage
▷reform. Her novels focus on the oppression that
women can suffer, yet Caird also creates bold
heroines who defy society's expectations. Much of
the fiction is polemical in tone, with long speeches
calling for changes in attitude. Caird herself saw
marriage as a patriarchal system of exchange, and
advocated equal rights to child custody, divorce,
and proper ▷education for women. Her novels
include *The Wings of Azreal* (1889), *A Romance of
the Moors* (1891) and *The Daughters of Danaus*
(1894). Her last work was *Stones of Sacrifice*
(1915). In the 1890s, her work was considered
▷'New Woman' fiction.
    ▷Feminism (19th-century Britain)
Bib: Cunningham, G., *The 'New Woman' and the
Fiction of the 1890s*; Stetz, M.D., 'Turning Points:
Mona Caird', *Turn of the Century Women* 2,
Winter 1985.

Cairns, Elizabeth (1685–1714)

Scottish Dissenting preacher and memoirist of
low social status. She looked after sheep, worked
as a servant and later ran a school and tended her
paralysed mother.
    ▷Women and work (18th-century Britain)

Cai Wenji ▷Cai Yen

Cai Yen (AD 177–?)

An aristocratic Chinese woman who lived in the
later Han dynasty (AD 25–220), Cai Yen, also
named Cai Wenji, was famous in her time for her
accomplishments in music and learning. Widowed
and childless, she was abducted by the Xunnu
tribes from north China during the civil unrest of

194–5 and made to marry one of the chieftains of the tribe. She lived for twelve years among the Xunnu people and bore two sons. Then she was released by the reigning minister as a favour to her father who had no other children. A famous painting depicts her at the moment of departure, torn between longing for her native land and love of her two sons, whom she had to leave behind. She composed the famous *Lamentations* in two versions, describing her feelings in moving terms. *Hu Jia Shi Ba Pai* are poems of lamentation, describing her capture by the barbarians and her life of exile, and mourning her separation from the two sons she left behind. It is a classic piece of Chinese poetry and enjoys a high place in the literary canon, though Cai's authorship is disputed. The story of Cai Wenji's exile and return has been the subject of many literary works, notably the play *Cai Wenji* by Guo Muoruo (1892–1978), China's leading poet, dramatist and man of letters of modern times.

Cajal, Rosa María (born 1920)
Spanish novelist. Born in Zaragoza, Cajal deals with feminist and Existentialist themes in her novels, which include *Juan Risco* (1948); *Primera derecha* (1955) (*Apartment 1-R*), and *Un paso más* (1956) (*Just One Step More*).

Cajou (1961)
This second novel by the Caribbean writer, ▷Michèle Lacrosil, is the diary of the mulatto, Cajou, who has been living in France for a while. Convinced of her inferiority because she is not white, she suspects the motives of those who would befriend or promote her, and also those of her white lover, Germain. The diary, written over a period of four evenings, closes as she departs for the Seine, pregnant and intending to drown herself. The colour of the skin as a factor which gives, or rather denies, ▷identity is a motivating feature in *Cajou*, as it is in all three of Lacrosil's novels (see also ▷*Sapotille et le serein d'argile*, 1960, and ▷*Demain Jab-Herma*, 1967).
▷*Folie Antillaise*

Caju ▷Júlia, Francisca

Caldwell, Taylor (born 1900)
US novelist. Of Scottish descent, Caldwell graduated from the University of Buffalo in New York in 1931. During World War I she served in the US Naval Reserve and, more recently, in the Department of Immigration and Naturalization. A prolific and popular writer, she voices her political conservatism in romances, historical romances and religious stories. Novels like *Captains and the Kings* (1973) focus on upper-class US industrialists and their family dynasties. Hungry for power, her protagonists are contemptuous of the lower classes. They resent social legislation designed to help the lower classes because they believe it curtails their own freedom.

Other works include: *The Eagles Gather* (1939), *The Arm and the Darkness* (1942), *The Final Hour* (1944), *This Side of Innocence* (1946), *Tender Victory* (1956), *A Pillar of Iron* (1965), *No One Hears But Him* (1966), *Dialogues with the Devil* (1968), *Testimony of Two Men* (1968) and *Glory and the Lightning* (1974).

Callaghan, Mary Rose (born 1944)
Irish novelist. Born in Dublin, she studied at University College, Dublin, and now divides her time between Ireland and the USA. Having taught for several years, she is now a full-time writer and freelance lecturer. Her novels are: *Mothers* (1982), *Confessions of a Prodigal Daughter* (1985), *The Awkward Girl* (1990) and *Has Anyone Seen Heather?* (1991), a teenage novel. Her biography, *Kitty O'Shea – A Life of Katherine Parnell*, appeared in 1989.

Callender, Hannah (1737–1801)
North American diarist. Probably born in Philadelphia, Pennsylvania, she was raised in Burlington, New Jersey, until her marriage to Samuel Sansom in 1762, when she resettled in the city of her birth and resided there the remainder of her life. She maintained a diary (▷'Extracts from the Diary of Hannah Callender') between the ages of twenty and twenty-five. She travelled a good deal in the years preceding her marriage, and her diary reveals a woman of good education and lively personality. Little is known of Callender after marriage, when her diary entries stopped.

Callwood, June
Influential Canadian journalist who has written numerous books on the legal and social position of women in Canada. They include *Love, Hate, Fear, Anger and the Other Lively Emotions* (1964), *The Law is Not for Women!* (with Martin Zuker, 1973), *Portrait of Canada* (1981), *Emma* (1984), *Emotions* (1986), and *Twelve Weeks in Spring* (1986). A social activist and public spokesperson, she is renowned for her work with the Civil Liberties Association, for her work on behalf of AIDS victims, and for founding a hostel for women.

Calvo de Aguilar, Isabel (born 1916)
Promoter of Spanish women's writing and novelist. Calvo de Aguilar is better known for founding the Associación de Escritoras Españolas (Association of Spanish Female Writers) in the 1950s than for her novels. Written mainly to entertain, her novels include romantic tales of unrequited love in exotic settings. Among her titles are: *El misterio del palacio chino* (1951) (*The Mystery of the Chinese Palace*); *La isla de los siete pecados* (1952) (*The Island of the Seven Sins*), and *La danzarina inmóvil* (1954) (*The Motionless Dancer*).

Calypso
The term, of particular relevance in Caribbean writing, by which the carnival songs of ▷Trinidad are known. Calypso is part of an oral tradition

(▷oral history, Caribbean) of verbal arts and biting commentary in the Caribbean. It is historically linked to the post-emancipation development of ▷carnival as a festival of celebration by the freed slaves. The songs are characterized by the use of personal ribaldry and licentious material. They often contain moral insights, and serve as social commentary. They are seen as an instrument of social criticism. The antecedents of the calypso were the praisesongs and songs of derision originating in West African tribal life.

▷*Picong*; Carnival; Calypsonian

Calypsonian

A singer of ▷calypso, the carnival songs of ▷Trinidad, with the ability to improvize on a selected topic, and to weave lyric, melody rhythm, phrasing and pantomime into a complete work of art so that the calypso song is identified with the personality of the singer. This term is of relevance in Caribbean writing.

Cambridge, Ada (1844–1926)

Australian novelist and poet. Cambridge was born in England, married a young curate, George Frederick Cross, in 1870, and emigrated to Victoria, where Cross served as an Anglican minister in various country parishes. She returned to England twice, but settled in Victoria in 1917, after her husband's death. Cambridge's life and works present many contradictions. Her autobiographical writings, *Thirty Years in Australia* (1903) and *The Retrospect* (1912), provide an admirable chronicle of colonial life. The second of her three volumes of poetry, ▷*Unspoken Thoughts* (1887), was published anonymously, but almost immediately withdrawn. Cambridge published thirty romances between 1865 and 1914, nine of which were serialized in the *Australasian*. Her best-known novels are ▷*A Marked Man* (1890, reprinted 1987), *A Woman's Friendship* (1889, republished 1988), ▷*The Three Miss Kings* (1891, reprinted 1987), *Not All in Vain* (1892), *A Marriage Ceremony* (1894), *Fidelis* (1895), *A Little Minx* (1893) and *Materfamilias* (1898).

Cambridge's reputation has suffered from the 20th-century prejudice against ▷romance fiction, and her stereotyped plots and characters, as well as her Anglocentric views, have been criticised. Such criticism, however, ignores the strength of Cambridge's writing, the validity of her concern with domestic issues such as courtship and marriage, which were all-important to her readers, and the strong element of social satire in the novels.

▷Short story (Australia); *From the Verandah; Peaceful Army, The; On Her Selection*

Cameron, Anne (born 1938)

Canadian novelist, poet and screenwriter, also known as Cam Hubert, born in British Columbia. She is the author of numerous works, many of them celebrating west-coast native myths and stories. *Dreamspeaker* won the 1978 Gibson Award

for Literature, and the film version won seven film awards; it portrays a delinquent boy who runs away and is adopted by two Native Canadian shamans, the Dreamspeaker and his companion, He Who Would Sing. Deep in the forests of British Columbia, they teach him the mystical power of the spirit world, and the courage to face his demons. Cameron's other books include: *Daughters of Copper Woman* (1981), *Child of Her People* (1987), *How Raven Freed the Moon, How the Loon Lost Her Voice* (1985), *Orca's Song, Raven Returns the Water*, and *Spider Woman* (1988). Many of these stories use Native Canadian content, but since their appearance she has stated publicly that she feels it is no longer appropriate to use Native Canadian voice. Later works are *Stubby Amberchuk and the Holy Grail* (1987) and *Women, Kids & Huckleberry Wine* (1989). *Earth Witch* (1982) and *The Annie Poems* (1987) are books of poetry. Anne Cameron uses goddess mythology and the mythology of Amazons, from Celtic to African, in her powerful parables. She lives in Powell River, British Columbia.
Bib: Scheier, L., Sheard, S. and Wachtel, E. (eds), *Language in Her Eye*.

Cameron, Eleanor (born 1912)

Canadian children's writer, born Eleanor Butler in Winnipeg, Manitoba. She wrote a number of fantasies exploring the intersection of histories. *A Room Made of Windows* (1971), *Julia and the Hand of God* (1977), *That Julia Redfern* (1982), and *Julia's Magic* (1984) are engaged with a developing writer. *The Green and Burning Tree* (1969) is a collection of essays on children's literature.

Campan, Jeanne-Louise-Henriette Genest (1752–1822)

French prose writer. Born in Paris, at fifteen she entered the royal household as reader to the youngest daughters of Louis XV. After her brief marriage she became first lady's maid and companion to Marie Antoinette. Having survived the Revolution (1789) she founded a national institution for the education of young women before being made director of Napoleon's Maison d'Education de la Légion d'Honneur in Ecouen in 1807. With the fall of the empire, she was accused of having collaborated with Napoleon and betraying the queen. Her *Mémoires* (1822) may in part have been written to counter such allegations. They provide an interesting testimony to life under the ancien régime and during the Revolution while focusing on the private life of Marie Antoinette (1755–1793). The tone, generally polite and respectful, occasionally becomes vitriolic; the style is pre-romantic, emphasizing sensibility and the emotions. Her other published texts, mainly related to her work as an educationalist, include educational plays and a manual for young mothers. The memoirs have most recently been published as *Mémoires de Madame de Campan, première femme de chambre de Marie Antoinette, 1774–1792 (Memoirs of Madame*

de Campan, Principal Lady-in-Waiting to Marie Antoinette, 1774–1792) (1988).
Bib: Montagu, V. M., *The Celebrated Mme Campan*; Reval, G., *Madame Campan*.

Campbell, Grace MacLennan (1895–1963)

Canadian novelist and short story writer, born Grace Grant in Williamstown, Ontario. After her marriage she lived in Saskatchewan, Quebec, and Ontario. Her best-known works, *Thorn-Apple Tree* (1942) and *The Higher Hill* (1944) celebrate the Glengarry community of Scots Highland settlers.

Campbell, Maria (born 1940)

Born June Stifle in Saskatchewan, Canadian author of the powerful autobiography, ▷*Halfbreed* (1973), the first book to articulate the oppressions and frustrations of Canadian Metis women. Campbell's story confronts the brutality of a life of alcoholism, drug addiction, and prostitution with a calm lack of bitterness. It was Cheechum, her Cree great-grandmother, whose strength and spirituality sustained Campbell through her personal journey and inspired her to reclaim her dignity. *Riel's People* (1978) and *People of the Buffalo* (1976) are Metis historical stories written for children. *The Book of Jessica* (1989) is an account of the writing of a screenplay with non-Native Canadian actress Linda Griffiths. Campbell now writes mostly drama and screenplays. 'One of the reasons I like drama is that it, like storytelling, involves the exchange of energy between the storyteller and audience.' She lives at Gabriel's Crossing, Batoche, Saskatchewan.
Bib: Godard, B. in ▷*A Mazing Space*; Lutz, H. in *Contemporary Challenges: Conversations with Canadian Native Authors*.

Campbell, Marion (born 1948)

Australian novelist and short fiction writer. Campbell's two novels, *Lines of Flight* (1985) and *Not Being Miriam* (1989), question the nature of reality, the relationship of art to reality, and the relationship of the speaking subject to the generated art form. Central to *Lines of Flight* is the relationship of the female hero, the young Australian artist Rita Finnerty, a student at the *Institute des Beaux Arts* in Aix-en-Provence, to her male mentors, a psychocritic, Raymond, and his semiotician protegé Sébastien, who is writing a thesis on discourse analysis. Considerable comedy is generated as each character enacts her or his ideological commitment. The novel concludes with a reviewer's judgement of Rita's exhibition in Perth.

Not Being Miriam is an ostensibly realist novel in that it does attempt to write about the personal experiences of women in a particular time and place (Perth), but it also deploys a variety of experimental techniques to disrupt traditional realist expectations and provide a more authentic realism: one which is closer to female experience.

Campbell, Meg (born 1937)

New Zealand poet. Meg Campbell has worked as a librarian and bookseller, mostly in the Wellington region. She is married to the poet, Alistair Campbell. Her work focuses on domestic, familial and personal relationships, with particular reference to the times she has suffered from depression and hospital treatment, and to the Maori and Polynesian dimension of her life. Her publications are *The Way Back* (1981) and *A Durable Fire* (1982).
▷Maori literature

Campion, Sarah (born 1906)

Australian novelist, pseudonym of Mary Rose Coulton. Campion was born in Eastbourne, England, married a New Zealander and lived briefly in Australia from 1938 to 1940. She is chiefly celebrated for her Australian-based trilogy, *Mo Burdekin* (1941), *Bonanza* (1942) and *The Pommy Cow* (1944), lively accounts of the life of Mo Burdekin, the only survivor of a pioneering family drowned in a torrential flood in the great Burdekin River of tropical Queensland. Mo Burdekin discovers gold and later travels to the Boer War, where he meets an English girl, the 'pommy cow' of Campion's third volume.

Canadian Woman Studies (1978–present)

Begun as *Canadian Women's Studies*, a feminist quarterly founded with the goal of making current writing and research in Canada available to women, as well as making a space for women to publish. It is actively aimed towards a middle ground between the scholarly and the popular, between theory and practice. It has had, for example, a special issue in honour of ▷Margaret Laurence, guest-edited by ▷Clara Thomas. Bilingual, it is produced by an editorial board at York University, Ontario.

Cancioneiro da Ajuda (1904)

The oldest of all the ▷*cancioneiros* or 'songbooks' in the Galician-Portuguese tradition. Dating back to the late 13th century, it is made up exclusively of ▷*cantigas de amor*. In 1904 the scholar ▷Carolina Michaëlis de Vasconcelos published a two-volume critical edition of the manuscript, in which she provides important information on the role of women in the creation of medieval Portuguese verse.

Cancioneiro Geral (1516) (*General Songbook*)

Organized by the poet and historian Garcia de Resende (c 1470–1536), this collection contains much of the verse produced in Portugal during the 15th century. Written in Portuguese and Spanish, the poems were authored by and destined for individuals in the royal court. Often referred to as 'palace poetry', many of the compositions are lively *desafios* (duels), demonstrating the verbal dexterity of the poets, a few of whom are women.
▷*Cancioneiros*; Almada, Filipa de, Dona

Cancioneiros

Collections recording some of the earliest poetic compositions in Portuguese. The oldest collection, the ▷*Cancioneiro da Ajuda*, dates back to the 13th century. Many of the poems in these volumes are called ▷*cantigas* (songs), and are subdivided into the following categories: ▷*cantigas de amigo*, ▷*cantigas de amor*, and ▷*cantigas de mal dizer e escárnio*.
  ▷*Cancioneiro Geral*

Candler, Ann (More) (1740–1814)

English poet from the labouring class. Her husband's enlisting in the army and his drinking led her to put four children in the workhouse. She followed him to London, but returned to the Ipswich workhouse. She wrote poems in the Ipswich journal and eventually, in 1802, ▷patrons (including ▷Elizabeth Cobbold) settled her in a cottage and published her *Poetical Attempts* (1803).

Canne al vento (1913) (Reeds in the Wind)

Italian novel by ▷Grazia Deledda. She creates a ▷fantastical narrative around the realistic story of the decline of a Sardinian village and one family in particular. The aristocratic Pintor family, now made up of three single sisters, is sliding deep into poverty. Noemi, the youngest sister, conceives an unwise passion for their nephew, Giacinto, who precipitates the ruin of the family. Yet it is to the character of Efix, the family servant, that Deledda specifically draws the reader's attention and sympathy. Efix, the personification of loyalty, sees Noemi's passion as a form of retribution on him for a crime committed long ago. It transpires that Efix is devoted to the women because he perceives it as his duty to protect them. He has killed their father, albeit in self-defence, and spends his life, in the manner of a typical Deledda character, trying to expiate his sin. The novel is striking in its depiction of the countryside, its emphasis on the role of tradition, and its representation of death. Death, for Efix, is finally a liberation. For Deledda, it is that point where goodness triumphs over sin; both are concepts in which she firmly believes.

Cannon, Moya (born 1958)

Irish poet. Born in County Donegal, she studied history and politics at University College, Galway and at Corpus Christi College, Cambridge. She now lives in Galway, where she teaches in a school for travelling children. Her poems have been included in numerous anthologies, and have also been set to music by the Irish composer Jane O'Leary. She published her first collection, *The Oar*, in 1990.

Canon (literary)

A term which designates the body of literary texts conventionally included for study on literature courses. In the 1970s Anglo-American feminist critics drew attention to the sexual politics of the canon of great literature, arguing that is was a patriarchal construction dominated by male writers. In *A Literature of Their Own* (1977), ▷Elaine Showalter attempted to construct a separate tradition of women's writing. Since then, lesbian and black feminist critics have attacked both traditional and mainstream feminist literary canons for their ▷heterosexist and racist assumptions. They have gone on to argue the need to distinguish lesbian and black traditions of women's writing.
  ▷Lesbian feminist criticism; Black feminist criticism

Canth, Minna (1844–1897)

Finnish ▷realist prose author and dramatist. She grew up as a daughter of working-class parents who bought a shop in Kuopio. There she went to a Swedish girls' school. She attended the first Finnish teacher's college, founded in 1863, but did not finish her education. She married one of her teachers in 1865 and had seven children. She wrote some minor articles for journals, but when she saw her first play in a theatre she knew that she wanted to write for the stage. Her first play was performed in 1882, *Murtovarkens* (*The Burglary*).

Meanwhile, her husband had died in 1879. She had to earn money, and travelled to Kuopio with her children to save her father's shop from bankruptcy. At the same time she studied current literature and social theory. She began to write naturalist propaganda literature: the drama *Työmiken vaimo* (1885) (*The Workman's Wife*), describing the economic and moral dilemma of a woman whose husband is legally entitled to drink away his wife's property and make a young girl pregnant. She also wrote short stories about the lives of the poor and of women.

In the 1890s, after she had read the Russian novelist Tolstoy (1878–1910), she began to describe middle-class psychology and questions of belief and religion, trying to compromise between the old and new standards of morality. She is famous for being the first Finnish realist writer, and she is synonymous with the ▷modern breakthrough in Finland. She had the literary skills to write in a new way about the most important themes of her time.

Cantiga

Term used to describe an early form of Portuguese poetry which was originally sung.
  ▷*Cancioneiros*

Cantiga de amigo

An early verse form produced in Portugal, examples of which can be found in the ▷*cancioneiros*. The narrator is always a woman, and the theme of the poem is love. Sometimes the narrator is speaking to another woman – usually her mother or a friend; other times she is addressing her beloved. These poems are often classified according to their geographic setting – the seaside (*barcarolas*), the countryside (*pastorelas*), etc. – or particular events such as pilgrimages (*romarias*), dances (*bailaradas*).

Cantiga de amor

One of the three principal categories of lyrics found in the early Portuguese ▷*cancioneiros*. The speaker of the poem is a man, and his 'song of love' is addressed to an aristocratic lady, who is often married and indifferent.

▷*Cancioneiro da Ajuda*

Cantigas de mal dizer e escárnio

These early 'songs of vilification' were generally humorous and sometimes obscene. Those found in most ▷*cancioneiros* and later anthologies of Portuguese poetry are ironic and amusing. The poet ▷Natália Correia published some of the more bawdy and scandalous ones in her controversial collection *Antologia da Poesia Portuguesa Erótica e Satírica* (1965).

Canto, Estela (born 1919)

Argentinian novelist, journalist and translator. She directed and collaborated on several magazines. *El hombre del crepúsculo* (1953) (*Man of the Twilight*) centres on the high bourgeoisie and its past opulence. This work, along with the novels *El retrato y la imagen* (1950) (*The Portrait and the Image*) and *El estanque* (1956) (*The Pool*), mark the psychological side of her fiction. In *Borges a contraluz* (1989), about Argentinian writer Jorge Luis Borges (1899–1986), Canto claims that Borges was in love with her. The book is regarded as rather scandalous, but Borges's dedication of his story 'El aleph' to Canto may indicate that there is some truth in her claim.

Other works: *El muro de mármol* (1945) (*The Marble Wall*), and *Los espejos de la sombra* (1945) (*Mirrors of the Dark*).

Canto delle sirene, Il (1989) (The Sirens' Song)

Italian novel by ▷Maria Corti. The sirens' song is the unifying thread of this narrative, through which stories of various navigators and various kinds of navigation are told. There are autobiographical elements here, in the tale of Celestina, a young Milanese scholar who tries to juggle her academic writing with her creative work. This is at once a fictional tale, a treatise, and an intellectual autobiography, and it is handled with consummate skill by Corti.

Bib: West, R., review, *Annali d'Italianistica*, 7 (1989), pp. 493–6.

Can Xue (born 1953)

Chinese writer. A native of Hunan in south China, Can Xue discontinued her studies after middle school and, while in her early twenties, set up a tailor's shop with her husband. She began to write in 1985 and won critical attention for the surrealist elements in her work. *Performance of Breakthrough*, a novel, and *Dialogues in Paradise* (translated in 1989 by R. Janssen and Zhang Jian), a collection of short stories, reveal the influence of Latin-American ▷magic realism.

▷Xi Xi

Canzoniere (1544)

A collection of poetry, written by Italian poet Vittoria Colonna. In the ▷Petrarchan tradition, it was republished several times during her lifetime, and throughout the 1700s, 1800s and 1900s. The theme of the poetry is, for the most part, one of sadness and mourning. In this poetry, Colonna expresses her grief at the loss of her husband, and of her father: '*Scrivo sol per sfogar l'interna doglia*' ('I write only to relieve my inner pain'), she says. She laments the inadequacy of her words to do justice to the two men whom she has loved. Yet the poetry is also a celebration of the happiness of the past, in which the poet claims for the female poet, as well as for women in general, a right to use all the expressions of love normally the prerogative of the male poet of this period.

Caoineadh Airt Úi Laoghaire ▷Lament for Art O'Leary, The (1921)

Cape, Judith ▷Page, Patricia K.

Capécia, Mayotte (1928–1953)

Novelist from the French Antilles in the Caribbean. She was born and educated in Martinique, and spent most of her later years in France. Capécia wrote two novels, *Je suis Martiniquaise* (1948) (*I Am Martiniquan*) and *La Négresse Blanche* (1950) (*The White Negress*), both of which focus on the love of a coloured woman for a white man. Condemned by the Martiniquan doctor and psychiatrist Franz Fanon for pandering to the white man's ethnocentric conception of self, her work was used in his study *Black Skins, White Masks* as case studies in the psychoneurosis of race relations. Although Capécia's novels portray a black woman defining herself through her relationship with a white man, they also depict relations between coloured women and men of any colour, such as those between masters and slaves. Her novels close with the Caribbean woman poised, ready for flight to France, a promised land of *liberté, égalité, et fraternité*. She was one of the first women to map out the quest of the black heroine within a white world, whereby the woman's awakening comes in the conflict of her relationship with a white man (▷identity, Caribbean).

▷Lacrosil, Michèle

Capmany Farnes, Maria Aurèlia (born 1918)

Spanish feminist writer. Capmany Farnes read philosophy at the University of Barcelona, and is now one of the leading figures of Catalan feminism. Her studies, such as *La dona a Catalunya* (1966) (*Woman in Catalonia*), and *El femenisme a Catalunya* (1973) (*Feminism in Catalonia*), are cornerstones of feminism in Spain. Her main novels are: *Necessitem morir* (1952) (*We Must Die*); *L'altre ciutat* (1955) (*The Other City*); *Tana o la felicitat* (1956) (*Tana, or Happiness*); *La pluja als vidres* (1963) (*Rain on the Windowpane*); *Un lloc entre els morts* (1969) (*A Place Among the Dead*); *Vitrines d'Amsterdam* (1970) (*Showcase of*

Amsterdam); *Quim/Quimà* (1971); *El jaqué de la democracia* (1972) (*The Tuxedo of Democracy*); *El malefici de la reina d'Hongria* (1982) (*The Enchantment of the Queen of Hungary*); and ▷*Lo color més blau* (1982) (*The Bluest Colour*).
▷Catalan women's writing

Cappiello, Rosa (1942)
Australian novelist. Cappiello was born in Naples, Italy, and came to Australia in 1971. She is one of Australia's most significant migrant writers. Her autobiographical novel, *Paese Fortunata* (1981) (*Oh Lucky Country*), dealing with migrant experience in Australia in the 1970s, was first published in Italy and won the Italian Premio Calabria award for 1982. An English version, translated by G. Rando, was published in 1985. Cappiello has also published (in Italian) *I Semi Negri* (1977) (The Black Seeds).
▷Migrant women's writing (Australia)

Captivity narratives
Accounts of kidnappings of European settlers by Native Americans. The earliest, and in many ways the most significant, captivity narrative in North America was written in 1682 by ▷Mary Rowlandson, a Puritan; it established what became an almost requisite style of captivity, trials and humiliation, and eventual 'restoration', that acted as the narrative structure and religious analogy of the genre for the next century. Although some men employed this genre, it was largely the realm of women writers and was one of the first acceptable ways in which a woman might publish her writings. The publication of ▷Elizabeth Meader Hanson's narrative in 1728 is seen as the transitional moment in the genre; since Hanson was a Quaker, her narrative is less an explanation for her community than it is a personal address to an individual reader. Thereafter, numerous fictionalized versions of the captivity narrative appeared, most notably ▷Ann Eliza Schuyler Bleecker's *History of Maria Kittle* (1791), Mary French's 'A Poem Written by a Captive Damzel' (1706) and Mary Kinnan's *A True Narrative of the Sufferings of Mary Kinnan* (1795).
▷'Bars Fight'

Carbery, Ethna (1866–1911)
Irish poet and journalist. Born in County Antrim, she was the daughter of a staunchly Fenian (nationalist) Belfast man. Shortly before her death she married the Irish poet Seamus MacManus, and is also known as Anna MacManus. Her poems appeared in all the prominent nationalist magazines of the period, and her first collection of poems and songs, *The Four Winds of Erin* (1902), was constantly reprinted. Her most important contribution to writing, however, was her editorial collaboration with ▷Alice Milligan on the monthly journal *The Northern Patriot*, later called *The Shan Van Vocht* (*The Old Woman of Ireland*), which they produced between 1894 and 1899. Her contribution to the development of Irish

writing still remains to be adequately assessed and valued.

Carbet, Marie-Magdeleine ▷*Au Peril de toi Joie*

Carby, Hazel V. (born 1948)
British feminist critic of 19th-century black women's writing. *Reconstructing Womanhood: The Emergence of the Afro-American Woman Novelist* (1987) is a landmark book in black feminist historical and literary criticism. Carby challenges the existence of a homogeneous African-American ▷female tradition, and the corresponding assumption that black women write out of a shared experience. In place of these generalizations, Carby makes a case for producing specific histories which stress historical differences in black women's writing, and distinguish between black women and black feminists.

Cardinal, Marie (born 1929)
French novelist, born in Algeria. Marie Cardinal's most famous novel, *Les Mots pour le dire* (1975), (▷*The Words to Say It*, 1983), is typical of the confessional, semi-autobiographical style which she adopts, but its account of the heroine's experience of ▷psychoanalysis has won more critical attention than her other works. Cardinal's novels often seem to conform to the conventions of the feminist confessional ▷*Bildungsroman*, in that her heroines/narrators describe moments of crisis and transition in their lives, which lead to greater independence or wholeness. Despite their awareness of their oppression, particularly as mothers, Cardinal's heroines never fundamentally question conventional heterosexuality or marriage. One of the crises in Cardinal's life which is reflected in her work is her loss of her childhood home, Algeria, and of the apparently secure political values and identity of her colonial family and class background.
Cardinal's writing has always focused on the situation of women, and this interest has developed as a result of the women's movement. She collaborated with feminist activist ▷Gisèle Halimi in *La Cause des femmes* (1973) (▷*The Right to Choose*, 1977) and with ▷Annie Leclerc in *Autrement Dit* (1976) (*In Other Words*), a sequel to and commentary on *The Words to Say It*. As the title of this work suggests, Cardinal is particularly interested in women's relationship to language.
Other well-known novels are: *La Clé sur la porte* (1972) (*The Key in the Dor*), *Une vie pour deux* (1979) (*A Shared Life*), *Au pays de mes racines* (1980) (*In the Country of my Roots*), *Le Passé empiété* (1983) (*The Past Encroached*), and *Les Grands Désordres* (1987) (*Devotion and Disorder*, 1991).

Carduccianesimo
A poetic school/inheritance, based on the works of Giosuè Carducci (1835–1907), an Italian writer and literary critic. Recurrent themes of his works, and those of his followers, include an aspiration towards the ideal of human dignity, an exalted

view of Italy, and valorization of the arts in general, and poetry in particular. His *Odi barbare* of 1877 both respect Classical metre, and in some respects foreshadow a move towards free verse forms. Thematic and stylistic echoes of his work can be found in the poetry of ▷Amalia Guglielminetti and ▷Renata Vigano.

Carey, Mary (1609/12–c 1680)
English poet and writer of meditations from Berwick. She first married Pelham Carey (knighted 1633) when she was young, and lived for 'Masquing, Dressing, vaine Companye, going to Plays'. Her second husband was the paymaster to Parliamentary troops, and Carey lived in garrison towns with him. Only three of her many children survived, and she wrote elegies for the dead. On her miscarriage she wrote, 'What birth is this: a poor despissed creature? / A little Embrio; voyd of life, and feature.' She wrote her meditations in the 1650s.
Bib: Greer, Germaine, *et al.*, *Kissing the Rod*.

Carey, Rosa Nouchette (1840–1909)
English novelist. The eighth child of a ship-owner, she was born in Stratford-le-Bow, London, and educated at home and at the Ladies' Institute, St John's Wood. Her first published novel was *Nellie's Memories* (1868), a story she had originally told to her sister before transcribing it several years later. Carey was deeply religious and conservative, believing strongly that woman's role was domestic and maternal. This attitude is reflected in the numerous short stories she wrote for the *Girls' Own Paper* and in the thirty-nine novels she published between 1868 and 1909. Her works include *Wee Wifie* (1869); *Not Like Other Girls* (1884); *The Sunny Side of the Hill* (1908) and *Barbara Heathcote's Trial* (1909). She also produced a volume of biographies: *Twelve Notable Good Women of the 19th Century* (1899).

Caribbean Women Writers: Essays from the First International Conference (1990)
This volume edited by Selwyn R. Cudjoe contains essays based on presentations at the first conference of Caribbean women writers and critics held at Wellesley College, Massachusetts, USA, in 1988. The conference, organized by the Black Studies Department, aimed to provide a forum for over fifty writers to discuss their work and concerns. It includes contributions from ▷Opal Adisa, ▷Phyllis Allfrey, ▷Valerie Belgrave, ▷Erna Brodber, ▷Jean D'Costa, ▷Clara De Lima, ▷Beryl Gilroy, ▷Lorna Goodison, ▷Rosa Guy, ▷Merle Hodge, ▷Grace Nichols, ▷Marlene Nourbese Philip and ▷Olive Senior.

Carleton, Mary (?1633–1673)
English writer who adapted the codes and conventions of scandalous chronicle to her own case. In reality born in Canterbury in 1633 and already married, she moved to London claiming to be a German lady. She rapidly married John Carleton, but when it was discovered that neither of them had the estate they pretended, he accused her of bigamy. Both wrote tracts in their own defence, and a corpus of writings grew up around the case, from Carleton's publications in her own defence to fictions and plays including: *The Case of Madam Mary Carleton* (1663); *A True Account* (1663) and *An Historical Narrative*.
Bib: Bernbaum, Ernest, *The Mary Carleton Narratives*.

Carlyle, Jane Welsh (1801–1866)
British woman of letters and literary personality. She was born in Haddington, East Lothian, the daughter of a doctor who gave her a rigorous classical education from the age of five. At school, she impressed her tutor, Edward Irving, with her character and intelligence, and he introduced her to the historian and critic Thomas Carlyle in 1821. They were married in 1826, and became the centre of an intellectual and literary circle. Her greatest friend was ▷Geraldine Jewsbury, and she knew such figures as John Stuart Mill, Charles Dickens and Tennyson. She is celebrated as one of the greatest letter-writers in the English language, observant and caustic but generous and kind. Her subjects include travel, books, personalities and servants and her correspondence has been published in editions by J.A. Froude (1883); L. Huxley (1924) and T. Scudder (1931). Between 1834 and 1866, the Carlyles lived at Cheyne Row, Chelsea, though they were often apart. Their relationship was fraught and difficult; some biographers have suggested that sexual impotence contributed to the marital stress. In the early 1860s Jane's health collapsed and she lived in fear of a mental breakdown, dying suddenly in 1866.
Bib: Surtees, V., *Jane Welsh Carlyle*.

Carnival
Carnival is celebrated throughout the Caribbean, although notably in ▷Trinidad. Its origins lie in the pagan festivals of Europe which the Roman Catholic Church adopted as a pre-Lenten festival. The observance of carnival spread to those countries where Roman Catholicism was the dominant religion, and in this way carnival came to Trinidad and the Caribbean. Originally celebrated by the planter classes, carnival was appropriated by the freed slaves in the post-emancipation period as a ritual observance to symbolize their freedom. Carnival as both theme and form has been used to give shape to a number of West Indian novels. ▷Merle Hodge, for example, uses carnival as part of a world and a way of life in ▷*Crick Crack Monkey*, where the heroine's response to carnival mirrors her inner conflict and her divided self.

Carnival drama (Italy)
Performed at carnival time in Italy, these were humorous plays which operated on the principle of 'the world turned upside down'. The dramatist was thus allowed considerable liberty to include

scenes/events which would normally be judged to be too outrageous. Potentially, then, this kind of drama offered women writers such as ▷Suor Annalena Odaldi the opportunity to transgress traditional boundaries, and to allow women to play adventurous parts. As the world is turned upside down in these plays, so too is patriarchal power in her work.

Bib: Weaver, E. 'Convent Comedy and the World: The Farces of Suor Annalena Odaldi' in *Annali d'Italianistica*, 7, 1989, pp. 182–92, and 'Spiritual Fun: A Study of Sixteenth-Century Tuscan Convent Theater' in *Women in the Middle Ages and the Renaissance: Literary and Historical Perspectives*, ed. M.B. Rose.

See Errol Hill, *The Trinidad Carnival* (1972). ▷Calypso.

Caro, Pauline (1835–1901)
French novelist. The wife of the philosopher Elme-Marie Caro, this author's first novel was *Le Péché de Madeleine* (1864) (*Madeleine's Sin*), a short text which intrigued its readers and publisher because its authorship could not be discovered. Caro only admitted having written the novel in 1875, once its success was assured – a relatively common practice among 19th-century French women writers. Other works which she published around the same period and simply signed 'the author of *Le Péché de Madeleine*' were *Flamien* (1866); *Histoire du Souci* (1868) (*The Tale of the Marigold*) and *Les Nouvelles Amours de Hermann et Dorothée* (1872) (*The Latest Loves of Hermann and Dorothée*). After a gap of almost twenty years she began to write again, using her own name, and produced a series of novels with haunting titles, such as: *Amour de jeune fille* (1892) (*A Girl in Love*); *Fruits Amers* (1892) (*Bitter Fruits*); *Complice* (1893) (*Accomplice*); *Idylle nuptiale* (1898) (*Wedding Idyll*) and *Aimer c'est vaincre* (1900) (*Love Conquers All*).

Caro Maillén de Soto, Doña Ana (c 1590–1650)
Dramatist from Spain's Golden Age (*Siglo de Oro*). She wrote many plays, notably the successful chivalresque drama *El conde Partinuplés* (*Count Partinuplés*). Caro Maillén de Soto was a friend of ▷María de Zayas y Sotomayor, she was active in Seville academies, and is mentioned by the writers Luis Vélez and Matos Fragoso.

Carpinteri, Laura ▷Di Falco, Laura

Carr, Emily (1871–1945)
Born in Victoria, British Columbia, Carr is best-known as one of Canada's great painters, although her work did not receive acclaim until late in her life. She studied at the California School of Design in San Francisco (1891–1893), in England (1899–1904) and Paris (1910–1911), but spent the rest of her life in Victoria. Much of her inspiration came from her visits to Native Canadian villages up the west coast of Vancouver Island, and to the Queen Charlotte Islands in

Pacific Canada. The dense colour and powerful totemic images that she painted were not well-received by an audience accustomed to English landscape painters; she was forced to rely on other means of survival, including giving art lessons and running a boarding house. She did not receive the recognition she deserved until 1927, when the first major exhibition of her work was held at the National Gallery in Ottawa.

After 1937, when her health made it difficult for her to paint, Carr began to write seriously, although she had earlier taken some courses in short story writing. The title of her first book of autobiographical sketches, *Klee Wyck* (1941) (*Laughing One*), is the name she was given by the Nootka Indians; it won a Governor General's Award. In 1942 she published *The Book of Small*, which describes her childhood with a visual and ironic eye. *The House of All Sorts* (1944) is an episodic collection based on her experiences as a landlady and dog breeder. Her autobiography, *Growing Pains*, written between 1939 and 1944, was published posthumously in 1946. Several other books appeared posthumously as well. *Pause: a sketch book* (1953), supplemented by drawings and doggerel verse, describes people and events that Carr encountered during a convalescence from illness in the East Anglia Sanatorium in Suffolk (1903–1904). *The Heart of a Peacock* (1953) is a selection of stories and prose sketches; *Hundreds and Thousands: The Journals of Emily Carr* (1966) is a selection from her journals, written between 1927 and 1941. *An Address* (1955) contains a speech she made to the Women's Canadian Club in honour of the first exhibition of her paintings in her home city, Victoria. It was re-printed in *Fresh Seeing: Two Addresses by Emily Carr* (1972). Carr's unvarnished, humorous, and satiric writing style is the antithesis to her dark and aggressively windswept canvases; but her power to visualize made her both a great painter and a vivid writer.
▷McNeil, Florence

Bib: Blanchard, P., *The Life of Emily Carr*; Gowers, R., *Emily Carr*; Hembroff-Schleicher, E., *Emily Carr: the Untold Story*; Shadbolt, D., *The Art of Emily Carr*; Tippett, M., *Emily Carr: a Biography*.

Carrasco, Margarita ▷Alonso, Carmen de

Carta Atenagórica **(1690)**
Letter published by the Bishop of Puebla, Manuel Fernández de Santa Cruz, with a text by 'Madre Juana Inés de la Cruz' (▷Juana de Asbaje y Ramírez de Santillana), in which she opposes a sermon of 1650 by the Portuguese Jesuit priest Antônio Vieira (1608–1697), and which she writes down at the request of the bishop of Puebla, who had listened to her previously. His letter is signed by the obvious pen-name of Sor Filotea de la Cruz, and reprimands her for her ideas. Later she defends herself from this accusation of meddling with Church business in a famous autobiographical text, ▷ *'Respuesta de la poetisa a la*

muy ilustre Sor Filotea de la Cruz' ('Response of the Poetess to the Very Illustrious Sor Filotea de la Cruz'), published in 1691, and states that gifted women should be granted as much intellectual freedom as gifted men when it comes to thinking and to discussing theological matters.

Cartagena, Teresa de (c 1420–1470)

One of the earliest known women writers in Spain. Cartagena came from a *converso* family (converted from Judaism) that achieved prominence in literature and the Church. She studied at the University of Salamanca, and became a nun (probably a Franciscan). At an early age she was afflicted by deafness. Her two main works are ▷*Arboleda de los enfermos* (c 1450) (*The Grove of the Sick*) and ▷*Admiraçión operum Dey* (*Wonder at the Works of God*).

Cartas a Uma Noiva (1871) (*Letters to a Bride-to-be*)

Written by the Portuguese writer ▷Maria Amália Vaz de Carvalho (1847–1921) when she was twenty-three, this book is composed of a series of *cartas* (letters) directed towards the young middle-class woman and bride-to-be. In the preface the author claims that the letters were sent to her by someone whose identity she prefers not to reveal. The text is divided into two parts, the first of which might be described as a kind of marriage manual. In the second part the letters focus on women's education. Carvalho is highly critical of the instruction offered to women, but in advocating reform she is quick to warn women against becoming too independent and bringing about the dissolution of the family.

'Carte de Tendre'

The 'Map of Human Tenderness', title of a 17th-century French allegorical map of love and friendship devised by ▷Madeleine de Scudéry for the entertainment of her friends in her salon, and subsequently incorporated into the first volume of *Clélie, histoire romaine* (1654–1660) (▷*Clelia: An excellent new romance*, 1661). This map, now seen as a forerunner of such modern board-games as Monopoly, was tremendously popular in *précieux* society (▷Precious Women) as a metaphor for love. The novel tells us: *'l'on ne voyait personne à qui l'on ne demanda s'il voulait aller à Tendre'* ('absolutely everybody was asking each other whether or not they wished to proceed to Tenderness'). It can be read on a number of different levels, but its principal purpose was to invest the relationship between the sexes with a new dignity, by defining the topography of the 'land of tenderness' and advising men how best to approach the difficult route which leads from *'Nouvelle Amitié'* ('New Friendship') to the town of *'Tendre sur Reconnaissance'* ('Tender Recognition'). It was based on a very loosely drawn map of France. The lover has to proceed from south to north to win his mistress's affection by a series of carefully regulated moves which take him through all the provincial towns from *'Complaisance'*

('Pleasing the Other'), *'Soumission'* ('Submission to the Other's Will'), *'Petits Soins'*, *'Assiduïté'* and *'Empressement'* (various types of attentiveness) to *'Tendresse'* ('Tenderness'), *'Obéissance'* ('Obedience') and *'Constante Amitié'* ('Constant Friendship'). The principal dangers for any who dare to try to circumvent this arduous journey lie in the rocky Pyrenees or *'Orgueil'* ('Pride') to the south-west, the Bay of Biscay (*'Mer d'Inimitié'* or 'Sea of Enmity'), to the west, the Channel (*'La Mer dangereuse'* or 'The Dangerous Sea') to the north, and a much enlarged Lake Geneva (the *'Lac d'Indifférence'* or 'Lake of Indifference') to the east. Those who fell in love at first sight would inevitably be borne along on the river of Inclination bisecting the country, but the fast flow and dangerous currents threatened to take them far beyond the town of *'Tendre sur Inclination'* ('Tenderness-on-Inclination'), located about the latitude of Paris, and on across the Dangerous Sea to the Forbidden Territory of the Unknown Lands in the north, where England and perdition lie.

Carter, Angela (1940–1992)

Angela Carter

English novelist, short story writer, journalist, dramatist and critic. Born in Eastbourne, she moved to south Yorkshire during the war years, studied English at Bristol University, and lived in London. Carter's first novel, *Shadow Dance* (1966), introduces her characteristic interrogation of sexuality, extended in *The Magic Toyshop* (1967), which also develops an interest in Freudian accounts of sexual fantasy and sexual development, and a concern with myth, fairytale and the neo-▷Gothic. Significantly, the latter novel is characterized by Carter's application of ▷magic realism to these themes of sexuality and eroticism. *The Infernal Desire Machines of Doctor Hoffman* (1972) follows through these formal and thematic concerns, with a strong emphasis on the escalation of sexual fantasy, and an exploration of the relation between aggressiveness and erotic object choice.

A libertarian attitude to sexuality forms the basis of Carter's feminist polemic *The Sadeian Woman: an Exercise in Cultural History* (1979). This non-fiction text provides a reading of the Marquis de Sade (1740–1814), and of the codes of pornographic representation, to question culturally accepted views of sexuality and, more specifically, the gendering of sadistic and masochistic positions. It is a text that makes explicit Carter's exploration of erotic pleasure as part of the reading process; a similar analysis of voyeurism and seduction informs the 'rewriting' of well-known fairy-tales in *The Bloody Chamber* (1979). Carter's interest in the disruptive energy of androgyny forms the basis of an interrogation of mythic and socio-cultural inscriptions of gender in ▷ *The Passion of New Eve* (1977). Her concern with sexual politics remains central to the burlesque-picaresque novel ▷ *Nights at the Circus* (1984). In the late 1980s Carter's writings occupied a central position within debates about feminist pluralism and ▷ postmodernism. Carter spent two years living in Japan, which produced a series of largely cross-cultural essays, many of which are collected in *Nothing Sacred* (1982). She also translated *The Fairy Tales of Charles Perrault* (1979) and wrote the screenplay for the film *The Company of Wolves* (1984) with Neil Jordon. Other novels are: *Several Perceptions* (1968), *Heroes and Villains* (1969), *Love* (1971). Her last novel was *Wise Children* (1991). Story collections: *Fireworks* (1974), *Black Venus* (1985). Radio drama: *Come Unto These Yellow Sands* (1985).

▷ Barker, Pat; *Bad Sister, The*; Brophy, Brigid; Tennant, Emma
Bib: Duncker, P., 'Re-imagining the Fairytale' in *Literature and History* (Spring 1984); Harrenden, J., *Novelists in Interview*; Punter, D., *The Hidden Script: Writing and the Unconscious* and *The Literature of Terror*; Schmidt, R., 'The Journey of the Subject in Angela Carter's Fiction' in *Textual Practice* (Spring 1984).

Carter, Elizabeth (1717–1806)
English correspondent, poet, linguist and ▷ Bluestocking. Lived with her father (who was a preacher at Canterbury cathedral) in Deal, Kent. He taught her Latin, Greek and Hebrew, and she also learned French, Italian, Spanish, German and some Arabic. Skilled also in music, mathematics and geography, she spent her life studying. She translated Epictetus, published a volume of poetry, ▷ translations from French and Italian, wrote for Samuel Johnson's *The Rambler* (March 1750–March 1752) and *The Gentleman's Magazine* (to which Johnson also contributed), and displays a sharp critical intellect in her correspondence with Catherine Talbot and ▷ Elizabeth Montagu. She regarded ▷ Katherine

Philips's poetry about friendship between women as 'very moral and sentimental'.
Publications: *Poems on Particular Occassions* (1738); *Poems* (1762); *Letters from Mrs. Elizabeth Carter, to Mrs Montagu, between the Years 1755 and 1800* (3 vols) (1817); *Memoirs of the Life of Mrs Elizabeth Carter*, edited by Montagu Pennington (1807); *A Series of Letters between Mrs Elizabeth Carter and Miss Catherine Talbot from the year 1741 to 1770, to which are added, letters from Mrs Elizabeth Carter to Mrs Vessey, between the years 1763 and 1787* (4 vols) (1809).
▷ Fielding, Sarah

Cartland, Barbara (born 1904)
English popular novelist. Beginning her writing career as a gossip columnist for the *Daily Express* newspaper, Cartland published her first novel, *Jigsaw*, in 1925. Cartland has been a prolific writer of ▷ romantic fiction, frequently set in the 19th century, including titles such as *The Ruthless Rake* (1975), *The Penniless Peer* (1976) and *The Cruel Count* (1976). Her worldwide sales have exceeded 390 million copies. Cartland has also written several volumes of autobiography, including *We Danced All Night 1919–1929* (1971) and *I Search for Rainbows* (1967), and fictionalized biographies of historical figures, including *The Private Life of Elizabeth Empress of Austria* (1959), *The Private Life of Charles II: The Women He Loved* (1958) and *Josephine, Empress of France* (1961). Her many advice books, including *Love, Life and Sex* (1957), *The Etiquette Book* (1962), *Look Lovely, Be Lovely* (1958) and *Barbara Cartland's Book of Beauty and Health* (1971), controversially espouse notions of women's supportive, 'inferior' social role, and conservative views on women's infidelity.

Carvajal, María Isabel ▷ Lyra, Carmen

Carvajal de Arocha, Mercedes ▷ Palacios, Lucila

Carvajal y Saavedra, Doña Mariana de (c 1620–1680)
Spanish writer. Carvajal was born of a noble Granada family. She wrote a collection of eight novellas entitled *Navidades entretenidas* (1663) (*Christmas Entertainments*), as well as some plays which are now lost.

Carvalho, Maria Amália Vaz de (1847–1921)
Portuguese poet, novelist, essayist and historian. She is best known for her didactic literature on the subject of middle-class women. On such matters as women's education she held traditional views mixed with small doses of a liberal sentiment. She began her career writing poetry, and in 1867 she published a collection of romantic verse entitled *Uma Primavera de Mulher* (*A Woman's Spring*). But she reached her widest readership with books such as ▷ *Cartas a Uma Noiva* (1871) (*Letters to a Bride-to-be*) and *Cartas a Luíza* (?1886) (*Letters to Luíza*), which counselled women in the areas of education, family and

religion. She also wrote essays for the Lisbon newspaper *Diário Popular* under the pen-name Valentina de Lucena.

In 1874 she married the poet Gonçalves Crespo, who died nine years later. Left alone to support her two children, she increased her literary output, publishing two dozen works between 1885 and 1920, including volumes on education and social history as well as literature and literary criticism. Between 1898 and 1903 she published a biography of the Duke of Palmela (*A Vida do Duque de Palmela*). In 1912 she and ▷Carolina Michaëlis de Vasconcelos were the first women to be inducted into the Lisbon Academy of Sciences.

▷Costa, Emília de Sousa; *Escritoras de Portugal*

Carvalho, Maria Judite de (born 1921)

Portuguese short story writer and novelist. Following her studies at the University of Lisbon, Carvalho spent six years living in Belgium and France. In 1959 she published her first collection of short fiction, *Tanta Gente, Mariana (So Many People, Mariana)*. In the next few years two more collections followed: *As Palavras Poupadas* (1961) (*Frugal Words*) and *Paisagem Sem Barcos* (1963) (*Landscape Without Boats*). A major theme in Carvalho's works is women's struggle against the conservative values of pre-revolutionary Portuguese society – a theme especially important to her 1966 novel, ▷*Os Armários Vazios (The Empty Cupboards)*. Since the revolution Carvalho has published two short works, *A Janela Fingida* (1975) (*The Feigned Window*) and *Além do Quadro* (1983) (*Beyond the Picture*). She frequently writes for the Lisbon newspaper *Diário de Notícias*.

▷Nóbrega, Isabel da

Cary, Alice (1820–1871)

US fiction writer and poet. Alice Cary first began publishing in regional newspapers and magazines, before publishing in prestigious eastern journals, and moved to New York City in 1850. Best known for her ▷*Clovernook* series, which depicted the realities of life on the western frontier, Alice Cary was also respected as a poet and as a children's author. Her collected poems, sketches and novels number over a dozen volumes, including collections of her work with that of her sister, Phoebe Cary (1824–1871), a poet and humorist. Both Carys were in New York City after 1851 and established a literary salon which attracted the leading literary lights of the era.

Cary, Elizabeth Tanfield, Lady Falkland (1585–1639)

English translator, poet and dramatist. From the time she was a child she developed a reputation for learning and languages, mastering French, Spanish, Italian, Latin and Transylvanian. She also demonstrated a studiousness which her parents must have thought excessive. By the age of twelve Cary owed servants £100 for smuggling candles (a total of 800) to her bedroom so that she could read at night. At the age of fifteen, she married Henry Cary, Lord Falkland. In 1626 she secretly converted to Catholicism. Upon discovering Cary's recusancy, Lord Falkland attempted to force his wife to recant. When she refused to obey him, he abandoned her, denying her custody of their eight children, and leaving her to live in near-destitute conditions. Although Cary translated a number of works, (including all of those by Jacques Davy, Cardinal Du Perron) and composed several verse lives of saints, hymns to the Virgin, and dramatic works, all but a few of her works are lost. Her ▷translation of a French treatise on geography exists in manuscript and, even though her translation of Cardinal Du Perron's *Reply* to King James was ordered to be publicly burned, a few copies of it survived. Also extant are two unfinished versions of *The History of King Edward II* (including *History of the Most Unfortunate Prince King Edward the Second, Harleian Miscellany*, 1808, misattributed to Henry Cary), and her most important work, ▷*The Tragedie of Mariam*, (1613).

Bib: Murdock, K.B., *The Sun at Noon*; Simpson, R., *The Lady Falkland: Her Life*.

▷Renaissance, British; Companionate marriage

Cary, Mary (fl 1621–1653)

English prophet. She was writing during the English Civil War (1642–1646 and 1648–1651) and the Protectorate of Oliver Cromwell (1599–1658, lord protector 1653–1658). Her first publication was *The Resurrection of the Witness* (1648), but her best-known prophetic writing is *The Little Horns Doom and Downfall* (1651, reprinted 1653) published with *A New and Exact Mappe or Description of New Jerusalem*. In *Little Horns Doom* Cary uses Daniel 7:8 to read the events of the 1640s and 1650s, and is one of the distinctive political prophets of that period. She dedicated the book to important contemporary women.

▷Blaugdone, Barbara; Quaker women (England); Trapnel, Anna.

Bib: Smith, Hilda, *Reason's Disciples*.

Casa de los espiritus, La (1982) ▷*House of the Spirits, The* (1985)

Casanova de Lutoslawski, Sonia (1862–1958)

Spanish novelist. Born in the village of Almerias in La Coruña, in 1887 Casanova married a Polish nobleman and from that time on lived mainly outside Spain. Her work often centres on Russia or Russian characters. Her novels include: *Lo eterno* (1907) (*The Eternal*); *Princesa rusa* (1922) (*The Russian Princess*); and *Las catacumbas de Rusia roja* (1933) (*Red Russian Catacombs*).

Casa sul lago della luna, La (1984) ▷*House On Moon Lake, The*

Case, Sue-Ellen (born 1942)

North American feminist drama critic and teacher. Case teaches in the Department of English, University of California. She went back later in life to get her Ph.D., which she received at age 39. At 48 she is now a full professor, and an encouraging role model for older women returning to education. Case is author of *Feminism and Theatre* (1988). In the chapter on 'Radical Feminism and Theatre' she takes up ▷Adrienne Rich's concept of 'compulsory heterosexuality', showing how it works in the context of theatre. The chapter goes on to record how lesbian dramatists have challenged ▷heterosexism, and suggests that in the theatre, at least, 'lesbian' as a concept and set of experiences is distinguished from the broader definition of lesbianism as a ▷woman-identified experience. Case is editor of *Performing Feminisms: Feminist Critical Theory and Theatre* (1990), and co-editor of *Theatre Journal*.

Casely-Hayford, Adelaide (1868–?)

Sierra Leonean pioneer of women's writing. She was born in the mid-19th century into a well-known Sierra Leone mulatto family (the preferred term in anglophone West Africa for the offspring of an ethnically mixed union). Though she married a Ghanaian, she returned to Sierra Leone and worked at promoting women's education with an emphasis on African customs, as opposed to the prevailing Western cultural bias of the time. She established the Girls' Vocational School in Freetown. She wrote a brief memoir of her life, which she concluded at the age of 91, and which was published in 1969, and some literary work, which was first published in the 1950s in the *West Africa Review*. Her daughter, ▷Gladys Casely-Hayford, achieved a reputation as a poet.
Bib: Cromwell, A. M., *An African Victorian Feminist – The Life and Times of Adelaide Smith Casely-Hayford*; Okonkwo, Rina, *Heroes of West African Nationalism*.

Casely-Hayford, Gladys

Sierra Leonean poet. Her mother was the educationalist ▷Adelaide Casely-Hayford and her father the Ghanaian Joseph Casely-Hayford, author of the first African novel in English, *Ethiopia Unbound.* She herself is remarkable mainly for her adoption of the Sierra Leonean dialect, Krio, as a vehicle for some of her poetry, at a period when Western education had elevated English and the classics above African culture. Around 1948 she published *Take Um So (Take It Like That)*, a small collection of her poems, of which three are in Krio.
Bib: Dathorne, O.R., *African Literature in the 20th Century.*

Case of the Whigs, The (1783)

Essay written by ▷Letitia Cunningham at the end of the American Revolution. *The Case of the Whigs* forthrightly calls upon Congress to act with integrity and in favour of those Whigs 'who loaned their money on the public faith'. She also admonishes newspapers of the era for their passive responses to political events and calls on them to expose the 'daring truths' about political and governmental actions. Inspired by an earlier

essay pseudonymously written by a man ('Vox Populi'), she notes that 'I intend to pursue the path marked out by him much farther than he has done.' Angry about the refusal of the new government to honour interest due on loan office certificates, she writes with acumen and an amazing outspokenness for a woman in late 18th-century North America.

Casket Letters and Sonnets, The (c 1567)

Eight letters and twelve sonnets allegedly written by ▷Mary Stuart, Queen of Scots, and used against her as evidence of her complicity in the murder of her husband Robert Darnley. They have been treated primarily as historical documents rather than as literature. Their authenticity remains doubtful and Mary never acknowledged them as her own compositions. The writings were supposedly confiscated from one of Bothwell's (Mary Stuart's third husband) servants. Although Mary wrote in a number of languages, her first language was French. The originals of the ▷letters are lost and the original language of them unknown. Even those used against Mary in her trial in England were copies. The earliest version is of 1571, written in Scots dialect. During the Renaissance, they also appeared in Latin, English, and French versions.

Casper, Linda Ty

Filipino novelist. Married to North American writer and professor, Leonard Casper, she is now mainly resident in the USA, and is a lawyer by profession. She started writing fiction while waiting for the results of her Bar examinations. Her short stories have been collected in *The Transparent Sun and Other Stories* (1963) and *The Secret Runner and Other Stories* (1974). Her first novel, *The Peninsulas* (1964), is possibly her best. Set in the Spanish colonial Philippines during the British capture of Manila (c 1750–1753), it recreates in vivid detail the life and society of the time. The novelist herself has described it as 'the Filipino's search for identity in the 1750s, the confusion of motives and loyalties, the impulse to error and martyrdom'. Among her novels and novellas are *The Three-cornered Sun* (1979), *Dread Empire* (1980), *Hazards of Distance* (1981), *Fortress in the Plaza* (1985) and *Ten Thousand Seeds* (1987).

Cassandra. A Novel and Four Essays (1984)

Translation of *Kassandra. Vier Vorlesungen. Eine Erzählung* (1983), a novel by the East German writer ▷Christa Wolf. Cassandra, daughter of Priam, King of Troy, is a priestess and visionary. As she faces her own death and the destruction of her world at the end of the Trojan War, she thinks back to the time when she tried in vain to warn her father of the consequences of the war for which he was so blithely preparing.
The story is essentially a meditation on ▷patriarchy, war and the impotence of women. A parallel with the political situation of the 1980s is made evident. In the accompanying lectures, Wolf explores the nature of a literary work, the role of

the writer in society, and her own method of writing.

Cassian, Nina (born 1924)

Romanian poet. Cassian studied drama and painting in Bucharest. One of her earliest poems was published in the Communist Party journal *Romania Libera* in 1945, but her first cycle, *La scara 1/1* (*On the Scale 1/1*), was considered to be out of step with Party ideology. She has published over fifty books, including fiction and children's books, is a composer of chamber and symphonic music, and also a film critic.

Cassian had been a leading literary figure in Romania for over forty years when, during a visit to New York in 1985, her satires of the regime of President Nicolae Ceauçescu (1967–1989) were discovered copied into a friend's diary. The friend was tortured to death, Cassian's house was ransacked by the authorities and her work banned. Since then she has lived in New York, where she teaches creative writing at New York University. Her work in English has been published in *The New Yorker*, and in Britain in the books *Life Sentence* (1990), *Call Yourself Alive?* (1988) and *Cheerleader for a Funeral* (1992).

'Castaway, A' (1870)

A 600-line prose poem by ▷Augusta Webster. The poem is concerned with the issue of prostitution and the ▷'fallen woman', and ranges widely in its exploration of the sexual ideology of 19th-century Britain. Unlike D.G. Rossetti's 'Jenny', published in the same year, Webster's poem speaks from the perspective of the fallen woman rather than that of the voyeuristic observer. '[T]he silly rules this silly world/makes about women' are decried by a speaker who is branded by society as a 'thing of shame and rottenness, the animal/that feeds men's lusts'.

Caste

The hierarchical ordering of all Hindus into broad bands of ritual and social purity. There are four castes (more properly, *varnas*): Brahmins, Kshatriyas, Vaishyas and Sudras. Hindus not belonging to one of these four groups are called Untouchables (or Dalits). In spite of its apparent rigidity, the caste system did not preclude social mobility, as Westerners once thought, but any upward mobility was the work of an entire *jati* (or sub-caste) rather than that of an individual.

Discrimination on the basis of caste is illegal in modern India, but caste remains very influential in the distribution of employment, land and education. Attempts to improve the position of Untouchables, with quotas for school and university entry and reservation of government jobs, are often controversial.

▷Arranged marriage

Castellanos, Rosario (1925–1978)

Mexican poet, short story writer, novelist and critic. After spending her childhood in Comitán, Chiapas, she studied literature in Mexico City and in Madrid. In 1948 she published her successful first book of poems, *Trayectoria del polvo* (*Trajectory of Dust*) and also her second, *Apuntes para una declaración de fe* (*Notes for a Declaration of Faith*). All of her books of poetry, written between 1948 and 1957, have a deep metaphysical tint and deal with human and love's frailty, social injustice and patriotism. Her best-known prose works, the most important examples of 20th-century ▷indigenist literature, are the novel *Balún Canán* (1958) (▷*The Nine Guardians*, 1970) the short stories *Ciudad Real* (1960) (*Royal City*), and the novel *Oficio de tinieblas* (1964) (*Office of darkness*). *Balún Canán* takes place in Comitán, Chiapas, and is about a girl who fights social prejudice and the exploitation of the Indians in rural Mexico. Castellanos published in the national and foreign press, was a professor in Mexico and the United States, and was an ambassador to Israel.

Other works include: *De la vigilia estéril* (1950) (*The Barren Vigil*); *El rescate del mundo* (1952) (*The Recovery of the World*); *Poemas 1953–1955* (1957) (*Poems 1953–1955*); *Al pie de la letra* (1959) (*At the Foot of The Letter*); *Lívida luz* (1960) (*Pale Light*); *Los convidados de agosto* (1964) (*August Guests*); *Album de família* (*Family Album*), and *Poesía no eres tú* (1972) (*You Are Not Poetry*). She also wrote books of essays, including on feminism.

Castelloza, Na (early 13th century)

French poet, one of the most famous of the ▷*trobairitz*. She left three and possibly four *chansons* (songs) in Occitan. She is described in the *vida* as '*une dame très joyeuse, très instruite et très belle*' ('a very joyous, educated and beautiful lady'). 'Castelloza's lyrics depict a woman driven as much by exasperation as by *joi* (joy) to justify her breach of silence against the charge that she should not, in conscience, sing.'

Bib: Van Vleck, A.E., '"*Tost me trobaretz fenida*": reciprocating composition in the songs of Castelloza', in Paden, W.D. (ed.), *The Voice of the Trobairitz*.

Castillo, Ana

US poet and novelist. Castillo was born and raised a ▷Latina in Chicago, Illinois. Her writing explores the politics of the erotic. *Otro Canto* (1977) protests against the plight of the urban poor, and these poems take a Marxist revolutionary stance. *The Invitation* (1979) appropriates the erotic for the female speakers, who create their own metaphors to represent their experiences. Castillo differentiates between these metaphors and those inherited from texts which inscribe potential experience. *Women Are Not Roses* (1984) shows how lower-class women are placed in a double-bind. They must choose between the erotic relationship and class struggle, and between feminine and masculine symbolic arenas; in these self-contradictory situations women claim their own sexuality. ▷*The Mixquiahuala Letters* (1986) chronicles a woman's failed erotic quest, and challenges ▷heterosexist romantic ideology.

Castillo y Guevara, Madre María Francisca Josefa del (1671–1742)

Colombian religious poet and prose writer. Her father was Spanish, her mother Colombian. Four of her brothers were priests, and she became a nun when she was twenty. Her poetry was published posthumously, and, in spite of the repetitions, synonyms and the mixture of the forms '*tu*' and '*vós*', its deep melancholy made it into one of the best examples of this kind of poetry in the Spanish language, according to Joaquín Ospina (1927). Castillo y Guevara wrote her famous autobiography, *Vida* (1817) (*Life*), under the instructions of her confessor. Her prose manuscript *Sentimientos espirituales* (2 Vols, 1843, 1945–46) (*Spiritual Feelings*) was compared to the writings of St Teresa de Jesús. These volumes relate the most extraordinary events of her childhood, including her direction of the convent, in the form of an intimate journal. It has been suggested that she was 'the great mystic of Spanish American letters'. *Tres jornadas del cielo* (*Three Days' Journey in Heaven*) was inspired by the Psalms and the Bible. She was often compared to ▷Juana de Asbaje y Ramirez de Santillana, some of whose poems have been attributed to her, in spite of the difference in style.

Castle, Terry (born 1953)

North American feminist literary critic of 18th-century literature. Castle teaches at Stanford University. She is the author of *Clarissa's Ciphers: Meaning and Disruption in Richardson's 'Clarissa'* (1982) and *Masquerade and Civilization: The Carnivalesque in Eighteenth-Century English Culture and Fiction* (1986). *Masquerade and Civilization* uses the cultural phenomenon of the masquerade to present a case-history of 18th-century attitudes towards sexuality. Castle describes how the world of the masquerade disrupts sexual and social hierarchies. Her work on the representation of lesbianism is historically precise. She shows, for example, how in the 18th century lesbianism was most often represented by female transvestism. For a detailed analysis of Henry Fielding's satiric portrait of Mary Hamilton, an 18th-century woman who was tried and found guilty of impersonating a man and marrying a woman, see Castle's paper, 'Matters Not Fit to Be Mentioned: Fielding's *The Female Husband*', (*ELH* 49, 1982).
▷Lesbian feminist criticism

Castle Rackrent (1800)

This novel by ▷Maria Edgeworth gained her a reputation as 'easily the most celebrated and successful of practising . . . novelists'. The full title: *Castle Rackrent, an Hibernian Tale: Taken from Facts, and from the Manners of the Irish Squires, before the Year 1782*, published in London in 1880, is considered to be the first distinctively 'Irish' novel, playing a pivotal role in the development of the genre. The chronicle of a declining Ascendancy (Anglo-Irish aristocracy) family over several generations, it is highly innovative in its ▷realism, its use of colloquial language, the choice of a peasant servant, Thady Quirk, as the narrator, and in its subversion of the traditional domestic plot.

Castro, Fernanda de (born 1900)

Portuguese poet and novelist. Her first book of poems, *Ante Manhã (Pre-Morn)*, appeared in 1919 when she was just nineteen years old. She wrote of the countryside, village life, popular customs, love and God – themes in keeping with the growing nationalist spirit of the period. She published extensively over the next fifty years, but two of her volumes deserve special mention: *A Ilha da Grande Solidão* (1962) (*The Island of Great Solitude*), an autobiographical work; and *Africa Raíz (Africa Roots)*, published in the 1960s, a novel based on her experience as a child growing up in the colonies. Married to the writer António Ferro, an official in the Salazar government, Castro was a supporter of the regime. In the late 1980s she published a two-volume *memoire* entitled *Ao Fim da Memória (To the End of Memory)*.

Castro, Juana

Contemporary Spanish poet, journalist, and essayist; born in Villanueva, Córdoba. The main themes of her poetry are solitude, love, mysticism and the feminine universe. Narcisia, the myth of her last work, depicts the woman who is the beginning and end of her own being. Her main works are: *Cóncava mujer* (1978) (*Concave Woman*); *Del color y las alas* (1982) (*On Colour and Wings*); *Paranoia en otoño* (1985) (*Paranoia in Autumn*); and *Narcisia* (1986).

Castro, Públia Hortênsia de (1548–1595)

Portuguese scholar and orator. She disguised herself as a man in order to attend classes in Philosophy and Letters at the University of Coimbra, and was awarded a doctorate at the age of seventeen. Widely considered to be the first woman orator in Portuguese history, she authored numerous poems, none of which have survived. Employed in the court of Felipe II, she was regarded as one of the leading intellectuals of her day. The king was so impressed by her erudition that he awarded her a lifetime pension.
▷*Infanta Dona Maria de Portugal e as Suas Damas, A*

Castro, Rosalía de (1837–1885)

Spanish poet and novelist. Castro was born in Santiago de Compostela. She wrote in Galician and Castilian, and is now considered to be one of the most important poets of the 19th century.

Her first works – *La flor* (1857) (*The Flower*), a collection of poems, and a novel, *La hija del mar* (1859) (*Daughter of the Sea*) – were published in Castilian. Her subsequent novels – *Ruinas* (1867) (*Ruins*), *El caballero de las botas azules* (1867) (*The Gentleman with the Blue Boots*), and *El primer loco* (1881) (*The First Madman*) – established her reputation. However, it is for her poetry that she is famous, particularly the Galician works, such as *Cantares gallegos* (1863) (*Galician Songs*) and

▷*Follas novas* (1880) (*New Leaves*). Her last work, a collection of poems written in Castilian, *En las orillas del Sar* (1884) (*On the Shores of the Sar*), explores in greater depth two themes evident in her earlier work, namely, the love of nature and empathy with the female estate.

▷Galician women's writing

Castroviejo, Concha (born 1915)

Spanish novelist. Born in Compostela, Castroviejo lived in exile in Mexico from 1939 to 1950, but since then has resided in Madrid. Her two novels, *Los que se fueron* (1957) (*Those Who Left*) and *Víspera del odio* (1959) (*Eve of Hate*), are set against the backdrop of the Spanish Civil War (1936–9).

Català, Victor ▷Albert, Caterina

Catalan women's writing

After the Spanish Civil War (1936–1939), the special resistance that Catalonia had demonstrated against the nationalist advance led Franco to prohibit the expression of Catalonian nationalism, and to forbid the use of the Catalan language in any official capacity throughout his dictatorship (1939–1975). Although this prohibition was relaxed to a degree in the 1960s and, even more so, in the 1970s, it nevertheless damaged the status of Catalan as a literary language.

Despite the active resistance of the Franco regime, however, Catalan literature continued to flourish, particularly women's writing. No doubt this was partly a result of the influence of the many fine Catalan female writers of the previous era, such as ▷Caterina Albert. Another inspiration may have been the idea behind ▷Maria Aurèlia Capmany Farnes's observation that, 'since it was a suppressed language, it was no big deal to write in Catalan, and it therefore became a women's activity.' Whether or not Capmany's observation can be taken at face value, it is striking how many Catalan women writers there are in the modern period.

▷Anglada, Maria Angels; Aritzeta, Margarida; Arqiumbau, Rosa Maria; Bertrana, Aurora; Domenech i Escate, Maria; Escobedo, Joana; Guilló, Magdalena; Karr i Alfonsetti, Carme; Monserdà de Macía, Dolors; Montoriol i Puig, Carme; Murià i Romani, Anna; Oliver, Maria Antònia; Pàmies, Teresa; Pompeia, Núria; Riera, Carme; Rodoreda, Mercè; Roig, Montserrat; Serrahima, Núria; Simó, Isabel-Clara; Valentí, Helena; Ventós i Cullell, Palmira; Vicens, Antonia; Xirinacs, Olga; Basque women's writing; Galician women's writing.

Catching It (1983)

Poems by New Zealand writer ▷Lauris Edmond. Edmond published her first book of poems in her fifties; *Catching It* is her fifth collection, and was largely written while Edmond held the Katherine Mansfield Fellowship in Menton. All Edmond's poems focus on moments of intense experience, relationships, selfhood and her 'acute observation of the physical world' (E. Caffin, *Oxford History of*

New Zealand Literature, 1991). She has said in an interview that 'you write poetry to discover something.' Edmond typically uses loosely-structured lyric forms. The poems in *Catching It* deal with travel, foreignness and selfhood, and try to unpick the significance of personal experience and dislocation.

Catchpole, Margaret (1762–1819)

Australian letter-writer. Margaret Catchpole, who was born in England, was twice sentenced to death – for horse-stealing and for escaping from Ipswich gaol – and was transported to Australia. Pardoned in 1814, she became an exemplary citizen, keeping a small store at Richmond, near Sydney. Her letters, to her uncle and aunt in Suffolk and to her former mistress, provide a vivid and authentic account of colonial life and affairs, as well as of her own resourcefulness and energy. Now in the Mitchell Library, Sydney, Catchpole's letters have been much quoted and have formed the basis for three separate biographies.

▷*Penguin Anthology of Australian Women's Writing, The;* Letters (Australia)

Caterina da Siena, Santa (1347–1380)

Italian religious writer. From the age of six she expressed a wish to enter a convent, and finally did so in 1363–1364. At once a mystic and a politically active woman, she openly supported the Holy War of Pope Gregory XI in 1373, and in 1374 cared for plague victims in Siena. In 1376 she went to Avignon, and was supposedly instrumental in persuading the Pope to return the papacy to Rome. Throughout her life, Caterina had visions and ecstasies, and in 1375 received the stigmata. Caterina was unusual in her role as a militant, mystic woman. Although she did not, in fact, know how to write, she dictated her religious thoughts, and they now form an important part of the body of ▷mystical and ▷religious writings of the period. The language of her writings is strikingly vivid and often violent and sensual. Her most famous work, *Il dialogo della divina provvidenza* (▷ *The Dialogue of the Seraphic Virgin, Dictated by Her While in a State of Ecstasy in 1370*, published in English in 1896, 1907 and 1925) is all of these, yet it is also practical and radical in its wish to reform the structure of the Church, and especially in its recommendations to the Pope on how he should truly imitate Christ. Her other main work is *Lettere di santa Caterina da Siena, ridotte a miglior lezione e in ordine nuovo disposto* (1915, 1913–1920) (*Saint Catherine of Siena as Seen in Her Letters*), while other publications in English include: *The Orchard of Sion* (1966); *The Treatise on Purgatory* (1915) and *The Life and Sayings* (1964).

Cather, Willa (1873–1947)

US novelist and short story writer. Cather's work chronicles the settling of the Nebraska prairie by immigrant peoples. Her own family migrated from Virginia to Red Cloud, Nebraska, when Cather was nine. In 1895 she graduated from the

Willa Cather

University of Nebraska and lived in Pittsburgh, Pennysylvania, with Isabelle McClung, where she worked as a journalist. In 1906 Cather moved to New York to edit *McClure's Magazine*. Her lifelong companion was Edith Lewis. In 1922 Cather expressed a religious commitment by joining the Episcopalian Church.

Cather's fiction celebrates the work of women who civilized the prairie. ▷*O Pioneers!* (1913) and ▷*My Ántonia* (1918) recover a time when women were economically and socially central. ▷*The Song of the Lark* (1915) and *My Mortal Enemy* (1926) explore the tension between femininity and creativity. *A Lost Lady* (1923) and ▷*Death Comes to the Archbishop* (1927) explore tensions between Old World values and life in the New World. *Sapphira and the Slave Girl* (1940) looks at the relationships between Anglo-American and African-American women, and mothers and daughters. Cather won a Pulitzer Prize for *One of Ours* (1922), a war novel championing democracy.

Other works include: *The Troll Garden* (1905), *Alexander's Bridge* (1912), *Youth and the Bright Medusa* (1920), *April Twilights and Other Poems* (1923), *The Professor's House* (1925), *Shadows on the Rock* (1931), *Obscure Destinies* (1932), *Lucy Gayheart* (1935), *Not Under Forty* (1936), *The Novels and Stories* (1937–1941), *The Old Beauty and Others* (1948), *Willa Cather on Writing* (1949), *Early Stories* (1957), *The Kingdom of Art: Willa Cather's First Principles and Critical Statements, 1893–1896* (1966), *The World and the Parish: Willa Cather's Articles and Reviews, 1893–1902* (1970) and *Uncle Valentine and other Stories* (1973).
Bib: Kates, G.N. (ed.), *Willa Cather in Europe:*

Her Own Story of the First Journey; O'Brien, S., *The Stories of Willa Cather*; Shirley, J. (ed.), *Writings From Willa Cather's Campus Years.*

Catherine de Medici (1519–1589)
French poet and author of letters. Born in Florence, she married the future King Henri II (1519–1559) in 1533, and was befriended by ▷Marguerite de Navarre. Her influence as queen was eclipsed by Diane de Poitiers (1499–1566) until her husband's accidental death in 1559, when she assumed the regency. She assured continuity to France during the short successive reigns of her three sons – François II (1544–1560), Charles IX (1550–1574) and Henri III (1551–1589) – marred by the Wars of Religion and other troubles. In her youth, she wrote poetry in Italian and seems to have continued in French after her marriage, though attribution has been disputed. Her influence on the artistic and literary direction of the court, though less celebrated than her Machiavellian politics and attempts to control the Protestants, is just as important in its own way. Some of her letters offering advice on government to her sons and her *cantiques* (canticles or hymns) have been published separately. They are written in a hurried hand and abound in Italianisms, and grammatical and spelling errors. Her writing is phonetic and, to be understood, often has to be read aloud. It is her letters to her eldest daughter Elisabeth de Valois (1545–1568), ill-fated bride of Philip II of Spain (1527–1598), which reveal her heart.
Bib: Williamson, H.R., *Catherine de' Medici.*

Catherine II (1729–1796)

Catherine II

Also known as Catherine the Great. One of the greatest of Russian rulers, Catherine used literature as a political tool, an example of enlightenment, and a source of amusement. A German princess, she was fluent in French and, after her marriage to the heir to the Russian throne in 1744, worked tirelessly to master Russian and endear herself to her future subjects. After taking power in 1762, she contributed to early Russian satirical journals, produced comedies that castigated common vices and attacked Freemasonry, worked on librettos for comic operas, dabbled in history and linguistics, and wrote children's tales and readers for her grandsons. She was surrounded by courtiers and secretaries, and few if any of these works can be ascribed totally to her own hand. She was a prolific letter-writer, and used her correspondence with French philosophers to establish a reputation as an enlightened monarch. She named a woman, ▷Ekaterina Dáshkova, to head two national academies. Autobiographical manuscripts, devoted mainly to the early unhappy years in Russia, circulated in her lifetime; they had obvious propaganda value as justification of the coup that brought her to the throne. The autobiography was not published until 1859, when it appeared in England as the *Memoirs of the Empress Catherine II, Written by Herself.*

Catherine of Aragon (1485–1536)
English letter-writer and patron. Perhaps most famous for being Henry VIII's first wife, she was the daughter of Ferdinand and Isabella of Spain. As a result of her parents' strong belief in learning, Catherine was extremely well-educated. She studied under Erasmus (1466–1536), and was skilled in Latin. She commissioned for her daughter ▷Mary Tudor's education Juan Luis Vive's ▷*Instruction of a Christian Woman*, which became the most popular women's ▷conduct book at the time. Her ▷letters, written after ▷Anne Boleyn replaced her as Henry's wife and queen, still survive. They document her strength and dignity during a most sorrowful time in her life.
▷Humanism (England); Patronage.
Bib: Green, M.A.E. (ed), *Letters of Royal and Illustrious Ladies of Great Britain.*

Catherwood, Mary Hartwell (1847–1902)
US fiction and non-fiction writer. Catherwood concentrated on historically accurate treatments of the exploration and settlement of the American Midwest. She was one of the earliest US writers of historical romances, and she prided herself on her research and factual correctness – arguing to editors that her work was worthwhile for even the least-educated readers, since they learned something of their country's history. ▷*The Romance of Dollard* (1889) established her reputation. She was a frequent contributor to the national literary magazines, and one of the few women who obtained advances and travel expenses for research projects; most notably, she procured financing of a European trip from ▷*The Century Illustrated Monthly Magazine* in order to prepare *The Days of Jeanne d'Arc* (1897). Other works include: *The Story of Tonty* (1890); *The Lady of Fort St John* (1891); *The Spirit of an Illinois*

Town (1897); *Mackinac, and Other Lake Stories* (1899); *The Queen of the Swamp, and Other Plain Americans* (1899).

Cato, Nancy (born 1917)
Australian novelist, journalist and art critic. Cato is best known for her trilogy, *All the Rivers Run* (1958), *Time, Flow Softly* (1959) and *Green Grows the Vine* (1960), all set against the background of the Murray River and later combined under the title ▷*All the Rivers Run* (1978). Cato has also published six novels, a volume of short stories and two of poetry, as well as five full-length non-fiction works, and has been extremely active in Australian literary circles.She has been made Member of the Order of Australia.

Cat's Eye (1988)
▷Margaret Atwood's *Kunstlerroman* (a ▷*Bildungsroman* about an artist), about a painter, Elaine Risley, who comes to artistic achievement through a complex enactment of memory. She paints the ordinary objects associated with women's lives, but also tries to visualize women's spiritual engagement with time. The novel represents the cruelties and dangers of childhood with powerful intensity; it also asserts the primacy of the personal over the political in the making of art.

Caumont de la Force ▷La Force, Charlotte Rose Caumont de

Cause des femmes, La (1972) ▷Right to Choose, The (1977)

Caution to Such As Observe Days and Times . . ., A (1763)
In this religious tract, ▷Sophia Wigington Hume argued that North American Christians' attention to worldly issues was distorting their understanding of God's power and that he might visit great sufferings upon them if they did not redeem their ways. Hume advocates that North Americans turn inward and live from the heart, not for the world.
▷*Exhortation to the Inhabitants of the Province of South Carolina, An; Extracts from Divers, Antient Testimonies; Justly Celebrated Mrs Sophia Hume's Advice, The;* Early North American Quaker women's writings

Cavalry Maiden, The (1988)
Journals by Russian writer ▷Nadezhda Dúrova, originally published in 1836. Dúrova's edited journals of her years (1807–1816) in the Imperial light cavalry during the Napoleonic Wars became the first important Russian autobiography published by a living author. It remains a rare first-hand account in any literature of a woman's life outside the female sphere, and was translated into English in 1988. Her pioneering introductory memoir, 'My Childhood Years', roots her adult rebellion in youthful experience: ruthless restriction by an unhappy mother, leavened by

worship of a weak but amiable father. Dúrova's focus on private adventures and free wanderings distinguishes her journal from contemporary military reminiscences. Her observations of fellow officers range from mildly amused to highly exasperated. Eager for female companionship despite her male disguise, she records numerous vignettes of women of different classes and nationalities. *Notes* (1839) is Dúrova's loose compilation of left-over journal entries; some of the anecdotes became the plots or narrative framework of her fictional tales.

Bib: Heldt, Barbara, *Terrible Perfection*; Zirin, M., 'A Woman in the "Man's World": The Journals of Nadezhda Dúrova' in *Revealing Lives*.

Cave (Winscom), Jane (c 1754–1813)

Welsh poet of Nonconformist parents (her father was an exciseman). Her *Poems on Various Subjects* (1783) was published (with 2,000 subscribers) before her marriage to John Winscom. It suggests that she worked, possibly as a teacher. The 1786 edition included 'An Elegy on a Maiden Name', including the lines, 'Forgive, dear spouse, this ill-timed tear or two, / They are not meant in discrespect to you; / I hope the name which you have lately given / Was kindly meant and sent to me by heaven. / But ah! the loss of Cave I must deplore, / For that dear name the tend'rest mother bore.' In 1789 and 1794 her *Poems* were reissued with additions. She suffered badly from repeated and agonizing headaches, which she made a subject of some of her poetry, and after living in Bristol, she died in Newport in Monmouthshire.

Cavendish, Lady Jane (1621–1669) and Lady Elizabeth (1626–1663)

English aristocrats, daughters of Sir William Cavendish, Duke of Newcastle who later married ▷Margaret Cavendish (née Lucas). During the Civil War, between 1644 and 1646, they wrote a book of poems and two plays, *The Concealed Fansyses* and *A Pastoral*. The first is a comedy of courtship, but the second registers more closely the circumstances of Civil War as troopers roam the countryside.

Bib: Starr, Nathan Comfort (ed.), *The Concealed Fansyses, PMLA*, 1931; Greer, Germaine, *et al.*, *Kissing the Rod*.

Cavendish, Margaret, Duchess of Newcastle (1623–1673)

English aristocrat who produced scientific treatises, letters, poetry, orations, utopias, drama and memoirs. Born in Colchester, she met and married William, Duke of Newcastle, at the court of Henrietta Maria, and shared his self-imposed exile after the Royalist defeat at the battle of Marston Moor (1644) during the English Civil War (1642–1646). During her exile, she began to write and to publish her writings, which included anti-empiricist scientific speculatioons as well as orations, letters and books of plays. Her best-known prose writing is her *Life* of her husband,

Frontispiece of The World's Olio *(1671): engraving of Margaret Cavendish by Abraham van Diepenbeke*

though the *Sociable Letters* (1664) are enjoyable and varied. She also wrote the extraordinary utopia, *The Blazing World*. During the 1650s she wrote plays, but various mishaps delayed publication until the Restoration. They draw on romance conventions as well as dramatic ideas, and demonstrate the ambivalence of Cavendish's attitude to women's action – on the one hand she sees noble women as unfairly constrained and on the other hand she represents citizen's wives as a social abomination. *The Convent of Pleasure* is perhaps the most theatrical of her plays, but all of them have theatrical elements. Cavendish wrote of them, 'For all the time my Plays a making were, / My brain the Stage, my thoughts were acting there.'

Other publications: *Poems and Fancies* (1653); *Philosophical Fancies* (1653); *Nature's Pictures Drawn by Fancy's Pencil* (1656); *The Worlds Olio* (1655); *Orations* (1662); *Playes* (1662), and *Playes* (1668).

▷Halkett, Lady Ann

Bib: Grant, Douglas, *Margaret the First*;

Heller Mendelson, Sarah, *The Mental World of Stuart Women.*

Caylus, Madame de (1673–?)

French memoir-writer. Born into a Protestant family, she was later converted to Catholicism when taken to live with her aunt, Madame de Maintenon, who was responsible for her education. At thirteen she was married to the Marquis de Caylus. Witty and outspoken, she was twice banished from the court at Versailles. Her memoirs, re-edited as *Les Souvenirs de Madame Caylus* (1986) (*Recollections of Madame Caylus*), originally published in 1770 by Voltaire (1694–1778), portray the court of Louis XIV from 1709 to 1715.
▷Hausset, Nicole du; Lambert, Marquise de; *Mémoires*

Cecil, Mildred Cooke (1526–1589)

English translator, the eldest daughter of Anthony and Anne Fitzwilliam Cooke. Along with her sisters, ▷Anne Cooke Bacon, ▷Elizabeth Cooke Hoby Russell, and Katherine Cooke Killigrew, she was well-educated. Educationalist Roger Ascham (1515–1568) described her as one of the two most learned women living in England (the other being ▷Jane Grey, 1537–1554). She was apparently extremely modest. She is said to have translated part of St Chrysostom, but upon hearing that a man was translating the same work, she refused to publish her own.
▷Vere, Anne Cecil de; Humanism (England); *Instruction of a Christian Woman*; Translation

Cecilia (1782)

A novel by ▷Fanny Burney, which analyzes its heroine's relationship to wealth, autonomy (around the issue of keeping her surname in marriage), morality and female dependence on others.

Cederna, Camilla (born 1921)

Italian essayist and journalist. She took a degree in Classics from Milan University. One of the founders of the weekly publication *L'Europeo* in 1945, she worked there for eighteen years. In 1956, she joined *L'Espresso* magazine, writing reports from Italy and from abroad. An ironic and observant writer, her work has been published in several collections. She writes critically of middle-class society, exemplified by *Noi siamo le signore* (1958) (*We are the Ladies*) and by *Signore e signori* (1966) (*Ladies and Gentlemen*).

Her other work includes: *La voce dei padroni* (1962) (*The Voice of the Bosses*); *Fellini otto e mezzo* (1965) (*Fellini's 8½*); *Callas* (1968); *Sparare a vista* (1975) (*Shoot on Sight*); *Cronaca di una strage* (1979) (*Diary of a Massacre*); *Il mondo di Camilla* (1980) (*Camilla's World*); *Vicino e distante* (1984) (*Near and Far*); *De gustibus* (1986).

Cellier, Elizabeth

English midwife who became a Catholic. Arrested for taking part in a plot in 1679, but acquitted in 1680, she published *Malice Defeated* and an attack on Thomas Dangerfield, *The Matchless Picaro* (reissued as 'rogue'). An unsympathetic contemporary account of her trial called her a 'Prodigy of Impudence'. She also proposed a foundling hospital to James II, and defends women midwives in *To Dr— an answer to his Queries Concerning the Colledge of Midwives* (1688).

Cely, Margery (late 15th century)

English letter-writer. The Cely papers form the largest surviving archive of a medieval English merchant firm, and provide much detailed information on the export trade in raw wool. The papers include documents on domestic as well as business matters, and preserved among them is a personal letter (in English) from Margery Cely to her husband George. Margery, at home while her husband is on his business travels, writes to him in Calais in 1484. She encloses a gold ornament, and tells him she misses him.
Bib: Hanham, Alison (ed.), *The Cely Letters, 1472–1488.*

Cena (8th century)

A letter from a certain Cena to ▷Boniface is preserved in the English Boniface Correspondence. Cena was apparently settled in a remote province of Germany. Her letter sends Boniface her greetings and affection, and asks if she can be of any help to any of his people who might come to her country.

Censorship (Ireland)

The work of many modern Irish writers, including the novelist James Joyce (1882–1941), the dramatist Sean O'Casey (1880–1964) and many others, has been banned under the terms of the Censorship of Publications Act (1929), which prohibits the publication of work considered 'indecent or obscene' or which advocates birth control. ▷Kate O'Brien's ▷*The Land of Spices* (1941) and *Mary Lavelle* (1936), ▷Maura Laverty's *Touched by the Thorn* (1943) and virtually all of ▷Edna O'Brien's fiction published during the 1960s were banned. Edna O'Brien – one of the few writers of her generation to protest openly against censorship – recently commented that 'banning is only the tip of the iceberg. Keeping our psyches closed is the real bogey.'

Although much less readily invoked now, the censorship legislation is still in place, and books can be banned for a period of twelve years.

Centeno, Yvette Kace (born 1940)

Portuguese poet, novelist and critic. She received a degree in German philology from the University of Lisbon. In addition to her volumes of poetry, which include *Opus I* (1966), *Poemas Fracturados* (1967) (*Fractured Poems*), *Sinais* (1977) (*Signs*) and *Perto da Terra* (1984) (*Close to the Earth*), Centeno has written several novels. Her works *Quem Se Eu Gritar* (1965) (*Who If I Scream*), *Não Só Quem Nos Odeia* (1966) (*Not Only Who Hates Us*) and *As Palavras, Que Pena* (1972) (*Words, What a Shame*) constitute a kind of trilogy in which the themes of love, womanhood, and the land are examined. In the last few years Centeno has written several important monographs on the poetry of Fernando Pessoa. She resides in Lisbon, where she is a professor at the New University.

Center for Editions of American Authors
US university-based publishing enterprise which produces fully edited and notated definitive scholarly editions of the works of US authors.

Centlivre, Susanna (Carroll) (1666–1723)
English comic dramatist who was also a poet and journalist. Her first play *The Perjur'd Husband* (1700) was an unsuccessful tragicomedy, and in the same year she published the first of two volumes of letters, *Familiar and Courtly Letters of Monsieur Voiture*. Her first success came with *The Gamester* (1705), followed by *The Busie Body* (1709) and *The Wonder: a Woman Keeps a Secret* (1718), spreading her greatest hits over a fairly long career writing for the stage. She wrote more than a dozen other plays, including *A Bold Stroke for a Wife* (1718), and took to publishing them anonymously because of what she felt was a severe prejudice against women writing for the theatre. She dedicated *The Platonick Lady* (1706) to 'all the Generous Encouragers of Female Ingenuity', saying that once plays were found out to be authored by women they were despised: 'But if by chance, the Plot's discover'd, and the Brat found Fatherless, immediately it flags in the opinion of those that extoll'd it before, and the Bookseller falls his Price, with this reason only, *It is a Womans*.'
Other works: *The Bassett-Table* (1705); *The Nine Muses* (1700).
▷Bluestocking; Pix, Mary; *Nine Muses, The*; Wiseman, Jane

Century Illustrated Monthly Magazine, The (1881–1930)
US periodical devoted to North American literature, including topical non-fiction. Edited throughout the 19th century by Richard Watson Gilder (1844–1909), *The Century* provided a high-paying and prestigious market for US authors, and was noted for its outstanding, original, serialized novels, such as ▷*Through One Administration*. While Gilder was often accused of using a stringent ▷parlour table standard, he published the most innovative literature of his time, along with a goodly amount of pap. Gilder's correspondence with contributors is fascinating for its record of writers resisting or accepting editorial intervention in their texts. Among writers published in *The Century* were ▷Frances Eliza Hodgson Burnett, ▷Mary Hartwell Catherwood, ▷Mary Hallock Foote, ▷Alice French, ▷Helen Hunt Jackson and ▷Edith Matilda Thomas.

Century of Dishonor, A (1881)
US non-fiction by ▷Helen Hunt Jackson. A historical indictment of US government policy toward and treatment of ▷Native Americans, *Century* was one of the earliest book-length critiques of prejudiced bureaucracy and practice.

Ceo (del Cielo), Sor Maria do (1658–?)
Spanish poet. Ceo was born in Lisbon, and was a nun from the age of eighteen. Mainly known for her poetry, Ceo also wrote five plays on *Triunfo do Rosario* (1740) (*Rosario's Triumph*), which she published posthumously under the pseudonym Sor Marina Clemencia.

Černínová z Harasova, Zuzana (1601–1654)
One of the best-known Baroque letter-writers in Czech literature. She was the daughter of a landowner, and in 1621 she married the depressive noble, Jan Černín z Chudenic. Her two daughters, Eliška and Eva Polyxena, married army officers, and her sons, Humprecht Jan and Heřman Václav, both played significant roles in the development of Bohemia during the Counter-Reformation. Her correspondence has been published frequently since 1869.
Her letters exemplify the lot of noblewomen during the Thirty Years War (1618–1648), managing large estates, being taxed heavily by both sides (since the ordinary people were pauperized by the war), being forced to billet soldiers, having her crops ravaged and her stores plundered. Occasionally she manifests anger at her lot, and at the lot of her country (she was something of a Bohemian patriot), but mainly she shows herself to be an astute businesswoman, a particularly affectionate mother, and someone who longed most of all for peace. For her the war was particularly wrong, because Christians were fighting Christians.

'Certain Familiar Epistles and Friendly Letters' ▷*Sweet Nosegay, A*

Cervantes, Lorna Dee (born 1954)
US poet. Cervantes was born in San Francisco, California, into the 'welfare class', and she learned poetry at the houses her mother cleaned. By age twenty she had devoted herself to writing. As editor of *Mango*, she helped other Chicana writers, and her own poetry responds to the Chicana's alienation from both Mexican and US culture. The poems in *Emplumada* (1981) trace her emerging identity as woman, Chicana and poet. The first section depicts the social determinism of gender and class roles. 'Uncle's First Rabbit' and 'Cannery Town in August' emphasize the single individual's inability to overcome these roles. In the second section poems like 'Starfish' concern the loss of the Spanish language and cultural continuity. Poems such as 'Visions of Mexico While at a Writing Symposium in Port Townsend, Washington', in the third section resolve the conflicts of cultural dislocation through the act of writing. Cervantes sees writing as the way of synthesizing the Chicana's private and public worlds.
▷Latina women's writing

Césaire, Ina

This ethnologist and dramatist from Martinique
in the French Antilles wrote her thesis on the
aesthetic sense of the nomadic Peul people. She
has co-edited with Joëlle Laurent a collection of
Creole tales, *Contes de mort et de vie aux Antilles*
(1976) (*Tales of Death and Life in the Antilles*), and
has also worked in film. She has produced two
ethnographic documentaries, one showing
preparations for ▷Carnival in Martinique, and
the other contrasting two fishing communities.
Césaire's first play, *Mémoire d'Isles* (1988) (*Memory
of the Islands*), deals quite simply with two
grandmothers who sit on the veranda and
reminisce about times past. Like ▷Schwarz-Bart
and ▷Bebel-Gisler in their novels, she uses the
collected life-histories of elderly women of
Guadeloupe and Martinique. In her second play,
L'enfant des Passages ou La geste de Ti-Jean (1987)
(*The Fear of Ti-Jean*), Césaire weaves together
Creole and French elements from folktales.
Orphaned and destitute, her folktale hero, Ti-
Jean, encounters a series of magical adventures,
an initiation which prepares him for the duel with
the beast who has stolen the sun. His victory
earns him both princess and kingdom.

César, Ana Cristina (1952–1983)

Brazilian poet, chronicle writer, literary critic and
translator. She did postgraduate work in Rio de
Janeiro and London, and belonged to the 1960s
alternative group of poets called the 'mimeograph
generation', though she wrote with an
intellectually refined, feminine voice. Her four
poetical pamphlets were assembled in *A teus pés*
(1982) (*At Your Feet*), and were reprinted several
times after her suicide in 1983. In 1985 *Dispersos e
esparsos* (*The Dispersed and Scattered*) confirmed her
success.

Ce sexe qui n'en est pas un (1977) ▷ *This Sex Which Is Not One*

Céu, Maria do, Sóror (1658–1753)

Portuguese poet and prose writer. She entered the
convent when she was eighteen; there she wrote
religious, didactic and allegorical works which she
signed Marina Clemência. Several of her works
were written in Spanish, and like many writers of
the period she wrote an elaborate, conceptualized
kind of poetry in the tradition of the Spanish poet
Góngora. Her literary production also includes
autos (plays), comedies, apologies and
hagiographies. Among her major works are: *A
Preciosa I* (1731), *II* (1933) (*The Precious One*) and
Enganos do Bosque, Desenganos do Rio (1741) (*Errors
of the Forest, Disillusionments of the River*).
    ▷*Conceptismo*

Céu, Violante do, Sóror (1601–1693)

Portuguese poet. Prior to entering the convent her
name was Violante Montesino; she took vows to
be a Dominican nun in 1630. One of the major
poets of the ▷Baroque period, many of her
poems appear in ▷*Fênix Renascida* (*Phoenix*

Reborn), a five-volume collection containing the
best of 17th-century Portuguese verse. Because of
the amorous nature of some of her poems, she
signed them 'by an anonymous poetess'. Religious
and profane love were prominent themes in her
work. The sonnet was her preferred form,
although she also composed odes, *romances*,
madrigals and *décimas*. Historians frequently
classify her poetry as *conceptista*. Her principal
collections include *Rimas Várias* (1646) (*Various
Rhymes*) and the two-volume *Parnaso Lusitano de
Divinos e Humanos Versos* (1733) (*Lusitanian
Parnassus of Divine and Human Verses*). So
accomplished was she as a poet that she was
frequently called the 'phoenix of Lusitanian
ingenuity'.
    ▷*Conceptismo*

Chacel, Rosa (born 1898)

Spanish writer. Chacel was born in Valladolid,
and studied painting and sculpture in Madrid.
During the 1920s she was a disciple of Ortega y
Gasset. Her first novel, *Estación, ida y vuelta*
(1930) (*Station/season, Round Trip – estación* in
Castilian means both station and season; the title
implies both terms), is a minute analysis of an
unfortunate love affair. After the Spanish Civil
War (1936–9) she published a book of sonnets, *A
la orilla de un pozo* (1936) (*On the Edge of a Well*).
Her novel *Memorias de Leticia Valle* (1945) (*The
Memoirs of Leticia Valle*) focuses on adolescent
love. One of Chacel's major works is *La sinrazón*
(1960) (*Unreason*), which later won the prestigious
Premio de la Crítica. Tracing the life of an
individual, Santiago Hernández, from 1918 until
his death in 1941, the novel skilfully explores
inner psychology through the form of a diary.
Barrio de Maravillas (1976) (*Maravillas
Neighbourhood*) and *Acrópolis* (1984) are the first
two parts of a trilogy largely based on
autobiographical material. Chacel has also
published numerous essays, a collection of short
stories, *Icada, Nevda, Diada* (1971), and a
collection of four novel projects: *Novelas antes de
tiempo* (1981) (*Novels Ahead of Time*).

Chacón Nardi, Rafaela (born 1926)

Cuban poet. She graduated in education at the
University of Havana, and pursued post-graduate
courses in Chile and France. She received several
scholarships, including one from UNESCO in
1963. She became Director of Educational
Extension, and represented Cuba in several
countries. Her work has been published in
numerous Latin American magazines. *Viaje al
sueño* (1948) (*Journey into Sleep*), *Viaje al sueño*
(1957) (*Journey into Sleep*) and *De rocío y de humo*
(1965) (*Of Dew and Smoke*), her books of poetry,
have been translated into various languages. She
has also published books on history, art,
architecture and education.

Chaibi, Aïcha

Tunisian novelist. Her novel *Rachid* (1975)
criticizes the *nouveau riche* society in Tunisia, by

depicting a young man, accustomed to the Europeanized values of the city, rediscovering traditional ways of life in the country. The novel denounces the loss of cultural identity. It was one of three novels that appeared in the context of Tunisian Women's Day, a yearly celebration introduced by Habib Bourguiba (born 1903), former president of Tunisia. The celebration, on 8 August, focuses on women's rights in every aspect of life.

Chaine of Pearle, Or a Memoriall of the peerles Graces, and Heroick Vertues of Queene Elizabeth, A (1630)

English poem written by Diana Primrose. The work is dedicated to 'all Noble Ladies and Gentlewomen' as an example for their own behaviour. Composed in rhymed couplets, the poem commemorates ten public and private virtues of Queen Elizabeth I. Each of the ten virtues or 'pearls' (religion, chastity, prudence, temperance, clemency, justice, fortitude, science, patience and bounty) is set off in a stanza of its own. The title page of Primrose's work identifies her as a 'Noble Lady'. Nothing else is known of the author of this work.

Challans, Eileen Mary ▷Renault, Mary

Chalmers, Alexandria

New Zealand novelist. Born in Southland, Alexandria Chalmers has worked as a teacher and educational administrator in North America, and now lives in Christchurch, New Zealand. She has written one novel, *The Wintering House* (1989), and a number of stories. Her writing focuses on gender roles, conflict and violence associated with economic and class inequity, emerging subjectivity, and repressed emotion.

Chambers, Charlotte (died 1821)

North American diarist. She was originally a resident of Chambersburg, Pennsylvania, but her religious commitment carried her at the end of the 18th century to Cincinnati, Ohio, where she worked for the Bible Society of Ohio. ▷*The Memoir of Charlotte Chambers*, which comprises the diary she kept from December 1796 to April 1821, reflects her dedication to the Bible Society and her social life as a member of a religious community.

Chamblit, Rebekah (died 1733)

North American author of advice literature. Her fame rests on her one known written statement, ▷*The Declaration, Dying Warning and Advice of Rebekah Chamblit*, which she was coerced into writing before she was executed for infanticide on 27 September 1733. Although she recounted her requisite guilt and remorse, her declaration contains an underlying record of the consequences of a society that seeks to repress sexual desires. She only briefly details the birth and murder of her infant, but she expansively acknowledges the social pressures on 'my Sex'.

The declaration is a tragic account of a young woman who sought desperate means to hide her child's illegitimate birth.

Champseix, Léodile ▷Léo, André

Chand, Meira (Angela) (born 1942)

British novelist. She was born in London to a Swiss mother and Indian father, and educated in England. Her first four novels are set in the closed and complex society of Japan, where she has lived with her Indian husband since 1962: *The Gossamer Fly* (1979), *Last Quadrant* (1981), *The Bonsai Tree* (1983) and *The Painted Cage* (1986). Her main characters are frequently expatriates or outsiders, and her themes those of alienation and the clash of Eastern and Western cultures, particularly for those of mixed blood. Her fifth novel, ▷*House of the Sun* (1989), was written after a long stay in India, and is set in Bombay. It was adapted for the stage and produced in London by the Tamasha Theatre Company in 1991.

Chandler, Elizabeth Margaret (1807–1834)

US poet, essayist and journalist. A Quaker who began publishing in her teens, Chandler was among the earliest US women writers to focus on African-Americans, ▷Native Americans and women. Like ▷Lydia Maria Child, Chandler used her poetry and prose to direct her readers to humane acts. Like African-American writers of the 18th century, she focused on the horror of enslavement and the human and cultural dignity of Africans. Her most famous poem is 'The Captured Slave'. A regular contributor to the abolitionist periodical, *The Genius of Universal Emancipation*, she urged economic, social and personal action to help the oppressed. Her periodical publications were collected posthumously and published by the editor of *The Genius* as *The Poetical Works of Elizabeth Margaret Chandler* (1836) and *Essays, Philanthropic and Moral* (1836).

Chang, Diana

US novelist and poet. Born in New York, Chang was raised in China by her Eurasian mother. Her work often moves beyond ethnicity in examining issues of identity and the self. In the poem 'On Gibson Lane, Sagaponack', cultural differences are subsumed. It emphasizes the experiences of life which are shared by the Chinese and Anglo-American girls. The poems in *What Matisse Is After* (1984) explore the evolution of the self. To achieve wholeness the self must integrate the inner and outer selves, as in 'A Dialogue with My Own Temperament'; the spiritual and the material, as in 'On Seeing My Great Aunt In a Funeral Parlor'; and the animalistic and the human, as in 'Twelve-Year-Olds'. Chang emphasizes the spectrum of possibilities for the fulfilment of being.

Other works include: *The Frontiers of Love* (1956), *A Woman of Thirty* (1959), *A Passion for Life* (1961), *The Only Game in Town* (1963), *Eye to*

Eye (1974), *A Perfect Love* (1978) and *The Horizon is Definitely Speaking* (1982).

▷ Asian-American writing

Chang, Eileen ▷ Zhang Ailing

Changes (1991)
The second novel by Ghanaian writer, ▷ Ama Ata Aidoo. Its heroine, Esi, a contemporary middle-class Ghanaian woman, lives in Accra and is married to Oko. She divorces him because she resents his demands on her time and wants to devote herself more to her work and her daughter. In taking this course of action, completely unacceptable in the eyes of her own society, Esi is shown to be extremely unconventional. Aidoo plays on the ▷ romance genre with its strain of fantasy, the longing it crystallizes in many women for an alternative way of being. Thus, though she demurely 'apologizes' for going back on the promise she once gave not to write about lovers in Accra, Aidoo presents us with a love story of great subversive potential. Esi falls for Ali, and they have an idyllic romance, though Aidoo's ironic style constantly reminds the reader of the different meanings of 'romance' for men and women. She agrees to become his second wife, in a bold attempt to combine commitment and independence. However, the moment they are married, the relationship is in the public arena and Esi loses her fascination for Ali. She emerges from the extreme suffering this entails to a new resolve – that if Ali cannot meet her idea of love, she will remain alone rather than compromise. The humour and deceptive simplicity of Aidoo's style deflect attention from the very serious and subversive point she is making: that whereas at one time women's silence and acquiescence helped to perpetuate a male-defined and socially restricted form of gender relations, this is no longer the case.

Channel, Elinor (fl 1654)
English prophet of the Civil War period (1642–1651). She became dumb with the burden of prophecy until her husband allowed her to go to London, where her prophecy was written down and distorted by Arise Evans as *Message From God by a Dumb Woman* (1654). Evans tried to turn her material complaints into Royalist propaganda. Compare
▷ Trapnel, Anna; Cary, Mary; Poole Elizabeth

Chansons de femme
French term meaning 'women's songs', referring to a medieval genre also known as *chansons de toile* (spinning songs) because they were sung in the places where women were occupied with weaving and spinning. Such songs were distinguished by the fact that they were not only sung *by* women but usually sang *of* women, too. Their subject was not the ideal and distant woman of the male poets' songs of '*fin'amor*' (courtly love), but a passionate young girl, the object of whose love was often unobtainable. Characterized by their lightness of form and content and the absence of any metaphysical dimension, such songs were often sung to dance rhythms.

Chantal, Jeanne de (1572–1641)
French author of numerous letters and grandmother of ▷ Madame de Sévigné. Following the death of her husband in a hunting accident when she was only twenty-eight, Jeanne de Chantal was left to bring up her four children and run the family château in Bourbilly alone. Inspired by a sermon of St François de Sales (1567–1622), Bishop of Geneva, she left in 1610 to found the Congregation of the Visitation of Sainte-Marie in Annecy under his direction. She was herself later canonized.

Chapel Perilous, The (1972)
Australian play by ▷ Dorothy Hewett. This was first performed in Perth in 1971, and could be seen as a feminist parallel of Sir Lancelot's search for the grail and his confrontation with the knights guarding the Chapel Perilous in Malory's *Morte D'Arthur* (c 1469/70). The heroine, Sally Banner, portrayed from the age of fifteen to 61, is in search of a sense of self-worth, and a sense of her own immortality. She consistently flouts the conventions of her society, is judged and condemned by its authority figures, is betrayed by her lovers, and finally arrives back at 'that lonely place' where she began. The mood of the play ranges from lyrical to satirical; its mode is impressionistic and its pace is lively. Although it has always had a controversial reception, *The Chapel Perilous* is regarded as a highly significant Australian drama.

Chapone, Hester (Mulso) (1727–1801)
English poet, letter-writer and ▷ Bluestocking. She learned languages, music and later, French and Latin. In 1745 she published the poem 'To Peace. Written during the late Rebellion, 1745'. For Samuel Johnson's periodical *The Rambler* (March 1750–March 1752) she wrote fictional epistles, and she also contributed to *The Adventurer* (1753). She had influence on and opinions about her contemporaries – among men, Samuel Richardson (▷ Richardson, influence of), whom she admired and Samuel Johnson (1709–1784), among women, ▷ Elizabeth Carter, ▷ Mary Wollstonecraft, ▷ Elizabeth Montagu. She married John Chapone in 1760, and he died within a year. She wrote on, producing *Letters on the Improvement of the Mind* (1773) dedicated to Montagu, *Miscellanies in Verse and Prose* (1775) and *A Letter to a New-Married Lady* (1777). Her works were published as *Works* (1807, 4 Vols) and *Posthumous Works* (1807, 2 Vols).

Charixena
Ancient Greek poet. Apart from the name, we know only that she was reputedly a musician or composer or lyric poet. The Greek expression 'from the time of Charixena' meant something was very out of date.

Charke, Charlotte (1713– c 1760)

English actress, autobiographer, writer, one of the offspring of actor and dramatist Colley Cibber (1671–1757). Educated at Mrs Draper's school in Westminster, and then within the household. In her youth she went hunting and shooting – practices which the neighbours found unacceptably unfeminine. Charlotte married Richard Charke, but left him because of his infidelity, and started a series of careers, first as an actress playing both men and women. Her first role at Drury Lane was in *The Provok'd Wife* (1730), and she also played Harlequin in her own unpublished *The Carnival* (1735). She was thrown out of Drury Lane for scandalous conduct, and her farce, *The Art Of Management, or Tragedy Expell'd* (1735), mocked her ex-employer, advising him, 'if any Gentleman feels himself but slightly glanced at, let me advise him to keep his sentiments to himself. A prudent man wou'd I'm sure.' She worked with English dramatist and novelist Henry Fielding's (1707–1754) troupe and then worked in grocery, puppetry and other ventures. She began to wear men's clothes, and became Mr Brown, an itinerant actor, printer and show-assistant who worked with Mrs Brown. She published her *A Narrative of the Life of Mrs Charlotte Charke* (1755), an 'account of her unaccountable life', in eight instalments. Describing teenage life in Hillingdon, she writes that she would 'divert myself with Shooting; and grew so great a Proficient in that notable Excercise, that I was like the person described in *The Recruiting Officer*, capable of destroying all the Venison and Wild Fowl about the Country'. She also wrote a novel, *Henry Dumont and Charlotte Evelyn*.
▷Bennett, Anna Maria; Haywood, Eliza
Bib: Ferguson, Moira, *First Feminists*.

Charlotte, a Tale of Truth (1791)

Novel by North American writer ▷Susanna Haswell Rowson. Better known by the title of *Charlotte Temple*, used in later editions, this novel not only was Rowson's bestseller but, with more than 200 editions, remained North America's bestseller until the mid-19th century. An impressionable fifteen-year-old, Charlotte flees England with her lover, Lieutenant Montraville, who subsequently abandons her although she is pregnant. The story is also an indictment of corrupt teachers who encourage romantic fantasies in their young students, as Charlotte's teacher had abetted her interest in Montraville. It is also a moral tale – of the consequences for a young woman who seeks to escape the moral guidance of her parents and community, but also of the consequences for a society that allows a double standard of morality for young men and women to prevail. In the end, Charlotte must, of course, die; as Rowson concludes, Charlotte's death was 'a striking example that vice . . . in the end leads only to misery and shame'. The North American public, however, adored Charlotte and relished her tragic fate, making her one of the most popular tragic heroines in North American literature.

Charlotte's Daughter; or, The Three Orphans: A Sequel to Charlotte Temple
▷*Lucy Temple*

Charlotte Temple ▷*Charlotte, a Tale of Truth*

Charman, Janet (born 1954)

New Zealand poet. Janet Charman's poetry reflects her working life as a nurse, receptionist and member of the 'service' professions. Her poetry first appeared in feminist publications such as *Broadsheet*, and represents itself as explicitly feminist in subject and language strategies. She has published one collection, *Two Deaths in One Night* (1987).

Charrière, Isabelle-Agnès-Elisabeth van Tuyll van Serooskerken van Zuylen de (1740–1805)

Swiss writer of Dutch origin. The aristocratic French-speaking Madame de Charrière explored every literary genre, producing novels, plays, poetry, and political pamphlets now collected in the ten-volume *Oeuvres complètes* (1979–1984) (*Complete Works*). Her earlier works, including the three novels *Lettres de Mistress Henley* (1784) (*The Letters of Mistress Henley*), *Lettres neuchâteloises* (1784) (*Letters from Neuchâtel*) and *Lettres écrites de Laussane* (1785) (*Letters Written from Lausanne*) 1799), portraying relationships in her restrained social circle, revealed her independent, non-conformist turn of mind, and won her a scandalous yet successful literary reputation. The writings of her last twenty years, individualistic and cosmopolitan in the assessment offered of the Revolution (1789), caused outrage, due to the fact that she was a woman expressing her opinions in the exclusively male domain of politics. Her Republican sympathies are moderated by a commitment to a broad set of humanitarian principles and the politics of tolerance: see the pamphlet collection *Observations et conjectures politiques* (1787–1788) (*Political Remarks and Proposals*) and her comedies, representing such figures as the immigrant, the fallen aristocrat, and the political hypocrite. Her novel, *Lettres trouvées dans des portfeuilles d'émigrés* (1793) (*Letters from an Émigré's Wallet*), looks at the causes of the Revolution, and includes a project for a Constitution. Other works include a comic opera, *Les Femmes* (1790) (*Women*), and the novel *Trois Femmes* (1797) (*Three Women*), which explores the Kantian notion of duty. An English translation of four of her stories (*Four Tales by Zélide*) appeared in 1925.
Bib: Beauvoir, S. de, *The Second Sex*; Deguise, A., 'Trois Femmes'. *Le monde de Mme de Charrière*; Farnum, D., *The Dutch divinity, a biography of Mme de Charrière*; Vissière, I., *Isabelle de Charrière*,

Une aristocrate révolutionnaire; Wood, D. M., *The Novels of Mme de Charrière*.

Chárskaia, Lidiia Alekséevna (1875–1937)

Pen-name of the Russian prose writer, poet, and actress L.A. Churilova. Between 1901 and 1916 she published about 80 books, and became the most famous children's writer in Russia. She also acted in character roles for the Aleksandrinskii Theatre between 1898 and 1924. Anyone this prolific could not possibly sustain a high level of quality, and the majority of her books seem to have been dashed off. Her books for children include historical novels such as ▷*A Daring Life* (1905) about Nadezhda Dúrova. The books most popular among children were the collections of adventure stories, for example, *Princess Dzhavakha* (1903), based on Caucasian legends, and *The Little Siberian* (1910). Several novels follow young girls' lives in institutions (*Notes of a Boarding School Girl*; *The Foundlings*). Her stories are formulaic: the sufferings and adventures of a lonely protagonist, the intervention of a noble person, a happy resolution. Their appeal to young people stems from their combination of entertaining and surprising plotlines. Her heroines lead intense emotional lives, form strong female friendships, and act according to such firm moral and religious principles as honesty, forgiveness, compassion for others, and repentance. Chárskaia also wrote four autobiographical novels, beginning with ▷*For What?* (1909). After 1917 her books were removed from libraries and she was not allowed to publish under her own name. In 1924 the Aleksandrinskii Theatre dismissed her. Her work had not been republished in the USSR until 1990, when a private publisher brought out *Princess Dzhavakha*. That it sold out immediately indicates the enduring appeal of her books.

English translations of her works include: *Little Princess Nina* (1924); *Fledglings* (1926); *The Tartar Princess* (1926); *The Little Siberian* (1929).

▷*Happiness*

Chartroule, Marie-Amélie (1850–?)

French erotic novelist. A free-thinker with a lively interest in the erotic literature of the past, her own writings caused her to fall foul of the law on several occasions; notably after her publication of *Les Vestales de l'Eglise* (*Vestals in the Church*), in 1877. This text offended because of its anti-clericalism, rather than its licentiousness, having been written in order to attack a group of nuns who had ensured that Chartroule spent eight days in prison the previous year. After two further works, *Les Dévoyés* (*The Delinquents*) and *Mme Ducroisy* appeared in 1879, she was condemned to four months' imprisonment; her sentence provoked a scandal and led her to publish a polemical pamphlet entitled *Mme Ducroisy, la presse et la justice* (*Mme Ducroisy, Justice and the Press*). Chartroule is unusual among women erotic writers of 19th-century France in that she

favoured a male pen-name, writing as Marc de Montifaud.
Bib: Brécourt-Villars, C., *Écrire d'Amour*

Chastenay de Lenty, Louise-Marie Victorine de (1770–?1838)

French memoir-writer, essayist and translator. A member of the French nobility, Chastenay was an accomplished musician, botanist and historian. Although she never married, her position as canoness enabled her to take the title of Madame, and allowed her to live independently. She was familiar with the ideas of the *philosophes*, and was said to have been Republican-minded. Imprisoned during the Terror, she was known later, under the Directoire, as *citoyenne Victorine* (Citizen Victorine). Her *Mémoires*, re-edited in 1987, span the tumultuous period from 1771 to 1815. Her other main works include the *Calandrier de Flore* (*Calendar of Plants*) (1802–1803) which combines botany with sentimental moral reflections, and the scholarly works *Du génie des peuples anciens* (1808) (*On the Genius of Ancient Peoples*), *Les Chevaliers normands en Italie et en Sicile* (1816) (*The Normans in Italy and Sicily . . .*) and *De l'Asie* (1833) (*Asia*). She also published several translations including ▷Ann Radcliffe's ▷ *The Mysteries of Udolpho* (1794) and Oliver Goldsmith's *The Deserted Village* (1770).

Châtelet-Lomont, Gabrielle-Emilie Le Tonnelier de Berteuil, Marquise du (1706–1749)

French essayist and translator of Issac Newton. Born in Paris, married to a high-ranking officer and engaged in a long, intimate and intellectual relationship with the French writer and philosopher Voltaire (1694–1778), she lived relatively independently of both at the Château de Cirey. Here she had a laboratory and studied mathematics, physics and geometry. In 1744 she published her first work, *Dissertation sur la nature et la propagation du feu* (*Essay on the Nature and Spread of Fire*) written for a competition held by the Academy of Sciences in 1738. Her major work, *Institutions de physiques*, appeared in 1740. She attempted to synthesize the theories of Newton (1642–1727) and Gottfried Leibniz (1646–1716), although she emphasized her support for Leibnizian vitalism and metaphysics. In the polarized climate of debate this work brought her into conflict with Cartesians on the one hand and radical Newtonians on the other. These works, and her translation of Newton's *Principia Mathematica* (*The Principles of Mathematics*), which remains the unique basis for French editions to date, made scientific thought accessible to the non-specialist. In her *Réflexions sur le bonheur* (1796) (*Reflections on Happiness*) she argued that the knowledge and – especially for women – the independence derived from study are essential foundations for happiness.

A modern edition of *Institutions de physiques* is available in facsimile reprint (1988).

▷Graffigny, Madame de

Bib: Didier, B., *Emilie, Emilie*; Ehrman, E., *Mme du Châtelet*; Wade, I.O., *Voltaire and Mme du Châtelet*.

Chauncy, Nan (1900–1970)

Australian author of children's fiction. Chauncy was born in England, and went as a child to live in Tasmania, where all her books are set, and remained there for the rest of her life. Three of her fourteen novels for children, *Tiger in the Bush* (1957), *Devils' Hill* (1958) and *Tangara* (1960), won Children's Book of the Year Awards.
▷ Children's literature (Australia)

Chauvet, Marie (1916–1973)

One of Haiti's best-known novelists, Chauvet (also known as Marie Vieux) depicts in two of her earliest novels, ▷ *Fille d'Haïti* (1954) (*Daughter of Haiti*) and ▷ *Amour* (1968) (*Love*), women who suffer from a sense of fragmentation, threatened from the inside by a sense of worthlessness, and from the outside by the violent social and political climate of Haiti. Lotus of *Fille d'Haïti* finds liberation and security in a kind of madness, while Claire in *Amour* is also a misfit, and withdraws into an obscure world of fantasies (compare the heroines of the Guadeloupian novelist, ▷ Michèle Lacrosil). Chauvet changes the focus in her novel *Fonds des Nègres* (1961) to the country, and, in the manner of some members of Haiti's indigenist school, decries the dire misery of the Haitian peasantry. Marie-Ange is a Haitian woman formed and deformed by society. In her posthumous novel, *Les Rapaces* (1986) (*Birds of Prey*), published under her maiden name, Marie Vieux, Chauvet offers a horrifying image of Haiti's misery, in which human values have vanished, and violence has dehumanized both the oppressed and the oppressors. Chauvet turns in *La Danse sur le volcan* (1957) (*Dance on the Volcano*) to Saint-Domingue on the eve of revolution, but also describes the horrors of slavery.

Chavez, Denise (born 1948)

US short story writer. A ▷ Latina of Mexican descent, Chavez was born in Las Cruces, New Mexico, and grew up in a household of women without men. She earned a Master's degree in creative writing at the University of New Mexico. She is a community-oriented artist, claiming her work is for the poor and the forgotten. *The Last of the Menu Girls* (1986) is a book of seven related stories, focusing on Rocio' Esquibel, an adolescent New Mexican girl. The stories concern Rocio's rites of passage into womanhood and her protests against the traditional serving roles society prescribes for women. She chooses to live as an artist writing about the lives of women in her neighbourhood. These stories give meaning to the woman's emotionally turbulent lives.

Chawaf, Chantal

French fiction writer. She is associated with ▷ *écriture féminine* (*feminine writing*) and, at the beginning of her career, was associated with the French women's group, ▷ *Psych et Po*. In her writing, Chawaf attempts to articulate 'The Body', a pre-Oedipal, pre-verbal discourse which explores the nature of 'the feminine'. She has published fifteen texts to date, including: *Retable* (*Reredas*), published together with *La Rêverie* (*The Daydream*) in 1974; *Chair chaude* (1976) (*Hot Flesh*); *Crépusculaires* (1981) (*Twilights*); *L'Intérieur des heures* (1987) (*Inside the Hours*); *Rédemption* (1989) (*Redemption*) and *L'Eclairage* (1990) (*Illumination*).

Chedid, Andrée (born 1921)

Egyptian-French poet, dramatist, novelist and short story writer. She was born in Cairo, of Lebanese parents, and went to a French language school. She graduated from the American University in Cairo in 1942, and has lived in Paris since 1946, with periodic visits to the Middle East. She started writing poetry in English. An early selection, *Trials Of My Fancy*, was published in Cairo in the 1940s, but the bulk of her work is in French. She draws on Egyptian and Lebanese material from both the past and the present, and it is this that gives her work its particular distinction. She has published nineteen volumes of poetry, of which two volumes, published in 1976, stand out: *Fraternité de la Parole* (*Brotherhood of Words*) and *Cérémonial de la Violence* (*Ceremony of Violence*). She was awarded the Louis Lajeier and the Mallarmé Awards for poetry in 1976. Her first collection of plays includes: *Berenice d'Egypte*, *Les Nombres* (*Numbers*), *Le Menteur* (*The Liar*) and *Echec à la Reine* (*Check to the Queen*). Her novels include one on Nefertiti, wife of the tragic pharaoh Akhenatun, who dreamt of a new political and social order with more justice for his subjects and the worship of One God.

Altogether, Andrée Chedid has published nine novels and three collections of short stories, in which the characters carry 'the stamp of death': living the trauma of disease, war and violence, with domestic violence presented as worst of all. These 'traumas invested with both laughter and tears', however, have a universal resonance in the tragedy of a frustrated wife in ▷ *Le Sommeil Délivré* (*From Sleep Unbound*) or a desperate grandmother. *La Maison Sans Racines* (1985) (*The House Without Roots*) is about the civil war in Lebanon, concentrating on the sacrificial act of two girls, who make their gesture against the sectarian war and are shot in consequence. Andrée Chedid was awarded the Royal Belgian Academy's Grand Prize for French Literature in 1975, and the Goncourt Prize for her collection *Les Corps et Le Temps* (1978) (*Bodies and Time*). In 1988 she was awarded an honorary doctorate by the American University in Cairo.

Translations of *La Maison Sans Racines*, *Le Sommeil Délivré* and *Le Sixième Jour* (*The Sixth Day*) have been published.
▷ Beirut

Cheeseman, Clara (1852–1943)

New Zealand novelist. Clara Cheeseman published only one novel, but new stories and articles appeared in Australian and New Zealand journals during the 1880s and 1890s. She held firm views about the content of colonial fiction, believing that colonial writers, and especially women writers, often breached propriety in their work. In her fiction she attacked materialism and acquisitiveness in colonial settlers. Her three-volume novel *A Rolling Stone* (1886) has been described as essentially a 'love story whose hero survives various pioneering vicissitudes' (Joan Stevens, *The New Zealand Novel*, 1961).

Cheevers, Sarah ▷Evans, Katherine and Sarah Cheevers

Chen Duansheng (18th–19th centuries)

Chinese writer. Chen lived during the Qing dynasty, and is chiefly remembered as the author of the highly popular romance in the *pintan* form (verse narrative sung to accompaniment), *Tale of the After Life*. It is supposed to be the story of characters resurrected from a previous narrative, hence the title. According to scholars, the whole work– 80 chapters in twenty volumes – was written between 1736 and 1820. The story is set in the Yuan dynasty and centres on a young girl, Meng Lijun, who goes through various adventures in male disguise. Chen completed the work up to volume fourteen, and at her death the thread of the narrative was picked up by another woman, Liang Desheng, who had travelled widely in her youth, and added a more colourful background to the story. The whole was later edited by a third woman, Madame Hon Xiangye (born c 1766), before being published.

Chen Jingrong (born 1917)

Chen Jingrong

Chinese poet and translator, native of Sichuan. From the 1930s Chen was involved with the writers' united front against Japanese invasion and worked as teacher, editor, and translator in various parts of the country. Meanwhile, she kept on writing and publishing poetry. Self-taught in foreign languages, Chen translated many works into Chinese, including Hans Christian Andersen's (1805–1875) *Fairy Tales* in six volumes, Victor Hugo's *Nôtre-Dame de Paris* (1831), and poems by Rainer Maria Rilke (1875–1926) and Charles Baudelaire (1821–1867).

Chen Jo Hsi ▷Chen Ruoxi

Chen Naishan (born 1946)

Chinese novelist and short story writer. A native of Shanghai, Chen taught English for many years, and 'Poor Neighbourhood', published in *The Blue House and Other Short Stories* (1989), reflects her experiences as a teacher. The novella, *The Blue House* (1983), is about the remnants of the vanishing old Shanghai 'gentility' in their struggle to adapt to the new regime, and the varying fates of the descendants through the vicissitudes of war and revolution. *The Piano Tuner* (1989), in English translation, collects some of her best-known stories, for example 'Hong Taitai'. Chen is the only writer to portray the business class in a sympathetic light, seen in such stories as 'No. 2 and No. 4 of Shanghai'. She is also China's only Christian writer, and is a member of the board of the YMCA, Shanghai branch. Stories such as 'In My Heart There Is Room for Thee' reflect her Christian sentiments.

Chen Ruiqing (born 1932)

Chinese writer of film scripts and short stories. Chen joined the communist revolution in 1947 and had worked mainly in films, writing and editing film scripts. She is now script writer for the Beijing Film Studio. Chen was labelled a 'rightist' (enemy category) in 1957 for outspokenness, and remained a political outcast for twenty-two years. Since rehabilitation in 1978 in the post-Mao era when many of the abuses of the Maoist political campaigns were being set to rights, she has published *The Great Northern Wilds*, a semi-autobiographical series reminiscent of her years of political exile.
Bib: 'Guessie Grows Up', a chapter of *The Great Northern Wilds*, is translated in *The Serenity of Whiteness*, selected and translated by Zhu Hong.

Chen Ruoxi (born 1938)

Taiwan-born Chinese writer. Chen Ruoxi (also known as Chen Jo Hsi) majored in English at the University of Taiwan and later received higher degrees at Mount Holyoke College and Johns Hopkins University in the US. Her early works were explorations in individual psychology, with a touch of the ▷Gothic. She went to mainland China in 1966, left in 1973 and is now teaching at Berkeley, USA. Chen has published novels and short stories about life in China during the 'cultural revolution' (1966–1976) with the intimate observation of a firsthand witness and the critical

perception of the detached writer. Representative works include *The Execution of Mayor Lin (1978)* and *The Old Man and Other Stories* (1986). Her works reveal different aspects of life in China: the violence of the 'cultural revolution' and the violation of basic individual rights even under normal circumstances.
Bib: (trans.) Ing, Nancy and Goldblatt, Howard, *The Execution of Mayor Lin, and Other Stories from the Great Cultural Proletarian Revolution.*

Chen Zufen (born 1943)

Chinese writer of documentary realism. A graduate of Shanghai Drama Institute, Chen was implicated in her father's political problems and moved to Beijing to work in a district cultural centre. She started writing poetry in 1976, but later turned to reportage. She is best known for reportage on patriotic themes. 'My Native Land, the Supreme Call', about the vicissitudes of a scholar returned from Germany, is one of her better-known pieces.

Chéri (1951)

Translation of *Chéri* (1920), one of French writer ▷Colette's most famous novels. *Chéri* describes the end of a six-year affair between a middle-aged woman, Léa, and a young man, Chéri, when the latter decides to marry. One of the most striking aspects of this novel is its questioning of gender stereotypes and its exploration of female sexuality; from the first page, Chéri, wearing silk pyjamas and Léa's pearls, is the object of the gaze, a languorous and delicate creature, whom the maternal Léa literally nurtures. Léa is also very capable of nuturing herself, and although taken by surprise by the pain of the loss of Chéri, and fully aware of the negative aspects of the ageing process, she demonstrates all the survival skills which Colette associates with femininity.
▷*Last of Chéri, The* (1951)

Chéron, Elisabeth-Sophie (1648–1711)

French poet. She was also a painter and sculptress and member of the Académie Royale de la Peinture et de la Sculpture and of the Academy of the Ricovrati. An anonymous collection of her psalms and *cantiques* (canticles or hymns) was published in 1694. 'La Gloire du Val de Grâce' ('The Glory of the Val de Grâce'), a verse piece, is attributed to her.
Bib: Grente, G. (ed.), *Dictionnaire des lettres françaises.*

Cherry, Frances (born 1937)

New Zealand story writer and novelist. Frances Cherry has spent most of her life in Wellington, where she teaches creative writing. Cherry began publishing occasional stories in the late 1970s and early 1980s, and a collection, *The Daughter-in-Law and Other Stories*, appeared in 1986. Cherry's fiction is focused on family relationships, especially the investigation of gender roles. Her novel, *Dancing with Strings* (1989), is based partly

on her own life, particularly the communism of her parents.

Cherryh, C.J. (Caroline Janice) (born 1942)

US novelist. Cherryh grew up in Lawton, Oklahoma, watching the ▷science fiction serial, *Flash Gordon*. She earned a Master's degree in classics at Johns Hopkins University. For eleven years she taught Latin and ancient history in Oklahoma City schools. She has published two major series of science fiction novels. The Morgaine series, which includes *Gate of Ivrel* (1976) and *Well of Shiuan* (1978), features a woman warrior, Morgaine, who leads the fight to save human worlds from destructive aliens. The Faded Sun trilogy – *The Faded Sun: Kesrith* (1978), *The Faded Sun: Shon'Jir* (1978) and *The Faded Sun: Kutath* (1979) – provides an extended study of an alien race. The novels depict various complex cultures.

Cherryh emphasizes that culture shapes the whole of life, and she examines the use of power and presents autocratic societies sympathetically. Her novels portray women in positions of absolute power.

Other works include: *Brothers of Earth* (1976), *Hunter of Worlds* (1977), *The Fires of Azeroth* (1979), *Hestia* (1979), *The Green Gods* (1980), *Serpent's Reach* (1980), *Downbelow Station* (1981), *Chernevog* (1990) and *Yugenie* (1991).

Chervínskaia, Lidiia Davydovna (1907–1988)

Russian poet who emigrated to Paris. She published three collections of poetry, in 1934, 1937, and 1956. Her lyric style is restrained, condensed, with a deceptively straightforward use of an almost prosaic colloquial language. Her poetry is concentrated on the self, rather than the external world; it is contemplative, moody, analytical. Chervínskaia will at times end a lyric with an unexpected break in the final stanza by reducing it to fewer lines or breaking off in the middle of a line, a formal imitation of the implied theme of incompleteness or indefiniteness.
Bib: Pachmuss, T. (trans.), *A Russian Cultural Revival: A Critical Anthology of Emigre Literature before 1939*; Markov, V. and Sparks, M. (eds), *Modern Russian Poetry.*

Chesebro', Caroline (1825–1873)

US children's and adult fiction writer and novelist. Like many other 19th-century US women writers, Chesebro' began her career writing sketches and short fiction for regional and specialized magazines, moving up and on to magazines like ▷*Harper's Monthly Magazine* and ▷*The Atlantic Monthly*. Her first book, *Dream-Land by Daylight* (1852), was a collection of these periodical pieces, but she progressed quickly to the novel, sustaining regular publication and a literary career. The novels are a curious mixture: strong, developed women characters, often in women-centred worlds; conventional morality; serious questioning of convention; didacticism; and an often egregious style. Chesebro' is one of the 19th-century women novelists who can truly be charged with purple prose – and with seemingly endless prose disquisitions rather than fictionalizing – but, at the same time, her topics and characters are among the most interesting of her era, and for our time. Her works include: *Isa, A Pilgrimage* (1852); *The Children of Light* (1853); *Getting Along, A Book of Illustrations* (1855); *Victoria, or The World Overcome* (1856); and *Peter Carradine* (1863).

Chesnut, Mary Boykin Miller (1823–1886)

US diarist. Wife of a southern US plantation-owner, daughter of a southern US senator, and resident in the south during the Civil War and Reconstruction, Chesnut produced the most extensive extant diary recording these years. She wrote from her singular perspective as a southerner sympathetic to African-Americans, but supportive of the states rights position of the southern Confederacy. Published in part as *A Diary from Dixie* (1905), the complete text was republished as *Mary Chesnut's Civil War* and won the 1981 Pulitzer Prize for history. It has become the definitive text for the southern US establishment woman's view of slavery and the Civil War.

Chézy, Helmina von (1783–1856)

German novelist. Her parents having divorced, she spent much of her childhood with her grandmother, a writer ▷Anna Louisa Karsch. She began an early literary career by moving to Paris and publishing the journal *Französische Miscellen* (1803–1807) (*French Miscellany*). A book about cultural life under Napoleon (1805–7) was confiscated by the French censors. Her marriage to the orientalist de Chézy lasted five years, after which she took up a semi-itinerant lifestyle, travelling through German-speaking Europe and meeting literary people everywhere. She wrote her libretto for Franz Schubert's (1797–1828) *Rosamunde* (1820). Her eventful life is in part evoked in her novel, *Emmas Prüfungen* (1817) (*The Trials of Emma*), and in the memoirs she dictated to her niece when she was old and blind.

Chidley, Katherine (fl 1641)

English polemicist who first published a defence of IIndependent Churches, *The Justification of the Independent Churches of Christ* (1641). This was followed by *a New Years Gift, or a Brief Exhoration To Mr Thomas Edwards* (1645) – Edwards attacks her in *Gangraena*. She also wrote *Good Counsel to Petitioners that they May Declare Their Faith Before They Build Their Church* (1645), and may have been the leader of the women's petition for the release of the Leveller John Lilburne in 1653.

▷Quaker women (Britain)
Bib: Gregg, Pauline *Free-Born John*; Hobby Elaine, *Virtue of Necessity*.

Child, Lydia Maria Francis (1802–1880)

US author of fiction, non-fiction, poetry and biography; editor of the first US children's periodical, the *Juvenile Miscellany*. Child is principally noted for her work in the abolitionist movement and her early sympathetic treatment of ▷Native Americans in ▷*Hobomok* (1824).

All of Child's writing reflects her interest in reform, her sympathy for women and minorities, and her desire to lead her readers to humane and moral action. Most read today is *Hobomok*, but also among her historical fiction are *The Rebels, or Boston Before the Revolution* (1825), dealing with North American colonials' response to British taxation, and *The Romance of the Republic* (1837), presenting abolitionist values and characters. She preceded ▷Catharine Beecher's ▷*Treatise on Domestic Economy* (1841) with her 1829 *The Frugal Housewife*, a guide to household management. With these and the *Juvenile Miscellany*, Child was either the first or the first significant US figure in a variety of popular genres.

In terms of national history and her own reputation, Child's anti-slavery and women's rights non-fiction had the greatest impact. Her *Appeal in Favor of that Class of Americans Called Africans* (1833) and *History of the Condition of Women in Various Ages and Nations* (1835) brought her favour and converts on the one hand, acrimony and loss of audience on the other. She valiantly continued promotion of the African-American cause, not only through her own writing and editing (the *National Anti-Slavery Standard*), but also through publication of works by or for African-Americans. These included her own *Correspondence* (1860) and the *Freedman's Book* (1865), as well as her edited edition of ▷Harriet A. Jacobs's ▷*Incidents in the Life of a Slave Girl*. From the 1830s to the 1860s, Child published scores of works, most focused on African-Americans, Native Americans and women. She pioneered the use of biographies of minorities and women as inspiring role models, a technique which has become common in literature directed to empowerment and equal rights.

Childhood (Caribbean)

A theme of Caribbean writers. For example, see ▷Jamaica Kincaid (▷*Annie John*), ▷Zee Edgell (▷*Beka Lamb*), ▷Merle Hodge (▷*Crick Crack Monkey*) and ▷Olive Senior (▷*Summer Lightning*).

Child marriage

The practice, once common among many middle and high-ranking Hindu ▷castes in India, of marrying girls before the age of puberty to boys or men chosen by their parents. The object was to secure a husband from a good family for one's daughter, and to ensure that she grew up knowing what would be expected of her in her in-laws' household. Child brides were rarely expected to live with their in-laws or have sexual relations with their husband before the onset of puberty, but they could be widowed while they were still virgins. The prohibition that the same social groups observed on widow remarriage then condemned these girls to a life of servitude, and often destitution. In the 19th century the British and many Indian social reformers attempted to popularize a minimum age of marriage for girls (and also to establish a meaningful age of consent to sexual intercourse). The Child Marriage Restraint Act of 1929 was one legislative move towards achieving this, but the work of changing popular practice still goes on today.

▷ Dowry; Arranged marriage

Children of Heaven (1962)

Translation of *Les Petits Enfants du siècle* (1961) (also translated as *Josyane and the Welfare*, 1963), novel by French writer ▷ Christiane Rochefort. Through the medium of her adolescent first-person narrator, Josyane, Rochefort satirizes the French government's post-war policy of providing family allowances in order to increase the national birth-rate, by describing its effects on a working-class family who produce children in order to acquire consumer goods. The education system, the disastrous urban development of the 1950s and 1960s, the motor car and romantic love also become targets for ironic comedy. The novel is unusual in its attempt to render something of the quality of colloquial spoken French through the use of clichés, slang and repetitions, and in its explicit depiction of Josyane's discovery of her sexuality. The novel ends pessimistically with Josyane succumbing to romantic love and continuing the cycle of child production.

Children of Nature (1968)

Japanese writer Kanai Mieko (born 1947) originally entitled this work *The Fruits of the Sea*. Out of nostalgia adults are often attracted to innocent children playing. In this story, written in a literary style approaching verse, everything at the seaside – fish, birds, hotel guests and even a drowned body – is fascinating to senior elementary schoolchildren who are spending the summer holiday with their mothers. The ten- and eleven-year-olds feel no threat from the future, and yet, while they enjoy swimming, they are aware of the water's resistance, representing some kind of restricting future hurdle.

Children of Violence (1952–1969)

Sequence of five novels by British writer ▷ Doris Lessing. The individual volumes are *Martha Quest* (1952), *A Proper Marriage* (1954), *A Ripple from the Storm* (1958), *Landlocked* (1965) and *The Four-Gated City* (1969). Lessing described the sequence as a ▷ *Bildungsroman*; the volumes chart the 'life-journey' of Martha Quest, the central figure throughout *Children of Violence*. Many of the stages of Martha's life have strong correspondences with Lessing's own experiences.

The first three volumes recount Martha's story from adolescence to young adulthood in the years before and during World War II. Brought up in a white farming community in Southern Rhodesia, Martha embarks on an uneasy rebellion against her society's conformism and racism. Lessing focuses in particular on the tensions between

Martha and her mother, May Quest, and the struggles between mother and daughter are a crucial aspect of the novel sequence as a whole. Martha's quest for freedom is both individual and transpersonal. Lessing follows her through everyday life and everyday rebellions – sexual, social and political – but also, in *Martha Quest*, opens up the world of Martha's dreams and visions. In subsequent volumes Martha struggles to bring her visionary glimpses of the future into being through the only channels available to her – the 'wisdom of the dream' becomes submerged. In the second volume of the sequence, *A Proper Marriage*, we see Martha marrying and bearing a child as war breaks out. Her brief marriage is empty and loveless, and Martha leaves her husband and child. *A Ripple from the Storm* follows Martha through a period of intense political involvement and a further failed marriage to a communist activist. She reaches an impasse and, in the fourth volume of the series, is literally and metaphorically 'landlocked' as she waits to leave for England. During this time – the months during which the war comes to its end – Martha's lover Thomas Stern is one of a number of men she has loved who dies amid a violence in which she is implicated: 'She could no more dissociate herself from the violence done her, done by her, than a tadpole can live out of water.'

In the final volume of the sequence, *The Four-Gated City*, Martha has arrived in London. Lessing uses Martha's position as an outsider to point up the hypocrisy and corruption of English society, as divided in class terms as Rhodesia is in racial ones. Martha takes up a post as housekeeper in the home of Mark Coldridge, a writer, and his disturbed and damaged family. Caring for them seems to become her destiny, the fulfilment of an earlier dream or vision of a middle-aged woman in a house full of children whose faces 'as they turned them towards her' were 'tortured and hurt'. These are the new generation of the 'children of violence' in an increasingly dystopian society.

The Four-Gated City was written after ▷ *The Golden Notebook* (1962) and shares a number of its themes and concerns; mental breakdown (both novels were influenced by the anti-psychiatry movement of the 1960s), the relationship between politics and psychiatry, the end of belief in collective political action, the place of the writer in the modern city, the role of the novel, and the limits of ▷ realism. *The Four-Gated City* ends with a nuclear accident, and an appendix in which Lessing presents the prophetic and mystical beliefs to which she had become increasingly drawn, and the modes of ▷ science fiction which she has turned to in her subsequent work.

Children's Hell (1944)

A collection of short stories by Greek writer ▷ Lilika Nakou. Published first in French and later in Greek (in Alexandria), it recounts the horror Greek children lived through during the German occupation of Greece in World War II.

Although fictional, the stories' basis in facts made a great impression upon the first readers. The heroism of the children leads through the horrors of the war to a sense of liberation.

Children's Hour, The (1934)

US play by ▷Lillian Hellman which brought her fame and money. Although hugely successful on Broadway, it was banned in Chicago, Illinois, Boston, Massachusetts, and London, England. It contains an overt lesbian theme: two women, Karen and Martha, have set up a private boarding school for girls, and a student, Mary Tilford, accuses Karen and Martha of having a lesbian affair. Mary is a spoiled and vicious problem-child and she convinces her grandmother that her story is true. Mary's lies culminate in the school's failure, Karen's broken engagement and Martha's suicide. Hellman's play reflects her aesthetic of political commitment and portrays the life-destroying power of money and the impact of sexual issues on women's lives.

Children's literature

Australia: Women have traditionally been the most prolific writers of Australian fiction for children and adolescents. The first recorded book for children in Australia is Charlotte Barton's *A Mother's Offering to her Children* (1841), published anonymously by 'A Lady Long Resident in New South Wales'. The classics of Australian children's literature include Ethel Pedley's ▷*Dot and the Kangaroo* (1899), ▷Ethel Turner's ▷*Seven Little Australians*, the ▷*Snugglepot and Cuddlepie Series* by ▷May Gibbs, the ▷*Billabong Series* by ▷Mary Grant Bruce, the ▷*Blinky Bill Series* by Dorothy Wall, ▷Jeannie Gunn's *The Little Black Princess* (1905) and ▷*We of the Never-Never* (1908), books which appeal to both adults and children, and ▷Louise Mack's *Teens* (1897) and *Children of the Sun* (1904). Among the many significant modern writers of children's fiction have been Eve Pownall (*The Australia Book*, 1952), ▷Patricia Wrightson (*The Crooked Snake*, 1955; *The Nargun and the Stars*, 1973; *The Ice is Coming*, 1977; *The Dark Bright Water*, 1978), ▷Nan Chauncy (*Tiger in the Bush*, 1957; *Devil's Hill*, 1958; *Tangara*, 1960), ▷Kylie Tennant (*All the Proud Tribesmen*, 1959), Eleanor Spence (*The Green Laurel*, 1963), ▷Hesba Brinsmead (*Pastures of the Blue Crane*, 1964; *Longtime Passing*, 1971; *Longtime Dreaming*, 1982), Mavis Thorpe Clark (*The Min-Min*, 1966), Annette Macarthur-Onslow (*Uhu*, 1969), Ruth Manley (*The Plum-Rain Scroll*, 1978), ▷Ruth Park (*Playing Beatie Bow*, 1980), Nance Donkin (*Yellowgum Gil*, 1976; *Nini*, 1979; *Two at Sullivan Bay*, 1985), ▷Robin Klein (*Thing*, 1983; *Thingnapped*, 1984; *Snakes and Ladders*, 1985), ▷Elyne Mitchell (*Silver Brumby*, 1958), and ▷Nadia Wheatley (*Dancing in the Anzac Deli*, 1984; *The House That Was Eureka*, 1985).

19th-century Britain: Children's literature flourished in 19th-century Britain and women writers produced some of the most popular and enduring books. The stress on woman's maternal role in the Victorian period meant that writing children's books was less controversial for women than attempting to enter the 'serious' literary marketplace. It was viewed as an extension of their 'natural' sphere rather than a transgression. Apart from moral tales, intended as instructional guides for young minds, a large number of adventure stories, tales of magic and fantasy, and animal stories were published. ▷Martha Sherwood's *History of the Fairchild Family* (1818–47) was influential in creating a market for children's literature, but most of the famous children's books by women belong to the latter half of the century. ▷Anna Sewell's classic horse-story, *Black Beauty*, appeared in 1877, ▷Frances Hodgson Burnett's ▷*Little Lord Fauntleroy* in 1886, and *The Story of the Treasure Seekers*, the first of ▷Edith Nesbit's long line of successful children's books, in 1899. Other notable writers of children's literature include ▷Anna Eliza Bray, ▷Sara Coleridge, ▷Rosa Nouchette Carey, ▷Juliana Ewing, ▷Jean Ingelow, ▷Margaret Gatty, ▷Christina Rossetti, ▷Catherine Sinclair, ▷Hesba Stretton, ▷Jane and Ann Taylor, ▷Mrs Humphry Ward, ▷Harriet Martineau and ▷Maria Louisa Molesworth.

Denmark: Children's literature in Denmark began as an influence from Germany. In the 19th century, Hans Christian Andersen (1805–1875) and others began to write fairytales for children, but there has not been an established children's literature in Denmark until the 20th century.

The first women writers of literature for children were Anna Baadsgaard (1865–1954) and Ingeborg Vollquartz (1866–1930), well-known from popular literature. But with authors like Bertha Holst (1881–1921), Caja Rude (1884–1949), Marie Andersen (1876–1941) and Estrid Ott (born 1900), a new tradition for girl's books was established. This ▷realist literature had a new emphasis on equality between the sexes, and it had a social and political awareness.

With ▷Karin Michaëlis's books about Bibi (1929–1939) this realist tradition developed in a Utopian direction. Bibi is a wild girl, brought up in an anti-authoritarian manner by her father; she has no mother. She is a predecessor to ▷Astrid Lindgren's Pippi Longstocking. The series about Bibi became famous worldwide, and was translated into more than twenty languages.

Today, the best-known woman writer for children in Denmark is Cecil Bødker (born 1927) with her series of books about the fantastic outsider-hero Silas (1967).

The Netherlands: After 1960, authors such as Thea Beckman, Miep Diekman (on racial discrimination), Alet Schouten and Tonny Vos-Dahmen von Buchholz described the past, drawing parallels between the present and the past, and creating characters that can easily be identified with by children. Translations include: Thea Beckman, *Crusade in Jeans* (1973); Tonke Dragt, *The Towers of February* (1975); An Rutgers van der Loeff-Basenau, *Children of the Oregon Trail* (1974) (and others), and Alet Schouten, *Flight into Danger* (1972) (and others).

Yvonne Keuls writes books on problems that older children may encounter, such as drugs or children's homes, in *Anybody and his Mother* (1979) and *The Mother of David S.* (1985). Els Pelgrom's books, too, contain social criticism, as in *The Winter When Time was Frozen* (1980).

For many years now, Annie M.G. Schmidt has been the most important Dutch writer of poetry and stories for children. She created a revolution in literature for children with her insistence on relationships on equal terms between children and adults, her subjects (the reader is introduced to a 'topsy-turvy world'), and her use of language (called 'anarchistic': language which no longer knows class distinctions between words). In 1950, her poetry collections *Het fluitketeltje* and *Wat dan nog?* were published. With *Huishoudpoëzie* she indicated her own place in poetry (the title translates as *Household Poetry*). The famous *Jip en Janneke* series from the 1950s has been translated in English as *Bod and Jilly*, and the *Floddertje* series has been translated as *Dusty* and *Smudge Keep Cool* (and many others). Her method is demonstrated in *Minoes* and *Pluk van de Petteflet*: Minoes is an unmarried lady who used to be a cat (and still is to some extent), and who begins a cat's press service for a journalist in order to fight injustice. *Pluk*, who shares a tiny penthouse with his cockroach, succeeds in saving the animals in the park by, as it were, reversing the order in the city. Among the many prizes Schmidt has been awarded is the 1988 Hans Christian Andersen Prize, 'the Nobel Prize for children's literature'.

New Zealand: Women writers have always been prominent in the production of children's literature. Early writers such as ▷Edith Howes (*Silver Island*, 1928), ▷Isabel Maud Peacocke (*Little Bit o'Sunshine*, 1924) ▷Esther Glen (*Six Little New Zealanders*, 1917) and ▷Mona Tracey (*Piriki's Princess*, 1925) all wrote prolifically and used the conventions of children's literature (family stories, school stories, fantasy) to address specifically New Zealand questions of race, culture and identity. Later writers such as Clare Mallory or Phillis Garrard also deal with the kinds of questions raised by colonial culture while focusing on conventional narrative subjects such as schools. Many women wrote for the *School Journal* which fostered writing for children from the 1950s, and acted as a breeding ground for school readers, many of which were written by established writers. The relationship between education and children's literature has also been important for Maori writers such as ▷Katarina Te Heikoko Mataira. ▷Mararet Mahy, who is one of New Zealand's best known writers overseas, has written for an international audience, but her contempories such as ▷Tessa Duder (*Alex*, 1987), Joan de Hamel (*The Third Eye*, 1987) or Anne de Roo (*Moa Valley*, 1969) have tended to focus more on a local readership. There are now great numbers of women writers

writing for children, continuing one of the dominant literary traditions established by women.

▷Allen, Pamela Kay; Dallas, Ruth; Dodd, Lynley Stuart; Locke, Elsie Violet; Macdonald, Caroline; Grace, Patricia; Penfold, Merimeri; Shaw, Helen; Sutton, Mary Evelyn; Maori writing

Norway: Children's literature in Norway began in the 19th century. Dikken Zwilgmayer (1853–1913) wrote nineteen books between 1890 and 1911, and became very popular for her character Inger Johanne. Inger Johanne is an active girl with a will of her own and strong feelings. With this character, Dikken Zwilgmyer created the modern girl's book in Norway.

Barbra Ring (1870–1955) continued the tradition, and wrote books about Peik and Fjeldmus (Mountain Mouse). She was a very productive and widely translated writer.

There was a large group of women writers who wrote for teenage girls up until 1940: Marie Hamsun (1881–1969), Hanne Henriette Bryn (1880–1963), Ranka Knudsen (1886–1966) and Karin Holst (born 1899).

Eva Bøgenæs (1906–1985) was very productive: from 1928–1974, she wrote books for young girls about life and love. Her characters are either lonely outsiders, or active and extrovert.

Since 1945, the best-known woman writer for children has been ▷Anne-Cath Vestly. She has written books for small children, eg the *Ole Alexander* series, and has introduced realism and urban life into Norwegian children's literature.

Southern Africa: Children's literature of the 19th century, apart from that of ▷oral tradition, was dominated by male writers, but during the course of the 20th century texts by women writers began to appear: in English, *Platkops Children* (1935) by ▷Pauline Smith and *The South African Twins* (1953) by ▷Daphne Rooke, for example, along with a number of books by Fay Goldie (also known as Fay King, born 1903), from the early *Fanyana the Brave* (1950) to the more recent *Zulu Boy* (1968). Two of the most prolific and successful among contemporary children's authors are Lesley Beake and Jenny Seed. In Afrikaans, the better-known writers who have published children's books are ▷M.E.R., Freda Linde, ▷Henriette Grové, and ▷Wilma Stockenström. In recent children's literature there has been a return to African mythology and narrative to provide texts for children, notably by the writers Marguerite Poland, with her collection *The Mantis and the Moon* (1979), for example; Diana Pitcher, with *The Calabash Child* (1980), and Phyllis Savory, with *The Little Wild One: African Tales of the Hare* (1990). ▷Fatima Dike staged a particularly interesting children's play in the 1970s, and ▷Gcina Mhlophe has composed both plays and stories for children. An organization called READ, based in Johannesburg, makes stories on tape available to children in black primary schools, who would otherwise not have access to English.

Contemporary writers are starting to make a particular effort to educate children out of the racism produced for them in daily life. Karen Press's stories and non-fiction for children are notable in this regard.

Sweden: Children's literature in Sweden began in the 18th century, mostly as an influence from Germany. After 1842, when school attendance became compulsory, a genuine Swedish literature for children developed, with Jenny Nyström (1854–1946), Ottilia Adelborg (1855–1936), and Elsa Beskow (1886–1853), who became famous as writers and illustrators of children's literature. From the beginning, there was a very close connection between pictures and text. After 1900, ▷Ellen Key wrote forty-two picture books and her aunts Green, Lilac and Brown are known by every Scandinavian child, as is ▷Selma Lagerlöf's *Nils Holgersens underbara resa genom Sverige I–II* (1906–1907) (▷*The Wonderful Adventures of Nils*).

Today, this vivid tradition is followed by such authors as Astrid Lindgren, with characters such as Pippi Longstocking, Mio and the Brothers Lionheart. But Maria Gripe (born 1923) and Gunnel Linde (born 1924) are also worthy heirs, with their fantastic realism, and they are translated into many languages.

▷Fenno-Swedish literature

West Africa: The role of women as carers for children, teachers and purveyors of culture, as well as traditional storytellers, provides the platform for writing for children. The fact that many successful adult writers, both men and women, have also written children's books (▷Ama Ata Aidoo, ▷Véronique Tadjo, ▷Nafissatou Diallo, ▷Ifeoma Okoye, Chinua Achebe, Cyprian Ekwensi, ▷Mabel Segun) indicates the importance attached to entertaining and educating children through literature. This is in a context where, until relatively recently, African children only had access to books produced and published in the West. The proliferation of African-authored children's books results from a deliberate attempt to provide younger readers with culturally relevant material. It no doubt also reflects the morally instructive function of traditional storytelling, which in the towns has largely been superseded by print and television.

Childress, Alice (born 1920)

US dramatist and novelist. Born in Charleston, South Carolina, Childress grew up in Harlem, New York, and in 1943 she began acting in the original American Negro Theatre in Harlem. As in *Like One of the Family . . . Conversations from a Domestic's Life* (1956) her work emphasizes the African-American struggle to maintain dignity under oppressive circumstances. Childress's plays examine how dominant Anglo-American social values distort perceptions of African-Americans. In *Wedding Band: A Love/Hate Story in Black and White* (1973) an inter-racial couple must hide their ten-year love affair, and in *Wine in the Wilderness: A Comedy-Drama* (1969) an African-American artist learns to see the real essence of African-American womanhood and beauty. As in

A Hero Ain't Nothin' But a Sandwich (1973), Childress's children's fiction depicts the ghetto child's struggle with aloneness.

Other works include: *Troubled in Mind* (1955), *Mojo and String: Two Plays* (1971), *When the Rattlesnake Sounds* (1975), *Let's Hear It for the Queen* (1976), *A Short Walk* (1979) and *Rainbow Jordan* (1981).

Chiuminá, Ol'ga Nikolaevna (1865–1909)

Russian poet, translator, dramatist, and prose writer. Although Chiuminá began publishing original poetry in 1882, in the 1880s she was mainly known as a talented translator. Her first volume of collected verse and translations appeared in 1889; her second received an honorable mention from the Imperial Academy of Sciences in 1897 and was reissued in 1900. She used a masculine persona to which some critics objected. In her early poetry there are echoes of the poets Nekrasov and Nadson, and the dominant mood is elegiac. In 1888 the Aleksandrinskii Theatre in St Petersburg staged her verse drama, *Temptation*, the first of several of her plays to enter its repertoire; they were published in 1904.

In the 1890s Chiuminá also turned to prose: the novels *For Life and for Death* (1895) and *For the Sins of the Fathers* (1896), and stories in *In the Glow of the Footlights* (1898), deal with theatrical life, and tend to be strongly moralistic. In 1901 she received the Pushkin Prize from the Imperial Academy. Two more collections, *New Poems* and *Autumn Whirlwinds*, were published in 1905 and 1908 respectively. Under the pseudonym 'Optimist' she published *In Expectation*, a collection of verse satires. This is her best work, formally and thematically inventive, witty, and artful. She could skilfully parody the ▷modernists, such as Maeterlinck. Under another pseudonym, 'Boycott', in 1906, she published two satirical pamphlets commenting on the political events of 1905. Like that of ▷Barýkova, ▷Shchépkina-Kupérnik, and ▷Gálina, Chiuminá's poetry is in the 'civic' tradition.

▷Bashkirtseff, Marie; Gurévich, Liubov'

Choiseul-Meuse, Félicie de (19th century)

French erotic novelist. Nothing is known about the background of this author, who signed her work anonymously or pseudonymously, and who claimed, in the preface to her best-known novel, *Julie ou j'ai sauvé ma rose* (1807) (*Julie, or I Saved my Rose*), to have retired from fashionable society while in the full flower of her beauty and desirability in order to write her racy stories. *Julie* recounts the sexual adventures of a woman determined to preserve her power over men by preserving her virginity, and has a strong lesbian subtext. Two other very successful works by Choiseul-Meuse, *Amélie de Saint-Far ou la Fatale erreur* (1802) (*Amélie de Saint-Far, or The Fatal Mistake*) and *Entre chien et loup* (1809) (*Between the Dog and the Wolf*) chronicle respectively the

relations between a debauched older woman and a virtuous young girl, and the erotic experiences of seven women intent on relating these to each other in as frank a manner as possible. All three works were placed on the Index, which did not prevent them from being reprinted several times. Her other novels include: *Cécile ou l'élève de la pitié* (1816) (*Cécile, or the Child of Pity*) and *Les Amants de Charenton* (1818) (*The Lovers of Charenton*).
Bib: Brécourt-Villars, C., *Écrire d'Amour*; Frappier-Masur, L., 'Marginal Canons: Rewriting the Erotic', *Yale French Studies*, Vol. 75; Foster, J., *Sex Variant Women in Literature*.

Cholmondeley, Mary (1859–1925)
English novelist, born in Hodnet, Shropshire, the daughter of Emily Beaumont and the Rev. Hugh Cholmondeley. She never married and lived all her life with her family. Her first novel, *The Danvers Jewels* was published in 1887. *Charles Danvers* (1889); *Diana Tempest* (1893) and *The Devotee* (1897) followed. These were popular, but it was ▷*Red Pottage* (1899) that brought Cholmondeley public recognition. Its satirical treatment of the clergy caused a minor scandal, with churchmen denouncing the book, while critics and journalists defended its humour and accuracy. None of Cholmondeley's six later novels was as successful. She faded from view, and published her last book, *The Romance of His Life* in 1921.
▷ Ghost stories (19th-century Britain)
Bib: Lubbock, P., *Mary Cholmondeley: A Sketch from Memory.*

Chopin, Kate O'Flaherty (1851–1904)
US short fiction writer and novelist. Though living most of her life in St Louis, Missouri, Chopin is principally known for regional fiction focused on the Louisiana Creole and Cajun society that she knew through her marriage and residence in Louisiana before her husband's death in 1882. She was the foremost woman writing about this region. Her collections, ▷*Bayou Folk* (1894) and ▷*A Night in Acadie* (1897), contain the most human, memorable and ironic treatments of clashing values of sex, love, class and race in Louisiana society. An equally consistent theme in Chopin's writing is women's oppression and suppression of self. While her last novel, ▷*The Awakening* (1899), is the most sustained, famous and infamous treatment of this theme, earlier work like 'The Story of an Hour' shows Chopin's habitual exploration of what women would feel and do in the absence of their husbands' (and society's) oppressive expectations and dictates.

Christ, Lena (1881–1920)
German novelist. The illegitimate daughter of a cook, she spent a happy childhood with her grandparents in rural Bavaria. Her first novel, *Erinnerungen einer Überflüssigen* (1912) (*Memoirs of a Superfluous Woman*), tells of the hard times that followed when, at the age of eight, she had to join her mother, who had married an innkeeper. She

is principally known for her humorous stories about village life; her novel *Rumpelhanni* (1916) was made into a successful film. She committed suicide by taking cyanide after she had been accused of forgery.

Christaller, Helene (1872–1953)
German novelist and short story writer. A Protestant parson's wife in southern Germany, she sought to earn money with her stories when her husband lost his position. She achieved great popular success as a writer of stories and novels about village life in the Black Forest, and accounts of the fortunes of her own family.

Christen, Ada (1839–1901)
Austrian poet. From an impoverished middle-class family, she became an actress, living in extreme deprivation until her marriage in 1864. After the death of her husband and child in 1866, she tried to support herself by publishing poetry. Her poems, *Lieder einer Verlorenen* (1868) (*Songs of a Lost Woman*) achieved notoriety because of their erotic and socially radical, naturalist explicitness. After a second marriage in 1873 she continued to publish poems about social misery, notably *Aus der Tiefe* (1878) (*From the Abyss*). She also became known for her vivid descriptions of ordinary life in Vienna.

Christensen, Inger (born 1935)
Danish lyric poet. She was born in the town of Vejle, became a teacher, and made her début as a poet with the collection *Lys* (1962) (*Light*) which she followed with *Græs* (1963) (*Grass*). But she became famous with the beautiful collection *Det* (1969) (*It*), where the human being as the creator of forms is finally dominated by her own creations, and by the new order which is also the order of isolation. Only the song, the poets and love can break this domination.

Christensen is a ▷ modernist; her work consists of system-poems, and uses writing itself as a theme, eg in her novel *Azorno* (1967). Her systems are made up of mathematical or grammatical structures, creating the complex order of a labyrinth.

This modernism of the 1960s became an important inspiration for a group of young lyric poets in the 1980s, eg ▷ Pia Tafdrup.

Christensen continues to write. *Alfabet* (1981) (*Alphabet*) has Pisan mathematician Leonardo Fibonacci's (1180–1250) sequence of numbers as its labyrinth structure. In the 1980s she has experienced an international breakthrough, and is considered the leading woman writer in Denmark.

Other publications: *Del af labyrinten* (1982) (*Part of the Labyrinth*).

Christian, Barbara (born 1943)
North American critic and lecturer. She is Professor of Afro-American Studies at the University of California, Berkeley, and member of the Women's Studies Board there. She is author of *Black Women Novelists: The Development of a*

Tradition, 1892–1976 (1980) and *Black Feminist Criticism* (1985). Christian's critical approach is ▷humanist in so far as she focuses on individual self-discovery in fiction, and historical in the attention paid to the specific and changing importance of 'big house' novels and slave narratives in the developing tradition of black women's writing. Christian argues for the importance of recognizing the distinct identity of an African-American tradition, but adds that this should be theorized as tradition of change and one that is in process. ▷Black feminist criticism; female traditions.

Christie, Agatha (1890–1976)

English ▷detective novelist. Born into an upper-middle-class family, Christie often presents in her novels a nostalgic portrayal of the pre-World War I period. Her first mystery novel is *The Mysterious Affair at Styles* (1920), which introduces one of her key sleuths, Hercule Poirot. Miss Marple, whose techniques rely on her feminine, spinster identity, first appears in *The Murder at the Vicarage* (1930). Her other detectives include Superintendent Battle and Tommy and Tuppence Beresford, who first appear as a young couple in *The Secret Adversary* (1922) and who, considerably older, make a final appearance in *Postern of Fate* (1973). **Bib**: Keating, H. (ed.), *Christie: First Lady of Crime*; Morgan, J., *Agatha Christie: A Biography*; Sanders, D., and Lovallo, L. (eds), *The Agatha Christie Companion*.

Christine de Pisan (1364/5–?1434)

French lyric poet and and prose writer. Champion of the cause of her sex, she is sometimes viewed as the first professional writer, because she had to write in order to live. Born in Venice, she came to Paris in 1368 when her university-educated father, Tommaso di Benvenuto da Pizzano, was appointed astrologer to Charles V (1337–1380). Following the early death of her husband, Estienne de Castel, a court notary, Christine de Pisan was left with three children, no inheritance, and interest to pay on her husband's debts. She turned to writing with great energy. Most of her shorter compositions, like the *Cent Ballades, Virelays, Rondeaux*, were written in the first decade after her husband's death. The first twenty *ballades* are profoundly marked by her grief, and the most frequently anthologized begins: 'Seulette sui et seulette vueil estre / Seulette m'a mon douz ami laissie' ('A woman alone am I and alone I wish to be, my sweet friend has left me alone'). Her remaining work shows an increased tendency to experiment with other themes and lyric forms. Christine conceived of her literary career as a learned continuation – in the vernacular – of the achievement of the Roman poet Virgil (70–19 BC). She earnestly followed 'le long chemin de l'estude' ('the long path of study'), though she was quite willing to admit when she had recourse to translations.

   La Cité des Dames (1405) (*The Book of the City of Ladies*, 1521) is now considered the most

Christine de Pisan presenting her work to the Duc de Berry, 1450

important of her works, since it is the earliest book written in French in praise of women to be written by a woman. It is presented as a new history of pagan and Christian women, and its title recalls St Augustine's City of God. The affinity of women and learning is both its vehicle and its message. *Le Trésor de la Cité des Dames* (1405) (*The Treasure of the City of Ladies*) is a continuation of her analysis of the female condition by the listing of examples. It gives a detailed classification of women's role in contemporary society in three sections: exhortation and advice to (1) queens, princesses and noble women; (2) women of the court and lesser nobility; (3) bourgeois women and common women. Although she was a highly respected and widely disseminated voice on the status of women in her day, Christine de Pisan's significance was the subject of debate in later centuries, when she was regarded as a mere compiler of received notions. It is now accepted that her reorganization of sources, such as *De claris mulieribus* by the Italian writer Boccaccio (1313–1375), is original in itself. She also produced a vast corpus of other works in verse and prose, and displays a technical mastery of various well-established genres of the day, and an astonishing poetic versatility. Her prose style, modelled on Latin, is difficult, experimental and innovative. Christine de Pisan was also one of the first vernacular writers to supervise the copying and illuminating of her own books. She received several important commissions from the royal family, producing the official biography of Charles V, *Le Livre des fais et bonnes moeurs du sage Roy Charles V* (*The Book of Deeds and Morals of the Wise King Charles V*), published in 1404. In the name of a peaceful kingdom, she also wrote several other semi-political educational treatises, intended as manuals of good government for the Dauphin, the future Charles VI, (1368–1422), whose reign proved to be the most calamitous in the whole of French history.

Her first works in prose appear to have been *Epistres du débat sur le Roman de la Rose* (1401–1403) (*Letters on the Debate on the Romance of the Rose*). She became the chief correspondent in the so-called '*Querelle de la Rose*' ('Quarrel of the Rose'), taking on some of the most formidable Parisian ▷humanists of her day in her attack on Jean de Meung's 13th-century continuation of this central work of medieval French literature, which she considered immoral in its slanderous misogyny. In her letters and subsequent treatises she sought to demonstrate that women possessed natural affinities for all areas of cultural and social activity. She wanted women to make better use of their opportunities, but not to question their place in society. Her allegorical autobiography, the *Avision-Christine* (1405), is the principal source of information on her life. She also founded a poetic Order of the Rose to reward knights who defended the honour of women. With *Le Ditié de Jehanne d'Arc* (1429), her last known composition, Christine de Pisan broke an eleven-year silence to write the only eulogy of Joan of Arc (1412–1431) to be written in French during her lifetime.
Bib: Solente, S., 'Christine de Pizan', *Revue d'histoire litteraire de France*, 40 (1974), pp. 335–422; Christine de Pisan, *The Book of the City of Ladies*; Willard, C.C., 'The Franco-Italian Professional Writer: Christine de Pizan' in Wilson, K.M., *Medieval Women Writers*, pp. 333–65.

Christine de Pisan: Middle English translations

French writer ▷Christine's reputation was established early in England, and there are Middle English translations of several of her works. Hoccleve (c 1368–1426) translated the 'Letter of Cupid'; the 'Epistle of Othea to Hector' was translated by Stephen Scrope (c 1396–1472) by an anonymous author, and, later in the 15th century, by Anthony Babygnton; there is a translation of her *Corps de policie*; Caxton printed a translation of her *Faits d'armes*; her *Proverbes* were translated and printed by Caxton in 1478, and there is an early 16th-century translation of the *Cité des dames*.
Bib: Bornstein, Diane, *Ideals for Women in the Works of Christine de Pizan*.

Chronicles of Carlingford, The

The collective title of a group of novels by ▷Margaret Oliphant, including *Salem Chapel* (1863); *The Rector and the Doctor's Family* (1863); *The Perpetual Curate* (1864); *Miss Marjoribanks*

(1866) and *Phoebe Junior* (1876). *The Chronicles* were Oliphant's most popular works, focusing mainly on religious life in a country town. They show the influence of Walter Scott, Anthony Trollope and ▷George Eliot, although like much of Oliphant's work, they appear somewhat hurriedly written.

Chudleigh, Lady Mary (1656–1710)

English poet and polemicist who replied to John Sprint's misogynist sermon *The Bride-Woman's Counsellor*. Although Alice Browne thinks such extreme cases of the insistence on male superiority were read as a joke, Chudleigh replied seriously with *The Ladies Defence* a verse defence of women, published in the second edition of her *Poems on Several Occassions* (1703). Also published were her *Essays Upon Several Occassions* (1710). She wrote *The Ladies Defence* for women, she says, 'out of the tender Regard I have for your Honour, joyn'd with a just Indignation to see you so unworthily us'd'. The poem borrows the character of Sir John Brute from Vanbrugh's *The Provok'd Wife*, a play dealing in the misfortunes of mismarriage, Sir John is suitably brutal, but the Parson more legalistically insidious, asserting that for women, 'Love and Respect, are, I must own, your due; / But not'till there's Obedience paid by you.'
▷Eugenia
Bib: Ferguson, Moira, (ed.), *First Feminists*; Browne, Alice, *The Eighteenth Century Feminist Mind*.

Chughtai, Ismat (1915–1991)

Indian dramatist, novelist and short story writer. Educated at Aligarh University, she was one of India's foremost Urdu writers. She was an active campaigner for Indian independence, and a formative influence in the ▷Progressive Writers' Association. After independence, she continued to campaign for social reform and civil liberties. Her best-known novel is *Terhi Lakir* (1944) (*Crooked Line*), the life-story of an Indian Moslem girl. A short story, 'Tiny's Granny', translated from the Urdu, appears in ▷*Truth Tales*, and a collection is now available in English as ▷*The Quilt and Other Stories*.

Chukóvskaia, Lidiia Kornéevna (born 1910)

A Russian fiction writer, memoir-writer and editor, Chukóvskaia is a courageous dissident who was silenced in 1969 and expelled from the ▷Soviet Writers' Union in 1974 for her agitation on behalf of repressed authors. The arrest and murder of her husband, scientist Matvei Bronshtein, underlies her two compelling novellas of the purges of 1937 and the renewed persecutions of 1949, ▷*Sofiia Petrovna* and ▷*Going Under*, which were written at great personal risk in the terrible times they described, and were first published abroad years later. She befriended ▷Anna Akhmátova and helped that persecuted author by memorizing poems that risked seizure by the authorities. Her two-volume

Notes about Akhmátova records the day-by-day course of their alliance. Over the past twenty years Chukóvskaia has devoted herself to preserving the legacy of her father, Kornei Chukóvskii.

▷ *tamizdat*

Churchill, Caryl (born 1938)

English dramatist. Born in London, she was educated in Montreal, Canada, and at Lady Margaret Hall, Oxford, where she wrote her first plays. *Downstairs* (1958) and *Having a Wonderful Time* (1960) were produced before Churchill graduated. During the mid-1970s she was resident dramatist at the Royal Court Theatre, London. Plays written there include *Objections to Sex and Violence* (1975), in which a woman employed as a caretaker is subjected to physical assault and sexual harassment.

Churchill's writing identifies itself strongly with feminist politics. Plays such as *Vinegar Tom* (1976) which uses 17th-century witch-hunts to explore the social demonizing and pathologizing of unorthodox femininity, and *Floorshow* (1977), a women's cabaret, were produced in association with the feminist theatrical company Monstrous Regiment. *Owners* (1972) looks at the intersection of capitalist and patriarchal value systems in a domestic scenario.

Her best-known play, *Serious Money* (1987), a comedy about stock exchange swindles and the effect of the 'Big Bang' in the City of London, was a collaboration with Joint Stock Theatre Company, with whom Churchill has maintained a long and successful partnership. Historical perspectives on political themes are provided in *Light Shining in Buckinghamshire* (1976), which explores thwarted social idealism in the context of the English Civil War, and ▷ *Cloud Nine* (1978), which alternates a colonial with a post-colonial context, to examine the intersection of race, class and gender oppression. Churchill's plays are Brechtian in style, incorporating music-hall elements and 'allegorical' or demystifying use of historical material for contemporary social comment. Other plays include: *Schreber's Nervous Illness* (1972), *Moving Clocks Go Slow* (1975), *Traps* (1977), *Three More Sleepless Nights* (1980), ▷ *Top Girls* (1982), *Fen* (1983), *Softcops* (1984) and *A Mouthful of Birds* (1986).

Bib: Cousin, G., *Churchill: The Playwright*; Fitzsimmons, L., *File on Churchill*; Keyssar, H., *Feminist Theatre*.

Cialente, Fausta Terni (born 1898)

Italian novelist and journalist, born in Cagliari. Her life was full of upheaval when growing up because her father's work necessitated constant movement. She married in 1921 and settled in Egypt until the end of World War II when she returned to Italy. During the Fascist period and the war, she was involved in radio broadcasts against the regime from Cairo. Many of her narratives are set in Egypt. Her writings have been seen as part of the *realismo magico* (▷ Magic realism) school. Her best-known work is probably

Ballata levantina (▷ *The Levantines*) of 1961, one of the Egyptian novels, in which Cialente pitilessly dissects male–female relationships. *Un inverno freddissimo* (*A Very Cold Winter*), written in 1966 and set in Milan, centres on the character of Camilla who tries to come to terms with her role as an independent woman, made so by the war. In this novel various roles are posited for the female characters, represented by Regina who ultimately figures as mother-type, and Alba who represents the alternative of prostitution. For Camilla, neither is possible. Most significantly, none of these female characters is happy, and all must face their ultimate aloneness and loneliness. The position of her female characters preoccupies Cialente throughout her work, not least in the semi-autobiographical *Le quattro ragazze Wieselberger* (*The Four Wieselberger Girls*) of 1976.

Her other works include: *Natalia* (1930, 1982); *Pamela e la bella estate* (1935, 1962) (*Pamela and the Beautiful Summer*); *Cortile a Cleopatra* (1936) (*A Court for Cleopatra*); *Il vento sulla sabbia* (1972) (*The Wind Blowing Over the Sand*); *Interno con figure* (1976) (*Interno with Figures*).

Circulating libraries

Libraries in Britain from which books were borrowed by the (mostly female) reading public. The most famous of these in 19th-century Britain were Mudie's, W.H. Smith's and Boots. The three-volume or 'three-decker' novel of the 19th century was largely supported by these libraries, although rigorous censorship was enforced.

▷ Publishing and publishers; Jewsbury, Geraldine

Cisneros, Sandra (born 1955)

US poet, short-story writer and novelist. A ▷ Latina writer, Cisneros teaches that art and talent survive the most adverse conditions, and her fiction features Chicanas who take control over their lives. Born of Mexican-American descent, Cisneros graduated from the Loyola University of Chicago in 1976. In 1978 she earned a Master's degree in creative writing at the University of Iowa Writers' Workshop. In 1982 and 1988 she received fellowships from the National Endowment for the Arts. She teaches at a variety of colleges. *My Wicked Wicked Ways* celebrates a woman's appropriation of her own sexuality. Cisneros has liberated herself from sexually repressive cultural traditions. Nevertheless, ▷ *House on Mango Street* (1984) evinces her sense of ethnic responsibility. *Women Hollering Creek and Other Stories* (1991) gives voice to women's repressed anger as it focuses on abused women who struggle to escape their stereotypical roles.

Čisté dni (1990) (*Clear Days*)

Fourth collection of poems by Slovak writer Míla Haugová (born 1942). It is typical of 'women's intimate poetry'. An emphasis on the feminine principle of love is obviously the most noticeable feature of Haugová's poetry. However, her love poetry is not simply an expression of intimate feelings. It also contains rational analysis. Haugová notices the drama of everyday, sometimes banal, situations. She introduces themes of necessary responsibility, self-knowledge, and coping with the pains caused by life. However, her main achievement is her ability to concentrate her ideas. The compactness of her verse reminds one of Chinese or Japanese poetry.

Cixous, Hélène (born 1938)

French feminist, dramatist and novelist. An Algerian Jew of French and German parentage, she is author of over thirty books, numerous essays, and several radio and stage plays. She is Professor of Literature at the University of Paris VIII-Vincennes, and Director of the Paris Centre des Recherches en Etudes Féminines, which she founded in 1974. Among English-speaking readers, Cixous is known for her theory of ▷écriture féminine. She urges women to release in writing the sexual pleasure of a feminine ▷imaginary which patriarchal societies have historically repressed. Écriture féminine is a political writing which ▷deconstructs the binarism of patriarchal definitions of sexual difference by freeing the ▷bisexuality of each person's gender identity. Although characterized as feminine, Cixous locates écriture féminine in men's writing too. Works translated into English include her doctoral thesis, published in France in 1968 and in England as The Exile of James Joyce (1972). She is joint author with ▷Catherine Clément of ▷The Newly Born Woman (1986) (La Jeune Née, 1975). Her experimental psychological novels include Angst (1977), translated into English in 1985, and Vive L'Orange (1979) (To Live the Orange). 'The Laugh of the Medusa' (1976) ('Le Rire de la Méduse') and 'Castration or Decapitation?' (1976) ('Le Sexe ou la Tête?') have been her most influential essays in Britain and North America. Cixous's writing for the theatre includes: Portrait de Dora (1976) (▷Portrait of Dora, 1991), Le Nom d'Oedipe: chant du corps interdit (1978) (The Name of Oedipus), La Prise de l'école de Madhubai, L'histoire terrible mais inachevée de Norodom Sihanouk, Roi du Cambodage (1985) and L'Indiade ou L'Inde de leurs rêves (1987). Collections from Cixous's seminars, together with readings of her work, can be found in Susan Sellers (ed.), Writing Differences: Readings from the Seminar of Hélène Cixous (1988); and Helen Wilcox (joint ed.) The Body and the Text: Hélène Cixous, Reading and Teaching (1990).
Bib: Conley, V.A., Hélène Cixous: Writing the Feminine; Shiach, Morag, Hélène Cixous.

Clacy, Ellen ▷Lady's Visit to the Gold Diggings of Australia in 1852-1853, A; Journals (Australia)

Claire-Solange, âme africaine (1924) (Claire-Solange, African Soul)

Written by the Guadeloupean (French Antilles) writer Suzanne Lacascade, this work met with indignation in Guadeloupe when it was first published. Lacascade's heroine is a Martiniquan mulatto, daughter of an Antillean mother, and a father who was a French colonial administrator. From her arrival in Paris, the heroine perpetually criticizes France in favour of Martinique. Claire-Solange claims with pride her African heritage and glories in the title of Négresse, causing some to identify in this novel sentiments which characterized the later ▷négritude movement. Claire-Solange, however, claims only royal African ancestors.

Clappe, Louise Amelia Knapp Smith (1819–1906)

US non-fiction writer and humorist. Clappe's literary reputation is based on a single work, letters written home to New England by 'Dame Shirley' (Clappe's persona and pseudonym), who, like Clappe, went west to California for the ▷gold rush. Written in the 1850s as a magazine serial, Clappe's letters were collected in The Shirley Letters (1922). Scrutinizing gold rush pretensions and realities from a woman's perspective, Clappe's Shirley Letters have become a significant document for both cultural historians and readers of personal narrative and literary humour.

Clara Morison: A Tale of South Australia During the Gold Fever (1854)

Australian novel by ▷Catherine Helen Spence. One of the first Australian novels written by a woman and highly praised by the critic, Frederick Sinnett, in his 'The Fiction Fields of Australia' published in the Journal of Australasia in 1856. It concerns the vicissitudes of a fatherless heroine, Clara, sent to the colony of South Australia to seek a position as governess. Unable to find an appropriate position and without patronage, she goes into demeaning service, and falls in love with a squatter, Charles Reginald, whom she marries, but only after a series of misunderstandings. The plot is stereotyped, but the novel is redeemed by the resilience of its heroine, and by the acute social observation of the author, particularly in regard to life on the goldfields and the gold-fever which gripped Melbourne in the 1850s.

Clark, Catherine Anthony (1892–1977)

Born Catherine Smith, in London, England, she emigrated to Canada in 1914. She published her first book, The Golden Pine Cone (1950), at the age of 58. It is the story of two children who journey to an 'inner world' to find their lost dog and return a magic pine cone. The Sun Horse (1951), The One-Winged Dragon (1955), The Silver Man (1959), The Diamond Feather (1962), and The Hunter and the Medicine Man (1966) all concern a journey to a fantasy world. Clark's writing is much influenced by Native Canadian legend, and the physical setting of the Kootenay, British Columbia, wilderness. She was Canada's first major fantasy writer for children.

Clark, Joan (born 1934)
Canadian writer of both children's and adult
fiction. Born in Liverpool, Nova Scotia, she
graduated from Acadia University, and later
taught school in the Maritimes and in Alberta.
Her children's books, *The Hand of Robin Squires*
(1977), *The Leopard and the Lily* (1984), *Wild Man
of the Woods* (1985), and *The Moons of Madelaine*
(1987), are strongly-plotted adventure stories. Her
adult short stories, *From a High Thin Wire* (1982)
and *Swimming Toward the Light* (1990), capture
the relationships of women with family and
friends. Her novel, *The Victory of Geraldine Gull*
(1988), which won the Canadian Authors Award
for Fiction, is a compassionate portrayal of the
conflict and hardship of life for a Native Canadian
community in northern Ontario. She lives in St
John's, Newfoundland.

Clarke, Mary Cowden (1809–1898)
British critic, novelist and poet, born in London.
She was the daughter of composer Vincent
Novello and Mary Sabilla Hehl, and was educated
at home and in France. Her father's literary
acquaintances included Keats, Leigh Hunt, and
Charles Cowden Clarke, whom she married in
1828. In 1829 she began a project that was to
occupy her for sixteen years. *The Complete
Concordance to Shakespeare* was eventually
published in 1845, and remained the standard
concordance until the end of the 19th century.
Other work on Shakespeare includes *Shakespeare
Proverbs* (1848) and a collection of stories based
on *The Girlhood of Shakespeare's Heroines* (1852).
She also wrote several volumes of verse;
biographies of her father and her husband; an
autobiography, *My Long Life* (1896); a series of
novels and a collection of *Short Stories in Metrical
Prose* (1873). She was the editor of the *Musical
Times* from 1853–6.
Bib: Altick, R.D., *The Cowden Clarkes*.

Claudine en ménage (1902) ▷ Claudine Married
(1960)

Claudine Married (1960)
Translation of *Claudine en ménage* (1902), third of
the 'Claudine' novels by French writer ▷Colette.
Written with the 'assistance' of Colette's first
husband, Willy, the Claudine novels achieved
immediate celebrity, generating a cult of
Claudine, and a whole range of Claudine
products. *Claudine Married* concentrates less on
the heroine's love for her husband Renaud, than
on her passionate affair with her woman friend,
Rézi. One senses the influence of Colette's
husband in those passages which are clearly
designed to titillate, and it is perhaps no
coincidence that the narrator, Claudine, expresses
her discomfiture at Renaud's voyeuristic interest
in the physical passion between herself and Rézi.
Despite this sense that the lesbian interludes are
written from the perspective of the male voyeur,
the novel does allow its heroine the carefee
sensuality which is normally a masculine preserve.

Colette begins her association of feminine
strength with retreat from love when, at the end,
Claudine flees to her country home, and to the
healing qualities of her garden and cat.

Clavers, Mrs Mary ▷ Kirkland, Caroline
Matilda Stansbury

Cleitagora (? 6th–5th century BC)
Ancient Greek poet. Her place of origin is
variously given as Sparta, Thessaly and Lesbos.
She wrote drinking songs for the *symposia* that
were popular in 5th-century BC Athens. Some
traditions make her a courtesan, but this may be a
guess as no women except courtesans and slaves
were allowed at the parties where her songs would
be sung.
Bib: (text & trans.) Edmonds, J.M., *Lyra Graeca*.

Clelia: An excellent new romance (1661)
Translation of the ten-volume
French novel, *Clélie, histoire romaine* (1654–1660),
by ▷Madeleine de Scudéry. *Clélie* was, if
anything, even more popular than *Le Grand Cyrus*
(▷*Artamenes, or The Grand Cyrus*), at least in the
first few years of its publication. It is in many ways
very similar to the plot and narrative structure of
Le Grand Cyrus and represents the same kind of
mid-17th-century gallantry, according to the
fashion in salon society. This time, however, the
novel is set in Rome in the 6th century BC, and
there is rather less emphasis on the historical
background. Battles on the epic scale are also
rather more intermittent. There is greater
emphasis on female society, partly because the
main character is a woman, based on the
legendary example of Roman womanly virtue,
Cloelia. The most important part of the narrative
is the gallant conversation which is conducted in
Clélie's salon or *ruelle*, the contemporary
readership clearly delighting in this anachronistic
fusion of legend and life. The ▷'Carte de Tendre',
an allegorical map of love, which had a
tremendous impact in the salons of the day, was
inserted in the first volume. The final volumes of
the novel are increasingly concerned with the
bourgeois society of '▷Sappho' or Madeleine de
Scudéry herself, and mark the beginning of the
end of the fashion for multi-tomed novels in
France.

Clélie, histoire romaine (1654–1660) ▷ Clelia:
An excellent new romance

Clemence of Barking (12th century)
Nun and translator in England. Clemence wrote a
verse *Life of St Catherine* in ▷Anglo-Norman, c
1163–1169. This was a modernized adaptation of
a standard Latin life of the popular saint,
Catherine of Alexandria. (The early Middle
English version of the 'Katherine Group' was
translated independently, and slightly later.) St
Catherine, famously threatened with torture on a
wheel before her execution, was said to have
overcome the most learned philosophers of

Alexandria in debate. The legend, which has no historical foundation, may originally have been based on, or composed as a response to, the story of ▷Hypatia. Clemence adapts the Latin fairly freely, making courtly additions, presumably to suit the tastes of her convent audience, and curtailing some of the more tedious passages. The work appears to have been popular, since it was frequently copied. It was one of the two verse saints' lives in Anglo-Norman produced at ▷Barking Abbey, an Anglo-Saxon foundation with a tradition of learning.
Bib: Burgess, G.S. and Wogan-Browne, Jocelyn (trans.), *Clemence of Barking's Life of St Catherine*; MacBain, William (ed.), *The Life of St Catherine by Clemence of Barking*.

Clemencia, Sor Marina ▷Ceo (del Cielo), Sor Maria do

Clément, Catherine
French university lecturer, journalist, diplomat and co-editor of the journal *L'Arc*. She contends, in the Marxist line, that the class struggle is more fundamental than the struggle between the sexes. Equally versed in political and ▷psychoanalytic theory, she became known for her part in the controversy which divided French feminists in the 1970s, and for ▷*La Jeune Née* (1975) (*The Newly Born Woman*), written in collaboration with ▷Hélène Cixous. This key text of ▷post-structuralist French feminist theory seeks to determine the connections between sexuality and writing. Clément's work includes specialist studies in psychoanalysis: *Les fils de Freud sont fatigués* (1978) (*The Weary Sons of Freud*), *Vies et légendes de Jacques Lacan* (1981) (*Lives and Legends of Jacques Lacan*), *Claude Lévi-Strauss ou la Structure du malheur* (1970) (*Claude Lévi-Strauss or the Structure of Adversity*); popular works on feminist themes: *L'Opéra ou la défaite des femmes* (1979) (▷*Opera, or the Undoing of Women*, 1981) and novels: *La Sultane* (1981) (*The Sultan's Wife*), *Le Maure de Venise* (1983) (*The Moor of Venice*), *Bleu panique* (1986) (*Panic Blue*). Though not as radically innovative as Hélène Cixous in her handling of fiction, she conveys experiences which are felt to take place outside patriarchal discourse.
▷Psychoanalysis

Cleobulina (6th century BC)
A poet and philosopher born in Lindos, she was the daughter of the Greek philosopher Cleobulus, one of the Seven Sages. She was renowned for her intelligence: her father nicknamed her Eumetis ('Of good counsel'). She was famous for her riddles, written in elegiac metre, some of which survive, including one about the year. Her fame led her to be satirized in Athenian comedy. The comic dramatist Cratinus (5th century BC) wrote a play entitled *Cleobulinas*.
▷Philosophers, ancient Greek and Roman women

Clermont, Catherine de (16th century)
French minor poet. She was the wife of the Maréchal de Gondi, Duc de Retz, the governor of the royal children, and was well-educated in mathematics, philosophy and history. She expressed herself with equal eloquence in Latin and French. On the visit of the Polish ambassador to the court of Charles IX (1550–1574) in 1573, Catherine de Clermont translated his address into French and replied in his native language.
Bib: Feugère, L., *Les Femmes poètes au XVIe siècle*.

Clèves, Marie, Marquise d'Isles (1426–1487)
French minor poet. The wife of the poet Charles d'Orléans (1391–1465), she played an important cultural role at the court of Burgundy, welcoming and assisting poets, who celebrated her beauty in verse. She also herself participated in literary competitions. Only two *rondeaux* remain.

Cliff, Michelle (born 1946)
This Caribbean-born writer and teacher left ▷Jamaica at the age of three for the USA, where she spent her childhood in the Jamaican communities of New York. She studied at the University of London. She considers herself to be 'a mixed blood Jamaican'. She is concerned with the ▷diasporic experience and a multi-ethnic identity, attempting to forge wholeness from what appears to be fragmented.
Her published work includes *Abeng* (1984), *The Land of Look Behind* (1985) and *No Telephone to Heaven* (1987). Her work is included in ▷*Creation Fire*.

Clifford, Lady Anne (1590–1676)
English diarist. She records her struggle to inherit lands from her father, which he willed to his brother rather than her. Her diary records the tenacity with which she clung to what she regarded as her rights, resisting the suasions of James I, among others. She finally inherited the land when she was 56. There is an 18th-century copy of the diary for 1603 and 1616–1619, and is of interest for records of what she read (Edmund Spenser's *Faerie Queene*, as well as the Bible) and for details of daily life and the minutiae of power struggles within her marriage. Two days before she died she recalled her legal battles: 'I remembered how this day 60 years I and my blessed Mother . . . gave in our answer in writing that we would not [relinquish]. . . . the lands of mine Inheritance, which did spin out a great deal of trouble to us, yet God turned it for the best.' The diary and *Books of Record* give a picture of her life, with gaps, from 1603 to the day she died.
Bib: Clifford, D.J.H. (ed.), *The Diaries of Lady Anne Clifford*.

Clift, Charmian (1923–1969)
Australian novelist, short story writer and journalist. Clift married writer George Johnston in 1947 and collaborated with him on three novels: *High Valley* (1949), which won first prize in the 1948 literary competition of the *Sydney Morning*

Herald; The Big Chariot (1953); and *The Sponge Divers* (1956), which was published in the USA as *The Sea and the Stone*. A selection of their short stories, *Strong Man from Piraeus and Other Stories*, was published in 1986.

Clift was born in Kiama, New South Wales, but lived in England and Greece for fourteen years, leading an unconventional life with her husband and their literary friends. The character Cressida Morley in George Johnston's work is loosely based upon Clift's life and death. On her own account she published two novels, two non-fiction works based on the family's experiences in Greece and two volumes of essays. On her return from Greece she wrote a weekly column for the *Sydney Morning Herald* and wrote regularly for other newspapers and magazines. She also adapted her husband's novel, *My Brother Jack*, for television.

Clifton, Lucille (born 1936)

US poet. Clifton was born in Depew, New York. She attended Fredonia State Teachers' College in New York and Howard University in Washington, DC. Her work emphasizes an awareness of African-American heritage, telling the stories of ordinary African-American women: *Good Times* (1969) and *Good News About the Earth* (1972) describe adversities in the ghetto and, portraying the ghetto as home, they convey a sense of optimism. *An Ordinary Woman* (1974) presents an image of the family as redemptive, focusing on women who are examples of survival through adversity. These poems convey ordinary women's disappointment that their lives are unfulfilled, although Clifton validates their traditional experiences as mothers. *Two-Headed Women* (1980) explores the self's search for spiritual relief from life's adversities.

Other works include: *Some of the Days of Everett Anderson* (1969), *The Black BC's* (1970), *Everett Anderson's Christmas Coming* (1971), *All Us Come Cross the Water* (1973), *Don't You Remember?* (1973), *Good, Says Jerome* (1973), *The Boy Who Didn't Believe in Spring* (1973), *Everett Anderson's Year* (1974), *The Times they Used to Be* (1974), *My Brother Fine with Me* (1975), *Three Wishes* (1976), *Everett Anderson's Friend* (1976), *Generations* (1976), *Amifika* (1977), *Everett Anderson's 1-2-3* (1977), *Everett Anderson's Nine Month Long* (1978), *The Lucky Stone* (1979), *My Friend Jacob* (1980), *Sonora Beautiful* (1981) and *Everett Anderson's Goodbye* (1983).

Clitoridectomy/infibulation (West Africa)

These practices, found predominantly in the Arab north of Africa, are widespread in black Africa. Clitoridectomy, the excision of the clitoris, and infibulation, the sewing up of the vulva so that only a tiny hole remains, are traditional practices relating to girls' initiation rites. Because, in the cultures where they occur, a girl is considered unclean, unfit for marriage, without them, they have proved hard to eradicate. Apart from being an agonizing and traumatic experience for the young girl, the operation, performed without anaesthetic by a traditional midwife, all too often leads to horrific complications and infection, and frequently to death. One way of counteracting this is to have the operation performed surgically, under sterile conditions. More radically, some health workers and activists are campaigning for its abolition, including the British-based organization FORWARD (Foundation for Women's Health Research and Development). *The Hidden Face of Eve* by the Egyptian writer ▷Nawal el Sadaawi, and ▷*La Parole aux négresses* (*Speak Out, Black Sisters*) by the Sengalese ▷Awa Thiam, are both concerned with clitoridectomy and infibulation.
▷*Khitan*

Clod, Bente (born 1946)

Danish poet and prose writer. For Clod, a commitment to feminism was the force that made her write and come out as a lesbian.

Her début was the collection of essays *Det Autoriserede danske samleje* (1975) (*The Authorized Danish Sexual Intercourse*), but her breakthrough in reaching a wider female audience came with her novels *Brud* (1977) (*Breaks*) and *Syv sind* (1980) (*In Two Minds*), depicting an autobiographical female character, her identity crisis and development, later continued in a novel about three generations of women *Vent til du hører mig le'* (1983) (*Wait till you Hear me Laugh*). Clod's prose style is realist.

Clod also writes poems; the first collection *Imellem os* (1981) (*Between Us*) talks of lesbian love, the second *Gul engel* (1990) (*Yellow Angel*) is more experimental in form and themes.

She is an important author within the realist feminist movement of the 1970s.

Cloud Nine (1978)

Play by English dramatist ▷Caryl Churchill. A two-act play which poses the problem of representation; its exploration of the legacy of Victorian views on sexual and cultural difference exploits and politicizes the theatrical convention of transformations. The first act is set in a British colony in Africa during the late 19th century and focuses on Clive, a colonial administrator, and his relations with his family. Churchill's own alienation technique draws attention to adopted roles and assumed identities. Clive's wife is played by a man, his black servant by a white actor and his daughter by a life-size dummy. The second act is set in London some 75 years later, but, for the characters, only twenty-five years have effectively passed. Although many of the characters are now played by actors of the 'appropriate' gender, Clive's son Edward is played by a woman, and the emphasis is again on gender disruption. Churchill's play dramatizes the durability of Victorian values, and the tensions between public and private selves, by addressing the family unit as a microcosm of social rules and values.

Clovernook, Or Recollections of Our Neighborhood in the West (1852)

US personal narrative by ▷Alice Cary. This account of frontier life was applauded in the 19th century and is still notable for its realistic depiction of the hardship and deprivation which were the price of life on the frontier. *Clovernook* and its successors, *Clovernook Children* (1855) and *Pictures of Country Life* (1859), are unequalled in showing the frontier from the perspective of a woman insider, rather than an emigrant or observer.

Clyde, Constance (1872–?)

New Zealand novelist. With her contemporary, ▷Louisa Baker, Constance Clyde questioned the position of women, especially within marriage. In her novel *A Pagan's Love* (1905) she sets her heroine against convention by depicting her contemplating an extra-marital relationship with a man. However, like the other 19th-century women writers, Clyde opts for retaining conventional marriage but suggests alternatives to female dependence, both in questioning convention and in suggesting that self-sufficiency is a narrative possibility for women.

Cneoburg (8th century)

Abbess of an English religious house. A letter (in Latin) addressed to ▷Boniface from the heads of three religious communities was composed by Cneoburg. The fact that she can speak for an abbot as well as another abbess is a measure of the standing of Anglo-Saxon abbesses.

Cobbe, Frances Power (1822–1904)

British essayist and ▷travel writer. Born in Newbridge, Dublin, she was educated by ▷governesses until 1836 when she went to school in Brighton. Her first published work, *Essays on the Theory of Intuitive Morals* appeared anonymously in 1855. One reviewer described it as 'the work of a lofty and masculine mind'. Cobbe wrote prolifically on religious and moral issues and was deeply involved in social ▷reform, advocating women's ▷suffrage and arguing that women were not contributing all that they might to society. Her works include *Essays on the Pursuits of Women* (1863); *The Cities of the Past* (1864); *Italics* (1864); *Darwinism in Morals and Other Essays* (1872); *The Moral Aspects of Vivisection* (1875); *The Duties of Women* (1881); *The Scientific Spirit of the Age* (1888) and an autobiography, *Life of Frances Power Cobbe* (1904).

Cobbold, Elizabeth (c 1764–1824)

English poet and helper of other women (▷Ann Candler and ▷Margaret Catchpole), born Elizabeth Clarke. In Manchester she published *Poems on Various Subjects* (1783) and *Six Narrative Poems* (1787). She married William Clarke in 1790, but he died six months later. In 1791 she published a novel, *The Sword, or Father Bertrand's History of His Own Times*, and later married John Cobbold from Ipswich. She continued to publish after the marriage, in Ipswich magazines, and in *The Ladies Fashionable Repositry*.

Codina, Iverna

Argentinian poet, novelist, short story writer and essayist. Born in Chile, she moved to Mendoza as a child and became an Argentinian citizen. Her first book was a collection of poems, *Canciones de lluvia y cielo* (1946) (*Songs of Rain and Sky*). Her first novel, *La luna ha muerto* (1957) (*The Moon Has Died*), dealt with the conflicts between spirituality and a life of pleasure, and cosmopolitanism and a rural life, a theme she later developed. *Detrás del grito* (1962) (*Behind the Shout*) brought her fame. It portrays the violence and poverty typical of the Mendoza region, where superficial richness often hides much conflict. This novel also follows the tradition of Latin American 'land novels'. *Los guerrilleros* (1968) (*The Guerrillas*) was written after the author interviewed the guerrilla members of the Salta region. She has written for both the national and the foreign press, and has worked in radio.

Coeur-Brûlant, Vicomtesse de ▷Mannoury d'Ectot, Madame de

Coeur d'Alene (1894)

US novel by ▷Mary Hallock Foote. One of the first US novels to address organized labour in the western mining industry. Set in Colorado, *Coeur* combines type characters in a union conflict for control of the mine with a fairly traditional romantic subplot involving the mine manager's daughter.

Cogewea, the Half-Blood: A Depiction of the Great Montana Cattle Range (1927)

US novel. ▷Mourning Dove's *Cogewea* is the first novel written by a ▷Native American woman, and it is also the first to incorporate oral traditions into a literary work. Cogewea is caught between the world of Native Americans and that of Anglo-Americans, between tradition and assimilation. The Anglo-American man she has married betrays her, devaluing her and her Native American rituals. She learns from Stemteena's storytelling to rely on the teachings of tradition to counteract Anglo-American racism. Stemteena teaches her that preserving tradition ensures the survival of Native Americans. In her novel Mourning Dove preserves the traditions of the Okanogans.

Coicy, Madame de (18th century)

French essayist, who published the text *Les Femmes comme il convient de les voir* (1785) (*How Women Should be Seen*). She argues that she is one of the first writers to record women's achievements, ignored by official history, and to show what they could be capable of if given access to a full education.

Coignard, Gabrielle de (died 1594)
French religious poet from Toulouse. A noble by birth, she was widowed early. Her poems are inspired by a passionate mysticism.
Bib: Moulin, J., *La poésie feminine du XII au XIXe siècles*.

Coit, Mehetabel Chandler (1673–1758)
North American diarist. A resident of New London, Connecticut, she began keeping a diary at the age of fifteen. Published more than a century after her death, ▷*Mehetabel Chandler Coit, Her Book* covers at least the next 60 years of her life during which she recorded, often briefly, notable family events.

Colaço, Branca de Gonta (1880–1944)
Portuguese poet and literary critic. Daughter of the poet Tomás Ribeiro, she married the painter Jorge Colaço in 1898, and their home became a gathering place for artists and writers. She published her first book of poems, *Matinas* (*Matins*) in 1907, and between 1912 and 1926 four more volumes appeared. Although she wrote during the ▷modernist period, her poetry has more in common with 19th-century verse. She also authored two important critical works: *Poetas de Ontem* (1915) (*Poets of Yesterday*) and *Cartas de Camilo Castello Branco a Tomás Ribeiro* (1922) (*Letters from Camilo Castello to Tomás Ribeiro*).

Cold Comfort Farm (1932)
Novel by English writer ▷Stella Gibbons. Her first, it won the Femina Vie Heureuse Prize for 1933. The novel's heroine, Flora Poste, goes to stay with her relatives, the Starkadders, at Cold Comfort Farm in Sussex. She finds the family living in pre-modern discomfort, and extravagantly indulging in emotional intensity and religious fanaticism. By the end of the novel, the indefatigable and thoroughly rational Flora has brought them all into the 20th century. The novel is a brilliant satire on the 'primitivist' novels of D.H. Lawrence (1885–1930) and Thomas Hardy (1840–1928), and the historical romances of the 1920s: its particular inspiration was probably ▷Mary Webb's ▷*Precious Bane* (1924).
▷Kaye-Smith, Sheila

Coleman, 'Kit' (Kathleen) (1856–1915)
Canadian Journalist. Born Catherine Ferguson in Ireland, she married Thomas Willis in 1876. When both her husband and an infant daughter died in 1883, she was left without support. She went first to London and then to Canada (1884), changed her name and age, married again (unhappily), and in 1888 again had to support herself and two children. She worked as a journalist for the Toronto *Mail*, and in 1898 succeeded in getting permission to go to Cuba to cover the Spanish–American War. That same year she married Theodore Coleman, a mine doctor, and moved with him to Copper Cliff, Ontario, continuing her journalism by mail. In 1904 they moved to Hamilton, Ontario. Coleman was

against suffrage, although she firmly believed in women working.
Bib: Campbell, S., & McMullen, L. (eds), *New Women*; Freeman, B., *Kit's Kingdom: The Journalism of Kathleen Blake Coleman*.

Coleridge, Mary (1861–1907)
English poet, novelist and critic, the daughter of Mary Anne and Arthur Duke Coleridge, and great-great niece of Samuel Taylor Coleridge. She grew up in a literary and scholarly atmosphere; her parents knew Tennyson, Browning and Ruskin, and she was taught by an ex-Eton schoolmaster. She first published at the age of twenty, when an essay appeared in ▷Charlotte Yonge's *Monthly Packet*. She continued to write for periodicals such as *Merry England*, and later for the *Times Literary Supplement*. *The Seven Sleepers of Ephesus* (1893) was her first novel; her first volume of verse *Fancy's Following*, published under the ▷pseudonym Anodos in 1896. Her best-known work is her novel *The King With Two Faces* (1897), although more attention is now being paid to her poetry, which varies between lyrics reminiscent of the ▷Pre-Raphaelites, distinctive poems of urban life, and concentrated, spare lyrics that anticipate 20th-century imagism. Coleridge also wrote a biography of Holman Hunt (1908), a collection of essays, *Non Sequitur* (1900), and other novels, including *The Lady on the Drawing Room Floor* (1906). *The Collected Poems of Mary Coleridge*, edited by T. Whistler (1954), is the most recent edition.

Coleridge, Sara (1802–1852)
English writer, the daughter of Samuel Taylor Coleridge. She educated herself, with the help of Robert Southey, acquiring six languages and a good knowledge of Classics and philosophy. Wordsworth described her as 'remarkably clever'. In 1822 she translated Dobrizhoffer's Latin *Account of the Abipones* and in 1825 the *Memoirs* of the Chevalier Bayard. She married her cousin, Henry Coleridge, in 1829, and lived in Hampstead, London, where she wrote *Pretty Lessons in Verse for Good Children* (1834) and the fantastical poem *Phantasmion* (1837). In 1843 Henry died, after which Coleridge devoted herself to organizing, editing and annotating her father's works, a task which she performed with great skill. She was greatly admired in London literary society, and her *Memoir and Letters* was published in 1873.
Bib: Wilson, M., *These Were Muses*; Woolf, V., 'Sara Coleridge' in *Death of the Moth and Other Essays*.

Colet, Louise (1810–1876)
French poet and novelist. The daughter of a wine merchant from Lyons, Colet married a composer who taught at the Paris Conservatoire, and from whom she later separated. A sensual, ill-humoured and vindictive woman, who on one occasion stabbed the critic Alphonse Karr after he

insulted her, Colet had affairs with the Academician Victor Cousin, with Alfred de Musset (1810–1857) and with the novelist Gustave Flaubert (1821–1880). Two of her works, *Une Histoire de soldat* (1856) (*A Soldier's Story*) and *La Servante* (1854) (*The Maidservant*) are usually considered to represent attacks upon Flaubert, with whom she enjoyed a long and stormy liaison that ended in 1854. Four of her poems, 'Le Musée de Versailles' (1839), ('The Versailles Gallery'), 'Le Monument de Molière' (1843) ('Molière's Monument'), 'La Colonie de Mettray' (1852) ('The Mettray Colony') and 'L'Acropole d'Athènes' (1854) ('The Athens Acropolis') were awarded prizes by the ▷Académie Française, but critics have attributed this to the influence of Victor Cousin, and have dismissed Colet's poetry as mediocre in the extreme. Her first collection of verse, *Les Fleurs du Midi* (1836) (*Flowers of the Midi*), is well written, but Flaubert's assertion that her work is characterized by a combination of philosophism and vagueness is, nevertheless, justified. Towards the end of her life she came to see herself as a champion of feminism, and planned to create a magnum opus entitled *Poème de la femme* (*The Poem of Women*). However, the three volumes of this which were published – *La Paysanne* (1853) (*The Peasant Woman*), *La Servante* and *La Religieuse* (1856) (*The Nun*) – contain few practical suggestions regarding the emancipation of women. Her other works include: *Les Chants des vaincus, poésies nouvelles* (1846) (*Songs of the Vanquished, New Poems*); *Ce qui est dans la coeur des femmes* (1852) (*Secrets of the Female Heart;*) *Ce qu'on rêve en aimant* (1854) (*What Love Dreams*) and *Lui* (1860) (*He*). This last represents a kind of counterpoint to ▷George Sand's *Elle et lui* (*He and She*).

Bib: Crosland, M., *Women of Iron and Velvet*; Sullerot, E., *Women on Love*; Albistur, M. and Armogathe, D., *Histoire du féminisme français*; Bellet, R., *Autour de Louise Colet*; Clébert, J., *Louise Colet; la Muse*.

Colette, Sidonie Gabrielle (1873–1954)

French author of plays, novels, film scripts, reviews and short stories. Colette produced over 70 texts between 1900 and 1949, and is one of the few French women writers to have gained a place in the ▷canon, despite the fact that her writing has sometimes been described as 'feminine' in a pejorative sense, and that at times more interest has been shown in her life than in her writing.

Colette's early works, the 'Claudine' novels (▷*Claudine Married*, 1960) were written under the aegis of her first husband, Willy, but they nonetheless contain some of the elements of her later work. In *Les Vrilles de la vigne* (1908) (*The Tendrils of the Vine*), a collection of short prose poems and dialogues, Colette's lyrical style begins to develop, particularly in the evocation of childhood and nature.

In Colette's mature works two broad thematic areas can be identified: in texts such as *La Maison*

Colette

de Claudine (1922) (*My Mother's House*, 1953), *La Naissance du Jour* (1928) (▷*Break of Day*), and ▷*Sido* (1929), Colette depicts a luminous and peaceful world where sexual love is renounced in favour of recollections of childhood, natural beauty, and the constant and reassuring strength of the maternal presence. Novels such as *La Vagabonde* (1911) (▷*The Vagabond*, 1954), *L'Entrave* (1913) (*The Shackle*, 1964), ▷*Chéri* (1920), *Le Blé en herbe* (1923) (▷*The Ripening Seed*, 1955), *La Fin de Chéri* (1926) (▷*The Last of Chéri*, 1951), *La Seconde* (1929) (▷*The Other One*, 1960), and *La Chatte* (1933) (*The Cat*, 1953), explore a darker, more painful universe dominated by love. These novels focus on the struggle between independent identity and passionate love, on times of transition, such as adolescence and middle-age, and on the delicate equilibrium of the *ménage à trois*.

Most of Colette's heroes and heroines exist on the margins of society; many are androgynous, so that her work is imbued with an implied questioning of traditional gender roles and of relationships between the sexes. In *L'Étoile vesper* (1946) (*The Evening Star*, 1973), and *Le Fanal bleu* (1949) (*The Blue Lantern*, 1963), Colette depicts her existence in old age, and, following the tradition of her mother/the character Sido, focuses increasingly on the small pleasures of everyday life, and on her role as social observer. Colette's work evades generic classification, and the use of the character/narrator 'Colette', and of a combination of real and fictional characters in many of the texts, constantly questions the relationship between autobiography and fiction, and contributes to her exploration of the nature of female identity.

Bib: Eisinger, E. and McCarty, M., *Colette: The Woman, The Writer*; Hinde Stewart, J., *Colette*; King, A., chapter on Colette in *French Women Novelists: Defining a Female Style*; Marks, E.,

Colette; Sarde, M., *Colette Free and Fettered*; Ward ouve, N., *Colette*.

Coligny, Louise de, Princesse d'Orange (1555–1620)

French author of a substantial collection of letters. The daughter of Admiral Gaspard de Coligny (1519–1572), she was extremely fortunate to escape from the scene of her father's dreadful assassination during the St Bartholomew's Day massacre of Protestants which was instigated by ▷Catherine de Medici and the Guise family. She took refuge in Switzerland, and thus began her life of exile and wandering which led her to write many letters to her family and powerful Protestants who might be of assistance, such as Queen Elizabeth I of England (1533–1603). She led a retired existence, but in 1583 she married William, Prince of Orange, who was assassinated the following year. Her letters reveal the depth of her suffering and of her affection for her children. She returned to France after the assassination of Henri IV (1553–1610), but quickly returned to The Hague. She died at the Château de Fontainebleau. Some 200 of her letters from the period 1573 to her death are extant.
Bib: Marchegay, P. (ed.), *Correspondance de Louise de Coligny* (1887).

Collected Essays of Yamakawa Kikue (1981–1982)

Yamakawa Kikue (1890–1980) was a socialist feminist in pre-war Japan. This collection was published in ten volumes. She not only introduced socialist theory on women's issues to Japan, but also gave active support to the women's socialist movement and fought for equal rights for women workers, when she was head of the Bureau for Women and Youth at the Ministry of Labour.

Collector of Treasures, The (1977)

A volume of thirteen short stories by Southern African writer ▷Bessie Head which largely focus on contemporary village life in Botswana. Her title story presents a woman who is seen as a collector of treasures for her ability to find gold amidst the ash, beauty amidst destruction. With her gentle but powerful hands, this woman castrates her brutal husband, and turns to a community of loving and creative women, as well as to a man who knows how to look after children and does not abuse women. Clearly a figure for the author, this woman excises male cruelty and selfishness from the community, shaping a space more hospitable to women than the world of Western and African oppression generally allows. Incorporating a variety of oral gestures and modes into the stories, and using the village storyteller of the ▷oral tradition, Head firmly places her text into the oral tradition, drawing on community memory, gossip and hearsay for her authority, and generally avoiding authorial judgement. The standard trajectory of the stories is to open and close with a wide-angle focus on the community, with individual voices typically emerging from and slipping back into communality.

Collet, Camilla (1813–1895)

Norwegian novelist and essayist. Collett was born in Christianssand in Norway. Her father was a minister, her brother the poet Henrik Wergeland. Collett's upbringing was cultured and open-minded. As a young girl she fell in love with the poet Welhaven, an antagonist of her brother and father.

In 1841, Collet married the lawyer Jonas Collett and had four sons with him. At the age of thirty-eight she became a widow and broke up her home. From then on she became a traveller, a writer and a cultural critic. She was a very 'modern' woman for her times.

She wrote for nearly fifty years, and her first work was an essay in 1842, but the real début, written anonymously, was *Amtmandens Døtre* (1855) (▷*The Governor's Daughter*) which was the first social novel to appear in Norway, and the first literary work to introduce a heroine who questioned conventions of education and marriage. She also wrote short stories, eg *Fortællinger* (1861) (*Stories*), memoirs, *I de lange Nætter* (1863) (*Through the Long Nights*), and six volumes of essays: *Sidste Blade* (1868, 1872, 1873) (*Last Pages*), *Fra de stummes Lejr* (1877) (*From the Camp of the Mute*) and *Mod Strømmen* (1879, 1885) (*Against the Stream*).

In 1873 she at last gave up her anonymity and put her own name on the title page. She saw literature as the mirror of life, and her own literature shows her as a woman swimming against the tide, as a pioneer for women's rights, but also for a social literature full of wit.

Colleville, Anne-Hyacinthe de Saint-Léger de (1761–1824)

French novelist and dramatist. Born in Paris, the daughter of a doctor. Colleville published her first work, an epistolary novel, *Lettres du chevalier de saint Alme et de Mlle de Melcourt* (*Letters of the Knight of Saint Alme and Mlle de Melcourt*) in 1781. Her later novels include *Alexandrine ou l'amour est une vertu* (1782) (*Alexandrine, or Love is a Virtue*), two novels dealing with the life of a woman of independent means, *Mme de M***, ou la rentière* (1802) (*Mme de M***, or the Woman of Independent Means*) and the sequel, *Victor de Martigues* (1804), and a novel ostensibly addressed to husbands, *Salut à MM. les maris ou, Rose et d'Orsinval* (1806) (*Greetings to Husbands or, Rose and d'Orsinval*). Her last work, *Coralie* (1816), bears the subtitle, '. . . or the danger of relying on one's self'. She also published three one-act plays: *Le Bouquet du père de famille* (1783) (*Father's Bouquet*), composed for her father, *Les deux soeurs* (1783) (*The Two Sisters*) and *Sophie et Derville* (1788), which were favourably received when performed in Paris. She is said to have burned the manuscript of a later work, *Le Porteur d'eau*, (*The Water Carrier*) about a victim of the Revolution.

Bib: Prudhomme, L.M., *Répertoire universel historique et biographique des femmes célèbres*.

Collier, Jane (1710–1754/5)

English writer and social critic who knew Latin and Greek, and numbered ▷Sarah Fielding among her friends, as well as Samuel Richardson (▷Richardson, influence of) whose *Clarissa* she criticized. Anonymously, she published *Essay on the Art of Ingeniously Tormenting* (1753) – 'general instructions for plaguing all your acquaintance'. This demonstrates the power of satire and burlesque in pointing to the need for social change. For instance, she advises the tormenting of female servants; 'Always scold her, if she is the least undressed or dirty; and say you cannot bear such beasts about you. If she is clean and well-dressed, tell her that you suppose she dresses out for the fellows.' In the next chapter she advises on the patroness's treatment of her humble female companion, noting, 'there is some difficulty in giving rules for tormenting a dependant, that shall differ from those laid down for plaguing and teazing your servants, as the two stations differ so little in themselves.' With Sarah Fielding she wrote *The Cry: a New Dramatic Fable* (1754).

Collier, Mary (1679–after 1762)

English poet who worked as a rural labourer, washerwoman, brewer and later, housekeeper. She paid for the publication of *The Woman's Labour* (1739), and in the reprinted version of 1762 argued that she wrote it in reply to the labourer-poet Stephen Duck's *The Thresher's Labour*. Her poem testifies to the drudgery of women's field labour: 'When night comes on, unto our home we go, / Our Corn we carry, and our Infant too; / Weary indeed! but 'tis not worth our while / Once to complain, or rest at every Stile; /We must make haste, for when we home are come, / We find again our Work but just begun.' Her poetry is a determined selfconscious articulation of the particular interlocking circumstances of gender and status. She later published, by subscription, *Poems on Several Occasions* (1762).

▷Leapor, Mary; Little, Janet; Whitney, Isabella; Yearsley, Ann.

Bib: Landry, Donna, *The Muses of Resistance*; Lonsdale (ed.), *Eighteenth Century Women's Poetry*.

Collins, An

English poet. Her *Divine Songs and Meditations* (1653) record spiritual experiences as well as negotiations with associates. She writes of herself as a bad poet, but a good example of a soul searching after God: 'If any pious friend / Will once vouchsafe to read them to the end; / Let such conceive if error here they find, / 'Twas want of art, not true intent of mind.'

Collins, Jackie (born 1937)

British novelist. Born in London but now living in California, Collins began to write at the age of eight. During a rebellious adolescence Collins was expelled from school at fifteen, when she went to Los Angeles in search of a film career like her sister, Joan Collins. Her real interest, however, was in writing and by the age of twenty-seven she had published her first bestseller, *The World is Full of Married Men* (1968). Since then she has produced twelve novels, including *The Bitch*, *Chances*, *Hollywood Husbands* (1986), *Hollywood Wives* (1983), *Lucky* and most recently *Lady Boss* (1991). Collins's immensely popular ▷romance fiction is about power, sex, relationships and success, and her characters come from the world of Hollywood. Her style is deliberately fast-paced and colloquial, that of a 'street writer', as she herself says. She describes herself as, 'an insider who can write like an outsider about the inside'. *Chances* and *Lucky* have both been made into television mini-series, and her novel *The Stud* (1969) was made into a film starring Joan Collins.

Collins, Merle

Merle Collins

This Caribbean poet, novelist, editor and lecturer was born and educated in ▷Grenada. She worked as a teacher and researcher, and was a member of the National Women's Organization in Grenada until 1983 and the US invasion. She now lives in Britain, where she is a lecturer at the Polytechnic of North London. She has an interest in drama and is a member of African Dawn, a group which performs dramatized poetry fused with Afro-Caribbean music. She has contributed to four anthologies of poetry and published one collection, *Because the Dawn Breaks, Poems Dedicated to the Grenadian People* (1985), with an introduction by Ngugi Wa Thiong'o, who places her poetry in three distinct traditions: the oral, the revolutionary and the folk. She is the co-editor, with Rhonda Cobham, of a collection of new black writing in Britain, *Watchers and Seekers* (1987). Her first novel, ▷*Angel*, appeared in 1987. Her most recent publication is a collection of short stories, *Rain Darling* (1990).

Collins lists Caribbean politics and society and the Grenadian revolution as major influences on her as a writer.

Colombi, la Marchesa (1846–1920)

Italian novelist; real name Maria Antonietta Torriani. She was married to Eugenio Torrelli Viollier, the founder and editor of *Corriere della Sera*, from whom she was later separated. One of her main interests was in the education of women, for which she worked and campaigned throughout her life. She wrote for children, as well as for adults. Her concern about the exploitation of women workers was revealed in her most famous work, *In risaia* (1878) (*The Rice Field*), in which she graphically described the dreadful working conditions. Also deservedly popular was her analysis of an unhappy marriage, *Un matrimonio in provincia* (1885) (*A Provincial Marriage*).

Colombine ▷Burgos Seguí, Carmen de

Colonia, Regina Célia (born 1940)

Brazilian poet and short story writer. In 1976 she won the Jabuti Prize for Poetry, one of the most important in Brazil, for her book *Sumaimana*, in which she uses Inca language. Her short stories and poems are concerned with South American Indian culture. She is currently Consul in Washington.

Other works: *Canção para o totem* (1975) (*Song for the Totem*), and *Os leões da Luziânia* (1985) (*The Lions of Luziânia*).

Colonna, Vittoria (1490–1547)

Italian poet and friend of Michelangelo. She married Ferrante Francesco d'Avalos, Marquis of Pescara. She passed her youth surrounded by literary and military men, as her father had been a captain. Following the death of her husband in 1525, she withdrew from the world and spent time in various convents in Rome, Orvieto and Viterbo. Her ▷*Canzoniere* laments the death of her husband, and of her father, and is very religious in tone. There were many reprints of her work. Her poetry is imitative of the style of Petrarch (▷Petrarchism)

Color més blau, Lo (1982) (*The Bluest Colour*)

A novel by the Spanish writer ▷Maria Aurèlia Capmany Farnes, generally considered to be her masterpiece. It is an ▷epistolary novel concerned with the lives of two women, Olivia and Delia, separated from each other at the conclusion of the Spanish Civil War in 1939. The novel traces their parallel but different lives, and in the process analyzes the impact of the civil war and its consequences for Catalonia.

Color Purple, The (1982)

Novel by US writer ▷Alice Walker. Walker's Pulitzer Prize-winning novel celebrates the survival of African-American women. On publication, the book immediately sparked controversy, provoking angry responses from all sides. The white moral majority in Oakland, California, attempted to ban the book as sexually offensive, liberals argued that the use of a rural Southern dialect was degrading to African-Americans, and some African-American men protested that Walker's portrayal of relations and lesbian sexuality was a betrayal of the black community. A central focus of the novel is the oppression of African-American women by African-American men, which Walker attributes both to socio-economic inequality and polarized gender roles. Walker uses the life-story of Celie, who suffers physical and sexual abuse from her stepfather and her husband, to expose the inter-relationship of racism and sexism. Walker thus emphasizes the political nature of intimate relationships and explores the possibility of radical social change through the transformation of personal relationships. Celie learns to value herself through her lesbian relationship with her husband's lover, a blues singer called Shug.

While celebrating African-American sisterhood as empowering Celie's liberation, *The Color Purple* also works to revise the macho masculinity which she critiques. Epistolary in form, the novel tells Celie's story in her own words by means of letters addressed first to God, and then to her sister, Nettie. Nettie's replies, although withheld until late in the novel, establish an alternative cultural and racial model through her experiences as a missionary in Africa. Without idealizing African society, Walker uses it to contextualise the experiences of the African-American characters and validate the restructuring of the nuclear family which the characters achieve by the end. The book was made into a controversial but popular feature film by Steven Spielberg in 1985.

Coloured People (1964)

A novel by Japanese writer ▷Ariyoshi Sawako. Shoko falls in love with a black soldier of the occupying troops in post-war Japan. She decides to live in the USA, 'Land of Liberty', because her baby is mocked for his skin colour. There she finds complicated, entangled discrimination against Italians and Jews as well as blacks. Through her experience of raising children, Shoko comes to realize that discrimination is not only based on a difference of colour, but on something else as well. She then decides to live completely as a black. Although Ariyoshi's idea of racism is clear, Shoko's struggle against the double discrimination faced by both yellow and black people is just beginning.

Columna, Sor Francisca de la (c 1600–1660)

Early 17th-century Spanish nun, author of a play entitled *Nacimiento de Cristo* (*The Nativity*), known only from a reference.

Colville, Elizabeth Melville (fl 1599–1603)

Scottish poet. Born in the late 16th century in Halhil, Scotland, very little is known about Colville. Sometime before 1599 she married John Colville of Culross. She had at least one surviving child, Alexander Colville, and probably died after 1640. Although Alexander Hume praised Colville's poetic abilities in his dedication of a book of hymns to her, ▷'Ane Godlie Dreame Compylit in Scottish Meter' (1603) is her only surviving work.

Comedia de encargo, Una (1988) (A Commissioned Play)

A play by the important contemporary Spanish dramatist ▷Pilar Pombo. The play was highly successful when staged in Madrid. It describes how two middle-aged women make a living by ghost-writing plays which must conform to a set pattern, and allegorizes the phantom of the male tradition which haunts women writers and forces their work to echo the patriarchal mode.

Come in Spinner (1951)

Australian novel by ▷Dymphna Cusack in collaboration with Florence James. It deals with the disillusioning experiences of a group of women, most of whom work in the beauty salon of the Hotel South-Pacific in wartime Sydney, which was occupied at the time by the North American forces. Come in Spinner won the Daily Telegraph Prize for 1948 and became a popular television series in 1989.

Cometh Up as a Flower (1867)

A novel of ▷sensation by British author ▷Rhoda Broughton. The heroine, Nell le Strange, is left as the head of a motherless household and delights in her father's affection. She is later attracted to a handsome guardsman, but he is already married and Nell has to accept a marriage of convenience to a rich old man, Sir Hugh. The novel is noteworthy for its description of Nell's revulsion, both at her aged husband and her situation as a 'bought' woman. She decides not to leave Sir Hugh after reading ▷Mrs Henry Wood's ▷East Lynne, and eventually dies of consumption.

Coming of Age in Mississippi (1969)

US novel. Anne Moody's semi-autobiographical work recounts what it means to grow up in Mississippi as an African-American woman. Born in 1940, Moody lived in poverty in an abusive household. At age fifteen she began to hate people: Anglo-Americans for bombing and killing African-Americans, and African-Americans for not standing up to Anglo-Americans. A top student, she earned a scholarship to Tougaloo College, an African-American college, and she became an activist in the civil rights movement. She concludes that the movement was not globally big enough to make significant changes.

Other works include Mr Death (1975).

Coming Out from Under: Contemporary Australian Women Writers (1988)

Australian critical work by Pam Gilbert. This provides a comprehensive discussion of the work of ▷Helen Garner, ▷Kate Grenville, ▷Elizabeth Jolley, ▷Barbara Hanrahan, ▷Robin Klein, ▷Thea Astley, ▷Jessica Anderson, ▷Jean Bedford, ▷Olga Masters, and ▷Antigone Kefala.

Coming to Birth (1986)

Novel by Kenyan writer ▷Marjorie Oludhe Macgoye. Coming to Birth is set in Nairobi in 1956 and interweaves the story of a failed marriage and a woman's struggle to be self-supporting with the politics of Kenyan independence.

Commedia di Nannuccio e quindici figliastre (1600) (The Comedy of Nannuccio and Fifteen Stepdaughters)

Written by Italian dramatist ▷Suor Annalena Odaldi, the story is of Nannuccio, a widower with fifteen daughters, who wishes to marry again. His wife's dowry has attracted a young woman to him. The daughters, however, claim that they, too, have a right to marry, as well as a right to their mother's dowry, and the judge ultimately rules in their favour, spoiling Nannuccio's plans. This is, in a sense, a play of social protest, as much as it is a comedy, in that it draws attention to a lack of paternal responsibility. Women are given more dialogue in the play than are the male characters, whom they considerably outnumber. Much of the humour in the play may well come from its author's own experience of being one of a very large family.

Community writing (20th-century Ireland)

The development of a vibrant community arts movement in Ireland dates from the 1980s. While severely lacking in resources, community arts groups are extremely active in a wide range of spheres. Writing groups, mainly initiated by women, are especially productive, enabling and encouraging many women to write who would never otherwise have done so, and challenging the 'canonical' or hierarchical notions of 'literature'. While some groups are predominantly middle-class and urban, many more are working-class, or have a rural base. Some recent publications from writing groups include: Notions – A Collection of Short Stories and Poems from the Kilbarrack Writers Group (1987); Tallaght Miscellany (annual, from 1984); The Box Under the Bed (Cork Women's Poetry Circle) (1986), and Hidden Talent (1990).

▷Bradshaw, Máire

Companionate marriage

A development of ▷humanism and the ▷Protestant Reformation, the ideal of companionate marriage proved a major argument in favour of educating women during the Renaissance. Whereas medieval Catholicism tended to idealize chastity and virginity, 16th-century Catholic humanists, and especially Protestant reformers, theoretically revised the status of marriage. To the earlier reasons for marriage, the prevention of fornication and the procreation of children, was added the third goal of companionship. As a result, women had to be educated in order to be fit wives and companions to their husbands. Although the ideal of companionate marriage was a prime motive for educating women, it also strictly limited the scope of women's learning to subjects that would not conflict with their chastity, obedience and piety. Although companionate marriage opened up the possibility of a wife finding her husband incompatible, this possibility was for the most part suppressed. Attempts by women to leave incompatible husbands often resulted in disaster.

▷Askew, Anne; Cary, Elizabeth; Lumley, Joanna

Company of Women, The (1980)
US novel. ▷Mary Gordon's book focuses on an ideologically liberated Catholic, Felicitas Taylor. Her mother's circle of friends see her as the heir to their devout Catholicism. Felicitas's brush with death occasions her to declare her spiritual independence and to leave the circle. The victim of a love affair, she learns the value of friendship among women. Gordon undermines the idealization of love and sex, and she celebrates the enduring community of friendship.

Compiuta Donzella, la (13th century)
Italian poet. A woman about whom there exists almost no biographical information, though it is generally believed that she lived in Florence in this period. She is thought to have been the writer of three beautiful sonnets, which certainly give voice to a female point of view. The first sonnet '*A la stagion che 'l mondo foglia e fiora*' ('In that season when the world is all in bloom') tells of a woman's desire not to be married off. The second sonnet '*Lasciar vorria lo mondo, e Dio servire*' ('I wish to leave the world to serve God') is not a religious sonnet, but rather a complaint about men. The third and final sonnet is addressed to another poet, and takes the form of a love poem. Her poetry reflects a knowledge of poetry of the Provencal school, as well as that of the *Scuola Siciliana* (▷Poetry).

Complete Works of May Ziyadah, The (1982)
Arabic writings of ▷May Ziyadah, the first professional Arab woman writer, including lectures, essays, criticism, studies of the life and work of pioneering women writers in Arabic, and translations from English, French and German, all published between 1911 and 1940.

The two volumes give the reader today a good idea of the wide range of Ziyadah's writings and the reason for the very high place she was accorded by her contemporaries. The first volume includes feminist essays which expound the ideas of Quasim Amin (1863–1908) in his ▷*Liberation of Women* (1899) and *The New Woman* (1900), and call upon her male readers and audience to support the necessary reforms in women's

education. She often addresses the women themselves, calling upon them to educate themselves properly, change their way of life and take more interest in social and cultural changes.

Her collection of essays *Bayna al-mad wa la-jazr* (*In and out with the Tide*) includes her articles on problems of language and literature. A series of brilliant essays starting in early 1919 discuss the relation between classical Arabic and the regional vernaculars. Two essays on music in the same collection show her appreciation of both Oriental and Western music.

The *Complete Works* also includes a book on *Equality*, which describes the history and philosophy of the systems of both government and economy through which humanity has passed. The last essay is supposed to be a letter to the author, where the male correspondents proposes and describes a programme of items or laws for social reform, along similar lines to the welfare states established more than thirty years later in Europe. She concludes by stressing the importance of recognizing individual differences as to talent, temperament and capacity for achievement. Her work also includes writings on the history of Europe and translations from German, English and French.

'Composed About Six Weeks Before Her Death, When Under Distressing Circumstances' (1759)
This 167-line poem, composed by ▷Esther Allen Hayden, a North American, was published posthumously in *A Short Account of the Life, Death and Character of Esther Hayden*. This tribute to Hayden, collected by a relative, begins with two anonymous texts by relatives – a biographical testimonial and a long poem – and concludes with Hayden's own poetic record of her religious struggles during the last weeks of her life. Hayden's poem is notable for her acknowledgement of a longing for reassurance of her salvation to stave off her 'fear of the Pow'r of Death'.

Comptes amoureux, Les (1530–1540) ▷Flore, Jeanne

Compton-Burnett, Ivy (1884–1969)
English novelist. Born in Pinner, and educated privately, she went on to read classics at Royal Holloway Women's College, London. Shre acted as governess to her younger siblings and became manager of the family household following her mother's death in 1911, assuming the same tyrannical method of authority previously adopted by her mother. Her closest brother died shortly before she completed her BA, another brother died in World War I, and her two youngest sisters committed joint suicide in 1918. Compton-Burnett suffered from a long physical and mental breakdown during the early 1920s, and the first novel to suggest the characteristic hallmarks of her fiction, *Pastors and Masters* (1925), was produced after her illness. Her first novel, *Dolores*

(1911), has little in common with her subsequent novels and was later disowned by the author.

Compton-Burnett's novels are generally narrated almost entirely through dialogue, and their epigrammatic quality places them in a strong English tradition of verbal artifice and sardonic humour, common reference points being ▷Jane Austen and the Restoration stage. The style of her novels was regarded as highly original by contemporary critics, and in formal terms her fiction has been likened to both cubism and post-impressionism in the visual arts, although her work now tends to stand aside from the main formal *and* thematic innovations of literary ▷modernism. Her consistent topics are parental tyranny, and conflicts over power and property in late Victorian and Edwardian upper-class households, as explored in her best-known novels, *A House and Its Head* (1935) and *A Family and a Fortune* (1939). *Manservant and Maidservant* (1947) examines the effect of power and authority on each level of the domestic hierarchy. Her concentration on the claustrophobic relationships within extended families seemingly cut-off from the outside world additionally appeals to the framework and motifs of Greek tragedy, as in *Brothers and Sisters* (1929) which has incest as its central theme and plot dynamic.

Other novels include: *Men and Wives* (1931), *More Women Than Men* (1944), *Daughters and Sons* (1937), *Parents and Children* (1941), *Elders and Betters* (1944), *Two Worlds and Their Ways* (1949), *A Heritage and Its History* (1959), *A God and His Gifts* (1963), *The Last and the First* (1969).
Bib: Burkhart, C., *The Art of Ivy Compton-Burnett: A Collection of Critical Essays*; Greig, C., *Ivy Compton-Burnett: A Memoir*; McCarthy, M., *The Writing On The Wall*; Sprigge, E., *The Life of Ivy Compton-Burnett*; Spurling, H., *Ivy When Young: The Early Life of Ivy Compton-Burnett 1884–1919* and *Secrets of a Woman's Heart: The Later Life of Ivy Compton-Burnett 1920–1969*.

'Compulsory Heterosexuality and Lesbian Existence' (1980)

US lesbian-feminist poet and theorist, ▷Adrienne Rich's influential essay was first published in the feminist journal ▷*Signs*, was reissued as a pamphlet by Onlywomen Press in 1981, and collected in Rich's *Bread, Blood and Poetry* (1986) with an afterword. There are two strands to Rich's essay. She argues that heterosexuality needs to be seen as an institution fundamental to ▷patriarchy, as well as a form of sexual relationship. Heterosexuality is imposed on women ideologically and by force, and is not a free choice or a biological necessity. This argument supports Rich's central theory of 'Re-Vision', or rewriting of partriarchal history and culture from a lesbian-feminist perspective. The project involves reformulating assumptions by redefining a lesbian as a 'woman-identified woman', that is, a woman who forms close emotional and intellectual bonds with other women. Sometimes a sexual relationship is

involved, but not always. The concept of a woman-identified woman leads Rich to assert the existence of a 'lesbian continuum', which is defined as the historical and continuing presence of woman-identified experience.

Comtesse de Tende, La (1723) ▷Lafayette, Marie-Madeleine Pioche de la Vergne, Comtesse de

Conan, Laure (1845–1924)
▷Pseudonym of French-Canadian Marie-Louise-Félicité Angers, important as Quebec's first woman novelist. Born at Murray Bay, Quebec, she attended school there, and at the Ursuline Convent in Quebec City. She led a solitary and semi-retired life at Murray Bay, writing as a means of making a living. Much of the thematic content of her work is attributed to an unrequited love, and it is true that she did not marry. Her best-known work is an epistolary novel, *Angéline de Montbrun* (1884, translated under the same title, 1974). In *A l'Oeuvre et à l'épreuve* (1891, translated as *The Master-motive: a Tale of the Days of Champlain*), Conan draws on the missionary period of New France as historical background to explore the psychological relation between heroism and disappointment. Although not much of her work has been translated, she is important for her depiction of a French-Canadian sensibility and history. She also wrote numerous moral and religious articles, for example, the dialogue *Si les Canadiennes le voulaient* (1886) (*If Canadians Wished It*) enjoining women to use their familial positions to enhance the quality of public life. She is an astonishing example of a woman who survived by her pen in a restrictive moral and political climate.
Bib: Blodgett, E.D., in *A Mazing Space*; Dumont, M., in *The Clear Spirit: Twenty Canadian Women and Their Times*; Gallays, F., in *Traditionalism, Nationalism and Feminism: Women Writers of Quebec*.

Conceptismo
Portuguese literary tendency associated with the ▷Baroque period. A highly intellectualized form of poetry, it involves a subtle, complex play of contrasting ideas.
▷Céu, Maria do, Sóror; Céu, Violante do, Sóror; *Fênix Renascida*

Condé, Maryse (1937–)
This novelist, dramatist, critic, short story writer and writer of children's fiction from Guadeloupe in the French Antilles is a professor at the University of Paris IV. Condé has won recognition for a wide range of literary activity, and is one of the only Antillean women writing in French who is simultaneously an essayist-scholar-critic and creative writer. Condé's two-volume cycle of novels, ▷*Segu*, has probably been her greatest commercial success. Africa has been the setting for several of her fictional works, which deal in various ways with the problematic relationship

between Africans of the Mother-Continent and Afro-Caribbeans. Both ▷*Heremakhonon* and ▷*A Season in Rihata* are concerned with the confrontation of an educated, bourgeois, black Antillean with a 'real' Africa very different from the Africa of the prophets of ▷*négritude*. Condé turns to the USA for *Moi Tituba, Sorcière Noire de Salem* (1986), the reconstruction of the life of the black witch of Salem, ignored by history. Her recent novel, *La Vie scélérate* (1987) (*Life is Wicked*), which translates the reality of the ▷diaspora by blending fragments of the black experience throughout the world. *Moi Tituba* won the Grand Prix Litteraire de la Femme. Two of Condé's plays, *Dieu nous l'a donné* (1972) (*God Gave Him to Us*) and ▷*Mort d'Oluwémi d'Ajumako*, are concerned with the manipulation of social mores and myths by individuals seeking political power and influence. Condé is also the author of numerous critical articles and reviews of both anglophone and francophone writers.

For a more complete bibliography of Condé's work, see Vivienne Liley (thesis), and for a bibliography of Condé's non-fictional writing see ▷Berrian.
▷Identity, Caribbean

Conde Abellán, Carmen (born 1907)

Spanish poet, novelist and critic. Conde was born in Cartagena. She was the first woman to be admitted to the Spanish Academy, to which she was elected in 1978 at the age of 71. Her early poetry, such as *Júbilos* (1934) (*Jubilations*), and *Ansia de gracia* (1945) (*Desire for Grace*), showed echoes of surrealism. She has also published novels, such as *En manos del silencio* (1950) (*In The Hands of Silence*); *Las oscuras raíces* (1953) (*Dark Roots*); *Creció espesa la yerba* (1979) (*Thick Grew the Grass*), and *Soy la madre* (1980) (*I'm the Mother*). Her work centres on problems of conscience, spiritual dilemmas and social issues.

Condict, Jemima (1754–1779)

North American diarist. Raised on a farm in Essex County, New Jersey, she adhered to the Presbyterian faith in which she was raised. During the turbulent early years of debate over North American independence and the entry into war, she maintained a diary (▷*Jemima Condict, Her Book*) that reflects an inner battle she was waging as she entered her marriageable years. She ultimately married a Mr Harrison, but she died shortly thereafter.

Conduct literature (Britain)

During the 16th and 17th centuries there was a proliferation of books on conduct for women, such as William Gouge's *Of Domesticall Duties*. These prescribed the way in which a woman should behave in all circumstances, and often gave very detailed guides to personal conduct, from sexual behaviour to appropriate reading.

▷Advice literature (18th-century Britain); Epistolary novel

Confession of faith

Under the influence of the ▷Protestant Reformation, confessions of faith took on great importance as each sect tried to establish itself as a unified Church. Confessions of faith were an important means of establishing membership in a religious community, and of testing for orthodoxy. They frequently made up part of examinations for heresy, such as ▷Anne Askew's and ▷Elizabeth Young's. Literate parishioners, including women, were encouraged to write formal confessions of faith. They were also instrumental to religious instruction, and therefore frequently published. Recognizing this potential, ▷Catherine Parr published her ▷*Lamentation or Complaint of a Sinner* (1547) in the hopes of winning converts to Protestantism. Many male religious leaders and reformers also encouraged their followers to write and publish confessions of faith. ▷Katherine Stubbes's 'A Most Heavenly Confession of the Christian Faith' (1592) was published by her husband after her death.

Confession of Faith or, A Summary of Divinity, A (1704)

Written in 1677 by ▷Sarah Symmes Fiske as preparation for admission into her Massachusetts congregation, this North American autobiographical work is a highly conventional confession of Puritan beliefs, but it is notable for its detailed, logical structure. In explaining her beliefs, for instance, she notes that 'the sin which follows [Adam's] Fall, is either *Original*, or *Actual*'; then both original and actual sin are defined and distinguished. Fiske's *Confession* remained popular among her friends after her death in 1692; it was finally published in Boston, Massachusetts, in 1704 as a model for other young parishioners seeking Church admission.

Conlon, Evelyn (born 1952)

Irish fiction writer. Born in County Monaghan, she travelled for a number of years in Australia and Asia, and now lives in Dublin. She has been active in the women's movement in Dublin since the 1970s. Her direct and drily humorous narratives express the difficulties and dilemmas of women seeking to reach a sense of themselves in a deeply conservative, misogynistic society. *My Head is Opening*, a collection of short stories, appeared in 1987, and *Stars in the Daytime*, a novel, in 1989.

Conrad, Christina (born 1942)

New Zealand poet. Christina Conrad is best known as a painter. Until recently she has published poetry under the name Christina Beer. Her publications are *This Fig Tree Has Thorns* (1974), and inclusion in an anthology of women poets, ▷*Private Gardens* (1977). Both Conrad's painting and poetry focus on the female body and

Evelyn Conlon

female sexuality figured graphically and metaphorically.

Consciousness-raising
Consciousness-raising is a practice generally associated with all-woman discussion groups, who since the 1960s have met to raise feminist awareness by politicizing the personal aspects of women's lives and encouraging women to identify with each other rather than competing to achieve standards set by men.

In the 1970s a group of semi-autobiographical novels appeared which aimed to raise the reader's consciousness of women's oppression, by charting the personal and political development of their fictional female protagonists. Examples include ▷Kate Millett's *Flying* (1974) and ▷Marilyn French's bestselling novel, *The Women's Room* (1977).

Conservationist, The (1974)
A novel by Southern African writer ▷Nadine Gordimer, whose central protagonist is a white businessman named Mehring. He has bought a farm which serves both as a tax-dodge and a weekend retreat, but also living on the farm is a set of black labourers and their families, and, on its outskirts, an Indian family who keep a store. The novel juxtaposes the sterile and increasingly paranoid consciousness of this wealthy white South African with a Zulu world just beginning to tap its rich resources of ritual and mythology. The symbolism of burial is central to the novel: the body of a black man lies half-buried on the land, signifying on the one hand the fantasies and fears of the white subconscious and, on the other, the means whereby the half-forgotten connection between the Zulus and their ancestors will be restored. While the novel's use of symbolism and its intense focus on the mind of an individual who

is increasingly divorced from reality represents a shift away from realism in Gordimer's writing, the materiality of the body, and its place in Zulu religion, challenges this shift. Readers have mistakenly read the ending of the novel in terms of Mehring's literal death, but it is, rather, a descent into madness, the fitting conclusion to the solipsism with which he has lived his life.

Constantia Neville; or, The West Indian (1800)
Sentimental novel by the North American author ▷Helena Wells. The novel presents the character of Mrs Hayman as the epitome of a proper woman. In direct addresses to the reader, Mrs Hayman advocates dutifulness and a woman's subordination of her life to her husband. Although Wells seems to agree with her character's advice, the events of Mrs Hayman's life reveal the brutality of her husband and thus, ironically, the consequences of such advocacy. Unlike the novels of ▷Hannah Webster Foster, which questioned such consequences, *Constantia Neville* was never reprinted.

Constant Nymph, The (1924)
Novel by English writer ▷Margaret Kennedy. Her second, it was an outstanding success, selling more copies than any other novel of the 1920s. Albert Sanger, a famous composer, lives in Bohemian disarray in Austria with his family, and assorted artists and writers. Fourteen-year-old Tessa, the 'constant nymph' of the title, is in love with composer Lewis Dodd. When their father dies, the Sanger children are taken to England by their beautiful but conventional cousin, Florence, whom Lewis marries. Bourgeois English life suits neither Lewis nor Tessa, however, and they finally run away together to Belgium. The story ends tragically. A powerful romantic fiction, it was dramatized for the stage and filmed four times.

Contemporary Verse 2
Canadian feminist poetry journal that declares itself as a forum for social action and change. It seeks to publish feminist writing: poetry, criticism, reviews, and artwork. It is edited by a collective in Winnipeg, Manitoba.

Continents noirs (1987) (Black Continents)
An analytical work by the Senegalese social scientist and feminist ▷Awa Thiam, which explores further the issues raised in her first book, *La Parole aux négresses* (1978) (▷ *Speak Out, Black Sisters*). Here she attempts an analysis of the ideological framework within which black women's lives are contained – what she calls the 'ideology of blackness'. She examines critically Freud's concept of the woman as 'dark continent', and the parallels this sets up between colonization and gender oppression, and gives an historical overview of attitudes adopted by the white, Western world toward blacks. Though lacking the urgency and immediately of her earlier work, this text seeks to place the concrete issues previously

raised by the author in a theoretical perspective that will enable a coherent strategy to emerge.

Contrabando (1961)
A long poem by Greek writer ▷Melpo Axioti. It is a confession of her love and nostalgia for Greece and the things she missed while exiled for her political ideals. The poem expresses humanistic ideas and the pure feelings of love people have for their roots.

Conversations et proverbes ▷Maintenon, Françoise d'Aubigné, Marquise de

Conversations of Cow, The (1985)
More an extended allegorical fable than a novel, *The Conversations of Cow* by Indian writer ▷Suniti Namjoshi follows an encounter between the lesbian narrator, Suniti, and Bhadravati, a lesbian Brahmin cow and goddess. Bhadravati goes through a series of transformations. Two of these metamorphoses, a sexist North American man called Baddy, and a stereotypical husband, Buddy, demonstrate the social power attached to conventional masculinity, and also that individuals are not reducible to social categories. In another metamorphosis Bhadravati becomes a disconcertingly beautiful woman with whom Suniti becomes lovers. These transformations teach Suniti a freer and more flexible form of being.

Conversion narratives (17th-century Britain)
Autobiographical memoirs written for private or public consumption by Protestants (and especially Puritans), examining themselves and their experiences. Often men and women attempting to join gathered (Dissenting or radical) Churches would present, either in writing or orally, the story of how they came to turn to God and recognize the way of the Church. Often structured around a dynamic encounter with temptation, the narratives move away from spiritual diaries (such as that of ▷Margaret Hoby) to present a rather more shaped version of a Christian life as a journey. Also related to spiritual autobiography, such as that of Richard Baxter.
▷Allen, Hannah; ▷Trapnel, Anna
Bib: Watkins, Owen C., *The Puritan Experience*; Smith, Nigel, *Perfection Proclaimed*.

Conway, Viscountess Anne (1631–1679)
English philosopher who corresponded with contemporary philosophers, including Englishmen Henry More and Joseph Glanvill, responded to French philosopher René Descartes (1596–1650), and influenced German philosopher Baron von Leibnitz (1646–1716). She knew Latin, Greek and Hebrew, and her *The Principles of the Most Ancient and Modern Philosophy* was published in Latin in 1690 and English in 1692.
Bib: Merchant, Carolyn, *Journal of the History of Philosophy*.

Cook, Eliza (1818–1889)
English poet, essayist and ▷feminist. The youngest of eleven children, she was born in London and grew up in Horsham, Sussex. She educated herself and published her first verses, *Lays of a Wild Harp*, in 1835. The collection was well-received, and encouraged her to contribute poems to the *Metropolitan Magazine*, the *New Monthly Magazine* and the *Weekly Dispatch*, the last of which printed her most famous poem, 'The Old Arm Chair', in 1837. Her work varies between ▷sentimental, domestic verse, fiery political ballads and satirical poetry. Her second collection, *Melaia and Other Poems* (1838), sold well both in Britain and North America, and three further volumes followed: *Poems: Second Series* (1845); *I'm Afloat: Songs* (1850) and *New Echoes, and Other Poems* (1864). From 1849–1854 she wrote and edited ▷*Eliza Cook's Journal*, a feminist miscellany addressing topics such as work, marriage and the law. The 1860 publication *Jottings From My Journal* includes much of this material. Cook also wrote a collection of aphorisms, *Diamond Dust* (1865). She never married, but was passionately attracted to Charlotte Cushman, an actress.
Bib: Hickok, K., *Representations of Women: 19th Century British Women's Poetry*.

Cooke, Rose Terry (1827–1892)
US short-story, religious non-fiction and children's writer, novelist and poet. Principally regarded for her ▷local color short stories of New England, Cooke was a major contributor of stories to the national literary magazines. She was critically esteemed in her time for her realism, telling use of dialect and distinctive characterization, developing the New England type characters of spinsters and farm people with humour and humanity. Like other New England women, she criticized the emotional and moral straitjacket of the Puritan tradition, focusing on strong, self-defined women characters with a more humane morality. Among her most frequently anthologized stories is 'How Celia Changed Her Mind'. Other works include: *Somebody's Neighbors* (1881); *Root-Bound, and Other Sketches* (1885); *Huckleberries Gathered from New England Hills* (1891).
▷*Galaxy, The*

Cookson, Catherine (born 1906)
English popular novelist. She also writes under the pseudonym Catherine Marchant. She was born in South Shields and grew up in East Jarrow. Cookson did not begin writing novels until she was in her forties. Cookson's ▷romantic fiction is extremely popular, and has been adapted for British television. Her novels tend to fall into a formulaic pattern whereby a woman and man meet, have little attraction or respect for one another initially, but gradually fall in love. The 'Mallen' series is a family saga which focuses on an aristocratic dynasty, but many of her novels

depict the local working community of Northumberland, where she now lives.

Coolbrith, Ina (1842–1928)

US lyric poet. Coolbrith was associated with the San Francisco *Overland Monthly* magazine and with the literary group that included US writers Bret Harte (1836–1902) and Samuel Clemens ('Mark Twain', 1835–1910). She was California's first state poet laureate. Her poems are collected in *A Perfect Day, and Other Poems* (1881); *The Singer of the Sea* (1894); and *Songs from the Golden Gate* (1895).
▷ Gold rush

Coonardoo: The Well in the Shadows (1929)

Australian novel by ▷ Katharine Susannah Prichard. *Coonardoo* deals with the previously forbidden subject of a sexual relationship between a white man and an Aboriginal girl. The subject is handled with great delicacy and the inference is that Coonardoo, the Aboriginal woman who has borne Hugh Watt's son, would be a more appropriate wife for him in every way than Mollie, the white girl he marries. Mollie resents the isolation and loneliness of the station, Wytaliba, where the novel is set, and eventually leaves Hugh. Hugh then takes Coonardoo as his woman but is unable, through misplaced delicacy, to renew his sexual relationship with her. He beats her and banishes her from the station after she has been raped by another white man. She becomes a prostitute among the Japanese pearl divers at Broome and, after Hugh has lost the station to his enemy, Sam Geary, Coonardoo returns to Wytaliba to die alone. Throughout the novel she is seen as the spirit of the land. Rather than embrace her, Hugh has rejected her, and this leads to the loss of his station and the ruin of both. Because of its philosophy and its sensitive depiction of their relationship, this is a very significant, though still controversial, novel.
▷ Aborigine in Australian women's writing, The

Cooper, Anna Julia Haywood (1858–1964)

US essayist, whose works mark the beginning of African-American feminism and of feminist racial consciousness. Born a slave, a lifelong and highly educated teacher, Cooper brought her own experience and formidable skills to the task of educating the USA to the perceptions of the ▷ 'other'. Her most noted work is *A Voice from the South by a Black Woman of the South* (1892), which includes her famous preface, 'Our Raison d'Etre'.

Cooper, Edith ▷ Field, Michael

Cooper, Mary Wright (1714–1778)

North American diarist. She lived her entire life in the Oyster Bay region of New York state. Married at fourteen to a farmer, and a religious mother of six, she devoted her life to the habits of agrarian life, including both field and household productivity. Her brief, staccato writing style in

▷ *The Diary of Mary Cooper* reflects how rare were her opportunities for the leisure of diary-writing; yet her six-year memoir also reveals a stalwart determination to record, however sparingly, her life-story.

Cooper, Susan Fenimore (1813–1894)

US writer of nature journals and biography, the latter in introductions to the work of her father, US writer James Fenimore Cooper (1789–1851). Her most noted work is *Rural Hours* (1850).

Copeland, Ann

Canadian short story writer, born in Hartford, Connecticut, and educated in Connecticut and Cornell University, New York State. She has taught literature and writing, and now lives in Sackville, New Brunswick. Her books include *At Peace* (1978), *The Back Room* (1979), and *Earthen Vessels* (1984). *The Golden Thread* (1989) is a powerful collection of stories about life inside a convent.

Copy of a Letter, lately written in meeter, by a Yonge Gentilwoman to her Unconstant Lover, A (?1567)

Verse epistle by ▷ Isabella Whitney. It is an early example of love poetry written in English by a woman. According to critic Betty Travitsky, it is 'the first published work in which an Englishwoman criticizes men'. Whitney's poem consists of thirty-five four-line stanzas written in the tradition of Ovid's *Heroides*. The female narrator addresses her ▷ letter to the lover who has abandoned her to marry another woman. The poem features a catalogue of faithless men, drawn from classical sources. Whitney skilfully maintains a consistently good-humoured tone while demonstrating a keen awareness of the sexual double standard of men's freedom and women's enforced passivity.
Bib: Travitsky, B., 'The Lady Doth Protest', *English Literary Renaissance*, 14 (1984).

Coquette; or, The History of Eliza Wharton, The (1797)

Epistolary novel by the North American novelist ▷ Hannah Webster Foster. Writing under the pseudonym of 'Lady of Massachusetts', Foster drew upon the factual history of Elizabeth Whitman's tragic life for the creation of this work. Whitman, who becomes the fictional Eliza Wharton, was seduced, left her home in Hartford, Connecticut, to give birth to an illegitimate child, and died shortly thereafter. In Foster's fictional rendering of this young woman's 'fall' from social grace, she draws upon the English tradition of seduction novels but converts the tale into a study of contemporary North American society, especially in terms of the double standard of morality that prevailed for women. As Eliza Wharton vacillates between her two suitors, the seemingly proper Reverend Boyer and the rake Major Sanford, she discovers that the counsel of family and friends is often at odds with the actions and attitudes of society. *The Coquette* was extraordinarily popular, going through thirteen editions in Foster's lifetime.

Coralina, Cora (1890–1985)

Brazilian poet, short story writer and chronicle writer, whose real name was Ana Lins dos Guimarães Peixoto Bretas. She lived all her life in Goiás Velho, a small 18th-century village. Her naïve poetry followed the oral tradition which was derived from the troubadours' art. *Meu livro de cordel* (1982) (*My Pamphlet Book*) is perhaps the best example of this. Other works include: *O cântico da volta* (1956) (*Song of Return*), *Poemas dos becos de Goiás e estórias mais* (1965) (*Poems of the Goiás Backwaters and Other Histories*) and *O vintém de cobre, as confissões de Aninha* (1982) (*The Copper Coin, the Confessions of Aninha*).

Corbin, Lucidor (18th century)

Creole political activist. Wrote the 'Hymne des citoyens de couleurs' ('Hymn of the Coloured Citizens') to the tune of the Marseillaise, which was published, together with her speech on universal freedom, 'Discours au Temple de la Raison' ('Speech at The Temple of Reason'), in *Les Femmes dans la Révolution française* (1982) (*Women in the French Revolution*).

▷French Revolution: pamphlets, registers of grievances, petitions and speeches

Cordelier, Jeanne

French novelist. Cordelier's most successful novel, *La Dérobade* (1976) (translated as *The Life*, 1978), is based on her own experiences as a prostitute in Paris. Written with Martine Laroche, the text provides a firsthand documentary of life 'on the game', and the violence of its language and content contrasts with the love and solidarity among the prostitutes themselves.

Corelli, Marie (1855–1924)

▷Pseudonym of British novelist, born in London and named Mary Mackay, the daughter of Scottish songwriter Charles Mackay. Although she had intended a career as a concert pianist, her first novel, *A Romance of Two Worlds* (1886) was so successful that she became a professional writer. Of her twenty-eight bestselling novels, *The Sorrows of Satan* (1895) did the most spectacular business, selling more copies than any other late-Victorian novel. Her fiction is ▷romantic and sensational as well as deeply religious. After 1901 she lived with her friend, Bertha Vyver, in Stratford-upon-Avon, and never married.

▷Sensation and sensational
Bib: Coates, E.G., *Life*.

Corinna (? 5th or 3rd century BC)

Poet, from Tanagra. There is much debate over her date, but most incline to the earlier. She wrote choral lyric poems in local dialect on local subjects (▷Myrtis). These included 'Boetus', the 'Seven Against Thebes', 'Eurynomie', 'Iolaus and the Return of Orion' and the poem *Orestes*.

Pausanias (2nd century BC) tells us her use of local dialect made her more popular than her male contemporary, Pindar (c 518–438 BC) of nearby Thebes. Surviving anecdotes have it that she jokingly told Pindar (who wrote very mythical poetry) to use more mythical material, and that she beat him five times in competition. The latter arises from a misunderstanding of a poem of Pindar's.

Three main fragments of Corinna's work survive. One describes a song contest between two famous Greek mountains, Cithaeron and Helicon, both connected with poetry. The second foretells the marriage of the daughters of Asopus. The third tells us the Muse of Dance called upon her to sing to the women of Tanagra. A lesser fragment refers disapprovingly to ▷Myrtis's rivalry, as a woman, with the male poet Pindar. Antipater of Thessalonica (2nd century BC) includes her as one of his nine women ▷Muses; her poetry was admired by the male Roman elegist Propertius (1st century AD). The Roman poet Statius (1st century AD) also admired her refined style.

▷Myia (II)
Bib: (text & trans.) Edmonds, J.M., *Lyra Graeca*.

Corinne, or Italy (1987)

Translation of ▷Madame de Staël's novel *Corinne ou l'Italie* (1807). A first-person retrospective narrative, its portrayal of Corinne illustrates the unease and suffering of a female genius unable fully to exercise her talents in a period when the hopes of women were being dashed on all sides. The novel also examines differences in national cultures, and includes lengthy dissertations on aesthetics and politics, while occasionally reading like a travelogue. The Anglo-Italian Corinne is crowned on the Capitol as the best Italian poet. She meets the melancholic Englishman, Oswald, a true romantic hero in the style of Werther, and helps him to discover Italy. Both are highly educated and sensitive, but their fundamentally different outlooks on life make them incompatible. Corinne, independent and unconventional, seeks to love freely, and refuses to bind Oswald to her. He returns to England to marry Lucille Edge, a paragon of conventional domesticated femininity. Corinne, the exceptional woman, dies alone and in despair.

Modern editions of this work are, in French, *Corinne ou l'Italie*, edited by S. Balayé (1985), and in English, *Corinne or Italy*, edited and translated by A. Goldberg (1987).

Corinne ou l'Italie (1807) ▷ *Corinne, or Italy* (1987)

Cornelia (2nd century AD)

Roman letter writer. Mother of two famous sons, Tiberius and Gaius Gracchus, and second daughter of Scipio Africanus, the conqueror of Hannibal. Cornelia was held as a model of Roman motherhood and was included in Plutarch's (c120–46 BC) *Lives of the Gracchi*. She bore twelve children, of whom only two sons and one daughter reached adulthood. She did not remarry after her husband's death, devoting her time to her children. Her culture was often noted; she knew Greek literature and spoke a Latin admired for its purity.

The Roman orator and politician Cicero (106–43 BC) mentions that her letters were the model of style. Two letters, but of dubious authenticity, survive under her name. They discourage her son Gaius from exacting violent revenge for the murder of his brother. Their tone leads some to judge them later fictions, as they conform to patterns of other such dissuasions that were a literary exercise at Rome. None the less they confirm her image as ideal Roman mother. The state tomb inscription reputedly ran simply 'Cornelia, mother of the Gracchi'.

Cornford, Frances (1886–1960)
English poet. She was born, and lived, in Cambridge. Cornford's verse has suffered from being critically regarded as 'modest', yet her style and subject matter should be viewed in terms of a dialogue with the poetry and poetics of her male peers in Cambridge, including her close friend, Rupert Brooke. *Collected Poems* (1954) includes the well-known triolet 'To a Fat Lady Seen from the Train'. Her other volumes include: *Autumn Midnight* (1923), *Travelling Home* (1948) and *On a Calm Shore* (1960).

Coronado, Carolina (1823–1911)
Spanish writer and polemicist, who opposed religious intolerance and pointed out the dangers for women who attempted to compete with men in cultural and humanistic pursuits. She lucidly portrayed the effects for women of double moral standards. Best known for her *Poesías* (1843) (*Poetry*), although she also wrote plays and novels.

Corpi, Lucha (born 1945)
US poet and short story writer. A ▷Latina, Corpi was born in Jaltipan, Veracruz, Mexico. At nineteen she emigrated to the US with her husband. Corpi graduated from the University of California at Berkeley. She helped found two Chicano arts organizations. Poems in *Palabras de mediodia/Noon Words* (1980) describe the woman writer's dilemma and the conflict between assuming domestic responsibilities and writing. Corpi's poetry portrays women's lives as shaped by circumstances. It features women who assume the responsibility of choice and who take all possible action before accepting their fate. In the four 'Marina' poems Corpi reinterprets historical circumstances from a woman's perspective, depicting Marina as a victim caught between two cultures, not an evil sorceress. In the story 'Los cristos del alma' (1983) Corpi describes the circumstances that exile a woman from her native culture.

Other works include: *Delia's Song* (1989).

Corps en pièces, Le (1977) (Body in Pieces)
A novel by the Algerian writer Zoulikha Boukortt. It is a description of the body of women in general, and Algerian women in particular. This body expresses life, claims an existence, asks for more respect and demands more rights.

Corpus, Aileen (born 1950)
Australian Aboriginal poet. Corpus's poems are mainly concerned with the double inequality of being black and being a woman. Her poems such as 'taxi conversation' – ('have you tried white men?/ why?/ how do they compare?/ compare with whom?/ with black men or do you only black?') – mostly deal with urban life in Redfern, a suburb of Sydney. 'blkfern jungle' attempts a phonetic transcription of Aboriginal speech. Both these poems appear in ▷ *The Penguin Book of Australian Women Poets*.

▷Aboriginal women's poetry in Australia

Correia, Hélia (born 1939)
Portuguese novelist. Like her contemporary, ▷Lídia Jorge, Correia writes about village life in 20th-century Portugal, drawing on myths and indigenous folklore to describe people living on the fringes of the modern industrialized world. But, unlike Jorge, Correia seems less concerned with historical or political issues and less inclined to a radical estrangement of novelistic technique. She focuses instead on the emotional lives of provincial characters, and her novels employ a Gothic, psychological mode – sometimes involving Gothic themes in the context of realistic social satire and sometimes blending them with fantastic or folkloric motifs. By this means she attempts to suggest what Freud called the 'return' of the repressed, especially in the sexual lives of women in small puritanical communities.

Her first two novels, *O Separar das Águas* (1981) (*The Parting of the Waters*) and *O Número dos Vivos* (1982) (*The Number of the Living*), focus on middle-class women brought up in the claustrophobic environment of the family and the home. The issues of maternity, female sexuality and oppression raised in these two novels reappear in a slightly different form in Correia's third and most interesting book to date, *Montedemo* (1983) (*Devil Mountain*), about an entire village's reaction to a forbidden sexuality. This novella was so successful that it was dramatized and performed on stage in Lisbon in 1987.

Correia, Natália (born 1923)
Portuguese poet, novelist and dramatist. Born on the island of São Miguel in the Azores, Correia was educated in Lisbon. A flamboyant figure and prolific writer, she began her career in 1947 with the publication of a book of poems, *Rio de Nuvens* (*River of Clouds*). Identified with the surrealist movement in Portugal, she edited the collection *O Surrealismo na Poesia Portuguesa*. Her most recent volume of poems, *Sonetos Românticos* (1990), is devoted to the theme of *saudade* (longing), a motif

in 19th-century Portuguese verse. In addition to poetry Correia has also written a number of important plays, one of which, *O Encoberto* (*The Concealed One*) was banned by the government in 1969. An outspoken opponent of the Salazar dictatorship, she was responsible for publishing the controversial *Novas Cartas Portuguesas* (▷ *The Three Marias: New Portuguese Letters*) – an act for which she could have been imprisoned. Correia's articles and creative writing can be found in most of the major literary reviews and journals in Portugal. Long associated with the political left, she is currently an independent representative in the Portuguese parliament.

▷ *Cantigas de mal dizer e escárnio*

Correspondence of Maria van Rensselaer, 1669–1689 (1935)

This North American text collects the twenty-year correspondence of ▷ Maria van Cortlandt van Rensselaer who, after her husband's death, was administrator of the colony of Rennsselaerswych in New Netherland (later New York). Unlike most 17th-century women in the New World, van Rensselaer had a position of authority, however tenuous. The correspondence collected in this text details how she supported her position through her intelligence and an awareness of her property rights, and her struggles against the declining future of the colony, which was about to come under British control.

▷ Early North American letters

Correspondences: A Family History in Letters (1974)

Poem sequence in epistolary form by British-based American poet ▷ Anne Stevenson, *Correspondences* traces the history of the Chandlers, a representative middle-class New England family, from 1828 to 1972. The sequence is made up of letters, journals, obituaries, a news report and a family tree, creating a powerful mixture of documentary ▷ realism and poetic force. The form allows Stevenson to investigate the history of both the family and the US society for which it is a metaphor, from the viewpoint of the women whom that history has traditionally marginalized. A series of letters convey, the tension between the intellectual vigour of the women and the futility of their ambitions in the face of familiar obligations and respectability. Only the contemporary poet Kay Boyd escapes after a disastrous marriage and mental breakdown, writing to her sister and father from a self-imposed exile in Britain: 'Kay Boyd, the woman, the writer, has survived' but 'It is a poem I can't continue. / It is American I can't contain'.

Stevenson is noticeably happiest with the figure of the serious intellectual woman, by contrast with the frivolous Southern Belle who has the misfortune to marry a Chandler. However, the letters from the Chandler men are extremely successful explorations of the relationship between a rigid puritan morality and the business principles of the Victorian family. *Correspondences*

remains Anne Stevenson's most formally experimental and exciting work.

Cortegiane oneste

An Italian term meaning 'honest courtesans' used by certain women poets of the 16th century to define themselves. Some of these writers are generally considered as courtesans, free to move in the upper echelons of society as a result of their sexual favours. The women poets themselves claim that their *onestà* (honesty) resides in the fact that they rarely used their sexuality indiscriminately. In other words, these were intelligent, artistically gifted, physically attractive women who claimed their right to be free of restrictive relationships, and who appear to have simply exercised sexual self-determination in a time when this was well outside the norm. ▷ Tullia D'Aragona, ▷ Veronica Franco, and ▷ Gaspara Stampa are arguably the three most famous women poets to define themselves in this way.

Bib: Bassanese, F.A., 'What's in a Name? Self-naming and Renaissance Women Poets', *Annali d'Italianistica*, 7, 1989, pp. 104–16.

Corti, Maria (born 1915)

Italian philologist, literary critic and writer of fiction. Primarily known, until very recently, for her academic work, Maria Corti's research interests include the history of the Italian language, ▷ poetry of the *stil nuovo*, and the Neapolitan lyric tradition of the 1400s. She began to write literary criticism in 1947, and extended her scope to include literature in 1962. She lectured in Italian at the University of Pavia, and is now professor emeritus. Her first work of fiction, *L'ora di tutti* (1962) (*Everyone's Time*), centres on a southern Italian community under the shadow of invasion. Her other non-academic works return often to the topic of the relationship between criticism and creative writing, and the difficulties of doing both. This theme surfaces in ▷ *Il ballo dei sapienti* (1966) (*The Dance of the Sages*), and also in one of the stories in *Il canto delle sirene* (1989) (*The Sirens' Song*).

Corti's other works include articles on Guido Cavalcanti, on *stil nuovo* poetry, and on Dante, as well as the collection *Voci dal Nord Est* (1986) (*Voices from the North-east*), subtitled *American Notebook*.

Cortines, Júlia (1868–1948)

Brazilian poet whose full name was Júlia Cortines Laxe. She was brought up on a farm by her grandmother, then moved to Niterói, Rio de Janeiro, where she studied by herself, becoming a teacher at twelve. Her first book of poems, *Versos* (1894) (*Verses*), was Parnassian. She published impressions of her travels in Europe in a column called 'Across a Life', in the newspaper *O País*. She remained unmarried.

Cosima (1937)

Published posthumously, this novel written in Italian by ▷Grazia Deledda tells, in fictional third-person form, the story of the author's childhood, adolescence and youth, including the tale of her unhappy first love (Cosima was her second name). It is particularly interesting in its chronicling of the difficulties faced by a woman who also wants to be a writer, growing up in a hostile environment. It is unusual in that it is the only one of Deledda's works which can truly be said to have a strong autobiographical content. It includes a lyrical description of the countryside and validates the existence of a dream-world, full of legend.

Cosson de La Cressonière, Charlotte Cathérine (1740–1813)

French poet. Born in Mézières, she added the aristocratic-sounding de La Cressonière to her name, evoking a watercress spring of which she was fond. In 1768 she went to Paris to join her student brother. Penniless after his death, she made money by writing poetry on public events, such as *Lamentations sur la mort du dauphin*, (1766) (*Lament on the Death of the Dauphin*) and *Ode sur l'incendie de l'Hotel-Dieu de Paris* (1773) (*Poem on the Fire at the Hotel-Dieu in Paris*). Her poetry, ballads, allegories and vaudeville pieces were published in several journals, including the *Mercure de France*, *Journal des Dames* (*Ladies' Journal*), *L'Année littéraire* (*The Literary Year*) and the *Journal de la littérature* (*Literary Review*). She is thought to have collaborated on a pedagogical essay, *De l'éducation physique et morale des femmes* (1799) (*On the Physical and Moral Education of Women*), which includes an alphabetical listing of 'illustrious women'.

Bib: D'Hébrail, J., *France littéraire*; Bouillot, l'abbé, *Biographie Ardennaise*.

Costa, Emília de Sousa (1877–?)

Portuguese biographer, essayist and author of children's literature. She is perhaps best known for her children's books which appeared in the series *Biblioteca Infantil (Children's Library)* and *Biblioteca dos Pequeninos (Little Ones' Library)*. She also translated *Grimms' Fairy Tales* into Portuguese. In addition to biographical studies of the 19th-century Portuguese poet Guerra Junqueiro and ▷Maria Amália Vaz de Carvalho, she wrote several feminist works, among them *Idéias Antigas da Mulher Moderna* (1923) (*Ancient Ideas of the Modern Woman*) and *Olhai a Malícia e a Maldade das Mulheres* (1932) (*Look at the Maliciousness and Evil of Women*). She worked as a teacher and formed an organization to subsidize the education of poor and working-class girls.

Costa, Maria Velho da (born 1938)

Portuguese novelist and short story writer. One of the ▷'Three Marias', whose collaborative book ▷*Novas Cartas Portuguesas* was banned by the Salazar/Caetano regime. Unlike ▷Barreno and ▷Horta, Costa felt that both women and men were oppressed in Portuguese society, and she disassociated herself from *Novas Cartas Portuguesas* when, following the revolution, feminist groups used the book as a banner for their cause. Prior to writing *Novas Cartas Portuguesas*, she had authored a volume of short fiction and the novel *Maina Mendes* (1969). From 1975 to 1978 she served as President of the Portuguese Association of Writers, and in 1978 she was awarded the City of Lisbon Prize for her novel *Casas Pardas (Brown Houses)*. Costa is widely regarded as one of Portugal's pre-eminent novelists; her works experiment with literary form, and most, like her highly successful novel *Lúcialima* (1983), focus on the lives of middle-class women. Her novel *Missa in Albis* (1988) is considered by many to be her best work to date. A lecturer at King's College in London for several years, she recently finished a term as Portugal's cultural attaché in Cape Verde.

Costumbrismo

In the Spanish American novel, a literary style that realistically describes the customs of a region or country. In Brazil this type of novel is called the *romance de costumes*. During the 19th century, the style was used in both romanticism and ▷realism-naturalism. It can refer to the colonial natives, as in ▷*criollismo*. In the mid-20th century this genre also became evident in newspapers. Women writers who excelled in this style in the 20th century were the Argentinian ▷Ema de la Barra de Llanos, who published ▷*Stella* (1905) under the pen-name César Duayen, describing Buenos Aries in picturesque detail, and the Venezuelan ▷Teresa de la Parra, whose ▷*Ifigenia* (1924) is a lively portrait of Caracas.

Cottenjé, Mireille (born 1933)

Flemish prose writer and dramatist. She worked as a nurse in Zaire, and described her experiences in the novel *Lava* (1973). In her first novel, *Dagboek van Carla* (1968) (*Diary of Carla*), a young woman breaks free from the enslaving bonds of marriage, a theme further explored in her later work. Her second, and best, novel, *Eeuwige zomer* (1969) (*Eternal Summer*), was written to rid herself of the frustrations that had resulted from a hiking tour through Lapland with the writer Jef Geerarts. *Met 13 van tafel* (1978) (*Thirteen Women Stepping Out*) and *Dertien mannen van tafel* (1980) (*Thirteen Men Stepping Out*) are collections of interviews with divorced men and women. Cottenjé joined the emancipation movement, and is a socially-involved writer. In addition to collections of stories, she published the novels *Muren doorbreken* (1980) (*Breaking Through the Walls*), *De verkeerde minnaar* (1982) (*The Wrong Lover*) and *Wisselspoor* (1991) (*Swith Rail*). Her last books can be compared with novels of Yvonne Keuls.

▷Children's literature (The Netherlands); Meinkema, Hannes

Cottin, Sophie (1770–1807)

French novelist. Brought up in Bordeaux, and married young, Cottin was widowed at twenty-three, after which she lived in Paris. Her life, particularly her emotional life, was turbulent, and her five novels, which were very popular, are sentimental in the extreme. All deal with the theme of passion and its effects. In *Claire d'Albe* (1799) she recounts, in fictionalized form, romantic episodes from her own life. *Mathilde, ou mémoires tirés de l'histoire des Croisades* (1805) (*Mathilde, or Memoirs from the History of the Crusades*) was the product of her friendship with the historian Joseph Michaud (1767–1839). *Elisabeth ou les exilés de Sibérie* (1806) (*Elisabeth, or the Siberian Exiles*) retraces the journey of a young girl who travels from Siberia to St Petersburg to plead with the tsar for an end to her father's exile. Cottin also wrote *Malvina* (1804) and *Amélie Mansfield* (1803). The poet Victor Hugo (1802–1885) noted in 1817 that she was considered by many to be the most accomplished novelist of her time.

Coudray, Madame Le Boursier du (18th century)
French midwife. Madame du Coudray, appalled by women's general lack of knowledge about their own bodies, travelled throughout France with an articulated doll which she designed herself, teaching the principles of her profession. The manual which she published, *Abrégé de l'art de l'accouchement* (1773) (*A Summary of the Art of Childbirth*), included colour plates and was praised by contemporary doctors as admirably clear and competent.
Bib: Albistur, M. and Armgathe, D., *Histoire du féminisme français*.

Counterfeit Life, A (1975)
▷Inna Varlámova's novel, written in Russian and translated into English in 1988, uses the cancer hospital as a psychological crucible (▷Voznesénskaia's ▷*The Women's Decameron*). Undergoing a mastectomy forces Nora, a writer, to reassess a life that Varlámova portrays as a summary of the Soviet experience of exile, repression, and physical labour. The rough camaraderie of the hospital brings her friendship with women of various classes and types. As Nora comes to realize the hollowness of her marriage to a conforming journalist, a saintly Romanian fellow patient offers her love and validation of her desirability despite the loss of her breast.

Country Doctor, A (1884)
US novel by ▷Sarah Orne Jewett. A largely autobiographical account of Jewett's childhood with her physician father, the novel follows the life of Nan Prince as she naturally develops a talent for medicine and ultimately chooses a life as a physician over marriage to a most eligible suitor. The tone and technique of *A Country Doctor* change in the course of the novel, fittingly paralleling the plot, and recalling and forecasting the course of US fiction. The opening shows Nan's dissolute mother carrying her child, as she staggers across fields in a storm, attempting to

bring her child home to her mother before her own collapse and death. The melodrama, Gothic elements, traditional morality and sentiment mark an earlier era in US fiction, though some of these effects are undercut by the fine characterization and realism which come to dominate the book. By the end of the novel, increasing lyricism, focus on nature and triumphant bonding between Nan and nature presage the later work of ▷Willa Cather, especially Cather's ▷*My Antonia* (1918).

Country Girl Again and Other Stories (1985)
Short stories by Australian writer ▷Jean Bedford. These stories exemplify the realist tradition in contemporary Australian women's writing. They are also within a tradition of discontinuous narrative – a series of interconnected stories involving the same characters – in Australian fiction, for the stories present aspects of the lives of a group of related characters. In their grim realism concerning life in both the bush and the city they challenge any easy, optimistic version of Australian life.
▷Short story (Australia)

Country of the Pointed Firs, The (1896)
US collection of New England sketches by ▷Sarah Orne Jewett. The stories are narrated by a summer boarder who much resembles the author. Set in Jewett's native Maine, these sketches of character, place and the economic decline of a New England seaport town are considered the finest examples of US ▷local color literature, notable for their perfection of style, description and characterization. ▷Willa Cather thought this collection one of the finest examples of US literature. Like Jewett's other work, it shows crossed and long-delayed love; characters trapped in themselves and their traditional ideas, disengaged from humanity and symptomatic of New England's decline; and characters whose native dignity and humanity are small versions of the heroic.

Coup de grâce (1957)
Translation of *Le Coup de grâce* (1939), novel by French writer ▷Marguerite Yourcenar. In this early novel, three young aristocrats play out their personal and social dramas against the background of the Bolshevik Revolution (1917) in Central Europe, and a neat parallel is drawn between sexual politics and large-scale power games.

Courths-Mahler, Hedwig (1867–1950)
German popular novelist. The illegitimate child of a farmer's daughter, she grew up neglected and ignored. She began to write at an early age, modelling herself on ▷Eugenie Marlitt, but her first novel *Scheinehe* (1905) (*Phoney Marriage*) did not appear until she was thirty-eight. From then on, she published more than 200 novels, in editions totalling over 40 million copies, and she remains, to this day, the most widely-read of German novelists. Her plots are invariably

fantasies about petty bourgeois heroines who achieve happiness by marrying rich and aristocratic men.

Coutinho, Sônia (born 1939)

Brazilian short story writer, novelist, journalist and translator whose full name is Sônia Valquíria de Sousa Coutinho. She has lived in Rio since 1968. Her novel *O jogo de Ifá* (1980) (*The Game of Ifá*) presents the split between past and present; Bahia, where she was born, and Rio; negro and white civilizations, and male and female roles. The stories of *Os venenos de Lucrécia* (1978) (*The Poisons of Lucretia*) and *O último verão de Copacabana* (1985) (*The Last Summer of Copacabana*) and the novel *Atire em Sofia* (1989) (*Shot in Sofia*) focus on emancipated women characters and postmodernism.

Couvreur, Jessie (1848–1897)

Australian colonial novelist. The daughter of Anglo-French and Dutch parents and born in London, Couvreur was brought to Tasmania in the 1850s. Her marriage to Charles Frazer in 1867 broke down through his gambling and infidelity and they were divorced in 1883. She married Belgian politician and journalist Auguste Couvreur and settled in Brussels, where she succeeded her husband as Brussels correspondent for *The Times*. She also lectured in France and Belgium on Australian affairs and was prominent in political, social and philosophical circles on the continent.

Writing usually under the pseudonym of 'Tasma', Couvreur contributed to the *Australasian* and the *Australian Journal*, the *Melbourne Review* and other annuals. Her six novels, ▷ *Uncle Piper of Piper's Hill* (1889), *In her Earliest Youth* (1890), *The Penance of Portia James* (1891), *A Knight of the White Feather* (1892), *Not Counting the Cost* (1895) and *A Fiery Ordeal* (1897) are largely concerned with problems within marriage, particularly the plight of women married to boorish, brutal, domineering or weak husbands. She also published *A Sydney Sovereign and Other Tales* (1890) and *Incidents and Scenes in Melbourne Life* (1892). 'Tasma' is usually grouped with ▷ Ada Cambridge and ▷ Rosa Praed, other romance writers of Australian colonial times.

▷ Short story (Australia); *From the Verandah; On Her Selection; Peaceful Army, The*

Couzyn, Jeni (born 1942)

South African poet who left for England in 1966, living first there, and more recently in British Columbia. She has published her poetry in six volumes: *Flying* (1970), *Monkeys' Wedding* (1972), *Christmas in Africa* (1975), *The Happiness Bird* (1978), *House of Changes* (1979), and *Life by Drowning* (1983). The last volume reprints some earlier work, as well as a powerful new sequence of poems on carrying and giving birth to a child. She also compiled *The Bloodaxe Book of Women's Poetry*, which includes some South African material.

Couzyn's poetry, strikingly passionate and often agonizingly beautiful, is deeply personal and familial, and yet also profoundly political: reaching back to her childhood, for instance, as well as dealing with the ordinary terrors of everyday adult life in a world beyond decency. In other poems, she celebrates joy and beauty. Equally at home in the narrative and lyric modes, her formal technique is closely aligned with her sense of subject. Her poetry retains a surprisingly strong South African feeling, despite its British and North American influence, and its affinities with ▷ exile.

Coward, Rosalind

British ▷ poststructuralist feminist critic, journalist and lecturer, who has taught visual communications at Goldsmith's College, London, and media studies at Reading University. Coward regularly contributes to the *Guardian* newspaper's women's page. *Female Desire: Women's Sexuality Today* (1984) analyzes the role of popular culture (romantic fiction, women's magazines, fashion, food and photography) in constructing and marketing female desire and identity. A concern with ▷ mass culture extends to the popularizing of theory itself, which is presented in a highly readable form.

Other publications include: (with John Ellis) *Language and Materialism* (1977), an early revision of traditional Marxist ideology in the light of poststructuralist theories of language and subjectivity; *Patriarchal Precedents* (1983), a critical history of the family and sexual relations since the 19th century, and *The Whole Truth: The Myth of Alternative Medicine* (1989), a critique of self-help therapy.

Cow-Boy, Le (1983) ▷ Cow-Boy, The

Cow-Boy, The (1987)

Translation of *Le Cow-Boy* (1985), first novel by Algerian writer, ▷ Djanet Lachmet. A French boy dresses up as a cow-boy for a school party and becomes an object of desire for Lallia, an Algerian girl. Lallia comes from a well-known family, is influenced by the Muslim Algerian society on one hand and her French education on the other. She also becomes aware of the Algerian struggle for independence. Lallia's mother identifies with her class and tradition and is very much a role model for Lallia. The traditional world of women is very well described in the *hammam* (the turkish bath) which symbolizes femininity. These women can feel free to give attention to their bodies, despite the fact that the intention of this beauty care in the *hammam* is to please men.

Lallia's relationships with René, the French boy, and two working-class Algerian girls, Zineb and Kheira, symbolize the opposing values of the colonizers and the indigenous (colonized) people. According to Judith Still, they 'have to do with the unknown'. Although it traces Lallia's growing awareness of the politics of liberation, the novel ends in a confusion of death, nightmare and

sadness. The clear sentences and uncomplicated syntax of *The Cow-Boy* give a calculated impression of simplicity and naïvety.
Bib: Still, Judith, *Body and culture: The representation of sexual, racial and class differences in Lachmet's Le Cow-Boy.*

Cowles, Julia (1785–1803)
North American diarist. She was born on 18 October 1785 in Farmington, Connecticut, to Mary Lewis and Zenas Cowles. The Cowleses' advocacy of education led them to send her to Sarah Pierce's Female Academy in Litchfield when she was eleven years old. At that time she began the journal that she would maintain until her death at the age of eighteen. ▷ *The Diaries of Julia Cowles* detail the manner of education that young women received at the better academies, her leisure reading and, obviously of most interest to her, her social life. As she becomes aware of her failing health, however, the diaries become more focused on issues of mortality.

Cowley, Cassia Joy (born 1936)
New Zealand novelist and story writer. Joy Cowley began writing when pregnant with her fourth child, her ambition being to publish a story in *The New Zealand Listener*. Her first novel was published when she was in her thirties and received much critical attention in New Zealand and elsewhere. Since then Cowley has published five more novels, many short stories, and contributed more than fifty children's reading books to the Price Milburn (PM) School Readers System. This is now widely used outside as well as in New Zealand, and features a huge range of graduated stories, many by established writers.
Cowley's adult fiction centres on the lives of (often elderly) women, investigating what she has referred to as 'that heart of being which is cosmic and eternal' ('Prologue', *Heart Attack and Other Stories*, 1985). Cowley's characters are often located on the margins of conventional society, and all her fiction implies the fragility as well as the value of domestic and family life.
Publications include: ▷ *Nest in a Falling Tree* (1967); *Man of Straw* (1970); *Of Men and Angels* (1973); *The Mandrake Root* (1975); *The Growing Season* (1978); *The Silent One* (1981).

Cowley, Hannah (Parkhouse) (1743–1809)
English dramatist and poet. Her first play was *The Runaway* (1776), followed by successful comedies, such as *The Belle's Stratagem* (1780) and *A Bold Stroke For a Husband* (1783). She also wrote a revised version of ▷ Aphra Behn's *The Lucky Chance* (1686), called *A School for Greybeards* (1786).

Cowman, Roz (born 1942)
Irish poet. Born in Cork, she lived in East and West Africa for several years, and now teaches in adult education in Cork. She received an Irish Arts Council Bursary in 1982, and was awarded the Patrick Kavanagh Poetry Prize in 1985. Her first collection, *The Goose Herd*, appeared in 1989.

Craddock, Charles Egbert ▷ Murfree, Mary Noailles

Craig, Christine
Caribbean poet, short story writer and dramatist. She was born and educated in Jamaica, where she graduated with an honours degree in English from the University of the West Indies. She has worked with the Jamaican Women's Bureau. She was awarded a Fellowship to the International Writers Programme at Iowa University, USA. Her first published works were the texts for two full-colour children's books produced by her artist husband (1970). She has produced several non-fiction publications and training manuals on feminist and health topics, as well as radio and television scripts. Her first collection of poems, *Quadrille for Tigers*, was published in 1984. Her poetry is included in ▷ *Jamaica Woman*, ▷ *Creation Fire*, and one of her short stories is in ▷ *Her True True Name*.

Craik, Dinah Mulock (1826–1887)
British novelist and essayist, also wrote poetry and short stories. She was born in Stoke-on-Trent and helped to support her family by writing prolifically. She married George Craik in 1865. Her first novel was *The Ogilvies* (1849), and her most famous ▷ *John Halifax, Gentleman* (1856). Craik's fiction is predominantly ▷ sentimental and romantic, but it also questions traditional sex roles and often depicts female characters attempting to discover autonomous identities. Her novels include *The Head of the Family* (1852); *Agatha's Husband* (1853); *Christian's Mistake* (1865) and *The Woman's Kingdom* (1869). Her non-fiction includes *A Woman's Thoughts About Women* (1858); *Plain Speaking* (1882); and *Concerning Men and Other Papers* (1888). These essays address the need for female self-reliance, offering advice to women on ways to gain independence. She was not a radical writer, but nevertheless contributed to the exploration of woman's role in the Victorian period.
Bib: Foster, S., *Victorian Women's Fiction: Marriage, Freedom and the Individual.*

Crampton, Mary ▷ Pym, Barbara

Crampton, Tom ▷ Pym, Barbara

Cranch, Elizabeth (1743–1811)
North American diarist. Born in Braintree, Massachusetts, on 21 November 1743, she was the niece of ▷ Abigail Smith Adams and had many connections with the Adams family and other politically and religiously oriented families. In 1785, while visiting another aunt in Haverhill, she began ▷ *The Journal of Elizabeth Cranch*. Although not contemplative, the journal details the everyday life of an upper-class young woman in the post-revolutionary years. She eventually

married a clergyman and raised a family in Weymouth.

Cranford (1851–1853)

A novel by ▷Elizabeth Gaskell, published serially in *Household Words* (edited by Charles Dickens). The best-known of Mrs Gaskell's works, it is set in the town of Cranford, based on Knutsford in Cheshire where the author grew up. The book describes the predominantly female society of the town, centring on two main characters, Miss Deborah Jenkyns and her sister Miss Matty, daughters of the former rector. The novel became an instant success, enjoyed for its humorous observations and sensitive portraits. More recently, it has been re-read by feminist critics, who have focused on the community of women in Cranford and argued that Gaskell depicts an alternative, cooperative vision. A discussion of recent feminist criticism of the novel can be found in Patsy Stoneman's *Elizabeth Gaskell* (1987).

Craven, Pauline (1808–1891)

French novelist and historical and autobiographical writer. A Frenchwoman born in London, Craven began her literary career at the age of 58 with the excessively spiritual *Récit d'une soeur, souvenirs de famille* (1866) (*Tale of a Sister: Family Recollections*). This work recounts the history of her brother's marriage to a Swedish woman of the Lutheran faith. It was enormously successful (especially in religious circles) and was followed by two other publications in the same vein: *Le Travail d'une âme, étude d'une conversion* (1877) (*A Soul in Travail: Account of a Conversion*) and *Une Année de méditations* (1881) (*A Year of Meditation*). Craven also wrote the novels *Anne Séverin* (1868), *Fleurange* (1871), *Le Mot de l'Enigme* (1874) (*The Key to the Riddle*), *Eliane* (1882), and *Le Valbriant* (1886), and biographical and historical studies. The mood of her writing is contemplative, and at times rather sombre.

Crawford, Isabella Valancy (1850–1887)

Canadian poet, born in Dublin. Her family emigrated first to Wisconsin in the United States, and then to Canada in 1857, living in Paisley and Lakefield, where they were acquainted with ▷Catherine Parr Traill, and later in Peterborough, Ontario. Crawford's writing was essential to support her impoverished family, which suffered adversity because of her father's alcoholism and his abuse of public funds. In her early twenties she won a $600 prize in a short story competition. Her father died in 1875, and she and her mother moved to Toronto. Her literary reputation is based largely on her narrative poems, although she wrote short stories and novellas for US magazines, her work appearing from 1872 on. In her lifetime she published, at her own expense, only one book, *Old Spookses' Pass, Malcolm's Katie, and Other Poems* (1884), which was a critical but not a commercial success. Her poetry is uncollected, although four volumes were made available: *Old Spookses' Pass* (1884,

reissued in 1886 and 1898, but full of errors), a carelessly edited *The Collected Poems of Isabella Valancy Crawford* (1905), the selected anthology *Isabella Valancy Crawford* (1923), and *Hugh and Ion* (1977), a poem found by ▷Dorothy Livesay buried in Crawford's manuscript material at Queen's University. Crawford's fiction is also uncollected, with only a small portion available through the work of various editors in *Selected Stories of Isabella Valancy Crawford* (1975), *Fairy Tales of Isabella Valancy Crawford* (1977), and *The Halton Boys: a Story for Boys* (1979). Her fiction reveals a skilful employment of 19th-century devices for suspense and resolution. She is most famous for the narrative poem, 'Malcolm's Katie', which employs Indian legends to position a love story. Her writing is now recognized as a powerfully mythopaeic vision of the Canadian landscape, and as revealing 'profound and original insight into the complexities of her age', but there is much work still to be done on her. She died in poverty.

Bib: Burns, R., *Isabella Valancy Crawford and Her Works*; Tierney, F. (ed.), *The Isabella Valancy Crawford Symposium*.

Creation Fire: A CAFRA Anthology of Caribbean Women's Poetry (1990)

A ▷CAFRA initiative, this anthology of Caribbean poetry, edited by ▷Ramabai Espinet includes poems in English, Spanish, Dutch and French, accompanied by translations into English of those originally written in other languages.

Creider, Jane Tapsubei

Kenyan writer and artist now living in Canada. Creider grew up near Lake Nyanza in Kenya and went to live in Canada after working in Kisumu and Nairobi. She is married with two children and works as an artist in clay sculpture in Ontario. She has written an introduction to Nandi culture and a dictionary of the Nandi language. Her articles on Nandi language and culture have appeared in the *Journal of African Languages and Linguistics* and *Anthropos*. She plans to write stories for children in the Nandi language. Her *Two Lives: My Spirit and I* (1986) is two autobiographies in one; the life of the author and that of the first Tapsubei, of whom she believes she is a reincarnation.

'Creidhe's Lament'

▷Old Irish poem. A verse lament of Creidhe for her husband, Caol, who has been drowned while fighting against foreigners. The story is part of the Fenian Cycle, one of the Old Irish prose sagas. These prose narratives were interspersed with lyrics and verse dialogues.

▷'Deirdre's Farewell to Scotland'; 'Liadain and Curithir'

Crenne, Hélisenne de (1510/1520–c 1550)

French novelist and translator. Pen-name assumed by Marguerite de Briet, who was born in Picardy and was married at a very young age to a *'petit seigneur de Cresnes'* and may have spent much of her time at the court of François I (1494–1547). She apparently herself chose the unusual name Hélisenne, which she also gave to the semi-autobiographical heroine of her three-part novel, known by the title of the first volume *Les Angoisses douloureuses qui procedent d'amours* (1538) (▷ *The Painful Anxieties Which Proceed from Love*), which enjoyed an immediate success. The novel tells the adventures of a bored young wife, who falls in love with an attractive young man, Guinelic. Held prisoner in a tower by her husband, she decides to write her own story. Municipal and legal documents of the time indicate that much of part I is factual, and has been called the first feminine journal in French. The second and third parts of the novel, in the tradition of chivalric fiction, were less popular. The second book, *Les Epistres familieres et invectives* (1539) (*Familiar and Invective Letters*), narrated by Guinelic, retells the adventures of part I in epistolary form, and has been described as the first attempt at the progressive construction of a story through letters, without the use of a connective frame.

There is a marked feminism in Crenne's work. She was the first French woman writer to have dedicated her work to a whole sex of '*lisantes*' (women readers) and to '*toutes honnestes dames*' ('all honest ladies'), and continually to address her female reader throughout the text. Anticipating the ▷ *Heptaméron* of ▷ Marguerite de Navarre, Hélisenne de Crenne also condemned sexual passion and defended a neo-platonic view of love. She appropriated extensively from the work of male writers and the widely shared male tradition of courtly love, where the woman is frequently held captive by a cruel husband. Paule Demats's edition of the text provides a twenty-page list of borrowings from just three sources: the French translations of *Fiametta* by the Italian writer Boccaccio (1313–1375); *Peregrino* by Caviceo; *Les Illustrations de Gaule et singularitez de Troie* by Jean Lemaire de Belges (1473–?1515). However, it has been persuasively argued that deliberate use of male sources and traditions makes *Les Angoisses douloureuses* a woman's counter-text. As she herself reworked in captivity the text her husband had burned, Crenne defended the woman's role as a writer and intellectual and the right of her sex to '*monster leurs louables oeuvres*' ('show their praiseworthy work'). The work closes with Guinelic's friend's discovery of Hélisenne's book. Crenne had a sound classical education and also produced the first prose translation of Books I–IV of the *Aeneid* in French (1541), dedicated to François I.

Bib: Stone, D., *From Tales to Truths: essays on French fiction in the XVIth century*; Ching, B., 'French Feminist Theory, Literary History, and Hélisenne de Crenne's *Les Angoysses douloureuses*', in *French Literature Series*, XVI (1989).

Creole
A term often used in the Caribbean region to describe white people born in the Caribbean.

Historically the term has undergone different meanings, in the past being applied to both blacks and whites born in the Caribbean. Both ▷ Jean Rhys and ▷ Phyllis Shand Allfrey were ▷ Dominican-born whites and are termed Creoles.
▷ Nation language; Language continuum

Creolized
This term indicates the process of change involved in adapting to the new Caribbean environment. African, European and other imported influences were subject to such changes as they fused with each other and with the ancestral cultures of the region, and evolved as a unique culture and language. This term is of relevance to an understanding of Caribbean writing.

Crepuscolarismo (Italy)
A term coined in 1910 by critic Giuseppe Antonio Borgese, using the image of the *crepuscolo* (sunset/twilight) to describe what he saw as the slow agony of Italian poetry of the period. It became widely used to define the then popular style of subdued tone, colloquial structure and colourless language, which accompanied the poet's sense of detachment from the world around her/him, and her/his uncertainty about the value of poetry itself. Women poets who used this genre include ▷ Maria Borgese Freschi and ▷ Amalia Guglielminetti.

Créqui, Renée-Caroline-Victoire Froulay, Marquise de (1714–1803)
French woman of letters. Born into an aristocratic family, she was orphaned at an early age, and raised by her maternal grandmother. Widowed in 1741, in middle age she was reputed to be a moderate, tolerant and religious woman. Her views on the position of women were conservative, and she was critical of the more progressive ideas of ▷ Stéphanie de Genlis. Among her friends were Rousseau and Sénac de Meilhan. Her letters to the latter for the period 1782–1789 were published in 1856 with a preface by Sainte-Beuve. The *Souvenirs de la marquise de Créqui* (1834–35) (*Recollections of the Marquise de Créqui*) are generally regarded as inauthentic, and have been attributed to the male author Causen.
Bib: Henriot, E., *D'Héloïse à Marie Bashkirtsseff*; Lescure, M. de, *Les Femmes philosophes*; Tisseau, P., *La Marquise de Créqui*.

Crick Crack Monkey (1970)
In this novel by the Caribbean writer ▷ Merle Hodge, the heroine, Tee, grows up amid the class and cultural confusions in ▷ Trinidad in the mid-20th century. Intelligent and sensitive, she suffers from insecurity and self-rejection when moved from a humane lower-class world into the artificial and prententious world of the middle classes. The novel deals with Trinidadian socio-political realities, the central role of education and the aspirations and attitudes reflected in the education

system. Hodge uses ▷Carnival to explore the two worlds her heroine is forced to occupy. Tee's response to Carnival becomes a mirror of her inner conflict and divided self.

See Roy Narinesingh's critical introduction to the 1981 paperback edition (Heinemann) for a useful explanation of the novel's major concerns.
▷ *Fifty Caribbean Writers*

Crimes of the Heart (1979)

US dramatist Beth Henley won a Pulitzer Prize for this play, which has also been made into a successful film. She was born in Jackson, Mississippi, in 1952.

Set in Hazelhurst, Mississippi, *Crimes of the Heart* focuses on the McGrath sisters. When they were children, their father abandoned them and their mother hung herself. Raised by grandparents, the sisters are struggling against partiarchal strictures on the ▷Southern lady. Because she cannot bear children, Lenny forsakes romance to care for her grandfather. Feeling she cannot allow herself to care, Meg forsakes romance for an unsuccessful singing career. Babe cannot tolerate her domineering husband, and eventually shoots him. Each sister learns not to subordinate herself to pleasing Southern patriarchy, and to define and pursue her own happiness. Having been emotionally crippled by this ▷patriarchy, they discover they can love. At the end of the play they are able to overcome their differences to celebrate their sisterhood.

Other works include: *Am I Blue* (1973), *The Miss Firecracker Contest* (1980), *The Wake of Jamey Foster* (1982), *The Debutante Ball* (1985) and *The Lucky Spot* (1986).

Criollismo

The *criollo* (possibly from the verb *criar* to raise, to suckle) is a native of Spanish America who is descended from the Spanish. The term is related to ▷ *costumbrismo* and to ▷regionalism in Brazil, where the term *criollismo* is not employed. The masterpiece of *criollismo* is *Don Segundo Sombra* (1926), by the Argentinian Ricardo Güiraldes, one of the founders of the magazine ▷*Martín Fierro* with another Argentinian, Jorge Luís Borges. Its stalwart Chilean defenders in the period 1917–1925 were Mariano Latorre and ▷Marta Brunet, with her famous novel *Montaña adentro* (1923) (*Mountain Interior*). This literary movement was created by the Venezuelan Rufino Blanco-Fommona as an exaggerated portrayal of popular customs, human types and popular language, and has dominated regionalist literature in Venezuela and Colombia since 1900.

Crisi, Maria ▷Ginanni, Maira

Critic, The (1881–1906)

US literary magazine, weekly (1881–1898), then monthly (1898–1906). Based in New York, it was founded and edited by ▷Jeanette Gilder and her brother, Joseph Gilder (1858–1936). As its editor and reviewer, Jeanette Gilder was the first national publisher of Joel Chandler Harris (1848–1908) and the principal magazine publisher of the prose of Walt Whitman (1819–1892), as well as some of his poetry. While never attaining the wide national circulation of the major national magazines, *The Critic* was a staunch and never stuffy advocate of US writers and commentator on the literary scene.

Crocker, Hannah Mather (1752–1829)

US essayist. A descendant of the famous New England Mather family of Puritan clergy, Hannah Mather Crocker developed into an effective social observer and sometime advocate of reform. Her principal work, *Observations on the Real Rights of Women, with their appropriate duties, agreeable to Scripture, reason and common sense* (1818), argues that women succeed through calm persuasion, taking a supportive but essential role in sustenance of the family and the nation. Other works include *A Series of Letters on Free Masonry* (1815) and *The School of Reform; or, The Seaman's Safe Pilot to the Cape of Good Hope* (1816).

Crocombe, Marjorie Tuainekore

Short story writer, editor and historian from the Cook Islands. Instrumental in the development of the South Pacific Creative Arts society to encourage artists and writers from the region, Marjorie Crocombe has had an enormous influence on the emergence of Oceanian literature in the last twenty years. Formerly director of the Extension Services department of the University of the South Pacific, Crocombe, who grew up in Rarotonga, is now the director of the Centre for Pacific Studies at Auckland University. She has published a number of short stories in local journals, particularly *Mana*, and has written several books on history.

Publications include: *If I Live: The Life of Ta'unga* (1977); *The Cook Islanders* (1967); edited *Cannibals and Converts: Radical Change in the Cook Islands* by 19th-century writer Maretu (1983). Short stories published in *Mana*, *Kovave* and *Lali: a Pacific Anthology*, ed. Albert Wendt (1980).

Croly, Jane Cunningham (1829–1901)

US (British-born) journalist, columnist, contributor to and editor of many newspapers and magazines. She was best known for her personal essays on domestic life and domestic tyranny and for her role as a founder of Sorosis, the literary club which started the women's club movement in the USA.

Through her writing and her work with the growing ranks of women's clubs, Cunningham Croly was a prominent and effective advocate of women's rights and women writers. She was among the first to recognize and write the women's history of women's organizations, using both her writing and her public persona to focus attention on women's potential through organization. She often wrote under the pseudonym Jennie June. Her volume publications include: *For Better or Worse: A Book for Some Men* and *All Women* (1875) and *The History of the Women's Club Movement in America* (1898).

Crônica

The word 'chronicle' refers to a historical account narrated in chronological order. One of the most famous chroniclers in Portuguese literature is Fernão Lopes (c 1380–1460), who wrote historical narratives on the Portuguese kings. In more contemporary terms, the word refers to a short commentary or 'sketch' based on a real or fictional circumstance and written for newspapers or reviews. The *crônica* is a popular literary genre in both Portugal and Brazil.

▷Caiel (Alice Pestana); Lisboa, Irene do Céu Viera

Crónica del desamor (1979) (Chronicle of Falling Out of Love)

A novel by ▷Rosa Montero, one of the most significant of the Spanish New Wave women writers. It follows an autobiographical format and concentrates on feminist issues, many of which were taboo during the Franco regime, such as contraception, abortion, homosexuality, and the single mother.

Cross, Amanda ▷Heilbrun, Carolyn

Cross, Zora (1890–1964)

Australian poet and journalist. Cross worked as a freelance journalist, had a long relationship with the poet David McKee Wright and published three volumes of love poetry which deal frankly with sexuality and motherhood: *A Song of Mother Love* (1916), *Songs of Love and Life* (1917) and *The Lilt of Life* (1918). She also published short stories, a number of romantic novels, works for children and an *Introduction to the Study of Australian Literature* (1922).

▷Literary criticism (Australia)

Crossroad, The (1913)

An epistolary novel in verse by the Russian poet ▷Poliksena Solov'ëva, which consists of eight letters from a brother to his sister. They are composed of iambic tetrameter with lines of alternating rhyme. Solov'ëva used the setting of summer on a country estate that was frequently found in 19th century fiction and plays. The theme of the novel is the difficulty faced by those who want to bring about changes in basic human behaviour. As in several other works by women (eg ▷Lókhvitskaia, ▷Verbítskaia, and ▷Stólitsa), a central motif in the work is the heroine's ecstatic dancing, in the manner of Oscar Wilde's *Salome* (1893), or Isadora Duncan. One critic found it entertaining and terse, but weak in the dialogues, while another found it unpretentious, light and sonorous.

Crothers, Rachel (1878–1958)

US dramatist. Born in Illinois, Crothers began writing at the Stanhope-Wheatcroft School of Acting in New York. Her plays concern the modern woman's search for freedom in a man's world. *The Three of Us* (1906) introduces a new heroine on the US stage; Rhy MacChesney is a ▷New Woman who revolts against double standards. *He and She* (1920) emphasizes women's achievements in spheres other than traditional female ones and warns how women undermine their success through self-imposed barriers. *Mary the Third* (1923) ushers in a new code of sexual and social conduct, challenging the sham and hypocrisy of the traditional values of love and marriage. *When Ladies Meet* (1932) and ▷*Susan and God* (1937) examine the potentially disastrous consequences of women indulging their freedom. Crothers presents women who refuse to sacrifice self-respect and integrity for unworthy men.

Other works include: *Criss-Cross* (1904), *The Rector* (1905), *A Man's World* (1915), *Old Lady 31* (1923), *A Little Journey* (1923), *Expressing Willie* (1924), *39 East* (1925), *The Heart of Paddy Whack* (1925), *Mother Carey's Chickens* (1925), *Once Upon a Time* (1925), *Let Us Be Gay* (1929), *Everyday* (1930), *As Husbands Go* (1931) and *Caught Wet* (1932).

Crowe, Catherine (?1800–1872)

English novelist and short story writer, born in Kent. She married Lt Col John Crowe in 1822 and moved to Edinburgh until the death of her husband in 1860, after which she went to live in Folkestone. A prolific writer, she is best-known for her collection of supernatural stories, *Night Side of Nature or Ghosts and Ghost Stories* (1848), which ran to several editions. She also wrote plays, her first work being the tragedy *Aristomedus*, published anonymously in 1838. Her novel *Susan Hopley* (1841) was successfully adapted for the stage, and *The Cruel Kindness* (1853), a ▷drama, was performed at the Haymarket Theatre. Other novels include *Manorial Rights* (1839); *Linny Dawson* (1847) and, for children, *Adventures of a Monkey* (1861).

Bib: Sergeant, A., *Women Novelists of Queen Victoria's Reign*.

Crow Eaters, The (1978)

Comic novel by Pakistani writer ▷Bapsi Sidhwa. Set in what is now Pakistan, this is the story of a Parsee (Zoroastrian) businessman attempting to build up his family's fortune. The Parsees were once a very wealthy and influential community in India, but their power has declined in the 20th century. Sidhwa found that individual families were often still wealthy enough to excite jealousy from their non-Parsee neighbours in Pakistan, but that they themselves felt their community to be failing. She hoped that her novel, written from the perspective of an insider, might provide some insights for all Pakistanis into a minority community's way of looking at itself.

Crozier, Lorna (born 1948)

Canadian poet. Born in Swift Current, Saskatchewan, she was educated at the Universities of Saskatchewan and Alberta, then taught at high school in Swift Current for seven years before turning to writing full-time. Her work is very much engaged in the landscape of sexuality. She has published *Inside is the Sky* (1975), *Crow's Black Joy* (1978), *No Longer Two People* (1979, with Patrick Lane), *Humans and Other Beasts* (1980), *The Weather* (1983), *The Garden Going On Without Us* (1985) and *Angels of Flesh, Angels of Silence* (1988).

Crusat, Paulina (born 1900)
Spanish novelist. Crusat was born in Barcelona into an upper-middle-class family. Her fiction, *Aprendiz de persona* (1956) (*Apprentice Person*), and *Las ocas blancas* (1959) (*The White Geese*), is centred in Barcelona and is highly autobiographical.

Cruz, Agata ▷Machado, Luz

Cruz, Sor Juana Inés de la ▷Juana de Asbaje y Ramirez de Santillana

Cry of a Stone, or a Relation of Something Spoken in Whitehall by Anna Trapnel, The (1654)
English verse prophesies. ▷Anna Trapnel fell into a trance and uttered prophesies which were written down and later published with a brief biography of their author. Her words use biblical allusion to prophesy political change, and condemn Oliver Cromwell (1599–1658). Her *Report and Plea* (1654) tells of her trial after subsequent trances and prophesies in Truro, Cornwall.
▷Cary, Mary; Lead, Jane; Wentworth, Anne

Cuando amas aprendes geografía (1973) (When You Love You Learn Geography)
An important collection of poems by the Spanish writer ▷Gloria Fuertes. Fuertes is one of the outstanding female poets of the post-war era. As the title to this collection suggests, Fuertes's poetry is inward-looking and is concerned with exploring the potential expressiveness of the female body. Her poetry is characterized by a word-play reminiscent of James Joyce, which gives her work a ▷postmodern edge.

Cuarto de atrás, El (1978) (The Back Room)
Outstanding Spanish post-war novel, by ▷Carmen Martín Gaite. The novel is dedicated to Lewis Carroll, and begins with the novelist's attempt to fall asleep while reading Todorov's work on the literature of the fantastic. She is woken up at midnight by the appearance of a stranger who reminds her that she had arranged an interview with him. The mystery of his identity grows as the novel progresses. The text weaves together the author's reminiscences of her childhood, the literature of the fantastic, and the '*novela rosa*' (sentimental romance). When she is woken up early next morning by her daughter, the narrator realizes the whole episode must have been a dream, but discovers that the novel she had been working on is now sitting, completed, on her desk. A year after publication, *El cuarto de atrás* was awarded the prestigious National Prize for Literature.

Cuestión palpitante, La (1883) (The Burning Question)
Extended essay by ▷Emilia Pardo Bazán, one of Spain's most significant novelists of the 19th century. It is a study of the theory of naturalism, and reveals Pardo Bazán as a proponent of Zolaesque naturalism. *The Burning Question* is important in the context of Pardo Bazán's own work, but is also useful as a barometer of the state of the polemic around naturalism in Spain at that time.
▷Realism

Cueva y Silva, Doña Leonor de la (c 1600–1660)
Spanish poet and dramatist. Cueva wrote a sonnet on the death of Isabel de Borbón (1645), as well as a play, *La firmeza en la ausencia* (*Constancy in Absence*).

Culleton, Beatrice
Canadian Metis novelist who grew up in and around Winnipeg, Manitoba. Her novel, *In Search of April Raintree* (1983) is about two Metis girls who are torn between assimilation into the dominant white world, and their sense of pride in their Metis heritage. She has also written a novella, a play, and a film script.

Cummins, Maria Susanna (1827–1866)
US popular novelist. Author of the enormously popular ▷*The Lamplighter* (1854), a ▷woman's novel directly echoing ▷Susan Bogert Warner's ▷*The Wide, Wide World*, Cummins typified her generation of New England women writers. After gaining fortune with this first bestseller, she established a career with periodical contributions and novels in volume publication – *Mabel Vaughn* (1857); *El Fureidis* (1860); *Haunted Hearts* (1864) – each different in setting, but all women-centred.

Cunard, Nancy (1896–1965)
English poet. A prominent member of English and French ▷avant-garde literary circles during the 1920s, Cunard was a good friend of ▷Virginia Woolf who published the poetry collection *Parallax* (1925). Cunard's first poems were published by ▷Edith Sitwell in the magazine *Wheels* (1916). The establishment of her own The House Press is described in *These Were the Hours* (1969). Cunard was considered an 'indomitable rebel', and the hostility and controversy surrounding her relationship with black musician Henry Crowder prompted the oppositional piece *Black Man and White Ladyship* (1931) and the civil liberties plea *Negro* (1934). Other collections include: *Outlaws* (1921) and *Sublunary* (1923).

Cunitz, Maria (1610–1664)
German writer and mathematician. The daughter of a physician in Silesia, in 1650 she published *Urania propitia – Newe und Langgewünschete/leichte Astronomische Tabelln* (*Propitious Urania – New and Much-desired/easy Astronomical Tables*), a work comprising more than 600 pages of tables and text in Latin and German. In this book she explained, and considerably developed, the work of the scientist Johannes Kepler (1571–1630).

Cunningham, Letitia (fl 1783)
North American essayist. She is known only through one extant essay, ▷*The Case of the Whigs*, that she published in Philadelphia in 1783. From her writing, it is obvious that she was well-educated, politically astute and powerfully outspoken. Few women of the era wrote with such rhetorical authority.

Curzon, Sarah Anne (1833–1898)
Born Sarah Vincent in Birmingham, England, she married Robert Curzon, and emigrated with him to Canada in 1862. She was a strong advocate of suffrage and education, contributed to many journals, and wrote a column on women's issues. *Laura Secord, the Heroine of 1812: A Drama, And Other Poems* (1887) and *The Story of Laura Secord, 1813* (1891) are both historical representations of Laura Secord's heroic actions in crossing enemy lines to warn the British of impending American attack in the war of 1812. The earlier volume includes *The Sweet Girl Graduate*, a comic play about a woman who disguises herself as a man in order to graduate from the University of Toronto.

Cusack, Dymphna (1902–1981)

Dymphna Cusack

Australian novelist and dramatist. Cusack was a prolific and popular novelist, dramatist, and writer of non-fiction whose works invariably reflected her social commitment. Cusack was a lifelong member of the Communist Party of Australia, and active in women's rights and the peace movement. Of her twelve novels ▷*Come In Spinner* (1951, in collaboration with Florence James) is the most famous. Other novels have been concerned with racism, the Vietnam war, alcoholism and fascism in post-war Germany. Her novels have been translated into fifteen languages, published in thirty-four countries, and are especially popular in Russia. Her plays also reflect her commitment to social problems, and one, ▷*Red Sky at Morning*, became a film in 1944. Cusack was awarded the Elizabeth II Coronation Medal in 1953 and was made Member of the Order of Australia.
▷New Theatre, The; ▷*Peaceful Army, The*

Cussons, Sheila (born 1922)
South African Afrikaans poet. Born in Piketburg, Cape, Cussons studied art in Pietermaritzburg, London and Amsterdam; in 1955 she moved to Barcelona and converted to Roman Catholicism. Since 1982 she has lived in Cape Town. Her first collection of poetry, *Plektrum* (1970, *Plectrum*), contains poems written over a period of twenty-five years. In many of these poems, Cussons enters into a dialogue with the work of the important Afrikaans poet, N.P. van Wyk Louw (1906–1970). Since an accident in which she was severely burnt, Cussons has written poetry which is religiously inspired and mystical; in *Die Skitterende Wond* (1979) (*The Brilliant Wound*) and *Omtoorvuur* (1982) (*Transfiguring Fire*), the poet's disfigurement through burning is used as a metaphor for the transforming power of her religion. Cussons has translated short stories by Jorge Luis Borges into Afrikaans under the title *Die Vorm van die Swaard en Ander Verhale* (1981) (*The Shape of the Sword and Other Stories*). *Die Woedende Brood* (1981) (*The Furious Bread*), was awarded the South African CNA (Central News Agency) Prize, and she has written an autobiographical account, *Gestaltes 1947* (1982) (*Configurations*, 1947). Some of her early poems appear in English translation in *The Penguin Book of South African Verse* (1968), and others in *Poems: A Selection* (1985), in parallel English and Afrikaans text. Her most recent collection, *Die Knetterende Woord* (1990) (*The Crackling Word*) includes some poems written in English.

Her other works are: *Die Swart Kombuis* (1987) (*The Black Kitchen*); *Verf en Vlam* (1978) (*Paint and Flame*); *Die Sagte Sprong* (1979) (*The Gentle Leap*), and *Die Somerjood* (1980) (*The Summer Jew*).

Custom of the Country, The (1913)
US novel by ▷Edith Wharton which focuses on Undine Spragg, who is the counterpart to Lily Bart in Wharton's ▷*The House of Mirth* (1905). Undine, who comes to New York from the Midwest, represents the values of the entrepreneur and speculator. She rises into the leisure class through a series of marriages. Wharton suggests that it is US custom for men to lavish their fortunes on wives, and this custom

damages women by turning them into commodities. Untroubled by passion, Undine is the perfect commodity, and her sole concern is marketing herself for marriage. Wharton observes that women can survive in a pecuniary society by destroying others instead of being destroyed themselves. Her second husband kills himself and Undine neglects her son.

Cyniburg (8th century)

English abbess. A letter of c 740 (in Latin) to this otherwise unidentified English abbess from Lull and others is preserved in the ▷Boniface Correspondence. The writers wish to place themselves in her care when they visit England, and they write with evident affection and deference.

Czrtoryska, Princess Izabela (1746–1835)

Polish poet. She wrote the first popular histories of Poland, *Pielgrzym w Dobromilu* (1818) (*The Pilgrims of Dobromil*), and in 1800 founded the Temple of Sybyl, a museum for Polish antiquities.

Dąbrowska, Maria (1889–1965)

Polish novelist and the country's best epic narrative writer. Dąbrowska grew up in a family of impoverished landowners on a farm near Kalisz. She studied natural sciences in Switzerland and Belgium. Her first stories were for children and display her firsthand knowledge of peasant life. Her style has been described as '▷realism deprived of any condescension'.

Her greatest work is *Noce i Dnie* (1932–1934) (▷*Nights and Days*). *Rozdroze* (1937) (*Crossroads*) looked at the peasant question, and demonstrated the need for agrarian reform.

Although Dąbrowska was courted by the post-war communist regime, in part by republishing her pre-war novels in mass editions, she stayed aloof and was silent during the Stalinist period, although she published her translation of Samuel Pepys's diary in 1948. In 1955 a volume of short stories *Gwiazda zaranna* (*The Morning Star*) came out. It portrays the Polish people's efforts to rebuild Warsaw after the war and the German occupation, and it shows her great faith in the people's ability to remain steadfast despite the vicissitudes of history.

She wrote literary studies on Gogol, Tolstoy, Chekhov, Conrad and Bolesław Prus, as well as plays and history books. She worked for fifteen years on the novel *Przygody cztowieka myslacego* (*Adventures of a Thinking Man*) which is set in Hitler's Poland.

Dacier, Anne Le Ferre (1651–1720)

French classical scholar, educated by her ▷humanist father at his Protestant teaching academy in Saumur. After the death of her first husband and her father, she moved to Paris, and later married a fellow scholar, André Dacier; both were converted to Catholicism. In Paris she was engaged to produce editions of classical literature, and then began to translate Greek and Latin texts into French. These included the first French translation of ▷Sappho, in *Les Poésies d'Anacréon et de Sappho* (1681) (*The Poems of Anacreon and Sappho*), with a preface on her life, and comedies by Plautus, Terence and Aristophanes. She progressed to translations of Homer's *Odyssey* and *Iliad*, with prefaces exalting classical literature and disparaging contemporary culture. When La Motte published his provocative translation of Homer, his preface took the opposite point of view. They became engaged in the second phase of the celebrated quarrel between the 'Anciens' and the 'Modernes'. Dacier published her reply in the form of a 600-page pamphlet, *Des causes de la corruption des goûts* (1714) (*On the Causes of the Corruption of Tastes*), and in *Homère défendu* (1716) (*In Defence of Homer*), condemning the '*faux romans*' ('false novels') of *Artamène, ou Le Grand Cyrus* (1649–1653) (▷*Artamenes, or The Grand Cyrus*, 1653–1655) and *Clélie, histoire romaine* (1654–1660) (▷*Clelia: An excellent new romance*, 1661) (▷Madeleine de Scudéry). Both of these texts have recently been republished (Slatkine reprints, 1970 and 1971). A comment by Voltaire offers an interesting insight into contemporary notions of writing and gender; comparing the thorough refutation of each argument by Madame Dacier to La Motte's more moderate style of reply, he concluded that one would think Madame Dacier's writing the work of a male scholar, while La Motte's might pass for that of an intelligent woman. Unlike her husband, she was not honoured by a place in the ▷Académie Française. She was, however, made a member of the Ricovrati Academy in Padua.

▷Lambert, Marquisede

Bib: Farnham, F., *Madame Dacier: scholar and humanist*; Hepp, N., *Homère en France au XVIIIe siècle*; Howells, R., 'Rewriting Homer . . .', *Romance Studies* 17 (1990).

Daddy Was a Number Runner (1970)

US novel in which Louise Meriwether celebrates African-American women who take responsibility for themselves and their families. Like her character, Francie, Meriwether lived in Harlem, New York, during the Depression. Her father also became a number runner when he could not find work. Meriwether depicts the problems of ghetto life: unemployment, poverty, slum-housing, black crime and child molestation, and she portrays the sense of communal powerlessness and despair generated by the ghetto. She also chronicles the breakdown of the African-American family. Francie's mother's work as a maid humiliates her father, who abandons the family. Francie learns from her mother to survive with dignity through co-operation.

Meriwether earned a Master's degree in journalism at UCLA in 1965. She was an activist in the civil rights movement. She has written books about famous African-Americans for elementary schoolchildren.

Other works include: *The Freedom Ship of Robert Smalls* (1971), *The Heart Man: Dr. Daniel Hale Williams* (1972) and *Don't Ride the Bus on Monday: The Rosa Park Story* (1973).

d'Agoult, Marie   ▷Flavigny Marie de

Dai Houying (born 1938)

Chinese novelist. Dai Houying is a teacher in the Chinese department of Shanghai University. Her first novel, *Stones of the Wall* (1981), describes the persecution of academics and the reversal of basic human values against the background of the 'cultural revolution' (1966–1976). With *Death of a Poet* (1982) and *Footsteps Echoing in the Void* (1986), she has completed a trilogy on the fate of intellectuals in China.

Bib: (trans.) Wood, Frances, *Stones of the Wall*.

Dai Qing (born 1941)

Chinese writer and journalist. Child of a revolutionary martyr, Dai Qing (born Fu Ning) followed the communist-led army across the length and breadth of China all through the war years of the 1940s. A graduate from the Harbin Institute of Military Technology in 1966, Dai

Qing first worked as a technician in Beijing, but later became a reporter. Her first short story, 'Anticipation' (1979), describes the trampling of talent and disregard for human values through the tragedy of one middle-aged couple. Readers' response was so strong that it elicited the greatest number of letters in the history of the national daily newspaper in which it was published.

Continuing to write through the 1980s, Dai Qing again won national acclaim for her series of interviews of noted intellectuals, among them the physicist and political dissident, Fang Lizhi. Her reports of controversial subjects, such as the Three Gorges Hydro-Electric Project, which raised concerns about ecological problems, her series of investigative reports on various types of Chinese women (from prostitutes to political prisoners), entitled *Series on Women*, and her outspokenness against social evil combined to make her one of the most prominent and controversial writers in China. Dai Qing was arrested following the Tiananmen Square crackdown on 4 June 1989, and released a year later.

Bib: Translation of 'Anticipation' in Link, Perry (ed.), *Roses and Thorns*; translation of 'The Unexpected Tide' in *The Serenity of Whiteness*, selected and translated by Zhu Hong.

Dakar Childhood, A (1982)

Translation of *De Tilène au Plateau: une enfance dakaroise* (1975), an autobiographical account by the Senegalese writer, ▷Nafissatou Diallo. Autobiography as a mode of expression is particularly significant in ex-colonized countries as part of the movement of cultural self-assertion. There are still very few autobiographies by women, especially Moslem women. The author depicts her comfortable childhood in a middle-class family dominated by her grandmother and father. Side by side with her formal education, Safi receives a training in traditional morality from her grandmother. She herself, growing up in the years after World War II, is part of a generation for whom change is paramount. Her story ends on this note, with her marriage, the death of her father, and her departure for Paris.

Dalibard, Françoise-Thérèse Aumerle de Saint-Phalier (died 1757)

French poet, dramatist and writer of prose fiction. Her first published works, the two novels *Le Portefeuille rendu, ou lettres historiques* (1749) (*The Returned Wallet, or Historical Letters*) and *Les Caprices du sort, ou l'histoire d'Emilie* (1750) (*The Whims of Fate, or the Story of Emilie*) bore only the initials of her maiden name (Mlle S*** and Mlle de St. Ph***), as did the collection of her poetry, *Recueil de poésies* (1751) (*Collected Poems*). *La rivale confidente* (*The Rival Confidante*) a three-act comedy, was performed in 1752 at the Théâtre Italien in Paris, and published in the same year, along with her last published work, *Murat et Turquia*, also attributed to ▷Lubert or ▷Marguerite de Lussan.

Bib: Prudhomme, L.M., *Répertoire universel historique et biographique des femmes célèbres*.

Dall, Caroline Wells Healey (1822–1912)

US essayist and lecturer. A prolific writer on women's issues, Healey Dall moved from early opposition to women's political roles to feminist advocacy of equal educational and labour opportunities for women. Especially effective in tracing the history and causes of women's oppression, she wrote or edited more than a dozen books, including *Woman's Right to Labor: or Low Wages and Hard Work* (1860) and *Sex and Education* (1874).

Dalla parte di lei (1949) ▷ Best of Husbands, The

Dallas, Ruth (born 1919)

New Zealand poet and novelist. Ruth Dallas was born in Invercargill and now lives in Dunedin, and her work reflects a strongly regional and historical focus. For some years she was involved with *Landfall*, New Zealand's major literary journal, when it was edited by Charles Brasch, who promoted many New Zealand writers. Dallas has published six novels for children, mostly about pioneering. These include *The Children in the Bush* (1969), *The Wild Boy in the Bush* (1971), *The Big Flood in the Bush* (1972) set in Longbush near Invercargill, *The House on the Cliffs* (1975) and *Shining Rivers* (1979), an 1860s gold-mining tale. She has also published eight collections of poetry. Although Dallas's work shows a strong subject interest in the history of southern New Zealand, it has also described being drawn to 'Buddhist influences in literature, Indian, Chinese, Japanese', particularly in her poetry. In 1978 Dallas received an honorary Doctorate in Literature from the University of Otago. She was further honoured in 1989 with a CBE.

Publications include: *Country Road and Other Poems 1947–52* (1953); *The Turning Wheel* (1961); *Day Book* (1966); *Shadow Snow* (1968); *A Dog Called Wig* (1970); *Walking on the Snow* (1976); *Song for a Guitar and Other Songs* (1976); *Steps of the Sun* (1979); *Holiday Time in the Bush* (1983); *Collected Poems* (1987); *Curved Horizon* (autobiography, 1991).

▷Children's literature, New Zealand; France, Ruth

D'Alpuget, Blanche (born 1944)

Australian novelist, biographer and journalist. D'Alpuget married and lived overseas for nine years, including four in Indonesia and one in Malaysia. Her novels, *Monkeys in the Dark* (1980) and *Turtle Beach* (1981), deal with Asian themes, and *Winter in Jerusalem* (1986) with the Middle East. She is particularly noted for her 'warts-and-all' biography of the Australian Prime Minister, *Robert J. Hawke, a Biography* (1982). She has also published *Mediator, a Biography of Sir Richard Kirby* (1977).

Daly, Ita (born 1955)

Irish novelist. Born in County Leitrim, studied at University College, Dublin, and now lives in Dublin. Her collection of short stories, *The Lady with the Red Shoes*, was published in 1980, and was followed by three novels: *Ellen* (1986), *A Singular Attraction* (1987) and *Dangerous Fictions* (1990). The winner of two Hennessy Literary Awards, she has also written children's books.

Dame Shirley ▷Clappe, Louise Amelia Knapp Smith

Dana, Jacqueline

French novelist and journalist. Dana has written essays on family life and parenthood, but is known mainly for the romantic novels which she has produced steadily throughout the 1980s. These could be described as 'post-feminist' romantic fiction, in that Dana's heroines often enjoy the external signs of liberation – a media job, a flat, an education – while remaining in the grip of the ideology of beauty and heterosexual romance. The symbol of oppression in the novels is a stifling, possessive mother, and/or a childhood trauma, and the hero is associated with independence. *Tota Rosa* (1983) and *Appelle-moi Emma* (1990) (*Call me Emma*) close in the traditional manner with the promise of happy love, though, significantly, ▷*Les Noces de Camille* (1987) (*Camille's Wedding*), in which the heroine is forty, has a sting in the tail.

Dancing on Coral (1987)

Australian novel by ▷Glenda Adams. An exuberant, witty, and experimental piece of work. Lark Watter is a naive Sydney student who meets a charming but patronizing North American, Tom Brown, a scholar, political activist and insufferable egotist. Lark concludes that Australia is not big enough to contain her thirst for true love and adventure, and hitches a ride to North America on a freighter. Her quixotic, often perilous journey leads her to the Manhattan of her dreams, where she learns many lessons. *Dancing on Coral* was awarded not only the Miles Franklin Award (Australia's most prestigious literary award) for 1987, but also the New South Wales Premier's Award for that year. In a controversial decision the money which usually accompanies the Premier's Award was withheld because Adams was not resident in Australia.

Dane, Clemence (1887–1965)

English dramatist and novelist. ▷Pseudonym of Winifred Ashton. Initially an actress, Ashton turned to writing after her health deteriorated during World War I. Her plays include *A Bill of Divorcement* (1921), which focuses on a mother–daughter relationship, *Will Shakespeare* (1921), about the writer's life, and *Wild Decembers* (1932), about the ▷Brontës. *Regiment of Women* (1917) is a novel set in a girls' school, and explores the megalomaniac tendencies of the schoolmistress, Claire Hartill. *Legend* (1919) reconstructs its deceased central character, a romantic novelist, through other people's impressions. *Fate Cries Out* (1935) is a volume of short stories, and *The Women's Side* (1926) a collection of essays.

Dangarembga, Tsitsi (born c 1958)

Zimbabwean novelist, born and brought up in colonial Rhodesia. She was educated at the multiracial Arundel School in Harare (then Salisbury), and then at Oxford University, where she studied medicine and psychology. She is currently studying film at the Berlin film school. She has written one play, *She No Longer Weeps*, and a novel, *Nervous Conditions* (1989), for which she received the Commonwealth Prize (Africa section).

Nervous Conditions is set in the eastern highlands of Rhodesia, some twenty years before its independence. The story focuses on the adolescence of two Shona girls: Tambudzai, who has been brought up on one of the rural reserves, and her cousin, Nyasha, whose father runs the local mission, and who has spent some years in England. Nyasha searches fretfully for a way of defining her place in Africa, for she has lost touch with her own language and people. Her period abroad, combined with a penetrating intelligence, gives her a sharp eye for the *petit bourgeois* world of her father's mission, and the way her mother has been sacrificed to it. She is deeply mistrustful of what she and her family have acquired through education, thus acting as a foil to her cousin Tambu, who desires education above all else. Tambu, the narrator of the novel, learns from Nyasha that the world is less simple and considerably more painful than she once believed.

The novel is also about the contradictions of neo-colonialism. The title is taken from Jean Paul Sartre's introduction to Frantz Fanon's *The Wretched of the Earth*: 'the condition of the native is a nervous condition.' In different ways, all the characters are in some stage of psychological damage due to colonization. Although the novel is not nostalgic, and does not propose a return to a prior world, it searches for alternative forms of what it calls 'expansion' rather than 'emancipation'. In this regard, Tambu's aunt Lucia is a crucial figure, and a prototype of African feminism.

Dangerous Age, The (1910)

Translation of the world-famous novel *Den furlige Alder*, by the Danish prose writer ▷Karin Michaëlis (1872–1950), translated into more than twenty languages, and filmed twice.

Elsie Lindtner, the protagonist, is forty years old. She is described as a woman who sees her gender as destiny. She divorces her rich, friendly husband, and isolates herself on an island, in a white house with a glass roof over her bed. Here she writes letters and a diary, telling the reader of her hysteria during menopause. The loss of femininity is analysed both as biological destiny and as a result of woman's place in society. Elsie loses her femininity as she loses her power over men. But in the second volume, *Elsie Lindtner* (1912), she finds a new life, together with an adopted son and female friends. After 'the dangerous age', a new woman-centred life can begin.

The novels created great public debate, especially in Germany. Feminists found them provocative, because they saw women as beings with sexual desires, even after the menopause. German feminists demonstrated outside the halls where Michaëlis spoke. The novels are theoretically built on Otto Weininger's (1880–1903) conceptions of the 'Feminine' (*Geschlecht und Character*, 1903, *Sex and Character*), but Michaëlis proved that important traits of femininity are created by society and not founded in gender.

Daniel Deronda (1876)

The last of English novelist ▷George Eliot's novels. It has two central characters, Gwendolen Harleth and Daniel Deronda. Gwendolen's once-wealthy family have become impoverished, and in order to save them from destitution she marries the arrogant aristocrat, Henleigh Grandcourt, despite the fact that she is aware of his long-standing affair with Lydia Glasher. The marriage is miserable, and the once-proud and vain Gwendolen suffers from guilt and an intense feeling of enslavement. She finds spiritual sustenance in Daniel, the adopted son of an English aristocrat, whose idealism and integrity inspire her. Daniel, it is gradually revealed, is actually the son of an internationally-known Jewish woman singer, Alchirisi. This strengthens Daniel's connection with the young singer, Mirah, and her Jewish nationalist brother, Mordecai. Eventually Daniel and Mirah marry and he devotes himself to the Jewish cause. An important theme in the novel is the nature of personal and artistic dedication, set against the monomaniacal and obsessive behaviour exhibited by several of the characters. Recent critics have emphasized Eliot's unconventional use of stereotypically 'masculine' and 'feminine' qualities, and highlighted the novel's depiction of the racism suffered by Daniel, Mirah and Mordecai.

D'Annunzianesimo

A term taken from the name of Italian writer, Gabriele D'Annunzio (1863–1938), and associated with ▷decadentism. D'Annunzio was a nationalistic, bellicose writer who exalted Italy in his writings, and was in favour of Italian colonialism. A creator of his own myths – aestheticism, patriotism, the 'superman' (inspired by Nietzsche), the cult of violence – his work was extremely influential. He wrote both poetry and prose. Stylistically, D'Annunzio's work is marked by his choice of rare words, antiquated/technical vocabulary, piling up of images and esoteric references. He is also a deeply misogynistic writer.
Bib: Klopp, C., *Gabriele D'Annunzio*.

Daong Khin Khin Lay (born 1913)

Burmese novelist. She was born in Mandalay, and took up writing as a career when she was thirty. Her prolific output includes about 600 novels and short stories in Burmese, and she also wrote for films. She published the *Yuwadi Journal* in 1946 and founded the *Yuwadi Daily Newspaper*.

Daring Life, A (1905)

A novel by the Russian children's writer ▷Lidiia Chárskaia. Though ostensibly based on the life of ▷Nadezhda Dúrova, the biography conforms to many of Chárskaia's fictional works about troubled, misunderstood teenage girls. Chárskaia was probably moved to write about Dúrova because of the patriotic feeling stirred up by the Russo–Japanese War (1904–5), but she may also have been attracted to the story of another woman with a deep attachment to her father (▷*For What?*). To make Dúrova's fascinating and strange life palatable for a young audience, Chárskaia recasts it into the mould of Joan of Arc, with whom Dúrova is made to identify. Thus Dúrova's idiosyncratic behaviour is justified by her patriotism, and the controversial issues of women's restricted roles, sexual role reversals, and transvestism implicit in her story are diffused. Chárskaia also makes her rebellion sympathetic by contrasting the silly, insensitive and superficial indoor world of her mother and sister with the male domain outdoors in nature that she longs to join. After Dúrova runs off to join the military, she makes a series of male friends who accept her as an equal. Once the Napoleonic Wars break out, Dúrova is shown to believe unwaveringly in the ultimate victory of the Russian forces. Yet she never loses touch with her 'feminine soul', and yearns to be accepted and reintegrated into society.
▷*Daughter of the People*

Dark, Eleanor (1901–1985)

Australian novelist. Dark was born in Sydney, the only daughter of the writer Dowell O'Reilly. She married Dr Eric Dark in 1922 and subsequently lived in the Blue Mountains to the west of Sydney. One of Australia's bestselling serious novelists, Dark published ten novels between 1932 and 1959, of which *Prelude to Christopher* (1934) and *Return to Coolami* (1936) won the Australian Literary Society's Gold Medal. In 1987 Dark was awarded the Australian Society of Women Writers' Alice Award; she has also received the Order of Australia. Her historical trilogy, ▷*The Timeless Land* (1941), was adapted for ABC Television in 1979. She also published poems, short stories and occasional pieces.
▷*Peaceful Army, The*

Daryush, Elizabeth (1887–1977)

English poet. The daughter of Poet Laureate Robert Bridges, she was brought up with a professional and technical interest in poetic form. Her seven volumes of poetry are experimental with verse forms and technically accomplished.

She uses a variety of metrical forms, ranging from accentual syllabic to an accentuated rhythm imitative of Gerard Manley Hopkins's (1844–1889) 'sprung rhythm', as well as syllabic verse, some of which comprises translations of Persian poetry. Daryush described her aim 'to build up subtler and more freely-followed accentual patterns than can be obtained either by stress-verse proper, or by the traditional so-called syllabic metres'. Her formal brilliance has not won her many readers, but W.B. Yeats (1865–1939), the US critic Yvor Winters and the British poet Roy Fuller (born 1912) were warm admirers. Fuller described her as 'a pioneer technical innovator' whose poems 'grapple with life's intensest issues'. Her works include: *Charitessi* (1911), *Verses* (1916), *Sonnets from Hafez and Other Verses* (1921), *The Last Man and Other Verses* (1936), *Verses: Seventh Book* (1971), *Selected Poems, Verses I-VI* (1972), which is the poet's own selection of her work, and *Collected Poems* (1976).

Das, Kamala (born 1934)
Indian poet and journalist. She was born in the south Indian state of Kerala, into a noted literary family. Her mother, Balamani Amma, was a famous Malayali poet, as was her grandfather. She had little formal education, and was married at fifteen. She lives in Trivandrum, Kerala. She is a former poetry editor of the *Illustrated Weekly of India*, former president of the Jyotsna Art and Education Academy, Bombay, and a founding member of the Bahutantrika Group of Artists.

Das writes in both English and Malayalam. Many of her short stories in Malayalam are published under the pseudonym Madhavi Kutty. She is well-known in India for her frank and outspoken exploration of female sexuality, and her poems are often a rebellion against the sexual self-denial which many cultures force on women. Her poetry collections include: *Summer in Calcutta* (1965), *The Descendants* (1967), ▷ *The Old Playhouse* (1973) and *Tonight, This Savage Rite: The Love Poems of Kamala Das and Pritish Nandy* (1979). *Collected Poems* was published in 1984. In 1963 she won the PEN Asian Poetry Prize, and in 1970 the Kerala Sahitya Akademi Award for a collection of short stories. A short story, 'Summer Vacation', translated from the Malayalam, is in ▷ *The Inner Courtyard*. Her candid autobiography, ▷ *My Story*, was published in 1976.
Bib: Raghunandan, Lakshmi, *Contemporary Indian Poetry in English*; Rahman, A., *Expressive Form in the Poetry of Kamala Das*.

Das, Mahadai
Caribbean poet, born in ▷ Guyana, Das is a member of the younger generation of Indo-Guyanese poets. Her work deals with feminist and radical nationalist perspectives. She studied at the University of Chicago, but became seriously ill and returned to Guyana, where she now lives and continues to write. Her published work includes *I want to be a Poetess of my People* (1976), *My Finer Steel Will Grow* (1982) and *Bones* (1989).

Her work is discussed by Jeremy Poynting in ▷ *Caribbean Women Writers*.

Dash (1804–1872)
▷ Pseudonym of French novelist Gabrielle-Anne Cisterne. A self-styled countess, whose marriage to an army officer proved unhappy, Dash turned to literature in order to support herself and her son. She worked as a journalist before devoting herself in 1839 to the writing of novels, of which she produced an enormous quantity. She tended to the ▷ sentimental, was fond of historical subjects and came close to salaciousness at times. Some of her most popular works were: *L'Écran* (1839) (*The Screen*); *La Marquise de Parabère* (1842); *Les Bals Masqués* (1842) (*The Masked Balls*); *La Marquise Sanglante* (1850); *La Comtesse de Bossut* (1855); *La Duchesse de Lauzun* (1858); *Un Amour à la Bastille* (1862) (*A Love Affair at the Bastille*) and *L'Arbre de la vierge* (1872) (*The Tree of the Virgin*).

Dáshkova, Ekaterina Romanovna (1743–1810)
Russian publicist, dramatist, and memoir-writer. Born into the powerful Vorontsov clan, Ekaterina Dáshkova had a long and complicated relationship with her patron, ▷ Catherine II, which began in plans for the coup that brought the empress to the throne in 1762. Widowed in 1764, Dáshkova travelled extensively in succeeding years, pursuing a stringent course of self-education wherever she went in western Europe; from 1776–1779 she lived in Edinburgh, Scotland, while her son attended the university. In the 1770s, anonymously and under the pseudonym 'A Russian Woman', Dáshkova began writing magazine articles on ethics and other civic topics. She was also the author of several comedies castigating contemporary morals. Her appointment in 1783 as Director of the Academy of Sciences and founding president of the Russian Academy was no mere sinecure: her eleven-year tenure was marked by organizational and educational reforms and, under her direction, the Russian Academy issued the first major dictionary of the Russian language and a forty-three-volume collection of Russian plays. As Barbara Heldt points out in *Terrible Perfection*, Dáshkova's *Memoirs*, which she wrote in French in 1804–1805, are marked by the lifelong struggle to balance the demands of the private and public woman, the mother and the citizen. First published in 1840, the *Memoirs* were published in a new English edition in 1957.

das Neves, Hilário ▷ Sousa, Auta de

Daubié, Julie (1824–1874)
French working-class feminist writer. The daughter of a book-keeper, Daubié received little in the way of formal education. However, she was taught Latin and Greek by her brother, who was a priest, and later became a governess. In 1858 she entered a competition organized by the Académie

de Lyon. The work which she submitted, and which won first place, was *La Femme pauvre au XIXe siècle* (*Poor Women in the 19th Century*), a wide-ranging study of female poverty and of the ways in which it might be resolved. One of the judges was so impressed with her 450-page essay (published in 1866) that he encouraged her to sit for the *baccalauréat* examination. She did so, despite opposition from the Ministry of Education, and in 1861 became the first *bachelière* in France. She subsequently obtained a degree from the Sorbonne.
Bib: Albistur, M. and Armogathe, D., *Histoire du féminisme français*; Moses, C., *French Feminism in the 19th Century*.

Daudet, Julia (1844–1940)
French poet and essayist. The wife of Alphonse Daudet (1840–1897), she was herself a prolific author, whose best-known works are *L'Enfance d'une Parisienne* (1883) (*The Childhood of a Parisian Girl*) and *Fragments d'un livre inédit* (1884) (*Fragments from an Unpublished Book*). These texts contain a series of impressions and pen-sketches drawn from the author's childhood and adult life, and were considered charming by Daudet's contemporaries. She also published critical articles under the pseudonym Karl Stern, some of which are contained in the volume *Impressions de nature et d'art* (1879).

Daughter of Mumbi (1969)
Fictionalized childhood autobiography by Kenyan writer ▷Charity Waciuma. *Daughter of Mumbi* traces the erosion of Kikuyu traditions as a result of colonial oppression and missionary Christianity. The episodic structure is designed to show varied aspects of Kikuyu culture as well as charting the breakdown in communication between whites and Kikuyu which led to the Mau Mau movement, culminating in the Emergency (1952–6). Waciuma's sensitive study offers fascinating insight into the ideological conflict between colonial values and those of an emergent nationalism. Her hope for the future is clearly education, and Wanjiku's rise up the educational ladder offers a role model for the new Kenyan woman.

Daughter of Time, The (1951)
▷Detective novel by ▷Josephine Tey. Her best-known work, it exploits the concept of crime detection as historical reconstruction. In hospital after a serious fall, Inspector Grant turns to history to pass the time. He becomes fascinated with a portrait of Richard III, and then with his story. Grant sets out to show, with the help of a research student in history, that Richard was innocent of the murder of the Princes in the Tower, and that his successor, Henry VII, was guilty of the crime. This thesis was not original to Tey, but her novel helped to popularize it. *The Daughter of Time* reveals Tey's lifelong interests in history (she refers in the novel to the play *Richard of Bordeaux*, written under her other

▷pseudonym, Gordon Daviot), and in physiognomy as a central aspect of detective work (Grant reads Richard III's character in his face).

Daughter of the People (1903)
A play by the Russian writer ▷N.P. Ánnenkova-Bernár about Joan of Arc. Originally intended as a benefit performance for Vera Komissarzhevskaia, it was staged at the St Petersburg Maly Theatre, where Ánnenkova-Bernár herself performed the title role. The play combines a muted feminist protest with the ▷Silver Age interest in mystical religion and the Middle Ages. In alternating scenes, the court and Church are each shown to be corrupt. Joan is associated with the peasantry, and the play emphasizes their hard lot. Depicted as an innocent young girl, Joan, as the play opens, is under pressure to get married. Ánnenkova-Bernár humanizes her by depicting Joan's military leadership comically at times, and presenting her Christianity as iconoclastic. At the same time Joan retains her charisma and her devotion to the cause of freedom and justice for the French people. The figure of the unconventional woman warrior appears again in ▷Chárskaia's novel, ▷*A Daring Life* (1905), and ▷Barkóva's play ▷*Nastas'ia Kostër* (1923).

Dauthendey, Elisabeth (1854–1943)
German writer. She was born in St Petersburg, where her father was court photographer. She was interested in psychological and ethical questions, especially as they relate to women. To explore such issues, she wrote fairytales, novellas and novels, and in particular the widely-read *Vom neuen Weibe und seiner Liebe. Ein Buch für reife Geister* (1900) (*Of the New Woman and Her Love-life. A Book for Mature Spirits*). This book argues that lesbian relationships can offer women emotional and social fulfilment which goes far beyond 'mere' sex.

Daviot, Gordon ▷Tey, Josephine

Davis, Rebecca Harding (1831–1910)
US fiction writer. Davis was among the most prominent and highly regarded 19th-century US writers of realist regional fiction. Coming to public attention with the publication of ▷*Life in the Iron Mills* in the April 1861 issue of ▷*The Atlantic Monthly*, Harding Davis brought a new perspective and new subject matter to US literature. Each of her works ventured new subjects, ranging from the economically and intellectually impoverished workers of New England to middle-class women who must sacrifice artistic talent and romantic love if they choose practical marriages and traditional roles as supportive wives and mothers. Harding Davis continually drew attention to the waste of human potential under capitalism and patriarchy.
  A lifelong voracious reader, Harding Davis first discovered literature with US subject matter when she read Nathaniel Hawthorne (1804–1864). Dedicated to finding her own subjects in the study

of common life, Harding Davis was a staunch proponent of the realism of the everyday, the tragedy in the lowly and the unconsidered.

Her finely crafted stories and novels were regularly published in the major national literary magazines, and she was one of the most valued contributors of *The Atlantic Monthly*. Her books include novels such as ▷*Margaret Howth* (1862); *Waiting for the Verdict* (1868), which addressed racism in North America, and *John Andross* (1874), which focused on capitalism's corrupting effect on 'democratic' politics; as well as collected short stories, *Silhouettes of American Life* (1892); and an autobiography.

▷'Anne'; *Appleton's Journal*; *Galaxy, The*

Davy, Sarah (Roane) (c 1639–1670)

Englishwoman who wrote a Baptist ▷conversion narrative, a genre which organized the narration as events leading towards the subject turning to Christ. Her narrative, *Heaven Realized, or the holy pleasure of daily intimate communion with God* (1670), was published as an example by her minister. She puts her experiences in religious terms, and uses biblical echoes to describe her feelings and eventual conversion by 'one that I never saw before, but of a sweet and free disposition'.

Bib: Graham, Elspeth, *et al.*, *Her Own Life.*

Davys, Mary (1674–1732)

Dramatist and novelist, originally from Dublin. She married the Reverend Peter Davys, and through him knew English satirist Jonathan Swift (1667–1745). Her husband died in 1698, and she came to England, where she lived by writing. Her first fiction was *Amours of Alcippus and Lucippe* (1704, republished 1725), and she writes about Ireland in *The Fugitive* (1705, rewritten 1725). Life in York, in the north of England, is worked into her comedy *The Northern Heiress, or the Humours of York*, which was staged in 1716. She set up a coffee-house in Cambridge, and published later works by subscription, *The Reform'd Coquet, or Memoirs of Amoranda* (1724) and *Works* (1725), which includes revisions of earlier writings. She also wrote the poem 'The Modern Poet' and other fictions and comedies, including *The Accomplish'd Rake, or Modern Fine Gentleman* (1727).

Bib: Lonsdale, Roger (ed.), *Eighteenth Century Women Poets.*

Daw Khin Myo Chit (born 1915)

Burmese writer. She began her career in the 1930s writing short stories for magazines and weekly journals, later joining the editorial staff. In the pre-war years she was involved with the independence movement, and during the war she supported the partisans. Afterwards, she gained a BA at Rangoon University and started writing short stories and magazine columns in English, working for the *Guardian Daily* and *Working People's Daily*. Her short story '13-carat Diamond' was included in *50 Great Oriental Stories* (1965),

published in the USA, and translated into Italian, German, Yugoslav and Gujarati. She has also won an award for another short story, *Her Infinite Variety*, and has written a historical novel, *Anawrahta of Burma.*

Daw Mi Mi Khaing (1916–1990)

Burmese writer. She was born in Minhla, a town in mid-Burma, educated at a convent, and obtained a BA (Hons) from Rangoon University and a BSc from King's College, London. She established, and was principal of, a private co-educational school in the Shan states from 1951 to 1953, and married a Shan chieftain. Writing in English, she produced a number of books, although her first, *Burmese Family* (1946), describing traditional Burmese family life, is probably the one for which she is best known. She went blind following a brain tumour, but learnt Braille and continued to read and write with the aid of her family.

Daw San San ▷Moe Moe (Inya)

D'Costa, Jean (born 1937)

Children's writer, poet, critic, educated at schools in Jamaica, the University of the West Indies, University College, London and the University of Oxford and Indiana. She is currently a lecturer in English at the universities of the West Indies. Her first children's book, *Sprat Morrison*, was published in 1972. She has since published several others and edited with ▷Velma Pollard an anthology of stories, *Over Our Way* (1981). Her experimentation with linguistic variety and Jamaican Creole is discussed in an essay by Joyce Johnson in *Wasafiri*, No. 5 (1986).

Deamer, Dulcie (1890–1972)

Australian novelist, journalist, poet and actor. Born in New Zealand, she was known as the 'Queen of Bohemia' for her association with the literary and artistic circle centred on Australian artist Norman Lindsay and the journal *Vision*, and with the bohemianism of the inner-city suburb, Kings Cross. She published a book of short stories, six novels, two volumes of poetry and one play, none of which is concerned with Australian life.

Death Comes to the Archbishop (1927)

US novel by ▷Willa Cather, which reflects her disgust with contemporary and materialistic values. It also reflects her interest in the story of the Catholic Church in the South-west. As in her pioneer novels, it focuses on an immigrant to the New World, presenting a fictionalized account of Archbishop Lamy's life. In the mid-19th century Jean Latour, a French missionary priest, is appointed bishop in New Mexico, where he tends to the neglected parishes of the diocese and unifies them. His work perpetuates the values of the Old World in the new one, and his search for integrity takes him to the frontier where Cather's heroines find their strength.

Death of a City, The (1976)

A collection of short stories by the Indian author ▷Amrita Pritam, translated from the original Punjabi. In the title story the narrator tells of her parents' outrage at her sexual encounters with her boyfriend. Although she escapes the admonitory marriage they had planned for her with an aged widower, her existence as a lonely teacher in London now resembles that of the city of Pompeii, smothered and lifeless in spite of its apparent corporeality.

Death of the Heart, The (1938)

Novel by Irish writer ▷Elizabeth Bowen. Portia, a sixteen-year-old orphan, comes to stay with her wealthy half-brother and his wife, Thomas and Anna Quayne, in their London house. The childless Anna finds Portia an unwelcome addition to her life; the novel is centrally concerned with the difficult relationship between the two women, surrogate mother and (unwanted) surrogate daughter. Portia falls in love with Eddie, a young man working for Thomas Quayne's advertising firm, who 'has to get off with people because he can't get on with them'. The novel charts Portia's repeated disappointments in her attempts to make her world conform to her needs. She comes to feel betrayed by Eddie and Anna; Anna feels watched and 'persecuted' by her. The novel ends with an intimation of an uneasy truce between the two women.

The two central motifs of *The Death of the Heart* are houses and Portia's diary. The novel contrasts two domestic spaces: the London house and the seaside villa, 'Waikiki', where Portia spends a holiday. Bowen suggests that the seeming stability and safety of the London house is rendered increasingly illusory, not only by the tensions of the family relationships it harbours, but by a world soon to be at war. Portia feels more at home in 'Waikiki' because it does not pretend to provide a stable, ordered existence. By making the ideology of the home explicit, Bowen exposes the obsolete conventions of the domestic novel she would otherwise appear to be writing.

The novel begins just after Anna has found and read Portia's diary, and has become furious, not only with its content, but with the very fact of Portia's observing consciousness. She complains to her novelist friend St Quentin Miller. Bowen subtly contrasts different kinds of writing and writer: the established male novelist, and the young female diarist attempting to give shape to confusing experiences and relationships. Along with its surface realism, then, the novel interrogates the construction of stories and histories.

Débat de Folie et d'Amour, Le ▷Labé, Louise

de Beauvoir, Simone (1908–1986)

French writer. Simone de Beauvoir was born in Paris in 1908 to bourgeois parents. The elder of two daughters, she was educated at Catholic schools and at the Sorbonne, where she read philosophy and qualified as a teacher of the subject. While a student, she met philosopher Jean-Paul Sartre (1905–1980), who was to be her lifelong companion. Together, they developed the philosophical system of Existentialism, and its essential themes (of the limits and possibilities of human freedom and choice) inform de Beauvoir's novels and her philosophical essays, including her study of women, ▷*The Second Sex.*

Until 1943 de Beauvoir earned her living as a secondary school teacher, working first in Marseilles and subsequently in Rouen and Paris. Her first novel, *L'Invitée* (▷*She Came to Stay*) was published in 1943, and in the following years she was to produce a considerable number of novels and essays, together with five volumes of autobiography. In 1954 her novel ▷*The Mandarins* won the prestigious Prix Goncourt.

Until the 1970s her engagement with feminism was largely intellectual, but then she became involved with the French feminist movement and began to be a vocal champion of women's rights, particularly on issues such as abortion and sexual violence. Political involvement, however, was nothing new for de Beauvoir, since in the years after the end of World War II she had taken a consistently left-wing (and at times personally perilous) stance on French policy in Algeria and the involvement of the USA in Vietnam.

Sartre died in 1980, and the final years of de Beauvoir's life were marked by sometimes bitter disputes with Sartre's adopted daughter, Arlette Elkaim. However, she also enjoyed the rich rewards of friendship with many women, and an international reputation as one of the major feminist writers of the 20th century.

▷*All Said and Done*; *Blood of Others, The*; Delphy, Christine; *Force of Circumstance*; *Memoirs of a Dutiful Daughter*; *Old Age*; *Prime of Life, The*; *Very Easy Death, A*; *Woman Destroyed, The*
Bib: Bair, Deidre, *Simone de Beauvoir*; Evans, Mary, *Simone de Beauvoir. A Feminist Mandarin*; Fallaize, E., *The Novels of Simone de Beauvoir*; Okely, Judith, *Simone de Beauvoir: A Re-reading*; Whitmarsh, Ann, *Simone de Beauvoir and the Limits of Commitment.*

Debeche, Jamila

Algerian novelist, born in Ghiras. She launched a feminist review *L'Action* (1947). She is among the first feminist crusaders of her generation in Algeria, who fought for education and women's right to vote. She wrote two novels: *Leila, jeune fille d'Algérie* (1947) (*Leila, Maid of Algeria*) and ▷*Aziza* (1955). They both deal with women's revolt against tradition and a society frozen by ancestral taboos. Debeche writes in a journalistic and straightforward style.

De Brémont, Comtesse Anna (1864–1922)

British/South African novelist, short story writer and poet, born of Irish parents in Cincinatti, Ohio, USA. She settled in London in 1889 and, after marrying and separating from a French count, emigrated to the Witwatersrand. She wrote two romances: *The Gentleman Digger: A Study of Johannesburg Life* (1891) and *A Son of Africa* (1899), also issued under the title *Was It a Sin?* (1906); a set of short stories, *The Ragged Edge: Tales of the African Gold Fields* (1895), and some poems: *Love Poems* (1889), and *Sonnets and Love Poems* (1892). Virtually forgotten now, her works are not reprinted, but she nevertheless has an important place in mining or diggers' literature, otherwise written by men. *The Gentleman Digger* presents a critique of the gold-mining industry, its violence and brutality. However, her gentleman digger is not quite as remote from violence as she might suggest. Blond as a Norse god, Hector proves his prowess by beating an already prostrate Zulu: according to the text, the surrounding Zulus 'felt the utmost respect for a Baas who could do his own flogging'.

Other work: *The World of Music* (1890).

Debyasuvan, Boonlua Kunjara ▷Boonlua

Decadentism (Italy)
A late 19th- and early 20th-century movement, usually most associated with Gabriele D'Annunzio (1863–1938) and his writings. It was anti-positivist and anti-bourgeois in inspiration. Decadentism exalted sensuality, and the cult of beauty. Women writers in this genre include ▷Maria Borgese Freschi, ▷Luisa Giaconi, ▷Amalia Guglielminetti and ▷Grazia Deledda.

▷*D'Annunzianesimo*

De Cespedes, Alba (born 1911)
Italian novelist, poet and journalist. She has lived in Paris, Havana and Washington. During the German occupation of Italy in World War II, she worked with the partisan Radio Bari. She founded the journal *Mercurio* in 1944 and has contributed to many Italian magazines and newspapers. She was concerned in her writing to draw attention to women's position in the family, which she saw as particularly problematic. Both ▷*Nessuno torna indietro* (1938) (*No-one Goes Back*), and *Dalla parte di lei* (1949) (*The Best of Husbands*), tell stories of male defects and female disappointments. Written in 1952, *Quaderno proibito* (*The Secret*, published in English in 1957) is a novel presented in diary form, in which the protagonist tells of her disappointments, and blames her husband and children for stifling her. The 1955 *Prima e dopo* (*Between Then and Now*, published in English in 1959) presents us with a female character in a somewhat more positive scenario, in that she does finally manage to achieve independence and freedom, after much earlier pain and suffering. De Cespedes is a writer who has achieved both critical and popular acclaim.

Her other main works include: *L'Anima degli altri* (1935) (*The Souls of Others*); *Concerto* (1937); *Fuga* (1940) (*Flight*); *Invito a pranzo* (1955) (*Invitation to Dinner*); *Il rimorso* (1963) (▷*Remorse*, published in English in 1967); *Nel buio della notte* (1976) (*In the Dark of the Night*). Poetry includes:

Prigionie (1936)(*Captivity*) and *Chanson des Filles de Mai* (1969) (*Songs of the May Girls*). *Quaderno proibito* was reworked as a play in 1962, and was produced as a TV play in 1980, while de Cespedes co-wrote *Gli affetti di famiglia* (*Family Ties*), another play, in 1952.

Déclaration des droits de la femme (1791)
▷*Rights of Woman, The* (1989)

Declaration, Dying Warning and Advice of Rebekah Chamblit, The (1733)
Published upon ▷Rebekah Chamblit's execution in Boston, Massachusetts, for the murder of her new-born, illegitimate child, this early North American writing is a complex record of community expectations and personal tragedy. Although it follows the traditional forms of criminal confessions, it emphasizes Chamblit's awareness that females in Puritan Massachusetts were under extraordinary pressures to deny their sexuality. It also reveals Chamblit's awareness of human beings' capacity for guilt – it was, she asserted, less the act of murder than the 'Guilt of this undiscover'd Sin lying upon my Conscience' that tortured her.

Deconstruct
To tease out traces of otherness in what appears to be single and self-identical, and thereby display the impossibility of meaning ever becoming complete. In practice, feminist critics have deconstructed literary texts in order to expose how repressed or excluded meanings return to destabilize and fragment apparently dominant ones. See, for example, ▷Barbara Johnson's essay on 'Gender Theory and the Yale School' in *A World of Difference* (1987 and 1989), where the feminine ▷other is shown to produce a particular anxiety in a school of criticism which is predominantly male and pretends to a patriarchal self-assurance.
▷Deconstruction

Deconstruction
A practice of reading developed by the French philosopher and founder of the International College of Philosophy in Paris, Jacques Derrida (born 1930). Derrida's influential use of deconstruction, a word he first used in *De la Grammatologie* (1967) (*Of Grammatology*, 1976) challenges the basis of the Western philosophical tradition and its reliance on grounding principles. His revolutionary views on language insist that pure intelligibility is never possible, because meaning is not anchored in concepts outside language, but is the effect of linguistic ▷differance. Language, according to deconstruction, always reveals the mark of the ▷other in what appears to be single and self-identical. As a result, ▷binary oppositions, including sexual ones, are rendered indeterminate and radically unstable.

Feminist theory has been influenced in particular by Derrida's recognition that the tradition of Western thought is ▷phallogocentric, and by his use of femininity and feminine undecidability as deconstructive figures which displace the possibility of final meaning.

▷French feminist critics have used a deconstructive analysis to displace the hierarchical binary oppositions which produce gender difference and women's oppression. Other deconstructive feminists, for example ▷Gayatri Spivak, have employed a deconstructive analysis to critique both sexual and racial hierarchies, and to begin to formulate alternative readings of the literary ▷canon. Derrida's decipherment of the *idea* of the woman, given in *Spurs: Nietzsche's Styles* (1979), is expanded in ▷Spivak's work; and Derrida's *Positions* (1981) contains a short and relatively accessible account of his work on language.

▷Barbara Johnson
Bib: Culler, J., *On Deconstruction*; Norris, C., *Deconstruction*; Sturrock, J., *Structuralism and Since*; Derrida, Jacques, *Writing and Difference*; *Dissemination*, and *Margins of Philosophy*.

Deephaven (1877)

US collection of ▷local color sketches by ▷Sarah Orne Jewett. Jewett's first published collection, *Deephaven* uses a narrator who is a summer visitor to a Maine town and who describes the declining seaport and the variety of characters and classes found there. In many ways, it anticipates Jewett's more accomplished work of the same kind in ▷*The Country of the Pointed Firs*.

Deerbrook (1839)

The only novel by journalist and feminist ▷Harriet Martineau, *Deerbrook* is set in a tranquil English village in the early 19th century. Two orphaned sisters, Hester and Margaret Ibbotson, come to stay with their cousins, the Grey family. The personal lives of the sisters become entwined with the life of the village – portrayed as a hotbed of personal rivalries, gossip and intrigue. The sisters are contrasted in personality: Hester is beautiful but prone to jealousy, Margaret less physically attractive but more intelligent. Romances develop between the sisters and the two most eligible men in the village. The novel also contains ▷feminist sentiments, expressed mainly by Maria, the crippled ▷governess, who protests against the restricted opportunities available to middle-class women. *Deerbrook* was well-received, being favourably compared to ▷Jane Austen's novels. ▷Charlotte Brontë later claimed that Martineau's honest portrayal of passion had influenced her own writing.

Deffand, Marie de Vichy-Chamrond, Marquise du (1697–1780)

French epistolary writer and salon hostess. As a young woman unfettered by social or religious moral prejudice, du Deffand enjoyed the fashionable society at the court of the Regent, and subsequently at the court of the Duchesse de Maine at Sceaux. After the death of her husband, from whom she had separated, she moved to the rue Saint-Dominique. There she held her powerful salon, receiving both intellectuals and aristocrats. Later, the blindness from which she suffered led her to invite the young ▷Julie de Lespinasse to become her reader and companion. She corresponded with a wide range of figures, including the philosophers d'Alembert (1717–1783) and Montesquieu (1689–1755), the Duchesse de Maine, and ▷Madame de Staal-Delaunay. Most frequently commented on are her letters to Voltaire (1694–1778) and to Horace Walpole (1717–1797), the distant younger man to whom she became passionately attached in later years. Her language is classical, her style spontaneous and natural. Her acerbic and incisive psychological portraits are frequently quoted. Beyond their merit as entertaining historical documents, these letters represent the means by which a woman, who felt intimidated by other forms of writing due to a lack of formal education, wrote with dry wit of the scepticism of the period and of her own profound experience of *ennui*.

Her works include: *Correspondance complète* (1865, 1867) (*Complete Correspondence*); *Correspondance inédite* (1809, 1859) (*Unpublished Correspondence*); *Lettres de Mme du Deffand à Horace Walpole* (1912) (*The Letters of Mme Du Deffand to Horace Walpole*), and a feminist edition of the correspondence with Voltaire, *Cher Voltaire* (*Dear Voltaire*), presented by I. and J. Vissière (1987).

English translations of her works include: *Letters to and from Mme Du Deffand and Julie de Lespinasse* (1938) and *H. Walpole's Correspondence with Mme du Deffand* (1939).

▷*Journal des Dames*
Bib: Duist, L., *Mme du Deffand épistolière*; Lescure, M. de, *Les Femmes philosophes*; Rageot, G., *Mme du Deffand*; Tallentyre, S.G., *The Women of the Salons*.

Deforges, Régine

French novelist. Deforges has worked in publishing, journalism and cinema, and in 1968 became the first woman to own a publishing house. She has written erotic stories, *Les Contes pervers* (1980) (*Tales of Perversity*), and historical romances set in various periods, but is most well-known for the trilogy set in World War II, *La Bicyclette bleue* (1981) (*The Blue Bicycle*). The sensual appetites of the heroine, Léa, earned Deforges, the label 'a real little French woman' from one reviewer. Mainly through Léa, the novels construct a French identity based on patriotism, the pleasures of sex and food, and attachment to the land. Recently, however, Deforges has been involved in a court case because of the novels' striking resemblance to the plot of ▷*Gone with the Wind*.

de Gabriak, Cherubina (1887–1928)

Pseudonym of Russian poet Elizaveta Ivanovna Dmitrieva. After Dmitrieva's early poems were rejected by the ▷avant-garde journal *Apollo* in

1908, she sent a selection to the poet Maksimilian Voloshin. He thought that her modest, unimpressive appearance was discordant with her neo-romantic poetry, and the two of them decided to disguise the real poet with an exotic-sounding pseudonym, Cherubina de Gabriak. She mailed *Apollo* a cycle of poems, along with a fictional autobiography, and it was published in 1909. Even after the 'mystification' was revealed, *Apollo* published another cycle of Cherubina's poems in 1910, and on the page next to them, a poem by Elizaveta Dmitrieva. De Gabriak's poems are filled with mystical symbolism and borrowings from Roman Catholicism. She used the fashionable forms of the sonnet and chain verse. After the exposure, Dmitrieva worked for *Apollo* as a translator, but no more of her poetry appeared in print. She joined the Theosophical Society in 1908 and, after she married and left St Petersburg in 1910, became active in the Anthroposophy Society. Around 1915 she started writing poetry again.

After the 1917 Revolution, she and the children's writer Samuil Marshak helped found a children's theatre in Krasnodar, and together wrote children's plays based on fairytales. In 1922 they moved to the Theatre for Young Spectators in Petrograd. Dmitrieva's last cycle of poetry, 'The Little House Under the Pear Tree', was written in 1927 under the pseudonym of Li Sian Tszy, to whom she also gave a fictional biography. In the same year she was arrested and exiled to Tashkent, probably because of her involvement with anthroposophy. She died a year later.

Dmitrieva acknowledged the influence of ▷Karolina Pávlova, ▷Mirra Lókhvitskaia, and ▷Elena Guró. Her poetry deals with the themes of fate, faith and love. From the poems that have thus far appeared, it is clear that over time she was maturing as a poet, but, since much of her work is still in manuscript, it remains difficult to assess.

Bib: Pachmuss, T. (trans.), *Women Writers in Russian Modernism*; Graham, S. (trans.), 'A Concourse of Poets: Unpublished Sonnets by Gumilev and E.I. Dmitrieva', *Scottish Slavonic Review* 1 (1983).

De Girondo, Norah Langue ▷Lange, Norah

de Hoyos, Angela (born 1940)
US poet. Born in Mexico, de Hoyos began composing poems at age three while recuperating from burns. Her family later moved to San Antonio, Texas. She has served as general editor for M&A/Manda Publications and *Huchuetitlan* magazine. To her, poetry is a social activity and can give voice to those who have been marginalized and who are unable to speak for themselves. *Arise, Chicano and Other Poems* (1975) exhorts migrant workers to rebel against their exploitation and to reinstate their race's dignity. *Chicano Poems for the Barrio* (1975) re-examines history and reminds Texas of its Hispanic heritage. The poems express the fear that Chicanos are losing their identity as they acquire Anglo-American values. De Hoyos mixes Spanish and English in her poetry to express this bi-cultural reality.

'Deirdre's Farewell to Scotland' (15th century)
Irish poem. The author of this elegiac poem is unknown. The story of Deirdre belongs to the ▷Old Irish Ulster Cycle. The speaker in this poem expresses her longing for the land she has left.
Bib: Jackson, Kenneth Hurlston, *A Celtic Miscellany*.

Dejanović, Draga (1843–1870)
Serbian poet. Known as the apostle of the Serbian feminist movement, Dejanović lived an active twenty-seven years as a poet, translator and actress. She also wrote articles, such as 'Are Women Capable of Being Equal with Men?' (1870), and about elections, education and other issues. She was a political activist in the United Serbian Youth Movement. Her poems, contained in the slim *Collection* (1869), are, on the whole, patriotic. She also left, in manuscript, a play based on one of the poems of the Serbian epic tradition.

Deken, Aagje (1741–1804)
Poet and prose-writer from the northern Netherlands, also known as Agatha Deken. Having lost her parents at an early age, she lived in an Amsterdam orphanage, and became a servant. While employed by the Bosch family, she befriended their daughter, Maria, with whom she wrote pietist and devout poetry, published under the title *Stichtelijke gedichten* (1775) (*Devotional Poems*). A letter to ▷Betje Wolff, full of reproach because of her supposedly worldly behaviour and mockery of religious matters, led to friendship and a lifelong literary co-operation. During their latter years in The Hague, Deken published *Mijn offerande aan het vaderland* (1799) (*My Sacrifice to the Native Country*), *Liederen voor den boerenstand* (1804) (*Songs for the Peasants*), and posthumously, *Liederen voor ouders en kinderen* (1805) (*Songs for the Parents and Children*).
▷*Sara Burgerhart*

De Kok, Ingrid (born 1951)
South African poet. Born and educated in Johannesburg, she lived in Canada for some years, and has now resettled in Cape Town, where she works as an educational administrator. She has published a number of poems in South African and Canadian magazines under the name Fiske as well as De Kok, and also some critical writing, and, on a few occasions, has read her poetry at political mass-meetings.

Her first and only volume of poetry to date, *Familiar Ground* (1988), reveals the work of a distinct poetic voice, careful and assured, at once intense and drily ironic. Like some of the other emerging South African writers, De Kok is responsive to the possibilities of multiculturalism, liberated from its fragmentation and repression under apartheid. Her poetry offers a direct and intelligent examination of a white, middle-class consciousness, both accepting the responsibilities of that social position and distancing herself from it through irony. While her poetry is deeply political, its interest is in the human suffering caused by apartheid and its repercussions: De Kok's voice is often the voice of grief.

She has spoken of the need for white South African poets to open themselves to local influences: to ▷performance poetry, for instance. While her work sometimes bears the marks of such influence, it has, at the same time, the grammatical limpidity and precarious tonal balance to be found also in ▷Margaret Atwood's poetry.

Delafield, E.M. (1890–1943)

E.M. Delafield

English novelist, journalist and short story writer of French descent. Delafield anglicized her name to prevent confusion with her mother, the novelist Mrs Henry de la Pasture. Delafield's writings are largely autobiographical, following the advice of her mother. *The Pelicans* (1918) is based on her relationship with her sister and *The War Workers* (1918) draws on her experience as a Voluntary Aid Detachment nurse during World War I. The majority of her novels are comedy-of-manners narratives, often satirizing women's vanity, and her novels are frequently concerned with women's complicity in their own subjection and domination. These novels focus on Edwardian upper-middle-class 'society', and are founded on Delafield's own experiences as a débutante. They include *The Way Things Are* (1927), *Thank Heaven Fasting* (1931) and *Late and Soon* (1943). Her

best-known work is ▷*The Diary of a Provincial Lady* (1931).

De la Littérature (**1800**) ▷*Treatise on Ancient and Modern Literature, A* (1803)

De l'Allemagne (**1810**) ▷*On Germany* (1813)

Deland, Margaret Wade Campbell (1857–1945)

US novelist. Deland set most of her works in her native Pennsylvania, but her use of place went beyond ▷local color to anticipate the archetypal places of later US fiction, eg William Faulkner's (1897–1962) Yoknapatawpha County. Most memorable for her well-developed characters, Deland usually plotted characters' conflicts between belief or emotion and convention – posing increasingly risky and innovative conflicts throughout her career. Her 19th-century works include: *John Ward, Preacher* (1888); *Sidney* (1890); *Philip and His Wife* (1894).

Delaney, Shelagh (born 1939)

English dramatist and short story writer. Delaney was born in Salford, Lancashire, and her working-class background forms the basis of much of her writing. Her best-known play is *A Taste of Honey* (1958), which she wrote at the age of eighteen. The play focuses on sexuality and teenage pregnancy within a working-class Manchester family, and was later made into a successful film for which Delaney provided the screenplay. Other film scripts include *Charlie Bubbles* (1968), about a writer returning to his 'authentic' northern roots, and *Dance with a Stranger* (1985), a carefully researched study of Ruth Ellis, the last woman to be hanged in England. Other writings include: *Sweetly Sings the Donkey* (1964), a collection of short stories, and the play *The Lion in Love* (1961).

Delany, Mary (1700–1788)

English poet and ▷Bluestocking. Married to a drunken husband (who died in 1724), she knew ▷Hester Chapone, ▷Fanny Burney and others, and wrote letters to Jonathan Swift (1667–1745). She also wrote poetry, and the unpublished *Marianna*.

Delarue-Mardrus, Lucie

French writer. She belonged to the aristocratic circle of Anna de Noailles and the Princesse de Polignac, who mixed with the most famous people of their day: Gide, Proust, Valery, and Rodin. Although kept within the bounds of propriety, her sexual preferences are hinted at in her poetry, *Horizons* (1905), in novels, and in a play, *La Prêtresse de Tanit* (1907) (*The Priestess of Tanit*).

De Lauretis, Teresa (born 1938)

Italian-born feminist poststructuralist and film theorist working in North America. Now Professor of the History of Consciousness at the University of California, Santa Cruz, de Lauretis is editor of *Feminist Studies/Critical Studies* (1986); and co-editor (with Stephen Heath) of *The Cinematic Apparatus* (1980). She is author of *La Sintassi del desiderio* (1976), *Umberto Eco* (1981), and *Alice Doesn't: Feminism, Semiotics, Cinema* (1984). De Lauretis's latest book, *Technologies of Gender: Essays on Theory, Film and Fiction* (1987), brings together work on cinematic representations of women with a concern over the exclusion of lesbian sexuality from feminist theories of gender difference. In contrast to the work of the lesbian critic ▷Adrienne Rich and the feminist historian ▷Lillian Faderman, de Lauretis argues that sexuality is absolutely central to any definition of lesbianism.

▷Lesbian feminist criticism

Delay, Florence

French novelist and dramatist. Her work shows a redirection of fiction away from ▷*nouveau roman* radicalism. Her works include: *Minuit sur les jeux* (1973) (*Midnight on the Games*), *Riche et légère* (1983) (*Rich and Light*), *Les Dames de Fontainebleau* (1987) (*The Ladies of Fontainebleau*), *Extemendi* (1990), *Graal Théâtre* (1977) (*Graal Theatre*) and *José Bergamin* (1989), with Jacques Roubaud.

Delbée, Anne

French theatre producer who founded the Gô theatre company. Her novel, *Une femme* (1982) (*A Woman*), and her play of the same name, combine biographical detail with fictional narrative in the 'herstory' of the 19th-century French sculptress, Camille Claudel.

Deledda, Grazia (1871–1936)

Italian novelist. Probably one of the most well-known Italian women writers, and the only one to receive the Nobel Prize for literature (in 1926). She was born in Sardinia, and the countryside in which she grew up occupies an important place in much of her writing. She had little formal education as a child, as little was offered to girls on the island. She was, however, an avid reader. As a young girl, family responsibilities weighed particularly heavily on her, since she seems to have been the only one of her large family to escape misfortune in the form of illness or involvement in crime. Her work enjoyed critical acclaim from her earliest writings, but it was after her marriage in 1900, which took her from Sardinia to Rome, that she produced her best work: she felt, like many writers, more free to write of what she knew best when at one remove from it. Her work is often considered to fall between ▷*verismo* and ▷decadentism. A prolific writer, she dealt with the problems of human passions, earthy and elemental, versus the demands of morality and the consequent sense of failure or guilt arising from the inevitable predominance of one over the other. *Canne al vento* (1913) (▷*Reeds in the Wind*), apparently her own favourite piece of work, tells the story of a family in decay, and centres mainly on the guilt of the servant, resulting from an event long past. *La madre* (1920) (▷*The Mother*) tells the story of an intense mother–son conflict. ▷*Cosima* (1937) is Deledda's autobiography in fictional form. She produced one volume of poetry in 1897, *Paesaggi sardi* (*Sardinian Landscapes*), translated Balzac's Eugénie Grandet into Italian in 1930, and some of her work was adapted by her, in collaboration with others, for the theatre.

The rest of her prolific output includes: *Amore regale* (1891)(*Regal Love*); *Fior di Sardegna* (1892) (*Sardinian Flower*); *Racconti sardi* (1894) (*Sardinian Stories*); *Anime oneste* (1895) (*Honest Souls*); *Il tesoro* (1897) (*The Treasure*); *Il vecchio della montagna* (1900) (*The Old Man of the Mountains*); *La regina delle tenebre* (1902) (*Queen of the Shadows*); *Dopo il divorzio* (1902) (*After the Divorce*), translated into English in 1905; *Elias Portolu* (1903); *Cenere* (1904) (*Ashes: A Sardinian Story*), translated into English in 1908; *Nostalgie* (1905) (*Nostalgia*), translated into English in 1905; *L'edera* (1908) (*The Ivy*); *Il nuovo padrone* (1910) (*The New Boss*); *Le colpe altrui* (1914) (*The Guilt of Others*); *Marianna Sirca* (1915); *Il Dio dei viventi* (1922) (*The God of the Living*); *La fuga in Egitto* (1925) (*The Flight into Egypt*); *Annalena Bilsini* (1927); *La casa del poeta* (1930) (*The Poet's House*); *Sole d'estate* (1933) (*Summer Sun*); *La chiesa della solitudine* (1936) (*The Church of Loneliness*). She also wrote a study of customs in the village in which she was born, *Tradizioni popolari di Nuoro in Sardegna* (1895).

Délia ▷Bormann, Maria Benedita Câmara de

De Lima, Clara Rosa (born 1923)

A Caribbean novelist, short story writer and radio journalist, De Lima was born in ▷Trinidad of Spanish descent. She was educated at schools in ▷Barbados, Trinidad and Baltimore, USA. She attended Long Island University, USA, where she began writing short stories. She travelled extensively throughout South America, and wrote her first novel (unpublished) concerning events in Guatemala. Her published novels include ▷*Tomorrow Will Always Come* (1965), *Not Bad, Just a Little Mad* (1975), *Countdown to Carnival* (1978), *Currents of the Yuna* (1978) and *Kilometre Nineteen* (1980).

Delle Grazie, Marie Eugenie (1864–1931)

Austrian poet. Daughter of a German mother and a Venetian father, she published her first collection of poems when she was seventeen and won a writer's grant. Her lyrical verse, her epic poem, 'Robespierre' (1894) and, above all, *Schlagende Wetter* (1899) (*Firedamp*), her play about a mining disaster, established her fame at the turn of the century.

Delphine (1802)

First of ▷Madame de Staël's major novels (see also ▷*Corinne, or Italy*), *Delphine* deals with one of de Staël's main preoccupations: the conflict between society and the individual. The events take place between 1790 and 1792, and the book is dedicated to the 'France of Silence'. This epistolary novel portrays an exceptional woman, betrayed by an unexceptional man who is unable to live in her shadow. The heroine, Delphine d'Albémar, is a young widow, intelligent, highly educated, sensitive, spontaneous, and of independent means and mind. The hero, Léonce, arriving from Spain in order to contract a marriage with her cousin, Mathilde, falls in love with Delphine. She reciprocates his feelings, but their relationship meets personal and political obstacles. Léonce's subsequent death at the hands of revolutionaries represents the crumbling of the old social structures and conventions he had been unwilling to challenge. The unconventional Delphine commits suicide, the victim of a pernicious social system she has failed to overcome. De Staël's analysis of France incorporates a challenge to the Catholic position on suicide, and argues in favour of divorce.

A modern edition of this work is S. Balayé, S. and L. Omacini, (eds), *Delphine* (1987).

Delphy, Christine (born 1941)

French writer and full-time researcher in sociology for the National Council for Scientific Research in Paris. She founded the journal *Nouvelles questions féministes* (*New Feminist Issues*) with ▷Simone de Beauvoir in 1977 to provide a forum for socialist feminism and shot to fame with her attack on ▷Annie Leclerc's ▷ *'Parole de femme'* (1974) ('Woman's Word') as essentialist. This led to the French Women's Liberation Movement splitting into feminist and class-struggle tendencies (▷MLF). She has published two important texts: *L'Ennemi principal* (1970) (*The Main Enemy*, 1974), and *Close to Home* (articles published in French 1970–1981; published as a collection in English only in 1984) materialist analyses of oppression, dealing with the domestic mode of production and the sexual division of labour.

Bib: Barrett, M. and McIntosh, M., 'Christine Delphy: Towards a Materialist Feminism?' *Feminist Review*, No. 1, (1979); Delphy, C., 'A Materialist Feminism is Possible' *Feminist Review*, No. 4, (1980).

Delta, Penelope (1871–1941)

Greek novelist and children's writer. Born in Alexandria, the daughter of the Greek benefactor, Emanuel Benaki. From an early age she dedicated herself to literature, her work mainly inspired by Greek tradition. She specialized in writing for children, in whom she wanted to foster an appreciation of literature and a love for everything Greek. Her first published work of fiction was *For the Motherland* (1909). Her long historical novel *In the Time of Vulgaroktonos* (1911) dealt with the Byzantine past in Macedonia. *The Secrets of the Swamp* (1937) was a novel about the struggle against the Turks in Macedonia during the War of Independence (1821–9). She wrote many more stories and novels, making use of a beautiful vernacular language (rather than the more formal literary language used by other writers). Her literary talents were much admired by Greek writers and critics.

Delta Wedding (1946)

US novel by ▷Eudora Welty which emphasizes the central power of womanhood. It constitutes a pastoral hymn of fertility as it focuses on the Fairchild family, who mythologize their Southern past, seeking a retreat from the modern world in that past. The marriage of Troy Flavin to Dabney Fairchild revitalizes the Fairchild family's outmoded world, and the wedding initiates the nine-year-old Lauren McRaven into the eternal cycles of fertility. Welty reveals the matriarchal tradition that lays obscured behind Southern patriarchy, a tradition which empowers Laura to become an assertive woman. Welty highlights the need to balance independence with a sense of community, and she celebrates the traditional domestic sphere of women's lives.

Demain Jab-Herma (1967) (*Tomorrow, Jab-Herma*)

Cragget, the protagonist of this third novel by a French Antilles writer from Guadeloupe, ▷Michèle Lacrosil, is a mulatto who works on the plantation, Pâline. Cragget is the male counterpart of the heroines of Lacrosil's two earlier novels, ▷*Sapotille* and ▷*Cajou*. Like them, Cragget is trapped by the historic (literary) obsession with whiteness of mixed-race characters and, like them, he is caught on the fringes between the two worlds of the Békés (white Creoles) and metropolitans (who own the plantation) and the blacks (who work on the land). With its dedication to ▷Simone de Beauvoir and Jean-Paul Sartre, Lacrosil's final novel is clearly informed by an Existential interpretation of the self–other relationship.

Démar, Claire (1800–1833)

French feminist essayist. Very little is known about this working-class writer, who was involved with the ▷Saint-Simonian feminists, but was not fully integrated into their group. She was the author of two radical texts: *Appel d'une femme au peuple sur l'affranchissement de la femme* (1833) (*A Woman's Appeal to the People on Women's Emancipation*) and *Ma loi d'avenir* (1834) (*My Law for the Future*), which was published posthumously by ▷Suzanne Voilquin. In the first, Démar denounces the innate sexism of the Napoleonic code. The second, also on the theme of female emancipation, argues in favour of free love, and demands that children should be raised in such a way that motherhood might cease simply to signify oppression and enslavement. Her writings reveal her strong (and at the time, even to fellow feminists, highly shocking) belief in the need to liberate woman's sexual desire and pleasure. Démar drowned herself with her lover, Perret Delessart, who was ten years her junior, and left behind a note declaring that she had been 'too daring'. Her published works and correspondence

are collected in the Payot edition *Textes sur l'affranchissement de la femme* (1976) (*Writings on Women's Emancipation*).
▷Saint-Simonism and Saint-Simonian feminism
Bib: Albistur, M. and Armogathe, D., *Histoire du féminisme français*; Moses, C., *French Feminism in the 19th Century*; Sullerot, E., *Histoire de la presse féminine en France, Women on Love*.

Demesne of the Swans, The (1957)
A collection of 60 poems by the Russian poet ▷Marina Tsvetáeva, dedicated to the subject of the Russian Civil War (1917–1921). *Demesne* is a diary-like cycle which begins on the day of Tsar Nicholas II's abdication in March 1917, and ends late in 1920, when the anti-communist White Army, in which her husband Sergei Efron was fighting, was finally defeated. The 'swans' of the title refers to the volunteers in the White Army. Although the poems are based both on personal and public events, Tsvetáeva succeeded in generalizing the content by grounding them in history, especially Russian history. There are also stylistic and metric devices derived from Russian folk poetry. Underlying the collection are Tsvetáeva's basic pacifist sympathies and her identification with the underdog, rather than any monarchist political urgings. Though some individual poems were published as early as 1921, the collection as a whole appeared only in 1957.
Bib: Kemball, R. (trans.), *The Demesne of the Swans*.

De Mist, Augusta (1783–1832)
South African Dutch diarist, born in Kampen, Netherlands. Her time at the Cape was recorded in a diary. Originally written in Dutch, and translated first into French, and then into English under the title *Diary of a Journey to the Cape of Good Hope and the Interior of Africa in 1802 and 1803*, it was published in 1953 and again in 1975. The diary is a vivid account of the 167 days spent accompanying her father, commissioner-general during Batavian rule at the Cape, on his journey to inspect the colony. In a context of trouble between the Dutch settlers and indigenous people in the Southern African interior, this eighteen-year-old narrator condemns the 'Hottentots' as lazy, the 'Bushmen' as brutal, but the 'Kafirs' come off better: for their physical strength and grace, the 'liveliness of their understanding and the precision of their judgment', by which she confessed herself surprised. Although her translator and editor passes her diary off as 'the whims and fancies of a selective feminine mind', comparing it unfavourably to that of the male traveller Martin Hinrich Karl Lichtenstein (1780–1857), it offers interesting views of Cape Town, the Moravian missionaries and the people of Swellendam, with lively anecdotes about, for instance, lion-shooting. She has, moreover, a sharp eye for the Cape's patriarchal way of life.
Augusta de Mist sailed with her father to America in 1805, and returned to Holland the same year, where she married.
▷Diaries and journals (Southern Africa)

Dennie, Abigail Colman (1715–1745)
North American poet. She was born on 14 January 1715, the daughter of a Calvinist minister. Her life stands as a stark contrast to that of her pious sister, ▷Jane Colman Turell. Both were poets but, unlike Turell, she rejected her father's patriarchal definitions of 'filial duty'. Her life-story is a tragedy, representative of the consequences women faced if they attempted to be independent in a society that condemned such desires. After an unhappy marriage that had been entered into in order to escape her father's control, she ended her short life on having to return to his household, where she died in May 1745. Because her father did not value her poetry as he did his pious daughter's writings, only one poem remains extant: ▷'Lines from a Letter to Her Sister, Jane Colman Turell, March 23, 1733'.

Deraismes, Maria (1828–1894)
French feminist author. Deraismes was an educated and wealthy woman, who began by writing theatrical works which are contained in the collection *Théâtre chez soi* (1863) (*Theatre at Home*). She was more interested in political activism, however, and during the late 1860s and 1870s she wrote for the newspaper *Le Droit des femmes* (*Women's Rights*) and helped set up the feminist ▷Association pour le droit des femmes. One of the more important feminist public speakers of the period, she gave a series of lectures, ▷*Les Bas-bleus* (Bluestockings) in which she attacked male writers and critics, like Alexandre Dumas (1802–1870), and Barbey d'Aurevilly who dismissed women as inferior beings, and in which she also spoke forcefully about the role and condition of women in France. A number of these lectures are to be found in *Eve dans l'humanité* (1891) (*Eve in Humanity*). A keen secularist and Freemason, she campaigned in the 1880s for the separation of Church and State. Her other published works include: *Nos principes et nos moeurs* (1868) (*Our Principles and Morals*); *Eve contre M. Dumas fils* (1872) (*Eve versus M. Dumas the Younger*); *France et progrès* (1873) (*France and Progress*) and *Oeuvres Complètes* (1896) (*Complete Works*).
▷Feminine/feminist journalism (France)
Bib: Albistur, M. and Armogathe, D., *Histoire du féminisme français*: Moses, C., *French Feminism in the 19th Century*.

Dermoût, Maria (1888–1962)
Dutch prose writer. Maiden name: Helena Antonia Maria Elisabeth Ingerman. She was born into a Dutch family that had lived in the Dutch East Indies for generations. When she was twelve, she was sent to the Netherlands to be educated, returning to her native land in 1905, where she married in 1907. She lived in Java and the

Moluccas until 1933, when she settled in the Netherlands. Dermoût did not make her début until 1951, with the novel *Nog pas gisteren* (*Yesterday*, 1959, *Days before Yesterday*, 1960); the title refers to the evocation of the past, just like the epigraph of her second and final novel, *De tienduizend dingen* (1955) (*The Ten Thousand Things*, 1983), published in the series *The Library of the Indies*, ed. E.M. Beekman. 'When the ten thousand things have been seen in their unity, we return to the beginning and remain where we always have been.' In style, Dermoût's novels and stories are closely related to the Indonesian storytellers (▷Beb Vuyk); she derived her material from existing stories and her own reminisces. Her characters are lonely, and they try to find a position from which they can confront the world and their own fate, sometimes reaching beyond the limits of death and time. Dermoût's books have been translated in many languages, and she received several literary prizes. Her collected works (*Verzameld Werk*) appeared in 1970 and 1974 .

Derrida, Jacques ▷Deconstruction

Dervis, Suat (1905–1972)
Turkish novelist, journalist and political activist, who has been publishing since she was fifteen. Her father, a professor of medicine, sent her to Berlin, where she studied literature at the university. In Berlin she wrote in German for newspapers and magazines. She returned to Istanbul in 1932, and worked as a journalist. She started editing a new socialist literary organ, *Yeni Edebiyat* (*New Literature*) in 1940, in which she was greatly helped by her husband. Their work in publishing and politics had to stop with the government's imposition of martial law. She went to France in 1953 but returned in 1963. She wrote two more novels before her death, which were translated into German and widely reviewed in Europe. Many of her works were first published in Europe and became widely known before their publication in Turkish. For example, *Arkara Mahpusa* (1968) was already widely known in its German version (1967). Other novels by Suat Dervis include: *The Black Book* (1920), *Neither Voice Nor Breath* (1923), *Night of Crisis* (1924), *As The Heart Wills* (1928), *Emine* (1931), *Nothing* (1939) and *Like a Madman* (1945).

D'erzell, Catalina (born 1897)
Mexican dramatist. In the beginning of the 20th century there were very strong, and autonomous theatre movements in Mexico and Argentina in which D'Erzell, who wrote about ten dramas, played an important role. In her comedies she dealt with the moral and social problems of her sex.
Works: *La Inmaculada* (*The Immaculate Woman*); *Apasionadamente* (*Passionately*), *Cumbres de nieve* (1923) (*Snow Peaks*); *Chanito* (1923); *Esos hombres* (1924) (*Those Men*); *El pecado de las mujeres* (1925) (*The Sin of Women*); *El reloj azul* (1925) (*The Blue Clock*); *La sin honor* (1926) (*The Woman Without Honour*); *La razón de la culpa* (1928) (*The Reason for Guilt*); *Los hijos de la otra* (1930) (*The Sons of the Other Woman*); *Lo que sólo el hombre puede sufrir* (1936) (*What Only Men Can Suffer*); *Maternidad* (1937) (*Maternity*), and *El* (1938) (*Him*).

Desai, Anita (born 1937)

Anita Desai

Indian novelist and short story writer. Born in Delhi to a Bengali father and a German mother, her writing has had a significant impact outside India. For her novel *Fire on the Mountain* (1977) Desai received the Royal Society of Literature's Winifred Holtby Prize and India's National Academy of Letters Award (1978). *Clear Light of Day* (1980) was nominated for the Booker Prize. She is married and has four children. She is a member of the Advisory Board for English, Sahitya Akademi, New Delhi, a Fellow of the Royal Society of Literature, and a member of the National Academy of Letters, New Delhi. In 1988 she was awarded the title Padma Shri by the President of India.

Desai's novels frequently depict the attempts of urban middle-class women to harmonize the needs of the self with the demands traditionally made of Indian women by the family, ▷caste and society. In addition to the novels above, two children's books and a collection of short stories, *Games at Twilight* (1978), she has published *Cry the Peacock* (1963), *Voices in the City* (1965), *Bye-bye, Blackbird* (1971), *Where Shall We Go This Summer?* (1975), ▷*In Custody* (1984), and *Baumgartner's Bombay* (1988).
Bib: Goel, Kunj Bala, *Language and Theme in Anita Desai's Fiction*; Jena, S., *Voice and Vision of Anita Desai*; Srivastava, R.K., *Perspectives on Anita Desai*.

Desbordes-Valmore, Marceline (1785–1859)

French poet. Born in Douai, the daughter of an impoverished craftsman, Desbordes-Valmore's childhood was harsh. After her mother's death, she began to act for a living, and travelled widely throughout France. She fell desperately and unhappily in love with the writer Henri Latouche, bore his child, and began to write poetry, much of which expresses her emotional anguish. Her son died in 1816, and she married a kindly but talentless actor, Prosper Valmore. Her life continued to be difficult – the daughters she bore Valmore also died, and her material resources were always limited – but literature offered her some consolation, and her poems still feature in French anthologies of verse. That she achieved such lasting recognition is a remarkable feat, given that women poets were, and still are, largely excluded from the French critical ▷canon. In 1959 an exhibition at the Bibliothèque Nationale in Paris marked the centenary of her death.

The volumes of poetry she published are: *Elégies et Romances* (1819) (*Elegies and Ballads*); *Elégies et poésies nouvelles* (1825) (*Elegies and New Poems*); *Les Pleurs* (1833) (*Tears*); *Pauvres Fleurs* (1839) (*Poor Flowers*) and *Bouquets et Prières* (1843) (*Bouquets and Prayers*). Her poems are characterized by a melancholic, elegiac tone, which recalls the work of other Romantic poets. However, they avoid the clichés that dogged much of the lyrical poetry produced during the Romantic era, and display a syntactical and lexical simplicity and originality which makes them seem remarkably modern. The North American critic Danahy has discerned in her poetic writing an emphasis upon intersubjectivity, and an attempt to ▷deconstruct or transform subject/object, self/other divisions which are also indicative of the modernity (and even the 'femininity') of her work. Critics have suggested, moreover, that her use of rhythm influenced Verlaine and the symbolist poets, and Verlaine did indeed view Desbordes-Valmore as the only woman worthy of the title of '*poète maudit*' ('damned poet'). Her work was also acclaimed by contemporaries like Baudelaire (1821–1867), and literary critic and historian Sainte-Beuve (1804–1869). In the last years of her life she wrote novels, short stories and children's poetry, and volumes of her correspondence were published in 1896, 1911 and 1924. Recent editions of her poems appeared in 1983 (Gallimard) and 1985 (Editions d'Aujourd'hui).

▷Blanchecotte, Auguste Malvina
Bib: Danahy, M., 'Marceline Desbordes-Valmore and the Engendered Canon', *Yale French Studies*, Vol. 75; Albistur, M. and Armogathe, D., *Histoire du féminisme français*; George-Day, 'Romantisme et poésie féminine', *Europe*; Jasenas, C., *Marceline Desbordes-Valmore devant la critique*.

Descard, Maria (1847–1927)

French novelist. Born in Brest, the daughter of one sea captain, and later the wife of another, she travelled widely, and put many of her experiences into her books. She wrote her first novel, *Mlle de Kervallez*, at the age of thirty, under the pseudonym Maryan, an amalgam of the Christian names of her English maternal grandmother. Quantities of others followed it, all of which were intended to entertain and instruct young ladies. Her works, which include *En Poitou* (1878) (*In Poitiers*); *Anne du Valmoët* (1880); *Les Chemins de la vie* (1882) (*The Paths of Life*); *La Cousine Esther* (1889) (*Cousin Esther*) and *Annie* (1890), won her the title of *lauréate* of the ▷Académie Française, despite the fact that she was quite lacking in literary ambition.

'Description of Cooke-ham, The' ▷*Salve Deus, Rex Judaeorum*

Desert Encroaches, The (1985)

A play by Nigerian writer ▷Tess Onwueme. Using the tradition of comic festival masks, the author addresses the issue of the arms race as it then was. Allegorical figures – Bear, Donkey, Dove, Hyena, and others – attend a summit conference to discuss the division of the world into two major blocs. Besides the issue it ostensibly addresses, the play also satirizes the new North–South division, and the failure of humankind to act while disaster looms – the desert encroaches.

Desert of the Heart (1977)

Canadian writer ▷Jane Rule's lesbian love story about two women who meet in Reno, Nevada, and discover themselves in one another. Evelyn Hall has gone to Reno to get a divorce; Ann Childs works there as a change girl in a casino. Their meeting and subsequent connection is gently developed, the setting of the desert and the gambling casinos effectively used to counterpoint the 'voluntary exile' both women inhabit. It was made into a feature film, *Desert Hearts* in 1985.

Deshoulières (Des Houlières), Antoinette du Ligier de la Garde (1637–1694)

French poet, philosopher and social critic. She had an affinity with some of the more independent thinkers of the 17th century, taught by the philosopher Pierre Gassendi (1592–1655). Madame Deshoulières was also an occasional dramatist, who even tried her hand at opera. There is a superficial philosophy of the French *libertines* (free-thinkers) in her early work, but in her later work she preaches faith in God and sometimes seems more like the severest moralist. She advocated the suppression of physical appetites '*par un effort de raison*' ('by intellectual effort'), and condemned in women '*le dessein général de plaire / [qui] Fait que nous plaisons beaucoup monis*' ('the general desire to please, which makes us less pleasing'). Her first collection of verse, *Les Moutons* (*The Sheep*), published in the *Nouveau Mercure galant* in 1677, is impregnated with pastoral nostalgia. The *Epître à Mlle de la Charce* (*Letter to Mademoiselle de la Charce*) deplores the superficiality of relationships between

men and women at court. The final years of her life were devoted to religious contemplation, and she wrote a series of odes attacking the obsession with rank and the accumulation of wealth. Her '*Ode à M. de la Rochefoucauld*' investigates the variety of positions adopted by philosophers on the afterlife. Her second series of *Réflexions diverses* (*Various Reflections*) are dominated by meditations on death, drawn from her reading of the Roman philosopher Seneca (c 3 BC–AD 65) and the Roman poet Lucilius (149–103 BC), either in translation or in the original, and of the French essayist Montaigne (1533–1592). She was a declared enemy of the *faux dévots* (religious hypocrites). She admired the work of the French dramatist Pierre Corneille (1606–1684) and was a member of the cabal which in 1677 condemned *Phèdre*, the tragic drama by Jean Racine (1639–1699). Anxious '*d'avoir du précieux et du hardi, [et] de mêler dans son bel esprit un grain d'esprit fort*' ('to be both precious and bold and to combine wit and intellectual acumen'), Madame Deshoulières held her own salon, frequented by the dramatists Thomas Corneille (1625–1709), his brother Pierre, and Philippe Quinault (1635–1688), the poet Isaac de Benserade (1613–1691) and the founder member of the Académie Française, Valentin Conrart (1603–1675) among others. The correspondence between Madame Deshoulières, her daughter and the eloquent priest, Esprit Fléchier (1632–1710), was published in 1671.
Bib: Perkins, W., 'Mme Deshoulières', *Newsletter of the Society for French Seventeenth-Century Studies* (1983), pp. 125–33.

Deshpande, Shashi (born 1938)
Indian novelist and short story writer. She was born in Dharwad, India, into a family renowned for its Sanskrit scholarship. She holds degrees in Economics and Law from the Universities of Bombay and Bangalore. She is married, has two sons, and lives in Bangalore. She did not begin writing seriously until she was thirty, when, as a housewife with young children, she found the urge to express herself overwhelming. She took a course in journalism, and completed an MA from Mysore University. Her short stories were first published in various English-language periodicals in India, but some have since appeared in the collections *The Legacy* (1971), *The Miracle* (1986) and *It was Dark* (1986). 'My Beloved Charioteer', from *It was Dark*, can also be read in ▷*The Inner Courtyard*. Among her novels are *The Dark Holds No Terrors* (1980), which has been translated into Russian and German, *Come Up and Be Dead* (1983), *It was the Nightingale* (1986) and ▷*That Long Silence* (1988). *Roots and Shadows* (1983) was awarded the 1984 Thirumathi Rangammal Prize for the best Indian novel in English. She has also written several books for children.

Desjardins, Marie-Catherine Hortense (1640–1683)
French writer, more commonly known as Madame de Villedieu. She was the first woman novelist to sign her name and recognize her works. She wrote under her maiden name, Desjardins, until 1667, and thereafter under that of the man whom she hoped to force to marry her, Antoine Boësset de Villedieu (1632–1668). As a professional writer, she does not seem to have been at all held back by the fact that she was a woman, and frequently approached distinguished patrons before she began a new work. Born into a heavily indebted, but fairly well-connected, family of the minor nobility, Madame de Villedieu was the victim of one and possibly two invalid marriages, becoming, according to legend, an unmarried mother at the age of nineteen. She lived a libertine existence, mostly in Paris, but she also travelled quite widely in France, Belgium and Holland, where she had many influential friends. She was a polygraph, who wrote a wide range of poetry, portraits, novels, short fiction (▷*nouvelles*), plays, and a collection of love letters published against her will. Her publisher, Barbin, also encouraged her to 'ghost' a collection of love stories which appeared anonymously in 1670 under the title *Le Journal amoureux* (*The Journal of Love*). Her works were very popular in their day, but most of her writing is situated in the marginal zone of *littérature de divertissement* (literary entertainment).

The sonnet, '*Jouissance*' (1658) ('Enjoyment'), her first successful poem, set the tone of her life and work, causing a minor scandal because a woman writer had dared to write a form of gallant love-poetry, or *poésie galante*, reserved for men. In 1659 she claimed general public attention with her *Farce des Précieuses* (1659) (*Farce of the Precious Woman*), satirizing the *Précieuses* (▷Precious Women) and the satire by the comic dramatist Molière (1622–1673), *Les Précieuses ridicules* (1659) (*The Ridiculous Precious Women*). This ensured her notoriety, but seems to have been well enough appreciated by Molière himself. In addition to an unfinished novel, a *nouvelle* written to amuse ▷Mademoiselle de Montpensier at Saint-Fargeau, she wrote various circumstancial pieces celebrating the court of Louis XIV (1638–1715) in the early 1660s, including a court ballet in honour of the Dauphin, dedicated to his governor, Monsieur de Montausier (1610–1690), which was probably never performed, and a successful tragedy, *Manlius* (1662) which was not without its detractors. Following the success of her last play, *Le Favory* (1665) (*The Favourite*), performed by Molière's troupe at Versailles with music by the Italian-born composer Jean-Baptiste Lully (1632–1687), on the controversial subject of a disgraced minister, Madame de Villedieu was promised a royal pension of 1500 *livres*, but received nothing before 1676, when she was given a *brevet* for under half the original sum. For a woman in 17th-century France this was still a singular honour.

In 1668, at the height of her fame, she found herself in serious financial difficulties, following Villedieu's marriage to another, and wrote a quick succession of lucrative novels and *nouvelles*. These works of fiction, which are often an amalgam of letters, sonnets, madrigals and other fashionable types of verse are, like her plays, an interesting combination of the old and the new. The best, like *Les Désordres de l'amour* (1677) (▷*Disorders of Love, Truly Expressed in the Unfortunate Lives of Givry with Mlle de Guise*), which contains a confession scene that may have inspired ▷*La Princesse de Clèves* (1679) (*The Princess of Clèves*) (▷Madame de Lafayette), are set in the 16th century and based on a thorough study of contemporary historians and memoir-writers. In her exotic tales, like *Les Nouvelles africaines* (1673) (*African Stories*), *Les Galanteries grenadines* (1673) (*Gallantries of Granada*) or *Les Annales galantes de Grèce* (1687) (*The Gallant Annals of Greece*), she allows her extravagant imagination free rein, and proceeds, with little or no thought for chronology, according to her own interpretation of the gallant annals of the past. Her prefaces contain information and references which seem successfully to have confused her readers about the historical accuracy of her fiction. The writer Pierre Bayle (1647–1706), who seems to have appreciated her work, singled her out as the originator of this fashion, which threatened the position of the official historians of the day.

Withdrawing to a convent at the height of her success in 1672, Madame de Villedieu wrote the semi-autobiographical novel *Mémoires de la vie d'Henriette-Sylvie de Molière* (1672–1674) (▷*Memoirs of the Life of Henriette-Sylvie de Molière*), which, together with *Le Portefeuille* (1674) (*The Portfolio*), is now considered her most interesting work. After a religious conversion, she married the wealthy Claude-Nicolas de Chaste (died 1679), chevalier and Sieur de Chalon, in 1677, but their marriage was kept secret and she seems to have retained the name Villedieu at least for a time.

Bib: Cuénin, M., *Roman et société sous LXIV: Mme de Villedieu (Marie-Catherine Desjardins) 1640–1683* (2 vols).

Desolación (1922) (Solace)

The first book of poems by the Chilean poet ▷Gabriela Mistral. In 1945 Mistral received the Nobel Prize, due in great part to the fame achieved by this lyrical book, as well as for her work as an educator in Chile. It was written after the tragic suicide of her one-time fiancé – a simple administrative officer who had married another – when he was accused of having committed a theft. In the novel, she begs God to forgive his suicidal soul and offers instead to suffer in his place. A clear dialogue emerges between a feminine narrator and an absent 'you', a beloved and idealized man. The deep emotion of this book, where the poet is gripped by maternal feelings, is continued in *Ternura* (1924) (*Tenderness*), which is dedicated to peace and love for children, but is present in all her work. Although Mistral published *Desolación* in 1922, when works by James Joyce (1882–1941), ▷Gertrude Stein, Ezra Pound (1885–1972) and

T.S. Eliot (1888–1965) were also appearing and ▷*modernismo* was surfacing in Brazil, the book has no relationship to the ▷avant-garde tones conveyed in these voices and in other movements present in Europe and Latin America, such as futurism and Surrealism. Mistral's tone is of a post-symbolist poet, and her book became a model of abstract and spiritual imagery that spread to other women poets in Latin America, such as the Brazilians ▷Cecília Meireles and ▷Gilka Machado, and the Uruguayan ▷Juana de Ibarbourou.

Désordres de l'amour, Les (1677) (Disorders of Love) ▷Desjardins, Marie-Catharine Hortense; Disorders of Love Truly Expressed in the Unfortunate Lives of Givry with Mlle de Guise

De Souza, Eunice (born 1949)

Indian poet and art critic. She was born in Goa, a former colony of Portugal famous for its syncretic Indo-Catholic culture, and was educated at the University of Bombay and Marquette University, Wisconsin. She taught in schools in England for two years, and at Loreto College, Darjeeling. Having completed her doctorate in 1989, she is now a lecturer in English at St Xavier's College, Bombay. She has co-edited an anthology of Indian prose in English, and has published children's tales, articles in arts journalism and three volumes of poetry, the most recent being *Ways of Belonging* (1990). With her years spent in the West, De Souza is an exemplary Goan, and her poetry, taut and sharp in its observations, often deliberately picks out and juxtaposes the different European and Indian strands of Goa's diverse cultural heritage.

De Stefani, Livia (born 1913)

Italian novelist, short story writer and poet. Born in Palermo, she read widely as a child, and wrote her first poetry at the age of ten. She married at seventeen and moved to Rome, where she contributed regularly to Italian newspapers and magazines. Her best-known work is her first novel of 1953, *La vigna delle uve nere* (*The Vineyard of the Black Grapes*). Set, as are her later narratives, in the Sicilian countryside, it tells the story of an incestuous relationship between a sister and brother. The father ultimately forces his daughter to kill herself because the son must inherit the land and uphold the family name. De Stefani is interested in developing the dramas of female protagonists, as *La Signora di Cariddi* (1971) (*The Woman from Cariddi*) further underlines in its tale of female psychological self-analysis, but she is also concerned with linguistic experimentation, and with creating a magical atmosphere in her narratives.

Her other works include: *Preludio* (1940) (*Prelude*); *Gli affatturati* (1955) (*The Bewitched*); *Passione di Rosa* (1958) (*Rosa's Passion*); *Viaggio di una sconosciuta e altri racconti* (1963) (*Journey of an Unknown Woman and Other Stories*).

Detective fiction

A genre of popular fiction in whose development women writers have played a central part. There is currently considerable critical interest in women's detective fiction. Critics are exploring the place of women writers in the history of the genre, the spread and popularity of feminist detective fiction, and the history of the woman detective in fiction from the 19th century onwards in the work of male and female writers.

The first detective novel written by a woman is often said to be the US writer ▷ Anna Katherine Green's *The Leavenworth Case* (1868), which introduces the female amateur detective Amelia Butterworth. This location of a literary origin depends, of course, on how the definitions and boundaries of the genre are made and drawn. The ▷ sensation fictions of the 1860s could be seen as early examples of the genre, and the North American Seeley Regester's sensation novel *The Dead Letter* (1867) has strong claims to be the first women's detective novel. The first women detectives in fiction appeared in the 1860s; the stereotype of women's 'nosiness' and obsessive interest in gossip and trivia was often used to explain the female detective's skill in ferreting out crimes and criminals. The history of the female sleuth in fiction is complicated by the number of forms in which this character appears – as spy, police officer, amateur detective and private eye. Michele Slung's *Crime On Her Mind* and Mary Cadogan and Patricia Craig's *The Lady Investigates* provide detailed accounts of the field.

By the end of the 19th century a number of women writers were producing detective and mystery fiction for an increasingly profitable market. Early 20th-century practitioners include the Hungarian-born Baroness Orczy who, in addition to her novels about the 'Scarlet Pimpernel', wrote a number of short stories featuring Lady Molly of Scotland Yard. She also invented an amateur 'armchair' detective, of unprepossessing habits and appearance, known as the 'Old Man in the Corner', who solves crimes deductively in collaboration with a female journalist. Orczy's contemporary, Marie Belloc Lowndes, wrote a number of crime and detective novels, including *The Lodger* (1911) (a fictionalized version of the Jack the Ripper case) and *The Terriford Mystery* (1913).

Women crime and detective writers came into greater prominence from the 1920s onwards, in the period known as the 'Golden Age' of detective fiction. This is usually dated from the first novel of ▷ Agatha Christie (*The Mysterious Affair at Styles*, 1920) to the last by ▷ Dorothy L. Sayers (*Busman's Honeymoon*, 1937). Other 'Golden Age' writers include ▷ Ngaio Marsh and ▷ Margery Allingham; ▷ Josephine Tey is often included in the category, although her post-war fiction, including ▷ *The Daughter of Time* (1951), is perhaps her most interesting. An account of women detective novelists from the 1920s onwards should also include the work of ▷ Georgette Heyer, Josephine Bell, Christianna

Brand (1909–1988), Hilda Lawrence and ▷ Gladys Mitchell, writers whose careers extend into the 1940s and 1950s.

Any attempt to describe why women are so good at crime writing should include the fact that detective fiction offered women writers a way into popular genre fiction free of the structures, preoccupations and language of romance; although novels like ▷ Daphne du Maurier's ▷ *Rebecca*, which combine the conventions of crime and romance writing should not be overlooked. Women writers' use of the 'crime puzzle' should also be distinguished from the bloodier forms of much male crime and thriller writing.

The period of the 'Golden Age', of course, maps onto the period between the wars, and critics have explained the popularity of detective fiction in the 1920s and 1930s as a response to the horrors of World War I. There is no simple cause and effect relationship, however; detective fiction is variously described as 'escape' literature, or as a way of negotiating anxieties about death and violence. The Detection Club, founded by Dorothy Sayers and others in 1930, set up rules for 'fair play' in detective fiction which not only relate to formal developments in the genre but could be said to express a fantasy of control over the means of death.

Similar complexities arise over the question of the 'conservative' or 'subversive' nature of the genre, and the work of Christie and Sayers is of particular salience here. While some women critics have seen Sayers as the creator of a feminist role-model in her writer/detective Harriet Vane, others are dismissive of her 'snobbery with violence'. Opinions are equally split over Christie. Critic Alison Light, for example, claims that Christie's writing is free of much of the nostalgia for 'traditional' English rural life played on by the enormously successful television dramatizations of her novels; her attitudes were, in fact, as 'populist' as her fiction is popular. On the other hand, her fiction is said to portray highly conservative views of 'natural justice' and of an innate disposition in human beings towards good or evil. More generally, opinions divide over the question of whether the genre itself is inherently conservative – crime is uncovered and punished and the community is made safe; or inherently subversive – criminality is the focus of interest and, possibly, sympathy. A topic of related interest, but with specific reference to women detective writers, is the portrayal of the 'spinster' – the elderly, unmarried, amateur detective typified in Christie's Miss Marple. Marion Shaw and Sabine Vanacker argue that, although Miss Marple escapes the despised status of 'spinster' in her role as detective, she contributes to the maintenance of relations of property and inheritance which have always disadvantaged the single woman. In this account, the conventional detective novel is an ambiguous and even, to borrow Cora Kaplan's phrase, 'an unsuitable genre for a feminist'.

Before discussing recent *feminist* crime and detective fiction, the work of ▷Ruth Rendell, ▷P.D. James and Patricia Highsmith should be mentioned. These very successful writers – the 'literary' qualities of whose writing have given detective fiction a new pedigree – are linked by their uses of ▷social realism, psychological approaches to the genre in which characterization is often as important as plot, and their rejection of 'formulaic' approaches to violence, murder and criminality. P.D. James comes closest to the work of recent feminist detective novelists in her depiction of contemporary social issues and her creation of female detectives Cordelia Gray and Kate Miskin. As Shaw and Vanacker point out, however, James's detective heroines 'do not see their work as constituting a critique of patriarchal society'.

This critique – central to what Jenny Turner more cynically describes as 'right-on leisure novels' – emerges in the work of numerous contemporary British and US detective novelists, the best-known of whom include ▷Amanda Cross (born 1926), ▷Valerie Miner, Frances Fyfield, ▷Barbara Wilson, Mary Wings, Gillian Slovo, Hannah Wakefield, Joan Smith, ▷Katherine V. Forrest, Sarah Dreyer, Val McDermid and ▷Sara Paretsky (born 1947). There are, of course, differences between the works of these writers. Paretsky, Forrest and Wings use, and subvert, the conventions of the thriller and the 'private eye' novel, whereas Cross, Miner and Smith play with the conventional setting of the closed community and/or the woman academic as detective. (Cross's mannered fictions are heavily indebted to the novels of Sayers.) Wilson, Wings, Dreyer, McDermid and Forrest write explicitly lesbian detective fiction, in which the 'marginality' of the detective is given a specific inflection, and in which identity, particularly sexual identity, becomes part of the scene to be investigated. Shared concerns include, however, the relationship of the work of detection to self-knowledge, the concept of 'corporate' and political crime (rather than criminality as the province of the lone killer), and violence as violence against women. This last aspect has been offered as a more general reason for women's attraction to and competence in the genre, 'an attraction which probably reflects the fact that the crime novel works over current fears and preoccupations about violence, victimisation and protection'. More positively, it could be claimed that women writers have found a way of revitalizing the genre, by politicizing its plots, and rewriting and transforming its tired old gender scripts and its stereotypical representations of femininity.

▷Grafton, Sue; Adaora Lily, Ulasi

Bib: Coward, R. and Semple, L., 'Tracking down the past: women and detective fiction', in Carr, H. (ed.), *From My Guy to Sci-Fi*; Light, A., *Forever England*; Turner, J., 'Right-ons', *London Review of Books*, 24.10.1991, pp. 22–23; Kaplan, C., 'An Unsuitable Genre for a Feminist?', *Woman's Review*, no. 8, June 1986, pp. 18–19; Shaw, M. and Vanacker, S., *Reflecting on Miss Marple*.

Norway and Sweden: Detective fiction writing has traditionally been a man's genre. Lalli Knutsen (1905–1981) is considered the first woman writer of detective novels in Norway; she wrote eight of them, together with her husband, Fritjof Knutsen.

Two contemporary women writers are well-known: Gerd Nyquist (1913–1985) was a very talented writer in the tradition of the US novelist Edgar Allan Poe (1809–1849). Her detective, Martin Brekke, is a lecturer, an anti-hero, and her novels are precise in their description of social surroundings, but also conservative in their restoration of law and order.

Ella Griffiths (1925–1990) was also a very productive writer. In the period from 1945 to 1985 forty-four detective novels were written by women writers in Norway, sixteen of them by Ella Griffiths. She wrote thirty novels in all, 70 short stories and thirteen books for children. Many of her detective novels are psychological thrillers, where the difference between hero and criminals is very blurred.

Kim Småge (born 1945, real name Karin Thorhus) has written a number of thrillers with great success. She writes freely with graphic descriptions of sex. Her début, the novel *Nattdykk* (1983) (*Night Diving*), is a feminist thriller, one of the first in Scandinavia, while *Origo* (1984) (*Orion*) is a political thriller, which has been filmed.

The Swedish detective novel is influenced by works from Britain and the USA. Swedish women writers did not take up this genre until the 1940s, but since then it has become very popular.

Kjerstin Göransson-Ljungman (born 1901) was the first woman writer to use the detective novel successfully. She wrote several novels in the British tradition, but set in Swedish surroundings.

Maria Lang (1914–1991) has written many novels, and has reached a very wide audience. Her first novel *Mördaren ljuger inte ensam* (1949) (*Not Only the Murderer Lies*) attracted attention. However, Lang does not transform the genre in any way, and writes in a rather stereotyped manner.

▷The Swedish novelist Kerstin Ekman started her career as an author of detective fiction in 1959, but gradually she shifted to psychological thrillers, and eventually abandoned detective fiction altogether.

Maj Sjöwall (born 1935) has written ten detective novels with her husband, Per Wahlöö (1926–1988). The novels depict Swedish society becoming increasingly political and corrupt. The novels are as much political novels in the ▷social realist tradition as they are detective novels. In 1990 she published a new detective novel, *Kvinnan som liknade Greta Garbo* (*The Woman who Looked Like Greta Garbo*) with a Dutch writer, Tomas Ross.

Detective's Album: Recollections of an Australian Police Officer, The (1871)

Short stories by ▷Mary Fortune ('Waif Wander'). This is the first book of detective stories published in Australia and is composed of six stories originally published in the *Australian Journal*.

De Tilène au Plateau: une enfance dakaroise (1975) ▷*Dakar Childhood, A*

Deuxième Sexe, Le (1949) ▷*Second Sex, The*, (1953)

Devanny, Jean (1894–1962)

New Zealand novelist. Jean Devanny grew up in a small mining town in the South Island. Her father was a miner and her mother the daughter of a British colonel, a difference which may be reflected in the class focus of Devanny's fiction and political life. Devanny married young, and she and her husband, also a miner, became deeply involved in political activity as Marxists. All five of Devanny's novels published in New Zealand are engaged with political and class questions and are overtly feminist in their critique of the status of women, particularly in their attack on the sexual conventions which lock women, emotionally and economically, into marriage. Devanny's first novel ▷*The Butcher Shop* (1926) was banned in New Zealand, Australia, Boston and Germany, both for its 'frank portrayal of farm conditions' which it was thought might affect immigration and because of its claim that a woman has autonomy over her body.

In 1929 the Devannys left for Australia where Jean Devanny became a political activist and toured the country lecturing for the Communist Party. Suffering from poverty and grief at the death of their eldest child, Devanny and her husband agreed to dissolve their marriage although they did not divorce. Devanny's work for the Party was extremely exhausting and time-consuming, and her publication of novels fell dramatically. Her later novels are polemics of political commitment and, apart from *Sugar Heaven* (1936), which deals with the Queensland sugar cane strikes, fail to produce complex narratives. Devanny's history with the Communist Party was troubled; she was expelled for no given reason in 1940, readmitted in 1944 and resigned in 1950, but remained committed to Marxism till the end of her life.

Devanny's work has received a lot of attention, especially from feminists, over the last twenty years, and establishes her as one of the most radical and interesting women novelists of 20th-century Australian and New Zealand writing.

Publications include: *The Butcher Shop* (1926); *Lenore Divine* (1926); *Old Savage and Other Stories* (1927); *Dawn Beloved* (1928); *Riven* (1929); *Bushman Burke* (1930); *Devil Made Saint* (1930); *Poor Swine* (1932); *All for Love* (1932); *Sugar Heaven* (1936); *Paradise Flow* (1938); *The Killing of Jacqueline Love* (1942); *Cindie* (1949).
▷*Gender, Politics and Fiction*

Devi

The mother goddess in the Hindu cosmos, sometimes referred to as Mahadevi, the great goddess. She takes many forms, each one with specific attributes, *eg* Kali, Durga.
▷Shakti

Devi, Ashapurna (born 1909)

Indian novelist, who writes predominantly in Bengali. She has had no formal education, and lives in Calcutta. She has written over 250 novels and short stories, and is one of India's most decorated writers. In 1966 she won the Bengal Government's Rabindra Award, and in 1977 she won the Sahitya Akademi Jnanpith Award for *Pratham Pratisruti*. In 1976 the President of India conferred the title of Padma Shri on her. Her writing provides lively and sympathetic insights into the world of middle-class Bengalis, often with a focus on the tradition-bound woman who is just beginning to learn of a life outside family responsibilities.

Many of Ashapurna Devi's short stories have been published in ▷*Manushi*.

Devi, Mahasveta (born 1926)

Indian novelist, dramatist and social activist. She writes in Bengali, using her fiction to campaign for a more just and humane society. Her career as an author was influenced by her early association with Gananatya, a group of politically active writers and actors who took the revolutionary step of performing plays in the villages of Bengal in the 1930s and 1940s. Her work as an activist and anthropologist in turn provided more raw material for her fiction. She has also written historical works in which she attempts to bring to life for Indians today the great figures of their past. Among these works is *Jhansi Rani*, (1956), the story of the Rani (Queen) of Jhansi, who died leading her troops into battle against the British in the Indian Rebellion of 1857.

▷*Five Plays* (1986) is a collection translated and adapted from some of her Bengali short stories. *Agnigarbha* (1978) (*A Womb of Fire*) is a collection of long stories which deal with the great Marxist uprising of the Naxalites in eastern India in the 1960s. A short story, 'The Wet Nurse', translated from the Bengali, appears in ▷*Truth Tales*, and several others are translated and published in *Of Women, Outcasts, Peasants and Rebels* (1990).

▷Spivak, Gayatri Chakravorty

Devi, Maitreyi (born 1914)

Indian poet and social worker, who writes predominantly in Bengali. She is a world-renowned authority on the poetry of Rabindranath Tagore, a legacy of her early personal contact with him as his pupil. She has written eight books on Tagore, thus earning for herself the sobriquet 'the

Boswell of Tagore'. She was awarded the Tagore Centenary Medallion by the USSR in 1961, and also the Soviet Desh Jawaharlal Nehru Prize in 1968. She has received other awards for her humanitarian work among socially oppressed groups in India.

Her first anthology of poems, with an introduction by Tagore, was published when she was sixteen, and has since been followed by many others. She has translated one of her novels, *Na Hanyate* (1974), into English as ▷*It Does Not Die* (1974). She has been the editor of *Nabajatak*, a Bengali literary journal, since 1964.

de Vilmorin, Louise (1906–1969)
French novelist and poet. She grew up in an aristocratic and intellectual family who encouraged her to write, and she produced several novels and collections of poetry related to her social milieu, or set in romantic surroundings. They include *Le Retour d'Erica*, (1948) (*Erica's Return*), *La Lettre dans un taxi*, (1960) (*The Letter in a Taxi*) and *Madame de . . .* (1954), filmed by Max Ophuls.

Devil's Doll, The (1911)
Russian novel by ▷Zinaida Gíppius. For her novel of ideas about the political 'reaction' in Russian society, Gíppius took Fyodor Dostoevsky's *The Possessed* (1871–1872) as her model. She creates a dominant, attractive hero, Iurii Dvoekurov, who voices a hedonistic credo with which she disagreed. Her depiction of radical revolutionaries who use terror is mostly negative, although several are presented sympathetically as having doubts about their movement. It is a man in sympathy with a third group which aims to combine revolution with Christianity who calls Iurii the 'Devil's Doll' at a public gathering. Gíppius also questions Iurii's philosophy through the agency of his half-sister Litta, who, like many 19th-century Russian heroines, understands intuitively the falseness of his credo.

Iurii explains that the aim of each person's life is his own happiness, defined in materialistic terms, while causing the least harm possible to others. Yet he does a lot of harm, especially to women. Iurii does not believe in love, because love involves putting consideration of another's welfare before one's own. The course of the novel shows his destructive relationships with several women, mostly from other classes. He gets the servant-girl Mashka pregnant, then forgets about her; in the novel's last chapter, Mashka is seen burying her child, the offspring of the 'Devil's Doll'. Natasha, a woman of his own class who has left the revolutionary movement, is one of the few women to escape from him: she flees abroad to make a new life for herself. Gíppius emphasizes the hard lot of women in a chapter entitled 'The Salty Sea and the Green Sea.' As the peasant Varvara explains, the salty sea is women's tears, and the green sea the wine their menfolk drink.

As with all of Gíppius's writing, this novel is marked by a careful use of language and attention to structural detail. There is some fine satire on contemporary aestheticism. However, in 223 pages Gíppius falls short of Doestoevsky's mastery of grounding multiple ideologies in personalities fleshed out in psychological and emotional depth.

Devlin, Anne (born 1951)
Irish writer. Born in Belfast, Devlin now lives in England. Her television, radio and stage plays have won a number of awards and include *A Woman Calling* (1984), *The Long March* (1984), *Ourselves Alone* (1985) and *Naming the Names*. Her first collection of short stories, *The Way Paver*, appeared in 1986. She describes herself as 'continually torn between writing about the "Troubles" and wishing to ignore them; resenting the grip of history and bowing to its inevitability'.

Devlin, Polly (born 1944)
Irish novelist and short story writer. Born in County Tyrone, she now lives in England. Her childhood, spent on her family's small farm on the shores of Lough Neagh, provided the material for her first two books, *All of Us There* (1983) and *The Far Side of the Lough: Stories from an Irish Childhood* (1983), evocative accounts of growing up in Northern Ireland in the 1950s. Her most recent novel, *Dora*, appeared in 1990.

Devocionario (1986) (Prayerbook)
Highly acclaimed collection of poems by Spanish poet ▷Ana Rossetti, one of the outstanding female poets of the post-Franco era. It is typical of much of her work in that it fuses sexual and religious codes. Rossetti's poetry is distinctive for its frank, confessional treatment of female eroticism, and its obsession with death and eroticized religious images.

Devojka za sve (1940) (Jill of All Trades)
Serbian novel by Milka Žicina (1902–1984). Based on the author's own experiences, this is the story of a peasant girl who sets out to lead an independent life. She works as a servant in a nearby village and then in a small town, and finally saves enough for her train fare to Belgrade. There, disillusion and humiliation follow, as she becomes just one woman among crowds seeking work. She goes into service in various households, and is finally taken on in the kitchen of a hotel restaurant. Žicina describes the relationships of the women who work there. Although tendentious, like her other autobiographical novel, *Kajin put* (1934) (*Kaja's Journey*) (Žicina later became an ardent communist), it is fresh and well-observed, and the work is lifted above its description of immediate experience by recurrent imagery which evokes another world, that of the girl's childhood in her home village.

Devotional Papers (1773)
Written by the North American Puritan, ▷Sarah Prince Gill 'in her solemn hours' and published two years after her death, they reveal her excellent education and astutely logical mind. The ten

papers address issues such as Christian magnanimity and God's loving kindness; papers seven to ten are her personal reflections on gaining 'a renewed Heart'. Also appended is a letter written in 1755 and enclosed in an envelope with the notation that it should not be opened until after her death; the letter is a word of counsel to 'all my young Acquaintance' to seek salvation without delay.

Devourers, The
Translated into English from *I divoratori* (1910), a novel by Italian writer ▷Annie Vivanti, divided into three sections. The novel highlights both the pitfalls of parental ambition for children, and the pain of having, and raising, children. There is a very keen observation of the cruelty of children, who are the devourers of the title. In each of the three tales told, children devour their mothers particularly and prevent them from doing anything else, such as developing their own talents. Above all, Vivanti seems to stress, children kill the artistic impulse in the mother. This novel is at once strikingly poetic, in the manner one might expect from a poet who is also a novelist, and outstandingly stark in its crushing portrayal of motherhood.

Devout Treatise on the Pater Noster, A (1524)
▷Margaret More Roper's ▷translation of Desiderius Erasmus's (?1466–1536) commentary on the Lord's Prayer. It is one of the earliest English translations of Erasmus's writing. Roper probably completed it in 1523. Her work was first published in 1524, and twice more during the following six years. Roper's skillful translation intensifies the already existing meditative and conversational tone of Erasmus's Latin treatise. It belongs to the ▷humanist agenda for disseminating ideas.
Bib: Verbrugge, R.M., 'Margaret More Roper's Personal Expression in the *Devout Treatise on the Pater Noster*' in Hannay, M, *Silent but for the Word*.

Dewees, Mary Coburn (fl 1787–1788)
North American travel diarist. Little is known of her life, except as noted in the diary (▷*Mrs Mary Dewees's Journal from Philadelphia to Kentucky*) that she maintained for the edification of her Philadelphia relatives while she and her family undertook the arduous journey to a new home in the recently opened lands of Kentucky. Her eye for detail and her poetic descriptions enhance her record of the family's pioneering journey.
▷Early North American letters

De Wet, Reza (born 1953)
South African dramatist writing in Afrikaans and English; born in the Orange Free State, she lives in Grahamstown in the Eastern Cape. De Wet's first published work is *Diepe Grond* (1986) (*Deep Earth*), a play set on a Free State farm, where a brother and sister, cared for by a black woman, re-enact their relationship with the parents they murdered. De Wet has said in an interview that the black woman symbolizes the regenerative force of African culture, and offers gentle mothering, in contrast to the ▷patriarchal culture of the white father. This somewhat romanticized view of Africa recurs in her work *Nag, Generaal* (1988) (*Night, General*). *Op Dees Aarde* (1987) (*What on Earth*) is similarly concerned with the oppressiveness of Afrikaner Calvinist values. De Wet's recent play in English, *In a Different Light* (produced in 1989), has not yet been published.

D'haen, Christine (Elodia Maria) (born 1923)
Flemish poet and essayist. After graduating in Germanic philology in Ghent, she continued her studies in Edinburgh, becoming a teacher in Bruges, and then worked for the Gezelle-archive until 1983. She made her début with the narrative poem 'Abailard and Heloys' (1948). For this and other collected poems (*Gedichten 1946–1958*) she was awarded literary prizes. In 1976 she became a member of the Royal Academy of Dutch Linguistics and Literature, and in 1991 she received the Anna Bijns Prize. D'haen stands apart, even isolated, in the literary world; her poetic aesthetic does not look for its norms and values in contemporary society, but in Western tradition (classical, biblical, mythological), and, later, in non-Western cultures. Her work reverts back to the classical names in literature (she has derived some titles from the 17th-century-writer Vondel). Some of her collections are: *Ick sluit van daegh een ring* (1975) (*I Close a Ring Today*), *Onyx* (1983) and *Mirages* (1989). In 1989 she also published *Zwarte sneeuw* (*Black Snow*), stories that vary widely in character, providing a fragmentary picture of a personal past. Translations of her work have appeared in *Poetry in Flanders: A Pen Edition* (1982).

Dhingra, Leena (born ?1940)
Indian freelance writer and novelist, now based in Britain. Her family were made refugees by the ▷Partition of India in 1947, and they moved to Paris. She has worked as a film technician, publicity officer and teacher. An autobiographical piece, 'Breaking out of the Labels', appears in the anthology *Watchers and Seekers* (ed. R. Cobham and M. Collins, 1987). It describes her attempts to break free of the labelling that she has encountered as someone considered different. These themes of self-discovery and definition are explored in a fairytale-like short story, 'The Girl Who Couldn't See Herself' in the anthology ▷*Right of Way* and in her first novel, ▷*Amritvela* (1988).

Dia dos Prodígios, O (1980) (The Day of Wonders)
This first novel by Portuguese writer ▷Lídia Jorge received widespread critical attention for its intelligent portrayal of the impact of the 1974 revolution on an isolated community in the southern Algarve. In some respects Jorge seems to have been influenced by the ▷'magical realism' of

Latin American fiction of the sixties. The novel depicts fantastic events, and, in order to convey the oral culture of a village community, it experiments with unusual forms of typography.
Bib: Sadlier, Darlene J., *The Question of How: Women Writers and New Portuguese Literature.*

D'iákonova, Elizaveta Aleksandrovna (1874–1902)

Russian diarist, prose writer, and poet. Like ▷Marie Bashkirtseff to whom she was frequently compared, D'iákonova was known primarily for her posthumously published ▷*Diary*. She too died young: at the age of twenty-eight she committed suicide in the Swiss Alps. D'iákonova also had artistic ambitions, but, unlike Bashkirtseff, she lacked the self-confidence and secure environment that made the former's strides possible.

From her diary we learn that D'iákonova came from a tradition-bound merchant family in Nerekhta (the milieu of ▷Liubov' Stólitsa's novel ▷*Elena Deeva*). After she completed secondary school in Iaroslavl', she wanted to go on to higher education ('women's courses') in St Petersburg, but her despotic mother prevented her doing so until she was twenty-one and could enrol without parental permission. She had seen education as an escape, and the reality of the courses was a grave disappointment. While still enrolled, D'iákonova began her literary career and published articles and fiction, including the article 'Women's Education', in the journal *Women's Cause*. In 1900 she went to Paris to enrol in the Sorbonne law school. According to an obituary, she was buried in her home town of Nerekhta.

After D'iákonova's death, her *Diary*, two stories and three sketches she wrote between 1898 and 1899, and some poems appeared in print. The first story 'The Shot', ends with the heroine's suicide, an eerie foreshadowing of D'iákonova's own death. The sketches deal primarily with the themes of people's insensitivity to each other. D'iákonova's experiments with different kinds of narrative, and her use of irony and dialogue indicate that she might have matured into a serious writer had she had the self-confidence and resourcefulness to persist.

Dial, The (1840–1844)

US small-circulation quarterly. It was edited by ▷Margaret Fuller from 1840 to 1842, and then by the US writer Ralph Waldo Emerson (1803–1882). The voice of the transcendentalist movement (▷transcendentalism), *The Dial* under Fuller celebrated variety and even contradictions. Its principal women contributors were Fuller herself, who became a 'martyr' to the journal, and Elizabeth Palmer Peabody (1804–1894).

Diallo, Nafissatou (1941–1982)

Senegalese autobiographer and novelist. A pediatrician and midwife at the Centre de Protection Maternelle et Infantile in Ouagou-Niaye, Senegal, she came to public attention with the publication in 1975 of her autobiographical account, *De Tilène au Plateau: une enfance dakaroise* (▷*A Dakar Childhood*). Five years later she published a novel, *Le Fort maudit* (1980) (*The Cursed Fortress*), an historical fiction which traces the role of Thiane, the heroine, in its epic events. Both texts centre on a young female protagonist moving from an idyllic childhood into womanhood. Her last book, *Awa, la petite marchande* (1981) (*Awa, the Little Shop-Girl*) is aimed at young girls growing up under the constant threat of disgracing themselves by giving way to pressure from men for sexual favours. It seeks to demonstrate that there is another way to survive, even when poverty makes ▷prostitution look like an easy solution.

Dialogo della divina provvidenza, Il (1378)

▷*Dialogue of the Seraphic Virgin, Dictated by Her While in a State of Ecstasy in 1378, The*

Dialogue of the Seraphic Virgin, Dictated by Her While in a State of Ecstasy in 1378, The (1896)

Translation of *Il Dialogo della divina provvidenza*. This work was dictated to her disciples by Italian writer ▷Santa Caterina da Siena in 1378, while, as the title implies, in a state of ecstasy. She learned to read and write herself only later in life. It has been reprinted many times, with varying titles. Using the structure of a dialogue between the soul and God, Caterina analyses the nature of Truth, the role of the Church and the Pope, and the nature of the world. This is a work which reveals Caterina's religious passion, her mysticism, her political understanding, and her strength of character, as well as being full of the most vivid metaphors and vigorous language. It is outstanding in the ▷religious literature of the period, as an example of one woman's contribution to an ongoing religious debate.

Diaries (Ancient Greek and Roman)

Some classical Greek and Roman women were credited with memoirs. The erotic work of ▷Philaenis may have taken this form, as may that of the scandalous Roman empress ▷Agrippina the Younger. In the Christian period we find ▷Perpetua recording her visions in prison before martyrdom and ▷Egeria chronicling her Christian pilgrimage for the benefit of her sister nuns.

Diaries and journals (Southern Africa)

In Dutch writing, fragments remain of a diary written in 1797 (as well as a cash book) kept by Johanna Margaretha Duminy, which gives a lively account of life on a farm near Caledon in the Western Cape. The first sustained accounts are ▷Anne Barnard's ▷*Journal of a Tour into the Interior* (written 1798, published 1849) and ▷Augusta de Mist's *Diary of a Journey to the Cape of Good Hope and the Interior of Africa in 1802 and 1803* (1953).

At the end of the 18th century a strong pietist

tendency existed at the Cape. Chief among these writers is Catharina Aldegonda van Lier (1768–1801), whose diary in Dutch, *Dagboek, Gemeenzame Brieven en Eenzame Overdenkingen* (1804) (*Diary, Familiar Letters and Solitary Musings*), is a mystical, poetic work which makes no mention of public events in the Cape. The writings of the Bosman sisters, Susanna (1711–1755) and Elisabeth (1720–1784), also provide interesting testimony to the pietism of Dutch women in the Cape.

Of the 1820 British settlers, a number of diaries and journals are available, among them *The Journals of Sophia Pigot* (1974), and Mary Elizabeth Barber's *Wanderings in South Africa by Sea and Land*, published in the *Quarterly Bulletin of the South African Library*, December 1962–December 1963. The wives of missionaries often kept journals, sometimes presenting accounts of the active roles played in their husbands' work, but sometimes also focusing on their husbands' lives to the exclusion of their own experiences and feelings, as in *The Journals of Elizabeth Lees Price*. *The Recollections of Elizabeth Rolland* recounts her work at the Beersheba mission station in the Orange Free State.

Two accounts of the Great Trek exist, in Afrikaans: one is a memoir by Anna Elisabet Steenkamp, dated 1843, collected in *Voortrekkermense* (*Voortrekker People*), edited by G. S. Preller, and the other an unpublished diary written later by Susanna Catharina Smit, who gives an account of her religious experiences with barely a reference to daily Trek life. A journey to the Cango Caves forms the substance of the first article published by a South African woman in a periodical: Petronella Sophia Faure (1787–1868) describes her travels and visit in *Het Nederduitsch Zuid-Afrikaansch Tijdschrift*, December 1824. The diary of Alida Margaretha Jacoba Badenhorst (1867–1908) was translated into English by Emily Hobhouse (1860–1926), appearing under the title *Tant Alie of Transvaal, her Diary, 1880–1902* (1923). This forms an important part of ▷Anglo–Boer War writing.

Although memoirs and reminiscences of white women abound, the tradition of publishing diaries *per se* virtually fell away in the 20th century, the six-volume *War Diaries, 1944–1948* of ▷Sarah Gertrude Millin standing as a rare example. The unpublished 1913–14 South African journal of ▷Pauline Smith gives an interesting account of one of her return trips to the world of her childhood, rapidly changing with industrialization, poverty and incipient racial conflict.

Diaries of Julia Cowles: A Connecticut Record 1797–1803, The (1931)

▷The North American Julia Cowles's diaries begin when, at the age of eleven, she was sent to Sarah Pierce's Female Academy in Litchfield, Connecticut. The purpose of diary-keeping, she noted, was to 'relate the events of my youth'. For Cowles, that meant the lessons learned each day, the leisure reading indulged in on rainy Saturdays,

the Sunday sermons, and the intricacies of group socials that became increasingly important to her. Most notable is the maturing of Cowles's ideas and her writing. In the later diaries, Cowles recognized that her health was failing, and her tone shifts to one of meditation. Preferring not to record the 'vain pleasures' that had occupied her youth, Cowles observes, "Tis only by searching that we can know ourselves . . . and correct our faults.' Whether she is discussing classes or social events or attending church, Cowles now describes her processes always in terms of 'preparing' – most explicitly, for the next life.

Diario e lettere: dal mio diario (1945) (Diary of a Woman)

A collection of Italian writings which covers the events of ▷Sibilla Aleramo's life, and her work, and which explores the relationship between the two. To read this alongside Aleramo's fiction, and most particularly alongside ▷*A Woman*, helps the reader towards a greater understanding both of Aleramo's writing, and of the way in which she viewed her work. She explains her writing here as a means of striving towards self-fulfillment, following on from the traumatic experiences of her early life as a young woman.

'Diary and Letters of Elizabeth Murray Inman, The' (1901)

Excerpts from ▷Elizabeth Murray Campbell Smith Inman's diary (1769–1771) and letters (1775–1783) are included in the biography of her brother, *Letters of James Murray, Loyalist*. A North American woman of initiative and wealth, Inman married three times, ran a business in Boston, Massachusetts, for several years, and managed the family estate and withstood Patriot troops during the revolutionary years when her husband was detained during the siege of Boston. In a travel diary that Inman maintained on a journey to Scotland ('the land of my nativity'), she repeatedly notes in moving prose the significance of embracing the memory of women who were important in her life. In subsequent years, Inman maintained a correspondence with family members throughout the American Revolution, in which she records in striking detail her attempts to manage their Cambridge estate. When friends advised her to leave the estate, she remarked with her usual spirit, 'I told them with a cheerful countenance we could die but once, and I was a predestinarian, therefore had no personal fear.' In the final letter of the collection, written shortly before her death, her spirit remains defiant, though her health was virtually gone.
▷Early North American letters

Diary kept by Elizabeth Fuller (1915)

Written between October 1790 and December 1792 by fifteen-year-old ▷Elizabeth Fuller, this diary reveals little about the thoughts or emotional development of a North American teenager, but it is rich in details of Fuller's domestic life at the end of the 18th century, her training in spinning and weaving, and the social gatherings that drew her attention. The text also includes some poems probably written by Fuller.

Diary of Anaïs Nin: 1931–1974, The (1966–1980)

According to the US novelist and diarist ▷Anaïs Nin, she began her diary at age eleven as a response to her father's desertion. In all there are 150 volumes, of which only a small proportion have been published. Seven collected books appeared between 1966 and 1980, covering Nin's life in France, New York and California. The earlier years between 1914 and 1920 were first published under the title *Linotte* (1978). Since then three more volumes cover the years 1920–1931.

The diaries are famous for their representation of Nin's bisexual relationship with Henry and June Miller, between whom she acted as what Ann Snitow calls an 'androgynous go-between'. Nin invites the reader into the intellectual and artistic milieu of 1930s Paris and her later life in the US. However, the documentary aspect of the diary is less significant than the investigation of the links between gender, sexuality and creativity.

The diary constructs a version of female subjectivity which is secret and private; bedroom writing, as against the multiple female roles Nin plays in her public life. She describes her diary as 'the only steadfast friend I have, the only one which makes life bearable', and she writes that it is her 'one place of truth, one dialogue without falsity'. But Nin also represents the diary's relation to her self in terms of 'illusion', describing it as like an opium pipe. The moment of writing is the moment 'when I relive my life in terms of a dream . . . an endless story'.

A truly ▷modernist work; textuality, sexuality and the unconscious are all entwined, and the stability of the self is undermined even as it is asserted.

Diary of Anna Green Winslow, A Boston School Girl of 1771–3 (1894)

The diary actually covers the years 1771–3 while its North American author ▷Anna Green Winslow attended a finishing school in Boston, Massachusetts. Winslow records her initial insecurities of separation from family, her developing friendships and religious training, and the everyday lessons of boarding-school life. Set against the backdrop of the British occupation of Boston on the eve of the American Revolution, the diary details not only a young woman's proper education but her reactions to the beginnings of war.

Diary of a Provincial Lady, The (1931)

Novel by English writer ▷E.M. Delafield. Comprising diary extracts which first appeared in instalments in the feminist journal *Time and Tide*, *The Diary* is an acute, extended, comedy of manners focusing on provincial or 'county' lifestyles of the aristocratic and upper middle classes. Followed by three sequels, the journal follows its unnamed heroine from her domestic role as wife, mother and household manager, through to an independent life in wartime London. The text illustrates Delafield's characteristic sharp observation of manners and social mores, and its episodic form reflects the fragmented life of the woman writer.

Diary of Christiana Leach, of Kingsessing, 1765–1796, The (1911)

Translated from ▷Christiana Leach's native German, this North American diary presents in brief notations Christiana's life in Massachusetts from 1765 to 1796. The diary highlights her brother's pre-war travel to London to meet the king and queen, family events such as the birth of her children and grandchildren, Leach's piety, the American Revolution ('a sad and troublesome time'), and the yellow fever epidemic in Philadelphia that claimed the life of her eldest son. Though non-reflective, in the cumulative record Leach's entries provide a surprisingly clear sense of the changes in one woman's life which spanned crucial years in North America's history.

'Diary of Elizabeth Porter Phelps, The' (1891)

Published in an edited collection of colonial writings, *Under a Colonial Roof-Tree*, the North American ▷Elizabeth Porter Phelps's diary covers entries from October 1763 until April 1812, five years before her death. Brief entries chronicle life in Hadley, Massachusetts, in the revolutionary and early federal periods.

Diary of Elizaveta D'iákonova, The (1904–1905)

This two-volume diary covers Russian writer ▷D'iákonova's life from the age of twelve to the last year of her life. Published posthumously, beginning in 1904, two years after her suicide, it was a great success. By 1912 four editions had appeared. The work is divided into three parts. In the first, 'The Diary of One Girl Out of Many: 1886–1895', she appears as a naïve religious child from a merchant family. The second part, 'Diary at the Higher Women's Courses: 1895–1899', describes her years at university, her loneliness and disenchantment. Her loss of faith in the cause of helping 'the people' leads her to abandon the idea of opening a school for peasant children. She also describes student unrest in 1899. The third section, 'Diary of a Russian Woman: 1900–1902', covers her life in Paris, her introduction to the Bohemian lifestyle of Russians abroad, her desperate crush on a French psychologist, her return home, and an attempted suicide. With no other goal in view, D'iákonova began dreaming of a writing career. This may explain the abrupt change to a more literary style in the third part, with dramatized dialogues and set scenes. Her literary ambitions were thwarted in part by her own lacerating self-doubts.

Widely reviewed, the *Diary* was not valued for

its literary merits, but rather for its presentation of a young woman's life that was seen as symptomatic of the 'enervating times.' After all, D'iákonova herself had said she was just 'one of many'. Negative reviewers dismissed it as a *succés de scandale*. The similarities between the *Diary* and ▷Marie Bashkirtseff's were noted: the age at which the two girls began writing, the unsparing self-analysis, the artistic ambitions, and the search for love and empathy.

Diary of Frances Baylor Hill, The (1967)

Written in 1797 by a young North American woman from Virginia, ▷Frances Baylor Hill's diary is not personally reflective but it does offer numerous details about her activities on a daily basis. As such it has historical value, although it is of little literary interest.

Diary of Grace Growden Galloway (1931)

During the American Revolution, ▷Grace Growden Galloway and her husband remained Loyalists; when conditions made it essential for her husband and daughter to leave North America, Galloway remained behind in an attempt to protect their property as their daughter's rightful inheritance. During the crucial year of June 1777 to July 1778, Galloway maintained a daily diary in which she recorded her bitter distress ('so I find I am a beggar indeed I expect every hour to be turn'd out of doors & where to go I know not') and her evolving recognition that no support would be forthcoming from her husband or the British government. Although of little literary significance, the diary is a historically compelling record of the fate of a Loyalist woman left to confront the social, economic and political consequences of such a political alliance during the American Revolution.
  ▷Early North American Quaker women's writings

Diary of Lady Margaret Hoby, 1599–1605, The

The earliest extant diary recording daily personal events by a British woman, ▷Margaret Hoby's diary is a record of her life from August 1599 to July 1605. Her entries document, but do not describe in any great detail, the many events in her daily management of a large household. The diary also enumerates the ▷letters written, visitors received, and books read. She also mentions, without detail, the medical treatments she administered, and her own personal illnesses. The diary seems rather impersonal, in that Hoby was apparently not interested in recording her feelings about the people she knew or about contemporary events (eg inflation and taxes, the Plague of 1603–1604, the Essex Rebellion). Hoby seems rather to have kept her diary primarily to assist in religious self-examination.
Bib: Meads, D.M. (ed.), *Diary of Lady Margaret Hoby, 1599–1605* (1930).

Diary of Lady Mildmay, The

Diary written by ▷Grace Sherrington Mildmay between about 1570 and 1617. The account covers not only the actual time during which it was written, but also (through retrospect) Mildmay's life from childhood to the early years of her marriage, when she began to write. Although her marriage to Anthony Mildmay was apparently an unhappy one, Mildmay seems to have genuinely liked her father-in-law, Walter Mildmay, the Puritan founder of Emmanuel College, Cambridge. Mildmay's diary contains approximately 1,000 pages, mostly filled with undated meditations. It is especially interesting for its extensive description of one Elizabethan woman's ideas concerning education. The preface to her work is entitled 'Experience I conned to my child', and expresses her belief in the importance of intellectual endeavours, knowledge of the scriptures, national history, and classical philosophy. She recommends to her daughter the four books her own mother had given to her: the Bible, John Foxe's *Book of Martyrs* (1563), ▷*The Imitation of Christ*, and Wolfgang Musculus's *Commonplaces*. Mildmay apparently admired her mother, and felt gratitude for her instruction, even though many lessons were reinforced with beatings. Her diary also attests to her fondness and admiration for her own teacher, Mrs Hamblyn, from whom she received her training in such skills as writing and knowledge of 'phisick and surgurie'.
Bib: Weigall, R., 'An Elizabethan Gentlewoman', *Quarterly Review*, 215 (1911), pp. 119–38.

Diary of M. Ambler, 1770 (1937)

The journal is a record of the North American author ▷Mary Cary Ambler's journey from Jamestown, Virginia, to Baltimore, Maryland, in her endeavour to have her children inoculated against smallpox. It details the process of inoculation, the landscape of 18th-century Baltimore, and the arduousness of travel for women and children during this period.

Diary of Mary Cooper: Life on a Long Island Farm 1768–1773, The (1981)

In brief notations, the North American author ▷Mary Wright Cooper details her agrarian lifestyle over a six-year period. The diary captures the importance of weather in a wheat farmer's life and the significance of religious devotion in Cooper's attempts to stave off the loneliness of her harsh life.

'Diary of Mrs Martha Moore Ballard (1785–1812), The' (1904)

Appended to *The History of Augusta First Settlements and Early Days as a Town*, the North American author ▷Martha Moore Ballard's diary is an extraordinary and yet representative account of what one scholar has called 'women's work in eighteenth-century Maine'. For work was the heart of Ballard's everyday life: as a midwife, a farmer, a wife and a mother of eight children.

Covering a twenty-seven-year period from 1785 until shortly before her death in 1812, the diary reveals both the mundane and the fantastic elements of North American women's lives in the post-revolutionary years. From producing clothing to baking to delivering children and generally acting as the local nurse, Ballard explicitly accounts for her daily chores but rarely includes her emotional life. 'Productivity' was the reality and the literary style of Martha Moore Ballard as she registered the complex details of 18th-century housewifery and midwifery.

Diary of Trifling Occurrences, A (1958)

During the American Revolution, ▷Sarah Logan Fisher, a Loyalist Quaker, recorded in her diary and later in her Letter Book what she called the 'trifling occurrences' of her life; in fact, it is a record of the emotional toll of being a Loyalist in Philadelphia during the Patriot uprising. While her husband was imprisoned in Virginia, Fisher struggled to care for her family and found solace in her religious beliefs.

Diaspora

This term, which is of particular relevance in Caribbean writing, is the name given to communities of people living away from their original homeland in particular the Jewish people living outside Israel. The African diaspora includes the Caribbean, North and South America, and Europe.

Díaz Lozano, Argentina (born 1912)

Honduran novelist and short story writer. In her most important novel, *Mayapán* (1950) the Maya Indians, living in their peaceful environment of Yucatán, face a cultural conflict with the shipwrecked Spaniards Gonzalo Guerrero and Jerónimo de Aguilar. The theme provides a melodramatic topic for a 19th-century plot. *Peregrinage* (1944) (*Henriqueta and I*, 1944) is an autobiographical novel. Other works include: *Perlas de rosario* (1930) (*Rosary Beads*); *Luz en la senda* (1935) (*Light on the Path*); *Topacios* (1940) (*Topaz*); *Y tenemos que viver* (1963) (*And We Must Live*); *40 dias en la vida de una mujer* (1950) (*40 Days in the Life of a Woman*), and *Fuego en la ciudad* (1966) (*Fire in the City*).

Dickens, Monica (born 1915)

English novelist and writer for children. The autobiographical *One Pair of Hands* (1939) launched Dickens's writing career, and personal experience consistently informs her fiction. The semi-autobiographical *Mariana* (1940) followed, and work in an aircraft factory during World War II is the basis for *The Fancy* (1943). A regular contributor to the magazine *Woman's Own* for twenty years, Dickens also worked with a number of charitable organizations, which provided further first-hand material. *Cobbler's Dream* (1963) emerges from her work with the RSPCA, and *The Listeners* (1970) from work with the Samaritans. The substantially researched *Kate and Emma*

(1964) looks at child abuse, and *The Heart of the Land* (1961) addresses alcoholism and social deprivation. Books for children include the popular 'Follyfoot' series, tales of horses and farming communities.

Dickinson, Emily (1830–1886)

US poet and letter-writer. Explosive, elliptical, fragmented and dazzling, Emily Dickinson's poetry has retained its enigmatic force through decades of attempts to explain (and contain) it through literary legend.

Born in Amherst, Massachusetts, to a family well known for educational and political activity, Dickinson saw, as she once put it, 'New Englandly'. The precise effect of her Puritan heritage may be debated; its power within her work seems undeniable. Often written in the metre of hymns, her poems deal not only with issues of death, faith and immortality, but with nature, domesticity, the uncertain relations between ecstasy and terror, eroticism and renunciation, captivity and liberty, and the power and limits of language. Dickinson's letters, which often incorporate poems, are similarly terse and suggestive. Her language can be as deceptively simple as her tone is complex; her formulations of the most conventional themes often render them alien and startling.

'Circumference is my business,' Dickinson once wrote. The poet's passion for abstraction and expansion – for the 'circumference' part of this statement – was not recognized for some time. The deliberate and perhaps even ruthless 'business' of her artistry took even longer to be recognized, in part because long before the poet's work itself was fully available she herself was firmly established as a figure of popular legend. Thomas H. Johnson's three-volume authoritative edition of the *Poems of Emily Dickinson* appeared in 1955, to be followed in 1958 by a three-volume edition of the *Letters of Emily Dickinson*, edited by Johnson and Theodora Ward. These editions, along with meticulous studies of Dickinson's biography and reading, helped prepare the way for major critical shifts that led to the challenging popular conceptions of the poet as a fey, reclusive, ethereal figure who was too eccentric, heart-broken and naive to recognise even her own brilliance. Not only does a still-growing tradition of scholarly and critical writings assert Dickinson's intellectual and artistic sophistication, but a counter-legend has arisen around the figure of a spunky poet-heroine who insists upon solitude as her only access to the ecstasies of art.

Feminist criticism, which has been in great part responsible for the growth of this dubious counter-legend, is also creating a lively and complicated tradition of readings of the poet's work and her cultural significance. In attempts to demystify Dickinson's ahistorical status as an Exceptional Woman, scholars have explored her relationships to her culture in general and to other 19th-century women in particular – addressing not only her passionate relationship with her sister-in-law, Sue Gilbert, her admiration for ▷Elizabeth Barrett Browning's work or her affection for ▷Helen Hunt Jackson; but her familiarity with lesser-known writers, her use of themes and stances common to the more conventional feminine poetry of her time, and her work's potential use as a means of developing more sophisticated readings of the verse of other women, both within and beyond her century. Feminist critics have also shifted and expanded the canon of frequently considered poems, focusing, for example, on fragmented or duplicitous treatments of poetic power and inspiration; on erotic poems and the expression of lesbian passion; or on Gothic interplays of entrapment and explosion. Questioning of conventional constructions of subjectivity and understandings of representation has also led to dramatic alterations in the readings of well-known poems. In the past, Dickinson's shifting personae, her elision of gender markers (her speakers' movements, not only from child to queen to mouse, but from 'he' to 'she' to 'it') and her more subtle violations of linguistic expectations have often been read as evidence of coyness, lack of control, or at most a subversive duplicity. Such strategies now play central roles in theoretical readings that attribute far-reaching aesthetic, intellectual and political implications to the poet's disruption of her culture's conventions of (self-) representation.

▷Rich, Adrienne
Bib: Donoghue, Denis, *Emily Dickinson*; Juhasz, Suzanne (ed.) *Feminist Critics Read Emily Dickinson*; Rupp, Richard H. (ed.) *Critics on Emily Dickinson*; Sewall, Richard B. (ed.) *Emily Dickinson: A Collection of Critical Essays*.

Didion, Joan (born 1934)
US novelist, essayist and journalist. Didion was raised as an Episcopalian in Sacramento, California, and in 1956 she graduated from the University of California at Berkeley. She was feature editor of *Vogue* until 1963, and subsequently worked as a contributing editor on *Life*. She also wrote for the *Saturday Evening Post* and *Harper's*. Very much a professional writer, Didion also collaborated on the script for the film *A Star is Born* (1976) starring Barbara Streisand. Her work evokes a sense of cultural despair, suggesting that contemporary North American culture is disintegrating because it lacks seriousness. In *Slouching Towards Bethlehem* (1968), for example, Didion argues that North America lacks a sense of past. This essay collection includes material on California in the 1960s and the Haight-Ashbury (in San Francisco) 'flower children'. *Play It As It Lays* (1970) describes a woman's mental breakdown, as she becomes unable to maintain an identity in the absence of sustaining moral values. *A Book of Common Prayer* (1977) depicts the breakdown of the mother–daughter relationship. Set in Boce Grande, a Central American dictatorship on the verge of crisis, the novel blends a series of stories

and histories into a ▷postmodern fiction. Although in 1972 Didion published an essay in the *New York Times Book Review* criticizing feminism for its narrowness, her novel *Democracy* (1984) suggests that the patriarchal ideals of US democracy work to exclude women.

Other works include: *Run River* (1963), *Telling Stories* (1978), *The White Album* (1979), *Salvador* (1983), *Miami* (1987) and *Joan Didion: Essays and Conversations* (1984).
Bib: Henderson, K.U., *Joan Didion*.

Die (Dia), Béatrice, Comtesse de (late 12th century)
One of the most famous of the French ▷trobairitz. She is described in the Béziers *chansonnier* (anthology of 'songs') as 'the wife of Sir Guilhem de Peitieus, a beautiful lady and good, who fell in love with Sir Raimbaut d'Aurenga, and made for (and about) him many good love-songs'.
Bib: Brunel-Lobrichon, G., 'Images of Women and Imagined Trobairitz in the Béziers Chansonnier' in Paden, W.D., *The Voice of the Trobairitz*, pp. 211–25.

Dies Buch gehört dem König! (1843) (This Book Belongs to the King!)
A novel by the German romantic writer ▷Bettina von Arnim (1785–1859). This is not so much a novel as a complex analysis of the social and political issues of the day, as seen from a woman's point of view. The book is addressed to King Friedrich Wilhelm IV of Prussia (1795–1861), so that he may take matters into hand and improve the lot of the poor. As a political statement it is an extraordinary example of public courage by one individual at a time of intense political repression and paranoia, and it bears witness to the intensity of Arnim's social and political commitment.

Dieulafoy, Jane (1851–1916)
French novelist and travel writer. Born in Toulouse, she married Marcel Dieulafoy in 1870, and accompanied him on diplomatic missions to Persia (1870–1887) and archaeological visits to Spain and Morocco. While travelling she wore male clothes for comfort, and obtained legal authorization so that she could continue to do so once back in Paris – a necessary procedure for 19th-century French women who wished to cast off their corsets. Apart from the travelogues her journeys inspired, the most famous of which was *La Perse, la Chaldée et la Susiane* (1886), (*Persia, Chaldea and the Sudan*) she wrote novels, including *Parysatis* (1890), which won a prize from the ▷Académie Française, *Volontaire* (1892) (*Volunteer*) and *Déchéance* (1897) (*Decline*). She also gave lectures on Greek and French literature at the Théâtre de l'Odéon.

Di Falco, Laura (born 1910)
Italian novelist and painter; real name Laura Carpinteri. She grew up in Syracuse, and then moved to Pisa, where she completed a philosophy

degree. She taught for many years in a teacher-training college in Rome. A regular contributor to *Il Mondo*, between 1950 and 1966, she has won a number of literary prizes for her work. Her most important work, *Le tre mogli* (1967) (*The Three Wives*), is set in the Sicilian countryside which she knows so well, and covers a long timescale, from the unification of Italy to the period just prior to the outbreak of World War II, evoked through the stories of her female characters.

Her other works include: *Paura del giorno* (1954) (*Fear of the Day*); *Una donna disponibile* (1959) (*An Available Woman*); *Tre carte da gioco* (1962) (*Three Playing Cards*); *Miracolo d'estate* (1971) (*Summer Miracle*); *L'inferriata* (1976) (*The Grille*); *Piazza della quattro vie* (1982) (*The Square with Four Streets*).

Differance

Spelt with an 'a' to distinguish it from ▷difference, differance is a development by French philosopher Jacques Derrida (born 1930) of Ferdinand de Saussures's (1857–1913) account of language as a system of differences with no positive terms to suggest that meaning is produced not only from the difference between words but also by deferral. Which is to say that the sense of a single meaning is deferred in the play of signification from other (absent) meanings. The deferral of meaning destabilizes the boundaries which appear to make meaning purely an effect of difference.

▷Deconstruction

Difference

The term is important in the Swiss linguist Ferdinand de Saussure's (1857–1913) theory of linguistic meaning. De Saussure, in his influential work *Course in General Linguistics* (posthumously published 1916), described language as a system of differences with no positive terms. He argued that meaning is not inherent in words, nor does it arise from any reference to things outside language; rather the meaning of a word arises from its difference from other words.

▷Women's language

Dike, Fatima (born 1948)

South African dramatist, born in Langa, Cape Peninsula, educated in the Transvaal, and now living in Cape Town. In 1975 she became stage manager of the Space Theatre, a fringe theatre complex in Cape Town, at the height of its most creative period, and between 1976 and 1979 was resident dramatist there. Her first play, ▷*The Sacrifice of Kreli* (1978), originally staged at the Space in 1976, promotes black resurgence through contact with the past, while her second, ▷*The First South African* (1979), staged in 1977, sees the individual in terms of conflicting racial identities. Her children's play, *The Crafty Tortoise* (produced in 1978, and not published), is based on Ekwefi's story in Nigerian novelist Chinua Achebe's *Things Fall Apart* (1958). The play is an animal fable in which the guileless birds get their reward and the mighty tortoise, who tries to do them out of their birthright, is brought to justice.

In 1980 Dike went to the Iowa Writers' School, also spending some time in New York, where she acted in her play *The Glass House* in the theatre of St Peter's Church. Hitherto unpublished, *The Glass House* reflects on the friendship between a middle-class black woman and a rich white woman, through which they transcend difference.

Dike stopped writing for some years, until *Two Weeks in September* was produced under the auspices of 'The Kafka Project', a German-funded venture promoting South African theatre. She has also recently published a short story, 'Township Games', which appeared in the anthology *Women in South Africa* brought out by Seriti sa Sechaba, the only ▷publishing company in Southern Africa devoted to writing by women. The tale is a bleak presentation, in the documentary tradition, of a gambler whose luck runs out when he kills a policeman.

Dillard, Annie

US essayist, poet and fiction writer. Born in Pittsburgh, Pennsylvania, Dillard grew up in affluence. She studied writing at Hollins College and graduated Phi Beta Kappa in 1967. She then worked in an anti-poverty program and wrote poetry. She won a Pulitzer Prize for her book of poetic essays ▷*Pilgrim at Tinker Creek* (1974). Her work reflects her urgent longing for a hidden God; as in *Pilgrim at Tinker Creek*, Dillard searches for God in commonplace, natural events. Her writing is characterized by her careful and attentive observations of nature. In *Holy the Firm* (1977) Dillard struggles with the metaphysical problem of pain, and the narrator reconciles herself to human suffering through her faith in God's connection to the world; like Dillard, she dedicates herself to serve as God's visionary through her art.

Other works include: *Tickets for a Prayer Wheel* (1974), *An American Childhood* (1987), *Encounters with Chinese Writers* (1985), *Teaching a Stone to Talk* (1982), *Living by Fiction* (1982) and *The Living* (1992).

Dime novel

US 19th-century popular genre of thriller fiction and, occasionally, fictionalized history. These inexpensive, individually bound, thrillers usually cost a dime (10 cents) or less. Published by Beadle and Adams and others, the dime novels focused on action plots, heroic individualistic characters, and distinctively US settings and situations. Seen by some literary and social critics as sensational literature for the masses, the dime novels were enormously popular, especially among audiences who read little other literature. ▷Ann Sophia Stephens's ▷*Malaeska: The Indian Wife of the White Hunter* (1860) is generally considered the first dime novel.

di Michele, Mary (born 1949)

Poet, born in Lanciano, Italy, she emigrated to Canada with her family in 1955. She attended the

Universities of Toronto and Windsor, where she worked with ▷Joyce Carol Oates. Her poetry has won numerous awards, including the CBC Literary Competition. Her books include *Tree of August* (1978), *Bread and Chocolate/Marrying Into the Family* (1980, with ▷Bronwen Wallace), *Mimosa and Other Poems* (1981), *Necessary Sugar* (1983), *Immune to Gravity* (1986) and *Luminous Emergencies* (1990). She combines the strengths of an ethnic and feminist positioning; her work exercises an elegaic power in its approach to both the familial and the political. In 1984 she edited an anthology of Canadian women poets, *Anything is Possible*. She lives in Toronto.

Dimitrova, Blaga (born 1922)

Leading contemporary Bulgarian poet. Blaga Dimitrova was born in Bijala Slatina, north-west Bulgaria, in 1922. She studied Slavonic philology at Sofia University and at the Gorki World Literature Institute in Moscow. She is an editor with the Narodna Kultura publishing house in Sofia, and in October 1991 was elected to Parliament. She has twenty poetry books to her name, numerous novels, plays and works of criticism.

Much of her early work recounts her childhood in Turnovo. *Requiem* mourns her father. There is a warmth and clarity in her lyrics, a sense of wonder from a searching mind. She inherits The feminism of the earlier Bulgarian poet ▷Elisaveta Bagryana. Her works include: *Stihove za vojda* (1950) (*Poems about the Leader*), *Pesni za Rodopite* (1954) (*songs on the Rhodope Mountains*), *Na otkrito* (1956) (*In the Open*), *Ooutre* (1959), *Expeditsia kum idiya den* (1962)(*Expedition Towards Tomorrow*) and *Osudeni na lyubiv* (1967) (*Sentenced to Love*). Works translated into English include: *Journey to Oneself* (1971), *The Last Imperial Eagle* (1992) and poems in the anthologies *Poets of Bulgaria* (1988), edited by William Meredith, and *The Devil's Dozen: Thirteen Contemporary Bulgarian Women Poets* (1992).

Dinesen, Isak ▷Blixen, Karen

Ding Ling (1905–1986)

Chinese novelist and short story writer. One of the most important figures in modern Chinese literature, Ding Ling was born Jiang Bingzhi, a native of Hunan province. Largely influenced by the liberal ideas of the May Fourth Movement (1919), she was far ahead of her time in leading an independent life and in exploring the psychology of women in her writing. Her best work of this period, ▷*Miss Sophie's Diary* (1928), raised a critical furore by its portrayal of an educated young woman who confronts the fact of her own sexuality.

Ding Ling joined the League of Leftist Writers in Shanghai and edited its magazine, *The Great Dipper*. The execution of the father of her child for his revolutionary activities precipitated her further to the left, and she joined the communist base in Yenan after release from detention in

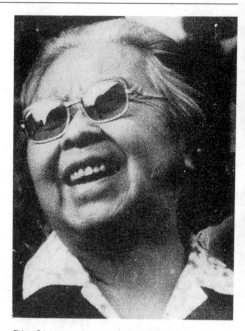

Ding Ling

Nanjing. In Yenan she tried to conform to Party aesthetics, but her short story 'When I was in Xia Village' (1940) drew criticism with its story of a peasant girl, who had been raped by the Japanese occupying troops and then used as a spy by the communists. Ding Ling also came under attack for her bitterly ironic article 'Thoughts on March 8' (1942), which exposes the subtle discrimination against women in a communist community. She conformed to socialist realism in her novel about land reform, *Sun Over Sanggan River* (1948), but was labelled a 'rightist' (enemy category) in 1957 and suffered many years in silent exile. She was rehabilitated in the late 1970s in the post-Mao era, when many of the abuses of the Maoist political campaigns were being corrected, and resumed writing. Widely translated, she will be best remembered for her earlier works.

Bib: Jenner, W.F. (trans.), *Miss Sophie's Diary and Other Stories*; Barlow, Tani (ed.), *I Myself Am a Woman: Selected Writings of Ding Ling*; Yi-tsi Mei Fuerwerker, *Ding Ling's Fiction*.

Ding Ning (born 1924)

Chinese writer. Ding Ning currently works at the Ministry of Culture. With limited formal education, Ding joined the communist revolution in 1938 and worked onstage as an actress and stage director. She also managed to publish prose and fiction and a number of lyrics and skits. Her main publications are *The Poetic Soul of Youyan* and *An Ox for the Young*, and she is much admired for her poetic prose style.

Dionyse de Munchensy (13th century)

English patron. Walter of Bibbesworth compiled a manual in the late 13th century for Lady Dionyse to help her teach her children French (▷Anglo-Norman). She was evidently literate in two languages: English and French.

Dionysia (fl c 1200)

English patron. Guischard de Beaulieu, a monk of Beaulieu Priory (a cell of St Albans), wrote the ▷Anglo-Norman *Sermon en Vers*, or *Romaunz de Tentaciuns de Siècle* in about 1200, for a 'Dame Dionisi'. His patron may have been Dionysia, the wife of Walter Hacon, a nobleman of the district. The work, whose subject is the decay of the world, is written in the metre of the *chansons de geste* ('songs of deeds'), made familiar by the *Song of Roland* (the text of which was copied out in England, c 1125–1150).

Diosdado, Ana (born 1938)

Spanish dramatist. Diosado is one of the few contemporary female dramatists to have had her work performed in the 1970s. Her main works are *Olvida los tambores* (1970) (*Forget the Drums*), *El Okapi* (1972) and *Usted también puede disfrutar de ella* (1973) (*You Can Enjoy Her As Well*). The last play pointed to the moral bankruptcy of the advertising industry in its promotion of the ideal woman.

Di Prima, Diane (born 1934)

US poet, dramatist and diarist. Di Prima was born in Brooklyn, New York, into a lower socio-economic class; her parents were first-generation Italian-Americans. She quit college to pursue a love affair, later moving to Greenwich Village, where she became the female voice of the rebellious Beat generation.

Her *Memoirs of a Beatnik* (1969) chronicles the bohemian lifestyle of the 1950s. In 1961 she began publishing a poetry newsletter, *Floating Bear*, with LeRoi Jones. Later in the 1960s she established Poets Press. *This Kind of Bird Flies Backward* (1958) reflects her self-expressive engagement with daily experience. In *Dinners and Nightmares* (1961), using a series of meals to hook memories, Di Prima explores psychic and symbolic states to consider personal feeling. Her work documents her awakening feminist consciousness. In *The New Handbook of Heaven* (1963) Di Prima integrates the process of childbearing into her writing. *Revolutionary Letters* (1971) protests against the Vietnam War and oppression.

Other works include: *Murder Cake* (1960), *Paideuma* (1960), *The Discontentment of the Russian Prince* (1961), *Like* (1964), *Poets Vaudeville* (1964), *Monuments* (1968), *Hotel Albert: Poems* (1968), *Earthsong: Poems 1957–1959* (1968), *L.A. Odyssey* (1969), *Kerhonkson Journal, 1966* (1971), *Discovery of America* (1972), *The Calculus of Variation* (1972), *Freddie Poems* (1974), *Whale Honey* (1975), *Selected Poems 1956–1975* (1975) and *Loba: Parts I–VIII* (1978).

Discord (1887)

Russian novella by ▷Anastasiia Verbítskaia. This is an important story because it touches on many of the concerns that women prose writers were to centre on in the next three decades. It is a transitional work, mixing the ideology of the women's movement of the 1860s with that of the nascent ▷Silver Age. The heroine bears the name Valentina L'vovna Kameneva: the middle name, or patronymic, literally means 'Lev's daughter', but can also signify the 'lion's daughter'; the last name is derived from the Russian word for rock or stone, so that both names denote strength. A chance encounter with a young governess – emblematic of the importance of ties between women – gives Valentina a chance to sum up her lifelong struggle in the advice she gives the girl. The gist of her testament is a rejection of love and family life for the sake of independence and the development of one's individuality. But this message is coupled with the exhortation to work for the public welfare and leave the 'warm' shelter of the home for the 'cold and darkness of the street'. This call was part of the populist ideology, and was repeated by women writers with left-wing political sympathies well into the 1920s. Although Valentina has children whom she clearly loves, they are most often depicted in the tale as a burden that competes with and even hinders her pursuit of a career. Thus her story opposes female accomplishment in work to marriage, sex, and children. Other women writers, including Verbítskaia herself, would reiterate this opposition. Still others vary the combinations, although none of them portrays a happily married, sexually fulfilled woman with both a career and children.

▷Krestóvskaia, Mariia

Discords (1894) ▷*Keynotes* and *Discords*

Discourse, Delivered on Saturday . . ., A (1769)

Sermon by the travelling Quaker preacher, Rachel Wilson (fl 1769). This discourse was taken down in shorthand by a member of the audience and published without prior permission from Wilson. Her sermon was presented to a meeting-house in Dutches County, New York, on 10 August 1769. It emphasized the religious duties of 'Children and Servants, People in General, and Preachers of the Gospel'. Although intended to be democratic in approach, it retains a social hierarchy by counselling servants not to blame masters for their lack of goodness but to seek to become 'good and faithful servants' to God.

Diski, Jenny (born 1947)

English novelist. Born in London, Diski is the author of four novels, all of which focus on the psychological experience of the outsider. Her first, *Nothing Natural* (1986), traces a woman's discovery of sexual pleasure in a dangerous sado-masochistic relationship. The novel uses a first-person narration by an unexceptional single mother to draw the reader into an understanding of the precariousness of our ideas of normality. This is a technique she again uses in *Rainforest* (1987), which investigates the arbitrary nature of the categories that organize our view of the world and our sense of self. Since *Rainforest* she has published *Then Again* (1990) and *Like Mother* (1988), a chilling exploration of Frances, whose life of intense emptiness is narrated by her baby born without a brain. The baby is called Nony, 'short for Nonentity', in a fitting metaphor for Frances's insecure sense of identity.

Disorders of Love Truly Expressed in the Unfortunate Lives of Givry with Mlle de Guise (1677)

Translation of *Les Désordres de l'amour* (1677), a French novel by Madame de Villedieu (▷Marie-Catherine Hortense Desjardins). The novel is in four parts, containing three stories which portray the different stages of the Wars of Religion during the reigns of Henri III (1551–1589) and Henri IV (1553–1610). The historical setting has been fairly carefully researched, but the theme which is constantly reiterated is that the political causes given for events are but the pretext. The real explanation is to be found in the tangled love affairs of the time woven by Givry and Mademoiselle de Guise, Madame de Sauve, the King of Navarre and the Duc de Guise, which are supposedly the true explanation of the disagreements and rivalry dividing the high nobility of the time. In general, Madame de Villedieu gives a much fuller account of the campaigns of both the Protestants and the Catholic 'League' than most novelists of the time. She is particularly effective on the siege of Paris of 1589, which echoes with allusions to the *Frondes* (1648–1653), the civil wars of her own times, but the emphasis on love distorts the official historical events almost beyond recognition, even where they are presented.

D'Istria, Dora (1828–1882)

Romanian writer of Albanian origin. Dora D'Istria was the ▷pseudonym of Helena Gjika, who was born in Bucharest of an aristocratic family from Macedonia. Her uncle was Grigore IV, *voivode* (local ruler) of Walachia. As a young girl she travelled with her parents to the courts of Vienna, Dresden and Berlin. In 1849 she married Prince Alexander Masal'sky and went to Russia with him. In 1855 they separated, and she moved to Switzerland, travelling to Greece in 1860, and finally settling in Italy.

D'Istria was devoted to the causes of national minorities in the Austro-Hungarian Empire, to equality for women, and to education for the masses. Her essay 'La nationalité albanaise d'après les chants populaires' ('The Albanian Nationality According to Popular Songs'), which was published in *Revue des deux mondes* (*Two Worlds Review*)in Paris in 1863, made an impact on the Albanian nationalist movement in the period of *Rolindja* (a renaissance of culture,

nationalist ideology and literature which occurred between 1878 and independence from the Ottoman Empire in 1912). It was soon translated into Albanian and Italian.

'Distaff, The'

Poem by ▷Erinna. According to the 10th-century AD biographical work, the *Suda*, the poem originally comprised 300 lines. An extant papyrus fragment offers parts of approximately 54 lines. The poem is a pathetic lament for the girl Baucis. The poet recalls their childhood games together and then Baucis' cruel early death. The title may be a nickname: it might come from Erinna's coupling the metaphor of the thread of fate with a mention of woolworking as a female occupation.
Bib: (text & trans.) Page, D.L., *Greek Literary Papyri*.

Ditlevsen, Tove (1918–1976)

Danish lyric poet and prose writer. Ditlevsen was born into a working-class family with no tradition of education. In her early writing she described her feeling of not fitting into her surroundings. She wrote about her longing for love and her fear of losing it. Her writing is painful, cultivating a self-destructive femininity.

In 1939 she made her début with the collection of poems *Pigesind* (*Girl's Mind*) and in 1941 she published the novel *Man gjorde et barn fortræd* (*A Child has been Molested*). She was very well-received by the literary critics, but her poetry is rather conventional, with a tendency to sentimentality. She was married four times, with children from three of the marriages, and was periodically in psychiatric hospital, once to be cured from drug addiction. Her life tends to shadow her writings, but even today she is very popular, and some of her early poems have been set to music and sung by rock and folk singers.

In her later works, the fictional memoirs *Ansigterne* (1968) (*The Faces*), *Gift* (1971) (*Married*) and *Wilhelms værelse* (1975) (*Wilhelm's Room*), she described her life as an adult, her experiences with psychosis, and the conflicts of being a mother, a wife and a writer. In 1976 she committed suicide.

Ditlevsen stands as a symbol of a female longing for symbiosis – with children, with men, or within writing. Her literature puts the reader into a position of total identification, which has a strong appeal for many women.

Diviners, The (1974)

Canadian writer ▷Margaret Laurence's magnificent culminating novel about a writer grappling with the needs of the self in conflict with the demands of others. The ambiguity and duality of the past and the way that it enters the present is beautifully evoked by the central image of the river flowing both ways, 'ahead into the past, and back into the future'. The motif of water-divining serves as a unifying principle for the multiple and shifting perspectives of the novel, often denoted by 'Memorybank Movies'. The main character, Morag Gunn, orphaned early in life, is adopted and raised by the town garbageman and his wife. Writing enables Morag to move beyond the limitations of her physical world, first to escape her outcast childhood and the narrow confines of Manawaka itself, then to escape from an oppressive marriage, finally to escape from her own selfconsciousness. Throughout the novel, Morag's conscience is represented by the voice of ▷Catherine Parr Traill. Writing is also the vehicle by which Morag comes to understand the multiple texture of the prairie and its people. Her relationships with the Metis, Jules Tonnere, and their daughter, Piquette, become gestures of intersection with her Canadian history, so that she finally recognizes where she is located as artist and woman.

Diving Into the Wreck (1973)

Poems by US writer ▷Adrienne Rich. *Diving into the Wreck* is a collection of overtly feminist, often angry poems. When Rich was awarded the Pulitzer Prize for the book, she insisted on sharing it with the other finalists ▷Audre Lorde and ▷Alice Walker, who were then not famous names. The books show a poet consciously at war with patriarchy, tackling the problem of transforming her own and others' experience into poetry without mythologizing it. The experience of society's victims is the theme of 'Meditations for a Savage Child', which cross-cuts between the history of the 'Wild Boy of Aveyron' and the oppression of women. The title poem relates a dream of an underwater journey in which the poet explores a wrecked ship. This quest leads the poet into the depths of her own identity, encountering the masculine and feminine archetypes of her drowned self, but her search for 'the damage that was done / and the treasures that prevail', also takes her to a collective past of women, forgotten in the 'book of myths / in which / our names do not appear'. The rediscovery of female identity is also the subject of the marvellous, puzzling poem, 'The Mirror in Which Two Are Seen As One'. The other side of Rich's emphasis on female selfhood is accompanied by her eloquent rage against patriarchy and North American imperialism. This is seen particularly in poems like 'Rape', 'The Phenomenology of Anger' and 'Trying to Talk with a Man'. The book has an extraordinarily vital combination of anger, compassion, learning and imaginative energy.

Divoratori, I (1910) ▷Devourers, The

Dix, Dorothea Lynde (1802–1887)

US non-fiction writer. A former teacher and nurse whose writing focused on investigating and reforming institutions – prisons, poor-houses, insane asylums – Dix attracted attention with her writing on prison reform. Her *Memorial to the Legislature of Massachusetts* (1843) is especially interesting in contrast to the later exposé of ▷Nellie Bly, ▷*Ten Days in a Mad House* (1887).

Dizhur, Bella Abramovna (born 1906)

Russian poet. Dizhur was born in Kiev to an assimilated Jewish family, grew up in Leningrad, spent most of her adult life in the Ural industrial city of Sverdlovsk, and from 1980 lived on the Baltic coast near Riga. In 1987, after years of waiting, the widowed poet received an exit visa to join her son, the famous *émigré* sculptor Ernst Neizvestny, in New York. Her long narrative poem, 'Janusz Korczak' (1944), recounts the true story of the heroic Polish doctor, director of a boys' orphanage in Warsaw, who chose to accompany his 200 Jewish charges to their death in the Treblinka concentration camp; translated into Polish and Yiddish after the war, the poem brought her the bitter fame of becoming the Sverdlovsk ▷Akhmátova – the writer singled out to be attacked in the renewed postwar repression as a 'rootless cosmopolite' by the local Writers' Union, of which she had long been a member. The selection of her poetry published in Russian and English in 1990 as *Shadow of a Soul* shows her to be a poet with a distinctive feminine voice, a humane spirit, and a gift for impressionistic imagery.

Djebar, Assia (born 1936)

Algerian novelist and film-maker, whose real name is Fatima-Zohra Imalayene. She was the first Algerian woman to be admitted to L'Ecole Normale Supérieure de Sèvres. She collaborated with the anti-colonial FLN (National Liberation Front) newspaper *Moudjahid* by conducting interviews with Algerian refugees in Morocco during the liberation war. She wrote her first novel *La Soif* (1957) (*The Mischief*) in two months during the student uprising in 1956. Among other novels she wrote ▷*Les Enfants du nouveau monde* (1962) (*Children of the New World*), an account of the war of liberation. Most of her work deals with the impact of the war on people's minds, and particularly women's. Through her novels she demands the right for women to occupy the same public sphere as men. Her first film, *La Nouba des femmes du mont Chenoua* (*The Celebration of the Women of Mount Chenoua*), was awarded the critics' prize at the Venice Biennale in 1979. Film-making is her means of reaching those who cannot read, especially women. Further, the Arabic dialect she uses in her films is the only medium comprehended by all Algerians, as the use of French or classical Arabic would reduce the audience. Djebar's other publications include: *Les Impatients* (1958) (*The Impatient Ones*), *Les Alouettes naïves* (1967) (*The Innocent Larks*), *Les Femmes d'Alger dans leur appartement* (1980) (*The Women of Algiers in Their Apartment*), *L'Amour, la fantasia* (1985) (▷*Fantasia: An Algerian Cavalcade*), *Ombre Sultanes* (1987) (▷*A Sister to Sheherazade*, 1989). The last two novels constitute the first two parts of a projected quartet.
Bib: Déjeux, Jean, *Assia Djebar, romancière algérienne, cinéaste arabe*; Djebar, Assia, *Woman at Point Zero* translated by Nawal el Sa'dawi as *Ferdaous: une voix à l'enfer*.

Dmitrieva, Elizaveta Ivanovna ▷De Gabriak, Cherubina

Dmítrieva, Valentina Ionovna (1859–1948)
Russian fiction writer. The daughter of an educated serf, Dmítrieva was one of the rare Russian women writers who portrayed peasant life from inside. Her peripatetic childhood and younger years are described in her 1930 autobiography, *The Way It Was*. Her determination to get an education led her to secondary school in Tambov and then to medical courses in St Petersburg. She began writing to support herself in her school days and during the long years she, a dedicated revolutionary, spent in exile in Tver' and Voronezh. Known for realistic psychological sketches of peasant and proletarian characters ('Akhmet's Wife', 1881; 'In Different Directions', 1883; 'Khves'ka the Hospital Watchman', 1900; 'Everybody Knows Her', 1900; 'Wolves', 1902), she published many novels and stories in provincial ▷'thick journals' and newspapers between 1880 and 1914. Her 1894 novella 'Gomochka' (the heroine's nickname), translated as *Love's Anvil*, reflects her own years in radical student circles. 'Through the Villages' (1896) is a memoir of work as an epidemic doctor. Dmítrieva also wrote crime novels which, like ▷Kapitolina Nazár'eva's, offered a disguised opportunity for social criticism ('Ill Will', 1883; 'Prison', 1887). Her short novel *The Volunteer* (1889) is the portrait of a provincial town during the 1877–1878 War in the Balkans. In 1902 Dmítrieva used male pseudonyms to publish abroad two wrenching stories of official abuses: 'For God, Tsar, and Country' about army life, and 'Lipochka the Priest's Daughter' about a girl raped by a prison interrogator. After the 1905 upheavals, stories like 'Humming Bees' became an open call to revolt. Ironically, after the 1917 Revolution Dmítrieva lost her readers; in the first ferment of the new society there was little interest in her realistic, committed fiction. Her 1896 children's story, 'A Kid and His Mongrel', has been a perennial favourite.
▷Gurévich, Liubov'

Dobson, Rosemary (born 1920)
Australian poet. The granddaughter of the English poet and essayist Austin Dobson, Dobson worked as an art teacher and editor for Angus & Robertson. Her lifelong interest in art and in classical themes is reflected in her poetry. Her poems, characterized by lucidity, elegance and grace, frequently appear in anthologies and have been translated into a number of languages. She has received several literary prizes including the *Sydney Morning Herald* Prize for *The Ship of Ice* (1948); the Christopher Brennan Award from the Fellowship of Australian Writers for 1979; and the Victorian Premier's Award for poetry in 1985. Dobson has written and edited non-fiction, and her volumes of poetry include: *In a Convex Mirror* (1944), *The Ship of Ice* (1948), *Child with a Cockatoo* (1955), *Cock Crow* (1965), *Greek Coins: A Sequence of Poems* (1977), *Over the Frontier* (1978), *The Continuance of Poetry* (1981) and *The Three Fates and Other Poems* (1984).
▷Poetry and Gender

Dr Zay (1882)
US novel by ▷Elizabeth Stuart Phelps (Ward). Developing a popular theme among US realist women writers in the 1880s, *Dr Zay* focuses on an early woman physician, the conflicts between marriage and profession forced upon her, and her difficult choice about whether to marry. ▷Sarah Orne Jewett's ▷*A Country Doctor* is in many ways similar.

Dodd, Lynley Stuart (born 1941)
New Zealand picture book illustrator and author. The huge success of her collaboration with her cousin, Eve Sutton, on *My Cat Likes to Hide in Boxes* (1973), winner of the New Zealand Library Association's Esther Glen Medal in 1975, catapulted Dodd into the world of books. Since the publication of her own first book *The Nickle Nackle Tree* (1976) she has not only received a Choysa Bursary and an award for her illustrations in *Druscilla* by Clarice England (1980), but also won the New Zealand Picture Story Book of the Year Award three times for books in her series about a terrier, Hairy Maclary. These books reflect her knowledge of animals and their habits and show her characteristic style: vigorous, fun, rhyming texts enhanced by freshly-coloured, busy, comical illustrations.
▷Children's literature, New Zealand

Dodge, Mary Abigail (1833–1896)
US editor, non-fiction writer, poet and biographer. Strongly associated with writing on women's issues and US party politics, Dodge was a forceful advocate. From an early stint as editor of the periodical *Our Young Folks*, she moved increasingly into writing addressed to inequities she found in US society. Among a large number of works in a prolific career, her *Country Living and Country Thinking* and *Woman's Wrongs* in the 1860s established Dodge as a proponent of more independent roles for women. In literary history, she is famous for a suit and satire against New England publishers: *A Battle of the Books* (1870). She published under the pseudonym Gail Hamilton; *Gail Hamilton's Life in Letters* was published in 1901.
▷*Harper's Bazar*

Dodge, Mary Elizabeth Mapes (1831–1905)
US children's writer and editor. Coming to literature through a rather late-starting career in magazine editing, Dodge established a significant audience and reputation with children's novels like *Hans Brinker: or, The Silver Skates* (1865). Mostly a fiction writer but also a poet, Dodge was the first editor of the Century Company's *St Nicholas Magazine*, soon the most prestigious children's magazine in the USA. Other works include: *A Few Friends and How They Amused*

Themselves (1869); *Donald and Dorothy* (1883); *The Land of Pluck* (1894); *When Life is Young* (1894).

Dohm, Hedwig (1833–1919)
German dramatist, short story writer and feminist essayist. Born in Berlin, the eleventh of eighteen children. Unlike her brothers, she had to leave school at fifteen, and fiercely resented having to do so. Her rebellion coincided with the revolutionary year of 1848, and triggered her interest in politics. After marrying the editor of the satirical paper *Kladderadatsch* (*Hoo-ha, Hot Air*) in 1852, she met many left-wing intellectuals, including Lassalle Ferdinand (1769–1859), Alexander Humboldt (1825–1864), Varnhagen (1785–1858) and ▷Fanny Lewald. In 1872 she published the first of her many radical essays, *Was die Pastoren von den Frauen denken* (*What Pastors Think of Women*), in which she argued for the economic, political and spiritual independence of women. Her plays and stories, and in particular her novella, *Wie Frauen werden – Werde, die Du bist* (1894) (*How Women are Made – Become the Woman You Are*) and the trilogy *Sibilla Dalmar* (1896–99), are penetrating analyses of women's oppression. During World War I, at the age of 85, she published an essay *Der Mißbrauch des Todes* (*The Misuse of Death*), which passionately denounces European militarism.

Dok Mai, Sod (1905–1963)
Pen-name of Thai writer M.L. Bubpha Kunjara Nimmanhemin, the half-sister of ▷Boonlua. She is credited as one of the writers who inaugurated modern Thai literature with her novel *Sattru Khong Chao Long* (1929) (*Her Enemy*). It won popular acclaim when it first appeared in serial form in a magazine, *Thai Kasem*, as did her two subsequent novels, *Nit* (1929–1930) and *Karma Kao* (1932) (*Karma in the Past*). However, it is *Khwam Phit Khrang Raek* (1930) (*The First Mistake*), published in the magazine *Narinat* just before the 1932 coup, which is generally considered her first major work. After 1933, her novels appeared only in book form, the first of these being *Sam Chai* (*The Three Men*) followed by *Ubattihet* (1934) (*The Accident*); *Chai Chana Khong Luang Naruban* (1935) (*The Triumph of Luang Naruban*), *Phu Di* (1937) (*The Genteel*); *Ni Lae Lok* (1940) (*This is Life*), which has been translated into English, and an unfinished novel, *Nung Nai Roi* (1962) (*One in a Hundred*). She has also written two collections of short stories, and her short story, ('Phonlamuang Di') ('The Good Citizen') has appeared in English translation in an Australian literary magazine, *Span* (1958), and is reprinted in *Treasury of Thai Literature: the Modern Period* (1988).

Her novels depict the conflict between new Western-influenced 'modern' perceptions, and traditional Thai customs and values, as embodied by female characters and protagonists of the class which considered itself elite, bred to be *phu di* (genteel), upholding traditional ideals in personal and social bearing, including relationships between the sexes.

'Dolefull Lay of Clorinda, The' (c 1586)
Pastoral elegy written by ▷Mary Sidney Herbert on the death of her brother, the poet Philip Sidney (1554–1586). It was long misattributed to Edmund Spenser (?1552–1599), who first printed it in 1595 along with other authors' elegies for Sidney. Herbert's elegy combines both classical and Christian traditions. She adopts the persona of a shepherdess grieving for the loss of her shepherd, Astrophel (the persona her brother had adopted in his famous sonnet sequence, *Astrophel and Stella*, 1591). The poem's vision moves from the earthly landscape of a mutable and fallen world robbed by death, to an assertion of Astrophel's attainment of eternal heavenly bliss. The poem ends with the narrator's grief for those remaining in the earthly world who have been left behind by Astrophel's death.
Bib: Freer, C., 'Countess of Pembroke: Mary Sidney' Wilson, K. (ed.), in *Women Writers of the Renaissance and Reformation*.

Dolgorúkaia, Natal'ia Borisovna (1714–1771)
Russian autobiographer. In December 1729 Princess Natal'ia Sheremeteva's engagement to Ivan Dolgorúkii, the close companion of Peter the Great's son and successor, Peter II, promised her a brilliant future. A month later the young tsar died, and the scheming, ambitious Dolgorúkii clan fell into disgrace. Natal'ia chose to marry Ivan anyway and follow him and his family into exile. After her husband's execution in 1739, she returned to Moscow to raise her two sons. In 1758 she entered the Frolov Convent in Kiev, and in 1767 she wrote her artless Russian reminiscences of her girlhood, hasty marriage, and five-month journey to Siberia. The work was the first woman's autobiography published in Russia, and Dolgorúkaia became a popular subject of laudatory poems and semi-hagiographic fictions. These in turn influenced the development of a still-persistent cult of self-sacrificing Russian womanhood. Her self-portrait in the *Memoirs* (1810) as a person with all-too-human complexities and frailties has been largely overwhelmed by the myth.
Bib: Townsend, Charles E., *Memoirs of Princess Natal'ja Borisovna Dolgorukaja*.

Dollmaker, The (1954)
US novel by ▷Harriette Arnow which depicts the corrosive effects of modern industrialism on the human spirit. Self-reliant, inarticulate Gertie Nievels moves her family from the Kentucky hills to a housing project in Detroit, Michigan. Her family's economic and physical survival depends upon her husband's job at the defence plant during World War II, and therefore upon the industry of killing. The secular self betrays the sacred self in its struggle for money, and Gertie betrays her artistic self to feed her family when she destroys the figure of Christ she tried to carve

in order to mass-produce ugly painted dolls. Arnow affirms, nevertheless, the sacred self when Gertie sees Christ in her neighbours.

Domenech i Escate de Canellas, Maria (1877–1952)
Spanish writer. Domenech was an advocate of better education for women; she founded a union for Catalan working women. Her main works are *Contrallum* (1917) (*Against the Light*) and *Confidències* (1946) (*Secrets*), a collection of nine short stories.
▷Catalan women's writing

Domestic novel
US 19th-century genre, including autobiographical fiction. Choosing domestic settings, assigning a high value to women's role in the home and community, these popular novels showed women using moral and religious values to establish woman, family and home as centres of virtue, principle and humanity. As women writers often began their careers publishing in magazines directed to women subscribers, personal narratives on domestic subjects admitted authors to literature and introduced women authors to their audiences.

Earlier 20th-century literary histories frequently conflated the domestic novel with the ▷woman's fiction tradition named and defined by critic Nina Baym in *Woman's Fiction* (1978). While both genres value domestic life, woman's fiction, which Baym dates from ▷Catharine Maria Sedgwick's *A New-England Tale* (1822), shows the dangers of dependency, and ultimately assigns the positive values of home to those who work to attain such values – frequently by achieving success and self-determination through public roles. The more traditional domestic novel allows for private, dependent lives and a separate sphere for women. Women characters confront others' prejudice, amorality and limitations with empathy, imagination, resilience, religion, conventional morality and often self-sacrifice.

Domestic novels have often been dismissed as sentimental and conformist popular literature, the novelists as advocates of traditional religion, constrained women's roles and the ▷feminization of US cultural life.

Domin, Hilde (born 1912)
German novelist and poet. Of Jewish origin, she interrupted her studies in Cologne in 1932, fled fascist Germany, and gained her doctorate in Florence. For fourteen years she worked as a teacher and translator in the Dominican Republic. Upon her return in 1954, she published poetry and novels which explore the theme of exile, both political and metaphysical. Her main works are *Höhlenbilder, Gedichte 1951–1953* (1968) (*Cave Paintings, Poems 1951–1953*); *Abel steh auf. Gedichte, Prosa, Theorie* (1979) (*Rise Up, Abel. Poems, Prose, Theory*); a story, *Die andalusische Katze* (1971) (*The Andalusian Cat*) and the novel *Das zweite Paradies. Roman in Segmenten* (1968)

(*The Second Paradise. A Novel in Segments*), which was totally revised in 1980.

Dominguez, María Alicia (born 1908)
Argentinian novelist, short story writer, essayist and children's dramatist. Her first work was *La Rueca* (1925) (*The Distaff*), a book of poetry, which together with *Crepúsculos de oro* (1926) (*Golden Twilights*) and *Música de siglos* (1927) (*Music of Centuries*), is filled with images of pantheism and pleasurable life. She reached her most purified and lucid style in *Campo de luna* (1944) (*Moon Land*), *Al aire de tu vuelo* (1949) (*To the Air of your Flight*), *Siete espadas* (1959) (*Seven Swords*) and *Las muchas aguas* (1967) (*Great Waters*), but was more transcendental in *Redención* (1933) (*Redemption*) and *La cruz de la espada* (1942) (*The Cross of the Sword*). Her work amounts to thirty volumes, many of which have been translated and have received awards.

Dominica
This geographical region of the Caribbean is both French- and English-speaking. It is the birthplace of ▷Phyllis Shand Allfrey; Elma Napier (1893-?) and ▷Jean Rhys.

Domna, H. (fl c 1220–1240)
French ▷*trobairitz*. The use of an initial instead of a proper name may indicate a woman of some respectability who wished to cloak her identity. She participates in a lovers' debate, in Provençal *tensos*, with one Rosin or Rofin, who by taking the opposite point of view forces her to defend a mildly scabrous position in the judgement of two lovers, one of whom shows the excess of his passion by making love to his lady despite his promise.

Dönhoff, Marion (born 1909)
German journalist and political writer. The daughter of a Prussian landowner, she was born during the last years of near-feudal society in East Prussia. She became an alert witness to political events in 20th-century Germany, and her books have established her as the foremost chronicler of German cultural history. Her main works include: *Namen die keiner mehr kennt* (1962) (*Names Which No One Remembers*); *Weit ist der Weg nach Osten: Berichte und Betrachtungen aus fünf Jahrzehnten* (1970) (*Long is the Way to the East: Reports and Reflections from Five Decades*); and *Preußen – Maß und Maßlosigkeit* (1990) (*Prussia – Constraint and Excess*).

Donna, Una (1906) ▷*Woman, A*

Donna con tre anima, Una (1918) (*A Woman with Three Souls*)
An original and unusual novel, by Italian writer ▷Rosa Rosà. Georgina Rossi, the protagonist, is a married woman who undergoes three metamorphoses in the course of her story. She is, to begin with, an ordinary middle-class housewife who suddenly starts to see the world around her

with new eyes. She becomes sexually liberated and androgynous. From this point, she undergoes more change, to become intellectually free: she suddenly acquires a poetic talent, and writes science fiction-type narratives. She ultimately returns to her old self, but is not the same person because of her discovery of these other selves. Rosà, writing outside the mainstream of the ▷futurist movement as far as her representations of women are concerned, is interesting for her concept of the female divided self (▷dualities).

Donna e il futurismo, La (1941) (*Woman and Futurism*)
Italian autobiographical narrative by Maria Goretti which is, in a sense, a history of the position of the ▷futurist movement on women. Woman, Goretti stresses, is most fulfilled when a mother, and should not, in any sense, compete with man. ▷Fascism is defined here as the defence of the family. The work is of the mainstream of the futurist movement, and is interesting as such.

Donna in guerra (1975) (*Woman at War*)
A novel in Italian by ▷Dacia Maraini, which is not about war, but about motherhood. It is written in diary form, and begins at its chronological end with the statement 'Now I am alone and I must start over again.' From here, we move back into the past of the protagonist, Vanna, who is a teacher, married and pregnant. She is subordinate to her husband, Giacinto, and is trapped in a routine of boring and repetitive tasks. A number of negative images of motherhood are paraded before us in the narrative: mothers are always isolated, and in some way treated as not quite human. When Vanna meets Suna, she teaches her to challenge society's view of women. Vanna, having considered her options and her future, decides to terminate her pregnancy. Motherhood is, for Maraini, an issue of choice. She does not necessarily present motherhood as negative in itself; it is society's treatment of mothers which makes it so.

Donna sbagliata, La (1950) (*The Woman Who Made a Mistake*)
Italian novel, by ▷Lea Quaretti, written in an autobiographical/confessional format, about a woman married to a man whom she does not love. Fragmentary because of its confessional structure and its constant time shifts, it is an introspective novel full of pain. It is interesting for both its psychological analysis and its form.

Donne muoiono, Le (1952) (*Women Are Dying*)
A collection of four Italian short stories by ▷Anna Banti, which have as a common thread running through them the isolation of women. The first story 'Conosco una famiglia' ('I Know a Family') is a portrait of a bourgeois family, with women and children at the centre of the narrative. It is a tale of matriarchy, maliciously told. 'I porci' ('The Pigs') has a 16th-century setting against which Lucilio and Priscilla, a brother and sister, flee the Sack of Rome. He is overcome by harsh reality, she becomes a convent superior. It is ▷fantastical in tone. 'Women Are Dying', the title story, is a futuristic tale set in a time when men can remember the past, while women cannot. This leads to incomprehension between the sexes. Life and death come to mean different things to them, as men have a sense of immortality, while women do not. Men are the historians of this world, while women are the poets and musicians whose imagination has free rein. It is an odd combination of Utopia and Dystopia. 'Lavinia fuggita' ('Lavinia Fled') is another narrative of female isolation, of jealousy, fantasy and competition between Orsola, Lavinia and Zanetta. The stories all address women's present reality even where they are set in the past, thus giving a timeless sense of women's lives.

Dorcey, Mary (born 1950)
Irish poet, short story writer and journalist. Dorcey was raised in County Dublin, Ireland. She has lived in England, France, the US and Japan, but presently spends part of her time in Dublin and part on the west coast. Politically active in Ireland, Dorcey was a co-founder of Irish Women United – a national feminist group in Dublin, and the Irish Gay Rights Movement. She has also worked on the feminist papers *Banshee* and *Wicca*. Her work is published by the independent feminist publishers, Onlywomen Press. Her first collection of poems, *Kindling*, appeared in 1982 and her short story collection, *A Noise From the Woodshed*, in 1989. Her work has also been widely published in journals and anthologies in Ireland, Britain and the US, including *Bread and Roses* (ed. Diana Scott), *In the Pink*, (ed. Raving Beauties), *Beautiful Barbarians* and *Mad Bad Faeries*. Dorcey writes love poems about women, from the lyrical eroticism of 'Sea Flower' to the emotional depth of 'First Love', a mother–daughter poem. She writes of her work that 'as much as our world is conditioned by words, written and spoken, we women can use words to change reality.'

Dot and the Kangaroo (1899)
Australian children's book by Ethel Pedley. A consistent motif in Australian colonial literature has been that of the child lost in the bush, indicating an overwhelming fear of the featureless wilderness. *Dot and the Kangaroo*, a classic in Australian children's literature, marks a significant progression in the oft-repeated story. The child, Dot, the daughter of an outback settler, instead of being found just too late and dead of thirst (as is almost invariably so in earlier stories) is rescued by the bush creatures, indicating a new and more benign attitude towards the bush. It is now a nurturing environment rather than one to be feared. A red kangaroo carries Dot to safety in its pouch, introducing her on the way to a platypus, a koala and a kookaburra. The story was adapted

for the stage in 1924 by Stella Chapman and Douglas Ancelon, and made into a film in 1977.
▷ Children's literature (Australia)

'Do Thou, O God, in Mercy Help' (1738)
Poem by North American writer ▷ Rebecca Richardson. Published in the *American Weekly Mercury*, this poem records Richardson's bitter assertion that her property was illegally confiscated and that, in spite of winning a lawsuit in England, it was never returned to her. In the poem, published on 10 January 1738, she calls upon God to recognize the way in which 'man my life pursues: / To crush me with repeated wrongs' and to 'Let thy just wrath (too long provok'd) / This impious race chastise.' It is Richardson's only known poetry.

Double Hook, The (1959)
Considered the most essentially modern and tremendously influential Canadian novel, *The Double Hook* was written out of ▷ Sheila Watson's experience of teaching at Dog Creek, a remote village in central British Columbia. The novel is brilliantly and imagistically truncated, and focuses on an isolated and incestuous community that must come to terms with its own damnation and salvation. Utilizing Native Canadian, Christian and classical mythology, Watson fragments any expectation of unified plot, and yet develops the notion that all mythologies repeat and complete themselves. It opens with the main character, James, killing his powerful mother, and then attempting to run away from the community that he feels burdened by; but he makes his own flight impossible, and returns, 'freed from freedom', and ready to face his responsibilities.

Double Life, A (1987)
Sketch by Russian poet ▷ Karolina Pávlova, originally published in 1848. Pávlova's novella-length sketch is a remarkable experiment in genre, intermingling an acerbic ▷ society tale in prose with the psychological profile in verse of a girl awakening to womanhood. By day, Cecily von Lindenborn – the foreign name suggests her alienation from Russian life – is a doll-like young lady dominated by her mother, a woman steeped in the empty mores of ▷ Moscow high society, and striving to reproduce herself in her daughter. At night, however, Cecily's poetic dreams come under the aegis of a male mentor who teaches her to tap the resources of her loving soul. In her last dream, on the eve of her wedding to a fortune-hunter, Cecily is already uneasy about the future, but is spiritually armed to face its vicissitudes.

Double-talk
A feature of Caribbean orality, this involves using words in a way intended to conceal their true meaning. It often implies sexual innuendo, and is a feature of ▷ calypso songs in particular.

'Doubt of Future Foes, The' (c 1568)
Poem by Elizabeth I (▷ Elizabeth Tudor). The poem consists of sixteen lines of poulter's measure (a twelve-syllable line alternating with a fourteen syllable line). It is regarding, if not addressed to, her Catholic cousin, ▷ Mary Stuart, Queen of Scots, who had escaped to England after her subjects rebelled and imprisoned her. In the poem, Elizabeth forcefully refuses to grant safe harbour to the fleeing queen. In spite of the seeming harshness of Elizabeth's refusal, she made it with good reason. As the granddaughter of Henry VII, Mary Stuart posed a continuous threat to Elizabeth's position on the throne until Mary was executed in 1587.

Dougall, Lily (1858–1923)
Novelist and essayist, born in Montreal, Canada, of Scottish descent, and educated in private schools. Determined to be a writer, she studied literature and philosophy at the Universities of Edinburgh and St Andrews, and in her lifetime wrote ten novels, eight theological works, and a collection of short fiction. Her first novel, *Beggars All* (1891), won considerable attention. Deeply religious, her concern with moral ambiguity is present in both her fiction and her essays. *What Necessity Knows* (1893) concerns the tension between Old and New World social mores in an immigrant community, and how different character types adapt to the challenges of Canada. Dougall's female characters are interesting and strong-willed; their relationship to nature is symbolic of balance and harmony.
Bib: McMullen, L., in ▷ *A Mazing Space*.

Douglas, Lady Eleanor Davies (1590–1652)
English aristocratic prophet and predictor of political events. She married Sir John Davies in 1609, and Sir Archibald Douglas in 1626. In 1625 she claimed that God began to issue her with direct instructions, some of which turned out to be true: she predicted her husband's death, and that of the First Earl of Buckingham, in 1628, which angered Charles I, as Buckingham was a royal favourite. She uses anagrams, especially ELEANOR AUDLEY (her maiden name) – REVEALE O DANIEL, and makes predictions using anagrams. She was fined, imprisoned and her works burned. The works themselves are many, beginning with *A Warning to the Dragon* (1625) and including *The Restitution of Prophecy*, continuing to the year of her death.
▷ Cary, Mary; Trapnel, Anna; Channel, Elinor
Bib: Berg and Berry in, *1642: Literature and Power in the Seventeenth Century,*Barker *et al.*; Hindle, C.J., *A Bibliography of . . . Lady Eleanor Douglas.*

Douglas, O. (1878–1948)
Scottish novelist. Pseudonym of Anna Buchan. Brought up in a staunch Free Church of Scotland household. Her first novel, *Olivia in India* (1912), is based on a visit to her younger brother in Calcutta. A fictional travelogue composed of

letters, the novel is firmly cross-cultural, with the narrator reflecting on Scotland as much as on her impressions of India. Her depiction of Scottish 'Church' communities, as in *The Setons* (1917) and *Ann and Her Mother* (1922), is a characteristic of her novels, and her portrayal of the contented spinster active in community affairs is central to *Penny Plain* (1920) and *Pink Sugar* (1924). Buchan's autobiography is *Unforgettable, Unforgotten* (1945).

Douka, Maro (born 1947)
Greek novelist. She was born in Hania, Crete, the daughter of a labourer who died when she was ten years old. In 1966 she went to Athens to study archaeology. In 1967, while Greece was under the dictatorship of the 'Colonels', she was imprisoned for her leftist views and resistance activities. Her early books – *The Well* (1974) and *Where Are the Wings?* (1975) – are collections of short stories, which received a somewhat mixed response from the critics. Her subsequent novels, *Karré Fix* (1976), *Fool's Gold* (1979) and *Floating City* (1984), are novels of contemporary Greek life, depicting women in unsatisfactory marital situations which they bear with resignation and depression. Many of the characters appear in different stories, which reveal the varied facets of human life. Douka began writing in her youth, but it was Marxism that, as she puts it, 'liberated the energies/dynamics of my soul', giving her creative insight into the life she observed around her. Her work covers the post-war years, the period of the junta (1967–1974), the student uprising against the 'Colonels', and the restoration of democracy in 1974. Douka makes effective use of the modern Greek vernacular to shape appropriate colloquial voices for her characters.

Douleur, La (1986)
Translation of *La Douleur* (1985), six texts by French writer ▷Marguerite Duras, originally published in 1985. Duras says she wrote five of these texts during or just after World War II, and forgot about them, finding them forty years later. The first is in diary form. It tells of Duras's agonized wait for the return of her husband, Robert L., from the Dachau concentration camp, his arrival, starved and barely alive, and his gradual recovery. The second is the account of Duras's meetings with the Gestapo officer she calls Rabier, who arrested her husband. She keeps in contact with him because he is the only possible link with her husband, and also to pass on any information he gives her to the Resistance cell of which she is a member. After the war he is tried and, presumably, shot. The third and fourth texts are about a woman called Thérèse, who, Duras says, is herself. The third tells of how Thérèse and other members of the cell torture an informer. The fourth concerns a young collaborator, arrested by Thérèse and her friend D., to whom Thérèse is attracted. The fifth text is the story of a meeting between a 'stranger', a child and a working man and the tension that arises

between them. The sixth text was written more recently, and is a conversation during an air raid between a little Jewish girl, Aurélia Steiner, and the woman to whom she was handed by her fleeing mother just before the arrival of the Gestapo.

Downie, Mary Alice (born 1934)
Born in Illinois, Downie grew up in Toronto, Canada, where she attended the University of Toronto. With her husband and others, she has written a number of children's books, often using a historical background: *Honor Bound* (1971, with John Downie), *Dragon on Parade* (1974), *The King's Loon* (1979), *The Last Ship* (1980), *And Some Brought Flowers* (1980, with Mary Hamilton), *Jenny Greenteeth* (1984) and *Alison's Ghosts* (1984, with John Downie). *The Witch of the North: Folktales of French Canada* (1975) is a collection of Quebec folktales. She edited, with Barbara Robertson, *The New Wind Has Wings: Poems from Canada* (1984). She is editor of *Northern Lights*, a history series for young children. She lives in Kingston.

Downing, Lucy Winthrop (1600/1601–1679)
North American letter-writer. She was born into the renowned Winthrop family of England on 9 January 1600/1601. Her early education was steeped in the tenets of Puritan Calvinism but, in academic terms, was exceptional for an early 17th-century girl. On 10 April 1622 she married a well-established lawyer, Emanuel Downing. The ▷*Letters of Mrs Lucy Downing* detail the deteriorating conditions for Puritans in England and her brother John's decision to lead the first major resettlement of Puritans to the Massachusetts Bay Colony. In 1638, after much deliberation, she and her family left for Boston, later settling in Salem. Her letters from the New World during the crucial early decades of the colony are beautifully written and unusually forthright for a Puritan woman; they offer a highly perceptive woman's perspective on well-known events and rare insights into the daily struggles of settling a new land. Some time after 1654, the Downings moved to Scotland because of Emanuel's alliance with Cromwell. After her husband's death, she returned to England, where she died.

▷Winthrop, Margaret Tyndal; *Winthrop Papers*; *Some Old Puritan Love Letters*; Early North American letters

Dowriche, Anne ▷*French Historie, The*

Dowry
In India, the custom among Hindus of presenting the bride to her husband's family with clothing and jewellery for herself, and items for the receiving household. Where once it was regarded as a token of love and affection given according to the ability of the woman's parents, in the 20th century it has become a right demanded by the parents of the groom. The killing of young wives

by their in-laws because they brought insufficient dowry is one of the most disturbing social phenomena in urban India today. The demanding of dowry has been outlawed by the Indian government, but many women's groups argue that the policing of the legislation is insufficient, and that too many murders are covered up as accidental deaths.

The giving of dowry was never a custom observed by all Hindus. Among lower-class and ▷caste groups in which women traditionally worked out of doors, a daughter was seen as an economic asset, and a prospective husband would be required to pay bride-price to her family before he could take her away.

Drabble, Margaret (born 1939)

English novelist, short story writer and critic. Born in Sheffield, sister of the novelist ▷A.S. Byatt, she read English at Newnham College, Cambridge. She has three children from her marriage to Clive Swift, which ended in divorce, Drabble marrying the biographer Michael Holroyd in 1982. Realism rather than formal experimentation characterizes Drabble's fiction, and her writing has strong affinities with both popular ▷romance fiction and a strong English novelistic tradition concerned with social *mores*. A strong influence, both stylistically and in terms of her view of her own work as social history, is novelist Arnold Bennett (1867–1931), and critics have frequently detected the influence of ▷George Eliot.

Drabble's protagonists are frequently young women graduates embarking on careers and relationships. A large proportion of her novels, from the early *A Summer Bird Cage* (1963) to the more recent *The Middle Ground* (1980), are concerned with the psychological and social impact of extramarital relations. *The Millstone* (1965) explores women's autonomy and independence, as does ▷*The Waterfall* (1969), which links these issues to sexual love and the symbolic as well as the physical importance of a woman's orgasm. The middle-period novels retain similar themes, but these are now translated as struggles between metropolitan and provincial identities. Drabble's concern with place and setting is foregrounded in *The Ice Age* (1977), which presents a disturbing picture of modern urban Britain, and is explored further in *A Writer's Britain: Landscape in Literature* (1979). Drabble has also written a number of short stories and a biography of Arnold Bennett (1974), and recently edited the fifth edition of the *Oxford Companion to English Literature* (1985).

Other writings: *A Summer Bird Cage* (1963), *The Garrick Year* (1964), *Wordsworth* (1966), *Jerusalem the Golden* (1967), *The Needle's Eye* (1972), *Virginia Woolf: A Personal Debt* (1973), *The Realms of Gold* (1975), *For Queen and Country: Britain in the Victorian Age* (1978), *The Tradition of Women's Fiction: Lectures in Japan* (1982), *Radiant Way* (1987) and *The Middle Ground* (1980).
  ▷*L-Shaped Room, The*

Bib: Packer, J., *Margaret Drabble: An Annotated Bibliography*; Hannay, J., *The Intertextuality of Fate: A Study of Margaret Drabble*; Salzmann-Brunner, B., *Amanuenses to the Present: Protagonists in the Fiction of Penelope Mortimer, Margaret Drabble and Fay Weldon*.

Dracopoulou, Theony (1883–1968)

Greek poet who used the pseudonym Myrtiotissa. Born in Constantinople, the daughter of the Greek consul, in her early youth she went to Athens, where she worked as an actress and as an elocution teacher in the Greek Conservatoire. She wrote for various Athens literary magazines, and in 1919 published her first collection of poetry, *Songs*. *Yellow Flames* (1925) and *Kravges* (1939) Cries were her best collections of poetry. The death in 1912, in World War I, of the poet Lorenzos Mavilis, with whom she was in love, made her poetry pessimistic and self-involved. But later she came out of herself, engaging with women's struggle for freedom from their condition. Her collection *Songs of Love* (1932) won her an award from the Academy of Athens, while *Kravges* gave her the National Poetry Prize. Later she wrote poems about the Greek civil war (1944–9), *I'll Never Forget*, and about the liberation from German occupation in World War II, *Liberation*. Her poetry expressed not a personal search for fulfilment but rather a general female critique of society's attitude towards women. She also translated into Greek the French *Poems of the Countess of Noailles* (1928) and she published a *Children's Anthology* (1930), which contained both her own and various foreign poems. Some of her poetry has been translated into English.
Bib: Dalven, Rae (ed.), *Modern Greek Poetry*; Karontonis, A., *Introduction to Myrtiotissa's Collected Work*; Tarsouli, A., *Greek Poetesses*.

Drake, Judith (fl 1696)

English polemicist who probably wrote *An Essay in Defence of the Female Sex*, which appeared anonymously in 1696 (for a discussion of the attribution, see Moira Ferguson ed., *First Feminists*). If Judith Drake did write it, then she may have had a medical practice, and is probably the sister of the eminent physician James Drake, and edited his works. The *Essay* uses characters – 'a Pedant, a Squire, a Beaus, a Vertuoso, a Poetaster, a City-Critick' – and Drake introduces the essay as if it were a puppet show. In the it itself she notes that Dutch women take a greater part in the public sphere than their English counterparts, and ridicules the vanity of men.

Drake-Brockman, Henrietta (1902–1968)

Australian dramatist, novelist and historian. Her considerable experience in the Western Australian bush is reflected in her novels – *Blue North* (1934) which deals with the pearling industry in Broome, *Sheba Lane* (1936), *Younger Sons* (1937), *The Fatal Days* (1947), *Sydney or the Bush* (1948) and *The Wicked and the Fair* (1957) – as well as in her successful plays and non-fiction works. Her play

Men Without Wives won the drama section of the New South Wales Sesquicentenary competition in 1938.

▷Dramatists (Australia)

Drakulić, Slavenka (born 1949)

Slavenka Drakulić

Prominent Croatian journalist, noted feminist, and novelist. Several of her articles were published as a book with the title *Smrtni grijesi feminizma* (1984) (*The Deadly Sins of Feminism*). They cover issues such as sex education in schools, media exploitation of women, and prostitution. She has her own theory, which she calls 'testicology', describing a dominant male ideology based on sexism, tradition and totalitarianism.

Her most compelling work, *Holograms of Fear* (1992), charts her experience of a kidney transplant when, coming close to death, she reappraises her life. Her *Mramorna Koža* (1989) (*Marble Skin*), examines an intense mother–daughter relationship in a steamy atmosphere of jealousy and fantasy involving the mother's lover. The daughter is a sculptress who expresses all her violent and confused emotion in a marble sculpture of her mother. A collection of journalistic essays, *How We Survived Communism and Even Laughed*, was published in English in 1992.

Drama

Arab Middle East: There have been many Arab women working on the stage since the introduction of this new art form to the Arab world early in the 20th century. Apart from actresses, for the last thirty years Arab women have worked in the theatre as set designers and as directors – but there are very few writers. Some of them are described below.

Nihad Gad (1937–1989), an Egyptian, who wrote the only play by a woman to achieve commercial success, which ran for over two years. *Street Scene*, originally published as *The Bus Stop*, is a daring modern play full of sharp political and social criticism. It is also makes a feminist point through the situation of Safiyya, the central character, who is the victim of her husband's deception and exploitation. He stands for the new class of dishonest middle-men who have thrown the country open to international con-men. An earlier play, *Adila*, was a monodrama performed at the Tali'a Theatre in Cairo in 1981, as part of a feminist celebration. The play, about the frustrations and petty ambitions of a woman's life, was written by a woman, directed by a woman and acted by a veteran actress against a set designed by a woman. Nihad Gad had degrees from both Cairo and Indiana Universities, and was a successful journalist and short story writer. The success of *Street Scene* might have been the beginning of a brilliant career in the theatre had she not died of cancer in 1989.

Fat hiya al-'Assal (born 1933) started by writing for radio between 1960 and 1970. She had little formal education, and read Arabic only. The authentic colloquial dialogue of her working-class urban characters made her radio plays a great success. In 1970, her first play, *The Seesaw*, was staged by the Egyptian state-funded theatre. The first explicitly feminist play on the Egyptian stage, it dramatizes a story common enough in a fast-changing society: the skilled workman who makes good, sets up his own business and takes a new wife, a fashionable modern girl who makes terrible demands on his time and money. His original wife, the mother of his children, appears and wrecks the new establishment. The writer was encouraged to present more technically daring plays by the popularity of translations of Brecht (1898–1956), Pirandello (1867–1936) and Ionesco (born 1912), which were staged by the Egyptian Public Sector Theatre in the 1960s and 1970s. An interesting play, *No*, was televised in 1975, but her best work for the stage was *The Unmasking* (1982), a feminist dramatization of 'the plight of women in modern Egypt'. The influence of Pirandello is evident in the appearance of the author to address her characters: 'You know how critics are . . . you wouldn't like them to say "she is just a woman! Women cannot write drama!"'

Fat hiya al-'Assal and many other women working in the media are now fully engaged in writing TV drama, for which there is a rapidly expanding market, with so many Arabic television services extending from the Persian Gulf to the Atlantic Ocean. Al-'Assal has been one of the most active and successful with this new medium. She has written ten television plays and some twenty serials. She started with specifically feminist problems, but soon widened her scope to cover socio-political problems involving the whole community.

In Lebanon, Therese 'Awwad (born 1933) was already an established poet when she turned to drama. Her poetic drama *al-Bakara* (1973),

created an uproar even in Beirut, with its unmasking of the relationship between men and women. She went on to write a play about madness in the home, but the greater madness of Beirut has not allowed great drama to flourish.
19th-century Britain: 19th-century literature is not known for its outstanding drama. Although popular forms such as melodrama flourished in city theatres, few serious plays of the period have lasting value. Nevertheless a number of 19th-century British women wrote plays, including ▷Joanna Baillie, ▷Catherine Crowe, ▷Catherine Gore, ▷Michael Field, ▷Felicia Hemans and ▷Augusta Webster. In addition, many women's ▷sensation novels were translated into highly successful melodrama, including ▷Mary Elizabeth Braddon's ▷*Lady Audley's Secret* and ▷Mrs Henry Wood's ▷*East Lynne*. ▷Winter, John Strange
Italy: Italian drama has a long and varied history, from the pastoral works and the *Commedia dell'arte* of 16th-century theatre with its masks and stock characters, to the present. The great names of Italian theatre, are traditionally recognized to be those of Carlo Goldoni (1707–1793), Luigi Pirandello (1867–1936) and, most recently, Dario Fo (born 1926). Women, whose names rarely feature in Italian anthologies of theatre, nevertheless wrote and produced theatrical pieces from the 1500s (▷Suor Annalena Odaldi) onwards. It is often the case that these women produced work in other genres as well. Prominent women dramatists, some of them better known for their other literary productions, include ▷Matilde Serao, ▷Natalia Ginzburg, ▷Dacia Maraini and ▷Franca Rame.

Dramatic Studies (1866)
The first collection of poetry by ▷Augusta Webster, including the much-admired poem 'Snow-Waste'. The dramatic monologues of the collection show the influence of Robert Browning, but Webster's subjects tend to be related specifically to women's experience, as in 'By The Looking Glass', a poem about spinsterhood. The ▷realism and directness of the verse disturbed some Victorian critics.

Dramatists (Australia)
Among the earliest who made their mark on the Australian theatre in the 20th century were Helena Sumner Locke and Agnes Gwynne, whose first plays were staged in 1908. Later came Millicent Armstrong, Helen Simpson and Dora Wilcox in the 1920s and 1930s, the dramatists of the ▷New Theatre movement, and ▷Henrietta Drake-Brockman, ▷Dorothy Hewett, ▷Alma de Groen, Doreen Clarke (famous for *Farewell Brisbane Ladies*, 1981); Eunice Hanger, who has produced at least fourteen plays and has edited volumes of plays; Patricia Johnson (*Gladbags*, 1984); Vasso Kalamaras (five plays, all with a Greek theme); Colleen Klein (*From Blacktown to St Ives, Two Plays*, 1978); Therese Radic (*Some of my Best Friends Are Women*, with L. Radic, 1983,

Madame Mao, 1986, *A Whip Round for Percy Grainger*, 1986); and ▷Jill Shearer. Musette Morell has written many plays for children, and Eva Johnson (*Murras: Plays from Black Australia*, 1989) is a successful Aboriginal dramatist.

Draupadi
In the Hindu classic, the ▷*Mahabharata*, the wife to all five of the Pandava brothers. She is a model of chastity, devotion, quiet wisdom and justice. She was gambled away by her principal husband, Yudhishthira, but the god Krishna saved her from the dishonour of a forced disrobing by her husbands' enemies by clothing her in an endless sari.
▷*Pati vati dharm*

Drawn in Colour (1960)
Autobiographical work by South African writer, ▷Noni Jabavu. It presents the return journey of this British-educated Xhosa woman to South Africa on the occasion of her brother's death, as well as an account of her life in Uganda. Much of its interest is provided by her attempt to fix up her sister's marriage in Uganda, which leads the narrator to confront the alien sexual mores of the Baganda, whose unfavourable comparison with those of the Xhosa leads Jabavu into nostalgia regarding the patriarchal social relations of her childhood. As one who straddles British and African life, the narrator compares whites' fear of blacks, as a fear of the unknown, with her own attitudes towards the Baganda, whom she feels are primitive. Because of this book, she was called the 'new un-African' by a reviewer in *The New African*.

Dream of a Common Language: Poems 1974–1977, The (1978)
Poems by US writer ▷Adrienne Rich. This is, as its title suggests, Rich's most lyrical and utopian book. Its poems set the exhilaration and tenderness of women against the impoverished or murderous actual world of patriarchal capitalism; they celebrate women surviving and creating against the odds, and they mourn the silenced and victimized. Whereas in her later poetry Rich has scrutinized the differences of class and race that divide women, *The Dream of a Common Language* celebrates the idea of a female world, its 'common language' representing nothing less than a transformation of the terms of North American culture. So 'Power', the first poem in the book, insists that women have to redefine power or else be destroyed by it, and the last poem, the celebrated 'Transcendental Etude', culminates in the imagined creation of a feminist art inspired by love between women, which, 'with no mere will to mastery', lovingly reassembles the precious fragments of existence. The book begins with eight poems centred on the difficulties, tragedies and occasional glories of women's experience; these include the famous 'Phantasia for Elvira Shatayev' and 'To a Poet'. The middle consists of 'Twenty-One Love Poems', a free-verse lesbian

version of the sonnet sequence (a form which traditionally celebrated a male poet's love for an idealized woman): lesbian experience is thus made literally central to the book. The third part is a series of ambitious poetic meditations, of which 'Natural Resources' is perhaps the finest, about the possibility of recovering the past and of transforming the future.

Dred (1856)

US anti-slavery novel by ▷Harriet Beecher Stowe. Stowe's next novel after ▷*Uncle Tom's Cabin*, *Dred* provides stronger African-American male characters, including the title character based on Nat Turner (1800–1831), a black North American slave who led a slave revolt in 1831. Parallel plots show whites driving slaves off into a dismal swamp, demonstrating to Stowe's public how slavery not only harms blacks but also leads whites to intolerable brutality.

▷Slaver narratives (19th-century US)

Drewitz, Ingeborg (1923–1986)

West German dramatist and novelist. With her play *Alle Tore waren bewacht* (1951) (*All the Gates Were Guarded*), she was the first German to write about the concentration camps. Her later novels, such as *Oktoberlicht* (1969) (*October Light*), the semi-autobiographical *Gestern war Heute – Hundert Jahre Gegenwart* (1978) (*Yesterday was Today – A Hundred Years in the Present*) or *Eis auf der Elbe* (1982) (*Ice on the Elbe*), are vivid evocations of the moral and cultural disarray of 20th-century Germany. In particular, Drewitz was concerned with the plight of women who struggle to cope with the conflicting demands of marriage, family and work. She also wrote a seminal study of ▷Bettina von Arnim in 1969.

Drewsen, Jette (born 1943)

Danish novelist. Drewsen was born in the countryside near Vejle in Jylland, where her father was a vet. She studied psychology at Copenhagen University, then she married and had three children.

In 1972 she divorced, and published her first novel *Hvad tænkte egentlig Arendse?* (1972) (*What did Arendse Actually Think?*) about a young, suburban housewife with an educated husband and small children. The woman is depressed and aggressive, she feels lonely and stupid. The novel is short, but sharply depicted, and it became a cult book of the feminist movement in Denmark. With the novels *Fuglen* (1974) (*The Bird*) and *Pause* (1976) (*Pause*), Drewsen reached a wide audience. She wrote exactly the right novels at exactly the right time, describing the ambivalent attitudes of young women towards love and work.

Her later work maintains her high artistic standards of writing, for example, *Midtvejsfester* (1980) (*Midway Celebrations*), *Ingen erindring* (1983) (*No Recollection*) and *En Smuk Mand i Farver* (1989) (*A Beautiful Man in Colours*).

She continues to write about her own generation, now disillusioned, alcoholic and so on,

and yet her novels give the impression of beauty and greatness because of the sharpness of detail and the flexibility of her language.

Drif, Zohra (born 1941)

Algerian novelist, Drif is the daughter of a Moslem judge (*cadi*), and herself studied law for a period. She was active in the FLN (National Liberation Front). In 1967 she was arrested by the French colonial government and sentenced to twenty years' hard labour. Like Djamila Bouhired and ▷Djamila Amrane, Drif was accused of participating in bomb attacks during the battle of Algiers. At the time, newspapers reported that Zohra Drif, the '*poseuse de bombes*' ('bomb-carrier'), was a brilliant law student. During the struggle for independence she was given the name 'Farida'. Today she is very involved in the struggle for Algerian women's rights, especially concerning the '*code de la famille*' (the family code, sporadically repeated and reinstated from the 1960s onwards, a government decree – which purported to set down the rights of women, but which was, in fact, restrictive) on the one hand, and Moslem Fundamentalism which sees the emancipation of Algerian women as an example of Western decadence on the other. Her novel, *La Mort de mes frères* (1960) (*Death of My Brothers*) is an account of the cruelty of the Algerian war.

Drinker, Elizabeth Sandwith (1734–1807)

North American diarist. A lifelong resident of Philadelphia, she was raised in one of the leading merchant families in the city and married into another in 1761. In 1758 she began keeping a journal, a project she continued for the next fifty years; a large portion of the journal was published in the 19th century in ▷*Extracts from the Journal of Elizabeth Drinker*. Her perspective is decidedly that of an upper-class, pious woman. For several years during the American Revolution she brought up her five children alone while maintaining a correspondence with her husband who had been imprisoned for refusing to serve in the military and to pay war taxes. In the post-war years, she was able to devote her journal writing to more pleasant issues of interest to her – the financial and spiritual progress of her family and, most notably, her prolific reading. The relative leisure of her last years allowed her to engage in the intellectual pursuits that most fulfilled her. She had a remarkably keen mind and philosophical perspective.

Droste-Hülshoff, Annette von (1797–1848)

German poet. Of Westphalian aristocratic descent, she grew up secluded from the world, in an atmosphere of strict Catholic conservatism. Her early poetry was derivative, but by 1820 she had developed her own style, and composed a cycle of religious verse, *Geistliche Jahre* (1851) (*Spiritual Years*). Contact with the romantic movement sharpened her literary acumen, but in 1820 a 'guilty' love affair put a stop to her public ambitions, and she retreated into writing the autobiographical fragment, *Ledwina*, which was not published until her *Collected Works* appeared in 1878. A collection of poems published semi-anonymously in 1838 found no success.

In 1840 Droste-Hülshoff became mentor to twenty-six-year-old Levin Schücking, and his admiration for her work galvanized her into feverish creativity. Poems of this period, such as 'Der Knabe im Moor' ('The Boy on the Moor') or 'Am Turme' ('On the Tower'), are powerful evocations of emotions, set against a sensual, often haunted, Westphalian landscape. Her masterly novella, *Die Judenbuche* (1841) (▷ *The Jew's Beech*, 1958), half-thriller, half ghost story, emerged as the most accomplished text of poetic realism in 19th-century German literature. In it she combines a realistic portrayal of pre-revolutionary rural Westphalia with a mystical vision of the human race lost in an enigmatic universe. A second collection of poems and ballads consolidated her fame in 1844.

▷ Huch, Ricarda; Reuter, Gabriele

Dualities/Doubles
Women writers often express dualities through the medium of two female characters (a female 'first self' and a female 'second self'). 19th-century women writers seem to have found in the device of the double a means of portraying a more complete representation of woman, with one character socially acceptable and the other not so. The free and uninhibited second self is, indeed, often presented as monstrous. Having stepped outside the boundaries of the conventional feminine, this self mobilizes those aspects of the female not sanctioned by conventional society. Women writers who make effective use of the device are ▷ Emma, ▷ Matilde Serao, ▷ Rosa Rosà and ▷ Emma Tennant.
Bib: Fanning, U., 'Angel v. Monster: Serao's Use of the Female Double', *Women and Italy: Essays on Gender, Culture and History*, ed. Z.G. Barański and S.W. Vinall.

Duayen, César ▷ Barra de Llanos, Ema de la

Dubsky, Countess ▷ Ebner-Eschenbach, Marie von

Duckworth, Marilyn (born 1935)
New Zealand novelist. Sister of the poet ▷ Fleur Adcock, Duckworth's writing career also began early; she published her first novel when she was twenty-four. Widowed once and married four times, Duckworth has said that most of her writing was done between relationships, because of the conflict between meeting her own needs and those of others. Unsurprisingly, her fiction mostly focuses on this conflict, though in her earlier novels her female characters are unable to act to alter their circumstances but remain inescapably dependent on men. Duckworth has said in an interview that for a woman to be a writer she must put her needs first, which goes against all her female conditioning. Duckworth

stopped writing for fifteen years after her fourth novel appeared, and her later novels, while still domestic in focus, have more reference to topical events and a wider contemporary scene.

Publications include: *A Gap in the Spectrum* (1959); *The Matchbox House* (1960); *A Barbarous Tongue* (1963); *Over the Fence is Out* (1969); *Other Lovers' Children* (poetry) (1975); *Disorderly Conduct* (1984); *Married Alive* (1985); *Rest for the Wicked* (1986); *Pulling Faces* (1987); *A Message from Harpo* (1989); *Explosions on the Sun* (stories) (1989).

Duder, Tessa (born 1940)
New Zealand journalist, non-fiction writer and children's author. Duder became a journalist in the 1960s and began writing fiction in the 1980s. With four teenage daughters, she felt the need to write stories which not only reflect contemporary urban attitudes and lifestyles, but which also present strong female characters and positively explore issues and situations faced by young women. A midnight inspiration resulted in her first children's book, a yachting adventure story *Night Race to Kawau* (1982). *Jellybean* (1985), exploring the ups and downs in life of a musical child, was an American Library Association 'Notable Book' and finalist in the New Zealand Goodman, Fielder, Wattie Award in 1986. She really became well known with *Alex* (1987), which won both the New Zealand Library Association's Esther Glen Medal and Children's Book of the Year Award in 1988, and its award-winning sequel, *Alex in Winter* (1989).
▷ Children's literature, New Zealand

Dudley, Dorothy (fl 1775–1776)
North American diarist. A resident of Cambridge, Massachusetts, during the initial years of the American Revolution, she was an eyewitness to the war. In detailed and dramatic fashion, she records the tragedies of war, the heroic postures of the Patriot leaders (most notably, Martha and George Washington), and the spirit of resistance that prevailed even during the siege of Boston. Among her final entries to her diary, which is extracted in ▷ *Theatrum Majorum*, is a testimony of her own commitment to the newly stated Declaration of Independence.

Dudley, Jane ▷ Grey, Jane

Duffy, Carol Ann (born 1955)
Scottish poet and dramatist. Born in Glasgow and brought up in England, Duffy has written extensively while occupying writer-in-residence posts in schools in East London. A characteristic of Duffy's poetry is her concern with diasporic and culturally alienated voices, as typified in the volume *Thrown Voices* (1988). *Standing Female Nude* (1985) has received much critical acclaim, and other volumes include: *Selling Manhattan* (1987), *The Other Country* (1990). Plays include: *Cavern of Dreams* (1984) and *Little Women, Big Boys* (1986).

Duffy, Maureen (born 1933)

English novelist, dramatist, poet and critic. Born in Worthing, Sussex, and read English at King's College, London. After graduating, she worked as a school-teacher for five years. Duffy's writings consistently focus on themes of social and sexual oppression, particularly the social pressures on lesbian identity in England. Another significant characteristic is Duffy's exploration of women's eroticism. Her first novel, *That's How It Was* (1962), is an autobiographically-based account of the relationship between a daughter and her mother faced with the hardships of life as a single-parent family. *The Microcosm* (1966) uses a fragmented narrative with alternating styles to portray the heterogeneity of lesbian identities, but in focusing on a lesbian underworld, the novel is also concerned to portray the social constraints on sexuality. The dualism of social/anti-social behaviour also informs *The Paradox Players* (1967). The story of an experimental half-man half-gorilla hybrid in *Gor Saga* (1981), together with *I Want to Go to Moscow* (1973), about anti-vivisectionists, highlight Duffy's commitment to animal rights, a concern followed up in *Men and Beasts: An Animal Rights Handbook* (1984). In addition to her critical work *The Erotic World of Faery* (1972), Duffy's study of ▷Aphra Behn was significant in reviving interest in this dramatist. *Collected Poems* was published in 1985.

Other novels include: *The Single Eye* (1964), *Wounds* (1969), *Love Child* (1971), *Capital* (1975), *Housespy* (1978), *Scarborough Fear* (as D.M. Layer, 1982), *Londoners: An Elegy* (1983), *Change* (1987), *Illuminations* (1991). Plays: *The Lay Off* (1962), *The Silk Room* (1966), *A Nightingale in Bloomsbury Square* (1973). Also: *A Thousand Capricious Chances: A History of the Methuen List 1889–1989* (1989).

Dufrénoy, Adelaïde (1765–1825)

French poet. Born in Nantes, and married at fifteen, she was obliged to leave France with her husband (a member of the royal entourage) after the Revolution (1789) and only returned in 1812. Her first published work of note was a collection of *Elégies* (1807) (*Elegies*), which was very popular with her contemporaries, and was reprinted several times. Her witty, sensitive and intermittently erotic verse was crowned by the ▷Académie Française in 1815, and earned her the title of the 'French Sappho' – a sobriquet which, according to the critic Claudine Brécourt-Villars, was highly appropriate given the presence in her writing of a distinct homosexual subtext. She also published novels and educational texts, and edited collections of literary works for women. Her writings include: *Etrennes à ma fille* (1815) (*New Year's Gift to my Daughter*); *La Petite Ménagère* (1816) (*The Little Housewife*); *Biographie des jeunes demoiselles* (1816) (*Biography of Young Ladies*); *Les Françaises nouvelles* (1818) (*The New Frenchwomen*); *Les Conversations maternelles* (*Maternal conversations*), and *Le Livre des femmes* (1823) (*The Women's Book*).

▷Tastu, Amable
Bib: Brécourt-Villars, C., *Écrire d'Amour*; Sullerot, E., *Women on Love*; Carton, H., *Histoire des femmes écrivains de la France*.

du Fresne, Yvonne (born 1929)

New Zealand fiction writer. Yvonne du Fresne's grandfather arrived in New Zealand in 1890. A French Huguenot, he joined the large Danish settlement in the Manawatu. Du Fresne grew up in a culturally distinctive community which retained its Danish connections within New Zealand society. All du Fresne's work reflects a double cultural identity and engages with post-colonial questions about settlement and origin. Her stories also focus on gender questions, and reflect her experience as a school teacher, as well as a female child bridging cultures. Du Fresne's first collection of stories won the PEN International Best First Book of Prose Award.

Publications include: *Farvel and Other Stories* (1982); *The Book of Ester* (1982); *The Growing of Astrid Westergaard and Other Stories* (1985); *Frédérique* (novel) (1987); *The Bear From the North* (1989).

Duggan, Eileen May (1894–1972)

New Zealand poet. Eileen Duggan grew up at Tua Marina, on the edge of the Wairau Plains. She was gifted academically, and was considered by the Foundation Professor of Classics at Victoria University of Wellington to have been a 'brilliant' student. She led an extremely retired life after the death of her parents, publishing five volumes of poetry over thirty years. Duggan's Irish ancestry, her Catholicism and her nationalism are the preoccupying subjects of her formally conventional verse. Writing mostly ballads or short lyrics, Duggan's poetry has been instrumental in the conception of 'New Zealand Literature' both at home and internationally, though she chose to set herself apart from the major male poets of the 1940s represented in Allen Curnow's *A Book of New Zealand Verse 1923–45*, declaring, 'Their New Zealand is not mine.' She wrote much about the area she grew up in, and her work is largely celebratory in its impulse.

Publications: *Poems* (1922); *New Zealand Bird Songs* (1929); *Poems* (1937); *New Zealand Poems* (1940); *More Poems* (1951).

Duley, Margaret (1894–1968)

Canadian novelist, born in St John's, Newfoundland. After attending Methodist College in St John's, she enrolled in the Royal Academy of Drama and Elocution in London, but World War I interrupted her studies, and she was forced to return to Canada. She was active in the Newfoundland suffrage movement, one of the founders of the Women's Franchise League, and her novels are about female characters who rebel against the confinement of propriety. She wrote primarily for money, and did not receive much recognition in her lifetime. Her books include *The*

Eyes of the Gull (1936), *Cold Pastoral* (1939), *Highway to Valour* (1941) and *Novelty on Earth* (1942). Her work is now being critically re-evaluated and reissued.

Bib: Feder, A., *Margaret Duley: Newfoundland Novelist.*

Dullemen, Inez van (born 1925)

Dutch prose writer. Her mother was a writer, and she is married to a theatre director. She made her début in the late 1940s, and was influenced by her frequent stays abroad. Her travel stories excel because of her very personal view on life in the United States, Canada and Kenya. Having written several novellas in a careful and florid style, she began a closer examination of her own motives with two collections of travel letters from the United States, the country that is also the setting of her novel *Luizenjournaal* (1969) (*Lice Logbook*), describing the settlement of the Mormons in Salt Lake City. *Vroeger is dood* (1976) (*The Past is Dead*) is the sober and evocative description of the physical decay and death of her parents; it is also a fierce indictment of the abominable treatment of the elderly in retirement homes. The history of a schizophrenic woman is the subject of *De vrouw met de vogelkop* (1979) (*The Woman with the Bird Head*). In the 1980s van Dullemen again distanced herself from her subjects. The stories in *Na de orkaan* (1983) (*After the Hurricane*) describe people who have just experienced a critical event in their lives. Her recent work includes the travel stories *Eeuwig dag, eeuwig nacht* (1981) (*Eternal Day, Eternal Night*), *Een zwarte hond op mijn borst* (1983) (*A Black Dog on My Chest*), *Viva Mexico!* (1988) and *Huis van ijs* (1988) (*House of Ice*), as well as the novel *Het gevorkte beest* (1986) (*The Forked Beast*).

du Maurier, Daphne (1907–1989)

English novelist, dramatist, short story writer, and biographer. Born in London, educated at home and privately in Paris, du Maurier lived in Cornwall for most of her life. That area formed the setting for her most well-known novels, beginning with her first publication, the 19th-century romance *The Loving Spirit* (1931). The subsequent Cornish novels, *Jamaica Inn* (1936), ▷*Rebecca* (1938), *Frenchman's Creek* (1941) and *My Cousin Rachel* (1952) are all romantic historical novels. *Rebecca* typifies du Maurier's characteristic blending of romance and ▷Gothic, a strong tradition in English women's fiction (▷*Jane Eyre*), and one which produces a tension between the possible reproduction of gender stereotypes and their subversion. A preoccupation with the irruption of the supernatural in the everyday is taken up again in *My Cousin Rachel*, whose central female character is haunted by a previous marriage. Her short stories include 'Don't Look Now' (1971), which explores the interface of ▷psychoanalytic and Gothic treatments of the irrational, focusing on a male protagonist, unwilling to acknowledge the process of mourning, who struggles to maintain his sense of

Daphne du Maurier

reason amid the confusion of psychic explanation and/or the externalization of psychic trauma. Her other writings include a study of her family, *The Du Mauriers* (1937), a biography of Branwell Brontë (1960) (the brother of ▷Anne, ▷Emily and ▷Charlotte Brontë), and two autobiographical volumes, *Growing Pains* (1977) and *Myself When Young: The Shaping of a Writer* (1978). She has also edited a selection of her father's letters, *The Young George Du Maurier 1860–67* (1951) and produced two books on Cornwall, *Vanishing Cornwall* (1981) and *Enchanted Cornwall: Her Pictorial Memoir* (1989). Du Maurier's work has formed the basis of a number of successful feature films.

Bib: Foreman, M., *Daphne Du Maurier's Classics of the Macabre*; Light, A., 'Rebecca', *Feminist Review* (1984).

Dumont, Carlotta ▷Matto de Turner, Clorinda

Dunbar, Christine, Countess of March (late 14th, early 15th century)

Scottish letter-writer Christine was the wife of George Dunbar, Earl of the Scottish March. Dunbar had quarrelled with the Earl of Douglas (each wanted his daughter to be married to the heir to the Scottish throne), and subsequently sided with Henry IV of England. A letter from Christine survives, written in 1403 (in French) to Henry IV, asking for help in their poverty and exile in England.

Bib: Moriaty, Catherine, *The Voice of the Middle Ages in Personal Letters 1100–1500.*

Duncan, Sandy Frances (born 1942)

Canadian children's writer, born in Vancouver, British Columbia. She attended the University of

British Columbia, then worked as a child psychologist until 1972, when she began writing. Her books include *Cariboo Runaway* (1976), *The Toothpaste Genie* (1981), *Finding Home* (1982) and *Kap-Sung Ferris* (1977). *Dragonhunt* (1981) and *Pattern Makers* (1989) are both allegorical fantasy novels. She lives in Vancouver.

Duncan, Sarah Jeannette (1861–1922)

Canadian travel writer, novelist and journalist, born in Brantford, Ontario. She attended the Toronto Normal School, and became a schoolteacher for a short time, but abandoned that occupation for the more interesting work of journalism. In 1884 she set off for the New Orleans Cotton Exhibition, having arranged with Canadian newspapers to write a series of travel letters. She worked for the *Washington Post*, and on her return to Canada was the first woman to work in the editorial department of a Canadian newspaper (1886, the Toronto *Globe*). She was a columnist for the Montreal *Star* and *The Week*, using the ▷pseudonym Garth Grafton. She was attracted to journalism for the freedom and independence it offered, since she believed that women should enjoy careers and independence. Her first book, *A Social Departure: How Orthodocia and I Went Round the World by Ourselves* (1890), was based on a series of sketches and articles written on a round-the-world trip that she undertook in 1888 with fellow journalist Lily Lewis, starting west on the recently completed Canadian Pacific Railway, and ending with two years in England. In India she met Everard Cotes, a museum curator, whom she later married (1890). She spent the next twenty-five years in India, but travelled to England and Canada frequently.

Duncan wrote twenty-two books that reflect the range of her experience, particularly her awareness of the tenuousness of colonialism, as in *The Simple Adventures of a Memsahib* (1893), about a young Englishwoman entering Indian society, and *His Honour and a Lady* (1896), about Indian politics. She is best-known for ▷ *The Imperialist* (1904), which portrays small-town Ontario, with its narrow and paternalistic interests of religion and politics. *An American Girl in London* (1891) and *Cousin Cinderella; or A Canadian Girl in London* (1908) both approach the question of social stratification and the interaction of Europe and North America, although the latter is by far the more sophisticated book. *A Daughter of Today* (1894) explores the life of a woman making unconventional choices and struggling to support herself as an artist in Paris and London; *The Path of a Star* (1899) has an actress as its protagonist. That Duncan portrayed women in unconventional roles is certainly a reflection of her own less than conventional life; her books frequently feature an emancipated heroine. Her autobiographical works reveal her capacity for acerbic analysis of social conventions. *On The Other Side of the Latch* (1901) describes Duncan's falling ill with tuberculosis in Simla, while *Two in a Flat* (1908) is about her

time in Kensington, London. *The Pool in the Desert* (1903) is a collection of short stories. Her last two Indian novels, *Set in Authority* (1906) and *The Burnt Offering* (1909), both focus on the rise of Indian nationalism and the challenge to imperialistic attitudes. Her subsequent books continued to combine international politics and social commentary: *The Consort* (1912), *His Royal Happiness* (1914), *Title Clear* (1922) and *The Gold Cure* (1924). She also wrote a number of plays. Duncan's work often confronts the clash between conformism and unconventionality. Her awareness of contemporary issues, and her keen observations of manners and customs, make her an important writer of her time. An edited *Sarah Jeanette Duncan: Selected Journalism* was published in 1978. She died in England.
Bib: Dean, M., *A Different Point of View: Sara Jeanette Duncan;* Fowler, M., *Redney: The Life of Sarah Jeanette Duncan;* Tausky, T., *Sarah Jeannette Duncan: Novelist of Empire.*

Duncombe, Susanna (1725–1812)

English poet who lived in Canterbury, and was encouraged in her writing by her husband, John Duncombe, whom she married in 1761, and who praised her verse allegory – now lost – in his *Feminiad* (1754) (see also ▷Mary Scott). Her poems survive in anthologies edited by others.
Bib: Mild, Warren, *Proceedings of the American Philosophical Society*, No. 122 (1978).

Dunlap, Jane (fl 1771)

North American poet. A devout Bostonian follower of the Great Awakening preacher, George Whitefield (1714–1770), she wrote and published ▷*Poems, Upon Several Sermons, Preached by the Rev'd . . . George Whitefield* in 1771. Although much of the poetry reflects her Puritan training as to woman's sphere, her interest in writing is notable. She concludes the book with the requisite apology for her 'homely stile', but only after having asserted in the introduction that, if her work is well received, she could be induced to write more.

Dunlop, Eliza Hamilton (1796–1880)

Australian poet. Before emigrating to Australia at the age of forty-two, Eliza Dunlop had contributed to a number of journals in Ireland, where she was born. She published extensively in Australian newspapers, her best known poem being 'The Aboriginal Mother', published in *The Australian* on 13 December 1838, and based upon the notorious Myall Creek massacre of that year. She became familiar with Aboriginal languages and culture and was the first Australian poet to attempt transliterations of Aboriginal songs. Her manuscript collection of poems, *The Vase*, is in the Mitchell Library, Sydney, and '*The Aboriginal Mother' and Other Poems* was published by Mulini Press, Canberra, in 1981.
▷Aborigine in non-Aboriginal Australian women's writing, The

Dunn, Nell (born 1936)

Nell Dunn

English novelist, dramatist and journalist. Born
into a wealthy, upper-middle-class family, Dunn
turned away from her own family background in
her twenties, and while living in Battersea,
London, began writing her demotic,
documentary-style narratives of working-class life.
Her short stories, first published in *New
Statesman*, were published in 1963 as ▷*Up the
Junction*. Her first novel, *Poor Cow* (1967), was an
acclaimed bestseller, and focuses on life as a
single parent, depicting a young mother and
factory worker whose husband is in prison. The
play *Steaming* (1981), which looks at the
community and solidarity of women who use a
Turkish bath under threat of closure, was a West
End hit. Other writings include the play *The Little
Heroine* (1988); *I Want* (1971), an epistolary novel
co-written with the poet Adrian Henri; *Different
Drummers* (1977), and *The Only Child* (1978). She
has also published a collection of interviews,
Talking to Women (1965).

Dunne, Mary Chavelita ▷Egerton, George

du Noyer, Anne-Marguerite Petit, (1663–1720)

French journalist. Born to Protestants in Nîmes,
she renounced her faith and married into a
distinguished family. When the marriage failed,
she went to Holland with her two daughters in
order to practise and preach her Protestantism
more freely. Her early *Mémoires* (1710)
concerning her marriage were later republished,
together with a satirical play about her and her
husband, *Le Mariage précipité* (*The Hasty Marriage*).
Whilst living in Holland she produced – between

1716 and 1730 – the periodical *La Quintessence des
nouvelles historiques critiques et politiques* (*The
Quintessence of Historical, Critical and Political
News*).

Other works: *Lettres historiques et galantes* (1704)
(*Letters on History and Love*); *Oeuvres mêlées* (1711)
(*Various Works*); *Evénements des plus rares, ou
l'histoire du S. abbé de Buquoy* (1719) (*Strange
Events, or the Story of the Abbot of Buquoy*).

▷*Journal des Dames* (*Ladies' Journal*)
Bib: Fabre, M., *Voltaire et Pimpette de Nîmes*;
Pailleron, M., 'Histoire de deux unions mal
assorties', *Revue des deux mondes* I (1920).

Du Plessis, Menán (born 1952)

South African novelist born and educated in Cape
Town. Co-founder and later national chairperson
of National Youth Action, which campaigned
against racial discrimination in education, she was
also involved in the United Democratic Front, a
mass-based anti-apartheid organization. She has
published poetry and criticism in magazines, as
well as two novels, *A State of Fear* (1983), which
won the Olive Schreiner Prize in 1985 and the
Sanlam Literary Prize in 1986, and *Longlive!*
(1989). These continue in the tradition
established by ▷Nadine Gordimer, where the
personal and political become deeply interfused in
the life of a white South African woman.

A State of Fear is mediated through the
consciousness of Anna Rossouw, a young white
schoolteacher teaching at a 'coloured' school
during the 1980 school boycott. The title refers
not only to the increasingly threatening police and
military presence within which schoolchildren and
schoolteachers exist, but also to Anna's state of
mind. Her concern for two children for whom she
provides refuge from the police is profoundly
related to her attempt to negotiate the ambiguities
of her existence. In her upbringing, she is part of
the society against which they are reacting, but at
the same time she is wholly sympathetic to them.

The second novel, *Longlive!*, set in November
1985, deals with political action on a broader
canvas. Written in the third person, it views events
through the minds of four major characters. One
of these characters is André Binneman, whose
name (*binne* means 'inside' in Afrikaans) is just
one signal of the author's continuing interest in
the way an intensely self-reflexive consciousness
functions in the context of political crisis. The
intense subjectivity of the first novel gives way to
the representation of a community whose voices
are multiple and various: political slogans, street-
vendors' cries, religious chants, graffiti, and so on.
These voices fuse the personal and political, as
well as individual and community; the particular
mode of existence represented in the text serves to
break down the categories of apartheid at least at
one level of lived reality, some years before its
official abolition by the state.

Du Plessis is one of the new wave of South
African writers, who, along with ▷Ingrid de Kok,
▷Antjie Krog, ▷Welma Odendaal, and others, is
engaged in creating a world whose political

direction is clear, in the sense that it is away from racism and other forms of oppression, and yet whose particular steps are often put under question.

Dupuy, Eliza Ann (1814–1881)

US writer of historical romances. She was best known for *The Conspirator* (1850), one of many 19th-century US novels focused on Aaron Burr (1756–1836), Thomas Jefferson's (1743–1826) competitor for the US presidency in 1800.

Durand, Cathérine, (died 1736)

French novelist. Although her married name was Bédacier, she preferred to retain the maiden name under which she had begun her writing career. Her first novel, *La Comtesse de Mortane (The Countess of Mortane)*, was published in 1699. In the following year two historical novels based on the intimate stories of royal and aristocratic figures were published: *Histoires des amours de Grégoire VII, du duc de Richelieu, de la princesse de Condé et de la marquise d'Urfé (The Love Affairs of Gregory VII, The Duke of Richelieu, The Princess of Condé and The Marchioness of Urfé)* and *Mémoires secrets de la cour de Charles VII, roy de France (Secret Memoirs from the Court of Charles VII, King of France)*. Two important later works show a continued interest in the intrigues surrounding sexual affairs: *Les petits soupers de l'été de l'année 1699* (1702) (*Intimate Suppers in the Summer of 1699*), and her fictionalized accounts of the famous courtesans of ancient Greece, *Les Belles Grèques* (1712) (*Greek Beauties*), which are followed by dialogues between contemporary 'galantes'.

Other works: *Le Comte de Cardonne, ou la constance victorieuse, histoire sicilienne* (1702) (*The Count of Cardonne, or Triumphant Constancy, a Sicilian Story*) and *Henry, duc des Vandales* (1714) (*Henry, Duke of the Vandals*).

Duranti, Francesca (born 1935)

Italian novelist. Her first work, *La bambina* (1976) (*The Little Girl*), is a recreation of her childhood, a kind of self-examination. It is also a vivid evocation of the experience of the war, in the setting of the Italian countryside. Her work frequently addresses the nature of writing and the role of the writer. *Piazza mia bella piazza* (1978) (*My Beautiful Square*), for instance, tells the story of Paola, who creates herself as an independent individual through her writing. For this freedom, she pays the price of losing her lover. Her best-known work, *La casa sul lago della luna* (1984) (▷ *The House on Moon Lake*, 1987), and her most recent work, *Effetti personali* (1988) (*Personal Effects*), in which a woman tries to find and interview an eastern European writer who does not exist, also deal with this theme of writing and writers. Duranti also wrote *Lieto fine* (*Happy Ending*) in 1987, and has translated ▷ Virginia Woolf's short stories. She is currently one of the most widely read of Italian writers.

Francesca Duranti

Duras, Claire de (1778–1828)

French novelist. After a much-travelled childhood, a four-year sojourn in Martinique, and marriage to the Duc de Duras, this author established a salon in London which became a meeting place for the French aristocratic exiles who flocked there after the Revolution (1789). Following her return to France in 1807, she met the writer Chateaubriand (1768–1848) who inspired in her a deep but platonic devotion, and whose career she furthered. His liaison with another woman, Madame Récamier, left Duras with time on her hands, and she compensated for her new solitude by writing two novels, *Ourika* (1823) and *Edouard* (1825). Both focus on the theme of impossible, thwarted passion. *Ourika* recounts the story of a black servant girl, who falls hopelessly in love with a white man, and eventually retires to a convent. The novel highlights the barriers erected by racial difference, and also, on a symbolic level, chronicles the resistance women encounter when they attempt to step out of the place allotted them by society. *Edouard* tells the tale of two socially unequal lovers who die because they are prevented from following their hearts' inclination. The underlying moral of both texts, particularly the second, is that passion rather than convention must serve as a reliable and felicitous guide to human conduct. Duras's writing bears some resemblance to that of Samuel Richardson (1689–1761) and Jean-Jacques Rousseau (1712–1778); it belongs, moreover, to a body of 'feminine literature' produced in France during the early years of the 19th century, which lost its vogue but is being rehabilitated by modern critics. A third novel of hers, *Olivier ou le secret* (*Olivier or the Secret*), deals with the theme of impotence, and explains, perhaps why Madame de Duras had a rather scandalous reputation. This work was not published until 1971.

▷ Genlis, Stéphanie de
Bib: Crichfield, C., *Three Novels of Mme de Duras*; Merlant, J., *Le Roman personnel de Rousseau à Fromentin*.

Duras, Marguerite (born 1914)

French writer and film-maker, who has written novels, short stories, plays, screenplays and articles. Born Marguerite Donnadieu in French Indo-China, she moved to France permanently at the age of nineteen to study law. Her first novel, *Les Impudents*, which she has since withdrawn, was published in 1943. Over the next fifteen years she published a number of novels and stories, all fairly traditional in style, notably *Un barrage contre le Pacifique* (1950) (▷ *The Sea Wall*, 1986), which drew on her experience of growing up in Indo-China. ▷ *Moderato Cantabile* (1958) provided the first real example of the sparse and limpid, yet suggestive, style which gives her perennial themes of sexual desire, love, death and memory their stark power. This style and the themes it conveys are also at work in her celebrated screenplay for Alain Renais's film *Hiroshima, mon amour* (1960) (*Hiroshima, My Love*). Over the next decade her style developed, in plays and, notably, in the novels *Le Ravissement de Lol V. Stein* (1964) (▷ *The Ravishing of Lol V. Stein*, 1986) and *Le Vice-consul* (1965) (▷ *The Vice-Consul*, 1968), which seem to be slightly conflicting episodes of a story which recurs throughout Duras's work. Her use of language was to be much discussed by feminists from the 1970s onwards as embodying ▷ *écriture féminine* (*feminine writing*).

After 1971 Duras concentrated on making films, distinctive in their oblique relation of spoken soundtrack to image, and published mainly screenplays, notably ▷ *India Song* (1973) and *Le Camion* (1977) (*The Lorry*). In the 1980s she diversified once more with the successful play *Savannah Bay* (1982), her Goncourt Prize-winning autobiography *L'Amant* (1984) (▷ *The Lover*, 1985) the reworked collection of early short stories, ▷ *La Douleur* (1985), a number of adaptations of work by Henry James and Strindberg, and some shorter 'narratives' and collected articles.

▷ *Square, The*; *Woman to Woman*
Bib: Selous, Trista, *The Other Woman: Feminism and Femininity in the Work of Marguerite Duras.*

Dúrova, Nadezhda Andréevna (1783–1866)

Russian author of fiction and autobiography. In 1806 Dúrova enlisted in the Russian cavalry, masquerading as a boy. When her gender and courage in combat against Napoleon became known to Alexander I the next year, he gave her a commission in the Hussars and a pseudonym drawn from his own name (Alexandrov). She retired in 1816, but defended her hard-won independence with semi-masculine dress and mannerisms. Edited excerpts from the journals she kept during her years of military service, ▷ *The Cavalry Maiden*, appeared in print in 1836.

In the late 1830s Dúrova began publishing fiction. The extravagant rhetoric and melodramatic plots of her works reflect her late 18th-century upbringing on English ▷ Gothic and ▷ sentimental literature. Some tales are narrated by a female cavalry officer whose curiosity uncovers terrible secrets: the degradation and death from syphilis, clinically described, of a girl married at thirteen to a dissolute man ('Elena, the Beauty of T.', 1837, revised as 'Play of Fate', 1839); the lethal outcome of a Polish priest's guilty love for his ward ('The Pavilion', 1839). She wrote stories from the history and legends of her native Ural region: 'Treasure Trove' (1840), 'Cheremiska', and 'Nurmeka' (1839), which features a transsexual masquerade. Her ▷ society tale, 'The Nook' (1840) describes a love kept alive only by extended deception. *A Year of Life in St Petersburg* (1838), Dúrova's memoir of literary fame, reveals bitterness at her treatment as a curiosity in the drawing-rooms of the capital. In 1841 she returned to obscurity, ending her life as an amiable eccentric in the remote Ural town of Elabuga where ▷ Tsvetáeva committed suicide in 1941.

▷ *Elena Deeva*

Dust Roads of Monferrato, The (1990)

Translation of *Le strade di polvere* (1987), a saga by Italian writer ▷ Rosetta Loy. This work covers almost 100 years in the life of generations of a Monferrato farming family. The broad 19th–20th-century panorama is impressively handled, and the novel also deals in depth with family emotions and events of everyday life. Loy recreates the world of her childhood here but, despite its historical dimension, the novel ultimately almost achieves a sense of timelessness.

Dusty Answer (1927)

Novel by English writer ▷ Rosamond Lehmann. Her first, it was acclaimed by critics, although its 'explicit' references to sexual passions were also decried. The novel tells the story of Judith Earle from childhood to young adulthood. Judith is the only and lonely daughter of wealthy, emotionally distant (or physically absent) parents, and is educated at home. Her life is chiefly centred on the Fyfe 'family-next-door', a group of cousins and siblings who come to stay during the holidays. The most vivid moments of her childhood are in their company; after a long absence, they return when Judith is nearly eighteen, and her life becomes caught up with theirs again.

At Cambridge, Judith begins a passionate friendship with another student, the beautiful, ebullient Jennifer. The extent to which Lehmann intended the friendship to be seen as a lesbian romance is unclear. The 'type' of the masculine lesbian is clearly depicted, however, in the older woman for whom Jennifer abandons Judith. On leaving Cambridge, Judith consummates an earlier passion for one of the Fyfe boys, Roddy, who makes love to her and then rejects her ardent protestations of love for him. In turn, she rejects Martin Fyfe's proposal of marriage. Become beautiful and more cynical, Judith recognizes that 'none of the children next door had been for her.' Alone at the end of the novel, she is prepared to discard her past and to ask 'what next?'

Dusty Answer has been described as a 'beginner's novel', naïvely romantic in its attitudes and its language, and inconsistent in its tone. For other readers, however, Lehmann succeeds in depicting the transition from childhood to adult awareness, displaying the skill, which she was to develop in her later work, of portraying the individual consciousness and its processes. Moreover, while the inner world of Lehmann's characters may appear a small one, her novels are never without a larger sense of the ways in which history, culture and, in particular, social mores impinge upon individual lives.

Dutt, Toru (1856–1877)

Indian poet. She was born in Calcutta to a wealthy and cultivated family, and educated at home with her sister, Aru. Her parents were converts to Christianity. In 1869 the family travelled to Europe, and Toru and Aru supplemented their education by attending a convent in Nice. When the family moved to Cambridge, England, in 1871 both women attended the higher lectures for women started by philosopher Henry Sidgwick (1838–1990) and other liberal dons. The Dutts returned to Calcutta in 1873, where Toru continued to write poetry and translate portions of the great Hindu classics the ▷*Ramayana* and the ▷*Mahabharata* from the Sanskrit into English. Like her mother and sister, she died of tuberculosis at a young age.

Toru Dutt was a pioneer in the field of women's writing at a time when few Indian women put their thoughts on paper, let alone got them published. She published a novel in French in 1879, *Le Journal de Mlle. d'Avers* (*The Diary of Mille d'Avers*). Her other volumes are *A Sheaf Gleaned in French Fields* (1875), and two works published postumously, *Bianca; or the Young Spanish Maiden* (1878) and *Ancient Ballads and Legends of Hindustan* (1882).

Dutton, Anne (fl 1743)

North American letter-writer. She was residing in Bristol, Pennsylvania, during the Great Awakening, and in 1743 published ▷*A Letter from Mrs Anne Dutton . . . to the Rev. Mr G. Whitefield.* The document provides little biographical information about her, but suggests an excellent education and a pious perspective.

▷Early North American letters

E

Eadburg (Bugga), Abbess of Minster in the Isle of Thanet (8th century)

English abbess. Eadburg is the recipient of letters (in Latin) from ▷Boniface and Lull. These mention gifts and books which she has sent them. A request for her to copy out in gold the epistles of St Peter indicates the degree of skill to be found in her scriptorium (manuscript workshop).

Early North American letters

While diaries and autobiographies have been recognized by late 20th-century feminists as non-traditional literary genres of significance for women, little attention has been directed toward the aesthetics of letter-writing by women. Because most societies within early North American culture discouraged the publication of writings by women as 'unwomanly' and outside of 'woman's sphere', the letter offered women a legitimate means of expressing their philosophies, frustrations and accomplishments. Although 'private' in the sense of not being published, letters exchanged with close friends or family members actually allowed women a mock-publication of their opinions. From the earliest aristocratic Puritan and Dutch correspondents, such as ▷Margaret Tyndal Winthrop (c 1591–1647) and ▷Lucy Winthrop Downing (1600/1601–1679), ▷Maria van Cortlandt van Rensselaer (1645–1689) and ▷Alida Schuyler van Rensselaer Livingston (1656–1727), the letter was a means of establishing a community with other women and of retaining contact with family and friends who remained in the Old World.

This is a genre that notably crosses all religious and political sects, as well as all classes, in early North America. ▷Mary Willing Byrd (1740–1814) used her letters to express the outrage she felt when her political affiliations were questioned during the American Revolution. The slave-poet ▷Phillis Wheatley (c 1753–1784) corresponded with other enslaved Africans as a way of sharing their lives, and the letters of ▷Deborah Read Rogers Franklin (1708–1774), who was nearly illiterate, demonstrate that the slightest education allowed women access to this genre. For women who found the isolation of a new environment almost unbearable, the letter acted both as a link with their native communities and as a record of the differences they encountered in their new settings. Thus ▷Elizabeth Brown Brown (1753–1812) corresponded with women in her home town of Concord, Massachusetts, after she had resettled in the 'wilderness', and ▷Mary Coburn Dewees (fl 1787–1788) did the same when she travelled from Philadelphia to settle in the newly opened lands of Kentucky.

But isolation was not always physical. For ▷Elizabeth Ann Bayley Seton (1774–1821), founder of the Sisters of Charity and the first North American saint in Catholic religious history, the isolation was as much psychological as physical. In this, Seton represents the typical sense of value that women placed on the letter as a means of community. But the letter also had an overt literary value: for dramatist and poet ▷Mercy Otis Warren (1728–1814), her correspondence with her friend ▷Abigail Smith Adams (1744–1818) enabled her to develop literary tropes that she could refine and incorporate into her literary productions. Thus the letter was one of the most prolific and significant forms of writing for early North American women.

Early North American narratives of witchcraft cases

In late 17th-century New England the mass hysteria instigated by psychologically disturbing and oppressive religious zeal led to numerous charges of witchcraft against both sexes, but women were far more often charged with conduct that was deemed unusual and therefore suspect. Nineteen people were executed in Massachusetts after being found guilty of witchcraft. Most accounts of the trials are transcripts taken down by a member of the audience, but ▷ *The Petition of Mary Easty* (1692) is a remarkable statement from an accused woman. It is highly literate and literary, and it suggests the great loss of life in this period of communal irrationality.

Early North American Quaker women's writings

Because their culture valued education of women as well as of men, and because women were more openly integrated into the formation of the community of ideas that shaped their faith, Quaker women wrote and published much more prolifically than did their counterparts in Puritan New England or non-Quakers in the mid-Atlantic and southern states. Undoubtedly, the most famous Quaker woman in early North America was ▷Hannah Callowhill Penn (1671–1726), whose marriage to the proprietor of Pennsylvania cast her into the annals of history. But Penn was a businesswoman as well as an aristocrat, as her turn-of-the-century correspondence reveals.

Letter-writing was an important means for Quaker women to express their political opinions to community leaders as well as to family and other Friends. As early as 1660, ▷Mary Traske (fl 1660) admonished the Puritan leaders of her Massachusetts community for their repression of differing religious faiths. ▷Hannah Griffitts, on the other hand, used correspondence as a way of exchanging her poetry with other women of her faith, whereby there developed a circle of literary critics and political commentators among these early Pennsylvania women.

While a few women, such as ▷Bathsheba Bowers (c 1672–1718) and Hannah More (1745–1833), published their religious and historical tracts, most early Quaker women relied upon detailed and often years-long endeavours to record their lives in the privacy of diaries and journals. Writers such as ▷Sarah Eve (1749/1750–1774) and ▷Ann Head Warder (c 1758–1829) used their diaries for capturing the everyday beauty and hardship of their environment, the social clashes and accomplishments of their communities, and the day-to-day experiences that marked Quaker women's lives in early North America.

During the American Revolution, when Quakers' pacifist beliefs put them in jeopardy with both sides during the war, faithful Quakers such as ▷Margaret Hill Morris (1737–1816) used their diaries as a means of confronting their beliefs and assuaging the psychological trauma of accusations from both sides. So, too, do such diaries capture the contributions of these pacifist women to the health and survival of the English and North American soldiers and their efforts to build the new nation at the war's conclusion.

Other notable early North American Quaker women writers include ▷Elizabeth Ashbridge; ▷Hannah Callender; ▷Grace Growden Galloway; ▷Hannah Hill, Jr; ▷Jane Fenn Hoskens; ▷Sophia Wigington Hume; ▷Mildred Morris Ratcliff; ▷Anna Rawle; ▷Elizabeth Webb and ▷Sarah (Sally) Wister.

East Lynne (1861)

A novel of ▷sensation by ▷Mrs Henry Wood. Lady Isabel Vane mistakenly believes her husband to be having an affair, and runs away with rakish Frank Levison. Her fate as a ▷'fallen woman' is one of the most appalling in Victorian literature. She has a child, is deserted, crippled in a train crash and reported dead, then returns home in disguise to become governess to her own children. In the meantime, her husband has married the woman Isabel believed he was involved with. Her final punishment is having to watch her son die without revealing her identity to him. The book was favourably reviewed in *The Times*, sold over 2½ million copies by 1900, was translated into several languages and adapted into a stage melodrama. Conventional Victorian values towards marriage and the family are forcibly driven home, and Wood displays an almost sadistic relish in her punitive treatment of Isabel.
▷*Cometh Up as a Flower*

Eastman, Mary Henderson (1818–1880)

US novelist and non-fiction writer. Eastman wrote a fictional response to ▷Harriet Beecher Stowe's ▷*Uncle Tom's Cabin*. Her *Aunt Phillis's Cabin; or, Southern Life as It Is* (1852) was quite popular in the south and partly provided the impetus for Stowe's compiling *A Key to Uncle Tom's Cabin* (1853). The warring novels – Stowe's *Uncle Tom* and Eastman's *Aunt Phillis* – marked an interlude in US anti-slavery literature in which novelists defended their fiction for its representational accuracy and documented their sources.

Eastman is also significant for her early writing on Native Americans, among whom she lived as a military wife. Among these works are *Dacotah* (1849), *The Romance of Indian Life* (1852) and *Chicora, and Other Regions of the Conquerors and Conquered* (1854). Not among the Native Americans' most sympathetic chroniclers, Eastman focused on the topic probably more as a result of opportunity and discovery of a publishable – because unusual – subject.

Eaubonne, Françoise d' (born 1920)

French historian, essayist, poet and feminist theorist. D'Eaubonne has written historical novels, a fictionalized biography of ▷Madame de Staël, and a feminist Utopia. Her historical novel, *Comme un vol de gerfauts* (1947) (*A Flight of Falcons*) and extracts from her essay 'Feminism or Death' in *New French Feminisms* (1974) have been translated into English. As the title of this essay suggests d'Eaubonne could be described as an ecological feminist.

Ebner, Christine (1277–c 1355)

German writer and visionary nun, also known as Christina von Engelthal. She entered the Dominican Convent of Engelthal at the age of twelve, and stayed there all her life. Her two books became exceedingly popular in 14th-century Germany. Her *Büchlein von der Gnaden Überlast* (*The Little Book on the Unbearable Weight of Grace*) follows the tradition of earlier chronicles of Dominican foundations, and describes the history and mystical experiences of the nuns at Engelthal. Her second book was inspired by the example of ▷Mechthild von Magdeburg, whose work had reached Engelthal in 1351. *Leben: Geschichte der Christina Ebnerin* (*A Life: Visions of Christina Ebner*) is an account of her own visions and mystic life. She was one of the best-known women mystics of her time, and received many visits from notable figures of the day, including the Holy Roman Emperor Charles IV (1316–1378).
▷*Visionsliteratur*

Ebner, Margarethe (c 1291–1351)

German visionary writer. Of noble birth, as a child she entered the Dominican Convent of Maria Medingen in southern Germany, and began to have religious visions after an illness in 1312. Encouraged by Heinrich von Nördlingen (c 1310–before 1387), a priest with whom she corresponded for many years, she noted down her *Offenbarungen* (1882) (*Revelations*). Written in Swabian dialect, they record her life long mystical confrontations with Christ.
▷*Visionsliteratur*

Ebner-Eschenbach, Marie von (Countess Dubsky) (1830–1916)

Austrian short story writer. She grew up in Vienna and on the family estate of Zdislawitz in Moravia, and in 1848 she married her cousin, an engineer and scientist. Despite her family's disapproval, she began to write at an early age. She dreamt of a career as a dramatist at the Vienna Burghtheater, but her plays met with failure, and eventually she found an alternative creative outlet in the novella form. It was not until 1883 that she achieved a first success with a collection of regional stories, *Dorf- und Schloßgeschichten* (*Stories from Village and Castle*), in which, with realism and gentle humour, she investigated contemporary social problems and their psychological repercussions. A Catholic ▷humanist with a great sympathy for the helpless, the oppressed and the poor, her best-known work includes the story of a dog, ▷*Krambambuli* (1875) and the novel, *Das Gemeindekind* (1887) (*Child of the Community*), which describes the struggle of a murderer's son against social ostracism. An admirer of ▷Louise von François, and a friend of ▷Betty Paoli and ▷Enrica von Handel-Mazzetti, Ebner-Eschenbach created many sensitive portraits of women, as in *Frauenbilder. Sechs Erzählungen* (1875) (*Images of Women: Six Stories*), or *Božena* (1876), the story of a housemaid. Famous also for her aphorisms, she became in later life a *grande dame* of Viennese cultural life, and was the first woman to receive an honorary doctorate from the University of Vienna.

Eclipsed: Two Centuries of Australian Women's Fiction (1988)

An anthology edited by Connie Burns and Margai McNamara, contains extracts from the writings of fifty Australian women, from ▷Catherine Helen Spence to Margaret Coombs.
　▷Anthologies (Australia)

Écriture féminine

Feminine (female) writing associated with ▷Hélène Cixous and ▷Luce Irigaray, who separately inscribe the different style of women's writing in metaphors of the female body. For both Cixous and Irigaray 'writing the body' is a form of female liberation.

Edgell, Zee

Caribbean novelist and teacher, born in Belize, where she was educated in the 1940s and 1950s. Her first job was as a reporter for the *Daily Gleaner* in Kingston, Jamaica. From 1966 to 1968 she taught in Belize, during which time she was also editor of a small newspaper in Belize City. She has travelled extensively with her husband and children, having lived in Britain, Nigeria, Afghanistan, Bangladesh and the USA. She was Director of the Women's Bureau in Belize until 1982, and now lives with her family in Somalia.
　She published ▷*Beka Lamb* in 1982. It won the Fawcett Society Book Prize, and was the first novel by a Belizian to reach an international audience. The novel focuses on the coming to consciousness of a young girl, and as such mirrors the 'making of Belize', articulating the country's social relations, its class and ethnic character. It received good critical reception in national literary reviews.
　See articles on Edgell in the *New Statesman* and *Wasafiri* (1985).

Edgeworth, Maria (1768–1849)

Irish novelist and educationalist, born in England. Edgeworth was taken by her father to Edgeworthstown, the family's Irish estate, in 1782. She remained there until her death. Most of her early writings were moral stories and educational essays written in collaboration with

her father, or strongly influenced by his belief in the doctrine of utilitarianism (propounded by the contemporary English lawyer and philosopher, Jeremy Bentham, 1748–1832). Her lively defence of women's education, *Letters to Literary Ladies*, was published in 1795, just five years before her outstanding novel, ▷*Castle Rackrent* (1800), on which her reputation is based. The theme of the declining Ascendancy class (the Anglo-Irish aristocracy) and especially the landlord-tenant relationship, so brilliantly handled in her first novel, returns in her subsequent fiction: *Ennui* (1809), *The Absentee* (1812) and *Ormond* (1817). Although skilful, the later novels tend to be rather didactic. Her last novel, *Helen*, appeared in 1834.
　▷'Big House', The

Edib, (Adivar) Halide (1883–1964)

Turkish nationalist leader and novelist, dramatist, memoirist and lecturer. She was the first Moslem Turkish girl to graduate from the American College, Istanbul. She worked for some time as a teacher, but later was the first Turkish woman to lecture at the university in Istanbul. She travelled to Egypt and England in 1909. She was active in the nationalist movement from 1910 to 1912, visited Syria during World War I and started Turkish schools in Damascus and Beirut. She took part in the War of Independence against Greek armies in Izmir, and later with the Kemalist forces in Anatolia. She was among the nationalist leaders to be sentenced to death by the commander of the British Force.
　After the establishment of the Republic in 1923 she and her husband, Professor Adnan Adivar, did not see eye-to-eye with their old colleagues, now in authority. They left in 1924 and lived in England and France for fifteen years. They visited India and North America, and Halide lectured in universities in these countries. She continued writing for newspapers in Europe and the USA, and also wrote novels and memoirs. In 1939 she returned home and taught English language and literature at the University of Istanbul. She was elected to the Turkish Parliament for Izmir in 1950. On the death of her husband in 1954 she retired from public life and concentrated on writing.
　Halide Edib was influenced by the ideas of the Turkish poet-philosopher Zia Gokalp (1876–1929), looking back to the early pastoral history of Turan. Edib's book *Turkey Faces West* (1930), has this epigraph by Gokalp: 'We come from the East / We go toward the West.' In the introduction, she explains his ideas important to her because he 'always claimed that men and women shared all rights, political and otherwise, in Turkish society. His evidence was fairly strong and authentic. The Turks and Mongols (of the pagan period) claimed descent from a virgin who bore a son without a father and without sin. Further, the ancestor worship of the Turks was not limited to the souls of grandsires; the souls of women ancestors were also included.' Halide Edib wrote many novels of Turkish life, concerning the

whole range of Turkish women's problems in a time of fundamental change. The best-known of her novels, *Sinekli Bakkal* (1938), appeared first in English, as *The Clown and His Daughter* (1935). In 1942 the novel won the first State Prize for the Turkish Novel, and a French translation was published in Istanbul as *Rue de l'Epicerie aux Mouches* (1944). It covers Turkish life from 1887 to 1907, and was supposed to be the first part of a trilogy; the second part *Tatçik* (*The Sandfly*) was published in 1940. Her works include: *Memoirs of Halide Edib* (1926), *The Turkish Ordeal, Being the Further Memoirs of Halide Edib* (1926), *Turkey Faces West: A Turkish View of Recent Changes and Their Origin* (1930), *The Daughter of Smyrna* (1941), *The Conflict of East and West in Turkey* (1963) and *Masks or Souls, A Play in Five Acts* (1953).

Edible Woman, The (1969)

Canadian writer ▷Margaret Atwood's first novel, about Marian MacAlpin, a young woman who works for a consumer company, and who is at a juncture where she has to decide what role she wants to play in her future. She attempts to flee from being fixed by her camera-pointing fiancé, makes friends with a feckless graduate student, and becomes so sickened by consumerism that she stops eating. The change in point of view from Marian as manipulable object to Marian as a subject who refuses to be packaged and consumed is effective. This novel is both funny and terrifying.

Edith (Eadgyth) (died 1075)

Queen of Edward the Confessor, and English patron. Edith was the daughter of Godwin, Earl of Wessex, and she appears to have been well-educated. She married Edward in 1045, and because they had no children, on Edward's death in 1066 Edith's brother, Harold, succeeded to the throne. Harold was defeated eight months later by William of Normandy in the Battle of Hastings. Edith commissioned the *Life of Edward the Confessor* (in Latin prose) during Edward's lifetime, and it was begun in 1065–1066, but also covers the period following his death. Edward is presented as a holy man, and Edith and her family are highly praised. Edith may have wanted the work to help safeguard her future after the death of her husband, so the commission may be seen as political propaganda. The *Life* influenced the view of Edward held by following generations.
Bib: Barlow, F., *Vita Ædwardi Regis*; Stafford, Pauline, *Queens, Concubines and Dowagers*.

Éditions des femmes

French publishing house. Established by the ▷*Psych et Po* group in 1973, and therefore concentrating on psychoanalytically-inspired texts, this is the only overtly feminist publishing house in France. Éditions des femmes has published the works of ▷Hélène Cixous, and it still exists in Paris as a publisher and bookshop.

Edmond, Lauris Dorothy (born 1924)

Lauris Edmond

New Zealand poet and prose writer. Lauris Edmond was born and grew up in Hawkes Bay and has described being a child in the major Napier earthquake of 1931 in the first volume of her autobiography, *Hot October* (1989). Trained as a teacher, Edmond spent her married life in educational work. She began publishing poetry late in life, but has described writing poems continually through the years of raising a family, only to stow them in a cupboard. Since her first book appeared in 1975, she has published nine volumes of poetry, a novel, an autobiography and has written several plays. In 1985 she won the Commonwealth Poetry Prize for *Selected Poems*, concerned with gender roles and with metaphysical questions about the individual's relationship to material and spiritual life. Edmond has been said to be the 'representative woman of her generation', particularly in the way her family commitments led to her late emergence as a writer.

Publications include: *In Middle Air* (1975); *The Pear Tree: Poems* (1977); *Wellington Letter: A Sequence of Poems* (1980); *Seven: Poems* (1980); *Salt from the North* (1980); ▷*Catching It: Poems* (1983); *Selected Poems* (1984); *Seasons and Creatures* (1986); *Summer Near the Arctic Circle* (1988); *High Country Weather* (1984); *Hot October* (1989); *Bonfires in the Rain* (1991).

Education

19th-century Britain: During the pre-Victorian period, middle-class girls' education took place either under the tutelage of ▷governesses or family members, or at schools where 'feminine accomplishments' were taught. The education of working-class girls was even more limited and haphazard. It was possible to attend a Church school and receive elementary instruction, but the majority did not.

The 1830s saw the first significant protests against the inadequacy of educational opportunity, but as with the ▷suffrage campaign, these protests tended to issue from the middle-classes who were generally unconcerned about their poorer sisters. Campaigners were primarily interested in improving the education of governesses; this group formed the majority of students at Queen's College in London when it opened in 1848. Queen's was more like a secondary school than a college, but it nevertheless offered a range of courses previously unavailable to women. It was also open to all 'ladies' over the age of twelve, and among its first students were ▷Jean Ingelow and ▷Adelaide Procter.

In 1862, Emily Davies launched the campaign for higher education; in the same year ▷Frances Power Cobbe read a conference paper calling for 'University Degrees for Women'. Despite fierce resistance from large sections of society who felt that women were constitutionally incapable of intellectual achievement, the campaigners slowly gained ground. In 1878 London University awarded its first degrees to women. 1892 saw the universities of Edinburgh, Glasgow, St Andrew's and Aberdeen following suit, but Oxford and Cambridge, although both had affiliated women's colleges, did not give degrees before 1920 and 1921 respectively. Women writers actively involved in campaigning for education include ▷Mathilde Blind, ▷Barbara Bodichon, ▷Mona Caird, ▷Harriet Martineau, ▷Emily Pfeiffer, ▷Catherine Sinclair and ▷Elizabeth Wolstenholme-Elmy.

▷'Woman Question, The'
Bib: Kamm, J., *Hope Deferred: Girls' Education in English History.*
Caribbean: Education has a preponderant importance throughout the Caribbean because it is often the only vehicle for social advancement. In practice, education can become an alienating force in relation to issues of class, language and ▷identity. It forms a central theme of much Caribbean writing (▷ *Crick Crack Monkey*, ▷ *Beka Lamb*, ▷ *Angel*). ▷Merle Collins also discusses the theme of education in women's writing in her article 'Themes and Trends in Caribbean Writing Today' in Helen Carr (ed.), *From My Guy To Sci-Fi* (1989).
Italy: Until the late 1800s in post-Unification (▷ *Risorgimento*) Italy, there was no national policy on the education of female children. Prior to this, individual women of the upper and middle classes were lucky to receive any education. This general lack of formal training for women is reflected in both the numbers, and the social class, of women writers prior to this period. Individual women of the higher social classes might indeed have received an excellent education, depending on the attitude of their family, and hence produced

interesting work, but these women were in the minority and were, in any case, dependent on fate. School programmes set up by the new Italian government in the 1870s opened up education to female children (and, thus, ultimately contributed to the burgeoning numbers of women writers from this point onwards). The curriculum, undeniably paternalistic, gradually widened its base from its original stress on domestic hygiene and domestic economy to the study of Italian language and literature, science, history, studies of exemplary lives, geography, basic physics and philosophy. Women were, even at this recent point in Italian history, educated largely for the purpose of facilitating the education of their children. In the 20th century, ▷fascism curtailed women's educational opportunities.

Edufa (1967)
A play by the Ghanaian dramatist ▷Efua Sutherland, dramatizing the dangerous consequences of forsaking the communal tradition for a selfish individualism. Edufa, obsessed with his own longevity, consults a diviner, who says his death can be averted if he can find someone to take his place. When he asks his household to pledge their love by saying they would die for him, his wife, Ampoma, ignorant of his evil intent, agrees. Even as she sickens towards death, she demonstrates, in her acceptance and her concern for others, her life-giving qualities. Edufa transgresses the Akan belief in the sanctity and communality of life, grasping at life for himself alone. The play clearly demonstrates the strengths of the traditional concepts of interdependence and the vacuity and negativity of individualism.

Edwards, Amelia (1831–1892)
British novelist, short story and ▷travel writer. She was born in Weston-super-Mare and educated at home by her mother. After working as a journalist, she published her first novel, *My Brother's Wife*, in 1855. She subsequently wrote several more romantic novels and two historical works, *The History of France* (1856) and *A Summary of English History* (1858), before editing a collection of poetry, *Home Thoughts and Home Themes* (1865). She contributed a number of notable ▷ghost stories to leading periodicals of the day before turning her attention to travel writing in the 1870s. *A Thousand Miles up the Nile* (1877) was a highly successful account of her journey through Egypt to the Nubian desert. Edwards then became an enthusiastic and learned Egyptologist, publishing a further work, *Pharaohs, Fellahs and Explorers* (1892), as well as translating a manual on Egyptian archaeology and lecturing on the subject in Britain and North America, earning herself an honorary doctorate from Columbia University.

Edwards, Sarah Pierpont (1710–1758)
North American spiritual autobiographer. She was born and married into Puritan ministerial families in Connecticut and Massachusetts. She and her

husband, Jonathan Edwards, a leader of the Great Awakening evangelical movement of the 1740s, were exceptionally close and raised eleven children together. In 1742, during the height of the Awakening, she experienced an almost mystical religious conversion which, at her husband's request, she recorded. Her husband published his version of her experience, asserting that it was a model of piety and conversion; her own account, ▷*Mrs Edwards . . . Her Solemn Self-Declarations*, was not published until 1830 and then was embedded in the biography of her husband's life. Her 'self-declaration' is an extensive record of one woman's personal journey toward religious salvation. She died from dysentery while she was visiting Philadelphia in October 1758. Her daughter ▷Esther Edwards Burr, was also a diarist.

Efuru (1966)

The first published novel by an African woman, ▷Flora Nwapa, inspired, the author admits, by Chinua Achebe's *Things Fall Apart* (1958). However, instead of dramatizing the conflict between colonialism and tradition, Nwapa concentrates on the village setting, with only incidental references to the changing world outside. The narrative is very close to the ▷oral tradition, being rich in Igbo greetings, proverbs and stories. Nwapa attributes the genesis of the story to conversations overheard in her mother's sewing shop. She says that Efuru, her heroine, is therefore 'not one single woman' but a composite of many stories. Within the novel, too, the collective voice is given prominence, so that what emerges is as much the story of a community as of an individual. Nevertheless, Efuru herself is a remarkable woman, not least for the way she retains respect and status despite her inability to bear more children after the death of her only daughter.

▷Infertility/childlessness (West Africa)

Ega, Françoise (1920–1976)

This novelist from the French Antilles was born and educated in Martinique but moved to France in 1946. She entered the French Air Force, and worked in Indo-China, Djibouti and Madagascar. She has published two novels. The first, *Les Temps de Madras* (1966) (*Days of Madras*), is autobiographical, and depicts childhood and adolescence in a small village near to Martinique's volcano, Mount Pélée. Ega's second novel, *Lettres à une Noire* (1978) (*Letters to a Woman of Colour*), is epistolary. Working as a cleaning woman in Marseille, Maméga writes to Carolina relating the injustices of modern slavery in France.

Egburg (Ecgburg) (8th century)

English abbess. A letter from Egburg to Boniface, of c 716–718, survives in the ▷Boniface Correspondence. She expresses her regard for him and asks for his prayers.

Egeria (5th century AD)

Diarist. There remain fragments of a diary, in Latin, describing a three-year pilgrimage made by Egeria to Jerusalem. She may have been a nun from Spain, but even her name is uncertain, for few personal details are revealed in the fragments. However, as she addresses her readers as 'sisters', we know she wrote primarily for women readers.

The work shows a great interest in historical and Christian matters. But the structure seems formulaic: each new site visited is recorded, with associated passages from the Bible and descriptions of the guides and the beauty of the site. One rare reference to a contemporary is to another woman: the deaconess Marthana. Pervasive throughout the work is the Christian theme of humility. Only about one-third survives. Some have thought it an idealized, fictional pilgrimage, but this seems an unnecessarily sceptical view.

▷Diaries, Ancient Greek and Roman

Egerton, George (1859–1945)

The ▷pseudonym of British novelist and short-story writer Mary Chavelita Dunne. She was born in Melbourne, Australia, and travelled widely as a young woman. In 1887 she eloped with Henry Higginson to Norway. She later married George Egerton Clairmonte and moved to Ireland where she began to write seriously. Her most successful works were two volumes of short stories, ▷*Keynotes* (1893) and *Discords* (1894). The stories challenged patriarchal attitudes, and Egerton became associated with the ▷'New Woman' movement. Her later writing did not live up to her early potential and she faded from view. Later works include *Fantasias* (1898); *Rosa Amorosa* (1901) and *Flies in Amber* (1905).
Bib: Cunningham, G., *The New Woman and the Fiction of the 1890's.*

Eggleston, Kim (born 1960)

New Zealand poet. Eggleston's poems reflect the rural and unconventional life she has led in the remoter parts of the South Island, especially the west coast. Heterosexuality, alcohol, itinerancy, violence and bodily life are the recurring subjects and reference points of her work, which is written in a loosely-linked informal ballad style.

Publications include: *From the Face to the Bin: Poems 1978–1984* (1984); *25 Poems: The Mist Will Rise and the World Will Drip with Gold* (1985); *The Whole Crack* (1987).

Egual, Doña María (1698–1735)

Spanish dramatist. Egual was born in Castellón and died in Valencia. She wrote two *comedias de bastidores* with music, *Los prodigios de Thesalia* (*The Prodigies of Thesalia*) and *Triunfo de amor en el aire* (*Triumph of Love in the Air*).

Egymásra nézve (1980) ▷*Another Way*

Ehrmann, Marianne (1753–1795)

German-speaking Swiss writer, journalist and editor of women's journals. Born in Rapperswil near Zurich, she became, after a first, short-lived marriage, a governess and then an actress in Vienna. In 1781 she married the writer T.F. Ehrmann, helped him with a journal, and began to supplement their meagre income with poems, stories and novels for serialization in magazines. In 1790 and 1793 she set up two new women's magazines: *Amaliens Erholungsstunden* (*Amalie's Recreation Time*) and *Die Einsiedlerin aus den Alpen* (*The Woman Hermit from the Alps*). In these journals, traditional notions of womanhood often competed with progressive political and ideological thought. Ehrmann's main works of fiction are *Amalie, eine wahre Geschichte in Briefen* (2 vols, 1787) (*Amalie, a True Story Told in Letters*) and the autobiographical *Antonie von Warnstein. Eine Geschichte aus unserem Zeitalter* (2 vols, 1796–1798) (*Antonie von Warnstein. A Story of Our Time*).

Eighth Wife, The (1972)

Novel by Kenyan novelist and biographer ▷Miriam Were. *The Eighth Wife* explores generational differences through the story of Kalimonje, who is caught in a love triangle between the old village chief and his eldest son. She marries Shalimba, a brave young warrior, instead of becoming the eighth wife of the chief.

Eight Voices of the Eighties: Stories, Journalism and Criticism by Australian Women Writers (1989)

Anthology edited by Gillian Whitlock. This contains a selection of the short fiction of eight women writers who represent the upsurge of women's writing in Australia in the 1980s. The fiction is supported by a selection of their criticism, reviews, interviews and commentary, including previously unpublished material. The writers are ▷Kate Grenville, ▷Barbara Hanrahan, ▷Beverley Farmer, ▷Thea Astley, ▷Elizabeth Jolley, ▷Jessica Anderson, ▷Olga Masters, and ▷Helen Garner.
▷Anthologies (Australia)

Eisheiligen, Die (1979) (Saints of Ice)

Novel by East German writer, ▷Helga Novak. It is the semi-autobiographical account of a girl's childhood and adolescence during the Third Reich, the Soviet occupation, and the establishment of the German Democratic Republic. The main focus of the novel is the young heroine, Erika's, difficult relationship with her cold and brutish stepmother, herself a product of the old-fashioned 'Prussian educational drill'. In an effort to escape this influence, Erika searches for an alternative family: first in the ranks of the Nazi youth movement, and later in the East German Socialist Party. Each time she exchanges one kind of tyranny with another. In Erika's increasingly frustrated bid for liberation, writing becomes the only way she can find release. *Die Eisheiligen* has a sequel in *Vogel Federlos* (1982) (*Featherless Bird*) which covers Erika's experiences in the 1950s.

Novak's novels are an important contribution to the retrospective analysis of the role played by the individual in fascist Germany. By centralizing the mother–daughter relationship, the works illuminate the German trauma from an interesting and unusual angle.

Ekman, Kerstin (born 1933)

Swedish prose writer. Ekman grew up at Katrineholm in a wealthy family, her father being a manufacturer. She went to Uppsala University, and in 1957 received an MA.

For a time she wrote short film features for educational purposes, and worked as a literary critic. She taught Swedish and literature at a traditional high school, and worked as a freelance author. She has received many prizes and awards.

In 1959 she made her début as a writer of ▷detective fiction, but her major work is a tetralogy about smalltown people in central Sweden from the 1890s to the 1970s. The first volume was *Häxringarnal* (1974) (*The Witches' Circles*, 1983) the last *En Stad av Ljus* (1983) (*A Town of Lights*). Ekman tells the story of the development of the modern Swedish welfare state. She creates a very individual world of precisely observed details, written in a very expressive and vital language. The reader is drawn into her dark Swedish forests. Ekman has been called the foremost ▷realist of the 1970s, but her language is much more than realistic. The fact that she sees everything from a woman's perspective is apparent in her use of language and imagery.

In her latest works, *Röverna i Skuleskogenl* (1988) (*The Robbers in the Forest of Skule*) and *Knivkastarens kvinna* (1990) (*The Knife Thrower's Woman*), there is a sense of a fantastic black humour, not so much at the story level, but in the way they are told, with wit, despair and beauty.

Elder, Anne (1918–1976)

Australian poet. Elder was born in Auckland, New Zealand, and became a ballet dancer with the Borovansky Ballet Company. She published two very impressive volumes of poetry, *For the Record* (1972) and *Crazy Woman and Other Poems* (1976).
▷Poetry and Gender

Eldershaw, Flora (1897–1956)

Australian novelist and historian. Eldershaw collaborated with ▷Marjorie Barnard on a number of literary projects, writing under the pseudonym of M. Barnard Eldershaw. She was the first woman president of the Fellowship of Australian Writers in 1935, and an active member of the Commonwealth Literary Fund. The collaboration produced five novels, a number of non-fiction works and one play. Eldershaw's non-fiction works, under her own name, include *Contemporary Australian Women Writers* (1931) and (edited) ▷*The Peaceful Army: A Memorial to the*

Pioneer Women of Australia 1788–1938 (1938).
Both were extremely influential.
▷Literary criticism (Australia)

Eldershaw, M. Barnard ▷Marjorie Barnard;
Flora Eldershaw; Literary criticism (Australia);
Peaceful Army, The

Eleanor of Aquitaine (c 1122–1204)

Queen, successively, of Louis VII of France and
Henry II of England, and patron. Eleanor was
powerful and politically active; she was imprisoned
in 1173 for plotting with her sons against her
husband, Henry II. After being released on
Henry's death in 1189, she remained a political
force during the reigns of her sons, Richard I
(Coeur de Lion) and John. The English court had
become a centre of literary and scholarly activity
with the accession of Henry and Eleanor in 1154.
Eleanor's patronage played an important part in
the transmission of the Celtic material into the
French and English vernaculars. Wace presented
to Eleanor his *Roman de Brut* (which included the
story of Arthur), a translation into ▷Anglo-
Norman, completed in 1155, of Geoffrey of
Monmouth's (1100–1153) Latin *History of the
Kings of Britain*. The *Tristan*, a popular and
influential romance in Anglo-Norman by Thomas,
was probably written for her. The historian and
romance poet, Benôit de Sainte-Maure, dedicated
to her his Anglo-Norman *Roman de Troie*, in
which the story of Troilus and Briseida (Criseyde)
makes what is apparently its earliest vernacular
appearance (see also ▷Marie de France).
Eleanor's daughters, Eleanor, Matilda and Joan,
were responsible for the spread of the literary
ideas of her court (including the stories of Tristan
and Arthur) to Spain, Germany and Sicily,
through the marriages arranged for them by
Henry II. A letter from Eleanor of Aquitaine, as
widow of Henry, is translated from the Latin by
Wood (▷Letters, England, Middle Ages):
Eleanor wrote to Pope Celestinus in 1192, asking
that her son Richard be freed from captivity. Her
scribe was Peter of Blois.

Eleanor of Provence (1223–1291)

Queen of Henry III of England, and patron.
Eleanor was the daughter of the Aragonese Count
of Provence, Raimon-Berengar, a 'poet-prince';
she married Henry in 1236. After the death of her
husband and accession of her son Edward I in
1272, she retired to the nunnery at Amesbury,
Wiltshire. Henry and Eleanor's court at
Westminster was a centre of artistic and literary
culture, both English and continental. Matthew
Paris's poetic *Estoire de Seint Aedward le Rei*, an
▷Anglo-Norman translation of the prose Latin
life of Edward the Confessor, was dedicated to
Eleanor (1250). The illuminated text was
circulated among her aristocratic female friends.
John of Hoveden, who usually composed in Latin,
completed for her (by 1274) an elegant poem in
Anglo-Norman on the life and passion of Christ
and the assumption of the Virgin, entitled

'Nightingale' ('Rossignos'). This was a version of
his Latin 'Philomena'. Two letters from Eleanor,
one in Latin to her husband (1254), the other in
French to her son (1286), are translated by Wood
(▷Letters, England, Middle Ages).

Elegies (Old English)

A group of ▷Old English poems in the late 10th-
century manuscript, the *Exeter Book*, have
traditionally been referred to as 'elegies', although
they are not elegiac in the classical or post-
Renaissance sense. They are widely distributed
throughout the manuscript, and are on a variety of
subjects. The poems are untitled in the
manuscript, and the titles (such as 'The
Wanderer', 'The Seafarer', 'The Ruin'), are
editorial. They have often been discussed as a
group because they share an awareness of
transience and mortality, and a preoccupation with
loss and suffering. We know nothing about
authorship or date of composition. Two of the
poems have women speakers, ▷'The Wife's
Lament' and ▷'Wulf and Eadwacer'.
Bib: Greenfield, Stanley, B. and Calder, Daniel,
G. *A New Critical History of Old English Literature.*

Elena Deeva (1916)

Russian novel in verse by ▷Liubov' Stólitsa,
written in 1914, just after ▷Poliksena Solov'ëva's
verse novel ▷*The Crossroad*. Stólitsa dedicated
Elena Deeva to Pushkin, and her work resembles
his famous novel in verse, *Eugene Onegin* (1825–
1831), in having eight chapters, the set being of a
capital city (here Moscow, in Pushkin St
Petersburg) and a country estate, and dealing with
unrequited love. Stólitsa's narrator, like Pushkin's,
is witty and conversational, and includes many
details about contemporary culture and mores.
Technically, however, Stólitsa uses a different
stanza, a different meter – trochaic tetrameter –
which Pushkin used in fairytales but not in
Onegin, and a number of proximate rhymes.
    The plot of Stólitsa's novel is closer to Leo
Tolstoy's *Anna Karenina* (1875–1877): a loveless
marriage, an unfaithful spouse, an unhappy lover
who goes off to war, and the death of the heroine.
Yet the author introduces some important role
reversals that have a feminist subtext. The
heroine, Elena, and her older sister, Anna, both
fall in love with the same man, Danilo. Anna is
married off to him by her imperious, old-
fashioned grandmother. But Danilo loves Elena,
and when Anna discovers their mutual love she
commits suicide. Out of guilt, Danilo becomes a
monk; like ▷Nadezhda Dúrova, Elena eventually
joins the Russian army in disguise. She dies in
battle.
    Stólitsa attempts to create a national heroine:
cultured, religious, and brave, but modern. Elena,
like Pushkin's Tat'iana, is steeped in Russian
national feeling, yet modern enough to be
comfortable with European life. The narrator
stresses the need for modern women to have
freedom of choice in matters of love.
    ▷*Diary of Elizaveta D'iákonova*; D'iákonova,
Elizaveta

Eleonore von Österreich (1433–1480)

German writer. She was a daughter of James I of Scotland (1394–1437), spent some time at the court of Charles VII of France (1403–1461) and, upon marrying Duke Siegmund of the Tyrol, became a vigorous promoter of the arts. In the 1450s she transcribed the French *chanson de geste*, *Pontius et la belle Sidonie*, into the didactic German novel ▷*Pontus und Sidonia*. It was to become very popular in 17th-century Germany.

Elephantis (? 3rd century BC)

Ancient Greek writer of erotica. No details of her life or works are known. The female name may be attributed to her works of erotica simply for literary reasons (▷Pornography, Ancient Greece; ▷Philaenis. 'She' is referred to by the Roman writers Martial and Suetonius (2nd century AD). The Greek doctor Galen (AD c 131–201) mentions a work *On Cosmetics* written by an Elephantis, but this author is perhaps a different one.

Elie de Beaumont, Anne-Louise Morin-Dumesnil (1730–1783)

French novelist, born in Caen. Her one novel, *Lettres du marquis de Roselle* (1764) (*Letters of The Marquis de Roselle*), which ran to several editions, relates the story of an opera chorus girl who almost succeeds in marrying a young marquis, only to lose him to a wealthier and ostensibly more virtuous woman. The novel criticizes convent education and early marriage. The family of ▷Madame de Tencin asked Elie de Beaumont to complete her *Anecdotes de la cour et du règne d'Edouard II* (*Anecdotes from the Court and Reign of Edward II*) which were then published in 1776.

Eliot, George (1819–1880)

George Eliot

▷Pseudonym of English novelist Mary Ann (or Marian) Evans. She was the daughter of a land-agent in Warwickshire, and attended school at Coventry between 1832 and 1835. At school she became a convert to Evangelicalism, but abandoned this creed in her early twenties after meeting Charles Bray, a free-thinking Coventry manufacturer. She demonstrated intellectual prowess early in life and read widely, her earliest works being translations from the German of Strauss's *Life of Jesus* and Spinoza's *Tractatus theologico-politicus*. In 1850 she began contributing to the *Westminster Review*, and from 1851–4 worked as its assistant editor. Her translation of Feuerbach's *Essence of Christianity* appeared in 1854, the year in which she began to live with George Henry Lewes. Their unconventional union caused some difficulties (Lewes was married and unable to obtain a divorce from his wife), but the couple remained together until Lewes's death in 1878. Eliot began to write fiction in 1856, her first stories appearing in *Blackwood's Magazine* in 1857. These were later collected as ▷*Scenes of Clerical Life* (1858). The major novels then followed: ▷*Adam Bede* (1859); ▷*The Mill on the Floss* (1860); ▷*Silas Marner* (1861); ▷*Romola* (1862–63); ▷*Felix Holt* (1866); ▷*Middlemarch* (1871–72) and ▷*Daniel Deronda* (1876). She also wrote poetry, though this is not well-regarded. Her last publication was the collection of essays, *Impressions of Theophratus Such* (1879). In 1880 she married John Cross, but died in the same year. She is generally regarded as one of the greatest of English novelists. Her comprehensive treatment of English society, her intelligence, imaginative sympathy and philosophical understanding are often commented upon. She dominated the Victorian novel in the 1860s and 1870s and was both popular and critically acclaimed. Her work has generated much recent feminist criticism.

▷'Silly Novels by Lady Novelists'; Regional novel, The; Historical novel, The
Bib: Haight, G.S., *Life*; Leavis, F.R., in *The Great Tradition*; Bennett, J., *George Eliot: Her Life and Art*; Hardy, B., *The Art of George Eliot*; Uglow, J., *George Eliot*; Beer, G., *George Eliot*.

Elisa, Henriqueta (died 1885)

Portuguese poet. Little-known writer of the 19th century. In 1864 she published the volume *Lágrimas e Saudades* (*Tears and Longings*), in the ▷ultra-romantic style made popular by writers such as ▷Maria Browne.
▷Romanticism (Portugal)

Elisabeth von Nassau-Saarbrücken (1397–1456)

Bilingual French and German writer. The first woman author of secular literature in Germany, she was the daughter of Duke Friedrich V of Lorraine and ▷Margarete von Vaudemont. In 1412 she married Philipp I, Count of Nassau-Saarbrücken (1368–1429) and, upon her husband's death in 1429, assumed power until her son came of age in 1438. All her family were greatly interested in literature; her brother was a poet at the court of Charles of Orléans (1391–1465), and her mother collected transcriptions of French *chansons de geste*, four of which, *Sibille, Herpin, Loher und Maller* and ▷*Huge Scheppel*, Elisabeth translated into German. These are tales of courtly heroes who, having been unjustly accused, fall from grace, only to be eventually restored to their rights. The transactions became immensely popular in 15th- and 16th-century Germany, and were often abridged into folktales.

Elisabeth von Schönau (c 1129–1164)

German nun and visionary writer. She entered the Benedictine Convent of Schönau in Hesse at the age of five, and stayed there until her death. A frail woman, suffering from depression, she began to confess to having visions in 1152, possibly as a result of her contact with the work of ▷Hildegard von Bingen, whose visionary text *Scivias* (1142–1152) (▷*Know the Ways*, 1986) volumes of which had by then been in circulation for four years. Encouraged by her brother, Ekbert, a monk and priest at the neighbouring monastery of Schönau, Elisabeth wrote an account and interpretation of her visions in *Liber viarum Dei* (*Book of the Ways to God*), in which she clearly emulates Hildegard, with whom she entertained a correspondence. Her *Liber revelationum* (*The Book of Revelations*), which contains an account of the martyrdom of St Ursula and the 11,000 virgins, and *De resurrectione* (*On Resurrection*), which is about the life of the Virgin Mary, were among the most popular religious texts of the time. Her works were handwritten and copied by nuns; they were finally typeset and published in 1884.
▷*Visionsliteratur*

Élise or the Real Life (1970)

Translation of *Élise ou la vraie vie* (1967), novel by French writer ▷Claire Etcherelli. This, Etcherelli's first novel, has become so famous in France that the phrase 'the real life of Élise' has even been used by politicians. The narrative is written in the first person and divided into two parts: in the first, Élise recounts her enclosed, poverty-stricken, provincial life, in which the only passions are her love for her more politically educated brother, Lucien, and her dreams of 'the real life'. In the second part, Élise follows Lucien to Paris, takes a job on the assembly line of a car factory, and begins a relationship with an Algerian worker, Arezki, thus discovering that 'the real life' is connection with other human beings, and increased political awareness, acquired through experience.

The novel is unusual in its concentration on the divisions between oppressed groups, and the absence of worker-hero or heroine. Élise herself, though an admirable character, has flaws: she colludes with Lucien's cruelty towards his wife, Marie-Louise, and her relationship with Arezki jolts her out of her naïve lack of awareness of racism in herself and others. The novel can thus be seen as a ▷*Bildungsroman* of Élise's development, but, unlike many of its feminist

successors of the 1970s, it is concerned with class and race as well as gender.
Bib: Atack, M., 'The Politics of identity in *Elise ou la vraie vie*' in Atack, M. and Powrie, P., (eds), *Contemporary French Fiction by Women: Feminist Perspectives*

Élise ou la vraie vie (1967) ▷*Élise or the Real Life* (1970)

Elisheva (1888–1949)

Hebrew poet. Elisheva was the pseudonym used by Elisaveta Ivanovna Zirkowa. She was born in Russia to a Christian family. From 1907 she lived in a Jewish community, and hence developed an interest in Jewish culture and the Hebrew language. She emigrated to Palestine with her Jewish husband in 1925. She began writing verse in Russian and translated English literature into Russian. Later she wrote Hebrew.

Elisheva's writing is greatly influenced by Russian and German literature. The characters she portrays are estranged individuals, uprooted from their world. Her works include *Kos Ketana* (1926) (*Small Cup*).

Elizabeth I ▷Elizabeth Tudor.

Elizabeth Tudor (1533–1603)

Elizabeth Tudor

English orator, translator, devotional writer and poet. The daughter of Henry VIII and ▷Anne Boleyn, she became Queen Elizabeth I in 1558. Although celebrated as the namesake for one of England's most prolific literary periods, Elizabeth I was a competent writer and scholar in her own right. Under the influence of her stepmother, ▷Catherine Parr, and the tutelage of John Cheke and Roger Ascham, she received an exceptional ▷humanist education. Her writings, especially her ▷translations, attest to her fluency in Latin and Greek, as well as a number of romance languages. She composed a personal *Book of Devotions* (c 1570s) in English, French, Italian, Latin and Greek. Perhaps her most famous translation is that of ▷Marguerite de Navarre's *Le Miroir de l'Ame Pecheresse* (▷*Mirror of the Sinful Soul*). Among the other works she translated are Petrarch's 'Triumph of Eternity', the second chorus of Seneca's *Hercules Oetaeus*, Horace's (65–8 BC) *Art of Poetry*, Plutarch's (AD 46–?120) *On Curiosity*, and Boethius's (475–524) *Consolation of Philosophy*, which she undertook at the age of 60. Although sixteen poems have been attributed to her, only six are almost surely hers. These include the ▷'Woodstock poems', ▷'The Doubt of Future Foes', 'On Monsieur's Departure', two lines on fortune, and four lines on suspicion written in her psalter. More than a dozen of her speeches survive, some of which Elizabeth herself prepared for publication. They frequently contain a politically astute mixture of regal formality and loving parentalness. Stylistically, they are characterized by plain diction and long but balanced sentences. Two of her most famous speeches are her ▷'Speech to the Troops at Tillbury' (1588) and her 'Golden Oration' to her last Parliament (1601).

▷Herbert, Mary Sidney; Humanism (England); *Instruction of a Christian Woman*; Letters (Renaissance Britain); *Monument of Matrones, The*; *Morning and Evening Praiers*
Bib: Bradner, L. (ed.), *Poems of Queen Elizabeth I*; Fox, A. (ed.), *A Book of Devotions*; Pemberton, C. (ed.), *Queen Elizabeth's Englishings*; Rice, G. (ed.), *The Public Speaking of Queen Elizabeth I*.

Eliza Cook's Journal (1849–54)
A journal written and edited (almost single-handedly), by ▷Eliza Cook, English poet and essayist. It was aimed at middle-class women and attempted to inform and entertain as well intervene in debates around the ▷'Woman Question'. It included reviews, essays, poetry and sketches, and treated such subjects as the position of working women, the need for legal ▷reform, the construction of the 'old maid' and the inadequacy of girls' ▷education. It ceased publishing after five years due to Cook's ill-health, but much material was later included in *Jottings from My Journal* (1860).

Ella Norman, or A Woman's Perils (1864)
Australian colonial novel by Elizabeth Murray, republished in 1985. Murray spent four years in Victoria when her husband was sent there as a commissioner on the goldfields. In this melodramatic romance the heroine travels to Victoria with her family, who subsequently lose their money. The novel is redeemed by its satirical exposure of colonial institutions, of the treatment of governesses by bush families, of the plight of penniless unmarried women who often have no option but prostitution, and of the social and political structure of the settlement.

Ellerman, Annie Winifred ▷Bryher

Elle sera de jaspe et de corail: journal d'un misovire (1983) (*She will be of jasper and coral: diary of a manhater*)
A work by the Cameroonian writer ▷Werewere Liking, combining elements of drama, poetry and the novel. The story of a *misovire*, a word coined by the author to parallel 'misogynist', which describes a woman who is unable to find a man to admire, perceiving all men as limited and lacking in inspirational power. It is above all a game of words, rhythms and song, breaking with the conventions of genre and challenging artistic preconceptions. In this respect, Liking, along with ▷Ama Ata Aidoo, ▷Véronique Tadjo and one or two others, is one of the few African women writers who consciously experiment with form, and dare to deviate from linguistic clarity and linear narrative.

Elliot, Sarah Barnwell (1848–1928)
US novelist and biographer. Elliot's sympathetic portraits of rural life in the border states, especially Tennessee, contributed to the growing range of regional subjects in US fiction after the Civil War. Her work became increasing realistic in treatment and technique. Among her novels are *The Felmeres* (1879), *A Simple Heart* (1887) and *Jerry* (1891).

Ellis, Alice Thomas (Anna Haycraft) (born 1932)
Novelist, columnist and cookery writer. Author of a number of novels, including *The Sin Eater* (1977), *The Birds of the Air* (1980), *The 27th Kingdom* (1982), *The Other Side of the Fire* (1985), *Unexplained Laughter* (1985), *Home Life* (1986), and a recent trilogy: *The Clothes in the Wardrobe* (1987), *The Skeleton in the Cupboard* (1988) and *The Fly in the Ointment* (1989). Ellis's characteristic mode is the satirical representation of family life, lifted out of realism by elements of the supernatural, and Christian mysticism. A number of her novels are set in Wales, whose culture Ellis tends to represent as mysterious, ancient and 'primitive', the source of a number of nasty shocks for rich city-dwellers pursuing their fantasies of the rural life. The image of the powerful, witch-like woman frequently occurs. Her writing has been linked with that of ▷Muriel Spark, with whom she shares an emphasis on the author as the godlike manipulator of his or her characters, and on God as puppeteer.

Ellis, E. ▷Wolstenholme-Elmy, Elizabeth

Ellis, Ellen (1829–1895)
New Zealand novelist. Ellen Ellis's only novel is an autobiographical narrative, *Everything Is Possible to Will* (1882), which presents the author's social convictions. Born in England to a strict Methodist

family of seventeen children, Ellis came to New Zealand in 1859 and lived the rest of her life in Auckland. Ellis believed in prohibition and was a member of a Temperance organization, the Good Templars, but, more importantly, saw the prohibition of alcohol as part of women's struggle for equality. Ellis was unusual for her time in connecting the oppression of Maori by European people with the subordination of women by men. She sought to raise the standards of female education and establish equal pay and equal legal status for women.

Ellis, Sarah Stickney (1799–1872)

English novelist and writer of ▷conduct books. She was born in Holderness, Yorkshire, and married William Ellis, a missionary, in 1837. The author of over thirty books, her non-fiction emphasized the superiority of the male sex and the duty of women to stay in the home and obey their husbands. In *The Wives of England* (1843), she addressed her female readers thus: 'It is quite possible you may have more talent, with higher attainments, and you may also have been generally more admired; but this has nothing whatsoever to do with your position as a woman, which is, and must be, inferior to his as a man.' Ellis's best-known conduct books include *The Women of England* (1838); *The Daughters of England* (1842) and *The Mothers of England* (1843). She was disapproving of fanciful, romantic fiction, and her own novels tended to be morally educative, although, as in her conduct books, the contradictions of women's lives often surface in the course of a narrative. Novels include: *Pique* (1850); *The Brother, or, The Man of Many Friends* (1855); *The Mother's Mistake* (1856) and *The Widow Green and her Three Nieces* (1865).
▷'Woman Question, The'
Bib: Showalter, E., ▷*A Literature of Their Own*; Helsinger, E. (ed.), *The Woman Question*.

Elsner, Gisela (born 1937)

German novelist. Her works are stylistically elaborate, often grotesque, satires on modern life. Her characters have lost all connection with reality, and struggle along as prisoners of their own absurd ideologies. Her main novels are: *Die Riesenzwerge* (1964) (*The Giant Dwarfs*), *Der Punktsieg* (1977) (*Victory on Points*), *Abseits* (1982) (*Elsewhere*), *Das Windei* (1987) (*The Wind-egg*).

Elstob, Elizabeth (1683–1756)

Anglo-Saxon scholar and translator, Elstob was born in Newcastle upon Tyne, and by 1691 both her parents were dead. Although her guardian opposed women's education, Elstob published *An English Anglo-Saxon Homily, on the birth-day of St Gregory* (1709), having gone to Oxford with her brother. She may have established a day school. She regarded herself as the first woman to study Anglo-Saxon, and in the preface to the *Homily* she justified women's learning: 'it will be said, What has a Woman to do with Learning? This I have known urged by some Men, with an Envy unbecoming that greatness of Soul, which is said to dignify their Sex. For if Women may be said to have Souls, and their Souls are their better part and that what is best deserves our greatest Care for its Improvement. We must retort the Question. Where is the fault in Womens seeking after Learning?' She also published *The Rudiments of Grammar for the Anglo-Saxon Tongue, first given in English with an apology for the study of northern antiquities* (1715).
Bib: Ferguson, M., *First Feminists*.

Emancipated Woman, The (1910)

The first Greek feminist novel, by ▷Kallirroi Parren, publisher of ▷*The Ladies' Newspaper*. It describes the life of a woman in Constantinople (Istanbul), who studied and became a painter in order to live an independent life. Left alone after an unsuccessful love affair, she carried on her life in a dignified manner with great success. The book is not sentimental, but rather attacks social injustice, the unfair treatment of women, and documents their stand against it.

Emecheta, Buchi (born 1945)

Nigerian novelist. Possibly the most prolific woman writer to have emerged from West Africa, Emecheta has lived in London since her early twenties. Her experiences as an immigrant are described in her autobiographical novels *In the Ditch* (1972) and *Second Class Citizen* (1974), published together as *Adah's Story*. Three other novels are set in Nigeria in the period from the early days of colonialism to World War II, drawing on the recollections of her mother and grandmother to depict women adapting to changing circumstances. These are ▷*The Bride Price* (1976), ▷*The Slave Girl* (1977) and *Joys of Motherhood* (1979). *Destination Biafra* (1982) is an ambitious attempt to tell the story of Nigeria's Civil War from a woman's point of view.

Emecheta has since set up her own publishing company, Ogugwu Afor, and publishes herself. *Double Yoke* (1983) came out of her experiences as a writer in residence at the University of Calabar and concerns the double standards and sexual exploitation women have to deal with in their pursuit of education. *Rape of Shavi* (1983) is a futuristic tale of an encounter between a group of Europeans fleeing the nuclear holocaust and an untouched, arcadian, traditional African village society. Her latest novel, *Gwendolen* (1989), deals with a young girl's transition from the Caribbean to England.
▷Slavery (West Africa)

Eminent Women of the Age (1869)

US collection of capsule biographies, edited by James Parton, husband of ▷Sara Payson Willis Parton (Fanny Fern). Including many biographies of US women writers written by other US women writers, this collection is one of the few not produced by very conservative, establishment publishers and editors. It is therefore fascinating for who is included and what is noted as achievement.

Emma (1844–1929)

Italian novelist and essayist; pseudonym of Emilia Ferretti Viola. A writer concerned with recording the social realities of her time, who often, nonetheless, chose the medium of the fable to do so, thus anticipating the narrative style of Italo Calvino (1923–1985). She was a regular contributor to the periodical *La Nuova Antologia*. Her most important work was ▷*Una fra tante* (1878) (*One Among Many*), on prostitution. She also wrote another novel, *Mediocrità* (1884) (*Mediocrity*).

Emma (1816)

A novel by English novelist ▷Jane Austen. Emma Woodhouse is confident, powerful, wealthy and attractive, greatly admired in society and satisfied with herself. She is, however, often blind to her own failings and does not recognize the dangers of opinionated judgements. In a gesture which Emma imagines to be purely generous, she takes under her wing Harriet Smith, an orphaned girl of unknown parents. Emma fantasises about Harriet's origins and decides that the girl should marry the vicar Mr Elton, dissuading her from accepting an eligible young farmer, Robert Martin. Emma becomes aware that Mr Elton is in love with herself, and her self-assurance is temporarily ruffled. Later in the novel Emma attaches herself to Frank Churchill, assuming that he is in love with her when in reality he is engaged to another woman, Jane Fairfax. Harriet, meanwhile, has misunderstood some encouraging words from Emma, and is cultivating an attachment to Mr Knightley, Emma's real love. Emma eventually realizes that she is being used by Churchill, and that her interference in Harriet's affairs threatens her own happiness. Again, she is repentant and humbled, and subsequently marries Mr Knightley. The marriage of Emma and Knightley is unconventionally represented in that both partners maintain autonomous interests and friendships. This reflects an important theme in the novel, that of female power, filtered through a series of strong, controlling women characters. Another central preoccupation is the father–daughter relationship, explored through the relationship between Emma and Mr Woodhouse, where the contemporary ideal of the devoted daughter is shown to have dangerous ramifications.

Emma of Normandy (Ælfgifu) (died 1052)

Queen, successively, of Ethelred II of England and Cnut of England. Emma was the daughter of Richard I of Normandy and Gunnor. She married Ethelred ('the Unready' – meaning 'the ill-advised') in 1002. After his death in 1016 she married Cnut. Cnut died in 1033. Emma remained politically active in her widowhood: she supported Harthacnut, her son by Cnut, for the throne in 1035, and later opposed Edward (the Confessor), one of her sons by Ethelred. The *Encomium Emmae Reginae* was written (in Latin, probably by a Flemish monk) for Emma at her request after Harthacnut's accession in 1040. The work presents Emma favourably, and justifies her actions, although it cannot be described as a biography of her: one of its aims was to demonstrate Harthacnut's right to the throne, although in doing so it suppresses all mention of Emma's first marriage. Nevertheless, the *Encomium* is important for the light it sheds on English and Scandinavian history in the early 11th century.

Bib: Campbell, Alistair, *Encomium Emmae Reginae*; Stafford, Pauline, *Queens, Concubines and Dowagers*.

Enchi Fumiko (1905–1988)

Japanese novelist. She was born the daughter of Ueda Kazutoshi, a famous scholar of Japanese literature, in downtown Tokyo's Asakusa. Enchi grew up enjoying Japanese classical culture, such as *Kabuki* and *Joururi*, and novels written by authors such as Takizawa Bakin and Ryutei Tanehiko in the Edo era. She left high school for health reasons, and took private lessons in English, French and Chinese literature. Consequently, she was absorbed in the aesthetic world of other writers without having friends of her own age. She was a contributor to *Art for Woman* (1930). While publishing dramas such as *Hometown* and *A Windy Night in Late Spring*, she married and had a daughter. After the publication of *A Lament over the Passing of Spring* (1935), she began to write a novel, *Starved Years*, which won a literary prize in 1953 when she was forty-eight and had suffered some years of misfortune. Subsequently *The Waiting Years* won the Noma Prize for Literature in 1958. This work describes the dreary life of a wife who is forced to live with the two mistresses of her husband, who rapes his daughter-in-law. Her autobiographical novels, *Robber of My Brightness*, *Wounded Wings* and *A Rainbow and Hell* won the Tanizaki Junichiro Prize. *A Vengeful Spirit*, based on the lives of powerful aristocrats in the 10–11th centuries, led to the ten-volume translation of the Genji Tales into contemporary Japanese. In ▷*Home Without a Table* she covers social problems such as the relationship between society and the home. *Like a Loving Child of Chrysanthemums* and *A Wandering Spirit*, published in her old age, sympathetically describe the sparkling love and sexual expression of an aged woman – a topic rarely discussed in Japan.

Ener, Güner (born 1935)

Turkish writer and designer. She studied art in Istanbul, and later went to London and Cambridge, where she studied English language and literature. On her return home she taught for some time, then devoted herself to writing and illustrating. Her books, novellas and short stories were published in magazines between 1960 and 1964. *September Tiredness*, a collection of short

stories, was published in 1969. She has also
published *Translations from English* (1966).

Enfants du nouveau monde, Les (1962)
(Children of the New World)

Novel by the Algerian writer ▷Assia Djebar. The
author depicts women from different backgrounds
who took part in the Algerian war of liberation
between 1954 and 1962. The novel shows women
collaborating and working as equals with men for
a common national cause. While her previous
novels dealt with women's self-realization in a
hostile society, in this novel Assia Djebar shows a
sense of optimism, for women have passed the
stage of the search for identity. They are
portrayed as politically aware and more concerned
with national issues than personal ones.

Engel, Marian (1933–1985)

Canadian novelist and short story writer, born
Marian Passmore in Toronto. She attended the
Universities of McMaster and McGill, where she
worked with ▷Constance Beresford-Howe and
the major Canadian novelist Hugh MacLennan
(1907–1990). After teaching in Montreal and
Montana, she travelled in Europe, married
Howard Engel in 1962 (divorced 1977), and
worked in London and Cyprus before returning to
live in Toronto in 1964. Engel's spare style and
tremendous unity of structure make her books
superlative in their economy. Her first novel, *No
Clouds of Glory* (1968, later published as *Sarah
Bastard's Notebook*), is a fierce, funny analysis of a
woman academic who 'operates from bastard
territory', her Ph.D. on Australian/Canadian
literature failing to save her from incipient
disaster. *The Honeyman Festival* (1970) takes place
during one night in the life of a pregnant wife and
mother, reliving her past relationship with
Honeyman, a famous film director. *Monodromos*
(1973, re-issued as *One-Way Street*) is set on
Cyprus, and, against that island background, tells
the story of a character trying to gather her much-
scattered self together within the expatriate
experience and the double alienation of living as a
sister with her homosexual ex-husband. First
commissioned as a radio novel for Canadian
Broadcasting Corporation, *Joanne* (1975)
chronicles the death of an an eighteen-year
marriage, and Joanne's recognition that life may,
despite grave financial difficulties and two
children, be simpler on her own. ▷*Bear* (1976) is
Engel's most famous, or notorious novel; it is a
pastoral fable about a woman's love affair with a
bear, 'an attempt to inscribe female sexuality on
the wilderness'. It caused considerable
controversy, and won the Governor General's
Award for fiction. Following it, *The Glassy Sea*
(1978) seemed to suggest that women retreat to
figurative nunneries as a refuge from the war
between men and women; this angry and irascible
novel has been much maligned and never clearly
analyzed. *Lunatic Villas* (1981) is a relaxed and
uncharacteristically light-hearted novel about a
complex extended family led by a single parent.

Engel's short fiction, *Inside the Easter Egg* (1975)
and *The Tattooed Woman* (1985, published
posthumously) reiterate her somewhat cynical
vision. The title story of *The Tattooed Woman* is a
particularly striking example of a woman literally
carving her sense of degradation at the hands of
her husband onto her own body.

Engel published two children's books, *Adventure
at Moon Bay Towers* (1974) and *My Name is Not
Odessa Yarker* (1977), as well as a non-fiction text
for *Islands of Canada* (1981). Her early death in
1985 silenced a writer who was willing to write
merciless portrayals of the differences between
men and women, of motherhood and sisterhood,
and of the scars that women carry. She showed
that it is necessary for women to search for
themselves in order to achieve fulfilment. She was
awarded the Order of Canada in 1982.
Bib: Special issue of ▷*Room of One's Own*, Vol. 9,
No. 2; Gibson, G., *Eleven Canadian Novelists*;
Howells, C., *Private and Fictional Words*; Irvine,
L., *Sub/Version*.

Engel, Regula (1761–1853)

German-speaking Swiss writer. A native of
Zurich, and the wife of a soldier in the French
Army during the Napoleonic Wars, she went with
him on campaigns all over Europe and North
Africa, gave birth to twenty-one children and, on
occasions, even took part in the fighting. When
her husband and two of her sons were killed at
the Battle of Waterloo, she returned to
Switzerland and, in order to support herself,
began publishing her memoirs. Her writings were
reprinted in 1977 as *Frau Oberst Engel. Von Cairo
bis Neuyork, von Elba bis Waterloo. Memoiren einer
Amazone aus napoleonischer Zeit* (*Madame Colonel
Engel. From Cairo to New York, from Elba to
Waterloo. Memoirs of an Amazon in the Age of
Napoleon*).

Èngel'gárdt, Sof'ia Vladimirovna (1828–1894)

Russian prose writer. Using the pseudonym Ol'ga
N, between 1853 and 1892 Èngel'gárdt published
over forty brisk, sardonic novellas and stories that
were a virtual catalogue of the life of ▷Moscow
middle-level gentry. Her sister, Ekaterina
Novosil'tseva (1820–1885), was an even more
prolific popular historian under the pseudonym T.
Tolycheva. Èngel'gárdt's early works often used
popular sayings for titles, and the plots were
correspondingly schematic: 'You Can't Escape
Your Destined Mate' (1854); 'Morning Is Wiser
than Evening' (1853); 'You Can't Please
Everyone' (1855). Later stories are more complex.
Historical events and current political and social
trends form their background, but the dilemmas
are private ones. 'Fate or Character?' (1861) asks
which force guides women's lives and decides that
women of character are likely to end up alone. In
'The Touchstone' (1862) a young widow finds her
Slavophile suitor no more respectful of her
personal integrity than her Francophile husband
was. 'In the Homeland' (1870) traces the
disillusionment of a young man brought up

abroad, as he faces the sad facts of life in Russia. Stories like 'The Old Faith' (1879) and 'Neither the First Nor the Last' (1883) depict the negative side of the revolutionary movements of the 1870s and 1880s.

Engelhard, Magdalene Philippine (1756–1831)
German poet. She came from a large, middle-class family in Göttingen. A first collection of her rather conventional poems appeared in 1778, under her maiden name, as *Gedichte von Philippine Gatterer (Poems by Philippine Gatterer)*. After her marriage to Engelhard, she wrote poems for her ten children, *Neujahrsgeschenk für liebe Kinder* (1787) (*A New Year's Gift for Good Children*). A further collection appeared in 1821 as *Neue Gedichte von Philippine Engelhard geborene Gatterer (New Poems by Philippine Engelhard, née Gatterer)*.

Engelthal, Christina von ▷Ebner, Christine

Enlightenment
Or 'Age of Reason'. An 18th-century philosophical movement that sought to make reason the premise of all political action and thought, as a way of combating religious prejudices, political dogma and irrational beliefs, such as superstition. A belief that all human beings are innately rational, regardless of class and sex distinctions, led to the universal demand for individual liberty and equality.
▷Mary Wollstonecraft

En'owkin School of International Writing (1989–present)
Situated in Penticton, British Columbia, this was the first Canadian centre for aboriginal people to study writing and publishing with aboriginal teachers. Founded to develop a curriculum for schoolchildren, it grew into a training centre for Native Canadian literature and voice, and functions primarily as a collective in association with the creative writing programme at the University of Victoria, British Columbia.
▷Jeanette Armstrong is its founding director, and others involved include ▷Lee Maracle.

Enracinement: prélude à une déclaration des devoirs envers l'être humain, L' (1949) ▷*Need for Roots, The* (1952)

Enríquez de Guzmán, Doña Feliciana (c 1580–1640)
Spanish poet and classical scholar. Born in Seville late in the 16th century, Enríquez went on to study at the University of Salamanca. She wrote *Los jardines y campos sabeos (Sabean Gardens and Fields)*, a tragicomedy in two parts, which were published in 1624 and 1627. Part I was performed before Philip IV in 1624.

Ensing, Riemke (born 1939)
New Zealand poet. Riemke Ensing was born in Groningen in the Netherlands, and emigrated to New Zealand as a child. Much of her work refers directly or indirectly to periods of transition and to cultural difference. Educated in Auckland, Ensing has been prominent as an academic at the University of Auckland, writing and lecturing on New Zealand literature. In 1977 Ensing edited the first anthology of women poets in New Zealand, ▷*Private Gardens*. Ensing is represented in all the major anthologies of New Zealand poetry and has published widely in literary magazines. Her work is formally innovative and reflects current cultural questions.

Publications include: Edited *Private Gardens* (1977); *Making Inroads* (1980); *Letters – Selected Poems* (1982); *Topographies* (1984); *Spells from Chagall* (1987).
▷Anthologies, New Zealand

Eon de Beaumont, Charles Geneviève Louise Auguste André Timothée, Chevalier d' (Chevalière d') (1728–1810)
French prose writer. An enigmatic figure, due to the ambiguity surrounding his/her sex, d'Eon is currently thought to have been either hermaphrodite or male, although 19th-century biographers included the name in volumes on women writers. D'Eon had a varied career as lawyer, reader to the Empress of Russia, diplomat, officer of the dragoons, and royal spy in London, and was known as a swordsman of unrivalled skill. Various diplomatic and personal quarrels led to the accusation that d'Eon was female. The French court insisted that the *chevalier* renounce military uniform and live unambiguously as a woman, which d'Eon did from 1755 to 1810. A scholarly writer on the history of finance, d'Eon also published texts on diplomacy which included sensitive material banned in France: see especially *Lettres, mémoires et négotiations particulières du chevalier d'Eon* (1764) (*The Private Letters, Memoirs and Dealings of the Knight of Eon*) and *Les Loisirs du chevalier d'Eon* (1774) (*The Pastimes of the Knight of Eon*). Two texts were presented as works by the female *chevalière*: a reply by 'Mlle d'Eon' to Beaumarchais (1778), who had been sent to London to silence the outspoken spy, and a text on the theatre, which includes a 'defence of women', where d'Eon is referred to as, 'a woman proud to be the chevalier of her sex'. Woman, man, hermaphrodite or transvestite, the case of d'Eon, from which English psychologist Henry Havelock Ellis (1859–1939) coined the term eonism, which ▷Mary Wollstonecraft cited as exemplary of prejudice against women, presents fertile material for gender studies.
Bib: Briquet, F., *Dictionnaire historique, littéraire et bibliographique des françaises*; Cox, C., *The Enigma of the Age*; Decker, M. de, *Mme le chevalier d'Eon*; Prudhomme, L.M., *Répertoire universel historique et biographique des Femmes célèbres*; Telfer, J.B., *The Strange Career of the Chevalier d'Eon*; Nixon, E., *Royal Spy*.

Ephelia
The name used by a late 17th-century poet writing in English, whose identification is made all

the more difficult by the fact that it is a name frequently used by other writers, or as the name of the recipient of a poem. How much weight we give to the internal evidence of poems – such as the poems to 'Strephon' – depends on how literally we imagine these poems can be related to a 'life'. The guesses at the identity of this author have included ▷Katherine Philips's daughter, Elizabeth Mordaunt.

Publications attributed to this name include: *Panegric to the King* (1678); *Female Poems on Several Occassions* (1679), and *Advice to His Grace* (1681/2).

Bib: Greer, Germaine *et al.*, *Kissing the Rod*.

Epigram, Ancient Greek

A favourite literary genre for women poets of the 4th–2nd centuries BC. These short poems are often only one or two couplets in length, but can be longer. They are characterized by neat word-play, tight structure, and emotion, often pathos.

▷Nossis; Anyte; Moero; Parthenis; Religion, Ancient Greek and Roman, women and

Epinay, Louise-Florence-Pétronille Tardieu d' (1726–1783)

French novelist and essayist. A central figure among the Enyclopaedists (a group which produced the twenty-eight volume *Encyclopédie* between 1751 and 1775). Alongside Grimm, her long-term lover, and Denis Diderot (1713–1784), she contributed unsigned articles to the periodical *Correspondance littéraire* (*Literary Correspondence*). Her collection of writings in *Mes moments heureux* (1759) (*My Happy Times*), which she dedicated to herself, show her establishing her independence through writing. The integral edition of her major work, the largely autobiographical novel *Histoire de Mme de Montbrillant*, (*The Story of Mme de Montbrillant*) was only published in 1952. Earlier adapted editions presented the text as her memoirs. In this text she gives her version of the events surrounding the rupture between Jean-Jacques Rousseau (1712–1778) and the Encyclopaedists, which differs from Rousseau's account in his *Confessions*. It has been republished as *Les Contre-confessions* (1989) (*Counter-confessions*), and praised as a Balzacian portrayal of 18th-century French life. As self-analysis, the text aims to explain and justify an individual woman's rejection of a conventional feminine identity, and her attempts to forge a new model. D'Epinay's views on the position of women as mothers and daughters are expressed in her educational writings, *Lettres à mon fils* (1759) (*Letters to My Son*) and *Les Conversations d'Emilie* (1774) (*The Conversations of Emily*, 1785), and in her letters to the abbé de Galiani. She emphasizes the role of mothers in the education of their daughters and suggests that through serious study women could cultivate the inner resources needed to survive their restrictive social condition. *Memoirs and Correspondence of Mme d'Epinay* was published in English in 1930.

▷*Journal des Dames*

Bib: Aury, D., 'Les dangers de la vertu' in *Nouvelle Revue Française*, February 1983; Badinter, E., *Emilie, Emilie*; Gréard, V.C.O., *L'Education des femmes par les femmes*; Thomas, Diderot, *d'Epinay*; Badinter, E., *Qu'est-ce qu'une femme?*; Valentino, H., *Une femme d'esprit sous Louis XV*.

Epistolary novel

The tradition of reading narratives structured in letters has both sacred origins in biblical epistles (such as those of St Paul) and secular antecedents in famous letter cycles, such as those between Héloïse and Abélard. In the 18th century *Letters From a Portuguese Nun* – five letters from a nun called 'Mariana' to her lover – can be set alongside guides to how to write (such as those given by ▷Hannah Wolley), both stimulating a genre of fiction structured in letters and closely associated with Samuel Richardson (▷Richardson, influence of), for example in his *Clarissa* (1747–1748), and used by ▷Aphra Behn and ▷Fanny Burney. In the French fiction *Les Liasons Dangereuses* (1782) by Choderlos de Laclos (1741–1803) the genre can be seen operating in order to generate a sense of complexity.

Bib: Spencer, Jane, *The Rise of the Woman Novelist*; Kamuf, Peggy, *Fictions of Feminine Desire*.

Erbil, Leyla (born 1931)

Turkish short story writer and novelist. A 'new' Turkish woman in many senses, she had a chequered career in work and education. She abandoned her study of literature at the University of Istanbul to work for a foreign airline, and later as a translator for various foreign consulates in the city. When she married she moved to Izmir, where she had a child before returning to Istanbul. She was writing at the same time. She favoured the short story, which she considered 'a most intelligible form of self-expression'. She contributed significant innovations in its form and the use of language. She was popular in the 1960s, and her verse and short stories were widely published in magazines. Her novels include *Hallaç* (1961), *At Night* (1962) and *A Strange Woman* (1971).

Erdrich, Louise (born 1954)

US short story writer and novelist. Of Chippewa ▷Native American descent, Erdrich was raised in Wahpeton, North Dakota. Her maternal grandmother was Tribal Chair on Turtle Mountain Reservation. Both of Erdrich's parents worked in the Bureau of Indian Affairs boarding school. In 1972 she graduated from Dartmouth College and later earned a Master of Arts degree at Johns Hopkins. At Dartmouth she worked with Michael Dorris, whom she eventually married. Erdrich's trilogy – ▷*Love Medicine* (1984), *Beet Queen* (1986) and *Tracks* (1988) – celebrates Native American survival. Her novels depict the sordid circumstances of Native Americans' lives, although they envision a means of transcending these circumstances through spiritual values and the careful integration of old traditions and ways of life with present-day realities. Erdrich portrays a culture that is not dying but is still evolving.

Other works include *Jacklight* (1984), *Baptism of Desire* (1989), and with Michael Dorris, *The Crown of Columbus* (1991).

Ere du soupçon: essais sur le roman, L' (1956)
▷*Age of Suspicion: Essays on the Novel, The*, (1963)

Erinna (? 4th century BC)
A poet from the island of Telos. Most famous for her poem ▷'The Distaff', which comprised hexameter lines, 54 of which are extant. An epigram (anonymous) records that she died at nineteen. Three of her epigrams survive, all concerning women: one is about a girl's portrait and two are inscriptions for the tomb of Baucis, the same woman mourned in 'The Distaff'. The biographical dictionary, the *Suda* (10th century BC), says, probably mistakenly, that she was a contemporary of ▷Sappho. Its entry on her naively uses her poetry for biography. While she employs some dialect forms like Sappho's, her general style is much closer to that of writers from the 4th–2nd century BC. An anonymous Greek epigram maintains Erinna was best at hexameter poetry, Sappho at lyric.
▷Muses; Parthenis

Erinni ▷Borgese Freschi, Maria

Eriphanis
Ancient Greek poet of mythical date. Reputedly a writer of lyric poetry and lover of the hunter Menalcas, she is credited with the invention of a type of pastoral poetry. The Greek writer Clearchus (4th century BC), in a book on *Love Matters*, says she was the first to compose love poetry. Only one line survives, quoted by the Greek writer Athenaeus (2nd century AD).

Erlenberger, Maria
German writer. Her novel, *Der Hunger nach Wahnsinn* (1977) (*Hunger for Madness*) is the diary of a woman in a psychiatric hospital who has been trying to starve herself to death. The book is an important example of a genre of German novels from the 1970s, in which illness becomes a metaphor for female anger and alienation. Three subsequent works expand the same theme and offer biting Existential analyses of the lone woman's struggle. The 1979 essay, '*Die Literathure*', a pun on the words 'literature' and 'whore' expresses Erlenberger's distrust of the value of art in a society that oppresses women.

Ernaux, Annie
French novelist. Ernaux teaches literature in a secondary school near Paris, and has written five largely autobiographical novels. The style is that of the intimate journal or confessional, and the claim to authenticity is underlined by the author's description of her most recent novel as 'neither a novel or a biography, perhaps something between literature, sociology and history'. *Les Armoires vides*

(1974) (*The Empty Cupboards*) is a vivid first-person account of the narrator's childhood and adolescence. It focuses on the feelings of dislocation and inadequacy which the experience of being educated out of one's class can entail, and on the resulting confusion in relation to identity and sexuality. In *La Femme gelée* (1981) (*The Frozen Woman*), the theme of oppression and inequality within bourgeois marriage is perhaps more typical of feminist confessional writing. *La Place* (1983) (*The Square*, translation forthcoming) is a history of her father's rise from agricultural labourer to café owner, and in *Une Femme* (1987) (*A Woman's Story*, 1990) Ernaux reflects on her mother's life, her final years and on their relationship. In the final pages we are told that Ernaux's mother died eight days before ▷Simone de Beauvoir, and there are clear parallels with the latter's description, in ▷*A Very Easy Death* (1966), of the painful combination of a deep emotional and physical bond between mother and daughter and the distance created by the daughter's intellectual emancipation.
Bib: Day, L., 'Class, sexuality and subjectivity in Annie Ernaux's *Les Armoires vides*' in Atack, M. and Powrie, P. (eds), *Contemporary French Fiction by Women: Feminist Perspectives*

Eschstruth, Nataly von (1860–1939)
German dramatist and popular novelist. She began her literary career writing plays, but later found a much wider readership for her stories about aristocratic families and life at court. Her best novels include *Der Majoratsherr* (1898) (*Master of the Estate*) and *Die Bären von Hohen-Esp* (1902) (*The Bears of Hohen-Esp*), a book that was commissioned by the German kaiser himself.

Escobedo, Joana (born 1942)
Spanish novelist born in Barcelona. Her novels, *Silenci endins* (1979) (*Silence Towards the Centre*) and *Amic, amat* (1980) (*Friend, Beloved*), portray the search for identity within the individual and within society.
▷Catalan women's writing

Escoffery, Gloria (born 1923)
Caribbean poet, painter, journalist and teacher, born and educated in ▷Jamaica. She went on to study at McGill University, Montreal, Canada, and the Slade School of Fine Arts, Britain. She lived for many years in Britain before returning to Jamaica. She currently teaches English at a rural community school, paints and exhibits her work, and writes as an art critic, contributing regularly to *Jamaica Journal*. She has always been active in promoting art, literature and music in the Caribbean. Her awards include the Order of Distinction in 1976 from the Jamaican government for her services to the arts, and poetry awards from the Jamaica festival in 1970 and 1973. Her poetry has appeared in a number of anthologies: *Breaklight* (1972), *Caribbean Voices* (1978) and *The Penguin Book Of Caribbean Verse* (1986). She has published poems and stories in

▷*BIM*, *Jamaica Journal*, *Focus* and *Arts Review*. Her published poetry includes *Landscape in the Making* (1976). Her output has been small but of high quality.

There has been little analysis of her work, though an interesting interview appears in *Jamaica Journal*, Vol. 5, No. 1 (1971).

Escott, Margaret (born 1908)

New Zealand novelist. Margaret Escott was born and educated in Britain but emigrated to New Zealand with her parents in 1926, partly as a result of World War I. Escott and her family spent some time on a farm in the Waikato before settling in Auckland, but Escott returned alone to London two years later, where she wrote her three novels – *Insolence of Office* (1934), *Awake at Noon* (1935) and *Show Down* (1936) – while working at the Times Book Club. After the publication of *Show Down*, Escott returned to New Zealand, where she worked as a teacher and librarian for the rest of her life. *Show Down*, her only novel set in New Zealand, is written from a male point of view and focuses on rural life and marriage. It represents its central character as inarticulate and emotionally deep, and experiments with a 'male' language that was seen as innovative and Hemingwayesque at the time. *Show Down* also focuses on economic and social inequity.

Escribo tu nombre (1965) (I Write Your Name)

Novel by one of Spain's most outstanding female post-war neo-realist novelists, ▷Elena Quiroga. It takes its title from a longer epigraph, which reads in full: 'On the School Exercise Books, Liberty, I Write Your Name.' The novel concentrates on life at a convent school, which becomes an allegory of society as a whole, which at the time was itself attempting to voice a muted cry for freedom.

Escritoras de Portugal (1924) (Women Writers from Portugal)

A two-volume study of women's writings from the 16th century to the early 1900s, written by Teresa Leitão de Barros. The first history of its kind, it includes commentaries on well-known writers, such as ▷Maria Amália Vaz de Carvalho and ▷Florbela Espanca, as well as numerous figures who have been neglected by subsequent scholarship.

Espanca, Florbela (1894–1930)

Portuguese poet. A major figure in 20th-century Portuguese literature, and one of the few women to appear in the established canon. Despite the pervasive avant-garde and modernist experiments in Portuguese verse during the 1900s and 1920s Espanca's poems were conventional in style and theme. Her first volume, *Livro de Mágoas*, (*Book of Sorrows*) appeared in 1919, and four years later, in 1923, she published *Livro de Sóror Saudade* (*Book of Sister Longing*), which shows her preference for the sonnet. Among the themes that recur in these and later volumes are nature, the divine, unrequited love, and spiritual disillusionment. Her love poems, especially those of a mystical-erotic nature, are among her most admired and compelling works.

Although Espanca is highly regarded as a poet, most of the scholarship about her tends to focus on her life as opposed to her works. Married three times, she nonetheless led a sad, somewhat isolated existence. Throughout her adult life she suffered from mental and physical illnesses, which worsened significantly following the accidental death of her brother, Apeles. She died on her thirty-sixth birthday, and historians generally describe her death as a suicide.

▷*Escritoras de Portugal*; Bessa-Luís, Agustina
Bib: *Longman Anthology of World Literature by Women*, pp. 326–28.

Espelho de Cristina (1518) (Christine's Mirror)

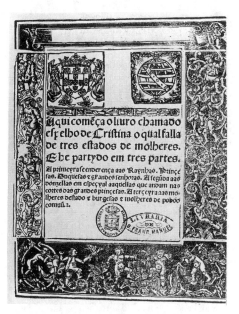

Frontispiece from Esphelo de Christina

Portuguese translation of ▷Christine de Pisan's *Livre des Trois Vertues*. The translation was carried out in the period 1447–1455, and the manuscript was originally titled *Livro das Três Virtudes*. According to one scholar, there are differences between the manuscript and the published version.

▷Leonor, Queen of Portugal; Isabel, Queen of Portugal
Bib: Willard, Charity Cannon, *A Portuguese Translation of Christine de Pisan's* 'Livre des Trois Vertues'.

Espina, Concha (1869–1955)

The first Spanish woman to earn her living exclusively from her writings, Espina has won many prizes for her work. Author of novels, plays and poetry, Espina is most closely associated with the regional slant of realism. Among her best and most successful novels is *La esfinge maragata* (1914) (*The Sphinx*). Set in Léon, this novel focuses on the plight of women in that region. As a result of her experiences during the Spanish Civil War (1936–9) she became pro-Franco, and her later fiction reflects this change.

Espinassy, Louise-Florence-Pétronille Tardieu d'Esclavelle, Marquise d' (died 1777)

French educational writer. Her published works include *Essai sur l'éducation des demoiselles* (1764) (*Essay on the Education of Young Ladies*), where she argues that the early years of the child's education are not important and can be safely consigned to a governess and nurse. She later published the pedagogical text *Nouvel Abrégé de l'histoire de France* (1767) (*New Summary of French History*).

Espinet, Rambabai (born 1948)

Caribbean poet, writer and researcher, born in ▷Trinidad, Espinet now lives in Canada, where she is a writer and researcher in literature and women's studies. She has been active in the women's movement in both the Caribbean and Canada. Her publications include essays, and her poetry has been published in ▷*Creation Fire*, *Trinidad and Tobago Review*, *Woman Speak*, *Fireweed*, *Toronto and South Asian Review* and *Jahaji Bhai*.

Essay to Revive the Antient Education of Gentlewomen, An (1673)

A prospectus for a school at Tottenham, just north of London, by ▷Bathsua Pell Makin. This prospectus is also an argument for women's education, and is an early part of the debate about the education of women in literacy, numeracy and languages (see also ▷Catharine Macaulay, ▷Mary Wollstonecraft, ▷Sarah Fielding). The tract confines itself to the education of gentlewomen, never suggesting that education should spread throughout society, but does make a significant argument for broadening the accepted curriculum for girls to place more emphasis on languages and literacy. She also situates her argument historically (note the word 'revive' in the title) and this serves to remind readers of a tradition of women's education before the English Civil War (1642–1646 and 1648–1651).

Essentialism

A term frequently used in feminist theory and criticism to characterize arguments which define gender and sexuality as innate. Essentialist theories are usually rooted in a biological determinism, and derive the central characteristics of femininity and masculinity from the anatomical differences between the sexes rather than from the social meanings given to anatomy. The view that women are naturally suited to child-rearing because of their reproductive role is a frequently-used example.

Essentialism also includes any argument about the nature of femininity which rests on the belief that there is an essence which is historically unchanging and culturally universal. Thus, essentialism may be psychological as well as biological. US radical feminists such as ▷Adrienne Rich and ▷Mary Daly have often been accused of essentialism because of their attempt to produce a general theory of ▷patriarchy to account for women's oppression across different historical periods and cultures. The French ▷post-structuralist feminists, such as ▷Luce Irigaray and ▷Hélène Cixous, have also been accused of essentialism because of their arguments about the relationship of a feminine desire to the woman's body. In each case, radical feminist or New French Feminist, the charge seems to rest on a mischaracterization of the specific social, political and intellectual contexts in which these thinkers have worked. Recently, feminist theories have started to rethink the concept by looking at the contexts in which different feminist theories have been developed. It has even been suggested that essentialism is a necessary, if not inevitable, risk for feminism.
Bib. Braidotti, Rosi, 'The Politics of Ontological Difference' in Teresa Brennan (ed.), *Between Feminism and Psychoanalysis*.

Estate di Anna, L' (1955) (Anna's Summer)

A psychological novel by Italian writer ▷Lea Quaretti, which analyses the world of its female protagonist in some detail, through her haze of mental illness. The plot unfolds through the painful memories of this central character, and the tone is at once striking and sympathetic in its portrayal of the protagonist's progressive degeneration. It is interesting for its suggestion that mental illness in women is socially constructed to some degree.

Estienne, Nicole d' (c 1544–c 1596)

French poet, also known as '*la dame Liébaut*'. Of illustrious birth, Nicole d'Estienne was a member of a highly cultivated humanist family. She adopted the ▷pseudonym 'Olympe' and was the fiancée and inspiration of the poet Jacques Grévin (1538–1570). She wrote a humorous *Apologie ou défense pour les femmes* (*Vindication or Defence of Women*), published by Claude Le Villain sometime after 1595. This text is also known as the *Misères de la Femme Mariée* (*Miseries of the Married Woman*). Nicole d'Estienne here reproaches men for their numerous faults. She calls upon the chaste Muses to favour her '*tant que je puisse descrire / Les travaux continus & le cruel martire / Qui sans fin nous talonne en ce sejour nuptial*' ('for as long as I may continue to describe the continuous work and cruel martyrdom which endlessly pursues us during our time as wives'), and the verses oppose married and monastic life according to patristic tradition. Her sonnets seem to have enjoyed a certain notoriety among her circle, though they were never published.

Bib: Guillerm, J.P., Guillerm, L., Hordoir, L., and Piejus, M.F., *Le Miroir des femmes*.

Etcherelli, Claire (born 1934)

French novelist. Etcherelli's first novel, *Élise ou la vraie vie* (1967) (▷*Elise or the Real Life*, 1970), won immediate acclaim, culminating in the award of the Prix Femina. Of working-class origins herself, Etcherelli writes about the experience of poverty and oppression, and her characters' struggle to find an identity, or 'real life', is inextricably linked to the growth of their political awareness. Without idealizing the political potential of art, Etcherelli has a clear political commitment to show how her characters are socially constructed, and in her most famous novel, *Élise*, to explore the relationship between different kinds of oppression. One of this novel's most important features is the depiction of racism, both in the outside world – Paris at the time of the Algerian War – and in the character/narrator Élise herself. In Etcherelli's sober descriptions there are no simplistic oppositions of oppressor/oppressed.

Her two later novels, *A Propos de Clémence* (1971) (*About Clémence*) and *Un Arbre voyageur* (1978) (*A Travelling Tree*), form a trilogy with *Élise*, united by common themes – the depiction of French society between the 1950s and the 1970s, and by the character, Anna, who is present in all three. The latter two novels, particularly *Un Arbre voyageur*, are more experimental in narrative form than *Élise*, but neither has achieved the popularity of the first novel. Etcherelli has also edited a collection of anti-racist poetry: *Cent poèmes contre le racisme* (*One Hundred Poems Against Racism*) with G. Manceroni and B. Wallon, 1986).

Ethan Frome (1911)

US novel. ▷Edith Wharton's book satirizes New England rural life as emotionally impoverished, focusing on the tragic plight of Ethan Frome. Ethan is dominated by his wife, Zeena, who stifles his manhood. He falls in love with a younger woman, Mattie, but burdened by his sense of responsibility, he cannot escape Zeena. He and Mattie try to commit suicide together but fail; Ethan is then left with two complaining women to support. Wharton emphasizes that her narrator has fabricated his own version of Ethan's story. The male narrator puts the man in the position of the oppressed, and he expresses his own fear of male castration if women are not controlled. Wharton analyzes how the patriarchal family shapes the social and economic exchanges between the sexes.

Ethelmer, Ellis ▷Wolstenholme-Elmy, Elizabeth

Etude et le rouet, L' (1989) ▷*Hipparchia's Choice* (1991)

Eudocia Augusta (5th century AD)

Poet. Daughter of the sophist Leontius, she became the wife of the Roman emperor Theodosius II (AD 401–450) in AD 421. She left Theodosius to go to Jerusalem, and died in AD 460. She wrote epic poetry in hexameters, in Greek, combining pagan and Christian ideas; a poem on *The Victory of the Troops of Theodosius over the Persians* (in AD 421–422), a *Paraphrase of the Octateuch* (which the Byzantine writer Photius says was well written, with no digressions and no mixture of fact and fiction), a *Paraphrase of the Prophecies of Daniel and Zachariah*, a *History of the Martyrdom of Cyprian and Justina*, and centos made up of verses and half-verses of Homer, telling of the fall of man, and his salvation by Jesus Christ. One fragment praises baths and healing springs.

Eugenia

Name used by a writer who attacked John Sprint's *The Bride-Woman's Counsellor* (1699) in *The Female Advocate* (1700), arguing that, although the woman is bound to passive obedience, yet 'I defy the meekest woman in the world, if she meets with an unreasonable, domineering, insolent creature . . . to forbear wishing it otherwise.'
▷Chudleigh, Lady Mary
Bib: Browne, Alicia, *The Eighteenth Century Feminist Mind*.

Evanescence (1988)

Work by Japanese writer Yoshimoto Banana (born 1964). The narrator, Toriumi Mermaid, is a girl who lives with her mother, the second wife of a particular man. She meets his son, Arashi, and feels a fleeting love for him. Her mother tried to commit suicide after travelling to Nepal with her patron. Toriumi muses that 'the future is in the dark, and life is unbearably endless . . . people try to close their eyes when endlessness becomes too big for them . . . I am happy to help my mother, who has been so oppressed with loneliness. I want to find brightness beyond Arashi.' Her narrative style has a gentle dream-like quality, which appeals to many young women.

Evans, Augusta Jane (1835–1909)

US popular novelist. A native southerner, Evans first used her experience and background to develop distinctive perspectives in historically-based fiction. After a first unsuccessful novel, *Inez: A Tale of the Alamo* (1855), the public responded to *Beulah* (1859) – though Evans lost some audience with her next, explicitly secessionist, *Macaria; or Altars of Sacrifice* (1864).

Her claim to lasting fame is as the author of ▷*St Elmo* (1867), one of the most popular novels of the 19th century. While Evans's work drew on classic elements of popular literature – rags-to-riches plots, melodramatic adventure – and required its hero's reform before a proper happy ending, *St Elmo* presaged a new era of assertive heroines who acknowledged their own sexuality and sexual attraction. With its wealthy rake hero,

St Elmo provided sexual tension and fantasy for the masses and generated some of the first-recorded US consumer-products advertising campaigns based on the appeal of literary characters. Never again approaching the blockbuster success of *St Elmo*, Evans was less prolific than many 19th-century women writers. Her other works include: *Vashti* (1869); *Infelice* (1875); *At the Mercy of Tiberius* (1887).

Evans, Katherine (died 1692) and Sarah Cheevers

▷Quaker preachers, travellers and visionaries who preached in England, Scotland, Ireland, Wales and abroad. In 1658/9 they set off to follow the footsteps of Paul the Apostle. On the way to Alexandria their boat stopped at Malta, where they were handed over to the Italian Inquisition by the English representative. They remained in prison for more than three years, and left a record of their sufferings and refusals to capitulate. The account (originally published by a male friend before their return) interprets behaviour, and even natural phenomena, in biblical terms: 'And in the time of our great trial, the sun and earth did mourn visibly three days, and the horror of death and pains of hell was upon me.' The document records what the Inquisition asked the Quaker women, and what they said in return. It also records their behaviour at Roman Catholic services, making it a fascinating close study of mutual incomprehension.

Their publications are: *This is a Short Relation of Some of the Cruel Sufferings, for Truth's Sake, of Katherine Evans and Sarah Cheevers, in the Inquisition in the Isle of Malta* (1662), and *A True Account* (1663).

▷Blaugdone, Barbara
Bib: Graham, Elspeth *et al.*, *Her Own Life*

Evans, Mary Ann (Marian) ▷Eliot, George

Evbu, My Love (1980)

A ▷romantic novel by the Nigerian journalist and novelist, ▷Helen Ovbiagele. The heroine, Evbu, is first encountered at Lagos airport, where, newly married, she waits for a plane to take her and her black North American husband, Steve, to the USA. She is described in terms of the classic stereotype: a sexy, glamorous, successful woman. The novel is the story of how she achieves this, from humble beginnings in a village in Bendel State. To escape marriage to an elderly schoolteacher, she runs away to Lagos to be with her boyfriend, Jide, but he is preoccupied by his own elitist education and leaves her to her own resources. Evbu's story is realistic and familiar. To survive, she is forced into earning money as a call-girl, using the money to pay for a secretarial training. Ovbiagele shows the manifold ways in which women are exploited – as workers, as lovers, as objects of desire for men. Evbu, however, attains absolution on all levels: first, from her father before he dies; second, from Jide who, having married someone else, realizes his

mistake but is killed in a car crash; third, through her marriage, in a white dress, to the perfect man, a foreigner who enables her to escape to a society where the relations between the sexes are not purely materialistic. In this fantasy ending, Ovbiagele expresses a collective yearning for something other than the current status quo in Nigeria.

▷Prostitution (West Africa)

Eve, Sarah (1749/1750–1774)

North American diarist. Born to Anne Moore and Oswell Eve, she resided in Philadelphia all her life. Well-educated and bearing a notable imagination, she seemed on the brink of a renowned life through her own talents and her engagement to Dr Benjamin Rush when she died at age twenty-four after a long illness. ▷*Extracts from the Journal of Miss Sarah Eve* (which covers 1772–1773 and is addressed to her father, a sea captain) is a well-written record of an educated young Quaker woman's inner thoughts and of her witty and intelligent critiques of pre-revolutionary Philadelphian society.

▷Early North American Quaker women's writings

Evelina: or, the History of a Young Lady's Entrance Into the World (1778)

▷Fanny Burney's best-known novel, although she published it anonymously. An epistolary tale, largely told in letters from Evelina to her guardian the Reverend Mr Villars. Set in London and Bristol, Evelina, a beautiful sixteen-year-old is introduced to the perils of public space – such as the gardens at Vauxhall – and the delights of the town, including opera. Perpetually socially embarrassed by her 'low' grandmother, Madam Duval, and her silversmith relatives, the Branghtons of Snow Hill, Evelina rises above such connections to be reclaimed by what remains of her family and a more than suitable marriage. As readers we are invited to enjoy the humiliation of an older woman with pretensions to beauty when Captain Mirvan disguises himself as a highwayman to abuse Madame Duval physically and mentally (compare the humiliation of the mother in Oliver Goldsmith's *She Stoops to Conquer*, 1773), and we are invited to identify with the artless and deserved rise of Evelina and the wit of her friend, Mrs Selwyn.

Evelyn, Mary (1634–1709)

English letter-writer from 1667 onwards She preferred ▷Katherine Philips to ▷Margaret Cavendish, whose eccentric behaviour and teacherly manner repelled her. Mary Evelyn wrote of women's aspiration, 'her fate commonly exposes her to wonder, but adds little of esteem'. Her daughter, also Mary Evelyn, also wrote, and John Evelyn seems to have encouraged a circle of women correspondents.

Bib: Grees, Germaine *et al.*, *Kissing the Rod.*

Ewing, Juliana Horatia (1841–1885)
English writer of ▷children's literature. Born in
Ecclesfield, Yorkshire, the daughter of
▷Margaret Gatty. Her first published story was
in ▷Charlotte Yonge's *Monthly Packet* in 1861.
She also contributed to her mother's periodical
for children, *Aunt Judy's Magazine*, taking over its
editorship in 1873. She was an extremely prolific
writer and very popular in her time, though her
▷sentimental and moralizing tone makes her less
liked by children today. Her stories include: *Mrs
Overtheway's Remembrances* (1866–68); *The
Brownies* (1865); *Jan of the Windmill* (1872) and
Jackanapes (1879).
　▷Ghost stories (19th-century Britain)
Bib: Eden, Mrs H.F.K., *Juliana Horatia Ewing
and her Books.*

Excellent Women (1952)
Novel by English writer ▷Barbara Pym. Gentle
comedy of manners seen through the eyes of its
protagonist, Miss Lathbury, 'an unmarried
woman, just over thirty who lives alone and has no
apparent ties'. As with many of Pym's novels, the
narrative explores middle-class femininity in the
1940s and 1950s, particularly through the lives of
women on the periphery of academic and Church
life. In exploring the stereotypical 'emptiness' of
the spinster's life, the novel is also concerned with
notions of order and acceptance, and ironically
portrays Miss Lathbury's social improprieties
(being caught in the act of wearing the 'wrong'
clothes, or not using the appropriate china). Pym's
narrator declares she is 'not at all like Jane Eyre,
who must have given hope to so many plain
women who tell their stories in the first person'
(▷*Jane Eyre*). Although Miss Lathbury desires a
'full life', satisfaction and fulfilment come through
being acknowledged as one of those 'excellent
women' who are capable, reliable, supportive of
men who could not manage their lives without
them, and respected and esteemed within the
community.

**Exhortation to the Inhabitants of the
Province of South Carolina . . ., An (1748)**
The first publication of North American preacher
and essayist ▷Sophia Wigington Hume, *An
Exhortation* is addressed to 'Friends and
Neighbours' in her home province of South
Carolina; Hume cautions them against their
prejudicial attitudes towards Quakers and
counsels them to observe their own backsliding.
Hume directly counters the 'Smile of Contempt'
or the pity at her 'Folly' that she knows will result
from her decision to publish her opinions. The
reasoned, intelligent and literate text of *An
Exhortation* remains a testament to her 'right' to
voice her beliefs.
　▷*Extracts from Divers, Antient Testimonies*; *Justly
Celebrated Mrs Sophia Hume's Advice, The*; *Caution
to such as Observe Days and Times . . ., A*; Early
North American Quaker women's writings

**Exiles at Home, Australian Women Writers
1925–1945 (1981)**
Critical work by Australian writer Drusilla
Modjeska. It examines the careers of a number of
Australian women writers in the 1930s: ▷Miles
Franklin, ▷Katharine Susannah Prichard, ▷M.
Barnard Eldershaw, ▷Eleanor Dark, ▷Jean
Devanny and others. The Depression made the
life of the woman writer doubly precarious, and
the awareness of the rise of ▷fascism in Europe
and Asia strengthened the close relationship
between these women, all of whom were
committed socialists.

Exile writing (South Africa)
During the turbulent period of the 1950s, with its
political trials and life sentences, and during the
1960s, with house arrests, bannings and
detentions without trial, a number of people left
South Africa, sometimes to evade arrest,
sometimes with an 'exit permit' after a period in
prison, and sometimes simply because they could
no longer countenance life like this. Out of such
experience has come a body of writing consisting
largely of political ▷autobiographies and, more
specifically, ▷prison memoirs, as well as fiction
and poetry. Much of the writing is linked by its
need to continue to protest against apartheid, and
to bear witness to the endurance of the
opposition.
　Phyllis Altman's novel *Law of the Vultures*
(1952), banned in South Africa until 1987, when
it was reprinted, is written from the perspective of
a white woman looking at the limited
opportunities for black South Africans in
Johannesburg. ▷Mary Benson and ▷Hilda
Bernstein first wrote autobiographies about their
political activism which then became reworked
into fiction. Ruth First's *117 Days* (1965)
concentrates on the period spent in solitary
confinement in prison. Her story is amplified in
the novel *Ties of Blood* (1989) and the film script
and film-diary, *A World Apart* (1988), written by
her daughters, Gillian and Shawn Slovo,
respectively, who are second-generation exiles.
　Among the South Africans who went into
'voluntary' exile during this period are Rose Moss,
Caroline Slaughter, and Barbara Trapido.
Trapido has written various interesting and
successful novels, *Brother of the More Famous Jack*
(1982) being one of them. Moss's *The Terrorist*
(1979) recounts the story of a young white liberal,
called, by some, a 'traitor to his race', sentenced
to death for an act of sabotage in which people are
killed. (The book was reprinted in South Africa in
1981 under the title *The Schoolmaster*.) Moss, who
settled in the US and has written many short
stories and essays, published an earlier novel, *The
Family Reunion* (1974), as well as the non-fictional
Shouting at the Crocodile (1990), which reproduces
the voices of those involved in the lengthy Delmas
Treason Trial (1985–1988). Carolyn Slaughter
has established herself as a writer in Britain, and
in only some of her books returns to South
African experience: *The Innocents* (1986) is an

interesting novel about a rural family's reaction to the resettlement, under apartheid, of its labouring force. Another writer who left during the 1960s was ▷Bessie Head, although she refused to call herself an exile writer since, she said, racist South Africa had never been a home. Set in Botswana, where Head had refugee and not citizen status, her writing reflects the exile's prevailing sense of homelessness.

The concept of home is a particularly interesting one in exile writing by black South African writers, which is less nostalgic than desirous of constructing a home denied them by a grid of laws and economic necessities. ▷Lauretta Ngcobo, who left the country during the 1970s in order to escape arrest, is the first writer to focus on women in the so-called 'homelands', to which 63 per cent of black women have been confined, together with some 8 million children. The category of exile writing is expanded, then, by the dislocation caused by systematic racial and economic oppression and exploitation: black South Africans have been placed in a permanent state of exile in their own land. The title of ▷Zoë Wicomb's *You Can't Get Lost in Cape Town* (1987) is an ironic reminder of this dislocation, at both a geographical and a psychological level.

Lindiwe Mabuza, the African National Congress's chief representative in the US, as well as a poet and short story writer, has edited a collection called *One Never Knows: An Anthology of Black South African Women Writers in Exile* (1989). This contains two stories by Dulcie September (1953–1988), killed, like Ruth First, by agents of the South African state, and a story by Rebecca Matlou, among others. The anthology *Somehow We Survive* contains poems by Baleka Kgositsile and Barbara Masekela. In 'For My Unborn Child' Kgositsile speaks with the voice of the mother giving bloody birth to a new country, whereas Masekela, in 'Phantoms', connects the lost country with a lost lover. Other writers in exile are Maggie Resha and Agnes Sam (prose) and Ilva Mackay and Christine Douts, whose poems appear in magazines. Amelia House, writing from the US, has published short stories in *Staffrider*, as well as a volume of poems, *Our Sun Will Rise* (1989). Most exile poetry by women is written primarily by black women, although ▷Jeni Couzyn is an important exception.

Expedition to the Baobab Tree, The (1983)

Translated from the Afrikaans (*Die Kremetartekspedisie*, 1981) by South African writer J.M. Coetzee, this is ▷Wilma Stockenström's third novel, and the only one available in English. Written in the first person, the narrative belongs to a young woman who had once been enslaved. She now lives in the interior of a baobab tree, her last refuge, from which she recalls her series of owners, the children she bears, and her passage from being the merest sexual plaything to being the head slave-girl of the richest man. On the death of the last owner, she leaves the city with an explorer, travelling with him and the son of her

previous owner, along with an entourage of slaves. The eldest son and the slaves abandon her and her companion, taking all their provisions and leaving them to die. Subtly, the novel shifts into the story of a life after death: the narrator is pure spirit, waiting for a time hospitable to her, endlessly enduring.

While colonial writers had typically presented the African landscape as a world to be penetrated, mapped and possessed, this novel seeks to present the landscape differently. To the extent that the land is body in the colonial tradition, it has been humiliated and degraded by colonial appropriation. But for Stockenström the land is also mind, or spirit, a feminine being who thus withstands masculine domination.

Extracts from Divers, Antient Testimonies (1766)

As a South Carolinian convert to Quakerism, the North American author ▷Sophia Wigington Hume's dedication to preaching and writing about her chosen faith is nowhere better exemplified than in this work. Concerned that the textual history of Quakerism be preserved, Hume gathered in this impressive collection numerous 'Antient Testimonies' of the faith of a persecuted sect. Thus *Extracts* remains a significant document in the religious history of the Society of Friends.

▷*Exhortation to the Inhabitants of the Province of South Carolina . . ., An*; *Justly celebrated Mrs Sophia Hume's Advice, The*; *Caution to such as Observe Days and Times . . ., A*; Early North American Quaker women's writings

'Extracts from the Diary of Hannah Callender' (1888)

Written between 1757 and 1762, the North American ▷Hannah Callender's diary entries capture the culture of the numerous Quaker communities in New York and New Jersey that she visited as a young woman. Mostly brief entries, the diary occasionally broadens into detailed records, especially of the travels and the landscapes observed. Most notable is her account of visiting the Moravian community in Bethlehem, Pennsylvania. Callender's diary ends upon her marriage in 1762.

▷Early North American Quaker women's writings

Extracts from the Diary of Mrs Ann Warder (1893–1894)

▷Ann Head Warder's diary, written for her sister Elizabeth who lived in England, covers her arrival in North America in 1786 and the next forty-four years of her life. At first interested in recording details about the alien society into which she had ventured with her North American husband, Warder soon adjusted to Philadelphia's Quaker society, and her talent as a writer is especially notable as she describes the beauty of the Pennsylvania countryside.

▷Early North American Quaker women's writings

Extracts from the Journal of Elizabeth Drinker (1889)

For almost fifty years (1758–1807) ▷Elizabeth Sandwith Drinker, a lifelong Philadelphian, maintained a journal in which she recorded family events, her attitudes on the American Revolution and the leisure activities of an upper-class 18th-century North American Quaker. Resistant to all war activities, Drinker records her disdain for the efforts of war alongside accounts of her assistance in nursing the wounded. Perhaps most interesting, however, are her comments on her reading during the post-war years; although she felt somewhat guilty about the time she devoted to reading, Drinker asserts that it was an activity in which she found 'consolation'. Her reading included novels, poetry and biographies as well as the works of Erasmus (1466–1530), Thomas Paine (1737–1809), Voltaire (1694–1778), Jean-Jacques Rousseau (1712–1778), ▷Mary Wollstonecraft and John Bunyan (1628–1688).

Extracts from the Journal of Miss Sarah Eve (1881)

Written during 1772–1773, ▷Sarah Eve's journal covers the everyday aspects of her life in 18th-century North America: gardening, social obligations, and the consequences of increasing poverty. 'Poverty without pride is nothing,' she wrote, 'but with it, it is the very deuce!' Yet her writings also reveal a keen intelligence, a sharp wit, a love of poetry and her hopes for the future. Writing on the brink of the American Revolution, Eve also detailed the irony of the Penn family's last display of political power.

'Extracts from the Journal of Mrs Ann Manigault 1754–1781' (1919–1920)

The North American diarist ▷Ann Ashby Manigault was 53 years old when she began to keep a journal of her active social life in Charleston, South Carolina. For the next twenty-seven years she notes in brief passages the numerous dinner parties and social gatherings that she attended and carefully records the various illnesses of family members.

Eybers, Elisabeth (born c 1915)

South African Afrikaans poet, born in the town of Klerksdorp, Transvaal, who has lived in Amsterdam since 1961. Eybers is the first significant woman poet in Afrikaans: a member of the *Dertigers* (writers of the 1930s), who included the poets Uys Krige and N.P. van Wyk Louw. With the poet Olga Kirsch she compiled a selection for English translation from her first four volumes of poetry: *Belydenis in die Skemering* (1936) (*Confession in the Twilight*); *Die Stil Avontuur* (1939) (*The Quiet Adventure*); *Die Vrou en Ander Verse* (1945) (*The Woman and Other Poems*), and *Die Ander Dors* (1946) (*The Other Thirst*); the selection appears under the title *The Quiet Adventure* (1948), the adventure referred to being that of the woman as wife and mother. Eybers's early poetry is characterized by its examination of women's lives: she draws from religion and mythology for her metaphors, portraying women as nurturing mothers and passive lovers. From *Die Ander Dors* onwards, her dissatisfaction with these traditional roles is increasingly explored.

During her 'Dutch period' she has published prolifically: *Tussengang* (1950) (*Mediation*), *Die Helder Halfjaar* (1956) (*The Bright Halfyear*), *Neerslag* (1958) (*Sediment*), *Balans* (1962) (*Balance*), *Onderdak* (1968) (*Shelter*), *Kruis of Munt* (1973) (*Heads or Tails*), which won the South African CNA (Central News Agency) Prize; *Einder* (1977) (*Horizon*), *Bestand* (1982) (*Permanence*), *Dryfsand* (1985) (*Quicksand*), and *Rymdwang* (1987) (*Forced Rhyme*). These works are mainly concerned with the artist's craft; some of the poems have been included in *Afrikaans Poets with English Translations* (1962). Two of her short stories appear in *Kwartet* (1957) (*Quartet*).

She has received numerous awards for her work, among them the Hertzog Prize, the most prestigious Afrikaans-language prize, which she received in 1943 and again in 1971. In 1990 she received the distinguished Dutch P.C. Hooft Prize.

Her other works are: *Gedigte: 1936–1958* (1978) (*Poems: 1936–1958*), and a volume of critical essays *Voetpad van Verkenning* (1978).

▷Herzberg, Judith; Vasalis, M.

F

Fabricius, Sara Cecilia Margareta Gjörwell
▷Sandel, Cora

Faccio, Rina ▷Aleramo, Sibilla

Faderman, Lillian (born 1940)
North American lecturer and writer of books on ethnic minorities and lesbian history. Born in New York, Faderman received her BA from Berkeley in 1962 and her Ph.D. in English from the University of California at Los Angeles in 1967. She is Distinguished Professor of English at California State University, Fresno. In *Surpassing the Love of Men* (1981), a history of romantic friendship between women from the Renaissance to the present, Faderman countered the absence of lesbianism in mainstream feminist history by expanding the traditional definition of lesbian to embrace women writers who had strong emotional attachments to other women without having sexual relations with them.

Other publications include: *Scotch Verdict* (1985), about the trial of two 19th-century women whose lesbianism was not legally recognized by Victorian society, and (joint ed.), *Lesbian Feminism in Turn-of-the Century Germany* (1980). She has published two books on ethnic minorities: (joint ed.), *Speaking for Ourselves: American Ethnic Writing* (1969), and (ed.), *From the Barrio: A Chicano Anthology* (1973).
▷Lesbian feminist criticism

Fage, Mary ▷*Fames Roule* (1657)

Fagnan, Marie-Antoinette (died 1770)
French prose fiction writer. Of Fagnan herself little is known, but her parodic fairy tales are especially interesting. The lewd tone of the scatalogical *Miroir des princesses orientales* (1755) (*Mirror of the Eastern Princesses*) and the incisively ironic style of her other works mark a departure from the stereotypes of conventionally feminine writing prevalent in the period. Her other tales include: *Kanor, conte traduit du sauvage* (1750) (*Kanor, a Tale from the Wild*), set by the River Amazon; *Histoire et aventures de Mylord Pet* (1755) (*The History and Adventures of Mylord Pet*), and *Minet-Bleu et Louvette* (1768) (*Blue-kitty and Little Wolf*), which takes the same theme as Perrault's *Riquet à la houppe* (*Riquet with a Feather in his Cap*): a pair of lovers are handicapped by the fact that for five days a week the woman is ugly but intelligent, and prone to falling in love, while the man is handsome but stupid and insensitive. On the remaining two days the situation is reversed.
Bib: Robert R., *Contes parodiques du XVIIIième siècle.*

Fairbairns, Zoë Ann (born 1948)
English novelist, short story writer and journalist. An overtly political writer, in her early fiction Fairbairns highlights the forms of contract which exist, or should exist, between the individual and the community. Later novels address women's issues by interweaving contemporary and historical narratives. *Stand We at Last* (1983) is a family saga set against the backdrop of the women's movement from the late 19th century onwards. The conflict between societal pressures and feminist consciousness is explored in *Here Today* (1984) and *Closing* (1987). Other novels include: *Benefits: A Novel* (1988) and *More Tales I Tell My Mother* (1987). She has also contributed to the anthology ▷*Tales I Tell My Mother* (1978). Non-fiction writings include: *Study War No More: Military Involvement in British Universities* (1974).
▷Maitland, Sara; *One Foot on the Mountain*

Fakunle, Funmilayo
Nigerian novelist. A Yoruba from the south-western town of Oshogbo, she aims her three novels specifically at a local audience. Fakunle is a trained sociologist, and her subjects are the everyday stuff of life in contemporary Yoruba families. Written with a strong didactic purpose, her novels *The Sacrificial Child* (1978), *Chasing the Shadow* (1980) and *Chance or Destiny?* (1983) deal with such issues as ▷infertility, ▷polygamy, conflicting religious beliefs, intra-ethnic suspicion, seduction and sexual jealousy, marriage, the influence of the extended family, superstition and ▷witchcraft, corruption and ostentatious living, all within a framework of romantic idealism and Christian morality.
▷Romantic fiction (West Africa)

Falco, João ▷Lisboa, Irene do Céu Viera

Falcón, Lidia (born 1935)
Spanish feminist writer. Born in Madrid, Falcón is a major intellectual and activist leader of Spanish feminism. She founded Spain's first Feminist Party in 1979, and also the feminist magazine, *Vindicación feminista* (1976–79) (*A Vindication of Feminism*). Her novels, such as *Los hijos de los vencidos* (1979) (*Children of the Defeated*) and *En el infierno* (*Ser mujer en las cárceles de España*) (1977) (*In Hell: A Woman in Spanish Jails*), have an autobiographical basis. One of her main themes is the exploitation of women by men. Falcón has also written feminist plays.

Falconnet, Françoise-Cécile de Chaumont (1738–1819)
French dramatist. Born in Nancy, she was educated by her mother. Her father had been in the service of the Polish king. Ambroise Falconnet, a member of the judiciary in Paris, was her second husband. Her plays – two comedies, *La Folle Enchère* (1771) (*The Crazy Offer*) and *L'Heureuse Rencontre* (1771) (*The Happy Meeting*), and the unusually sub-titled *L'Amour à Tempé, pastorale érotique* (1773) (*Love at Tempé, an Erotic Pastoral*) – were well-received. Prudhomme (see bibliography) refers to a large body of poetry which does not appear in current bibliographies.
Bib: Prudhomme, L.M., *Répertoire universel historique et biographique des femmes célèbres.*

Fall, Kiné Kirama

Senegalese poet. She began to write some years after leaving school to get married at fourteen. With the encouragement of the ▷*Négritude* poet Leopold Senghor, who prefaced her book, she published a collection of poems under the title *Chants de la rivière fraîche* (1976) (*Songs of the Pure River*). Her poetry celebrates the natural world, but also expresses a longing for love, suggesting dissatisfaction with polygamous marriage.

Fallaci, Oriana (born 1930)

Italian journalist and novelist. As a reporter, she has worked for *Il Mattino*, been a special correspondent for the journals *Epoca* and *L'Europeo*, and has written articles for *The New York Times*, *Corriere della sera* and *Life*. She has won several awards for her journalism in Italy, and in North America where she is now based. She has worked as a university lecturer in Yale, Harvard, Chicago and Columbia. Fallaci has written repeatedly on the nature of war; sometimes it is the central focus, as in her most recent novel, ▷*Insciallah* (1990), set in Beirut (the title means 'If God Is Willing'); sometimes she accords the theme significance in novels which ostensibly cover other ground. *Lettera a un bambino mai nato* (1975) (▷*Letter to a Child Never Born*), for example, deals with the nature of life, the issues of abortion and motherhood, and death. *Penelope alla guerra* (1964) (*Penelope At War*, translated into English in 1966), is another novel which deals with this theme. *Niente e cosi sia* (1969) (*Nothingness: So be It*), and *Intervista con la storia* (1974) (*An Interview with History*), both deal with war and with the nature and abuse of power. The nature of relationships between the sexes is also a recurrent theme in Fallaci's work, as we see in *Il sesso inutile* (1964) (*The Useless Sex*), *Letter to a Child Never Born* and *Un uomo* (1980) (*A Man*, translated into English in 1981). While Fallaci is obviously a writer who sees social analysis as part of her brief, and is willing to write on the politics of sexuality, power and parties, she is also a poetic writer who traffics in the currency of dream, illusion and fantasy.

Her other works include: *Gli antipatici* (1965) (*Limelighters*, translated into English in 1967) and *Se il sole muore* (1965) (*Should the Sun Die*, translated into English in 1967).

'Fallen Woman, The'

A number of British women writers addressed the subject of the 'fallen woman' in the latter half of the 19th century. Sympathetic representations include ▷Elizabeth Gaskell's ▷*Ruth*, and Marion Erle in ▷Elizabeth Barrett Browning's ▷*Aurora Leigh*. Both these works brought attention to the sexual double standard, and both figure maternal love as the path of redemption for the woman. In other novels such as ▷Mrs Henry Wood's ▷*East Lynne* the errant woman was cruelly punished in the course of the narrative, serving as a warning to women readers.

▷'Castaway, A'; *Father and Daughter, The*; Orphans; Sentiment and sentimental; Webster, Augusta

Fall Franza, Der (1979) (The Franza Case)

A novel by the Austrian writer ▷Ingeborg Bachmann, the first of a trilogy entitled *Todesarten* (*Ways of Dying*). It was published five years after her death. It is the story of a 'murderous marriage' in which Franziska, wife of a successful Viennese psychiatrist, is destroyed by her husband who surreptitiously reduces her to being a 'case study'. Even when she escapes, and travels through Egypt and the Sudan with her brother, Franziska cannot shake off the choking grasp of her husband's influence. The novel is Bachmann's most haunting evocation of a woman victimized.

Fames Roule (1657)

Collection of acrostic poems written by Mary Fage. All that is known of Fage is, as she tells us, that she was the 'wife of Robert Fage, the younger, gentleman'. Apparently of the middle class, Fage seems to have been fairly well-educated. Her work provides an exaggerated example of ▷patronage-seeking by a Renaissance author. *Fames Roule* consists of 420 verses in which Fage presents 'the names of . . . King Charles, his Royal Queen Mary, and his most hopefull posterity: Together with the names of the Dukes, Marquesses, Earles, Viscounts, Bishops, Barons, Privie Counsellors, Knyghts of the Garter, and Judges of his three renowned Kingdomes, England, Scotland, and Ireland: Anagrammiz'd and espressed by acrosticke line on their names'. The incredible number of addresses, combined with the excessiveness of Fage's poetic flattery, suggest that she was a professional writer.

Familiar Letters Written by Mrs Sarah Osborn, and Miss Susanna Anthony (1807)

These letters, written between 1740 and 1779, are a major contribution to studies of women's epistolary exchanges and to women's roles in late 18th-century North American religious circles. The early exchanges acted as impetus to the founding of a religious revival by ▷Sarah Haggar Wheaten Osborn in the 1760s, modelled on the Great Awakening. Out of an exchange of life-histories, the two women developed an egalitarian religious philosophy that, while traditional in its Puritan adherence to submission and humility, moved far beyond the earlier Awakening to include women and African-Americans in the revival meetings.

▷*Life and Character of Miss Susanna Anthony, The*; Early North American letters

Familie Seldorf, Die. Eine Erzählung aus der französischen Revolution (2 vols) (1795–1796) (The Seldorf Family. A Story from the French Revolution)

A novel by the German author ▷Therese Huber (1764–1829). Although the plot develops against the background of the French Revolution (1789), this is not a historical novel. Instead, the story shows how political strife and social turmoil affect women who are hopelessly dependent on men and a stable social fabric. The heroine, Sara Seldorf, is very nearly destroyed as she tries to face dilemmas of morality and loyalty when the political events in France polarize and divide her friends and family. The novel makes an important early statement about the situation of women in a society determined by men.

Family sagas (Iceland)
In the family sagas, from around the year 1000, women writers are mentioned, such as Thórdís skjaldkvinde på Gnupufell (Thórdis the Scaldic Woman at Gnupufell), Thorfinna skjaldkvinde på Thorvaldsstadur (Thorfinna the Scaldic Woman at Thorvaldsstadur) and Thorúnn skjaldkvinde i Surtsdal (Thorúnn the Scaldic Woman of Surtsvalley). However, none of their works have been preserved for posterity.

Family Sayings (1967)
Translated into English from Italian writer ▷Natalia Ginzburg's *Lessico famigliare* (1963). This novel is perhaps the author's most famous work, and won the Strega Prize of 1963. It is a novel which deals, in essence, with Ginzburg's own life in the years before, during, and after World War II. This is a close examination of a family and, as the title suggests, its language. It is, not surprisingly, very much a 'spoken' text, one in which dialogue is of great importance. The exploration of a personalized family vocabulary is at the heart of the novel. Certain characters, such as the authoritarian father, recur in Ginzburg's fiction. The institution of the family is neither sanitized nor glamorized in this novel, which depicts both violent family quarrels and warm reconciliations.

Family Spear (1973)
Play by the Ugandan poet and dramatist ▷Elvania Namukwaya Zirimu. *Family Spear* describes the slow erosion of family ties, and conflict between the generations, in a society in which traditionally the father has the right of the first night with his son's new bride.

Fanshawe, Lady Ann (1625–1680)
English memoirist, whose main concern was to record lineage for her son. In her opening address she advises him to 'endeavour to be as innocent as a dove, but as wise as a Serpent'. She records her life with the statesman and translator Richard Fanshawe, who worked for the return of Charles II, and briefly held the post of ambassador to Madrid. Much of the interest of the diary is from the effect of historical circumstances on her life.
▷Halkett, Lady Ann.
Bib: Loftis, John (ed.); *The Memoirs of Anne, Lady Halkett and Ann, Lady Fanshawe*.

Fantasia (1883) ▷*Fantasy*

Fantasia: An Algerian Cavalcade (1989)
English translation of *L'Amour, la fantasia* (1985) by Algerian novelist ▷Assia Djebar. After an interruption of many years, during which Djebar made films and taught history at the University of Algiers, she resumed her writing with this novel, the first part of a proposed quartet about Algerian women, past and present. It is partly autobiographical, for Djebar draws upon her own life and her subsequent experience in the city of her homeland and in Paris, equating writing with the act of love. But the novel has many voices; the 'Fantasia' in the title refers to the patterned exercises of the Algerian cavalry, and also to a contrapuntal European musical form that suggests an improvisational character. The parts of the novel are punctuated with the sounds of old indigenous tunes; an air on the *nay* (the Arab flute) closes the novel, mixing old memories and modern fears.

The voices from the past are drawn from meticulous research into the memoirs of both soldiers and fellow-travellers of the invading French army of 1830, as well as official accounts in Arabic, French, Turkish, and sometimes Spanish. She includes a famous incident of 1845, when a whole tribe suffocated in mountain caves, where they had taken refuge. It is reconstructed from an account published in a Spanish newspaper, written by a Spanish officer fighting with the French Army. The Spaniard describes the flames, 200 feet high, enveloping the El-Kantara promontory. The soldiers, he states, shoved wood into the cave like into an oven to keep the furnaces stoked throughout the night.

From the detailed accounts of battles, raids and sieges, she picks out what happens to the women, often raped and robbed, not only by the invading French soldiers, but by men of their own warring tribes.

Of the voices of the present, she picks those of the peasant women, highlighting their part in the war of independence (1954–1962). Many are the voices of widows or bereaved mothers, some the proud relatives of the few survivors. When the fighting is over, men and women resume their former, polarized positions, and a widow speaks: 'I wait amid the scattered sheef of sounds, I wait, foreseeing the inevitable moment when the mare's hoof [of the old cavalry dance] will strike down any woman who dares to stand up freely, will trample all life that comes out into the sunlight to dance . . . I hear the death cry in the *Fantasia*.'

Fantastical literature (Italy)
An umbrella term, used to describe writings as varied as those of ▷Grazia Deledda and ▷Gianna Manzini. It refers, most obviously, to a non-realist mode of representation. It may include, for instance, an extensive use of mythological features, or an attempt to disorientate the reader by setting the narrative in a strange, unrecognizable locus or by playing with shifting time-frames. Other writers defined as fantastical include ▷Anna Banti, ▷Oriana

Fallaci, ▷Elsa Morante and ▷Anna Maria Ortese.
▷Magic realism

Fantástico no Feminino (1985) (Fantastic in the Feminine)

Since the 1974 revolution women writers in Portugal have been drawn to science fiction and fantasy literature as a way of commenting on women and society. This volume contains examples of work in this area by fourteen well-known writers. One of the best selections in the volume is by new writer Clara Pinto Correia (born 1960), who is also a biologist. Her 'A Molécula do Prazer' ('The Pleasure Molecule'), in the form of a conference paper, parodies the bizarre scientific findings of the academic community.

Fantasy (1890)

Translated from the Italian Fantasia (1883). A novel, by ▷Matilde Serao, in the ▷sentimental genre, it contains many references to Flaubert's Madame Bovary (1857). Like its French predecessor, it concentrates in part on the effect of an inferior education on female sensibility. It departs from the French novel, however, in that it tells the story of the passionate relationship between two female schoolfriends, Lucia and Caterina. Lucia is an imaginative and passionate character, while Caterina is pleasant, passive and pedestrian. Caterina marries Andrea, with whom Lucia eventually falls in love and runs away. Serao inverts Flaubert's plot here, by allowing Lucia to escape unpunished and by having Caterina, the saintly character, commit suicide. The novel also subverts Flaubert's work by making the central issue of betrayal here that of the betrayal of one female by another.

Fanthorpe, U.A. (born 1929)

English poet. A writer concerned with the hierarchies and injustices of the social system. In her first volume of poetry, Side Effects (1978), Fanthorpe treats the socially suppressed voices of psychiatric patients. Standing To (1982) looks at warfare as an analogue of work, and addresses the lives and experiences of soldiers. The poems in this volume, which address masculinity viewed from the 'woman's angle', anticipate Fanthorpe's later interest in feminity, in language as power (see Voices Off, 1984) and, in The Watching Brief (1987), with the linked issue of women and creativity. Selected Poems was published in 1986.

Farewell, Love! (1892)

Translation into English (1892) of Addio, Amore (1890), a novel by Italian writer ▷Matilde Serao. Written in the ▷romantic/▷sentimental genre, it was very popular when first published. It tells the tale of two orphaned sisters, Anna and Laura Acquaviva, both of whom fall in love with Cesare, their harsh tutor/guardian, who functions in the novel as a father-substitute. Anna marries Cesare, who then has an affair with Laura. The novel culminates in Anna's suicide. This is, in effect,

constitutes part one of a two-part story, in that Castigo (Punishment) of 1893 tells of the ensuing troubled and ill-fated relationship between Cesare and Laura. The novel is interesting for its reversal of the stereotypical femme fatale figure (Laura), and for its depiction of the female relationship here, despite the traditional plot, as one of kinship and similarity instead of opposition.

Farley, Harriet (1813–1907)

US writer, and editor of ▷The Lowell Offering from 1842 to 1845. An industrial worker in the textile mills of Lowell, Massachusetts, Farley dedicated herself to demonstrating the capabilities of ▷mill girls by editing the Offering, which published their writing. Farley concentrated the Offering on literature and refused to involve it in the Female Labor Reform Association's organizing of mill-workers, a stand for which she was criticized in ▷The Voice of Industry. Farley and other Offering contributors continued writing after the periodical's demise; her own work is collected in Shells from the Strand of the Sea of Genius (1847) and Happy Nights at Hazel Nook (1852).

Farmar, Eliza (fl 1774–1783)

North American letter-writer. Born in England, she came to North America some time during the decade preceding the American Revolution. Settling in Philadelphia, she sympathized with the Patriot cause, as the ▷'Letters of Eliza Farmar to Her Nephew' reveal; but, as a recent citizen of England, she also brought an objective eye to the war situation.

Farmer, Beverley (born 1941)

Australian novelist and short story writer. Farmer has worked as teacher and waitress and spent three years in Greece. She is a celebrated short story writer who has won several awards, including first prize in the Canberra Times National Short Story Award 1980, and the New South Wales Premier's Award for Fiction in 1984 for the short story collection Milk (1983). Home Time (1985) is her second collection of short stories.
▷Short story (Australia); Eight Voices of the Eighties

Faroese literature

Faroese literature began with the medieval ballads, but as the Faroese language only gained its orthography in 1854 and Danish was the official language until 1948, modern Faroese literature made its appearance only recently.

Modern Faroese literature has been dominated by male writers, the first and only well-known woman poet being Gudrid Helmsdal Nielsen (born 1941), who has been successful with her sensitive, ▷modernist poems in the Scandinavian tradition originating from ▷Edith Södergran (1892–1923).

There is, however, a growth in modern Faroese

culture, especially among women writers who are just beginning to articulate themselves.

Farquharson, Martha (1828–1909)
Pseudonym of Martha Finley, US children's novelist. An extraordinarily prolific writer, Farquharson was the author of nearly 100 children's novels, including *Elsie Dinsmore* (1867) and the twenty-seven succeeding Elsie novels which traced the character's life, eg *Elsie's Holidays* (1869) and *Elsie's Girlhood* (1872). Equally popular in the USA and Britain, the Elsie books were moral and religious and thus met the objections of those who devalued children's novels as entertainment. Recalling a semi-mythical US south before the Civil War, the setting and characters are as stereotyped and unrealistic as Elsie's sweetness and piety. In Elsie's overcoming adversity and finding fortune the series mirrored its effects on the author's own fortunes. Millions of readers provided Farquharson with one of the highest US authors' incomes of the 19th century.

Farrell, M.J. ▷Keane, Molly

Fascism (Italy)
From about 1925 until the demise of the fascist government at the end of World War II, fascism set back any progress made by Italian ▷feminism in earlier years, and militated against further improvements in the position of women. Women's presence in the workforce became less visible, in accordance with the pro-natalist policies of fascism. In 1938, women's employment was limited by the government to ten per cent of the national total, and it was not until the post-war period (in 1946, precisely) that Italian women were finally admitted to ▷suffrage, at least twenty years later than most of their European counterparts. Benito Mussolini's (1883–1945) government was also against women's education, and against women as educators. In 1927, women were forbidden to teach letters and philosophy in Italian secondary schools.
Bib: Caldwell, L. 'Reproducers of the Nation: Woman and the Family in Fascist Policy', *Rethinking Fascism: Capitalism, Populism and Culture*, ed. D. Forgacs, and *'Madri d'Italia': Film and Fascist Concern with Motherhood'*, *Women and Italy: Essays on Gender, Culture and History*, ed. Z.G. Barański and S.W. Vinall.

Fashion (1850)
US drama by ▷Anna Cora Mowatt, first produced in 1845. Generally considered the best US comedy of manners of the 19th century, *Fashion* employed type characters: the honest US Yankee, the (fake) fortune-hunting European aristocrat, the social-climbing US woman who valued tawdry European values and suitors over virtuous North American ones, whose essence was revealed in their names, eg Trueman, Snobson. Plot and subplot combine romantic and financial frauds – all resolved with the victory and value

assigned to worthy, upright, distinctively US character and characters.

Fashionable Novel, The (The 'Silver-fork' School)
A genre popular in Britain between 1825 and 1850. Typically, such novels concentrate on describing the lives of the wealthy and feature glamorous heroines in search of love, marriage and luxury. A significant aspect of the genre is its focus on contemporary fashion; the novels often served as handbooks on the latest styles, referring explicitly to particular London shops and dressmakers. Practitioners of the genre include ▷Susan Ferrier and ▷Catherine Gore. In *The Silver Fork School: Novels of Fashion Preceding Vanity Fair*, M.W. Rosa discusses the work of male and female 'fashionable' authors and argues that the genre reached its apotheosis in Thackeray's *Vanity Fair* (1847–8).

Fasting
A practice of self-denial commonly observed by many Hindus, Buddhists, Jains, Sikhs and Moslems in southern Asia. While fasting may have a particular purpose, such as showing respect for a god on a certain day, it can be a regular ascetic practice designed to suppress the needs of the body and enhance the search for spiritual betterment.

Father and Daughter, The (1801)
A novel by ▷Amelia Opie. Described as a 'Simple Moral Tale', it tells the story of Agnes Fitzhenry who leaves her loving father to elope with Captain Clifford. Clifford then seduces and abandons her, and Agnes returns home full of repentance. Her father, meanwhile, has gone insane as a result of her action. Agnes devotes herself to nursing him, sacrificing herself entirely. He recovers on his deathbed and blesses her, then both father and daughter die almost at the same moment and are buried together. The novel was hugely successful, running to ten editions by 1844.

Faugeres, Margaretta V. Bleecker (1771–1801)
North American poet, dramatist and essayist. Born on 11 October 1771, in Tomahanick, New York, she was the daughter of the poet and novelist ▷Ann Eliza Schuyler Bleecker and John Bleecker. Although she was born into one of New York's most notable families, she suffered repeated tragedies – her mother's death when she was twelve, her father's rejection of her marriage to Peter Faugeres in 1792, and an abusive marriage partner who squandered the Bleecker family fortune. Drawn to Peter's revolutionary ideals, she soon learned that the man was quite different from his political espousals. Four years after their marriage, Peter abandoned her and their daughter. After struggling against dire poverty, she became a schoolteacher in New Brunswick and later in Brooklyn. She could not

overcome the toll of numerous hardships, however, and died on 14 January 1801 at the age of twenty-nine. Yet in her short life she accomplished a great deal. As a tribute to her mother, she collected and published ▷ *The Posthumous Works of Ann Eliza Bleecker* (1793), to which she appended several of her own creative works. In the 1790s she published poetry in magazines such as the *New York Monthly*, which reflected her fundamental belief in human liberty. But her greatest work was a tragedy entitled ▷*Belisarius* (1795) – the drama is a testimony to her political ideals as well as her literary talents.

Fauques, Marianne-Agnès Pillement, Dame de (1721–1773)

French prose fiction writer. Born in Avignon, and forced to become a nun by her family, she succeeded in having her vows annulled after ten years of convent life. Rejected by her family, she moved to Paris, where she began writing. The first three of her novels are presented as exotic in origin: *Le Triomphe de l'amitié*, 'translated from the Greek' (1751) (*The Triumph of Friendship*); *Abbassaï*, 'an Oriental story' (1753); and the *Contes du sérail*, 'translated from the Turkish' (1753) (*Tales from the Harem*). Her other works focus more on contemporary morals: *Les Préjugés trop bravés et trop suivis* (1755) (*Prejudices Defied: Prejudice Sustained*), *La Dernière Guerre des bêtes* (1758), (*The Animals' Last War*) and *Le danger des préjugés, ou les mémoires de Mlle d'Oran* (1774) (*The Danger of Prejudices, or The Memoirs of Mlle d'Oran*). She also wrote on contemporary figures: *Frédéric le Grand au temple de l'Immortalité* (1758) (*Frederick the Great at the Temple of Immortality*), *L'Histoire de Mme la marquise de Pompadour* (1759) (*The Story of Mme de Pompadour*). Her last published work was a collection of short prose pieces, *Dialogues moraux et amusans* (1777) (*Entertaining Dialogues*).

Fauset, Jessie Redmon (1882–1961)

US novelist, short-story writer, poet and essayist. Fauset was born in New Jersey to a poor African-American family, and her father was a Methodist Episcopal minister. In 1905 she graduated from Cornell University with honours, and began teaching French at a public high school in Washington, DC, the following year. In 1919 she earned a Master's degree at the University of Pennsylvania. She moved to New York and became literary editor of *Crisis*, an African-American journal, giving her an important publishing role in the ▷Harlem Renaissance.

There is Confusion (1924) addresses the limited vocational opportunities African-American women, like herself, face. It implies that African-Americans achieve racial superiority through their endurance of discrimination. *Chinaberry Tree* (1931), set in a black community in a New Jersey village, revises notions of the values of life, arguing that the facts of life are more important than social rules of living; it exposes society's limited and limiting false values.

Bib. Sylvander, C.W., *Jessie Redmon Fauset, Black American Writer*.

Fear of Flying (1973)

US novel by ▷Erica Jong which is considered a milestone for US fiction. It portrays a sexually liberated woman, chronicling her adventures in blunt, earthy language. Isadora Wing escapes the socially-prescribed roles for women through sex. She wants to experience sex without guilt, but equates feelings of guilt with being a woman and being Jewish. Writing poetry helps her to escape her sense of persecution. Poetically, she violates tradition by writing about women's sexuality. Sexually, she violates the taboos of womanhood. Nevertheless, the novel emphasizes a lack of fulfillment, and Jong suggests that women's freedom is not found in imitating male roles.

Feinstein, Elaine (born 1930)

English poet, novelist and translator. Best-known as a poet and a translator of high calibre, she published her first book of poems, *In a Green Eye*, in 1966. She is also the author of eight novels. Feinstein situates her work within the US rather than the English tradition of poetry, including ▷Emily Dickinson, Wallace Stevens (1879–1955) and William Carlos Williams (1883–1963). The latter's influence is evident in Feinstein's belief that poetry is about 'trying to make sense of experience'. She has also been heavily influenced by the work of the Russian poet ▷Marina Tsvetayeva. She translated *The Selected Poems of Marina Tsvetayeva* in 1971 and in 1987 published her biography, *A Captive Lion*. Feinstein's work is often marked by her strong Jewish identification, in, for example, *The Celebrants and Other Poems* (1973) and the novels *The Ecstasy of Dr Miriam Garner* (1976), *The Shadow Master* (1978) and *The Border* (1984). Other works include *Some Unease and Angels: Selected Poems* (1977), *Bessie Smith* (1985) and *Badlands* (1986).

▷Tennant, Emma

Felix Holt, the Radical (1866)

A novel by ▷George Eliot. It is set in 1832, the year of the new ▷Reform Bill and a period of intense political ferment. Felix Holt is a talented, idealistic and initially egotistical young man who, though well-educated chooses the life of an artisan, aiming to stir his fellow workers to a sense of their own worth. Harold Transome is also a radical politician, but he pursues a more conventional political career. The two men are rivals for Esther Lyon, the heroine of the story who, like so many of Eliot's female characters, struggles to reconcile her public and private selves. Eventually, Esther opts for poverty with Felix rather than financial comfort with Harold. The other central female figure in the novel is Mrs Transome, who conceals her son's illegitimacy (he is in fact the son of the hated lawyer, Jermyn). Although Mrs Transome is a demanding and arrogant woman, she suffers principally through her relationships with men, finding that her emotional investments both in Jermyn and Harold are not reciprocated. The novel's treatment of male–female relations is centrally concerned with the different ways in which the sexes exert power, yet, despite its title, the novel does not promote radical politics of any kind, but reflects the conservatism of Eliot's later years.

Fell, Alison (born 1944)

Alison Fell

Scottish poet, novelist and journalist. Co-founder of the feminist Women's Street Theatre group. Fell's writings, from journalism to poetry, articulate a strong Marxist-feminist orientation. Her poetry additionally voices the concerns of others (groups and individuals) confronting political oppression. Poetry collections include: *At the Edge of Ice* (1983), *Kisses for Mayakovsky* (1984). *Every Move You Make* (1984) is an autobiographical novel, which was followed by *The Bad Box* (1987). Fell has also written a children's novel, *The Grey Dancer* (1981), and edited the anthology of short stories by women *The Seven Deadly Sins* (1988) as well as *Hard Feelings: Fiction and Poetry from Spare Rib* (1979).
▷ *One Foot on the Mountain*

Fell, Margaret (1614–1702)

English ▷ Quaker writer. Fell was from Lancashire, and after her conversion by George Fox (1624–1691) she made her house, Swarthmore Hall, a centre of Quaker activity. Fox later became her second husband, and she shared imprisonment with him in Lancaster gaol. Fell was a prolific pamphleteer, and continued to take an active part in the Quaker movement, despite its segregation of women after the Restoration. Like other Quakers and sectaries, she wrote in favour

of women's preaching, and published *Women's Speaking Justified* (1666) in the difficult years after the Restoration of Charles II, whom she visited in person. She argued that 'women were the first that preached tidings of the Resurrection, and were sent by Christs own command.'

Other publications: *A Testimonie of the Touch-stone* (1656); *A Loving Salutation to the sted of Abraham and the Jewes*; *An Evident Demonstration to God's Elect* (1660); *This is to the Clergy* (1660), and *A Brief Collection of Remarkable Passages . . . Relating to Margaret Fell* (1710).

Felman, Shoshana

North American ▷ poststructuralist Lacanian feminist theorist. Felman is Professor of French and Comparative Literature at Yale University. Influential in reintroducing Freud, via Jacques Lacan's re-reading, (▷ psychoanalysis), to a feminist audience, Felman's work is more than a good exegesis of Lacan's difficult theories. It employs Lacanian theory to re-read literary texts from a feminist perspective in ways that expose the patriarchal blind spots in traditional literary criticism and its concept of knowledge. A good example is 'Woman and Madness: the Critical Phallacy' (*Diacritics* 5, 1975), which shows how critics of Honoré de Balzac's (1799–1850) *Adieu* have historically effaced the role of the woman in the story, thereby associating the author's 'realism' with men and reason. Women are displaced beyond the 'real' world, and relegated to the realm of madness and ignorance.

Felman's alternative reading of *Adieu* demonstrates how madness as a concept disrupts the boundary between knowledge and ignorance, revealing them to be massively contradictory and unstable categories; by extension, so are the definitions of gender difference they produce. Felman is editor of *Literature and Psychoanalysis: the Question of Reading: Otherwise* (1982), and author of *The Literary Speech Act: Don Juan with Austin, or Seduction in Two Languages* (1983), *Writing and Madness: Literature/Philosophy/ Psychoanalysis* (1985) and *Jacques Lacan and the Adventure of Insight: Psychoanalysis in Contemporary Culture* (1987).

Female Has Seven Sins (1990)

This work by Japanese writer Horiba Kiyoko (born 1930) is a history of the role of women in Okinawa prefecture. It was awarded the Aoyama Nao Prize. Inhabitants of Okinawa have been oppressed throughout the district's existence. Women in particular have suffered from customs such as *Senkotu* and *Totome* which discriminate against them. *Senkotu* is the custom whereby a woman has to clean the corpse of a family member a couple of years after burial. *Totome* refers to a family mortuary tablet on which only the names of men are inscribed. Both customs are deeply connected with the patriarchal system in Okinawa. Women started the movement to abolish Totome in 1980, and after efforts by the women's movement, Senkotu began to be phased-out in pre-war Japan. Horiba describes in detail how the women's movement is urging the Japanese to overcome the conventional view of the female role in society.

Female Man, The (1975)
US novel. In this ▷science-fiction story ▷Joanna Russ portrays five alternate realities, examining polarities such as the individual and society, and women and men. On contemporary earth, women are losing their fight for equality, and they gain their personhood by becoming a female man. On an alternate contemporary earth, women gain their sense of existence from men, indulging in fantasy to escape from social constraints. On one future world, women create their own society apart from men; they are violent warriors waging biological warfare on men. On another future world, Whileaway, individual women's needs are met with minimal social constraints, and men are perceived as patronizing aliens. The narrator's world contains all possibilities of past, present, and future. She enables women to be heroes and find fulfilment regardless of social constraints.

Female Quixote, The (1752)
English writer ▷Charlotte Lennox's best-known fiction. It parodies and mocks romance, using the heroine, Arabella.

Female Quixotism: Exhibited in the Romantic Opinions and Extravagant Adventures of Dorcasina Sheldon (1801)
Novel by North American writer ▷Tabitha Gilman Tenney. Tenney's novel satirizes the limited education available to upper-class young women in 18th-century North America, and the sentimental fiction that aggrandizes those limitations while leaving women in a state of perpetual childishness. The well-developed characterization of Dorcasina Sheldon, whose choices in life are shaped by her reliance upon the dictates of popular sentimentalism, exposes both the vapidity of such dictates and the severe consequences of believing in this kind of 'education'. Dorcasina's life is a model of the foolishness of advocating innocence into perpetuity for women. A bitingly witty and deeply textured satire, the novel broadens its sphere to include the society that values only innocence and ignorance in the female sex.

Female traditions
These are accounts of women's literature and history, where women are included by virtue of their sex, not their feminism. The construction of separate female traditions is a common project in North American feminist criticism of the mid-1970s. Representative examples from the white mainstream feminist canon are ▷Elaine Showalter's *A Literature of Their Own* (1977), and ▷Sandra Gilbert and ▷Susan Gubar's *The Madwoman in the Attic* (1979). At the time these books appeared in North America, black and lesbian critics criticized the lack of attention to,

and in some cases the absence of, their different traditions. In the 1980s, feminist critics of various sexual and ethnic groups began to differentiate female traditions from feminist ones.
▷Black feminist criticism; Lesbian feminist criticism; Carby, Hazel V.

Feminine/feminist journalism (France)
In the 19th century, women increasingly turned to journalism, even if only to write for the fashion journals, of which there were a considerable number. The first feminist journal of the period was the short-lived *Athénée des Dames* (1808), a journal run, and subscribed to, soley by women. Its mainstay was Sophie de Senneterre and it also received contributions from ▷Constance de Salm-Dyck. The purpose of the journal was to instruct as well as to entertain, and it demanded that women should have access to better education; thus they might cease merely to be charming, flowery creatures, and become men's intellectual equals. The *Athénée* was a remarkably radical publication for its time, but infinitely more radical was the *Tribune des femmes (Women's Tribune)*. This working-class feminist paper appeared between 1832 and 1834, and was run by proletarian ▷Saint-Simonian feminists who were growing disenchanted with Enfantin. The *Tribune* was mainly edited by ▷Suzanne Voilquin. The women who wrote for the journal, including Pauline Roland, Jeanne Déroin, and Désirée Veret, signed articles with their first names only, and had an extremely strong sense of class solidarity. They were ridiculed by male journalistic contemporaries, and were also disliked by the more moderate women journalists of the bourgeois, Christian ▷*Journal des Dames (Ladies' Journal)*, a paper which the Saint-Simoniennes in their turn mocked for being elitist and frivolous. In fact, the *Journal des Femmes (The Women's Journal)* a relatively feminist publication which was launched in 1832, was initially edited exclusively by women and only became a trivial '*journal de modes*' (fashion journals) between 1835 and 1838. Its contributors included ▷Louise Belloc, ▷Alida de Savignac, ▷Anaïs Ségalas, ▷Amable Tastu and ▷Constance Aubert, all of whom, according to Evelyne Sullerot, were driven to journalism by an almost aggressive desire to educate and moralize, which was related to the intellectual frustrations imposed upon their sex by society. Another bourgeois feminist paper of the period was the *Gazette des Femmes (Women's Gazette)*, which was run by both men and women, appeared every month between 1836 and 1838, and campaigned for equal civil, educational and professional rights for women. Meetings of the *Gazette*'s editors and subscribers took place on Thursdays and were attended by, among others, ▷Hortense Allart, ▷Flora Tristan, Anaïs Ségalas and ▷Eugénie Niboyet. Niboyet subsequently edited the *Voix des femmes (Women's Voice)*, which came out six days a week between March and June of 1848 and contained, among other things

articles by women who had previously written for the *Tribune*, including Voilquin and Roland.

In the second half of the 19th century, feminist publications flourished. The most important of these was *Le Droit des femmes* (1869–91) *(The Rights of Women)* , edited by Léon Richer and ▷Maria Deraismes. The aim of the paper, which received articles from ▷André Léo and ▷Julie Daubié, was to promote the civil emancipation and political education of women, but it avoided fully addressing the issue of feminine suffrage – a fact which encouraged ▷Hubertine Auclert to set up the suffragist *La Citoyenne (The Women Citizen)* in 1881. The last decade of the century witnessed the publication of even more feminist papers, the best-known of which is *La Fronde (The Insurrectionist)*, a Republican and secularist daily that dealt with a wide range of issues related to the campaign for women's rights.

▷Renneville, Madame Sophie de
Bib: Albistur, M. and Armogathe, D., *Histoire du féminisme français;* Sullerot, E., *Histoire de la presse féminine en France.*

Feminine Plural (1968)

Translation of *Le féminin pluriel* (1965), novel by french writers ▷Benoîte and ▷Flora Groult. Written by two sisters, the text takes the form of a double first-person narrative which recounts the thoughts of two women friends who are in love with the same man. Through this triangular relationship, the novel considers the different kinds of women's love, and the plurality of the female experience. The narrative itself combines the style of popular fiction with frequent allusions to canonical literary texts.

Féminin pluriel, Le (1965) ▷Feminine Plural

Feminism

Australia: Australian women were among the first in the world to achieve the vote, federally in 1901, in South Australia in 1894, and in the other states at varying times. Many 19th-century Australian feminist activists were either writers or were concerned in other ways with the literary scene. They include ▷Louisa Lawson, Rose Scott, (1847–1925) Vida Goldstein (1869–1949) Alice Henry (1857–1943), ▷Catherine Helen Spence, ▷Miles Franklin, Adela Pankhurst Walsh (1888–?), ▷Jean Devanny (1894–1962), and Jessie Street (1889–1970).

Recent feminist accounts of Australian experience form the background to feminist works of fiction and feminist literary criticism. These include *Damned Whores and God's Police* (1975) by Anne Summers (born 1945), ▷ *The Real Matilda: Women and Identity in Australia, 1788–1975* (1976) by Miriam Dixson, *The World Moves Slowly* (1977), a documentary history illustrating many of the arguments of Summers and Dixson, *My Wife, My Daughter and Poor Mary Ann* (1975) by Beverley Kingston (born 1941), *Uphill All the Way* (1980) by Kay Daniels, and *Women's Role in Aboriginal Society* (1970), edited by Fay Gale.

19th-century Britain: The stereotypical image of Victorian womanhood as passive, self-sacrificing and contented ignores the wide-ranging efforts and achievements of scores of activist women. 19th-century campaigns for women's ▷suffrage, better ▷education, social ▷reform and wider vocational opportunities brought women together in radical circles. Although 'feminist' was not a term in general use, we may use it to describe such writers as ▷Lucy Aikin, ▷Mathilde Blind, ▷Barbara Bodichon, ▷Mona Caird, ▷Sarah Grand, ▷Harriet Martineau, ▷Elizabeth Wolstenholme-Elmy and others. All of them were passionately concerned with the position of women in society, and published works which exposed the hypocrisies, and protested against the injustices, of Victorian patriarchy. For the most part, however, Victorian feminism was a solidly middle-class movement which did not engage with wider analyses of social structures. It also rarely challenged the dominant view that men and women are *essentially* different, and many feminists still felt that motherhood was woman's supreme function in life. Campaigns around issues of sexuality generally aimed to curtail male sexuality rather than free female libido. For many feminists religion was a strong motivating force.

▷'Woman Question, The'; Bethan-Edwards, Matilda; Norton, Caroline; Procter, Adelaide; Webster, Augusta
Caribbean: In the Caribbean context the use of the term 'feminism' or 'feminist' in relation to women's writing has been questioned. Frequently the ideology of feminism has stemmed from North American or western European theories; there is a danger, therefore, in respect of women's writing from previously colonized regions, of this language becoming another form of cultural imperialism. This debate is discussed at length in the Preface to ▷ *Out of the Kumbla: Caribbean Women and Literature*, in an introductory dialogue entitled 'Talking it Over: Women, Writing and Feminism', pp. ix–xix.
Italy: The feminist movement was active in Italy during the post-Unification period (▷ *Risorgimento*), but it was somewhat less organized than its European equivalents, and was restricted in its appeal, which was, to begin with, largely confined to the middle classes, and to northern Italy. It was middle-class women entering the workforce in the 1870s who first began to be aware of being disadvantaged in terms of pay and conditions on the grounds of sex. By 1911 various women's groups had embarked on ambitious programmes for women's education, setting up nurseries, libraries, summer schools, and evening classes for women workers. During World War I, women became a significant part of the Italian working class, increasingly politicized, involved in unions and strikes. The progress of organized feminism in Italy was slow but sure, until the advent of ▷fascism. In the post-war period, the Italian feminist movement has been one of the most active in Western Europe. The divorce law was passed in 1970, contraception

advertising allowed in 1971, abortion legalized in 1973 and family law revised in 1975.
Bib: Caldwell, L., 'Italian Feminism: Some Considerations', *Women and Italy: Essays on Gender, Culture and History*, ed. Z.G. Barański and S.W. Vinall.

Feminist literary criticism (Australia)
▷Germaine Greer, with *The Female Eunuch* (1970), is the most notable Australian feminist writer, but any listing must include Carole Ferrier, editor of ▷*Hecate* and of ▷*Gender, Politics and Fiction* (1985); Susan Sheridan, who has written many articles on colonial women's fiction and has published a critical book on ▷Christina Stead; Susan Magarey, Elizabeth Webby, ▷Dale Spender, Helen Daniels, Kay Schaffer, Bronwen Levy, Gillian Whitlock, Delys Bird, Brenda Walker, and many others. Specific books on feminist literary issues also include *Exiles at Home: Australian Women Writers 1925–1945* (1981) ▷Drusilla Modjeska, *Who Is She? Images of Woman in Australian Fiction* (1983), edited by Shirley Walker, ▷*Poetry and Gender* (1989), edited by Brenda Walker and David Brooks, ▷*A Bright and Fiery Troop* (1988), edited by Debra Adelaide, *Contemporary Australian Women Writers*, by Pam Gilbert, *Women and the Bush: Forces of Desire in the Australian Cultural Tradition* (1988), by Kay Schaffer, and *Writing a New World: Two Centuries of Australian Women Writers* (1988), by Dale Spender.

Feminist Press, The (1970)
US publisher. Founded in 1970, The Feminist Press is a non-profit-making educational and publishing organization, dedicated to eliminating sexual stereotypes in books and schools, and to providing a vision of a more humane society. The press began by publishing literature of working-class African-American and Anglo-American women, including ▷Josephine Herbst, ▷Edith Summers Kelley, ▷Meridel Le Sueur, ▷Tillie Olsen, and ▷Agnes Smedley. The press also publishes portraits of what it means to grow up female, and the writers of these portraits include ▷Mary Austin, ▷Paule Marshall and ▷Jo Sinclair. Other works by writers like ▷Susan Glaspell and ▷Helen Hull focus on friendships between women. The press is recognized for publishing reprint editions of many rediscovered 19th-century North American writers.

Feminist publishing (Britain)
The history of feminist publishing in Britain can be traced back to the mid-19th century, when Emily Faithfull founded the Victoria Press (1860), going on to co-found, with Emma Anne Paterson, the Women's Printing Society in 1876. The latter had a distinct agenda with clearly defined feminist goals. The women's ▷suffrage movement had the greatest generating effect for feminist publishing. The Woman's Press was responsible for publishing the work of the Women's Freedom League, and the Women Writers' Suffrage League, founded in 1908 by ▷Cicely Hamilton and Bessie Hatton, published many pamphlets for the suffrage cause – most notably ▷May Sinclair's 'Feminism' (1912). In the 1920s, the small press movement had a key role in the publication of work by women ▷modernists, but the main period of heightened activity runs parallel to the development of feminism and feminist criticism. The rediscovery of a neglected corpus of women's writing has demanded that numerous texts be republished, and in Britain the three main feminist publishers of both contemporary and earlier material are Pandora (which closed in the early 1990s), Virago and The Women's Press. Sheba and Onlywomen Press have also been very important as publishers of black, lesbian and working-class writing by women.

Feminization
US term of cultural criticism. Introduced by Ann Douglas in *The Feminization of American Culture* (1977), it works off traditional distinctions between high culture and popular literature. Douglas describes the 19th century as a period when popular women writers and clergymen combined – and confused – the roles of religion and literature, promoting traditional values and thereby 'feminizing' culture.

Femme dans le monde moderne, La (1970)
▷*Women, Society and Change* (1971)

Femme rompue, La (1968) ▷*Woman Destroyed, The*

Femmes algériennes dans la guerre, Les (1991) (*Algerian Women in the War*)
A study of the role of women in the war of liberation, by Algerian writer ▷Djamila Amrane. Amrane's research is based on two sources: on the file of 10,949 militant women, registered in the Ministère des Anciens Moudjahidines, and on 88 interviews in French and Algerian Arabic. She also includes a large number of Berber poems (many in the Berber language as well as in translation). The work is illustrated with photographs, and she also uses letters, articles, etc. Her work starts with women in the 1950s, at the beginning of the women's movement, and their involvement in Algerian politics. She noticed that of 10,949 militant women, only six had a specifically political (communist) background. Those involved include Algerian, French *Pieds-Noirs* (French nationals born in the Maghreb) as well as Jewish women. Amrane writes that, in contrast to the European women who went to meetings mostly attended by men, the Algerian women met each other in their homes. The work includes information on women in education, politics, family and work.

The second chapter is the main chapter, and concerns the Algerian struggle for independence. It is about the participation of women in the *maquis* (the guerrilla force in the cities) as well as in the fight for liberation, in demonstrations and in prison, based on interviews with women. Amrane shows that although the FLN (the National Liberation Front) used women as nurses or *poseuses de bombes* (bomb-carriers), it was very surprised to see them demonstrating on the street in 1960. Contrary to Franz Fanon, Amrane does not believe that the Algerian Liberation Movement was predominantly rural.

The third part of her work concerns the different kinds of women fighters, and in the fourth part she deals with *l'apres-guerre* (the aftermath of war), which is notable for the non-involvement of women. Amrane is disappointed that women have been forgotten and that the Algerian Family Code has made sure that they do not even have many rights. The situation of women at present is hardly mentioned in her book. The participation of women in the Algerian Liberation Movement is still ignored by historians as well as politicians. Amrane wants to redress the balance.

Femmes d'Alger dans leur appartement, Les (1980) (*Women of Algiers in their Apartment*)

Stories in French by Algerian ▷Assia Djebar. In her introduction the author explains that the stories were written over a period of twenty years, 1958 to 1978. In them she reworks her problem of expressing the discourse of the Arab women of Algeria in French. The female voice she attempts to catch in these stories carries back to the past, in a line of 'whispered' memories that shows the plight of women unchanging across times of war and revolution.

The life of Algerian women does not seem to change. A family living in exile in Tunis loses brothers and other male members during the war of independence, but the girl is 'inspected for marriage' by two women in the same old way. Even when she speaks out and says to the matchmakers' faces that she does not want to get married, nobody takes it into account, and preparations go on in the normal way. In another story, a girl just out of the French prison after independence finds that she, her family and the whole neighbourhood keep *Ramadan*, the month of fasting, in the old way, as if nothing had happened.

A postscript explains the source of the title story. The author tells the story of how the painter Delacroix (1789–1863), arrived in Algiers in 1832, and how the master of the harbour persuaded one of his employees, a former *rais* (captain), to allow the painter to penetrate the ▷*harem* and glimpse his 'women in their apartment'. After crossing a dark corridor, Delacroix came unexpectedly on the *harem* bathed in an almost unreal light. He later made sketches and noted down names of women, and took home articles of women's clothing. The result was his famous picture. He returned to the subject fifteen years later, and produced another version which he presented at the Salon of 1849. The author

concludes that, if it was once possible to find in the fixed image of the 'Women of Algiers' the yearning for happiness or the softness of submission, what strikes us most today is the bitterness of despair.

Feng Keng (1907–1931)

Chinese writer. A native of Guangdong province, Feng had been active in leftist student politics from an early age. She first wrote poetry to protest against the 1927 Shanghai massacre of communists and leftist sympathizers. She joined the underground Communist Party in 1929, and was arrested and executed in 1931. Feng Keng is best remembered for her realistic portrayal of the downtrodden in her short stories 'The Salt Miner' and 'The Child Pedlar'.

Feng Yuanjun (1900–1974)

Chinese writer and scholar. A native of Henan, Feng was deeply influenced by the liberal ideas of the May Fourth Movement (1919). She taught Chinese literature at various universities while publishing fiction which shocked the public by its outspoken revolt against tradition. Feng's themes were mostly love and marriage and the disparities between the ideal and reality. Feng studied at the Sorbonne and received a doctorate in literature in 1935. After returning to China, she settled at Shandong University, where she served as vice-chancellor. Her main scholarly publications include *History of Chinese Poetry, History of Chinese Literature, Short History of Chinese Classical Literature* (all co-authored with her husband, Professor Lu Kanru) and other studies of Chinese classical drama and poetry.

Feng Zhongpu ▷Zong Pu

Fênix Renascida (1716–1728) (*Phoenix Reborn*)

One of the most important anthologies of 17th-century Portuguese poetry. Compiled by Matias Pereira da Silva in a five-volume format, it was published over a twelve-year period. A highly diversified collection, it contains lyric, epic, satirical and religious verse. The influence of the 16th-century Portuguese poet Luís Vaz de Camões is especially evident. Among the poets appearing in this collection is ▷Sóror Violante do Céu.

▷Baroque; *Conceptismo*

Fenno, Jenny (fl 1791)

North American poet and essayist. Her life is known only through the sparse biographical details revealed in her spiritual writings. A resident of Boston when she wrote ▷*Original Compositions in Prose and Verse*, her poetry and essays are conventional in form, but her explicit challenge to those who would censure women's expressions raises this collection above the norm of religious writings at the end of the 18th century.

Fenno-Swedish literature

From the 12th century to 1809, Finland was governed by Swedish officials, and Swedish was the political and cultural language. After 1917, when Finland became an independent nation after having been a member of the Russian Empire, the cultural language for a long time continued to be Swedish, or the particular version of Swedish now spoken in Finland. Today, only a small group in Finland speaks Swedish, but an extensive body of literature is still written in Fenno-Swedish.

The first influential Fenno-Swedish woman writer was Helene Westermarck (1857–1938), a writer of the 1880s, and a liberal feminist. She wrote some very sensitive portraits of women from former times.

It was Fenno-Swedish literature that brought ▷modernism to Scandinavia, and ▷Edith Södergran and ▷Hagar Olsson (1893–1978) were the writers who introduced it: Södergran in her poems, Olsson in her literary essays and criticism.

In the 1960s it was the Fenno-Swedish women writers who introduced new feminist insights, eg ▷Märta Tikkanen. Children's literature was dominated by the world-famous ▷Tove Jansson. She was originally an artist, but has written more than twenty-five books. Many have been filmed, or published as cartoons, eg the Moomin series, and many of her books are also read by adults.

Irmelin Sandman Lilius (born 1936) is another talented writer for children. She writes in the tradition of the sagas, and most of her books may be read by adults as well as by children. She has been widely translated and has won international fame.

Christina Andersson (born 1936) also writes in the tradition of the sagas, with fantastic modern tales for children. Her books are children's literature in the classical sense.

Marita Lindqvist (born 1918) writes about children and everyday life, and is well-known for her characters Malene and Kotten. She has initiated a new realistic trend in Fenno-Swedish literature for children.

Today, Fenno-Swedish literature is extensive and full of life despite its diminishing background in the population.

▷Children's literature (Denmark, Norway and Sweden)

Ferber, Edna (1885–1968)

US novelist. Ferber was born in Kalamazoo, Michigan, and her parents' lives provide the formula for much of her fiction, including the Pulitzer Prize-winning ▷So Big (1924) and Cimarron (1930), where a practical, far-sighted woman married to a man of lesser intelligence successfully takes over managing the family business. In 1909 Ferber suffered a breakdown related to the conflict between her need for independence and her parents' emotional demands. During her last ten years she suffered from tic douloureux. She wrote fiction to be productive. Ferber's Jewishness was important in enabling her to both glorify and criticize US culture. Her work recognizes also the importance of working women to the development of the US. It focuses on women like Emma McChesney, the travelling petticoat saleswoman and single mother in The Business Adventures of Emma McChesney (1913) and Emma McChesney and Company (1915). Ferber emphasizes also the importance of work to women's own growth, and she champions women's need for self-fulfilling careers.

Other works include: Roast Beef Medium (1911), Fanny Herself (1917), The Girls (1921), Show Boat (1926), American Beauty (1931), A Peculiar Treasure (1939), Saratoga Trunk (1941), Great Son (1945), Giant (1952), Ice Palace (1958) and A Kind of Magic (1963).

Fergusson, Elizabeth Graeme (1737–1801)

North American poet and translator. She was the daughter of Anne Keith and Thomas Graeme, one of the wealthiest and most prominent families in Philadelphia. At seventeen she became engaged to Benjamin Franklin's son, William. Although heartbroken when the engagement was broken, she was sent to London at this time which had remarkable benefits for her. She spent three years translating Fénelon's ▷Telemachus (1766–1769) and gained fame as a notable poet in her own right; upon her return to Philadelphia, she was recognized as the leading lady of letters in the city for works such as ▷Paraphrases of the Psalms of David (1766–1767) and numerous poems published in newspapers. Her marriage to Hugh Henry Fergusson was not a happy one; he supported the British during the American Revolution, and they soon separated. The accusation that she herself aided the Tories destroyed her reputation, and she lived the remainder of her life at Graeme Park, the family estate. She died there on 23 February 1801.

▷Griffitts, Hannah; Smith, Anna Young; Stockton, Annis Boudinot

Ferland, Barbara (born 1919)

Caribbean poet. Felland was born and educated in ▷Jamaica, before departing for, England, where she worked in the British Council Theatre Department. She was a regular contributor to the BBC World Service 'Caribbean Voices' programme during the 1950s. Her output of verse has been small but impressive. No full collection of her poetry has been published, but her published work includes 'Vestel', 'Orange', and 'Jasmine' in ▷BIM, Nos 15 and 16 (1976), and 'At the University', 'Expect No Turbulence' and 'Le Petit Paysan (Modigliani)' in Caribbean Voices (1970).

Fern, Fanny ▷Parton, Sarah Payson Willis

Fernández Cubas, Cristina (born 1945)

Spanish writer. Fernández was born in Barcelona. She has published two short-story collections: Mi hermana Elba (1980) (My Sister Elba) and Los altillos de Brumal (1985) (The Year of Grace). Her fiction probes the dividing line between madness and sanity.

Fernandez Morales, Juana ▷Ibarbourou, Juana de

Fernando, Chitra

Sri Lankan prose writer and academic. Since 1968 she has taught linguistics at Macquarie University, Sydney. She is the author of several books for children. With Ranjini Obeyesekere she has co-edited *An Anthology of Modern Writing from Sri Lanka* (1981), and with Roger Flavell she has written *On Idiom: Critical Views and Perspectives* (1981). Other published works include *Glass Bangles* (1968) and *Three Women* (1983).

Fernando, Gilda Cordero (born 1930)

Filipino writer. She comes from Manila and authentically describes her own background – the urban upper middle class. Her stories, collected in *The Butcher, the Baker and the Candlestick Maker*, are told with sophisticated wit and can be mercilessly satirical. They focus on women who both fully accept and have internalized the ▷patriarchal codes and values of Philippine society. Even as their lives seem to be spent validating these values, they are revealed as unconscious victims of a dominant male culture.

After collaborating with Alfredo Roces in the publication of a ten-volume encyclopaedia of Philippine history, culture and the arts, she ventured into publishing coffee-table books such as *Streets of Manila* (1977), *Turn of the Century* (1978), and *Jeepney* (1979), which serve as a useful illustrated document of aspects of Philippine cultural history.

Fern Leaves from Fanny's Portfolio (1853)

US collection of sketches, essays and newspaper columns by ▷Sara Payson Willis Parton (Fanny Fern). Parton's bestselling first book, *Fern Leaves* is interesting for its mixture of pieces. Traditional, sometimes sentimental, work reveals the standard of periodical writing in the 1850s and provides an informative contrast to the rest of the collection: Parton's distinctive satiric writing on the status and treatment of women. Parton's columns, while seemingly topical, are still humorous today, eg her comment upon seeing a 'MEN WANTED' sign: 'Well; they have been "wanted" for some time; but the article is not in the market, although there are plenty of spurious imitations.'
Bib: Fern, Fanny, *Ruth Hall & Other Writings*, ed. Joyce W. Warren (1986).

Ferraud, Anna Bellinzani, Président Michel (1657–1740)

French novelist. Her one novel, *L'Histoire des Amours de Cléante et de Bélise avec le recueil de ses Lettres* (1691) (*History of the Love of Cléante and Bélise with a Collection of their Letters*), idealizes the woman in the tradition of courtly love and *préciosité* (▷Precious Women), making the heroine superior to her lover.

Ferreira de la Cerda, Doña Bernarda (1595–1644)

Spanish dramatist and poet. Ferreira was the daughter of a Portuguese courtier. She lived in Lisbon, and was admired by Philip III. She wrote some unpublished plays, a poem, *España libertada* (1618) (*Spain Liberated*) and a volume of lyric poetry, *Soledades de Buçaco* (*Buçaco Solitudes*).

Ferrier, Susan (1782–1854)

Scottish (▷Scotland) novelist. The youngest of the ten children of James Ferrier and Helen Coutts, she was born and educated in Edinburgh, and introduced to literary society by Sir Walter Scott, a friend of the family. Her first novel, ▷*Marriage*, was published in 1818; many critics assumed it to be the work of Scott. ▷*The Inheritance* appeared next in 1824, and *Destiny*, considered Ferrier's weakest novel, in 1831. All these books were published anonymously, as were Ferrier's *Works* (1841), although it was reissued under her name in 1851. Her novels were enormously popular and she was paid large sums for them by Blackwood, her publisher. Her satirical treatment of Scottish high society caused her to be compared to ▷Jane Austen and ▷Fanny Burney, though her fame dwindled during the 19th century. She is nevertheless an important figure in the history of Scottish women's writing, demonstrating a strong identification with her country.
Bib: Sackville, M., 'Introduction' to 1970 edition of *Works*.

Fiamengo, Marya (born 1926)

Canadian poet, born in Vancouver, and educated at the University of British Columbia, where she now teaches in the Department of English. She has published a number of books of poetry: *Quality of Halves* (1958), *The Ikon: Measured Work* (1961), *Overheard at the Oracle* (1969), *Silt of Iron* (1971) and *In Praise of Older Women* (1976). *North of the Cold Star* (1978) collects much of her best material. Her poem, 'In praise of old women' condemns patriarchal shunning of older women, and argues for the natural strength of ageing. She also writes about the immigrant experience and the cultural differential between Canada and the USA.

Field, Michael (Katherine Bradley, 1846–1914 and Edith Cooper, 1862–1913)

Katherine Bradley moved to the home of her niece, Edith Cooper, in 1865, and thereafter the two women were devoted and constant companions until the death of Edith in 1913. Although they sometimes wrote individually, publishing under the ▷pseudonyms Arran (Katherine) and Isla (Edith) Leigh, they also collaborated on more than twenty-five tragic ▷dramas and eight volumes of lyrics. The dramas are mostly on classical and historical subjects, and only one was ever performed, but their poetry is notable for its sensuousness, passion and mysticism. Their collections of verse include *Long*

Ago (1889), based on poems by ▷Sappho;
Underneath the Bough (1893); *Wild Honey from
Various Thyme* (1908); *Poems of Adoration* (1912),
written by Edith, and *Mystic Trees* (1913), written
mainly by Katherine. The two women also co-
wrote a journal, *Works and Days*, extracts from
which were published in 1934.
Bib: Hickok, K., *Representations of Women: 19th
Century British Women's Poetry*; Faderman, L.,
Surpassing the Love of Men.

Field, Rachel (1894–1942)
US novelist. Field was raised in Stockbridge,
Massachusetts, by her widowed mother, and she
was the first woman to receive the Newbery
Medal for children's literature. Her novels explore
feelings not often dealt with in books for girls. As
in ▷*All This and Heaven Too* (1938), Field
provides the social history of the period in which
her novels are set. In her children's books – *Little
Dog Toby* (1928) and *Polly Patchwork* (1928) – she
presents a protagonist who solves a particular
problem. In her adolescent books – ▷*Hitty, Her
First Hundred Years* (1931), *Calico Bush* (1931) and
Hepatica Hawks (1932) – she features independent
heroines who accept or control their destinies. In
her adult novels – *Time Out of Mind* (1935) and
And Now Tomorrow (1942) – Field raises the issue
of class barriers.

Fielding, Sarah (1710–1768)
English novelist, translator and writer of one of
the earliest fictions for the education of children.
The sister of the English novelist Henry Fielding
(1707–1754), Sarah's West Country childhood
was troubled by disputes between her
grandmother and her father: her grandmother
sent her to a boarding school. Her writing career
probably began with contributions to her brother's
Joseph Andrews (1742) and she published her first
and best-known novel, *The Adventures of David
Simple* (1744), with an explanation that 'distress in
her circumstances' was what induced her to write.
A sequel, *Familiar Letters Between the Principal
Characters in David Simple, and Some Others* (1747)
was published by subscription and with 'help'
from her brother. In January 1749 her book for
children, ▷*The Governess, or the Little Female
Academy* became one of the earliest books
designed for children (especially girls). She
published *David Simple, Volume the Last* in 1753,
and her brother, Henry, died in 1754, the same
year in which she published *The Cry: A New
Dramatic Fable* with her close lifelong friend,
▷Jane Collier. She published fictional biography
in *The Lives of Cleopatra and Octavia* (1757) and
Countess of Dellwyn (1758), probably *The History of
Some Penitents in the Magdalen House* (1759) and
The History of Ophelia (1760), as well as the
successful translation of *Xenophon's Memoirs of
Socrates* (1762) – the only published piece to
which she put her name. She admired Samuel
Richardson's novels (▷Richardson, influence of)
and she and Jane Collier were his friends

(although he was satirized by her brother) and she
knew and was read by ▷Elizabeth Carter.

Fields, Annie Adams (1834–1915)
US essayist, literary biographer and hostess. A key
figure in the literary circle of Boston,
Massachusetts, in the second half of the 19th
century, Adams Fields was the second wife of
James T. Fields (1817–1881), publisher and
editor of ▷*The Atlantic Monthly* from 1861 to
1871. As friend and confidante to many women
writers, especially ▷Sarah Orne Jewett, Adams
Fields served as centre for a supportive literary
group. Among her many books are those like
▷*Authors and Friends* (1896) which provide a vivid
record of 19th-century US literary life. In the
correspondence and travels of 19th-century US
women writers, Adams Fields is an almost
constant factor and friend. Subjects of her literary
biographies include ▷Harriet Beecher Stowe and
Adams Fields's husband, in *James T. Fields:
Biographical Notes and Personal Sketches* (1893). She
is the subject of M.A. DeWolfe Howe's *Memories
of a Hostess* (1922).
▷Thaxter, Celia Laighton

Fiennes, Celia (1662–1741)
English Protestant travel writer, and daughter of a
regicide. She travelled around the English
counties alone and accompanied, riding and using
a coach. Descriptions combine the interests of a
traveller with details which make the familiar
social territory strange – for example, her vivid
story of the recovery of a human relic in the
abandoned monastery at York. Her 'Book' was
first published in part in 1888.

Fifty Caribbean Writers: A Bio-Bibliographical Critical Sourcebook (1986)
This volume, edited by Daryl Cumberdance,
provides a comprehensive study of fifty Caribbean
writers, introducing the authors and their works,
and giving full biographical, critical and
bibliographical information. It includes articles on:
▷Phyllis Shand Allfrey, ▷Louise Bennett,
▷Dionne Brand, ▷Erna Brodber, ▷Jean
D'Costa, ▷Merle Hodge, ▷Jamaica Kincaid,
▷Jean Rhys and ▷Sylvia Wynter.

Figes, Eva (born 1932)
Novelist and critic. Born in Berlin of German
Jewish parents, Figes has since taken British
citizenship. Concerned to develop in her novels a
formal distinction from the 'English' novel, she
identifies itself with, and incorporates into much
of her fiction, mainland European experimental
forms. *Ghosts* (1988) alludes strongly to Henrik
Ibsen's (1828–1906) play of the same title, and
contains sections of the lyrical or poetic prose
which now characterizes Figes's fiction. *Light*
(1983) makes explicit its impressionist reference
point through its depiction of the character
Claude, based on Monet (1840–1926). *The Seven
Ages* (1986) focuses on a thousand years of
women's history. Her non-fiction writings include

Patriarchal Attitudes (1970) and *Sex and Subterfuge: Women Writers to 1850* (1982).

Figuli, Margita (born 1909)

Slovak prose writer and dramatist. She was a member of the Slovak Lyrical Prose school. Her first collection of short stories *Pokušenie* (*The Temptation*) was published in 1937. The 1940s were the most important period of her work, when her brief novel ▷ *Tri gaštanové kone* (1940) (*Three Chestnut Horses*) and the long, allegorical novel ▷ *Babylon* (1946) were published.

Figuli tried to create her own conception of the world and history, in which woman represents the stable element, and preserves values. Her female characters are not active. They are presented only in the sphere of partner-relationships, in which they rely on intuition, and are led by a love which is understood ethically rather than erotically. Figuli's work contains many legendary, fairy-tale and biblical elements.

Fille d'Haïti (1954) (*Daughter of Haiti*)

In this novel by the Haitian novelist, ▷ Marie Chauvet, Lotus, the protagonist is threatened by a sense of fragmentation similar to that suffered by Claire in her earlier novel ▷ *Amour* (1968) (*Love*). The daughter of a 'successful' prostitute, Lotus is caught within a tangle of social and personal contradictions. Appearing to the people of the street as a mulatto who can enjoy the privileges of a bourgeois life, Lotus is viewed by the bourgeoisie as bearing the mark of her mother's trade. She belongs nowhere. Chauvet shows Lotus finding liberation and security in a kind of madness, luring men, whom she hates, and rejecting them when they would possess her.

Filleul, Jeanne (1424–1498)

French poet, one of the so-called 'poetesses of the north'. We know little about her except that she was lady-in-waiting to Marguerite Stuart (1424–1444), who was the daughter of James of Scotland, and the abandoned wife of the future Louis XI (1423–1483), and who encouraged such poets as Alain Chartier (1385–1433). A single rondeau survives, where profound suffering is expressed in the form of light verse.
Bib: Wilwerth, E., *Visages de la littérature féminine*.

Finas, Lucette (born 1921)

French professor of classical literature, and experimental writer. She has published many critical essays, notably in her collection *Le Bruit d'Iris* (1978) (*The Sound of Iris*), which includes readings of texts by ▷ Hélène Cixous and ▷ Nathalie Sarraute. Of her writings, only the confessional novel *L'Echec* (1958) has been translated into English (as *The Faithful Shepherd*, 1963). Her other experimental novels include *Donne* (1976) (*Give*) and *Le Meurtrion* (1968) (*The Murderer*). She has also written *La Crue* (1972) (*The River Rising*), an essay on French literary theorist Georges Bataille, and *La Toise et le vertige*

(1986) (*The Height Chart/Vertigo*), an essay published by ▷ Éditions de femmes.

Finch, Anne, Countess of Winchelsea (1660–1720)

English poet, at present best-known for her 'A Nocturnall Reeverie', esteemed by William Wordsworth (1770–1850). With ▷ Anne Killigrew she was a Maid of Honour to Mary of Modena and married Heneage Finch. After James II fled, they moved to Kent and she wrote poetry. Only some was printed, but she published *Miscellany Poems on Several Occassions* (1713). Finch uses the natural world in a distinctive and subtle way in her poetry, linking landscape and state of mind in a way that blends the features of the inner and outer worlds, politics and place. She also had a vein of sharp satire – in 'Unequal Fetters' she wrote: 'Marriage does but slightly tye men / Whil'st close Pris'ners we remain / They the larger slaves of Hymen / Still are begging Love again / At the full length of all their chain.'

Fin de Chéri, La (1926) ▷ *Last of Chéri, The* (1951)

Findern Anthology (15th and 16th centuries)

English verse anthology. The *Findern Anthology* (or *Findern Manuscript*) is a collection of secular and religious verse in English (some dating from the 14th century, some later), thought to have been compiled informally by and for the prominent Derbyshire family after which it is named, and their friends. The names of five women appear in the manuscript: Fraunces Crucker; Margery Hungerford; Elizabeth Koton; Elizabeth Frauncys, and Anne Schyrley. They may be the names of those who copied out some of the texts from other manuscripts. However, some of the lyrics and short pieces unique to this manuscript may also have been composed by these women. The collection is a product of the growth in vernacular literacy in 15th-century England.
Bib: Beadle, Richard and Owen, A.E.B., *The Findern Manuscript*.

Finnigan, Joan (born 1925)

Born Joan MacKenzie in Ottawa, this Canadian poet studied at Carleton University, Ottawa, and Queen's University. Her poetry is reflective and personal. She has published *Through a Glass Darkly* (1957); *A Dream of Lilies* (1965); *Entrance to the Greenhouse* (1968); *It was Warm and Sunny When We Set Out* (1970); *Living Together* (1976); *A Reminder of Familiar Faces* (1978), and *This Series has Been Discontinued* (1980). *I Come From the Valley* (1976), *Some of the Stories I Told You Were True* (1981), *Look! The Land is Growing Giants* (1983), *Laughing All the Way Home* (1984) and *Legacies, Legends and Lies* (1985) all reflect Finnigan's interest in regional localities. She also wrote the script for a National Film Board movie, *The Best Damn Fiddler from Calabogie to Kaladar* (1969).

Fire-Dwellers, The (1969)

▷Margaret Laurence's Canadian novel about the domestic miseries of Stacey MacAindra (sister of Rachel Cameron, main character in ▷*A Jest of God*, 1966). Manawaka is part of Stacey's youth; now, in Vancouver, she watches a nuclear world lowering over her children, and middle age closing in around her. She has a brief affair, but ultimately chooses to stay within her marriage.

Fireweed (1978–present)

Canadian feminist quarterly from Toronto. It covers a range of women's issues, often literary. Special issues have focused on writing by Quebec women, feminist aesthetics, and women of colour. ▷Gay Allison was its founding editor.

First, Ruth ▷Autobiography (Southern Africa); Exile writing (South Africa); Prison writing (South Africa)

First Examynacyon of Anne Askewe, Lately Martyred in Smythefelde, The (1546)

The details of her examination and trial during March of 1545, written by Englishwoman ▷Anne Askew. John Bale published Askew's account with his own lengthy preface and conclusion, as well as extensive commentary inserted at frequent intervals in Askew's own narrative. During the seven days of her first arrest, Askew was questioned by Christopher Dare, a number of chancellors, and the mayor. The majority of the questions dealt with the sacrament of communion and transubstantiation. Her account attests to her courage and spirited responses to her inquisitors' questions, many of which seemed posed to entrap her. She also demonstrated a daring wit in her refusals to answer what she considered inane questions. Her inquisitors were especially frustrated by their inability to make her answer according to their liking. Nevertheless, after signing a ▷confession of faith that was agreeable to the authorities, and after much delay, Askew was released from prison. Within the next year, however, she was arrested again. Her account of this final imprisonment and the trial leading to her execution was published by John Bale as ▷*The Lattre Examynacyon of Anne Askew* (1547).
▷Protestant Reformation

First South African, The (1979)

A play by South African dramatist ▷Fatima Dike, written and produced in 1977 when Dike was resident dramatist at the Space Theatre in Cape Town. The title of the play recalls a South African literary tradition deeply concerned with the question of identity: Sir Percy Fitzpatrick, for instance, who won the first South African general election as a figure committed to the unification of the four South African colonies, and whose biography in 1971 was called *The First South African*. Dike's 'first South African' is instead, the author says, a man who looks white, has the heart of a black, and is classified 'coloured'. Zwelinzima, nicknamed '*Rooi*', 'Red' (or ochre-coloured, earth-coloured), and later renamed Ruben, is the child of a black woman and a white man, himself torn between desire for a black woman and a white woman; he leaves his home to take up the life of a white man, supervising black labour and denying his past. However, he returns at the end of the play, crazed, a man without a secure sense of self.

Fischer, Caroline Auguste (1764–1834)

German poet, novelist and writer of short stories. After her divorce from a Danish court preacher, she had a long-standing relationship with the writer Christian August Fischer (1771–1829), by whom she had a son. They were married in 1808, but separated soon afterwards. She tried to make a living by running a school in Heidelberg and a library in Würzburg, and she published short stories and novels, either unsigned or under various pseudonyms. Her work constitutes an important link between pre-modern and modern woman's literature in Germany. In *Honigmonathe* (1802–1804) (*Honey-months*), for example, she argued against the prevalent ideal of self-denying, suffering womanhood that was glorified in ▷Karoline Wobeser's bestselling *Elisa, oder das Weib, wie es sein sollte* (*Elisa, or Woman as She Should Be*), published in 1802.
▷*Bildungsroman*

Fisher, Sarah Logan (1751–1796)

North American diarist. The calmness of her life as a member of a well-to-do Philadelphia Quaker family was disrupted with the outbreak of the American Revolution. An ardent Loyalist, she recorded her political admonitions of the events in a Letter Book that she maintained in the 1770s and 1780s and which she termed ▷*A Diary of Trifling Occurrences*. When her husband was imprisoned in Virginia, she found personal strength in her religious practices.
▷Early North American Quaker women's writings

Fiske, Ingrid ▷De Kok, Ingrid

Fiske, Sarah Symmes (1652–1692)

North American spiritual autobiographer. Born in Charleston, Massachusetts, she entered an orthodox Puritan family. Her mother died shortly after her birth, but both her father and grandfather were ministers. In 1671 she married Moses Fiske; they had fourteen children. In 1677, as preparation for admission into her Church, she wrote ▷*A Confession of Faith or, A Summary of Divinity*. She was only twenty-five years old, but she had learned the tenets of her faith so well that her testimony was published in 1704 as a model for all young persons seeking Church membership.

Fitnat-Khanim (c 1725–1780)

Turkish poet, personal name Zubeyda, who was regarded as the greatest woman poet of the Ottoman school. She came from a learned family in Constantinople. Her father was Sheikh al-Islam, who was also talented in music. Early in life she married a much older man of high position, who was intellectually her inferior. Their union was the subject of many literary anecdotes by her contemporaries. Her lyric poetry dealt mainly with love and a philosophical approach to life. The scholar, E.J.W. Gibb, describes the language of her verse as 'original and graceful' and places her among the leading poets of the romantic period. The 'directness and spontaneity' of her verse was greatly admired by her contemporaries and she exchanged *ghazels* (Persian odes) and repartee with male poets who thought highly of her verse. She used conventional imagery derived from Persian models:

> Arise, my prince, the garden land hath
>   wonder-joy in fair array;
> And hark, the plaintive nightingale is singing
>   on the rosy spray
> The tender bud will blush for shame whene'er
>   it doth thy cheek survey.
> Arise, and to the garth thy gracious air and
>   cypress mien display.

Bib: Gibb, E.J.W. (trans.), *A History of Ottoman Poetry.*

Fitzgerald, Penelope (born 1916)

English novelist. Fitzgerald's first publication was a biography, *Edward Burne-Jones* (1975), followed by another, a biography of her uncles, *The Knox Brothers* (1977). Her first novel, *The Golden Child* (1977), is a thriller set in a museum, which explores the ethics of displaying counterfeit objects, while also commenting on the public consumption of the purloined treasures of other cultures. The Booker Prize-winning *Offshore* (1979) elaborates Fitzgerald's preoccupation with the effect of immediate environment. Set among houseboat communities, the novel looks at social interaction in this microcosm of community relations. Other novels include: *Human Voices* (1980), *At Freddie's* (1982), *Innocence* (1986) and *The Gate of Angels* (1990).

Fitzgerald, Zelda (1900–1948)

US journalist, short story writer and novelist. Fitzgerald was born in Montgomery, Alabama, into a well-established, distinguished family, and she was legendary in her rebellion against conventional behaviour. In 1918 she married the writer F. Scott Fitzgerald (1896–1940). Later she became the spokeswoman for the flapper, a liberated playgirl with moral courage. In France in 1924 she had an affair with a French aviator, and in 1929 she began writing the 'Girl' sketches, which focus on women struggling for identity and achievement. In 1930 Fitzgerald suffered a breakdown and began living in sanatoriums.

Her autobiographical novel, *Save Me the Waltz* (1932), centres on Alabama Beggs, who tries to discover herself through artistic expression. Like Fitzgerald, Alabama competes with her husband for a successful artistic career, and struggles to find her own identity separate from that of her husband.

Other works include: *Bits of Paradise* (1974) and *Scandalabra* (1980).
Bib: Milford, Nancy, *Zelda.*

FitzGilbert, Constance (Custance) (fl mid-12th century)

English patron. Constance was a Lincolnshire noblewoman, wife of Ralph FitzGilbert. She borrowed Geoffrey of Monmouth's (c 1100–1153) *History of the Kings of England (Historia Regum Britanniae)* from her husband, and gave it to Gaimar (probably a clerk of her husband), in about 1150, to translate into French. The first part of Gaimar's ▷Anglo-Norman verse chronicle, a *Brut* (named from Brutus the Trojan, the legendary founder of Britain), is now lost. The second part, a sequel bringing the story up to date, for which he made use of the Anglo-Saxon Chronicle, survives. Gaimar was the first to translate a *Brut* into a vernacular. The combination of a *Brut* and sequel provided the pattern for popular history for the following three centuries. Constance's patronage therefore had lasting consequences.

Fitzhugh, Louise (1928–1974)

US novelist. Born in Memphis, Tennessee, Fitzhugh fled the South to attend Bard College in New York. Considered controversial, her children's fiction attacks prejudice and conformity while respecting individuality.

Like Harriet in ▷*Harriet, The Spy* (1964), Fitzhugh is painfully honest in noting human inadequacies. The adults in her novels are self-centred and too rigid to change. However, when the adults reveal their cruelty, the adolescent heroines learn to love themselves. In *The Long Secret* (1965) Beth Ellen, abandoned by her mother, rediscovers the self she had kept secret when she sees her mother's self-indulgence. *Nobody's Family Is Going Change* (1974) depicts the effects of prejudice on an African-American girl whose father has internalized racial hatred. Fitzhugh emphasizes the need for humility and charity in attitudes to the self and others.

Other works include: *Bang, Bang You're Dead* (1969).

Five Little Peppers and How They Grew, The (1881)

US children's novel, the first of a popular series, by ▷Harriet Mulford Stone Lothrop. The Pepper family of five siblings are living in their 'little brown house' so close to absolute poverty that they must save their candle stubs. A fortuitous meeting moves them to the household and fortunes of a wealthy patron, and the Peppers virtually become his wards.

Five Plays (1986)

A collection of plays by Indian writer ▷Mahasveta Devi, translated from the original Bengali. All the plays are dramatizations of short stories, and they share a theme of the historical, self-perpetuating nature of exploitation. *Mother of 1804* comes from the Bengali short story '*Hajar Churashir Ma*' (1973). It tells of the awakening of an apolitical woman, Sujata, who is the mother of corpse number 1804, one of the bodies found in the wake of the Marxist Naxalite uprisings in eastern India in the 1960s and 1970s. It takes Sujata two years to see the link between her son's death and the waves of economic exploitation and deprivation that her people have always suffered. Only when she has made these links can she come to terms with her grief and begin to experience a new kind of fulfilment.

Flanner, Janet (1892–1978)
US journalist and novelist. Janet Flanner's 'Letters from Paris', published in the *New Yorker* from 1925 to the outbreak of World War II, present a fascinating document of Parisian life, art and politics. Having perhaps more in common with the style of Baudelaire's *flâneur* (detached observer of modernity) than her contemporaries, journalists Eugene Jolas and Ernest Hemingway (1899–1961), Flanner's letters take us through the streets of Paris, into the markets, cafés and bars, through to the salons, theatres and opera houses, juxtaposing fleeting impressions with shrewd political and social observation. Writing about Paris fashions with the same ease as she analyzes the ▷avant-garde or French feminism, Flanner's letters present an early challenge to the dichotomy between popular and high culture. Just as the city of Paris provides a structure and a setting for her letters, her only published novel, *The Cubical City* (1926) uses the architecture of New York to frame a critique of repressive North American mores and manners. 'I should have liked to be a writer,' Flanner modestly replied to a questionnaire in *The Little Review*. She was undoubtedly that, and one, moreover, with a highly original slant on the history which was being created around her. As Flanner herself puts it, 'history looks queer when you're standing close to it, watching where it is coming from and how it is being made.'

Other works include: *An American in Paris: Profile of an Interlude between Two Wars* (1940), *Men and Monuments* (1957), *Paris Journal, 1944–65* (ed. W Shawn, 1966), *Paris Journal, 1965–71* (ed. W. Shawn, 1971), *Paris was Yesterday, 1925–1939* (ed. I. Drutman, 1972), *London was Yesterday 1925–1939* (ed. I. Drutman, 1975), *Janet Flanner's World: Uncollected Writings 1932–75* (ed. I. Drutman, 1979).

Flavigny, Marie de, Comtesse d'Agoult (1805–1876)
French novelist, autobiographer and historical/political writer, who used the ▷pseudonym Daniel Stern. The daughter of a French father and a German mother, and one of the leading figures of fashionable society, Marie de Flavigny found marriage stultifying, and in 1835 eloped with the composer Franz Liszt (1811–1886), by whom she had two daughters. When the couple separated in 1844 she began to write in earnest, producing studies of political and intellectual life in Germany (1803–1882), and an article on Emerson for the *Revue des deux mondes* and the *Revue Indépendante*. In 1846, she published a semi-autobiographical novel, ▷*Nélida*, in which she treats her former lover harshly and intimates that passion is a chimera which hampers women from leading fulfilling lives. Although, like ▷Hortense Allart, she was wary of ▷Saint-Simonian feminism, there is evidence of a feminist consciousness at work in at least two of her texts, *Essai sur la liberté* (1847) (*Essay on Freedom*) and *Esquisses morales* (1849) (*Moral Sketches*), in which she denounces sexual inequality and argues for feminine emancipation through education. The latter is a collection of reflections on the society and mores of her time, and has been considered her most original work. Also of interest are her *Histoire de la révolution de 1848* (1851) (*History of the 1848 Revolution*), which offers insight into the political and social climate of mid-19th-century France, her studies of Mary Stuart (1856) and Joan of Arc (1856), and her novella *Valentia* (1883), a feminist narrative which presents marriage as a vehicle for legalized rape. More at ease with historical and biographical writing than with fiction, she produced a volume of memoirs, *Mes Souvenirs* (*My Memories*), which were published posthumously in 1877. With his customary harshness, Barbey d'Aurevilly (▷*Les Bas-bleus*) described her as an 'intellectual Amazon, devoid of not one but two breasts' and as a 'traitor to her sex'.

Bib: Albistur, M. and Armogathe, D., *Histoire du féminisme français*; Crosland, M., *Women of Iron and Velvet*; Desanti. D., *Daniel ou le visage secret d'une comtesse romantique*; Rabine, L., 'Feminist writers in French Romanticism', *Studies in Romanticism*, Vol. 16; Vier, J., *La Comtesse d'Agoult et son temps*.

Fleißer, Marieluise (1901–1974)
German dramatist, novelist and short story writer. Her first play, *Fegefeuer in Ingolstadt* (*Purgatory in Ingolstadt*), was staged by Bertolt Brecht (1898–1956) in 1926, and was so successful that she was offered a contract by the publisher Ullstein. A second play, *Pioniere in Ingolstadt* (1928) (*Pioneers in Ingolstadt*), in which Brecht was instrumental in shaping some sexually explicit scenes, became the scandal he had anticipated, and ended her career as a dramatist. In all her work, but most notably in stories such as *Die Stunde der Magd* (1925) (*The Hour of the Maid*) or *Ein Pfund Orangen* (1927) (*A Pound of Oranges*), she offers a penetrating analysis of everyday life blighted by conservative and patriarchal attitudes.

Fleming, May Agnes (1840–1880)
Novelist and short story writer, born May Early in Portland, New Brunswick. She published her first story at the age of fifteen, while still attending school at Sacred Heart Convent. She was the first Canadian to achieve success as a popular

▷romance writer, selling short stories and serialized novels to various US and Canadian outlets. Her first works were published under the name, Cousin May Carlton, but after her marriage in 1865, she published as May Agnes Fleming. From 1865 she managed to write three novels a year for *Saturday Night*. Usually, her works were republished after their initial appearance in periodicals; she became sufficiently independent to leave her alcoholic husband, and move with her children to Brooklyn. Her work was so popular that her stories (some written by another, but attributed to her) continued to appear after her premature death. Her tales are generally romantic fantasies about poor women (teachers, seamstresses) who manage to marry good, prosperous men, often at the expense of a defiant, passionate competitor. They include: *La Masque; or, The Midnight Queen* (1863), *A Mad Marriage* (1875), *Kate Danton; or, Captain Danton's Daughters* (1877) and *The Heir of Charlton* (1878). Her last novel, *Lost for a Woman* (1880), is about a woman who has the courage to leave an unhappy marriage. She died of Bright's disease.

Fließende Licht der Gottheit, Das (1250–1260) ▷*Revelations of Mechthild, The* (1953)

Flight Against Time (1987)

English translation by Issa Boulatta of Lebanese writer ▷Emily Nasralla's novel first published in Arabic (1981). The 'flight against time' is the flight of an old man, Radwan, who leaves his village in Lebanon for the first time to see his children in Canada. The journey is all arranged and paid for by his children, but he feels lost and scared.

The Lebanese community in Prince Edward Island, Canada, is composed of prosperous small businessmen, administrators and academics. They are well integrated, and give the old couple a warm welcome, putting forward their Lebanese façade – the Lebanese food and songs, the Arab coffee with cardamom, drunk in small cups – but soon the pattern of the new alien life takes over. Radwan's worst disappointment is his grandchildren, who do not speak or understand Arabic.

His wife, who has accompanied him, is content to stay indoors, but the old man is restless. He visits New York to look for news of his two brothers and sister, who landed there fifty years earlier, and finds nothing but a city that sucked up his siblings and transformed their names, so that they are lost without a trace.

Among two gifts from two Lebanese villagers to Radwan's children is one from the madwoman of the village, who insisted on his carrying her gift, a handful of dust wrapped in a dirty piece of cloth. They receive it with enthusiasm. They promise to put it in a crystal vase and position it in the hall, a shrine to the homeland. The homeland is enshrined in their hearts and homes, but they will never return. When news of the civil war worsens (the date is 1975), they meet anxiously and collect money to help 'the victims of the war'. Only old Radwan insists on rushing back home, and is kidnapped and killed the day after his homecoming. At his funeral the villagers turn out to bid him farewell; he is mourned equally by his neighbours dressed in black (the Christians) or in white (the Shi'a Moslems).

Nasralla's most recent collection of short stories, *Our Daily Bread* (1990) covers similar issues.

Flore, Jeanne (early 16th century)

French author of fiction or ▷*nouvelles* (novellas). We have no trace of her existence other than the two sets of *nouvelles* attributed to her, to which remarkably few other writers refer directly. Some critics have argued that they were in fact written by a man. The choice of *devisantes* (female narrators) rather than *devisants* (male narrators), the virulent defence of the female sex and the feminine sensuality of *Les Comptes amoureux* (*Tales of Love*) and the *Pugnition de l'Amour contempné* (*Punishment of Despised Love*) belie this theory. Both texts, which seem to be interrelated, were published in Lyon between 1530 and 1540 and appear incomplete. The framework is similar to that employed by the Italian writer Boccaccio (1313–1375), but, although ten narrators are assembled at the beginning of the *Comptes amoureux*, only seven tales remain. Jeanne Flore exploits the chivalric tradition, but is perhaps most effective in her portrayal of the scorned lover. She has been accused of cynicism, immorality and licentiousness, yet her *nouvelles* have a morality of their own. Condemning '*l'impareil mariage*' ('unsuitable marriages') between young women and old men '*qui ont déjà un pied dans la fosse*' ('with one foot already in the grave'), Jeanne Flore claims the woman's right to free love. In the verse conclusion to her work, she is careful to remind her reader that it has all been but a poetic fiction.
Bib: Wilwerth, E., *Visages de la littérature féminine*.

Florentino, Leona (1849–1884)

Generally considered the first Filipino woman poet. She was born into a wealthy family, learning Spanish from the parish priest, but she began writing poetry in Iloko, a major language of her native Ilocos Sur in Northern Luzon, at the age of ten, later becoming a prolific poet and dramatist. Although not written for publication, her works nevertheless became famous throughout the region. They soon reached the national capital, Manila, and were published along with their Spanish translation in the major newspapers. Her work tends to be didactic and satirical, but she also wrote love lyrics and poems celebrating friends' birthdays, engagements and weddings.

Through the efforts of her eldest son, Isabelo de los Reyes, founder of the Philippine Independent Church, some of her work was exhibited in the *Exposition Internationale* of 1889, held in Paris. Her name and some of her works were also included in the *Bibliothèque Internationale des Oeuvres des Femmes*, edited by Madame Andzia

Wolska in 1889, and her works were more recently included in the *Exposición Filipino* held in 1987 in Madrid.

Floresta, Nísia (1810–1885)

Brazilian poet, novelist, essayist and translator who used various pseudonyms, including Une Brésilienne, Telesilla, Floresta Augusta Brasileira, Madame Floresta A. Brasileira, Madame Brasileira Augusta, and N.F.B.A. She wrote for newspapers, and owned a school called Augusto, in Rio de Janeiro (1838–1849). She often travelled in Europe, and finally moved to Paris. She wrote didactic works, was one of the forerunners of the feminist movement in Brazil, and was an early abolitionist. Her works include: *Daciz, ou jovem completa* (1847) (*Daciz, or a Complete Youth*); *A lágrima de um caéte* (1849); *Dedicação a uma amiga* (1850) (*Dedication to a Friend*); *Itineraire d'un voyage en Allemagne* (1857) (*Travels in Germany*); *Scintille d'un ánima brasiliana* (1859) (*The Spark of a Brazilian Soul*); *Trois ans en Italie suivis d'un voyage en Grèce* (1864) (*Three Years in Italy Followed by a Trip to Greece*), and *Fragments d'un ouvrage inédit* (1878) (*Fragments of an Unpublished Work*).

'Floure and the Leafe, The' (15th century)

This English verse allegory, courtly and chivalric in its themes, is written as if by a woman, although the authorship is a matter for speculation. It is composed in Rhyme Royal (the stanza form used, for example, by Chaucer for 'Troilus and Criseyde'). It is part of a long tradition of allegorical vision poetry, but the writing remains fresh. Until about 1870 the poem was thought to have been by Chaucer, and was till then highly praised; it was paraphrased by Dryden, among others.
Bib: Pearsall, D.A. (ed.), *The Floure and the Leafe and The Assembly of Ladies.*

Flygare-Carlén, Emilie (1807–1892)

Swedish prose writer. She was born on the Swedish coast, the youngest of fourteen children, and her father was a rich ship-owner. She did not receive a formal education, but was self-educated. She married a poor and elderly physician, Axel Flygare. By the age of twenty-seven she had borne four children, two of whom died very young, and she was a widow. She fell in love with another man and became pregnant, but the man died and she bore her daughter clandestinely and had her adopted. The daughter was the author Rosa Carlén (1836–1883).

Emilie began to write, and in 1838 she published *Waldemar Klein*, a salon novel (▷Literary salons, Scandinavia). In 1841 she married the writer Johan Gabriel Carlén. She is known as the first regional writer in Sweden. She had a wide audience, and made herself a fortune from her thirty-one volumes. Her principal work is the realistic *Ett köpmanshus i skärgården* (1860) (*A Merchant's House in the Archipelago*).

Folie Antillaise, La

La folie Antillaise is a recurrent motif in the literature of the French Antilles. ▷Simone Schwarz-Bart describes this particular 'madness' in her ▷*The Bridge of Beyond*: 'When, in the long hot blue days, the madness of the West Indies starts to swirl around the air above the villages, bluffs, and plateaus, men are seized with dread at the thought of the fate hovering over them, preparing to swoop on one or another like a bird of prey, and while they are incapable of offering the slightest resistance' (p. 23).

Madness threatens Zétou in Warner-Vieyra's ▷*As the Sorcerer Said* and ▷*Juletane*. In the case of Zétou and Juletane, and also ▷Michèle Lacrosil's ▷*Sapotille* and ▷*Cajou*, Schwarz-Bart's Mariotte, ▷Jacqueline Manicom's Madévie, Fanny in ▷*Au Peril de ta joie*, confession or journal-writing emerges as an attempt to control and correct personal history, and to explain apparent madness. This madness may be viewed as a defence mechanism, or a sense of splitting of the inner and outer self. It may also be seen as a crisis caused by the difficulty of entering into, or staying within, an order which has been established by a different culture, and in which the all-important framework of language has been established by a colonial power. Evelyn O'Callaghan suggests French Antillean writers are using psychic damage and distorted self-image as metaphors 'for a kind of pervasive "illness" to which [West Indian] societies are prone as a result of the colonial encounter' ('Interior Schisms Dramatized' in ▷*Out of the Kumbla*, p. 104).
▷Identity, Caribbean

Foligno, Angela da (c1248–1304)

Italian religious writer. As a young woman, she lived a full, worldly life, and was married with children. In 1283 she appears to have undergone a profound spiritual crisis, following the deaths in that year of her mother, husband and children. She entered the Franciscan order in 1290–91, and claimed to have had a vision of the Trinity during this period. She had many disciples. Her 'writings' are, in fact, dictations to her confessor/secretary, Brother Arnaldo. For the most part, they consist of her memoirs and her mystical experiences and theories. Her most significant work is the *Liber sororis Lelle de Fulgineo, de tertio ordine sancti Francisci* (1292–1296) translated as *The Book of Visions and Instructions as Taken Down from Her Own Lips by Brother Arnold* (1871). She also wrote many letters, prayers and didactic essays. Her *Libro delle mirabili visioni e consolazioni* appeared in Italian in 1922, and was translated into English as *The Book of Divine Consolation* in 1909 and 1966.

Follas novas (1880) (New Leaves)

One of the most outstanding books of poetry published in 19th-century Spain. It was written in the Galician language by ▷Rosalía de Castro. In her poetry, Rosalía de Castro combined a sensitive use of traditional metre with a peculiarly Galician structure of feeling, epitomized by *saudade*, a term which covers both longing for an absent loved one and nostalgia for one's homeland.

Fontaines, Marie-Louise-Charlotte de Pelard de Givry, Comtesse de (died 1730)

French novelist. Daughter of the Marquis de Givry. She published two novels: *Histoire d'Aménophis, prince de Lydie* (1728) (*The Story of Amenophis, Prince of Lydia*) and the better-known *Histoire de la comtesse de Savoie* (1726) (*The Story of the Countess of Savoy*). The latter has been cited as a source for the tragedy *Tancrède* by Voltaire, who praised the 'natural ease' of Fontaine's prose.

▷Lambert, Marquise de

Bib: Cioranescu, A., '*Tancrède* de Voltaire et ses sources', *Revue de Littérature Comparée* XIX (1939).

Fonte, Moderata (1555–1592)

Italian poet, religious writer and dramatist; real name Modesta Pozzo. She was born in Venice, where her parents both died the year after her birth, probably of plague. She received an exceptionally good education for a female child, and was fortunate to be able to continue this education after her marriage to Giovanni Nicolò Doglioni, who encouraged her both to study and to write. She died in childbirth. Her most famous work is ▷*Il Merito delle Donne* (*Woman's Worth*), a treatise on the superior nature of women, published in 1600, which formed an important part of an ongoing debate between the sexes in this period.

Her other works include: *Tredici canti del Floridoro*, a collection of poetry (1581); *Le feste. Rappresentazione avanti il Serenissimo Principe di Venezia Nicolò da Ponte* (1581) (*The Celebrations. A Dramatic Work Performed Before His Serene Highness, The Prince of Venice, Nicolo da Ponte*).

Fontette de Sommery, Mademoiselle (18th century)

French essayist and novelist. She published several essays on contemporary morals and received ideas: *Brochure morale* (1769), *Doutes sur les opinions reçues dans la société* (1782) (*Doubts about Received Opinions in Society*) and *Doutes sur les différentes opinions . . .* (1783) (*Doubts about Different Opinions . . .*). Her fictional works include two ▷epistolary novels, *Lettres de Mme la comtesse de L*** à M. le comte de R**** (1785) and *Lettres de Mlle de Tourville à Mme. la comtesse de Lenoncourt* (1788), and two tales, *L'Oreille* (1789) (*The ear*) and *Le Rosier et le brouillard* (1791) (*The Rosebush and the Mist*). She also published *Lettre à Delon* in 1784.

Fool's Gold (1979)

A novel by Greek writer ▷Maro Douka. This story about the world of modern Greece, featuring characters from every walk of life, is humorous, ironic, sarcastic and eventually self-negating. The varied characters represent Douka's own personal characteristics, and reveal in their actions the environment and the world they come from. The book lacks a continuous story and a close relationship between the people, who seem to accept isolation as their ideal condition. The language is simple and sharp. The book was received with enthusiasm because it seemed to express modern anxieties and isolated lifestyles.

Foote, Mary Hallock (1847–1938)

US novelist, short-story writer and illustrator. Initially renowned as an illustrator for magazines and books, Hallock Foote is most significant for her regional fiction set in the American west. Like many of her contemporaries she was rewarded – with publication and popularity – for bringing unique subject matter into the national literature. Hallock Foote's most memorable treatments of western mining camps and organized labour combined realistic treatment of economic and social conditions with plots which placed lovers in conflict with warring economic interests. Author of more than a dozen volumes and numerous magazine pieces, her works include: *The Led-Horse Claim* (1883); *The Chosen Valley* (1892); ▷*Coeur d'Alene* (1894).

▷*Century Illustrated Monthly Magazine, The*

Footprints in the Quag ▷Soweto Stories

Force de l'âge, La (1960) ▷Prime of Life, The, (1962)

Force des choses, La (1963) ▷Force of Circumstance

Forced Marriage, The (1845)

The publication of ▷Evdokiia Rostopchiná's Russian poem created a scandal in St Petersburg in 1846. Subtitled 'Ballad and Allegory', in eight ten-line stanzas the work presents the complaint of an 'old baron,' who accuses his wife of perfidy and sedition, and then gives her response. Married against her will, forbidden to speak her native language, suffering the exile of loyal servants, she finds her husband's marriage gifts to be 'shame, persecution, and slavery'. The poems"medieval setting fooled the censorship, but, when gossip about its allegorical subtext of Russian–Polish relations reached Nikolai I, he banned Rostopchiná from the court.

Bib: Pedrotti, L., 'The Scandal of Countess Rostopchiná's Polish-Russian Allegory', *Slavic and East European Journal* 20, 2.

Force of Circumstance (1965)

Translation of *La Force des choses* (1963), third volume of the autobiography of French writer, ▷Simone de Beauvoir. This book describes her life in the period between 1945 and 1960. Two major themes are central to the work: de Beauvoir's account of her relationships with Nelson Algren and Claude Lanzmann, and her growing involvement in left-wing politics. The two themes are only implicitly related. Algren introduced de Beauvoir to the realities of racism and poverty in the United States, Lanzmann was responsible for demonstrating to de Beauvoir the extent of European anti-Semitism. Partly as a result of these influences, de Beauvoir became involved in opposition to French policy in Algeria, and subsequently to the United States's involvement in Vietnam. The 'circumstances' of the book's title are the personal and global politics with which de Beauvoir became concerned.

for colored girls who have considered suicide/when the rainbow is enuf (1975)

US choreopoem. ▷Ntozake Shange's popular theatre piece combines poetry, music and dance to celebrate African-American womanhood. Seven African-American women chronicle their history of abuse by men and they reveal their vulnerability to socio-economic oppressive forces. But Shange emphasizes their ability to survive, and the seven women find a source of strength in their collectivity, which is expressed in the poem's formal interweaving of voices, and then publicly validate their lives. Shange shows the characters discovering their own sense of self-worth as African-American women.

Ford, Cathy (born 1952)

Canadian poet, born in Lloydminster, Saskatchewan, and educated at the University of British Columbia in Vancouver. Her poetry is very much concerned with the background of women's goddess or witch mythology, as well as with the physical body. She has published *Blood Uttering* (1976), *The Womb Rattles its Pod Poems* (1981), *Affaires of the Heart* (1982), *By Violent Means* (1983) and *Saffron, Rose and Flame* (1988). She lives on Maine Island in British Columbia.

Ford, Elbur ▷Plaidy, Jean

Forest (1985)

The autobiography of Japanese novelist ▷Nogami Yaeko. The story centres on a group of people involved with Meiji high school for girls, where Nogami was a student and which, from the 1880s to the 1900s, was a nerve-centre for people trying to improve the social status of women. The characters in her reminiscences are vividly portrayed, and this work is a useful resource for research on social, as well as women's, history.

For Love Alone (1944)

Australian novel by ▷Christina Stead. Stead's novel is concerned with the life of Teresa Hawkins, an idealistic girl obsessed with love and sex, who falls in love with the contemptible Jonathan Crow. She starves herself almost to death to save the money to follow him to London, only to discover his egocentric indifference and sadistic personality. She is saved by the love of James Quick, who restores her dignity and makes her conscious of her sexual power as a woman, which she tests in a sexual adventure with Quick's friend, Harry Girton. This surprising interlude, towards the end of the novel, makes the point that

women should have, and must exercise, their sexual freedom. *For Love Alone*, like Stead's other well-known work, ▷*The Man Who Loved Children*, is concerned with the dynamics of power within relationships and with the necessity for women, in particular, to achieve their individuality and sexual autonomy.

Fórmica, Mercedes (born 1918)

Spanish novelist. Born in Cádiz, Fórmica was one of an elitist bourgeois family. After graduating in 1945, she practised law. Her best-known novels, *La ciudad perdida* (1951) (*The Lost City*) and *A instancia de parte* (1955) (*On Behalf of the Third Party*), criticize a *machista* society which alienates women and victimizes men.

Forrest, Katherine V.

US novelist and short story writer. Katherine Forrest writes bestselling lesbian mystery novels featuring Kate Delafield. Kate is a homicide detective with the Los Angeles Police Department and, as a lesbian, she struggles to keep her private and public lives separate. She not only solves murder mysteries but also explores the erotic through a series of lesbian relationships, although arguably the sex scenes fail to find a convincing language for the representation of female eroticism, and are caught within the codes of ▷romantic fiction and pornography. Forrest's novels raise socio-political issues. *The Beverly Malibu* (1989) examines the effects of the house Un-American Activities Committee's loyalty investigations. As in *Murder at the Nightwood Bar* (1987), Forrest considers the present discrimination against gays and lesbians.

Other works include: *Curious Wine* (1983), *Daughters of a Coral Dawn* (1984), *Amateur City* (1984), *An Emergence of Green* (1986), *Dreams and Swords* (1987) and *Murder by Tradition*.
▷Detective fiction

Forrester, Helen (born 1919)

Pseudonym of June Bhatia, Canadian novelist, born in Hoylake, Cheshire who has written of her experiences growing up poor in England. Her autobiographical books (*Twopence to Cross the Mersey*, 1974; *Minerva's Stepchild*, 1979; *By the Waters of Liverpool*, 1981, and *Lime Street at Two*, 1985) portray her struggle to escape the domestic prison of her family. She married Avadh Behari Bhatia in 1950, and emigrated to Canada with him. Her novels continue to address the situation of women who must balance the demands of home and family with their own desires. They include *Most Precious Employee* (1976), *Liverpool Daisy* (1979), *The Latchkey Kid* (1985), *Thursday's Child* (1985) and *Yes, Mama* (1988). She lives in Edmonton, Alberta.

Forsh, Ol'ga Dmitrievna (1873–1961)

Russian prose writer, dramatist, and script writer. Although early in her life she studied art and even taught drawing at high-school level, Forsh became best-known for her historical novels, which she

began publishing in 1924. She first appeared in print in 1907, and published stories in pre-revolutionary ▷'thick journals', while continuing to teach drawing. In the first decade of the 20th century, Forsh, like a number of other women writers, became interested in occultism, and in Elena Blavatskaia's theosophy in particular. This brief interest is reflected in the stories 'The Knight from Nuremberg' (1908) and 'Children of the Earth' (1910). Forsh also wrote film scripts (eg *Palace and Fortress* about the revolution) and plays (eg *Copernicus' Death*, 1919). Her first historical novel, *Clad in Stone* (1924), in which she used a diary form, is set in Russia of the 1870s and 1880s. Like all her novels, it is structured around a moral and psychological opposition. Her next novel, *The Contemporaries* (1926), opposes the artistic genius of Gogol' and the painter Aleksandr Ivanov to a Salieri-like character. Three others dealt with the more recent past which she personally witnessed: *The Hot Shop* (1926) about the 1905 Revolution, *The Mad Ship* (1931) – many consider this her best work – about the Petrograd literary world of the 1920s, and *The Symbolists* (1933), about the literary world before the revolution. The trilogy *Radishchev*, published between 1932 and 1939, concerned the 'dissident' writer who was exiled to Siberia by ▷Catherine II. Her last full-length novel, *Pioneers of Liberty* (1953) was about the Decembrist rebellion of 1825.
Bib: Goscilo, H. (trans.), *Russian and Polish Women's Fiction*; Solasko, F. (trans.), *Palace and Prison*; Wilson, K. (ed.), *An Encyclopedia of Continental Women Writers*, Vol. I; Weber, H. (ed.), *Modern Encyclopedia of Russian and Soviet Literature*.

Forster, Margaret (born 1938)
English novelist. A writer who concentrates on family relationships, and particularly that between mother and daughter, Forster is also concerned with socially inscribed gender roles and alternative feminine identities. *Dames' Delight* (1964) is set in an all-women Oxford college, and follows the career of the unorthodox and non-conformist Morag. *Georgy Girl* (1966), made into a successful film, features another protagonist who refuses to subscribe to traditional notions of femininity. *The Park* (1968) focuses on six women with different experiences of being wives and mothers. The rewards and pitfalls of close relationships is examined in *The Seduction of Mrs Pendlebury* (1974). Non-fiction writings include: *Significant Sisters: The Grassroots of Active Feminism 1839–1939* (1984). Her most recent novel, *Lady's Maid* (1990), tells the story of ▷Elizabeth Barrett Browning through her maid.

Fortune, Mary
The first Australian woman writer of detective fiction who wrote under the name 'Waif Wander' or 'W.W.' . Waif Wander's identity was carefully hidden until the research of Lucy Sussex revealed the bizarre life-story of a resourceful and

energetic woman who surmounted, sometimes by dubious means, the misfortunes which could accompany life in the colonies for a woman without male protection. ▷*The Detective's Album* (1871) is the first book of detective stories published in Australia. Other publications in serial form included *Navvie's Tales: Retold by the Boss* (1874–5), *The Secrets of Balbrooke* (1866), *Twenty-Six Years Ago, or the Diggings from '55* (1882–3). They all appeared in the *Australian Journal*.
▷Short story (Australia); *From the Verandah; Peaceful army, The*

Fortunes of Richard Mahony, The (1930)
Australian novel by ▷Henry Handel Richardson. It details the life of the hero, Richard Mahony, an Irish-born doctor, against a dense and realistic background of life on the goldfields of Ballarat, and also in Melbourne, Geelong, and various other locations in rural Victoria. Richard Mahony is a tragic figure, whose characterization and life-story is based upon that of Richardson's father. Mahony's fortunes suffer from his impulsive and often unwise decisions, and his mental health is unstable. Because of the strength of its characterization, its panoramic picture of a dynamic colonial society, and its working out of a classical pattern of tragedy in the life of its protagonist, this is one of Australia's most significant novels. It was first published in three volumes, *Australia Felix* (1917), *The Way Home* (1925) and *Ultima Thule* (1929), and in one volume as *The Fortunes of Richard Mahony*.

Fortunes of War, The
Collective title of two trilogies of novels by ▷Olivia Manning. *The Balkan Trilogy* comprises *The Great Fortune* (1960), *The Spoilt City* (1962) and *Friends and Heroes* (1965). Its sequel, *The Levant Trilogy*, comprises *The Danger Tree* (1977), *The Battle Lost and Won* (1978) and *The Sum of Things* (1980). Based on Manning's own experiences during World War II, the novels centre on Harriet Pringle, newly married to Guy Pringle, a British Council lecturer. *The Balkan Trilogy* is set in Bucharest and Athens, *The Levant Trilogy* in Egypt. The first trilogy charts the effects of the war on the Balkan countries and, more specifically, on the group of British delegates and expatriates who stay on despite worsening conditions and increasing dangers. Manning paints a particularly vivid portrait of the likeable scrounger in Prince Yakimov, a Russian-Irish émigré fallen on hard times. She shifts between points of view in the novels, although the narrative most often stays with Harriet. Frequently left alone by the gregarious Guy, for whom social and political life are all-important, Harriet observes and acts in the local dramas of civilian life while territories are progressively annexed by Nazi Germany and lives are destroyed. At the end of *The Balkan Trilogy* Guy and Harriet escape from Athens and are evacuated to Cairo. Manning returned to their stories when she published *The Levant Trilogy* more than a decade later. Central to

this trilogy is the story of Simon Boulderstone, a British officer who fights in the Battle of Alamein.

For What? (1909)

The first of a series of four autobiographical novels by the Russian writer ▷Lidiia Chárskaia. In the foreword, Chárskaia says that she wrote this book because it might be of use to children. The fictional heroine's strong attachment to her father is echoed by the real Chárskaia's dedication of the book to her 'dear father and friend.' The heroine, Lidiia Voronskaia, comes home on vacation from an exclusive boarding school for girls and finds that her father has remarried. Lidiia reacts negatively to this news and to the birth of a step-sister whom she sees as a competitor for her father's attention. The turning point comes when she is temporarily blinded with smallpox. She is cared for by a certain 'Sister Anna' who leads Lidiia to question her hatred for her stepmother. For the first time she understands her father's need for a wife and companion, and realizes how egocentric she has been. When Lidiia's bandages are removed, she discovers that Sister Anna is her stepmother. Like most of Chárskaia's works, this one is infused with a strong moral lesson, a minute depiction of a strong-willed young heroine's emotions, especially the feeling of being unjustly misunderstood, a yearning to belong to a group of people, and a happy ending. The other three volumes in the series follow the heroine through boarding school and on to careers in the theatre and literature.

Fosso, Il (1949) (The Trench)

A quartet of short stories by ▷Laudomia Bonanni. All four narratives show characters engaged in a desperate struggle to survive. Bonanni is especially interested in the kind of choices which great poverty forces women to make. The subject is particularly relevant to Italy in the post-war period.

Foster, Hannah Webster (1758–1840)

North American novelist. The daughter of Hannah Wainwright and Grant Webster, she was born in Salisbury, Massachusetts, on 10 September 1758. Her early education must have been exceptional because her novels reveal a well-rounded knowledge of literature, history and philosophy. In 1785 she married John Foster. When her five children had reached a certain self-sufficiency, she began the career that would make her one of early North America's most popular (if not profitable) authors. ▷The Coquette (1797), an epistolary novel of seduction drawn from a well-known case in Massachusetts, appeared in thirteen editions. Her second novel, ▷The Boarding School (1798), not surprisingly, could not live up to the success of The Coquette but it reflected her ongoing interest in women's education. For several years thereafter, she limited her writing to newspaper articles; when her husband died, she resettled in Montreal with two of her daughters, Eliza Lanesford Cushing (1794–

?) and Harriet Vaughan Cheney (1796–?), both of whom had followed in their mother's literary footsteps. She died in Montreal on 17 April 1840. The Coquette, recently recovered, has won new audiences and scholarly interest in the late 20th century.

Fothergill, Jessie (1851–1891)

English novelist, born in Chetham Hill, Manchester. She was sent to boarding school in Harrogate after her father's death, and began her literary career with Healey (1875). Eleven novels followed, including The First Violin (1877); The Lasses of Leverhouses (1888) and her last work, Oriole's Daughter (1893). Much of her fiction concerns romantic involvements between people of different social classes.

Fouqué, Karoline Freifrau de la Motte (c 1773–1831)

German writer. The only daughter of a Prussian landowner, she married an army officer and compulsive gambler who, shortly before their divorce was finalized, shot himself because of debts. In 1803 she married the romantic writer Friedrich de La Motte Fouqué (1777–1843), and began to publish a series of unsigned fairytales, novels and novellas. She also wrote letters and essays on the education and social role of women, including Briefe über Zweck and Richtung weiblicher Bildung (1810) (Letters on the Purpose and Direction of Female Education) and Die Frauen in der großen Welt. Bildungsbuch beim Eintritt in das gesellige Leben (1826) (Women in the Wider World. A Guide for Entering Society).

Fourqueux, Madame de (18th century)

French novelist. She published three works, all concerned with female destinies: Zély ('or the difficulty of being happy, an Indian novel') (1775); Julie de Saint-Olmont 'or the first illusions of love') (1805) and Amélie de Tréville ('or the solitary woman') (1806).

Fowke, Edith (born 1913)

Born Edith Marshall in Lumsden, Saskatchewan, she was educated at the University of Saskatchewan and taught folklore as an English professor at York University, Toronto. Canada's premier folklorist, she has published many books that detail various aspects of Canadian folklore. Folk Songs of Canada (1954, with Richard Johnston), Canada's Story in Song (1960, with Alan Mills), More Folk Songs of Canada (1967), The Penguin Book of Canadian Folk Songs (1986) and Lumbering Songs from the Northern Woods (1985) are all collections of folksongs. She is famous for her extensive work on fables and stories, as in Folklore of Canada (1976) and Tales Told in Canada (1986). Folktales of French Canada (1979) is an excellent collection that makes an attempt to emulate the style of the original French narrators. She also published *A Bibliography of Canadian Folklore in English* (1981), which is the first comprehensive listing of all the different genres of Canadian folklore, an important aspect of social history.

Frabotta, Biancamaria (born 1947)

Italian poet and academic. Born in Rome, Frabotta has earned acclaim for her poetry and her literary criticism. She is a lecturer in the fields of modern and contemporary literature at the University of Rome, and is active in the Italian feminist movement. Much of her academic work has been in the field of feminist theory, including *Femminismo e lotta di classe* (1973) (*Feminism and Class Struggle*); *La politica del femminismo* (1976) (*The Politics of Feminism*) and *Letteratura al femminile* (1980) (*Literature in the Female Mode*). Her most recent work, *Velocità di Fuga* (1989) (*The Speed of Flight*), is stylistically novel, and feminist in inspiration.

Her other works include: *Carlo Cattaneo* (1969); *Affeminata* (1977) (*Feminate*); *Il rumore bianco* (1982) (*White Noise*) and *Appunti di volo e altre poesie* (1986) (*Notes on Flight and Other Poetry*). **Bib:** 'Left Hand, White Poetry', *Annali d'Italianistica*, 7, (1989) pp. 340–54.

Fraenkel, Naomi (born 1920)

Israeli novelist. Fraenkel was born in Berlin and emigrated to Palestine in 1933. She studied at the Hebrew University. Fraenkel's trilogy of novels, *Saul Ve'Yohana* (1956–1967) (*Saul and Johana*), reflects the awareness of Israeli writers in the late 1950s of the historical memory of the nation. The novels follow a Jewish-German family through three generations, linking the past in Germany with the present in Israel.

Frame, Janet Paterson (born 1924)

New Zealand novelist. Janet Frame is New Zealand's greatest novelist. One of five children of a railway worker, she grew up in Oamaru. She was academically successful but lived in conditions of considerable poverty and difficulty. Frame's account of her life in her autobiographical trilogy fully documents both her family's situation and the development of her intellectual and creative life. Two of Frame's sisters died young by drowning and her brother's life was affected by epilepsy, events which had consequences in her life and are frequently referred to in her writing. She went to Dunedin Teachers College 1943–4, but left teaching in 1945 and became a voluntary patient at Seacliff Mental Hospital in 1947. She spent the next seven years in various mental hospitals and during this time published a collection of stories, *The Lagoon* (1951), which won the Hubert Church Memorial Award.

From 1954 to 1955 Frame lived on the property of the New Zealand writer, Frank Sargeson, and wrote her first novel ▷*Owls Do Cry*. She left New Zealand on a State Literary

Janet Frame

Fund grant in 1956, and lived in Spain and England for the next seven years, publishing three novels and two collections of stories. She returned to New Zealand in 1963, and has lived there, with extended visits to the United States since then, working full-time as a writer.

Frame has published eleven novels, four collections of stories, a collection of poems, three volumes of autobiography which have been made into a film (*An Angel at My Table*, 1990) and has won all New Zealand's major literary awards. The direction of Frame's fiction is, as she puts it in her autobiography, 'toward the Third Place, where the starting point is myth' (*To the Is-land*). Although her fiction begins in ▷realism, Frame's concern with language and its relation to truth, and her suspicion of conventional 'realities', has led to her development of a unique kind of narrative which explores the process by which 'reality' is created.

Frame has an international reputation and several of her later novels are set in the US, but she is also an important regional writer, documenting New Zealand's cultural history and identity.

Publications: *The Lagoon* (stories) (1951); ▷*Owls Do Cry* (novel) (1957); *Faces in the Water* (novel) (1961); *The Edge of the Alphabet* (novel) (1962); *Scented Gardens for the Blind* (novel) (1963); *The Reservoir* (stories) (1963); *Snowman, Snowman* (stories) (1963); *The Adaptable Man* (novel) (1965); *A State of Siege* (novel) (1966); *The Pocket Mirror* (poems) (1967); *The Rainbirds* (novel) (1968); *Mona Minim and the Smell of the Sun* (children's book) (1969); *Intensive Care* (novel) (1970); *Daughter Buffalo* (novel) (1972); *Living in the Maniototo* (novel) (1979); *To the Is-land* (autobiography) (1983); *An Angel at My Table* (autobiography) (1984); *You Are Now Entering the Human Heart* (stories) (1984); *The Envoy from*

Mirror City (autobiography) (1985); *The Carpathians* (novel) (1988).

France, Ruth (1913–1968)
New Zealand poet and novelist. France originally wrote under the pseudonym Paul Henderson. Like her contemporary ▷Ruth Dallas, she wrote landscape poetry in which the landscape is a metaphor for emotion. As 'Henderson', France published two collections of poetry as well as two novels under her own name.

Publications: *Unwilling Pilgrim* (1955); *The Race* (1958); *The Halting Place* (1961); *Ice Cold River* (1961).

Franchi, Anna (1866–1954)
Italian journalist, novelist, essayist and critic. Born in Livorno, she lived through, and recorded in her work, many crucial phases of Italian history, such as the post-unification period, World War I, ▷fascism, World War II and the immediate post-war period. Her critical works include studies on art and art history, such as *Arte ed artisti toscani dal 1850 ad oggi* (1902) (*Tuscan Art and Artists from 1850 to the Present*); *I macchiaioli toscani* (1945) (*The Tuscan Impressionists*); *G. Fattori. Studio biografico* (1910) (*A Biographical Study of G. Fattori*); historical works such as *Caterina de'Medici regina di Francia* (1933) (*Caterina de' Medici, Queen of France*), *Storia della pirateria nel mondo* (1953) (*A World History of Piracy*), and literary works such as *Luci dantesche* (1955) (*Reflections of Dante*).

Her other works include: *I viaggi di un soldatino di piombo* (1901) (*The Travels of a Little Lead Soldier*); *Decadente* (1901); *Un eletto del popolo* (1909) (*Chosen by the People*); *Dalle memorie di un sacerdote* (1910) (*Memories of a Priest*); *Mamma* (1912); *Il figlio della guerra* (1917) (*Son of War*); *Ironie* (1919) (*Ironies*); *La torta di Mele* (1927) (*Apple Tart*); *Dono d'amore* (1931) (*Gift of Love*); *Cose d'ieri dette alle donne d'oggi* (1946) (*Sayings of Yesterday for Women of Today*); *La mia vita* (1947) (*My Life*); *Santa Margherita da Cortona* (1947); *Polvere del passato* (1953) (*Dust of the Past*).

Franciscan literature (Italy)
Saint Francis was born in Assisi in about 1182 of a noble and wealthy family. After a serious illness as a young man, he devoted himself to a religious life of privation. His writings are ▷mystical in style. His most famous work, *Il cantico di Frate Sole* (*Brother Sun's Canticle*), also known as *Laudes creaturarum*, inspired a particular genre of religious writing. ▷Angela da Foligno joined the Franciscan order and wrote poetry which is partly inspired by the writing of Saint Francis.

Franco, Veronica (1546–1591)
Italian poet. An accomplished ▷'cortegiana onesta', celebrated for her writing and her beauty. Born in Venice, she spent her life there, married a doctor and had one son, but was widowed early in life. She was a friend and correspondent of many of the famous men of politics and letters of her day. Critics have long been divided over Franco's

possible reformation late in life. The only evidence of this, however, is that she certainly founded a hostel for 'fallen women' in 1577. In none of her poetry, nor in her letters, does she ever express guilt or regret for her life as a courtesan. On the contrary, her writing celebrates her way of life. At least one Italian critic, Francesco Flora, has taken exception to the celebration of female sexuality in Franco's work, describing it as 'bestial'. Her two most famous volumes are her *Terze Rime*, a collection of poetry of 1575, and her *Lettere* (*Letters*) of 1580. Her poetry, like her letters, tells the story of her life, and, in this concentration on personal experience, has similarities to the poetry of Petrarch (▷Petrarchism). In the poetry (reprinted in 1738 and 1913), she makes of herself a goddess figure and explicitly links herself with images of sexuality and fertility. She plays on her name, describing herself as a character both '*vera*' (true) and '*unica*' (unique). Throughout this poetry, she rejects images of female chastity. Her claim that women should be free and independent is strikingly different from the female submission demanded in most of the poetry of the period. Her *Letters*, however, contain one particularly revealing missive, addressed to a mother who wished her daughter to become a courtesan. In this letter, Franco dwells on the harshness of the courtesan life, and criticizes the mother who would subject her daughter to such an existence, thus revealing another side to the life she had led.

François, Louise von (1817–1893)
German short story writer and novelist. A native of Saxony who was largely self-educated, she was introduced to literature by ▷Fanny Tarnow, and in 1855 began publishing novellas under the pseudonym L.v.F. Her stories are set in 18th- and 19th-century Saxony, and centre on themes of self-sacrifice and renunciation, nurtured by a strict Protestant ethos. Her greatest success was the novel, *Die letzte Reckenburgerin* (1871) (*The Last Woman of the Rechenburgs*).

Frank, Anne (Annelies Marie) (1929–1945)
German-Jewish diarist whose parents moved to Amsterdam in order to escape the Nazis. *The Diary of Anne Frank* won instant fame on its publication in 1947, two years after the death of its author in Belsen. The diary charts the years between 1942 and 1944 when she and her family were forced into hiding by the German invasion of Holland. The diary begins just before the family retreated into their 'Secret Annexe' and records some of the restrictions faced by Dutch Jews under the Nazis.

The poignancy of the diary is increased by Anne Frank's use of an epistolary form. The letters are addressed, in the absence of a 'real friend', to the imaginary 'Kitty'. Her record of the hardships of life in hiding is entangled with the experiences of an ordinary adolescent coming to terms with puberty under extraordinary circumstances. Anne Frank revised the diaries herself while still in hiding, after listening to a radio broadcast from London about the importance of war diaries and letters. In August 1944 the Gestapo discovered the family's hiding place, and Anne Frank was sent to the Dutch concentration camp, Westerbork, and from there to Belsen, where she died in March 1945.

Frankenstein, or the Modern Prometheus (1818)

A ▷Gothic tale of terror by English novelist ▷Mary Shelley, informed by contemporary philosophical debate and structured as an ▷epistolary novel. Frankenstein is a student of natural philosophy who discovers the secret of imparting life to inanimate matter. He creates a monster of gigantic proportions and endowed with supernatural strength. The monster is benevolent, and seeks human company, but his appearance is so terrifying and repellent that he cannot be accepted by human society. Frankenstein refuses to create a female mate for the monster, who then turns against him, murdering Frankenstein's friend, Clerval, and fiancée, Elizabeth. Frankenstein pursues the monster to the Arctic in an attempt to destroy it, but dies in the pursuit. In the Preface, Mary Shelley states that she began writing the novel in the summer of 1816, when she, Percy Bysshe Shelley and Byron agreed to write a ▷ghost story apiece. Hers was the only one to be completed. The tale has been absorbed into popular culture, and numerous film versions have been made, but the novel has also generated much critical comment in recent years. It has been read as a critique of ▷Romantic individualism, as a philosophical discussion of human nature indebted to Rousseau, as a semi-autobiographical work, and as a representation of the position of women in society. Feminist criticism includes Anne K. Mellor's *Mary Shelley: Her Life, Her Fiction, Her Monsters*; Margaret Homans's, *Bearing the Word*, and *The Proper Lady and the Woman Writer* by Mary Poovey.

Frank Leslie's Popular Monthly (1876–1906)

US illustrated periodical. It was the flagship magazine of the Frank Leslie publishing empire, which included more than a dozen other specialized journals. Along with topical articles, the monthly published poetry, travel, essays, short stories and serialized novels – some of the literature pirated from British magazines. Among the US contributors (who were paid) were ▷Harriet Prescott Spofford and ▷Amelia Huddleston Barr.

Franklin, Deborah Read Rogers (1708–1774)

North American letter-writer. Although little is known of her early life, she became a part of national history when her common-law husband, the North American statesman Benjamin Franklin, detailed their courtship in his now classic *Autobiography*. Raised in Philadelphia, she had a stormy courtship with Franklin, and when he went to England she married John Rogers; it

was an unhappy marriage, and they soon separated. Though never divorced, she was reconciled with Franklin upon his return to North America, and they lived as man and wife for the remainder of her life. Her correspondence, collected in *The Papers of Benjamin Franklin*, reveals the great difference in education between herself and her husband; her writing is often phonetically spelled and full of the details of her life in North America while Benjamin was in Europe on business. The letters also reveal the courage and heartiness with which she withstood abuses from North American citizens who disagreed with Franklin's actions abroad and with her husband's constant admonitions to be frugal, in spite of his own luxurious lifestyle in the royal courts of England and France. Very ill in her later years, she often pleaded with her husband to return to North America; he did not do so until one month after she had died. Perhaps no couple of the American Revolution so blatantly symbolized the gender differences in education and opportunity that prevailed, even in a country that advocated democratic principles.

▷'Letters of Deborah Read Rogers Franklin, The'

Franklin, Miles (1879–1954)

Miles Franklin

Australian novelist; full name Stella Maria Miles Franklin, also used the pseudonym 'Brent of Bin Bin'. Franklin was born at Talbingo, New South Wales, and lived at Brindabella near Canberra, then on a poverty-stricken farm near Goulburn as the family fortunes declined, but spent her adult life in Sydney, Chicago and London, and finally returned to Sydney. Her first novel, ▷*My Brilliant Career*, written when she was eighteen, was published in 1901, and was enthusiastically received both in Australia and overseas. Franklin was active in the Australian feminist movement and, after moving to Chicago in 1906, worked in a secretarial and editorial capacity for the National Women's Trade Union League until 1915. She served with the Scottish Women's Hospital in Serbia from 1917 to 1918; worked with the National Housing and Town Planning Council in London from 1919 to 1925; and returned permanently to Australia in 1934. *Childhood at Brindabella* (1963) and *My Career Goes Bung* (1946) are semi-autobiographical; *Some Everyday Folk and Dawn* (1909), *Old Blastus of Bandicoot* (1931), *Bring the Monkey* (1933), and ▷*All That Swagger* (1936), are romances of mixed quality; and six pastoral romances appeared under the pseudonym of 'Brent of Bin Bin'. Franklin bequeathed her estate to establish the prestigious annual Miles Franklin Award.

▷Autobiography (Australia); Feminism (Australia); *Gender, Politics and Fiction*; Literary criticism (Australia); *Peaceful Army, The*

Frapan, Ilse (1849–1908)

German novelist and short story writer. A teacher in Hamburg, in her twenties she began to write and travel widely, taking up the study of natural sciences in Zurich in 1882. She was principally known for her witty stories about everyday life in Hamburg, but novels such as *Wir Frauen haben kein Vaterland* (1899) (*We Women Have No Homeland*) or *Arbeit* (1903) (*Labour*) are serious investigations of the nature of women's oppression.

Fraser, Sylvia (born 1935)

Canadian novelist, born Sylvia Meyers in Hamilton, Ontario. She was educated at the University of Western Ontario and, until 1968, travelled widely and worked as a journalist. Her first novel, *Pandora* (1972), covers eight years in a young girl's life, and reflects on the politics of childhood. Curiously, in its intensely detailed recounting of a child's point of view it is a fictional prefiguration of Fraser's powerful and courageous memoir of paternal incest, *My Father's House: A Memoir of Incest and Healing* (1987). *The Candy Factory* (1975) is a strange fantasy set in a candy factory, and reflecting a whole range of sexual politics. *A Casual Affair: A Modern Fairytale* (1978) depicts the personal brutality and manipulation of an extra-marital affair. *The Emperor's Virgin* (1980) is an historical work about a Roman woman who breaks her vow of chastity. *Berlin Solstice* (1984) shifts to World War II, and the trade-offs that people must make to survive. Fraser lives in Toronto.

Bib: Irvine, L., *Sub/Version*.

Frau Emma kämpft im Hinterland (1929)

A play by the German writer and dramatist ▷Isle Langner. Set at the time of World War I, it depicts women's struggle for survival in a country close to social collapse and famine. The central figure is the working-class mother, Frau Emma. While her husband is in the trenches, Emma becomes a ruthless and resourceful survivor and protector of her children. When he returns, she does not readily relinquish her newly-found independence. This was the first anti-war play written by a German woman, and it is also an important statement about how women may sometimes gain power to resist the destructive forces of male-dominated society.

Freeman, Mary E. Wilkins (1852–1930)

US short story writer, novelist, poet and dramatist as well as writer of poems and stories for children. The leading US writer on New England, she is principally known for her stories, first published in the prestigious national literary magazines and then collected in volumes including ▷*A Humble Romance* (1887), ▷*A New England Nun* (1891) and *Edgewater People* (1918). Her novels include *Jane Field* (1893), *Jerome, A Poor Man* (1897), *The Heart's Highway* (1900) and her finest, ▷*Pembroke* (1894). She is also the author of a remarkable play on the Salem witch trials: ▷*Giles Corey, Yeoman*.

Many of Wilkins Freeman's plots centre on the difficulties of marriage, especially of two individuals bringing themselves to marry and living together afterwards. Among her marriages are many odd couples. She is noted for her realism, for her finely developed characters, and for her insights into people, communities and cultures. Wilkins Freeman was critically esteemed in her own time and is generally regarded as one of the finest fiction writers of the 19th century.

▷*Harper's Bazar*

French, Alice (1850–1934)

US short-story writer and novelist. Primarily known for her ▷local color stories, set in Arkansas and Iowa, French was a regular and significant contributor to national literary magazines, especially ▷*The Century Illustrated Monthly Magazine*. An unusually effective negotiator with editors, French insisted on the integrity of the language and thought of her Arkansas characters. Her stories are collected in a number of volumes, including *Knitters in the Sun* (1887) and *Stories of a Western Town* (1893); novels include *Expiation* (1890) and *The Man of the Hour* (1905). She is also significant, along with ▷Mary Hallock Foote, for her treatment of labour issues in the American west. French published under the pseudonym Octave Thanet.

French, Anne (born 1956)

New Zealand poet. Anne French grew up and was educated in Wellington. After a short time spent in university teaching she worked in publishing. French won the 1972 Young Writers Award for Poetry but did not publish a collection until 1987. Her work is characterized by a strong formal control, experimentation with metrical structures, language play and a sharply satirical view of social, and especially gender, relations.

Publications include: ▷*All Cretans are Liars* (1987); *The Male as Evader* (1988); and *Cabin Fever* (1990).

French, Marilyn (born 1929)

US novelist and essayist. French was born in New York into a poor family of Polish desent. She left college to marry, and after raising two children she earned a doctoral degree at Harvard University. In her controversial novels French vents her anger at women's fate under ▷patriarchy. *The Women's Room* (1977), which was French's most popular novel, tells the stories of suburban housewives and depicts the limitations and emptiness of their lives, where men are seen as impediments to their wives' lives. French posits that US culture is founded on contempt for women. *The Bleeding Heart* (1981) examines the failure of marriage in an industrialized society. French suggests that emotions are starved in a society that emphasizes power, as such a society denies the self its true nature. French's protagonists assert their independence from their victimization.

Other works include: *Beyond Power: On Women, Men and Morals* (1985), *Her Mother's Daughter* (1987) and *The War Against Women* (1992).

French, Mary (fl 1703)

North American poet. In the summer of 1703 she was captured by Native Americans and taken from her home in Deerfield, Massachusetts, to Canada, where she was detained by French captors. In▷'A Poem Written by a Captive Damsel', she addresses her teenage sister and counsels her to have faith during this moment of trial. This is one of the rarer poetic forms of the early North American ▷captivity narratives.

French Expedition to Egypt (1798–1801)

This expedition first opened the country to modern exploration and scientific study. The army of French *savants* had a great impact on knowledge of the country, though the expedition was a military failure. French orientalists in the service of the army set up an Arabic printing press which published leaflets and army commands in Arabic. In spite of the huge volume of documentation on all aspects of this expedition, there is hardly any information on whether it had any impact on the cloistered lives of the women of the country. One solitary incident is reported concerning a woman of the *Ashraf* class (the descendents of Prophet Muhammad through the children of his daughter Fatima): Zaynab al-Bakriyya donned European dress and apparently mixed freely with the infidel French. Her father cut his throat in public after the evacuation of the French army, thus washing out his *'ar* (shame, disgrace) with blood and vindicating his *sharaf* (honour).

French feminism, influence of

Although in a geographical sense the term includes all French feminists, it is usually taken to designate women writing after 1968, whose work employs ▷poststructuralist theories of language and subjectivity. The exception is ▷Simone de Beauvoir. French feminists whose work has been translated into English and who are therefore most influential in the English-speaking world are: ▷Hélène Cixous, ▷Luce Irigaray, ▷Julia Kristeva and Monique Wittig. Despite other differences, the influence of ▷psychoanalysis can be seen in each of these theorist's work, as well as writing by other French feminists.

▷MLF (Mouvement de Libération des Femmes)
Bib: Marks, E. and de Courtivron, I. (eds), *New French Feminisms*; Moi, T., *French Feminist Thought.*

French Historie, The (1589)

Long narrative poem by English writer Anne Dowriche. Little is known of the author, other than that she was the daughter of Peter Edgcumbe, and that she was married first to Hugh Dowriche and then to Richard Trefusis. *The French Historie*, written during Dowriche's first marriage, is her only known work. Consisting of approximately 2,400 lines of poulter's measure (a twelve-syllable line alternating with a fourteen-syllable line), Dowriche's poem is based on Thomas Timme's English prose translation of Jean de Sarre's *Commentaries* on the French Civil Wars. The strongly Protestant tale concerning the recent tribulations of the Huguenots unfolds through two male personae, an Englishman (the narrator) and the French exile he encounters while out on a walk. Dowriche's Frenchman recounts an often exciting narrative of battles between the Protestant righteous and the villainous Catholics, the French King Henry and ▷Catherine de Medici who are in council with the devil. Central themes are the exile and righteousness of Protestant godliness in the face of Catholic suppression. Dowriche's reasons for composing her work were threefold: self-edification, the defense of poetry and the edification of others by delighting with the glory of God.

▷Prefaces (16th– and 17th–century Britain); Protestant Reformation

French Revolution: pamphlets, registers of grievances, petitions and speeches

During the French Revolution (1789), women began to write and to make their opinions heard in new areas. They made speeches which were printed, and they published pamphlets, brochures, manifestos and petitions. One of the forms adopted was the *Cahiers de doléances* (▷Register of Grievances), published by groups and individuals claiming or defending their rights: the *Cahiers de doléances et réclamation des femmes* (1789) (*Register of Women's Grievances and Complaints*) for example, published by the anonymous Madame B*** B*** These women demanded acceptance of the principle of equality, and called for legislation to enshrine and protect political and civil rights, particularly in regard to participation in legislative and executive processes, divorce, illegitimacy, inheritance and work. Other demands included free education, professional training, and the right to join the army. Many of the women extended their arguments to include other oppressed groups, arguing for equality regardless not only of sex but also race and class. The analyses of the economic and political situation are shrewd, and propositions are precise and concise. However prudent the women were, they set out their demands firmly and rigorously.

▷Corbin, Lucidor; Aeders, Etta Palm d'; Gouges, Marie Gouze de (Olympe de); Jodin,, Mademoiselle; Lacombe, Claire; Léon, Pauline; Roland, Madame; Théroigne de Méricourt, Anne-Joseph.
Bib: Didier, B., *Ecrire la Révolution;* Duhet, P., *Les Femmes et la Révolution.* Editions of collected documents include: Duhet, P. (ed.), *Cahiers de doléances des femmes et autres textes (Register of Women's Grievances and Other Texts*); *Les femmes dans la Révolution française (Women in the French Revolution*), (1982); Levy, Applewhite and Johnson, *Women in Revolutionary Paris.*

French-speaking North Africa

When francophone Maghrebian literature is mentioned, one is more likely to read about male writers, such as Driss Chraîbi, Katib Yacine and Mohammed Dib, than women writers like ▷Taos Amrouche, ▷Assia Djebar, ▷Béji Hélé and others. This unfortunate ignorance, if not exclusion, of francophone women writers in North Africa is due largely to the difficulties they have in making their voices heard.

Of the three countries of the Maghreb (Morocco, Algeria and Tunisia), Algeria has produced the largest literary output by both men and women. In each country, the use of French as a means of expression is due to the colonial legacy, and especially the French colonial policy of assimilation. This policy was meant to drive a wedge between the Maghrebian people and their own languages and cultures. It succeeded, in that most writers read and write very little classical Arabic (if any at all). Women writers, like their male counterparts, come mostly from the middle and upper social classes with access to French education. Most of them continued their higher education in the French metropolis.

Maghrebian women's writing came to be known as early as 1947 with Taos Amrouche's novel *Jacinthe noire (Black Hyacinth).* The theme of biculturalism that predominates in her work has been continued by later generations of women writers.

Women's writing (especially in French) did, and still does, meet with less enthusiasm at home than in France. The Maghrebian reading public considers women writers to be alien to their own culture. Their cool reception by the literary milieu, which is predominantly male, is attributable to their daring to enter the public sphere and voice their concerns in print. The literate elite in Maghrebian society demonstrates an ambiguous contradiction between public attitudes and private practice. While by its Westernized education it claims to be '*evolué*'

(advanced), its family values, and specifically the position of women, remain within the realm of Moslem and conservative tradition.

When Assia Djebar published her first novel *La Soif* (1957) (*The Mischief*), the reception was hostile. The critics reproached her for her concern with sexuality at a time when the whole country was fighting for liberation. Concerned mainly with the revolution against French rule, the critics failed to see *The Mischief* as another form of revolution, namely the reclamation of the female body.

Maghrebian women writers have voiced common concerns and preoccupations, such as the right of women to education and recognition of their political, economic and social status. However, their efforts have not reached as wide a spectrum of the population as would potentially benefit from such awareness. This is because women's writing in the Maghreb has certain weaknesses. Their straightforward, semi-autobiographical and introspective style lacks aesthetic value. The problem of illiteracy, especially among women, makes their work available only to a limited reading audience. The use of French doubles the handicap. Conscious of the problem of language, Assia Djebar turned to film-making. With *La Nouba des femmes du mont Chenoua* (1979) (*The Celebration of the Women of Mount Chenoua*) she managed to overcome the problems of language and literary, reaching the illiterate masses through the use of Arabic.

Censorship is another obstacle that hinders literary production in the Maghreb. The large publishing houses are state-controlled (SNED in Algeria, Dar-al-Kitab in Morocco). Smaller private publishing houses tend to die very quickly (such was the fate of the literary review *Souffles* and the literary magazine *Kalima* in Morocco). Because of this, most writers publish in France, and a good number of them also live there so as to have more freedom of expression. The lack of this freedom is a major handicap for women's literary production in the Maghreb. Censorship and self-censorship weaken the credibility of their work. This is one of the reasons why non-fiction writers like the Moroccan sociologist ▷Fatima Mernissi, attract a bigger audience than their fiction-writing sisters. Women who write are more likely to be personally identified with their characters and judged accordingly. Hence the use of ▷pseudonyms by some, such as Assia Djebar and ▷Aicha Lemsine.

Unfortunately, in the face of these obstacles, many writers give up. With very few exceptions, Maghrebian women writers tend to fall silent after one or two publications.

Freud, Sigmund ▷Psychoanalysis

Friedan, Betty (born 1921)

US feminist writer and social psychologist. Born in the Midwest, Friedan graduated from Smith University, and went on to do research in psychology at the University of California at

Berkeley. She became a freelance writer after her marriage and the birth of her children, writing for magazines such as *Harper's, Good Housekeeping* and *Mademoiselle,* as well as *Reader's Digest.* In 1966 she became one of the co-founders of the National Organization for Women, and its first president; NOW was the first national organization of the new women's movement, 'Although', Friedan recently commented at its Silver Anniversary Celebration, 'it wasn't called the Women's Movement at the time . . . I always considered it the Unfinished Movement'.

She is best-known for *The Feminine Mystique* (1963), which was the first investigation of the social and cultural construction of femininity of the contemporary women's liberation movement in the US. An immensely influential book, it asked why, after the feminist gains of the early 20th century and the impact of World War II on women's opportunities, the 1950s found middle-class women back in the home. Her project was to account for the 'strange discrepancy between the reality of our lives as women and the image to which we were trying to conform, the image that I came to call the feminine mystique'. The book is remarkable for its chapter on women's magazines as an early example of feminist consideration of popular culture and ideology. Although criticized now by some feminists for its sociological approach to gender roles, it remains a classic of its time.

Other works include her autobiography, *It Changed My Life* (1976), and *The Second Stage* (1982).

Fringe Dwellers, The (1961)

Australian novel by ▷Nene Gare. This novel deals with the problems of two part-Aboriginal girls, Noonah and Trilby Comeaway, who persuade their parents to move into a housing development where assimilation is encouraged. The family is unable to escape its background – the drinking, gambling and freeloading of the relatives. They are evicted and return to a one-roomed house on a native reservation, where Trilby becomes resigned to the squalor and emptiness of the life of a fringe-dweller.

▷Aborigine in Australian women's writing, The

Frischmuth, Barbara (born 1941)

Austrian novelist. After her father had been killed during World War II, she was raised by her mother, who struggled to look after her while running a hotel. Frischmuth's works are preoccupied with childhood, from her early novel *Klosterschule* (1968) (*Convent School*), onwards. Fairytale fantasy and ▷realism are mingled together in her semi-autobiographical trilogy of ▷Bildungsromane: *Die Mystifikationen der Sophie Silber* (1976) (*The Mystifications of Sophie Silber*); *Amy oder die Metamorphose* (1978) (*Amy or the Metamorphosis*); and *Kai und die Liebe zu den Modellen* (1979) (*Kai and the Love of Models*). Her interest in myth, the miraculous and the exotic

also colours her novels *Das Verschwinden des Schattens in der Sonne* (1973) (*The Disappearance of the Shadow in the Sun*), set in Istanbul, and *Mörderische Märchen* (1989) (*Murderous Fairytales*). Always partially autobiographical, her books revolve around women's yearnings and searches for fulfilment – a quest she re-examines in each successive novel. Her works display a vivid plasticity of language, and powerful narrative inventiveness. More recent novels include ▷*Über die Verhältnisse* (1987) (*Beyond One's Means*) and *Einander Kind* (1990) (*One-another Child*).

Frohberg, Regina (1783–1850)

German writer. Born into a Jewish family in Berlin, she converted to Christianity, changed her name to Saling, and in 1813 moved to Vienna, where she belonged to a number of literary circles. After a first novel, *Schmerz der Liebe* (*Pain of Love*), published anonymously in 1810, she wrote many other novels and novellas under the pseudonym 'F'. They include *Die Entsagung* (1824) (*The Renunciation*), *Eigene und fremde Schuld* (1837) (*One's Own and Someone Else's Guilt*) and *Vergangenheit und Zukunft* (1840) (*Past and Future*). She also translated and edited French plays, published as *Theater* (*Drama*) in 1818.

Frölich, Henriette (1768–1833)

German novelist. Born into the large family of a court employee, she supplemented a basic education with her own reading programme, and began to write poetry at the age of ten. After her marriage to a lawyer, by whom she had ten children, her house in Berlin became a place where progressive thinkers could congregate. In 1792 the family moved to a country estate, but lost everything when they were ransacked twice during the Napoleonic wars. Influenced by the ideals of the French Revolution (1789), she wrote a utopian novel, *Virginia oder die Kolonie von Kentucky* (1818–19) (*Virginia or the Colony of Kentucky*).

From a Garden in the Antipodes (1929)

Poems by New Zealand writer ▷Mary Ursula Bethell: Published under the pseudonym Evelyn Hayes, *From a Garden in the Antipodes* is a loosely connected collection of poems written about Bethell's garden in the Cashmere Hills south of Christchurch. The poems resist rhetorical flourishes in their close focus on the activities of the garden, but in her use of botanical language and carefully-judged metaphor Bethell creates a suggestive set of connections between gardening and larger views of landscape, time and belief. It has been said of Bethell that New Zealand was not really discovered until she raised her head from digging and saw it; although her poems raise the colonial question of separation and 'home' they also create a very specific locality.

From Man to Man (1926)

A novel by South African writer ▷Olive Schreiner. Schreiner started *From Man to Man* when she was eighteen but, according to her husband, left it unfinished at her death forty-seven years later. He published it in 1926, adding a short postscript giving the ending he said his wife had suggested. More recently, however, critics have argued that its open-ended structure was what the writer indeed wished for, her inability to proclaim the novel finished indicating her covert desire not to provide a conventional happy ending. The story centres on two women, Rebekah and Bertie. It is, as Schreiner once put it, 'the story of a prostitute and of a married woman who loves another man, and whose husband is sensual and unfaithful'. In the Prelude, called 'The Child's Day', and one of the most powerful sections of the text, Rebekah tells stories to her newly-born little sister, whom she does not know is dead. Growing up into a highly intelligent woman, continually eager to educate herself and to improve her knowledge of the natural sciences, Rebekah marries a man who belittles and limits her, is unfaithful, and refuses her a divorce. In another of the novel's powerful scenes, Rebekah writes him a lengthy letter setting out her view of male–female relationships, which he never reads. This story ends with Rebekah's deepening friendship with Mr Drummond, a friendship which signifies the gender equality Schreiner's writing so constantly and so hopelessly drives toward.

The text's other story is about Bertie, who is seduced by a visiting tutor, and subsequently jilted by her fiancé when she confesses this tale of her past. Bertie then becomes the mistress of a Jew who takes her to London, Rebekah later hearing that she has become a prostitute. Bertie comes to represent the feminine as it turns towards the humiliating parasitism Schreiner lambasted in her *Woman and Labour* (1911). Alternately tender and sarcastic towards 'Baby-Bertie', Schreiner uses her to expose the social injustice of a situation which condemns a woman, whether for the loss of her virginity before marriage or for prostituting herself, yet turns a blind eye to irresponsible male behaviour. Moreover, Bertie's status as mistress and, supposedly, prostitute, casts its shadow over Rebekah's marriage, posing questions about the possibilities for gender equality in a situation of economic dependence.

This is an uneven book. Huge chunks of it were added throughout Schreiner's life, with older parts sometimes remaining incompletely matched to the new, but it is, nevertheless, arguably her most powerful and affecting work, vastly underrated by critics.

From Purdah to Parliament (1963)
Autobiography of ▷Shaista Ikramullah, the first woman to sit in Pakistan's Constituent Assembly when it was convened in 1948. Ikramullah writes engagingly of her shift between three political and cultural eras, that of the declining Mughal courtly culture of Dacca which her grandfather attempted to preserve, the heyday of the British Empire in which she grew up, and the fight for

independence and the birth of Pakistan which she witnessed as an adult. The book is interesting for its generous appraisal of the life behind the veil which her mother and her female cousins observed, and also for Ikramullah's explanation of her passionate commitment to a separate homeland for India's Muslims.

From the Verandah: Stories of Love and Landscape by Nineteenth Century Australian Women (1987)
Anthology edited by Fiona Giles, contains stories by ▷Jessie Couvreur ('Tasma'), ▷Rosa Praed, Ellen Augusta Chads, Ellen Liston, ▷Mary Fortune ('Waif Wander'), ▷Ethel Turner, Flora Beatrice, ▷Ada Cambridge, Mura Leigh, Ellen Clacy, Agnes Rose-Sorley, Lala Fisher, ▷Louise Mack, ▷Barbara Baynton, Ethel Mills, ▷Mary Gaunt, and Mary Hannay Foott. The stories are arranged under four headings – 'Mysteries, Some Solved', 'Laughing Matters', 'Four Country Heroines and a Hero', 'Loss', and 'Stories Remembered' – and demonstrate the range of interests of Australian women short story writers in the 19th century.
▷Anthologies (Australia)

From Which Place (1965)
An autobiographical novel by Japanese writer Setouchi Haroumi (born 1922). The narrator elopes, leaving her infant daughter with her husband, when she falls in love with the husband's student. She finds herself in difficulties after she parts from her lover and encounters a middle-aged writer living in obscurity. The narrator devotes herself to writing novels for ten years while they live together from time to time. Her desolate mental condition during this period leads her to adopt a religious way of life eight years later.

Frost in May (1933)
Novel by English writer ▷Antonia White. Described by ▷Elizabeth Bowen as a girls' school story for adults, the novel details the four years spent by the protagonist, Nanda Gray, at Lippington Convent School. Arriving at the age of nine, Nanda is asked to leave at thirteen following the discovery of the manuscript of her 'dissident' novel. The engagement of *Frost in May* with themes of waywardness and rebelliousness is set within an exploration of the 'outsider', and particularly of Roman Catholicism as an 'aristocratic' faith founded on blood and lineage. Nanda Gray represents the '*nouveau*' Catholicism of the recent convert – her friend Léonie points out 'You understand a lot of things, but you simply don't understand that specific Catholic something. I don't mean dogmas and all that.' Crucial to the novel's analysis of these issues is that Lippington represents a hermetic community. The moment of the protagonist's rebellion and

ostracization is simultaneously the realization of her dependence on it and its values.

Fru-Fru ▷Parra, Teresa de la

Fuchs, Anna Rupertina (1657–1722)
German poet. Orphaned when young, she grew up with relatives in Nuremberg, and all her life wrote and recited poetry with amazing virtuosity. A play about Job appeared in 1714 under the pseudonym 'Daphne' and was followed, in 1720, by an anthology of poems, *Poetischer Gedancken-Schatz* (*Poetic Treasure*). This collection contains examples of an awakening awareness of the conflict between the individual's struggle for freedom and the demands of society. Her collected works, *Poetische Schriften* (*Poetic Writings*), were published posthumously in 1726.

Fuertes, Gloria (born 1918)
One of the most significant poets of post-war Spain. Her main works are: *Isla ignorada* (1950) (*Unknown Island*); *Aconsejo beber hilo* (1959) (*I Advise Drinking Thread*); *Todo asusta* (1958) (*Everything is Frightening*); *Que estás en la tierra* (1962) (*Who Art on Earth*); *Poeta de guardia* (1968) (*Poet on Guard*); *Cómo atar los bigotes al tigre* (1969) (*How to Tie up the Tiger's Whiskers*); and ▷*Cuando amas aprendes geografía* (1973) (*When You Love You Learn Geography*).

Fugard, Sheila (born 1932)
South African novelist and poet who came to South Africa in 1937, originally from Birmingham. She studied Speech and Drama at the University of Cape Town, and later married the dramatist Athol Fugard. Her first novel, *The Castaways* (1972), received two prestigious local prizes, the CNA Prize in 1972 and the Olive Schreiner Prize in 1973. This novel was followed by *Rite of Passage* (1976), and *A Revolutionary Woman* (1983), which strives to insert a feminine voice into the official South African story, a tale told by 'the thugs and strong men of history'.

Fugard's poems, collected under the titles *Threshold* (1975) and *Mythic Things* (1981), show a particular interest in forms of madness and in mysticism. In *Threshold* she examines the barriers between sanity and insanity, meaning and meaninglessness, in a largely pessimistic record of personal despair and social injustice. *Mythic Things* once again experiments with form in order to explore the ways in which image and language explain ourselves and the world. These dense, complex, visionary poems explore nature and history in a strikingly original way.

Fuller, Elizabeth (1775–1856)
North American diarist. Born in Princeton, Massachusetts, at the beginning of the American Revolution, she was the daughter of the Reverend Timothy Fuller. At about age fifteen, she began keeping a diary (▷*Diary kept by Elizabeth Fuller*) in which she recorded the details of her life over a

two-year period. Fuller is not known to have married; she died at the age of 80.

Fuller, Margaret (1810–1850)
US editor, non-fiction writer, feminist and intellectual – the key woman figure in US ▷transcendentalism. Through her development of US feminism and her literary and cultural criticism, Fuller changed the face of the United States in the 1830s and 1840s. Convener of the famous Boston 'conversations' on feminism which led to her ▷*Woman in the Nineteenth Century* (1845), editor of ▷*The Dial* (1840–1842) and a prolific critic, Fuller was at the centre of US intellectual life before the Civil War, and the most effective purveyor of ideas to a larger community. Among her volume publications are ▷*Summer on the Lakes in 1843* (1844), *Papers on Literature and Art* (1846) and the posthumously published collections, *At Home and Abroad* (1856) and *Life Without and Life Within* (1859).
  ▷Howe, Julia Ward

Fumelh, Madame de (18th century)
French prose writer. She published the novel *Miss Anysie* (1788), and, during the Revolution, a *Discours à la nation française* (1789) (*Discourse for the French Nation*). Her collected works, *Oeuvres diverses*, were published in Geneva in 1790.

Funnyhouse of a Negro (1962)
US play by ▷Adrienne Kennedy which dramatizes the psychic torment of an African-American women student. Sarah lives in a society where Anglo-Americans ridicule African-Americans; she is unable to accept her blackness. Having internalized racial hatred, Sarah goes mad and commits suicide. Considered avant-garde, the play focuses on Surrealistic and expressionistic images rather than plot. The other characters represent various aspects of Sarah's psyche and they materialize in fantasies that reveal her preoccupation with problems of identity. Kennedy presents a portrait of the isolation and solitude of African-Americans living in the US. She asks how African-Americans can achieve self-discovery and self-development and, in doing so, comments on issues of assimilation, integration, black nationalism and Pan-Africanism.

Fuoco grande (1959) (*The Great Fire*)
An unfinished novel co-authored by Italian writers ▷Bianca Garufi and Cesare Pavese. Written in 1944, it takes the form of a diary, with alternate chapters ostensibly written by a man and a woman about the same events, seen from their different perspectives. Garufi wrote the female part, Pavese the male part, and the tone of the novel is both morbid and decadent. It caused something of a literary scandal as it was incorrectly believed by many critics that Pavese had written all of the work or, at the very least, that he had substantially revised Garufi's contribution. It is interesting as a literary experiment, as well as for the differences between the styles of the two writers.

Füruzan (born 1935)

Turkish novelist and short story writer (born Selçuk, married name Yerdelen). She left school early on the death of her father and worked as an actress. After the failure of her marriage she began to use her personal name, Füruzan, as a pen name, and published two novels and three collections of short stories. The short stories were particularly admired by readers and critics. In 1977 she was invited to visit West Germany, and wrote a series of articles on the conditions of Turkish workers there. In her work she shows deep sympathy for the poor and the weak. One of her stories. 'The River', is included in *An Anthology of Modern Turkish Short Stories*.

Fussenegger, Gertrud (born 1912)

Austrian novelist. The main themes in her prolific writing are the concepts of faith, love, fate, motherhood and guilt – notions which she explores through complicated plots which often chart the destiny of a child. Her best work includes: the story of her own family, *Das Haus der dunklen Krüge* (1951) (*The House of the Dark Jugs*); the novel, *Zeit des Raben, Zeit der Taube* (1960) (*Time of the Crow, Time of the Dove*), which is an account of the lives of Marie Curie and Leon Bloy, and a biography of the Austrian empress, *Maria Theresia* (1980).

Futurism (Italy)

An early 20th-century avant-garde movement, whose leading light was Filippo Tommaso Marinetti (1876–1944). It was anarchic in its approach to language, literature and art, but hardly so in its view of human sexuality. In most areas, the futurists (as the name implies), rejected the beliefs, systems, and customs of the past. They gloried in the increasing industrialization of Italian society and the cult of the machine. In Italy, futurism was strongly nationalistic, bellicose and right-wing, ripe to be useful to ▷fascism. In their poetry, the futurists espoused free verse forms, set out to destroy logical connections in writing, and practised the abolition of punctuation. A central tenet of futurism, and one which ensured a paradoxical continuity with the past, was the *disprezzo della donna* (contempt for woman), which made futurism perhaps the most misogynistic 20th-century literary movement. This created obvious problems for women writers who formed part of the futurist group, and they resolved these problems in different ways. ▷Benedetta and ▷Enif Robert-Angelini responded with relatively conformist approaches, while ▷Maria Ginanni and ▷Rosa Rosà were more feminist in their work.
Bib: Re, L., 'Futurism and Feminism', *Annali d'Italianistica*, 7, 1989, pp. 253–73.

Fyge, Sarah (1669/72–1722/3)

English author of the verse *The Female Advocate, or an Answere to a late Satyr against the Pride, Lust and Inconstancy etc., of Women* (1686), which she claimed to have written when she was fourteen. This was a reply to an attack on women by Robert Gould (1683), 'written by a lady in vindication of her sex'. The defence begins with a reworking of the much-disputed question of the nature of Eve – 'The Devil's strength weak Woman might deceive, / But Adam only tempted was by Eve, / She had the strongest Tempter, and least Charge; / Man's knowing most, doth make his sin more large.' Fyge claims in a poem (published in *Poems on Several Occassions, together with a Pastoral*, 1703) that in the 1680s her father banished her to a village far from the comfort of friends. She wrote one of the elegies in ▷*The Nine Muses* (1700) and had two husbands, first Field, and then the Reverend Thomas Egerton, to whom she was unhappily married. In 'The Liberty' she writes, 'My daring Pen, will bolder Sallies make, / and like myself, an uncheck'd freedom take.'
▷Manley, Delarivier
Bib: Medoff, Jeslyn, 'New Light on Sarah Fyge (Field, Egerton)', *Tulsa Studies in Women's Literature*, 1, 2 (1982) pp. 155–75.

G

Gacon-Dufour, Madame Marie Armande Jeanne (1753–?1835)

French novelist and writer on a diverse range of subjects, from agronomy and domestic economy to philosophy and history. Born in Paris, she lived in Brie-Comte-Robert. Her novels include: *L'Homme errant fixé par la raison* (1787) (*The Wandering Man Fixed by Reason*), *Le préjugé vaincu* (1787) (*Prejudice Overcome*), *Georgeana* (1798), *Melicrete et Zirphile* (1802), and *Les Dangers de la prévention* (1806) (*The Dangers of Foresight*). *La Femme-grenadier* (1801) (*The Woman Grenadier*) is a counterpoint to Sylvain Maréchal's *La Femme-abbé* (*The Woman Priest*). She wrote a *Mémoire pour le sexe féminin contre le sexe masculin* (1787) (*Defence of the Female Sex Against the Male*), opposed Maréchal's proposed legislation prohibiting women from learning to read in *Contre le projet de loi de S.M.* (1801) (*Against the Law Proposed S.M.*) and published an essay on women's rights to education, *De la nécessité de l'instruction pour les femmes* (1805) (*On the Need for Education for Women*). She edited several collections of correspondence, among them that of Madame Châteauroux (died 1744), and wrote anecdotes about the courts of Catherine de Medicis (1519–1589) and Louis XIV (1638–1715). She also published practical manuals on rural economy and housekeeping, and trade manuals for *pâtissiers*, soap-makers and perfumiers. She was co-founder of the Bibliothèque Agronomique.

Gagneur, Marie-Louise (1832–1902)

French novelist and polemical writer. The wife of the socialist writer and thinker Just Charles Gagneur (who proposed before even making her acquaintance after he had read a pamphlet she wrote about pauperism), she published novels in which she condemned the oppression of women: *Le Calvaire des femmes* (*Women's Calvary*); *Les Réprouvées* (1867) (*The Condemned*) and *Les Crimes de l'amour* (1874) (*The Crimes of Love*), and the corruption of the clergy: *La Croisade noire* (1866) (*The Black Crusade*); *Un Chevalier de sacristie* (1881) (*The Knight of the Sacristy*); *Le Roman d'un prêtre*, (1881) (*A Priest's Story*), and *Le Crime de l'abbé Maufrac* (1882) (*The Crime of the Father Maufrac*). The publication in *La Constitution* of an article of hers opposing militarism caused that journal to be banned in 1872. She campaigned in favour of divorce law reform, and another text she wrote in 1872, *Le Divorce*, helped prepare the ground for the decree permitting the dissolution of civil marriage passed in 1884.

Gai Oni (1982) (*Valley of my Strength/Grief*)

Israeli novel by ▷Shulamit Lapid. *Gai Oni* is based on authentic documents and depicts a period of transition in the history of Israeli society. Through its woman protagonist, Fania, it describes the change from early pioneering days to an established society. The female perspective provides an unusual insight, since historians have tended to neglect the role of women at this time.

Galaxy, The (1866–1878)

US New York monthly magazine, publishing non-fiction, fiction, serial novels and literary criticism. A New York alternative to Boston's ▷*Atlantic Monthly*, *The Galaxy* saw itself as more open and more innovative, but in fact it shared many of the same US contributors and interests. *Galaxy*'s serials, however, were mainly reprints of British novels – in contrast to the *Atlantic*'s customary first publications of US works. Among *Galaxy* contributors were ▷Rebecca Harding Davis and ▷Rose Terry Cooke.

Galgóczi, Erzsébet (1930–1989)

Erzsébet Galgóczi

Hungarian novelist. Born into an extremely poor peasant family near the country town of Györ in western Hungary, Galgóczi was of the post-war generation which was educated under the new communist regime and rose during the 1950s to be its brightest lights. Her books deal with peasant life, and with her own passage from it to literary success in Budapest. She was an accomplished journalist, who also worked in films, and was awarded the Joszef Attila Prize in 1976 and the Kossuth Prize in 1987 for her work. She was a Member of Parliament until her death which, considering the fact that she was an open lesbian in a country where homosexuality is hardly mentioned, is perhaps surprising. Her books include *A Közös Bün* (1976) (*Common Sin*), *A törvényen belül* (1980) (*Inside the Law*), which contains the novella *Egymásra nézve* (▷*Another Way*, 1986), and *Vidravas* (1984) (*Otter Trap*) whose revelations about the uprising of 1956, and the similarity of some of its characters to persons still living, caused a scandal in Budapest. She died of cancer in 1989.

Galician women's writing

The language of Galicia, like Spain's other vernacular languages, Basque and Catalan, was banned from public use during Franco's regime (1939–75). This censorship applied to literature as well as the spoken word. While this has clearly hindered the emergence of a Galician literary tradition, especially women writers, nevertheless, some women writers have continued to write in *gallego*, consciously drawing inspiration from the great 19th-century Galician woman writer ▷Rosalía de Castro.

▷Herrera Garrido, Francisca; Queizán, María Xosé; Torres, Xohana; Basque women's writing; Catalan women's writing

Gálina, G.A. (1870/73–1942)

Pen-name of the Russian poet and children's writer Glafíra Adol'fovna Mamoshina (by marriage Èinerling and Guseva-Orenburgskaia). After finishing secondary school she worked in a telegraph office from 1890 to 1896. Her first poems were published in 1895, and from 1899 her works appeared in several ▷'thick journals'. In 1901 she also began composing verses and fairytales for children. She published two collections of poetry, *Poems* (1902) and *Pre-Dawn Songs* (1906), and two of fairytales (1903, 1909). Gálina wrote 'civic' poetry in the 19th-century populist tradition, using simple language and imagery, at times sentimental and clichéd, and remaining formally and thematically untouched by the ▷modernist movements in poetry. The poems in the second collection exhibit a greater thematic variety than those of the first, although both were generally criticized. Gálina was widely anthologized, particularly in books of poetry with a political principle of inclusion, and her poems were set to music by Rachmaninov and Glière. She is most noted for 'They're cutting down the woods – the young, still green woods . . .' composed in 1901 in response to the government's repression of student activists. She was banned from St Petersburg for a year for reading it aloud. The poem circulated in handwritten copies and was first published abroad in 1905. A poem on the Boer War (1899–1902) became a folk song. Her last known publications were two poems in a Latvian newspaper in 1942. One source claims that, after the 1917 Revolution, she and her second husband emigrated.

Galindo, Beatriz ('La Latina') (?1474–1534)

A distinguished Spanish ▷humanist. Galindo taught Latin to the Queen of Spain, wrote good Latin verse, notes on classical authors, and a commentary on Aristotle.

Gallant, Mavis (born 1922)

Canadian short story writer and novelist, born Mavis de Trafford Young in Montreal, Quebec. Fluently bilingual in French and English, by the time she completed high school she had attended seventeen different schools in Quebec, Ontario, Connecticut, and New York. She never attended

Mavis Gallant

university. Her father disappeared when she was very young, and her mother remarried; Gallant felt that she was sent to school to get her out of the way. In 1941 she returned to Montreal, worked as a social secretary, in the real estate business, for Canadian National Railways, with the National Film Board, and finally for *The Montreal Standard* (1944–1950). She married John Gallant in 1943, and divorced in 1946. Her first stories were published in *Preview* and *The Standard*, and were produced on radio by the Canadian Broadcasting Corporation. In 1950, discovering that she was not paid as much as men in comparable positions, she left *The Montreal Standard*, and began submitting stories to *The New Yorker*. At first the magazine found her work too Canadian in flavour, but soon accepted a story, which gave Gallant the confidence to undertake her plan of travelling in Europe and giving herself two years to establish herself as a writer. Since then, most of her short stories have appeared in *The New Yorker*.

Between 1950 and 1954 Gallant travelled widely in Europe, and in 1960 settled in Paris, but continued to travel, and to consider herself very much a Canadian. In her own words, 'I've arranged matters so that I would be free to write.' She is best-known for her finely crafted short stories, which often address cross-cultural alienation, personal dislocation, and the expatriate experience. They depict situations from a frequently irritable and detached standpoint, but their sting is mitigated by the compassion of Gallant's close observational powers. They are collected in: *The Other Paris: Stories* (1956); *My Heart is Broken: Eight Stories and a Short Novel* (1964); *The Pegnitz Junction: A Novella and Five Short Stories* (1973); *The End of the World and Other Stories* (1974); *From the Fifteenth District: A Novella and Eight Short Stories* (1979); *Home Truths: Selected Canadian Stories* (1981); *Overhead in a Balloon: Stories of Paris* (1985), and *In Transit* (1988). The 'Linnet Muir' stories in *Home Truths*, which won a Governor General's Award, are a somewhat autobiographical portrayal of an independent woman. Gallant has also published, less successfully, novels, including *Green Water, Green Sky* (1959) and *A Fairly Good Time* (1970), as well as an incisive, politically astute collection of non-fiction, *Paris Notebooks: Essays and Reviews* (1986). Her first play, *What Is to Be Done?* (1983) was produced in Toronto.

Bib: Besner, N., *The Light of Imagination: Mavis Gallant's Fiction*; Grant, J.S., *Mavis Gallant and Her Works*; Howells, C., *Private and Fictional Words*; Irvine, L., *Sub/Version*; Kulyk Keefer, J., *Reading Mavis Gallant*.

Gallardo, Sara (born 1934?)

Argentinian novelist. She also has been a journalist, and now lives in Rome. Her first novel, *Enero* (1958) (*January*), is considered to be one of the most memorable portraits of rural Argentinian life. It is the sincere love story of a girl in the countryside, through which flows the undercurrents of rural conflict due to crisis and class conflict. In *Pantalones azules* (1963) (*Blue Trousers*), these conflicts become even more visible. *Los galgos, los galgos* (1968) (*The Greyhounds, The Greyhounds*) is technically and stylistically her most ambitious and innovative novel. It is divided into four parts, which are narrated by the character Julián. The greyhounds (*galgos*) represent the humans (Julián and Lisa), the sun and the moon, and the novel shows how different dreams are from reality.

Other works include: *Teo y la TV* (1974) (*Teo and the TV*) and *La rosa en el viento* (1978) (*The Rose in the Wind*).

Galloway, Grace Growden (died 1782)

North American diarist and poet. Her family was one of the wealthiest Quaker families in Philadelphia, and her father, Lawrence Growden, was a political leader. In 1753 she married a wealthy Marylander, Joseph Galloway, apparently as much at the behest of her father as through her own devotion; they had four children, but only one, a daughter, survived beyond infancy. When her husband's Loyalist proclivities forced him to flee Philadelphia with their daughter and eventually to settle in England, she remained in Philadelphia in an attempt to protect their vast property holdings as her daughter's rightful inheritance. From 1778 until her death, she recorded in ▷ *The Diary of Grace Growden Galloway* her struggle against increasing poverty and her failed hopes for a British victory and a reunion with her family. In minute daily entries, her mental and physical decline are detailed, as is her increasing wrath at the failure of the British government – and her husband – to uphold her rights. She died in 1782 without seeing her child again and without achieving success in her endeavours to retain the Galloway estate or her inheritance.

Galvão, Patrícia (1910–1962)

Brazilian poet, novelist, journalist, teacher, translator and painter who used the names Pagu, Mara Lobo, and GIM. She was a correspondent for Brazilian and French newspapers in Asia and Russia, writing on art, architecture, drama, literature and politics. In 1923 she met Oswald de Andrade, and married him in 1930. As the muse of the modernist movement (▷ *modernismo*) she had the poem 'Coco de Pagu' written for her by Raul Bopp. She joined the Communist Party in the 1930s, and because of this her 'proletarian novel' *Parque industrial* (1933) (*Industrial Park*) was published under the pen-name of Mara Lobo, as it was considered to be psychological rather ▷ social realist. It described the women workers' routine in a factory, and used her husband Oswald de Andrade as the model for a bourgeois protagonist. She was arrested several times for her political views in Europe and in Brazil. *A famosa revista* (1945) (*The Famous Journal*) was published with Geraldo Ferraz, her second husband, and was a reconsideration of her previous political views.

Galvarriato, Eulalia (born 1905)

Spanish novelist. Galvarriato was born in Madrid, where she has resided most of her life. Her best-known novel, *Cinco sombras* (1947) (*Five Shadows*), tells the story of a tyrannical father who struggles to control his five daughters. Galvarriato has also published a collection of brief fiction, lyric essays and prose poems, *Raíces bajo el tiempo* (1986) (*Roots Beneath Time*).

Gambara, Veronica (1485–1550)

Italian poet, of noble family. She married in 1509 and had two sons. Her husband died in 1518 and, though in deep mourning, she took over the management of her state (Correggio) and family. She was greatly respected by her subjects, not least for her success in holding off the army of Galeotto Pico della Mirandola in 1538. Gambara counted among her friends and acquaintances many political and literary figures of the time, including Bernardo Tasso, Pietro Aretino, Pietro Bembo, and the Emperor Charles V. Her poetry was ▷ Petrarchist in inspiration and style. As a young woman, she wrote mainly love poetry, and later religious verse. Alongside her poetry, she wrote many letters. The most complete edition of her writings is to be found in *Rime e lettere di Veronica Gambara* (*Poetry and Letters of Veronica Gambara*), published in 1759 and again in 1879.

Gambaro, Griselda (born 1928)

Argentinian dramatist, short story writer and novelist. Her first book, *Madrigal en ciudad* (1963) (*City Madrigal*), consisted of three short novels. The play *El Campo* (1968) (*The Camp*) was adapted for a Swedish radio broadcast in 1978. It takes place in a Nazi camp, which works as a metaphor for life and death. *Los Siameses* (1967) (*The Siamese*) was adapted for French radio in 1979. Many of her books of short stories and plays won prizes. She was granted several scholarships, and often travels abroad.

Other works: *El Desatino* (1964) (*Foolishness*); *Una felicidad con menos pena* (1967) (*Happiness with Less Trouble*); *Nada que ver con otra historia* (1972) (*Nothing to Do With Another Story*); *Sólo un aspecto* (1974) (*Only One Aspect*); *El Nombre* (1976) (*The Name*); *Sucede lo que pasa* (1976) (*Whatever Happens Happens*); *Ganarse la muerte* (1976) (*To Escape Death*); *Dios no nos quiere contentos* (1979) (*God Does Not Want Us to be Happy*); *Las paredes* (1963) (*The Walls*); *Viejo matrimonio* (1965) (*Old Matrimony*); *El desatino* (1965) (*Foolishness*); *Los siameses, Decir Sí* (1981) (*The Siamese, To Say Yes*); *La malasangre* (1982) (*The Bad-blood*); *Real envido* (1983) (*Royal Envoy*); *Del sol naciente* (1984) (*The Rising Sun*), and *Lo impenetrable* (1984) (*The Impenetrable*).

Gan, Elena Andreevna (1814–1842)
Russian prose writer. Gan was the middle link in three generations of remarkable Russian women: her mother, Elena Fadeeva (1788–1860), was a botanist with international ties; her daughters were the writer Vera Zhelikhovskaia (1835–1896), and Elena Blavatskaia (1831–1891), a founder of the worldwide theosophist movement. Gan married an army officer and followed him from post to post; much of her subject matter was derived from her consciousness of being an outsider in philistine provincial circles, a woman with intellectual aspirations, the equivalent of the ▷'superfluous man'. She devoted the last six years of her life to writing novellas which appeared in print under the pseudonym Zenaida R-va. Her exalted diction, improbable plots, exotic settings, and her idealistic protagonists' incredible nobility are typical of the last gasp of Russian romanticism. In *Utballa* (1838) Gan's half-Kalmyk heroine knowingly accepts a horrible fate in exchange for six days of love. In *Dzhellaledin* (1843, originally published as *The Moslem*, 1838) a Crimean Tartar renounces his heritage to win a Russian beauty who betrays the sacrifice. In 'Society's Verdict' (1840) a man lets false gossip destroy his faith in the woman he loves. Gan's late tales (*Teofaniia Abbadzhio*, 1841 and ▷*A Vain Gift*) show a developing social pathos and a movement towards realism cut short by her premature death.

Gándara, Carmen (1900–1977)
Argentinian novelist, short story writer, essayist and critic. She exploits the psychological, the supernatural and the metaphysical. Her narrative is shadowed by indeterminism and doubt, as in her novel *Los espejos* (1951) (*The Mirrors*). This work plays with narration itself and with aesthetics. Other works include *El lugar del diablo* (1947) (*The Devil's Place*) and *La figura y el mundo* (1958) (*The Figure and the World*), both books of short stories.

Ganga (the river Ganges)
A major river in India, revered by Hindus as a great goddess. There are many famous sites of pilgrimage on its banks. In Hindu scripture the river is said to originate in heaven, and so it mediates between the divine and mundane worlds. The river's personification as Ganga Ma, literally 'Mother Ganges', draws on both its spiritual and agricultural reputation as a giver of life.

Gánina, Maiia Anatolievna (born 1927)
Russian prose writer. Gánina has published regularly since her novella *First Trials* appeared in the prestigious ▷'thick journal' *New World* in 1954. She is an active member of the ▷Soviet Writers' Union, and uses her position to promote women's concerns. Gánina is a prolific writer who concentrates on modern urban life. Her prose falls within the realist tradition. She has a feminine, even feminist, perspective on family problems, and her fiction is full of strong, independent heroines. Many of her stories deal with the modern Soviet variant of subjects found in fiction by Russian women since the 19th century: the difficulty of balancing the different roles that women can take on; the sometimes successful search for fulfilment through one's work and the failure to find fulfilment in relations with men; the temptation of material comfort, and the central emotional importance and supportive role of female friendship.
Bib: Goscilo, H. (trans.), *Balancing Acts: Contemporary Stories by Russian Women*; Gánina, M., *The Road to Nirvana*; Schneidman, N.N., *Soviet Literature in the 1980s: Decade of Transition*.

Gant, Phyllis
New Zealand novelist. Born in Australia, Phyllis Gant has spent most of her adult life in New Zealand. She has published two novels, *Islands* (1973) and *The Fifth Season* (1976), and a number of stories. A ▷realist writer, Gant has also worked as a journalist. Her novels and stories mostly focus on the difference between female ambition, talent or need and the conventional expectations of others, which results in confusion, isolation, or conflict.

García Marruz, Fina (born 1923)
Cuban poet. She became interested in literature when young. She was part of the committee of the magazine *Clavileño* (1943), and organized the group '*Orígenes*', which produced a publication under the same name, and to which she often contributed. She has worked as a literary researcher at the Department of Cuban Collection of the National Library José Martí in Cuba.

Other works: *Poemas* (1942) (*Poems*); *Transfiguración de Jesús en el Monte* (1947) (*The Transfiguration of Jesus on the Mount*); *Las miradas perdidas 1944–1950* (1951) (*The Lost looks 1944–1950*), and *Visitaciones* (1970) (*Visitations*). She also wrote essays.

García Morales, Adelaida
Contemporary Spanish novelist. García was born in Badajoz, grew up in Seville, and studied at the University of Madrid. *El sur* (1983) (*The South*) is

a phantasmagoric love story; the film version directed by Víctor Erice was a resounding success. *El silencio de las sirenas* (1985) (*The Silence of the Sirens*) likewise focuses on a love affair, this time between a young woman from an isolated village in the Alpujarras in Andalusia, and a man she barely knows.

Garden Party and Other Stories, The (1922)

Stories by New Zealand writer ▷Katherine Mansfield. The last volume of stories to be published during Katherine Mansfield's lifetime, *The Garden Party and Other Stories* established her standing as a modernist writer and contains many of her most accomplished stories: 'At the Bay', 'The Daughters of the Late Colonel', 'Miss Brill', 'Her First Voyage'. Two years before she died in 1923 she remarked of *The Garden Party*: 'I hope the book on which I am now engaged will be more worthy of the interest of the public [than *Bliss*].' *The Garden Party* attracted a great deal of enthusiastic comment, so much so that ▷Virginia Woolf noted in her diary, 'So what does it matter if K.M. soars in the newspapers and runs up sales sky high?' All the stories in *The Garden Party* were written between 1920 and 1921, many of them while Mansfield was living at the Villa Isola Bella in Menton. A number of the stories focus on the lives of lonely or isolated women; commentators have referred these stories both to Mansfield's own situation and that of her unmarried friend Ida Baker ('L.M.'). Several of the stories also refer back to her childhood in New Zealand, particularly the famous 'At the Bay'. In 1922 Mansfield wrote to William Gerhardi, an author associated with the ▷Bloomsbury Group, that in 'The Garden Party' she had tried to convey the 'diversity of life and how we try to fit in everything. Death included.' Less than a year after the collection was published Mansfield died at Fontainebleau.

Gardner, Helen (1908–1986)

English literary critic. University Reader in Renaissance English Literature, Oxford, and later Merton Professor of English Literature, Oxford, Gardner was a specialist in late 16th- and early 17th-century English poetry. Her views on the function of the critic are set down in *The Business of Criticism* (1959), and Gardner generally held the view that neutrality and objectivity were crucial to good criticism. Closely aligned with the critical views held by the poet T.S. Eliot (1888–1965), who was also drawn to the metaphysical poets, Gardner believed that literary texts could deliver up stable, accessible meanings. Despite the organicism and formalism this approach may suggest, Gardner's criticism favoured a linguistically-based form of historical contextualization. Publications include: *The Divine Poems of John Donne* (1952), *The Metaphysical Poets* (1957), *T.S. Eliot and the Poetic Tradition* (1966), *Religion and Literature* (1971) and *In Defence of the Imagination* (1982).

Gardners Kalender, The (1772)

Written by the North American author ▷Martha Daniell Logan, a resident of South Carolina, *The Gardners Kalender* is a treatise on gardening. Scientific in nature but presented in lay terms, it was very popular and was reprinted in several late 18th-century North American almanacs.
▷*Letters of Martha Logan to John Bartram*

Gare, Nene (born 1919)

Australian novelist. Her first novel ▷*The Fringe Dwellers* (1961) is a powerful exploration of the failure of part-Aborigines in their attempts to integrate with white society and is one of the most perceptive books written about Aboriginal life by a white woman. Other works include *Green Gold* (1963), set in Carnarvon, Western Australia; *Bend to the Wind* (1978), short stories concerned with Aboriginal life; and two autobiographical accounts, *A House with Verandahs* (1980) and *An Island Away* (1981).
▷Aborigine in non-Aboriginal Australian women's writing, The

Garg, Mridula (born 1938)

Indian novelist, short story writer and columnist. She was born in Calcutta, and has a, MA in Economics. She lives in Delhi. She has chosen to write for an Indian audience, and hence has published most of her works in Hindi, although she has translated many of them into English. She has published five novels, five collections of short stories and a play, all in Hindi, and an English novel. For her novel *Uske Hisse ki Dhupa*, translated as *A Touch of the Sun* (1982), she won the 1975 M.P. Sahitya Parishad Award.

Garner, Helen (born 1942)

Australian short story writer and novelist. Garner has worked as a teacher, journalist and as writer-in-residence at a number of Australian universities. Her first novel, the prize-winning ▷*Monkey Grip* (1977), was followed by *Honour and Other People's Children: Two Stories* (1980), *Moving Out* (with Jennifer Giles, 1984) and *The Children's Bach* (1984). *Postcards from Surfers* (1985) won the New South Wales Premier's Award for Fiction in 1986.
▷Short story (Australia); *Coming Out from Under*; *Eight Voices of the Eighties*

Garro, Elena (1920)

Mexican writer. Her main novel, *Los recuerdos de porvenir* (1963) (*Recollections of Things to Come*, 1969), is a successful combination of ▷realism and magical events in a story that takes place in a small town of post-revolutionary Mexico.

Garufi, Bianca (born 1920)

Italian novelist and Jungian analyst. Born in Rome, she completed a thesis on Jung in 1950, and later began to practise as an analyst. She was one of the founders of the Einaudi publishing house and worked there for some time. A contributor to many periodicals, she worked with

Cesare Pavese on the novel ▷*Fuoco grande* (1959)
(*The Great Fire*), a novel incorrectly thought by
many critics to be almost entirely the work of
Pavese. It was not until she published *Il fossile*
(*The Fossil*) in 1962 that her literary ability was
recognized in this tale of a depressed young
woman, unable to get away from a claustrophobic
existence in the south of Italy. Her other
important work, *Rosa cardinale* (1968) (*Cardinal
Pink*), also centres on a depressed female
character unable to make sense of her life.

Gaskell, Elizabeth (1810–1865)
British novelist and short story writer. Elizabeth
Cleghorn Stevenson was the daughter of a
Unitarian minister and spent her childhood living
with her aunt in Knutsford, Cheshire, after her
mother's death in 1811. In 1832 she married
William Gaskell, also a Unitarian minister, based
in Manchester, with whom she had four daughters
and a son who died in infancy. Mrs Gaskell's first
novel, ▷*Mary Barton*, appeared in 1848. It won
the attention of Charles Dickens, and most of her
later work was published in his periodical
magazines *Household Words* and *All the Year
Round*. ▷*Cranford* began to appear in 1851, and
▷*Ruth* in 1853. This latter novel caused a scandal
in its sympathetic treatment of a ▷'fallen woman'.
Social issues are also at the heart of ▷*North and
South* (1854–55) and many of Gaskell's short
stories. In 1863 the ▷historical novel ▷*Sylvia's
Lovers* appeared, and ▷*Wives and Daughters*,
though unfinished, was published posthumously
between 1864 and 1866. Other works include the
celebrated biography of ▷Charlotte Brontë
(1857), and ▷ghost stories, a selection of which
has recently been reprinted as *Lois the Witch and
Other Stories* (1989).

Mrs Gaskell's works reveal a commitment to
humanitarian principles and to Unitarianism. The
'social problem' novels call for reconciliation
between employers and workers, for Gaskell was
always reformist rather than radical. She
advocated motherhood as woman's mission in life,
but her fiction often exposes the contradictions in
Victorian attitudes and calls for more 'nurturing'
men. Recent feminist critics have re-assessed
Gaskell's portrayal of 'marginalized' women – the
spinsters, widows, ▷orphan girls and madwomen
who figure largely within her work.
Bib: Gerin, W., *Gaskell: A Biography*; Stoneman,
P., *Elizabeth Gaskell*.

Gates Ajar, The (1868)
US novel by ▷Elizabeth Stuart Phelps (Ward).
An extraordinarily popular book both in the USA
and internationally, it moves from a novelistic
focus on a young woman unable to console herself
for the war death of a loved one to recording her
aunt's consolatory conversations depicting an
afterlife and heaven – a very specifically and
concretely detailed place. While some critics have
remarked on the uncanny resemblance between
this heaven and the 19th-century USA, others
have noted that *Gates Ajar* and Phelps's two

succeeding books on the afterlife, *Beyond the Gates*
(1883) and *The Gates Between* (1887), outline a
vision of a less patriarchal, more equal world.

Gatty, Margaret (1809–1873)
British writer of ▷children's literature and a keen
botanist. She was born Margaret Scott in
Burnham vicarage, Essex, and moved to Yorkshire
after marrying the Rev. Alfred Gatty in 1839. Of
her ten children, ▷Juliana Horatia Ewing worked
most closely with her on *Aunt Judy's Magazine*, a
periodical for children. Gatty's works include *The
Fairy Godmothers* (1851); *Parables from Nature* (a
series of five books published between 1855 and
1871); *Aunt Judy's Tales* (1859); *Christmas Crackers*
(1870), and a two-volume *History of British
Seaweeds* (1863), which became the standard
source of information about seaweeds for the next
80 years. Gatty's writing for children reveals a
good sense of humour, but contains too much
moralizing to appeal to 20th-century readers. She
was, however, highly popular in her day.

Gaudy Night (1935)
▷Detective novel by English popular writer
▷Dorothy Sayers. The third of four detective
novels featuring Lord Peter Wimsey and Harriet
Vane, it takes Harriet back to Oxford on academic
research. Mysterious events in her old college
lead to her employment as a detective. Despite a
weak denouement, indicative of Sayers's
conservative views on social class, the novel's
representation of a closed female community, and
its meditations on the merits and disadvantages of
marriage for women, add fascinating tensions to
the detective plot.

Gaunt, Mary (1861–1942)
Australian novelist, short story writer, travel writer
and journalist. The daughter of a judge, Gaunt
was one of the first two women students at the
University of Melbourne. After the death of her
husband, Dr Hubert Miller, she lived in London,
where most of her novels were written and
published. She wrote romances, short stories and
travel books. Of at least twenty romances, the
best-known is ▷*Kirkham's Find* (1897) which has
a pronounced feminist theme.
▷*From the Verandah; On Her Selection*

Gauthier, Xavière (born 1942)
French writer, lecturer at Paris University, editor
of the feminist journal *Sorcières* (*Witches*), author
of novels and essays. In *Surréalisme et sexualité*
(1971) (*Surrealism and Sexuality*), she critically
examines the mythologizing of women by the
Surrealists, and the basic ambivalence of their
attitude to women's sexuality – liberating it, but
imposing their own interpretation of it – is
exposed. In *Dire nos sexualités: contre la sexologie*
(1976) (*To Speak on Sexuality: Against Sexology*),
she undertakes a ▷deconstruction of Freud's
approach to female sexuality (▷psychoanalysis),
paving the way for the construction of sexual
difference through new psychoanalytic

perspectives. *Les Parleuses* (1974) (▷*Woman to Woman*, 1987) is the transcription of unscripted interviews with ▷Marguerite Duras, ranging over the latter's novels and films, and establishing the limits of her affinities with the feminist movement.

Gautier, Judith (1846–1917)
French novelist. The eldest daughter of Théophile Gautier (1811–1872), she was briefly married to the poet Catulle Mendès, but separated from him and devoted herself to writing. She was also a friend of Richard Wagner's, and sought to bring his music to the attention of the French public. The vast majority of her novels have Oriental settings, since she was fascinated by Eastern civilizations and had a considerable knowledge of Oriental culture. This was due in part to her acquaintance with the Chinese scholar Tin-Ton-Li, whom her father had welcomed into his home, and from whom she learnt Chinese. The vision of the East which emerges from her novels – which include *Le Livre de Jade* (1867) (*The Book of Jade*); *Le Dragon impérial* (1869) (*The Imperial Dragon*); *La Soeur du soleil* (1875) (*Sisters of the Sun*) and *La Femme de Putiphar* (1884) (*Potiphar's Wife*) – is nevertheless a somewhat mythical, exoticized and decadent one. The books seem extremely old-fashioned to modern readers, and it is abundantly clear that Gautier never visited the lands she evoked so lovingly. She also wrote plays and critical articles, and was elected to the Académie Goncourt.
Bib: Brécourt-Villars, C., *Ecrire d'Amour*; Camach, M., *Judith Gautier: sa vie et son oeuvre*.

Gaviota, La (1849) (*The Seagull*)
Novel by the Spanish writer ▷Cecilia Böhl von Faber. It tells a tale of love in a rural setting: a young German surgeon, Stein, falls in love with, transforms and marries a beautiful peasant girl, Marisalada. When her husband dies, Marisalada returns to her native village and marries the barber. *La Gaviota* is considered to be an important precedent of Spanish ▷realism.

Gay, Sophie (1776–1852)
French novelist. The mother of ▷Delphine de Girardin, Gay published her first novel, *Laure d'Estelle*, in 1802, without initially acknowledging authorship. This work, which provoked strong reactions among the reading public, has a highly melodramatic plot that centres on the amorous adventures of a young woman who believes her husband to have been killed in battle. When Gay's own husband was posted to Aix-la-Chapelle, a rich spa town, she began to hold a literary salon, which she maintained after her return to Paris, and which was one of the most celebrated of the period. Widowhood turned writing from a hobby into a necessity, with the result that after 1822 she produced a string of historical and society novels, including *La Duchesse de Chateauroux* (1834) (*The Duchess of Chateauroux*); *Un mariage sous l'Empire* (1832) (*A Marriage During the Empire*); *La Comtesse*

d'Egmont (1836), and *Marie de Mancini* (1840). She also published articles and plays.

Ge Cuilin (born 1930)
Chinese writer for children. Ge has published many fairy tales, children's verses and drama, the best-known being *The Clever Daughter-in-Law* (1956), a fairy tale, and *Little Hero of the Steppes*, a play. Labelled a 'rightist' (enemy category) in 1957, she was rehabilitated twenty years later and now works on writing, editing and anthologizing works for children.

Gedge, Pauline (born 1945)
Novelist, born in Auckland, New Zealand who moved to England and then settled in Canada. Her novels are essentially popular historical fiction. *Child of the Morning* (1977) is about the life of Hapshepsut, the Egyptian pharaoh; *The Eagle and the Raven* (1978) is about Celtic Britain. *Stargate* (1982) is science fiction. In *Twelfth Transforming* (1984) and *The Scroll of Saggara* (1990) Gedge returns to ancient Egypt as a setting for her fiction. She lives in Alberta.

Gee, Maggie (born 1948)
English novelist. After completing postgraduate research on Surrealism, and a doctoral thesis on the modern novel, Gee published her most experimental novel, *Dying, in Other Words* (1981) which explores the manner in which the death of a woman is treated within varying stories and forms of reportage. Gee's commitment to pacifism and nuclear disarmament is voiced in *The Burning Book* (1983), about nuclear holocaust, and *Grace* (1988), concerned with a peace campaigner under surveillance. Gee has also edited *For Life on Earth* (1982), an anthology of pacifist writings. *Where Are the Snows* was published in 1991.

Gems, Pam (born 1925)
British dramatist and novelist. Gems's plays explore women's experiences of a male-dominated world. Several of her plays, like *Our Country's Good* (1988) by ▷Timberlake Wertenbaker and ▷*Top Girls* (1982) by ▷Caryl Churchill, allow the voices of previously silenced women to speak out: she has reclaimed the stories of Marguerite Gautier (from Alexandre Dumas's *La dame aux camélias*, 1852, *The Lady of the Camellias*), Edith Piaf and Queen Christina from myth or sentimentality.

In *Camille* (1984) Gems gives Marguerite a voice and physical presence, liberating her from the text of Dumas's novel, which is set after Marguerite's death, and in which her actions and feelings are mediated through the double screen of the narrator and her lover, Armand. Gems's play, unlike Dumas's novel, criticizes property- and money-oriented bourgeois society, which both requires and despises prostitutes, and paints Marguerite's tragedy as one of an individual forced into ill health and unhappiness by male values.

Gems's plays include *Piaf* (1973), *Dusa, Fish,*

Stas and Vi (1975), *Queen Christina* (1977) and *Loving Women* (1984). She has also created her own versions of Anton Chekhov's *Uncle Vanya* (1979) and Henrik Ibsen's *A Doll's House* (1980).

In 1989 Gems produced her first novel. *Mrs Frampton* is the tale of a woman who retires to Spain with her husband. Mrs Frampton's adventures continue in *Bon Voyage, Mrs Frampton* (1990).

Gender, Politics and Fiction: Twentieth Century Australian Women's Novels (1985)

Collected criticism edited by Carole Ferrier. A superb introduction, 'Women Writers in Australia', is followed by readings of 20th-century Australian women's fiction from socialist and/or feminist standpoints. The book reconsiders the novels in the context of the economic, political and social situation of women and women writers in Australia, making a major contribution to the current state of criticism in this area. Writers reviewed in depth are ▷Miles Franklin, ▷Nettie Palmer, ▷Katharine Susannah Prichard, ▷Jean Devanny, ▷Eve Langley, ▷Christina Stead, ▷Elizabeth Harrower and ▷Shirley Hazzard. As well, there are essays on ▷migrant women writers and Australian women novelists of the 1970s.
▷Feminist literary criticism (Australia)

Genlis, Stéphanie-Félicité Ducrest, Countesse de (1746–1830)

French educational writer and novelist. The daughter of an aristocratic but impoverished family, she married the wealthy Charles de Genlis in 1763, was presented at court, became the mistress of the Duc de Chartres (later the Duc d'Orléans and Philippe-Egalité), and was eventually appointed as governess to his children. In 1779 she published the first of over 80 books, a collection of uplifting plays for the young entitled *Théâtre à l'usage des jeunes personnes* (*Theatre for The Young*). This was followed by (*Adèle et Théodore, ou lettres sur l'éducation* (1782) (▷*Adelaide and Theodore, or Letters on Education*, 1783) and *Les Veillées du Château* (1784) (*Tales of the Castle*, 1785). These texts, which are among her best known, need to be read in tandem, since the first is a novel which explicates de Genlis's educational vision, and the second a series of moral tales destined to show how her pedagogical method works. In the 1790s she travelled widely throughout Europe, and lost both her husband and the Duc d'Orléans to the guillotine. She was by this point an object of such suspicion to the Republican régime that she published an exculpatory *Précis de la conduite de Mme de Genlis depuis la Révolution* (1796) (*Summary of the Conduct of Mme de Genlis Since the Revolution*), the purpose of which was to facilitate her return to France. She also continued to produce moral and educational works, notably *Leçons d'une gouvernante à ses élèves* (1791) (*Lessons from a Governess to Her Pupils*), and wrote fiction, including the novella *Mademoiselle de Clermont* (1802). Critics have rated this last, which has the same theme as ▷Claire de

Duras's *Edouard*, her most accomplished literary work. Bonaparte became fascinated by her, and gave her a handsome pension, but requested her to write on moral and literary subjects only. Under his patronage she published historical novels glorifying the *ancien régime*: *La Duchesse de la Vallière* (1804), which was a huge success, *Mme de Maintenon* (1806) and *Mlle de Lafayette* (1813). She claimed later to have breathed new life into an otherwise moribund genre. After the fall of Napoleon she continued to write prolifically, and her last work was a ten-volume set of *Mémoires* (1825). One of the most fascinating women of 19th-century France, she was admired by some contemporaries and loathed by others, particularly by those who disliked her attacks upon the *philosophes*. Although first and foremost a doggedly determined educationalist, her fictional writing is far less insipid and derivative than hostile critics have suggested.
▷Savignac, Alida de

Bib: Broglie, G. de, *Mme de Genlis*; Laborde, A., *L'Oeuvre de Mme de Genlis*; Moers, E., *Literary Women*.

Genteel tradition

US 19th-century cultural concept. It was named by the Spanish-born US philosopher George Santayana (1863–1952) in a 1918 address, 'The Genteel Tradition in American Philosophy'. Santayana and later cultural critics used the term 'genteel tradition' to describe what the 19th century had called simply 'gentility': an emphasis on what was decorous, proper, refined, religious, moral, traditional – high culture separated from the realities and diversity of everyday life. Many 19th-century US writers decried the national literary magazines' enforcement of gentility, complaining that real life generally, and sexual attraction specifically, had no place in US periodical literature, which was restricted to a ▷parlour table standard.

Geoffrin, Marie-Thérèse Rodet (1699–1777)

French woman of letters and salon hostess. Born in Paris of modest origins, orphaned at an early age and raised by her maternal grandmother, she was married at fourteen to François Geoffrin, some thirty years her senior. The marriage brought her substantial wealth and, after his death in 1749 she began to hold her salon in the rue St Honoré, attended by artists such as Soufflot, Bouchardon, Boucher, Vernet and Van Loo, and literary figures and *philosophes* including Montesquieu, Fontenelle, Marivaux and d'Alembert. She encouraged and helped finance the project of the Encyclopaedists. Geoffrin's *Correspondance* (1875) with Empress Catherine II of Russia, King Stanislas of Poland and the Abbé de Berteuil relates her travels throughout Europe.
Bib: Aldis, J., *Mme Geoffrin, her Salon and her Time*; Goodman, D., 'Filial Rebellion in the Salon: Madame Geoffrin and her daughter', *French Historical Studies*, 16: 1 (1989); Lescure, M. de, *Les femmes philosophes*.

Gerhardt, Ida (Gardina Margaretha) (born 1905)

Dutch poet. She was a teacher of classical languages from 1939 to 1963, and graduated with a translation of Lucretius's *De Rerum Natura*. She began with nature poetry, focusing on self-recognition in nature. Nature was seen in images, which developed into symbols (she expanded especially the symbol of water), a reflection of a reality that has a higher meaning. Her poetry is rhetorical, shunning the commonplace and incidental, giving it a particular character in post-war Dutch poetry. Gerhardt is ranked among the most prominent Dutch poets of this century. The award of the P.C. Hooft Prize for her complete works was celebrated with the publication of her collective poems, *Verzamelde gedichten*, in 1980. Work from the period 1940–1956 was published in *Vroege verzen* (1978) (*Early Verse*). 1972 saw the appearance of her translation of the Psalms, *De Psalmen*, translated from Hebrew by Ida Gerhardt and Marie H. van der Zeyde. Recent work includes: *Dolen en dromen* (1980) (*Wandering and Dreaming*), *De zomen van het licht* (1983) (*Seams of Light*) and *De adelaarsvarens* (1988) (*The Bracken*).

German-speaking Swiss writers

Switzerland is a small multi-cultural and multi-lingual country which, since its foundation in 1291, has been pursuing political and cultural separatism vis-à-vis its powerful neighbours. Swiss-Germans, unlike their French and Italian compatriots, are further separated from their natural cultural sphere because of their language. Spoken Swiss-German differs considerably from the standard German which must be learnt in school. This meant that until the late 19th century only a tiny élite of particularly well-educated writers could reach a readership beyond the Swiss border.

The first known Swiss woman writer was ▷Elisabeth Stagel, a 14th-century nun from Zurich. No other Swiss-German woman writer reached fame until ▷Marianne Ehmann established herself as editor of educational women's journals in the late 18th century. In the 19th century didacticism and regionality were the prime characteristics of emerging writers such as ▷Lisa Wenger, ▷Cécile Lauber, ▷Isabella Kaiser, ▷Maria Waser, ▷Cécile Ines Loos, ▷Olga Meyer and ▷Johanna Spyri, whose children's novel, *Heidi* (1880) became world famous.

A sign that horizons were beginning to widen was the publication in 1825 of ▷Regula Engel's travelogue about the Napoleonic Wars. It was a genre further developed this century by ▷Lina Bögli, ▷Annelisa Rüegg and ▷Annemarie Schwarzenbach. The struggle for recognition continued right up to the 1960s when interest in liminal artistic expression finally reached Switzerland and initiated new appraisals of neglected writers, ▷Franziska Stöcklin and ▷Gertrud Wilker amongst them. Since then there has been an unprecedented surge of literary

activity with novelists such as ▷Maja Beutler, ▷Margrit Schriber, poets such as ▷Erika Burkart and ▷Silja Walter and a vigorous ▷*avant-garde* represented by ▷Erica Pedretti, ▷Verena Stefan and ▷Gertrud Leutenegger.

Gersão, Teolinda (born 1940)

Teolinda Gersão

Portuguese novelist. Born in Coimbra, she received a doctorate in German philology and is currently a professor at the New University in Lisbon. Gersão's fiction is highly introspective and focuses on the relationships between middle-class men and women. Her first novel, ▷*O Silêncio* (1981) (*The Silence*), is a difficult work that conveys the problem of 'speaking' in a world dominated by a patriarchal language. Like her contemporary ▷Lídia Jorge, Gersão also writes about historical matters, but her treatment of history is far more oblique – as can be seen in her second novel, *Paisagem com Mulher e Mar ao Fundo* (1981) (*Landscape with Woman and the Sea in the Background*), which deals with such themes as women's independence, the dictatorship and the colonial war in Africa. Her *Os Guarda–Chuvas Cintilantes* (1984) (*The Scintillating Umbrellas*) is an experimental novel in diary form. Her most recent novel is entitled *O Cavalo de Sol* (1989) (*The Sun Steed*).
Bib: Sadlier, Darlene J., *The Question of How: Women Writers and New Portuguese Literature.*

Gertrude the Emigrant: A Tale of Colonial Life (1857)

Early Australian novel by ▷Louisa Atkinson. The adventures of the emigrant heroine are interspersed with improving verses, moralistic messages, and warnings against transgression and strong drink. This novel gives a fascinating glimpse of emigrant attitudes towards colonial-born women ('I see her now, whistling the dogs, and cracking her stockwhip'), towards the convict heritage ('the tainted stock from which they spring') and towards the Aborigines, to whom it is on the whole sympathetic.

Gertrud von Helfta (1256–1302)

German nun and mystical writer. She was one of the foremost members of the Cistercian Convent of Helfta in Saxony, citadel of mysticism in 13th and 14th-century Germany. Also known as Gertrud the Great and St Gertrud, she was canonized in 1739. An exceptionally gifted child, she entered the convent at the age of five, and was educated under the guidance of the abbess, Gertrud von Hackeborn. When she was twenty-five she began to have visions, which some nine years later she described in *Legatus divinae pietatis* (*Life and Revelations of Saint Gertrude: Virgin and Abbess of the Order of St Benedict*, 1871), a text complemented and edited by the nuns after her death. She also wrote a guide to spiritual exercise, *Exercitia spiritualia* (*Exercise*, 1956). Together with her spiritual leader, ▷Mechthild von Hackeborn, she initiated the cult of the adoration of the Sacred Heart.

▷*Visionsliteratur*

Gértsyk, Adelaida Kazimirovna (1870–1925)

Russian poet, prose writer and literary critic. The themes of Gértsyk's earliest poetry, published from 1908, recall those of ▷Gíppius: an aversion to the mundane, a yearning for the absolute, and a concentration on the conflicts within the self. She later became close to the Moscow group of symbolists and reviewed books in their journal *Scales* under the pen-name 'Sirin' (1905–6). Between 1907 and 1918 Gértsyk published poetry in almanacs, journals, and anthologies. Reviewers of her only book, *Poems: 1906–1909*, called her a sibyl and prophet. It shows her to be a mystical, musical poet whose metrically experimental verse borrows repetitions, parallelisms, dactylic endings, noun doublets and nature symbolism from genres of folk poetry like the lament, incantation and song. This influence of folklore on her poetry links her to her contemporary, ▷Liubov' Stólitsa. Gértsyk met ▷Marina Tsvetáeva in 1911, and during World War I she was the centre of a circle that included women poets such as Tsvetáeva and ▷Sofiia Parnók. Influenced by Gértsyk's poetry, Tsvetáeva remembered her as 'Deaf, unattractive, no longer young – and – irresistible'. Gértsyk's late poems, most of which have yet to be published, became even more imbued with a religious and moral content. Her prose is lyrical, highly psychological, and autobiographical. The story cycle 'Basement Sketches', published posthumously in 1926 in a Latvian journal, reflects her experience during the Civil War in the

Soviet Union (1918–21), when she was arrested and spent three weeks in jail.

Bib: Pachmuss, T. (trans.), *Women Writers in Russian Modernism*; Burgin, D., 'The Life of Adelaida Gertsyk', *Russian Literature Triquarterly* 23 (1990); Weber, H. (ed.), *The Modern Encyclopedia of Russian and Soviet Literature*, Vol. 8; Tsvetáeva, M., *A Captive Spirit: Selected Prose*.

Geschichte des Fräuleins von Sternheim (1771) (The Story of Fraulein von Sternheim)

A novel by the German writer ▷Sophie La Roche. Written in letter form, it relates the story of the orphan Sophie, who, in escaping her aunt's intention to make her a prince's mistress, falls for a rogue, the English Lord Derby, who does not love her, but tricks her into a mock-marriage and abducts her to Scotland. With the help of friends she takes charge of her own destiny, becomes first a teacher of young girls, and then the companion to a noblewoman. She is again abducted, and very nearly killed, by her ex-husband, but virtue triumphs, and she eventually marries the reputable Lord Seymour, who truly loves her.

As the first woman's novel in German, the book created a sensation in 18th-century Weimar. Women, in particular, received it with enormous enthusiasm, and it became the standard against which many other women writers measured their work.

Getting of Wisdom, The (1910)

Australian novel by ▷Henry Handel Richardson. In this Richardson fictionalizes her experiences at the Presbyterian Ladies' College, Melbourne between 1883 and 1887. It is one of a number of Australian works which have been seen as a female ▷*Bildungsroman*. It concerns the stages in the development of its heroine, Laura Ramsbotham, to a sense of self and a knowledge of reality. As Laura is a potential writer, it also concerns her growth to artistic maturity and a knowledge of the relationship between truth, reality and art. *The Getting of Wisdom* was made into a successful film in 1977.

▷Autobiography (Australia)

Ghalem, Nadia

Algerian novelist and poet. At eighteen she became a radio and television reporter, and today she lives in Canada. Her collection of poems *Exil* (1980) (*Exile*) was published in Quebec. In 1981 she published two novels: *Le Jardin de cristal* (*The Crystal Garden*) and *L'Oiseau de fer* (*Iron Bird*). This last novel is about the struggle of an Algerian girl to come to terms with her traumatic memories of the Algerian war. The girl, Chafia, finally emerges from the schizophrenic state into which these memories had propelled her.

Ghost stories (19th-century Britain)

In the latter half of the 19th century, many British women writers contributed to the burgeoning genre of the ghost story. Tales of the supernatural and eerie usually appeared in periodicals such as

Dickens's *All the Year Round*, *The Saturday Review*, *Cornhill*, *The Belgravia* (founded by ▷Mary Braddon) and *Argosy* (founded by ▷Mrs Henry Wood). The genre held a similar appeal for women to that of the ▷Gothic. Supernatural narratives allowed women writers and their female readers to explore fears and fantasies which could not find overt expression in the dominant Victorian literary mode, ▷realism. The ghost story provided an opportunity to represent conventionally marginalized figures such as the madwoman or the witch, and to release repressed feelings about maternity, childbirth and male/female relations. Another important dimension of the form was its ability to call into question conventional (and perhaps patriarchal) notions of reality and time, which were often disrupted or fractured in narratives produced by women. Practitioners included Braddon, ▷Rhoda Broughton, ▷Mary Cholmondeley, ▷Catherine Crowe, ▷Amelia Edwards, ▷Juliana Horatia Ewing, ▷Elizabeth Gaskell, ▷Vernon Lee, ▷Eliza Lynn Linton, ▷Louisa Molesworth, Rosa Mulholland, ▷Edith Nesbit, ▷Margaret Oliphant, Mrs Riddell and Mrs Henry Wood.
Bib: Uglow, J., *The Virago Book of Ghost Stories*.

Giacobbe, Maria (born 1928)
Italian novelist. Born in Sardinia, she studied in Rome then moved to Copenhagen with her Danish husband, who was also a writer. She has also edited and translated anthologies of poetry and fiction. Her works are often short but striking, and tend to contain autobiographical elements. A favourite theme for her is adolescence and its problems, often presented through the memories of her characters. Her first novel, *Diario di una maestrina* (1957) (*A Schoolteacher's Diary*), tells the story of a female teacher, and makes much use of memory and flashback. *Piccole cronache* (1961) (*Little Stories*), tells the story of the childhood of a little girl who perceives herself as an outsider because of her family circumstances. *Il mare* (1967) (*The Sea*), is another novel of memory and adolescence, seen through the eyes of the protagonist, Rosa. Giacobbe has written about ▷Grazia Deledda, another Sicilian woman writer from the same village, Nuoro (*Grazia Deledda*, 1974). *Le radici* (1978) (*Roots*) is also about the place of the past in the present.

Giaconi, Luisa (1870–1908)
Italian poet. Born in Florence, she grew up in a fairly impoverished family and had a somewhat unstable childhood, as her father's work involved constant moving. She received a diploma from the *Accademia delle belle arti* in Florence, and from then on made a living from painting copies of paintings. She published very little in her lifetime. There are echoes of ▷D'Annunzianesimo in her poetry, yet she was also influenced by the English Pre-Raphaelites. Her writings are collected in the *Tebaide*, published posthumously in 1909, and again in 1912.

Gibbons, Stella (1902–1989)
English novelist, poet and journalist. Gibbons's first publication was a volume of poetry, *The Mountain Beast* (1930), which contains many 'nature' and pastoral poems. Her first novel, ▷*Cold Comfort Farm* (1932), turns these modes on their head, satirizing the pretensions and aspirations of Fleet Street, while also parodying the primitivist/naturalist vogue popularized by writers such as ▷Mary Webb. A hallmark of Gibbons's fiction is astute social observation, and her comedy-of-manners novels include *A Pink Front Door* (1959) and *The Snow-Woman* (1969). *Starlight* (1967) and *The Charmers* (1965) focus on cross-class relations. She also published *Collected Poems* (1951) and two volumes of short stories, *Christmas at Cold Comfort Farm* (1940) and *Conferences at Cold Comfort Farm* (1949).
▷Kaye-Smith, Sheila

Gibbs, May (1877–1969)
Australian children's author and illustrator. Her first Australian children's book, *Gumnut Babies*, published in 1916, created characters such as Bib and Bub and Snugglepot and Cuddlepie, who were personifications of Australian wild flowers, and who appeared in a succession of immensely popular juvenile books and cartoon strips. The ▷*Snugglepot and Cuddlepie Series*, together with ▷*Dot and the Kangaroo* (1899) by Ethel Pedley and the ▷*Blinky Bill Series*, by Dorothy Wall, created an indigenous literature for young children, based upon the flora and fauna of the Australian bush.
▷Children's literature (Australia)

Gibson, Margaret (born 1948)
Canadian short story writer, born and raised in Toronto, Ontario. She did not finish high school, and has suffered from mental illness for much of her life. She was hospitalized for the first time at the age of fifteen, and for several years after refused to speak. The power of Gibson's fiction has much to do with the effect of silence, and she frequently writes about silenced people. 'Making it', from *The Butterfly Ward* (1976), was the basis for Craig Russell's film *Outrageous*. *Considering Her Condition* (1978) develops her lucid and terrifying observations of a world encroaching with menacing determination; the fine line between madness and sanity is one that Gibson blurs in her intricate fiction.

Gift book
Widely popular US anthology form. In the pre-Civil War USA, before the development of national literary magazines, these annuals collected poetry, fiction, art and essays in often sumptuous bindings. Designed to be gifts, most of these anthologies necessarily avoided the controversial and the very topical. Both established and new writers published in the gift books, which were an important source of authors' income.
▷Souvenir; Miscellany

Gilbert, Florence Ruth (born 1917)

New Zealand poet. Ruth Gilbert is one of a number of women writers who have published regularly but have not been represented in major anthologies of New Zealand poetry. One of the contributors to ▷*Private Gardens* (1977), a pioneering anthology of women poets, Gilbert makes use of biblical stories and fables, and celebrates both natural and human landscapes. Gilbert's collection *The Luthier* (1966) focuses on the connection between instruments, their makers, and the songs they produce, a link that is metaphorically explored in much of her work.

Publications: *Lazarus and Other Poems* (1949); *The Sunlit Hour* (1955); *The Luthier* (1966).

▷Anthologies, New Zealand

Gilbert, Sandra (born 1936)

North American poet, critic and Professor of English at the University of California at Davis. She has collaborated with ▷Susan Gubar on a number of projects. Together they made an important contribution to the ▷woman-centred criticism of the 1970s, which aimed to construct a tradition of women's writing. Of chief importance is *The Madwoman in the Attic: The Woman Writer and the Nineteenth-Century Literary Imagination* (1979). This has been followed by *No Man's Land: The Place of the Woman Writer in the Twentieth Century*, published in three volumes. *The War of the Words*, Vol. 1 (1988) focuses on the middle of the 19th century to the present; *Sexchanges*, Vol. 2 (1989) reviews the period from the 1880s to the 1930s; *Letters from the Front*, Vol. 3 is forthcoming. Gilbert and Gubar have jointly edited *Shakespeare's Sisters: Feminist Essays on Women Poets* (1979), *The Norton Anthology of Literature by Women: the Tradition in English* (1985) and *The Female Imagination and the Modernist Aesthetic* (1986). They have collaborated on a number of essays.

Gilbert's poetry offers a personal record of her political development as a feminist. It moves from invoking male modernists in *In the Fourth World* (1979), to making allusions to a feminine world of domesticity in *The Summer Kitchen* (1983), and to female poets in *Emily's Bread* (1984). *Poems in Blood Pressure* (1988) employs sensuous and bodily metaphors to describe the passage from childhood experience to an adult sexual awareness.

▷Female traditions

Gilded Age

US era of growth, inflation and corruption which followed the Civil War. The term is often associated with land speculation and dishonourable manipulation of and by national and local politicians.

Gilder, Jeanette Leonard (1849–1916)

US editor, critic and columnist. A literary editor with long experience at the *New York Herald* and other publications, Gilder, along with her brother Joseph, founded ▷*The Critic* (1881–1906), for which Jeanette Gilder was the principal and,

finally, the sole editor. Of her own writing, perhaps the most lasting and significant is her column, 'The Lounger', which provided a generation of readers with book reviews, commentary and literary opinion from a distinctly US perspective.

Giles Corey, Yeoman (1893)

US drama by ▷Mary E. Wilkins Freeman. Wilkins Freeman's play on the Salem witch trials is extraordinary for its decade: a forceful drama with developed characters as well as realistic motivation and dialogue.

Gill, Sarah Prince (1728–1771)

North American essayist. The daughter of a Englishwoman, Deborah Denny, and a North American Puritan minister, Thomas Prince, she was raised in strict piety and was known for 'her eminently good genius and education'. During the evangelical revivalism that swept New England during the 18th century, she maintained private ▷*Devotional Papers*; two years after her death, they were published in Norwich, Connecticut, as models of Puritan piety and theology.

Gilman, Charlotte Perkins (1860–1935)

US fiction and non-fiction writer, poet, editor and feminist theorist. Most of Perkins Gilman's work is about the status and oppression of women. She saw early and consistently that economic dependence often meant physical and emotional slavery and that the moral prescription of women's roles as mothers and homemakers was a prescription for both personal and cultural incapacity.

Among her feminist works are short stories, including her frequently anthologized autobiographical short story ▷'The Yellow Wallpaper', and an early poetry collection, *In This Our World* (1893). Her definitive ▷*Women and Economics* (1898) was one of the first analyses to describe US society as 'androcentric' and to question the history and economic validity of women's dependence – a theme she continued in *Concerning Children* (1900) and *The Home* (1904), works which posed alternative social and economic models. In the 20th century she edited and wrote most of the women's rights periodical, *The Forerunner*, and published a number of non-fiction works and novels, including *The Crux* (1910).

Gilmore, Dame Mary (1865–1962)

Australian poet, journalist and social activist awarded the DBE. Gilmore grew up in the bush, then taught at Silverton, near Broken Hill. Here she was exposed to the radical unionism of the miners, and later, when she taught in Sydney schools, she actively supported the shearing and maritime strikes of the 1890s. In 1896 Gilmore joined the William Lane expedition to found a Utopian settlement (New Australia) in Patagonia, married there, but returned to Australia with her husband and son when the experiment failed.

From 1908 to 1931 she edited the women's page of the Sydney *Worker*, arguing always for feminist rights and responsibilities, for a return to the values of the pioneer founders of Australia, and spoke up for the outcasts and socially disadvantaged in society. Modern scholars have pointed to the conflict between her adulation of the pioneers and her recognition, in her autobiographical volumes, ▷*Old Days: Old Ways* (1934) and *More Recollections* (1935), of the fact that the settlement of Australia was based upon the massacre and dispersal of the Aboriginal race. A passionate lyricist with a considerable gift for the epigrammatic, her published poems include *Marri'd and Other Verses* (1910), *The Tale of Tiddley Winks* (1917), *The Passionate Heart* (1918), *The Tilted Cart* (1925), *The Wild Swan* (1930), *The Rue Tree* (1931), *Under the Wilgas* (1932), *Battlefields* (1939), *The Disinherited* (1941), *Pro Patria Australia and Other Poems* (1945), *Selected Verse* (1948) and *Fourteen Men* (1954). *Letters of Mary Gilmore* (1980) have been edited by W. H. Wilde and T. Inglis Moore, and W. H. Wilde's biography *Courage a Grace* (1988) is excellent.

▷'No Foe Shall Gather Our Harvest'; *Peaceful Army, The*

Gilroy, Beryl (born 1924)

Caribbean children's writer, novelist, teacher and psychotherapist. Gilroy was born and spent her childhood in ▷Guyana; she trained as a teacher there and worked for Unicef (United Nations International Children's Emergency Fund) before leaving for Britain in 1951, where she obtained a BSc at London University, and an MA at the University of Sussex. She has remained in Britain, has worked as a freelance journalist, and became the first black headteacher at a North London primary school. Between 1970 and 1975 she wrote a series of children's books, and in 1970 published *Black Teacher*, a chronicle of her experiences as a black headteacher. In 1982 she won the Greater London Council Creative Writing Prize for Ethnic Minorities, and a further literary award for her novel, *Frangipani House* (1986). She has also published *Boy-Sandwich* (1989).

There has been little criticism of her writing to date. *Frangipani House*, a powerfully written novel, is set in Guyana. It explores the theme of women and old age, telling the story of Mama King, who is trapped by age and infirmity. Her relatives send her to an institution, from which she eventually escapes, but not before she has suffered humiliation and been driven close to madness. Gilroy expresses a firm protest at a society where the traditional roles of women have been undermined by cultural forces from outside, and which denies respect and responsibility to the weak. Beryl Gilroy talks about the composition of this novel on a video which is part of the Institute of Contemporary Arts (London) series.

GIM ▷Galvão, Patrícia

Ginanni, Maria (1892–1953)

Italian poet, novelist and dramatist; real name Maria Crisi. Part of the ▷futurist movement. Born in Naples, she married the futurist painter and writer, Ginna. She edited the series of volumes, *Libri di valore* (*Worthwhile Books*) produced by *L'Italia futurista*, which Ginna illustrated. Her images of women were not, on the whole, as reactionary as those put forward by ▷Benedetta, yet neither did she really form part of the feminist wing of the futurist movement. ▷*Montagne trasparenti* (*Transparent Mountains*) of 1917 is a collection of writings in which her ambivalent attitude to woman's role is discernible. Sexual images, of which the phallus is the most prevalent, abound in her work. She co-wrote a three-act play with Emilio Settimelli, *La macchina* (*The Machine*), and her other works are *Luci trasversali* (*Transverse Lights*), written in 1917, and *Il poema dello spazio* (1919) (*The Space Poem*).

Gínzburg, Evgeniia Semënovna (1896–1980)

Russian memoir-writer and essayist. Evgeniia Gínzburg's gripping autobiography became a ▷*samizdat* bestseller in the 1960s, was widely translated abroad (English versions are *Into the Whirlwind*, 1967; *Within the Whirlwind*, 1981), and was at last published in the USSR in the late 1980s. A professor of history at Kazan' University married to a high communist official, Gínzburg was swept up in the Stalinist repressions in 1937 and spent eighteen years amid the unimaginable torments of prison, labour camps and exile. Her reminiscences, as she herself described them, are a ▷*Bildungsroman*, the 'cruel journey of a soul'. Willing 'to die for the Party – not once but three times', her ordeal brought her to the realization that she was the victim of a mad state experiment in the humiliation and destruction of innocent citizens. The bleak horror of Gínzburg's tale is relieved by her portraits of the people with whom she shared the ordeal and who kept love, poetry and humour alive in her heart.

Gínzburg, Lidiia Iakovlevna (1902–1990)

Gínzburg was a major Russian literary critic whose theoretical works stress the complex interrelations of life and art, and offer an alternative to Western schools that deal with the text as an ahistorical, hermetic unit. She was born into an intellectual Jewish family in Odessa, and greeted the 1917 Revolution wholeheartedly. In 1922 she enrolled in the Leningrad State Institute of History of the Arts, where she received a solid grounding in formalism. In talks with North American critic Jane Gary Harris (*Slavic Review*, Winter 1990) Gínzburg, with her 'unfailing . . . honesty and unflagging analytical bent', denied that she had exhibited any special moral courage in the Stalin epoch: 'we should not have any illusions, no one escaped unscathed.' Despite this appealingly modest disclaimer, she passed through the years of repression with integrity intact. She lived and worked in ▷Leningrad throughout the Nazi siege of World War II. Her most prolific

years began with the appearance of *On the Lyric* (1964), and her last two decades brought acclaim for ▷*On Psychological Prose* (1971, revised 1977; English translation 1991), and *On the Literary Hero* (1979). In recent articles, US critic Sarah Pratt has used the scholar's own theories to demonstrate the autobiographical core of works like Gínzburg's fictional sketch ▷'The Siege of Leningrad' and the critical articles collected as *About the Old and the New* (1982), *Literature in the Search for Reality* (1987), and *A Person Seated at a Desk* (1989). A selection of Gínzburg's writings appeared in English in 1992 as *Notes from the Leningrad Blockade and Other Writings*.
▷*tamizdat*

Ginzburg, Natalia (1916–1991)

Natalia Ginzburg

Italian novelist, short story writer and dramatist. Born in Palermo, she has spent much of her life and set much of her work in Turin. Her father was Jewish, her mother Catholic; as a result she was brought up an atheist, and this apparently made her feel special, and different from the other children with whom she mixed. As the youngest child in the family, she also felt different from her siblings, sometimes in a positive sense, but sometimes negatively. Her childhood appears to have been marked by strong feelings of isolation. The environment within which she was raised was strongly anti-fascist, and her marriage to Leone Ginzburg, who was imprisoned by the regime, and who died mysteriously while in prison in 1944, strengthened her political position. They had three children. Very much a part of the Italian literary scene, Ginzburg was a friend of Pavese,

Calvino and ▷Elsa Morante. In her earliest writings, she consciously rejected any autobiographical style or elements, which she saw as characteristic of what she called 'feminine' writing, but she soon discovered that it was through writing of her personal experiences in a fictionalized form that she succeeded best in expressing herself. Many of these autobiographical works, such as *Tutti i nostri ieri* (1952) (▷*All Our Yesterdays*), *Le voci della sera* (1961) (*Voices in the Evening*, translated into English in 1963), and *Lessico famigliare* (1963) (▷*Family Sayings*), are novels which rely on memory and evocation of the past, particularly the time of Ginzburg's youth in Turin. She has translated some of the works of Vercors and Proust, and her *La famiglia Manzoni* (1983) (*The Manzoni Family*), a literary and historical study beautifully told, and as concerned with family memories as any of her other works, was deservedly popular in Italy. She remains one of the most highly respected Italian writers of today, and her output has been considerable.

Her other work includes: *La strada che va in città e altri racconti* (1942) (*The Road to the City and Other Stories*, translated into English in 1952); *È stato così* (1947) (*That's How It Was*); 'La madre' (1948) (▷'The Mother'); *Valentino* (1957) (*Valentine*); *Le piccole virtù* (1962) (*Small Virtues*); *Cinque romanzi brevi* (1965) (*Five Short Novels*); *Ti ho sposato per allegria* (1966) (*I Married You For Fun*); *La segretaria* (1967) (*The Secretary*); *Mai devi domandarmi* (1970) (*Never Must You Ask Me*, translated into English in 1973); *Paese di mare* (1972) (*Village by the Sea*); *Caro Michele* (1973) (*Dear Michael*); *Sagittario* (1975) (*Sagittarius*); *La città e la casa* (1985) (*Town and House*).

Giorno e mezzo, Un (1988) (*A Day and a Half*)

An Italian novel by ▷Fabrizia Ramondino, which describes a weekend in the lives of a group of Neapolitan friends. Ramondino concentrates mainly on the feelings and experiences of the female characters. The novel is set in 1969 against the background of student unrest and political militancy, but is equally concerned with relationships and emotions. Stylistically, it could be classified as part of the genre of *realismo magico* (▷Magic realism).

Giovanni, Nikki (born 1943)

US poet. Born in Knoxville, Tennessee, to an African-American middle-class family, Giovanni was raised in Ohio. In 1967 she graduated with honours from Fisk University, where she was active in SNCC (Student Non-Violent Coordinating Committee), and in 1969 she chose to have a child out of wedlock. She became an activist in the African-American community, and in 1971 Giovanni recorded her poetry on a best-selling album, *Truth Is On Its Way*.

Her work reflects her sense of responsibility to her own people, and her early poetry affirms the beauty of blackness, envisioning a violent, revolutionary liberation of African-Americans in the contemporary US. In *My House* (1972) Giovanni focuses on the personal and the familial. *The Women and the Men* (1975) emphasizes self-realization, and celebrates African-American women's creativity. *Cotton Candy on a Rainy Day* (1978) reflects Giovanni's sense of loneliness and emptiness.

Other works include: *Black Feeling, Black Talk* (1967), *Black Judgement* (1968), *Re:Creation* (1970), *Gemini: An Extended Autobiographical Statement on My First Twenty-Five Years of Being a Black Poet* (1971), *Spin a Soft Black Song Poems for Children* (1971), *A Dialogue: James Baldwin and Nikki Giovanni* (1975), *Ego-Tripping and Other Poems for Young People* (1973), *A Poetic Equation: Conversations Between Nikki Giovanni and Margaret Walker* (1974), *Vacation Time: Poems for Children* (1980), *Those Who Ride the Night Winds* (1983) and *Sacred Cows and Other Edibles* (1988).

Gíppius, Zinaida Nikolaevna (1869–1945)

Russian poet, prose writer, dramatist, and critic. Gíppius published from 1888, but her serious career began with 'Song' (1893), 'Impotence' and 'Flowers of Night' (1894). These poems, influenced by western European 'decadent' trends, express a preference for possibility over attainment, a sense of earthly life as entrapment, and a disdain for moderation and materialism. Gíppius's poetry is full of unexpected epithets, daring images, and synesthesia. She was a bold innovator in rhyme, and a pioneer in the use of complex rhythm, including free verse and the three-beat *dol'nik* later popularized by Aleksandr Blok (1880–1921) and ▷Akhmátova.

Gíppius made a personal and professional assault on perceived biological sexual differences. Aware that the feminine created restrictive expectations, she used masculine and androgynous personae in her poetry, or avoided gendered voice altogether. For the most part, she ignored the expected woman's theme – love – and wrote an intellectual, abstract, sometimes aphoristic poetry. In both verse and prose she explored the nature of human sexuality, including homosexuality, lesbianism and androgyny. In this area she anticipated ▷Marina Tsvetáeva's poetry, and prose by ▷Zinóv'eva-Anníbal and ▷Anna Mar. Gíppius's early realistic fiction gradually became more abstract, philosophical and didactic. Her first story, 'The Ill-Fated Girl' (1890) retells Karamzin's 1792 'Poor Liza' from the girl's point of view. The semi-literate, lower-class girl betrayed by an upper-class cad reappears in the story 'Two Hearts' and the novel ▷*The Devil's Doll* (▷Mariia Krestóvskaia and ▷Ol'nem). Other stories present a rejection of marriage and material security ('The Blue Sky', 'The Lonely One'). In 'An Ordinary Event' (1904), Tolstoy's influence shows in the praise of intuitive understanding and acceptance of death. Gíppius used varied narrative strategies and crafted well-plotted, suspenseful stories (eg 'Outside Time: An Old Etude'). She portrayed strivings for a spiritual

as well as political revolution in the *The Devil's Doll* (1911) and the play ▷*The Green Ring* (1914).

Noted for outrageous behaviour and outbursts of exhibitionism, Gíppius was at the height of her poetic achievement and personal fame in Russia between 1910 and 1917. She influenced the poetry of Briusov, Blok, and ▷Adelaida Gértsyk, and was a model for women writers (▷Solov'ëva, Liudmila Víl'kina, and ▷Shaginián). In 1920 she and her husband, Dmitrii Merezhkovskii, settled in Paris, where they conducted a Sunday salon in their apartment between 1925 and 1940, and founded the literary and philosophical society 'The Green Lamp', which lasted from 1927 till the mid-1930s. In emigration Gíppius published poetry, memoirs (*Living Faces*, 1925), criticism, and a biography of her husband (1951).

▷Gurévich, Liubov'; Lókhvitskaia, Mirra; Odóevtseva, Irina; *Tragic Menagerie, The*
Bib: Pachmuss, T. (trans.), *Women Writers in Russian Modernism*; Pachmuss, T. (trans.), *Selected Works of Zinaida Gippius*; Pachmuss, T. (trans.), *A Russian Cultural Revival*; Markov, V. and Sparks, M., *Modern Russian Poetry*; Proffer, C. and E. (eds), *The Silver Age of Russian Culture*; Koteliansky, S. (trans.), *The Green Ring*; Zlobin, V., *A Difficult Soul: Zinaida Gippius*; Matich, O., *Paradox in the Religious Poetry of Zinaida Gippius*; Gibson, A., *Russian Poetry and Criticism in Paris from 1920 to 1940*; Weber, H. (ed.), *The Modern Encyclopedia of Russian and Soviet Literature*, Vol. 8; Wilson, K., *An Encyclopedia of Continental Women Writers*, Vol. 1; Rosenthal, C., 'The "Silver Age": Highpoint for Women?' in Edmundson, L. (ed.), *Women and Society In Russia and the Soviet Union*.

Girardin, Delphine de (1804–1855)

French poet, dramatist, novelist and journalist. Daughter of the novelist ▷Sophie Gay, she is best-known for her elegiac *Essais poétiques* (1824) (*Poetic Essays*) and *Nouveaux Essais poétiques* (1825) (*New Poetic Essays*), which are characterized by the spirituality and sensitivity typical of early French romantic writing, and for the witty and occasionally malicious *Lettres parisiennes* (*Parisian Letters*), a series of chronicles published under the pseudonym of Vicomte de Launay between 1836 and 1848 in the newspaper *La Presse*, which was owned by her husband, Emile de Girardin. After her marriage she established a salon which became even more famous than her mother's, and wrote plays, including *Judith* (1843); *Cléopâtre* (1847); *Lady Tartufe* (1853), and the innocuous *L'Ecole des journalistes* (1839) (*School for Journalists*) which was nevertheless banned. She was also the author of a collection of short stories entitled *La Canne de M. Balzac* (1836) (*M. Balzac's Walking Stick*). An early poetic work, 'Le Dévouement des médecins français et des soeurs de Ste Camille dans la peste de Barcelone' (1822) ('The devotion of the French Doctors and the Sisters of St Camille during the Plague in Barcelona') was crowned by the ▷Académie Française.
Bib: Malo, H., *La Gloire du Vicomte de Launay*.

'Girl of the Period, The' (1868)

An essay by ▷Eliza Lynn Linton, published in *The Saturday Review*. It caused much controversy, was sold worldwide and was described as 'an epoch-making essay'. The 'Girl of the Period' is depicted as a frivolous, extravagant creature 'who dyes her hair and paints her face . . . whose sole idea of life is fun' and who shows no respect for men, marriage or motherhood. Linton laments this 'pitiable mistake and . . . grand national disaster' and calls for a return to a past ideal of womanhood. The essay does not touch upon issues central to women's lives in the 1860s such as higher ▷education, work, or ▷suffrage, but it caused a furore and sparked numerous imitations.

Girl's Life Eighty Years Ago: Selections from the Letters of Eliza Southgate Bowne, A (1888)

Beginning with her school years, including her education under the tutelage of ▷Susanna Haswell Rowson, ▷Eliza Southgate Bowne's selected correspondence from 1797 to 1809 details the upper-class life of a remarkably witty and intelligent young North American woman. One of her favourite correspondents was her cousin, Moses Porter, with whom she discussed the vagaries of courtship and openly professed her dismay at the number of loveless marriages among North Americans. She adamantly rejected parental matches and argued that only when 'equal affection' existed could a marriage prosper. She tells Porter, 'I congratulate myself that I am at liberty to refuse those I don't like, and that I have firmness enough to brave the sneers of the world and live an old maid, if I never find one I can love.' Bowne did marry, at the age of twenty, but her correspondence reveals that she retained her independent spirit after marriage.

▷Early North American letters

Girls of Slender Means, The (1963)

A novel by Scottish writer ▷Muriel Spark. Set in London at the end of World War II, when 'all the nice people in England were poor', the novel describes the lives and relationships of a group of young women in a residential club. The light, spare surface of the novel coexists with Spark's characteristic preoccupations with good and evil, egotism and sacrifice.

Giroud, Françoise

French journalist and broadcaster, editor of *L'Express*. She was nominated Secretary for the Status of Women as part of Giscard d'Estaing's 'New Deal' in 1974, and accepted the post, in spite of the fact that she disagreed with his politics. She resigned in 1976. Her published works, which have been translated into English deal mainly with the reality of male political power, of which she gives a privileged insider's view, and include *Ce que je crois* (1975) (*I Give You My Word*), *La Comédie du pouvoir* (1977) (*The Comedy of Power*) and *Le Bon Plaisir* (1983) (*The Wish*).

Glasgow, Ellen (1873–1945)

US novelist, short-story writer and poet. Glasgow was born in Richmond, Virginia, into one of the oldest colonial families. Her mother was the perfect embodiment of the ▷Southern lady. When her mother died, Glasgow assumed her role in Richmond's social life. Glasgow defends Southern womanhood while criticizing the tradition of the ideal Southern lady. Her work emphasizes the conflict between women's biological destiny and women's instinct for freedom, and it celebrates women's inborn strength and moral courage – their vein of iron. ▷*Virginia* (1913) protests against the idealism of romantic love, while *Life and Gabriella* (1916) envisions Southern women fabricating new identities for themselves through work.

▷*Barren Ground* (1925) and ▷*Vein of Iron* (1935) feature women who reject the ideal of romantic love and channel their creative energies into their work. *The Sheltered Life* (1932) cautions women against locating their identities in their sensuality. Glasgow's Pulitzer Prize-winning work, *In This Our Life* (1941), advocates experimenting with the construction of sexual relationships. Thus Glasgow envisions a mediation between femininity and independence.

Other work includes: *The Descendant* (1897), *The Battle-Ground* (1902), *The Deliverance* (1904), *The Wheel of Life* (1906), *The Builders* (1919), *One Man in His Time* (1922), *They Stooped to Folly* (1929), and her autobiography, *The Woman Within* (1954).

Bib: Thiebaux, Marcelle, *Ellen Glasgow*.

Glásnost'

Glásnost' ('public discussion') was the more successful of the two policies (the other being *perestroika*, or economic restructuring) under which Mikhail Gorbachëv came to power in 1985. It brought a virtual end to censorship and government monopoly of publication (▷Soviet Writers' Union) and introduced Soviet readers to forgotten and suppressed writers. After over fifty years of subservience to the strictures of ▷socialist realism, Russian literature is now free, but must compete with other free media and the surge of interest in non-fictional truth-telling.

▷Barkóva, Anna; Lisniánskaia, Inna; *samizdat*; 'Woman Question' (Russia)

Glaspell, Susan (1876–1948)

US dramatist and novelist. The descendant of pioneer settlers, Glaspell was born in Davenport, Iowa. In 1899 she graduated from Drake University, and in 1913 she married George Cook. They founded the Provincetown Players with the dramatist Eugene O'Neill (1888–1953) and started New York's little theatre movement. Glaspell's work features women who do not conform to social norms. Her first novel, *The Glory of the Conquered* (1909), celebrates the power of romantic love; *Fidelity* (1915) considers the conflict between personal and social values; *Brook Evans* (1928) explores the pulls between desire and duty. *Judd Rankin's Daughter* (1945) examines liberalism versus conservatism. Glaspell's plays ▷*Trifles* (1916) and *The Outside* (1917) emphasize sisterhood in the struggle to save women's lives. *The Verge* (1921) looks at women's fight to transcend the limitations of biology. Glaspell received a Pulitzer Prize in Drama for ▷*Alison's House* (1930).

Other works include: *The Visioning* (1912), *Lifted Masks* (1912), *Inheritors* (1921), *Bernice* (1924), *Tickless Time* (1925), *The Road to the Temple* (1926), *The Comic Artist* (1927), *Fugitive's Return* (1919), *Ambrose Holt and Family* (1931), *The Morning Is Near Us* (1940) and *Norma Ashe* (1942).
Bib: Waterman, Arthur E., *Susan Glaspell.*

Glass, Joanna (born 1936)
Canadian dramatist, born Joanna McClelland in Saskatoon, Saskatchewan. She studied acting at the Pasadena Playhouse, and began to write in the late 1960s. She married Alexander Glass in 1959, but divorced in 1975. She gained recognition with the two one-act plays, *Canadian Gothic* and *American Modern*, which were produced at the Manhattan Theatre Club in 1972. Although radically different in setting, they both deal with contemporary despair. Her first novel, *Reflections on a Mountain Summer*, appeared in 1974. *Artichoke*, produced in 1975, has been performed in Canada, the USA and London; it is a comedy about a middle-aged woman on a prairie farm who decides to undertake adultery as a summer project. *The Last Chalice* was commissioned by the Manitoba Theatre Centre in 1977; it portrays an alcoholic home. *To Grandmother's House We Go* was produced in 1981, *Play Memory* in 1984. *Woman Wanted*, her second novel, appeared in 1985. She lives in Guilford, Connecticut.

Glen, Alice Esther (1881–1940)
New Zealand children's author and editor; journalist. While working in an office, Glen wrote freelance stories and verse for New Zealand, Australian and English magazines, and wrote for children. Her first book *Six Little New Zealanders* (1917) and its maturer sequel *Uncles Three of Kamahi* (1926) were set on a sheep station in South Canterbury near the Rangatata River where Glen and her siblings had enjoyed childhood holidays. Not only important for their local rather than English settings, these stories are also pacy, exciting, and refreshing for their lack of didacticism, and depiction of young characters who talk and act like real children. *Robin of Maoriland* (1929) is also set in New Zealand and draws on Glen's family life. On the radio, and as 'Lady Gay', editor of the children's page in local newspapers, Glen became a 'guiding star' to hundreds of children in New Zealand, encouraging their literary efforts, particularly by visits and contributions from writer friends like ▷Edith Howes and ▷Mona Tracy. Her life and work for children are remembered in the Esther Glen Medal, an annual award by the New

Zealand Library Association to a New Zealand citizen for a distinguished work of fiction for children.
▷Children's literature, New Zealand

Gleaner, The (1798)
A three-volume collection of the *Massachusetts Magazine* writings by the North American feminist, ▷Judith Sargent Murray. Included in *The Gleaner* are essays advocating religious and marital egalitarianism as well as nationalistic political and literary critiques, a novella ('The Story of Margaretta') and two dramas. The narrator is 'Mr Vigilius' or 'The Gleaner'; by maintaining a male persona, Murray found the freedom to express her radical views in a public forum, but the essays also repeatedly challenge stereotypical definitions of what is 'masculine' and 'feminine'. The essays also call for the development of North American literary styles and genres; in 'Panegyric on the Drama', the 'flowery' language of English traditions is satirized and abandoned in favour of a more pragmatic literary style. This collection constitutes the first major feminist writings by an early North American woman.

Glinska, Teofila (?1765–1799)
Polish poet. Her poem, '*Hymn Pervanów o smierci*' (1785) ('The Peruvian Hymn to the Dead') was adapted from *Incas*, a novel by Marmontel. Her poem *Sczorse* (1785) combines didactic and descriptive elements.

Glória, Madalena da, Sóror (1672–176?)
Portuguese poet. A nun, she used the pen-name Leonarda Gil da Gama to sign her works, including an allegorical novel, *Reino de Babilônia* (1749) (*Reign of Babylon*); *Orbe Celeste* (1742) (*Celestial Orb*), a collection of poems; and her two-volume fiction *Brados do Desengano contra o Profundo Sono do Esquecimento* (1739; 1749) (*Cries of Disillusionment Against the Deep Sleep of Forgetfulness*).

Glück, Louise (born 1943)
US poet. Born and educated in New York, Glück graduated from Columbia University in 1965, has been twice married, has one son, and has taught at Williams College Massachusetts since 1983. The main setting for Glück's poetry is domestic, but it is a domesticity riven with difficulties, fractured and often broken apart by death, abandonment and loss, sometimes redeemed by the innocence of children, or the hope of love between men and women. The poems are often narrative in form, but these narratives are allusive, concise and spare rather than circumstantial, often drawing on mythical or biblical stories for their starting-point. In *The House on Marshland* (1975) these themes are marked by resignation and pervasive melancholy; *Descending Figure* (1980) contains many poems dealing with the withdrawal from life and descent of the dying and the fear of death. Glück has also treated such subjects as

anorexia and sexual violence, detailing the cost of femininity and sexual inequality in relationships.

Other work includes: *Firstborn* (1968), *Teh* (1976), *The Garden* (1976), *The Triumph of Achilles* (1985), *Ararat* (1990).

Glückel von Hameln (1645–1724)

Yiddish-speaking German writer. Her memoirs are the earliest known Yiddish texts by a German woman. Born in Hamburg, she married Chaim of Hameln when she was fourteen, and had fourteen children. To alleviate her grief at her husband's death in 1689, she undertook to write her memoirs and the history of her family in seven books: *Zikhroynes marat glikl hamil 1645–1719*, German translation: *Die Memoiren der Glückel von Hameln 1645–1719* (*The Memoirs of Glückel of Hamelin*, 1977). She had completed five volumes when, in 1700, she relucantly remarried. Widowed for a second time in 1712, she had completed the remaining two volumes of her history by 1719.

Glümer, Claire von (1825–1906)

German writer of travel books and short stories. Her family had to flee Germany because of her father's involvement with the liberal movement. In 1841 she returned to work, first as a governess and then as a parliamentary reporter. She was caught trying to help her brother escape from gaol, and was herself imprisoned for three months. Her first novel *Fata Morgana* (1848) was followed by many stories and novellas, but she became best known for her translation of ▷George Sand's autobiography and for a description of her travels in the Pyrenees, entitled *Aus den Pyrenäen* (1854) (*From the Pyrenees*).

Goblin Market and Other Poems (1862)

The first published collection of poems by British poet ▷Christina Rossetti. The title poem is a narrative concerning two sisters, Laura and Lizzie, one of whom is tempted to eat the fruit of the rapacious goblin men, while the other saves her sister in an act of sacrifice. The poem is a rich blend of fantasy, allegory, fairytale and moral tale, erotically suggestive and linguistically complex. It has generated much feminist criticism, being interpreted as a lesbian fantasy, as a female myth, and as a poem concerned with women's relationship to language. It is Rossetti's most famous work. Other notable poems in the collection include the enigmatic and elusive 'Echo' and 'Winter: My Secret', and 'A Triad', in which Rossetti criticizes the amatory possibilities available to women. The collection established Rossetti as a significant voice in Victorian poetry.

Godden, Rumer (born 1907)

English novelist, poet and writer for children. Godden lived in India as a young child, was educated in England, returned to India, and after another educational visit to England, opened a ballet school in Calcutta. Much of her writing uses her knowledge of Indian and Chinese history and legend. Her early novels include *Chinese Puzzle* (1936), a collection of stories of an ancient mandarin reincarnated as a pekinese dog. The commercially successful *Black Narcissus* (1939) focuses on missionary nuns working in the Himalayas. Her other novels include the well-known *The Greengage Summer* (1958), narrated from a child's point of view; her many books for children include *The Mousewife* (1951), based on a character found in the journals of ▷Dorothy Wordsworth. Godden has also written *The Tale of Tales: The Beatrix Potter Ballet* (1971). Her autobiography is *A Time to Dance, No Time to Weep* (1987).

Godey's Lady's Book (1830–1898)

The best-known 19th-century US women's magazine. It was famed for its fashion illustrations and for establishing middle-class standards of taste. Edited for most of its life by ▷Sarah Josepha Hale, the magazine became the conservative authority promoting such concepts as women's separate sphere of influence and the 'Cult of True Womanhood'. While Hale promoted women's education, she opposed women's suffrage.

▷*Peterson's Magazine*; *Una, The*; Whitcher, Frances Miriam Berry; *American Ladies' Magazine*

Godley, Charlotte (1821–1907)

New Zealand correspondent. Charlotte Godley sailed from Plymouth for New Zealand in 1849 with her husband J.R. Godley who was on his way to prepare for the Canterbury Association's (the organization responsible for the settlement of Christchurch, Canterbury, New Zealand) first settlers. Godley's letters to her mother, Mrs Charles Wynne, written until the Godleys returned to England in 1853, form a record of her experience in the early colonizing days of New Zealand. *Letters from Early New Zealand* was privately printed in 1936, and published in the centenary year of the Canterbury settlement (1951). Charlotte Godley died in London in 1907.

'Godlie Dreame Compylit in Scottish Meter, Ane' (1603)

Allegorical poem by English writer ▷Elizabeth Colville. Written in Scottish dialect, it consists of stanzas of *ottava rima* (an eight-line stanza, figuring a b a b a b c c). Although Colville's poem is reminiscent of medieval dream vision poetry, it is a staunchly Protestant work. The narrator, deeply distressed over personal sins as well as those of the mortal world, falls asleep and begins to dream. She encounters an angelic guide (Christ) who comforts her with a vision of a heavenly castle of silver and gold which she cannot enter until she has accompanied him on a journey through the afterworld. In their journey they pass over the smoky black pit of Hell, which she mistakes for the 'papist purgatory'. The dreamer is corrected by Christ, who provides her with a lesson in the Protestant doctrine of justification by faith rather than works. The poet's courage and grip on her guide falters, and she begins to plummet toward Hell, but her guide rescues her as she awakes. Melville's poem underwent ten printings during the 17th century and several more during the 18th century.

▷Protestant Reformation

Bib: Laing, D., *Early Scottish Metrical Tales*.

Godoy Alcayaga, Lucila ▷Mistral, Gabriela

God's Mercy Surmounting Man's Cruelty, Exemplified in the Captivity and Redemption of Elizabeth Hanson (1728)

▷Captivity narrative by North American writer ▷Elizabeth Meader Hanson. One of the few such texts by a North American Quaker, *God's Mercy* follows the prescribed narrative structure of Hanson's capture, negotiations for her freedom, and ultimately her literal and spiritual redemption. Hanson's account is notable, however, for her descriptions of the involvement of the French in the slaughter and kidnappings, and for the account of her captors' longstanding refusal to free Hanson's marriage-aged daughter, Sarah.

God's Step-Children (1924)

A novel by South African writer ▷Sarah Gertrude Millin, which has received notoriety because of its treatment of 'miscegenation'. A recurring theme in South African English literature, and touched on by other South African writers, such as ▷Olive Schreiner, ▷Ethelreda Lewis, and William Plomer, it was dealt with obsessively by Millin. The story is a saga of generations, centring on an English missionary, Andrew Flood, his union with a black ('Hottentot') woman, and their line of descendants, which issues finally in Barry Lindsell. Barry, to all appearances 'white', goes to Oxford to take holy orders, and returns to South Africa with an English bride. His jealous half-sister reveals the secret of his ancestry to his wife, who returns to England, and Barry, resuming contact with his family in Griqualand West, realizes that his true home is with them, the 'brown people'. He thus returns to the mission field of his ancestor in an attempt to wipe out what Millin calls this 'tragedy of blood'.

Millin's novel, however disturbing, must be read not merely as a hotchpotch of colonial prejudices, as one critic has put it, but more seriously as the reflection of scientific and historical thought regarding evolution and degeneration; thought recently current in Britain and rigorously pursued in racist South Africa.

Godwin, Gail (born 1937)

US novelist. Born in Birmingham, Alabama, Godwin was raised by her mother and grandmother in North Carolina. Her mother supported the family by teaching romantic literature and writing love stories. In 1971 Godwin earned a Doctoral degree at the University of Iowa. Her fiction focuses on women undergoing a transformation; they reject the prescribed role of the ▷Southern lady and forge a new identity for themselves. In *The Odd Woman* (1974) a professor decides not to abandon her career for her lover; in *Violet Clay* (1978) an artist finds her own, specifically female, muse, and her art celebrates women instead of rendering them victims. In *A Mother and Two Daughters* (1982) three women take control over their destinies. As in *The Finishing School* (1985), Godwin emphasizes the self's limitless possibilities.

Other work includes: *The Perfectionists* (1970), *Glass People* (1972) and *A Southern Family* (1987).

Godwits Fly, The (1938)

Novel by New Zealand writer ▷Robin Hyde. Based on the author's own life, *The Godwits Fly* has been described as the novel which encapsulates the concerns of the writers of the 1930s. The novel is a narrative of the lives of the Hannay family, focused on one of the daughters, Eliza Hannay, and her reflection on the relationships and events she is involved in. *The Godwits Fly* is set in Wellington and records the history of a particular region, but its main focus is on family relationships as well as the shift of a young girl away from family and into more complex social and sexual relationships. As Eliza grows to individuality and adulthood she learns, through a series of painful relationships, the rewards and costs of subjectivity, and particularly the subjectivity of the artist. Well received when it first appeared, *The Godwits Fly* came to be seen as a major New Zealand novel with the 'rediscovery' of Hyde's work in the 1970s.

Goethes Briefwechsel mit einem Kinde (1835) ▷ Goethe's Correspondence with a Child

Goethe's Correspondence with a Child (1837)

Translation of *Goethes Briefwechsel mit einem Kinde* (1835) by ▷Bettina von Arnim. This is an autobiographical novel in letter form, very loosely based on her own correspondence with Goethe (1749–1832) from 1807 to 1811, when she was a young woman and he was thirty-five years her senior. In mixing original text from letters with fiction and interpretation, she evolved a style that was unique to herself.

Going Under (1972)

Russian novella by ▷Lidiia Chukóvskaia. Written between 1949 and 1957, and published in English in 1972, *Going Under* describes Soviet life at the start of the new wave of arrests and persecution of 1949. The setting is a sanitarium-retreat for writers, into which the turmoil outside gradually penetrates: the matron's sister disappears from her place of exile; a Yiddish poet is arrested. In contrast to ▷*Sofiia Petrovna*, which portrayed the 1937 purges through the eyes of a simple woman with faith in the Soviet system, here Chukóvskaia uses the first-person viewpoint of a sophisticated narrator, a translator and writer who recites classical Russian poetry on her walks in the snow.

'Going under' is the process by which the heroine tries to penetrate intuitively the experience of her husband, who has been missing since his arrest in 1937. From the novelist Bilibin, she learns that imprisonment 'without right of correspondence' is a euphemism for execution, and that her husband is undoubtedly dead. In a rare mark of confidence, Bilibin shares with her his own experiences of prison and labour camp. The integrity of Russian literature is an important theme of the novella: the narrator reacts with outrage to Bilibin's use of people and incidents from his ordeal in a construction novel tailored to the dictates of ▷socialist realism. In the end, she must also question her right to judge the compromises others make with conscience.

Goldberg, Lea (1911–1978)

Lea Goldberg

Israeli poet, critic, dramatist and translator. Born in Kovna, Lithuania, Goldberg studied at the universities of Kovna, Bonn and Berlin. She settled in Palestine in 1935 and immediately became part of the main literary circles of the time. She played a central role in the Hebrew literary world, as a creative poet, academic (she was head of the Department of Comparative Literature at the Hebrew University) and translator.

Goldberg's poetry shows strong tendencies towards the symbolists of both eastern and western Europe. But although she was associated with the ▷modernist movement of the 1930s, she used traditional verse and limited the symbolic content of her poems by using a simplicity of expression. Her themes are universal and the poems are personal and introspective.

Her numerous translations into Hebrew include works by Dante, Petrarch, Baudelaire, Tolstoy, Chekhov, Ibsen and Shakespeare. She wrote a play, *Ba'alat Ha'armon* (1974) (*The Castle Owner*), was a popular children's writer and published

articles and books of literary criticism. Her main poetic works are: *Taba'ot He'Ashsn* (1935) (*Rings of Smoke*), *Im Ha'Layla Haze* (1967) (*With This Night*) and ▷*Mukdam U'Meuchar* (1970) (*Early and Late*).

▷*Anthology of Modern Hebrew Poetry*; *Penguin Book of Hebrew Verse, The*; *Voices Within the Ark*

Golden Age of Russian poetry, The

In literary history the appellation 'Golden Age' was given to the period from the 1810s to 1840 when Aleksandr Pushkin (1899–1937) and the groups of remarkable poets surrounding him were active. It was the culmination of 100 years of intensive absorption of western European culture, and the slow transformation of the written language from a frozen Slavonic dialect to a flexible colloquial Russian.

The Golden Age is sometimes portrayed as a community of aristocratic writers who met at the salons of attractive ▷St Petersburg and ▷Moscow hostesses to read their sentimental and romantic fiction and inscribe graceful epistles and lyrics in ladies' albums, but the democratic, socially focused element that has marked Russian literature throughout its history was present as well. After the Napoleonic Wars, liberal soldiers, writers, and intellectuals formed secret societies dedicated to reforms ranging from abolition of serfdom to constitutional monarchy. The abortive 1825 Decembrist Revolution which they led ended in an epoch of repression under Nicholas I. ▷Nadezhda Teplóva was the first noted woman poet of the period, and ▷Evdokiia Rostopchiná and ▷Karolina Pávlova both began their careers in the Golden Age. By the end of the period, prose had replaced poetry as the dominant genre, and an aggressive generation of professional writers from a broad spectrum of classes had appeared.

Bib: Todd, W.M., *Fiction and Society in the Age of Pushkin: Ideology, Institutions, and Narrative.*

Golden Cangue, The (1943)

Novella by Chinese writer ▷Zhang Ailing (Eileen Chang). *The Golden Cangue* creates the image of a formidable woman who evokes our compassion even as she destroys the life around her in a desperate attempt to assert herself.

Chi-ch'iao is the daughter of a sesame oil dealer who is able to move up the social ladder by marrying into a mandarin family, her husband being an invalid. By openly flaunting their conventions of speech and behaviour she holds her own among her well-born in-laws who despise her. When her husband and her mother-in-law die, Chi-Ch'iao lives with her son and daughter. Her brother-in-law, who had formerly repulsed her advances, now approaches her, but she suspects him of being after her money – the money that she sold herself for – and she drives him away. She rules her son and daughter with an iron hand. To keep her son under control, she lures him into smoking opium and gives him a concubine, driving her daughter-in-law, and eventually the concubine, to suicide. She humiliates her daughter so that she has no social life at all. When the girl finally finds a partner, Chi-chi'iao lays a devilish plot to expose her to her fiancé as an opium addict, and ruins the affair. 'For thirty years, she had worn a golden cangue. She had used its heavy edges to chop down several people; those that did not die were half killed.' In lonely old age, when facing death, Chi-chi'iao thinks of the young men in her own station in life that she might have married; a teardrop strays down her cheek and dries by itself.

There are great psychological depths in this portrait of a woman who is hard, bitter, even evil, but who is also presented as strong and resourceful, a woman who has managed to rise above her circumstances only to be cheated out of what is truly worthwhile in life.
Bib: Lau Joseph M., Hsia, C.T. and Lee, Leo, O. (eds), *Modern Chinese Stories and Novellas, 1919–1949.*

Golden Chariot Does Not Go Up To Heaven, The (1991)

Arabic novel by Egyptian writer ▷Salwa Bakr. In Egypt in the 1980s there had been a number of cases of women killing their husbands or lovers. In two of the cases the women had cut up the body and disposed of the pieces in plastic bags. The Egyptian press made it appear as if every male in Egypt was in danger, and the plastic bag became for caricaturists and columnists a symbol of the knife hanging over their collective head.

Salwa Bakr's novel, set in the women's prison in Cairo, was written against the background of this lunatic fit in the media, though none of the characters in her novel are based on the unfortunate women whose names, photographs and circumstances had been widely publicized.

All previous accounts of the women's prison in memoirs or fiction had been written by political prisoners. Bakr had also had first-hand experience of the women's prison as a 'political suspect', and shows that the 'politicals' are a truly marginal group in the women's prison. It is an inferno of ordinary women; most of them are poor and ignorant people who have come to the end of their tether.

There is no sentimentality in her presentation of characters, though the majority are victims of men and of society at large. The structure is that of ▷ *The Arabian Nights*: one story leading into another, and divergent voices speaking, telling their own stories, digressing, commenting – it is matter-of-fact, but in other ways unreal, because it is discourse in hell. The style is also that of *The Arabian Nights*; ungrammatical, mainly colloquial, changing with the narrative change of voice, and often brilliantly illuminating a character through the narrator, who makes no pretence of detachment, but seems to speak from deep within each character. Many of the inmates suffer from *ishq* (the Arabic for 'love that possesses the soul'), and are devoted to the image of their loved ones,

though they may be doing time or life for murdering him.

The life of the inmates is depicted with detailed realism, at the same time revealing the variety of worlds of suffering, as well as the fantasy behind the novel.

Golden Honeycomb, The (1977)

A novel by Indian author ▷Kamala Markandaya. Set in India during the Raj, the novel charts the fortunes of a princely state whose rulers have gradually lost more and more power to the British. The 'honeycomb' of the title refers to the glowing but essentially hollow and fragile network of princely alliances with the British in pre-independence India. Markandaya's novel is not only a cry against exploitation of the poor by the rich and the Indians by the British; it provides a quite subtle delineation of generational change and conflict, and of the ties of conjugal and filial love binding families together.

Golden Notebook, The (1962)

Novel by British writer ▷Doris Lessing. 'The point is,' says Lessing's heroine, Anna Wulf, in the opening lines of *The Golden Notebook*, 'the point is that, as far I can see, everything is cracking up.' Indeed, it is precisely the 'cracking-up' or fragmentation of female subjectivity that Lessing's novel so strikingly dramatizes, through a series of four 'notebooks' each, purportedly, taking a different aspect of Anna's experience. Thus the 'black book' explores her life as a writer; the 'red', politics; the 'yellow' fictionalizes Anna's experiences, whilst the 'blue' is a type of 'diary'. But the point is not that each book divides up Anna's life in order to reconcile it into a new 'whole', but that the borders between the books do not hold, the different fictions of female subjectivity do not make a coherent narrative and, as the book's double-ending demonstrates, the contradictions that lie at the heart of Lessing's heroine's relation to her own history can, at best, be thought through in a form of affirmative undecidability. This key text for 'second-wave' feminism became a classic in its time, and the questions it raises – about women's writing, politics, history, psychoanalysis, narrative and sexual relations – are just as relevant to feminism today.

Gold rush

US (California). Frantic emigration from the eastern USA (and much of the world) to California and the US west coast followed the discovery of gold in 1848. The adventure, polyglot population and rapid growth of towns and cities spawned a distinctive literature: 'letters' home from the gold-fields published in eastern periodicals; a rich diary literature still being explored, especially in so far as it records women's experience; ▷local color fiction; humour, eg ▷Louise Clappe's *Shirley Letters*; and the San Francisco literary group and periodicals associated with ▷Ina Coolbrith.

Goll, Claire (1891–1977)

German poet. After an unhappy childhood in a wealthy Jewish family in Nuremberg, followed by a brief marriage, she went to Geneva to study philosophy. During World War I she was drawn to Expressionism and pacifism, had an affair with the poet Rilke (1875–1926), and met her future husband, the poet Ivan Goll (1891–1950). In addition to some prose pieces, notably the feminist anti-war stories *Die Frauen erwachen* (1918) (*Women Awake*), she published two volumes of Expressionist poetry in 1918 and 1919. After the war she moved with Goll to Paris, where their flat became a meeting place for members of the avant-garde, such as the writers James Joyce (1882–1941) and André Gide (1869–1951), and the painters Georges Braque (1882–1963) and Picasso (1881–1973), as well as members of the Surrealist group. Under the influence of literary cubism and Surrealism, in 1925 the Golls issued a collection of their mutual love poems in French, in which words assume a new associative power within an unconstrained form. During World War II they emigrated to the USA, returning to Paris in 1947. After her husband's death, Claire resumed her literary career, publishing poetry, stories and autobiographical texts, such as *Der gestohlene Himmel* (1962) (*The Stolen Heaven*), *Memoiren eines Spatzen des Jahrhunderts* (1978) (*Memoirs of a Sparrow of this Century*) and *Ich verzeihe keinem* (1981) (*I Forgive No One*). These texts tell the story of her childhood, and reflect her unremitting hatred for her mother.

Gom, Leona (born 1946)

Canadian poet and novelist. Born near Hines Creek in isolated northern Alberta, where her parents were homesteaders, she attended the University of Alberta, wrote her MA thesis on ▷Margaret Laurence and worked closely with ▷Dorothy Livesay. She taught English and Creative Writing at Kwantlen College in Surrey, British Columbia, from 1973 until 1988, and for ten years was editor of the Canadian literary magazine, *Event*. She was initially known as a poet, publishing in dozens of literary journals in Canada, the USA and Australia. Her poetry collections include: *Kindling* (1972), *The Singletree* (1975), and *Land of the Peace* (1980). *NorthBound* (1984) collects the best of her poetry, about place and the hardship of homesteading in an isolated rural community, from the earlier books. In *Private Properties* (1986) Gom's focus shifts to women's relative powerlessness in the face of what is imposed on them (including anorexia, incest and rape), balanced against the demands of 'appropriate behaviour'. Her fiction is strongly feminist in its examination of the various traps in which women are caught. Her first novel, *Housebroken* (1986), tells the story of an agoraphobic housewife; *Zero Avenue* (1989) is about an incest victim and her unresolved relationship with her complicitous mother. Despite the seriousness of Gom's subject matter, there is a sly wit to her characters and their dialogue which leavens their victimization. *The Y Chromosome* (1990) is a futuristic novel about a woman-centred world where the male gene has become completely recessive. She lives in White Rock, British Columbia.

Gomez, Madeleine-Angélique Poisson, Dame Gabriel de (1684–1770)

French dramatist and writer of prose fiction. Born in Paris, daughter of the actor Paul Poisson, she married a penniless Spanish actor, and earned her living by writing. Gomez was one of the few women to write for the theatre and to have her plays performed at the Comédie Française. The first of her tragedies to be produced, *Habis* (1714), was one of the most successful plays in the period 1700–1715, and achieved the rare honour of being revived in 1732. The second, *Marsidie, reine des Cimbres* (1735) (*Marsidie, Queen of the Cimbri*), was not staged, but her subsequent tragedies, *Semiramis* (1707, performed 1716) and *Cléarque, tyran d'Héraclée* (1717) (*Cléarque, Tyrant of Héraclée*) were. These political tragedies all focus on the spectacle of the suffering of proud women whose heroism lies in their refusal to submit to the tyranny which threatens them. During the remainder of her prolific writing career, Gomez produced many volumes of prose fiction. Of her volumes of short prose pieces, *Journées amusantes* (1722–31) (*Amusing Days*) enjoyed something of a European vogue. *La Belle Assemblée* (1750) (*Gathering of the Fair*) ran to eight editions, and the *Cent nouvelles* (1811) (*One Hundred New Short Stories*) ran to eighteen volumes. These popular collections of romances, fictionalized historical stories and exotic tales owed much to earlier heroic and baroque traditions, but were also influenced by the new taste for sensibility in the vein of ▷Richardson and Prévost.

Bib: Mish, C., *Revue de Littérature Comparée* XXXIV (1960) pp. 213–25; Lancaster, H. C., *Sunset: A History of Parisian Drama in the Last Years of Louis XIV, 1701–1715*; Showalter, Jr., E., 'Writing Off the Stage: Women Authors and Eighteenth-century Theatre' in Dejean, J., and Miller, N. K. (eds), *Displacements*.

Gómez de Avellaneda, Gertrudis (1814–1873)

Spanish dramatist. Although born in Cuba, Gómez left the island in 1836 to settle in Madrid. She is the author of a collection of romantic poetry, *Poesías* (1841), and three novels: *Sab* (1841), *Dos mujeres* (1842) (*Two Women*), which attacks the institution of marriage, and a historical novel, *Guatemocín* (1846). She is most renowned, however, for her historical plays – *Alfonso Munio* (1844), *El Príncipe de Viana* (1844) (*The Prince of Viana*), and *Egilona* (1846) – and two biblical dramas – *Saúl* (1849) and *Baltasar* (1858), her masterpiece. Gómez de Avellaneda is notable for her anti-slavery stance, her attack on prisons and the ills of the criminal justice system, and her presentation of women as victims of society's laws.

Gómez Ojea, Carmen (born 1945)

Contemporary Spanish novelist. Born in Gijón, she has published three novels to date. *Cántiga de agüero* (1982) (*Canticle of Ill-Omen*) is a complex family saga set in Galicia, with mythical and magical overtones. *Otras mujeres y Fabia* (1982) (*Other Women and Fabia*) narrates the daily lives of women in a lower-middle-class neighbourhood from the viewpoint of the schoolteacher, Fabia. *Los perros de Hecate* (1985) (*Hecate's Hounds*) has a timeless atmosphere in spite of its almost contemporary time frame.

Gonçalves, Olga (born 193?)

Portuguese novelist and poet. Born in Angola, she was educated in Portugal and England. Gonçalves began her career writing poetry and has published five volumes of verse, but she is primarily known for her novels. Two of her best works, *A Floresta em Bremerhaven* (1975) (*The Forest in Bremerhaven*) and *Este Verão o Emigrante Là-bas* (1978) (*This Summer the Emigrant Over There*) are concerned with the issue of emigration. Her 1982 novel, *Ora Esguardae* (*Now Take Heed*), is a fragmented, montage-like text about the Portuguese revolution. A more recent novel, *Armandina e Luciano, O Traficante de Canários* (1988) (*Armandina and Luciano, the Canary Trafficker*), is about drug trafficking and prostitution in Lisbon.

Gondal

An imaginary world created by British writers ▷Emily and ▷Anne Brontë around 1834 when they broke away from ▷Charlotte and Branwell, who were engaged in the creation of ▷Angria. None of the prose writings of Gondal survive, although many of Emily's poems take on the persona of a Gondal character such as Augusta Geraldine Almeda or Julius Brenzaida. Gondal continued to be a source of imaginative engagement for Emily and Anne as late as 1845, when Emily was twenty-seven and Anne twenty-five.
Bib: Ratchford, F., *Gondal's Queen.*

Gone With the Wind (1936)

US novel set against the US Civil War (1862–1865), ▷Margaret Mitchell's *Gone With the Wind* protests against war. A 1937 Pulitzer Prize-winner, it upholds the tradition of Southern agrarianism against the industrialism that arose after the war. However, that tradition generated conflict in the ▷Southern lady. In Scarlett O'Hara the desire to be male-identified conflicts with the need to be stereotypically feminine. Scarlett is sexually attracted to the pragmatic, selfish Rhett Butler, but romantically drawn to the idealistic, chivalrous Ashley Wilkes. Ashley's wife, Melanie, represents the Southern lady who rebels against conventional mores for a higher, Christian ideal. But the civilization Ashley and Melanie represent cannot survive in the industrialized South. In Mitchell's view, survival means finding a balance between self-reliance and dependence.

The fame of *Gone With the Wind* was guaranteed when it was made into a film in 1939.

Good Earth, The (1931)

US novel. A Pulitzer Prize-winner, ▷Pearl S. Buck's story depicts a Chinese farmer's rise from poverty to wealth. Wang Lung's prosperity derives from his close relationship to the land. Lung knows the virtue of industry and responsibility that those corrupted by wealth do not. *The Good Earth* affirms Buck's belief in the human ability to rise through ambition and the willingness to strive, and it stresses the importance of free will in overcoming obstacles.

Goodhue, Sarah Whipple (1641–1681)

North American spiritual autobiographer. Born into a devout Puritan family in Ipswich, Massachusetts, she married Joseph Goodhue at age twenty and bore eight children. In 1681 she experienced a 'strong persuasion' that she would die in childbirth; rather than confide in her family, she penned ▷*A Valedictory and Monitory Writing*, which follows traditional Puritan spiritual autobiographical patterns but reveals a poetic nature to her style, and her strong desire to leave an instructional record for her children. She died on 23 July 1681, after giving birth to twins.

Goodison, Lorna (born 1947)

Poet, painter and short story writer from the Caribbean. Goodison was born in ▷Jamaica, and trained as a painter at the Jamaica School of Art and in New York. She has been Writer in Residence at the University of the West Indies and at Radcliffe College, Massachusetts and recipient of the Bronze Musgrave Medal and Centenary Medal from the Institute of Jamaica for poetry. Best-known as a poet of great power and presence, she has published three collections, *Tamarind Season* (1980), ▷*I Am Becoming My Mother* (1986), *Heartease* (1988) and *Baby Mother and the King of Swords* (1990). Her poems have been translated into French, Hebrew, German and Spanish. Goodison's work is remarkable for its examination of inner and outer worlds. Her language revels in the long continuum of Jamaican English.
See an interview with Goodison in *Wasafri*, No. 12 (1989) and Edward Baugh's article, 'Lorna Goodison in the Context of Feminist Criticism', *Journal of West Indies Literature*, Vol. 4, No. 1.

Good Man is Hard to Find and Other Stories, A (1955)

US short stories. ▷Flannery O'Connor's work emphasizes the self's need for Christian faith. The title story and 'The Artificial Nigger' criticize Anglo-American Southern pride for its false piety. O'Connor claims that such pride must be destroyed for the individual to know grace. 'A Temple of the Holy Ghost' and 'Good Country People' both feature Anglo-American Southern women who are punished for their pride in their independence; O'Connor suggests that their rebellion against the role of the ▷Southern lady renders them freaks. In 'A Temple of the Holy Ghost', female independence entails a martyrdom to sexual innocence, and in 'Good Country People' Joy-Hulga's independence is usurped by her sexuality; soon her pride is smashed by violent, aggressive male sexual behaviour. Such behaviour exposes Joy-Hulga's helplessness before God, and her punishment enables the dominant social values to be restored.

Good Morning Midnight (1939)

This novel by the Caribbean writer ▷Jean Rhys uses a modified ▷stream-of-consciousness technique to portray the consciousness of sensitive, emotionally scarred and ageing Sasha Jensen who, back in Paris for a 'quiet, sane fortnight', reviews her life; her past, her present, and to some extent her future. Like a wounded animal, vulnerable, weakened and in retreat from the world she is a woman living in shadow. It was the adaptation of this novel by Vaz Dias for the BBC in 1959 which led to Rhys's rediscovery.

For critical analysis see Carole Angier, *Jean Rhys Life and Work* (1990) and Carole Ann Howells *Jean Rhys* (1991).

Goodness of St Rocque and Other Stories, The (1899)

US story collection by ▷Alice Moore Dunbar Nelson. Set in New Orleans, these stories are perhaps Dunbar Nelson's best – finely plotted, and showing the humanity and dignity of characters dealing with adversity. The collection is especially significant for its place as one of the earliest-published story collections by an African-American woman.

'Good Wife Taught Her Daughter, The' (14th century)

This English poem survives in six manuscripts dating from c 1350 to the end of the 15th century. It contains a mother's instruction to her daughter on such matters as churchgoing and almsgiving; behaviour towards a suitor (later husband); moderation, particularly with regard to drink and pastimes; the avoidance of pride, covetousness and quarrelling with one's neighbours; domestic economy; vigilance over servants; and the care of children. It is the earliest surviving instruction in English written for lay women (as opposed to religious women, such as anchoresses), and may have been composed by a woman (compare ▷Christine de Pisan's manuals of instruction) or a cleric. It is of interest also because the setting is middle-class rather than aristocratic. 'The Good Wyfe Wolde a Pylgremage' (which survives only in one 15th-century manuscript) is similar in metre and content: a mother going away on a pilgrimage advises her daughter. However, unlike the earlier poem, there is no advice concerning the duties of a married woman.
Bib: Mustanoja, T.F. (ed.), *The Good Wife Taught her Daughter*.

Gorbanévskaia, Natal'ia Evgen'evna (born 1936)

Russian poet and memoir-writer. Gorbanévskaia's earliest poems date back to the 1950s. Only nine of her poems were published in official journals (in 1966), but her poetry circulated in ▷*samizdat* from 1961, and two collections were published in the West, one in Russian in 1969 and one in English in 1972. She became known first for her political activity rather than her poetry. She was a civil rights activist who help to create the unofficial publication *Chronicle of Current Events*. She participated in a demonstration in Red Square against the Soviet invasion of Czechoslovakia in 1968. Arrested in 1969, she was placed in a psychiatric prison hospital in 1970, freed in 1972, and allowed to emigrate in 1975. She lives in Paris where she is a deputy editor of the journal *Continent*.

In exile, Gorbanévskaia has struggled with the problem of becoming a 'provincial' Russian poet by blurring specific references to give them a more general character. Though her poetry is personal and non-public, she has the ability to universalize her suffering. As in much *émigré* poetry, one finds in Gorbanévskaia's a deep religiosity. Thus her view of evils that have befallen her and her country is religious rather than political.
Bib: Weissbort, D. (trans.), *Selected Poems*; Lieven, A. (trans.), *Red Square at Noon*; *Russian Literature Triquarterly* 6–7 (1973) and 9 (1974); Glad, J. and Weissbort, D. (eds), *Russian Poetry: The Modern Period*; Wilson, K., *An Encyclopedia of Continental Women Writers*, Vol. 1; *Free Voices in Russian Literature 1950s–1980s: A Bio-Bibliographical Guide*; Smith, G.S., 'Another Time, Another Place' *Times Literary Supplement* 4395 (1987).

Gordimer, Nadine (born 1923)

South African novelist and short story writer; her mother of British descent and her father a Jewish jeweller originally from Latvia. She was born and grew up in Springs, an East Rand mining town outside Johannesburg which provides the setting for her first novel, *The Lying Days* (1953). Often kept at home by a mother who imagined she had a weak heart, she began writing from the age of nine. By her twenties she had had stories published in many of the local magazines, and in 1951 the *New Yorker* accepted a story, publishing her ever since.

The Lying Days was followed by *A World of Strangers* (1958), *Occasion for Loving* (1963), *The Late Bourgeois World* (1966) and *A Guest of Honour* (1970). In these first novels Gordimer looks sharply at the master–servant relations characteristic of South African life, at the spiritually and sexually claustrophobic existence bequeathed to white South Africa by the racial paranoias of colonialism, and, increasingly, at the political responsibilities of privileged white South Africans. In ▷*The Conservationist* (1974), which marks the transition between what critics call her 'liberal' and 'radical' phases, and also in ▷*Burger's*

Daughter (1979), ▷*July's People* (1981), and her novella *Something Out There* (1984), she shifts into explicit political critique, and becomes preoccupied with the politics of revolution. Always deeply committed to the craft of writing, she now begins to move slightly away from a realist mode, although in the end she does not make a full move into postmodernist strategies. Still engaged with the crisis of liberalism in South African politics, she widens her focus to include black South Africans more fully than before, posing important questions about racist domination. Her novels are engaged with the present, and occasionally cast forward into a possible future, as in *July's People*. So, too, in *A Sport of Nature* (1987), which extends in time from the 1950s to an independent black South Africa in the near future. The novel deploys a mock-historical tone which casts its shadow over the Utopian ending. Her most recent novel is *My Son's Story* (1990).

Feminists have sometimes been disappointed by her public dismissal of feminist issues in a country dominated by racism. Yet her writing explores the complicated intertwining of racism with sexism, and in other ways, too, reveals a strong interest in women, albeit never romanticized. Her work is politically committed and formally innovative, seeking out narrative strategies by which to combine European and African cultures, and investigating with cool detachment the links between personal and political life.

Her stories have received less critical scrutiny than the novels, but are at least equally fine. Some act as blueprints for the novels, but also represent an autonomous and highly skilled part of Gordimer's career. Her collections are *Face to Face* (1949), reprinted in an expanded edition under the title *The Soft Voice of the Serpent* (1952), *Six Feet of the Country* (1956), *Friday's Footprint* (1960), *Not for Publication* (1960), reprinted under the title *Some Monday for Sure* (1976), *Livingstone's Companions* (1971), *No Place Like* (1979), *A Soldier's Embrace* (1980), *Crimes of Conscience* (1991), and *Jump, and Other Stories* (1991).

Gordimer has also made a name for herself as an essayist. She has published a large number of essays in major international publications as well as smaller magazines. These include essays on writing, politics, travel, as well as autobiographical pieces. A large selection of these appear in her book *The Essential Gesture: Writing, Politics and Places* (1988). She is also to be remembered for her commitment to black writers who often lack the possibilities for advancement open to white writers. Her early friendships with black writers of the 1950s were sustained through the separatist years of ▷Black Consciousness, during which time she engaged in writers' workshops and readings, to encourage less practised writers. She is a founding member of Congress of South African Writers, as well as a member of the African National Congress.

Her work has won local and international awards too numerous to list, among them the South African CNA (Central News Agency) Prize

on three occasions, and has shared the British Booker Award for *The Conservationist* (1974). Above all, she won the Nobel Prize for Literature in 1991.

Bib: Clingman, Stephen, *The Novels of Nadine Gordimer: History from the Inside*; Cooke, John, *The Novels of Nadine Gordimer: Private Lives/Public Landscapes*; Heywood, Christopher, *Nadine Gordimer*; Newman, Judie, *Nadine Gordimer*.

Gordon, Caroline (1895–?)

US short-story writer and novelist. Born in Kentucky, Gordon was educated by her father, and in 1916 she graduated from Bethany College in West Virginia. She married Allen Tate, a conservative Southern agrarian, and in 1947 she converted to Catholicism.

Her work depicts the conflict between the values of agrarianism and industrialism, supporting a hierarchical social order by emphasizing the irresponsibility of individualism. Her first novel, *Penhally* (1931), traces the decline of pre-war Southern culture. *Aleck Maury, Sportsman* (1934) suggests a man's identity derives from his social role; Aleck loses his identity when his heritage is abolished. *Green Centuries* (1941) considers the role of civilization in restraining the masculine principle; without civilization the men indulge their will to dominate. In *The Strange Children* (1951) and *Malefactors* (1956) Gordon envisions salvation from this destruction through Catholicism.

Other works include: *None Shall Look Back* (1937), *The Garden of Adonis* (1937), *The Women on the Porch* (1944), *The Forest of the South* (1945) and *How To Read a Novel* (1957).

Gordon, Mary (born 1949)

US novelist. Gordon was born to devout Catholics in Long Island, New York. Her mother supported the family and her father taught her to be a scholar. She attended Catholic schools and studied under ▷Elizabeth Hardwick at Barnard College. In 1973 she earned a Master's degree in creative writing at Syracuse University. Gordon's fiction celebrates a female tradition rooted in the Catholic tradition. *Final Payments* (1978) focuses on a failed Catholic, Isabel Moore. Sexually guilt-ridden, Isabel tries to absolve herself by caring for her former housekeeper. Enduring spiteful treatment, she thinks she does her father's will in denying herself pleasure, but she finds salvation through an intellectual life with women. ▷*The Company of Women* (1980) emphasizes the sanctity and permanence of friendship over sexual love.

Other works include: *Men and Angels* (1985); *Temporary Shelter* (1987) and *The Other Side* (1990).

Gore, Catherine (1799–1861)

English novelist and dramatist who also wrote under several ▷pseudonyms: Mrs Charles Gore, C.D., C.F.G., Albany Poyntz. She was born in Nottinghamshire, the daughter of a wine merchant, and married Captain Charles Gore in

1823. The same year she published her story in
verse, *The Two Broken Hearts*. She went on to
write prolifically until her old age, producing more
than 70 volumes. Her works include ▷*Women as
They Are, or, The Manners of the Day* (1830);
▷*Mothers and Daughters* (1831); *Mrs Armytage, or,
Female Domination* (1836) and *Cecil, or, The
Adventures of a Coxcomb* (1841). Gore's first play,
The School for Coquettes, was published and
produced at the Haymarket theatre in 1832, while
▷*Quid Pro Quo, or, The Day of the Dupes* (1843)
won a £500 prize for 'English comedy', but was
not a box-office success. Her novels belong to the
▷'silver-fork' school of fiction, concerned with
high society mores. Gore offers advice on the
latest styles of dress, while centring her narrative
action on marriage. She had no sympathy with
▷feminist ideas, and claimed that extending
women's rights would produce 'injurious effects
upon the female character'. Her last work,
Heckington: A Novel, was published in 1858.
Bib: Moers, E., *Literary Women*; Rosa, M.W., *The
Silver Fork School: Novels of Fashion Preceding
Vanity Fair*; Anderson, B., 'The Writing of
Catherine Gore', *Journal of Popular Culture* 10
(1976).

Gore-Booth, Eva (1870–1926)
Irish poet and dramatist. Born in County Sligo,
she was a sister of the famous Irish nationalist
Constance Markievicz, the 'rebel Countess'. She
spent most of her adult life in Manchester,
England, where she worked as a social worker.
Her poetry was collected by her friend, Esther
Roper, and published in 1929 as *Poems of Eva
Gore-Booth*. Her poem, 'The Waves of Breffny', a
lyrical if sentimental evocation of the pleasures of
the Irish landscape, first included in an anthology
in 1903, was on the Irish school curriculum for
many years.

Gormonda de Monpeslier (? 13th century)
French ▷*trobairitz*. Nothing is known about her
other than that she was responsible for the only
Provençal *sirvente* (verse satire) to be attributed to
a woman and 'the first French political poem by a
woman'. The poem is a response to the *sirventes* of
Rome by Guilhem Figueira, with which it should
be contrasted. Gormonda makes it clear in the
first stanza that she opposes the heresies attacking
the source of all goodness, salvation and faith. She
uses the concepts of courtly conventions even
when she is expressing religious or moral ideas.
Numerous allusions to historical events such as
the death of Louis VIII in 1226 make it possible
to determine the approximate period of the
poem's origin.
Bib: Stadtler, K., 'The *Sirventes* by Gormonda de
Monpeslier' in Paden, W. (ed.), *The Voice of the
Trobairitz*, pp. 129–57.

Gorriti, Juana Manuela (1816–1892)
Argentinian novelist. She was the first woman
novelist in Argentina. The daughter of a rebel of
the Argentinian Independence cause, in 1831 she
emigrated with her family to Tarija, Bolivia,
where, at fourteen, she married General Manuel
Isidoro Belzú. The two had three children, then
separated in 1843, while he was President of
Bolivia. He was later murdered. Gorriti moved to
Arequipa, then to Lima, Peru, where she became
a teacher and held important literary evenings
where intellectuals met. Her novel *La Quena*
(1845) (*The Flute*) appeared first in *Revista de
Lima*, and later obtained recognition in other
countries. In 1874 she moved to Buenos Aires,
where she founded the international magazine *La
Alvorada del Plata*. She wrote many tales, short
stores, legends and autobiographical and historical
narratives. The two volumes of her *Panoramas de
la vida* (1876) (*Views of Life*) consisted of fantastic
narratives and *costumbrista* (▷*costumbrismo*)
vignettes, and a supernatural structure resembling
the ▷*Arabian Nights*. Its themes were love,
jealousy, and the South American Indian
tradition. For critics, her novels are important not
only as an expression of a woman's feelings, but
also as a portrayal of an epoch.

Go Shizuko (born 1929)

Go Shizuko

Japanese novelist. *Requiem* won the Akutagawa
Prize in 1972. The narrator, a seventeen-year-old
schoolgirl, reflects on the deaths of members of
her family in World War II. Her mother was
killed by shell fire, her father was gaoled for his
anti-war attitude and died in prison, and her elder
brothers were killed at the front during the air-
raid on Yokohama, her birthplace. She also dies
young, from tuberculosis. This work reveals Go's
strong resistance to war. Her other novels include
Ghost and *Outside the Fence*.

Gothic
Britain: An 18th-century genre, originating in
England. Features of the Gothic include: a sense

of impending doom, premonitions of evil, suspense techniques, confusions of identity, the use of doubles, incest motifs, the omnipresence of death and occult manifestations, to name but a few.

Most significant, particularly for later Gothic works, is the manner in which the reader is encouraged to identify with the protagonist. This identification may partly explain the 'not quite respectable' literary reputation acquired by the Gothic.

Many notable 19th-century British women writers adopted and adapted the form. ▷Mary Shelley's ▷*Frankenstein* is the most famous example. ▷Charlotte and ▷Emily Brontë also utilized Gothic conventions in ▷*Jane Eyre*, ▷*Villette* and ▷*Wuthering Heights*, and a number of women writers including ▷Elizabeth Gaskell wrote horror and ghost stories. The Gothic was also an influence on the ▷sensation novels of the 1860s and the horror fiction of the 1890s.
Italy: The genre was also adopted in continental Europe, enjoying a later revival in Europe in the early 1900s. With its concentration on female protagonists and women's dilemmas, Gothic seems to have held a fascination for women writers well into the 19th century, and even the 20th century. Italian women writers, like their European counterparts, used this genre fruitfully until relatively recently. ▷Carolina Invernizio and ▷Matilde Serao were perhaps the best-known Italian women writers to present their public with the Gothic as serious art, but Gothic themes and structural features abound too in the ▷*romanzo d'appendice*, with which both of these writers are also associated.

▷Lee, Harriet; Lee, Sophia; Radcliffe, Ann; Reeve, Clara

Gotlieb, Phyllis (born 1926)
Canadian writer, born Phyllis Bloom in Toronto, Ontario, and educated at the University of Toronto. She is primarily known for her science fiction, although she was first recognized as a poet. She uses her Jewish heritage and her knowledge of children to good effect. *Who Knows One* appeared in 1961, *Within the Zodiac* in 1964, and *Ordinary, Moving* in 1969. Since 1959 she has published science fiction stories and novels. *Sunburst* (1964), her best, is a novel about mutant children and their sinister capacity for telepathy. *Why Should I Have All the Grief* (1969) is about a Holocaust survivor. *O Master Caliban!* (1976) explores genetic mutation. *A Judgment of Dragons* (1980), *Emperor, Swords, Pentacles* (1982) and *The Kingdom of the Cats* (1985) have as their protagonists a pair of crimson cats. With Douglas Barbour, she has been an editor of *Tesseracts*, 1987.

Gottsched, Luise Adelgunde Victorie (1713–1762)
German writer and translator. The childless wife of the influential writer and critic Johann Christoph Gottsched (1700–1766), she spent her life working for her husband, copying and translating texts from French and English, acting as his secretary, and accompanying him on lecture tours. She became famous in her own right with comedies such as *Die Pietisterey im Fischbein-Rocke* (1736) (*Pietists in Whalebone Corsets*) – an attack in the French mode on the Pietists' hold over gullible bourgeois women – and a collection of poems, *Kleinere Gedichte* (*Little Poems*), edited by her husband in 1761. She had a lifelong intense friendship with Henriette von Runckel, who, after Gottsched's death, published a collection of her remarkable letters in *Briefe der Frau Louise Adelgunde Victorie Gottsched gebohrne Kulmus* (1771–1772) (*Letters of Mrs Louise Adelgunde Victorie Gottsched, née Kutmus*).

Goudvis, Bertha (1876–1966)
South African dramatist, novelist and short story writer. Born Bertha Cinamon in Barrow-in-Furness, Cumbria, England, she came to South Africa in 1881 as part of the first major wave of Jewish immigration. Working with her husband as a hotelier in South Africa, Southern Rhodesia and Mozambique, she also established a career as a journalist, starting with an account of the 1893 Matabele Rebellion, 'Bulawayo under Arms: A Lady's Experiences'.

The play *A Husband for Rachel* (1924), reprinted under the title *The Way the Money Goes and Other Plays* (1925), presents a young Jewish woman, intent upon escaping an arranged marriage, who falls in love with a man with whom her marriage has been secretly arranged, after all. Nevertheless, Rachel is given space to speak out against arranged unions. Goudvis's short stories, first written during the 1940s and later added to and collected in *The Mistress of Mooiplaas and Other Stories* (1956), revolve around energetic and successful women. Her only novel, *Little Eden* (1949), presents a petty bourgeois society only dimly aware of its role in an emergent racist capitalist society. Based in Louwsberg on the Zululand border, where she lived from 1905–1911, the action stems from the visit of a Rand magnate on the lookout for minerals on a nearby farm, and follows the fortunes of Frances Laurens, an efficient and independent businesswoman who stands for women's rights.

Extracts from Goudvis's unpublished memoir *South African Odyssey* have appeared in *South African Rosh Hashana Annual and Jewish Year Book, 1932, Jewish Affairs 1956*, and *South African PEN Yearbook 1956*. Her first publication, a cookbook entitled *Belinda's Book for Colonial Housewives* (c 1909) is not extant.
Bib: Leveson, Marcia, 'Bertha Goudvis: Time, Memory and Freedom', in Clayton, Cherry (ed.), *Women and Writing in South Africa* (1989).

Gouges, Marie Gouze (1755–1793)
French dramatist and revolutionary writer. Born in Montauban, the daughter of a butcher and a washerwoman, she denied the rumour that she was the illegitimate daughter of an aristocrat.

Once widowed, she left for Paris, adopted a ▷pseudonym Olympe, and began her career as a dramatist. All her works were dictated as she never learned to write herself. By the 1780s she was producing plays and airing contentious political views for which she was heckled. *L'Homme Généreux* (1786) (*A Generous Man*) raised the issue of women being debarred from positions of power; *Zamor et Mirza* (1788) and *L'Esclavage des noirs* (1792) (*Black Slavery*) argued for the abolition of slavery, while *Le couvent* (1792) (*The Convent*) highlighted the problem of women forced into taking religious vows. During the revolutionary period she produced over thirty political pamphlets, posting her opinions on placards when unable to have them published. She proposed a luxury tax to pay for improved maternity facilities, and refuges for orphans and the old. She also suggested the founding of a second National Theatre for women. In her celebrated *Déclaration des droits de la femme* (1791) (*The Rights of Women*), written a year before ▷Mary Wollstonecraft's *Vindication of the Rights of Women*, she welcomed the Republic but condemned all bloodshed, and sided with the moderate Girondin party, calling for a plebiscite on the king's fate. When the king was beheaded she continued to write and speak out against Robespierre and Marat. In July 1793 she was arrested. Her execution took place on 3 November 1793.

▷French Revolution: pamphlets, registers of grievances, petitions and speeches
Bib: Kelly, L., *Women of the French Revolution*; Levy, Applewhite and Johnson, *Women in Revolutionary France*.

Gournay, Marie de Jars (1565/6–1645)

French writer and editor, who called herself Marie de Jars de Gournay. Editor of the *Essais* (*Essays*) of the French philosopher Michel de Montaigne (1533–1592), and author of a treatise on the equality of the sexes, and autobiographical texts, Mademoiselle de Gournay is considered the first French woman to have taken a serious interest in literary research, though in her day she was regarded as rather an eccentric pedant. The eldest daughter of Guillaume de Jars, secretary of the King's Chamber, and Jeanne de Hacqueville, she never married. After her father's death in 1577, the family removed to Gournay in Picardy, where Marie largely educated herself, proving rather more successful with Latin than with Greek. Her early passion for Montaigne's *Essais* was so excessive that it made her a laughing stock among her acquaintances, but was much appreciated by the author himself. In response to her request to see him while on a visit to Paris, Montaigne offered her '*l'alliance de père à fille*', the status of an adopted daughter. In return, she provided him with the services of secretary and proof-corrector while he prepared the second edition of the *Essais* at Gournay. Encouraged by her mentor, she published her first text in 1589, *Le Promenoir de Monsieur de Montaigne* (*The*

Promenade of Montaigne). She also corresponded with The Belgian scholar Lipsius (Juste Lipse, 1547–1606), another of Montaigne's great admirers, who complimented her on her intelligence, unusual in one of her sex. On Montaigne's death in 1592, Mademoiselle de Gournay became his sole literary executor, producing two revised editions of the *Essais* in 1596 and 1598, while living with Montaigne's widow and daughter. During the following decade she travelled in the Low Countries, returning to Paris to receive a royal pension, though she always lived a simple life.

The object of considerable jealousy for her success and independence, Mademoiselle de Gournay was much criticized, and even accused of witchcraft for having dabbled in alchemy. She became increasingly involved in literary debates, defending Pierre de Ronsard (1524–1585) and other 16th-century poets against François de Malherbe (1555–1628) and the literary purists who wished to refine the language of poetry and who opposed the ▷*Pléiade*'s exalted concept of the poet. She is therefore sometimes considered rather old-fashioned for her fidelity to Renaissance language and ideas. She also criticized the emergent forms of *Préciosité* (▷Precious Women), refusing to cramp her style to follow '*le train des donzelles à bouche sucrée*' ('the manner of sickly-sweet-voiced girls'). In 1600 she presented Henri IV (1553–1610) and Marie de Medici (1573–1642) with an educational treatise entitled *De l'education des enfants de France* (*On the Education of the Children of France*), which she complemented in 1608 with another entitled *La Bienvenue à Monseigneur le duc d'Anjou* (*Welcome to the Duke of Anjou*). Following the king's assassination in 1610, she also published a short treatise in defence of the Jesuits, and for her pains was ridiculed in a satirical tract entitled *L'anti-Gournay, ou Remerciement des beurrières de Paris au sieur de Courbouzon Montgommery* (*Anti-Gournay, or Thanks from the Butter-Sellers of Paris to Monsieur Courbouzon Montgommery*). Undaunted, she produced her third edition of Montaigne's *Essais*, with translations of his Latin and Greek quotations and a subject and author index. In the 1620s she produced two feminist texts: *Egalité des hommes et des femmes* (1622) (*Equality of Men and Women*), dedicated to Anne of Austria (1601–1666), wife of Louis XIII (1601–1643); and *Le Grief des dames* (1626) (*The Ladies' Grievance*). In response to a practical joke, a letter purporting to be from James I of England (1566–1625) requesting details of her life and a portrait, she agreed to write her autobiography. In 1626 she produced a self-portrait in alexandrines, entitled *Peincture de moeurs*, (*Portrayal of Manners*), to complete an earlier *Apologie pour celle qui escrit* (*Defence of She Who Writes*) written in prose. The same year, she published a compilation of her own work under the title *A l'ombre de la demoiselle de Gournay* (*In the Shadow of Mademoiselle de Gournay*). This work was apparently dispatched to England, much to everyone's astonishment there.

A revised edition, with additional essays, entitled *Les Advis ou les presens de la demoiselle de Gournay* (*The Advice or the Presents of Mademoiselle de Gournay*), was published in 1634.
Bib: Dezon-Jones, E., *Les Ecritures feminines.*

Governesses

The governess was a familiar figure to Victorians, as she is to readers of ▷*Jane Eyre* and ▷*Agnes Grey* today. Governesses were drawn from the ranks of the middle classes; from families whose economic circumstances demanded that their daughters seek employment, yet remain respectable. The range of professions deemed suitable for middle-class women narrowed during the early 19th century so that by the Victorian period governessing was virtually the only path open to them. Pay and conditions, however, were often poor, as the ▷Brontë novels testify. In 1841 a Governesses' Benevolent Institution was founded to assist the unemployed and needy. It was increasingly recognized that the 'plight' of the governess was a social problem, and many periodical essayists addressed the issue during the 1840s. It was the governess's status as a middle-class woman that fired such concern; no similar attention was directed to working-class women's conditions of employment. The preoccupation with the figure of the governess crucially linked to the ideal of womanhood that she was supposed to embody and reproduce in her charges. The anomaly of her position was that at the same time as she ideally conformed to all the standards of middle-class femininity, she was competing for jobs in the marketplace and therefore threatened to undermine the ethos of separate spheres of activity for women and men upon which Victorian society depended. Practically as well as ideologically she was often in a difficult position – barely educated herself yet required to teach others. The need for governesses to be better informed led to a series of evening lectures held at King's College, London, in 1847. These fed directly into the campaign for higher education for women, and in 1848 Queen's College for women was founded in London.

▷Jameson, Anna; Education; *Deerbrook*; *Lady Audley's Secret*; *Shirley*; *Villette*

Governess, or the Little Female Academy, The (1749)

Children's stories by English writer ▷Sarah Fielding. It was one of the earliest books designed for education. It preceded the spate of educational children's books published by the bookseller John Newberry, and sparked off a sequence of imitators. The gently moralistic and amusing stories are set in a school for girls of between eleven and fourteen, run by the clergyman's widow, Mrs Teachum. It opens with a fight over who shall have the largest apple – 'they fought, scratch'd and tore, like so many Cats', so that by the end they have in their hands shreds of garments and clumps of hair. Mrs Teachum has

terrible punishments, but we never learn what exactly they are – apparently Fielding's way of concealing her opposition to beating from the ever-strong lobby in favour of whipping. Influenced by Fénelon's *Instructions for the Education of a Daughter* (1687, translated into English 1707) and John Locke's *Some Thoughts Concerning Education* (1693).

▷More, Hannah

Govier, Katherine (born 1948)

Canadian novelist and short story writer. She was born in Edmonton, Alberta, attended the Universities of Alberta and of York in Toronto, and worked as a journalist in Canada, England and the United States. Her fiction depicts ordinary women trying to accommodate a range of possibilities in their lives, and to manage often unsatisfactory relationships. *Random Descent* (1979) is a generational novel, which was followed by *Going Through the Motions* (1982), an interesting situational conflict about a stripper charged with assault for kicking a drunk in the jaw. *Between Men* (1987) slides between the story of a contemporary woman trying to make choices about her future and the story of a Native Canadian woman murdered in 1889. *Hearts of Flame* appeared in 1991. Govier's short fiction is stylistically more accomplished and satisfying in its tension than her novels; her collections include *Fables of Brunswick Avenue* (1985) and *Before and After* (1989).

Grace, Patricia (born 1937)

New Zealand novelist, short story writer and children's author. Patricia Grace (also known as Ngati Toa, Ngati Raukawa and Te Ati Awa) was born in Wellington where she still lives. She trained as a teacher, specializing in English as a second language, and began writing stories in her twenties while bringing up her seven children and teaching in a small country school. When Grace published her first collection *Waiariki* in 1975 she became the first Maori woman writer to publish a collection of stories in English, and later the first Maori woman novelist when *Mutuwhenua* (1978) appeared.

Grace has produced fiction steadily since 1975 for both adults and children and has won numerous awards for her work including the prestigious Scholarship in Letters. She has said that all through her schooling she never read books about people who were brown or black and if there were black characters there was always something wrong with them. She wrote about Maori, as did many Maori writers, in order to make them visible and to help create a ▷Maori literature. Her work has become more explicitly political in recent years, exposing race and class questions in New Zealand society. Like the work of many Maori writers, Grace's fiction focuses on the family, especially the extended family, and its relationship to the environment, to Maori myth and oral narrative. She has said she always writes about relationships, but personal relationships in

Grace's fiction extend into political relationships between races, and the implications of social change on ethnic peoples. She is a well-known children's writer and has written some highly successful picture books, as well as a number of Maori language readers for children.

Publications include: *Waiariki* (stories) (1975); *Mutuwhenua* (novel) (1978); *The Dream Sleepers* (stories) (1980); *The Kuia and the Spider/Te Kuia me te Pungawerewere* (children) (1982); *Wahine Toa: Women of Maori Myth* (with Robyn Kahukiwa) (1984); *Watercress Tuna and the Children of Champion Street/Te Tuna Watakirihi me nga Tamariki o te Tiriti o Toa* (children) (1984); ▷*Potiki* (novel) (1986); *Electric City* (stories) (1987).

▷Children's literature, New Zealand

Graduate, The (1980)

Novel by Kenyan writer ▷Grace Ogot. *The Graduate* combines an examination of the problems faced by the 'educated' woman trying to establish herself in the modern world, with the theme of post-colonial European dominance of the Civil Service. Juanina Karungaru makes a success of her public life, becoming a political activist and being offered a cabinet post by the president, but neglects her domestic life. Ogot clearly supports women's quest for a political role but chastises her character, who fails to combine this with family duties.

Graffigny, Françoise d'Issembourg d'Happoncourt de (1695–1758)

French novelist and dramatist. Daughter of an officer in the Duke of Lorraine's gendarmerie, de Graffigny suffered an extremely unhappy marriage, her husband being imprisoned for the violence he used against her. She stayed with the ▷Marquise du Châtelet-Lomont at Cirey, and when they quarrelled sought refuge with the Duchesse de Richelieu. Her major work was ▷*Lettres d'une Péruvienne* (1747) (*Letters of a Peruvian Princess*, 1818), an important text in the evolution of the ▷epistolary novel, and the development of the theme of the solitary woman writing to an absent lover. The text also echoes Montesquieu's *Lettres persanes* (1721) (*Persian Letters*) in that two cultures, here French and Peruvian, are compared. After the success of this novel, Graffigny wrote and produced the play *Cénie* (1751) (*Cenia, or The Oppressed Daughter*, 1752) which was well received and ran for twenty-five performances. Focusing on the problem of illegitimacy, the play portrays the humiliations and sufferings of an unmarried governess, Orphise, and her daughter, Cénie. *La Fille d'Astride* (1759) (*Astride's Daughter*) features, in a Greek setting, a woman forced to sell herself into bondage as an act of self-sacrifice in order to pay off her benefactor's debts: a situation which dramatically evoked the sacrifices demanded of women contracted into arranged marriages so as to solve their family's financial problems. Her other works include: *Le mauvais exemple, nouvelle espagnole* (1745) (*The Bad Example, a Spanish Story*); *Ziman et Zenise, comédie* (1749) (*Ziman and Zenise, a Comedy*), and *Vie privée de Voltaire et de Mme du Châtelet* (1820) (*The Private Life of Voltaire and Mme du Châtelet*).

▷Monbart, Madame de Lescum Marie-Joséphine

Bib: Noel, G., *Une primitive oubliée*, and *Vierge du Soleil*; Showalter Jr., E., 'Writing Off the Stage: Women Authors and Eighteenth-century Theatre' in Dejean, J., and Miller, N. K. (eds), *Displacements*.

Grafton, Sue (born 1940)

US novelist. Born in Louisville, Kentucky, Grafton graduated from the University of Louisville in 1961. She wrote *A is for Alibi* (1982) while involved in a custody battle. Grafton's murder mysteries feature a contemporary, Californian detective, Kinsey Millhone, who helps women who have been victimized. Millhone is an intelligent, independent, autonomous and moralistic woman, and it bothers her to kill a murderer in self-defence. Millhone is also a sexual woman. Grafton undermines the masculinist division in ▷detective novels between professional and personal life.

Other works include: *Kezish Dane* (1967), *The Lolly-Madonna War* (1969), *B is for Burglar (1985)*, *C is for Corpse* (1987), *D is for Deadbeat* (1987), *E is for Evidence* (1989), *F is for Fugitive* (1989), *G is for Gumshoe* (1990), *H is for Homicide* (1991) and *I is for Innocent* (1992).

Graham, Ennis ▷Molesworth, Louisa

Grahn, Judy (born 1940)

US poet and critic. Born in Chicago, Illinois, Grahn was raised as a Protestant in New Mexico. An Anglo-American, she attended an African-American college. She was co-founder of the Woman's Press Collective in Oakland, California, and her work has been published mainly by independent women's presses. These include *Edward the Dyke and Other Poems* (1971) *The Common Woman, She Who – A Graphic Book of Poems* (1977), *A Woman is Talking to Death* (1974) and *Confrontations with the Devil in the Form of Love*, all collected in *The Work of a Common Woman* (1978), with an introduction by ▷Adrienne Rich . Grahn's work is committed to the development of an accessible feminist and lesbian working-class aesthetic. She writes about ordinary women, such as the waitress, secretary and meat-wrapper in *The Common Woman Poems*, using a range of imagery which is both drawn from their lives and refutes their victim status. Grahn's poetry is characterized by a sense of defiance and irreverence. Although given little academic recognition, Grahn's poetry is experimentally innovative, mixing prose dialogue and poetry, and drawing on ▷Native American forms to create secular chants, for example, in *She Who*.

Other works include: *True to Life Adventure*

Stories (1978), *The Queen of Wands* (1982), *Another Tongue: Gay Words, Gay Worlds* (1984), *The Highest Apple: Sappho and the Poetic Tradition* (1985), *The Queen of Spades*.

Gramcko, Ida (born 1924)

Venezuelan poet, dramatist, short story and essay writer. She graduated in philosophy. Her name became revered in Venezuelan poetry, especially after the publication of *La vara mágica* (1948) (*The Magic Wand*), which was translated into French and Russian, and *Poemas* (1952) (*Poems*). She refuses to be called a poetess, for she wants her poetry to express universal themes rather than female love or passion. She participated in the ▷*Viernes* Group, with ▷Luz Machado, ▷Ana Enriqueta Terán and ▷Enriqueta Arvelo Larriva, among other poets. Venezuelan poetry has gained an epic dimension and a new sense of aesthetics with the recalling of its legends and myths, and the attention being given to its landscapes, peoples and history. Gramcko's prose and poetry works within this framework and combines elements of dream, folklore and reality to achieve both intimacy and universality. She revealed her long period of mental illness in *Poemas de una psicótica* (1964) (*Poems of a Psychotic*), and more mystically in *Lo maximo murmura* (1965) (*The Loudest Murmur*).

Granata, María (born 1921)

Argentinian poet, novelist and journalist. She wrote for newspapers and magazines such as *Conducta, La Nación* and *Selecta*. Her book, *Umbral de tierra* (1942) (*Land Threshold*), is written with the same rigour as her poems. *Color humano* (1966) (*Human Colour*) is an objective exposition of human problems. Her novel *Los viernes de la eternidad* (1971) (*The Fridays of Eternity*) was filmed in 1981. She has also written tales and novels for children.

Grand, Sarah (1854–1943)

▷Pseudonym of British novelist Frances McFall, née Clark. She was born in Donaghadee, County Down, and moved to Yorkshire after her father's death in 1861. At sixteen she married Major David McFall, a surgeon. She later left her husband and moved to London where she became involved in ▷feminist activity. Her first novel was *Ideala* (1888), her second ▷*The Heavenly Twins* (1893), which was a sensational success. It attacked the sexual double standard in marriage, called for emancipation and protested against the immorality of the Contagious Diseases Act. She is said to have coined the term ▷'New Woman' in 1894. In 1897 her semi-autobiographical novel ▷*The Beth Book* appeared. In 1898 she became President of the Tunbridge Wells branch of the National Union of Women's ▷Suffrage Societies, and between 1922 and 1929 was mayoress of Bath. She died in Bath at the age of 88.
Bib: Kersley, G., *Darling Madame: a Portrait of Sarah Grand*; Cunningham, G., *The 'New Woman'*

and the Fiction of the 1890s; ▷Showalter, E., *A Literature of Their Own*.

Grandes, Almudena

Spanish author of popular erotic novels, such as *Las edades de Lulú* (1989) (*The Ages of Lulu*), and *Te llamaré viernes* (1991) (*I'll Call You on Friday*).

Grandmother, The (Yai)

Novel by Thai writer ▷K. Surangkhanang. An old woman, disregarded by her four prosperous children and tolerated in the home of the fifth and poorest only because of the income she brings in as an intinerant hawker, is sustained by her Buddhist faith that good deeds and patience in this life may earn her a better life in her next incarnation. Her unwitnessed death epitomizes her anonymity and the suffering of countless women like her, left behind by economic progress and its erosion of family values. Surangkhanang describes moral corruption even within the religious orders, as when the monks view the grandmother's meagre food offerings with contempt, and she fears to impose her presence on a son, an abbot, because of comments by the other monks that she is only there for the food.

'Grania's Lullaby' (12th century)

The authorship of this ▷Old Irish poem is unknown, but the speaker is a woman, Grania, who sings a lullaby to her lover, Diarmid. There also survives a verse from a 9th- or 10th-century version of the story of the elopement of the two, in which Grania expresses her longing for her lover. Yeats wrote a poem based on the lullaby.
Bib: Greene, David and O'Connor, Frank (eds.), *A Golden Treasury of Irish Poetry AD 600 to 1200*.

Grass is Singing, The (1950)

First novel by British novelist ▷Doris Lessing. Set in Southern Rhodesia, the book's theme and tone is encapsulated in the epigraph from T.S. Eliot's *The Waste Land* (1922) with which it opens; the quotation encompasses the frustration and barrenness of drought with the hope of renewal. Lessing brings a range of power relationships concerning race and gender into sharp focus through the murder of a white woman, Mary Turner, by the black 'houseboy', Moses.

The book opens with the newspaper announcement of the murder, the motive of which is attributed to stealing, and then traces the true history of the event. The woman's frustration as the wife of an unsuccessful farmer in a remote rural area, and her difficulty with the ▷otherness of the black servants she is supposed to master, climax in her relationship with Moses, with whom she is entrapped in the violent and erotic master–slave relationship which leads to her death. The novel explores the position of the white woman as guardian of the honour of the white masters, and the eroticism generated by unequal power relationships under white supremacist rule in Rhodesia.

Grau, Shirley Ann (born 1929)

US novelist and short-story writer. Grau was born of part Creole ancestry in New Orleans, Louisiana, and she graduated from Sophie Newcomb College, a women's college, in 1950. Her early work focuses on the primitive people in Louisiana's Cajun country. In *The Black Prince and Other Stories* (1955) and *The Hard Blue Sky* (1958) the characters' lives are controlled by the harshness of nature. Her later work centres on sophisticated Anglo-Americans who also lack control over their lives. In *The House on Coliseum Street* (1961) and *The Condor Passes* (1971) the characters are shaped by their wealth. In the Pulitzer Prize-winning ▷ *The Keepers of the House* (1964) the characters' lives are dictated by racism. Grau's work reveals the difficulty of living a meaningful life in the face of these obstacles.

Other work includes: *Nine Women* (1985).

Gravity and Grace (1952)

Translation of *La Pesanteur et la grâce* (1947) essay by French philosophical and political writer ▷ Simone Weil. This work constitutes Weil's spiritual testimony. Her central idea is that the very impossibility of justifying the Creation as the effect of God's grace testifies to the existence of the transcendental: the only explanation for suffering is to believe that beyond death lies infinite grace. Her thought was rooted in gnosticism, a mystic philosophy which flourished in the first six centuries of the Church, and combined Greek and Oriental philosophy with Christianity.

Gray, Oriel (born 1920)

Australian dramatist. Gray was a member of the Communist Party of Australia until 1950 and was closely associated with the Sydney ▷ New Theatre. She wrote numerous plays for radio and television as well as for the theatre. Her autobiography, *Exit Left: Memoirs of a Scarlet Woman*, was published in 1985.

▷ *Penguin Anthology of Australian Women's Writing, The*

Gray, Teresa Corinna ubertis ▷ Teresa

Great Feast, The (1981)

English translation of the Hindi novel *Mahabhoj* (1979) by the Indian author ▷ Mannu Bhandari. Unlike Bhandari's previous works, *The Great Feast* is a detailed reconstruction of the harshness and corruption of political life in India. It was intended as a commentary on contemporary Indian politics, but Bhandari shifted the setting back to 1942, an important year in India's struggle for independence, to show how even the purest of ideals could be corrupted by greed and disrespect for fellow humans. The novel's themes of spiritual decay and death are presaged by the Hindi title which refers to the feeding of Brahmin priests at the death-rite feasts observed in Hinduism. The story itself tells of unprincipled politicking between rival election candidates over the death of a village boy.

Great Love, A (1981)

Translation of a novella by Russian writer ▷ Aleksandra Kollontái, originally published in 1923. *A Great Love* harks back to the years between 1908 and 1917 when, in flight from arrest in her own country, she worked as a propagandist in western Europe. Its subject is an affair between a woman much like herself and a leader of the Russian revolutionary movement abroad. Her married lover's jealousy and demands for secrecy, and his failure to acknowledge the importance of her work, inevitably combine to kill her 'great love'. The work has strong autobiographical elements, but commentators have also noted the resemblance the leading characters bear to Lenin and his close associate, Inessa Armand.

Great Nordic dispute on chastity, The

The dispute, which was central to the ▷ modern breakthrough in Scandinavia, is important because of its early discussion of issues concerning sexual morality as the most important question of modernity. From 1882–1888, nearly every poet in Denmark, Norway, Finland and Sweden was involved in the debate about polygamy, monogamy, marriage and prostitution: the sexual question.

Georg Brandes (1842–1927) attacked the bourgeois sexual double standard: that men could be discreetly polygamous and, for example, visit prostitutes, while women had to be chaste until marriage, after which they had to be monogamous. While Brandes proclaimed free love, Bjornstjerne Bjornson, in his play *En Handske* (1883) (*A Glove*), demanded that not only woman but man, too, be chaste until marriage, and the writer August Strindberg (1849–1912) in his *Giftas* (1884) (*Getting Married*) opposed Bjørnson, and marriage as an institution.

▷ Victoria Benedictsson and ▷ Amalie Skram also criticized conventional marriage, but most women writers in the debate agreed with Bjørnson, and had good reasons to do so: the threats of pregnancy, syphilis and financial disaster were too evident not to be taken into consideration.

The battle showed how crucial the sexual question was to the formulation of a modern, ▷ realist literature.

Bib: Bredsdorf, E., *The Great Nordic War of Sexual Morals*.

Green, Anna Katharine (1846–1935)

US detective novelist. Green wrote ▷ *The Leavenworth Case* (1878), the first US formula detective novel, which established the genre. She was an extraordinarily prolific writer, author of more than three dozen ▷ detective novels after *Leavenworth*, though none equalled the popular appeal of this first bestseller. Many of the later novels made repeated use of the same detective characters. Among the most memorable are *The Milly Mystery* (1886), *The Forsaken Inn* (1890) and *That Affair Next Door* (1897).

While critics disagree over whether Green was the first US woman writer in the mystery or detective genre, she is clearly responsible for distinctive elements of the detective novel formula. She focused on the detective, and her detectives included now classic types: the working-class policeman, the elderly woman and the girl detective. Her plot elements and techniques are definitive, including the wealthy man killed in his library, the butler, the detective's revelatory scene, rules of evidence, etc.

Green, Dorothy (born 1915)

Australian poet and critic, born Dorothy Auchterlonie. Dorothy Green has worked as a teacher, academic, journalist, essayist and reviewer, and was Senior Lecturer in English and Australian Literature at Monash University, the Australian National University, and was Honorary Visiting Fellow at the Royal Military College, Duntroon. She has been awarded the Medal of the Order of Australia. As well as her trenchant reviews of all aspects of Australian literature, Green is well-known for her three volumes of poetry, *Kaleidoscope* (1940), *The Dolphin* (1967) and *Something to Someone* (1984); her biographical and critical study *Ulysses Bound: Henry Handel Richardson and her Fiction* (1973); her collection of critical essays *The Music of Love, Critical Essays on Literature and Life* (1984); and her revision of the two-volume *A History of Australian Literature 1789–1950* (1985), originally published in 1961 by her husband, H.M. Green.

▷Literary criticism (Australia); *Poetry and Gender*

Greene, Catharine Ray (?1731–1794)

North American letter-writer. She was in her early twenties when she met the North American statesman Benjamin Franklin, almost thirty years her senior, but after a short trip together (in which he acted, as a favour to his brother, as her travel companion to Newport, Rhode Island, so she could visit a sister) they became lifelong correspondents. Through Franklin she also became acquainted with ▷Jane Franklin Mecom, and they too became friends and correspondents. In ▷*Benjamin Franklin and Catharine Ray Greene: Their Correspondence 1755–1790*, her evolution from flirtatious youth to politically committed adult is revealed. She lived in Warwick, Rhode Island, after her marriage, and died there in 1794.

Green Ring, The (1914)

Play by the Russian poet ▷Zinaida Gíppius. Originally held up by censors for alleged immorality, it was first staged in 1915 at the Aleksandrinskii Theatre in Petrograd by the famous director Vsevolod Meyerhold. In an afterword, Gíppius stresses that the central idea of the play is one of togetherness, of community. Characters are organized by generation. The young people reject the ways of their parents, displaying their concern for others' well-being and for relationships that are based on freedom rather than habit or emotional coercion. The one older character, who is 'freer' and therefore allowed to attend meetings of the Green Ring Society, is affectionately called Uncle Mike; the one member of the younger generation who is 'old' in attitude and whose struggle to become free is the central conflict of the play is Sof'ia, his niece. As often in Gíppius's prose, there is a fine portrayal of servants, the country girl Marfusha, and the snobbish St Petersburg Matrëna, who goes under the fancy name Mathilda. In contrast to Turgenev's novel *Fathers and Sons*, which also dealt with generational conflict and portrayed the young as ushering in a new way of life, Gíppius portrays her young people as compassionate toward the hopelessly constrained older generation.

Bib: Koteliansky, S.S. (trans.), *The Green Ring*.

Greenwell, Dora (1821–1882)

British poet, essayist and theological writer. She was born in Lanchester, Co. Durham and educated at home by a ▷governess. Her first published work was a volume of *Poems* (1848), reprinted in 1850 as *Stories That Might Be True and Other Poems*. Further collections appeared in 1861 and 1867, followed by *Carmina Crucis* (1869); *Songs of Salvation* (1873); *The Soul's Legend* (1873) and *Camera Obscura* (1876). Greenwell's interest in religious, spiritual and social questions informs her poetry as well as her prose works, which include *A Present Heaven* (1855) and *Two Friends* (1863).

▷Hymns (19th-century Britain)

Greenwood, Grace ▷Lippincott, Sara Jane

Greenwood, Lisa (born 1955)

New Zealand novelist. Lisa Greenwood began writing in 1983, establishing a weekly routine of five hours a day. Her first novel, *The Roundness of Eggs* (1986), deals with female subjectivity and its relation to creativity and gender roles. Greenwood's second novel, *Daylight Burning* (1990), won her the Katherine Mansfield Memorial Fellowship for 1990.

Greer, Germaine (born 1939)

Australian feminist literary critic, reviewer and broadcaster. Born in Melbourne, Greer took a BA from Melbourne University in 1959, an MA from Sydney in 1963 and a Ph.D. from Cambridge in 1968. She lectured in English at Warwick University from 1968 to 1973, and wrote for various publications, including the *Sunday Times* and *Private Eye* (under the pseudonym Rose Blight). She has also contributed articles to *Harpers*, the *Listener*, the *Spectator* and *Esquire*. In 1979 Greer founded the Tulsa Center for the Study of Women's Literature at the University of Tulsa, Oklahoma. She now lives in Europe.

Greer emerged as a dominant voice in feminist

Germaine Greer

criticism when she published *The Female Eunuch* (1970). Translated into twelve languages, the book analyzes sexist representations of women in society and literature; and it is this, rather than the advancement of a specific feminist theory, which comprises Greer's critique of patriarchy. Like much ▷'images of women' criticism, *The Female Eunuch* wears its theoretical sophistication lightly, enlisting the general reader's understanding with its witty, accessible prose.

Later works, *The Obstacle Race* (1979), a history of women and painting, and *Sex and Destiny: The Politics of Human Fertility* (1984), critically explore sexual relations and familial structures from a feminist perspective, although *Sex and Destiny* has been criticized by some feminist readers for advocating a return to the extended family. *Daddy: We Hardly Knew You* (1989) studies family life again, as Greer records her attempt to discover her own father's identity. Her feminist literary criticism includes: *Shakespeare* (1986); *The Madwoman's Underclothes: Essays and Occasional Writings 1968–1985* (1986); (joint ed.), *Kissing the Rod: An Anthology of 17th Century Women's Verse* (1988). Her other publications include: *Darling Say You Love Me* (1965); (as Rose Blight), *The Revolting Garden* (1979); 'Women and Power in Cuba' in *Women: a World Report* (1985).

Gregory, Lady Augusta (1852–1932)

Anglo-Irish dramatist and folklorist. A member of the Protestant ascendancy in Ireland, and owner of the famous ▷big house, Coole Park, Lady Gregory was prominent in fostering Irish cultural nationalism through the foundation of the Abbey Theatre in Dublin. However, it has been suggested that her model of Irishness was, perhaps inevitably, compromised by the ambiguous cultural position of the ascendancy. In

1893 she began to collect local Galway folk tales and legends, which she then published. Her later dramatic style was influenced by this work. Her translations of Gaelic epics, *Cuchulain of Muirthemne* (1902) and *Gods and Fighting Men* (1904) gave this Irish material a new audience and provided W.B. Yeats (1865–1939) with material for his plays. Lady Gregory collaborated with Yeats on his controversial play *Cathleen ni Houlihan* (1902) for the Abbey Theatre, although she has received little credit for her contribution. She went on to write regularly for the Abbey. Her plays take in a wide range of dramatic genres. They include *Twenty-Five* (1902) and the comic one-act plays *The Jackdaw* (1902), *Spreading the News* (1904) and *Hyacinth Halvey* (1906), based on farce; the tragicomedies *The Canavans* (1906), *The White Cockade* (1905), *The Deliverer* (1911); the miracle plays *The Travelling Man* (1909) and *Dave* (1927); a ghost play, *Shanwalla* (1915), and children's plays *The Jester* (1918) and *The Dragon* (1919). *Kincora* (1905), *Devorgilla* (1907) and *Grania* (1911) are epic tragedies with powerful heroines at their centre. Other works include: *Gods and Fighting Men* (1904); *The Kiltartan Moliere* (1910); *Irish Folk History Plays*, first series and second series (1912); *In Our Irish Theatre* (1913); *Lady Gregory's Journals 1916–1930*; *Visions and Beliefs in the West of Ireland* (1922); *The Coole Edition of Lady Gregory's Writings* (1970), and *Seventy Years* (1974).

Greiffenberg, Catharina Regina von (1633–1694)

Austrian poet. She came from one of the rare branches of Protestant Austrian gentry, and was given an enlightened Renaissance education. In 1658 her uncle, who wanted to marry her, published a first volume of her poems, which bear witness to a religious awakening triggered by the death of her sister in 1651, but also to moral torment in view of her benefactor's wishes. In 1653 she consented to marrying her uncle, and in 1662 established her fame with a collection of poems, *Geistliche Sonnette/Lieder und Gedichte* (*Spiritual Sonnets/Songs and Poems*). In 1675 her pastoral poem, *Tugend-Übungen sieben Lustwehlender Schäferinnen* (*Virtuous Exercises of Seven Exquisite Shepherdesses*) appeared together with *Sieges-Seule der Buße und des Glaubens* (*Victory Monument of Penance and Faith*), a religious epic inspired by the war against the Turks. After her husband's death in 1677 she fled the political persecutions, constrictions and spiritual isolation of a Protestant in Austria, and went to Nuremberg, where she assumed a central role as a female poet in a flourishing artistic climate.

Greki, Anna (1931–1966)

Algerian poet. Anna Greki is the ▷pseudonym of Colette Anna Grégoire (married name Melki). She was born in the Aurès mountains, and went to school in east Algeria. Greki continued her studies in Paris, but decided to return to Algeria before their completion, where she was arrested

and tortured in 1957. She remained in prison for
a year, after which she was deported to France.
She died only eight years later, in 1966, while
giving birth. Her poetry focuses on the struggle
for Algerian independence, her involvement as a
woman activist, and her experiences in prison.

Grékova, I. (born 1907)

The distinguished Russian mathematician Elena
Sergeevna Venttsel became the fiction writer I.
Grékova (the pseudonym stands for *y*, 'an
unknown quantity') relatively late: her first story,
'Behind the Checkpoint', which depicted life in a
secret laboratory, was published in 1962. A keen
observer, Grékova's stories are rich in quiet
humour, a feeling for detail that suggests the
texture of everday life, and a strong dose of social
criticism. Her story, 'On Manoeuvres' (1967,
1986), which depicts army exercises in 1952 at a
remote testing-ground, enraged military
authorities (Adele Barker, 'Irina Grékova's "Na
ispytaniiakh": The History of One Story,' *Slavic
Review*, Fall 1989). 'Masters of Their Own Lives'
(*Soviet Women Writing*) is a man's story of the
vicissitudes of the Stalin era, written in 1960 but
published only in 1988. Grékova's themes are
drawn largely from her own experience as a
widowed mother and a professional; her heroines
are often women who derive great psychological
satisfaction from their careers. In 'Ladies'
Hairdresser' (*Russian Women*, 1963) a director of a
scientific institute, the mother of two charming
but spoiled sons, becomes attached to a
stubbornly honest young hairdresser as dedicated
to his craft as she is to mathematics. In 'A
Summer in the City' (*Image of Women in
Contemporary Soviet Fiction*, 1965) Valentina
Stepanovna, a single mother, is faced with her
daughter's pregnancy. Two longer works, ▷ *The
Hotel Manager* and ▷ *The Ship of Widows*, depict
the lives of groups of women linked by
circumstance and affection.

Grenada

This geographical region of the Caribbean is
English-speaking, and the birthplace of ▷ Merle
Collins.

Grenville, Kate (born 1950)

Australian novelist and short story writer.
Grenville was educated at the University of
Sydney and the University of Colorado. She has
worked as a typist, teacher, journalist, film writer
and subtitles editor for multicultural television,
and now writes full-time. A writer of great
originality, she was runner-up in the Vogel/
Australian Award 1983 for her short story
collection *Bearded Ladies* (1984), and winner in
1984 with ▷ *Lilian's Story* (1985). Her other
publications are *Dreamhouse* (1986) and *Joan
Makes History* (1988).

▷ Short story (Australia); *Coming Out from
Under*; *Eight Voices of the Eighties*

Gress, Elsa (1919–1989)

Danish prose writer, dramatist, script writer and
debater. Member of the Danish Academy from
1975 till her death. In her memoirs, *Mine mange
hjem* (1965) (*My Many Homes*), *Fuglefri og fremmed*
(1971) (*Free as a Bird and Strange*) and *Compania
I–II* (1976), she described her childhood, which
was unconventional. Her father was a neurotic,
and unable to work. Gress described herself and
her brother, who committed suicide, as outsiders.
Her standpoint when she was involved in public
debates was always provocative and different. She
wrote against ▷ Simone de Beauvoir (1908–1989)
in *Det uopdagede kon* (1964) (*The Undiscovered Sex*),
and then wrote and spoke out against the new
feminists in the 1970s. She wrote from the
position of a human being, rather than as a
woman. In Danish literature she forms a link
between ▷ Karen Blixen and ▷ Suzanne Brøgger,
but she does not reach the same literary level,
except perhaps in her memoirs.

Grève des battu, La (1979) ▷ *The Beggars' Strike*

Gréville, Alice (1842–1903)

French novelist and journalist. Unusually well
educated, she was the daughter of a journalist
who became Professor of French at the University
of St Petersburg. She spent fifteen years in
Russia, learned the language, and wrote numerous
articles about Russian culture under the
pseudonym Henry-Gréville. Her novels, whose
titles betray her preoccupation with things Russian
– *Les Koumiassine* (1877); *Les Epreuves de Raïssa*
(1877) (*The Trials of Raïssa*); *Un Violon Russe*
(1889) (*Russian Violin*), and *Louk Loukitch* (1890)
– were very popular with French readers, but have
lapsed into obscurity. She also wrote an *Instruction
morale et civique des jeunes filles* (1881) (*Moral and
Civil Education for Girls*) which, like the majority
of texts of this kind, was put on the Index.

Grey (Dudley), Jane (1537–1554)

The granddaughter of Henry VIII's sister Mary,
Jane Grey is best known as England's 'nine days'
queen'. Edward VI and John Dudley, Grey's
father-in-law, attempted to subvert the succession
order established in Henry's will by naming Jane
Grey the heir over both ▷ Mary and ▷ Elizabeth
Tudor. The plan failed when Mary Tudor was
peaceably crowned. Jane Grey and her husband,
Guilford Dudley, were imprisoned and sentenced
to death. Grey was well-educated by ▷ humanist
tutors, and lived briefly in ▷ Catherine Parr's
household. The only surviving works by Grey are
those written during her six months'
imprisonment in the Tower of London before her
execution. Her works, which were recorded in
John Foxe's *Actes and Monuments* (also known as
the *Book of Martyrs*, 1563), include a ▷ prayer
made before her death, her scaffold speech, a
poem written on her cell wall, and her
examination by Dr Fecknam. Also written during
this time were letters to a reprobate friend, and to
her father and her sister, Katherine Grey. Her

Lady Jane Grey

writings demonstrate a zealous Protestantism, and a poignantly mature courage in the face of death.
▷Letters: *Monument of Matrones, The*

Griffen, Vanessa (born 1952)
Short story writer and editor from Fiji. Like ▷Marjorie Crocombe, Vanessa Griffen has been crucial to the emergence of Oceanian literature. Griffen helped to establish the writing group University of the South Pacific Arts Centre (UNISPAC) in the early 1970s and has been deeply involved with the South Pacific Creative Arts Society and its journal *Mana*. Griffen has published many short stories in journals (*Mana*, *Pacific Islands Monthly*) and in collections of Pacific writing. In recent years she has edited two reports on Pacific women's conferences, focusing on political and social questions associated with development, and a health handbook for Pacific women. She writes social realist stories which focus on women's lives and their place in post-colonial Pacific society. Her fiction is uncollected.

Griffitts, Hannah (1727–1817)
North American poet and letter-writer. She lived her entire life in Philadelphia and never married. The daughter of Mary Norris and Thomas Griffitts, she had the educational advantages afforded young women of wealthy Quaker families in the early 18th century. A talented, prolific poet and letter-writer, she corresponded with several other women poets, including ▷Elizabeth Graeme Fergusson, and exchanged poems and criticism with them. Concerned with crafting and revising her poetry, she chose not to publish it; manuscripts are in the Library Company of Philadelphia (an archive established by US statesman Benjamin Franklin). Two of her most

notable poems are ▷'On Reading Some Paragraphs in "The Crisis", April '77' and ▷'To the Memory of My Late Valuable Friend Susannah Wright'. Her poetry shows considerable talent and deserves attention.
▷Early North American Quaker women's writings

Grignan, Françoise-Marguerite, Comtesse de (1646–1705)
French author of letters to her mother, ▷Madame de Sévigné. Almost all were apparently burnt in 1784 on the last orders of her daughter, Pauline de Simiane (1674–1737). Mademoiselle de Sévigné's marriage to the twice-married Comte de Grignan in 1668 took her to Provence, where her husband was the effective viceroy, though he never received the emoluments that went with the office. It is not generally recognized that Madame de Grignan initiated the correspondence with her mother, who in her first letter to her daughter refers to *'l'émotion et la joie que m'a donnée . . . votre lettre'* ('the joy and emotion which your letter gave me'). Madame de Sévigné also frequently compliments Madame de Grignan on her style, and says she has read out extracts from the letters to her friends in Paris. It is, however, difficult to assess the daughter's epistolary talents when all that remains of her writing are a few notes to her uncle, Roger de Bussy-Rabutin (1618–1693), and her husband, which were salvaged before all the other originals were destroyed by a young cousin as a final mark of respect for Madame de Simiane, who had feared that certain passages in the correspondence might cause gossip about the family.
Bib: Duchêne, J., *Françoise de Grignan*; Sévigné, Madame de, *Correspondance*, ed. R. Duchêne (3 vols).

Grimké, Angelina Emily (1805–1879)
US non-fiction writer, distinguished for her work in the causes of abolition of slavery and women's rights. Along with her sister, ▷Sarah Moore Grimké, Angelina Grimké was one of the principal documenters of slavery, and proponents of women's essential role in achieving social justice. A southerner herself, Grimké spoke from and to a unique perspective: a southern woman charging other southern women to act in *Appeal to Christian Women of the Southern States* (1836), a southern woman calling on northern women in *An Appeal to the Women of the Nominally Free States* (1837). Grimké was ahead of her time in a number of ways: more than a decade before the US author Henry David Thoreau (1817–1862) wrote his famous 'Civil Disobedience', Grimké was urging women to civil disobedience; more than a decade before ▷Sojourner Truth's famous 'Ain't I A Woman?' speech, Grimké was urging the sisterhood of all women – black and white. Her work is a distinctive mixture of feminism and religious argument.

In addition to her pamphlets and other separately published works for the abolitionist cause, Grimké published a series of letters in abolitionist journals, and with her sister Sarah produced *American Slavery As It Is: Testimony of a Thousand Witnesses* (1839), one of ▷Harriet Beecher Stowe's sources in writing ▷*Uncle Tom's Cabin*.

Grimké, Charlotte L. Forten (1839–1914)
US poet and diarist. *The Journal of Charlotte L. Forten* (published 1953) was written in the decade 1854–1864; it is one of the earliest journal records of an African-American woman, and the first published. In her poetry, which appeared in abolitionist periodicals – eg *The Liberator* (which also published ▷Angelina Emily Grimké) – Forten Grimké urged action: 'We must educate the heart, – /Teach it hatred of oppression.'

Grimké, Sarah Moore (1792–1873)
US non-fiction writer. Along with her sister, ▷Angelina Emily Grimké, Sarah Grimké was a formidable advocate of abolition of slavery and women's rights. In *An Epistle to the Clergy of the Southern States* (1836) she makes a religious argument for human equality that anticipates Martin Luther King's much later and much more famous 'Letter from the Birmingham Jail'. Sarah Grimké wrote regularly for periodicals, but only one collection of this work was published as a volume: *Letters on the Equality of the Sexes and the Condition of Woman* (1838). With her sister, she produced *American Slavery As It is: Testimony of a Thousand Witnesses* (1839).

Grinévskaia, Izabella Arkad'evna (1864–1944)
Russian dramatist, poet, prose writer and literary critic. Grinévskaia began her literary career as a translator from Polish, Italian, German and French in the early 1890s. In 1895 a play, *The First Storm*, appeared, and she began publishing original stories, poems, and articles on literature. A series of her one-act plays ran on the Imperial stages and were published twice in the early 20th century (*A Collection of Plays and Monologues*). The five-act verse drama ▷*Bab*, which was staged at the ▷St Petersburg Malyi Theatre in 1904, was her most successful work. According to *Responses of the Press About the Dramatic Poem 'Bab'* (1910), Grinévskaia received a letter from Tolstoy about the play. She wrote two other verse dramas, *Harsh Days* (1909), about the 18th-century Pugachëv Rebellion, and *Bekha-Ulla* (1912), a sequel to *Bab*. In 1900 Grinévskaia published *The Little Lights*, a collection of stories, poems, and plays; in 1904, *Poems*; in 1915 another collection of poems, *Salute to Heroes*, and a collection of stories, *From the Book of Life*. After the 1905 Revolution, Grinévskaia produced a pamphlet, *The Right of Books*, arguing against censorship. Her last known work was a thirty-two-page collection of poems, *Poems* (1922). Other post-revolutionary publications include pieces in two poetry anthologies and a short story in 1927.

Grinévskaia was most famous as a dramatist but she displayed a keen intelligence and thoughtfulness in everything she wrote. Her verse style is graceful, if conventional. At the very least some of her plays and criticism deserve to be republished. It would also be beneficial to learn more about her activities after the 1905 Revolution, and the contents of her large archives.

Griot
A term originating in West Africa, and of particular relevance in Caribbean writing, a *griot* is the living memory of the people, a walking cultural encyclopaedia of the community. A *griot* is musician, storyteller, singer and poet in one person. A *griot's* reportoire is huge, containing simple stories, ancient myths, historical traditions and poetry.

Gritsi-Milliex, Tatiana (born 1920)
Greek novelist, poet and short story writer. Born in Athens, she began writing during the German occupation of Greece in World War II. Her first novel, *Thision Square* (1947), and two short stories (also 1947), explore with acute observation and great sensitivity the theme of Greek resistance against the Germans. She was involved in the Greek Women's Movement, and in 1945 represented Greece at an international women's conference in Paris. Since 1964 she has worked for Greek radio and also written articles for Athenian and Cypriot newspapers. She began writing again in 1957. Typically her novels are based on personal experiences, expanding outwards from concrete situations to embrace a whole world of moral and social ideas. Despite its pessimism her writing is not nihilistic, but on the contrary shows how human dignity can survive the most shattering situations and the darkest frustrations. *Lacerations* (1981) is a volume of fictional narratives, and *Retrospectives* (1982) a collection of eighteen short stories. She has also published collections of her poems. Much of her work has been translated into other European languages.
Bib: *Macmillan Guide to Modern World Literature*; Robinson, Christopher, review in *World Literature Today*, 57, No. 4 (Autumn 1983).

Groen, Alma de (born 1941)
Australian dramatist. De Groen was born in New Zealand, and her plays have been produced in Australia, London and Canada and she has received an AWGIE (Australian Writers' Guild) award in 1985 for the best television adaptation. Her published plays include *Chidley* (1977), *Going Home*, *The Joss Adams Show* and *Perfectly All Right* (1977), and *Vocations* (1983). Other plays include *The Sweat-proof Boy* (1972), *The After Life of Arthur Craven* (1973), *Decade* (1980), *Man of Letters* (ABC Television, 1984) and *The Rivers of China* (1987). De Groen has dealt with a range of subjects, from marital relationships to child abuse, to the lives of eccentric individuals such as William James Chidley and the fictional Arthur Craven, nephew of Oscar Wilde.
▷Dramatists (Australia)

Grogger, Paula (1892–1984)

Austrian novelist and short story writer. Local colour, religious feeling and historical themes characterize her writings, and combine most successfully in her novel *Das Grimmingtor* (1926) (*The Griming Gate*), which is the chronicle of an Austrian family during the Napoleonic Wars. She was a great admirer and imitator of ▷Enrica Handel-Mazzetti, to whom she dedicated her story *Das Gleichnis von der Weberin* in 1929 (*The Parable of the Weaver-woman*).

Grossmann, Edith Searle (1863–1931)

New Zealand novelist. Grossmann is the most distinguished of the female Temperance novelists of the late 19th century and her work reflects, perhaps most accurately, the connection between alcohol, women and colonialism that is central for women writers. Women were usually excluded from higher education, and their dependence on the industry, skill and moral value of men became extreme in a colonial environment; Grossmann's novels simultaneously raise colonial and feminist questions. Her best-known novel is her last, ▷*The Heart of the Bush* (1910), in which a romance structure is used to highlight the differences between a New Zealand and British environment. The novel is particularly sharp on the education of women, but resorts to traditional re-affirmation of marriage. Grossmann was well educated herself, having an MA from Canterbury College, and was active as a voice for the professional equality of women.

Publications: *Angela, A Messenger* (1890); *In Revolt* (1893); *A Knight of the Holy Ghost* (1907); *The Heart of the Bush* (1910); *Life of Helen Macmillan Brown* (biography of the 'first woman to graduate with Honours in a British university' and a celebration of her work as an educator of women) (1905).

Grossmann, Judith (born 1931)

Brazilian poet, short story writer, novelist and essayist. She is a professor of literature in Bahia. Her writing is Existential and anguished, as is most writing by women of her generation. Her short stories, which are narrated by female protagonists, are gathered in two collections: *Omeio de pedra* (1970) (*The Middle of the Rock*) and *A noite estrelada* (1977) (*The Starry Night*). Her poetry employs concretism, a kind of rational poetry coming after the ▷1945 Generation, as is seen in *Linhagem de rocinante* (1959) (*Lineage of Rocinante*).

Grotte éclatée, La (1979) (The Shattered Cave)

A novel by the Algerian writer, ▷Yamina Mechakra. This novel about the Algerian war is set in the Aurès mountains. A cave provides refuge for injured *maquisards* (guerrillas). After the bombing of this cave by French soldiers, the heroine, a nurse, and her son, who have been wounded, are taken to a hospital in Tunisia. There they stay until the end of the war. The use of the first-person singular gives this work the feeling of an autobiography. The novel is interspersed with different stories, memories, pictures, dreams. Some of these are incomplete, to give a sense of lost memories.

Groult, Benoîte (born 1921)

French writer, born in Paris. Has written articles for a number of magazines, including a regular column in *F. Magazine*, which she co-founded with Claude Servan Schreiber in 1978. She has co-written several novels with her sister, ▷Flora Groult, of which *Journal à quatre mains* (1962) (*Diary in Duo*, 1965) and *Le féminin pluriel* (1965) (▷*Feminine Plural*, 1968) have been translated into English. Independently, her writings include the successful novel, *La part des choses* (1972) (*All Things Considered*), as well as feminist analyses of the condition of women, notably in ▷*Ainsi soit-elle* (1975) (*So Be It*) and *Le Féminisme au masculin* (1977) (*Feminism in the Masculine*).

Groult, Flora (born 1925)

French writer, born in Paris. She has written a large number of novels, the most successful of which are those written together with her sister, ▷Benoîte Groult. These collaborative texts include *Journal à quatre mains* (1962) (*Diary in Duo*, 1965), *Le féminin pluriel* (1965) (▷*Feminine Plural*, 1968), and *Il était deux fois* (1967) (*Twice Upon a Time*), which won the Prix Gallia.

Group, The (1775)

Play by the North American dramatist, ▷Mercy Otis Warren. *The Group* satirizes North American Tories as unprincipled individuals who sold out for personal profits. British military leaders, such as Brigadier Hateall, are revealed as corrupt and manipulative, and essayists such as 'Massachusettensis', who support the Tories, are ridiculed for writing with an 'oily tongue'. The play concludes with the intervention of 'a Lady nearly connected with one of the principal actors in the group' but who rejects the group's treasonous actions. Her final monologue laments the deaths of North Americans that will be required to gain Columbia's freedom. It is a notable play and the best of Warren's numerous dramas.

▷*History of the Rise, Progress and Termination of the American Revolution*; *Ladies of Castille, The*; *Poems, Dramatic and Miscellaneous*

Grové, Henriette (born 1922)

South African Afrikaans novelist, dramatist and short story writer, born near Potchefstroom, Orange Free State, who has also published popular fiction under the name of Linda Joubert. In her writing, which often ends in conflict and disillusionment, she speaks of longing to escape from the constrictions of middle-class morality. Her literary career began with short stories, published in *Kwartet* (1957) (*Quartet*) along with stories by ▷M.E.R., ▷Elisabeth Eybers, and Ina Rousseau. Her most important works are her novel *In die Kamer was 'n Kas* (1989) (*In the Room There was a Cupboard*), along with her stories collected in *Jaaringe* (1966) (*Growth Rings*), and *Winterreis* (1971) (*Winter Journey*), the first of which was awarded the South African CNA (Central News Agency) Prize, as was her novel.

She has also written a number of plays, for which she was awarded the most distinguished award in Afrikaans writing, the Hertzog Prize. These are: *Die Jaar* (1958) (*The Good Year*), *Die Glasdeur* (1959) (*The Glass Door*), *Halte 49* (1962) (*Stop 49*), *Toe hulle die Vierkleur op Rooigrond gehys het* (1975) (*When They Raised the Transvaal Flag on British Ground*), and *Ontmoeting by Dwaaldrif* (1981) (*Meeting at Dwaaldrif*), along with a farce, *Die Onwillige Weduwee* (1965) (*The Unwilling Widow*).

Grové's less interesting work includes two children's books, *Die Verlore Skoentje* (1948) (*The Lost Shoe*), and *Bimbo en Prins* (1950) (*Bimbo and Prince*); two novels, *Meulenhof se Mense* (1961) (*The People of Meulenhof*) and *Die Laat Lente* (1962) (*Late Spring*); and a collection of short stories, *Roosmaryn en Wynruit* (1962) (*Rosemary and Rue*). Many other short stories have appeared in magazines. None of her writing has been translated into English.

Grumbach, Argula von (c 1492–1563)

German religious and political polemicist. She came from the Bavarian nobility, was orphaned by the plague, and, after marrying Friedrich von Grumbach, lived in Dietfurt in Franconia. Influenced by the new ideas of the Reformation, she distributed tracts, and wrote letters to the court in Munich and the University of Ingolstadt, arguing her religious beliefs, and attacking the clergy for its abuse of religious and secular power. Her endeavours met with indifference, and indeed hostility; at one point the university sent her a spinning wheel to put her in her place. Having lost his job because of his wife's activities, Argula von Grumbach's husband left her and their four children.

Grumbach, Doris (born 1918)

US biographer and novelist. Grumbach was born in New York. She earned a Master's degree specializing in medieval literature at Cornell University in 1940, and has worked as a university professor and a journalist. A respected literary critic, Grumbach wrote a controversial literary biography on ▷Mary McCarthy, *The Company She Kept* (1967).

Grumbach's fiction focuses on women struggling for a sense of self in a hostile culture. In *Chamber Music* (1979) Caroline MacLaren died emotionally when she married, and after her husband's death, she passionately awakens in a lesbian love affair. In *The Missing Person* (1981) Franny represses herself after being sexually abused as a child; transformed later into a Hollywood sex symbol, she remains lost to herself. In *The Ladies* (1985) Grumbach features women who find themselves in loving each other.

Other work includes: *The Spoil of the Flowers* (1962), *The Short Throat, The Tender Mouth* (1964) and *The Magician's Girl* (1987).

Grymeston, Elizabeth Bernye (died 1603)

English anthologist and poet. Born sometime before 1563, Grymeston was the daughter of Martin and Margaret Flynte Bernye. She was raised in a strongly Catholic environment. Her father had been fined as a recusant in 1587, and in 1592/3 Grymeston, herself was fined for recusancy. By 1584 she was married to Christopher Grymeston who was apparently still a student at Caius College, Cambridge. Her only surviving work is ▷*Miscelanea, Meditations, Memoratives*, which she wrote for her son, Bernye. The materials she collected in *Miscelanea* indicate she was well-educated, and familiar with Italian, Latin and Greek writings. Grymeston's life was apparently fraught with hardship. Although she gave birth to nine children, only one survived. In her prefatory letter to her son, she also indicates a rift between Grymeston's own mother, Dorothy (whom she feared was attempting to murder Christopher Grymeston), and herself and her husband, possibly over religion or inheritance.
Bib: Beilin, E.V., *Redeeming Eve: Women Writers of the English Renaissance*; Fletcher, B.Y. and Sizemore, C.W., 'Elizabeth Grymeston's *Miscelanea, Meditations, Memoratives:* Introduction and Selected Texts', *The Library Chronicle* 47 (1981), pp. 53–83; Huey, R. and Hereford P., 'Elizabeth Grymeston and her *Miscelanea*', *The Library Chronicle* 15 (1934), pp. 61–91.

Guacci Nobile, Maria Giuseppa (1808–1848)

Italian poet. Born in Naples, she addresses her collected poetry, the *Rime* (*Rhymes*) 1832, to Neapolitan women. The Italian critic, De Sanctis, defined her poetry as masculine because it is full of scientific references, adheres strictly to form and is serious in tone. Ironically, in the light of De Sanctis's views, not only is Guacci Nobile addressing herself to a female audience, she also discusses women's role and, through her rewriting of the *Canto delle Sirene* (▷*The Sirens' Song*), she deconstructs a traditional representation of women.

Guatimozín, el último imperador de Méjico (1846) (*Guatomozín, The Last Emperor of Mexico*)

A novel by the Cuban-Spanish writer ▷Gertrúdis Gómez de Avellaneda about the conquest of Mexico and the life of Hernán Cortés, the Spaniard who conquered it. She pitifully defends the vanquished Indian civilization. Gómez Avellaneda calls the book a 'sad anecdote', in which she tells the reader a historical secret about a 'sad night': Marina, Cortés's lover drowns Gualcazintla, the widow of the Mexican *caudillo* (chief) Guatimozín, and she claims that her spirit, after her death, will join Guatimozín's, and together they will claim revenge against Cortés.

Gubar, Susan (born 1944)

North American critic and Professor of English at Indiana University. With ▷Sandra Gilbert she is author of *The Madwoman in the Attic* (1979) and *No Man's Land* (1988–1989). She has co-edited *Shakespeare's Sisters* (1979); *The Norton Anthology of Literature by Women* (1985); *The Female Imagination and the Modernist Aesthetic* (1986); and (with Joan Hoff), *For Adult Users Only. The Dilemma of Violent Pornography* (1989). Her published essays include '"The Blank Page" and the Issues of Female Creativity' (1981), which employs the title of Isak Dinesen's short story as a controlling metaphor to address women's special relationship to writing and creativity.

▷Woman-centred

Guellouz, Souad (born 1937)

Tunisian novelist. Has been teaching French in a number of schools in Tunis since 1969. Her first novel, *La Vie simple* (1975) (*The Simple Life*), was written in 1958. Guellouz is better known for her second novel, *Les Jardins du nord* (1982) (*Gardens of the North*). This novel, set in the 1940s, is an observation of family life, its traditions and evolution.

Guerra, Olga Alves

20th-century Portuguese playwright. Born in the Azores, she is one of the few women playwrights to have her work staged in theatres in Lisbon. Her first play, entitled *Tempos Modernos* (1940) (*Modern Times*), was critical of the institution of marriage. A review of the play by the critic Adolfo Casais Monteiro referred to it as '*uma revelação*' (a revelation). Three other plays by Guerra appeared in theatres in Lisbon and the Azores: *O Desaparecido* (1942) (*The Disappeared*), *Vidas Sem Rumo* (1945) (*Lives Without Direction*) and *A Rapariga do Bar* (1956) (*The Girl in the Bar*).

Guérillères, Les (1971)

Translation of *Les Guérillières* (1969), second novel of French writer ▷Monique Wittig. It depicts a feminist Utopia, where the battle against ▷patriarchal culture is fought both by the warrior women of the title and by the novel's experimentation with language and form. Wittig's text is intersected by lists of female names, and circles, possibly representing female genitalia and/or the zero-point from which a post-patriarchal culture must begin afresh. Wittig describes female genitalia in positive and poetic terms, and simultaneously criticizes this as a lapse into essentialism. Rewritten fairytales such as 'Sleeping Beauty' and 'Snow White' are woven into the text and at the end the victorious women are joined by young men eager for re-education.

Guérin, Eugénie de (1805–1848)

The daughter of provincial aristocrats, Guérin was born (and died) in the Château de Cayla in the Tarn region of France. Her life and writing is usually linked by critics with that of her dandyish brother, Maurice, a poet who predeceased her,

and whose *oeuvre* was far more sensual – and better-known – than hers. She led a retiring, almost monastic life, which is described in her *Journal* (1862), written between 1834 and 1840. This work provides a detailed account of her thoughts, prayers and the books she read, and is spiritual and poetic in tone. She also wrote a vast number of elegant, quasi-mystical letters to her brother which were published in 1864 by the critic Barbey d'Aurevilly (▷*Les Bas-Bleus*), an intimate family friend who approved of Eugénie because she was not in his view a Bluestocking, but rather a 'virgin mother'. Texts by both de Guérins are to be found in a 1965 edition, *Textes Choisis* (*Selected Passages*), and Eugénie de Guérin's journal was reprinted in 1976.
Bib: Bannour, W., *Eugénie de Guérin ou une chasteté exemplaire*; Giraud, V., *La Vie chrétienne d'Eugénie de Guérin*.

Guesnerie, Charlotte-Marie-Anne Charbonnière, de la (1710–1785)

French novelist. Published four ▷sentimental tales praised for their elegance of style, which were popular with her contemporaries: *Mémoires de Milady B* (1760), also attributed to ▷Madame Riccoboni; *Iphis et Aglae* (1768); *Mémoires de Milady Varmonti* (1778), also attributed to an unidentified. 'Mme. L.', and *Les Ressources de la vertu* (1782) (*The Resources of Virtue*).

Guette, Madame de la (1613–1676)

French writer of ▷*mémoires*. Born Catherine Meurdrac, and a member of the *noblesse d'épée* ('nobility of the sword', that is of high nobility) by birth, she received the usual education for young ladies but was also trained in the the martial arts, at her own request. She was also said to be quite unlike other women in her temperament. Although the mother of ten children, Madame de la Guette manifested a preference for '*la guerre aux exercices tranquilles de mettre les poules à couver & de filer la quenouille, quoique l'on dise qu'une femme ne doit savoir que cela*' ('war rather than the tranquil occupations of tending chickens and spinning, although it is said that a women should know only that and no more'). The *Mémoires de Mme de la Guette*, first published in 1681, are of remarkable documentary interest for the private and public life of the very troubled period of the *Frondes*, the civil wars of 1648–1653 caused by rebellions against the French crown. The *Mémoires* are modern in style and reveal a woman of action with a very forceful ego. A royalist, secretly married to one fiery-tempered *frondeur* (rebel) and the mother of another, she condemned all those who challenge the crown as '*mauvais Français*' ('bad Frenchmen'), but remained loyal to her husband. She often dressed as a man to act as emissary between the *frondeurs* and the royalists. Greatly distressed by the death of her disgraced husband in 1665, Madame de la Guette dedicated the rest of her life to establishing her children, with whom she spent her final years in The Hague. It was perhaps there that – dependent

upon the generosity of William of Orange (1650–1702), future King of England – she turned to writing to supplement the family income.
Bib: Cuenin, M. (ed.) *Mémoires de Mme de la Guette 1613–1676* (1982); Watson, F., 'Le Moi et l'histoire dans les Mémoires de Mme Motteville, Mme de la Guette et Mlle de Montpensier', *Papers on French Seventeenth-Century Literature* XVIII, No. 34 (1991).

Guglielminetti, Amalia (1885–1941)

Italian poet, novelist and dramatist. Born in Turin. Of wealthy bourgeois origins, she strove from an early age to create her own identity, separate from that of her family. At the age of eighteen she published her first collection of poetry, *Voci di giovinezza* (1903) (*Voices of Youth*), reminiscent of Carducci's (▷*Carduccianesimo*) work. She was involved in two grand passions, one with Gozzano while she was still quite young, and later with the novelist Pitigrilli. The latter relationship ended unhappily with her institutionalization. She died tragically from a fall during an air raid in World War II. In her writing, as in her life, Guglielminetti sought to create an image of female independence not divorced from sensuality. Her *Vergini folli* (*Crazed Virgins*) of 1907 was ▷D'Annunzian in inspiration. Somewhat more felicitous was her ▷*Le seduzioni* (1909) (*Seductions*), which depicted modern woman striving for independence on her own terms. Her prolific output included books for children, and she contributed to various periodicals, including *La Stampa* and *La Donna*. The correspondence between Guglielminetti and Gozzano was published in 1951, and covers the period 1907–1910.

Her other work includes: *Emma* (1909); *L'amante ignoto* (1911) (*The Unknown Lover*); *L'insonne* (1913) (*The Sleepless One*); *I volti dell'amore* (1913) (*The Faces of Love*); *Fiabe in versi* (1916) (*Verse Fables*); *Gli occhi cerchiati d'azzurro* (1918) (*Dark-circled Eyes*); *Le ore inutili* (1919) (*Wasted Hours*); *La porta della gioia* (1921) (*The Gate to Joy*); *La rivincita del maschio* (1923) (*The Revenge of the Male*); *Il baro dell'amore* (1926) (*Love's Cheat*); *Quando avevo un amante* (1924) (*When I Had a Lover*); *Il pigiama del moralista* (1927) (*The Moralist's Pyjamas*); *I serpenti di Medusa* (1934) (*Medusa's Snakes*).

Guibert, Elisabeth (1725–1788)

French poet and dramatist who received a royal pension. Guibert was noted as a particularly reactionary writer, especially for the comedy *La Coquette Corrigée* (*The Reformed Coquette*) which preaches against encouraging women's independence. This text, together with *Le Rendez-vous* (*The Meeting*) and *Les triumvirs*, was published in *Poésies et oeuvres diverses* (1764) (*Poems and Other Works*). Two comedies in verse were published in 1768, *Les Filles à marier* (*Unmarried Daughters*) and *Le sommeil d'Amynthe* (*Amynthe's Sleep*), followed by *Pensées détachées* (1771) (*Detached Thoughts*). The poem *Les philéniens ou le patriotisme* was entered in the 1775 ▷Académie Française competition. Her poems were also published in the periodical *Almanach des Muses*.
Bib: Sullerot, E., *Women on Love*.

Guibert, Louise-Alexandrine, Comtesse de (?1765–1826)

French novelist. After the death of her husband (1790) she devoted herself to editing his works and to writing her own novels. These were published as if translations from English, and include *Margaretha, comtesse Rainsford* (1797), *Agatha ou la religieuse anglaise* (1797) (*Agatha, or the English Nun*) and *Fedaretta* (1803). In 1806 the pedagogical *Leçons sur la nature* (*Lessons on Nature*) was published. She is perhaps most renowned for editing *Lettres de Mlle de Lespinasse au comte de Guibert, 1773–1776* (1809). A collection of her own correspondence, *Lettres inédites* (*Unpublished Letters*), was published in 1887.

Guidacci, Margherita (born 1921)

Italian poet. Born in Florence, she attended the University there, graduating with a thesis on Giuseppe Ungaretti. After her marriage she moved to Rome, where she taught English language and literature. She has contributed to several literary journals, and has translated writers from Spanish, English and Latin, including Blake, Conrad, ▷Emily Dickinson, James, ▷Sarah Orne Jewett, Pound, and ▷Edith Sitwell. She has also written critical studies of various English, North American and Italian writers. Much of her poetry is religious, mystical, even visionary, and she has won many literary prizes. Guidacci's most striking work is perhaps *Neurosuite* (1970), a collection of rather horrific poems, redolent of depression. Her earlier work, particularly, makes use of images of pain and negativity. Even in 1980, with *L'altare di Isenheim* (*Isenheim's Altar*), she deals with painful themes (among them the death of her husband and the tragedy of Hiroshima). One of her most recent works, ▷*Inno alla gioia* (1983) (*A Hymn to Joy*), is in many ways the total opposite of her earlier work in its celebration of life. The two most significant themes of her poetry are life and death.

Her other main works include: *La sabbia e l'angelo* (1946) (*The Sand and the Angel*); *Morte del ricco* (1955) (*Death of a Rich Man*); *Paglia e polvere* (1961) (*Straw and Dust*); *Poesie* (1965) (*Poems*); *Un cammino incerto* (1970) (*An Uncertain Path*); *Terra senza orologi* (1973) (*A Land Without Time*); *Taccuino slavo* (1976) (*Slav Notebook*); *Il vuoto e le forme* (1977) (*Emptiness and Form*); *La via crucis dell'umanità* (1984) (*Humanity's Way of the Cross*); *Poesie per poeti* (1987) (*Poetry for Poets*); *Il buio e lo splendore* (1989) (*The Darkness and the Light*). *A Book of Sibyls* (1989) is available in English.

Guido, Beatrix (born 1924)

Argentinian novelist, short story writer and dramatist. She studied philosophy and literature in Buenos Aires, Rome and Paris. She is one of the best-known authors in Argentina, and her books have been widely published. Adolescence is the theme in several of her novels: *Las casa del ángel* (1954) (*The House of the Angel*), *La caída* (1956) (*The Fall*), *El secuestrador* (1958) (*The Kidnapper*) and *Fin de fiesta* (1958) (*End of the Party*). In these stories, the young people are trapped between sexual guilt and innocence. *Fin de fiesta* takes place in Buenos Aires, during the years 1930–1945, and reveals the dark side of a powerful family of the local oligarchy. The 'party' is a symbol of revolution, violence, sexual crimes, decadence, and bad habits in the Church and the government. Her prize-winning first novel is *La casa del ángel*. *La caída* her second novel, as well as *El Secuestrador*, became films directed by Torre Nilsson, whom she married in 1959. In 1961 the film of *La mano en la trampa* (*The Hand in the Trap*), which was published the same year, won the first prize in the Film Festival at Cannes. Her play *Homenaje a la hora de la siesta* (*Homage to Siesta Time*) was filmed and competed in the Venice Festival. Widowed in 1979, she was appointed Argentinian Cultural Attaché in Spain in 1984.

Guiducci, Armanda (born 1923)

Italian poet, novelist and essayist. She studied in Milan and contributed particularly to left-wing journals. Her work is concerned with the relationship between art and society, as is obvious in both *La domenica della rivoluzione* (1961) (*Revolution Sunday*), and *Dallo zdanovismo allo strutturalismo* (1967) (*From Zdanovism to Structuralism*). She has written on Pavese more than once, in ▷*Il mito Pavese* (1967) (*The Myth of Pavese*) and *Invito alla lettura di Pavese* (1972) (*A guide to Reading Pavese*). Her other abiding concern is that of woman's role in society, and its constrictions. Many of her writings rework this theme from different angles. Some of the most interesting are ▷*La mela e il serpente* (1974) (*The Apple and the Serpent*), a supposedly autobiographical tale which tells the story of a female character in first-person narrative, and *La donna non è gente* (1977) (*Woman Is Not Human*).

Her other works include: *Poesie per un uomo* (1965) (*Poetry for a Man*); *A colpi di silenzio* (1982) (*In Deafening Silence*); *Donna e serva* (1983) (*Woman/Servant*); *A testa in giù* (1983) (*Head Down*).

Guillet, Pernette du (c 1520–1545)

French poet. Of aristocratic birth, she was the mistress of the poet Maurice Scève (1501–c1560) and a friend of ▷Louise Labé. She was both musically talented and an accomplished linguist. Pernette du Guillet's poetry is bound up with the poet whom she loved and whose talent she considered much greater than her own. The *Rymes de gentille et vertueuse dame Pernette du Guillet, Lyonnoise* (*Rhymes of the Noble and Virtuous Lady Pernette du Guillet, of Lyon*), published shortly after her death, contain a number of epigrams, *chansons* ('songs') and elegies in neoplatonic and ▷Petrarchan styles. Her work explores the paradoxical interplay between a female poet and a male poetic tradition. In her second elegy, she seeks, but ultimately fails, to achieve a simultaneous love for the ▷Muses and her own beloved. Du Guillet tried to assert herself as a poet worthy of recognition in her own right, but was overwhelmed by Scève's talent. After her death, Scève, who had immortalized du Guillet in his famous poem in 440 *dizains* (ten-syllable lines), '*Délie*' (1544), rewrote much of her verse. Critics have noted the paradoxical contrast between her two poetic identities. Silent and alarming as the object of Scève's love, she is contented and modest as a lover-poet.
Bib: Guggenheim, M., *Women in French Literature.*

Guilló, Magdalena (born 1940)

Spanish novelist. Guilló read mathematics at university, and since 1972 has resided in Salamanca. Her first book was published in Catalan – *En una vall florida al peu de les espases* (1977) (*In a Flowering Valley*). She also writes in Castilian, in which she has published two books, both dealing with Judaic themes: *Entre el ayer y el mañana* (1984) (*Between Yesteryear and Tomorrow*) and *Un sambenito para el señor Santiago* (1986) (*Penitent's Garb for Santiago*).
▷Catalan women's writing

Guimarães, Elina (1904–1991)

Portuguese lawyer. She was in charge of the legal division of the National Council on Portuguese Women in the 1930s and 1940s, and wrote extensively on women's rights. Among her books are *Dos Crimes Culposos* (*Of Serious Crimes*), *A Lei em que Vivemos* (*The Law in which We Live*), *Coisas de Mulheres* (*Women's Things*) and *Mulheres Portuguesas Ontem e Hoje* (1979) (*Portuguese Women Past and Present*). In 1985 she was awarded the Portuguese Order of Liberty. She wrote on women's legal status for the *Diário de Notícias* and other publications.

Guizot, Pauline (1773–1827)

French novelist. A cultivated woman whose father was ruined by the Revolution (1789), Mme Guizot turned to writing to support her mother and sisters. She published some early novels based on English models, including *La Chapelle d'Ayton* (1800) (*The Chapel of Ayton*), her best-known fictional piece. She also worked as a literary journalist on the *Publiciste* (*Advertiser*). In 1812 she married the historian and politician François Pierre Guizot, who was fourteen years her junior, and went on to have several children. After marrying, she produced a number of highly moral educational texts, including *Les Enfants* (1812) (*Children*); *L'Ecolier* (1821) (*The Schoolboy*); *Nouveaux contes* (1823) (*New Tales*) and her *Lettre de famille sur l'éducation domestique* (1826) (*Family Letter on Home Education*), a treatise on the instruction of women which won a prize of 8,000 francs. Like ▷Claire Rémusat, she was keen to extend the scope of women's education so that they might rear their children more easily, run their homes more efficiently, and thereby escape some of the drudgery and oppression of domestic life.

Gulbadam, Begum (16th century)
Daughter of Babur, the first Mughal emperor of India (reigned 1526–?). She was India's first female historian, and in her Persian work *Humayun Nama* (c 1580) (▷ *The History of Humayun*, 1902), she provides unique insights into the domestic lives of the first two Mughal emperors.

Günderrode, Karoline von (1780–1806)
German poet. Her mother persuaded her to enter a convent for high-born ladies, but she disliked living there, and spent much time travelling and visiting friends, especially ▷Bettina von Arnim, who later wrote a biography of her. Fascinated by the ideas of the French Revolution (1789) and in love with Friedrich Creuzer, a married man and scholar of mythology, she too became interested in myths and the study of alternative, particularly matriarchal, societies. Finding it more and more difficult to integrate herself in everyday life, she envisaged a Utopia in which her creative femininity would fuse harmoniously with man and with nature. Her poems, collected in *Gedichte und Phantasien* (1806) (*Poems and Fantasies*) and *Melete* (1806), evoke an alienation from life so extreme that, in order to survive, the poet needs to dream away the present and live only in the imagination. When love did not bring her the happiness that she yearned for in reality, and her liaison with Creuzer lapsed, she killed herself with a dagger. In *Kein Ort, Nirgends* (1979) (*No Place on Earth*, 1982, 1983) ▷Christa Wolf reinterpreted Karoline von Günderrode's predicament in modern feminist terms.

Gunn, Jeannie (1870–1961)
Australian novelist. After her marriage to Aeneas Gunn in 1901, Jeannie Gunn accompanied her husband to Elsey Station on the Roper River in the Northern Territory. After his death in 1903 she returned to Melbourne and published *The Little Black Princess* (1905) and ▷*We of the Never-Never* (1908). These two books were immensely popular with both adults and children, but modern critics have objected to the patronizing depiction of the Aborigines, who were seen as the equivalent of naughty children to be educated into white ways by the 'young missus'.

▷Children's literature (Australia)

Gunnars, Kristjana (born 1948)
Poet, short-story writer and novelist, born Kristjana Gunnarsdottir in Reykjavik, Iceland, who emigrated to the USA in 1964, and then settled in Canada in 1969. She taught in rural Iceland in 1973–1974, studied at the Universities of Regina and Manitoba, and is active in Canada's literary and Icelandic communities as an editor and translator. Her poetry is remarkable for its moving eloquence and its tactile visualizations. She has published *Settlement Poems 1 and 2* (1980); *Wake-Pick Poems* (1981); *One-Eyed Moon Maps* (1980); *The Night Workers of Ragnarök* (1985), and *Carnival of Longing* (1989). A stark evocation of loss makes Gunnars's poetry overwhelming. Her fiction is even more extraordinary for its lyrical intensity and her ability to unfold the terrifying complexities of narrative. *The Axe's Edge* (1983) is a collection of short stories that melds the author's Icelandic heritage with her Canadian experience. *The Prowler* (1989) is a densely textured and yet lucid novel about Icelandic starvation during World War II and its aftermath. *Zero Hour* (1991) is an autobiographical account of a daughter's vigil over her father's dying. Her work is a powerful example of ethnic sensibility brought to bear on the Canadian mosaic. Her usage of Norse mythology and Icelandic folklore within a different cultural mosaic addresses the pervasive influence of origins. She translated the poems of Stephan Stephansson (1853–1927), the famous Icelandic poet who lived in Canada, which were published in 1988, and has edited a collection of essays on ▷Margaret Laurence. She lives in Edmonton, Alberta, and teaches Creative Writing at the University of Alberta.
Bib: Owens, J., in *Contemporary Manitoba Writers*.

Gur, Batya
Israeli novelist. Gur introduced the detective novel into Israeli literature. Through her protagonist, a lonely police officer who appears in all her novels, she provides an insight into various aspects of Hebrew society. In her latest novel, *Linah Meshoutefet* (1991) (*Cohabitation*), a murder is committed on a kibbutz. The investigation conducted by the police officer reveals personal as well as ideological conflicts, through which the author examines kibbutz life and beliefs.

Gurévich, Liubov' Iakovleva (1866–1940)
Russian editor and publisher, literary critic and historian, fiction writer, and translator. Gurévich received a university-level education at the Bestuzhev Courses for Women in St Petersburg. ▷Bashkirtseff's *Diary*, which began appearing in French in 1885, lent support to her desire for independence and her rebellion against bourgeois morality. Her article, 'M.K. Bashkirtseva: A Biographical and Psychological Study' (1888), analyzed the artist with sympathy and approval.

As publisher and co-editor of the *Northern Herald* (1891-98) with Akim Volynskii, Gurévich set out to 'modernize' Russian tastes and give women a greater role in the cultural world. The journal published stories by Tolstoy and Chekhov, along with 'decadent' prose writers and poets (▷Lókhvitskaia, ▷Gíppius, Sologub, and Bal'mont) to whom other journals remained hostile. Among women writers, the *Herald* found room for works by ▷Krestóvskaia, ▷Vengérova, ▷Kovalévskaia, ▷Veselítskaia, ▷O. Shapír, ▷V.

Dmítrieva, E. Letkóva, ▷Chiúmina, and ▷Lou Andreas-Salome. A number of articles highlighted women and their concerns. Despite attacks by critics hostile to the idealist and aestheticist positions of the *Herald*, by the time it closed in 1898 Gurévich had become a role model for younger critics like Elena Koltonóvskaia. She worked as a literary and theatre critic, and her collected essays on individual figures and theoretical topics, *Literature and Aesthetics*, appeared in 1912. The political upheavals in Russia in 1905 galvanized her into political activity. She worked on behalf of civil rights, collaborated in running meetings for working women, and published two pamphlets, *The 9th of January* (about the 1905 upheavals) and *Why Women Must Be Given All Rights and Freedom*, both in 1906. Discouraged by the feminists' lack of success and forced to earn a living for herself and her daughter, Elena (Gurévich never married), she dropped out of political activity. In 1904 Gurévich met Stanislavskii, and much of her later career was connected with him and the theatre. From 1911 to 1913 she worked as a critic for two newspapers, and in 1914 she went with the Moscow Art Theatre to Germany. After the 1917 Revolution, Gurévich edited Stanislavskii's theoretical writings, collaborated with him on his memoirs, *My Life in Art* (1926), and published *The Actor's Art: On the Nature of the Actor's Artistic Experiences on Stage* (1927) and *The History of Russian Theatrical Life* (1939). When she died she left the manuscript of a book on Molière. Gurévich also translated works of foreign literature and philosophy including Bashkirtseff's diary, Spinoza, Maupassant, Stendhal, Anatole France, Baudelaire, Proust, Schnitzler, and Hauptmann.

▷Silver Age, The

Bib: Rabinowitz, Stanley (trans.), 'The Farsighted Ones: Bryusov's *Fiery Angel* and Kuzmin's *First Book of Stories*' in *The Noise of Change: Russian Literature and the Critics (1891–1917)*.

Guró, Elena Genrikhovna (1877–1913)

Russian poet, prose writer and dramatist. Trained as an artist, Guró began publishing in 1905. Her book, *Hurdy-Gurdy* (1909), unites art, poetry, and prose. That same year she became involved with the newborn Russian futurists, who regarded her as the 'First Female Futurist'. Her play *Autumnal Dream*, with an epigraph from ▷Adelaida Gértsyk, was published in 1912. A second edition of *Hurdy-Gurdy* and a collection of her work, ▷*The Little Camels of the Sky*, were published in 1914.

Her entire *oeuvre* is united by particular images, devices, and themes. A frequent image is that of the unappreciated, awkward loner, both male and female, under assault from philistines or simply the 'norms' of social behaviour (eg Harlequin in her play *Harlequin the Beggar*, and the female figure in the poem 'Caustic'). Guró expressed this compassion for the vulnerable as a maternal urge: 'Sometimes I think that I'm mother to everything'

(*Little Camels*). Her work tends to break down such conventional categories as the animate and inanimate worlds, past–present–future time distinctions, and the rubrics of poetry, prose, and drama: her prose is often 'poetic', foregrounding lyrical impressions and moods, filled with imagery and a heightened emotional diction, lacking a narrative base and a proper ending, and divided into short stanza-like paragraphs; her poetry is often 'unpoetic' free verse. Like a number of her contemporaries (▷Chiúmina, ▷Gíppius, ▷Solov'éva, ▷Tsvetáeva), she sometimes used the masculine voice for her lyric persona. Her favourite devices are personification and metonymy, which tend toward fragmentariness, and combine concrete reality with abstraction and fantasy, both on the semantic (noun-epithet combinations) and content level. Perhaps because of her training as an artist, she often stresses the act of perception: in the poem 'Daytime' we learn at the end that the speaker is lying down and looking up; in the prose piece 'Arrival in the Country' the child describes the landscape and objects as she moves away from them in a wagon (both in *Hurdy-Gurdy*). Guró anticipates Iurii Olesha (1899–1960) and Vladimir Nabokov (1899–1977) in her attention to colours and the play of light, shadows, and reflections.

Various indigenous and foreign influences have been seen in Guró's creative development, including the Russian symbolists Andrei Bely (1880–1934), Aleksandr Blok (1880–1921) , western Symbolists Friedrich Nietzsche (1844–1900) and Norwegian writer Knut Hamsun (1859–1952). She in turn influenced writers like ▷de Gabriak and ▷Mariia Shkápskaia. Guró's two books were almost completely ignored by critics, and much of her work remains to be published and assessed.

Bib: Kaun, A. (trans.), *Soviet Poets and Poetry*; O'Brien, K. (trans.), *Little Camels of the Sky*; Banjanin, M. (trans.), 'An Impulse', *Russian Literature Triquarterly* 9; Henderson, L., 'The Merging of Time and Space: "The Fourth Dimension" in Russia from Ouspensky to Malevich', *The Structurist* 15–16; Jensen, K., 'Russian Futurism, Urbanism, and Elena Guro'; Nilsson, N., 'The Sound Poem: Russian Zaum and German Dada', *Russian Literature* 10, No. 4; Banjanin, M., 'Of Harlequins, Dreamers, and Poets', *Russian Language Journal* 36, Nos. 123–24; 'Looking Out, Looking In: Elena Guro's Windows', *Festschrift fur Nikola R. Pribic*, and 'Nature and the City in the Works of Elena Guro', *Slavic and East European Journal* 30; Bowlt, J., 'Esoteric Culture and Russian Society', *The Spiritual in Art, Abstract Painting, 1890–1985*; Nilsson, N., 'Russia and the Myth of the North: The Modernist Response', *Russian Literature* 21 and 'Elena Guro: An Introduction', *Elena Guro: Selected Prose and Poetry*.

Gutridge, Molly (fl 1778)

North American poet. She is known only through the poem she published as a broadside, ▷'A New

Touch on the Times', one of the numerous 'Daughter of Liberty' poems published during the American Revolution. A resident of Marblehead, Massachusetts, she noted in her poem the devastating effects of war on a seaside community dependent upon trade for its survival.

Guy, Rosa (born 1925)

This Caribbean novelist, short story writer, children's writer and activist was born in ▷Trinidad, but in 1932 moved to the USA. She grew up in Harlem. She left school at fourteen and became involved with unions at her workplace, and then in the wider struggles for black liberation. She went on to study at New York University, where she first began to write plays and stories. The play *Venetian Blinds* was first produced in 1954. But her early writing was repeatedly rejected until her work for young adults gained her recognition. A co-founder of the Harlem Writers' Guild, she is the award-winning author of ten novels, including ▷*Bird At My Window* (1965), the trilogy *The Friends* (1973), *Ruby* (1976) and *Edith Jackson* (1978), and *My Love, My Love, or the Peasant Girl* (1985). *A Measure of Time* (1983), was her first novel for adults. Impressive and captivating, it is based on the character of her stepmother. Her work bears a close relationship to that of ▷Maya Angelou and ▷Paule Marshall.

For further references see Jerrie Norris, *Presenting Rosa Guy* (1988).

Guyana

This geographical region of the Caribbean is the most racially mixed of all the English-speaking Caribbean. Those of Indian descent form over half of the entire population. There are marked distinctions between the African and Indian racial groups, and there is a history of violent clashes between these groups. It is the birthplace of Jacqueline De Weever, Evadne D'Oliviera, (born 1942) ▷Grace Nichols, ▷Janice Shinebourne, Rajkumari Singh and ▷Shana Yardan.

Guyart, Marie ▷Marie de l'Incarnation

Gu Ying (born ?1945)

Chinese writer. A native of Yunnan, Gu worked for many years in museums and as an art teacher before she turned to writing. She is author of many short stories and works for children, but is best-known for the short story 'Jingjing is Born', about the horrendous experience of women in labour during the turmoil of the 'cultural revolution' (1966–1976).
Bib: Zhu Hong (trans.), 'Jingjing Is Born' and 'The Serenity of Whiteness' in *The Serenity of Whiteness*.

Guyon, Marie-Jeanne Bouvier de la Motte (1648–1717)

French autobiographer, poet and mystic. Following the early death of her husband and her own physical disfigurement by smallpox, she gave a lecture tour of Savoy between 1681 and 1686, signing her publications on the subject of a form of religious mysticism emphasizing passive devotion to God. After she returned to Paris she was frequently imprisoned, but formed a close relationship with the philosopher, the Abbé Fénelon (1651–1715), whom she enlightened on the doctrine of '*pur amour*' ('pure love'), provoking a dispute with the bishop and writer Bossuet (1627–1704). Madame Guyon, who entrusted the education of her own five children to others so that she might give more attention to her apostolic mission, was one of the formative influences on the foundation of the girls' college at Saint-Cyr, until she and Fénelon fell out of favour with ▷Madame de Maintenon. Madame Guyon's works, amounting to some forty volumes of poetry and treatises, including *La Vie de Mme Guyon écrite par elle-même* (*The Life of Madame Guyon Written by Herself*), composed in 1688, were condemned in 1694. The following year she was arrested. When released from the Bastille in 1703, she formed a quietist circle in Blois. Her poetry is marked by mystical fervour.
Bib: Dumas, F., *Fénelon et les Saintes Folies de Mme Guyon*; Wilwerth, E., *Visages de la littérature féminine*.

Gyllembourg, Thomasine Buntzen Heiberg Ehrensvärd (1773–1856)

The first Danish psychological and realist prose writer. Gyllembourg was born into a wealthy family in Copenhagen. She received a good education at home, and in 1790 she married her teacher, the writer and philologist P.A. Heiberg. The marriage was not a happy one, and in 1799, when he was expatriated, she wanted a divorce, a very radical step at that time. She had fallen in love with the Swedish Baron Gyllembourg, whom she married in 1801. In 1815 he died, and for long periods she lived with her son, the dramatist Johan Ludvig Heiberg (1791–1860), and his wife, the famous actress Johanne Luise Heiberg (1812–1890), who has described this *ménage à trois* in her memoirs.

In 1827, when she was 58 years old, she had her anonymous literary début in her son's periodical with the story '*Familien Polonius*' ('The Polonius Family'). During the following seventeen years she wrote twenty-eight short stories, plays and novels, always stories of everyday life, of woman's idealized role in the bourgeois family, written in a realist, psychological prose, eg *En Hverdags-Historie* (1829) (*A Story of Everyday Life*).

Gyllembourg was ambivalent. She never gave up her anonymity. The structure of her stories was conventional for the moralizing literature of her time, but her psychological insights into the systems of morality were strikingly modern, and made her expand her own limits to become one of the first realist authors in Denmark.

Gynocritics

A term coined by ▷Elaine Showalter to distinguish reading representations of women, armed with men's theoretical tools, from the type of feminist criticism Showalter proposes (gynocriticism), which is concerned with '*woman as writer* – with woman as the producer of textual meaning, with the history, themes, genres, and structures of literature by women'.

Bib: Showalter, E., 'Toward a Feminist Poetics' and 'Feminist Criticism in the Wilderness'.

Gyp (1850–1932)

The ▷pseudonym of Gabrielle de Mirabeau, Comtesse de Martel de Janville, French novelist and an aristocrat descended from the revolutionary politician Mirabeau. She was brought up in the Lorraine by her grandfather, and published her first novels, *Petit Bob* (*Little Bob*) and *La Vertu de la baronne* (*The baroness's Virtue*), in 1882. These were followed by some 100 others, many of which she also illustrated, signing her drawings 'Bob'. Her *oeuvre*, which is witty, irreverent and frequently satirical, offers insight into the world of rich, fashionable French society under the Second Empire and the Third Republic. She was especially fond of depicting young, cheeky and tomboyish heroines, who have been seen by critics as precursors of those created by ▷Colette. Her novels, which contain an inordinate amount of dialogue, often couched in slang language that has long since fallen into disuse, were extremely popular with both the French and the English, but are no longer read; her volumes of memoirs – *Souvenirs d'une petite fille* (1927–8) (*Memories of a Little Girl*); *Du temps des cheveux et des chevaux* (1928) (*Time of Hair and Horses*) and *La Joyeuse Enfance de la III République* (1931) (*Happy Childhood in the Third Republic*) – are, however, of greater interest to today's reader because of the sociological data they provide. An ardent nationalist, Gyp became very involved in the Dreyfus affair, and her writings, however amusing, show such evidence of her racism that R.F. Byrnes describes her as 'the most important and influential anti-Semitic novelist' of the late 19th century. Her other novels include: *Autour du mariage* (1883) (*About Marriage*); *Ce que femme veut?* (1883) (*What a Woman Wants?*); *Elle et Lui* (1885) (*She and He*); *Mlle Loulou* (1888); *Pas jalouse!* (1893) (*Not jealous!*) and *Bijou* (1896) (*Jewel*).

Bib: Byrnes, R.F., *Anti-Semitism in Modern France*; Crosland, M., *Women of Iron and Velvet*; Missoffe, M., *Gyp et ses amis*.

H

Hacker, Marilyn (born 1942)

US poet. Born in New York, she is the author of *Separations* (1976), *Presentation Piece* which won the National Book Award for poetry in 1975, *Taking Notice* (1980) and *Love, Death and the Changing of the Seasons* (1986). She has lived in New York, San Francisco and London, and has taught creative writing at several universities.

Hacker has a distinctive poetic voice. She is expert with traditional metric and stanzaic forms, from the sonnet and rondeau to the sestina, but takes pleasure in reworking these forms in a modern urban North American idiom. 'Three Sonnets for Iva' in *Taking Notice*, for example, explores in unrhymed sonnets the life of the writer who is also a single mother, and the mother–daughter relationship. The juxtaposition of the sonnet form with 'the Pamper / full of mustardy shit', and moments of anger and violence towards the child, undercut the traditional ideals of romantic love, and the romantic male poet secure on his 'mountaintop'. *Love, Death and the Changing of the Seasons* also uses a flexible sonnet form to create a long sequence comparable to Dante's *La Vita Nuova* (1920–1924) and the work of Sidney and Shakespeare. The sonnets chart a passionate lesbian relationship from start to finish.

In some ways similar to ▷Adrienne Rich's 'Twenty-one Love Poems' because of the subject matter and the challenge to heterosexual romantic love poetry, Hacker's work celebrates and explores the intensity and pleasurable discomfort of sexual desire, whereas Rich's interests are more in the political context which informs and destroys the lover's relationship. Hacker's poems allude to such a context but use the sheer energy of the passion between the two women as an iconoclastic tool and as a matrix for the rest of the speaker's life.

Other works include *Assumptions* (1985), *The Hang-Glider's Daughter: New and Selected Poems* (1990) and *Going Back to the River* (1990).

Hades (1984–1985)

A work by Japanese writer Saegusa Kazuko (born 1929). The narrator, Akiko, is travelling around the ruins of ancient Greece, having parted from a man whom she had loved for almost twenty years, and also having left her job as a high-school teacher. She bade him farewell just as he began to want marriage, a baby and a happy home, despite the fact that she had previously had an abortion. Akiko is determined to die alone. Standing in front of a dreary ruin, she reflects that her man wants a family, and yet was not at all concerned about the blood shed when she had an abortion, and does not consider himself a murderer; their relationship is just the same as the strife of matriarchy and ▷patriarchy in a Greek tragedy.

Hadewych (born mid-13th century)

Poet and prose-writer from the southern Netherlands. Very little is known about her. From her work and from the influence she has exercised, it appears that she lived in Brabant and was active in a group of women devoted to God. A late tradition places her in Antwerp. From her youth, rhymed letters have survived. With her forty-five *Strophic Poems* she created a whole new genre of mystic love poetry, written in the vernacular. For the format of her verses she often turned towards the French troubadours. Her fourteen *Visions* contain reminiscences of gifts of mercy that she had received in the past. In her thirty-one *Letters*, at times true treatises, Hadewych addresses the women devoted to God to whom she gave spiritual guidance. The hermetic form and somewhat eccentric content of her work mean she is little-read. A choice from her work has appeared in *A Selection of Early Dutch Poetry*.
▷*Visionsliteratur*

Haesaert, Clara (born 1924)

Flemish poet. Full name: Claire Haesaert-Weyens. Employed at the Ministry of Education and Culture, she is co-founder of an artistic-literary magazine, as well as of the Brussels art centre, Taptoe. Her first collections include *De overkant* (1952) (*Other Side*) and *Omgekeerde volgorde* (1963) (*Reverse Order*); these titles give some indication of their themes: discovering new spheres of life, and the reversal of norms and values. Initially she discussed the dialectical man–woman relationship in classical verse. Gradually, she switched to free verse, and her language became more sober in style. In her collection *Met terugwerkende kracht* (1977) (*With Retrospective Effect*) the reflection on the process of phrasing receives more attention, also in a thematical way, while the imagery is related to Surrealism. Her other collections include: *Onwaarschijnlijk recht* (1967) (*Improbably Straight Forward*), *Spel van vraag en aanbod* (1970) (*Game of Supply and Demand*), *Medeplichtig* (1981) (*Accessory*) and *Bevoorrechte getuige* (1986) (*Privileged Witness*). Some of her poetry has appeared in translation in *Poetry in Flanders: A Pen Edition* (1982).

Hafsia, Jalila

Tunisian novelist. Little is known about the life of this writer, but according to Jean Déjeux's *Dictionnaire des auteurs Maghrebins des langues Françaises* (1984) she has worked at the 'Tahar Haddad', a cultural club in Tunis. Her novel *Cendre à l'aube* (1978) (*Ash at Dawn*) draws on her social situation as a middle-class woman who is constrained by her family. *Visages et rencontres* (1981) (*Faces and Encounters*), Hafsia's second book, is composed of interviews with North African and European writers.

Hagar (1913)

US novel by ▷Mary Johnston which traces a girl's growth to womanhood, and a society's growth to maturity. Mentally, Hagar confronts her ▷Southern society to determine her own destiny. She sees that the South is doomed by its rigid, hierarchical social order, and that the way her

Southern culture defines women, men and society also destroys them. For the survival of her region and herself, Hagar advocates the rejection of hierarchies. She connects capitalism with women's lack of selfhood, and socialism with women's freedom, and envisions a future where new men and women direct their own lives. Johnston examines the construction of gender based on biological assumptions and sociopolitical analyses. She urges her readers to support the women's movement to create a humane future.

Hagedorn, Jessica Tarahata

US poet and short story writer. At an early age Hagedorn emigrated to the US from the Philippines. Her work explores how non-white US immigrants lose their cultural identity. The poem 'Song for My Father' describes how Filipinos immigrated to escape martial law. The story 'The Blossoming of Bong Bong' examines how Filipinos remain strangers in the USA; Bong Bong and Pearl cannot understand Anglo-American culture and its contradictions. They are confronted with violence, deprivation, cruelty, loneliness and indifference, and they begin buying things to subsist. Hagedorn sees US consumerism as a panacea for rage. Eventually, Bong Bong forgets who he is. As an alternative, the Filipina in 'Smokey's Getting Old' identifies with African-Americans. Hagedorn's poetry examines why Anglo-Americans try to possess or destroy the beauty of non-white people. It posits that racists do so to relieve their loneliness.

Other work includes: *Dangerous Music: The Poetry and Prose of Jessica Hagedorn* (1975), *Petfood and Tropical Apparitions* (1981) and *Dog Eaters* (1990).
▷ Asian-Americam writing

Hagiwara Yoko (born 1920)

Japanese novelist and essayist. She was born in Tokyo, the daughter of a famous poet, Hagiwara Sakutaro. *My Father, Hagiwara Sakutaro*, in which the narrator describes a true picture of the poet, won the Essayist Club Prize in 1960. *A Flower in Heaven – Miyoshi Tatsuji* (1966), which won the Tamura Toshiko Prize and the Shincho Prize for Literature, portrays the poet Miyoshi Tatsuji, who married her aunt. *The House Twisted by Nettles* describes in detail the complicated relationships in her parents' home and her own life, and won a literary prize in 1974.

Hahn, Ulla (born 1946)

German poet. A Marxist literary critic, she initially took the view that modern poetry must be political. She published some tough political verse, but during the 1970s she came to change her outlook radically. Her poems of the 1980s, in *Herz über Kopf* (1981) (*Heart over Head*), *Spielende* (1983) (*Players*) and *Freudenfeuer* (1985) (*Fires of Joy*), speak in the traditional imagery and forms of non-political individualism, of love and of loss. They reflect her interest and admiration for an earlier, all but forgotten tradition of women's

poetry, by writers such as ▷ Ricarda Huch, ▷ Else Lasker-Schüler and ▷ Gertrud Kolmar. *Ein Mann im Haus* was published in 1991.

Hahn-Hahn, Ida von (1805–1880)

German poet, novelist and travel writer. Of aristocratic descent, she tried to supplement her income by publishing poems and short stories after her divorce in 1830. She led an unconventional life, travelling in Europe and the East with her lover, Count von Bystram, and achieved popularity with her many travelogues. Her novels of this period reflect the influence of contemporary French liberalism, and the effervescent spirit of 'Young Germany', a radical left-wing and political movement of the 1830s. They were, at the time, considered rather scandalous. After 1848, horrified by the revolutions that had broken out across Europe, and shaken by the death of Bystram, she converted to Catholicism, entered a convent, and henceforth devoted herself to writing Catholic literature. While reflecting the changes in her outlook, her novels are invariably about aristocratic women of great beauty, moral strength and intelligence who yearn for emotional freedom. Her main works are: *Gräfin Faustine* (1840) (*Countess Faustine*); *Orientalische Briefe* (1844) (*Oriental Letters*); *Maria Regina* (1860); see also her autobiography, *Von Babylon nach Jerusalem* (1851) (*From Babylon to Jerusalem*).

Halamová, Masa (1908–1986)

Slovak poet. Halamová produced three collections of intimate lyric verse: *Dar* (1929) (*The Present*), *Červený mak* (1932) (*The Red Poppy*) and *Smrt' tvoju žijem* (1966) (*I Am Living Your Death*). She worked as a clerk and as an editor in a Bratislava publishing house.

Halamová saw poetry as a means to self-knowledge. Her verse was influenced by Slovak symbolism, the proletarian poetry of the 1930s, and the oral tradition. Her constant themes were family, home, love, nature, remembrances of mother and husband, and travel impressions. Her verse is simple and sensitive, concerning love, patience and pity. She also wrote several short stories and fairy-tales, and translated works from Russian, Czech and Serbian.

Halbtier! (1899) (*Half-animal!*)

A novel by the German writer ▷ Helene Böhlau. As its title suggests, its theme is the degradation of women. The heroine, Isolde Frey, is the daughter of an autocratic and patriarchal writer and his self-effacing wife. An inheritance allows her to achieve temporary independence and emotional fulfilment as a practising artist; yet she cannot allow herself to ignore the terrifying destiny of women like her sister, Marie, who dies in childbirth and, as a corpse, is exposed to the cynical jokes of medical students. Isolde rejects the Women's Movement as 'the strangest slaves' revolt', finding it to be no more than an excuse for empty bickerings. Although Böhlau offers no alternatives to patriarchal society, she does allow her heroine a final dramatic act of rebellion.

Hale, Keron ▷Lyttleton, Edith

Hale, Lucretia Peabody (1820–1900)
US humour and fiction writer, journalist and social reformer. She is primarily known for her splendid humorous stories, first published in the magazines *Our Young Folks* and *St Nicholas*, and later collected in ▷*The Peterkin Papers* (1880) and *The Last of the Peterkins, with Others of Their Kin* (1886). Aside from the Peterkin books, Hale's career represents the various kinds of literary work available to 19th-century US women: co-authored novels, religious texts, compendiums of crafts, and stories for children.

Hale, Nancy (born 1908)
US novelist, short story writer and biographer. With distinguished painters as parents, Hale formally studied art in Boston, Massachusetts, and when she married, she moved to New York. She started writing at *Vogue* magazine. In 1933 she was assistant editor at *Vanity Fair* magazine, and in 1935 she became the first woman reporter at the *New York Times*. Her writing captures, and often satirizes, specific social manners and attitudes. *The Young Die Good* (1932) satirizes the heroine who indulges in glamour, fun and sexual freedom without considering social practicalities. Novels like *Dear Beast* (1959) focus on the conflict between a New Englander and a Southerner. As in ▷*Prodigal Women* (1942), Hale's writing also portrays women's conflict with their inner selves and the outer world. In her autobiographies and biographies she comes to understand the inner world of women artists.

Other work includes: *New Any More* (1934), *The Earliest Dreams* (1936), *Between the Dark and the Daylight* (1943), *The Sign of Jonah* (1950), *The Empress's Ring* (1955), *Heaven and Hardpan Farm* (1957), *A New England Girlhood* (1958), *The Pattern of Perfection* (1960), *The Realities of Fiction* (1962), *Black Summer* (1963), *The Life in the Studio* (1969), *Secrets* (1971), *Mary Cassatt* (1975) and *The Night of the Hurricane* (1978).

Hale, Sarah Josepha (1788–1879)
US editor, fiction writer, poet, dramatist and novelist. Best known as the forceful editor of the ▷*American Ladies' Magazine* and, for forty years, of ▷*Godey's Lady's Book*, Hale represented the conservative values of women's separate sphere and the cult of true womanhood. While she endorsed women's education, and reform movements for women and children, her reputation was built solidly on achievement within traditional roles and literary forms. Among her most recognized works are *Poems for Our Children* (1830), which includes her famous rhyme 'Mary Had a Little Lamb'; the novel ▷*Northwood* (1827), and *Sketches of American Character* (1829).
▷*Una, The*

Halfbreed (1973)
▷Maria Campbell's autobiographical chronicle of a Canadian Metis woman's struggle to overcome various obstacles. It addresses Campbell's own alcoholism, drug addiction and prostitution, and paints an unflinching portrait of the pervasive racism and sexism that inhibit the potential of Canada's aboriginal peoples. As the first public engagement with this much-effaced cultural genocide, *Halfbreed* is an extremely important book.

Halil, Rasiah (born 1956)
Singaporean poet. Bilingual in English and Malay, she has an MA in Malay Studies and some of her poems in English and in English translation can be found in the *Anthology of ASEAN Literatures: The Poetry of Singapore* (1985). She is the only Singaporean Malay woman to have published a volume of poetry – *Perbualan: Buku Catatan Seorang Gipsi* (1988) (*Conversations: Notebook of a Gypsy*). She also has a recent collection of short stories *Orang Luar* (1991) (*The Outsider*), whose main themes are alienation and marginalization.

Halimi, Gisèle (born 1927)
French lawyer, born in Tunisia. She was defence attorney for the FLN (Algerian Liberation Front) during the Franco–Algerian war, and co-founder, co-president and legal counsel for Choisir, La Cause des femmes ('The right to choose'), the association which challenged the abortion laws in a test case in 1972. She is the co-author (with ▷Marie Cardinal) of *La Cause des femmes* (1973) (▷*The Right to Choose*, 1977), *Le Lait de l'oranger* (1988) (*Milk of the Orange Tree*), and co-author of *Le Programme commun des femmes* (1978) (*The Common Programme for Women*).

Halkett, Lady Ann (1623–1699)
English memoirist, born Ann Murray. She wrote a memoir of her earlier life in 1677–1678. In 1647 she fell in love with Colonel Joseph Bampfield, a Royalist agent. In 1648 she helped with the plan to aid the escape of the Duke of York (the second son of Charles I), who rewarded her with a pension when he became king. Rumours that Bampfield's wife was still alive disturbed her, but she believed his version of events until 1653, when she discovered conclusively that his wife was still alive. In 1652 she met Sir James Halkett, whom she later married. But before they were married she ran into Bampfield again in London. Her description of their exchange is typical of the engaging way in which the memoir tells the story of her past: 'He [Bampfield] said he desired me only to resolve him one question, which was whether or not I was married to Sir J.H. [Halkett]. I asked why he inquired. He said because if I was not, he would then propose something . . . both for his advantage and mine . . . I said nothing a little while, for I hated lying, and I saw there might be some inconvenience to tell the truth, and (Lord pardon the equivocation) I said, "I am" (out

loud, and secretely said, "not").' She later became a teacher.

▷Cavendish, Margaret; Fanshawe, Lady Ann; Hutchinson, Lucy
Bib: Loftis, John (ed.), *The Memoirs of Anne, Lady Halkett and Ann, Lady Fanshawe.*

Hall, Anna Maria Fielding (1800–1881)
Irish writer. Born in Dublin, she spent most of her life in London. A commercially successful novelist and short story writer, she also wrote for the stage. Progressive in her views about Ireland, she also believed strongly in women's rights. *The Whiteboy*, her pro-Irish, nationalist novel, appeared in 1845.

Hall, Bernadette (born 1945)
New Zealand poet. Hall lives in Christchurch and published in journals there, particularly *Untold*, for some time before publishing a collection, *Heartwood*, in 1989. Her poems are often addressed to particular people and gather around an image or set of images. She often uses formal structures to draw attention to language in her verse.

Hall, Elisa
Guatemalan novelist. Her two novels, *Semilla de mostaza* (1938) (*Mustard Seed*) and *Mostaza* (1939) (*Mustard*), are a historical appraisal of the Spanish conquerors in Guatemala, based on the life of the 17th-century gentleman Don Sancho Alvarez de Asturias. In *Semilla de mostaza*, Don Sancho prepares his departure to the realm of 'Goathemala'. Elisa Hall's aim was to reconstruct the Spanish scene and language of the time, but because of the perfection of her style, she was accused of having found a manuscript of some male ancestor. Several writers defended her, and she wrote *Mostaza* to prove the authenticity of her narrative. The novel is so-called because she compares a small mustard seed with a grown-up man.

Hall, (Marguerite) Radclyffe (1880–1943)
English poet and novelist. The child of a tempestuous marriage, her mother remarried in 1883 and her father died in 1898, leaving Hall financially independent. In 1906 she paid for the publication of her first volume of poetry, '*Twixt Earth and Stars*. Her second volume, *A Sheaf of Verses* (1908), was published shortly after she began living with her lover, Mabel Veronica Batten ('Ladye'), and was the first of her writings to disclose lesbian themes. Subsequent poems continued to present Hall's love for women, frequently, and uncritically, drawing on dominant poetic figures and motifs of femininity. In 1915 she met Una Vincent Troubridge, who soon became her lover and her companion after the death of Batten in 1916.

Hall's first novel, *The Unlit Lamp* (1924), explores the emotional hold of mother on daughter, through the relationship between an elderly woman and the spinster daughter who is unable to capitalize on her one opportunity to escape her obligations. The following novels, *The Forge* (1924) and *A Saturday Life* (1925), are comic portrayals of married life, while the next novel, *Adam's Breed* (1926), a narrative of religious, rather than merely spiritual, awakening, was an outstanding critical success, winning the James Tait, Black Memorial Prize and the Prix Femina. The largely autobiographical ▷ *The Well of Loneliness* (1928) is another coming-to-consciousness narrative, one that marks Hall's first attempt to deal openly with lesbian identity in the novel form. Prosecuted for obscenity, the novel was subsequently suppressed, despite the support of many writers including ▷Virginia Woolf and ▷Vera Brittain. The following novels, *The Master of the House* (1932), a Christian typology, and *The Sixth Beatitude* (1936), whose protagonist is a heterosexual woman, are often seen as Hall's attempt to compensate for the controversy that surrounded the trial of the earlier novel. *Miss Ogilvy Finds Herself* (1934) is a collection of stories written over the previous decade. Una Troubridge published *The Life and Death of Radclyffe Hall* in 1945.
Bib: Baker, M., *Our Three Selves*; Brittain, V., *Radclyffe Hall: A Case of Obscenity?*; Dickson, L., *Radclyffe Hall at the Well of Loneliness*; Francks, C., *Beyond 'The Well of Loneliness': The Fiction of Radclyffe Hall.*

Hall, Sandi
New Zealand writer of futurist fiction. Sandi Hall is one of a number of feminist (often lesbian) futurist writers who have appeared internationally over the last ten years. Her two novels are utopian, radical and about lesbians, and so directly challenge and offer alternatives to conventional heterosexual social models and roles. Hall has led an itinerant life, moving from England as a child to Australia, Africa, New Zealand and elsewhere.

Publications: *The Godmothers* (1983); *The Wingwomen of Hera* (1987).
▷Lesbian writing, New Zealand

Halpern, Marjorie Stela Agosin ▷Agosin, Marjorie

Hamilton, Cicely (1872–1952)
English novelist, dramatist and suffragist. Educated in England and Germany, Hamilton returned to England, and became a theatre actress and dramatist. Her most successful play was *Diana of Dobson's* (1908), a comedy that also contains a sharp commentary on the drudgeries of working women's lives. She first became involved with the ▷suffrage campaign in 1907, and was a founder-member of the Women Writers' Suffrage League and the Actresses' Franchise League in 1908, working closely with the actress and dramatist ▷Elizabeth Robins and with Christopher St John (Christabel Marshall), co-author of Hamilton's suffrage play *How the Vote Was Won* (1909). Her most influential work, the polemic *Marriage as a Trade* (1909), expounds the

view that women become wives not from choice but economic necessity, and mounts a forceful argument for women's autonomy. Hamilton also explored these issues in her plays *Just to Get Married* and *The Cutting of the Knot* (published as a novel entitled *A Matter of Money* in 1916).

During World War I Hamilton worked as an administrator in a French military hospital, and helped organize wartime entertainment. Her book *Senlis* (1917) described the destruction of the French town and its civilian population by the German Army. The first of her war novels, *William – An Englishman*, won the Femina Vie Heureuse prize in 1919. Here Hamilton explores the moral dilemmas with which war confronts individuals, particularly the issues of pacifism and of the importance of the suffrage movement within the context of the injustices of war. The novel *Theodore Savage* (1922) portrays a war-torn society reverting to savage survivalism.

Hamilton returned to feminist activism in the 1920s as a journalist, commentator and member of a number of organisations working for women's rights, including the right to contraception and abortion. She also continued to write plays and novels and, in the 1930s and 1940s, political writings about war and democracy. Her treatise *Lament for Democracy* was published in 1940. Hamilton's autobiography is *Life Errant* (1935).

▷Feminist publishing (Britain)

Hamilton, Gail ▷Dodge, Mary Abigail

Hamilton, Virginia (born 1936)
US novelist and biographer. Hamilton grew up on the farm in Yellow Springs, Ohio, that her grandfather purchased after escaping from slavery. Her children's fiction focuses on the survival of the African-American in the US. Hamilton weaves elements of traditional African folklore and mythology into the realistic social contexts of her novels. In *Zeely* (1967) a girl learns to look at daily life realistically without sacrificing her imagination, and in *The Planet of Junior Brown* (1971) two friends survive by living for each other. In *M.C. Higgins, The Great* (1974) Higgins decides to fight the environmental menace threatening to destroy his family. ▷*Sweet Whispers, Brother Rush* (1982) has a ghost who helps Tree to survive by revealing the painful secrets of her family's past. Hamilton creates African-American characters who foster feelings of self-worth.

Other work includes: *The House of Dies Drear* (1968), *W.E.B. DuBois: A Biography* (1972), *Tales of Jahdu, Paul Robeson: The Life and Times of a Free Black Man* (1974), *Justice and Her Brothers* (1978), *The Magical Adventures of Pretty Pearl* (1983), *Dustland* (1980), *The Gathering* (1981), *Willie Bea and the Time the Martians Landed* (1983) and *A Little Love* (1985).

Han Aili (born 1937)
Chinese writer. Born in Japanese-occupied Shanghai, Han graduated from Peking University and was assigned to work at the North China

Kunqu (a form of classical Chinese opera) Theatre Company, where she had written scripts for Kunqu. Han is best-known for her collection of short stories, *Swept Away* (1979), based on her observations of the cruelties of the 'cultural revolution' (1966–1976).

Handel-Mazzetti, Enrica von (1871–1955)
Austrian writer of Catholic historical novels, who used the pseudonym Marien Kind. She was brought up carefully by her mother, the Protestant widow of a Catholic officer, and the two women lived together until her mother's death in 1901. Her first success came with the publication of *Meinrad Helmpergers denkwürdiges Jahr* (1900) (*Meinrad Helmperger's Memorable Year*), followed by the powerful historical novel, *Jesse und Maria* (1906). Two main themes characterize these and all her subsequent writings: the confrontation between Catholicism and Protestantism in a historical setting, and the role of women, suffering but powerful, as ultimate moral arbiters. Her work was received ambivalently, even in Catholic circles. Welcomed for upholding the Catholic spirit, it was also criticized for its obsession with conflict and suffering, and for its graphic descriptions of cruelties.

▷Ebner-Eschenbach, Marie von

Handfasted: A Romance (1984)
Utopian novel by Australian author ▷Catherine Helen Spence (1825–1910). *Handfasted* was rejected for publication during Spence's lifetime, the publishers fearing that it 'was calculated to loosen the marriage tie – it was too socialistic, and consequently dangerous', but was published by Penguin in 1984. It purports to be the journal of Marguerite Keith, the founder of the country of Columba, where 'handfasting', trial marriages of a year and a day, are the custom, and illegitimacy has no stigma. Unwanted children of parents who decide not to marry become the administrative élite of Columba, for they are the only ones taught to read and write. The custom of 'handfasting' undermines the 19th-century ideals of chastity, monogamy, and legitimacy which is necessary for inheritance through the patriarchal line. Columba is obviously a feminist paradise.

Handful of Holesome (though homelie) Hearbs, A (1584)
Book of private devotions by Anne Wheathill. Almost nothing is known about the author of this work except her status as a gentlewoman of the middle class. In her ▷preface she states that her work was composed 'in the state of [her] virginitie or maidenhood', and she apologizes for having collected her ▷prayers 'without the counsell or helpe of anie'. Although her work is addressed to women, she obviously fears the censure of men. Wheathill's book contains forty-nine prayers for daily use, as well as on various other occasions. It belongs to the tradition of Reformist collections of

private devotions. Most of her prayers are derived from scripture, especially the Psalms.

▷Protestant Reformation

Handful of Rice, A (1966)

A novel by Indian writer ▷Kamala Markandaya. Set in Madras, this tells of the gradual erosion of a village boy's integrity by the wealth and glamour promised in the city. The hero, Ravishankar, having left his poverty-stricken village, finds that his meagre education has put him above working with his hands, but has not qualified him sufficiently to compete for clerkships with the better-educated city boys. If he could accept the humble but honest existence of a tailor, then he and his marriage would survive, but the promise of illicit wealth eats away at his capacity for work, and he sinks into the apathy and poverty that had so irritated him in his home village.

Handmaid's Tale, The (1985)

▷Margaret Atwood's terrifying dystopic novel about a possible future where women are valued only for their ability to reproduce. In the regressive theocracy of the Republic of Gilead, all the freedoms that women have gained are revoked. This is the story of one Handmaid, Offred, who cannot erase the past from her memory, and who reads for us the bizarre censorship of a world where language is forbidden to all but the male élite. Atwood pushes to their ultimate conclusion censorship and essentialism, resulting in a mordant and corrosive parable. She includes in her parodic dissection not only feminism and fundamentalist religions, but the inability of academia to read even a squarely visible text. This is a brilliant, devastating novel that underscores the power of language and the potential misuse of censorship.

Handzová, Viera (born 1931)

Slovak prose writer and translator. Handzová read Slovak and Russian at Bratislava University, and then worked as an editor and freelance writer. Her first collection of short stories, Madlenka, was published in 1957. Her best books are the collection of short stories Kamaráti do zlého počasia (1977) (Friends for Bad Weather) and the novels Zrieknite sa prvej lásky (1965) (Renounce Your First Love) and Lebo sme vedeli, čo činíme (1969) (Because We Knew What We Were Doing).

Handzová depicts the relationships of ordinary people, especially women. Her female characters are mature, intelligent and independent, but often disillusioned and sceptical. The dominant theme of her work is the confrontation between an ideal (childhood, youth) and the reality of life for contemporary women. Unfortunately, Handzová tends towards the stereotypical. In her attempt to defend traditional moral values she often falls into depicting contrived, melodramatic, sentimentalized situations.

Hang Ying (born 1944)

Chinese writer of short stories and plays. Hang was first trained as a stage designer. In her writing she specializes in the Chinese stereotype of the feminine ideal, which combines socialist principles with traditional virtues. The trilogy, The Oriental Woman (1985), The Red Ribbons and If There Were No Fourth Wall, is typical of her style. The heroine in the first of the series forgives her husband's philandering and cares for his illegitimate child. The erring husband conveniently dies while his mistress, the 'fallen woman', drags out her days in misery.

Bib: Translation of 'The Saleswoman' in Prize-Winning Stories from China 1980–81 (1985).

Hanke, Henriette (1785–1862)

German novelist. The third wife of the Protestant pastor Gottfried Hanke, she wrote lively tales about contemporary family life. They became so popular that, after her husband's death, she was able to support all five of his children by her writing. Her work comprises 126 volumes of novels and stories.

Hanrahan, Barbara (born 1939)

Australian artist, novelist, and short story writer. Hanrahan was educated at Adelaide Teachers' College, the South Australian School of Arts and the Central School of Art, London. Her paintings and prints have been exhibited throughout Australia and in London and Florence, and she is represented in the Australian National Gallery and most Australian state galleries. She lives with the sculptor Jo Steele. Hanrahan began writing in 1968 with the fictionalized autobiography The Scent of Eucalyptus (1973). Her novels are notable for their melding of realism, fantasy and the grotesque. Against a nostalgic and realistic setting, usually Adelaide and its environs, Hanrahan portrays a cosmic struggle between good (usually represented by an innocent child) and evil (depraved and sexually predatory adults). Her novels include Seagreen (1974), The Albatross Muff (1977), Where the Queens all Strayed (1978), ▷The Peach Groves (1979), The Frangipani Gardens (1980), Dove (1982), Kewpie Doll (1984), Annie Magdalene (1985), A Chelsea Girl (1988) and Flawless Jade (1989). Dream People (1987) is her first book of short stories.

▷Short story (Australia); Coming Out from Under; Eight Voices of the Eighties

Hansberry, Lorraine (1930–1965)

US dramatist, journalist and essayist. Hansberry was born in Chicago, Illinois to middle-class African-American parents. She studied at the University of Wisconsin, Roosevelt College, and the School of Art Institute of Chicago. In 1950 she worked for Freedom, a radical African-American newspaper, in New York City, which brought her into contact with black intellectuals such as Paul Robeson, Langston Hughes and W.E.B. DuBois. She continued to write and speak on both race and gender issues, for example, her speech 'In Defense of the Equality of Men', which is published in *The Norton Anthology of Literature by Women*, edited by ▷Sandra M. Gilbert and ▷Susan Gubar.

With *A Raisin in the Sun* (1959), Hansberry became the first African-American woman to have a play produced on Broadway, and the first black dramatist ever to win the New York Drama Critics Circle Play of the Year Award. The play celebrates the African-American struggle for freedom and equality. Racism has consigned the Younger family to life in the ghetto until the death of the family patriarch offers an opportunity for the family to overcome their oppression. The mother uses his legacy to buy a house in an Anglo-American neighbourhood. The family confront Anglo-American racism with pride and dignity when they are offered money to stay out. The play addresses issues of racism and the tension between racial assimilation and separatism. Her play *The Sign in Sidney Brustein's Window* (1964) focuses on a Jewish intellectual, and challenges assumptions about appropriate subjects for African-American writers.

Other works include: *The Movement: Documentary of a Struggle for Equality* (1964), *To Be Young, Gifted and Black: Lorraine Hansberry in Her Own Words* (1969), and *Les Blancs: The Collected Last Plays of Lorraine Hansberry* (1972).
Bib: Bond, Jean Caron (ed.), *Lorraine Hansberry: Art of Thunder, Vision of Light*, a special issue of *Freedomways* magazine.

Hanson, Elizabeth Meader (1684–1737)

North American spiritual autobiographer. What is known of her life-story begins in 1724 when she was taken captive at her New Hampshire home by French and Native American marauders. A victim of the political disputes between the English and French, she is one of the few known Quaker authors of an early North American ▷captivity narrative. As the title of her narrative attests (▷ *God's Mercy Surmounting Man's Cruelty*), her record is as much of her faith in God as of her experiences.

Happiness (1897)

Russian novel by ▷Tat'iana Shchépkina–Kupérnik. *Happiness* is interesting both in terms of Shchépkina-Kupérnik's career and as a reflection of the ferment of the 1890s (a second edition was published in 1903).

While still a gymnasium student, Marusia Nezvatseva marries one of her teachers. The depiction of this period resembles other women writers' stories about life in girls' secondary schools (▷Krestóvskaia, ▷Lukhamánova, ▷Chárskaia). As the marriage turns sour, Marusia meets a female mentor (as in ▷Verbítskaia's ▷ *Discord*, in which the heroine acts as a mentor to a younger girl). Liudmila, a young widow described as aesthetic, well-educated, and bold, advises Marusia that happiness should consist of more than love for just one person, and describes the exciting possibilities for women in ▷Moscow or ▷St Petersburg. Marusia moves to the city and becomes a piano student. Tempted by a false female mentor, Patti, who preaches a cult of sensuality influenced by the French Decadents, she returns briefly to her husband before accepting Liudmila's teachings and a life devoted to art. At the end, Marusia, happily pregnant, informs her husband of her plans for a divorce.

Happiness is finally defined in terms of exclusively female relations, motherhood and art. The influence of Tolstoy is palpable, not only in the emphasis on women and motherhood and the hostility towards French ▷modernism, but also in novelistic devices: the protagonist who goes astray, lured by superficial beauty and sensuality; the innocent who sees the absurdity of a highly conventional art form.

Harada Yasuko (born 1928)

Japanese novelist. Her novels often portray women with too keen a sensibility, founded on her own experience of a weak youth and the ruin of her parents' home. *An Elegy* (1956), which pictures sorrowful love between an architect, his wife and a fascinating girl, was a dominant influence for some years after its publication. Her other main works are *Yameru Oka* and *Kita no Hayashi*.

Hara'ir

Arabic term, plural of *hurra*, 'a free woman', both adjective and noun. The poetry of *hara'ir* in the golden age of the Abbasids was mostly written by women of the royal family. They were competent in poetry, but did not have the opportunity of mixing with other poets enjoyed by the ▷*jawari* (concubines). Their poetry was personal, speaking of love often suppressed or unrequited. The name of the beloved could not be mentioned (he was in some cases an inferior, a servant in the household), and the stricken poet had to use a female name. 'Ulaya-bint al-Mahdi, Harun al-Rashid's sister is the best-known of this class of poets.

In more general usage the word *hurra* means a woman who is proud, chaste and strong in character. As an Arabic saying goes: 'A *hurra* would die rather than eat with her thighs' (in other versions breasts).

In contemporary discourse, *hurra* is used in arguments for female emancipation, particularly against ▷*hijab* (the veil): a free woman does not need the veil to guard her honour/chastity.

Harbou, Thea von (1888–1954)

German novelist. A poet turned actress, she married the film director Fritz Lang (1890–1976) in 1921, and subsequently supplied him with all his film scripts. She also worked with Carl Dreyer (1889–1968), F.W. Murnau (1889–1931) and von Gerlach. She wrote many gripping adventure stories, though she preferred action and sentimental cliché to psychological insight.

Hardwick, Elizabeth (born 1916)

US novelist and essayist. A native of Lexington, Kentucky, Hardwick graduated in 1939 with a Master's degree from the University of Kentucky and moved to New York. From 1949 to 1972 she was married to poet Robert Lowell. Hardwick began her successful career as a social and literary critic with liberal sentiments at the *Partisan Review*. In 1963 she co-founded *The New York Review of Books*, a leading intellectual and controversial journal. The essays she contributed on women in literature revise mistaken notions of women's lives as essentially tragic. Her novels, *The Ghostly Lover* (1945) and *Sleepless Nights* (1979), focus on women who re-invent their lives.

Other works include: *The Simple Truth* (1955), *A View of My Own: Essays in Literature and Society* (1962), *Seduction and Betrayal: Women in Literature* (1974), and eighteen volumes of *Rediscovered Fiction by American Women* (1977), which Hardwick edited.

Harem, harim

Originally *haram*, an Arabic word for 'sanctuary, a sacred place to be protected against invaders or intruders', it came to mean the separate quarters for women in Moslem households (*anderun* in Persian). In most cases it simply referred to the wife or wives of a man, or collectively to the womenfolk of the house. Most houses had a *mandara*: a room or two on the ground floor near the entrance to the house, where male guests were received.

In contemporary usage, *harim* has come to mean: (a) women in a subordinate position, dependent on and restricted by male relatives; (b) women who use their sexuality to manipulate men and can think of themselves only as sexual objects; (c) the compartments in a tram or train set aside for women, rather like the 'ladies' room' in a London railway station.
Bib: Sha'arawi, Huda, *Harem Years: The Memoirs of an Egyptian Feminist*, translated and edited by Margot Badran; Tuqan, Fadwa, *Mountainous Journey*, translated by Olive Kenny.

Harford, Lesbia (1881–1927)

Australian poet and novelist. Harford graduated in Arts and Law from the University of Melbourne in 1916, and worked as an art teacher, a clerk, and in a clothing factory to better understand the conditions for women workers. Her poems were collected by ▷Nettie Palmer, published posthumously as *Poems* (1941), and republished as *The Poems of Lesbia Harford* (ed. ▷Drusilla Modjeska and Marjorie Pizer, 1985). A novel, *The Invaluable Mystery*, was published in 1987.

Harjo, Joy (born 1951)

US poet and screenwriter. Born in Tulsa, Oklahoma, Harjo is of the Creek (Muscogee) tribe of ▷Native Americans. After attending the Institute of American Indian Arts, she graduated from the University of New Mexico in 1976. She earned a Master of Fine Arts degree from the

Joy Harjo

Iowa Writers' Workshop in 1978. Since then she has taught at the University of Colorado and at the University of Arizona. Harjo's poetry is concerned with spiritual as well as social connections. It expresses her anger at the duality of modern life, and explores worlds inside which this polarity does not exist, enabling her to emphasize the spirituality of the female body. Harjo seeks to reconcile dualities into a harmonious, balanced whole. Her 1983 volume *She Had Some Horses* celebrates the spiritual survival of Native American women, proclaiming the renunciation of fear. This was followed by *Secrets from the Center of the World* (1989) and *In Mad Love and War* (1990). Harjo's work mixes Native American myth with contemporary settings and events, for example the political murder of the American Indian Movement activist, Anna Mae Acquash, to forge an authoritative and politically committed poetics.

Other works include: *The Last Song* and *What Moon Drove Me To This?*.

Harlem Renaissance

The influx of people into northern industrial centres of the US, such as Pittsburgh, Chicago and Harlem, in the period following World War I accentuated racial and social tension. Gradually Harlem emerged from the riots and unrest as a symbol for the struggle of African-Americans. During the 1920s the creativity of African-Americans was celebrated in literature and music, for which Harlem became a focal point. The work of Harlemites, writers and poets such as ▷Alice Dunbar Nelson, Langston Hughes, Claude McKay, ▷Jessie Fauset, ▷Angelina Grimké, Countee Cullen, Jean Toomer, Sterling Brown, Mary White Ovington and ▷Zora Neale Hurston, was influential in the

US and internationally, for instance, upon African and West Indian students in Paris who later initiated the ▷*Négritude* movement.

Although women were central within the Harlem Renaissance, the names which define the movement are usually male. This is in part because the writers frequently depended on a patronage system which tended to exclude women. Patrons such as Alain Leroy Locke, who fostered the work of Langston Hughes, were overtly misogynist. The bar culture which was so much a part of the Renaissance also presented difficulties for women because it was incompatible with ideals of respectable femininity. Racist assumptions about black women's loose sexuality made the social codes particularly tricky for the women artists of the movement.

Women who played a central role in the Harlem Renaissance include Alice Dunbar-Nelson, Angelina Grimké, the Washington-DC-based writer ▷Georgia Douglas Johnson, Jessie Fauset, ▷Nella Larsen, ▷Gwendolyn Bennett, Zora Neale Hurston, Helene Johnson, Ethel Ray Nance, Regina Anderson, Effie Lee Newsome, Gladys Mae Casely Hayford and Anne Spencer. These women contributed to the outpouring of poetry, fiction, plays and essays, but also held intellectual evenings, promoted and supported the work of their contemporaries, and worked as editors; for example, Jessie Fauset was literary editor for *The Crisis*, and Ethel Ray Nance secretary at *Opportunity*.

Bib. Hull, Gloria T., *Color, Sex and Poetry: Three Women Poets of the Harlem Renaissance*.

Harlequin romances

Cheaply-priced North American paperbacks which follow the formulaic demands of the ▷romantic narrative. Harlequin insists that the narratives are written in 'good taste' (that is, with no sexually explicit material) and that they end 'happily', usually in marriage. The protagonists of the stories are nearly always white, Western and exclusively heterosexual women. Harlequin began reprinting romances for the mass market in 1949. Harlequin's British counterpart is Mills and Boon. Equally popular in North America and Britain, the romances were strongly criticized by feminists in the 1970s for shoring up patriarchal attitudes. ▷Germaine Greer takes this line in *The Female Eunuch* (1970). More recently, ▷Tania Modleski and ▷Janice Radway have suggested that it is possible to read popular romances against the grain, and to see them as symptomatic of women's dissatisfaction with their lives under partriarchy.

Harley, Lady Brilliana (c 1600–1643)

English letter-writer and Puritan, called Brilliana after Brill, her birthplace in Holland. The third wife of Sir Robert Harley, she lived at Brampton Castle in Herefordshire. She wrote to her husband from 1625 onwards, and (affectionately) to her eldest son from 1638 onwards, when he went to study at Oxford. She was also famous for defending Brampton Castle against siege by Royalists in 1643 during the English Civil War (1642–1646, and 1648–1651), a task which she saw as given by God. A contemporary described her as full of 'religion, resolution, wisdom and warlike policy'.

▷Cavendish, Margaret; Hutchinson, Lucy; Osborne, Dorothy
Bib: Eales, Jacqueline, *The Harleys of Brampton Bryan and the Outbreak of the English Civil War.*

Harper, Frances E.W. (1825–1911)

US poet, novelist, and advocate of women's rights and the abolition of slavery. A well-known lecturer for the abolitionist cause, the first African-American woman to publish a novel, and a popular poet, Harper also probably published more books than any other African-American woman of her century. These include: *Forest Leaves* (c 1845), *Poems on Miscellaneous Subjects* (1854), *Moses* (1869), *Sketches of Southern Life* (1872), ▷*Iola Leroy* (1892) and *The Martyr of Alabama and Other Poems* (c 1894). She focused on black women and on education, and wrote as she spoke to lecture audiences – with a passionate urging for a better life.

Harper's Bazar (1867–present)

US women's magazine. It began publication as a weekly in 1867 and became a monthly in 1901. Its name was changed to *Harpers Bazaar* in 1929. Designed as a complement to *Harper's Weekly* and ▷*Harper's Monthly Magazine*, the *Bazar* was subtitled 'A Repository of Fashion, Pleasure, and Instruction'. Modelled on the Berlin *Der Bazar*, from which it took its fashion plates, the US magazine concentrated on vogues in clothing, domestic decoration and home issues – while printing and paying well for choice US and British non-fiction and fiction. Among its contributors were ▷Mary E. Wilkins Freeman and ▷Mary Abigail Dodge.

Harper's Monthly Magazine (1850–present)

US magazine, based in New York, and established by Harper & Brothers, the leading national US publisher of the mid-19th century. The Harpers developed the *Monthly* as a commercial venture to promote authors and readership. Initially publishing a large amount of British literature, the *Monthly* gradually became a major market for US writers, including ▷Elizabeth Stuart Phelps (Ward), ▷Caroline Chesebro' and ▷Sarah Orne Jewett. Its book reviews were influential, as were its editorial essays on new literature.

Harp in the South, The (1948)

Australian novel by ▷Ruth Park. *The Harp in the South* won the 1946 *Sydney Morning Herald* novel competition and was a bestseller in Australia and overseas. It is a sensitive account of the hardships of a poverty-stricken Irish-Australian family, the Darcys, and their neighbours in the slums of Surry Hills in Sydney. The novel focuses on the eldest daughter, Roie, her love affair with the

Jewish Tommy Mendel, and finally her pregnancy and miscarriage after being beaten up in a drunken brawl. The story of the Darcys is continued in Ruth Park's next novel, *Poor Man's Orange* (1949).

Harp-Weaver and Other Poems, The (1923)

US poetry. ▷Edna St Vincent Millay received the Pulitzer Prize for this collection. The title poem is representative of Millay's use of a child's voice and conveys a child's sense of wonder and belief in magic, emphasizing the cultural legacy that mothers pass on to their children. 'Oh, Oh, you will be sorry for that word' is indicative of Millay's rebellion against conventions that inhibit women's freedom. As in 'I, being born a woman and distressed', Millay proclaims women's sexual liberation. She points to the inevitable loss of romantic love in 'The Betrothal' and 'Sonnets from an Ungrafted Tree'. In 'Euclid alone has looked on Beauty bare' nature's beauty provides comfort against death. Millay's poetry affirms life.

Harriet, The Spy (1964)

US novel. In ▷Louise Fitzhugh's controversial children's books, Harriet Welsch spies on her neighbours. Without compassion or respect she records the weaknesses she observes in others, and her brutal honesty reveals her own rigidity and lack of humility. Nevertheless, she chooses to learn to live with who she is; she would rather be freakish and friendless than be charitable and hypocritical. Through the character of Harriet Fitzhugh explores issues of individuality and conformity, self-indulgence and social acts.

Harris, Christie (born 1907)

Canadian children's writer, born Christie Irwin in Newark, New Jersey, who emigrated with her parents to Canada in 1908. She grew up in a British Columbia log cabin, attended the University of British Columbia, and sold her first stories in the 1920s. She taught at school and did freelance work for the Canadian Broadcasting Corporation while raising her five children (she married Thomas Harris in 1932). At the age of fifty she began writing books for children and young adults, and has since then published more than twenty books, including *Once Upon a Totem* (1963), *Raven's Cry* (1966), *Mystery at the Edge of Two Worlds* (1978), *The Trouble with Princesses* (1980) and *The Trouble with Adventures* (1982). Her stories range from historical fiction and Native Canadian legends retold for the modern reader to contemporary novels for young adults. She is perhaps most noted for her series of books on 'Mouse Woman' (*Mouse Woman and the Vanished Princesses*, 1976; *Mouse Woman and the Mischief-Makers*, 1977, and *Mouse Woman and the Muddleheads*, 1979), a supernatural character who comes out of the mythology of the Northwest Coastal Indians. Her writing employs Native Canadian folklore and legends a great deal, but with unusual sensitivity and care; she does not confine her research to historic and anthropological texts, but has spent much time with aboriginal people. Her humorous ▷realism, combined with a wealth of detail and history, have earned Harris's writing a revered place within children's literature. She lives in Vancouver.

Harris, Claire (born 1937)

Trinidad-born poet who emigrated to Canada in 1966, having studied at St Joseph's Convent, Port of Spain, University College, Dublin, and the University of Nigeria in Lagos. Her first book of poetry was called *Translation into Fiction* (1984). *Fables from the Women's Quarters* (also 1984) won the Canada and Caribbean Area Commonwealth Prize for Poetry. *Travelling to find a Remedy* appeared in 1986, and *The Conception of Winter* in 1989. Harris's work deals with prisons and metamorphoses in the lives of women; she is also acutely aware of the position of the black writer in Canada. She has said that 'to reclaim sensibility black women have to discover/define two aspects of the self: the authentic female self and the authentic black self' which have been separated by black history and experience in the Americas. Harris lives in Calgary, Alberta, where she is a schoolteacher.
Bib: Neuman, S. and Kamboureli, S. (eds), ▷*A Mazing Space*.

Harrison, Constance Cary (1843–1920)

US writer of essays, fiction, satire and autobiography. A North American who later moved to Britain, Harrison's best and most appreciated work satirizes North Americans in Europe, from *The Anglomaniacs* (1890) to *Good Americans* (1898). Her autobiography is *Recollections Grave and Gay* (1911).

Harrison, Susie Frances (1859–1935)

Canadian poet, short story writer and musician, born Susie Riley in Toronto, and educated there and in Montreal. She married a professional musician, and became known as a pianist, vocalist, and expert on old French-Canadian folksongs. Under the pseudonym Seranus she wrote stories which depicted particular Canadian characteristics and settings, published as *Crowded Out! and Other Sketches* (1886). Her best-known poetry collection, *Pine, Rose, and Fleur de Lis* (1891), includes a monody on ▷Isabella Valancy Crawford, but concentrates on the villanelle form, although in her content Harrison seeks to express an authentic Canadian representation.

Harrower, Elizabeth (born 1928)

Australian novelist. Harrower was born in Sydney, grew up in industrial Newcastle, Australia, worked as a clerk, and studied psychology before becoming a writer. She spent the years from 1951 to 1959 in London, then worked for the Australian Broadcasting Commission in Sydney, for a publishing firm and as a reviewer for the *Sydney Morning Herald*. Harrower's four novels, *Down in the City* (1957), *The Long Prospect* (1958), *The Catherine Wheel* (1960) and ▷*The Watch*

Tower (1966), are all concerned with psychological struggle, and particularly with women and children caught up in power struggles within the family. They are all novels of extraordinary intensity and force.

▷ *Gender, Politics and Fiction*

Hart, Julia Catherine (1796–1867)

Born Julia Beckwith in Fredericton, New Brunswick, Canada, she is the author of the first novel published in British North America to be written by a person born there. She moved from Fredericton to Kingston, then Upper Canada, in 1820, married George Henry Hart soon after, and ran a boarding school for girls. *St Ursula's Convent; or, The Nun of Canada* appeared in 1824; as might be expected from its title, the novel is a typically sentimental and rather contrived account of Quebec religious and seigneurial life, filled with melodrama and mistaken identity. *Tonnewonte; or The Adopted Son of America*, which appeared after the Harts moved to the United States in 1824, is a patriotic ▷ romance as well, comparing North American democracy to Napoleonic chaos. In 1831 they returned to Fredericton, where Hart wrote short fiction for the local papers and worked on *Edith; or, the Doom*, an unpublished novel. Very much a product of her colonial time and place, she is nevertheless important for her recognition of landscape and history as intrinsic elements of fiction as a cultural marker.

Hartigan, Anne Le Marquand (born 1931)

Irish writer and visual artist, born in England of an Irish mother and a Jersey father. Hartigan grew up in England, and trained there as a painter. She settled in Ireland in 1962, and began writing while raising her six children. Her paintings and batik works have been exhibited in Ireland and abroad, and have won several awards. She is a poet as well as a dramatist and fiction writer, and her work has appeared in numerous anthologies. Both of her plays, *Beds* (1982) and *La Corbière* (1989), were performed at the Dublin Theatre Festival. Her long narrative poem, 'Now is a Moveable Feast', was broadcast on Irish national radio and published in 1991. She has published two collections of poetry, *Long Tongue* (1982) and *Return Single* (1986). Her work is both sensuous and direct, with a strong sense of the personal and historical forces which shape women's lives.

Hartlaub, Geno (born 1915)

German novelist. Myth, fantasy and psychological analyses characterized her early novels, *Noch im Traum* (1943) (*Still Dreaming*) and *Anselm, der Lehrling* (1947) (*Anselm, the Apprentice*). Later works, such as the novella, *Der Mond hat Durst* (1963) (*The Moon is Thirsty*), are concerned with gender issues. More recent novels, such as *Lokaltermin Feenreich* (1972) (*Fairyland in Local Terms*), have a realistic setting, and deal with the theme of Nazism and its links with contemporary German society.

Harvest, The (1928)

Translation of *Mors tua* (1926) by ▷ Matilde Serao. A strongly anti-war novel, it was widely believed to have cost its author the Nobel Prize of that year because of Mussolini's antagonism to its message. The novel is set in World War I, and is unusual for the almost exclusively female perspective it adopts on the war. This is a tale of maternal anguish, of families destroyed, and ultimately of wasted lives.

Harwood, Gwen (born 1920)

Gwen Harwood

Australian poet. Harwood also wrote under the names of Francis Geyer, Walter Lehmann, T.F. Kline and Miriam Stone. Harwood studied music and was organist at All Saints' Church in Brisbane. She married William Harwood in 1945 and moved to Tasmania, where she began to write poetry in her late thirties. Harwood is one of the most powerful, thoughtful and intellectual of Australian women poets, and her intense lyrics often reflect personal experience, such as the dissatisfaction with the lack of fulfilment within a sexual relationship or in motherhood. At the same time the poems are intensely reflective and often philosophically complex (their dependence upon the philosophy of Wittgenstein has been noted by Harwood herself, as well as by the critics). She has written librettos for Larry Sitski's operas, and has written for other prominent composers. Her literary awards include the *Meanjin* Poetry Prize for 1958 and 1959, the Robert Frost Award for 1977 and the Patrick White Literary Award for 1978. Volumes of poetry include *Poems* (1963), *Poems: Volume 2* (1968), *Selected Poems* (1975), *The Lion's Bride* (1981) and *Bone Scan* (1988). A volume of her letters, *Blessed City*, edited by Alison Hoddinott, was published in 1990.

▷ Letters (Australia); *Poetry and Gender*

Ha'Sefer Ha'shlishi (1969) (The Third Book)
Book of verse by Israeli poet ▷Dalia Ravikovitch.
Already established as one of Israel's leading
writers, Ravikovitch considered *Ha'Sefer
Ha'shlishi*, her third book, to be her best. Critics
have praised its versatility. In addition to the use
of strong imagery and myth, which dominates her
earlier books, Ravikovitch here introduces
conversational verse. What seem to be occasional
monologues become forceful expressions,
intensifying the deep sense of loss which
permeated her poetry.

Hashim, Khalidah (born 1945)
Malay popular fiction writer. Her writing is less
bleak than ▷Salmi Manja's because her women
characters are the products of the Malayan post-
Independence socio-political environment: better-
educated, more self-assertive, and thus less
constrained by circumstances. In *Badai Semalam*
(1968) (*Yesterday's Tempest*), her most highly
regarded work, Mazni dutifully accepts her
parents' match for her, but studies part-time after
her marriage, and later suffers her husband's
philandering. She perseveres with her medical
studies, and when her husband is killed in an
accident, is able confidently to embark on her own
career.

However, Hashim's themes are wider, focusing
as well on Malay poverty, the side-effects of
modernization on Malay individuals and society,
and the qualities needed for progress. Thus in
Pelangi Pagi (1971) (*Morning Rainbow*), a teenage
girl, Norani, plays truant frequently, mixing with
hippie, drug-taking drop-outs. Her worried
parents seek her teacher's help only to have her
fall in love with him, and when he marries, Norani
responds badly and would have failed her exams
but for the teacher's stratagems which challenge
her to pass, which she does. Her award-winning
novel, *Merpati Putih Terbang Lagi* (1972) (*The
White Dove Flies Again*), translated into English by
Harry Aveling (1985), is also about the will to
improve. A diligent, ambitious youth establishes
his own business. His enterprise galvanizes the
other villagers to similar effort, and puts to shame
his civil servant brother and father, who represent
backward conservatism. He is rewarded for his
progressiveness by being nominated as a candidate
in the elections.

Among her other novels are: *Jalan Ke Kubur*
(1969) (*Road to the Cemetery*); *Belum Masanya*
(1976) (*It's Not Time Yet*); *Di Tengah Kabus* (1980)
(*In the Midst of Mist*); *Mira Edora* (1984); *Bila dan
Di Mana* (1981) (*When and Where*), and *Bujang
Kota* (1985). A religious teacher, then a journalist
with Malay newspapers, she is also known for her
short stories, many of which, like 'Aku Anak
Menteri' (1980) ('I, the Minister's Child') have
won her the *Hadiah Sastera* (National Literature
Prize) many times.

Hassan, Zurinah
Malay poet. Her poetry tends to be didactic; she
herself has noted, for instance, that her 'earlier

poems [those written in the early 1960s] have
social themes, especially those concerning
peasants and fishermen. At the time, I was deeply
interested in being a social critic.' Her volumes
Sesayup Jalan (1974) (*Desolate Road*) and *Di Sini
Tiada Perhentian* (1977) (*No Waiting Place Here*)
trace her progress towards a more private and
lyrical emphasis.

English translations of her poems may be found
in *Selections of Contemporary Malaysian Poetry*
(1978) and *Modern Malaysian Poetry* (1980). She
deservedly has the largest selection of poems in
the latter, two of which, 'We Must Speak After
Silent So Long' and 'Greetings from a Woman in
Prison' illustrate her capacity for fusing public and
personal concerns: 'she wants to speak/but has no
voice/for the words of a woman/endanger herself
. . . together with her sisters/in their march
towards death/for fear has long/killed them.' She
is remarkable, too, for her frank love lyrics and
exploration of personal problems. As one critic
has remarked, 'Although Malaysian literature does
not discriminate against women poets . . . because
of certain attitudes of propriety and feminity, the
really vocal individual woman poet is a rare
person.'

Hatherly, Ana Maria (born 1929)
Portuguese poet, prose writer and critic. Born in
Oporto, she studied music in Portugal, France
and Germany. In 1958 she published her first
collection of poems, *Um Ritmo Perdido* (*A Lost
Rhythm*), and since then she has written over a
dozen volumes. In the 1960s she participated in
Poesia Experimental – an avant-garde group
interested in the relationship between written
verse and graphic art. In 1981 she published *Po.
Ex.*, which contains the principal theoretical
writings and other documents of this movement.
Her *tisanas* (short prose pieces) were recently
compiled in *A Cidade das Palavras* (1988) (*The City
of Words*). Hatherly has described these short
narratives as fables, anti-fables, fairy tales and
subverted or reinterpreted myths. Currently she is
a lecturer in the Portuguese department at the
New University of Lisbon.
Bib: *Longman Anthology of World Literature by
Women*, p. 787.

Hauková, Jiřina (born 1919)
Surrealist poet from Moravia, Czechoslovakia. For
most of the 1970s and 1980s her work was
banned. Her first collection, *Přísluní* (1943)
(*Perihelion*) is predominantly verse about nature,
though the last section contains some love poetry.
All that is remarkable about *Přísluní* is the
gentleness of the phrasings and imagery. The
best-known of her collections, *Země nikoho* (1970)
(*No Man's Land*), concerns history, history-
consciousness and identity. Echoes of the Czech
poet Halas and of 'concrete poetry' are palpable,
but Hauková attempts to go beyond Halas, British
poet T.S. Eliot (1888–1965) and North American
poet e.e. cummings (1894–1962). She tries to say
the unsaid, and displays a mystical theory that the

primary roots of existence and conscious identity lie in dreams. Modern society, she believes, subverts communication. Hauková's *Motýl a smrt* (1990) (*Butterfly and Death*) pursues the same theme as *Země nikoho*, but less intensely. However, *Molýl a smrt* evokes pessimism, whereas her verse hitherto had, however strong the scepticism, at least supported the possibility of optimism.

Haunting of Hill House, The (1959)

Novel by US writer ▷Shirley Jackson. Jackson's experience writing for women's magazines is evident in her creation of the ▷Gothic counterpart of an ideal 1950s North American family home. Hill House is a comfortable, solid, self-cleaning structure that takes care of its inhabitants in both senses of the phrase. Jackson investigates the pretend family which inhabits the house, managing to invoke the characters' fantasies of domestic fullfilment only to reveal them as impossible. The house recognizes Eleanor, the novel's heroine, as the weak link and draws her fully into its insanity whereby it creates manifestations to order, from the desires of the inhabitants. Eleanor's death is the horrific enactment of feminine self-sacrifice at its most dubious. The message of the novel is that families kill, and kill women most efficiently.

Haushofer, Marlen (1920–1970)

Austrian novelist. She had a Catholic upbringing, and spent two unhappy years in a convent school, an experience to which her work repeatedly alludes. All her writing, but in particular the novels, *Die Tapetentür* (1957) (*The Door in the Wallpaper*) and *Die Wand* (1958) (*The Wall*), takes as its theme the alienation of the individual in the modern world. In their laconic, nightmarish illumination of the banal and the absurd, her novels are reminiscent of Franz Kafka, (1883–1924), Robert Walser (1878–1956) and Samuel Beckett (1906–1990).

Hausset (Haussay), Nicole Colleson du (1713–1801)

French writer of memoirs. Born in Vitry-le-François, the daughter of a provincial tanner, she was orphaned at an early age and raised in a convent. Her marriage to a minor aristocrat enabled her to enter the royal household after his death where she became lady's maid, companion and confidante to Madame de Pompadour. Her *Mémoires*, first published in 1809 and recently re-edited (*Mercure de France*, 1985), provide a detailed picture of the private lives of Louis XV and Mme de Pompadour at the court of Versailles. Although memoirs in general are often regarded simply as interesting historical documents rather than as literary works, du Hausset appears to be conscious that her writing is part of a genre already practised by women. In her introduction, she mentions the precedent of the memoirs of ▷Madame de Caylus (1770).
Bib: Lemoine, H., 'Mme. Du Hausset' in *R. Hist.*

Versailles (1937); Saintville, G., *La Confidente de Mme de Pompadour. Mémoires*

Häutungen. Autobiografische Aufzeichnungen, Gedichte, Träume, Analysen (1975) ▷*Shedding* (1978)

Hawken, Dinah (born 1943)

New Zealand poet. Hawken began writing after many years working as a student counsellor and group therapist for women. Much of her published collection *It Has No Sound and Is Blue* (1987) was written during a four-year stay in New York, and her poetry reflects cross-cultural stress and the articulation of difference related to living in New York. Hawken's poetry is explicitly feminist and political and exploits topical events to uncover issues. She has used the work of North American poets John Ashbery (born 1927) and ▷Adrienne Rich as models for her own poems. Hawken's collection won the Commonwealth Writers Award for 1989.

Hayashi Kyoko (born 1930)

Japanese novelist. Born in Nagasaki prefecture, she spent her youth in Shanghai in China where her father worked. From there, she was evacuated back to Nagasaki where she was atom-bombed. *The Ritual of Death* describes the agony caused by her fear of serious radiation-induced disease, and her estrangement from her husband. It won the Gunzo Prize for a New Writer and the Akutagawa Prize in 1975. She continues to write about the nuclear threat. Her other main works are *Round Dance* and *Home in This World*, which won the Kawabata Yasunari Prize.

Hayashi Mariko (born 1954)

Japanese copywriter and novelist, born in Yamanashi prefecture. She stopped writing copy for advertisements after the publication of her novel *Let's Go Home Happily* ('Runrun' wo katte Ouchini kaero) (1982). 'Runrun' immediately became a vogue word. This work is a light portrayal of a young woman who wants to marry, although she loses one love after another. Hayashi won the Naoki Prize in 1985 with *For the Last Train* after *Stellar, A Deep Impression of Grapes* and *The Home of Nuts* had been previously considered for the prize. *The Emperor, Meiji and Shimoda Utako* (1990) which pictures an eminent woman, Shimoda Utako, in the Meiji era is popular in Japan today.

Hayden, Anna Tompson (1648–post–1720)

North American poet. She was born into the literary Tompson family of Braintree, Massachusetts. The only poem that can be assuredly attributed to her is the memorial, ▷'Verses on Benjamin Tompson', her brother-poet who had recently died. The poem evidences little literary talent.

Hayden, Esther Allen (c 1713–1758)
North American poet. She was probably born in
1713; her father was Samuel Allen, but her
mother's identity is unknown. She and her
husband, Samuel Hayden, settled in Braintree,
Massachusetts, and raised nine children. In 1758,
shortly before her death, she composed a 167-line
poem from her death-bed. Intended for family
and friends, the poem, ▷'Composed About Six
Weeks Before Her Death, When Under
Distressing Circumstances', is poignant in its
honest revelation of Hayden's doubts, even on her
death-bed, about personal salvation.

Hayes, Evelyn ▷Bethell, Mary Ursula

Hays, Mary (1760–1843)
English writer of poetry, fiction, essays and letters.
Her parents were Dissenters and she also wrote
against the Church of England. She met ▷Mary
Wollstonecraft, and was in correspondence with
English novelist William Godwin (1756–1836)
about her *Memoirs of Emma Courtenay* (1796). Her
novels, including *A Victim of Prejudice* (1799),
advocated egalitarian and radical positions. In
1783 she published (anonymously) *Appeal to the
Men of Great Britain on Behalf of the Women*, in
which she wrote, 'To point out the frequent . . .
abuses of this authority, would be to draw a
picture of what many an amiable woman suffers
from it; and many an unamiable one too. For
though men are apt . . . to suppose, that these two
characteristics merit very different treatments; yet
they should consider, that all have the feelings of
right and wrong.' She also published *Female
Biography* (1803) on earlier women and their
achievements.

Other publications: *Cursory Remarks* (1791);
Letters and Essays (1793).
Bib: Hill, Bridget, *Eighteenth Century Women.*

Haywood, Eliza (?1690/3–1756)
English novelist, poet, dramatist and journalist.
Born in London, she married the Reverend
Valentine Haywood, but reappeared in 1714 as an
actress in Dublin. Her first novel, *Love in Excess,
or the Fatal Enquiry* (1719–1720) was successful,
and she published by subscription *Letters From a
Lady of Quality to a Chevalier* (1720). Her husband
spurned her in 1721. Novels poured from her
pen, *British Recluse* (1722), *The Injur'd Husband*
(1722) and *A Wife to be Lett*. Like ▷Delarivier
Manley, she wrote narrative politics and scandal –
Memoirs of a Certain Island . . . Adjacent to Utopia
(1724), *The Court of Caramania* (1727) and the
political *Eovaai* (1736). Attacked as 'the nymph
Corinna' by satirist Jonathan Swift (1667–1745)
and in Alexander Pope's *Dunciad*, (1728), she
published an attack on Swift in *The Female
Dunciad* (1729). She acted with ▷Charlotte
Charke in the 1630s, and wrote *Anti-Pamela, or
Feign'd Innocence Detected* (1741) in response to
Samuel Richardson's *Pamela* (1740). After a
scandalous youth she moved into morals as editor
of the periodical *The Female Spectator* (1744–1746)

and *Miss Betsy Thoughtless* (1751). ▷Clara Reeve
summed up her career in *The Progress of Romance*
(1785) as one who had 'the singular good fortune
to recover a lost reputation'.
▷Richardson, Samuel, influence of

Hazzard, Shirley (born 1931)
Australian novelist and short story writer. Hazzard
was born in Sydney, and has lived in Hong Kong,
New Zealand, Europe and the USA since 1947.
She worked for the United Nations in New York
for ten years, and her first non-fiction work,
*Defeat of an Ideal: A Study of the Self-destruction of
the United Nations* (1973), is an account of her
disillusion with that institution. Hazzard is
married to the writer, Francis Steegmuller. Her
novels are polished, urbane and cosmopolitan, and
are all to some extent concerned with the
achievement of and loss of love. Two short novels
with an Italian setting are *The Evening of the
Holiday* (1966) and ▷*The Bay of Noon* (1970), and
her long novel, ▷*The Transit of Venus* (1980),
deals with the complex relationship between love
and destiny. *Cliffs of Fall* (1963) is a collection of
her stories from the *New Yorker* and *People in
Glass Houses* (1967) deals with the sterile
atmosphere at the United Nations.
▷Short story (Australia); *Gender, Politics and
Fiction*

H. D. (Hilda Doolittle) (1886–1961)

H.D.

US poet, novelist, short-story writer and essayist.
The question that H.D's poems and novels
consistently pose is that of what it means to
represent female sexuality. The relation between
art and female creativity is explored in her

autobiographical account of her upbringing in Bethlehem, Pennsylvania, *The Gift* (1969), which dramatizes a tension between what H.D. later refers to as her 'father's science' and her 'mother's art', and which cuts across all her work. H.D's literary and intellectual 'fathers' are formidable. Her early novel, *HERmonione* (1981), written in 1928, represents a struggle between the poet Ezra Pound's (1888–1972) influence and her own explorations of writing and sexuality. It was Pound who assured her reputation as an imagist poet, shortening Hilda Doolittle to H.D. and giving her an exemplary status within the imagist movement; the reasons for such exemplarity are evident in the pioneering imagist collection *Sea Garden* (1916).

Sometime wife of English poet Richard Aldington (1892–1962) and long-term lover of Bryher (Winifred Ellerman), H.D. was introduced to film by the latter, resulting in the collaboration in 1930 on the film, *Borderline*, which connects issues of gender and sexuality with those of race and class. Another influential 'father' (although often also a reluctant 'mother' according to H.D.) was Sigmund Freud (1856–1939). H.D.'s analysis with Freud is documented in her *Tribute to Freud* (1956), but the questions ▷psychoanalysis poses about narrative and mythical origins, representation and sexuality are most strikingly developed in the explorations of myth in both ▷*Trilogy* (1973) and ▷*Helen in Egypt* (1961). The former strikingly intertwines the 'mother's art' or, more precisely, the maternal body, with the wider historical and political theatre of World War II. Her poetry from 1912 to 1944 has been published in *Collected Poems*, edited by Louis L. Martz (1983). A prolific writer, much of H.D.'s work remains as yet unpublished.

Other works include: *Hymen* (1921), *Heliodora and Other Poems*, (1924), *Palimpsest* (1926), *Hippolytus Temporizes, Hedylus* (1928), *Red Roses for Bronze* (1931), *Kora and Ka* (1934), *Nights* (1935), *The Hedgehog (1936). Euripides' Ion* (1937), *By Avon River* (1949), *Bid Me to Live*, (1960), *Hermetic Definition* (1972) and *The Selected Poems of H.D.* (1957).

Bib: Friedman, Susan Stanford, *Psyche Reborn; The Emergence of H.D.*; Guest, Barbara, *Herself Defined: The Poet H.D. and Her World*; DuPlessis, Rachel Blau, *H.D.: The Career of that Struggle*; Buck, Claire, *H.D. and Freud: Bisexuality and a Feminine Discourse.*

Head, Bessie (1937–1986)

Southern African novelist, short story writer and non-fiction writer. Born in Pietermaritzburg to a mother classified white and a father classified black under apartheid legislation, she was reared partly by foster-mothers and partly in an orphanage: these and other early biographical events enter her fiction in tortured ways. Head worked as a journalist in Johannesburg and Cape Town before leaving the country for Botswana in 1963 on an exit permit. She is among Africa's finest writers, ambitious, energetic and challenging. One of her major contributions is the creation of an indigenous voice, rooted in Africa, even while looking to European writers like German dramatist Bertolt Brecht (1898–1956) for inspiration. Another is her sympathetic representation of 'ordinary' people, without simplification or patronization. As a woman writer, her attitude to male domination is highly critical, although it must also be said that her texts sometimes betray a yearning for a benevolent patriarchalism.

Her first two novels – ▷*When Rain Clouds Gather* (1967) and ▷*Maru* (1971) – engage with contemporary Botswana, on the one hand presenting a critique of its gender and racial oppressions, and on the other hand constructing an ideal rural community out of the potentialities of the past and present. ▷*A Question of Power* (1973) looks inward. A novel of breakdown, which Head has called autobiographical, it deals partly with the psychological baggage lugged from a racially and sexually violent South Africa, and partly with what had to be confronted in contemporary Botswana. For her next book, *Serowe: Village of the Rain Wind* (1981), Head interviewed and gathered stories from the inhabitants of her village. This venture provided the germs for some of her short stories in ▷*The Collector of Treasures* (1977). Together, the two books represent the less tortured and less introspective mode briefly glimpsed at the end of *A Question of Power. The Collector of Treasures* extends Head's narrative technique into a masterly literary creation of ▷oral tradition, a mode which also informs the last book to be published in her lifetime, ▷*A Bewitched Crossroad* (1984).

Two collections of her writing have been posthumously published: *Tales of Tenderness and Power* (1989), and *A Woman Alone* (1990). They contain essays, sketches and stories, with much autobiographical material. A collection of letters between her and Randolph Vigne, friend and one-time editor, *A Gesture of Belonging: Letters from Bessie Head, 1965–1979* (1991), gives an intimate view of this complex and brilliant woman, and provides insight into the material and psychological realities that fed into her writing.

Head's literary remains are at the Khama III Memorial Museum, Serowe. More of her correspondence is likely to be published in due course, as well as an early novel. Although her literary reputation is sound, and critical work on her is interesting and useful, her writing still awaits the detailed and rigorous critical scrutiny accorded ▷Olive Schreiner and ▷Nadine Gordimer, for example.

Bib: Abrahams, Cecil (ed.), *The Tragic Life: Bessie Head and Literature in Southern Africa*; Gardner, Susan and Scott, Patricia, *Bessie Head: A Bibliography*; MacKenzie, Craig, *Bessie Head: An Introduction.*

Heap, Jane ▷*Little Review, The*

Heart Is a Lonely Hunter, The (1940)
US novel by ▷Carson McCullers which focuses
on Mick Kelly, a tomboy faced with impending
womanhood. She desires to be a famous musician.
However, accepting her womanhood means
conforming to a social role and stifling her
ambition. Mick feels like an outsider – a freak.
She identifies with others who are socially
alienated or marginalized: a deaf mute, a socialist
reformer, a black doctor working to uplift his
people and a Jew. McCullers thereby relates
sexism to classism, racism and disablism, and
depicts the anxiety caused by female sexuality
which relegates women to prescribed social roles.

Heart of the Bush, The (1910)
Novel by New Zealand writer ▷Edith Searle
Grossman. Edith Searle Grossmann wrote four
novels of which *The Heart of the Bush* is the last. In
her work Grossman investigated the way in
which social, religious and political structures
affected women, particularly in marriage. Two of
her novels address the questions involved in the
Married Women's Property Act of 1884, and
more generally her fiction deals with conventions
she saw as worn out and oppressive for women
(essentially male control of women's assets and
activities), and the illustration of the 'purer'
morality she proposes in *The Heart of the Bush*. *The
Heart of the Bush* describes the marriage of
Adelaide Borlase, toast of the English social set,
to her father's farm manager Dennis McDiarmid.
In the course of the novel Dennis and Adelaide
are educated about each other and their marriage
comes to be based on mutual respect and the
recognition of each other's individuality. Changing
the status and basis of marriage would,
Grossmann believed, do more for women and
their husbands than other forms of social change.

Heat and Dust (1975)
A novel by ▷Ruth Prawer Jhabvala, winner of the
1975 Booker Prize. Set in India, this novel broke
with the tradition of Jhabvala's previous ones by
spanning fifty years, and several generations of
British experience in India. In 1923 the young
Olivia goes to India with her husband, Douglas,
only to desert him and the boredom of a
memsahib's life for the glamour of an Indian
prince. Fifty years later, Douglas's granddaughter
makes the same journey to trace out Olivia's
scandal. All the people of Olivia's time are
paralleled in the people that Douglas's
granddaughter meets, and the latter, like the
former, finds herself pregnant to an Indian lover.
The granddaughter, however, is able to make a
solution for herself, whereas Olivia had to
surrender all claims to her own society and
culture.

Heat of the Day, The (1949)
Novel by Irish writer ▷Elizabeth Bowen. The
most 'plotted' of Bowen's novels, it is set in 1942,
and explores the insecurity and intrigue of the war
period. Stella Rodway, a divorced forty-year-old

woman, is pursued by the mysterious Harrison,
who reveals to her that Robert Kelway, her lover
and fellow worker for the wartime security
services, is a Nazi agent. She is thus confronted
with the fact that love is not a realm of freedom,
but deeply bound up in danger and deceit.
Although Bowen herself described aspects of the
novel as 'point-blank melodrama', the novel is a
powerful evocation of life in wartime London, and
an exploration of women's difficult emotional and
sexual lives. The politically contentious aspect of
the novel is Bowen's representation of Robert as
both a fascist and a sensitive, 'civilized'
Englishman, whereas Harrison, on the side of law
and the state, is a vulgar, and at times menacing,
intruder. It has been suggested that this is less a
question of Robert's implausibility as a character
than one of Bowen's own questioning of the post-
war consensus, and of the view that 'civilization'
resides with the democratic victors of the war.

Heaton, Hannah Cook (1721–1794)
North American spiritual autobiographer. Born in
Long Island, New York, she settled in North
Haven, Connecticut, after her marriage in 1743 to
a farmer from that community. As a member of
the Congregational Church in North Haven, she
was drawn into the Great Awakening revivalist
movements of the 1760s and 1770s. Her
autobiographical writings, which remain in
manuscript form, are excerpted in ▷*The World of
Hannah Heaton*. Her spiritual meditations capture
both the 'delightsome' and the devastatingly
rigorous battles she waged against the devil in
order to be saved.
▷Osborn, Sarah Haggar Wheaten

Heavenly Twins, The (1893)
A novel by British novelist ▷Sarah Grand. The
first half of this immensely successful book
describes the lives of two twins, Angelica and
Diavolo. As children they are both irrepressible,
energetic and daring, but as they grow older they
are forced to take different paths. Diavolo is given
a good ▷education and finally leaves home for an
army career, while Angelica follows a
conventionally female path and becomes trapped
in domestic routine. The second half of the book
concentrates on two women, Edith and Evadne.
Religious and naive, Edith unknowingly marries a
syphilitic naval officer, and both she and her child
contract the disease. After a period of mental
degeneration, Edith dies. Evadne, who has studied
anatomy, physiology and pathology, refuses to
consummate her marriage after discovering that
her husband has had a previous affair, and lives a
sexless life. She is frustrated as a result and has a
mental breakdown, but she recovers from this
after the death of her husband and marries again.
Like Grand's ▷*The Beth Book*, the novel explicitly
addresses sexual/political issues. The lives of the
twins reflect the inequality of educational
opportunity, while Edith and Evadne represent the
'old' and ▷'New Woman' respectively. Despite
Evadne's learning, however, she becomes trapped

in a life of repression after promising her husband that she will not become active in the women's movement.

Hébert, Anne (born 1916)

French-Canadian novelist, poet and short-story writer. Born in Sainte-Catherine-de-Fossambault, Quebec, she spent her early years in Quebec and studied in Quebec City, but since the mid-1950s has lived in Paris. Her first collection of poems, *Les Songes en Équilibre* (*Dreams of Equilibrium*), appeared in 1942. It is a rigorous but relatively traditional collection, in marked contrast to her first collection of short stories, *Le Torrent* (1950, translated as *The Torrent*), which is a powerful evocation of repression and revolt. In her next collection of poetry, *Le Tombeau des Rois* (*Tomb of the Kings*), Hébert explores this reaction further, particularly in relation to a Quebec dominated and oppressed by king and clergy. Her first novel, *Les Chambres de Bois* (1958, translated as *The Silent Rooms*, 1974) which won the Prix France-Canada, is again about a woman who revolts against her marital prison. Hébert's next books of poetry are very much works about the enlightenment of language, the word as sun; *Poèmes* (1960, translated as *Poems*, 1975) won a Governor General's Award. She is best-known for her four-novel cycle that addresses the violent and repercussive nature of insular and isolated Quebec, especially in relation to its Gothic darkness. *Kamouraska* (1970, translated under the same name, 1973) begins the cycle in 19th-century Quebec, and is based on a historical murder. It was made into a motion picture, and awarded the Prix des Libraires in France. *Les Enfants du Sabbat* (1975, translated as *Children of the Black Sabbath*, 1977) takes as its subject a family who practise black magic; the main character, Julie, despite her convent calling, is dedicated to sorcery and lives out a perverse version of the virgin birth. In *Héloïse* (1980, translated under the same title, 1983), Hébert shifts her location to Paris, and her focus to a woman succubus who haunts the underground and sucks the blood of Métro passengers. *Les fous de Bassan* (1982, translated as *In The Shadow of the Wind*), which was awarded the Prix Femina, returns to an English-speaking village in the Gaspé, and the voices of a community trying to unravel how two beautiful young girls were killed. The strange violence and yet dramatic tenderness of Hébert's fiction is difficult to reconcile, but it speaks to her overall vision of passivity and entrapment as a precedence to revolt and necessary, if shocked, awareness. Hébert has also written plays.

Bib: Lacôte, R., *Anne Hébert*; Lemieux, P., *Entre Songe et Parole: structure du Tombeau des Rois d'Anne Hébert*; Pagé, P., *Anne Hébert*; Russell, D., *Anne Hébert*; Paterson, J., *Anne Hébert: Architexture Romanesque*.

Hebrew Short Stories ▷*Anthology of Modern Hebrew Poetry* and *Hebrew Short Stories*

Hecate: A Woman's Interdisciplinary Journal

Australian literary magazine. *Hecate*, edited by Carole Ferrier of the University of Queensland, has been published, usually twice a year, since 1975, and is the foremost vehicle for ▷feminist literary criticism in Australia.

Hedyle (? 3rd century BC)

Athenian poet. The Greek writer Athenaeus (2nd century AD) records both Hedyle and her mother, ▷Moschine, as poets. She was the mother of the male epigrammatist Hedylus. She wrote a mythological poem called *Scylla* – of which one quote survives – describing the sea god Glaucus.

Heilbrun, Carolyn (born 1926)

US essayist and novelist. Born in East Orange, New Jersey, Heilbrun graduated from Wellesley College in 1947. In 1959 she earned her PhD in English literature at Columbia University. Mother of three, she is a feminist scholar and professor at Columbia and on the editorial board of the feminist scholarly journal, ▷*Signs*. Under the pseudonym Amanda Cross, Heilbrun writes mystery novels featuring Kate Fansler, an English professor and amateur detective. Heilbrun's work is noted for its eruditeness. Novels like *The James Joyce Murder* (1967) and *The Theban Mysteries* (1972) centre on literature, and Heilbrun satirizes US society to emphasize issues of sex, as in *Death in a Tenured Position* (1981); class, *The Question of Max* (1976), and race, *A Trap for Fools* (1989). Her work also examines relationships between women.

Other fictional works include: *Poetic Justice* (1979), *In the Last Analysis* (1981), *Sweet Death, Kind Death* (1987) and *No Word From Winifred* (1988). Her critical works include: *The Garnett Family* (1961), *Towards a Recognition of Androgyny* (1973) and *Reinventing Womanhood* (1979).

▷Detective fiction

Heir of Redclyffe, The (1853)

A novel by English writer ▷Charlotte Yonge, informed by the religious principles of the ▷Oxford Movement and much admired by prominent literary figures of the day such as Tennyson, D.G. Rossetti and William Morris. The novel contrasts genuine and superficial goodness of character through the story of two cousins, Guy and Philip Morville. Guy appears brash, but is deeply generous and ultimately self-sacrificing, whereas Philip is greatly admired but undeserving of accolades. Philip's machinations almost succeed in thwarting Guy's marriage. Guy later nurses Philip through a fever, catches it himself and dies. Philip repents of his sins and inherits the ancient house of Redclyffe.

Hélé, Béji (born 1948)

Tunisian novelist, born in Tunis to a French mother. Taught literature at the University of Tunis. Now living in Paris and working at UNESCO. She wrote a critical analysis of decolonization, *Le Désenchantement national* (1982) (*National Disenchantment*), and a powerful novel

▷*L'Oeil du jour* (1985) (*The Day's Eye*) which expresses a young woman's internal conflicts with regard to her original and adopted cultures.

Helena

Ancient Greek poet, of mythical date. Ptolemy Hephaestion, quoted by the Byzantine writer Photius, records that she wrote an epic *Trojan War*. Tradition made her one of the women poets from whom Homer borrowed his ideas (▷Manto, ▷Phantasia). She was also either the mother or daughter of the mythical poet Musaeus.

Helen in Egypt (1961)

Poem sequence by US poet ▷H.D.. *Helen in Egypt* is a highly intricate rewriting of the myth of Helen of Troy. The three sections which comprise the sequence, 'Pallinode', 'Leuke', and 'Eidolon', transform the classic epic genre by interleaving short lyrics with prose headnotes. The poem charts the multiple and contradictory myths which surround Helen as a cultural icon of femininity: wife of Menelaus; mother of Hermione; *femme fatale* who caused the Trojan War; phantom 'substituted for the real Helen, by jealous deities' while she was 'transposed' to Egypt; dead on the walls of Troy; the lover of the military hero Achilles. The proliferation of these incompatible stories in *Helen in Egypt* has provoked equally contradictory readings from feminist critics. Although the poem invites us to identify with Helen as an oppressed victim of ▷patriarchy, and indeed has frequently been read as presenting a matriarchal alternative to monotheism. H.D.'s representation of Helen is more complex and ambivalent than this. She uses her reading and experience of ▷psychoanalysis to represent Helen not so much as the oppressed, but as the *repressed* of Western civilization. From this perspective, her idealization in Western culture is figured as part of a denial of what is held to be deeply threatening about her. To identify with Helen, as H.D.'s poems vividly demonstrate, is therefore not a straightforward gesture against patriarchy. It also forces the reader to negotiate for oneself the twin poles of dealization and repudiation. *Helen in Egypt* represents H.D. at her most demanding, as its complex interweaving of questions of history, narrative and female sexuality demonstrate that the return of the repressed' is never simply an occasion for celebration. It also raises for women the vexed question of their origins and identifications.

Hellman, Lillian (1906–1984)

US dramatist and screenwriter. Hellman was born in New Orleans, Louisiana, to Jewish parents, but was shaped by her African-American nurse, Sophronia. In 1925 Hellman stopped attending New York University and married Arthur Kober. She became a New York play reader and a Hollywood scenario reader. After divorcing Kober in 1932, she began living with Dashiell Hammett, the bestselling ▷detective story writer. Hellmann,

Hammett and her friend ▷Dorothy Parker were left-wing political activists. In the 1950s Hellman was blacklisted by the House Un-American Activities Committee for her leftist politics.

Hellman characterized herself as a morality writer. ▷*The Children's Hour* (1934) and ▷*The Little Foxes* (1939) depict the impact of socio-economic forces on women's lives. Set in the US, *Watch on the Rhine* (1941) protests against fascism in the prelude to the entry of the US into World War II. *The Autumn Garden* (1951) and *Toys in the Attic* (1960) emphasize accepting social and moral responsibilities. Hellman's memoirs include *An Unfinished Woman* (1969), *Pentimento* (1973) and *Scoundrel Time* (1976).

Other works include: *Days to Come* (1936), *The North Star: A Motion Picture about Some Russian People* (1943), *The Searching Wind: A Play in Two Acts* (1944), *Another Part of the Forest: A Play in Three Acts* (1947), *Montserrat: Play in Two Acts* (1950), *The Lark* (1956), *Collected Plays* (1972) and *Maybe* (1980).

Bib: Lederer, Katherine, *Lillian Hellman*.

Hemans, Felicia (1793–1835)

Anglo-Irish poet and dramatist, born in Liverpool and educated at home by her mother, Felicity Wagner. Her father, George Browne, was a merchant. She was encouraged to write by her parents, who arranged the publication of her first volume of *Poems* (1808). *The Domestic Affections* (1812) was her first mature collection. She married Captain Alfred Hemans in 1812 and had five sons in six years, after which the couple separated. Hemans went on to support her sons through writing. Her volumes of verse include *The Forest Sanctuary* (1825); *Records of Woman* (1828) and *Songs of the Affections* (1830). She also wrote essays and two plays: *The Siege of Valencia* and *The Vespers of Palermo* (both 1823). Hemans's poetry mainly consists of ▷sentimental love lyrics, and in her day she was considered a model of feminine charm and was extremely popular. Recent feminist readings have reconsidered her relationship to ▷Romanticism.

▷Drama (19th-century Britain); Ballad (19th-century Britain)

Bib: Hickok, K., *Representations of Women: 19th Century British Women's Poetry*.

Hendel, Yehudit (born 1926)

Israeli novelist and short story writer. Born in Warsaw, Hendel was taken to Palestine as a baby by her parents. She studied in Haifa, and began her literary career in the 1950s. Hendel's writing reflects the change in the Israeli self-image, from the certainty and uniformity of the 1940s to the problematic, complex Israeli society of the present. In her novels she portrays the difficult interaction between conflicting sections of society. Her novels include: *Anashim Acherim Hem* (1950) (*They are Different People*) and *Rechov Ha'Madregot* (1956) (*The Street of Steps*).

Henderson, Paul   ▷France, Ruth

Henderson, Zenna (born 1917)

US novelist. Born in Tucson, Arizona, Henderson was raised in a strongly religious environment. In 1954 she earned a Master's degree in literature at Arizona State University. She has taught elementary school in a variety of contexts. Her science fiction novels, *Pilgrimage: The Book of the People* (1961) and *The People: No Different Flesh* (1966), focus on the People, a race of aliens endowed with psychic powers and an acute moral sense. Humans have persecuted and exiled them for these differences but, by serving as models, they teach humans to transcend prejudice and ignorance. *The Anything Box* (1965) suggests the necessity of using the imagination's power responsibly. Henderson celebrates humanity's potential for compassion and respects the sanctity of the individual.

Other works include: *Holding Wonder* (1971).

Henley, Beth ▷ *Crimes of the Heart*

Henning, Rachel (1826–1914)

Australian letter-writer. Henning was born in England, visited Australia from 1854 to 1856, and settled permanently in 1861. The next year she and her sister joined their brother, Biddulph, on his station, inland from Bowen in Queensland. Her letters written to her sisters Etty and Amy, dated from 1853 to 1882, detail her first visit, her second visit and her experiences in the outback of Queensland, and her marriage to her brother's overseer; a marriage which was opposed by Biddulph because of the lower status of the groom in colonial, or English society. The popular publication, *The Letters of Rachel Henning* (1962), edited by David Adams and illustrated by Norman Lindsay, provides an enthralling account of a resourceful Englishwoman's response to the Australian landscape and to pioneering life. Much is revealed of Henning's own personality, invariably cheerful and coping with all difficulties in a positive manner, and living as much as possible as if she were at 'home' in the civilized counties of her native England.

▷Letters (Australia); *On Her Selection*

Hennings, Emmy (1885–1948)

German actress and writer. She began her career as a member of an itinerant theatre group, and by the age of twenty-three was widely-known for the power of her poetic recitals. She was interested in Expressionism, and joined the artistic cabaret show *Simplicissimus* (*Simpleton*) in Munich, where she met her future husband, the poet Hugo Ball (1886–1927). In 1913 she published her collection of poems, *Die letzte Freude* (*The Last Pleasure*), and in 1916–17 participated with Ball in the Zurich Dada movement. After Ball's death in 1927, she converted to Catholicism, edited his work, and wrote fairytales, legends and autobiographies.

Henningsen, Agnes (1868–1962)

Danish prose writer, mostly known for her memoirs. She was born on the island of Fyn, her mother died early, and to get away from home she married a teacher in 1887, while already pregnant. In 1895 he emigrated to the USA, and she lived alone with her four children, one of whom had another father. The image of the sexually free woman who is able to establish relationships with many men was not only lived by Henningsen but also written about. As a cultural leftist she was influenced by Georg Brandes (▷Modern breakthrough), an influence she described in *Polens Døtre* (1901) (*The Daughters of Poland*). Her principal works are the trilogy *Kærlighedens Aarstider* (1927–1930) (*The Seasons of Love*), and her memoirs in eight volumes from 1941–1955 *Let Gang paa Jorden* (*To Tread Lightly*).

In Danish literary history, Henningsen is usually regarded as one of the three amazons of sexual, cultural and political freedom, together with ▷Karin Michaëlis and ▷Thit Jensen. Her prose is witty and elegant in style, and her female characters are sexual beings more than anything else.

Bib: Wamberg, B., *The Prize of Improvidence.*

Heptaméron, L' (1559) ▷ *Heptaméron de Marguerite of Navarre, The*

Heptaméron of Marguerite de Navarre, The (1654)

Translation of the French book *L'Heptaméron* (1559) by ▷Marguerite de Navarre. Begun in 1542, it is an unfinished collection of tales in imitation of the form of the *Decameron* (1352) by the Italian writer Boccaccio (1313–1375). The Prologue introduces a group of ten storytellers of noble birth, five men and five women, who have together taken refuge from terrible floods in the monastery of Notre Dame de Serrance in the Pyrenees, and who there agree to recount ten tales apiece, one each on each of ten consecutive days. The most important of the narrators is Parlamente, who speaks for Marguerite herself and has a lofty view of love. The author had completed some 72 of these ▷*nouvelles* at her death in 1549, arranged in seven 'days', each comprising ten *nouvelles* and the first two tales of the eighth day. The tales were all supposedly true, of recent date, brief, natural and interesting. They emphasize the predicament of isolated individuals in conflict with convention. Several of the heroines are shown to fight for the right for self-determination in a hostile world. Although frequently salacious, the tales are presented by their author as moral *exempla* in the commentaries which follow each tale, and which are sometimes more important than the tales themselves.

Herbert, Mary Sidney, Countess of Pembroke (1561–1621)

English translator, poet, and patron. Herbert was the daughter of Henry and Mary Dudley Sidney. At the age of fourteen she moved into ▷Elizabeth

Tudor's household at the queen's request. Two years later, she married Henry Herbert, Earl of Pembroke. Herbert was extremely close to her brother, Sir Philip Sidney (1554–1586), and they worked in various degrees of collaboration together. In 1580 Philip dedicated to her *The Countess of Pembroke's Arcadia*, which he had written at her suggestion. At about this same time Herbert and Sidney began working together on a verse ▷ translation of the biblical ▷ *Psalms of David* (one to forty-three by Sidney, the remaining 107 by Herbert). Herbert, however, was forced to finish the work alone when her brother was killed in 1586. In 1590 William Ponsonby printed without authorization the first edition of Sidney's *Arcadia*. In reaction, Herbert published in 1593 her own edition of her brother's work, which she had revised, dividing it into five rather than three books, adding new sections from manuscripts in her possession, and even rewriting some sections. In 1598 she revised and published *Arcadia* for a second time.

Herbert also composed a number of works on her own. She was known for her translating skills, having studied Latin, Greek, Hebrew and French. In 1592 she published two English translations of French works – Plessis du Mornay's 'A Discourse of Life and Death', and Robert Garnier's *Tragedie Antonie* which Herbert rendered into blank verse, adding some choral lyrics of her own composition (▷ *The Tragedie of Anthonie*, 1590). In 1593 she translated Petrarch's *Triafs della Morte* (1470) as ▷ *Triumph of Death*. In 1595 Edmund Spenser (?1552–1599) appended her poem, ▷ 'The Dolefull Lay of Clorinda,' to his own 'Astrophel'.
▷ Hoby, Margaret; Patronage

Herbst, Josephine (1892–1969)
US novelist. Born in Sioux City, Iowa, Herbst worked as a special news correspondent in the 1930s, and she investigated political dissent in the US, Cuba, Germany and Spain. She was a social and political activist. In *Nothing Is Sacred* (1928) and *Money for Love* (1929) Herbst depicts the US middle class as lacking in moral values. She emphasizes that her characters are victims of capitalism and its materialistic values, and she shows how money perverts romantic relationships.

In her trilogy – *Pity Is Not Enough* (1933), *The Executioner Waits* (1934) and *Rope of Gold* (1939) – Herbst depicts the evolution of US society from the Civil War to the Depression. She shows how capitalism perverts the human personality and claims that capitalism causes social disintegration. Herbst's fiction is characterized by its collective technique.

Other works include: *Satan's Sergeants* (1941), *Somewhere the Tempest Fell* (1947) and *New Green World* (1954).
Bib: Lange, Elinor, *Josephine Herbst: The Story She Could Never Tell*.

Here Lies (1939)
US short-story collection by ▷ Dorothy Parker, of stories previously published in *Lament for the*

Living and *After Such Pleasures*. These stories criticize the predicament of women in heterosexual relationships and depict how prescribed gender roles leave women economically and emotionally dependent on men. In doing so, they examine the disintegration of heterosexual relationships. 'Mr Durant' indicts male chauvinism and womanizing; 'Big Blonde' and 'The Waltz' portray the plight of women who satisfy social expectations and risk an unfulfilling relationship rather than risk being alone; 'Too Bad' chronicles the disintegration of a marriage when a woman lacks a meaningful occupation.

The collection also includes new stories reflecting Parker's radicalism in the 1930s. 'Clothe the Naked' focuses on the helplessness of poor African-Americans. Parker's stories claim that heterosexual relationships disintegrate as a result of a power imbalance.

Heremakhonon (1982)
Translation by Richard Philcox of the novel by the French Antilles writer, ▷ Maryse Condé, *Hérémakhonon* (1976). The protagonist of Condé's first novel is Veronica Mercier, a middle-class academic originally from Guadeloupe. In search of racial contentment, she left Guadeloupe for France, and now she has left her French lover for Africa. During the three months Veronica spends in Africa, she has an affair with Ibrahima Sory, brother-in-law of her colleague Saliou, and Minister of the Interior. Ibrahima's villa is called 'Hérémakhonon', or 'Await Happiness'. Sory becomes the 'nigger with ancestors' for whom Veronica had been searching. The affair is set against a background of political unrest, and Veronica's friends and students are arrested. Saliou dies. Realizing that she is not African and does not need to look for her ancestors on that continent, Veronica eventually returns to France. An intricate and experimental novel, *Heremakhonon* relies upon the wealth of allusion in Veronica's silent monologue, and upon cinematic perspectives and contrapuntal structures to depict the Guadeloupean woman's quest for ▷ identity.

Héricourt, Jenny d'
French feminist writer. A friend of ▷ Juliette Adam, d'Héricourt wrote the two-volume *La Femme affranchie* (1860) (*The Emancipated woman*) in which she analyzes and/or attacks the views on women expressed by Proudhon (▷ Proudhonism), Michelet and the ▷ Saint-Simonians. She also puts forward suggestions for social reforms which would contribute to women's emancipation, and condemns, amoung other things, the need for women to abandon their names upon marriage. Like Adam, d'Héricourt was a bourgeois feminist who did not become involved in the wave of feminist activity that was launched in the late 1860s.

Hermeticism (Italy)
A term frequently applied to post-World War I poetry. Hermeticist poetry attempts to reduce

language to its essentials, to avoid excessive rhetoric. It may be written in either free or traditional verse form. Its preferred themes are those of human existence, and it often denounces notions of power and progress as delusory. The poetry of ▷Maria Luisa Spaziani is described as hermeticist.

Hermodsson, Elisabet Hermine (born 1927)

Swedish multi-media artist, poet, prose writer, visual artist, composer and singer. Hermodsson was trained as a visual artist, but also studied philosophy and, at an early age, began to write poetry. In 1966 she had her literary début with the collection of poems *Dikt=ting* (*Poem=Thing*). She likes to work in more than one medium: she writes music for her ballads, and illustrates her own poems.

Hermodsson is an artistic philosopher. She is religious, and a political activist. She often depicts opposite tendencies in a creative tension and dialectical complexity. Her most popular work is *Disa Nilssons visor* (1974) (*Disa Nilsson's Ballads*), which introduced a critical female voice into the Swedish ballad tradition. Hermodsson describes the oppositions between nature and technology, art and science, in female–male terms. Some reviewers see her in the tradition of ▷Elin Wägner and the theologian Emilia Fogelklou (1878–1972), both of whom also combined feminism and religion.

Hernández, Luisa Josefina (born 1928)

Mexican dramatist and novelist. She focuses her work on the Mexican middle class. The performance of her first two plays, *Aguardente de caña* (1951) (*Rush*) and *Los surdomudos* (1953) (*The Deaf-mutes*), brought her success. The latter symbolizes the lack of understanding, perspective and autonomy of the dumb and deaf heroine's family. Her play *Popol Vuh* (1966) is based on the famous sacred book of the Mayas. Her novels include: *El lugar donde crece la hierba* (1959) (*The Place Where the Grass Grows*); *La Plaza de Puerto Santo* (1961) (*Puerto Santo Square*); *Los palacios desertos* (1963) (*The Deserted Palaces*); *La noche exquisita* (1965) (*The Exquisite Night*), and *El valle que elegimos* (1965) (*The Valley We Chose*).

Herophyle

Poet. No dates are known, although she allegedly lived before the Trojan War. There are various traditions associated with her name. She was connected with several places: Marpessus, Erythrae, Samos and Delphi. At one of the sites holy to the god Apollo – Delos or Delphi – she wrote a *Hymn to Apollo*, in which she calls herself the sister, wife and daughter of the god. She is said to have prophesied through dream interpretation. The Greek travel writer Pausanias (2nd century AD) records four lines of a tomb inscription from Gergis in the Troad.

Herrad von Landsberg (c 1130–1195)

German nun, artist and writer. She succeeded her teacher, Relindis, as abbess at the Convent of Hohenburg in Alsace. With her assistance she compiled the exquisitely-illustrated *Hortus Deliciarum* (*The Garden of Delights*), an encyclopaedia of contemporary general knowledge. Enriched with anonymous poetry, it was used for the instruction of the nuns in the convent.

Herrera Garrido, Francisca (1869–1950)

Spanish novelist and poet. Herrera was born in La Coruña, into a wealthy aristocratic family. Like ▷Rosalía de Castro, she wrote in both Castilian and Galician. Her output included poetry; novels, such as *Néveda* (1920), *Pepiña* (1922), *Réproba* (1926) and *Familia de lobos* (1928) (*Family of Wolves*), and short stories, such as *A ialma de Mingos* (1922) and *Martes de antroido* (1925).

▷Galician women's writing

Hertha (1865)

The most famous novel of the Swedish writer ▷Fredrika Bremer. In the novel, Bremer protested against ▷patriarchy. She criticized the fact that women in Swedish society could get no education or training, but had to get married. The novel was widely discussed, and generated a new debate about the women's question (▷woman question) in Sweden. In *Hertha*, conventional marriage is exposed as a financial transaction. The novel pleaded for reforms; it demanded that unmarried women could come of age without a man as a guardian.

Hertha was seen as an immoral novel. Many bourgeois daughters were not allowed to read it. But for the Swedish Women's Liberation Movement the novel was of fundamental importance. Bremer thought that woman was chosen by God to save the world. This was and is an important trend in Western feminism, as represented by ▷Ellen Key and many others.

Her True True Name: An Anthology of Women's Writing from the Caribbean (1989)

This volume, edited by ▷Pamela Mordecai and Betty Wilson, includes writing by thirty-one women from throughout the Caribbean region, including ▷Guyana, Belize, ▷Jamaica, ▷Haiti, ▷Dominican, Puerto Rico, ▷Antigua, ▷Barbados, ▷Grenada, and ▷Trinidad and Tobago.

Hervey, Elizabeth (c 1748–?1820)

English novelist. She was half-sister of William Beckford (1759–1844), who wrote the Gothic novel *Vatheck*, and married Colonel William Hervey in 1774. He died leaving her with his debts in 1778. *Melissa and Marcia, or the Sisters* (1788) came out anonymously. Her brother attacked her, but she continued to write, producing at least four more novels, including *Julia* (1803) and *Amabel* (1813).

Herwegh, Emma (1817–1904)

German writer. In 1848 she accompanied her husband, the poet and revolutionary Georg Herwegh (1817–1875), on a campaign to raise support for the Revolution in Germany. She later published an account of her experiences in *Zur Geschichte der deutschen demokratischen Legion aus Paris. Von einer Hochverräterin* (1849) (*On the History of the German Democratic Legion from Paris. By a Woman Accused of High Treason*).

Herz, Henriette (1764–1847)

German writer. From an Orthodox Jewish family, and a childhood friend of ▷Dorothea Schlegel, she married at thirteen, and was educated by her husband, who introduced her to the sciences and let her study several languages. Intelligent and interested in the romantic movement, she opened a salon that became an important centre for literary and philosophical discussion in early 19th-century Berlin. She wrote two novellas which she later burnt, but her memoirs and letters have recently been republished in *Henriette Herz in Erinnerungen, Briefen und Zeugnissen* (1984) (*Henriette Herz: Memoirs, Letters and Testimonies*).
▷Salon culture (Germany and Austria)

Herzberg, Judith (Frieda Lina) (born 1934)

Dutch poet, dramatist and prose writer. Daughter of the writer Abel Herzberg, from 1941 to 1945 she stayed at various undercover addresses, subsequently returning to Amsterdam where she had been born. Since 1983 she lives alternately there and in Israel. She has written for many literary magazines, publishing her first poetry in 1961, and has written plays for the stage and television, texts for musical theatre, libretti for chamber operas, and film scripts. She was awarded the Joost van de Vondel Prize for her complete works in 1981. Her first collection of poetry, *Zeepost* (1963) (*Seamail*), was well received because of its blending of concrete observations and tentative reflections. Herzberg makes use of the reality of objects and animals, her own emotional life, and nature, but she also writes emotional lyrics that are quite intimate in character and narrative in tone. *Leedvermaak* (1982) (*Malicious Pleasure*) is the best of her plays: against the background of a wedding reception, fourteen people are talking with, about, and mostly past, each other. Poetry collections include *Beemdgras* (1968) (*Meadow Grass*). *Vliegen* (1970) (*Flying*), *Strijklicht* (1971) (*Skimming Light*), *Botshol* (1980), and *Dagrest* (1984) (*A Day's Remnant*). Some of her work has been translated into French and English, including *That Day May Dawn* (1977), *But, What* (1987) and *Selected Poems* (1988); her work has appeared in *Nine Dutch Poets* (1982), *Quartet: an Anthology of Dutch and Flemish Poetry* (1987), *Writing in Holland and Flanders*, 38 (Spring 1981), *The Shape of Houses* (1974) and *Dutch Interior* (1984).

Heterosexism

The assumption that heterosexuality (sex between a man and a woman) is the only 'normal' and 'natural' form of sexual expression, and the consequent classification of gay and lesbian sexuality as 'perverse'.
▷Case, Sue-Ellen; de Lauretis, Teresa; Rich, Adrienne; Lesbian feminist criticism

Hewett, Dorothy (born 1923)

Dorothy Hewett

Australian poet, novelist, dramatist and autobiographer. Hewett was educated at the University of Western Australia and, despite a privileged rural background, joined the Communist Party of Australia at nineteen. She supported herself by writing for an advertising agency, and factory work which provided the material for her novel *Bobbin Up* (1959). Hewett is probably most famous for her many plays, the best known being ▷*The Chapel Perilous* (1972), *This Old Man Comes Rolling Home* (1976) and ▷*The Man from Muckinupin* (1979). She has also published at least seven volumes of poetry, of which *Rapunzel in Suburbia* is the most celebrated, and has recently published her autobiography, ▷*Wild Card* (1990). Hewett is a writer of considerable frankness, vision and skill who has won many literary awards including the ABC National Poetry Prize for 1945 and 1965, two AWGIE (Australian Writers' Guild) Awards for 1974 and 1981, the Australian Poetry Prize 1986 and the Grace Leven Award for poetry for 1989. She has also been awarded the Order of Australia.
▷Dramatists (Australia)

Heyer, Georgette (1902–1974)

English novelist. She was educated at seminary schools and Westminster College, London, married in 1925, lived in East Africa from 1925 to 1928, and Yugoslavia from 1928 to 1929. She was author of nearly 60 historical romances and detective novels, the first of which she wrote at the age of seventeen.

Heyer is best-known for her historical romances, most of which are set in the Regency period (1811–1820). A careful historical researcher, Heyer filled her novels with details of Regency fashion, manners and slang, and created a further sense of authenticity through the introduction of historical figures (Beau Brummell, the Prince Regent) among her fictional characters. Her romantic plots usually employ the stock figures of the aristocratic rake, the virtuous, though spirited, heroine, and a supporting cast of Regency fops and blades. Heyer claimed ▷Jane Austen as her literary model, and sought to emulate her ironic tone, though there is little of Austen's social satire in Heyer's work.

Heyer's dozen ▷detective novels are less well-known, although they contribute interestingly to the development of the detective genre in the 1920s and 1930s. The novels are set in the confined worlds of the country house or the London party, and the family becomes the source and location of the drama, with inheritance usually revealed as the motive for murder. Subplots are reminiscent of Heyer's Regency romances, with the hero-rake being ultimately cleared of suspicion and declaring his love for the spirited heroine.

Heyer's writing has been criticized for its conventional plots and characterizations and 'escapist' qualities or, alternatively, lauded for its wit and period 'feel'. Such discussions have overlooked other aspects of Heyer's novels which link her firmly to a tradition of women's popular romances, and in which the portrayal of relationships between the sexes suggests a different reason for her popularity. For example, in one of Heyer's best-known historical romances, *Regency Buck*, the heroine is 'tamed' by her guardian, and love and marraige come with female submission to this stern but dashing hero. Sexual fantasy is arguably a more important element in Heyer's fiction than has been allowed for.

Heyking, Elisabeth von (1861–1925)
German novelist and painter. The granddaughter of ▷Bettina von Arnim, she lived for twenty years with her husband in Peking, Valparaiso, Cairo, New York and Calcutta. This itinerant life was described in her bestselling novel *Briefe, die ihn nicht erreichten* (*Letters which Never Reached Him*), published anonymously in 1903.

Heymair, Magdalena (c 1545–after 1586)
German teacher and author of school books. Little is known of her life except that she wrote and taught in various places in southern Germany to supplement the meagre earnings of her husband, also a teacher. Her four books, *Die Sontegliche Epistel* (1566) (*The Sunday Epistle*), *Jesus Sirach* (1571), *Die Apostel Geschicht* (1573) (*The Story of the Apostles*) and *Das Buch Tobiae* (1580) (*The Book of Tobias*), are didactic renderings of biblical texts in the form of songs for children. They were extremely popular and were widely used by teachers in 16th-century Germany.

Hibbert, Eleanor ▷Plaidy, Jean

Higgins, Rita Ann (born 1955)
Irish poet, born in Galway. She left school early and only began to read seriously at the age of twenty-two while recuperating from tuberculosis. Higgins started writing poetry in 1982, and her first collection, *Goddess on the Mervue Bus*, was published in 1986. *Witch in the Bushes* followed in 1987, and *Collected Poems* in 1990. With its strong images and its colloquial, satirical, acerbic and passionate language, her poetry is a powerful indictment of class and sex oppressions. Her work has been performed by Galway Theatre Workshop, on radio and on television.

Higiro, Joy
Kenyan poet. Her autobiography *Voice of Silence* (1975) contains the First Makerere Arts Festival Song of 1968 and poems on black consciousness.

Hijab
Arabic noun for 'curtain, screen, cover', now used for a woman's veil and wraps. The polemic on *hijab* still active in some Islamic societies involves two major issues: first, the proper clothing for women out of doors, and even indoors in the presence of male adults who are not immediate relatives. Second, the question of women taking part in public life, their segregation or non-segregation in education, in the work place and in public transport.

On the issue of dress, the reference for all arguments has been a number of verses in the *Qur'an* that call upon the women of the prophet to cover their charms and behave modestly in public. Writers on the emancipation of women since Qasim Amin's ▷*Liberation of Women* (1899) have repeatedly pointed out that the *Qur'an* did not mention covering the face, and that the veil was not originally an Arab or Islamic custom. The Prophet Muhammad did not lock up his women or ban them from public life. *Sufur* or 'unveiling' became a major issue for feminist movements in Islamic countries in the first half of the 20th century. Huda Sha'rawi (1879–1947), founder of the Egyptian Feminist Union, and Saiza Nabarawi (1897–1985) signalled the issue by publicly unveiling in Cairo railway station on returning home from an International Women's Conference in Rome in 1923.

When unveiling was imposed 'from above' by statute, as was the case in Iran (1936) or by colonial authorities as in North Africa, a strong backlash in favour of veiling and *hijab* in general is seen as part of radical nationalist resistance to practices imposed by Western imperialism. *Hijab* is then promoted, not just as a religious or ideological stance, but as resistance to the economic interests of manufacturers of cosmetics, women's clothes, fashion magazines and advertising agencies that exploit women and their unveiled bodies for commercial ends.

The question of providing education and work opportunities for women under conditions of strict *hijab* has resurfaced in the last twenty-five years because of the growth of fundamentalism in some Islamic countries. On the other hand, oil-rich Saudi Arabia has actually managed to provide women's education that is 'equal but separate' from men. In higher education no expense is spared to hire female academics from all corners of the globe. Modern technology provides closed-circuit television and one-way screens by means of which male instructors can teach the women without offence to their *hijab*. A network of telephones, fax machines and a fleet of cars assures the smooth running of administration and communication with the outside world. It is, however, a costly ideal which most Islamic states cannot afford.

▷ *Hara'ir*
Bib: Beck, Lois and Keddie, Nikki (eds), *Women in the Moslem World*; Jayawardena, Kumari, *Feminism and Nationalism in the Third World*; Mernissi, Fatima, *Beyond the Veil*; Rahnavard, Zahra, *The Message of Hijab*; Sha'arawi, Huda, *Harem Years*, translated and edited by Margot Badran.

Hijos muertos, Los (1958) (The Lost Children)
Novel by Spanish writer ▷Ana María Matute. It is a good example of the neo-realism characteristic of the post-war novel in Spain. This novel meticulously traces the conflicts within three generations of the Corvo family, leading up to the tragedy of the Spanish Civil War (1936–9), expressed by means of the Cain and Abel theme.

Hilda of Whitby (614–680)
English abbess and patron. Hilda was the distinguished abbess of the important monastery of men and women at Whitby, Yorkshire. The English historian Bede (673–735) tells of the wisdom for which Hilda was consulted, by kings and noblemen as well as ordinary people. The library at Whitby appears to have been well stocked; the anonymous *Life of Pope Gregory I* (the Great), one of the earliest known to have been written in England, was produced there (680–704). Bede records the tradition that Hilda discovered and then cultivated the poetic gift of Cædmon, a lay-brother working in the monastery at Whitby; and so began the composition of Christian poetry in Old English.
Bib: Colgrave, Bertram and Mynors, R.A.B. (eds and trans.), *Bede's Ecclesiastical History of the English People*.

Hildegard von Bingen (?1098–1179)
German nun, scholar, poet, visionary and prophet. A famous, near-mythic, personality of medieval Germany, she became also known as 'the Sibyl of the Rhine', and was canonized in the 15th century. She belonged to a noble family and, at the age of eight, entered the Benedictine Convent at Disibodenberg, where she received a thorough education, especially in Latin and Botany. In 1136 she became abbess, and in 1147 founded her own convent in Rupertsberg near Bingen.

From the age of three Hildegard had visions, throughout her life experienced many episodes of religious ecstasy, and correctly predicted the advent of the three Popes in the Great Schism of 1378. She described and interpreted her visions in the mystic trilogy *Scivias* (1142–1151) (*Know the Ways*, 1986), *Liber vitae meritorum* (1158–1163) (*Book of the Lives of the Worthy*) and *Liber divinorum operum* (1163–1173) (*Book of Divine Works*), a work greatly admired by the progressive religious thinker, Bernard of Clairvaux (?1090–1153). Thus endorsed, she was able to play an active part in contemporary events by exercising some influence on the notables of her time, including Pope Eugenius III (died 1153) and the Holy Roman Emperor, Frederick Barbarossa (c 1125–1190).

Hildegard was also an accomplished orator, musician and writer, and, besides inventing a secret calligraphy and language, she composed songs, hymns, poems and passion plays which found wide popularity at the time. Her scientific writings deal with a broad variety of subjects, ranging from human anatomy and pathology to studies of animal and plant life and mineralogy. These works reveal her as a scholar of outstanding erudition and thoroughness.

Hill, Ernestine (1900–1972)
Australian novelist and travel writer. Hill is best known for her only novel, *My Love Must Wait* (1941), a fictional account of the life of the explorer Matthew Flinders, which was enormously popular in Australia, England and the USA. A tireless traveller, Hill also wrote a number of excellent travel books, including *The Great Australian Loneliness* (1937).

Hill, Frances Baylor (fl 1797)
North American diarist. Her life is known only through the diary she maintained in 1797 when she was a young woman. Raised in a well-to-do Virginia family, she was part of a socially active milieu. She spent her hours in domestic activities such as sewing and reading and visiting neighbours or attending social gatherings with other young people of her age. ▷*The Diary of Frances Baylor Hill* offers a detailed account of these everyday activities that filled the lives of so many young Southern women at the end of the 18th century.

Hill, Hannah, Jr (1703–1714)
North American religious tract writer. A devout Quaker, she desired to leave a record upon her death that would act as a guide for other young people. In ▷*A Legacy for Children*, her final sayings are interwoven into testimony from family and friends as to her goodness and charity.

▷Early North American Quaker women's writings

Hill, Susan (born 1942)

English novelist, short story writer and radio dramatist. Hill's first novel, *The Enclosure* (1961), was published before she graduated from London University. Following a career in literary journalism, Hill took to writing fiction full-time, and her novels characteristically treat themes of loneliness, isolation and despair. *In the Springtime of the Year* (1974) addresses the process of mourning, while her best-known novel, *I'm the King of the Castle* (1970), overturns assumptions of childhood innocence. *The Woman in Black* (1983), also staged as a play in the London West End, is a ghost story, in which a mother seeks revenge for the death of her child. *The Cold Country* (1975) is a collection of radio plays. Her short-story collections include: *The Albatross* (1971) and *The Custodian* (1972).

Hillern, Wilhelmine von (1836–1916)

German novelist. The daughter of the dramatist ▷Charlotte Birch-Pfeiffer, she first worked as an actress, but found her vocation, and a wide readership, by writing novels and stories for the popular magazine *Gartenlaube* (*Gazebo*). A powerful spokeswoman for conservative values, her most interesting novel is *Ein Arzt der Seele* (1869) (*Physician of the Soul*), in which an intelligent and ambitious girl is encouraged by an evil uncle to become a scientist and an atheist. When she succumbs to brain fever, she is rescued by a good man who teaches her to accept her true role as a woman.
▷*Bildungsroman*

Hillesum, Etty (Esther) (1914–1943)

Dutch prose writer. Of Jewish descent on her father's side, she studied law, Slavonic languages and psychology in Amsterdam. She worked for the Jewish Council until she and her family were transported to Auschwitz from the internment camp at Westerbork in 1943. Her diaries and letters, written between 1941 and 1943, were rediscovered in 1981, and published as *Het verstoorde leven*. Their literary, human and historical qualities were immediately recognized. Her writings bear testimony of an unyielding faith in people, a radical ethic, and stoic resignation. In 1982 the letters *Het denkende hart van de barak* were published. In 1984 new diary notes appeared under the title *In duizend zoete armen* (*In a Thousand Gentle Arms*), and a scholarly edition of her complete works was published in 1986. Translations of her writing created international interest in her work *A Diary* (1985), *An interrupted Life* (1985), *Letters from Westerbork* (1986).

Hills of Hebron, The (1966)

This novel by Caribbean writer ▷Sylvia Wynter is set in ▷Jamaica, and concerns the aspirations of Prophet Moses and his people, who, seeking to overcome 'three centuries of placelessness', leave the corrupt world of the past (colonialism) to found a new colony in Hebron where 'the black man could walk proud'. Against the background of the anti-colonial struggle of the 1950s and 1960s, the novel heralds a time of radical reorientation, and explores the possibilities posed by a move towards self-government. Wynter explores the folk culture and the phenomena of religious revivalism in Jamaica to examine the complex forces affecting Jamaican society, capturing the vital instinct of the Caribbean people to survive and create.

Critics have noted that the novel is 'invested with so much that the message tends to overwhelm the story'. In spite of this weakness, however, *The Hills of Hebron* possesses some notable features: Wynter's use of language and dramatic effects, the central role of women, and the depiction of the rural Jamaican landscape.

See the article on Sylvia Wynter in ▷*Fifty Caribbean Writers* for details of reviews and criticism.

Hilst, Hilda (born 1930)

Brazilian poet, short story writer, novelist and dramatist. Her style is intricate, and she employs intimate language on Existential topics, such as the suffering of women. She belonged to the ▷1945 Generation. Her poetry has a metaphysical and philosophical dimension, combined with all kinds of esoterisms. She defined two of her most recent books of poems as 'pornographic'. Her dramas have been performed, but not published. Her works include *Balada do festival* (poetry) (1955) (*Festival Ballad*); *Poesia 1959/1967* (anthology) (1967) (*Poems, 1959/1967*); *Qadós* (short stories) (1973); *A obscena Senhora D* (novel) (1982) (*The Obscene Mrs D*); *Cantares de perda e predilsção* (poetry) (1983); *Com meus olhos de cão e outras novelas* (short stories) (1986) (*With My Dog's Eyes, and Other Stories*).

Hindmarch, Gladys (born 1940)

Born in Ladysmith, British Columbia, Hindmarch was part of the upsurge of writing on the west coast of Canada in the 1960s. She has published *Sketches* (1970), *A Birth Account* (1976), *The Peter Stories* (1976) and *The Watery Part of the World* (1988). Her stories are physical and visual; many are based on her experiences as a cook and a messgirl.

Hineira, Arapera (born 1932)

New Zealand poet and story writer. Arapera Hineira grew up at Rangitukia on the east coast of New Zealand. Educated at the University of Auckland, Hineira worked as a teacher in the Auckland area. Under the name Arapera Blank (she has also been known as Ngati Porou, Ngati Kahungunu, Rongowhakaata and Te Aitanga-a-Mahaki), Hineira published stories in *Te Ao Hou* and other important journals, and her stories and poems have appeared in all major anthologies of New Zealand poetry and ▷Maori writing. Like the work of ▷Patricia Grace, Hineira's fiction focuses on the extended Maori family as the respository of communal values and distinctive culture. Her poetry, which is written in Maori as well as English, has become more overtly political, but also focuses on race and culture difference as exemplified in the family.

Hingano: Selected Poems 1966–1986 (1987)
Poems by ▷Konai Helu Thaman from Fiji. *Hingano* is a collection of new poems and selected material from Thaman's two earlier published collections, *You, The Choice of My Parents* (1974) and *Langakali* (1981). Thaman's poems are occasional, informally constructed, personal lyrics that reflect the cultural contexts of their writing, but are mostly addressed to friends or family. The earlier poems have a political edge and reflect Thaman's years spent in New Zealand and the United States, but the later material uses more accomplished forms and celebrates the poet's relationships, and in particular the landscapes and mythology of Fiji and other Pacific islands.

Hipparchia (4th century BC)
Possibly Athenian. A philosopher herself, she was the wife of the Greek philosopher Crates the Cynic (4th century BC), brother of another Cynic, Metrocles (4th century BC). Hipparchia is the only woman to earn a separate chapter in Diogenes Laertius's *Lives of the Philosophers* (3rd century AD). From that we learn she was of wealthy background but abandoned all to follow the ascetic philosophy of the Cynics. Male sources (in satire and comedy) found her adoption of male philosophic dress more interesting than her philosophy. The biographical dictionary, the *Suda* (10th century AD), lists her written works as *Hypotheses, Preliminary Proofs*, and *Propositions against Theodorus the Atheist*. Some letters from her to her husband survive, but they do not reveal anything of her beliefs and act purely as context for letters, allegedly from Crates to Hipparchia, urging moderation, fortitude, and care of their child.
▷Philosophers, Ancient Greek and Roman women

Hipparchia's Choice (1991)
Translation of *L'Etude et le rouet* (1989), a major work by French philosopher ▷Michèle Le Doeuff. It is structured around a detailed comparison of the philosophies of Jean-Paul Sartre and ▷Simone de Beauvoir, and combines a feminist critique of the philosophical tradition with discussion of theoretical and practical feminist issues. In her endeavour to reintroduce feminist ideas into philosophy in a way that meets philosophical standards, Le Doeuff reveals that those standards have always been unstable, since philosophy is a constant process of reorientating thought. The last section of the book stresses the responsibility of the state in women's oppression, and criticizes its incapacity and unwillingness to promote a society in which both sexes can participate equally.

Hiraiwa Yumie (born 1932)
Japanese novelist and scriptwriter. She was born in Tokyo, the eldest daughter of the chief priest of a Shinto shrine. Hiraiwa began to write novels in 1957, basing them on her experience of Japanese classical entertainment such as *Buyou*, *Nagauta* and *Tsuzumi*. *A Swordsmith* (1959) won the Naoki Prize. This work describes the delicate feelings of men whose swordsmanship is being judged. Her other main works are *Huko* and *The Inn Called Kawasemi*.

Histoire et mythologie de l'amour: huit siècles d'écrits féminins (1974) ▷*Women in Love: Eight Centuries of Feminine Writing* (1980)

Historical novel, The (19th-century Britain)
A novel set in a period before the author's lifetime, often representing historical events with a cast of real and fictional characters. In the 19th century, Walter Scott developed the form, although he acknowledged his debt to ▷Maria Edgeworth. ▷George Eliot's ▷*Romola* and ▷Mary Shelley's *Valperga* are both examples of such fiction. Other practitioners of the form include ▷Lucy Aikin, ▷Anna Eliza Bray, ▷Elizabeth Gaskell, ▷Eliza Lynn Linton, ▷Margaret Oliphant and ▷Charlotte Yonge.

Historical novelists
The Netherlands: The best-known 19th-century historical novelist is Truitje Bosboom-Toussaint (1812–1886). In her novels she presents various political, religious and social ideals: *De graaf van Devonshire* (1838) (*The Earl of Devonshire*), *Het huis van Lauernesse* (1840) (*The House of Lauerness*), *Leycester-cyclus* (1846–1855), and *De Delftse wonderdokter* (1870) (*The Delft Miracle Doctor*). A novel on Hugo de Groot and Maria Reigerberch, entitled *Vaderland in de verte* (*Native Country in the Distance*), written by ▷Annie Romein-Verschoor, appeared in 1948. The most important female historical novelist of this century is Hella Haasse (born 1918). Initially she wrote beautiful, though traditional, historical novels, like *Het woud der verwachting* (1949) (*In a Dark Wood Wandering*), a romantic life of Charles d'Orléans (1394–1465), and *De scharlaken stad* (1952) (*The Scarlet City*), describing 15th-century Rome. Later, her work consisted mainly of commentaries on historical documents; later she returned to a narrative style. In *Mevrouw Bentinck of De onverenigbaarheid van karakter* (1978) (*Mrs Bentinck or Incompatibility of Character*) and *De groten der aarde of Bentinck tegen Bentinck* (1981) (*The Great of the Earth or Bentinck versus Bentinck*) Haasse paints a vivid picture of the life of an 18th-century noble married couple. *Een vreemdelinge in Den Haag* (1984) (*Sophie, a Stranger in The Hague*) contains the correspondence of Queen Sophie of the Netherlands. *Schaduwbeeld of Het geheim van Appeltern* (1989) (*Silhouette or the Secret of Appeltern*) is a biographical novel on the

life of an 18th-century patriot. Haasse's work gained international recognition through many translations.

Helene Nolthenius (born 1920) wrote historical novels. *Duecento* (1951) is a study embracing music and society in 13th-century Italy; the city of Florence in the 14th century is the subject of *Renaissance in mei* (1956) (*Renaissance in May*); and in *De man uit het dal van Spoleto* (1988) (*The Man From the Valley of Spoleto*) she explores the life of Francis of Assisi. Her most recent historical novel is *Babylon aan de Rhône* (1991) (*Babylon on the Rhône*).

The first historical novel of Nelleke Noordervliet (born 1945), *Tine of De dalen waar het leven woont* (1987) (*Tine or the Valleys Where Life Lives*), tells the story of Everdine van Wijnbergen, first wife of the 19th-century Dutch writer Multatuli.

Scandinavia after 1900: At the beginning of the century the historical novel provided a chance for women writers to escape the pressure to write realistically. ▷Sigrid Undset and ▷Thit Jensen both wrote about very modern sexual conflicts in medieval settings, because this gave them an opportunity to unfold their Utopian visions. Ingeborg Refling Hagen (1895–1989) is also notable.

Since 1970, a new kind of historical novel has emerged. Women now rewrite history, especially in relation to female characters, in the light of new feminist research. This literature has found a wide audience. In Sweden, ▷Sara Lidman, ▷Kerstin Ekman and Marianne Frederiksson (born 1926) have become very popular; in Norway, Karin Bang (born 1928), and in Denmark, ▷Dorrit Willumsen and Anne Marie Eirnæs (born 1946).

One group of novels describes famous women from history, or women from royal families. Another group describes everyday life of a historical period. Both groups tend to create incredibly strong female characters, evidently influenced by the new gender and sexual roles after 1970.

History: A Novel (1977)

Translation of *La storia* (1974) by Italian writer ▷Elsa Morante. Set in Rome during the 1940s, it tells the story of what can only loosely be described as a family. Ida is raped by Gunther, a German soldier, and gives birth to Useppe, the protagonist, as a result. Useppe inherits epilepsy from his mother, and eventually dies of it. The tale of these individuals, their isolation, fear, poverty and pain is offset against received history. The novel charts a progression of disasters in the lives of its characters.

History of Emily Montague, The (1769)

▷Frances Brooke's ▷epistolary novel about garrison life in Quebec City in the 1760s is considered to be the first Canadian novel, although Canada as such did not yet exist. Brooke spent five years with her husband, who was chaplain with the British Garrison at Quebec City,

and her experience informs this seminal work. The epistolary form permits Brooke to use different points of view, and it is the characters' descriptions of the New World that are interesting, more so than their very colonial courtships and romances. One of the main correspondents, Arabella Fermor, Emily Montague's best friend, praises the lives of Native Canadian women because they are free to travel where they please, without asking permission of any male. Although she later retracts her desire for this difference when she learns that they are not free to choose their own husbands, the ambiguous nature of freedom and choice for women is raised in interesting relation to early colonialism. The 228 letters which comprise the novel describe well the dichotomy between the natural and societal world, and question the whole division of civilization and savagery as constructed by a garrisoned occupier.

History of Humayun, The (1902)

English translation of the Persian chronicle *Humayan Nama* (c 1580) by the 16th-century princess ▷Begum Gulbadam. In addition to providing detailed histories and genealogies of the first two Mughal emperors of India, Babur and Humayun, it gives precious insights into the lives of the Muslim women of the court. No male chronicler of the time would ever have been allowed to peer into the secluded lives of the royal women, but as the Begum shows in her history these women were often very powerful political figures in their own right.

History of Maria Kittle, The (1791)

Epistolary novel by North American writer ▷Ann Eliza Schuyler Bleecker. First published in the *New-York Magazine* and subsequently in *The Posthumous Works of Ann Eliza Bleecker* (1793), this novel blends the traditions of the early North American ▷captivity narrative and the sentimental novel. Drawing on her own experiences of having to flee danger during the American Revolution (which, in one instance, cost the life of her infant daughter), Bleecker transfers the source of danger to Native Americans, whom she describes as 'barbarians'. In such a depiction, Bleecker was at the forefront of novelists who described the North American frontier as a wilderness inhabited by savages where the new North American heroes – or, importantly, in Bleecker's case, heroines – were formed.

History of Mary Prince, A West Indian Slave, Related by Herself (1831)

In this unique document, first published by the ▷*Anti Slavery Reporter* in 1831, the Caribbean writer ▷Mary Prince vividly recalls her life as a slave in ▷Bermuda, Turks Island and ▷Antigua. She tells of her rebellion against physical and psychological degradation, and her eventual escape in London in 1828. A central element of the text revolves around her religious conversion, which provided her with a sense of her worth.

Dictated by Mary Prince, this narrative forms part of the abolitionist literature of the period. Since the narrative (like others) was intended as propaganda to correct a social wrong, the text conformed to a formula. Women were censored so as not to suggest any moral degradation, thus in Prince's text her experience of sexual abuse is encoded within accounts of angry jealous mistresses and a master who forced her to wash him naked.

See Ziggi Alexander's preface and Moira Ferguson's introduction to the 1987 edition of *The History of Mary Prince*.

History of the Marquis de Cressy, The (1765)

A translation of ▷Riccoboni's third novel, *Histoire de M. le Marquis de Cressy* (1758). It portrays a male lover who, despite being well-intentioned and eventually repentant, proves untrustworthy, and ruins the lives of three women. In love with Adélaide, he recognizes that a marriage with her would not be a good match, and abandons her for a wealthy widow, Madame de Raisel, who is in love with him. Once married, he betrays her with her young protégée, Hortense. De Raisel commits suicide, poisoning her own tea and having him serve it to her. Hortense retires to a convent. The novel reiterates Riccoboni's view of the unbridgeable nature of the gap between the sexes: men are morally and psychologically weaker than women who, for the most part, are inherently sincere, but are slow to recognize male duplicity and their own capacity for self-delusion in love.

History of the Rise, Progress and Termination of the American Revolution (1805)

▷Mercy Otis Warren's three-volume history of the American Revolution. Twenty-five years in the writing, it includes biographical sketches of military and political leaders of the era, many of whom she knew personally. Her 'moral observations' and anti-federalist biases are not eliminated from the history, but it was highly praised and remained the seminal work in its field for decades after its publication.

▷*Group, The; Ladies of Castille, The; Poems, Dramatic and Miscellaneous*

Hitty, Her First Hundred Years (1931)

US novel. ▷Rachel Field's *Hitty* was the first children's book written by a woman to win the Newbery Medal. Hitty is a wooden doll carved early in the 19th century. With Hitty, Field creates a heroic, adventurous heroine, and her adventures include a whaling expedition, and meeting island savages and a missionary family in India. Through the historical and regional settings Field provides, Hitty introduces the young reader to different times and places, and accepts her destiny while eagerly anticipating the next adventure.

Ho, Minfong (born 1951)

Singaporean writer. She was born in Burma in 1951 to a Singapore Chinese family, and educated in Thailand and the USA, where all her books were first published. She frequently lives and works with her North American husband in South-east Asia, which also provides the setting for her novels; her writing tends to be feminist in approach. Her first novel, *Sing to the Dawn* (1975) won the Inter-racial Books for Children Council's Prize. Set in Thailand, it relates how a farmer's daughter bravely makes it to school in the city, despite family and social pressure to give up her scholarship to her brother. *Rice Without Rain* (1986), a socially-engaged novel about two young Thai sisters whose village and lives are changed by leftist Thai student political activists, especially a female medical student, won Singaporean, North American and Commonwealth book awards. A recent novel, *The Clay Marble* (1991), set in a Thai border refugee camp, focuses on the courage, tragic lives and survival instincts of Cambodian refugee children. Her prize-winning short story, 'Tanjong Rhu' ('Casuarina Headland'), however, is set in Singapore, based on childhood memories of her home and grandfather.

Hobbes, John Oliver (1867–1906)

▷Pseudonym of British novelist, dramatist and journalist, born Pearl Morgan Richards, the daughter of a wealthy American businessman. She came to England as a baby, was educated in London and Paris, and married Reginald Craigie, a banker, in 1887. The marriage lasted until 1891, when Hobbes and her child returned to the parental home. She became a Catholic in 1892. Her first novel *Some Emotions and a Moral* (1891) was highly successful, and set a pattern for her subsequent fiction in its treatment of ill-matched marriages and disillusioned idealism. Both Hobbes's fiction and her drama display wit and frivolity, but the novels also demonstrate a greater depth of thought and a melancholy wisdom. Works include: *The Sinner's Comedy* (1892); *Journeys End in Lovers Meeting* (1894); *The School for Saints* (1897), and *Robert Orange* (1900). Her last work was *The Dream and the Business* (1906).
Bib: Maison, M., *Life*; Richards, J.M., *Life*.

Hobhouse, Emily ▷Anglo-Boer War writing

Hobomok: A Tale of Early Times (1824)

US novel by ▷Lydia Maria Child. Child's earliest book, *Hobomok* is a historical treatment of early Massachusetts. Its romantic plot, pairing and marrying the Puritan heroine Mary Conant with the noble Native American, Hobomok, evidenced Child's sympathy and support for ▷Native Americans – and raised some controversy at the time. The book's conclusion pales with Mary and her son's return to the white world.

Hoby, Margaret Dakins Devereux Sidney (1571–1633)

English diarist. The only daughter of Arthur and Thomasine Gye Dakins, she was raised in the strongly Puritan household of Catherine Hastings. Sometime before 1589 she married Walter Devereux, who died two years later. Within less than a year she married Thomas Sidney, the brother of Philip Sidney (1554–1586) and ▷Mary Herbert. Sidney died in 1595 and the following year she married Thomas Posthumous Hoby, the son of ▷Elizabeth Cooke Russell. ▷ *The Diary of Lady Margaret Hoby, 1599–1605* is probably the earliest extant diary in English.

Hockby, Stephen ▷Mitchell, Gladys

Hodge, Merle (born 1944)

Caribbean novelist, children's writer, lecturer and journalist. Hodge was born, and received her early education, in ▷Trinidad. She read French at University College London, where she obtained BA and MA degrees. She has worked and studied in France and Denmark, travelled extensively in Europe, West Africa and the Caribbean, and worked in ▷Grenada under the socialist regime of Maurice Bishop, as Director of Curriculum Development. She now lives in Trinidad, where she lectures part-time at the University of the West Indies, St Augustine, and is working on her second novel. Her first novel was ▷ *Crick Crack Monkey*, but she has also written short stories for children and numerous articles and reviews. *Crick Crack Monkey*, like many first novels by Caribbean writers, is a novel of ▷childhood. See the introduction to the Heinemann 1981 edition for a useful explanation of the novel's major concerns.

Hodge has been an important voice in the womanist debates concerned with the historical oppression of Caribbean women. Her two non-fiction essays, 'The Shadow of the Whip: A Comment on Male–Female Relations in the Caribbean' (1974) and 'Young Women and the Development of Stable Family Life in the Caribbean' (1977) reflect her political views.

An essay on Hodge is included in ▷*Fifty Caribbean Writers*, and this provides full biographical details and critical references.

Hodgkins, Sarah Perkins (?1750–1803)

North American letter-writer. A resident of Ipswich, Massachusetts, she was left to manage the family household while her husband, Joseph Hodgkins, participated in the American Revolution. ▷'The Hodgkins Letters' constitute a collection of twenty letters that she sent to her husband between May 1775 and January 1779.

'Hodgkins Letters, The' (1958)

Between May 1775 and January 1779, ▷Sarah Perkins Hodgkins of Ipswich, Massachusetts, wrote twenty letters to her husband, Joseph, who was serving in the Continental Army during the American Revolution. The letters reveal Hodgkins's love for her husband, her daily activities and thoughts as she was thrust into the role of head of the household, and her reliance upon religious faith as guidance. The letters were not collected until 1958, as part of *This Glorious Cause*.
▷Early North American letters

Hodrova, Daniela (born 1946)

Czech novelist and literary critic. Hodrová is the wife of the prose writer Karel Milota and, although they both became generally known only after the collapse of communism in November 1989, she was active in intellectual life throughout the 1980s from her base as a research worker in the Academy Institute of Literature. Fragments of her novels did appear in France, but her first works of prose fiction, *Kukly* (*Masks or Pupae*) and *Podoboji* (*In Both Kinds*) were published only in 1991. These labrynthine novels, written with exquisite verbal precision, presently a world where the living and the dead co-exist, have become recognized as the greatist achievements in Czech prose since World War II. She translated Russian literary theory, particularly Mikhail Bakhtin (1895–1975), but her one book of literary criticism/theory, *Hledání románu* (1989) (*Seeking the Novel*), was emasculated by the authorities. Even so, it showed her to be the most original contemporary Czech thinker about literature. (*Hledání* is an anagram of Daniela H.) She rejects pure theory and pure literary history, but produces a persuasive account of the development of the novel in Russian and western European (and Czech) literature. She conceives of the novel (or romance) as having two fundamental types: the 'novel-as-invention' and the 'novel-as-reality'; these two types each have, potentially, eight sub-types.

Hofmo, Gunvor (born 1921)

Norwegian lyric poet. She is a prominent figure in modernist lyrical poetry in Norway. Her writing speaks of her own generation and its feelings of powerlessness and despair. The female 'I' is confronted with pain, anxiety and death. The poems are written as a reaction to chaos, to World War II and the new post-war era.

Her début was *Jeg vil hjem til menneskene* (1946) (*I Want to go Home to People*) which used a rather conventional style with rhymes, stanzas and a fixed rhythm, but from the next book onwards, she developed a more experimental, modernist style: *Fra en annen virkelighet* (1948) (*From Another Reality*), *Blinde nattergaler* (1951) (*Blind Nightingales*), (*I en våkenatt*) (1954) (*During a Night's Watch*) and *Testamente til en evighet* (1955) (*Testament to an Eternity*).

Hofmo was then silent for sixteen years. In the 1970s she began to publish again with *Gjest på jorden* (1971) (*Guest on Earth*). Her themes are now historical, political or social, but her tone and style remain the same: the Existential struggle, the longing for a different world, religious pain and ecstasy. She has published seventeen books of lyrical poems.

Hogan, Linda (born 1947)
US novelist and dramatist. A Chichascuo
▷Native American, Hogan grew up in Colorado
and Oklahoma. She gained a Master's degree in
1978 from Colorado University, and since 1984
has taught at the University of Minnesota-Twin
Cities at Minneapolis. Her work underlines the
importance of protecting the natural world and
the land for the survival of Native American
culture. The historical novel *Mean Spirit* (1990)
tells the story of the brutal exploitation of Native
Americans for their oil-rich lands in the 1920s
and 1930s, and shows how, despite this, Native
Americans resisted forced assimilation into Anglo-
American culture by sustaining family and tribal
relationships and traditions. Hogan retrieves this
history to show that spirituality, respect for the
environment and politics are inseparable in Native
Americans' struggles to reclaim land and cultural
traditions.
   Other works include: *A Crate of Wooden Birds*,
Seeing Through the Sun (1985).

Holden, Helene (born 1935)
Canadian novelist. A Montrealer of Greek-French
descent, her writing approaches the tensions of
relationships between men and women, while
retaining an enigmatic economy. *The Chain* (1969)
was translated into French by the author in 1970.
Goodbye, Muffin Lady (1974), *After the Fact* (1986)
and *Snow* (1990) are imagistic etchings balanced
on an intricate bilingual awareness.

Holiday House (1839)
A novel for children by Scottish writer
▷Catherine Sinclair, which helped to develop a
taste for books representing mischievous rather
than moral children. Sinclair described her
intentions thus: 'In these pages the author has
endeavoured to paint that species of noisy,
frolicsome, mischievous children, now almost
extinct, wishing to preserve a sort of fabulous
remembrance of days long past, when young
people were like wild horses on the prairies,
rather than well-broken hacks on the road.'
   ▷Children's literature (19th-century Britain)

Hollar, Constance (1881–1945)
This Caribbean poet, born in ▷Jamaica, was an
active member of poetry circles in Jamaica during
the late 1930s and early 1940s. Her poetic output
was prolific and impressive, although some critics
now regard her style as 'dated'. Her best-known
books include the collection *Flaming June* (1941)
and her contributions to the *Independence Anthology
of Jamaican Literature* (1962) and *Caribbean Voices*
(1966).

Hollingsworth, Margaret (born 1940)
Dramatist, born in London, England, who
emigrated to Canada in 1968, and received an
MFA in theatre and creative writing from the
University of British Columbia in 1974.
Hollingsworth's drama has been produced in
England and Canada, and has been given

international radio and television exposure. Her
one-act stage plays include *Alli Alli Oh* (1979),
Bushed and *Operators*, published together in 1981;
they succeed in evoking unified moments through
an intensely realized brevity. *Mother Country*
(1981) and *Ever Loving*, produced in 1980, both
deal with Canada as second home: the former is
about Canadians who are more English than the
English, the latter about three war brides and
their adjustment to Canada. Hollingsworth has
also published a collection of short fiction, *Smiling
Under Water* (1989). Her multilingual sense of
language and its boundaries informs the acute
observations of her characters.

Holt, Victoria ▷Plaidy, Jean

Holtby, Winifred (1898–1935)
English journalist, novelist, dramatist and social
reformer. Born in Yorkshire, Holtby read history
at Somerville College, Oxford, but her degree was
interrupted during World War I when she joined
the Women's Auxiliary Corps. She returned to
Somerville in 1919 and became close friends with
▷Vera Brittain, both women becoming active
campaigners for pacifism and women's rights.
Holtby's commitment to pacifism and feminism
forms the basis of much of her journalism,
particularly for the *Manchester Guardian*, the *News
Chronicle* and the feminist weekly *Time and Tide*,
of which she became a director in 1926. Holtby
was also a fierce spokesperson for the unionization
of black workers in South Africa, a cause for
which she continued to fight throughout her life.
   Holtby's first novel, *Anderby Wold* (1923),
focuses on the Yorkshire farming communities of
her childhood, while her next novel, *The Crowded
Street* (1924), introduces Holtby's concern with
women's issues and experiences, highlighting the
shallowness of the everyday lives of bourgeois
women. *Mandoa Mandoa!* (1933) satirizes the
travel industry, and looks at the attempts to
market a central African principality for European
consumption. Holtby won the James Tait Black
Memorial Prize with ▷*South Riding* (1936), which
explores the relationship between regional policy-
making and its effect on the concrete
circumstances of the local community. Her non-
fictional writings include an early critical study of
▷Virginia Woolf (1932) and *Women in a Changing
Civilization* (1934), a history of the changing social
role of women. Holtby's correspondence with
Vera Brittain is collected in *Letters to a Friend*
(1937).
   ▷*Testament of Youth*
Bib: Brittain, V. *Testament of Friendship*; Handley-
Taylor, G. *Winifred Holtby: A Concise and Selected
Bibliography*; White, E. *Winifred Holtby As I Knew
Her*.

**Holy Anchoress of Mansfield, The (15th
century)**
English anchoress. Anchoresses were women who
chose to live of prayer and meditation in seclusion
rather than in a community of nuns. The 'cells' in

which they were enclosed were often attached to churches, and their contact with the outside world was very restricted. However, their advice and guidance was often sought (▷Julian of Norwich). They would have had books to aid them in their devotions, and it is quite possible that more anchoresses than we know of may have written. A poem to the Virgin Mary, 'The Five Joys of Our Lady' is ascribed in one of the manuscripts to the prolific writer Lydgate (c 1370–1449/50), and in another to 'a holy Ancresse of Mansfield'.
Bib: Brown, C. (ed.), *Religious Lyrics of the Fifteenth Century.*

Holyoke, Mary Vial (1737–1802)

North American diarist. An only child, she married Edward Augustus Holyoke, a physician, and produced twelve children of whom only three survived beyond youth. Her forty-year diary, published in a family collection, ▷*The Holyoke Diaries, 1709–1856*, was begun shortly after her marriage. From January 1760 to December 1799, she recorded the events of her life as a prominent member of society in Salem, Massachusetts. Secular in theme, the diary is a collection of short entries that constitute a community record from the pre-revolutionary era through the decades of the nation's emergence.

Holyoke Diaries, 1709–1856, The (1911)

Included in this North American family collection is the forty-year diary of ▷Mary Vial Holyoke of Salem, Massachusetts. Holyoke renders her life only in snippets of daily activities and family events ('My Dear Child Buried. Mr Brown went to new port', 'Violent Storm N.E. News of Gen. Lee's Being taken'), but the cumulative effect is an account of her upper-class community's day-to-day activities. Two female relatives' diaries are also included in the collection.

Home, Cecil ▷Webster, Augusta

Home Girls, The (1982)

Australian short story collection by ▷Olga Masters. This collection of short stories ruthlessly exposes the unfortunate situation of women and children in the Australian bush. 'The Home Girls', the title story, deals with orphan children shunted from one uncaring home to another, and 'The Snake and Bad Tom' with the Dickensian plight of a boy who is hated, victimized and whipped by his father, the 'snake' of the title. Masters's writing is skilful, economical and savage.

Home Without a Table (1978)

Japanese writer ▷Enchi Fumiko based this novel on a memorable incident when the radical students' group (the Allied Red Army) inflicted brutal punishment to the point of death on some of their members at Asama Cottage in 1972. She writes in an afterword: 'I am motivated by such a horrendous affair to describe the image of a man who continues to struggle for his belief, while his

family is broken and nobody gathers around the table. I am happy if readers notice there is a close relationship between society and family.' Enchi has pinpointed a serious problem which is central to modern society.

Honeymoon for Three (1979)

Novel by Ugandan writer ▷Jane Bakaluba. In this work of popular fiction Bakaluba attempts to bring together traditional and modern elements in society through the device of a marriage between Naiga and Muwa.

Hope Leslie (1827)

Popular US novel by ▷Catharine Maria Sedgwick. Using a historical setting in Puritan Massachusetts, and many historical characters and incidents, *Hope Leslie* adopts the conventions of the ▷captivity narrative, but within a romantic conception of the ▷Native American. With a number of paired characters, plots, and reports from different points of view, Sedgwick achieves some complexity through the dualities. The Puritan household of the story encompasses two young Native Americans and two white sisters, the title character, Hope, and her sister, Faith – who is captured by the Native Americans, marries, and refuses to return to the white Puritan world. To the degree that Native American and Puritan settler views are set parallel, *Hope Leslie* is distinctive and innovative – but the dialogue is stilted and the emotion often stereotyped.

Hopkins, Sarah Winnemucca (c 1844–1891)

US non-fiction writer. Hopkins was among the earliest-published ▷Native American women writers. Her periodical publication and her autobiographical *Life Among the Paiutes: Their Wrongs and Claims* (1883) reflect the mixture – and conflict – of cultures that made up her life. Descended from tribal chiefs, she was educated in California and knew Spanish as well as English. A vigorous proponent of Native American rights, she also was an involved participant in white North American culture – causing some to question her allegiances.

Hora violeta, L' (1980) (The Violet Hour)

Novel by Spanish writer ▷Montserrat Roig. It explores the evolution of two families in Barcelona by focusing on the relationship between two female protagonists. *L'Hora violeta* sets the relationships of a number of women within the historical frame of the Spanish Civil War (1936–9) and the Franco years (1939–75), and evaluates the various ways in which women seek solidarity in a world which disenfranchises them from birth.
▷Catalan women's writing

Horovitz, Frances (1938–1983)

English poet. She was educated at Bristol University and the Royal Academy of Dramatic Arts. Following an early career as an actor, Horovitz became a well-known reader of contemporary poetry for radio and television. Her first volume of poetry, *Poems* (1967), was followed by *The High Tower* (1970). *Water over Stone* (1980) and *Some Light, Water Light* (1983) are distinctive for their evocative representations of Northumberland landscapes and natural habitat, revealing also a strong interest in ancient history and myth. *Collected Poems* (1985) was edited and published posthumously.

Horta, Maria Teresa (born 1937)

Portuguese poet, novelist and journalist. Author of more than twenty books, Horta is best known as one of the ▷'Three Marias'. In the sixties she was an active participant of *Poesia 61*, a movement opposed to ▷neo-realism; she was also involved in experimental film-making with the ABC Cine Club. In 1971 she published *Minha Senhora de Mim* (*Milady of Me*), a slim volume of poetry which was banned by the regime for its graphic descriptions of physical love. This incident was the catalyst for the collaborative ▷*Novas Cartas Portuguesas*. After the April 1974 revolution Horta joined the Communist Party, and, since then, she has devoted much of her time to political activism. In 1977 she published the volume of poems *Mulheres de Abril* (*Women of April*), in which images of working-class women figure prominently. Among her most recent works are the novel *Ema* (1985) and the poetry collections *Minha Mãe, Meu Amor* (1986) (*My Mother, My Love*) and *Rosa Sangrenta* (1987) (*Bleeding Rose*) – all of which focus on the female body and sexuality. For several years Horta was editor of the magazine *Mulheres* (*Women*), the principal publication of the Movimento Democrático de Mulheres, the largest women's association in the country. She currently writes for the literary supplement *Jornal de Letras*.
▷Costa, Maria Velho da; Barreno, Maria Isabel

Hortensia (1st century BC)

Orator. The daughter of the celebrated Roman politician and orator Quintus Hortensius (2nd century BC), she delivered a speech in 42 BC protesting against a proposed law that women's possessions be taxed to fund civil war. She claimed that women, who were not allowed to hold office or take part in politics, ought not to be forced to pay for men's mistakes. Her speech greatly impressed her audience, many remarking how, through the daughter, the father lived again, and it was successful. The Roman writer Quintilian (1st century AD) says her speech, then still extant, was worthy to be read 'not simply for its honour towards women'. No fragments survive, but the Greek historian Appian (1st century AD) has his own version which may be based on the original.

Hosain, Attia (born 1913)

Indian journalist, novelist and short story writer. She was born in Lucknow to an aristocratic *taluqdari* (land owning) family, and was the first

Attia Hosain

woman from this background to obtain a university education. Her schooling in Lucknow combined the Western liberalism of La Martiniere School for Girls and Isabella Thoburn College, with the traditional lessons in Arabic, Persian and Urdu at home which enabled a high-class Moslem girl to make her way in Lucknow's courtly culture. As a young adult she was greatly influenced by the political ideals of the Indian National Congress and the ▷Progressive Writers' Association, and she could not accept the proposal of a separate land for India's Moslems. When independence in 1947 was accompanied by ▷Partition, she chose to make London her home rather than stay in India or move to the new state of Pakistan. There she presented her own women's programme on the BBC's Eastern Service, appeared on the West End stage, and television. A collection of short stories, ▷*Phoenix Fled*, was published in 1951, and it was followed by a novel, ▷*Sunlight on a Broken Column*, in 1961. Both were republished in 1988.

Hoskens, Jane Fenn (born 1694)

North American spiritual autobiographer. Born in London, she was reared in the teachings of the Church of England. Struck by illness at age sixteen, however, she promised God that if she survived she would dedicate her life to him. It was a promise she kept, first in her travels to the New World and her conversion to Quakerism, and then in her journeys as a public preacher, all of which are detailed in her autobiography, ▷*The Life and Spiritual Sufferings of That Faithful Servant of Christ, Jane Hoskens* (1771). Described as 'a tender spirit, but weighty and awful in prayer', she chose to write her autobiography as a spiritual and literal travel record of her many public preachings in New England, Virginia, the Carolinas,

Barbados, and in England and Ireland. Controversial in her own day, she remains an important figure in women's religious and literary history.
▷Early North American Quaker women's writings

Hospital, Janette Turner (born 1942)

Janette Turner Hospital

Australian-born novelist and short story writer who emigrated to Canada in 1971, but has also lived in the USA, England, and India. She continues to spend some time in Australia, and her fiction frequently takes as its subject the dislocated character, unsure of where home is. She graduated from the University of Queensland, and taught at high school in tropical Australia, before moving to Boston, where she was a librarian at Harvard University for four years. After coming to Canada, she received an MA in medieval English literature from Queen's University, and she has been a lecturer and writer-in-residence at various institutions. In 1982 she won the Seal Award for *The Ivory Swing*, a novel which employs India as a site for a character's pivotal moment of struggle and self-recognition, an outsider able to achieve only temporary intersection with an alien world. *The Tiger in the Tiger Pit* (1983) engages a cross-geographical family, split in time and inclination, as their parents celebrate their fiftieth anniversary. *Borderline* (1985) is a sophisticated novel that questions narrative positioning and determinacy with considerable skill: three characters who intersect at the Canadian–US border in an illegal crossing are interrogated by a highly selfconscious text, which is primarily about art and denial. *Charades* (1989) is less effective, but nevertheless

strongly allusive in its apprehension of disguise and damage. Hospital's short story collections, *Dislocations* (1986) and *Isobars* (1990), are sensitive to the yearnings of wandering and homeless characters.
▷Short story (Australia)
Bib: Howells, C., *Private and Fictional Words*.

Hossain, Begum Rokeya Sakhawat

Indian writer and social activist. Her lifelong campaign against purdah (the veil) and for female education brought her fame as a pioneer reformer among Bengali Moslem women. She published, in both Bengali and English, many articles condemning the oppression of women in India. In 1909 she opened the Sakhawat Memorial Girls' School, and in 1916 she founded the Anjuman-i-Khawatin-i-Islam to promote education among all classes of women. She also presided over the Bengal Women's Educational Conference, and led a session of the Indian Women's Conference. Her short story, 'Sultana's Dream' (1905), has been acknowledged as one of the first self-consciously feminist pieces of Utopian writing.

Hotel du Lac (1984)

Novel by English writer ▷Anita Brookner. Her fourth novel, it won the Booker Prize for 1984, and finally established her reputation as a writer of fiction. Her heroine, romantic novelist Edith Hope, goes to stay in a Swiss hotel, in disgrace, we discover as the plot unfolds, for leaving Geoffrey, the man she is supposed to marry, standing on the registry office steps. She is in love with David, who is married and does little to alleviate the loneliness of her life. At the hotel, she writes him long letters which, it transpires at the end of the novel, she never sends. These are primarily about the other hotel guests, the majority of whom are women – widowed, single or separated from their husbands. The issues that concern the reserved, 'ladylike' but ironical Edith are 'the question of what behaviour most becomes a woman', and the seeming impossibility of combining love and marriage – she has been offered both, but not by the same person.

Brookner's controlled, precise writing gives a vividness to the narrative. She works in a ▷realist mode, but the novel contains complex, self-reflexive moments in which Edith's romantic novels are implicitly contrasted with the story Brookner herself is telling. The novel also contains faint echoes of ▷Virginia Woolf's ▷*Mrs Dalloway* (1925).

Hotel Manager, The (1976)

Russian novella by ▷I. Grékova. In this Soviet variant of Chekhov's *The Darling*, I. Grékova traces Vera Butova's life from her poverty-stricken childhood on the Black Sea to her sixtieth birthday in the 1970s. The skills Vera learns during twenty-seven years as the submissive wife of a rigid military man enable her to make a success of a later career runing a hotel in her

home town. Male characters are mere stereotypes in Grékova's picture of the contradiction between the demands they make on women, and the nexus of love and support women create for each other, as well as the psychological satisfaction they draw from everyday activities. Somewhat saccharine twists in the plot are redeemed by well-realized scenes and delightful details. The work appeared with 'The Ladies' Hairdresser' in translation as *Russian Women* (1983).
(1925).

'Hottentot Eve'

Term coined by critic Stephen Gray in his book *Southern African Literature: An Introduction*, to refer to the figure of a Khoi woman, used by male travel writers and critics to represent anarchic or bestial sexuality. Gray charts the representational 'journey' of this figure, from a play by Andrew Geddes Bain called *Kaatje Kekkelbek or Life among the Hottentots* (first produced in 1838), to the play *Boesman and Lena* (1969) by contemporary dramatist Athol Fugard, by which time history has transformed the figure into an abject version of her original self.

Gray includes the real-life Krotoa in this representational complex, for white, male preconceptions shaped the fate of real women too. Krotoa (renamed Eva) was the first Khoikhoi woman to live among the Dutch colonizers at the Cape. Sent by the Cochoqua to act as official interpreter between the Dutch and the Khoikhoi, and also acting as unofficial spy, probably to both groups, she gradually assimilated into the Dutch people. She lost her position of authority with the Khoikhoi, and, after her Danish husband's death, was also rejected by the Dutch for her unseemly behaviour. By the time of her death, aged twenty-two, having apparently borne six children, she had given herself over to a life spent wandering drunkenly around the dock area, singing the Khoikhoi songs of her youth. Krotoa's story, first given in the journals of Jan van Riebeeck (1952–62), has been recently rewritten in a long poem by the South African poet Karen Press as well as in a children's book, *Krotoa* (1990), revisionist texts which give substance and voice to a figure once apparently controlled by white, male fantasy.

Houdetot, Elisabeth-Françoise-Sophie de La Live de Bellegarde, Comtesse de (?1730–1813)

French writer of occasional verse. Born in Paris, she belonged to a family of financiers. Her marriage in 1748 to the Comte de Houdetot was unsuccessful, and they separated amicably five years later. She was the cousin of ▷Madame d'Epinay and, while staying with her, met Rousseau (1712–1778), who wrote of his passion for her in his *Confessions* (1781). Her poetry was published in a volume of the work of the poet Saint-John Crèvecoeur in 1833.
Bib: Lescure, M. de, *Les Femmes philosophes*; Perroud, R., 'Mme d'Houdetot', *Revue de lettres Modernes* III (1952).

Houri-Pasotti, Myriam

Tunisian Jewish novelist. Her *Contes de ghzala* (1980) (*Tales of Ghzala*), a collection of short stories, includes tales about animals and traditional figures in Arabic literature like 'J'ha'. It also draws on Bedouin and Jewish traditions, and some of the stories are about the lives of African slaves. Her other novel *Habib, petit arabe de Tunisie* (1971) (*Habib, Little Arab of Tunis*) is a portrait of a boy from Tunis who discovers a more traditional life when he goes to visit his grandparents in the country. This novel focuses on two different ways of life, which it shows need not necessarily be exclusive of each other.

Householder, The (1960)

A novel by ▷Ruth Prawer Jhabvala. Set in India, this is a gentle domestic comedy on the strivings of a newly-married couple for mutual understanding. Prem and Indu begin married life beset by many difficulties, not the least of which is Prem's well-meaning mother. Only when Prem begins to assert himself does he begin the long road to becoming a householder, one of the four important stages in a Hindu man's life. Jhabvala produced a screenplay from the book for the Merchant-Ivory team, and the resulting film received much acclaim.
anging transient self.

Household management and child rearing, Ancient Greek

These subjects provided the theme of many ancient Greek prose works concerning, and sometimes by, women. In the classical Greek world a woman's place was indoors, but there she had considerable power over slaves and the domestic economy. She also held sway regarding the upbringing of her children. These themes are especially common in Pythagorean writing.
▷Pythagorean women; Theanor (I); ▷Myia (I); Melissa; Phintys; Aspasia

Housekeeping (1981)

US novel by Marilynne Robinson (born 1944) which follows an adolescent girl's journey to selfconsciousness, tracing Ruth's alienation from her sister Lucille after their mother's suicidal drowning. Each sister chooses a different way of coping with the loss and change. Lucille restores normalcy in her life by fitting into society and conforming; Ruth adopts her aunt Sylvie's view of life and death. Sylvie, an eccentric drifter, accepts transience. She feels 'the life of perished things', believing that 'what perished need not be lost'. Her housekeeping undermines any normalcy by allowing the outside (dead leaves, animals) to come inside. Ruth and Sylvie resist pressures to conform, and invent a new life of drifting. Robinson presents an alternative view of life that can accommodate a changing transient self.

House of Incest (1936)

Prose poem by US writer ▷Anaïs Nin. In *House of Incest* Nin follows an unnamed woman's search for psychic wholeness through a withdrawal into her unconscious. Combining Surrealist and ▷stream-of-consciousness techniques, the prose poem uses the house to represent the psyche through which the narrator wanders, while incest stands as an image of inertia and entrapment. In *The Diary of Anais Nin* (1966–1977), Nin argues that woman must reject her definition by and identification with man. Man has destroyed his psychic unity by creating a consciousness divorced from the unconscious. She gives woman the role of restoring unity by recovering an unconscious. In order to accomplish this woman must first return to the womb to 'expose its secrets and its labyrinths' and recover her origins. But then she must return to the world to articulate this unconscious. Otherwise she would die psychically as the 'characters' in the house of incest. This seems to be the process in which the narrator in the poem engages. However, a more pessimistic reading is possible. The feminist critic Shari Benstock, for example, argues in *Women of the Left Bank: Paris 1900–1940* that the work refuses unity and offers 'a nightmare vision'. Nin's own publishing house, Siana Editions, first published *House of Incest*, and it was reprinted immediately by the Obelisk Press, a company publishing sexually controversial works banned in England and North America such as ▷Radclyffe Hall's ▷*Well of Loneliness* and Henry Miller's *Tropic of Cancer* (published in France in 1934). *House of Incest* is central to Nin's *oeuvre*, and she described it as the 'seed of all my work'.

House of Liars (1951)

English translation of *Menzogna e sortilegio* (1948), a lengthly first novel by ▷Elsa Morante. Set in the south of Italy, it covers three generations of a family. Like many of Morante's narratives, it is at once ▷realistic and ▷fantastical in style. Its subject matter is love and adolescence. Elisa, the narrator, is twenty-five years old, and she is trying to reconstruct the history of her family. Along the way, she uncovers much deceit. Elisa herself is something of a dreamer, but her discovery of family truths and lies allows her to be more realistic. Mothers, as in Morante's later works, are important figures here, not so much from their perspective as from that of the children concerned. To be mothered, Morante implies, is vital. Another theme that prefigures Morante's later writing is that of memory, and of the recreation of the past.

House of Mirth, The (1905)

US novel by ▷Edith Wharton which traces the decline of Lily Bart, an unmarried woman in turn-of-the-century New York Society. Lily's impoverished, widowed mother resolves to recover her lost fortunes through her daughter, and Lily learns to barter her beauty for a wealthy husband. Ultimately, however, she cannot compromise herself and marry for money, although having learned to love luxury, she lives off of the wealthy. But when she fails to marry, this society casts her out. She falls into hopeless poverty and commits suicide. Wharton exposes the frivolity of the wealthy that destroys women like Lily, and examines how women are turned into ornamental objects and commodities. In Wharton's analysis, marriage functions as the market where these commodities are bought and sold.

House of the Spirits, The (1985)

Translation of *La casa de los espiritus* (1982), the first and internationally recognized novel by Chilean ▷Isabel Allende. It brings about a counterbalance to the success of Gabriel García Marquez's *One Hundred Years of Solitude* in its vivid use of ▷magic realism as it tells an imaginative history of Chile and the saga of the Trueba family through the vision of a female narrator. The book is an important landmark in women's literature, and was generally well-received by the critics. The protagonist, Alba, employs her dreamy and imaginative grandmother Clara's notebooks of writing as an interwoven, intertextual narrative with her own. The two versions reveal the repressed but spiritually happy life of the grandmother, who was the rich owner of a city mansion and a farm with her patriarchal husband, Esteban Trueba, and Alba's voice. The stories combine into two different perspectives of life that are separated by history and a dictatorship. Isabel Allende presents life in Chile as the union of a dreamlike reality and a repressive military government, which Alba can barely understand and face.

House of the Sun (1989)

Comic novel by British author ▷Meira Chand. It is set in a crowded tenement in Bombay which is home to a community of Hindu Sindhis, refugees from Pakistan at the time of ▷Partition. The various Sindhi households, of differing levels of wealth, are united by the twin obsessions of making money and marrying off their daughters. The main themes are those of displacement and the sense of cultural loss felt by older members of a displaced community as they witness the adaptation and assimilation of the young in a new environment.

House on Arnus Square, The (1988)

Novel by Syrian writer ▷Samar 'Attar, in which she contrasts the old ways of life in Damascus with those of modern, Europeanized women. The old Damascene house with its fountain and enclosed garden, in a style lovingly remembered by many Syrian writers, represents a way of life that is disappearing:

> The great old Damascus houses were being torn down and nobody objected . . . I should have seen how my friend Nadia's house fell apart . . . how the fig trees had been cut down, and also the cherry trees, and how the Yazid River filled up with earth and no one even objected . . . When Nadia returned to Damascus after being away for years she

discovered a stranger living alone in her house. How many rooms were there? She could not even remember . . . In Nadia's garden there had been rose-bushes and trees which the Arabs had known for centuries . . . nobody objected when the trees were cut down and the fountains were covered over with dirt and the houses decayed . . . antique dealers were sending their men to houses that were being demolished to find bits of tile or the remains of painted walls with intricate designs.

The narrator is the sister who has escaped, made a clean break with the old house. Rima, the one who stayed, tries to make a life for herself as an individual, independent working woman who wears Parisian clothes and listens to western European classical music. She lives in the family home, however, and has to support the family hangers-on, playing the role of a man, a breadwinner.

House on Mango Street (1984)

US novel by ▷Sandra Cisneros which won the 1985 Before Columbus Foundation's American Book Award. It consists of forty-four short, inter-related stories from Esperanza's girlhood. A Chicana, Esperanza is an aspiring writer anchored to the socio-political reality of the *barrio* (the Chicano ghetto). She desires a house that can give her a sense of dignity. But, Cisneros emphasizes, minorities are deprived of adequate housing under US capitalism. As a woman, Esperanza sees the *barrio* as threatening, with men controlling or appropriating female sexuality through violence. She learns from other women to transcend domestic oppression through art; they also teach her to assume her social obligation to the community. In her art she will always return to the *barrio*. Esperanza embodies female possibilities.
  ▷Latino women's writing

House on Moon Lake, The (1987)

Translation into English of *La Casa sul lago della luna* (1984), this is a novel in three parts by ▷Francesca Duranti. Each part ostensibly centres on a female character (Fulvia, Maria and Petra respectively), but the central narrative consciousness of the text is that of Fabrizio, the male character who, in a sense, invents all of the female characters. He invents a version of Fulvia which does not tally with other perspectives of her given in the text; Maria is wholly a creature of his imagination, and Petra could arguably be seen as a delusion. The plot revolves around Fabrizio's translation of a German novel, self-consciously entitled *Das Haus am Mondsee*, and his invention of a character, the aforementioned Maria, as a mistress for his author. His fabrication proves his undoing, as Petra claims to be Maria's granddaughter, and to have letters relevant to his work. When he goes to see her, he is gradually stripped of his will and effectively becomes her

prisoner. This is a cleverly constructed novel about the relationship between fiction and reality and the creative process.

Howe, Fanny (born 1940)

US poet and novelist. Howe's sister, ▷Susan Howe also writes poetry, and their parents were a Harvard Law School professor and an Irish dramatist and actress. Howe has written seven novels including *First Marriage* (1974) and *In the Deep North* (1988). Her collections of poems include *Poems from a Single Pallet* (1980), *Alsace-Lorraine* (1982), *Robeson Street* (1985), *Introduction to the World* (1986), *The Lives of a Spirit* (1987), *The Vineyard* (1988) and *In the Deep North* (1988).
  The British poet ▷Wendy Mulford described Howe's work as primarily 'concerned with ways of speaking the unspeakable, speaking spiritual experience'. Howe moves away from expressive and representational modes: 'You are always in the way of yourself / Too big, or small, until you or it disappears'. Nevertheless her poetry has a lyricism which makes it unexpectedly accessible, compared to the work of the language poets with whom she is grouped, such as Lyn Hejinian, ▷Susan Howe and Rae Armantrout.

Howe, Julia Ward (1819–1910)

US poet, dramatist and non-fiction writer. A prolific author, primarily known for her poetry, including the highly popular ▷'Battle Hymn of the Republic', Ward Howe was the most outspoken woman contributor to the US literary magazines. Accusing ▷*Atlantic Monthly* editors James Russell Lowell (1819–1891) and James T. Fields (1817–1881) of rejecting, mistreating and underpaying her because she was a woman, Ward Howe had contentious relations with publishers, so eventually directed her career away from poetry and, to some degree, away from literature, as she increasingly became involved in social movements, women's suffrage and the establishment of US women's clubs.
  A lifelong feminist, Ward Howe found conflict not only with the publishing establishment but also with her husband, who resented his wife's career and fame, if not her money. Her first poetry collection, *Passion Flowers* (1854), thus appeared anonymously, though later volumes – *Words for the Hour* (1857), *Later Lyrics* (1866) and *From Sunset Ridge* (1898) – were printed under her own name. Only some of her extensive periodical publications were collected, and her plays and much of the non-fiction are out of print and unavailable. Near the turn of the century she devoted more time to biography, with publications including a volume on ▷Margaret Fuller, and her own *Reminiscences* (1899).

Howe, Susan

US poet and critic. Howe's mother is an Irish dramatist and actress, and Howe herself was an actress, stage designer and a radio producer. Until 1971 she was also a painter and graphic artist, but gradually gave this up in favour of writing. She has published nine books of poetry, including *A Secret History of the Dividing Line* (1978), *Cabbage Gardens* (1979), *Pythagorean Silence* (1982), *The Defenestration of Prague* (1983), *Articulation of Sound Forms in Time* (1987) and *Singularities* (1990).

Howe claims the Black Mountain poet Charles Olsen as an influence, and her fascination with the interrelationship of topography, history and language demonstrates this. Influences such as Cotton Mather and other early Puritan writers, and ▷Emily Dickinson, of whom she has written the critical study, *My Emily Dickinson* (1986), suggest her interests in gender, culture and tradition, and their relationship to voice and identity. About Emily Dickinson and ▷Gertrude Stein, Howe writes that their writing 'accomplishes the disintegration of conventional meaning in the voice of a remote-seeming narrator', and represents 'a feminine penchant for linguistic decreation and re-creation'. These concerns with the nature of the poet's voice or authority, and the possibilities of kidnapping language from its conventional modes of syntax and meaning in order to find 'an order beyond mere sexual gender', best represent the concerns of Howe's poetry.
▷Howe, Fanny

Howes, Edith Annie (1872–1954).

New Zealand children's author. Born in London, Howes came to New Zealand as a child. She became a teacher, and successfully pioneered the use of Montessori teaching methods. Inspired by a 'didactic instinct', but hampered by the lack of books with which to teach children, she wrote her own, and became established as a writer of books blending science and fairy fantasy. From 1917 to 1919 she taught in Wellington and published critical accounts of conditions in New Zealand schools in *Tales Out of School* (1919). Also very active in women writers' groups, Edith Howes received the MBE in 1935 and the George VI Coronation Medal in 1937 for her literary work.
▷Children's literature, New Zealand

Howes, Mary (born 1941)

A practising nurse, and a fiercely energetic Canadian poet and performance artist living in Edmonton, Alberta, whose poems address a powerful and violent sexuality with acerbic humour. *Lying in Bed* (1981) totalizes frustration and desire, while *Vanity Shades* (1990) underwrites the hospital as the culminating zone of pleasure and death.

Hoyers, Anna Ovena (1584–1655)

German poet. The daughter of an astronomer, she spoke and wrote Latin and Greek, and read Hebrew. At fifteen she married Hermann Hoyer, and had nine children. After her husband's death in 1622 she entered public life, and began to take part in the religious debates between the Lutherans, the Anabaptists and the Mennonites.

She wrote numerous religious pamphlets and songs, as well as didactic and satirical poems, some of which were collected in *Geistliche und Weltliche Poemata* (1650) (*Spiritual and Secular Poems*). Decried as a heretic by orthodox Protestants, her writings were proscribed, and she died in exile in Sweden.

Hrdinovia (1918) (*The Heroes*)

Novel by Slovak realist writer ▷Timrava. *The Heroes* portrays the effect of outside events (in this case World War I) on the psychology of its characters. The main character, an idealistic young notary, is forced to join the army after the beginning of war. The novel ends with his death. Timrava is interested in the immediate reactions of people faced with sudden changes in their everyday routine. She is fascinated by revealing hidden emotions. She traces people's motivation, confrontates them, and reveals their vacillation between hypocrisy, proclaimed national and political ideas, and truth. The result of this merciless confrontation is a certain sarcasm, noticeable in the title of the novel. The novel is generally considered to be a work of 'psychological naturalism'.

Hrotsvith von Gandersheim (c 935–after 973)

Germany's first woman writer and dramatist. Probably of noble descent, she was in charge of the school in the Benedictine Nunnery of Gandersheim, the first religious establishment for women in Saxony, and an important cultural centre. Her pious legends, such as the story of *Dionysius*, who becomes St Denis, patron Saint of Paris, or St Agnes, the virgin martyr, were to become part of popular Christian mythology for centuries. These Latin stories were written in dactylic hexameters, and show her ability to draw on both religious and secular (classical) source material. She was, however, best-known for her six plays: *Gallicanus*; *Dulcitius*; *Callimachus*; *Abraham*; *Paphnutius*; and *Sapientia* (translated as *The Plays*, 1923, and *The Plays of Hrotswitha of Gandersheim*, 1979). Written in Latin rhyme, and probably never performed, these plays display an accomplished dramatic talent, and tell, often in cruelly realistic detail, of the conversions and martyrdoms of early Christians. She also wrote a number of epic poems and two verse histories: one of Gandersheim itself, and one of Otto I (912–973), Holy Roman Emperor.

Huang Qingyun (born 1920)

Chinese writer of children's stories. Influenced by Hans Christian Andersen (1805–1875), Huang started writing for children in 1941 and edited a children's magazine. She wrote about the poor, deprived children of old China and later on the struggles of the Communist Party for subject matter. Huang published a notable fairytale 'Annals of a Fossil' (1980), drawing a parallel between the 'Gang of Four' (Jiang Qing, Mao's wife, and her associates) and four varieties of

vicious animal. She leaves the identity of the 'Great Fossil Tortoise' to the reader's conjecture.
Bib: Link, Perry (trans.), 'Annals of a Fossil' in *Roses and Thorns*.

Huang Zongying (born 1925)

Chinese writer, journalist and actress, Huang comes from a talented family which has produced more than one artist/writer. She studied at Yenching University in Beijing and started acting in the 1940s in Shanghai. She married Zhao Dan, the famous actor and spokesman for artistic freedom. Always fluent with her pen, Huang combined writing with her acting career. Her best-known works, *The Flight of the Wild Geese* (1978) and *The Little Wooden Cabin* (adapted for television) pay tribute to professional women who suffer for their dedication.
Bib: 'The Flight of the Wild Geese' in *Seven Contemporary Chinese Women Writers*.

Huber, Marie (1695–1753)

French essayist. A Protestant born in Geneva, Huber later lived in France. Her first work, *Le Monde fou préféré au monde sage* (1731) (*Madness is Better than Wisdom*) takes the form of discussions between three friends – a philosopher, a lawyer and a businessman. Her deist text, *Lettres sur la religion essentielle* (1738, 1754) (*Letters About Basic Religion*), which was translated into English and German, is opposed to dogma and the Church. It precedes the deism and sentimental philosophy of her compatriot Jean-Jacques Rousseau (1712–1778).

Her other works are: *Le Système des anciens et des modernes concilié . . .* (1738, 1739) (*Ancient and Modern Systems Reconciled . . .*), and *Réduction du 'Spectateur anglais'* (1753).
Bib: Monod, A., *De Pascal à Chateaubriand*.

Huber, Therese (1764–1829)

German novelist. She had no formal education, but as the daughter of a university professor in Göttingen she came into contact with intellectuals who stimulated her literary interests. In 1785 she married the writer Georg Forster (1754–1794), but later fell in love with Ludwig Huber (died 1804), a friend of her husband, and a fellow Jacobin. In 1793 she divorced Forster and married Huber. Her first novel ▷*Die Familie Seldorf* (*The Seldorf Family*), appeared in 1795 under the name of her husband. An early example of a woman's ▷*Bildungsroman*, it recounts the heroine's coming of age, both politically and emotionally, during the French Revolution (1789). Huber went on to publish regularly, but until her husband's death in 1804 all her stories, novels and plays, in which she emulated French and English models, appeared under his name. In 1816 she became editor of the newspaper *Morgenblatt* (*Morning Paper*).

Huch, Ricarda (1864–1947)

German novelist, poet, critic and historian. From a merchant family in Braunschweig, she studied history in Zurich, obtaining her doctorate in 1891. Her early adult life was overshadowed by her love for her sister's husband, her cousin, Richard Huch. Her neo-romantic poems, *Gedichte* (1891) (*Poems*), and two semi-autobiographical novels, published while she was working as a teacher in Zurich, established her literary reputation, which was consolidated in 1899 and 1902 by two scholarly works on the romantic movement. After a brief first marriage and the birth of a daughter, she married her cousin in 1907, but they parted three years later.

A prolific writer, her best-known story today is the gripping novella, ▷*Der letzte Sommer* (1910) (*The Last Summer*). Her historical writings tend to focus on rebels and rebellions, such as (1483–1546), Garibaldi (1807–1882), Luther, Bakunin (1814–1876), and the 1848 Revolutions. Her work on ▷Rahel Varnhagen, ▷Caroline Schlegel-Schelling and ▷Annette von Droste-Hülshoff revived public interest in important women of German culture. Sensitive to the threat of German militarism, in 1912–14 she published a penetrating analysis of the Thirty Years War (1618–1648). In 1931 she became the first woman member of the Prussian Academy of Literature, but left two years later in protest against Hitler's cultural policies. Her last poems are collected in *Herbstfeuer* (1944) (*Autumn Bonfires*). She died while still working on a history of the Munich Resistance of 1943.

Huge Scheppel (c 1450)

A novel translated into German by ▷Elisabeth von Nassau-Saarbrücken from a French *chanson de geste*. It relates the adventures of Hugh Capet, son of a knight and a butcher's daughter, who saves the daughter of the murdered King Ludwig from the wicked designs of Count Savari. With the help of ordinary Parisians, Hugh thwarts Savari's illegal bid for power, wins the princess's hand, and becomes King of France. One of the earliest secular German narratives, the novel is reminiscent of a fairytale, in which social mobility of the hero is perfectly acceptable. Written in an entertaining and easily accessible style, the story became very popular and, together with two of Elisabeth's other novels, *Herpin* (1437) and *Loher und Maller* (1437), was reprinted many times, often in an abridged form. It thus became part of the German folk-tale heritage.

Hughes, Monica (born 1925)

Author of children's fiction, born in Liverpool, England. She lived in Cairo, then London and Edinburgh, served in the WRNS in World War II, then worked as a dress designer and bank clerk in London and Rhodesia. In 1952 she emigrated to Canada, and lived in Ontario before settling in Edmonton, Alberta in 1964. Hughes is one of Canada's premier writers for young people, especially of popular science fiction. Her work is valued for the way that she understands the dilemmas of the adolescent; her writing portrays a reverence for nature, as well as the importance of social conscience within a cultural context.

Her books include: *Earthdark* (1977); *Crisis on Conshelf Ten* (1977); *The Tomorrow City* (1978); *Beyond the Dark River* (1979); *Keeper of the Isis Light* (1980); *The Guardian of Isis* (1981); *Hunter in the Dark* (1982); *Ring Rise, Ring Set* (1982); *Space Trap* (1983); *My Name is Paula Popowich!* (1983); *Devil on my Back* (1984); *Sandwriter* (1985); *The Dream Catcher* (1986), and *Blaine's Way* (1986).

Hulda (1881–1946)

Pseudonym of Unnur Benediktsdóttir Bjarklind, an Icelandic neo-romantic lyric poet. She was brought up in a cultured home. Her father was a librarian, and she received an excellent education at home, which included foreign languages. When she was twenty she had her first poems published and, although she became a busy housewife and had poor health, she wrote seven collections of poems, the last of which was published posthumously in 1951. Her first volume was *Kvædi* (1909) (*Poems*). She wrote about many subjects, and during her own life she was recognized as an important lyric poet.

She also wrote very popular pastiches of some of the Icelandic popular poetry, eg rhapsodies and nursery rhymes. She published more than ten volumes of prose of this kind, including novels. In this respect she was a great inspiration to many younger writers.

In her own time, she was hailed as a star of the neo-romantic movement, although today her short stories seem idealized and overly romantic.

Hull, Eleanor (early 15th century)

English translator. Eleanor Hull was connected with the court, and, in common with other court women, her spiritual director was probably a confessor at Sion Abbey, a Bridgettine house at Twickenham founded by Henry V in 1415. Bridget (▷Birgitta av Vadstena) had encouraged biblical translation, and the use of vernacular devotional books. Eleanor Hull translated – as a pious exercise, it has been suggested – from French into English, a commentary on the seven penitential psalms and meditations on the seven days of the week. Certain prayers are also attributed to her.
Bib: Barratt, Alexandra, *Women's Writing in Middle English*.

Hull, Helen Rose (1888–1971)

US novelist and short story writer. Born in Albion, Michigan, Hull earned a PhD in English at the University of Chicago. Teaching at Wellesley College in 1912, she met her lifelong companion, Mabel Louise Robinson. In 1916 Hull joined the faculty at Columbia University and became an active feminist. Her early stories dealt with such issues as spousal abuse, illegitimate birth and rape. Her novels accuse the white middle-class North American family of victimizing women. *Quest* (1922) and *The Surry*

Family (1925) focus on adolescent girls who pledge to live differently to their mothers. ▷*Islanders* (1927) explodes the myth of female dependence that underlies the family. Hull's work is noted for its feminist models of growth.

Other works include: *Labyrinth* (1923) and *Last September* (1988).

Hulme, Keri (born 1947)

Keri Hulme

New Zealand novelist and poet. Keri Hulme became one of New Zealand's best-known writers when she won the Booker Prize in 1985 for her novel ▷*the bone people*. Born in Christchurch, Hulme has spent most of her life in the South Island doing various kinds of seasonal and itinerant work as well as writing. Okarito in Westland, where she now lives and supports herself by fishing and writing, is famous for its bird life and is at the centre of environmental questions which figure in Hulme's work. All her writing is concerned with questions of race, culture, gender and environment, and her work both celebrates and challenges New Zealand landscape and society and the forces which shape and threaten it. Hulme is of Kai Tahu descent, and her writing is fundamentally engaged with Maori cultural identity both past and present.

Publications: *The Silences Between [Moeraki Conversations]* (poems) (1982); ▷*the bone people* (1984); *Lost Possessions* (1985) *Te Kaihau/The Windeater* (stories) (1986).
▷Maori literature

Humanism

Italy: The term was originally associated with the Renaissance, and had its beginnings in Italy, where in the 15th century humanist writers gathered round the courts of Venice, Rome, Florence and Naples. Because of the nature of humanist study, which included the dissemination of classical Greek and Latin, only a very few, privileged women had access to it (▷Education, Italy). Two women writers who did contribute to the movement are Lucrezia Tornabuoni de' Medici (1425–1482) and Antonia Giannotti Pulci (c1452–?).

England: Philosophical and literary movement which, in a general sense, places Man (the individual) at the centre of thought and meaning. Meaning is thus located outside language, culture, history and also outside woman (who is, of course, not Man).

The influence of humanism reached England in the 16th century. The humanists' emphasis on education extended to women, and English humanists put their theories into practice with regard to their own daughters and the daughters of families for whom they served as tutors. However, the terms and goals of their educational theories were ultimately limiting. Whereas the goal of men's education was to enable them to enter into public life, the goal of women's learning was to teach them the virtues of chastity, obedience and piety necessary to their place in the domestic realm. Humanists believed in instructing women so as to enable them to converse intelligently with their husbands, but always within the privacy of the home. That Renaissance Englishwomen composed primarily devotional works and ▷translations is largely due to their training, which focused on subjects in keeping with feminine domesticity and piety. Vives's ▷*Instruction of a Christian Woman*, for example, prohibited women from reading 'dangerous' works such as romances and poetry (that is, imaginative literature). A number of women trained by humanists became relatively important writers, especially as translators. Sir Thomas More's daughter, ▷Margaret Roper, is perhaps the most famous, but other 'daughters of humanism' include Roper's own child, ▷Mary Basset, as well as Anthony Cooke's children, ▷Anne Bacon, ▷Mildred Cecil, and ▷Elizabeth Russell. Also included among the women educated by humanist tutors are ▷Jane Grey and ▷Elizabeth Tudor.

In the 18th century, in the period known as the ▷Enlightenment, or 'Age of Reason', humanist philosophers attempted to ground the origin and end of meaning in rational principles. For radical thinkers, such as Tom Paine (1737–1809), this led to calls for the granting of political rights to mankind, and for democratic government and national independence. Feminist writers in the 18th century, most notably ▷Mary Wollstonecraft, argued that women, no less than men, were capable of acting on rational principles and should therefore be given equal civil and political rights.

▷Ascham, Margaret; Lumley, Joanna; Protestant Reformation
Bib: Holm, J.B., 'The Myth of Feminist Humanism: Thomas Salter's *The Mirrhor of Modestie*' in Levin, C. and Watson J. (eds), *Ambiguous Realities: Women in the Middle Ages and Renaissance*; Kelso, R., *Doctrine for the Lady of the Renaissance*; Lamb, M.E., 'The Cooke Sisters: Attitudes Toward Learned Women in the Renaissance' in Hannay, M. (ed.), *Silent But for the Word*; Wayne, V., 'Some Sad Sentence: Vive's Instruction of a Christian Woman' in Hannay, M. (ed.), *Silent But for the Word*.

Humanism, modern critiques of
19th– and 20th–century philosophical movements have contributed to challenging a humanist emphasis on individual autonomy. These include Marxism, ▷psychoanalysis, ▷poststructuralism and ▷deconstruction. For feminism generally, humanism has been a two-edged concept: on the one hand, in historical practice at least, it has placed man at the centre of the world, but on the other, a humanist emphasis on the self has enabled feminist thinkers to construct theories of human beings as free, autonomous political agents. In the US a debate is currently taking place among feminists over what is seen in some quarters to be the anti-humanist and therefore politically disempowering tendencies of poststructuralist and ▷postmodernist theory. See, for example, the journal *Praxis International* No. 11 (1989) and Linda J. Nicholson (ed.), *Feminism/ Postmodernism* (1990).

Human Toll (1907)
Australian novel by ▷Barbara Baynton. This melodramatic novel details the life of Ursula, an orphaned heiress in the Australian bush, and the efforts of the bush inhabitants to secure her inheritance either legally or illegally. The biblical and pastoral parallels are obvious as Ursula is repeatedly seen as a 'motherless lamb' threatened by wolves, in particular the predatory clergyman, Mr Civil. Ursula's lover, Andrew, is won by the deceitful Mina, who tricks him into a sexual encounter by plying him with strong drink, and becomes pregnant by him. Ursula saves the baby when Mina threatens to kill it and escapes with it into the inhospitable Australian bush. The novel ends with an impressionistic dream or ▷stream-of-consciousness sequence intended to depict madness and either death or rescue (both options are possible). Critics have hailed this sequence as modernistic in both theme and technique and an anticipation of the wasteland themes of 20th-century fiction.

Humayun Nama (c 1580) ▷*History of Humayun, The* (1902)

Humble Romance, A (1887)
US story collection by ▷Mary E. Wilkins Freeman. Set in New England, the stories are typical of US ▷local color in their concentration on distinctive regional characters, environment and situations. The plots make more use of surprise, coincidence and misunderstanding than Wilkins Freeman's later works. Especially notable is 'An Independent Thinker', a sketch of a grandmother who deftly reconciles her

independent religious beliefs with social requirements for conformity.

Hume, Anna (fl 1644)

Scottish poet who translated Petrarch's *Trionfo della Morte* (1476) as *The Triumphs of Love: Chastitie: Death* (1644), following the example of other learned women, including ▷Elizabeth Tudor and (famously) ▷Mary Sidney Herbert, Countess of Pembroke.

Hume, Sophia Wigington (1702–1774)

North American preacher and essayist. Born in South Carolina to Susanna Bayley and Henry Wigington, she received an exceptional home education. At age nineteen she married Robert Hume, a prominent attorney; but in 1737, when Robert died, she was left as the sole support of two young children. This crisis led her to reconsider her religious beliefs, ultimately rejecting her father's Anglicanism and embracing her mother's Quaker practices. Her maternal grandmother, Mary Fisher (c 1623–1698), had been a renowned Quaker preacher, and she soon followed in Fisher's footsteps. After several years with the Society of Friends in England, she returned to her 'native Country' in 1747; the following year she began her career as an author, publishing ▷*An Exhortation to the Inhabitants of the Province of South Carolina*. Her later publications continued her cautionary note, as in ▷*A Caution to Such as Observe Days and Times* (1763), and captured her concern for the preservation of the history of her chosen faith, as in ▷*Extracts from Divers, Antient Testimonies* (1766). Commended by John Woolman for her commitment and piety, she lived to see her counsel published in ▷*The Justly Celebrated Mrs Sophia Hume's Advice* (1769). A major figure in the North American Quaker movement, she died in England, the country of her apprenticeship, on 26 January 1774.

▷Early North American Quaker women's writings

Humo de Beleño (1985) (Henbane Smoke)

Play by the post-war Spanish dramatist ▷Maribel Lázaro. Set in 17th-century Galicia, it describes the struggle between the Inquisition and a group of women accused of withcraft. In one scene, which caused great controversy when the play was staged in Madrid, the witches enact a sexual ritual which parodies church ritual, lubricating their genitals with holy oil.

Hunting the Wild Pineapple (1979)

Australian short story collection by ▷Thea Astley. Set in tropical north Queensland, where the luxuriant and slovenly excesses of nature match the activities of her characters, this is one of Astley's most enjoyable books. Her collection of hippies, dropouts, eccentrics and do-gooders display to the full their prejudices, selfishness and self-preserving fictions.

Huntington Letters, The (1905)

This collection of letters by ▷Anne Huntington Huntington and her daughter, Rachel Huntington Tracy, spans two generations of early North American women's lives in Connecticut. Anne's letters, directed almost solely to her husband from 1774 until shortly before her death in 1790, are a record of domestic matters and neighbourhood news. However, Rachel's letters, written before her marriage, focus on her lively social activities, her travels and women's fashions, and are directed to her sisters. The letters are particularly interesting for generational differences between women who lived through the American Revolution and those who were raised in the aftermath of national independence.

▷Early North American letters

Huntington, Anne Huntington (?1740–1790)

North American letter-writer. A member of the Huntington family of Norwich, Connecticut, she was a prolific correspondent from 1774 until her death. While her husband was employed at the seat of government, she corresponded with him, delivering news of local events and family matters. ▷*The Huntington Letters*, which also include several letters from her daughter Rachel, detail two generations of women's lives in late 18th-century Connecticut.

Huo Da

Chinese journalist and writer of children's stories, film scripts and novels. Huo Da is a Muslim, and winner of the Mao Dun Literary Prize of 1991 for her novel *Muslim Funeral*. Based on painstaking research, the novel describes the lives of ordinary Muslims in Beijing. It has historical, sociological as well as literary value and has been translated into many languages. Huo Da has also won a prize for the novella *A Woman of the Streets* (1986), in which a former prostitute who sincerely wants to lead a new life is driven to suicide.

Hurst, Fannie (1889–1968)

US novelist. In 1909 Hurst graduated from Washington University in St Louis, Missouri and the next year she moved to New York to establish herself as a writer. Unlike the characters in her books, Hurst had both a successful career and marriage. Her bestseller, *Back Street* (1931) focuses on a married man's mistress. Left penniless upon his death, Ray dies alone in her room; typical of Hurst's characters, Ray sacrifices herself for a weak, egocentric, cruel man. Hurst compels her reader to identify and empathize with women who have been dominated, used and destroyed. Another bestseller, ▷*Imitation of Life* (1933) emphasizes that professional success is not emotionally fulfilling without male companionship. Hurst's novels suggest women are conditioned to be emotionally dependent on men.

Other works include *A Passionata* (1926), *Five and Ten* (1929), *We Are Ten* (1937), *Anywoman* (1950), *Anatomy of Me* (1958) and *God Must Sad* (1961).

Hurston, Zora Neale (c 1901–1960)

Zora Neale Hurston

US novelist, short story writer, folklorist and journalist. Hurston was born in the first self-governing black town of Eatonville, Florida. In the 1920s she worked as secretary to the popular novelist ▷Fannie Hurst. Although she had little early formal education she went to Howard University, where she was a contemporary of the poet ▷Georgia Douglas Johnson, and later studied anthropology with Franz Boas at Barnard College. During the 1920s Hurston was part of the ▷Harlem Renaissance movement, and her short story 'Spunk' appeared in both *Opportunity* and Alain Locke's famous collection *The New Negro* in 1925. Other stories such as 'Sweat' and 'Gilded Six-Bits' also appeared in *Opportunity*. During this period she also wrote plays, such as *Color Struck* (1926) and *The First One* (1927).

Boas encouraged Hurston to undertake research in African-American folklore of the South. This work was variously funded by a fellowship and by Hurston's white patron, Charlotte Osgood Mason, who cultivated an interest in primitivism. The material about customs, stories, superstitions, games and songs appeared first as essays for ▷Nancy Cunard's *Negro: An Anthology* (1934), and eventually in Hurston's *Mules and Men* (1935). It also formed the basis of some musical revues written by Hurston, such as *The Great Day* which was first performed in 1932. During the late 1930s Hurston was offered a fellowship in anthropology and folklore at Columbia University, and she worked for the Federal Theater Project in New York and travelled in the Caribbean collecting material for *Tell My Horse* (1938), her second volume of folklore. She also worked for the Federal Writer's Project in Florida.

Hurston wrote four novels in all: *Jonah's Gourd Vine* (1934), about an 'itinerant preacher', ▷*Their Eyes Were Watching God* (1937), *Moses Man of the Mountain* (1939) and *Seraph on the Sewanee* (1948), which looks at the life of a Southern white woman. Her most famous is undoubtedly *Their Eyes Were Watching God*, which uses material from her folkore research to construct a specifically African-American Southern culture and to examine the place of women within it.

Despite her established reputation today, from the late 1940s until her death Hurston found it increasingly difficult to get her writing published, and she was forced to work at a range of jobs from supply teacher and domestic to freelance writer. She suffered poor health and was shaken by a false accusation of child abuse. In 1959 she died in poverty in Florida, and it was only in the 1970s that her work was rediscovered by African-American women writers and critics, Helen Hunt Washington and ▷Alice Walker, and her biographer, Robert Hemenway. Walker edited a reader of her work, *I Love Myself When I am Laughing . . . and Then Again When I am Looking Mean and Impressive* (1979), which includes the important essay 'How it Feels to be Colored Me'.

Other works include Hurston's play *Singing Steel* (1934) and her autobiography *Dust Tracks on the Road* (1942).

Hutchinson, Lucy (?1620–post 1675)

English memoirist. In 1638 she married John Hutchinson, and lived near Nottingham. Hutchinson became a Parliamentary Colonel in the English Civil War (1642–1646, and 1648–1651) and signed King Charles I's death warrant, for which he was imprisoned in 1663. He died in prison in 1664, and she wrote a memoir of him, *Memoirs of the Life of Colonel Hutchinson* (not published until 1806), ostensibly for her children and 'to moderate my woe'. It is full of fascinating detail and opinions about the Civil War, and indicates the active part played by women, though written in a very self-effacing style. Of her husband's signing of the warrant she says, 'As for Mr Hutchinson, although he was very much confirmed in his judgement concerning the cause, yet herein being called to an extraordinary action, whereof many were of several minds, he addressed himself to God by prayer.' She also translated part of Virgil's *Aeneid* and Lucretius's *De rerum natura*, and wrote *On the Principles of the Christian Religion*, first published in 1816.

▷Halkett, Ann; Harley, Brilliana; Venn, Anne

Hu Xin (born 1945)

Chinese writer. Hu Xin is the author of the short story 'Four Women of Forty'. Winner of a national prize, it is one of the earliest works to honestly reveal sexual inequality in contemporary China. The four educated women in the story are all victims – of political campaigns, of the double standard in sexual matters, and of limited opportunities.

Bib: Zhu Hong (trans.) of 'Four Women of Forty' in *The Serenity of Whiteness*.

Huxley, Elspeth (born 1907)
British novelist and travel writer. She was brought up on a coffee farm in Kenya, and studied agriculture at university before working as a journalist and a farmer. Her novels are attuned to her experience of colonialism and voice the necessity for cross-cultural tolerance. They depict colonial Africa, using her early life in Kenya for material. Best-known is the autobiographical *The Flame Trees of Thika* (1959) which was made into a television series. Huxley also wrote crime fiction, such as *Murder on Safari* (1938). Her own travel writing is reflected in *Livingstone and His African Journeys* (1974) and *Florence Nightingale* (1975), and her work editing ▷M.H. Kingsley's *Travels in Africa* (1976). In 1962 Huxley was awarded the CBE.

Among her many works are *White Man's Country* (1935), *Murder at Government House* (1937), *Red Strangers* (1938), *East Africa* (1941), *The Mottled Lizard* (1962), *Back Street New Worlds* (1964), *A Man From Nowhere* (1964), *The Challenge of Africa* (1971), *The Prince Buys the Manor* (1982), *Out in the Midday Sun* (1985) and *The African Poison Murders* (1986).

Hyde, Robin (1906–1939)
New Zealand novelist, poet and journalist. Robin Hyde was the pseudonym of Iris Guiver Wilkinson, who was born in Cape Town of English and Australian parents and came to New Zealand as an infant. Her family settled in Wellington, a city extensively described in Hyde's novel ▷*The Godwits Fly* (1938) and her poem sequence *Houses by the Sea* (1952). On leaving school Hyde became a journalist, a profession which supported her for the rest of her life, and in which she made her mark as a feminist, challenging gender-based inequity and social stereotypes. She suffered from a long illness which left her lame, and also from depression and drug addiction, which meant she spent much of her life in poverty. She had two children (one stillborn) but did not marry. In 1938 she left for England, detouring to China *en route*, where she worked as a war correspondent. She committed suicide in London the following year, aged 33.

Hyde's work reveals both her free thinking and her reliance on conventional literary models. Her poetry moved from semi-mystical celebrations of nature and emotion to ironic and sharp commentary on the foreign landscape of China or Hong Kong in her last poems. Hyde's novels and autobiographical writing have received a lot of attention from feminists in recent years, particularly for the way in which they challenge received assumptions about gender roles. Her fiction also challenges convention and was very widely read in its time. Hyde's more experimental writing, such as the fantasy *Wednesday's Children* (1937) and travel book *Dragon Rampant* (1938),

have recently come back into print and have been the subject of critical attention, which has restored Hyde as one of New Zealand's major woman writers. Her time in relative obscurity is suggestive of the kinds of political and historical contexts within which literary traditions are created.

Publications include: Poetry *The Desolate Star and Other Poems* (1929); *The Conquerers and Other Poems* (1935); *Persephone in Winter* (1937); *Houses by the Sea*, ed. Gloria Rawlinson (1952). Prose: *Check to Your King* (1936); *The Godwits Fly* (1938); *Passport to Hell* (1936); *Wednesday's Children* (1937); *Nor the Years Condemn* (1938); *Journalese* (1934); *Dragon Rampant* (1938).
▷Rawlinson, Gloria

Hyder, Qurratulain (born 1927)
Indian novelist and journalist. She is the daughter of the Urdu novelist S.H. Yildarim, and writes in Urdu herself. She was born and educated in Lucknow, but moved to Pakistan after the ▷Partition of India in 1947. She returned to live in India some years later, and has become one of the country's leading authorities on Urdu literature. She has travelled all over the world, and has been a broadcaster with the Urdu section of the BBC. She was the managing editor of *Imprint*, Bombay, from 1964 until 1978, and has been on the editorial staff of the *Illustrated Weekly of India* since 1968. Her collection of short stories, *Patjhar ki Awaz* (*The Voice of Autumn*), won the Sahitya Akademi Award in 1967. Her novel, *Aag ka Darya* (1959) (*River of Fire*), received great acclaim for its allegorical retelling of India's history. It has been translated into all the principal Indian languages.

Hygeburg (Hugeburc, Huneburc) (8th century)
English nun and hagiographer. Hygeburg was an English nun connected with the ▷Boniface mission, who settled in Heidenheim, Germany, shortly after 761. She wrote the *Life of Saints Willibald and Wynnebald* in an elaborate Latin prose. This describes a journey made by Willibald to the Holy Land and eastern Mediterranean between 723 and 729, and is based on what he reported. The work has been described as eccentric (because of its style); however, it is not only a fascinating travel book, but also reveals Hygeburg's own curiosity, about the holy places Willibald visited, and concerning such natural phenomena as volcanic eruptions. It is also of interest from a literary point of view, since Hygeburg displays her interest in cryptography – literary game-playing. The work is the only account which survives from the 8th century of a pilgrimage to the Holy Land.
Bib: Talbot, C.H. (ed. and trans.), *The Anglo-Saxon Missionaries in Germany*; Dronke, P., *Women Writers of the Middle Ages*.

Hymns (19th-century Britain)
A number of 19th-century British women writers wrote hymn lyrics. ▷Christina Rossetti's 'In the

bleak mid-winter' and ▷Sarah Flower Adams's 'Nearer, My God, to Thee' are among the best-known. Many of ▷Dora Greenwell's poems in *Songs of Salvation* (1873) were also sung as hymns.

Hypatia (AD 370–415)

Philosopher. A pagan, Hypatia was the daughter of the Alexandrian mathematician Theon, who educated her in mathematics, astronomy and Neoplatonist philosophy. She is most famous for her dramatic murder, by Christians envious of her influence in Alexandria, recounted by the ecclesiastical historian Socrates (5th century AD). Socrates rated her above all contemporary philosophers, and she had a large number of pupils. Eleven letters from her pupil Synesius to Hypatia survive, but none of her replies (except one letter, obviously specious, as it deals with matters after her death). Synesius's letters are full of respect for Hypatia, whom he once calls 'mother, sister, mistress and benefactress'. The biographical dictionary, the *Suda* (10th century AD), combines several confused stories, but lists her works as: *Commentary on Diophantus* (on algebra), *Astronomical Canon* (the movement of the planets), *On the Conics of Apollonius* (mathematics). An epigram by Palladas (5th century AD) develops her interest in astronomy into a metaphor, calling her 'the flawless star of wise learning'.

▷Philosophers, Ancient Greek and Roman women

Hyvrard, Jeanne

A French-speaking writer associated with Guadeloupe (French Antilles), little is known of Hyvrard, a very private woman who refuses public appearances and interviews. She has published some poetry, scattered prose pieces and five novels. Her texts are impossible to summarize as each is a delirious, non-stop meditation on the female condition that flows into all the others as the others ebb and flow into it. Dedicated to '*le soldat inconnu*' ('the unknown soldier'), Hyvrard's first novel, *Les Prunes de Cythère* (1975) is the interior monologue of a woman with paralysed legs who spends her days locked up (voluntarily or involuntarily?) in her room, who may (or may not) have miscarried (or aborted). The protagonist of both *Les Prunes de Cythère* and *Mère la Mort* (1976) (*Mother Death*) is apparently viewed by others as 'mad'. The identity of these women fluctuates, so that they are simultaneously themselves, their mothers, the child they have not had, and they also merge with other Antillean women. In their supposed madness, they see their alienation afresh, especially through language. Other works by Hyvrard include *La Meurtritude* (1977) (*The Bruising*), *Les Doigts du figuier* (1977) (*The Fingers of the Fig Tree*) and *Le Corps défunt de la comédie* (1982) (*The Defunct Body of Comedy*).

I Am Becoming My Mother (1986)

The winner of the 1986 Commonwealth Poetry Prize, this is the second book of poetry by the Caribbean writer ▷ Lorna Goodison. In this collection Goodison writes with an intense honesty, exploring the nature of women's lives, whether private or political. In the poem 'Bedspread', which describes a police raid on Winnie Mandela's house, she reveals with striking dexterity how the police succeed in arresting only a bedspread woven with the colours of the ANC (African National Congress); the danger, however, is that while 'They arrested the bedspread / They and their friends are working / to arrest the dreams in our head'. 'Survivor' provides a sardonic look at the notion of woman as the creature of male consciousness. 'On Becoming a Mermaid' explores the full embracing of women's sexuality. The title of this collection has two levels of meaning: one concerns a woman's sense of identity through identification or ▷ bonding with the mother and the female line of ancestry, the other concerns the sense of having to produce oneself, to become one's own mother. The poem 'I am Becoming my Mother' serves to celebrate the recognition of a woman's inheritance as artist, focusing on the metaphoric sense of rebirth and metamorphosis of the self which is the dominant theme of this collection.

See Edward Baugh's article in *Journal of West Indian Literature*, Vol. 4, No. 1, for a discussion of Goodison's work.

Ibáñez, Sara de (1909–1971)

Uruguayan poet. In 1945 she was appointed a professor of literature. She became renowned with her first collection of poems, *Canto* (1940) (*Song*), which contains a prologue by Pablo Neruda (1940–1973) stating that she employs 'passion subjected to rigour', in the manner of ▷ Juana de Asbaje y Ramirez de Santillana. Ibáñez's following volumes of poetry received favourable criticism. She was very strict in the form of her love poems, and used unconscious and hermetic symbols in them. She also dealt with death and patriotism in, for example, *Artigas* (1952). *Hora ciega* (1943) (*Blind Hour*) reveals the influence of Neruda, and is strongly metaphysical. *Pastoral* (1948) is written in three 'movements', each with a different tone and stanzaic form. Its flowing form differs from ▷ *modernismo*, for it is cruel, visionary, anguished and enchanting, as in French symbolism.

Other works include: *Las estaciones y otros poemas* (1957) (*The Stations, and Other Poems*); *La Batalla* (1967) (*The Battle*); *Apocalipsis XX* (1970) (*Apocalypse XX*), and *Canto póstumo* (1973) (*Posthumous Song*).

Ibarbourou, Juana de (1895–1979)

Uruguayan poet. She received the title of 'Juana de América' in 1929 in recognition of her popularity. Born Juana Fernández Morales, she was brought up in a convent, and at eighteen married a soldier and moved to Montevideo. Her vocabulary is naïve, and deals with nature and love as seen through the mirror of her erotic and healthy body. Her first book of poems, ▷ *Las lenguas de diamante* (1919) (*Tongues of Diamond*), achieved immediate success. In *Raíz salvaje* (1922) (*Savage Root*) she refers intimately to love and to a tamed nature, especially to water and fire. Hedonism relates to pleasurable words like fruit, flower, to images of plants and animals, and to feeling alive. Time is a symbol for the anxious expectation of the beloved. It has been said that her poetry an 'act of narcissism', which is filled with femininity, coquetry and commotion. In her sonnet '*Rebelde*', she imagines her own triumphal nakedness in the realm of the dead. In '*Vida-Garfio*' she feels like a 'defying nymph'. The different phases of her poetic work are organized as are the cycles of life – birth, youth, maturity and old age – or the hours of the day and the seasons of the year. However, *Perdida* (1950) (*Lost*) written after twenty years of silence, mourns the passage of time and the loss of youth, which have taken away her jubilant narcissism. Her religious evolution reveals itself in *Estampas de la Biblia* (1934) (*Imprints of the Bible*) and in *Loores a Nuestra Señora* (1934) (*Praise to Our Lady*). *Chico-Carlo* (1944) is the story of her happy childhood in Melo.

Ibingira, Grace

Kenyan novelist, author of *Bitter Harvest* (1980). This novel is about autocratic tyranny in Uganda, with annihilation of opposition, mock trials and torture by the secret police, concluding with the overthrow of the tyranny itself.

Icaza, Carmen de (born 1899)

Novelist, born in Madrid, the daughter of the well-known Mexican writer Francisco A. de Icaza. She published her first novel, *La boda* (1916) (*The Wedding*) at the age of seventeen. In 1936 came her first commercial success with *Cristina de Guzmán, profesora de idiomas* (1936) (*Christina de Guzmán, Foreign Language Teacher*). Icaza's works belong to the *novela rosa* genre of ▷ sentimental romance.

Ice breaker Poems (1980)

Poems by New Zealand writer ▷ Jan Kemp. A cycle of twelve poems prefaced by 'Ice breaker', Kemp's *Ice breaker Poems* use the metaphor of a voyage to chart a love affair. Characterized by spare, tight, short lyrics, Kemp's sequence makes the most of its metaphorical structure by leaving connections implicit, building up a larger unspoken metaphor about what is concealed or lies below the surface of the poems.

Icelandic literature in modern times

The economic boom during World War I also manifested itself in Iceland. In Reykjavík a wealthy, conservative middle class emerged, parallel to a new proletarian employed in the fishing industry. Icelandic poetry, which around 1900 had been largely traditional and romantic, moved towards a greater ▷realism and stylistic flexibility after 1920. An intense cult of the self, the present and sexuality emerged, together with a greater political consciousness. After World War II, the best-known Icelandic woman writer is ▷Svava Jakóbsdóttir (born 1930) who writes works of grotesque realism. Jakobína Sigurdardóttir (born 1918) writes prose attacking the alienation of the modern world.

Women writers have become predominant in recent years. Ingibjörg Haraldsdóttir (born 1942), Alfrún Gunnlaugsdóttir (born 1950) and Steinunn Sigurdardóttir (born 1950) are writing as urban women in a ▷modernist tradition. They are representatives of a new, female identity, just like Vigdís Grímsdóttir (born 1953), who has a fascinating lyrical style.

Idées antiproudhonniennes sur l'amour, la femme et le mariage (1858) (*Anti-Proudhonist ideas on Love, Women and Marriage*)

Political/philosophical work by ▷Juliette Adam. This text constitutes a refutation of the anti-feminist opinions of Pierre-Joseph Proudhon (1809–1865) (▷Proudhonism), and was published only four months after his *De la justice (On Justice)*. In the first part of her work, Adam dismisses a number of Proudhon's doctrines, especially those regarding love and women, which she found particularly obnoxious because they 'express[ed] the general feeling of men who, regardless of the faction to which they belong – progressive or reactionary, monarchist or Republican, Christian or pagan, atheistic or religious – would be delighted if a method were found which would allow the reconciliation of their egotism and their conscience and would create a system that enabled them to preserve the advantages of an exploitation [of the opposite sex] based upon strength, without having to worry about protests based upon strength, without having to worry about protests based on right'.

After ▷deconstructing Proudhon's discourse on femininity, Adam goes on to outline her own views regarding the status of women, and to call for equal rights and opportunities in key areas such as education, medicine and public affairs. She was also keen – keener than most of her feminist contemporaries – on working towards divorce-law reform; a fact which undoubtedly reflects the unhappiness she endured during her first marriage. What is most significant about Adam's thesis is that she distinguishes between sexual equality and total identity, and makes it very clear that, as far as she was concerned, certain social functions and roles had to be the province of men rather than women, or vice versa. Her aim, in other words, was the creation of what she describes as a 'functional equality' between the sexes, while her conviction that women and men have separate, albeit equally worthwhile, capacities reflects the influence upon her of ▷Saint-Simonism.

Identity (Caribbean)

One of the central preoccupations in women's writing from the Caribbean has been a concern with the discovery or quest for an authentic identity, one that can transform boundaries of race, class and gender. This quest often takes the form of a literal or metaphorical journey, whether to another country or a voyage into the self. Frequently this involves an exploration of different and alternative states of consciousness and language in order to subvert and transform dominant stereotypes and discourses. For example, see ▷Jean Rhys (▷*Voyage in the Dark*), ▷Jamaica Kincaid (▷*Annie John*), ▷Erna Brodber (▷*Jane and Louisa Will Soon Come Home*), ▷Grace Nichols (▷*i is a long memoried woman*) and ▷Joan Riley (▷*The Unbelonging*).

Women's writing from the French Antilles (▷essay, French Antilles) shares this concern, which is common to West Indian writing in general, through its re-viewing and re-writing of the past. Journeying creates a sense of displacement, which motivates the reconstruction of a social and imaginary world, as in ▷*Heremakhonon* and ▷*Sapotille*. This physical and psychological voyaging in the search for an authentic motherland and consciousness is also central in the work of ▷Maryse Condé, Myriam Vieyra, ▷Simone Schwarz-Bart and ▷Mayotte Capécia.

Idu (1970)

The second novel by Nigerian writer ▷Flora Nwapa, who was the first African woman novelist ever to be published. Like her first novel, ▷*Efuru*, *Idu* is set in a traditional village environment based on the author's lakeside home, Oguta, in eastern Nigeria. Although Idu is the heroine, the novel is really a portrait of a community. It is concerned with the social dynamics of communal interaction and survival, including the propagation of culture, belief and custom, the strict limits which define acceptable behaviour, and how people are sustained by these things. Nwapa's technique is as close as possible to the ▷oral tradition, the narrative being conveyed through conversation – between women, or between husband and wife. Every event is reported in the form of 'gossip', here an essential part of communal caring, and the means by which people keep in touch with each other's problems. The use of proverbs, songs and stories by women shows them as articulate propagators of social culture. As in her earlier novel, this technique serves the important purpose of reclaiming for fiction those aspects of traditional society which are ignored by famous male writers like Chinua Achebe, and making them central.

Ifigenia: Diario de una señorita que escribó porque se fastidiaba (1924) (*Ifigenia: Diary of a Lady Who Wrote Because she was Bored*)

First published in 1922 as *Diário de una señorita que se fastidiaba* (*Diary of a Lady Who Was Bored*) by the Venezuelan ▷Teresa de la Parra. Her first book, it received a prize in Paris in 1924, and was translated into French in 1929. She next wrote *Memórias de Mamá Blanca* (1929) (▷*Mama Blanca's Souvenirs*, 1959). *Ifigenia* takes place in the half-Republican, half-colonial environment of Caracas at the beginning of the 20th century, and is the journal of a young lady called María Eugenia Alonso, who belongs to the city's old aristocracy, very much like the writer herself did. María unhappily cries and bores herself, but also defies the habits of Caracas in her time, making acute observations about its customs and providing a *costumbrista* (▷*costumbrismo*) picture of the city. Looking to Proust, Parra uses time as an almost palpable topic for her fiction, and, in elegant and objective prose, presents realistic descriptions with fine humour and irony. She employs acute subjectivism in the description of psychic life, while evoking the old aristocracy, her childhood and the scenes, events and people of her time. The critic Luis Correa considers *Ifigenia* as probably the most important Latin American novel by a woman.

'Ignota' ▷Wolstenholme-Elmy, Elizabeth

Iguana, L' (1965) (The Iguana)
A short novel by ▷Anna Maria Ortese. A political fable in which the iguana of the title is a monstrous being, half-woman, half-animal. The iguana is a metaphor for the impossibility of a positive relationship between humankind and nature. The story told is of the violent revolt of a woman who has been metaphorically trodden on by a corrupt society. The world, however, remains a place where there is no escape from injustice and unhappiness. The love story within the novel (the Aleardo–iguana relationship) is tragic. The novel is typical of Ortese in its polemic against a harsh world which respects only winners and destroys losers.

i is a long memoried woman (1983)
The first collection of published poetry by the Caribbean writer ▷Grace Nichols, which was winner of the Commonwealth Poetry Prize in 1983. The poems celebrate for the first time the black woman's progress and evolution in the New World. The poems are Nichols's imaginative rendering of the consciousness of the black woman as she responded and adjusted to life in the Caribbean. These poems chart the survival of the enslaved black woman as mother, daughter, warrior and priestess. This collection, which has been compared to that of the Caribbean writer E.K. Brathwaite, *The Arrivants* (1973), gives voice to the black woman's experience of the ▷Middle Passage and slavery. Nichols's verse is beautifully crafted, and her technical command of both English and creole language indicate a poet of considerable ability.

Ikramullah, Shaista (born 1915)
Indian-born Pakistani writer and politician. Her autobiography ▷*From Purdah to Parliament* (1963)

records her extraordinary progress from seclusion to a public life of great prominence. She was born in Calcutta into two different lifestyles. Both her parents came from the Urdu-speaking aristocracy of Bengal, but, whereas her mother's family stuck to the old ways of the Mughal culture, her father and his brothers were rapid modernizers. She was educated in English, Arabic and Urdu, and agreed willingly to an ▷arranged marriage. She only came out of *purdah* (the veil) at her husband's request. In the 1940s she received a Ph.D. from the University of London for her dissertation on the development of the Urdu novel and short story. Back in India she enthusiastically supported the campaign for Pakistan, and sat as a member in its first Constituent Assembly in 1948. She was also a member of Pakistan's delegation to the Third Session of the UN in 1948. As a politician she became known for her work on education and among the millions of refugees that flooded into Pakistan at the time of its creation.

'Images of women' criticism
Criticism which focuses on representations of women in literary texts as part of a critique of patriarchy. 'Images of women' criticism was popularized, if not initiated, by feminist readers of the 1960s and 1970s. ▷Kate Millett's exposure of the patriarchal and sexist representations of women in novels by D.H. Lawrence (1885–1930) and Henry Miller (1891–1980) is a good example of how this type of criticism challenges the argument of traditional literary criticism that literature is politically neutral.
▷Greer, Germaine

Imaginaire philosophique, L' (1980) ▷*The Philosophical Imaginary* (1984)

Imaginary
In the work of French psychoanalyst Jacques Lacan (1901–1981), the imaginary is the condition of illusory unity and mastery, where the child sees its *image* in the mirror and experiences an imaginary oneness of self, prior to the ▷Oedipus complex and entry into the ▷symbolic order of language and ▷difference. ▷Hélène Cixous and ▷Luce Irigaray are two French feminist theorists who have separately attempted to construct a specifically feminine imaginary. In Cixous's poetic revision of Lacanian theory, the imaginary becomes woman's spiritual and linguistic home: it is a place before the (masculine) law, where female creativity is positively and spontaneously expressed. For Irigaray, however, feminists need to rethink women's relation to the imaginary as other than a place of refuge for those rendered homeless in the symbolic order, and to formulate it as a political and social sphere where change can occur.

Imitation of Christ, The (1504)
▷Margaret Beaufort's ▷translation of the fourth book of Thomas à Kempis's Latin work. She commissioned William Atkynson to translate the

work. He translated the first three books from Latin, and she translated from a French version the fourth book which discusses the sacrament. All four books were printed by Wynkyn de Worde (died 1534) in 1504. Atkynson's and Beaufort's work is the second known English translation of this popular devotional work, and the first to be printed in England.
Bib: Ingram, J.K. (ed.), *The Earliest English Translation of . . . De Imitatione Christi.*

Imitation of Life (1933)
US novel. ▷Fannie Hurst's bestselling book chronicles a woman's rise from rags to riches. A widowed mother, Beatrice Chipley, with the help of her African-American maid, Delilah, establishes a successful chain of waffle restaurants using Delilah's syrup recipe. She also markets Delilah's stereotypical, maternal image. Beatrice's commercial success, however, does not compensate for her lack of romantic love. Hurst shows that, without this 'man love', women's lives are considered to be only imitations. Respecting Beatrice's accomplishment, Hurst shows how women have been made emotionally dependent on men. She shows the complexity of inter-racial relationships between women that are both exploitative and affectionate.

Imperialism (19th-century Britain)
The desire to establish an empire beyond the home country and to colonize and dominate other lands and peoples. Victorian Britain controlled the largest empire in world history; an unquestioned assumption of cultural superiority was extremely prevalent amongst the English. In turn, this attitude permeated the literature of the age. Women were as deeply involved in the ideology of imperialism as were men: ▷Queen Victoria was the figurehead of the empire, and the construction of the Victorian woman as an ▷'Angel in the House' contributed to imperialist belief by stressing the moral and spiritual perfection of the middle-class English woman. The imperialist context in which 19th-century literature was produced has become a key focus for critical discussion in recent years.

Imperialist, The (1904)
Germane to Canadian literature, ▷Sarah Jeannette Duncan's *The Imperialist* is a portrait of Canada within a larger Victorian Empire. Written while Duncan was living in India, it examines the ideal of Empire in a rhetorical yet realistic way. The community of Elgin is unfolded through the device of courtship, but the liaisons portrayed serve as political and religious metaphors for the Canadian small town's idealism and abnegation. This novel is convincing as a powerful example of social realism, despite verging on sentimentality. The differing love stories conflict with and amplify the overall political thrust of a fiction that addresses the insidious influence of the United States on Canada's moral relationship to the British Empire. *The Imperialist* is strongest for its

representation of community, and how community's structure can effect a profound difference in history's impervious cadence.

Inber, Vera Mikhailovna (1890–1972)
Russian poet, short story writer, and journalist. Inber's long career began with several volumes of light lyrics influenced by symbolism (*Melancholy Wine*, 1914; *Bitter Delight*, 1917; *Fleeting Words*, 1922). In ▷Moscow from the early 1920s she joined the constructivist movement, and adapted its theories of a utilitarian, compressed art to her poetry (*The Goal and the Journey*, 1925), and in humorous short stories and sketches which described the clash of the old and new in Soviet life – 'Nightingale and Rose' (*North American Review* 266, 1924) and 'Garlic in His Suitcase' (1927, *Literary Review*, Winter 1991). Many of these stories dealt with children's perceptions, and Inber also addressed the psychology of childhood with great empathy in memoirs and fiction based on her own youth in an intellectual family in Odessa – 'Death of the Moon' (1928) and 'How I Was Little' (1953) – and in an essay on children in wartime, 'On Leningrad Children' (1942–1943). Her experiments in writing for theatre include opera libretti and a verse comedy, *Mother's Union* (1938). As a journalist, Inber reported on life in the Transcaucasus; like ▷Aligér and ▷Shaginián, she used verse to describe her journeys (*Travel Diary*, 1939; *Waterway*, 1951). In 1941 she chose to accompany her doctor-husband to Leningrad and work there during the 900-day siege; her epic poem, *Pulkovo Meridian* (1941–1943) and her journals *Almost Three Years* (English translation *Leningrad Diary*, 1971), are classic accounts of the city's ordeal. Inber's 1957 *Inspiration and Mastery* is a meditation on the driving forces behind creativity.
　　▷Leningrad

Inchbald, Elizabeth (1753–1821)
English actress and writer. She began writing with the farce *Mogul Tale*, in which she also acted. She wrote twenty plays, often successful, and a novel, *A Simple Story* (1791). She also wrote for periodicals, and prefaces to plays, and knew the anarchists Thomas Holcroft (1745–1809) and William Godwin (1756–1836).

Incidents in the Life of a Slave Girl, Written by Herself (1861)
US personal narrative by ▷Harriet A. Jacobs. Edited by ▷Lydia Maria Child, the first edition of *Incidents* was published without the author's name. The correspondence of the fictionalized characters and events to Jacobs's own life has since been documented by Jean Fagan Yellin, editor of the current reprint edition of *Incidents*, published by Harvard University Press in 1987. The narrative details Jacobs's life in and escape from slavery. It is notably honest in its treatment of her own sexuality, and straightforward in its treatment of racism and women's rights.

Incomplete Works of Ghada al-Samman, The (1978)

Miscellaneous works in Arabic by Syrian novelist and journalist ▷ Ghada al-Samman. They were collected by the author from periodicals after the originals were destroyed in the first year of the Lebanese civil war (1975). Fourteen volumes were published by 1988, covering some of her earlier stories, her reporting, her criticism, some of her verse and many interviews she gave to the Arabic press over some twenty-five years.

Volumes twelve to fourteen are devoted to a selection from hundreds of such interviews, which make very interesting reading. Adept at self-advertising and self-dramatizing, Ghada al-Samman has used those press interviews to state her position as a serious professional writer who remains undeterred by the shocked reactions of some of her readers. When accused of 'writing like a man' – that is, writing frankly of sex, politics and drugs, her standard reply is that she writes 'like a human being, a product of the Third World, but also a well-travelled citizen of the world'. When questioned about her readings, Ghada al-Samman shows she belongs to a category of writers that today exists only in Third World countries. Assimilating her own cultural heritage from the *Qur'an* to modern Arabic poetry, she learned to read French as a child and majored in English in the University of Damascus. Quotations from Shakespeare (1564–1616), Goethe (1749–1832), ▷ Virginia Woolf or ▷ Simone de Beauvoir come to her as naturally as the proverbial Arabic saying.

The author's choice of titles for her books is often ingenious: the three volumes of interviews are *The Tribe Questions the Victim* (a particularly good title in Arabic as tribe in Arabic is *gabila*, and *gatila* is 'female victim'), *The Sea Tries a Fish* (1986) and *Loitering inside a Wound* (1988).

Incredible Journey, The (1923)

Australian novel by ▷ Catherine Martin. This novel provides a particularly sympathetic treatment of Aboriginal life. It deals with Aboriginal culture, with their dispossession and, in particular, with the white practice of removing Aboriginal children from their parents. It tells the story of an Aboriginal mother, Iliapa, and her search through the Australian outback for her son, who has been kidnapped by a white man. The novel was republished by Pandora Press in 1987.
▷ Aborigine in non-Aboriginal Australian women's writing, The

In Custody (1984)

A novel by Indian author ▷ Anita Desai. It charts the physical and moral peregrinations of a man abandoning the haven of his small-town home in India for a grand metropolis, and ultimately discovering a new kind of dignity for himself. The novel is a delicate study of the subtle degrees of displacement that can be experienced within one culture, and a celebration of the small victories that self-discovery brings.

Indentured labour (Caribbean)

In the early days of colonization, field labour was supplied mainly by indentured workers brought from Britain. This involved a labour contract for a fixed period of time (normally five years) whereby workers sold themselves to the highest bidder. At the end of the period of service most indentured labourers acquired land of their own. As the demand for labour increased, this system was replaced by slavery. With the abolition of slavery in the British West Indies in 1834 the indentured system revived. From the 1840s to 1917 (when this system ended) over half a million indentured workers were brought from India (mainly) to ▷ Trinidad and ▷ Guyana. See D. Dabydeen and Brinsley Samaroo (eds), *India in the Caribbean* (1987).

Indiana (1832)

Novel that founded the reputation of French novelist ▷ George Sand. The story brings together a double claim for the freedom of passion and the right to social justice, exploring the shackles of conventional marriage and the social prohibitions on love that crosses class boundaries. Indiana is trapped in an arranged marriage to a man much older than herself. Her Creole maid, Noun, has been seduced with promises of marriage by an unscrupulous nobleman, Raymon de Ramière. Raymon falls in love with Indiana; the pregnant Noun drowns herself in despair; Indiana falls in love with Raymon, and finds herself confronting her husband with passionate pleas for her freedom: 'I know that I am the slave and you are the master. You are master by the law of the land. You can bind my body, tie fast my hands, rule my every action. You have the right that belongs to the strong, and society confirms it; but, Sir, you have no power over my will, which God alone can bend and break.' In the first version, Indiana's radical intransigence leads naturally to her death. In the second, more circumspect (and more in tune with Sand's later reformism in both feminist and socialist arenas), she finds a happy ending in marriage with her childhood friend and cousin, Sir Ralph, retreating from fashionable society and devoting herself to the emancipation of black slaves.

India Song (1976)

Translation of the 1973 screenplay by French writer ▷ Marguerite Duras for the 1975 film of the same name. The screenplay is the staging as a memory of the story recounted in ▷ *The Vice-consul*. Anne-Marie Stretter shows sympathy for the ostracized Vice-Consul of Lahore, but refuses to allow him to stay with her after a reception at the embassy, and later kills herself at her island residence. This story is interwoven with that of a mad beggarwoman who has walked to Calcutta from Laos. The voices of two women question each other about what happened in these stories, and their dialogue is intercut with conversations and snatches of dialogue between characters from Anne-Marie Stretter's story itself.

Indigenism (*Indigenismo*)

In Spanish-speaking countries (in Brazil *indianismo*), indigenism is the literature having the Indian peoples as its topic. Although the Indian peoples constitute the main theme of this literature they are depicted from the point of view of the dominant culture. Important 19th-century Latin American indigenist novels by women writers are ▷ *Guatimozín* (1846) and *El cacique de Turmequé* (*The Chief of Turmequé*) by the Cuban ▷ Gertrúdis Gómez de Avellaneda (1814–1873), and *Aves sin nido* (1889) (▷ *Birds without a Nest*, 1968) by the Colombian ▷ Clorinda Matto de Turner (1854–1909). In Brazil, ▷ Maria Firmina dos Reis (1825–1917) wrote a short story, 'Gupeva' (1861), set in a romantic plot. In this century, ▷ Rosario Castellanos (1925–1978) has written on the 20th-century Mexican Indian, especially in the novel *Balún Canán* (1958) (▷ *The Nine Guardians*, 1970).

Infanta Dona Maria de Portugal e as Suas Damas, A (1902) (*The Infanta Dona Maria of Portugal and Her Ladies*)

A biography of the ▷ Infanta Dona Maria and the women of her court. Written by ▷ Carolina Michaëlis de Vasconcelos, this study gives specific information on little-known Portuguese women writers and scholars of the 16th century, such as ▷ Luisa Sigea, Ángela Sigea and Paula Vicente. It also contains a section on the scholar and orator ▷ Públia Hortênsia de Castro. In general terms, the book provides important insights into the history and literary culture of Renaissance Portugal.

Infertility/childlessness (West Africa)

This is a recurring theme in writing by African women, and understandably so, for a woman is valued very much according to her ability to bear children. Women's suffering as a result of childlessness is treated by numerous writers. Significantly, the heroines of ▷ Flora Nwapa's ▷ *Efuru* and ▷ *Idu* are both childless women who rise above their disability. The trials undergone by ▷ Ifeoma Okoye's heroine in her novel *Behind the Clouds* have a happy conclusion when it turns out to be the husband who is at fault. This is a wish-fulfilment fantasy, considering that it is always presumed to be the woman's problem.

Ingelow, Jean (1820–1897)

English poet, novelist and writer of ▷ children's literature, also published under the ▷ pseudonym Orris. She was born near Boston, Lincolnshire and educated at home. Although she wrote poetry as a child, she did not begin publishing until compelled by financial need in the 1850s. She has been described as 'A lost ▷ Pre-Raphaelite', who failed to gain a place in literary history despite her contemporary popularity. Her second volume of *Poems* (1863) ran to thirty editions, and her 1883

poem, 'High Tide on the Coast of Lincolnshire, 1571', was very well-known. Among her friends were ▷ Christina Rossetti and ▷ Jane and Ann Taylor. Ingelow's writing for children includes *Mopsa the Fairy* (1869). *Off the Skelligs* and *Sarah de Berenger* (both 1879) are among the novels she wrote in later life.
Bib: Peters, M., *Jean Ingelow, Victorian Poetess*; Hickok, K., *Representations of Women: 19th Century British Women's Poetry*.

Inglewood, Kathleen (1876–?)

New Zealand novelist. Kate Isitt, who wrote under the pseudonym Kathleen Inglewood, was the daughter of a Methodist minister and came from a family strongly associated with prohibition. She worked as a journalist for many years and wrote one novel, *Patmos* (1905), in which she describes the political history of the prohibition movement and associates the prohibition of alcohol with religion. After the 1902 election, she left for England where she continued to work as a journalist.

Inglis (Kello), Esther (1571–1624)

English calligrapher. She was born in France to Marie Prissott and Nicholas Langlois (the name was later changed to Inglis or Inglish). Her family was Protestant, and in 1572 they fled to England following the St Bartholomew massacre (during which French Protestants were killed by Roman Catholics). In 1596 she married Bartholomew Kello who was listed as 'Clerk of all Passports', and for whom Inglis worked as scribe. She probably learned calligraphy from her mother as early as thirteen. Until her death at the age of 53, Inglis worked actively and accurately as a calligrapher, producing hand-illuminated works for wealthy patrons. Although over forty of her manuscripts remain extant, none have been reproduced during the 20th century.
▷ Patronage
Bib: Jackson, D., *Esther Inglis: Calligrapher 1571–1624*.

Inheritance, The (1824)

The second work of ▷ Scottish novelist ▷ Susan Ferrier. Like all her books, it was published anonymously by Blackwood. The plot revolves around an heiress, Gertrude St Clair, who is abandoned by her father and cheated of her inheritance because he suspects she is not his daughter. Gertrude finds support from her uncle, Adam Ramsay, who takes her in and enables her to marry the man she loves. The novel was influenced by the work of ▷ Jane Austen and ▷ Maria Edgeworth, and contains good comic scenes.

In Hope of Better Days (1860)

Russian writer ▷ Nadezhda Khvoshchínskaia's novel is among her best works. A contemporary critic described her sardonic study of an aristocratic family in the period just before the abolition of serfdom as 'incomparably more significant than [Goncharov's] *Oblomov* and [Turgenev's] *On the Eve*'. An egotistic matriarch, Princess Desiatova, is smugly convinced that her ancient lineage and wealth give her the right to impose her will on the relatives and covey of dependent women assembled for the summer at her country estate. In the battle for her favour, her precociously sly schoolboy grandson, Vas'ia, outwits his older cousin, Ivan, a guards officer preoccupied with simultaneous love affairs with a married neighbour, Katerina Aleksinskaia, and Polina, a parasitic hanger-on in the Desiatov household. The only positive characters, Aleksinskaia's husband and the steward on her estate, are depicted as helpless bystanders. A clever touch in the novel is the running motif of women's crafts – the useless embroidery that occupies the hands of the princess and her dependents, contrasted with the frantic sewing and laundry that Polina's mother must undertake to keep her daughter smartly turned out.

Inman, Elizabeth Murray Campbell Smith (c 1724–1785)

North American diarist and letter-writer. Born in Scotland, she joined her brother James in North America when she was orphaned at the age of fourteen. She ran a millinery business in Boston for several years, and in 1755 married Thomas Campbell, a Scottish merchant, who died only a few years later. She married twice more – in 1760 to James Smith and in 1771 to Ralph Inman, both prosperous Boston merchants. After Smith's death in 1769, she returned to Scotland for restoration of her spirits. During the two years she remained in her homeland, she maintained a journal of her travels there. After returning to North America and marrying for the final time, she settled into a comfortable, upper-class life in Cambridge, Massachusetts. When the American Revolution began, however, her and her husband's Loyalist alliances brought about the confiscation of their property. In a diary kept during these years, she details her management of their estate while her husband was trapped in the siege of Boston. The end of the war brought the beginnings of peace, but she died shortly thereafter, on 25 May 1785. Her diary and letters are collected in *The Letters of James Murray, Loyalist (1901)*.
▷ 'Diary and Letters of Elizabeth Murray Inman, The'

Innamorata, L' (1893) (A Woman in Love)

A largely autobiographical novel, by ▷ Contessa Lara. Leona, the protagonist, falls in love with a man who uses her and disappoints her. Love is viewed here in a negative light as something that can only lead to disappointment. The novel is interesting for its celebration of the erotic from a female point of view.

Inner Courtyard, The (1990)

A collection of short stories, edited by Lakshmi Holstrom, which brings together Indian women writers from India, Britain and North America. Although some of the stories were written in English, many are translations from Indian regional languages, including Hindi, Urdu, Tamil and Malayalam. There is a glossary of culturally specific terms. There are contributions from: ▷ Lalitambika Antarjanam, ▷ Vaidehi, ▷ Kamala Das, ▷ Qurratulain Hyder, ▷ Mrinal Pande, ▷ Lakshmi Kannan, ▷ Ambia, ▷ Ismat Chughtai, ▷ Mahasveta Devi, ▷ Attia Hosain, ▷ Anita Desai, ▷ Shashi Deshpande, Shama Futehally, Vishwapriya Iyengar, ▷ Padma Perera, Rukhsana Ahmad, ▷ Anjana Appachana and ▷ Suniti Namjoshi.

Inner Harbour, The (1979)

Poems by New Zealand writer ▷ Fleur Adcock. *The Inner Harbour* is Adcock's sixth published collection. Divided into four sections, 'Beginnings', 'Endings', 'The Thing Itself', and 'To and Fro', *The Inner Harbour*, in a more focused way than Adcock's earlier collections, deals with cross-cultural experience in the life of the poet. All Adcock's work is preoccupied with writing and its contexts: relationships, knowledge, cultural and historical identity, the cool analytical tone of the poet contrasting with the often intimate experiences and emotions she recounts. Her poems are frequently replies to letters or conversations, or addressed to a particular person, and so give the impression of a continuing reconstruction of her daily and intellectual life. The poems refer to an explicitly British context but also recall New Zealand and other ideas of 'home', especially in the suggestive title poem and the last section 'To and Fro'. Adcock's poems exemplify aspects of post-colonial discourse while at the same time participating in a distinctively cultured and knowledgeable British tradition.

Inno alla gioia (1983) (A Hymn to Joy)

A collection of Italian poetry by ▷ Margherita Guidacci, and a departure from her largely negative earlier work. Guidacci says, 'I had to choose this title, in spite of its deplorable lack of originality and the formidable Schiller-Beethoven precedent, because it was the only one perfectly compatible with the content of my book: indeed, if it hadn't already existed, I think I could have invented it.' Appropriately, it is a collection which celebrates the victory of life over death. In many ways, it overturns, or at least revises, Guidacci's *Neurosuite* (1970) in that negative images from that collection become positive in this. Wind, for example, a demonic force in the earlier work, is a blessed one in this. The conclusion, too, is wholly positive and looks hopefully to the future. This is a text full of joy, of love poetry and of images of light. 'Joy' is the most frequently recurring word in the text.

Insciallah (1990)

A novel, by ▷ Oriana Fallaci, which focuses on the international peace-keeping force in Beirut. Like much of Fallaci's work, it is an anti-war piece which apportions both pity and blame. It is also akin to her earlier work in that it addresses the question of what it means to be a man. This is perhaps the most self-consciously literary work that Fallaci has yet produced, with its novel-within-the-novel, which reveals itself late in the text. Ostensibly, the novel we are reading is being written by one of Fallaci's (male) characters. (Readers familiar with modern Italian writers may be reminded of Bradamante in Calvino's *Non-Existent Knight*.) Yet, in some respects, the novel also appears to be quite traditional. For instance, Fallaci polarizes her male and female characters according to the familiar culture/nature split, with no apparent irony intended. This novel is stylistically interesting for its mingling of the ▷fantastical and the ▷realistic.

In Search of Our Mother's Gardens: Womanist Prose (1983)

Essays by US writer ▷Alice Walker. The key themes of this groundbreaking collection are encapsulated in the title. Walker defines a form of feminism which challenges the biases of the white, women's movement, without discarding feminism as a politics and philosophy. She replaces the term feminist with that of womanist. The title essay reworks ▷Virginia Woolf's project in ▷*A Room of One's Own* to think back through our mothers, and examines the specific conditions of African-American women's writing and creativity. Taking Woolf's minimum requirement of a room of one's own and £500 a year, Walker asks what that could mean for ▷Phillis Wheatley, 'a slave, who owned not even herself', and then uses Woolf's example to establish a model of creativity rooted in women's domestic work: gardening, quilting, sewing and cooking.

Walker also espouses oral traditions, explaining that her stories are her mother's stories. Storytelling provides a model for the majority of Walker's essays. In '*One* Child of One's Own' she uses a third-person version of her own life to explore the relationship between writing and motherhood, racism, and the biases of white literary criticism. Other essays recover a tradition of African-American women writers, such as ▷Zora Neale Hurston, Phillis Wheatley, and Rebecca Jackson, a 19th-century itinerant minister and letter-writer. Walker examines the marginalization of these writers, and the effects on contemporary African-American women writers of an imposed ignorance of their predecessors. She emphasizes a spiritual interconnectedness of life which could encompass the divisions of race and gender.

Inside the Haveli (1977)

Novel by Indian writer Rama Mehta, and her only major work. Set in the house (*haveli*) of a traditional Indian extended family, the novel tells of a young bride's rise from the lowly status of daughter-in-law to the supreme position of mistress of the household. It begins with the birth of her daughter, and ends when the daughter has reached a marriageable age. The novel's emphasis on the wife's relations with her female in-laws rather than on those she has with her husband is an accurate reflection of the priorities which a bride entering an extended family must observe. It is the success of her relationship with her elders that will determine ultimately whether her marriage is deemed a successful one. Filial love rather than conjugal love takes priority.

Instruction for Christians, An ▷Martin, Dorcas

Instruction of a Christian Woman (1529)

Translation of a Latin treatise on women's education by Juan Luis Vives, tutor in the household of ▷Catherine of Aragon, who commissioned the work for her daughter ▷Mary Tudor in 1523. In 1529 Richard Hyrde, a tutor in the household of Thomas More (1478–1535), translated the work into English. It went through more than forty editions and translations in the 16th century. The work was particularly influential to the education of women such as ▷Elizabeth Tudor, ▷Anne Bacon, ▷Mary Basset, ▷Margaret Roper, ▷Mildred Cecil, and ▷Elizabeth Russell, who were reared in ▷humanist families. It is divided into sections covering the three stages of female life: virginity, marriage, and widowhood. When compared with contemporary discussions of education for men, including his own, Vives's work seems more like a ▷conduct book than an educational treatise. It stresses household management, morality, and the three virtues of silence, obedience, and piety. Although Vives treated seriously the notion that women were educable and not innately wicked, he nevertheless maintained the misogynist belief in woman's defective nature. Education, according to Vives, was a way of controlling and therefore protecting women's easily misled virtue, by keeping their attention away from worldly evils. The extreme and common ambivalence expressed by humanist educators such as Vives regarding women frequently manifested itself in Renaissance women's own ambivalence about their skills and writings.
Bib: Wayne, V., 'Some Sad Sentence: Vives' Instruction of a Christian Woman' in Hannay, M. (ed.), *Silent But for the Word*.

In the Eye of the Sun (1992)

Novel in English by Egyptian writer ▷Ahdaf Soueif. Exploring the ramifications of lives lived across national boundaries, across language barriers and diverging cultures. Asya, a young Egyptian girl, is jolted into consciousness of the world with the shock of the Arab defeat of June 1967. She lives between cultures: an Arab girl nurtured on English literature. Her story is told in many voices, and carries the reader where Asya travels: Cairo, Alexandria, Akhmim, Beirut, Rome, Vienna, Paris, London and New York.

In New York Asya finally breaks with her habitual sense of obligation, of having to do things she does not desire or believe in, and finally frees herself from her English lover, Gerald.

Though Asya's life between 1967 and 1982 is at the centre of the novel, there are other lives, a diverging, criss-crossing network of relatives, siblings, close friends, schoolmates and acquaintances. This vast novel tries to capture their variety, highlighting Asya's husband, Saif, and the mirage or puzzle he comes to represent to her.

Intimate Strangers (1937)
Australian novel by ▷Katharine Susannah Prichard. *Intimate Strangers* is a good example of that conflict between romanticism and the principles of socialist realism which the critics have discerned in Prichard's work. It charts the marital breakdown between Greg and Elodie Blackwood, Elodie's decision to run away with a romantic adventurer, and the less than credible reconciliation between Greg and Elodie when they agree to sink their differences and work together for the good of the socialist revolution. It is said that the suicide of Prichard's husband, Hugo Throssel, a war hero and the model for Greg, influenced the ending of this novel. It has been made into a successful ABC Television series.

Inuit literature
The Greenland Inuit (Eskimos) had no written language before they came into contact with literate Europeans in the 18th century. A dictionary and a grammar were then written.

Much of the oral literature has been collected and written down by Danes. While women were storytellers, and maybe also creators in the oral tradition, only very few women writers have published modern Inuit literature, although some women have written lyrics to popular modern rock songs.

Today, some womens' groups are participating in the cultural debate, but this is a new development. Some women have written about their encounter with the Danish culture, eg Mâliâraq Vebæk (born 1917) in her novel *Búsime nâpinek* (1981) (*The Meeting on the Bus*).

Invernizio, Carolina (1858–1916)
Italian novelist. She lived for most of her life in Florence, and produced numerous novels. In her own time she was an extremely popular writer, yet after her death her writing was increasingly trivialized, and even vilified. Recently, feminist critics in particular have looked at her work in a different and altogether more positive light. Many of her novels followed the ▷*romanzo d'appendice* format. She wrote for a mainly female audience, and addressed issues of particular interest to her readers, such as the nature of romantic love and motherhood. She celebrated the sufferings of women in her work, and often presented her characters in a horrific/▷Gothic setting. The title of her collected works sums up her subject matter and her approach in an apt fashion: *Romanzi del peccato, della perdizione e del delitto* (1970) (*Novels of*

Sin, Perdition and Crime). The titles of individual works are also revealing.

Her other work includes: *Le figlie della duchessa* (1889) (*The Duchess's Daughters*); *La bastarda* (1892) (*The Bastard*); *Cuor di donna* (1894) (*A Woman's Heart*); *Dora la figlia dell'assassino* (1895) (*Dora, the Assassin's Daughter*); *I drammi dell'adulterio* (1898) (*Dramas of Adultery*); *I disperati* (1904) (*The Despairing*).

Invitée, L' (1943) ▷*She Came to Stay* (1949)

Iola Leroy, or Shadows Uplifted (1892)
US novel by ▷Frances E.W. Harper. Set during the Reconstruction era after the US Civil War, *Iola Leroy* is one of the earliest novels by an African-American woman. It re-visioned for its readers the 19th-century experience of US people of color – showing what its audience had not known before: the experiences of African-American soldiers, the color line within the African-American community, the potential conflicts between upward mobility and identification with community and race.

Iordanidou, Maria (born 1897)
Greek novelist. She was born in the city which for Greeks was still Constantinople (Istanbul). As a young woman she went to Stavropol, in Russia, and afterwards came to Athens, where she still lives. She did not begin writing until the age of 65. Her first book, the autobiographically based novel ▷*Loxandra* (1960), was received with great enthusiasm in Greece and went through numerous editions. It is based on her life at the beginning of this century, when Istanbul was still as much a Greek as a Turkish city and all the places had their Greek names. The book deeply moved all those Greeks who had been forced to leave Turkey in 1922 and who still retained vivid memories of their former homes. Loxandra, the name of her grandmother, is an unsentimental, but a vibrant, loving, down-to-earth character who represents the vanished world of Greek Asia Minor. *Vacations in the Caucasus* (1985) is the story of Loxandra's granddaughter's experiences in the Caucasus. *Like Crazy Birds* (1978) is a story about life in Greek Alexandria and Athens. Her last novel, *The Circle's Turnings* (1982), concerns the period of the German occupation of Greece in World War II. Iordanidou's books, based on real historical events, have been very popular in Greece, expressing as they do, the nostalgia felt by all Greeks for the lost homeland of Constantinople and Asia Minor.

Iphigenia at Aulis (1909)
Abridged prose ▷translation by ▷Joanna Lumley (c 1532–1576/77) of Euripides's Greek tragedy. Lumley's translation, made in about 1550 when she was only thirteen years old, is the earliest surviving English translation of a Greek drama. Although she probably translated from an edition in which Desidenius Erasmus's (?1466–1536) Latin translation of the play was printed alongside

the Greek text, her accomplishment is significant given the primitive state of knowledge concerning Greek during the mid-16th century. Her choice of story is also interesting. Agamemnon, who has promised to sacrifice his daughter to ensure victory against the Trojans, summons Iphigenia to Aulis under the pretence of arranging her marriage to Achilles, a man she had never met. Lumley's elimination of most of the choruses focuses the play's tension on Iphigenia's patriotic decision to sacrifice herself for the good of her country. Her translation remained unpublished until the Malone Society printed it in 1909.
Bib: Child, H.H. (ed.), *Iphigenia at Aulis, c. 1550*; Crane, F.D., 'Euripides, Erasmus, and Lady Lumley', *Classical Journal* 39 (1944), pp. 223–8; Greene, D.H., 'Lady Lumley and Greek Tragedy', *Classical Journal* 36 (1941), pp. 537–47.

Iremonger, Lucille (born 1921)
This Caribbean novelist and collector of folktales was born and educated in ▷Jamaica. She won the Jamaican Scholarship, and proceeded to higher education in Britain. She has published seven novels spanning the period 1951–1962, many of which are now out of print. An extract from her first novel, *Creole* (1951), was published in the *Jamaican Independence Anthology* (1962). A collector of folklore, she has published a range of material for children focusing on traditional ▷Anancy Stories.

Irigaray, Luce (born 1930)
French feminist, psychoanalyst and philosopher. A French national born in Belgium, Irigaray's influence extends beyond academic circles; she is a regular contributor to the newspaper of the Italian Communist Party, and is now Director of Research in Philosophy at the National Centre for Scientific Research, Paris.

Since her first book, *Le Langage des déments* (1973) (*The Language of the Demented*), a study of linguistic collapse in senile dementia, Irigaray's work has been at the forefront of psycho-linguistic enquiry, and is particularly concerned with the relationship between gender and language. Her doctoral thesis, published in France in 1974 and translated into English as ▷*Speculum of the Other Woman* (1985), resulted in her expulsion from Jacques Lacan's École Freudienne.

Irigaray critically re-reads Freud in the light of Jacques Derrida's critique of ▷binary thought. And she challenges Lacan's writing on feminine sexuality: Lacan theorized the difference of female sexuality and women's consequent relation to language in terms of ▷lack; Irigaray locates women's ▷otherness more positively, crediting them with a multiple sexuality and a distinctly feminine psycho-linguistic economy, which she calls '*parler femme*', a form of ▷*écriture féminine*. Irigaray's ideas on feminine sexuality and writing can be found in ▷*This Sex Which Is Not One* (1985), which is a more accessible book than *Speculum*. Her work discusses sexual relations alongside the laws of capital. Her publications include: *Amante marine. De Fredrich Neitzsche* (1983); *L'Oubli de l'air. Chez Martin Heidegger* (1983); *Ethique de la différence sexuelle* (1984); *Parler n'est jamais neutre* (1985); *Sexes et Parentés* (1987).
▷Deconstruction; Psychoanalysis
Bib: Grosz, Elizabeth, *Sexual Subversions: Three French Feminists*; Moi, T., *Sexual/Textual Politics*; Whitford, Margaret, *Luce Irigaray: Philosophy in the Feminine*.

Irwin, P. K. ▷Page, Patricia K.

Isabella (early 13th century)
French ▷*trobairitz* of the third period. Possibly a fictitious female voice, she engaged in poetic 'jousting' with Elias Cairel in Provençal and has been identified as Isabella Pallavicini, though some regard this hypothesis as highly improbable.
Bib: Cherchi, P., 'The Troubled Existence of Three Women Poets' in Paden, W.D. (ed), *The Voice of the Trobairitz*, pp. 197–209.

Isabel of Warenne, Countess of Arundel (mid-13th century)
Patron. The ▷Anglo-Norman poetic *Life of St Edmund* (*La Vie de Saint Edmond, Archeveque de Cantorbery*) by Matthew Paris was translated for and dedicated to Isabel, after 1250. Ralph Bocking dedicated to her the *Life and Miracles of Richard of Chichester* (a Latin Life of the Bishop of Chichester, in whose diocese Isabel lived, and who was canonized in 1262).

Isabel, Queen of Portugal (died 1455)
Married to King Afonso V, who reigned from 1448–1481. She was deeply interested in religion, history and literature. In 1445 she requested Portuguese translations of Ludolph von Sachen's *Vita Christi* and ▷Christine de Pisan's *Livre des Trois Vertues*. Isabel's brother, the Infante Pedro (1429–66), wrote a biography of her life, *Tragédia de la Insigne Reyna Dona Isabel* (1457), which was edited by ▷Carolina Michaëlis de Vasconcelos in 1901.
▷*Espelho de Cristina*; Leonor, Queen of Portugal

Isaia, Nana (born 1934)
Greek poet and translator. She was born in Athens, where she studied painting at the School of Fine Arts. She exhibited her work at six of the 'Panhellenic' exhibitions, and in 1974 gave her first private exhibition. In 1969 she published her first collection of poetry, *Poems. A Glance*, another collection, appeared in 1974. In the same year she published her translation of poems by ▷Sylvia Plath, with her own introduction. Further collections include *Alice in Wonderland* (1977), *Form* (1980), *In the Tactics of Passion* (1982) and *Consciousness of Oblivion* (1982). She has contributed articles and poems to a number of non-Greek periodicals. Her poetry is somewhat pessimistic in tone, much of it based on unhappy love affairs and traumatic personal experiences.

Isharaza, Grace Birabwe
Ugandan poet, teacher in Tororo, Uganda.
Bib: Calder, A., Mapanje, J. and Pieterse, C.
(eds), *Summer Fires: New Poetry of Africa*.

Ishigaki Rin (born 1920)
Japanese poet. Born in Tokyo, she lost her
grandmother and two sisters after her mother died
when she was only four. She worked at a bank
from the age of fourteen until her retirement and
started to write poems at school. Her first poetry
collection, *The Kettles and Burning Fire in Front of
Me*, appeared in 1959. Her second collection was
A Nameplate and Others (1969), and *The Poetry
Collection of Ishigaki Rin* (1971) won the Tamura
Toshiko Prize. She pursues the significance of life
and death through a realistic description of daily
lives, and excels at satire. A five-volume collection
of her poetry was published in 1987.

Islanders (1927)
North American novel by ▷Helen Rose Hull
which documents the effects of economic and
technological changes on women's lives. Ellen
Dacey experiences the isolation and powerlessness
in shifting from an agrarian to a cash economy.
An unmarried woman, she is rendered dependent
on a family which exploits her. Hull emphasizes
that to operate, the middle-class household
victimizes women. Ellen escapes this by turning to
nature and to other women for nurturing. Hull
posits that women must assume responsibility for
retaining their integrity in order to survive
institutionalized victimization.

Ismail, Siti Zainon
Malay poet. The world she expresses and exploits
in her poems is intensely personal, the imagery
almost obscure, so private is the experience. An
Indonesian-trained *batik* artist, her poetry also
emphasizes artistic values and interests, drawing
upon the world of myth for her images as in
'Profil Cinta' ('Profile of Love') from her first
volume *Nyanyian Malam* (1976) (*Night Songs*),
where the dancer eloquently expresses her love:
'Fingers and nails / her heart, eyes mournful /
she's my Sita / like a wave in the dance.' Her
second volume, *Puisi Putih Sang Kekasih* (1984)
(*White Poems for My Love*), continues with
introspective poems about love, friendship and
personal emotions, some startlingly frank,
illustrating how far the modern, educated Malay
woman in the 1980s has shattered the stereotype
of the shy, submissive maiden of the past.

Isobel, Countess of Argyll (15th century)
Scottish author of two courtly love lyrics in
Scottish Gaelic. Isobel's authorship of these
expressive poems on conventional secular themes
indicates how far women's literacy had developed
by the 15th century in aristocratic circles, in
Scotland as in England.

Bib: Jackson, Kenneth Hurlston, *A Celtic
Miscellany*; MacQueen, John, *Ballatis of Luve*.

Isola di Arturo, L' (1957) ▷*Arturo's Island*

'Ita and the Infant Jesus'
▷Old Irish poem. Ita was a Munster saint of the
6th century who was said to have been granted the
privilege of nursing the infant Jesus. She is made
the speaker of this poem.
Bib: Greene, David and O'Connor, Frank (eds),
A Golden Treasure of Irish Poetry AD 600 to 1200.

Italics Are Mine, The (1969)
Autobiography of the Russian-American writer
▷Nina Berbérova, published in Russian in 1972
and 1983. Berbérova covers her life from
childhood on the family estate and in pre-
revolutionary St Petersburg, through emigration to
the West in 1922 and eventual settlement in the
United States. At the outset, Berbérova
emphatically states that she is writing an
autobiography, not a memoir, probably to dampen
expectations that the focus would be on the
famous and infamous people she knew in Russia,
Berlin, Prague, Sorrento, Paris and the US,
among them Maxim Gor'kii (1868–1936),
Vladimir Nabokov (1899–1977), Ivan Bunin
(1870–1953), ▷Akhmátova, ▷Tsvetáeva,
▷Gíppius, and Kerenskii. In describing others,
she is best on those, like Nabokov and Gor'kii, for
whom she felt an aesthetic or personal sympathy.
Berbérova has a fiction writer's ability to set up
scenes, complete with dialogue, the apt gesture,
and the telling detail. Her autobiography is an
important record of a painful, but significant part
of Russian history. It portrays well the dilemma of
émigrés trying to sustain a culture while living in
exile, and the particular importance of Nabokov's
work in validating the effort.

It Does Not Die (1974)
Translation of the Bengali novel *Na Hanyate*
(1974) by the Indian writer ▷Maitreyi Devi. Subtitled 'A Romance', it is the story of the
relationship between a young foreigner and a
Bengali girl from a cultured Calcutta family. Set
in the 1930s when the struggle for independence
was gathering momentum, the novel incorporates
many of the prominent political and social figures
of the time. The Bengali title refers to a verse in
the '*Bhagavad Gita*' ('Song of the Lord')
(▷*Mahabharata*) which describes the immortality
of the soul, so that in spite of the strong historical
placement of her romance, Devi indicates that it is
with the understanding of eternity and eternal love
that she is most concerned.

it/det (1969)
Collection of verse by ▷Inger Christensen. The
book is one long poem with a very rigid structure:
the first part is composed of 66 verses, the second
of thirty-three multiplied by two, the third of
twenty-two multiplied by three, and so on, until

the poem consists of single lines. There is a relationship between the structure and the content of the poem. It is a poem of genesis, a secular world comes into existence. At first, we see inorganic development, which grows into increasingly differentiated organic beings and a more and more detailed description of the cultural world: the city, the houses, the couples and finally, in the single verses, the individual. In this evolution, man as creator has been dethroned by his own creations. The structures have taken on their own life and man is isolated and defined by them, not only physically but also psychologically and in language. Only the outsiders, the insane, are able to stand up against the *logos*. Their song becomes the catalyst of change.

The poems have been, and still are, a major influence in modern Scandinavian ▷modernist, lyrical writing.

I Testify Against the Wind (1987)

Arabic poetry by Syrian writer ▷Ghada al-Samman. The voice speaking in this collection of verse is the same voice confessing, 'declaring' love in earlier collections: *I Declare Love on You* (1976), *Capturing a Fugitive Moment* (1979) and *Love in the Veins* (1980). The persona behind the voice asserts the power of love as a fortified, 'electrified' island in a sea of hatred and ugliness. Love is shored against the violence and carnage surrounding us all. The earlier volumes explore all the moods of a woman in love, conventional and infinite in their variety. The last collection sounds a new note, a woman accepting and in control. The conversational, almost colloquial lines belong to the school of ▷Nizar Qabbani, a cousin of Ghada al-Samman, who helped her publish her first piece of writing when she was in her teens.

Jabavu, Noni (born 1919)

Noni Jabavu

South African autobiographer, whose two books, ▷*Drawn in Colour: African Contrasts* (1960) and ▷*The Ochre People: Scenes from a South African Life* (1963), present a rare view of Eastern Cape life, mediated through the nostalgic eyes of one of its daughters. Jabavu was born into an academically distinguished Xhosa family, her mother a teacher at Lovedale college, and her father professor of African Languages and Latin at Fort Hare University. As a young girl she was sent to Britain to be educated (Mount School in York, followed by the Royal Academy of Music), and subsequently married an Englishman, Michael Cadbury Crosfield, whose work as a film director led them to various parts of Africa, and to settle for a while in Uganda. The first autobiography compares Ugandan and Xhosa life, and the second presents a more sustained look at Xhosa life.

Like early Xhosa literature by, for example, Walter Rubusana, John Henderson Soga, and A.C. Jordan, Jabavu's writing is aimed at capturing a heritage disintegrating under an alien government. Her interest in representing the Xhosa community as equal in civilization to British and other European communities leads her into a set of stylistic and rhetorical choices which set her texts apart from other contemporary black South African writing.

▷Autobiography (Southern Africa)

Jackson, Helen Maria Hunt (1830–1885)

US poet, novelist, short-story, non-fiction and children's writer. She sometimes used the pseudonym Saxe Holm. While Hunt Jackson established her literary career with conventionally themed but technically adept poetry, she is most memorable for her ▷local color short stories published in the national literary magazines and for a number of significant novels. Her experience in the west as a military wife and her sympathetic treatment of ▷Native Americans brought a distinctive new subject matter and sensibility to US literature in ▷*A Century of Dishonor* (1881) and ▷*Ramona* (1884). Like ▷Emily Dickinson, Jackson received support for her poetry from Thomas Wentworth Higginson (1823–1911), perhaps the basis for her fictionalized biography of Dickinson, ▷*Mercy Philbrick's Choice* (1876).

▷*Century Illustrated Monthly Magazine, The*

Jackson, Shirley (1919–1965)

US short-story writer and novelist. Jackson was born into a professional family in San Francisco, California. In 1940 she graduated from Syracuse University where, with the critic Stanley Hyman, she had co-founded the magazine *The Spectre*. Jackson wrote psychological thrillers in which the distinction between fantasy and reality is blurred. 'The Lottery' (1948), published in *The New Yorker*, depicts a modern community enacting an ancient scapegoat ritual. The community unquestioningly conforms to conventions and habits. In *Hangsaman* (1951) Jackson also shows the impact of small communities on the female psyche, when Natalie Waite retreats into schizophrenia as a response to patriarchal authority. In *The Bird's Nest* (1954) Jackson investigates the treatment and 'healing' of a woman with multiple personality disorder. In ▷*We Have Always Lived in the Castle* (1962) the female psyche is rendered sociopathic. The book had a brief four-day life as a Broadway play. She is also, however, the author of domestic humour sketches, collected with Jackson's articles in *Life Among the Savages* (1953) and *Raising Demons* (1957), and children's books, including *Famous Sally*.

Other works include: *The Road Through the Wall* (1948), *The Sundial* (1958), ▷*The Haunting of Hill House* (1959), *The Magic of Shirley Jackson* (1966) and *Come Along with Me* (1968).

Bib: Friedman, Lenemaja, *Shirley Jackson*.

Jacobs, Harriet Ann (1813–1897)

US non-fiction writer of newspaper pieces and personal narrative of her life in slavery. Jacobs was born and raised in slavery and had two children by a white lover. Pursued by her owner for sexual favours and threatened with the loss of her children, she went into hiding in the south, eventually escaping north once she was able to secure the freedom of her children. In New York City, Boston, Massachusetts, and Rochester, New York, she became involved in the anti-slavery and women's rights causes, publishing first anonymous newspaper accounts of her experiences and then, in 1861, her ▷*Incidents in the Life of a Slave Girl, Written by Herself*.

Jacobus, Mary (born 1944)

British feminist literary critic. After teaching at Oxford University for many years, Jacobus now works at Cornell University in North America, where she is Professor of English and Women's Studies. Jacobus's essay 'The Difference of View', which is in the anthology she edited, *Women Writing and Writing About Women* (1979), was one of the first pieces of British feminist literary criticism to use ▷deconstruction and ▷psychoanalysis to theorize gender difference in literature. The essay ▷deconstructs the gendered opposition between reason and madness in the context of a discussion about the specificity of women's writing. The same essay employs Freud's theory of the unconscious to analyze textual uncertainties and contradictions. Jacobus's later work owes as much to the French psychoanalyst Jacques Lacan (1901–1981) as it does to Freud. *Reading Woman: Essays in Feminist Criticism* (1986) exemplifies Anglo-American feminist appropriations of Lacanian theory in order to produce a theory of woman and her writing as a figure that exceeds the boundaries of patriarchy and renders its meanings unstable. Also a critic of romanticism, Jacobus is author of *Tradition and Experiment in Wordsworth's Lyrical Ballads 1798* (1976) and *Romanticism, Writing and Sexual Difference: Essays on The Prelude* (1989). She has co-edited *Body-Politics: Women and the Discourse of Science* (1989).

Jakobsdóttir, Svava (born 1930)

Icelandic prose writer and dramatist. She was a member of the Icelandic Parliament from 1971 to 1979. Woman and her role in society is the main theme in Jakobsdóttir's writings, but she does not write traditionally ▷realistic literature; she uses grotesque effects and modernist disruptions. Jakobsdóttir has published three collections of short stories: *12 konur* (1965) (*12 Women*), *Veizla undir grjótvegg* (1967) (*Party under a Stone Wall*) and *Gefið hvort öðru* (1982) (*Each Given to the Other*), and a novel, *Leigjandinn* (1969) (*The Lodger*). She has had five plays produced on stage and on the radio in Iceland, and is the best-known modern woman writer there.

Jalandoni, Magdalena (1891–1978)

Filipino novelist who authored 66 volumes, including twenty-four novels, short stories and poems. Despite her mother's opposition, authorship not being considered a suitable occupation for women of her rank and time, she became the first Filipino woman novelist, writing in Hiligaynon, the language in Iloilo (in the Western Visayas) where she was born and lived all her life.

Her first novel, *Ang Tunuk Sang Isa Ka Bulak* (1907) (*The Thorns of a Flower*) was written when she was only sixteen. Influenced by the *corrido* (metrical romance) which drew its material from European medieval romance, her novels belong to the romantic-didactic tradition and, in fact, her first work, written at the age of ten and subsequently published, was a *corrido*. Her narrative skill, vivid portrayal of her times and her espousal of traditional moral values have made her works widely read in her region to this day.

Three of her novels have been published in English: *Ang Bantay Sa Patio* (*The Watchman at the Graveyard*), *Juanita Cruz*, and *Ang Dalag sa Tindahan* (*The Lady in the Market*). This last, set during the Philippine Revolution (1896) has a heroine who is stronger and more independent than her usual romantic heroines.

Despite the traditional world view of her chosen field in her lifetime, Jalandoni not only single-mindedly became a professional writer, but also fought for women's suffrage in the late 1920s and 1930s, during the first wave of Philippine feminism, and was an active nationalist and charity worker. She was honoured with many awards, some posthumously.

Jalna (1927)

The first of the sixteen 'Jalna' books, which won the Canadian novelist ▷Mazo de la Roche the $10,000 Atlantic-Little, Brown Prize, it uses romantic ▷realism to develop a sometimes sentimental generational saga. Jalna is both family and place, and the story is full of complex intrigue and allegiance, with romance as the governing principle. One of the strongest characters is Adeline, the proud matriarch. Members of the Whiteoaks family are genealogically rotated, yet together they form almost a set or backdrop for their larger representation as part of the Jalna tribe.

Jamaica

This geographic region of the Caribbean is the largest of English-speaking Caribbean islands. It is the birthplace of ▷Vera Bell, ▷Louise Bennett, ▷Valerie Bloom, ▷Jean Binta Breeze, ▷Erna Brodber, Beverley E. Brown, ▷Michelle Cliff, ▷Christine Craig, ▷Jean D'Costa, Alice Durie (born c 1909), ▷Gloria Escoffery, ▷Barbara Ferland, ▷Lorna Goodison, Jean Goulbourne, ▷Lucille Iremonger, ▷Mary F. Lockett, ▷Una Marson, ▷Pamela Mordecai, ▷Velma Pollard, ▷Marsha Prescod, ▷Joan Riley, ▷Mary Seacole, ▷Olive Senior, ▷Pamela C. Smith, ▷Clarine Stephenson, Mitzie Townsend (born 1935) and ▷Sylvia Wynter.

Jamaica Woman: An Anthology of Poems (1980)

This collection of Caribbean poetry, edited by ▷Pamela Mordecai and Mervyn Morris includes contributions by ▷Christine Craig, ▷Jean D'Costa, ▷Lorna Goodison, ▷Velma Pollard, ▷Olive Senior and ▷Pamela Mordecai.

Jamaica Labrish (1966)

This volume is the best-known collection of the poetry of the Caribbean poet, ▷Louise Bennett. It illustrates her main objective as a folk poet, to communicate, in dialect or creole, subjects which were everyday concerns to ordinary people.

Although the text is presented in written form, the importance of performance and the effect of the spoken word is an essential element of Bennett's work, as Rex Nettleford emphasizes in his introduction. Written originally for her newspaper column, these poems have been described as 'a sort of comic-verse-journalism'. Many deal with topical issues, such as 'Capital City', concerning the ▷West Indies Federation, and 'Back to Africa', in which Bennett questions the wisdom of those Jamaicans who wish to go back to Africa, a prevalent ambition of the Rastafarians in the 1940s. Poems such as 'Street Boy', 'Candy Seller', 'Dry Foot' and 'Back to Africa' are good examples of Bennett's early work. Humour is an integral part of her style. Her text often takes the form of a dramatic monologue which may address a number of different people in a range of tones of voice, and in which the talent of derision and ridicule is exercised against neighbours, friends and people in authority. 'Colonization in Reverse' is a classic example of Bennett's 'brand of satire and the biting irony of the situation', whereas poems such as 'Perplex', 'Obeah Win de War', 'White Pickney', and 'Pass Fe White', give a good sense of the everyday concerns that Bennett poeticized.

See ▷*Fifty Caribbean Writers* for critical references.

Jambrišak, Marija (1847–1937)

Croatian teacher and women's rights campaigner. Born in Karlovac, Jambrišak trained as a teacher in Zagreb, taught at a convent as a volunteer, and then became a full-time teacher in Krapina. At the 1871 First General Teachers' Conference in Zagreb she made a firm feminist stand for equal pay for women teachers, and demanded recognition for women as professionals on an equal footing with men. The director of the Vienna Pedagogium, was, so the story goes, enchanted with her appearance, and offered her a place at his institution, from which she, its first woman student ever, graduated with top marks. However, she refused a teaching job at the institution, and patriotism brought her back to Zagreb.

She taught at a girls' high school in Zagreb from 1874 to 1892, then moved on to the newly-founded Girls' Lyceum as a teacher of history, geography and methodology. She published articles in several magazines and books, and was the instigator and a founder member of the Croatian and Slovenian Ladies' Association for Women's Work and Education.

James, Alice (1848–1892)

US diarist. She was the younger sister of the writer Henry James (1843–1916) and the philosopher William James (1840–1910). Her posthumously published diary has become a touchstone for feminist analysis of 19th-century invalidism and of gender's influence on the family members' lives and careers. In addition to the diary, Alice James's letters and a biography were published in the 1980s, drawing attention to her as one of the 'silenced' voices of the 19th century. Her devastating story shows a world in which marriage is the only viable woman's occupation, with vocation a possibility for some, and suicide or death the only hope for others. James welcomed her own death, from breast cancer.

Bib: Strouse, Jean, *Alice James, A Biography*; Yeazell, Ruth Bernard, *The Death and Letters of Alice James*.

James, Elinor (fl 1681–1715)

English polemicist and pamphleteer. The wife of a printer, and a printer herself, she became a self-publicizing giver of advice to James II, and, a supporter of the Stuarts in general. She printed unsolicited advice and commentary in her *Vindication of the Church of England* (1687), addressed the House of Lords and was sent to prison for her unruly conduct.

James, P.D. (Phyllis Dorothy) (born 1920)

English ▷detective novelist. A civil servant from 1949, James worked initially as a hospital administrator (1949–1968) and between 1972 and 1979 in the Criminal Policy Division. Medical institutions frequently form the murder setting, and her knowledge of hospital and forensic procedures is crucial to the development of her novels during the 1970s. James's first novel, *Cover Her Face* (1962), introduces her regular detective, Adam Dalgliesh. The complications and jealousies of love form the central motif in *Death of an Expert Witness* (1976) and *Unnatural Causes* (1967). *An Unsuitable Job for a Woman* (1972) promotes the twenty-two-year-old detective Cordelia Gray over Dalgliesh. Another woman detective, Kate Miskin, is introduced in *A Taste for Death* (1986). James's work has been adapted for both film and television.

Jameson, Anna Bronwell (1794–1860)

Born in Dublin, Ireland, in 1794, Anna Bronwell Murphy moved to England in 1798. She worked as a ▷governess from the age of sixteen until she married Robert Jameson in 1825. She is famous as a travel writer, biographer, essayist and critic, and she devoted her life to writing. Her letters are particularly revealing: she had intense relationships with Ottilie von Goethe, ▷Jane Carlyle, ▷George Eliot, ▷Fanny Kemble and, especially, ▷Elizabeth Gaskell. Estranged from her husband, she did not join him during the period when he was Chief Justice of Dominica, but when he became Attorney General of Upper Canada, she travelled to Toronto, and spent a winter and the following summer there. Her ▷*Winter Studies and Summer Rambles in Canada* (1838) is easily the best-known and the most convincing of all Canadian travel books of that period. Although she stayed in Upper Canada for only eight months, separating from her husband in September of 1837, Jameson succeeded in evoking the spirit and the physical setting of Canada in counterpoint to a woman's inner journey, charting her response to what she encountered in Canada in fragments of a journal addressed to a friend. Indeed, her writing was characterized by her commitment to women's experience and its validation. Her 'blasphemous defiance of the hegemonic discourse' infiltrated all her work.

Her works include: *Characteristics of Women* (1832); *Winter Studies and Summer Rambles in Canada* (1838); *Memoirs and Essays on Art, Literature and Morals* (1846); *Sacred and Legendary Art* (1848–52). Her political essays on women's position include *The Relative Position of Mothers and Governesses* (1846) and *The Communion of Labour* (1856). She was a friend of writers such as ▷Elizabeth Barrett Browning, and sponsored the ▷feminist reformers ▷Barbara Bodichon and ▷Adelaide Procter.
Bib: Fowler, M., *The Embroidered Tent: Five Gentlewomen in Early Canada;* Friewald, B., in ▷*A Mazing Space;* Nestor, P., *Female Friendships and Communities: Charlotte Brontë, George Eliot, Elizabeth Gaskell;* ▷Thomas, Clara, *Love and Work Enough: The Life of Anna Jameson.*

Jameson, Storm (1891–1986)
English novelist and critic. Her first novel, *The Pot Boils* (1919), and others written in the early twenties, including *The Clash* (1922) and *The Pitiful Wife* (1924), deal with the effects of World War I on the relations between men and women. During World War II Jameson worked for European refugee writers, and her anti-fascist writings of this period include *The Writer's Situation* (1941) and *The End of This War* (1941). Her other novels focusing on occupied Europe include *Europe to Let* (1940) and *Cousin Honoré* (1941). Among her forty-five novels, Jameson produced two family saga trilogies, and the three novellas *Women against Men* (1933–1937) have recently been republished. *Journey from the North* (1969–1970) is a two-volume autobiography.

Jane and Louisa Will Soon Come Home (1980)
The first novel by the Caribbean writer ▷Erna Brodber, this was originally conceived as a case study in abnormal psychology. It tells the story of Nellie, a young woman who travels to 'foreign' to study. On her return she suffers a crisis of 'unbelonging', which is only resolved for her by a re-examination of her past and the distorted perceptions she acquired during ▷childhood concerning her female ▷identity. Remarkable for its stylistic versatility, it is considered a revolutionary and innovative novel in which Brodber weaves ▷autobiography, poetry, ▷psychoanalysis, historical documentation and a range of narrative voice to explore images of Caribbean womanhood. She draws upon Jamaican folk traditions using ▷Anancy Stories, children's ring games and the image of the *kumbla* in the structuring of this novel, and as metaphors to signify Nellie's growing awareness of herself and the women of her family. (A *kumbla* is a Jamaican

concept which suggests a disguise or a place to hide oneself, and signifies both safety and entrapment.)

For critical analysis and further references see Leslie Humphrey, 'A Myriad of Circles: The Kumbla Image in Jane and Louisa Will Soon Come Home', *ACLALS Bulletin*, Eighth Series, No. 1 (1989), ▷*Caribbean Women Writers* and ▷*Out of the Kumbla.*

Jane Anger, her protection for women (1589)
First defence of women written by an English woman. It was written in response to a now-lost work entitled *Boke his Surfeit in Love* (1588). Anger frequently employs Latin quotations and phrases, as well as allusions to classical stories and authors, to defend women. She emphasizes the evils of male lust; argues that the female is superior because she was created last, and is therefore purer; and she argues that women are indispensible for the domestic services they provide (eg as nurturers, nurses, and housewives). Although Jane Anger sounds like a ▷pseudonym and the author makes numerous puns upon it, the name was not uncommon; records exist of at least six Joan or Jane Angers who could have been the author of this pamphlet.
Bib: Shepherd, S. (ed.), *The Women's Sharp Revenge*; Henderson, K.U. and McManus, B.F., *Half Humankind: Texts and Contexts of the Controversy about Women in England, 1540–1640.*

Jane Eyre (1847)
A novel by ▷Charlotte Brontë. The best-known and most popular of her works, it follows the life and experiences of the ▷orphaned and penniless Jane from childhood to marriage. At the start of the novel Jane is living in the home of her aged and unsympathetic aunt, Mrs Reed. She is later sent to a charitable school, Lowood (based on Cowan Bridge, which Charlotte and her sisters attended), after which she joins the household of Mr Rochester to work as a ▷governess. She becomes increasingly attracted to the Byronic Rochester, and finally agrees to marry him. Unbeknownst to her, however, he has a mad wife locked in the attic, who escapes the evening before the wedding and destroys Jane's veil. In church the next day, Rochester is exposed as a potential bigamist by the first Mrs Rochester's brother. Jane flees, finding sanctuary with Mary, Diana and St John Rivers. She is later sought in marriage by St John, a clergyman of cold and passionless nature. Jane refuses him after a telepathic communication from Rochester, to whom she returns, discovering that his house has been burned down and that he has been blinded trying to save his wife. Finally, she marries him.

The novel is a mixture of ▷Romantic, ▷Gothic and ▷realist forms, a female ▷*Bildungsroman* that challenged contemporary attitudes in its portrayal of a 'strong-minded' and desiring woman. Recently, it has been re-read by feminist critics, notably ▷Gilbert and ▷Gubar in *The Madwoman in the Attic*, who see Bertha Mason as Jane's repressed self. Another re-reading occurs in ▷Jean Rhys's ▷*The Wide Sargasso Sea* (1966) which tells the story from the perspective of the first Mrs Rochester. ▷Gayatri Chakravorty Spivak's important essay: 'Three Women's Texts and a Critique of Imperialism' re-examined the book in the light of Victorian ▷imperialism.

Janés, Clara (born 1940)

Spanish novelist, poet, translator, essayist and biographer. Born in Barcelona. Her main poetic works are: *Las estrellas vencidas* (1964) (*The Conquered Stars*); *En busca de Cordelia y Poemas Rumanos* (1975) (*Searching for Cordelia and Romanian Poems*); *Libro de alienaciones* (1980) (*Book of Alienations*); *Vivir* (1983) (*Living*); *Fósiles* (1984) (*Fossils*); *Kampa* (1986), and ▷Lapidario (1988) (*Lapidary*). Janés has also published two novels: *La noche de Abel Micheli* (1965) (*The Night of Abel Micheli*), and *Desintegración* (1969) (*Disintegration*).

Janitschek, Maria (1859–1927)

Austrian poet, novelist and short story writer. Her work contains three main themes: relationships between men and women; the social subordination of women, and social misery. Her collection of poems *Irdische und unirdische Träume* (1889) (*Earthly and Unearthly Dreams*), contains the notorious '*Ein modernes Weib*' ('A Modern Woman'), in which a dishonoured woman challenges a man to a duel and shoots him.

Jan Lobel aus Warschau. Erzählung (1948) (Jan Lobel From Warsaw. A Tale)

A novella by the German writer ▷Luise Rinser. It is a first-person narrative about three women who give shelter to a young Polish Jew who has escaped deportation to a concentration camp. All three women fall in love with him, but continue to live together peacefully. Their idyll is destroyed when the husband of one of them returns. He takes over command of the situation, whereupon the young man leaves and dies.

One of the first post-war stories to deal with the German war experience, this novel is a beautifully-written poetic statement, made more notable by its latent feminist-pacifist content.

Janny, Amélia (1838–1914)

Portuguese poet. Often called the 'Poetess of the Mondego', a reference to the river that flows through the city of Coimbra in central Portugal. Admired by some of the most famous writers of the period, she wrote largely for magazines and reviews, among them the *Almanaque de Lembranças* (*Almanac of Memories*). Many of her poems reveal her liberalism; for example, she wrote verse on behalf of *Progresso* (Progress), and dedicated one of her poems to Gonzaga, the Brazilian revolutionary-poet.

▷Romanticism (Portugal)

Jansenism

Theological tendency important in France and Holland in the 17th century. Following the teachings of Cornelius Jansen (1585–1638), Bishop of Ypres in Flanders, Jansenism maintained that the human will was by nature perverse and unable to achieve goodness. It emphasized the infirmity of human nature as a result of the Fall of Man, and claimed that only the grace mediated by the Catholic Church could offer an escape. In France, Jansenism was supported by the Arnauld family and the theologians of Port-Royal. It was opposed by the Jesuits, and condemned by the Sorbonne and the Pope. In the second half of the 17th century, French Jansenists were severely persecuted, and many took refuge at the abbey of Port-Royal. A number of French women writers supported or had links with Jansenism, including ▷Agnès Arnauld, ▷Jacqueline Arnauld, ▷Gilberte Pascal, ▷Jacqueline Pascal, ▷Madame de Sablé, ▷Madeleine de Scudéry and the ▷Marquise de Sévigné.

Jansson, Tove (born 1914)

Fenno-Swedish writer of children's literature. She was born in Helsinki, and her parents were artists. She studied art in Helsinki, Stockholm and Paris and, since 1943, has had several exhibitions.

In 1945 and 1946 she published two books for children which did not receive much attention, but experienced a breakthrough in 1948 with *Trollkarlens hatt* (*The Magician's Hat*). Since then she has written a number of books about the Moomin Family. In the course of time her books have changed, and today she writes for adults as well as for children. Jansson has created her own idyllic world. Many of her Moomin books have been filmed or published as cartoons.

In her books for adults, Jansson writes about the relationships between adults and children. The autobiographic *Bildhuggarens dotter* (1968) (*The Sculptor's Daughter*) is written from a child's point of view, while the much-translated *Sommarboken* (1972) (*The Summer Book*) describes the friendship between an old woman and a her granddaughter.

Jansson has also published psychological short stories, eg *Dockskåpet* (1978) (*The Doll's House*), and a psycho-thriller *Den ärliga bedragaren* (1982) (*The Honest Deceiver*).

▷Fenno-Swedish literature

Jardine, Alice A. (born 1951)

North American feminist literary theorist. Jardine is Associate Professor of Romance Languages and Literature at Harvard University, where she teaches feminist theory and contemporary literary criticism. She has become known as a sophisticated theorist of ▷postmodernism and feminism since the publication of *Gynesis: Configurations of Woman and Modernity* (1986).

'Gynesis' is a term Jardine coins to convey 'the putting into discourse of "woman"'; it is the manifestation in discourse of the threat which uncertainty, traditionally associated with women, poses to patriarchal history, knowledge, and truth. In this context, gynesis exemplifies the postmodern crisis resulting from the disintegration of master-narratives; that is, those universal historical, political and philosophical discourses which shore up patriarchy and privilege the concepts 'Man', the ▷Subject, 'Truth', 'History', and 'Meaning'. Gynesis is of interest to feminism because it designates a new theoretical, though arguably Utopian space, free from patriarchal domination. Jardine is co-translator of ▷Julia Kristeva's *Desire in Language* (1980), co-editor with Hester Eisenstein of *The Future of Difference* (1980), and co-editor with Paul Smith of *Men in Feminism* (1987), which addresses the controversy arising from the increasing involvement of men in feminist criticism.

Jarnević, Dragolja (1812–1875)

Croatian diarist. Her diary highlights two familiar sources of tension for women in the 19th century: the conflict between intellectual activity and household chores, and the conflict between independence and sexual desire. She was unconventional in solving the latter problem by, in 1854, engaging a young peasant boy, buying him a cottage, and later arranging a marriage for him. She wrote: 'It is an impulse of the flesh that has control of me and it is such that it dominates my reason – but I would follow it, follow it for at least a year or two, that would not be too much for a whole lifetime! . . . I have defended myself all my life against accusations of loose living; now it has come against my will.' In addition to her diary, which was originally written in German, she wrote stories, poems, plays and a novel.

Jawari

Arabic term, plural of *jariya*, originally meaning simply 'a girl', later popularly used for 'concubine or slave-girl'. Some famous *jawari* of the Abbasid courts of Baghdad (8th and 9th centuries) were carefully educated and financed by their master-owners along the same lines as the star system in sport and entertainment today. They had the advantage over 'free women' of being able to mix with men and attend literary and musical soirées in the houses of the grandees of the city. They participated in poetry and musical contests. The popular tradition has exalted one of them, Tawaddud al-Jariya, to the pinnacle of beating learned men and theologians in a debate covering all branches of learning. Historically, some notably accomplished *jawari* had their private establishments, extended patronage and largesse and exchanged *ruq'as* (cards of verse) with poets of the city. Some of their compositions have survived in the famous medieval anthologies of Arabic literature and have attracted the attention of modern researchers and compilers.

The terms *jawari* and ▷*harim* are used in contemporary feminist discourse to indicate the inferior status of the woman in marriage (see ▷Sahar Khalifa's *Lasna Jawari Lakum*, 1974, *We Are Not Your Concubines*). The same terms are used by men in contempt for women who exploit their sexuality.

Jelinek, Elfriede (born 1946)

Austrian poet, dramatist and novelist. A pessimistic Marxist, she writes intensely acerbic fiction satirizing class structures and the power of men. Her most widely-read novel, *Die Liebhaberinnen* (1975) (*The Women Lovers*), tells of two factory girls whose lives are blighted by their work and the men with whom they come into contact. *Die Klavierspielerin* (1983) (*The Woman Piano-player*) is a merciless exploration of a mother–daughter relationship. Her disturbing, near-pornographic, novel *Lust* (1989) has added a new kind of notoriety to her reputation.

Jellicoe, Ann (born 1927)

English dramatist, Jellicoe began her theatre career in repertory, where she combined the roles of actress, manager and director. She later founded the Cockpit Theatre Club in the 1950s, and with the production of ▷*The Sport of My Mad Mother* (1958) her reputation for experimental and innovative theatre was established. *The Knack* (1962) is a comedy focusing on three men with different attitudes to sex and personal relationships. As a writer who often privileges dramatic elements other than dialogue, her subject matter is diverse. *The Reckoning* (1978) and *The Tide* (1980) are among several interactive community-based projects.

Jemima Condict, Her Book (1930)

Diary by North American ▷Jemima Condict. For seven years during the American Revolution, Condict recorded in a private diary her ruminations on religion and marriage as she moved towards adulthood. Her text, and her sense of herself ('I a poor misarible Creater'), are controlled by the dictates of Presbyterianism in which she was reared. Biblical passages and summaries of sermons fill many entries; yet the diary also proved to be a means for Condict to express her grief during a period of great loss. On one occasion she composed a poetic dirge, occasioned by the death of a female relative.

Jenkinson, Biddy (born 1929)

Irish poet, who lives in County Wicklow and uses Biddy Jenkinson as a pseudonym. She is highly regarded as one of the finest poets now writing in Irish. Her collections are *Baisteach Gintli* (1986) and *Uisci Beatha* (1988).

Jennings, Elizabeth (born 1926)

English poet. She was educated at Oxford where she met the Movement poets, with whom she is often associated because of her combination of traditional verse form and modern idiom. Subsequently she worked in publishing in London. Jennings was raised as a Roman Catholic, and her poetry is defined by her active religious belief. She has drawn a parallel between the act of prayer and the writing of poetry in terms of an aspiration to the 'loss of self'. Her nervous breakdown has also been an important influence on her poetry since the 1960s, such as

Recoveries (1964) and *The Mind Has Mountains* (1966). However, she distinguishes herself from confessional poets, such as ▷Sylvia Plath and ▷Anne Sexton, arguing that 'any belief *does* demand a looking inward but that perusal is for examining your conscience not your identity.' Writing, for the most part, within traditional forms, Jennings, like T.S. Eliot (1888–1965), is selfconscious about her relationship to tradition. She stands in a line of religious poets from George Herbert (1593–1633) and Henry Vaughan (1622–1695) to Gerard Manley Hopkins (1844–1889) and Eliot. Her book *Every Changing Shape* (1961) is about mystic poetry. The formal and linguistic control of Jennings's poetry is often in fruitful tension with her depiction of isolation, despair and passion.

Her other works include: *Poems* (1953), *A Way of Looking* (1955), *A Sense of the World* (1958), *Song for a Birth or a Death* (1961), *Christianity and Poetry* (1965), *Collected Poems* (1967), *Lucidities* (1970), *Growing Points* (1975), *Seven Men of Vision: An Appreciation* (1976), *Consequently I Rejoice* (1977), *Extending the Territory* (1985) and *Collected Poems* (1986).

Jensen, Thit (1876–1957)

Danish prose writer and debater. She received many prizes and awards. Jensen was born at Farsø in Northern Jylland. Her father was a vet, a man with a deep interest in many spiritual phenomena. The family had eleven children, and Thit had to help her mother a great deal, whereas her brother, the famous writer Johannes V. Jensen, was allowed to read and study. The two of them were rivals for the rest of their lives.

Thit Jensen went to Copenhagen, and from 1912 to 1918 she was married to the painter Gustav Fenger. In 1903 she published her first novel *To Søstre* (*Two Sisters*) and she wrote several novels about her own time, but after 1909 she won fame because of her many lectures on motherhood and contraception. As a writer she had her real breakthrough with her ▷historical novels, eg *Stygge Krumpen* (1936). Here she created a fantastic story of love, the battle of the sexes, and fertility, in a historical setting.

Jensen's prose is large in scale. Her characters are larger than life, especially the historical ones, and she was not afraid to use big words or symbols. Her contemporary novels are 'smaller', with women who are split between love and work, or politics, in, for example, *Gerd* (1918) and *Aphrodite fra Fuur* (1925) (*Aphrodite from Fuur*).

▷Michaëlis, Karin; Henningsen, Agnes
Bib: Andersen, J., *Den sidste Valkyrie*.

Jen o rodinných záležitostech (1965) (*Only Family Matters*)

Czech novel by Jaromíra Kolárová (born 1919). It is an evocative, terse, sometimes lyrical, novel about two enthusiastic communists caught up in the 1950s show trials. One, a Jew, is condemned to twenty-five years in prison, the other, a Communist Party fanatic, to fifteen years. The fanatic, Jaroslav, had been involved in underground activities during the German occupation and, after the communist take-over, becomes a senior official in Silesia. His wife is just as fanatical, but his daughter, Naděžda ('Hope') is not. His mistress, the glamorous Monika, is a colleague from the League of Anti-Fascist Fighters. The Jew, Stein, had lost his wife and two daughters in Auschwitz because he had waited for Communist Party permission to leave Czechoslovakia. He himself manages to get to England after their disappearance. When he returns, however, he finds himself in an unpleasant situation for a communist – he is very rich because all his relations have been killed by the Germans. Still, he gets a senior position in a ministry.

The novel does not attack the Communist Party, or even the system, but just the way the system worked under Stalin. Kolárová's great achievement is to make the reader feel respect and sympathy for people who became victims of the system which they had themselves helped to set up. She avoids all sentimentality.

Jesse, F. Tennyson (1888–1958)

English novelist and dramatist, and editor of several volumes in the *Notable British Trials Series*. Jesse's interest in criminology is the foundation of much of her writing, including *A Pin to See the Peepshow* (1934). In *Murder and Its Motives* (1924) Jesse classifies murderers according to her theory of six distinct types of motive. Other writings include *The Lacquer Lady* (1929), a cross-cultural narrative which follows the protagonist Fanny from Brighton to an exoticized Mandalay. Jesse was one of the few women war correspondents during World War I, and her journalism is published in *Sword of Deborah: First-Hand Impressions of the British Women's Army in France* (1919).

Jest of God, A (1966)

Novel by Canadian writer Margaret Laurence, about a woman finally daring to pour out her love and grief. Much has been made of Rachel Cameron's role as a spinster who learns to transcend her inhibitions through a brief but torrid affair. But the power of the novel resides not in its focus on transformation, but on the way that eulalic language is used to show both the confinement and the ultimate release of a woman crying out for contact with a judgmental world that has pasted her into a spinster schoolteacher scrapbook. The subtext of mortality, Rachel's father having been both the town drunk and undertaker, is neatly undercut by Rachel's overcoming her body's betrayal. That she is finally able to cry out, that she dances with the tongues of the gods, is the truly exhilarating achievement of this powerful rendition of loneliness. *A Jest of God* was published as *Now I Lay Me Down* (1969) in England, and was made into a motion picture entitled *Rachel, Rachel* (1968), under which name it was also republished. It is perhaps the most underestimated of Laurence's Manawaka novels. **Bib.**: van Herk, A., 'The Eulalias of Spinsters and Undertakers' in Gunnars, K. (ed.), *Crossing the River* .

Jesus, Carolina Maria de (1914–1977)
Brazilian novelist and chronicle writer. In the Canindé slum, in São Paulo, she lived by picking up papers and selling them. *Quarto de despejo – diário de uma favelada* (1960) (*Children of the Dark*, 1960) consists of notebooks with her everyday impressions. Journalist Audálio Dantas, from the newspaper *A Noite*, discovered her, and probably edited the text heavily. It is an impressive journal and the unique voice of a poor woman from the slums. She tried to move from the *favela* with her four children, as she tells in *Casa de alvenaria – diário de uma ex-favelada* (1961) (*House of Bricks – Journal of an Ex-Slumdweller*), but had to return. *Diário de Bitita* (1986) (*Journal of Britita*) is translated from an interview in French. However, her fame was already past.

Jeune née, La (1975) ▷ *The Newly Born Woman*

Jewett, Sarah Orne (1849–1909)
US short-story writer, novelist, poet and children's writer. One of the best of the regional realist writers, Jewett, along with ▷ Mary E. Wilkins Freeman, marks the highest point of the ▷ local color tradition. Her finely crafted New England stories chronicle both country and town life, though Jewett's love of nature and preference for the rural is always clear. Extremely well respected in her own time, Jewett contributed to the prestigious national literary magazines, collecting her stories in a series of critically lauded volumes, including ▷ *Deephaven* (1877), *A White Heron* (1886) and ▷ *The Country of the Pointed Firs* (1896). Her novels include ▷ *A Country Doctor* (1884) and *The Tory Lover* (1901), the latter marking a late-career turn to historical romance.

In both her stories and her novels, women characters and women's lives are central, with considerable attention to the bonding between different types of women and different generations. Jewett definitely saw herself in relation to other women. ▷ Annie Adams Fields was an essential part of Jewett's life, and provided an alternative home for Jewett in Boston, Massachusetts, an essential connection to literary circles and cultural life. Jewett also claimed that ▷ Harriet Beecher Stowe's example inspired her own subject matter and technique, as ▷ Willa Cather later claimed Jewett as her model and mentor.
▷ *Harper's Monthly Magazine*

Jewish Enlightenment
During the period 1760 to 1881 Jewish life in eastern and central Europe experienced great changes. The Enlightenment movement was formed, the aim of which was to change traditional life in the closed, self-sufficient Jewish communities. The Enlightenment aimed at modernizing Jewish life, enabling involvement in non-Jewish society, but without losing the Jewish identity. It lead to flourishing cultural creativity and the revival of modern Hebrew. Politically, the Enlightenment had a cosmopolitan, humanistic vision which was shaken by the pogroms of 1881–1882 in Russia. This led to emigration, and the creation of the Zionist movement by writers and social leaders, which aimed at reconstituting a Jewish state in Israel.

Jew's Beech, The (1958)
Translation of *Die Judenbuche* (1842) by ▷ Annette von Droste-Hülshoff. It is one of the most accomplished novellas in 19th-century German literature. The story is set in a remote Westphalian village, and recounts the mysterious circumstances surrounding the murder of a Jew. In a plot where much remains unexplained, the main themes are the notions of individual and communal guilt, and the mysterious workings of divine retribution. The book is written in a style which endows a realistic milieu with haunting intimations of the demonic, the mythic and the eternal.

Jewsbury, Geraldine (1812–1880)
English novelist, critic and journalist. She was born in Measham, Derbyshire, the fourth of six children. Her first novel, *Zoe*, was published in 1845, followed by *The Half-Sisters* (1848) and ▷ *Marian Withers* (1851). Jewsbury moved to London in 1853 in order to be close to her great friend, ▷ Jane Welsh Carlyle. She contributed articles and reviews to periodicals such as *The Westminster Review* and *The Athenaeum* and was a reader for the ▷ publisher Bentley, influencing the choice of books selected for Mudie's ▷ circulating library. She wrote three further novels: *Constance Herbert* (1855); *The Sorrows of Gentility* (1856) and *Right or Wrong* (1856), as well as two stories for children. She was well-known for her brilliant wit and conversation, and in 1892 *A Selection from the letters of Geraldine Jewsbury to Jane Carlyle* was published (edited by Mrs A. Ireland). Both women had wanted their letters destroyed. ▷ Virginia Woolf wrote an article, 'Geraldine and Jane', for *The Times Literary Supplement* (28 February 1929) concerning the women's friendship.
Bib: Howe, S., *Geraldine Jewsbury*.

Jhabvala, Ruth Prawer (born 1927)
Novelist and screenplay writer, formerly based in India. She was born in Cologne to Jewish Polish parents who fled to Britain in 1939. She was educated at Queen Mary College, University of London. In 1951 she went to live in India with her husband, C.S. Jhabvala, an architect, with whom she had three children. India remained her principal home and the primary source of material for her novels until 1975, when she moved to New York.

Her novel *To Whom She Will* (1955) was the

first of many. Others include *The Nature of Passion* (1956), ▷*The Householder* (1960), *Get Ready for Battle* (1962), *A Backward Place* (1965) and *A New Dominion* (1972). *In Search of Love and Beauty* (1983) is set in New York. There are several collections of short stories including: *Like Birds, Like Fishes* (1963) and *A Stronger Climate* (1968). In an introductory essay to another collection, *How I Became a Holy Mother* (1971), Jhabvala has discussed her profoundly ambivalent reactions to life in India, as it is lived by both Indians and Westerners. Much of her fiction explores post-colonial India and relations between Western and Indian peoples in this context. Cross-cultural narratives such as *Esmond in India* (1958) directly address Western assumptions and prejudices about Indian urban life. The 'outsider's' ambivalence towards cutural differnce and dislocation is examined in the Booker Prize-winning novel ▷*Heat and Dust* (1975), as well as the shory story collections *An Experience of India* (1971) and *Out of India* (1986). Her novels and stories have been widely praised by Western critics, but her dry and witty observations on the foibles and aspirations of middle-class Indians have made some Indian critics uncomfortable. Her acute sense of being an outsider – even after many years in India – has encouraged Indian critics to equate her authorial detachment with old-fashioned Western superiority.

Jhabvala has made a second career for herself as a screenplay writer with the Ivory-Merchant team. In addition to the screenplay (1983) of her own novel *Heat and Dust*, she has written, among others, the screenplays for *Shakespeare Wallah* (1965), *Autobiography of a Princess* (1975), *The Europeans* (1979) and *Room with a View* (1986), for which she won an Academy Award. In 1978 she won the Neil Gunn International Fellowship.
Bib: Gooneratne, Yasmine, *Silence, Exile and the Cunning: The Fiction of R.P. Jhabvala*; Williams, H.M., *The Fiction of Ruth Prawer Jhabvala*.

Jiles, Paulette (born 1943)
Canadian poet and novelist. Jiles was born in the Missouri Ozarks, emigrating to Canada in 1969. From 1973 to 1983 she worked in the Arctic and sub-Arctic regions, and taught creative writing in Nelson, British Columbia. Her work is innovative and daring, ranging far beyond metaphor and imagery. Her poetry includes *Waterloo Express* (1973), *Celestial Navigation* (1984) and *The Jesse James Poems* (1988). *Celestial Navigation* won the Governor General's Award, the Gerald Lampert Memorial Award, and the Pat Lowther Award, the first time one volume has garnered all three major Canadian prizes. Her novels, *The Late Great Human Road Show* (1986) and *Sitting in the Club Car Drinking Rum & Karma-Kola* (1987), are eccentric refusals of conventional fiction. The former is a post-nuclear fantasy, and the latter a picaresque parody of feminist dimensions. *Blackwater* (1988) and *Song to the Rising Sun* (1989) collect poetry, prose, and radio writing. Jiles speaks of herself as a 'Third Force Feminist',

a writer who trusts to what she calls 'quiet feminism,' rather than political and theoretical positioning.
Bib. Scheier, L., Sheard, S. and Wachtel, E. (eds), *Language in Her Eye*, Special Issue of *The Malahat Review* 83, (Summer 1988).

Jin, Meiling (born 1956)
Caribbean poet, short story writer and children's writer. Jin was born in ▷Guyana of Chinese parents. She emigrated to Britain in 1964, and was educated there. She visited China in 1981 and was deeply moved by this experience. The author of several children's stories, as well as a collection of poetry entitled *Gifts from My Grandmother* (1985), she is also a contributor to an anthology of women's writing edited by Rhonda Cobham, *Watchers and Seekers* (1987). Her poetry is included in ▷*Creation Fire*.

Joceline, Elizabeth (1596–1622)
English writer. Her parents separated, and she was brought up in London by Bishop Caderton, who believed in Protestant education for women. *The Mothers Legacie* was written when she was pregnant with a child that survived her, and was published in 1624 by her husband as an indication of wifely piety. She writes to her child, 'I know all the delight a Parent can take in a childe is hony mingled with gall. But the true reason that I have so often kneeled to God for thee, is, that thou mightest be an inheritour of the Kingdome of Heaven.'

Jodin, Mademoiselle (18th century)
French revolutionary speaker. The daughter of a clockmaker from Geneva, she collaborated on the *Encyclopédie*. Her speech, *Vues legislatives pour les femmes* (*Legislative Prospects for Women*), discussing divorce and addressed to the Assemblée Nationale (1790), appears in modern collections of women's Revolutionary documents (▷French Revolution: pamphlets, registers of grievances, petitions and speeches).

Modern editions of her work con be found in P. Duhet, (ed.), *Cahiers de doléances des femmes et autres textes (Register of Women's Grivances and Other Texts)*; English translations in Levy, Applewhite and Johnson, *Women in Revolutionary Paris*.

Joenpelto, Eeva (born 1921)
Finnish prose writer. Pseudonyms: Eeva Antare and Eeva Hella. Eeva Joenpelto grew up in a middle-class family in the semi-rural town of Lohja. She graduated from high school in 1940, and studied at the College of Social Sciences. She became a professor of the arts in 1980. She had her breakthrough with her third novel *Johannes vain* (1952) (*Just Johannes*) which describes the relation between material and spiritual values, conflicts that also dominate her later works. She writes in a concise style without sentimentality. The novels *Neito kulkee vetten päällä* (1955) (*A Maiden Walks on Water*) and *Kipinöivät vuodet*

(1961) (*Sparkling Years*) explore the contrast between old and new lifestyles on a farm situated between an expanding city and a disappearing village.

In her historical novels about the years of the Finnish struggle for independence, she succeeds in drawing some very fine psychological portraits, eg *Ritari metsien pimennosta* (1966) (*The Knight from the Dark Forests*), and *Kuin kekäle kedessä* (1976) (*Like Holding a Red-Hot Coal*).

Joenpelto's prose describes the contrasts of modern life: countryside and town, the generations and the sexes. She depicts surburban life and often shows weak men and strong women.

Johansen, Hanna (born 1939)

German novelist. She was born in Bremen, studied literature, and now lives in Switzerland. *Die Stehende Uhr* (1978) (*The Silent Clock*) is preoccupied with the conflict between an individual's inner and outer experiences. Cultural differences form the theme of *Zurück nach Oraibi* (1986) (*Back to Oraibi*), and the novels *Trocadero* (1980) and *Der Mann vor der Tür* (1988) (*The Man Outside the Door*) examine the relationship between the sexes.

John Halifax, Gentleman (1856)

A highly successful novel by British writer ▷Dinah Mulock Craik. The tale is narrated by Phineas Fletcher, a crippled man of sensitive character. He relates the story of John Halifax, who begins his working life as a tanner's apprentice, but rises in the world through his hard work, heroic deeds and good fortune. By the end of the novel he has married an heiress, bought property and a business, and is given the opportunity to run for Parliament. Phineas Fletcher, unable to pursue the material rewards of the world as a result of his physical disability, has been seen as symbolizing women's position in society. Phineas does not, however, revolt against his lot, but shows profound admiration for the achievements of Halifax.

Johnson, Amryl

Caribbean poet and novelist she came to Britain from ▷Trinidad at the age of eleven to join her parents, having been brought up by her grandmother at home. She took a degree in African and Caribbean studies at the University of Kent, and is active in Britain as a teacher and workshop leader. She has published two separate collections of poems with the same title, *Long Road to Nowhere*, (1982, 1985). Her first novel, *Sequins for a Ragged Hem* (1988), focuses on a return to the landscape of her childhood.

See Lauretta Ngcobo, *Let it Be Told: Black Women Writers in Britain* (1988) for biographical information and critical comment.

Johnson, Barbara (born 1947)

North American feminist deconstructionist, born in Boston and educated in Ohio and at Yale. She is Professor of French and Comparative Literature at Harvard University. Johnson has made a major contribution to deconstructive theory by raising the issue of sexual difference within deconstruction's concern wider concern with ▷differance. In *A World of Difference* (1987 and 1989) Johnson rigorously defends ▷deconstruction as a political and feminist critical practice. Her work teases out gendered oppositions in literary texts and ▷deconstructs them to the point of collapse.

An example of this process at work can be found in the essay 'Teaching Ignorance', from *A World of Difference*, where Johnson deconstructs the opposition knowledge/ignorance in Moliere's play *L'Ecole des femmes* (*The School of Women*) in a way that reveals ignorance to be an integral part of knowledge, not its ▷binary ▷other. Ignorance, which traditionally connotes woman, is thus shown to be both the condition of knowledge and its undoing. The deconstructive potential of ignorance as a concept which is displaced by and displaces knowledge is analogous to the discursive displacement of women in patriarchy which brings them into a close relationship with deconstruction. Johnson states, 'It seems to me that women are all trained, to some extent to be deconstructors. There's always a double message, and there's always a double response.' Johnson is translator of Jacques Derrida's *Dissemination* (1981), and author of *Défigurations du Langage Poétique: La Seconde Révolution Baudelairienne* (1979) and *The Critical Difference: Essays in the Contemporary Rhetoric of Reading* (1980).

Johnson, Georgia Douglas (c 1880–1966)

US poet and dramatist. Born in Atlanta, Georgia, Johnson attended Howard University and Oberlin Conservatory of Music. Her training in music was to be influential on her poetry: 'Into my poems,' she wrote, 'I poured the longing for music.' Johnson married a distinguished Washington, DC, lawyer and politician. After her husband's death in 1925, and with two sons, Johnson combined her literary career with various government jobs. Noted for her love poetry, she was one of the first African-American women poets to gain public recognition.

The Heart of a Woman and Other Poems (1918) emphasizes a woman's inability to secure a place in the world for herself. Trapped in traditional female roles, she 'tries to forget it [her heart] has dreamed of the stars'. The poems in *Bronze: A Book of Verse* (1922) address the racial and social problems facing the African-American woman. They chronicle African-American history from a woman's perspective. Protesting against racism, Johnson celebrates the African-American struggle for freedom and equality. These two books use mainly traditional verse forms, but with *An Autumn Love Cycle* (1928) Johnson makes greater and more effective use of free-verse to write about passion. Her first play, *Blue Blood* (1927), confronts the rape of black women by white men, while *A Sunday Morning in the South* (1934) protests against lynching.

Part of the ▷Harlem Renaissance movement of the 1920s, although located in Washington, Johnson also played an important role as a literary hostess, drawing together fellow writers such as ▷Angelina Weld Grimké, ▷Jessie Fauset, Langston Hughes, Countee Cullen, Anne Spencer and ▷Alice Dunbar-Nelson.

Other works include: *Plumes: a Play in One Act* (1927), *Frederick Douglass Leaves for Freedom* (1940) and *Share My World: A Book of Poems* (1962).
Bib. Hull, Gloria T., *Color, Sex and Poetry: Three Women Poets of the Harlem Renaissance*.

Johnson, Pamela Hansford (1912–1981)

English novelist and critic. Johnson has been described as 'quintessentially British', and her realist novels of the 1930s and 1940s advance the association of the English realist tradition with notions of Englishness, and, particularly during the 1940s, with peculiarly 'British' characteristics. Her fiction often lacks a psychological dimension, and novels such as *This Bed Thy Centre* (1935), which makes an attempt at sexual frankness, and *Winter Quarters* (1943) are characterized by emotional detachment and the distancing of the reader's involvement. Her more experimental writings of the 1950s such as the 'Six Proust Reconstructions' for radio broadcast, coincide with her works of criticism including *Ivy Compton-Burnett* (1953) (▷Ivy Compton-Burnett).

Johnson, (Emily) Pauline (1861–1913)

Best-known as a poet, Johnson was born on Canada's Six Nations Reserve near Brantford, Ontario, daughter of a Mohawk Indian chief (George Johnson) and an English mother (Emily Howells). She was schooled in both the 19th-century English Romantic tradition and the legends and tales of her Native Canadian grandfather. At the turn of the century Johnson was easily the most famous Native Canadian writer and performer; she enjoyed considerable public attention, and in 1886 adopted the name Tekahionwake. Her poetry first appeared in New York in *Gems of Poetry*, 1885, and in W.P. Lighthall's 1889 anthology, *Songs of the Great Dominion*. Praised for the authentic aboriginal voice in her poetry, Johnson more and more took on the popular persona of 'The Mohawk Princess'. At the same time, she was clearly aware of the tension between the indigenous and European cultures, and recognized her own ambiguous position. Her narrative poetry to some extent idealizes and commodifies her Native Canadian heritage. She first published *The White Wampum* (1895) in England, followed by *Canadian Born* (1903). After ill health forced her to stop performing, she published *Legends of Vancouver* (1911), based on tales told to her by her Squamish friend, Joe Capilano, and *Flint and Feather* (1912), her most famous collection. *The Shagganappi* and *The Mocassin Maker*, both prose collections, were published after she died in Vancouver in 1913.

Bib. Keller, B., *Pauline;* McRaye, W., *Pauline Johnson and Her Friends*.

Johnson, Stephanie (born 1961)

New Zealand short-story writer. Stephanie Johnson was one of very few women contributors to Michael Morrissey's *The New Fiction* (1985), an anthology of ▷postmodern writing. Johnson's stories invert and satirize gender roles, particularly in the field of sex workers, and are both feminist and innovative in form.

Publications: *The Glass Whittler and Other Stories* (1988).

Johnston, Jennifer (born 1930)

Irish novelist, born in Dublin into an Anglo-Irish, Protestant family. Her parents, Shelagh Richards, actress and theatre director at the Abbey Theatre, Dublin and Denis Johnston, were associated with the Irish poet and dramatist, W.B. Yeats (1865–1939) and the Irish Revival (the Irish nationalist and cultural movement which flourished in the late 19th century and early 20th century). She lived for some time in London, and now lives in Derry in Northern Ireland. Her novels explore the roots and evolution over time of political, social and cultural tensions in Ireland. While the ▷'Big House' is a recurrent setting and a central metaphor in her work, she has also written about the Northern Irish working class (*Shadows on Our Skin*, 1977). Internationally acclaimed as one of Ireland's finest contemporary novelists, *The Old Jest* (1979) won the Whitbread Award in 1979. Her other novels are: *The Captains and the Kings* (1972), *The Gates* (1973), *How Many Miles to Babylon?* (1974), *The Christmas Tree* (1981), *The Railway Station Man* (1984), *Fool's Sanctuary* (1987) and *The Invisible Worm* (1991).

Johnston, Mary (1870–1936)

US novelist and essayist. Johnston wrote historical romances of colonial Virginia, social criticism and mysticism. Born in Virginia of Scottish ancestry, Johnston was a frail child. She was educated by a governess, and after her mother died in 1889, she managed the household. After her father died, Johnston lived with two of her sisters in Virginia where she was involved in pacifist and socialist organizations.

Johnston was committed to an 'adventure in consciousness'. She emphasizes that humanity participates in an evolutionary process, and as a ▷Southern lady, she experienced the tragic limitations of the past; as a woman she envisioned a perfectible future. In novels like ▷*To Have and To Hold* (1900) and ▷*Hagar* (1913) Johnston rejects social hierarchies. She put forth the idea of a universal, spiritual unity combined with social action.

Other works include: *Lewis Rand* (1908), *The Long Roll* (1911), *Cease Firing* (1912), *Witch* (1914), *Eanderes* (1917), *Foes* (1918), *Michael Forth* (1919), *Sweet Rocket* (1920), *Silver Cross* (1922) and *Drury Randall* (1934).

'Joint Letter from Mary Traske and Margaret Smith . . . to . . . John Endicott' (1660)
Written by two North American Quakers in Massachusetts, ▷ Mary Traske and Margaret Smith (fl 1660), who had been incarcerated for eight and ten months in a Boston gaol, charged with religious dissension for having freely expressed their opposing beliefs, the letter attacks the 'Spirit of Error' that the Puritans pursued in their Calvinism and their persecution of other faiths. It outspokenly asserts the tenets of Quakerism as the true faith and seeks to shame the leaders of Massachusetts for unjustly restraining them 'from our children and habitations'. The 'Joint Letter' is an important document in the religious disputes of 17th-century Massachusetts Bay Colony and for its exposure of the role that women played in those debates.
▷ Early North American letters

Jolley, Elizabeth (born 1923)

Elizabeth Jolley

Australian novelist and short story writer. Jolley was born in England and came to Western Australia in 1959, soon establishing a reputation as a contemporary writer of great brilliance. She has been a salesperson and a nurse as well as a teacher of creative writing and literature at the Fremantle Arts Centre, at the University of Western Australia and at Curtin University, where she is currently employed as a part-time tutor. Jolley is interested in the eccentric and the

grotesque, and her novels are textually experimental. Lesbianism is a constant theme, in the context of exploitation within personal relationships. Her literary awards include the *Age* Book of the Year Award 1982 for *Mr Scobie's Riddle* (1983), the New South Wales Premier's Award for Fiction 1985 for *Milk and Honey* (1984) and the Miles Franklin Award 1987 for ▷ *The Well* (1986). Other novels are *Palomino* (1980), *The Newspaper of Claremont Street* (1981), ▷ *Miss Peabody's Inheritance* (1983), *Foxybaby* (1985), *The Sugar Mother* (1988), *My Father's Moon* (1989) and *Cabin Fever* (1990). Books of short fiction are *Five Acre Virgin and Other Stories* (1976), *The Travelling Entertainer* (1979), and *Woman in a Lampshade* (1983).
▷ Lesbian writing (Australia); Short story (Australia); *Coming Out from Under; Eight Voices of the Eighties*

Jones, Gayle (born 1949)
US novelist, poet and dramatist. An African-American, Jones was raised in Lexington, Kentucky when schools were segregated. After graduating from Connecticut College, she studied creative writing at Brown University and went on to lecture at the University of Michigan. Her work focuses on the psychological damage inflicted by an oppressive history of racism and the abuse of women. In *Corregidora* (1975) an African-American woman, Ursa, is bequeathed a legacy of hatred for men through a maternal history of slavery and sexual exploitation. Ursa is herself unable to have children and sublimates this painful history into the blues and the story she tells. In doing so she recontextualizes the hatred it generated within a history of racism and sexism. Jones suggests that women possess a violent sexual power in their passivity, and paradoxically recognizes the sexual vulnerability of the victimizer in the act of victimization. In *Eva's Man* (1987), Ursa Medina Canada uses her sexual power to rebel against male domination, sexually dismembering her man. The novel is narrated by Eva from a psychiatric prison, portraying the logic of her insanity as a response to emotional and sexual abuse by a series of men. Discussing the importance of storytelling in her work, Jones explains that it enables her to comment indirectly on 'language . . . politics and morality and economics and culture' without having to 'isolate them and therefore freeze them'.
Other works include: *White Rat and Other Short Stories* (1977), *Song for Anninho* (1981), *The Hermit Woman* (1983) and *Xargue and Other Poems* (1985).

Jong, Dola de (Dorothea Rosalie) (1911–?)
Dutch prose writer and journalist. She ran away from her conservative Jewish father, becoming a ballet dancer and a journalist. *Dans om het hart* (1939) (*Dance Around the Heart*), the story of a ballet dancer, was her first novel. Just before the German occupation in 1940 she left the country, finally settling in the USA and gaining US citizenship in 1946, though she returned to the

Netherlands in 1972. She was instrumental in stimulating literary contacts between the USA and the Netherlands and Flanders. Her most important work is a war novel about refugees, *En de akker is de wereld* (1946) (*The Field*). Her last novel, originally written in Dutch, *De thuiswacht* (1954), describing the relationship between a lesbian and her friend, was translated into English only after many years as *The Tree and Vine*, (1961). Many of her children's books and novels, including the thriller-like *The Whirling of Time* (1964), were first published in the US, being subsequently translated into Dutch.

Jong, Erica (born 1942)

US poet and novelist. Jong was born into a family of Jewish artists and intellectuals, and was raised in New York. In 1965 she earned a Master's degree in English literature at Columbia University. Jong's work is characterized by humour and she uses language traditionally considered unfeminine. The poems in *Fruits and Vegetables* (1971) declare women's sexual and intellectual equality with men. They express Jong's anger at the plight of the woman poet. Poems in *Half-Lives* (1973) show how women suffer from the lack of human intimacy; they envision women gaining control of their own destinies through their bodies. The heroine of the novel ▷*Fear of Flying* (1973), Isadora Wing, seeks her freedom through the erotic. In the novel *Fanny* (1980) Jong shows women's boldest potential. She celebrates women's power and locates it in a matriarchal tradition.

Other works include: *Loveroot* (1975), *How To Save Your Own Life* (1977), *At the Edge of the Body* (1979), *Witches* (1981), *Ordinary Miracles* (1983), *Parachutes and Kisses* (1984), *Serenissima* (1989) and *Any Woman's Blues* (1990).

Jongleuse, La (1900) ▷*Juggler, The* (1990)

Jonker, Ingrid (1933–1965)

South African Afrikaans poet. Born in Douglas, near Kimberley, Cape Province, she and her sister spent part of their youth in an orphanage after the deaths of their mother and grandmother, later being looked after by their father. Writing poetry from a very early age, Jonker submitted a first collection to a publisher which was not accepted. However, it brought her encouragement and advice from the publisher's reader, the established Afrikaans poet D.J. Opperman. Her work is informed by surrealism, and exhibits a preoccupation with loss and bereavement. In this regard it has been compared to that of ▷Sylvia Plath. Her love poems, for which she is most famous, are sometimes sentimental. She produced two volumes of poetry during her lifetime, *Ontvlugting* (1956) (*Flight*) and *Rook en Oker* (1963) (*Smoke and Ochre*) – the second highly acclaimed – with one posthumously published, *Kantelson* (1966) (*Westering Sun*). Her *Selected Poems* (1968) offers English translations of her work by Jack Cope and William Plomer. She also

wrote a one-act play '*n Seun na my Hart* (1970) (*A Son After My Own Heart*), and a number of short stories.

After several suicide attempts, she killed herself by drowning at age 32.

Bib: Cope, Jack, 'Poet against the System' in *The Adversary Within: Dissident Writers in Afrikaans*.

Jordan, June (born 1936)

US poet, children's writer, dramatist and essayist. Jordan was born in Brooklyn, New York, to Jamaican immigrant parents, with whom she had a troubled relationship. Best-known for her poetry, she is a prolific writer and has produced a number of plays in collaboration with Adrienne B. Torf. While her poetry draws stylistically on the mainstream of North American poetry in its personal vision and syntactic and thematic inventiveness, her subject matter stems from an uncompromising concern with politics in its widest sense. In exploring the complexities of the African-American experience, history and culture, her work manifests a spiritual vision of wholeness and humanity whilst testifying to the devastating effects of racism and economic exploitation. Collections such as *New Days: Poems of Exile and Return* (1974) and *Things That I Do in the Dark* (1977) focus in particular on the position of African-American women – often through writing about her mother – in a world which is dominated and controlled by men. In the essays in *Civil Wars* (1981), Jordan suggests that poetry is a form of mothering of African-American culture. Her political essays engage with a wide variety of issues, including ecology and internationalism, as well as government abuses of power in the US.

Other work includes: *Who Look at Me?* (1969), *Some Changes* (1971), *His Own Where –* (1971), *Dry Victories* (1972), *Fannie Lou Hamer* (1972), *Poem: On Moral Leadership as a Political Dilemma* (1974), *New Life: New Room* (1975), *Kimako's Story* (1981), *Freedom Now Suite* (1984), *The Break* (1984), *The Music of Poetry and the Poetry of Music* (1984), *Living Room: New Poems 1980–84* (1985), *Bobo Goetz a Gun* (1985), *On Call: New Political Essays 1981–85* (1985), *Bang Bang Uber Alles* (1986), *Naming Our Destiny: New and Selected Poems* (1989) and *Moving Towards Home: Political Essays* (1989).

Jorge, Lídia (born 1946)

Portuguese novelist. She was born in Boliqueme, a village in the southern Algarve, and much of her fiction concerns that part of the nation. In 1980 she published ▷*O Dia dos Prodígios* (*The Day of Wonders*), about the coming of the 1974 revolution to a remote village community. Her second novel, *O Cais das Merendas* (1982) (*Picnic Quay*), deals with villagers who have left their homes to work in a fashionable tourist hotel on the southern coast. In both of these books Jorge is preoccupied with the impact of modernization and cultural colonialism on the lives of a traditional population. Her novel *Notícia da Cidade Silvestre* (1984) (*News from the Sylvan City*) was awarded the Lisbon

Lídia Jorge

Municipal Prize in 1984. Four years later she published *A Costa dos Murmúrios* (*The Coast of Murmurs*), a novel about the colonial wars in Africa. Stylistically innovative, Jorge is one of the most prominent figures in the post-revolutionary generation.

▷Correia, Hélia

Bib: Sadlier, Darlene J., *The Question of How: Women Writers and New Portuguese Literature.*

Joseph, Vivienne (born 1948)

New Zealand poet. Vivienne Joseph was born in Wellington, where she has spent most of her life. Her poetry places personal relationships, especially the gendered roles of mother, daughter and wife, in a culturally specific context of films, books and constructed fictions; a context that acts as an ironic commentary on emotion.

Publications: *A Desirable Property* (1985).

Jotuni, Maria (1880–1943)

Pseudonym of Maria Tarkiainen, a Finnish novelist and dramatist. She received little attention during her lifetime, but has recently been rediscovered and republished. She is now regarded as the greatest dramatist in Finland. She was born in Kuopi, and at the beginning of the 20th century she studied literature. Her earliest short stories were written in a laconic, understated style, which gives room not only for psychological insight but also for a sort of tragic destiny. Later she refined her technique in modernist writing. In 1905 she made her début with *Suhteital* (*Relationships*), stories about her home-village, Kuopi. In 1927 she published the pessimistic *Tyttö ruusutarhassa* (1927) (*The Girl in the Rose Arbour*), a collection of short stories.

It is as a dramatist that she has received most attention. In 1910 she published *Vanka koti* (*The Old Home*), and thereafter: *Miehen kylkiluu* (1914)

(*Adam's Rib*), *Kultainen vvasikka* (1918) (*The Golden Calf*), *Tahvelisankarin rouva* (1924) (*The Henpecked Husband's Wife*), a tragedy (1929) and a comedy (1942).

Joubert, Elsa (born 1922)

South African Afrikaans novelist and travel writer, born in Paarl, Cape Province, best-known for *The Long Journey of Poppie Nongena* (1980), also published as *Poppie* (1981), originally published as *Die Swerfjare van Poppie Nongena* (1978). This book fits most interestingly into an ▷autobiographical tradition where white women write the stories told to them by black women. Her career began with journalism and travel writing, which fuses with her fiction, in that all her work searches for knowledge about Africa. Her fiction, in turn, may be read as new journalism. Apart from *Poppie*, only her first novel, *Ons Wag op die Kaptein* (1963) (*To Die at Sunset*, 1982), has been translated from the Afrikaans. Later novels are *Die Wahlerbrug* (1969) (*The Wahler Bridge*) and *Bonga* (1971), which won the CNA (Central News Agency) Prize. While her collection of short stories *Melk* (1980) (*Milk*) explores racial tension in contemporary Southern Africa, her latest work *Missionaris* (1988) (*Missionary*) turns back to the experiences of the early 19th-century missionary, Aart Antonij van der Lingen.

Her travel books are: *Water en Woestyn* (1956) (*Water and Desert*); *Die Verste Reis* (1959) (*The Furthest Journey*); *Die Staf van Monomotapa* (1964) (*The Staff of Monomatapa*), *Swerwe in die Herfsland* (1968) (*Wander in the Autumn Country*), and *Die Nuwe Afrikaan* (1974) (*The New African*).

Bib: Schalkwyk, David, 'Elsa Joubert: Women and Domestic Struggle in *Poppie Nongena*' in Clayton, Cherry (ed.), *Women and Writing in South Africa* (1989).

Joubert, Linda ▷Grové, Henriette

Joudry, Patricia (born 1921)

Canadian dramatist and novelist. Joudry was born in Spirit River, Alberta, but her family moved to Montreal in 1925. She began to write scripts for public radio in Toronto in 1940, then lived in New York (1945–1949) where she co-authored a radio serial. She returned to Toronto in 1949, and wrote material for radio and television. *Teach Me How to Cry* (1955), about two star-crossed lovers who re-play *Romeo and Juliet* with a more sensible conclusion (that is, life), is one of the most commercially successful Canadian stage plays ever written. Joudry wrote a number of adaptations of ▷*Anne of Green Gables* for radio. In 1957 she moved to England with her second husband, and continued to write plays, the best of them dealing with domestic strife. For a time she believed that George Bernard Shaw (1856–1950) was 'transmitting' plays through her; later she wrote a wry account of this period when she suffered from 'religious delusion', called *Spirit River to Angels' Roost: Religions I Have Loved and*

Left (1977). She returned to Canada in 1973 but, disillusioned with prospects for the production of Canadian drama, she wrote two novels, *The Dweller on the Threshold* (1973) and *The Selena Tree* (1980).

Journal amoureux, Le (1670) (The Journal of Love) ▷Desjardins, Marie-Catherine Hortense

Journal and Letters of Eliza Lucas (1850)
Early North American texts by ▷Eliza Lucas Pinckney. Chronicling Pinckney's years of managing plantations and slave labourers in the West Indies, raising a family in England and South Carolina, and her final years, these texts from 1739–1762 are of major significance in the literary history of 18th-century South Carolina. As a well-educated, independent young woman, Pinckney rejected the idea of marriage for economic profit and insisted that she would prefer to remain single rather than marry without equality and affection. Her independent spirit propels her private records, whether discussing family issues or her agricultural experiments.
▷Early North American letters

Journal des Dames (1759–1778) (Ladies' Journal)
Eighteenth-century periodical which had three female and six male editors. It was unique in that for a time it was written by and for women, whereas contemporary periodicals written by women were not overtly women's journals, for example, the ▷Dame du Noyer's, *La Quintessence des nouvelles* (1712–1727) (*The Quintessence of the News*), ▷Marie-Anne Barbier's, *Les Saisons littéraires* (1714) (*Literary Seasons*) and ▷Marie Le Prince de Beaumont's *Nouveau magasin français* (1750) (*New French Shop*) (although the anonymous editor of the fifteen-issue feminist *La Spectatrice*, 1728–1729, *The Woman Spectator*, may have been a woman).
The *Journal des Dames's* founding male editor (1750–61), Thorel de Champigneulles, intended to publish 'delicious nothings' for women, while the second editor, M. de Loupitière (1761), invited contributions from women in the hope of finding a wife. He did not expect the serious copy he received from women such as ▷Madame de Puisieux, and ▷Madame de Beaumer, who became the journal's first woman editor in 1761. Her assertively feminist editorship, calling for radical and speedy reforms, resulted in the censors forcing her to hand over to Pierre Du Rozoi, who alienated both former contributors and subscribers. The paper's feminist content was reinstated by Madame de Maisonneuve who acquired it in 1763 and enlisted two male oppositional journalists: Mathon, who became the next editor, and Louis-Sébastien Mercier. Suspended between 1769 and 1774, the paper was resurrected by ▷Marie-Emilie de Montanclos, another bold feminist and popularist editor, who then passed it on to the radical Mercier (1775–76). He was forcibly replaced by

Dorat, the last editor, who, keen to appease the authorities, changed the name to *Mélanges littéraires* (*Literary Miscellany*). Despite his efforts to sever the journal's links with its radical past, it was nevertheless finally suppressed in 1778. Over the years the paper had attacked established institutions, and fought for widespread social and political change, encouraging contributions and active participation from women, especially those from the provinces and lower classes. These female journalists were condemned by the aristocratic and upper-middle-class women of the salons, such as the ▷Marquise Du Deffand, ▷Louise d'Epinay and ▷Julie de Lespinasse as 'crass, unseemly and too virile in their pretentions'. But they passed on a tradition of feminist action which had been present in the Fronde, carried on throughout the Revolution, and would later be embodied in the 19th-century women's journal which called itself *La Fronde* in acknowledgement of these origins.
▷Antremont, Marquise de; Beauharnais Countesse de ; Bourette, Charlotte Rouyer; Feminine/feminist journalism (France); Savignac, Alida de
Bib: Adburgham, A., *Women in Print*; Gelbart, N.R., *Feminine and Oppositional Journalism in Old Régime France: le Journal des Dames*.

Journalgyaw Ma Ma Lay (1916–1985)
Burmese writer. She was born in Pyapon, and embarked on a literary career in 1937. She worked as publisher and managing editor for the weekly newspaper, *Thunderer*, and the *Peoples' Forum Daily Literary Journal*, and was appointed President of the Burmese Writers' Association in 1955. Her best-known novel is the prize-winning *Not Because of Hatred*.

Journalism
West Africa: Whereas achieving publication in book form is an arduous process, journalism is an area where women have been relatively visible in West Africa. In Ghana, the short story writer Mabel Dove-Danquah, who was also the first woman elected to Parliament in 1952, had a column in the *West Africa Times* under the name Marjorie Mensah. The Nigerian writers ▷Adaora Lily Ulasi and ▷Mabel Segun were also both journalists in the early post-independence era. Today, journalism is probably second only to teaching as the most popular profession for women writers. The Cameroonian writer Lydie Dooh-Bunya (▷*La Brise du jour*) is a journalist, and the ▷romantic fiction writer ▷Helen Ovbiagele is women's page editor of *Vanguard*, a Nigerian national daily newspaper. Though there is a tendency for women to be relegated to women's pages and 'women's issues', these can also provide a useful space for expression. The *Vanguard* women's page, for example, has for several years now made a feature of its regular weekly serial, 'Treena Kwenta: diary of a fun-loving but hard-working single parent'. Under the guise of that most ephemeral of formats, the

gossip column, and sheltered by her anonymity, the fictional author/subject gives a remarkably frank insight into the intrigues and scandals of middle-class Lagos life, including her own romantic involvements.

The quality of the press is not uniform throughout West Africa. No other country in Africa can equal Nigeria for the number and variety of its newspapers and magazines, but nowhere else has a 110 million-strong population to sustain such abundance. Elsewhere, Senegal has a thriving press, while in Ghana the press is government-controlled and heavily censored. Though many Ghanaian women are attracted to journalism, there are very limited opportunities for them to progress, and many, like the writer and freelance journalist Ajoa Yeboah-Afari, are driven into different fields. Deputy editor of the *Mirror* for ten years until 1986, she was known for her column of social and political comment, 'Native Daughter'. A collection of her articles has been published as *Thoughts of a Native Daughter* (1988), and her volume of short stories, *The Sound of Pestles*, is forthcoming.

In a climate where information is tightly controlled, alternatives to newspapers take on a more significant function. In Ghana, the women's magazine *Obaa Sima* ('ideal woman'), started by Kate Abbiam in 1971, is a remarkable survival story. With a staff of one, it continues to appear, providing a forum, not only for information, but for creative writing. Among many others, Kate Abbiam's own romance, *Beloved Twin*, was serialized in the pages of her magazine.

Apart from print journalism, radio and television also provide outlets for women, and a great deal of poetry and drama is generated in this way. But it is in the nature of these media that what they produce is ephemeral and very little is accessible in any concrete form. It does mean, however, that one should look beyond the printed book for evidence of women's creative activity.
Italy: It was in the second half of the 19th century that the newspaper began to exert its cultural and socio-political force on Italian life. Women contributors were, at first, few and far between. ▷Contessa Lara, Olga Ossiani and ▷Matilde Serao are among the first women writers to make their presence felt in this sphere and, of these three, Serao is undoubtedly the most significant because of her power first as co-editor and co-proprietor of various newspapers (mainly in Naples), and later as editor and proprietor of her own papers. In the 20th century, women journalists such as ▷Maria Bellonci, ▷Camilla Cederna, ▷Alba de Cespedes, ▷Oriana Fallaci and ▷Dacia Maraini have brought their considerable talents to bear on Italian newspapers.

Journal of a Tour into the Interior (1798)

Eighteenth-century journal written by ▷Lady Anne Barnard, important in the tradition of writing by South African colonial women partly because it stands as a 'first' in English. Addressed to her sisters in England, the journal records a journey from Cape Town over the Hottentots Holland mountains to the Moravian mission at Genadendal, and then to Swellendam in the east, returning via Saldanha Bay in the west. Travelling by wagon drawn alternately by horses and oxen, depending on the terrain, Barnard was part of a group consisting of her husband and his younger sister, her seventeen year-old cousin, the 'Cape Malay' driver of the wagon, and a small entourage of servants and slaves.

Written in an intelligent and lively manner, the journal tries to come to terms with a landscape and a people hitherto virtually unrepresented in travellers' tales. For Barnard, the landscape lacks the picturesque qualities upon which contemporary aesthetics were founded. Constantly seeking features reminiscent of England, she seizes upon a cluster of rocks, a clump of thorn trees, or an occasional pool of water around which to focus her composition, seldom finding the accommodation she seeks in this alien environment. Longing to view a 'Hottentot' woman in her 'natural' state, her eye discovers, with unconscious contradiction, 'Pharaoh's daughter in the brook before me, washing her royal robes and perhaps one of the most picturesque creatures it was possible to see'.

As the journal proceeds, however, Barnard starts investing the landscape with a history. A few pointed stones give her the grave of 'Hottentot heroes slain in battle', and an oddly-shaped rock leads her to imagine a turreted castle and an urn, 'the sarcophagus of some giant' slain by 'the king of the Caffres'. Grieved to find that it had no such history, Barnard resolves to give it one, set to 'Hottentot music', and celebrating the prince's rescue of a damsel in distress. Just as Barnard's compositional mode was directed by the picturesque, so was her narrative mode directed by a ▷romantic and ▷Gothic tradition.

Barnard's presentation of the Dutch is respectful when she finds signs of good manners, but otherwise patronizing or downright contemptuous. She contrasts the brutality of the local Dutch slave-owners to the behaviour of Moravian missionaries, who respect the converts as fellow human beings, if subordinate, and who teach them 'religion, industry and good order'.

The published *Journal*, which first appeared in *Lives of the Lindsays* (1849), and later as an addition to *The Letters of Lady Anne Barnard Written to Henry Dundas* (1973), is an extract from the original journal of a tour into the interior, which itself forms a small section of a five-volume journal (hitherto unpublished) detailing Barnard's sea journey to the Cape of Good Hope, her residence there from 1797 to 1802, and her return journey to Britain.

Journal of a Young Lady of Virginia 1782 (1871)

Although dated 1782, ▷Lucinda Lee's diary was actually written in the year 1787. Lee, a member of the old-guard Virginia aristocracy, relates for her friend, Polly Brent, the intricacies of her social activities and opinions on issues of importance to a young North American woman – marriage, fashion, novels and prospective beaux.

Journal of Elizabeth Cranch, The (1944)

Written in 1785–6 during a visit to relatives living in Haverhill, Massachusetts, ▷Elizabeth Cranch's journal notes reading, games and day-trips, and includes weather reports and accounts of the numerous visitors who called socially. It is of little literary value but details the social and domestic lives of North American upper-class youths in the post-revolutionary years.

Journal of Esther Edwards Burr 1754–1757, The (1984)

When she moved to New Jersey after her marriage, the North American Puritan ▷Esther Edwards Burr made a pact with her friend, Sarah Prince of Massachusetts, to maintain journals in order to track the progress of each other's lives, especially in terms of spirituality. The journal exposes Burr's devout Puritan beliefs but also her frustrations at the exhausting duties that often required her to forgo her own intellectual interests in order to entertain her husband's visitors. As the spouse of the President of the College of New Jersey, Burr had the opportunity to record the intricate workings of the Puritan patriarchy, but she was equally interested in issues concerning 'The Sisterhood'. Because the journal was maintained in the rare snippets of time she could find for such endeavours, it is sometimes breathless in nature; but it is most often a detailed account of an upper-class North American woman's daily life and occasionally includes long meditations on her religious beliefs.

Journal of Mrs John Amory, The (1923)

From May 1775 to March 1777, ▷Katherine Amory recorded her reactions as a Loyalist to the American Revolution. Opposed to the War for Independence, Amory sailed for London in 1775, and her journal is an informative record of her life as an expatriate in London.

Journals (Australia)

The journals of colonial women provided both a utilitarian and a recreational function. Numerous journals and diaries survive and are discussed in Lucy Frost's ▷*No Place for a Nervous Lady: Voices from the Australian Bush* (1984), and in 'Letter Writing and Journal Scribbling', an essay by Dorothy Jones published in ▷*A Bright and Fiery Troop: Australian Women Writers of the Nineteenth Century* (1988), edited by Debra Adelaide. Diaries and journals range from practical and necessary records of farming life to genteel accounts of the social round. Often journals and letters were interchangeable; the journals providing the material for letters 'home', and letters and diaries quite often forming the basis for memoirs which were published later, such as Ellen Clacy's ▷*A Lady's Visit to the Gold Diggings of Australia in 1852–53* (1853). Among the more famous

journals were those of ▷Annie Baxter, ▷Annabella Boswell, and ▷Georgiana McCrae. A most interesting diary which is quoted by Lucy Frost is the illiterate yet lively and authentic journal of Sarah Davenport, a working-class emigrant woman. One of her children is accidently scalded on the emigrant ship. He dies two days later, and the shock causes her to go into labour: 'i had what was caled purmature labour and that babe was throne in the sea i was almost Dumb with grief.' Her life when she reaches the colony is scarcely more fortunate.

Journals, diaries and memoirs of Australian women are listed in the bibliography of ▷*Stories of Herself When Young: Autobiographies of Childhood by Australian Women* (1990), by Joy Hooton, while a selection of extracts from contemporary diaries and letters is given in *Angry Women: Anthology of Australian women's writing* (1989), edited by Di Brown, Heather Ellyard and Barbara Polkinghorne.

Journals of Madam Knight, The (1825)

Although not published until 1825, ▷Sarah Kemble Knight's account of her travels on horseback from Boston to New York was written in 1704–5. The journals are notable for Knight's picaresque sketches of colonial North American roadside life, many of which prefigure the wit and astuteness of Samuel Clemens's (also known as Mark Twain, 1835–1910) 19th-century sketches of North American types. Knight's journey was undertaken as part of an estate sale that she, as a talented businesswoman, was undertaking for a widowed relative. Leaving in October 1704 and not returning until the following March, Knight travelled through Rhode Island and Connecticut, often hiring guides and trusting to the hospitality of strangers for a night's rest. In addition to her witty prose accounts of the frustrations of such travel, Knight relied upon the process of writing poetry – 'my old way of composing my resentments' – to alleviate some of her fears and disappointments as she endeavoured to complete a journey unprecedented for a colonial woman. The literary quality and delightful characterizations of herself as well as of the people she met on her journey have made Knight's journal a classic North American text.

Journals of Susanna Moodie, The (1970)

Canadian writer ▷Margaret Atwood's poetic re-visioning of ▷Susanna Moodie's life, from her disembarkation at Quebec to after her death, making her appearance as 'an old woman on a Toronto bus'. Atwood said that she dreamed about Susanna Moodie before she had read Moodie's books: 'I was alone in the theatre; on the empty white stage, a single figure was singing.' When she did read Moodie's work, what struck her was Susanna Moodie as a representative immigrant to Canada. In three parts, Atwood articulates first the Moodies' struggle, then the period in Belleville, and finally Susanna Moodie underground, reflecting on the 20th century going on above her. Full of doubleness and death, the poems insist on resurrection even in the strangeness of Canada, 'these vistas of desolation'.

Juana de Asbaje y Ramirez de Santillana (1651–1695)

Mexican poet and dramatist whose pen-name was Sor Juana Inés de la Cruz. She is one of the most important women poets of the Spanish-speaking world. She was a nun, known as the '*monja de México*' ('the nun of México') or as the 'tenth muse', who acquired an extraordinary fame for her work and her feminist ideas. Probably an illegitimate child, which prevented her from making a good marriage, for a time she was a lady of honour in the court of the Marquise of Mancera. She then entered the Convent of the Unshod Carmelites in 1677, and in 1699 joined the less rigid order of St Jerome. In her ▷'*Respuesta de la poetisa a la muy ilustre Sor Filotea de la Cruz*' (1691) ('Response of the Poetess to the Very Illustrious Sor Filotea de la Cruz'), she stated that at three she learned how to read and at seven she wanted to enter the university disguised as a man. In her cell she conducted scientific experiments, composed music, kept a 4,000-volume library – one of the best in the vice-kingdom – and received intellectuals of the court for literary evenings. '*Respuesta de la poetisa a la muy ilustre Sor Filotea de la Cruz*' is an extraordinary autobiographical letter, in which she defends her ▷'*Carta Atenagórica*' (1690), which the Bishop of Puebla published under the pen-name of Sor Filotea de la Cruz. The bishop rebukes her for her opinions in a document that he published with the '*Carta*'. In the latter she had expressed opposition to the ideas of a sermon by the Jesuit priest Padre Antônio Vieira (1608–97). In her '*Respuesta*' she defends herself for becoming involved in worldly and political matters. Probably as a result of the bishop's reprimand, she stopped writing in 1694 and sold her library and her musical and scientific instruments. She died in the convent after treating her fellow sisters during a plague epidemic. She exalted the rights of women, and defended slaves and South American Indians in her texts. Among her plays, *Los empeños de una casa* (1683) (*The Obligations of a House*) is a parody of Calderón's *Los empeños de un acaso* (*The Obligations of an Accident*). *Primero sueño* (*First Dream*), a 'silva' of 975 verses, is one of her most important poems, written in gongoristic style.

▷*Prótesta que, Rubricada con su sangre, hizo de su fe y amor a dios*
Bib: Paz, O., *Sor Juana, or, the Traps of Faith*.

Judenbuche, Die (1842) ▷*Jew's Beech, The* (1958)

Juggler, The (1990)

Translation of *La Jongleuse* (1900), novel by French writer ▷Rachilde (Marguerite Eymery). A fantasy of how a strong woman might negotiate and turn to her own advantage *fin de siècle* representations of the feminine. The novel is a perceptive and vivid evocation of how women are defined by appearances, and are required to produce themselves, through dress, décor and social rites and rituals, as objects of pleasure for men. To this Rachilde adds a flamboyant and ultimately unconvincing claim that women who are aware of the games being played can juggle with men's fantasies as a means to procure power of their own.

The heroine, Eliante, both Salomé and Herodias, seduces the young medical student, Léon, by incarnating in rapid, dazzling succession all the images of his desire, while refusing to allow him to possess her physically. The text, like its author, is riddled with bad faith. Eliante maintains that her authority and integrity remain absolute, even though she has clearly given herself over entirely to definition by the male gaze, turning herself into another commodity in the glittering Decadent shop window. For all her frenetic masking, age and familiarity must depreciate her value. Her niece, Missie, the cigarette-smoking, sporty, bluestocking New Woman, may well be the object of her bitter contempt, but she has the advantage of youth. Eliante, having chosen to live by the sexual market values of her contemporaries, must also die by them, as she confesses with her final suicide, stabbing herself to fall symbolically across the bed where she has tricked Léon and Missie into sleeping together. Inexplicably, the novel is nowadays presented as a feminist text (reprinted as such by the Editions des Femmes, 1982).

Juletane (1987)

Translation of the second novel by the French Antilles (Caribbean) writer, Myriam Warner-Vieyra, *Juletane* (1982). This novel is the diary of an Antillean woman, Juletane. It has been handed over to Hélène, an Antillean about to be married to an African, by a psychiatrist who tried unsuccessfully to help Juletane. After marrying Mamadou in France, the orphaned Juletane goes with him to Senegal, where she discovers that her husband already has a wife and child. Mamadou divides his time between his two wives. Juletane becomes progressively more distraught each time he goes to his other wife. After her miscarriage and Mamadou's third marriage, Juletane joins the other wives and children in the family compound, where she becomes a recluse and is seen as being mad. Bearing similarities to ▷Mariama Bâ's *Une si longue lettre* (see essay on West Africa), *Juletane* presents the drama of an Antillean woman whose self-identity is compromised to the extent that she becomes submerged under a web of neuroses and phantasms. The contact with Africa portrayed by Warner-Vieyra provides a sharp contrast with the Edenic return to sources announced by proponents of the ▷*négritude* movement.
▷*Folie Antillaise*

Júlia, Francisca (1871–1920)

Brazilian poet. Her full name is Francisca Júlia da Silva Munster, and she wrote under the pen-names Maria Azevedo and Caju. A teacher and didactic writer, she wrote for several Rio and São Paulo newspapers. Her Parnassian poems made her famous, especially *'Musa impassivel'* ('Impassive Muse'), from her first collection, *Marmores* (1895) (*Marble*). This had a preface by João Ribeiro, who, doubting that a woman could have written some of her poems, originally attributed them to Raimundo Correia. *Esfinges* (1903) (*Sphinxes*) revealed symbolist tendencies. After her marriage in 1909 she retired from literary life, and her death may possibly have been suicide.

Other works: *Livro da infância* (1899) (*Book of Childhood*); *Alma infantil*, with Júlio César da Silva (1912) (*Childish Soul*), and *Poesias* (1961) (*Poems*).

Julian of Norwich (c 1342–after 1416)

English mystic. Julian was probably born in Norwich, and may have been educated by Benedictine nuns at the convent of Carrow. In May 1373 she suffered a critical illness (in answer to her prayer) during which she experienced a series of 'showings', or revelations. She afterwards became an anchoress, and lived for over 20 years in a cell adjoining the Church of St Julian in Norwich. She gained a reputation as a spiritual advisor; among her visitors was ▷Margery Kempe. Through her *Revelations of Divine Love* Julian has gained recognition both in the history of English mysticism and as a writer of English prose. Her showings are recorded in a 'short' version, set down with the help of a scribe soon after her experience; and a 'long' version, written twenty or so years later, adding the insights she had gained into her experience through years of meditation and reflection. Julian's carefully constructed account of each showing reveals considerable rhetorical skill. Notable, too, is her use of 'homely', everyday imagery. Julian's experience of divine love embraces the feminine (in her development of the image of Christ as mother) as well as the masculine; and an unusual acceptance is shown, both of the feminine in humanity, and of the human body. Julian's voice and her spirituality have continued to echo in the 20th century, as in T.S. Eliot's 'Little Gidding': 'And all shall be well and / All manner of things shall be well'; and in Aldous Huxley's *Eyeless in Gaza*.

Bib: Colledge, E. and Walsh, J., *A Book of Showings to the Anchoress Julian of Norwich*; Wolters, C., *Revelations of Divine Love*; Petroff, E.A., *Medieval Women's Visionary Literature*.

July's People (1981)

A futuristic novel by Southern African writer ▷Nadine Gordimer. The central character, Maureen Smales, who has fled war-torn Johannesburg with her husband, Bam, and their two small children, is taken with her family into the country by July, their servant of many years' standing. The text scrutinizes the family's increasing dependence on July, deploying the symbolism of car, gun and key, among other

things, to signify shifts in power. Gender stereotypes also receive scrutiny, along with those of race, most powerfully in the relationship between Maureen and Mwawate (July's own name). In the relationship between Maureen and her husband, whose world now lacks all that was once made possible by the 'master bedroom', gender roles become unstable.

The novel purposely opens with references to the bushveld as sea, offering the Smales's flight as another colonial journey, one that is truly into Africa rather than into a European version of Africa. But at the end of the novel, Maureen's direction is unclear. The world suddenly becomes hard to read, recalling earlier textual hints regarding fiction, reality and represented image. Although the novel points to a new epoch for South Africa, it at the same time recognizes the impossibility of its representation.

June, Jennie ▷Croly, Jane Cunningham

Jurado, Alicia (born 1915)

Argentinian novelist, short story writer and essayist. She studied abroad and received several foreign scholarships and prizes. Her first novel is *La cárcel de los hierros* (1961) (*The Prison of the Irons*). Her second, *En soledad vivía* (1967) (*In Solitude I Lived*), takes place on Victoria Island in Lake Nahuel Huapí. Both novels stress the contrast between love and unhappiness, and perfection and the possible. In 1980 she became a member of the Argentinian Academy of Letters.

Other works include two collections of short stories: *Lenguas de polvo y sueño* (1965) (*Tongues of Dust and Sleep*) and *Los rostros del engaño* (1968) (*The Faces of Deceit*).

Jurić, Maria ▷Zagorka

Justly Celebrated Mrs Sophia Hume's Advice, The (1769)

Near the end of her life, the North American preacher and essayist ▷Sophia Wigington Hume had become renowned for her dedication to her chosen faith, Quakerism. This volume of her collected advice reveals her keen intelligence and a dedication, not only to her own salvation but to that of all people.

▷*Exhortation to the Inhabitants of the Province of South Carolina, An*; *Extracts from Divers, Antient Testimonies*; *Caution to Such As Observe Days and Times . . ., A*; Early North American Quaker women's writings

Juvonen, Helvi (1919–1959)

Finnish lyric poet. Juvonen worked as a teacher, a bank clerk and a translator. For ten years she wrote very mature, spiritual poetry. Juvonen wrote of the religious mysticism of God's presence in nature, and was inspired by studying the German mystics. Her first collection of poems, *Kääpiöpuu* (1949) (*The Dwarf Tree*), was melancholic, but her later collections described the harmony of the universe, and were influenced both by the Bible and by Finnish hymns, eg *Kuningas Kultatakki* (1950) (*King Goldcoat*) and *Kalliopohja* (1955) (*Bedrock*). Her later collections became more intense and tightly composed, eg *Pohjajäätä* (1952)

(*Deep Ice*) and in *Päivästä päivään* (1954) (*From Day to Day*) she used a simple ballad-like style.

She is both traditional and modern in her use of symbolic language, and is considered the most important writer of the modernism of the 1950s.

Kadaré, Elena (born 1943)

Reputedly the first Albanian woman to publish a novel. Elena Kadaré was born in Fier, educated in Elbasan, and graduated from the University of Tiranë. She worked as a journalist and editor, and married fellow-author Ismail Kadaré.

Her work has dealt with the problems of women's emancipation in a socialist society. She published a collection of stories called *Turn off the Light, Vera!* in 1965 and her novels include *A Difficult Birth* (1970), *The Bridge and the State of Siege* (1978) and *The Spouses* (1981).

Kaffka, Margit, (1880–1918)

Hungarian novelist. Margit Kaffka grew up in an impoverished, genteel and strictly Catholic family in eastern Hungary. She became a teacher, and started writing poems. Her early works of shorter fiction include *Quiet Crisis* (1909) and *Nyár* (1910) (*Summer*).

Kaffka's most famous work is *Színék és évek* (1912) (*Colours and Years*), in which she describes the decline of an old family, the struggle of women with their role, and the question of marriage. The book focuses on the young Magda Pórtelky, who has lost touch with her traditional woman's role. Kaffka was an ardent advocate of social equality.

In *Maria évei* (1912) (*Maria's Years*) the heroine is a young woman who studies and has a career, but who is moved by social conventions. Her life ends in tragedy and suicide. *Allomások* (1917) (*Stations*), a *roman-à-clef*, depicts the unsettled Bohemian life of a group of Hungarian writers known as the Nyugat Circle. The heroine is a liberated woman who manages her own life and steps out of her disastrous marriage. Independent again, she enters a new relationship with a married man. But does love provide companionship or only a sexual bond between man and woman? Then she plunges ambitiously into the cultural life of the fast-expanding pre-World War I Budapest. *Hangaboly* (*Ant Hill*) is an anti-clerical and pessimistic autobiographical novel about a girlhood at a restrictive convent school.

All Kaffka's characters can be said to be self-portraits at different stages of the author's life. Her early death came at a time when she was making great strides for contemporary Hungarian literature. She died in an epidemic of influenza at the end of World War I.

Kahana-Carmon, Amalia (born 1930)

Leading Israeli writer. Kahana-Carmon's lyrical style is reminiscent of ▷Virginia Woolf's writing, both for its sensitive, rich language and for its close examination of the self. Her main characters, mostly women, are individuals trying to break free from their loneliness through a meaningful contact with the 'other'. The mysterious nature of male–female relationships is her central theme. Characters might experience a mystical, true contact, but this is but a momentary revelation before they fall back into their previous

Amalia Kahana-Carmon

existence. Women are usually shown as the victims of love, or of their desire for this contact. Her published books include: ▷*Bichfifa Achat* (1966) (*Under One Roof*), *Ve'Yareach Be'Emek Ayalon* (1971) (*And the Moon in the Ayalon Valley*), *Sadot Magnetim* (1977) (*Magnetic Fields*) and *Lema'alah Be'Montifer* (1984) (*Up in Montifer*).

Kairi, Evanthia (1799–1866)

Greek dramatist and translator. Born on the island of Andros. She studied philosophy and ancient Greek under her brother, the famous philosopher Theophilos Kairis. She taught classics and history at the famous school for girls in Kydonies in Greek Asia Minor (now Turkey). She translated into Greek various French works on education and on the counselling of young women. In 1826, when Missolonghi fell to the Turks, she wrote *Nikiratos*, a play dedicated to the Greek women who had sacrificed their lives in the struggle. On the outbreak of the Greek uprising against Turkish rule in 1821, she appealed for help to women's organizations in Europe. Through her personal contacts and intellectual influence she created a strong philhellenic movement in Europe among women intellectuals. Following Greek Independence she settled on her native Andros, where she founded a home and school for war orphans.

Kaiser, Isabella (1866–1925)

Bilingual Swiss novelist. She was thirteen when her family moved from Geneva to German-speaking Switzerland. At eighteen she won a prize for her French novella, *Gloria victis* (*Glory to the Vanquished*), a success she consolidated with the poems in *Ici-bas* (1888) (*Down Here*), and the semi-autobiographical novels *Coeur de femme* (*Rahels Liebe*) (1891) (*Heart of Woman, The Love of Rahel*) and *Die Friedensucherin* (1908) (*Marcienne de Flue*, 1909). From 1902 she lived as a literary recluse on Lake Lucerne, receiving only a few select friends, and enjoying a legendary, if short-lived, reputation abroad. Her best works are the novellas collected in *Wenn die Sonne untergeht* (1901) (*When the Sun Sets*), especially *Der Herr Marquis* (*The Marquis*) and *Auf dem Leuchtturm* (*Up the Lighthouse*).

Kalasanda (1965) Kalasanda Revisited (1966)

Collections of Ganda village tales by the Ugandan novelist, short story writer and writer of children's literature ▷Barbara Kimenye. The tales are sustained by the author's sense of comedy, sharply-observed characters and shrewd eye for the snobberies and tensions of village life. Commentators have noted her condescending tone and the essentially conservative values of the deeply traditional society which she describes.

Kali for Women

India's first feminist publishing house, founded in 1984. It aims to present a variety of women's creative writing while producing academic titles which reflect and contribute towards the debates and issues facing women in India today. Kali is a blood-thirsty and independently-minded manifestation of Hinduism's supreme goddess. When in the form of Kali, the goddess rarely has a male consort.

Kannan, Lakshmi (born 1947)

Indian poet, novelist, critic and translator. She writes in both English and Tamil, her works in the latter language being published under the ▷pseudonym Kaaveri. She has taught English at university level for over ten years and has also worked as the Tamil expert on a national lexicon covering sixteen of India's languages. She has published many academic articles on English, North American and Indian literature. A book of short stories, *Rhythms*, which she translated from the Tamil, was published in 1980 and a volume of poetry, *Impressions*, in 1974. Her short story '*Munniyakka*', translated from the Tamil, appears in ▷ *Truth Tales*.

Kantûrková, Eva (born 1930)

Czech novelist. Kantûrková is the daughter of a journalist father and writer mother (Bohumila Sílová, 1908–1957). Her husband became head of Czech television. She worked mainly as a journalist until 1967, when she became a freelance writer. Her first book of short stories, *Jen si tak maličko povyskočit* (*Just a Little Leap*) was published in 1966. She was banned during the post-1968 Soviet occupation of Czechoslovakia, and in 1981 was arrested for sedition and held in custody for a year. She became an active politician during November 1989. Her comic novel, *Pozůstalost pana Ábela* (*Mr Abel's Legacy*) (whole 1971 printing pulped, published abroad in 1977), is a clumsy satire on wheeling and dealing, and suffers from unconvincing optimism. *Černá hvĕzda* (1981) (*Black Star*) is the fictional autobiography of a communist journalist who, though no hard-liner, manages to keep his head above water because he has the patronage of the Communist Party leader. The journalist's intellectual frustration is expressed by his difficulties with women. The novel is important for its over-long evocation of the atmosphere surrounding the show trials of the 1950s, and for its statements on the Czech character.

Kantûrková is best known for her slightly condescending account of her 1981 imprisonment, *Přítelkynĕ z domu smutku* (1987) (*Friends from the House of Sadness*, 1984), which is narrated in readable, 'housewifely' Czech. She glosses over her interrogations, and concentrates on characterizing the various types of criminal women she meets (she is particularly interested in the gyspy, Majka) and on the types of human amorality and immorality her cellmates display.

Karelli, Zoe (born 1901)

Greek poet, dramatist, essayist and short story writer. She was born Chryssoula Argyriadou in Thessaloniki, where she studied foreign languages and music. A weak child, she was first educated at home. Inspired by a love for the ancient world, she learned ancient Greek. She also became fluent in English, French and Italian. She was forty before she published her first collection of poems; fear of criticism had deterred her from publishing it before. Karelli writes in a highly individual style, surrealistic and metaphysical. Her language, which mixes Byzantine hymnology with modern demotic Greek, expresses the dislocation and anxiety of her time, searching for meaning within a world of declining values. But Karelli believes in the freedom and self-determination of the person. Her characters live isolated within their own bodies, which through the twin demands of flesh and spirit become sources of doubt about what exists around them. Yet through this same double constitution of the body they locate a pulse of spiritual life; searching deep within themselves they are able finally to transcend themselves. In 1935 Karelli published her first short story, *Moods*, and in 1940 her first collection of poetry, *Pathway*. She has published other collections of poetry as well as a number of plays and essays. She has been twice awarded the national poetry award. She is a member of the Greek National Academy.

Karodia, Farida (born ?1942)

South African novelist and short story writer who emigrated to Canada in 1969. Her first novel, *Daughters of the Twilight* (1986), evokes small-town life as lived by a South African Indian community forced out of their homes by apartheid legislation. The novel traces the gradual destruction of one family's livelihood, as seen through the eyes of the younger daughter, giving an account of the subtle tensions within the family under the brutal impact of external forces. Her collection *Coming Home and Other Stories* (1988) explores a wide variety of South African themes and settings: life on a Boland wine farm (the novella *Coming Home*), a township necklace-murder ('The Necklace'), and

the materialist obsessions and inhumanity of a
member of the white Zimbabwean elite ('The
World According to Mrs Angela Ramsbotham').
The stories delineate the alienation and
dislocation in the personal relationships and
individual life-histories of South Africans living in
a fractured society. Karodia has also had several
radio dramas broadcast in Canada.

Karr i Alfonsetti, Carme (1865–1943)
Spanish fiction writer. Based in Barcelona, Karr
was active in the *Modernisme* movement. She
published two collections of brief fiction: *Bolves,
quadrets* (1906), and *Clixíes, estudis en prosa* (1906)
(*Snapshots: Studies in Prose*), which portrays
women as being trapped by their circumstances.
She also published a short novel, *La vida d'en Joan
Franch* (1912) (*The Life of John Franch*), *Cuentos a
mis nietos* (1932) (*Stories for my Grandchildren*), and
El libro de Puli (1958) (*Pauline's Book*) – cautionary
tales for children.

Karsch, Anna Louisa (1722–1791)
German poet. She was born in Silesia, the
daughter of an innkeeper who died when she was
six. For four years she lived with an uncle, who
taught her to read and write, whereupon she was
returned to her mother, who had remarried. At
sixteen she married a weaver, who abused her
abysmally and then divorced her while she was
pregnant with their third child. To avoid
destitution she married a tailor named Karsch,
who was an alcoholic. She tried to alleviate their
utter poverty by earning a little money writing
poems for patriotic and family occasions. The
beauty of her poetry, and her exceptional talent
for improvisation, soon became well-known in the
region, and attracted the attention of literary
figures such as Lessing Gotthold (1729–1781),
Moses Mendelssohn (1729–1786), Herder (1744–
1803), and later even Goethe (1749–1832).
Famed as 'Sappho Resurrected' (▷Sappho), she
began to find sponsors, and was even granted an
audience by Friedrich II of Prussia (1712–1786)
The poet Gleim (1719–1803) arranged for the
publication of her poems in 1764. When her
passionate love for Gleim was rejected, she
established herself in Berlin, and became the first
woman writer in Germany who could support
herself and her children by her writings.
   Her works include: *Auserlesene Gedichte* (1764)
(*Selected Poems*); *Einige Oden über verschiedene hohe
Gegenstände* (1764) (*Some Odes on Various Elevated
Subjects*); *Poetische Einfälle, Erste Sammlung* (1764)
(*Poetical Ideas, First Collection*); *Kleinigkeite* (1765)
(*Little Nothings*), and *Neue Gedichte* (1772) (*New
Poems*).
   ▷Chézy, Helmina von

Kaschnitz, Marie Luise (1901–1974)
German novelist, short story writer and poet. A
prolific writer, she made a name for herself in the
1930s with psychological novels, such as *Liebe
beginnt* (1933) (*Love Begins*) and *Elissa* (1937).
After the war she broached the subject of

Marie Luise Kaschnitz

Germany's recent history with the poems
Totentanz und Gedichte zur Zeit (1947) (*Dance of
Death and Poems for Our Time*), which evoked the
devastated city of Frankfurt in traditional,
grandiloquent and elegiac verse. As her distress
about the fascist past combined with
disillusionment about the development of post-
war Germany, Kaschnitz's poetry was increasingly
characterized by a fragmentation of form and
syntax. '*Zoon Politikon*' ('Political Zone'), written at
the time of the Auschwitz trials, and which
coincided with her husband's death in 1962,
poignantly combines, in abrupt laconic lines,
private mourning and public distress about the
past. These themes remain dominant in all her
poetry, through to the last collection, *Kein
Zauberspruch* (1972) (*No Magic Formula*). She also
wrote radio plays and short stories, many of which
have a haunting quality, created by a subtle shift
towards the unreal and the enigmatic.

Kassam, Jeanette Leboeuf
Kenyan poet and artist working in Nairobi.
Bib: Calder, A., Mapanje, J. and Pieterse, C.
(eds), *Summer Fires: New Poetry of Africa*.

Kassandra. Vier Vorlesungen. Eine Erzählung
(1982) ▷*Cassandra. A Novel and Four Essays*
(1984)

Katharina von Gebweiler (died c 1340)
German nun and chronicler. She was a member
of the Dominican Convent of Unterlinden, near
Colmar in Alsace. Her *Vitae sororum* (*The Lives of
the Sisters*), written in sophisticated Latin, traces
the spiritual lives of a number of nuns in her
convent. It is one of the first examples of what was
to become a common genre in the Dominican

convents of southern Germany in the 14th century.
▷*Visionsliteratur*

Katherine of Sutton (died 1376)

English religious dramatist. Katherine was abbess of ▷Barking Abbey from 1363 to 1376. Her plays are the earliest known to have been written by a woman in England. They are in Latin, and are closely based on the Easter liturgy, and were designed to arouse the devotion of worshippers during the Easter festival. They are original and inventive in their staging. Their use of nuns, at times, rather than always male clerics, appears not to have been the practice in England, although it was sometimes found on the continent.
▷Hildegarde of Bingen
Bib: Cotton, Nancy, *Women Playwrights in England, c 1363–1750.*

Kaus, Gina (1894–1985)

Austrian dramatist, novelist and biographer. She had a first success in 1917 with the comedy *Diebe im Haus* (*Thieves in the House*) which was performed in the prestigious Vienna Burgtheater. With this introduction into Viennese literary circles, she came to know writers such as Franz Werfel (1890–1945), Hermann Broch (1886–1951), Robert Musil (1880–1942) and Karl Kraus (1874–1936), became a friend of the ▷psychoanalyst Alfred Adler (1870–1937), and in 1920 married the writer Otto Kaus, though they were divorced in 1926. She ran an advisory service and a journal for women, wrote numerous stories, and had a second major success with her novel, *Die Überfahrt* (1932) (*The Crossing*) which, like most of her subsequent novels, was immediately translated into English and made into a film. Her biography of ▷Catherine the Great, *Katharine die Große* (1935), remained a bestseller for several years. Under Hitler her books were banned, and she emigrated first to Switzerland and then to France, and after the war went to settle in Hollywood, USA. There she met up with other exiled German and Austrian writers, such as Bertold Brecht (1898–1956) and ▷Vicki Baum.

Kautsky, Minna (1837–1912)

Austrian novelist. An actress who was married to a theatre painter, and a mother of three, she started to read widely when her health began to fail in her thirties. She became interested in the ideas of Karl Marx (1818–1883) and Friedrich Engels (1820–1895) and in women's rights, and began to publish stories which aimed to educate working-class readers. Her novels, of which *Stefan vom Grillenhof* (1879) (*Stefan from Grillenhof Farm*), *Victoria* (1889), *Helene* (1894) and *Im Vaterhause* (1904) (*In Father's House*) are the best, are about contemporary working-class heroes and heroines whose awakening to socialist ideas transforms them in every way. Her stories were often serialized in progressive papers and political journals, and she became widely known as 'Red

Marlitt' (a left-wing incarnation of the novelist ▷Eugenie Marlitt).

Kavanagh, Julia (1824–1877)

Anglo-Irish novelist, historian and biographer. She was born in Thurles, Ireland, but lived most of her life in France and settled in London in 1844. France provided the inspiration for many of Kavanagh's novels, including *Madeleine* (1848) and *Nathalie* (1850), which has been seen as an influence on ▷Charlotte Brontë's ▷*Villette*. She was a popular writer as well as a good biographer and historian, and much of her work focuses on women. Her non-fiction includes *Woman in France in the 18th Century* (1850); *Women of Christianity* (1852); *French Women of Letters* (1862) and *English Women of Letters* (1863). Other novels include *Rachel Grey* (1856); *Beatrice* (1865); *Dora* (1868); *Silvia* (1870) and *Bessie* (1872). Her last work was *Forget-me-nots* (1878), published a year after her death.
Bib: Colby, R., *Fiction with a Purpose*; Foster, S., *Victorian Women's Fiction: Marriage, Freedom and the Individual.*

Kay, Jackie (born 1961)

Scottish poet and dramatist. In 'So you think I'm a mule?' Kay writes about the racism which cannot encompass her as black, Scottish and from Glasgow. She writes politically engaged poetry that deals with the inter-relationship of race, sexuality and gender in British society. 'Remi', for example, explores the literal violence and 'image-murder' of racism, in order to build up a position of resistance. 'And I still cannot believe it' and 'Tulips' celebrate black lesbian sexuality. Kay comments that 'Writing is very important to me because it helps me to define what I want to change and why.' Her poems first appeared in *Artrage* and *Feminist Review*, and then in *A Dangerous Knowing: Four Black Women Poets* (1983) from the ▷feminist publishers Sheba. Her short stories have been published in *Everyday Matters 2* (1984) and *Stepping Out* (1986). In 1986 the Theatre of Black Women performed her first play, *Chiaroscuro*, which has since been published in *Lesbian Plays*, edited by Jill Davis (1987). Her most recent published work is a poem sequence, *The Adoption Papers* (1991), which uses multiple points of view to explore the story of the adoption of a black child by white parents.

Kaye-Smith, Sheila (1887–1956)

English regional novelist and poet, born in Sussex, where she lived most of her life, farming and writing. She converted to Catholicism in 1929. Her first publication was *The Tramping Methodist* (1908). Her many novels include *Starbrace* (1909), *Sussex Gorse* (1916) which, like ▷Mary Webb's ▷*Precious Bane* (1924), tells the story of a farmer whose ambition destroys his family, and *The History of Susan Spray the Female Preacher* (1931). Her best-known novel, *Joanna Godden* (1922), tells the story of a woman who inherits and runs a farm, but leaves it rather than marry a man she does not love, the father of her child. Kaye-Smith also wrote three volumes of autobiography: *Three Ways Home* (1937), *Kitchen Fugue* (1945) and *All the Books of My Life* (1956). Her brand of fiction – rural and at times melodramatic – was parodied by ▷Stella Gibbons in ▷*Cold Comfort Farm* (1932).

▷Stern, Gladys Bertha

Kazantzaki, Galateia (1886–1962)

Greek novelist and poet. She was the older sister of ▷Elli Alexiou. Born in Crete into a cultured and progressive family whose rich library drew her towards literature, she first published in local magazines under various pseudonyms, writing poems inspired by religion and mysticism. In Crete she met the writer Nikos Kazantzakis, with whom she went to Athens, where they lived together for a time before getting married. Her first book, *Ridi Pagliacco* (1909), takes the form of a diary written by an intellectual woman in love. Starting as a story about personal weakness and intense sensuality, the book progresses to the plane of social criticism. In 1922 she published *Sonetta*, a collection of poems. The eroticism of her poems is not a personal expression but seems to come out of social conditions she detests. Her long poem *The Sinful One* (1931) is a portrait of a prostitute in a decadent society.

Her short stories are contained in three volumes: *11 a.m. till 1 p.m.* (1929), *Men* (1934) and *Crucial Moments* (1933). The first describes life in government ministries when they are open to the public; the second tells stories of men who cannot cope with women's modern demands; the third relates stories of women coping with difficult domestic circumstances. After divorcing Kazantzakis she married Marko Avgeri, a famous Greek critic and poet, with whom she lived a very happy and fulfilled life. In her mainly autobiographical *Men and Supermen* (1957) Kazantzaki writes with great subjective intensity about her first husband, with whom she disagreed ideologically.

Kazantzis, Judith (born 1940)

English poet, short-story writer and feminist. A self-described anti-establishment figure, Kazantzis is a member of the Women's Literature Collective, and regularly reviews women's poetry for the feminist journal *Spare Rib*. Her poetry characteristically explores traditional/canonical representations of femininity in poetry, myths and fairytales, and is concerned to rewrite narratives of women's creativity. *Touch Papers* (1982) was written together with ▷Michèle Roberts and ▷Michelene Wandor. Other volumes include: *Minefield* (1977), *Let's Pretend* (1984), *A Poem for Guatamala* (1986) and *Flame Tree* (1988).

▷*One Foot on the Mountain*; canon

Kazir, Yehudit (born 1963)

Israeli short story writer. Kazir studied at Tel-Aviv University, where she now teaches creative writing. She is also a reader for one of Israel's main publishing houses. A striking feature of her short stories is the authentic use of local Tel-Aviv vocabulary, through which she portrays a contemporary social context. Her characters, women, are ordinary individuals who are forced out of their inertia by experiences such as loss or disappointment in love. Her novel *Sogrim Et Ha'Yam* (*Closing the Sea*) was published in 1990.

Keane, Molly (born 1904)

Molly Keane

Irish novelist, born in County Kildare, into an Ascendancy (Anglo-Irish aristocratic) family. Between 1928 and 1956 she wrote several successful plays and eleven novels using the pseudonym M. J. Farrell. The best-known of her novels of this period was *Devoted Ladies* (1934). Following a scalding review of her last play, and her husband's sudden death (leaving her to raise a young family), she gave up writing altogether for twenty years. She made a sensational comeback in 1981 with *Good Behaviour*, a much-praised black comedy of Anglo-Irish life in the 1920s, followed in 1983 by *Time After Time*.

▷'Big House, The'

Keepers of the House, The (1964)

US novel. In ▷Shirley Ann Grau's Pulitzer Prize-winning book an Anglo-American woman is victimized by her town's racism; Abigail Tolliver's father, a wealthy, Southern landowner, had secretly married an African-American woman. When this marriage is revealed, Abigail's husband abandons her. Using her economic power, Abigail emerges victorious against the townspeople's violent attacks. Grau revises notions of ▷Southern history in presenting a legitimate inter-racial marriage. She also shows how the South's legacy can empower its daughters to fight racism.

Keeshing-Tobias, Lenore

Ojibway poet from Cape Croker Reserve in Ontario, she is an active spokeswoman on behalf f Native Canadian writers. She graduated from ork University with a Bachelor of Fine Arts egree, and has been an editor for *The Magazine ʾ Re-Establish the Trickster*. Her work is concerned ʾith orality and the Native Canadian tradition, nd she speaks strongly against appropriation. She as written and recorded many stories for hildren. Her most recent books are *All My ʾelations: Sharing Native Values Through the Arts ꞁ988)* and *Word Magic* (1990).

ꞁeesing, Nancy (born 1923)
ꞁustralian poet, freelance writer and editor. ꞁeesing has published two volumes of poetry, two hildren's books, a number of critical, iographical and non-fiction works, including *ꞁouglas Stewart* (1965) and *Australian Post-War ꞁovelists* (1975), and has edited a number of olumes, including *Australian Bush Ballads* (1955, ʾith Douglas Stewart).

ꞁefala, Antigone (born 1935)
ꞁustralian poet and novelist. Kefala was born in ꞁomania of Greek parents, and has lived in ꞁomania, Greece, New Zealand and Australia. ꞁer poetry and stories have appeared in a number ʾf magazines and collections. She has taught ꞁnglish and been a member of the Literature ꞁoard of the Australia Council. Kefala has ublished two volumes of poetry, *The Alien (1973)* nd *Thirsty Weather (1978)*, and three of fiction, ʾhe First Journey* (1975), *The Island* (1984) and ꞁlexia* (1984). She has also translated John ꞁoutsoleras's *Men for the Rights of Men, Rise ꞁ974)*.

▷Migrant women's writing (Australia); *Coming ʾut from Under; Penguin Anthology of Australian ꞁomen's Writing, The; Poetry and Gender*

ꞁelley, Edith Summers (1884–1956)
ꞁS novelist. Born in Toronto, Canada, Kelley ꞁraduated with honours from the University of ʾoronto in 1903. After moving to New York, she ꞁed at Helicon Hall, an experimental, co-perative community. She actively promoted ꞁminism and socialism. She unsuccessfully tried ꞁrming in Kentucky and California with her ꞁecond husband. ▷*Weeds* (1923) and *The Devil's ꞁand* (1974) emphasize the physical hardships nd economic uncertainties of farming. Kelley hows how they sap women's vitality. Kelley's own ʾriting career was constrained by financial ꞁressures and domestic responsibilities.

ꞁello, Esther ▷Inglis (Kello), Esther

ꞁellow, Kathleen ▷Plaidy, Jean

ꞁelly, Gwen (born 1922)
ꞁustralian short story writer, poet and novelist. ꞁelly has worked as a teacher, academic and ʾriter. Her published work has appeared in ꞁagazines and journals since the mid-1950s and ʾhe has won the Henry Lawson Prose Award four ꞁmes and the Hilarie Lindsay Award 1981 from

the Society of Woman Writers. Kelly's fiction includes *There is No Refuge* (1961), *The Red Boat* (1968), *The Middle-Aged Maidens* (1976) and *Always Afternoon* (1981) and her poetry has been published in *Fossils and Stray Cats* (1980). *The Happy People* (1988) is a collection of her short stories.

Kelly, Maeve (born 1930)
Irish poet, short story writer and novelist. Born in Dundalk, Maeve Kelly qualified as a nurse, and worked in England for some time. She now lives in Limerick, and was for many years administrator of Adapt, the Limerick Centre for Abused Women, of which she was co-founder. She has published a collection of short stories, *A Life of Her Own* (1976), a poetry collection, *Resolution* (1986), and two novels: *Necessary Treasons* (1985) and *Florrie's, Girls* (1989). Her fiction is a perceptive and shrewd record of the subtle shifts and changes in contemporary Irish women's lives.

Kelly, Rita (born 1953)

Rita Kelly

Irish writer, born in Galway. She has been writing fiction, poetry, criticism and drama in both Irish and English for many years. Her first collection of short stories, *The Whispering Arch and Other Stories*, appeared in 1986. Her poetry collections are: *Dialann sa Diseart* (1981) (*Desert Diary*), which she wrote with her husband, Eoghan O Tuairisc, *An Bealach Éaodóigh* (*The Way of Despair*) (1984) and *Fare Well/Beir Beannacht*, a bilingual collection (1990).

Kemble, Frances (Fanny) (1809–1893)
English actress, poet and autobiographer, born in London. She was the niece of actress Sarah Siddons and the daughter of actor-manager Charles Kemble. In 1832 she left Britain to tour North America with her father, recording her experience in her *Journal* (1835). She married Pierce Mease Butler in 1834, but the relationship became problematic when Fanny realized that her

husband was a slave-owner. She was horrified by a visit she made to his Georgia plantation in 1838, and became increasingly estranged from him. Eventually they separated in 1845 and were divorced in 1849. In 1863 she published *Journal of a Residence on a Georgia Plantation*, in which she attacks ▷slavery, describes the living and working conditions of the people and decries her own unwitting involvement in the system. For the rest of her life, she travelled between Europe and North America, writing and giving public readings. Her works include *Poems* (1844); *Records of a Girlhood* (1878); *Records of Later Life* (1882), and *The Adventures of Mr John Timothy Homespun in Switzerland* (1889).
Bib: Driver, L.S., *Life*; Marshall, D., *Life*.

Kemp, Jan (born 1949)

New Zealand poet. Jan Kemp began publishing poetry during the 1970s, when she was one of a number of New Zealand poets seen to take a new direction, affected by the poetry coming from the USA. Kemp has taught English as a second language in a number of Asian and Pacific countries in the 1980s and 1990s, an itinerancy which is reflected in her work. With poems like 'A New World: Homage to Wallace Stevens' Kemp's work continues an association with North American writing but focuses more generally on personal experience.

Publications: *Against the Softness of Woman* (1976); *Diamonds and Gravel* (1979): ▷*Ice breaker Poems* (1980); *Five Poems* (1988).

Kempe, Margery (c 1373–after 1439)

English composer of spiritual autobiography in English. Margery was born into a prosperous merchant family in Lynn, Norfolk, and married at about twenty. She first dictated the *Book of Margery Kempe* some twenty years after her first religious experience. It opens with an account of the emotional and spiritual crisis lasting several months which followed the birth of the first of her fourteen children, and from which she was restored by a vision of Christ. It goes on to describe the temptations and adversities she encountered in the course of her life. She wished to live austerely, in contrast to her previous ostentation and indulgence. She persuaded her husband (eventually) to relinquish sexual relations with her. She was accused more than once of heresy, but was always able to defend herself when questioned. Margery's devotion, particularly to Christ's passion, was characterized by 'plentiful tears and many loud and violent sobbings', which brought her the opprobrium of many around her, at home and abroad: she was abandoned by her fellow pilgrims on pilgrimage to the Holy Land. However, many (including ▷Julian of Norwich) recognized holiness in her. Although unlettered, Margery had a retentive memory, and was familiar with the Bible and works of medieval spirituality. She had less in common, temperamentally, with English medieval piety, than with the continental women mystics of the 13th and 14th centuries,

such as St Bridget of Sweden (▷Birgitta av Vadstena), whom she mentions, and Dorothea of Prussia.
Bib: Windeatt, B.A. (trans.), *The Book of Margery Kempe*; Petroff, E.A., *Medieval Women's Visionary Literature*.

Kennedy, Adrienne (born 1931)

US dramatist. Kennedy grew up in an ethnically integrated neighbourhood in Cleveland, Ohio. She encountered profound racial hostility while attending the Ohio State University and became indifferent to her studies. Writing was an outlet for the psychological confusion she experienced. Most of her ▷avant-garde plays, like ▷*Funnyhouse of a Negro* (1962) and *The Owl Answers* (1963), dramatize an African-American woman's search for an identity. Her characters struggle with internalized social and cultural forces.

Kennedy portrays the imprisonment and powerlessness of African-American women through images from the subconscious, and she uses historical and symbolic figures as characters to portray her characters' psychoses. Kennedy dramatizes the repressed fears, anger and desires hidden beneath the pretences of racial harmony. She won an Obie Distinguished Play Award for *Funnyhouse of a Negro*.

Other works include: *A Lesson in a Dead Language* (1964), *A Rat's Mass* (1965), *A Beast's Story* (1966), *A Movie Star Has to Star in Black and White* (1976) and *People Who Led to My Plays* (1987).

Kennedy, Anne (born 1959)

New Zealand novelist. Anne Kennedy began publishing stories and winning awards for them in the 1980s. She is a formally innovative writer, using discontinuous narrative to suggest connections and associations which are often implicitly feminist. *100 Traditional Smiles* (1988) i a multidirectional broken narrative based on the activity and imagery of knitting.

Kennedy, Margaret (1896–1967)

English novelist and dramatist. Kennedy's first novel, *The Ladies of Lyndon* (1923), introduces her preoccupation with the resistance of social expectations and conventions. This is often treated through characters who opt for a Bohemian lifestyle over the creative impotence and philistinism that surrounds them, as in *The Game and the Candle* (1926) and *The Oracles* (1955). Her interest in the complexity and difficulties of family relations informs both ▷*The Constant Nymph* (1924) and *Together and Apart* (1936), which focuses on the child at the centre o divorce proceedings.

Kennett, Margaret Brett (fl 1723–1725)

British/American travel writer. The daughter of a well-to-do English clergyman, she combined piety with a strong determination to fulfil her desire for adventure and travel. In 1719 she married a Mr

Kennett; together they planned a journey to the plantations of South Carolina. Leaving England approximately four years after her marriage, she and her husband settled in Charles Town. Directing her correspondence to her mother, she captured both the excitement and factionalism of the port town as well as the personal endeavours of her husband and herself to establish a business in the area. Although her stay in North America probably lasted no more than two years, her astute observations in ▷*An Account of Charles Town in 1725* constitute a significant contribution not only to our understanding of that region in the pre-revolutionary years but also to the art of New World 'propaganda' literature from early settlers.

Kerslake, Susan (born 19?)

Canadian fiction writer who emigrated to Halifax, Nova Scotia from the United States in 1966. Her first novel, *Middlewatch* (1976), apprehends the terrifying disjunction between silence and language, developed even further in her densely textured language novel about a remote island asylum, *Penumbra* (1984). The short story collections *The Book of Fears* (1984) and *Blind Date* (1989) develop the stark poetic vision of characters again and again stricken by silence.
Bib. Kulyk Keefer, J., in *Under Eastern Eyes*.

Keulen, Mensje van (born 1946)

Dutch prose writer and poet. Full name: Mensje Francina van Keulen-van der Steen; ▷pseudonym: Josien Meloen. She went to Britain in 1965, attending painting classes in London, returning to Amsterdam in 1966, where she worked as an artist for numerous magazines. Her first novel, *Bleekers zomer* (1972) (*Bleeker Is Summer*), was well-received. A collection of stories, *Allemaal tranen* (*Only Tears*), appeared in the same year, followed by the novel *Van lieverlede* (*Little by Little*) in 1975. Van Keulen's work is narrative in style, and usually sober; it stands in the tradition of pessimism. *Van lieverlede*, especially, is a very melancholic book. Van Keulen gives a minute description of a world of vulnerable individuals dominated by physical and spiritual decay. The reader is presented with the inescapable suggestion that life is a continuing condition of doom. Her third novel, *Overspel* (1982) (*Adultery*), about fidelity and infidelity, contains more action than her previous work. Her fourth novel appeared in 1987 (*Engelbert*). Her most recent collection of stories (*De lach van Schreck*, 1991 (*The Laugh of Schreck*) tells about war and gruesome deeds (its epigraph is: 'Death's a good fellow and keeps open house', Poe). 1977 saw *Lotgevallen* (*Vicissitudes*), eleven ballads about the grief and suffering of people and animals, while in 1980 a sample of burlesque, narrative poetry appeared, entitled *De avonturen van Anna Molino* (*The Adventures of Anna Molino*).

Keun, Irmgard (1905–1982)

German novelist. She had a sensational popular success with her first two novels: *Gilgi – eine von uns* (1931) (*Gilgi – One of Us*) and *Das kunstseidene Mädchen* (1932) (▷*The Artificial Silk Girl*). Both books are about the fortunes of *petit-bourgeois* heroines who, during the Depression of the 1930s, try to become successful, independent women. Told with wit, authenticity of speech and a sharp eye for milieu, the novels expose the moral hypocrisy and exploitive materialism of the urban *petite-bourgeoisie*. Her books were banned as immoral by the Nazis, and Keun went into exile in 1936. Largely forgotten after the war, her work has enjoyed a revival as a result of the surge of interest in women's literature in the 1970s and 1980s.

Key, Ellen (1849–1926)

Swedish prose writer and intellectual. Key was born at the manor house in Sundsholm. Her father owned the estate, and was a politician. In 1868 the family moved to Stockholm, and Ellen was educated as a teacher. She taught until 1900, and from that time on she wrote and lectured in Sweden and abroad. In 1910 she returned to Sweden and built the manor of Strand, where she lived until her death.

In her writings Key idealized woman as mother. She thought that women should stay in the home with their children, and that women without children should involve themselves politically as mothers of society, fighting for peace. She saw woman, earth and peace as a trinity. Her principal works are about the psychology of women and the life of children, for example, *Barnets århundrade* (1900) (*The Century of the Child*). She developed an anti-authoritarian method of teaching which has had a very great impact on Scandinavian pedagogy.

Her *Lifslinjer I–III* (1903–1906) (*Life-Lines*), which describes a philosophy of morals, tells of a woman with a vivid intellectual life and a strong personality.

Key was a religiously-inclined evolutionist who was close to mysticism in her concept of motherhood. Her primary laws were duty, self-discipline, fidelity and beauty – in hearts and homes, but especially in and through women and mothers.

Ke Yan (born 1929)

Chinese poet and writer. Ke Yan is the author of many works for children, of which the plays *Taking Off from Earth* and *The Crystal Cave* were successfully staged in the 1950s. Ke Yan gained national acclaim for her poem 'Where are you, Premier Zhou?' (1976) which expressed the collective sorrow of the Chinese people for the loss of their beloved premier, and which was also read as a veiled protest against the current political situation. *Retrieval of Time Lost*, her novel about adolescent delinquency, was successfully adapted for television.

Keynotes and *Discords* (1893 and 1894)

Two volumes of short stories by British writer ▷George Egerton which explore female oppression as well as celebrating women's potential. Notable stories in *Keynotes* include 'Now Spring Has Come', which deals with the transitory nature of romance, 'The Spell of the White Elf' and 'A Cross Line'. The *Discords* collection is graver and darker, focusing on women's anger and describing the effects of women's emotional and economic dependence on men. In 'Gone Under' a woman's lover arranges to have their illegitimate child murdered by the midwife, in 'Wedlock' a women murders her three stepchildren because her husband has separated her from her own child. 'Virgin Soil' describes the lasting damage caused to a young girl by her lack of sex education. Egerton's writing is characterized by a use of symbolism influenced by Ibsen and Strindberg.

▷'New Woman, The'

Keys to Happiness, The (1908–1913)

Six-volume novel by Russian writer ▷Anastasiia Verbítskaia. The first two volumes were intended as a finished work ending with the heroine's suicide, but after they became immediate bestsellers, Verbítskaia resurrected her protagonist in four sequel volumes which are much diminished in quality.

Like most of Verbítskaia's work, *Keys* combines popular entertainment with a serious attempt to embody ideas in fiction. Her model to some extent is Chernyshevskii's ▷*What Is To Be Done?*. The ascetic hero of that novel is here transformed into Jan, who, along with an earlier female mentor, sets the heroine-artist, Mania, on the road to liberation. Jan's ideology is a hodgepodge of socialism and a popularized form of Nietzsche's ideas, that involves rejection of self-denial and obligations to family or society; he encourages Mania to follow her 'passions and dreams' wherever they may lead her.

The setting of the first two volumes contrasts dark, cold Moscow, where Mania is born, and sunny, warm Ukraine, where romance is born. Mania is given a history that includes a mad mother and a pair of miserable, self-sacrificing older siblings. Sexual passion, always an enslaving urge in Verbítskaia's work, draws Mania to the far-right antithesis of Jan, Nelidov, with whom she commits suicide. Although Verbítskaia also 'killed off' her artist-heroine in her first story, ▷*Discord*, *Keys* is the more pessimistic, because the heroine of *Discord* dies feeling that she has left a testament for future generations of liberated women. Some of the best scenes consist of arguments about the burning issues of the day, grounded in the characters' personal psychology and situation. The novel also embodies the issue of anti-Semitism in the 'good' Jew Shteinbakh.

▷Bashkirtseff, Marie
Bib: Brooks, J., *When Russia Learned to Read: Literacy and Popular Literature, 1861–1917*; Clowes, E.W., *The Revolution of Moral Consciousness: Nietzsche in Russian Literature, 1890–1914*.

Khadiga and Sawsan ▷'Ashur, Radwa

Khalifa, Sahar (born 1941)

Palestinian novelist born in Nablus, where she still lives. Her work depicts the life of Palestinians in Jerusalem and the West Bank. The life of poor people in cities and on farms, which becomes progressively more deprived and oppressed, runs parallel to the discussions, misgivings and prison experiences of the politicized intellectuals. Sahar Khalifa has no illusions about the male chauvinism of many freedom fighters and colleagues engaged in the national or class war. Her first novel, *Lasna Jawari Lakum* (1974) (*We Are Not Your Concubines*), records the feminist revolt of her protagonist against the traditional duel of the sexes played out in the modern setting of a great artist's studio. Her second novel, *The Cactus* (1976), marked a breakthrough in contemporary Palestinian fiction. Her characters are the Arab *sabras* (natives) dispossessed in their own homeland, but surviving as the cactus survives in the parched desert. It has been translated into French, German and English. A sequel, *Sunflowers* (1980) is a great imaginative statement on the life of the old Arab city, Nablus, under occupation. It is mainly the women who provide the day-to-day action of making a life for themselves and for their multiplying children. There are two protagonists: Rafif, the journalist, fighting for equal rights with her 'progressive' male colleagues who believe that feminist issues are a distraction at a time of national crisis, and Sa'ddiya, the working-class widow of a 'martyr', who has to brave the gossip and disapproval of the neighbours and go out to the prosperous Israeli city to get work to support her orphaned children: 'I tied up my hair and sat in mourning for months and no one gave the children anything; what could I do?' She saves money to get out of the old narrow alley, to buy a plot in the country and build a house in the sun, but it is no good. The land is listed for a new Israeli settlement and the soldiers arrive with arms and bulldozers. It is there that the two protagonists meet, the journalist on the scent of a story, and the deranged Sa'ddiya who has lost everything. A fourth novel, ▷*Memoirs of an Unrealistic Woman*, was published in ▷Beirut in 1986. It concentrates on the plight of a woman as a daughter and a wife, supposedly away from the political conflict. Her last novel ▷*Bab al-Saha*, the name of a square in the old city of Nablus, carries the story to the time of the *Intifada*.

▷*Jawari*
Bib: Le Gassick, T. and Femea E. (trans.), *Wild Thorns*.

Khamis, Zabiya (born 1958)

Gulf poet, born in Abu Zabi. Having obtained a BA in Philosophy and Political Science in the United States, she worked for the Ministry of Planning in the Emirates, contributed to periodicals at home and abroad, and published her poetry, mainly in ▷Beirut. She began by writing verse in traditional measures, then started experimenting with new forms, and is now considered an ultra-modernist. ▷'Modernism' is not favoured in the Gulf, and Zabiya had to leave – ostensibly to read for a PhD in London. She lived in London, Paris and other European cities for some time, and now lives in Cairo. She has published five collections of poetry and one of short stories.

A Step Over the Earth (1981), *I Am the Woman, the Earth and all the Ribs* (1983), *Yearnings of the 'Umani Mare* (1985), *Love Poems* (1985), *Veins of Lime and Henna* (1985) and *The Sultan Stones a Woman Pregnant with the Sea* (1988) were all published in Beirut or London. Her latest writings are termed 'prose poems' because of her experimentation with form, but it is mainly her celebration and concrete imagery of the flesh that have lined both the critics and the authorities against her. Images of an ocean seething with life and promise as well as danger, the expansive parched desert in contrast to 'cement streets' are common in her work, as well as that of other Gulf poets. Hers is a distinct voice, however, asserting the female body: pregnant, menstruating or copulating. Her poem 'A song for the flesh', published in 1986, was the only poem from the Gulf included in a sweeping attack on the dangers posed by modernity to the traditions and values of an Islamic society in a conference on 'Poetry and Tradition' in Riyadh in 1990.

Bib: Jayyusi, Salma K. (ed.), *The Literature of Modern Arabia*.

Khanim, Leyla (died ?1847/8)

Turkish poet at the close of the last purely Oriental period of Turkish poetry – before the introduction of European languages. She was born in Constantinople and was related to a famous statesman and man of letters, 'Izzat Mollah, who tutored her in literature. Leyla was married when she was quite young, but was soon separated from her husband, and 'gave herself up entirely to literature and the pursuit of pleasure.' Her *diwan* (collection of poetry) reflected her love of fun and her *ghazels* (Persian odes of 12 lines) were written in the Persian tradition of extolling love and wine, singing of nature and protesting against the envious detractors of love: 'The merry feast prepare; let them say whate'er they will. Sip the wine with yonder fair; let them say whate'er they will. Leyla, seek a nook apart, fall at yonder fairy's feet, Unto her thy troth declare, let them say whate'er they will.' She experimented with other verse forms besides the traditional *ghazel*. She daringly tried her hand at imitating famous classical poems, usually considered an exercise of great skill.

Bib: Gibb, E.J.W., *A History of Ottoman Poetry*.

Khitan

Arabic noun used equally for male circumcision and female clitoridectomy. The former, originally a Jewish practice adopted by Islam together with other customs connected with cleanliness and food intake, is encouraged and lawfully performed by members of the medical profession. Attendant trauma is reduced nowadays by the use of anaesthaetic, or by circumising the boy in his first week of life, which divests the operation of its ritualistic aspects and classifies it with vaccination as part of the medical care of a newborn baby boy. For a description of the festivities attending circumcision in the 19th century see: E. W. Lane, *Manners and Customs of Modern Egyptians* (1836).

In the case of girls, the subject is clouded by mists of ignorance and taboo on the one hand, and polemic on the other. No reliable information is set before the lay reader or the puzzled parent. The custom is certainly not Islamic; it is sometimes described as 'heathen', African or Pharaonic, but there is no study of its various forms, locales or its real effects. As it is discouraged by doctors, it was, and one would assume, still is performed by practitioners of alternative medicine, or itinerant female *ghagar* (gypsies whose trade is to circumcise and tattoo).

▷Nawal El Sa'dawi, physician and feminist writer, was one of the first women writers to speak frankly on the subject and depict the operation as part of the traumatic experience of some of her female characters. ▷Alifa Rif'at has also given prominence to it in her short stories. It will be noted that both these writers are Egyptian, and in fact, female circumcision is only practised in a very few Arab countries, namely, Egypt, Yemen and Somalia, and is unknown in the rest of the Middle East.

▷Clitoridectomy/infibulation

Khuri, Colette (born 1937)

Syrian novelist, poet, short story writer, teacher and journalist. The granddaughter of a famous statesman and man of letters, she went to school in Damascus and Beirut and graduated from the University of Damascus with a degree in French. Her first publication was a collection of verse in French: *Twenty Years* (1957), followed by *Tremors* in 1960. In the meantime, her Arabic novel *Days With Him* (1959) had exploded upon the Arabic literary scene. There were echoes from French poetry and from the poetry of ▷Nizar Qabbani in the powerful account of a young aristocratic girl's hopeless affair with a married man. On the tide of the uproar created by her first novel, she published a second, *One Night* (1950), recounting the experience of a one-night-stand on a Paris train for a repressed young Arab wife. The choice of topic suggests the influence of ▷Françoise Sagan. By 1987, when she published her first collection of Arabic verse, she had fifteen works to her name and a number of them had gone through several editions. Like many Syrian writers, she celebrates her birthplace in *Damascus My Big Home* (1969). The change that has come over Damascus is painfully noted by the writer in her 'passage-to-Europe' novel, *A Summer Passes* (1975): 'Damascus the eternal woman, living only in my dreams . . . how often I have searched and not found her in reality . . . I found a woman with scared eyes, unkempt hair and ragged clothes . . . they gave her money and love . . . she took the money and did not buy any clothes . . . she traded the love and continued to live with illusions in the ruins of an old prison.'

Khvoshchínskaia, Nadezhda Dmitrievna (1824–1889)

Russian poet, fiction writer, critic, and translator. From the 1840s to her death Khvoshchínskaia became the widely-read author of more than 100 poems (published under her own name from 1842 to the late 1850s), ten novels, and over forty shorter prose works (under the male pseudonym V. Krestovskii), literary criticism (under other male names), and translations from French and Italian. Kvoshchínskaia was the mainstay of an extended family, and most of this literary activity took place in her home in Riazan'. (Not coincidentally, much of her fiction is set in a dreary provincial city she dubs 'N.'.) She spent only her last five years in St Petersburg. Her younger sister ▷Sof'ia Khvoshchínskaia was also a talented artist and writer, and a third sister, Praskov'ia, (pseudonym: S. Zimarova) produced a volume of stories about the horrors of domestic life, *In City and Country* (1881).

Like those of any prolific author, Khvoshchínskaia's works vary in quality and interest, but she deserves more attention in Russian literary history than she has yet received. Her writings intersperse personal and civic themes. Much of her poetry is elegaic, similar in tenor to prose stories that deal pessimistically with the struggle for autonomy of Russian gentry women (▷superfluous man). ▷*Ursa Major* (1870–1871) was a widely discussed part of the debate over women's emancipation. The best of her early fiction has a strong satirical bite; examples include: 'A Few Summer Days' (1853), about a girl's flirtatious exploitation of male ideals; 'Brother Dear' (1858), in which an egotistical man takes malicious delight in ruining his family's life; and the novel ▷*In Hope of Better Days* (1860). Stories like those in the *Album* cycle of the 1870s contrast idealists who remain true to the liberal and revolutionary causes of their youth with cynics who exploit those ideals. As a literary critic, Khvoshchínskaia belonged to the prescriptive school, more interested in liberal ideas than artistic execution.

▷Society tale

Khvoshchínskaia, Sof'ia Dmitrievna (1828–1865)

Russian writer ▷Nadezhda Khvoshchínskaia's younger sister, Sof'ia, was an artist and writer who used the ▷pseudonym Iv. Vesen'ev. Both sisters drew much of their material from the provincial capital of Riazan', where they lived. Her apt 'physiological sketches' under titles like 'A Provincial's Lament' (1861), 'Earthly Joys and Joys of Our Back Street' and 'A Little about Our Customs' (1862), and 'Our Urban Life' (1864), presented a slightly pompous, idle male narrator (Vesen'ev). He observes the mores and opinions of a provincial Russian town in the years after the

emancipation of the serfs, and mourns the apathy, self-absorption, and ignorance that boded ill for Alexander II's reforms. Her story 'City Folk and Country Folk' (1863) has an independent heroine who remains an amused observer of the glib liberalism of a posturing visiting city man and the hypocritical religiosity of a spongeing female relative. Khvoshchínskaia's reminiscences of a ▷Moscow boarding school, published under the initial 'N.' in 1861, depict an artificial and restrictive existence that could only warp the girls subjected to it; the story 'Aunty's Legacy' (1858) shows the same life through the eyes of a horrified male observer. Her promising career was cut short by early death.

Kidman, Fiona (born 1940)

New Zealand novelist, poet and dramatist. Fiona Kidman grew up in Hawera, a small town represented in her bestselling novel ▷*A Breed of Women* (1979). A prolific writer, Kidman wrote 60 radio plays before publishing her first collection of poetry when she was thirty-five. Her first novel, *A Breed of Women*, which has been said to have turned the tide for women writers in New Zealand, opening the way for publishing opportunities, was described as the 'thinking woman's Mills and Boon', but established a narrative pattern common to Kidman's novels; the female character who chooses against social convention and for self-possession in one form or another. All Kidman's work has reflected the preoccupations of mainstream cultural feminism – celebration of the female, widening of choice, rejection of conventional gender expectations – and has consequently found a wide audience. Her longest novel, *The Book of Secrets* (1987), explores family and cultural origins in the form of a family saga. Kidman has also published three collections of poetry and short stories.

Publications: *Search for Sister Blue* (play) (1975); *Honey and Bitters* (poems) (1975); *On the Tightrope* (poems) (1978); *A Breed of Women* (novel) (1979); *Mandarin Summer* (novel) (1981); *Mrs Dixon and Friend* (stories) (1982); *Paddy's Puzzle* (novel) (1983); *Gone North* (non-fiction) (1984); *Going to the Chathams* (poems) (1985); *The Book of Secrets* (novel) (1987); *Unsuitable Friends* (stories) (1988); *True Stars* (novel) (1990).

Kiengsiri, Kanha ▷Surangkhanang, K.

Killigrew, Anne (c 1660–1685)

English poet and painter. She was praised for her piety, and was greatly admired by her circle of aristocratic contemporaries. She was Maid of Honour to the Duchess of York. *Poems by Mrs Anne Killigrew* (1686) were published posthumously.

▷Finch, Anne, Countess of Winchelsea

Kilpi, Eeva (born 1928)

Finnish lyric poet and prose writer. She was born at Hiitola and now lives at Esbo. Her father was a businessman. From 1949 to 1966 she was married to the writer Mikko Kilpi, and had three sons. She has studied literature and languages, and has worked as a teacher. She was director of the Finnish PEN-Club from 1970 to 1975, and has received many prizes and awards.

Kilpi's work falls into two categories: the early happy and straightforward books of childhood, eg her début, the collection of short stories *Noidaulukko* (1959) (*The Witch Lock*) and the principal work of the early years, the emigrant novel *Elämä edestakaisin* (1964) (*Life, There and Back*). For a period she wrote about despair and the destructiveness of love for women, eg the short stories in *Rokkanden ja kademan pöytä* (1967) (*The Table of Love and Death*), but since then she has written simple texts, easy to read, but not to forget, for example, *Tamara* (1972), an erotic novel about a woman and a disabled man. She has also published poems and self-portraits, including *Ihuisen ääni* (1976) (*The Voice of Man*) and *Elämän evakkona* (1983) (*The Evacuee of Life*).

Kilpi's principal character is often the woman who stands alone during or after a divorce – outside the nuclear family. Her women find their strength in the roots of their family or in nature itself.

Kimenye, Barbara (born 1940)
Ugandan novelist, short story writer and writer of children's literature. She has worked as a journalist in Uganda and Kenya and for the government of the Kabaka of Buganda. Her two collections of Ganda village tales ▷*Kalasanda* (1965) and ▷*Kalasanda Revisited* (1966) are sharply observed, often amusingly satirical vignettes of village life, describing the slow pace of social change and continuity of tradition. She has also produced a series of graded readers for East African elementary and secondary schools.

Kincaid, Jamaica (born 1949)
Caribbean novelist, short story writer and journalist, born in ▷Antigua. She was born Elaine Potter Richardson, but she assumed the name Jamaica Kincaid when she began writing. Educated at government schools in Antigua under the colonial system, she left without formal qualifications to live and study in the USA at the age of sixteen. She worked as a freelance journalist, and published her first articles for *Ingenue* magazine, later becoming a regular contributor to the *New Yorker*, where she has continued as staff writer since 1976, and where most of her early stories were first published. Her first collection of short stories, ▷*At the Bottom of the River*, contains seven stories first published in the *New Yorker*. Her first novel, ▷*Annie John*, was published in 1985. She has also written a non-fiction study of Antigua, *A Small Place* (1988). She has recently published a novel set in the USA entitled *Lucy* (1991).

There has been little critical study of her work, but see Bryant Magnum's essays in ▷*Fifty Caribbean Writers* and ▷*Caribbean Women Writers*.

Kind, Marien ▷Handel-Mazzetti, Enrica von

Kindheitsmuster (1976) ▷*Patterns of Childhood* (1984)

Kindred (1979)
US novel. In ▷Octavia Butler's science fiction story, an African-American woman must rescue her white oppressor. The heroine is snatched from her home in 1976 and she finds herself enslaved on a Southern plantation in the early 19th century where the plantation owner's white son can summon her when he is in danger. She must save him, her great-grandfather, to ensure her own family's existence. Butler shows the similarities between the power relationships of the 19th century and contemporary USA.

King Emene (1974)
A play by Nigerian dramatist ▷Zulu Sofola. Set in the Igbo-speaking part of Bendel State where the author herself comes from, it depicts the organization of traditional society and the penalties for non-observance of custom. King Emene has been warned by the elders not to perform certain rites because a crime has been committed in the palace. Unknown to him, he has only attained the kingship because of the murder of the rightful heir by his mother. He accuses the elders of plotting against him, but his intransigence leads to his being driven from the shrine and to his suicide. The message of the play is unmistakably in support of tradition.

Kingsley, Mary (1862–1900)
English ▷travel writer and ethnologist. She was born in Islington, London, the daughter of Mary Bailey and George Henry Kingsley, and niece of the novelist Charles Kingsley. She is remembered today as an explorer of West Africa, having travelled widely in that area between 1893 and 1895. She recorded her experiences in *Travels in West Africa, Congo Francaise, Corisco, and Cameroon* (1897), in which she writes of the customs and traditions of peoples such as the Ajumba, Adooma and Fan, as well as describing natural environments in great detail. Two further works, *The Story of West Africa* (1899) and *West African Studies* (1899), are respectively historical and anthropological in focus. Kingsley died of enteric fever in Cape Town in 1900, during her third trip to Africa. She was celebrated as a great ethnologist; a society was founded in her name to promote the study of African peoples and culture. **Bib:** Campbell, O., *Mary Kingsley: A Victorian in the Jungle;* Clair, C., *Mary Kingsley, African Explorer;* Stevenson, C., 'Female Anger and African Politics: The Case of Two Victorian "Lady Travellers"', *Turn-of-the-Century Women* 2,1, Summer 1985.

Kingsley, Mary (1852–1931) ▷Malet, Lucas

Kingston, Maxine Hong (born 1940)
US novelist. Kingston was born in the United States of Chinese immigrant parents, and she grew up in the Chinatown of Stockton, California.

In 1962 she graduated from the University of California at Berkeley. She married that same year. In 1967 she moved to Hawaii: halfway between the two cultures competing for her loyalties. There she taught in a high school, the Mid-Pacific Institute, and at the University of Hawaii. ▷ *The Woman Warrior: Memoirs of a Girlhood Among Ghosts* (1976) which won the National Book Critics' Circle Award for non-fiction, contains Kingston's autobiography. In it Kingston constructs an identity as an ▷Asian-American woman. *China Men* (1980), her second novel, gives the Chinese-American view of North American history through its blend of personal memory, family history, Chinese folklore and North American immigration law. In the process of charting the Chinese search for the mythic 'Golden Mountain', and the brutal realities of immigrant experience, Kingston weaves the Chinese-American into the making of modern North America. The book's challenge to singular, homogenous models of both narrative and history is fundamental to its refutation of sexist and racist stereotypes.

Other work includes: *Tripmaster Monkey: His Fake Book* (1989).

Kinkel, Johanna (1810–1858)

German writer. As a pianist and composer she moved in the progressive circles of Berlin and Bonn, and knew ▷Bettina von Arnim and ▷Malwida von Meysenbug. After the Revolution of 1848, she and her husband went into exile in England. She wrote beautifully-crafted stories on musical themes, and a novel, *Hans Ibeles* (1860), about life in exile.

Kinnan, Mary (1763–1848)

North American autobiographer. Little is known of her life in Virginia before her captivity. As ▷*A True Narrative of the Sufferings of Mary Kinnan* reveals, she was captured by the Shawnees in 1791 and held against her will for more than three years. One of the last accounts of captivity in this genre, her autobiography comes at a time when many women were questioning their social roles, and her life was a record of one woman's capabilities for survival and ultimately for control over her own life. She died on 12 March 1848 in New Jersey, where she had settled after being freed.

▷Captivity narratives

Kirkham's Find (1897)

Australian novel by ▷Mary Gaunt. The independent heroine, Phoebe Marsden, refuses to marry for money and becomes financially independent as a bee-keeper. The background includes prospecting in the Northern Territory and clashes with the Aborigines. This is more than just a romance; it is a strong statement of a woman's right to value herself and find her own place in society. Phoebe is the 'find' of the title, in contrast to the gold which men seek. The novel

was republished in 1988, with an introduction by ▷Kylie Tennant.

Kirkland, Caroline Matilda Stansbury (1801–1864)

US non-fiction and fiction writer. While Kirkland had a diverse career, she is notable for her writing on life on the western US frontier. Her ▷*A New Home – Who'll Follow?* (1839), published under the protective pseudonym Mrs Mary Clavers, attracted critical and popular attention for its realistic portrayal of women's trials and its humorous characterization of people and customs. The community depicted was unappreciative of Clavers's judgements about its lack of culture and amenities. Her later publications – including *Forest Life* (1842) and *Western Clearings* (1845) – are less fresh and humorous.

Kirpíshchikova, Anna Aleksandrovna (1848–1927)

Russian fiction writer. Kirpíshchikova's works concentrate on the Ural region where she spent her entire life. She was the daughter of a serf-clerk at a factory in Perm province, and married a teacher at the same establishment. The implicit social critique of her lively chronicles was in tune with the reformist spirit of Russian realism; under initials and her maiden name (Vydarina) they appeared in leftist ▷'thick journals' from the mid-1860s. 'Petrushka Rudometov: Sketches from Life at the Mines' (1878) is typical in tracing the fate of a single individual within his harsh milieu. Three short works, 'The Past' (1876), 'Not Long Ago' (1877) and 'Twenty Years Ago' (1889) form an autobiographically-based trilogy.

Kirsch, Sarah (born 1935)

German poet and short story writer. Brought up in East Germany, her early collections of poems, such as *Laundaufenthalt* (1967) (*A Stay in the Country*), *Zaubersprüche* (1973) (*Magic Spells*) and *Rückenwind* (1976) (*With the Wind Behind*), are often terse displays of private and public pain, anger and disillusionment. She emigrated to the West in 1977, when her poetry entered a new phase with *La Pagerie* (1980). In this collection of luminous prose poems she relates an idyllic stay in Provence. Her stories *Blitz aus heiterem Himmel* (1980) (*Thunderbolt out of the Blue*) and *Allerlei-Rauh* (1988) (*Many-pelts*) examine the divisiveness of political and gender differences. Her most recent poetry, *Erdreich* (1982) (*Earth Kingdom*) and *Katzenleben* (1985) (*Cat's Life*), displays a new, more contemplative involvement with people, animals and nature.

Kitchen Table: Women of Color Press

US publisher. This independent press was co-founded by ▷Cherrié Moraga in 1981 and it is the only US press run by and for women of color. Kitchen Table produces works of artistic quality that can contribute to the liberation of women of color and it publishes such anthologies as ▷*This Bridge Called My Back: Writings by Radical Women of Color* (1981), *Cuentos: Stories by Latinas* (1983) and *Home Girls: A Black Feminist Anthology*. Writers published include Cherrié Moraga, ▷Mitsuye Yamada and ▷Hisaye Yamamoto. Both Yamamoto and *This Bridge Called My Back* have won awards from the Before Columbus Foundation. In 1986 the press moved to the Albany Urban League/NAACP building in Albany, New York. It has formed a coalition with the oldest civil rights organizations in the US.

Klein, Robin (born 1936)
Australian children's author. Klein left school at fifteen and has worked as a telephonist, nurse, library assistant and teacher, and is the mother of four children. She is one of Australia's most popular and prolific children's authors, with several bestselling works to her credit. She won the Australian Junior Book of the Year Award 1983 for *Thing* (1982), and has published at least twenty-four other books for children, including *The Giraffe in Pepperell Street* (1978), *Sprung* (1982), *Hating Alison Ashley* (1984), and a series of Penny Pollard books beginning with *Penny Pollard's Diary* (1984). The most recent in the series is *Penny Pollard in Print* (1986).
▷Children's literature (Australia); *Coming Out from Under*

Klepfisz, Irena (born 1941)
US poet. A Polish Jew, Klepfisz was born in Warsaw during World War II and emigrated to New York in 1949. She was educated at City College, New York, and the University of Chicago. She writes 'as much out of a Jewish consciousness as I do out of a lesbian / feminist consciousness'. Both identities are defined by Klepfisz in terms of alienation and marginality.
    Keeper of Accounts (1982) contains 'From the Monkey House and Other Cages', which uses the metaphor of the zoo to explore both Jewish and lesbian experience. Other works, such as the prose poem 'Bashert', deal explicitly with the history of Jews in Europe. It is because of her painful material about wartime Europe, anti-Semitism and the migrant experience that she claims the poetic identity of a 'keeper of accounts'. 'The Journal of Rachel Robotnik' is the fictional account of a working woman, a '*robotnik*', who is attempting to get her journal published. It mixes an editorial preface with news-clippings, fiction, and journal entries about poverty, work, family relationships and lesbian love.
    Klepfisz was also a founding editor of the feminist journal *Conditions*, and she contributes fiction, political essays and poetry to a range of Jewish, feminist and lesbian-feminist magazines, including *Sinister Wisdom*. Her work is collected in *Different Enclosures: Poetry and Prose of Irena Klepfisz* (1985).

Knight, Sarah Kemble (1666–1727)
North American travel journalist. Born in Boston, Massachusetts, on 19 April 1666 to Elizabeth Trerice and Thomas Kemble, she is an example of New England 'industry and frugality': she owned a home in which she boarded family and lodgers; she managed a shop out of her home, and she was a scrivener and witness for estate documents. In conjunction with her estate work, she made a round-trip journey on horseback from Boston to New York in the winter of 1704–1705. The first woman to accomplish such a feat, she employed wit and considerable narrative talent to describe the adventures and hardships of such travel in ▷*The Journals of Madam Knight*, now a classic North American text. After 1713, she resettled in New London, Connecticut, and died there on 25 September 1727.

Knížka s červeným obalem (1986) (*The Little Book with a Red Cover*)
Collection of short stories by Czech writer Alexandra Berková (born 1949). It is a series of episodes, in varied styles, about a woman who, having grown up in the 1960s, becomes, slightly late in life, a writer. The work's irony ranges from the jolly to the caustic. However pessimistic it is, the reader ends up with the impression that life is rather fun. The book is a comic account of growing up, and a bizarre depiction of the various states people call 'love'. The work concerns the nature of human, particularly female, identity, but rejects the 1960s' pre-occupation with the 'identity crisis'. Indeed, Berková satirizes the identity crisis myth. Although one might say that Berková's text relies on collage, allusion, quotation and intertextuality, she is also a sound observer of dialogue and most forms of outward behaviour.

Knjeginja iz Petrinjske ulice (1910) (*Princess from Petrinskja Street, The*)
Croatian novel by ▷Zagorka. One theme permeates the whole of this novel: the unpredictability and irrationality of love. This is shown as its greatest good and, potentially, its greatest evil. The theme is developed to good effect, showing love as merciless in its annihilation of obstacles and liquidation of opponents. The narrative is objective, with lively dialogue and confessional monologues. It stands apart from the majority of Zagorka's novels, which generally contain complex plots, action and tension, and are almost like historical detective stories.

Know the Ways (1986)
Translation of *Scivias* (1142–1152), a Latin text by the German nun ▷Hildegard von Bingen. It is the first volume of her mystic trilogy, and ranks amongst the most important and sophisticated texts from medieval Germany. Conceived in three sections, with each part revolving around a particular theme, the book describes the author's visions, and offers their interpretation.

Knox, Elizabeth (born 1959)
New Zealand novelist. Elizabeth Knox's first novel was largely written while she was still a student, and since then she has been a full-time writer. Her novels have been widely praised and have

won awards. *After Z-Hour* (1987) mixes the historically-documented voice of a Gallipoli soldier with the chance inhabitants of a lonely house, displacing realities, while *Paremata* (1989) is an investigation of children's sexuality.

Kobiakóva, Aleksandra Petrovna (1823–1892)
Russian novelist. Kobiakóva, who lived in the Volga port of Kostroma, was one of the rare Russian woman writers to emerge from the merchant class notorious for its conservative patriarchal mores. The brief autobiography which appeared in the radical ▷St Petersburg journal *Russian Word* in 1860 is a gloss on her novel *The Podoshvin Household* (printed there earlier in the year), in which, as she wrote, she 'tried to explain the consequences of despotic and incoherent upbringing'. In general, her sometimes clumsy fiction combines what one editor called 'artless simplicity that often rises to art' with vivid characterization, plots as chaotic as the life they depict, and a gift for dialogue reminiscent of Ostrovsky's plays about the 'dark kingdom' of the merchantry. Later stories like 'Gingerbread' (1871) deal with the life of impoverished gentry and peasants.

Koea, Shonagh (born 1939)
New Zealand short story writer and novelist. Shonagh Koea has spent most of her life in the North Island of New Zealand. She is a journalist and published a number of short stories in local journals before publishing a collection, *The Woman Who Never Went Home and Other Stories*, in 1987. Her sharp, ironic stories, which reflect a ▷postmodern environment of travel and change, have appeared in many anthologies. Her first novel, *The Grandiflora Tree*, was published in 1989.

Kogawa, Joy (born 1935)
Canadian poet, novelist and children's writer of Japanese extraction, born Joy Nakayama in Vancouver, British Columbia. Her family was transported to an internment camp in central British Columbia, then removed to Coaldale in southern Alberta. She attended the University of Alberta, the Toronto Conservatory of Music, and the University of Saskatchewan, before moving permanently to Toronto. Her poetry books, which circle the uneasy ground of home and death, include *The Splintered Moon* (1967), *A Choice of Dreams* (1974), *Jericho Road* (1977), and *Woman in the Woods* (1985). ▷*Obasan* (1981), which won both the Books in Canada First Novel Award and the Canadian Author's Association Book of the Year Award, is a complex historiographic novel about the internment of the Japanese in Canada in World War II. Rewritten for children as *Naomi's Road* (1986), *Obasan* is a spare and haunting combination of document, fiction, and political examination.
Bib. Howells, C.A., *Private and Fictional Words*.

Kola, Pamela
Kenyan short story writer. Kola was educated in Kenya and later studied for a Diploma in Education at the University of Leeds. She is at present head of a nursery school in Nairobi. Since 1968 she has been publishing traditional folk tales in a series known as the *East Africa When, How and Why Stories*.
Bib: James, Adeola, *In Their Own Voices, African Women Writers Talk*.

Kolb, Annette (1870–1967)
German novelist and essayist. The bilingual child of a Parisian concert pianist and a German architect, she achieved fame with her novel, *Das Exemplar* (1913) (*The Example*). for which she received the Fontane Prize. She became a passionate pacifist during World War I, and continued throughout her life to campaign for Franco-German reconciliation. Her novels, *Daphne Herbst* (1926) and *Die Schaukel* (1934) (*The Swing*), are vivid evocations of European society at the turn of the century.

Kollontái, Aleksandra (1872–1952)
Russian diplomat and writer. Kollontái, an active revolutionary from an aristocratic family, became famous for her demands in polemics and prose fiction (▷*The Love of Worker Bees*; ▷*A Great Love*) for a radical reconstruction of personal and family relations. She was an early member of the Soviet government, active in women's affairs. Becoming an embarrassment to the essentially puritanical Bolsheviks, she was sent abroad in 1922 as Soviet ambassador to Norway, Mexico, and Sweden. It was in Oslo that she began writing novellas and stories that owe a lot in style and diction to the popular novels of pre-revolutionary writers like ▷Verbítskaia and ▷Lukhmánova about women's thirst for love and autonomy. The ambiguous resolutions of her works suggest that, in a society of unreconstructed men, the struggle of the sexually emancipated 'new woman' to realize her ideals is almost certainly doomed.
▷Woman Question (Russia)

Kollwitz, Käthe (1867–1945)
German sculptor, graphic artist, diarist and letter-writer. The expressive power of her sculptures, woodcuts and etching has established her as one of the most important German artists of the 20th century. Naturalism was the formative influence on her work, and her art takes as its theme war and social injustice, especially as they affect women and children. Her letters, memoirs and diaries are collected in *Ich sah die Welt mit liebevollen Augen* (1970) (*I Saw the World with Love-filled Eyes*).

Kolmar, Gertrud (1894–?1943)
German poet. Born into a wealthy Jewish family, she lived all her life in Berlin. After the death of her mother in 1930 she became a near-recluse in the family home, nursing her father, and developing an interest in Zionism, Eastern

religions and the French Revolution (1789). A collection of early poems was published in 1917, and in 1933 two of her poems were included in an anthology of women's poetry edited by ▷Elisabeth Langgässer. Despite the restrictions of the Third Reich, she was able to publish two further collections of poems, *Preußische Wappen* (1934) (*Prussian Coat of Arms*) and *Die Frau und die Tiere* (1938) (*Woman and Animals*). Her poetry first evokes images of the woman poet as sick and blind, a 'troglodyte', 'toad' or 'hyena', although this notion is gradually transformed into a triumphant and defiant anthem to 'otherness' and to Judaism. In 1943 she was deported to Auschwitz.

Køltzow, Liv (1945)

Norwegian prose writer. Liv Køltzow was born in Oslo, and studied history and literature at Oslo University. She worked as a teacher, and has been active in theatre and literary magazines.

She made her literary début in 1970 with a collection of short stories *Øjet i treet* (*The Eye in the Tree*), and had her breakthrough with the novel *Hvem bestemmer over Bjørg og Unni* (*Who Decides for Bjørg and Unni?*), which became a classic of ▷realist Scandinavian women's prose of the 1970s. The two young women in the novel decide to take more active control of their lives. This means public and private confrontations.

The novel *Historien om Eli* (1975) (*Eli's Story*) is a classical ▷Bildungsroman, with a female character. Her process of self-discovery is depicted as a way out of her fatalistic acceptance of the female role. In the novel *Løp, mann* (1980) (*Run, Man*) a group of more mature teachers and intellectuals make compromises between the ideals of their youth and living an endurable life.

Køltzow's later works are the two collections of short stories, *April, November* (1983) and *Hvem har ditt ansikt?* (*Who Has Your Face?*). They are more experimental, and have not gained the wide audience of her earlier works. It seems that she is working on a new way of writing, more influenced by ▷modernism.

Køltzow's early prose is straightforward; she tells her stories in an everyday narrative voice, with an undertone of melancholy danger.

Kolychev's Patrimony, The (1911)

A novel by Russian writer ▷Mariia Veselkóva-Kil'shtét, first serialized and then published as a separate book in 1912. This long (over 600 pages) two-part work is a cross between family chronicle and historical novel that tells the story of three generations of the Kolychev family from the mid-19th century to the early 1880s. As family history, the novel records the personal and financial downfall of the noble Kolychevs and the rise of one of their serf families. Each generation of Kolychevs makes the fatal error of falling in love with the wrong person. This love object involves the second and third generations in fatal political activities. The story of the second generation takes place against the background of the

liberation of the serfs and the Polish uprising of the 1860s. The romance of the third generation upfolds against the revolutionary terrorist movement which carried out the assassination of Alexander II in 1881.

The Kolychev family is presented as generous to a fault, faithful, high-minded, religious, and patriotic. These qualities make them vulnerable to schemers: the manipulative Polish Catholics Zosia Juszkewicz and her father, Roman, and the equally objectionable 'nihilist' Vasilii Iashnev. The novel features fine observations of life on a country estate, as well as honest depictions of childbirth and women's fears and concerns about it. But its conservative political agenda – in terms of women's roles and character, Russian nationalism, and autocracy – is embodied in characterization that is schematically divided into good and evil. Thematically – the degeneration of a gentry family, the infatuation of a nihilist with a beautiful woman who does not share his views – the work is reminiscent of novels and stories by Ivan Turgenev (1818–1883), Fyodor Dostoevsky (1821–1881), Anton Chekhov (1860–1904), Ivan Bunin (1870–1953) and, among Veselkóva-Kil'shtét's female contemporaries, ▷Ol'nem and ▷Krestóvskaia.

Komaróva, Varvara Dmitrievna (1862–1942)

Using the ▷pseudonym Vladimir Karenin and writing in both her native Russian and in French, Komaróva devoted most of her life to a major four-volume biography, ▷*George Sand, sa vie et ses oeuvres* (*George Sand, her life and her Works*). She also occasionally wrote well-crafted prose fiction in Russian. Her novel, *Musia* (1888), is eerily low-key in its depiction of a young woman, like Komaróva herself from a well-connected, intellectual St Petersburg family, who finds in marriage no outlet, either for her talents or emotional needs. In the 1912 story 'Poison' Komaróva shows the impact of revolutionary violence on children from the families of both the government official killed by a bomb and the terrorist group responsible. 'Broken Windows' (1914) is the equally understated tale of a promising Jewish musician's murder in a provincial pogrom.

König, Alma Johanna (1887–?1942)

German-Jewish novelist, born in Prague, and who lived in Vienna. Her first novel, *Der heilige Palast* (1922) (*The Holy Palace*), attracted much attention because of its erotic explicitness. *Die Geschichte von Half, dem Weibe* (1924) (*The Story of Half, A Woman*), about a Viking woman, earned her the literary prize of the city of Vienna. Of special interest is her autobiographical novel, *Leidenschaft in Algier* (1932) (*Passion in Algiers*). When the Nazis marched into Austria, she was first persecuted, and finally deported. She disappeared in the Minsk ghetto in 1942.

Königsdorf, Helga (born 1938)

East German novelist. A trained mathematician, and suffering from Parkinson's disease, she became one of the leading figures in East German literature. Her collections of stories *Meine ungehörigen Träume* (1978) (*My Unseemly Dreams*), *Lauf der Dinge* (1982) (*The Run of Things*), *Lichtverhältnisse* (1988) (*Relationships of Light*) and *Die geschlossenen Türen am Abend* (1989) (*The Closed Doors at Evening*), share a characteristic theme – of a dismal, lacklustre world suddenly transformed by the will-power of a heroine.

Konopnicka, Maria (1842–1910)

Polish poet, positivist and campaigner for women's emancipation and rights to education and work. Konopnicka was born in a small town, the daughter of a lawyer, and she was brought up among the gentry. At school she became friends with ▷Eliza Orzeskowa (then Eliza Pawlowski), and their mutually supportive friendship was sustained in letters for years. She married an older man, a landowner, bore six children, then rebelled and fled to Warsaw.

Konopnicka was a radical – she deplored the conditions of the working class and denounced the Church. As a result she often attracted hostility during her literary career from landowners, clergy and tsarist censors. Her poems are really populist novelettes in verse on the plight of the oppressed and the lives of peasants, workers and Jews. Her epic poem *Pan Balcer w Brazylji* (*Mr Balcer in Brazil*) took her twenty years to write and, by following the modest village blacksmith Balcer to Brazil, where he finds work clearing primeval forests, argues the pros and cons of emigration.

Kono Taeko (born 1926)

Japanese novelist. Born in Osaka she came Tokyo not only to work, but to write novels. *Hunting for Children* won the Shincho Prize in 1962, and *Crabs* won the Akutagawa Prize in 1963. These works describe the inner life of a woman who is caught by loneliness after being subjected to masochism and sadism. *Unexpected Voice* (Hui no Koe) won the Yomiuri Prize for Literature in 1968. ▷*Bizarre Story of a Husband and Wife during Wartime* (1990) describes the unusual sexual love between a husband and wife during wartime. This novel is a summation of all her work. She is Director of the Japan Association for Writers and Director of the Museum of Modern Japanese Literature.

Korean Women Divers Forced to Work in Japan – A Visit to Boso Peninsula (1988)

This work is by Kim Yon and Yan Junya, two second-generation Korean women living in Japan. Searching for their identity as Koreans, they visited various Korean women in their sixties and asked them about their life history. These women, who used to dive for sea grass and shells, had been forced to work during the period of Japanese colonization. This work is an inspiration for Japanese women considering their own identity.

Kostash, Myrna (born 1944)

Canadian journalist and writer of creative non-fiction, Kostash was born and raised in Edmonton, Alberta, and steeped in her parents and grandparents' Ukrainian-Canadian cultural tradition. After her education at the University of Alberta, the University of Washington, and the University of Toronto, she worked in Toronto as a successful freelance journalist before returning to Alberta. *All of Baba's Children* (1977), a generational exploration of Ukrainians in Canada, was one of the first ethnically-centred texts to contraversialize multicultural issues. Through her creative cultural critiques, Kostash pushes against the boundaries of straight journalism. *Long Way From Home (The Story of the Sixties Generation in Canada)* (1980) is a somewhat derivative exploration of the failure of 1960s idealism in Canada. *No Kidding (Inside the World of Teenage Girls)* (1987) is a focused and articulate study of the cultural pressures on teenage girls to conform. Kostash is both energetically political, and astute in her readings of contemporary society.

Kottanner, Helene (1400–after 1470)

German writer of historical memoirs, and the first bourgeois woman known to have written in German. The widow of a burgomaster of Odenburg, she married Johann Kottanner, a Viennese court official in 1432. She became the confidante of the Duchesse Elisabeth, daughter of the Hungarian-German Emperor Sigismund (1368–1437) and wife of Albrecht V of Austria, who died in 1439 while his wife was nine months pregnant. Helene's memoirs, *Denkwürdigkeiten der Helene Kottannerin* (1450) (*Noteworthy Memoirs of Helene Kottanner*), are an excellent historical source. They also contain a gripping account of how, in order to safeguard the throne of Hungary for Elisabeth's baby son, Ladislaus, Kottanner stole the Hungarian crown from the heavily-guarded treasury in Plintenburg on a dark night in February 1440.

Kouza, Loujaya M.

Poet from Papua New Guinea. Described by *Manoa: A Pacific Journal of International Writing* (Vol. 1, No. 1, Spring 1990) as one of Papua New Guinea's outstanding women poets, Kouza published a collection of poetry while still at high school. She has also published poems in *Ondobondo* 6, and currently works as a journalist.

Kovalévskaia, Sof'ia Vasil'evna (1850–1891)

The career of the prize-winning Russian mathematician and professor at Stockholm University, Sof'ia Kovalévskaia, was a source of inspiration for ambitious young women all over Europe. In her last years she wrote reminiscences (▷*A Russian Childhood*) and fiction which suggest that her premature death of pneumonia cost Russian literature a promising talent. In 1886 Kovalévskaia published a reminiscence of two visits to ▷George Eliot in which she dealt frankly and sympathetically with the English novelist's late marriage to a young friend. She and the Swedish writer Anne Charlotte Leffler collaborated on a set of two plays under the blanket title *Struggle for Happiness*, which depict the same characters in circumstances governed by different ethical choices, one leading to disaster and the second to a rational, happy life. Her novella *The Nihilist Girl* (1890) was based on the true story of an idealistic girl who married a stranger convicted of revolutionary agitation in order to spare him a potentially fatal sentence to hard labour; he would be allowed to live in exile with his wife instead. The contrast of Kovalévskaia's lively voice with her heroine's own triumphant narrative shows notable gifts as a storyteller.

▷ Gurévich, Liubov'; *What is to Be Done?*
Bib: Chapman, Raymond and Gottlieb, E., 'A Russian View of George Eliot', *Nineteenth-Century Fiction* 33; Koblitz, Ann Hibner, *A Convergence of Lives. Sofia Kovalevskaia: Scientist, Writer, Revolutionary.*

Krall, Hanna (born c. 1933)
Polish journalist and novelist. Krall's work blurs the border between journalism and fiction. Her interview with the last survivor of the Warsaw Ghetto uprising, Marek Edelman, *Shielding the Flame* (1986), was published in Poland in 1977. It is an extraordinary, all-encompassing dialogue about the Holocaust.

Her novel *The Subtenant* is also concerned with history, in this case the life of a Jewish girl surviving World War II concealed in a succession of Polish homes. It is the story of Krall's own childhood. In 1986 it was awarded the Solidarity Cultural Prize for fiction. An extract is published in English in *Storm: New Writing from East and West*; Vol. 1, edited by Joanna Labon.

Krambambuli (1875)
A novella in *Seven Stories* (1986) by ▷ Marie von Ebner-Eschenbach. It is about a dog, Krambambuli, who dies of a broken heart because he is forced to serve two masters. Told with economy of language and perfection of style, the story offers suggestive glimpses into human psychology within the feudal milieu of 19th-century rural Austria. It is to this day considered one of the best short stories in 19th-century German literature.

Krandiévskaia, Anastasiia Romanovna (1865–1938)
Russian prose writer. Krandiévskaia worked for newspapers and journals in the 1880s, but her first serious story, 'The Gold Medal', appeared only in 1896. By 1900 she had published a collection of stories, *That Happened in Early Spring*, followed by two other volumes in 1905 and 1911. In the 1910s Krandiévskaia tried other genres, short philosophical prose pieces, 'Aphorisms of an Insomniac' (1915), and a political novel, *The Secret of Joy* (1916), which became her last known publication.

Many of Krandiévskaia's stories are didactic.

Her most popular story, 'Only an Hour', starts out well, as the narrator describes with heavy irony the naivété of a female reporter who has come to a coal mine to collect material for an article. Her hour amid the horrors of the mine, which changes her forever, is described in fine naturalistic detail, but the rest of the story drags as the narrator hammers home the message of the human cost of 'progress'. *The Secret of Joy* is centred on the Verkhovskii family and, like ▷ Gíppius's ▷ *The Devil's Doll*, is set against the 1905 Revolution. Critics noted the influence of Dostoevsky.

Krandiévskaia started a dynasty of women writers: her daughter ▷ Nataliia Krandiévskaia-Tolstáia was a poet, and her great-granddaughter, ▷ Tat'iana Tolstáia is a Russian short story writer.

Krandiévskaia (-Tolstáia), Nataliia Vasil'evna (1888–1965)
Russian poet. Krandiévskaia came from a literary family. Her mother was the prose writer ▷ Anastasiia Krandiévskaia, and her father published the *Bulletin of Literature and Life*. Her home was frequently visited by well-known literary figures. Her second husband was the writer Aleksei Tolstoi, and she is the grandmother of the contemporary prose writer ▷ Tat'iana Tolstáia.

Krandiévskaia began writing poetry as a young girl. She published her first collection in 1913 and two more in 1919 and 1922 (the latter in Berlin). After the Revolution Krandiévskaia and her family spent more than four years abroad before returning to the USSR. After a hiatus of several decades, she started publishing again. In 1959 her memoirs were published (*I Remember*; second edition *Memoirs*, 1977). Posthumous collections of her poetry were published in 1972 and 1985. Her poems are in the 'feminine' tradition of short lyrics which often revolve around the theme of love. Her other subjects include intimations of mortality, memory, and the stages of life. She tends to use traditional metre and verse structure. Her most accomplished poems show a mastery of sound orchestration, apt epithets, and the imaginative use of metaphor, particularly synecdoche.

Krantz, Judith (born 1928)
US novelist. Born in New York, Krantz graduated from Wellesley College in 1948. She was the fashion editor at *Good Housekeeping* magazine from 1949 to 1956. At age fifty Krantz published her first novel, *Scruples* (1978), a bestseller. Commercial successes, Krantz's novels are preoccupied with sex, fame and power and they expose the politics behind such glamour industries as fashion and film-making. Their women characters are strong, independent and powerful survivors. The heroines of *Scruples* and *Princess Daisy* (1980) overcome abusive circumstances. They pursue successful careers: one in retail and the other in advertising, and they find ultimate personal happiness in a heterosexual romantic relationship. The heroines of *I'll Take Manhattan*

Judith Krantz

(1986) and *Dazzle* (1990) also succeed in the male-dominated professional world.
Other works include: *Mistral's Daughter* (1982) and *Till We Meet Again* (1988).
▷Romance fiction

Krechel, Ursula (born 1947)

German dramatist and poet. She achieved instant fame with her play, *Erika* (1974), the story of a woman who leaves her husband in order to seek self-fulfilment. After a series of emotional adventures she returns to him, and the couple decide to care together for the child Erika has conceived in an extramarital affair. Her poems, in *Nach Mainz* (1977) (*To Mainz*) and *Verwundbar wie in den besten Zeiten* (1979) (*Vulnerable at the Best of Times*), are further investigations of feminist issues.

Krestóvskaia, Mariia Vsevolodovna (1862–1910)

Russian prose writer. Krestóvskaia was the daughter of the historical novelist Vsevolod Krestóvskii. She first tried acting, but by 1885 was publishing fiction about life in the provincial theatre. Her first major novel, *Early Storms* (1886), typifies her work. It is a minute dissection, unfolding at a snail's pace and suffering from prolixity, of the break-up of a marriage and the effect on the couple and their daughter, told from the point of view of all three. Krestóvskaia's novella *Outside Life* is a searing depiction of the crippling of a young girl and her gradual transformation into a monster. The novel *The Actress* (1891) again describes the slow evolution of a relationship: the heroine renounces her love for a highly placed civil servant for the sake of art. ▷Verbítskaia had dealt with the same theme in ▷*Discord* (1887), but, to the outrage of male critics, Krestóvskaia's actress more openly indulges in 'free' love.

By the mid-1890s Krestóvskaia had published several volumes of prose and seemed to be groping for a new narrative approach. She started an epistolary novel, *Woman's Life* (1894–95), supposedly based on actual letters between her aunt and her aunt's cousin, presented as typical Russian women. Her last two stories are far from her best: 'The Wail' (1900) and 'Mytishchev's Confession' (1901) both use a diary form and oppose 'decadent' behaviour – egocentricity, materialism, neurosis – to populist moral norms. In 1905 she published travel notes and diary entries, *To the Sunshine!*, which included a visit to ▷Mariia Bashkirtseff's family in Paris.
Bib: Moller, P.U., *Postlude to 'The Kreutzer Sonata': Tolstoj and the Debate on Sexual Morality in Russian Literature in the 1890s.*

Krestovskii, V. ▷Khvoshchínskaia, Nadezhda

Krisan, Asokesin (born 1931)

Pen-name of Thai novelist Sukanya Yanaranop. She has written about 100 novels, and as many short stories, which record the rise of the new social class and the problems attendant upon ruthless ambition. Apart from literary awards for novels such as *Rua Manut* (1968) (*The Human Ship*) and *Tawan Tok Din* (1972) (*The Sun Sets*), she received the National Artist Award for Literature in 1988.

Kristeva, Julia (born 1941)

Bulgarian linguist who writes in French and is Professor of Linguistics at the University of Paris VII. In the 1960s she was a key contributor to the left-wing Maoist journal *Tel Quel*. Now a practising psychoanalyst, her work, although not explicitly feminist, has greatly influenced areas of feminist theory concerned with analyzing the acquisition of gender identity in language from the perspective of ▷psychoanalysis. Kristeva's books about language and gender translated into English include: ▷*Revolution in Poetic Language* (1984), published in France in 1974 and *Desire in Language: A Semiotic Approach to Literature and Art* (1980).
They analyze the representation of motherhood in Western culture, and introduce Kristeva's influential theory of the ▷subject 'in process', which proposes that subject identity is perpetually changing. ▷*Powers of Horror* (1980), ▷*Tales of Love* (1987), *Soleil noir: dépression et mélancholie* (1987) (*Black Sun: Depression and Melancholy*) and *Strangers to Ourselves* (1991) offer cultural histories of the inscription and effects of horror, love and madness and foreignness in the West. They show in practice how feminists might interpret and resist culturally constructed myths of gender. Her influential essay 'Women's Time' (1979) ('Le Temps des Femmes') is translated in ▷*Signs* 7 (1981).
Bib: Benjamin, Andrew and Fletcher, John, *Abjection, Melancholia and Love: The Work of Julia Kristeva*; Grosz, Elizabeth, *Sexual Subversions:*

Three French Feminists; Lechte, John, *Julia Kristeva*; Moi, T., *Sexual/Textual Politics* and *A Kristeva Reader*; Pajaczkowska, C., 'Introduction to Kristeva', *m/f*, (1981).

Kristin Lavransdatter (1920–1922)

▷Sigrid Undset wrote these four volumes about the late Middle Ages in Norway as a mirror of the political and religious anxiety and social upheaval that dominated the years between World Wars I and II in Scandinavia. The ▷historical novel was a very suitable genre for women neo-realists. In the setting of the 14th century, Undset was able to create an optimistic female character who succeeded in both loving deeply and in being religiously active. In 1928 she was awarded the Nobel Prize for *Kristin Lavransdatter*. The novel is a love-story, and depicts female love as a strong and positive force. It is told in traditional styles, from Nordic ballads to European courtly poetry and religious literature. The hero, Erland, is a weak but charming knight, who saves a woman's virtue and makes her love him despite social and parental conventions. Love is a destiny that must be obeyed even if it means that earthly rules are broken. Love and marriage are here combined in a very modern way, where sexuality is the axis of love. Marriage is the framework of a passionate love that can be continued after death in another heavenly version, because it is seen as a mysterious, even religious force. It has to be paid for by the heroine, Kristin, who devotes herself to nursing the victims of the Black Death. On the one hand she has her sexuality and individual freedom, on the other, social responsibilities and religion. This discrepancy is prominent in all the works of Sigrid Undset.

The historical setting in the novel is very precise and detailed, the language is of great richness, and the novel continues to win many readers.

Křížová cesta kočárového kočího (1979) (The Coachman's Coach Crusade)

the first novel by Czech journalist Eda Kriseová (born 1940). The writer's importance has been enhanced in the popular mind by her affiliation with the dissident organization Charter 77. The novel consists of a series of seemingly dotty episodes, whose only link is a mental hospital. The importance of the work is, in fact, political rather than literary. For example, the character Hanuš infuriates a group of villagers by maintaining that the 1945 uprising against the occupying Germans means the end of World War II. The same cowardly Czechs later gather to force him to join the collective farm. He refuses, but loses his land and is imprisoned. Kriseová thus explicitly links the Nazis with the communists, a link at the time very rare in Czech literature, though well known to the Slovaks.

Krog, Antjie (born 1952)

South African Afrikaans poet, born in Kroonstad, Transvaal, where she now lives. She has published seven volumes of poetry (none translated into English). She published *Dogter van Jefta* (1970) (*Daughter of Jefta*) while she was a schoolgirl, its explicit eroticism causing a local stir. Her early collections share the theme of adolescent love, sometimes sentimentally treated; these are: *Januarie-suite* (1972) (*January Suite*), *Mannin* (1975) (*Virago*) and *Beminde Antarktika* (1975) (*Beloved Antarctica*). *Otters in Bronslaai* (1981) (*Otters in Watercress*) contains poems on the experiences of mother and wife in the tradition of ▷Elisabeth Eybers. This collection also casts back to a 19th-century tradition of writing by women, for it includes the cycle of poems 'Die leeu en die roos' ('The lion and the rose') which are based on the diary of the mystic, Susanna Smit. Her most recent collection, *Lady Anne* (1989), calls upon ▷Anne Barnard as muse: in these highly self-conscious poems, the modern poet measures against the earlier writer her own situation as artist, as woman, and as politically committed South African. Krog has also opened herself to African ▷oral tradition, deploying some of the formal patterning of Sotho oral praise poetry, as in her poem 'Lovesong After the Music of K.E. Ntsane', published in *From South Africa* (1987), ed. David Bunn and Jane Taylor.

Her other works are: *Eerste Gedigte* (1984) (*First Poems*); *Jerusalemgangers* (1985) (*Pilgrims to Jerusalem*), and a children's book, *Mankeplank en ander Monsters* (1985) (*Mankeplank and Other Monsters*).

Kronauer, Brigitte (born 1940)

German novelist and essayist. It was the publication of her first novel, *Frau Mühlenbeck im Gehäus* (1980) (*Mrs Mühlenbeck in her Shell*), which brought her fame overnight. Her unique and sovereign command of language caused critics everywhere to wonder how her equally sophisticated earlier prose pieces, such as *Der unvermeidliche Gang der Dinge* (1974) (*The Unavoidable Way of Things*) and *Die Revolution der Nachahmung* (1975) (*The Revolution of Imitation*), could have passed unnoticed. Since then her stories, collected in *Die gemusterte Nacht* (1981) (*Patterns of the Night*), and the novels, *Rita Münster* (1983) and *Berittener Bogenschütze* (1986) (*Archer on Horseback*), have established her as one of the most challengingly innovative and cerebral writers in Germany. She delights in inventing near-mathematical linguistic constructions on the themes of modern life and human desire.

Krüdener, Barbara Juliane von (1764–1824)

Writer in German and French. Born in Riga on the Baltic, she married at the age of fourteen. After a divorce, she became devoutly mystical, and travelled Europe as a preacher, drawing huge crowds for her sermons. An outspoken critic of European aristocracy and a spokeswoman on behalf of the poor, she became increasingly unwelcome in many countries. Her novel, *Valérie* (1803), although written in French, owes much to German romanticism. Modelled on Goethe's

Werther (1774), it is the tale of a young hero's fatal love for an unattainable woman. It was translated by ▷Dorothea Schlegel and ▷Helmine von Chézy in 1804. Krudener's work has also been compared to that of ▷Adèle de Souza.
Bib: Ley, F., *Mme de Krudener et son temps*; Merlant, J., *Le Roman personnel de Rousseau à Fromentin*.

Krusenstjerna, Agnes Julie Fredrika von (1894–1940)

Swedish prose writer. She came from the aristocracy, her father being a military person, with insanity in the family. She had to leave her girl's school in the sixth grade because of nervous breakdowns, and never gained an education. At the age of twenty she was engaged, but after a breakdown broke off the engagement. Up until 1921, when she married the critic David Sprengel, she suffered further breakdowns.

Her début was in 1917 with *Ninas dagbok* (*The Diary of Nina*), a talented girl's book, which was followed by a trilogy, *Tony* (1922–1926). During her erotic awakening, Tony emancipates herself from her parents but ends up in mental hospital.

It is the seven books about the *Misses von Pahlen* (1930–1935) and female sexuality that made Krusenstjerna infamous. ▷The Krusenstjerna Debate in the 1930s included very violent personal attacks on the author. Her last four volumes of *Fattigadel* (1935–1938) (*Poor Nobility*) are about feminine destructiveness, mothers repressing their daughters as they themselves had been repressed.

Krusenstjerna's style is clear and lyrical, although occasionally over-romantic and long-winded. She brought two new themes into Swedish literature: the young woman's sexual awakening, and mental illness.

Krusenstjerna (or Pahlen) Debate, The

In the 1930s, the Swedish writer ▷Agnes von Krusenstjerna wrote seven volumes about the *Misses von Pahlen – Den blå rullgardinen* (1930) (*The Blue Blind*), *Kvinnogatan* (1930) (*Women's Street*), *Höstens skuggor* (1931) (*The Shadows of Autumn*), *Porten vid Johannes* (1933) (*The Gate of Johannes*), *Älskande par* (1933) (*Loving Couples*), *Bröllop på Ekered* (1935) (*Wedding at Ekered*) and *Av samma blod* (1935) (*Of the Same Blood*). The series gave rise to an intense debate in the newspapers, in particular the fifth volume, *Loving Couples*, with its very direct descriptions of sexual variations. Von Krusenstjerna was accused of having written pornography, and the attacks on her were so harsh and personal that she never quite recovered from them. The debate lasted for more than two years, and its central subject was obscenity in literature.

The volumes of the *Misses von Pahlen* do describe female sexuality, but they also unfold a mystical, matriarchal Utopia influenced by the ideas of French philosopher Saint-Simon (1760–1825).

The seven volumes are considered the principal work of Agnes von Krusenstjerna.

Kúl'man, Elisaveta Borisovna (1808–1825)

Elizaveta Kúl'man

Russian poet and translator. Kúl'man's widowed mother, left poor and with a number of children to raise, still managed to encourage her daughter's extraordinary talents. A family friend, German teacher K.V. Grossheinrich, tutored Kúl'man, and later wrote a monograph about her upbringing; the director of the St Petersburg Mining Academy taught her along with his own daughters. By sixteen she knew German, French, Italian, Latin, Church Slavonic, classical and modern Greek, English, Spanish and Portuguese, and practised these languages by translating poetry into them, and from them into Russian, and then writing original poems in the national literary idiom. She translated 18th-century Russian classical tragedies into German and retold Kievan epic folk songs in modern Russian. Revering Homer and Pausanius, and steeped in the culture of classical Greece, Kúl'man wrote a series of poems in which she attempted to reproduce intuitively the spirit of the lost Greek poet ▷Corinna. A selection of her poems in German, Italian, and French was praised by Goethe (1749–1832) and won her a place in German literary history. Her preference for unrhymed verse and adoption of foreign styles set her apart from mainstream Russian literature, however, and in her homeland Kúl'man's story was often used as a cautionary model of a girl driven to an early grave by intellectual over-stimulation. Kúl'man died at seventeen from consumption brought on by poverty and exposure to the St Petersburg flood of 1824, but the evidence is that, far from languishing under her tutor's goad, she relished life and learning to the last. ▷Gan's ▷*A Vain Gift* is a sympathetic tale of a girl genius.

Kulyk Keefer, Janice (born 1952)

Canadian fiction writer, poet and critic. Kulyk Keefer studied at the University of Toronto and the University of Sussex in England. Her short stories are sure-footed renditions of tone and detail, European in their focus on moments of language. Her first collection, *The Paris–Napoli Express* (1986) establishes the timbre of private epiphany that her later collections, *Transfigurations* (1987) and *Travelling Ladies* (1990), develop. Her novel, *Constellations* (1989), is a parodic description of community bondage and outsiderhood. *White of the Lesser Angels*, a poetry collection, appeared in 1986. An active and practising scholar, Kulyk Keefer has also published a critical reading of Maritime fiction called *Under Eastern Eyes* (1987) and a critical study of ▷Mavis Gallant, *Reading Mavis Gallant* (1989). She lives in Eden Mills, Ontario.

Kumin, Maxine (born 1925)

US poet, children's writer and essayist. Kumin was born in Philadelphia, Pennsylvania to Jewish parents, and educated at Radcliffe College, where she earned her MA in 1946. She has since taught at Tufts and Columbia Universities, and is the National Poet Laureate. Kumin and her husband live on a farm in New Hampshire. She was close friends with ▷Anne Sexton and both read each other's work. However, she is not a 'confessional' poet, but instead uses traditional poetic forms as a way of containing the pain and chaos of the world. She has said that it is a poet's function to name things, and her work details the features of everyday life – domesticity, family stories, gardening, cooking – that provide a bulwark against suffering. Mother–child relationships have also figured largely in her work. Particularly important, especially since *Up Country* (1972), which was awarded the Pulitzer Prize, has been humanity's troubled relationship with the natural world, and nature's domination and exploitation by humans.

Other works include: *Halfway* (1961), *Follow the Fall* (1961), *A Winter Friend* (1961), *Spring Things* (1961), *Summer Story* (1961), *Mittens in May* (1962), *No One Writes a Letter to the Snail* (1962), *Eggs of Things* (1963), *The Beach Before Breakfast* (1964), *More Eggs of Things* (1964), *Speedy Digs Downside Up* (1964), *Through Dooms of Love* (1965), *The Privilege* (1965), *Paul Bunyan* (1966), *Faraway Farm* (1967), *The Passions of Uxport* (1968), *The Wonderful Babies of 1809 and Other Years* (1968), *When Grandmother Was Young* (1969), *When Mother Was Young* (1970), *The Nightmare Factory* (1970), *When Great-Grandmother Was Young* (1971), *The Abduction* (1971), *The Designated Heir* (1974), *House, Bridge, Fountain, Gate* (1975), *The Wizard's Tears* (1975), *What Color is Caesar?* (1978), *The Retrieval System* (1978), *To Make a Prairie* (essays) (1979), *Our*

Ground Time Here Will Be Brief (1982), *In Deep: Country Essays* (1987) and *Nurture* (1989).

Kumina

An Afro-Jamaican religious cult of particular relevance in Caribbean writing. For a full discussion see *Dictionary of Jamaican English* and Maureen Warner-Lewis, 'The Nkuyu: Spirit Messengers of the Kumina', *Savacou*, 1977, pp. 76–7. The Kumina cult derives originally from African religious practices in which there is a veneration of ancestors, and harmony with the spiritual world is created by a close relationship with the ancestral spirits. A sense of continuity is created between the past, the present and the future. For the influence of Afro-Jamaican folk elements in women's writing, see Carolyn Cooper's essay in ▷*Out of the Kumbla* and in Susheila Nasta (ed.), ▷*Motherlands: Black Women's Writing from Africa the Caribbean and South Asia*.

Kunstseidene Mädchen, Das (1932) ▷*Artificial Silk Girl, The* (1933)

Kuntsch, Margaretha Susanna von (1651–1716)

German poet. The well-educated daughter of a courtier, she married a councillor and had fourteen children, of which only one daughter survived. After her death, her grandson published a collection of her poems, principally laments on the deaths of her children.

Kurahashi Yumiko (born 1935)

Japanese novelist, who was born in Kochi prefecture. *Partei* (1960), published when she was a student at Meiji University, has been praised by the critic, Hirano Ken. This satirical work depicts the revolutionary movement against the Japan–US Security Treaty, describing the conflict between individuals and a party. Kurahashi faced a clash of ideologies when she wrote an Existentialist experimental novel, *The Adventures of Sumiyakist Q* (1969). *Engagement* was followed by *A Dark Travel*, which won the Tamura Toshiko Prize in 1963. *The Floating Bridge of Dreams* (1971), *A Castle Among Castles* (1980) and *Exchange* (1989) are works in which she tries to create a completely fictitious world, taking spouse-swapping as one of her themes. In *Two Ways to Amanon*, she criticizes feminism. She is a writer of rare distinction, with an acerbic style.

▷*Sacred Girl, A*

Kurz, Isolde (1853–1944)

German poet, novelist and short story writer. She was educated by her mother, a revolutionary free spirit, who taught her to swim, dance, and speak and read several languages, while also introducing her to German classicism as well as new, socialist ideas. At odds with the conservative atmosphere of provincial Germany, she moved to Florence in 1880, where, at last, she felt able to realize her artistic potential. Her first poems, *Gedichte*

(*Poems*), appeared in 1888 when she was thirty-five. They were followed by a collection of stories, *Florentiner Novellen* (1890) (*Novellas from Florence*), and, together, these works established her as one of the most accomplished poets and writers of late 19th-century Germany. Her work, while reflecting her lifelong interest in the Italian Renaissance, includes evocative images of life in Italy and her native Swabia, and often revolves around an intense exploration of the inner self. One of her last novels, the semi-autobiographical *Vanadis* (1931), was at the time fiercely criticized by progressive women for its glorification of the heroine's self-sacrifice.

▷*Bildungsroman*

Kuznetsóva, Galina Nikolaevna (1902–1976)
Russian poet, prose writer, and memoir-writer. Kuznetsóva was born in Kiev, but emigrated to the West in 1920, living in Prague, Paris and, from 1949, the United States. She published continually from her debut in 1926 in Paris. Considered to be one of Ivan Bunin's pupils, in 1927 she went to live in Grasse, France, with the writer and his wife. Like Bunin (1870-1953), she wrote both poetry and prose, and in the 1930s she published a book of short stories, *Morning*, a novel, *Prologue*, and a collection of verse, *Olive Grove*. In 1967 *Grasse Diary*, a memoir of her life with the Bunins, appeared. It gives an interesting portrait of Bunin and the significance his winning the Nobel Prize held for the beleaguered *émigré* community, and shows Kuznetsóva herself, like Bunin, to be preoccupied with the visual and sensual beauty of earthly life and the dread of death.
Bib: Karlinsky, S. and Appel Jr, A., (eds), *The*
Bitter Air of Exile: Russian Writers in the West, 1922–1972.

Kuzwayo, Ellen (born 1914)
South African autobiographer and short story writer, born in Thaba Patchoa, Orange Free State, and generally known as 'the mother of Soweto' for her wide-ranging social work and fearless political activity (she was detained without trial in 1977, aged 63). Her autobiography *Call Me Woman* (1985) was the first book by a black South African writer to win the prestigious CNA (Central News Agency) Prize: here Kuzwayo carefully expands the philosophy and practice of ▷Black Consciousness to accommodate the aspirations and achievements of women, and also organizes her narrative in such a way that the individual story is bound up with the story of a people. Kuzwayo subsequently published a volume of short stories, *Sit Down and Listen* (1990), which calls upon ▷oral tradition for its narrative mode, and contemporary black life for its content. She has also been involved with the making of two films, *Tsiamelo: A Place of Goodness* (1984), which is about the forced removal of her extended family from their rural home, and *Awake from Mourning* (1981).

▷Autobiography (Southern Africa); Black literature

Kyk-over Al (1945–1961)
One of the first literary magazines to be published in the West Indies, *Kyk-over Al* provided a forum for short stories and poetry.

Kyme, Anne ▷Askew (Kyme), Anne

Labé, Louise Charlin Perrin (1520–1566)

French poet. She was known as '*la belle cordière*' ('the beautiful ropemaker'), because she was the daughter and wife of ropemakers in Lyon, and was praised by Renaissance poets and historians for her extraordinary beauty. She received the same education as her two half-brothers, following her father Pierre Charly's reading of the 1509 treatise on education by the philosopher Cornelius Agrippa (1486–1533), which defended '*la noblesse et l'excellence du sexe féminin*' ('the nobility and excellence of the female sex'). The poet Maurice Scève (1501–c 1560), fresh from a stay in Italy, was appointed her tutor, encouraging her to read the Italian writers Boccaccio (1313–1375), Petrarch (1304–1374), Dante (1265–1321) and Castiglione (1478–1529). She supposedly participated in a tournament in honour of Henri II (1519–1559) and in the siege of Perpignan, disguised as a man, under the ▷pseudonym *Capitaine Loys* (Captain Louise). Louise Labé was the author of three elegies, twenty-four sonnets, of which the first is in Italian, and *Le Débat de Folie et d'Amour* (*The Debate between Folly and Love*), a courtroom dramatization of the irrationality of the emotions. Labé published her *Euvres* (*Works*) herself in 1555, having applied for the *privilège du roy* (king's privilege) in person. The Epilogue assembled a series of verses by others in praise of 'L.L.L.', but by addressing the sonnets to a lover, probably the poet Olivier de Magny (1529–1561), she had created a scandal. At the end of their affair, Magny belittled Labé and her old husband in the vituperative *Ode à Sire Aymon*, and she seems to have gone into an early decline.

Her reputation evolved to her detriment after her death, but much of the criticism directed against her may have been simply because she had dared to write love-poetry. This 'indiscretion' is now thought to be the key to her feminism. Her poetry challenges the courtly ideal of woman and men's misogynistic views. The elegies are a form of manifesto for women and writing. The first and third are devoted to a defence of writing about love. In the third, she seeks the sympathy of other women, who may come to suffer as she has done: '*Quand vous lirez, ô dames Lionnoises, / Ces miens escrits pleins d'amoureuses noises / . . . Ne veuillez pas condamner ma simplesse, / Et jeune erreur de ma folle jeunesse, / Si c'est erreur*' ('When you read my writings full of amorous sounds, O ladies of Lyon, be so good as not to condemn my simplicity and the youthful error of my mad youth, if indeed it is an error'). Labé was conscious of her role of champion of her sex against male oppression, but she was modest about her own talents. The sonnets she selected for publication, which may be merely a token of her actual poetic production, by turns light-hearted and melancholic, erotic and ambiguous, protest her poetic genius. They challenge the artificiality of the ▷Petrarchan conceit and insist on the force of the woman poet's emotional experience. The final sonnet begins: '*Ne reprenez, Dames, si j'ay aimé: / Si j'ai senti mille torches ardentes, / Mille travaux, mille douleurs mordentes*' ('Do not criticize me, Ladies, if I have loved: if I have felt a thousand burning torches, a thousand travails, and a thousand times sharp pain').

She formed a literary circle in the garden of her house in Lyon, frequented by most of the poets known as the 'School of Lyon', including her close friend ▷Pernette du Guillet up to her death.

Bib: Cameron, K., *Louise Labé: Renaissance Poet and Feminist*; E. Dezon-Jones, *Les Ecritures féminines*.

Lacan, Jacques ▷Psychoanalysis

Lachmet, Djanet (born 1953)

Algerian novelist, from a well-known family. She received a French education in Algiers and today lives in France. Her first novel, *Le Cow-Boy* (1983) (▷*The Cow-boy*, 1987), raises important issues to do with women in general and Algerian women in particular. Lallia, the heroine, who comes, like Lachmet, from a wealthy background, undergoes a common experience of cultural conflict, as a result of the traditional teaching of her mother as against her formal education at school.

Lack

A term used by French psychoanalyst Jacques Lacan (1901–1981) to characterize the condition of subjectivity. Entry into the ▷symbolic order means the sacrifice of the human being's organic nature in exchange for subjectivity. The subject, however, no longer 'whole', can never be the source of meaning but only its (unstable) effect. The subject's exclusion from the ▷imaginary state (characterized by plenitude), which precedes entry into the symbolic order, is responsible for introducing to the subject the lack that gives rise to desire. Women are doubly lacking on account of not having a penis; they are therefore unable to fully identify with the symbolic power of the phallus.

Lacombe, Claire (1765–?)

French revolutionary activist. Born near Arxiège, she worked as an actress. In Paris she became president of the Société des citoyennes républicaines révolutionnaires. She was imprisoned briefly from 1794 to 1795, before returning to the stage. One of her speeches, 'Petition des femmes de la société des Républicaines' ('Women's Petition from the Society of Female Republicans') has been published in modern collections of documents relating to women's revolutionary activities (▷French Revolution: pamphlets, registers of grievances, petitions and speeches).

Modern editions of her work can be found in P. Duhet, (ed.) *Cahiers de doléances des femmes et autres textes* (*Register of Women's Grievances and of the Texts*). English translations in Levy, Applewhite and Johnson, *Women in Revolutionary Paris*.

Lacrosil, Michèle (born 1915)

This novelist from the French Antilles was born in Guadeloupe. ▷*Sapotille et le Serein d'argile* (1960) (*Sapotille and the Clay Canary*), ▷*Cajou* (1961) and ▷*Demain Jab-Herma* (1967) (*Tomorrow, Jab-Herma*) provide eloquent illustrations of a sense of alienation due to skin colour engendered by the racism of colonialism. A motif in all three novels is the gaze of one who has returned, an image used to highlight a sense of otherness. Lacrosil's first two novels place her in the wake of the tradition exemplified by ▷Mayotte Capécia, dealing with protagonists who have an inferiority complex and an obsession with skin colour, and who have affairs with white or high mulatto men in an attempt to escape their situation in the Antilles. In her third novel, the focus is no longer upon the female self, and Lacrosil turns to an interpretation of history.

▷Identity, Caribbean

Ladies' Newspaper, The

A Greek newspaper published from March 1887 until 1917. It was published weekly up to 1907 and, after that, fortnightly. It was very successful from the beginning and, according to statistics, in 1892 it was the newspaper with the second highest circulation both in Athens and throughout Greece. It was the first newspaper based on subscription and including advertising. It was published by ▷Kallirroi Parren, a teacher and journalist at that time, who was particularly interested in the position of women in Greece. The paper was the first to introduce feminist issues in Greece, attacking current views on women, and certain writers in particular. Its main function was to affirm female qualities and skills which could be used in the public sphere. It included advice on bringing up children, and introduced new books, but mainly it promoted ideas about sexual equality and reported international feminist conferences. The paper was run by women only, and was the first to offer space for women to express themselves and publish work not accepted elsewhere. Kalliopi Kehayia, ▷Myrtiotissa, Irene Athenea, ▷Athena Tarsouli and other educated women and teachers contributed articles recounting the difficulties of their position, claiming their rights and supporting women's causes. It generally created an ideological climate which helped women to organize mutual support groups and to struggle for political and social rights. It also made men aware of women's demands and helped gain their support.

Ladies of Castille, The (1790)

A tragedy in five acts, it was one of two dramas published in the North American author ▷Mercy Otis Warren's ▷*Poems, Dramatic and Miscellaneous*. Although most of her plays were set in North America, this one was written when a friend requested she try another setting. She does not, however, abandon her themes of independence over tyranny and personal activism, and the setting for the play is the period of Charles V's tyrannical rule in 16th-century Spain. The notable characterization is that of Donna Marcia, an activist and a woman who refuses to see herself as limited because of her sex: 'But for myself – though famine, chains, and death / Should all combine – . . . / I ne'er will yield, / Nor own myself a slave.'

▷*History of the Rise, Progress and Termination of the American Revolution; Group, The*

Ladies of Llangollen, The

Two Irish women, journal and letter-writers Lady Eleanor Butler (1739–1829) and Sarah Ponsonby (1755–1831) were firm friends who ran away from diverse fates – one a convent, the other an ageing but amorous bachelor planning his next marriage. In 1780 they set up house at Plas Newdydd, Llangollen, where they spent their life in companionship and scholarly pursuits. Lady Eleanor kept a journal and wrote letters, Sarah Ponsonby kept a journal for a brief period, recording their first visit to Llangollen. Lady Eleanor's journal observes natural phenomena, and often follows the format of a timetable, giving details of daily activities. On 1 January 1788 it ran, 'Soaking rain. Gloomy heavy day. Three. Dinner. Roast Beef. Plum Pudding. Half past three till 9. Still close night. Reading – making an accompt book. Then reading Sterne to my Beloved while she worked on her Purse, 9–12 in dressing-room reading . . . A day of Sensibility and Sweet Respose'. The code-diarist ▷Ann Lister was among their visitors.

▷Astell, Mary

Lady Audley's Secret (1862)

A novel of ▷sensation by British writer ▷Mary Braddon. Abandoned by her husband, the heroine deserts her child, leaving it to the care of her father. She adopts a new identity and gains work as a ▷governess, later accepting an offer of marriage from Sir Michael Audley and thereby becoming a bigamist. When her first husband returns, she attempts to murder him by pushing him down a well, but he survives and Lady Audley is discovered. She is sent to a lunatic asylum, having pleaded hereditary insanity. The novel was a huge success and has been dramatized, filmed and adapted for television. Feminist critics have read the work as a subversive attack on domestic ideals and feminine stereotypes, and commented on Braddon's use of an angelic-looking blonde as a deviant woman.

Bib: ▷Showalter, E., *A Literature of Their Own.*

Lady Bridget in the Never-Never Land (1915)

Australian novel by ▷Rosa Praed. The story is that of an impulsive Irish aristocrat, Lady Bridget O'Hara, and her romance in the Never-Never Land (western Queensland) with a bushman, Colin McKeith, with whom she strives to build a relationship based on equality and respect. It is also concerned with controversial social issues of the time such as marriage and women's rights, unionization of labour and the treatment of Aborigines in 19th-century Australia.

Lady Oracle (1976)

▷Margaret Atwood's bizarre ▷Gothic comedy about Joan Foster, a woman who fakes her own suicide in order to escape her fame and fortune as a celebrated poet and become her double, the historical ▷romance writer, Louisa K. Delacourt. Joan, who feels that she is an imposter, tries to avoid the confluence of her many personae, but finally must face her own constructedness and her fear. Through flashbacks, Joan's story as a fat and ungainly child comes to light, and we begin to understand why she would choose the superficiality of a heroine with 'a costume rustling discreetly over her breasts'. Lady Oracle is both angry and hilarious; finally, it is a story about a woman inhabiting her own story.

Lady's Visit to the Gold Diggings of Australia in 1852–1853, A (1853)

Australian journal by Ellen Clacy, republished in 1963. This is a vivid contemporary account of life on the Victorian goldfields. Ellen Clacy arrived in Victoria a year after gold was discovered, and spent only a year in the colony. As well as the above account, she published Lights and Shadows of Australian Life (1854). Both works are sensationalized treatments of life in the goldfields, the bush, bushrangers, the Aborigines, and the emigration experience.

▷Journals (Australia)

Laelia (2nd century BC)

Orator. Daughter of the Roman orator Gaius Laelius, she was said by the Roman writer Quintilian (1st century AD) to reflect his ability. Laelia was the elder of two daughters and was nicknamed 'the Wise'. She was famed for the conservative purity of her Latin, which was admired by the Roman politician and orator Cicero (1st century BC).

Lafayette, Marie-Madeleine Pioche de la Vergne, Comtesse de (1634–1693)

French novelist and author of historical fiction and ▷mémoires. Known as the author of the first modern French novel, Madame de Lafayette also wrote two historical ▷nouvelles (short fiction), a Spanish romance in the tradition of the Scudérys (▷Madeleine de Scudéry) and memoirs of the French court. As wife of François, Comte de Lafayette, with whom she spent the minimum of time, she was sufficiently conscious of her noble status to deny authorship of all the main texts that now bear her name. However, her defence of ▷La Princesse de Clèves (1679) (The Princess of Cleves) in a letter to a friend describing it as an authentic collection of memoirs, which should not be classified as a novel, is, in the rhetoric of 17th-century novelists, tantamount to a signed confession. She was related through her mother's second marriage to the family of the ▷Marquise de Sévigné, with whom she corresponded for over forty years. Like the marquise, Madame de Lafayette was guided in her learning by her friend and tutor, the scholar Gilles Ménage (1613–1692), who taught her Latin. She also benefited from the social and literary atmosphere of the salons of her day, notably that of Madame Plessis-Guénégaud (died 1677), where she was known as the Nymphe de l'Allier (Nymph of Allier).

Her first work, the only one to appear with her name during her lifetime, was the literary portrait of Madame de Sévigné which she composed for the amusement of ▷Mademoiselle de Montpensier and her friends, published with similar works by Madame de Villedieu (▷Marie-Catherine Hortense Desjardins) and others in La Galerie des Portraits (The Portrait Gallery) in 1659. The quality of her court fiction is so striking because it follows directly on from Madeleine de Scudéry's ancient-historical salon extravagances. It is based on a close reading of 16th-century historical memoirs, many of which had, like those of Brantôme (c 1540–1614) and Michel de Castelnau (1520–1592), been published for the first time in the second half of the 17th century. The enduring fascination of texts like La Princesse de Clèves and the earlier nouvelle, La Princesse de Montpensier (1662) (The Princess of Montpensier), is the rigorous analysis of the thoughts and feelings of a young and beautiful heroine, caught in an impossible dilemma between her husband and the man she loves. In their day, however, both these texts were equally appreciated for their historical atmosphere. They reveal a subtle understanding of the period in which they are set with remarkable concision. In her clever fusion of the court of the Valois and the court of Louis XIV (1638–1715), Madame de Lafayette set a new precedent in standards of historical fiction. La Comtesse de Tende (The Countess of Tende) (published posthumously in 1723), the shortest of all her works of fiction, is a final abridgement of the novelist's bitter philosophy of the married woman's predicament at court. Although it has been argued that she may have modelled much of her fiction on her own emotional experiences, there was an abundance of historical and contemporary examples of unhappily married women on which she could draw. Also published posthumously, La Vie de la Princesse (Henriette) d'Angleterre) (The Life of Princess Henrietta of England) – whose marriage to Louis XIV's brother was fraught with infidelities on his part, flirtations on hers and frequent childbirth, and who died suddenly in mysterious circumstances – is remarkably reminiscent of La Princesse de Clèves. In 1669 Madame de Lafayette published Zaïde, histoire espagnole (▷Zayde; a Spanish History Written by M. de Segrats, 1678), a Spanish romance in the old style which is in many ways the odd one out in her work as a whole.
Bib: Lafayette, Madame de, Romans et Nouvelles, ed. A. Niderst (1989); Duchêne, R., Mme de Lafayette.

Lafite, Marie-Elisabeth Bouée de (?1750–1794)

French educational writer and translator. Lafite resided in La Haye with her husband, a Protestant preacher, with whom she collaborated on the periodical, *Bibliothèque des sciences et des beaux arts* (*Library of Science and Fine Arts*). She published two volumes of educational prose fiction and plays, *Entretiens, drames et contes moraux* (1778) *Conversations, Dramas and Moral Tales* and *Eugénie et ses élèves* (1787) (*Eugenie and her Pupils*) and a collection, *Lettres sur divers sujets* (1775) (*Letters on Various Subjects*). Her translations include *Essais sur la physionomie* (1787), (*Essays on Physiognomy*), from the German by Lavater, and also the novel by Sophie de la Roche, *Miss Lony* (1792).

Lafitte y Pérez del Pulgar, María de los Reyes (born 1902)

Spanish novelist. Lafitte was born in Seville, where she resided until her marriage in 1922 to a grandee of Spain. Her most famous work is *La guerra secreta de los sexos* (1948) (*The Secret War of the Sexes*), a philosophical study of women throughout history, which emphasizes feminine phychology, women's position in society, and women's reactions to men. Her novel *La flecha y la esponja* (1959) (*The Arrow and the Sponge*), explores the same themes using Freudian psychoanalysis.

La Force, Charlotte Rose Caumont de (1650–1724)

French author of novels and fairytales. A member of an illustrious family which had been close to Henri IV (1553–1610), Mademoiselle de La Force spent a very free youth and had many love affairs. At thirty-four she made an effort to conform by marrying de Briou, nine years her junior, but the family objected and locked up the young man. She stole into his bedroom, dressed as a bear with a travelling troupe, and managed to escape with him, but the pair were caught and brought to justice. The marriage was annulled. A few years later, she was implicated in the publication of satirical verses and given the choice between exile and the convent. She chose the latter and began to publish novels and fairytales to support herself. The latter were published in *Les Contes des contes* (*Tales of Tales*) in 1697 under the pseudonym Mademoiselle de X. Some are based on 16th-century rewritings of medieval *chansons de geste* (verse chronicles of heroic deeds) and chivalric poems. She also wrote various pseudo-historical novels which have received less critical attention. Between 1694 and 1703 she published the secret histories of Marie de Bourgogne (1457–1482), Henri IV, King of Castille (1454–1474), Marguerite de Valois (1552–1615) and Catherine de Bourbon, which is more reminiscent of the novel *L'Astrée* (*Astrea*) by Honoré d'Urfé (1567–1625) than any history. Admitting that critics may object to the episodes that she has invented, she appends a scrupulous list of sources

to this novel, but makes no distinction between historical and fictitious texts.

Bib: Barchilon, J., *Le Conte merveilleux français de 1690 à 1790*; Robert, R., *Le Conte de fées littéraire en France de la fin du XVIIe à la fin du XVIIIe siècle.*

Laforet, Carmen (born 1921)

Spanish novelist, born in Barcelona. Laforet was the first woman novelist to come to the public's attention in the post-war period. Her fame largely rests on her novel ▷*Nada* (1944) (*Nothing*), which is a rewriting of the masculinist format of the ▷*Bildungsroman*. Laforet's other novels are: *La isla y los demonios* (1952) (*The Island and the Devils*); *La mujer nueva* (1955) (*The New Woman*), and *La insolación* (1963) (*Sunstroke*). She has also published collections of short fiction: *La muerta* (1952) (*The Dead Woman*); *La llamada* (1954) (*The Call*); and *La niña y otros relatos* (1970) (*The Child and Other Stories*).

Lage de Volude, Béatrix-Etiennette Renart de Fuchsamberg d'Omblimont, Marquise de (1764–1842)

French memoir-writer. Born in Paris, she was one of the many French aristocrats to flee the country during the Revolution (1789). Her *Souvenirs d'émigration* (*Memories of Exile*) were published by the Baron de La Mornière in 1869.

Bib: Chuquet, A., *Episodes et portraits.* Vol. 1.

▷*Mémoires*

Lagerlöf, Selma Ottilia Lovisa (1858–1940)

Swedish novelist. She received the Nobel Prize in 1909, and was the first woman ever to enter the Swedish Academy. She was born and died at the manor house of Mårbacka. She was disabled, and had a very protected childhood. She became a teacher, and was deeply affected when her father had to give up Mårbacka in the 1880s. She wrote about an era she felt had disappeared, and in 1891 she published the saga-novel *Gösta Berlings Saga* (▷*The Story of Gösta Berling*) in lyrical prose which broke with the naturalism of the 1880s. She won a wide audience with the novels about Dalar farmers, *Jerusalem I–II* (1901–1902), written in the style of the Icelandic sagas.

In 1901 she was asked to write a schoolbook on geography, which she finished between 1906–1907 as *Nils Holgerssons underbara resa genom Sverige I–II* (▷*The Wonderful Adventures of Nils*).

With her Nobel Prize award she bought back Mårbacka, and lived there with her many prizes and awards, often in ill-health. From 1922 to 1932 she wrote about Mårbacka in her autobiography, but her most important later work is the trilogy *The Ring of Löwenskölds* (1925–1928), where the female characters are strong and optimistic in their realism.

Lagerlöf had a growing interest in spiritualism and life after death, eg *Herr Arnes penningar* (1904) (*Herr Arne's Hoard*, 1925), but her social concern and interest in strong female characters also persisted.

Lagorio, Gina (born 1930)

Italian novelist and critic. She taught Italian literature and history in her native Liguria for many years, but eventually moved to Rome where she began to work for *Radio-audizioni italiene* (RAI), and to contribute regularly to Italian newspapers and magazines. *Approssimato per difetto* (1971) (*By Default*), is perhaps her best-known work. It recounts her own life and her husband's death from cancer. It is at once her story, his story, a story of illness and of death, as well as of love. She has recently allied herself with a growing band of self-consciously female Italian writers, keen to identify a tradition of Italian women writers. She has done this most notably through her association with *Racconta*, a collection of writings published by the feminist publishing house *La tartaruga* (Tortoise Press). Her contribution to this collection, *Arcadia*, presents the relationship between an elderly couple engaged in mutual psychological torment in their opulent mansion. The female character of the couple is still forward-looking, and wishes more of life. Her male counterpart is embittered, and elderly in his approach. It is she who finally has the courage to break free of their destructive bond. Many of Lagorio's works deal with women alone, and she has won many literary prizes. *Tosca dei gatti* (1983) (*Tosca and her Cats*), tells the sad story of a lonely, isolated woman, who lives – and dies – for her cats. In the end, Tosca chooses to die because she cannot stand the loneliness of her life. Lagorio uses here the technique of the novel-within-the-novel, as what we read is ostensibly the work of a writer/character who observes Tosca closely. *Il golfo del paradiso* (1987) (*Paradise Bay*), is a similar tale, in that we are presented here with an old painter who can live in harmony with nature, but who is quite withdrawn from the world. *Fuori scena* (1979) (*Off Stage*), is the tale of a return to the past in an attempt to achieve understanding. Much of Lagorio's work is concerned with the old, their past, and the isolation of the individual from society.

Her other works include: *Fenoglio* (1970); *Cultura e letteratura ligure del 1900* (1972) (*The Literature and Culture of Liguria in the 20th Century*); *La spiaggia del lupo* (1977) (*Wolf's Beach*); *Qualcosa nell'aria* (1980) (*Something in the Air*); *Giotto. La storia di Gesu* (1983) (*Giotto. The Story of Jesus*); *Penelope senza tela* (1984) (*Penelope Without a Web*); *Le nouvelle di Simonetta* (1988) (*Simonetta's Stories*).

Lagrave, Comtesse de (18th century)

French novelist. She published some ten novels, mostly ▷ sentimental, with the exception of the Gothic *Le Château d'Alvarino, ou les effets de la vengeance* (1799) (*Alvarino's Castle, or the Results of Revenge*). Her other works include: *Minuit, ou les aventures de Paul de Mirebon* (1798) (*Midnight, or the Adventures of Paul de Mireton*); *Sophie de Beauregard, ou le véritable amour* (1798) (*Sophie de Beauregard, or True Love*); *Zabeth, ou la victime de l'ambition* (1798); (*Zabeth, or the Victim of Ambition*); *La Chaumière incendiée* (1802) (*The Burnt-out Cottage*) M. *Ménard ou l'homme comme il y en a peu* (1802) (*M. Ménard, or the Exceptional Man*); *Hector de Romagny, ou l'erreur d'une bonne mère* (1803) (*Hector de Romagny or the Error of a Good Mother*); *Juliette Belfour, ou les talens récompensées* (1803) (*Juliette Balfour, or Talents Rewarded*), *Paulina* (1804); *La Méprise du coche, ou à quelque chose malheur est bon* (1805) (*The Error of the Coach, or the Usefulness of Suffering*), and *La Méprise de diligence* (1820) (*The Error of Zeal*).

Laguiller, Arlette (born 1940)

French Member of Parliment and author. A long-term militant for the Communist Party (Trotskyist tendency), she has been an MP since 1981, and ran as the first woman candidate for the presidency in the 1974 elections. She is the author of *Moi, une militante* (*My Life as a Militant*).

Lagum (1991) (*The Cavern*)

Serbian novel by Svetlana Velmar-Janković (born 1933). The novel is an account of the social transformation and upheaval in Yugoslavia after World War II, when shopkeepers and caretakers became landlords, and property was confiscated from former owners, who now became tenants. The narrative ranges from the 1930s to 1984. It is narrated in the first person by a middle-class woman married to a professor of art history who decides to collaborate with the Fascist government in order to save lives. She disagrees with him, but remains loyal. After the war he is arrested and executed, and she is left to live in only two rooms of their once finely-furnished flat, supporting herself and her children by working as a translator.

The work is composed in layers of reminiscence. It is a series of 'nows' which are used to introduce other characters. The most important of these is the orphan peasant girl, Zora, taken on as a maid by the husband, who becomes a communist, and ends up occupying most of the flat. There is also a university art critic who, as a partisan, is wounded and then sheltered secretly by the narrator while he recovers. Both characters are brutalized by the Communist Revolution, and incapable of responding to the narrator's straightforward and modest appeal to be allowed to retain one painting of great sentimental value to her, incapable, that is, until she is buried and Zora wails at her graveside. This dignified statement leaves an enduring impression that nothing of value was gained from the social upheavals which cost so much in terms of human spirit.

Laina, Maria (born 1947)

Greek poet. Born in Patras, she studied law in Athens. Inspired by the poetry of Kavafis (Constantine Cavafy, 1863–1933), George Seferis (1900–1971) and Karyotakis, she began writing her own poems, quickly establishing her own style and voice. Her first collection, *Coming of Age* (1968), contains poems of great profundity and sensitivity. Her poetry expresses the themes of love, death and innocence, not through the voice of individual characters but in the context of social situations and problems. *Change of Place* (1974) is a collection of love poems. *Punctuation Marks* (1979) and *Her Own* (1985) are further collections on the theme of love and death. She has also translated English literature into Greek.

Lair, Clara (born 1895)
Puerto Rican poet, real name Mercedes Negron Muñoz. She uses a deeply melancholy rhythm, and her style ranges from ▷*postmodernismo* to ▷*modernismo*. She belongs to the 'Feminine Parnasse' of the 1930s. Her first book, *Arras de cristal* (1937) (*Glass Pledge*), shows high lyricism, as evidenced in the poem 'Lullaby mayor'. Her eroticism prompts a fantasy of forgetfulness, as in the poem '*Fantasia del olvido*', from *Trópico amargo* (1950) (*Bitter Tropic*). In this book she is 'erotic, passionate, daring in her confidences on surrender to the male and solitude in the midst of such fires', according to E. Anderson Imbert in *Spanish-American Literature* (1969).

Laisse, Madame de (18th century)
French prose fiction writer. She published collections of anecdotes, tales and proverbs, with songs: *Recueil d'anecdotes* (1773) (*Collected Anecdotes*); *Nouveaux Contes Moraux* (1774) (*New Moral Tales*); *Ouvrage sans titre* (1775) (*Untitled Work*); *Proverbes dramatiques* (1777) (*Dramatic Proverbs*) and *Nouveau Genre de Proverbes dramatiques* (1778) (*New Kind of Dramatic Proverbs*). A letter in response to a criticism by ▷Dame Montanclos in the ▷*Journal des Dames* (*Ladies' Journal*) appeared in the periodical *Mercure*, in August 1774.

Lake, Claude ▷Blind, Mathilde

Lakshmi
The Hindu goddess of wealth, good fortune and beauty. She is the consort of Vishnu, the preserver of life in the Hindu cosmos, but unlike the consorts of the other main gods, Shiva and Brahma, she is often worshipped in her own right. Her ability to bring good luck is closely related to her wifely devotion and obedience. ▷Sita, the wife of Rama, is a manifestation of Lakshmi.

Lamas, Maria (1893–1983)
Portuguese feminist activist, essayist and editor. In 1925 she became editor of the women's magazine *Modas e Bordados* (*Fashions and Embroideries*), a position she held for twenty years. In the 1940s Lamas assumed the leadership of the National Council of Portuguese Women and opened its membership to the proletariat. She lost her job at *Modas e Bordados* when she objected to the government's order to close the Council in 1946. Prior to going into exile, she wrote a book about working women in urban and rural Portugal entitled *Mulheres do Meu País* (1948) (*Women of*

My Country), and a sociological overview entitled *A Mulher no Mundo* (1952) (*Woman in the World*).

Lamb, Lady Caroline (1785–1828)
English novelist, daughter of the third Earl of Bessborough. At the age of sixteen she married William Lamb, who later became Lord Melbourne. The marriage grew difficult when Caroline developed an obsessive infatuation with the poet Byron, with whom she had a brief affair in 1812. Her first novel, *Glenarvon* (1816), was published anonymously and created a minor scandal. The character of Glenarvon was based on Byron, and the story is a ▷Gothic tale of passion and ▷romance. Her other novels include *Graham Hamilton* (1820) and *Ada Reis* (1823). Always tending towards mental instability, Caroline's final breakdown occurred after she caught sight of Byron's funeral procession in 1824. She separated from her husband and retired to live in the country until her death four years later.

Lambert, Anne-Thérèse de Marguenat de Courcelles, Marquise de (1647–1733)
French essayist and salon hostess. Educated by her stepfather, she was reputed to be a serious young woman who disapproved of her mother's frivolity. Married at nineteen and widowed at thirty-nine, Lambert struggled for twenty years to secure her disputed inheritance. The salon she inaugurated in her sixty-third year, considered as an antechamber to the ▷Académie Francaise, enabled her to wield a considerable amount of power. The formal assemblies and academic debates were attended by many intellectual women including the ▷Comtesse Fontaines, ▷La Force, ▷Murat, ▷Bernard, ▷Caylus, ▷d'Aulnoy, ▷Dacier and ▷Staal-Delaunay. Her writings include *Réflexions nouvelles sur les femmes* (1727) (*New Reflections on Women*), *Traité de l'amitié* (1736) (*Treatise on Friendship*) and *Traité de la vieillesse* (1736) (*Treatise on Old Age*), all addressed to women. The respect for Christian moral values in her work has earned her a reputation as a moralist, to the detriment of the feminist import of her writing; the two are, however, inextricably linked. Although she deplored a certain moral degeneration in women, she blamed it on culturally reinforced notions of innate inferiority, inadequate education and, in particular, Molière's ridicule of female intellectual endeavour. In arguing for women's right to study, she noted that the relative freedom of women in France, restricted to the domain of the frivolous, did not include the right to pursue self-development. Women, alienated from themselves, needed to become conscious of their own specific qualities: imagination, sensitivity and taste, which she claimed increased their capacity for effective reasoning. Encouraged to study and to be more ambitious, women would gain access to a happier and more dignified existence, and be less inclined to seek relief from boredom and anxieties in dissipated lifestyles. The argument in favour of

moral rectitude is used to make the feminist demand for a right to self-improvement.

Other works: *Lettres d'une dame à son fils sur la vraie gloire* (1726) (*Letters from a Lady to Her Son on True Glory*); *Avis d'une mère à son fils et à sa fille* (1728) (*A Mother's Advice to Her Son and Daughter*); *Lettres sur la veritable éducation* (1729) (*Letters on True Education*), and *Métaphysique de l'amour* (1729) (*Metaphysics of Love*).

Recent edition of her works include: *Réflexions nouvelles sur les femmes*, with a Preface by P. Milagro, (1989).
Bib: Dauvergne, R., *La Marquise de Lambert à l'hôtel Nevers*; Fassiotto, M-J., *Mme de Lambert ou le feminisme moral*; Reynold, G. de, *Le XVIIième siècle*; Zimmerman, J.P., 'La Morale laïque au commencement du XVIIIième siècle-Mme de Lambert' in *Revue de l'Histoire Littéraire* (1917).

Lambert, Betty (1933–1983)
Canadian dramatist and novelist. Born Betty Lee in Calgary, Alberta, Lambert grew up listening to radio plays from the Canadian Broadcasting Corporation, and conceived the ambition to write drama. She attended the University of British Columbia, and travelled extensively before returning to Canada. In her lifetime, she wrote over fifty radio, stage, children's and television plays, the bes-known being *The Visitor* (1970), *Song of the Serpent* (1973) and *Sqrieux-de-Dieu* (1976). *Jennie's Story* (1981) takes as its subject the enforced sterilization of a woman considered mentally deficient. Her novel, *Crossings* (1979), is a savagely brilliant metafiction that explores a battered woman's textualization of her physical experience. She was Associate Professor of English at Simon Fraser University in British Columbia until her death.
Bib: van Herk, A., in ▷*A Mazing Space*.

Lamentation or Complaint of a Sinner, The (1547)
English writer ▷Catherine Parr's vehemently Protestant work. It formed not only a confession of her past sins, but also a repentance of her past ignorance of faith (that is, her earlier Catholicism). Hoping to edify others and further the ▷Protestant Reformation, she published her work under her own name rather than anonymously. Parr's *Lamentation* strongly denounces Catholicism and the Pope, espouses a belief in justification by faith rather than works, and praises Henry VIII as a religious reformer. The work went through three editions between 1547 and 1563.
▷Confession of faith
Bib: *Harleian Miscellany* I (1808), p. 286–313.

Lament for Art O'Leary, The (1921)
Translation of *Caoineadh Airt Úi Laoghaire* by ▷Eibhlín Dubh Ní Chonaill. In this famous long lament, considered to be the finest love poem in the Irish language, Eibhlin Dubh tells the story of her husband's death, and expresses her grief at his loss in deeply moving terms: 'On my heart is such sorrow / That all Munster could not cure it, / Nor the wisdom of the sages.' Many translations have been made of the poem, including those by Sean O Cuír (1923), Frank O'Connor (1959) and that by Eilis Dillon, which is the subject of this entry.

Lamplighter, The (1854)
US novel by ▷Maria Susanna Cummins. Moralistic, improbable, wildly popular, *The Lamplighter* captured the woman's version of the rags-to-riches saga. Gerty, a scruffy and untamed orphan, is taken up by Trueman, the lamplighter. She learns piety and virtue, becomes educated and refined, and so gets – and deserves – marriage to the most deserving friend of her youth. While *The Lamplighter* was almost an archetype of melodramatic plot, its writing was vivid, its dialogue real and its scenes memorable. It was modelled on its bestselling predecessor ▷*The Wide, Wide World*.

Lancaster, G.B. ▷Lyttleton, Edith

Land of Cockayne, The (1901)
English translation of *Il paese di Cuccagna* (1891), a broadly ▷realist novel by ▷Matilde Serao. It is, in essence, a study of Naples in the grip of the lottery, and shows how all social classes are affected by gambling. Yet it is also a narrative which highlights female strength, in which women save their families and businesses. It is a tale of how women support men, but equally demonstrates how they support each other. There is a fascinating ▷Gothic family subplot here which traffics in madness, delirium and visionary trances, and runs counter to the overall style of the narrative. Yet both Gothic and realist plot ultimately tell the same story of strong female bonds. The most powerful relationships in this novel are those between mothers and daughters, a recurrent feature of Serao's fiction.

Land of Spices, The (1941)
This remarkable novel by ▷Kate O'Brien is a beautifully understated study of the ways in which the lives of an austere English woman, Reverend Mother of a Catholic convent school, and a young Irish schoolgirl, Anna Murphy, become interwoven, and of how each, almost unwittingly, helps the other to grow in human understanding, compassion and courage. Anna moves towards womanhood under the loving but always distant gaze of Mère Marie Hélène, herself struggling to resolve the conflict she experiences between the need for love and the dangerously seductive pleasures of intellectual and spiritual self-containment. The novel was banned in Ireland because of a single, if pivotal, sentence referring to a male homosexual act. The ban has now been lifted.
▷Censorship (Ireland)

Landon, Letitia (1802–1838)

English poet, also wrote under the ▷pseudonym
L.E.L. She was born in Chelsea, London, and her
first work appeared in the *Literary Gazette* in 1820.
Between 1821 and 1828 she published five
volumes of verse: *The Fate of Adelaide* (1821); *The
Improvisatrice* (1824); *The Troubadour* (1825); *The
Golden Violet* (1827) and *The Venetian Bracelet and
Other Poems* (1828). Her work was extremely
popular, seeming to combine a lightweight
▷Romanticism with delicate feminine sentiments
and melancholic expression. She had many
admirers but eventually married George Maclean.
The couple left for Africa, where George was a
governor, and a few months later Letitia was
found dead. It is not known whether she
committed suicide or was murdered. Her other
works include five novels and many miscellaneous
pieces. Landon was seen by other Victorian
women poets as an important precursor, and both
▷Elizabeth Barrett Browning and ▷Christina
Rossetti wrote poems dedicated to her.
  ▷Ballad (19th-century Britain)
Bib: Hickok, K., *Representations of Women: 19th
English Women's Poetry.*

Land Without Thunder (1968) *The Island of Tears* (1980)

Short stories by Kenyan writer ▷Grace Ogot.
The first of these is a collection of short stories in
which Ogot gives full rein to her profound feeling
for the macabre and the fantastic. *The Island of
Tears* is a later collection, the title-story mourning
the death of Tom Mboya, the Kenyan political
leader assassinated in 1969. Ogot's Christian
values are evident in 'The Wayward Father' from
the later collection, a story of adultery and
reconciliation which powerfully reveals the central
position the man holds in the new Kenyan
middle-class family.

Lange, Norah (1906–1972)

Full name Norah Langue De Girondo.
Argentinian poet, novelist and essayist of
Norwegian descent. She participated with her
husband, Oliverio Girondo, in the ▷*Martín Fierro*
Group of poets, as well as moving in the most
cultivated circles of Buenos Aires, and publishing
several ▷avant-garde magazines. *La calle de la
tarde* (1924) (*Afternoon Street*), poems, was her first
book, and was tied to memories of childhood and
to literature, topics also present in her other books
of poetry, *Los días y las novelas* (1926) (*Days and
Novels*) and *El rumbo de la rosa* (1930). Her
experimental novel *Personas en la sala* (1950)
(*People in the Room*) also follows these themes. Its
protagonist, an adolescent narrator, projects her
magic imagination onto the world. Lange's first
novel, *45 días y 30 marineros* (1933) (*45 Days and
30 Sailors*), describes the journey of a woman
alone on a freighter from Buenos Aires to Oslo.
Although perhaps not typical of her mature work,
it does reflect the feminist effervescence of a rich
girl. One of her most outstanding novels is *Los dos
retratos* (1956) (*Two Portraits*), especially for its
ability to give a concise idea of time and feelings.
Discursos (1942) (*Discourses*), her speeches at the
meetings of the *Martín Fierro* Group, are
outstanding in that genre.

Langgässer, Elisabeth (1899–1950)

German poet and novelist. Her poetry, collected
in *Wendekreis des Lammes* (1924) (*Tropic of the
Lamb*), *Tierkreisgedichte* (1935) (*Zodiac Poems*) and
Der Laubmann und die Rose (1947) (*The Forester
and the Rose*), is steeped in both Christian and
pagan imagery, and deals with the individual's
yearning for redemption in a world where nature,
and in particular the poet's own homeland of
Rheinhessen, assumes mythical dimensions. As
she was half-Jewish, Langgässer was banned from
publishing after 1936, and it was during the
following years that she composed her most
powerful work, *Das unauslöschliche Siegel* (1946)
(*The Indelible Seal*). This novel, though
experimental in form and style, develops within a
very clearly-defined framework of Christian
ideology. She also wrote evocative stories about
women's experiences in World War II, collected
in *Der Torso* (1947) (*The Torso*), and a further
novel about the quest for redemption, *Märkische
Argonautenfahrt* (1950) (*The Quest*, 1953).
  ▷Kolmar, Gertrud

Langley, Eve (1908–1974)

Australian novelist. Langley is best known for her
epic novel ▷*The Pea Pickers* (1942), an
imaginative first-person narrative of feminine
adventure. It deals with the adventures of two
young women, 'Steve' and 'Blue' who, in male
disguise, seek excitement and love during their
rovings among the seasonal workers in rural
Gippsland. *The Pea Pickers* won the S.H. Prior
Memorial Prize for 1941. Its sequel, *White Topee*
(1954), is less interesting. Eve Langley's life was
as bizarre as any fiction. She spent her last years
in isolation in a bush shack in the Blue Mountains
to the west of Sydney, dressed in male clothes and
obsessed with the personality of Oscar Wilde.

Langmann, Adelheid (died 1375)

German nun and visionary writer. Little is known
of her life, other than that she entered the
Dominican Convent of Engelthal after the death
of her fiancé. Like the mystic writer ▷Christine
Ebner, who died in the same convent around
1355, she had many visions, which she recorded
in *Offenbarungen* (*Revelations*).
  ▷*Visionsliteratur*

Langner, Ilse (1899–1988)

German dramatist, poet and novelist. A prolific
writer, she first achieved fame in 1929 with
▷*Frau Emma kämpft im Hinterland* (*Emma Fights
on the Home Front*), the first anti-war play written
by a German woman. Her novel *Die purpurne
Stadt* (1937) (*The Purple Town*) was proscribed by
the Nazis. After World War II she contributed to
Germany's *Trümmerliteratur* (literally, 'rubble-
literature') which examined the recent fascist past

and wartime devastation. To this period belong the poems in *Zwischen Trümmern* (1948) (*Among the Rubble*) and the plays *Trümmerstücke* (*Bits of Rubble*) and *Heimkehr* (1949) (*Homecoming*). Langner's work generally is most interesting when it deals with immediate, topical issues; the play, *Métro*, written in Paris in 1952, deals evocatively with the fear, prevalent during the Cold War, of a sudden nuclear holocaust, while the novel, *Die Zyklopen* (1960) (*The Cyclops*), discusses the problems surrounding atomic power.

Language continuum

The term used to denote the span of language forms present in the Caribbean. These range from the ancestral language of the ▷Native Americans and the imperial language of the colonizers (English, French, Dutch and Spanish) to the adaptation of these languages in the form of creole. Creole(s) developed out of the fusion of European languages with the imported languages of the enslaved Africans and indentured workers.

Where possible, slaves were isolated from their common language group and transported and sold in 'mixed lots' as a deliberate means of eliminating the possibility of revolt. The policy of language suppression was continued on the plantations wherever it could be implemented. The result was that within two or three generations (and sometimes less) the only language available to the Africans for communication either among themselves or with the master was a form of the European language, or a new code in which the language of the European predominated. Creole is thought to have reached Guadeloupe and Martinique around 1635. A language which started as an unstable and precarious system for exchanges, creole quickly became established as the oral linguistic tool of the descendant of the African, while French remained as the means of (spoken and written) linguistic mastery of the European in these islands.
▷Nation Language

Language in Her Eye: Writing and Gender (1990)

Edited by Libby Scheier, Sarah Sheard, and Eleanor Wachtel, *Language in Her Eye* was conceived as a discussion of the current debates about feminist theory, and the effect that feminism has on the writing and publishing environment in Canada. A range of Canadian women writers were invited to respond to questions about the connection between politics and writing, including issues of voice and appropriations. The result is a many-faceted book of reflections, with individual pieces from writers as diverse as ▷Marlene Nourbese Philip, ▷Margaret Atwood, and ▷Gail Scott. Articulating as it does a range of opinions on gender and writing, it has caused controversy and debate since its publication.

Lanyer, Aemilia (1569–?1640)

English poet. Lanyer (born Bassano) is best known for ▷*Salve Deus, Rex Judaeorum* (1611) and 'The Description of Cooke-ham'. Lanyer was the daughter of Baptista Bassni, a court musician, and she married another musician, Alfonso Lanyer. A poem about her youth, 'To the Ladie Susan, Countess Dowager of Kent', indicates that the Countess was her patron. She was not weathly and it seems that her volume of poems, *Salve Deux, Rex Judaeorum*, was published in hope of obtaining patronage, and it was accompanied by several dedications. Indeed, it seems that she adopted the format in which her book was published for different patrons. In *Salve Deux, Rex Judaeorum* she writes of the execution of Christ in the way which insists on universal oppression: 'Things reasonable, and reasonlesse possest / The terrible impression of this fact: / For his oppression made them all opprest.' The poem also contain 'Eve's Apologie in Defence of Woman'. 'The Description of Cooke-ham' was produced in praise of Margaret Clifford, Countess of Cumberland, who married the Earl of Dorset in February 1609. The poem uses the idea of place, and, like some other 17th-century poems on country houses, uses the house to figure nostalgia and loss, beginning, 'Farewell (sweet Cooke-ham) where I first obtain'd / Grace from that Grace where perfit Grace remain'd; / And where the Muses gave their full consent, / I should have powre the virtuous to content.' Critic A.L. Rowse has contended that Lanyer was the 'dark lady' of Shakespeare's sonnets, but there is no evidence to support this.

Lapauze, Jeanne (1860–1920)

French novelist, poet and dramatist who used the ▷pseudonym Daniel Lesueur. Lapauze began writing in 1882, published a collection of poems entitled *Fleurs d'Avril* (*April Flowers*), which were crowned by the ▷Académie Française, and then turned to novels, producing one a year until 1912. These have evocative titles like *Névrosée* (1890) (*The Neurotic*); *Justice de femme* (1893) (*Women's Justice*); *Haine d'Amour* (1894) (*Aversion to Love*); *L'Honneur d'une femme* (1901) (*A Woman's Honour*) and *Le Masque d'Amour* (1904) (*The Mask of Love*), and were feminist in tenor, as were her dramatic works (see for example her *Théâtre féministe*, 1899, *Feminist Theatre*). She was the first woman to be awarded the *Légion d'honneur* for literature (1910).

Lapid, Shulamit (born 1934)

Israeli novelist and short story writer. Lapid was born in Tel-Aviv and studied at the Hebrew University. She was the chairwoman of the Hebrew Writers' Association, and is the author of short stories, novels, plays and children's books. Lapid's writing surprises readers with its constantly changing perspectives. Women and feminist issues are central themes. In her acclaimed novel ▷*Gai Oni* (1982), the protagonist, a woman, represents the women neglected by historians of Israel's pioneering period. Her novels include: *Ka'Cheres Ha'Nishbar* (1984) (*Like a Broken Vessel*); *Iton Mekomi* (1989) (*Local paper*), and *Akavishim Smechim* (1990) (*Happy spiders*).

Lapidario (1988) (*Lapidary*)

Collection of poetry by ▷Clara Janés, one of Spain's most significant female poets. She focuses at once on the identity created through language as well as the identity created by society. Janés's poetry depicts a feminine identity which does not depend on an autonomous ego, but which is created through a fusion with 'other' identities.

Láppo-Danilévskaia, Nadezhda Aleksandrova (1875/76–1951)

Prose writer and dramatist. Láppo-Danilévskaia was one of several Russian women who became popular for their entertaining and melodramatic prose before and during World War I. Her characters move in the upper-class world of balls and fancy dress, her heroines and heroes are all handsome and well-groomed, love drives her plots, and, although her young ladies may rebel against the restrictions of their lives, in the end they accept their place in society. Their grandmothers are the source of moral education, mothers being either corrupt or self-absorbed. The villains in her world are women.

This formula served her so well that several of her novels went through multiple editions. ▷*Michail or The Heart of a Russian* (Russian title: *A Russian Gentleman*), first published in 1914, appeared in at least six editions of 36,000 copies in all. *The Minister's Wife* (1913) and *In the Mist of Life* (1911) came out in five editions, and the former was republished a sixth time in Latvia in 1931. After 1917 Láppo-Danilévskaia emigrated to western Europe, where she continued to publish novels, stories and plays until at least 1937. But her audience was much reduced: copies of her novels now numbered 2,000, and there was a second edition of only one, *Barren Flowers* (1928). Her work is representative of one aspect of the popular fiction market that existed for a brief time during the ▷Silver Age.
▷Bashkirtseff, Marie

Lara, Contessa (1849–1896)

Italian poet and novelist. Born in Florence, she lived much of her life in Rome, where she moved in the literary and journalistic circles of the period. As a child she was taught English, French and Spanish by her father, and music by her mother. She married Eugenio Mancini, and with him lived a life of aristocratic pleasure in Naples and Milan. A prolific writer, her somewhat sensational novels tragically mirrored her life. One of her lovers was killed by her husband in a duel, and she herself was finally murdered by a painter with whom she was living. Her lifestyle had earned her considerable moral censure, echoed even in her obituaries. Her novel ▷*L'innamorata* (*A Woman in Love*) may be seen as at least semi-

autobiographical. She also wrote tales for children.

Her other works include: *Canti e ghirlande* (1867) (*Songs and Garlands*); *Versi* (1883) (*Verses*); *E ancora versi* (1886) (*More Verses*); *Nuovi Versi* (1897) (*New Verses*), a collection published posthumously.

Larcom, Lucy (1824–1893)

US poet and autobiographer. One of the Lowell ▷mill girls who went on to a literary career, Larcom is most significant for her autobiographical *A New England Girlhood, Outlined from Memory* (1889), reprinted in 1924 and available now in a 1986 edition. While Larcom was always a rather self-effacing writer – her preface to *A New England Girlhood* begins: 'The following sketch was written for the young, at the suggestion of friends' – her record is important for its insider's account of the effects of industrialism both on the community and on the young women industrial workers.

La Roche, Guilhem (1644–1710)

French minor novelist. A Protestant who took refuge in England after the revocation of the Edict of Nantes in 1685 which removed Protestants' rights, she has a reputation as a mediocre novelist, who imitated ▷Madeleine de Scudéry and Madame de Villedieu (▷Marie-Catherine Hortense Desjardins). If works like *Almanzaïde* (1674), *Arioviste, histoire romaine* (1674) and *Singis, histoire tartare* (1692) are best forgotten, the comedy *Rare en tout* (*Rare in Everything*), performed in Whitehall in 1677, is rather more worthy of interest.

La Roche, Sophie (1730–1807)

German novelist, letter-writer and editor. From a cultured family, she was the one-time fiancée of the writer Christoph Wieland (1733–1813), but married Councillor La Roche in 1754, and had five children. In 1771, when her children were nearly grown up, she published anonymously the epistolary ▷*Geschichte des Fräuleins von Sternheim* (*The Story of Fräulein von Sternheim*), the first woman's novel in Germany. After her husband's death she began to travel, and wrote travelogues, novels and stories. She started her own periodical, *Pomona*, in 1783, and carried on a lively correspondence with many writers of her time. When her daughter, Maximiliane, died leaving twelve orphans, she took on the care of the younger ones, one of whom was ▷Bettina von Arnim.

Larpent, Anna Margaretta (fl 1815–1830)

English diarist who recorded her life from the age of fifteen onwards. She married John Larpent, Examiner of Plays. She continued her diary after marriage and noted events in theatre and in letters. Her diary ends in 1830.

Larreta de Gándara, Carmen Rodríguez
▷Gándara, Carmen

Lars, Claudia ▷Brannon, Carmen

Larsen, Nella (1891–1964)
US novelist. Larsen was born a mulatta in
Chicago, Illinois, and when her father died, she
became the only African-American in her
immediate family. Like Helga Crane in *Quicksand*
(1928), Larsen first moved south, and then on to
Denmark, where she went to the University of
Copenhagen. In 1912 she began working as a
nurse in New York, and later became a librarian.
In 1919 she became the socialite wife of a
physicist. She is usually, although not comfortably,
identified with the ▷Harlem Renaissance.
   Quicksand depicts the conflict of cultural
loyalties resulting from mixed ancestry. Helga
seeks to fulfil her potential but is caught in the
intersection of race and gender. She cannot find
her identity in either white or black communities.
A modern woman without money or family, she
questions prescribed gender roles. However, by
the end of the novel she is entrapped in a
marriage with a rural Alabama preacher. ▷*Passing*
(1929) focuses also on an African-American
woman committed to Anglo-American middle-
class values. Larsen's work concerns the
relationship between the African-American
middle class and their heritage.
Bib: Bone, R., *The Negro Novel in America*;
Bontemps, A. (ed.), *The Harlem Renaissance
Remembered*.

Lask, Berta (1878–1967)
German poet and dramatist. She was born in
Galizien, a German province between Hungary
and Poland, of wealthy middle-class parents.
Inspired by the Russian Revolutions, she
developed strong feminist and pacifist convictions,
which were expressed in two collections of poems:
Stimmen (1914) (*Voices*) and *Rufe aus dem Dunkeln*
(1921) (*Cries from the Dark*). In 1923 she joined
the Communist Party and with polemical plays,
such as *Leuna* (1921) and *Thomas Münzer* (1925),
became Germany's most important socialist
dramatist after Bertolt Brecht (1898–1956). She
also wrote didactic stories for children, and the
autobiographical novel *Stille und Sturm* (1955)
(*Calm and Storm*).

Lasker-Schüler, Else (1869–1945)
German poet. From a wealthy Jewish family, she
was privately educated because of her nervous
disposition. The death of her parents in the 1890s
disoriented her greatly, and, after a brief marriage,
she began to lead an unfettered, Bohemian life in
the cafés of Berlin. With her black bob and her
oriental dress, she became a well-known figure
and met many poets and artists, Georg Trakl
(1887–1914), Franz Marc (1880–1916), Gottfried
Benn (1886–1956) and Karl Kraus (1874–1936)
among them. Her collection of poems, *Styx*
(1902), was received both as 'perverse' and a

'work of genius'. Calling herself 'Prinz von
Theben', 'Tino von Bagdad' and many other
exotic names, she created a colourful poetic world
for herself, in which her life, her family and her
religious feelings were reinvented in exotic and
mythic terms. In 1906 she published *Das Peter
Hille Buch* (*The Peter Hille Book*), a strongly
idealized portrait of her friend and companion,
the vagabond poet Peter Hille. After a brief
marriage to Georg Levin, editor of the
Expressionist journal *Der Sturm* (*The Storm*), she
led a lonely, poverty-stricken life, at one stage
courting Gottfried Benn with a series of intense
love poems. She fled Germany in the 1930s, and,
after an itinerant life, settled in Jerusalem in 1939.
Her best poems are collected in *Hebräische
Balladen* (1913) (*Hebrew Ballads*) and *Mein blaues
Klavier* (1943) (*My Blue Piano*).

Lasoen, Patricia (born 1948)
Flemish poet and essay writer. She studied
Germanic philology in Ghent, contributed to
literary magazines, and worked as a reader of
Dutch and English in Bruges. She represented
Flanders at the Poetry International Festival in
1975 and 1977. Lasoen made her writing début in
1968 with *Ontwerp voor een Japanse houtgravure*
(*Design for a Japanese Woodcut*). Gradually she
aquired the reputation of being a writer of easily
accessible verse in a neo-realistic style. She
believes strongly in the need for communication,
in the importance and the re-evaluation of the
objects surrounding us, and in the possibility of
expressing ideas through description. The basic
theme of her poetry is the contrast between the
realization of hopeless absurdity and a sympathetic
attention to the tiny details of life. Thus, life is
opposed to death, familiarity to alienation, routine
to wonder, and restlessness to rigidity, as in her
collection *Veel Ach & een beetje O* (1978) (*Much Ah
& a Little Oh*). In 1981 a selection of her poetry
from 1965 to 1980 (*Landschap met roze hoed*;
Landscape with a Pink Hat) was published,
followed by *De witte binnenkant* (1985) (*White
Interior*), while in 1990 her first novel, *De geur van
rood* (*The Scent of Red*), appeared. Translations of
her poetry have appeared in *The Shape of Houses*
(1974), *Five Contemporary Flemish Poets* (1979) and
in *Quartet: an anthology of Dutch and Flemish Poetry*
(1987).

Last Man, The (1826)
A novel by English writer ▷Mary Shelley. It is set
in the late 21st century and portrays a republican
England. The first part is concerned with the
interaction of six characters, but the real narrative
does not begin until the second volume, which
describes the gradual destruction of the human
race by plague. The story is narrated by Lionel
Verney who becomes the sole surviving man,
writing the tale amidst the ruins of Rome. The
two sections of the novel are not satisfactorily
bridged and the work as a whole is inconsistent,
but its fantasy of the total corrosion of patriarchal
order and its description of nature reclaiming the

world in revenge against 'man' contains traces of the radical vision of Shelley's ▷*Frankenstein*.

Last of Chéri, The (1951)

Translation of *La Fin de Chéri* (1926), novel by French writer ▷Colette. In this continuation of the story of Léa and Chéri, the latter has returned from World War I indifferent to life. The novel can be seen as an attempt to portray the despair and disillusionment of a generation and period. It is not his wartime experience, however, but his dependency on Léa, which he resisted and finally avowed in the first novel, which leads to Chéri's suicide. He is unable to reconcile the Léa of his fantasy with the 60-year-old reality. The sequel again contrasts Léa's strength and will to live with Chéri's moribund fragility, and thus depicts masculinity as beautiful, but self-destructive and superficial. Even Chéri's young wife, Edmée, who suffered from his detachment in the first novel, has now found a vocation in hospital work, the very smell of which repulses Chéri. Whereas Léa's thoughts and feelings dominated the first novel, the focus here is on Chéri, and on the contrast between Chéri's romanticism and Léa's earthiness. The narrative confines itself to a detailed account of the nuances of emotion which Chéri experiences, and makes no moral judgement on either side.

▷*Chéri* (1951)

Latakia (1979)

Canadian writer ▷Audrey Thomas's brilliant metafictional novel about a woman who falls in love and has a '*Latakia*,' a hopeless affair with a married man. Part travelogue and part writers' exploration, it is about a man and woman, Rachel and Michael, who decide to spend a winter in Greece. Both writers, their affair is fraught not only with sexual jealousy but with creative jealousy, and although the novel plays with the notion of being a 'tragedy' about a man and two women, it is more accurately a comedy about two writers and the one language that they struggle to control. The conjunction between sexuality and art is powerfully evoked, and against the background of Greece and Syria the play of love and language slides gently and savagely towards the ultimate untranslatability of both.

Latina women writers (20th-century US)

The literature of Latina writers calls for cultural and political change, depicting the everyday life of working-class people whose families emigrated to the US from Puerto Rico, Mexico and Latin America. It concentrates on the process of assimilation to North American values, and the consequent cultural losses, exposing the contradiction in the ideology of the American Dream. Latina writers are engaged in challenging stereotypes and definitions of Latina women by dominant Anglo-American society. They also undertake the more fraught project of confronting the sexism within their own community.

In Latina writing the mother–daughter relationship is often a focus for the issues of cultural inheritance and femininity. The women recover and celebrate their maternal inheritance, but the relationship is also the locus of a cultural and generational confrontation. Language is a key dilemma for Latina writers, who explore the fragmentation created by linguistic migrancy, but affirm and define their intercultural selves by writing in a mixture of Spanish and English. They locate their writing as part of a collective Latina cultural tradition which they both draw on and transform. Informed by their culture's oral traditions, they blur the boundaries between poetry and prose, short story and novel.

Latina writers include ▷Gloria Anzaldua, ▷Ana Castillo, ▷Lorna Dee Cervantes, ▷Denise Chavez, ▷Sandra Cisneros, ▷Lucha Corpi, ▷Angela de Hoyos, ▷Nicholasa Mohr, ▷Cherrié Moraga, ▷Evangelina Vigil and ▷Helen Maria Viramontes.

La Tour du Pin, Henrietta Lucy Dillon de (1770–1853)

French memoir-writer. A descendant of Irish and English Jacobites, her memoirs, originally written for her sole surviving son, Aymar, were published in 1906 and re-edited sixteen times in the next few years. She wrote from the age of fifty until her death, covering her childhood, life at the court of Louis XVI, the Revolution (1789), her years of exile in North America and England, and the first year of the Restoration. The text intertwines historical memoirs with a record of family life. The current French edition was reprinted in 1989. There are two editions of the English translation by F. Harcourt; *Escape from Terror* (1979) and *Memoirs of Mme de la Tour du Pin* (1985).

▷*Mémoires*

Lattre Examynacyon of Anne Askew, The (1547)

English writer ▷Anne Askew's account of her final imprisonment at Newgate and her examination and trial before Henry VIII's council. Askew's account continues to document her strength and wit during sessions of interrogation, some of them lasting more than five hours. The work includes a ▷confession of faith, unambiguously asserting her belief in the symbolic nature of the sacrament. She bravely points out her inquisitors' hyper-literalism by providing them with examples of other material things in addition to bread and wine by which Christ was signified in the Bible (for example, a door, a vine, a lamb). Towards the end of her trial she was transferred to the Tower of London, where she was tortured on the rack until she fainted. She was revived and then questioned for two more hours while she sat upon the floor. These questions were aimed primarily at getting her to name other 'ladies and gentelwomen of her sect'. In spite of the torture that crippled her body so badly she had to be carried to the place of execution, Askew either would not or could not name other Reformist women. Moreover, she would not recant her Protestant beliefs. Her *Lattre Examynacyon* exhibits a keener awareness of the imminent danger of death than in ▷ *The First Examynacyon*. She repeatedly expresses her desire for continuing strength in maintaining her convictions in the face of martyrdom. John Bale published *The Lattre Examynacyon*, providing a lengthy preface and conclusion, and interruptive commentary.

▷ Prayers; Protestant Reformation

Lauber, Cécile (1887–1981)

German-speaking Swiss writer, novelist, dramatist and poet. The relationship between humans and nature is the theme of all her work. In her novel, *Die Wandlung* (1929) (*Metamorphosis*), she describes how a butcher develops an empathy with the animals he slaughters. *Stumme Natur* (1939) (*Silent Nature*) is the story of the colonization of an island by a farmer, his wife and their crippled child. In the four volumes of *Land deiner Mutter* (1946–57) (*Land of Your Mother*) she compiled a cultural history of Switzerland for the young.

Launay, Vicomte de ▷ Girardin, Delphine de

Laurence, (Jean) Margaret (1926–1987)

Margaret Laurence

Born Jean Margaret Wemyss in Neepawa, Manitoba, perhaps no fiction writer in Canada enjoys a more revered status than Margaret Laurence. Both her parents died early, and she was raised by an aunt. She attended United College (now the University of Winnipeg), and after graduating with a BA in English, worked as a reporter for the *Winnipeg Citizen*. In 1947 she married Jack Laurence, an engineer, and with him moved, first to England (1949), and then to Somaliland and Ghana. There she developed strong anti-colonial feelings, and translated some Somali writing, which appeared in 1954 as *A Tree for Poverty: Somali Poetry and Prose*. She also began

to write fiction. The Laurences returned to Vancouver, British Columbia, in 1957. Her first novel, *This Side Jordan*, appeared in 1960, and her first collection of short stories, *The Tomorrow-Tamer*, in 1963. Both are set in Africa, as is her memoir, *The Prophet's Camel Bell* (1963).

After she separated from her husband in 1962, Laurence lived with her children in Buckinghamshire, England, and there, within ten years, wrote the five novels (all located around the fictional prairie town of Manawaka) that made her reputation. ▷ *The Stone Angel* (1964), which won the Governor General's Award for Fiction, has been frequently cited as the best-known and greatest of all Canadian novels. Told from the point of view of a recalcitrant old woman, it recounts Hagar Shipley's inner conflict between pride and rejoicing, her fierce determination in the face of her own death. ▷ *A Jest of God* (1966, republished as *Rachel, Rachel*, also the name of the 1968 film) is a passionate exploration of the stymied passion of Rachel Cameron, a spinster schoolteacher, and daughter of the town undertaker. ▷ *The Fire-Dwellers* (1969) relates the story of Stacey, Rachel's sister, and her dissatisfaction with domestic life. *A Bird in the House* (1970) is an interconnected cycle of stories which unveil the town of Manawaka and its historical peregrinations through the eyes of the adolescent narrator, Vanessa MacLeod. Finally, ▷ *The Diviners* (1974), which again won the Governor General's Award for Fiction, brings all of the 'Manawaka' novels together in an exploration of writing and its commitment to place, to a solid ground. The 'Manawaka' books are powerfully-realized attempts to understand the experience of women in relation to a larger universe. Laurence is keenly aware of the doubleness of narrative and memory, the enigma of articulation in the face of time and decorum. At the same time, her work is movingly particular; she does not recoil from the sexual or the spiritual, and the compassion with which her characters' failures are drawn takes her writing far beyond the limitation of realism. She also published several children's books, *Jason's Quest* (1970), *Six Darn Cows* (1979), *The Olden Days Coat* (1979) and *The Christmas Birthday Story* (1980). Her essays, *Long Drums and Cannons: Nigerian Dramatists and Novelists 1952–1966* (1968) and *Heart of a Stranger* (1976), as well as her autobiographical memoir and celebration of motherhood, *Dance on the Earth*, which was published posthumously in 1989, speak of a writer whose vision was generous and magnificent. Laurence returned to Canada in 1974, and lived at Lakefield, Ontario, until her death.

▷ Wiseman, Adele

Bib: Gunnars, K. (ed), *Crossing the River: Essays in Honour of Margaret Laurence*; Hind-Smith, J., in *Three Voices*; Howells, C.A., *Private and Fictional Words*; Morley, P., *Margaret Laurence: The Long Journey Home*; New, W.H. (ed.), *Margaret Laurence, the Writer and Her Critics*; Thomas, Clara, *The Manawaka World of Margaret Laurence*;

Woodcock, G. (ed), *A Place to Stand On: Essays By and About Margaret Laurence*; ▷*Canadian Woman Studies* Vol. 8, No. 3; *Journal of Canadian Studies* Vol. 13, No. 3.

Lavant, Christine (1915–1973)

Austrian poet. She came from a large family of miners near St Stefan, worked as a knitter, and hardly ever left her home. Her poems have strong rhythms and clear rhymes, and have been called 'blasphemous prayers', since they use biblical models of language and imagery to create visions of personal distress and despair. In the collections *Die Bettlerschale* (1956) (*The Beggar's Bowl*), *Spindel im Mond* (1959) (*Spindle on the Moon*) and *Der Pfauenschrei* (1962) (*The Cry of the Peacock*), she uses images of a rural world in which dark, severe landscapes form the backdrop to terrifying mystical experiences.

Lavater-Sloman, Mary (1891–1980)

German-speaking Swiss novelist and biographer. Born in Hamburg, she met her husband, Emil Lavater, in St Petersburg, and after 1922 settled in Winterthur near Zurich. She achieved great success with her many well-researched and captivating biographical novels, based on the lives of great women such as Lucrezia Borgia, ▷Queen Elizabeth I, Joan of Arc, ▷Catherine the Great, and ▷Annette von Droste-Hülshoff.

Laverty, Maura (1907–1966)

Irish novelist, journalist and broadcaster, born in County Kildare. During her twenties Laverty lived in Spain, working as a governess, a secretary, and later as a journalist in Madrid. She returned to Ireland in 1928, where she again worked as a journalist. In addition to two influential and popular cookery books, *Flour Economy* (1941) and *Full and Plenty* (1960), she wrote plays, including *Liffey Lane* (1947) and *Tolka Row*, later adapted by RTE, the national broadcasting station, as a soap opera. *Never No More* (1942) and *No More than Human* (1944) are semi-autobiographical novels. *Touched by the Thorn* (1943) received the Irish Women Writers Award, but was banned for some years by the censors. Her other novels are: *Alone We Embark* (1943), *Lift Up Your Gates* (1946) and *Green Orchard* (1949).
▷Censorship (Ireland)

Lavin, Mary (born 1912)

Irish short-story writer and novelist, born in Massachusetts, USA. Lavin and went to live in Ireland with her Irish mother when she was nine years old. She is one of the very few Irish women writers of her generation to live continuously in Ireland and to write about it. Considered one of Ireland's greatest living writers, she has received many prizes and awards for her work and was President of the Irish Academy of Letters from 1972 to 1974. She is an extraordinarily prolific writer, and her short story collections include: *Tales from Bective Bridge* (1942), *The Long Ago* (1944), *At Sally Gap* (1946) *Patriot Son* (1956), *A*

Single Lady (1956), *The Great Wave* (1961), *In the Middle of the Fields* (1967), *Happiness* (1969), *A Memory and Other Stories* (1972) and *The Shrine and Other Stories* (1976). Her *Collected Stories* appeared in 1985. Her novels are *The House in Cleve Street* (1945), *The Becker Wives* (1946), *Mary O'Grady* (1950) and *A Likely Story* (1957). Major themes of this rich and challenging *oeuvre* are the constraints of convention, and the dilemmas of private conscience in a repressive society.

Lawes Resolution of Women's Rights, The (1632)

English book on the legal position of 17th-century women by one 'T.E.' It offers an analysis of women's place under the law, which it summarizes as follows: 'Women have no voice in Parliament, they make no laws, they abrogate none. All of them are understood either married or to be married, and their desires are subject to their husbands', adding the comment – 'I know no remedy, though some women can shift well enough.' The extent to which this legal formulation, whereby women were always defined in relation to men (as maids, wives or widows), was followed has been disputed, but it is certainly true that the legal status of women affected their economic powers and rights throughout the 17th and 18th centuries. In the event, women who were lucky enough to inherit property or money more often than not relinquished it to their husbands.
Bib: Hogrefe, Pearl, *SCJ* 3 (1972), p. 97–105; Ezell, Margaret *The Patriarch's Wife*.

Lawless, Emily (1845–1913)

Irish novelist, poet and historian, born in Kildare, the eldest daughter of Lord and Lady Cloncurry. A fine horsewoman and swimmer, she achieved the even more unusual distinction for a woman of the award of D.Litt. from Trinity College, Dublin. Both her poetry (republished in 1965) and her fiction express a powerfully nationalist vision of Ireland in naturalist terms. *Hurrish* (1886), praised by the British statesman and scholar, W.E. Gladstone (1809–98) for portraying 'a living reality, the estrangement of the people of Ireland from the law', is a study of the causes and effects of peasant violence. *Grania* (1892) is the tragic story of a woman's search for autonomy and freedom in an introverted island community. This remarkably feminist novel marks Emily Lawless as one of the most significant early Irish women writers.

Lawson, Louisa (1848–1920)

Australian feminist, publisher, editor, journalist and poet, the mother of Henry Lawson. She married Norwegian sailor Peter Larsen in 1866, had five children and moved to Sydney in 1883 where she edited the *Republican* in 1887 and founded and published the *Dawn*, Australia's first feminist journal, from 1888 to 1905. Lawson was active in the women's suffrage movement, established the Association of Women in 1889,

and worked in association with Rose Scott and the Womanhood Suffrage League from 1891 onward. As well as her editorial work and articles for the *Dawn*, Louisa Lawson published *Dert and Do* (fiction, date uncertain) and *The Lonely Crossing and Other Poems* (1905). *Louisa* (1988), Brian Matthews's imaginative reconstruction of Louisa Lawson's life, has won many literary awards.
▷Feminism (Australia); *On Her Selection*

Laxe, Júlia Cortines ▷Cortines, Júlia

Lay Down Your Arms! (1892, 1972)
Translation of *Die Waffen nieder! Eine Lebensgeschichte* (1889), a German novel by the pacifist, ▷Bertha von Suttner. Written as a first-person narrative, this accessible and emotive work is related by a woman who tells of the miseries of the European wars between 1859 and 1871. She evokes the senseless sacrifices on the battlefields, the loss and sorrow experienced by the families left behind, and the absurdity of war in general. The book was an extraordinary success, and was widely translated, becoming a key work for the European peace movement at the turn of the century.

'Lay of Sorrow, The' (c 1500)
Anonymous Scottish poem. This lyrical lament of a woman who has lost her love is found in a 15th-century manuscript which appears to have been made for Henry, third Lord Sinclair (fl 1488–1513). The conventional theme is treated expressively and with technical skill.
Bib: Wilson, K.G., *Speculum* 29 (1954), pp. 708–724).

Lázaro, Maribel (born 1948)
Contemporary Spanish dramatist. Lázaro is one of the few female dramatists to have had her work performed in the 1980s. Her most celebrated play, ▷*Humo de Beleño* (1985) (*Henbane Smoke*), caused great controversy when staged in Madrid.

Lazarová, Katarina (born 1914)
Slovak prose writer. Lazarová worked for Czechoslovak Radio, and as a freelance writer. Her first book, *Kamaráti* (1949) (*Friends*), deals with the Slovak uprising of 1944, in which she had taken part. The novel *Osie hniezdo* (1953) (*The Wasps' Nest*) depicts the collectivization of the 1950s. Her novels of this period are ▷social realist and were praised by critics.
In subsequent works Lazarová threw off her black-and-white picture of the world and became more critical towards society. After several unsuccessful works she left topical themes and real events, and wrote popular ▷detective novels, for example, *Kňažná z Lemúrie* (1964) (*The Princess of Lemúria*), *Interview s labuťami* (1966) (*Interview With the Swans*), *Kavčie pierko* (1967) (*The Jackdaw's Feather*). These can be understood as an indirect comment on the situation at the time.
In the 1970s she wrote a semi-autobiographical

novel, *Vdovské domy* (1977) (*The Houses of Widows*), about village life during World War I. Lazarová's work is interesting, more because of its discussion of established ideology than for its literary value.

Leach, Christiana (fl 1765–1796)
North American diarist. From February 1765 to May 1796, she maintained a diary of her life in Kingsessing, Pennsylvania. Although ▷*The Diary of Christiana Leach* consists only of short notations at intervals of several months, it is a rare account of an apparently upper-class German woman whose interests range from her brother's meetings with the king and queen of England to the botanical arts in which her brother was employed. The diary, and our knowledge of her life, ends on 10 May 1796, with a typical account of family affairs.

Lead, Jane (1624–1704)
English mystical writer. Her mysticism contrasts with the radical political potential of earlier prophets, such as ▷Anna Trapnel and ▷Mary Cary.
Her publications include: *The Heavenly Cloud New Breaking* (1681); *The Revelation of Revelations* (1683); *The Enochian Walks with God* (1694).

League For Women's Rights, The (1920)
A Greek feminist organization started by Avra Theodoropoulou, a musician, at the instigation of the International Union for Women's Suffrage. Many educated women took part in it and contributed substantially to its activities for women's political rights. On 16 April 1923 they launched their magazine, *Women's Struggle*, which lasted until 1935. The organization publicized the urgent need for political rights for women, primarily the vote, and at the same time dealt with women's work, education, refugees fron Asia Minor, unmarried mothers, prostitution, and especially with family law, which was under amendment at the time. Many feminist women from this organization formed 'The Little Andante for Women', a feminist group which made contact with similar organizations in Romania, Yugoslavia, Czechoslavakia and Poland. They also took part in international feminist conferences and brought ideas and tactics back to Greece.

Leakey, Caroline Woolmer (1827–1881)
Australian novelist and poet, also known as Oliné Keese. Leakey, a member of a prominent evangelistic family, was born in England but spent five years in Tasmania, returning to England to write ▷*The Broad Arrow: Being Passages from the History of Maida Gwynnham, a Lifer* (1859). A volume of poems, *Lyra Australis* (1854), was published during her stay in Tasmania. Her life, told in the memoir, *Clear Shining Light*, published in 1882 by her sister, is a record of ill-health and the demands of a particularly extreme form of

evangelical Christianity. Leakey also published a great number of religious tracts.

▷*A Bright and Fiery Troop*; On Her Selection

Leapor, Mary (1722–1746)
English poet. She was from the labouring classes, and worked as a kitchen maid. She was able to write poetry with the support of a patron, Bridget Fremantle, and *Poems upon Several Occassionns* (1748, 1751) was first published after Leapor died of measles. It included the ironical 'Essay on Woman', commenting '*Hymen* lifts his sceptered Rod, / and strikes her glories with a fatal nod.' Her verse often uses a figure called 'Mira' to explore the familial and sexual problems of women, and she strongly associates poetry with sleep and dream. In 'The Cruel Parent: a Dream' ▷Gothic elements interwine with labouring-class problems, including starvation. In 'a Verse Epistle to a Lady' she describes the working woman poet who 'rolls in treasures till the breaking day: . . . till the shrill clock impertinently rings, / and the soft visions move their shining Wings'. She also wrote a blank-verse tragedy, but died while its staging was being discussed. She left a library of only sixteen or seventeen volumes, including some Pope and Dryden.

▷Collier, Mary; Little, Janet; Whitney, Isabella; Yearsley, Ann; Women and work
Bib: Landry, Donna, *The Muses of Resistance*.

Learned literature in Sweden
The tradition was founded by ▷Birgitta av Vadstena, but was resumed with Queen Christina (1626–1689), who wrote in the style of the French *précieuses* (▷Precious women), and had a literary salon like them (▷Literary salons in Scandinavia). It was also a religious literature. Examples include the work of Agneta Horn (1629–1672), who wrote an autobiography, in the form of a devotional history, about finding one's way to God. It was completed on her eighteenth birthday, when she got married.

Sophia Elisabeth Brenner (1659–1730) was also a learned woman, famous in her own time but since forgotten. She was called the 'Sappho of the North' (▷Sappho) because of her religious poems written in different languages, such as Swedish, Italian, Latin, French and German.

Later learned women were also active in literary salons, eg Hedvig Charlotta Nordenflycht (1718–1763) and Anna Maria Lenngren (1754–1817). They also participated in intellectual debates, eg Ellen Key.

Leavenworth Case, The (1878)
US first popular detective novel by ▷Anna Katharine Green. Like the ▷dime novel, the detective novel formula was originated and developed by a woman, but became identified as a male genre.

Leavis, Q.D. (1906–1981)
English literary critic. Leavis's doctoral dissertation, published as *Fiction and the Reading Public* (1932) looked at patterns of consumption of novels from the 17th to the 20th century, and was based on 'scientific' principles of empirical research. After marrying the critic F.R. Leavis (1895–1978), she published no major study in her own right, and although she made numerous editorial contributions to the journal *Scrutiny*, these were never acknowledged. Her critical method differed from that of her husband in that her emphasis was more historical, and Q.D. Leavis constantly urged the broadening of the canon and the inclusion of certain women writers. Both critics shared a belief in the decline in 'taste' and 'standards', and while they argued strongly for the centrality of English literature in British culture, they believed the canon could only be sustained by the evangelical zeal of informed, highly trained critics. Other works include: *Dickens the Novelist* (1971), with F.R. Leavis, and *Collected Essays* (1983).

Leavisite criticism
A school of criticism which emerged in Britain out of the work of F.R. (Frank Raymond) Leavis (1895–1978) in Cambridge during the 1930s. Leavis, who taught at Cambridge, defined and defended the narrow literary ▷canon of largely male writers that is still influential today. For Leavis, 'Great Literature' is written by 'great authors' who somehow manage to express the quintessential truths of life which transcend differences of class, sex, culture and creed. Leavisite critics would dismiss feminism as a political ideology that, like all ideologies, has little bearing on artistic greatness. In the 1930s and 1940s, fearing that mass literacy was producing an explosion of popular but inferior literature, Leavis defended tradition against innovation in *Mass Civilization and Minority Culture* (1930). Feminist critics such as ▷Germaine Greer and ▷Tania Modleski have challenged Leavis's definition of 'Great Literature', and have argued the importance of fiction of all kinds for a feminist politics of change.

Leavis published his views in the influential journal *Scrutiny* (1932–1953), which he edited. *New Bearings in English Poetry* (1932) and *The Great Tradition* (1948) are two of his best-known books.

▷Leavis, Q.D.
Bib: Eagleton, T., *Literary Theory: An Introduction*; Widdowson, P. (ed.), *Re-Reading English*.

Leben und Abenteuer der Trobadora Beatriz nach Zeugnissen ihrer Spielfrau Laura. Roman in dreizehn Büchern und sieben Intermezzos (1974) (Life and Adventures of the Troubadour Beatriz According to the Testimony of her Minstrel Laura. A Novel in Thirteen Books and Seven Intermezzi)
A novel by the East German writer, ▷Irmtraud Morgner. Initially intended as the first part of a trilogy (the second volume is about a witch, *Amanda: Ein Hexenroman*, 1983, *Amanda: A Witch's Novel* – the third was never finished), it is

a long and complex work centring on the quest for self-fulfilment by the heroine, Laura Salman, a woman from East Berlin. The story intially revolves around the fortunes of the 12th-century female troubadour Beatriz, who, dissatisfied with her own position as a woman artist, invokes her magical powers to travel through time and space to join forces with Laura in the 'Promised Land' of socialist Germany. In a careful montage of short chapters, the novel intermingles the realistic and the fantastic, fact and fiction, in an extravagant bid to reinterpret, indeed to reinvent, the world in non-linear, non-patriarchal terms.

This novel is one of the most interesting texts to grow out of the youth movement of 1968, and rigorously reflects the ideas of the late 1960s. It met with great acclaim, particularly in West Germany.

Le Camus, Madame (17th century)
French poet. She published poetry in the *Mercure galant*, but little else is known about the other than the laudatory introduction by the editor Donneau de Visé (1638–1710) of his latest author: '*Tout Paris est informé [de la délicatesse de son esprit], toute la cour en est convaincue & c'est assez de nommer Mme Le Camus pour faire penser à une femme toute admirable*' ('All Paris knows her reputation for delicate wit, all the court is convinced of it, and it is enough to name Madame Le Camus to bring to mind an admirable woman'). She wrote a witty piece for the Comtesse de Guiche on her jubilee in 1677 and addressed a *Madrigal impromptu* to the Duc de Saint-Aignan in 1679 to which he promptly replied.
Bib: Vincent M., *Donneau de Visé et le 'Mercure galant'*.

Leclerc, Annie (born 1940)
French philosopher and teacher. She has written for a number of journals, including *Les Temps modernes* (*Modern Times*). Her first novel, *Le Pont du nord* (1967) (*The North Bridge*), was followed by a large number of philosophical writings, essays and short stories. Of her essays, the most widely-read are ▷'*Parole de femme*' (1974) ('Woman's word') and *La Venue à l'écriture* (1977) (*The Road to Writing*), written with ▷Hélène Cixous and the French-Canadian author Madeleine Gagnon.
▷Cardinal, Maire

Le Doeuff, Michèle (born 1948)
French philosopher, currently a researcher at the Centre Nationale de la Récherche Scientifique. Her work has generated interest among both feminists and professional philosophers. She is known by some as an author of essays on 17th-century philosophy who relaunched Baconian studies in France, and by others for her work on the way in which philosophy produces an imagery of its own, as discussed in her first book, *L'Imaginaire philosophique* (1980) (▷ *The Philosophical Imaginary*, 1989). Yet others know her as a caustic though scholarly feminist philosopher, the author of several articles on the

position of women in philosophy and of an important book, *L'Etude et le rouet* (1989) (▷*Hipparchia's Choice*, 1991). Le Doeuff is a popular spokeswoman on practical feminist issues who enjoys challenging the French government. She has worked in the theatre, on the play *La Soeur de Shakespeare* (1978) (*Shakespeare's Sister*) with the Théâtre de l'Aquarium, and with her translation and stage adaptation of Shakespeare's *Venus and Adonis* (1986).

Leduc, Violette (1907–1972)
French author of autobiographies and fictionalized confessions, which focus on her illegitimate birth, her mother's rejection of her, and her sense of marginality. Acclaimed by feminists as an authentically feminine voice, the protégée of ▷Simone de Beauvoir, her works are a landmark in the treatment of explicit sex between women, blending factual account with surrealist hallucinations. Her best-known novels are ▷*La Bâtarde* (1964) and *Ravages* (1955) (*Devastation*).

Lee, Harper ▷ *To Kill a Mockingbird*

Lee, Harriet (1757–1851)
English novelist and dramatist. Her fiction includes *Canterbury Tales for the Year 1797*, co-written with her sister, ▷Sophia Lee. Her *Kruitzer, the German's Tale* (1801) was reworked by the poet Byron (1788–1824) as *Werner* (1821).
▷Gothic (Britain); Radcliffe, Ann

Lee, Lucinda (fl 1787)
North American diarist. She was a member of the Virginia Lees, one of the most prominent Southern families in 18th-century North America. In the ▷*Journal of a Young Lady of Virginia 1782*, she addresses her friend, Polly Brent, and captures for Polly all of the excitement of her social life among the Lees, the Washingtons and other notable Virginians.

Lee, Sophia (1750–1824)
English novelist and dramatist, elder sister of ▷Harriet Lee, and friend of ▷Ann Radcliffe. Her historical fiction included *The Recess, or a Tale of Other Times* (1783–5), and she co-wrote *Canterbury Tales for the Year 1797* with her sister.

Lee Tzu Pheng (born 1946)
Singaporean poet. A university lecturer, she began publishing her poems in Singaporean and international journals in the late 1960s. Her first volume, *Prospect of a Drowning* (1980) was followed by its companion volume, *Against the Next Wave* (1988), and recently, *The Brink of an Amen* (1991). The poems record a journey from youthful idealism, expressed in poems of social observation, to increasing introspection about personal suffering, friendship and disillusionment. After she had converted to Roman Catholicism, her poems became more religious in the second volume. Apart from two national literary awards,

she was also the recipient of the SEA (South-East Asia) WRITE Award in 1987.

Lee, Vernon (1856–1935)

▷Pseudonym of English essayist, novelist and short story writer Violet Paget. She was born near Boulogne, France, and travelled around Europe as a young girl, receiving her education from various ▷governesses. Lee's literary career was full of eccentric oscillations between fame and infamy. Her first major work was *Studies of the 18th Century in Italy* (1880), which was a great success, but her first novel (*Miss Brown*, 1884) damaged her reputation, as did the short story 'Lady Tal' (*Vanitas*, 1892), which contained an ill-considered and barely disguised portrait of novelist Henry James. Thereafter she turned her attention to essays, and *Genius Loci: Notes on Places* (1899) was a success. During the World War I she wrote a pacifist trilogy, *Satan the Waster* (1920), which was generally condemned, although it was better received when re-issued in 1930. Lee left England to avoid the disapproval of her family and friends for her lesbianism. In Paris she was a frequent visitor at ▷Natalie Barney's famous Rue Jacob salon. Other works by the prolific Lee include *Gospels of Anarchy* (1908); *The Tower of Mirrors* (1914), and two volumes of *Supernatural Tales*, published posthumously in 1955 and 1956.
▷Ghost stories (19th-century Britain)

Leffler, Anne Charlotte ▷Kovalévskaia, Sof'ia; Modern breakthrough in Scandinavia, The

Le Fort, Gertrud von (1876–1971)

German Catholic novelist. From an old Huguenot family, she studied Church History and Philosophy in Heidelberg, and converted to Catholicism in 1926. Her first poems, from 1899, are neo-romantic, almost playful explorations of religious and fairytale themes. With her increasing interest in the Catholic faith, her writings assumed a deeper, more philosophical dimension. Her *Hymnen an die Kirche* (1924) (*Hymns to the Church*) are psalm-like, metaphysical investigations into the devout soul's relationship with the Church. In her fiction she explored religious issues within the timelessness and universality of somewhat hazy historical settings. She first achieved fame with *Das Schweißtuch der Veronika* (1928) (*Veronica's Cloth*), a novel in which she explores the role of women as bringers of solace and redemptive forces in a society on the brink of spiritual collapse. *Die Letzte am Schafott* (1931) (*The Last Woman to the Scaffold*) relates how Divine Grace helps the heroine to overcome fear in the face of the guillotine during the French Revolution (1789). Representing the spirit of conservative resistance, initially to Hitler and later to the literary cynicism of the post-war period, she became one of the great old ladies of Adenauer's Germany.

Left Bank and Other Stories, The (1972)

This is the first published collection of stories by the Caribbean writer ▷Jean Rhys. They illustrate the major themes of her work – denial, rejection, alienation and vulnerability. The introduction by Ford Madox Ford makes little reference to Rhys, but provides the setting of the Left Bank mentioned in the title. Although every story has its own setting – a room or a café in Paris, Vienna, Budapest or ▷Dominica, a prison cell or a street, Rhys's concern is with the passion, hardship and emotions of her characters. These stories are told from the perspective of the 'others', who are usually female (though occasionally they are disadvantaged male colonials or foreigners), and they present a variety of constructions of women; with tales of revenge, mutual exploitation, suicidal desperation and female romantic fantasies. These stories illustrate Rhys's use of a variety of narrative forms, including sketches and dramatic monologues.
For critical analysis, see Carole Angier, *Jean Rhys Life and Work* (1990) and Carole Ann Howells, *Jean Rhys* (1991).

Legacy for Children, A (1714)

Written by the eleven-year-old American ▷Hannah Hill, Jr, shortly before her death, *A Legacy* offers advice for other young people and reveals Hill's Quaker beliefs in working for the 'General Good and Wellfare' of all people, regardless of their religious sect or race. Published shortly after Hill's death, the popular *Legacy* appeared in three editions in North America.
▷Early North American Quaker women's writing

Le Garrec, Evelyne

French feminist writer and journalist. Le Garrec has published two important social documentaries based on interviews with women: the first, *Un Lit à soi* (1979) (*A Bed of One's Own*) is an analysis of the experiences of single women in a society dominated by heterosexual couples and families, while the second, *Des Femmes qui s'aiment* (1984) (*Women Who Love Each Other*), presents the experience of lesbians living in France. She has also written *Séverine: une rebelle* (1982) (*Séverine: A Rebel*), a fictionalized biography of the 19th-century radical journalist; an autobiographical work dealing with the problem of her own mixed German and French ancestry, *La Rive allemande de ma mémoire* (1980) (*The German Side of My Memory*), and *Les Messagères* (*The Messengers Women*), published by ▷Éditions de femmes in 1976.
▷Séverine

Legend of Marcello Mastroianni's Wife, The (1981)

Poems by New Zealand writer ▷Elizabeth Smither. As its title suggests, Elizabeth Smither's collection of poems is a series of carefully constructed stories on subjects ranging from ▷St

Theresa to Casanova; Smither's poetry deals with
a highly textual and intellectual world. She has
been described as a 'distinctive and idiosyncratic
poet' (E. Caffin, *Oxford History of New Zealand
Literature*, 1991), and her distinctiveness consists
in the highly formalized short poems she writes,
which focus on the play of ideas (usually
philosophical and textual but ranging, as in *The
Legend of Marcello Mastroianni's Wife*, over various
media) rather than personal experience. It is
unusual to find Smither writing about herself, and
her collections tend to resemble a gathering of
reflections and inventions on a variety of subjects.

Legends of holy women (Scandinavia)

From about 1250 to 1500, legends of holy women
were widely read in Scandinavia. The legends
concerned women martyred or tortured for their
Christian beliefs, and sprang up especially as a
result of the establishment of the Bridgettine
Order by ▷Birgitta av Vadstena. The Bridgettines
worshipped the Virgin Mary and her mother, who,
according to tradition, was St Anne.

The legends are similar in many respects to
Latin versions circulating elsewhere in Europe.
They can be read in collections of *Holy Women*,
▷prayer books and in manuscript form. Some of
the later legends, for example, *The Legends of St
Katherina of Siena*, written in 1488 by the monk
Nils Mogensen at the request of the nun
Elizabeth Hermansdaughter, included semi-erotic
versions of the holy women's ecstatic marriages to
Christ.

Leggott, Michele (born 1956)

New Zealand poet. Educated in New Zealand and
the United States, Michele Leggott is a poet and
academic at Auckland University. She has
published a study of the work of North American
poet Louis Zukofsky (1904–1978), and is the
poetry editor for *Landfall* and *Rambling Jack*.
Leggott's poetry was widely published in New
Zealand journals and anthologies before her first
collection, *Like this?*, appeared in 1988. Her work
reflects her interest in Zukofsky in that it uses
sharp images, language play and minimalist forms
in a multi-referenced context of 'aural delight',
focusing attention on the multiple meanings and
suggestions of similar sounds. The suggestiveness
of Leggott's poems cannot be reduced to the
singularities of voice, subject or narrative, nor
does her work entirely abandon more conventional
frames of meaning. Instead it places the reader in
an unresolved but delightful dialogue with the
poem. Her most recent collection is *Swimmers,
Dancers* (1991).

Le Givre de Richebourg, Madame (18th century)

French writer of prose fiction. Her first published
work was a tragi comic short story, *La Veuve en
puissance de mari* (1732) (*The Widow Under Her
Husband's Control*). The majority of her other
works are Spanish-inspired: *Aventures de
Clamandès et Clarmonde* (1733) (*The Adventures of*

Clamandès and Clarmonde); *Aventures de Flores et de
Blanchefleur* (1735) (*The Adventures of Flores and
Blanchefleur*); *Aventures de Dom Ramire de Roxas et
de Dona Leonone de Mendoce* (1737) (*The Adventures
of Don Ramirez de Roxas and Dona Leonone de
Mendona*), and *Persiles et Sigismond* (1737),
adapted from Cervantes. The exception to the
Spanish-inspired works is *Aventures de Zelin et de
Damasine*, ('an African story') (1735) (*The
Adventures of Zelin and Damasine*). The works were
signed with initials only, which have also been
interpreted as '*La Grange de Richebourg*' and '*le
gendre de Richebourg*'.

Le Guin, Ursula (born 1929)

US novelist, short story writer and essayist. Le
Guin was born and raised in Berkeley, California.
She studied Romance literature at Radcliffe
College and Columbia University. Settling in
Portland, Oregon, she began publishing while
working and raising three children.

Le Guin invents new cultures that represent
new possibilities for society and the self, and her
▷science fiction and fantasy literature criticizes
contemporary US society. 'The Ones Who Walk
Away from Omelas' exposes the contradiction
between a society's democratic beliefs and its
exploitative actions. Her work is informed by a
sense of ecological balance: a balance between
irrationality and rationality in *The Tombs of Atuan*
(1971) and *The Farthest Shore* (1972); male and
female in *The Left Hand of Darkness* (1969);
technologically advanced and less advanced
civilizations in *Always Coming Home* (1985).

Other works include: *Rocannon's World* (1966),
Planet of Exile (1966), *City of Illusions* (1967), *A
Wizard of Earthsea* (1968), *The Lathe of Heaven*
(1971), *The Dispossessed* (1974), *The Wind's Twelve
Quarters* (1975), *Wild Angels* (1975), *The Word for
World is Forest* (1976), *Very Far Away from
Anywhere Else* (1976), *Orsinian Tales* (1976), *The
Language of the Night: Essays on Fantasy and Science
Fiction* (1979), *Malafrena* (1979), *The Beginning
Place* (1980), *The Compass Rose* (1982), *Dancing at
the Edge of the World* (1989) and *Searoads: The
Chronicles of Klatsand* (1991).
Bib: Bucknall, Barbara J., *Ursula K. le Guin*.

Lehmann, Rosamond (born 1901)

English novelist, short story writer and translator.
Daughter of R.C. Lehmann, Liberal MP, writer
and editor, and Alice Lehmann; sister of John
Lehmann, writer and editor. Educated privately
and at Girton College, where she studied modern
languages. Lehmann married twice – both
marriages ending in divorce – and maintained a
long-term friendship with the poet C. Day Lewis
(1909–1972). Lehmann's novels consistently
articulate the themes of women's sexuality and
passion, engaging also with a thematic and stylistic
concern with feminine expression. Her first novel,
▷*Dusty Answer* (1927), explores the realm of
adolescent infatuation, a topic to which Lehmann
frequently returns, as with *Invitation to the Waltz*
(1932). *Dusty Answer* also produced controversy

through its latent lesbianism, a subject treated more overtly in *A Note in Music* (1930). Later novels, such as *The Ballad and the Source* (1944), work around the destructive aspects of relationships. Lehmann's use of 'impressionistic' techniques of narration, and her concern with the representation of feminine consciousness, has been linked with that of ▷Virginia Woolf.

Lehmann's daughter, Sally, died of poliomyelitis while in Jakarta in 1958; this event had a profound effect on Lehmann's writing. Her preoccupation with mysticism and spirituality, developed in *The Ballad and the Source* (1944), was drawn into an analysis of bereavement in *The Swan in the Evening* (1967). The death of Lehmann's daughter also provides a frame for contextualizing her interest in the paranormal in her final novel, *A Sea-Grape Tree* (1976). Lehmann's short stories are collected under the title *The Gypsy's Baby* (1946), and she also translated Cocteau's *Les Enfants Terribles*, published in 1955. Other writings: ▷*The Weather in the Streets* (1936), *No More Music* (1939), *The Echoing Grove* (1953), *Letters from Our Daughters* (with O.H. Sandys, 1972).
Bib: Dorosz, W., *Subjective Vision and Human Relationships in the Novels of Rosamond Lehmann*; Kaplan, S.J., *Feminine Consciousness in the Modern British Novel*; Sturgeon, D.E., *Rosamond Lehmann*; Tindall, G., *Rosamond Lehmann: an Appreciation*.

L.E.L. ▷Landon, Letitia

Leland, Mary
Irish short-story writer and novelist, born in Cork. Having worked with the *Cork Examiner* and *The Irish Times*, she is now a freelance writer. Her first novel, *The Killeen*, appeared in 1985, and was followed by a collection of short stories, *The Little Galloway Girls* (1986) and a second novel, *Approaching Priests* (1991).

Lélia (1833)
Novel by French writer ▷George Sand: a *succès de scandale*, confirming the reputation established with ▷*Indiana* (1832). Sand wrote two versions of this story of the passion of the young poet Sténio for an older woman. Both are founded on the romantic commonplace of the pain of unattainable desire, whose object is variously named as truth, beauty, and divine and human love. The difference lies in the importance attributed to the latter, which marks a shift of focus from private to public world: from passion to politics. In the 1833 version, the poet Sténio's devotion to Lélia is platonic, while she is more inclined to earthly love. The version of 1839 presents Sténio as selfish seducer and Lélia as the aspirant to heroic purity, whose ambitions are not for personal satisfaction, but for the improvement of society at large. This version carries a feminist message: that women be held educated and their minds sharpened for higher goals. Lélia takes refuge in a convent, where she immediately becomes abbess,

and which she turns into a protected enclave where a new kind of woman can come into being.

Under the influence of Pierre Leroux and Lamennais (1782–1854), Sand uses her novel to explore the scope for social change offered by the institution of the Catholic Church. The enterprise fails, because Lélia's ambitions turn out to be too high-minded and élitist for the small-minded religious establishment in which she finds herself. Like her author, she ends in scepticism, firmly rejecting the insufficiencies of contemporary society, but with no clear notion of what an alternative world might be.

Lemoine-Luccioni, Eugénie (born 1912)
French literary critic and translator, now a psychoanalyst and member of the École Freudienne established by Jacques Lacan (▷psychoanalysis) She has published two collections of short stories, *Cercles* (1946) (*Circles*) and *Marches* (1977) (*Marches*) and a number of psychoanalytic works. Under the pseudonym Gennie Lemoine, she is also a regular contributor to a number of psychoanalytic journals. Her book *Partage de femmes* (1976) (*The Dividing of Women or Women's Lot*, 1988) is her only work so far translated into English. It is based on analyses of pregnant women, and develops her view that women's psychic organization is fundamentally dual because women have two distinct sexual organs, are the same sex as their mothers, whom they thus mirror, and become mothers themselves, splitting into two people. The result, she says, is that women fear losing part of themselves, as happens when they give birth, and respond to this fear by becoming intensely narcissistic and/or dependent on a man to restore their loss.

Her other works include: *Le Psychodrame* (1968) (*Psychodrama*), in collaboration with Paul Lemoine, *La Robe* (1983) (*The Dress*); *Psychanalyse pour la vie quotidienne* (1987) (*Everyday Psychoanalysis*), and *Une politique de la psychanalyse* (*A Politics of Psychoanalysis*).

Lemsine, Aicha (born 1942)
Algerian novelist. Born in Nemencha. Her name is a ▷pseudonym constructed out of the Arabic letters 'L' (*Lem*) and 'S' (*Sin*). Her novels, *La Chrysalide* (1976) (*Chrysalis*) and (*Ciel de Porphyre*, 1978) (*Beneath a Sky of Porphyry*), deal with the liberation movement in Algeria. In her first novel she takes an optimistic view of the situation of women in her country, whom she portrays as playing a major role in the war of liberation. However, her second novel is more circumspect, with women depicted as the subordinates of men. Aicha Lemsine now lives in Mexico.

Lenclos (Lanclos), Anne (Ninon) de (1620/ 1623–1704/1705)
French author of numerous letters, notably to Saint-Evremond (1614–1703). Only a few dozen authentic examples have survived. Ninon de Lenclos (more correctly, Lanclos) was the most notorious courtesan of the 17th century. Probably

Aicha Lemsine

prostituted by her mother, she never actually attended the court, but she is supposed to have had love-affairs for over 60 years with the most important men at court. There have been attempts to reconstruct her life to make her into a *courtisane philosophe* ('philosopher-courtesan'), since she studied the philosopher Michel de Montaigne (1533–1592) and others. A noticeable change in her status occurred between 1662 and 1670, when she became known as Mademoiselle de Lenclos, and was increasingly valued for the quality of her wit and her art of conversation by such people as ▷Madame de Lafayette, ▷Madame de la Sablière and ▷Madame de Maintenon. Nevertheless she always needed money from men in order to survive, receiving 2,000 *livres* as a life pension from the statesman Cardinat de Richelieu (1585–1642) during an earlier liaison. The memoir-writer Tallemant des Réaux (1619–1692) tells us she used to write to her favourites and then ask for her letters back. At any rate, since she never prepared them for publication, her epistolary style can be assumed to be as it stands. In his study of her letters Roger Duchêne suggests that she prolonged her emotional, intellectual and sexual adventures in and through her writing. There were several 18th-century apocryphal editions of her love-letters, notably with the son of the ▷Marquise de Sévigné, with whom she is said to have had a tempestuous affair at a very great age, much to his mother's chagrin, since Ninon had also been her husband's mistress at the time of his early death in a duel. No authentic letters have survived from the correspondence between Ninon and the future Madame de Maintenon. Ninon's *libertinage* (immoral free-thinking) and disrespect for religion is manifest in every line of her correspondence with the writer Saint-Evremond. By no means

devoid of wit, she was responsible for the definition of the *Précieuses* (▷Precious Women) as '*les jansénistes de l'amour*' ('the Jansenists of love'). The letters which have been preserved contain few literary references, but show her vulnerability, particularly to age. At the end of her life, even women flocked to the social gatherings at Ninon's house in the rue des Tournelles in Paris, where she also supposedly received the young Voltaire (1694–1778).
Bib: Duchêne, R., *Ninon de Lenclos: la courtisane du grand siècle*; Colombey, E., *Correspondance authentique de Ninon de Lenclos*.

Lendorff, Gertrud (1900–1986)
German-speaking Swiss novelist. Born in Basle, she wrote stories for children and young women, thrillers, and historical novels about Basle. Women's destinies are a central theme in her work, which includes *Die salige Frau* (1935) (*The Special Woman*) and *Timdala* (1937), a biography of the scientist Sybilla Merian. She also wrote the prize-winning radio play *Frau Oberst* (1953) (*Madam Colonel*).

L'Engle, Madeleine (born 1918)
US novelist and poet who wrote for both children and adults. Born in New York, L'Engle graduated from Smith College in 1941. Her novels emphasize the right and the responsibility of the individual to make choices; her characters search for a theology by which to live. ▷*A Wrinkle in Time* (1962), the first of L'Engle's ▷science fiction trilogy for children, uses time travel to explore the tension between good and evil. Evil is symbolized by a disembodied brain called IT which turns one of the characters into a robot. The overcoming of evil is thus tied to a belief in the individual.
The Small Room (1945) explores the conflicts between career, romance and marriage for a young woman who has inherited her mother's musical genius. In the sequel, *A Severed Wasp* (1982), the same woman, at the end of a successful career, is the centre of a network of relationships in which the key motif is the search for self-reconciliation. The novel mixes past memories with the present.
L'Engle also experimented with verse drama in her biblical story *The Journey with Jonah* (1967), and her poems were published in *Lines Scribbled on an Envelope and Other Poems* (1969). *A Circle of Quiet* (1972), *The Summer of the Great Grandmother* (1980) and *Walking on Water: Reflections on Faith and Art* (1980) are all non-fiction works based on her journals. L'Engle's works are linked by a challenge to conventional religious pieties and an assertion of the dignity and creativity of each individual.
Other works include *Ilsa* (1946), *The Moon By Night* (1963), *The Arm of the Starfish* (1965), *The Young Unicorns* (1968), *Dance in the Desert* (1969), *The Other Side of the Sun* (1971), *A Wind in the Door* (1973), *Prayers for Sunday* (1974), *Dragons in the Waters* (1976), *The Irrational Season* (1977), *A*

Swiftly Tilting Planet (1978), *The Anti-Muffins* (1981), *Camilla* (1981), *The Sphinx at Dawn: Two Stories* (1982), *And Both Were Young* (1983), *And It Was Good: Reflections on Beginnings* (1983), *The Love Letters* (1983), *A House Like a Lotus* (1984), *The Twenty-Four Days Before Christmas: An Austin Family Story* (1984), *Trailing clouds of Glory: Spiritual Values in Children's Books* (1985), *Many Waters* (1986), *A Stone for a Pillow: Journeys with Jacob* (1986) and *The Crosswicks Journal* (1988).

Lenguas de diamante, Las (1919) (*Tongues of Diamond*)

First book by the leading Uruguayan poet ▷Juana de Ibarbourou (1895–1979), who received the name 'Juana de America' in 1929 after the success of her erotic, narcissistic poetry. In contrast to the abstract mother-like love expressed by Chilean ▷Gabriela Mistral in her ▷*Desolación* (1922) (*Solace*), Ibarbourou expressed in her book, which was compared to spring, all the superb eroticism related to sensual body. Her following books were compared to summer, *Raiz salvaje* (1922) (*Savage Root*), to an autumn afternoon, *La rosa de los vientos* (1930) (*The Rose of the Winds*), and to the decline of old age, or a winter night, in *Perdida* (1950) (*Lost*), where the voice is that of a sad, secluded widow who does not like to appear in public. In *Tongues of Diamond*, sensuousness is openly expressed.

Leningrad

Leningrad, the name by which ▷St Petersburg was known from 1924 to October 1991, lost much of its aura of patriarchal power and intrigue when the capital was moved back to ▷Moscow, away from Russia's northern border, during the upheavals of the 1918–1920 Civil War. The 900-day siege of Leningrad by the Germans in World War II has been described by ▷Lidiia Gínzburg (▷*The Siege of Leningrad*) and ▷Vera Inber (*Leningrad Diary*, 1971). The state's crackdown on even the mild measure of pluralist opinion permitted as propaganda during the war began with an attack on two Leningrad writers, Mikhail Zoshchenko and ▷Anna Akhmátova.

Lennox, Charlotte (Ramsay) (?1729–1804)

English novelist, poet, dramatist and unsuccessful actress; daughter of an English army officer (she may have been born in Gibraltar) she grew up in the environs of New York. Her father died when she was in her mid-teens and she came to England. Her patrons for her early writings, such as *Poems on Several Occassions* (1647), included Lady Isabella Finch, but she was later known to the powerful male literary establishment, including Samuel Johnson, Samuel Richardson, Henry Fielding and Horace Walpole. Her poem, 'the Art of Coquetry' offended ▷Elizabeth Carter, presumably because of its advice to 'form your artful looks with studious care' so that 'caught by these arts, with pride and hope elate, / the destined victim rushes on his fate.' Her husband, Alexender Lennox, did little to support

her or their children, and she wrote for money. Her first novel was *Harriot Stuart* (1750), and ▷*The Female Quixote* (1752) was well received, but she was never financially successful, and throughout the 1750s she worked as a translator and editor of Shakespeare. In 1758 she published *Henrietta*. She edited *The Ladies Monthly* (1760–1761) but continued to be very poor. She achieved some success when the theatrical producer David Garrick (1717–1779) staged her *Old City Manners* (1775, adapted from the well-known comedy *Eastward Hoe*, 1605), but plans to raise money by issuing subscription versions of her poems repeatedly foundered. She published her last novel, *Euphemia* in 1790, finally left her husband in 1792 and remained in dire poverty as her applications to the Royal Literary Fund testify.
Bib: Lonsdale, R. (ed.) *Eighteenth-Century Women Poets*.

Lenski, Lois (1893–1974)

US novelist. Born in Springfield, Ohio, Lenski infused children's literature with a socio-economic realism. After graduating from Ohio State University in 1915, she studied art in New York and London, England. In 1936 she published *Phebe Fairchild: Her Book*, the first in a series of historical novels. Each novel interprets the social and intellectual climate of a particular place and time, and it does so by focusing on one family's everyday life.

In 1943 Lenski published *Bayou Suzette*, the first in her regional series that includes ▷*Strawberry Girl* (1945). She emphasizes the importance of knowing and understanding people different from oneself.

Other works include: *Little Engine that Could* (1930), *Fireside Poems* (1930), *Indian Captive: The Story of Mary Jemison* (1941), *Judy's Journey* (1947), *Mr and Mrs Noah* (1948), *Cotton In My Sack* (1949), *I Like Winter* (1950), *Prairie School* (1951), *Davy and His Dog* (1958), *Shoofly Girl* (1963), *Adventures in Understanding* (1968), *More Mr Small* (1979), *Bound Girl of Cobble Hill, Lois Lenski's Big Big Book of Mr Small* (1985), *Sing for Peace* (1985) and *Sing a Song of People* (1987).

Léo, André (1824–1900)

Pseudonym of French novelist and journalist Léodile Champseix. A founder member of the feminist ▷*Association pour le droit des femmes* established in the 1870s, and a regular contributor to the radical newspaper *La Sociale*, Léo only became a militant feminist during the ▷Paris Commune, 1871 – partly because she was horrified by the misogyny of the Communards. Her novels *Un mariage scandaleux* (1862) (*A Scandalous Marriage*) and *Un divorce* (1866) (*A Divorce*), while placing the institution of marriage on trial, were written primarily in order to support her family, rather than to further the feminist cause. However, her *Les Femmes et les moeurs* (1869) (*Women and Morals*) is a more radical work, in which she refutes the anti-feminism of ▷Proudhonism and its followers,

derides the traditionalist visions of femininity cherished by her male socialist contemporaries, and demands equal political rights for women. Barbey d'Aurevilly (▷*Les Bas-bleus Bluestockings*) observed, unsurprisingly, that she was a bluestocking of the worst kind.
Bib: Albistur, M. and Armogathe, D., *Histoire du féminisme français*; Moses, C., *French Feminism in the 19th Century*.

Leoba (Lioba, Leobgyth) (died 779)
English nun. Leoba was abbess of Bischofsheim in the diocese of Mainz. According to her biographer, Rudolph, a monk of Fulda (who wrote her life in 836), Leoba went to Bischofsheim at the request of ▷Boniface. Rudolph records, among other qualities and gifts, her love of scholarship. Her only surviving poetic composition is an early verse of four lines at the end of a letter (in Latin) to Boniface.

León, María Teresa de (born 1904)
Spanish novelist, essayist and translator. Wife of the poet Rafael Alberti. Her early works, such as *Cuentos para soñar (Stories for Dreaming)*, were written with children in mind. An active member of the Spanish Communist Party, she played a vital role in the Republican cultural machine during the Spanish Civil War (1936–1939) as director of the Teatro de las Guerrillas and organizer of the Republic's effort to save Spanish art treasures from the effects of war. After her experience of the civil war, her work became more politicized: *Cuentos de la España actual* (1937) (*Tales of Present-day Spain*); *Contra viento y marea* (1941) (*Against Wind and High Seas*); *Morirás lejos* (1942) (*You'll Die Far Away*); *Las peregrinaciones de Teresa* (1950) (*Teresa's Wanderings*), and *Fábulas del tiempo amargo* (1962) (*Fables of the Bitter Time*). A main theme of León's later work is the exposure of social injustice.

Leon, Pauline (1769–?)
French revolutionary activist. Born in Paris, she worked with her mother in their chocolate factory. She was co-founder of the Société des citoyennes républicaines révolutionnaires in 1793. When the women's clubs were dissolved in 1793 she returned to the factory. Imprisoned for five months in 1794, she was released after the fall of Robespierre. Her speech, 'Adresse des citoyennes de la capitale' ('Speech to the Women Citizens of the Capital'), has been published in recent collections of documents relating to women's revolutionary activities (▷French Revolution; pamphlets, registers of grievances, petitions and speeches).

Recent editions of her work can be found in P. Duhet, (ed.), *Cahiers de doléances des femmes et autres textes (Registers of Women's Grievances and Other Texts)*; English translations in Levy, Applewhite and Johnson, *Women in Revolutionary Paris*.

Leonardos, Stela (born 1923)
Brazilian poet, short story writer, novelist and children's writer. Leonardos, whose full name is Stela Leonardos da Silva Lima Cabassa, published her first book of poetry, *Palmares* (1940) (*Palm Groves*), at the age of seventeen. She combines a precise knowledge of history with the popular tradition of Brazil to write romance poems as in the *Romanceiro do Bequimão* (1986) (*Tales of Bequimão*). Influenced by the ▷1945 Generation, her poems are full of abstract ideas and spiritualism.

Other works include: *Passos na areia* (1940) (*Steps in the Sand*), *A grande visão* (1942) (*The Grand Vision*), *Poesia em três tempos* (1956) (*Poetry in Three Times*), *Estátua de sal* (1961) (*Statue of Salt*) and *Cancioneiro catalão* (1971) (*Catalan Songs*).

Leonor, Queen of Portugal (1458–1525)
Married to King João II, whom she survived, Queen Leonor was a strong supporter of letters and the arts; she is perhaps best known for her patronage of Gil Vicente, an important Portuguese dramatist. She is generally credited with having brought the printing press to Portugal, and with the publication of the Portuguese translation of ▷Christine de Pisan's *Livre des Trois Vertues*.
▷*Espelho de Cristina*; Isabel, Queen of Portugal

Léonora, l'histoire enfouie de la Guadeloupe (1985) (Léonora, the Vanished Story of Guadeloupe)
This novel by the French Antilles (Caribbean) writer, ▷Dany Bebel-Gisler is a transcription from Creole to French of the life-history of an elderly Guadeloupean woman. Léonora emerges as a resilient woman who struggles to bring up her family, and who, after successive betrayals by her partners, chooses to live alone, turning to political activity and to religion. Through the title of her novel, Bebel-Gisler suggests a link between woman and island which ▷Simone Schwarz-Bart also sets up in her ▷*The Bridge of Beyond*.

Leontium (2nd century BC)
Philosopher; consort and pupil of the Athenian philosopher Epicurus (341–270 BC). Sources say she wrote a work decrying the philosopher Theophrastus's view that philosophers should not marry. She is mentioned in the *Life of Epicurus* by Diogenes Laertius (3rd century AD), but even here she is referred to only in relation to Epicurus, and as a courtesan, prone to sexual licence. The Roman Cicero (1st century BC) disparagingly refers to her as a 'little prostitute' who dared to write the work on marriage. But he admits her good Attic Greek style. The Elder Pliny (1st century AD) records that there was a statue of her 'thinking', by Theodorus. Some of Epicurus's surviving letters are addressed to Leontium, but none of her replies survive. Tradition records a daughter, Danae, a courtesan.
▷Philosophers, Ancient Greek and Roman women

Le Prince de Beaumont, Marie (1711–1718)

French writer of educational prose fiction. Le Prince de Beaumont was born in Rouen, and educated at the Convent of Ernemont, which, unusually for the period, specialized in preparing young women for teaching. She earned her living as a ▷governess and after an unsuccessful marriage left for England. There she published several volumes of moral tales for children, which appeared in periodical form in *Le Nouveau Magasin français* (1750) (*The New French Shop*), *Magasin des enfants* (1758) (*The Children's Shop*), and in two collections of *Contes Moraux* (1744, 1776) (*Moral Tales*). She also provided plans and material for the education of both boys and girls, as well as adolescents, and one collection for 'craftsmen, the poor and people of the countryside'. The works became the handbooks for governesses throughout a century. Her method of using fiction as a pedagogical tool was regarded as progressive, and her practice anticipates some of Jean-Jacques Rousseau's (1712–1778) theories. Her fairytales continue to be re-edited in France, her most well-known work being her version of *The Beauty and the Beast*, which she adapted from the original by ▷Gabrielle de Villeneuve. The full bibliography of her published prose fiction, which also included novels and later poetic tales more attuned to the style of the romantic period, runs to some 70 volumes.
Bib: Clancy, P.A., 'Mme Le Prince de Beaumont: founder of children's literature in France', *Aust. Journal of French Studies*, XVI (1979); Hazard, P., *Les Livres, les enfants et les hommes*; Robert, R., *Le Conte de fée*; Reynaud, M.A., *Mme Le Prince de Beaumont*.

Leprohon, Rosanna (1832–1879)

Canadian novelist, born Rosanna Mullins in Montreal. She attended convent school and, encouraged by the nuns to write, began publishing fiction at the age of seventeen. She married Jean-Lucien Leprohon, a medical doctor, and had thirteen children with him. Her five novels are so convincing in their evocation of 19th-century French Canada that it was assumed she was French, although she wrote and published in English. *Antoinette de Mirecourt; or, Secret Marrying and Secret Sorrowing: A Canadian Tale* (1864), is a romantic novel about an heiress who marries secretly, but is miserable until her husband is killed and she is free to marry her real love. *Armand Durand; or, A Promise Fulfilled* (1868) is suspicious about the ideal of marrying for love; nevertheless, Leprohon advocates both marriage as a partnership, and the education of women. Leprohon's popular romances traversed the French–English separation, and succeeding in conveying 'essentially Canadian' themes.
Bib: Gerson, C., *Three Writers of Victorian Canada and Their Works*.

Lesbian continuum ▷Rich, Adrienne

Lesbian feminist criticism

The question of definition is a constant concern for lesbian feminist critics. Early lesbian feminists began by retrieving lost texts and re-reading canonical ones for inclusion in a history of affective (lesbian) bonding between women: an example is ▷Lillian Faderman's history of women loving women, *Surpassing the Love of Men* (1981). ▷Adrienne Rich also produced a broad definition of a lesbian as a ▷woman-identified woman. ▷Teresa de Lauretis, among others, has argued for a more precise meaning of lesbianism, insisting that sexuality should be the basis of its definition. In an early essay, 'Toward a Black Feminist Criticism' (1970), Barbara Smith drew attention to the exclusion of black lesbianism as a concept from both black female traditions and white lesbian ones. Since the 1980s ▷French feminism, especially Monique Wittig's theory and fiction, has theorized lesbian sexuality within the context of ▷*écriture féminine*.
▷Case, Sue-Ellen; Castle, Terry
Bib: Hobby, E. and White, C., *What lesbians do in Books*; Smith, B., 'Toward a Black Feminist Criticism'.

Lesbian Images (1975)

Canadian writer ▷Jane Rule's evocative and declarative essays about the lesbian experience of twelve women writers, including ▷Vita Sackville-West, ▷Colette, ▷Radclyffe Hall, and ▷Gertrude Stein. In her introduction Rule identifies the difficulties she has had in being known as a lesbian writer, but asserts that, despite her occasional anger, she is 'proud to be in such company, to share such a risk and such a heritage'.

Lesbian pulp fiction

US lesbian pulp fiction is a phenomenon of the 1950s. Hundreds of paperback novels about lesbians were sold in drugstores, supermarkets and bus stations across the US. The phenomenon began with Tereska Torres's *Women's Barracks* (1950), published by Faucett Crest, a mainstream press. Pulp fiction writers include ▷Ann Bannon, Paula Christian, Vin Packer, Artemis Smith and Valerie Taylor. The novels are set in girls' schools and college sororities, suburbs and lesbian bars. They feature the lesbian coming-out process. The lesbian character knows she violates a sexual taboo in loving another woman, and she struggles with her own internalized oppression. The novels often end tragically and moralistically in suicide, accidental death, insanity or marriage. Pulp fiction gave way to fiction by openly lesbian authors, like ▷Rita Mae Brown. ▷Naiad Press reprints some of these pulp novels.

Lesbian writing

Australia: The earliest Australian novel with a lesbian theme is probably ▷Rosa Praed's *Affinities: A Romance of Today* (1886), while more modern examples include *All That False Instruction* (1975) by Elizabeth Riley, *Alone* (1980) by

▷Beverley Farmer, *A Gap in the Records* (1987) by
Jan McKemmish (born 1950), *Remember the
Tarantella* (1987) by Finola Moorhead (born
1947), *Working Hot* (1989) by Mary Fallon, *Surly
Girls* by Susan Hampton (1989), *Saturn Return* by
Louise Wakeling (1989), and *Easy Come, Easy Go*
by Pamela May (1990). The lesbian theme is
pervasive in much of ▷Elizabeth Jolley's fiction,
and is explicit in *Palomino* (1980), ▷*Miss
Peabody's Inheritance* (1983) and ▷*The Well*
(1986). Anthologies such as ▷*The Penguin Book of
Australian Women Poets* (1986), edited by Susan
Hampton and Kate Llewellyn, and *Moments of
Desire: Sex and Sensuality by Australian Feminist
Writers* (1989), edited by Susan Hawthorne and
Jenny Pausacker, also contain depictions of a wide
variety of female erotic experience, including
lesbian experience.
New Zealand: The first anthology of lesbian
writing in New Zealand, *The Power and the Glory*
edited by Mirian Saphira, appeared in 1987.
Since then there have been a number of texts
which feature lesbianism, among them plays by
▷Renée and novels by ▷Sandi Hall, and a
number of stories have appeared in mainstream
collections. Typically lesbian writing challenges
heterosexual institutions (particularly marriage and
the family) and conventions, while remaining fairly
conventional in form, for instance rewriting the
▷romance as lesbian. Since its appearance
lesbian writing has become less separatist in its
publishing outlets.
  ▷McCauley, Sue; Te Awekotoku, Ngahuia

**Lespinasse, Julie-Jeanne-Eléonore de (1732–
1776)**
French woman of letters and salon hostess. Born
in Lyon, the illegitimate daughter of the Comtesse
d'Albon. Educated by her mother and orphaned at
sixteen, she became governess to the children of
her sister, the Marquise de Vichy Chamond, who
was married to the youngest brother of the
▷Marquise du Deffand. In 1752 du Deffand,
suffering from the loss of her sight, invited de
Lespinasse to live with her as a companion and
reader. The arrangement came to an abrupt end
when du Deffand learned that the regulars of her
own salon met with de Lespinasse before visiting
her. Lespinasse moved out and was helped by the
philosophe d'Alembert (1717–1783), and other
members of the Encyclopaedist group, who
thereafter attended her Salon. Literary historians
have celebrated de Lespinasse as Muse of the
Encyclopaedists and tragic victim of two
passionate affairs, one with the Marquis de Dorat,
the other with the Comte de Guibert. The
published correspondence with Guibert, re-edited
by Editions d'aujourd'hui and presented by J.
Pascal (1978), has often been read as a unique
testimony of love in the 18th century, and the
vehemence in her writing has led to Lespinasse
being portrayed as a heroine prone to hysteria.
Only recently has the correspondence been
situated, by the critic S.L. Carrell, as a literary
work in the tradition of the monophonic

▷epistolary novel. Equally, her correspondence
with women has traditionally been dismissed as
only of secondary interest; it was described by one
critic as preparatory exercises for the writing
addressed to male lovers. The *Lettres de Julie de
Lespinasse à Condorcet: 1769–1776* were re-edited
by Desjonquères in 1990.
  ▷*Journal des Dames*
Bib: Castries, Duc de, *Julie de Lespinasse: le drame
d'un double amour*; Carrell, S.L., *Le Soliloque de la
passion féminine*; Truc, G., *'Julie de Lespinasse'* in
*Aimer en France, Actes du colloque de Clermont
Ferrand.*

Lessico famigliare (1963) ▷*Family Sayings*

Lessing, Doris (born 1919)
British novelist and short story writer. Through
both her involvement in the Communist Party and
the peace movement in political life, and in her
prolific and varied literary output, the problem
that Doris Lessing continually probes is that of
the representation of political questions from a
woman's point of view. It is a question that has
led Lessing to adopt a variety of political
perspectives and, in her literary work, through an
equally wide range of literary genres, such as
political realism, ▷science fiction, fantasy and
feminist ▷*Bildungsroman*. Although born in Persia
(Iran), Lessing spent the early part of her life in
South Africa, where she became involved in the
both the Communist Party and black politics. This
environment provides the staging for her
disturbing representation of the interrelation
between racial and sexual politics in ▷*The Grass
is Singing* (1950). With her move to London in
1949, Lessing's vision takes an epic and mystical
turn with the ▷*Children of Violence* series, opening
with *Martha Quest* (1952) and comprising five
novels, written over seventeen years. It is,
however, in her famous ▷*The Golden Notebook*
(1962), that Lessing's concern with female
subjectivity most strikingly begins to break up
novelistic form; a process which culminates in the
dazzling and complex *Briefing for a Descent into
Hell* (1972). Such experiments with style, time and
structure continue, albeit in a slightly different
direction, in her science fiction novels, the
Canopus in Argos: Archives series, (1979–1982) and
in her dystopic *Memoirs of a Survivor* (1979). By
way of contrast, *The Good Terrorist* (1985) offers a
devastating critique of the naïvity and exploitation
endemic in political activism. Claims that this
book represents a 'return to realism' on Lessing's
part, however, have been challenged by her latest
'fantastic' novel, *The Fifth Child* (1986), which
provides a timely exploration of female
reproductive sexuality.
  Other works include: *Five Short Novels* (1953),
A Proper Marriage (1954), *Each His Own Wilderness*
(play) (1958), *In Pursuit of the English* (1960),
African Stories (1964) and *Four-Gated City* (1969).
Bib: King, Jeannette, *Doris Lessing.*

Lesueur, Daniel ▷Lapauze, Jeanne

Le Sueur, Meridel (born 1900)

US journalist, novelist, short story writer, poet and biographer. Born in Murray, Iowa, Le Sueur grew up in Texas, Oklahoma and Kansas. She was raised by her socialist step-father and by women who espoused radical politics, which was reflected in her writing for labour and left-wing magazines. The radical scope of Le Sueur's writing can be gauged by the range of journals in which she was published: *Dial, Daily Worker, Partisan Review, New Masses, Pagany, Scribner's* and *Anvil*. Le Sueur lived a varied life which included working as an actor in early Hollywood films, directing the Little Theater of Sacramento, California and at one time living in an anarchist commune with Emma Goldman (1869–1940). After World War II Le Sueur was informally blacklisted as a communist sympathizer. A social historian, she records the stories of ordinary anonymous people. *North Star Country* (1945), for example, is significant for its use of the local language of its Midwest setting and its grounding in oral material. Her early stories describe the lives of working-class and pioneer women, and after the birth of her first daughter in 1928 her stories began to emphasize women's role in the continuity of life. Her later writing celebrates a sense of solidarity among women. Collected in ▷*Ripening: Selected Work of Meridel Le Sueur* (1982) her work envisions a social regeneration through women. Le Sueur's writing for children develops a native tradition in works such as *Nancy Hanks of Wilderness Road* (1949), *Sparrow Hawk* (1950) and *The River Road: A Story of Abraham Lincoln* (1954).

Other works include: *Annunciation* (1935), *Salute to Spring* (1940), *Crusaders* (1955), *Corn Village* (1970), *Harvest: Collected Stories* (1977), *Rites of Ancient Ripening* (1975), *The Girl* (1978), *Song for My Time, Women on the Breadlines* (1978), *Harvest: Collected Stories and Essays 1926–58* (ed. John F. Crawford, 1990).

Letessier, Dorothée (born 1953)

French novelist. Letessier is a working-class woman who worked in a factory for several years before writing her first and most well-known novel, *Le Voyage à Paimpol* (1980) (translated as *A Breath of Air*), which recounts the narrator's brief escape from the constraints of her responsibilities as worker, wife and mother. The confessional tone of the novel is supported by the note of 'authenticity' provided by the author's own background. Letessier's other novels are *Loïca* (1983), *La Belle Atlantique* (1986) (*The Beautiful Atlantic*), *Jean-Baptiste ou l'éducation vagabonde* (1988) (*Jean-Baptiste: Learning to Be a Wanderer*), and *La Reine des abeilles* (1989) (*The Queen Bee*).

Lettera a un bambino mai nato (1975)
▷*Letter to a Child Never Born*

'Letter . . . by Mary Stafford to her Kinswoman, A' (1980)

Written in 1711, it details ▷Mary Stafford's poverty as the cause of her family's departure from England and resettlement in South Carolina, her first experiences in the colony, and her impressions of the American South. The letter is one of the few extant early North American documents that details the plight of the lower economic classes.
▷Early North American letters

Letter from Elizabeth Webb to Anthony William Boehm, A (1781)

This forty-four-page document consists of a letter and spiritual narrative from the North American Quaker minister, ▷Elizabeth Webb, to Anthony William Boehm, chaplain to Prince George of Denmark, with whom she became friends during a visit to England in 1712. *A Letter* was written while she was in England; she notes that her respect for Boehm compels her to communicate further with him and to share her spiritual experiences. She emphasizes her egalitarian philosophy of religion, insisting that she does not 'see HIM through particular forms, sects, party-impressions'. In Boehm's reply, which is attached, he relates his 'great satisfaction' with the letter and the fact that he has shared it with numerous friends who have copied it for their own edification. It was probably one of these copies that served as the source for the 1781 publication in Philadelphia.
▷Early North American letters; Early North American Quaker women's writings

Letter from Mrs Anne Dutton . . . to the Rev. Mr G. Whitefield, A (1743)

Published in Philadelphia during the Great Awakening, this letter by the North American ▷Anne Dutton begins by thanking God for bringing the Reverend Whitefield to Bristol, Pennsylvania, where foolish people have assumed 'that they have not *Sinned* in thought, Word or Deed for Months!' In an otherwise formulaic text, Dutton emphasizes that salvation is a process: the Apostle did not say humans '*are* like [Christ] . . . but we *shall* be like him'. This eleven-page letter is her only known publication.
▷Early North American letters

Letters

Australia: A great many collections of letters written by Australian women survive in Australian libraries. 19th-century Australia was a land of emigrants and the prevalence of letter-writing, and the preservation of collections of letters, is explained by desperate homesickness, by the necessity to reassure relatives left behind, and by the urge to describe the emigrant's life in a picturesque and exciting new land. As is explained by Lucy Frost, in ▷*No Place for a Nervous Lady: Voices from the Australian Bush* (1984), the quality of the prose varies from the literary and genteel to the uneducated and unpunctuated, but each is authentic in its own way.

Well-known collections of letters are those of ▷Margaret Catchpole, a convict woman; of Elizabeth Macarthur, who arrived with the

Second Fleet, and was the wife of one of Australia's wealthier pioneers; of ▷Eliza Brown, an early settler in the Swan River colony in Western Australia; of ▷Rachel Henning; and of Georgiana Molloy, one of the first white settlers on the Blackwood River in Western Australia and an accomplished botanist who discovered and recorded many of the unique plants of her region. Extracts from all these letters appear in many Australian anthologies, and they tell of the rigours and joys of life on emigrant ships, of women's reactions to the Aborigines, of childbirth in the bush, and of the death of mothers in childbirth and the loss of their infant children. Letter-writing is not a lost art in Australia, as is shown by a recent publication: *Blessed City: Letters to Thomas Riddell* 1943 (1990) by ▷Gwen Harwood, edited by Alison Hoddinott.

Britain, Middle Ages: ▷Boniface Correspondence; Margery Cely; Paston Letters; Plumpton Correspondence; Stonor Letters.
Bib: Wood, Mary Anne Everett, *Letters of Royal and Illustrious Ladies of Great Britain*; von Thal, Herbert, *The Royal Letter Book*; Legge, M. Dominica, *Anglo-Norman Letters and Petitions*; Moriarty, Catherine, *The Voice of the Middle Ages in Personal Letters 1100–1500*.

Renaissance Britain: Letters by Renaissannce Englishwomen are much more likely to survive than any other genre of women's writing, including poems and religious compositions. In part this is due to the fact that most of the extant letters are either by women of note (for example queens such as ▷Catherine of Aragon, ▷Anne Boleyn, ▷Jane Grey and ▷Elizabeth Tudor) or by women in correspondence with famous men. The latter group includes, for example, ▷Anne Bacon's letters to her sons, ▷Anne Locke's to John Knox, and ▷Margaret Roper's to her father Thomas More and to Erasmus. Although some letters by middle-class women exist, most of them remain as unedited manuscripts. As historical documents, women's letters form an important source of information regarding their personal ideas and their status in Renaissance society. Moreover, they form an important body of literary endeavours in which, perhaps more than anywhere else, women could speak in their own voices. The acceptability of women writing conventional letters opened the way to later fictionalized epistles. ▷Isabella Whitney's verse epistles appended to ▷*A Sweet Nosegay* (1573) are an early example of fictionalized letter-writing by an Englishwoman.

▷Lisle, Honor; Stuart, Mary
Bib: Green, M.A.W. (ed.), *Letters of Royal and Illustrious Ladies of Great Britain*.
Southern Africa: Letters, like ▷diaries and journals, form an important part of women's writing, particularly at a time when women shied away from other literary genres. The earliest preserved writing is Dutch: Johanna Maria van Riebeeck, granddaughter of the first Dutch governor at the Cape, wrote a set of letters between 1709 and 1711, which were edited and

published in 1952, in Dutch. Letters were also written by British travellers, and, later, settlers. Lady Lucie Duff Gordon (1821–1869) wrote a set of letters home during a brief visit to the Cape in 1861–62, made in the hope of curing her chronic bronchitis. Like ▷Lady Anne Barnard's, the letters betray the intense desire to classify and rank people ethnically that marks the South African colonial enterprise. Yet they are noteworthy for their sympathetic depiction of the Cape Moslems (called Malays because of the origin of some of them), in her view considerably more civilized than white South Africans. First published in 1863 in Francis Galton's *Vacation Tourist*, Lady Gordon's letters were also included in her book *Last Letters from Egypt* (1875), together with a memoir by her daughter, with a definitive edition *Letters from the Cape* appearing in 1927, edited by South African writer Dorothea Fairbridge. Emily Hobhouse's visit to the Cape during the Anglo–Boer War (1899–1902) issued in a set of *Boer War Letters* (1984, edited by Rykie van Reenen), which form an important part of ▷Anglo–Boer War writing by South African women.

Early missionary experience was often recounted in letters: those of Mary Moffat, for instance, which have been used to form her biography, *Beloved Partner: Mary Moffat of Kuruman* (1974). Emma Murray's letters have been used in a similar way in *In Mid-Victorian Cape Town* (1953) and in *Young Mrs Murray Goes to Bloemfontein 1856–1860* (1954), which provides a fascinating account of a Dutch Reformed Church household in the early part of the 20th century. Other settler accounts were given in epistolary form, most notably by Rhodesian writer Sheila MacDonald, best known for a collection of letters written during 1907–1911, which provide conventional but amusing accounts of homesteading and housewifery in primitive bush conditions. Published under the title *Sally in Rhodesia* (1927, reprinted 1970), the book went into nine editions, becoming something of a Rhodesian institution.

Some of the early South African novelists left letters as part of their literary remains, notably ▷Olive Schreiner, ▷Sarah Gertrude Millin, and ▷Pauline Smith. Schreiner's letters were first selected and edited by her husband in 1924, some in censored form, and the first volume of a projected two-volume collection appeared, with notes, in 1987 (edited by Richard Rive).

Letter-writing also occurs as an interesting if small strand of black Southern African literary tradition. The first letters known to have been written by a black South African woman were by Emma Sandile, the daughter of a Xhosa chief, who was sent for her education to a mission boarding school in the Cape in the late 19th century. A very few of these are reprinted in Janet Hodgson's *Princess Emma* (1987). Then, from 1949 to 1951, a young girl, given the name Lily Moya by her editor in order to protect her identity, corresponded with educationist Dr Mabel

Palmer, from whom she wanted assistance in gaining further education; these letters are collected in *Not Either an Experimental Doll* (1987), edited by Shula Marks, along with a few letters between Palmer and Sibusisiwe Makhanya on the topic of 'Lily'. The letters tell a story of aspiration, misunderstanding, and interpersonal failure which has significant political implications. By Lily Moya's own account, Mabel Palmer gave her a scholarship to Sterkfontein, the notorious mental institution for black South Africans.

The letters of ▷Bessie Head, who died in 1986, and wrote prolifically about her fiction to publishers and friends, are just starting to be released to the public. They are remarkable for the detail and honesty with which they present her relationships and state of mind, as well as the intellectual boldness with which they discuss Southern African history, politics and everyday life.

'Letters and Journal of Hannah Bulfinch, The' (1896)

Excerpted in *The Life and Letters of Charles Bulfinch, Architect*, the North American writer ▷Hannah Apthorp Bulfinch's correspondence and journal was maintained during the years after the American Revolution, when the Bulfinches had been reduced to poverty. Hannah noted in 1797 that, although born into well-established families, they had been reduced to sharing a home with friends. Addressing her journal to her children, she wrote, 'Read, my children, the wanderings of your mother, who once thought herself plac'd by fortune far above these vicissitudes.'

▷Early North American letters

Letters from Juliette Catesby (1786)

Translation of *Letters de milady Juliette Catesby* (1759), a novel by French writer ▷Marie-Jeanne Riccoboni. The letters, sent to a female confidante, read as a journal of a journey undertaken by Juliette, and include mordant portraits of people and places. In form the text resembles ▷Samuel Richardson's *Pamela* (1740). Juliette has been deserted two years previously by her fiancé, Mylord d'Ossery, who has married Jenny Monfort. Recently widowed, he now pursues Juliette. Although she still loves him, she formally rejects him as unworthy, and attempts to put him out of her mind. Finally a reconciliation is effected, after he sends a letter explaining his actions. A passing infidelity with Jenny had resulted in pregnancy, and he had married her, but as he is now widowed he sees himself as free to marry his original fiancée. The novel is typical of Riccoboni's works, with its focus on the female point of view and an analysis of the difficulties women have in relating to the male characters. A modern edition of this work is *Lettres de milady Juliette Catesby*, edited by S. Menant (1984).

Letters of a Portuguese Nun, The (1929)

Translation of *Lettres Portugaises* (1669), one of the earliest examples of epistolary prose and a major work of world literature. The five letters in the collection were purportedly written by a Portuguese nun, ▷Sóror Mariana Alcoforado, to her soldier-lover, Noël Bouton, who was Chevalier of Chamilly and Marshall of France. The letters describe her despair as a result of having been abandoned by Bouton, who returned to France. The letters were published in Paris by Guilleragues, who had supposedly translated them from the Portuguese. Later, scholars uncovered evidence proving that Guilleragues was the author of the work.

▷*Three Marias: New Portuguese Letters, The*; 'Three Marias', The

Bib: Kamuf, Peggy,'Writing like a Woman' in *Women and Language in Literature and Society* ; Kauffman, L.S., *Discourses of Desire: Gender, Genre and Epistolary Fictions*; Perry, Ruth, *Women, Letters and the Novel* ; Sadlier, Darlene J., *The Question of How: Women Writers and New Portuguese Literature*.

Letters of Benjamin Franklin and Jane Mecom, The (1950)

Although best-known as the younger sister of the North American statesman Benjamin Franklin (1706–1790), ▷Jane Franklin Mecom lived a very different life from that of her brother. Poorly educated, she was married at a young age to a man of little ambition, and her life was a struggle against poverty and loss. The letters, beginning in 1758 and ending one year before Mecom's death in 1794, include numerous passages of praise for her brother's accomplishments, but they also articulate the difficulties of her life and her concerns for the welfare of her children and herself during the American Revolution. If her 'Dear Brother' was 'the whol worlds friend', Mecom was obviously a treasured sister and friend to Franklin as well.

▷*Benjamin Franklin and Catharine Ray Greene*; Early North American letters

'Letters of Deborah Read Rogers Franklin, The' (1959–)

Collected in *The Papers of Benjamin Franklin*, the letters of ▷Deborah Read Rogers Franklin, common-law wife of the North American statesman, were written between 1755 and her death in 1774. Though of little literary value, they are historically significant, capturing the extraordinary events of the American Revolution from the perspective of a woman whose husband was deeply involved in the formation of the new government but whose own life was one of hardship, near illiteracy, and imposed frugality that was often taken to extremes. Thus her letters and her life symbolize the disparity between the hopes and opportunities of the dominant culture in the newly-formed nation and that of women and other oppressed groups whose futures offered little hope for reform.

▷Early North American letters

'Letters of Eliza Farmar to Her Nephew'
(1916)
Written between 1774 and 1783, these letters by
▷ Eliza Farmar, an Englishwoman, who settled in
North America shortly before the American
Revolution, attest to her advocacy of the Patriot
cause, but also to a lingering and heartfelt
sympathy for her homeland. During the invasion
of Philadelphia by the British in 1783, she did not
alter her faith with the North American movement
for independence and thus faced many hardships,
as she relates to her nephew who remained in
England.
  ▷ Early North American letters

Letters of Eliza Wilkinson (1839)
The twelve extant letters of ▷ Eliza Wilkinson, a
South Carolina widow during the American
Revolution, cover the years 1779 to 1782 and
recount her experiences of the invasion of the
region around Charleston by British troops.
Written on reflection because 'I mean never to
forget', she creates a local history of the war.
Exceptionally well-written, they reveal not only
her ardent patriotism but also her attitudes toward
the slaves whom she employs to aid her escape.
They are an above-average example of 18th-
century North American women's epistolary
writings.
  ▷ Early North American letters

'Letters of Hannah Callowhill Penn, The'
(1981–1987)
Collected in the *Papers of William Penn*, the letters
of ▷ Hannah Callowhill Penn reflect her
impressive input in the maintenance of the Penn
family's proprietorship of Pennsylvania in early
18th-century North America. Yet the letters are
also decidedly woman-centred; interspersed with
business directives are detailed concerns over the
maintenance of the family estate. The letters from
North America begin in the summer of 1700 and
reveal the myriad complications of upper-class life
in early Pennsylvania.
  ▷ Early North American letters

'Letters of Josiah and Mary Bartlett, of
Kingston, New Hampshire, 1775–1778, The'
(1980)
Appended to a study of *The Old Revolutionaries*,
▷ Mary Bartlett's letters offer a representative
picture of women's lives during the American
Revolution. While her husband is attending the
Continental Congress, Bartlett manages their
farm, supervises hired workers, gives birth to her
twelfth child, and acts as a local historian for her
husband by detailing all the news from their
community of Kingston. She reports the local
attitudes towards war, especially enlistment, and
relates the town's concern over smallpox
epidemics and weather conditions that one minute
promote and the next destroy the crops and thus
their livelihood. Bartlett's endeavours reveal the
significance of women's work during the

American Revolution in maintaining local
economies and in supporting the war efforts.
  ▷ Early North American letters

Letters of Martha Logan to John Bartram,
1760–1763 (1958)
▷ Martha Daniell Logan, American author of
▷ *The Gardners Kalender*, was a regular
correspondent with the noted botanist, John
Bartram (1699–1777), during the early 1760s.
Logan's letters catalogue the seeds and roots that
she exchanged with Bartram and include accounts
of her experiments in raising various shrubs and
flowers in her native South Carolinian climate.
  ▷ Early North American letters

'Letters of Mary Willing Byrd' (1950–)
Written during the American Revolution but not
published until 1950 and after, as part of *The
Papers of Thomas Jefferson*, ▷ Mary Willing Byrd's
letters are her eloquent defence against charges
that she had collaborated with the enemy by
supplying them goods from her Virginia
plantation. Rather than allow her reputation to be
defamed, she wrote directly to Jefferson, outlining
how the confusion arose and defending her own
actions. Detailing her acts of loyalty, she
demanded of Jefferson, 'What am I but an
American?' Her passionate and articulate self-
defence were listened to, and the charges against
her were dropped.

Letters of Mrs Lucy Downing (1871)
The letters of ▷ Lucy Winthrop Downing, an
English Puritan who resettled in the
Massachusetts Bay Colony in North America in
1638, begin in 1626 during the turbulent years
when Puritans were increasingly persecuted for
their beliefs. They include the more than sixteen
years she lived in Boston and Salem and a brief
period spent in Edinburgh, Scotland, and
conclude after her return to England. The last
letter in the collection is dated 1674. Downing's
epistolary style, indebted to the very rich Puritan
tradition of 'plain style', is notable for the use of
highly literary techniques, including tropes,
typology and alliteration. The letters reveal
Downing's political awareness, as she counsels her
brother on the necessity of establishing a
university in the New World, and they detail the
extensive responsibilities of a domestic life in a
developing colony. Many of the letters are written
to her daughters and to her sister-in-law,
▷ Margaret Tyndal Winthrop, whom she
addressed as 'Moste worthy Sister'. The latter
letters are especially significant, for they reveal the
necessities of sisterhood in surviving the
establishment of a new patriarchy.
  ▷ *Winthrop Papers*; *Some Old Puritan Love
Letters*; Early North American letters

'Letters of Molly and Hetty Tilghman' (1926)
Written between 1782 and 1789, these letters are
highly detailed accounts to a female cousin of two
late 18th-century North American young women's

concerns about courtship, marriage and motherhood. Only two are written by Henrietta Maria Tilghman (1763–1796), but ▷Mary (Molly) Tilghman's letters add information about her sister's life as well. They are notable for the underlying sense of obligations to family that, at times, bore heavily on Molly, as she considered her prospects for marriage.

▷Early North American letters

'Letters of Susanna Symmes, The' (1956)

Published in *The Intimate Letters of John Cleves Symmes and His Family*, these letters by the North American ▷Susanna Livingston Symmes detail her unhappiness in her marriage and her decision to act for her own benefit rather than succumb to her husband's will. When he attempted to deny her the promised right of control over her own money, she sought legal action; letters to an attorney, who denied her confidence and revealed her concerns to her husband, are included.

Letter to a Child Never Born (1976, 1982)

English translation of *Lettera a un bambino mai nato* (1975), a novel by Italian writer ▷Oriana Fallaci which essentially tells a tale of loss. The novel centres, for the most part, on the dilemma of an unmarried woman who finds herself unexpectedly pregnant. Thus, the author considers the issues of abortion, of woman's right to choose, and the bond between mother and unborn child. This is a work which was adopted by both pro- and anti-abortionists in the 1970s in Italy, each side claiming that it supported their case. On the one hand, this text analyses patriarchal discourses (of the baby's father, the woman's employer and the doctor), and subjects radical feminist dogma (the narrator's friend's approach) to the same harsh scrutiny. Pregnancy is, nevertheless, presented in terms of a metaphor for illness, which literally confines and entraps woman. It is, in fact, a threat to this woman's life. The mother is finally forced to choose between her own life and that of the baby. This is also a stylistically complex narrative, in that dreams and fairytales continually break into the surface narrative structure.
Bib: Pickering-Iazzi, Robin, 'Designing Mothers: Images of Motherhood in Novels by Aleramo, Morante, Maraini and Fallaci', *Annali d'Italianistica*, 7 (1989) pp. 325–41.

Lettres de mistress Fanni Butlerd (1757) (Letters from Mistress Fanny Butlerd)

French writer ▷Marie-Jeanne Riccoboni's first novel. It is in the form of letters written by Fanny to her lover, Alfred. The early letters detail Fanny's gradual seduction as she and Alfred exchange letters. The correspondence continues during a period of separation when Alfred is away on a military campaign. On his return it is revealed that he is to marry another woman, and the final letters record the disintegration of the relationship. The form of the novel focuses attention on the female point of view and the psychology of letter-writing: the tendency to idealize the absent addressee, a greater attachment to the letters and the writing of them than to the lover. In the letter of rupture Fanny announces her intention to publish the correspondence, as if she seeks to free herself of her dependency on the male lover by becoming a public writer and re-addressing herself to a wider audience – including other women. A modern edition of this work is *Lettres de Fanni Butlerd*, edited by J.H. Stewart-Hind (1979).

▷Epistolary novel

Lettres d'une Péruvienne (1747) (Letters of a Peruvian Princess)

▷Madame de Graffigny's ▷epistolary novel, re-edited forty-two times in the 18th century and translated into six languages, including English: *Letters from a Peruvian Princess* (1818). An Inca virgin, Zilia, captured by the Spanish, arrives in Paris. She writes to her estranged male lover at first using the *quipos* (cords knotted to notate language), until she learns French. This figure of the abandoned woman writing to the absent lover is part of a tradition in French literature (for example, Guilleragues, *Lettres portugaises*), as is the ingenuous foreigner commenting on another culture (for example Montesquieu, *Lettres persanes*). The natural world without a written language is privileged over the corrupt civilization of France, in the manner of Jean-Jacques Rousseau (1712–1778). The novel deals with the learning of language, communication, and cultural and sexual differences. The combining of the two traditions leads to a critique of the social system in France, and of the oppression of women. The novel ends on an optimistic note: Zilia, sustained by a positive sense of her own existence ('I am, I live, I exist') is shown as capable of inventing her own destiny.

A modern edition of this work is *Lettres portugaises, Lettres d'une péruvienne et autres romans d'amour par lettres*, edited by B. Bray and I. Landy-Houillon (1983).

▷Monbart, Madame Marie-Joséphine

Lettres Portugaises (1669) ▷Letters of a Portuguese Nun, The

Letzte Sommer, Eine Erzählung in Briefen (1910) (The Last Summer. A Story Told in Letters)

A novella in German by ▷Ricarda Huch. Set during the eve of the Russian Revolution (1905), it tells, in letter form, of the plot to assassinate the head of an aristocratic Russian family. The writer of the letters is a young anarchist secretary who has devised an ingenious plan to blow up his employer using a typewriter. However, his task becomes increasingly difficult as he gets involved with the beautiful daughters of the family.

The gripping story is interesting, not only as a period piece, but also as an example of political fiction written by a German woman.

Leutenegger, Gertrud (born 1948)
German-speaking Swiss novelist. Her novels are contemplative and lyrical, loosely structured around a single, significant event: ▷*Vorabend* (1975) (*On the Eve*) describes a stroll through streets on the eve of a political demonstration; *Ninive* (1977) (*Nineveh*) recounts the exhibition of a whale in a Swiss village; and *Meduse* (1988) (*Medusa*) portrays an encounter with a floating, transparent, amorphous jellyfish.

Levantines, The (1963)
Translation of *Ballata levantina* (1961). This novel, by Italian writer ▷Fausta Terni Cialente, was the first of her works to be seriously considered by both public and critics alike. It is divided into five sections, and its main concern is the process of memory. The first part of the work, 'La nonna' (the grandmother) recreates the life of the upper class in Egypt during the *belle époque*. The character Daniela links the other parts of the work, and her love affair functions as comparison and contrast with the earlier unhappy love affair of the grandmother. The novel provides the reader with a broad canvas of the history and mores of a section of society in Egypt during the period.

Levertov, Denise (born 1923)
US poet and essayist. Levertov was born in Ilford, Essex, England. Her father was a Russian Jew who became an Anglican minister. She was largely educated by her Welsh mother, who introduced her to poetry. In 1946, after publishing her first book, she married a North American GI and novelist and emigrated to North America. There she found her 'American' poetic voice and was influenced by William Carlos Williams (1883–1963) and ▷H.D. Using her own version of free verse forms, her work is preoccupied with the immediate and actual, the moment of heightened perception and its imaginative correlation in the poet's 'inscape'. During the 1960s Levertov became politically active in the anti-Vietnam War movement, and her poems of this period, collected in *To Stay Alive* (1971) reflect this. *Sorrow Dance* contains a poignant sequence of poems inspired by her sister Olga's death. She continues to attempt to balance her two poetic styles – political and imaginative/mystical – and is interested in the idea of pilgrimage. She is a prolific essayist and translator and is poetry editor of the *Nation*. Whilst not identifying herself as a feminist, she has shown a continuing interest in the complexities of female identity and self-definition.
Other works include: *The Double Image* (1946), *Here and Now* (1956), *Overland to the Islands* (1958), *With Eyes at the Backs of Our Heads* (1960), *The Jacob's Ladder* (1961), *O Taste and See* (1964), *Relearning the Alphabet* (1970) *Footprints* (1972), *The Poet in the World* (prose) (1974), *The Freeing of the Dust* (1975) *Life in the Forest* (1978), *Light up the Cave* (1981), *Candles in Babylon* (1982), *Breathing the Prayers* (1986), *Breathing the Water* (1987).

Bib: Wagner, Linda, *Denise Levertov*; Wagner, Linda (ed.), *Denise Levertov: In Her Own Province*, Slaughter, William, *The Imagination's Tongue: Denise Levertov's Poetic*; Middleton, Peter, *Revelation and Revolution: The Poetry of Denise Levertov*; Marten, Harry, *Understanding Denise Levertov*.

Levesque, Louise Cavelier (1703–1743)
French writer of prose fiction and poetry. Born in Rouen, the daughter of a public prosecutor, she later lived in Paris. Her early work, *Le Prince des Aigues-Marines* (1722) (*The Prince of the Aqua Marines*), the first fantastic tale by a French woman, begins with a primitive scene of ritualized killing carried out to decide the succession of power on an unnamed island. Her novels, with their historical, contemporary and allegorical settings, brought her a measure of celebrity. In 1738 she also published three poetical works: *Augustin, pénitent*; *Minet*, and *Sancho Pança, gouverneur*.
Her other works are: *Lettres et chansons de Céphise et d'Uranie* (1731) (*Lettres and Songs of Céphise and Uranie*); *Célénine* (1732); *Lilia, ou histoire de Carthage* (1736) (*Lilia, or a Story of Carthage*); *Le Siècle, ou les mémoires du comte de S**** (1736) (*This Century, or Memoirs of the Count of S****); *La Vie de Job en vers* (1736) (*The Life of Job in Verse*); *Remarques critiques sur l'histoire de Don Quichotte* (1738) (*Critical Observations on the Story of Don Quixote*).
Bib: Baratte, L.H., *Poètes normands*.

Levinson, Luisa Mercedes (born 1914)
Argentinian short story writer, novelist and dramatist. Her first novel, *La casa de los Felipes* (*The House of the Felipes*), was published in 1951. *Concierto en mi* (1956) (*Harmony in Myself/E Major*) is an intense soliloquy. *La pálida rosa de Soho* (1959) (*The Pale Rose of Soho*) contains eighteen stories, among which the title story '*El Alba*' ('Dawn') and '*El Porto*' ('The Door') are outstanding. She has won many literary prizes, including the French Academy Palms (1982) and the Konex Foundation Prize (1984), and her short stories and plays have appeared in anthologies abroad. She has lectured abroad and travelled widely, and was appointed Professor *Honoris Causa* at John F. Kennedy University.

Levy, Amy (1861–1889)
Jewish novelist and poet, the daughter of Lewis Levy and Isabelle Levin, she was born in Clapham, London, and was the first Jewish woman to attend Newnham College, Cambridge. While still a student, she published her first volume of poetry, *Xantippe and Other Verse* (1881). *A Minor Poet and Other Verse* appeared in 1884, and in 1888 *The Romance of a Ship* and *Rueben Sachs*, a novel describing the London Jewish community in which she grew up. *Miss Meredith* and *A London Plane Tree and Other Verse*, both published in 1889, mark the end of Levy's literary career. She killed herself in the same year. She

was actively involved in ▷feminist and radical debates as well as deeply concerned about the position of Jewish people in Europe.

Lewald, Fanny (1811–89)

German novelist. Born into a Jewish family, she converted in 1828 to Lutheranism, hoping to marry a young theologian, but he died before the marriage could take place. For seventeen years she tended her parents' house, languishing with unrequited love for a cousin, and refusing any marriage of convenience. In 1842 she published her first novel, *Clementine*. Its success was matched by the publication, a year later, of *Jenny* and, in 1845, *Eine Lebensfrage* (*A Question of Life*). These novels are important studies of women's social position, marriage and divorce. Her success meant that she could begin to travel widely. She met literary figures such as ▷Bettina von Arnim, ▷Therese von Bacheracht and ▷Luise Mühlbach, and set up house in Berlin with the novelist Adolf Stahr (1805–1876), a married man whom she married in 1854 after his divorce. Her novel, *Diogena* (1847), attracted much attention because it ridiculed the work of ▷Ida von Hahn-Hahn, a literary *grande dame* of the time. In articles, such as *Osterbriefe für die Frauen* (1863) (*Easter Letters for Women*) and *Für und wider die Frauen* (1870) (*For and Against Women*), she argued for education for women. She also wrote travelogues and family sagas. Her autobiography, *Meine Lebensgeschichte* (1861) (*My Life Story*), is to this day a document of great interest to social historians.

Lewis, Ethelreda (1875–1946)

South African novelist. Born in Matlock, Derbyshire, England, she came to South Africa in 1904. Besides contributing poems and short stories to local newspapers and magazines, she produced three novels under her married name – *The Harp* (1924), *The Flying Emerald* (1925) and *Mantis* (1926) – and four under the pseudonym R. Hernekin Baptist – *Four Handsome Negresses* (1931), *Wild Deer* (1933, reprinted 1984 under her own name), *Love at the Mission* (1938) and *A Cargo of Parrots* (1938). She also edited the highly successful *The Life and Times of Trader Horn*, published in three volumes: *The Ivory Coast in the Earlies* (1927), *Harold the Webbed* (1928) and *The Waters of Africa* (1929).

Four Handsome Negresses, subtitled *The Record of a Voyage*, tells the story of four women, captured from the coast of Guinea in the 15th century, whose voyage down the African coast brings varieties of abuse at the hands of the Portuguese crew. Although the text stands as an exposé of the worst horrors of imperialism, it has been criticized for unconsciously reproducing the oppositions of the 'civilized' and the 'primitive' on which imperialism is based.

Lézardière, Marie Charlotte Pauline (1754–1835)

French historian. Daughter of a French nobleman who devoted himself to his children's education.

Lézardière's *Théories des lois politiques de la monarchie française* (*Theories on the Political Laws of the French Monarchy*) was published in 1844 by her brother, almost all pre-existing copies having been destroyed during the Revolution (1789). The fourth part is lacking, but the first three analyze three epochs: imperial law prior to Clovis, legislation by popular consensus sanctioned by the monarchy from Clovis to Charles le Chauve, and feudal customs extending to the early 14th century.

Lezay Marnezia, Charlotte Antoinette de Bressy, Marquise de (died 1785)

French novelist. She entertained a literary circle at her home in Nancy, but was not known as a writer. The *Lettres de Julie à Ovide* (1753) (*Letters from Julie to Ovid*) were published anonymously and attributed to Marmontel, until Lezay Marnezia's son revealed them as the work of his mother.

Lezioni d'amore e altre commedie (1982) (Lessons in Love and Other Plays)

A collection of six plays by Italian writer ▷Dacia Maraini, In which the dramatist strives to find a new theatrical language. 'Lezioni d'amore' tells the story of a young man, Melo, initiated into both the secrets of the theatre and those of love by a mature and fascinating actress. 'Mela' is the tale of a grandmother who loves life, her politically militant daughter, Rosaria, and her cynical granddaughter, Carmen; it is a representation of three generations of women in conflict. 'Reparto speciale antiterrorismo' ('Special Anti-terrorist Division') analyses both the harshness and the weakness of representatives of public order. 'Fede o della perversione matrimoniale' ('Faith, or Marital Perversion') considers how the past complicates the relationship between a couple, and is self-conscious in its alternation of 'real' and 'fantasy' characters. 'Felice Sciosciammocca' tells of a Neapolitan masque revisited. 'Bianca Garofani' investigates identity through the drama of an amnesiac, searching to recreate herself. All of the plays deal, to an extent, with the problem of appearance versus reality.

Lhériter de Villandon, Marie-Jeanne (1664–1734)

French author of fairytales, stories and novellas. Her tales were published in the *Mercure galant*, including the first version of 'Sleeping Beauty', '*La Belle au bois dormant*' (1695). She was the niece of Charles Perrault (1628–1703), the author of the most famous collection of French fairytales, who may have been an important influence on her work. Some tales, like '*Riquet à la houppe*' ('Riquet with the Topknot'), are common to both collections and to others by, for example, ▷Madame de Murat. One of her best creations, *L'Adroite Princesse, ou les Aventures de Finette* (*The Clever Princess, or the Adventures of Finette*), was mistakenly attributed to Perrault for 150 years. Mademoiselle Lhériter was interested in the

theory of tale-telling, insisting on the Gallic origins of her works and sometimes referring to manuscript sources, but most of her tales are *contes de vieilles* (old wives' tales), related by some old wet-nurse or servant. She promoted the role of the educated narrator in the creative transmission of the tale, believing that ordinary people '*salissaient*' or 'dirtied' the tales they told. She presents herself in the tales as champion of the 'fair sex'. A frequent theme in her collection is that women are worth as much if not more than men. Transvestism – perhaps partly under the influence of the Abbé de Choisy (1644–1724), with whom she collaborated – is another. She considered his transvestism a homage to her sex. The heroine of *Marmoison or L'Innocente tromperie* (1695) (*The Innocent Deception*) dresses as a boy. The *Histoire de la Marquise-Marquis de Banneville*, published separately in 1723, disguises the sex of both the hero and the heroine, and both are remarkably similar in their physical appearance. Yet Mademoiselle Lhéritier, who refused all offers of marriage and was known for her virtue, was the primmest of tale-tellers and had a tendency to excessive moralization. At first she maintained her anonymity, but after 1720 she willingly signed her books, though her tales still appeared without attribution in the *Mercure galant*. Included among the nine ▷ Muses of the Academy of the Ricovrati in Padua, she also held her own salon where the tales were part of the collective entertainment. Among her closest friends were ▷ Madame Deshoulières and ▷ Madeleine de Scudéry in old age. In the *Querelle des Anciens et des Modernes* (*Quarrel of the Ancients and Moderns*) she resolutely took the part of Perrault and the Moderns.
Bib: Soriano, M., *Contes de Perrault*.

'Liadain and Cuirthir'
▷ Old Irish poem. The lament of Liadain, the Cork poet and nun, for the poet Cuirthir, whom she refused.
  ▷ 'Deirdre's Farewell to Scotland'; 'Creidhe's Lament'.
Bib: Greene, David and O'Connor, Frank (eds.), *A Golden Treasure of Irish Poetry AD 600 to 1200*.

Li Ang (born 1952)
Chinese writer. A native of Taiwan, Li received her higher degree in the USA. She is best known for the novella ▷ *The Butcher's Wife* (1983). Li Ang had been struck by an old report of a sensational murder in Shanghai, in which a woman had killed her husband, not for a lover, as presumed by the public, but because of his abuse. Li Ang changed the background to her own native seacoast town in Taiwan to write a stunningly powerful story of a wife's revenge. In the story, the woman kills and dismembers her husband, just as he does his pigs. The story concerns not only wife abuse, but – in the writer's own words – 'larger issues of humanity, such as hunger, death, sex' and 'human nature in general'.
Bib: Goldblatt, Howard and Young, Ellen (trans.), *The Butcher's Wife*.

Liberal feminism
Probably the oldest strand of mainstream feminism in British history. It is a theory of women's individual political and social rights, and was first described at length in ▷ Mary Wollstonecraft's ▷ *Vindication of the Rights of Woman* (1792).

Liberation of Women (1899)
Treatise by liberal Egyptian judge Qasim Amin (1863–1908), which was the first important call for a drastic change in the education and social position of women. He argues in the *Liberation of Women* (1899) and *The New Woman* (1900) that the subordinate position of women at the time was not Islamic, and that ▷ *hijab* (the veiling, and consequently, the segregation of women) as it was then practised was not originally an ordinance of Islamic *Shari'a*. He was the first Arabic writer to take the position that you cannot have freedom in a society when half the population, the women, are behind walls. He called for a programme of reform in the marital and social status of women.
  Above all, Qasim Amin's name is associated with the education of women in Arab countries, which has grown far beyond the liberal programme he called for. As a legislator, he proposed regulating a man's right to divorce his wife at will and his right to take more than one wife. Legislation in Arab countries is battling with this question to this day. A number of codes for personal affairs have been passed, amended – and in some cases repealed – in a number of Moslem countries, in accord with the tightening or relaxation of the grip of fundamentalist opinion. In North Africa the change of women's status was first urged by Tahir Haddad in *Women in Islamic Law and Society* (1930).
  Qasim Amin's carefully formulated arguments against *hijab* formed the groundwork for all later discourse on the subject. The Moroccan feminist sociologist ▷ Fatima Mernissi uses the same discourse to prove that Islam in its early 'pure' form did not prescribe the veiling of women, nor did it confine them within the walls of a ▷ *harem*. Amin's name remains a red rag to Moslem fundamentalists, whose polemics are absurdly abusive of a man who has been dead for almost a century.

Libro de la vida, El (1588) (The Book of Her Life)
World classic by ▷ Santa Teresa de Ávila, the Spanish mystic. The style of this work is plain, simple and direct and echoes the rhythms of everyday speech. Santa Teresa does not theorize, but conveys her experience of God in a language rich in popular idiom with metaphors drawn from everyday life, such as water in a fountain, rooms within a house, the flame of a candle, and the image of a silkworm which is transformed into a moth.

Li Ch'ing–chao ▷ Li Qingzhao

Lichnowsky, Mechthilde (1879–1958)

German writer. The great-granddaughter of the Austrian empress, Maria Theresa, she travelled widely in pre-war Europe and Egypt, and first became known for her travelogue, *Götter, Könige und Tiere in Ägypten* (1913) (*Gods, Kings and Animals in Egypt*). Her prose, plays and essays are all eloquent discussions of the decline of an aristocratic European culture. In *Gespräche in Sybaris* (1946) (*Conversations with Sybaris*) she gives vent to her total disdain of Nazi ideology.

Lidman, Sara Adela (born 1923)

Swedish prose writer and essayist. She was born in Vasterbotten in a religious environment. She took the General Certificate by correspondence, and later studied in Uppsala.

Her work falls into three categories. The early novels about Västerbotten: *Tjärdalen* (1953) (*The Tar Pit*), *Hjortronlandet* (1955) (*Cloudberry Country*), *Regnspiran* (1958) (*The Rainbird*) and *Bära mistel* (1960) (*To Wear Mistletoe*). These early novels depict a region, and introduce an interest in the ambivalence and confrontation between individuals and social forces, a theme that points to her political travel essays and reports about Africa, Vietnam and Sweden, where she was concerned with social problems and the conflicts between rich and poor. After 1977 she wrote a new series about Västerbotten, when she moved back to the country of her childhood, eg *Vredens barn* (1978) (*The Children of Wrath*) and *Järnkronan* (1985) (*The Iron Crown*). Here again she writes of her region, but now traces its development back to the time before the railways and industrialization came to the provinces of Sweden.

Sara Lidman has also written plays, but it is her novels about Västerbotten, about the women and the landscape, about hard work and industrialization, and about the deeply felt religiousness in a remote corner of Sweden, that make her an excellent writer.

Liebmann, Irina (born 1943)

German writer. Born in Moscow, she lived in East Germany until 1988, when she moved to West Berlin. She had a first success with *Berliner Mietshaus* (1983) (*Block of Flats in Berlin*), an account of the lives of people in an old block of flats in East Berlin that was half fiction, half documentary. Her poems, *Mitten im Krieg* (*In the Midst of War*), published in 1989 shortly before the sudden reunification of Germany, are concerned with the post-war division of the country.

Liebrecht, Savyon (born 1948)

Israeli novelist. Liebrecht was born in Germany, the daughter of Holocaust survivors, and has lived in Israel since early childhood. In her writing she expresses the experiences of those whose birth and childhood took place under the shadow of trauma and terror. Her novels represent the need to break the silence over these experiences. Her women characters, at the centre of her writing, are strong, independent and lead purposeful lives. Her novels include: *Tapuchim Me'Hamidbar* (1986) (*Apples from the Desert*) and *Susim Al Kvish Geha* (1988) (*Horses on Geha Road*).

Life and Adventures of Jonathan Jefferson Whitlaw, The, (1836)

An anti-slavery novel by ▷Frances Trollope. J.J. Whitlaw, who sees ▷slavery as a 'most righteous and Christian-like' doctrine, works as an overseer for Colonel Dart, the owner of a plantation in Louisiana ironically named 'Paradise'. Whitlaw attempts to increase his prosperity through marriage to Selena Crofts, but she rejects him. He then discovers that Selena has black ancestors, and threatens to expose her unless she gives him land. Selena kills herself. At the end of the novel, Whitlaw is lured into a forest by Selena's grandmother, Juno, and murdered by the slaves. The novel is one of the earliest examples of anti-slavery fiction.

Life and Character of Miss Susanna Anthony, The (1796)

In this life of Susanna Anthony (1726–1791) by the renowned North American Puritan minister and biographer, Samuel Hopkins (1721–1803), extracts from Anthony's own writings constitute the majority of the text. A devout Quaker, Anthony's intellectual epistolary exchanges with her friend, ▷Sarah Haggar Wheaten Osborn, acted as the means for her development of a deeply felt theology. Covering a twenty-year period from 1749 to 1769, during which her community of Newport, Rhode Island, experienced a widespread but controversial religious revival, Anthony's religious meditations are a valuable record of the intellectual and communal involvement of women in 18th-century North American religious circles.
▷*Familiar Letters Written by Mrs Sarah Osborn, and Miss Susanna Anthony*; Osborn, Sarah Haggar Wheaten; *Memoirs of the Life of Mrs Sarah Osborn*

Life and Death of Harriett Frean (1922)

Novel by English writer ▷May Sinclair. This novel condenses into fifteen brief chapters the 70-odd years of one Victorian woman's life. The ▷stream-of-consciousness narrative style is deceptively simple, bleak even, and no direct explanation of characters' psychological motives is offered. The novel reflects the influence of both Sinclair's involvement in the women's ▷suffrage movement and her interest in the introduction of Freudian ▷psychoanalytic techniques into Britain. In *Life and Death of Harriett Frean*, Sinclair displays her sympathy with the non-essentialist (▷essentialism) account of sexual identity which psychoanalysis offers, but also an acute awareness of the profound difficulties of Freud's account of femininity. Harriet Frean obeys the implicit paternal injunction to repress desire and to identify with an apparently self-denying mother. She is unable to express even the most minimal sexual desire involved in acquiescence to marriage with Robin, a man desired by her schoolfriend, Priscilla Heaven. The result of the repeated self-denials which Harriett believes are enjoined on her by the paternal edict always to 'act beautifully' is that her repressions eventually find symbolic and physical expression in psychogenic disease – a deathly cancer. In this way she finally achieves the terms of the Freudian ▷oedipal injunction to identify with her mother, and she dies from the same terminal disease. On her deathbed, Harriett believes that her tumour is a dead baby and, finally, that she herself is once again the baby that her mother desired. In Sinclair's relentless pursuit of both the Victorian and the Freudian logic of heterosexual feminine identity and desire, Harriett achieves 'proper' femininity in having the baby and identifying with her mother. However, in this bleakest of novels, that 'achievement' is portrayed as a self-consuming and deathly sickness.

Life and Loves of a She-Devil, The (1983)
Novel by English writer ▷Fay Weldon. Weldon's treatment of the 'revenge of the spurned spouse' narrative questions gender stereotypes and competing feminine identities. The protagonist, Ruth Patchett, is at the outset a 'six feet two, tall and clumsy, patient and practical, wife and mother', whose husband leaves her for the romantic novelist Mary Fisher, 'small and pretty and delicately formed'. Examining the suburban social pressures on women to conform to a particular physical type, the novel opens with the collapse of a marriage in which 'it was obvious to both of them it was Ruth's body which was at fault.' Turned 'she-devil', Ruth determines to exact her revenge on her husband and his lover, and through a series of strategies beginning with arson and culminating in extensive plastic surgery, Ruth destroys their careers, identities and relationship to emerge as the victor, grotesquely transformed into the physical replica of her husband's lover. By exploiting and parodying both the notion of romantic love and the women's romance genre, the novel deploys and reverses romance conventions, at the heart of which is generally the submissive feminine figure. The disempowering of the plastic surgeons working on Ruth's transformation, coupled with her conviction that she is 'remaking herself' and her consistent refrain 'I like to control nature and make things beautiful', plays with the notion of free will at the same time as it questions a reading of the ▷Frankenstein theme as a direct enactment of male authority and power.

Life and Spiritual Sufferings of That Faithful Servant of Christ, Jane Hoskens, a Public Preacher among the People Called Quakers, The (1771)
Autobiographical account by the North American, ▷Jane Fenn Hoskens. Hoskens's account of her decision to come to the New World and of her conversion to Quakerism is also a record of the spirit of community among travelling Quaker women preachers. As she recounts her journeys throughout New England, the North American mid-Atlantic and southern colonies, as well as in England and Ireland, Hoskens is careful to record the names and habits of her sister travellers, whom she affectionately describes as 'true yoke-fellows; sympathizing with each other in, and under, the various exercises whether of body or mind, which we had to pass through'.
▷Early North American Quaker women's writings

Life Before Man (1979)
Canadian writer ▷Margaret Atwood's novel about the distemper of modern marriage uses a diary form, but shifts from character to character in a limited omniscient point of view that reflects the narrowed objectivity of the characters themselves. Museum specimens in the larger archive of human history, the three main characters of this novel catalogue themselves in relation to potential happiness, and in relation to potential extinction, like the dinosaurs in the museum where two of the characters work.

Life in the Iron Mills (1861)
US novella by ▷Rebecca Harding Davis. It focuses on the wasted lives and talents of oppressed mill-workers and vividly brings to life the horrific physical, social and economic conditions of industrializing New England. Published in ▷ The Atlantic Monthly, the novella both introduced Harding Davis to the US reading public and introduced in US fiction the subject of the economic and human effects of industrialism. The story of an untrained sculptor who forms the spectre of the Korl Woman from the waste materials of the mills, Iron Mills addresses not only the oppression of workers under capitalism but the oppression of all artists. Harding Davis's work generally focuses on talented and misplaced souls who seek for more but are unable to develop their minds and arts – or, sometimes, unable even to survive.
Bib: Olsen, Tillie (ed.), Life in the Iron Mills and Other Stories.

Li Huixin (born 1937)
Chinese short story writer. A practising doctor, Li kept up writing throughout her medical career in Beijing. During the 'cultural revolution' (1966–1976), she travelled with an itinerant medical team over the remote impoverished regions of north and south-west China, where some of her stories are based. Li is best-known for the much-anthologized short story 'The Old Maid' (1980). It is a moving exposé of the combination of cultural tradition and political norms which are brought to bear on an unmarried young doctor who is banished to a remote village for her 'bourgeois' family background.

Likimani, Muthoni

Muthoni Likimani

Kenyan novelist and poet. Formerly a popular broadcaster and producer, she has an advertising and promotion business in Nairobi. Her publications include *Women in Kenya;* ▷ *They Shall Be Chastised* (1974), which explores the conflict between traditional values and missionary Christianity over the practice of female circumcision; ▷ *What Does a Man Want?* (1974) a series of poetic monologues about the problems of women in modern Kenya; *Shangazi na Watoto*; and *Passbook Number F47927: Women and Mau Mau in Kenya* which examines the Mau Mau revolutionary war (1952–6) from a woman's perspective.
Bib: James, Adeola, *In Their Own Voices, African Women Writers Talk.*

Liking, Werewere
Cameroonian dramatist. Originally from Cameroon, she lives and works in Côte d'Ivoire, where she runs the experimental Ki-yi Mbock Theatre, part of a cultural project which includes a museum, a gallery and a communal lifestyle for its participants. She has created a form she describes as 'ritual theatre', which she evolved partly through her partnership with Marie-Jose Hourantier, a French researcher and practitioner of 'ritual theatre'. Together they published *Orphée Dafric* (1981) (*African Orpheus*), a recreation of the Orpheus´myth in an African setting, which includes both a novel by Liking and a piece of ritual theatre by Hourantier. Their collaboration, since ended, also produced *Spectacles rituels* (1987) (*Ritual spectacles*), consisting of two plays by Liking, *Les Mains veulent dire* (*The Hands Mean to*

Say) and *Rougeole arc-en-ciel* (*Rainbow of Measles*), which were produced by Hourantier in the early 1980s.

Liking's other publications include *On ne raisonne pas avec le venin* (1977) (*One Doesn't Argue with Poison*), a book of twenty poems in which she speaks as the mouthpiece of the people of Africa; ▷ *Elle sera de jaspe et de corail: journal d'un misovire* (1983) (*She will be of jasper, and coral: diary of a manhater*), a fusion of genres which explores a future Africa; the novel *L'Amour-cent-vies* (1988) (*Love of a Hundred Lives*); and plays, initiation stories and several ritual dramas such as *La Puissance de Um* (1979) (*The Power of Um*), and *Du sommeil d'injuste* (1980) (*Of the Unjust Sleep*).
▷ Aidoo, Ama Ata; ▷ Tadjo, Véronique

Liksom, Rosa, (born 1958)
Prose writer born in Finnish Lapland. Her name is a ▷ pseudonym: 'Rosa' the colour; '*Liksom*', a Swedish word for 'like'; her real name is not known. Born as the youngest child of six, Liksom ran away from home when she was fifteen. Since then she has been travelling around, calling herself an urban anthropologist. For years she had her headquarters in Copenhagen, where she wrote her first two books. She is still writing in Finnish, and now lives in Finland to keep up with her language. Twice she has been nominated for the Nordic Council's Award for Literature, a sign of her quality.

She writes short works, always telling of the dark and brutal sides of Nordic urban life. Her language is raw and anarchic. She made her début with the collection of short stories *Stopover for One Night* (1985) and her latest book, from 1990, is called *Paradise on a Lonely Road*.

She is an exponent of a new, hard-boiled urban brutality, where visions are few and depression rules in style and tone, as well as in theme.

Lilian's Story (1985)
Australian novel by ▷ Kate Grenville. *Lilian's Story* is loosely based upon the life of a Sydney personality, Bea Miles. The Lilian Singer of the novel is unloved by her mother, is raped by her father, and becomes a bizarre and eccentric adult. Splendidly obese and self-confident, she recites Shakespeare in the streets for a shilling, demands taxi rides, abuses the drivers if they demand a fare, and falls in love with her own fantastic projection of 'Lord Kitchener'. The novel, which won the Vogel/Australian Award for 1984, is as energetic and exuberant as its heroine.

Lily, The (1848–1854)
US periodical focused on women's suffrage and, to a lesser degree, temperance issues. Its publisher was Amelia Bloomer (1818–1894), who is perhaps better known as the inventor of trousers-like garments for women, 'bloomers'.

Lim, Catherine (born 1942)
Singaporean short story writer. Although she was born in a small Malaysian town, she had her

Catherine Lim

tertiary education in Singapore, became a school teacher, a lecturer in linguistics, and is now a full-time writer. Her first two volumes of short stories, *Little Ironies: Stories of Singapore* (1978), and *Or Else the Lightning God* (1980), containing vignettes and slices of Singaporean life – seen mostly from an ironic perspective – immediately struck a chord with Singaporean and other readers. Her sole novel, *The Serpent's Tooth*, an expansion of the title story of her second volume, describes the clash of values between a traditional Chinese mother-in-law and the modern English-educated wife of her eldest son, within the context of a large extended family. *They Do Return* (1983) is a rather weak collection of ghost stories, while *The Shadow of a Shadow of a Dream* (1987) is a collection of Singapore love stories, usually bleak. A recent collection, *O Singapore!* (1989), is of satirical fantasies which hilariously represent some typical Singaporean institutions and foibles, and in the early 1990s she was working on a sixth collection, *The Woman's Book of Superlatives*.

Lim, Shirley Geok-lin (born 1944)
Malaysian-born US poet and short story-writer. In 1980 Lim was the first Asian (▷ Asian-American writing) and the first woman to win the Commonwealth Poetry Prize. *Crossing the Peninsula and Other Poems* (1980) explores the complexities of a multi-cultural self. Of Chinese ancestry, Lim was born and raised in Malaysia, and at age twenty-four she began teaching in the US. Poems like 'Adam's Grief' record the self's painful separation from its native country.

▷ *No Man's Grove* (1985) chronicles Lim's decision to live imaginatively in both countries: old and new. She focuses on women's lives, especially mother–daughter relationships. *Another Country* profiles Chinese-Malaysian women of different ages and social classes who look back over their lives to their childhood. Lim co-edited *Making Waves: An Anthology of Writings By and About Asian-American Women* (1989), the first such anthology.

Other works include: *Chinamerican Reflections* (1984) and *Modern Secrets* (1988).

Lin, Nora ▷ Alonso, Dora

Lindgren, Astrid (born 1907)
Swedish writer of children's books. Lindgren is a dominant figure in modern ▷ children's literature in Sweden and in Scandinavia. She seems to have had a wonderful childhood, she expresses as much in interviews, and her books seem to be drawn from her own childhood, eg the children of *Bullerby* (1947–1952) and *Madicken* (1960, 1976).

In 1944 Lindgren published *Britt-Marie lättar sitt hjärta* (*Britt-Mary Unburdens her Heart*); in 1945 she became world-famous with *Pippi Långstrump* (*Pippi Longstocking*), a powerful character, and a real 'father's daughter'. Her new character, *Ronja Rövardotter* (1981) (*Ronja Robber's Daughter*) is a modern and more complex variation of the same figure. Ronja is her mother's daughter, and her father, despite his physical strength, is a weak person.

Astrid Lindgren has also written more melancholic books: *Mio, min Mio* (1954) (*Mio, My Son*) and *Bröderna Lejonhjärta* (1973) (*The Brothers of Lionheart*), move between life and death, mediating an unendurable life with the fear of death in a romantic and dualistic fantasy which appeals to the feelings of children.

An extensive literature on Astrid Lindgren's books exists in many languages.

Line in Water, A (1975)
Translation of the Punjabi novel *Chhak Nambar Chhati* by ▷ Amrita Pritam. A poetic love story which describes the relationship between an artist and his student. Although an important backdrop, the rural setting enhances the focus upon Kumar's denial of the need for love and his love for Alka.

'Lines . . . Dedicated to the Rev. Mr Gilbert Tennent' (1741)
The North American poet ▷ Sarah Parsons Moorhead, a resident of Boston, Massachusetts, published this poem in the *New England Weekly Journal* of 17 March 1741, at the height of the Great Awakening. Less admonishing than her poem, ▷ 'To the Rev. James Davenport' (1742), 'Lines' is meritorious poetically and is significant as a record of the religious and literary role that women played in the revivalist movement of the 1730s and 1740s.

'Lines from a Letter to Her Sister, Jane Colman Turell, March 23, 1733' (1860)
Written by the American poet ▷ Abigail Colman Dennie ('The unfortunate Celia') to her sister, poet ▷ Jane Colman Turell ('lovely Delia'), this poem reflects the very different lives the two

sisters chose. Turell aligned herself with her father's strict Calvinist piety, while Dennie rebelled and sought independence. If the poem acknowledges the unhappiness Dennie faced as a consequence of her choices, it also reveals her abiding love for her sister; the different treatment each sister received from their father is not reflected in her attitude towards the 'fortunate' sister. 'Not all my woes', Dennie asserts, 'can make me wretched while / My Delia does vouchsafe on me to smile.'

Ling Shuhua (born 1904)

Chinese prose and short story writer. Ling studied at Yenching University in Beijing. She was first associated with the Western-orientated 'New Crescent' school of writing. Her prose and stories are collected in *The Flowery Temple, Women, Two Little Brothers* and other volumes, many of them concerned with the lives of women. 'The Helpmate' reveals the boredom of 'upper-class' women imprisoned in their daily routine of spending. *Love Through Life and Death*, a tale of love defying tradition and society, was reprinted on the mainland with great success. Published in both Chinese and English, Ling's stories show subtle craftsmanship, while her prose is greatly admired for classical allusions and literary elegance.

Lin Haiyin (born 1919)

Chinese writer, Lin was educated in Beijing and moved to Taiwan in 1948. She worked as editor and journalist for various magazines, and later started her own publishing house to promote high culture. She has published many collections of essays, *A Stranger in the US* (1966) being one of the better known. Novels include *The Story of a Marriage* (1963), *Green Weeds and Salted Eggs* (1958) and *Tales of Old Peking* (1960), the last of which has been successfully filmed on mainland China.

Linton, Eliza Lynn (1822–1898)

English novelist, journalist and poet, born in Keswick, the daughter of the Rev. James Lynn. Her mother died when she was five months old and despite receiving no formal education she taught herself and learned several languages. At twenty-three she moved to a boarding house in London and in 1858 married William Linton, though the relationship ended in separation not long afterwards. A prolific writer, she is best remembered today for her sensational essay ▷'The Girl of the Period' (1868). Other works include novels which attack the hypocrisy of the church (*The True History of Joshua Davidson, Christian and Communist*, 1872, and *Under Which Lord?*, 1879; ▷historical novels (*Azeth the Egyptian*, 1846, and *Amymone*, 1848) and works addressing the ▷'Woman Question' (*Sowing the Wind*, 1867, and *The One Too Many*, 1894). Linton was often fiercely anti-feminist but she never consistently maintained a position, varying her line depending upon her readership. Despite her intense attachments to other women, she condemned lesbianism explicitly in *The Rebel of the Family* (1880). Interestingly, her ▷*Autobiography of Christopher Kirkland* (1885) records her own life, but from the perspective of a male.

▷Ghost stories (19th-century Britain)
Bib: Anderson, N.F., *Woman Against Women in Victorian England: A Life of Eliza Linton*.

Lionheart Gal: Life Stories of Jamaican Women (1986)

Published by the Women's Press, this collection of Caribbean life stories marked an important stage in the work of the ▷Sistren Collective. Since 1977 the women of Sistren had been exploring the lives of the Caribbean working class; the book brings together the life stories of fifteen women, and is an invaluable record of the oral history of the community. The stories are based on tapes collected over several years and edited by Honor Ford-Smith. As the introduction to the collection says, the stories are testimony to 'the terms of resistance in women's daily lives' and reveal the ways in which women can move from the 'apparent powerless of exploitation to the creative power of rebel consciousness' (p. *xiii*). The use of ▷nation language throughout is discussed in a paper by Carolyn Cooper published by the Institute of Commonwealth Studies, University of London (*Aspects of Commonwealth Literature*, Vol. 2).

Lipkin, Jean (born 1926)

South African poet, born in Johannesburg, who left for England in 1960, and has lived and worked in London since then. Lipkin began writing poetry at university, and her earliest poems appeared in *Jewish Affairs* in Johannesburg, as well as in North American and British magazines. In her two volumes, *Among Stones* (1975) and *With Fences Down* (1986), her writing is predominantly lyrical, employing image and symbol to convey a sense of the pain and beauty of existence. Her first concern is with language, and in elegant, intense poems she explores the extent to which deeply felt moments can be captured.

Lipperini, Guendalina ▷Luanto, Regina di

Lippincott, Sara Jane (1823–1904)

US poet and essayist. Lippincott is typical of mid-19th-century US women writers. A successful poet, journalist, travel writer and essayist, both she (known by her pseudonym, Grace Greenwood) and her work were popular with the reading public. Her best collection from periodical publication was *Greenwood Leaves* (1850).

Li Qingzhao (?1084–?1151)

Chinese poet of the Song dynasty (960–1279), also known as Li Ch'ing-chao. China's greatest woman poet, she excels in the *ci* (an irregular form of poetry intended to be sung to musical accompaniment). Born to a prestigious family in what is now the capital of Shandong province, Li was married at twenty to Zhao Mingchen, an imperial university student. The couple shared their love of writing and their passion for collecting books, paintings and art objects. Li Qingzhao's early poetry reflects this period of marital bliss, interspersed with the pangs of temporary parting and its varying moods.

The latter part of Li Qingzhao's life was clouded by her husband's early death following a barbarian invasion and enforced removal of the imperial seat to southern China in 1127. In the turbulence Li's vast collection of books was destroyed and she ended her life a homeless exile. Her later poetry expresses her loneliness and melancholy. She has also left astute criticism of the poetry of her contemporaries. Record has it that, after her death, her works were collected in seven volumes of prose and six volumes of verse, though only thirty poems survive.
Bib: Translation in Birch, Cyril (ed.), *Anthology of Chinese Literature.*

Lisboa, Henriqueta (1904–1985)

Brazilian poet and essayist. She wrote for journals and newspapers, and contributed to literary anthologies. She lived in the state of Minas Gerais, then for a while in Rio de Janeiro, and later returning to Minas Gerais, to the city of Belo Horizonte. She also worked as a translator and as a teacher. In her poetry, she was a neo-symbolist who did not adopt ▷modernism. Unlike some, she never gave herself to exaggerated regionalisms or colloquialisms. In 1963 she was the first woman to be elected to the Minas Gerais Academy of Letters. *Flor da noite* (1949) (*Flower of the Night*) and *Madrinha lua* (1952) (*Godmother Moon*) won prizes. She was awarded, for her complete work, the Minas Gerais Academy Medal (1955), and the Brasília Prize (1971), as well as the Machado de Assis Prize from the Brazilian Academy of Letters (1964). She preferred poetry of a more imagistic and musical character, and turned to word-games and enchantment, but with a certain colloquial and very personal view of poetry in *Madrinha lua*. She has been compared to ▷Cecília Meireles for the abstractness of her thought and the style of her verse form.
Bib: Lobo, Filho, B., *The Poetry of Emily Dickinson and Henriqueta Lisboa.*

Lisboa, Irene do Céu Viera (1892–1958)

Portuguese prose writer and poet. She was a teacher and inspector in the Lisbon public school system. In the 1930s she openly opposed the Salazar regime, and was branded a communist. To avoid further persecution she used the pen-names João Falco and Manuel Soares on all her literary and pedagogical publications. In 1940 she was forced to resign her position in the school system. Two years later, in 1942, she published *Esta Cidade!* (*This City!*), her first book to appear since 1926 under her own name.

Lisboa is best known for her fictional works about daily life in the capital. Solitude – especially in the lives of middle-class women – is a prominent theme in many of her works, including her widely – acclaimed ▷*Solidão* (1939). Somewhat like the ▷neo-realists, she sympathized with the poor and working class, and she was often critical of the bourgeoisie. Lisbon was the setting for most of her fiction, although towards the end of her life she wrote a volume of stories set in the Serra da Estrela, a mountainous region in the interior.

Lisboa was critical of the novel as a literary form, feeling that it was artificial and bourgeois. She opted for shorter modes, such as ▷*crônicas, reportagens* (reports), *diários* (diaries), *historietas* (mini-stories) – all of which which tended to avoid linearity and closure. A good example of her unconventional style is her book of jottings and notes, entitled *Apontamentos* (1942) (*Memoranda*), which contains interesting meditations on literary style. Her fiction and poetry can be found in *Presença, Seara Nova, O Diabo* and other important magazines and journals of the period.
Bib: Sayers, Raymond S., 'Irene Lisboa as a Writer of Fiction', *Hispania* (1962); *Longman Anthology of World Literature by Women*, pp. 295–302.

Lisle, Honor Grenville Basset (c 1495–1566)

English letter-writer. She was the daughter of Thomas and Isabella Gilbert Grenville. In 1515 she married John Basset, who died in 1528. The following year she married Arthur Plantagenet, Lord Lisle. Her husband served as Deputy of Calais between 1533 and 1540, when he was recalled to England, arrested, and charged with complicity in a plot to turn Calais over to the Pope. He was imprisoned in the Tower of London for two years, and although he was pardoned in 1542, he died before he could be released. During her husband's imprisonment, Honor Lisle remained in Calais, under surveillance and separated from her daughters. At the time of Lisle's arrest, all of his official and personal papers, including thousands of letters to and from members of the Lisle family, were seized as evidence. Although the confiscated papers proved Lisle's innocence, they also revealed him to be an incompetent government official. The letters written by Honor Lisle demonstrate her skill in promoting and negotiating her husband's political career in spite of his inabilities. They also attest to her love and care for her husband and family, her piety, and her relations with numerous contemporary figures, including Thomas Cromwell (1485–1540, chief minister of Henry VIII), Henry VIII and ▷Anne Boleyn.
Bib: Byrne, M. (ed.), *The Lisle Letters.*

Lisniánskaia, Inna L'vovna (born 1928)

Russian poet. Lisniánskaia began publishing poetry in 1948. Her best friend was the poet, ▷Mariia Petrovýkh, to whom she wrote several poems, and who apparently offered her critical support. Her daughter is the writer ▷Elena Makárova. Between 1957 and 1978 she published five volumes of poetry. However, she had trouble with the censor over the fourth volume (*At First Hand*, 1966) and there was a gap of twelve years before the fifth appeared. Shortly thereafter Lisniánskaia, along with ▷Bella Akhmadúlina, contributed six poems to the ▷*samizdat Metropol* almanac, and was able to publish only abroad until the onset of ▷*glásnost*'. Two collections appeared in the West in 1983–84. Since 1987 Lisniánskaia has published in various periodicals in the USSR. An article in the Russian *Literary Review* (1989) is part of a larger study on ▷Akhmátova's ▷'Poem Without a Hero'.

Lisniánskaia's poems are often meditative lyrics in a style that can combine informal, colloquial Russian and mundane details with abstract words and concepts. Those she first published in the USSR centre on ethical issues: the writer's duty to bear witness and show courage, the fear of losing the genuine self. In her later work, Lisniánskaia has shown herself to be a religious and philosophical poet, concerned with time and the eternal.

Bib: Kasack, W., *Dictionary of Russian Literature Since 1917*; Wilson, K., *An Encyclopedia of Continental Women Writers*, Vol. 2; Aksyonov, V., *et al.* (eds), *Metropol: Literary Almanac*.

Lispector, Clarice (1925–1977)

Clarice Lispector

Brazilian short story writer, novelist and chronicle writer. She is one of the most outstanding Brazilian woman writers, and a leading exponent of ▷postmodernism. Her parents left the Ukraine for Recife when she was two months old. As an adolescent she moved to Rio, studied law (1944) and became a journalist. Married to a diplomat, she lived in Europe, but returned to Rio in 1959. At nineteen she published her first and very successful novel, *Perto do coração selvagem* (1944) (*Close to the Savage Heart*), a psychological insight into a woman's inner life. Her style has a peculiar,

feminine outlook on everyday trivialities, which become real entities, in the light of Heidegger's and Sartre's philosophies. *Laços de família* (1960) (*Family Ties*, 1972) and *Legião estrangeira* (1964) (*The Foreign Legion*, 1986) show this trait well. *A paixão segundo G.H.* (1964) (▷*The Passion According to G.H.*) brings the human conflict of a housewife and her exploited maid to an almost unbearable tension, seeing it from the point of view of civilized–uncivilized, tame–untame, and cosmopolitan-wild. Her works are written in the first person, with the use of epiphanic moments and ▷stream-of-consciousness. With a philosophical look, she rediscovers objects and subtly denounces women's subjection to patriarchal society, a theme pursued in her novel *Uma aprendizagem ou o livro dos prazeres* (1969) (*An Apprenticeship or the Book of Delights*, 1986). After the late 1970s, she challenged the rules of the genre with her prose fragments. Her last novel, *A hora da estrela* (1977) (*The Hour of the Star*), which was successfully filmed, shows the socioeconomic problems of a naïve, proletarian girl.

Lister, Anne (1791–1840)
Diarist and traveller from Halifax. Her diary, written in code, records local life, travel and lesbian love. She visited the ▷Ladies of Llangollen. The decoded diary has recently been published.

Literary criticism (Australia)
▷Zora Cross's *Introduction to the Study of Australian Literature* (1922), ▷Nettie Palmer's *Modern Australian Literature* (1924), and ▷M. Barnard Eldershaw's *Essays in Australian Fiction* (1938), were the earliest systematic attempts by Australian women critics to account for a developing literary canon and include discussion of both male and female writers. ▷*The Peaceful Army* (1938) edited by ▷Flora Eldershaw, an explicitly female text containing poems and essays by women in honour of pioneering women, includes literary criticism, while ▷Miles Franklin's *Laughter, Not for a Cage* (1956) has much to say on the same subject. Significant Australian women literary critics, apart from those listed in the entry ▷Feminist literary criticism (Australia), include ▷Dorothy Green for her study of ▷Henry Handel Richardson and her revision of H.M. Green's *A History of Australian Literature*; ▷Nancy Keesing for her *Australian Postwar Novelists* (1975); and ▷Judith Wright for her *Preoccupations in Australian Poetry* (1965) and *Because I Was Invited* (1975).

Literary salons (Scandinavia)
The literary salon was created on inspiration from the French fashion for salon culture in the 17th century. It was a forum in which intellectual women could meet each other and see famous artists. It was a place where many wealthy women refined their tastes and education. It became an important forum for criticism before regular media criticism was developed. The salon was

always centred around one woman. In Scandinavia there were aristocratic and bourgeois salons.

Around 1800 there were three important literary salons in Denmark, and very many minor salons at the manors up and down the country. Charlotte Schimmelmann (1757–1816) was one of the leading ladies in Denmark, married to the Minister of Finance, Ernst Schimmelmann. She had a literary salon where many European guests could meet leading Danish writers and artists. During the summer the salon was at the manor of Sølund; in the winter it was at the palace in Copenhagen. She wrote thousands of letters in French, a selection of which has been published.

Friederike Brun (1765–1832) was Schimmelmann's most important competitor. She was married to the rich businessman Constantin Brun, and for many years she travelled in Europe. She had a wide acquaintance, and even though she was not in the same position as Schimmelmann, her salon won the competition and became the most popular in Denmark.

Kamma Rahbæk (1775–1829) was neither an aristocrat nor rich. Her salon became the first and most important bourgeois salon in Copenhagen. Her house still exists as a museum (Bakkehuset). She wrote many letters, some of which have been preserved and published.

The French *précieuses* (▷Precious women) had a great influence on the salons in Sweden in the 18th and 19th centuries. But in Sweden this influence was developed in a new bourgeois literary milieu. Hedvig Charlotta Nordenflycht (1718–1763) was an intellectual woman, the centre of the Tankebyggerordenen (Society of Thought Builders), the first literary salon in Sweden. Nordenflycht was a highly productive writer in the tradition of the ▷Enlightenment and the French philosopher Jean Jacques Rousseau (1712–1778), whom she also wrote against in her *Fruntimrets försvar* (1761) (*In Defence of Woman*).

Anna Maria Lenngren (1754–1817) was a pietist, and had a learned upbringing. In 1780 she married Carl Peter Lenngren, who published periodicals in which his wife began to write anonymously. Their home was a literary salon. Mrs Lenngren tried, in spite of her learnedness and her outstanding satires, to describe herself as the perfect housewife, the only acceptable model for women, but in fact she was not.

Quite different was Magdalena (Malla) Silverstolpe (1782–1861). Very early on she had an interest in the new German romantic literature. After the death of her husband in 1819 she created a literary salon in Stockholm which became the centre of literary life there. In her *Memoirs* (1908–1911), Malla Silverstolpe wrote about Swedish salon life and female identity.

▷Salon culture (Germany and Austria)

Little, Janet (1759–1813)

Scottish labouring-class poet who wrote in Gaelic and English. She did not have more than a 'common education' before becoming a domestic servant to Frances Wallace Dunlop of Dunlop,

the patron of Scottish poet Robert Burns (1759–1796). She later married John Richmond. She went to work in the dairy at Loudoun Castle, and her employer showed some of her poetry to Burns. In 1792 *The Poetical Works of Janet Little* was issued. Incisively aware of her own 'impudent' status as a poet, she refuses to accept received pronunciation, and threads her writing with changes in linguistic mode. She wrote, 'But what is more surprising still, / A milkmaid must tak' up her quill; / An' she will write, shame fa' the rabble / That thinks to please with ilka bawble.' She continued to write after the publication of the book.

▷Collier, Mary; Leapor, Mary; Yearsley, Ann; Women and work
Bib: Landry, Donna, *The Muses of Resistance.*

Little, Jean (born 1932)

Born Jean Llewellyn in Formosa (Taiwan), she was educated in Canada, graduating with a BA from the University of Toronto in 1955. Blind at birth, Little has only partial vision, but was fortunate in that her parents never treated her as a handicapped child, and encouraged her to transcend the limits of her physical world through reading. She has since become one of Canada's most important writers of juvenile literature, and takes a special interest in disabled children. Her first book, *Mine for Keeps*, won the Little, Brown Canadian Prize in 1962. Since then she has published numerous children's books: *Home From Far* (1965); *Spring Begins in March* (1966); *When the Pie was Opened* (1968); *Take Wing* (1968); *One to Grow On* (1969); *Look Through my Window* (1970); *Kate* (1972); *From Anna* (1972); *Stand in the Wind* (1975); *Listen for the Singing* (1977); *Mama's Going to Buy You a Mockingbird* (1984), and *Lost and Found* (1985). In her writing she tries to depict children working through difficult situations, to understanding and self-acceptance. She received the Canada Council Children's Book Award in 1977, and her books have been translated into many languages.

Little Camels of the Sky, The (1914)

A collection of prose and poems by Russian author ▷Elena Guró, written in the last three years of her life. They are all fragmentary, lyrical, impressionistic pieces that often read like diary notes. Some of Guró's favourite motifs can be found in the book: the idealist and dreamer, often identified as a poet, who is doomed to suffer, or who is vulnerable to the philistines and the modern urban world ('The Little Star', 'May your fame resound . . .', 'At last they took in the poet . . .'); the child's closeness, in naïveté and vivid imagination, to immortality ('Mama, was Don Quixote kind?', 'Your violin's gone slightly mad'), and the blurring of borders between the animate and inanimate world, the real world and that of imagination or dream. When the book was published posthumously, it was reviewed by only one person, the poet Briusov, who was positive.
Bib: O'Brien, K., *The Little Camels of the Sky.*

Little Eva

Saintly child character in North American writer
▷Harriet Beecher Stowe's famous anti-slavery
novel, ▷*Uncle Tom's Cabin*. Little Eva became the
literary embodiment of a number of 19th-century
US attitudes toward children and women. A
special child doomed to a short life on earth, Eva
represented the caring, religious and transcendent
values associated with the idea of women and
home as bastions of higher values and morality.
This woman's sphere was opposed to the
commercialism, dissolution and self-interest of the
male, social world. Eva was also the dying child,
too good and too pure for this earth – values
which were transposed to woman as pure, as
sexless, as physically weak instead of, or because,
morally strong.

Little Foxes, The (1939)

US play by ▷Lillian Hellman which focuses on
the power struggle within the Hubbard family.
The Hubbard siblings vie with each other to buy
the controlling interest in a cotton mill. Regina,
the sister, embodies the plight of the ▷Southern
lady, being totally dependent on her husband for
money. Rather than give her the money, he
decides to loan it to her brothers; when he suffers
a heart attack, Regina refuses to give him his
medicine, and she allows him to die. Regina
blackmails her brothers to gain the largest share
of the mill.

Regina becomes the son her father always
desired, and assumes patriarchal power. Hellman
examines the life-destroying socio-economic
forces on the Southern woman, as well as the
impact of the forces of industrialism on the South.

Little House on the Prairie (1935)

US novel. ▷Laura Ingalls Wilder's
autobiographical work describes the arduous tasks
a pioneer family performs to establish a home on
the Kansas frontier. It also chronicles the threats
to their sense of security. The child narrator
depicts the complexities of growing up. Although
Laura perceives herself as naughty, she is
struggling against the restrictive role of women as
bearers of civilization. Empathetic to ▷Native
Americans, Wilder portrays them as people who
have been uprooted from their land.

Little Karoo, The (1924)

A collection of eight short stories written by South
African writer ▷Pauline Smith, with two more
added in 1930. The title refers to the Little Karoo
region of the Cape Province, which is around
Oudtshoorn and the Long Kloof valley. In this
rural world, the people are poverty-stricken, either
scratching a precarious living as *bijwoners* (tenant
farmers), or desperately trying to save their own
land from economic ruin. They are, moreover,
bowed under a punitive Calvinist God. Some of
the stories focus on the subordination of women
in this patriarchal world: in 'The Sisters', for
instance, Marta de Jager is the object of exchange
between her father and a richer, neighbouring

farmer. In 'The Miller', Andries Lombard's
insecurity as a *bijwoner* is turned into a feeling that
God has abandoned him. In retaliation, he
victimizes his wife, but at the moment of death
realizes that his treatment of her is structurally no
different from the way Jews were treated in
Eastern Europe.

Smith's interest in the structures and
perpetuation of oppression led her to refer to a
variety of unequal social relations, and, most
obliquely, to those between black and white.
'Ludovitje', which tells the story of a young
evangelist and his conversion of 'Maqwasi the
Kaffir', establishes a subtle connection between
Afrikaners and Africans: both groups have had
occasion to see themselves as God's Israelites, the
'Chosen People'. In a context of developing
Afrikaner nationalism, profoundly based on a
religious belief in being elected by God, the story
is a powerful one. 'The Sinner', moreover,
presents a man who had once counted himself
among the elect, but now knows himself to be
damned.

Despite the oblique, didactic comments,
Smith's interest in these rural Afrikaners is a
deeply sympathetic one, which recognizes their
own oppression by the English settlers at the
Cape, and their precarious existence in a world
being overtaken by industrialization. Her writing
incorporates the speech-patterns of the Afrikaans
language, and in other ways keeps close to its
subject. However, it occasionally veers into
idealization and sentimentality, as in her lead story
'The Pain'.

Little Lord Fauntleroy (1886)

A story for children by Anglo-American writer
▷Frances Hodgson Burnett. It was hugely
successful in Britain and North America, and
started a new fashion for dressing boys in
'Fauntleroy' velvet suits. It was also, however,
ridiculed and derided as cloyingly ▷sentimental.
The tale is straightforward, with the unnaturally
angelic boy hero going from rags to riches by
inheritance. The story remains popular today, was
famously filmed by Hollywood, and has been
serialized on television.
▷Children's literature (19th-century Britain)

Little Review, The (1914–1929)

Pioneering ▷modernist magazine, edited by
Margaret Anderson (1886 to 1973) and Jane
Heap (died 1964). Running from 1914 to 1929
and published, variously, in Chicago, Paris and
New York, the magazine was less Ezra Pound's
(1885–1972) 'official organ' (what, in his words,
he imagined it to be) than, in Jane Heap's words,
a forum which gave space to 'twenty-three new
systems of art representing nineteen countries'.
The 'Art for Art's sake' credo of the magazine
came chiefly from Margaret Anderson's conviction
that 'people who make art are more interesting
than those who don't.' This guiding aesthetic
principle, however, did not prevent the magazine
from exploring diverse fields such as philosophy,

psychoanalysis, feminism and politics. Indeed, the list of contributors reads like a 'who's who' of early 20th-century art and letters and includes Sherwood Anderson, Richard Aldington (1892–1962), ▷Djuna Barnes, Hart Crane, T.S Eliot (1888–1965), Emma Goldman, ▷H.D., James Joyce (1882–1941), Wyndham Lewis (1882–1957), ▷Dorothy Richardson, William Carlos Williams, and W.B. Yeats (1865–1939). In 1918 *The Little Review* began to serialize James Joyce's *Ulysses* and subsequently found itself in an obscenity trial in 1920 which Anderson and Heap lost. More than the editorial backbone to the artists they promoted, Anderson and Heap consistently attempted to push back the limits of art and literature. 'But thank Heaven *I* can still get some ecstasy out of life!' Anderson said in a dialogue with Heap recorded in 1922, to which Heap replied, 'Why limit me to ecstasy?'

Other works by Anderson include: *My Thirty Years War* (1930), *The Fiery Fountains* (1951), *The Little Review Anthology* (ed.) (1953) and *The Strange Necessity* (1970).

Little Women (1868, 1869)

US novel by ▷Louisa May Alcott, originally published in two parts. One of the all-time internationally popular and lasting US novels for children and adults, *Little Women* begins the chronicle of the March family. In its celebration of family and women's relationships through the characters of the mother, Marmee, and the four daughters, Meg, Amy, Beth and Jo, the novel vividly portrays the personalities and possibilities of 19th-century women – from genteel domesticity to feminist independence.

Liu Nienling (born 1934)

Chinese-American writer and critic publishing under the pseudonym of Mulin Chi. Liu was born in China but settled in the US at an early age. Educated in Berkeley, Columbia, Harvard and Cambridge, Liu chooses to think of herself as a 'marginal' being, practising her art as a writer while making the observation and participation of life into an art form. Liu writes with great sensitivity about displaced intellectuals in the US, as seen in her book of short stories, *The Marginal Man* (1987). The novel *The Image in the Bamboo Grove* (1983) is a historical and literary reconstruction of the lives and times of the 'Seven Sages of the Bamboo Grove' (c AD 200–300), known for their anti-establishment views and unconventional lifestyles. Liu Nienling edits the only Chinese language literary magazine in North America, *Convergences*, which brings together essays, poems, short stories and *belles lettres*.

Liu Suola (born 1955)

Chinese writer. Born in Beijing, Liu studied music, and still composes and performs. She also writes fiction. Her first novella, *You Have No Choice* (1985), was a critical success. Its theme, the writer explained, is 'the new music of China, and the new generation of composers'. This was followed by *Blue Sky and Azure Sea* (1985) and *In Search of the King of Singers* (1986). As a musician and performer, Liu is swayed by her musical instincts and tries to apply the principles of composing to her writing.

Liu Zhen (born 1930)

Chinese writer. Born to a destitute peasant family whose male members had been killed for their association with the communists, Liu left home and followed the communist army in 1939, when she was a ragged little girl. She learned to read and write in the army. As she grew up she kept a diary, and later began to publish reports and short pieces. One of her best stories, 'The Winding Stream' (1962), is about a young woman who dedicates herself to the revolutionary war and suffers neglect after being disabled. It was publicly attacked as 'demoralizing'. Liu also exposed the deceptions of the 'Great Leap Forward' (a nationwide movement in 1958 to industrialize the country overnight, resulting in famine and economic disaster) in another striking story 'The Black Flag' (1978). It was one of the earliest works to question the ultra-leftism that dominated policy in China even before the disaster of the 'cultural revolution' (1966–1976).

Live or Die (1966)

North American writer ▷Anne Sexton describes her collection of poems as reading 'like a fever chart for a bad case of melancholy'. All the poems, written between 1962 and 1966, use a first-person voice constructing the confessional aesthetic for which Sexton is famous. Poems about mental breakdown, family history and children are punctuated by poems about suicide, including Sexton's famous poem 'Sylvia's Death' about ▷Sylvia Plath.

In accordance with the opposition established by the book's title, the identity of Sexton's poetic persona is precariously secured through the elaboration of a fantasy about death. The science and rituals of suicide, to be found in poems such as 'Imitations of Drowning' and 'Wanting to Die', permit an illusory control over both selfhood and life. The poems also map the relationship of mental breakdown, 'the scene of disordered senses', to family history. In poems such as 'And One for My Dame', about her travelling salesman father, 'Mother and Jack and the Rain' and 'Those Times' the speaker searches out an identity from the memories and relationships of her childhood. The influence of Freudian psychoanalysis in post-war North America is marked here, and in the disturbing link between childhood, family and sexuality which emerges. The best-known poem in the collection, the celebratory, 'Little Girl, My String Bean, My Lovely Woman', about her daughter's growth into womanhood, links maternal love to erotic love. The book was awarded the Pulitzer Prize.

Lively, Penelope (born 1933)

English novelist and writer for children, born in Cairo. A characteristic of Lively's writings is her

Penelope Lively

interest in the ordering of events in time, and a preoccupation with a metaphysical foreboding or evil which disturbs the everyday world. Her children's fiction is frequently based on folklore and legend, and her child characters often believe in the presence of ghosts. *Astercote* (1970), *The Ghost of Thomas Kempe* (1973) and *The Revenge of Samuel Stokes* (1981) are all concerned with the irruptive force of previous events. Lively's adult fiction, as in *Treasures of Time* (1979) and *According to Mark* (1984), is similarly concerned with the interpenetration of personal and public history and its effect on the present. She won the Booker Prize with *Moon Tiger* (1987).

Livesay, Dorothy (born 1909)

Born in Winnipeg, Livesay is one of Canada's most respected poets, although she has also been a journalist, teacher, social worker, broadcaster and political activist. She studied literature at the University of Toronto (1931) and the Sorbonne in Paris (1932) before joining the Communist Party of Canada, and entering the School of Social Work at the University of Toronto (1934). Her prolific writing career began with *Green Pitcher* (1928) and *Signpost* (1932), imagistic works, followed by more powerful political poetry in *Day and Night* (1944) and *Poems for People* (1947), both of which won Governor General's Awards.

Although Livesay withdrew from leftist politics after her marriage in 1937, she never stopped her activism on behalf of feminism and peace, and as a founding member of the League of Canadian Poets and Amnesty International (Canada). *Call My People Home* (1950), a radio documentary poem about the dispossession of the Japanese-Canadians in World War II, was followed by *New Poems* (1955), *Selected Poems, 1926–1956* (1957) and *The Colour of God's Face* (1964). The *Unquiet Bed* (1967), *Plainsongs* (1971), *Ice Age* (1975), *The Woman I Am* (1977) and *The Phases of Love* (1983) are moving explorations of the range of woman's sexuality and capacity for love, 'bright wound that will not heal'. *The Documentaries: Selected Longer Poems* (1968) show Livesay working in the long poem format before it became fashionable. She has also published *Disasters of the Sun* (1971), *Nine Poems of Farewell* (1973), *The Raw Edges: Voices From Our Time* (1981), *Feeling the Worlds: New Poems* (1984), and *The Self-Completing Tree: Selected Poems* (1986). In her foreword to *Collected Poems: the Two Seasons* (1972), Livesay talks about 'the pull between community and private identity that is characteristic of being a woman'; and in her non-fiction book *Right Hand Left Hand* (1977) she explores the political influences on her voice as a woman and a poet. *A Winnipeg Childhood* (1973), revised as *Beginnings* (1988), brings together her autobiographical short stories. *The Husband: A Novella* appeared in 1990. She has written plays and has also been an active editor, founding the poetry journal, *Contemporary Verse 2*, and editing two volumes of poetry by women, *Forty Women Poets of Canada* (1972) and *Woman's Eye: 12 B.C. Poets* (1974). The National Film Board of Canada has released a documentary, *The Woman I Am* (1982), about her. Livesay, who lives on Galiano Island, British Columbia, continues to be a catalyst for Canadian women's poetry
▷Webb, Phyllis
Bib: Denham, P., *Dorothy Livesay and Her Works*; Thompson, L. B., *Dorothy Livesay*; ▷*Room of One's Own* Vol. 5, no. 1/2, 1979.

Lives of Girls and Women (1971)

Canadian writer ▷Alice Munro's ground-breaking portrait of the artist as a young girl, striving to see clearly her detailed and intricate world. Del Jordan grows up in the town of Jubilee, constantly re-evaluating her place there as daughter, sister, lover, neighbour. Episodic in development (indeed, the novel takes the form of a series of separate though interlocked incidents), it is nevertheless a wholly integrated account of a young woman's coming of age in sensibility as well as sexuality. Munro's style has been described as beautifully transparent; in this novel it is not only that but consummately satisfying.

Livingston, Alida Schuyler van Rensselaer (1656–1727)

North American letter-writer. The daughter of Margaretta van Schlechtenhorst, whose family directed Rensselaerswyck, the family estate, in the colony of New Netherland (now New York), and Philip Peterse Schuyler, a wealthy merchant, she was born at Fort Orange. At age nineteen, she married Nicholas van Rensselaer, who was at least twice her age; it was a marriage of families rather than individuals. After Nicholas died, she married Robert Livingston, who had been director of Rensselaerswyck. In this marriage, she found a true partnership. In the ▷*Business Letters of Alida Schuyler Livingston, 1680–1726*, her life in an egalitarian marriage and in an entrepreneurial partnership is played out over almost fifty years of married life. Her husband retired in 1726, but she continued to manage their manor until her death the following year.

Livingston, Anne (Nancy) Shippen (1763–1841)

North American diarist. Born 24 February 1763 in Philadelphia, she was raised in a wealthy and socially active family. As her private writings (▷*Nancy Shippen, Her Journal Book, 1783–1791*) suggest, however, her training was very much that of the conservative school of thought about 'woman's sphere'. When she desired to marry, her father's will prevailed and she married for economic reasons rather than love. The consequences are detailed in her moving, well-written journal, as is her awakening to an understanding of the need to break from tradition. Her life-story constitutes a tale of courage and self-discovery; perhaps most poignant – and ultimately fulfilling – is her decision to educate her daughter to the realities of life and to a sense of independence and ability, whether or not she should marry.

▷Early North American letters

Li Xiaojiang (born 1951)

Chinese writer. Native of Jiangxi province, Li Xiaojiang was among the generation of young people caught by the 'cultural revolution' (1966–1976) and obliged to work in the country and the factories.

Li later earned an MA in Western literature at Henan University, and while teaching courses in Western literature at Zhengzhou University, where she is now based, she has gradually moved into women's studies. In 1985, she set up the first non-governmental association of women's studies in China; in 1987 she set up and headed the first research centre for women's studies in an institution of higher learning – the Women's Studies Centre of Zhengzhou University.

Li's own publications have played a key role in introducing Western feminist theories into China and applying modern feminist theories to the study of the current situation of women in China. She edited the Chinese translations of *Documents of the Women's Rights Movement in the West* (1987) and ▷*The Second Sex* (1991). Li's published writings include *The Search of Eve* (1987), *The Gender Gap* (1988), *The Way Out for Women* (1989), *Women, a Beautiful, Long-Lost Legend* (1989) and *Inquiry into Female Aesthetics* (1990).

Li Xiaoyu (born 1951)

Chinese poet. Li was born into a literary family and was attracted to poetry at an early age. She was recruited into the army after middle school and started to publish poetry when serving as a nurse in the army. She later moved to the editorial staff of *Poetry* magazine, and has published two anthologies of lyric poems, *Song of Swallows* (1979) and *The Red Scarf* (1983).

Lizars, Kathleen MacFarlane (died 1931)

Canadian novelist. Born at Stratford, Ontario, she was for some time private secretary to John Robson, Premier of British Columbia. She wrote articles and historical accounts for newspapers, as well as a comedy about the Rebellion of 1837 called *Humours of '37, Grave, Gay, and Grim* (1897), and *Committed to His Charge: A Canadian Chronicle* (1900), a novel about a small town.

Lobo, Mara ▷Galvão, Patrícia

Local color

US descriptive literary term or 19th-century US genre, usually applied to fiction but sometimes to poetry and non-fiction. Local color focuses on subject matter, theme, character and language on what is unique, distinctive and native in a particular locale. Associated with the US desire for a national literature separate from the British tradition, local color used dialect, regional folkways and customs, particularized character types and descriptions of the natural environment to bring new subjects to literature. Sometimes associated with a nostalgic and romantic re-creation of the past, local color at its best went beyond verisimilitude to become realism on regional subjects. In 20th-century literary criticism, local color is sometimes a reductive term, and regionalism a term of higher status. Feminist literary criticism sees local color as a woman's tradition in US literature. Among writers associated with the local color genre are ▷Alice Brown; ▷Rose Terry Cooke; ▷Rebecca Harding Davis; ▷Margaret Wade Campbell Deland; ▷Mary E. Wilkins Freeman; ▷Helen Hunt Jackson; ▷Sarah Orne Jewett; ▷Sarah Pratt McLean; ▷Mary Noailles Murfree; ▷Harriet Beecher Stowe; ▷Sarah Keating Wood, and ▷Constance Fenimore Woolson.

▷Gold rush

Lochhead, Liz (born 1947)

Scottish poet, dramatist and performance artist. Lochhead began her writing career while a lecturer in fine art, and her first publications were the screenplay *Now and then* and poetry collection *Memo for Spring* (both 1971). After winning a Writers Exchange Fellowship which enabled her to visit Canada, she became a full-time writer. She has since occupied numerous writer-in-residence posts. *Dreaming Frankenstein and Collected Poems* (1984) contains sustained critiques of patriarchy, and illustrates Lochhead's characteristic cutting irony. The collection *The Grimm Sisters* (1981) comprises poems that rework the sexual politics of fairy tales. Her plays include: *Mary and the Monster* (1981), retitled *Blood and Ice* (1982), about ▷Mary Shelley, and recently, *Jock Tamson's Bairns* (1989), a study of 'Scottish' identity and psychology. The scripts of her live performances are included in *True Confessions and New Clichés* (1985).

▷Tennant, Emma

Locke (Dering Prowse), Anne Vaughan (fl 1556–1590)

English translator and letter-writer. The daughter of Stephen Vaughan, she was probably influenced by her Protestant step-mother Margery Brinklow. Although Anne Vaughan had three husbands, she is most frequently referred to by her first husband's name. She married Henry Locke sometime between 1550 and 1556. About one year after Locke's death in 1571, she married the radical Protestant preacher Edward Dering. After Dering's death in 1576, she married Richard Prowse sometime before 1583. During her first marriage she came under the spiritual guidance of the Scottish reformer John Knox, whom she met in 1552. Thirteen ▷letters from their correspondence between 1556 and 1562 still exist. During Queen Mary's reign, Knox persuaded a number of Protestants to flee persecution. In December 1556 Knox wrote to convince Locke to join other Protestant exiles in Geneva. She arrived in May 1557 with her infant son and daughter and a maid, but without her husband. By 1559 Anne Locke had returned to England and her husband. Her first ▷translation, Calvin's ▷*Sermons upon the Songe of Ezechias* (1560), was completed during her exile in Geneva. She translated her second work, John Taffin's ▷*Of the Markes of the Children of God* (1590), during her marriage to Richard Prowse.

▷Protestant Reformation

Bib: Collinson, P., 'The Role of Women in the English Reformation Illustrated by the Life and Friendships of Anne Locke', *Studies in Church History* 2 (1965) p. 258–72; Laing, D. (ed.), *The Works of John Knox*.

Locke, Elsie Violet (born 1912)

New Zealand author of children's historical novels, history and non-fiction. She was educated in Waiuku, then at the University of Auckland in 1933. In the late 1930s Locke was editor of *Woman Today*, a progressive women's magazine, but after her marriage in 1941 she found little time for writing until the 1950s. An article in the December 1958 issue of *Landfall*, a notable literary journal, won her the Katherine Mansfield Non-Fiction Award in 1959 and set her upon a writing career. Locke's first and classic story *The Runaway Settlers* (1965) is about a 19th-century Australian family fleeing from a drunken, brutal father to New Zealand. In *Journey Under Warning* (1983) and *The End of the Harbour* (1968) Locke explores Maori/European relations. Concerned at the 'distorted' way writers of New Zealand history have portrayed Maori and women, Locke consciously tries in her books to 'even up the score'. Her New Zealand histories are *The Kauri and the Willow* (1984) and *Two Peoples, One Land* (1988).

Publications include: *Moko's Hideout* (1976); *The Boy With Snowgrass Hair* (1976); *Explorer Zach* (1978); *The Gaoler* (1978); *Student at the Gates* (autobiographical) (1981); *A Canoe in the Mist*

(1984); *Mrs Hobson's Album* (1990); *Peace People* (1991).

▷Children's literature, New Zealand; Maori literature

Lockett, Mary F. (born 1872)

This Caribbean novelist and poet, born in ▷Jamaica, published her first novel, *Christopher*, in 1902.

Logan, Martha Daniell (1702–1779)

North American author of botanical tracts and correspondence. Born on 29 December 1704, she was the daughter of the Deputy Governor of South Carolina. In 1719 she married George Logan. Little is known of her married life, but after she was widowed she established a gardening business in her home, selling seeds, flowers and other gardening materials. In the 1760s she corresponded regularly with John Bartram (1699–1777), the renowned botanist, and the ▷*Letters of Martha Logan to John Bartram, 1760–1763* expose the scientific bent of her mind. In 1772 she published ▷*The Gardners Kalender*, a treatise on gardening that was reprinted in numerous almanacs during the late 18th century.

Logocentrism

A system of thought which according to French philosopher Jacques Derrida (born 1930) describes a tradition of Western philosophy that centres on the power of the *logos*, or concept, to make present in language meaning which is believed to originate outside it, in the mind of an individual or God. ▷Difference displaces the illusion of the presence of meaning in words.

Lókhvitskaia, Mirra (Mariia) Aleksandrovna (1869–1905)

Russian poet and dramatist. Her younger sister was the writer ▷Tèffi. By the age of fifteen Lókhvitskaia had already decided on her vocation. In 1892 she married and, over the next few years, had five children. She published five volumes of verse between 1896 and 1904, and in 1908 a posthumous volume of her poems appeared under the title *Before Sunset*. Lókhvitskaia was the first modern woman poet whose reputation was enhanced by the ▷Silver Age's tendency to blur the distinction between the created persona and the real person. Her popularity was no doubt enhanced by her beauty and charm, her scandalous affair with the poet Konstantin Bal'mont in 1896–98, and her widely successful appearances at poetry readings.

Lókhvitskaia was the quintessentially 'feminine' poet – her poetic persona was always womanly, and much of her subject matter was the confessional poetry about love and other intimate matters expected of women. But she extended the terms that women poets could use in speaking of love to include overt sensuality, self-absorption, and even physical details of the male love object. Lókhvitskaia's verse is characterized by an accomplished, melodic line. In her first collection,

Poems (1896), she wrote about the joy of motherhood, another 'feminine' subject. This book won her the Pushkin Prize in literature from the Imperial Academy of Sciences, and she was awarded another, posthumously, in 1905 for her fifth volume of poetry.

Her second volume of poetry, *Poems 1896– 1898*, was written during her affair with Bal'mont, and the love theme becomes contaminated with a sense of sin and destruction. Bal'mont's collected poems, *Let's Be Like the Sun* (1903), was dedicated to Lókhvitskaia ('To the artist of Bacchic visions, the Russian ▷Sappho, who knows the secret of sorcery'), lending the relationship a further taint of scandal. Henceforth she was labelled 'the Russian Sappho.' In her last three volumes of poetry, published between 1900 and 1904, Lókhvitskaia continued to concentrate on the theme of love, though the treatment becomes more problematic, and negative feelings like jealousy more often appear. At the same time she moved into other genres, writing both verse dramas and extended narrative poems. Her dramas include: *On the Road to the East*, with the Queen of Sheba as the heroine, *Immortal Love*, set in the Middle Ages, and the historical tragedy *In nomine Domini* (*In the Name of the Lord*), set in 17th-century France. The last, in unrhymed iambic pentameter, has two powerfully drawn female characters: one, a *femme fatale*, is tormented by the conflict between religious duty and passion; the other, a religious fanatic, is motivated by envy and given to violence.

Lókhvitskaia died from tuberculosis. Because she has been more or less forgotten today, it is important to emphasize that in the early 20th century she was the standard against which other women poets were measured. For example, when ▷Mariètta Shaginián reviewed ▷Tsvetáeva's first book of poetry, *Evening Album* (1910), she compared her lyric voice to Lókhvitskaia's. There are themes and images in her poetry that anticipate, ▷Akhmátova, and ▷Tsvetáeva, and it was she, not Akhmátova, who 'taught women how to speak' (Markov), as ▷Cherubina de Gabriak has acknowledged in her recently published autobiography.

▷*Crossroad, The*; *Bab*; Gurévich, Liubov
Bib: Pachmuss, T. (trans.), *Women Writers in Russian Modernism*; Anglo-Russian Literature Society, *Proceedings* 80 (1917); Markov, V. in Moskovich, Wolf, et al. (eds), *Russian Literature and History: In Honour of Professor Ilya Serman*; Cioran, S., 'The Russian Sappho: Mirra Lokhvitskaia', *Russian Literature Triquarterly* 9.

Lolly Willowes (1926)
▷Sylvia Townsend Warner's very successful first novel. Laura ('Lolly') Willowes is a middle-aged spinster living a dull existence with her brother's family. She finally decides to break away, and takes lodgings in the small village of Great Mop. Communion with nature leads to communion with Satan, and Laura discovers that Great Mop is a haven for witches like herself. To Satan, disguised

as a gamekeeper, Laura describes the constraints women endure: 'Women have such vivid imaginations and lead such dull lives.' As in ▷*Summer Will Show* (1936), Warner is concerned with women's lack of independence in society, and their need to live in conditions of their own choosing. *Lolly Willowes* was selected as the first Book-of-the-Month choice of the new American Book Club, and nominated for the Prix Femina.
▷*Opus 7*

Lombarda (13th century)
French ▷*trobairitz* from Toulouse. Her existence is attested in a charter of 1206. She exchanged *coblas* with Bernart Arnaut, Count of Armagnac (1219–1226), possibly her husband, who confesses: '*Lombartz volgr'eu esser per na Lombarda*' ('I would like to be a Lombard for Lady Lombarda'). Lombarda replies that she does not want to give up her identity for a man's: '*no'm volgr'aver per Bernard na Bernarda / e per n'Arnaut n'Arnauda appellada*' ('I would not wish to be called Bernarda for Bernard or Arnauda for Arnaut'). It has been suggested that Lombarda plays on feminine forms of names as a way of asserting her own distinctive voice.
Bib: Paden, W.D. (ed.), *The Voice of the Trobairitz*.

Longhi Lopresti, Lucia ▷Banti, Anna

Loos, Cécile Ines (1883–1959)
German-speaking Swiss novelist. Born in Basle, she was orphaned while young, and worked abroad as a governess until she had a first success with her novel *Matka Boska* (1929) – an intense metaphysical exploration of womanhood and motherhood. Women's destinies are central to all her work. *Die Rätsel der Turandot* (1931) (*The Enigmas of Turandot*) is a romantic biography of the dancer Turandot Manoville, and *Der Tod und das Püppchen* (1939) (*Death and the Little Doll*) tells of the experiences of a young girl in the Jura mountains. Its sequel, *Hinter dem Mond* (1942) (*Behind the Moon*), is the story of a woman sacrificing herself for the good of her family. Much of Loos's work remains unpublished.

Lopes de Janeiro Almeida, Júlia Valentina
▷Almeida, Júlia Lopes de

López de Córdoba, Leonor (c 1362–1412)
Spanish author of one of the classics of medieval literature, ▷*Memorias* (*Memoirs*). López was born in Calatayud. In 1366 she and her family were left in Navarre as hostages for the fulfilment of a treaty with Pedro I of Castile. She was married at the age of seven to Ruy Fernández de Hinestrosa, son of King Pedro's Chancellor of the Secret Seal.

Lord, The (1986)
A novel written in English by Soraya Antonius, a Palestinian born in Jerusalem, who now lives in Europe. The scene is Jaffa and the coast of Palestine extending north to Mount Lebanon,

with ruins of Crusader castles that serve as tourist attractions and a reminder of the wars over the Holy Land. The name of 'Our Lord' is evoked from the start, but his example is never truly followed. The time is the early 1930s, culminating in the first Arab revolution of 1936. Palestine is governed by British forces under a mandate from the League of Nations and the British officials, civil and military, could have been transferred live from E.M. Forster's (1879–1970) India. Their attitude to the missionary schools that educate the children of the 'meek childish Arabs' is reminiscent of the whites in ▷Doris Lessing's African novels. The voices in the narrative are multiple, cleverly caught by the main narrator, a journalist. She is researching the story of a man pursued and executed by the British authorities, described by many as 'the magician', but addressed by the local shopkeepers as *Sayyidna* (Our Lord).

Another voice is that of Miss Alice, the teacher at the Missionary School who arrived with her father at the turn of the century, fell in love with the country and the people and stayed. She too was betrayed by one of her compatriots, the High Commissioner's assistant, who fell in love with the pretty teacher, but finally married money to further his career. Tareq, the executed man, had been one of her favourite pupils, but neither she nor her father believed him when he protested that the knowledge he showed in his final exam was given to him from a source he did not know or understand. They accused him of cheating, and would not grant him the certificate that would have secured him a job with the government. Tareq has an Arab's characteristic reverence for his teacher, and comes to her when she is alone to show her proof of the extraordinary power that he possesses. She is troubled by the evidence, but has not enough faith to speak out in his defence.

The irony of the 'High Commissioner's thunder' pursuing the Man from Tarshiha', as the thunder of the Romans had pursued Jesus, is lost on the British police chief exercising his skills as sleuth and huntsman, though it is cynically pointed out to him by the Moslem sheiks, who refuse to help try the man for blasphemy.

Lorde, Audre (born 1934)

This Caribbean poet, novelist, essayist, lesbian, feminist and activist was born in the USA of Grenadian parents. Educated at the University of Mexico, Columbia University and Hunter College, she has been Professor of English at Hunter College since 1980. Her poetry has appeared in numerous periodicals and anthologies. Her published works include: *The First Cities* (1968); *Cables to Rage* (1970); *From a Land Where Other People Live* (1973) (which was nominated for the National Book Award for Poetry in 1974); *New York Head Shop and Museum* (1975); *The Black Unicorn* (1978); *The Cancer Journals* (1980) (in which she charts her own experience of, and struggle against, cancer); *Chosen Poems: Old and New* (1982); her

Audre Lorde

autobiographical novel, ▷*Zami: A New Spelling of My Name* (1982), and *Our Dead Behind Us* (1986). She has two significant collections of essays, ▷*Sister Outsider* and *A Burst of Light* (1988), which include discussion of the relationship of poetry to politics and the erotic.

For critical analysis of her poetry see Mari Evans (ed.), *Black Women Writers* (1983) and Barbara Christian, *Black Feminist Criticism* (1985).

Lothrop, Amy ▷Warner, Anna Bartlett

Lothrop, Harriet Mulford Stone (1844–1924)

US author of an endearing and enduring bestselling series of children's books about the 'Five Little Peppers'. The first Pepper book, ▷*The Five Little Peppers and How They Grew* (1881), focuses on the five siblings' childhoods. The subsequent Pepper books in the series follow the children's fortunes as they grow to adulthood in the rural USA. The Pepper books have sold millions of copies and retained their popularity for a century. Lothrop provided a rags-to-(almost)-riches variant of the male-centred, urban Horatio Alger series (Alger, 1832–1899, wrote over 100 books for boys). Lothrop's novels also featured more developed characters and plot. Her pseudonym was Margaret Sidney.

Louise de Savoie (1476–1531)

French author of a journal and poetic pieces. Daughter of Philippe, Duc de Savoie, and Marguerite de Bourbon, she married Charles de Valois, by whom she had two children: ▷Marguerite de Navarre and François I (1494–1547). The early deaths of Charles VIII (1470–1498), his four children and Louis XII (1462–1515), who had no male heirs, allowed her to realise her main ambition and bring her son to the throne. Her motto, *libris et liberis* (for books and children), indicates her interest in learning and the family. She ensured the education of her children by the best available scholars. Beautiful and intelligent, she was also grasping, and was involved in considerable political intrigue. She did not have enough money to assemble many important writers around her at the Château de Cognac in her youth, and it is said that she always preferred to take than to give. She played an important role in the Treaty of Cambrai in 1529 and was greatly missed by her son, if by few of the others who composed verses and funeral orations in her honour. Her *Journal* is written in a heavy rhetorical style and reveals her fierce egoism. Three poetic pieces have been attributed to her, and the only genuine sentiment in them seems to be maternal affection for her son.

Louw, Anna M. (born 1913)

Anna M. Louw

South African Afrikaans novelist, dramatist, short story writer and travel writer, born in the Calvinia district in the Cape. Her allegorical novel *Kroniek van Perdepoort* (1975) (*Chronicle of Perdepoort*), awarded the prestigious Hertzog Prize, chronicles the decline of a farming family engaged in re-burying the paterfamilias. She has written one book in English, *20 Days that Autumn* (1963): an account of four people's reactions to disturbances in the black townships of Langa and Nyanga in Cape Town, following the shootings at Sharpeville in 1960. This brought her the Olive Schreiner Prize for prose in 1964. She has also produced

two historical novels about Paul Kruger – *Die Banneling: Die Lyfwag* (1964) (*The Exile: The Bodyguard*) and *Die Groot Gryse* (1968) (*The Great Grey One*) – both critiques of Afrikanerdom.

Louw's first published work is the play *Goud* (1948) (*Gold*), followed by a radio drama, *Oom Kolie Gee Raad* (1965) (*Uncle Kolie Advises*). She has also written short stories, collected as *'n Geseënde Dag* (1969) (*A Blessed Day*), and three travel books, *Agter My 'n Albatros* (1959) (*An Albatross Behind Me*), *Die wat met Fluite Loop* (1967) (*Those Who Walk with Flutes*), and *Die Derde Tempel* (1978) (*The Third Temple*).

Her other novels are: *Die Onverdeelde Uur* (1956) (*The Undivided Hour*), *Die Koms van die Komeet* (1957) (*The Advent of the Comet*), *Die Voortreflike Familie Smit* (1962) (*The Excellent Smit Family*) and *Op die Rug van die Tier* (1981) (*Riding the Tiger*).

Love Affairs (1978)

Work by Japanese writer Mori Yoko (born 1940). Yoko is a housewife aged thirty-five. She has an English husband and a daughter, but her husband shows no interest in her, and she frets over her vanishing youth. She starts to love another man, keeping her family secret from him. She wants to recover the sparkle in her life, but when her family situation is disclosed their love affair ends. Nothing is changed and there is nothing left for her. The empty feeling in her heart continues to grow while she stays at home.

Löveid, Cecilie (born 1951)

Norwegian prose writer, lyric poet and dramatist. She grew up in Bergen with her grandparents, because both her parents worked at sea for long periods. She began to train as an artist but broke it off. At seventeen she had a baby. She made her début in an anthology in 1969 with young poets from Bergen. Today she is the only Norwegian dramatist with an international reputation. She is unique as a social modernist and has received many prizes for her work.

Her real début was the prose-lyrical novel *Most* (1972). She had an international breakthrough with the novel *Sug* (1979) (*Sea Swell*) in which she described a young woman as the prototype of a whole European generation of women, but in a 'new' language, a broken, lyrical voice, speaking as though from a psychotherapist's couch.

In the 1980s she has had a very big influence on modern European drama, with poetic plays about woman's desire as in *Måkespisere* (1983) (*Seagull Eaters*).

Love Letters Between a Nobleman and His Sister

Epistolary fiction by ▷Aphra Behn, based on the story of the adulterous and quasi-incestuous elopement and affair of Lady Henrietta Berkely and her brother-in-law, Forde, Lord Grey of Werke, and transposing the scene to France. The novel was originally published in three volumes from 1684 to 1687. Part one concentrates on the story of Sylvia and Philander, the second part follows Philander to Cologne, and the third part ends with the execution of the Duke of Monmouth after his attempt to depose James II.

Loveling, Virginie (1836–1923)

Flemish poet and novelist. Following the death of her father in 1846, the family lived in Ghent. Together with her sister, Rosalie (1834–1875), she made her début with ▷realistic, perceptive poems, usually with a sentimental undertone, *Gedichten* (1870) (*Poems*). The sisters also published two collections of short stories and impressions on the subjects of rural life and townspeople: *Novellen* (1874) (*Short Stories*), and *Nieuwe novellen* (1876) (*New Short Stories*). After Rosalie's death, Virginie Loveling's writings included the political vignettes *In onze Vlaamsche Gewesten* (1877) (*In Our Flemish Region*), and the novel *Sophie* (1885), describing a crisis of faith during the conflict over schools and religion. *Een dure eed* (1891) (*A Dear Oath*) gained her critical acclaim. Her later work included naturalistic novels with a more pessimistic view. In *Een revolverschot* (1911) (*A Gunshot*), among the best of her novels, the central theme is an ill-fated love affair. She also made a name for herself as a writer of children's books and essays. Together with her cousin, Cyriel Buysse, she wrote *Levensleer* (1912) (*A Philosophy of Life*), a humorous novel about the Frenchified bourgeoisie of Ghent.

Love Medicine (1984)

US novel by ▷Louise Erdrich which counters the romantic view of the doomed ▷Native American Indian as victim. It traces the lives of two Chippewa Native American families from 1934 to 1984. Each individual chapter is narrated from a particular character's point of view. The novel's structure reflects the Native American world view of the interconnection of all life. Erdrich emphasizes that the Native American's survival depends upon integrating past and present, masculine and feminine. The hunter / warrior tradition fails when it is not integrated with present-day realities, and it survives when it is integrated with a modern North American political sensibility. The hunter / warrior tradition also fails when it traps characters in gender-based roles; it can carry on when typically masculine traits such as power are integrated with feminine traits like nurturing.

Love of Worker Bees, The (1977)

This book, originally published in 1923, contains two novellas and a brief tale, 'Sisters', by the Russian revolutionary and diplomat ▷Aleksandra Kollontái. As the title suggests, all three deal in somewhat soap-opera fashion with the dilemmas of the Soviet 'new woman.' In 'Vasilisa Malygina', the eponymous heroine finds that her dedication to Bolshevik ideals does not mesh with her marriage to an anarchist turned slippery businessman under the New Economic Policy of the 1920s. In the end, pregnant, she leaves her husband to a more conventionally feminine rival and returns to agitational work in a factory, planning to set up a communal nursery for her baby. 'Three Generations' contrasts the lives of women who are progressive for their times: a populist grandmother who puts fulfilment in love above everything; her Marxist daughter, Olga, who finds different kinds of love in shared idealism with her revolutionary husband and passionate attraction to an 'unsympathetic and unprincipled' businessman, and tries to hold on to both; and her granddaughter, Zhenia, who practises a cheerful promiscuity. Zhenia regrets having sex with her mother's young lover, 'a true proletarian', solely for the pain it causes Olga, the only person whose love is important to her.

Lover, The (1985)

Translation of *L'Amant* (1984), autobiographical narrative by French writer ▷Marguerite Duras. It is structured around the story of a sexual relationship she had at the age of fifteen with a rich young Chinese man in Indo-China, which ended when she left the colony. This story of sexual passion is intermixed with reflections on Duras's family: her difficult relationship with her mother, and the latter's obsessive love for her wayward elder son. In this book, which won the Prix Goncourt, Duras discusses some of the ideas implicit in her other writings.

Lowell, Amy (1874–1925)

Amy Lowell

US poet and critic. Lowell was born into a distinguished Boston, Massachusetts, family. She was expected to lead a genteel life, but became celebrated for her eccentric personal behaviour, such as smoking cigarillos and wearing masculine clothing. After studying on her own in her father's library, she devoted herself to poetry.

Her first volume of poems, *A Dome of*

Many-Colored Glass (1912), was conventional in style and was influenced by Keats, whose biography she wrote in 1925. *Sword Blades and Poppy Seeds* (1914) and *Can Grande's Castle* (1918) display the influence of the ▷modernist Anglo-American poetry movement, imagism. Identifying herself particularly with the work of ▷H.D., Lowell experimented with language and rhythm, and adopted the idea that poetry should present an image. Her most interesting work experiments with unrhymed cadence, and develops what she calls 'polyphonic prose'. Lowell's venture into orientalism with her experimental translations of Chinese poetry in collaboration with Florence Ayscough in *Fir-Flower Tablets* (1921) are usually seen as less successful. She is best known as a promoter of imagism and modernist poetry, playing a key role in the production of three imagist anthologies, besides lecturing and writing criticism.

Her love poems, such as 'The Letter' (1919) and 'Madonna of the Evening Flowers' (1919), were composed for her collaborator and companion, Ada Dwyer Russell. 'The Sisters' in *What's O'Clock* (1925) chronicles a history of women poets. Lowell posthumously received a Pulitzer Prize for *What's O'Clock*.

Other works include: *Dream Drops or Stories from Fairy Land by a Dreamer* (1887), *Six French Poets* (1915), *Tendencies in Modern American Poetry* (1917), *Pictures of the Floating World* (1919), *Selected Poems* (1928), *Poetry and Poets* (1930) and *Complete Poetical Works of Amy Lowell* (1955).

Lowell Offering, The (1840–1845)
US literary periodical written by textile mill-workers in Lowell, Massachusetts. The New England ▷mill girls lived in the boarding-houses established by their employers. Growing out of workers' self-improvement societies, the *Offering* became internationally celebrated as testimony to the literary and educational potential of labourers and of women. Eventually rocked by conflict over whether the magazine should stay 'literary' or support workers' interests against management, the *Offering* folded and then became the *New England Offering* (1847–1850), a periodical much like the original, but with a broader range of contributors. Selections from the *Offering* were published in ▷*Mind Amongst the Spindles* (1844).
▷Farley, Harriet; Larcom, Lucy; *Voice of Industry, The*
Bib: Eisler, Benita (ed.), *The Lowell Offering: Writings by New England Mill Women (1840–45)*.

Lowther, Patricia Louise (1935–1975)
Canadian poet, born Patrica Tinmuth in Vancouver, British Columbia, where she spent her life. Lowther was murdered in September 1975, and her second husband, who died in prison in 1985, was convicted of the crime. Lowther had left school early, and worked at various clerical jobs. An active socialist and feminist, her short life was characterized by hardship and poverty. *This Difficult Flowering* (1968) contains poems exploring

women's experience; it was followed by a limited edition called *The Age of the Bird* (1972). *Milk Stone* (1974) shows a fully realized poetic voice. Lowther was profoundly affected by the work of Pablo Neruda, and *A Stone Diary* (which appeared posthumously in 1977) contains a sequence of 'letters' dedicated to his memory. Her poetry is lyrical and intensely personal, despite its political commitment and its struggle with pervasive injustice and violence. Although her corpus of work is small, it continues to exert a meaningful presence. A memorial prize is given every year in her name.

Loxandra (1960)
Greek novelist ▷Maria Iordanidou wrote this book in her late 60s. It was reissued many times because Greeks loved the direct vernacular language with which she described her life at the beginning of this century in Istanbul, when much of its population was still Greek. The book, despite the unhappy events it describes, is written with humour and love for the places lost to Greek inhabitants.

Loy, Mina (1882–1966)
English poet, painter and dramatist. She studied art in Munich, London and Paris, and later moved to Florence. Immersed in, and influenced by, the futurist movement, Loy insisted on a feminist reading of futurist aesthetics and cultural politics, as detailed in 'Aphorisms on Futurism' in *Camera Work* (1919). Loy later rejected futurism following the alignment of this movement with fascism. The collection of poems *Lunar Baedecker* (1923) looks at specifically female experiences. Her contributions to a variety of magazines are collected in *Lunar Baedecker and Time-Tables* (1958), and *Last Lunar Baedecker* (1982) forms her collected verse. Other works include the unfinished volume *Anglo-Mongrels and the Rose* (1925).

Loy, Rosetta (born 1931)
Italian novelist. Based in Rome, she is a highly respected writer who has won many literary prizes for her work. Her experience of growing up during the war years in the Italian countryside is chronicled in her writing. Perhaps her best-known work is *Le strade di polvere* (1987) (▷ *The Dust Roads of Monferrato*, translated into English in 1990), which chronicles the lives of a family of small farmers in 19th-century northern Italy. In her novels, frail human ambitions are offset against a strong and indifferent Nature.

Other works: *La bicicletta* (1974) (*The Bicycle*); *La porta dell'acqua* (1976) (*The Door to the Water*); *L'estate di Letuquè* (1982) (*Summer in Le Touquet*); *All'insaputa della notte* (1984) (*Unknown to Night*).

'Loyalist's Account of Certain Occurrences in Philadelphia . . ., A' (1892)
The North American diarist ▷Anna Rawle's account of Patriot reactions to the announced surrender of General Cornwallis at Yorktown on

22 October 1781. Although a Quaker, she was not without allegiances in the war and lamented the mistreatment of Loyalists in reaction to Cornwallis's surrender, envisaging it as the end of Philadelphia as 'that happy asylum for the Quakers that it once was'. Brief but well written, it is an interesting acknowledgement of the Quakers' declining control over Pennsylvania.

▷ Early North American Quaker women's writings

Loynaz, Dulce María (born 1903)

Cuban poet. She studied at home and published her first verses in *La Nación*, in 1920. In that year she also visited the United States. She was adopted by a general of the Cuban revolutionary army, Enrique Loynaz del Castillo, whose son, Enrique Loynaz del Castillo, was also a poet. Her poetry is part of ▷ *postmodernismo*, and is subjective and contemplative, showing an influence from the Spaniard Juan Ramón Gómez de la Serna (1888–1963). She was a lawyer until 1961. Her works include *Versos, 1920–1938* (1938) (*Verses, 1920–1938*); *Versos del agua y del amor* (1947) (*Verses of Water and Love*); *Jardín* (1951) (*Garden*), and *Últimos días de una casa* (1958) (*Last Days of a House*).

Loynes, Antoinette and Camille de (16th century)

Minor French poets. Antoinette de Loynes was the daughter of an ardent ▷ humanist and friend of the Dutch scholar Erasmus (1466–1536), who encouraged her in her studies. Shortly before 1544 she married Jean de Morel (1511–1581), the poet and orator. Praised for her exceptional beauty by many of the leading poets of her day who frequented the Morel salon in Paris, she produced a number of poems and sonnets, minor compositions and letters in Latin, few of which have survived. She wrote less than she might have, because of her diligent attitude to household duties and her desire to leave her husband free of such occupations in order to allow him to devote more time to study. Among other pieces, she composed an epigram on the death of a family friend, the poet Joachim Du Bellay (1522–1560), in keeping with the popularity of funeral verse in the salons of the period. The Morel household was known as the '*temple des Muses*' ('seat of the Muses'), where the whole family recited their verse compositions in Latin and French.

Camille de Loynes was the most celebrated of Antoinette's three daughters, known collectively as the '*trois perles du XVI siècle*' ('the three pearls of the 16th century'). A poetic dialogue with Du Bellay, entitled *Joachimi Bellaii et Camillae Morellae Dialogismus extemporalis*, survives. Camille also wrote a poetic lament on the death of Henri II (1519–1559) in Latin.

Bib: Keating, L.C., *Studies on the Literary Salon in France*.

L-Shaped Room, The (1960)

A novel by English writer ▷ Lynne Reid Banks. Her best-known work, it tells the story of Jane

Graham, an unmarried woman in her mid-twenties, whose first, joyless, sexual encounter makes her pregnant. Although this is the stuff of Victorian novels, as is her father's casting her out of his home, Jane's subsequent experiences are thoroughly modern ones. She decides to have the baby, gives up her job, and goes to live in a squalid London bed-sit – the L-shaped room of the title. There she befriends the other tenants in the house: the prostitutes in the basement; the scheming landlady, Doris; John, the jazz-player, whose blackness is such a novelty to Jane that for a long time she does not realize that he is gay, and the Jewish struggling writer, Toby, who becomes her lover. Much of the novel is given over to Jane's physical and emotional experiences of pregnancy and, as in ▷ Margaret Drabble's *The Millstone* (1965), Banks endorses her decision to be a single mother rather than to have an abortion (the only option for ▷ Rosamond Lehmann's heroine in ▷ *The Weather in the Streets*, 1936) or to agree to a marriage of convenience (when Jane again meets Terry, the father of her child-to-be, she refuses his chivalrous proposal). At the close of the novel, Jane gives birth to a son, and returns to her father's home, her relationship with Toby in suspension. Banks thus holds open the possibility of a 'happy' romantic ending, while refusing to give her heroine a safe and respectable closure in the shape of marriage and the family.

The great success of the novel was in large part due to its tapping into the images and concerns of its period – sex and the single girl, bed-sitter land, non-English identities such as the black man and the Jew, and aberrant sexualities. The depiction of John the 'negro' now seems ridiculous as well as racist – he is presented as 'primitive' and childlike – but Banks's intentions in giving him 'feminine' qualities (he is also domestic and nurturing) may have been to counter myths of the sexually threatening, aggressive black male. Throughout the novel, Banks shows her middle-class heroine being progressively liberated from her former prejudices and fears; her 'condition', which places her outside respectable suburban society, is the means to her enlightenment.

Banks produced a sequel a decade later, *The Backward Shadow* (followed by *Two's Company* in 1974), which picks up Jane's story from the point at which *The L-Shaped Room* leaves it. The comparative failure of the sequel reinforces the sense of *The L-Shaped Room* as a novel of its time, not 'to be continued'. It was made into a film, starring the French actress Leslie Caron – the film-makers, for reasons which merit speculation, turning the English heroine of the novel into a French woman in London.

Luanto, Regina di (?1862–1914)

Italian novelist. Her pseudonym is Contessa Anna Roti, partly an anagram of her real name Guendalina Lipperini. She married, but soon separated from her husband. She was too liberal, and too questioning, to fit into a traditional family structure, and lived an extravagant and independent life, mainly based in Florence and Rome. The society which she depicts in her novels is that aristocratic society to which she belonged, but she never fails to present it from a questioning and non-conformist point of view which analyses the conflicts between the desires of the individual, particularly the female individual, and the regulations of society. Luanto's literary output was prolific. She wrote of hysteria in *Salamandra* of 1892, of murder and madness in *Un martirio* (*Martyrdom*) of 1894, and of the hidden sexual drives of apparently virtuous and devoted wives in *Le virtuose* (*The Virtuous Ones*) of 1912. The conflict between socially sanctioned appearance and messy, complicated reality is a constant theme which runs throughout her work.

Lubert, Mlle de (?1710–?1779)

French writer of prose fiction. The daughter of a parliamentary president, she chose not to marry, and lived quietly in the country. Her works, published anonymously, consist mainly of fairytales, and the 1743 edition of the tale of the misogynist prince *Tecserion* (an anagram of *sec et noir*, dry and black) includes an '*Apologie des contes de fées*' ('In praise of fairytales'). The most successful of her tales, *La Princesse camion* (1743) (*The Waggon Princess*), was published in the collection *Cabinet des fées* (*The Fairies' Boudoir*) of the same year. Her short novel, *Léonille* (1755), was acclaimed in her lifetime.

her other works are: *Le Prince glacé et la princesse étincelante* (1743) (*The Frozen Prince and the Sparkling Princess*); *La Princesse couleur de rose et le prince Céladon* (1743) (*The Pink Princess and Prince Porcelain*); *La Princesse sensible et le prince Typhon* (1743) (*The Tender Princess and Prince Typhoon*); *La Princesse Coque d'Oeuf et le prince Bonbon* (1745) (*Princess Eggshell and Prince Sweet*); *La Veillée Galante* (1747) (*The Romantic Evening*); *Amadis des Gaules* (1750) (*Amadis of Gaul*); *Les hauts faits d'Esplandion* (1751) (*The Noble Deeds of Esplandion*); *Blancherose* (1751) (*Rose White*); *Mourat et Turquia* (1752) (also attributed to ▷Lussan or ▷Dame Dalibard); *Histoire secrète du prince Croqu'éton et de la princesse Foirette* (*The Secret Story of Prince Croqu'éton and Princess Foirette*).
Bib: Robert, R., *Le Conte de fée*.

Lucy (1991)

Novel by Caribbean writer ▷Jamaica Kincaid. *Lucy*, unlike Kincaid's two previous works of fiction which are set in the Caribbean, focuses on the life of a nineteen-year-old West Indian girl who goes to work as an *au pair* in New York. During this period in the USA, Lucy explores her relationship with her mother and her island, as well as her own sexuality.

Lucy Temple (1828)

US novel by ▷Susanna Haswell Rowson. Also known as *Charlotte's Daughter; or, The Three Orphans: A Sequel to Charlotte Temple*. Rowson's ▷*Charlotte Temple* (1791), near the beginning of her career, was the first US bestselling novel. *Lucy Temple*, marking the end of Rowson's career, continues the story through the next generation.

Ludlow, Johnny ▷Wood, Mrs Henry

Ludwig, Paula (1900–1974)

German poet. From a poverty-stricken broken family, she spent her youth looking after her brothers and sisters, and working as a maid. At seventeen she had a son and became a painter's model and an actress. In 1920, she published a volume of singularly original, dreamlike verse, *Die selige Spur* (*The Holy Tracks*). Her love poems, *Dem dunklen Gott* (1932) (*To the Dark God*), are the result of her long-standing relationship with the poet Ivan Goll (1891–1950).

Luft, Lia (born 1938)

Brazilian novelist, chronicle writer, poet, literary critic and translator. She writes in an intimate, Existential mode. Her novel *O quarto fechado* (1984) (*The Closed Room*) centres on the failed life of a woman who abandoned her art as a piano player to get married and to have children. She has twins, whom she does not understand, and one of which dies, reflecting the stifling domestic ambience and perhaps the conflicts existing beteween the Brazilian and the German cultures in the southern part of the country, an area in which Luft has lived. She has won poetry prizes, among them the Alfonsina Storni Prize in Buenos Aires.

Other works include: *Canções de limiar* (1963) (*Songs of the Threshold*), *Matéria do cotidiano* (1978) (*Everyday Matters*), and *A asa esquerda do anjo* (1981) (*The Left Wing of the Angel*).

Lukhmánova, Nadezhda Aleksandrovna (1840–1907)

Russian prose writer, dramatist, and essayist. Lukhmánova came to literature late in her life, but in a short time she wrote over twenty books and many plays that were popular in their day. As she wrote in 1900, 'As a woman I tried to write specifically for women and as far as I could arouse in them the best and most honest feelings . . .' Widowed in 1873, she worked as a translator, and wrote for children. In 1893 she began publishing adult fiction with 'Twenty Years Ago (From Life in an Institute)', the first of three autobiographical tales. Like many early works by women writers, it describes the final years of girlhood and the transition to womanhood. In it, Lukhmánova touches on some of her abiding themes: scorn at the absurdity of girls' education and the strict discipline in boarding schools; a high regard for marriage and motherhood. Her pamphlets and essays include *On the Position of Unmarried Daughters Within the Family* (1896); *On Happiness* (1898); and the handsomely produced *A Woman's Guide* (1898) which had sections on professions (artists, doctors, mathematicians), short biographies of famous women including ▷Bashkírtseff and ▷Harriet Beecher Stowe, women's organizations, and women's education. Her popular and slick stories were usually centred on a crisis in love. Occasionally she wrote a beautiful tale like 'The Miller's Wife' (*Eternal Questions*, 1896), which depicts the complex figure of a village priest who manages to reconcile Church doctrine and his own humane promptings.

At the turn of the century, Lukhmánova gave public lectures on women's issues, her travels abroad, and other popular topics. During the Russo–Japanese War (1904–1905), she worked as a volunteer nurse.

▷Kollontái, Aleksandra; *Happiness*

Lumley, Joanna Fitzalan (c 1537–1576/77)

English translator. She was the eldest of the two daughters of Henry and Katherine Grey Fitzalan. About 1549 she married John Lumley, a schoolmate of her brother at Cambridge. John Lumley, himself a scholar, translator, and book collector – he owned one of the largest private libraries of the day – apparently favoured his wife's scholastic and literary endeavours. Lumley is best-known as the first translator of a Greek drama into English. Her work, an abridged prose ▷translation of Euripides, ▷*Iphigenia at Aulis*, exists in a rough copy book, also containing some Latin letters to her father, and translations of Isocrates out of Greek into Latin.

▷Companionate marriage; Humanism (England)

Lunga vita di Marianna Ucria, La (1990) (*The Long Life of Marianna Ucria*)

A novel by Italian writer ▷Dacia Maraini, set in 18th-century Sicily. Marianna, the protagonist, is deaf and dumb as the result of shock following her rape as a child. The rape was committed by her uncle, whom she then married, according to the wishes of her family, at the age of thirteen, unaware that he was, in fact, the rapist. After the death of the authority figures in her life (her father and husband) Marianna is free to depart with the peasant girl who is her only friend. They leave for Europe on a voyage of self-education. Maraini appears to be making some interest points here about male–female relationships, in that society and that period, at least. She clearly advocates female ties as facilitative of learning and self-knowledge, while male characters in the text are both violent and authoritarian. She draws attention to the female silence imposed by men and, for Marianna, the only way to break through this silence is to write. The novel underlines Maraini's versatility as a writer and is at once informative and absorbing. It won the Campiello Prize in 1990.

Lunn, Janet Louise (born 1928)

Canadian children's writer. Born Janet Swoboda in Dallas, Texas, she emigrated to Canada in 1946, and was educated at Queen's University. She is the mother of five children, and was children's editor at Clarke Irwin Publishers in Toronto from 1972 to 1975. Her books include

Double Spell (1968), a psychic mystery that explores the potential of creative power; *The Twelve Dancing Princesses* (1979), a fairy tale; *Larger than Life* (1979), a history; *The Root Cellar* (1981), about the American Civil War; *Shadow in Hawthorn Bay* (1986); *Amos's Sweater* (1988), and *One Hundred Shining Candles* (1990). Lunn succeeds in writing children's books that are both sophisticated and satisfying. She lives in Hillier, Ontario.

Luo Shu (1903–1938)

Chinese writer. First educated along classical lines in early youth, Luo Shu later studied literature in France. She attracted wide-spread attention by the publication of her novel *Wife of Another Man* (1936), a grim tragedy of a peasant who sells his wife. After her death in childbirth, Luo Shu's stories were collected and published by the prestigious writer, Ba Jin.

Lurie, Alison (born 1926)

US novelist and critic. Born in Chicago and raised in New York, Lurie graduated from Radcliffe College, and currently teaches at Cornell University. Immensely popular, her fiction is sometimes compared to ▷Jane Austen's because of its focus on social mores and its skilled use of irony.

The theme of adultery runs through Lurie's early novels. *Love and Friendship* (1962) and *The War Between the Tates* (1974) take up the theme of adultery within a campus setting. The latter, written in the present continuous, sets marital breakdown and generational conflict against the political upheavals of US campuses in the 1970s, through the story of the effects of a university professor's affair with his hippy graduate student, Wendy. The reader's sympathies are mobilized in favour of his wife, Erica, faced with approaching middle age, her appallingly fractious children and the disappointment of the marriage. *Only Children* (1979) exploits a *faux naif* perspective, viewing the games of a group of adulterous adults on a country weekend through the eyes of a child.

Foreign Affairs (1984) uses a US academic's research trip to London to explore isolation, middle age and social manners. Lurie comically mixes seemingly incompatible worlds, through the unexpected liaison between the aggressively spinsterish Virginia Miner, a researcher in schoolchildren's folk-rhymes, and Chuck Mumpson 'an engineer from Tulsa specializing in waste-disposal systems'. Her 1988 novel, *The Truth about Lorin Jones*, explores the nature of biography and the obsessive nature of writing about another's life, when Polly Alter, a lesbian-feminist art historian, tracks the life of a dead artist, Lorin Jones. Interesting for the staging of this obsession, the novel is problematic in that the process returns Polly to respectable heterosexuality.

Other works include: *The Nowhere City* (1965), *Imaginary Friends* (1967) and *Real People* (1970), and the non fiction works *Fabulous Beasts* (1981),

The Language of Clothes (1982) and *Don't Tell the Children: Subversive Children's Literature* (1990).

Lusarreta, Pilar de (1914–1967)

Argentinian dramatist and novelist. She lectured, translated, and wrote art criticism for the press and literary criticism for the radio. Her first play, *Casa en venta* (*House for Sale*), was performed in 1925, and she published her first book of narratives, *Job el opulento* (*Job the Rich*) in 1928. She won several prizes for her theatre, cinema and narrative productions, and many of her manuscripts were published posthumously.

Other works: *La herencia del bárbaro* (1929) (*The Inheritance of The Barbarian*); *Celimena sin corazón* (1935) (*Celimena Without a Heart*); *Iconografía de Manuelita* (1937) (*Iconograph of Manuelita*); *El culto de los héroes* (1939) (*The Cult of The Heroes*); *El amor a los sesenta* (1942) (*Love at Sixty*); *Cristina o la gracia de Dios* (1943) (*Cristina, or The Grace of God*); *Alondra* (1943) (*Skylark*); *Cinco dandys porteños* (1943) (*Five Dandies from Buenos Aires*). Novels: *El espejo de acero* (1944) (*The Steel Mirror*); *La gesta de Roger de Flor* (1945) (*The Epic of Roger de Flor*); *Niño Pedro* (1955) (*Boy Pedro*); *Potro blanco* (1961) (*White Colt*); *El manto de Noé* (1965) (*Noah's Cloak*); *Los sueños de unos días de verano* (1970) (*The Dreams of Some Summer Days*), and *Hombres en mi vida* (1971) (*Men in my life*).

Lussan, Marguerite de (1682–1758)

French writer of prose fiction. Believed to be the illegitimate daughter of the Comte de Soisson, who provided for her education. An obituary, often cited, insists on the unfemininity of her voice and appearance. Noted for her lively intellect, she was encouraged in her work by Le Huet. The merit of her writing led to rumours of male collaborators, especially regarding her first (and successful) novel *L'Histoire de la comtesse de Gondez* (1730) (*The Story of the Countess of Gondez*). She produced a collection of magical fairytales, *Les Veillées de Thessalie* (1731) (*Evenings in Thessaly*), and turned in later life to historical subjects: *Anecdotes de la cour de Phillipe-Auguste* (1733–38) (*Anecdotes from the Court of Phillipe-Auguste*); *Anecdotes de la cour de Childéric* (1736) (*Anecdotes from the Court of Childéric*); *Anecdotes de la cour de François Ier* (1748) (*Anecdotes from the Court of François I*); *Anecdotes de la cour d'Henri II* (1749) (*Anecdotes from the Court of Henry II*); *Marie d'Angleterre* (1749) (*Mary of England*); *Histoire et règne de Charles VI* (1753) (*The Life and Reign of Charles VI*); *Histoire et règne de Louis XI* (1755) (*The Life and Reign of Louis XI*); *Histoire de la révolution du royaume de Naples* (1757) (*History of the Revolution of Naples*), and *Vie de Louis Bable Bertonde Crillon* (1757) (*The Life of Bable Bertonde Crillon*). Her tale, *Mourat et Turquia* (1752) is also attributed to ▷Lubert or ▷Françoise-Thérèse Dalibard.

Lussu, Joyce Salvadori (born 1912)

Italian poet and novelist. Brought up in an anti-fascist family, she was involved in political struggle from the time of her adolescence. She became a captain in the *Giustizia e libertà* (Justice and Freedom) ▷Resistance group. Her political experiences of this period form the backdrop to *Fronti e frontiere; Collana della liberazione* (1945) (*Freedom Has No Frontier*, translated into English in 1969). She studied philosophy at Heidelberg University, and went on to work in the niversities of the Sorbonne and Lisbon. A contributor to many Italian magazines, with essays on both literature and politics, Lussu has translated the work of many other poets, and is especially interested in those of the Third World. A feminist, she is concerned with struggles against colonialism, and is also active in the ecology movement. These interests are reflected in her writings, as the titles often, indicate.

Her other works include: *Liriche* (1939) (*Poetry*); *Donne come te* (1957) (*Women Such As You*); *Poesie d'amore di Nazim Hikmet* (1965) (*Love Poems by Nazim Hikmet*); *Tradurre poesia* (1967) (*Translating Poetry*); *Le inglesi in Italia* (1970) (*English Women in Italy*); *Padre, Padrone, Padreterno* (1976) (*Father, Master, Eternal Father*); *L'acqua del 2000* (1976) (*Water in the Year 2000*); *L'uomo che voleva nascere donna* (1978) (*The Man Who Would Have Been Female*); *Che cos'è un marito?* (1979) (*What Is a Husband?*); *Il Libro Perogno su donne, streghe e sibille* (1981) (*Women, Witches and Sibyls*); *Donne, guerra e società* (1982) (*Women, War and Society*).

▷Neorealisn (Italy)

Lütken, Hulda (1896–1947)

Danish lyric poet and prose writer. Lütken was born in Jylland, and had gipsy blood in her veins, which she used to create her own personal mythology. Her temper was as violent as her art. Her sources of inspiration were numerous: ▷psychoanalysis, surrrealism, Expressionism, but also ▷social realism. She was a young girl when she had her first poems published. In the years from 1927 to 1945 she wrote nine collections of poems; often love poems where love contains death, desire is overwhelming, and the lover leaves the female character. The fear of losing love leads to the death of love.

As a prose writer, her principal book is *Mennesket paa Lerfødder* (1943) (*Man on Clay Feet*), a very experimental, introspective novel, where the female character has to change into a son and be crucified to join her father. Together with Bodil Bech (1889–1942), Hulda Lütken is the most important ▷modernist, experimental writer in the years between World Wars I and II. Her modernism is linked to a mystical religiousness, and expresses a universe where the sexes are not fixed, and desire is the driving force.

Luxemburg, Rosa (1870–1919)

German-Polish revolutionary, feminist, pacifist and one of the founders of the German Communist Party. The daughter of a cultured Jewish family, she joined a revolutiorary group at her high school in Warsaw, and had to flee to

Switzerland when she was only eighteen years old. She studied economics and law in Zurich, and in 1896, in order to gain German citizenship, married the anarchist Gustav Lubecks. Together with Karl Liebknecht (1871–1919) and ▷Clara Zetkin (1857–1933) she ran the revolutionary Spartacus Movement, and generally led the campaign for socialism in Germany until she was murdered by the police in 1919. A gifted and lucid writer, she composed powerful political tracts, such as *Massenstreik, Partei und Gewerkschaften* (1906) (*Mass Strike, Party and Trade Unions*), as well as important works on economics, such as *Die Akkumulation des Kapitals* (1912) (*The Accumulation of Capital*) and *Einführung in die Nationalökonomie* (1912) (*An Introduction to Economics*). She spent most of World War I in prison, where she wrote moving personal letters to friends, as well as the stirring clandestine pamphlet *Junius* (1915), which is a penetrating analysis of the failings of Social Democracy.

Lu Xin'er (born 1949)

Chinese novelist and short story writer. Lu graduated from the Central Institute of Drama and is now settled in Shanghai. She specializes in women's themes, and her earlier works were fired by idealism and filled with images of women who overcome obstacles by pure strength of will and individual striving. *Oh, Bluebird!* (1982) and *The Structure of Beauty* are typical of this phase. Her later works, such as the short stories 'The One and the Other' and 'The Sun Is Not Out Today', are tinged with irony and take apart the myth of the 'liberated' woman for a closer look. Her latest stories are collected in *Born Woman* (1990).
Bib: Translation of short stories in *The Serenity of Whiteness*, selected and translated by Zhu Hong, and *Chinese Literature*, Winter 1990.

Lu Yin (1899–1934)

Chinese writer. An active participant in the May Fourth Movement (1919), Lu Yin started to write and publish while working as a teacher and administrator in various parts of China. Themes of love and struggle against destiny abound in her stories, as well as the inner conflicts of a generation on the threshold of change. A note of melancholy pervades her work, though on the whole she brings out forcefully the rebellious spirit of the new woman of the age. *The Ivory Ring* (1934), *Autobiography*, *The Homecoming Cranes* (1931) and *Heart of Women* (1933) are some of her most popular titles. Her career was cut short by death in childbirth. Highly regarded in her time, Lu Yin's reputation was on a par with ▷Bing Xin, her contemporary.

Lyall, Edna (1857–1903)

▷Pseudonym of British novelist Ada Allen Bayly. She was born in Brighton, Sussex, and after the deaths of both her parents moved to her uncle's home in Caterham. Lyall supported woman's ▷suffrage, was a committed Liberal and involved herself in charitable and social work. Her novels

reflect her Christian religious views, but are more than simple moral tracts. With her second work, *Donavan* (1882), she became an extremely popular writer and her subsequent works ran to numerous editions. *We Two* (1884) and *Hope the Hermit* (1898) were especially successful. Other works include *Doreen* (1894), in which she supported the movement for Irish Home Rule, and her last novel *The Hinderers* (1902), which protested against the Boer War.
Bib: Escreet, J.M., *Life*; Payne, G.A., *Life*.

Lymberaki, Margarita (born 1910)

Greek novelist, dramatist and poet. She studied law and painting. Her first novel, *The Trees*, published in 1945, was not received with any great enthusiasm by the critics. But her second novel, *The Straw Hats* (1946), was hailed as a masterpiece. In 1950 it was published in French, also to great acclaim. It is the story of three young girls pursuing different paths in life. The style is characteristic of many of the novels of adolescence written at that time. Lymberaki was the first woman to write about women in this style. She subsequently went to France, where she wrote a novel in French, *The Secret Bed* (1950). She also wrote there, in Greek, *The Other Alexander* (1950), a novel completely modern in style. Lymberaki had learned Greek and French simultaneously, something she admits had made her feel as if she were living on the margins of both the Greek and French worlds, never feeling completely part of either. The main character in her play *The Holy Prince* is similarly trapped in a dual consciousness of East and West. Lymberaki makes great use of myth in her work, which she says 'corresponds to personal imagery'. *Erotica* is a novel about conflicts between the two sexes which never reach a peaceful solution. She has also written scripts for films, such as *Phedra*, a modern version of the famous myth of the rejected lover. In 1972 she published a collection of poems. She now lives in Paris.
Bib: Sachinis, A., *Our Contemporary Literature*.

Lynch, Marta (1925–1985)

Argentinian novelist and short story writer. Her participation in Arturo Frondisi's government (1956–1958) provides the background for her first novel, *La alfombra roja* (1962) (*The Red Carpet*), considered by many to be a *roman à clef* of Argentinian politics. Others consider it a psychological study of an election campaign. After Doctor Aníbal Rey, the protagonist, is elected president and stands alone in his residence, the writer revives the myth of the *caudillo* (chief) and questions the judiciousness of having too much concentration of power. Her novel *La Señora Ordoñez* (1968) was widely-read. She committed suicide in 1985.

Other works: *Al Vencedor* (1965) (*To the Winner*); *Cuentos tristes* (1966) (*Sad Stories*); *El cruce del río* (1970) (*The River Crossing*); *Cuentos de colores* (1972) (*Stories of Colours*); *La penúltima versión de la colorada Villanueva* (1978) (*The*

Penultimate Version of the Coloured Villanueva); *Los años de fuego* (1980) (*Years of Fire*); *Toda la función* (1982) (*The Whole Show*); *Informe bajo llave* (1983) (*Report Under Lock and Key*); *Páginas de Marta Lynch seleccionadas por la autora* (1983) (*Pages from Marta Lynch, Selected by the Author*); *El cruce del río* (1948) (*The River Crossing*), and *No te duermas, no me dejes* (1985) (*Don't sleep, don't leave me*).

Lyra, Carmen (1888–1951)

Pseudonym of Costa Rican novelist and journalist María Isabel Carvajal. She guided the intellectual direction of the Communist Party, but, in spite of her knowledge of Marxist theory, she never wrote explicitly about politics in her books. After the 1948 revolution she lived in exile. Her style is simple, derived from popular language, and realistic. She is part of the important group of Spanish American women writers who appeared after the advent of ▷*modernismo*. She wrote children's books, such as the novel *Las fantasías de Juan Silvestre* (1918) (*The Fantasies of Juan Silvestre*), and the famous book of short stories *Los cuentos de mi tía Panchita* (1920) (*The Stories of My Aunt Panchita*), taken from different popular sources. The novel *En una silla de rodas* (1918) (*In a Wheelchair*) presents a poetic and sentimental version of ▷*costumbrismo*. It is based on the idea that all of us are in part or entirely linked to a wheel-chair. The book takes place during a time-span of twenty years, and is narrated by Sérgio, who is handicapped because of poliomylitis in his childhood. Sérgio uses the third-person singular or his journals, letters or recollections to tell the story. The South American Indian Canducha, who serves him, feels that she is linked to the house, for, were she taken away from it, she would die like a seed. The author establishes a certain intimacy with the reader by using diminutives of familiarity and warm emotions.

Lyrics (Middle English, secular)

There are many anonymous Middle English lyrics in which the speaker is female, and some, at least, of these may have been composed by women: for example laments, cradle songs, songs of betrayed maidens etc.
Bib: Brown, C. and Robbins, R. H. (eds.), *Index of Middle English Verse*; Robbins, R. H. and Cutler, J. L. (eds.), *Supplement to Index of Middle English*

Verse; Barratt, Alexandra, *Women's Writing in Middle English*.

Lysenko, Vera (1910–1975)

Pen-name of Vera Lesik, Canadian novelist, journalist and social historian, who was born in Winnipeg to Ukrainian parents who had emigrated to Canada in 1903. She attended the University of Manitoba (1930), and published, under various ▷pseudonyms, political articles informed by her ethnic, immigrant and working-class experience. *Men in Sheepskin Coats: A Study in Assimilation* (1947) is a feminist and politically astute study of Ukrainian Canadians, the first to be written in English by an Ukrainian-Canadian. *Yellow Boots* (1954) and *Westerly Wild* (1956) both have a strong ethnic focus, and develop interesting and unusual heroines.

Lyttleton, Edith (1874–1945)

New Zealand novelist and poet. Edith Lyttleton was born in Tasmania and moved to New Zealand as a child. Lyttleton wrote and published stories and poems extensively while resident in New Zealand, always under a pseudonym (first 'Keron Hale' and later 'G.B. Lancaster') as her family 'hated publicity in men and denied it to women'. The Lyttleton family were part of the New Zealand and Australian colonial squattocracy, and her novels and stories often focus on questions of class. However, writing under a pseudonym which implies masculinity meant that Lyttleton also wrote stories and novels which focused on the activities and society of men, in the manner of Henry Lawson or Rudyard Kipling. After they left New Zealand in 1908, the Lyttleton family spent a member of years travelling in Europe and the Americas, and this movement is reflected in the novels Lyttleton wrote, often family-sagas focusing on the history of a particular region. Lyttleton's last known (Lancaster) novel *Pageant* was particularly successful in the USA. During the war Lyttleton was busy with war work.

Works (a selective list): *Sons O'Men* (stories) (1904); *The Tracks We Tread*, (1907); *A Spur To Smite*, (1905); *Jim of the Ranges*, (1910): *The Honorable Peggy*, (1911); *Pageant*, (1933); *The World is Yours*, (1933); *Promenade*, (1938); *Grand Parade*, (1945).
▷Romance writing, New Zealand

M

Macaulay, Catharine (1731–1791)
English historian and Whig radical. In 1760 she married the physician George Macaulay, and in 1763 began to publish her long 'anti-Royalist' *History of England from the Accession of James I to that of the Brunswick Line* (1763–1783) (compare, for example, ▷Mary Astell's Tory history). Her husband died in 1766, and she became ill, but went to France in 1777 and visited the US in 1784, staying with President George Washington (1732–1799). She was abused for her second marriage to the younger William Graham. She responded to philosopher Thomas Hobbes (1588–1679) and Edmund Burke (1729–1797), and again took issue with Burke's *Reflections on the Revolution in France* (1790). Her *Letters on Education* (1790) influenced ▷Mary Wollstonecraft's ▷*Vindication of the Rights of Woman*. In the *Letters* (addressing 'Hortensia') she wrote, 'The situation and education of women . . . is precisely that which must necessarily tend to corrupt and debilitate both the powers of mind and body.'
▷*Essay to Revive the Antient Education of Gentlewomen, An*
Bib: Ferguson, Moira (ed.), *First Feminists*.

Macaulay, Rose (1881–1958)
English poet, novelist, travel writer and critic. Born into an Anglo-Catholic family, Macaulay reworked her dissatisfaction with home life in her first novel, *Abbots Verney* (1906). Her clandestine relationship with the married writer Gerald O'Donovan caused her to sever all connections with the Church. Macaulay produced twenty-three novels, many of which are concerned with themes of reluctant exile. Her novels of the 1920s, including *Potterism* (1920) and *Dangerous Ages* (1921), are social satires. *Orphan Island* (1924) interrogates the notion of civilization, an issue taken up again in *The World My Wilderness* (1950), which explores ▷modernist notions of urban and moral desolation. The semi-autobiographical *The Towers of Trebizond* (1956) won the James Tait Black Memorial Prize. Her criticism includes studies of the poet Milton (1934) and the novelist E.M. Forster (1938), and her letters have been collected in three volumes, including *Letters to a Friend* (1961).

Macdonald, Caroline (1948)
New Zealand children's author resident in Australia. Macdonald began writing fiction in 1982, and in 1983 a Choysa Bursary led to her first novel, *Elephant Rock*, about a twelve-year-old coming to terms with her mother's terminal illness. This won the New Zealand Library Association's Esther Glen Medal in 1984. *Visitors* (1984), a haunting extra-terrestrial story, was New Zealand Children's Book of the Year in 1985. For a futuristic story, *The Lake at the End of the World* (1988), Macdonald was runner-up in the *Guardian* Children's Fiction Award in 1990. The author believes that child protagonists, a little out of step with the organized adult world and thus more open to suggestions of fantasy, allow her to experiment with future fiction, science fiction, the mystical and supernatural. Her protagonists are also frequently isolated from their peers, so relate mainly to adults, allowing Macdonald to explore parent–child relations.

Macdonald, June Elizabeth Gostwycke (1864–1922)
Canadian poet and short story writer, born June Roberts, sister of the poet Charles G.D. Roberts. She was educated in Fredericton, and at the University of New Brunswick, and taught at the School for the Blind in Halifax in 1891. She married her cousin and went west in 1912, but separated from him and returned to Ottawa in 1915. Her poems, collected in *Poems* (1885), and *Northland Lyrics* (1899) celebrate nature.

MacEntee, Máire ▷Mhac An tSaoi, Máire

MacEwan, Gwendolyn (1941–1987)
Canadian poet and fiction writer, born in Toronto, Ontario, who left school at the age of eighteen determined to write. Two pamphlets of poetry, *The Drunken Clock* and *Selah*, appeared in 1961, followed by a large number of poetry collections: *The Rising Fire* (1963); *A Breakfast for Barbarians* (1966); *The Armies of the Moon* (1972); *Magic Animals* (1974); *The Fire-Eaters* (1976); *The T.E. Lawrence Poems* (1982), and *Earthlight* (1982). She twice received the Governor General's Award for Poetry, for *The Shadow-Maker* (1969), and posthumously for *Afterworlds* (1987). Her poetry is strongly mythopoeic. She published two novels, *Julian the Magician* (1963) and *King of Egypt, King of Dreams* (1971), as well as two collections of short fiction, *Noman* (1972) and *Noman's Land* (1985), which reflect her acknowledged fascination with the interface between the 'real' world and a dream or fantasy world. Her engagement with myth, metaphor, and symbol led her to travel in the Mediterranean, out of which she wrote a memoir, *Mermaids and Ikons: A Greek Summer* (1978). She adapted Euripides's *The Trojan Women* for the stage in 1978, and published the translation in 1981. She also wrote three books for children.
Bib: Bartley, J., *Invocations: The Poetry and Prose of Gwendolyn MacEwan*.

Macgoye, Marjorie Olhude (born 1928)
Kenyan poet and novelist, Macgoye was born in Southampton in 1928. After studying at Royal Holloway College and Birkbeck College she went to Kenya in 1954 as a missionary bookseller and has had various jobs as a bookseller, editor and teacher. She started publishing stories in magazines in the mid-1960s and, later, two collections of her poetry and a novel were published in East Africa. She is married to a Luo doctor, is the mother of four children, and took up Kenyan citizenship in 1964 after independence. She is deeply committed to her Luo community. *Growing up at Lima School* (1970)

is a novel for children, *Murder in Majengo* (1972) an acclaimed thriller which began the Oxford University Press New Fiction from Africa series, and *Song of Nyarloka* (1977) contains lyric poems. ▷*Coming to Birth* (1986), winner of the 1986 Sinclair Prize of Fiction, parallels the emergence of a new type of Kenyan woman and the emergence of a new nation as it traces the female protagonist's development between 1956 and 1978. Her latest novel, *The Present Moment* (1987), centres on elderly women from different tribes as they talk about their lives and about being caught between the old Africa and the new. In *Street Life* (1987) Nairobi street characters are revealed in their struggle to live 'decently' on the pavement. *The Story of Kenya* (1986) is non-fiction.

MacGregor, Mary Esther (1876–1961)
Canadian novelist, born Mary Miller. She was educated in Toronto, then taught at Orillia, where she married the Reverend D. MacGregor. She wrote religious biographies and moralistic, uplifting novels under the pseudonym Marian Keith.

Machado, Gilka (1893–1980)
Brazilian poet. She began to write poetry as a child, and as an adult supported her family by working for the Rio Railway Company. Her first book, *Cristais partidos* (1915) (*Broken Crystals*), gave new life to the post-symbolist style, combining her literary abilities with erotic writing. Initially, her poetry was attacked as immoral, but later critics recognized her literary value. In 1979 she won the Machado de Assis Prize from Academia Brasileira de Letras.

Other works: *A revelação dos perfumes* (1916) (*A Revelation of Perfumes*), *Estado de alma* (1917) (*Condition of the Soul*); *Poesias (1915–1917)* (1918) (*Poems, 1915–1917*); *Mulher nua* (1922) (*Naked Woman*); *Meu glorioso pecado* (1928) (*My Glorious Soul*); *Sublimação* (1938) (*Sublimation*); *Velha poesia* (1965).

Machado, Luz (born 1916)
Venezuelan poet, essayist and journalist, who also writes under the names Luz Machado de Arnao and Agata Cruz. At university she studied law, philosophy and letters. Besides writing for the Venezuelan press, she was a member of the ▷*Viernes* Group of poets. She stated that she wanted her books to be universal, not feminist. Her long epic poem 'Canto al Orinoco' (1953) ('Song to the Orinoco'), which has been translated into French (1955), was inspired by the myths and legends of her native land. From 'Ramón Medina' (1962), a poem in her first collection, to *Ronda* (1941) (*Round*), to *Sonetos nobles y sentimentales* (1956) (*Notable and Sentimental Sonnets*), she has sustained an essentially lyrical tone that combines the natural elements of the Venezuelan world with human truth as she sees it.

Other works: *Variaciones en tono de amor* (1943) (*Variations in a Love Tone*); *Vaso de resplandor* (1946) (*Radiant Glass*); *La espiga amarga* (1950)

(*The Bitter Seed*); *Crónicas sobre Guyana, 1946–68)* (1984) (*Reports From Guyana, 1946–68*); *Cartas al señor tiempo* (1959) (*Letter to Mr Time*); *La casa por dentro* (1965) (*The Inside of The House*); *Sonetos sueltos* (1965) (*Free Sonnets*); *Poemas sueltos* (1965) (*Free Poems*); *A la sombra de Sor Juana Inés de la Cruz* (1966) (*In The Shadow of Sor Juana Inés de la Cruz*); *La ciudad instantanea* (1969) (*The Instant City*), and *Retratos y tormentos* (1973) (*Portraits and Torments*).

Machado de Arnao, Luz ▷Machado, Luz

Machar, Agnes Maule (1837–1927)
Canadian moral crusader and author of poetry, fiction, history and biography. She was born and lived in Kingston, Ontario. She first published poems and Sunday School stories, then proceeded to patriotic and historical works. A Christian socialist of sorts, she was active in the fight for labour reform, and temperance. Her works include *Lays of the 'True North' and Other Canadian Poems* (1899), and *Roland Graeme, Knight: A Novel of Our Time* (1892).
Bib: Gerson, C., *Three Writers of Victorian Canada*.

Macinghi Strozzi, Alessandra (1407–1471)
Italian letter-writer. Born in Florence, she married Matteo Strozzi, with whom she had eight children. She might never have been known as a woman of letters, had it not been for the fact that her husband was exiled from Florence when Cosimo de' Medici returned to power in 1434. Her male children were also subject to this decree as soon as they reached maturity. The family moved to Pesaro, but there Matteo and three of the children conracted plague and died. Alessandra then returned to Florence with her remaining five children. Thus, as her children grew up and left Florence, she began to write long and informative letters to them. These letters today paint a picture of life in Florence at that time, written in simple, clear prose. They are packed with detail, and full of emotion. Her letters were first published in 1877, and again in 1914, in a collection entitled *Lettere di una gentildonna fiorentina del secolo XV ai figliuoli esuli* (*Letters of a Florentine Lady of the 15th Century to her Sons in Exile*).

Mack, Louise (1874–1935)
Australian children's author, novelist and journalist. Mack collaborated with ▷Ethel Turner on the girls' magazine, *The Parthenon*, and worked on the *Bulletin* as author of its 'A Woman's Letter' from 1896 to 1901. *The Bulletin*, established in 1880, was an extremely influential weekly journal of general affairs with a strong literary interest. It had a wide circulation, was known as the 'Bushman's Bible', and discovered and fostered many of Australia's leading writers, particularly between 1890 and 1910. Mack lived in England and Italy and was in Belgium at the outbreak of World War I, an experience which formed the basis of her *A Woman's Experiences in the Great*

War (1915). Mack married twice but survived each husband, and eventually returned to Sydney. She published a number of adult novels, usually light romances, and a book of poems, but is best known for her extremely popular books for girls, including *The World is Round* (1896), *Teens* (1897), *Girls Together* (1898), *Children of the Sun* (1904), *Teens Triumphant* (1933) and *The Maiden's Prayer* (1934).

▷Children's literature (Australia); *From the Verandah*

Mackay, Jessie (1864–1938)

New Zealand poet. One of the best-known Victorian poets writing in New Zealand, Jessie Mackay has seemed, to later commentators, typical of the worst aspects of 19th-century colonial writing. Widely published in magazines, such as *The New Zealand Illustrated Magazine*, and anthologies, Mackay wrote 'awful pseudo-Scottish stuff' (Patrick Evans, *The Penguin History of New Zealand Literature*, 1990), often with a ▷Maori subject, as in the much-reproduced 'The Noosing of the Sun-God', in an attempt to establish a national literature. She also wrote moral articles for Temperance magazines or other publications intended to educate poor women.

Publications: *The Spirit of the Rangatira and Other Ballads* (1889); *The Sitter on the Rail and Other Poems* (1891); *Land of the Morning* (1909); *From the Maori Sea* (1908); *The Bride of the Rivers and Other Verses* (1926); *The Girl of the Drift* (1928); *Vigil* (1935).

Mackay, Shena (born 1945)

Scottish novelist and short story writer. Mackay's fiction characteristically treats macabre and discomforting themes in a Surreal frame. Her explicit analysis of violence, found in her early novels such as *Toddler On the Run* (1964), is maintained in *Old Crow* (1967) with the violent death of the protagonist. In *An Advent Calender* (1971) Mackay picks up her concern with animal rights issues. The story revolves around the anxieties of a central character who inadvertently consumes human flesh. Her best-known novel, *Music Upstairs* (1965), focuses on a suprising *ménage à trois* against the backdrop of London bed-sit land. Short-story collections are: *Babies in Rhinestones* (1983) and *Dreams of Dead Women's Handbags* (1987). Other novels include: *Redhill Rococo* (1986), *A Bowl of Cherries* (1984).

Mackintosh, Elizabeth ▷Tey, Josephine

MacManus, Anna ▷Carbery, Ethna

MacMurchy, Marjory

Canadian journalist and writer. As well as being literary editor of *The News*, Toronto, MacMurchy published widely in *Saturday Night*, *Harper's Bazaar* and *The Bohemian*. She was elected President of the Canadian Women's Press Club from 1909 to 1913. *Women of Today and Tomorrow* (1919) examines the rapidly changing roles of women. Described as one of the ablest of Upper Canada's women journalists, she later became Lady Willison.

Macpherson, (Jean) Jay (born 1918)

Canadian poet. Macpherson was born in London, England, but was taken to St John's, Newfoundland, at the age of nine, and moved to Ottawa in 1944. She attended University College in London, returning to Canada in 1952 to study at McGill University, and then the University of Toronto, working under Northrop Frye. She later became Professor of English at Victoria College there. Her first collection, *Nineteen Poems*, appeared in 1952. Her second, *Oh Earth Return*, was published as a booklet in 1954, and later reprinted as a section of her most important book, ▷*The Boatman* (1957), which received the Governor General's Award. It employs Christian mythology and archetypal displacement, reminiscent of Blake (1757–1827). *Welcoming Disaster* was printed privately in 1974; it was republished, together with *The Boatman*, as *Poems Twice Told* (1981), illustrated by the author. Macpherson's work is concerned with the transformative aspects of the metaphysical. She has also published a revised version of classical mythology for young people, *Four Ages of Man: the Classical Myths* (1962).

Bib: Weir, L., in *Gynocritics*.

Mactier, Susie

New Zealand novelist. Very little is known about Susie Mactier's life beyond the publication of her three novels. Her first novel, *A Far Countrie*, published in 1901 claimed to be a 'true story of domestic life at home and in the bush'. Like her contemporaries ▷Kathleen Inglewood and ▷Ellen Ellis, Mactier wrote novels which recorded domestic environments, worked out romantic narratives and made an association between alcohol, the unequal status of women, and Christian belief. For Mactier, alcoholism is evidence of moral corruption for both men and women, though in her novel *The Hills of Hauraki* (1908) it is clear that women are driven to intemperance by the moral failure of a man. Her final work was *Miranda Stanhope*, published in 1911.

Madre, La (1920) ▷Mother, The

'Madre, La' (1948) ('The Mother')

A striking short story by Italian writer ▷Natalia Ginzburg, this tale of modern motherhood analyses family life. The protagonist is a young mother (never named) whose husband has died. She has two sons, and lives with her parents-in-law. The relationship between the grandparents and the children is positive, warm and strong; that between the mother and her children is uncertain and often cold. The mother loves her children, but longs for a life of her own. She feels restricted and censured by her husband's parents. The narrative perspective is that of the children, who cannot understand their mother, her work, her appearance, or her comings and goings. The woman finally commits suicide in a hotel room, and life goes on without her. The story's strength lies in Ginzburg's successful adoption of the point of view of a child, while, retaining an adult perspective which does not compel the reader to share the child's opinions.

Madre e figlia (1980) (Mother and Daughter)

A novel by Italian writer ▷Francesca Sanvitale which explores the dynamics of the mother–daughter relationship. This is, in essence, the story of a daughter who has lost herself in her mother. Sonia, the daughter, is at once the protector and the reflection of her mother, Mariannina. Sonia recreates her mother's past and her own childhood through flashbacks. In many respects, the text reads like a fable. The narrative is selfconscious, with asides to the reader. Sanvitale also investigates femininity in biological terms here: the experiences of mastectomy, abortion, pregnancy and birth are central to the narrative. The paternal role in the text is viewed as entirely negative: authoritarian, unreliable and untrustworthy. Yet the maternal role is a source of deep conflict as well as one of deep affection. One of the most telling statements in the book is that of Sonia when she admits: '*solo il corpo di mia madre è per me un corpo d'amore*' ('only my mother's body is a loving body, for me').

Magic realism

20th-century Britain: Descriptive term first applied to the work of a number of German artists of the 1920s whose paintings combined an interest in the irrational and improbable with the formal execution of a recognizably realist mode. As a literary critical term, it is frequently used to describe the fiction of a number of Latin American novelists, such as Jorge Luis Borges (1899–1987), Gabriel García Márquez (born 1928) and Alejo Carpentier (born 1904), whose novels explore the unexpected, supernatural and fantastic within a realist frame of reference. A strong tradition of magic realism has developed in England from the 1970s, and is associated with the writings of ▷Angela Carter and ▷Emma Tennant, as well as other writers, including Salman Rushdie (born 1947) and John Fowles (born 1926). Carter's and Tennant's use of this technique typically incorporates elements of dream, fantasy, myth and fairytale within ostensibly realist narratives.

Italy: *Realismo magico* is used to describe a narrative which presents the reader with a recognizable representation of contemporary society (often rendered in considerable detail), alongside which all kinds of fantastical and unlikely events take place. Writers of these works often draw heavily on myth and symbol for their distinctive effects, and the language is frequently lyrical. The works of ▷Elsa Morante, ▷Fausta Terni Cialente, ▷Anna Maria Ortese and ▷Fabrizia Ramondino have been associated with magic realism.

Mahabharata (400 BC–AC 400)

With the ▷*Ramayana*, one of Hinduism's two greatest epics. A mixture of history, legend and spiritual instruction, the *Mahabharata* was composed over many centuries, and it was in existence as an oral form long before it began to be consolidated on paper from 400 BC to AD 400. It tells of the conflict between the Pandavas and the Kauravas, two branches of the famous Vedic tribe of the Bharatas, from which India takes her name *Bharat*. Although the Pandavas are the ultimate victors and are accorded greater respect in the epic, there is no simple division between good and evil. Yudhishthira, the eldest of the five Pandava brothers, is shown to have a very human failing when he loses his saintly wife ▷Draupadi to the Kauravas in a game of dice. The long-suffering Draupadi remains today one of the most popular images of womanhood in India. Gandhari, the mother of the Kauravas, is another representation of a strong woman in the *Mahabharata*. She sympathizes with the Pandavas because she believes their cause to be just, and rebukes her husband for being weak with their own sons.

The famous '*Bhagavad Gita*', or 'Song of the Lord', is a relatively late addition to the *Mahabharata*. It is a discourse on the rights and duties of people in a world where the boundary between good and evil is not always clearly discernible. It is written in the form of advice given by the god Krishna to Arjuna, one of the Pandavas, who, on the eve of the great battle with the Kauravas, is uncertain about the rightness of killing his kinsmen.

Mahabhoj (1979) ▷Great Feast, The (1981)

Mahfuz, Nagib, influence of

Egyptian novelist and short story writer, born in 1911, Nobel Prize laureate for literature in 1988. His novels, published between 1938 and 1988, established the art of the novel in Arabic, and developed it along many new tracks followed by later novelists. The world of Mahfuz's novels is mainly that of the contemporary urban Egyptian middle class, with emphasis on the lower ranks as well as the intellectuals. Apart from the lessons in technique that women writers may have learned from Mahfuz, the images of his women characters have become part of the consciousness of all Arabic speakers.

Mahfuz's female characters range from the selfless, loving mother to the frustrated, sharp-tongued unmarried daughters and sisters, or the liberated entertainers/prostitutes who supply his male characters with congenial company. In his later novels he introduced 'New Women': well-educated professional women, journalists, teachers and doctors, but they are not as convincing as his more traditional types. In *Zuqaq al-Midaq* (1947) (*Midaq Alley*), Hamida, the beauty of the *zuqaq* (alley), is interpreted by many critics as representing Egypt. The author does not object to the interpretation, but insists it had not originally been his intention. She is poor and ambitious and is seduced by a 'wolf', not for his own use, but for an expensive brothel for officers of the Allied Forces in Cairo during World War II.

In *Miramar* (1967), Zahra, a peasant girl from the province of Beheira, leaves her village, refusing to marry the old man proposed by her family. She goes to Alexandria to work in the Pension Miramar; the male residents all try to seduce or befriend her according to their political and social positions and their individual characters.

In his *Trilogy* (1957–8) Mahfuz created a character whose name has become a synonym for an authoritarian patriarch, Sayyid Ahmad abdel Gawwad, addressed by his wife as 'Si al-Sayyid'. He is loved but dreaded by all members of his family, who speak in hushed tones whenever he is in the house. His wife is not allowed outside the door without his permission, and then only to visit her mother or her daughters. His life outside his house is completely different: he is full of jokes and quips, he drinks and sings, and has a mistress in a world which he believes is completely separated from his family. 'Playing Si al-Sayyid' is an expression fully understood in Arabic today, while the name of his wife, Amina, stands for the fully subjugated wife who cannot breathe a word of protest to or about her husband, but guards his image before his children, although she smells his drunken breath when he returns home in the early hours of the morning.
Bib: Le Gassick, T. (trans.), *Midaq Alley*; Moussa-Mahmood, Fatima (trans.), *Miramar*; Hutchins, W. M. and Kenny, Olive (trans.), *Palace Walk*.

Mahjar poetry

Arabic poetry written in the early decades of the 20th century by Lebanese and Palestinian emigrants to the United States and Brazil. They were poor men who wrote mostly in Arabic for their compatriots at home, and sent their compositions to two important monthlies published in Cairo, *al-Hilal* and *Muqtataf*. Khalil Gibran (1883–1931) is probably the only one of them who made a name for himself in western European literature with *The Prophet* and other works. Gibran and his friends, who founded an Arab Pen Association in New York in 1920, brought a revolutionary new idiom to Arabic writing, introducing the ideas of Emerson (1803–1882) and Walt Whitman (1819–1892), and the adoration of nature of the English romantics. They experimented with measures of Arabic poetry, and one of them, Amin Rihani, advocated the use of free verse or 'prose poems'. Another, Elia Abu-Madi, introduced a tone of scepticism and questioning in easy, light verse, that was then set to music and had a large audience in the Arab world.

Mahy, Margaret May (born 1936)

New Zealand children's author. Mahy did not begin writing full-time until 1980, but had her first work published when she was still at school. From 1961 onwards her stories and poems appeared in the *New Zealand School Journal* and her first book, *A Lion in the Meadow* (1969), won the New Zealand Library Association's Esther Glen Medal in 1970. Her many other picture books show her gift for exaggeration and fantasy. She also writes television scripts, novels, school readers, poems and plays. She has won many awards, including the *Observer* Teenage Fiction Award in 1987 for *Memory* (1987), based on her aunt's experience of Alzheimer's disease.

Mai devi domandarmi (1970) ▷ *Never Must You Ask Me*

Maiga-Ka, Aminata (born 1940)

Senegalese novelist Author of three novels, *La voie du salut (Way of Health)*, *Le miroir de la vie (Mirror of Life)* and *En votre nom et au mien* (1989) (*In Your Name and Mine*), she is also a technical adviser at the Ministry of Education in Dakar. She is concerned to show how women fight to maintain their dignity and autonomy, in spite of societal pressures.

Maillet, Antonine (born 1929)

French Canadian writer, born in Bouctouche, New Brunswick. Acadian novelist and dramatist Maillet was educated at Moncton, New Brunswick, and the Universities of Montreal and Laval in Quebec. She has published more than twenty-five books, which have garnered many literary prizes, and of which a large number have been translated into English. *La Sagouine* (1971, translated with the same title in 1979) is the story of 'a scrubwoman, a woman of the sea, who was born with the century, with her feet in the water'. This striking slattern is a 72-year-old vindication of orality, 'all together a glossary, a race and the other side of the coin'. *Don L'Original* (1972, translated as *The Tale of Don L'Original*, 1989) engages a range of fantastic storytellers, embodied by occupation. *Pélagie-la-Charette* (1979, translated as *Pélagie: the Return to a Homeland*, 1983) won the Prix Goncourt for its evocation of a group of French Acadians, driven by the British into exile in the southern United States, who make the long trek back to their burned and long-deserted homeland. *Crache à Pic* (1984, translated as *The Devil Is Loose!*, 1986) is a hilarious story of bootlegging and smuggling in Acadia. *Le Huitième Jour* (1986, translated as *On the Eighth Day*, 1989), fabulously transcends the original seven days of creation. Maillet frequently uses crude and working-class characters; their Acadian-Rabelaisian drama and exuberance are without equal.
Bib: Fitzpatrick, M.A., in *Traditionalism,*

Nationalism and Feminism: Women Writers of Quebec; Kulyk Keefer, J., *Under Eastern Eyes*.

Maintenon, Françoise d'Aubigné, Marquise de (1635–1719)

French author of a voluminous correspondence. Granddaughter of Agrippa d'Aubigné (1552–1630), the Calvinist writer, Françoise d'Aubigné was born in prison and spent the first part of her life in impoverished circumstances in Guyana, following her father's disgrace. At the age of seventeen, she returned to France to marry the crippled dramatist, comic novelist and poet, Paul Scarron (1610–1660), with whom she had corresponded from the Caribbean. This unsuitable marriage at least allowed her to meet some of the wittiest urbane writers of her day. She continued to receive her husband's royal pension after his death in 1660, and in 1674 was appointed governess of the illegitimate children of Louis XIV (1638–1715). She quickly replaced Madame de Montespan (1640–1707) in the king's affections and, as the king's official mistress, accumulated sufficient fortune to purchase the territory of Maintenon, and was raised to a marquisate in 1678. Six years later the Marquise de Maintenon and Louis XIV were secretly married, though there is no extant proof of the ceremony. The king's morganatic second wife enjoyed considerable political influence in the day-to-day running of the country, as her considerable correspondence confirms, though the king continued to act alone in the most important affairs.

There were 80 volumes of her letters in all, of which forty were still extant at the end of the 18th century; 4,000 letters remain in existence today. Most of her most intimate correspondence with the king and close friends has been lost, but we still have many of her numerous letters to relations and friends, her religious guides, servants and the girls and Mothers Superior at the convent of Saint-Cyr, where she endowed an educational establishment for young girls of good family. There has never been a complete edition of her correspondence. The only edition published in the 18th century in nine volumes is not authentic. Madame de Maintenon also wrote instructions for the girls at Saint-Cyr in the first person, giving an account of her interviews with the girls and their teachers. Her final work was *Conversations et proverbes*, a series of one-act dialogue plays intended for the moral and civic instruction of the girls.

Her pension of 48,000 *livres* was renewed by Philippe d'Orléans (1640–1701) upon the king's death, even though she had deliberately hampered the constitution of the Regency. She spent the final years of her life in reclusion at Saint-Cyr. Usually held responsible for the lugubrious atmosphere of excessive religiosity in the final decades of Louis XIV's reign, Madame de Maintenon was a fascinating character, as revealed in a recent biography published in the form of pseudo-memoirs.

Bib: Chandeganor, F., *L'Allée du roi*; Dyson, C.C., *Mme de Maintenon: Her Life and Times*; Langlois, M., *Madame de Maintenon*; Mermaz, L., *Madame de Maintenon*.

Maitland, Sara (born 1950)

English novelist, short story writer and historian. Educated at St. Anne's College, Oxford, Maitland developed a commitment to Anglo-Catholicism alongside her engagement with feminism and socialism. Maitland's fiction is frequently concerned with exploring the relevance of Christian thinking for feminism and the relationship of feminism and Christian orthodoxy. *Daughter of Jerusalem* (1978) looks to the explanatory capabilities of Old Testament narratives to make sense of contemporary women's concerns. *Virgin Territory* (1984) addresses the conflict between religious devotion and lesbian love. A co-founder of the Feminist Writers Group with ▷Zöe Fairbairns, ▷Michèle Roberts and ▷Michelene Wandor. The results of their collaborations include ▷*Tales I Tell My Mother* (1978). Maitland and Wandor have also co-authored the novel ▷*Arky Types* (1987). Her other writings include *Very Heaven: Looking Back at the Sixties* (1988) and *Three Times Table* (1990). She has edited *The Rushdie File* (1989) with Lisa Appignanesi.

▷Tennant, Emma

Majerová, Marie (1882–1967)

Czech novelist. She began as a well-heeled anarchist, then became a communist, was thrown out of the Communist Party in 1929, only to become one of the most self-compromising of the hardliners in the 1940s and 1950s. Her first major novel, *Náměstí republiky* (1914) (*Place de la République*), is a rhapsodic work describing and, mainly between the lines, analysing the life of the Parisian anarchists of the period 1906–1907. Majerová here lays into the rationalism which governed anarchism. She rewrote the novel in the 1940s and omitted one character, a Russian anarchist, Nasta, who strangles her cat before leaving for her socialist paradise, New Zealand.

Majerová's experimental novel suggesting, unconvincingly, idealist communism, *Přehrada* (1932) (*The Dam*), displays the influence of futurism and Surrealism, and she attempts to keep rank with the ▷avant-garde. *Havířská balada* (1938) (*Miners' Ballad*), is *littérature engagée* (politically committed literature), demonstrating social injustice. Majerová's depiction of miners as all one family is persuasive, generally avoiding the political tendentiousness of the cause in whose service she is usually claimed to have been writing.

Makárova, Elena Grigor'evna (born 1951)

Makárova, the daughter of Russian poet ▷Inna Lisniánskaia, is a prolific short-story writer. A teacher of art to kindergarten children in Moscow, in the late 1980s she served as co-curator of an exhibition in Prague and Jerusalem of artwork by children from the Terezin concentration camp. Her work with children is reflected in the story 'Treasure', which relates the break-up of a marriage as it is perceived by the couple's five-year-old daughter. More typically, as US critic Nancy Condee has pointed out (*Institute of Current World Affairs*, NPC-9), Makárova deals not with 'the woman writer's "eternal triangle" – work-love-progeny' but with its 'pre-history': the world of young women seeking to define themselves, often in unrealistic terms and with unattainable goals; in this preoccupation Condee finds Makárova's 'literary ancestors' to be the 19th-century writers ▷Gan and ▷Pávlova. In Makárova's 'Herbs from Odessa' (*Balancing Acts*) Lenka seeks a curative potion for her dying grandfather. 'Uncle Pasha' (*Nimrod*, 33, 2) portrays a talented, insecure art student through the eyes of a lonely old male artist's model who befriends her. Makárova's ability to find a striking idiom to express her protagonist's character gives her stories depth and appeal.

Makin, Bathsua (born 1600)

English poet, linguist and defender of women's education. She published poetry in languages including Greek, French, Hebrew and Spanish. She married Richard Makin in 1622, and became tutor to Charles I's daughter, Princess Elizabeth, before the outbreak of the Civil War. She corresponded with the famous scholar ▷Anna Maria von Schurmann. At the Restoration she probably published ▷*An Essay to Revive the Antient Education of Gentlewomen. In Religion, Manners, Arts & Tongues* (1673), which is in part an advertisement for a school. Complaining that 'a Learned Woman is thought to be a Comet', she wrote of 'the Barbarous custom to breed Women low', and argued that in the past, gentlewomen were educated in 'the knowledge of Arts and Tongues'. Makin's argument is addressed to the upper echelons of society and her examples of feminine learning include Queen Elizabeth I (▷Elizabeth Tudor), the masque-loving Queen Christina of Sweden. She wrote, 'persons of higher quality, for want of this Education, have nothing to imploy themselves in, but are forced to Cards, Dice, Playes and frothy Romances merely to drive away the time.' Makin was one of the earliest to theorize the necessity for women's education, and to offer a school in which it could be carried out. Compare ▷Hannah More, ▷Mary Wollstonecraft and ▷Sarah Fielding.

Other publications: *Musa Virginea* (1616); *Index Radiographer*.

▷Astell, Mary

Bib: Myers, Mitzi, *Studies in Eighteenth-Century Culture*, No. 14, (1985).

Maksimović, Desanka (born 1898)

Serbian poet. A lyric poet who began to write very young, Maksimović has been a prominent figure in Serbian cultural life for the last 60 years, continuing to write with unflagging energy well into her nineties. Her verse, predominantly

personal in tone, is intimately linked with the culture and history of her native Serbia. She is perhaps best known for a number of lyric poems connected with World War II in Serbia, and for the cycle *Tražim pomilovanje* (1964) (*I Seek Clemency*), a 'dialogue' with the 14th-century Tsar Dušan's Code of Laws.

Malaeska: The Indian Wife of the White Hunter (1860)

US historical novel by ▷Ann Sophia Stephens. A bestselling work, *Malaeska* combined the conventional characters of Stephens's earlier historical novels with the romance and thriller action of the US frontier. Her success inspired a new style of publishing and of advertising books, especially sensational adventure stories – a style that became the US genre of the ▷dime novel.

Malange, Nise (born 1960)

South African performance poet and dramatist. Born in Clovelly near Cape Town, she grew up and was educated in various parts of the Cape, part of a generation whose schooling was deeply bound up with political involvement. Many of her peers were killed in clashes with police, and with black conservative vigilantes, known as *witdoeke* for their white armbands and headbands. In 1982, Malange moved to Howick, Natal, and the following year started working for trade unions in Durban. She is now an organizer for the Transport and General Workers' Union, part of COSATU (Congress of South African Trade Unions), and engaged in its cultural unit, writing/making plays as part of a more general movement in ▷popular theatre, as well as composing poetry for ▷performance. The presence of women in COSATU's various cultural units has been sporadic: Malange's participation thus represents a significant historical moment. Her poem, 'I, the Unemployed', connects women's economic marginalization with COSATU's campaign for a living wage. This poem is to be found in *From South Africa: New Writing, Photographs, and Art*; others are to be found in *Black Mamba Rising* (1985). They are composed and delivered in English.

Malet, Lucas (1852–1931)

▷Pseudonym of British novelist Mary Kingsley, the daughter of novelist Charles Kingsley. The pseudonym was adopted to avoid capitalizing on the family's literary fame. *Mrs Lorimer: A Sketch in Black and White* (1882) was Malet's first novel, and she continued to write until her death, producing more than twenty works, including *Colonel Enderby's Wife* (1885); *The Wages of Sin* (1891); *The Gateless Barrier* (1900); *The Far Horizon* (1906); *Deadham Hard* (1919); *The Survivors* (1923) and *The Dogs of Want* (1924). Her style is prolix and often ▷sentimental, her characterization and detail typically 19th- rather than 20th-century, yet her contribution to literature was recognized when she was awarded a civic pension in 1930.

Mallet-Joris, Françoise (born 1930)

Belgian-French novelist. Born in Anvers in 1930, Mallet-Joris grew up in Belgium, and visited the USA before settling in France. As a member of the jury of the Prix Femina, and, since 1970, of the Académie Goncourt, she has become part of the literary establishment, as well as a well-known popular novelist. Her first novel, *Le Rempart des Béguines* (1951) (*The Illusionist*, 1952), is written as the intimate journal of an adolescent girl who has a lesbian relationship with her father's exotic and dominant mistress, Tamara. The relationship is represented as perverse, if pleasurable, and the novel rapidly became a bestseller.

Since then Mallet-Joris has produced novels illustrating moral or religious dilemmas such as *Les Signes et les prodiges* (1966) (*Signs and Wonders*, 1966), historical romances such as *Les Personnages* (1961) (*The Favourite*, 1962), family melodramas, such as *La Tristesse du Cerf-Volant* (1988) (*The Sadness of the Kite*), a biography of Marie Mancini, and two autobiographical works: *Lettre à moi-même* (1963) (*Letter to Myself*, 1964) and *La Maison de papier* (1970) (*The Paper House*, 1971). These consist of reflections on various subjects, including the author's Catholic faith, and the tensions between the demands of her domestic life as mother of four children and her work as a writer. Mallet-Joris has also written songs in collaboration with singer/songwriter Marie-Paule Belle.

Malraux, Clara (born 1900)

French novelist, translator, autobiographer and children's writer. She has written travelogues of the many countries she visited with her husband, and has translated ▷*A Room of One's Own* into French, as well as some of Freud's writings (▷psychoanalysis). Of the six volumes of her memoirs, two have been translated into English as *Memoirs* (1963). Her novel, *Portrait de Grisélidis* (1945) (*A Second Griselda*, 1947), combines fiction with autobiography in a pre-feminist tale of a woman's struggle for independence and equality.

Mama Blanca's Souvenirs (1959)

Translation of *Las Memórias de Mamá Blanca* (1929), the second novel by the Venezuelan ▷Teresa de la Parra – probably her masterpiece. A book of memoirs, it centres on an old woman called '*Mamá Blanca*' ('White Mum'). As in her first novel ▷*Ifigenia* (1924), the character recalls episodes in her life through realistic, or ▷costumbrismo, pictures, with a sense of humour as well as an impressionistic style. These recollections of a happy childhood in a sugar-cane farm are filled with a melancholic sensibility, imagination and sympathy for the people. The book seems purely spontaneous, but has a highly elaborate structure, filled with metaphors.

Mamduh, Aliya ▷*Mothballs*

Mancini, Marie de (1640–1715) and Hortense de (1646–1699)

French memoir-writers. The nieces of Cardinal Mazarin (1602–1661), the five Mancini sisters followed their uncle from Italy to France where first Olympe (1639–1708) and then Marie were courted by Louis XIV (1638–1715). The king was forced by his prime minister, Mazarin, to abandon Marie on the point of marriage. She later married the Duc de Colonna, quickly separated from him and was shut up in a convent by Louis XIV on her return to France. Hortense, who took the title Duchesse de Mazarin, married the wealthy Duc de La Meilleraye, became the mistress of the Duc de Rohan and then went to England, where she was for a time the mistress of Charles II (1630–1685) and founded a society of witty libertines, of which the writer Saint-Evremond was a member during his exile. The *Mémoires de M.C.D.L. [duchesse de Mazarin]* were published in 1675, while she was still in England, and those of her sister Marie, the Connétable de Colonna, in 1678. The circumstances of publication were somewhat unusual, since the memoirs first appeared in pamplet form, where the author denigrated herself, and then in two later editions, where she tells us that she was forced to write her account of her life, although her status and '*conduite assez bien réglée*' ('relatively quiet life') should have spared her, because she received a letter from France informing her '*qu'il courait une histoire de [sa] vie, qu'on supposait avoir été écrite [d'elle-même]*' ('that a story of her life was in circulation, supposedly written in her own hand'). These two sets of memoirs have also been attributed to the historical novelist, Saint-Réal (1639–1692).
Bib: Hipp, M., *Mythes et réalités: Enquête sur le roman et les mémoires 1660–1700*; Doscot (ed.) *Mémoires de Madame la Connétable de Colonna*.

Mandarins, The (1957)

Translation of *Les Mandarins* (1954), novel by French writer ▷Simone de Beauvoir. *The Mandarins*, for which de Beauvoir won the Prix Goncourt, is, like much of her fiction, based on her own life. The heroine (the de Beauvoir character) is involved with a North American writer (in real life the US novelist Nelson Algren) but refuses to marry him because of the prior claims of her husband (who represents Jean-Paul Sartre). Other loosely disguised individuals who appear in the novel are Albert Camus and Arthur Koestler. The personal dramas are set against a backdrop of French left-wing politics in the years immediately after 1945. The novel established de Beauvoir's reputation as a major French novelist.

Mandel, Miriam (1930–1982)

Canadian poet, born Miriam Minovitch in Saskatchewan. She attended the University of Saskatchewan in Saskatoon, where she met and married the poet Eli Mandel. Following the births of her children (1955 and 1959), and her divorce (1967), she was frequently hospitalized for depression. *Lions at Her Face* (1973), an entextment of psychological suffering, was published with the encouragement of ▷Sheila Watson, and won the Governor General's Award for Poetry. *Station 14* (1977) describes 'the world – deaf, dumb, and blind' of the psychiatric ward. *Where Have You Been* (1980) compiles a series of located and dated diary poems. After Mandel's death, Sheila Watson edited *The Collected Poems of Miriam Mandel* (1984), which brings together the earlier published and unpublished material. Watson maintains that these poems are really a long sequence which work toward their own transgressive silencing, concluding, 'This darkness – / a / veil of heavy black lace / lowered / tight / over my face. / I do not breathe.'

Mandel'shtám, Nadezhda Iakovlevna (1899–1980).

Russian memoirist and essayist. Mandel'shtám's ruthlessly honest *Reminiscences* and *Second Book* (English translations, *Hope Against Hope*, 1970; *Hope Abandoned*, 1974 – the Russian titles play on the name Nadezhda, meaning hope) are centred on her husband, the poet Osip Mandel'shtám (1891–1938), and represent the trauma of an entire generation of poets repressed or destroyed by the Soviet state. The first volume deals with the period between Osip's arrest and exile to Voronezh in 1934 and his re-arrest and disappearance into the camps in 1938. The second describes their younger years and Nadezhda's struggle, after Osip's death, to preserve her life and his poetry. The work is also a masterpiece of autobiography: Nadezhda's free spirit and earthy scepticism are clearly expressed. In tones ranging from gentle humour to withering scorn, her sharply observed vignettes bring to life a variety of people – writers, bureaucrats, landladies, convoy guards – who helped the couple or served as agents of Osip's destruction. In later years Mandel'shtám taught English and wrote a dissertation on Anglo-Saxon linguistics. *Mozart and Salieri* (English translation 1973) is an analysis of the nature of poetic inspiration that draws on the ideas and example of her husband and their close friend ▷Anna Akhmátova. Mandel'shtám died secure in the knowledge that her husband's poetry had been collected and published in ▷*samizdat* and ▷*tamizdat* editions. A *Third Book* in the series came out in Paris in 1987.

Mander, Jane (1877–1949)

New Zealand novelist. Jane Mander began writing while she was a student at Columbia University, during her twenty-year absence from New Zealand. Her first novel was ▷*The Story of a New Zealand River* (1920), and it was followed by five more. In 1923 she moved to London, and eventually back to New Zealand in the 1930s, where she spent the rest of her life. All Mander's fiction is preoccupied with social politics. She wrote complicated ▷romance narratives which illustrate the demands that social expectation and convention make upon women, and in general terms attack puritanism and materialism. Her novels progressively move away from marriage and family as an inevitable environment for women, suggesting instead the possibilities of careers and extramarital relationships. Mander's novels feature outsiders and challenge narrow conceptions of morality, duty and gender roles, and in her New Zealand novels (her last two are set in New York and London) an association is made between physical and spiritual environments. Mander is the first woman novelist to have gained any real status in New Zealand literary history, and several of her novels have been republished in recent years.

Publications: *The Story of a New Zealand River* (1920); *The Passionate Puritan* (1921); *The Strange Attraction* (1923); *Allen Adair* (1925); *The Besieging City* (1926); *Pins and Pinnacles* (1928).

Man From Muckinupin, The (1979)

Australian play by ▷Dorothy Hewett. Hewett wrote this play to celebrate Western Australia's sesquicentenary in 1979, and also to celebrate her reconciliation with her home state. It is set in a wheatfields town in Western Australia, 'east of the rabbit-proof fence', on the eve of World War I, and is concerned both with young love and with race relationships in a small town. A set which suggests archetypal harvest festivals, a cast of wholly believable eccentrics and a superb plot have made this one of Australia's most successful plays.

Mangal sutra

A necklace of black beads strung on gold which is presented by a Hindu groom to his bride at the conclusion of their wedding ceremony. It signifies the union of the married couple, and the acceptance into the husband's family of his new wife. It is only worn by married women, and hence has become a symbol of a Hindu woman's status.

▷*Sindoor*; *Pati vrata dharm*

Manicom, Jacqueline (1938–1976)

A novelist from the French Antilles. Manicom was the eldest of twenty children in a poor Indian family in Guadeloupe. She gained both a law and a medical degree, and became a midwife. With her husband she founded the Guadeloupe Association for Family Planning. She led a movement to make abortion legal and was also co-founder of the group 'Choisir' ('Choice'). In both her novels she focuses on the triple problems of class, race and gender, and she is critical in both of modern medicine's (particularly white male doctors') treatment of female bodies, in particular those of lower-class or women of colour. Her concern with the issues of contraception and abortion are evident in her second novel, *La Graine: Journal d'une Sage-Femme* (1974) (*The Seed: The Diary of a Midwife*), but it is for her first novel, ▷*Mon Examen de Blanc* (1972) (*My Exam in Whiteness*), that she has received the greatest critical attention.

Manigault, Ann Ashby (1703–1782)

North American diarist. A resident of South Carolina, she was ensconced in the upper-class social circles of fashionable Charleston. Although she did not begin keeping a diary until after age fifty, thereafter she briefly noted the details of her life for the next twenty-seven years. Selections are included in ▷'Extracts from the Journal of Mrs Ann Manigault'.

Manja, Salmi (born 1939)

Pen-name of Saleha Abdul Rashid, Malay religious teacher, poet, short story writer, novelist and journalist. Born in Singapore, she is married to the well-known Malay writer and journalist, A. Samad Said, with whom she has published a joint short story collection, *Daun-daun Beguguran* (1962) (*The Leaves are Falling*). Another collection is *Badan Piatu Di Rantau Orang* (1965) (*Alone in a Foreign Land*). A selection of her poems in English translation features in *Modern Malay Verse, 1946–61* (1963), where she is the only woman poet to be included. One of the more prolific women writers, she was most productive in the 1960s, being best known for her novels, which at first sight seem a throwback to the novels of the 1950s. This is reflected in their preoccupation with the helplessness of women trapped in unhappy arranged marriages (polygamy adding to their woes), or as divorcees, victims of authoritarian and unfeeling fathers, male religious teachers and husbands, with no recourse to justice because of the culturally sanctioned inferior position of women in Malay society. But the writing conveys a strong note of protest rather than portraying submissiveness as a sign of female moral superiority.

Her first novel was the autobiographical *Hari Mana Bulan Mana* (1960) (*On Which Day, In Which Month*). Other titles are: *Dari Mana Punai Melayang* (1961) (*From Where the Dove Flies*), the only one with a happy ending (the mother relents and enables her daughter to marry the man she loves); *Hendak Hujan, Hujan Sekali* (1967) (*Let It Rain Once and For All*) which realistically captures the accents of women's conversation; *Entah Mengapa Haiku Duka* (1968) (*For No Reason My Heart Is Sad*); *Rindu Hilang Di Tapak Tangan* (1968) (*Love Lost in the Palm of the Hand*); *Sayang Ustazah Sayang* (1968) (*A Pity, Female Religious Teacher, A Pity*), and *Entah Mengapa Hatiku Duka* (1968) (*Why This Sadness*).

Manley, Delarivier (1663–1724)

English novelist, dramatist, Tory political journalist and writer of political and scandalous memoirs. She married Sir Roger Manley, who died in 1687, then her cousin, John Manley, who turned out to be already married. She later took lovers. In 1700 she edited ▷*The Nine Muses*, but later quarrelled with ▷Sarah Fyge and attacked both Fyge and ▷Mary Pix in *The Secret Memoirs of the New Atlantis* (1709); she also pilloried ▷Catherine Trotter. She used scandalous narrative to political ends. She was the editor of the periodical *The Examiner* (following Jonathan Swift, 1667–1745). In the memoir-novel, *The History of Rivella*, Sir Charles Lovemore begins the story by saying, 'There are so many Things Praise, and yet Blame-worthy in *Rivella*'s Conduct, that as her Friend I know not how with a good Grace, to repeat.' Her play *The Lost Lover* was unsuccessfully staged in 1696. Her other plays include *The Royal Mischief* (1696).

▷Haywood, Eliza.

Manner, Eeva-Liisa (born 1921)

Finnish lyric poet and dramatist. She was born in Helsinki, where her father was an editor. She worked in the insurance business, and as an editor herself. She has received many awards and prizes for her poems, for her work as a translator and for her plays. She now lives at Tammerfors and in Spain.

She had her breakthrough with *Tämä matka* (1956) (*This Journey*) but she was first published in 1944, and since 1946 she has made a living as a writer. She writes about loneliness and loss, but also about nature and her connection with it. Another of her principal works is a fantasy about atomic disaster, *Fahrenheit 121* (1968). Here she writes from her self-elected exile in Spain, and speaks with an open egocentricity. The result is very intense. *Kuollet vedet* (1977) (*Dead Water*) continues the theme of man and death, but now in a free, cheerful style. She has also written satires and plays.

Manner often combines rationalism with a Taoist philosophy. She has managed to write through the decades without disruptions and has for a long time been considered a leading ▷modernist in Finnish literature.

Mannin, Ethel (1900–1984)

English novelist, short story and travel writer of Irish descent. Committed to the women's movement and a member of the Independent Labour Party during the 1930s, Mannin was a prolific writer, and many of her 100 publications (fiction and non-fiction) deal with women's oppression. In *Women and the Revolution* (1938) she argues that only the overthrow of capitalism will fully emancipate women, but Mannin's politics later shifted from socialism to anarchism. The novel *Red Rose* (1941) is based on the life of Emma Goldman. Her interest in child-rearing and child psychology is detailed in *Common Sense and the Child* (1931). Travel writings include *Women Also Dream* (1937) and *South to Samarkand* (1936). Autobiographical writings include *Confessions and Impressions* (1930), *Privileged Spectator* (1939) and *Stories from My Life* (1973).

Manning, Olivia (1908–1980)

Anglo-Irish novelist, short story writer and literary journalist. Manning was born in England, but spent much of her early life in Ireland; this gave her 'the usual Anglo-Irish sense of belonging nowhere'. As an adult she lived in London, where she began her friendship with ▷Stevie Smith.

After her marriage to a British Council lecturer she lived abroad until 1946, in Bucharest, Egypt, where she was press officer to the US embassy in Cairo, and Jerusalem, where she was press assistant to the Public Information Office. Her life abroad provided material for her two major trilogies: *The Balkan Trilogy*, which included *The Great Fortune* (1960), *The Spoilt City* (1962) and *Friends and Heroes* (1965), and *The Levant Trilogy*, comprising *The Danger Tree* (1977), *The Battle Lost and Won* (1978) and *The Sum of Things* (1980). These were televised as ▷ *The Fortunes of War*. Both trilogies explore the lives and marriage of a civilian couple, Harriet and Guy Pringle, during the World War II years. Manning's other work includes *The Wind Changes* (1937), her first published novel, which deals with Irish politics at the time of the 1921 settlement; *The Remarkable Expedition* (1947); *Growing Up* (1948); *The Doves of Venus* (1955); *The Play Room* (1969), an autobiographical novel set in the Isle of Wight; *Extraordinary Cats* (1967), and *The Rain Forest* (1974). Manning also wrote for newspapers and journals, such as *The Sunday Times*, *The Observer*, *Spectator*, *The New Statesman* and *Horizon*, and her ▷romantic fiction was serialized in magazines. In 1976 she was awarded the CBE.
Bib: Allen, W., *Tradition and Dreams*; Staley, T., (ed.) *Twentieth-Century Women Novelists*.

Mannoury d'Ectot, Madame de (19th century)

French erotic novelist. Little is known about this author, except that she had a château near Argenton, entertained many artists and writers, and was obliged to turn to literature – and, apparently, to open a matrimonial agency – because of straitened financial circumstances. She wrote two erotic texts: *Les Cousines de la colonelle* (1880) (*The Colonel's Wife's Cousins*), which was signed '*La Vicomtesse de Coeur-Brûlant*', and *Le Roman de Violette* (*The Story of Violette*), which was published anonymously in the early 1880s, although (falsely) dated 1870. The first is extremely vulgar, but its language sheers away from the directly explicit, and it is oddly respectful of bourgeois morality. The second consists of a series of lascivious set-pieces, depicts erotic activity, especially lesbianism, in a very stereotypical way, and is reminiscent of 18th-century French erotic writing.
Bib: Brécourt-Villars, C., *Ecrire d'Amour*; Frappier-Mazur, L., 'Marginal Canons; Rewriting the Erotic', *Yale French Studies*, Vol. 75.

Mano tagliata, La (1912) ▷*Severed Hand, The*

Mansfield, Katherine (1888–1923)

New Zealand short story writer. Born Kathleen Beauchamp to a middle-class New Zealand colonial family, Katherine Mansfield is New Zealand's most famous writer. Her life and work have been exhaustively documented, from her own letters, journals and notebooks kept by her husband John Middleton Murry, to biographical versions of her life. She continues to be a figure of great fascination to a contemporary audience, as much for the life she led as the fiction she wrote.

Kathleen Beauchamp was born in Wellington, the third of six children. She grew up in a landscape which she painstakingly and vividly reconstructed in her famous stories, 'At the Bay', 'The Doll's House', 'Prelude', and 'The Garden Party': a semi-pastoral landscape of large colonial houses, and beach. When Kathleen was four her father moved the family to a large house in the then rural environment of Karori, where they lived for six years. The Beauchamp children attended the local school, and the class structure of a new society which Mansfield experienced as a child is represented in her fiction. When the elder Beauchamp girls were teenagers they were taken to London to attend Queen's College. On her return to New Zealand in 1906, Mansfield pined for London and her friends there, particularly Ida Baker ('L.M.'), who was to remain close to her all her life, and managed to persuade her parents to allow her to return in 1908. Mansfield never visited New Zealand again.

In London she led a much-commented upon 'bohemian' life, marrying George Bowden and leaving him the next day, touring with a musical company and writing a little. Her first collection of stories was written while she was in Germany in 1909, where she suffered a miscarriage. On her return to London in 1910 she became ill with an untreated sexually transmitted disease, a condition which contributed to her weak health for the rest of her life. Around this time Mansfield began writing for A.R. Orage's *The New Age*, a journal which had its roots in the Theosophical movement, and submitted stories to *Rhythm*, a new journal edited by the man she eventually married, John Middleton Murry. Through this work Mansfield met people who were to influence and help her, among them ▷Virginia Woolf, ▷Ottoline Morrell and D.H. Lawrence.

Mansfield and Middleton Murry lived and worked together for a number of years before their marriage in 1918, during which time Mansfield's health broke down and she suffered the loss of her only brother in World War I, a loss which stimulated and focused her writing about New Zealand. Mansfield spent much of her time in France, seeking relief from tuberculosis, and developed her distinctive type of short fiction over the years between writing for *Rhythm* and her death in 1923. Lonely, unwell, and separated from family and friends for long periods of time, she nevertheless managed to produce a body of work that helped establish modernism as a primary literary movement and permanently changed the genre of short fiction.
Publications: *In a German Pension* (1911); *Prelude* (1918); *Bliss and Other Stories* (1921); ▷*The Garden Party and Other Stories* (1922); *The Doves' Nest and Other Stories* (1923); *Poems* (1924); *Something Childish and Other Stories* (1924); *The Journal of Katherine Mansfield*, ed. J.M. Murry

(1927); *The Letters of Katherine Mansfield*, ed. J.M. Murry (1928, 1929).

Mansfield Park (1814)

A novel by English writer ▷Jane Austen, concerned with the confluence of different moral orders and the conflicts that arise as a result. Sir Thomas Bertram of Mansfield Park represents a cold, authoritarian and conservative order, while his niece, Fanny Price, although seemingly child-like, is sensitive, rational and exemplarily wise. The wealthy and independent sister and brother, Mary and Henry Crawford, embody a metropolitan degeneracy that threatens to subvert the social order, and when Bertram is away they virtually take over Mansfield Park in order to rehearse a popular play of the period, Kotzebue's *Lover's Vows*. Later, Henry Crawford proposes to Fanny, but she refuses him in spite of the financial security he offers, provoking the astonished anger of Sir Thomas. Fanny in fact loves Sir Thomas's son Edmund, whose hand in marriage she eventually wins. The novel has often been considered deficient in Austen's characteristic irony, but recent feminist revaluations have contested this view, arguing that the author consistently satirises society's attitudes to women, as represented by characters such as Sir Thomas and Henry Crawford, and in the drama of Kotzebue. Austen's concern with morality has a feminist focus in *Mansfield Park*, for she demonstrates the hypocrisy and prejudice of a society that denies women full moral stature while lauding itself as a land of liberty and justice.

Mansilla, Daniel García ▷ Mansilla de García, Eduarda

Mansilla de García, Eduarda (1838–1892)

Argentinian novelist, short story writer and dramatist. Born in Buenos Aires, she also wrote under the pen-names Daniel García Mansilla and Alvar. As Alvar she published chronicles in *El Plata Illustrado* (1871–1872). At seventeen she married the diplomat Manuel Rafael García, and lived for a time in the United States and Europe. She wrote and published many of her books in French, and her brother translated them into Spanish. Her first novel, *El médico de San Luis (1860) (The Doctor of San Luis)*, was published under her son Daniel's name, to hide her female identity. Although it was highly praised, it was in fact closely based on *The Vicar of Wakefield* (1766) by the Irish dramatist, novelist and poet Oliver Goldsmith (1728–74) . Her novel *Pablo où la vie dans les pampas (1869) (Pablo or Life in the Pampas)* was first published in serial form in *L'Artiste*, and was translated into many languages.

In Buenos Aires, her house was a meeting-point for intellectuals and politicians. She tended to write popular serials rather than great literary works, but they serve as a useful reminder of life in Argentina at the turn of the century.

Other works: *Lúcia Miranda* (1860); *Creaciones*

(1883) (*Creations*), and *La marquesa de Altamira* (1881) (*The Marchioness of Altamira*).

Mansour, Joyce (1928–1987)

French writer. Born in England of Anglo-Egyptian parents, she settled in France, and all her works are written in French. Closely linked to the post-war group of Surrealists who popularized Freudian concepts (▷psychoanalysis), her poetry and texts convey the repressed violence of female sexuality. *Les Rapaces* (1960) (*Birds of Prey*), *Les Gisants satisfaits* (1958) (*The Contented Effigies*), *Carré blanc* (1965) (*Flash Card*), *Ça* (1970) (*That*) and *Faire signe au machiniste* (1977) (*Signal to the Driver*) are written in language akin to automatic writing, and cover themes of eroticism, death and anguish.

Manto

A mythical Ancient Greek poet and seer. Some say she was the daughter of the mythical seer Teiresias. Diodorus Siculus (1st century BC) records that she wrote oracles which were well composed. She is one of the women poets from whom Homer borrowed his ideas.

▷Helena; Phantasia; Boio

Manushi

An influential journal about Indian women and their place in Indian society, set up by journalist Madhu Kishwar in New Delhi in 1979. Its consistently high quality and regularity of publication is a tribute to its editors and their staff (many of them volunteers) and to the financial support it has received from well-wishers around the world. It is published in both Hindi and English editions, and has pioneered the translation of much writing by women in other Indian languages into these two languages. It has been in the forefront of the campaign against ▷dowry and dowry-deaths, and it addresses a wide range of political, social and economic issues from a woman's perspective. Contributors of poetry and prose to *Manushi* have included ▷Ambia, ▷Suniti Namjoshi, ▷Amrita Pritam, ▷Ashapurna Devi and ▷Mrinal Pande.

Man Who Loved Children, The (1940)

Australian novel by ▷Christina Stead. This is undoubtedly the most powerful novel written by an Australian woman. Set in Washington DC, but in reality reconstructing much of Stead's early life in Watson's Bay and around Sydney Harbour, it presents the unforgettable Pollit family: father Sam, a geologist in the public service and a loquacious know-all; his wife, Henny, an incompetent manager and mother of many; and Louie, the fat and unattractive child of Sam's first marriage, who is (at least potentially) a literary genius. The novel is concerned with the power-play within the family, which develops to the point where Louie prepares poison for her parents, which Henny deliberately drinks. The ending is ambivalent, for although Louie gathers the courage to walk away from the family, it is not clear whether she will fulfil her destiny. Underpinning the characterization of Louie is the philosophy of Nietzsche, particularly the notion of the artist as the 'superman' (or -woman) who is beyond conventional morality.

▷Autobiography (Australia)

Man/Woman: The One is the Other (1989)

Translation of *L'Un est l'autre* (1986), by French historian ▷Elisabeth Badinter. In this work Badinter draws on a wide field of research in anthropology and sociology in order to show the evolution of the relations between the sexes. She covers a range of cultures, going back to prehistory, in an attempt to discern the impact of the dramatic changes which have taken place in the 20th century.

Many Thing Begin for Change (1971)

A detective novel by the Nigerian writer ▷Adaora Lily Ulasi, the sequel to *Many Thing You No Understand* (1970). The first novel establishes the grounds for conflict between the rival authorities of the Igbo chiefs in eastern Nigeria and the colonial administration. It tells the story of what happens when, in accordance with tradition, twenty human heads are buried with a dead chief, and this flouting of colonial law is discovered after a relative of one of the victims complains. The second novel concerns the attempt by the colonial authorities to trace the perpetrators of the crime, in the course of which the District Officer is murdered. Ulasi takes delight in ridiculing British habits and customs, while portraying her African characters as either dim-witted or wily and underhand.

Many Thing You No Understand ▷*Many Thing Begin for Change*

Manzini, Gianna (1896–1974)

Italian novelist. Born in Pistoia, she went to university in Florence, and lived much of her life in Rome, contributing regularly to several Italian magazines. A recurrent theme of her work is the link between personality and surroundings. She considers this in the light of her own move to Rome in two works, *Lettera all'editore* (1945) (*Letter to the Editor*), and *Forte come un leone* (1944) (*Strong as a Lion*). Her lyrical style has been compared with that of ▷Virginia Woolf, as well as with D'Annunzio (▷*D'Annunzianesimo*), Proust and Joyce. Other descriptions of her writing are ▷surreal and ▷fantastical. Another recurrent theme of much of her work is the loneliness of women, and the comfort brought by memories and dreams. The typical shifting timescale of her narrative can be seen in ▷*Allegro con disperazione* (1965) (*Allegro, Despairingly*). Perhaps her most significant work is ▷*La sparviera* (1956) (*The Hawk*), an autobiographical novel. Also autobiographical, in a sense, is her *Ritratto in piedi* (1971) (*Portrait, Standing*), a memorial to/portrait of her father, which is full of warmth.

Other works: *Tempo innamorato* (1928) (*The Time of Love*); *Incontro col falco* (1929) (*Meeting the Hawk*); *Rive remote* (1940) (*Distant Shores*); *Carta d'identità* (1945) (*Identity Card*); *Ho visto il tuo cuore* (1950) (*I Have Seen Your Heart*); *Cara prigione* (1951) (*My Dear Prison*); *Animali sacri e profani* (1953) (*Sacred and Profane Animals*); *Il valtzer del diavolo* (1953) (*The Devil's Waltz*); *Arca di Noè* (1960) (*Noah's Ark*); *Un'altra cosa* (1961) (*Something Else*); *Sulla soglia* (1973) (*On the Threshold*).

Maori Literature

The pre-European Maori literary tradition is an oral tradition in which rhetorically formal songs and oratory express a traditional range of occasions and emotions. While some of the oral forms were written down, sometimes by Europeans, Maori written literature did not begin to appear in any kind of quantity until the 1950s, when it was actively encouraged, in both Maori and English, by the establishment of journals, particularly *Te Ao Hou*, catering for a Maori readership. Despite the numbers of Maori who wrote for these journals, book-form publication by Maori writers did not appear until the 1970s and remains a small, though actively sought, part of New Zealand book publication. The work of one of these writers, ▷J.C. Sturm, was eventually collected as *The House of the Talking Cat* in 1983, and ▷Patricia Grace published her first collection of stories, *Waiariki*, in 1975. The emergence of Maori women writers in English increased dramatically during the 1980s and 1990s, with the international success of ▷Keri Hulme's ▷*the bone people* and the appearance of a number of new writers, but proportionately the number of publications in Maori or English by Maori writers is still small. Maori women tend to write about family and gender roles and celebrate the significant identity of an individual within a group, partly in order to combat the perceived threat to Maori community presented by European society.

▷Bridger, Bub; Campbell, Meg; Hineira, Arapera; Mataira, K. Te Heikoko; Menzies, Trixie Te Arama; Te Awekotuku, Ngahuia; Orbell, Margaret; Penfold, Merimeri; Potiki, Roma; Sturm, J.C.

Mar, Anna (1887–1917)

Pen-name of Anna Iakovlevna Brovar (married name, Lenshina), Russian prose and film-script writer. Mar also wrote a column for the magazine *Journal for Women* under the pseudonym 'Princess Daydream', answering readers' inquiries. Her first works were short prose pieces collected as *Miniatures* (1906). Their themes are philosophical, religious, and sexual. The stories about sexuality often reverse roles: the female characters are blatantly seductive but a number of male characters are undone by sensuality. In 1912 another volume of collected stories, *The Impossible*, appeared. The novella *Passers-by* deals with some of her favourite themes: obsessive, unrequited love, attraction to suffering, religious salvation, and the plight of poor women who turn to prostitution. The novella *For You Alone I Sinned* (1914) is set abroad, where the young, widowed, tubercular heroine, Mechka, meditates on the affinity of religious fervour, sensuality, and beauty. She falls in love with the priest who helps her to regain her Catholic faith and senses that the feeling is returned. She realizes she must pay dearly for his love: 'And, purchasing her happiness with suffering, she rejoiced, for there is nothing more tasteless and vulgar than a blind, satisfied happiness.' Unlike Mar's short works, the narrative is loose and unfocused. The short stories and 'post cards' collected in 1916 as *Blood and Rings* include portraits of a number of sensual women and explore aspects of love that include its closeness to hatred and elements of sadomasochism. The 'post cards' are short monologic confessions, often by a male speaker. In 'Notes personnelles' the female narrator, a writer, argues with her readers who demand moral and 'useful' works and confuse her writing with her person. Mar also wrote scripts for ten successful films and a play, *When Ships Are Sinking* (1915). Her last published work was the novel ▷*Woman on the Cross*, published in a heavily censored version in 1916, and in two more complete editions in 1917 and 1918. In 1917 Mar poisoned herself over an unhappy love affair.

Dacia Maraini

Maracle, Lee (born 1950)

Canadian Metis orator and writer, who grew up in Vancouver, British Columbia. As a young woman she drifted between California, Toronto and Vancouver, experiences recounted in *Bobbi Lee: Indian Rebel* (1975, republished in 1990). *I am Woman* (1988) is a further literary monograph of her struggle. She published a book of poetry, *Seeds*, and in 1990 co-edited *Telling It: Women and Language Across Cultures. Sojourner's Truth and Other Stories* (1990) (▷Soujourner Truth) relies to a large extent on principles of Native Canadian oratory. Maracle's work is rhetorically engaged with the political situation of Native Canadian women.

▷En'owkin School of International Writing
Bib: Lutz, H., *Contemporary Challenges: Conversations with Canadian Native Authors.*

Maraini, Dacia (born 1936)

Italian novelist, dramatist, poet and journalist. Maraini was born in Florence, but while still a child she lived in Japan and Palermo, finally moving to Rome. A contributor to many Italian journals and periodicals. She lived with the writer Alberto Moravia after the end of his relationship with ▷Elsa Morante. Her writing often addresses feminist themes, such as the role of women in society, issues of choice and alternative ways of living. Many of her narratives centre on female protagonists. Her first work, *La vacanza* (1962) (*The Holiday*, translated into English in 1966), has as its main theme female sexual freedom, explored through the character of Anna, a young girl whose first sexual experiences take place against the backdrop of World War II. *L'età del malessere* (*The Age of Discontent*, published, and translated into English, in 1963) also deals with female sexuality. Her relationship with her father comes under scrutiny in *Crudeltà all'aria aperta* (1966) (*Cruelty in the Open*), a collection of poetry. She is probably one of the most widely read and most respected of contemporary Italian writers, though she has never shrunk from controversy. Her most recent novel, ▷*La lunga vita di Marianna Ucria* (1990) (*The Long Life of Marianna Ucria*), set in 18th-century Sicily, won the Campiello Prize in 1990, and indeed her work has won many literary awards over the years. Her theatrical work has also enjoyed considerable success. She has produced essays on the theatre (*Fare teatro*, 1974, *Theatre*), on poetry (*Cento anni, poesia giapponese*, 1968) on Japanese poetry and on striking female figures of mythology and history (*I sogni di Clitennestra*, 1981, *Clytemnestra's Dreams*).

Her other works include: *Le figlie del defunto colonello* (1962) (*The Dead Colonel's Daughters*); *A memoria* (1967) (*By Heart*); *Mio marito* (1968) (*My Husband*); *Il ricatto a teatro e altre commedie* (1970) (*Blackmail in the Theatre and Other Plays*); *Memorie di una ladra* (1972) (*Memories of a Female Thief*, translated into English in 1973); *E tu chi eri?* (1973) (*And Who Were You?*); *Viva l'Italia* (1973); *Donne mie* (1974) (*Women*); *Dialogo di una prostituta col cliente* (1975) (*A Prostitute Talks with Her Client*); *La donna perfetta* (1975) (*The Perfect Woman*); *Donna in guerra* (1975) (*Woman at War*); *Don Juan* (1976); *Mangiami pure* (1978) (*Do Eat*

Me); *Lettere a Marina* (1981) (*Letters to Marina*); ▷*Lezioni d'amore e altre commedie* (1982) (*Lessons in Love and Other Plays*); *Isolina* (1985).

Maranhão, Heloísa (born 1925)

Heloísa Maranhão

Brazilian novelist, short story writer, dramatist and poet, whose full name is Heloísa dos Reis Maranhão. She is also a translator and a professor of drama. In her most important novel, *Lucrécia* (1980), she interweaves the voices of two women – the boisterous Lucretia Borgia and the sacred Santa Teresa d'Avila. The novel dramatically portrays a confrontation between the sacred and the profane, questioning truth, and parodying the accepted social rules for women's behaviour. The same pattern is followed in *A rainha de Navarra* (1986) (*The Queen of Navarra*), in which a delirious woman, dressed like a queen and holding the flag in a samba school, is under the delusion that she really is a queen. In *Florinda* (1982) she was influenced by the folklorist Câmara Cascudo.

Other works: *Paixão da terra* (1957) (*The Earth's Passion*); *Negra Bá* (1959) (*Bá the Negress*); *Inês de Castro, a rainha morta* (1975) (*Inês de Castro, the Dead Queen*); *Tiradentes* (1970); *A Cobra* (1977) (*The Snake*; *Castelo interior e moradas* (1973) (*Interior Castle and Dwellings*); *Dona Leonor Teles* (1985), and *Adriana* (1990).

Maratti Zappi, Faustina (c1680–1745)

Italian poet. Born in Rome. Like many female poets of the period, she used her poetry to confront intensely personal issues, such as the death of her son, to whom she addressed much of her work. She also wrote love poetry, expressing her possessiveness and jealousy. Yet her poetry stands out for her celebration of her own strength and courage, and her readiness to face whatever misfortune fate might send her way. She wrote a variety of ▷Arcadian poetry: *canzoni*, madrigals, sonnets and elegies. Her poetry was published along with that of her husband in a collection, *Rime dell'avvocato Giovanni Battista Felice Zappi e di F. Maratti sua consorte* (1723, 1736) (*Poetry by Giovanni Battista Felice Zappi and by F.Maratti, His Consort*). Her position in this anthology is obviously secondary to that of her husband, but this is not true of her poetry.

March, Susana (born 1918)

Spanish poet and novelist from Barcelona. Her most important novel is *Algo muere cada día* (1955) (*Something Dies Within Us Every Day*), which describes the disintegration of a male–female relationship and indirectly criticizes the social conventions which restrict individuals' lives. Her other works are: *Narraciones* (1945) (*Narrations*); *Nina* (1949); *Canto rodado* (1944) (*Rolling Stone*), and *Nido de vencejos* (1945) (*Nest of Swallows*).

Marchant, Catherine ▷Cookson, Catherine

Márchenko, Anastasiia Iakovlevna (1830–1880)

Russian fiction writer and minor poet. Of Polish-Ukrainian parentage, Márchenko grew up in happy freedom on a rural Ukrainian estate, experienced poverty in her youth in Odessa, and taught music to support her family. In 1855 she married a military officer named Kir'iakov and moved to St Petersburg. Between 1847 and 1859 she published four novels, at least fifteen shorter prose works, and a number of poems. In the 1860s she disappeared from public view. A precocious, self-willed child, Márchenko began writing young, and published her first novellas in Odessa under the deceptive title *Travel Notes* and the pseudonym 'T. Ch.'. They received unprecedented acclaim for their fresh voice and feminine viewpoint and opened the pages of ▷St Petersburg ▷'thick journals' to her. The influence of ▷George Sand can be seen in her unstereotyped heroines and, like most other women writers of the period, she is better at portraying women than men. In 'The Governess' her young protagonist must choose between remaining a burden to her impoverished parents, marrying without love, or finding a way to earn a living. In Márchenko's stories love is rarely reciprocated. 'Too Late!' deals with a chain of love affairs in which poor but proud Aleksandrina is the odd woman out. In 'Around and About' Margarita finds the idle young Kereutov unable to meet the challenge of her direct personality. In the effective novella *Hills*, artificial sledding slopes become a metaphor for the ups-and-downs of St Petersburg life as an independent provincial girl experiences it.

▷Society tale

Mare non bagna Napoli, Il (1953) ▷*Bay Is Not Naples, The*

Margaret Howth: A Story of Today (1862)

US novel by ▷Rebecca Harding Davis. It was serialized in ▷*The Atlantic Monthly* as 'A Story for To-day' shortly after Davis's début there with ▷*Life in the Iron Mills*. *Atlantic Monthly* editor James T. Fields (1817–1881) objected to the gloom of the story, but, while Harding Davis offered to revise it, her gloomy portrait and ending remained fairly intact. She published the story with an introductory explanation that digging into 'commonplace . . . vulgar American life' led us to see 'new and awful significance'.

Margaret Howth brings together many subjects and themes that characterize US fiction for the rest of the century: the working conditions of industrial workers, a romantic subplot with the lovers separated by economic interests, racial prejudice, and Utopian schemes to improve conditions for workers. Margaret Howth loses her lover and works in the mill for lack of traditional family support, befriends an African-American woman who suffers from her own experience of poverty and the work in the mill, and gains increasing recognition of the economic and racial causes of workers' unrest in the USA.

Margaret, Duchess of Burgundy (Margaret of York) (1446–1503)

Scribe presenting Boethius' Consolation of Philosophy *to Margaret of York, Flemish illustration, 1476*

English patron Margaret was the third daughter of Richard, Duke of York, and Cecily Neville. She married Charles, Duke of Burgundy in 1486. She commissioned a variety of books: translations into French; copies of devotional works; and she was a collector of richly illuminated manuscripts.

Among the recipients of her patronage was the translator and printer William Caxton (died 1492). Caxton had begun a translation from French into English of the *History of Troy* in 1469. He resumed it again with Margaret's financial support, and printed it – the first printed book in English – in 1476.

Margaret of Anjou (1430–1482)

Daughter of the Duke of Anjou, queen of Henry VI of England, letter-writer. Margaret of Anjou was married to Henry in 1445. She was politically active, and played a leading role on the Lancastrian side in the Wars of the Roses (1455–1485). Eventually defeated (with her son Edward killed, and Henry later murdered), she ended her life in poverty in Anjou. Some letters written by her (in English) are preserved, which are of interest both from the point of view of politics and power, and for what they reveal of her other interests and pleasures, such as hunting.
Bib: Wood, Mary Anne Everett, *Letters of Royal and Illustrious Ladies of Great Britain*; Moriarty, Catherine, *The Voice of the Middle Ages in Personal Letters 1100–1500*.

Marghieri, Clotilde Betocchi (1897–1981)

Italian novelist and essayist. Born in Naples, she attended the University of Florence, and lived in Rome for most of her life. She was a regular contributor to *Il Mondo* and *Corriere della Sera*. She began to write rather late in life, and her fiction is experimental in style. She won literary prizes for all of her work, and was popular with both the reading public and literary critics. Memory as recreation of time past is the recurrent theme of her work. Her most important publications, *Vita in villa* (*Life in a Country House*) of 1963, *Le educande di Poggio Gherardo* (*The Female Boarders in Poggio Gherardo*) of 1963, and *Il segno sul braccio* (*The Marked Arm*) of 1970, are collected in ▷*Trilogia* (*A Trilogy*) of 1982.

Marguerite d'Autriche (1480–1530)

French occasional poet. The daughter of Maximilian I of Austria (Emperor 1493–1519) and Marie de Bourgogne (1457–1482), she was brought up at the French court to marry Charles VIII (1470–1498). Abandoned in favour of Anne de Bretagne (1477–1514), she eventually married Philibert le Beau, Duc de Savoie (the brother of ▷Louise de Savoie), who died in 1504. Marguerite was inconsolable, but took as her motto *Fortune infortune fort une* (Fortune and misfortune are all the same to me). She became governor of the Low Countries, and a major political figure on the European stage, signing the Treaty of Cambrai with Louise de Savoie in 1529. She held court at Malines, where she was a generous patron of the arts. Her library contained much French fiction and poetry, and she left three manuscript albums of light verses on love and piety of which one piece has been positively attributed to her: '*C'est pour jamais qu'un regret me demeure*' ('One regret remains with me for ever').

Bib: Grente, G. (ed.) *Dictionnaire des lettres françaises.*

Marguerite de Navarre (d'Angoulême), Duchesse d'Alençon (1492–1549)

French poet and short story writer. The sister of François I (1494–1547), she was the author of *L'Heptaméron* (1559) (▷ *The Heptameron of Marguerite de Navarre*, 1654) one of the most famous French narratives written in the style of the Italian author Boccaccio (1313–1375), and produced an enormous range of religious and secular texts, including four Biblical comedies and seven other plays. A marriage of convenience in 1509 to Charles, Duc d'Alençon, proved unsatisfactory because he had never read or studied. When he died in 1525, she married Henri d'Albert, King of Navarre, in 1527, but her letters and poems suggest that she may have only really loved her brother, who shared her passion for literature. As writer and patron, and a cultivated woman of letters, she played an important role in the development of the French Renaissance, and was surrounded by the great writers of her day: François Rabelais (c 1483–1553), Clément Marot (1496–1544) and Robert Estienne (1503–1559). Her education was supervised by her mother, ▷ Louise de Savoie. Marguerite was attracted to evangelism, and was acquainted with the religious reformer Jean Calvin (1509–1564). She knew Latin, Italian and Spanish, and enough Greek to study the Bible in the original. The Bible represented for her the supreme authority, leading to various controversies with the Church. She was profoundly marked by mysticism and the neoplatonism of the Italian ▷ humanist Marsilio Ficino (1433–1499). Marguerite and her mother were involved in the government of France during François I's imprisonment in Spain. At court she impressed all the ambassadors who conversed with her.

The *Miroir de l'âme pécheresse* (1531) (*The Mirror of the Sinner's Soul*), the most important of her poetic works, was translated by the future ▷ Elizabeth I (1533–1603). Her famous poem, the '*Triomphe de l'Agneau*' ('The Triumph of the Lamb'), was a pious but controversial meditation on the Fall of Man, and was condemned by the Sorbonne. She also wrote *Marguerites de la Marguerite des Princesses* and its 'sequel', *Suyte des Marguerites de la Marguerite des Princesses*, containing several plays and a large number of poems, published in Lyon in 1547. The death of her brother in that year led her to write a number of mournful poems and notably '*Le Navire*' ('The Ship') and '*Les Prisons*' ('The Prisons'), first published by Abel Lefranc at the end of the 19th century. 'The Prisons' is one of the most remarkable poems of the 16th century. It presents the poet's spiritual odyssey as he is held captive in three successive prisons: 'Love', 'Ambition' and 'Science'. Free once more, the former captive exchanges the torments of intellectual and worldly aspirations for the happiness of the contemplation and adoration of God.

The *Heptaméron*, begun in the last decade of Marguerite's life, was left unfinished and published posthumously in 1558 and 1559. It can be seen as the first essays in French literature on the relationship between the sexes. The deeds of men are of only incidental interest in the narrative, which discusses how women's honour is threatened by men's conduct. Although women are not presented as entirely innocent, it is the men who are blamed for seeking to indulge '*[le] plaisir qui gist a deshonorer les femmes*' ('the pleasure to be found in dishonouring women'). In the *Heptaméron*, Marguerite de Navarre presents a high ideal of marriage, stating of one of her heroines: '*si amour et bonne volonté fondée sur la craincte de Dieu, sont les vraiz et seurs liens de mariage, elle estoit si bien lyée que fer, ne feu, ne eau ne pouvaient rompre son lien, sinon la mort*' ('if love and goodness founded on the fear of God are the true and sure bonds of marriage, she was so firmly bonded [to her husband] that neither the sword, nor fire, nor water could break that bond, and only death could come between them'). Although she has been accused of immorality, her work promotes a neoplatonic view of love founded '*sur Dieu et sur honneur*' ('on God and honour').
Bib: Marguerite de Navarre, *Oeuvres choisies*, ed. H.P. Clives, 1968; Telle, E., *L'Oeuvre de Marguerite d'Angoulême reine de Navarre et la Querelle des Femmes.*

Marguerite de Valois (1553–1615)

French memoir-writer. She was also known as Marguerite de France and 'Queen Margot', and often rather confusingly called Marguerite de Navarre after her marriage in 1572 to the future Henri IV (1553–1610). The daughter of Henri II (1519–1559) and ▷ Catherine de Medici, she was the great-niece of ▷ Marguerite de Navarre, the author of the *Heptaméron* (1559) (▷ *The Heptaméron of Marguerite de Navarre*, 1654). Her marriage to Henri de Navarre did not achieve the intended reconciliation between Catholics and Protestants on either a personal or a national level. After their separation it was annulled. Known for her beauty and powers of seduction, she had a reputation as a nymphomaniac, and was exiled from the court by Henri III (1551–1589) for her political and amorous intrigues, but she held a brilliant court at Nérac before being imprisoned at Usson in the Auvergne from 1587 to 1605. She is glowingly portrayed by Brantôme (c 1540–1614), to whom she dedicated her own ▷ *Mémoires* (1628) in recognition. Although short, her record of the '*malheurs de mon temps*' ('misfortunes of my time') are very interesting and were much appreciated in the 17th century, being frequently republished. They are the only memoirs source, for instance, which ▷ Mademoiselle de Montpensier openly acknowledged. Her poetry and letters in French and in Latin were also much praised for their eloquence, and she was celebrated by Pierre de Ronsard (1524–1585), among other poets.

Marguerite d'Oingt (1286–1310)
French religious biographer and author of letters. Not much is known of her life other than that she was the daughter of Guichard, Seigneur d'Oingt in Beaujolais, and that she became a nun in the Carthusian convent of Poleteins in the Ain, of which she became prioress, and which she never left. A highly cultivated woman, she wrote mainly in Latin, but her other extant writings, such as a life of Beatrice of Ornacieu and fragments of letters to her directors of conscience and another lady in Lyon dialect, were written in French.
Bib: Grente, G., *Dictionnaire des lettres françaises.*

Maria (1954)
A novel by Italian writer ▷Lalla Romano. It tells the story of Maria, a poor girl, a housekeeper, whose main characteristic is unshakeable loyalty. The novel reads like a blend of poetry and prose, with a rapid succession of images following one upon another in the narrative. This work won the Veillon Prize in the year it was published.

'Maria del Occidente' ▷Brooks, Maria Gowen

Maria de Portugal, The Infanta, Dona (1521–77)
The daughter of King Manuel and Queen Leonor of Austria. With the death of King Manuel in 1521, Maria's step-brother succeeded his father to the throne. The new king, João III, refused to allow Leonor to leave Portugal with Maria – this despite a prenuptial agreement, signed by Manuel, giving permission to his foreign-born wife to depart with any children they might have in the event of his death. Leonor left Portugal without her daughter in 1523, and later married Francisco I of Spain. Meanwhile Maria came under the care of the new queen of Portugal, Catarina. Leonor spent the rest of her life trying to arrange a marriage for Maria, the only way she could legally get her daughter out of the country. João III rejected her earliest attempts, claiming that Maria was too young, and he warded off later proposals. Finally, in 1547, a contract was signed between the Infanta and Felipe, son of Carlos V, the king of Spain. But just prior to Maria's departure for Spain in 1553, the contract was rescinded for political reasons, and the following year Felipe married Mary Tudor, who had become queen of England.

According to ▷Carolina Michaëlis de Vasconcelos, Maria rejected later marriage contracts, resolving to remain single. She presided over her own household from the age of sixteen, and surrounded herself with some of the most learned women in the country. Her palace was often referred to as the 'home of the muses' and the 'female university'. The women of her court included the Latin scholars ▷Luisa Sigea and Joana Vaz; the musicians and teachers Paula Vicente and Ángela Sigea; and Leonor de Noronha, translator of the *Chronica do Mundo.*
▷*Infanta Dona Maria de Portugal e as Suas Damas, A*

Marian Withers (1851)
A novel by English writer ▷Geraldine Jewsbury. Considered to be her best work of fiction, it is concerned with issues such as female ▷education and societal expectations of women. Set in Manchester, the narrative focuses on the life of Marian Withers, detailing her social background and describing her passage to maturity.

'Maria of the West' ▷Brooks, Maria Gowen

Marie (13th century)
English nun and hagiographer. Marie may have been a nun of Chatteris, Cambridgeshire, an Anglo-Saxon foundation connected with Ely. She wrote an ▷Anglo-Norman verse life of St Audrey (the Anglo-Saxon Æthelthryth), virgin patroness and former abbess of Ely. Her Life is a free adaptation (which has been described as 'rather dry') of the Latin account found in the *History of Ely* by the monk Thomas, although Marie names Bede (the Anglo-Saxon historian) as her source. Marie is one of the three women known to have written Anglo-Norman religious verse.
▷Barking, Anonymous nun of; Clemence of Barking
Bib: Södergård, Östen (ed.), *La Vie Seinte Audrée: Poème Anglo-Normande du XIIIe siècle.*

Marie de France (12th century)
French poet. She was the first woman to write in a European vernacular, perhaps the greatest woman author of the Middle Ages, and the creator of the finest medieval short fiction before the Italian and English writers Boccaccio (1313–1375) and Geoffrey Chaucer (?1345–1400). Despite intriguing efforts to determine her identity, she remains a mystery. The extreme view is that the name Marie was added by a scribe, and that the author may have been a man. All that can be asserted with conviction is that at least one poet by the name of Marie was writing in the second half of the 12th century, but she was not called Marie de France. This poet, who seems to have written mainly at the English court, probably during the 1170s and 1180s, has been variously associated with women of the period with this name: Marie de Champagne (daughter of Eleanor of Aquitaine, 1122–1204) and Patroness of the poet Chrétien de Troyes (c 1135–c 1190)); Marie, Abbess of Shaftesbury in Dorset (fl 1181–1215, the illegitimate daughter of Geoffrey Plantagenet and half-sister to Henry II of England (1133–1189); Marie, Abbess of Reading; Marie (1140/50–?), eighth child of Waleran de Meulan (who married into a family with lands in England and Normandy); and ▷Mary, Countess of Boulogne (?1154–?, daughter of Stephen of Blois, and Abbess of Romsey in Hampshire). The prominence of the motif of adultery and evident

interest in the chivalric life suggest that her poetic tales were not written by someone who had led a monastic life.

The most impressive documentation for identifying her is to be found in her collection of *'vers de lais, Ke ne sunt pas del tut verais'* ('verse lays which are not all true') by which we know of her existence. Until the late 18th century, Marie was known as the '13th-century' author of *L'Ysopet*, a collection of fables, an adaptation of a Latin translation of an English version of Aesop's *Fables*, (Greek, 6th century BC) which were an inspiration to Jean de La Fontaine (1621–1695). Although the fables have recently been reappraised, she is now much better known as the author of twelve *Lais* (*Lays*), in the Breton tradition, first published in 1819. These lays are marked by their brevity and the intensity with which they portray passion. As a form of short story, the lay was traditionally associated with a musical performance, but Marie's *lais*, varying in length from a hundred lines to over a thousand, were not apparently intended to be sung, and represent a more literary stage in the development of the genre. Many of the *lais* tell of frustrated young women who have been married off to older men because of their child-rearing capacities, and contrive to see their lovers at regular intervals, despite the risk. The author also has an evident interest in the welfare of infants. Marie intervenes frequently in the first person, and is proud of her literary talents and reputation. She may nevertheless have had to work in secret: *'Soventes fiez en ai veillé'* ('I have often stayed awake at night working on them'). She also wrote *'Espurgatoire de Saint-Patrice'* ('St Patrick's Purgatory'), a 2,300-line account of the knight Owein's descent into the Otherworld through a cavern on Station Island in Lough Derg (County Donegal in Ireland), based on the *Tractatus de Purgatorio Sancti Patricii* (*Treatise on St Patrick's Purgatory*), written some time after 1189.
Bib: Burgess, G., *The Lais of Marie de France*; Marie de France, *Fables*, ed. H. Spiegel.

Marie de l'Incarnation (1599–1672)

French author of two autobiographical narratives and numerous letters. Born Marie Guyart, she married Claude Martin in 1618 and, widowed the following year, left for Canada, founding the first Ursuline convent there, later becoming Mother Superior. Her autobiography was written in two stages, twenty years apart, the first in Tours in 1633 and the second in Quebec in 1653. These *Relations* (*Accounts*) were published together with her letters in 1681, and are remarkable for their accurate reflection of the world beyond the monastery walls.
Bib: Grente, G., *Dictionnaire des lettres françaises*.

Marin de Gibraltar, Le (1952) ▷ Sailor from Gibraltar, The (1966)

Marín del Solar, Mercedes (1804–1866)

Chilean poet. One of the first romantic women poets in Chile, she wrote under the influence of the Spanish-Cuban writer ▷Gertrúdis Gómez de Avellaneda. She refused to be taught domestic activities, and instead learned French, read French books and studied the Venezuelan philosopher Andrés Bello (1781–1865). Her main work, *Canto fúnebre a la muerte de don Diego Portales* (1837) (*Funeral Song on The Death of Don Diego Portales*), a daring poem praising the hero of the Chilean Republic, was published (anonymously) by *El Araucano*, even though she was a woman and the daughter of Don Gasper Marín, secretary of the First Governmental Council. Her collected poems were compiled by her son, Enrique del Solar, and published posthumously in 1874.

Marinelli Vacca, Lucrezia (1571–1653)

Italian poet and essayist. Born in Venice, she began writing poetry at about the age of twenty. Her father was a doctor and a philosopher, and she was well-educated. She married late in life. A religious woman, she wrote both heroic and religious poetry. She is, indeed, generally judged to be the greatest female heroic poet of the period. In terms of literary influences, traces of Poliziano, Ariosto and Tasso can be detected in her work. Her heroic poetry includes *'Enrico ovvero Bisanzio acquistato'* (1653) (Henry or Byzantium Gained), written in celebration of the Doge of Venice, Enrico Dandolo, and his Crusades. Her religious writings include *La vita del serafico e glorioso San Francesco* (1595) (*The Life of the Seraphic and Glorious Saint Francis*), *Il libro di Maria Vergine, imperatrice dell'universo* (1602) (*The Book of the Virgin Mary, Empress of the Universe*), *Rime sacre* (1603) (*Religious Poetry*), *Vita di Santa Giustina* (1606) (*The Life of Saint Justine*), *Dei gesti eroici e della vita meravigliosa della serafica Santa Caterina da Siena* (1624) (*On the Heroic Gestures and the Wondrous Life of the Seraphic Saint Catherine of Siena*). She also wrote allegorical and mythical poetry, one example of which is *Amore innamorato ed impazzito* (1618) (*Love in Love and Maddened*), in which Love wounds himself accidentally, and so falls in love with Ersilia. Yet Marinelli is perhaps most famous for her contribution to the debate on the nature of women and men current in the 16th century (▷16th-century treatises on women). In this debate, she took the side of women, and extolled female virtue while criticizing men. Her *La nobiltà e eccelenze delle donne, et i difetti e mancamenti de gli huomini* (*On the Nobility and Excellence of Woman and the Defects and Failings of Man*) was published in 1600, and reprinted several times. It is a large tome, in two sections, the first of which defends women while the second highlights male inadequacies.

Other works: *La colomba sacra* (1595) (*The Holy Dove*); *Arcadia felice* (1605) (*Joyful Arcadia*); *Le vittorie di Francesco il serafico* (1644) (*The Victories of Francis the Seraphic*); *Il canto d'amore della vergine Santa Giustina* (1648) (*The Love Song of the Virgin Saint Justine*).

Marini, Marcelle

French psychoanalyst who questions Freudian theory from a feminist viewpoint, and particularly its relation to language as developed by French psychoanalyst Jacques Lacan (1901–1981) (▷psychoanalysis). The focus of her research into femininity is the work of ▷Marguerite Duras, which she explores in ▷*Territoires du féminin, avec M. Duras* (1977) (*Feminine Territories, With M. Duras*). This led to her independent enquiry into Lacanian theory, *Jacques Lacan* (1986); unlike ▷Luce Irigaray, she does not argue from the point of view of a former member of Lacan's École Française de Psychanalyse.

Marion, artista del caffè concerto (1891) (Marion, a Singer)

Italian novel, by ▷Annie Vivanti, which tells the story of Marion, a child who grows up in a theatrical environment. She loses her mother at the age of twelve and, forced to sing for a living thereafter, is repeatedly exploited. This story is made more complex by the inclusion of the character Anna, a middle-class child raised in comfort. Unlike Marion, she is not particularly intelligent. The two finally meet and Marion, in a sort of trance, kills Anna. By this act, she takes revenge on society. This novel ultimately investigates the difficult position of the woman who is also an artist.

Markandaya, Kamala (born 1924)

Indian novelist and journalist. She was educated at the University of Madras, and emigrated to Britain in 1948, where she has lived since. Her ▷social realist novels include *Some Inner Fury* (1955), *A Silence of Desire* (1960), *Possession* (1963), ▷*A Handful of Rice* (1966), *The Coffer Dams* (1969), *The Nowhere Man* (1972), *Two Virgins* (1973), ▷*The Golden Honeycomb* (1977) and *Pleasure City* (1982). Her writing often explores the inability of rustics to survive the onslaught of modern sophisticates, as in *Nectar in a Sieve* (1955), and all her works examine critically what she sees as the poor record of interaction between the East and the West.
Bib: Joseph, M.P., *Kamala Markandaya*; Krishna Rao, A.V., *The Indo-Anglian Novel and the Changing Tradition*; Srivastava, R.K., *Six Indian Novelists in English*.

Marked Man, A (1890)

Australian novel by ▷Ada Cambridge. *A Marked Man* is considered to be the finest novel Cambridge produced during her long and distinguished writing career. Set in the English fens and in Sydney, it explores, through two generations of the Delavel family, the opposition between love and religious difference and class distinction. In the marriage of Richard and Annie Delavel love is destroyed by petty materialism, and Richard takes refuge in a near-adulterous relationship with Constance, and with periodic escapes to an artist's camp near Sydney. The novel was republished by Pandora in 1987.

Marlatt, Daphne (born 1942)

Canadian poet, prose writer, editor and critic, born Daphne Buckle in Melbourne, Australia. She lived in Malaysia and England before emigrating with her parents to Canada in 1951. Marlatt graduated from the University of British Columbia in 1964, then moved with her husband to Bloomington, Indiana, where she received an MA from the University of Indiana (1968), returning permanently to Vancouver after her marriage ended in 1970. Her first book, *Frames of a Story* (1968), combines prose and poetry, and predicates the direction her writing would take in its inter-genre movement. *leaf leaf/s* (1969) employed a rigorously pared poetic line; but it was clear early on that Marlatt was edging toward the runaway ongoing line of her strongest work. *Rings* (1971), which engages the author's experience of motherhood and marital disintegration, was later republished in expanded form as *What Matters: 1968–1970* (1980). *Vancouver Poems* (1972) celebrates that city and its history as an evocative, sensual experience. She goes further into evocation of place in *Steveston* (1974, republished 1984) and *Steveston Recollected* (1975), poetic and aural renditions of a Japanese fishing village located at the mouth of the Fraser River in British Columbia. *Our Lives* (1975) utilizes Marlatt's experience of living in a communal house for its narrative. *Selected Writing: Net Work* (1980) is a selection of her early work and re-emphasizes her concern with the local and the communal in the texture of language. *Zócalo* (1977), a journal-novel, reads the foreign territory of the Yucatán.

Marlatt's work continues to explore the elements of orality and travel; *How to Hug a Stone* (1983) uses voice transcriptions of narrative vernacular she encountered on a journey to England. *Double Negative* (1988, with ▷Betsy Warland) is about a doubly reflected journey to Australia. ▷*Touch to My Tongue* (1984) outlines Marlatt's relationship to the living body of language; it includes her important essay, 'Musing with Mothertongue', which signals her engagement with feminist literary theory. The blurring between essay and poem is here articulately sensual; this piece enables her to explore a feminist and lesbian erotics of etymology. *Ana Historic* (1988) is a deconstructive novel of women's historical silencing. *Salvage* (1991) re-examines two decades of feminist experience. During the 1970s Marlatt worked as a teacher; she edited for *Capilano Review* and *Periodics*, as well as *Island*. More recently, her association with ▷Nicole Brossard and ▷Louky Bersianik is evident in her collective work on the feminist theory journal ▷*Tessera*. Marlatt is one of the most brilliant writers engaged in experiment and feminist theory in Canada today.
Bib: Ricou, L., in ▷*A Mazing Space*; Special Issue, *Line* (1989).

Marlitt, Eugenie (1825–1887)

German novelist. From a cultured merchant family, she was a talented musician and, as a young woman, sang in the theatres of Leipzig, Linz and Graz until, in 1853, deafness put an end to her promising career. She became a lady's companion, and began to write stories in instalments for the popular journal, *Gartenlaube* (*Gazebo*), whose circulation doubled as a result. Her novels, of which *Goldelse* (1867) (*Golden Else*) was the first and the best, were translated into many languages. With her plots about poor but beautiful heroines whose virtue is always rewarded with wealth and fame, she created a tradition of ▷sentimental women's fiction, which, in this century, found its continuation in the work of ▷Hedwig Courths-Mahler.

Marni, Jeanne (1854–1910)

▷Pseudonym of Jeanne Marnière, French novelist and dramatic author. After a precocious literary début – a short story of hers was published in *Le Monde illustré* (*Illustrated World*) when she was only eight – she began an acting career, but became disenchanted with the theatre, and, after losing her husband in 1858, turned back to writing. A series of early novels, for example, *La Femme de Silva*, 1887 (*The de Silva Woman*), and *L'Amour coupable*, 1889 (*The Guilty Love Affair*), were followed by articles, dialogues and humorous pieces which first appeared in journals of the period and were subsequently published, in volume form, by Ollendorf. These included *Comment elles se donnent* (1895) (*Women's Devotion*); *Comment elles nous lâchent* (1896) (*How Women Cast Us Off*); *Les Enfants qu'elles ont* (1897) (*The Children Women Have*); *Leurs Péchés Capitaux* (1897) (*Their Mortal Sins*), and *Celles qu'on ignore* (1899) (*Women Ignored*). Later novels, the best-known of which are *Pierre Tisserand* (1907) and *Souffrir* (1909) (*Suffering*), deal with the theme of marital unhappiness, and condemn the lack of control Frenchwomen of the late 19th and early 20th centuries had over their own lives. Marni also wrote plays, often based upon her dialogues, which were well-received.
Bib: Waelti-Walters, J., *Feminist Novelists of the Belle Epoque*

Maron, Monika (born 1941)

East German novelist. Her novel *Flugasche* (1981) (*Flying Ash*), was the first to deal with the issues of pollution and ecology in East Germany. It established her as an important member of a new, more rebellious and critical generation of East German writers. *Die Überläuferin* (1986) (*The Turncoat*) describes the psychological collapse of a young woman who is part of a dehumanized and dehumanizing state. *Stille Zeile Sechs* was published in 1991, and in 1992 she won the prestigious Kleist Prize.

Maróthy-Soltesová, Elena (1855–1939)

Slovak novelist. She was the first female Slovak literary critic, and was editor of the magazine *Živena* from 1910 to 1922. With ▷Terézia Vansová she was a pioneer of the Slovak women's movement, and was Chair of the women's society,

Živena, founded in 1871. She was born into the family of the romantic poet Daniel Maróthy, and was influenced by the atmosphere of Turčiansky Svätý Martin, centre of the Slovak national movement.

Her first short story, *Na dedine* (*In the Village*) was published in 1881. She wrote the novels ▷*Proti prúdu* (1894) (*Against the Stream*) and *Moje deti* (1923–1924) (*My Children*), and a book of memoirs *70 rokov života* (1925) (*70 Years of Life*). In her works she tried to achieve so-called 'ideal realism' – realism based on the co-existence of community and the ideal. In her later works she denied this principle and wrote ▷social realism. She contributed to both Slovak and Czech women's periodicals, and worked for women's education and women's participation in the national movement. She also wrote reviews and essays on literary theory.

Marquets, Anne de (died 1588)

French poet. Known as '*la belle religieuse*' ('the beautiful nun'), she was celebrated by the poet Pierre de Ronsard (1524–1585). She was a native of the Comté d'Eu, but came to live in Paris, before retiring to the monastery at Poissy. Her talents were best demonstrated at the conference at Poissy in 1561, where the principal ecclesiastics of the period met to try to resolve the religious differences which were to result in the outbreak of civil war the following year. Anne de Marquets's prayers and verses addressed to the main representatives of the Catholic faith at the colloquium were published in 1562 and dedicated to the Cardinal of Lorraine. In 1569 she published a translation of the sacred works of Flaminio as a tribute to the supremacy of Italian literature, followed by a collection of her own verses dedicated to ▷Marguerite de Valois. A collection of spiritual sonnets was published in 1605.
Bib: Feugère, L., *Les Femmes poètes au XVIe siècle*.

Marriage (1818)

A novel by Scottish (▷Scotland) writer ▷Susan Ferrier, published anonymously by Blackwood. The first Scottish novel of manners, it centres on the lives of Lady Juliana Courtland and her two daughters, Adelaide and Mary, and describes the advantages and disadvantages of love-matches in marriage. The story is set in London, Edinburgh and the Scottish countryside, and is satirical in tone. Most literary critics assumed it to be the work of Sir Walter Scott, who was a friend of Ferrier's. A recent feminist reading of the work is N.L. Paxton's 'Subversive feminism: a reassessment of Susan Ferrier's *Marriage*', *Women and Literature* 4 (Spring 1976).

Marriage of Anansewa, The (1975)

A play by the Ghanaian dramatist ▷Efua Sutherland, embodying her principles of using indigenous African aesthetics in art. Anansewa is the daughter of Ananse, a figure based on the Akan spider god. The trickster is an essential

element of African folklore, taking different forms
– he may be a tortoise or, as in African-American
folklore, Brer Rabbit. The spider trickster, who
spins webs to ensnare the unwary, here takes the
form of a wily old man who is out to test the
suitors for his daughter's hand. In playing them
off against each other, he narrowly avoids
becoming enmeshed in his own plot, but emerges
triumphant, having ascertained who really loves
his daughter. Sutherland not only ˒˒es a
traditional motif to explore a universal human
situation, but draws on the ▷oral technique of
inviting the audience's reaction. A storyteller
stands outside the action and mediates between
the actors and the audience, thus breaking down
the distance between them. Finally, in its didatic
moral purpose, the play adheres closely to the
primary functions of oral literature: to educate
while entertaining.

Marriott, Anne (born 1913)

Canadian writer, born and educated in Victoria,
British Columbia. She was a poetry columnist and
editor, then script editor from 1945 to 1949 for
the National Film Board in Ottawa. Her long
narrative poem, *The Wind, Our Enemy* (1939), a
lament for the prairies during the 1930s drought,
was her first publication . *Calling Adventurers*
(1941) won a Governor General's Award; *Salt
Marsh* (1942) and *Sandstone and Other Poems*
(1945) followed. After a long silence she
published *Countries* (1971), *The Circular Coast:
New and Selected Poems* (1981) and *Letters from
Some Islands* (1985). *A Long Way to Oregon* (1984)
collects her short fiction. She lives in Vancouver,
British Columbia.

Marron, Marie Anne Carrelet, de (1725–1778)

French painter and dramatist. Born in Dijon,
Marron was a talented painter, and one of her
works was hung in the Eglise de Notre Dame in
her home town. She also designed porcelain. At
the age of forty-two she began to write plays in
verse. Of her eight tragedies and two comedies
(which Voltaire is reputed to have read and
praised) only one was published: *La Comtesse de
Fayel* (1770), 'a society tragedy', well received by
the critics.

Marryat, Florence (1838–99)

English novelist, the daughter of Captain
Frederick Marryat, author of *Children of the New
Forest.* (1847) Florence was educated by
▷governesses and at sixteen married T. Ross
Church, with whom she had eight children. A
prolific writer of ▷sensation novels, her first
work, *Love's Conflict*, was published in 1865.
Between 1865 and 1899 she wrote over forty
volumes, including works on spiritualism such as
There Is No Death (1891) and *The Spirit World*
(1894). Marryat's novels are mostly melodramatic
▷romances with stereotypical characters who
become involved in crimes of passion. They
include *Woman Against Woman* (1865); *Her Lord

and Master* (1871); *A Crown of Shame* (1888) and
How Like a Woman (1892).

Marseille d'Althouvitis (16th century)

French poet. The daughter of one of the
mistresses of Henri III (1551–1589) and a noble
of Florentine descent, she was closely involved
with the Valois court, but took the name Marseille
from the town where she spent most of her life.
Before her early death, she wrote a number of
circumstancial pieces of which only one remains.
In this she celebrates Provençal poetry and those
who tried to revive it.
Bib: Feugère, L., *Les Femmes poètes au XVIe siècle.*

Marsh, Ngaio (1895–1982)

New Zealand writer of ▷detective fiction. Ngaio
Marsh, the only child of an English father and
New Zealand mother, was brought up in
Christchurch, New Zealand, where she continued
to live as an adult when not in England. Marsh,
whose fiction is internationally known, began
writing detective novels in London in the 1920s.
Most of her thirty-two novels are set in England
and all were published there, but despite the
English qualities of her writing – its formula plots,
especially the 'country house murder', its reliance
on class structure and a British social environment
– Marsh always thought of herself as a New
Zealander. The four novels she set in New
Zealand show a sympathy for ▷Maori, and a love
of the landscape. Marsh began detective writing
almost by chance, but her other lifelong activity,
for which she was very well known in New
Zealand, was theatrical production. She founded
the Little Theatre in Christchurch and produced
a play, often Shakespeare, almost every year, as
well as writing novels.
　　Publications: (a selective list of her New
Zealand-set novels): *Colour Scheme* (1943); *Vintage
Murder* (1937); *Died in the Wool* (1944); *Black
Beech and Honeydew* (autobiography) (1966).

Marshall, Joyce (born 1913)

Canadian novelist, short story writer and
translator. Born in Montreal, Quebec, and
educated at McGill University, she currently lives
in Toronto, Ontario. Her first novel, *Presently
Tomorrow* (1946), set in the Eastern Townships of
Quebec, is an elegant delineation of character
motivation, which Marshall developed even
further in *Lovers and Strangers* (1957). The short
stories of *A Private Place* (1975) exhibit her best
writing; the collection addresses both the strength
and vulnerability of urban women. 'So Many Have
Died' is a particularly powerful character piece
about tenacious old age. Marshall translated three
works by ▷Gabrielle Roy into English; she was
awarded the Canada Council Translation Prize
(1976) for her translation of Roy's *Cet Ete qui
Chantait* (1972), *Enchanted Summer* (1976).

Marshall, Paule (born 1929)

This novelist, short story writer and journalist was
born in Brooklyn, USA, her parents having

emigrated from ▷Barbados during World War I. She studied at Hunter College, New York, and later at Brooklyn College, where she graduated with a degree in English. She began working on the small black journal, *Our World Magazine* as a researcher and feature story writer. She has travelled throughout Latin America and the Caribbean. Her first novel, ▷*Brown Girl, Brownstones* (1959), was adapted for a CBS Television Workshop and she was awarded a Ford Foundation grant. She has taught creative writing at Yale, Columbia, the University of Massachusetts in Boston and at the Iowa Writers' Workshop, and lives in New York. She has published three other novels, *The Chosen Place, the Timeless People* (1969), ▷*Praisesong for the Widow* (1983) and *Daughters* (1991), and several collections of short stories, including *Soul Clap Hands and Sing* (1961), *Merle, a Novela and Other Stories* (1983) and *Reena and Other Stories* (1984).

Marson, Una (1905–1965)

The first major Caribbean woman poet, Marson was also a dramatist and journalist. Innovative for its period, her poetry pioneered both the pursuit of feminist issues, examining the nature and ▷identity of the black woman, and explored the use of a variety of language forms as a means of expression. Born and educated in ▷Jamaica, she left for Britain in 1932 and became secretary to the League of Coloured People in London and later private secretary to Haile Selassie during his period of exile. A political activist, she worked with the Women's International League for Peace and Freedom and the International Alliance of Women. She returned to Jamaica in 1936, where she wrote plays for production, helped launch various literary journals, and founded the Reader's and Writer's Club. Back in Britain in 1938 she worked for the BBC World Service, launching 'Caribbean Voices', the programme which provided international recognition for Caribbean writers. She left Britain for Jamaica in 1945 and worked there as a publisher, journalist and social worker until her death.

She published four collections of poetry, *Tropic Reveries* (1930), *Heights and Depths* (1932), ▷*The Moth and the Star* (1937) and *Towards the Stars* (1945).

Her plays produced in Jamaica include: *At What a Price* (1932), *London Calling* (1937) and *Pocamania* (1938).

Her poetry is included in O.R. Dathorne (ed.), *Caribbean Verse*, (1967), J. Pearn's *Poetry in the Caribbean* (1985) and Paula Burnett (ed.), *The Penguin Book of Caribbean Verse* (1986).

Critical material is in J.E. Clare McFarlane, *A Literature in the Making* (1956) and Rhonda Cobham's article in ▷*Out of the Kumbla*.

Märten, Lu (1879–1970)

German dramatist, poet and essayist. A sickly child, she educated herself at home and, early on, became interested in the workers' movement and women's rights. She began her literary career with the poems, *Meine Liedsprachen* (1906) (*The Languages of My Song*), stories for children, and essays on women artists such as ▷Käthe Kollwitz and ▷Ricarda Huch. In 1909 she achieved international fame with the play *Bergarbeiter* (1909) (*Miners*), which offers a gripping yet sensitive psychological portrait of the miner and strike leader Jakob Burger. Also in 1909 she published *Torso. Das Buch eines Kindes* (*Torso, The Book of a Child*), an account of her childhood. From then on she dedicated herself to writing essays on socialist and feminist issues, such as *Die Frau als Künstlerin* (1914) (*Woman as Artist*) and *Revolutionäre Dichtung in Deutschland* (1920) (*Revolutionary Poetry in Germany*). In 1920 she joined the Communist Party.

Martereau (1959)

Translation of *Martereau* (1956), by French writer ▷Nathalie Sarraute, originally published in 1953. *Martereau* retains a measure of plot to illustrate Sarraute's conception of reality versus appearances; it opposes a character seen from outside, who can clearly be identified with a first-person narrator, and his family group. Conflict over the purchase of a house reveals that Martereau is psychologically identical to the rest of the group.

Martin, Catherine (1847–1937)

Australian novelist and journalist. Martin was brought from the Isle of Skye to South Australia by her parents in 1855, and later married Frederick Martin. As well as a serial, *The Moated Grange*, which has not been published as a book, Martin published four novels, two of which, ▷*An Australian Girl* (published anonymously in 1895) and ▷*The Incredible Journey* (1923), are particularly significant.

▷Aborigine in Australian women's writing, The; *On Her Selection*

Martin, Claire (born 1914)

French Canadian translator and novelist. Born Claire Montreuil in Quebec, she writes under her mother's maiden name. Prolific in the 1960s and 1970s, her work has been translated, but has not received the attention it perhaps deserves. *Doux-amer* (1960, translated as *Best Man*, 1983) is a complex frame story; *Quand j'aurai Payé ton Visage* (1962, translated as *The Legacy*, 1986) is about a love triangle. Her memoirs, *Dans un Gant de Fer* (1965) and *La Joue Droite* (1966), translated together as *In an Iron Glove* (1986), depict a traumatic childhood. She has translated works by ▷Margaret Laurence and Robertson Davies into French.

Martin, Dorcas Eglestone (16th century)

English tranlator of devotional works. Nothing is known of this 'godlie Matrone and Gentlewoman named Mistresse Dorcas Martin'. Her only known work is a ▷translation of a French book of ▷prayers, meditations, psalm verses, and religious instructions. In his ▷*Monument of Matrones*,

Thomas Bentley printed her work under the title of *An Instruction for Christians conteining a fruitful and godlie exercise, as well in wholsome and fruitfull praiers, as in reverend discerning of Gods holie Commandements and Sacraments*. Interesting sections in Martin's collection include a discussion of 'how to examine such yong persons as be willing to receive the Supper of our Lord', which is written in the form of a dialogue between mother and child, and how to examine children regarding the sacraments, obedience, and confession.

Martin, Violet Florence ▷ Ross, Martin

Martineau, Harriet (1802–1876)

English novelist, critic, journalist and essayist. She was born in Norwich, the sixth child in a family of eight. Her youth was marked by illness and poverty; her puritanical Huguenot parents insisted on educating the children to earn their own living, which became essential after the father went bankrupt in 1826. As a young woman, Martineau was a devout Unitarian, and in 1823 she published *Devotional Exercises for the Use of Young Persons*, followed by *Addresses with Prayers* (1826). In 1830 she won all three prizes in an essay competition set by the Central Unitarian Association. Between 1832 and 1834 she published a series of social reformist tales, *Illustrations of Political Economy*, influenced by the ideas of J.S. Mill, Jeremy Bentham and David Ricardo. The tales were highly successful, as were her stories for 'Brougham's Society for the Diffusion of Useful Knowledge'.

Martineau became a literary celebrity, and was consulted on social and economic matters by her politician friends (increasingly, she turned away from religion). She travelled to North America in 1834, supporting the Abolitionists despite threats to herself, and published *Society in America* (1837) and *A Retrospect of Western Travel* (1838). From 1839 to 1844 she was an invalid, but during these years she produced a novel, ▷ *Deerbrook* (1839), an historical work, *The Hour and the Man* (1840), and children's stories collected in *The Playfellow* (1841). *Life in the Sick Room* appeared in 1843, and *Letters on Mesmerism*, an account of the treatment that she claimed had cured her illness, in 1845. She settled in the Lake District in 1845, visiting Palestine in 1846–7. Other publications included numerous articles for the *London Daily News*, a radical *History of the Thirty Years' Peace* (1849–50), and the anti-theological *Laws of Man's Social Nature and Development* (1851). Her free translation, *The Positive Philosophy of Comte*, appeared in 1853, and her *Autobiography*, begun in 1855, was eventually published in 1877.

▷ Children's literature (19th-century Britain); Reform; Slavery; Travel writing; Education; Feminism
Bib: Miller, F., *Life*; Pichanick, V.K., *Harriet Martineau: The Woman and Her Work*; Webb, R.K., *Harriet Martineau: A Radical Victorian*.

Martínez Sierra, Maria de la O (1874–1974)

Spanish novelist. Born in a small town in northern Spain called San Millán de la Cogolla, Martínez was the eldest child of a large family of scientists and intellectuals. In 1897 she began writing in collaboration with her future husband, Gregorio Martínez Sierra, producing works such as *Almas ausentes* (1900) (*Absent Souls*), and *Pascua florida* (1903) (*Easter Sunday*). Their most celebrated novel is *Tú eres la paz* (1906) (*You Are Peace*), which is typical of much of their work in that it depicts the female protagonist as independent, intelligent and nurturing.

Martín Fierro Group of poets

An Argentinian group, named after the epic poem (1872–1879) by José Hernández (1854–1886), which supported the avant-garde ▷ Ultraism movement, founded by the Argentinian writer Jorge Luís Borges (1899–1986). At the beginning of her poetical career, in the early 1920s, ▷ Norah Lange was a member of the group, and it was her husband, Oliverio Girondo, who wrote its manifesto in 1924. The poets founded the magazine *Martín Fierro*, which appeared from 1924 to 1927.

Martín Gaite, Carmen (born 1925)

One of Spain's most significant female authors. Martín Gaite was born in Salamanca in 1925, and completed a doctoral thesis in Romance Philology at the University of Madrid. Her thesis on *Usos amorosos del dieciocho en España* (1973) (*Amorous Behaviour in 18th-Century Spain*), 'shocking' for the time (early Franco period), focuses on sexual customs in past times, but with an eye on the repressed present. Her first novel, *El balneario* (1954) (*The Spa*), was awarded the Café Gijón Prize. A major work followed with *Entre visillos* (1957) (*Between the Blinds*), which describes with great insight the life of a girl growing up in Franco's Spain. Other novels also met with success, such as: *Las ataduras* (1960) (*Bonds*); *Ritmo lento* (1962) (*Slow Motion*); *Retahílas* (1974) (*Threads*); and *Fragmentos de interior* (1976) (*Glimpses of an Interior*). Her undisputed masterpiece, however, is ▷ *El cuarto de atrás* (1978) (*The Back Room*).

In recent years Martín Gaite has directed theatrical productions of Golden Age drama in Madrid. Her most recent work, *Caperucita en Manhattan* (1991) (*Little Red Riding Hood in Manhattan*), explores the connections between fairytale motifs and Hollywood symbology.

Martinson, Moa (1890–1964)

Swedish proletarian politician, prose writer, and poet. Martinson was born an illegitimate child of a working-class mother. Very early in life she had to make her own living. In 1910 she married a smallholder, with whom she had five sons, two of whom later drowned. In 1928 her husband committed suicide. In 1929 she married Harry Martinson, who was fifteen years younger than her, but who had already made his name as a lyric poet. In 1940 they were divorced.

Martinson became politically engaged and began to write in the 1920s. At first she wrote for Social Democratic newspapers, but in 1933 she published the novel *Kvinnor och äppelträd* (*Women and Appletrees*). Many of her twenty books describe her own and her mother's life, taking up the oral tradition of story telling. Her books have been seen as naïve and ▷realist, whereas her husband, Harry Martinson was regarded as a very talented modernist. New readings have pointed out the modernist traits in Moa Martinson's novels, and have shown her to be a talented artist.

Martinson described the everyday life of proletarian women in Sweden. Her women are strong because of their co-operation and moral support, but also because of their ability to enjoy aesthetics and the beauty of their surroundings. Their feeling of self-worth is often expressed symbolically in a scrap of luxury that they cling to.

The seemingly unpolished tone in Martinson's novels is exactly what distinguishes them as 'modern'.

Maru (1971)

Southern African writer ▷Bessie Head's second and most hauntingly beautiful novel, set, like her others, in Botswana. Maru and his brother, Moleka, are both in line for the chieftaincy. Sometimes taking on the stature of god-like figures, they represent two opposed forces (sun and moon, for example) in the moment of chaos before creation. On a realistic level, the novel focuses on a schoolteacher called Margaret, who is one of the Basarwa people, the despised 'Bushman' (!Xam or San) race. The Basarwa, traditionally the slaves of the Batswana, are treated like animals. When the Batswana of the village discover that Margaret is a Basarwa, she loses her job. However, Maru and Moleka, along with Margaret's friend Dikeledi, recognize her humanity. Both Moleka and Maru fall in love with her, until Maru persuades Moleka to love Dikeledi instead, so that he can fulfil his destiny by marrying Margaret.

On both the realistic and allegorical planes of the story, romantic love sets a new world in motion. First, Moleka's monogamous marriage with Dikeledi heralds a new type of existence for women (away from polygyny). Secondly, Maru's marriage to Margaret gives the chieftain an occasion to counter the racism of his people. In a process called 'segmentation' by anthropologists, Maru and Margaret leave the village to set up a new community, free of racism. A door thus opens for the Basarwa people, the wind of freedom blowing.

The novel's creation myth takes a particularly tantalizing direction as regards Margaret's role as artist, magnificently rendered in the text. Her creative vision gives substance to Maru's dreams. Yet once she is married, her task is no longer to draw and create, but instead to bear the brunt of her husband's strange moods. What the text does not quite say is that the door of freedom has yet to open for women.

▷Polygamy

Maruoka Hideko (1903–1990)

Japanese critic. She was born in Nagano prefecture. Her first publication, *The Problems of Women Farmers in Japan* (1937) is the first systematic research on the heavy workload of women farmers in Japan. She tried to eliminate feudal sexual discrimination as a leader of the mother's movement in post-war Japan. She co-edited the ten-volume *Archive Series of Women's Issues in Modern Japan* (1976–80).

Maryan   ▷Descard, Maria

Mary Barton (1848)

The first novel by British writer ▷Elizabeth Gaskell, subtitled *A Tale of Manchester Life*. The background of the story is Manchester in the 'hungry forties', a decade in which working-class protest came to the attention of the middle classes. Mary Barton is the daughter of a militant Chartist, John Barton, who is employed by the Carson family as a mill-hand. In the course of the novel Barton assassinates Henry Carson, one of the most unpopular employers, but Jem Wilson becomes the principal suspect. Mary has been involved with both Henry and Jem, lured by the appeal of Henry's middle-class prosperity, but ultimately saving working-class Jem from the death penalty and recognizing her real love for him. The novel provoked much hostility from Manchester mill owners and the Tory press, yet it has also been criticized by Marxist commentators who find the ending of the tale ▷sentimental and naive in its treatment of class struggle. Recent feminist readings have emphasized the novel's critique of masculinist politics of confrontation, its exploration of the processes of socialization, and its call for an ethics of caring and nurturance in the community which is seen to bind women and the working class.

Mary, Countess of Boulogne (died 1181)

English letter-writer. Mary was the daughter of King Stephen of England (reigned 1125–1154). She became prioress, first of Lillechurch, a nunnery founded for her by her father, and later of the celebrated abbey of Romsey. She had a rich inheritance, however, for which she was much in demand, and her cousin King Henry II of England (reigned 1154–1189) made her marry Matthew, son of the Earl of Flanders, in order to secure an alliance with Matthew's family. A letter survives, dated 1168, addressed to King Louis VII of France, which expresses Mary's bitterness towards Henry. Mary's husband permitted her to re-enter the religious life in 1169, after nine years of marriage.

Bib: Wood, Mary Anne Everett, *Letters of Royal and Illustrious Ladies of Great Britain*.

Mary, nun of Amesbury (1278–1332)

Daughter of Edward I of England. Mary entered the nunnery at Amesbury, Wiltshire (a priory in the order of Fontevrault) in 1284, where her grandmother, ▷Eleanor of Provence, acted as her guardian. Mary enjoyed a far from enclosed life, travelling and visiting the court. The Dominican friar Nicholas Trevet composed an ▷Anglo-Norman chronicle for Mary (completed in 1334, after her death), which was subsequently translated into Latin. A section of Trevet's work was apparently the principal source for Chaucer's (c 1340–1400) *Man of Law's Tale*.

Mary Olivier: A Life (1919)

English novel by ▷May Sinclair which charts the life of Mary Olivier, the only daughter in a middle-class family in late Victorian England. In common with ▷Radclyffe Hall's *The Unlit Lamp* (1924), *Mary Olivier* deals with the dilemma of an intelligent and independent girl, who reads Kant, Hegel and Spinoza with enthusiasm, but is suppressed by the demand to conform to Victorian models of femininity. Mary Olivier remains unmarried and bound by her mother's needs throughout. However, unlike Hall, Sinclair constructs a more optimistic narrative in which her heroine retains an autonomous sense of self, conveyed to the reader through a ▷stream-of-consciousness narrative technique. Despite the outward constraints of Mary's life, in her late thirties she becomes a successful poet and translator. Moreover, Sinclair flirts with a romantic fulfilment to Mary Olivier's life, allowing her a passionate sexual relationship with a writer, Richard Nicholson, whom she refuses to marry on the grounds that domesticity would only spoil their love. Instead she is left at the end, after her mother's death, with a house of her own and 'inconceivable freedom', in a challenge to the traditional romantic ending. In line with Sinclair's interest in the new Freudian ▷psychoanalysis, the main focus of the novel is, however, Mary's tortured relationship with her mother, and her desire for the exclusive love which is inevitably directed to her eldest brother. Ultimately her mother acknowledges 'that I was jealous of you, Mary. And I was afraid for my life you'd find it out'.

Mary (Marie) Stuart, Queen of Scots (1542–1587)

Scottish poet, letter-writer and essayist. The daughter of James V of Scotland and Mary of Guise, Mary Stuart was made queen when less than one year old. Because of threats to her position as an infant on the throne, Mary was sent to the French court. There she was stongly influenced by Catholicism, ▷Catherine de Medici, and Diane de Poitiers. She was well-educated and skilled in a number of languages. In 1558 she married the French dauphin, later Francis II. When Francis died, a year and a half after their marriage, Mary returned to reign as a Catholic queen in Protestant Scotland. During her residence at Edinburgh she assembled a library of some 300 volumes. In 1564 she strengthened her claim to the English throne by marrying her relative, Robert Darnley (who was next in line behind her as heir). Three months after Darnley's murder in 1567, Mary Stuart married John Hepburn, Earl of Bothwell. Upon her marriage to Bothwell, one of the conspirators in Darnley's murder, Mary's Scottish nobles rebelled, and imprisoned her. In 1568 she escaped and fled to England in the hopes of finding assistance from her cousin ▷Elizabeth Tudor. Because Mary stood as a potential rival for the English throne, however, Elizabeth imprisoned her. Mary was executed in 1587. Most of Mary's writings, including her ▷letters and essays, are in French. Brought up at the court of the Valois, Mary Stuart used the French form of her name in her signature throughout her life. She delighted in poetry and poets, particulary Pierre de Ronsard (1524–1585) and Joachim Du Bellay (1522–1560). She wrote poignant lines on the death of her first husband at the tender age of sixteen, and verses to Ronsard. Impressed by her beauty, Ronsard maintained that he kept Marie's portrait continually before him in his library, but he later wrote a quatrain suggesting that her cousin, Elizabeth I, could rival her charms. At the time of her flight into England, she composed a French sonnet to Elizabeth which may have inspired ▷'The Doubt of Future Foes' in response. Also extant is a Latin poem written on the morning of her execution (1587). Although less certainly hers, the most famous works attributed to her are ▷*The Casket Letters and Sonnets* which were used to implicate her in the murder of her husband, Robert Darnley. The poem most commonly attrributed to her, 'Adieu, plaisant pays de France', has been exposed as the work of an 18th-century French journalist.
Bib: Bax, C., *Letters and Poems by Mary Stuart*; Travitsky, B., *The Paradise of Women: Writings by Englishwomen of the Renaissance*.

Mary Tudor (1516–1558)

English translator and letter-writer. As the daughter of Henry VIII and his first wife, ▷Catherine of Aragon, Mary's status as heir to the throne fluctuated greatly according the whims of first her father and then her brother, Edward VI. In connection with his divorce from Catherine of Aragon, Henry had Mary declared illegitimate. Later he changed his mind, even naming her as heir to the English throne after her brother Edward. When her brother took the throne as Edward VI, however, he named the Protestant ▷Jane Grey as his heir, favouring her over his Catholic sister (as well as his other sister, ▷Elizabeth Tudor). Grey's reign, however, lasted only nine days, and Mary Tudor was crowned Mary I in 1553. In 1554 she married Philip of Spain. In spite of the turbulence of her life, especially after her parents' divorce, Mary was well-educated. Catherine of Aragon had taken a keen interest in her daughter's learning, hiring

Mary Tudor

▷humanist scholars as tutors, and organizing a school of girls and women at court. She also commissioned Juan Luis Vives '▷*Instruction of a Christian Woman* for Mary's education. Mary was skilled in several languages. In 1548 her ▷translation of Desiderius Erasmus's (?1466–1536) paraphrase of the Gospel of John was published, sponsored by Mary's stepmother ▷Catherine Parr.

Mason, Bobbie Ann (born 1940)

US short story writer and novelist. Born near Mayfield, Kentucky, Mason grew up on a dairy farm. She was national president of the Hilltoppers Fan Club and after graduating from the University of kentucky in 1962, she wrote for fan magazines. In 1972 she earned a PhD degree at the University of Connecticut. Collected in *Shiloh, And Other Stories* (1982), her stories depict the changes Mason observed as rural Kentucky became urbanized, emphasizing the tension between history and progress that is left unresolved. Her characters are working-class people who feel a desperation they cannot articulate. Samantha Hughes, the protagonist of *In Country* (1985), tries to know her father, who died in Vietnam. A recent high-school graduate, she searches the past for answers to her future, but she discovers that she cannot learn from history.

Other work includes: *Nabokov's Garden: A Guide to Ada* (Mason's dissertation) (1974) and *The Girl Sleuth: A Feminist Guide to the Bobbsey Twins, Nancy Drew, and Their Sisters* (1975).

Mass culture

Mass culture is popular culture which includes literature, film, art, television serials and soap operas, designed to appeal to a wide, predominantly female audience. Traditional

literary critics, such as F.R. Leavis (1895–1978) (▷Leavisite criticism) have argued that mass culture is detrimental to literary and artistic standards. In recent years, however, feminist critics like ▷Rosalind Coward have challenged Leavis's category of 'great literature' worthy of study by taking mass culture seriously and analyzing the special appeal it has for women. ▷Tania Modleski and ▷Janice Radway have argued further that, in so far as popular romance enables women to vicariously experience a personal power and emotional fulfilment denied to them by partriarchy, it both resists and is an effect of patriarchal sexual politics.

Masters, Olga (1919–1986)

Australian novelist, short story writer and journalist. Masters was married to a teacher and reared seven children, all of whom are prominent in Australian cultural and sporting affairs. She worked for many years on country and then suburban newspapers, notably the *Manly Daily* (Sydney). She began writing fiction in her late fifties and wrote five works (the last two were published posthumously): ▷*The Home Girls* (1982), *Loving Daughters* (1984), *A Long Time Dying* (1985), *Amy's Children* (1987) and *The Rose Fancier* (1988). Masters's fiction is notable for its frank, often savage, depiction of the situation of women and children in Australian society. A collection of her journalism, *Reporting Home* (1990), has been released.

▷Writers for film and television (Australia); Short story (Australia); *Coming Out from Under, Eight Voices of the Eighties*

Mastoraki, Jenny (born 1949)

Greek poet and translator. She was born in Athens, where she studied Byzantine and Medieval Greek literature. She began writing poetry when very young. Her first collection of poetry, *Tollgates*, appeared in 1971. These near-autobiographical poems, which fall outside traditional conventions of form and style, express a sensitive female voice struggling to communicate and to escape the alienation that separates her from others. In 1978 Mastoraki published *The Clan*, a collection of poems dealing with the experience of growing up in a family which offers love and support but stifles freedom of expression. Another collection, *Stories of the Deep*, appeared in 1983. Some of her poetry has been translated into English. Mastoraki has also translated North American, Italian and German works into Greek.

Mataira, Katarina Te Heikoko (born 1932)

New Zealand children's author and illustrator. Mataira's special interest and contribution to New Zealand literature has been to promote the Maori language through writing, innovative teaching methods (which draw upon the knowledge and initiative of native Maori speakers), and publishing. To this end she has worked within educational and traditional Maori groups, and bodies like the Maori Language Commission and the Broadcasting Corporation of New Zealand. Her first children's book was *Maui and the Big Fish* (1972), and in 1975 *Maori Legends for Young New Zealanders* and *Te Atea*, a story in Maori about a nuclear holocaust, were published. Her many other books include *The Oxford Maori Picture Dictionary* (1978), and she contributes to Maori-language journals, including *Te Ao Hou*. Recently, Katarina Mataira began what has been described as a 'new wave of writing', mostly in Maori, and is working with young writers in this field.

▷Children's literature, New Zealand; Maori literature

Matamoros, Mercedes (1851–1906)

Cuban poet. Her full name was Mercedes Matamoros y del Valle, and she wrote under the pen-name Ofelia. Her mother died when she was three, and she studied at home with her father. For a while she was a teacher, and she published literary essays and poetry in the Cuban press, including the poems of *Armonías cubanas* (1897) (*Cuban Harmonies*). She translated well-known lyrical poets into Spanish, and became known as 'the blind lark'.

Other works: *Poesías completas* (1892) (*Complete Poems*) and *Sonetos* (1902) (*Sonnets*).

Matchless Orinda ▷Philips, Katherine

Matilda, Countess of Winchester (died 1252)

English patron. Matilda was the third wife of Roger de Quincy. Matthew Paris, the chronicler and artist of St Albans, planned (or produced) an illustrated psalter or Book of Hours for Matilda, in Latin, with verses in ▷Anglo-Norman to accompany the pictures.

Matilda, Empress (1102–1167)

Matilda was the daughter of Henry I of England. Her first husband was the Holy Roman Emperor, Henry V (died 1125); her second, Geoffrey V Plantagenet, Count of Anjou (died 1150). A letter from Matilda, written (in Latin) in 1165 at the request of Pope Alexander III, attempted to mediate in the dispute between her son, King Henry II of England, and the Archbishop of Canterbury, Thomas à Beckett.

Bib: Wood, Mary Anne Everett, *Letters of Royal and Illustrious Ladies of Great Britain*.

Matriarchal society

A society in which rule by women is the norm, and where the mother, not the father, is head of the family. In the Caribbean context, the figure of the 'matriarch' or strong woman is a common stereotype; women are frequently depicted as such in literature by male authors, the folk matriarchal figure being the most common example, as in Sam Selvon's portrayal of Tanty in *The Lonely Londoners* (1956). The term 'matriarchal' is, however, often misused: while women are frequently the bearers of culture and tradition within the family, they hold little social or economic power outside. See ▷Beryl Gilroy

(*Frangipani House*, 1986), ▷Zee Edgell (▷*Beka Lamb*, 1982) and ▷Olive Senior's discussion of the role of Caribbean women in society in *Kunapipi* (1985). The term ▷matrifocal more accurately depicts the nature of women's roles in Caribbean society.

Matrifocal society

A society which focuses on and relies on the central importance of women in the transmission of cultural values and the creation of a sense of continuity within the family. In the Caribbean context, partly because of the nature of plantation slavery, the father had no official role to play within the family; the children belonged to the slave-owner, and the mother was the only officially recognized parent. Marriage was not possible under this system, and has not, therefore, among the poorer communities, become institutionalized in the 150 years since Emancipation. Caribbean women traditionally often assumed the roles of both mother and father because the father was absent for one reason or another. As ▷Olive Senior has put it, 'the myth of the black matriarch projects an image of Caribbean woman as strong and powerful . . . but the myth disguises the fact of her powerlessness in the wider society . . . women have little share in the formal power structures.'

▷Matriarchal society

Matto de Turner, Clorinda (born 1909)

Peruvian novelist, biographer, essayist, travel writer and dramatist. She wrote some of her work under the pen-name Carlotta Dumont. *Tradiciones cusqueñas* (1884–1886) (*Traditions from Cuzco*), written in two volumes, was influenced by *Tradiciones peruanas* (first series, 1872) (*Peruvian Traditions*) by the Peruvian writer Ricardo Palma (1833–1919). She used various sources and, like Palma's work, her stories can be interpreted at several levels, describing, in particular, customs, legends and historical tales in a romatic way. In a long letter to Pastor S. Obligado, she drew a complete geographical, socio-historical and psychological picture of her country, from Tucumán to Guayaquil, from the Incas to modern times. Like others before her, Clorinda Matto de Turner defended the Indian cause in *Aves sin nido* (1889) (▷*Birds Without a Nest*, 1968), which is probably her best novel, and was the first indigenous novel of contemporary South American Indian life.

Other works: *Indole* (1890) (*Kind*); *Hima-sumac* (1892); *Leyendas y recortes* (1893) (*Inscriptions and Cuttings*); *Herencia* (1893) (*Inheritance*), and *Borealis, minaturas y porcelanas* (1902) (*Northern Lights, Minatures and China*).

Matutani Miyoko (born 1926)

Japanese writer of children's literature. Born in Tokyo, she evacuated to Nagano prefecture, and her experience of country life there was the starting-point for her writing. *The Child Who Became A Shell* (1951) won the Association of

Writers of Children's Literature Prize for a New Writer. Her masterpiece is *Taro, The Child of a Dragon* based on the folklore of Nagano, which won the International Andersen Prize and two other prizes. She also pursues the theme of war experience as contemporary folklore in *Two Iidas*. Her complete works appear in *Collection of Matsutani Miyoko* (1971–72) (fifteen volumes).

Matute, Ana María (born 1926)
Spanish novelist. Born in Barcelona into an upper-middle-class family, Matute is recognized as being one of the major female novelists of the 20th century. Her early works, such as *Los Abel* (1948) (*The Abel family*), *Fiesta al noroeste* (1952) (*Celebration in the North-west*), and *En esta tierra* (1955) (*In This Land*), are historically based. Her most celebrated novel is ▷*Los hijos muertos* (1958) (*The Lost Children*). Her other works are: *Primera memoria* (1960) (*First Memory*); *Los soldados lloran de noche* (1964) (*Soldiers Cry at Night*); *La trampa* (1969) (*The Trap*), and *La torre vigía* (1971) (*The Watchtower*).

Matvéeva, Novella Nikolaevna (born 1934)
Russian poet. Matvéeva's poetry began appearing in the early 1960s, and she has published several volumes since, taking pains to develop a distinctive poetic voice. Selecting for imagery objects of everyday, domestic life such as gutters, meat grinders and pantries, she expands them into moral and philosophical symbols. While there is no overt political commentary in her lyrics, unspecified forces of evil inform them. Some of her poetry is delightfully whimsical, and her heroine often experiences a sense of wonder at the mysterious world around her. Matvéeva combines strict poetic forms with an informal, colloquial Russian, and tends to use repetitions to create a rhythm and a heightened emotional tone.
Bib: Reavey, G. (trans.), *The New Russian Poets: An Anthology*; Glad, J. and Weissbort, D. (eds), *Russian Poetry: The Modern Period*; Proffer, C. and E. (eds), *The Ardis Anthology of Recent Russian Literature*; *Soviet Literature* 6 (1967) and 12 (1979); Markov, V. and Sparks, M. (eds), *Modern Russian Poetry: An Anthology with Verse Translations*; Brown, D., '"Loud" and "Quiet" Poets of the Nineteen Sixties', *Papers in Slavic Philology* 1.

Maud (died 1198)
Daughter of Henry II of England. Maud became Abbess of ▷Barking. William Adgar, who may have been chaplain to the nuns at Barking, addressed his popular collection of *Legends of St Mary* to his audience and 'Lady Maud'.

Maud (Edith) (1079–1118)
First wife of Henry I of England, and patron. Maud was a royal princess, the orphan daughter of St Margaret of Scotland and Malcolm Canmore. She was well-educated (she had been brought up by her aunt, Christina, Abbess of Romsey and later of Wilton), and was praised for her learning as well as her beauty and piety. She was pressed into a political marriage with Henry I (reigned 1100–1135). Her court at Westminster attracted poets and musicians, and Maud particularly encouraged writing in French. Benedeit translated his Latin *Voyage of St Brendan* into ▷Anglo-Norman verse at the queen's request. Five letters (in Latin) from Maud to Anselm, Archbishop of Canterbury, survive. She supported the archbishop against the king. She also wrote a formal and ornate letter to Pope Paschal II, in about 1103.
Bib: Wood, Mary Anne Everett, *Letters of Royal and Illustrious Ladies of Great Britain*.

Maude, Caitlín (1941–1982)
Irish poet. Born in Connemara, County Galway, she studied at University College, Galway, taught for many years, and also worked as a singer of traditional songs and as a translator. She was active in the Gaeltacht civil rights movement in the 1970s. Her work is entirely in Irish. She was considered one of the most interesting of contemporary Irish poets. Her work was collected and published posthumously as *Caitlín Maude, Dánta* (1984) (*Caitlín Maude, Poems*). She also wrote a play, *An Lasair Choille*, (*The Spark in the Wood*), with poet Michael Hartnett and made a recording of folk-songs and readings from her own work, *Caitlín* (1975).

Mavet Ba'geshem (1982) (*Death in the Rain*)
Israeli novel by ▷Ruth Almog. Her second novel, it continues a central theme of her writing – the struggle of individuals with their fate. The novel portrays four characters, two men and two women, caught up by strong emotions and living under the shadow of death. A young, ambitious academic reconstructs the puzzle of their lives through their diaries and letters. Through its continual shifts in point of view, the novel unfolds a story of complex of human relationships.

May 1968
The events of May 1968 in France were part of the youth movement which began at Berkeley University in California and quickly spread across Europe. In France, the movement gained support from students dissatisfied with the French university education, and spread to the whole social system, bringing it to a standstill for a month. Although the movement failed to 'change life' in terms of immediate concrete results, it gave people a chance to voice their grievances against a repressive society and to define alternatives.

The ▷MLF (French Women's Liberation Movement) seized this opportunity to build on the success of the 1967 Neuwirth law which had legalized contraception, and to publicize their demands for more radical changes in the status of women. The Veil bid to legalize abortion in 1972 shows that positive results soon followed. However, women were angered to find that the left-wing activists of May 1968, who rejected traditional party politics, denied them any real responsibilities or power of decision in the issues being discussed. This led to a split within the MLF between those who identified the women's struggle with the class war, and those who saw women as a separate class, having to fight men as well as the rest of society.

Mayor, Flora M. (1872–1931)

English novelist and short story writer who also wrote under the pseudonym of Mary Stafford. The twin daughter of intellectual parents, and born into an Anglican clerical household that respected women's education, Mayor was educated at Surbiton High School and Newnham College, Cambridge. She initially pursued an acting career without parental consent. Mayor's first publication appeared during this period, a collection of short stories entitled *Mrs Hammond's Children* (1901). Mayor's career as an actress was terminated through illness, brought on by the sudden death of her fiancé in 1903. Mayor never married, and lived largely in the company of members of her family.

Mayor's writings champion the rights of middle-class unmarried women and widows at a time when the English spinster was regarded as a problem by political commentators and the women's movement alike. Her first two novels take as their central theme different facets of spinsterhood, focusing particularly on psychological issues. In *The Third Miss Symons* (1913) Mayor explores the stereotype of the 'spurned' and unlikeable spinster in relation to a sensitive apprehension of the self-destructive effects of apparent social, sexual and emotional failure. *The Rector's Daughter* (1924) redresses the stereotype, detailing the complexity of the unconsummated but reciprocated passion between Mary Jocelyn and the neighbouring clergyman. *The Squire's Daughter* (1929) formulates an analysis of the disintegration of late-Victorian class boundaries, a concern which draws attention to Mayor's own conservative political beliefs. Mayor's novels are significant in their close examination of the inner life of women, and interestingly straddle late 19th- and early 20th-century gender ideologies. Mayor's only other publication is *The Room Opposite and Other Tales of Mystery and Imagination* (1935).
Bib: Oldfield, S., *Spinsters of this Parish* (1990); Williams, M., *Six Women Novelists* (1987).

Mayoral, Marina (born 1942)

Spanish novelist. Born in Mondoñedo (Lugo), Mayoral now lectures in Spanish Literature at Madrid's Universidad Complutense. Her main works are: *Cándida otra vez* (1979) (*Candida Again*); *Al otro lado* (1981) (*On the Other Side*); *La única libertad* (1982) (*The Only Freedom*) and *Contra muerte y amor* (1985) (*Against Love and Death*). A major theme in her novels is personal liberty.

Mayreder, Rosa (1858–1938)

Austrian essayist and poet. A gifted young painter, she hoped in vain to be allowed to follow her brothers into higher education. She began to frequent the artistic circles in Vienna, and found a new career as a writer when her libretto, *Der Corregidor* (*The Chief Magistrate*) (completed in 1897, but never performed) was put to music by the composer Hugo Wolf (1860–1903). In 1893 she founded the Austrian Women's Association and, besides continuing to write fiction and poetry, published a series of penetrating analyses on the cultural position of women. They included *Zur Kritik der Weiblichkeit* (1905) (*Towards a Critique of Femininity*) and *Geschlecht und Kultur* (1923) (*Gender and Culture*).

Mayröcker, Friederike (born 1924)

Austrian poet and writer. A teacher living in Vienna, she first published her elusive poetry in ▷avant-garde journals in the 1950s, establishing herself as one of the most original and experimental of modern poets. Her prolific writing also includes novels, prose and radio plays, as well as children's books. In her works, the themes of transience, paradox and absurdity are evoked in a flamboyant, extravagant style. Her main publications include: *Larifari, Ein konfuses Buch* (1956) (*This and That, a Confused Book*); *Minimonsters Traumlexikon* (1968) (*Minimonster's Dictionary of Dreams*); and *Reise durch die Nacht* (1984) (*Journey Through the Night*).

Mazing Space: Writing Canadian Women Writing, A ▷*A Mazing Space: Writing Canadian Women Writing*

Mba, Nina ▷*Nigerian Women Mobilized*

McAlpine, Rachel (born 1940)

New Zealand poet, novelist and dramatist. One of six daughters of an Anglican clergyman, Rachel McAlpine's early life was spent moving around New Zealand. After some years spent bringing up her own children and teaching part-time, she began to write after hearing a male New Zealand poet talk about the lack of women poets in print. McAlpine was determined to 'do something about' the way women were not represented in literature, and published her first collection of poems in 1975, International Women's Year. Since then she has written many poems, novels and plays. McAlpine's work has always had a strong feminist direction, seeking particularly to recuperate the domestic and the personal as legitimate and major subject areas of writing. Much of her later work has satirized gender roles and male preconceptions about women, and has celebrated female sexuality and activism, as in her recent novel about the suffragette movement in New Zealand, *Farewell Speech*.

Publications include: *Lament for Ariadne* (poems) (1975); *Stay as the Dinner Party* (poems) (1977); *Recording Angel* (poems) (1983); *Driftwood* (play) (1985); *Selected Poems* (1988); *Power Play* (play) (1990); *Farewell Speech* (novel) (1990).

McBreen, Joan (born 1944)
Irish poet, born in Sligo, and now lives in County Galway. Her first collection, *The Wind Beyond the Wall* (1991), explores the often conflictual interplay of the traditional and the modern in the lives of contemporary Irish women.

McCafferty, Nell (born 1944)
Irish writer and journalist, born in Derry. After taking her degree at Queen's University, Belfast, she travelled extensively and then returned to Derry, where she became active in the civil rights movement. She moved to Dublin and became involved in the women's movement there, and joined *The Irish Times* where she worked for a number of years. She is now a freelance journalist, and lives in Dublin. Described as a 'passionate witness' of contemporary Ireland, she is internationally renowned as Ireland's most eloquent and acerbic journalist, and as an indefatigable campaigner on radical and feminist issues. Her books include two collections of journalism, *The Best of Nell* (1983) and *Goodnight Sisters* (1987); *A Woman to Blame: The Kerry Babies Case* (1985), and *Peggy Deery: A Derry Family at War* (1988). *A Worm in the Heart* (1990), her first play, was performed in both Dublin and London.

McCaffrey, Anne (born 1926)
US novelist. Born in Cambridge, Massachusetts, McCaffrey graduated from Radcliffe College in 1947. She is mother to three children, and is the first woman to win the Hugo Award for ▷science fiction; in 1968 it was awarded to the first novella in her Dragonriders of Pern series, *Weyr Search* (1967). Her novella *Dragonrider* (1968) won the 1968 Nebula Award. In emphasizing relationships, McCaffrey made emotion and love respectable subjects for science fiction. Her novels introduced active heroines into science fiction.

Other works include: *Restoree* (1967), *Decision at Doona* (1969), *The Ship Who Sang* (1969), *Dragonquest* (1971), *The Mark of Merlin* (1971), *Ring of Fear* (1971), *To Ride Pegasus* (1973), *The Kilterman Legacy* (1975), *Get off the Unicorn* (1977), *The White Dragon* (1978), *Norilka's Story* (1986) and *The Renegades of Pern* (1989).

McCarthy, Mary (born 1912)
US novelist, short story-writer and essayist. McCarthy was born in Seattle, Washington and raised by relatives after her parents' death in 1918. *Memories of a Catholic Girlhood* (1957) recalls the severity, rigid Catholicism and emotional deprivation of her childhood. She graduated with honours from Vassar College in 1933 and moved to New York, where she moved in left-wing and intellectual circles. She was encouraged to write by her second husband, Edmund Wilson (1895–1972), and has since produced a large output of fiction and non-fiction. Her first book, *The Company She Keeps* (1942),

satirizes this left-wing intellectual milieu and tells the story of a divorced woman seeking an independent identity. Her best-known novel, *The Group* (1963) charts the lives of a group of women college graduates. Criticized at the time for its 'feminine gossip', it delineates the enclosed and restricted values and world of middle-class, educated women. McCarthy's detached, satiric writing looks to sense rather than sensibility as its watchword, and engages with the shortcomings of North American liberalism. As important as her fiction are criticism and political reporting, such as *The Mask of State: Watergate Portraits* (1971), which have formed a large part of her work.

Other work includes: *The Oasis* (1949), *Cast a Cold Eye* (1950), *The Groves of Academe* (1952), *A Charmed Life* (1955), *Sights and Spectacles 1937–1956* (1956), *Venice Observed: Comments on Venetian Civilisation* (1956), *The Stones of Florence* (1959), *On the Contrary* (1961) *The Humanist in the Bathtub* (1964), *Vietnam* (1967), *Hanoi* (1968), *The Writing on the Wall and Other Literary Essays* (1970), *Winter Visitors* (1970), *Birds of America* (1971), *Medina* (1972), *The Seventh Degree* (1974), *Cannibals and Missionaries* (1979), *Ideas and the Novel* (1980), *The Hounds of Summer and Other Stories* (1981), *On the Contrary* (1981), *Child Traffic Accident in Ireland* (1985) and *How I Grew* (1987).
Bib: Hardy, Willene S., *Mary McCarthy*; Geldeman, Carol, *Mary McCarthy: A Life*.

McCauley, Sue
New Zealand novelist. Sue McCauley grew up on a farm and wanted to be a cowboy. After an unorthodox childhood she became a journalist. Her first novel, *Other Halves* (1982), is about a European woman's relationship with a Maori teenager fifteen years her junior, and is partly based on McCauley's second marriage. The novel received a lot of publicity when it appeared, as it was one of the first novels to deal with racial inequity in an unconventional setting. McCauley's second novel *Then Again* (1986) features lesbianism but, like many women writers, her narrative focus is the family dynamic, particularly unconventional versions of the family which raise wider social questions.
▷Lesbian writing, New Zealand

McClung, Nellie Letitia (1873–1951)
Canadian feminist, novelist, short story writer, activist and broadcaster, born Nellie Mooney in rural Ontario. In 1880 her family moved to a Manitoba homestead. McClung was thirsty for knowledge, and although she did not start school until age ten, within six years she was enrolled in Winnipeg's Normal School. She taught school, and decided early to use her abilities to effect social change. Active in the Women's Christian Temperance Movement, she married in 1896, and had five children, but nevertheless determined to do all she could for the causes of temperance and suffrage. Her first novel, *Sowing Seeds in Danny* (1908), about an ordinary

community, was an enormous success; it sold more than 100,000 copies. Its heroine, Pearlie Watson, becomes an independent suffragist in the subsequent novels, *The Second Chance* (1910) and *Purple Springs* (1921). McClung also published *The Black Creek Stopping-house and other Stories* (1912) and *When Christmas Crossed 'The Peace'* (1923), both short story collections. *Painted Fires* (1925) reflects the writer's interest in immigrant groups; its protagonist is a Finnish girl. McClung's social messages do intrude on her fiction, but it is difficult to resist the spirited impulse of her writing. Her best-known feminist polemic is *In Times Like These* (1915, republished in 1972 with an excellent introduction by Veronica Strong-Boag).

McClung was engaged in the fight for the enfranchisement of Manitoba women; and after the family moved to Edmonton, Alberta, in 1914, she campaigned tirelessly for both suffrage and prohibition there. She was elected to the Alberta provincial legislature in 1921 (defeated in 1925), was one of the five women engaged in the famous legal fight over the 'Persons Case' (see Emily Murphy), and was Canadian delegate to the League of Nations, 1938. Her newspaper columns are collected in *Be Good to Yourself* (1930), *Flowers for the Living* (1931), *Leaves From Lantern Lane* (1936) and *More Leaves From Lantern Lane* (1937). *Clearing in the West* (1935) and *The Stream Runs Fast* (1945) are autobiographical. McClung was a powerful tonic for the time that she lived in, and she made her mark on the political configuration of western Canada, especially in terms of the rights of women.

▷Salverson, Laura Goodman
Bib: Benham, M.L., *Nellie McClung*; Savage, C., *Our Nell: A Scrapbook Biography of Nellie L. McClung*; Cleverdon, C.L., *The Woman Suffrage Movement in Canada*.

McCrae, Georgiana Huntley (1804–1890)
Australian diarist. McCrae was born in London, the illegitimate daughter of George, Marquis of Huntley, later the fifth Duke of Gordon. An accomplished linguist, musician and portrait painter, Georgiana married Andrew McCrae, a lawyer, in 1830 and emigrated to Victoria in 1841. She became prominent in literary and cultural circles in Melbourne. Her journals, covering the period 1838–1865, supplemented by those of George Gordon McCrae, her son, were edited by her grandson, the poet Hugh McCrae, and published as *Georgiana's Journal* (1934).
▷Journals (Australia)

McCullers, Carson (1917–1967)
US novelist and short story writer. Born in Colulmbus, Georgia, McCullers was raised in a strong maternal environment. She suffered bouts with rheumatic fever which compelled her to relinquish a musical career. In 1934 she went to New York and studied writing at Columbia University. Typically McCullers focuses on Southern tomboys who are assertive and

Carson McCullers

independent, but who are terrified by puberty and the passage to womanhood; marginalized, they see themselves as freaks. Like Mick Kelly in ▷*The Heart Is a Lonely Hunter* (1940) and Frankie Addams in ▷*Member of the Wedding* (1946), they have artistic ambitions. But these ambitions violate the standards of femininity, especially those of the ▷Southern lady. As did Amelia Evans in ▷*The Ballad of the Sad Café* (1951), McCullers herself cultivated a masculine identity to pursue her career.

Other works include: *Reflections in a Golden Eye* (1941), *The Square Root of Wonderful* (1958), *Clock Without Hands* (1961), *Sweet as a Pickle and Clean as a Pig: Poems* (1964) and *The Mortgaged Heart* (1971).
Bib: Spencer Carr, Virginia, *The Lonely Hunter: A Biography of Carson McCullers*; Westling, Louise, *Sacred Groves and Ravaged Gardens: The Fiction of Endora Welty, Carson McCullers and Flannery O'Connor*.

McCullough, Colleen (born 1937)
Australian novelist. McCullough qualified as a neurophysiologist and practised in Sydney, England and Yale University's School of International Medicine from 1967 to 1976. Her novels, *Tim* (1974) and *An Indecent Obsession* (1981), have been made into successful films, and ▷*The Thorn Birds* (1977) was serialized for television. McCullough's other publications include *A Creed for the Third Millenium* (1985), *The Ladies of Missalonghi* (1987) and *The First Man in Rome* (1990), the first of a proposed six-volume series set in Roman times. McCullough now lives on Norfolk Island with her husband, Ric Robinson.

McDermid, Val

Scottish detective fiction writer, dramatist and journalist. McDermid's three ▷detective novels create Lindsay Gordon, reporter turned sleuth, out of her wide experience as a journalist. Since 1975 she has worked on newspapers such as the *South Devon Times*, *The Sunday Independent* (Exeter), the *Scottish Daily Record* and, currently, the *People* in Manchester. Her three novels, *Report for Murder* (1987), *Common Murder* (1989) and *Final Edition* (1991), belong to a recent trend in feminist writing which co-opts the detective genre to investigate a ▷patriarchal society. ▷Heterosexism and the English view of Scotland are particular targets for McDermid's lesbian Glasgow-based detective. McDermid has also had two stage plays performed, and The Scottish Society of Playwrights made her radio play *Like a Happy Ending* its first publication.

McFall, Frances ▷Grand, Sarah

McGuckian, Medbh (born 1950)

Irish poet, born in Belfast. She was educated in a Catholic convent school, and at Queen's University, Belfast, where she subsequently spent a year as Writer-in-Residence. Highly acclaimed in Ireland, Britain and the USA, she won the British National Poetry Society competition (1979), and the Rooney Prize and the Alice Hunt Bartlett Award (1983). Her collections of poetry are: *Single Ladies* (1980), *Portrait of Joanna* and (1980), *The Flower Master* (1982), *Venus and the Rain* (1984) and *On Ballycastle Beach* (1987). The recurrent themes of her work – female experience, the loss of identity, the omnipresence of conflict and tension, her refusal to be bound by linear syntax, and her search for a language free of the constraints of syntax – mark her as one of the most adventurous of Irish poets.

McIlwraith, Jean Newton (1859–1938)

Canadian novelist, critic and biographer. Born and educated in Hamilton, Ontario, she worked for a publisher in New York from 1902 to 1922. Best-known for her historical romances *The Curious Career of Roderick Campbell* (1901), *A Diana of Quebec* (1912) and *Kinsmen at War* (1927), she also wrote children's books, and a comic opera.

McLean, Sarah Pratt (1856–1935)

US fiction writer of New England ▷local color, especially of the Cape Cod area. McLean is typical of the minor women writers of her era, claiming her fame from her distinctive portraits, often autobiographical, of a particular area and its characteristic culture and personalities. Best known are her *Cape Cod Folks* (1881) and *Last Chance Junction* (1889).

McNeil, Florence (born 1937)

Canadian poet and editor, born and educated in Vancouver, British Columbia. Her poetry, collected in *A Silent Green Sky* (1967), *The Rim of*

the Park (1972), *Ghost Towns* (1975), *A Balancing Act* (1979) and *Barkerville* (1984), is concerned with time in transition, and the visual texture of nature. *Emily* (1975) is about painter ▷Emily Carr. *Miss P. and Me* (1982) and *All Kinds of Magic* (1984) are children's books.

McNeill, Janet (born 1907)

Irish writer. Born in Dublin, she was educated in England and Scotland and later settled in Lisburn, near Belfast. She has written children's books, plays and several novels, including *A Child in the House* (1955), *The Other Side of the Wall* (1957), *As Strangers Here* (1960), *The Early Harvest* (1962) and *The Maiden Dinosaur* (1964). These stylish, woman-centred accounts of life in Protestant Belfast have never received the recognition and serious critical attention they deserve.

McPherson, Heather (born 1942)

New Zealand Poet. Heather McPherson was trained as a teacher and completed her university education in New Zealand. Since the 1970s she has been publishing poetry in local journals and magazines, and has also been active in feminist publishing. She was editor of the feminist literary magazine *Spiral* for some years. Her work is explicitly feminist and focuses particularly on the feminist interest in alternative theologies, and on traditionally 'female' activities, as in poems like 'Theology and a Patchwork Absolute'.

Publications: *A Figurehead, A Face* (1982); *The Third Myth* (1986).

McQueen, Cilla (born 1949)

New Zealand poet. Cilla McQueen was born in England but has spent her working and professional life in New Zealand. Unusually for New Zealand, McQueen works full-time as a poet and publishes regularly in local and overseas literary magazines. She lives in Dunedin and there is a strongly regional flavour to much of her work. Her most persistent subject, however, is the process of perception; her poetry often represents landscape by means of cognitive visual referents – painting, perspective, reflection, geography. She also writes satirical verse about gender relations or roles, nationalism, her role as a poet; her work challenges sacred cows of all kinds. McQueen does not use conventional metrical forms often, but her verse is highly structured and controlled.

Publications include: *Homing In* (1982); *anti-gravity* (1984); *Wild Sweets* (1986); *Benzina* (1988).

Meatless Days (1989)

Autobiography of a Pakistani woman, Sara Suleri, an academic. It explores the break-up and dispersal of her family, and serves as an elegy for her dead sister, Ifat, who was killed in a hit-and-run accident in the early 1980s in what may have been a revenge attack on the family for her fathers opposition to General Zia's regime. Primarily *Meatless Days* is the story of a girl growing to maturity in Lahore in the 1960s and 1970s.

Although the tumultous political events of those years, which included the military coup in Pakistan led by General Zia al-Haque, are not given prominence in the memoir, they hover in the background as the parallel story of a young nation's loss of innocence. A theme which is prominent in much writing from the Indian subcontinent, the dissonance of Eastern and Western cultures, appears in *Meatless Days* in the author's account of her Pakistani father's relationship with her Welsh mother.

Mechakra, Yamina (born 1953)

Algerian novelist. Born in the Aurès mountains, she studied psychiatry and medicine. Her novel ▷*La Grotte éclatée* (1979) (*The Shattered Cave*) is about a young nurse who is a fighter in the Algerian liberation movement. She tends injured Algerian fighters in a cave, concealed in the Aurès mountains, until one day the cave is bombed and the refuge destroyed.

Mechtel, Angelika (born 1943)

German novelist and writer of short stories. She established her theme and reputation in 1968 with a volume of finely-crafted short stories, *Die feinen Totengräber* (*The Delicate Gravediggers*). Terse, laconic language, quasi-Surreal montage techniques and complex narrative structures evoke the brutality of modern 'macho' society, and present woman as a symbol for all that is oppressed and repressed. Her other works include: *Die Blindgängerin* (1974) (*The Explosive Woman*); *Die Träume der Füchsin* (1978) (*Dreams of the Vixen*); and *Gott und die Liedermacherin* (1983) (*God and the Singing Woman*).

Mechthild von Hackeborn (1241–1299)

German nun and visionary writer. At the age of seven she joined her sister, Gertrud von Hackeborn (1232–1299), in the Cistercian Convent of Rodersdorf in Saxony. After her sister became abbess, the whole foundation moved to Helfta in 1258, and from then on developed into one of the foremost centres of mysticism in Germany. Mechthild enjoyed a good education, and became a teacher in the convent school. Like so many women of her time and lifestyle, she had, from an early age, many religious visions, but kept them secret until, at the age of fifty, she confided them to her fellow nuns. She also encouraged the young ▷Gertrud von Helfta to note down her own visions, which were to become famous and earn her a sainthood. Indeed it was Gertrud who, together with other nuns, wrote down Mechthild's account of her visions in *Liber specialis gratiae* (*The Book of Special Grace*) (first published in Paris in 1877), a strikingly visual account, which makes particular use of colours and light. A translation, *The Boke of Gostely Grace* (ed. T.A. Halligan) was owned by Cicely, Duchess of York (died 1495), the mother of Edward IV and Richard III of England.

▷Mechthild von Magdeburg; Visionsliteratur

Mechthild von Magdeburg (c 1212–1294)

German nun and visionary poet. Of noble descent, she became a ▷Beguine in Magdeburg at the age of twenty, and in 1270 entered the convent of Helfta in Saxony, an important centre of learning and mysticism at the time. She had religious visions from her childhood onwards, but kept them secret until, between 1250 and 1260, she began to write about them in *Das fließende Licht der Gottheit* (▷*The Revelations of Mechthild*). This book, written in Swabian dialect, comprises numerous short paragraphs, which contain accounts of visions, autobiographical data, prayers, hymns and dialogues, as well as textual analyses. Unique in 13th-century German literature, the book became widely known throughout German-speaking Europe, and also had an important influence on the writings of ▷Gertrud von Helfta and ▷Mechthild von Hackeborn, her younger contemporaries at Helfta.

▷*Visionsliteratur*

Mecom, Jane Franklin (1712–1794)

North American letter-writer. Born in Boston on 27 March 1712, she was the daughter of Abiah Folger and Josiah Franklin. Early in life she forged a special bond with her older brother, the future statesman Benjamin Franklin. In the summer of 1727 she married Edward Mecom, a saddler; together they raised twelve children, but Edward was never an adequate provider for the large family. Thus she not only raised the children but also took in boarders to supplement their income. If her life was one in which 'Sorrows roll upon me like the waves of the sea', she found respite in her lifelong correspondence with Benjamin. In ▷*The Letters of Benjamin Franklin and Jane Mecom*, several of her letters detail her life and her perspective on the American Revolution. She died in Boston in May 1794.

▷*Benjamin Franklin and Catharine Ray Greene: Their Correspondence 1755–1790*; Greene, Catharine Ray; Early North American letters

Medio, Dolores (born 1914)

Spanish novelist and short-story writer. Born in Oviedo, Medio worked first as a teacher and then went into journalism and creative writing. Her autobiographical novel, *Nosotros los Rivero* (1953) (*We Riveros*), won the Nadal Prize. Her subsequent works operate within the conventions of the social novel common at that time, such as: *Funcionario público* (1956) (*Civil Servant*); *El pez sigue flotando* (1959) (*The Fish Keeps Afloat*), and *Diario de una maestra* (1961) (*Diary of a Schoolmistress*). Medio has also published several collections of short stories, including *Compás de espera* (1954) (*Waiting Time*). Her work is characterized by integrity and altruism, and a keen appreciation of the ironies of everyday life.

Meehan, Paula (born 1955)

Irish poet. Born in Dublin, she studied at Trinity College, Dublin, and took an MA in Fine Arts at Eastern Washington University, USA. She has published three collections of poems: *Return and No Blame* (1984), *Reading the Sky* (1986) and *The Man who was Marked by Winter* (1991).

Megalostrata (? 6th century BC)
Poet. From Sparta, she was praised by the Spartan lyric poet Alcman (7th century BC), whom tradition made fall in love with Megalostrata because of her intelligent conversation. But this may derive from a fragment of Alcman's verse which praises her for her beautiful hair.

Mehetabel Chandler Coit, Her Book, 1714 (1895)
Although titled '1714', the diary covers the North American author ▷Mehetabel Chandler Coit's life from 1688 until some time around 1749. Published privately at the end of the 19th century, Coit's day-to-day account of her life in New London, Connecticut, is in the form of brief notations kept on an irregular basis. *Her Book* also includes two letters by Coit that reveal her concerns about the behaviour of her daughter.

Mehta, Gita
Indian novelist educated in India and at Cambridge. She has worked on several television films; her publications include *Karma Cola* (1979) and ▷*Raj* (1989).

Meijsing, Doeschka (Maria Johanna) (born 1947)
Dutch prose writer and poet. She studied literary theory in Amsterdam and works as literary editor of a national weekly magazine. Important themes in her work are the inescapable domination of the past, the search for identity and the relationship between reality and appearance. Her novels and stories usually possess a complex structure of meanings. In her first collection of stories, *De hanen en andere verhalen* (1974) (*The Cocks and Other Stories*), the main characters are confronted with the vague borderline between fantasy and reality. Her most widely-read novel is *Robinson* (1976), describing the vicissitudes of a grammar-school girl who experiences the exploration of her own identity as a form of isolation. In the novel *De kat achterna* (1977) (*Following the Cat*) the narrator is confronted with an inaccessible past. *Tijger, tijger!* (1980) (*Tiger, Tiger!*) is a patchwork of reflections, letters, conversations and reminiscences. In *Utopia of De geschiedenissen van Thomas* (1982) (*Utopia or the Tales of Thomas*) the question of the power and impotence of the imagination is raised. Her first collection of poems came out in 1986 (*Paard Heer Mantel; Horse Gentleman Cloak*). The stories in *Beer en jager* (1987) (*Bear and Hunter*) form a meaningful fairytale. *De beproeving* (1990) (*The Ordeal*) gives an authentic image of the mental desperation of a man who lost, together with his love, also his belief in the world.

Meinkema, Hannes (born 1943)
Dutch prose-writer and poet. ▷Pseudonym of Hannemieke Stamperius, the name she uses for her scholarly writings. She studied Dutch and literary theory and took her doctorate in 1977. By that time, her first novel, *De maaneter* (1974) (*The Mooneater*), about relational problems, and a collection of stories, *Het wil nog maar niet zomeren* (1975) (*Summer is Slow to Come*), had already been published. The death of her mother and her involvement with feminism considerably influenced her life. Together with ▷Ethel Portnoy and Hanneke van Buuren, she founded the literary women's magazine *Chrysallis* (1978–1981), offering young writers an opportunity to publish. Main themes in Meinkema's work are the triangular love affair, the different ways in which men and women experience sexuality, and the complex mother–daughter relationship, as in the collection of stories *De naam van mijn moeder* (1980) (*The Name of My Mother*). Her characters usually live their lives knowing that no real contact is possible between people; a recurring theme is the discrepancy between people's behaviour and their thoughts. *Het persoonlijke is poëzie* (1979) (*Personal Matters are Poetry*) is a collection of poems. Her novels include *En dan is er koffie* (1976) (*And Then There is Coffee*), *Het binnenste ei* (1978) (*The Innermost Egg*), *De driehoekige reis* (1981) (*The Triangular Journey*), *Te kwader min* (1984) (*Loving Insincerely*) and *Mooie horizon* (1989) (*Beautiful Horizon*). An English translation of part of her work was published in 1981, in *Real Life* and *Sex and Sensibility*.

Meireles, Cecília (1901–1964)
Brazilian poet, chronicler and prose writer. Orphaned at a young age, she was brought up by her Portuguese grandmother, who came from the Azores. A teacher, she became a professor in 1940, and travelled widely. She is considered Brazil's greatest woman poet.

Between 1919 and 1927 she contributed to the magazines *Arvore Nova*, *Terra do Sol* and the transcendental and spiritualist magazine *Festa* (1927), but she always retained symbolist traits. Her first book, *Espectros* (1919) (*Spectrums*) was Parnassian, and has been described as 'an airy and vague poetry, languid and fluid, set in an intimate atmosphere of shadows and dreams'. However, *Viagém* (1939) (*Voyage*) and *Mar absoluto* (1942) (*Absolute Sea*) were her most successful books. She had a perfect command of the poetic form. Holding a mirror to the world, she tackles the sadness of death with figurative language and a lively poetic imagination.

Romanceiro da Inconfidência (1953) (*Poet of the Inconfidence*), written in the style of Iberian folksongs, centres on the first colonial attempt at Brazilian Independence, in Minas Gerais, and the leader, Joaquim José da Silva Xavier, who has been hailed as another Jesus Christ. She won major literary prizes for much of her work.

Other works: *Obra poética* (1958) (*Poetic Work*); *Nunca mais . . . e poema dos poemas* (1923) (*Never*

Again . . . and Poem of Poems); *Balada para El-Rei* (1924) (*Ballad for El-Rei*); *Vaga música* (1942) (*Vague Music*); *Retrato natural* (1949); *Amor em Leonoreta* (1952) (*Love in Leonoreta*); *Doze noturnos da Holanda* (1952) (*Twelve Dutch Nocturnes*); *O Aeronauta* (1952) (*The Aeronaut*); *Pequeno oratório de Santa Clara* (1955) (*Little Oratory of St Claire*); *Pistóia, cemitério militar brasileiro* (1955) (*Pistóia, Brazilian Military Cemetery*); *Espelho cego* (1955) (*Blind Mirror*); *Romance de Santa Cecília* (1957) (*The Romance of St Cecilia*); *A Rosa* (1957) (*The Rose*); *Metal rosicler* (1960) (*Rosicler Metal*); *Poemas escritos na India* (1961) (*Poems Written in India*); *Solombra* (1964); *Inéditos* (1967) (*Unpublished Works*); *Flor de poemas* (1972) (*Flower of Poems*).

Mela e il serpente, La (1974) (The Apple and the Serpent)

A novel by Italian writer ▷Armanda Guiducci, told in the first person. The subtitle of the novel is 'Female Self-analysis'. Divided into three parts, it maps out the life of its female narrator. The first part of the work, entitled 'A Woman's Blood', considers menstruation as both a wound and a single event which destroys childhood. From this the narrator moves on to set up a notion of women as a Third World group, a subculture. Part II, entitled 'Taking on the Role', envisions the role of woman as a part to be played; in this section the protagonist discovers the use of food as a *weapon* through which she may gain control over her life. The third section, '*Mater mystica*', considers woman as mother. The protagonist loves her son, and is proud of him, but dwells with horror on how she is taken over by an alien being during pregnancy. This novel is at once the story of an individual and of women in general, both a narrative and a history (or, indeed, herstory). It tells of woman's struggle with society's images of the feminine, and also of her struggle with herself. It addresses the fact that it is easier to go along with the dominant mode than to fight against it, yet in so doing to be forced to recreate oneself, and to reject myths of femininity.

Melissa (? 3rd century BC)

Possibly Athenian philosopher. She is one of the women credited with being a Pythagorean philosopher (▷Pythagorean women, ▷Philosophers, Ancient Greek and Roman women). There survives a letter, written to another woman, Clearete, discussing the desirability of sober dress. She confirms that manners, not beauty or wealth, make a woman attractive. Wisdom is to govern a household well (▷Household management and child rearing, Ancient Greek).

Melissanthi (born 1910)

Greek poet. She was born Eve Chougia-Skandalaki in Athens, and studied at the French Academy there. She taught French in Athens and wrote literary articles for Greek newspapers and journals. Her first poems, *Insect Voices* (1930), followed traditional poetic forms and were, in her own words, 'stepping stones which helped me to stand on my own feet as a writer'. But this is true of their form only, since what characterizes her poetry is the element of 'personal agony' about metaphysical questions which transcends 'the agony of mere expression' so characteristic of her generation. Her earliest poems were religious, preoccupied with sin and the search for God's forgiveness; these were written using strict poetical forms. But after World War II Melissanthi turned to more intellectual subjects and also used free verse forms. She moved away from emotional and lyrical writing towards a more Existentialist poetry. But her belief in love and human dignity always illuminates her work, dispelling any sense of gloom. Her works include *Burning Bush* (1935), *Hosanna* (1939), *Lyrical Confessions* (1945), *Human Form* (1961) and *New Poems* (1976). Her poetry has been translated into a number of European languages.
Bib: Friar, Kimon, *Greek Poetry*.

Melville, Pauline (born 1948)

Actress, poet and short story writer, born in ▷Guyana. She is based in Britain, but maintains strong links with the Caribbean. Her poetry is included in the anthology ▷*Creation Fire*.

Member of the Wedding (1946)

US novel by ▷Carson McCullers which depicts the psychological trauma suffered by Frankie Addams when she must accept her womanhood. A twelve-year-old tomboy, Frankie dreams of becoming a great poet. When she is not permitted to accompany her brother on his honeymoon, she is forced to face the facts of adult sexuality. Frankie identifies with the African-Americans in her town who strain against circumscribed social roles. However, fearful of being freakish, she accepts the limits of her sexuality. She submits to the role of the ▷Southern lady. McCullers emphasizes that a woman's sexuality traps her into conformity.

Mémoires

A French type of memoirs. Originally notes for history written in the third person, *mémoires* developed as an increasingly personal literary genre in France during the 16th and 17th centuries. Written mainly by nobles, distanced from the court by disgrace, age or illness, or in secret within the walls of the Louvre or Versailles, *mémoires* were not usually destined for publication by their authors, who hoped, nevertheless, to rewrite the history of events and establish their innocence for posterity. While most *mémoires* were written by men, the genre also appealed particularly to aristocratic women writers and women writers with aristocratic pretensions such as ▷Madame d'Aulnoy, ▷Madame de la Guette, ▷Madame de Lafayette, ▷Duchesse de Montpensier, ▷Madame de Motteville, ▷Madame de Murat, ▷the Duchesse de Nemours and ▷Marguerite de Valois. Such unofficial historical accounts were an invaluable

source of reference for late 17th-century novelists, who imitated their subject, form and style.
▷*Memoirs of the Life of Henriette-Sylvie de Molière*

Mémoires d'une jeune fille rangée (1958)
▷*Memoirs of a Dutiful Daughter*

Memoir, Letters and Journal, of Elizabeth Seton (1869)
This text collects and excerpts the public and private writings of the first North American saint ▷Elizabeth Ann Bayley Seton, one of the founders of the Sisters of Charity in North America. Although narrated by a male minister who edited her writings, complete letters and expansive excerpts of autobiographical narratives are included. The letters to her friend, Julianna Scott, are notable for the private side they reveal of a publicly renowned woman.
▷Early North American letters

Memoir of Charlotte Chambers, The (1856)
▷Charlotte Chambers's memoirs from December 1796 until April 1821 denote her life's work for the Bible Society of Ohio in North America. Chambers moved from Pennsylvania to Cincinnati, Ohio, to dedicate herself to the Bible Society's mission. Her twenty-five-year record reflects in its brief notational style the rigorous schedule she maintained in her commitment to her religious work and in a busy social life within the religious community.

Memoir of Miss Hannah Adams (1832)
The North American writer ▷Hannah Adams's memoir reflects an immense modesty against the backdrop of extraordinary accomplishments. Adams chronicles the influence of her research, as well as her own experiences, on her changing religious attitudes. A dedicated historian, Adams maintains an objectivity about her own life that is tempered by her heartfelt attention to the people and events that shaped her life. She relates 'the difficulties . . . encountered, while writing for the press', most of which developed because of her insistence upon including contemporary controversial issues and, as she carefully noted, because she was a woman. In spite of criticisms from her peers, Adams continued to write, declaring that she need only answer to herself and a 'few friends whose opinion I most highly prized'; otherwise, she proclaimed, 'I was comparatively indifferent to the censure or ridicule of the world in general.' Adams's *Memoir*, published the year after her death, is appended with a less objective tribute 'By a Friend'.
▷*Alphabetical Compendium of the Various Sections*; *Summary History of New England, A*

Memoirs of a Dutiful Daughter
Translation of *Mémoires d'une jeune fille rangée* (1958), by French writer ▷Simone de Beauvoir. In this, the first volume of her autobiography, de Beauvoir tells of her childhood and adolescence as

the elder daughter of a French bourgeois family in the years just before and after World War I. Originally prosperous, de Beauvoir's family became reduced to relative poverty by 1918, and a major theme of the book is the tension within the family caused by lack of money and declining social status. More than that, the book is an outstanding document of a girl's struggle to acquire higher education and emancipate herself from the strictures of a conventional upbringing. As de Beauvoir makes clear, she was saved – by her family's poverty – from the life of a dutiful daughter.
▷*Mémoires*

Memoirs of an Unrealistic Woman (1986)
Arabic novel by Palestinian writer ▷Sahar Khalifa. Khalija's novel is regarded by her critics as more interested in feminist issues than in the national cause. The 'unrealistic woman' in question is 'Afaf, daughter of a school inspector, a respectable educated man. He suppresses his taste for literature and his love for singing as his children grow up because of the necessity to impose discipline and strict morality among the youngsters. 'Afaf (her name means modesty and chastity, necessary requirements in females) is described by her father as *hawaiya* (ethereal). When she looks it up in the dictionary, she is glad to find it has to do with air, breath, the necessary element of life. Later, she realizes that it can also mean weak, changeable, undependable, which was probably what her father meant. The girl loves singing and dancing, and listens enthralled to the old stories narrated in the evenings by her grandmother, but she soon realizes that there is some kind of taboo on enjoyment, on pleasure of the senses. There is some relationship between a girl showing off her beauty and femininity, and her being killed by her people for 'honour'. The growing girl is frightened at signs of her blossoming femininity, and develops into a mixed-up adolescent.

She had asked why the birth of a male was a cause for celebration and the birth of a girl was an occasion for condolences. When she tried to be a tomboy she was told to be 'realistic'.

At seventeen, 'Afaf is married off to a man in his forties, because she was caught walking in a country lane with a romantic boy, a neighbour's son. Her husband is a tradesman, and she is now simply referred to as the merchant's wife, as she used to be addressed as 'Miss Inspector'. She lives as a prisoner in a modern flat, which she keeps immaculately clean. Still she cannot be 'realistic', hoping one day to get a divorce and make a fresh start. Trying to induce an abortion, she damages her womb and joins the ranks of the really damned – an Oriental woman who can never give birth to a child. She finds refuge with her widowed mother; her brothers have 'eaten' her inheritance, her sisters live cowering in the protective shade of their respective husbands. The boy of her adolescent dreams is married, unhappily he says. He is glad to see her, still loves her, but he will not divorce his wife. There is nothing for her to do in her home town, so changed under Israeli occupation, and the reader is left in the dark as to 'Afaf's future.

Memoirs of Hadrian (1954)

Translation of *Les Mémoires d'Hadrien* (1951), by French writer ▷ Marguerite Yourcenar. Translated into fifteen languages, these fictional memoirs of a lesser Roman emperor (AD 76–138) constitute Yourcenar's chief claim to fame. Dealing with the emperor's passionate relationship with Antinous, they show male sexuality from a woman's viewpoint and the corrupting influence of power. *Les Mémoires* provided a generation traumatized by war and weary of *engagement* with solace drawn from its cultural heritage.

Memoirs of Mrs Abigail Bailey (1815)

Published posthumously, the North American author ▷ Abigail Abbott Bailey's memoirs were probably written in the early 1790s when she sought approval from the Congregational Church to divorce her husband Asa. Although Bailey had endured her husband's infidelity and physical abuse for twenty-five years, she was compelled to take action when she discovered that her husband had committed incest with their daughter, Phebe. Bailey's account of her discovery is remarkably straightforward in detailing her husband's infidelities, his abuse of Phebe, and her own initial unwillingness to believe he was capable of incest. Finding strength in her faith and support from her congregation, Bailey divorced her husband in 1793. The memoir is a rare document of abuse and incest in early North American domestic relations.

Memoirs of the Count of Comminge (1756)

A translation of *Mémoires du Comte de Comminge* (1735) a novel by ▷ Claudine de Tencin. Dealing with the conflict between love and duty, the text denounces the abusive power wielded by families in respect of their offspring. The psychological portraits of the lovers suggest there are also internal obstacles which would threaten their relationship even if they were free to do as they wished. The text is presented, as was often the convention, as a retrieved manuscript published without alteration. It is a retrospective narrative written by the eponymous hero. He meets by chance Adélaïde de Lussan, they fall in love, he fights a duel for her, and saves her from an accident. However, since their fathers, who are cousins, have long been embroiled in a family feud, the narrator's father will not permit a marriage and has his son incarcerated. In order to secure the young Comte's release and to prove her love for him, Adélaïde chooses to marry Benavides, the least attractive of her suitors. The Comte, released, gains entry to the Benavides' house disguised as a painter and, although Adélaïde remains faithful to her husband, Benavides finds the two in a compromising situation. The Comte wounds Benavides, runs

away and takes refuge in a monastery to mourn his lost love. Years later he is present at the last confession of a dying monk, who is revealed as Adélaïde in disguise. After the death of her husband, who had locked her away and pretended she was dead, she had been drawn to the monastery, and remained there, concealing her identity so as not to unsettle the Comte. Having lost Adélaïde a second time, he remains in retreat to grieve and write his memoirs. The novel has been read as a text with subversive potential, due to the lovers' sacrilegious use of the institutions of marriage and the monastery (see M. Delon's preface to 1967 edition in the *Mémoires du comte de Comminge*, published by Decottignies).

Memoirs of the Life and Death of the Pious and Ingenious Mrs Jane Turell ▷ *Religuiae Turellae et Lachrymae Paternal*; Turell, Jane Colman

Memoirs of the Life of Henriette-Sylvie de Molière (1672–1674) (Mémoires de la vie d'Henriette-Sylvie de Molière)

French fictional autobiography by Madame de Villedieu (▷ Marie-Catherine Hortense Desjardins). It helped to popularize the genre of ▷ *mémoires*, or pseudo-memoirs, in the latter part of the 17th century. The heroine is a modern adventurer in the tradition of the kind of hero found in the picaresque novel, but many of the adventures she experiences are more reminiscent of the baroque novel of the first part of the 17th century. Unlike most early French fiction, the action of the novel is contemporaneous with the period when it was written. Real characters are also included, and the work contains a description of the first great festivals at Versailles, *Les Plaisirs de l'Ile enchantée* (*The Pleasures of the Enchanted Island*) of 1664. The heroine's vicissitudes involve her not only in dilemmas of conscience but also in inheritance suits.

Memoirs of the Life of Martha Laurens Ramsay (1812)

Published the year after the North American diarist ▷ Martha Laurens Ramsay's death, the *Memoirs* collect testimonies to her as well as excerpts from her diary (July 1791 to June 1808) and correspondence from the last years of her life. Presented in the traditional format of 'memoirs of the life of . . .' that were so popular at the turn of the century, it reveals her pious, self-reflective nature. If traditional in religious attitudes and presentation, it does capture the personal strength and integrity of this South Carolina woman.

Memoirs of the Life of Mrs Sarah Osborn (1799)

This text is an expansion of the North American writer ▷ Sarah Haggar Wheaten Osborn's earlier autobiographical narrative, ▷ *The Nature, Certainty, and Evidence of True Christianity* (1755). It is unknown how much of the revisions were completed by Osborn herself and how much her

minister, Samuel Hopkins, who acted as editor of the manuscript, altered the text. It draws on the voluminous diaries that Osborn maintained from 1744 to 1767. As the leader of a major evangelical revival in the 1760s, in her memoirs she captures the spirit of revivalism as well as woman-centred concerns with spirituality and social constructs. Meditative in nature, yet replete with plot structures that suggest the influence of novel-reading, these memoirs are a major contribution to early North American theology and literature.
▷*Familiar Letters Written by Mrs Sarah Osborn, and Miss Susanna Anthony*; *Life and Character of Miss Susanna Anthony, The*; *World of Hannah Heaton, The*; Heaton, Hannah Cook

Memoranda and Correspondence of Mildred Ratcliff (1890)

Excerpted journal entries and correspondence of this North American Quaker preacher detail her life of travel and exhortation from 1799 until 1838. Unlike many women preachers' autobiographical narratives from this era, ▷Mildred Morris Ratcliff included detailed accounts of her role in meetings and her positions on current religious debates within the Society of Friends.
▷Early North American letters; Early North American Quaker women's writings

Memorias (Memoirs)

Written by Spain's ▷Leonor López de Córdoba, this is one of the classics of medieval literature. The memoirs deal with two periods of her life, the first when she was locked up in the Atarazanas prison as a result of political intrigue, and the second a period of particularly bitter family quarrels. Though López cannot always be relied on for factual accuracy, her memoirs are moving and provide a privileged insight into a woman's experience in the Middle Ages.

Memories of the Past, by a Lady in Australia (1873)

Diaries by ▷Annie Maria Baxter. Based on thirty-five volumes of Baxter's diary covering the period 1834–1865, the diaries record her steadily deteriorating first marriage and increasing poverty, her life in various parts of Australia, her husband's suicide in 1855 and a subsequent disappointing marriage to Robert Dawbin. They give a vivid account of colonial society and an insight into their vivacious and indomitable author. Lucy Frost's ▷*No Place for a Nervous Lady* (1984), includes a selection from Baxter's diaries.

Mendels, Josepha (Judica) (born 1902)

Dutch prose writer. For ten years she was headmistress of a pedagogical centre for Jewish girls. Since 1936 she has lived in Paris, being attached to the Dutch Embassy after the war. She purposely chose to be an unmarried mother. She wrote psychological novels, usually against the background of her Orthodox Jewish education. In 1947 she surprised the literary world with *Rolien*

and Ralien, the story of a girl who falls victim to her *alter ego* and tries to exclude the evil outside world by means of exorcism rituals. *Als wind en rook* (*As Wind and Smoke*), which followed in 1950, centres on the problem of being half-Jewish, a theme that recurs in her novel *De speeltuin* (1970) (*The Playing Garden*). There is no happiness in love in her other books, with the exception of *Je wist het toch . . .* (1948) (*But You Knew*). *Welkom in dit leven* (*Welcome to this Life*), published in 1981, is autobiographical. Together with ▷Anna Blaman she worked on a novel that remained unfinished. 1986 saw the collection of stories *Joelika en andere verhalen*. Because of the independent and frank position she adopted, she is sometimes regarded as a forerunner of modern feminism. She was awarded the Anna Bijns Prize 1985.

Menebhi, Saïda (1952–1977)

Moroccan poet, born in Marrakech. She taught English in Rabat, and was an active member of the National Union Of Moroccan Students (UNEM) as well as the Marxist-Leninist organization *Ila Al Amam*. She was arrested in January 1976 and condemned to seven years solitary confinement in the civil prison of Casablanca. She died as a consequence of a hunger strike while in prison. Her poems and prose in *Poèmes, Lettres, Ecrits de Prison* (1978) show a profound and an unshaken belief in the principles of democracy.

Meneres, Maria Alberta (born 1930)

Portuguese poet and author of children's literature. A graduate of the University of Lisbon, she has taught in secondary schools for many years. She has also published more than three dozen books – most of them volumes of poetry. Her best-known collections of verse are *Intervalo* (1952) (*Interlude*), *Água-Memória* (1960) (*Water-Memory*) and *O Robot Sensível* (1978) (*The Sensitive Robot*). In addition, Meneres has written children's literature and produced a children's programme for Portuguese Radio and Television. In 1971 she and her husband, the poet E.M. Melo de Castro, edited *Antologia da Novíssima Poesia Portuguesa*, one of the most important anthologies of contemporary Portuguese verse. She has collaborated on a number of journals and reviews, and has continued to edit anthologies which call attention to a wide range of poets.

Meneses, Doña Juana Josefa de (1651–1709)

Spanish writer of both verse and prose. She was the third Condesa de la Ericeira. Her published works are: a poem in Castilian *octavas* (eight-syllable lines), *Despertador del alma al sueño de la vida* (1695) (*Rouser of the Soul to the Dream of Life*); two plays, *Dividido imperio de amor* (*Divided Empire of Love*) and *El duelo de las finezas* (*The Sorrow of Kindness*); and two *autos sacramentales* (Spanish religious plays popular in the 17th century, celebrating one of the Christian sacraments). She also wrote two prose works translated from the French, and much poetry in manuscript.

Men Without Ears (1984)

A novel by the Nigerian writer ▷Ifeoma Okoye. Chigo returns from several years in Tanzania to find himself out of key with the rampant materialism and corruption of oil-boom Nigeria. Try as he will to maintain his integrity, the whole society is against him. His only ally is his brother's wife, Anny, for whose sake he decides to remain in Nigeria when her husband dies as a result of his own underhand dealings. The author's choice of a male protagonist may arise from a feeling that only through a man could she realistically portray certain aspects of the society. Despite this, her hero is strongly woman-identified, both in his relationship with his sister-in-law, and in his own personality and behaviour. The novel won the Association of Nigerian Authors Award in 1985.

Menzies, Trixie Te Arama (Tainui) (born 1936)

New Zealand poet. Trixi Te Arama was born in Wellington, was educated at Auckland University, and taught at Otahuhu College in Auckland. Menzies' two collections of poems are published by Waiata Koa (a publishing group whose name translates as Dawn Chorus – Songs of Joy) a branch of Karanga, a national Maori women's group of artists, musicians and writers. Menzies' poetry combines feminism with *Maoritanga* (Maori culture); the foreword to *Papakainga* (1988) describes her poems as *waiata*, the memory-songs of knowledge which the woman poet guards. Menzies' work has been represented in a number of recent anthologies.
▷Maori literature

Menzogna e sortilegio (1948) ▷*House of Liars*

M.E.R. (Maria Elisabeth Rothmann) (1875–1975)

South African Afrikaans writer, who was born and died in Swellendam in the Cape. Taking an Arts degree at the University of the Cape of Good Hope in 1896, she qualified as a teacher, later working as a journalist and editor on *Die Boerevrou* (*The Boer Woman*), the first Afrikaans women's magazine, and on *Die Burger* newspaper, where she was first editor of its women's page. Her appointment in 1928 as secretary of the ACVV (Afrikaans Christian Women's Organization) led to her publishing its history in 1954: *Ons Saamreis* (*Our Journey Together*) and *Ons Voortgang* (*Our Progress*). As a social worker, and the only woman member of the Carnegie Commission into the poor-white problem in South Africa, she conducted a sociological study of the problems of mothers and daughters in poor white families, dispelling myths about white Afrikaners but still limited by her racial focus.

Her writing reflects these two careers. It began with children's stories, *Kinders van die Voortrek* (1920) (*Children of the Voor Trek*), based on firsthand information from Afrikaners who left the Cape for a life free from British rule. Her adult fiction exhibits the concerns of the welfare worker, the narratives often interrupted by moralizing digressions or didactic passages. Perhaps the most interesting of this fiction is *Na Vaste Gange* (1944) (*By Set Ways*), in which the young white widow of a rich Indian man uses her inheritance to educate young white girls to become worthy mothers of the Afrikaner race. She also wrote three stories, *Drie Vertellings* (1944) (*Three Narratives*) whose content is comparable to that of ▷Gertrude Stein's ▷*Three Lives*, although not as stylistically innovative.

Prolific in non-fiction as well, she translated, from Dutch into Afrikaans, that classic of ▷Anglo–Boer War (1899–1902) literature, *Tant Alie van Transvaal* (1939) (*Tant Alie of the Transvaal: Her Diary, 1880–1902*, 1923); published three volumes of essays and sketches; edited her brother's diary, and wrote an autobiography *My Beskeie Deel* (1972) (*My Humble Contribution*). With her daughter, Anna, she wrote *The Drostdy at Swellendam* (1960), her only English work. Her letters to her daughter were published posthumously in two volumes, *Familiegesprek* (1976) (*Family Conversation*) and *'n Kosbare Erfenis* (1977) (*A Valuable Inheritance*).

Her other works are: *Onweershoogte* (1927) (*Stormy Height*), *Die Kammalanders* (1928) (*Those of the Never-Never Land*), *Jong Dae* (1933) (*Young Days*), *Die Sondagskind* (1920) (*The Sunday Child*), *Uit en Tuis* (1946) (*At Home*), *Die Eindelose Waagstuk* (1948) (*The Endless Risk*), *Die Gevers* (1950) (*The Givers*), *So is Onse Maniere* (1965) (*These are Our Customs*), *Vroue Wat Jesus Geken Het* (1965) (*Women who Knew Jesus*); *Hanne en die Bessiekinders* (1972) (*Hanne and the Berry Children*).

Merard de Saint-Just, Anne-Jeanne-Félicité d'Ormoy (1765–1830)

French novelist. Her first main prose work, *Rosine et Colette*, whose subtitle declares that 'happiness is only to be found in the equality of conditions', appeared in the *Journal Littéraire de Nancy* (1784) and was followed by the published diary *Mon journal d'un an* (1787) (*A Year From My Diary*). Her later works include the prose fictions *La Corbeille de fleurs* (1795) (*The Basket of Flowers*); *Démence de Mme de Panor* (1796) (*The Madness of Mme de Panor*) and *Le Chapeau noir* (1799) (*The Black Hat*). Her novel *Six mois d'exil* (1805) (*Six Months in Exile*) is a testimony for the 'orphans of the Revolution'.

Her other works are: *Les Quatre Ages de l'homme, poème* (1782) (*The Four Ages of Man, a Poem*); *Bergeries et opuscules* (1782) (*Pastorals and Short Works*); *Histoire de la baronne d'Alvigny* , and (1788) (*The Story of the Baroness d'Alvigny*); *Le Petit Lavater, almanach* (1800).

Mercoeur, Elisa (1809–1835)

French poet. The illegitimate daughter of a Breton lawyer, Mercoeur's precocious intelligence enabled her to master Greek and Latin, and to learn enough English by the age of twelve to give lessons in it and support her mother. She published her first collection of poems at sixteen, and was awarded various literary prizes for them. However, her poetry, which was precious and tended to the pedantic, fell out of vogue after 1830, and she was obliged to earn a living as a literary journalist. A tragedy of hers was rejected by the Théâtre Française, but appears in her *Oeuvres complètes* (1843) (*Complete Works*) along with her poems and essays. Her life was a short and largely unhappy one.

Mercy Philbrick's Choice (1876)
US fictionalized biography of US poet ▷Emily Dickinson by ▷Helen Hunt Jackson. Hunt Jackson was one of Dickinson's few women friends, and the woman writer to whom Dickinson showed her poems. Jackson's account is selective and sympathetic, if somewhat romantic.

Mereau-Brentano, Sophie (1770–1806)
German poet and novelist. The wife of a professor of jurisprudence, Friedrich Mereau (died 1801), she lived in Jena, one of the most active cultural centres in Germany at the time. She met many of the leading figures of the burgeoning romantic movement, published poetry in the literary journals, of the poet Schiller (1759–1805) and, early on, established her economic independence by translating important literary texts from English, Spanish, Italian and French, most notably Boccaccio (1313–1375) and ▷Madame de Staël. She was the editor of several progressive journals and the author of a courageous appraisal of the 17th-century French intellectual ▷Ninon de l'Enclos, whose letters she published. In this work, Mereau argues for the erotic emancipation of women, an issue she also explores in novels such as *Das Blüthenalter der Empfindung* (1794) (*The Blossoming of Sensitivity*) and *Amanda und Eduard* (1803). After divorcing Mereau in 1801, she married the poet Clemens Brentano (1778–1842) in 1803, and died in childbirth three years later.

Meredith, Gwen (born 1907)
Australian dramatist and novelist. Meredith is best known for her ABC Radio serial, *The Lawsons*, which ran from 1943 to 1949, and was succeeded by her *Blue Hills*, which ran for twenty-seven years. Both serials were immensely popular, dealing with the lives of typical yet idealized characters in the Australian bush, and with their personal relationships and problems. For over thirty years Meredith both depicted and helped to shape the contours of Australian rural society. She has received an MBE.
▷Writers for film and television (Australia)

Meredith, Louisa (1812–1895)
Australian poet, novelist, botanist and non-fiction writer. Meredith was born in England and emigrated with her husband, Charles Meredith, to Tasmania in 1839, where he was a member of the

Tasmanian Parliament from 1860 to 1879. Meredith is celebrated for her exquisite drawings and paintings of Australian flora and fauna, for her accounts of life in the colonies, including *Notes and Sketches of New South Wales* (1844), ▷*My Home in Tasmania During a Residence of Nine Years* (1852) and *Over the Straits: A Visit to Victoria* (1861), and for her illustrated books of poetry for both adults and children. She was a prominent figure on the Tasmanian literary and cultural scene until her death in 1895.
▷*On Her Selection*

Merian, Maria Sibylla (1647–1717)
German writer and scientist. Born in Frankfurt, she was the daughter of Matthäus Merian, author of *Topographien* (1642) (*Topographies*) and *Historia naturalis* (?1653) (*Natural History*). In 1679 and 1683 she published two volumes of *Der Raupen wunderbare Wandelung und sonderbare Blumen-nahrung* (*The Marvellous Metamorphosis, and Especial Sustenance from Flowers, of Caterpillars*), an extensive investigation into the biological and ecological systems relating to caterpillars. Her most famous work, *Metamorphosis Insectorum Surinamensium* (1705) (*Metamorphosis of Insects in Surinam*), was the result of a research expedition to South America undertaken with her daughter from 1699 to 1701.

Merian, Svende (born 1955)
German novelist. Her first and only novel, *Der Tod des Märchenprinzen* (1980) (*The Death of the Fairy Prince*) became an instant popular success in feminist circles. In the fashionable idiom of contemporary street culture, the author tells, with little critical distance, of her own development away from a lover, towards an imagined ideal of sexual, emotional and intellectual autonomy.

Meridian (1976)
Novel by US writer ▷Alice Walker. *Meridian* takes a critical look at the US Civil Rights Movement and its aftermath from the viewpoint of the African-American woman. Meridian Hill is a young African-American girl growing up in the South. After a teenage pregnancy and hasty marriage force her to drop out of high school, Meridian joins the Civil Rights Movement, leaves both her son and her marriage and goes to university. Her relationships with her lover, Truman Held, a white Jewish woman, Lyndsey, with whom Held has a child, and other activists of the movement provide the forum for Walker's exploration of the gender and race conflicts which structure these relationships. The power of the book emerges from the complexity of its narrative structure, 'like a crazy quilt' according to Walker. Brief episodes, told from different narrative viewpoints, are juxtaposed rather than chronologically ordered, the book opening long after the Civil Rights movement has ended. The result is a questioning of the dominance of official histories of the movement, whether Anglo-American or male African-American. Instead, the

novel exposes the reader to the difficulties and contradictions of the racial and sexual histories it confronts, and explores questions about maternity, non-violence, spirituality, and the influence of a past that cannot be left behind or easily encompassed. At the centre of the book Meridian focuses Walker's strategies. She is the recipient of the fantasies and definitions of those who surround her, yet persistently refuses and eludes their categorizations.

Merito delle donne, II (1600) (Woman's Worth)

Subtitled 'In Which It Will Clearly Be Shown How Much More Worthy and Perfect They Are Than Men', this tract by Italian writer ▷Moderata Fonte forms part of an ongoing 16th-century debate (▷16th-century treatises on women). Fonte has created here a community of women, made up of one queen, three accusers and three defenders of men. Corinna, the most anti-male of the group, is normally identified with Fonte herself. One of the most interesting arguments put forward here is the charge levied against men that they have appropriated language for themselves. Fonte here reclaims that language for women. Marriage is criticised as an institution by the women, while chastity, in Corinna's view, facilitates her writing and allows her control over herself and her body. Ironically, this book was completed just before Fonte died in childbirth.

Meriwether, Louise ▷Daddy Was a Number Runner

Merken, Lucretia Wilhelmina van (1721–1789)

Poet and dramatist from the northern Netherlands. This pious, Remonstrant-reformed woman was considered to be the greatest artist of her time by her contemporaries (for example ▷Betje Wolff) because of her long didactic poem *Het nut der tegenspoeden* (1762) (*The Use of Adversity*), and the ambitious epic poems *David* (twelve books, 1768) and *Germanicus* (16 books, 1779). In its typically 18th-century Protestant content, as well as in its constrained style, this work is characteristic of late classicism in the Netherlands. Van Merken also wrote plays following the French classicist model, celebrating episodes from national history (including *Beleg der stad Leyden*, 1774), (*Siege of the City of Leyden*). She also wrote seventeen metrical psalms that were in use for a considerable time. *Toneelpoezij* (1774–1786) contained plays of both hers and her husband's. *De mare geluksbedeeling* (*The Bestowal of True Happiness*) appeared posthumously in 1792.

Mernissi, Fatima (born 1940)

Moroccan feminist writer. A professor of sociology at Rabat, she grew up in Fez, and obtained a PhD in sociology from the United States. A prolific writer, she has published work in Arabic, French and English. A regular contibutor to national and international conferences on women, and an active member of the editorial boards of a number of periodicals, she has given wide publicity to her brand of Islamic feminism. Making a thorough study of the *Qur'an* and of the history of the first Islamic period (during the life of the Prophet Muhammad and his immediate successors) and sifting the volumes of Tradition (the sayings of the Prophet) and the writings of early Moslem thinkers, she came up with the thesis that the subordinate status of women in Moslem countries is not a feature of the 'natural', model Islam of the early phase. Muhammad's message was equality between the sexes; later developments grew out of political and social conditions.

Mernissi's investigations into the conditions of contemporary women in Morocco, her interest in folklore, and her articulation of the unheard voices of the masses of uneducated women make fascinating reading for the non-specialist. Her publications include: *Beyond the Veil: Male-Female Dynamics in a Modern Moslem Society* (1975), *Doing Daily Battle: Interviews with Moroccan Women* (1988), *Le Harem Politique (Le Prophète et les Femmes)* (1987) (*The Political Harem, The Prophet and Women*), *Chahrazad n'est pas marocaine* (1988) (*Shahrazad is not Morrocan*) and *Sexe Idéologie Islam* (1983) (*Sex Ideology Islam*).

Merril, Judith (born 1923)

Born Josephine Juliet Grossman in New York City, she is a science fiction writer and anthologist who emigrated to Canada in 1968, and now divides her time between Toronto and Jamaica. She has been married and divorced three times, but her prodigious energy is evident in her work as editor. She is a leading authority on science and speculative fiction, and has edited more than twenty science fiction anthologies, including the series, *SF: The Year's Best* and *Tesseracts*. Her own works include *Daughters of Earth and Other Stories* (1968), *The Best of Judith Merril* (1976) and *Survival Ship and Other Stories*. She successfully employs a woman's point of view in this very male genre.

Mess Mend: Yankees in Petrograd (1923)

An international adventure story by the Russian writer ▷Mariètta Shaginián writing under the pseudonym Jim Dollar. Set in Russia and a totally imaginary New York, the hero, Mike Thingsmaster, aided by his faithful dog, Beauty, leads a secret workers' union and performs magical feats of resistance to evil capitalists. Shaginián described the work as a parodic treatment of western European detective fiction, with grafted elements of the Russian fairytale plot about grateful animals. Serialized ▷detective stories had been enormously popular in pre-revolutionary Russia, and they often featured foreign settings and foreign heroes, including pirated Sherlock Holmeses, Nat Pinkertons, and Nick Carters (*cf*, J. Brooks, *When Russia Learned to Read*). The work shows Shaginián's sense of fun and her thorough acquaintance with the devices and motifs of this genre.

Shaginián wrote the tremendously popular *Mess Mend* (and its two less successful sequels) in response to the interest in literary parody and well-plotted narratives expressed by Russian formalist critics and writers who were casting about for a literature to match the new Soviet reality. Some of the most famous male authors of the time were suspected of being the author of the trilogy before Shaginián revealed her identity in 1926 in a pamphlet, *How I Wrote Mess Mend*.
Bib: Cioran, S. (trans.), *Mess Mend: Yankees in Petrograd*.

Metalious, Grace ▷ *Peyton Place*

Meulenbelt, Anja (born 1945)
Dutch prose writer. She lives in Amsterdam as a mother and lesbian. Having been involved in the Dutch feminist movement since 1970, she has written many articles on the subject, taught female sciences at the University of Amsterdam, and lectured on female social work. In order to demonstrate that feminism is not a theory but a way of life (though full of conflicting emotions, in which self-pity and rancour play their parts, but not shame), she wrote the autobiographical *De schaamte voorbij* (1976) (English edition: *The Shame is Over: a Political Life Story*, 1980), which had a considerable impact. In addition to books on feminism, her work includes the novels *Alba* (1984), *Een kleine moeite* (1985) (English edition: *A Small Favour*, 1989) and *De bewondering* (1987) (*The Admiration*). Translations of her work include *For Ourselves: From Women's Point of View: Our Bodies and Sexuality* (1981).

Meurdrac, Catherine (1613–1676) ▷ Guette, Madame de la

Mew, Charlotte (1869–1928)
English poet and short story writer. Born in London to a genteel middle-class family, Mew's life was shadowed by the mental illness of two siblings and the death of her father, which was to leave her impoverished in her late twenties. In 1928, after the death of her closest sister, Mew committed suicide by drinking Lysol. Mew wrote poems and short stories for journals such as *The Egoist*, *The English Woman* and *The Yellow Book*. Her work impressed a number of better-known contemporary writers, including Thomas Hardy (1840–1928), Siegfried Sassoon (1886–1967), Ezra Pound (1885–1972), Harold Monro, John Masefield (1878–1967) and Walter de la Mare (1873–1956). Their recognition gained her a civil pension in 1923. Despite being excluded from the Georgian poetry anthologies, her work is frequently linked with this early 20th-century poetic movement because of the naturalistic form of her poetry. This, however, fails to do justice to the complexity of Mew's use of the dramatic monologue, in poems such as 'The Farmer's Bride', 'In Nunhead Cemetery', 'The Quiet

House' and 'Madeleine in Church', to explore gender relations, frustrated and obsessive sexuality, loss and extreme psychological isolation. Her book of poems, *The Farmer's Bride*, appeared in 1916 and was enthusiastically reviewed by the US poet ▷ H.D. and ▷ Rebecca West. It was reissued in an expanded version in 1921, appearing in the USA as *Saturday Market*. *The Rambling Sailor* (1929) was published posthumously. ▷ Virginia Woolf described her as 'the greatest living poetess' in 1924. However, Mew ended her life in obscurity, and only later was her work collected and reissued, first in *Collected Poems of Charlotte Mew* (1953), and recently in *Mew: Collected Poems and Prose* (1982).

Meyer, Olga (1889–1972)
German-speaking Swiss novelist. The gifted child of a postman, she became a teacher in one of the poorer districts of Zurich. In order to educate her pupils, she wrote over thirty novels, of which the story *Anneli: Erlebnisse eines kleinen Landmädchens* (1918) (*Anneli: Experiences of a Small Country Girl*), became particularly popular. It describes the effects of the Industrial Revolution in rural Switzerland, and was influential for generations of Swiss children.

Meynell, Alice (1847–1922)
English poet and essayist, born in Barnes, London, and educated at home by her father. She converted to Catholicism in 1868, a faith shared by her concert-pianist mother. Her first volume of verse, *Preludes*, was published in 1875, attracting praise from ▷ George Eliot and from the author and editor Wilfred Meynell, whom she married in 1877. Further volumes followed, including *Poems* (1893); *Other Poems* (1896); *Later Poems* (1902); *Poems on the War* (1916) and *Last Poems* (1923). Meynell's lyrical and mystical poetry gained her a high reputation, particularly among writers, and after Tennyson's death she was proposed as Poet Laureate. She had eight children, and supported the family by writing for periodicals and newspapers, including *The National Observer* and *The Pall Mall Gazette*. Her essays were collected under various titles, which include *The Rhythm of Life* (1893) *The Colour of Life* (1896) and *The Spirit of Place* (1899). She also wrote translations, produced editions and wrote biographies of Holman Hunt (1893) and Ruskin (1900). She was active in the ▷ suffrage movement in the early years of the 20th century.
Bib: Michalik, K., *Meynell: Her Life and Works*; Badeni, J., *Life*.

Meysenbug, Malvida von (1816–1903)
German writer. An active and enthusiastic supporter of the 1848 Revolution, she was forced to leave Berlin in 1852. She lived in England, Paris and Rome, and opened salons where she entertained many important figures, including the Italian revolutionary Garibaldi (1807–1882), the German philosopher Nietzsche (1844–1900), and ▷ Lou Andreas-Salomé. Meysenbug's writings

are for the most part autobiographical, and include *Eine Reise nach Ostende* (1849) (*A Journey to Ostend*) and *Memoiren einer Idealistin* (1876), published in English as *Rebel in Bombazine: Memoirs of Malwida von Meysenbug* (1936).

Mhac An tSaoi, Máire (Maire MacEntee) (born 1922)

Irish poet, born in Dublin. She was educated at University College, Dublin, and at the Sorbonne, Paris. Called to the Bar in 1944, she also obtained an MA in classical modern Irish, and then joined the Irish Department of External Affairs, serving in Paris and Madrid. She has written short stories, essays and many scholarly articles, and collaborated with her husband, the Irish politician and writer, Conor Cruise O'Brien (born 1917), on *A Concise History of Ireland* (1972). She has also translated Irish works for publication. She is best known for her Irish-language poetry. Her collections include: *Margabh na Saoire* (1956) (*Freedom Fair*), *A Heart Full of Thought* (translations from the Irish) (1959), *Codladh an Ghaiscigh* (1973) (*The Hero's Sleep*), *An Galar Dubhach* (1980) (*The Black Disease*) and *An Cion go dtí Seo* (1987) (*Affection Until Now*).

Mhlophe, Gcina (born 1958)

South African dramatist, short story writer, poet and storyteller. She was born in Hammarsdale, near Durban, and went to school in the Transkei. Some aspects of her childhood are written into her play *Have You Seen Zandile?* (1989): she was brought up by her grandmother, of whom she became very fond, until she was taken away by her mother, whom she barely knew. Mhlophe has also published a few, very fine, short stories: 'The Toilet', 'It's Quiet Now' (these are available in the anthology *Sometimes When It Rains*) and 'Nokulunga's Wedding' (available in the anthologies *LIP from Southern African Women*, and *In a Land Apart*). 'The Toilet' deals with the genesis of a writer, whose initial writing space is a toilet in a park. In 'Nokulunga's Wedding', she offers a critique of traditional African ▷patriarchy, casting her story in such a way as to reflect on tales from ▷oral tradition. In her role as resident director at the Market Theatre in Johannesburg, Mhlophe instituted an annual story festival, designed to recreate the oral storytelling tradition of rural South Africa, lost to urban children. She has also worked with a group at the Market Theatre in a ▷popular theatre production called *Inyanga: About Women in Africa* (staged in 1989). In her poetry, as in her fiction and drama, Mhlophe takes account of both racial and gender oppression. Her forceful poem 'Say No', addressed to black women, exhorts them to refuse all forms of subordination, exploitation and abuse. Mhlophe has also written two children's books, *The Snake with Seven Heads* (1989) and *Queen of the Tortoises* (1990).

Michael, Julia Warner (1879–?)

Born in the Bahamas, she was one of the first poets to publish verse in the Caribbean. Her *A*

Memory of New Providence Island (1909) is an early collection of Caribbean poetry. She was a contributor to J. Culmer (ed.), *A Book of Bahamian Verse* (1930). There is little information available on this writer.

Michaelis, Hanny (born 1922)

Dutch poet and essay writer. She lost her Jewish parents in 1943. After the war she worked as an editor, translated children's books, and also worked for the Amsterdam Arts Council between 1957 and 1984. From 1948 to 1959 she was married to the writer G.K. van het Reve. Her first collection of poems, *Klein voorspel* (1949) (*Modest Invitation*), describes a woman's emerging consciousness while growing to maturity against the backdrop of the German occupation. The poems in *Water uit de rots* (1957) (*Water From the Rocks*) are variations on the theme of lack of a loved one. In *Tegen de wind* (1962) (*Against the Wind*), the death of the lover is the central theme. Attempting to put grief in perspective dominates the collection *Onvoorzien* (1966) (*Unforeseen*), while *De rots van Gibraltar* (1969) (*The Rock of Gibraltar*) centres on the conflict between spontaneity and growing awareness. Her last collection, *Wegdraven naar een nieuw Utopia* (1971) (*Hurrying Towards a New Utopia*), contains poems on the disappointment that creates a longing for a new Utopia. From then on Michaelis wrote only literary essays. In 1989 a selection of her poetry appeared, *Het onkruid van de twijfel* (*The Weeds of Doubt*). Translations of her poetry have been published in: *Change of Scene: Contemporary Dutch and Flemish Poems in English Translation* (1969); *The Shape of Houses: Women's Voices from Holland and Flanders* (1974), and *Dutch Interior: Postwar Poetry of the Netherlands and Flanders* (1984). *Selected Poems* appeared in 1984.

Michaëlis, Karin (1872–1950)

Danish prose writer. She also wrote under the pseudonym Karin Michaëlis Stangeland in the years between 1912 and 1917. Michaëlis was born at Randers. Her parents were poor, but had bourgeois pretensions. She was an ugly and clumsy, but helpful and intelligent child, as she described herself in her memoirs *Trået på Godt og Ondt* (1924–1930) (*The Tree of Good and Evil*) and *Vidunderlige Verden* (1948–1950) (*Wonderful World*). Karin went to Copenhagen when she was twenty, where she met the poet Sophus Michaëlis (1865–1932), married him (till 1911), lived a bohemian life and began to write. In 1902 she had her first international breakthrough with the novels *Barnet* (*The Child*) and *Lillemor* (*Mummy*). From then on, she lived part of the year in Vienna, and wrote in Danish and German. She became one of the most famous people in Denmark, and involved herself in politics, always as the advocate of women and the poor.

Her second international breakthrough came with *Den farlige Alder* (1910) (▷ *The Dangerous Age*), the third came with the books about Bibi, the wild girl who lives alone with her father and travels around Denmark, and the fourth with her memoirs.

During World War II, Michaëlis helped many German Jews, Communists and artists to escape to Denmark. Her own books were burned and her money lost. From 1940 to 1945 she lived alone and in poverty in New York. She was forgotten until the 1980s, when her many books were re-read by feminist scholars. Her work is uneven. She was the first to introduce the ▷stream-of-consciousness style, and she created the wild, Scandinavian girl in children's literature. Some of her books were reprinted in the 1980s.

▷Children's literature (Denmark, Norway and Sweden)

Michail or The Heart of a Russian (1917)

Translation of the novel *A Russian Gentleman* (1914) by ▷Nadezhda Láppo-Danilévskaia, who is identified only as 'A Russian Lady'. The English publisher was William Heinemann, who also brought out the works of ▷Sarah Grand, apt company for Láppo-Danilévskaia. A typical product of the pre-revolutionary market for popular fiction in Russia, the novel is an entertaining, melodramatic work revolving around a love plot set in the highest society. It gives a great deal of information about clothing, coiffures, and interiors. The language is clichéd, and the reliable narrator leaves no doubt as to how the reader is supposed to regard the characters. The protagonist, Michail Gurakin, is the Russian nobleman at his best: a connoisseur of the arts, handsome, amiable, fun-loving, generous to a fault, ebullient, honourable, and brave. Women who act from misguided, selfish motives are the focus of evil. The moral centre of the novel, as in several of Láppo-Danilévskaia's works, is a grandmother, and the moral and political messages are equally predictable and superficial. The tsarist system is depicted with admiration, the 'good' protagonists exude a patriotism verging on chauvinism, and women know their place. *Michail* includes brief indications of the fashionable interest in spiritualism, and exposes religious hypocrisy. Sadly, it also displays anti-semitic attitudes.

Michel, Louise (1830–1905)

French socialist and feminist writer. An ardently Republican schoolteacher who is remembered as the 'Red Virgin' of the ▷Paris Commune, Michel was also, like ▷André Léo, a founder member of the ▷*Association pour le droit des femmes*. After the Commune was crushed, she was exiled from France to New Caledonia, and only returned after the amnesty of 1880. However, her involvement with the anarchist movement meant that she had to leave once more and spend time teaching in London. She died in 1905, in the middle of a lecture tour. Her writing bears witness to her political commitment and her feminism, especially her volume of *Mémoires* (1886); her *La Commune, histoire et souvenirs* (1898) (*The Commune, History and Memories*), and her novels *La Misère* (1881)

(*Poverty*), *Les Méprisées* (1882) (*Women Despised*) and *La Fille du peuple* (1883) (*Daughter of the People*). She also published collections of poetry.
Bib: Moses, C., *French Feminism in the 19th Century.*

Middleman, The (1989)

A collection of short stories by the Indian-born author ▷Bharati Mukherjee which won the 1989 National Book Critics Circle Award in the USA. Many of the stories examine the 'American Dream' from the perspective of immigrants and exiles who, in spite of their diverse origins, are often shown to have common expectations and disappointments.

Middlemarch, A Study of Provincial Life (1871–72)

A novel by English novelist ▷George Eliot, considered by many to be her finest work. It is set in the years immediately preceding the 1832 ▷Reform Bill, a time of unrest, agitation and intense political discussion. Dorothea Brooke is an intelligent, idealistic young woman who finds no immediate outlet for her passions. Her intellectual yearnings lead her to the pedantic scholar, Casaubon, who is attempting to write the definitive 'Key to All Mythologies'. Dorothea marries him, believing that she will find fulfilment, but quickly becomes disillusioned during her honeymoon in Rome, when she realizes that Casaubon is both unable and unwilling to satisfy her either intellectually or physically. A parallel marital story is that of Lydgate, a young doctor engaged in radical research, and Rosamund, his materialistic wife. Lydgate's arrogance in viewing women as ornamental reflections of himself blinds him to Rosamund's real personality, as Rosamund's social aspirations and romantic fantasies blind her to Lydgate's individuality. Lydgate's career is virtually ruined when he becomes involved in a scandal concerning Bulstrode, the banker, and he dies, as does Casaubon, having failed to achieve his ambitions. Dorothea's youthful desire is similarly thwarted, but at the end of the novel she seems to find happiness with Will Ladislaw, a young relative of her husband's. Through the portrayal of these characters, and others such as the Garth family, Cadwallader, Chettam and Brooke, Eliot analyses the social and political upheavals of the early 19th century and exposes the sexual prejudice that permeated the society of the day. The limitations imposed upon women's lives are highlighted in the case of Dorothea, while the danger of immersing oneself in the ideologies of femininity is explored through Rosamund. The detailed and thorough analysis of gender in the novel has not prevented some critics from arguing that at the heart of Eliot's vision is a conservatism that emphasizes the need for individuals to curb their own desires in the face of social duty.

▷Realism (19th-century Britain)

Middle Passage

The name given to the journey of slave ships across the Atlantic from Africa to the Caribbean and North and South America. It is of particular relevance for Caribbean writing. During the period of the slave trade over 75,000 enslaved Africans were transported each year across the Atlantic, crammed and chained into the hold of slave ships.

Miegel, Agnes (1879–1964)

German poet. Born in Königsberg, she drew on the folklore and history of East Prussia as inspiration for her highly successful stories and ballads. In 1924 she was awarded an honorary doctorate for her historical research. During the 1930s she earned the approval and encouragement of the Nazis with her celebrations of her native land in the poems *Deutsche Balladen* (1935) (*German Ballads*), and collections of stories such as *Gang in die Dämmerung* (1934) (*Into the Twilight*) and *Unter hellem Himmel* (1936) (*Under the Bright Sky*).

Mieza, Carmen (1931–1976)

Spanish novelist. Mieza was born in Barcelona. Her two novels are based on her experience of exile in Mexico as a result of the Spanish Civil War (1936–9): *La imposible canción* (1962) (*The Impossible Song*), and *Una mañana cualquiera* (1964) (*Any Morning*).

Migrant women's writing (Australia)

The term 'migrant writing' is usually applied to the works of those non-Aboriginal women for whom English is a second language. The difficulty of negotiating another language and thus entering an alien system of signification, as well as the often false suppositions which the Anglo-Saxon reader brings to the text, have been persuasively argued by the critic, Sneja Gunew. Significant migrant writers in Australia include ▷Rosa Cappiello, Anna Couani (born 1948), Margaret Diesendorf (born 1912), Vasso Kalamaras (born 1932), ▷Antigone Kefala, Wolla Meranda and Ania Walwicz (born 1951). *Beyond the Echo: Multicultural Women's Writings* (1988), edited by Sneja Gunew and Jan Mahyuddin, provides a selection of prose and poetry by settler women, and their works are listed in Lolo Houbein's *Ethnic Writings in English from Australia: A Bibliography* (1976) and included, along with male migrant writings, in Peter Skrzynecki (ed.), *Joseph's Coat: An Anthology of Multicultural Writing* (1985).

Mihri Khatun

Turkish poet of the last quarter of the 15th century and the early decades of the 16th century. There is no record of the exact date of her birth or death, but stories told by her contemporaries and by historians of Turkish literature associate her with the court of Prince Ahmad, son of Bayazid, who was governor of her native town Amasiya (1491–1512). She composed traditional *ghazels* (Persian odes) and directed her love poetry to three gentlemen, one of whom was a minor poet of the same court. Her poetry was greatly admired by writers on Turkish literature and, as in the case of the Andalusian ▷Wallada bint al-Mustakfi, some of those authors defended her 'honour': 'Maiden came she to the world and maiden went she. For all her love of youth, none ever had his wish of her . . . neither did any greedy hand ever reach to her hidden treasure . . .' Lady Mihri herself was defiant in a world of so many male competitors: 'Since they cry that woman lacketh wit alway, / Needs must they excuse whatever word she say. / Better for one female, if she worthy be, / Than a thousand males, if all unworthy they.' The reference is to a description of women attributed to the Prophet Muhammad as 'lacking in reason and religion'.

Of Mihri's *diwan* (collection) only twenty-eight *ghazels* have survived in manuscript; they are typical of the classical tradition at its best: 'Aid! Aid! for thou hast smit me, O physician of the soul! / Quoth he, "Tis my wont to leave the lover all unhelped to die" / Never rose hath bloomed on earth's parterre but still the thorn was by / We shall die, but never, Mihri, shall we leave to love the fair; / Let him speak who will, without a loved one ne'er shall we aby.'
Bib: Gibb E.J.W. (trans.), *A History of Ottoman Poetry.*

Mikulich, V. ▷Veselítskaia, Lidiia

Milani, Milena (born 1922)

Italian novelist, short story writer, poet, journalist, dramatist, painter and ceramicist. Born in Savona, she read Letters at the University of Rome, and has contributed to many Italian periodicals and journals. She has won many literary prizes for her writing, which is confrontational, especially in relation to sexuality and gender. *La ragazza di nome Giulio* (1964) (*A Girl Called Jules*, translated into English in 1968), is a very controversial novel about the nature of gender identity, which led Milani to be charged with writing immoral books; however, she was cleared of this charge in the subsequent trial. Her *Storia di Anna Drei* (1947) (▷ *The Story of Anna Drei*, translated into English in 1970) was a very popular novel, cleverly constructed, about the nature of female identity and relationships between women, as well as between the sexes.

Other works: *Ignoti furono i cieli* (1944) (*Under Unknown Skies*); *L'estate* (1946) (*Summer*); *Uomo e donna* (1952) (*Man and Woman*); *La ragazza di fronte* (1953) (*The Girl Opposite*); *Italia sexy* (1967); *La mattina è diventata sera* (1970) (*Morning Has Turned Into Evening*); *Io donna e gli altri* (1972) (*I, a Woman, and the Others*); *Miei sogni arrivederci* (1973) (*Goodbye to My Dreams*); *New York amatissima* (1975) (*Beloved New York*); *Soltanto amore* (1976) (*Only Love*); *Oggetto sessuale* (1977) (*Sex Object*); *Mi sono innamorata a Mosca* (1980) (*I Fell in Love in Moscow*); *Umori e amori* (1982)

(*Moods and Love*); *L'angelo nero e altri ricordi* (1984) (*The Black Angel and Other Memories*).

Mildmay, Grace Sherrington (1552–1620)
English diarist. The second of three daughters of Henry Sherrington, she was educated by a cousin named Mrs Hamblyn, who served as governess. Around 1567 she married Anthony Mildmay, who had to be persuaded with threats by his father to go through with the marriage. She is best-known for ▷ *The Diary of Lady Milmay*, a journal which she began writing within a few years of her marriage, and continued until a few years before her death. In addition to her journal, Mildmay also left numerous medical prescriptions and herbal recipes which her only child, Mary Fane, collected and copied into a volume entitled 'For the Workhouse'.

Milítsyna, Elizaveta Mitrofanovna (1869–1930)
Russian prose writer. Milítsyna began publishing stories in a newspaper in 1896 and, supported by Korolenko and Gorky, was soon writing for ▷'thick journals'. Her early stories are Tolstoyan depictions of the peasantry as stoic, accepting their fate and submitting to God. She denounces the upper classes and the Orthodox Church for opposing the education of the peasants.

Milítsyna's collected stories (1905) centred on village life, especially women's lot; a few concern the urban poor. Two volumes of her collected works were published in 1910 by Gorky's 'Knowledge' publishing house and brought her wide attention. A third volume was halted by the censor in 1913, and Milítsyna was brought to court for 'setting one class against another in print'. Among the stories included in these volumes are 'The Village Priest' (Russian title 'The Idealist', 1904) which gives a positive picture of the title figure, and 'The Old Nurse'. The latter is the first-person story of a woman discarded by the family she has served, despite the mutual devotion that she and the children feel. The third volume also contained some 'prose poems' influenced to some extent by the ▷modernist movement.

During World War I, Milítsyna served as a volunteer nurse at the front and wrote the anti-war *Notes of a Nurse* (1916), which was prohibited by censorship. She also produced an 'oral history', *In A Prisoner-of-War Camp: From the Worlds of P.Z. Bakhmetov, Formerly Imprisoned*. After the Revolution, Milítsyna published little. She joined the Communist Party in 1920, but was criticized for insufficient understanding of the underlying class antagonisms among the peasantry.
Bib: Tollemache, B.L. (trans.), *The Village Priest and Other Stories from the Russian of Militsina and Saltykov*.

Millay, Edna St Vincent (1892–1950)
US poet and dramatist. Millay was born in Rockland, Maine, and was the eldest of three girls brought up by their divorced mother, who encouraged her to develop her creativity. She graduated from Vassar College in 1917 and moved to Greenwich Village in New York, where she acted and wrote journalism as well as poetry and plays. In 1923 she married the widower of the feminist Inez Mulholland. Millay's work was hugely popular in the 1920s but has become less so, partly due to her use of conventional non-experimental verse forms. However, her ballads, lyrics, sonnets and verse plays use traditional metrical and formal structures to counterpoint the emotional intensity and passion of her poetic voice. *A Few Figs From Thistles* (1920), her most popular collection, demonstrates how this combination of the cerebral and passionate vividly imagine a womanhood that is unconventional, exuberant, forthright and rebellious. Millay was interested in socialist and feminist politics, as well as trying to shape her life against conventional ideas of femininity, and many of her later poems reflect this interest, as well as her pacifist verse play *Aria da Capo* (1920).

Other works include: *Renascence and Other Poems* (1917), *Second April* (1921), *Two Slatterns and a King* (1921), *A Distressing Dialogue* (1924), *The King's Henchman: A Play in Two Acts* (1927), *Fear* (1927), *The Fatal Interview, Sonnets* (1931), *The Princess Marries The Page: A Play in One Act* (1932), *Wine From These Grapes* (1934), Vacation Song (1936), '*There Are no Islands Any More*' (1940), *Make Bright The Arrows: 1940 Notebook* (1940), *Invocation to the Muses* (1941), *The Murder of Lidice* (1942), *Poem and Prayer for an Invading Army* (1944), *Mine the Harvest* (1954).
Bib: Gould, Jean, *The Poet and her Book*; Brittin, Norman A., *Edna St. Vincent Millay*; Prasad, Pramod, *The Aesthetics of Tension: A Study of the Poetry of Edna St. Vincent Millay*.

Miller, Anne (1741–1781)
English poet, patron and travel writer. She held poetry evenings in her excessively expensive villa at Bath, during which poems would be thrown into an antique vase and then each taken out and read aloud. Some were published in *Poetical Amusements at a Villa near Bath* (1775–1781), and the preface emphasizes 'the Vase, and Sprigs of Bay and Myrtle alluded to in these poems are not emblematical, but real'. When ▷Fanny Burney visited her, she called her 'a round plump coarse-looking dame'. Miller also wrote *Letters From Italy* (1776–1777).
▷Seward, Anna

Miller, Ruth (1919–1969)
South African poet, born in Uitenhage, Cape Province, whose first volume of poetry, *Floating Island* (1965), won the Ingrid Jonker Memorial Prize. Intensely, even cruelly, self-conscious in the manner of ▷Sylvia Plath and ▷Ingrid Jonker, these poems also chart a South African landscape hostile to the European consciousness, making an important break with colonial precedents. In bold, explorative poetry, she goes where no other (woman) poet in South Africa has gone before.

However, in 'Discoveries', she disclaims any pioneering responsibility in lines which also distance themselves from the colonial enterprise: 'To signify not triumph, but defeat / I plant my flag, in already scuffed-up ground.'

Just before Miller's death, her *Selected Poems* (1968) was published, revealing a terrible despair – mediated by means of metaphysical conceit and wit – given occasion in the poems through the death of her fourteen-year-old son and her own approaching death from cancer. Her poems are intensely private, and not always immediately accessible. Some repay a feminist reading, as in 'Galatea', where Prometheus's sculpted woman says: 'I was before you touched me. I.'

Miller's writing has been collected in *Poems, Prose, Plays* (1990), ed. Lionel Abrahams, which includes the two published collections, most of her uncollected poems, two verse plays for radio, a short story, a short essay, and an introduction by contemporary writer Lionel Abrahams.

Millett, Kate (born 1934)
North American feminist activist, novelist, and literary critic. Born in St Paul, Minnesota, Millett graduated from the University of Minnesota in 1956, and read English at St Hilda's College, Oxford in 1958. Her thesis for her Ph.D., awarded by Columbia University in 1970, later became *Sexual Politics* (1970). Now a feminist classic, *Sexual Politics* expands the concept of the political to give a generalized analysis of sexual power relations in literature and society. Millett relates ▷ sexism in literature to a wider patriarchal culture, insisting that literature cannot be read in isolation from ideology and history. Her political readings of literature went against the grain of the dominant ▷ 'New Criticism', which specified that literature should be analyzed without reference to authorial intention or politics. Two novelists Millett attacks in particular are Henry Miller (1891–1980) who holds a major position in the ▷ canon of North American literature, and British writer D.H. Lawrence (1885–1930). Millett criticizes the misogynist and sexist attitudes of Miller's novels, the sexual episodes of which repeatedly portray women in degrading and humiliating ways. Lawrence's novels are ridiculed by Millett for glorifying the awesome power of the man's penis, and presenting woman as the passive partner in the sexual act.

An early publication, *Token Learning* (1967), published by ▷ NOW (National Organization for Women), is a political critique of the curricula in women's colleges. Her later work is increasingly concerned with the contribution made by women's autobiographies to a feminist political history. This can be seen in *Three Lives* (1970), a documentary directed by Millett, which allows women to tell their stories in their own words; *The Prostitution Papers* (1971), which collects prostitutes' narratives, and two autobiographical novels, *Flying* (1974) and *Sita* (1977). Both novels are ▷ consciousness-raising and ▷ woman-centred narratives. Her other publications include:

The Basement (1979), *Going to Iran* (1982), and *The Loony Bin Trip* (1991).

Mill girls
US 19th-century mill girls were young women who left their paternal homes to work in the New England textile mills and to live communally in boarding-houses. A phenomenon of particular prominence in the 1840s, they were the first generation of free US women to be employed in industry, rather than in domestic service. Primarily daughters of uneducated, rural, lower-middle-class North Americans, these women worked long hours in the mills but dedicated their evenings to education, to self-improvement and to writing – producing the first US literary journal by and for industrial workers, ▷ *The Lowell Offering*.

As mill-owners abandoned benevolent paternalism, reducing wages and forcing productivity, US families became reluctant to send their daughters to the mills. The Female Labor Reform Association's attempts to organize mill labour created additional conflict with New England's traditional individualistic, anti-union culture.

▷ Larcom, Lucy; Farley, Harriet; *Mind Amongst the Spindles*; *Voice of Industry, The*
Bib: Robinson, Harriet Jane (Hanson), *Loom and Spindle; or, Life Among the Early Mill Girls. With a sketch of 'The Lowell Offering' and some of its contributors*, Introduction by the Honorable Carroll D. Wright (1898); republished with an introduction by Jane Wilkins Pultz in 1976.

Milligan, Alice (1866–1953)
Irish poet, journalist and lecturer. She was born in County Tyrone, and educated in Belfast at Methodist College, and at King's College, London. She co-founded and edited *The Northern Patriot*, later called *The Shan Van Vocht* (*The Old Woman of Ireland*) with her friend, ▷ Ethna Carbery. Like Ethna, she was an active and articulate nationalist, and committed, through her writings, to furthering the cause of Irish freedom. In addition to poetry, widely published in nationalist magazines, she wrote a novel, *A Royal Democrat* (1892), and a biography of the Irish patriot, Wolfe Tone (1898). She was one of the dramatists at the Abbey Theatre, Dublin, and two of her plays were performed by the Irish Literary Theatre and by the Abbey Theatre: *The Last Feast of the Fianna* (1900) and *The Daughter of Donagh* (1920). Her work is largely of historical interest today.

Millin, Sarah Gertrude (1888–1968)
South African novelist, short story and non-fiction writer. Born in Lithuania into a Russian Jewish family, she came to South Africa as a baby, and spent her childhood, adolescence and early adulthood in or near Kimberley and the Vaal River diamond diggings, a locale to which her fiction often returns.

After her marriage she lived in Johannesburg, where she moved in liberal political, legal and literary circles. Besides writing essays and reviews for local and sometimes overseas newspapers and magazines, she wrote seventeen novels, two sets of short stories, two autobiographies, two political biographies, and other non-fiction, as well as extensive diaries and letters. Her best-known work is ▷*God's Step-Children* (1924), which became a bestseller in the United States. The novel deals with the theme of miscegenation so common in South African writing. In Britain, her reputation depended rather more on the novel *Mary Glenn* (1925), and *The South Africans* (1926), her first work of non-fiction, which also brought her acclaim in South Africa.

From her first novel, *The Dark River* (1919), Millin reveals an obsession with what she later calls the tragedy of blood, blood being, for her, the vehicle of either racial purity or taint. A similar theme is pursued in *Adam's Rest* (1922) and *The Jordans* (1923). She returned repeatedly to what she saw as degraded forms of life, largely symbolized in her fiction by white men's cohabitation with black women, and their creation of 'half-caste' children. In *God's Step-Children* the 'tainted', mixed-blood hero renounces his white community and returns to the place of his origin, seeing this as the only means to put a stop to the 'tragedy' of the so-called 'coloured' race.

Millin's racial attitudes reveal, at best, charitable paternalism towards black South Africans, and, at worst, uncontrolled abhorrence regarding racial mixing. She failed to make the analogies between different forms of racism that other South African writers sometimes made, ▷Pauline Smith, for example, and, later, ▷Mary Benson. Yet Millin was horrified at the Nazi appropriation of *God's Step-Children*, and refused permission for more of her work to be translated into German after Hitler's rise to power. *The Herr Witchdoctor* (1941, published in America as *The Dark Gods*) warned against the penetration of South Africa by Nazi propaganda. Her own writing is continually overtaken by its metaphors of 'taint' and 'flaw'. By the time she wrote *King of the Bastards* (1949), *The Burning Man* (1952) and *The Wizard Bird* (1962) her work had become imaginatively enfeebled by its reiterated paranoia. Because of her racial attitudes, she has lost status as a writer.

Yet Millin's significance as a writer has also to do with her evocation of the social and political tensions of South Africa at the time. If she was unable to overcome racial prejudice, she was also a victim of one of her major fictional strategies, which was to transform class into race, and thus to transplant to South African soil one of the standard British novelistic themes and structuring devices. In some novels, her interest in class, urbanization, and social mobility produces an interesting evocation of small-town life, as in *Mary Glenn* (1925), for instance, though the novel still bears the marks of social prejudice. Similarly, in a group of stories known as the 'Alita' stories, mostly published in *The Atheneum* and *The Adelphi* in the early 1920s and collected in *Two Bucks*

Without Hair (1957), Millin manages to prevent her racist prejudices from dictating her writing. These stories are based on the experiences which Alita, a domestic worker of Sotho origin, brings into the white narrator's home. Despite the patronization, the stories show some sensitivity to the problems of the relations between white 'madam' and black 'maid'. Other short stories are collected in *Men on a Voyage* (1930).

The Sons of Mrs Aab (1931) gives a particularly desolate view of poverty and deprivation. Caroline Aab bears numerous children; two survive and only one is fit to earn a living. This son, unable any longer to care for his mother and his mentally retarded brother, proposes to send them to government institutions instead, whereupon the mother kills both herself and her dependent son.

A prolific writer, and an insomniac, Millin also published two autobiographies, *The Night is Long* (1941) and *The Measure of My Days* (1955), and a number of other non-fiction works. *The South Africans*, offering an impressionistic rather than historically documented account, contains some fine descriptions of South African life. It was later revised as *The People of South Africa* (1951). *Rhodes* (1933) is a critical biography of Cecil John Rhodes, whom she admired deeply, although she was offended by what she called his 'aggressive nationalism'. The two-volume *General Smuts* (1936) is, by and large, a celebration of a man who was also a close friend. Smuts, by that time Prime Minister of South Africa, encouraged her to keep a detailed account of World War II, which was later published as *War Diaries 1944–1948*.

Other novels: *Middle-Class* (1921); *The Artist in the Family* (1927); *The Coming of the Lord* (1928); *The Fiddler* (1929); *Three Men Die* (1934); *What Hath a Man?* (1938), and *Goodbye, Dear England* (1965).

Other works of non-fiction: *South Africa* (1941).
Bib: Rubin, Martin, *Sarah Gertrude Millin: A South African Life*; Coetzee, J.M., 'Blood, Flaw, Taint, Degeneration: The Case of Sarah Gertrude Millin', *English Studies in Africa* 23.1 (1980).

Mill on the Floss, The (1860)

A novel by English novelist ▷George Eliot. The two principal characters, Maggie Tulliver and her brother, Tom, are children of the miller of Dorlcote Mill on the Floss. Maggie is headstrong, passionate and intelligent, whereas Tom, to whom she is devoted, is a narrow-minded, conventional and overbearing older brother. Maggie's frustrations in attempting to communicate with Tom lead her to seek intellectual companionship with Philip Wakem, the disabled son of a local lawyer. When Maggie's liaison is discovered, Tom forbids her to continue the friendship because their father despises Philip's father. Later in the novel Maggie goes to St Ogg's to visit her cousin Lucy, who is happily engaged to Stephen Guest. Maggie and Stephen become very attracted to one another, and though both attempt to resist, they are increasingly drawn together. The association between the two eventually causes a scandal, and Maggie is rejected not only by the community at St Ogg's, but also by Tom, who turns her out of the house in disgust. Maggie and her mother take refuge with an old family friend. The situation seems irredeemable, but in a melodramatic denouement at the end of the novel, a flood descends, Maggie rescues Tom from the mill and brother and sister are reconciled before they drown. Although much is left unresolved at the end of the work, its power has always been acknowledged, particularly Eliot's representation of the psychological turmoil experienced by Maggie. In the provincial environment in which she grows up, Maggie is never free to follow her desires, but is forced to internalize all her intellectual and spiritual energies. Many women readers have identified with Eliot's semi-autobiographical portrayal of Maggie; ▷Simone de Beauvoir once wrote that the novel 'seemed to translate my spiritual exile into words'.

Mimochka Gets Married (1883), *Mimochka at the Spa* (1891), *Mimochka Took Poison* (1893).

The Russian writer ▷Lidiia Veselítskaia's lively trilogy of novellas plays on the romantic genre of the ▷society tale. In the first sardonic episode, the energetic mother and aunts of a passive, narcissistic girl from a ruined family, marry her to a rich middle-aged general. The second novella echoes Lermontov's 'Princess Mary' (*A Hero of Our Time*, 1840) in its depiction of Russian society at Caucasian spas and Mimochka's seduction by an accomplished rake. Tolstoy, in his late moralistic period, loved Veselítskaia's satire, and in return the author introduced into 'Mimochka at the Spa' the Tolstoyan figure of young cousin Vava, whose striving for a useful life has made her the family problem child. In 1893 the first two episodes appeared in English as *Mimi's Marriage*. The third and longest episode interweaves a scornful picture of moneyed middle-level ▷St Petersburg society with Mimochka's attempt at suicide after her French lover, her son's tutor, deserts her to marry a rich young woman with education and intellectual interests similar to his own.

Mimo mar todos los veranos, El (1978)
▷*Same Sea as Every summer* (1990)

Minco, Marga (born 1920)
Dutch prose writer. ▷Pseudonym of Sara Menco. Her parents were Jewish, and when her relatives were deported during World War II, she was forced to go into hiding. She made her début with short stories and television plays. The sober but unusually moving chronicle of her personal experiences during the persecution of the Jews, told in *Het bittere kruid* (1957) (*Bitter Herbs*, 1960), was very well received. Other books characterized by her tragic experiences and her quiet style include: *De andere kant* (1959) (*The Other Side*), *Een leeg huis* (1966) (*An Empty House*; English

Marga Minco

edition 1990), *De val* (1983) (*The Fall*; English edition 1990) and *De glazen brug* (1986) (*The Glass Bridge*; English edition 1988). Her work has been translated into fourteen languages.

Mind Amongst the Spindles (1844)
US collection, reprinting writing by textile ▷mill girls, originally published in ▷*The Lowell Offering*. Volume publication of selections from a current periodical was unusual for the time, and testimony to the national and international interest in working women as writers. Much of the market for the volume was outside New England, and prompted partly by some critics' questioning whether mill girls could indeed be the writers of the refined poetry and prose of the *Offering*.

Mirabai (16th century)
Indian *bhaketi* poet, or saint-poet. She was a Rajput princess who was determined from very early in her life to have no other husband than the Hindu god Krishna. Her marriage into a neighbouring Rajput household was something of a fiasco as she refused to bow down before her in-laws or their deities and she appears to have maintained her virginity. Attempts by her in-laws to poison her are said to have failed because of the divine intervention of Krishna on her behalf. When her husband died she became free to join an ascetic community of Krishna worshippers at Brindavan, the god's birthplace.

Her devotional poems are sung all over India today, even in the south where little other Hindi is known. They tell of her extreme love for Krishna, and of the ennobling nature of love. Many of them dwell on emotions arising from specifically female experiences, such as the anxiety of a new bride and the loneliness of separation from one's

husband. Often she casts herself as a *gopi*, one of Krishna's numerous milkmaid consorts.
Bib: Alston, A.J., *The Devotional Poems of Mirabai*; Hawley, J.S. and Juergensmeyer, Mark, *Songs of the Saints of India*.

Mirage (1895)

Five-act comedy by ▷Anastasilia Verbítskaia, staged in 1895–96 at the Malyi Theatre in Moscow. Set in the early 1890s, the play presents four pairs of characters: two mothers, two young women, two young men, and two cooks. The plot revolves around obstacles to true love, as the wrong couple pairs off for most of the action. Their supposed love is one of several 'mirages' in the play. The most effective figures are the two mothers, who resemble neoclassic comic characters. One is a liar and social climber who produces a daughter, Lëla (Elena), who is also a liar, idler, and materialist. The other mother is a sycophantic hypocrite and coward whose son, Egor', is in her image. As in neoclassic comedy, there are *raisonneurs* to explain the play's message. One is Vera, who exposes a populist ideology of 'serving the working class' and, in contrast to her friend, Lëla, is self-sacrificing, hard-working, and financially independent. The issue of women's education is broached, as the frivolous Lëla is sent to an exclusive boarding school, while Vera goes to the university to study biology and become a physician's assistant. Another issue is motherhood: Vera is a good mother who aids the feckless Lëla with her sickly son. The second young man is Vladimir Variagin, a *fin-de-siècle* version of the ▷superfluous man. True to type, he is smart enough to see through his own mirages and unmask Egor's pretensions to 'serve the people'.

The best scenes demonstrate Verbítskaia's gift for individualized speech and satire.
Bib: Pachmuss, T. (trans.), 'Mirage', *Women Writers in Russian Modernism*.

Miremont, Anne d'Aubourg de La Bove, Comtesse de (1735–1811)

French novelist and educationalist. Her one published novel, *Mémoires de la marquise de Crémy* (1766) (*Memoirs of the Marschioness of Crémy*), is reputedly autobiographical. The seven-volume *Traité de l'éducation des femmes* (1779–89) (*Treatise on Women's Education*), which includes a complete course of lessons, is her main work.

Miremont, Jacqueline de (late 16th century)

French poet. One of the better-known Parisian women poets of the Renaissance, she was of noble birth, was admired for both her wit and her learning, and was a fairly prolific writer. Her first collection of verses was rather bizarrely entitled *Le Petit Nain qui combat le monde* (*The Little Dwarf Who Fights the World*). 'n her next poem, '*La Part de Marie, soeur de Marthe*' ('On Behalf of Mary, Sister of Martha'), she praised the virtues of a contemplative life and attacked vice. Among her other works was a play which she used to introduce a verse panegyric of James VI of Scotland (1566–1625).
Bib: Feugère, L., *Les Femmes poètes au XVIe siècle*.

Miró, Pilar

Contemporary Spanish film writer and director. Her film *El crimen de Cuenca* (1979) (*The Crime of Cuenca*) was initially banned because it exposed a miscarriage of justice, whereby two men were committed on the basis of confessions extracted by police torture. Her other works, *Gary Cooper que está en los cielos* (1980) (*Gary Cooper Who Is in Heaven*) and *Halblamos esta noche* (1983) (*We Talked Tonight*) were also widely acclaimed.

Mirror of the Sinful Soul (1548)

▷Elizabeth I's prose ▷translation of ▷Marguerite de Navarre's *Le Miroir de l'ame pecheresse*. In 1544 the eleven-year-old princess Elizabeth presented her work as a New Year's gift to her stepmother, ▷Catherine Parr. The work begins as a meditation on sin and the unworthiness of the human soul. In a move away from despair, however, the work develops images of familial relationships through which the love of God can be understood. These consist almost entirely of biblical references to women, among the most interesting of which are the allegories of the Christian soul as mother, daughter, sister, and wife. Elizabeth's *Mirror* was published by John Bale in 1548 as *A Godly Meditation of the Christian Soul Concerning a Love Toward God and his Christ*.
Bib: Ames, P. (ed.), *Mirror of the Sinful Soul*; Prescott, A.L., 'The Pearl of the Valois and Elizabeth I: Marguerite de Navarre's *Miroir* and Tudor England' in ▷Hannay, M.P. (ed.), *Silent But for the Word*; Salminen, R. (ed.), *Le Miroir de L'Ame Pecheresse*.

Mirrour of Princely Deedes and Knighthood, A (1578)

English writer ▷Margaret Tyler's ▷translation of Diego Ortunez de Calahorra's Spanish chivalric romance. The tale is set in Greece after the time of Consantine. Tyler's translation is prefaced by a lengthy epistle to the reader, in which Tyler justifies not only the value of the work she has chosen to translate but also her position as a woman translating a romance rather than a religious work. Her reasoning shows her awareness of both the popularity of the romance genre and of women as the targeted market for them. She argues that if women can have romances dedicated to them, and if they can read them, then they ought to be allowed to translate such works themselves.
▷Patronage; Prefaces (16th- and 17th-century Britain)
Bib: Krontiris, T., 'Breaking Barriers of Genre and Gender: Margaret Tyler's Translation of *The Mirrour of Knighthood*', *English Literary Renaissance*, No. 18 (1988), pp. 19–39.

***Miscelanea, Meditations, Memoratives* (1604)**
English book of devotions and mother's advice
composed by ▷Elizabeth Grymeston. The book
consists of fourteen chapters of ▷prayers, staves,
madrigal odes and moral maxims, gathered
together by Grymeston for the edification of her
only son, Bernye. The materials she collected are
drawn especially from the Church fathers, and
recusant authors such as Robert Southwell and
Richard Rowlands, but she also drew upon the
classics, poets Edmund Spenser, (?1552–1599)
Samuel Daniel (1562–1619), *A Mirror for
Magistrates* (1559), and Ludevico Ariosto's *Orlando
Furioso* (1532). Yet *Miscelanea* is more than simply
an anthology of the works of others. Critic Ruth
Huey notes that, although much of the material
included is borrowed to varying degrees from
other authors, 'the general style of the prose
throughout is the same, even in passages of
especial eloquence, so that it is hardly too much
to say that she made the borrowings very much
her own.' Grymeston's reasons for composing her
book, outlined in her dedicatory ▷letter to her
son, place her work within the context of
Renaissance mother's legacies.
Bib: Huey, R. and Hereford, P., 'Elizabeth
Grymeston and her *Miscelanea*', *The Library*, No.
15 (1934), pp. 61–91.

Miscellany
US 19th-century anthologies of miscellaneous
poetry, prose and illustrations. Very popular,
particularly in the first half of the century, these
anthologies printed both established writers and
new voices – serving for some women writers as
their first publication and publicity. Often
unthemed and uncategorized, such anthologies
occasionally inspired writers to publish
miscellanies of their own work.

***Miss Peabody's Inheritance* (1983)**
Australian novel by ▷Elizabeth Jolley. Jolley's
novel deals with the correspondence between
Dotty Peabody, a lonely and frustrated clerical
worker in England, and an Australian woman
novelist, Diana Hopewell, during which the text of
Hopewell's erotic and melodramatic lesbian novel
is forwarded in fragments to Miss Peabody, who
eventually inherits the author's task. Considerable
irony is generated by the parallels between the
novel, the correspondence, and the developing
relationship between Peabody and Hopewell. This
is a powerful and original tale of female love and
loneliness, presented in a distinctly modernist
mode which cleverly erases the distinction
between truth and fiction, reality and art.

***Miss Sophie's Diary* (1928)**
Novel by Chinese writer ▷Ding Ling. On the
book's publication, the young author found herself
instantly famous – or infamous – for depicting a
young girl's sexual consciousness.
   Sophie is an educated young woman, living
alone with her thoughts, her boredom and her
frustrations. She is consumptive, and spends most

of her time in bed, sometimes masturbating,
sometimes fantasizing. The hotel where she lives
is full of irritating noises, and she feels imprisoned
by the whitewashed blank walls, which stand as an
emblem of her life: 'Wherever you sit, they block
your view. If you try to escape by lying on your
bed, you're crushed by the ceiling, which is
whitewashed too.'
   Wei, the weepy young man who professes to
love her, does not have a clue to what is going on
in her head, and only arouses her sadistic instincts
to torture him.
   Sophie falls in love with a tall, handsome
stranger, and for the first time becomes aware of
male beauty. She fights against her sexual
obsession, fully aware that the man is completely
worthless. She analyses herself incessantly:
'Fortunately my life is mine alone in all the
universe to play with.'
Bib: Jenner, W.F. (trans.), *Miss Sophie's Diary and
Other Stories*.

***Mistaken Identity* (1988)**
Novel by Indian author ▷Nayantara Sahgal. Set
in pre-independence India, the novel charts the
course of Bhusan Singh after he returns home to
India in 1929 and is gaoled on conspiracy charges.
The growing Hindu–Muslim tension of the 1930s
looms as a threatening backdrop to Singh's life-
story. As in her other novels, Sahgal's
achievement here is to relate in the form of the
history of an individual something of the complex
history of modern India.

***Mr Hogarth's Will* (1865)**
Australian novel by ▷Catherine Helen Spence.
Two young women, Jane and Alice Melville, are
given a 'masculine' education in accountancy,
mineralogy and agricultural chemistry by their
uncle, Mr Melville, in Scotland, and are then
disinherited by him so that they will become
independent women. They emigrate to Australia
where they eventually go into service below their
station; Jane as a governess/companion and Alice
as a lady's maid, until both are liberated by happy
marriages.

Mistral, Gabriela (1889–1957)
Chilean poet, prose and letter writer. She is a
prolific, and perhaps the most important, Chilean
poet, and she was awarded the Nobel Prize for
Literature in 1945. Born Lucila Godoy Alcayaga,
she adopted her pen-name as homage to the
Italian writer Gabriel D'Annunzio (1863–1938)
(▷*D'Annunzianesimo*) and the Provençal poet
Frédéric Mistral (1830–1914). She became a
teacher at the age of fifteen, and achieved
recognition with the publication of her first – and
some critics say her greatest – book, ▷*Desolación*
(1922) (*Solace*), written in response to the tragic
suicide of her one-time fiancé.
   Mistral never married, but adopted a boy, who
to her deep sorrow, also committed suicide at the
age of fifteen. Her passionate, and maternalistic
poetry, especially '*Ternura*' (1924) ('Tenderness'),

is dedicated to peace and love for the children. Mistral's post-symbolist poetry is full of pertinent, soul-searching metaphors. Love, but not erotic passion, is her main topic.

In *Tala* (1938) (*Grazing*) she changed her style, using more complex imagery and technique, and achieving a more abstract vision of nature. The title is a reference to a children's play, and in it she describes the devestation of the Cordillera forest, 'lain down like a lover'. Unusually, *Lagar* (1954) (*Wine Press*) contains very concise poems.

Mistral lived in Europe between 1922 and 1938. She worked for the United Nations with the Polish-born French physicist Marie Curie (1867–1934) and the philosopher Henri Bergson (1859–1945). She was a consul in Brazil in 1945, and after 1948 taught in North American universities, eventually settling in Santa Barbara, California.

Mrs Almy's Journal (1880)

Written in the summer of 1778, ▷ Mary Gould Almy's journal reflects both the realities of war and, in style, the rising influence of sentimental literature in North America. Almy recorded the events of the American Revolution from a decidedly Loyalist point of view that summer as the Patriots, aided by French troops, besieged Newport, Rhode Island.

Mrs Dalloway (1925)

English writer ▷ Virginia Woolf's fourth novel details the lives of a number of diverse characters, all connected on one particular day to the 'event' of Clarissa Dalloway's party. The action is restricted to a single day, but the novel relies heavily on recollection, memory and random thought processes to build a collage of subjective characterizations. Throughout, the clock time of Big Ben is placed in tension with the alternative duration of memory and consciousness. In addition to the novel's interrogation of temporality, Woolf's treatment of the political and sexual milieu of bourgeois London society is produced in relation to a strong thematic of impotence and sterility. From the vivid image of Clarissa Dalloway's bedroom to the thwarted career prospects of Richard Dalloway, the novel draws out the impositions of gender and class, and interrogates the legacy of Victorian gender ideologies. *Mrs Dalloway* is the second of Woolf's novels to utilize the ▷ stream-of-consciousness narrative technique and, together with the preceding novel, *Jacob's Room* (1922), assured Woolf's position as a leading ▷ modernist writer.
　▷ *Hotel du Lac*

'Mrs Edwards . . . Her Solemn Self-Declarations' (1830)

Account of her religious conversion, by North American ▷ Sarah Pierpont Edwards. In the early 1740s, few North American families were as involved in the Great Awakening as that of Sarah Pierpont Edwards and her husband Jonathan, a spiritual leader of the movement. Edwards's own narrative of her religious conversion has been subordinated historically by her husband's well-known tribute to her piety. Edwards's narrative testifies to her Calvinist faith but also to her own writing talents. Resulting in a 'sense of the beauty and excellency of divine things', Edwards's conversion narrative details her process of recognizing her own worth – even if she were to lose the goodwill of her husband and community.

Mrs Mary Dewees's Journal from Philadelphia to Kentucky, 1787–1788 (1904)

The North American diarist ▷ Mary Coburn Dewees's travel journal covers her arduous five-month journey with her family undertaken in order to resettle in Kentucky. Dewees recounts for relatives in Philadelphia the beauty of Kentucky and her own pioneering spirit in hoping to find 'better days' in the new territory.

Mitchell, Eleyne (born 1913)

Australian children's author, novelist and non-fiction writer. Mitchell is most famous for her many novels for children, usually dealing with life in the Australian Alps and with a love of animals, particularly horses. The best-known of these is *Silver Brumby* (1958).
　▷ Children's literature (Australia)

Mitchell, Gladys (1901–1983)

English novelist of Scottish descent. A writer primarily of ▷ detective fiction, Mitchell wrote under her own name and, between 1930 and 1950, also adopted the male pseudonyms Stephen Hockby and Malcolm Torre. Her first novel, *Speedy Death* (1929), introduces the remarkable character Dame Beatrice LeStrange Bradley, Home Office psychiatrist and sleuth. Mitchell's writing occupies an area between classic detective fiction and a parody of its conventions; this gives her novels a high degree of originality, although not all are successful. Mitchell's detective novels include *The Saltmarsh Murders* (1934), *Death at the Opera* (1934) and *The Rising of the Moon* (1945). She was a prominent member of the Detective Club and also wrote several children's books.
　▷ Sayers Dorothy L.

Mitchell, Margaret (1900–1945)

US novelist. The daughter of a suffragist, Mitchell identified herself primarily as a Southerner. Throughout her life, this conflicted with her identity as a woman. When her mother died in 1918, Mitchell left Smith College and assumed her role in the upper-crust of Atlanta, Georgia society. In 1922 she became a reporter for the *Atlanta Journal*. When she married in 1925 she quit her job. From 1926 to 1929 she wrote ▷ *Gone With the Wind*, dressing in boys' trousers while writing. It was not published until 1935 when she first showed it to an editor. Mitchell died after being hit by a car.
Bib: Farr, Finis, *Margaret Mitchell of Atlanta: The Author of 'Gone With the Wind'*.

Mitchison, Naomi (born 1897)

Scottish novelist and poet. She was born in Edinburgh, daughter of the suffragist Kathleen Louise Taylor and the physiologist John Scott Haldane. She began a science degree as a 'Home Student' at Oxford, but gave this up to become a Voluntary Aid Detachment nurse. In 1916 she married G.R. Mitchison, who became a Labour MP, and became involved with the Labour Party as well as the pacifist and women's movements. She was also an early campaigner for women's birth control. Mitchison's literary career commenced with poems and plays, although she has now gone on to write more than 80 novels. Her first novel, *The Conquered* (1923), is based on her wartime experiences, a subject she returned to again after World War II in the diary *Among You Taking Notes* (1985). *Cloud Cuckoo Land* (1925) is the first of many historical novels, although Mitchison has proved herself to be a prolific and varied novelist. Another historical novel, *The Corn King and the Spring Queen* (1931), set in the small state of Marob, explores the conflict between native culture and the imperialism of Athenian power and culture.

Mitchison's most controversial novel, *We Have Been Warned* (1935), confronts sexual behaviour frankly and explicitly, and, owing to its radical depiction of seduction, rape and abortion, was rejected by leading publishers and ultimately censored. In 1937 Mitchison returned to Scotland, and *The Bull Calves* (1947) identifies her involvement in the Scottish Renaissance movement. Later writings include science fiction novels, such as *Memoirs of a Spacewoman* (1962), and a volume of travel writing, *Mucking Around* (1981). She has written three volumes of autobiography, *Small Talk* (1973), *All Change Here* (1975) and *You May Well Ask* (1979).
Bib: Benton, J., *Naomi Mitchison: A Century of Experiment in Life and Letters*; Caldecott, L., *Women of Our Century*; Hart, F.R., *The Scottish Novel: A Critical Survey*.

Mitford, Mary Russell (1787–1855)

English essayist, dramatist, novelist and poet, born in Alresford, Hampshire. She is remembered today as the author of ▷*Our Village* (1824–32), a series of essays depicting rural life. Her collections of poetry include *Miscellaneous Poems* (1810) and *Narrative Poems on the Female Character in the Various Relations of Life* (1813). Her most successful play was *Rienzi* (1828), produced at the Drury Lane theatre in London in 1828 to critical acclaim.
Bib: Watson, V., *Life*; Astin, M., *Life*.

Mitford, Nancy (1904–1973)

English novelist, historian and journalist. Born in London and educated at home, Mitford lived in France after World War II. Mitford's preferred form is the comedy of manners, and many of her novels describe youthful Bohemianism in upper-class society. Her first successful novel was *The Pursuit of Love* (1945), which explores the fascinations and pitfalls of love, drawing a dichotomy between bohemian hedonism and authoritarian parental control. Subsequent novels, including *Love in a Cold Climate* (1949) and *The Blessing* (1951), focus on similar themes, while *Noblesse Oblige: An Enquiry into the Identifiable Characteristics of the English Aristocracy* (1956) exploits her astute observation of social nuance and ear for dialogue. *Wigs on the Green* (1935) attacks the British Fascist Movement, in which her sisters Diana and Unity were involved. Other publications include the biographies *Madame de Pompadour* (1954) and *Voltaire in Love* (1957) and the novels *Highland Fling* (1931), *The Blessing* (1951), *Don't Tell Alfred* (1960). Mitford has edited two volumes of family correspondence: *The Ladies of Alderley* (1938) and *The Stanleys of Alderley* (1939).

Mito Pavese, Il (1967) (*The Myth of Pavese*)

A critical study of Cesare Pavese by Italian writer ▷Armanda Guiducci. The text analyses Pavese, his place in Italian culture, and European and North American influences on his work. The book is interesting, both as a study of an influential Italian writer of the period and for Guiducci's analysis of the relationship between myth and poetry. The work sheds light on Guiducci as a poet, as well as on Pavese.

Miura Ayako (born 1922)

Japanese novelist. Miura was born in Asahikawa in Hokkaido. She suffered from caries for thirteen years from the age of twenty-four, and was baptized a Christian in the face of death. *The Freezing Point* won a prize for the *Asahi* newspaper in 1963 and was popular at the time. It describes a couple who are beset with troubles when they adopt a girl whose father kills their eldest daughter. Religion pervades many of Miura's works; her latest novel is *Days in the Hand of God*.

Mixer, Elizabeth (fl 1707–1720)

North American spiritual autobiographer. A resident of Ashford, Massachusetts, she was the daughter of devout Puritans; in 1720, when she was about thirteen, she experienced a series of 'raptures' or visions. Her account of these experiences was transcribed by her minister and published in 1736 under the title ▷*An Account of Some Spiritual Experiences and Raptures*. Her rapturous descriptions of Christ appearing to her on three occasions garnered her admittance into Church membership.

Mixquiahuala Letters, The (1986)

US novel. ▷Ana Castillo won the 1987 Before Columbus Foundation's American Book Award for this book. The book is written as a series of letters. Tere recollects to her travelling companion, Alicia, their travels together ten years ago. These travels represent their failed erotic quest as, filled with illusions and ideals, they actively explored their sexuality and expected to find heterosexual erotic bliss.

Tere wants to define herself sexually, but she operates under a heterosexist ideology. Similarly, she wants to define herself as a North American, but is of Mexican descent. Castillo provides several different sequencing charts for reading the letters and suggests that readers choose where to read according to their own ideological needs. Her book questions the ideologies which entrap characters and readers.

Miyao Tomiko (born 1926)
Japanese novelist. She was born the daughter of a geisha master in Kochi prefecture. *An Oar* (1973) depicts the world of a geisha house, and is based on the life of her mother, who unwillingly succeeded to her father's business. She sympathizes with those who are subjected to discrimination such as prostitutes and gangsters in such works as *An Oar* and *Yokiro*. *A Koto with One String* won the Naoki Prize in 1978. Her other main works are *Mai* and *Kinone*.

Mizuta Tamae (born 1929)
Japanese historian of feminist thought in Europe. Mizuta was born in Tokyo and is Professor of Economics at Nagoya University. She has greatly influenced the development of women's liberation theory in Japan through her books, such as *A History of Women's Liberation Thought* (1979).

MLF – Mouvement de Libération des Femmes
The French Women's Liberation Movement grew out of the ▷May 1968 disturbances, and rapidly divided into three main groupings.

The Class Struggle Tendency, which had a dual allegiance to the women's movement and to various mixed extreme-left organizations, had disappeared by the mid-1970s, though the question of the relationship between feminism and Marxism clearly remains significant.

The ▷*Psych et Po* (*Psychanalyse et Politique*) group, deeply influenced by Lacanian ▷psychoanalysis, aims to cultivate feminine difference through cultural separatism rather than political action. In 1975 *Psych et Po* registered the logo 'MLF' as their own property, thus generating years of conflict and court cases between feminists. With the departure of its leader, Antoinette Fouque, to the USA, the group has lost its former importance.

Finally, 'non-aligned' feminists, orginally, *Féministes Révolutionnaires*, reject theoretical frameworks, whether Lacanian or Marxist, in favour of specific struggles and diversity of opinion. The journal *Questions féministes* (*Feminist Issues*), which has been particularly critical of *Psych et Po*'s tendency to ▷essentialism, was produced by 'non-aligned' feminists. The group's fundamental belief that 'the personal is political', and their emphasis on women's experience, and on non-hierarchical organization, place them more in the mainstream of the feminist movement internationally than *Psych et Po*.

African and Caribbean women living in France did not begin to organize separately until the 1980s, with the creation of *Nanas Beurs*, an organization by and for second-generation North African immigrants, and of *Modefen* (Movement for the Defence of Black Women's Rights).
Bib.: Duchen, Claire, *Feminism in France – From May 1968 to Mitterand.*

Moderato Cantabile (1966)
Translation of *Moderato Cantabile* (1958) by French writer ▷Marguerite Duras. Duras's seventh novel is a story of desire involving a rich woman, Anne Desbaresdes, and Chauvin, a working man. Anne meets Chaurin in a café after they have both been present at the murder of a woman by her lover, and the text describes their subsequent meetings in the café. The tension increases until the final 'consummation', intercut with scenes of Anne's recalcitrant son's piano lessons, and a scene where Anne returns late and drunk to a lavish dinner party at her home. The language is simple and clear, its power lying as much in what is not said as in what is actually described.

Modern breakthrough in Scandinavia, The
In 1883 the Danish literary critic Georg Brandes (1842–1927), who translated J.S. Mull's *The Subjection of Women* in 1869, took stock of the new realist literature which he had inspired in Scandinavia by writing *Det moderne Gjennembruds Mænd (The Men of the Modern Breakthrough)*. No women writers are to be found in this book, but the modern breakthrough was also a breakthrough for women writers in Denmark, and the most important question in the modern realist literature was the one of sex, as seen in ▷the great Nordic dispute on chastity. Pil Dahlerup, in her *Det moderne gennembruds kvinder 1–2*, (1983) (*The Women of the Modern Breakthrough*), suggests that women's literature changed from the maternal image of woman to a sexualized one. She also stated that women writers in general can be said to have been in a state of depression, and that this depression was linked to their realism.

Central women writers of the modern breakthrough in Denmark are: Adda Ravnkilde (1862–1883), Emma Gad (1845–1922), Erna Juel-Hansen (1845–1922), and the Norwegian ▷Amalie Skram.

In Finland there was a breakthrough of a new realistic literature, and of a Finnish literature in opposition to the dominant Swedish culture. The influence of Georg Brandes also came to Finland, thanks to ▷Minna Canth, who translated his work, and seems to have been personally influenced by his programmes and aesthetics. Canth was the leading figure in the modern breakthrough in Finland; her topics were woman's emancipation and the plight of the poor. She is still considered the most notable Finnish dramatist, but also started many contemporary, now forgotten, women on a career of writing, eg Maila Talvio, Selma Anttila and Elsa Heporanta.

The modern breakthrough in Norway took

place from around 1877 to 1892, as a result of the ▷modern breakthrough in Denmark. In this period Norway was still rural, and the radical and Bohemian tendencies seen in Denmark and Germany were concentrated in Oslo and Bergen. In 1883 the poet Bjørnstjerne Bjørnson wrote 'A Glove' as an appeal to men to remain chaste until marriage, as women had to. Many women writers agreed with him because of the threat of syphilis. This led to the ▷great Nordic dispute on chastity.

New, realist women's writing appeared. Hanne Winsnes (1789–1872), ▷Camilla Collett (1813–1895) and Magdalena Thoresen (1819–1903) all wrote realist prose about everyday life and the women's question (▷woman question). The most famous woman writer in the Norwegian modern breakthrough was Amalie Skram.

The modern breakthrough in Sweden was dominated by male writers but, as in the other Scandinavian countries, the women's question was also an important theme for male writers, eg August Strindberg (1849–1912), who participated in the ▷great Nordic dispute on chastity with the collection of short stories *Giftas* (1884) (*Getting Married*).

Some Swedish women writers, like ▷Victoria Benedictsson, took part in the modern breakthrough in Sweden. She was deeply influenced by Georg Brandes, but is today also considered as a part of the female breakthrough in Swedish literature in the 1880s, together with Anne Charlotte Leffler (1849–1892), Alfhild Agrell (1849–1923) and Mathilda Malling (pseudonym: Stella Kleve, 1864–1942). Leffler was the most productive prose writer and dramatist, and she wrote about female sexuality and women's right to a life of their own.

Modern Hebrew Literature (1970)
A study of the history of Modern Hebrew literature by Simon Halkin. The book covers the period from the ▷Jewish Enlightenment (1870–1880) until the 1950s. The author, an acclaimed poet, novelist and critic, describes and analyzes writers and their writing from a literary and historical perspective.

Modern Hebrew Poem Itself, The (1965)
A book of 69 poems, presented in the original Hebrew, in transliteration and in literal translation into English. The general introduction is comprehensive and each poem is analyzed by various critics and translators of Hebrew verse. Women writers included are ▷Yocheved Bat-Miriam and ▷Dalia Ravikovitch.

Modernism
The term 'modernism' is associated with a broad-based international artistic movement emerging in the 1890s and reaching its height in the 1920s (high modernism). Modernism is usually seen as a challenge to, or reaction against, both the formal dominance of ▷realism and any uncritical investment in 'rationality' as the governing interpretative principle. The modernist aesthetic is highly selfconscious, and expresses an innovative movement attuned to contemporaneous developments in other fields, the most notable being Freudian ▷psychoanalysis and its theorizing of the Unconscious, the psychology of Jung, Bergson's theory of temporality, and the analysis of cultural repositories associated with anthropology and mythology. A further significant characteristic is the articulation of a sense of historical discontinuity: the characteristic modernist bracketing of the immediate past alongside a rejection of its values and assumptions is identifiable with a dependence on myth as the dominant structuring device. In fiction, the merging of these interests is clearly seen in the ▷stream-of-consciousness novel, a technique which also reformulates the definitional parameters of mimesis. The 'anti-realist' aesthetic practices of modernism, the privileging of 'subjective' reality and dismantling of the boundary between 'art' and 'life', are articulated in the work of many women writers – prominently, ▷Virginia Woolf, ▷Dorothy Richardson, ▷May Sinclair, ▷H.D. – as a concern with a peculiarly feminine aesthetic and interrogation of women's consciousness. The argument as to whether modernism is a completed project is central to current debates on ▷postmodernism.

▷Compton-Burnett, Ivy; Sitwell, Edith
Bib: Benstock, S., *Women of the Left Bank*; Hanscombe, G. and Smyers, V., *Writing for Their Lives*; Jardine, A., *Gynesis*; Wolff, J., *Feminine Sentences*.

Latin America: In the Spanish-speaking parts of Latin America, this literary movement was founded by the Nicaraguan poet Rubén Darío (▷pseudonym of Félix Rubén García Sarmiento) (1867–1916). In their work, the modernists abandoned previous, traditional rules and forms, tried to find beauty in everything, and rejected didactic art and literature. There were four phases of modernism in Brazil, mainly dominated by male writers and artists, but because they do not correspond to the modernist phases in Spanish America, this can be misleading when considering modernism in Latin America as a whole. Modernism in Brazil corresponds to ▷postmodernism in Spanish America.

The first, most revolutionary phase of Brazilian modernism was instigated by the Week of Modern Art held at the São Paulo Town Theatre in February 1922, when poets, painters and musicians disgusted audiences with their innovative work. During this first phase the poet ▷Cecília Meireles actively conrtibuted to the literary developments, writing for the magazine *Festa*. The second phase of modernism was marked by the ▷1930s social novels, and among women the work of ▷Raquel de Queirós in particular. ▷Postmodernism in Brazil describes the third phase, which was developed by the ▷1945 Generation of poets, and the fourth, final phase, when writers experimented with more contemporary themes and the use of language.

The main female exponent of modernism at this time was ▷Clarice Lispector.

Premodernism in Brazil (1912–1922) (when *postmodernismo* began to flourish in Spanish America) was initiated when European trends such as Dadaism, futurism and Surrealism were gradually introduced, mainly by men returning from travels abroad. A strong reaction against these influences resulted in writers re-examining the importance of South American Indian culture, with the Brazilians determined to retain an identity free from European influences.
Portugal: Portuguese modernism is generally divided into two movements: *orphismo* (1915–1927), a radical, experimental phase influenced by futurism, cubism and Expressionism, which produced such poets as Fernando Pessoa and Mário de Sá-Carneiro; and *presencismo* (1927–1940), a more reflective, critical and high-cultural phase which transformed some of the early modernists into canonical authors. In Portugal, as elsewhere, modernism was characterized by intense concern with literary form, and by a certain deconstruction of romantic subjectivity.

Modernismo

In Spanish-speaking countries, this literary movement corresponds most closely to symbolism and other trends that flourished towards the end of the 19th century. The most notable Spanish American exponent was the Nicaraguan Rubén Darío (pen-name of Félix Rubén García Sarmiento, 1867–1916), followed by the Chilean Magallanes Moure (1878–1924).
▷Modernism (Latin America)

Modjeska, Drusilla (born 1946)

Australian historian, critic and novelist. Modjeska was born in London and came to Australia in 1971 after spending three years in New Guinea. She is best-known for her critical study, *Exiles at Home: Australian Women Writers 1925–1945* (1981), her editing (with M. Pizer) of *The Poems of Lesbia Harford* (1985) and (with S. Dermody and J. Docker) of *Nellie Melba, Ginger Meggs and Friends: Essays in Australian Cultural History* (1982). Modjeska, who teaches at the University of Technology (Sydney), has recently published an autobiographical novel, *Poppy* (1990), which focuses upon the life of her mother.
▷Feminist literary criticism (Australia)

Modleski, Tania (born 1949)

North American professor of film and literature at the University of Southern California. A theorist of popular culture, in common with ▷Rosalind Coward and ▷Janice Radway, Modleski argues that popular culture plays an important role in shaping women's understanding of themselves and their place in the world. In *Loving with a Vengeance: Mass Produced Fantasies for Women* (1982), a study of ▷harlequin romances, ▷Gothic novels and television soap operas, Modleski explains that these mass-produced narratives have an especial appeal to women because they answer a set of desires and needs which are produced by, but cannot be fulfilled within, patriarchal culture. Modleski challenges F.R. Leavis's (▷Leavisite criticism) denunciation of ▷mass culture as trivial and unimportant, suggesting by implication that he failed to consider the specificity of a feminine literary response. She is editor of *Studies in Entertainment: Critical Approaches to Mass Culture* (1986), and author of *The Women Who Knew Too Much: Hitchcock and Feminist Theory* (1988).

Moe Moe (Inya) (1944–1990)

Pen-name of Burmese writer Daw San San. She began her literary career while still at school, and then worked as a magazine editor. In 1974, 1980, 1982 and 1986 she won National Literary Awards for her collections of short stories and novels written in Burmese. Her books include *Lost and Wandering, Ngapali Story, A Thing Called Love, A Hundred Wild Flowers and We Live in Burma*. She died suddenly of a cerebral haemorrhage, leaving two manuscripts unfinished.

Moero (4th–3rd century BC)

Poet. Sometimes known as Myro, she came from Byzantium and was the mother of the grammerian and tragic poet Homerus. Two Greek ▷epigrams and ten lines of epic hexameter survive, but the biographical dictionary, the *Suda* (10th century AD), also records that she wrote lyric poetry. The two epigrams are for dedications to gods, one being for some grapes. The hexameters concern the Pleiades, who were women transferred to heaven as stars by the god Zeus as a reward for helping him when he was young. Moero also wrote a work entitled *Memory*, which does not survive.
▷Praxilla; Anyte; Sappho; Muses; Parthenis

Mogador, Céleste (1824–1909)

French autobiographer and novelist. A working-class woman, who was raped in adolescence by one of her mother's suitors, she became a courtesan and a dance hostess. After marrying an aristocratic lover, Lionel de Chabrillan, she published her memoirs, *Adieux au monde* (1853–54) (*Goodbye World*). These scandalized the public – despite her avowed intention to use the depiction of vice in order to encourage virtue – because they dealt with the murky world of prostitution. The memoirs proved, however, to be a bestseller, and Mogador's publishers insisted on producing a second edition, in spite of her unwillingness to allow their reissue (her husband had become French Consul-General in Melbourne, and she wished to avoid compromising his reputation further). Obliged to live by her pen after de Chabrillan's death, she published novels including *Les Voleurs d'or* (1857) (*The Gold Thieves*), her first and most successful fictional work, and *Sapho* (1858). Her brief period in the literary limelight did not prevent her from dying a pauper.
Bib: Brécourt-Villars, P., *Ecrire d'Amour*; Carton,

H., *Histoire des femmes écrivains de la France*;
Haldane, C., *Daughter of Paris: the Life Story of Céleste Mogador*.

Mohr, Nicholasa (born 1935)
US short story writer and novelist. Mohr was born
of Puerto Rican parents and lived in a ghetto in
New York. Her juvenile and young-adult fiction is
noted for its realism. Mohr shows in *Nilda* (1973)
what it feels like to grow up poor and belonging to
a despised minority.

In *El Bronx Remembered* (1975) and *To Nueva
York* (1977) Mohr traces the Puerto Rican
migrant's process of assimilation and
demonstrates how migrants become victims of
racism in their search for a better life. Many
resort to crime for their survival. Mohr describes
such problems in the *barrio* as drug usage, illegal
gambling and teenage pregnancy. Mohr suggests
US-born offspring inherit a false legacy as they
envision Puerto Rico as an island paradise. Mohr
chronicles the legacy of a people who have been
colonized throughout history.

Other works include: *Felita* (1979), *Rituals of
Survival: A Woman's Portfolio* (1985) and *Going
Home*.

Moi, Toril (born 1953)
Norwegian-born feminist theorist who publishes
in English. After holding the post of Director of
the Centre for Feminist Research in the
Humanities at the University of Bergen, Norway,
Moi is now Adjunct Professor of Comparative
Literature at Bergen, and Professor of Literature
at Duke University in the US. She is author of
Sexual/Textual Politics: Feminist Literary Theory
(1985); and *Feminist Literary Theory and Simone de
Beauvoir* (1990). Moi has edited and introduced
two influential introductions to French feminist
theory: *The Kristeva Reader* (1986); and *French
Feminist Thought: A Reader* (1987).

Moix, Ana María (born 1947)
Born in Barcelona, Spain, Moix is a poet,
journalist, translator, novelist and short story
writer. She is the sister of the well-known gay
novelist Terençi Moix. Her first novel, *Julia*
(1970), portrays the world of the Catalan
bourgeoisie in the post-war period, and examines
the ways in which society can warp individual
identity. A similar theme emerges in a collection
of short stories, *Ese chico pelirrojo a quien veo cada
día* (1971) (*That Red-headed Boy I See Every Day*).
Moix continues her satire of the Catalan
bourgeoisie in *Walter, por qué te fuiste?* (1973)
(*Walter, Why Did You Leave?*), and *Las virtudes
peligrosas* (1985) (*Dangerous Virtues*). Her three
books of poetry have been reissued under the title
A imagen y semejanza (1983) (*In the Image and
Likeness*).

Molesworth, Mary Louisa (1839–1921)
British novelist and writer of ▷children's
literature, also wrote under the ▷pseudonym
Ennis Graham. She married Major Richard

Molesworth in 1861, but the couple separated in
1878. Her first works were three novels: *Lover and
Husband* (1870); *She Was Young and He Was Old*
(1872) and *Cicely* (1874), all of which were
concerned with the problem of women and
marriage. She was advised to write for children by
Sir Noel Paton, an illustrator, and concentrated
on this market for the rest of her life. Works for
children include *Carrots* (1876); *The Cuckoo Clock*
(1877); *The Adventures of Herr Baby* (1881) and
The Carved Lions (1895). Molesworth's stories are
mostly lively blends of magic and ▷realism,
featuring female characters in central roles.

▷Ghost stories (19th-century Britain)
Bib: Green, R.L., *Life*.

Molloy, Frances (born 1947)
Irish novelist. Born in Derry, she now lives in
England. Her first novel, *No Mate for the Magpie*
(1985), is the story of a young woman, a Catholic,
growing up in Northern Ireland in the 1950s and
1960s. Her style is marked by humour, irony and
vividly colloquial dialogue.

Monbart, Marie-Joséphine de Lescun (Madame Sydow) (1758–?)
French novelist and essayist. Born in France, she
later lived in Germany, and the majority of her
works were published in Berlin. These include
two collections of verse and prose pieces, *Les
Loisirs d'une jeune dame* (1776) (*The Pastimes of a
Young Lady*) and *Mélanges de littérature* (1799).
Two of her works focus on the education of
women: *Sophie, ou l'education des filles* (1777)
(*Sophie, or Education for Girls*) and *De l'education
d'une princesse* (1781) (*The Education of a Princess*).
The last of her published works, the novel *Lettres
taïtiennes* (1786) (*Tahitian Letters*), was written as a
sequel to ▷Madame de Graffigny's ▷*Lettres
d'une péruvienne* (1747) (*Letters of a Perurian
Princess*, 1818).

Monck, Mary (c 1680–1715)
Irish poet and translator who wrote *Marinda:
Poems and Translations upon Several Occassions*
(1716), which included original writing and
translations.

Monday Night (1938)
US novel by ▷Kay Boyle which focuses on an
idealist overpowered by circumstance. Wilt is a
frustrated writer who procrastinates and drinks,
and the story traces his search for a renowned
French toxicologist. He surmises that the
toxicologist is responsible for the imprisonment of
innocent people. Wilt has the material therefore
for his masterpiece but another reporter prints the
story first. Typical of Boyle's characters, Wilt
struggles against oppressive forces although he
does try to reach out to identify with humanity.

Mondo salvato dai ragazzini, II (1968) (*The World Saved by Little Children*)
A collection of poetry by ▷Elsa Morante. In the
main, this is poetry of social protest. Morante

denounces war, fascism, and the manner in which society tries to repress the individual. Madness, she suggests, is a condition brought about by society. She declares that she stands apart from society, has no wish to be part of it, and will allow only children (who are still interested in important things) to be part of her separate world.

Mon Examen de Blanc (1972) (*My Exam in Whiteness*)

In this first novel by the French Antilles writer ▷Jaqueline Manicom, Madévie, the Guadeloupean heroine, takes her 'exam' in whiteness through an affair with Xavier, a racist and sexist medical student in Paris. This relationship with a white man is that of subject–object, master–slave. Madévie is Xavier's exotic sexual toy. The novel traces Madévie's cathartic confessions concerning the affair, and the abortion of the child conceived from the union to Cyril, the white surgeon who is her colleague in Guadeloupe. Cleansed by her confession, Madévie becomes involved with Gilbert, a black revolutionary, and through him with his political group. The novel concludes with his death in the shooting by the police of those involved in the 1967 strike of sugar-cane workers in Pointe-à-Pitre. Madévie is left alone. Like other French Antillean writers such as ▷Michèle Lacrosil, ▷Mayotte Capécia, ▷Maryse Condé and M-M Carbet (▷*Au Peril de toi Joie*), Manicom is thus dealing with the problem of white prejudice and alienation, using the well-worn plot of the racially mixed affair.
▷Identity, Caribbean.

Monkey Grip (1977)

Australian novel by ▷Helen Garner. *Monkey Grip* portrays the difficult relationship between the narrator, Nora, and a heroin addict, Javo, who is her lover. It won the National Book Council Book of the Year Award 1978, and was made into a successful film in 1981.

'Monna Innominata' (1881)

A sequence of sonnets by British poet ▷Christina Rossetti, published in ▷*A Pageant, and Other Poems* (1881). In the Preface to the sequence, Rossetti refers to Beatrice and Laura, the female muses of Dante and Petrarch respectively. She writes that the muses 'have come down to us resplendent with charms, but . . . scant of attractiveness', and speculates about what might have been 'Had such a lady spoken for herself'. The sequence then enacts a rewriting of amatory poetic tradition, using a female speaker as subject rather than object of the verse. The sequence does not straightforwardly reverse sexual power relations, however, but rather defines the female self through renunciation, dwelling on loss and on unfulfilled desire.

Monnet, Marie Moreau (1752–1798)

French prose fiction writer. Born in La Rochelle, the daughter of a wigmaker, her husband was a chemist and inspector of mines. She wrote two volumes of oriental tales, *Contes orientaux* (1772) (*Eastern Tales*) and *Histoire d'Abdal Mazour* (1784) (*The Story of Abdal Mazour*), inventing the character of Caleb, an itinerant Persian sage. Caleb was also the addressee of her next work, *Lettres de Jenny Bleinmore* (1787) (*The Letters of Jenny Bleinmore*). These were well received, and she was referred to as Caleb, after her character. Diderot made the traditional comparison between Monnet and ▷Sappho, adding that she was less tender but more beautiful than her predecessor.

Her other works are: 'Les Deux hermites' ('The Two Hermits') in *Mercure*, Feb. 1787; *Essai en vers* (1788) (*Essay in verse*), and 'La Piété maternelle' ('Maternal Piety') in *Mercure*, June 1789.
Bib: Fabien-Pillet, 'Notice sur la vie de Marie Moreau Monnet', *Mercure*, IV (1790).

Monplaisir, Emma (born 1918)

This French Antilles writer, the daughter of a French mother and a Martiniquan father, came very early to Martinique. Her semi-historical novel, *La Fille du Caraïbe* (1960) (*The Daughter of the Carib Indian*), is interesting not only for its descriptions, based on Monplaisir's research, of the situation in Martinique, but also for the importance it gives to heredity and to syncretism. The novel's protagonist is Winna, daughter of a Carib and a European. She eventually falls in love with the Carib Indian Twalheitou, leaving the 'slavery of civilization' to join her 'savage' partner. After the death of Twalheitou, Winna realizes that it was only through her love that she was able to live with the Caribs. On leaving, she meets the mulatto Terramen, son of a *béké* (white Creole), and with him she conceives the child who symbolizes the Antillean race, combining European, African and Indian heritage. Monplaisir was also interested in the folklore of Martinique, and published *Martinique et ses danses* (1962) (*Martinique and Her Dances*) and *Cric Crac Martinique* (1957). Nine years after the publication of *La Fille du Caraïbe*, Monplaisir published the first volume of her romantic *Christophe Colomb chez les Indiens*.

Monserdà de Macía, Dolors (1845–1919)

One of Spain's Catalan writers, who wrote broadly realist novels. She was interested in depicting the working class and the problems of working women. Her work is also significant for her exposé of materialism and amorality in the upper classes.
▷Catalan women's writing

Monsieur Vénus (1884) (*Mr Venus*)

The first successful novel by French writer ▷Rachilde (Marguerite Eymery). Subtitled 'a materialist novel' and dedicated 'To physical beauty', it fell foul of the censor on first publication in Brussels in 1884. The French edition of 1889 was made safe by a preface from Maurice Barrès, who pointed out the Decadent frisson to be gained from what he described as the innocently vicious fantasies of a twenty-year-old virgin. Rachilde's heroine, the wealthy, high-born and coldly sadistic Raoule de Vénérande, turns the tables on men by taking as her lover a poor young painter from the popular classes, humiliating and tormenting him and turning him into an effeminate plaything. The class bias in the book is crass; the writing and philosophy are locked derivatively into the Decadent mode; the plot and scenes are pure melodrama, often to the point of ludicrousness. Nevertheless, there is a feverish power in the book which holds the reader's attention. This comes partly from the intensely sensuous and idiosyncratic detail of Rachilde's vision, but most of all from the clarity with which she sets out the patterns of exploitation within which contemporary male and female sexual desire is constructed.

Montagne trasparenti (1917) (Transparent Mountains)

A collection of Italian ▷futurist writings by ▷Maria Ginanni, characteristic of most futurist writing of the period in its view of women. Ginanni is involved here in an investigation into the nature of the self. The masculine point of view is frequently privileged as, for example, in the statement: 'it is good to take a woman, just like that, with the hands of a predator.' The text is packed with sexual imagery, with the phallus notably featured. Sexuality has violent connotations in this work, which also includes images of motherhood as favoured by the futurists. It is presented as an exemplary, ideal role for women.

Montagu, Elizabeth (1720–1800)

English intellectual, critic and letter-writer, known as 'Queen of the Blues' (▷Bluestockings). She married Edward Montagu in 1742. Her letters are decorous, and mildly sententious: ' "Virtue alone is happiness below." Much praise should be given to Mr Pope for making morality speak by the voice of divine poetry.' She wrote the last three of Lord George Lytton's Dialogues of the Dead (1760–1765), and the well-known Essay on Shakespeare (1769). She was a crucial link in a network of women attempting to find a role for the female English intellectual.

▷Chapone, Hester; More, Hannah; Piozzi, Hester Thrale; Scott, Sarah

Montagu, Lady Mary Wortley (1689–1792)

English letter-writer, dramatist, commentator, poet and Whig polemicist. Aristocrat and grandaughter of the diarist John Evelyn (her mother was Elizabeth Pirrepoint). She wrote from an early age, copying out her works in Poems, Songs &c in 1703. She prefaced it with a justification that 'all these was writt at the age of 14.' A tortuous courtship and eventual elopement (1712) with Mr Edward Wortley Montagu brought an arid marriage. She went with him when he became ambassador to Turkey, and wrote the letters which became her best-known writing under the title Embassy to Constantinople. She also introduced the Turkish practice of inoculation against smallpox into England. Once in England again, she fell out with the poet Alexander Pope (1688–1744), with whom she had been friendly (she cruelly satirized him in the poem she and Lord Hervey wrote on his 'Imitation of the Second Book of Horace' in 1733). In the 1730s she adapted her play Simplicity from the French of Marivaux, and from 1737 to 1738 ran her own polemical periodical The Nonsense of Common Sense (anonymously). One issue commented '(contrary to all other Authors) I see with a favourable Eye the little vanitys with which [women] amuse themselves, and am glad they can find in the imaginary Empire of Beauty, a consolation for being excluded every part of Government in the State.' In 1736 she went abroad, secretly hoping to live with Francesco Algarotti, but when this failed she stayed abroad in Venice, Avignon and, Rome. Her letters to her daughter date from this period. She returned to England when her husband died in 1761.

Editions of her work include: Halsband, Robert (ed.), Essays and Poems and Simplicity, A comedy (1977); Murphy, Dervla (ed.), Embassy to Constantinople.

▷Astell, Mary; Carter, Elizabeth; Richardson, Samuel, influence of

Montanclos, Marie-Emilie Maryon de, Baronne de Prinzen (1736–1812)

French journalist and dramatist. Born in Aix, she was married twice, widowed once, and legally separated from her second husband. In 1774 she succeeded Madame de Maisonneuve as editor of the women's periodical the ▷Journal des Dames, (Ladies' Journal) associated with subversive writers such as Louis-Sébastien Mercier. Throughout her life she insisted on her right to a career as a journalist and dramatist. She aimed to use the Journal des Dames to address 'all classes of female citizens and to uphold their sex, without which the arts and sciences would still be in chaos'. The paper criticized the frivolity of the court, and Montanclos dedicated it to Marie-Antoinette to enlist her support for the cause of women and against social injustices in general. Under her editorship the Journal began to re-evaluate motherhood as a serious occupation, requiring women to be not only the tender mother envisaged by Rousseau, but also enlightened educators of their children. After a second year, when the paper became bolder in its oppositional stance, it was sold to Mercier. Montanclos's plays include Le choix des fées (1782) (The Fairies' Choice), Le fauteuil (1799) (The Armchair), Robert le bossu (1799) (Robert the Hunchback), Alison et Silvain (1803) and La Bonne maîtresse (1804) (The Good Mistress). Her prose writing was published as Oeuvres diverses (1791) (Diverse Works). Certain feminist articles published during the Revolution, in papers such as Etrennes nationales des Dames

(*New Year's Gift for Women*), signed Madame de M., may have been the work of Montanclos.
   ▷Laisse, Madame de
Bib: Gelbart, N.R., *Feminine and Oppositional Journalism in Old Régime France: le Journal des Dames; Marquiset, A., Les Bas-bleus du premier Empire.*

Montero, Rosa (born 1951)

Spanish novelist. Born in Madrid, Montero is closely associated with *El País*, and is one of Spain's best-known media interviewers. She is now considered to be one of the most significant of the New Wave of women writers. Her main novels are: ▷*Crónica del desamor* (1979) (*Chronicle of Falling Out of Love*); *La función Delta* (1981) (*The Delta Function*), which uses two interrelated diaries to analyze women's Existentialist problems; *Te trataré como a una reina* (1983) (*I'll Treat You Like a Queen*), which portrays the decadent atmosphere of a Madrid nightspot in the red-light district; *Amado amo* (1988) (*Beloved Master*), which likewise focuses on the male-female relationship, and ▷*Temblor* (1990) (*Trembling*).

Montesson, Charlotte-Jeanne Béraud de La Haye de Riou, Marquise de (1738–1806)

French dramatist and poet. Born in Paris, she was a member of a distinguished Breton family. Married at sixteen and widowed in 1769, she later secretly married the Duc D'Orléans. After his death she was imprisoned during the Terror, but later found favour with Napoleon's government, from which she received a pension. Another writer protected by Napoleon, the ▷Comtesse de Beauharnais, was a close friend. Her dramatic works were performed at the Palais Royal, and later in her own home. *Mme de Chazelle* was performed at the Théâtre Français (1785). Her poetry was published as *Mélanges de poésie* (1782) (*Various Poems*). Only twelve copies of her seven volumes of plays, *Oeuvres anonymes* (1782–85) (*Anonymous Works*), were published.
Bib: Turquan, J., *Souverains et grandes dames*; Olah, L., *Une grande dame, auteur dramatique et poète au XVIIIe siècle.*

Montgomery, Lucy Maud (L.M.) (1874–1942)

Canadian novelist, born in Prince Edward Island. L.M. Montgomery was raised by her maternal grandparents after her mother died. She joined her father briefly in Prince Albert, Saskatchewan, but he had remarried, and she returned to Prince Edward Island. She gained her teacher's licence, and began to teach, at the same time sending out various stories and poems. In 1895 she enrolled at Dalhousie College in Halifax to study literature, but in 1896 went back to Cavendish, Prince Edward Island, to take care of her now-widowed grandmother, and to concentrate on writing. In 1904 her notebook entry, 'Elderly couple apply to orphan asylum for a boy. By mistake a girl is sent them', gave rise to what would become her most famous novel, ▷*Anne of Green Gables*, which she wrote and rewrote before it finally appeared in

1908, after rejection by several publishers. Thereafter followed incredible success, and much pressure on Montgomery to produce sequels, which, in rapid succession, she did. After her grandmother died (1911), she married Ewan Macdonald, a Presbyterian minister, and went with him to live in rural Ontario. Despite marriage and children, she managed to continue her writing, producing a book every other year (more than twenty novels and a large number of short stories), until three years before her death. In 1925 the family moved to Norval, near Toronto, then in 1935, after Macdonald's retirement, to Toronto, where Montgomery died.

   Considered primarily a writer of stories for adolescent girls, the tremendous and continuing attraction of Montgomery's heroines is not to be discounted. Not only the 'Anne' books, but *Emily of New Moon* (1923), *Emily Climbs* (1925), *The Blue Castle* (1926) and *Emily's Quest* (1927), have had a profound effect on eager young readers. Montgomery's heroines are frequently motherless, but adventurous, imaginative, and determined, with a bright intensity that has made them as resilient to time as Alice in Lewis Carroll's *Alice's Adventures in Wonderland* (1865) or Mark Twain's *Huckleberry Finn* (1884). Although her work has, in the past, been dismissed by critics for its reliance on sentiment, new evaluations are doing greater justice to her ability to evoke the ambivalence of adolescence. Her books have been widely translated, and her work and her life continue to be a source of interest. Her letters to fellow aspiring writers and penfriend Ephraim Weber were published in 1960, and those to G.B. MacMillan in 1980. The two-volume *The Selected Journals of Lucy Maud Montgomery* appeared in 1985 and 1988.
Bib: Gillen, M., *The Wheel of Things: A Biography of L.M. Montgomery*; Ridley, H.M., *The Story of L.M. Montgomery*; Sorfleet, J.R. (ed.), *L.M. Montgomery: an Assessment*; Urquhart, J., 'Afterword' to *Emily Climbs* (1925); Waterston, E., in *The Clear Spirit: Twenty Canadian Women and Their Times.*

Montifœud, Marc de ▷Chartroule, Marie-Amélie

Montolieu, Pauline (1751–1832)

French-speaking Swiss novelist and translator. Born in Lausanne, she began her literary career in 1786 by writing the novel *Caroline de Lichtfield*. The author of a vast number of translations of German and English literary works, and of novels of the same type, she is best-known for her translation into French of Johann David Wyss's *The Swiss Family Robinson* (1813), to which she wrote a sequel in 1824.

Montoriol i Puig, Carme (1893–1966)

A Catalan dramatist, novelist and poet, Montoriol lived in Barcelona most of her life. Her works concentrate on the problems of family relationships. Her main works are two plays,

L'abisme (1933) (*The Abyss*) and *L'huracà* (1935) (*The Hurricane*), and a novel, *Teresa o la vida amorosa d'una dona* (1932) (*Teresa, or the Love Life of a Woman*). An active feminist during the Second Republic, Montoriol did not write after the Spanish Civil War (1936–9), partly because the Franco regime prohibited the use of Catalan.

▷Catalan women's writing

Montpensier, Anne-Marie-Louise d'Orléans, Duchesse de (1627–1693)

French novelist and author of personal memoirs. The daughter of Gaston d'Orléans (1608–1660), younger brother of Louis XIII (1601–1643), she became known as the *Grande Mademoiselle*, partly for her height, and partly for the difficulties she had in finding a suitable husband. She was the wealthiest woman in all France, and entertained hopes of an excellent marriage with a succession of princes, including Louis XIV (1638–1715) and even the Holy Roman Emperor, but was disappointed on every occasion. Her lover, the notorious Duc de Lauzun (1632–1723), imprisoned on the eve of their first wedding ceremony, may have eventually married her in secret late in life, when she had already lost all her illusions about him. They quickly separated. For her ambitious projects to make herself Queen of France and other countries, and for ordering a volley of cannon to be fired on the king's troops from the Bastille during the civil war known as the *Frondes* (1648–1653), Mademoiselle de Montpensier spent much of her life in exile at the Château de Saint-Fargeau. It was there that, gathering a coterie of men and women of letters around her in imitation of the salon of the Marquise de Rambouillet (1588–1665), she turned to writing. Her early correspondence with ▷Madame de Motteville presents a pastoral Utopia – rather like the Forez of the pastoral novel *L'Astrée* (*Astrea*) by Honoré d'Urfé (1567–1625) – which she wished to re-create in Saint-Fargeau and the literature associated with it.

In 1653 she completed *La Vie de Mme de Fouquerolles* (*The Life of Mme de Fouquerolles*). *La Galerie des portraits de Mlle de Montpensier* (*The Portrait Gallery of Mlle de Montpensier*) to which ▷Madame de Lafayette and Madame de Villedieu (▷Marie-Catherine Hortense Desjardins) contributed, included the princess's own portrait of her cousin, Louis XIV. It was published in great secret in 1659 in a very high-standard volume by her secretary, Jean Regnauld de Segrais (1624–1701), and the Abbé Huet (1630–1671) in Caen for the exclusive readership of the court at Saint-Fargeau. The same year Mademoiselle de Montpensier, an avid reader of the novels of Gomberville (1600–1674) and the Scudérys (▷Madeleine de Scudéry) as well as *L'Astrée*, published a highly imaginative romance entitled *L'Histoire de la princesse de Paphlagonie* (*The Story of the Princess of Paphlagonia*), without revealing her identity. In both these works, the influence and interventions of her secretary, Segrais, are clearly discernible. The poor spelling

and syntax in her *Mémoires*, which she had begun in 1652 during her first period of exile but never sought to publish, are indicative of her uncultured early life and the fact that she probably did not show this very private work to Segrais. She did, however, order a member of her household to correct her manuscript, recognizing the illegibility of her own hand. Written in three phases covering '*tout ce qu'[elle] a vu et même ce qui [lui] est arrivé*' ('everything which she saw and indeed which happened to her'), her 2,000-page account is the most extensive set of memoirs to be written in the 17th century. The record of her private and public affairs begins in the early 1630s, and breaks off with a conversation with the king in the grounds of Versailles in the 1680s. The first phase has an oral tone, suggesting that the memoirs were written to be read aloud in response to the demand of the princess's ladies-in-waiting. The second stage, begun after a succession of domestic quarrels, is much more personal. The princess writes: '*Je ne m'amuse à ces mémoires que pour moi. Ils ne seront peut-être jamais vus de personne, au moins de mon vivant.*' ('I am only writing these memoirs for my own amusement. They will perhaps never be seen by anyone else, at least not during my lifetime'). In fact, she increasingly addressed her remarks to posterity. It may be said in conclusion that Mademoiselle de Montpensier's *Mémoires* offer a merciless observation of the court of Versailles, with little respect for chronological order, as was the custom with this kind of literary souvenir. Towards the end of her life, she wrote various religious meditations.

▷*Mémoires*
Bib: Garapon, J., *La Grande Mademoiselle mémorialiste: une autobiographie dans le temps.*

Montrelay, Michèle

French psychoanalyst, living in Paris. Author of *L'Ombre et le Nom* (1977) (*The Shadow and the Name*), a collection of essays on 'femininity'. The text identifies two distinct stages in the development of the little girl's 'femininity': the first, associated with the metaphor of the 'shadow' (*l'ombre*), acknowledges a primary female identity based on the girl's realization that she has a vagina. The second stage coincides with the girl's entry into the Lacanian ▷Symbolic Order (outlined by psychoanalyst Jacques Lacan, 1901–1981), and is linked to the metaphorical 'Name' or 'No' (*le nom*), suggested by the Lacanian Law of the Father.

▷Psychoanalysis

Montvid, Aleksandra Stanislavovna (born 1845)

Russian fiction writer. In the 1880s and 1890s under the name Shabel'skaia, Montvid published a number of stories united under the rubric 'Pencil Sketches'. The best of them form ethnographically apt, sympathetic cycles about life in the Ukrainian countryside, in which the meticulously depicted villages and estates themselves become players in the plot. In

'Paraska' social pressure drives the tragic conflict between a strong patriarch and his equally determined daughter-in-law. The merchant who buys an estate allows the dispossessed gentry mother and daughter to live in a rundown tavern nearby ('Naked Lady'); the stench of past debauchery which hangs over a summer pavilion on the estate ('Nagornoe') seems to lead inevitably to a rape. In 'The Legend,' set in a provincial city, a Russian girl's friendship with a family of poor Jews teaches her hard lessons about anti-semitism. Scattered works by Montvid appeared in the 1900s under a variety of ▷pseudonyms, but her later fate is unknown.

Monument of Matrones, The (1582)
Anthology of devotional writings compiled for women by Thomas Bentley. Although the work consists primarily of writings by men and the 'words' and songs of biblical women, it is important as an early anthology containing a relatively large number of writings by women. In addition to work by the queens ▷Elizabeth Tudor, ▷Catherine Parr, and ▷Jane Grey, Bentley also anthologized the works of Elizabeth Tyrwhit (*Morning and Evening Praiers, with diverse Psalmes, Hymnes and Meditations*), Frances Aburgavennie (▷*Prayers made by the Right Honorable Lady Frances Abergavennie*), ▷Anne Askew, Mistress Bradford (▷'Praier that Maister Bradfords Mother Said'), and ▷Dorcas Martin.
▷Prayers; Protestant Reformation; Translation

Moodie, Susanna (1803–1885)
The youngest of the literary Strickland sisters, born in Suffolk, England, Susanna Moodie lived near Southwold until her emigration to Canada in 1832. Her sisters, Agnes and Elizabeth, wrote *Lives of the Queens of England* and other biographies; her other sister, ▷Catherine Parr Traill, wrote many natural history books. Moodie published early, contributing her stories, poems and sketches to various annuals. Suzanna and Agnes, collaborated on a poetry volume called *Patriotic Songs* (1830), and Susanna published her own *Enthusiasm; and Other Poems* in 1831, the same year she married John Wedderburn Dunbar Moodie. A year later the couple emigrated to Upper Canada (Ontario). In *Flora Lyndsay; or, Passages in an Eventful Life* (1854) Moodie offers a fictionalized version of the arduous journey, concluding with the trip up the St Lawrence River. Her best-known works are ▷*Roughing it in the Bush; or, Life in Canada* (1852) and *Life in the Clearings Versus the Bush* (1853), considered autobiographical but written using strong elements of fiction. Susanna Moodie as writer is effectively able to distance herself from Susanna Moodie as narrator. Both books detail the harshness of trying to wrest a living out of the uncleared wilderness. In essence, the Moodies were ill-equipped to deal with the demands of pioneer life, failed at farming, and moved to the town of Belleville in 1840, where Dunbar Moodie was appointed sheriff.

Despite her isolation, Suzanna Moodie did not curtail her literary aspirations. She wrote serialized fiction for *The Literary Garland*, which was published in Montreal. In 1847 to 1848, the Moodies together edited *The Victoria Magazine* in Belleville. Susanna also wrote a number of sentimental novels, much less interesting than her Canadian material: *Mark Hurdlestone; or, the Gold Worshipper* (1853), *Matrimonial Speculations* (1854), *Geoffrey Moncton; or, the Faithless Guardian* (1855) and *The World Before Them* (1868). Although Moodie has been the recipient of much critical vitriol for her desire to warn potential settlers of what awaited them in Canada, her story is remarkable for its courageous endurance in the face of hardship. After her husband's death in 1869 she lived mostly with her family in Toronto.
▷*Journals of Susanna Moodie, The*
Bib: Dahl, E.H., '*Mid Forests Wild': A Study of the Concept of Wilderness in the Writings of Susanna Moodie, J.W.D. Moodie, Catherine Parr Traill and Samuel Strickland*; Fowler, M., *The Embroidered Tent: Five Gentlewomen in early Canada*; Morris, A., *The Gentle Pioneers: Five Nineteenth-Century Canadians*; Murray, H., in ▷*A Mazing Space*; Shields, C., *Voice and Vision*; ▷Thomas, Clara, in *The Clear Spirit*.

Moody, Ann ▷ Coming of Age in Missisipi

Moore, Jane Elizabeth (1738–?)
English poet and memoirist of fairly low social status, born of French parents in London. She married in 1761, and was arrested for her husband's debts when he died twenty years later. She wrote poems and *Genuine Memoirs* (1786). She went to Dublin, where *Miscellaneous Poems on Various Subjects* (1796) was published.

Moore, Julia A. (1847–1920)
US poet. Moore is remarkable because she typifies the qualities of sentimentality, pathos and poetic ineptness often charged against most US women poets, especially popular poets. Associated with the state of Michigan, both by her residence and by the title of her first collection, *The Sweet Singer of Michigan Salutes the Public* (1876), Moore became known as 'the sweet singer of Michigan'. She was well-known in her time because Samuel Clemens ('Mark Twain', 1835–1910) and other US writers made fun of her verse, and so publicized it. *The Sweet Singer* was republished as *The Sentimental Song Book; A Few Words to the Public* (1878) is a second poetry collection.

Moore, Marianne (1887–1972)
US poet, translator, dramatist and critic. Born in Missouri, Moore was raised in Pennsylvania. Her mother supported the family after Moore's father was institutionalized for mental illness. In 1909 Moore graduated with a degree in biology and histology from Bryn Mawr College, where she had already come into contact with ▷modernist art. She lived with her mother in New York until her mother's death in 1947, and was in contact with

poets such as William Carlos Williams. After working as a librarian Moore became editor of *The Dial* magazine in 1925, and this position gave her a significant role over the next few years in publishing the work of writers such as Paul Valery, T.S. Eliot, Hart Crane, Ezra Pound and Ortega y Gasset.

Moore's own work was first published in the *Egoist*, an important British forum for modernist poetry. *Poems* (1921) was also first published in Britain, followed in 1924 by ▷*Observations*, her first US collection. *Collected Poems* (1951) won the Pulitzer Prize and the National Book Award in 1952 and the Bollingen Prize in 1953. In 1968 Moore threw out the first ball for opening day at the Yankee Stadium, testifying to her status as a North American poet. One of the best metaphors for her work comes from baseball; she said that she would have liked to have invented the 'eight-shaped stitch with which the outer leather is drawn tight on a baseball'.

Although Moore is widely recognized as one of the most innovative of modern poets, this has been somewhat to her disadvantage. To characterize her work in terms of its experimentation with syllabic metrics and stanzaic form, or its modernist precision and economy, does not do justice to the range of her concerns. She is best-known for poems which use animals, from the common or garden snail in 'To a Snail' to the exotica of 'The Jeboa', 'The Pangolin' and the extinct birds of 'He "Digesteth Hard Yron"', in order to explore questions of aesthetics and the power of the creative imagination. However, Moore's concerns also encompass the nature of North American values, such as democracy and liberty, in poems like 'Viriginia Britannica', 'Rigorists' and 'Granite and Steel', and the problems of marriage for women in her long poem of that title.

In addition to her own poetry Moore has also published a translation of *The Fables of La Fontaine* and *The Absentee: A Comedy in Four Acts* which is a dramatic version of ▷Maria Edgworth's 1812 novel. Her critical essays on writers such as ▷Louise Bogan and Ezra Pound, are collected in *Predilections* (1955).

Other works include: *Selected Poems* (1935), *The Pangolin and Other Verse* (1936), *What Are Years?* (1941), *Nevertheless* (1944), *A Face* (1949), *Like a Bulwark* (1956), *O to Be a Dragon* (1959), *Idiosyncrasy and Technique* (1959), *A Marianne Moore Reader* (1961), *Poetry and Criticism* (1965), *Tell Me, Tell Me* (1966) and *The Complete Poems of Marianne Moore* (1967) and *The Accented Syllable* (1969).

Bib. Costello, Bonnie, *Marianne Moore: Imaginary Possessions*; Phillips, Elizabeth, *Marianne Moore*.

Moorhead, Sarah Parsons (fl 1741–1742)
North American poet. A resident of Boston during the Great Awakening, she offered through her poetry, such as ▷*To the Rev. James Davenport* and ▷'Lines . . . Dedicated to the Rev. Mr Gilbert Tennent', a balanced voice in the midst of rapturous evangelicalism. Cautioning against excessive zeal, she also admonished those who disparaged the movement. Although a devout Puritan, she was not afraid to address in her poetry these leaders of the movement and advise them on what she deemed the proper conduct of a New Light minister.

Moosdorf, Johanna (born 1911)
German poet and novelist. She was born in Leipzig, and in 1932 married the writer Paul Bernstein, who died in Auschwitz in 1944. Her early poetry, *Brennendes Leben* (1947) (*Burning Life*) won her several prizes, but in post-war East Germany she was not considered a reliable socialist writer, and in 1950 she moved to West Berlin. Her works explore the issues of fascism, past and present, and the situation of women in an aggressive male world. Her novels include: *Flucht nach Afrika* (1952) (*Escape to Africa*); *Die Nachtigallen schlagen im Schnee* (1953) (*Nightingales Sing in the Snow*); *Nebenan* (1961) (*Next Door*); *Die Andermanns* (1969) (*Other Folk*); and *Die Freundinnen* (1977) (*The Woman Friends*)

Moraga, Cherrié (born 1952)
US poet, essayist, dramatist and editor. Moraga writes as a lesbian and a ▷Latina conscious of class differences. Born in Whittier, California, she grew up listening to women telling stories. In 1980 she earned a Master's degree at San Francisco State University. ▷*This Bridge Called My Back* (1981), which she edited with Gloria Anzaldua, emphasizes the common experiences of women of color.

With *Cuentos* (1983) she helped found a Latina literary tradition. Her poetry examines how the female body is colonized, and attempts to reclaim it. *Giving Up the Ghost* (1986) stresses women's desire for independence in their sexuality. In her essays Moraga argues that her lesbianism is not a betrayal of her race. In *Loving in the War Years*) she equates loving other women with reclaiming her mother's race. She co-founded ▷Kitchen Table: Women of Color Press.

Morandini, Giuliana (born 1941)
Italian critic and novelist. Author of an informative study on 19th- and early 20th-century women writers (*La voce che è in lei*, 1980, *The Voice Within Her*), as well as a study on the conditions of women in mental hospitals (*E allora mi hanno rinchiusa*, 1977, *Then They Locked Me Up*). Her own creative writing centres on women's dilemmas. Yet, despite the problems encountered by her characters, they face the future with a degree of optimism.

Her other works include: *I cristalli di Vienna* (1978) (*Viennese Glass*); *Caffè specchi* (1983) (*Café Mirrors*); *Angelo a Berlino* (1987) (*An Angel in Berlin*); *Da te lontano* (1989) (*Far from You*).

Morante, Elsa (1912–1985)
Italian novelist. Morante began to write at the age of thirteen. She lived in Rome for most of her life,

and was very involved in the Roman literary scene. Yet she was equally a very private person who did not, on the whole, give interviews about her work, despite her prominent place in Italian literature. She published her first short stories in the 1930s. In 1941 she married Alberto Moravia, one of the few Italian writers as famous abroad as in Italy. The marriage ended in 1962, but the couple never divorced, partly, it seems, because of Morante's intense Catholicism. Her writing blends ▷fantasy and ▷realism in the semi-mythical worlds she creates. From her earliest collection of stories, *Il gioco segreto* (1941) (*The Secret Game*) onwards, her work has been located in the tradition of *realismo magico* (▷magic realism). Her first novel, *Menzogna e sortilegio* (1948) (▷*House of Liars*), was acclaimed by both critics and public, and it won the Viareggio Prize for that year. It is, in essence, a long novel about the nature of reality and fantasy and the recuperation of the past. Her second novel, *L'isola di Arturo* (1957) (▷*Arturo's Island*), deals with similar themes presented through the character of Arturo as he comes to grips with his childhood, adolescence and familial relationships. *Lo scialle andaluso* (1963) (*The Andalusian Shawl*) is another collection of short stories which, once again, mingle fantasy and reality. In 1968 Morante published ▷*Il mondo salvato dai ragazzini* (*The World Saved by Little Children*), a collection of poetry which won more literary awards. It is a fantastical work, enriched by literary allusions, and informed openly by Morante's personal beliefs. Her novel *La storia* (▷*History: A Novel*) of 1974 investigates, through the character Useppe, the relationship between received history and reality. ▷*Aracoeli* of 1982 again deals with recovery of the past, and the forging of personal identity. Morante's work is not, on the whole, positive in its view of life. She creates a magical universe paradoxically filled with harsh reality.

Other works: *Le bellissime avventure di Caterì dalla trecciolina* (1941) (*The Wonderful Adventures of Kate*); *Alibi* (1958); *Pro e contro la bomba atomica* (1987) (*For and Against the Atom Bomb*); *Opere* (1988) (*Collected Works*).
Bib: Caesar, M., 'Elsa Morante', *Writers and Society in Contemporary Italy*.

Mordecai, Pamela (born 1942)
Caribbean poet, editor, children's writer, broadcaster and educator. Born in ▷Jamaica and educated there and in the USA, she attended the University of the West Indies, has taught English at school level, and worked as a radio, television and film interviewer and presenter. Her particular interests are in the development of curriculum materials in language arts for the Caribbean. She currently works as publications officer for the School of Education at the University of the West Indies. Her poems have been published in ▷*BIM*, *Savacou*, *Jamaica Journal*, *Arts Review*, *Caribbean Quarterly*, and in the anthologies *The Caribbean Poem* (1976) and *Ambakaila* (1976). She is the editor of the *Caribbean Quarterly*, and co-editor

and contributor to a collection of women poets ▷*Jamaica Woman*. Women's issues are a strong feature of her poetry.

More, Hannah (1745–1833)
English writer in many genres, including plays, poetry, commentary, pious essays and education. She was taught at a school run by her sisters in Bristol, and learned Latin. She wrote the play *The Search after Happiness* (1773) at the age of fifteen; a tragedy, *The Inflexible Captive* (1774), was performed at Bath. She was assured of a living by her former fiancé, who paid her an annuity after breaking his engagement with her. In 1773 she went to London with an introduction to actor and dramatist David Garrick (1717–1779), with whom she became a great favourite. She also met ▷Elizabeth Montagu and Samuel Johnson (1709–1784), and began a career which was to make her wealthy. After Garrick died in 1779 her theatrical career drew to a close, and she began to regret her engagement with the stage. She went on to have an equally successful career campaigning against social inequality – against the slave trade, attacking the aristocracy (in *Thoughts on the Importance of the Manners of the Great to General Society*, 1788). *Strictures on the Modern System of Female Education* (1799) and *Hints* (1805) were both conservative and progressive writing on women's education. In *Strictures* she wrote, 'An early habitual restraint is peculiarly important to the future character and happiness of women. A judicious, unrelaxing but steady and gentle curb on their tempers and passions can alone ensure their peace and establish their principles . . . They should very young be enured to contradiction.' Her commercially successful *Cheap Repository Tracts* (1795–1798) aimed to help the poor to read. She attempted to be a patron to ▷Ann Yearsley, and was a friend of portrait painter Joshua Reynolds (1723–1792), Elizabeth Montagu, ▷Hester Chapone, and ▷Elizabeth Carter. She also knew the Burneys (▷Fanny Burney).

Other publications: *Village Politics* (1792); *Works* (1801).
▷Bluestocking

More, Mary (died 1713/5)
English polemicist who wrote *The Womans Right or Her Power in a Greater Equality to Her Husband proved than is allowed or practised in England*.
Bib: Ezell, Margaret, *The Patriarch's Wife*.

Morel, Madame de ▷Loynes, Antoinette and Camille de

Morency, Barbe-Suzanne-Aimable Giroux de (Madame Bertrand Quinquet) (1770–?)
French novelist. There are no records of her life, except for a few autobiographical elements in her first published novel, *Illyrine, ou l'écueil de l'inexpérience* (1799–1800) (*Illyrine, or The Danger of Inexperience*), which chronicles the life of a courtesan during the Terror. This appears to be the first novel written by a woman in the tradition

of first-person erotic narratives published by men earlier in the century. It differs from these in that the heroine neither renounces her independent life in favour of marriage, nor retreats to a convent but, instead, decides to write her memoirs. The tension surrounding the notion of women as writers is reflected in the fact that Morency's writing scandalized her contemporaries more than her reputation as the '*courtisane du Directoire*'. Her later novels include *Lise, ou les hermites du Mont-Blanc* (1801) (*Lise, or the Hermits of Mont-Blanc*), *Rosellina, ou les méprises de l'amour et de la nature* (1801) (*Rosellina, or Misapprehensions of Love and Nature*), *Euphémie, ou les suites du siège de Lyon* (1802) (*Euphémie, or the Consequences of the Siège of Lyon*), *Orphana ou les enfants du hameau* (*Orphana, or the Children of the Hamlet*) and *Zephira et Figdella, ou les débutantes dans le monde* (1806) (*Zephira and Figdella, or Beginners in Society*). Modern editions of her work include: *Illyrine, ou l'écueil de l'inexpérience*, with a preface by C. Brécout-Villars (1983).
Bib: Monselet, C., *Les Oubliées et les dédaignées*.

Moreno, Virginia R. (born 1925)

Filipino poet and dramatist, While at the University of the Philippines, she was known as the 'literary dictator' of the prestigious UP Writers' club and was to become the first director of the University's Film Center. Familiar with the Western aesthetic tradition (her own work being influenced by the French symbolists) and ▷avant-garde literary trends, her impeccably crafted poems and plays are nevertheless steeped in Philippine history and culture.

She has published one volume of poems, *The Batik maker and Other Poems*. Of her poetic dramas, the best-known is *Itim Asu* (*The Onyx Wolf*), first staged in 1972 and later made into a full-length ballet. For this she won not only an award from the Cultural Center of the Philippines, but also the SEATO (South-East Asian Treaty Organization) literary prize. Under the title *La Louve Noire* it has been listed as the sole Philippine entry in *Avant-garde Staging Around the World*, published in Paris.

Morgan, Lady ▷Owenson, Sydney

Morgan, Sally (born 1951)

Australian Aboriginal writer and artist. Morgan married in 1972 and has three children. Her first work, *My Place* (1987), is an attempt to reconstruct the past of her family, particularly of the Aboriginal women in her family who were exploited by white men. She has also published *Wanamurraganya* (1989), the biography of her uncle. Both books have been bestsellers and have done much to promote an understanding of Aboriginal history among the white community.
▷Aboriginal women writers in Australia

Morgner, Irmtraud (1933–1990)

East German novelist. The daughter of a train driver, she was one of the beneficiaries of the socialist government's policy of sending workers' children to university. She studied German in Leipzig, and then worked as an assistant editor of a literary journal. Her early fiction was conceived within the limitations of ▷socialist realism, but she attracted attention outside her own country with *Hochzeit in Konstantinopel* (1968) (*Wedding in Constantinople*) and *Die wundersamen Reisen Gustav des Weltfahrers* (1972) (*The Marvellous Travels of Gustav the Globetrotter*). In a strikingly individual manner, she explores the dilemmas of modern life using fantasy and experimental narrative structures, with exceptional linguistic virtuosity. Her greatest achievement is the Salman trilogy. The first volume, ▷*Leben und Abenteuer der Trobadora Beatriz nach Zeugnissen ihrer Spielfrau Laura* (*Life and Adventures of the Troubadour Beatrice According to her Minstrel Laura*), appeared in 1974; the second volume, *Amanda: Ein Hexenroman* (*Amanda: A Witch's Novel*) was published in 1983. The third volume was never finished due to Morgner's untimely death. Through the story of Laura Salman, single mother, half-witch and train driver in modern-day East Berlin, Morgner sets out to reinterpret the whole of Western culture in modern feminist terms. One of the most energetically imaginative writers in Germany this century, her reputation has yet to be consolidated internationally.

Mori Mari (1903–1987)

Japanese novelist and essayist. She was born in Tokyo, the daughter of the novelist Mori Ogai. When her essay collection *My Father's Hat* won the Japanese Essayist Club Prize in 1957, she took up her career as a novelist. *The Forest for Lovers*, which describes homosexual love, won the Tamura Toshiko Prize in 1961. *The Room Filled With Sweet Honey* also won the Izumi Kyouka Prize in 1975. Her unique romanticism and sense of the erotic characterize this work. Her single life and her aesthetic judgement have fuelled many anecdotes about her.

Morisaki Kazue (born 1927)

Japanese documentary writer and novelist. She was born in Kumamoto prefecture where many miners lived, and spent her youth in Korea during the period of Japanese colonization. Her works are based on these experiences. Concerning miners, *Pitch* describes the life of women miners' based on oral history. *Prostitute* and *A Pale Afterglow at Sea* are sympathetic towards people who are subjected to discrimination.

Mórits, Iunna Petrovna (born 1937)

Russian poet. An original, talented poet who rewards repeated reading, Mórits has been publishing since 1954. The influence of ▷Marina Tsvetáeva is evident in her poetry. Mórits frequently combines almost grotesque realistic description with a fantastic symbolic imagery and realized metaphor. Repeated themes include mortality, loneliness, fate and childhood.
Bib: *Soviet Literature* 3 (1975); *Russian Literature*

Triquarterly 9 (1974); Feinstein, E. (trans.), *Three Russian Poets: Margarita Aliger, Yunna Moritz, Bella Akhmadulina*; Dobson, R. and Campbell, D. (trans.), *Seven Russian Poets*; Glad, J. and Weissbort, D. (eds), *Russian Poetry: the Modern Period*; Wilson, K. (ed.), *An Encyclopedia of Continental Women Writers*, Vol. 2; Kasack, W. (ed.), *Dictionary of Russian Literature Since 1917*.

Morning and Evening Praiers, with diverse Psalmes, Hymnes, and Meditations (1582)

Book of private devotions composed by Elizabeth Tyrwhit, sometime governess to the princess ▷Elizabeth Tudor. Her inclusion in Bentley's ▷*Monument of Matrones*, as well as George Ballard's quotation of the testimony given by an Elizabeth Tyrwhit during the investigation made into the possible poisoning of ▷Catherine Parr, suggest that Tyrwhit was probably associated with Parr's household. *Morning and Evening Praiers* is a conventional collection of ▷prayers for different occasions and times of day, contemplations and meditations, and hymns.

Bib: Beilin, E.V., *Redeeming Eve: Women Writers of the English Renaissance*; Ballard, G., *Memoirs of Several Ladies of Great Britain*.

Morrell, Lady Ottoline (1873–1938)

British literary patron and memoirist. Born in Tunbridge Wells to an army family, Ottoline Morrell became a well-known figure in artistic and intellectual circles. In 1913 she and her husband, the Liberal MP Philip Edward Morrell, bought Garsington Manor in Oxfordshire. Here Morrell entertained some of the leading writers, artists and thinkers of the early years of the 20th century.

Visitors to Garsington included ▷Virginia Woolf, D.H. Lawrence, Bertrand Russell, Aldous Huxley, Augustus John and T.S. Eliot. Ottoline Morrell's patronage is depicted in both Huxley's *Chrome Yellow* (1921) and Lawrence's *Women in Love* (1921), where she is parodied as Hermione Roddice. From 1924, Morrell lived in Bloomsbury, and her house in Gower Street is marked with a commemorative plaque. Her writings are collected in *Ottoline* (1963), ed. R. Gathorne-Hardy, and *Ottoline at Garstone: Memoirs 1915–18* (1974).

Morris, Margaret Hill (1737–1816)

North American diarist. A widow from Burlington, New Jersey, she maintained a record, the ▷*Private Journal of Margaret Morris* (1836), of the tumultuous events she witnessed in war-torn Burlington from December 1776 until the summer of 1778. Addressed to one of her sisters, the lively account details the landing of Hessian troops near her home and her attempts, as a Quaker, to maintain a neutral stance on the American Revolution.

▷Early North American Quaker women's writings

Morrison, Toni (born 1931)

Toni Morrison

US novelist. Morrison was born in Lorain, Ohio, to working-class parents. Her father held three jobs simultaneously for many years. She graduated from Howard University and took a Masters degree at Cornell University in 1955; she then married and had two sons. She is an editor for the publisher Random House and has also taught at universities. Morrison's novels focus on the African-American community, and are typically set in towns resembling her birthplace, a crossing point between North and South, 'neither plantation nor ghetto'. Her novels focus on the unique cultural inheritance of African-Americans through the complexities of ethical issues, memory, and inter-personal relationships, and searchingly explore the African-American family and codes of femininity. ▷*The Bluest Eye* (1970) and ▷*Sula* (1973) in different ways focus on the traumatic process of growing up an African-American woman. In *Song of Solomon* (1977) friendship and memory, and the recovery of family and community history through folklore are interwoven in the story of Milkman Dead. *Tar Baby* (1981) narrates the conflicting searches of Jadine and Son for identity and security and the tensions of desire. ▷*Beloved* (1987) uses Morrison's extraordinary and experimental language to explore the relation between history and memory, identity and empowerment, loss and healing.

Her most recent works are the novel *Jazz*

(1992) and *Playing in the Dark: Whiteness and the Literary Imagination* (1992).
Bib: Holloway, Karla F.C. and Demetrakopoulos, Stephanie A., *New Dimensions of Spirituality*; Samuels, Wilfrid and Hudson-Weems, Cleonora, *Toni Morrison*.

Mors tua **(1926)** ▷*Harvest, The*

Mort d'Oluwemi d'Ajumako (1973) (*The Death of Oluwemi*)
The second play by the French Antilles writer, ▷Maryse Condé, this shows Oluwemi, an aged father and traditional ruler, who shirks his responsibility by avoiding his own ritual death, and runs away with Sefira, a young woman. We soon learn that he and Ange, his Western-educated son, both love the same woman. A conflict between father and son becomes unavoidable when Ange joins the runaways in their hiding place. Ange not only informs his father of his discovery of the latter's scheme to avoid death, but also succeeds in replacing his father in Sefira's arms. With the shrewd intervention of a much-travelled stranger (a symbol of wisdom), Oluwemi finally decides to return to his kingdom to face certain death. The play is a transparent allegory of post-colonial Africa, characterized by a seemingly unavoidable generational and ideological struggle. The son 'wins' in the end, but only in the sense that older generations cannot help but make way (however painful an experience this proves to be) for the younger ones.

Mortem Margaritas Valesiae, Navorrum Reginae (1550)
Elegiac poem. In 1549 Anne, Jane, and Margaret Seymour, the three eldest and well-educated daughters of Anne Stanhope and Edward Seymour, composed 104 Latin couplets commemorating the death of ▷Marguerite de Navarre. The poem, which develops the image of Marguerite as bride of Christ, was translated into Greek, French and Italian. It was printed in French in 1551 under the title *Le Tombeau de Marguerite de Valois Royne de Navarre* (*The Fall of Marguerite de Valois, Queen of Navarre*).

Mortimer, Penelope (born 1918)
Welsh novelist. A freelance journalist bringing up young children, Mortimer published her first novel, *Johanna* (1947), shortly before her marriage to the writer John Mortimer. Subsequent novels generally assume a semi-humourous portrayal of domestic relationships, exploring in particular the traps and ties of married life. The central character of *The Pumpkin Eater* (1962) is a woman obsessed with pregnancy and child-rearing, and the novel explores the break-up of her fourth marriage. Her other writings include a travel book *With Love and Lizards* (with John Mortimer, 1957), *The Home* (1967), *Long Distance* (1974) and *About Time: An Aspect of Autobiography* (1979).

Morton, Sarah Wentworth Apthorp (1759–1846)
North American poet and essayist. Born into a wealthy family in Boston, Massachusetts, she received an extensive education, which is reflected in her neo-classical verse. Resisting her family's Loyalist proclivities during the American Revolution, she devoted herself to the Patriot cause. She remained an activist throughout her life, advocating the repeal of her state's restrictive theatre laws, arguing for abolition, espousing nationalistic political and literary perspectives, and supporting the emergence of young North American writers. Her poetry – ▷*Ouabi; or, The Virtues of Nature* (1790), ▷*Beacon Hill* (1797) and ▷*The Virtues of Society* (1799) – as well as her collection of essays, sketches and poetry, ▷*My Mind and its Thoughts* (1823), reflect these ideals, and her poetry was notably popular at the turn of the century.

Mort très Douce, Une (1966) ▷*Very Easy Death, A* (1966)

Moruedi ▷Surangkhanang, K.

Moschine (4th century BC)
An Athenian-born poet and the mother of the woman poet ▷Hedyle. Nothing survives of her work.

Moscow
One of the sources of the richness of Russian literature has been the existence of Moscow and ▷St Petersburg as two governmental and cultural capitals of very different physical profile and ideology. Moscow, located in the Russian heartland and centred around the medieval architecture and onion-domed churches of the Kremlin, was the capital of an ever-expanding Russia from the 14th to the 18th centuries when St Petersburg usurped its governmental role. In the 19th century, Moscow was pictured in literature as the locus of traditional, conservative Russian values. In a poem which begins 'We're contemporaries, Countess, Both daughters of Moscow', ▷Pávlova contrasts her quiet life there to ▷Rostopchiná's glittering cosmopolitan existence in St Petersburg and abroad. Moscow ▷'thick journals' fostered the talents of other mid-century writers (eg ▷Sof'ia Èngel'gárdt and ▷Evgeniia 'Tur'). ▷Marina Tsvetáeva was a Muscovite, while ▷Akhmátova's poetic image is firmly connected to St Petersburg. During the 1918–1920 Civil War the government returned to Moscow, and its image took on more ominous overtones with the increase of state repression.
▷*Double Life, A*: *Happiness*; Golden Age of Russian poetry, The; Our Crowd; Seifúllina, Lidiia.

'Most Heavenly Confession of the Christian Faith, A' (1592)
Deathbed ▷confession of faith made by English writer ▷Katherine Stubbes. When Stubbes began

dying from complications related to childbirth, she called her neighbours together to make public confession to them. Her three reasons for doing so were: to move others to conversion; to ensure that none could say she did not die a perfect Christian, and to continue her Christian duty to bear witness to her religious convictions. Her confession outlines her religious beliefs, which were staunchly Puritan and anti-Catholic. These include her disbelief in purgatory, her belief in justification by faith alone, predestination, and the two sacraments of baptism and communion – both of which are 'signs and not the things themselves'. In 1592 Stubbes's husband, Philip, published a record of her last words along with 'A Most Wonderful, Conflict betwixt Sathan and her Soule' in his memorial tribute, *A Christal Glas for Christian Women*. In the account of her soul's battle against Satan, she successfully resists his temptation of her toward despair because she is a sinner and unworthy to approach God. The work was extremely popular, undergoing twenty-two editions between 1592 and 1665.

▷Protestant Reformation

Moth and the Star, The (1937)

This is the third published collection of poetry by the Caribbean writer ▷Una Marson. It illustrates her growing awareness of ▷feminist issues and questions of racial identity in West Indian society. The poems 'Kinky Hair Blues' and 'Cinema Eyes' examine defined images of beauty. Her concern with the position of the single woman in society is illustrated in poems like 'Repose', 'The Heart's Strength' and 'Fulfillment', in which she asserts the positive values of self-reliance and platonic love. A number of poems in this collection illustrate the early use of ▷Nation Language and rhythm, and show Marson's search for a mode of expression which gives voice to her concerns and the challenges of post-war Jamaican society.

For a critical analysis see Selwyn Cudjoe's introductions to ▷*Caribbean Women Writers* and ▷*Out of the Kumbla*.

Mothballs (1986)

Novel by Iraqi journalist and novelist Aliya Mamduh. *Mothballs* is a remarkable contribution to the genre of the feminist novel in Arabic. The city is Baghdad, and the characters are mainly women: the grandmother, the mainstay of the household; the young aunt; the sick mother who goes home to her own people when it is clear that she will never recover from tuberculosis; and other women of the quarter. The subject is the women's world in the crowded city of Baghdad; their life is controlled by men, the breadwinners, who are physically absent from the day-to-day life of their women and children. Huda, the little girl who grows up in the course of the novel, will refuse to be kept in mothballs in a closed house, as happens to her aunt. She is active and curious, 'her clay mixed with devilish water'. Following her progress in the company of women, we explore their life, the housework and the cooking, the preparations for a wedding, the new rooms built and furnished for the bride, the visit to the public bath, the visits to the holy mosques, the funerals and the wakes, the visit to the holy city of Karbala, and finally, on her own with her little brother, a visit to the absent father at his post. He is the commandant of a prison, a suitable profession for the part he plays in the novel. The men figure almost as ogres in the imagination of the little girl, but the women are vindicated: the silent, frustrated aunt turns into a virago, and the frightening father turns to the bottle, falls into a depression but wakes up finally to throw the gate of the prison open, set the prisoners free and trample the picture of the Regent underfoot.

Mother, The (1922)

Translation into English of *La Madre* (1920). A novel by Italian writer ▷Grazia Deledda, it depicts, in detail, the conflict between a mother and her son, the former having dedicated her life to the latter. She has worked hard as a servant and made many sacrifices so that he may become a priest. He, however, is unhappy and sees his unhappiness reflected in the barren land around him. He falls in love, and thus begins the struggle between mother and son, as well as that between the two women, which seems to take place inside him. The son is finally victorious in one sense, in that he overtly conquers his earthly passion; however, he is vanquished in that he is still possessed by the woman he loves, and has lost his struggle with his mother. The mother is victorious in that she has beaten her son, but vanquished in that she dies as a result of the strain of the struggle. Deledda here, as so often, makes the point that in the struggle of life there are no real winners, simply degrees of loss. The narrative is reminiscent of a classical tragedy in tone.

Mother–daughter relationships (Caribbean)

A predominant theme in Caribbean writing, for examples of which see ▷Lorna Goodison (▷*I am Becoming My Mother*), ▷Jamaica Kincaid (▷*Annie John* and ▷*At the Bottom of the River*), and ▷Jean Rhys (▷*Wide Sargasso Sea*).

Motherlands: Black Women's Writing from Africa, the Caribbean and South Asia (1991)

An important collection of critical essays, edited by Susheila Nasta, and published by Woman's Press, which attempts to draw links between women's writing from Africa, the Caribbean and southern Asia. The fifteen contributors re-examine the mythology of motherhood already well-explored in feminist literary debate, and apply these ideas to the post-colonial situation. The themes of mothercountry, motherculture and mothertongue are examined from a variety of cultural perspectives as women writers from these areas attempt to subvert the colonial image of the 'mothercountry' and retrieve authentic voices through their own representation of culture and consciousness. The essays in the book are exemplary, and have wide reverberations in post-colonial women's writing. Authors discussed include ▷Jean Rhys, ▷Jamaica Kincaid, ▷Michelle Cliff, ▷Paule Marshall, ▷Lorna Goodison and ▷Olive Senior.

Mother (Mat') Mariia (Elizaveta Iur'evna Kuz'mina-Karavaeva) (1891–1945)

Russian poet. Mother Mariia was born into a gentry family in St Petersburg. Early on she showed a dual interest in literature and social activism. A member of the Social-Revolutionary Party before 1917, she also took part in such modernist literary groups as the 'Poets' Guild'. Her first two collections of poetry, *Scythian Crocks* (1912) and *Ruth* (1916) show her inclination toward mystical and theosophical themes.

In 1919 Kuz'mina-Karavaeva emigrated to France. Her religious interests were evident in her two-volume collection of saints' lives (1927) and her book on the Russian religious philosopher Vladimir Solov'ëv (1929). In the early 1930s she became a nun, taking the name 'Mariia'. She continued to write primarily religious poetry, while serving the Russian *émigré* community. Her active part in the French Resistance in World War II cost her her life. In 1947 a posthumous collection of her work was published. She has been the subject of two biographies, one published in France in 1980, and a fictionalized life published in the USSR in 1983 and 1988. Since the advent of ▷*glásnost*', articles on her poetry have also appeared in the USSR.

Bib: Terras, V. (ed.), *Handbook of Russian Literature*; Wilson, K., *An Encyclopedia of Continental Women Writers* 2.

Mothers and Daughters: A Tale of the Year 1830 (1831)

A novel by ▷Catherine Gore, belonging to the 'silver-fork' school of ▷fashionable fiction, like Gore's earlier work ▷*Women as They Are* (1830). The central characters are Lady Maria Willingham and her two daughters, Claudia and Eleanor. The action revolves around the women's schemes for attracting aristocratic or wealthy men, and goes into great detail about the fashions of the day and the social milieu of the wealthy and privileged.

Mothers of Maya Diip, The (1989)

Collection of fables and poems by the Indian feminist ▷Suniti Namjoshi.

Mothertongues

The idea of mothertongues in Caribbean women's writing relates to the notion of discovering an authentic mother language as opposed to a language acquired as a result of the influence of colonialism or other patriarchal forces. Many women writers are seeking to discover alternative and new voices which subvert or challenge the dominant discourse. See ▷Jamaica Kincaid's *In a Small Place* (1988).

▷*Motherlands*

Mots pour le dire, Les (1975) ▷*Words to Say It, The* (1983)

Motteville, Françoise Bertaut, Madame de (1615/1621–1689)

French memoir-writer. A confidante of Anne of Austria (1601–1666) and niece of the poet Jean Bertaut (1552–1611), she spoke Italian and Spanish at an early age, since her mother had been at the Spanish court with Anne of Austria before her marriage to Louis XIII (1601–1643). She was much liked by Queen Anne and received a pension at the age of seven. Out of favour with Cardinal de Richelieu (1585–1642), who was suspicious of their special relationship with the queen, the family spent eleven years in Normandy. Widowed in 1640, Madame de Motteville returned to court and was given the *brevet* of one of the queen's ladies-in-waiting, receiving a pension of 2,000 *livres*. Her *Mémoires pour servir à l'histoire d'Anne d'Autriche* (*Memoirs Serving as a History of Anne of Austria*) contain some of the most useful documentary evidence on Anne's regency. Madame de Motteville began taking notes for them in 1643 and, in the tradition of memoir-writers, insists: '*ce que j'ai mis sur le papier je l'ai vu et je l'ai ouï*' ('What I have put down on paper is what I have seen and heard'). She gives the following justification of her decision to write: '*J'ai donné à cette occupation les heures que les dames ont accoutumé d'employer au jeu et aux promenades; Je ne sais si j'ai mieux fait que les autres; mais il me semble qu'on ne sauroit plus mal employer son temps que de le passer à ne rien faire*' ('I have devoted to this occupation the hours which ladies usually give to gambling and promenades; I do not know where I have done better than them; but it seems to me that there is no worse way of spending time than to do nothing'). She also exchanged letters with ▷Mademoiselle de Montpensier concerning her project for a bucolic paradise on the banks of the Loire. Withdrawing to the Convent of the Visitation after nursing Anne of Austria through her final illnes, Madame de Motteville spent her last years writing treatises on religion and death, which seem to have exhausted her.

▷*Mémoires*

Bib: Hipp, M., *Mythes et réalités*.

Mountain Lion, The (1947)

US novel in which ▷Jean Stafford explores the tension between the inner and the external world. Molly Fawcett must choose either psychic or cultural integration. Unlike Stafford's other heroines, Molly decides not to sacrifice her inner self. However, she is unable to accept her sexuality, and withdraws into the world of her imagination. Her brother mistakes her for a lion and kills her. Stafford suggests that the self can only retain its psychic identity and innocence through death.

Mouré, Erin (born 1955)

Canadian poet, born in Calgary, Alberta. Mouré studied at the Universities of Calgary and British

Columbia. She lived and worked on the Canadian transcontinental passenger train (VIA Rail) at Vancouver from 1978. In 1984 she moved to Montreal to work in management. Her early poems, *Empire, York Street* (1979) and *The Whiskey Vigil* (1981) are concerned with work, friendship, and survival. In *Wanted Alive* (1983) Mouré begins to stretch her connection between language and the physical world; it includes a superb sequence of poems about the Supercontinental, the train as metaphor for the heart. With *Domestic Fuel* (1985), she began to collapse motion and desire, the violence of language; *Furious* (1988) won the Governor General's Award for Poetry, and Mouré enters, 'furiously', a feminist aesthetic of language. *WSW (West South West)* (1989) returns to a memory of body and rootedness. There is a physical immediacy and attentiveness to Mouré's writing that reflects the dissimilation of contemporary language. She has close connections with many women writers, especially ▷Gail Scott.

Mourning Dove (Hum-Ishu-Ma) (1888–1936)
US novelist. Born in Idaho, Mourning Dove was the first ▷Native American woman novelist. She was raised by her grandmother, who instilled in her the respect for the traditions of her Okanogan tribe. Mourning Dove attended the Sacred Heart Convent in Ward, Washington, for three years. In 1912 she enrolled in business school to improve her English and to learn to type, while working on ▷*Cogewea, the Half-Blood* (1927). In 1914 she met Lucullus V. McWhorter, an Indian rights advocate, who became her literary collaborator. He urged her to collect and preserve Okanogan folktales. A migrant worker, she travelled with her typewriter and wrote at night. To help finance the novel's publication Mourning Dove worked longer hours in the field. She was elected an honorary member of the Easter Washington State Historical Society. Mouning Dove's work made her culture's world view accessible to the dominant Anglo-American culture in the US.

Moutza-Martinengou, Elisavet (1801–1832)
Greek autobiographer, poet, dramatist and translator. Born in Zakinthos, the daughter of a wealthy nobleman, on an island still under Italian and British occupation, she spent a secluded childhood educating herself in her father's library. When still very young she asked for a tutor to teach her ancient Greek and Latin. She began writing plays and poems, as well as translating Homer's *Odyssey* and Aeschylus's *Prometheus* into modern Greek. An extract from these translations appeared in a local newspaper in 1947. She also wrote two treatises, one on economics and another on the art of poetry. All her work was unfortunately burnt in Zakinthos in a great fire after the earthquake in 1953. She was married against her own will and died during the birth of her first child. Her main work was her autobiography, a fascinating book containing details of her strict upbringing, and preserving an image of life in an aristocratic home of that period. But above all it is the true feminist voice of a woman reacting against family oppression and the stifling of creativity that went with it. She laments her life as a woman, describing how she even tried to escape to Italy, to a convent, where she felt would have been free to write and educate other women. Her autobiography is a sincere and revealing book, unique at a time when Greek women had no education at all. When it was published by her son in 1881 it made a great impression on Greek writers and intellectuals.

Moving Image, The (1946)
Australian poems by ▷Judith Wright. The Platonic epigraph to this volume, 'Time is a moving image of eternity', indicates that, although the poems deal with uniquely Australian experience, their true concern is metaphysical. The main theme of the volume is that of the poet's awareness of time, death, and evil on a universal scale (most of the poems were written in wartime). Two poems in particular, 'Bullocky' and 'South of my Days', celebrate Australia's pioneering past, and are justly famous, having been frequently anthologized and translated into many other languages. 'Bora Ring' and 'Nigger's Leap, New England' deal with the massacre and dispersal of the Aboriginal tribes, and many other poems, such as 'The Trains', take the threat of the war in the Pacific as their subject. Because of their lyrical beauty and technical excellence, these poems made a tremendous impact on publication, and, together with those of the next volume, ▷*Woman to Man*, they confirm Wright's place as Australia's leading woman poet.
▷Aborigine in non-Aboriginal Australian Women's writing, The

Mowatt, Anna Cora (1819–1870)
US dramatist, non-fiction writer, novelist and autobiographer. Coming to the stage with varied writing experience, Mowatt soared to prominence with her drama ▷*Fashion* (produced 1845), probably the best and most popular US comedy of manners of the 19th century. With her success as a dramatist, Mowatt began a career on the stage, one of the first established, middle-class US women to do so. She continued writing drama – *Armand, the Child of the People* (1847) – and autobiographical non-fiction: *Autobiography of an Actress* (1854), *Mimic Life* (1856) and *Twin Roses* (1857). Her descriptions of 19th-century life in the theatre remain a source for US dramatic history.

M'Rabet, Fadéla
Algerian novelist. Her real name is Abada. She taught in different schools in Algiers. Her radio programmes on women's problems attracted a large audience. She has been living in France for many years. Her novels, *La femme Algérienne* (1964) (*Algerian Woman*) and *Les Algériennes* (1967) (*The Algerians*), were strongly criticized for their openness. In them she breaks taboos and

denounces the condition of women in a repressive and conventional society.

Mugo, Micere Githae (born 1942)

Kenyan poet, dramatist and academic. Mugo was born in the Kirinyaga District of Kenya. She studied drama under ▷Rebeka Njau at the Alliance Girls' High School and afterwards at Makerere University, where she won the best actress award at the Uganda Drama Festival; she gained an MA from the University of New Brunswick, Canada, and a PhD from the University of Toronto. Her PhD dissertation was published as *Visions of Africa: The Fiction of Chinua Achebe, Margaret Laurence, Elspeth Huxley and Ngugi wa Thiong'o* (1978).

Mugo began writing while at an all-white school in Limuru (1961–2) and published poetry and a short story in the student literary magazine, *Penpoint*, while at Makerere. She has been influenced by the Ugandan poet Okot p'Bitek (born 1931) and encouraged by Nigerian novelist Chinua Achebe (born 1930). She is a Marxist, concerned with the fate of Africa since independence, and uses her writing as part of the revolutionary process. She was senior lecturer and Dean of the Faculty of Arts at the University of Nairobi, but like her close colleague, Ngugi wa Thiong'o, she has been exiled from her homeland since 1982 for political reasons. She is now teaching at the University of Zimbabwe.

Publications include a collection of poetry, *Daughter of My People, Sing!* (1976) and two plays, *The Long Illness of Ex-chief Kiti* (1976) and (jointly with Ngugi wa Thiong'o) ▷*The Trial of Dedan Kimathi* (1976), as well as her work of criticism, *Visions of Africa*.
Bib: See interviews with Nancy Owano in *African Woman 6* (1976); Brenda Berrian in *World Literature Written in English* 21 (1982); Adeola James in *In Their Own Voices*.

Mugot, Hazel (de Silva) (born 1947)

Kenyan novelist and poet. Mugot was born in Nairobi, of mixed Sri Lanka and Seychelles parentage, and was educated in Kenyan schools before studying liberal arts in the USA and social sciences in Britain. She taught at the University of Nairobi before moving to Mahe, Seychelles, where she writes, paints and works with batik and ceramics. In ▷*Black Night of Quiloa* she explores the theme of inter-cultural marriage (1971), and later works include *Makongo, the Hyena* and *Sega of the Seychelles* (1983), a poetic narrative written under the name de Silva, treating the complex roles of women in these islands.
Bib: Taiwo, Oladele, *Female Novelists of Modern Africa* ; Bruner, Charlotte H. (ed.), *Unwinding Threads, Writing by Women in Africa*.

Muhando, Penina (born 1948)

Tanzanian dramatist and academic. Muhando was educated at the University of Dar es Salaam. She writes in Kiswahili in order to communicate with a Tanzanian and East African audience. She is committed to writing plays that are directly concerned with social problems, and feels that as a woman writer she has a responsibility to highlight women's issues. Publications include: *Hatia* (Guilt); *Tambuene Haki Zetu* (*Recognize Our Rights*); *Heshima Yangu* (*My Respect*); *Pambo* (*Decoration*); *Talaka si mke wangu* (*Woman, I Divorce You*); *Nguzo-mama* (*Mother Pillar*); and *Harakati za Ukombozi* (*Liberation Struggles*), co-authored with Lihamba and Balisidya. She is at present professor and head of the Department of Theatre Arts at the University of Dar es Salaam.

Mühlbach, Luise (1814–1873)

German novelist. A wealthy and cultured society woman, she kept a salon in Berlin which was frequented by the aristocracy, and where ▷Fanny Lewald, among many others, came to be introduced to society. Mühlbach's own work, which comprises 290 volumes of travelogues and social and historical novels, was extremely popular at the time, not least because of the attraction of her stories about high-born characters. However, behind these extravagant narratives, Mühlbach touches upon the problems of women's emancipation, divorce and social oppression. One of her most interesting novels is the fictionalized 1849 biography of the English 17th-century dramatist, ▷Aphra Behn.
▷Salon culture (Germany and Austria)

Mukdam U'Meuchar (1970) (Early and Late)

A collection of poems by Israeli poet ▷Lea Goldberg. It contains poems from earlier books of verse, with the addition of some new poems. Although Goldberg's poems are strongly influenced by the symbolist poets, especially the Russians, they are constructed in traditional forms. This creates an effect of direct, simple and rhythmical expression. The collection covers a complex web of topics, from the intimate to the philosophical, which characterizes Goldberg's verse.

Mukherjee, Bharati (born 1938)

Indian novelist and short story writer. Born in Calcutta, India, Mukherjee moved to the US in 1961. In 1969 she earned a PhD at the University of Iowa and has subsequently received grants for her writing from the National Endowment for the Arts and the Guggenheim Foundation. She has taught creative writing at Columbia University and City University of New York and at the University of California at Berkley. In *The Tiger's Daughter* (1972) a Westernized Indian returns to India. Raised in a genteel Brahmin family, the heroine now sees poverty and hunger. In *Wife* (1975), the heroine violently vents her rage at oppressive cultural traditions, unable to reconcile the Bengali ideal of the passive wife with life in New York City. *The Middleman and Other Stories* (1988) won the National Book Critics Circle Award. In 'The Middleman' an Iraqi Jew learns to survive in a dog-eat-dog world. 'Jasmine' portrays an enterprising adolescent from Trinidad who is oblivious to her own exploitation. Mukherjee's fiction shows how immigrants are transformed by the idea of living in the US. *Darkness: Days and Nights in Calcutta* (1977), co-authored with her husband Clarke Blaise, contains stories based on her experiences while resident in Canada for a short period.

Other works include: *The Sorrow and the Terror* and *Jasmine* (1990).

Mukoda Kuniko (1929–1981)
Japanese essayist, born in Tokyo. She started her career as a scriptwriter for television while she was an editor of a film magazine. Her works depict everyday life with a humorous touch, and she is a forerunner in this field. *My Father's Letter of Apology* (1978) is a remarkable essay written after her father's death and her fight with cancer. *Memory of Cards* won the Naoki Prize in 1980. She was killed in an aeroplane accident during a trip to Taiwan.

Mulder de Draumer, Elisabeth (born 1904)
Spanish writer of prose and poetry. Mulder was born in Barcelona of a South American mother and a Dutch-born father. Her early works were collections of poetry, but she is mainly remembered for her fiction, which is nostalgic and sentimental, often telling the story of an impossible, romantic love, as in *Crepúsculo de una ninfa* (1942) (*Twilight of a Nymph*). Her best works are: *Preludio de la muerte* (1946) (*Prelude to Death*) and *Luna de las máscaras* (1958) (*Moon of the Masks*), which contrast with the social ▷realism common in the post-war period. Her work forms the *novela rosa* (sentimental romance) backdrop to ▷Martín Gaite's ▷*El cuarto de atrás*.

Mulford, Wendy (born 1941)
Welsh poet and critic. A lecturer on women's writing and feminist criticism, Mulford was also a member of the Communist Party of Great Britain, and is active in the women's peace movement. The concerns expressed in her poetry, with questions of subjectivity, language and particularly with the polysemic potential of language, are written within a distinct feminist agenda. *Bravo to Girls and Heroes* (1977) was followed by *Reactions to Sunsets* (1980) and *Late Spring Next Year* (1987). Mulford has co-authored *No Fee: A Line or Two for Free* (1978) with ▷Denise Riley.

Mulin Chi ▷Liu Nienling

Mulkerns, Val (born 1925)
Irish fiction writer. Born in Dublin, she worked as a civil servant for several years, and was assistant editor of one of Ireland's most influential literary magazines during the 1950s, *The Bell*. Her short story collections include: *Antiquities* (1978), *A Friend of Don Juan* (1979) and *An Idle Woman* (1980). Her novels are: *A Time Outworn* (1951), *A Peacock Cry* (1954), *The Summerhouse* (1984) and *Very Like a Whale* (1986).

Müller, Clara (1861–1905)
German poet. The daughter of a Protestant parson, she worked first as a teacher, and then in the editing rooms of left-wing journals. She was sympathetic to the workers' movement, and expressed her views in politically committed poems such as 'Fabrikausgang' (1899) ('Factory Exit') or 'Den Ausgesperrten' (1907) ('To Those Locked Out'). Her autobiographical novel, *Ich bekenne* (*I Confess*), appeared in 1904.

Mulock, Dinah ▷Craik, Dinah

Munro, Alice (born 1931)

Alice Munro

Canadian short story writer, born Alice Laidlaw in Wingham, Ontario. She attended the University of Western Ontario, then married and moved to British Columbia, where her children were born, and where she and her husband established a successful bookstore in Victoria. Her first story was published in 1951, but she did not publish a collection, *Dance of the Happy Shades*, until 1968. It won the Governor General's Award for Fiction. ▷*Lives of Girls and Women* (1971), a cycle of linked stories about a young girl who wants to become a writer, is frequently treated as a novel. It established Munro's reputation as a writer of extraordinary perceptiveness, especially with regard to the detailed failures and allegiances of women in a world where they are measured mostly in relation to men. *Something I've Been Meaning to Tell You* (1974) and ▷*Who Do You Think You Are?* (1978, published in the USA and UK as *Beggar Maid*) consolidated Munro's fictional virtuosity; her stories began to appear regularly in *The New Yorker*. Meanwhile, she had divorced and remarried, moving back to her familiar territory of southern Ontario. Subsequent books include *The Moons of Jupiter* (1982), *The Progress of Love* (1986) and *Friend of My Youth* (1990). She has been widely translated, has received the Governor General's Award for Fiction three times, and is veritably revered as a Canadian Chekhov. She can be positioned as a regional writer, articulating the Gothic sensibilities of her characters through a kind of photographic hyper-realism and paradoxical modification. Although she does not claim an explicitly feminist stance, her primarily female characters enact the powerful drama of women's understated lives. **Bib:** Dahlie, H., *Alice Munro and Her Works*; MacKendrick, L.K. (ed.), *Probable Fictions: Alice Munro's Narrative Acts;* Martin, W.R., *Alice Munro: Paradox and Parallel;* Miller, J. (ed.), *The Art of Alice Munro: Saying the Unsayable;* Rasporich, B.J., *Dance of the Sexes: Art and Gender in the Fiction of Alice Munro.*

Murat, Henriette-Julie de Castelnau, Comtesse de (1670–1716)

French author of memoirs, novels, *nouvelles* (short fiction) and fairytales. Born in Brest, in Brittany, she was orphaned at an early age and brought up by her grandmother. With her Breton costume, she became the '*coqueluche de la cour*' ('the darling of the court') when she arrived in Paris. However, her involvement in a slander of ▷Madame de Maintenon resulted in a period of exile at Loches from 1694 to 1715. She admits that boredom was a major factor in her decision to begin a sentimental chronicle of her existence at that time, which was published in 1697. The first part of these memoirs conveys her nostalgia for her lost childhood and her early passion for the romances of the day, reflected in all her writings. After an unhappy marriage, from which she tried unsuccessfully to escape, the work of Guez de Balzac (1597–1654) became a powerful influence on her education. Her memoirs show that she was fully conscious of her literary vocation: '*Je me trouvai même assez de dispositions pour apprendre les langues & à écrire avec un peu plus d'exactitude que la plupart des femmes*' ('I even found myself quite well disposed towards the learning of languages and to writing with a little more correctness than most women'). Letters are frequently inserted in these memoirs, which also include a narrative written by an unnamed '*Dame de Province*' romantically involved with the Marquis de Fleury. Her tales reject the popular tradition and remove love from the power of the fairies. Their most curious quality is the insistent emphasis on plant life. Her fairy kingdom is composed of trees, plants, flowers, perfumes and colours.
Bib: Hipp, M., *Mythes et réalités*; Wilwerth, E., *Visages de la littérature féminine.*

Murder of Roger Ackroyd, The (1926)

▷Detective novel by ▷Agatha Christie, featuring Christie's Belgian detective, Hercule Poirot. It has been described as a perfect example of the crime-puzzle, the detective story as conundrum. Its interest for historians of the detective genre and narrative theorists alike lies in its use of a criminally unreliable narrator.

Murdoch, Iris (born 1919)

Anglo-Irish philosopher and novelist. Born in Dublin, Murdoch grew up in London, and remained a frequent visitor to Ireland. She was educated at the Froebel Institute, London, and Somerville College, Oxford, where she read classics, ancient history and philosophy. After completing postgraduate work at Newnham College, Cambridge, Murdoch returned to Oxford at the end of World War II, and in 1948 became fellow of St Anne's College.

Murdoch was raised as a Protestant, but calls herself a 'Christian fellow traveller'. Her main philosophical writings include *The Sovereignty of Good* (1970), *The Fire and the Sun: Why Plato Banished the Artists* (1977) and *Sartre: Romantic Rationalist* (1953). Murdoch's novels engage strongly with philosophical preoccupations, being strewn with philosophical motifs and references, as in ▷*The Bell* (1954), which comically handles the ethical dilemma of giving up one's seat to someone else. Although Murdoch herself rejects the critical privileging of this influence, much of her early fiction is cast in terms of a general dialogue with Existentialist concerns, and her central characters are frequently placed in what is to them an absurd, incomprehensible world.

Her first novel, *Under the Net* (1954), has as its protagonist the Sartrean hero Jake Donague, and forms a critique of his concern with essences rather than materiality. Together with ▷*A Severed Head* (1961), which exploits Jungian theories of archetypes, it has been criticized for the weighting of its theoretical template over and above a concern with characterization and character fidelity. Yet Murdoch's chief concern seems to be the desire to tackle head-on everyday ethical or moral concerns, and to explore the function of myth in the process of making sense of one's life. This is reflected in novels such as *The Accidental Man* (1971), where Murdoch's formal concern with pattern and structure forms, at the same time, an exploration of its arbitrariness. *A Fairly Honourable Defeat* (1970) and *The Good Apprentice* (1985) play on Wittgenstein's theory of language games, while syntactical logic is a central concern of *The Flight from the Enchanter* (1956). Murdoch won the Booker Prize with *The Sea, the Sea* (1978). Other writings include: *The Time of the Angels* (1966), *Bruno's Dream* (1969), *The Servants and the Snow* (1970), *The Black Prince* (1973), *The Sacred and Profane Love Machine* (1974), *A Word Child* (1975), *Art and Eros* (1980) and *The Book and the Brotherhood* (1987).
▷Bowen, Elizabeth; Byatt, A.S.; Spark, Muriel
Bib: Begnal, K., *Iris Murdoch: A Reference Guide*; Byatt, A.S., *Iris Murdoch* and *Degrees of Freedom* (1965); Dipple, E., *Iris Murdoch: Work for the Spirit*; Hague, A., *Iris Murdoch's Comic Vision*; Ramanathan, S., *Iris Murdoch: Figures of Good*; Todd, R., *Iris Murdoch: The Shakespearian Interest.*

Murfree, Mary Noailles (1850–1922)

US ▷local color short-story writer and novelist. Murfree published under the pseudonym Charles

Egbert Craddock, and for some time concealed her true identity from her editors and readers. Her stories concern her native Tennessee and are exceptional for their accurate and effective use of dialect and their realistic depiction of mountain characters and folk customs. A prolific writer and frequent contributor to the national literary magazines – especially *Lippincott's* and ▷*The Atlantic Monthly* – Murfree also collected her stories in a number of volumes, including *In the Tennessee Mountains* (1884), *The Mystery of Witch-Face Mountain, and Other Stories* (1895) and *The Phantoms of the Foot-Bridge, and Other Stories* (1895). She also wrote historical novels, eg *Where the Battle Was Fought* (1884) and *The Story of Old Fort Loudon* (1899).
▷Kollontái, Aleksandra; *Happiness*

Murià i Romani, Anna (born 1904)
Born in Barcelona, Murià is a novelist, political activist and journalist. Exiled from Spain in 1939, she subsequently married Agustí Bartra, a celebrated Catalan poet. She finally returned to Catalonia in 1970. Her most ambitious novel is *Aquest serà el principi* (1985) (*This Will Be the Beginning*), spanning the declaration of the Republic (early 1930s), the exile years and the period of return to Catalonia. Her other works are: *Joana Mas* (1933); *La Peixera* (1938) (*The Fishbowl*), and *Res no és veritat, Alicia* (1984) (*Nothing is True, Alicia*).
▷Catalan women's writing

Muriel (?), nun of Wilton (late 11th century)
English poet. Wilton Abbey (Wiltshire), a Benedictine nunnery, was a wealthy Anglo-Saxon royal foundation of the 9th century. No works by Muriel are known to have survived, and it is not known in which language she wrote; but she is described in a 12th-century account as 'the famous poetess'.
Bib: Tatlock, J.S.P., 'Muriel: The Earliest English Poetess', *PMLA* (*Publications of the Modern Language Association of America*) 48 (1933), pp. 317–21.

Muriel at Metropolitan (1975)
▷South African writer Miriam Tlali's first novel, it was originally published by South Africa's Ravan Press in 1975, and then in a longer version by Longman in 1979. The book details the daily experiences of a young woman working for Metropolitan Radio in central Johannesburg, a business which sells furniture and household appliances, as well as radios, at iniquitous hire-purchase rates to black South Africans compelled by poverty to sign such contracts. Muriel's task is to join in the company's enterprise of squeezing as much money as possible out of her fellow black workers, and of repossessing furniture when the payments cannot be made. Written in the first person, and avowedly autobiographical, the book charts Muriel's growing unease at capitalist exploitation and racism, at the humiliation of African 'boys' old enough to be her father, and at

the sniggering responses of Metropolitan's white employers to customers' letters. Offered as a naïve account – 'I do not profess great knowledge. I am not a writer. But I do not have to be any of these to know about Africans' – the novel ends with Muriel writing her letter of resignation, in a handwriting whose certainty and strength she compares with the wavering hand of the resignation notes she had tried to write before: 'I would never again place myself in a position in which I had to ask for pass-books or be "loyal to the firm".'
The two different texts of this novel pose an interesting critical problem. Tlali's original manuscript was heavily edited for the Ravan edition, primarily by South African writer ▷Sheila Roberts; Longman restored the text to the longer version of its original form, keeping, for instance, some of Tlali's anti-Semitic references, although a number of stylistic changes were made.

Murphy, Dervla (born 1931)
Irish travel writer, born in County Waterford, where she still lives. Her first book, *Full Tilt* (1965), an account of her journey by bicycle from Dublin to India, was an Alternative Book Society Choice, and an immediate success. Her subsequent travel books include: *Tibetan Foothold* (1966), *The Waiting Land* (1967), about Nepal, *In Ethiopia With a Mule* (1968), *On a Shoestring to Coorg: an Experience of South India* (1976), *Where the Indus is Young: a Winter in Baltistan* (1977) and *Eight Feet in the Andes* (1983). Her autobiography, *Wheels within Wheels*, appeared in 1979. She has also written about Irish and international political issues: *A Place Apart*, about Northern Ireland, appeared in 1978, *Race to the Finish? The Nuclear Stakes* in 1982, and *Changing the Problem: Post-Forum Reflections* in 1984.

Murphy, Emily Gowan (1868–1933)
Canadian journalist, fictional autobiographer and activist. Born Emily Ferguson, in Cookstown, Ontario, Murphy was the first woman in the British Empire to be appointed a Magistrate. She married an Anglican minister, Arthur Murphy, in 1887, and travelled with him to England and Germany in 1898. Out of that experience she wrote *The Impressions of Janey Canuck Abroad* (1902), an irrepressible description of what she observed. After moving west to Edmonton, Alberta, in 1907, Murphy was actively involved, along with ▷Nellie McClung, in the women's suffrage movement, and in the passage of the Dower Act (1911), which ensured that wives had some title to their husband's property. Appointed a Magistrate in 1916, Murphy's authority was challenged on the grounds that women were not 'persons' and could not hold public office. In the 'Persons Case', with other women, she fought for that interpretation to be changed: in 1929 the British Privy Council ruled that women *were* 'persons.' Her other books include *Janey Canuck in the West* (1910), *Open Trails* (1912) and *Seeds of Pine* (1914), as well as *Black Candle* (1922), a

carefully researched book on the evils of narcotics. Although she is more famous as an activist than a writer, her enthusiasms and motivations to change the situation of women are a lasting legacy.
Bib: James, D., *Emily Murphy*; Mander, C., *Emily Murphy: Rebel*; MacEwan, G., *And Mighty Women Too: Stories of Notable Western Canadian Women;* Sanders, B.H., *Emily Murphy*.

Murray, Judith Sargent (1751–1820)
North American essayist, poet, dramatist and novelist. Born in Gloucester, Massachusetts, on 1 May 1751, she was North America's first major feminist. A prolific author, noted for her wit and intelligence, she advocated equality for women (modelled in her own egalitarian marriages, first to the sea captain John Stevens and, after Stevens's death, to the founder of the American Universalist Church, John Murray) and was ardent in her demands for women's education. She published under the pseudonyms 'Constantia' and 'Honoria' and occasionally under 'Judith Stevens'. In her seminal essay, ▷'On the Equality of the Sexes' (1790), she satirizes sexual stereotyping and appends a revisionist reading of Eve and the 'Fall'. Her breadth of interests and intellectual engagement are revealed in the three-volume collection of her magazine writings, ▷*The Gleaner* (1798), in which her nationalistic philosophy is brought to bear upon models of industriousness, the rise of North American drama and, most notably, a concern that the literary contributions of women authors such as ▷Mercy Otis Warren be recognized and preserved. She died in Natchez, Mississippi, on 6 July 1820, one of the few early North American women authors who gained national recognition during her lifetime.

Musa, Gilda (born 1926)
Italian poet, novelist and essayist. A student in both Milan and Germany. She has a wide knowledge of German literature and poetry, and has translated some German poetry into Italian, particularly that of the post-war period. She has been a literary reviewer for *Paese Sera*. She was, at first, best known for her own poetry, but her fiction is now equally valued. Most of her narratives are ▷fantastical, and she has contributed to anthologies of ▷science fiction.

Works include: *Il porto inquieto* (1953) (*An Unquiet Haven*); *Amici e nemici* (1961) (*Friends and Enemies*) ; *La notte artificiale* (1965) (*False Night*); *Berliner Mauer* (1967) (*The Berlin Wall*); *Strategie* (1968) (*Strategies*); *Lettere senza francobollo* (1972) (*Letters With No Stamp*); *Giungla domestica* (1972) (*The Domestic Jungle*); *Festa sull'asteroide* (1975) (*Asteroid Party*); *Marinella Super* (1978); *Dossier extra terrestre* (1979) (*Extra Terrestrial Dossier*, with her husband I. Cremaschi); *Esperimento donna* (1979) (*Woman Experiment*).

Muses
The nine deities of the Arts, daughters of the Greek god Zeus and the goddess Mnemosyne ('Memory'). They are appealed to by poets and philosophers for inspiration. General sponsors of the Arts in the Greek period, the Romans differentiated them by topic: Calliope (epic poetry), Clio (history), Euterpe (lyric poetry and music), Terpsichore (song and dance), Erato (erotic poetry and mime), Melpomene (tragedy), Thalia (comedy), Polyhymnia (solemn hymns), Urania (astronomy). The word 'museum' means 'place of the Muses' and to the Greeks signified any school.

Antipater of Thessalonica (2nd century BC) speaks, in an epigram, of nine women poets as the nine human Muses: ▷Praxilla, ▷Moero, ▷Anyte, ▷Sappho, ▷Erinna, ▷Telesilla, ▷Corinna, ▷Nossis and ▷Myrtis

Musgrave, Susan (born 1951)
Poet and novelist, born in California to Canadian parents who moved to Vancouver Island in 1954. Bored, she left school in Grade Ten, and ran away from home to be a writer. She published poems by the age of sixteen, and lived in California, Ireland, England, and the Queen Charlotte Islands. Her poetry collections, including *Songs of the Sea-Witch* (1970), *Grave-Dirt and Selected Strawberries* (1973), *The Impstone* (1976), *A Man to Marry; a Man to Bury* (1979), *Tarts and Muggers* (1982) and *Cocktails at the Mausoleum* (1985), celebrate animism, and take a macabre delight in death and morbidity. Her work is both fascinating and repellent for its secondment to robbers, vampires, executioners, and outlaws, but is, at its best, transformed by evocative mythologies. Lacking her poetry's immediacy of image and density of phrase, Musgrave's fiction is far less successful. *The Charcoal Burners* (1980) is a savagely brutal tale in which a young woman is raped and cannibalized. *The Dancing Chicken* (1987), a satire on small-town madness, is mordantly unfunny. Despite the textual victimization of her fictional characters, many of Musgrave's poems affirm the power of female archetypes. She has published two books for children, *Gullband* (1974) and *Hag Head* (1980), and her non-fiction is collected in *Great Musgrave* (1989). She lives in Sidney, British Columbia with her daughter and her third husband.

Mvungi, Martha
Tanzanian novelist and short story writer, Mvungi spent her early childhood among the Hehe people, though she herself is a Bena, and was educated at the Universities of Edinburgh and Dar es Salaam, where she did research and teaching in the education department before becoming a teacher in southern Tanzania. Fascinated by the oral tradition of storytelling, she has collected tales from her mother and grandmother; her pupils' participation in 'story time' at school inspired her to collect and record folk tales from her immediate environment. She has produced a collection of Hehe and Bena folk

tales in English translation, *Three Solid Stones* (1975), and a novel in Swahili, *Hana Hatia*.

My Ántonia (1918)

US novel. ▷Willa Cather creates an American legend in the character of Ántonia Shimerda, daughter of an immigrant farming family. Ántonia's story, set on the Nebraska plains in the 1890s, is interpreted and explained by Jim Burden, a neighbour. Jim celebrates Ántonia as earth mother. Ántonia survives the hardships of her life: her father's suicide, farm work, employment as a hired girl, and an illegitimate pregnancy. She gains her strength from the frontier before distinctive gender roles become prescribed, where her work is economically and socially central. But, unlike Alexandra in Cather's ▷*O Pioneers!* (1913), Ántonia surrenders to sexual desire and the ideal of romantic love. Cather emphasizes that these betray a woman. Ántonia eventually marries and has children, and she loses autonomy in assuming a prescribed gender role. From Jim's masculine point of view, her role is limited then to that of mother.

My Australian Girlhood (1902)

Australian autobiography by ▷Rosa Praed. Praed's book tells of her life on outback stations in Queensland and later in Brisbane, where her father was a public servant and politician. *My Australian Girlhood* demonstrates conflicting attitudes towards the destruction of the Aboriginal peoples: on the one hand admiring the ceremonies and myths of the Aborigines, which Praed saw as part of a diffuse, Platonic world religion, and on the other demonstrating a fear and distrust of the Aborigines. This probably stems from Praed's childhood experience when she lived on a cattle station near where the Hornet Bank massacre of a white family had occurred.
▷Aborigine in non-Aboriginal Australian women's writing, The

My Barren Song (1980)

Collection of poems by Ugandan poet ▷Grace Akello. The title poem of this collection, together with 'The Barred Entry', are long, dramatic poems offering a bleak vision of the Uganda of Idi Amin. The other fifty-odd poems in the collection are also concerned with the Uganda of that period.

My Brilliant Career (1901)

Australian novel by ▷Miles Franklin. *My Brilliant Career* is the story of a bush girl, Sybylla Melville, child of impoverished dairy farmers at Possum Gully, whose literary ambitions are hampered by poverty and family circumstances. Sybylla has a taste of gracious living on her grandmother's station property Caddagat, but this ends abruptly when she is sent as governess to the slovenly M'Swat family to pay off her father's debts. She rejects all forms of slavery, including marriage to the handsome and rich Harry Beecham, in favour

of freedom to develop her individuality and to write. At the time of publication this novel was compared favourably with ▷Emily Brontë's ▷*Jane Eyre* and ▷Olive Schreiner's ▷*The Story of an African Farm*. It is much loved in Australia because of its affectionate but realistic picture of bush life, and its depiction of the frustration of life in the bush for women and children. An Australian film of the book was made in 1979.
▷Autobiography (Australia)

'My Country'

Australian poem by Dorothea Mackellar (1885–1968). This much-loved patriotic poem was first published as 'Core of my Heart' in the London *Spectator* in September 1908, then as 'My Country' in the *Sydney Mail* in October of that year. It celebrates the Australian landscape, 'a sunburnt country/ A land of sweeping plains/ Of ragged mountain ranges,/ Of droughts and flooding rains.', and contrasts it with the softer English landscape of 'field and coppice,/ Of green and shaded lanes'.
▷*On Her Selection*

My Father's Daughter (1965)

An autobiographical account of growing up in western Nigeria, written for children by Nigerian writer ▷Mabel Segun. While it is in no way comparable to Wole Soyinka's account of his childhood, *Aké*, these two are the only available personal reminiscences of childhood in colonial Nigeria. Daughter of a clergyman who was also the village postmaster, Mabel Segun was intensely proud of her father and adopted him, rather than her sweet, self-effacing mother, as her model. The story ends with her father's death and the removal of the family. A slight work, it is nevertheless significant for its depiction of a vanished way of life, and the pre-adolescent consciousness of a Nigerian girl.

My Grandmother's Cactus: Stories by Egyptian Women (1991)

English translations of stories by eight Arab short story writers, all born between 1942 and 1953, introduced and translated by Marilyn Booth. The title, introduction and fleeting references in some of the tales pay tribute to the grandmother, a very important repository of tales of wonder for Arab children. The earliest grandmother is invoked by Neamat al-Behiri, and is Isis, the mother goddess of the whole Egyptian valley.

The political and social upheavals of the late 20th century are reflected in the ugliness and poverty eroding the lives of the women depicted, the cancerous growth of prefabricated houses and ugly cement blocks all testifying to the 'modernity' of their surroundings. Their consciousness, however, is as old as their grandmothers'. The 'grandmother's cactus' of the title appears in 'I Saw the Date-Palms' by ▷Radwa 'Ashur, in which a cutting from the narrator's grandmother's cactus plant is used as a symbol of continuity and endurance.

The cactus plant in Arabic is *Sabbar* (the patient one). It is planted next to graves, in courtyards and in the little gardens on rooftops that were the recreation areas of housebound women. It is a 'blessed plant', symbolizing endurance, surviving for generations on little moisture; it serves as an emblem of the life and culture of these women, tenaciously surviving for generations in all kinds of environments.

My History as a Woman Textile Worker (1980)

The autobiography of Takai Toshio (1902–1983). She was the daughter of a charcoal-burner and started work at a textile factory at the age of twelve. She married Hosoi Wakizo, a fellow worker, who published *A History of Women Textile Workers* (1925) with her assistance. After World War II she worked as a casual labourer and helped establish the Japan Trade Union of Daily-Employed Labourers.

My Home in Tasmania During a Residence of Nine Years (1852)

Australian autobiographical work by ▷Louisa Meredith. Meredith details the slaughter of white settlers ('the aged woman and the helpless child alike fell victims to their ferocity') by the Tasmanian Aborigines, led by 'Mosquito', a Sydney Aborigine. In this way she excuses the systematic destruction of the Tasmanian Aborigines, and the removal of the pitiful remnant to Flinders Island. This should be compared with ▷Caroline Leakey's account in ▷*The Broad Arrow* which is entirely sympathetic to the Aborigines and suggests that the whites will eventually pay dearly for the way in which they have acquired the 'blood-soaked' island of Tasmania.
   ▷Aborigine in non-Aboriginal Australian women's writing, The

Myia (I) (3rd century BC)

Philosopher from Croton in southern Italy. The wife of a Milo, she was one of the women Pythagoreans (▷Pythagorean women, ▷Philosophers, Ancient Greek and Roman women). Some sources designate her Pythagoras's daughter. There survives a letter to another woman, Phyllis, discussing various aspects of child rearing: the careful choice of a nurse, healthy diet, and moderation in everything.
   ▷Household management and child rearing, Ancient Greek and Roman

Myia (II)

Sometimes known as Mynna, she was a lyric poet from Sparta. The Greek writer Lucian (2nd century AD) says she was celebrated for her beauty and learning. She composed hymns to the deities Apollo and Artemis, according to the biographical dictionary, the *Suda* (10th century AD). Her identity is unknown. Myia is also sometimes an eponym for ▷Corinna.
Bib: (text & trans.) Edmonds, J.M., *Lyra Graeca.*

My Life-History (1974)

The autobiography of the Japanese suffragist Ichikawa Fusae (1893–1981). A teacher by training, she established the organization for female suffrage, Fujin Sanseiken Kakutoku Kiseidomei in 1924. She was an active member of the Upper House, as well as a central organizer of womens' movements after the realization of female suffrage in 1946.

My Mind and its Thoughts, in Sketches, Fragments, and Essays (1832)

The North American writer ▷Sarah Wentworth Apthorp Morton's only work to be published under her name, it is the culmination of her poetic and social vision, rendered in a variety of literary forms from the sketch to poetry and essays. The collection includes reprints of some earlier works as well as new writings. It is significant as a collected work by a prolific poet but, with the rising tide of 'cult of domesticity' literature, it is also as an assertion of woman's capacity for reason and reflection.

Mynna ▷Myia (II)

My Place (1987)

Australian autobiography by ▷Sally Morgan. This is a deeply moving account of Morgan's search for the truth of her Aboriginal ancestry, back through the lives of her mother and grandmother. Aboriginal women who have been in domestic service, have been coerced into sexual relations by white men, often their masters, robbed of the children of these unions and have finally decided to pass as Indian, rather than as the despised Aborigine. Despite the despair and pain which Morgan recounts, this is a work of great humour and courage which says much for the heroism of the Aboriginal spirit. The book, which has become an Australian bestseller, is beautifully crafted, with a complex narrative structure.
   ▷Aboriginal women writers in Australia

Myrtiotissa ▷Dracopoulou, Theony

Myrtis (6th–5th century BC)

From Anthedon in Boeotia, she is the earliest Boeotian lyric poet, but no fragments of her work survive. The biographical dictionary, the *Suda* (10th century AD), describes her as the teacher of the male lyric poet Pindar and the woman poet ▷Corinna. But such sources often invent the teacher–pupil relationship between similar writers. She is called 'sweet-sounding' by the epigrammatist Antipater of Thessalonica, and 'clear-voiced' by Corinna. The Christian writer Tatian (2nd century AD) records a statue of her by Boiscus.
   Our knowledge of her work comes only from a prose paraphrase by the Greek writer Plutarch (2nd century AD). He tells of a woman, Ochna, jilted by a man, Eunostus. She lies to her brother, saying that she was raped, and her brother

promptly kills the innocent man. Guilt then leads Ochna to kill herself by jumping off a cliff.
▷Muses
Bib: (text & trans.) Edmonds, J.M., *Lyra Graeca.*

My Shining Room (1978)
Work by Japanese writer Tushima Yuko (born 1947). The heroine, a divorcee, lives with her daughter in a room with four windows facing different directions. The room is on the third floor, at the top of an old building. Every night her daughter cries, keeping her awake. Despite her lack of sleep, the woman is driven to visit the amusement quarters, trying to tempt a young unknown man. Tushima portrays her as a liberated woman with a new image.

Mysteries of Udolpho, The (1794)
▷Gothic novel by English writer ▷Ann Radcliffe. Radcliffe interweaves concentration on the picturesque, mystery and feeling, following the fashion set by Horace Walpole in *The Castle of Otranto* (1764). The novel was reviewed by poet Samuel Taylor Coleridge (1772–1834) when it was first issued, and was very popular in the late 18th and early 19th centuries. The novel is set in the early 16th century. On the death of her parents the heroine, Emily, suffers a reversal of fortune which exposes her to the foolishness of her aunt, compounded by her aunt's second marriage to the autocratic Montoni, who removes the entire family to his seat in the Appenines, the Castle of Udolpho. The castle is constructed of dark and labyrinthine passages and dungeons, and inhabited by strange echoes and rumours of ghosts. While Emily yearns for her beloved Valmont (who is meanwhile in Paris with his regiment), her chastity and fidelity are tested by a range of brutal suitors.

Mystical writings (Italy)
Written in the 13th and 14th centuries, these differ from straightforward religious texts/tracts in that they involve a highly selfconscious use of fantastical and supernatural events. They traffic in visions and other-worldly devices. Viewed simply as literature, these works may be seen as the products of highly creative imaginations. Women writers have been able to give free rein to their most extravagant literary impulses through this form of writing. Examples of women writers in this genre include ▷Santa Caterina da Siena and ▷Angela da Foligno.

My Story (1976)
Autobiography of Indian poet ▷Kamala Das. She began writing her life-story when she was hospitalized with a heart disease and believed that she was dying. She was determined to tell all about her life, even at the risk of offending friends and family and upon publication *My Story* was hailed and reviled alike for its sexual candour. It explores one woman's journey from naïvety to a degree of self-understanding, and from a dissatisfaction with marital life to experimentation with extra-marital affairs.

Myth of Motherhood, The (1981)
Translation of *L'Amour en plus* (1980), by French historian ▷Elisabeth Badinter. In her first work, Badinter traces the origins of what she calls the 'myth' of maternal instinct and its development in social consciousness, from the 18th to the 20th century. She bases her research on records of child-rearing practices and infant mortality in France.

Nada (1944) (Nothing)

Novel by Spanish writer ▷Carmen Laforet. It is a female rewriting of the male format of the *Bildungsroman*. It recounts the life of an adolescent, Andrea, who arrives in war-ravaged Barcelona from the Canary Islands to study at the university. In its depiction of poverty, hunger, and unemployment, *Nada* has been read as a socio-historical document. The subtle exploration of the incest motif within the family unit in Laforet's novel leads one to suspect that the novel can also be read as an allegory of Spain, cut off economically and diplomatically from the rest of the world and thrown back on its own resources.

Nagródskaia, Evdokiia Apollonovna (1866–1930)

Russian prose writer, poet, and script writer. Nagródskaia's mother was the writer ▷Avdot'ia Panáeva, and her father the journalist Apollon Golovachev. Her first book, the novel ▷*The Wrath of Dionysus*, published in 1910, became an immediate bestseller and went through ten editions by 1916. Her later works included poetry, four novels, short story collections, and a screenplay. After the 1917 Revolution, she and her husband emigrated to Paris. She published four more novels, including the trilogy of historical novels *The River of Time* (1924–26), which bears the imprint of her activity in the Masonic movement. Her themes are those common in the literature of the ▷Silver Age: love in its various guises, androgyny, a faith in mystical insights, a distrust of reason, and salvation from an ugly reality through dreams, fantasy, beauty and art. Her prose is well-plotted and moves at a brisk pace with no time for digressions and descriptions.
Bib: (trans.) *La Dame et le Diable* (play); *Der Zorn des Dionysos*; *Die bronzene Tur*.

Na Hanyate (1974) ▷*It Does Not Die* (1974)

Naheed, Kishwar (born 1940)

Pakistani Urdu poet, journalist and translator. She was born in Bulandshahr, India, and educated at Pakistan University. She is the director of the Lahore Arts Council, and is considered one of the leading women poets in Urdu. English translations of her poems appear in *The Penguin Book of Modern Urdu Poetry* (ed. Mahmood Jamal, 1986), *Modern Urdu Poets from Pakistan* (ed. Anis Nagi, 1974) and ▷*We Sinful Women* (1991). *The Price of Looking Back* (1987) is a volume of her poems translated from the Urdu by Baidar Bakht and Derek M. Cohen.

Naiad Press

US publisher. Located in Tallahassee, Florida, Naiad publishes works with lesbian themes. It was begun in 1973 by Barbara Grier and Donna McBride, life partners. Grier had been editing and publishing *The Ladder*, the first national US lesbian periodical. Anyda Marchant and Muriel Crawford, fans of *The Ladder*, gave Grier $2000 to found Naiad. In 1974 Naiad published *The Latecomer*, a romance by Sarah Aldridge, Anyda Marchant's pen-name.

Naiad's publications reflect a variety of literary tastes, including ▷Gothic romances, ▷detective fiction, ▷science fiction, westerns and ▷lesbian pulp fiction. It publishes such works as *Lesbian Nuns: Breaking the Silence* (1985) and writers like ▷Ann Bannon, ▷Katherine V. Forrest, ▷Helen Hull, ▷Vivien Renee and ▷Jane Rule. Naiad reassures any lesbian that she is not alone. It promotes positive images of lesbians and has helped to create a lesbian culture.

Naidu, Sarojini (1879–1949)

Indian poet. She was born to a high-caste Bengali family, and was sent to England to be educated at King's College, London, and Girton College, Cambridge, when it appeared that she was determined to marry a man who was neither Bengali nor of her caste. In England she was exposed to and influenced by the poetry of the romantics Wordsworth and Keats. In England, as in India, she was popular for her vivacity and lively wit. Upon her return to India in 1898 she married the man her parents had hoped she would forget in her absence. Throughout her life she continued to write sentimental verse, but she is remembered more in India now for her prominent role in the struggle for independence. Upon her death in 1949 the Prime Minister, Jawaharlal Nehru, saluted her as a national figure.

Her published volumes of poetry include: *The Bird of Time: Songs of Life, Death and Spring* (1912), *The Broken Wing: Songs of Love, Death and Destiny, 1915–16* (1917) and ▷*The Sceptred Flute: Songs of India* (1928).
Bib: Dwivedi, A.N., *Sarojini Naidu and Her Poetry*; Khan, Izzat Yar, *Sarojini Naidu: The Poet*; Naravane, V.S., *Sarojini Naidu*.

Naissance du jour, La (1928) ▷*Break of Day* (1961)

Naked Poems (1965)

Canadian writer ▷Phyllis Webb's sparse and delicious love poems, which locate themselves on the white space of the page with italicized delicacy. The conjunction of lyric and narrative is beautifully non-linear, and exemplifies the joy and sorrow of the questions that both love and poetry must ask.

Nakou, Lilika (born 1903)

Greek biographer, novelist and essayist. She was born in Athens but grew up in Geneva. She studied philosophy and piano in Geneva and then worked as a piano teacher in Athens. In her early youth she became a socialist, influenced by Barbusse and others. For Nakou socialism and humanism were identical, since both were equally concerned with the suffering and the oppressed. She lived for a time in Paris, where she met many scientists and intellectuals, under their influence becoming a writer. She knew Gide, Einstein, de

Unamuno and Rolland amongst others. In Paris and Greece she wrote for the Greek newspaper *Akropolis*. She also worked for the Greek women's movement, recording details about the living standards of Greek women. Her first collection of short stories *The Deflowered Maiden* (1931) created a considerable stir when it first appeared. It tells, in a first-person narrative, the story of a woman's hard life under male oppression and strict social conventions. ▷*Children's Hell* (1944) is a series of short stories about the suffering and deprivation endured by children during the German occupation in World War II. In 1954 her novel *Nausika* appeared in French and in Greek simultaneously. *Madame Doremi* (1953), a novel of great spontaneity and humour, shows the characteristic virtues of her writing: sensitivity to human nature and optimism in the face of life's struggles. Nakou has also written plays for children's puppet theatre.

Naksa

Arabic term meaning 'setback or relapse', a euphemism used by Arab politicians to refer to the defeat of the Arabs in the six-day war of June 1967. The shock and bitterness resounded in the writings of Arab women (as well as men) from ▷Khanatta Binnuna in Morocco to ▷Ghada al-Samman in ▷Beirut. That disillusionment marks Arabic literature to this day. ▷Emily Nasralla, in her novel on the disaster of Beirut, *Those Memories* (1980), recreates the memory of the old wound: 'I learned in the days that followed, that a long time will pass before that open wound in my breast may heal.' Some translations from the Arabic confuse the *naksa* with the *nakba* (disaster or catastrophe): the term used to refer to the United Nations resolution on the partition of Palestine (1947), the creation of the state of Israel, and the defeat of Arab armies (1948), resulting in the transformation of Palestinians into refugees or exiles.

The *Nakba* of the *Baramika* (the Barmacides of *The Arabian Nights*) was a coup engineered by Harun al-Rashid against his friend and *wazir* (minister, chief adviser), Ja'far al-Barmaki, probably in a bid to stem the rising influence of Persia in the politics of Baghdad. Ja'far was executed, all his family and dependants were massacred, and their property – including some star ▷*jawari* (concubines) – was confiscated.

Namjoshi, Suniti (born 1941)

Indian poet and prose writer. She was born in Bombay, and educated at the Universities of Poona and Missouri. She completed her doctorate at McGill University, USA, in 1972. With her mother, Sarojini, in 1968 she translated into English (1968) the poems of Govindagraj, an early 20th-century Marathi poet. She is most well-known for her witty feminist renditions of traditional fairy stories, such as 'Bluebeard' and 'Beauty and the Beast'. Her collections of fables include *Feminist Fables* (1981), ▷*The Conversations of Cow* (1985), *Aditi and the One-Eyed Monkey* (1986), *The Blue Donkey Fables* (1988) and The *Mothers of Maya Diip* (1989). Several volumes of poetry have been published, including *The Jackass and the Lady* (1980), *The Authentic Lie* (1982), *Flesh and Paper* (1986) and *Because of India* (1989). Her writing has been praised for its complex, dreamlike quality, and its paradoxical ability to enlighten rather than obscure Namjoshi's subject matter. Drawing on her roots in a society that has a strong tradition of story-telling and oral renditions of the past, Namjoshi appropriates all types of inherited knowledge to her writing: legends, literary allusions, and even nursery rhymes from both Indian and European sources.

Nancy Shippen, Her Journal Book, 1783–1791 (1935)

One of the most extensive and moving private accounts of an upper-class early North American woman's life. ▷Anne Shippen Livingston begins her journal with the collapse of her marriage, which had been decided according to her father's will. As she struggles to find a life for herself outside this abusive marriage, she reveals the psychological processes of an evolving feminism. She not only chooses a reclusive life over her socially acceptable but humiliating marriage but also comes to recognize that she must educate her daughter to realize her own potential and her right to choose her own lifestyle. The book has earned a lasting place in 18th-century North American autobiographical literature.

Nannestad, Elizabeth (born 1956)

New Zealand poet. Nannestad is by profession a doctor, and her writing began appearing in local journals in the mid-1980s. Her first collection, *Jump* (1987), was co-winner of the New Zealand Book Award for Poetry in 1987. Nannestad writes ironic, delicately judged lyrics which reflect an international context and landscape, and often refer explicitly to travelling.

Naranjo, Carmen (born 1931)

Costa Rican poet, novelist, short story writer and essayist. Naranjo's novels deal with rural life, like most Costa Rican literature, but they also describe the urban middle class, office workers and bosses, and they criticize industrial society, 'where consumerism and bureaucracy alienate and dehumanize people'. She experiments by writing from different perspectives, and dramatizes the voice of the anonymous masses. Whether fantasy or realistic, her short stories are ironic, humorous and critical.

Naranjo's latest novel, *Sobrepunto* (1985) (*Overpoint*), centred on female characters, describes the difficulties women face in society, showing how they frequently function only as objects. The protagonist's fate is destruction and suicide – a result of her victimization by the ▷patriarchal society. As in *Misa a escuras* (1967) (*Mass of Dark*), she gives a realistic view of society, with no religious or spiritual explanations for the living conditions in Latin America.

Other works: *América* (1961) (*America*); *Canción de la ternura* (1964) (*Songs of Tenderness*); *Hacia tu isla* (1966) (*Towards Your Island*); *Los perros no ladraron* (1966) (*The Dogs Didn't Bark*); *Camino al mediodia* (1968) (*Midday Road*); *Memorias de un hombre simbolo* (1968) (*Memories of a Symbolic Man*); *Responso por el niño Juan Manuel;* (1972) (*Response by The Child Juan Manuel*); *Diario de una multitud* (*Diary of a Crowd*); *Hoy es un largo día* (1974) (*Today is a Long Day*); *Por las páginas de la Biblia y los caminos de Israel* (1976) (*For The Pages of the Bible and the Roads of Israel*); *Cinco temas en busca de un pensador* (1977) (*Five Ideas in Search of a Thinker*); *Mi guerrilla* (1984) (*My Guerilla*); *Nunca hubo alguna vez* (1984) (*There Never Was Another Time*), and *Ondina* (1985)

Nasralla, Emily (born 1938)

Lebanese novelist and short story writer. Born in a village in south Lebanon, she graduated from the American University in ▷Beirut. She had to earn her living by writing while she was reading for her BA, a new pattern for Arab women. Her first novel, *Birds of September* (1962) imaginatively recreates the life of a poor village in Lebanon, where the young men leave but the young women, tied down by old customs, stay. Her next novel, *The Oleander Tree* (1967), is a further exploration of the plight of women in a rural environment. The village is Christian and there is no ▷*hijab* (segregation) between the sexes, but the mores are the same: love is taboo and women should be kept in their place. 'Women love strength, they thrive on beating,' the men agree. Raya, the heroine, is a rebel because she wants to get out to the larger world – but she is helpless; *she* is the beautiful, poisonous oleander tree.

Emily Nasralla lived in Beirut, and her work reflects the wanton destruction of the city by the civil war since 1975 and the savage bombing during the Israeli invasion of 1982. *Those Memories* (1980) is an attempt by two women to recreate the past and explain the present. One, whose house has been destroyed in the war, says: 'I am like my family home, ruins of burnt walls, windows like open wounds and a ceiling that has fallen in.' The house should be repaired but who is there to repair it? Farid, the wealthy husband, has taken his business to Europe; he and their sons are happy living abroad.

In ▷*Flight Against Time*, her first novel to be translated into English in 1981, the old theme of emigration is tied to the new theme of the civil war. Radwan, an old villager on a visit to his children in Canada, insists on returning home on hearing the bad news. He makes the long flight to be kidnapped and murdered by masked 'armed elements'. His body is found 'crucified' on the crossroads. In his funeral, attended by crowds of mourners, his children see a smile on his face and imagine him whispering, 'Father, forgive them for they do not know.' Emily Nasralla suffered many losses in her Beirut ordeal, and has not written any new novels since 1981, but she has written short stories. Her collection *The Lost Mill* (1985)

is presented with the 'taste of ashes', stories written from 1981 to 1984. *Women in Seventeen Stories* (1984) is a collection of 'feminist stories'. Emily Nasralla now lives in Cairo.

▷*Naksa*

Bib: Cooke, Miriam, 'Women Write War: The Feminization of Lebanese Society in the War Literature of Emily Nasralla' in *British Society for Middle Eastern Studies Bulletin,* 14 (1988) pp. 52–67; *War's Other Voices: Women Writers on the Lebanese Civil War*.

Nastas'ia Kostër (1923)

A play by ▷Anna Barkóva, set in 17th-century Russia. Its subject is a popularly-based rebellion against the gentry, led by the heroine, Nastas'ia Kostër. Her last name means 'bonfire' and symbolizes both her sexual passion and her apocalyptic political movement. It is not clear whether Barkóva knew of the historical figure of Alëna Arzamasskaia, who led a popular uprising between 1670 and 1673. The play can be seen as an attempt, as in Barkova's 1922 collected poems *Woman*, to tie the theme of revolution to that of love. Nastas'ia is a sexually assertive Joan of Arc, who makes the fatal error of falling for a man from the enemy camp. Although she is consciously fighting a class war, she is not above using a magic icon to win over the people. Some of the best scenes treat the priesthood and its divisions over her call for rebellion. Barkóva's characters speak a Russian based on northern dialects and folklore. In 1925 *Nastas'ia Kostër* was recommended for production in professional theatres, but, in view of its ideological defects, not in amateur ones. It is interesting to note Russian women writers' enduring interest in the warrior-heroine, previously depicted in ▷Ánnenkova-Bernár's play ▷*Daughter of the People,* ▷Stólitsa's play *The Blue Carpet,* and in ▷Tsvetáeva's poetry.

Nation, The

US weekly magazine. Founded in 1865, it was dedicated to reform (education, civil rights for freed slaves, good government) and to elevated standards of cultural and literary criticism. Modelled on the London *Spectator, The Nation* soon made its book reviews definitive and critical, eschewing the sympathetic style that had characterized many of its predecessors. While *The Nation's* reviewers were varied, they were rarely women, and women writers often felt the sting of its criticism.

National Velvet (1935)

Novel by English writer ▷Enid Bagnold. A classic of children's literature, it tells the story of horse-mad fourteen-year-old Velvet Brown, who dresses as a man to ride in, and win, the Grand National on a horse she wins in a raffle. *National Velvet* may well be the originator of the 'pony story', but its interest goes beyond this, notably in its depiction of a working-class family, the bonds betwen mother and daughter, and its portrayal of the power and courage of women.

National Women's Poetry Competition (20th-century Ireland)

Literary prizes specifically for women are rare, but an Irish community arts group, The Works, based in Wexford, has established the annual National Women's Poetry Competition. Two anthologies of the competition entries have been compiled: *Women's Work* (1990) and *Women's Work is Never Done* (1991).

Nation language

A term coined by Edward K. Brathwaite award-winning poet, dramatist, lecturer and critic from ▷Barbados. He uses 'nation language' in his *History of the Voice* (1984) to describe the language spoken by the ordinary people of ▷Jamaica. The terms 'dialect' and 'creole' are felt to contain notions of inferiority in relation to 'standard English'. 'Nation language' relocates the language used within the context of African modes of expression and the African oral traditions which have adapted to the Caribbean experience. A significant feature of nation language is its orality, and the recognition of rhythms, sound and performance is an important aspect of this. ▷Louise Bennett was a noted pioneer in the use of nation language in her poetry, but it is now widely used in both poetry and prose by writers throughout the Caribbean.

▷Language continuum

Native American legends

In many Native American cultures the woman acted as the local 'archivist', that is, she memorized the tribe's historical events and spiritual beliefs and then retold these events to the next generation so that the community's legends would be preserved. Not only did the myths and legends of each tribe become a way of preserving their customs in the face of increasing oppression by Spanish, French and English colonial settlers, but oral traditions also related to the youth of the tribe what were acceptable behaviour and values within the community. In 'The Maiden of Deception Pass', for instance, the young maiden learns that to gain honour and become a spiritual guide she must satisfy the demands of both her husband and her community. In other legends, however, women are also depicted as powerful determiners of cultural events and as tricksters who achieve personal satisfaction while meeting the requirements of communal service. Not unlike the later Euro-American advice literature, Native American oral traditions both historicized a community's values and codified gender-determined behaviours, while at the same time establishing woman's vital role in the processes of culture formation and communication.

▷*Ouabi; or, The Virtues of Nature*; Morton, Sarah Wentworth Apthorp

Native Americans

19th century: Distinctive oral forms of Native American culture were imperfectly recorded in 19th-century translations in Anglo-European languages. The first widely read sympathetic portrayals of Native Americans came from 19th century US women writers outside Native American culture in ▷captivity narratives, ▷Lydia Maria Child's ▷*Hobomok* (1824), and ▷Helen Hunt Jackson's ▷*A Century of Dishonor* (1881) and *Ramona* (1884). In 1883 ▷Sarah Winnemucca Hopkins – Native American lecturer, educator, and the subject of pamphlets by social reformer Elizabeth Peabody (1804–1894) – published her *Life Among the Paiutes*, the first 19th-century volume by and about Native Americans by a Native American woman writer.

20th century: The history of Native American women's writing in the 20th century cannot be divorced from the longer history of the colonization of North America. The indigenous peoples were dispossessed of their land, suffered genocide, and were subjected to redefinition as 'savage' and 'primitive' by the colonizers. This process of dispossession and relocation extended well into the 20th century, and has included the urban migration enforced often by the poor economic conditions found in the land reservations. The earliest writers – Humishuma (▷Mourning Dove), Ella Cara Deloria, Zitkala-Sa, Mary TallMountain, Sarah Callahan, and the Canadian ▷E. Pauline Johnson – were motivated by the need to preserve the oral traditions of their culture. Humishuma and Deloria both worked in the field of ethnography and folklore, making use of the early Anglo-American interest in primitivism to do their own work. Other women narrated stories to ethnographers who then published them, as did the Chippewa Delia Oshogay, who told the story 'Oshkikwe's Baby' to Ernestine Friedl in 1942.

▷Paula Gunn Allen, an important contemporary writer, describes Native Americans as writing 'out of tribal traditions, and into them', suggesting the complex interplay in their writing between oral and written forms, and between Anglo-American and Native American aesthetics, where myths, legends and stories interweave with contemporary experience. Values at odds with the dominant culture are central to Native American writers such as Gunn Allen, ▷Louise Edrich, ▷Leslie Marmon Silko, ▷Joy Harjo, Chrystos, ▷Carol Lee Sanchez, Vickie Lee Sears, LeAnne Howe and ▷Linda Hogan. They write from a sense of collective experience, denying the values of individualism, and out of this emphasis on community there emerges a concern with the individual's correct relationship to family, tradition and nature. Writers such as the poet Chrystos, in her collection *Vanishing*, depict the effects of urbanization and economic oppression on Native Americans, writing about alcoholism, drugs, homelessness and alienation.

The political activism of Native Americans also feeds into their writing, as in Harjo's poem 'For Anna Mae Pictou Aquash', about an activist in the American Indian Movement who was murdered by the FBI. The poetry of Harjo, Chrystos and Hogan is also representative in its focus on a female voice and on relationships between women. In connection with this, Rayna Green, poet, short-story writer and editor of a collection of Native American women's writing, *That's What She Said*, has written about the link between feminism and the 'matriarchal and matrifocal' traditions of many tribes. Green's anthology is one of several influential collections which have appeared recently and which mark the self-definition of Native American women writers as a group. Others are Paula Gunn Allen's *Spider Woman's Granddaughters: Traditional Tales and Contemporary Writing by Native American Women* (1989) and *A Gathering of Spirit: Writing and Art by Native American Women*, edited by Beth Brant (1984).

Bib: Allen, Paula Gunn, *The Sacred Hoop: Recovering the Feminine in American Indian Traditions*; Green, Rayna, *Native American Women: A Contextual Bibliography*.

Nature, Certainty, and Evidence of True Christianity, The (1755)

This fifteen-page spiritual autobiography by the North American writer ▷Sarah Haggar Wheaten Osborn, although published in 1755, reflects upon the decade from 1743 to 1753 when she was developing her philosophy of religion as a new member of the Congregational Church in Newport, Rhode Island. The work was reprinted in the 1790s and expanded into the ▷*Memoirs of the Life of Mrs Sarah Osborn* at the end of the century.

▷*Familiar Letters Written by Mrs Sarah Osborn, and Miss Susanna Anthony; Life and Character of Miss Susanna Anthony, The*; *World of Hannah Heaton, The*; Heaton, Hannah Cook

Naubert, Christiane Benedikte Eugenie (1756–1819)

German translator and novelist. She came from a medical family in Leipzig, had a good education, and began her literary career by translating English novels. Her large output of fiction often draws upon medieval legends and folk-tales, transcribing this material into sophisticated and captivating narratives which explore women's ambitions, sensuality and suffering. Tales such as *Der kurze Mantel* (*The Short Coat*) and *Ottilie* (published as *Zwei Volksmärchen, Two Folktales*, in 1819) are masterpieces of the genre. The four volumes of her collected tales, *Die neuen Volksmärchen der Deutschen* (1789–1793) (*The New German Folktales*), were certainly known to the Brothers Grimm, and served as a source of inspiration to the romantic author E.T.A. Hoffmann (1776–1822). Other writings include *Heerfort und Klärchen* (1779); *Velleda. Ein Zauberroman* (1795) (*Velleda. A Novel of Magic*); and *Walter, von Montbarry, Großmeister des Tempelordens* (1786) (*Walter von Montbarry, A Grand Master of the Templars*).

Naudé, Adèle (1910–1981)

South African poet and travel writer, born in Pretoria, who wrote in both English and Afrikaans. After studying at the University of Cape Town, she worked as a freelance journalist, radio script writer and broadcaster, and also travelled widely with her husband through North America, Europe and the Middle East. After producing two travel books in Afrikaans, *Strooihoed en Sonbril* (1965) (*Straw Hat and Sunglasses*) and *Tousandale aan my Voete* (1968) (*Sandals on My Feet*), she published four volumes of poetry in English: *Pity the Spring* (1953), *No Longer at Ease* (1956), *Only a Setting Forth* (1965), and *Time and Memory* (1974). Her poetry is primarily concerned with seasons and time, and the ways in which they may undermine beauty and order. Crafted in fairly traditional verse forms, her poems are enriched by her travel experiences, and a set of classical and South African references. Her descriptive veracity and subtle technique lend her work a quiet, poignant originality.

After writing her childhood reminiscences in *Rondebosch and Round About* (1973), she published *Cape Album* (1979), a set of historical photographs of early 19th-century life in the Cape.

Navales, Ana María (born ?1945)

Spanish writer of both poetry and prose. Navales was born in Zaragoza, and wrote a doctoral thesis on the Spanish epistolary novel. Her first published work was poetry, with: *En las palabras* (1970) (*In the Words*); *Junto a la última piel* (1973) (*Next to the Last Skin*), and *Restos de lacre y cera de vigilias* (1975) (*Remains of Lacquer and Wax from the Midnight Candle*). She also published fiction: a short-story collection, *Dos muchachos metidos en un sobre azul* (1976) (*Two Kids in a Blue Envelope*), and two novels, *El regreso de Julieta Always* (1981) (*The Return of Juliet Always*) and *El laberinto de Quetzal* (1985) (*The Labyrinth of Quetzal*).

Naylor, Gloria (born 1950)

US novelist. Naylor was born and raised in New York. After graduating from Brooklyn College, she earned a Master's degree at Yale University. She has taught writing and literature at various universities.

The Women of Brewster Place (1982) received the American Book Award for best first novel. It consists of seven stories, and although each focuses on a different African-American woman, the women's lives are interlocked; collectively, they depict the shared experience of the African-American urban woman. Naylor emphasizes the communal tragedy that occurs when the women reject a lesbian, and she examines the fears of heterosexual women about lesbians.

Mama Day (1988) concerns a matriarch whose psychic powers are tested by her emancipated great-niece. Naylor emphasizes the redemptive power of African-American women's maternal heritage. *Linden Hills* (1985) explores the destructive consequences of the adoption of the 'American Dream' and bourgeois aspirations by African-Americans.

Nazár'eva, Kapitolina Valer'ianovna (1847–1900)

Popular Russian fiction writer and dramatist, derided as a 'muchwriter' who ran up her works on a sewing machine. Beginning in 1879, Nazár'eva, under her own name and fifteen known male and female pseudonyms, published a great number of sketches and stories in the ▷'thick journals' and thin magazines of her native ▷St Petersburg. Over twenty of her novels appeared in separate editions during her lifetime. Nazár'eva had no artistic pretensions, but her works, which dealt with a wide range of topical issues and contemporary character types, made light, often engrossing reading. Her first sketch, 'Specialist', was a recipe for getting a divorce. In crime novels like *In the Grip of Poverty* (1885), she combined procedural ▷detective fiction, romantic love story, and naturalistic exploration of the underside of St Petersburg life. Her polished plays, with their taut, melodramatic plots drawn from contemporary life, were staged in ▷Moscow in the 1890s.

▷Dmítrieva, Valentina

Ndiaye, Marie (born 1967)

Franco-Senegalese novelist, born in Pithiviers. She has produced four novels to date, including *Quant au riche avenir* (1985) (*Thoughts on the Rich Future*) and *En famille* (1990) (*With the Family*). In *La Femme changée en bûche* (1989) (*The Woman Turned into a Log*), the distinction between fantasy and reality is blurred in the supernatural tale of a woman who calls upon the devil to take vengeance on her husband. Her most successful novel, *Comédie classique* (1987) (*Classical Play*), is an exercise in style, a text composed of a single sentence, which recounts the events of a single day in the narrator's life.

Necker, Suzanne Cruchod (1737–1794)

French-Swiss essayist and salon hostess. Educated by her father, the evangelical minister Louis Cruchod, she went to Paris after his death and worked as a ladies' companion. In 1764 she married the wealthy Swiss banker Joseph Necker. Her Parisian salon was attended by many of the *philosophes* and Encyclopaedists. She herself educated her daughter Germaine, later ▷Madame de Staël. Her writing was published as *Mélanges extraits des manuscrits* (*Various Extracts from Manuscripts*) in 1798 and *Nouveaux Mélanges* (*Further Extracts*) in 1801, and included essays on charitable hospices and on divorce. She was of the opinion that the differences between the sexes were the result of education, and argued in favour of encouraging women to study. In her *Réflexions sur le divorce* (*Reflections on Divorce*), marriage is presented as requiring mutual sacrifices in the fulfilling of conjugal duties. She also suggests that a court of women be set up to adjudicate requests for legal separations.

Bib: Gréard, O., *L'Education des femmes par les femmes.*

Nedobytá vítězství (1910) (*Unfulfilled Triumphs*)

A collection of three stories by Czech writer Božena Benešová (1873–1936). The anti-sentimental stories are set in little Moravian country towns where behaviour is governed by a set of tedious rules against which people revolt in youth, but to which they soon submit once youth has passed. Women can hope for little more from love and marriage than disappointment. Women may not, realistically, remove their frustrations, but they can, with a little rational effort, come to terms with them by not expecting too much from the world of the emotions. Benešová does not, however, try to impose some ideology of practicality. The stories of *Nedobytá vítězství* demonstrate the psychological misery that is all too easily imposed by a rationalistic approach to living.

Nedreaas, Torborg (1906–1987)

Norwegian prose writer and literary critic. She grew up in Bergen, her parents divorced, and she lived with her mother and stepfather. She trained as a pianist, lived in Paris for a year, married a rich man, and began to write short stories for magazines. At the beginning of World War II she divorced, and lived with her two sons and her mother, whom she supported financially. In 1945 she made her début with the two collections of short stories *Før det ringer tredje gang* (*Before the Third Bell*) and *Bak skapet står øksen* (*Behind the Cupboard Stands the Axe*), war stories without heroism. World War II found Nedreaas a sympathizer with the communists, and she married a leading communist in Norway.

Her most famous character is Herdis from the short stories *Trylleglasset* (1950) (*The Magic Glass*) and the novels *Musikk fra en blå brønn* (1960) (*Music from a Blue Well*) and *Ved neste nymåne* (1971) (*At the Next New Moon*), a story which, though never finished, is a masterpiece of style and psychological insight. Herdis is followed in her development from fantasy-struck child to a young woman, after the outbreak of World War I.

Av måneskin gror det ingenting (1947) (*Nothing Grows from Moonlight*) is considered another of her major works. Here a woman who is broken physically as well as psychologically as a result of repeated abortions, poverty and a self-destructive love affair, is shown in a one-night conversation with a stranger.

Nedreaas's prose is direct and sensual, but never sentimental.

Need for Roots, The (1952)

Translation of *L'Enracinement: prélude à une déclaration des devoirs envers l'être humain* (1949), by French philosophical and political writer ▷Simone Weil. Together with ▷*Oppression and Liberty*, this is Weil's major contribution to political science and social ethics. In it she examines the relationship between the individual and the collective, and develops her thoughts on the conditions needed for the harmonious integration of men and women, particularly manual workers, within society.

Neera (1846–1918)

Pseudonym of Anna Radius Zuccari, Italian novelist and poet. Born in Milan, she lost her mother while still quite young, and thus she was brought up in the country by elderly aunts. As a child, she appears to have been somewhat sad and solitary, but she was an avid reader. She married in 1871, and had two children, a son and a daughter. She produced many works in the course of her life, some of which recreate the countryside of her childhood and her memories of it. Her work is poetic, with a strong vein of moral conservatism running through it. Though concerned with women's problems in the society of her time, she was an avowed anti-feminist who wrote many moral tracts. She was a very independent person, much given to solitude and was, she once claimed, only bored in the company of others. Benedetto Croce described her, in terms commonly used to describe good women writers of the age, as a woman writer who revealed a capacity for masculine thought! Neera's work often centres on female protagonists (of all classes), and, through her narratives of unhappy love, she appears to warn women against seeing themselves solely in sexual terms. Yet, other narratives, such as ▷ *Teresa* (1886) and *L'indomani* (*The Following Day*), subtly undermine this message when they present romantic love as the only possible means of self-fulfilment. She is, in fact, a writer whose enormous output of work is full of contradictions.

Her other work includes: *Vecchie catene* (1878) (*Old Chains*); *Un romanzo* (1880) (*A Novel*); *Dizionario d'igiene per le famiglie* (1881) (*A Dictionary of Family Hygiene*); *Il marito dell'amica* (1885) (*A Friend's Husband*); *Voci della notte* (1893) (*Night Voices*); *Anima sola* (1984) (*The Soul of an Artist*, translated into English in 1905); *Poesie* (1898) (*Poems*); *La vecchia casa* (1900) (*The Old House*); *Le idee di una donna* (1903) (*A Woman's Ideas*); *Conchiglie* (1905) (*Shells*); *Una giovinezza del XIX secolo* (1919) (*Growing Up in the 19th Century*); *Fiori* (1921) (*Flowers*). Her collected works appeared in 1943.

Negri, Ada (1870–1945)

Italian novelist and poet. Ada Negri was a teacher, from a working-class family. She grew up in considerable poverty, exacerbated by the death of her father, and claimed that as a child she took refuge in study to escape from her environment. She married, and had one daughter. She lived in Switzerland after her separation from her husband. This period of her life furnished her with material for some of her fiction. During World War I she returned to Italy and worked in a hospital. For the most part, she lived a somewhat reclusive life. Her poetry, at first packed with socio-political comment, gradually became less politically vocal. She did appear to be linked with the fascists in the beginning, but had distanced herself from them by the time World War II broke out. Much of Negri's writing has a religious tone, though her later works concentrate on women's role in society. She won many literary prizes for her work, and was a member of the *Accademia d'Italia*. Her first collection of poetry, *Fatalità* (1892) (*Fate and Other Poems*, translated into English in 1898), catapulted her into the public eye and received critical praise. The collection *Tempeste* (*Storms*) of 1894 addressed a number of issues, from her passion for social justice to her memories of family and childhood. *Maternità* (1904) (*Maternity*) looks at woman's role and experience as mother. *Le solitarie* (1917) (*Solitary Women*), and *Sorelle* (1929) (*Sisters*), works of poetry and prose respectively, both consider woman's role, problems and destiny. *Stella mattutina* (1928) (*Morning Star*), is an autobiographical text, which presents us with the pains of Negri's childhood and her attempts to rise above them. Much of her work deals specifically with women's experience of pain, but it is a lyrical evocation of this pain. Her collected works are available in *Poesie* (1948) (*Collected Poetry*), and *Prose* (1954) (*Collected Prose Writings*).

Négritude

The term *négritude* was first used by Aimé Césaire in *L'Etudiant Noir* (*The Black Student*), a journal launched in 1934 in Paris by three students; Leopold Senghor (Senegal), Leon Damas (Guyana) and Aimé Césaire (Martinique). Originally a refusal of cultural assimilation and a rejection of a certain image of the black person as passive and incapable of building a civilization, *négritude* became an expression of the ideas in which the cultural renaissance of francophone black people would take seed. Césaire's *Cahier d'un retour au pays natal* (1939) (*Return to My Native Land*) has been one of the most influential expressions of *négritude*.

Négritude is a quintessentially masculine ideology which relegates woman to a position of wordless passivity. Critic Clarisse Zimra observes, 'Liberation was started by men and the *négritude* prophets who stood in its vanguard were all men. The liberation of one sex was subsumed under that of one race and thereby deferred' ('*Négritude* in the Feminine Mode', *Journal of Ethnic Studies*, 12, 1, 1984). In Senghor's famous poem, 'Black Woman', Africa is described as feminine, vegetable, procreative, recumbent, a source of poetic inspiration.

Though a powerful tool for colonized intellectuals of that era, *négritude* is also a philosophical conundrum. Influenced by Marxism, Existentialism and Surrealism, it follows the binary opposition at the basis of Western rationalism. In accepting the duality of black/white, self/other, it sought to recover for the Black Other the qualities of warmth, sensuality, fecundity, musicality and intuition, in opposition to the cold, rational and technological associated with White. Stressing integration and wholeness over analysis and dissection, it asserted that black culture was emotional rather than rational, thus adopting stereotypes which reflect European prejudice and reinforcing racial stereotypes. In the Antillean context, the doctrine of *négritude* privileges the admittedly predominant 'African' or 'Black' component in Antillean society to the exclusion of the Tamoul Indian, Native American, Chinese and European-*béké* (white Creole) elements.

Negron Muñoz, Mercedes ▷ Lair, Clara

Nei mari estremi (1987) (In Heavy Seas)

A novel in Italian by ▷ Lalla Romano, which tells of her relationship with her husband, from the moment they meet to the time of his death. The process of failing in love is lyrically evoked. The tale is one of a meeting of minds as well as of hearts. Detailed flashbacks bring the couple vividly to life, while the narrative pace slows towards the end, as life flows away from one of the two protagonists. It is a very human work, full of joy and sadness conveyed with immediacy, and in this it is typical of Romano's work as a whole.

Nélida (1846)

A novel by ▷ Marie de Flavigny under the pseudonym Daniel Stern. This work is de Flavigny's only novel, and was written after the end of her affair with Franz Liszt. It provides a fictionalized account of their liaison, and one, moreover, that reveals the bitterness to which she succumbed after she broke off with her lover in 1844. Although *Nélida* was apparently intended to give an objective version of what passed between de Flavigny and Liszt, it resembles more closely an attempt at self-justification, and contains a contemptuous denunciation of the faults and inadequacies of the man to whom its author had been passionately attached.

The novel tells the story of the proud, spiritual Mademoiselle de la Thieullaye, who, after an adolescence spent in the rarefied atmosphere of a convent school, a brief brush with the superficial, frivolous world of Parisian aristocratic society, and marriage to the faithless Timoléon de Kervaëns, elopes with a young working-class artist, Guermann, her former childhood companion, with whom she falls deeply in love. He proves, however, to be her moral and intellectual inferior, and eventually betrays the ideal love Nélida believed they shared by compromising himself with the ex-mistress of Nélida's husband. Although the lovers are reconciled shortly before Guermann's death, Nélida comes, with the help of the radical socialist Mère Elisabeth (the former Mother Superior of the convent in which she was educated), to see that intellectual reflection and good works are the path to true happiness for idealistic women such as herself. While the narrator of the novel coyly refuses to tell us what becomes of Nélida after Guermann's death, the reader cannot help but assume that she embraces the kind of life Mère Elisabeth has recommended. *Nélida* is a romantic, excessively melodramatic

story which enables the reader to see why de Flavigny felt ill at ease with fiction. It reveals, nevertheless, her capacity for lucid political analysis (Guermann preaches ▷ Saint-Simonism, albeit incoherently, and Mère Elizabeth and her fellow conspirator, Férez, are mouthpieces for Republican radicalism) and contains a subtle but forceful critique of the passivity and ignorance to which 19th-century aristocratic women were condemned. If *Nélida* is the product of de Flavigny rage at Liszt, the novel also offers a telling account of the privileged yet restricted existence led by the majority of the author's female contemporaries. Significantly, the relationships which are shown in the novel to be fulfilling and undamaging are those that exist between women.

Nelken i Mausberger, Margarita (1898–1936)

Spanish essayist. Nelken was an influential feminist during the Second Republic. She went into exile following the end of the Spanish Civil War (1936–9). She wrote some fiction, but is best-known for her essays, such as: *La condición de la mujer en España* (1922) (*The Condition of Women in Spain*), and *Las escritoras españolas* (1930) (*Spanish Women Writers*).

Nellie Bly's Book: Around the World in Seventy-Two Days (1890)

US travel book, first-person journalism, by ▷ Nellie Bly (Elizabeth Cochrane Seaman). The volume publication of Bly's account of her record-breaking world tour, sponsored by the New York *World* newspaper, the book attracted international attention, as did the tour itself.

Nell'ingranaggio (1885) (Caught in the Wheel)

A novel by Italian writer ▷ Bruno Sperani, set in the increasingly important banking world in Milan. The protagonist, Gilda, a teacher, takes a post as governess in a Milanese banking family. Signora Pianosi is a former actress who has an expensive lover to maintain; Signor Pianosi is entirely caught up in his work, and Gilda unfortunately falls in love with him. He eventually leaves Milan for a political career in Rome, and Gilda drowns herself. The thesis of this novel is that the emotional and spiritual life is destroyed by capitalism. Fashion, appropriately for Milan even then, becomes an important index of consumerism. The novel also contains a very finely observed portrait of Milanese society.

Nelson, Alice (Ruth) Moore Dunbar (1875–1935)

US fiction writer, poet, editor, journalist and activist. An extraordinarily versatile writer who marked African-American first achievements in many areas, Dunbar Nelson followed both her artistic talents and her commitment to social justice. She was significant as an editor, political activist and columnist. Her most notable literary works are collected in *Violets, and Other Tales*

(1895) and ▷*The Goodness of St Rocque, and Other Stories* (1899), which are some of the first collections of stories by an African-American woman. She focused foremost on her characters' humanity rather than their race, and wrote memorable pieces on woman's oppression in conventional roles outside the world of work. A constant worker herself, she moved in the 20th century to editing collections of African-American writing, including her own.

Dunbar Nelson is often remembered for her first marriage to writer Paul Laurence Dunbar (1872–1906); she later married Robert J. Nelson, and so published under a series of names: Alice Ruth Moore, Alice Dunbar, Alice Dunbar-Nelson, Alice Dunbar Nelson.

Nemes Nagy, Ágnes (1922–1991)

Hungarian poet. Agnes Nemes Nagy grew up in Budapest, and graduated from university in Hungarian and Latin. From 1945 to 1953 she worked on an educational magazine, then as a secondary school teacher until 1958. From then on she lived from her writing. In 1969 she was awarded the prestigious Joszef Attila Prize, and in 1983 the Kossuth Prize. Lorant Czigány, in his survey of Hungarian literature, comments on her sparse, articulate poetic statements, which use traditional forms, and often refer back to the horrific images of World War II. She is concerned with reasons for the existence of colours, objects or sounds. Her many works include *Kettös Világban* (1946) (*Dual World*) *Szárazvillám* (1957) (*Dry Lightning*) and *A Lovák és az angyalok* (1969) (*Horses and Angels*).

Nemours, Marie d'Orléans, Duchesse de (1625–1707)

French writer of memoirs. She was the daughter of Henri, Duc de Longueville, and Louise de Bourbon-Soissons, and stepdaughter of the sister of the Prince de Condé (1621–1686). She regretted her father's involvement in the *Frondes* (the civil wars of 1648–1653), but was, like him, opposed to Mazarin (1602–1661). Her *Mémoires*, which contain portraits of the principle *frondeurs* (those who rebelled against the crown), give a fascinating picture of this troubled period, and can be usefully compared with those of the Cardinal de Retz (1613–1679).

Neo-realism (Portugal)

Literary movement in Portugal dating from the late 1930s, when the term *neo-realismo* first appeared in *O Diabo* (*The Devil*), a literary review. Influenced by a world-wide tendency towards social realism in the 1930s, the movement focused on the economic problems of the poor and working class. The Brazilian Northeastern novel was particularly important to the development of neo-realist literature in Portugal, and Brazilian writers such as Jorge Amado, Graciliano Ramos and Amando Fontes were widely read. *Gaibéus* (1940) by Alves Redol, about workers in the Ribatejo area in Portugal, is regarded as the first

neo-realist novel. The neo-realist movement dominated Portuguese poetry and prose until the advent of Existentialism in the 1950s.
▷Horta, Maria Teresa; Lisboa, Irene do Céu Viera

Neorealism (Italy)

The definition of Italian neorealism has always been problematic. It arose largely as a cinematic and literary response to Italy's experience of ▷fascism, and chronicled, for the most part, the events of the Italian ▷Resistance. Most critics are agreed that its temporal boundaries span roughly the years 1945 to the mid-to-late 1950s. Yet neorealist novels which hark back to this period of Italian history continued to appear well into the late 1960s. Neorealist writers strove to portray the experience of ideological indoctrination and the horror of war, rejecting notions of heroism and romanticism. Stylistically, they wished to reproduce a language close to spoken Italian. Those male writers most celebrated in the genre (Vittorini, Pavese, Calvino, Fenoglio and Carlo Levi) were also concerned to deal with the dilemma of the male intellectual in this turbulent period. Women writing in this genre, on the other hand, witnessed the experience of women, and not exclusively middle-class women. The most notable women writers of the genre were Renata Fusè, ▷Caterina Percoto, ▷Anna Maria Ortese, ▷Renata Viganò, ▷Alba de Cespedes, ▷Joyce Lussu and ▷Giovanna Zangrandi.

Nesbit, Edith (1858–1924)

British writer. She was born in London and educated in France and Germany as well as England. Through her elder sister, Mary, she met the ▷Rossettis, Swinburne and William Morris, and published her first poem in *The Sunday Magazine* in 1876. She married the journalist, Hubert Bland, in 1880, and both became founder members of the Fabian Society in 1884. Hubert was a notorious womanizer, but Edith allowed his illegitimate offspring to live in the household along with her own four children (H.G. Wells satirized the couple's unconventional lifestyle in his *Experiment in Autobiography*). Financial difficulties forced Nesbit to abandon poetry and write popular fiction and books for children – her first stories about 'the Bastable family' appeared in 1898. Three 'Bastable' novels quickly followed: *The Story of the Treasure Seekers* (1899), *The Wouldbegoods* (1901) and *The New Treasure Seekers* (1904). Her blend of ▷realism and magic proved highly popular, and her other famous children's novels include *Five Children and It* (1902); *The Phoenix and the Carpet* (1904); *The Railway Children* (1906) and *The Enchanted Castle* (1907). Her other published work includes early collections of poetry, political verse such as *Ballads and Lyrics of Socialism* (1908), a study of childhood, *Wings and the Child* (1913) and several ▷ghost stories. Her last novel, *Lark*, appeared in 1922.
▷Children's literature (19th-century Britain)

Bib: Moore, D.K., *Life*; Briggs, J., *A Woman of Passion*.

Nessuno torna indietro (1938) (No-one Goes Back)

The first novel by Italian writer ▷Alba De Cespedes. It won great critical acclaim both in Italy and abroad. The novel centres on the family as a microcosm of society and, as all of the characters are in some sense paralyzed, incapable of making anything of their lives, it is hardly surprising that it did not meet with a positive response from the Fascist government which censured it. The novel also deals specifically with the relationship between women and society, and anticipates many feminist ideas. It was widely translated, and also adapted for the cinema.

Nest in a Falling Tree (1967)

Novel by New Zealand writer ▷Joy Cowley. *Nest in a Falling Tree* is Cowley's first novel, and was widely praised on its appearance. A narrative about an unmarried woman, Maura, who takes care of her mother and falls into an ungovernable passion for a seventeen-year-old boy, *Nest in a Falling Tree* highlights the isolation and wastefulness of a life given to the service of parents. The train of events that are put in motion by Maura's discovery of her emotional and sexual self can only be destructive and, as the title suggests, refuge or home is illusory.

Neufvic, Madame de (17th century)

French translator. A *femme d'esprit* (woman of keen intellect), she made a verse translation from the Spanish of the novel *Diana* by Jorge Montemayor (1520–1561). She supported efforts to purify the French language.
Bib: Fukui, Y. *Raffinement précieux dans la poésie française du XVIIe siècle.*

Never Must You Ask Me (1973)

Translation into English of *Mai devi domandarmi* (1970), a collection of writings by ▷Natalia Ginzburg, mainly taken from her publications in *La Stampa* in the 1960s. They are almost a diary of memories and thoughts, collected chronologically. The subject matter varies from memories of house-hunting to the process of writing; character sketches are to be found alongside memories of trips abroad. The title piece is an analysis of Ginzburg's complicated relationship with opera, and is taken from *Lohengrin*. These writings are interesting for what they have to say about morality, education, and society, as well as for the insight they offer into Ginzburg herself.

New Criticism

A school of literary criticism which came to the fore in North America in the 1940s and 1950s in work by the US scholars Cleanth Brooks, John Crowe Ransom, W.K. Wimsatt and others. New Criticism rejects authorial intention and historical context as keys to understanding literary meaning, and attends instead to the words of the text, insisting that meaning inheres in linguistic patterns of ambiguity, irony and paradox.
▷Millet, Kate.

New England Nun, A (1891)

US story collection by ▷Mary E. Wilkins Freeman. ▷local color sketches, they are generally realistic in technique. Most of them focus on women characters whose lives and romantic possibilities are deflected by the situations in which they find themselves. The title story concerns a woman who establishes a domestic life of her own, and so finally declines to marry her lover, after years of waiting for his return from Australia.

New Home – Who'll Follow? or, Glimpses of Western Life, A (1839)

US semi-fictional personal narrative of Michigan frontier life by ▷Caroline Matilda Stansbury Kirkland, published under the pseudonym Mrs Mary Clavers. As a newly arrived pioneer, Kirkland offered an outsider's unsentimental account of the hardships and rudeness of frontier life, along with characterizations of some of its distinctive personalities – none of them flattering. Popular upon publication, the book created something of an uproar in Michigan. It was reissued as *Our New Home in the West* (1874).

New Letters of Abigail Adams 1788–1801 (1947)

This selection of letters by ▷Abigail Smith Adams, who married the North American statesman and president, John Adams (1735–1826), is devoted to correspondence with her sister, Mary Cranch. Detailing her White House years, the letters blend Abigail Adams's incisive political analyses with the exacting details of her home life, representing the two worlds that she occupied as one of 18th-century North America's most prominent women. She describes the conundrums of managing the household in the ill-equipped White House with the same fervour and insights into human nature that she employs to detail her role as First Lady among the nation's most renowned – and often contentious – political leaders.
▷*Adams Family Correspondence*; *Adams–Jefferson Letters*; *Book of Abigail and John, The*; Early North American letters

Newly Born Woman, The (1986)

Translation of *La Jeune Née* (1975), written jointly by ▷Hélène Cixous and ▷Catherine Clément. Through their reading of historical, literary and psychoanalytic accounts they explore what is hidden and repressed in culture, and define 'woman's place' through a series of oppositions where she is seen as the negative to man's positive set of values. The originality of this work resides in its fusion of poetic language and ideological content, avoiding the traditional opposition between academic and fictional language. In *The*

Guilty One, Clément explores the image of the witch and the hysteric as exemplary female figures. In *Sorties (Forays)* Cixous makes some of the most forceful deconstructions of patriarchy to date.
▷Bisexuality; Deconstruction.

New lyric poetry of the 1980s (Scandinavia)
In Scandinavia a new generation of lyric poets emerged in the 1980s. They revolted against the ▷realistic literature of the 1970s, and made links with the ▷modernism of the 1960s, eg ▷Inger Christensen. Their genres were lyric poems or lyrical prose.

In Denmark the most well-known lyric poet of the 1980s is ▷Pia Tafdrup but many others should be mentioned, eg the poet Pia Juul (born 1962), the poet and dramatist Astrid Saalbach (born 1955), Merete Torp (born 1956), and Juliane Preisler (born 1959), who has written both poems and lyrical prose.

In the other Scandinavian countries, similar developments have been seen: in Finland with the prose writer ▷Rosa Liksom (born 1958); in Sweden with Anne Hermanson (born 1956), Ann Jäderlund (born 1955), Ingela Norlin (born 1959) and Inger Edelfeldt (born 1959), and in Norway with Lisbet Hiide (born 1942) and Eva Jensen (born 1955).

This is a generation of very well-educated women writers who often write 'meta-literature' and who revolt against the feminism of the 1970s. They write as women, but they want to be read because of their poetry not because of their gender – although their poems are often concerned with woman as a sexual being.

New Movement in modern Arabic poetry
There have been many attempts to revitalize Arabic poetry and produce 'new' verse in the 20th century. More specifically, however, 'modern poetry' refers to a watershed in Arabic poetry that was instigated in 1947 by ▷Nazik al-Mala'ika and Badr Shakir al-Sayyab (1926–1964) independently. Al-Mala'ika was the first to publish a poem, 'Cholera' (1947), in a ▷Beirut literary magazine, and question what was thought of as the backbone of Arabic verse. Al-Mala'ika argued, in the introduction of her next volume of poetry, that Arabic poetry had to break with the old verse forms and the cold, stilted language of the past. This introduction, dated February 1949, is an important manifesto for Arabic poetry. It states that it is the poets who will revitalize the language by 'exploding it from within'. The mono-rhyme, that millstone hampering the Arabic *qasida* (ode), should be discarded. She mentions English blank verse as a possible model. The *bait* (couplet), with its regular repetition of feet, should not serve as the unit for the poem, which should be the *tafila* (the foot). The new verse should be a proper vehicle for expressing the new thoughts, new anxieties and new sensibilities of new generations of Arab poets. Al-Malaika's position is summed up in the following quotation: 'I believe

that Arabic poetry stands on the brink of a stormy change which will sweep away the old forms; measures, rhymes, forms and doctrines will be shaken at the root. Diction will expand, poetic experience will look inward to the depths of consciousness . . . I say this is a logical consequence of our reading European literature and studying the latest theories of philosophy, art and psychology . . . I believe in the future of Arabic poetry. I believe it is going forward with all the strength and talent of our poets, to take its noble place in World Literature'.

The New Movement was fiercely opposed by traditional poets and critics, and even by men like 'Aqqad, who had in the 1930s introduced new ideas themselves. Most of the important Arab poets who made their debut in the 1950s and 1960s, however, contributed to the new verse form, but they are now superseded by younger generations of poets who look to the 'modernist' poets of Beirut for models. Al-Mala'ika and her Iraqi and Egyptian colleagues are now the 'Establishment' in Arabic poetry.
▷'Attar, Samar
Bib: Jabra, I., 'Modern Arabic Literature and the West' in *Critical Perspectives on Modern Arabic Literature*; al-Jayyusi, B. and Salma, K., *Trends and Movements in Modern Arabic Poetry*.

New-Norwegian literature
From the 19th century a constant battle has been taking place in Norway between *bokmål* (language of books) and *landsmål*. *Landsmål* is a language created to unite all the different local dialects of Norway, but as this proved impossible, different variations of *landsmål* still exist together with other dialects, eg urban dialects.

For many years *landsmål* literature was a radical literature, in opposition not only to *bokmål* but also to the dominant Danish culture in Norway. The best-known early *landsmål* woman writer is Hulda Garborg (1862–1934), but today many well-known women writers (and men, too) write in landsmål, eg ▷Aslaug Vaa (1889–1965) and ▷Halldis Moren Vessas (born 1907).

Gro Holm (1878–1949) had a more critical view towards the idealization of peasant life in *landsmål* literature. Modern *landsmål* literature is no longer an idyllic literature of Norwegian village life.

New Theatre, The
New Theatre (Australia) is a federal organization, formed in the early 1950s to promote a committed socialist drama. The Sydney and Melbourne groups were established in 1932 and 1936 respectively, and are still operational. ▷Australian women dramatists who were committed to left-wing politics and have written for New Theatre include ▷Betty Roland, ▷Katharine Susannah Prichard, ▷Oriel Gray, ▷Dymphna Cusack and ▷Mona Brand. Oriel Gray's autobiographical *Exit Left, Memoirs of a Scarlet Woman* (1985) records her involvement with the Communist Party and the New Theatre, and is a particularly interesting

account of the left-wing movement in Sydney during the war years.
▷Dramatists (Australia)

'New Touch on the Times, A' (c 1778)

This 84-line poem was written some time around 1778 by ▷Molly Gutridge, a resident of Marblehead, Massachusetts. The poem not only recounts Gutridge's patriotism during the American Revolution, but tempers that zeal with a realistic depiction of the consequences of war for a community dependent upon trade by sea: 'Our lives they all are tired here, / We see all things so cruel dear, / Nothing now-a-days to be got, / To put in kettle or in pot.' Although the byline notes only the anonymous 'Daughter of Liberty', the poem ends with the poet's assertion of authorship: 'MOLLY GUTRIDGE composition'. Published as a broadside, it emphasized women's contributions to the war with imprints of women working at the hearth and the traditional 'Daughter of Liberty' figure of a woman with Patriot's hat and musket; in these symbols and the subtitle ('Well adapted to the distressing Situation of every Sea-port Town'), 'A New Touch' is presented as representative of conditions in revolutionary North America.

'New Woman, The'

A term said to have been coined by British novelist ▷Sarah Grand in 1894. 'New Woman' fiction was a phenomenon of the 1890s, when women writers such as Grand, ▷George Egerton and ▷Mona Caird produced novels, stories and poems that looked forward to burgeoning opportunities for women in the century to come. Such fiction tended to suggest that woman's spiritual power was waxing and that female influence would dominate in the new age. In the eyes of society, the 'New Woman' was seen as liberated and bold, a rebel against the sexual ideology of the 19th century, a supporter of women's ▷suffrage and advocate of women's rights. This was partly a misreading, however, for the 'New Woman' tended not to seek sexual liberation, but the curtailing of 'rapacious' male sexuality. Some critics have seen the character of Sue Bridehead in Thomas Hardy's *Jude the Obscure* (1894–5) as representing the 'New Woman', although Sue disaffiliates herself from the struggles of her sex.
▷'Woman Question, The'
Bib: Cunningham, G., *The 'New Woman' and the Fiction of the 1890's*.
19th-century US: Late 19th-century characterization of individualistic, self-defined women who educated themselves for economic independence and public life. The New Woman was both a feature and an outgrowth of much 19th-century US women's fiction and non-fiction concerned with the dangers of women's dependence, oppressive marriage, self-sacrifice and wasted talents.

New Writing From Israel (1976)

A collection of translated works, both poetry and prose, by Israeli writers, edited by J. Sonntag. The book contains a general introduction by Professor S. Sandbank. Women writers included are ▷Dalia Ravikovitch, Shulamit Har-Even, ▷Zelda and ▷Yonah Wallach.

N.F.B.A. ▷Floresta, Nísia

Ngcobo, Lauretta (born 1932)

South African novelist who now lives in London. Beating the police by five hours, she left South Africa in the 1960s in order to escape political detention as a member of the banned Pan-African Congress. In England she wrote two novels: ▷*Cross of Gold* (1981), until recently banned in South Africa, and ▷*And They Didn't Die* (1990). Both concern the political turbulence of life for black South Africans in the 1950s and 1960s. *Cross of Gold* was written, Ngcobo has said, in the hope that it would help her understand herself and the world she had come from. Yet, she added, whenever she started using her own experience as a woman, her female character would die on her. She thus felt compelled to focus on the activities of a male revolutionary instead, who takes the action into a future South Africa marked by full-scale civil war. Brooding over the novel, nevertheless, is a powerful feminine presence, an idealized figure of compassion through whom, the text suggests, war might come to an end.

And They Didn't Die concerns a woman determined to take charge of her own life, who negotiates with difficulty a variety of racial and sexual abuse, to say nothing of the grinding poverty bequeathed her by apartheid South Africa. The trajectory of this novel differs from the first, in that the central female character, assuming a material rather than idealized or symbolic existence, takes the decision to fight back. The story ends with her killing the white man who has raped her daughter, in a gesture which signifies the importance of rebellion. The novel is particularly significant as the first representation by a black South African writer of rural women, left to take care of the homestead for eleven months of the year, while the men go to work in the cities.

Ngcobo has also edited a collection of essays by black women writers in Britain, *Let It Be Told* (1987), as well as writing critical essays on South African literature.

Ngurukie, Pat Wambui (born 1948)

Kenyan novelist. She completed her high school education in 1968 and qualified as a secretary in the same year. She has studied French and is currently pursuing journalism and public relations. Novels include *I Will Be Your Substitute* (1984) and *Soldier's Wife* (1989).

Nguya, Lydiah Mumbi

Kenyan novelist. Nguya is the author of *The First Seed* (1975), set in pre-colonial Kikuyuland, which questions the efficacy of traditional sacrifices and preoccupation with male lineage.

Niboyet, Eugénie (1797–1883)
French novelist and feminist journalist. Niboyet began her career by translating English novels, before embarking on her own original work, including *Les Deux Frères* (1839) (*The Two Brothers*), *Lucien* (1841) and *Quinze Jours de vacances* (1841) (*A Fortnight's Holiday*). A passionate defender of the poor and the oppressed, and an ardent pacifist, she was involved for a time with the ▷ Saint-Simonians, founded the socialist journal *La Paix des deux mondes* (*Peace in Both Worlds*) in 1844, and in 1848 set up the socialist feminist daily newspaper *La Voix des femmes* (*Women's Voice*). A keen and prominent supporter of women's suffrage, she was frequently lampooned by contemporary cartoonists. Her memories of 1848 are to be found in a late work, *Le Vrai Livre des femmes* (1862) (*The True Book of Women*). Her other works are her *Souvenirs d'enfance* (1841) (*Childhood Memories*); *Dieu manifesté par les oeuvres de la création* (1842) (*God as Manifested by the Works of the Creation*) and *Cathérine II* (1847).
▷ Feminist/feminine journalism (France)
Bib: Moses, C., *French Feminism in the 19th Century.*

Nichols, Grace (born 1950)

Grace Nichols

Caribbean poet, born and educated in ▷ Guyana. She worked there as a teacher (from 1967 to 1970), as a reporter for *The Chronicle* (1972–1973) and later (1973–1976) as an information assistant with Government Information Services, before going to Britain in 1977. She is married to the poet John Agard. She has published a number of children's books, as well as two collections of poetry and a novel. Her first collection, ▷ *i is a long memoried woman* won the 1983 Commonwealth Poetry Prize; her second, *The Fat Black Woman's Poems* was published in 1984. She is well known for her use of a variety of linguistic styles and registers in her poetry and for the presentation of black women's issues. Her first novel, *Whole of a Morning Sky* (1986), evokes the world of her own Guyanese ▷ childhood during the 1960s.

Her poetry is beginning to receive critical acclaim, and has been included in a number of anthologies: *A Dangerous Knowing: Four Black Women Poets* (1984), *News For Babylon* (1984), *Angels of Fire: Radical Poetry in the 80's* (1986) and *The Penguin Book of Caribbean Verse* (1986). Nichols's voice is considered to be one of the most authoritative among young black women poets.

Nichols, Ruth (born 1948)
Canadian writer of fantasies for children. Born in Toronto, she studied at the University of British Columbia, and at McMaster University. Her books, *A Walk out of the World* (1969), *Ceremony of Innocence* (1969), *The Marrow of the World* (1972), *Song of the Pearl* (1976) and *The Left-Handed Spirit* (1978), use fantasy landscapes, where the young girls who are their protagonists can experience freedom and confront their fears and doubts. Nichols is influenced by J.R.R. Tolkien (1892–1973), the Bible and C.S. Lewis (1898–1963), but succeeds in the magic transformations she effects. Her first adult book of historical fiction is *The Burning of the Rose* (1989).
Bib: Egoff, S., in *The Republic of Childhood.*

Ní Chonaill, Eibhlín Dubh (c 1743–c 1800)
Irish poet, born in Kerry, one of twenty-two children. Widowed after six months of marriage, Eibhlin Dubh she then eloped with a colonel in the Irish Brigade, Art O'Leary, by whom she had three children. Her only known work, *Caoineadh Airt Ui Laoghaire*, (▷ *The Lament for Art O'Leary*), was written following the death of her husband in painful circumstances. Because Art O'Leary was a Catholic, he was not entitled, under the Penal Laws then in force in Ireland, to own a horse worth more than £5. A Protestant neighbour, Morris, offered O'Leary £5 for his fine horse, which O'Leary could not, by law, refuse. Rather than sell his famous mare, O'Leary challenged Morris to a duel, for which Morris had him outlawed. O'Leary escaped, with Eibhlín Dubh's help, but was eventually ambushed and shot by soldiers in 1773. His bloodstained mare returned to Eibhlín Dubh, and guided her to where her beloved husband lay dead. The lament which she composed for him is considered to be the finest love poem in the Irish language.

Ní Chuilleanáin, Eiléan (born 1942)
Irish poet, born in Cork. She studied at University Colllege, Cork, and at Oxford, and now lectures

in English Literature at Trinity College, Dublin. Her first collection, *Acts and Monuments* (1972), won a Patrick Kavanagh Poetry Award. Subsequent volumes include: *Site of Ambush* (1975), *Cork* (1977) and *The Rose Geranium* (1981). *The Second Voyage: Selected Poems*, was published in 1977 and reissued in 1986. Her latest collection is *The Magdalene Sermon* (1989).

Ní Dhomhnaill, Nuala (born 1952)

Irish poet, born in England, who grew up in County Tipperary. Childhood holidays were spent with her mother's Irish-speaking family in County Kerry, where her knowledge of the language and of Irish folklore were nurtured. She studied at University College, Cork, then travelled widely, living in Holland and in Turkey, where she began to write in Irish. She has been awarded many bursaries and prizes for her poetry. Her collections include: *An Dealg Droighin* (1982), (*The Thorn of the Blackthorn*) and *Féar Suaithinseach* (1984) (*Marvellous Grass*). A bilingual selection, *Rogha Dánta/Selected Poems*, appeared in 1986, and *Pharaoh's Daughter* in 1990. One of the most innovative and revitalizing voices in modern Irish writing, her poetry gives central focus to female experience and the feminine, and is at once earthy, mystical, sensuous and witty. She holds 'the sincere conviction that poetry can change the world and that women's poetry *en masse* is about to do just that'.

Ní Dhuibhne, Éilís (born 1954)

Éilís Ní Dhuibhne

Irish novelist and poet, born in Dublin. She studied at University College, Dublin, and in Denmark, obtaining a Ph.D. for her research on Irish folklore. She is now a Keeper in the National Library of Ireland. A first collection of short stories, *Blood and Water*, appeared in 1988, and was followed in 1990 by a novel, *The Bray House*, and more short stories, *Eating Women is*

Not Recommended, in 1991. Her poetry has been published in magazines and anthologies. Her work combines a futuristic and visionary dimension with a sharply satirical evocation of the contexts of women's lives in contemporary Ireland.

Nieh Hualing (born 1925)

Chinese writer. Educated in China, Nieh moved to Taiwan in the late 1940s. Her short stories of this period, later collected in *Emerald Cat* (1959) and *A Little White Flower* (1963), probe beneath the complacency of middle-class life in Taiwan. She settled in the US in 1964 and started the International Writers' Project at the University of Iowa with her husband, the poet, Paul Engle. Her novella, *The Lost Golden Bell* (1961), tells the story of a young girl's initiation into adulthood through her unintentional participation in the unmasking of a clandestine affair. Other publications include a novel, *Mulberry and Peach: Two Women of China* (1976), translations from US literature and prose pieces.

Nigah, Zehra

Pakistani Urdu poet. She lives in London. *Sham ka Pahla Tara* (1980) (*The First Star of Twilight*) contains poems in Urdu with parallel text in English and quotations from Persian verse. Some of her poems have been anthologized in ▷ *We Sinful Women* (1991).

Nigâr (1862–1918)

Turkish poet and memoirist, one of the last great poets of the Ottoman period. She was the daughter of an important army general, who sent her to school in a convent. She was married early in life, but was unhappy and was soon divorced. She had a brilliant literary career after her divorce, travelled in Europe and started a new fashion in the Turkish capital. She hosted a famous Tuesday literary salon, attended by Turkish men of letters and foreign visitors. Pierre Loti (1850–1923) and Sully Prudhomme were two French authors who celebrated this aristocratic muse.

Nigâr's pen-name was *Uryan Kalp* (the naked heart), and she composed poetry suited to this appellation. Her first collection of poetry was called *Alas!* (1876–1890). Her collection *Fires* was published in 1890 and *Echoes* in 1900. A play, *The Abyss* was performed in 1912. Her letters were published in 1901 as *Weakness of a Heart*. After the Young Turks' Revolution in 1908, she led a retired life, compiling memoirs of the old regime. In 1959 her son published an abridged edition of 20 notebooks and diaries she had left him.

Nigerian Women Mobilized: Women's Political Activity in Southern Nigeria 1900–1965 (1987)

A study by the historian Nina Mba, examining the growth of women's political activity. Using documentation and interviews, it builds up a picture of how women organized traditionally, their role in the nationalist movement, and their

political involvement up to the period preceding the civil war between Nigeria and the seceded state of Biafra, which began in 1967. In particular, it gives an account of the Women's War of 1929, in which thousands of Igbo and Ibibio women in eastern Nigeria defied the colonial administration through attacks on warrant chiefs and local court offices. It also gives an account of the mass movement by the women of Abeokuta in 1946–1948 in protest at the imposition of poll tax, and includes interviews with the famous political activist and women's leader, Funmilayo Ransome-Kuti.
Bib: Van Allen, Judith, 'Aba Riot or Igbo Women's War?' in Hafkin, N. and Bay, E. (eds), *Women in Africa*.

Ní Ghlinn, Áine (born 1955)
Irish writer, born in County Tipperary. She lives in Dublin, where she works as a presenter and reporter for RTE, the national broadcasting station. Her poetry, in Irish, has appeared in numerous magazines and anthologies. She has published two collections of poems: *An Chéim Bhriste* (1984) (*The Broken Step*) and *Gairdín Phartais agus Dánta Eile* (1988) (*The Garden of Paradise and Other Poems*).

Night in Acadie, A (1897)
US story collection by ▷Kate Chopin. Chopin's second collection of Louisiana stories and sketches, this volume gives increasing prominence to the theme of women's self-discovery.

Nights and Days (1932–1934)
Translation of *Noce i Dnie*, Polish novel by ▷Maria Dąbrowska. In this *roman-fleuve* the story begins in the late 19th century, and tells the story of a husband and wife from the landed gentry, living on their estate. Financial troubles and conflicts inside the family illustrate the social transformation in Poland during the period from 1863 until World War I in 1914. It is a family saga in four volumes, focusing on the lives of one couple and on husband's awareness that his class – the gentry – is doomed to destruction in this changing society. The role of marriage is also questioned. The prose style is quiet and controlled, using rich but simple language. The novel has been serialized on British television.

Nights at the Circus (1984)
Novel by English writer ▷Angela Carter. Ostensibly a burlesque-picaresque novel that follows the winged protagonist, Fevvers – the 'most famous aerialiste of the day' – on a circus tour from London to Siberia, taking in the workers' struggle in pre-revolutionary Russia *en route*. It is also concerned with the plight of the US journalist, Walser – 'a war correspondent between wars and a passionate amateur of the tall tale' – who joins Fevvers by joining Captain Kearney's Grand Imperial Tour.

If the novel is concerned, as with so many of Carter's novels, with issues of sexuality and culturally prescribed gender roles, then the issues at stake here are rendered more complex through the novel's consistent fragmentation of 'readable' narratives. The description of Fevvers is that of the potentially liberated and empowered woman – a 'Mae West with wings' – and that of Walser the disempowered man whose political and moral journey is towards 'reconstruction'. Yet these surface gender identities are positioned within an interrogation of cultural mythologies of gender, as well as a questioning of the whole problem of 'authenticity': 'Am I fact or am I fiction?' asks Fevvers. *Nights at the Circus* consistently disrupts any simple 'reading off' of political or meaningful narratives. The novel's engagement with history is produced within a questioning of homogenizing narratives. On both counts, the novel occupies a central position in current debates on ▷postmodernism.

Nightwood (1936)
Novel by US writer ▷Djuna Barnes. Barnes's extraordinary novel tells the story of the marginal and estranged who populate the carnivalesque netherworld of pre-war Europe. Paris and Vienna provide the backdrop for Barnes's characters' sense of alienation and their futile, although often grotesquely comic, attempts to find love and, above all, make sense of sexual and racial identity. Thus, Dr Matthew O'Connor, with his box of gynaecological instruments, philosophizes on the characteristics of Irish and Jewish people, whilst the night finds him alone with his wig and woman's nightie. Baron Felix Volkbein thinks he finds love with the novel's anti-heroine, the enigmatic and beautiful Robin Vote, yet this doomed quest for aristocratic perfection is at the same time a symptom of the repression of his Jewish identity. Through Robin's own compelling lesbian love affair with Nora Flood, Barnes explores the possibility of redemption, but here too love gives way to obsession and melancholy. Barnes, like many of her contemporaries, gives us a picture of a degenerate and decaying world. *Nightwood* differs from other works which tackle the same themes, not only because of the humour of the novel and its unique prose-poetry, but also because of Barnes's consistent refusal to judge this world, or to suggest any value-laden cure for its 'maladies'.

Nikambe, Shevantibai M.
Indian novelist and social worker. She was dedicated to the cause of women's education and improving the lot of young married girls and widows in late 19th-century India. She founded a school to educate high-caste Hindu girls, and enrolled married girls and young widows in it. *Ratnabai: A Sketch of a Bombay High-Caste Hindu Wife* (1895) was a crusading novel with an explicitly reformist intention, aiming to influence public opinion in favour of women's education. It told of a girl married at the age of nine, whose father sends her to school against the wishes of her in-laws, while her husband is away in England

for higher education. On his return, the husband finds his young bride transformed by education into his true and equal companion.

▷Child marriage

Nils Holgerssons unberbara rese genom Sverige I–II (1906–1907) (The Wonderful Adventures of Nils and The Further Adventures of Nils)

In 1901 ▷Selma Lagerlöf was asked to write a schoolbook on geography. She had great difficulties, but at last, and after several journeys, the novel about Nils Holgersson appeared. Nils is put under a spell because he treats animals badly. He becomes so small that he can travel on the back of a goose. Through him, we come to see the flora and the fauna, the industry and the geography of Sweden. In a traditional style Lagerlöf has written a ▷*Bildungsroman*, demonstrating an optimistic faith in evolution. As in ▷*The Story of Gösta Berling*, work is shown to be the road to happiness. With this book Lagerlöf wanted to prevent emigration from Sweden. The book has become a classic, and even today it is read to and by most Scandinavian children.

Nimmanhemin, M.L. Bubpha Kunjara ▷Sod, Dok Mai

Nin, Anaïs (1903–1977)

US poet, novelist, short-story writer and diarist. In 1914, after her parents separated, she moved to New York City with her mother, and, in response to her father's leaving, began to keep her famous diaries. In 1923 she married Hugh Guiler, who later illustrated Nin's books under the pseudonym Ian Hugo. They moved to Paris, France, where she wrote *D.H. Lawrence: An Unprofessional Study* (1923). After Nin returned to the US she began printing her own books in order to ensure their publication. Nin's work takes the form of a sustained and often provocative exploration of the relationship between eroticism and identity. It is the study of this theme which linked her with novelist Henry Miller, and his wife June, with whom Nin developed a lifelong association, Surrealist writer Antonin Artaud, and novelist Lawrence Durrell. She also studied with the psychoanalyst Otto Rank and herself practised as an analyst.

She is best-known for her autobiographical works, such as ▷*The Diary of Anaïs Nin: 1931–1977*, which appeared in seven volumes (1966–1980) and *Delta of Venus: Erotica* (1977). Her work records a woman's immediate, emotional reaction to experience, but also investigates the mutability of the self. In her prose poem ▷*House of Incest* (1936), which was set to music by Varese, she describes the desire for psychic wholeness. In *The Winter of Artifice* (1939), a collection of stories, the central character is named after the writer ▷Djuna Barnes. The stories centre on women's need to separate themselves from psychic male domination. Djuna reappears in *Cities of the Interior* (1959).

Other works include: *Under a Glass Bell* (1944), *Realism and Reality* (1946), *On Writing* (1947), *Collages* (1964), *The Novel of the Future* (1968), *Paris Revisited* (1972), *A Woman Speaks: the Lectures, Seminars and Interviews of Anaïs Nin* (1975), *In Favour of the Sensitive Man and Other Essays* (1976), *Waste of Timelessness and Other Early Stories* (1977), which includes six novellas: *Ladders to Fire* (1946), *Children of the Albatross* (1947), *The Four Chambered Heart* (1950), *A Spy in the House of Love* (1954), *Solar Barque* (1958) and *Seduction of the Minatour* (1961); and *Linotte: The Early Diary of Anaïs Nin* (1978–1982).

Nine Guardians, The (1970)

Translation of the Mexican-Indian novel *Balún Canán* (1958) by ▷Rosario Castellanos. The story is set in the years 1934–1940, during the presidency of Cárdenas, who wanted to foster agrarian reform and literacy in Mexico. Castellanos describes the low condition of poor Mexican women, who submit to a ▷patriarchal model of colonization, and contrasts it with the white women of the upper classes who are against governmental political measures designed to change the status quo. At the same time, because of their Catholicism, these upper middle-class women are the victims of guilt, madness and death. The narrator of the book is '*la niña*' ('the girl'), who attempts to recover her subjective memories of the recent past. Meanwhile others – '*la naña*' ('the grandmother'), Uncle David, and the Indian girls Vicenta and Rosália – tell of the magical and mystical past before Spanish colonization. This past consists fo the mystical terror of devilish beings, such as the '*catashaná*', the '*dzulún*' and '*el sombrerón*'. According to the sacred book of the Mayas, *Chilán Balán*, the foreigner is identified with the tiger, or an 'Indian sucker'. *Balún-Canán* is the ancient name for Comitán, the Maya region, in the *tzeltal* idiom, and the name means 'the place where the wind dwells', a symbol for the imagination and for dreams. The kites with which the boys play represent the process of liberating one's imagination, and the wind is the intermediary between heaven and earth. The old Indian prophecies and superstitions work as forms of resistance, so that old cultural patterns may not be forgotten. The novel also depicts the personal conflicts of the family world, showing the girl as repressed for being a woman, and her brother, who finally dies, as privileged and the heir, for being a man. The story is both a cultural critique of the role of women in a Christian, patriarchal, and ethnically dominant society and a personal view of the Indian influences underlying Mexican culture.

Nine Muses, The (1700)

Book of elegies by English women writers to the poet John Dryden (1631–1700), edited by ▷Delarivier Manley, in which each muse laments his death. Contributors include: ▷Susanna

Centlivre, ▷Sarah Fyge, ▷Mary Pix, ▷Catherine Trotter and Lady Piers.

1900 Generation

The name given to a group of mostly male writers, including the Nicaraguan poet Rubén Darío (1867–1916), who developed the Spanish American ▷*Modernismo* or symbolism. The Uruguayan poets ▷Delmira Agustini and ▷Juana de Ibarbourou followed the literary trend they began, as well as being influenced by the French poets such as Victor Hugo (1802–1885), Charles Baudelaire (1821–1867) and Arthur Rimbaud (1854–1891).

1945 Generation

A Brazilian group of writers, especially poets, who came to the fore around 1945, during the third phase of ▷modernism, or ▷postmodernism, and followed the philosophical trend of the international poetry of the Irish poet W.B. Yeats (1865–1939), the US-born English poet T.S. Eliot (1888–1965), the Italian poet Guiseppe Ungaretti (1888–1970), and the Spanish poet Federico García Lorca (1899–1936). They rejected free verse, developed by some modernists, and chose to write with discipline, order, rigour and rhetoric in their poetry. In his *Antologia poética da gerarção de 45* (1966) (*Poetic Anthology of the 1945 Generation*) Godói Campos collected work by the most representative poets of the 1945 Generation – mainly men, but including ▷Stela Leonardos and ▷Hilda Hilst.

▷Cecília Meireles was a founder of the modernist magazine *Festa* (1927). The 1945 Generation's most significant journal was *Orfeu* (1947), whose manifesto was written by Péricules Eugênio da Silva Ramos in the first issue of the magazine *Revista Brasileira de Poesia* (1947) (*Brazilian Poetry Journal*).

1930s novel

In Brazil, this refers to a social novel of the 1930s, or a series of north-eastern social novels, which developed out of the 20th-century ▷*costumbrismo* literary style. The novels discussed rural problems in Brazil, the social conditions in the north-eastern states of the country, and especially the plight of poor tenants and workers emigrating from the hinterland to the coast during the dry season. These novels, written with ▷realism, formed part of the second phase of ▷modernism. The first 1930s novel was *A Bagaceira* (1928) (*Trash*), by José Américo de Almeida. ▷Raquel de Queirós was a noted exponent of the 1930s novel.

Nisanit (1990)

Novel written in English by Palestinian writer Fadia Faqir (born 1956). The subject is the Palestinians living under Israeli occupation after the Arab defeat of 1967. The novel is in three parts, and in each part time goes back and forth, depicting an incident in the light of earlier memories.

The novel is a web of tragedy, war, dispossession, violence, torture and death. At the centre of the web stands Eman, who, like the *nisanit* (a desert flower), will survive.

After the execution of her father, Eman's mainstay is her love for Shaheed. *Shaheed* in Arabic means 'martyr', and Eman's love is for a martyr of a special kind. Imprisoned by the Israelis, Shaheed goes mad. He develops a tenderness for an ant, his only living companion, which evokes comparison with a famous short story in Arabic by Yusuf Idris (1927–1991) in which the torturer drives his prisoner into madness by ordering him to make love to an ant.

Like ▷Sahar Khalifa in *The Cactus* (1976), Fadia Faqir tries to show the human side of some of the Israeli characters in the novel, but as the characters involved with the Arab inhabitants are mainly soldiers, policemen or prison officers, there is little chance for the portrayal of the their softer aspects. Shaheed's torturer, David, suffers torments at the results of his actions, but, as one reviewer commented, it does not bother him sufficiently to make him give up his job.

Niu Zhenhuan (born 1950)

Chinese short story writer. A native of Gansu province, Niu was recruited by the provincial ping-pong team in middle school, but had to give up sports during the 'cultural revolution' (1966–1976). She educated herself by reading, started to publish stories about her native Gansu, and later enrolled in a writing programme at Wuhan University. She now teaches creative writing at the Lanzhou Trade Institute and is a member of the Writers' Union. Her much-anthologized short story, 'Lost in the Wind and the Snow' (1980), describes how rural women sold themselves into marriage to help their families survive during the famine of the 1960s.

Bib: Zhu Hong (trans.), 'Lost in the Wind and the Snow' in *The Serenity of Whiteness*.

Njau, Rebeka (born 1932)

Kenyan novelist, short story writer, dramatist and teacher. Njau was educated at the University of Makerere and is now headmistress of Nairobi Girls' Secondary School. She has two children.

Her plays *In the Round Chain* (mimeograph) and ▷*The Scar* (1965) deal with the oppression of women and the Mau Mau period (during the revolt against white rule, 1952–6) in Kenya. Her powerful symbolic novel ▷*Ripples in the Pool* (1975) considers the conflict between old and new in post-independence Kenya, highlighting the suffering and frustration of women in their search for a new morality. *The Hypocrite* (1980) is a collection of short stories which explore themes of hypocrisy, jealousy, ingratitude and injustice.

Bib: Porter, Abiseh M. in *Ariel* 12 (1981); Schipper, Mineke, *Theatre and Society in Africa*; O'Barr, Jean F. in Jones, Eldred (ed.), *African Literature Today* 8, *Drama in Africa*, 1976; James, Adeola *In Their Own Voices*.

Noailles, Anna de (1876–1933)

French poet and novelist. The daughter of a Romanian prince and a Greek mother, the aristocratic and wealthy de Noailles began writing poetry while still very young. Her first published volumes, *Le Coeur innombrable* (1901) (*Greatheart*) and *L'Ombre des jours* (1902) (*The Shadow of Days*), received a rapturous reception, and her collections of verse (which include *Les Eblouissements*, 1907, *Dazzled*, *Les Vivants et les morts*, 1913, *The Living and the Dead*, and *Les Forces eternelles*, 1921, *Eternal forces*) continued to enjoy considerable popularity. In spite of her fondness for the romantics, particularly Victor Hugo, her own poetry is classical in its form. It is also highly lyrical, and is characterized by a rich (and at times excessive) use of adjectives. Her fondness for oriental themes – she represents the East as a paradise of warmth and sensuality – has been attributed by critics to her exotic background, and to the influence of the writer Maurice Barrès, with whom she was friendly. Another key thematic strand of her verse, which is particularly in evidence in the poems of *L'Honneur de souffrir* (1927) (*The Honour of Suffering*), revolves around man's fear of death and the melancholy this inspires. De Noailles also wrote novels, including *La Nouvelle Espérance* (1903) (*New Hope*), *La Domination* (1904), and *Le Visage emerveillée* (1904) (*The Astonished Face*). Although less striking than the novels of ▷Rachilde, these works have been likened to Rachilde's prose fiction because they display a preoccupation with the bleaker and more 'perverse' aspects of human sensuality. De Noailles was awarded the *grand prix de littérature* by the ▷Académie Française, and in 1922 became a member of the Belgian Royal Academy of language and literature.
Bib: Perche, L., *Anna de Noailles*; Cocteau, J., *La Comtesse de Noailles, oui et non*; Du Bos, C., *Anna de Noailles et le climat de génie*.

Nóbrega, Isabel da (born 1925)

Portuguese novelist and dramatist. Like her contemporaries ▷Fernanda Botelho and ▷Maria Judite de Carvalho, Nóbrega is drawn to the similar Existentialist theme of the impossibility of communication between individuals. In 1965 her book *Viver com os Outros* (*To Live with the Others*) was awarded Portugal's prestigious Camilo Castelo Branco prize for best novel. An unusual work, it is composed entirely of dialogue and has neither a recognizable plot nor a single narrative voice. Among Nóbrega's other books are the novel *Já Não Há Salomão* (1966) (*There's No Longer Any Solomon*) and a volume of short fiction, *Solo Para Gravador* (1973) (*Solo for the Recorder*). She writes regularly for newspapers in Lisbon.

Noce i Dnie (1932–1934) ▷*Nights and Days* (1932–1934)

Noces de Camille, Les (1987) (*Camille's Wedding*)

Fourth novel by French writer ▷Jacqueline Dana. Dana's heroine is a successful, forty-year-old

yuppie, who divides her time between the gym and the office, until she falls for twenty-five-year-old Sébastien. Marriage and a baby follow, but, in the end, Camille is not allowed to escape the generic requirement that the heroine should be young and beautiful: the promised happy ending is denied by the epilogue, which describes Camille resorting to a face-lift, and Sébastien's desiring gaze alighting on a young woman in the Métro.

'No Foe Shall Gather Our Harvest'

Australian poem by ▷Dame Mary Gilmore. This famous patriotic poem was published in the *Australian Women's Weekly* of 29 June 1940, and subsequently appeared in the collection *Fourteen Men* (1954). The poem, of four eight-line stanzas each concluding with the refrain: 'No foe shall gather our harvest,/ Or sit on our stockyard rail', lifted the morale of Australians during the darkest days of World War II when a Japanese invasion of Australia seemed imminent.

Nogami Yaeko (1885–1985)

Japanese novelist, essayist and dramatist. Born in Oita prefecture, she was a student at Meiji high school for girls in Tokyo, which was a centre for women's emancipation from the late 1880s to the 1900s. She married Nogami Toyoichiro, a scholar of English literature, who was under the guidance of Natsume Soseki and who influenced Yaeko's career. She contributed small essays to *Seito* (*The Bluestockings*), a journal for women's literature and women's emancipation. *The Neptune* (1922) portrays the psychology of people who are at the end of their tether. *Machiko* (1928) attracted attention because it describes young people caught up with the Marxist movement. *A Maze* (1958) took her thirty years to write. This work depicts the upper middle class in Japan at the time when fascism was on the rise and the left wing was being suppressed. At the age of 78 she published *Hideyoshi and Rikyu* which describes the conflict between a politician, Hideyoshi, and a tea-ceremony master, Rikyu, in the 16th century. She produced many essays, translations, novels and plays. In 1948 she was made a member of the Japan Academy of Arts, and she received a Cultural Medal in 1971. She died just before her hundredth birthday, while she was writing ▷*Forest*, her autobiographical novel. She had a profound knowledge of English literature as well as Japanese classical works, and always kept a fresh mind while keenly observing subjects from a ▷humanistic view. Her collected works appear in *The Complete Works of Nogami Yaeko* (twenty-six volumes).

No Man's Grove (1985)

US poetry and short story collection. In this book ▷Shirley Geok-lin Lim avoids the dilemma of 'Identity No Longer', as she journeys to her Chinese-Malaysian origins. 'Pantoun for Chinese Women' laments the injustice of female infanticide; 'A Dream of Duty' laments women losing their selves in domestic duties. The poet mourns her troubled relationship with her mother and the daughter struggles to keep her mother's image but, ultimately, she sees only her mother's defeat. In stories like 'Mr Tung's Girls' Lim challenges ▷patriarchy and focuses on women's sexuality. In 'Keng Hua' she shows how racial and sexual attitudes affect a Malaysian woman who fails to take advantage of an opportunity to bring good luck to herself.

Non c'è che te! (1919) (There's No-one But You!)

A ▷futurist novel, by ▷Rosa Rosà. Edvige, the protagonist, is trapped by marriage. She leaves her husband, as she feels it is impossible to be a modern woman and to be married. Rosà here criticizes marriage and the family as bourgeois institutions which have no relation to the needs of modern women. Yet Edvige goes on to be an actress, with all the traditional connotations of moral ambiguity that implies. Edvige is, in other words, in no sense an independent woman. She is conventionally liberated into sexuality. This is certainly an unusually positive novel of its kind, in relation to its prescriptions for women, yet it is still caught in stereotypes.

Noonuccal, Oodgeroo (born 1920)

Australian Aboriginal poet, writer and artist, also known as Kath Walker. Noonuccal received only a primary school education before being sent out to domestic service at thirteen. She was the first Australian woman writer of Aboriginal descent and is a committed Aboriginal activist who has established an Aboriginal cultural and educational centre on Stradbroke Island. She has lectured and tutored in several tertiary institutions, including the University of the South Pacific, and has won a number of awards including the Jessie Litchfield Award in 1975 and the Mary Gilmore Medal in 1970. She has also been awarded an MBE. Her poetry, which usually deals with her rich Aboriginal heritage and its threatened position in Australian culture, includes *We Are Going* (1964), *The Dawn Is at Hand* (1966), *My People* (1970) and *Father Sky and Mother Earth* (1985). She has also compiled *Stradbroke Dreamtime* (1972), which is based on the legends of her people.

▷Aboriginal women's poetry in Australia

No Place for a Nervous Lady: Voices from the Australian Bush (1984)

Criticism and anthology by Lucy Frost. Frost discusses the prolific letter- and journal-writing by 19th-century Australian women, then provides a fascinating collection of extracts from letters and journals, including those of ▷Annie Baxter (1843–1844), Penelope Selby (1840–1851), and Sarah Davenport (1840s).

▷Journals (Australia); Letters (Australia)

Norman, Marsha (born 1947)

US dramatist. Norman was born in Louisville, Kentucky, and her parents were strict Christian fundamentalists who isolated her from other children. In 1969 she earned a degree in philosophy from Agnes Scott College. Norman's plays are about the choices her characters make. *Getting Out* (1977) focuses on Arlene, a prostitute who chooses to work as a dishwasher; she kills her former self and rejects its world of incestuous abuse, neglect and poverty. *'night Mother* (1983) centres on a young woman, Jessie, who has decided to commit suicide, and who moves deliberately through the nightly schedule with Thelma, her mother. Realizing that Jessie means what she says, Thelma recognizes her powerlessness to prevent Jessie's suicide. This play won a Pulitzer Prize. Norman's work features women who take responsibility for their lives, and they also dramatize the powerlessness of characters to save those they care for.

Other works include: *Third and Oak* (1978), *Circus Valentine* (1979), *The Holdup* (1983), *Traveler In the Dark* (1984), *The Fortune Teller* (1987) and *The Secret Garden* (1992).

North and South (1854–1855)

A novel by British writer ▷Elizabeth Gaskell, published serially in Charles Dickens's periodical *Household Words*. *North and South* explores the contrast between the rural south and the industrial north of England, as the heroine, Margaret Hale, moves from Hampshire to Lancashire. During a dispute between workers and employers, she encounters Mrs Thornton and her son John, an inflexible and unsympathetic manufacturer. Margaret finds Thornton's attitudes repellent at first, but gradually the couple move closer together and are finally united. Margaret comes to appreciate and respect both the mill owner and his workers, while Thornton, through Margaret's influence, adopts a more humane attitude towards his employees. Like Gaskell's ▷*Mary Barton*, *North and South* was an important 'social problem' novel of the mid-Victorian period, but the work achieves an added richness through its exploration of religious doubt and its use of industrial unrest as a symbolic register of sexual awareness. Recent feminist critics have argued that it promotes the spread of maternal values outside the sphere of the home and into the commercial world.

Northanger Abbey (1818)

A novel by English novelist ▷Jane Austen, begun in 1798 but not published until after the author's death. In part a satire on popular ▷Gothic literature, particularly the work of ▷Anne Radcliffe, the novel also appropriates Gothic conventions in a progressive and politically significant way. The heroine, Catherine Morland, visits Bath, where she falls in love with Henry Tilney, the son of an officious General. Believing Catherine to be extremely wealthy, General Tilney approves the courtship and invites Catherine to Northanger Abbey, where she begins to fantasize that the General murdered his wife in the medieval abbey. This is shown to be a delusion, but the General is nevertheless presented as villainous: evil, duplicitous and repressive. So, although Austen parodies Gothic trappings, she retains the central Gothic figure – the tyrannical father – and makes him a well-respected pillar of the community and the nation. Austen also liberates her heroine from the codes of propriety that bound 18th-century representations of female characters, allowing Catherine to ask questions that reveal the oppressive and untrustworthy behaviour of paternal despots.

Northwood: A Tale of New England (1827)

US novel by ▷Sarah Josepha Hale. A widely popular, early anti-slavery novel, *Northwood* is notable for its contrasting of US regions. It was one of the first US novels to use the south as a foil for defining the distinctive character of the north.

Norton, Caroline (1808–1877)

British poet, novelist, dramatist and campaigner. She was the granddaughter of Richard Sheridan, and married George Norton in 1827. The marriage was disastrous, and in 1836 her husband brought an action for adultery against Lord Melbourn, who had frequented Caroline Norton's literary salon. The divorce case collapsed for lack of evidence, but Norton's sexual reputation was severely damaged. She then began a long struggle to gain access to and custody of her children, publishing *A Plain Letter to the Lord Chancellor on the Infant Custody Bill* (1839) under the ▷pseudonym Pearce Stevenson. Her efforts resulted in a change in the law in 1839. She later campaigned for the property rights of divorced women in *English Laws for Women in the 19th Century* (1854). She cannot be described as a ▷feminist, however, since she believed in male superiority and sought legal change only on the basis that individual cases existed in which men had failed in their responsibilities. Norton's novels, which were admired in her day, include *The Wife and Woman's Reward* (1835); *Stuart of Dunleath* (1851); *Lost and Saved* (1863). Poetry includes *The Sorrows of Rosalie* (1829); *The Undying One* (1830) and *The Dream* (1840).

▷Reform (19th-century Britain)
Bib: Ackland, A., *Life*; Perkins, J.G., *Life*.

Nossis (4th–3rd century BC)

Poet from the Greek colony of Locri, southern Italy. She composed epigrams (▷Epigram, Ancient Greek), which centre on the worship of the deities Hera and Aphrodite. Twelve of them survive; only two concern men. She refers to herself on three occasions. Once she compares herself with ▷Sappho. One epigram tells us her mother was Theophilis and her grandmother Cleocha. Three epigrams concern dedications to Aphrodite. Three concern portraits of women, one of whom is said to be very like her mother. One epigram is a prayer to the goddess Artemis for aid in childbirth. She inspired the imagist poet ▷H.D. to compose her *Nossis*.
▷Parthenis

Bib: (text & trans.) Paton, W.R., *The Greek Anthology*.

Nöstlinger, Christine (born 1936)

Austrian novelist. Best-known as an author of children's books, for example, *Die feuerrote Friederike* (1970) (*Bright-red Frederike*), her popular writing gives an authentic insight into children's experiences and contemporary Viennese life. Her novel for adults, *Die unteren sieben Achtel des Eisbergs* (1978) (*The Hidden Seven-eighths of the Iceberg*), describes the tragedies which lurk beneath the surface of an apparently ordinary Viennese family.

Nott, Kathleen (born 1909)

English poet and novelist. Generally concerned with philosophical issues, her four volumes of poetry, *Landscapes and Departures* (1947), *The Emperor's Clothes* (1953), *Poems from the North* (1956) and *Creatures and Emblems* (1960), are unified through their interrogations of life and death. Novels include *Mile End* (1938), based on her experience as a social worker in East London. Non-fiction writings include: *Philosophy and Human Nature* (1970) and *The Good Want Power* (1977), a study of liberalism. Other poetry: *Elegies* (1981).

Not Waving But Drowning (1957)

Collection of 68 poems by English writer ▷Stevie Smith. It opens with the eponymous poem, for which she is best known, and which has come to characterize her poetry: ironic, macabre, brief and tragicomic. Moving between commentary on the drowned man and his own post-mortem voice, the poem is about the perpetuation of a fatal misunderstanding: 'I was much too far out all my life / And not waving but drowning.'

Other poems in the collection are variants on the dramatic monologue. 'A Dream of Nourishment', for example, is an adult's recollection of childhood experience, that of the ecstacies of being nurtured, and the shock, whose effects are permanent, of being wrenched from the breast. The themes of death and religion are present in many of the poems, and here Smith is often reminiscent of ▷Emily Dickinson. Another central theme is that of the humiliation and ill-treatment that humans inflict on animals, as in 'Fafnir and the Knights', also an example of Smith's habitual use of ballads and fairytales.

Nouveau roman

Unlike drama or poetry, the novel has never been codified as a genre, and its practice has developed on unquestioned assumptions: that it is a story, told by an omniscient writer, its structure reflecting that of the society it depicts. This concept of the novel came under attack in France in the 1950s for not being 'realistic'. Simultaneously, the obligation for the novel to be simply a copy of reality was replaced by the view that it was a 'practice of writing', free from any narrative structures. The term *nouveau roman* refers to the works of ▷Nathalie Sarraute, Alain Robbe-Grillet, Michel Butor, Claude Simon and Robert Pinget; the inclusion of ▷Marguerite Duras's work is disputed. Of this group, only three have produced theoretical justification of their writing practice, namely Sarraute in ▷ *The Age of Suspicion*, Robbe-Grillet in *Towards a New Novel* (1963) and Butor in *Répertoire* (1960) (*Repertoire*) and *Essays on the Novel* (1964). These writers claim that it is the novels which produce the theory, and not the other way round. Sarraute and Duras show how the *nouveau roman* approach can be used to reflect feminine consciousness, the former by withholding the identity of the narrator, the latter by denying a voice to her central female protagonist.

Nouvelle

French form of short fiction. The *nouvelle* was particularly popular in France in the second half of the 17th century, following the demise of the so-called *grand roman*, or novel on the grand scale, around 1660. The revival of interest in this type of fiction is usually credited to *Les Nouvelles françaises* (1658) by Jean Regnauld de Segrais (1624–1701), but is in no small part related to the influence of conversational readings of individual tales in the long novels like *L'Astrée* (*Astrea*) by Honoré d'Urfé (1567–1625), *Artamène, ou le Grand Cyrus* (1649–1655) (▷*Artamenes, or The Grand Cyrus*, 1653–1655), and *Clélie, histoire romaine* (1654–1660) (▷ *Clelia: An excellent new romance*, 1661) in the women-dominated salons with which Segrais was also associated. Late 17th-century *nouvelles* were inspired by the dual Italian and Spanish tradition of the form. The continuing influence of the *société conteuse* or frame narrative in imitation of the Italian author Boccaccio (1313–1375) by such writers as ▷Marguerite de Navarre in the 16th century was a particularly significant influence on both long and short narrative, encouraging the return to the *nouvelle* form in the 1660s, which was by no means as abrupt as has been thought. *Nouvelles* were usually defined by their brevity, the fact that the story had happened only recently, and that the narrator stood guarantee for the accuracy and authenticity of the tale told. This form of narrative was particularly popular with female novelists such as ▷Madeleine de Scudéry, ▷Madame de Lafayette and Madame de Villedieu (▷Marie-Catherine Hortense Desjardins).

Novak, Helga (born 1935)

German poet and novelist. Born in Berlin, she studied journalism in Leipzig, and lived in Iceland, France, Spain and the USA before returning to East Germany. Her first collection of poems, *Die Ballade von der reisenden Anna* (*The Ballad of Anna on Her Travels*), distributed clandestinely in East Germany in 1958, was one of the earliest attacks on the repressive policies of the socialist government. In 1966 she was expelled from the East, and settled in West Germany. Political issues that evolve from personal experience are central to all her work, particularly her fictional, two-part autobiography, ▷*Die Eisheiligen* (1979) (*Saints of Ice*) and *Vogel Federlos* (1982) (*Featherless Bird*). Both books are important contributions to the debate on the Third Reich, World War II, and the post-war division of Germany.

Nováková, Teréza (1853–1912)

Czech novelist. The content of Nováková's works places her among an earlier literary generation, but her treatment of human beings as fundamentally political entities makes her a realist. She was born into a German family, though her civil servant father soon became interested in Czech matters. She married a Czech schoolmaster, and their son, Arne (1880–?) was to become the leading Czech literary historian of the First Republic (1918–1938). Her *roman à thèse Jiří Smatlan* (1906), sets out to demonstrate that the socialists were the natural descendants of the Bohemian Brethren (a Protestant Church founded in the late 15th century). In other words Nováková modifies T.G. Masaryk's notion of the spirit of Czech history. *Drašar*, published posthumously in 1914, is a fictional biography of the minor National Revival writer, Josef V.J. Michl (1810–1862), which turns into a novel about a 'beautiful loser'. Michl, the 'Drašar' of the title, is a dreamer whose dreaming does ill to himself and to others. In *Dva obrazy staropražské* (1921) (*Two Old Prague Portraits*) Nováková allows her neo-revivalist proclivities to run away with her.

Novas Cartas Portuguesas (1972) ▷*Three Marias: New Portuguese Letters, The*

Novelas amorosas y exemplares (1635) (Exemplary Love Stories)

Collection of stories by ▷María de Zayas y Sotomayor, one of the most distinguished female writers of 17th-century Spain. The stories depict a world in which the sexes are locked in conflict. In one of the stories a wife is immured by her husband, and released only when her flesh has been eaten away by worms. In another a woman is forced to drink from the skull of her ex-lover. Not surprisingly, Zayas's stories also depict female revenge against male tormentors.

Novel on Yellow Paper (1936)

Novel by English writer ▷Stevie Smith, which gained critical acclaim and established her as a writer. Its loquacious narrator, 'the talking voice that runs on', Pompey Casmilus, is also the heroine of *Over the Frontier* (1938). Plot in Smith's novels is subordinated to her delight in word-play and the expression of opinions – about death, love, sex, literature, friendship, work and marriage. 'This is a foot-off-the-ground novel that came by the left hand', Pompey warns the reader: 'And the thoughts come and go and sometimes they do not quite come and I do not embarrass them with formality to pursue them into a harsh captivity.' The novel combines direct address to the reader with interior monologue. At the time of its publication it was assimilated to ▷stream-of-consciousness techniques like those of ▷Virginia Woolf and ▷Dorothy Richardson, but Smith's narrative voice is far more colloquial than theirs, mimicking other tones and voices and relishing US slang. This voice is witty and acerbic (the novel contains superb parodies of ▷romantic novels and 'agony aunt' wisdoms), and at times offensive – Pompey's comments on her 'Jew-friends' grate on the modern ear, and are said to have angered her Jewish friends at the time. Pompey/Smith's preoccupation with Jews arose in part from her troubled thoughts on Germany, whose past culture she loved, but whose contemporary realities made her increasingly fearful as fascism advanced.

Novel on Yellow Paper is also about death and unrequited love, and running through the wit and cynicism is a sense of the difficulties facing women who want more from life than society is prepared to let them have. The novel is 'autobiographical' in that the experiences and friendships it describes were Smith's own, but its interest in this context is the way it ventriloquizes, rather than mirrors, the self.

NOW

National Organization for Women (USA), founded by Betty Friedan in 1966. The movement was characterized as middle-class and reformist by Robin Morgan, a lesbian feminist, who charged Friedan and her followers with adopting anti-lesbian sentiments in the interest of producing a respectable public image for feminism.
Bib: Morgan, R. (ed.), *Sisterhood is Powerful*.

Numeri e sogni (1887) (Numbers and Dreams)

Italian novel by ▷Bruno Sperani which, like the earlier ▷*Nell'ingranaggio* (1885) (*Caught in the Wheel*), is set in Milan, and tells the tale of a sad love affair which ends in the suicide of a female protagonist. Marietta, an artist's model, is in love with the painter, Adriano. Like her predecessor, Gilda, she is duped and exploited by the man she loves. This male character, however, is not a wealthy, powerful representative of the ruling class, but a member of the artistic avant-garde. He is also a doubly destructive character, in that he ruins not just Marietta's life, but also the life of his conventional wife, Filomena. Both female characters in this novel are socially oppressed, and when one compares this work with Sperani's earlier novel, it is easy to see how she constructs the relationship between the sexes as oppressive in itself for women.

Nunes, Maria Natália (born 1921)

Portuguese novelist. She was curator at the National Archives of the Torre de Tombo in Lisbon from 1957 to 1968. Despite having written many novels and volumes of short fiction in the 1950s and 1960s, she has been somewhat neglected by critics. Most of her protagonists are women, and romantic love is a prominent theme. Among her works are *Autobiografia duma Mulher Romântica* (1955) (*Autobiography of a Romantic Woman*); *Assembléia de Mulheres* (1964) (*Assembly of Women*) and the novella *O Caso de Zulmira* (1967) (*The Case of Zulmira*).

Nwapa, Flora (born 1931)

Flora Nwapa

Nigerian short story writer and novelist. The first African woman to publish a novel, she is from the lakeside town of Oguta in the Igbo-speaking part of eastern Nigeria. Her first two novels, ▷*Efuru* (1966) and ▷*Idu* (1970), are given traditional settings, but all her subsequent work has dealt with contemporary issues in Nigerian life, specifically the changing situation of women. She has published two collections of short stories, *This is Lagos* (1986) and *Wives at War* (1980), and two more novels, *One is Enough* (1981) and ▷*Women are Different* (1986). In the first novel, a woman leaves her husband because she is childless, and becomes a successful businesswoman in Lagos. Though she has children by another man, she refuses to marry him – 'One is enough.' The second novel is about a circle of women who were contemporaries at school – the author's own school at Elelenwa in eastern Nigeria – and how they cope with the conflicts and contradictions of life in the real world. Both stress the importance of women's autonomy and the need for a support network of other women.

▷Oral tradition (West Africa)
Bib: Adams Graves, A. and Boyce-Davies, C. (eds), *Ngambika: Studies of Women in African Literature*; Brown, L., *Women Writers in Black Africa*; Taiwo, O., *Female Writers of Modern Africa*; James, A., *In Their Own Voices: Interviews with African Women Writers*.

Oates, Joyce Carol (born 1938)

US novelist, short story writer, poet and essayist. Oates was born in Lockport, New York, and was raised a Catholic. While an English major at Syracuse University, she wrote a novel each term. In 1961 she earned a Master's degree at the University of Wisconsin, and also married. She has taught in a number of universities, including the University of Detroit and Princeton.

In her fiction Oates pushes naturalism beyond itself. Her work is characterized by its violence, and this violence emphasizes her characters' struggle to define themselves against their oppressive circumstances. In 'Where Are You Going, Where Have You Been?' (1974) and ▷*them* (1969) the violence is often associated with male sexual aggression. Women struggle against their socio-economic circumstances, but they become sexually victimized and lose their identity in the struggle, as in *Do With Me What You Will* (1973), and *A Garden of Earthly Delights* (1967), where a woman achieves social and economic status through marriage, but finds herself and her son caught in an alienating parody of the American Dream. *Bellefleur* (1980) and the *Bloodsmoor Romance* (1983) are historical novels which focus on women's roles.

Other works include: *By the North Gate* (1963), *With Shuddering Fall* (1964), *Upon the Sweeping Flood and Other Stories* (1966), *Expensive People* (1968), *Anonymous Sins and Other Poems* (1969), *The Wheel of Love and Other Stories* (1970), *Love and Its Derangements* (1970), *Cupid and Psyche* (1970), *Wonderland* (1971), *Marriages and Infidelities* (1972), *Angel Fire: Poems* (1973), *The Goddess and Other Women* (1974), *The Hungry Ghosts: Seven Allusive Comedies* (1974), *The Seduction and Other Stories* (1975), *The Assassins: A Book of Hours* (1975), *The Fabulous Beasts* (1975), *The Triumph of the Spider Monkey* (1976), *Childwold* (1976), *Son of the Morning: A Novel* (1978), *Women Whose Lives Are Food, Men Whose Lives Are Money* (1978), *The Step Father* (1978), *All the Good People I've Left Behind* (1979), *Queen of the Night* (1979), *Cybele* (1979), *Unholy Loves* (1979), *A Sentimental Education* (1980), *Contraries: Essays* (1981), *Angel of Light* (1981), *On Boxing* (1987), *American Appetites* (1989) and *Black Water* (1992). **Bib.** Friedman, Ellen G., *Joyce Carol Oates*.

Oba Minako (born 1930)

Japanese novelist. Born in Tokyo, she lived for eleven years in Alaska, where her husband had been transferred. *The Three Crabs*, which describes the endless emptiness of a wife, won not only the Ginzo Prize for a New Writer, but the Akutagawa Prize as well. *No Stereotype* won the Tanizaki Prize in 1980. Her perspective is free from the stereotyped view of dichotomies – such as man and woman, the world and Japan – as exemplified in her collection of critical essays *A Theory on Man from the Standpoint of a Woman. Tsuda Umeko* (1990), a biography of Tsuda Umeko, who went to the USA to study in 1871 and founded Tsuda College, exactly expresses her ideas. She is a prolific writer, and her collected works to date are soon to be published.

Obasan (1981)

▷Joy Kogawa's Canadian historical novel about the internment of Japanese-Canadians as enemy aliens in World War II. *Obasan* is a spare and haunting combination of document, fiction, and political examination. Through three powerful female characters, each of whom has differing ways of handling grief and pain, Kogawa explores the extended silence arising from the unjust persecution of the Japanese-Canadians, but she succeeds also in asserting the ambivalent identity of every Canadian. The central narrator in *Obasan* asks, 'Where do any of us come from in this cold country?' Her answer, 'We come from our untold tales that wait for their telling. We come from Canada, this land that is like every land, filled with the wise, the fearful, the compassionate, the corrupt', is not afraid to acknowledge the nature of racism and separation.

Obeah

This term is of relevance to Caribbean writing. The practice of witchcraft was brought to the Caribbean from Africa. *Obeah* is essentially a magical practice whereby an individual may obtain personal desires, eradicate ill-health, procure good fortune in life and business, evoke love, evince retribution or revenge and generally manipulate the spiritual forces of the cosmos. It is practised by both men and women throughout the Caribbean.

O'Brien, Edna (born 1932)

Irish novelist, short story and travel writer, born in County Clare. She studied in Dublin, and later moved to London, where she still lives. Her first novel, *The Country Girls* (1960), was a *succès de scandale* in Ireland for its frank and sensuous descriptions of women's sexuality and, not least, for its clearly autobiographical elements. A series of novels followed in rapid succession: *The Lonely Girl* (1962), filmed as *The Girl with Green Eyes*, *Girls in their Married Bliss* (1964), *August is a Wicked Month* (1965), *Casualties of Peace* (1966), *A Pagan Place* (1970), *Night* (1972), *Johnny I Hardly Knew You* (1977) and *Returning* (1982). *The High Road* (1988) is her most recent novel. Her short-story collections include: *The Love Object* (1968), *A Scandalous Woman and Other Stories* (1974), *Mrs Reinhardt and Other Stories* (1978) and *A Fanatic Heart* (1985). Her play about the life of ▷Virginia Woolf, *Virginia*, was first performed in 1981, and *Far From the Land* in 1989.

▷Censorship (Ireland)

O'Brien, Kate (1897–1974)

Irish novelist, biographer and travel writer. She was born in County Limerick, and educated at a convent boarding school and at University College, Dublin. She lived in London for a time, and then in Spain, where she developed a passionate and enduring love of Spanish literature

Kate O'Brien

characterizes her work. A poem such as 'An Octopus', about Tacoma, the ▷Native American name for Mount Ranier, shows Moore juxtaposing the languages of the romantic ode, the discursive essay and the tourist guide to investigate the myth of the North American wilderness and the relationship of man and nature. 'Marriage' interweaves fragmentary quotations which explore the fantasies accruing to the 'institution' of marriage. Other better-known poems, such as 'To a Snail' and 'To a Chameleon', explore aesthetics. Moore's interest in form as itself an interpretive process is already apparent here in poems such as 'The Fish' and 'Sea Unicorns and Land Unicorns'.

Ocampo, Silviana (born 1903)

Argentinian poet and short story writer. She is a sister of ▷Victoria Ocampo, and in 1934 married Adolfo Bioy Casares. They were friends of the Argentinian writer Jorge Luis Borges (1899–1986). However, despite these associations, her work is not very well-known outside her own country. Her family ancestors included some of Argentina's founding fathers, and she studied drawing and painting, as well as French, English, and her native Spanish.

Ocampo's first book of prose, *Viaje olvidado* (1937) (*Forgotten Journey*), places her in the vanguard of literature. Together with Borges and Casares she organized the important *Antología de la literatura fantástica* (1940), (*Anthology of Fantastical Literature*), and the *Antología poética argentina* (1941) (*Anthology of Argentinian Poetry*). Her first book of poetry, *Enumeracion de la patria y otros poemas* (1942) (*Enumeration of the Mother Country and Other Poems*), tackled the often opposing ideas of the infinite as opposed to apparent. She became more inward-looking in her following books of poetry *Poemas de amor deseperado* (1949) (*Poems of Desperate Love*) and *Lo amargo por dulce* (1962) (*Bitterness Through Sweetness*). The latter, written as an autobiography, exposes conflicting aspects of her own self, in a kind of 'intellectual extasis' and it won the National Poetry Award. *Espacios métricos (1945) (Metric Spaces)* is an anthology of more traditional poetry. In both *Informe del cielo y del infierno* (1969) (*Report From Heaven and Hell*) and *Autobiografía de Irene* (1948) (*Autobiography of Irene*) – part of which is included in the translation *Leopoldina's Dream* (1988) – Ocampo shows her indifference towards conventional values.

Her reputation as a short story writer was secured by the publication of her collections of short stories, *La furia* (1959) (*Fury*) and *Las invitadas* (1961) (*The Women Guests*). Symbolism, particularly mythological allusions and archetypes, pervades the short story '*Las invitadas*', who represent the seven deadly sins. In her twenty-four stories she goes beyond the intimacy of her poetry and explores aspects of everyday life, from the humble and beautiful, through trivialities to the grandiose. *Ulysses*, *The Furies*, and other examples, reveal her awareness of time, and her

and culture. Although her first play, *Distinguished Villa* (1926), had a successful run in a London theatre, it was her first novel, *Without My Cloak* (1931), which established her literary reputation, winning the Hawthornden Prize. A succession of beautifully crafted and superbly readable novels followed: *The Ante-Room* (1934), *Mary Lavelle* (1936), *Pray for the Wanderer* (1938), ▷*The Land of Spices* (1941), *The Last of Summer* (1943), *That Lady* (1946), *The Flower of May* (1953), *As Music and Splendour* (1958) and *Presentation Parlour* (1963). One of this century's great novelists, her fiction broke new ground in Irish writing by focusing on the prosperous Catholic bourgeoisie, and by giving central importance to women's struggle for selfhood and the dilemmas of identity and sexuality in a rigidly sex-stereotyped society. She is unique among Irish writers of her generation in her sensitive exploration of relationships between women. Ironically, two novels by this most understated of writers were originally banned in Ireland under the terms of the Censorship of Publications Act (1929). Of Anglo-Irish writing she remarked: 'We have made a literature, slowly and in some pain and confusion.'
▷Censorship (Ireland)

Observations (1924)

US poetry collection by ▷Marianne Moore which contains material from her first collection, *Poems* (1921), which was published in England by ▷H.D., ▷Bryher and Robert McAlmon without Moore's knowledge. Additional poems in the collection include 'Marriage' (1923) which had appeared the previous year, 'An Octopus' and 'Sea Unicorns and Land Unicorns'. Moore describes poetry as 'imaginary gardens with real toads in them', suggesting the blend of the fantastic and the accurately observed that use of the esoteric combined with ▷magic realism. Probably because of her wealthy background, she never dwelt on social problems in her work, nor on regional topics. She travelled and wrote, without the restraint of economic pressure. In the 1970s she concentrated mainly on writing for adolescents.

Other works: *Sonetos del jardín* (1948) (*Garden Sonnets*); *Los nombres* (1953) (*Names*); *Pequeña antología* (1954) (*Small Anthology*); *Los Traidores*, with J.R. Wilcock (1956) (*The Traitors*); *El pecado mortal* (1966) (*The Mortal Sin*); *Amarillo celeste* (1972) (*Heavenly Yellow*), and *Cornelia frente al espejo* (1988) (*Cornelia in Front of the Mirror*).

Ocampo, Victoria (1890–1979)
Argentinian novelist, historian and essayist. Her memoirs are considered an important record of her time. She had a fine education, often stayed in Europe, and studied at the Sorbonne in Paris. In 1931, she founded ▷*Sur* magazine, and later a leading publishing house with the same name. In 1939 she recited 'Perséphone' by the French novelist André Gide (1869–1951), accompanied by music by the Russian composer Igor Stravinsky (1882–1971). She performed at Stravinsky's invitation in Buenos Aires, Rio and Florence. In 1931 she visited the United States, invited by the Guggenheim Memorial Foundation, and in 1946 went to England and France as the guest of the British Council and French government. During the German occupation of France, she supported the journal *Lettres Françaises* in Buenos Aires. She lectured and taught in Argentina and abroad, and contributed to *La Nación* and other newspapers. She occupied several cultural positions and received many honours from France, India, England and Argentina. In 1976 she became the first woman to enter the Argentinian Academy of Letters. She translated several books, and recorded poetry in French.

Works: *De Francesca a Beatrice* (1924) (*From Francesca to Beatrice*); *La laguna de los nenúfares* (1924) (*The Poet of the Water Lilies*); *Testimonios* (1935, 1941, 1950, 1957, 1964, 1967, 1971, 1975, 1977) (*Testimonies*); *Domingos en Hyde Park* (1936) (*Sundays in Hyde Park*); *El viajero y una de sus sombras* (1951) (*A Traveller and One of his Shadows*); *Habla el Algarrobo* (1959) (*The Carob Tree Speaks*); *La bella y sus enamorados* (1964) (*The Beauty and her Lovers*); *Memorias: El Archipiélago* (1979) (*Memories: The Aschipelago*); *El imperio insular* (1980) (*The Island Emperor*); *La rama de Salzburgo* (1981) (*The Salzburg Branch*); *Viraje* (1982) (*Bend*), and *Figuras simbólicas, Medida de Francia* (1983) (*Symbolic Figures, Medida of France*).

Ochre People, The (1963)
Autobiographical text by South African writer ▷Noni Jabavu, first published in England, and reprinted in South Africa in 1982. The text looks lovingly at the rhetorical richness of the Xhosa language and, in particular, its capacity for tact: the languages of apartheid are brutal by contrast. It also pays homage to what is called 'that oblique

African laughter', whereby the disenfranchised deal with the crudities of life under white rule.

The book, whose ostensible aim is to celebrate Xhosa civilization, presents a journey through the Ciskei, from Middledrift, the author's paternal home, to Confluence Farm, the home of her maternal relations. The journey proceeds north to Johannesburg, where people are eking out an existence, many using old water-tanks as their homes, and where gangsterism is rife. The sharp contrast between this and the rural harmony, albeit poverty-stricken, of the earlier sections is modified by Jabavu's vision of a shadow city, not only versed in endurance but also holding on to what she sees as the standards of civilized life.

The dramatic tension of the autobiography pivots on the narrator's relation with her step-mother, whose presence functions symbolically as the barrier between daughter and father, and between the past and the present. The book manifests what one critic has called 'the pathos of lastness': a family life that cannot be retrieved, an idyllic communal past that lives only in the writer's imagination. In the preface to the new edition Jabavu pays tribute to the younger generation – who were born and grew up in the course of her prolonged absence from South Africa – for their revolutionary fervour, but in the original text she is uneasy with political activism. The distance between this Xhosa 'grandmother' and the post-1976 generation is also widened by her idealized representation of Xhosa life as homogeneous, and her apparently untroubled participation in its ▷patriarchal structures: both as experiencing self within her community and as narrating self, the critically-minded woman writer is surprisingly muted.

O'Connor, Clairr (born 1951)
Irish poet, dramatist and novelist, born in County Limerick, and educated at University College, Cork, and at St Patrick's College, Maynooth. She taught in London for several years, and then returned to Ireland, where she continues to work as a teacher. Her plays include: *Getting Ahead* (1987), broadcast on BBC Radio, *No Return*, and *House of Correction* (both 1988). *When You Need Them*, her first collection of poems, appeared in 1989, and *Belonging*, a novel, in 1991.

O'Connor, Flannery (1925–1964)
US short-story writer and novelist. Born a Roman Catholic in Georgia, O'Connor attended the Writer's Workshop at the University of Iowa. Suffering from disseminated lupus, a rare and incurable blood disease, she moved to Milledgeville, Georgia, where she lived with her mother, raising chickens and peacocks.

Like the daughters in ▷*A Good Man is Hard to Find and Other Stories* (1955), O'Connor rebelled against the role of the ▷Southern lady, criticizing conventional Southern pride for its false piety and moral blindness. Her fiction features grotesque characters to emphasize how pride perverts the self.

The novels *Wise Blood* (1952) and *The Violent Bear It Away* (1960) centre around prophetic figures who expose humanity's hypocrisies and limitation. O'Connor envisions an apocalyptic grace that smashes through this pride, and her work is characterized by violence to stress the need of the self for redemption.

Other works include: *Everything That Rises Must Converge* (1965), *Mystery and Manners* (1969), *The Complete Stories* (1972) and *The Habit of Being: The Letters of Flannery O'Connor* (1979).
Bib. Montgomery, Marion, *Why Flannery O'Connor Stayed Home*.

Odaga, Asenath Bole

Kenyan novelist, dramatist and children's writer. Odaga was educated at the University of Nairobi where she did research at the Institute of African Studies before becoming a full-time writer. Writing both in Luo and English, Odaga's publications include *The Villager's Son* (1971), *Jande's Ambition*, *The Shade Changes*, *A Bridge in Time* (1987), *Between the Years* (1987), *The Diamond Ring* and *Tutinda*. She has also published two works on oral traditions, *Yesterday's Today: The Study of Oral Literature* (1984), and jointly with K. Akivaga, *Oral Literature: A School Certificate Course* (1982). She is setting up a publishing house to encourage young writers to publish books in Kiswahili.

Odaldi, Suor Annalena (1572–1638)

Italian dramatist. Born Lessandra Odaldi in Pistoia, she was the sixth of a family of fifteen children. In 1585, she entered the Franciscan convent of Santa Chiara, and took her religious name. She had various tasks over the years in the convent, such as sacristan, bookkeeper and Mistress of Novices. She wrote comedy while in this last capacity, so that the novices could perform before an audience of nuns as part of the ▷Carnival festivities. All of the comedies, while they have a religious grounding, are secular in tone and plot. Essentially, they are satirical verse comedies, which deal with marriage and parental responsibility. Nuns are positively portrayed in her work, while marriage is anything but a peaceful haven. She wrote three plays: ▷*Commedia di Nannuccio e quindici figliastre* (1600) (*The Tale of Nannuccio and Fifteen Stepdaughters*), *Commedia di mastro Paoluccio medico* (1604) (*The Tale of Paul the Doctor*), *Commedia di tre malandrini* (1604) (*The Tale of the Three Rogues*).
Bib: Weaver, Elissa, 'Convent Comedy and the World: The Farces of Suor Annalena Odaldi', *Annali d'Italianistica*, 7, (1989) pp. 182–93.

Odendaal, Welma (born 1951)

South African short story writer and journalist, writing largely in Afrikaans. She was born in Vereeniging, Transvaal, and now lives in Cape Town. In 1973 she published her first collection of short stories, *Getuie vir die naaktes* (*Testimony for the Naked*), to considerable critical acclaim. Her second collection, *Keerkring (Tropic)*, published in 1977, was banned by the Directorate of Publications for its depiction of the political situation in the country. All the publisher's copies were destroyed and it has not yet been republished. At the time Odendaal was working at the South African Broadcasting Corporation Radio Service as a sub-editor on the national news programme, a position from which she was dismissed as a result of her political activities. Her most recent collection is *Verlate Plekke* (1991) (*Deserted Places*).

Odendaal's work is characterized by a semi-journalistic style. In many of the stories she examines the effect of the violence endemic in South African society, often representing some form of loss of innocence. Besides the awkward questions she asks about South African political morality, some of her stories focus on lesbianism, and thus fly in the face of the intense patriarchalism of Afrikaner culture. Short stories in English have appeared in *LIP from Southern African Women* (1983) and in *Tri/Quarterly*'s special issue on South African writing, *From South Africa* (1987), edited by David Bunn and Jane Taylor.

'Ode of Gratitude, An' (1790)

A North American poem written in the early 1770s, and addressed to the poet ▷Elizabeth Graeme Fergusson, ▷Anna Young Smith's tribute to her aunt's generosity in raising her and encouraging her literary talents is representative of the many poems she published during her short lifetime. Dying in childbirth when she was aged about twenty-three, she had not yet had the time to refine the beginnings of literary talent that are evident in this poem.

Odóevtseva, Irina Vladimirovna 1901

Pen-name of the Russian poet, prose writer and memoir-writer, Iraida Gustavovna Geinike. Odóevtseva began publishing poetry in 1920 as a pupil of Nikolai Gumilëv, from whom she learned poetic restraint and refinement, and the use of an accomplished but unobtrusive metre and rhyme. Some reviewers criticized her poetry as imitative. Her verse, like ▷Akhmátova's, often has a 'story' to it, based on love; in 1922 she published a book of ballads, *Court of Miracles*. That same year she emigrated to Paris with her husband, the poet Georgii Ivanov. She published four novels between 1927 and 1954. The last of them is *All Hope Abandon*, which is set among the élite in Soviet Russia on the eve of World War II. In the 1950s she returned to poetry. Vladimir Markov characterized her *émigré* verse as 'the dazzling lightness of Odóevtseva's delirious dreams' (*Modern Russian Poetry*: 1 xvi). It can also be tinged with irony, and display a unique combination of the real and surreal. Odóevtseva has published two memoirs, *On the Banks of the Neva* (1967) which covers the years 1918–22 and focuses on Gumilëv's tutelage, and *On the Banks of the Seine* (1983) which has a particularly interesting chapter on ▷Gíppius and her

husband, Dmitrii Merezhkovskii. In 1987
Odóevtseva returned to the USSR to live.
Bib: Nachshen, D. (trans.), *Out of Childhood*;
Reed, F. (trans.), *All Hope Abandon*; Pachmuss, T.
(trans.), *A Russian Cultural Revival*; Markov, V.
and Sparks, M. (eds), *Modern Russian Poetry*;
'Days with Bunin', *Russian Review* (1971), pp.
111–23, 226–39.

O'Donnell, Mary E. (born 1954)
Irish poet and short story writer. Born in County
Monaghan, she now lives in County Kildare, and
works as a theatre critic. Her first collection of
poems, *Reading Sunflowers in September*, appeared
in 1990, and a short story collection, *Strong
Pagans*, in 1991.

Oedipus complex
In Freud's account of psycho-sexual development,
little girls and boys must resolve the Oedipus
complex in order to acquire a sexual identity. This
happens in different ways for boys and girls, but
the boy's case is taken as the norm against which
the little girl's progress is measured. Infants of
both sexes take their mother as initial love object
(the Oedipus complex). For boys, the acquisition
of a masculine identity necessitates giving up
competition with the father for sexual possession
of the mother, and learning to identify instead
with the psycho-sexual position of the father,
which is authoritative and patriarchal. This shift is
mobilized by the fear of castration which occurs at
the moment when the boy child sees that his
mother and sister lack a penis (the castration
complex).

The resolution of the Oedipus complex in girls
is more complicated, and Freud is unclear exactly
how this occurs. Nevertheless, he suggests that
the acquisition of femininity for young girls turns
on the recognition that they are already castrated,
which provokes a disgust for the mother, whom
the girl blames for her inferior genitals, and
henceforth relinquishes as love-object,
transferring her desire instead to the father and
the promise of bearing a boy-child some time in
the future.
▷Penis envy; Psychoanalysis

Oeil du jour, L' (1985) (The Day's Eye)
A novel by the Tunisian writer, ▷Beji Hélé. The
narrator, who lives in Paris, goes back to her
native town, Tunis. She is enchanted with the
traditions of the Mediterranean and Arab culture
kept alive by her grandmother. With the
grandmother's death this whole world goes into
oblivion. With despair and nostalgia she sees her
native town transformed in a world of vice and
baseness. She condemns the elite for adopting
only the negative aspects of the modern West.

Oeuvre au noir, L' (1968) ▷Abyss, The (1976)

O'Faolain, Julia (born 1932)
Irish writer, born in London, the daughter of the
writer Sean O'Faolain (born 1900). She studied at
University College, Dublin, at the Sorbonne in
Paris, and in Rome, and now lives in the USA. A
prodigiously hard-working and prolific novelist
and short story writer, she has also made
translations from the Italian, and edited (with her
husband, Lauro Martines) a collection of
polemical writings about women, *Not in God's
Image: Women in History from the Greeks to the
Victorians* (1973). Her novels include: *Godded and
Codded* (1970) (published as *Three Lovers* in the
USA), *Women in the Wall* (1975), *No Country for
Young Men* (1980), *The Obedient Wife* (1982) and
The Irish Signorina (1984). Her collections of short
stories are: *We Might See Sights* (1968), *Man in the
Cellar* (1974), *Melancholy Baby* (1978) and
Daughters of Passion (1982). Her best-known novel
is probably *No Country for Young Men*, a satirical,
painful comedy about the punishing burdens laid
on Irish women by Church, state and history.

Ofelia ▷Matamoros, Mercedes

Of The Markes of the Children of God (1590)
English writer ▷Anne Locke's ▷translation of
John Taffin's French work. Taffin had composed
his treatise as a comfort to Protestants enduring
persecution in the Netherlands. Locke translated
Taffin's work in the belief that English Protestants
would soon be in need of similar comfort. In her
dedication to the Countess of Warwick, Locke
describes her sense of herself as a woman author
and religious instructor. 'Everie one in his calling
is bound to doo somewhat to the furtherance of
the holie buiding; but because great things by
reason of my sex, I may not doo, and that which I
may, I ought to doo, I have according to my
duetie, brought my poore basket of stones to the
strengthening of the walles of Iurusalem.'
▷Prefaces; Protestant Reformation

Ogot, Grace Akinyi (born 1930)
Kenyan novelist, short story writer and politician.
Ogot was trained as a nurse at St Thomas's
Hospital, London, was married in 1959 and
studied at Makerere University (1963–4). She
became an announcer for BBC Radio and
Principal of the Women's Training Centre,
Kisumu, Kenya. Her bride price on her marriage
in 1959 was 25 head of cattle. Ogot has worked in
the Kenyan media and is prominent in politics
and diplomacy: she has been a UN delegate, a
member of UNESCO and member of parliament.

Her publications include ▷*The Promised Land*
(1966), a story of Luo pioneers in Tanzania,
typical of Ogot in its blend of magic and realism;
▷*Land Without Thunder* (1968), short stories
about traditional life in rural East Africa; *The
Other Woman and other stories* (1976), which deals
with problems of modern life; ▷*The Graduate*
(1980), a novel about a graduate who goes to
America and returns home to find things have
changed; and *The Island of Tears* (1980), short
stories on a range of themes, the title story
commemorating the death of Tom Mboya, the
Kenyan political leader assassinated in 1969. She

has written a book of short stories, *Till*, and two novels, *Miaha* and *Simbi Nyaima*, in Luo. Ogot has translated *Miaha*, an interpretation of a Luo myth, as *The Strange Bride* (1989).
Bib: Interview in *Africa Report*, July–August 1972; Taiwo, Oladele, *Female Novelists of Modern Africa*; Bruner, Charlotte H. (ed.), *Unwinding Threads, Writing by Women in Africa*; Brown, Lloyd W., *Women Writers in Black Africa*; Berrian, Brenda F. (ed.), *Bibliography of African Women Writers and Journalists*; Hans, Zell, Bundy, Carol, and Coulon, Virginia (eds), *A New Reader's Guide to African Literature*.

Ogundipe-Leslie, Molara

Nigerian poet and critic. A Yoruba from Ijebu-Ode in western Nigeria, she has lectured at universities in Nigeria and the USA. She has published a volume of poetry, *Sew the Old Days* (1985), and two volumes of Essays: *African Women and Critical Transformations* and *Towards a Double-Gendered Cosmos: Essays on African Literature*. She is outspoken in her critique of patriarchy, debunking the cherished mythology of the traditional African woman in, for example, her essay *The Female Writer and her Commitment* (1983). She has made a statement of her feminist position in her contribution to *Sisterhood is Global* – 'Not Spinning on the Axis of Madness' (1984).
Bib: James, A., *In Their Own Voices: Interviews with African Women Writers*; Otokunefor, H., and Nwodo, O., *Nigerian Female Writers: A Critical Perspective*.

Ohara Tomie (born 1912)

Japanese novelist. Born in Kochi prefecture, she broke her engagement because was suffering from tuberculosis. Her fiancé was killed at the front. *A Cold Rain* (1935) won a prize from *Literature for Women*, a magazine edited by the feminist activist, Kamichika Ichiko. She started her career as a novelist after *Soldier Going to the Front* was considered for the Akutagawa Prize in 1938. *Deafness from Streptomycin* won the Prize for a Woman Writer in 1956. *A Woman Called En* (1960) describes the oppressive life of a woman in the 17th century. En Nonaka suffered house-arrest for forty years until all her brothers – and the family line with them – died. This work won the Noma Prize for Literature and the Mainichi Prize for Publication. She was baptized a Catholic in 1951. Her other main works are ▷*A Woman Travelling on the Earth* and *The Camp of Abraham*.

Okoye, Ifeoma

Nigerian novelist and children's writer. From the Igbo-speaking east of Nigeria, she has been a teacher and nursery-school proprietor and has written several children's stories, including *No School for Eze* (1980), *The Village Boy* (1981) and *Eze Goes to School* (1980). She is also the author of two adult novels *Behind the Clouds* (1982), dealing with a woman's suffering in the face of her inability to bear children, and ▷*Men Without Ears* (1984), a satire on the rampant corruption in oil-

Ifeoma Okoye

boom Nigeria. The latter won the Association of Nigerian Authors award in 1985. She is married to the well-known writer and politician, Mokwugo Okoye, and lectures in Mass Communications in Enugu.
  ▷Children's literature (West Africa); Infertility/childlessness (West Africa)

Old Age (1972)

Translation of *La Vieillesse* (1970), by French writer ▷Simone de Beauvoir. In this study of the process of ageing and the state of being old, de Beauvoir applies to the elderly much of the same understanding that characterized her earlier study of women, ▷ *The Second Sex*. The old have become the outsiders, the useless beings, in a society (largely that of Western capitalism) which has no respect for age. The author's sympathy for the old is obvious, but the thesis (like that of *The Second Sex*) rests upon a radical opposition between two categories, in this case the young and the old. Richly documented, the book is a pioneering study of a neglected issue.

Old Days: Old Ways (1934)

Australian autobiography by ▷Dame Mary Gilmore. Through her own and her family's reminiscences of Australian pioneering life Gilmore attempts to convey the heroic nature of the colonizing enterprise, but her pioneers stand condemned by her chilling account of atrocities committed against the Aboriginal people. A companion volume, *More Recollections*, was published in 1935.
  ▷Aborigine in non-Aboriginal women's writing, The

Old English

The language of the Anglo-Saxons, and the form of English used in England until after the Norman Conquest of 1066. Some of the earliest surviving vernacular literature in Europe is written in Old English.

▷Elegies, Old English; 'Wife's Lament, The'; 'Wulf and Eadwacer'

Old English Baron, The (1778)

Historical and ▷Gothic ▷romance by English writer ▷Clara Reeve, first published as *The Champion of Virtue: A Gothic Story* (1777). Sir Philip Harclay returns to England after serving Henry V, to discover that there have been strange deeds in the family of his friend, Lord Lovel, whose castle is now occupied by Lord Baron Fitz-Owen. A mystery begins to be unravelled around the well-bred but impoverished Edmund, and his banishment by an evil relative. Ultimately, the rightful claims of inheritance are asserted. In a preface, Reeve asserts that Gothic effects must 'be kept within certain limits of credibility'.

▷*Mysteries of Udolpho, The*; Radcliffe, Ann

Old Irish

The form of Irish used from about the 6th to the 12th century.

▷'Creidhe's Lament'; 'Deirdre's Farewell to Scotland'; 'Old Woman of Beare, The'; 'Liadain and Cuirthir'

Old Order, The (1958)

US short-story collection by ▷Katherine Anne Porter which focuses on the American South. It depicts characters who secure a place in the world by creating fictions. In the 'Miranda' stories, Porter juxtaposes the past with the present, exposing the South's use of mythology as a self-protective idealization. Miranda is a rebel in search of self-definition. In 'The Grave' she yearns for the femininity represented by the ▷Southern lady. Through her exposure to mortality she intuits the significance of becoming a woman and comes to a recognition that her family's romanticized vision of the past has shaped her desires. In 'Old Mortality' she tries to escape the familial bonds that have 'smothered her in love and hatred'. But Porter implies that Miranda cannot escape the past; it has shaped her character.

Old Playhouse, The (1973)

A collection of poems by the south Indian poet ▷Kamala Das. Renowned for her frankness about female sexuality, Das helped to break the mould that previous women poets in India, such as ▷Toru Dutt and ▷Sarojini Naidu, had set with romantic and sentimental verse. The poems in *The Old Playhouse* ask embarrassing questions about the conflicting standards that society, in particular traditional Indian society, expects from women in matters of sexuality. Das tackles head-on the male expectations that wives should be pure and yet sexually available, desirable and yet not desiring sexual fulfilment themselves.

'Old Woman of Beare, The' (or 'Nun of') (late 8th or early 9th century)

▷Old Irish poem. It is not known whether this disturbing and powerful poem was composed by a man or a woman, but the speaker is a woman. She looks back, in old age, on the time of her youth and beauty, when she was loved by kings.
Bib: Greene, David, and O'Connor, Frank, (eds. and trans.), *A Golden Treasury of Irish Poetry AD 600 to 1200*; Murphy, Gerard, *Early Irish Lyrics*.

Olenka ▷Savary, Olga

Oliphant, Margaret (1828–1897)

▷Scottish novelist, biographer and critic, born in Wallyford, Midlothian; also known as M.O.W. She married her cousin Francis Oliphant in 1852, but in 1859 he died of consumption, leaving Margaret with two children and expecting a third. She supported her family (and that of her widowed brother and his three children) by writing prolifically, becoming the author of over 100 works. She wrote fiction, biography and reviews, her best-known novels today being the ▷*Chronicles of Carlingford* series (1863–76). Her first work, *Passages in the Life of Mrs Margaret Maitland* (1849) was well-received, and this was followed by the ▷historical novel *Caleb Field* (1851) and *Merkland* (1851). *The Athelings* (1857) was a huge success, and is the best of Oliphant's many domestic ▷romances. In 1862, her biography of Edward Irving appeared, and in 1863 the first of the *Chronicles, Salem Chapel*. The other four novels in the series were *The Rector and the Doctor's Family* (1863); *The Perpetual Curate* (1864); *Miss Marjoribanks* (1866) and *Phoebe Junior* (1876). Another group of books, *Stories of the Seen and Unseen*, dealt with matters of death and the soul, and include *A Beleaguered City* (1880) and *A Little Pilgrim in the Unseen* (1882). Also in 1882, her much admired *Literary History of England* appeared, and, in 1897–8, *Annals of a Publishing House*, which commemorated her long association with *Blackwood's Magazine*, to which she was a frequent contributor. Oliphant's best writing is sharply humorous and vivid in description, and she has been compared to ▷George Eliot and Trollope, but the financial pressure to keep producing inevitably affected her work, not least since she was compelled to write scores of popular romances. Her posthumously published autobiography (1899) reveals the strain she was under, and records her struggle to meet financial obligations.

▷Ghost stories (19th-century Britain)
Bib: Coghill, H. (ed.), *Margaret Oliphant: the Autobiography and Letters*; Williams, M., *A Critical Biography*; Colby, V. and R., *The Equivocal Virtue: Margaret Oliphant and the Victorian Literary Market Place*; Cunningham, V., *Everywhere Spoken Against: Dissent in the Victorian Novel*.

Oliveira Campos, Narcisa Amália de
▷Amália, Narcisa

Oliveira, Marli de (born 1935)
Brazilian poet. She lived in Campos, Rio and Rome, studied in Europe, and travelled widely. Her first book of poems, *Cerco da primavera* (1957) (*The Siege of Spring*), was awarded two prizes, and she achieved recognition with her third book of poetry, *A suave pantera* (1962) (*The Gentle Panther*), which won the Brazilian Academy of Letters Prize. Her style is emblematic, symbolic and metaphysical – following the style of the Brazilian ▷1945 Generation of poets.

Other works: *Explicacão de Narciso* (1960) (*The Explanation of Narcissus*); *A vida natural/O Sangue na veia* (1967) (*The Natural Life/The Blood in the Veins*); *Contato* (1975) (*Contact*); *Invocacão de Orfeu* (1979) (*Invocation of Orpheus*); *Aliança* (1979) (*Alliance*); *A força da paixão/A incerteza das coisas* (1984) (*The Power of Passion/The Certainty of Things*), and *Retrato/Vertigem/Viagem a Portugal* (1986) (*Portrait/Vertigo/Journey to Portugal*).

Oliver, Maria Antònia (born 1946)
One of Spain's most significant female Catalan writers of the post-war period. Born in Manacor (Majorca), Oliver is known for her writing based on fantasy. Her early works, such as *Croniques d'un mig estiu* (1970) (*Chronicles of Half a Summer*), *Coordenades espai-temps per guardar-hi les ensaimades* (1975) (*Time-Space Coordinates for Keeping Pastries in*) and *El vaixell d'iràs i no tornaràs* (1976) (*The Ship That Never Returned*), are, in the main, set in Majorca, and have liberal recourse to fantasy. Her later works focus more clearly on women's Existential problems. For example: *Punt d'arròs* (1979) (*Knit-Purl*); *Vegetal i Muller que cerca espill* (1982) (*Vegetable and Women in Search of a Mirror*); *Crineres de foc* (1985) (*Manes of Fire*), and *Estudis en lila* (1987) (*Studies in Lilac*).
▷Catalan women's writing

Olivier, Christine
French psychoanalyst living in Aix-en-Provence. Author of *Les Enfants de Jocaste* (1980) (*Jocasta's Children*, 1989). This feminist rewriting of Freud's theories of sexuality reclaims the role of the mother, Jocasta, in the infamous 'Oedipus complex', emphasizing the fundamental differences in the sexual development of women and men.
▷Psychoanalysis

Ol'nem (1872–?)
Pen-name of Russian prose writer and journalist Varvara Nikolaevna Tsekhovskaia. Ol'nem was one of the best female fiction writers of the ▷Silver Age and regularly published unfailingly fine stories. From 1889 to 1895 she worked as a journalist in Kiev and edited the 'Local Chronicle' of a Russian-language magazine, an experience she later drew on in her fiction ('The Ant Hill', 'My First Steps', and 'The Editor's Anniversary'). Her first story, 'Warum' (1895) ('Why?'), deals with the Chekhovian theme of the downfall of the old aristocracy, and features one of her favourite structural devices: the encounter between a dissatisfied, ▷'superfluous man' and an eccentric, unusual woman.

By 1912 Ol'nem had published three collections of stories with a wide variety of themes and characters. Although a few stories consist primarily of internal monologue (eg, 'Without a Residence Permit', 1901), most of them use a third-person, objective narrator. She had a wonderful ear for individual speech, and her narrative style is lean and spare, focusing on character presented in abundant dialogue against a background of social commentary. She created some of the most memorable characters in the short fiction of the pre-revolutionary period: the two gaudy actresses in 'Without Illusions' (1904); the three brothers – each with a separate obsession – in 'Dynasty' (1910).

Reviewers noted the richness of character depiction and the ease of her style, and found her fiction to be lively and full of keen, even profound observations. She was criticized as being an imitator of Chekhov, but, although there are similarities, Ol'nem preferred flashier, more colourful characters. In 1911, one critic called her an 'aristocrat' by comparison with other writers and noted her elegant and rich language.

Ol'nem published a few short stories and brief plays for children between 1912 and 1914. Her last piece of serious fiction appeared in 1914. After that she worked for a few years as an editor of a liberal ▷'thick journal', *Russian Wealth*. Her last known publication was a 1923 article on the children's writer and populist, E.N. Vodovozova-Semevskaia (1844–1923).
Bib: McReynolds, L., 'Female Journalists in Prerevolutionary Russia', *Journalism History*, 14, 4.

Olsen, Tillie (born 1913)
US novelist, short story-writer and essayist. Olsen was born in Omaha, Nebraska to Russian-Jewish parents. After leaving school early, she held a series of manual and clerical jobs in Kansas and California, becoming a trade union organizer and political activist. She married in 1936 and has four daughters. Her novel *Yonnondio: From the Thirties* (1974) was begun before she married and was put aside because of the demands of being a working mother, and her work as a whole bears witness to the force of circumstance in thwarting the creativity of the working class, African-Americans and women. *Yonnondio* tells the story of the Holbrook family, concentrating on Maizie and her mother, and how their lives, dreams and aspirations are devastated by the economic effects of the recession, by sexism and sexual inequality. The stories in *Tell Me a Riddle* (1961) document in various ways the lost dreams and creativity of ordinary people struggling to make a place for themselves. In *Silences* (1978) Olsen theorizes the concerns that have shaped her fiction, emphasizing that those who write, particularly women, must speak for those whose voices have

been silenced. In recent years Olsen taught at various universities, where she has developed her working-class feminist analysis.

Other work includes: *Mother to Daughter/ Daughter to Mother: Mothers on Mothering* (1984), *Mothers and Daughters: That Special Quality – An Exploration in Photographs* (with Julie Olsen-Edwards and Estelle Jussim) (1987).
Bib: Pearlman, Mickey and Werlock, Abby H.P., *Tillie Olsen*; Orr, Elaine Neil, *Tillie Olsen and a Feminist Spiritual Vision*; Morton, Abigail, *Tillie Olsen*.

Olsson, Hagar (1893–1978)
Fenno-Swedish prose writer, lyric poet, dramatist and literary critic. Olsson introduced ▷modernism to Finland, together with ▷Edith Södergran. Olsson was born the daughter of a minister, and grew up at Viborg. She studied in Helsinki, where she lived as a critic, and soon began to write poems.

In 1916 she had her début with *Lars Thormann och döden* (*Lars Thormann and Death*), influenced by Buddhist mysticism. The longing for spiritual experience is also present in the lyrical prose of *Själarnas ansikten* (1917) (*The Faces of the Souls*) and in *Kvinnan och nåden* (1919) (*Woman and Grace*), a prose poem of the unity of life and death. But most important in her early work are the critical essays published in 1925 as *Ny generation* (*New Generation*). Her artistic breakthrough came with the novel *Chitambo* (1933), a partly autobiographical novel about a young girl, her eccentric father and her first love. It is a classic of ▷Fenno-Swedish literature. In her later work, she writes a dreamlike prose, closely connected to lyrical poetry. Her subjects are always young women, their powerlessness and conflicting desires.

Ombres, Rossana (born 1931)
Italian poet and novelist. She lived in the Piedmontese countryside and in Naples before settling in Rome. She contributed regularly to many Italian magazines, publishing short stories, literary criticism and translations. The recurrent themes of both her poetry and her prose are her Piedmontese childhood, and the harshness of women's lives. She mixes fantasy and reality in her poetry.

Her works include: *Principessa anche tu* (1956) (*You, Too, Are a Princess*); *Le ciminiere di Casale* (1962) (*The Chimneys of Casale*); *L'ipotesi di Agar* (1968) (*Agar's Hypothesis*); *Bestiario d'amore* (1974) (*A Bestiary of Love*); *Le belle statuine* (1975) (*The Beautiful Statues*); *Memorie di una dilettante* (1977) (*Memories of a Dilettante*); *Serenata* (1980) (*Serenade*).

Omoifo-Okoh, Julie
Nigerian dramatist. A lecturer in French at the University of Port Harcourt, she has so far published *Mask* (1988), a play on marital infidelity. Her declared aim is to demonstrate that the reality of women's existence is not the way it is generally depicted in the male-dominated Nigerian theatre.

One Foot on the Mountain (1979)
Anthology of British feminist poetry between 1969 and 1979, edited by Lilian Mohin. A survey of ten years of the effect of the women's liberation movement on women's poetry, the anthology looks at the development of a distinctly feminist poetry, and welcomes the intervention made by the feminist slogan 'the personal is political'. Working on the principle of 'redefinition', the poems in this collection illustrate the feminist necessity to change language, and thus also syntax, gendered metaphors, poetic stereotypes, and traditional academic standards of poetic craft. The feminist poetry included here promotes the view that 'Nothing is assumed to be inevitable or seen as "normal"', and this includes sustained explorations, celebrations and reassessments of relationships between women. The anthology includes work by writers who identify themselves firmly with the women's liberation movement – including ▷Alison Fell, Ann Oosthuizen, Thalia Doukas, Paula Jennings and Sheila Shulman – and work by other writers who challenge established assumptions. It contains poems by, among many others, ▷Judith Kazantzis, ▷Michelene Wandor, ▷Michèle Roberts and ▷Zöe Fairbairns.

On Germany (1813)
Translation of ▷Madame de Staël's *De l'Allemagne* (1810). De Staël's extensive critical analysis of German society and culture initiated French readers of her generation into German theatre and poetry, and provided them with their first manifesto for romanticism. De Staël here seeks to forge a new type of criticism, free of the aesthetic dogmas of classicism. The first section, on Germany and German morals, looks at the country region by region. In the second section, on literature and the arts, the writer examines the notion of taste, which she sees as relative rather than absolute. Recommending cultural exchange between France and Germany, she proceeds to outline past and present currents in German literature. The third section, on philosophy and morals, analyzes Kant (1724–1804), and attacks the materialist philosophies responsible, in de Staël's view, for the Terror, the *Directoire*, and Napoleon's repression of freedom of expression. The final section on religion and enthusiasm contains her definition of poetry.

On Her Selection: Writings by Nineteenth-Century Australian Women (1988)
Anthology edited by Lynne Spender. A valuable selection from the works of early Australian women writers. It contains extracts from the works of Georgiana Molloy, ▷Anna Maria Bunn, ▷Louisa Meredith, ▷Mary Vidal, ▷Annie Maria Baxter, ▷Catherine Helen Spence, ▷Annabella Boswell, ▷Rachel Henning, ▷Caroline Woolmer Leakey, ▷Mary Fortune ('Waif Wander'),

▷Louisa Atkinson, ▷Ada Cambridge, ▷Catherine Martin, ▷Jessie Couvreur ('Tasma'), ▷Louisa Lawson, ▷Rosa Praed, and ▷Mary Gaunt.

On Lies, Secrets and Silence: Selected Prose 1966–1978 (1979)

Essays by US writer ▷Adrienne Rich. This collection of essays declares Rich's interest in several areas: feminism, poetry, the feminist redefinition of language, the task of resurrecting and reclaiming forgotten or unknown poets, and the politics of lesbian identification. In the classic essay 'When We Dead Awaken: Writing As Re-Vision' (1971), Rich articulates a radical feminist theory of the woman poet's relation to tradition. Pointing out how disabling for women writers has been the 'image of Woman in books written by men', she reconstructs a half-buried tradition of women's poetry, at the same time telling her own story as an autobiographical parable of the woman writer's quest to discover new forms to articulate her own experience. 'Power and Danger', an essay introducing the poems of ▷Judy Grahn, is similarly full of a vision of the transformations of meaning made possible by lesbian feminist poetry. There are also admirable essays on ▷*Jane Eyre*. 'The Temptations of a Motherless Woman', on the poetry of ▷Emily Dickinson, and on the work of lesser-known poets like Eleanor Ross Taylor.

Rich's formulation of a radical feminist poetics of experience in *On Lies, Secrets and Silence* has been influential in shaping the terms of feminist debate about women's poetry and women's writing in general, particularly in North America: the book has been a focus of sometimes critical debate among feminist scholars such as Mary Jacobus, ▷Cora Kaplan and ▷Elaine Showalter. It remains an important landmark of feminist thinking not only about women and poetry but about the relation between experience, language and feminist politics.

On Psychological Prose (1991)

Literary critical work by Russian writer ▷Lidiia Gínzburg, originally published in 1970, revised in 1977, and published in English translation in 1991. This major work is a rigorous demonstration of the interrelationship between history and literature. Gínzburg shows the 'unbreakable chain linking artistic prose to [documentary] genres and ultimately . . . everyday life' through the 'aesthetic activity' all people perform in defining their personalities. She examines a wide range of French and Russian writings from the 17th to the 19th centuries in light of the contemporary psychological concepts and social pressures that inform them.

'On Reading Some Paragraphs in "The Crisis", April, '77' (1981)

Poem by the North American poet ▷Hannah Griffitts of Philadelphia. This poem questions the traditional acclamations afforded Thomas Paine (1737–1809), the English-born political philosopher. Paine had just received a paid governmental post so he could devote himself to his writings for the Patriot cause during the American Revolution. Although a Whig herself, Griffitts questioned Paine's motives: it was rumoured, she notes, that should 'Howe increase the scribbler's pension, / No more will Pane a whig be found.' Part of her disdain obviously came from Paine's writings about women: 'Of female manners, never scribble, / Nor with thy rudeness wound our ear . . . / The delicate is "not thy sphere".' None of her poems were published, but they were shared with female friends, which afforded her the outspokenness evidenced in this poem.

'On the Equality of the Sexes' (1790)

Serialized in the April and May 1790 issues of *Massachusetts Magazine*, this essay by ▷Judith Sargent Murray predates ▷Mary Wollstonecraft's ▷*Vindication of the Rights of Women* and constitutes one of North America's earliest feminist documents. Through astute argumentation and satirization, Murray challenges the idea that intellectual differences in men and women are 'natural' and asserts that they are the consequences of unequal education and opportunity. Appended to the essay is a letter, written in December 1780, in which a revisionist reading of the story of Eve and the 'Fall of Man' is presented to counter prevailing religious arguments against the rights of women.

On the Horizon (1985)

Work by Japanese writer Nakazawa Kei (born 1959). A boy kisses Izumi, a schoolgirl younger than him, after asking her permission and despite feeling no love towards her. Izumi is worried that he will not want to see her afterwards. He does, however, and begins to say that he loves her when she denies him. Through the eyes of a writer in her twenties, this work suggests that when a woman agrees to have sexual contact, she is openly accepting not only the unattractive aspect of a man's lust, but also his arrogant assumption that women should adopt a submissive role.

Onwueme, Tess (born 1955)

Nigerian dramatist and poet. From the Igbo-speaking part of Bendel State in mid-west Nigeria, Tess Onwueme is, like ▷Zulu Sofola, a university lecturer, at the Imo State University, Owerri, in the east. In common with her mentor, the dramatist Femi Osofisan, and with Sofola, the academic connection enables Onwueme to produce her own plays with student actors. She has written more than ten plays, including *A Hen Too Soon* (1983), *The Broken Calabash* (1984), *Mirror for Campus* (1987) and *The Reign of Wazobia* (1988). She has toured, taking productions of her work abroad, and in 1985 her play ▷*The Desert Encroaches* won the Association of Nigerian Authors prize for drama. Onwueme is an outspoken critic of the status quo, especially of the position of women in Nigeria. *The Broken Calabash* dramatizes the conflict between a young woman and her traditional father, who requires her to marry according to custom rather than love. In the ensuring tussle between opposing cultural values, modernity wins.

Bib: Otokunefor, H. and Nwodo, O., *Nigerian Female Writers: A Critical Perspective.*

Opening the Gates: a Century of Arab Feminist Writing (1990)

English anthology of modern Arab women's writings extending from Morocco to Iraq and the Sudan, edited by Margot Badran and Miriam Cooke. The majority of the texts are translations from Arabic, occasionally from French, but a few were originally written in English. Almost every Arab woman writer of note is represented in this collection, and there are stories by the liberated ▷Alifa Rif'at (Egyptian), the traditional Sophie Abdulla (Egyptian), the romantic Khayria al-Saqqaf (Saudi) as well as the Iraqi Daizy al-Amir and the Palestinian Samira 'Azzam. The contributions from North Africa are translated from French, and include a film script by Farida Benlyazid (Moroccan). The script, written in French (1987), was performed in Moroccan Arabic dialect as *Bab al-Sama Maftuh* (*The Gate of Heaven is Open*). It presents a girl's attempt to keep her inheritance against her brother's authority to sell the family home.

The few examples of verse included in the anthology represent the development of women's verse from the epistles on personal or social occasions, common in the writing of both men and women in the opening decades of this century, to the tortured, self-asserting rebellious outbursts Arab women have been composing occasionally after the defeats and setbacks of the last twenty-five years. Women's verse is well-represented, though only briefly, from the Syrian Warda al-'Yaziji's epistolary poem to Warda al-Turk (1867) to the Lebanese ▷Nadia Tueni's 'Who are you, Claire Gebeyli?' (1968) Claire Gebeyli, a Lebanese poet of Greek origin, struck a sympathetic note with her *Memorial d'exil* (1975) (*Memorial of Exile*), describing the pain of both Lebanon and Greece.

Opera, or the Undoing of Women (1981)

Translation of *L'Opéra ou la défaite des femmes,* (1979), a series of witty essays by French writer ▷Catherine Clément. Clément exposes the role of women as scapegoats or sacrificial victims in a genre which purports to cast them as heroines.

Opéra ou la défaite des femmes, L' (1979)
▷*Opera, or the Undoing of Women* (1981)

Opie, Amelia (1769–1853)

English novelist and poet. She began publishing by contributing articles to periodicals such as the *London Magazine.* Her first novel, *The Dangers of Coquetry,* appeared anonymously in 1790, followed by ▷*The Father and Daughter* under her own name in 1801. This was highly successful,

running to ten editions by 1844. Opie was already well-known in literary and artistic circles; she knew William Godwin and ▷Elizabeth Inchbald, and married the successful painter John Opie in 1798. Her novel ▷*Adeline Mowbray* (1804) is based on the life of ▷Mary Wollstonecraft. Opie's fame was not enduring, and as the 19th century progressed she was read less and less. This may be attributed to the fact that her novels of ▷sensibility were considered out of date. Her works include *Miscellaneous Poems* (1802); *Simple Tales* (1806); *The Warrior's Return and Other Poems* (1808); *Valentine's Eve: A Novel* (1816) and *Lays for the Dead* (1833).

Bib: Brightwell, C.B., *Memorials from the Life of Amelia Opie.*

O Pioneers! (1913)

US novel by ▷Willa Cather which celebrates the courage of pioneer women who civilized the frontier. It focuses on a time when women exercised their power and it emphasizes that in an agrarian economy, women's work is central. Alexandra Bergson's Swedish family emigrated to the prairie to make a new life. When her father dies, Alexandra assumes his role, and she inherits his strength of will to persevere. She finds happiness working with nature to make the land fertile. However, she denies her body and represses any sexual desire. Cather implies that romantic love would sap Alexandra's strength. Middle-aged, Alexandra reconciles herself to a safe marriage with her old friend, Carl Lindstrom. Cather shows how pioneer women released their creativity through domestic arts, like preserving vegetables.

Opoponax, The (1966)

Translation of ▷*L'Opoponax* (1964) the first novel of French writer ▷Monique Wittig. Childhood experience is presented without the controlling framework of adult interpretations, and the flow of unexplained sensations and experiences becomes a perfect vehicle for the creation of a non-linear narrative. The novel's main 'character' is a group of children, rather than an individual, and the emphasis is on the acquisition of skills and the exploration of nature by an oppressed group, rather than on individual psychology or characterization. Sexual difference is an insignificant part of the children's development, as one might expect, given Wittig's insistence on the culturally constructed nature of the former.

Oppression and Liberty (1958)

Translation of *Oppression et Liberté* (1955) by French writer ▷Simone Weil. This book examines the problems of authority and power, their use and misuse. With ▷*The Need for Roots,* it contains Weil's most central and considered theories on politics and society.

Oppression et Liberté (1955) ▷*Oppression and Liberty* (1958)

Optimist's Daughter, The (1972)

US Pulitzer-Prize-winning novel by ▷Eudora Welty which focuses on the troubled relationship between mother and daughter. An independent career woman, Laurel Hand, returns to Mississippi for her father's funeral where she must summon the courage to face the past to gain self-knowledge. She sees similarities between herself and her dead mother as they both had rebelled against their mothers to assert their own independence. Laurel learns to see her mother's values as nourishing and to use memory to help understand her own experiences. Welty emphasizes that the traditions of the past are empowering and she recovers a ▷Southern matriarchal tradition.

Opus 7 (1931)

Narrative poem by English writer ▷Sylvia Townsend Warner. A mock-pastoral written in rhyming couplets, the poem is set in the England of the Napoleonic Wars, and contains a powerful evocation of the horrors of war. Its main character, Rebecca, is an old village-woman who grows flowers that are much admired. She spends the income from their sale on gin, and the poem lyrically describes the beauty of flowers and the delights of intoxication. The theme of the subversive spinster was also explored by Warner in ▷*Lolly Willowes* (1926).

Oral history (Caribbean)

A term which encompasses the oral traditions of folklore, storytelling, recollections, legends, tales, songs, religious beliefs, customs, sayings and humour of the Caribbean people. See also ▷Anancy Stories and ▷Pamela C. Smith.

Oral tradition

West Africa: The European incursion into West Africa was characterized by a misapprehension, which still endures, that because nothing was written down, Africa had no history and no literature. The existence of an ancient oral tradition, extending to vast and complex genealogies and historical narratives, drama, poetry, song, storytelling, proverbs, elaborate greetings, jokes and abuse, is probably the most significant cultural difference between Africa and the West. But, despite Western education and the spread of literacy, it would be equally misleading to present this tradition as something archival, of mainly anthropological interest. Not only are the oral traditions alive, current, creative and contemporary, and still a primary means of culture, information and education for the majority of rural dwellers in West Africa, they have also gained new impetus from radio, television, film and the music industry. Broadcasting services in West African languages, using West African presenters, and indigenous artists and composers are promoted by public performance, the recording industry and media exposure. To appreciate West African literature, it is essential to understand that 'orature' (oral literature) is its bedrock, providing a philosophy and aesthetics essentially different from the Western literary tradition.

▷Nwapa, Flora; ▷*Efuru*, *Idu*; Sutherland, Efua; *Marriage of Anansewa, The*; Aidoo, Ama Ata; *Our Sister Killjoy*; *Stillborn, The*; Alkali, Zaynab

Southern Africa: In the oral tradition, as in writing, social norms and values, as well as symbols and conventions, are handed down from past to present. The present, by using and adapting its cultural inheritance, engages in turn with the past. In orature generally, as in writing, the values of the past are transmitted to the present, as part of the process of cultural representation and socialization. But in orature, unlike writing, the major medium of cultural representation is through stories and poetry *in performance*, so that gestures, facial expressions and other bodily movements play as important a part as speech. Indeed, some critics have argued that when we experience an oral performance, we are not simply hearing language but are also seeing speech. Gestures become language, and the relation between gesture and language rewrites language itself. This means that printed versions of oral tradition are poor substitutes for the performance.

Southern African women have played a central part in oral tradition. Critics have suggested that women have been officially responsible for prose narratives, while men have been responsible for the public performance of poetry, including epic poetry, praise poetry, poetry performed at funerals, weddings, initiations and so on. Epic poetry is concerned with communal history, while praise poetry provides individual genealogy, eulogizing those who embody social values, criticizing those who are anti-social. Thus poetry performances have often been used to mediate relations between ruler and ruled on public occasions. Although women do not assume the role of official praise poet, akin to a court poet in European tradition, there is evidence of their composing and performing poetry in public in the past, using it to exhort the men to battle, for instance, as indicated by Thomas Mofolo's (1876–1948) early Sotho novel, *Chaka* (1925; translated 1931). Women also take part in poetry performances among themselves, reciting their own praises, and praises for one another.

In their poetry, women use the highly figurative language typical of the genre, employing a robust ▷realism and explicit sexual reference. In the performance of a praise poem, the woman leaps to her feet and begins to dance and sing to the accompaniment of the other women, who then also take up the lines of her praise poem as she recites them. When she is finished, a second woman leaps up, enters the circle and launches into her praise poem. In this convivial atmosphere, appropriate lines are greeted with approval, amusement, and sometimes criticism. The following lines, translated from the Zulu, offer an example:

I am she who cuts across the game reserve
That no girl crosses
I am the boldest of the bold, outfacer of wizards
Obstinate perseverer.

Often highly stylized, poetry is an art form within which individual talent might emerge. Similarly, performers of oral narrative sometimes become renowned for their skill. Oral narrative builds on the nucleus of a well-known, oft-told story, passed down through the tradition along with various cultural symbols, images and character types. Since the audience is often familiar with the story-line itself, the specific artistry lies in the performance, and in the dynamic built up between performer and audience.

The storytellers are usually older women entrusted with the education of young boys and girls. Girls are often trained in storytelling, and receive derisive treament from their audience when their performative powers fail. Inevitably, the stories are conservative, and, as far as the representation of women is concerned, feminine destiny is bound up with motherhood, with marriages traditionally being arranged for the good of the community rather than according to personal desire.

It has been argued that indirect feminist protest is a part of oral narrative tradition. The narratives often have a complex structure, one, two or even three original stories being interwoven by the individual storyteller. Sometimes these parts comment on one another, the events or images in one part presenting ironic reversal of another. Some stories depict women, set upon by ogres and cannibals, who manage to outwit their adversaries, or women whose magic transformational powers permit escape from overbearing men. In the trickster tradition, the victimizer's ploy is neatly reversed, through an inversion of events and images, so that the original trick becomes turned against the trickster/ victimizer. Here, too, then, women have the opportunity for social comment and imaginative reparation.

Critics also argue that what has been largely preserved in oral tradition was at the behest of European missionaries, who transcribed and edited the texts for publication, perhaps selecting from the storehouse of tradition stories that bore out European expectations of Africanness. Hence the preponderance of animal stories, which closely resembled those which Europeans read to children.

Southern African oral tradition was first collected by missionary-anthropologists and others, some of whom were women. In the 19th century, working with the !Xam, W.H.I. Bleek (1827–1875) was assisted by Lucy Lloyd (1834–1914), who continued the work after his death. She was joined by her niece Dorothea Bleek (1867–1948), a self-trained philologist and anthropologist, who spent most of her life studying the language and beliefs of the !Xam

people, living among them in the Kalahari for long periods. She worked with Lloyd on a collection Lloyd and W. Bleek had initiated, called *The Mantis and His Friends* (1923), for which she wrote the introduction, and edited *Customs and Beliefs of the !Xam Bushmen* (1931–1935) in seven volumes, among other work. Lloyd published her own *Short Account of Further Bushman Material Collected* (1889).

There are numerous other collections of oral tradition. Henry Callaway collected Zulu tales in the late 19th century. A.C. Jordan (1906–1968), well-known as a Xhosa novelist and academic, recalled and rewrote stories from his childhood, which depended on the performances of women storytellers. During the last twenty-five years or so, Xhosa tales have been collected by Harold Scheub, who has written stirring accounts of the artistry of a performer called Nongenile Mazithathu Zenani (born c 1910), a senior woman in a Gcaleka community and famous for her art. Praise poetry performed by Zulu women has recently been collected, translated and interpreted by Elizabeth Gunner.

If the transcription of oral performance into printed form signifies loss, so, too, does translation. African languages are characterized by concordial relationships, ideophones, parallelisms, alliteration and tonal patterns that have been well-nigh impossible to render in English. The transcription and translation of oral tradition cannot possibly reproduce the richness of that tradition. In addition, Western technology and literacy have diminished the importance of oral tradition. Therefore it is all the more valuable that oral forms enter the present, whether in plays, ▷performance poetry, or stories. ▷Children's stories have been seen as hospitable to oral tradition.

Orature informs the writing of various contemporary writers in different ways: ▷Bessie Head, ▷Antjie Krog, ▷Gcina Mhlophe, ▷Nise Malange, and ▷Miriam Tlali, for instance. In one of Head's stories, a woman victimized by her extended family reaches back to oral tradition for a proverb which she is able to redirect for her own use: 'I agree with all that has been said about me. But I am a real woman and as the saying goes the children of a real woman do not get lean or die.' And in Tlali's ▷*Soweto Stories*, one of the stories recalls the ironic mode of the trickster motif, providing a way of subverting the surface message of capitulation to white authority.

Bib: Callaway, Henry, *Nursery Tales, Traditions and Histories of the Zulus*; Canonici, N.N., *Isinganekwane: An Anthology of Zulu Folktales*; Dube, Violet, *Wozanazo izindaba zika Phoshozwayo* (*Tell Us the Tales of Phoshozwayo*); Gunner, Elizabeth, 'Songs of Innocence and Experience: Women as Composers and Performers of Izibongo, Zulu Praise Poetry' in Clayton, Cherry (ed.), *Women and Writing in South Africa*; Jordan, A.C., *Tales from Southern Africa*; Scheub, Harold, 'The Art of Nongenile Mazithathu Zenani, A

Gcaleka Ntsomi Performer' in Dorson, Richard (ed.), *African Folklore*; Scheub, Harold, *The Xhosa Ntsomi*.

Oranges Are Not the Only Fruit (1985)

Novel by English novelist ▷Jeanette Winterson. An innovatively written novel that focuses on Winterson's own experiences of growing up in Lancashire within a strict working-class Evangelical family. The novel explores desire, passion, sexuality and lesbian identity within the 'great struggle between good and evil'.

Winterson's first novel introduces her characteristic method of interweaving and juxtaposing biblical, mythic and fairytale narratives, a technique which Winterson adopts to defamiliarize cultural codes and values. Concerned also to analyze the stability and meaning of history and interested in personal, alternative and competing histories, *Oranges* proposes that 'People like to separate storytelling which is not fact from history which is fact . . . Very often history is a means of denying the past . . . We are all historians in a small way.' The novel has recently been dramatized for television.

Orbell, Margaret (born 1934)

New Zealand translator. Margaret Orbell was trained as an anthropologist, but has been highly influential in the development of ▷Maori literature. In the early 1960s she edited *Te Ao Hou*, a journal published for a Maori readership, which sought to encourage Maori self-expression. Orbell's collection of work by Maori writers in *Contemporary Maori Writing* (1970) helped to introduce a non-Maori readership, to Maori writing. Orbell has spent the succeeding years working on translating 19th-century Maori writing.

Publications: (edited) *Maori: Folktales* (1968); *Contemporary Maori Writing* (1970); *Traditional Songs of the Maori* (1975); *Maori Poetry: An Introductory Anthology* (1978).

Orchid House, The (1953)

The author of this novel, the Caribbean writer ▷Phyllis Allfrey, describes it as 'a love story, by a woman in love with an island', it represents an important milestone in the development of West Indian fiction in the post-war years, reflecting a significant aspect of the West Indian experience which is sometimes forgotten: the experience of the white West Indian. Set in a fictional island modelled upon ▷Dominica, the story is narrated by Lally, the long-serving black nurse of a white family. Lally's memory spans three generations of the L'Aromatique family, and through her insights the novel provides an analysis of the family's decline. The ambivalence of the family relations reflects the confusion endemic within a society experiencing transition from colonial rule to the post-colonial world, where the power of the planter class is being displaced by the emergence of a new economic order and ruling class. It is the women of the orchid house, the three daughters,

who effect the family's survival during this period of transition, 'challenging their father's drug-induced torpor, revolting against the hold of the Roman Catholic clergy, struggling against the family's poverty and undermining the political hegemony of a privileged White minority'. Joan, Stella and Natalie serve to liaise between the old ▷Creole leadership and the emerging new leadership of the island.

See ▷*Fifty Caribbean Writers* for critical references.

Original Compositions in Prose and Verse. On Subjects Moral and Religious (1791)

The only extant work by the North American author ▷Jenny Fenno, this is a collection of religious and patriotic verse and essays. The text is notable for Fenno's assertion of her right as a woman 'to make public my private thoughts and reflections'.

Orlando (1928)

Novel by English writer ▷Virginia Woolf. Dedicated to ▷Vita Sackville-West, the novel is a historical fantasy and literary pastiche, parodying, among other literary texts, Sackville-West's *The Land* (1927). Written as the biography of its protagonist, Orlando, the novel charts the life of its central character from a masculine identity within the Elizabethan court to a feminine identity in 1928. *Orlando* provides an analysis of the historically constituted subject, and a critique of gender essentialism, while it explores, importantly, the issue of gender and creativity. Subjectivity is presented as a multifaceted multiplicity of conflicting elements, and the novel reiterates the key problematic within Woolf's analysis of sexual politics: the tension between androgyny and the articulation of sexual difference.

Ormoy, Charlotte Chaumet, Mme présidente d' (?1732–1791)

Novelist and dramatist. Born in Estampes, Ormoy was the mother of ▷Madame Mérard de Saint-Juste. She was a member of the Académie de Rome, where she was given the name Laurilla. She published two sentimental moralizing novels in succession: *Les Malheurs de la jeune Emilie* (1777) (*The Misfortunes of Young Emilie*) and *Journal de monsieur* (1779–80) (*A Gentleman's Diary*) and collaborated on the collective work *La Vertu chancelante* (1778) (*Threatened Virtue*). In 1780 her comic opera *Zelmis, ou la jeune sauvage* (*Zelmis, or the young savage*) was performed at Versailles. Her last two works, *Le Lama amoureux* (*The Lama in Love*), an 'Oriental tale' and a fairytale, *La Belle dans le souterrain* (*Beauty Below Ground*), were published in the following year.

Ormsby, Stephanie

Caribbean poet, born in ▷Jamaica. Her work is included in two volumes edited by J.E. Clare McFarlane, *Voices from Summerland* (1929) and *A Treasury of Jamaican Poetry* (1949), and in A.J. Hendriks and Cedric Lindo (eds), *The*

Independence Anthology of Jamaican Literature
(1962).

Her sister, M.M. Ornsby, is also a poet:
criticism her work can be found in 'Women in
Jamaican Literature' by Rhonda Cobham, in *Out
of the Kumbla: Caribbean Women and Literature*
(1990).

Oroonoko, or the Royal Slave (c 1688)

Novel by English writer ▷Aphra Behn. It is set in
the colony Surinam, and traces the fortunes of the
African 'prince' Oroonoko when he has been
made a slave, and follows his relationship with his
beloved, Imoinda. The narrative is ambivalent
about the morality of slavery and the position of
Oroonoko as a slave. The story moves between
romance and novelistic discourses.

Orozco, Olga (born 1920)

Argentinian poet, dramatist, journalist, critic and
translator. Her poetry is deeply spiritual, like that
of other contributors to the magazine *Canto*, and
has won prizes. For the critic Enrique Anderson
Imbert, she writes 'long dissolute verses, dark with
the strong emotions of a solitary'. Anguish and
sombre melancholy permeate her poetry since
Desde lejos (1946) (*From Afar*), her first book. *Las
muertes* (1952) (*The Dead*) further explores her
interest in nostalgia. She received two grants to
study spiritualism in modern poetry. In her novel
La obscuridad es otro sol (1967) (*Darkness is Another
Sin*) she reaches obscure depths with hallucinatory
visions: 'I elected deliria, magic and love.'

Other works: *Obra poética* (1979) (*Poetic Works*);
Los juegos peligrosos (1962) (*Dangerous Games*);
Museo selvaje (1973) (*Forest Museum*); *Ventinueve
poemas* (1975) (*Twenty-nine Poems*); *Canto a
Berenice* (1977) (*Song to Berenice*); *Mutaciones de la
realidad* (1979) (*Mutations of Reality*), and *La noch
a la deriva* (1984) (*The Night Adrift*).

Orphans

In mid-Victorian fiction, orphans frequently
appear as central characters. In an age when the
reading public responded to ▷sentiment, the
representation of orphans was sometimes used by
writers as a catalyst for pathos. This was often the
case with ▷Elizabeth Gaskell, for example, whose
novel ▷*Ruth* creates sympathy for the ▷'fallen
woman' by stressing initially the heroine's lack of
parental guidance. Alternatively the effects of
disinheritance and exclusion were illustrated
through an orphan, as ▷Emily Brontë
demonstrates with Heathcliff in ▷*Wuthering
Heights*. Authors seeking to challenge the
conventions of society often created orphaned
central characters in order to speak from a
marginalized position, to view society from
'outside'. The heroine of ▷Charlotte Brontë's
▷*Jane Eyre* is an example, although Jane, like
many other fictional orphans, eventually discovers
familial connections and financial support, thereby
gaining both security and power. The necessary
independence of orphans could also give rise to
the theme of individualism and self-help which

ran through the literature of the age, registering
an unacknowledged complicity with the values of
the middle classes. This paradoxical position is
exemplified by the heroine of ▷Elizabeth Barrett
Browning's ▷*Aurora Leigh*, who both resists as a
woman the constraints imposed upon her by
society and simultaneously advocates the
conservative ideology that has oppressed her.

▷*Professor, The*; Sherwood, Martha

Orphee, Elvira (born 1930)

Argentinian novelist and short story writer. She
studied literature in Buenos Aires and Paris. Her
criticism, essays and fiction have appeared in the
press, and her books have won many prizes. Her
first novel, *Dos veranos* (1956) (*Two Summers*),
echoes the US novelist William Faulkner (1897–
1962), but with *Uno* (1962) (*One*) and *Aire tan
dulce* (1967) (*Such Sweet Air*) she has achieved a
more personal style. Her novels describe the
inhabitants of northern Argentina as hiding a core
of polemics, passion and aggressiveness behind a
seemingly controlled appearance.

Other works: *En el fondo* (1969) (*At Heart*); *Su
demonio preferido* (1973) (*One's Preferred Devil*); *La
última conquista de El Angel* (1977) (*The Last
Conquest of the Angel*); *Las viejas fantaseosas* (1981)
(*The Old Dreaming Women*).

'Orris' ▷Ingelow, Jean

Orta, Teresa Margarida da Silva e (?1712–1793)

Brazilian novelist. In 1716 her family moved from
Brazil to Portugal, where she lived for the rest of
her life. At sixteen, she married against the wishes
of her family and was disinherited. Considered
one of the leading women intellectuals of the
period, she wrote a study on the expulsion of the
Jesuits from Brazil and Portugal. In 1752, inspired
by Fénelon's *Les Aventures de Télémaque* (1699),
and writing under the pen-name Dorothea
Engrássia Tavareda Dalmira, she published
*Máximas de Virtude e Formosura com que Diófanes,
Climeneia e Hemirena, Príncipes de Tebas, Venceram
os Mais Apertados Lances da Desgraça (Maximas of
Virtue and Beauty with which Diófanes, Climeneia
and Hemirena, Princes of Thebes, Overcame the Most
Rigorous Trials of Adversity*). The second edition of
the novel appeared with the title ▷*Aventuras de
Diófanes*. The 'feminism' often attributed to this
work stems in part from Orta's portrayal of strong
women characters and her commentaries in
support of better instruction for women. Orta's
liberalism is also manifested in her espousal of
other progressive social legislation as well as
reforms in the areas of agriculture and industry.

Ortese, Anna Maria (born 1914)

Italian novelist, short story writer and journalist.
Of a poor family, Ortese did not have a consistent
or thorough education, but she read voraciously as
a child. Born in Rome, she is one of the most
popular and highly respected Italian women
writers, and has won many literary awards. Ortese

has lived in many southern Italian cities, and has incorporated the flavour of southern Italian life into much of her work. She has contributed to many Italian newspapers and literary magazines, especially to the 'women's pages'. She specializes in ▷surrealistic studies of adolescence. Her first work, *Angelici dolori* (1937) (*Angelic Pains*), led to her inclusion by critics in that body of writers whose style can be defined as *realismo magico* (▷magic realism). However, there are also elements of ▷naturalism, lyricism and Existentialism in her work. Her dissection of Italian cities, including Milan and Naples, lays bare the myths that surround them, and reveals the reality. There is a strong poetic, almost visionary, feel to her prose. Her collection of short stories *Il mare non bagna Napoli* (1953) (▷*The Bay Is Not Naples*) is a typical mixture of her realistic and fantastical narrative. Much of her work is fabulous, in that it is constructed in the manner of the fable. Yet, for her, fabulous narrative is in no way opposed to realistic narrative. ▷*L'iguana* (*The Iguana*) of 1965 is typical of her fabulous/realistic style in its construction as a political fable, crammed with unlikely characters, which nevertheless addresses real dilemmas. *Poveri e semplici* (1967) (*The Poor and the Simple*) is set in Milan in the immediate post-war period, and is reminiscent of Vittorini in its moral concern and literary novelty.

Her other works include: *I giorni del cielo* (1958) (*Days of Heaven*); *Silenzio a Milano* (1958) (*Silence in Milan*); *La luna sul muro* (1968) (*The Moon on the Wall*); *L'alone grigio* (1969) (*The Grey Halo*); *Il porto di Toledo – Ricordi della vita irreale* (1975) (*The Port of Toledo – Memories of an Unreal Life*); *Il cappello piumato* (1979) (*The Plumed Hat*); *Il treno russo* (1983) (*The Russian Train*); *Il mormorio di Parigi* (1986) (*The Hum of Paris*); *La morte del folletto* (1987) (*The Death of the Sprite*); *Estivi terrori* (1987) (*Summer Terrors*); *In sonno e in veglia* (1987) (*In Sleep and Wakefulness*).

Ortiz, Lourdes (born 1943)

Born in Madrid, Spain, Ortiz is a journalist, translator, dramatist and novelist. She is acknowledged as an established member of the New Wave of female novelists who dominated the 1980s. Her first novel, *Luz de memoria* (1976) (*The Light of Memory*), tells the story of a man confined to a psychiatric hospital. *Picadura mortal* (1979) (*A Fatal Sting*) is a detective novel with the added attraction of a female detective. *En días como éstos* (1981) (*In Days Like These*) treats the theme of political violence. Generally acknowledged as her masterpiece is ▷*Urraca* (1982). Her more recent works are: *Arcángeles* (1986) (*Archangels*), which meditates on the political figures who held the reins of power in Spain during the 1960s, and *Los motivos de Circe* (1988) (*Circe's Motives*). A major theme of Ortiz's work is the inner destructiveness of violence, political or sexual.

Orvieto, Laura (1876–1953)

Italian children's writer. Although she wrote primarily for children, her books may be appreciated by adults as well. Of a Jewish family, Orvieto was hounded by the fascist regime. She wrote easily accessible historical works on Rome and Greece, collected in one volume as *Storia della Storia del mondo* (*Story of the History of the World*), published in 1953 and 1955.

Orzeszkowa, Eliza (1841–1910)

Polish writer and political activist. A self-taught writer, Orzeskowa earned a living with her pen at a time when few women had any financial independence. She was born Eliza Pawlowski on her family's estate near Grodno in Lithuania. She attended boarding school in Warsaw. At sixteen she married Piotr Orzeszk, and they moved to his estate. She was a political activist for the causes of national independence, democracy and the emancipation of the peasantry. After her divorce, both her and her husband's estates were confiscated or sold, and she returned to Grodno and supported herself. She founded schools, set up a Polish publishing house, and was active as a creative writer and publicist.

Osborn, Sarah Haggar Wheaten (1714–1796)

North American spiritual autobiographer and diarist. Born in London on 22 February 1714, she emigrated to North America at the age of eight; her family settled in Newport, Rhode Island, where she remained until her death. A devout Puritan Congregationalist, she was a prolific author of spiritual texts, beginning with ▷*The Nature, Certainty, and Evidence of True Christianity* (1755). As the leader of an evangelical revival in the 1760s, she brought her concerns for women's role in the Church and society and her abolitionist philosophy to bear upon her religious preachings, which were conducted in her home. As with Anne Hutchinson (1591–1643), who held informal religious meetings for women, these meetings caused great concern among the male clergy, especially when she integrated men and women's meetings and held meetings for African-Americans as well. In 1799 the ▷*Memoirs of the Life of Mrs Sarah Osborn* was published by her minister, and in the following century her correspondence with an equally devout friend were published as the ▷*Familiar Letters Written by Mrs Sarah Osborn, and Miss Susanna Anthony*. After a lengthy illness, she died in Newport on 2 August 1796, leaving a legacy of religious activism that acted as a model for women in decades to come.

▷*Life and Character of Miss Susanna Anthony, The*; Heaton, Hannah Cook; *World of Hannah Heaton, The*

Osborne, Dorothy, (1627–95)

English letter-writer. Her letters to her future husband William Temple, whom she married in 1654, are acerbic and witty, and she uses them to negotiate for herself an important material and emotional status for her forthcoming marriage. She corresponded with ▷Katherine Philips, but despised ▷Margaret Cavendish, commenting on

her poems, 'Sure, the poor woman is a little distracted, she could never be so ridiculous else as to adventure at writing books, and in verse too.'
Bib: Parker, K., *The Letters of Dorothy Osorne.*

Os habla Electra (1975) (Electra Speaking)
Novel by ▷Concha Alós, one of the most significant of the post-war female novelists currently writing in Spain. In this novel, which is a neo-Freudian study of the mother–daughter relationship so central to feminism, Alós uses the Electra myth to elucidate the tragedy of the female characters.

Ostenso, Martha (1900–1963)
Canadian novelist. Born near Bergen, Norway, her family emigrated in 1902 to the midwestern United States. At fifteen she moved to Brandon, and later to Winnipeg, Manitoba, in Canada, where she went to high school and, for a short time, to the University of Manitoba. She taught at school, and worked as a reporter for the *Winnipeg Free Press*, then in 1921 moved back to the United States. She studied, at Columbia University in New York, with Douglas Durkin, who became her lifetime associate. They eventually married in 1944. Ostenso is justifiably famous for her novel, ▷*Wild Geese* (1925, published in Britain as *The Passionate Flight*), set in the Interlake district of Manitoba, which depicts a passionate, headstrong female character, Judith Gare, who resists the tyranny of her abusive father in order to seize her own happiness. *Wild Geese* won, over more than 1,300 competitors, an enormous literary competition, jointly sponsored by Dodd, Mead, Famous Players, and *The Pictorial Review*, for the best first novel by a North American writer. Only two other of Ostenso's sixteen novels, *Prologue to Love* (1932) and *The Young May Moon* (1929), are set in Canada. She also published one book of poetry, *The Far Land* (1924). Much has been made of the extent to which Durkin and Ostenso apparently collaborated on the novels published under her name. If so, the joint authorship appears to have diluted the promise that Ostenso displays so vigorously in *Wild Geese*; her later novels, although they repeat features such as self-righteous fathers and rebellious women, are rather romantic counter-examples. Still, Judith Gare and her proud defiance remain a powerful example to subsequent female characters in Canadian fiction.
Bib: Fairbanks, C., *Prairie Women: Images in American and Canadian Fiction;* Harrison, D., *Unnamed Country: The Struggle for a Canadian Prairie Fiction;* Northey, M., *The Haunted Wilderness;* Thomas, C., *Canadian Novelists 1920–1945.*

Osório, Ana de Castro (1872–1935)
Portuguese feminist activist, essayist and author of children's books. Among her earliest publications were her children's books in the series *Para as Crianças (For Children)*. She also wrote pamphlets on educational matters, which appeared under the title *O Bem da Pátria (The Good of the Nation)*. One

Ana de Castro Osório

of the most active participants in the feminist struggle in Portugal, she was an early supporter of the republic and co-founded the Republican League of Portuguese Women. In 1917 she began the National Crusade of Portuguese Women, an organization in support of Portugal's role in the war effort.

Concerned with the welfare of women of all social classes, Osório was especially interested in helping to create progressive legislation. For many years she carried out the duties of *sub-inspectora de trabalho feminino*, an office concerned with women in the work force.

▷Cabete, Adelaide; *Alma Feminina*

Other
▷Simone de Beauvoir uses the concept of the other in *The Second Sex* (1949) to explain how patriarchal culture constructs woman as man's subordinate and derivative inferior. In ▷French feminism and ▷poststructuralism the concept has two main meanings. In contrast to de Beauvoir, the French feminists ▷Hélène Cixous and ▷Luce Irigaray celebrate women's otherness as a mark of their difference from men. According to French psychoanalyst Jacques Lacan's (1901–1981) poststructuralist theory of subjectivity, subject identity is acquired in the ▷subject's address *to* others and its address *by* others: for example, a man's encounter with a woman confers and confirms his gender identity. Lacan's Other (capital O) is the place of speech, of language.

Other One, The (1960)
Translation of *La Seconde* (1929) by French writer ▷Colette, a study of the relationship between Fanny, her dramatist husband, Farou, and their companion/secretary, Jane. The book is remarkable in that Fanny realizes that the pain of discovering the sexual relationship between Farou

and Jane is less disturbing to her than the possible loss of her female companion. There is as much emphasis on the physical proximity and emotional harmony of the two women as on the differences between them. The conclusion avoids tendentiousness by depicting the combination of closeness and ambivalence which their relationship now holds. The final phrase, which leaves them to 'nurture their newly born, sickly security' provides a fairly open ending.

Otto-Peters, Louise (1819–1895)

German novelist, poet and essayist. The fourth daughter of a Leipzig lawyer, she was orphaned at sixteen. With the help of her own intensive reading programme, she acquired a wide knowledge of history, literature and politics, and developed an interest in social issues. From the outset, her novels, such as *Ludwig der Kellner* (1843) (*Ludwig the Waiter*), dealt with the plight of the workers. Another early concern was the emancipation of women explored in *Kathinka* (1844). Both of these themes are also to be found in her poetry collection, *Lieder eines deutschen Mädchens* (1847) (*Songs of a German Girl*). During the 1848 Revolution she published articles, under the pseudonym Otto Stern, demanding the vote for women, and equal rights for all. In the years of reaction which followed, she suffered persecution and social ostracism. In 1849 she founded the first serious woman's journal in Germany, and went on to open schools of continuing education for women. She wrote many novels, novellas, stories, libretti and essays, of which the novels *Schloß und Fabrik* (1846) (*Castle and Factory*), *Die Schultheißentochter von Nürnberg* (3 vols) (1859–1861) (*The Daughter of the Mayor of Nuremberg*) and the polemic *Das Recht der Frauen auf Erwerb. Blicke auf das Frauenleben der Gegenwart* (1866) (*The Right of Women to Gainful Employment. A Book of Women's Lives Today*) remain the most interesting.

Ouabi; or, The Virtues of Nature: An Indian Tale in Four Cantos (1790)

Poem by the American poet, ▷Sarah Wentworth Apthorp Morton. *Ouabi* captures her concerns with the moral and social visions of the developing nation. One of the earliest poems about Native Americans, it was first published in 1790 under the authorship of 'a Lady of Boston'. *Ouabi* argues against the complacency and luxury of civilized life and calls for a return to natural virtues, which are exemplified in Native American culture where 'Ev'ry boon of life' resides.

'Ouida' (1839–1908)

The ▷pseudonym of Marie Louise de la Ramée. 'Ouida' began to write in the 1860s, contributing tales of high society life to *Bentley's Miscellany*. Flamboyant, extravagant and egotistical herself, 'Ouida's novels are ▷sensational ▷romances set amidst exotic surroundings, featuring much passion and intrigue within privileged social circles. 'Ouida' aspired to the aristocracy herself

and increasingly feared its pollution by middle-class vulgarity (though she was middle class herself). In *Moths* (1880), she describes the social hierarchy being eaten away by parasites and hypocrites. Other novels include: *Chandos* (1866); *Under Two Flags* (1867); *Pascarel* (1873); *Two Little Wooden Shoes* (1874) and *Princess Naxaprine* (1884). *Views and Opinions* (1895) and *Critical Studies* (1900) are collections of vituperative articles against female ▷suffrage, cruelty to animals, ▷publishers, and the *nouveaux riches*.
Bib: Ffrench, Y., *Ouida: A Study in Ostentation*; Bigland, E., *Ouida the Passionate Victorian*.

Our Crowd (1990)

English translation of novel by Russian writer ▷Liudmila Petrushévskaia. One of Petrushévskaia's most ambitious stories, *Our Crowd* (originally published in 1988, and translated by Helena Gascilo in *Glasnost: An Anthology of Literature under Gorbachev*, 1990) is a satirical depiction of the life of a rackety circle of ▷Moscow pseudo-intellectuals grouped around 'our Serge', a scientist who, according to the nameless narrator, has 'calculated the principle of flight for flying saucers'. Their Friday gatherings, devoted to liquor, amorous byplay, and cynical baiting of one another, offer a devastating contrast between the tenor of modern urban life and the idealistic 19th-century intelligentsia circles Russians are taught to revere. In headlong, breathless style, the unnamed protagonist, a self-described 'cruel person', relates how, desperate to puncture the group's callous selfishness, she resorts to a ruse to assure her son's future.

Our New Home in the West ▷New Home – Who'll Follow? or, Glimpses of Western Life, A

Our Nig: or, Sketches from the Life of a Free Black, in a Two-Story White House, North. Showing that Slavery's Shadows Fall Even There. By 'Our Nig' (1859)

US autobiographical novel by Harriet E. Wilson (c 1808–1870). One of the earliest-published novels by an African-American woman, *Our Nig* reveals the effects of slavery and racism on free blacks in the north, using some elements of the ▷domestic novel tradition but focusing on the character's struggles for racial and gender identity. Although published in 1859, *Our Nig* dropped out of sight for nearly a century and a half. It was reprinted in 1983 in an edition by Henry Louis Gates, Jr, which documents the correspondence between the narrative and Wilson's life.

Our Sister Killjoy (1981)

The first novel by Ghanaian writer ▷Ama Ata Aidoo, dealing with the encounter between Africans and Europe. She is critical of those who profess to love their country but are lured away by the material benefits of the developed world. The young heroine, Sissie, on the other hand, is disillusioned and alienated by her experiences in

Germany. Her friendship with a German woman is described in terms of seductive sensuality, particularly with regard to food. But when it teeters on the brink of a lesbian love affair, Sissie is disgusted. She perceives the loneliness and aridity which underlie the material opulence of German life, and decides to return to Ghana. Aidoo's narrative technique alternates between prose and poetry, with animated dialogue and direct appeals to the reader, in the manner of ▷oral storytelling.

Our Village (1824–1832)

A series of essays by ▷Mary Russell Mitford, describing the rural life of a village based on Three Mile Cross in Berkshire. The essays were greatly admired for their observations and vivid depictions of village existence, and although at times Midford creates an idealized image, she also portrays a community under threat because of increasing industrialization. The essays remain of interest today.

Out of the Kumbla: Caribbean Women and Literature (1990)

This collection of essays, edited by Carole Boyce Davies and Elaine Savory Fido, and with a foreword by ▷Pamela Mordecai, examines the image of women in Caribbean literature and the role of women writers in the redefining of this literature. Included are articles which discuss the work of ▷Erna Brodber, ▷Michelle Cliff, ▷Maryse Condé, ▷Jamaica Kincaid, ▷Paule Marshall, ▷Jean Rhys and ▷Zee Edgell.

Ovbiagele, Helen

Nigerian novelist. Born in Benin city, she has been a teacher, and is now editor of the woman's page of *Vanguard*, a national daily newspaper.

Despite the quality of her writing she has received little critical recognition because of her espousal of that quintessentially 'feminine' genre, the romance. Her five novels, all of which have been published in Macmillan's Pacesetter series, are interesting for the way they have adapted the romance formula to the Nigerian setting. Her divergence from the traditional formula followed by Western publishers like Mills and Boon, and writers like ▷Denise Robbins and ▷Barbara Cartland, suggests the contours of a culturally-specific fantasy of ideal love in an African milieu. For example, Ovbiagele's heroines are often not virgins, and may even be middle-aged and divorced. She takes a pragmatic view of sex and the practice, induced by harsh economic circumstances, of gaining material benefits, like funding an education, from sexual relationships. Alongside the fantasy of monogamy, faithfulness and a perfect man, runs the equally strong current of women's independence and self-sufficiency. She has so far published ▷*Evbu, My Love* (1980), *A Fresh Start* (1982), *You Never Know* (1982) and *Forever Yours* (1985).

▷Romantic fiction (West Africa); Journalism (West Africa); Prostitution (West Africa)

Owenson, Sydney (Lady Morgan) (c 1775–1859)

Irish novelist. Supposedly born at sea, she became a governess when her father lost his money. In 1809 she married a doctor, Charles Morgan, who was subsequently knighted. She led a colourful life, hosting an influential salon in Dublin and travelling widely in Europe. Her third novel, *The Wild Irish Girl* (1809), a romantic story of Gaelic Ireland, became a bestseller and established her, with ▷Maria Edgeworth, as one of the first distinctively Irish novelists. Her later novels (*O'Donnel*, 1814; *Florence McCarthy*, 1819; *The O'Briens and the O'Flahertys*, 1827), are historical ▷romances of Ireland's past, unashamedly nationalist, written with great verve and serious intent.

Owls Do Cry (1957)

Novel by New Zealand writer ▷Janet Frame. *Owls Do Cry* is Frame's first novel and it set the pattern for her later work. Written after a number of years in mental hospitals, *Owls Do Cry* is a non-realist novel about the Withers family and their lives in small-town New Zealand. The novel is focused on the four Withers children and reflects an unstable and potentially dangerous environment in which children suffer different kinds of threat. The narrative centres on the town rubbish dump, where the children find 'treasure', and on the 'treasure' of language which affects all their activities and perceptions. *Owls Do Cry* has attracted a great deal of critical commentary because of its complex structure, particularly the way Frame handles time and narrative voice, and for its radical questioning of language. In her three-volume autobiography *To the Is-land* (1982), *An Angel at My Table* (1984) and *The Envoy from Mirror City* (1985), Frame has made it clear how much *Owls Do Cry* is connected to the events of her life, but transformed by the medium of fiction. Considered to be one of Frame's finest novels, *Owls Do Cry* was written before she left for England, while she was resident with the New Zealand writer Frank Sargeson. Many of the novel's concerns reappear and are reworked in her later fiction.

Oxford Movement (Tractarian Movement)

A movement in the Church of England, centred at Oxford and initiated in 1833. The movement aimed to defend the independent, spiritual status of the Church against what was seen as increasing state intervention, by arguing that it was a divine institution descending directly from the medieval Catholic Church. The Tractarians (so-called because of 'tracts' written for *The Times* newspaper) attempted to tread a path between post-Reformation Catholicism and Protestantism. The movement was weakened, however, when several of its proponents converted to Catholicism, alienating the Anglicans. It was nevertheless highly influential and had significant literary repercussions. ▷Christina Rossetti, ▷Elizabeth Sewell and ▷Charlotte Yonge were committed supporters. The Tractarian emphasis on medieval and 17th-century Church history was reflected in the medieval setting of much Victorian poetry.

▷ *Robert Elsmere*

Oyarzún, Emilia Pincheira ▷ Oyarzún, Mila

Oyarzún, Mila (born 1912)

Chilean poet and novelist. The pen-name of Emilia Pincheira Oyarzún, who studied medicine and librarianship in Chile, but was ultimately a poet. She lectured on Chilean literature in much of Spanish America. Her first poetic work, *Esquinas del viento* (1941) (*Corners of the Wind*), was surpassed by *Estancias de soledad* (1946) (*Farms of Solitude*) which had much more harmonious poetic results. Her best-known novel is *Cartas a una sombra* (1944) (*Letters to a Shadow*).

Ozick, Cynthia (born 1928)

US novelist, short story writer and essayist. Ozick was born in New York to immigrant parents, and she graduated with honours from New York University in 1949. In 1950 she earned a Master's degree at Ohio State University.

Her work reflects her Jewish concerns, and her characters struggle between the pagan and the holy, between nature or art and Judaism. *The Pagan Rabbi and Other Stories* (1971) focuses on dislocated Jewish immigrants; Ozick emphasizes a sense of loss: of the Yiddish language, of the past, of virility, and of religion. 'Usurpation' from *Bloodshed and Three Novellas* (1976) centres on a woman artist; Ozick concludes that storytellers upstage God because storytelling is a forbidden, magic act. Stories in *Levitation* (1982) and the novel *The Cannibal Galaxy* (1983) portray mothers as usurpers of God in their creation of powerful daughters.

Other works include: *Trust* (1966), *Art and Ardor: Essays* (1983), *The Messiah of Stockholm* (1987) and *Metaphor and Memory* (1989).

Paalzow, Henriette von (1788–1847)

German novelist. After a brief marriage, she set up house in Berlin with her mother and brother, and maintained a lively contact with artists and intellectuals of her time. She became extremely popular as the author of historical novels, such as *Godwie Castle. Aus den Papieren der Herzogin von Nottingham* (1836) (*Godwie Castle. From the Documents of the Countess of Nottingham*) or *Sainte Roche* (1839). The plots of these novels revolve around the family life of aristocratic personalities.

Packer, Joy (1905–1977)

South African writer, whose melodramatic romances and personalized travel books have had great popular appeal, and have been extensively translated. Born Joy Petersen in Cape Town, she married Sir Herbert Packer, a naval officer (later an admiral) in Portsmouth, England, and, after a brief period with the *Daily Express*, travelled with him through the Far East, Turkey, Greece and Yugoslavia, an experience captured in *Pack and Follow: One Person's Adventures in Four Different Worlds* (1945). Three other similarly autobiographical volumes followed: *Grey Mistress* (1949), *Apes and Ivory* (1953) and *Home from the Sea* (1963). *Deep as the Sea* (1975), based on her husband's letters, tells the story of his naval career from 1907 to 1953.

The most popular of Lady Packer's fiction was the bestselling historical romance, *Valley of the Vines* (1955), which was turned into a South African television series, and *Nor the Moon By Night* (1957), made into a J. Arthur Rank film. Although Packer prided herself on racial tolerance, her novels romanticize apartheid as well as gender inequality, and beg to be examined for their uneasy inclusion of the colonial 'other' into the romance formula. The sentimental, sometimes Victorian dialogue is often oddly juxtaposed with the discourse of racial bigotry and bushveld jargon. Her work is occasionally reprinted.

Other novels: *The High Roof* (1959); *The Glass Barrier* (1961); *The Man in the Mews* (1964); *The Blind Spot* (1967, published in the USA in 1968 as *The Man Out There*); *Leopard in the Fold* (1969); *Veronica* (1970).

Travel books: *The World is a Proud Place* (1966); *Boomerang* (1972); *The Dark Curtain* (1977).

Paemel, Monika van (born 1945)

Flemish novelist. She has written several novels in an experimental, associative style, in which the story and subjective experiences are blended into a firm whole. The emphasis is always on a character's obsessional search for his/her own identity: as an individual in a community, as a woman in a male society, or as an author. *Amazone met het blauwe voorhoofd* (1971) (*Amazon With the Blue Forehead*), her first novel, won a literary prize, as did *Marguerite* (1976), a novel of the author's reminiscences of her grandmother. *De confrontatie* (*The Confrontation*) dates from 1974. She acquired a wider audience only when, after nine years of silence, she published *De vermaledijde vaders* (*The Cursed Fathers*) in 1985. This substantial novel is experimental in its shifts of style and point of view, ▷stream-of-consciousness narrative, and leaps in time. Essentially the book tells the story of a Belgian woman after World War II; it is a cynical social-political novel about post-war Belgium, 'the country that would never be a nation'.

Paese di Cuccagna, Il (1891) ▷*Land of Cockayne, The*

Page, Gertrude (1873–1922)

Early Rhodesian novelist, born in England and arriving in Rhodesia at the turn of the century. She wrote prolifically, achieving considerable popularity during her lifetime, particularly with '*The Edge o' Beyond*' (1908). Her seventeenth and last novel, *Jill on a Ranch* (1921), went into twelve editions. Her first novel, *Love in the Wilderness* (1907), subtitled *A Story of Another African Farm* after ▷Olive Schreiner's novel, sets the tone of what is to follow: a combination of sentimentalized Edenic pastoralism, harsh frontier racism in a ▷'realist' mode, and a mysticism about nature. The characteristic ideas of the Rhodesian settler novel of colonial fiction recur in Page's novels, as in those of her contemporary, ▷Cynthia Stockley, and in both novelists the colony becomes a liberatory space after the constraints and artifices of English life. Many of her books are published under her married name, Mrs G.A. Dobbin, and, with R.A. Foster-Melliar, she co-wrote *The Course of My Ship* (1918).

Other novels: *Paddy-the-Next-Best-Thing* (1908), *The Silent Rancher* (1909), *Jill's Rhodesian Philosophy* (1910), *Two Lovers and a Lighthouse* (1910), *The Rhodesian* (1912), '*Where the Strange Roads Go Down*' (1913), *The Pathway* (1914), *Follow After* (1915), *The Supreme Desire* (1916), *Far From the Limelight* (1918), and *The Veldt Trail* (1919).

Page, Patricia K. (P.K.) (born 1916)

Canadian artist and poet, also known as P.K. Irwin, and Judith Cape. Page was born in Dorset, England, and emigrated to Canada with her parents in 1919. She attended school in Calgary, Winnipeg and England, then worked in various cities as a sales clerk, filing clerk, historical researcher and radio actress, writing poetry, and developing a novel called *The Sun and the Moon* (published in 1944 under the pseudonym Judith Cape, republished with other fictions in 1973).

In the fall of 1941 she went to Montreal, where she became active in the writing community, and helped to edit *Preview*, a small magazine instrumental in the development of ▷modernist poetry in Canada. She published her first book of poetry, *As Ten, As Twenty* in 1946, and in the same year moved to Ottawa to work for the National Film Board (NFB). She met Arthur Irwin when he became Chairman of the NFB in 1950, and they married that year. He was named Canadian High Commissioner to Australia, during which time Page's second book, *The Metal and the Flower* (1954), appeared, and won the Governor General's Award for Poetry. Irwin's subsequent postings were to Brazil, Mexico and Guatemala; travelling with him, Page began to develop an interest in drawing and painting, which she studied seriously. She has had numerous exhibitions, and her work has been widely shown. After returning to Victoria, British Columbia, in 1964, she began to write poetry again, publishing *Cry Ararat!* (1967), *P.K. Page, Poems Selected and New* (1974), *Evening Dance of the Grey Flies* (1981) and *The Glass Air* (1985). *The Glass Air* elects her best work, and includes new material: it is almost crystalline in its articulation of baroque detail. Page is a modernist poet, working with symbols of the ideal, and striving for a transcendent dimension, but she is still at home in the garden of the self. Her beautifully written and observed *Brazilian Journal* (1987), a 'period piece' based on letters and journals kept while she lived in Brazil (1957–1959), is arresting for its lush transparency. It includes reproductions of a number of her paintings. She published *A Flask of Sea Water* in 1989.

▷Webb, Phyllis

Pageant, and Other Poems, A (1881)

A collection of poems by ▷Christina Rossetti, including the sonnet sequence ▷'Monna Innominata' and the important poems 'The Thread of Life' and 'An Old World Thicket', in which Rossetti explores her poetic and religious identity. Other noteworthy lyrics include 'An Immurata Sister', spoken from the perspective of a nun who seeks release from worldly (and gender-specific) constraints, and 'A Life's Parallels', an enigmatic poem addressing the mystery of death.

Paget, Violet ▷Lee, Vernon

Pagu ▷Galvão, Patrícia

Pahlen Debate, The ▷Krusenstjerna (or Pahlen) Debate, The

Painful Anxieties Which Proceed from Love, The (1538) (*Les Angoisses douloureuses qui procedent d'amours*)
Three-part French novel by ▷Hélisenne de Crenne, which enjoyed immediate sucess. This semi-autobiographical novel tells the adventures of a bored young wife, who falls in love with an attractive young man, Guinelic. She manages to resist him by reminding herself of the misfortunes of other famous lovers, such as Lancelot and Guinevere, and Tristan and Yseult. Having decided to love Guinelic from a distance as a friend, her frustration is reinforced by her husband's violent intervention. Held prisoner in a tower, she decides to write her own story, but when her journal of the affair is discovered, she is sequestered in the country by her jealous husband, putting an abrupt end to her account. Municipal and legal documents of the time indicate that much of Part I is factual. Part II, *Les Epistres familieres et invective* (1539) (*Familiar and Invective Letters*), narrated by Guinelic, retells the adventures of the first book in epistolary form. The heroine never yields to her lover, though he compromises her position on several occasions. After a final, desperate attempt to free her from her husband, Guinelic has to watch her die, and the title of the final chapter suggests that his own death is also imminent.

Palacios, Lucila (born 1902)
Venezuelan novelist, short story writer and dramatist. Born Mercedes Carvajal de Arocha, she adopted her pen-name in 1931. She was a politician and an ambassador in Uruguay. The critic Mancera Galetti best describes her work: she employs direct, communicative language in her theatre, and in her narratives she conveys the psychological traits and reactions of her characters in very clear situations and in pictures without undertones. Another critic, Juan Liscano, states that 'She is a writer who has a drive for change and with political sensibility, with little tendency for a formal and stylistic speculation, for confidence or melancholy evocation.' In her recent writing, Lucila Palacios has taken the sea as her main theme.

Work: *Desatemos el nudo* (1935) (*Let's Untie The Knot*); *Los Buzos* (1937) (*The Divers*); *Rebeldía* (1940) (*Rebelliousness*); *Orquídeas azules* (1942) (*Blue Orchids*); *Trozos de vida* (1942) (*Slices of Life*); *La gran serpiente* (1943) (*The Great Snake*); *Tres palabras y una mujer* (1944) (*Three Words and a Woman*); *El córcel de las crines albas* (1950) (*The Charger With the Dawn Mane*); *Cubil* (1951) (*Den*); *Niebla* (1952) (*Mist*); *Los Lunáticos* (1953) (*The Lunatics*); *El mundo en miniatura* (1955) (*The World in Miniature*); *Horas de vida. Juan se durmió en la torre* (1956) (*Hours of Life. Juan Slept in the Tower*); *El día de Cain* (1958) (*The Day of Cain*); *Signos en el tiempo* (1959) (*Signs of the Time*); *Tiempo de siega* (1960) (*Harvest Time*); *Poemas de noche y de silencio* (1964) (*Poems of Night and Silence*); *Ayer violento* (1965) (*Violent Yesterday*), and *La piedra en el vacío* (1970) (*The Stone in the Void*).

Palatine, Madame (1652–1722)

Pen-name used by Elisabeth-Charlotte von der Pfalz, French author of possibly the largest collection of letters of the period. Of German origin, she was married at the age of nineteen to Philippe d'Orléans (1640–1701), the homosexual brother of Louis XIV (1638–1715). Mother of two children and an excellent observer of the court of Louis XIV, she remained true to her German origins in her mannish comportment, dress and incurable '*scribo-manie*' ('writing-mania'). She once remarked: '*J'ai regretté toute ma vie d'être femme*' ('I have regretted having been born a woman all my life'), and chose to refer to herself as an '*esclave couronné*' ('a slave queen'). She bombarded her German relations and friends with letters about her youth in Germany and her position at the French court. However, at least a third of the 60,000 or so letters in her hand were written in French, a language which she wrote well. She sent at least 7,000 letters to her confidante, the Comtesse de Beuvron, and among her other regular French correspondents were the Duchesse de Lorraine, Sophie, Electress of Hanover (died 1714), three Spanish queens, and Madame de Ludre (1638–1726); 700 or more are still extant. Her library contained many early 'feminist' texts.
Bib: van der Cruysse, D., "'*J'ai regretté toute ma vie d'être femme*": Madame Palatine *féministe?*' in *French Literary Studies*, XVI (1989); van der Cruysse, D., *Mme Palatine, Princesse européenne*.

Palencia, Isabel de (1878–196?)

Spanish author of historical and social essays, memoirs, and novels. Palencia was born into a prominent family in Málaga. Her first novel, *El sembrador sembró su semilla* (1928) (*The Sower Sowed his Seed*), was inspired by contemporary reproductive theory.

Palestine

The area now called Israel is part of what was originally named Palestine (Palestina) by the Romans. It was known as such until the division of Palestine into Jewish and Arab states by the United Nations in 1947.

Paley, Grace (born 1922)

US short story-writer. Paley was born and lives in New York. She has two children, has been twice married and has taught at universities and colleges in New York. She comes from a socialist Russian-Jewish family and was surrounded by storytellers from an early age. Her stories are typically set in working-class and Jewish neighbourhoods of New York and highlight both the ordinariness and extraordinariness of their inhabitants' daily lives. The episodic stories in *Enormous Changes at the Last Minute* (1974) often focus on family relationships where men come and go but women look to children for hope and inspiration in their daily battles. In a wry and comic style, these episodes show moments of change in the characters' lives, narrating in a clear-eyed way the courage, pathos and joy with which they face 'the little disturbances of man'. Paley's ear for the speech of her city allows her to temper abstractions with colloquialisms, the authentic turns of speech that make her stories both poignant and celebratory. Paley is both a writer and a political activist, and her experience in the peace movement forms the backdrop for many of the stories in *Later the Same Day* (1985).

Other work includes: *The Little Disturbances of Man: Stories of Men and Women in Love* (1959), *Leaning Forward* (poems) (1985), *365 Reasons Not to Have Another War* (1989) and *Long Walks and Intimate Talks* (1991).
Bib: Taylor, Jacqueline, *Grace Paley: Illuminating the Dark Lives*.

Palma, Felip ▷Ventós i Cullell, Palmira

Palmer, Henrietta ▷Winter, John Strange

Palmer, Nettie (1885–1964)

Australian literary critic, poet and journalist. Palmer was born Janet Higgins in Bendigo, Victoria, and graduated MA from the University of Melbourne in 1912. She married the writer, Vance Palmer, in 1914 and their literary partnership was highly significant for Australia's cultural life. Palmer travelled extensively. She attended the Writers' Congress in Paris in 1935, and she and her husband were in Spain at the outbreak of the Spanish Civil War in 1936. She worked for the cause of world socialism, helping migrants and refugees from the war in Spain.

Her literary criticism was considerable, including not only *Modern Australian Literature 1900 to 1923* (1924), but also numerous articles in prestigious journals which did much to gain recognition for Australian literature and, in particular, Australian women's literature, during the first half of the 20th century. She was the first to recognize the importance of ▷Henry Handel Richardson, and published significant early critical studies of the works of ▷Barbara Baynton, ▷M. Barnard Eldershaw and ▷Katharine Susannah Prichard.

▷*Gender, Politics and Fiction*; Literary criticism (Australia)

Pàmies, Teresa (born 1919)

Spanish sociological writer.) Born in Balguer, in the province of Lérida, Pàmies was the daughter of a peasant farmer. She eventually became a left-wing militant. Most of Pàmies's writings are heavily autobiographical, and their interest is more sociological than literary. Her major works include: *La filla del pres* (1967) (*The Prisoner's*

Daughter) and *Testament a Praga* (1971) (*Testament in Prague*), which was written in collaboration with her father, Tomás Pàmies. Pàmies excels in the memoir genre, for example her *Quan érem capitans* (1974) (*When We Were Captains*), about the Spanish Civil War (1936–9). Also notable is her travelogue, *Rosalia no hi era* (1982) (*Rosalia Wasn't There*), which is based on her travels to Galicia in 1981, and her pilgrimage to the birth-place of ▷Rosalía de Castro, the celebrated 19th-century poet.

▷Catalan women's writing

Pamphila (1st century AD)

A historian from Epidaurus, of Egyptian family, Pamphila wrote in Greek. She was a scholar at Rome under the Emperor Nero (ruled AD 54–68). Her most famous work was a *Miscellaneous History*, of which only a summary, provided by the Byzantine writer Photius (AD c820–?892), survives. The work, in thirty-three books, was probably a source for several later writers of similar works (Favorinus, 1st century BC; Aulus Gellius, 1st century BC; Diogenes Laertius, 3rd century AD). Photius records that in her preface she states that she lived with her husband for thirteen years, never leaving his side for an hour. She wrote down whatever she heard from him or other men who visited the house, and what she herself read. She says she aimed deliberately at no unity of structure, but at diversity, like the varied flowers in the field. The biographical dictionary, the *Suda* (10th century AD), records she also wrote epitomes, or abridgements, of historical works, including that of Ctesias (in three books); *On Controversies* and *On Aphrodisiacs*. But her name, meaning 'She who loves all', was a common one and the latter work may not be by the same woman (▷Pornography, Ancient Greece).

Panáeva, Avdot'ia Iakovlevna (1819/20–1893)

Russian fiction writer and memoir-writer. Panáeva, the daughter of a ▷St Petersburg theatrical family, is best remembered in literary history for the company she kept: married to minor writer Ivan Panáev from 1837, she lived with his partner, the poet Nikolai Nekrasov, and played an active role in editing their liberal ▷'thick journal' *The Contemporary* from 1848 to 1863. At the famous Monday gatherings at the trio's apartment, she served tea and fed all the major writers of the time, including Tolstoy, Dostoevsky and Turgenev, and the radical critics (Belinsky, Dobroliubov, Chernyshevsky) who were reshaping Russian consciousness. Although her memory sometimes betrayed her as to details, Panáeva's *Reminiscences* (1889) are a valuable picture of the excitement of those years.

Using the male ▷pseudonym N. Stanitskii, she and Nekrasov produced two popular novels, *Three Countries of the World* (1848–49) and *The Dead Lake* (1851). Alone, she wrote the autobiographical novella ▷*The Tal'nikov Family* (1848) and a series of stories and sketches largely devoted to the position of women, of which her own stormy life, first with Panáev and then with Nekrasov, gave her unhappy experience. 'A Young Lady of the Steppe' (1855) deflates Turgenev's plots involving urban men and impressionable country girls. 'Woman's Lot' (1862) is a passionate protest against a false emancipation of young women that will only leave them vulnerable to corrupt men. Panáeva's daughter by a second marriage was the *fin de siècle* novelist ▷Evdokiia Nagródskaia.

Bib: Gregg, R., 'A Brackish Hippocrene: Nekrasov, Panaeva, and the "Prose of Love"', *Slavic Review*, 34, 4; Ledkovsky, M., 'Avdotya Panaeva: Her Salon and Her Life', *Russian Literature Triquarterly* 9.

Pande, Mrinal (born 1946)

Indian novelist, short story writer and journalist. She is the editor of *Saptahik Hindustan*, the Hindi edition of one of India's leading newspapers, *The Hindustan Times*. She is also the editor of *Vama*, a prominent Hindi-language women's magazine. Although she has taught English at university level, she has opted to write her fiction in Hindi to maximize her Indian audience. She has published several novels, plays and collections of short stories. 'Tragedy in a Minor Key', translated from '*Eka Nica Traijedi*' (1981), appears in ▷*Truth Tales*. Another short story, 'Girls', translated from the Hindi, is published in ▷*The Inner Courtyard*.

Pandora, the Musyque of the Beautie of his Mistresse Diana, ▷Vere, Anne Cecil de

Pankhurst, Christabel ▷Suffrage (20th-century Britain)

Pankhurst, Emmeline ▷Suffrage (20th-century Britain)

Pankhurst, Sylvia ▷Suffrage (20th-century Britain)

Panóva, Vera Fëdorovna (1905–1973)

Russian prose writer, dramatist, script writer, and memoir-writer. Panóva wrote poetry and prose from a young age, and began publishing in newspapers and magazines on a regular basis at the age of seventeen. Her first play, *Il'ia Kosogor*, was published in 1939. During World War II she began writing the factory novel *Kruzhilikha* (1947) and her first novella, which evolved into *Evdokiia* (1959). Assigned to write a brochure about a military hospital train, she also produced her first successful novel, *The Train* (1946), which won her a Stalin Prize. She won a second prize for *Kruzhilikha* despite criticism; in her third Stalin Prize novel, *The Bright Shore* (1949), Panóva followed the prescription for ▷socialist realism more faithfully.

Even in her made-to-order novels about

industrial and socialist construction, Panóva assigned a central importance to private life. As with many women writers, much of her best work was devoted to children, eg the cycle of stories *Serëzha* (1955), and used the device of seeing the adult world through the uncomprehending eyes of a child. Panóva's is a moral voice which emphasized the need for kindness and sympathy between people. Her novel, *The Seasons* (1953), one of the early works to signal the end of the Stalinist stranglehold on Russian literature, was criticized for its non-judgemental stance. In the 1960s and 1970s, Panóva wrote plays (*It's Been Ages*, 1966), several film scenarios, a variety of stories and novels, and memoirs.

Bib: Pomorska, K. (ed.), 'Seryozha,' *Fifty Years of Russian Prose* 2; Reeve, F.D. (trans.), 'It's Been Ages', *Contemporary Russian Drama*; Goscilo, H. (trans.), 'Evdokiia', *Russian and Polish Women's Fiction*; 'What Prompted Me to Write The Train', *Soviet Studies in Literature* 3 (1966–67); *Selected Works*; Traill, V. (trans.), *Span of the Year* (*The Seasons*); *The Bright Shore*; *The Factory*; Skvirsky, D. (tr.), *Looking Ahead*; Brown, E.J., *Russian Literature Since the Revolution*; Gasiorowska, Z., *Women in Soviet Fiction, 1917–1964*; Kreuzer, R.L., 'A New Bright Shore for Seryozha', *Slavic and East European Journal*, 27, 3; Wilson, K. (ed.), *An Encyclopedia of Continental Women Writers* 2; Terras, V. (ed.), *Handbook of Russian Literature*.

Paoli, Betty (1814–1894)

Austrian poet. Born in Vienna as Barbara Elisabeth Glück, the natural daughter of a Hungarian prince, she received a good education in the household of her step-father. When he died and her mother lost her fortune, she had to earn her living as a lady's companion, translator and poet. A great admirer of the poetry of ▷Annette von Droste-Hülshoff and ▷Latitia Elisabeth Landon, she began to write early, and from 1841 onwards published her poems in various collections: *Gedichte* (1841) (*Poems*); *Nach dem Gewitter* (1843) (*After the Thunderstorm*); *Neue Gedichte* (1850) (*New Poems*), and *Neueste Gedichte* (1870) (*Newest Poems*). Traditional in form and content, her poetry speaks of mental torment and tragic love. It was well-received by her contemporaries, who saw in her work evidence of 'pure genius' and 'true femininity'; the poet and dramatist Franz Grillparzer (1791–1872) declared her the 'foremost poet of Austria'. A gifted essayist who also wrote sensitive novellas about aristocratic women, she became the role-model and friend of ▷Marie von Ebner-Eschenbach.

Paolini Massimi, Petronilla (1663–1726)

Italian poet. As a young girl she led a very dramatic life. Her father was murdered when she was very young, and her mother was forced to flee with her daughter. They went to Rome, where Petronilla was sent to a convent to be educated. Because constant threats were made on her life, as she was heir to the family fortune, she was married by proxy at the age of ten to a much older relative. Her husband turned out to be violent, and he opposed her interest in literature. Eventually she left him and took refuge in the convent where she had been educated. He refused to allow her access to her money and her children, so she took him to court and succeeded in winning her case. She remained in the convent until her husband died, and then returned to the Abruzzi where she had been born. Her poetry was ▷Arcadian in style, and her Arcadian pseudonym was Fidalma Partenide. Her writing was enriched by her own personal experiences which she retold in poetic form. She also wrote much religious poetry. After her return to the Abruzzi she wrote joyously of her birthplace. Her poetry is included in the collection *Rime degli Arcadi* (1716, 1717 and 1722) (*Verses of the Arcadian Poets*). She also wrote some plays to be set to music. She was a feminist poet, who rejected the notion of love as the source of all joy, and registered her disapproval of the way women were treated by men. Her poetry celebrates women's strength in the face of destiny.

Papadat-Bengescu, Hortensia (1876–1955)

Romanian writer. In her acute analyses of urban and suburban life, Papadat-Bengescu is especially good at portraying mental abnormality among the *nouveau riche*, observing them with savage sharpness. *Drumul ascuns* (1933) (*Hidden Road*) is perhaps her best work.

Her works include: *Ape adînci* (1919) (*Deep Water*), *Sfinxul* (1920) (*The Sphinx*), *Batrînul* (1920) (*The Old One*), *Femeia în fata oglinzii* (1921) (*Women in the Mirror*), *Balaurul* (1923) (*The Dragon*), *Romantă provinciala* (1925) (*A Provincial Romance*), *Fecioarele despletite* (1926) (*Virgins' Flowing Hair*), *Desenuri tragice* (1927) (*Tragic Drawings*), *Concert din muzica de Bach* (1927) (*A Concert of Bach's Music*), *Logodnicul* (1935) (*The Fiancé*), *Radacini* (1938) (*Roots*).

Papadopoulou, Alexandra (1867–1906)

Greek short story writer, essayist, novelist and poet. She was born in Constantinople (Istanbul) into a rich Greek family, and became a teacher. At the age of twenty-one she became the co-editor of the *Ladies Almanac of Constantinople*, contributing short stories and essays dealing with the social life of the time. She also wrote, under various pseudonyms, for a number of local newspapers and magazines. In 1894 she published her novel, *Miss Lesviou's Diary*, the first ever written by a Greek woman at that time. It was received with enthusiasm by the Athenian literati, and subsequently, in 1895, some of her work was published in an anthology of short stories. Hers was the only work by a woman to be included in the anthology. In 1896, together with two male writers, she published the journal *Literary Echoes* and contributed articles written in *dimotiki* (modern Greek), thus supporting those who favoured the use of *dimotiki* against those who preferred writing in *katharevousa* (the 'pure' ancient Greek). Papadopoulou contributed about

200 articles and short stories to journals published in Athens, mainly dealing with the political and social problems of Greek society in Constantinople. Grigorios Xenopoulos, the famous writer from Athens who had corresponded with her for years, was greatly impressed by her liveliness of spirit when he eventually met her in Athens. She died aged 39.

Paraphrases of the Psalms of David (1766–1767)

Raised in the Anglican faith, the North American poet and translator ▷Elizabeth Graeme Fergusson was a devout woman. In these paraphrases of the Psalms, Fergusson's own poetic talents stand forth clearly, as does her engagement with the stylistic beauty of the Psalms. When the *Paraphrases* were published in Philadelphia, they added to Fergusson's growing reputation as the city's most renowned woman of letters.

Pardo Bazán, Emilia (1851–1921)

As Spain's most significant feminist in the 19th century, Pardo Bazán was also the greatest female writer of her time in Spain. She is one of the giants of 19th-century realism and naturalism, and ranks on a par with the best of her century, Galdós, Alas and Valera. She introduced her literary contemporaries to naturalism, notably in her study ▷*La cuestión palpitante* (1883) (*The Burning Question*). Her Catholic-naturalist novel, ▷*Los pazos de Ulloa* (1886) (*The House of Ulloa*), is without doubt one of the literary masterpieces of the past century. The sequel to this novel, *La madre naturaleza* (1887) (*Mother Nature*), which explored naturalist and feminist themes, was equally successful. She is also credited with having written the first novel in Spain dealing specifically with the female urban proletariat, ▷*La tribuna* (1883) (*The Female Orator*): research for this novel was carried out in a cigar factory in La Coruña which was mainly run by women workers.

Paretsky, Sara N. (born 1947)

US novelist. Born in Ames, Iowa, Paretsky earned both a PhD in history and a Master of Business Administration degree at the University of Chicago in 1977. In 1986, after working as a marketing manager for the CNA insurance company in Chicago, she decided to pursue writing as a full-time profession. She helped found Sisters in Crime in 1986 to promote women in the suspense field of writing. She became director of the National Abortion Rights Action League of Illinois in 1987.

Paretsky's ▷detective novels reflect her feminist concerns. She pits her private investigator, V.I. Warshawski, against anti-abortion fanatics, right-wing archbishops, a company dumping toxic waste, and Chicago's political machine. Paretsky explores the negotiation between the professional and the personal, independence and nurturing, and examines relationships between women. The

Sara Paretsky

novels are also distinctive in their portrait of a racially diverse and divided society. A feature film based on Paretsky's books, *V.I. Warshawski*, was released in 1991.

Other works include: *Deadlock* (1984), *Indemnity Only* (1985), *Killing Orders* (1985), *Bitter Medicine* (1987), *Blood Shot* (1989), *Burn Marks* (1990) and *Guardian Angel* (1992).

Paris Commune (March–May 1871)

A governing council set up in Paris by the revolutionary socialist insurrectionists who tried to seize power in France after the Franco-Prussian War (1871). The declared goals of the Communards were the emancipation of the working classes and the emancipation of women – but the 90-strong *Conseil de la Commune* (Council of the Commune) had no female members, and those women who were involved in the insurrection complained incessantly of the misogynistic attitudes of their male comrades. ▷André Léo went so far as to denounce the anti-feminism of the Communards in the journal *La Sociale*, and the aggressive tone of a number of the feminist tracts published in 1871 reveals the bitter disappointment experienced by many of the women who took part in the Commune in the hope of achieving greater sexual equality. After the violent coup known as '*la Semaine Sanglante*' ('the bloody week'), the Commune fell, there were arrests and executions, and both Léo and her fellow revolutionary ▷Louise Michel were exiled.

Park, Ruth (born c 1923)

Australian novelist and children's writer. Park was born in New Zealand and educated at the University of Auckland, and much of her early work deals with her New Zealand experience. She moved to Australia in 1942, living first of all in the outback, then in the slums of Surry Hills, the

Ruth Park

setting for ▷*The Harp in the South* (1948) and *Poor Man's Orange* (1949), published in the USA as *121/2 Plymouth Street* (1951). Other novels are *The Witch's Thorn* (1951), *A Power of Roses* (1953), *Pink Flannel* (1955), *One-a-Pecker, Two-a-Pecker* (1957), published in London as *The Frost and the Fire* (1958), *The Good Looking Women* (1961), published in 1962 as *Serpent's Delight*, and *Swords and Crowns and Rings* (1977), which won the Miles Franklin Award for 1977. Park was also a prolific writer of children's fiction, including *Playing Beatie Bow* (1980) which won the Children's Book of the Year Award for 1981, and *When the Wind Changed* (1980), which won the 1981 New South Wales Premier's Award. She is also known as the creator of *The Muddle-Headed Wombat*, a drama series for ABC Radio.

▷Children's literature (Australia)

Parker, Catherine Langloh (c 1855–1940)

Australian collector of Aboriginal legends and recorder of tribal life. Parker grew up on a property in the Darling Downs region of Queensland and, after her marriage, lived on properties in New South Wales and Queensland. She was the first woman to systematically collect and publish the legends of the Aborigines. Her works include *Australian Legendary Tales: Folklore of the Noongahburrahs* (1896), *More Australian Legendary Tales* (1898), *The Walkabouts of the Wur-Run-Nah* (1918), *Woggheeguy: Australian Aboriginal Legends* (1930) and *The Euhlayi Tribe: A Study of Aboriginal Life in Australia* (1905).

▷Aborigine in non-Aboriginal women's writing, The

Parker, Dorothy (1893–1967)

US short story writer, poet, essayist and journalist. Born in West End, New Jersey, to a Jewish father and Scottish mother, Parker was educated at an exclusive girls' school. She was raised by those she hated and feared, her father and stepmother. In the 1910s she was the drama critic for *Vanity Fair* and *Ainslee's*. After the publication of her first book of poetry, *Enough Rope* (1926), which was extremely successful, she left *Vanity Fair*. Her first three volumes of poems, which explore romance, sexuality and women's social role amongst other themes, were collected in *Not So Deep as a Well* (1936). The popularity of Parker's witty, satiric verse has not prevented critics from judging her work lightweight. During the 1920s, although she had extra-marital affairs, drank heavily and attempted suicide three times, she maintained her writing. In the 1930s she collaborated with her second husband on screenplays, including *A Star is Born* (1937). In the 1940s Parker was blacklisted for supporting radical causes; she left her estate to civil rights leader Martin Luther King, Jr.

Collected in ▷*Here Lies* (1939), her stories satirize the social conditioning that leaves women economically and emotionally dependent on men. In anguish, Parker's lonely women break with convention in order to fulfil social expectations. Targeting the upper class, Parker depicts the intellectual emptiness of women's lives.

Other works include *Sunset Gun* (1928), *Laments for the Living* (1930), *Death and Taxes* (1931), *After Such Pleasures* (1933), *Collected Stories of Dorothy Parker* (1942) and *Collected Poetry of Dorothy Parker* (1944).

Bib. ▷Hellman, Lillian, 'Dorothy Parker' in *An Unfinished Woman*; Kinney, Arthur F., *Dorothy Parker*.

Parker, Mary Ann (fl 1795)

English travel writer whose husband was a captain. Her book, *A Voyage Round the World in the Gorgon Man of War* (1795), was published by subscription when she found herself in distress after her husband's death. It recounts a journey to New South Wales on which she had accompanied her husband. She describes Australian convict settlements (at Paramatta they 'found everything perfectly quiet though surrounded by one thousand conviucts'), and is derogatory about Australian native peoples.

Parleuses, Les (1974) ▷Woman to Woman (1987)

Parlour table standard

US 19th-century catch-phrase used to describe the ▷'genteel' constraints imposed on literature by magazine publishers and editors. National family literary magazines, eg ▷*The Century Illustrated Monthly Magazine*, were the primary, lucrative market for authors in the last half of the century. Magazine editors' restrictions on treatments of sexuality, realistic language, vulgarity, religion, etc. were based on the standard that nothing should appear in the magazines which could not appear on the US middle-class family's parlour table. A variant statement of the standard, often expressed by editors, was that the magazines should not print anything that a father would be ashamed to read aloud to his young daughter – or to have her read herself. Hence developed the 'young girl' and 'parlour table' standards of decency. The national literary magazines were the primary market for literature, and the magazines generally printed only what would be acceptable on parlour tables.

Parnók, Sofiia Iakovlevna (1885–1933)

Russian poet, literary critic, and opera librettist. Parnók began her career as a translator and critic under the male ▷pseudonym Andrei Polianin; as a poet she developed slowly. Her sexual friendship with ▷Marina Tsvetáeva from 1914 until early 1916 forms the background of a series of poems written by both women. It was Parnók who introduced Tsvetáeva to the poetry of ▷Karolina Pávlova, and for both of them Pávlova's achievement in the 19th century became critical evidence of a female tradition in Russian poetry.

Parnók's best poetry is contained in three collections published in the 1920s. She particularly liked strict forms such as the sonnet and the rondeau. Often harking back to the 19th century, her poetry is one of statement, and tends to be directed outward towards other people, objects, and phenomena. Frequently she addresses a woman, and some of her best poems deal with searing love. Music was an abiding interest of hers, but her work as an opera librettist remains unexamined. After 1928 she was no longer allowed to publish, and she wrote no lyric poetry for several years after that. In her final years, inspired by a last love, Parnók produced two cycles of poems. Recently her work been printed in miscellaneous journals and Soviet anthologies of Russian sonnets. Collected works were published in the USSR in 1979, but Parnók's *oeuvre* still awaits the critical assessment it deserves.

▷Gértsyk, Adelaida
Bib: Shore, Rima (trans.), *Conditions* 6, (1980); Markov, V. and Sparks, M. (eds), *Modern Russian Poetry*; Burgin, D., 'After the Ball is Over: Sophia Parnók's Creative Relationship with Marina Tsvetáeva', *The Russian Review*, 4 (1988); Heldt, B., *Terrible Perfection: Women and Russian Literature*; Karlinsky, S., *Marina Tsvetaeva: The Woman, Her World, and Her Poetry*.

'Parole de femme' (1974) ('Woman's Word')

Bestselling essay by French philosopher and novelist ▷Annie Leclerc. Much quoted by women writers in France, the text challenges male domination of language (and French in particular), positively re-evaluates the female body, and sets out 'to invent a woman's word', in a quest for sexual difference. The politics and style of Leclerc's essay have been criticized by materialist feminists such as ▷Christine Delphy.

Paroliberismo (Italy)

A term which applies to the technique, used by ▷futurist writers, of breaking down logical connections in writing: a piling up of nouns, excision of adjectives, adverbs and punctuation; a way of expressing, through a layering of words with no conventional order, the feeling of facing the 'new' world of the first half of the 20th century.

Parr, Catherine (1512–1548)

Catherine Parr

English devotional writer, patron and religious reformer. She was the daughter of Thomas and Maud Green Parr. As the sixth and last wife of Henry VIII, she took an active part in the education of her three royal stepchildren, and probably influenced the developing Protestantism of the two youngest, Edward and ▷Elizabeth Tudor. In 1544 the eleven-year-old princess Elizabeth presented her prose ▷translation of ▷Marguerite de Navarre's ▷*Mirror of the Sinful Soul* as a New Year's gift to her stepmother 'for correction and improvement'. Parr also encouraged her eldest stepdaughter, ▷Mary Tudor, to publish her translation of part of Desiderius Erasmus' (?1466–1536) *Paraphrases* under Mary's name rather than anonymously. Following her own convictions, Parr published under her own name two works: ▷*Prayers, or Meditations* (1545) and ▷*The Lamentation or Complaint of a Sinner* (1547). As a promoter and ▷patron of Protestant ▷humanism, she commissioned a number of translations important to the English ▷Protestant Reformation, including Miles Coverdale's translation of the New Testament. After the death of Henry VIII in 1547, Parr married Thomas Seymour. She died in 1548, six days after the birth of her only child.

▷Confession of faith; *Monument of Matrones, The; Morning and Evening Praiers*
Bib: King, J.N., 'Patronage and Piety: The Influence of Catherine Parr' in Hannay, M.P.

(ed.), *Silent But for the Word*; Hogrefe, P., *Tudor Women of Action.*

Parr, Susanna (fl 1659)

English religious writer from Exeter in Devon. She published *Susanna's Apology Against the Elders* (1659), her version of a dispute with an Independent Church whose minister, Mr Lewis Stuckley, had excommunicated her in 1658. Parr gives a lively account of her part in discussing and formulating Church policy in the 1650s, and gives her version of leaving Stuckley's congregation. When he ignored the voices of women in his congregation because it suited him, she tells us, 'this serpentine subtlety of his I took special notice of, and did reprove him to his face.'
Bib: Graham, Elspeth *et al*, *Her Own Life.*

Parra, Teresa de la (1889–1936)

Venezuelan novelist and short story writer. Her full name was Ana Teresa Parr Sanojo, but she adopted the pen-name Fru-Fru. She was born in Paris, but soon her family returned to their farm in Tazón, near Cúa. In 1906 her father died, and the family moved to Valencia in Spain, where she attended a Catholic school. She returned to Venezuela to gather material for her books, travelled widely, and never married.

Her first book, *Diario de uma señorita que se fastidiaba* (1922) (*Diary of a Lady Who Was Bored*), republished as ▷ *Ifigenia* (1924) is the journal of a young lady from Caracas in ▷ *costumbrismo* style. However, her masterpiece is *Las Memórias de Mamá Blanca* (1929) (▷ *Mama Blanca's Souvenirs*, 1959), which centres on an old woman's recollection of her childhood on a sugar-cane farm.

In 1926 Parra formed a group of French and Latin American writers, and in 1927 she took up lecturing in Cuba on Bolívar and feminism. Her short stories appeared in the Caracas and Paris press, and her works were translated into many languages. She suffered from tuberculosis, and her remains were brought to Caracas eleven years after her death.

Other works: *Obras completas* (1965) (*Complete Works*); *Cartas* (1951) (*Letters*), and *Epistolario íntimo* (1953) (*Private Letters*).

Parra, Violeta (1917–1967)

Chilean poet, musician and painter. She travelled throughout small villages in Chile and abroad, singing popular lyrics of her own to the rhythm of boleros, *corridos* (which are fast) and *tonados* (Andes singsongs). She studied, in particular, the musical folklore of her parents region of the Nuble.

In Paris she recorded '*Cantos del Mundo*', and, in Chile, she founded the Museum of Popular Art at the University of Concerción. Also a ceramicist, her paintings were exhibited in the Louvre; her poems have been published in several languages. Her posthumous biography, *Veintieuno son los dolores* (1976) (*Twenty-one Sorrows*) by Bernado Subercaseaux and Jaime Londoño, which includes

one of her best-known songs '*Gracias a la Vida*' (*Thanks to Life*), was extremely successful. It compared her poetical work with ▷ Gabriela Mistral's, in spite of the contrast in tone and vocabulary.

Works: *Poésie populaire des Andes, Violeta* (1965) (*Popular Poems from the Andes, Violeta*); *Décimas* (1970) (*Stanzas*); *Toda Violeta Parra* (1974) (*The Complete Violeta Parra*), and *Violeta del pueblo* (1976) (*The People's Violeta*).

Parren, Kallirroi (1861–1940)

Greek journalist, novelist and teacher, born in Crete. For ten years she taught in girls' schools in Russia and in various Balkan countries. She spoke English, French, Russian and Italian. After her marriage to a French journalist working in Athens, she gave up teaching and settled in Athens, where in 1887 she began publishing ▷ *The Ladies' Newspaper*, a weekly journal run entirely by and for women. This paper was for thirty years the voice of female consciousness in a male world. Parren wrote numerous articles attacking the inequalities and injustices suffered by women in matters of legislation, prison conditions, social custom, family life, education and other areas. In 1894 she founded the Union for the Emancipation of Women, and in 1911 she founded the Lyceum of Greek Women, which offered support to women in the fields of education, employment, home economics and childcare. She ran a school to help widows and to teach orphan girls to read and write, and founded a hospital for people suffering from incurable diseases. She wrote two novels incorporating feminist ideas, a feminist play (never staged) and two studies, *The History of Woman* and *The History of Greek Women from 1650–1860*. In 1936 the Greek Academy awarded her the 'Golden Cross of the Saviour' for her long-standing activities on behalf of women.

Parshiyot (1968) (*Episodes*)

Israeli short stories by ▷ Devorah Baron. The stories are set either in the small Jewish towns of eastern Europe or in Israel. Baron is well-known for her east European stories, in which she reconstructed a world she knew well. Most of the stories are centred on women struggling against their frustrations in a restrictive society. The stories are realistic and economically written. Their dramatic effects derive from the use of unusual points of view.

Partenide, Fidalma ▷ Paolini Massimi, Petronilla

Partenide, Irminda ▷ Bergalli Gozzi, Luisa

Parthenay, Anne de (16th century)

French poet. She was celebrated by the poet Clément Marot (1496–1544), supposedly excelled in composing verses and music, and had an excellent voice. Her talents, founded on a sound study of classical languages and theology, captivated her contemporaries and were praised by the writer Théodore de Bèze (1519–1605).

▷Parthenay, Catherine de

Parthenay, Catherine de (died 1631)

French poet, dramatist, satirist and translator. She was the daughter of the Seigneur de Soubise, and niece of ▷Anne de Parthenay. Following the death of her first husband in the Saint Bartholomew's Day massacre of Protestants in 1572, she continued her correspondence with her mother in Latin to protect them both. In 1575 she married Viscount René de Rohan, Prince of Léon, and one of her sons was the famous general, Henri de Rohan (1579–1638). She was equally dedicated to the Calvinist cause, her children's education, and her own. She recorded her troubles in melancholic elegies, mourning the death of so many heroic men, including her husband and Admiral Gaspard de Coligny (1519–1572), in the terrible religious conflicts of the second half of the 16th century. One of her tragedies, *Judith et Holopherne*, performed at La Rochelle in 1573, is worthy of memory. The *Discours d'Isocrate à Démonique* illustrates that she had not only a brilliant imagination but also considerable depth of knowledge. As she was also known for her playful wit, it is not surprising that the satire *Apologie de Henri IV* (*Defence of Henri IV*) should have been attributed to her, though she also wrote an important poem to commemorate '*ce prince glorieux*' ('this glorious prince'), Henri IV (1553–1610), following his assassination after nineteen attempts in 1610. She showed considerable courage at the siege of La Rochelle in 1628, and died in captivity in Poitou, following her imprisonment at the Château de Niort.
Bib: Feugère, L., *Les Femmes poètes au XVIe siècle*.

Parthenis (? 3rd–2nd century BC)

Ancient Greek poet. We have only one mention of her name. The epigrammatist Meleager refers to her in a poem on Greek women poets, which includes ▷Sappho,   ▷Anyte, ▷Moero, ▷Nossis and ▷Erinna. She probably also wrote epigrams. ▷Epigram, Ancient Greek

Partition

The trauma of the Partition of the Indian subcontinent and the creation of Pakistan as a separate state when India became independent in 1947 has been a lasting theme in Indian and Pakistani literature. Many women writers have focused on the particular horrors inflicted on women during the communal riots and massacres of the 1940s, and the mass transfer in the west of Hindus and Sikhs to the Indian side of the new border, and of Moslems to Pakistan. Many women were abducted and raped, and were then rejected as 'unclean' or 'dishonoured' by their families when negotiations between the two countries had secured their return. They frequently turned to prostitution as their only means of livelihood. The fiction of the Punjabi novelist and poet ▷Amrita Pritam, such as ▷*A*

Line in Water (1975) and ▷*The Death of a City* (1976), and her autobiography, *Life and Times* (1989), reflect what the author witnessed as a refugee from Lahore to Delhi. Her novella, *The Skeleton* (1987), tells of a Hindu village girl, kidnapped by a Muslim, who herself chooses not to return to her family. The novel *Ice-Candy Man* (1988, published in the USA and Canada as *Breaking India*) by the Pakistani author, ▷Bapsi Sidhwa, approaches the theme with an unusually comic touch, relating the story of an abducted Hindu *ayah* (nanny) through the eyes of the young girl in her charge. As the child grows up in Lahore on the eve of independence, she learns not only of male predatoriness, but of the brutal hypocrisy of prevailing social attitudes towards women's sexual purity and probity.

Parton, Sara Payson Willis (1811–1872)

US non-fiction and fiction writer, satirist, and the earliest first-person columnist in US journalism. Pseudonym: Fanny Fern. Parton's work is so highly autobiographical that her life-story is accurately told in her first novel, ▷*Ruth Hall* (1855). She became a writer to support herself and her children on the death of her first husband. While her brother, N.P. Willis (1806–1867), was an influential author and editor, he refused to help her, and Parton worked her way from low-paid piece-work for local papers to become a highly paid columnist for the *New York Ledger* and a sought-after contributor in a range of periodicals.

Her first book, ▷*Fern Leaves from Fanny's Portfolio* (1853), collects these periodical writings, which contain wonderful satire on women's roles and overbearing husbands and relations, mixed with a number of sentimental pieces on domestic life. As Parton gained recognition, she was frequently attacked for unwomanly coarseness and unseemly revenge, as she pilloried family and associates in thinly disguised characterizations of their venality.

The wide reading public loved her and her writing. Her sentimental work remained popular in volumes for children: *Little Ferns for Fanny's Little Friends* (1854), *A New Story Book for Children* (1864) and another novel, *Rose Clark* (1856), again fictionalized autobiography. Parton's strong suit, however, was in her columns and personal essays which filled a series of additional volumes beginning with *Fresh Leaves* (1857). For directness, humour, forthright support of women and blunt assessment of their harassers, Parton was and is hard to match.

Parturier, Françoise (born 1919)

French novelist and journalist, born in Paris. Her essays, which challenge sexual and racial inequality, have appeared in numerous journals, including *Nouvelles littéraires* (*Literary News*) and *Le Figaro*. Her first novel, *Les Lions sont lâchés* (1958) (*Albertine in the Lion's Den*), written with Josette Raoul-Duval, was published under the ▷pseudonym Nicole, and discusses the nature of sexuality through an exchange of letters between two women friends. Subsequent works were published under Parturier's own name. These include a novel, *L'Amant de cinq jours*, (1959) (*The Five-day Lover*, 1961), and *Lettre ouverte aux hommes* (1968) (*An Open Letter to Men*), a pre-feminist essay which appeared shortly before the unrest of ▷May 1968. This was followed by *Lettre ouverte aux femmes* (1974) (*An Open Letter to Women*). More recently, she has written a three-act play, *La folle vie* (1977) (*This Crazy Life*), an essay on Générale de Gaulle, *La Lettre d'Irlande* (1979) (*Letter from Ireland*), and a novel, *Les Hauts de Ramatuelle* (1983) (*Ramatuelle's Heights*).

Parun, Vesna (born 1922)

Prolific Croatian poet. She began writing very young, and published her first poem at the age of ten. She spent much of her hard life living in Zagreb as a writer. *Zore i vihori* (1947) (*Dawns and Whirlwinds*) is a youthful work, a powerful evocation of the experience of childhood, and important because of its freshness in the general greyness of post-war ▷social realism. It was immediately attacked by the communist establishment because of its metaphysical tone. As such, it marked a turning-point in post-war Croatian literature, and her verse pointed the way forward for a whole generation of poets. Parun's work has remained a symbol of the rejection of convention. Expressly sensual and immediate in tone, it is rooted in the natural world, with vivid descriptions of nature (particularly the landscape of the Mediterranean) and inner states of being.

Pascal, Gilberte (1620–1687)

French biographer and editor. Elder sister of ▷Jacqueline Pascal and the philosopher, mathematician and scientist Blaise Pascal (1623–1662), she has been overshadowed by the reputation for intellectual and spiritual rigour of the rest of her family. Her father ensured her education was no less complete, and when she returned to Rouen after her marriage to Florin Périer, a lawyer, she and her husband were converted to ▷Jansenism. Their children were educated at Port-Royal. Gilberte supported her sister in the difficult days when their father was determined to prevent her from entering the abbey. She was also very closely involved in the preparation of Blaise Pascal's *Apologie de la religion chrétienne* (*Defence of the Christian Religion*), of which fragments were posthumously published as the *Pensées* (1670) (*Thoughts*). Both Jacqueline and Blaise died in her arms in successive years (1661 and 1662), and for several years thereafter she frequented Parisian intellectual circles, turning towards Jansenism, like the ▷Marquise de Sablé's salon, where she made quite a reputation for herself for the quality of her conversation, the best appreciated of the womanly arts. In honour of her brother and sister, she wrote their biographies – *Vie de la Soeur Saint-Eustache* and *Vie de Monsieur Pascal*. She also supervised the publication of Blaise Pascal's *Pensées* by the Committee of Port-Royal in 1670.

Bib: Gazier, C., *Les Belles Amies de Port-Royal*.

Pascal, Jacqueline (1625–1661)

French author of poetry, drama, letters and religious writings. Sister of the philosopher, mathematician and scientist Blaise Pascal (1623–1662), like her brother she was an infant prodigy. Jacqueline Pascal helped to write a comedy in 1636, and her publication of verse in collections won her a poetry prize at Rouen in 1640. Her conversion to ▷Jansenism was opposed by her father. After his death, she became a nun at Port-Royal in 1652, and was a vital influence on her brother's conversion. She is noted for her letters of devotion to ▷Agnès Arnauld, who tried to make her endure patiently the delays which her family forced on her religious vocation. Towards the end of her life, Jacqueline Pascal also wrote reflections on the death of Christ and instructions for the novices of Port-Royal. Although she tried to resist signing an official condemnation of Jansenism in 1661, her doctors advised her to give in, and she died three months later, a broken woman, who felt she had betrayed her faith.

Passing (1929)

US novel by ▷Nella Larsen which focuses on two middle-class African-American women. Irene is part of Harlem's middle class and craves security. Out of economic necessity, Clare married an Anglo-American by passing for white herself. Missing her African-American race, she risks her social position by socializing in Harlem. Irene sees Clare as a threat to her sense of safety. She resents Clare for having abandoned her African-American race but she also admires Clare for her nerve to pass.

Larsen shows her own ambivalence towards middle-class African-Americans who imitate Anglo-Americans, but she posits no alternative in the folk customs of rural blacks. Larsen presents African-American women in traditional roles. They assume responsibility for their lives, but they cannot find the way to develop their potential while experiencing a cultural conflict.

Passion According to G.H., The (1964) (A paixão segundo G.H.)

Novel by Brazilian writer ▷Clarice Lispector. This is her eighth book, fifth novel, and her masterpiece, but it has not yet been translated into English. As in her other work, Lispector continues to exploit the ▷stream-of-consciousness technique, writing the narrative in the first person. Each new chapter starts from where the previous one ended, and the book is a poetic rereading of St John's Passion in the Bible, seen through the eyes of a middle-class woman, who is probably based on the author's own personality, as in most of her novels and chronicles.

The protagonist discovers on the bedroom wall of her maid, whom she had recently dismissed, a charcoal drawing of a couple and a dog. Influenced by her knowledge of philosophical works by the German Martin Heidegger (1889–1976) and the French Jean-Paul Sartre (1905–1980), the heroine-author-narrator speculates over the find from the viewpoint of a housewife who had hitherto ignored the possible existence of another 'self', or given little consideration to the other person who had lived in her house for six months. The conclusion bears a strong similarity to the Austrian novelist Franz Kafka's *Die Verwandlung* (1916) (*Metamorphosis*), but in the end the protagonist crunches between her teeth a cockroach that she finds on the maid's wardrobe door. This last scene links a reinterpretation of the Catholic Bible through an Existential understanding of 'passion' or sacrifice, and a deeper consciousness of her own self as a cosmopolitan, educated, cultured woman removed from the primitive, ignorant, far-away woman of the lower classes. This novel by Lispector and (*Rosa Grande sertão: veredas*) (1963) (*The Devil to Pay in the Backlands*), by João Guimarães Rosa were landmarks of Brazilian ▷postmodernism, that is, the third phase of Brazilian ▷modernism, which brought change to the linguistic and semantic use of language.

Passion of New Eve, The (1977)

A novel by English writer ▷Angela Carter, described by her as an 'anti-mythic novel', 'a feminist tract about the social creation of femininity'. The main protagonist and narrator of this 'speculative fiction' is Evelyn/Eve, and the novel is set in a US of the (possibly near) future, torn by civil unrest and in a state of urban decay. In the opening sections the male Evelyn is in New York, having an affair with the black prostitute Leilah, a subject for his sexual fantasies and prey to his contempt for women. The narrative continues with his capture, imprisonment and castration by a community of women. The leader of this matriarchy, 'Mother', oversees Evelyn's physical and psychological transformation into the female Eve. Escaping from the community, and from further experimentation (Eve is intended to produce a 'New Eve', fertilized by the sperm of her former male self), Eve ends up as one of the 'wives' of the sadistic Zero, who submits her to sexual abuse and humiliation. Finally, Eve escapes and meets the screen idol Tristessa, the embodiment of the former Evelyn's fantasies of femininity, now revealed to be a transvestite male. Their love-making – which represents sex and love as ▷bisexual and fully reciprocal – results in Eve's impregnation. Tristessa is killed, Eve re-encounters Leilah/Lilith, the former prostitute, in fact a militant member of a new civil rights movement. She prepares Eve for her journey into an unknown future and shows her the dying 'Mother', whose demise may represent the end of essentialist notions of the feminine.

The Passion of the New Eve plays with myths and mythic figures – Eve, Lilith, Oedipus, Tiresias,

Frankenstein's monstrous creation – using and undercutting them. As in *The Infernal Desire Machines of Doctor Hoffman* (1972), Carter links myth and science, and reveals them both to be dangerous projections of human fantasies – 'Mother's' technological manipulations are part and parcel of her myth of the 'feminine'. Carter explores how femininity is constructed, provides a critique of 'the feminine', and questions fixed oppositions between male and female. The novel is closely related to feminist debates about the distinction between biological 'sex' and socially constructed 'gender'. Carter also sets up a contrast between myth and history, and the novel ends with Eve's release from static, mythic structures and images into history and temporality. The novel has interesting parallels in ▷Julia Kristeva's influential essay 'Women's Time'. A further aspect of the novel is Carter's brilliant manipulation of genres, including science fiction, dystopia, biblical narratives and romance.

Paston Letters (c 1420–1503)

English correspondence. This collection of letters is from the archives of the Paston family of East Anglia. They are concerned with matters connected with the family estates, with domestic, and with personal affairs. Nearly one-third are written by or addressed to women. Margaret Paston (married John Paston c 1440, died 1484) figures most largely; but the collection includes letters from Agnes (married William Paston 1420, died 1489); Elizabeth Paston, later Poynings, then Browne (1429–1488); Margery Brews (married John Paston III 1477, died 1495); and Margery Paston, later Calle (died not later than 1479).
Bib: Davis, Norman (ed.), *The Paston Letters; A Selection in Modern Spelling*; Barber, Richard (ed.), *The Pastons: A Family in the Wars of the Roses*.

Pati vrata dharm

The Hindu concept of wifehood. The husband is a god to his wife, and she should be entirely devoted to him. Such devotion is ultimately powerful because it nourishes an inner heat in the wife that both purifies her and provides her with a forceful weapon against those who would threaten her purity and her husband's welfare. In this way a Hindu wife is responsible for her husband's well-being; her chastity and devotion are seen to make him invulnerable. Sita exemplifies the ideal Hindu wife. In spite of her unswerving loyalty to her husband, Rama, she is repeatedly doubted, but her love survives being put to the pyre, and being cast out into the jungle when pregnant.
▷*Ramayana*

Patriarchal representations of women

Images of women in literature and society which, implicitly or explicitly, present women as inferior to men. To term such representations 'patriarchal' is to suggest that the production of images of women in writing and art is a cultural and political, not merely an individual phenomenon.

▷'Images of women' criticism; Patriarchy

Patriarchy

Taken from the Greek, patriarchy literally means 'the rule of the father'. A contemporary definition of patriarchy would be a system of unequal social, sexual and economic relations between the sexes which produces and maintains men's authority and power over women. Although patriarchy is a concept crucial to all forms of feminist theory as the term which names the oppression of women, various strands of feminist theory define its location and effects differently. It is not, of course, a single, unchanging essence, but a power relation which is differently instituted in different cultures.

Patronage (Renaissance England)

The now-familiar system by which authors are paid money by publishers for the publication of their compositions was unheard of during the Renaissance. If writers profited at all from their writing it was by means of patronage. Wealthy or powerful persons sometimes commissioned works, bestowing gifts upon the author in exchange. More commonly, however, authors prefaced their works with unsolicited dedications addressed to one or more persons in hopes of receiving a reward. Works were frequently addressed to prospective patrons who did not even know (personally or by reputation) the author. Writers often attempted to match the work with a person likely to make an appreciative and profitable audience. Persons of various kinds of importance were among the most likely to be solicited for patronage. Partly due to the huge numbers of them, not every dedication was likely to result in the hoped-for reward. For example, although Queen Elizabeth I (▷Elizabeth Tudor) had over 250 works dedicated to her, she was not a particularly generous patron. Royalty and aristocrats were most likely to be chosen by women as dedicatees. Although women were not expected to write, they were frequently encouraged to be patrons and buyers of books. The works most often dedicated to them included sermons, religious works, and conduct books. Some women, however, resisted the tendency of male authors to dedicate only religious works to them. ▷Margaret Beaufort, one of the earliest and most important Renaissance patrons of literature, supported the first English printers by commissioning not only devotional works but romances as well. By the end of the 16th century, as ▷Margaret Tyler notes in the ▷preface to her ▷*Mirrour of Princely Deedes* (1578), male authors considered women a prime market for romances. ▷Mary Sidney Herbert was also an extremely important literary patron. In addition to being a competent poet in her own right and a source of poetic advice, Herbert opened her residence at Wilton House to numerous writers, providing them with an extensive library, as well as an intellectual community within which to work.

Other important Renaissance patrons included ▷Catherine of Aragon and Margaret Clifford, to whom ▷Aemilia Lanyer dedicated her ▷*Salve Deus, Rex Judaeorum*.

▷*Fames Roule*; Inglis, Esther

Patrons (16th–18th-century Britain)

Wealthy and aristocratic women exercised power as patrons and sometimes gave literary and financial help, such as Henrietta Maria (1609–1669, queen of Charles I) and especially Elizabeth I (▷Elizabeth Tudor), had poems dedicated to them, but other patrons included Lucy Russell, Countess of Bedford, and ▷Mary Herbert, Countess of Pembroke.

Bib: Williams, Franklin B., *Index of Dedications and Commendatory Verses in English Books before 1641.*

Patterns of Childhood (1984)

Translation of *Kindheitsmuster* (1976), a novel by the East German writer ▷Christa Wolf. In this major novel, Wolf embarks on a full-scale investigation of recent German history, asking herself, 'How have we become who we are now?'. The fictional biography of Nelly, the heroine, is also that of the author/narrator. Wolf returns to her childhood memories in order to arrive at an analysis of her present identity. Moreover, she regards this investigation of her own childhood and coming of age as typical of the story of a whole generation of East Germans. Ultimately, the book is a metaphor for the development of Wolf's country from fascism to socialism.

Paul, Joanna (born 1945)

New Zealand poet, fiction writer and dramatist. Joanna Paul is a painter, photographer, film-maker and poet whose poems have been published occasionally in New Zealand journals for many years. She composes her poetry visually, as textual images, her published collections drawing attention to their status as aesthetic objects as much as written texts, referring to a deeply-felt emotional life. In this way her work constantly highlights more than one way of perceiving of language and is connected to the use of language by some New Zealand painters, notably Colin McCahon.

Publications: *Imogen* (1978); *Unwrapping the Body* (1980).

Paura d'amare, La (1911) (Fear of Loving)

A novel in Italian by ▷Carola Prosperi. It is, on the whole, very negative in the possibilities permitted to the female characters of the narrative. It tells the tale of the petty bourgeois Planis family which is full of unhappy women, disappointed in love. Illness seems the only solution to their tormented and guilt-ridden lives. The only positive element of the novel resides in the depiction of the mother–daughter relationship here: Benvenuta, the daughter, is cared for by her mother when she has become ill following the death of her lover. The mother, Elisabetta, in turn becomes ill and is cared for by her daughter, but she dies. Benvenuta's future is unremittingly bleak. Prosperi also includes more than a fair share of female madwomen in this text. Madness, she seems to imply, is a likely result of unhappiness.

Pávlova, Karolina Karlovna (1807–1893)

Karolina Pavlova

Pávlova was a major Russian poet, dedicated to her 'holy craft', which transformed bitter experience into lyrics permeated by a stoic philosophy. The daughter of a Russified German doctor, she grew up in ▷Moscow and received a fine education at home. An early romance with the Polish poet Adam Mickiewicz left melancholy traces. After she married in 1836, her husband, the minor writer Nikolai Pávlov, ran through her fortune and, in the scandal of their breakup in the early 1850s, the Moscow community sided with him against a woman who, unlike ▷Rostopchiná, did not mask her sense of vocation in feminine deference. In 1853 Pávlova enjoyed a rare period of emotional and intellectual fulfilment in an affair with a much younger law student. In 1856, disillusioned and isolated, she left Russia for good, and in 1858 settled in Dresden. There she translated Aleksei Tolstoi's historical dramas into German, and the poet in turn offered her friendship and moral support until his death in 1875. She died in poverty, her works forgotten.

Like ▷Elizaveta Kúl'man, Pávlova knew eight languages and saw her work praised by Goethe. Her first published volume was a collection of Russian poetry translated into German, along with eight original poems in that language (*Northern Lights*, 1833), and in 1839 her *Preludes* (Paris, 1839) offered a similar mixture of translation and original poems in French. At the same time, her lyrics in Russian began appearing regularly in Moscow ▷'thick journals'. In her introduction to the translation of Pávlova's ▷*A Double Life* (1978), US critic Barbara Heldt has pointed out that women's 'fate' in a society where men set the rules is a major theme for Pávlova. In lyrics ('Yesterday pages of a torn-up book . . .', 1843), in longer poems ('Quadrille', 1843–1859; 'Three Souls', 1845), and in *A Double Life* she depicts woman's life as one of inevitable submission to forces beyond her control, as a gallant but losing gamble ('Of the past, of the perished, the old . . .', 1854). As US critic Diana Greene points out, in Pávlova's short story 'At the Tea Table' (1859), her depiction of a reversal of sex roles foregrounds women's subordinate position. Her technical facility and gift for conveying complex ideas and changing moods in simple, exact terms brought her new fame in the ▷Silver Age.

▷de Gabriak, Cherubina; Golden Age, The; Parnók, Sofiia; Society tale; Woman Question (Russia)

Pazos de Ulloa, Los (1886) (*The House of Ulloa*)

Novel by ▷Emilia Pardo Bazán, Spain's greatest 19th-century female writer. This novel tells the story of how a fledgling priest, Julián, attempts to civilize Pedro, the Lord of the House of Ulloa, a decadent, philandering aristocrat. Julián's mission fails, after his attempts to protect Pedro's wife, Nucha, from harm are misinterpreted, and he is sent away in disgrace. In this novel Pardo Bazán combines naturalism with Catholicism, and infuses Zola's secular world-picture with an Augustinian sense of predestination, to produce a picture of mankind as irremediably 'fallen'. The novel focuses on the plight of women who are subordinate to the will of fathers and husbands, and exposes taboo subjects of the time, such as woman's pain in childbirth and the physical maltreatment of women by men.

▷Realism

Paz Paredes, Margarita (born 1922)

Mexican poet. Her full name is Margarita Camacho Baquedano, and her main concern lies in the social problems of simple people, as well as love, childhood and unhappiness. These topics are seen in an introspective, sombre light, particularly in *Andamios de sombra* (1950) (*Shadow Scaffolds*) and *Dimensión del siléncio* (1953) (*Dimension of Silence*), her two most important works.

Other works: *Sonaja* (1942) (*Little Bell*); *Oda a Constantino Oumanski* (1945) (*Ode to Constantino Oumanski*); *Voz de la tierra* (1946) (*Voice of the Earth*); *El anhelo plural* (1948) (*Manifold Desires*); *Retrono* (1948) (*Thunder*); *Génesis transido* (1949) (*Genesis Overcome*); *Elegía a Gabriel Ramos Millán* (1949) (*Elegy to Gabriel Ramos Millán*); *Canto a Mexico* (1950) (*Song to Mexico*); *Presagio en el viento* (1955) (*Omen in the Wind*); *Casa en la niebla* (1956) (*House in the Mist*); *Coloquio de amor* (1957) (*Love Talk*); *Cristal adentro* (1957) (*Glass Inside*); *Los amantes y el sueño* (1960) (*The Lovers and the Dream*); *Rebelión de ceniza* (1960) (*Ash Rebellion*);

Elegia a César Garizurieta (1962) (*Elegy to César Garizurieta*), and *Adám en sombra y noche final y siete oraciones* (1964) (*Adam in Shade and Final Night and Seven Prayers*).

Peaceful Army: A Memorial to the Pioneer Women of Australia 1788–1938, The (1938)

Anthology edited by ▷Flora Eldershaw. This was originally published to celebrate the sesquicentenary of white settlement in Australia and was re-published, edited by ▷Dale Spender, for the bicentennial in 1988. In *The Peaceful Army* a number of prominent Australian women writers including Flora Eldershaw, ▷Mary Gilmore, ▷M. Barnard Eldershaw, ▷Dymphna Cusack, Dorothea Mackellar (see ▷'My Country'), ▷Eleanor Dark, ▷Miles Franklin, and ▷Kylie Tennant, contribute poems or essays in honour of the pioneer women of Australia. This is one of the first Australian feminist collections, and Winifred Birkett's (1897–1966) article on 'Some Pioneer Australian Women Writers', where she discusses ▷Catherine Helen Spence, ▷Ada Cambridge, ▷Rosa Praed, ▷Jessie Couvreur ('Tasma'), and ▷Louisa Atkinson, is of great interest.
▷Literary criticism (Australia)

Peach Groves, The (1979)

Australian novel by ▷Barbara Hanrahan. Set in Adelaide and New Zealand in the 1880s, it melds realistic, fantastic and grotesque elements, with a melodramatic plot-line. The two children in the novel, Ida and Maud, dream of exotic New Zealand and their Uncle Harry who lives there, but their visit is fraught with danger for the pre-adolescent Maud, threatened not only by the lascivious Mr Maufe, but also by the witchcraft of the half-Maori Tempe. This novel exposes the genteel pretentions of colonial life and reveals its underlying violence and passion, including Mama's incestuous relationship with her brother, Uncle Harry.

Peacocke, Isabel Maud (1881–1973)

New Zealand author of children's and adult fiction (light romances), journalist. Peacocke began writing as a child, and wrote verse as a young woman, some of which appeared in the *Bulletin* (Sydney) and in her first book, a collection of poems, *Songs of the Happy Isles* (1910). From 1915 to 1936 she produced a children's book almost annually. With their urban settings and focus on human nature and relationships, particularly between adult and child, these novels differed from school stories, the trend of the day. A prolific writer, Peacocke also contributed to magazines and newspapers in New Zealand, Australia, Britain and North America, and she was active in women writers' groups from 1925. Her interest in writing children's novels declined after her husband's death in 1937.
▷Children's literature, New Zealand

Pea Pickers, The (1942)

Australian novel by Eve Langley. A picaresque novel dealing with the adventures of two sisters who dress up as boys, call themselves 'Blue' and 'Steve', and travel to Gippsland, Victoria, the home of their pioneer ancestors. Both girls yearn for love, but their fervid relationships with a series of males are painful, comic and unproductive. They pick peas and hops and maize, and see life, but remain virgins. *White Topee* (1954) is a sequel in which 'Steve' does achieve a measure of self-understanding.

Pedrero, Paloma (born 1957)

Spanish actor and dramatist. Born in Madrid, Pedrero studied drama, and since 1987 has acted and written for the theatre and for television. Her work combines a down-to-earth depiction of everyday life with a lyrical subplot. Her main works are: *La llamada de Lauren* (1987) (*Lauren's Call*); *Besos de lobo* (1987) (*Wolf's Kisses*), and *Invierno de luna alegre* (1987) (*The Winter of a Cheerful Moon*). The last work was awarded the Tirso de Molina Prize.

Pedretti, Erica (born 1930)

German-speaking Swiss writer and sculptor. Born in Czechoslovakia, she emigrated to Switzerland in 1945, and in 1952 married the sculptor Gian Pedretti. Her text, *Harmloses, bitte* (1970) (*Harmless Things, Please*), and the novels *Heiliger Sebastian* (1973) (*Saint Sebastian*) and *Valerie oder Das unerzogene Auge* (1986) (*Valerie or The Impertinent Eye*), are complex montages of realistic detail, associative thought processes, memories, and reflections on the issues of artistic identity and self-realization.

Pélandrova (1976)

The one work of Pélandrova Dreo, suggesting by its title a strongly autobiographical link with its author. The protagonist is a remarkable woman, a practitioner of traditional magic arts who is able to inveigle herself into colonial society through her affair with a French veterinarian. She is ruthlessly amoral, having apparently successfully evaded the conventional strictures on women in her society. The focus of the narrative is exclusively on the self-affirmation, the drive towards individual autonomy and self-definition, of its central figure.
▷Witchcraft (West Africa)

Pembroke (1894)

US novel by ▷Mary E. Wilkins Freeman. Wilkins Freeman's best novel, *Pembroke* is the story of the self-destructive repression and stubbornness of the New England Puritan character. Beginning with a falling-out between Barney Thayer and the father of Charlotte, his betrothed, the novel follows both families and the town as years pass and Barney is too 'set' to apologize and reclaim his love. On the night of the falling-out, Charlotte's aunt misses her long-time lover's weekly courting visit, and he also stubbornly abandons his love and happiness.

These two pairs of separated lovers are set against a vigorously detailed community of well-developed characters, with parallels in the lives of two other women characters. A sometime friend of Charlotte's pursues Barney. Barney's sister, who is forbidden contact with her love because he is related to Charlotte's family, meets him clandestinely, becomes pregnant before she is married and then is forced to marry. Both Charlotte and her aunt also marry by the end of the novel; each of their lovers returns only when outside pressures threaten to destroy the women – Charlotte by being excluded from the Church, her aunt by being taken off to the poorhouse, having 'lived out' the value of her homestead. The novel is finely detailed throughout, with a range of families and relationships that substantively question both the New England character and the roles and economic dependency of women.

Penfold, Merimeri (born 1924)

New Zealand poet and translator. Merimeri Penfold (also known as Ngati Kuri Ki Te Aupouri), born at Te Hapua, Northland, is one of the few Maori writers still to write in Maori. Penfold lectured in Maori Studies in Auckland, and has been active on Maori language questions throughout her life. Her poetry uses traditional Maori song-forms and subjects, and has appeared in major anthologies of New Zealand poetry. Penfold has also written extensively on Maori women artists, and collaborated in the production of bilingual children's books.

▷Children's literature, New Zealand; Maori literature

Penguin Anthology of Australian Women's Writing, The (1988)

Anthology edited by ▷Dale Spender. This selection includes work from forty Australian women. The balance favours the earlier writers, the book commencing with a letter written by the convict woman ▷Margaret Catchpole in 1801. Also included is an entire novel, *A Girl's Ideal*, by ▷Rosa Praed. The only two writers in this selection who were born after 1920 are ▷Antigone Kefala, and ▷Germaine Greer. The selection also contains plays such as *Brumby Innes* (1940) by ▷Katharine Susannah Prichard, and *The Torrents* (1965), by ▷Oriel Gray.

▷Anthologies (Australia)

Penguin Book of Australian Women Poets, The (1986)

Anthology edited by Susan Hampton and Kate Llewellyn. A selection from the poems of 89 Australian women poets, from tribal Aboriginal singers through to the present. It provides, for the first time, an overview of the traditions, the voices and the range of women's poetry in Australia. There are, according to the editors, 'poems about the selector's wife and daughter, factory work, prostitutes, social conventions, feminism, lovers, Japan, old age, happy marriage, the conflict between love and independence, and the Sydney Harbour Bridge . . . poems that do not exist in official histories, as well as poems that have come to be regarded as classics'. This anthology is a welcome corrective to the more traditional mixed-sex poetry anthologies in Australia which, statistically, have devoted only seventeen per cent of their space to the poetry of Australian women.

▷Aboriginal women's poetry in Australia; Anthologies (Australia)

Penguin Book of Hebrew Verse, The (1981)

An anthology of Hebrew poetry, from the Bible to present-day Israeli verse. Poems are presented simultaneously in the original and in English literal translation. The comprehensive introduction provides an in-depth study of Hebrew verse. Each poem is followed by a short analysis and biographical notes on the poet. Women writers included are ▷Lea Goldberg, ▷Zelda and ▷Dalia Ravikovitch.

Penis envy

According to Sigmund Freud (1856–1939), when a little girl sees a little boy's penis she becomes aware not only of her sexual difference but also of her inferiority. Freud suggests that girls instantly desire the penis the moment they see it. The feeling of inferiority girls experience because they lack a penis stays with them into adulthood, when they learn to replace the early desire for a penis with the wish for a baby. Freud's writing on penis envy can be found in *On Sexuality: Three Essays on the Theory of Sexuality and Other Works*, Vol. 7, Pelican Freud Library (1977). Freud's concept of penis envy has been criticized by feminist writers as diverse as ▷Kate Millett in *Sexual Politics* and ▷Luce Irigaray in ▷*Speculum of the Other Woman*. However, some ▷poststructuralist feminists have argued that the concept of penis envy needs to be reassessed within the context of French pschoanalyst Jacques Lacan's (1901–1981) theories concerning the relationship of the penis to his concept of the phallus, and its privileged position as primary signifier in the ▷symbolic order.

▷Oedipus complex; Psychoanalysis

Penn, Hannah Callowhill (1671–1726)

North American letter-writer. Born in Bristol, England, she lived in North America for less than two years but her impact as spouse of William Penn, the Proprietor of Pennsylvania, had lasting repercussions. Her correspondence with associates in the province's central government, The ▷'Letters of Hannah Callowhill Penn', reveals an astute business mind and a concern for the welfare of the proprietorship as well as the maintenance of Pennsbury, the family estate outside of Philadelphia. When her husband suffered a stroke after their return to England, she took over administrative duties of the province, conveying her decisions through correspondence with appointed officials in Pennsylvania over a fourteen-year period and, sporadically thereafter, until her death.

▷Early North American Quaker women's writings; Early North American letters

Penombra che abbiamo attraversato, La (1964) (*The Shadows Through Which We Have Passed*)

Italian novel by ▷Lalla Romano which, like all of her work, is full of autobiographical detail, lyrically fashioned. Romano returns to the terrain of Ponte Sturo, to her childhood world, retraces her steps alongside the geography of the place, and looks back on herself as a child. The past is eyed here with affectionate irony, and linked forward to the present.

Percoto, Caterina (1812–1887)

Italian short story writer. Born in Friuli, of a noble family, she confounded expectations by refusing to marry. Instead, she looked after her family's land and was very involved with the local community. Her writings are very regional in tone, and indeed, much of her later work is in dialect. Despite a retiring lifestyle, she acquired considerable literary prestige and was, in some respects, a very innovative writer. Her work is certainly in the ▷realist mode, and was republished as *Scritti friulani: L'inno della fame ed altri racconti* (*Writings from Friuli: The Song of Hunger and Other Stories*) in 1945, when ▷neorealism was at its height. She wrote the preface to Giovanni Verga's *Storia di una capinera* of 1871, and it seems that her work was very close to that of Verga, and may have prefigured his to some degree. A recurrent theme of her work is woman's lot in the society of the period.

Works: *Racconti* (1858) (*Short Stories*); *Ventisei racconti vecchi e nuovi* (1878) (*Twenty-Six Stories, Old and New*); *Novelle scelte* (1880) (*Selected Stories*); *La matrigna* (1881) (*The Step-Mother*); *Novelle popolari edite e inedite* (1883) (*New and Old Stories*).

Percy, Charles Henry ▷Smith, Dodie

Peregrina, La ▷Gómez de Avellaneda, Gertrúdis

Perera, Padma

Indian short story writer and academic, born in Madras, southern India. She was educated in India, and at the University of Michigan, Ann Arbor, USA, where she won the Hopwood Award for fiction. She lives in the USE, where she has taught in several North American universities, including the University of Colorado at Boulder. She is a classical Indian dancer in the Manipuri style, and has written several books on dance as well as one on traditional Indian handicrafts. She has published three collections of short stories, including *Coins of Vantage* (1972) and ▷*Birthday Deathday and Other Stories* (1985). An academic work, *The Challenge of Indian Fiction in English*, was published in 1975. Other short stories and non-fiction essays have been published in *The New Yorker, The Saturday Evening Post, Horizon* and *The Iowa Review*.

Performance poetry (Southern Africa)

A mode that has developed from ▷oral tradition in South Africa. Poetry is delivered rather than read, often along with bodily gesture and movement, at mass-meetings, trade union and community gatherings, funerals, and other public and political occasions. As in other genres within oral tradition, scripts, where they exist, cannot convey the dramatic power of the original, for the spoken words combine with chants, ululations, and songs, as well as eliciting popular responses from the audience.

Much performance poetry is in one of the African languages, although there is some in English. While most performer poets are men, a few women perform, among them Mavis Smallberg, ▷Gcina Mhlophe, and, most notably, ▷Nise Malange, who has been part of a group of worker poets associated with COSATU (Congress of South African Trade Unions) since 1983. They all use the declamatory mode which has come to characterize black South African verse (distinguishing it from the lyric and narrative verse of an English tradition), although Smallberg's poetry, unusually, is moved by narrative as often as by declamation. The poetic persona, too, is generally constructed not as an individual, but as a community figure: the 'I' inhabits multiple positions.

▷Ingrid de Kok has spoken of the need for white South African poets to open themselves to the most effective practices of performance poetry: its repetitions, parallel structures, alternating voices, and the lists it provides of martyrs and heroes, and of the places and dates that memorialize everyday experiences of suffering and triumph. Some of her poetry, as well as some of ▷Antjie Krog's, manifests this cross-cultural influence.

Perictione (? 4th–2nd century BC)

Philosopher. She was one of the ▷Pythagorean women, but her name is shared by the mother of the philosopher Plato (427–348 BC) and is not separately included in a list of women Pythagoreans in the *Life of Pythagoras* by Iamblichus (3rd century AD). Her date and even her existence are therefore uncertain. Her philosophy survives in letter form. *On the Harmony of Women* encourages women to study philosophy for the good of the household and the city. Sexual desires should be moderated and a husband's infidelities borne. Dress should be modest and without adornment. *On Wisdom*, perhaps not by the same woman, concerns knowing the true nature of things, their quantity and harmony.

▷Philosophers, Ancient Greek and Roman women

Bib: (trans.) Guthrie, K.S., *The Pythagorean Sourcebook and Library*.

Perilla

Roman poet. The sole record of her is a reference by the Roman poet Ovid (1st century AD). He says her poetry was surpassed only by that of ▷Sappho.

Periodicals (Britain)

The regular publication of newspapers began in the period of the English Civil War (1642–1646, and 1648–1651), and in the 17th and 18th centuries women began to be considered an important part of the audience who might buy periodicals in the vernacular. From the publication of John Dunton's *Athenian Mercury* (1691–1697) onwards, women were addressed in articles and in the correspondence pages, and there was soon a *Ladies Mercury*. There were also fiction periodicals marketed for women, such as *Records of Love*. Richard Steele's *Tatler* first appeared in 1709, and the first issue mentioned that it anticipated two audiences – male and female. Both the *Tatler* and the *Spectator* devoted space to letters, including those from women, and emphasized issues of conduct and virtue. Periodicals were also edited by women such as ▷Delarivier Manley. Some periodicals for women also came to be run by women – ▷Eliza Haywood edited *The Female Spectator* and ▷Charlotte Lennox edited *The Ladies Monthly*.

Peri Rossi, Christina (born 1941)

Uruguayan writer. She was born in Montevideo, the daughter of Italian immigrants, and her mother, a teacher, and a Communist uncle gave her a taste for reading. She graduated in letters at the University of Montevideo, and became a journalist and a teacher of literature. Persecuted by the government for her opposition to oppression, she moved to Barcelona in Spain in 1972.

Her first book, *Viviendo* (1963) (*Living*), consisted of three short stories about the sombre atmosphere which surrounds women, trapped as passive victims in a patriarchal society. *Los museos abandonados* (1969) (*The Abandoned Museums*), four short stories, won the Arca Prize for young Uruguayan authors in 1968. They describe the decadence of Uruguayan culture, and show the lack of communication between a couple, as in *Los extraños objectos voladores* (*The Strange Flying Objects*). Her novel *El libro de mis primos* (1969) (*The Book of My Cousins*) won a prize from *Marcha* magazine. The story is told by a child, with shifts in narration, and Peri Rossi uses visual devices and a mixture of prose and verse. The bourgeoisie is one of the targets for her satire, especially girls who are brought up with too much protection. *Indicios pánicos* (1970) (*Panic Signs*) is a collection of forty-six fragments, stories, poems, essays and aphorisms, which are characteristic of the age of repression in Uruguay. It was banned by the military when they took power in 1973.

After publishing poetry in magazines, *Evohé* (1971) was Peri Rossi's first book of poems. Like the Uruguayan poet ▷Juana de Ibarbourou, her poems are frequently a sensual, erotic celebration of the female body. Once she had become established in Barcelona, Peri Rossi published *Descripción de un naufragio* (1975), (*Description of a Shipwreck*), poems that stress political exile and love. These themes are in a way repeated in *Diáspora* (1976) (*Diaspora*), a book of poems written in manuscript form, which won the 1973 Inventarios Provisionales. The short stories in *La tarde del dinosaurio* (1976) (*The Afternoon of the Dinosaur*) and *La rebelión de los niños* (1980) (*The Children's Rebellion*) describe children who experience repression. In contrast *El muso de los esfuerzos inútiles* (1983) (*The Museum of Useless Endeavours*), published in Spain, is a collection of aphorisms on contemporary topics, such as loneliness, ▷psychoanalysis, war and political oppression, written in a humorous style that defies traditional literary classification. Also published in Spain, her novel *La nave de los locos* (1984) (*The Ship of Fools*) employs the 15th-century metaphor of a voyage of madness, but Peri Rossi compares it to injustice and oppression in contemporary life, where peace cannot be obtained, and where people have to live in a state of constant exile. *Una passión prohibida* (1986) (*A Forbidden Passion*) combines satire and mystery in its twenty prose pieces. While her books direct their criticism towards the political situation in Latin America in the 1970s in a metaphorical way, at the same time they employ many of the resources exploited by the Argentinian/French writer Julia Cortázar (1914–1984) and the Argentinian Jorge Luis Borges (1899–1986) as pioneers of ▷magic realism, but especially by the Columbian novelist Gabriel García Márquez (born 1928).

Other work: *Lingüística general* (1979) (*General Linguistics*).

Perpetua (3rd century AD)

Vibia Perpetua lived in Carthage, where she wrote memoirs. The anonymous *Acts of the Christian Martyrs* quotes from them regarding her stay in prison and the visions she experienced there. She was later canonized.

▷Diaries, Ancient Greek and Roman

Perrein, Michèle

French novelist and essayist. Perrein is quite a popular writer in France but, like many recent feminist writers whose novels conform to ▷realist conventions, she is scarcely known abroad. The first of Perrein's fifteen novels, *La Sensitive* (1956) (*The Sensitive Woman*), consists of the adolescent heroine Odile's unsent letters, describing the events leading to the suicide of one of her three male lovers. Perrein has recently added a postscript to the new edition, *La Sensitive ou l'innocence coupable* (1986) (*The Sensitive Woman, or Guilty Innocence*), in which an older and wiser Odile reflects on her former self, and on the constraints on female identity in the 1950s. The solitary heroine living on the margins of society and searching for self-expression, for her identity, or roots, is typical of Perrein's fiction, which is often set in her native country – the Bordeaux area. Identity and language are also major themes of her feminist essays, *Le Mâle aimant* (1975) (*The Loving Male*), *Entre chienne et louve* (1978) (*In the Female Twilight*), and *Ave Caesar* (with Adam Thalamy, 1982).

Other novels by Perrein are: *La Chineuse* (1970), *La Partie de plaisir* (1971) (*The Pleasure Party*), *Le Buveur de Garonne* (1973) (*The Drinker of Garonne*), *Comme une fourmi cavalière* (1980) (*Like a Soldier ant*), *Les Cotonniers de Bassalane* (1984) (*The Cotton Plants of Bassalane*), and *La Margagne* (1989).
Bib: Parker, G., 'Michèle Perrein: the parenthesis as metaphor of the female condition' in Atack, M. and Powrie, P.S. (eds), *Contemporary French Fiction by Women: Feminist Perspectives.*

Persaud, Lahkshmi

Caribbean poet and novelist, born and educated in Trinidad, but now living in London. Her writing focuses on the Indo-Caribbean experience which is her own cultural background. Little commentary on her work exists to date; her first published novel, *Butterfly in the Wind* (1990), concerns the experience of a young girl growing up in a traditional Hindu community; the fictionalized autobiography explores the effects of diverse social and cultural influences on the consciousness of Kamla, the central character.

See '"You want to be a Coolie Woman?": Gender and Identity in Indo-Caribbean Women's Writing' in ▷*Caribbean Women Writers*, pp. 98–105.

Persimmon Tree and Other Stories, The (1943)

Australian stories by ▷Marjorie Barnard. The stories in this volume are ironic, carefully-structured studies of inner experience and interpersonal relationships. The title story, 'The Persimmon Tree', is a delicate and haunting account of the psychological reaction of a woman who observes another's nudity and realises that the other is pregnant. *The Persimmon Tree*, reprinted in 1985, is a celebrated Australian classic.
▷ Short story (Australia)

Personal Recollections of the American Revolution: A Private Journal. Prepared from Authentic Domestic Records by Lydia Minturn Post (1859)

A lucid and warmly personal account of one woman's reaction to war. A North American Patriot, ▷Lydia Minturn Post recounts for her absent husband the invasion of her home by Hessian soldiers, her attempts to maintain a semblance of her old way of life in the face of life-threatening events, and her process of conversion to the Quaker faith. Her religious conversion was directly linked to her abhorrence of 'the warrior's craft'. *Personal Recollections* is also an important literary record of women's non-traditional contributions to the American Revolution.

Persuasion (1818)

A novel by English novelist ▷Jane Austen, published the year after the author's death. The heroine, Anne Elliot, is twenty-seven at the start of the story. Eight years previously, she had broken off an engagement to Frederick Wentworth, a naval officer, on the advice of her friend, Lady Russell, who thought him too easygoing and insufficiently well-off. Wentworth is now prosperous and successful and Anne realizes that she has made a mistake. The narrative then describes the obstacles placed in the lovers' path, including rivals for Wentworth's attentions (Louisa and Henrietta Musgrove) and a rival suitor for Anne (her cousin William Elliot). Eventually Wentworth and Anne are married. Their strength is seen to lie in their quiet and reticent conduct, contrasted with the showy but shallow characteristics of figures such as the duplicitous William Elliot. Throughout the novel, Austen represents old, established orders as out-dated in their emphasis on ancestry. She also creates a mature, independent heroine who frees herself from paternal authority through her bondings with other women characters such as Lady Russell, Mrs Smith and Mrs Croft. Austen's treatment of Mrs Croft is especially interesting, since this robust, rational and 'weather-beaten' woman is at no point ridiculed as anti-feminine or 'mannish'. Although *Persuasion* is not as formally accomplished as Austen's earlier works, its strengths lie in its representation of men and women as moral equals and in its inversion of the conventional roles of hero and heroine.

Pert, Camille (1865–1952)

▷Pseudonym of French novelist Louise Hortense Grillet. The author, whose talent was slim but whose output was enormous, wrote only on the theme of love, and published quantities of novels with telling titles like *Amoureuses* (1895) (*Women in Love*); *Amante* (1896) (*The Lover*); *Nos amours, nos vices* (1901) (*Our Loves, Our Vices*); *Les Amours perverses de Rosa Scari* (1905) (*The Wayward Love Affairs of Rosa Scari*); *Une Liaison coupable* (1907) (*A Guilty Liaison*); *Passionnette tragique* (1914) (*Tragic Little Affair*) and *Amour vainqueur* (1917) (*Love the Conqueror*). Her works typify the 'feminine' literature of late 19th-century France, and contain a virulent denunciation of the women of the period who were campaigning for female emancipation. An early novel, *Les Florifères* (1898) (*The Flowering Plants*), exemplifies Pert's anti-feminism.

Pesanteur et la grâce, La (1947) ▷ Gravity and Grace (1952)

Peseta, Tili

Short story writer and poet from Western Samoa. Tili Peseta has published a number of stories and poems in the journals *Mana*, *Unispac*, and *Pacific Islands Monthly*. Peseta's sketches and poems celebrate the natural environment, particularly its spiritual dimension.

Pestana, Alice ▷ Caiel (Alice Pestana)

Peterkin Papers, The (1880)
US satire by ▷ Lucretia Peabody Hale. Hale first introduced the Peterkin family in a series of stories published in juvenile magazines, *Our Young Folks* and *St Nicholas Magazine*. Satirizing Boston's distinctive culture of self-betterment, and introducing an enormously popular and varied family, tales of the Peterkins soon became a national amusement. A sequel collection, *The Last of the Peterkins, with Other of Their Kin* (1886), continued and enlarged the family and its adventures. They were among the first family-oriented humour in the USA.

Peterson's Magazine (1848–1898)
US wide-circulation women's magazine (called the *Ladies' National Magazine* and a variety of other titles before 1848). Developed by the publishers of the *Saturday Evening Post* and *Graham's Magazine* to compete with the more expensive ▷ *Godey's Lady's Book*, *Peterson's* popularity was based on a combination of fashion illustration and serialized fiction. It was advertised as a magazine by and for women, and its contributors included ▷ Louise Mary Alcott, ▷ Ann Sophia Stephens, ▷ Lydia Huntley Sigourney, and popular fiction writer and suffragist Elizabeth Oakes Smith (1806–1893).
▷ *Una, The*

Petit, Magdalena (born 1903)
Chilean novelist, short story writer, essayist, biographer, critic and dramatist. Her full name is Magdalena Petit Marfán, and her interests are music and the history of Chile. Her first work, *La Quintrala* (1930), is a historical novel about Doña Catalina de los Ríos, the 'Lucretia Borgia of Chile'. She is imaginative in her use of history, biography, and fictional situations, as in *Caleuche* (1946) and *Un hombre en el universo (confesión de un desorientado)* (1951) (*A Man in the Universe, Confession of a Lost Soul*). She writes for national and foreign periodicals, and has written a biography of ▷ Gabriela Mistral, several biographical novels and children's plays.
Other works: *Don Diego Portales (el hombre sin concupiscencia)* (1937) (*Don Diego Portales, The Man Without Sexual Desire*); *Los Pincheira* (1939), and *El patriota Manuel Rodríguez* (1951) (*The Patriot Manuel Rodríguez*).

Petition of Mary Easty, The (1692)
This petition by a North American woman charged with witchcraft during the Salem witch trials of 1692 is directed to Sir William Phips, judge of the trials. Rather than pleading her innocence, Easty asserts it and devotes her text to revealing her awareness of 'the wrong way' taken by those who prosecuted the accused. It is a beautifully written testament. Easty was one of nineteen persons executed during the 17th-century witch trials in North America.
▷ Early North American narratives of witchcraft cases

Petits Enfants du siècle, Les (1961) ▷ *Children of Heaven* (1962)

Petrarchism (Italy)
A poetic style derived from the writings of Francesco Petrarch (1304–1374). Petrarch wrote letters, treatises, historical works and Latin poetry, but is most famous for, and most influential in, his Italian poetry, particularly his *Canzoniere*. In this work he tells of his love for Laura, an unfulfilled and largely earthly passion, a story of desire and torment, which is transferred onto a higher, more celestial plain only after the death of the beloved. Stylistically, Petrarch's poetry is significant for its use of assonance, its imagery of nature, and its retelling of Classical myth. It is also poetry which deals, in a selfconscious manner, with the act of writing poetry, in which Laura is inevitably associated with the laurel, symbol of poetic achievement.

Petrarchism was already in existence in Petrarch's lifetime, and reached its height in the 16th century, in its attempts at formal perfection, its echoes of Classical poetry in Italian rather than Latin, and its concentration on personal feelings and experiences. Women poets were particularly keen to borrow Petrarch's style and subject matter, transforming it where necessary to suit their specific needs. Among the most famous practitioners of Petrarchism were ▷ Tullia D'Aragona, Laura Battiferri (1523–1589), ▷ Vittoria Colonna, ▷ Veronica Franco, ▷ Veronica Gambara, Chiara Matraini (1514–c1597), Isabella di Morra (1520–1548), ▷ Maria Savorgnan, ▷ Gaspara Stampa and Laura Terracina (1519–c1577).

Petrovýkh, Mariia Sergeevna (1908–1979)
Poet and translator. A friend of ▷ Akhmátova's between 1933 and 1965, she gave her shelter, help, kindness and devotion in the diverse roles of listener, critic, and editor. Akhmátova, in turn, spoke of her approvingly and cited her poem 'Give me a Rendezvous in This World' as a masterpiece of the 20th-century Russian lyric. She was also highly regarded by Mandel'shtám (who dedicated a poem to her) and Boris Pasternak. Despite these marks of esteem and her great poetic gifts, her own work long remained obscure and little published. In part, Petrovýkh's obscurity seems to have resulted from her own reticence, altruism, and reluctance to see her poetry into print.

She was known primarily for translation, particularly from Armenian, Polish and Yiddish. Although she began publishing in the 1920s, she brought out only one book of her work, *A Distant Tree* (1968) in Erevan, Armenia, composed both of original poems and translations. Two posthumous collections appeared: *Predestination*

(1983) and *The Line on the Horizon: Poems and Translations, Reminiscences of Mariia Petrovýkh* (also Erevan, 1986). Since *Predestination*, her poetry has received critical recognition in important Soviet literary journals. In Petrovýkh's poetry, nature acts as solace, the means through which she voices spiritual expression, and as a source of a rich metaphoric language. She is also the author of poems on the blessedness of motherhood and the power it bestows on the adult to cope with a dangerous, ugly world.

Bib: Kasack, W., *Dictionary of Russian Literature Since 1917*; Wilson, K., *An Encyclopedia of Continental Women Writers* 2; Proffer, C. and E. (eds), *The Ardis Anthology of Recent Russian Literature*

Petrushévskaia, Liudmila Stepanovna (born 1938)

Soviet dramatist and story writer. From the early 1970s to 1986 only seven of Petrushévskaia's stories appeared in print, and her plays were staged informally by a 'guerrilla' troupe of devoted actors. With the onset of ▷ *glásnost'*, her sardonic stories were welcomed in ▷ 'thick journals' and her unsparing, darkly humorous dramas of the Soviet daily grind became an immediate hit in official Moscow theatres. With ▷ Tolstáia, she has been hailed in the West as the vibrant forerunner of a new Russian literature. While Tolstàia dazzles with imagery and hyperbole, Petrushévskaia has a sensitive ear for idiolect, and grounds her plays and stories in what she calls 'urban folklore' – gossip and anecdote that she hears from neighbours and friends or overhears on the street (Nancy Condee, *Institute of Current World Affairs*, NPC-14). Her stories have almost no dialogue, and a breathless style that seems to embody the messy complications of everyday life. The narrator (sometimes pseudo-authorial, sometimes a character) seems oblivious to the implications of her tale; unlike ▷ Tókareva's heroines, she has no easy moral to share. In an interview with Sigrid McLaughlin (*Images of Women in Contemporary Soviet Fiction*), Petrushévskaia stressed the didactic impulse behind her art: 'My stories ask: can one really live that way?' Works like 'The Violin' (*Balancing Acts*, 1973), 'Nets and Traps' (*Images . . .*, 1974), ▷ *Our Crowd*, and her major play ▷ *Three Girls in Blue*, depict women who scrape out marginal lives and sacrifice their self-esteem to a futile search for love and security. The male who exploits their vulnerabilities is portrayed in 'The Overlook' (*Soviet Women Writing*, 1982).

Bib: Law, A. (trans.), *Four*.

Petry, Ann (born 1908)

US short story-writer and novelist. Born and raised in Old Saybrook, Connecticut, Petry developed a unique African-American perspective; her family was one of the few African-American families in town. During the 1930s she worked as a pharmacist in the family-owned drugstore. After marrying in 1938, she

moved to New York. She learned about Harlem while reporting for the newspaper *People's Voice*. In 1946 Petry graduated from Columbia University, where she studied creative writing. Her fiction depicts the way bigotry erodes its victims' personal lives.

'Like a Winding Sheet' (1945) shows how racial oppression induces a man to beat his wife. ▷ *The Street* (1946) is a novel of social protest which describes how an African-American woman, Lutie Johnson, struggles to survive in the harsh socio-economic environment of Harlem. *The Narrows* (1953) illustrates what happens when an African-American youth falls in love with an Anglo-American woman. Petry exposes how modern society erects barriers to meaningful human relationships. Petry was also a member of the American Negro Theater.

Other works include: *Country Place* (1947), *The Drugstore* (1949), *The Drugstore Cat* (1949), *Harriet Tubman, Conductor on the Underground Railroad* (1955), *The Common Ground* (1964), *Tituba of Salem Village* (1964), *Legends of Saints* (1970) and *Miss Muriel and Other Stories* (1971).

Peyton Place (1956)

US novel. Grace de Repentigny Metalious (1924–1964) was born in Manchester, New Hampshire. She married in 1942 and became the mother of three. Sexually titillating, *Peyton Place* was her sensational, controversial bestseller. The novel exposes the bigotry and narrow-mindedness of a small New England town.

It portrays the psychological, emotional and physical abuse women suffer from men and it criticizes sexual double standards, making a case for legalizing abortion. It subverts the conventional view of women as sexually passive. Some of the women in the novel take control over their lives and they succeed in realizing their ambitions. In addition to dealing with issues of sexism, *Peyton Place* also depicts the damaging effects of classism, such as alcoholism. The novel later became a cult television series.

Other works by Metalious include: *Return to Peyton Place* (1959), *The Tight White Collar* (1960) and *No Adam in Eden* (1963).

Pfeiffer, Emily (1827–1890)

Welsh poet and polemical writer, born in Montgomeryshire. Pfeiffer wrote ten volumes of poetry, including *Gerard's Monument* (1873); *Poems* (1876); *Sonnets and Songs* (1880); *The Rhyme of the Lady of the Rock* (1884) and *Flowers of the Night* (1889). Her work is informed by a Victorian ▷ feminist perspective, is sympathetic to marginalized women and addresses subjects such as marriage, rape, ▷ education, sexuality and work. Pfeiffer also wrote political essays including *Flying Leaves from East and West* (1885), written after a tour of Asia and America, and *Women and Work* (1887), where she protests against the limited vocational opportunities available to women. She died in 1890, leaving £2000 for higher education for women, which was used to

build accommodation for female students at University College, Cardiff.
Bib: Hickok, K., *Representations of Women: 19th Century British Women's Poetry*.

Pfeiffer, Ida (1797–1858)

Austrian writer of travelogues. Born in Vienna into an industrialist's family, she found it difficult, even as a girl, to submit to the restrictions imposed on the women of her time. When her mother refused to give permission for a love match, she married a man much older than herself, by whom she had two sons. After years of unhappy marriage, she began, at the age of forty-five, to undertake long and hazardous journeys, first to the Middle East, then to Scandinavia and Iceland, and later twice around the world. She financed her travels by publishing learned accounts of her experiences. Her books were widely-read, and attracted the admiration of contemporary explorers, such as Carl Ritter (1779–1859) and Alexander von Humboldt (1769–1859). In 1856 she became an honorary member of the Geographical Society of Paris and Berlin, and received a gold medal from the Prussian king. Her works include: *Reise einer Wienerin in das Heilige Land* (2 vols) (1833) (*Journey of a Viennese Woman to the Holyland*); *Eine Frauenfahrt um die Welt. Reise von Wien nach Brasilien, Chili, Otaheiti, China, Ostindien, Persien und Kleinasien*, (3 vols) (1850) (*A Woman's Voyage Around the World. From Vienna to Brazil, Chile, Otaheiti, China, East Indies, Persia and Asia Minor*), and *Meine zweite Weltreise*, (4 vols.) (1856) (*My Second World Tour*).

Phallocentrism

A term associated with ▷French feminism and Lacanian ▷psychoanalysis, defining the order of patriarchy and the ▷symbolic order, where the phallus is positioned as the primary signifier so that the feminine is subordinated to the masculine.

Phallogocentrism

A term associated with ▷French feminism and Lacanian ▷psychoanalysis, it conjoins the meanings of ▷phallocentrism and ▷logocentrism. French philosopher Jacques Derrida (born 1930) accuses French psychoanalyst Jacques Lacan (1901–1981) of phallogocentrism in the sense that it is the *meaning* of the phallus which exerts a determining effect on the subject.

Phanothea

Poet. The Christian writer Clement (2nd century AD) records that she was a priestess of Apollo at Delphi in Greece, and that she invented the hexameter verse.
▷Phemonoe

Phantasia

A poet from Egyptian Memphis or Naucratis, daughter of Nicarchus. The Byzantine writer

Photius (AD c820–?892) records that she wrote epic poetry, a *Trojan War* and an *Adventures of Odysseus*. She left her works in a temple of Hephaestus in Memphis, where Homer allegedly used them for his own epic poetry on the same subjects.
▷Helena; Manto

Phelps, Elizabeth Porter (1747–1817)

North American diarist. A resident of Hadley, Massachusetts, she began her diary in 1763, at the age of sixteen, and recorded the personal events of her life until 1812, five years before her death. She chronicles her experiences during the American Revolution and captures the excitement and tension of evolving political, religious and social attitudes in the federal era.
▷'Diary of Elizabeth Porter Phelps, The'

Phelps, Elizabeth Stuart (1815–1852)

US novelist, pseudonym H. Trusta, mother of ▷Elizabeth Stuart Phelps (Ward). Phelps began writing for religious periodicals and for children, emphases which stayed throughout her career. Her children's stories, eg *Little Kitty Brown and Her Bible Verses* (1851), and periodical literature are moralistic, and her claim to success and sales rests in her autobiographical fiction. While Phelps has often been dismissed as a religious sentimentalist, her novels realistically reveal women's lives and ambitions – as well as providing interesting insight into survival in a clergyman's family. Most notable are the enormously popular *The Sunny Side; or, the Country Minister's Wife* (1851) and ▷*The Angel Over the Right Shoulder* (1852).

Phelps (Ward), Elizabeth Stuart (1844–1911)

US fiction and non-fiction writer. Born Mary Gray Phelps, the daughter of ▷Elizabeth Stuart Phelps, she renamed herself on her mother's death. Phelps first gained popular attention with ▷*The Gates Ajar* (1868). An enormous seller, *Gates* led to sequels: *Beyond the Gates* (1883) and *The Gates Between* (1887). More lasting in their effect and interest are her novels that concentrate on women's resistance against convention and oppression. *Hedged In* (1870), ▷*The Silent Partner* (1871), ▷*The Story of Avis* (1877) and ▷*Dr Zay* (1882) show women defining themselves, seeking careers, forming communities with other women across class and race.

She also wrote realistic regional fiction: *The Madonna of the Tubs* (1886) and *Jack, the Fisherman* (1887). After marrying Herbert Dickinson Ward, she co-authored a number of books with him in an attempt to boost his career. Towards the end of her career she found less favour with publishers and increasingly varied her work to try to catch the fashion. Her autobiography is *Chapters from a Life* (1896).
▷*Harper's Monthly Magazine*

Phemonoe

Poet and priestess of Apollo at Delphi. Date unknown. She is credited by Eustathius to have been the inventor of the hexameter. Clement says she lived and wrote poetry twenty-seven years before (the mythical) first poet, Orpheus, Musaeus and Linus. She wrote on dream interpretation, and a work *On Augury* used by the Elder Pliny (1st century AD). An epigram by Antipater of Thessalonica (2nd century BC) refers to a statue of her in a cloak.

▷Phanothea

Philaenis (? 3rd century BC)

A writer of prose erotica, she is reputed to come from Samos, but the island was renowned for prostitutes and may be designated merely because it befits her subject. Even in antiquity one authority denied her authorship, attributing it to Polycrates (6th century BC) the sophist. Some papyrus fragments survive.

▷Pornography (Ancient Greece); Elephantis; Diaries, Ancient Greek and Roman

Philip, Marlene Nourbese (born 1947)

Caribbean writer, poet, lecturer and lawyer, born in Tobago, who has lived in Canada since 1968. In 1983 she was awarded the Canada Council Explorations Grant to write and produce a taped documentary, *Blood is for Bleeding (The Positive Values of the Menstrual Experience)*. She won the Casa de las Americas literary prize for poetry in 1988. She is the author of three books of poetry: *Thorns* (1980), *Salmon Courage* (1983) and *She Tries Her Tongue Her Silence Softly Breaks* (1989), plus one novel, *Harriet's Daughter* (1988). Her poetry and prose have been included in numerous anthologies. Her writing attempts to fuse the disparate threads that make up the New World experience; her most recent work is a prose poem entitled *Looking For Livingstone* (1991).

Philips, Katherine (1632–1664)

Welsh poet and dramatist working during the Interregnum (1649–1660), known as 'Orinda'. Her parents were Presbyterians, and in 1647 she married James Philips, a supporter of Olivor Cromwell (1599–1658). Philips herself was a Royalist, and her poems record the difference between her own views and those of her husband. She was fluent in several languages, and a prolific writer. Thus far, 116 poems, five verse ▷translations and translations of two plays comprise her canon. The performance of her translation of French dramatist Pierre Corneille's (1606–1684) *Pompey* in 1663 make her the first woman to have a play staged professionally in London. In 1651, her poems began to circulate in manuscript, and they were first published in 1651, prefixed to the poems of Henry Vaughan (1622–1695) and Thomas Cartwright. In 1664 an unauthorized edition of her poems was published, but an authorized edition appeared in 1667. Philips's 'Society of Friendship', a correspondence circle, seems to have begun in 1651 and lasted until 1661, and included Henry Vaughan, among others. Within the circle, each member was assigned a name from classical literature, and Philips was dubbed 'Matchless Orinda'. Her letters to Sir Charles Cotterell were published as *Letters from Orinda to Poliarchus* (1705). She also corresponded with ▷Dorothy Osborne. When she died of smallpox, her translation of *Horace* was unfinished. Philips was praised by her contemporaries as the ideal woman poet because of her modest choice of subjects (compare, for example, ▷Aphra Behn). The majority of her poetry is written for particular occasions or persons, and in many of them she transforms the conventional language of courtship and applies it to friendships between women: 'Our hearts are mutuall victims lay'd, /While they (such power in friendship ly's) / are Altars, Priests, and off'rings made, / And each heart which thus kindly dy's / Grows deathless by the sacrifise.'

▷Polwhele, Elizabeth

Bib: Greer, Germaine, *et al.*, Kissing the Rod; Hobby, E., *Virtue of Necessity*.

Phillips, Jayne Anne (born 1952)

US novelist and short story writer. Phillips was born in West Virginia, and educated at West Virginia University and at the University of Iowa, where she studied creative writing. In 1975 she published her short story, 'Fast Lanes', followed by *Sweethearts* (1976), *Counting* (1978), *Black Tickets* (1979) and the short-story collection *Fast Lanes* (1987).

Her work is usually associated with the school of dirty realism and writers such as ▷Bobbie Ann Mason. The stories in *Black Tickets* are often very short confrontational pieces about working-class lives in middle and urban North America. Frequently they deal with young girls' experience of abusive sexual exploitation, as in 'Sweethearts' and 'Lechery', using a spare and matter-of-fact style for impact, even while engaging with the dreams and fantasies of the characters. Other stories register political events through their impact on the lives of ordinary people. This is the strategy of Phillips's novel, *Machine Dreams* (1984), which traces a family from World War II, through Korea to Vietnam. The oxymoron of the title reflects the dual emphasis of the book on dreams and memories, and the technological transformation of post-war US society. Since the wars are mediated through the character's nightmares, and dreams often turn on the material of popular culture, this is by no means a simplistic opposition in Phillips's work.

Philosophers, Ancient Greek and Roman women

Many ancient Greek philosophical schools had, by tradition, a few women followers or pupils. The Epicureans had ▷Leontium, and other women who were reputedly courtesans: Hedeion, Mammarion, Boidion, Demetria, Erotion and Themista (all 3rd century BC). None of the latter are known to have written anything. The Cynics had ▷Hipparchia, wife of Crates. The literature of the Pythagorean revival (▷Pythagorean Women) includes some letters reputedly by women: ▷Theano, (I) ▷Perictione, ▷Melissa, ▷Myia (I), ▷Phintys and ▷Aesara. Aristippus' daughter ▷Arete was a philosopher. Plato (4th century BC) was said to have had two women pupils, Axiothea and Lasthenia, but neither are known as writers. In the 5th century AD we find ▷Hypatia.

▷Aspasia; Cleobulina

Philosophical Imaginary, The (1989)

Translation of *L'Imaginaire philosophique* (1980), first book by French philosopher ▷Michèle Le Doeuff. Philosophical discourse asserts that its status as philosophy consists in its break with figurative accounts of the world, such as those produced by myths, fables, poetry, or old wives' tales. Le Doeuff argues that philosophical texts are, in fact, full of images and little fables about islands, trees, comedies and Woman-as-Other. Through essays on philosophers such as Thomas More, Descartes and Kant, she shows that the bases of philosophy lie outside the strict confines of the discipline itself.

Phintys (3rd century BC)

A philosopher whose date and biography are unclear, she shares the name of a daughter of a Spartan admiral who died 406 BC. She is credited with a work in letter form *On the Temperance of Women* (▷Pythagorean women). In this she remarks that fundamental to a woman's virtue is the love and praise she gives her husband. A woman can achieve virtue by chastity, modesty of dress, discretion over when to leave the house, avoidance of unseemly religious festivals, and punctual and moderate sacrifices to gods. She concludes that a woman's greatest accomplishment is to produce children like their father.

▷Philosophers, Ancient Greek and Roman women; Household management and child rearing, Ancient Greek

Bib: (text & trans.) Guthrie, K.S., *The Pythagorean Sourcebook and Library.*

Phoenix Fled (1951)

A collection of short stories by the Indian writer ▷Attia Hosain. Published shortly after Hosain had migrated to England in the wake of the ▷Partition of India, the stories attempt to capture the momentous political and social changes which were taking place during the fight for independence. There is a nostalgia for the traditional, aristocratic way of life that Hosain had known as a girl in Lucknow, made all the more poignant by her acceptance that that sort of life had to go if Indians were to win their freedom from the British.

Pichler, Karoline (1769–1843)

Austrian poet, novelist and dramatist. The daughter of a courtier in Vienna, she had an excellent education, and was acquainted with many of the literary figures of her time. After her marriage to the state official Andreas Pichler in 1896, she opened a literary salon in Vienna, and met ▷Madame de Staël, ▷Henriette Herz, and the Schlegel brothers (Friedrich 1772–1829 and August Wilhelm, 1767–1845). She also had a longstanding friendship with ▷Dorothea Schlegel. Several of Pichler's historical plays were performed at the Vienna Burgtheater, but she also wrote aphorisms, poems and novels, such as *Leonore* (1804), *Frauenwürde* (1808) (*The Dignity of Women*), and the historical *Agathokles* (1808), which earned her great acclaim. A prolific writer, she was one of the most successful literary women of her day.

▷Salon culture (Germany and Austria)

Pickthall, Marjorie (1883–1922)

Poet and fiction writer. Born in Middlesex, England, she emigrated with her family to Toronto, Canada, in 1889. Once considered the best Canadian poet of her time, she has been relegated to anthologized obscurity. A talented child, she was encouraged by her parents. She sold her first story when she was fifteen, and in her early twenties published three juvenile novels of boys' frontier adventure: *Dick's Desertion: A Boy's Adventures in Canadian Forests; A Tale of the Early Settlement of Ontario* (1905); *The Straight Road* (1906), and *Billy's Hero; or, The Valley of Gold* (1908). Although troubled by illness throughout her life, Pickthall worked as a librarian; in 1912 she went to stay with relatives in England, and in World War I actively contributed to the war effort there as an ambulance driver. She attained some success as a novelist, but she is best-known as a premodernist poet, and it is perhaps her resistance to ▷modernism that has aroused such harsh criticism of her work. Critics claim that her best poetry is contained in her first collections, *The Drift of Pinions* (1913) and *The Lamp of Poor Souls, and Other Poems* (1916). Considered a pastoral poet and a romantic, she draws nature well, although she attributes a mysticism to the natural world that is difficult to actualize. Loneliness and grief are repeated motifs; there is a delicate and ethereal quality to her poetry. Her adult novels, *Little Hearts* (1915) and *The Bridge* (1922), are somewhat melodramatic. She also wrote a verse drama, *The Wood Carver's Wife* (1922). After her early death, her short stories were collected in *Angels' Shoes and Other Stories* (1923); *The Complete Poems of Marjorie Pickthall* (1927) was edited by her father; *Selected Poems* (1957) was edited by Lorne Pierce.
Bib: Pierce, L., *Marjorie Pickthall: A Book of Remembrance*; Williamson, J., in ▷*A Mazing Space.*

Picong

Derived from the French word *piquant* (stinging/insulting), this term is used in the Caribbean to

define the ▷calypso war (part of ▷Trinidad
▷carnival's calypso competition), during which
performers improvize verses ridiculing and
insulting each other in a good-natured way.

Piercy, Marge (born 1936)

US novelist, poet and essayist. Piercy was born in
Detroit, Michigan, to working-class Jewish
parents. She gained an MA in 1958 from
Northwestern University and has held various
creative writing fellowships at universities. She has
been married three times. Piercy's writing stems
from her political commitment, which began in
the anti-Vietnam War movement and women's
movement during the 1960s. Her early novels,
like *Small Changes* (1973) have been used as
historical documents in women's studies courses.
In contrast to the documentary approach of some
of her novels, the utopian ▷science fiction story
▷*Woman on the Edge of Time* (1976) makes a
critique of contemporary North America by
counterposing it to a future in which gender roles,
economic exploitation and abuse of the
environment are things of the past. While her
novels have been criticized for their lack of
stylistic sophistication, the rhythms of ordinary
North American speech allow her poetry to be
both accessible and innovative, both meditative
and didactic. Drawing on the same political
commitment that informs her fiction, Piercy's
poetry, such as *The Moon is Always Female* (1980)
explores both feminism and femininity, family
relationships and motherhood, myths, spirituality
and nature as well as the realities of the
oppressed.

Other works include: *Breaking Camp* (1968),
Hard Loving (1969), *Going Down Fast* (1969),
Dance the Eagle to Sleep (1970), *The Grand Coolie
Damn* (1970), *The Earth Smiles Secretly: A Book of
Days* (1970), *A Work of Artifice* (1970), *4-Telling*
(with others) (1971), *When the Drought Broke*
(1971), *To Be of Use* (1973), *Living in the Open*
(1976), *The Twelve-Spoked Wheel Flashing* (1978),
The High Cost of Living (1978), *The Last White
Class: A Play About Neighbourhood Terror* (with Ira
Wood) (1980), *Parti Colored Blocks for a Quilt*
(1982), *Circles on the Water* (1982), *Braided Lives*
(1982), *Stone, Paper, Knife* (1983), *My Mother's
Body* (1985), *Gone to Soldiers* (1987), *Fly Away
Home* (1984), *Available Light* (1988), *Summer
People* (1989) and *Mars and Her Children* (1992).
Bib: Walker, Sue and Hammer, Eugenie (eds),
Ways of Knowing: Critical Essays on Marge Piercy;
Thelman, Pia, *Marge Piercy's Women: Visions
Captured and Subdued.*

Pigeon Girl, The (1967)

Translation of *La Plaça del Diamant* (1962),
arguably the best novel written in post-war Spain.
Written by ▷Mercè Rodoreda, it has been
translated into several languages, including twice
into English, as ▷*The Pigeon Girl*, and *The Time of
the Doves* (1983). It tells the story of Natàlia and
her marriage to Quimet; when the latter is
reported killed in action during the Spanish Civil

War (1936–9), Natàlia experiences such poverty
that she contemplates killing herself and her two
children. Out of a desire for economic stability,
Natàlia remarries but she is haunted by the
possibility that Quimet may return, and she
gradually retreats from the world. Natàlia's story
is symbolic of many in Spain whose lives were
destroyed by the historical calamity of the civil
war, but it is specifically feminine in that it
unmasks the ▷patriarchal structures which
(mis)govern her life, especially in matters of love.

Pilgrimage (1915–1967)

Sequence of thirteen novels by English writer
▷Dorothy Richardson – her lifelong project.
Pilgrimage was first published as a series of
separate novels as follows: *Pointed Roofs* (1915),
Backwater (1916), *Honeycomb* (1917), *The Tunnel*
(1919), *Interim* (1919), *Deadlock* (1921), *Revolving
Lights* (1923), *The Trap* (1925), *Oberland* (1927),
Dawn's Left Hand (1931), *Clear Horizon* (1935)
and *Dimple Hall* was included in the first collected
edition (1938), *March Moonlight* with the second
collected edition (1967). The thirteen novels have
been reprinted in four volumes by Virago Press.

Pilgrimage is an autobiographical work, covering
the period in Richardson's life between 1891 and
1912 through the consciousness of her
autobiographical/fictional persona, Miriam
Henderson. It is also a woman's ▷*Bildungsroman*
or, perhaps, a *Künstlerroman*, for in the final parts
of *Pilgrimage* we see Miriam beginning to write
her story. It is, furthermore, a quest narrative,
using, as its title suggests, the metaphor of the
journey common to the literature of this period.
Written largely in the third person, although
occasionally moving into first-person narration, it
creates a literary space of its own between the
genres of the novel and autobiography.

Events and experiences described from the first
volume onwards include Miriam's father's
bankruptcy; her stay in Germany working as a
governess; her mother's suicide; her work in
London, first as a teacher and then a clerical
assistant; her involvement with the political,
philosophical and religious doctrines and groups
of the 1900's and her relationship with 'Hypo G.
Wilson' (in real life, novelist H.G. Wells, 1866–
1946), whose attitudes and aesthetics she
repeatedly pits herself against. *Pilgrimage* contains
a number of ironic rewritings of episodes in
Wells's ▷'New Woman' novel, *Ann Veronica*
(1909). Richardson refers, in the foreword to
Pilgrimage, to her desire 'to produce a feminine
equivalent of the current masculine realism'.
▷Virginia Woolf, in her review of *Revolving
Lights*, refers to Richardson's invention of a 'a
woman's sentence'. The issue of a gendered
language is one that Miriam herself debates in the
text; it could be seen as one of the dilemmas with
which she is confronted, rather than as a matter of
certainty on Richardson's part. In any case, the
questions of gender and language, and of the
possibility of a 'female aesthetic', are central to the
novel and to recent analyses of Richardson's work.

Richardson's own brand of ▷'realism' entails an immersion in her heroine's consciousness as it moves in and out of engagement with scenes, events and people. Space, movement, light and reflections are also primary focuses of attention. The perceiving consciousness is centrally important, but it is shown in a state of flux and process; as Jean Radford and Stephen Heath have pointed out, Miriam's name condenses the sense of a 'myriad I am's', of multiple identities.

Richardson's experiments with form and narrative method have now ensured her a place as a literary ▷modernist, although her work was neglected for a long time. The fascination of her writing also resides, however, in its engagement with cultural forms and historical consciousness, including, as Radford notes, the cultural discourses of its time – Darwinism, Fabianism, ▷suffrage feminism, literature and aesthetics. This immersion in the social and cultural field is also an aspect of *Pilgrimage*'s insistent focus on the self in relation to the world. These facets, among others, make their own case against the charge of narcissistic self-absorption levelled against the text by those writers and critics who have failed to understand the significance and magnitude of its project.

▷Sinclair, May

Pilgrim at Tinker Creek (1974)
US essays for which ▷Annie Dillard won a Pulitzer Prize. This collection of religious essays centres on an individual consciousness in relation to God. In each essay the narrator observes an everyday event in nature and tries to sense the relationship between the event and all of nature. In this way she hopes to feel God's connection to the world. Each event prompts a philosophical question that connects each essay with the next. An overriding concern is how to reconcile mystic encounters with nature's senseless horrors. The narrator concludes that beauty and death are branches of the same creek. Dillard blends scientific facts, theological musings and poetry in her study of nature.

Pilkington, Laetitia (c 1708–1750)
Irish poet and memoirist, born to parents of Dutch origin in Dublin. In 1725 she married the Reverend Matthew Pilkington and met satirist Jonathan Swift (1667–1745) and others. Swift helped Matwhew Pilkington to a chaplaincy in London, and when Mrs Pilkington followed she found that he was involved with an actress. In 1733 she returned alone to Dublin, already regarded as a woman of dubious character. In 1738 Pilkington divorced her for adultery. Pilkington did not supply much maintenance, and she and her children moved to London, where she tried to live by her writing. She began with the subject of masculine infidelity in *The Statues: Or, the Trial of Constancy* (1739) and accompanied writing with wild living. She found it hard to survive by her pen, and was imprisoned for debt, escaping to open a bookshop in St James's. She

returned to Dublin in 1747, and began to publish her *Memoirs* featuring stories of Swift and Samuel Richardson (▷Richardson, influence of), some of which settled old scores.

Her other publications include: *An Excursory View on the Present State of Things* and *Memoirs* (1748–1754).

Pinar, Florencia (c 1470–1530)
Spanish poet. Unlike ▷Teresa de Cartagena and ▷Leonor López de Córdoba, who also wrote during the Middle Ages, nothing is known of Pinar's life except that she had a brother who was also a poet. Some of her poems collected in Hernando del Castillo's *Cancionero general* (1511) are of the highest literary value. Particularly powerful is her poem 'Destas aves su nación' ('The Natural Heritage of these Birds') which draws a parallel between the woman in love and the female partridge imprisoned in a cage. Pinar's use of animal imagery gives her poetry a sexual dimension which was striking for the time.

Pinckney, Eliza Lucas (c 1722–1793)
North American letter-writer. Born in Antigua, West Indies, and educated in England, she was the daughter of wealthy South Carolinan plantation owners. An astute and imaginative businesswoman, she managed the family plantations in the West Indies beginning in 1740. Her experiments to improve the cultivation of indigo were major contributions to that crop's importance in the West Indian and American South's economies. The ▷*Journal and Letters of Eliza Lucas* details her life in the West Indies, her experiments with indigo, her attitudes towards marriage and her religious beliefs. After a life in which she continued her various agricultural experimentations and raised a family in South Carolina, she died in Philadelphia.

Piñon, Nélida (born 1936)
Brazilian novelist and short story writer. Her family emigrated from Galicia in Spain to Brazil early in the 20th century, a fact she retells in her latest novel, *A república dos sonhos* (1984) (*The Republic of Dreams*). Her literary career began with one of her most successful novels, *Guia-mapa de Gabriel Arcanjo* (1961) (*The Angel Gabriel's Guide-map*), written in an experimental, restless style. *A casa da paixão* (1972) (*The House of Passion*) is one of her simplest, most accomplished works. Her novel *Tebas do meu coração* (1974) (*My Agile Heart*) follows the style of Spanish American writers, such as Gabriel García Marquez (born 1928) and touches on ▷magic realism. She has travelled widely, won several prizes, and is a member of the Brazilian Academy of Letters. Her works have been translated, and many of her stories are included in foreign and Brazilian anthologies.

Other works: *Madeira feita cruz* (1963) (*Wood-made Cross*); *Tempo das frutas* (1966) (*Time of the Fruits*); *Fundador* (1969) (*The Founder*); *Sala de armas* (1973) (*The Armoury*); *A força do destino*

(1978) (*The Power of Destiny*); *O calor das coisas* (1980), and (*The Heat of Things*).

Piozzi, Hester (Lynch) (1741–1821)
English letter writer diarist, ▷Bluestocking and poet. She was brought up in Herefordshire and began writing poetry at an early age. In 1763 she married Henry Thrale and moved to London. In London she joined the literary circle around Samuel Johnson (1709–1784), and she recorded her meetings with ▷Fanny Burney and others in her journal. After her husband's death in 1781 she began to write seriously – most of her publications date from the 1780s onwards. In 1784 she married the Italian musician Gabriel Piozzi, scandalizing the Bluestocking community – even Johnson advised her against it, and the Burneys mocked her. She toured Italy and returned to Wales.

Publications: *Thraliana* (1942) (journal); *The Florence Miscellany* (1784); *Anecdotes of the Late Samuel Johnson* (1786); (ed.), Johnson's *Letters* (2 Vols, 1788); *Observations and Reflections*; *British Syonymy* (1794), and *Retrospection* (1801). Her edited *Letters* appeared in 1991.

Pirckheimer, Caritas (1467–1532)
German nun and writer. Descended from a long line of German ▷humanist scholars, she received an excellent education, and, at the age of sixteen, took vows in the Convent of St Klara in Nuremberg. She corresponded in Latin with intellectuals and notables and, as an abbess, became an important voice in German intellectual life. Besides writing a history of her convent, she also composed *Denkwürdigkeiten* (1524–1528) (*Memorabilia*), a meticulous documentation of the intellectual, political and relgious arguments of the Reformation in Nuremberg, where her convent became an increasingly beleaguered Catholic stronghold.

Pitt, Marie E.J. (1869–1948)
Australian poet. Pitt lived for a time in Tasmania, where her husband worked as a miner, and settled in Melbourne in 1902. She lived with the poet Bernard O'Dowd from 1919 onward, was a member of the Victorian Socialist Party, and edited its magazine. Her poetry reflects her political commitment. It includes *The Horses of the Hills and Other Verses* (1911), *Bairnsdale and Other Poems* (1922), *The Poems of Marie E.J. Pitt* (1928) and *Selected Poems* (1944). Her biography, *Doherty's Corner: the Life and Work of Australian Poet Marie E.J. Pitt* (1985), was written by Colleen Burke.

Pitter, Ruth (born 1897)
English poet. The first woman to receive the Queen's Gold Medal for Poetry (1955), Pitter was educated at a Christian charity school, and became an Anglican in her forties. Beginning with *First Poems* (1920), Pitter's poetry is characteristic for its use of strict metrical schemes and 'formal' language, a technique maintained in the later

volumes *Persephone in Hades* (1931) and *A Mad Lady's Garland* (1934). Later poems reveal a strong Christian quest for spiritual meaning. Other volumes include: *Poems 1926–1966* (1968) and *Collected Poems* (1969).

Pix, Mary (1666–1709)
English Restoration dramatist. She wrote a commendatory poem for *Sylvia's Revenge* (1688), and in 1696 published her only novel, *The Inhumane Cardinal, or Innocence Betrayed*. In the same year she wrote the farce *The Spanish Wives* and the successful tragedy *Ibrahim the Thirteenth*. She wrote ten more plays (tragedies and comedies), and translated a long poem from Boccaccio, *Violenta, or the Rewards of Virtue* as well as contributing to ▷*The Nine Muses* (1700). She knew ▷Susanna Centlivre, ▷Catherine Trotter, and complimented ▷Delarivier Manley's *The Royal Mischief*, calling Manley's writing 'Like *Sappho* Charming, like *Afra* Eloquent, / Like Chast *Orinda*, sweetly Innocent.'

Pizarnik, Alejandra (1936-1972)
Argentinian poet and critic. She lived in France for a long time, returning to Buenos Aires in 1960. Since her first book, *La tierra más ajena* (1966) (*The Most Foreign Land*), she has tended to use direct, rational, naïve language, and her poems are short. She used to write as though in a trance – repeating images – and her writing incorporates a sense of irony, mysticism and a feeling of solitude and emptiness. This lends a contemporary feel and an air of spontaneity to her language. Her poems were translated and published abroad. Pizarnik committed suicide at the age of 36. Her last poems were collected and organized posthumously by ▷Olga Orozco and Ana Becciú in 1982.

Other works: *La última inocencia* (1956) (*The Last Innocence*); *Las aventuras perdidas* (1958) (*Lost Adventures*); *Arbol de Diana* (1962) (*Tree of Diana*); *Los trabajos y las noches* (1965) (*Tasks and Nights*); *Extracción de la piedra de locura* (1968) (*Extraction of the Madness Stone*); *Los pequeños cantos* (1971) (*Little Songs*), and *El infierno musical* (1971) (*The Musical Hell*).

Pizarro, Agueda (born 1941)
Colombian poet. Her full name is Agueda Pizarro de Rayo, and although she was born in the United States, she descends from Colombian parents. She was recognized as a poet when she produced her book of poems *Sombraventadora* (1979) (*Shadow-winnower*). This has been translated into English, and the poems published simultaneously in both languages.

Pla, Josefina (born 1909)
Paraguayan poet, short story writer, critic and dramatist. Born in the Canary Islands, she arrived in Paraguay in 1927 with her husband, the ceramic craftsman Julián de la Herrería (1888–1937), became a Paraguayan citizen, and was totally committed to the life there.

Her literary career began when she wrote her comedy *Víctima preparatoria* (1927) (*Preparatory Victim*). In 1940, she emerged as an important figure in the ▷avant-garde generation of poetry, along with ▷Dora Acuña and Julio Correa (1900–1953), thus helping to revive Paraguayan literature.

Josefina Pla's poetry has as its main theme spiritual, not carnal, love, of an anguished, metaphysical, mystic nature – a form of eroticism that has spread through South America, as in the poems of ▷Juana de Ibarbourou, for example. She wrote several successful dramatic works in collaboration with Centurión Miranda; her comedy *Aquí no ha pasado nada* (1942) (*Nothing Has Happened Here*) is considered to be her best play. *Nino de alegría (Cenáculo Vy'á Raity) (Nest of Happiness)* is a play about a father who refuses to legitimize his five children. The title is a sentence in Guaraní. She also wrote essays on Paraguayan art, culture and literature.

Other works: *El precio de los sueños* (1934); *La raiz y la aurora* (1960) (*The Root and the Dawn*); *Rostros en el agua* (1963) (*Faces in the Water*); *La mano en la tierra* (1963) (*The Hand on the Ground*); *Invención de la muerte* (1965) (*Invention of Death*); *Satélites oscuros* (1966) (*Dark Satelellites); Antología de poesía paraguaya* (1966) (*Anthology of Paraguayan Poetry*), *and Antología poética* (1978) (*Poetry Anthology*).

***Plaça del Diamant, La* (1962)** ▷*Pigeon Girl, The* (1967)

Plaidy, Jean (born 1906)
English novelist. Pseudonym of Eleanor Alice Burford Hibbert, who also writes under the pseudonyms Victoria Holt, Ellalice Tate, Elbur Ford and Kathleen Kellow. Born in London and educated privately, Plaidy is a prolific writer of historical novels and family sagas. She originally wrote some thirty novels under her own name, but the pseudonym Jean Plaidy became virtually synonymous with British popular historical/▷romantic fiction. More than 80 novels have been published under the Plaidy name, and these include a dozen distinct 'series'. The pseudonym Victoria Holt was first used in 1961 with *The Mistress of Mellyn*; the Holt novels are ▷Gothic romances.

Planetarium, The (1960)
Translation of *Le Planétarium* (1959) by French writer ▷Nathalie Sarraute. The novel shows the same events from the point of view of several characters, emphasizing the gap between perception and reality. Female characters illustrate how women are brought up to see themselves as less important than males in the family.

Plassara, Katerina (born 1943)
Greek novelist. She was born in Athens, where she studied political science and drama. Growing up in a home where there was little communication, she began writing mainly as an

outlet for her ideas and feelings. In her books it is usually the subject matter that defines her style rather than any strictly personal concern. The interest of her writing lies in her efforts to make her ideas more comprehensible to readers. By creating a form of communication with imaginary persons she allows her readers to realize what is wrong around them and so perhaps make them want to change it. Her first novel, *Stony Summer* (1965), was followed by many others. *The Witch* (1977), a collection of short stories, won her a literary award. She has also worked in publishing, editing books by women authors.

Plath, Sylvia (1932–1963)
US poet and novelist. Sylvia Plath's uncompromisingly forces her readers to examine the links between the woman writer, madness and history, and the same themes return repeatedly in the fiercely contested debates over her life and work which have raged since her suicide in 1963 at the age of thirty. Plath's literary success came early, winning the *Ms* magazine College Fiction Contest and graduating with honours from Smith College. Her extraordinary novel, ▷*The Bell Jar* (1963) reveals, however, how her identity as a woman writer had a darker subtext in the form of her nervous breakdown. Whilst studying at Cambridge she married the poet Ted Hughes (born 1930); this relationship underpins much of her most astonishing and disturbing poetry, and today provides a major source of contention for biographers, academics, feminists and publishers. The poems collected in *The Colossus and Other Poems* (1962), prise open the relation between writing and the female body through their explorations of familial and sexual relations. The remarkable ▷*Ariel* (1965) connects up the themes of female subjectivity, suffering and negativity to the Holocaust and questions of racial identity. Plath's own consistent and unique challenge to the way we think about women's identity, writing and madness demands that we read her work beyond the stereotype of self-obsessed and indulgent 'mad-woman-writer' which so often accompanies readings of her life and work.

Other works include: *Crossing the Water* (1971), *Winter Trees* (1971), *Letters Home: Correspondence 1950–1963* (1975), *Johnny Panic and the Bible of Dreams* (1978) and *The Journals of Sylvia Plath* (1983).

Bib: Rose, Jacqueline, *The Haunting of Sylvia Plath*; Stevenson, Anne, *Bitter Fame: A Life of Sylvia Plath*.

Plato, Ann
US 19th-century African-American essayist, biographer and poet. Plato was the first African-American known to have published a volume of essays. Her *Essays; Including Biographies and Miscellaneous Pieces in Prose and Poetry* was self-published in 1841 in Hartford, Connecticut, something of a literary centre and a city in which most African-American inhabitants were free. Plato's essays are Christian and devotional – on

such topics as 'Benevolence,' 'Obedience' and 'Lessons from Nature' – with remarkably little race consciousness.

Pleasing Instructor, The (1799)

A classical literature anthology by the North American author, ▷Tabitha Gilman Tenney, it was directed to an audience of young women. Through subtle humour, it blended the processes of providing a reader with exposure to ancient texts and of establishing proper conduct for young women. An example of the vast body of conduct literature that proliferated at the turn of that century.

Pléiade

A group of 16th-century French poets originally referred to as 'La Brigade'. The term was borrowed from classical mythology and the Greek tragic poets, and was used to refer to the seven most important French male poets of the reign of Henri II (1547–1559), grouped around Pierre de Ronsard (1524–1585). They included in their number Jean-Antoine de Baïf (1532–1589), Joachim Du Bellay (1522–1560), Pontus de Tyard (1521–1605), Etienne Jodelle (1532–1573), Rémy Belleau (1528–1577) and Jean Dorat (1508–1588). From time to time the list was modified, but the objective remained the same: to refine French language and literature by enthusiastic imitation of the ancients, and to popularize new poetic forms in France, such as the ode, the sonnet and the epic.

Pleijel, Agneta (born 1940)

Swedish dramatist, cultural critic, poet and novelist. Pleijel was born in Stockholm into an intellectual family. Her father was a professor, her mother a writer. She studied at the university and gained her Ph.D. in 1973.

She was active as a cultural critic in the 1960s, and in the 1970s she began to write plays in a radical, modernist tradition, often in collaboration with other authors. In the 1970s she was active in the feminist movement, and began to write feminist literature with strong social criticism. Her most important plays are: *Ordning härskar i Berlin* (1970) (*Order Reigns in Berlin*), *Kollontaj* (1979), *Lycho-Lisa* (1979) (*Lucky-Lisa*), *Sommarkvällar på jorden* (1984) (*Summer Evenings on Earth*), and *Berget på månens baksida* (1984) (*The Mountain at the Back of the Moon*).

She has also published modernist poems, eg 'Änglar, Dvärgar' (1981) ('Angels, Dwarfs') and 'Ögon ur en Dröm' (1984) ('Eyes out of a Dream'). In the 1980s, her prose (for example, *Vindspejare*, 1987, *Chase a Wind*, and *Hundstjärnan*, 1989, *The Dog Star*) has developed into a meta-literature, where the self-reflection concerns the specific process of female creation. In this way the reader is reflected in the artistic creation.

Plessen, Elisabeth (born 1944)

German novelist. She first found acclaim in 1974, when she published (together with Michael Mann) the 'unwritten memoirs' of Katia Mann, wife of the German author Thomas Mann (1875–1955). She consolidated her reputation with the autobiographical novel *Mitteilung an den Adel* (1976) (*Message to the Noble*). This work describes how the heroine reappraises her image of her aristocratic father. Plessen treats her subject with thoughtful sensitivity, while also catching accurately the rebellious mood of young West Germans in the years immediately after 1968.

Plisson, Marie-Prudence (1727–1788)

French poet and prose fiction writer. Born in Chartres, she studied on her own, and later became a midwife in Paris. The majority of her work, including fantastic and allegorical texts reflecting on contemporary mores, was published in different periodicals, most prominently in the *Mercure*. Of these the short story, *La Promenade de province* (*Provincial Walk*), which was to have several sequels, was published in 1783, together with *Les Voyages d'Oromasis* (*The Travels of Oromasis*). Two volumes of her verse were also published: *Ode sur la vie champêtre* (1750) (*Ode to Country Life*), and *Stances à une amie* (1753) (*Stanzas to a Friend*). Her other works include a collection of moral maxims, a project to aid the poor in the countryside, and a critical essay on the problem of illegitimacy and late births – a subject on which she was cited as an authority.

Plönnies, Louise von (1803–1872)

German poet. The well-educated daughter of a doctor, she married a medic, and had nine children. After a journey to Belgium in the early 1840s, she began to translate Flemish literature and put together a first collection of her own sonnets, which appeared in 1844. Her work was well-received, and she went on to publish further collections of poetry and a number of epic poems and novels. In her lyric poems she tends to deal with contemporary issues: 'Glas' (1844) ('Glass') discusses child labour, and technological progress is the theme of 'Auf der Eisenbahn' (1844) ('On the Railway'). However Plönnies's epics and novels are based on material from myths and legends. *Maryken von Nimwegen* (1853), for example, tells the story of a female Faust figure.

Pluie et Vent sur Télumée Miracle (1972)

▷*Bridge of Beyond, The* (1974)

Plumpton Correspondence (1460–1548)

English correspondence. This collection from the archives of the Plumpton family of Harrogate, Yorkshire, includes letters from Agnes, wife of Sir Robert Plumpton (1502–1504); Isabell, his second wife; from Dorothy Plumpton to her father, Sir Robert; and letters from Edith Nevill (to Lady Plumpton), Ann Abbot, Katherine Chadderton and Mawd Rose.

▷Letters (England, Middle Ages)

Bib: Stapleton, Thomas (ed.), *Plumpton Correspondence*; Gray, Douglas (ed.), *The Oxford Book of Late Medieval Verse & Prose* (includes a letter from Dorothy Plumpton).

Po (1979) (After)

A brief novel by Slovak writer Alta Vášová (born 1939). Vášová is the only established female Slovak author of ▷science fiction. *After* is a story about the world after the extinction of mankind, and about its renewal by robots. Vášová offers a flashback to the development of human civilization and its limits. Human existence is treated as an absurd game, and yet it has some sense: it provides continuity. The struggle between man and machine eventually ends in harmony through the love of a man for a robot-woman, and by their return to a natural life. Love and nature are treated as the only eternal principles. Vášová's work is an attempt to show the alienation caused by advanced technology.

Poems (1844)

A collection of poetry by British poet ▷Elizabeth Barrett Browning, published after six years of invalidism during which Barrett (as she was then) focused her energies on poetic experiment. *Poems* (1844) is notable for its formal innovation (half-rhymes, metrical irregularity, compound words) and for the range of voices that surface in the collection. There is a mystical, opium-inspired voice in poems such as 'The House of Clouds' and 'A Vision of Poets'; a ▷sentimental voice, found in the popular ▷ballads and in poems such as 'To Flush, My Dog'. A concern with social class is evident in 'The Cry of the Children', a strategically sentimental protest poem about the working conditions of children. 'A Drama of Exile' reviews the Fall 'with a peculiar reference to Eve's allotted grief', while 'L.E.L.'s Last Question' and the pair of sonnets 'A Desire' and 'A Recognition' are poetic tributes to ▷Letitia Landon and ▷George Sand respectively. The collection established Barrett as a major Victorian poet.

Poems by Currer, Ellis and Acton Bell (1846)

The first published work by the British writers, the ▷Brontë sisters, which included poems by Charlotte (Currer), Emily (Ellis) and Anne (Acton). Charlotte organized the publication after 'discovering' Emily's poetry, which she considered 'not at all like the poetry women generally write'. The collection sold only two copies, but received a few favourable notices.

▷Pseudonyms (19th-century Britain)

Poems, Dramatic and Miscellaneous (1790)

Selected works by North America's premier dramatist, ▷Mercy Otis Warren. Dedicated to the first US president, George Washington (1732–1799), it includes two tragedies (*The Sack of Rome* and ▷*The Ladies of Castille*), short political commentaries, and several of Warren's best poems. The poems are political, historical and personal in nature, and many of them address her interest in women's literary and political abilities. In 'To Mrs Montague', she praises ▷Montague as a literary critic who enhances the male authors she reviews, from Shakespeare to Voltaire. 'If gentle Montague my chaplet raise', the poem concludes in an acknowledgement of the need for women's artistic endeavours to be noted as well, 'I'll take my stand by fam'd Parnassus' side, / And for a moment feel a poet's pride.'

▷*Group, The*; *History of the Rise, Progress and Termination of the American Revolution*

Poems on Divers Subjects (1757)

Written by the North American poet ▷Martha Wadsworth Brewster and published in New London in 1757, this collection is Brewster's life-story and thoughts recorded in verse. Noting that 'rare it is to see a *Female Bard*, / Or that my *Sex* in *Print* have e're appear'd', Brewster subverts the usual woman's stance of unworthy author; she also published under her own name rather than anonymously. Her verses are often religious in theme, but several poems ('A Farewell to some of my Christian Friends at *Goshen*', 'A Letter to my Daughter *Ruby Bliss*') reveal intimate details of Brewster's life in North America during the 1740s and 1750s. Also included in the text is a short prose piece, 'In the Year, 1744', which describes a religious experience she underwent shortly after her father's death. Although Brewster's poetry is inconsistent in quality, several pieces are worthy of further study.

Poems on Various Subjects, Religious and Moral (1773)

The African-American slave-poet ▷Phillis Wheatley's collection was first published in England, and in North America the following year. The poems range in theme from personal tributes to national figures such as George Washington to personal narratives and religious explications to pre-romantic studies in imagination. Although some poems, such as 'On Being Brought from Africa to America', reflect the biased Christian education she received that renders Africa a 'pagan land', other works more readily expose her poetic strengths and literary talents. 'On Imagination' is a beautifully rendered exploration of the power of imagination and the oppressive nature of this earthly life; the especially burdensome life of a slave is carefully embedded in the text. It could not be discussed openly because her audience would be the very people who had enslaved Africans, but slavery is symbolized in references to 'fetters' and 'iron bands' that stifle the imagination. In most of her poetry, the next world is envisioned as a place of imaginative freedom as reward for the limitations of one's earthly life. *Poems* offers a major North American poet's collected writings.

Poems, Upon Several Sermons, Preached by the Rev'd . . . George Whitefield, while in Boston (1771)

Written by the North American poet, ▷Jane Dunlap, this twenty-two-page collection is more interesting for its introduction and concluding poem than for the rather formulaic poetic interpretations of scripture used in Whitefield's sermons. In the introduction, she acknowledges that 'If what I have written should meet with favorable reception, I may perhaps in like manner, write a few lines' based on Whitefield's preachings when he was in Boston, Massachusetts, seven years earlier. The conclusion attempts, with questionable success, to define her skill as due merely to God's graciousness.

Poem Without a Hero (1940–1962)

Russian writer ▷Anna Akhmátova worked on this three-part poem for more than twenty years. Several versions of the long and complex work were circulated by Akhmátova in manuscript form, fragments were published in the USSR, one text came out in New York in 1960–61, and a complete version approved by the author herself appeared in England in 1967. These, and other versions published since, all differ in some respects. Most of the poem was written in the years 1940–42. When Akhmátova began writing it, the worst years of Stalin's terror had just ended; she continued to work on it after the start of the war, through the blockade of ▷Leningrad, and during her own evacuation to Tashkent.

The poem is divided into three parts – Akhmátova called it a 'triptych' – and trios figure prominently in its structure and content. Akhmátova cites the three cities – Leningrad, Tashkent, and Moscow – in which she worked on it. Van der Eng-Liedmeier has discerned a 'symphonic' structure to the poem: a dramatic first part, a light middle, and a dignified end. The poet ▷Inna Lisniánskaia sees the three parts as expressing guilt, expiation, and redemption. There is a tripartite time frame: past, present, and future. The first section, 'The Petersburg Tale', features a love triangle and a trio of poets, who have been identified as Blok, Kuzmin, and Vsevolod Kniazev. In Part II, the 'Intermezzo', the speaker calls the poem a box with a 'triple bottom.'

The work is filled with references to historical incidents and personages, and so many citations from the poetry of other writers, that the speaker herself refers to 'plagiarism.' These devices of indirection were a way of eluding the censorship and, more important, of projecting the essence of an era. Akhmátova's personal life, feelings, judgements, and career also come into this supra-personal story of the ▷Silver Age and Russian history in the 'real 20th century' through the voice of the speaker who guides us through the maze of associations and passes judgement – at first ambivalently, then more decisively – on the culture of her youth. The speaker implicates herself as a participant in this 'guilty' past by the presence of doubles, like the charming, but ultimately destructive, actress who is implicated in the suicide of Kniazev in 1913. The speaker eventually finds consolation, as she did also in ▷'Requiem', in an identification with the Russian nation and its national culture, especially its poetry.

The poem is a brilliant example of Akhmátova's capacity for innovation, her stylistic range, her skill at word placement and rhyme, as well as her ability to make new use of devices like ellipses and periphrases. For the poem, Akhmátova invented the stanza now dubbed the 'Akhmátovian stanza'. **Bib:** Reeder, R. (ed.) and Hemschemeyer, J. (trans.), *The Complete Poems of Anna Akhmátova*, 2; Proffer, C. (trans.), *The Silver Age of Russian Culture*; Eng-Liedmeier, J. van der and Verheul, K. (trans.), *Tale Without a Hero and Twenty-Two Poems by Anna Akhmátova*.

'Poem Written by a Captive Damsel, A' (1706)

Written on 23 December 1703 by ▷Mary French, a North American woman who had been taken captive during a Native American raid and who was being held by French accomplices, this 103-line poem was first published in excerpts by Cotton Mather in his collection of early North American ▷captivity narratives, *Good Fetch'd Out of Evil*. French emphasizes the 'Popish' beliefs of her Catholic captors. Traditional in theological perspectives, it is an interesting addition to the genre, both because it was written by a teenager and because, as a poem, it is a rarer form of the genre.

Poetry (Italy)

Poetry in the Italian language, as opposed to Latin, first appears in the early 13th century, and the only record we have of a woman writing in this period is that of the ▷*Compiuta Donzella*. Provençal poetry, which was widely influential in Italy at this time, treats the figure of the woman as the object of the poet's awe and admiration. Conversely, in the Sicilian school of poetry, woman was celebrated for her ability to give sensual pleasure to men. In the second half of the century, the poetry of the *dolce stil novo* (the sweet, new style) presented a further variation on the theme of woman as object: now she was seen to lead man to God, and was often associated with the figure of the angel. Woman has functioned, more or less constantly since then, as object for the Italian male poet. It is in the writings of ▷Vittoria Colonna, ▷Tullia D'Aragona, ▷Veronica Franco and ▷Lucrezia Marinelli that woman's representation of herself as subject, wrestling with the appropriation of the first-person 'I', and with the representation of woman in general, is consolidated in Italian poetry, and built on by 20th-century poets like ▷Biancamaria Frabotta.

Poetry and Gender: Statements and Essays in Australian Women's Poetry and Poetics (1989)

Anthology of criticism, edited by Brenda Walker and David Brooks. Introduced by Brenda Walker, this book contains a series of short and often provocative statements by women poets concerning their poetry and poetics, and essays on their work by leading Australian literary critics. It includes discussion of the poetry of Aboriginal women, of women poets in the 1920s and 1930s, of ▷Judith Wright, ▷Rosemary Dobson, Margaret Diesendorf (born 1912), Dorothy Auchterlonie (Green), ▷Gwen Harwood, ▷Fay Zwicky, ▷Judith Rodriguez, Ania Walwicz (born 1951), ▷Antigone Kefala, ▷Anne Elder, Kate Llewellyn (born 1940) and J.S. Harry (born 1939).

▷Aboriginal women's poetry in Australia; Migrant women's writing (Australia); Feminist literary criticism (Australia)

Pohanková, Jana (born 1944)
Czech poet. She was greeted with mocking condemnations, as a masochistic near-pornographer, when she published her first collection of verse, *Žena nůse píseň kost* in 1981. The title is a list of the four main declensions of feminine verbs in Czech, but also indicates the socially-accepted functions of woman: bearer of burdens, singer in all times, sex object. This collection constituted the first expression of entirely female feeling in socialist Czechoslovakia. It was attacked particularly for one poem which described the loss of virginity as unenjoyable. *Chůze střemlav* (1986) (*A Headlong Walk*) has nothing of the injured powerfulness of the first collection. Nevertheless, Pohanková still expresses an awareness that men can give very little to women. With the apocalyptic *Ataraktos* (1987) Pohanková appears to have joined the group of 'Angry Young Women' that emerged in Czechostovakia in the 1980s in condemning all modern civilization, while simultaneously finding solace in the possible revival of a humane Atlantis.

Pohvala Knezu Lazaru (1402) (Eulogy to Prince Lazar)
Serbian poem by Jefimija the Nun (c 1349-c 1405). This poem is regarded as among the finest texts of medieval Serbian literature. It was embroidered in gold thread on cloth in 1402 by Jefimija, and decorated simply with a border of vines and leaves. The text itself is strikingly patriotic and poetic. Prince Lazar was killed by the Turks at the Battle of Kosovo in 1389. It praises his qualities as a man and a ruler, and then makes a lengthy and passionate prayer for his help towards his descendants, for land and for the strengthening of the Orthodox Church. It apologizes for the modesty of the gift, and remembers with gratitude how Lazar took Jefimija into his court after her husband, the despot Uglješa, a minor ruler, had been killed in battle against the Turks in 1371. The last part is personal, immediate and dignified in tone.

Pointon, Robert ▷Rooke, Daphne

Polcz, Alaine (born 1921)
Hungarian novelist. Polcz works as a child psychologist in Budapest. She is married to the writer Miklós Mészöly. Her novel, *Asszony a Fronton* (*Woman on the Battlefront*), is a World War II memoir, and was published to great acclaim in Hungary in 1991. The book describes a woman's life on the front – the hunger, lice, cold and dirt – and the brutality of the occupying Russian soldiers towards women, which had been unmentionable under Soviet rule. A twenty-page extract from the novel is published in English in *Storm: New Writing from East and West* (Vol. 3), edited by Joanna Labon.

Poletti, Syria (born 1921)
Argentinian writer. She spent her childhood and adolescence in Italy, between the Dolomites and Venice, which strongly influenced her work. She emigrated to Argentina in 1945, and after experiencing harsh treatment as an Italian immigrant in several cities she moved to Buenos Aires. She graduated in Spanish and Italian in Cordoba, became a radio and newspaper journalist, and then began to publish in well-known magazines. She later became a distinguished professor at the University of Los Angeles.

In 1953 she won a contest with an anthology of children's literature, *Veinte cuentos infantiles* (1955) (*Twenty Infant Stories*). Her story *Rojo en la salina* (1964) (*Red in the Salt Mine*), afterwards included in *Historias en rojo* (1967) (*Stories in Red*), formed part of the anthology *Cuentos de crimen y misterio* (*Stories of Crime and Mystery*), together with work by Jorge Luis Borges (1899–1986). *Botella al mar* (*Bottle to the Sea*), another anthology of children's stories, won the Donzel Prize in Spain. Many of the stories were included in anthologies, such as *Así escríben las mujeres* (*Thus Women Write*), with work by ▷Silvina Bullrich, ▷Marta Lynch and ▷Olga Orozco, among others. The anthology of Latin American women writers *Puerta aberta* (1986) (*Open Door*) included her story '*Tren de medianoche*' ('Midnight Train'). *Gente conmigo* (1962) (*People With Me*) won the Losada International Prize and the second City Prize, was made into a film, and was also adapted for radio and television, as many of her works have been. It describes an old woman, probably based on her Italian grandmother, who sets an example and high values for the young girl in the story. This figure of an old woman is portrayed as a symbol of wisdom, imagination and security, and a means towards self-realization. She occurs in several of the author's short stories, and in her novel *Extraño oficio (Crónicas de una obsesión)* (1971) (*Strange Duty, Chronicle of an Obsession*). This saga of Italian immigrants in Argentina was highly acclaimed, and Poletti has often been acknowledged as an outstanding author on this topic. Two of her children's books deal with Italian immigration in Argentina: *Inambú busca novio* (1966) (*Inambú Seeks a Boyfriend*) and *El rey que prohibió los globos* (1987) (*The King who Forbade*

Balloons). *Taller de imaginería* (1977) (*Imagery Workshop*) is a collection of some of her short stories and newspaper interviews.

Since the 1970s she has mainly dedicated herself to young readers. The majority of her female narrators reminisce about their adolescence. Her style has been considered realistic and authentic, as in her short stories in *Gente conmigo*, and in her novel *Línea del fuego* (1964) (*Line of Fire*).

Other works: *Reportajes supersónicos* (1972) (*Supersonic Reports*) and *El juguete misterioso* (1977) (*The Mysterious Toy*).

Policy and Passion (1881)
Australian novel by ▷Rosa Praed. This is considered to be Praed's best novel and is set in Leichardt's Land (Queensland). It concerns the romance of Honoria Longleat, daughter of Thomas Longleat (ex-convict but now Premier of the state) and Hardress Barrington, a scheming Englishman. Barrington compromises Honoria, but she is saved from scandal by her faithful Australian suitor, Dyson Maddox. The pattern of a naive colonial girl seduced, or almost seduced, by a suave Englishman is a common one in Praed's work, and has been seen to symbolize the relationship between the old world and the new. Although the plot of *Policy and Passion* is the stereotyped one of romance, the novel is redeemed by the characterization of its heroine, and by its tough perception of colonial politics.

Polidouri, Maria (1902–1930)
Greek poet. Born in Kalamata into an educated family, her first poem appeared when she was only thirteen. At fifteen she published a whole anthology of poems, *Margerites*. Refusing her parents' plans to make her a teacher she went to Athens to study law, working in a municipal office. In Athens she lived a free and independent life, rebelling against the strict standards to which women were then expected to conform. She nevertheless wrote conventional romantic poetry. She fell in love with the famous poet, Kostas Karyotakis, who refused to marry her because he suffered from venereal disease. Deeply disappointed, she nevertheless maintained a good friendship with him. She became engaged to another man but left him and went to live in Paris, where she wrote many poems in the process of recovering from her love for Karyotakis. Suffering from tuberculosis, she returned to Greece, where after a short stay in a hospital she died in 1930. Her collections of poems, *Dying Trills* (1928) and *Echo and Chaos* (1929), reveal her quest for love, her disappointments and her retreat from life's expectations. Her writing is always personal and emotional, deeply charged with a sense of loss and disillusionment.

Polier, Marie-Elisabeth, Chanoinesse de Heiliggraben (1742–1817)
French-Swiss prose fiction writer, translator and journalist. Born in Lausanne, most of her published works are translations from German, including the novel by ▷Sophie de La Roche, *Eugénie, ou la résignation* (1795) (*Eugénie, or Resignation*). She was principal editor of the periodical *Journal littéraire de Lausanne* (*Literary Journal of Lausanne*) from 1794 to 1798. With J. de Maimieux she produced the short-lived *Bibliothèque germanique* (1800–1801) (*German Library*), *Midi industrieux* and *Gazette britannique* (*The British Gazette*).

Other works: *Recueil d'histoirettes* (1792) (*Collected Short Stories*); *Le Club des Jacobins, comédie* (1792) (*The Jacobin Club, a Comedy*); *La Sylphide ou l'ange gardien* (1795) (*The Sylph or the Guardian Angel*); *Mythologie des Indous* (trans.) (1809) (*Hindu Mythology*).

Polimita, D. ▷Alonso, Dora

Pollard, Velma (born 1937)
Caribbean poet, short story writer and critic, born in ▷Jamaica. She is currently Senior Lecturer in Education at the University of the West Indies. Her publications include three anthologies for schools. She has published a collection of poems, *Crown Point* (1988), and a volume of short stories, *Considering Women* (1989). Her work has also appeared in *Jamaica Journal*, *BIM*, *Arts Review* and *Caribbean Quarterly*. She is a contributor to ▷*Jamaica Woman: An Anthology of Poems* and ▷*Creation Fire*.

She is the sister of ▷Erna Brodber.

Pollock, Sharon (born 1936)
Canadian dramatist, director and actress, born Sharon Chalmers in Fredericton, New Brunswick. She attended the University of New Brunswick, and now lives in Calgary, Alberta. She taught at the University of Alberta in Edmonton, and the Banff School of Fine Arts, where she was head of the Banff Centre's Playwrights Colony for four years. She has written numerous plays with a strong social and political impulse, many of them embedded in historical incident. *Walsh* (1973) is about 19th-century government mistreatment of Canada's indigenous peoples; *The Komagata Maru Incident* (1976) explored an example of Canadian racism against Asians in 1914; *One Tiger to a Hill* (1979) relives a hostage-taking incident in a maximum security prison. *Blood Relations* (1981), a meta-drama on US axe-murderess Lizzie Borden, won the Governor General's Award for Drama. It serves as a bridge to *Whiskey Six Cadenza* (1983) and *Doc* (1984), plays that are concerned with more personal social issues. The women in these plays struggle against the linearity of a male-determined world.
Bib: Bessai, D., in ▷*A Mazing Space*.

Polluted Sea, Sufferers and the Pure Land (1965–1966)
Work by Japanese writer Ishimure Michiko (born 1927). Minamata is a city facing Ariake Bay, where chemical waste from the Chisso factory has caused a terrible disease, *Minamatabyo*, since the

1950s. Ishimure was born and grew up there, and feels very deeply about Minamata. After visiting the afflicted, she founded a society in order to confront the polluters. She describes suffering villagers and fisher-people – especially a boy, Yamanaka Kuhei, a blind child with a distorted body – contrasting them with the beautiful natural setting. Her creative approach connects the narrative, written in a regional dialect, with relevant social matters.

Polotan, Kerima
Filipino fiction writer, essayist and editor. Although she has raised ten children, she has consistently sustained her commitment to writing. Of the conflict between her writing career and her attempts to raise a family, she noted in 1975 that, once seated at the broken-down treadle sewing machine table that serves as her desk, she felt 'beyond the reach of many things, the small despairs that visit the young wife with not too much money but more children than she bargained for, trying valiantly to cope with a motherhood that she secretly resented'. Yet 'through my [family and marriage] I grew, as a woman and as a person'.

She has won several literary awards, including a major award for her novel *The Hand of the Enemy* (1961). Her other published works include *Stories* (1968), and two collections of her journalistic pieces and essays, *Author's Choice* (1971) and *Adventures in a Forgotten Country* (1975).

Polwhele, Elizabeth (?1651–1691)
English Restoration dramatist. Polwhele seems to have written three plays, *Elysium* (now lost) the rhymed tragedy *The Faythfull Virgins* (manuscript), and the comedy *The Frolicks*, performed at the Dukes Theatre in 1671. The play features a rake, Rightwit, who is the father of illegitimate children, and Claribell, a wity heroine. With ▷Katherine Philips and ▷Frances Boothby, she was one of the women writing for the stage in the early Restoration period.
Bib: Milhouse, J. and Hume R.D. (eds), *The Frolicks* (1977).

Polygamy (West Africa)
The practice of a man having more than one wife in traditional African societies was rooted in the need to produce many children as labour and to ensure the continuance of the family. A high rate of infant mortality meant that many more children were born than survived. There were undoubted benefits for women in a polygamous household – companionship, sharing of childcare and domestic work and so on – though the custom also bred rivalry and dissent.

While polygamy is intrinsic to Islam, the coming of Christianity to Africa brought with it the concept of monogamous marriage. There exists today an uneasy combination of traditional polygamy (having more than one wife) and polygyny (having several woman, who may not necessarily be wives). The aspiration of many educated women to a relationship of love and equality with a man is a dominant theme in women's writing, as is the disappointment and disillusion of the reality. ▷Mariama Bâ in *So Long a Letter* (1981) writes poignantly of the different responses to polygamy available to Moslem women – essentially either to leave the marriage or to accept it and suffer. ▷Ama Ata Aidoo's Esi in ▷*Changes* chooses to become a second wife as a practical alternative to the demands of a monogamous marriage, but she too discovers the reality is unacceptable.

Pombo, Pilar
Contemporary Spanish dramatist. Pombo was one of the few female dramatists to have her work staged in the 1980s. Her play ▷*Una comedia de encargo* (1988) (*A Commissioned Play*) was highly successful when put on in Madrid.

Pompeia, Núria (born 1938)
Spanish writer and newspaper cartoonist. Born in Barcelona into a well-to-do family. Pompeia's *Cinc cèntims* (1981) (*Five Cents*) is a collection of twelve short stories which satirize social conformism. Her novel *Inventari de l'últim dia* (1986) (*Inventory of the Last Day*) reflects lucidly on the Existential 'lostness' of her generation.
▷Catalan women's writing

Poniatowska, Elena (born 1933)
French-born Mexican fiction writer. Elena Poniatowska Amor's father was French, of Polish ancestry, and her mother, Paula Amor, was a Mexican raised in France. In 1942 she moved with her family to Mexico City. She studied in an English school, and later at a Catholic convent in Philadelphia, USA, talked French with her well-to-do family, and learned Spanish from their maids. She felt like a foreigner in Mexico, and lacked information on its cultural background. She therefore benefited from her friendship with the servants, and from her career as a journalist, working for the *Excélsior* and *Novedades*. This gave her a valuable insight into the use of language, and the knowledge necessary to become a social writer dealing with the less privileged classes of Mexico City.

Her first work, *Lilus Kikus* (1954), comprises twelve imaginative short-stories about the experience of a young girl conforming to society during adolescence. They were later expanded into twenty stories as *Los cuentos de Lilus Kikus* (1967) (*The Stories of Lilus Kikus*). With the publication of one of her main novels, *Hasta no verte, Jesús mío* (1969) (*Until We Meet Again*, 1987), about the Mexican-Indian voice, she established herself as one of the most important Latin American writers of this century. This novel, written in the present tense, is a first-person narration by Jesusa Palancares, a poor, illiterate woman born at the beginning of this century, who recalls her life in the 1960s. The book has been widely reviewed, and the protagonist has been considered a prototype for a lower-class heroine and social victim.

Other works: *Palabras cruzadas* (1961) (*Crossed Words*); *Todo empezó el domingo* (1963) (*It All Began on Sunday*); *La noche de Tlatelolco; testimonios de historia oral* (1971) (*Massacre in Mexico*, 1975); *Querido Diego, te abraza Quiela* (1976) (*Dear Diego*, 1986), *Gaby Brimmer* (1979); *Fuerte es el silencio* (1980) (*Silence is Loud*); *Domingo siete* (1982) (*Sunday the 7th*); *El último guajolote* (1982) (*The Last Idiot*); *La 'Flor de Lis'* (1988) (*The 'Fleur de Lis'*), and *Nada, nadie* (1988) (*Nothing, Nobody*).

Ponsonby, Sarah ▷Ladies of Llangollen, The

Pontus und Sidonie (c 1450)
A novel translated by ▷Eleonore von Österreich into German from a French *chanson de geste*, *Pontius et la belle Sidonic*. A tale of chivalry and courtly love, it relates the adventures of Prince Pontus, who woos Princess Sidonia. When suspected of trying to seduce her, he indignantly leaves the court for seven years, flees from the Moors, and arrives in Britain, where he successfully fends off their attack. Upon his return he marries Sidonia, but promises to consummate the marriage only after successfully reconquering his kingdom. The high moral tone of this novel found a very receptive readership in Germany, and between 1483 and 1792 it was reprinted twenty-four times.

Poole, Elizabeth (fl 1648)
English prophet who went before the General Council of the army at the end of the English Civil War (1642–1646 and 1648–1651) to argue that they should not try the king because he was as a husband to the kingdom. She wrote the famous lines 'You never heard that a wife might put away her husband, as he is the head of her body.' Compare ▷Elinor Channel.

Her publications include: *A Vision* (1648); *A Prophecie Touching the Death of King Charles* (1649), and *An Alarum of War* (1649).
Bib: Mack, Phyllis, in Eley G. and Lamont, W. (ed.), *Reviving the English Revolution*.

Poole, Fiona Farrell (born 1947)
New Zealand poet, fiction writer and dramatist. Fiona Farrell Poole has spent most of her life in New Zealand working as a secondary school teacher and writing. She has published stage and radio plays, collections of short stories, and poetry. Like many of her contemporaries, Poole challenges gender roles and investigates different ways of perception in her writing, often with a historical dimension focusing on the history of women. Her poetry often displays a narrative quality. Poole's short fictions have been included in a number of major anthologies and she has won several literary awards for fiction, including the American Express Award.

Publications: *Passengers* (play) (1986); *Cutting Out* (poems) (1987); *The Rock Garden* (1989).

Popp, Adelheid (1869–1939)
Austrian writer and feminist. The fifteenth daughter of a weaver, she left school at the age of ten, and from then on worked in factories and as a maid, supplementing her earnings with needlework, despite increasing exhaustion and ill health. In her twenties she joined the workers' movement and, in 1892, became one of the founders of a journal for women workers. She began publishing essays proclaiming radical socialist and feminist views, and as a result was repeatedly put into prison. In 1909 she published, anonymously, the autobiographical *Jugendgeschichte einer Arbeiterin, von ihr selbst erzählt* (*Story of the Youth of a Working Woman as Told by Herself*). It is one of the earliest firsthand accounts of the miseries endured by women workers in an industrialized country.

Popular theatre (Southern Africa)
Popular theatre is a continuation of African ▷oral tradition, whose religious rituals, praise poems and imaginative narratives included well-developed dramatic elements. Although this popular tradition expressed itself in urban areas from the early 20th century, it became a vibrant force of cultural resistance during the 1970s, with the rise of ▷Black Consciousness. Popular theatre includes plays staged at alternative theatres (the Market Theatre in Johannesburg, the Space Theatre in Cape Town, no longer in existence, and the Upstairs Theatre in Durban) as well as township drama, staged in community halls, and also includes productions taken into the rural areas. It originates in workshopped productions rather than script, and does not always issue in written form. It generally deploys song and dance, along with political slogans and direct political imagery, and blurs distinctions between dramatist, director and actor.
Unscripted drama developed as a way in which people might act out everyday experiences and issues, in order to formulate them and to reach out for consensus. It was also a way to avoid censorship. The history of popular theatre, at least until the 1990s, is fraught with political harassment of the severest kind: police hounded theatre group members, and troops sometimes closed down community halls, beating up or intimidating actors and audience. Far from receiving state support, popular theatre has operated despite the state's prohibitions and reactive violence. In the early days, productions moved constantly from venue to venue. Yet, in the face of all this, popular theatre has done more than any other cultural form to reach a wide, often not literate, audience, in the virtual absence of television, radio and film.

Because of its informal structure, it is difficult to gauge the extent of the role played by women in popular theatre. The first well-known production involving women was *Imfuduso*, created and acted by a group of women from Crossroads, a squatter village in Cape Town.

Staged at the Market and the Space in 1978, the play portrayed the experiences of Crossroads women who were forcibly removed from their homes under one of the state's resettlement programmes. A later, particularly well-known production was *You Strike the Woman, You Strike the Rock*, performed in 1986 at the Market, the Baxter Theatre in Cape Town (the Space having closed down), and later at the Edinburgh Festival, also travelling to the US in 1989. Workshopped by director Phyllis Klotz and the Sabikwa Players – Nomvula Qosha, Tobeka Maqhutyana, and Poppy Tsira – it presents the daily experiences of urban black women who are trying to support their families. Problems portrayed are specific to them as women, and it is thus that they find common strength. The play ends on a defiant note as they chant:

Hey Botha
Hey Botha man
What are you trying to do?
When you strike the woman
You strike the rock.

The last lines are the words used in 1956 by the women of FEDSAW (Federation of South African Women), when they marched, 10,000 strong, on the Union Buildings in Pretoria, campaigning against the Pass Law.

Among established women directors and groups, besides Klotz and the Sabikwa Players, are Saira Essa, director and dramatist who runs the Upstairs Theatre in Durban, ▷Gcina Mhlophe, who was recently placed as resident director at the Market Theatre, and Mavis Taylor of the University of Cape Town Drama School, whose Little Theatre Tours takes theatre to outlying areas. Essa's unit runs classes in literacy and communication as well as in drama. Much popular theatre has a direct educational function, as well as a rallying one. In Zimbabwe as well, leading up to and after independence, adult education programmes started using vernacular drama to achieve their ends. The Women's Action Group in Zimbabwe, established in the first part of the 1980s, used dramatic production as a way of establishing bonds between rural and urban women, for instance.

In many cases, actors involved in popular theatre are not paid, but decide to work together in the hopes of making a success of the production. This is the case with Doreen Mazibuko's *Qhewukani Magwalandini* (*Rise Up, Cowards*). The play examines the fate of a black family whose members come into contact with a black policeman, either as servants or suspects. In other cases, actors are employed by a specific theatre company, as is the case with the production, *Inyanga: Women in Africa* (*inyanga* means healer), directed by Barney Simon of the Market Theatre and workshopped and acted by Gcina Mhlophe, Jennifer Ferguson, Sophie Mcgina and Thembi Mtshali. In still other cases, trade union workers engage in dramatic

production as part of union activity. This is a male-dominated field, but since 1983, ▷Nise Malange has been part of such a group. Some of the plays are summarized in *Organize and Act: The Natal Workers' Theatre Movement, 1983–1987* (1989).

Some ▷children's and juvenile plays have been composed, by ▷Fatima Dike, Gcina Mhlophe and Hope Dube, who is originally from Zimbabwe.

Porete, Marguerite (died 1310)

French author of religious writing. She is said to be the most neglected of the great writers of the 13th century. Also known as Margarita de Hannonia, because she came from the Hainaut region, she is thought to have been born in Valenciennes. Marguerite was burnt at the stake in the first-known formal *auto-da-fé* ('act of the faith', burning of a heretic by the Inquisition) in Paris. She was identified as the author of the astonishingly popular *Mirouer des Simples Ames* (*Mirror of Simple Souls*), a work of poetic prose, dialogue and lyric written between 1285 and 1295 and condemned as heretical around 1300 by the Bishop of Cambrai. All known copies were burnt. The text, which has survived only in late manuscript copies and translations, advocates the 'complete and perfect passivity of the will in attaining the divine experience'. The sacramental ministry of the Church in the final stages of the soul's ascent to perfection was therefore rendered unnecessary. The book also gives an erotic depiction of divine love. Marguerite persisted, nevertheless, in sending it to prominent churchmen, even after she had been forbidden to disseminate her ideas further on pain of excommunication. In prison, she refused to reply to her inquisitors. Nothing is known of her social status, though it has been suggested that the support she received from several prominent churchmen indicates that she was well-born. Described at her trial as a '▷*béguine*', she was probably a lay follower of the apostolic life, and it is known that she belonged to the freer religious communities of the time. In imitation of Christ, Marguerite seems to have led a life of poverty and abstinence. Her work indicates that she must have been highly educated, especially in theology, and conversant with the court literature of her day.
Bib: Bryant, G., 'The French Heretic Beguine' in Wilson, K.M., *Medieval Women Writers*, pp. 204–27; Dronke, P., *Women Writers of the Middle Ages*, pp. 202–29.

Pornography (Ancient Greece)

Several authors of works of Greek erotica are purportedly women: ▷Elephantis, ▷Philaenis. They may have taken the form of courtesans' memoirs, like the 18th-century British writer John Cleland's *Fanny Hill* (1748 and 1749), and thus may not have been written by women.
▷Pamphila

Portal, Marta (born 1930)
Spanish journalist, literary critic and novelist.
The main themes of Portal's work are female
independence, female sexuality and adultery.
Her main works are: *A tientas y a ciegas* (1966)
(*Blindly, Gropingly*); *El malmuerto* (1967)
(*Killed in Error*); *A ras de las sombras* (1969)
(*Level with the Shadows*); *Ladridos a la luna* (1970)
(*Baying at the Moon*); *La veintena* (1973)
(*A Score of Tales*), and *Un espacio erótico* (1983)
(*An Erotic Space*).

Porte du fond, La (1988) (***The Far Door***)
Novel by French writer ▷Christiane Rochefort.
Written in confessional style, Rochefort's most
recent work explores the nature of sexual abuse.
The novel retains the colloquial language,
narrative structure and value system of her earlier
works, but light-hearted humour is replaced by
black comedy, and the feminist analysis of power
relations is more explicit.

Portefeuille, Le (1674) (***The Portfolio***)
▷Desjardins, Marie-Catherine Hortense

Porter, Katherine Anne (c 1890–1980)
US short story writer, novelist, journalist,
screenwriter and translator. Born in Indian Creek,
Texas, Porter was raised in poverty by her
paternal grandmother. She was educated in
convent schools, but at age sixteen she ran away,
was briefly married, and subsequently earned her
living as a journalist on newspapers in Chicago,
Illinois and Denver, Colorado.

From 1918 to 1921 she became involved
in revolutionary politics in Mexico, which
provided her with material for a number of short
stories and for *Outline of Mexican Popular Arts and
Crafts* (1922). The strand of primitivism
associated with Porter's Mexican-Indian and
Hispanic characters remained a feature of her
work. In the late 1920s she travelled in Europe,
settling in Paris during the early 1930s, where
she became friends with the English modernist
writer Ford Madox Ford. Porter also contributed
to leftist journals, such as *The New Republic* and
The Nation.

In 1966 her *Collected Stories* (1965) was awarded
the Pulitzer Prize. Like ▷*Ship of Fools* (1962),
stories in *Flowering Judas and Other Stories* (1930)
and ▷*The Old Order* (1958) reveal the self's
cultural displacement in the modern world.
Stories such as 'Flowering Judas', 'He' and 'The
Jilting of Granny Weatherall' feature women who
realize that they have deluded themselves about
their lives. Much of Porter's fiction focuses on
such a moment of epiphany.

Other works include *Noon Wine* (1937),
Pale Horse, Pale Rider (1939), *The Leaning Tower,
and Other Stories* (1944), *The Days Before* (1952),
A Defense of Circe (1955), *Holiday* (1962) and
Collected Essays and Occasional Writings (1970).
Bib. Givner, Joan, *Katherine Anne Porter: A
Life.*

Porter, Sarah (fl 1791)
North American poet. Believed to be a resident of
Plymouth, Massachusetts, she is known solely
through her one extant book, ▷*The Royal Penitent*
(1791). The writing reflects her Puritan values
and literary heritage, but she moves beyond
religious themes and enters the prevailing debate
on the establishment of a political order, asserting
the need for moral leadership.

Portnoy, Ethel (born 1927)
Dutch prose writer, dramatist and essay writer.
She was born in Philadelphia, and studied English
in New York and ethnology in Paris. She has been
married to the Dutch writer Rudy Kousbroek.
She worked for Unesco (United Nations
Educational, Scientific, and Cultural
Organization), but became a full-time writer in
1962. Portnoy published widely in magazines on,
among other subjects, female writers and, together
with ▷Hannes Meinkema and Hanneke van
Buuren, founded the literary-feminist magazine
Chrysallis (1978–1981). Her publications include
the collection of stories *Steen en been* (1971) (*Stone
and Bone*), 93 contemporary folk-tales, *Broodje Aap*
(1978) (*The Monkey Burger*), and stories and
sketches, *Vliegende vellen* (1983) (*Soaring Sheets*).
Travel stories appeared in *Vluchten* (1984)
(*Travels*) and *Rook over Rusland* (1990) (*Smoke Over
Russia*).

Portrait d'un inconnu (1948) ▷*Portrait of a
Man Unknown* (1958)

Portrait of a Man Unknown (1958)
Translation of *Portrait d'un inconnu* (1948), novel
by French writer ▷Nathalie Sarraute. In his
preface to the second edition of this work, Sartre
describes Sarraute as an 'anti-novelist'. A narrator
tries to look beyond words and appearances to
understand the true nature of a father–daughter
relationship which fascinates him. However, his
efforts prove completely unsuccessful.

Portrait of Dora (1991)
Translation of *Portrait de Dora* (1976). ▷Hélène
Cixous' dramatization of Freud's (1856–1939)
controversial case history, *Fragment of an Analysis
of a Case of Hysteria*, ('*Dora*'), which has been a
focus of feminist debate about the value of
psychoanalytic accounts of femininity and the
possibility of a feminine language and subjectivity.
Interweaving the voices of Dora, Freud, her father
and his lover, Frau K., Cixous's play investigates
and challenges the process by which Dora's sexual
identity is fixed through language and within
familial relationships. The staging of the case
history reveals the complicity of Freud and
▷psychoanalysis in that process. The feminist
critic Morag Shiach writes of *Portrait of Dora*,
'Cixous has tried to stage the process of sexual
differentiation, to show the possibility of refusal,
of transgression, of moving beyond the Law.'
Bib: Freud, Sigmund, 'Dora' Pelican Freud
Library, Vol. 8; Gallop, Jane, *Feminism and*

Psychoanalysis: The daughter's seduction; Shiach, Morag, 'Their "symbolic" exists, it holds power – we, the sowers of disorder, know it only too well' in *Between Feminism and Psychoanalysis*, ed. Teresa Brennan.

Possession: A Romance (1990)

Novel by English writer ▷A.S. Byatt. Winner of the Booker Prize for Fiction in 1990, the novel interweaves Victorian and contemporary narratives of the literary and literary critical industries. The central theme, suggested by its title, is that of ownership and obsession, and the novel foregrounds the complexity of the relationship between author and commentator. Combining references and allusions from literature, myth, history and the visual arts with a reconstruction of Victorian literary circles, Byatt examines the roles of the biographer and the critic: their treatment of the 'author' and the role of biographical material in traditional literary criticism and contemporary critical readings of literary texts, particularly those informed by ▷post-structuralist thinking and concerned with questions of identity and gender.

Post, Lydia Minturn (fl 1776–1783)

North American diarist. Excerpts from her journal have been collected in ▷*Personal Recollections of the American Revolution*, which details her experiences on Long Island during the revolutionary years. A strong Patriot, she recounts for her absent husband the intricacies of the political situation and her attempts to maintain some sense of normality in her life. Her journal also discloses her eventual conversion to Quakerism and pacifism.

Posthumous Works of Ann Eliza Bleecker, The (1793)

Collected by her daughter, the poet and dramatist ▷Margaretta Bleecker Faugeres, North American poet and novelist ▷Ann Eliza Schuyler Bleecker's late 18th-century writings are a study in one woman's use of her literary talents to assuage the psychological distress that embroiled her after the death of her infant daughter during the American Revolution. Included in the collection are a novel, ▷*The History of Maria Kittle*, and several poems. Often written for family members, Bleecker's poetry expresses her hatred of war, her despair at the tragic loss of her daughter, and her anger at friends who try to quell her grief, asserting that 'the mollifying hand of Time' never 'wipes off common sorrows' nor could 'cancel mine'. Appended to this collection are several works by Faugeres. The daughter's writings include poetry such as 'To the Moon' and 'The Hudson' that is romantic in style and content, and her 'Memoir', which details her life and her mother's.
▷*Belisarius: A Tragedy*; Captivity narratives

Postmodernism (Brazil)

In Brazilian literature, this corresponds to the third phase of ▷modernism, beginning with the abstract and metaphysical poetry of the ▷1945 Generation of poets and the fourth phase which included the novels of ▷Clarice Lispector, which experiment with language and literary techniques.

Postmodernism

A term, the meaning and very existence of which is much contested. Generally speaking, postmodernity is a condition where historical truth, tradition and authenticity are put into question. Debates surrounding the application of this term fall into three broad categories. To describe an artistic movement *after* ▷modernism, whose aesthetic is marked by the interpenetration of high/low cultures, fragmentation and multivocality, no longer secured by the unifying mythic structures of modernism. This cultural position apparently abandons the avant-garde for an ambivalent place in 'commercial' culture. Postmodernism is also used to refer to an historical epoch or phase of capitalism which necessarily incorporates the first category as one of its defining characteristics. In philosophy, postmodernism is related to a questioning of the ethics and politics of the Enlightenment, and the demand that philosophy be more attuned to 'difference'.

Feminist debates converge with definitions of postmodernism over the linkage with issues of heterogeneity and fragmentation. Feminism can either be read as representing a 'minoritarian' discourse that socially and culturally intervened to produce the condition of postmodernism, or, that postmodernism represents the questioning of feminism as an homogeneous category not itself attuned to the politics of difference. In both cases, the terms of postmodern debate are frequently contested on the basis of its potential destruction of the ground for a politics of agency or identity.

Feminists writing about postmodernism include ▷Alice Jardine, whose book *Gynesis: Configurations of Woman in Modernity* (1985) raises the possibility that 'woman' as a discursive concept exemplifies the instability and plurality of meaning that is the condition of postmodernity. In *Feminine Fictions: Revisiting the Postmodern* (1989), Patricia Waugh critically reviews male theories of postmodernity in the light of women's fiction, which is seen both to pre-empt and exceed postmodernism's insistence on the dissolution of the unified ▷subject. Waugh's main thesis is that, because women have always been displaced to a position on the margins of patriarchal culture, they do not display the same nostalgia for the unified subject that she detects in the writing of male postmodernists, such as Fredric Jameson.
Bib: François, J.L., *The Postmodern Condition*; Jameson, F., 'Postmodernism, or The Cultural Logic of Late Capitalism'.

Postmodernismo

In Spanish-speaking countries, the period 1910–1930. It differs from ▷postmodernism in Brazil. ▷Juana de Ibarbourou, ▷Alfonsina Storni and ▷Delmiro Agustini made a significant contribution to the movement.

Poststructuralism

Poststructuralism moves away from structuralism's quest for common patterns in language and culture towards an analysis of their difference. The term encompasses a range of developments in critical theory, including ▷psychoanalysis, ▷deconstruction and ▷French feminism. In poststructuralist theory, meanings are cultural and learned. In critical practice this produces a shift from the author as source of meaning to an analysis of how meanings are constructed in language. French feminism, for example, is concerned with the inscription of women's psychic difference in writing.

▷Coward; Rosalind; Felman, Shoshana
Bib: ▷Weedon, C., *Feminist Practice and Poststructuralist Theory*.

Potiki (1986)

Novel by New Zealand writer ▷Patricia Grace. *Potiki* is Grace's second novel. It was awarded joint third prize at the James Wattie Book of the Year Awards in New Zealand in 1986. Described as an 'impressionist' novel, *Potiki* uses a layered form of narration, and each chapter is narrated by a different character. Like all Grace's fiction, *Potiki* is concerned with the relationship of the family to the community, and of the individual to the group, as Maori culture values group identity as the basis of society. The novel is about the resistance of a coastal tribal community to developers who want to buy their land. Although offers of money are followed by violence and threats, *Potiki* represents Maori community as becoming stronger for its determination to retain its traditional lands and the cultural values they embody, and shows its resistance to development strengthening individual identity within a shared context.

▷Maori literature

Potiki, Roma (born 1958)

New Zealand poet. Roma Potiki (also known as Te Arawa) has been publishing occasional poetry since the mid-1980s, and her work has appeared in a number of major anthologies of New Zealand poetry. Potiki lectures in drama and women's studies at Victoria University, Wellington, has been active in Maori and experimental theatre groups, and has exhibited widely as a cloak maker, with cloaks held in several permanent collections. Her poetry is written in English and uses open form. She has said of her work: 'In my writing I seek a place for myself in relation to the world and within that world I include my *taha Maori* [a political term for "Maori culture"].'

▷Maori literature

Pougy, Liane de (1869–1950)

French novelist. De Pougy is a member of the group of lesbian writers who worked in Paris in the early years of the 20th century, and she also achieved celebrity as an upper-class prostitute or *demi-mondaine*. Her novel *Idylle Saphique* (1901) (*Sapphic Idyll*) has recently been republished by ▷Éditions des Femmes, and it is a thinly disguised account of her affair with ▷Natalie Barney. Annhine de Lys, the heroine, is a courtesan, who lounges in a boudoir full of lace and frills, but is disgusted by her work as a prostitute. She escapes into the arms of the adoring Flossie, dressed as a page. Their relationship is never consummated, and Annhine dies as a result of pregnancy, the 'poison' left by one of her lovers. The text represents lesbianism simultaneously as perverse and as a higher, ecstatic form of love. De Pougy's diaries, *Mes cahiers bleus* (*My Blue Notebooks*), were published in 1977.
Bib: Benstock, Shari, *Women of the Left Bank: Paris, 1900–1940*

Poulain, Mademoiselle (18th century)

French prose fiction writer, essayist and poet. She published a volume of *Anecdotes intéressantes* (1786) (*Interesting Anecdotes*) about 'conjugal love', and an epistolary novel, *Lettres de Mme la comtesse de la Rivière* (1776) (*Letters of the Countess de la Rivière*), as well as a pedagogical work, *Tableau de la parole* (1783) (*The Picture of Speech*), explaining how to use play in the teaching of reading. She also wrote an abridged history of Port-Royal (1786). Her last publication was a collection of her poetry, *Poésies diverses* (1787) (*Collected Poems*).

Powers of Horror (1982)

Translation of French psychoanalyst and cultural theorist ▷Julia Kristeva's *Pouvoirs de l'horreur* (1980) by Leon Roudiez. Kristeva looks at theology and anthropology as well as ▷psychoanalysis and literature, in order to demonstrate how the maternal is ritually repudiated, or 'abjected', across a wide range of cultural and social practices. While 'abjection' offers a powerful account of society's misogyny, Kristeva also, more contentiously, insists that a repudiation of the maternal is necessary in order to prevent the onset of an anti-social form of psychosis such as, for example, she discovers in the fascism of French writer Céline (1894–1961). Thus *Powers of Horror* stands as a forceful warning against the romanticization of the maternal which her earlier book ▷*Revolution in Poetic Language* (1984) might have been said to foster. Kristeva's emphasis lies here not so much in privileging the archaic and anarchic over the socio-symbolic (▷symbolic), but on the unsteady hold that cultural formations and artistic practices have on our desires.

▷*Tales of Love*

Pozzi, Antonia (1912–1938)

Italian poet. Born in Milan, she attended university there. She committed suicide at the age of twenty-six, having written some very promising poetry and a critical work on Flaubert. Her poetry, published posthumously, seems semi-autobiographical in tone, and is at once realistic and lyrical. ▷Elsa Morante wrote appreciatively of her work, praising its controlled emotion. Her works are: *Parole* (1939) (*Words*); *Flaubert: la formazione letteraria* (1940) (*Flaubert's Literary Make-Up*).

Pozzo, Modesta ▷ Fonte, Moderata

Prado, Adélia (born 1936)
Brazilian poet, short story writer and chronicler. Her full name is Adélia Luzia Prado de Freitas, and she describes life in the hinterland of Brazil from a feminine perspective, and in a spontaneous and naïve style. In her first book of poetry, *Bagagem* (1976) (*Luggage*), she places women in the domestic and unsophisticated environment of a housewife, and explores the pattern of spiritual relationships linking everyday life, the family and God.
    Other works: *A lapinha de Jesus*, with Lázaro Barreto (1971) (*Jesus's Grotto*); *O coração disparado* (1978) (*The Shooting Heart*); *Solte os cachorros* (1979) (*Release the Dogs*); *Cacos para um vitral* (1980)(*Fragments for a Stained-glass Window*); *Terra de Sante Cruz* (1981) (*Land of Santa Cruz*); *Os componentes da banda* (1984) (*The Members of the Band*); *O Pelicano* (1987) (*The Pelican*), and *A faca no peito* (1988) (*The Knife in the Breast*).

Praed, Rosa (1851–1935)
Australian novelist, autobiographer and dramatist; also wrote under the name Mrs Campbell Praed. Praed is often placed with ▷ Ada Cambridge and ▷ Jessie Couvreur ('Tasma') as a romance writer of the turn of the century. Born in southern Queensland, the daughter of Thomas Murray-Prior, a prominent pastoralist, public servant and politician, Praed was brought up on outback stations and in Brisbane, before marrying Arthur Campbell Praed. Her unhappy experiences of marriage and bush life on an isolated station are recorded in her first novel, *An Australian Heroine* (1880), in *The Romance of a Station* (1889) and in her autobiographical works, *Australian Life: Black and White* (1885) and ▷ *My Australian Girlhood* (1902). Her comments upon the Australian Aborigines are of great interest.
    Praed settled in London in 1875, was a prominent member of literary and occult circles, and a number of her novels (particularly *Affinities: A Romance of Today*, 1886), demonstrate her interest in the occult. All four of Praed's children died in tragic circumstances and, after leaving her husband, she lived with the spiritual medium, Nancy Haward, whom she believed to be the reincarnation of a Roman slave girl. Of her forty works of fiction, the best-known are ▷ *Policy and Passion* (1881), *The Head Station* (1885), *Affinities* (1885), which contains a portrayal of Oscar Wilde, *The Bond of Wedlock* (1887), which was dramatized as *Ariane* and performed in London in 1888, and was republished in 1987, *Outlaw and Lawmaker* (1893, republished in 1987), *Nulma* (1897), *Fugitive Anne* (1903), and ▷ *Lady Bridget in the Never-Never Land* (1915), which was republished in 1987.
    ▷ Aborigine in non-Aboriginal Australian

women's writing, The; *From the Verandah*; *On Her Selection*; *Peaceful Army, The*; *Penguin Anthology of Australian Women's Writing, The*

'Praier that Maister Bradfords Mother Said and Offered unto God in his Behalfe, a Little before his martyrdome' (1582)
▷ Prayer recorded by Thomas Bentley in his ▷ *Monument of Matrones*. Virtually no information exists about the woman who composed this prayer for her son, the Protestant martyr John Bradford (c 1510–1555). The prayer suggests that, while Bradford's death is not yet imminent, it will be the likely result of his religious convictions. Her prayer seeks forgiveness for her son's sins, and strength for his coming tribulation. Mistress Bradford's prayer stands as a moving testimony to her own religious convictions, as she imitates the biblical Hanna, offering up her son to God.
    ▷ Protestant Reformation

Prairie realism (Canada)
Authenticity is considered to be a staple of women writers on the prairies; the essential critical texts argue strenuously for prairie realism as a means of discerning the movement of women toward an articulation of their space. This critical emplacement has been used to demean the adventurousness of that regional writing, and fails to take into account the underlying argument of critic Henry Kreisel's famous essay: 'The Prairie: a State of Mind'. Certainly, merely capturing that imposing space, haunting and beautiful, in words requires the precepts of ▷ realism. But at the same time, the mirage-like quality of the landscape prohibits the usual simplistic application of replication. What is deemed to be prairie realism is often something quite different: ▷ Nellie McClung sustains a fierce polemical interrogation that can hardly be deemed realistic; ▷ Martha Ostenso arouses the rebellion of land against man; even ▷ Patricia Blondal, in ▷ Flannery O'Connor fashion, makes grotesque the characters in a prairie town. And ▷ Margaret Laurence, who is vaunted as the flag-bearer of prairie realism, exercises a sharp awareness of the act of writing, invention and tale-bearing within the context of her stories. ▷ Gabrielle Roy traces a nuanced subtext full of double language despite her faithfulness to the people and the landscape, and in the poetry of ▷ Anne Szumigalski there is the lively chatter of animal dance. Regional constrictions are almost always imposed on prairie writing, so the full impact of its magical space and its parodic reading of itself and its time is frequently missed by pedestrian critics. It is curious that early writers were more actively ironic in their portrayals than contemporary writers, who feel the weight of realism much more insistently, resulting in the heavy endurance of ▷ Sharon Butala's characters, and the detail of the plays of ▷ Gwen Pharis Ringwood. Perhaps these writers feel pressured to live up to what is expected of them in regional terms. Happily, the stranglehold of realism as a desirable literary end is being

actively undermined by writers like ▷Kristjana Gunnars, ▷Aritha van Herk, ▷Joy Kogawa, and ▷Sharon Riis.

Bib.: Fairbanks, C., *Prairie Women: Images in American and Canadian Fiction.*

Praisesong for the Widow (1983)

Novel by the Caribbean writer ▷Paule Marshall. It is concerned both with the literal journey of the widow, Avey Johnson, on her annual holiday cruise to the Caribbean from the USA, and with the personal and spiritual odyssey of the black, middle-aged, Americanized central character who explores the psychological effects of the traumatic history of the ▷Middle Passage for all those New World people connected with the Afro-Caribbean ▷diaspora. The novel is linked in theme to many other diaspora novels by women writers, such as ▷Michelle Cliff's *Abeng* (1984) and ▷Maryse Condé's ▷*Heremakhonon* (1982).

See Abena Busia, 'What is Your Nation?: Reconnecting Africa and Her Diaspora through Paule Marshall's *Praisesong for the Widow*' in Cheryl Wall (ed.), *Changing Our Own Words* (1989), pp. 196–211. Paule Marshall is celebrated by the noted Caribbean writer E.K. Brathwaite as a novelist of the 'African Reconnection'.

Prayer books (Scandinavia)

In the 13th and 14th centuries writing for prayer books was one of the few avenues open to women. Nuns were given the opportunity to study and write, and in Vadstena (▷Birgitta av Vadstena) it is still possible to read the nuns' version of nine miracles performed by St Anne, who by tradition is the mother of the Virgin Mary. The Bridgettine nuns from Vadstena were particulary active in following the cult of St Anne. The German nun ▷Mechthild von Hackeborn also included legends and prayers to St Anne in her work.

The style of the prayer books is highly emotional, often using a sexual vocabulary as an expression of the Bridgettines' longing to be the brides of Jesus Christ and live through his caresses.

▷Legends of holy women (Scandinavia)

Prayers

During the Renaissance, prayer books were an important element in the lives of literate Englishwomen. Several women composed books of prayer, some of which were addressed specifically to women and some to all readers. ▷Catherine Parr's ▷*Prayers, or Meditations* (1545) belongs to the first group. The prayers typically contained in collections composed specifically for women provide important insights into the quality of their lives. In addition to prayers that might be said by either male or female Christians, volumes of prayers by such women as ▷Dorcas Martin, Elizabeth Wheathill (▷*A Handful of Holesome (though homelie) Hearbes*), Frances Aburgavennie (▷*Prayers made by the Light and Honorable Lady Frances Aburgavennie*), and Elizabeth Tyrwhit (▷*Morning and Evening Praiers*)

include numerous prayers for the various stages of childbirth, the absence of husbands, and the prosperity of the household. Individual prayers, such as those by ▷Jane Grey and Mistress Bradford (▷'Praier that Maister Bradfords Mother Said'), frequently appeared in anthologies of religious writings not strictly devoted to prayers.

▷Protestant Reformation

Prayers made by the Right Honorable Lady Frances Aburgavennie (1582)

Book of devotions composed by Frances Manners Neville Aburgavennie. Very little is known of this English devotional writer. She was the daughter of the Earl of Rutland, wife of Henry Bergavenny, and the mother of Mary Fane. Her only surviving work is a collection of her ▷prayers and her ▷confession of faith written in prose and verse. Aburgavennie's composition covers various occasions (eg 'time of bloodie battell' and 'in time of plague'), mental states (eg covetousness), and times of day (eg upon rising, before meals). She dedicated her book as a dying mother's legacy to her only daughter, Mary Fane. The work ends with 'a prayer deciphering in Alphabet form, the name of the right worshipful Lady Fane' and an acrostic prayer forming her own name. In 1582 Thomas Bentley printed Aburgavennie's composition in his ▷*Monument of Matrones* under the title *Prayers made by the right honorable Lady Frances Aburgavennie, and comited at the hour of her death to the right worshipful lady Marie Fane (her only daughter) as a Jewell of health for the soule, and a perfect path to paradise very profitable to be used of every faithful Christian man and woman.*

Bib: Beilin, E.V., *Redeeming Eve: Women Writers of the English Renaissance.*

Prayers, or Meditations (1545)

A collection of private devotions used by ▷Catherine Parr. Parr published the work under her own name in the hopes of edifying her fellow Christians. Unlike her strongly Protestant ▷*Lamentation, or Complaint of a Sinner* (1547), *Prayers, or Meditations* is fairly Unitarian in its religious stance. It develops a theme of *de contemptu mundi* and is particularly influenced by Book III of Thomas à Kempis's ▷*Imitation of Christ*. Available in inexpensive editions, Parr's work was extremely popular during the Renaissance, undergoing fifteen editions between 1545 and 1608.

Praxilla (5th century BC)

Poet, from Sicyon. She is one of the nine women poets whom Antipater of Thessalonica called the nine mortal ▷Muses. Eight fragments survive of hymns and choral songs for the worship of Dionysus. She also wrote drinking songs popular in 5th-century BC Athens: one praises the mythical heroine Alcestis for her bravery. Her work uses a variety of metres, one of which was named after her: the Praxilleion. Her fragments are preserved because they often represent unusual versions of myths. Her *Hymn to Adonis* was admired by

Zenobius (2nd century AD). There was a statue of her in the 4th century BC.
▷Moero; Anyte; Sappho
Bib: (text & trans.) Edmonds, J.M., *Lyra Graeca*.

Précieuses ▷Precious Women

Préciosité ▷Precious Women

Preciosity ▷Precious Women

Precious Bane (1924)
Novel by English writer ▷Mary Webb, set in 19th-century Shropshire. The narrator, Prudence Sarn, an old woman, tells her story and that of her brother, Gideon. Prudence's bane is her hare-lip, Gideon's his lust for money. His greed finally destroys the Sarns' farm, the family and himself. Written in Shropshire dialect, celebrating mysticism and nature-worship, the novel was cruelly but brilliantly parodied by ▷Stella Gibbons in ▷*Cold Comfort Farm* (1932).

Precious Women
Translation of the French term *Précieuses*, applied to a group of literary women in the 17th century. The *Précieuses* were closely associated with the salon movement in the decade 1650 to 1660 and placed ever greater emphasis on refinement, or *Préciosité* in matters of social etiquette, literature and language in a bid to raise the status of women. Among the most notable were ▷Madeleine de Scudéry and the *bourgeoises* who frequented her *Samedis* or Saturday salons. The original sense of the term was positive, reaffirming that women were 'full of value', and designating such a woman as '*celle qui raffine sur le langage, qui sait quelque chose*', ('a woman who uses refined language and knows something'). The Precious Women accordingly placed great value on women's independence from men and questioned the institution of marriage. For their *romanesque*, or romantic, ideas and linguistic excesses, they were much ridiculed by the dramatist Molière (1622–1673) and others. In his *Dictionnaire des Précieuses* (1659) (*Dictionary of the Precious Women*), Somaize (1639–?) distinguished three sorts of women in French society: those with 'no knowledge and no conversation' ('*aucune connaissance, aucune conversation*'); those who were just as ignorant but engaged readily in conversation ('*aussi ignorantes, mais parlent avec promptitude*'); and those who, using their exceptional beauty to distinguish themselves from the crowd, read all the novels and verse they could in a bid to learn how to speak well. In his dictionary, Antoine Furetière (1619–1688) gives the following definition: 'The epithet *Précieuse* was formerly applied to exceptionally virtuous women, who were particularly knowledgeable about society and language. The word has been devalued by the excesses and affected manners of others, who have been called false *Précieuses* or ridiculous *Précieuses*, about whom a comedy has been written.' ('*Précieuses est aussi une épithète qu'on a*

donné ci-devant à des filles de grande vertu, qui savoient bien le monde et la langue: mais parce que d'autres ont affecté et outré leurs manières, cela a décrié le mot, et on les a appelées fausses précieuses, ou précieuses ridicules, dont on a fait une comédie.')

Prefaces (16th and 17th-century Britain)
Prefaces form an important genre in terms of writings by Renaissance Englishwomen because they were one of the few types of composition deemed suitable for women. Women writers during the 16th century produced primarily religious works and ▷translations (often of religious works). The woman devotional writer or translator could maintain a sense of private modesty even in her preface, because such works called for a less 'public' authorial persona. She could create the illusion of herself as a selfless vehicle for God's or the original author's words. An author's preface to her work, therefore, often provided an opportunity for expressing herself clearly and modestly as a writer. Prefaces also presented women with an acceptable opportunity for original composition. Some women boldly justified their writing even while employing the traditional humility topois, while others used prefaces for more general literary defences. In her ▷*The French Historie*, for example, ▷Anne Dowriche defended poetry for much the same reasons as Sir Philip Sidney (1554–1586) did; and ▷Margaret Tyler defended not only her right to translate a chivalric romance, but the right of women authors in general to work beyond the confines of devotional literature. Women writers such as ▷Margaret Ascham also wrote prefaces introducing the works of men.
▷Locke, Anne; *Salve Deus, Rex Judaeorum*

Preissová, Gabriela (1862–1946)
Czech dramatist. Although also a prose writer, Preissová is most important for two plays. *Gazdina roba* (1890) (*The Gaffer's Woman*), whose dialogue is mainly in Moravian Slovak, concerns the love of a strong, poor Lutheran girl, Evuška, and a rich weakling Roman Catholic boy, Marek. Each of them marries someone socially and religiously suitable, but their mutual love survives. Marek will not get a divorce, though Evuška goes with him to Austria, where she is labelled 'the gaffer's whore'. Although generally regarded as the first Czech feminist drama, *Gazdina roba* is primarily a play about human loyalty.
Preissová's next play, *Její pastorkyňa* (1891) was made into an opera by Leoš Janáček in 1904, known in English as *Jenufa*. It is a drama of elemental passions with an old-fashioned moral: that one should love people for their internal rather than external selves.

Pre-Raphaelite Movement
A movement in British poetry and painting in the mid-19th century. Known as the 'Brotherhood', it included artists, poets and critics such as Dante Gabriel and William Michael Rossetti, the brothers of ▷Christina Rossetti. Although she

was officially excluded from the 'Brotherhood', Christina Rossetti was one of the movement's earliest successes. Under the ▷pseudonym Ellen Alleyne she published five poems in the first two issues of the magazine *The Germ* which were seen as accomplished examples of the Pre-Raphaelite aesthetic.

▷Ingelow, Jean

Prescod, Marsha

Caribbean poet born in ▷Jamaica. She came to Britain in the 1950s, and was influenced by the Brixton Writers' Workshop, *Black Ink*. She began publishing her work by the 1980s, and her first collection of poetry was called *Land of Rope and Tory* (1985). Much of the poetry, as the title suggests, is wry, political satire.

Bib: Ngcobo, Lauretta (ed.), *Let It Be Told: Black Women Writers in Britain*.

Pre vybranú spoločnosť (a zvlášť Alenku) (1989) (*For Select Society, and Especially for Alice*)

A collection of poems by Slovak author Tat'jana Lehenová (born 1961). The poems had a mixed reception. One of them, 'Little Nightmare', published in the literary monthly *Romboid* in 1988, gave rise to a debate about the poet's good taste, and about the permissible bounds of the erotic. The collection attempts to break down the traditional taboos of Slovak woman's literature. The poet does not weep sentimentally over woman's lot, nor accept the illusion of emancipation and possible independence. Lehenová's poetry undoubtedly has two sides – she wants to win 'private' happiness, but she is unable to ignore the banality, despair and loneliness of life, which leads her to gentle sarcasm. She emphasizes rational, strictly anti-sentimental feelings. This collection, the poet's first, may be regarded as the expression of the feelings of a generation, or as an attempt to catch the attention of the public and to cause a sensation.

Prichard, Katharine Susannah (1883–1969)

Australian novelist, autobiographer and dramatist. Prichard was born in Fiji, the daughter of Tom Prichard, editor of the *Fiji Times*, but grew up in Tasmania and Melbourne. After living in England she returned to Australia in 1916, married the war hero Hugo Throssel, VC in 1919, and settled in Perth, Western Australia. A committed socialist, Prichard was a foundation member of the Communist Party of Australia and visited Russia in 1933. Her husband's suicide at this time is said to have affected the ending of ▷*Intimate Strangers* (1937). Prichard was also prominent in literary circles, being President of the Australian Writers' League in 1935.

Her novels reflect her socialist ideals, and critics have discerned a conflict between her tendency towards a Lawrentian romanticism and her commitment to the ideals of socialist realism. Her books have been translated into fifteen

Katherine Susannah Prichard

languages. The most significant are *Black Opal* (1921), *Working Bullocks* (1926), ▷*Coonardoo: The Well in the Shadow* (1929), which deals with the relationship between a white pastoralist and an Aboriginal woman, *Haxby's Circus* (1930) and *The Roaring Nineties* (1946). *Pioneers* (1937) and *Brumby Innes* (1940) are her two best-known plays, and *Child of the Hurricane: An Autobiography* (1963) records Prichard's early life.

▷Aborigine in non-Aboriginal Australian women's writing, The; Short story (Australia); New Theatre, The; *Gender, Politics and Fiction, Penguin Anthology of Australian Women's Writing, The*

Pride and Prejudice (1813)

A novel by English author ▷Jane Austen. One of the most popular of her works, it concentrates on the fortunes of the Bennet family, minor gentry who live at Longbourn near London. Mrs Bennet is shallow, foolish, and obsessively preoccupied with finding husbands for her five daughters. Mr Bennet, by contrast, is intelligent, witty, but uncommitted and withdrawn. The central focus of the novel is the story of Elizabeth Bennet and her relationship with Fitzwilliam Darcy. Darcy considers Elizabeth socially beneath him, but is nonetheless captivated by her and proposes to her, making it clear that he feels he is lowering himself. Elizabeth, 'prejudiced' by an inveterate dislike of the aristocracy and the false testimony of George Wickham, an untrustworthy army officer, indignantly rejects him. Elizabeth subsequently refuses the sycophantic clergyman, Mr Collins, who then transfers his affections onto Charlotte Lucas, a friend of Elizabeth's. In the course of the novel, Elizabeth and Darcy draw closer together as each others' character is revealed beyond the narrow prejudices of social class. Meanwhile the Bennet family learns that one of the daughters,

Lydia, has eloped with Wickham, an event which threatens to destroy the family name. Darcy comes to the rescue, helping to trace the runaways, arrange their marriage and provide for their futures. Finally Elizabeth and Darcy are married. *Pride and Prejudice* is often considered Austen's most lightweight work, but it nonetheless contains much astute social commentary. The heroine is by far the most intelligent character in the book, as well as being unconventional in her independence, physicality and liveliness. Recent feminist critics have emphasized Elizabeth's transgressions of the rules of propriety, and argued that Austen's treatment of Elizabeth and Darcy's relationship undermines conservative myths about gender and class.

Prime of Life, The (1962)
Translation of *La force de l'âge* (1960), second volume of French writer ▷Simone de Beauvoir's autobiography. Covering the period between 1929 and 1945, the book contains much that is of interest about French intellectual and social life between the wars, and about the experience of living in an occupied country between 1940 and 1945. Of most significance to many readers, however, will be the account in the book of the relationship between the author and Jean-Paul Sartre. The love affair, and the subsequent close friendship, are described by de Beauvoir with apparent openness, and yet persistent evasion. It is an extraordinary account of one of the most famous, indeed almost mythical, personal relationships of the 20th century.

Prime of Miss Jean Brodie, The (1961)
Novel by Scottish writer ▷Muriel Spark, which was later made into a popular film. Set in the Marcia Blaine School for girls during the period 1931 to 1938, Spark's novel follows a seven-year relationship between the schoolteacher, Jean Brodie, and her select or élite group of students, the 'Brodie Set'. Brodie's fascination with Mussolini and the rise of Italian fascism provides an integrated and parallel narrative to both her educational policies and her teaching career. Starting from Brodie's hypothesis 'give me a girl at an impressionable age and she is mine for life', Spark elaborates a complex scenario of seduction and desire, in which Brodie attempts to educate her students on the 'higher' aspects of 'culture'. Brodie's manipulative tendencies are cast within an exploration of love, obsession and sexual awakening, the specific context of love and fascism providing an intertwined interrogation of the dualities of idealism and materiality, of purity and impurity. Spark's use of shifting viewpoints and mixed chronology both disrupts and questions the basis of Jean Brodie's developmental schema.

Primrose, Diana (fl 1630)
English writer of a memorial poem to Elizabeth I (▷Elizabeth Tudor).
▷*Chaine of Pearle*

Prince, Mary (c 1788–?)
This early Caribbean writer, born a slave in ▷Bermuda, experienced all the harshness of the slave system. Employed to work in houses and tend children, she was sent to work in the salt ponds on Turks Island in 1805. She returned to Bermuda in 1810, where she was employed to care for her owner's children. She also grew crops. Around 1814 she moved to ▷Antigua with new owners, and lived there until 1827, when they took her with them to England. Once in England she petitioned for her freedom, and remained there when her owners returned to Antigua. She was employed by the editor of the ▷*Anti-Slavery Reporter*. Always a confident and spirited individual, she participated in 'active slave resistance' and was an outspoken campaigner against slavery. She had had five owners before she managed to free herself. She is historically important as the first black woman from the Caribbean to document and publish a record of her experience and eventual escape from slavery: ▷*The History of Mary Prince A West Indian Slave Related by Herself.* Her narrative was published by the Anti-Slavery Society in 1831, and it caused an outcry between pro- and anti-slavery supporters. See the introduction to the 1987 edition of *The History of Mary Prince* for further information.

Prince's Progress, and Other Poems, The (1866)
The second published collection of poetry by British poet ▷Christina Rossetti, including the quest narrative 'The Prince's Progress', 'The Iniquity of the Fathers Upon the Children' (a narrative poem spoken from the perspective of an illegitimate child) and 'L.E.L.', a lyric dedicated to ▷Letitita Landon. The simple diction and controlled poetic form which characterizes the collection reflects Rossetti's developing aesthetic of personal and artistic renunciation.

Princesse de Clèves, La (1679) (The Princess of Cleves)
A semi-historical novel by French writer ▷Comtesse de Lafayette. It is set at the court of Henri II, during the peace celebrations of the year 1558–1559. It was extremely popular during the reign of Louis XIV and has often been called the first modern French novel. Imitating the ▷*mémoires* form, this novel traces the tragic story of a triangular love affair, where the virtuous heroine is torn between her duty to her husband and her love for the Duc de Nemours, which she hardly dare admit, even to herself. Their growing passion for one another, which the princess ultimately denies, though her husband's sudden death from a broken heart might seem to free her to do as she pleases, is played out against the background of court ceremonial and intrigue, culminating in the King's death in a tournament. The final tragic act follows the reversal in power which brings the Guises, a French ducal family, to power and sets the scene for the Wars of Religion (1562–1598) to come. The novel is an important

early example of the *roman d'analyse* (psychological novel). It is also one of the first French novels to include an *aveu* (confession), remarkable in that it is addressed by a wife to her husband, and overheard by her lover.

Princesse de Montpensier, La (1662) (*The Princess of Montpensier*) ▷Lafayette, Marie-Madeleine Pioche de la Vergne, Comtesse de

Prison and Chocolate Cake (1954)
First volume of autobiography by the Indian novelist and journalist ▷Nayantara Sahgal. Born into a family of prominent nationalists, Sahgal provides an intimate portrait of many of the figures familiar in India's struggle for independence, including her famous uncle, Jawaharlal Nehru (1889–1964). Together with her sister, she grew up in an exciting but baffling atmosphere of wealth, privilege and foreign travel, tempered by the long absences of her parents when they were gaoled by the British for their political activities. Sahgal's second volume of autobiography, *From Fear Set Free* (1962), takes up her life-story after the formation of an independent India in 1947.

Prison writing (South Africa)
A number of South African women have been imprisoned for their part in the campaign against apartheid. Some of them have recounted the experience as part of ▷autobiographical writing, while for others it enters their fiction, often written in ▷exile. Ruth First's *117 Days* (1965) is a prison memoir recounting a period spent in solitary confinement in 1963 under the infamous 90-day detention clause. Arrested at the same time as African National Congress leader Nelson Mandela and others, she was the first woman detained under this clause. It allowed for anyone suspected of committing an offence against the state, or possessing information relating to an offence, to be detained, without charge or trial, without legal advice, and without visits from family or friends. The 90-day period might be renewed immediately upon the prisoner's release: this was the case with Ruth First. In 1982, after having continued her political work from abroad, mostly in Mozambique, she was assassinated by a letter bomb sent from South Africa.

117 Days is an intelligent and observant account of prison conditions, extending into political analysis. The book also gives poignant testimony to First's intense desire to endure solitary confinement and withstand interrogation for fear of betraying her friends. As in the case of Emma Mashinini, who wrote about her prison experience in her autobiography *Strikes Have Followed Me All My Life* (1989), the idea of collective solidarity sustained her during this period. According to Caesarina Kona Makhoere, First's account had some influence over her own prison memoir, *No Child's Play: In Prison Under Apartheid* (1988). Makhoere was a 'child' of ▷Soweto 1976, in detention for a year before she was sentenced to

five years' imprisonment under the Terrorism Act for recruiting for *Umkhonto we Sizwe*, the armed wing of the African National Congress. She sees herself as part of a community of heroes, and engages in establishing a unified black front against prison rule, politicizing criminals as well as drawing together political prisoners. This, plus certain particular forms of resistance developed under ▷Black Consciousness, keeps Makhoere strong, and in some way able to withstand the particularly brutal treatment meted out to her in prison.

▷Autobiography (Southern Africa); Exile writing (South Africa)

Pritam, Amrita (born 1919)
Indian poet, novelist and short story writer. She is one of India's leading writers in Punjabi. Pritam was born in Gujranwala, which is now in Pakistan, but opted to live in India after the ▷Partition of the Punjab. Since 1986 she has been a nominated member of the Rajya Sabha (the upper house of the Indian parliament). A prolific writer, she has published thirty novels, almost twenty volumes of poetry, and eight collections of short stories. She is also an authoritative critic on Punjabi literature, and edits the Punjabi monthly *Nagmani*. Many of her works have been translated into Urdu and other Indian languages.

Her poetry collection *Sunehere* (*Golden*) won the Sahitya Akademi Award in 1956, and a subsequent collection, *Kagaz te Kanwas* (*Paper and Canvas*) won the Bharatiya Jnanpith Award in 1981. She has also had the title of Padma Shri conferred upon her. *Teesri Aurat* (*The Third Woman*) is her best-known collection of short stories. Two volumes of stories are available in English translation, ▷*The Death of a City* (1976) and *The Aerial* (1978), as are several of her novels, including *Chhak Nambar Chhati* (1975) (▷*A Line in Water*) and *The Skeleton* (1987)
▷Partition

Private Gardens: An Anthology of New Zealand Women Poets (1977)
The tremendous growth in publication of books by women writers in the late 1970s in New Zealand was marked historically by the publication of *Private Gardens*, edited by ▷Riemke Ensing. *Private Gardens* represented the work of thirty-six women poets, and was responsible for initiating a reassessment of the place of women writers in literary history. ▷Mary Stanley, one of the writers featured in *Private Gardens*, has subsequently appeared in major anthologies, and a number of other writers who were included have gone on to become major figures in New Zealand writing, including ▷Lauris Edmond, ▷Anne French, ▷Elizabeth Smither and ▷Rachel McAlpine. Although *Private Gardens* has a rather defensive introduction, it established the beginnings of a new literary focus for women writers, and was succeeded by a wave of publications featuring women, including a later anthology of women

poets, *Yellow Pencils* (1988), edited by Lydia Wevers.
▷Anthologies, New Zealand

Private Journal of Margaret Morris (1836)
A highly detailed account of the early years of the American Revolution in Burlington, New Jersey, ▷Margaret Hill Morris's journal reflects her Quaker pacifism but also her activism in aiding the wounded on both sides and her courage in the face of Hessian troops that invaded her home. Her devout nature is reflected in her assertions that divine Providence was protecting her and her children during a conflict that would leave participants on both sides accountable for their acts of war. It is a well-written documentation of a Quaker woman's rejection of the necessity of war.

Prize Giving, The (1980)
A novel by the Turkish writer, Aysel Özakin, on modern Turkey as seen through the experience of Turkish women. The author is a Turkish feminist who now lives in Europe, writing and lecturing widely in women's circles. The novel telescopes the lives of three generations of Turkish women: Nuray, the protagonist, stands in puzzlement between her mother (a daughter of the Kemalist secular revolution of 1923 who thought she could do everything with her life, and subsequently kills herself out of depression) and her own daughter, Seçkin, a young student and socialist activist, who believes she knows all the answers. Seçkin leaves home and lives in a flat with her comrades; they plan demonstrations, write leaflets and believe in the power of the people. Nuray is shut out by the daughter who, with adolescent arrogance, looks down upon her mother's interests and on her achievement (writing a novel about the sufferings of a petty bourgeois woman and winning a prize for it). As a little girl, Nuray had been shut out by her mother, who had spent her last months looking at the ceiling; neither her daughter nor her husband could do anything for her. Nuray's life gives the lie to many cherished 'received ideas' about marriage, love and the roles of the sexes. Long excerpts from her prize-winning novel are included in the narrative, emphasizing the complex relationship between the past and the present, and the contrast between the romantic ideal and brutal reality.

The novel questions the institution of marriage in a modern society in flux. It is not just Nuray's marriage which fell to pieces under the first pressure from the outside world, it is the prosperous, modern married couples, the phoney patrons of art and literature, who shock Nuray into realizing how alienated she really is in the glitter of the luxury hotel where she meets them. Barefaced, brutal shooting and police violence bring the novel to a close; the husband is shot during a vain attempt to bring back the past; the daughter is certainly in danger, and Nuray's literary prize is meaningless in the face of such violence.
Bib: Kerslake, Celia (trans.), *The Prize Giving.*

Proba (4th century AD)
Poet. Faltonia Betitia Proba, a Christian, was the daughter of a Roman consul and the wife of a pagan prefect of Rome. Her one extant hexameter poem (694 lines) relates the Old Testament version of the Creation with the life story of Jesus Christ. But its remarkable feature is that it is a cento, namely comprised totally of lines and parts of lines taken from the Roman epic poet Virgil (1st century AD). Proba's preface falls into a conventional style of declaring that she has abandoned war poetry to write new poetry, here to sing of God and of how Virgil praised Jesus before Jesus was recognized. Her poem closes with an appeal to her pagan husband to follow in her worship. Proba's work was admired by the Roman Emperor Theodosius II (4th century AD) and Isidore of Seville (7th century AD). She was popular in the Middle Ages.

Procter, Adelaide (1825–1864)
English poet and ▷feminist, also wrote under the ▷pseudonym Mary Berwick. She was born in London, the daughter of the poet, Barry Cornwall. In 1853 she began to contribute poetry to *Household Words* and found an admirer in Charles Dickens, who wrote a foreword to her *Complete Works* (1905). A collected two-volume edition, *Legends and Lyrics* (1858 and 1861) includes her most popular verse, much of which is ▷sentimental. Procter was a dedicated feminist and helped to found the Society for Promoting the Employment of Women. The proceeds from *Chaplet of Verses* (1862) went to a homeless women's refuge. Procter also edited an anthology of miscellaneous verse, *Victoria Regia*, which was published by Emily Faithful's Victoria Press in 1861.

Prodigal Women (1942)
US novel. While working on this book, ▷Nancy Hale gave birth, divorced and suffered a nervous breakdown. Similarly, the novel's three heroines are caught in a conflict with their inner selves. They try to define their lives by heterosexual relationships and the need to fulfil a yearning for motherhood. Yet they struggle to establish their own separate identity and to acquire some power. The novel portrays the psychological impact on women who give themselves lavishly to men.

Proensa, Comtesse de (12th–13th century)
French ▷*trobairitz* of the third period. She has been identified as Garsenda de Forcalquier, daughter of Guillaume IV de Forcalquier, Countess of Provence by her marriage in 1193 to Count Alfonso II. Widowed in 1209, she entered a religious order in 1225. She exchanged a *cobla* with Gui de Cavaillon. The authors are not named in the texts, but are identified by a heading in one of the two manuscripts that preserve them.
Bib: Paden, W.D. (ed.), *The Voice of the Trobairitz.*

Professor, The (1857)

A novel by British author ▷Charlotte Brontë, written in 1846 but not published until after the author's death. In many ways it is an early version of ▷*Villette*, although it is not as sophisticated. The central character, William Crimsworth, is an ▷orphan who leaves England to seek his fortune in Brussels. He falls in love with Frances Henri, an Anglo-Swiss pupil-teacher, and eventually marries her. Their relationship is analogous to that of Lucy Snowe and Paul Emmanuel in *Villette*, although it is not drawn with as much complexity.

Progressive Writers' Association

A radical movement started in India during the struggle for independence by, among others, the famous Hindi and Urdu novelist, Premchand (1880–1936). They were strongly influenced by Gandhian ideals.

▷Chughtai, Ismat; Hosain, Attia

Promised Land, The (1966)

Novel by Kenyan writer ▷Grace Ogot. *The Promised Land* focuses on the perennial African theme of conflict between demands of family and those of personal ambition. Ogot subtitles this story of Luo pioneers who search for happiness and prosperity in Tanzania 'a true fantasy', indicating the combination of social realism and 'magical' elements which is typical of her writing. Important historically as the first novel to be published by East African Publishing House and the first by a woman writer in East Africa, *The Promised Land* is part social critique, part re-creation of the African past. Ogot's failure to explore human relationships convincingly has been noted.

▷Magic realism

Prosperi, Carola (1883–1975)

Italian novelist and short story writer. Born in Turin, she was a regular contributor to *La Stampa*, and published many short stories and serial novels in women's magazines. A prolific writer, she began her career with works which were little more than moral fables, but then moved on to write ▷*romanzi di consumo*. Typically of a writer of these kind of novels, she concentrates on women and their problems. Her work is full of tales of female unhappiness, just a few examples which are: ▷*La paura d'amare* (1911) (*Fear of Loving*), *Agnese, amante ingenua* (1934) (*Agnes, the Naive Lover*), and *Fiamme burgiarde* (1951) (*Flames of Deceit*). She wrote many works, and revealed her favourite subject matter to be love, and its overwhelming destructive power. Her female characters are usually severely restricted by their middle-class existence, and their fantasies of other lives lead them into impossible and unhealthy relationships with unsuitable men. On one level, Prosperi's narratives function as conventional moral warnings to her readers; on another they highlight the inherently wasteful nature of these women's lives.

Other works include: *La profezia* (1909) (*The Prophecy*); *L'estranea* (1915) (*The Stranger*); *La felicità in gabbia* (1922) (*Caged Happiness*); *La donna forte*(1935) (*The Strong Woman*); *La maschera d'amore* (1941) (*The Mask of Love*); *Racconti del Piemonte* (1954) (*Piedmontese Stories*).

Prostitution (West Africa)

A product of urbanization and the confusion of values brought about by the pace of city life, few women writers treat prostitution as openly as ▷Ken Bugul, or celebrate it in the manner of Nigerian writer Cyprian Ekwensi. The eponymous heroine of his novel *Jagua Nana* (1948) is one of the most unforgettable characters in West African literature. However, the phenomenon of the 'sugar daddy', or rich older lover who provides material comforts, is fully recognized and accepted even if not condoned, in novels such as ▷Helen Ovbiagele's ▷*Evbu, My Love*. The Nigerian pidgin term 'bottom power' also testifies to the prevalent strategy among women of finding their way through the use of sexual favours. This is an intrinsic part of a social system where polygyny (▷polygamy) is the norm, having many girlfriends is a man's right, and women are expected to pay for access to power or position.

▷Diallo, Nafissatou

Protestant Reformation

The dissolution of Catholicism, and the later radical Protestant movements in England, provided an unprecedented opportunity for women to learn, speak, and write – especially regarding spiritual matters. Protestants argued for spiritual democratization, in which salvation lay in the unmediated power of God working within the individual soul, and in which the Church consisted of a community of believers. The availability of English translations of the Bible made it possible for more women to gain access to the scriptures. Various forms of personal writing filled the gaps left by abolished Catholic practices, such as mass and priestly confession. The most important of these in terms of women's writings include the ▷confession or profession of faith, daily meditations and ▷prayers, the ▷letter, occasional poetry, and ▷translation. Like the ▷humanists, Protestant reformers played a key role in both the emergence and limitations of English women's writing. Renaissance Englishwomen whose writings were significantly influenced by the Protestant Reformation include ▷Catherine Parr, ▷Anne Askew, ▷Katherine Stubbes, and ▷Anne Locke.

▷Bacon, Anne; Companionate marriage; *Monument of Matrones, The*; Young, Elizabeth.

Prótesta que, Rubricada con su sangre, hizo de su fe y amor a dios (1694) (Protestation, Signed in Her Blood, of Her Faith in and Love of God)

Declaration made by Mexican poet ▷Juana de Asbaje y Ramirez de Santillana. It was kept in the Book of Professions of the Convent of St Jerome, which constituted the last document signed by Sor Juana Inés de la Cruz (her pen-name), where she recommends herself to her convent sisters and declares: 'To all I apologize for the love of God and his Mother. I, the worst in the world, Juana Inés de la Cruz.' This document is her defence against the Bishop of Puebla's rebuke on her intellectual freedom.

Proti prúdu (1894) (Against the Stream)

Slovak novel by ▷Elena Maróthy-Soltesová. The work was written with the purpose of proving the author's concept of 'ideal realism'. It concerns the possible contribution of the nobility towards any Slovak national struggle, which was the chief question of Slovak literature in the second half of the 19th century. The novel concentrates on two main spheres – national problems and family life. The main characters are simply pegs on which to hang ideas. They are idealized examples of people devoting themselves to their nation. Even, their names are symptomatic. 'Laskárová' suggests redemption through love. Her husband's name, 'Šavelský', suggests the conversion of Saul to Paul. The novel provoked great debate about its literary values, in particular about its verisimilitude, and the idealism of its suggested 'aristocratic' solution.

Proudhonism

Pierre-Joseph Proudhon (1809–1865) was a French socialist writer and thinker who strongly opposed the feminist cause and the campaign for female suffrage. He viewed woman as man's physical, moral and intellectual inferior, and believed that her role was primarily to help and complement her masculine companion. He naturally attracted the enmity of many female contemporaries, including ▷Juliette Adam, ▷Jenny d'Héricourt and ▷André Léo. His anti-feminism is made most apparent in his *La Justice dans la Révolution et dans l'église* (1858) (*Justice in the Revolution and the Church*).

Psalms of David, The (1823)

Verse ▷translations of the biblical psalms begun by Sir Philip Sidney (1554–1586) and completed by ▷Mary Sidney Herbert. Sidney had translated forty-three by the time he died in 1586. Herbert translated the remaining 107, and extensively revised her brother's work. It is one of the earliest and finest examples of post-Reformation collections of religious verse. Dazzling in its variety of stanzaic forms, the translation circulated in manuscript copies, and became relatively famous even though it remained unpublished for more than 200 years. Herbert's translation is particularly important in terms of Elizabethan versification and psalmody because it makes use of 164 unrepeated and distinct stanza forms and 94 different metrical patterns. In each psalm translated, she carefully combined form and meaning in accordance with Renaissance notions of poetic decorum. Poets John Donne (1572–1631) and Samuel Daniel (1562–1619) praised Herbert's work, and George Herbert's *The Temple* (1633) was strongly influenced by the collection. The translations were not published in their entirety until 1823, when an edition of only 250 copies was printed. A second edition appeared in 1963.

Pseudonyms

Many women writers have adopted pseudonyms for a variety of reasons. In common with male authors they have done so in the context of political censorship, as in the example of the 19th century African-American writer ▷Harriet Jacobs who published her *Incidents in the Life of a Slave Girl: Written by Herself*, under the name Linda Brent for reasons of safety. Similarly, the Chilean poet ▷Mercedes Marín del Solar anonymously published a poem in praise of the hero of the Chilean Republic, and the Brazilian ▷Patrícia Galvão was forced to use a pseudonym (Mara Lobo) by the Communist Party, which did not want her to attract adverse publicity on their behalf. More recently, in the 1950s ▷Ann Bannon, the lesbian pulp fiction writer, used a pseudonym presumably to avoid discrimination on the basis of her sexuality. Where women have adopted male pseudonyms this has arisen from their desire to have their writing judged on its literary merit rather than according to sexual prejudice. In 19th-century Britain the emergence of the pseudonym occurred during the 1840s when female novelists were becoming a recognizable professional group. In order to have their writing judged on its literary merit rather than according to sexual prejudice, many women attempted to conceal their identities. The ▷Brontë sisters first published under the androgynous pseudonyms Currer, Ellis and Acton Bell. Charlotte Brontë later admitted that 'a vague impression that authoresses are liable to be looked on with prejudice' had influenced the decision. ▷George Eliot pleaded with Charles Gray not to expose her identity after she published an article in the *Westminster Review* in 1855. 'The article appears to have produced a strong impression' wrote Eliot, 'and that impression would be a little counteracted if the author were known to be a *woman*'. Other examples might include Eliot's own influence, the French writer ▷Georges Sand, Australian writers ▷Henry Handel Richardson, ▷Miles Franklin, and ▷M. Barnard Eldershaw, a neuter and composite version of the two writers ▷Marjorie Barnard and ▷Flora Eldershaw. Cultural attitudes towards the proper role of women have also been important. In the 20th century, for instance, the Senegalese writer ▷Ken Bugul's French publishers, Les Nouvelles Editions Africaines, insisted that she used a pseudonym. Her answer was the Wolof for 'nobody wants it'.

▷Egerton, George; Field, Michael; Lee Vernon; Malet, Lucas; Winter, John Strange

Psych et Po

In full, *Psychanalyse et Politique*, French feminist movement. Founded in 1968 by Antoinette Fouque and backed by its own publishing house, ▷Éditions des Femmes, this movement generally claims to be the intellectual hub of ▷French feminism, and as such has acquired sole rights to the ▷MLF logo. *Psych et Po* are opposed to political involvement which, according to them, only leads women to seek power and duplicate male models. They seek to use the theories of ▷psychoanalysis and historical materialism to explore woman's Unconscious and to subvert society. The group's ideological position and definition of ▷*écriture féminine* is best exemplified by the writings of ▷Hélène Cixous.

Psychoanalysis

Sigmund Freud's (1856–1939) term for his theory of psycho-sexual development. As the hyphen linking the words implies, the unconscious and sexuality are inextricably interwined in psychoanalysis, and for all psychoanalysts the acquisition of subjectivity is at root a psychic and sexual development. Sexuality is therefore not something which is added on to human subjectivity, rather it is through sexuality and gender that subjectivity is formed.

Since the 1950s a new strand of psychoanalytic theory has emerged in France out of the work of Jacques Lacan (1901–1981) whose re-reading of Ferdinand de Saussure's (1857–1913) theory of language has influenced ▷poststructuralist schools of feminist criticism. Lacan privileges the signifier (or symbol), arguing that language is a figurative structure which only ever operates at the level of symbol and image. He argues, too, that language structures or shapes human identity. This implies both that there is no escaping language and that the autonomous individual of ▷humanist ideologies is an illusion. Lacan's insistence that ▷subject identity is acquired in language, or the ▷symbolic order of representation, releases sexual identity from the tyranny of biologistic definitions. Two important essays, by Lacan, on feminine sexuality, 'God and the *Jouissance* of the Woman: A Love Letter' and 'Seminar of 21 January 1975', have been translated, edited and introduced by Juliet Mitchell and Jacqueline Rose in *Feminine Sexuality: Jacques Lacan and the École Freudienne* (1982).

Hostility towards psychoanalysis characterizes feminist literary criticism in the 1970s. ▷Kate Millett presented a patriarchal Freud, arguing that he ignored the influence of contemporary historical and cultural prejudices on his work, and presented ▷heterosexist, bourgeois definitions of femininity and masculinity as universal norms. In particular, Millett attacked the role played by the dual concepts of ▷penis envy and the ▷Oedipus complex in Freud's theory of the acquisition of sexual difference. By the mid-1970s, however, feminists began re-evaluating psychoanalysis.

In *Psychoanalysis and Feminism* (1974), Juliet Mitchell argued that psychoanalysis explains how gender identity is acquired on the basis of repressing desires that are *culturally* unacceptable, and thus freed Freud from charges of biological determinism. Mitchell's re-evaluation of Freud is heavily influenced by Lacan's re-reading of his work.

Jacqueline Rose, who has worked with Juliet Mitchell, takes her defence of psychoanalysis a step further: in *Sexuality in the Field of Vision* (1986) Rose argues that Lacanian psychoanalysis is useful for feminism because it provides an account of sexual identity as culturally constituted and constantly resisted. ▷Julia Kristeva, ▷Hélène Cixous and ▷Luce Irigaray offer various important revisions and critiques of Lacanian theory. Lacanian feminist literary critics include ▷Shoshana Felman and ▷Mary Jacobus.
Bib: Freud, Sigmund, *New Introductory Essays on Psychoanalysis*; Lacan, Jacques, *Écrits: A Selection*; *The Four Fundamental Concepts of Psycho-Analysis*; Wright, Elizabeth, *Psychoanalytic Criticism*.

Publishing and publishers (19th-century Britain)

The publishing industry expanded enormously during the mid-19th century in response to the demands of a literate middle-class readership. Distribution of books and magazines was facilitated by the railway system which connected the centres of literary production with previously remote regions. Novels were published either in three-volume form or, since 'three-deckers' were relatively expensive to buy, in serial format in monthly magazines such as Dickens's *Household Words*. The serial form made particular demands upon narrative structure, since readers had to be encouraged to buy the next instalment. The cliff-hanging chapter endings, coincidences and contrivances so characteristic of Victorian fiction are inextricably linked to the context in which the work appeared. Literary production was also conditioned by the censorship exerted by publishing houses. Publishers' readers would reject work which transgressed the bounds of propriety, fearful of the effect of such fiction on a predominantly female readership. Novels were subjected to a second round of censorship at the hands of the ▷circulating libraries, which would refuse to stock 'morally questionable' literature.
▷Jewsbury, Geraldine; 'Ouida'

Publishing companies run by South African women

While no feminist press as such exists in Southern Africa, there have been and are publishing companies devoted to women writers and/or run by women. The first was the short-lived Silver Leaf Books, founded by Thelma Gutsche (1915–1984) and Marion Friedman, in the 1940s, which published only a few titles, including ▷Nadine Gordimer's *Face to Face* (1949). Chameleon Press was established in Cape Town in the mid-1980s, with the intention, in part, of publishing writing by women. The publisher, Lynne Bryer, has reprinted two of ▷Daphne Rooke's novels, out of print for many years, along with short stories by Afrikaans writer ▷Welma Odendaal. At much the same time, Seriti sa Sechaba, which translates as 'the nation's dignity', was launched in Johannesburg. This is a non-profit organization run entirely by black South African women (the publisher is Dinah Lefakane) and publishing only black women writers. It has not flourished so far because it is not affiliated to any of the organizations of the mass democratic movement: Lefakane was asked not long ago who gave her 'the mandate' to open a publishing house. COSAW (Congress of South African Writers) has recently established special publishing programmes for women's writing.

Puértolas, Soledad (born 1947)

Spanish journalist and novelist. The main themes of her work are friendship, responsibility for others, and the mysterious harmonies of life. Her main novels are *El bandido doblemente armado* (1980) (*Doubly Armed Bandit*); *Una enfermedad mortal* (1982) (*A Mortal Illness*); *Burdeos* (1986) (*Bordeaux*), and *Todos mienten* (1988) (*They're All Liars*).

Pugnition de l'Amour contempné (1530–1540) (Punishment of Despised Love) ▷Flore, Jeanne

Puisieux, Madeleine d'Arsant de (1720–1798)

French moralist and novelist. Born into the minor nobility of Paris, she was educated at Port-Royal. Puisieux's works reflect her preoccupations with social, political and psychological issues. Her first two published texts, *Conseils à une amie* (1749) (*Advice to a Friend*) and *Les caractères* (1750) (*Characters*), non-traditional and anti-clerical, deal with the social education required for young women and men. Her plan for extending education to all classes in the *Prospectus sur un ouvrage important* (*Prospectus for an Important Project*) and her revolutionary philosophy in general earned her a pension from the Convention. Her libertine tale, *Le Plaisir et la volupté* (1752) (*Pleasure and Sensuality*), is possibly a rewriting of Diderot's *L'Oiseau blanc* (*The White Bird*), on which she may have collaborated. The feminist essay *La Femme n'est pas inférieure à l'homme* (1750) (*Woman Is not Inferior to Man*) is attributed to her husband but may be her work, or a translation of a text by ▷Lady Mary Wortley Montagu. Her novels *L'Education du Marquis de **** (1753) (*The Education of the Marquis de ****), *Zamor et Almanzine* (1755), *Alzarac* (1762), *Histoire de Mlle de Terville* (1768) (*Story of Mlle de Terville*) and *Mémoires d'un homme de bien* (1768) (*Memoirs of a Good Man*) offer critiques of relationships between the sexes, French society and the rights of individuals, the court of Louis XV and religious intolerance, while in the play *Le Marquis à la mode* (1763) (*The Fashionable*

Marquis), she targets the nobility. A collection of poetry, *Une suite de poèmes* (1746) (*A Series of Poems*), remains in manuscript form at the Bibliothèque Nationale.

▷*Journal des Dames*

Bib: Garnier, C., *Mme de Puisieux: moraliste et romancière* and 'La femme n'est pas inférieure à l'homme (1750)', *R.H.L.F* July/August 1987, pp. 709–713; Laborde, A., *Diderot et Mme de Puisieux*.

Puja

The ceremonies used in worshipping a Hindu god or goddess. Puja can be on a very grand scale, at a temple and conducted by priests, but it can also be conducted in the home by individual worshippers in front of their household divinities.

Pusich, Antónia Gertrudes (1805–1883)

Portuguese poet, dramatist and editor. She spent her childhood in Cape Verde, where her father, a military officer, was stationed. Married and widowed twice, she supported herself and her two children with her writings, which included poetry and plays. A third marriage brought further difficulties: her husband was imprisoned for political reasons and she became the sole support of the family, which now included the children from this marriage.

She is perhaps best known as the founder and editor of several reviews, including ▷*A Assembléia Literária* (1849–1851) (*The Literary Assembly*), an instructional magazine for women. In addition to educational issues, the magazine also included articles on religion, literature and the arts, economics and politics.

Pym, Barbara (Mary Crampton) (1913–1980)

Barbara Pym

English novelist. Born in Shropshire and educated at St Hilda's College, Oxford, Pym lived at home after graduating, and wrote her first novel, *Some Tame Gazelle* (1950), in her twenties. Her novels are characterized by their ironic treatment of provincial life, spinsterhood, unrequited love, and the social and emotional centrality of 'institutions' such as the Church and the local library in the lives of educated, middle-class women. Following the late publication of her first novel, Pym began writing again in the 1950s, and her novels include: ▷ *Excellent Women* (1952), *Less Than Angels* (1955) and *A Glass of Blessings* (1958). During the 1960s and 1970s, Pym assumed the ▷ pseudonym Tom Crampton, but the novels from this period were consistently rejected by publishers. Interest was renewed later in the decade, and *Quartet in Autumn* (1977) and *The Sweet Dove Died* (1978) were published shortly before her death. Other novels: *Jane and Prudence* (1954), *A Few Green Leaves* (1980), *Crampton Hodnett* (1980), *An Unsuitable Attachment* (1982), *Civil to Strangers* (1987), *No Fond Return of Love* (1961).

Pythagorean women

The philosopher Pythagoras (6th century BC) started his school in Italy. It was revived in the 3rd–2nd centuries BC in Athens and Alexandria. From the revival period literature under women's names survives in letter form. Dating and female authorship are controversial, but the attribution of female names at least presupposes readers would not think such a phenomenon incredible. The works are also designed for female readership. Iamblichus's *Life of Pythagoras* lists sixteen women followers. Such women were the stuff of 5th-century BC Athenian comedies with the title *The Woman Who Pythagorizes*.

▷ Theano (I); Perictione; Myia; Phintys; Melissa; Philosophers, Ancient Greek and Roman women; Household management and child rearing, Ancient Greek

Q

Qabbani, Nizar, influence of

Born in 1923 in Damascus, Qabbani is the most widely-read poet in the Arab world. His poetry has been particularly influential in its openness about female sexuality: one of his first collections was called *Tufulatu Nahd* (1948) (*Innocence of a Breast*), and his poetry has been criticized for the explicitness of its imagery. His earlier poetry accuses women of sticking to the ▷*harem*, and later verse celebrates women's rebellion: 'Rebel against an East that sees you/A banquet sprawling on a bed.' The voice raised in protest in many of his poems is that of a woman addressing Middle Eastern Man.

Bib: al-Udhari, Abdullah (ed. and trans.), *Modern Poetry of the Arab World*; Mikhail, Mona, *Images of Arab Women*.

Qiong Yao (born 1938)

Taiwan-based Chinese writer. A precocious child, Qiong Yao started writing in her teens and has kept on writing and publishing ever since. A prolific writer of popular romances, she has now published over forty volumes, and has a huge following in both Taiwan and mainland China. Her novels include *Lucky Blade*, *I Am a Cloud* and *The Heart's Knots*.

Quaker women (England)

A vital tradition of preaching, prophecy and missionary work sprang from the radical sect emerging in England in the 1650s and led by James Nayler and George Fox (1624–1691). Initially Quakers were socially disruptive, refusing hat-honour (refusing to bare their heads as a gesture of respect) and disrupting Church services by invading 'steeple-houses' and testifying. Women took an active part in the movement from its inception, but after the Restoration of Charles II, the imposition of the so-called Clarendon Code made religious Dissent and Quaker activity even more difficult. In response to continued and escalating oppression, gaoling and debarment from public office, the Quaker leadership began to play down the sect's radicalism, and this brought a review of the position of women as preachers and as prophets, accompanied by a move to develop women's meetings. However, as the Quakers outlived other English Civil War period (1642–1651) sects, such as Independents ▷(Katherine Chidley), women were never fully silenced. Throughout the 17th and 18th centuries women continued to play a very important part as ministers, missionaries and preachers, often travelling vast distances in appalling conditions. Often their writings tell the story of their travels as a way of communicating with their fellow-believers or 'friends', and they also produced autobiography, polemic, records, pamphlets, sermons and poems.

▷Blaugdone, Barbara; Carey, Mary; Chidley, Katherine; Evans, Katherine; Fell, Margaret; Vokins, Joan

Bib: Hill, Christopher, *The World Turned Upside Down*, Hobby, Elaine, *Virtue of Necessity*.

Quaretti, Lea (born 1912)

Italian novelist. Born in Rigoso near Parma, she spent much of her life in Venice, and contributed regularly to Italian newspapers. The recurrent theme of her work is memory and the recreation of the past. Her prose style is lyrical. ▷*La donna sbagliata* (1950) (*The Woman Who Made a Mistake*), is a novel which, like many of her works, recreates the pain of the past (in this through the story of an unhappy marriage). ▷*L'estate di Anna* (1955) (*Anna's Summer*), is a novel of memory, and of psychological trauma. Her work deals, on the whole, with introspective characters.

Her other works include: *Il faggio* (1946) (*The Beech Tree*); *La voce del fiume* (1947) (*The Voice of the River*); her collected works were published in 1982.

Quarrel of the Ancients and Moderns

The *Querelle des Anciens et des Modernes*, a literary debate in France at the end of the 17th century as to the relative merits of Graeco-Roman and contemporary writers. The chief protagonists were the Academicians Nicolas Boileau (1636–1711), author of *L'Art poétique* (1674) (*The Poetic Art*), which attacked the 'Moderns', and Charles Perrault (1628–1703), who sought to defend them in the *Parallèle des Anciens et des Modernes* (1688–1697) (*The Parallel of the Ancients and Moderns*). Boileau and Perrault also differed in their views of women, though the latter's defence of them in *L'Apologie des Femmes* (*A Defence of Women*) is now considered as old-fashioned as Boileau's attack on them in the *Satire des Femmes* (1674) (*Satire of Women*).

▷Dacier, Anne Tanneguy Le Febvre.

Quartet (1928)

This novel by the Caribbean writer ▷Jean Rhys, originally entitled *Postures*, is considered to be an account of Rhys's affair with Ford Madox Ford. It tells the story of Marya, a young English woman who, unemployed and afraid of growing old meets and marries a Polish man who lives in Paris. She knows little to nothing about him, and when he is arrested she finds herself cast adrift in Paris. Alone and broke, she is taken up by an English couple, the Heidlers, who slowly overwhelm her with their own desires. In this novel Rhys provides a classic version of the fate of the innocent, helpless victim caught up in the duplicities of social and sexual games that she does not really understand.

For a critical analysis see Carole Angier, *Jean Rhys Life and Work* (1990) and Carole Ann Howells, *Jean Rhys* (1991).

Queechy (1852)

US novel by ▷Susan Bogert Warner. Like Warner's 1851 blockbuster novel ▷*The Wide, Wide World*, *Queechy* was an enormous success with the popular audience. Like other ▷woman's fiction, *Queechy* focuses on a young woman bereft of the protections and financial support presumed of the patriarchal family. Supporting herself and her family, the heroine faces conflicts between class expectations and economic realities and between her sense of self and traditional social expectations of young women.

Queiros, Diná Silveira de (1911–1983)

Brazilian novelist, dramatist, journalist, short story writer and chronicler. Born Diná Silveira de Castro Alves, she adopted this pen-name. Her most important novel is her first, *Floradas na serra* (1939) (*Blossoming in the Mountains*), which takes place in a sanatorium in Campos de Jordão, and centres on a love story. It was filmed in 1955, and subsequently two of her short stories and her novel *A Muralha* (1954) (*The Barricade*) were dramatized for television. Married to a diplomat, she helped to promote Brazilian culture abroad, and was awarded several medals. She also received several literary prizes, and was the second woman elected to the Brazilian Academy of Letters.

Other works: *A sereia verde* (1941) (*The Green Siren*); *Margarida La Rocque (A ilha dos demônios)* (1949) (*Margarida La Rocque, The Island of Demons*); *O oitavo dia* (1956) (*The Eighth Day*); *As noites do morro do encanto* (1956) (*The Nights of the Enchanted Hill*); *Eles herdarão a terra* (1960) (*They Will Inherit the Earth*); *Os invasores* (1965) (*The Invaders*); *Verão dos infiéis* (1968) (*Summer of the Unfaithful*); *Café da manhá* (1969) (*Breakfast*); *Comba Malina* (1969); *O livro dos transportes* (1969) (*The Book of Transportation*); *Eu venho (Memorial de Cristo I)* (1974) (*I Come, Memorial to Christ I*), and *Guida, caríssima Guida* (1981) (*Guida, Dearest Guida*).

Queirós, Raquel de (born 1910)

Brazilian novelist, dramatist, chronicler and short story writer. She moved from the family state in the hinterland of Ceará, to the capital, working as a journalist, and then to Rio. Often using her pen-name Rita de Queluz, she is an extremely active writer, working as a translator, and publishing in magazines, newspapers and journals. In 1977 she was the first woman to become a member of the Brazilian Academy of Letters. Her most important novel, ▷*O Quinze* (1930) (*The Fifteenth*) was the second novel of the north-eastern series of ▷1930s novels. Her style, like that of many ▷regionalists, is colloquial, straightforward, direct and simple. Her third novel, *As três Marias* (1963) (*The Three Marias*), is a psychological and dramatic analysis of the status of women in Brazilian ▷patriarchal society. De Queirós was a pioneer in the description of female characters with a rebellious and independent nature. Her fiction and chronicles reveal how her political views changed from socialism to conservatism. Her novel *Dora Doralina* (1974) has been made into a film and her work has been included in a number of anthologies. She has also written plays and stories for children.

Other works: *João Miguel* (1932); *Caminho de pedras* (1937) (*The Rocky Path*); *A donzela e a moura torta* (1948) (*The Damsel and the Crooked Post*); *O*

galo de ouro (1950) (*The Golden Cockerel*); *Lampião* (1953) *Três romances* (1957) (*Three Novels*); *100 crônicas escolhidas* (1958) (*100 Selected Titles*); *A beata Maria do Egito* (1958) (*Blessed Maria of Egito*); *O brasileiro perplexo* (1964); *O caçador de tatu* (1967) (*The Armadillo Hunter*); *As menininhas e outras crônicas* (1976) (*The Girls and Other Tales*).

Queizán, María Xosé (born 1938)

Spanish teacher, feminist, literary critic and novelist. She has published three novels: *A orella no buraco* (1965) (*On the Brink of a Hole*), a Galician rewriting of the *nouveau roman; Amantia* (1984), a feminist novel set during the Roman colonization of Galicia in the 4th century, and *O segredo da Pedra Figueira* (1985) (*The Secret of Figueira Rock*), which is a semi-fantastic novel in the vein of Tolkien's *The Lord of the Rings*.

▷Galician women's writing

Querelle des Anciens et des Modernes

▷Quarrel of the Ancients and Moderns

Question of Power, A (1974)

An avowedly autobiographical novel by Southern African writer ▷Bessie Head. The title refers, according to Head, to the possibility that, if the things of the soul are a question of power then anyone in possession of this power could be Lucifer. The novel presents its central character, Elizabeth, in an extended state of mental breakdown, tormented by her own mother's 'madness'. The child, daughter of a white mother and a black father, had been born in a mental hospital, her mother having been declared insane for falling in love with a black man. Raised first by a foster mother and then by a missionary bent on saving the heathen, Elizabeth has now entered Botswana on an exit permit from South Africa. She feels herself to be contaminated by her racist heritage, and is, moreover, forced to confront an imperfect social state in Botswana. Her psyche becomes a space for the warring forces of good and evil, whose distinctions are not always clear, and which are bound up in complicated ways with the pleasures and horrors of sexual desire. Outside, as part of village life, a team of international volunteer workers is helping the local people set up agricultural projects. At the end of the novel Elizabeth manages to re-enter that community: a world where plants grow, people help one another, and to which she finally belongs.

Quid Pro Quo, or, the Day of the Dupes (1843)

A play by English writer ▷Catherine Gore, which won a £500 prize for an 'English comedy'. The plot concerns social climbing, class division, and the political machinations of county folk. Although it was admired by the judges of the competition, it was a box-office failure, unpopular with both audiences and critics. It was Gore's last play.

▷Drama (19th-century Britain)

Quilt and Other Stories, The (1990)

A collection of fifteen stories by the Indian writer
▷Ismat Chughtai, translated from the Urdu by
Tahira Naqvi and Syeda S. Hameed. The stories
are set in India, principally among the Muslim
upper class and their servants. They are
distinguished by bold and innovative realism, the
use of rich metaphor and robust colloquialism,
and the subversive and ironic wit with which
Chughtai challenges convention, particularly
regarding the traditional status of women. The
title story, 'The Quilt', originally published in
1944, involved the author in a two-year obscenity
trial in Lahore, before the case was dismissed.
The story obliquely depicts a lesbian relationship
between a married woman and her maid, seen
through the eyes of a nine-year-old child.

Quimboiseur l'avait dit, Le (1980) ▷As the
Sorcerer Said (1982)

Quin, Ann (1936–1973)

English novelist. Quin's four published novels
deal with themes of personal alienation, death and
mental illness, and are written in an experimental
style influenced by the *nouveau roman*. *Berg* (1964)
won its author critical acclaim and two
scholarships, enabling Quin to travel to Europe
and the USA, where she lived for some years. It
was followed by *Three* (1966), *Passages* (1973) and
Tripticks (1972). *The Unmapped Country*, which
looks at life in a mental hospital, was left
unfinished when Quin was found drowned.

Quinze, O (1930) (The Fifteenth)

Novel by the Brazilian prose writer ▷Raquel de
Queirós, in which she tells the saga of north-
eastern hinterland immigrants in Brazil trying to
find food and surviving the drought in her native
state, Ceará, one of the poorest regions in the
country. Her experience as a journalist and her
sympathy for the Communist Party made it
possible for her to become the first woman to
enter the Brazilian Academy of Letters, to
sympathize with the immigrants, and write with
feeling about them. The book was the second of
the so-called ▷1930s Novels, as it was published
two years after the first book of this north-eastern
cycle, *A Bagaceira* (*Trash*), by José Américo de
Almeida.

Quiroga, Elena (born 1921)

One of Spain's leading female novelists of the
post-war generation. Born in Santander,
Quiroga's most celebrated novel is ▷*Escribo tu
nombre* (1965) (*I Write Your Name*). The main
themes in Quiroga's work are the Spanish Civil
War (1936–9), death, personal relationships, and
the female estate. Her other novels include: *La
soledad sonora* (1949) (*Sonorous Solitude*); *Viento del
Norte* (1951) (*Northwind*); *La sangre* (1952) (*Blood*);
Algo pasa en la calle (1954) (*Something's Happening
in the Street*); *La enferma* (1955) (*The Sick Woman*);
La careta (1955) (*The Mask*); *La última corrida*
(1958) (*The Last Bullfight*); *Tristura* (1960)
(*Sadness*), and *Presente profundo* (1973) (*Profound
Present*).

Raab, Esther (1899–1981)

Israeli poet. Born in Palestine, in one of the first Jewish settlements, Raab is a true poet of the Israeli landscape. The hard, rugged scenery is a major theme in her lyrical poetry. Her works include: *Kimshonim* (1930) (*Thorns*) and *Shirey Esther Raab* (1963) (*The Poems of Esther Raab*).
▷*Anthology of Modern Hebrew Poetry*; *Voices Within the Ark*

Rachel (1890–1931)

Pseudonym of Israeli poet Rachel Bluwstein, who was born in Russia and emigrated to Palestine in 1909. Although she later went to France and Russia, she returned to Palestine and settled in Galilee.

Her simple, lyrical poetry, much-influenced by Russian poets, became a symbol of the first *Halutzim* (Jewish pioneers) in Israel. The landscape of the Jordan valley and the experience of settling in the biblical homeland are her main themes. A victim of long-term illness herself, she also wrote about the personal pains of a woman deprived of love and children, facing death. Her verse appealed to a large audience, and made her one of the most popular Israeli poets. Her books include: *Saphiach* (1927) (*After Growth*); *Mineged* (1930) (*From Afar*); *Nevo* (1932); ▷*Shirat Rachel* (1961) (*Rachel's Poetry*).
▷*Anthology of Modern Hebrew Poetry*; *Voices Within the Ark*

Rachilde (1860–1953)

French novelist. Born Marguerite Eymery, she read widely during her adolescence (the works she came across included those of the Marquis de Sade), began a career in journalism, married Alfred Vallette, who was the editor of the *Mercure de France*, and published her first novel, ▷*Monsieur Vénus*, in 1884. This tale of gender role inversion and cross-dressing, which launched Rachilde upon a long literary career, was deemed by many of its readers to be pornographic and was banned in Belgium, where it was first published. In fact the novel is remarkably inoffensive, and is also very typical of French *fin de siècle* fiction, given its focus upon strange and 'perverse' forms of erotic activity. Other novels by Rachilde are characterized by a similar fascination with 'unnatural' sexuality, such as homo-eroticism and androgyny, and with the complexities of the human psyche: *Les Hors Nature* (1897) (*Nature's Outcasts*), for example, tells the tale of two incestuous brothers; *L'Heure sexuelle* (1898) (*The Sexual Time*) fictionalizes a case of erotic obsession described in psychiatrist Richard von Krafft-Ebing's *Psychopathia Sexualis* (1886); and *La Souris japonaise* (1912) (*The Japanese Mouse*) deals with paedophilia. Rachilde wore male clothing, a not uncommon practice among literary and artistic women of the period, but she also described herself as a 'man of letters' and adopted a mode of writing – that of the Decadents – which was intensely misogynistic. Her self-masculinization may be explained by the fact that the father, to whom she was devoted in childhood, longed for a son, and instilled in her a sense of the worthlessness of her femininity which emerges explicitly in her autobiographical pamphlet *Pourquoi je ne suis pas féministe* (1928) (*Why I Am Not a Feminist*). Other works by Rachilde include *Mme Adonis* (1888); *La Tour d'Amour* (1899) (*The Tower of Love*), *La Jongleuse* (1900) (▷*The Juggler*) and *L'Amazone rouge* (*The Red Amazon*).
Bib: Brécourt-Villars, C., *Ecrire d'Amour*; David, A., *Rachilde: homme de lettres, son oeuvre*; Santon, N., *La Poésie de Rachilde*.

Radcliffe, Ann (1764–1823)

English novelist. She was author of the renowned ▷Gothic novel ▷*The Mysteries of Udolpho* (1794). Her father seems to have been middle class, and she had relatives in the medical profession. In 1787, she married William Radcliffe, who gave up the law to run *The English Chronicle* and later became a Fellow of the Society of Antiquaries. Influenced by the writing of ▷Sophia Lee, she began writing, and earned money by her pen during her short writing career, which ended in 1795. Her life is said to have been so uneventful that ▷Christina Rosetti had to give up a projected biography for lack of material. Her fiction abounds in romantic description of scenery as well as terrors, and may well have influenced the poet John Keats (1795–1821). Certainly, her reputation was high and her novels extremely popular.

Other publications: *The Castles of Athlin and Dunbayne, a Highland Story* (1798); *A Sicilian Romance* (1790); *The Romance of the Forest* (1791); *The Italian* (1795); *A Journey through Holland and the Western Frontier of Germany* (1795), and *Gaston de Blondeville* (1826).
▷Reeve, Clara

Radha

Consort of the Hindu god Krishna. Like ▷Sita, she is understood primarily in terms of her relationship with her lord, but in this case the relationship is an adulterous one. Although married to another, she is passionately attracted to Krishna, and breaks all the social norms to pursue her love. Her popularity among Hindus arises from her putting her devotion to Krishna above all else, and she is often adopted as a model by Krishna devotees, male and female alike.

Radway, Janice A.

US Professor of American Civilization at the University of Pennsylvania. *Reading the Romance: Woman, Patriarchy and Popular Literature* (1984) adds to ▷Tania Modleski's re-evaluation of popular fiction. In place of the common feminist suspicion of romance, on the grounds that it reinforces women's dependence on men and enlists them within repressive ideologies, Radway argues that ▷romantic fiction can be read as a form of protest against and escape from the restricted roles ascribed to women in patriarchal culture.
▷Harlequin romances

Radzwiłł, Franciszka (1705–53)

Polish dramatist. Radzwiłł was born into a noble family, and lived in a castle at Nieswiez with a rich library, of which she made full use. She wrote plays for the theatre at Nieswiez which had been founded by her husband, who was passionate about drama. She was the first Pole to translate and adapt – quite freely – Molière's comedies. Her early plays are pastorals, mythological stories and fantasies. Her later drama is influenced by the French classical tradition – a transition characteristic of her epoch. A woman of the world, she did not shy away from strong language or bawdiness. She neglected to publish her novels, although they were brought out posthumously in *Komedie i tragedie* (1754) (*Comedies and Tragedies*).

Rafael Marés, Carmen de (born 1911)

Spanish novelist. Born in Barcelona into a cosmopolitan family. Her major work is the trilogy *Sic transit*, consisting of: *Al otro lado del mar* (1973) (*Beyond the Sea*); *El viaje* (1975) (*The Voyage*), and *El regreso* (1976) (*The Return*). The three novels reconstruct the history of three generations of Catalan emigrants and have autobiographical elements. The trilogy's strong points are its exploration of various personal dramas and its study of the problems of ageing. Her other novels include: *Duermen bajo las aguas* (1954) (*They Sleep Beneath the Waters*); *El desconocido* (1956) (*The Stranger*); *Detrás de la piedra* (1958) (*Behind the Rock*); *Al lado del hombre* (1961) (*Beside the Man*); *El becerro de oro* (1964) (*The Golden Calf*); and *Las algas* (1966) (*Seaweed*).

Rafanelli, Leda (1880–1971)

Italian novelist and short story writer. Born in Tuscany, she moved to Alexandria at the age of twenty. While in Egypt, she converted to Islam and espoused anarchism. On returning to Italy, she settled in Florence, then moved to Milan, and founded the publishing house *Società Editrice Milanese* as a means of publicizing anarchist ideas. She was particularly interested in women as revolutionaries. Hounded by the Fascist government, she nevertheless continued to write, though in a less overtly political style. In her work, she targets the Church, militarism and institutional oppression. ▷*Un sogno d'amore* (1905) (*A Dream of Love*) is typical of her narratives of social comment. *Seme nuovo* (1905–8) (*New Seed*) is a work which describes political activism and writing as parallel tools for the protagonist, Vera, to express her beliefs. Love, in this novel, is a means of domination as effective as political tyranny, and which requires as much resistance. *L'oasi. Romanzo arabo* (1929) (*Oasis. An Arabian Novel*) is an anti-colonialist work. *Una donna e Mussolini* (1946) (*A Woman and Mussolini*) is a denunciation of fascism, and an analysis of Mussolini, whom Rafanelli had met in 1913–1914.

Her other works include: *L'eroe della folla* (1920) (*Hero of the Crowd*); *Incantesimo* (1921) (*Enchantment*); *Donne e femmine* (1922) (*Women and Females*).

Raine, Kathleen (born 1908)

English poet, critic and translator, of Scottish origin. The youngest and only female member of the Cambridge Poets in the early 1930s, Raine sees her writing as the legacy of her Scottish ancestry, but was alerted to the idea of a specifically women's writing by ▷Virginia Woolf's ▷*A Room of One's Own*. Her poetry is informed by an anti-materialist viewpoint and includes *Stone and Flower* (1943), *The Hollow Hill* (1964), *Farewell Happy Fields* (1973), and *Collected Poems, 1935–80* (1981). She has published criticism on poets William Blake (1757–1827), S.T. Coleridge (1772–1834) and W.B. Yeats (1865–1939), as well as translations of Honoré de Balzac (1799–1850).

Raj (1989)

Novel by Indian author ▷Gita Mehta. It was the first Indian popular bestseller in the Indian subcontinent and Britain. It tells of a Rajput princess, Jaya Singh, who has to make her way as a royal wife in an Indian princely state during the years of the independence struggle. Her sympathies with the nationalist cause and her desire to improve the lives of her subjects repeatedly clash with the retiring behaviour expected of a traditional lady of the court. The book is, obliquely, a tribute to the many hundreds of independent princes who, in return for pensions that would enable their families to keep up the old royal obligations, surrendered their sovereignty to the new state of India. These pensions have since been clawed back by the Indian government.

Ramayana (200 bc–ad200)

With the ▷*Mahabharata*, one of the two great epics of Hinduism. It was written down in Sanskrit between 200 bc and ad 200, but many Indians today are more familiar with its story through the Hindi version composed by St Tulsi Das in the late 16th century. It tells the story of the god Rama, an *avatar* of Vishnu, and his struggles to conquer evil. Exiled from his kingdom of Ayodhya, he wanders for many years, accompanied by his brother, Lakshman, and his wife, ▷Sita. When Sita is captured by the demon Ravana, Rama and Lakshman call on the aid of the monkey god, Hanuman, to win her back, but their victory is tarnished by rumours of Sita's infidelity. In spite of her protestations of innocence, Rama has her burnt upon a pyre, and is only convinced of her chastity when the flames refuse to burn her. His doubts, however, are not quieted for long, and he eventually casts her out into the jungle where, pregnant, she gives birth to his twin sons. Years later, when Rama is still seeking proof of her fidelity, she opts instead for death, and cries out to Mother Earth to swallow her up.

Rame, Franca (born 1929)

Italian dramatist and actress. Much of her work is produced in collaboration with one of Italy's best-known dramatists, her husband Dario Fo. She targets the bastions of patriarchal society: the law, the state, the family and the church. Her *Tutto casa, letto e chiesa* (1978), translated into English in 1981 as *Female Parts: One-Woman Plays* has been performed throughout Europe (notably by Rame herself) with great success. At once hilarious, horrendous and hard-hitting, this collection of plays illustrates how the institutions at the core of society conspire to oppress women and restrict their freedom.

Ramée, Marie Louise de la ▷'Ouida'

Ramona (1884)

US novel by ▷Helen Hunt Jackson. Set in Mexican California, Mexico, and Native American villages, it positions an ultimately happy love story between a ▷Native American and an adopted Native American/Euro-American against the prejudice of the young woman's adoptive Mexican parents. Vividly depicting the oppression (and murder) of Native Americans as newer settlers take their land, *Ramona* was the first US novel to bring Native American rights – and wrongs – before a large reading public.

Ramondino, Fabrizia (born 1936)

Italian novelist and short story writer. Born in Naples, she has been recognized since the 1980s as one of the most popular and respected of Italian contemporary writers. Some of her work is based on her recreation of her own past. *Althènopis* (1981) is, in essence, the story of her family, and of her relationship with her mother during and after World War II. *Taccuino tedesco* (1987) (*A German Notebook*), is interesting for its style; it is part diary and part a tale of Ramondino's own education. ▷ *Un giorno e mezzo* (1988) (*A Day and a Half*), is set in 1969, and deals to an extent with politics, but also with friendships and memories, as a group of old friends plan a rendezvous. Ramondino produces her work with feminist publishing houses, and contributes to collections of short stories by Italian women writers. She is a self-conscious woman writer. Her other work is *Storie di patio* (1983) (*Patio Stories*).

Ramsay, Martha Laurens (1759–1811)

North American memoirist. She was a member of an upper-class family in Charleston, South Carolina. Deeply religious, she maintained a diary of her religious meditations and self-reflections from 1791 until 1808. She incorporated domestic events into her meditative entries, often finding religious analogies in personal experiences. She died in Charleston on 10 June 1811, at the age of 52.

▷*Memoirs of the Life of Martha Laurens Ramsay*

Rand, Ayn (1905–1982)

US novelist and essayist. Born in St Petersburg, Russia, Rand graduated in 1924 from the University of Leningrad, specializing in history. Unable to adjust to communism, she emigrated to the US in 1926 and was naturalized in 1931. She worked as a screenwriter in Hollywood until 1949 when she became a full-time writer and lecturer.

An atheist, Rand philosophically subscribes to objectivism, with its emphasis on reason, and politically to capitalism. Her novels, *The Fountainhead* (1943) and ▷*Atlas Shrugged* (1957) depict the victory of individualism in battle against collectivism. As outlined in *The Virtue of Selfishness: A New Concept of Egoism* (1964), the self's moral purpose in life is her own happiness. The individual must live for her own sake without sacrificing for others. Rand is a radical advocate for the inviolate supremacy of individual rights.
Bib: Branden, Barbara, *The Passion of Ayn Rand*.

Randhawa, Ravinder (born 1953)

Indian novelist and short story writer, based in Britain. Her writing is especially sensitive to the dilemmas faced by Asian immigrants to Britain. She is a founding member of the Asian Women Writers' Collective, and she has been involved in anti-racist campaigns and in establishing refuges and resource centres for Asian women in Britain. Her first novel, *A Wicked Old Woman*, was published in 1987. She has short stories in the collections *More to Life than Mr Right* (1985) and *A Girl's Best Friend* (1987).

Rank and Money (1838)

▷Evdokiia Rostopchina's *Rank and Money* is a quintessential example of a Russian ▷society tale. It recounts the story of a tragic romance between Vadim, a young man of noble heart and modest means, and a Moscow girl, ironically named Vera ('Faith'), who cannot resist the determination of her noble, rich parents to marry her to a man of equal or greater prestige and wealth. Its three sections – a letter from Vadim to his sister; passages from his diary; a third-person narrative of the denouement and its aftermath – are all in the exalted Sandian (▷George Sand) rhetoric which was a hallmark of hyper-romantic Russian fiction of the late 1830s by authors of both sexes.

Rashid, Saleha Abdul ▷Manja, Salmi

Rasp, Renate (born 1935)

German novelist and poet. Her first novel, *Ein ungeratener Sohn* (1967) (*A Spoilt Son*) is a powerful satire on the repressive nature of the West German education system. It earned her fame and notoriety as one of the 'angry young women' of 1968. The theme of youthful, poetic idealism and feminine vulnerability struggling against the middle-aged ▷patriarchy of the West German establishment is also explored in two collections of her poems: *Eine Rennstrecke* (1969)

(*A Race-track*) and *Junges Deutschland* (1978) (*Young Germany*).

Ratcliff, Mildred Morris (1773–1847)

North American memoirist and letter-writer. Although born shortly before the American Revolution, she devoted her life to religious rather than secular strifes. As an itinerant preacher, her nomadic lifestyle led her from Virginia to Ohio, Pennsylvania, and surrounding states. In the ▷*Memoranda and Correspondence of Mildred Ratcliff*, she recounts her participation in Quaker meetings and theological debates. Although married, she lived an autonomous life, yet one that was dedicated to saving the souls of others as well as herself.

▷Early North American Quaker women's writings

Rattazi, Maria (1830–1902)

French novelist and historical, political and geographical writer. The granddaughter of Lucien Bonaparte, she married the wealthy Comte de Solms, who abandoned her four years later. Linked with opposition to the empire, she lived in exile during the 1850s, returning in 1860 to France, where she subsequently worked as a journalist and editor. Rattazi married twice more, and produced a great many novels. Among these, some of the more noteworthy are the two that appeared under the collective title *Si j'étais reine* (*If I Were Queen*), which have a strong autobiographical flavour, and the erotic novel *Les Mariages de la Créole* (1866) (*The Marriages of a Creole Woman*), which was banned. She also left travelogues and a number of plays.

Ratushínskaia, Irina Borisovna (born 1954)

Poet and memoir-writer in Russian. Brought up in Odessa and educated as a physicist, Ratushínskaia was a lifelong rebel and, with her husband, Igor Gerashchenko, began taking part in the Soviet human rights movement in Kiev in 1980. In 1982 she was arrested and in 1983 sentenced to seven years in a camp and five in exile for anti-Soviet agitation – eg dissemination of her poems. Her plight attracted international attention, and in 1986 she and her husband were permitted to emigrate. Always interested in literature, Ratushínskaia dates her vocation from her discovery of the poetry of the ▷Silver Age in the late 1970s. Translations of her works include: dual-language short stories (*A Tale of Three Heads*, 1986); poems (▷*Beyond the Limit*, 1987); and her gallant memoirs of imprisonment (*Grey Is the Color of Hope*, 1988).

▷Tsvetáeva, Marina; Akhmátova, Anna

Rau, Santha Rama (born 1923)

Indian novelist and travel writer. She was born in Madras. Her father was a diplomat and her mother, Dhanvathi, a prominent social worker who campaigned for education and social and legal rights for Indian women. She was educated at St Paul's School, London, and Wellesley College, Massachusetts, and now lives in the USA. She has travelled extensively, recording some of these experiences in *View to the South-East* (1957) and *My Russian Journey* (1959). *The Cooking of India* (1970) is also written in the form of a travelogue. She has written three volumes of autobiography which draw extensively on her movements around the world, *Home to India* (1945), *East of Home* (1950) and *Gifts of Passage* (1961). Her travel writing has won praise for its liveliness and its empathy with her subjects. She is a frequent contributor to *The New York Times* and *Horizon*, and in 1960 adapted E.M. Forster's *Passage to India* for the stage. In 1976 she co-authored *A Princess Remembers* with Gayatri Devi of Jaipur. Her novel *Remember the House* (1955) draws on her experiences in Japan, the Philippines and China. Another novel, *The Adventuress*, was published in 1971.

Ravikovitch, Dalia (born 1936)

Israeli poet and short story writer. Born in Ramat-Gan, Israel, Ravikovitch was educated in Haifa and Jerusalem. Her first book of verse was published in 1959 and immediately established her as a leading Israeli poet. Her writing is deeply personal and conveys a strong sense of loss. In many of her poems, however, the personal hurt is portrayed in the form of an impersonal myth. Ravikovitch sometimes replaces the rich imagery of her writing with conversational tones, but the poems never lose their dramatic effect. She has also published a collection of short stories written in a lyrical style and portraying similar emotions. Her books include: *Ahavat Tapuach Ha'Zahav* (1959) (*The Love of a Golden Orange*); *Choref Kashe* (1964) (*Hard Winter*); ▷*Ha'Sefer Ha'shlishi* (1969) (*The Third Book*); *Ahava Amitit* (1987) (*True Love*); *Mavet Ba'mishpacha* (1990) (*Death in the Family*).

▷*New Writing From Israel*; *Modern Hebrew Poem Itself, The*; *Penguin Book of Hebrew Verse, The*; *Voices Within the Ark*

Ravishing of Lol V. Stein, The (1986)

Translation of *Le Ravissement de Lol V. Stein* (1964), ▷Marguerite Duras's ninth novel. The narrator, Jacques Hold, tells the story of the woman he loves, Lol V. Stein, as he has reconstructed it from what he has been told by her friend, Tatiana Karl, who is also his lover, and from his own imagination. When she is young, Lol loses her fiancé, Michael Richardson, to another woman, Anne-Marie Stretter, at a ball. For a while she appears mad, then recovers enough to marry and have children, living in a manner copied from her neighbours. After meeting Jacques, she starts following him, lying in a field outside the hotel where he goes with Tatiana. This three-way relationship in which she is the excluded witness returns Lol to the scene at the ball, which she constantly seeks to recapture. However when Jacques and Lol become lovers, his passion for her leads him to decide to break with Tatiana, and thus also to destroy the satisfaction Lol has constructed for herself.

Ravissement de Lol V. Stein, Le (1964)
▷*Ravishing of Lol V. Stein, The* (1986)

Rawle, Anna (fl 1781)
North American diarist. A Philadelphia Quaker
and Loyalist during the American Revolution, she
records her outrage at attacks against Loyalists in
▷'A Loyalist's Account of Certain Occurrences
in Philadelphia . . .'. The 'occurrences' were acts
of violence committed in reaction to General
Cornwallis's surrender on 22 October 1781, a
'surprizing and vexatious' event, to her mind.

Rawlings, Marjorie Kinnan (1896–1953)
US novelist and short story writer. At six Rawlings
began writing and publishing stories. In 1918 she
graduated Phi Beta Kappa from the University of
Wisconsin and became a journalist. She farmed
and wrote in Florida from 1928 until 1947, when
a neighbour sued her for libel. With the Pulitzer
Prize-Winning novel ▷*The Yearling* (1938) and
the autobiographical *Cross Creek*, Rawlings
established herself as a regionalist. She portrays
poor, proud, self-reliant farmers scratching their
subsistence from the Florida swamp.

Rawlinson, Gloria (born 1918)
New Zealand poet and fiction writer. Gloria
Rawlinson was born in Tonga and spent her early
childhood there. She began writing and
publishing poetry as a child and was interviewed
at a young age by the writer ▷Robin Hyde, with
whom Rawlinson and her mother maintained a
close friendship. Rawlinson has published
frequently over the years and still produces new
work. Her first volume was published when she
was fifteen. Rawlinson's work, like that of Robin
Hyde, was considered to be out of the main
literary tradition for most of her life, but has been
brought into new prominence by feminism,
although her work lacks the qualities – of
questioning, challenge to established ideas,
especially those of gender and literary innovation
– that have made Hyde's attractive to feminist
thinkers.
    Publications: *Gloria's Book* (1933); *The Perfume
Vendor* (1935); (edited) *Houses by the Sea: The
Later Poems of Robin Hyde* (1952); *The Islands
Where I Was Born* (1955); *Of Clouds and Pebbles*
(1963).

Realism
A catch-all term for literary and visual forms
which aim for the accurate reproduction of the
world as it is. There is a long tradition of
philosophical realism concerning the relationship
of individual phenomenon to abstract categories,
and the relationship of ideas to the real world.
Literary realism emerges in the late 18th and 19th
centuries concomitantly with the rise of the novel.
Nineteenth-century novels are often described,
from a 20th-century perspective, as classic realist
texts, a term devised by the film critic Colin
McCabe in 1974 to describe ▷George Eliot's
▷*Middlemarch* (1871–1872). Classic realism,

according to McCabe, who reverses the terms of
Lukacs's ▷socialist realist attack on
▷modernism, works by a sleight of hand, to hide
the constructedness of the world; the world of the
novel is presented to the reader as if it were a
direct mirroring or reflection of the real world,
rather than an ideologically saturated
interpretation of the real. The term most often
used to describe the strategy of the realist text is
transparency. The illusion of transparency created
by realism is then contrasted with modernist
writing, which supposedly foregrounds its
conventional status.
    ▷Virginia Woolf, as a modernist, wrote on the
need to break with realist and literary conventions.
In her essay 'Mr. Bennett and Mrs. Brown', she
constructed an important and witty argument for
the impossibility of writing about women outside
of the dominant definitions of femininity. Woolf
is, however, writing against naturalism, a late
19th-century form of realism, associated with the
French novelist Emile Zola. Naturalism emerged
out of an attempt to marry literary and scientific
discourses, and demanded a scientific and
empirical objectivity from writers, whose novels
were supposed to be laboratory experiments to
show how character is determined by
environment. In practice, as Woolf notes,
naturalism remained focused on the world as
external material appearance, and imposed a rigid
set of normalizing causal narratives. However, any
absolute distinction between modernism and
realism needs cautious treatment. Woolf's
modernist break with realism, was also done in
the name of delivering the real, and her criticism
of naturalism is based partly on the view that it
fails to do this, rather than on a critique of the
possibility of doing so. It is also important not to
conflate different forms of realism – for example,
classic realism, naturalism, socialist realism – and
to recognize they they presuppose different kinds
of relationship between the literary text and the
world.
    The dominant 20th-century critiques of realism
as a naturalization of ideological positions,
presenting them as if they were commonsense
perceptions or views, had the effect that realism
was seen as an inappropriate literary mode for
feminist writers. The need to challenge dominant
representations of gender led to a suspicion of the
many pleasures of realism and a valorization of
modernist and avant-garde representational
practices. Catherine Belsey's *Critical Practice*
(1980) and Toril Moi's *Sexual / Textual Politics*
(1985) are, in different ways, exemplary of this
position.
    Latterly, it has been argued that the polarization
of realism and modernism, and the rejection of
realism, has been too absolute. More work is
being done on the many varieties of realism, and
work on reading and fantasy suggests that earlier
views of how the classic realist text operated
assumed too simplistic a model of reading
practices and modes of reception. The urgent
need to theorize predominantly realist popular

culture forms which are read by the majority of women, such as ▷romance fiction, has also motivated this rethinking of realism. Rita Felski's recent book, *Beyond Feminist Aesthetics* (1989), is a good indicator of these trends.

▷Molesworth, Maria Louisa; Nesbit, Edith; Regional novel, The; Webster, Augusta

Italy: The preferred Italian form to describe this 19th-century movement is *verismo*. It came into being as a reaction to lyrical ▷romanticism, and was founded on the principle of 'objective' narrative representation. Giovanni Verga (1840–1922) is generally acknowledged to be the founder of the movement in Italy, as well as its greatest exponent. He strove to make the story read 'as if it had written itself', attempting to completely get rid of the authorial presence. Language is of crucial importance in debates on realism, as it is in the works of the realists themselves. These writers attempt to render as closely as possible the rhythms of spoken Italian, occasionally using dialect to achieve this. Italian realism is also a form of documentation of life at different levels of society, and functions as a challenge to the supposedly unified post-▷*Risorgimento* Italy. Many women writers as diverse as ▷Caterina Percoto, ▷Matilde Serao, Paola Drigo and, more recently, ▷Elsa Morante and ▷Oriana Fallaci, have either been defined as realist writers, or have been said to include elements of realism in their work.

Realismo magico ▷Magic realism

Real Matilda: Woman and Identity in Australia 1788 to the Present, The (1976)
Feminist history by Miriam Dixson. One of Australia's earliest and most respected feminist historical works. It argues that women have a lower standing in Australia than in comparable countries, that they are the 'doormats of the western world'. Dixson attributes this to Australia's formative past, its convict beginnings and its subsequent early history, where women were treated with both contempt and brutality. She considers that women are 'still deeply, if unconsciously, impoverished by this dominant cultural characteristic' and reminds Australians that their heroes are all misogynist; for example Ned Kelly, the notorious Australian bushranger and his gang; and the 'mateship' men at Gallipoli, 'eternal sexual adolescents, one feels, exuding wariness or fear about women, and often themselves virtually womanless'. 'Mateship' is a much-discussed Australian male ethic, supposedly evolved from the almost exclusively male society, and perhaps most clearly demonstrated in battle or sport – for example, at Gallipoli, where Australians fought with great courage in 1915. The mateship ethic is much resented by feminists. Dixson cites a considerable amount of documentary evidence in support of her theory, and the book has been revised and updated several times since its first publication.

Real Mothers (1981)
American-Canadian writer ▷Audrey Thomas's collection of short stories about motherhood and its fearful moments. These stories concern themselves with mothers in conflict with husbands, daughters or lovers; and with mothers very much alone. This is Thomas at her best: sharp, incisive, and parenthetically reflective, working within the difficult form of short fiction with finesse.

Rebecca (1938)
Novel by English writer ▷Daphne du Maurier. Its famous first line – 'Last night I dreamt I went to Manderley again' – establishes the pervasive tone of nostalgia and loss. The unnamed female narrator, in the novel's opening an exile from England, recounts in retrospect the story of her 'fairytale' marriage to the wealthy Max de Winter, who rescues her from impoverished middle-class drudgery and takes her to Manderley, his country estate. There her happiness is overshadowed by the difficulty of stepping into the place of the deceased first Mrs de Winter, the Rebecca of the title, who comes to be the embodiment of successful femininty for the narrator.

The second half of the novel becomes in part a crime and mystery story, in which Max de Winter is tried for Rebecca's murder. Although he is finally acquitted, he reveals to his wife that he was driven to kill Rebecca: 'She was vicious, damnable, rotten through and through.' This new version of events gives the narrator a freedom from Rebecca's power, which her own jealousy and insecurity had brought into being. The novel promises a happy ending, but in fact ends with the destruction of Manderley.

Rebecca is a powerful blend of ▷romance, ▷Gothic and thriller conventions; a romantic novel which submits romance to scrutiny, and demonizes sexual desire while invoking its power. A number of its themes and images are borrowed from ▷*Jane Eyre*. In 1940 Alfred Hitchcock made a hugely popular film of *Rebecca*.

Rebecca; or, The Fille de Chambre (1792)
Novel by the North American writer ▷Susanna Haswell Rowson. *Rebecca* draws upon autobiographical events such as a young woman's recognition of the realistic horrors of war, the perilous nature of sea journeys in the 18th century and the lasting effects of an impoverished childhood. Unlike the characterization of a young woman in her better-known novel, ▷*Charlotte, a Tale of Truth*, it presents a heroic young woman of fortitude and courage.

Recke, Elisabeth von der (1754–1833)
German poet and diarist. After a ten-year marriage to a much older man, and following the death of her only child, she obtained a divorce and began to travel among the courts of northern Europe, where she met many writers. An intense friendship with Sophie Becker-Schwarz led to an exchange of poems, published after Sophie's

death as *Elisens und Sophiens Gedichte* (1790)
(*Poems of Elise and Sophie*). Her extensive diaries
include essays on such issues as the French
Revolution (1879), the emergence of the German
middle class, the repression of women, and on the
dangerous attractions of a man like Alessandro
Cagliostro (1743–1795), a notorious Italian
alchemist, physician and confidence man. These
diaries were republished in 1984 as *Tagebücher
und Selbstzeugnisse* (*Diaries and Self-portraits*).

Red Pottage (1899)

A novel by English author ▷Mary Cholmondeley.
It centres on the lives of two women, Hester
Gresley and Rachel West. Hester is a writer who
lives with her bigoted clergyman brother and his
narrow-minded wife. Her efforts at literary
achievement are defeated when her brother burns
the only copy of her novel, claiming it to be
immoral. The story of Hester's friend, Rachel, is
a more conventional ▷romance. The novel
caused a minor sensation, being simultaneously
denounced by clergymen and celebrated as a
brilliant satire by journalists. Recent feminist
readings have emphasized the strength of the
relationship between Hester and Rachel, and
praised the novel's defence of women's friendship.
Bib: ▷Showalter, E., *A Literature of Their Own*.

Red Sky at Morning (1942)

Three-act Australian play by ▷Dymphna Cusack.
First produced in 1935, and published in 1942,
this is a drama of early Australian life. Set in
1812, it concerns the relationship between Alicia,
a high-born lady, and Michael, an Irish convict.
Alicia is fleeing from an officer in the New South
Wales Corps, with whom she has had an illicit
relationship, and who has, on an earlier occasion,
had Michael sadistically flogged for speaking to
Alicia. Alicia and Michael agree to escape to a
new life together, but are trapped and drowned
while attempting to cross a flooded river.
Historically accurate, but somewhat melodramatic,
this well-constructed play has had an excellent
critical reception.

Rees, Rosemary (1876–1963)

New Zealand romantic novelist. Rees was an actor
as well as romantic novelist; during World War I
she entertained New Zealand troops and
subsequently established her own company which
toured New Zealand until it collapsed in 1923.
She wrote her first novel in five weeks, and
altogether produced twenty-four romantic novels,
which are set in England, Australia and New
Zealand and which affirm marriage as the proper
destiny for young women. Rees's novels were
popular and widely-read during her lifetime: she
told ▷Robin Hyde that she was the most
successful woman writer in New Zealand, and she
employed the formulas and gender stereotypes
that govern romance. The dustjacket of *Wild, Wild
Heart* (1928) proclaims: 'Rosemary Rees' women
are true women – her men, real men.'
  Publications: (A selective list): *April's Sowing*

(1924); *Heather of the South* (1924); *Life's What
You Make It!* (1927); *Wild, Wild Heart* (1928);
Dear Acquaintance (1929); *Home's Where the Heart
Is* (1935); *Hetty Looks for Local Colour* (1935); *Little
Miss Independent* (1940); *I Can Take Care of Myself*
(1940); *The Mended Citadel* (1949).
▷Romance writing, New Zealand

Reeve, Clara (1729–1807)

Novelist, poet and critic who wrote the well-
known ▷Gothic novel ▷*The Old English Baron*
(1778). The daughter of a rector from near
Ipswich, one of eight children, who started writing
in the 1750s. She translated Barclay's romance,
Argenis, as *The Phoenix* (1772), and in *The Progress
of Romance* (1785) her characters comment on
romance in its different historical and
geographical incarnations – a process which
involves a discussion of women writers, including
Hortensius's opinion that the dead ▷Aphra Behn
is too risqué – 'I shall not disturb her, or her
works' – but a woman speaks up for ▷Oroonoko.
  Other publications: *Original Poems on Several
Occassions* (1769); *The Two Mentors* (1780); *The
School For Widows* (1791), and *Plans of Education*
(1792).
▷Radcliffe, Ann; Haywood, Eliza

'Réflexions sur l'Algérie – tu es descendue des montagnes' (1989) ('Reflections on Algeria – You have come down from the mountains)'

A poem by the Algerian poet ▷Nafissa Boudalia,
describing the euphoria of the Algerian
independence in 1962. The woman, dressed as a
bride, symbolizes Algeria as well as the liberation
from French oppression. The bride is waiting for
the bridegroom, who symbolises freedom. Instead
of being happy, the bride is disillusioned and
deprived of her jewels, which mean protection in
the Berber tradition. The events of 1988 are the
result of rape, and represent the disappointment
of the Algerian people, especially the women, who
have to suffer the consequences of the changing
situation: 'Your back is bent, you are not able to
walk anymore . . . your rags smell repugnant . . .
without living I do not call myself ALGERIA.'

Reform (19th-century Britain)

A series of legislative changes specifically affecting
women occurred in Britain during the 19th
century. The Infant Custody Bill of 1839, which
became law partially as a result of the efforts of
▷Caroline Norton, allowed a divorced woman
access to her children until they were seven years
old (previously, divorced women had no right of
access). Divorce, however, was not common, nor
was it equitable. The 1857 Divorce Act decreed
that a man could obtain a dissolution of his
marriage if he could prove one act of infidelity. A
woman seeking divorce could not sue on the
grounds of infidelity alone. She also had to prove
cruelty or violence on the part of her husband.
This Act, which reflected the sexual double
standard of Victorian society, remained the law

throughout the rest of the 19th century and into the 20th.

Before 1870, a married woman had no legal right to possess property or earnings. All her goods, her children and her body belonged to her husband under the doctrine of couveture – the idea that 'the very being or legal existence of the wife is suspended during the marriage or at least incorporated and consolidated into that of the husband under whose wing protection and cover she performs everything.' The Married Women's Property Bill of 1870 gave a married woman control over her earnings, but no other property.

The Parliamentary Reform Bills of the 19th century had no effect upon the status of women. The Bills of 1832, 1867 and 1884 progressively expanded the franchise so that by the end of the century all non-institutionalized male members of society had the right to vote. Despite the persistent campaigning for women's ▷suffrage, the franchise was not achieved until 1918.

▷*Eliza Cook's Journal*; Bodichon, Barbara; Caird, Mona; Power Cobbe, Frances; Martineau, Harriet; *Middlemarch*

Regionalism
In Brazil,▷*costumbrismo*.

Regional Novel, The (19th-century Britain)
A novel set in a real locality, accurately described. Regional novels became popular in Britain during the 19th century and many women writers used the form. ▷George Eliot, ▷Elizabeth Gaskell and the ▷Brontë sisters are notable examples; lesser-known writers include ▷Isabella Banks, nick-named 'The Lancashire novelist' as a result of her detailed local description.

▷Realism (19th-century Britain)

Reiche, Momoe Malietoa von
Samoan poet. Momoe Malietoa von Reiche was born in Western Samoa and educated in Samoa and New Zealand, training as a teacher in Wellington. Her work, like ▷Konai Helu Thaman's, is feminist and postcolonial, focusing on the conflicts of marriage and family and the loss of a distinctive cultural environment.

Publications: *Tai, heart of a tree* (1989).

Reidy, Sue
New Zealand short story writer. Best known as an illustrator and designer before her collection of stories, *Modettes*, appeared, Reidy has published occasional stories in major journals since the early 1980s. In 1985 her story 'Alexandra and the Lion' won the Bank of New Zealand Katherine Mansfield Award. Reidy's fiction is located around Asia and the Pacific and reflects a clearly-defined geographical region away from the Eurocentrism of earlier writers. Her stories feature independent, self-sufficient female characters and her narrative environment is usually ▷magic realism with reference to Asian belief systems.

Reimann, Brigitte (1933–1973)
East German novelist. Her novel *Ankunft im Alltag* (1961) (*Arrival in Everyday Life*) tells the story of three young workers who must learn to integrate themselves usefully into the new socialist workforce. The book became the paradigm for a whole series of similar stories by East German writers seeking to educate their readers into becoming good socialists. *Franziska Linkerhand* (1974), a novel which remained unfinished because of Reimann's untimely death, is a much more complex and thoughtful exploration of the difficult relationship between a woman's idealism, her search for freedom and self-expression, and the demands of everyday socialist reality.

▷*Bildungsroman*.

Reinig, Christa (born 1926)
German poet and novelist. A factory worker in Berlin during World War II, she entered university to study art history in the 1950s. She began publishing poetry in East German journals, but switched to West German publishers when censorship became too intrusive. In 1964 she left East Germany, and now lives in Munich. The main body of her work is characterized by a radical and uncompromising feminist stance, which declares war on men the state and on predatory society, in both East and West. Her main works include: *Die Ballade vom blutigen Bomme* (1972) (*The Ballard of Bloody Bomme*); *Entmannung* (1976) (*Castration*); *Mädchen ohne Uniform* (1981) (*Girl Without Uniform*), and *Feuergefährlich. Gedichte und Erzählungen für Frauen und Männer* (1982) (*Inflammatory. Poems and Stories for Women and Men*).

Reinsberg-Duringsfeld, Ida von (1815–1876)
German poet, essayist and novelist. A precocious talent, she wrote poetry while still in her teens. As the wife of the aristocratic Freiherr von Reinsberg, she later made a name for herself with novels and novellas, as well as essays on cultural and historical subjects. In recent years, interest in her has revived, chiefly because of her eulogistic poem, 'An George Sand' ('To George Sand'), which, in many ways, is an early exploration of many of today's feminist concerns.

▷Sand, George

Reinshagen, Gerlind (born 1926)
West German dramatist and novelist. A pharmacist by profession, she had a first success with *Doppelkopf* (1967) (*Double Head*), a satirical play about the way the German economic miracle entraps *petit-bourgeois* citizens in false hopes and disastrous situations. All her plays and novels criticize the stuffiness of modern life. Blinkered and confused, her protagonists delude themselves with hopelessly utopian aspirations. Her other important works include the plays *Himmel und Erde* (1974) (*Heaven and Earth*) and *Sonntagskinder* (1981) (*Sunday's Children*), and the novel, *Die flüchtige Braut* (1984) (*The Flighty Bride*).

Reis, Maria Firmina dos (1825–1917)

Brazilian novelist and poet. A poor, mulatto teacher in Guimarães, in Maranhão, she remained single but adopted several children. Her novel *Úrsula* (1859), published under her pen-name Uma Brasileira ('A Brazilian'), and discovered only this century, was the second novel written by a woman, and the first abolitionist novel, in Brazil. Its plot deals with a marriage made impossible because an intruding, powerful uncle kills Úrsula's fiancé and drives her to madness. She contributed to *Semanário Maranhense* (1867-1868), and wrote patriotic hymns and abolitionist poems in *Cantos à beira-mar* (1871) (*Seaside Song*). Her short stories *Escrava* and *Gupeva*, published in *Moraes Filho* (1975), are a defence of the slaves and South American Indians.

Other work: *Maria Firmina, fragmentos de uma vida* (1975)(*Maria Firmina, Fragments of a Life*).

Réisner, Larisa Mikhailovna (1895–1926)

Russian prose writer and journalist. Réisner's father was a professor of law, and she grew up in an intellectual atmosphere. She began writing poetry, and produced one poetic mystery play, *Atlantis* (1913), with the apocalyptic theme of a doomed people in pre-revolutionary St Petersburg. From 1915 to 1918 she wrote articles and theatre criticism for various periodicals. After the 1917 Revolution Réisner became active in cultural life on behalf of the new Soviet state. Married to a Bolshevik leader, Fëdor Raskol'nikov, she went with him to the eastern front, where she worked as a commissar. Her sketches of the Civil War were published in the book *Front* (1925). Life abroad in Afghanistan, and then in Germany, with her ambassador-husband resulted in more books of sketches: *Afghanistan* (1925), *Hamburg on the Barricades* (1924), *Berlin in the Year 1923* (1925), and *In Hindenburg's Country* (1926). She dealt with the industrialization drive in the Soviet Ural mountain region and the Donetsk River basin in *Iron, Coal, and Living People* (1925). At her premature death from typhoid fever, she was working on historical portraits of the participants in the uprising of 1825, *The Decembrists*. Réisner is cited as one of the innovators of the Soviet literary sketch – aestheticized reporting clearly identified with the communist cause.

Bib: Chapple, Richard (trans.) and Réisner, Larisa, *Hamburg at the Barricades, and Other Writings on Weimar Germany*.

Relation of the Melancholy Death of Six Young Persons . . . (1767)

When lightning struck and killed six young people in Hartland, Connecticut, in the summer of 1767 the North American poet ▷Consider Tiffany published a broadside about the event. Formulaic in its assertion that the deaths were a warning of God's disfavour, it calls for 'old and young' to 'spend our latest breath / In making Christ our friend'.

Religion

Ancient Greek and Roman, women and: From earliest times women held a prominent position in the organization of, and participation in, ancient religious cults. In classical Athens, where respectable women's public life was severely restricted, religion was practically the only sphere in which a woman could hold a civic position. The priest of Athena, the city's patron-deity, was a woman. At the oracle of Delphi, the mouthpiece of the god Apollo was a prohesying priestess. At Sparta, women were involved in the worship of the goddess Artemis. At Rome, too, even before it grew to power, women were important religious figures, as priestesses and prophetesses. The Vestal Virgins tended the sacred hearth-fire of Rome itself. The Roman empresses invariably possessed religious titles among the other honours bestowed them.

It is not, therefore, surprising that much of the earlier literature written by classical women, especially the Greek, comes from a religious background. Choral lyric for religious celebration by female performers is the first genre from which women's poetry survives. ▷Sappho wrote wedding hymns, and many women poets' commonplaces may also be seen to stem from other religious demands – for example laments for the dead (always specially associated with women in classical times), or epigrams (originally designed for tombstones).
▷Epigram, Ancient Greek

Christianity, Islam and traditional beliefs in West Africa: Both Christianity and Islam were imported to Africa as the ideological components of imperialist projects. The ancient belief systems that flourished in West Africa prior to the Arab incursion from the north or European colonization were perceived by both sets of invaders as 'pagan' and 'uncivilized', and therefore justified their obliteration. Traditional religion is, in the main, animist, infusing all living things with meaning and attaching great significance to the ancestors, and the links between the living, the dead and the unborn. It still flourishes, often alongside the 'official' religions, as described in ▷Zaynab Alkali's ▷*The Stillborn* (1984), set in a village in the Middle Belt of Nigeria, where all three belief systems coexist. In some cases, like that of the Yoruba people of south-west Nigeria, the elaborate mythology of the traditional religions is a rich source of creativity for contemporary artists and writers.

Religious poetry in Norway

The most important writer of religious poetry is Dorothe Engelbretsdatter (1634–1716), who made a living from writing hymns and devotional books, such as *Taare-Offer* (1685) (*Tear Sacrifice*). *Sjælens Sang Offer* (1678) (*A Singing Sacrifice from the Soul*) was reprinted twenty-four times, not least because the hymns were also poems and could be read as such. Engelbretsdatter was the first woman in a very male-dominated learned tradition, but not the last; among others were Ingeborg Grytten

(1668–?), Birgitte Christine Kaas (1682–1761) and Birgitte Lange (1714–1753). They all wrote religious and learned literature.

A less learned, but maybe more religious literature was written by women writers in the 19th century, such as Hanna Winsnes (1789–1872) and Berthe Canutte Aarflot (1795–1859), a simple farmer's wife who had a very big influence on the Norwegian hymn. Her hymns are sung even today.

Religious writings (Italy)

Most of the earliest writings in the Italian language were religious in tone and inspiration. The Church was accepted as an appropriate guide in all aspects of civil and moral life. Early 13th-century works in Italian (rather than Latin) are written largely by those in religious orders, and usually addressed to the laity. Saint Francis of Assisi (1182–1226) founded his ▷Franciscan order, which was of significance in the production of religious writings. Yet it is ▷Santa Caterina da Siena (1347–80) who is acknowledged to be the most interesting of the religious writers of the period, mainly for her mixture of religious ecstasy with sound practical and political acumen.

Reliquiae Turellae et Lachrymae Paternal (1735)

The writings of the North American poet ▷Jane Colman Turell, collected in a biographical memoir by her husband after her death. They are the only extant writings by her, and reflect her husband's interest in presenting her as a model of piety. Included are poems, essays and diary entries. Her poetry reveals interests far beyond the usual ken of Puritan women and is woman-centred in its themes and tropes. In 'On Reading the Warning by Mrs Singer', she reveals the encouragement she felt in discovering another woman writer of similar values: 'Surprised I view, wrote by a female pen, / Such a grave warning to the sons of men / . . . A woman's pen strikes the cursed serpent's head, / And lays the monster gasping, if not dead.' Often neo-classical, her poetry always integrates personalized reflections.

▷Dennie, Abigail Colman; 'Lines from a Letter to Her Sister, Jane Colman Turell'

Remorse (1967)

English translation of *Il rimorso* (1964), a novel by Italian writer ▷Alba de Cespedes. The plot centres on a group of male intellectuals, and analyses their characters and their attempts to come to terms with Italian life in the twenty years after the ▷Resistance. It deals with the significance of the past, and past actions, and is structured in a loosely episodic style.

Rémusat, Claire de (1780–1821)

French educational writer. A lady-in-waiting to the Empress Josephine and an habituée of the Parisian salons of the imperial era, Rémusat kept in contact with this fashionable milieu even after her husband, a government administrator, was posted to Toulouse and then Lille. The milieu resuscitated in her memoirs, which her grandson published in 1880. She was also the author of an *Essai sur l'éducation des femmes* (*Essay on Women's Education*), published posthumously, which urges its female readers to cultivate modesty and humility, and was intended, as critic Claire Moses observes, 'to help women achieve usefulness and dignity' through domestic competence.

Bib: Moses, C., *French Feminism in the 19th Century.*

Renaissance (Italy)

A key cultural movement in Italy between the 15th and 16th centuries which had widespread influence on European civilization as a whole. The Italian term *rinascimento* signifies rebirth, in this instance a cultural rebirth inspired by a rediscovery of classical culture. Earlier Italian works, too, were reassessed: the writings of Petrarch were seen as of particular importance (▷Petrarchism). Courtly literature (writings produced for, on, about the Italian courts, their courtiers and *dame di palazzo* – 'ladies of the courts') abounded, best exemplified, perhaps, in Castiglione's *Book of the Courtier* (▷16th-century treatises on women). The literature of the period harked back to the classical age, to formal elegance. The traditionally accepted 'great names' of the Renaissance are those of men: Castiglione, Machiavelli and Ariosto. Yet women writers, too, contributed much to the writings of this period, particularly in their poetry (▷Gaspara Stampa, ▷Tullia D'Aragona, ▷Vittoria Colonna, ▷Veronica Gambara, ▷Maria Savorgnan), and their treatises (▷Moderata Fonte, ▷Lucrezia Marinelli).

Renault, Mary (1905–1983)

South African/English novelist. Renault is acclaimed for her representations of life in classical Greece. Born in London, and educated at St Hugh's College, Oxford, she first wrote four novels about nursing life, published under her own name, Eileen Mary Challans. The last of these, *Return to Night* (1947), won her an MGM (Metro-Goldwyn-Mayer) Prize. In 1948 she emigrated to South Africa, where she began publishing historical novels about ancient Greece, after visiting Greece during her extensive travels.

Her reputation depends largely on the first two of her historical novels, *The Last of the Wine* (1956) and *The King Must Die* (1958), works of meticulous scholarship and imaginative historical evocation. *The King Must Die* reconstructs the youth of the legendary Greek hero Theseus, and his encounter with ancient Cretan culture, and attempts to strip the legend of its mythical embellishments. Theseus is identified as part of the rising patriarchal social order, ruled by male sky gods, at a time when matriarchal cultures and earth mother goddesses were waning in influence.

Part of Renault's interest in classical Greece is an interest in homosexuality, which recurs in her only mature novel set in modern times: *The*

Charioteer (1953). Her other Greek novels are: *The Bull from the Sea* (1962); *The Mask of Apollo* (1966); *The Persian Boy* (1972) (a trilogy on Alexander the Great); *Fire From Heaven* (1969), and *Funeral Games* (1981). Other early English novels are: *Purposes of Love* (1939, USA edition entitled *Promise of Love*); *Kind are Her Answers* (1940); *The Friendly Young Ladies* (1944); *The Middle Mist* (1945), and *North Face* (1948). She also wrote a history of ancient Greece, retold for young readers, *The Lion in the Gateway* (1964). She wrote no novels with a South African setting because, she said, trying not to offend anyone would require an impossible racial balancing act. Her work is occasionally reprinted.

Other works: *The Praise Singer* (1975), *The Nature of Alexander* (1975), and an unpublished play, *The Day of Good Hope* (written 1955). **Bib:** Wolfe, Peter, *Mary Renault*; Dick, Bernard F., *The Hellenism of Mary Renault*.

Rendell, Ruth (born 1930)

English novelist. An acclaimed and bestselling crime writer, her ▷detective novels feature the refined and sensitive Chief Inspector Reginald Wexford, and include *From Doon to Death* (1964), *No More Dying Then* (1971) and *A Sleeping Life* (1978). These have become the basis of a popular television series. Her other novels centre on murder and violent crime, focusing on a mass-murderer (*A Judgement in Stone*, 1977), a rapist (*Live Flesh*, 1978) and espionage mixed with child abuse in *Talking to Strange Men* (1986). *A Dark-Adapted Eye* (1986) and *House of Stairs* (1988) have been published under the name of Barbara Vine.

Renée (born 1929)

New Zealand dramatist and novelist. Born Ngati Kahungunu, one of three children of a Maori widow, brought up during the Depression, Renée left school and went to work aged twelve, but returned to academic work as an adult, achieving a BA after ten years extra-mural study. She has worked as a journalist and a teacher and has been active in the feminist publication *Broadsheet*. Since 1981 she has written ten stage and five television scripts, her plays including the well-known *Wednesday to Come* (1985), a play about four generations of working-class women, and its sequel *Pass It On* (1986). Renée has also published stories, *Finding Ruth* (1987), and a novel, *Willy Nilly* (1990). A committed feminist, her work generally reflects her description of *Wednesday to Come* as a 'passionate celebration of the contribution women have made to the politics of this country'. Her novel *Willy Nilly* is a move into satiric comedy of social conventions.
▷Lesbian writing, New Zealand

Renneville, Sophie de (1772–1822)

French novelist, who also wrote under her maiden name, de Senneterre. Born in Caen, Renneville was highly educated, and wrote mainly for young people. Her literary career, like those of many of her contemporaries, took off after she found herself obliged to support a family ruined by the Revolution. She was very prolific – her works fill twelve pages of the Bibliothèque Nationale catalogue – and her tales include *Lettres d'Octavie, une pensionnaire* (1806) (*Letters of Octavia, a Boarder*); *Contes à ma petite fille et à mon petit garçon* (1811) (*Stories for My Little Girl and Boy*); *La Mère gouvernante* (1811); (*The Governess Mother*); *Le Conteur moraliste* (1816) (*The Moral story-teller*) and *Les Secrets du coeur* (1816) (*Secrets of the Heart*). She was largely in charge of the *Athénée des Dames*, a journal edited by women, and feminist in its tenor. Although de Renneville is often viewed as one of the first women in 19th-century France to embrace the feminist cause, the preface to her novel *Zélie* (1820) informs her readers that, since woman is born to be dependent, she must cultivate docility and virtue, and derive her pleasure and her '*gloire*' (glory) from the love bestowed upon her by husband and children.
▷Feminine/feminist journalism (France)

Requiem (1935–1940)

This poem by Russian writer ▷Anna Akhmátova, first published in full in Munich in 1963 and in the USSR in 1987, belongs to Akhmátova's second major period of creativity, in which she increasingly turned to longer forms of poetry and a more elevated, sombre style. *Requiem* can be seen both as a cycle of poems and a single long poem connected by a narrative line.

The work is based on personal tragedies in Akhmátova's life: her former husband, the poet Nikolai Gumilëv, was shot as a counter-revolutionary in 1921; her friend and fellow poet, Osip Mandel'shtám, was arrested in 1934 (▷Nadezhda Mandel'shtám), as were her son, Lev Gumilëv, and her companion, Nikolai Punin, in 1935. Akhmátova projects her own story onto the entire group of Russian women who waited in line for news of loved ones during the Stalin terror. Her personal suffering as a woman, but particularly as a mother, is generalized to the nation as a whole, and Russia's anguish becomes part of the larger biblical drama of Mary and Christ. Akhmátova achieves the identity of the poet-mother with her nation by incorporating elements of Russian geography, history, and culture, including folklore and the Russian Orthodox religion into the poems. In particular, there are references to the great national poet Pushkin, and imitations of the 19th-century civic poet Nikolai Nekrasov, who also portrayed the sufferings of women. *Requiem* ends as the poet assumes the critical role of bearing the collective memory of the terrible events in her nation's history.
Bib: Reeder, R. and Hemschemeyer, J. (trans.), *The Complete Poems of Anna Akhmátova*.

Reschke, Karin (born 1940)

German writer. Her autobiographical *Memoiren eines Kindes* (1980) (*Memoirs of a Child*) describes the emotional confusion and helplessness of a girl who, five years old at the end of World War II, has to grow up dealing with the steadfast refusal of her mother and teachers to talk about the past. *Verfolgte des Glücks. Findebuch der Henriette Vogel* (1982) (*Pursued by Happiness. The Album of Henriette Vogel*) is a fictitious diary of the woman who committed suicide together with the late 18th-century dramatist Heinrich von Kleist (1777–1811).

Resino, Carmen (born 1941)
Contemporary Spanish dramatist. Resino was the first president of the Asociación de Dramaturgas Españolas (Association of Spanish Female Dramatists) which was founded in Madrid in 1987, and which numbers among its members: Marisa Ares, ▷Ana Diosdado, Yolanda García Serrano, ▷Maribel Lázaro, ▷Paloma Pedrero, ▷Pilar Pombo, María Manuela Reina, Concha Romero and Dora Sedano.

Resistance, and literature of the Resistance (Italy)
Women were involved in the Italian Resistance movement of World War II as much as men. They took an active part, but were often forced into supporting and nurturing roles, acting as messengers between different groups, or caring for the wounded.

The role of women in the Resistance movement is reflected much more thoroughly, and in much more detail, by those women writers who make the Resistance the subject of some of their work than it is by their male counterparts. Most of these women write from experience, and clearly have a vested interest in telling 'their' story. Included in the considerable number of women who write of their wartime experiences are ▷Renata Viganò, ▷Alba de Cespedes, ▷Joyce Lussu, Luisa Adorno (a Pisan novelist), ▷Natalia Ginzburg, ▷Lucia Tumiati and ▷Giovanna Zangrandi. In the works of the most celebrated male writers of the resistance (Vittorini, Pavese, Calvino, Fenoglio), woman is generally seen as the object, either sexualized, or mythologized as the eternal maternal/feminine. Women writers of the Resistance resolutely break this mould.

'Respuesta de la poetisa a la muy ilustre Sor Filotea de la Cruz' (1691) ('Response of the Poetess to the Very Illustrious Sor Filotea de la Cruz')
Autobiographical letter by Sor Juana Inés de la Cruz, the pen-name adopted by the Mexican poet, dramatist and nun ▷Juana de Asbaje y Ramirez de Santillana. This letter is one of the earliest examples of women's literature in the Spanish baroque, and one of the first autobiographical letters written. Juana lived in the wealthy Convent of St Jerome. In this letter, she defends herself from the accusations by the Bishop of Puebla, telling the reader that by the age of three she had learned to read by listening to her sister being taught, and that by the age of five she had learned how to write (women were frequently illiterate in South America until the

19th century). She also remembers that at six or seven she wanted her mother to send her to university disguised as a man. She defends the right of all women and men who are intellectually gifted to study science and theology.

Reuter, Gabriele (1859–1941)
German novelist. She grew up in Egypt and Germany, and wrote evocative stories about Alexandria, as well as erudite studies of ▷Annette von Droste-Hülshoff and ▷Marie von Ebner-Eschenbach. She took an active part in the women's movement, and achieved fame chiefly for her novels, which explore the psychological and social difficulties experienced by women of her time. Her most successful novel, ▷*Aus guter Familie* (1895) (*Of Good Family*), tells the story of a wealthy young woman's painful search for self-fulfilment. It became one of the most widely-read and fiercely discussed books among German women at the turn of the century.

'Revelation Respecting Purgatory, A' ('A Reuelacyone schewed to ane holy womane now one late tyme') (15th century)
This English prose work on a traditional visionary theme was apparently dictated by an unidentified 'holy woman' to the writer who introduces it. It describes the pains and punishments experienced in purgatory by men and women for various sins – for example, the pains of priests who had been lechers, and their partners; the tormenting by cats and dogs of one who had loved them immoderately on earth; and other punishments for pride, wrath and envy.
Bib: Horstmann, C. (ed.), *Yorkshire Writers*, Vol. I; Brewer, D.S. and Owen, A.E.B., *The Thornton Manuscript*.

Revelations of Mechthild, The (1953)
Translation of *Das fließende Licht der Gottheit* (1250–1260) by the mystic ▷Mechthild von Magdeburg. The book explores the author's relationship with God in a kind of spiritual diary. It takes the form of a series of short texts, some visionary and some meditative, which are interspersed with poems, polemics, prayers, litanies, narratives and interpretations of spiritual and secular texts. Making no distinction between physical and spiritual experience, Mechthild develops an intense discourse on love, and in particular upon the mystery of a *unio mystica* (mystic union) with a divine bridegroom. The original text was written in Swabian dialect and was lost. A retranslation into Allemanic German from Latin dates back to 1344. It stands unique in German medieval literature, and became popular and influential in 13th- and 14th-century Germany, especially amongst Mechthild's younger fellow nuns at the famous school and convent of Helfta in Saxony
▷*Visionsliteratur*

Reventlov, Franziska zu (1871–1918)
German novelist and diarist. The fourth child in a family that was part of the lesser Prussian aristocracy, she left home as she soon as she came of age, and went to Munich to become a painter. After a brief marriage she began to adopt an exuberantly unconventional, bohemian lifestyle, and earned a meagre living for herself and her young son with translations, and by writing fiction. Her novel, *Ellen Olestjerne* (1903), tells the story of her childhood and rebellious youth, while *Herrn Dames Aufzeichnungen* (1913) (*The Notebook of Herr Dame*) offers interesting insights into the workings of the Munich *demi-monde* at the turn of the century. *Von Paul zu Pedro* (1912) (*From Paul to Pedro*) is a collection of loosely-connected stories about a woman's sexual adventures. Her many diaries and letters give a vivid account of a woman's life lived outside the social conventions of her time.

Revolution in Poetic Language **(1984)**
Translation by Margaret Waller of French psychoanalyst and cultural critic ▷Julia Kristeva's *La Revolution du language poétique* (1974), in which she formulates the relation between art, the psyche and cultural politics in such a way as to challenge orthodox thinking. Based on her doctoral thesis, this book brings together linguistics, semiotics, ▷psychoanalysis, philosophy and history in order to theorize the subversive potential of ▷avant-garde literature. The English translation provides only the first, theoretical, part of the book. Here, Kristeva grafts the concepts of the drives and pre-Oedipality (▷Oedipus complex) from psychoanalysis on to a notion of signification formed by semiotics and phenomenology. The result is a twofold conception of discourse in which the stabilizing, ordering and social elements of language (▷symbolic order) are seen as underpinned by an archaic disordering, drive-related process of signification ('the semiotic'). Poetic language is 'revolutionary' in so far as it captures these libidinal, rhythmical, semiotic processes and, by disrupting meaning and signification, subverts structures of power and language.

Kristeva's stress on the simultaneous instability of language and human identity makes gender identity a key issue, and many feminists have been inspired by the way Kristeva associates the 'semiotic' with the drives that circulate around the mother's body. In the remaining sections of the book Kristeva offers a detailed study of avant-garde writers, in particular Lautreamont and Mallarmé, and analyzes the social and historical conditions that made this revolution in poetic language possible.
▷*Powers of Horror*; *Tales of Love*

Rhys, Jean (1890–1967)
Caribbean novelist, short story writer and poet. Jean Rhys was a central figure in Caribbean women's literature. Born Gwendolen Rees Williams into the minority white community of

▷Dominica, she travelled to England in 1907, and attended The Perse School, Cambridge, and the Royal Academy of Dramatic Art in London. She abandoned her education because of a lack of funds, and worked for a while as a chorus girl with a touring theatre company. She began writing under the patronage of Ford Madox Ford, whom she met in Paris, and published her first book ▷*The Left Bank and Other Stories* (1927) under the pen-name Jean Rhys. Her novels followed this: ▷*Quartet* (originally entitled *Postures*) (1928); *After Leaving Mr Mackenzie* (1931): ▷*Voyage in the Dark*; ▷*Good Morning Midnight* and ▷*Wide Sargasso Sea*. Her later works include a collection of short stories, *Sleep It Off Lady* (1976) and a posthumous autobiography, ▷*Smile Please*.

Little-known when she first began to publish, she gained international recognition in the 1950s when the BBC produced a dramatized version of *Good Morning Midnight*. She gained international acclaim with the publication of *Wide Sargasso Sea*.

A central focus of her writing is the exploration of the conflict she experienced as a white ▷Creole woman, both in the Caribbean and in England. Influenced by ▷autobiography, her fiction deals with the role of woman as victim and explores the theme of mothers, alienation and cultural roots.

For full biographical details and critical studies see Elgin W. Mellown, *Jean Rhys a Descriptive and Annotated Bibliography of Works and Criticism* (1984); ▷Jean D'Costa, 'Jean Rhys' in ▷*Fifty Caribbean Writers*; Teresa F. O'Connor, *Jean Rhys: The West Indian Novels* (1986).

Riaz, Fahmida (born 1946)
Pakistani poet. She was born in Meerut, India, and educated at Sind University. In addition to her poetry, she has published a work of literary criticism, *Pakistan: Literature and Society* (1986). Her poetry collection *Badan Dareeda* (*The Wounded Body*) shocked the Pakistani literary establishment with its overtly sexual themes and its open exploration of the nature of sensuality. English translations of her poems appear in *The Penguin Book of Modern Urdu Poetry* (ed. Mahmood Jamal, 1986), *Modern Urdu Poets from Pakistan* (ed. Anis Nagi, 1974) and ▷*We Sinful Women* (1991).

Riccoboni, Marie-Jeanne Laboras de Mézières (1713–1792)
French novelist. Of bourgeois origins, Riccoboni married an Italian actor in 1734, and began her own career as an actress. Later she left her husband, and lived the last thirty-nine years of her life with her friend, also an actress, Marie-Thérèse Biancolleli. Her literary career began when she successfully imitated the style of Marivaux, completing his novel *La Vie de Marianne* (1745) (*The Life of Marianne*). The first three of her eight novels, ▷*Lettres de mistriss Fanni Butlerd* (1757) (*Letters from Mistress Fanny Butlerd*). ▷*Histoire de M.le marquis de Cressy* (1758) (*The History of the Marquis de Cressy*) and *Lettres de Milady Juliette Catesby* (1759) (▷*Letters*

of Juliette Catesby 1786), brought sufficient financial reward to enable her to retire from the theatre. Her work was admired for its concision and the perceptive descriptions of love and friendship in domestic settings. She also produced plays, short stories, articles and translations of English drama. In her mainly ▷epistolary novels, Riccoboni's strong, proud and sincere heroines are confronted with morally inferior men. The male lovers are accused of betraying love and making vain promises, while women's capacity for self-deception is also highlighted. The gap between the two sexes repeatedly appears unbridgeable, and in a later novel, *Lettres de Milord Rivers* (1776) (*Letters of Lord Rivers*), the portrait of two Frenchwomen presents their relationship as preferable to love between men and women. However, in general, the critique rarely moves beyond the personal to the social, and the women's extensive self-analysis engenders no explicit revolt.

Her other works include: Prose fiction: *Histoire de Miss Jenny* (1762) (*The History of Miss Jenny*); *Histoire d'Adélaïde* (1766) (*The History of Adélaïde*); *Lettres d'Elisabeth-Sophie de Vallière* (1772) (*Letters of Elisabeth-Sophie de Vallière*); *Les Amours de Roger et Gertrude* (1780) (*Roger and Gertrude in Love*); *Histoire de Christine, reine de suabe* (1783) (*The History of Christine, Queen of Swabia*) *Histoire de deux jeunes amis* (1786) (*The Story of Two Young Friends*); Play: *Les Caquets* (1761) (*The Gossipers*). Correspondence: *Lettres de Mme R. à Diderot* (*Letters from Mme R to Diderot*) in Diderot, *Oeuvres* (1798); *Correspondance de Laclos et de Mme R.* (1864) (*The correspondence of Laclos and Mme R.*), and *Mme Riccoboni's Letters to David Hume, David Garrick and Sir Robert Liston 1764–1783* (1976).

▷Aïssé, Charlotte-Elisabeth Aïcha; Guesnerie, Charlotte de la
Bib: Demay, A., *Marie-Jeanne Riccoboni;* Hinde Stewart, J., *The Novels of Mme Riccoboni.*

Rice, Anne (born 1941)

US novelist. Rice was raised a Catholic in New Orleans, Louisiana. In 1971 she earned a Master's degree from San Francisco State University. She writes horror to emphasize the individual's alienation from society. *The Feast of all Saints* (1980) examines the alienation of free people of color in the 19th century. *Cry to Heaven* (1982) focuses on the castrated male opera sopranos of the 18th century. Her vampire chronicles – *Interview with the Vampire* (1976), *The Vampire Lesat* (1985) and *Queen of the Damned* (1988) – revise vampire mythology. In Rice's works vampires are social outcasts in search of an identity; she exploits the myth's erotic dimension. Rice's work considers the intersection between the living and the dead, suggesting this intersection reveals the individual's desire to participate in a community. Nevertheless, Rice's female characters often find power in their alienation.

Other works include: *The Mummy, Or Ramses the Damned* (1989). As A.N. Roquelaure, Rice has written erotic novels, including *The Claiming of Sleeping Beauty* (1983), and as Anne Rampling she is the author of *Exit to Eden* (1985) and *Belinda* (1986).

Rich, Adrienne (born 1929)

Adrienne Rich

North American poet and essayist. Rich was born into an intellectual, middle-class, Jewish family in Baltimore, Maryland, and was educated at Radcliffe College. She has taught on the SEEK and Open Admissions Program at City College, New York, and at Douglass College. Married for seventeen years, Rich left her husband in 1970 and now defines herself and her work as lesbian feminist. She and the poet ▷Michelle Cliff have edited the journal *Sinister Wisdom*. With ▷Audre Lorde and ▷Alice Walker, Rich is one of the best-known and most influential feminist poets writing today. Her first book, *A Change of World* (1951) won the Yale Younger Poets series, and was followed by *The Diamond Cutters and Other Poems* (1955). In ▷*On Lies, Secrets and Silence: Selected Prose 1966–1978* (1979) Rich characterizes this early poetry in terms of a masculine poetic tradition. Poems such as 'Storm Warnings' and 'Aunt Jennifer's Tigers' stress emotional restraint and detachment, 'neatly and modestly dressed', as poet W.H. Auden (1907–1973) described them.

It was another eight years before she published *Snapshots of a Daughter-in-Law*, which began the scrutiny of women's position, its psychic, emotional and political consequences, which has characterized Rich's work ever since. The strategy of the title poem is typical, simultaneously addressing a woman's difficulty in maintaining an identity, and the placing of women in literary tradition: 'When to her lute Corinna sings neither words nor music are her own.' The importance of ▷Emily Dickinson, who with ▷H.D. is a central influence on Rich's work, is also evident. The poems address, too, the divisions among women that undermine a sense of community.

In 1966 Rich moved to New York where she was active in the Civil Rights Movement and against the Vietnam War. The more formally experimental poetry of *Leaflets: Poems 1965–1968* (1969) and *The Will to Change* (1971) belong to this period. *Of Woman Born: Motherhood as Experience and Institution* examines the myths, history, and experience of motherhood through a mixture of medical history, politics, anthropology and personal memoir. Her prose from this period also includes the ground-breaking essay, ▷'Compulsory Heterosexuality and Lesbian Existence' (1980). ▷*Diving Into the Wreck* (1973) won the National Book Award in 1974 and Rich accepted it in the name of all women. ▷*The Dream of a Common Language: Poems 1974–1977*, which appeared in 1978, included her lesbian sonnet sequence 'Twenty-one Love Poems', originally published in 1976. These two volumes, and *A Wild Patience Has Taken Me This Far*, chart a consistent engagement with the relationship of women to language, and represent a project which demands the political transformation of language.

Since the 1970s her work has moved from a euphoric faith in women-identified relationships and communities to a tougher scrutiny of the potentially conflicting intersection of race, sexuality, gender and class. This has resulted in what she calls in *Blood, Bread, and Poetry: Selected Prose, 1966–1978* a poetics of location. Moreover, her recent works, *Your Native Land, Your Life* (1986), which reprints 'Sources', and *An Atlas of the Difficult World: Poems 1988–1991* (1991), explore her relationship to a Jewish heritage through an interweaving of personal and public histories. In 1991 Rich was awarded the Commonwealth Poetry Prize.

Other works include *Necessities of Life: Poems, 1962–1965* (1966), *The Fact of a Doorframe: Poems Selected and New, 1950–1984, Poems: Selected and New, 1950–1974.*

▷Case, Sue-Ellen; de Laurentis, Teresa; Heterosexism; Lesbian-feminist criticism
Bid: Gelpi, B.C. and A. Gelpi, *Adrienne Rich's Poetry: The Texts of the Poems, the Poet on Her Work, Reviews and Criticisms*; Juhasz, S., *Naked and Fiery Forms: Modern American Poetry by Women*; Montefiore, J., *Feminism and Poetry*; Ostriker, Alicia Suskin, *Stealing the Language.*

Rich, Mary, Countess of Warwick (1624–1678)

Aristocratic memoirist and diarist, daughter of Richard Boyle, first Earl of Cork, born at Youghal near Cork, Ireland. Having refused a suitor, she moved to London, where she stayed with her

brother and sister-in-law Elizabeth, 'reading romances . . . reading and seeing playes . . . going to court and Hyde Park and Spring Garden'. She met and married Charles Rich, the poor second son of the Earl of Warwick, 'I was convinced that it was time for me to give him a flat and final denial . . . but . . . my great kindness for him stopt it.' They lived in Essex, and her husband (who eventually inherited the title) was an MP during the English Civil War (1642–1651). She was involved in hiding arms from Royalist commanders at the siege of Colchester. She kept a daily religious diary from 1666 to 1678, and in 1672 she began her autobiography. She also collected materials for a biography of her father.
Bib: Mendelson, Sara Heller, *The Mental World of Stuart Women.*

Richardson, Dorothy Miller (1873–1957)

Dorothy Richardson

English novelist, journalist, translator. Third daughter of Mary Miller Taylor and Charles Richardson, an aspiring gentleman and intellectual whom Dorothy Richardson accompanied to meetings of scientific societies. The family became bankrupt in 1891, and Richardson earned her living first as a governess and as a teacher in Hanover, returning to teach in Britain after six months. In 1895 Richardson gave up full-time employment to nurse her mother, who committed suicide later that year. Now based in London, Richardson took a position as a secretary and then as a journalist.

Through her involvement with various ▷*avant-garde* societies she developed friendships with many prominent intellectuals, including H.G.

Wells (1866–1946) with whom Richardson had an affair in 1906, resulting in a miscarriage. Wells was an influential figure within Richardson's development as a writer, both in terms of her journalism and also as a springboard for Richardson's novelistic development of a 'feminine aesthetic'. Wells figures in Richardson's major work, ▷*Pilgrimage* (1915–1967), as the character Hypo G. Wilson, a paradigm of masculine vision and values, to which Richardson opposes a distinctively feminine consciousness and feminine aesthetic.

Richardson was the first English novelist to adopt the ▷stream-of-consciousness technique, her use suggesting its apparent commensurability with female experience, and her belief that a woman 'thinks flowingly'. Richardson elaborates her views on women and writing in the essay 'Women in the Arts' (1925), which appeared prior to ▷Virginia Woolf's formulation of similar concerns in ▷*A Room of One's Own*. Richardson occupies a central position among ▷modernist writers, and figures strongly within discussions of a feminist literary tradition.
Bib: Fromm, G., *Dorothy Richardson: A Biography*; Gregory, H., *Dorothy Richardson: An Adventure in Self-Discovery*; Hanscombe, G., *The Art of Life: Dorothy Richardson and the Development of Feminist Consciousness*; Powys, J., *Dorothy M. Richardson*; Rosenberg, J., *Dorothy Richardson The Genius They Forgot: A Critical Biography*.

Richardson, Ethel ▷Richardson, Henry Handel

Richardson, Henry Handel (1870–1946)
Australian novelist, real name Ethel Richardson. Richardson was educated at the Presbyterian Ladies' College in Melbourne, and her experience there is reflected in ▷*The Getting of Wisdom* (1910). She taught as a governess before proceeding to Leipzig in 1888 to study music. Her novel, *Maurice Guest* (1910), reflects her Leipzig experience. She married J.G. Robertson, later Professor of German at the University of London, and lived a life of deliberate isolation, looked after by her husband and her companion, Olga Roncoroni, in order to pursue her writing career. Her trilogy, ▷*The Fortunes of Richard Mahony* (1930), first published as *Australia Felix* (1917), *The Way Home* (1925) and *Ultima Thule* (1929), is based upon the life of her father, and is an Australian classic. Richardson was awarded the Australian Literary Society's Gold Medal for 1929 and was nominated for the Nobel Prize in 1932.

▷Autobiography (Australia); Short story (Australia)

Richardson, Rebecca (fl 1738)
North American poet. Like so many early American women who published in periodicals, she is known only by the details included in her published work. ▷'Do Thou, O God, in Mercy Help' recounts in poetic form allegations of the confiscation of her Philadelphia property. She sought recompense for the losses by travelling to England and bringing a law suit there. She won her case but was unable to enforce it in Philadelphia. The poem asks God to revenge her wrongs.

Richardson, Samuel, influence of
The novels of Samuel Richardson (1689–1761), *Pamela* (1740), *Clarissa* (1747–1748) and *Sir Charles Grandison* (1753–1754), influenced many contemporary and later novels by women, and received much serious discussion and consideration by women writing in the 18th century, *Clarissa* was perhaps the most discussed and reworked, rivalled in this only by Jean Jacques Rousseau's (1712–1778) *Julie, ou la nouvelle Héloïse* (1761), ▷Eliza Haywood, ▷Sarah Fielding and ▷Lady Mary Wortley Montagu considered and criticized *Clarissa*, and the heroine's conduct and rape became the focus of discussions on morality and sexuality. Responses, recensions and echoes can be found widely, for example, in Elizabeth Griffith, *The Delicate Distress*; Georgina Spencer, *Emma*; Sophia Briscoe, *Miss Melmoth or the New Clarissa*; ▷Anna Maria Bennett, *Agnes de Courci*, and Susannah Gunning, *Fashionable Involvements*.

▷Barbauld, Anna Laetitia
Bib: Browne, Alice, *The Eighteenth Century Feminist Mind*; Grundy, Isobel in Doody, Margaret Anne and Sabor, Peter (eds), *Samuel Richardson*; Spencer, Jane, *The Rise of the Woman Novelist*.

Rich Like Us (1985)
Novel by Indian author ▷Nayantara Sahgal, winner of the 1985 Sinclair Prize for Fiction. The novel is set in Delhi during the imposition of Emergency Rule in 1975–77 by the Indian Prime Minister (and Sahgal's cousin), Indira Gandhi. The narrator is Sonali, an Oxbridge-educated civil servant, who has been brought up on the ideals promoted during the struggle for independence and her father's firm belief in the separation of politics and government service. The novel opens with her demotion, effectively her dismissal, for refusing to grant an import licence to a foreign company favoured by a government minister, and charts her growing disillusionment with the corruption of the politicians around her. Nevertheless, *Rich Like Us* ends on a positive note. Offered a chance to research the 17th-century history of India for a British art exhibition, Sonali suddenly takes a step back from the turmoil of contemporary politics and looks at her country's development from a more distant perspective. At the same time, however, she sees that individual acts of integrity do count for something even when all is spoilt around, and she realizes that the Emergency will eventually end.

Ride on Stranger (1943)
Australian novel by ▷Kylie Tennant. A realist work which deals with the epic adventures of Shannon Hicks, a restless country girl engaged in a search, not only for a suitable occupation during

the Depression, but also for some meaning to her life. Her experiences in radio and in trade union circles are disillusioning, and she eventually marries an unambitious young farmer, John Terrill, who is killed in the war. *Ride on Stranger* gives a panoramic vision of Australian society in both Sydney and the bush during the Depression. It became a successful television series in the 1980s.

Ridler, Anne (born 1912)
English poet and dramatist. Ridler worked from 1935 as secretary to the poet T.S. Eliot (1888–1965), then as a junior editor. Her poetry is a contemplation of the nature of love, family and place, set within a Christian context. Among her volumes of poetry are *Poems* (1939), *Golden Bird* (1951), *A Matter of Life and Death* (1959), *Dies Natalis* (1980) and *New and Selected Poems* (1988). She has published several verse dramas, including *Cain* (1943), *Henry Bly* (1947) and *The Trial of Thomas Cranmer* (1956).

Riera, Carme (born 1949)
Born in Majorca, Riera writes novels and stories in Catalan, and literary criticism in Castilian. She is Professor of Castilian Literature at the Universitat Autònoma in Barcelona. She received a prize for her first short story, '*Et deix, amor, la mar com a penyora*' (1974) ('I Leave You, Love, the Sea as Token'), but her emergence as a writer belongs almost entirely to the post-Franco era (after 1975). Her literary works include two collections of short stories: *Jo pos per testimonis les gavines* (1977) (*For My Witness I Call the Seagulls*); *Epitelis tendríssims* (1981) (*Exquisite Epithelia*), and one novel, *Una primavera per a Domènico Guarini* (1980) (*A 'Primavera' for Domenico Guarini*).

The fictional world of Carme Riera is populated in a semi-Kafkaesque fashion by beings who lose at playing a game whose rules are unknown. The language employed ranges from standard Catalan to the Valencian and Majorcan dialects, from journalese to a more impersonal, literate style. She is fast proving to be one of the major novelists of the contemporary era.
▷Catalan women's writing

Rif'at, Alifa (born 1930)
Egyptian short story writer, who started publishing her stories only in the 1970s, but made an immediate impact because of the originality of her subject matter. Born into a conservative middle-class family, she had little formal education, and she was married early in life to her cousin, a policeman. She accompanied him to his postings in different parts of the country, thus gaining insight into the life of peasants as well as provincial government officials and their families. Her technique of narration is artless, almost naïve, and her discourse is 'feminine', almost non-literary. The lives of women, harassed and unfulfilled, labouring even to old age for husband and children, come alive in many of her short stories. She writes about women's sexuality and

the traumas and frustrations attending their awareness of it, and she explores the avenues of depression and neurosis into which it is often channelled. Her first two collections were published in Cairo in 1981: *Eve Returns with Adam* and *Who Can Be The Man?* The stories in the second volume have attracted particular attention, and have been translated into English and German. The women of her stories are not just passive victims of physical traumas: they have their cunning wiles and paid allies who can get them out of any scrape. Their worst scrapes are connected with 'honour' – synonymous with virginity in the context of a family's celebration of their daughter's marriage. An English translation of a number of her stories was published in London as *Distant View of a Minaret* (1984). Another collection, *A Long Winter Night*, has also been translated into English and German.

A story called 'The Eyes of Bahiya' was published in the Cairo monthly *al-Hilal* (1990). Bahiya is the name of a heroine in many Egyptian folk songs, possibly standing for Egypt itself. Alifa Rif'at had used the name for the young woman in the three stories of *Who Can Be The Man?* Bahiya, in the last story, comes from a different class; she is an old woman, and her beautiful green eyes, celebrated in the folk song, have grown dim with the tears she has constantly shed over her lot in life. Bahiya, speaking as an old woman, summarizes the life of the Egyptian *fallaha* (peasant), a life of hard work and little pleasure.
▷*Opening the Gates*, contains translations of the stories 'Who can be the man?' and 'Honour'.
▷*Khitan*

Right of Way (1988)
An anthology of writing by Asian women based in Britain brought together by the Asian Women Writers' Workshop. For many of the contributors this is their first experience of being published. Contributors include ▷Ravinder Randhawa and ▷Leena Dhingra. The theme of cultural marginality runs through many of the pieces, but it is explored from many different angles. Crime, unwanted pregnancies, old age and ▷arranged marriages are some of the topics addressed.

Rights of Woman, The (1989)
Translation of *Declaration des droits de la femme* (1791), ▷Marie Gouze (Olympe) de Gouges's famous challenge to the French Revolution's 'Rights of Man and Citizen', which excluded women. The pamphlet was addressed to the queen, whose support she sought to enlist. In her preface she upbraids the men of the Revolution for perpetuating patriarchal despotism. *The Rights of Woman* outlines twelve articles to ensure women's equal rights in public and private life, with concise arguments supporting each demand. Among these are equal access to work (including public appointments), accountability of ministers, and the right to establish the paternity of children born out of wedlock. The postscript, addressed to women, urges them to recognize that little has

been gained, and calls on them to rally under the banner of philosophy. It is argued that in the past, due to the constraints upon them, women have been 'contemptible but respected' and are now 'respectable but scorned'. Gouges draws an analogy between the status of women and the status of black slaves, calling for the freedom of both. She highlights problems linked to marriage, children and financial insecurity, and demands free state education, and reform of conjugal conventions. To this end she provides a 'form of the social contract between man and woman', setting out the equal social and financial responsibilities of both parties. Among other demands made are the right for priests to marry, the grouping of prostitutes in specific quarters, and the setting up of a constitutional monarchy. The text ends anecdotally with Gouges recounting her own quarrel with a cab-driver over a fare, and inveighing against the stupidity of state officials (a passage omitted in the English translation).

Recent editions. French: in P.M. Duhet (ed.) *Cahiers de doléances des femmes et autres textes* (*Register of Women's Grievances and Other Texts*) (1981).

Right to Choose, The (1977)

Translation of *La Cause des femmes* (1973). In a series of interviews given to ▷Marie Cardinal, ▷Gisèle Halimi describes her movement from student to ▷MLF activist, and her growing awareness, from personal experience, of the political dimension of women's oppression.

Riis, Sharon (born 1947)

Canadian novelist and screenwriter. Born in High River, Alberta, she received a BA in history from Simon Fraser University in British Columbia. She has lived in London, Paris, and Edmonton, and now resides in Saskatoon. ▷*The True Story of Ida Johnson* (1976) is a Canadian classic; it is set in Longview, Alberta, the oral, multifaceted story of a waitress who has deliberately murdered and burned her husband and children. It is also the story of friendship between women, a friendship that moves past survival. *Midnight Twilight Tourist Zone* (1989) is Riis's second novel. She has also written two feature films, *Latitude 55* and *Loyalties*. Bib: Perreault, J., in ▷*A Mazing Space*.

Riley, Denise (born 1948)

English poet. Active in the women's liberation movement in the 1960s, Riley has worked as a translator and completed a Ph.D. in philosophy at Sussex University. She has worked closely with the poet ▷Wendy Mulford, who collaborated with her on *No Fee: A Line or Two for Free* (1978) and published Riley's *Marxism for Infants* in 1977. Riley's poetry is ambitious in its attempt to link poetry, feminism and ▷post-structuralist ideas about the role of language in the construction of identity and sexuality. While this blend undoubtedly makes her poetry 'difficult', she mobilizes a powerful and evocative lyricism to expose the myths of domesticity, the nuclear

family and heterosexuality. *War in the Nursery* (1983) an historical work, was followed by the collection *Dry Air* in 1985. In 1987 she published the critical work *Am I That Name?*, which deals with the relation between feminist theory and women's identity.

Riley, Joan (born 1958)

Joan Riley

Caribbean novelist. Born the youngest of eight children, Riley spent her childhood in ▷Jamaica. She left for Britain, and studied at the University of Sussex, obtaining a BA in 1979, and an MA from London University in 1984. Actively involved in the black community, she works for a drugs advice agency and teaches black history. She is concerned with issues facing black women.

Riley's three novels, *The Unbelonging* (1985), *Waiting in the Twilight* (1987) and *Romance* (1988), involve a complex vision of the problems experienced by West Indian women living in Britain. Each deals with a distinct life stage. *The Unbelonging* explores the search for ▷identity by a young Jamaican girl brought to England to join her father and his new family, and her struggle against sexual and racial oppression, incest, family violence and mental illness. *Romance* portrays the lives of two young women as they develop from relative immaturity to full awareness of their adult responsibilities, and examines the influence upon them of their grandmothers, who offer a feast of folktales and the authority of matriarchal age. *Waiting in the Twilight* focuses on a mature woman crippled by a stroke who looks back at Jamaica and Britain in the 1950s and 1960s. Her memories of failure serve as a record of unending struggle for dignity and selfhood.

There has been little published criticism, but see Neisen de Abruna, 'The Sea Change of Our Sisters: West Indian Women Writing in England', University of London, Post Graduate Seminar, 4 March 1990, and the introduction to Lauretta Ngcobo, (ed.), *Let It Be Told: Black Women Writers in Britain* (1988).

Rime d'amore (1554) (Love Poems)

A collection of Italian poetry by ▷Gaspara Stampa. These poems are traditional in that their subject matter is love, and in that they are written in ▷Petrarchan form. Yet, in so far as Gaspara Stampa presents herself, the poet, as more important (drawing attention to her own nobility and excellence) than the male object of her love, they are unusual. The poetry is often sensual as, for instance, when she looks back on: *'le notti mie colme di gioia'* ('those past nights full of joy'), and she complains repeatedly of the coldness of men, again an unusual approach for a woman poet. She expresses, too, a desire to be in control of her life, and hopes to avoid passionate love for this reason. Her poetry was reprinted, along with that of ▷Veronica Franco, in 1738 and 1913.

Rime e lettere (1759) (Poems and Letters)

Written in Italian by ▷Veronica Gambara, the poetry was published in various collections in the 1500s, but was collected alongside her letters for the first time in 1759. Most of the early poetry is love poetry, ▷Petrarchan in style, in which she claims the right of women poets to express all of the emotions, conventionally associated with love. The recurrent themes of the poems are, nonetheless, sad. She is preoccupied by endings of relationships, death and decay. Her later work is religious in inspiration. She also wrote political sonnets, expressing her disapproval of the devastation of her country by war, thus extending her arena as a woman poet. In her letters, she writes of her desire for a peaceful and simple life. This collection was republished in 1879.

Rimorso, Il (1964) ▷Remorse

Ringwood, Gwen Pharis (1910–1984)

Dramatist, born Gwen Pharis in Washington. Her family moved to Alberta, Canada in 1913. Ringwood attended the University of Montana, and then the University of Alberta in Edmonton, where she worked with Elizabeth Sterling Haynes, a pioneer in community theatre, who produced Ringwood's first stage play, *The Dragons of Kent*, at the Banff School of Fine Arts in 1935. In 1937 she attended the Carolina Playmakers School at the University of North Carolina, where, influenced by 'folk drama', she wrote and produced a number of her best plays, including *Still Stands the House* (1939), about the Depression, and *Dark Harvest* (1945). She returned to Alberta in 1939, married, and lived in various places in Saskatchewan and Alberta, all

the while writing and producing plays. The best of this period are *The Rainmaker* and *Widger's Way*. Her work is located in, and celebrates, the regional, the small community. Modest and unassuming, her dramatic progression is evidenced by a finely honed comic sense, and a wider engagement with injustice. After settling in Williams Lake, British Columbia, in 1953, she wrote several plays about Canada's first people. She also published a novel, *Younger Brother* (1959). In her lifetime she wrote and produced more than 60 dramatic works, including musicals, comedies, radio plays, and children's plays, some of which are available in *The Collected Plays of Gwen Pharis Ringwood* (1982), with a foreword by ▷Margaret Laurence. She was a major influence on the development of Canadian drama, especially in the west.

Bib: Anthony, G., *Gwen Pharis Ringwood*; Anthony, G., in *Stage Voices*; Wagner, A. (ed.), *Canada's Lost Plays*.

Rinser, Luise (born 1911)

German novelist, short story writer, diarist and essayist. The daughter of devout Catholic parents, she studied psychology and became a teacher. During the 1930s she refused to join the Nazi Party, and in 1939 resigned her post. Her first book, *Die gläsernen Ringe* (1940) (*The Glass Rings*) is a ▷Bildungsroman about a woman growing up under national socialism. It was a great success when it appeared in 1941, but a second edition was banned, and she spent the last months of World War II in prison, accused of high treason, an experience she recorded in *Gefängnis-Tagebuch* (1946) (*Prison Diary*). After the war she published a number of novels in quick succession: *Hochebene* (1948) (*High Plateau*); *Die Stärkeren* (1948) (*Those Who are Stronger*), and, most notably, the masterly novella ▷*Jan Lobel aus Warschau* (1948) (*Jan Lobel from Warsaw*). With the publication of *Mitte des Lebens* (1950) (*Middle of Life*), she became one of the widest-read and best-known German writers of the immediate post-war period, both at home and abroad. Her success faded somewhat after the publication of two intensely devout Catholic novels, *Daniela* (1953) and *Die vollkommene Freude* (1962) (*Perfect Joy*).

All Rinser's work is determined by a strong Catholic faith. Her plots concentrate upon how women or children learn to cope with social, emotional and religious problems. In her later writings, such as *Baustelle. Eine Art Tagebuch* (1970) (*Construction Site. A Sort of Diary*), and *Kriegsspielzeug* (1978) (*Toys of War*), she adopts, often in diary form, a more universally ▷humanist, even socialist stance. Taking up topical, everyday issues, she argues for social justice and tolerance, and speaks out against all aspects of oppression. Her autobiography, *Den Wolf umarmen* (*Embracing the Wolf*), was published in 1981.

Rio de la Plata Group of Poets, The

A group flourishing in the region between Uruguay and Argentina in the early 20th century.

The group was mainly male, but included the Uruguayan poet ▷Delmira Agustini, who was active in the group during the years 1910–20, and who was also influenced by the ▷1900 Generation.

Ripening Seed, The (1955)
Translation of *Le Blé en herbe* (1923), novel by French writer ▷Colette. Originally written for serialization in the newspaper *Le Matin*, *The Ripening Seed* was considered scandalous when it was first published, because in the last chapter its sixteen-year-old heroine, Vinca, initiates her first sexual experience with her childhood sweetheart, Phil. In this novel, which invites comparison with Proust, Colette conveys the subtle details, particularly of smell and colour, which constitute experience of a place (in this case the Brittany coast) or a relationship. Colette explores those 'emotions which we lightly call physical', as they are experienced by a *ménage à trois* consisting of the adolescent lovers, Phil and Vinca, and the older woman, Madame Dalleray, who seduces Phil. This triangular relationship which juxtaposes an older woman with a young man and woman is found in several novels by Colette. It is often used to contrast two very different versions of femininity, and to explore mother–daughter and mother–son patterns of behaviour in sexual relationships. Madame Dalleray is, however, virile rather than motherly; *The Ripening Seed* is typical of Colette's mature work in its questioning of the nature of masculinity and femininity, through the androgynous qualities of the three main characters. The narrative point of view alternates between Phil, Vinca and the 'wise' narrator, though it is the point of view of the least stable character, Phil, which dominates; as a result this is a less traditional narrative than it would first appear, and the ending is open and ambiguous.

Ripening: Selected Work of Meridel Le Sueur (1982)
US writer ▷Meridel Le Sueur's work of social history reflects her belief that artists are activists and revolutionaries. Collected in *Ripening*, Le Sueur's work focuses on real US working-class women. 'Women on the Breadlines' (1932) documents the plight of millions of unemployed women and chronicles their psychological and economic suffering. *The Girl* (1939) testifies to the collective strength of a group of women who survive the Depression by living together, describing the sexual abuse they suffer as scapegoats for men's economic frustration; their suffering provides them with a source of solidarity. Le Sueur celebrates women's sexuality and reproductive capacities, identifying women with the earth. She emphasizes the interdependence of humans and nature, and espouses the 'female concept of nourishing' as a means to social regeneration.

Ripples in the Pool (1975)
Novel by Kenyan writer ▷Rebeka Njau.
▷Essay on East Africa

Risorgimento (Italy)
The movement to unite Italy, through political and military struggle, which succeeded in 1861. Much was written exalting and encouraging national pride in this period. Debates on the meaning of being Italian, and on the Italian language itself, flourished. Perhaps the most famous writer on many issues of Italian interest at this time was Alessandro Manzoni (1785–1873). Women writers such as Antonia Giacomelli and Rosina Muzio Salvo also wrote of the *Risorgimento*, and stressed both the pains and the gains of the process of unification.

Ritchie, Lady (Anne Thackeray) (1837–1919)
British novelist, short story writer and essayist, the daughter of William Makepeace Thackeray and aunt of ▷Virginia Woolf. Almost all the literary celebrities of the day were known to the family, including Dickens, Tennyson, Robert and ▷Elizabeth (Barrett) Browning, ▷Charlotte Brontë and ▷George Eliot. Ritchie wrote five novels: *The Story of Elizabeth* (1863); *The Village on the Cliff* (1867); *Old Kensington* (1873); *Miss Angel* (1875) and *Mrs Dymond* (1885). Her non-fiction includes *Toilers and Spinsters* (1874), which called attention to the plight of single, unemployed women, and *A Book of Sibyls* (1883), a collection of essays on women writers. Other works include *Records of Tennyson, Ruskin and Browning* (1892), and *Alfred Tennyson and his Friends* (1893). The *Letters of Anne Thackeray Ritchie* was published in 1924. The character of Mrs Hilbery in Virginia Woolf's *Night and Day* is based on Ritchie, and she was well-known to the ▷Bloomsbury Group.
Bib: Gerin, W., *Life*; Woolf, V., 'The enchanted organ: Anne Thackeray Ritchie' in *Collected Essays*, Vol. 4.

Ritter, Erica (born 1948)
Canadian dramatist essayist and stand-up comic, born in Regina, Saskatchewan. She attended the Universities of McGill and Toronto, then in 1975 began to work with Tarragon Theatre's playwriting workshop in Toronto. Her first play was *The Visitor From Charleston* (1974), but her comic intelligence is much more powerful in *The Splits* (1978) and *Automatic Pilot* (1980), which is informed by Ritter's experience as a stand-up comedienne. Her drama shows a shrewd awareness of the compromises that women make in order to survive. Her essays are collected in *Urban Scrawl* (1984) and *Ritter in Residence* (1987).
Bib: Lister, R.H., in *Gynocritics*.

Rivoyre, Christine de (born 1921)
French novelist. Having worked as a journalist for *Le Monde*, and then as editor of a women's magazine, de Rivoyre published several popular romantic novels. Two of these, *Le Petit matin* (1968) (*Morning Twilight*, 1970) and *La Mandarine* (1957) (*The Tangerine*, 1958), were later adapted into screenplays. Moving away from the formulaic prose of popular romance, her novel, *Boy* (1973, translated in 1974 with the same title), set against

the background of the Spanish Civil War, demonstrates her originality as a writer, in the tale of a spoilt boy's lack of generosity towards the women who love him. Her more recent novels include *Le Voyage à l'envers* (1977) (*Upside-down Journey*), *Reine-mère* (1985) (*Queen Mother*), and *Crépuscule, taille unique* (1989) (*Twilight, One size*).

Robert, Louise-Félicité Guinement de Kéralio (1758–1821)

French novelist, historian and translator. Born in Paris, she and her husband were members of the Société fraternelle des deux sexes (*Fraternal Society of the Two Sexes*). She translated works from both Italian and English into French. Her *Histoire d'Elisabeth, reine d'Angleterre* (1786–88) (*History of Elizabeth, Queen of England*) is the result of ten years' work. Another long-term project was an encyclopaedic collection of women's writing. She completed fourteen volumes entitled *Collection des meilleurs ouvrages français composés par des femmes* (1786–88) (*Collection of the Best French Works Composed by Women*) and had planned to continue with collections on English and Italian women. In 1789 she directed the political *Journal de l'État et du citoyen* (*Journal of the State and the Citizen*) and worked on the *Mercure national* (*National Mercury*) and the *Censeur universel* (*Universal Censor*). Her political writings include: *Observations sur quelques articles du projet de constitutions de M. Monnier* (1789) (*Observations on Some Articles by About the Project for Constitutions Proposed by M. Monnier*), *L.R. à M. Louret* (1789) (*L.R. to M. Louret*) (the published text of a speech), *Adresse aux femmes de Montauban* (1790) (*Address to the Women of Montauban*) (reflecting her enthusiasm for the Revolution and her valorisation of women's domestic duties), another address on hospitals in *Extraits des délibérations de la société fraternelle* (1795) (*Extracts from the Deliberations of the Fraternal Society*) and *Les Crimes des reines de France* (1830) (*The Crimes of Queens of France*). Her novels include: *Adélaide* (1782); *Amélia et Caroline ou l'amour et l'amitié* (1808) (*Amelia and Caroline, or Love and Friendship*); *Alphonse et Mathilde, ou la famille espagnole* (1809) (*Alphonse and Matilde, or the Spanish Family*), and *Rose et Albert ou le tombeau d'Emma* (1810) (*Rose and Albert, or Emma's Tomb*). **Bib:** Prudhomme, L.M., *Répertoire universel historique et biographique des femmes célèbres*; Michelet, J., *Les Femmes de la Révolution*.

Robert, Marie Anne Roumier (1705–1771)

French novelist, born in Paris. The most successful of her works was the novel *La Paysanne philosophe* (1762) (*The Peasant Woman Philosopher*). In this and a later novel, *Nicole de Beauvais* (1766), Robert traces the destinies of two heroines from their peasant origins through to their insertion into noble families. In both novels the injustices suffered by the heroines are examined. The virtues and values of the lower classes are praised, and social prejudice denounced. In the latter work, Nicole rejects the ideals of the nobility, and renounces love in favour of a life among a group of like-minded women. Robert's other works include: *La Voix de la nature* (1763) (*The Voice of Nature*) and the two fantastical tales: *Voyages de mylord Céton dans les sept planètes* (1765–66) (*Travels of Lord Céton through the Seven Planets*) and *Lesondins* (1768). **Bib:** Girou-Swiderski, M., 'Comment peut-on être parvenue?' *Etudes littéraires*, December 1979.

Robert-Angelini, Enif (1886–1976)

Italian writer and actress. A member of the ▷futurist movement. She wrote for futurist journals, and was, in some respects, one of the more feminist members of the futurist movement in that she spoke positively of women's strength and intelligence. In relation to her writing, too, she appears to be feminist, in so far as she puts forward the idea of a feminine writing which will not be governed by notions of romantic love. Ultimately, though, for Robert, as for most of the Futurist women writers, biology was destiny. Her co-writing, with Marinetti, of ▷*Un Ventre di donna* (*A Woman's Womb*) revealed her underlying negativity towards the condition of being female, and towards the female body itself.

Robert Elsmere (1888)

A novel by English writer ▷Mrs Humphry Ward. The protagonist, Robert Elsmere, is a clergyman who loses his faith through a study of the 'higher criticism' of Bible texts, and resigns his orders for a life of social service in the East End of London. His devout wife, Catherine, is distressed by his actions. The novel, like many other literary texts of the mid-Victorian period, deals with a crisis of faith. It evokes the atmosphere of religious debate that succeeded the demise of the ▷Oxford Movement, and supports the view that Christians should attend to their social obligations first and foremost. The novel was hugely successful, benefiting from a review written by the statesman, W.E. Gladstone, in *The Nineteenth Century*.

Roberts, Elizabeth Madox

US novelist. Born in Perryville, Kentucky, and a descendant of pioneers, Roberts continually struggled against ill health. Despite disruptions to her education, she eventually earned a philosophy degree in 1921 from the University of Chicago. She taught school in rural Kentucky to learn country speech and folk ballads.

Her historical novels, like *The Great Meadow* (1930), celebrate Kentucky women pioneers. Her protagonists struggle against nature and fate, but they discover the spirit and inner strength that enable them to endure. Her heroines undergo a search for self that follows a mythic pattern. In ▷*The Time of Man* (1926) Roberts appropriates *The Odyssey* and transforms it into a pioneer woman's epic. She chose to focus on the introspective lives of her protagonists rather than on sweeping historical events.

Other works include: *The Great Steep's Garden* (1915), *My Heart and My Flesh* (1927), *Jingling in the Wind* (1928), *He Sent Forth a Raven* (1935),

Black Is My Truelove's Hair (1938), *Songs in the Meadow* (1940) and *Not By Strange Gods* (1941). **Bib:** McDowell, Frederick P.W., *Elizabeth Madox Roberts.*

Roberts, Michèle (born 1949)

Michèle Roberts

English poet and novelist. As poetry editor of *Spare Rib* (1975–1977) and *City Limits* (1981–1983), Roberts has had a significant influence on the development of contemporary British poetry. She teaches creative writing, and regularly performs her work in readings and on radio and television. Among her volumes of poetry are: *Cutlasses and Earrings* (1976, with ▷Michelene Wandor), *Licking the Bed Clean* (1978) and *Smile, Smile, Smile, Smile* (1980). Her novels, which deal, often controversially, with issues of female sexuality and religion, include *The Visitation* (1983), *The Wild Girl* (1984) and *The Book of Mrs Noah* (1987).
 ▷Maitland, Sara; *Tales I Tell My Mother; One Foot on the Mountain*; Kazantzis, Judith

Roberts, Sheila (born 1937)

South African short story writer, novelist and poet. Roberts was born in Johannesburg, and is currently a professor at the University of Milwaukee-Wisconsin. While her short stories have won prizes in South Africa – her first set of short stories, *Outside Life's Feast* (1975), won the Olive Schreiner Prize – her first novel, *He's My Brother* (1977), received the more dubious honour of being banned in South Africa, later being reprinted in the USA under the title *Johannesburg Requiem.*

Roberts is interested in the decaying culture of white suburban life, on which she casts a satirical eye. *The Weekenders* (1981) is set in a casino in the fictional state of Tshithaba, a loosely-veiled Sun City, Bophuthatswana: here socialites from Johannesburg gather in an atmosphere of forced geniality which turns savage. In the one-act play *Weekend* (1977), a woman leaves her abusive and dictatorial husband, only to return: a scene set to recur again and again. Her poetry, *Lou's Life and Other Poems* (1977), and *Dialogues and Divertimenti* (1985), deals to a large extent with people and situations, thus reflecting the interests of a novelist and short story writer, and skilfully combining lyric and narrative modes. Apart from a third novel, *Jacks in Corners* (1987), and a second set of short stories, *This Time of Year and Other Stories* (1983), Roberts has published critical work on South African writing, as well as a book on contemporary South African writer Dan Jacobson (born 1929), and a collection of essays on women writers, *Still the Frame Holds* (1986).

Robertson, Heather (born 1942)

Canadian novelist and journalist, born in Winnipeg. She attended the Universities of Manitoba and Columbia, worked for the *Winnipeg Tribune*, the Canadian Broadcasting Corporation, and *Maclean's* magazines. Informed by history, her work successfully traverses the boundaries between journalism and fiction, 'the point at which a real human being becomes a "character" in a book'. Her early non-fiction works include *Reservations are For Indians* (1970), *Grass Roots* (1973), *Salt of the Earth* (1974) and *The Flying Bandit* (1981). Her novels, *Willie: A Romance* (1983) and *Lily: A Rhapsody in Red* (1986) are irreverent political meditations about the Mackenzie King era. *More Than a Rose: Prime Ministers, Wives, and Other Women* (1991) examines the evolving role of political women.

Robertson, Margaret Murray (1821–1897)

Canadian novelist. She was born in Aberdeenshire, Scotland, but after her mother died in 1932 the family emigrated to the United States and then moved to Sherbrooke, Quebec in 1836, where her father was a minister for twenty-five years. From 1866 she published more than a dozen family chronicles; her novels are ▷sentimental, and frequently feature sacrificial women. For example, the heroine of *Shenac's Work at Home: The Story of Canadian Life* (1868) matures through faith and suffering.

Robinson, Marilyn ▷*Housekeeping*

Roche, Mazo de la (1879–1961)

Popular Canadian novelist. Born Mazo Roche in Newmarket, Ontario, she was educated at Parkdale College, Toronto, and lived for some years near Clarkson, on the shores of Lake Ontario. There, with her beloved cousin and companion, Carolyn Clement, she wrote. Her first short story appeared in 1902, and her first collection of short stories, *Explorers of the Dawn*, in 1922. *Possession* was published in 1923, and *Delight* in 1926; both are realistic works. When

▷*Jalna* (1927) won the $10,000 Atlantic-Little, Brown Fiction Award and achieved tremendous success, she and Clement moved to England, where they adopted two children, and lived for ten years, returning to Toronto after the beginning of World War II. De la Roche's reputation is based on the dramatic Whiteoaks chronicle, the popular and readable family saga which includes sixteen volumes: *Jalna* (1927); *Whiteoaks of Jalna* (1929); *Finch's Fortune* (1931); *The Master of Jalna* (1933); *Young Renny* (1935); *Whiteoak Harvest* (1936); *Whiteoak Heritage* (1940); *Wakefield's Course* (1941); *The Building of Jalna* (1945); *Return to Jalna* (1948); *Mary Wakefield* (1949); *Renny's Daughter* (1951); *Whiteoak Brothers* (1953); *Variable Winds at Jalna* (1955); *Centenary at Jalna* (1958), and *Morning at Jalna* (1960).

Despite the author's attempts to escape from the Jalna series, her other works did not enjoy as much success. She wrote children's and animal stories: *Portrait of a Dog* (1930), *Beside a Norman Tower* (1934), *The Very House* (1937), *The Sacred Bullock, and Other Stories of Animals* (1939), *The Song of Lambert* (1955) and *Bill and Coo* (1958). Her other novels include: *Lark Ascending* (1932), *Growth of a Man* (1938), *The Two Saplings* (1942) and *A Boy in the House* (1952). Three of her one-act plays were performed in the 1920s – they are included in *Low Life and Other Plays* (1929). Some of her short fiction has been republished in *Selected Stories of Mazo de la Roche* (1979). Her work is judged largely in terms of 19th-century romance, with careful plotting and strong character development. She died in Toronto.
Bib: Givner, J., *Mazo de la Roche: The Hidden Life*; Hambleton, R., *Mazo de la Roche of Jalna*; Hendrick, G., *Mazo de la Roche.*

Rochefort, Christiane (born 1917)

French novelist and essayist. Rochefort is an accessible and, in France, a popular writer, whose second novel, *Les Petits Enfants du siècle* (1961) (▷*Children of Heaven*, 1962, *Josyane and the welfare*, 1963), is studied in schools and in higher education. Apart from two ventures into fantasy – a dystopian novel, *Une Rose pour Morrison* (1966) (*A Rose for Morrison*), and a Utopia, *Archaos ou le jardin étincelant* (1972) (*Archaos, or the Glittering Garden*), Rochefort's novels conform to realist conventions, and are often simultaneously confessional in tone and highly comic. The typical Rochefort narrative depicts the struggles of a social outcast against oppression, and ironic humour and irreverent colloquialisms are used to criticize the norms of conventional society and language. The repression of independent female sexuality, whether lesbian or heterosexual, and of sexuality, creativity and pleasure generally in contemporary society, are constant themes in all of Rochefort's writing, much of which has a markedly 1960s feel to it.

Her other novels are: *Le Repos du guerrier* (1958) (*Warrior's Rest*, 1959), *Les Stances à Sophie*, (1963) (*Cats Don't Care for Money*, 1965), *Printemps au parking* (1967) (*Spring in the Car*

Park), *Encore heureux qu'on va vers l'été* (1975) (*Still Happy that Summer is Coming*), *Quand tu vas chez les femmes* (1982) (*How to Deal with Women*), ▷*La Porte du fond* (1988) (*The Far Door*).
Bib: Holmes, D., 'Realism, fantasy and feminist meaning: the fiction of Christiane Rochefort' in Atack, M. and Powrie, P. (eds), *Contemporary French Fiction by Women: Feminist Perspectives.*

Roches, Madeleine Neveu des (1520–1587) and Catherine Fradonnet des (1542–1587)

French writers of poetry, prose and drama. A mother and daughter variously known as *les dames des Roches* or *les demoiselles des Roches* (the des Roches ladies), they were among the most respected and famous women authors of their day. They are now considered more important for the literary atmosphere that they created in and around their native Poitiers (a town neither ever left) than for their individual works. Their fame spread to Paris, where they were particularly renowned for the literary salon which they held in the parish of Saint-Michel for over twenty years. Supported by the first generation of ▷humanist scholars, it was described by the historian Etienne Pasquier (1529–1615) as '*une vraye escole d'honneur*' ('a true school of honour'), which rivalled the Parisian salons of the humanist Jean de Morel (1511–1581), and the courtiers Villeroy (▷Madeleine de l'Aubespine) and the Maréchale de Retz (Claude-Catherine de Clermont-Dampierre, ?1545–1603). Pasquier describes the daily routine of Mesdames des Roches thus: in the morning was their time to '*se mettre sur les livres, puis tantost faire un sage vers, tantost une épistre bien dictée, après avoir donné ordre à leur mesnage*' ('to take to their books, then to write a good verse, or a well-written epistle, after having put the house in good order').

Between them, they wrote both poetry and prose, and undertook various translations from Latin. Madeleine des Roches, who was twice widowed, had a melancholy temperament particularly suited to verse. Her daughter Catherine, who never married but shocked salon society by having two affairs, wrote mainly prose, as well as a number of sonnets under a ▷pseudonym, and a biblical tragicomedy entitled *La Tragédie de Tobie et Sarra* (*The Tragedy of Tobie and Sarra*). *Les Missives de Mes Dames Des Roches* (1586) (*The Letters of Mesdames des Roches*) was the first correspondence between women to be published in French. Both mother and daughter were well aware of the singularity of their position in a world where culture was the province of men, but there is no question of their challenging social structures of the role of women, except perhaps in their private lives. They claimed the woman's right to study, and Catherine is the more aggressive in her attitude towards men. Madeleine rejects '*le fuseau pour la plume*' ('the bobbin for the pen'), but does not want to flee the duties of her sex, hoping '*aux hommes faire veoir / Combien leurs loix nous font de violence*' ('to show men how much violence their laws do to us'). Catherine wishes to

convince men '*De faire estudier les dames du pays*' ('to get local women to study'). Her work implies the need for female solidarity. Both mother and daughter condemn tyrannical husbands, and in two sets of dialogues, *Placide et Sévère* and *Iris et Pasithaé*, oppose two types of father: one limits his daughters' education to '*le fuseau*' and '*la quenouille*' (the tools of spinning); the other gives them a liberal and eclectic education in philosophy, law, medicine, and sacred and ancient texts. Catherine des Roches notes: '*Il y a bien assez d'hommes qui escrivent, mais assez peu de filles se meslent d'un tel exercice & j'ay toujours desiré d'estre du nombre de peu*' ('There are quite enough men who write, but rather few girls who attempt such an exercise and I always wanted to be one of the few'). Although desirous of poetic immortality, the demoiselles des Roches are careful to explain that they have only written in '*le temps de [leur] plus grande oisiveté*' ('the time when they would otherwise have been completely unoccupied'). Both mother and daughter died on the same day, of the plague.
Bib: Diller, G.E., *Les dames des Roches: Etude sur la vie littéraire à Poitiers dans la deuxième moitié du XVIe siècle, Revue du XVIe siècle.*

Rochester, J.W. (1861–1924)
Pen-name of Russian novelist and short story writer Vera Ivanovna Kryzhanovskaia. Rochester specialized in popular occult and historical novels. She and her husband, Sergei Semënov, were actively involved in various spiritualist salons in ▷ St Petersburg, and her occult interests pervade her fiction. She first published in France in the mid-1880s and then in Russia in the 1890s. She was very popular: her novels appeared in editions of up to 10,000 copies, and were translated into English and other European languages. She wrote more than fifty novels altogether, as well as numerous short stories. In addition to tales of the occult, she specialized in historical fiction set in such exotic places as ancient Egypt and Rome. Her novels make for good entertainment, include fantastic elements, and end with the triumph of good over evil. Kryzhanovskaia emigrated to Latvia, where she died of tuberculosis in great poverty. After her death, her novels remained in print for another decade.
Bib: *The Torch-Bearers of Bohemia* (1917).

Rodoreda, Mercè (1909–1983)
Arguably Spain's best 20th-century female novelist. Born in Barcelona, Rodoreda was the only daughter of an upper-middle-class Catalan family. Before the Spanish Civil War (1936–9), Rodoreda wrote fiction, much of which she later repudiated. She went into exile after the civil war, residing first in Bordeaux, then Paris, and finally Geneva, where she settled until the time of her return to Catalonia after some twenty-three years in exile. Her masterpiece is *La plaça del Diamant* (1962) (▷ *The Pigeon Girl*, 1967). Her other novels include: *Vint-i-dos contes* (1957) (*Twenty-Two Tales*); *El carrer de les Camèlies* (1966) (*The*

Street of Camellias); *La meva Cristina i altres contes* (1967) (*My Christiana and Other Stories*); *Jardí vora el mar* (1967) (*Garden by the Sea*); *Mirall trencat* (1974) (*Broken Mirror*); *Semblava de seda i altres contes* (1978) (*It Seemed Like Silk and Other Stories*), and *Quanta, quanta guerra* (1980) (*So Much War*). Rodoreda's fiction is characterized by its swift-moving plots, precise characterization, and fundamental empathy with the female condition.
▷ Catalan women's writing

Rodriguez, Judith (born 1936)
Australian poet and short story writer. Rodriguez has worked as a teacher and academic. She was poetry editor of the Australian magazine *Meanjin* from 1979 to 1982, is now a lecturer at Macarthur Institute, Sydney, and is poetry reviewer for the *Sydney Morning Herald*. Her second marriage is to the prominent Australian poet, publisher and novelist, Thomas Shapcott. She received the South Australian Biennial Prize for Literature for *Water Life* (1978) and the PEN/Stuyvesant Prize for Poetry for *Mudcrabs at Gambaro's* (1980). Other volumes include *Nu-Plastik Fanfare Red* (1973), *Shadow on Glass* (1978) and *Witch Heart* (1982).
▷ Poetry and Gender

Roig, Montserrat (born 1946)
Spanish novelist. Born in Barcelona, Roig is a well-known journalist and television interviewer. She has published collections of interviews and a volume of feminist essays. Her short-story collection *Molta roba i poc sabó . . .* (1970) (*Lots of Clothes and Little Soap . . .*) won the important Victor Català Prize. Her novels explore the evolution of two Barcelona families, Miralpeix and Claret, between 1894 and 1979, concentrating on the women. They often consist of dialogues between two female protagonists, and reflect the testimonial orientation of a reporter-novelist. Her novels are: *Ramona, adéu* (1972) (*Goodbye, Ramona*); *El temps de les cireres* (1977) (*The Time of the Cherries*); ▷ *L'hora violeta* (1980) (*The Violet Hour*), and *L'opera quotidiana* (1982) (*Workaday Opera*).
▷ Catalan women's writing

Roland, Betty (born 1903)
Australian dramatist, novelist, non-fiction writer. Roland was born Elizabeth Maclean in Kaniva, Victoria, adopted her father's christian name of Roland, worked as a journalist and married in 1923. Her first play, *The Touch of Silk* (1928), was followed by *Morning* (1932). In 1933 Roland eloped with the prominent Australian communist, Guido Barrachi, and lived in Russia for a time. Returning to Australia, she became famous for socialist realist dramas such as *Are You Ready Comrade?* (1948), which won the Western Australian Drama Competition. Her play *Granite Peak* was televized in England in 1952, and the Australian television series *Return to Eden* (1983) was based upon her radio serial *A Woman Scorned*. Roland has also written children's books, travel

books and three novels, one of which, *Caviar for Breakfast* (1979) is based upon her experiences in Russia.

▷New Theatre, The

Roland, Marie-Jeanne Philipon (1754–1793)
French woman of letters, celebrated in the 19th century as a great romantic heroine. Born in Paris, the daughter of an engraver, she received a convent education, described in her correspondence with the Carnet sisters. During the Revolution (1789) she and her husband belonged to the moderate Girondist party. Her husband held several public offices, and participated in public political life, sitting in on conferences, drafting state papers, and contributing to the newsletters *Le Courrier de Lyon* and the *Patriote française*. In Paris she presided over a Republican salon, and was acquainted with all the leading figures on the left. A letter challenging the king, drafted by Madame Roland, made the couple national heroes but they lost public support when they voted against his execution. Madame Roland was arrested in June 1793, and executed the following November. During her imprisonment she wrote the *Mémoires* on which her literary reputation is based. The frankness with which she describes the attempt by one of her father's employees to abuse her sexually when she was twelve, the 'unpleasant surprises' experienced on her wedding night, and her attachments to her lover, Buzot, and her friend, Sophie Carnet, caused the memoirs to be viewed as scandalously indecent, and prompted comparisons with Rousseau's *Confessions* (1781). The *Mémoires* record a cynical view of the court at Versailles, and present a tableau of bourgeois life at the end of the *ancien régime*.

An English translation (abridged) of her *Memoirs*: E. Shuckburgh, *The memoirs of Mme Roland* (1989).

▷French Revolution: pamphlets, registers of grievances, petitions and speeches
Bib: Benrekassa, G., 'Le sein blessé de Clorinde' in *Littérature*, No. 69; Chaussinand-Nogaret, G., *Madame Roland. Une femme en Révolution*; Cornevin, M., *La Véritable Mme Roland*; Gelfand, E., 'A Response to the Void . . .' in *Romance Notes*; May, G., *Mme Roland and the Revolution*.

Roland Holst, Henriëtte (1869–1952)
Dutch poet, prose writer and dramatist; full name Henriëtte Goverdine Anna Roland Holst-van der Schalk. Daughter of a notary, she was educated for some years at a boarding school for girls. As a young woman, she rebelled against the materialism prevailing in her environment. Her first collection of poems appeared around the time of her marriage to the painter and essayist R.N. Roland Holst (*Sonnetten en verzen in terzinen geschreven*, 1896, *Sonnets and Verse Written in Terzets*). She joined the socialist movement, and opted for a radical Marxist position, exemplified by the poems in *De nieuwe geboort* (1903) (*The New Birth*) and the tragedy *De opstandelingen* (1910)

(*The Rebels*). After leaving the socialist movement, and following the death of her mother, she wrote the poems in *Verzonken grenzen* (1918) (*Submerged Borders*), and became a communist, though she rejected party discipline (*Tusschen twee werelden*, poetry, 1923: *Between Two Worlds*). *Heldensage* (1927) (*Saga of Heroes*) is a poetic homage to the Russian Revolution (1917). The cycle of poems *Vernieuwingen* (1929) (*Renewals*) is evidence of her growing religious feelings. Her autobiography, *Het vuur brandde voort* (*The Fire Burnt On*), was published in 1949.

Romance fiction
19th-century Britain: In Victorian Britain it was commonly assumed that romance and the novel were inextricably entwined. This association was significant for women writers, since affairs of the heart were seen as woman's domain. To write about love, therefore, was considered 'natural', in a way that writing about politics was not. Almost every 19th-century woman writer, from ▷Jane Austen onwards, worked within the conventions of romantic fiction to a greater or lesser degree. Commentators and critics, eager to separate and categorize the writing of women, praised their 'special' ability to portray love and linked this to an essential feminine nature. Behind such praise lay prejudice, however, for a focus on love was also viewed as a limitation. Women writers, it was argued, were unable to venture into abstract and intellectual areas of existence and represent 'universal' values. Women were, and ought to be, confined within the domestic and emotional in literature as well as life. This ideology was increasingly undermined as the century wore on, but romantic novels remained as popular with women readers as they are today.

▷'Silly Novels by Lady Novelists'; 'Woman Question, The'; Blind, Mathilde; Broughton, Rhoda

20th century: Although the romance emerged during the 18th century as a genre of popular fiction directed at women readers, the mass-market formula romance is a 20th-century phenomenon. Its distinguishing feature is the repetition, with minor variations, of the same formulaic plot, so that novels by different authors but from the same publisher can be purchased with the assurance that they will deliver an equivalent experience. The context for the appearance of mass-produced formula romance fiction can be found in the transformation earlier this century of the publishing industry by technological changes which permitted the production of cheap paperbacks on a large scale; by developing communications systems which made possible efficient marketing and distribution; and by the injection of capital and a modern competitive business ethos as conglomerates took over the older independent publishing houses. Although romantic fiction had been appearing in confession and romance periodicals since the 1920s, it was only in the 1950s that the big romance paperback publishers began to emerge. Mills and Boon, in Britain, became an exclusive romance publisher in 1957, while in the US ▷Harlequin Enterprises published its first romance title in 1958, and in Canada, Simon and Schuster sponsored Silhouette.

It was the ▷Gothic romance which dominated the field from the mid-1950s until the early 1970s. This immensely successful 'line' was modelled on ▷Daphne du Maurier's ▷*Rebecca*, which had remained in print since its first publication in 1938. Writers such as Victoria Holt (▷Jean Plaidy) and Phyllis Whitney led the way with a typical first print-run of 800,000. Between 1969 and 1972 thirty-five Gothic romance titles appeared a month in the US. In the 1970s the Gothic was superceded by the 'bodice-ripper' or 'sweet-savage romance', pioneered by Avon Books. The typical formula for this type of romance, derived from ▷Samuel Richardson and ▷Charlotte Brontë's ▷*Jane Eyre*, involves a young woman who falls in love with a rich, handsome, older man. The hero is cynical, cruel or cold, and often violent. The narrative follows the misunderstandings which keep them apart, and the eventual revelation that the hero loves the heroine; tender interior is often revealed beneath his tough masculine exterior. These books usually contain explicit sex scenes, although the place of sex in the romance is a controversial matter.

Today there are a variety of lines of romance designed to target multiple markets, rather than assuming a single female readership. ▷Catherine Cookson and ▷Georgette Heyer write Gothic and historical romances, while ▷Barbara Cartland maintains the soft-focus traditional romance, eschewing any sex scenes. ▷Jackie Collins exploits the racy glamour and scandal of the contemporary film and television worlds, as in *Hollywood Wives* (1983). A focus on women in the public and business sphere has also become an increasingly important aspect of the romance, pioneered in the 1970s by ▷Judith Krantz, whose books were set in multinational corporations, and equated sex, power and big business. Popular writers who have developed the novel in which strong women fight their way to power and success include ▷Barbara Taylor Bradford, Shirley Conran and Julie Burchill. Sally Beauman, like Bradford, writes novels in which women fight their way to power and wealth over several generations, but within more glitzy settings. The Australian Colleen McCullough's ▷*The Thorn Birds* has also been a massively successful generational saga. Other writers, such as ▷Danielle Steel, have attempted to adapt the romance to the new liberated and autonomous woman; her novel, *Full Circle* (1984) features a heroine who is involved with the 1960s civil rights and anti-Vietnam War movements in the US. However, all these books have in common the premise that women's fulfilment is to be achieved through romantic love, and many have been successfully adapted for television.

The popularity of romance fiction, Harlequin claiming for example that 16 million women in the US read their products, has posed a dilemma for feminist critics. Early feminist and Marxist criticism claimed that reading romances duped women by reconciling them to their subordinate role. Others have labelled romance reading as simply escapism.

These positions have been criticized as a patronizing dismissal of the interests and pleasures of the majority of women. Recent work pioneered by feminist critics such as ▷Tania Modleski in *Loving With a Vengeance* (1982) and ▷Janice A. Radway in *Reading the Romance* (1984) have challenged the view that women passively consume romance fiction. Modleski explores the role of fantasy in romance reading, and suggests that romances engage with the difficulties of heterosexual marriage for women. Radway takes a more empirical approach, examining women's own accounts of their experience of reading romance fiction. She argues that women use romance reading in a variety of ways that cannot be encompassed by traditional literary critical models of reading, such as an interpretative process aimed at finding the text's meaning.

A new area of interest is the spread of romance fiction in Africa, and other post-colonial countries. The marketing of Western romance fiction in these places raises questions about their ideological, political and economic relationship with the West, because of the different cultural norms concerning love, marriage, the family and gender. African writers such as ▷Helen Ovbiagele and ▷Pat Wambui Ngurukie have begun to rewrite the Western romance as a response.

Another conflict of norms, this time between heterosexual and lesbian sexuality, was evident in the development in the 1950s of a popular genre of lesbian romances (▷lesbian pulp fiction) by writers such as ▷Ann Bannon, and more recently ▷Jane Rule. However, there is a model for the lesbian romance in ▷Radclyffe Hall's deliberate exploitation of the romance genre in *Well of Loneliness* in 1928. Hall's work belongs to a long tradition of marriage between so-called serious fiction and the despised and lowly realms of popular culture, of which ▷Margaret Atwood's ▷*Lady Oracle* (1976) is one of the most recent and popular examples.
▷Romance (19th-century Britain)

New Zealand: In the late 19th century romance writing was a dominant form of literary production for women, and writers such as ▷Louisa Baker ('Alien') and G.B. Lancaster (▷Edith Lyttleton) were very well known. When realism replaced romance as a preferred mode of writing in the 1930s and 1940s, romance writing became the province of popular women writers, who have provided a continuous stream of narratives interpreting women's experience for a large audience, ranging from the immensely popular rural romances of ▷Mary Scott (*Breakfast at Six*, 1953, *Dinner Doesn't Matter*, 1957, and many others) and ▷Nelle Scanlan (*Pencarrow*, 1932, and its successors), to the gothic historical romances of Dorothy Eden (1912–1982) and the contemporary romances of Mills and Boon writers ▷Essie Summers, Robyn Donald and Daphne Clair. Romance writers are generally professionals and reach large audiences, helping to create a market for other kinds of fiction, and are often the only way that non-New Zealand readers of popular fiction experience regional settings.

▷Lesbian writing, New Zealand; Mander, Jane; Rees, Rosemary

West Africa: In West Africa there is a clear distinction between literature considered appropriate to the curriculum and accorded critical recognition, and popular fiction. The question of what constitutes the 'canon', and the aesthetics by which it will be judged, is a matter of heated debate in African literary criticism, in which the multinational publishers have inordinate influence. Indigenous publishers, however, have seen the market potential of popular fiction aimed at a less literate mass audience, and it is in this context that romantic fiction flourishes. The romance 'formula' of the Western genre has been modified in certain crucial respects to suit an African audience. The primacy of virginity, for instance, is displaced in cultures which set greater store by fertility, as is absolute fidelity in a context of polygamy and polygyny.

West African romantic fiction therefore tends to combine pragmatism and realism with fantasy, projecting the ideal of romantic love and monogamous marriage more as a trope for the repressed desire of women for change in the sexual status quo. Authors of popular romances include ▷Helen Ovbiagele, Rosina Umelo, Martina Nwakoby, Betty Manvers, Yemi Sikuade, ▷Funmilayo Fakunle and ▷Hauwa Ali in Nigeria; Christine Botchway and Kate Abbiam in Ghana; Ami Gad in Togo; Thérèse Kuoh-Moukouri in Cameroon, and Yemi Lucilda Hunter in Sierra Leone, while many others have written novels in which romance is a strong element.

Romance of Dollard, The (1889)

US historical romance by ▷Mary Catherwood. A magazine writer and novelist who prided herself on the research and accuracy of her works, Catherwood switched to historical romance in mid-career and had her first major success with *Dollard*. Like most of her historical work which followed, *Dollard* concerns the French and French Canadian exploration and settlement of the North American mid-west.

Romano, Lalla (born 1909)

Italian novelist, poet and translator. An extremely popular contemporary writer, indeed a best-seller, she has also won many literary awards for her work. She attended Turin University, from which she received a degree in Letters, and worked in Turin as a librarian and as a teacher. After the war, she moved to Milan. She has translated works by Flaubert, Delacroix and Beck into

Italian, and has contributed both poetry and short stories to many Italian literary magazines. All of Romano's narratives are in some respect autobiographical. A clear example of this is *Nei mari estremi* (1987) (▷*In Heavy Seas*), which retells the story of her life with her husband, from their first meeting, through his illness and death. ▷*La penombra che abbiamo attraversato* (1964) (*The Shadows Through Which We Have Passed*), is an earlier return to her childhood and youth. The much praised *Le parole fra noi leggere* (1969) (*Light Words Between Us*), tells of her complex relationship with her son. *Inseparabile* (1981) (*Inseparable*) , presents us again with the life of that same son, as his relationship with his wife ends and he, in turn, faces specific parental problems. Family relationships, their joys and pains, are usually to be found at the centre of any work by Romano. They are endlessly fascinating to her. She has produced many volumes of work, and defends her autobiographical approach by pointing out that she writes best of what she knows best.

Other works include: ▷*Maria* (1954); *L'uomo che parlava solo* (1961) (*The Man Who Spoke Alone*); *Diario di Grecia* (1974) (*A Greek Diary*); *Una giovinezza inventata* (1979) (*A Tale of Youth*); *La treccia di Tatiana* (1986) (*Tatiana's Plait*).

Romanticism

19th-century Britain: Women writers are rarely included in traditional accounts of literary Romanticism, but recent feminist criticism has reassessed the role of writers such as ▷Dorothy Wordsworth and ▷Mary Shelley, among others. Shelley's ▷*Frankenstein* may be read as a critique of Romantic individualism, while Wordsworth's ▷*Journals* indicate an uneasiness with Romantic abstraction. ▷Emily Brontë is clearly influenced by the tradition, as is ▷Elizabeth Barrett Browning, yet Brontë's poetry often demonstrates an ambivalence towards Romanticism's conception of the self. An unease is also evident in ▷Christina Rossetti's work, with poems such as 'The Thread of Life' and 'An Old World Thicket' challenging Romantic epistemology and modifying its view of nature. The Romantic poets were nevertheless major influences, especially William Wordsworth on Elizabeth Barrett Browning, ▷Felicia Hemans and ▷Letitia Landon, Lord Byron on the Brontës, and John Keats on Christina Rossetti. For a discussion of the effects of Romanticism on women writers, see Margaret Homans, *Women Writers and Poetic Identity* and Anne K. Mellor (ed.), *Romanticism and Feminism*.

▷*Jane Eyre*; Realism; *Wuthering Heights*

Italy: Literary, philosophical, artistic and political movement which spanned the end of the 18th century and the early 19th century. In literary terms, it is often referred to as the expression of the *mal du siècle*. It involved a re-evaluation of the past, an idealistic view of the people as depositories of an ancient knowledge, a positive reconsideration of religious values, and an exaltation of the imagination and the emotions (the sentimental, in essence) over the rational. The greatest exponent of romanticism in Italy is generally acknowledged to be Alessandro Manzoni, for both his novel *I promessi sposi* (1825–1827) (*The Betrothed*) , and his theoretical writings. No women writers have been included in the canon of Italian romanticism. Rosina Muzio Salvo was, perhaps, the most well-known woman writer in the genre, but her work is now out of print, even in Italian.

Portugal: Literary tendency dominating the period from the publication of Almeida Garrett's epic poem *Camões* in 1825, to the appearance of Antero de Quental's argument on behalf of literary ▷realism *Bom Senso e Bom Gosto* (*Good Sense and Good Taste*) in 1865. The ▷Marquesa de Alorna, who spent several years in Vienna and England, brought back to Portugal ideas associated with romanticism. She is credited with having influenced writers such as Alexandre Herculano, one of Portugal's most important novelists of the period. In political terms the Portuguese romantic movement coincides with one of the most turbulent periods in the nation's history, when monarchists and constitutionalists were battling for control. Romantic authors such as Garrett and Herculano participated in the struggle against absolutism, and much of their work is characterized by a fervent nationalistic spirit.

▷Ultra-romanticism; Browne, Maria da Felicidade do Couto; Elisa, Henriqueta; Janny, Amélia

Romanzo d'appendice (Italy)

A genre which had its origins in the second half of the 19th century, and which continued, in different forms, well into the 20th. Literally meaning a novel 'in appendix', the term refers to novels written for, and published in, newspapers in serial form. By virtue of their mode of production, these works tended to be thrilling, melodramatic tales. Their function was to bait the reader (to promote the circulation of the paper), encouraging him/her to read on, much in the style of the modern soap opera; hence the closure of each instalment/chapter with an exhausting cliff-hanger, so that readers would tune in again. Like the ▷*romanzo di consumo*, this genre attracted many women writers, no doubt in part because of its relatively quick financial pay-off. Perhaps its best known women practitioners, given their success in more traditionally acceptable literary genres, include ▷Carolina Invernizio, ▷Annie Vivanti and ▷Matilde Serao.

▷Gothic

Romanzo di consumo (Italy)

More or less translatable as 'literature for the masses'. In its 20th-century form, it includes the categories of ▷science fiction, detective stories and romantic novels/short stories. The *romanzo di consumo* had its origins in the late 1800s, and is closely related to both the ▷*romanzo d'appendice* and the ▷*romanzo popolare* of that period. It has,

from the beginning, had a relatively high number of women practitioners, from ▷Carolina Invernizio and ▷Carola Prosperi in the early days of the genre, to such respected, largely mainstream writers as ▷Elsa Morante in recent years. The very popularity of many of these women writers has often militated against their inclusion in the literary canon.

Romanzo popolare (Italy)

A genre which overlaps, to a certain extent, with the ▷*romanzo di consumo*. The term literally translates as the 'popular novel'. Again, many types of writing are covered by the definition *romanzo popolare*. In the 19th century, melodramatic, sentimental novels and crime novels formed the bulk of the genre. In its 20th-century form, crime novels, ▷detective fiction, romantic novels (▷romance) and ▷science fiction narratives would all claim inclusion. It has been suggested by various literary critics that all of these narratives are ultimately conventional, finally giving the seal of approval to socially sanctioned institutions (the judiciary, marriage), and supporting the primacy of good over evil. This has also been adduced as a reason for their popularity. This view may itself be somewhat simplistic and patronizing, and it fails to take into account those works in the genre which subvert all notions of authority.

Romein-Verschoor, Annie (Anna Helena Margaretha) (1895–1978)

Dutch prose writer. She grew up in Java (Dutch East Indies) and the Dutch naval port, Den Helder, and studied Dutch, history, and later, Russian, in Leiden. She married the historian Jan Romein. Her many publications in the field of sociology of literature and the history of culture are mainly Marxist in tenor. Following her 1935 thesis *De Nederlandsche romanschrijfster na 1880*, (or *Vrouwenspiegel*), (*The Dutch Woman Novelist After 1880*, or *Woman's Mirror*) her work included a government-commissioned survey of Dutch literature between 1920 and 1946, translated into French (*Alluvions et nuages*, 1947) and English (*Silt and Sky*, 1950). In the field of history, she published jointly with her husband. Also included in her considerable *oeuvre* are a historical novel on Hugo de Groot, *Met eigen ogen* (1953) (*With My Own Eyes*), a description of her stay in Indonesia, and reminiscences of her militant left-wing commitment, and dedication to woman's emancipation (*Omzien in verwondering*, 1970–1971; *Looking Back in Wonder*).

Romieu, Marie de (?1545–?1590)

French poet. Known as '*la quatrième des grâces*' ('the fourth Grace'), she was the author of the *Bref discours de l'excellence des femmes* (*Brief Discourse on the Excellence of Women*), written as a reply to her brother Jacques's invective against women. To prove the superiority of women in this verse treatise, now considered of little literary or documentary interest, Marie de Romieu brings to

bear religious, mythological and even aesthetic arguments, presenting her sex as '*chasse-mal, chasse-ennuy, chasse-dueil, chasse-peine*' ('a protection against evil, boredom, mourning and pain'). Since the first publication of *Stances du mariage* (*Stanzas on Marriage*) by the poet Philippe Desportes (1546–1606) in 1573, traditional Italian stanzas and alexandrines had been frequent media for feminist and anti-feminist tracts. Marie de Romieu also translated Alessandro Piccolomini's *Dialogo della bella creanza delle donne* under the title *Instruction pour les jeunes dames* (1573) (*Instruction for Young Ladies*). All her work was published by her brother and tutor, Jacques de Romieu. An apologetic preface to the *Premières oeuvres poétiques de Mademoiselle de Romieu* (1581) (*First Poetic Works of Mademoiselle de Romieu*), reminds him how little time an enlightened bourgeois woman has for writing poetry: '*Prenez en bonne part, mon Frère, ce mien brief discours que je vous envoye, composé à la hâte, n'ayant pas le loisir à cause de notre mesnage, de vacquer (comme vous dedié pour servir aux Muses) à chose si belle & si divine que les vers*' ('Take in good heart, my brother, this my brief discourse that I am sending you which like you is dedicated to serving the Muses, but has been composed in haste, for our household leaves me no free time to devote to so beautiful and divine a thing as verse, though I am no less dedicated').
Bib: Guillerm, J.P., Guillerm, L., Hordoir, L. and Piejus, M.F., *Le Miroir des femmes*.

Romola (1862–1863)
An ▷historical novel by English novelist ▷George Eliot, serialized in *Cornhill Magazine*. It is set in Florence at the end of the 15th century and describes the period and place in exhaustive detail. Machiavelli, Charles VIII and the reforming monk, Savonarola, are among the historical figures included, but the narrative action centres on the fictional character, Romola, a young woman whose story is one of salvation through self-denial. She marries an untrustworthy Greek scholar who betrays her, and becomes disillusioned by Savonarola, who falls away from his high-minded mission. Left isolated, Romola finds self-sacrifice the key to peace of mind. The novel is generally considered dull and is the least popular of Eliot's works.

Rooke, Daphne (born 1914)
South African writer of historical fiction and contemporary romance, born in Boksburg, Transvaal; she now lives in Australia. Her first three novels, *A Grove of Fever Trees* (1950, first published as *The Sea Hath Bounds* in 1946 under the pseudonym Robert Pointon), *Mittee* (1951) and *Ratoons* (1953) gave her an immediate popularity, especially in the USA. Her style is racy, and sometimes melodramatic. *Mittee* and *Ratoons* have both been reprinted, the former in South Africa in 1987, and in Britain in 1991, and the latter in South Africa in 1990. Her work is accordingly starting to receive its first serious critical scrutiny. Well-known writer and critic J.M.

Coetzee wrote an afterword, not altogether favourable, to *Mittee*.

Mittee, set in the late 19th century, is the story of two women, Mittee, the eponymous heroine, and her black servant, Selina. Unbeknown to Mittee, she and Selina share the same lover. This novel, like others by Rooke, is marked by an interest in sexual politics in a racist culture. As regards the robustness with which this sexuality is presented, Rooke breaks new ground in Southern African fiction. Particularly interesting is her presentation of the competitive yet intimate relations between white and black women. However, Rooke is not a selfconsciously political writer, on either racial or sexual grounds.

A Lover for Estelle (1961) is set in Zululand in the 1920s. As in Rooke's other texts, action and melodrama abound: drought, bankruptcy, adultery, sexual bondage, and murder. The lover who provides the title is first the doltish but rich Manie du Toit, to whom Estelle is in effect sold by her family to ward off financial ruin. She then flees across the Portuguese border with another man, Foley, after he has shot his wife and pretended to shoot himself.

Rooke's other novels are: *Wizards' Country* (1957), *Beti* (1959), *The Greyling* (1962), *Diamond Jo* (1965), *Boy on the Mountain* (1969), *Double Ex!* (1971) and *Margaretha de la Porte* (1974). She also wrote three children's books: *The Australian Twins* (1955), *The South African Twins* (1953), and *The New Zealand Twins* (1957). *Apples in the Hold* (1952) appeared under her ▷pseudonym Robert Pointon. A recent set of interviews is available from the National English Literary Museum, Grahamstown.

Room of One's Own, A (1929)
Essay by English writer ▷Virginia Woolf. An extended discussion of the question of women and writing in the form of a series of lectures to a women's college, *A Room of One's Own* is crucial to an understanding of Woolf's work as a whole. Woolf argues here that literature should explore feminine experience, and not form a comparative assessment of women's experience in relation to men's. She is primarily concerned with the problem of mimicry, and suggests that the majority of 19th-century writing by women is not yet 'women's writing'. Woolf is concerned that women writers should 'think back through their mothers if we are women. It is useless to go to the great men for help, however much we go to them for pleasure.' Woolf carefully presents a materialist analysis of women's marginalization, and the text provides a sustained analysis of British society as a ▷'patriarchy'. Her argument on the 'feminine sentence' proposes a definite connection between sexual difference and language, while the final section introduces Woolf's complex notion of 'androgyny'. Woolf's interest in androgyny, which seems to endorse both harmony and the unity of sexual difference as the ideal writing identity, has provoked a series

of debates as to its meaning within Woolf's feminist politics.

▷Malraux, Clara; Raine, Kathleen; Richardson, Dorothy; *Three Guineas*

Room of One's Own (1975–present)

Canadian feminist journal of literature and criticism, it originates out of Vancouver, British Columbia, and is edited by the Growing Room Collective. The title of the periodical comes from ▷Virginia Woolf's assertion that every woman must have a room of her own if she is to write, and it was established to provide women with an opportunity for publication. It has published special issues on ▷Marian Engel, ▷Carol Shields, and ▷Audrey Thomas, particularly valuable for the bibliographies that are supplied.

Roper, Margaret (More) (1505–1544)

English translator and letter-writer. She was the eldest child of Thomas (1478–1535) and Jane Colt More. Under the influence of the famous group of ▷humanists connected with her father's household, all of the More children were tutored in Latin and Greek, logic, philosophy, mathematics and religion. Thomas More took a special interest in his daughter, providing her with perhaps the best education received by a Renaissance woman. In 1521, she married William Roper. Roper is characterized in a number of contemporaneous writings, including those of her father and of his biographers, as the ideal example of a learned but modest woman of virtue. A family friend, Desiderius Erasmus (?1466–1536) called her 'the flower of all the learned matrons in England'. She is most famous for her ▷translation of Erasmus's ▷*Devout Treatise on the Pater Noster* (1524). Also extant are the ▷letters she wrote to her father between April 1534 and July 1535, when he awaited execution for his refusal to take the Oath of Supremacy.

▷Humanism (England); *Instruction of a Christian Woman*.
Bib: Rogers, E.F. (ed.), *The Correspondence of Sir Thomas More*.

Rosà, Rosa (1894–1978)

Pseudonym of Italian novelist, essayist, and illustrator Edyth von Haynau. Though she was born in Vienna, Rosà's work is very much in the context of the Italian ▷futurist movement. Her work stands out, however, from that of most male and female futurist writers because of her unashamedly feminist approach. In a series of articles for *L'Italia futurista*, she argued that the war was a positive experience for women in general, in that it could lead them to a new sense of independence and an awareness of their individual identity. Unlike most futurist women, she does not accept that woman's main role in a new Italy is the traditional one of mother. Her writing contains more complex female characters than most other futurist fiction. She wrote two short novels, ▷*Non c'è che te!* (1919) (*There's No-one But You!*), and *Una donna con tre anime* (1918)

(*A Woman With Three Souls*), both of which contain unorthodox female characters who react against patriarchal society and create new identities for themselves. Rosà seems to have been the only futurist woman writer who actively rejected whole segments of Marinetti's doctrine in relation to women.

Rosamalin ▷Surangkhanang, K.

Rosca, Ninotchka

Filipino writer. She was an activist during her student days in the 1960s at the University of the Philippines, and was arrested and held in a military detention camp when martial law was declared in 1972. Out of these experiences came her volume of short stories, *The Monsoon Collection* (1983). Before that, she had published her first collection, *Bitter Country and Other Stories*.

She is now resident in New York, where she is a freelance writer. Her novel *State of War* tries to make sense of Philippine history through the use of what she calls 'suprarealistic' techniques. She has also published a short story 'Epidemic', which was chosen as one of the USA's 100 best stories in 1986. Though refusing to be labelled a feminist, she sees her success in international writing and publishing as a triumph for the Filipino woman.

Ross, Martin (1861–1915)

Irish novelist, born in Galway; psedonym of Violet Florence Martin, née Ross. She was educated in Dublin at Alexandra College. She is best-known for her literary partnership with her cousin, ▷Edith Somerville, which produced a series of highly successful, light-hearted novels which poke malicious fun at the social vagaries of the Irish of all classes: *Some Experiences of an Irish R.M.* (Resident Magistrate) (1899), *Further Experiences of an Irish R.M.* (1908) and *In Mr Knox's Country* (1915).

Rosselli, Amelia (born 1930)

Italian poet. Born in Paris and educated in France, England and the USA, she writes in English and Italian, but all three languages enrich her poetry. She began to write in the early 1960s, encouraged by Pier Paolo Pasolini, and is arguably the most famous contemporary Italian woman poet. Rosselli strives in her poetry to articulate a feminine 'I', to define herself. Much of her work centres on the unconscious mind, on the *lapsus linguae* which reveal the inner self. She is one of those women writers for whom the whole area of self-definition is crucial, for whom identity is a shifting construct.

Her works include: *Variazioni belliche* (1964) (*War Variations*); *Serie ospedaliera* (1969) (*Hospital Series*); *Documento* (1976) (*Document*); *Primi scritti 1952–63* (1981) (*Earliest Writings*); *Impromptu* (1981); *La libellula* (1985) (*The Dragonfly*); *Antologia poetica* (1987) (*Poetry Anthology*); *Diario Ottuso* (1990) (*Obscure Diary*).

Rossetti, Ana (born 1950)

Contemporary Spanish poet. Rossetti established her reputation in the 1980s. Her collection *Los devaneos de Erato* (1980) (*Erato's Ravings*) won the Premio Gules de Poesía. Subsequent collections, such as *Dióscuros* (1982), *Indicios vehementes* (1985) (*Vehement Indications*), ▷*Devocionario* (1986) (*Prayerbook*), and *Yesterday* (1988), were also greatly acclaimed. She has also published a novel, *Plumas de España* (1988) (*Feathers of Spain*).

Rossetti, Christina (1830–1894)

British poet, younger sister of Dante Gabriel and William Michael Rossetti. Her father, Gabriele, was an Italian patriot who came to England in 1824, her mother Frances Polidori was half-English and a former ▷governess. Italian influence, particularly that of Dante, is noticable in much of Rossetti's work. She was educated largely at home, her first poetry being published privately when she was twelve. Five poems appeared under the ▷pseudonym Ellen Alleyne in the ▷Pre-Raphaelite Brotherhood's journal *The Germ* (1850). She broke off an engagement to the painter James Collinson when he joined the Catholic Church in 1850, for she was a devout High Anglican, much influenced by the ▷Oxford Movement. Although she was high-spirited as a child, she became increasingly reclusive and was plagued by illness, contracting Grave's disease in 1873.

Rossetti's best-known poem today is the sensual and complex ▷*Goblin Market*, published with other poems in 1862. ▷*The Prince's Progress, and Other Poems* appeared in 1866; ▷*Sing Song. A Nursery Rhyme Book* in 1872 and ▷*A Pageant, and Other Poems* in 1881. She also wrote religious prose works such as *Seek and Find* (1879); *Called to be Saints* (1881); and *The Face of the Deep* (1892). Her poetry often dwells on loss, renunciation and death, yet she is not limited to these subjects. The work ranges from fantasy verses to lyrics, ▷ballads, nonsense poems, devotional verse and sonnets, including the ▷'Monna Innominata' series (1881). The 'simple surface' of the poetry often conceals the complications beneath: Rossetti's best work engages profoundly with epistemological, spiritual and psychic concerns. Her work has suffered from reductive interpretations, but she is increasingly being reconsidered as a major Victorian poet.

▷Hymns (19th-century Britain)

Bib: Crump, R. (ed.), *The Complete Poems of Christina Rossetti* (3 vols); Kent, D.A. (ed.), *The Achievement of Christina Rossetti*; Rosenblum, D., *Christina Rossetti: The Poetry of Endurance*; Harrison, A., *Christina Rossetti in Context*.

Rostopchiná, Evdokiia Petrovna (1811–1858)

Rostopchiná was a rarity, a Russian woman writer who moved easily in aristocratic circles. Born Evdokiia Sushkova into a prominent ▷Moscow family, she received a sporadic education at home. Although she was a poet from adolescence, family prejudice against women writing kept her from

Evdokiia Rostopchiná

publishing until after her marriage to Count Andrei Rostopchin in 1833. Her facile gifts soon won her fame among the poets of the ▷Golden Age and, after Pushkin's death, a few of them even acclaimed her his successor. In early years Rostopchiná cloaked her sharp wit in charming chatter and her ego in 'feminine' self-deprecation. In lyrics like 'Temptation' (1839) she portrayed the inner conflict among the duties of motherhood, a feminine need for admiration and social life, and the intellectual demands of the poet's calling. Rostopchiná was reported to have called the works of Byron and Victor Hugo her 'gospels', and she carried their exalted romanticism and castigation of social hypocrisy into an increasingly prosaic and realistic Russian literature in tales such as ▷*Rank and Money* (1838), poems like 'The Circus of the Nineteenth Century' (1850), and the novel *A Fortunate Woman* (1851–1852). Her political allegory, ▷'The Forced Marriage' (1846), led to expulsion from ▷St Petersburg; she moved to Moscow, where her Saturday gatherings of writers soon became famous. In the blank verse play *An Unsociable Woman* (1849) the heroine becomes convinced of men's inability to devote themselves to love, and accepts a solitary life based on 'God, hope, and will . . . my firm will!'. 'Chatsky's Return' (1856), in which the hero of Griboedov's 1823 comedy *Woe from Wit* finds Moscow life still empty and banal, offended Muscovites on both sides of the political spectrum. Rostopchiná spent the last years of her life in increasingly bitter isolation.

Bib: Pedrotti, L., 'The Scandal of Countess

Rostopčina's Polish-Russian Allegory', *Slavic and East European Journal*, 30, 2, pp. 196–214.

Roth, Friederike (born 1948)

German poet, novelist and writer of radio plays and short stories. She holds a doctorate in linguistics and philosophy, and has become one of the most innovative young writers in Germany. Her work encompasses many themes and genres, from poetry and novellas to folk stories and dialect plays. All her writing experiments with language, images and forms, but this is particularly true of her poetry: *Tollkirschenhochzeit* (1978) (*Deadly Nightshade Wedding*); *Schieres Glück* (1981) (*Sheer Luck*), and *Schattige Gärten* (1987) (*Shady Gardens*). She is also author of a trilogy, *Das Buch des Lebens, ein Plagiat* (*The Book of Life, A Plagiarism*). The first volume, *Liebe und Wald* (1983) (*Love and Forests*), has a complex narrative structure, and aims to debunk many of the most commonly held notions about the nature of love.

Rothmann, Maria Elisabeth ▷M.E.R.

Roti, Contessa Anna ▷Luanto, Regina di

Roughing it in the Bush; or, Life in Canada (1852)

▷Susanna Moodie's story of pioneer hardship in southern Ontario, this is autobiography transformed by writing skill. The novel uses the form of the episodic memoir, written in the effective first-person voice of Moodie herself. It recounts the Moodies' emigration to Canada, and how, poorly equipped to deal with the hardship they meet, she and her husband lose almost everything, and retreat to Belleville, Ontario. Lacking the sunny pragmatism of her sister, ▷Catherine Parr Traill, Moodie paints a much less idyllic picture of life in Canada. The opening section of the novel, which describes the cholera epidemic in Quebec, is a carnivalesque *tour de force* that reveals Moodie's fascination with the very excesses she is repelled by. She claims at the end of the book that she will consider herself amply repaid for her toil if she deters even one family from going to the backwoods of Canada. ▷Margaret Atwood uses Moodie as the persona for her collection of poems, ▷*The Journals of Susanna Moodie*.

Rover, or the Banish'd Cavaliers The (1679)

Two-part comedy by ▷Aphra Behn. The first part is the best-known, and features the 'rover' Willmore and the young Hellena (who has disappeared by the beginning of the second play). Part I traces the fortunes of cavaliers abroad after the English Civil War (1642–1651), around a carnival, the making of three marriages and the bringing low of Blunt (an Essex gentleman). The plot also concerns the plight of Angellica, an élite courtesan, who imperils her identity and livelihood by falling in love.

Rowe, Elizabeth (Singer) (1674–1737)

English poet and journalist from Somerset – where her father had settled after being imprisoned for religious Nonconformity. Of Dissenting religious principles, she began to publish, and the Thynnes became her patrons (▷Frances Seymour, Countess of Hertford). Her *Poems on Several Occasions* (1696) contains several different kinds of poetry. In her preface she writes that male writers have the traditions of writing, and try to 'Monopolize Sence too' so that not 'so much as Wit should be allowed us'. She sees such assertion as 'Violations of the liberties of Free-born English women' – language which recalls the radical political associations of Nonconformist religion with the English Civil War (1642–1646 and 1648–1651). She married the writer Thomas Rowe (1710), and after his death in 1715 she lived in Frome, Somerset, working as a teacher. Religion became her topic in the *Friendship in Death* (1728) – letters from the dead to the living. More letters followed, *Letters Moral and Entertaining* (1729–33) and the verse *History of Joseph* (1736).

▷Scott, Mary (Taylor)

Rowlandson, Mary White (c 1636–post-1678)

North American spiritual autobiographer. Apparently born in England and brought to North America as a young girl, she was a resident of Lancaster, Massachusetts, in 1676 when her settlement was attacked by Native Americans participating in King Philip's War. While numerous family members were killed, she was taken captive and forced to travel with her captors for a period of eleven weeks. Her account of this experience, ▷*The Soveraignty and Goodness of God* (1682), became the model for a century of subsequent early North American ▷captivity narratives and for attitudes of the 'savage' nature of Native Americans. Her only publication, it stands today as a classic North American text of the 17th century.

Rowson, Susanna Haswell (1762–1824)

British/North American novelist, dramatist, poet and essayist. Born in Portsmouth, England, she was brought to North America at the age of five. Although she returned to England periodically thereafter, because of political persecution or economic need, she became one of North America's earliest and most popular novelists. Extraordinarily diverse in her literary talents, she published ten novels, including ▷*Victoria* (1786), ▷*Charlotte, a Tale of Truth* (1791), *Mentoria* (1791), ▷*Rebecca* (1792) and ▷*Lucy Temple: a Sequel to Charlotte Temple*; a dozen plays, most notably ▷*Slaves in Algiers* (1794); several collections of poetry, including ▷*A Trip to Parnassas* (1788); and numerous other miscellanies, including textbooks and historical accounts of famous women. Her novels combined traditional didactic seduction plots with a more 'feminist' treatment of women's situation. Acknowledging the power of sexuality and the dangers of women's economic dependency (especially dependency on those who prove unreliable), Rowson's fiction shows links with the later 19th-century ▷woman's novel formula.

She pursued various other careers during her life, including actress and songwriter; but, in addition to her literary career, her role as head of the Young Ladies' Academy was her most influential position. Intellectually demanding and yet warm and caring, she is cited in numerous private journals of the era as an excellent teacher. Although her life was one of constant financial hardship, it was also notable for her extraordinary literary productivity and attention to women's lives. She died on 2 March 1824.

▷Bowne, Eliza Southgate

Roy, Gabrielle (1909–1983)

French-Canadian novelist, born in St Boniface, Manitoba, to parents who migrated to western Canada from Quebec in the late 1800s. She attended a convent school, then taught school herself in rural Manitoba. In 1937 she travelled to London and Paris, returning to Quebec in 1939. After her marriage to Marcel Carbotte in 1947, and a few years in France, she lived the rest of her life in Quebec City. Her first novel, *Bonheur d'Occasion* (1945, translated as ▷*The Tin Flute*, 1947), set in an industrial neighbourhood of Montreal, is about a young woman who dreams of escape from her poverty-stricken family. It was the first French-Canadian novel to win France's Prix Fémina, and established Roy's prominent position in Canadian literature. Her subsequent novels and short stories are works of compassionate simplicity, marked by a profound understanding of human nature. They include *La Petite Poule d'Eau* (1950, translated as *Where Nests the Water Hen*, 1951), *Rue Deschambault* (1955, translated as *Street of Riches*, 1957), *Un Jardin au Bout du Monde* (1975, translated as *Garden in the Wind*, 1977), and *Ces Enfants de Ma Vie* (1977, translated as *Children of My Heart*, 1979). She also published essays, including *Cet Eté qui Chantait* (1972) (*Enchanted Summer*, 1976), and her autobiography, *La Détresse et l'enchantement* (1984, trans. *Enchantment and Sorrow: The Autobiography of Gabrielle Roy*, 1987), published posthumously. Most of her work has been translated, some by ▷Joyce Marshall. She was honoured with three Governor General's Awards, and many other prizes.

Bib: Babby, E.R., *The Play of Language and Spectacle*; Hesse, M.G., *Gabrielle Roy*; Lewis, P.G., *The Literary Vision of Gabrielle Roy*; Micham, A., *The Literary Achievement of Gabrielle Roy*.

Royal Penitent, in Three Parts, to Which Is Added David's Lamentation over Saul and Jonathan, The (1791)

In the neo-classical style, this poem by the North American writer ▷Sarah Porter runs to more than 300 lines and retells David's story of seduction and repentance. Integrated are political themes on the need for morality in government and the dangers of a ruling class–debates that flourished in post-revolutionary North America. It reveals Porter's considerable talent and her Puritan beliefs.

Roy de Clotte le Barillier, Berthe (1868–1927)

French poet and novelist who used the ▷pseudonym Jean Bertheroy. Born in Bordeaux, she began writing at nineteen, and her first published text was *Vibrations* (1888), a collection of verse. However, her fondness was for novels with historical or classical settings, and she wrote quantities of them for Ollendorf, a publishing house of the period that specialized in popular fiction. Many, including her best-known work, *La Danseuse de Pompéi* (1899) (*The Dancer of Pompeii*), are love stories which were viewed at the time as provocative and salacious, although they seem very tame today. She received three literary awards from the ▷Académie Française, but had a scandalous reputation. Her other novels include (*Cléopâtre*) (1891); *Ximénès* (1893); *Les Délices de Mantoue* (1906) (*The Delights of Mantua*), and *Sybaris* (1907).

Bib: Brécourt-Villars, C., *Ecrire d'Amour*.

Royer, Clémence (1830–1902)

French philosopher, natural scientist, and writer on economic and social matters. Born in Nantes, Royer travelled widely during her childhood and early adulthood. A keen advocate of improved education for women, she settled temporarily in Lausanne, where she established lecture courses on logic and philosophy for women, and later taught philosophy at the Sorbonne. She wrote an *Introduction à la philosophie des femmes* (*Introduction to Women's Philosophy*) in 1859, in which she denounced sexual inequality in the educational domain, and demanded that women should be taught science. Royer was a prolific author, whose writings include the French translation of Darwin's *Origin of the Species* and a philosophical novel, *Les Jumeaux d'Hellas* (1864) (*The Twins of Hellas*), which was banned in France. Her other works of interest are: *La Question religieuse* (1897) (*The Religious Question*); *La Constitution du monde* (1900) (*The Constitution of the World*) and *Le Bien et la loi morale* (1881) (*Goodness and Moral Law*).

Rozhovory s útěkem (1990) (Conversations with Escape)

Novel by the Czech pop singer Bara Basiková (born 1963). It was the most talked-about literary work in Czechoslovakia in 1989 (when it began to be serialized in the establishment Writers' Union monthly, as the literary establishment's demonstration of how broad-minded it was) and 1990, when reviews began to come out. It attempts to universalize the experiences of young Czech displaced women. The setting is never clear (it is meant to lie anywhere) but readers automatically assumed it was a picture of human, and then young female, despair in the last stages of socialism. The narrator is a semi-educated 'culture vulture' who goes through a series of crises, heterosexual, homosexual, heterosexual, and ends up simply wanting to be a single mother. The trouble is that she thinks she may be giving birth to some sort of Messiah.

Rubens, Bernice (born 1928)
Welsh novelist and short story writer, of Jewish parentage. Her writing deals with the nature of Jewishness, and also with marginality in general. Her novel *Madame Sousatzka* (1962) was successfully adapted for the screen by ▷Ruth Prawer Jhabvala. Her publications also include: *The Elected Member* (1969, winner of the Booker Prize); *Our Father* (1987) and *Kingdom Come* (1990).

Rubertino, Maria Luisa (born 1962)
Argentinian poet and dramatist. Her first book was *Memorias del bosque* (1946) (*Souvenirs from the Wood*). Many of her plays, essays, children's stories and film scripts earned her prizes. She also worked for the radio, and her poems and plays were often broadcast.

Other works: *El Silencio* (1946) (*Silence*); *Rostro distante* (1948) (*Distant Face*); *Está en nosotros* (*It Is In Us*); *El encuentro* (*The Meeting*), *La Cesta* (*The Basket*), *El Regreso* (1953) (*The Return*); *El cerco roto* (1957) (*The Broken Fence*); *El caballo en el espejo* (1957) (*The Horse in the Mirror*); *La Rueda* (1959) (*The Wheel*); *Las señales* (1961) (*The Signals*), and *Tantos muchachos, menos un ángel* (1964) (*So Many Boys Minus An Angel*).

Rubinstein, Renate (Ida) (1929–1990)
Dutch prose writer. Her family fled Germany in 1935, and her Jewish father was arrested at the beginning of the German occupation of the Netherlands. After the war she worked for a publishing company, and spent a number of years in Israel, adopting the pseudonym Tamar. From 1955 she studied in Amsterdam, wrote travel letters, and in 1962 began writing a weekly column in a magazine. These columns constitute a major part of her *oeuvre*, in addition to travel journals and books on subjects including nuclear arms, feminism, divorce (*Niets te verliezen en toch bang*, 1978, *Nothing to Loose but Still Scared*), and her fight against multiple sclerosis (*Nee heb je*, 1985, *Don't Take No*, 1988). Her outspoken ideas, and the firm stand she took on various subjects, made her a controversial figure. Even after her death she caused a stir, with the publication of *Mijn beter ik* (1991) (*My Better Self*), describing her secret love affair with a well-known Dutch writer.

Rubyfruit Jungle (1973)
US novel. ▷Rita Mae Brown's semi-autobiographical comic novel was originally published by a small press, Daughters Publishing Company. Four years later, it became the first lesbian novel to be published by a mainstream press, Bantam Books.

It traces the adventures of Molly Bolt, who exposes the obstacles that ▷patriarchy has erected to keep lesbians, women, and the poor, oppressed. Learning that success means conformity and dishonesty, Molly refuses to compromise. The book celebrates the beauty and power of the female body and lesbian relationships. Brown observes that lesbian relationships fail when they conform to a patriarchal model. She pays tribute also to the mothers against whom daughters rebel to establish their own autonomy; such a mother empowers her daughter to act out her own repressed desire for freedom from conformity.

Rudé západy (1904) (*Crimson Sunsets*)
Collection of symbolist verse by Czech poet Ruzena Sesenska (1863–1940). The impact of Mallarmé and the Czech symbolist Otakar Březina is evident, but the collection remains very much the poet's own statement. Furthermore, it is intimate verse, such as one does not generally link with symbolism. Love, often erotic masochism, forms the main theme. The god-figure who frequently appears is probably a beloved (either real or notional). Spirituality is to be found through sexuality. Expressions of unrestrained passion alternate with verse in which the meaning is conveyed acoustically rather than lexically.

Rue des Tambourins (1960)
Novel by Algerian writer ▷Marie-Louise Taos Amrouche, published under the name Marguerite Taos Amrouche. This autobiographical novel expresses the drama of Marie-Corail, the central character, who is split between Islam and Christianity. The sense of not wholly belonging to either creed enhances the heroine's confusion as to her identity. She is estranged and marginalized in her native Kabyle (Berber) environment, as well as in the western European culture she entered as a Christian convert.

Rüegg, Annelise (1879–1934)
German-speaking Swiss writer of travelogues. From a poor artisan's family, she travelled the world in search of a dignified way of making a living. She worked as a maid, waitress and nurse in many countries, and got into trouble with the police in Britain and the USA for making pacifist speeches during World War I. She recorded her adventures in *Erlebnisse einer Serviertochter* (1914) (*Experiences of a Waitress*) and *Im Kriege durch die Welt* (1918) (*Through the World in Wartime*).

Rukeyser, Muriel (1913–1980)
US poet, essayist, translator and dramatist. Born to an affluent Jewish family in New York, Rukeyser was educated at Vassar College, where she knew ▷Elizabeth Bishop and ▷Mary McCarthy, and at Columbia University. She was a social activist who was imprisoned during the Vietnam protests, and in her 60s flew to Hanoi to protest against the death sentence on the poet Kim Chi-Ha. To her, poetry has the power to encourage humans to realize their fullest potential. Her earlier work protests against such

injustices as the anarchists Sacco and Vanzetti's execution, and coal miners' lung disease.

Her first volume, *Theory of Flight* (1935), won the Yale Series of Younger Poets competition. Her work is located within an accessible democratic and radical tradition going back to Whitman and Milton. Rukeyser's later poetry reflects her experience as a single mother. In 'Body of Waking' (1958) and 'Breaking Open' (1973) the maternal counters the violence of the Vietnam wars. She creates authority for herself out of a series of female figures from myth and history, which in the words of the critics ▷Sandra Gilbert and ▷Susan Gubar 'counter the destructiveness she associated with American capitalism'. Rukeyser empowers the younger generation of women writers, such as ▷Anne Sexton.

Author of over twenty volumes, her poetry has been collected in *The Collected Poems of Muriel Rukeyser* (1978). She collaborated on a translation of Octavio Paz's *Selected Poems* (1963) and his *Sun Stone* (1963).
Bib. Kertesz, Louise, *The Poetic Vision of Muriel Rukeyser*.

Rule, Jane (born 1931)

Canadian novelist, essayist and short story writer. Born in Plainfield, New Jersey, she grew up in California and the US mid-west. In 1956 she moved to Vancouver, British Columbia, to live with partner Helen Sonthoff. She worked at the University of British Columbia, then moved to Galiano Island, British Columbia, in 1976. A lesbian activist and writer, Rule has had a powerful influence on feminist and lesbian awareness in Canada. ▷*Desert of the Heart* (1964, filmed as *Desert Hearts* in the 1980s) is about two women who meet and fall in love in Reno, Nevada. *This is Not For You* (1970) takes the form of a long, never-to-be mailed epistle about a woman's inability to resist convention in order to accept the love of another woman. *Against the Season* (1971) *The Young in One Another's Arms* (1977), *Contract With the World* (1980), *Memory Board* (1987), and *After The Fire* (1989) are novels celebrating connection and community, without losing sight of the politics of sexuality. Rule calls her characters 'deceptions in search of the truth'. Her short stories, collected in *Theme for Diverse Instruments* (1975), *Outlander* (1981), and *Inland Passage* (1985) explore relationships between lovers, families, and friends. Her essay collections, ▷*Lesbian Images* (1975) and *A Hot-Eyed Moderate* (1985), are sensitive explorations of what it means to be a lesbian.

Rumens, Carole (born 1944)

English poet and novelist. Rumens has been an advertising copywriter, a writer in residence and poetry editor of *Quarto* and *Literary Review*. Her poetry collections include: *A Strange Girl in Bright Colours* (1973), *A Necklace of Mirrors* (1979), *Unplayed Music* (1981), *Star Whisper* (1983), *Direct Dialling* (1985) and *From Berlin to Heaven* (1989).

Selected Poems was published in 1987, and Rumens has also edited *Making for the Open: The Chatto Book of Post-Feminist Poetry 1964–1984* (1985). Rumens has also written a novel, *Plato Park* (1987).

'Runaway Slave at Pilgrim's Point, The' (1850)

A poem by British poet ▷Elizabeth Barrett Browning. The speaker of the poem is a black woman slave who relates how she was torn from her lover and then raped by a white slave-owner. She bears a child, whom she murders and buries in a forest. The rage, grief and pain of the woman is chillingly conveyed in the first person narrative. The speaker cannot bear to see 'The *master's* look' on the child's face, yet is driven to frenzied distraction after the murder. Reconciliation is offered for the mother and child only 'In the death-dark where we may kiss and agree'. Barrett Browning's impassioned protest against ▷slavery made a considerable impact upon her contemporaries; it is still a powerful read.

Runeberg, Fredrika (1807–1879)

▷Fenno-Swedish prose writer. Runeberg was married to the well-known writer J.L. Runeberg. She was always primarily a wife and housewife, only later becoming a writer in her own right. But she was the first important woman writer in Finland.

Runeberg was very impressed by the German romantics, and she tried to write in their style. For many years she wrote small sketches and short stories in *Helsingfors Morgonblad* and a literary magazine. In 1861 they were published as *Teckningar och Drömmar* (*Drawings and Dreams*). She also wrote two historical novels.

She is famous for being in the shadow of her husband, almost erasing herself in living up to the image of the ideal loving wife, but it was a picture she herself nurtured and admired.

Runge, Erika (born 1939)

East German writer. The daughter of a judge, she studied art and literature in East and West Germany, obtaining a doctorate in 1962. She has made two important contributions to documentary literature: *Bottroper Protokolle* (1968) (*Bottrop Protocols*), a collection of edited tape recordings of conversations with workers in a coal mine, and *Frauen: Versuche zur Emanzipation* (1974) (*Women: Attempts at Emancipation*), in which seventeen women from different backgrounds talk about their lives and hopes for the women's movement.

Rúnova, Ol'ga Pavlovna (1864–1952)

Russian prose writer and poet. Rúnova began publishing in 1887 and, in 1890, the publishing company Intermediary (*Posrednik*) founded by Tolstoy for the mass reader, published Runova's story 'Accursed Gifts'. The ideology of her stories about provincial gentry and government officials is very close to Tolstoy's. Rúnova brought out two collections of stories in 1905 and 1912.

Though her early prose generally received negative reviews for its formlessness, plotlessness, and excessive detail which brought it close to ethnography, with time Rúnova became a better writer. Her improvement is evident from her most well-known piece of fiction from the pre-Soviet period, *Without a Commandment* (1913). Here the details are motivated by the theme of women's search for identity, though the novella often resembles a documentary of women's lives rather than a piece of narrative fiction. Most of it takes place at a clinic where women exchange their views on pregnancy and children, views which for their time were shockingly negative.

After the Revolution, Rúnova wrote a couple of short pamphlets on revolutionary women, Klara Tsetlin and Krupskaia, published her only novel, *At the Roots*, in 1926 (second edition in 1927), and her last collection of stories, also in 1927. She continued publishing, emphasizing in her stories the possibility of man's moral transformation.
Bib: Fen, E. (trans.), 'The Thief', *Soviet Stories of the Last Decade*.

Ruolan ▷Su Hui

Russ, Joanna (born 1937)
US novelist and prose writer. Born in New York, Russ graduated from Cornell University in 1957. In 1960 she earned a Master of Fine Arts degree at the Yale School of Drama. She writes ▷science fiction because it allows female characters to perform dramatic acts of bravery where they can achieve self-actualization independent of men.

In *Alyx* (1976) Russ establishes her basic precepts: to destroy dehumanizing bonds, like those of an oppressive marriage; to affirm the individual's free will to make choices, and to accept a moral obligation to educate the young. In *The Two of Them* (1978) she portrays the dehumanizing effects of a chauvinistic male society. All of Russ's novels, including ▷*The Female Man* (1975), explore polarities: the individual and society; the actual and the possible; women and men.

Other works include: *Picnic on Paradise* (1968), *And Chaos Died* (1970) and *How to Suppress Women's Writing* (1983).

Russell, Dora (1894–1985)
English feminist and social reformer. Educated at Girton College, Cambridge, Russell was involved in radical socialist and feminist circles in her early twenties, and became the lover of the philosopher Bertrand Russell (1872–1970), whom she later married. Together they wrote *The Prospects of Industrial Civilization* (1923). Russell was an early campaigner for birth control and maternity leave, and she co-founded the Workers' Birth Control Group (1924). *Hypatia: Or, Women and Knowledge* (1925) argued for sexual freedom and became a bestseller. She was later a founder member of the National Council for Civil Liberties. Other

publications include: *The Right to Be Happy* (1927) and *In Defence of Children* (1932).

Russell, Dora Isella (born 1925)
Uruguayan poet. Born in Argentina, she moved to Montevideo at the age of eight. She has been a teacher, a journalist, and has specialized in the poetry of ▷Juana de Ibarbourou, keeping an archive of her work. Russell's first book of poetry was *Sonetos* (1943) (*Sonnets*), but since *El otro olvido* (1952) (*The Other Oblivion*) she has employed a more colloquial, original language. Her subject is the tormented past, seen as an inescapable situation. Some of her poems were translated into French in 1951, and she has published many essays.

Other works: *El canto irremediable* (1946) (*The Incurable Song*); *Oleaje* (1949) (*Surge*); *Première anthologie* (1951) (*First Anthology*); *Antología poética* (1952) (*Poetry Anthology*); *Tríptico a Jean Aristeguieta* (1952) (*Triptych to Jean Aristeguieta*); *Los barcos de la noche* (1954) (*Ships of the Night*); *Del alba al mediodía (1943–1952)* (1954) (*From Dawn to Midday, 1943–1952*); *Elegía de juinio* (1963) (*June Elegy*); *Tiempo y memoria* (1964) (*Time and Memory*); *El tiempo del regreso* (1967) (*Time of Return*); *Los sonetos de Simbad* (1970) (*The Sonnets of Sinbad*); *Poemas hispanoamericanos* (1977) (*Spanish-American Poems*); *Memorial para Don Bruno Mauricio de Zavala*, and (1977) (*Memorial for Don Bruno Mauricio de Zavala*); *Los sonetos de Carass Court* (1983) (*Sonnets from Carass Court*).

Russell, Elizabeth Cooke (Hoby) (1540–1609)
English poet and translator. The daughter of Anthony and Anne Fitzwilliam Cooke, and sister to ▷Anne Cooke Bacon, she married Thomas Hoby in 1558. Famous for his translation of Baldassare Castiglione's *Il Cortegiano* (1528) (*The Courtier*, 1561), Hoby died in 1566. In 1574 Elizabeth Cooke Hoby married John Russell, upon whose death in 1584 she composed an effectively moving, dirge-like elegy. The elegy was inscribed on her husband's tomb at Westminster. She also wrote epitaphs for other relatives. Her most famous work is ▷*A Way of Reconciliation*, her ▷translation of John Ponet's French treatise on the sacrament.
▷Humanism (English); *Instruction of a Christian Woman*

Russian Childhood, A (1978)
Autobiography by Russian mathematician ▷Sof'ia Kovalévskaia, originally published in 1890. These lively reminiscences by the renowned mathematician intersperse personal memories – her feelings of being an unloved child and the development of her precocious talents – with sketches of the household: the glamorous, remote mother, the warm Russian nanny, the domineering English governess, and eccentric uncles. The last four chapters are focused on her restless elder sister, Anna Korvin-Krukovskaia's, attempts to escape from the boredom of life on a backwoods estate with self-dramatizing medieval

aestheticism, the revolutionary ideology of the 1860s as propagated by a local priest's son, and a career as a 'Russian authoress'. Two of Anna's stories were accepted for publication in Fyodor Dostoevsky's journal *The Epoch*, and Kovalévskaia ends with an account of the great writer's courtship of her sister in 1865, and her own infatuation with him. Kovalévskaia also wrote an interesting memoir of the Polish rebellion of 1863, which was published in Swedish in her lifetime and in the Soviet Union only in the 1960s.

Ruth (1853)

A novel by British writer ▷Elizabeth Gaskell. Ruth Hilton, an ▷orphan, is seduced by wealthy and self-interested Mr Bellingham and abandoned after a brief affair. She is taken in by the Dissenting minister, Mr Benson, and his sister, and assumes the identity of Mrs Denbigh, a widow, so that she and her illegitimate son will be accepted in society. Ruth finds employment as a ▷governess to the Bradshaw family, and later re-encounters her seducer, who is now the local MP, re-named Mr Donne. He offers to marry her, but she refuses, having determined to seek redemption for her sin. Later, her true identity is discovered, and Mr Bradshaw casts her out (Donne is not known to be the seducer). After many futile attempts to find employment she offers her services as a sick-nurse during a typhus epidemic, and through her devoted work becomes revered in the eyes of the community. Her last unselfish act is to nurse delirious Mr Donne through his fever, after which she catches typhoid and dies a martyr's death. The novel was burned by members of Gaskell's congregation and criticized both for its sympathetic treatment of the ▷'fallen woman' and for its unrealistically saintly portrayal of Ruth, who is throughout a picture of innocence, humility and Christian submissiveness. Flawed as it is by religiosity and narrative contrivance, *Ruth* nevertheless reveals the ideological contradictions of Christian and Victorian attitudes towards women.

Ruth Hall (1855)

US autobiographical novel by ▷Sara Payson Willis Parton, published under her pseudonym, Fanny Fern. One of the bestselling novels of the 19th century, *Ruth Hall* is fictionalized autobiography, recalling the trials and ultimate triumph of the title character. The novel continually reinforces the need for women's economic independence and self-assertion in order to achieve that independence – as it reveals the mean-spirited behaviour of Payson Willis Parton's own family and publishers.

The novel begins with Ruth's life as daughter in a patriarchal family, and follows her through a short marriage, happy except for the interference of in-laws and the death of her child, ended with the early death of her husband. Because of a lawsuit, her husband's death leaves Ruth and her children destitute and dependent on her father and her husband's family – both grudging and conditional in their support. While these early chapters are sometimes characterized by the religiosity, purple prose and emotional indulgence generally associated with sentimental literature, such effects are consistently undercut by Ruth's reflections and by alternating satiric scenes revealing the cruelty and self-interest of other characters in the families and community.

The hard-edged satire and telling revelation of character through dialogue become dominant, the prose becomes more straightforward and the tone more cynical, as the novel continues through Ruth's attempts to support herself amidst grinding poverty. Abandoned by her family – including an editor brother who refuses to help her earn a living as a writer – and by social acquaintances who refuse to visit, Ruth finds that traditional women's occupations like sewing can never provide enough income to support her and her children. Moving into periodical publishing, she is exploited by publishers. Only by dint of continual self-assertion, determination, and the emotional support of working-class friends and former servants, does Ruth come into her own – writing for increasingly larger audiences and higher pay as she negotiates her own contracts.

The overwhelming success of the novel brought the author personal attacks, as the family members and publishers exposed in the book revealed her true identity, previously hidden behind the pseudonym of Fanny Fern. Criticism acknowledged the very real mistreatment recorded in the book, its accuracy and its power, but concentrated on the author's unwomanliness in seeking revenge in public print.

Ru Zhijuan (born 1925)

Chinese short story writer, based in Shanghai. Ru Zhijuan joined the drama troupe of the communist-led army in the 1940s and started to write in her spare time. Drawing from her army experience for subject matter, Ru Zhijuan says that her stories, however, are mostly 'about the lives of women during different periods, and the changes in their ways of thinking and feeling'. Outstanding pieces, such as 'The Tall White Poplar', 'Lilies' and 'The Quiet Maternity Hospital', are collected into over ten volumes. At one time her writings were attacked for being overly concerned with tender emotions and family affairs. She responded by naming her next stories 'Tender Emotions' and 'Family Affairs'.
Bib: Short stories translated in *Lilies and Other Stories* and *The New Realism*, edited by Lee Yee.

Ryum, Ulla (born 1937)

Danish dramatist and prose writer. Ryum's writing is permeated by suppressed outsiders, her language is a modernist one of dreams, filled with associations and ambiguity.

Her début was *Spejl* (1962) (*Mirror*), where she depicted a man, paralysed inside a shell of his aggressions, while the novel *Natsangersken* (1963)

(*Night Singer*) told the story of a woman, a female Christ, victim of her own will. The gap between the sexes is unbridgeable, eg *Latterfuglen* (1965) (*The Laughing Jackass*) and the two collections of short stories *Tusindskove* (1969) (*Thousand-Forests*) and *Noter om idag og igår* (1971) (*Notes about Today and Yesterday*).

In the 1970s Ryums become known for being a dramatist whose plays attack the dehumanized world. She sees women and the specific powers of femininity as a critical standpoint in language, structure and theme.

She has received many prizes and awards and is the best-known Danish woman dramatist.

Sab (1839)

An anti-slavery novel, written in two volumes, by the Cuban-Spanish author ▷ Gertrúdis Gómez de Avellaneda. It is based on a romantic Cuban legend. A slave, who is in love with his landlady, sacrifices his life for her, even to the point of helping her to conceal her love affair with an unworthy gentleman. It has been considered Cuba's version of *Uncle Tom's Cabin* by ▷ Harriet Beecher Stowe.

Sablé, Madeleine de Souvré, Marquise de (1599–1678)

French author of maxims and letters. She was the daughter of the Marquis of Courtenvaux, governor of Louis XIII (1601–1643), and married at the age of fifteen. Mother of four children, she suffered from her husband's infidelities until his death in 1640. A highly cultivated *Précieuse* (▷ Precious Women) and a prominent member of the salon of the Marquise de Rambouillet (1588–1665), she was also a close friend of the philosopher, mathematician and scientist Blaise Pascal (1623–1662). Madame de Sablé was involved in various political intrigues during the civil wars of the *Frondes* (1648–1653), but remained loyal to the king. From 1650 on, she held her own more learned and philosophical salon in the Place Royale in Paris, where she received, among other brilliant writers, ▷ Madame de Lafayette and La Rochefoucauld (1613–1680), and rebellious nobles who despised the diplomat Cardinal Mazarin (1602–1661). She was a major influence on the taste for witty aphorisms among the literary élite during the reign of Louis XIV (1638–1715), and on the fashion for Spanish literature. Credited with having created the genre of *maximes* (maxims), she wrote one set of maxims on education and another on education. A partial collection was published in 1678 shortly after her death.

There is a noticeable cross-fertilization of ideas between these *Maximes* and those of La Rochefoucauld, who valued her judgement, as did the Great Arnauld (Antoine Arnauld, 1612–1694), who sent her a copy of the introduction to his *Logique* (1662) (*Logic*), inviting her to give her opinion. An anonymous letter to the *Journal des Savants*, critical of the misanthropic tendencies in La Rochefoucauld's maxims, has been attributed to her. Although she shared this author's fundamental pessimism and fine sense of irony, denouncing excessive self-esteem at every turn, Madame de Sablé's remarks are less misanthropic. In one of her maxims, she reflects: '*C'est une assez grande folie de s'écouter soi-même quand on s'entretient avec les autres, que de parler tout seul*' ('It is just as great a folly to listen to oneself speak when one is conversing with others as to talk to oneself'). She wrote a treatise on *Amitié* (*Friendship*). A gourmet, Madame de Sablé delighted in exchanging cookery recipes. She wrote many letters to ▷ Agnès Arnauld and others. Increasingly attracted to ▷ Jansenism, in 1655 she removed her salon to a house within the walls of Port-Royal, where she lived with her doctor, Valant, who kept all her papers. Their correspondence suggests that, with her constant concern for her health and demands for advice, she was a considerable nuisance to Mère Agnès and the other sisters in her old age, though her piety is not in doubt.

Bib: Tallemant des Réaux, *Historiettes*; Sainte-Beuve, *Causeries du lundi*; Cousin, V., *Mme de Sablé*; Crussaire, A., *Un Médecin au XVIIe siècle, le docteur Vallant. Une malade imaginaire, Mme de Sablé*; Picard, R., *Les Salons littéraires et la société française 1610–1769*).

Sablière, Marguerite de la (1636–1693)

French author of Christian maxims. Of Dutch Protestant origin, Madame de la Sablière was separated from the financier Rambouillet (no relation of the celebrated Marquise) but retained the magnificent house in Reuilly, where she held one of the most elegant and brilliant salons of the 17th century. The originality of her salon sprang from her own passion and aptitude for the sciences, particularly physics and astronomy. It was frequented by doctors, explorers and philosophers like Fontenelle (1657–1757), as well as her close friend, the writer Jean de La Fontaine (1621–1695), ▷ Madame de Lafayette, Madame Scarron (▷ Madame de Maintenon), ▷ Madame de Sévigné and the poet and critic Nicolas Boileau (1636–1711), with whom Madame de la Sablière quarrelled on a scientific detail. Her circle was famous for its bold discussion of the latest theories. Following her lover's abandonment of her for drink and an actress, she retired to a convent.

Bib: Sablière, Madame de la, *Ses Pensées chrétiennes et ses lettres à l'abbé de Rancé*, ed. V. Menjoy d'Elbenne.

Sabrina, ils t'ont volé ta vie (1986) (Sabrina, They Have Stolen Your Life)

A novel by Algerian writer, ▷ Myriem Ben. It portrays the hardship the heroine has to endure for the sake of love for Saber, her husband. Financially dependent on Saber's father, the couple has to live with the family, and the heroine has to endure their degrading treatment of her. The mother-in-law treats her like a maid. The father-in-law tries to rape her in order to save the reputation of his son, whom he knows is infertile. The richly-detailed narrative reflects the author's skills as a painter.

Sabúrova, Irina Evgen'evna (1907–1979)

Russian *émigré* fiction writer and poet. Sabúrova's family emigrated first to Finland in 1917. She lived in Latvia till 1943, and then settled in Munich. From the time of her first short story in Latvia in 1923, she worked for periodicals and at publishing houses, writing fiction, editing and translating. Her first collection of stories, *The Shadow of Blue March*, appeared in 1938. Sabúrova was a prolific writer, and other collections followed. She brought out a book of poetry, *Conversation in Silence* (1956), and three novels, *After. . .* (1960), *Ships of the Old City* (1964) and *About Us: A Novel* (1972).

In her concentrated short stories, Sabúrova uses symbols and motifs from folk belief and folk tale, numerology and nature to project human intuition and the workings of fate. These components are set against elements of the modern world, and set in a deceptively simple narrative structure. With this combination, she uncannily succeeds in getting the modern reader to suspend disbelief in the fantastic. Her stories most resemble those of Aleksandr Grin, one of her favourite Russian authors.
Bib: Pachmuss, T. (trans.), *Russian Literature in the Baltic Between the World Wars*, and *A Russian Cultural Revival: A Critical Anthology of 'Emigre' Literature before 1939.*

Sachs, Nelly (1891–1970)
German poet. Born into a comfortable and protective Jewish family, she initially wanted to become a dancer, but found her vocation in writing. She maintained an intense correspondence with the Swedish writer ▷Selma Lagerlöf, but for many years suffered from depression, a condition aggravated by the rise of fascism, and the prosecution and disappearance of Jewish friends. In 1940 she managed, with the help of Lagerlöf, to escape with her mother to Sweden, where she remained for the rest of her life. It was only in the 1960s that her poetry began to attract attention. Drawing on the Hebraic and Hassidic tradition, her poetry speaks of the Jewish condition and the Holocaust, and alludes to feelings of horror that cannot be expressed in mere words. In 1965 she received a peace prize for her collections *Fahrt ins Staublose* (1961) (*Journey into the Dust-Free Zone*), *Zeichen im Sand* (1962) (*Figures in the Sand*) *Glühende Rätsel* (1964) (*Red-hot Enigmas*). In 1966 she was awarded the Nobel Prize for Literature.

Sackville-West, Vita (1892–1962)
English novelist, poet and biographer. Daughter of the third Baron Sackville, she grew up at the family home of Knole, Kent, and was educated privately. In 1914 she married the civil servant Harold Nicolson and, while initially accompanying him when he was posted overseas, eventually chose to remain in England when her husband was abroad. In 1918 Sackville-West began an affair with ▷Violet Trefusis that lasted until 1921, and her close friendship with ▷Virginia Woolf, which inspired Woolf's ▷*Orlando*, has received much attention. Despite Sackville-West's affairs and Nicolson's own homosexuality, the unconventional marriage survived, and is described by their son Nigel Nicolson in *Portrait of a Marriage* (1973). The couple moved to Sissinghurst Castle in 1930, cultivating a joint passion for gardening, and the following year Sackville-West produced *Sissinghurst*, while *English Country Homes* appeared in 1941. Her disappointment at not being able to inherit the

family estate owing to her gender is described in *Knole and the Sackvilles* (1922), her preoccupation with patrimony being linked to a concern with genetics in her first novel, *Heritage* (1922).

Her reputation as a poet was established with the long pastoral poem *The Land* (1927), while *Solitude* (1938) displays a concern with the spiritual and mystical anticipated by the biography *Saint Joan of Arc* (1936). Her interest in women saints is maintained in *The Eagle and the Dove* (1943), a study of St Theresa of Avila and St Thérèse of Lisieux. Her most commercially successful novels are those focusing on the lives of the aristocracy. *All Passion Spent* (1931) deals with the independence and self-determination achieved in widowhood, and as a recognized feminist classic, provides an interesting gloss on Sackville-West's other writings on property and patrimony. Her letters have been published in two volumes: *Dearest Andrew* (letters to Andrew Reiber, 1951– 1962) (1980), *Letters of Vita Sackville-West to Virginia Woolf* (1984), and *Violet to Vita: The Letters of Violet Trefusis to Vita Sackville-West* (1984).

Other writings include: *Grey Wethers* (1923), *Passenger to Teheran* (1926), *Aphra Behn* (1927), *The Edwardians* (1930), *Invitation to Cast Out Care* (1931), *The Easter Party* (1953), *Daughter of France: The Life of Anne Marie Louise d'Orléans* (1959).
▷Bagnold, Enid
Bib: Glendinning, V., *Vita: The Life of Vita Sackville-West*; Steven, M., *Vita Sackville-West: A Critical Biography*; Trautmann, J., *The Jessamy Brides: The Friendship of Virginia Woolf and Victoria Sackville-West.*

Sacred Girl, A (1973)
Novel by Japanese writer ▷Kurahashi Yumiko. Miki's mother is killed in a car accident while Miki is driving. Miki loses her memory in the accident, and her notebook is sent to a youth called 'K' who happens to become acquainted with her. In the story in the notebook, Miki gets to know her father, from whom she was separated soon after her birth. Miki is attracted to her father and seduces him. K is also attracted to his elder sister. Kurahashi hypothesizes that incestuous love is a holy love, which will inevitably lead to a terrible decadence.

Sacrifice of Kreli, The (1978)
Produced at the Space Theatre in Cape Town in 1976 and published in 1978 in *Theatre One*, edited by Stephen Gray, this is the first play to be written by black South African dramatist ▷Fatima Dike. The play is set seven years after the ninth Frontier War between Kreli, King of the Gcalekas (part of the Xhosa people), and the British. Although the Gcaleka have been defeated, 500 men, including Kreli, refuse to surrender. Now, wishing to come out of exile, they need to propitiate their ancestors. Their sacrifice fails because it has been interrupted by a white reporter, and the diviner – left in the veld to die – sends a message of endurance and new hope to the people: 'our sun is rising'.

Dike has said that she wrote this play in order to give back to the 18 million black people in South Africa a past that had been wiped out by white South African historical writing. Like ▷Bessie Head, she turns back to the past in order to provide a future for black South Africa.

Sa'dawi, Nawal El (born 1930)

Egyptian feminist, novelist and short story writer. Trained as a medical doctor, she brought to her writings the frankness of her profession. One should separate the message of Sa'dawi concerning the customary physical and mental oppression of women in a traditional society from her attempts at presenting such material in novels or short stories. Her *Women and Sex* (1972) discusses problems of sexual fulfilment for women, the meaning of honour for women and men, the trauma of ▷*khitan* (cirrcumcision) for girls, family laws, the position of women in society: issues that she and others are battling to this day. The facilities of censor-free publishing offered by ▷Beirut made it possible for her message to circulate widely in the Arab world. Her works of fiction suffer from the qualities that make her a good defender of feminist issues. Critics complain of repetition, a limited vocabulary and a loose structure. Her first novel, *The Absent One*, presents the first female character in Arabic fiction to be explicitly sexually harassed: from the doorkeeper's abuse of the little girl sitting on the bench to her grown-up experience of males who try to take advantage of her. Bahia Shaheen, the heroine of *Two Women in One* (1975) is a traumatized woman who cannot, or will not, get any fulfilment from sex; she apparently seeks her 'double' in a sexual partner. Sa'dawi associates sexual oppression with social and political oppression and with religious authority. Hatred of the father and of all manifestations of patriarchal authority is the 'Thread' (title of one of her stories), that leads to the neurosis, the sickness of many of her characters. Two of her novels with explicit anti-religious material could only be published in Beirut: *Death of the Only Male on Earth* (1976) and *The Fall of the Imam* (1987). A number of Sa'dawi's works have been translated into English. They translate well because of the direct, simplified polemical discourse. Her non-fiction works include: *Women and Sex* (1972), *The Hidden Face of Eve* (1980), *Memoirs from the Women's Prison* (1987) and *Memoirs of a Woman Doctor* (1988). Among her novels are: *Woman at Point Zero* (1983), *The Circling Sun* (1989), *The Fall of the Imam* (1988) and *She has no Place in Paradise* (1991).

▷Djebar, Assia

Saenz-Alonso, Mercedes (born 1917)

Spanish literary critic, essayist and novelist. Saenz-Alonso was born into a noble family of San Sebastián. The family is a central theme of her narrative. Her main works are: *Bajos fondos* (1949) *(The Depths)*; *El tiempo que se fue* (1951) *(Time Gone By)*, and *La pequeña ciudad* (1952) *(The Small City)*.

Sagan, Françoise (born 1935)

French novelist who has also written plays and short stories. Sagan's first novel ▷*Bonjour Tristesse* (1954) was an immediate bestseller, and made its author famous in France and abroad. *Un Certain Sourire* (1956) *(A Certain Smile)* also became well-known. Since then, Sagan has produced a novel every two to three years, and several plays, dealing mainly with the themes of heterosexual love, the *ménage à trois*, solitude and almost Existential boredom in a middle-class milieu. Sagan uses the language of polite everyday speech to describe nuances of emotion. Her style, and hence the emotional world she evokes, are apparently simple and transparent, particularly in the first two novels. She is often relegated to the domain of lightweight romance by male critics, and it could be argued that her first two novels, in particular, deserve more critical attention.

Sahgal, Nayantara (born 1927)

Indian novelist and political journalist. She was born in Allahabad, into one of India's leading families, a niece of Jawaharlal Nehru (1889–1964), India's first Prime Minister, and the daughter of his sister, Vijaya Lakshmi Pandit, India's first Ambassador to the Soviet Union. She was educated in India, and at Wellesley College, Massachusetts. Her two early volumes of autobiography, ▷*Prison and Chocolate Cake* (1954) and *From Fear Set Free* (1962), which were enriched by her exposure to the dreams and personalities of the struggle for Indian independence, added a new dimension to Indian women's writing. In addition to her creative writing, she works in India as a journalist, and has given a high profile to the civil liberties movement there which evolved during the Emergency. She was Writer-in-Residence at the Southern Methodist University in Dallas, Texas, in 1973 and 1977, a visiting scholar at the Radcliffe Institute, Harvard University, in 1976, and a Fellow of the Woodrow Wilson Center in Washington DC in 1981–82. She was a member of the Indian delegation to the UN General Assembly in 1978. She has been married, and has three children.

Sahgal's best-known novel is ▷*Rich Like Us* (1985) which was awarded the Sinclair Prize for Fiction. *Plans for Departure* (1985) won the Commonwealth Prize for Fiction, (Eurasia category). Her other novels include *A Time to be Happy* (1958), *This Time of Morning* (1965), *Storm in Chandigarh* (1969), *A Voice for Freedom* (1977), *A Situation in New Delhi* (1977) and ▷*Mistaken Identity* (1988). Her interest in the destiny of contemporary India has also produced a history, *The Freedom Movement in India* (1970), and a study of her cousin, *Indira Gandhi: Her Road to Power* (1982).

Sailor from Gibraltar, The (1966)

Translation of *Le Marin de Gibraltar* (1952), third novel by French writer ▷Marguerite Duras. In this novel, the male narrator breaks up with his girlfriend and meets Anna, a wealthy woman. She sails the world in her yacht, looking for the sailor from Gibraltar, a man she loves who has disappeared. Anna and the narrator embark on a love affair, but continue the search for the sailor, as it is this other love of Anna's that keeps their own alive.

St Aubin de Téran, Lisa (born 1953)

English novelist. She married a Venezuelan land-owner at age sixteen, and de Téran managed their estate in the Andes for seven years. On returning to England, she initially concentrated on writing poetry, and in 1982 married the poet George Macbeth. The death of her mother and the break-up of her marriage to Macbeth provoked a nervous breakdown, an event which has influenced much of her later work. Novels include: *Keepers of the House* (1983), *Slow Train to Milan* (1984), *Black Idol* (1987), *Off the Rails, Memoirs of a Train Addict* (1989), *The Marble Mountain* (1989), *Joanna* (1990).

Saint-Chamond, Claire-Marie Mazzarelli, Marquise de La Vieuville de (1731–?)

French prose fiction writer, essayist and dramatist. Of modest Italian origins, she married into the French aristocracy. Her early writing appeared in periodicals: a self portrait in the *Mercure* in 1751, and a letter to Jean-Jacques Rousseau (1712–1778), accusing him of misanthropy in *L'Année littéraire* (1763) (*The Literary Year*) . She subsequently published two eulogies, *Éloge de Sully* (1763) (*In Praise of Sully*) and *Éloge de René Descartes* (1765) (*In Praise of René Descartes*). The tale *Camédris* was published in the same year. Her one published play, the comedy *Les Amants sans le savoir* (1771) (*The Unknowing Lovers*), was well received.

St Elmo (1867)

US novel by ▷Augusta Jane Evans (Wilson). A bestseller that became a cultural as well as a literary phenomenon, *St Elmo* is a curious, though highly successful, mixture of the various types and tensions in the popular 19th-century US novel. Like most ▷woman's fiction, *St Elmo* focuses on a young woman, Edna Earl, who must make her own way in the world and ends in a marriage of heightened domesticity. In between are the traditions and sexual risk of the seduction novel – but combined with the heroine's clear and physical attraction for the dissolute suitor, with the heightened incident and coincidence of melodrama, and with miscellaneous disquisitions on all manner of subjects. Critics have made very different sense of the novel's combination of conservatism and seeming feminism, and the text is varied enough – perhaps even in conflict with itself – for readers to find there what they will.

St Lucia

This geographical region of the Caribbean is French- and English-speaking.

St Petersburg

St Petersburg (renamed Petrograd in 1914 and ▷Leningrad from 1924 to 1991) was Peter I's 'window on the West'. The new capital was hacked by forced labour out of swamps on the Gulf of Finland in the early 18th century; its great palaces and administrative buildings, designed by Western architects, sit like a Venetian mirage in their northern setting. As capital, the city became the place where the most prestigious ▷'thick journals' were published and writers could make their careers. While women occasionally used the city as a setting for their works (▷Márchenko), until the late decades of the century ▷Moscow was the more hospitable locus for women writers, and relatively few (for example, ▷Búnina, ▷Panáeva) lived in St Petersburg. From the 1890s, symbolism and successive modernist movements drew heavily on the eerie St Petersburg atmosphere. ▷Akhmátova reconstructed the ▷Silver Age ferment of the city in ▷'Poem Without A Hero'.

▷*Bab;* Golden Age, The; *Happiness*; *Mimochka Gets Married*; Rochester, J.W.

Saint-Simonism and Saint-Simonian feminism

The Saint-Simonians were followers of the Comte de Saint-Simon, who formed one of the first French socialist groups, and were led in the late 1820s and 1830s by Prosper Enfantin. Christian and Utopian in its inspiration, the movement came to resemble a kind of Church, and Enfantin transformed himself into its Messiah. Although the Saint-Simonians advocated sexual equality and female emancipation, and called upon women to speak out for their rights and liberate themselves, the group's hierarchy became entirely male-dominated. The working-class women who had been drawn to the movement by its egalitarian complexion were irritated, both by Enfantin's views on morality and by his authoritarianism. In consequence, they were on the whole relieved at being excluded from the upper, masculine echelons of the movement, and formed their own feminist groups. One very significant result of this was the birth of the *Tribune des Femmes* (*Women's Tribune*), a journal run exclusively by Saint-Simonian women, which, as time went on, reflected Enfantin's ideas less and less. Saint-Simonian feminist propaganda died down after 1834, however, partly because a number of the women had joined the Saint-Simonian community that was established in Egypt.

▷Allart, Hortense; Arnaud, Angélique; Démar, Claire; Héricourt, Jenny d'; Niboyet, Eugénie; Voilquin, Suzanne; Feminine/feminist journalism (France)

Saison à Rihata, Une (1981) ▷*Season in Rihata, A* (1988)

Salete, Mademoiselle de (early 17th century)
French minor poet, who has left two poetic pieces written in response to Bertaut, a court poet. Nothing else is known about her life, though she was probably a maid of honour at the court of Henri IV (1553–1610). Her sober verses indicate that women were in the forefront of the movement for the purification of the French language.
Bib: Fukui, Y., *Raffinement précieux dans la poésie française du XVIIe siècle.*

Salis-Marschlins, Meta (1855–1929)
German-speaking Swiss writer and feminist. Rebelling against traditional ideas of how women should behave, she left her wealthy home at nineteen and, for a time, worked as a governess abroad. In 1887 she obtained a doctorate from the University of Zurich with a thesis on Agnes of Poitou. She was a fervent advocate of equal rights for all, and of women's rights in particular; these beliefs are explored in her writings, *Die Zukunft der Frau* (1886) (*The Future of Women*) and *Die Schutzengel* (3 vols) (1889–1891) (*Guardian Angels*). She compiled a collection of portrayals of outstanding women in *Auserwählte Frauen unserer Zeit, I und II* (1900 and 1916) (*Exceptional Women of Our Time, I and II*), and also wrote a monograph on the philosopher Nietzsche (1844–1900).

Salisachs, Mercedes (born 1916)
Spanish novelist. Passion and murder are a recurrent theme in Salisachs's work. Some of her stories with a romantic plot, such as *Concert of Confidences*, have been bestsellers. Her main works are: *Primera mañana, última mañana* (1955) (*First Morning, Last Morning*); *Carretera intermedia* (1956) (*Second-Class Highway*); *Vendimia interrumpida* (1960) (*Interrupted Wine Harvest*); *Adagio confidencia* (1973) (*Concert of Confidences*); *La gangrena* (1975) (*Gangrene*); *Viaje a Sodoma* (1977) (*Trip to Sodom*); *El proyecto* (1978) (*The Project*); *La presencia* (1979) (*Presence*); *Derribos* (1981) (*Demolition*); *La sinfonía de las moscas* (1982) (*Symphony of the Flies*), and *El volumen de la ausencia* (1983) (*The Volume of Absence*).

Sally Wister's Journal (1830)
Written during the early years of the American Revolution when ▷Sarah (Sally) Wister was in her early teens, it relates youthful impressions of the soldiers encamped near her family home, and reveals through its lively prose the intelligence and wit of its author. Wister's talent for characterization and comic sketches make this one of the best texts in its genre. In 1987 it was reprinted in a scholarly edition, *The Journal and Occasional Writings of Sarah Wister*, along with later writings, including religious essays, poetry and meditative journal entries. The flirtatious youth evolved into a philosophical woman. One of the few texts by early North American women writers that are readily available, it is an exceptional contribution to early North American literature.
▷Early North American Quaker women's writings

Salm-Dyck, Constance de (1767–1845)
French poet, dramatist and novelist. An extremely well-educated women with a reputation for intellectualism – the poet Marie-Joseph Chénier labelled her the 'Muse of Reason' – she was married first to a fashionable surgeon, then to a German botanist, the Prince of Salm-Dyck. She published a lyrical tragedy, *Sapho* (1794) and a series of epistles in verse (a collection appeared in 1811) which were feminist in tone despite having been written during the post-revolutionary era – a time when French feminism had been largely silenced. Of greatest interest are her *Souvenirs politiques et littéraires* (1833) (*Political and Literary Memories*) and her *Vingt-quatre heures d'une femme sensible* (1824) (*A Day in the Life of a Sensitive Woman*), a subtle and sensitively written study of the effects of jealousy.
▷Feminine/feminist journalism (France)

Salon culture (Germany and Austria)
The literary salon was a place where all kinds of people could meet on a regular but informal basis in order to exchange ideas, and discuss current affairs and cultural matters. The salon often enabled progressive thinkers to break out of social isolation, and salons became an increasingly important feature of intellectual life in 18th-century Germany, particularly in cities such as Berlin, Frankfurt and Weimar. One of the most successful salons was kept in Berlin by the Jewish hostess ▷Henriette Herz, until her establishment was gradually eclipsed by that of the young ▷Rahel Varnhagen at the beginning of the 19th century. A generation later, ▷Luise Mühlbach carried on the same tradition. Vienna too had a number of flourishing salons. Among the most successful was the one led by the writer ▷Karoline Pichler, and the salon of the Jewish sisters Cäcilie von Eskeles and Fanny von Arnstein (whose fictional biography was published by ▷Hilde Spiel in 1978). The family and cultural connections of these two women with Berlin ensured that lively contact was maintained between the Jewish salons of the Prussian and Austrian capitals. In Weimar ▷Johanna Schopenhauer led a salon associated with the court, dominated, even in his absence, by the figure of Goethe (1749–1852). The salons were especially important for literary-minded women such as ▷Bettina von Arnim, ▷Dorothea Schlegel and ▷Caroline Schlegel-Schelling; the salon afforded these writers a respectable context in which they could meet their contemporaries.
▷Literary salons (Scandinavia)

Salúcio, Ida
▷de Sousa, Auta

Salvan de Saliez le Viguier d'Albi (17th century)
French author of a *'Relation de l'entrée de M. l'Archevêque d'Albi dans la ville de ce nom'* ('Account of the Entry of the Archbishop of Albi into the Town of that Name'), published in the journal *Mercure galant*. She also wrote *La Princesse d'Isambourg* (*The Princess of Isambourg*), a short novel, and the *'Projet pour une nouvelle secte de philosophes en Faveur des Dames'* ('Plan for a New Sect of Philosophers in Favour of Ladies'), which appeared in the same publication in 1678 and 1681 respectively.
Bib: Vincent, M., *Donneau de Visé et le 'Mercure galant'*.

Salve Deus, Rex Judaeorum (1611)
Collection of poems by English writer ▷Aemilia Lanyer. In her prose epistle 'To the Vertuous Reader', she outlined both her reasons for writing her work, and how she believed it ought to be received. The volume contains a collection of nine dedicatory poems to contemporary women, the main dedication being to Margaret Russell, Countess of Cumberland. Lanyer praises the virtue of women by creating a poetic community of good women which extends through history, encompassing (a justified) Eve; good women of the Bible and of classical antiquity; the recently dead Elizabeth I (▷Elizabeth Tudor); the contemporary aristocratic women addressed in the poem's dedications, and ultimately, 'all vertuous Ladies in generall'. Distributed throughout the central poem's depiction of the crucifixion of Christ are Eve's apology in defence of women, Pilate's wife's plea for Christ, the tears of the daughters of Jerusalem, the Virgin Mary's sorrow, and numerous praises of the Countess of Cumberland. The final section of the poem, 'The Description of Cooke-ham', forms a farewell to the Countess of Cumberland's estate. Lanyer's 'Cooke-ham' is the first country house poem to be published in England, and might have been written before Ben Jonson's (1572–1637) 'To Penshurst' (long considered the first example of its kind).
▷Patronage; Prefaces (16th– and 17th–century Britain)
Bib: Barnestone, A., 'Women and the Garden: Andrew Marvell, Emilia Lanier, and Emily Dickinson', *Women and Literature*, No. 2 (1981), pp. 147–67; Beilin, E.V., *Redeeming Eve: Women Writers of the English Renaissance*; Lanyer, A., *Salve Deus Rex Judaeorum* (1978); Lewalski, B.K., 'Of God and Good Women: The Poems of Aemilia Lanyer', in Hannay, M.P. (ed.), *Silent But for the Word*.

Salverson, Laura Goodman (1890–1970)
Canadian novelist, born Laura Goodman in Winnipeg, Manitoba, to Icelandic immigrant parents. When she was ten, her family moved to Minnesota, where she first went to school and learned English, then began to write poems and stories. She married in 1913, and moved frequently around western Canada because of her husband's job with the railway. Determined to articulate herself through writing, Salverson was one of the first Canadian writers to address the problems of immigrant dislocation. Her first novel, *The Viking Heart* (1923), is a historical epic which reveals her immense pride in her Icelandic heritage. But her writing also displays an awareness of ethnic difference. Her strong pacificist and feminist sensibilities are expressed in *The Dark Weaver* (1937) and her autobiographical *Confessions of an Immigrant Daughter* (1939), both of which won Governor General's Awards. She dedicated *When Sparrows Fall* (1925) to ▷Nellie McClung. **Bib:** Fairbanks, C., *Prairie Women*; Gunnars, K., in ▷*A Mazing Space*.

Same Sea as Every Summer, The (1990)
Translation by Margaret Jones of the first novel of a trilogy by Spanish writer ▷Esther Tusquets, *El Mismo mar de todos los veranos* (1978). It describes the mid-life crisis of a nameless protagonist who, after the failure of her marriage, has a brief but intense affair with a student, Clara. This novel is striking not only for its frank treatment of feminine (and lesbian) sexuality, but also for its exploration of a new feminine language, which approaches ▷Hélène Cixous's notion of ▷*'écriture féminine'*.

Samian literature
For many hundreds of years the literature of Lapland (Samia) was an oral literature. This changed completely in the 1970s, a time of great activity in the Samian culture. In 1971 Kirsti Paltto (born 1947) from Finnish Lapland published the first Samian book written by a woman, the collection of short stories *Soagmu* (*Courting*), and in 1972, a Samian competition for short stories was set up, with several women participating. Samian women's literature is nostalgic and Utopian at the same time.
Lapland covers a vast area: Norway, Sweden, Finland and the Kola Isthmus, and the Samians speak many different languages. It is therefore not easy to speak of one literature; the oral traditions are old, but the genre of the *joiken*, a long, spoken narrative, with short, concise portraits has dominated for the last 100 years, and is still important in the written literature of today.
The best-known Samian woman writer today is the Finnish Rauni Magga Lukkari (born 1943) who now lives at Tromsø in Norway. She writes poems, and her first collection was *Jienat vulget* (1980) (*The Ice Breaks*).

Samizdat
A term which literally means 'self-publishing.' Since the imposition of official censorship by the tsarist government in the 18th century, Russian writers circulated their unacceptable writings privately. Despite harsh penalties, the practice of passing around handwritten, typed, mimeographed, or xeroxed manuscripts continued

and flourished in the Soviet period. With
▷*glásnost*', the need for *samizdat* virtually
disappeared.

▷Gínzburg, Evgeniia; Gorbanévskaia, Natal'ia;
Lisniánskaia, Inna; Mandel'shtám, Nadezhda;
Shchépkina-Kupérnik; *tamizdat*; Thaw;
Voznesénskaia, Iuliia

Sanchez, Carol Lee

Carol Lee Sanchez

US poet. Born in New Mexico, Sanchez is of
Laguna Pueblo and Sioux ▷Native American
descent, and was raised in a multicultural,
Catholic environment. In 1964 she began teaching
American Indian studies at San Francisco State
University. She has been active in the women's
movement.

Her poetry is abstract, reflecting the abstract
thinking practised by Native American women; its
rhythms resemble those of Pueblo music. Sanchez
explains that her artwork redefines and
reinterprets the symbols of her Native American
civilization; she sees it as her responsibility to
maintain a sense of traditional propriety. She
organizes her books – *Conversations from the
Nightmare* and *Message Bringer Woman* – to convey
a sense of ritual. Her work provides a connection
to the spirit world and provides a bridge back into
tradition.

Other works include: *Excerpts from a Mountain
Climber's Handbook*.

Sanchez, Sonia (born 1934)

US poet and dramatist. Born in Birmingham,
Alabama, Sanchez moved to Harlem, New York at
age nine, and in 1955 she graduated from Hunter
College. In 1972 she joined the Nation of Islam.
An African-American, Sanchez works for black
revolutionary causes in the US and abroad. In her
poetry she advocates black militancy in retaliation
for white violence.

Her poetry uses the language of popular
African-American street culture and of West
Africa. In the plays, *Sister Son/ji* (1972) and *Uh
Huh; But How Do It Free Us?* (1975), Sanchez
depicts the misogyny within the black
revolutionary movement. In autobiographical
writings, like *homegirls & handgrenades* (1984),
Sanchez reflects on her struggle for the
psychological freedom of contemporary African-
Americans, and she also chronicles her emotional
development. In *A Blues Book for Black Magical
Women* (1973) Sanchez recovers African-
American women's peculiar heritage.

Other works include: *Homecoming* (1969), *We a
BaddDDD People* (1970), *It's a New Day (poems for
young brothas and sistuhs)* (1971), *Ima Talken bout
the Nation of Islam* (1972), *The Adventures of
Fathead, Smallhead, and Squarehead* (1973), *Love
Poems* (1973), *A Sound Investment* (1980), *I've Been
a Woman: New and Selected Poems* (1981), *Crisis in
Culture – Two Speeches by Sonia Sanchez* (1983)
and *Under a Soprano Sky* (1987).

Sánchez de Cepeda y Ahumada, Teresa
▷Teresa de Ávila, Santa

Sand, George (1804–1876)

George Sand

French romantic novelist. Easily the best known
French woman writer of the 19th century, Sand
was born Aurore Dupin, the daughter of an

aristocrat, Maurice Dupin de Francueil, and of Sophie Delaborde, a woman of more humble social origin, whose character and lifestyle Sand's father's family viewed as morally dubious. Having lost her father at the age of four, Sand was brought up by her paternal grandmother, who encouraged her independent spirit, and oversaw her education until she was sent to the convent of English Augustine nuns in Paris to finish her schooling. Married at eighteen to the Baron Dudevant, she found conjugal life oppressive, and left him in 1831 to live with a young writer, Jules Sandeau, whose surname she adapted in order to provide herself with a pen-name. She subsequently enjoyed a string of extra-marital liaisons, the most famous of which were with the poet Alfred de Musset (1810–1857) ('recorded' in her novel *Elle et Lui*, 1859, *She and He*), and with composers Franz Liszt (1811–1886) and Frédéric Chopin (1810–1849). She played an active role during the political upheavals of 1848, but disassociated herself from radical feminist attempts to get her elected to the National Assembly, as she was a reformist rather than a revolutionary at heart. Although viewed for many years by contemporaries as highly scandalous, Sand's life became, towards its end, one of bourgeois respectability. She retired to her family château in Nohant-sur-Seine, devoted herself to writing and charitable works, and died peacefully at home in 1876.

Sand's literary production may be divided into a series of 'periods'. Her early novels, which include ▷*Indiana* (1832); *Valentine* (1833); ▷*Lélia* (1833) and *Jacques* (1834), are those to which she owes her reputation as a 'feminist' writer – primarily because they articulate her perception of marriage as 'one of the most barbaric institutions [society] has ever invented'. *Indiana* in particular denounces men's victimization of women, and best exemplifies the feminist dimension of Sand's writing. Some modern critics have dismissed Sand's feminism as sentimental and politically ineffective. However, these first works were courageous for their time, and represent a literary landmark in the history of the struggle for emancipation waged by 19th-century French women. The 'second phase' of Sand's writing coincided with her increased enthusiasm for humanitarianism, socialism and Christianity. During this period she produced novels in which her desire to see humanity regenerate itself through a combination of social change and adherence to the teachings of Christ is very apparent. These include *Spiridion* (1838); *Les Sept Cordes de la lyre* (1839) (*The Seven Strings of the Lyre*) and the related texts *Consuelo* (1842–43) and *La Comtesse de Rudolstadt* (1843–44). They were followed by the series of pastoral and/or socialist novels – *La Mare au Diable* (1846) (*The Devil's Pool*); *Le Péché de M. Antoine* (1847) (*The Sin of M. Antoine*); *La Petite Fadette* (1849) (*Little Fadette*); *François le Champi* (1850) (*François the Champ*) and *Les Maîtres Sonneurs* (1853) (*The Master Bell-ringers*) – for which their author is most famous,

and which reveal her tendency to idealize and idyllicize working-class rural life. In the mid-1850s she wrote other, less successful novels, and published her twenty-volume autobiography, *Histoire de ma vie* (1855, translated as *My Life*). Her *Oeuvres complètes* (*Complete Works*), published by M. Lévy, run to 105 volumes. Although George Sand's literary popularity has declined in the 20th century, her writing is still of major interest to feminist scholars.

▷Bentzon, Thérèse; Eliot, George

Bib: (selective) Barry, J., *George Sand ou le scandale de la liberté*; Cate, C., *George Sand: a Biography*; Crecelius, K.J., *Family Romances: George Sand's early Novels*; Dickson, D., *George Sand: A Brave Man, the most Womanly Woman*; Glasgow, J., *George Sand, Collected Essays*; Maurois, A., *Lélia ou la vie de George Sand*; Salomon, P., *George Sand*; Thomson, P., *George Sand and the Victorians*.

Sandel, Cora (1880–1974)

▷Pseudonym of Sara Fabricius, a Norwegian prose writer. Sandel was born into an unhappy marriage. As a young girl she wanted to become a painter; she studied painting with Harriet Backer, travelled to Paris in 1905, and was a talented artist. In 1913 she married the Swedish sculptor Anders Jönsson, and they had a son in 1917. By then she had stopped painting and begun to write. One of her conclusions was that women artists need to live alone. In 1926, at the age of forty-six, she separated from Jönsson, the same year in which she published her first novel, *Alberte og Jakob* (*Alberte and Jakob*). After that she lived alone. She was reticent, and unwilling to participate in the cultural market.

The ▷*Alberte* trilogy made her famous. But she also wrote short stories, such as *En blå sofa* (1927) (*A Blue Sofa*). Her work is modest but beautiful. She was very conscious of style in her writing, an impressionist who wrote in pointillist prose, in, for example, *Kranes Konditori* (1945) (*Krane's Café*, 1967). Another of her major works is *Kjøp ikke Dondi* (1958) (*The Leech*). Her characters are often talented and sensitive women, struggling desparately to realize their potential, but often they are hindered by an insensitive family or by social conventions.

Sandel was one of the most interesting writers in Scandinavia in the period between World Wars I and II.

Sanditon

An unfinished novel by English novelist ▷Jane Austen, written in the first three months of 1817, the year in which the author died. Charlotte Heywood is invited to stay with the Parker family in the seaside-village resort of Sanditon. She catches the attention of Lady Denham, the local aristocrat, with whom Clara Brereton is staying. Lady Denham's nephew, Sir Edward, plans to seduce Clara, but his aunt expects him to marry a West Indian heiress, due to visit Sanditon in the near future. The inhabitants of the village come to expect a huge entourage of visitors; in the event only four individuals arrive. Written when Austen was suffering from Addison's disease, the fragment is notable for its satirical treatment of hypochondriacs.

San Félix, Sor Marcela de (1605–1688)
Spanish poet. San Félix was the illegitimate daughter of Lope de Vega, the Golden Age dramatist, and the actress, Micaela de Luján. She began to write poetry at the age of ten; her literary talents were encouraged by her father. Her main works are *Poesías* (*Poetry*); and *Coloquios* (*Dialogues*).

Sang des autres; Le (1948) ▷*Blood of Others, The* (1948)

San Mao (born 1943)
Taiwan-based Chinese writer. Born Chen Ping, San Mao studied philosophy at university and travelled widely in the USA, Europe and parts of Africa. From the 1970s she started to publish exotic romances with autobiographical backgrounds, which were highly popular and translated into over a dozen languages; these include *Stories of Sahara*, *The Tender Night* and *Over Land and Sea*. She now teaches in Taiwan and continues to write.

Santiago, Elena
Contemporary Spanish journalist residing in Valladolid. She has published several novels, among which figure: *Acidos días* (1979) (*Acid Days*); *Una mujer malva* (1981) (*A Mauve Woman*); *Gente oscura* (1981) (*Obscure People*); *Manuela y el mundo* (1983) (*Manuela and the World*), and *Veva* (1988). Her work is concerned with the value of human relationships.

Sant Jordi, Rosa de ▷Arquimbau, Rosa Maria

Sanvitale, Francesca (born 1929)
Italian novelist, short story writer and journalist. Born in Milan, she studied in Florence, and is based in Rome. She worked for *Radio-audizione italiane* (RAI), for whom she wrote television plays and contributed to cultural programmes. Her first novel, *Il cuore borghese* (1972) (*The Middle Class Heart*), is a novel of self-analysis on the part of its intellectual protagonist. ▷*Madre e figlia* (1980, 1986) (*Mother and Daughter*), her second novel, is the study of an intense relationship between a mother and her illegitimate child, over their lifetime. The narrative traces the roots of the relationship in the mother's childhood. *L'uomo del parco* (1984, 1987) (*The Man in the Park*), is a psychoanalytical novel in which the protagonist, Giulia, analyses her life and searches for the truth about herself. Sanvitale's most recent publication, *La realtà è un dono* (*Reality Is a Gift*) of 1987, is a collection of short stories.

Sanz, María (born 1956)
Spanish poet. Her poetry has an intimate tone and focuses on female experience in relation to the natural world. Her main works are: *Aquí quema la niebla* (1986) (*The Mist Burns Here*); *Cenáculo vinciano y otros escorzos* (1985) (*Leonardo da Vinci's Aristic Circle and Other Foreshortenings*); *Contemplaciones* (1988) (*Contemplations*); *Jardines de Murillo* (1989) (*Murillo's Gardens*), and *Trasluz* (1989) (*Reflected Light*).

Sanzara, Rahel (1894–1936)
German novelist, whose real name was Johanna Bleschke. She trained as a dancer, had her film debut in 1917, and became a successful actress. Her first and only remaining novel, *Das verlorene Kind* (1926) (*The Lost Child*), describes the rape and murder of a four-year-old girl. The book created a great stir, especially because it had been written by a woman. It ran to several editions and was translated into eleven languages. Sanzara was even offered the Kleist Prize for this book, but refused it.

Sapotille et le Serein d'Argile (1960) (Sapotille and the Clay Canary)
In this first novel by the Guadeloupean (French Antilles) writer ▷Michèle Lacrosil, we are presented with the journal to which Sapotille, during a sea voyage from Guadeloupe to France, commits her thoughts. The journal is a review of Sapotille's life at school in Guadeloupe, and her relationships with her black husband and mulatto lover. Motivated by an Existential interpretation of the self/other relationship as one of insoluble conflict, the novel reveals a woman fleeing Guadeloupe, and a past there marked by racism and the alienation of French education. It also reveals a woman who believes she can find happiness in France.
▷*Cajou*; *Demain Jab-Herma*; *Folie Antillaise, La*; Identity, Caribbean

Sappho (Psappho) (7th–6th century BC)
Greek poet from Lesbos. Daughter of Scamandronymus and Cleis, and sister of three brothers. At some time she visited Sicily. The many anecdotes about Sappho's life, drawn from her works and from comic dramas written about her, make accurate biography impossible. She may have had a daughter, Cleis, although Sappho refers to her with a word that may simply be a term of affection. The stories that she committed suicide for love of Phaon probably come from 4th-century BC comic drama.

Her work is the largest corpus written by an ancient Greek woman, although very fragmentary. It shows, in a variety of metres, Sappho as leader of a band of young girls in worship of the goddess of love, Aphrodite. The *Hymn to Aphrodite*, in a metre called Sapphic after her, is an address to the goddess to aid her seduction of a young girl whom Sappho loves. It neatly employs traditional hymnic commonplaces to describe a female object of desire. A second fragment was preserved because it evocatively describes the symptoms of one in love, as she watches the woman she loves beside her bridegroom. Sappho wrote many

Sappho meets Alcaeus (calathos, c 480)

marriage songs and was famous for them in antiquity.

Other fragments include a description of the beauty of the woman Anactoria, a poem to her 'daughter' Cleis, good wishes to her brother as he sets out on a voyage, a narrative poem on the marriage of Hector and Andromache (epic characters) and a poem for a girl, Lydia, who is compared to the moon outshining the stars.

Sappho occasionally used epic metaphors and images of war to describe love, and thus played an important part in the development of the theme of 'love as war' in later Latin elegiac poetry. This literary transference of male war imagery to female love poetry is one further sign of her literary ability. Another is the variety of metres employed in her lyric poetry. She is correctly considered as good as, if not better than, the contemporary male lyric poet Alcaeus. Her poetry was translated into Latin and imitated by Roman poets such as Catullus and Horace in the 1st century BC. Antipater of Thessalonica (2nd century BC) includes her in his list of nine women poets, and another Greek ▷epigram styles her 'the tenth Muse' (▷Muses).

▷Anyte; Moero; Praxilla; Erinna; Parthenis; Perilla; Religion, Ancient Greek and Roman, women and

Bib: (text & trans.) Campbell, D.A., *Greek Lyric*; deJean, J., *Fictions of Sappho 1546–1937*.

Sara Burgerhart (1782) Historie van mejuffrouw Sara Burgerhart

In the preface to this epistolary novel by ▷Betje Wolff and ▷Aagje Deken, the authors address the *juffers* or young ladies of the Netherlands, marriageable girls of eighteen or nineteen from the upper middle classes. Their aim was to show that an excess of vivacity and too strong a desire for pleasure would plunge girls into misery. The main character of the novel, Sara Burgerhart, is such a girl, who falls victim to a wicked gentleman, although she escapes in the nick of time. The edifying tenor of the novel is evident: Sara's landlady makes her realize the importance of raising a family. She marries the serious Hendrik Edeling, who works in trade, the basis of the nation's prosperity. The novel, probably inspired by foreign examples like ▷Richardson's *Pamela*, and a new element in the Dutch literary tradition, was a great success.

▷Wollstonecraft, Mary

Saranti, Galateia (born 1920)

Greek novelist, short story writer and children's author. Born in Patras, she studied law in Athens. Her first book, *The Castle* (1942), deals with the world of Greek provincial town and family life. The strength of her writing rests less on the analysis of outward situations than on the effect these have on her characters' inner selves. *The Book of Johannes and Maria* (1952) is a love story set in German-occupied Athens. Her best novel is probably *Our Old House* (1959); it displays her writing abilities, rich in emotion and sympathy, in perfect form. In 1962 she published *Colours of Trust*, a collection of rather melodramatic short stories based on everyday life. Another successful novel was *The Boundaries* (1966), the story of a woman alienated from society. Saranti's main focus of interest is human relationships, especially in the lives of female characters who seem unable to fit in. She has also written three plays, as well as some short stories for children.

Sarasvati

The Hindu goddess of learning and poetic inspiration. She is the spouse of Brahma, the Hindu god of creation, and is rarely worshipped as an independent goddess.

Sarfatti, Margherita (1883–1961)

Italian essayist, journalist and novelist. Born in Venice. As a young woman, she was a member of the Socialist Party, but, in 1915, she left the party. From then on, she was involved in the fascist movement and was literary and artistic editor of the fascist newspaper, *Il Popolo d'Italia* (*The Italian People*). She worked closely with Mussolini, and produced a biography of him (*Dux*) in 1926. Ironically, because she was of a Jewish family, she was forced, after the introduction of the racial laws, to resign from her literary post and to emigrate to North America. She wrote her memories of this period in her life in 1955, in *Acqua passata* (*Water Under the Bridge*).

Her other works include: *La fiaccola accesa* (1919) (*Torchlight*); *Segni, colori e luci* (1925) (*Signs, Colours and Lights*); *Il palazzone* (1929) (*The Great Palace*); *Storia della pittura moderna* (1930) (*A*

History of Modern Painting); *Casanova contro Don Giovanni* (1950) (*Casanova vs. Don Giovanni*).

Sarraute, Nathalie (born 1902)

Nathalie Sarraute

French writer, leading exponent of the ▷*nouveau roman*. Born in Russia, she was raised in France, where she has spent most of her life. *Tropismes* (1939/1946) (▷*Tropisms* (1963), a precursor of the *nouveau roman* passed unnoticed, and it was not until publication of *Portrait d'un inconnu* (1948) (▷*Portrait of a Man Unknown*, 1958) that the public were alerted to the innovatory significance of Sarraute's work. ▷*Martereau* (1953) followed, and *L'Ere du soupçon: essais sur le roman* (1953) (*The Age of Suspicion: Essays on the Novel*, 1963) established her as the leader of a group of writers which included Michel Butor (born 1926), Claude Simon, Alain Robbe-Grillet (born 1922) and Robert Pinget, and which was championed by Éditions de Minuit.

In *The Age of Suspicion*, she heralded the death of the 'character' in fiction, to be replaced by 'a matter as nameless as blood, a magma'. Authorial presence becomes marginal, as the power of speech seems to derive paradoxically from its inefficiency as a means of communication. *Sous-conversation*, already exemplified by *Tropisms*, indicates that the words are the verbal translation of a non-verbal communication. Increasingly, in later works – *Les Fruits d'or* (1963) (*Golden Fruits*), *Entre la vie et la mort* (1968) (*Between Life and Death*) – the non-verbal signals are presented as speech; the voices no longer have an individual source of any kind; conversation and *sous-conversation* merge, as if the 'characters' were simultaneously transparent and opaque to each other. In the wake of ▷Virginia Woolf, her work

also addresses the issues of gender perception with subtle irony.

Her other works include *Le Planétarium* (1959) (▷*The Planetarium*, 1960) and plays, *Le Mensonge* (1967) (*The Lie*), and *Le Silence* (1967) (*Silence*). Her autobiography, *Enfances* (*Childhood*) was published in 1983.
Bib: Ross-Besser, Gretchen, *Nathalie Sarraute* ; Temple, Ruth, *Nathalie Sarraute* ; Watson Williams, Helen, *The Novels of Nathalie Sarraute*.

Sarrazin, Albertine (1937–1967)

French novelist, born in Algeria. One of the best modern prison writers, she faithfully documents the milieu of petty crime and prostitution, combining autobiography with fiction. Her depiction of her personal growth from delinquent to author led her to be compared to Genet, though the brevity of her career leaves this judgment open to conjecture. She wrote novels: *L'Astragale* (1965) (▷*Astragal*, 1967), *La Cavale* (1969) (*The Runaway*), *La Traversière* (1966) (*The Crossing*); journals: *Biftons de prison* (1977) (*Notes from Prison*), *Journal de Fresnes* (1984) (*Fresnes Diary*), and poems.

Sarton, May (born 1912)

US novelist, poet and essayist. Originally from Belgium, Sarton's family fled to Cambridge, Massachusetts, when World War I began. Her mother was a painter. Having declined a college scholarship, she eventually founded and directed the Associated Actors Theater in 1933. In 1936 she turned from her work in the theatre to a full commitment to her career as a writer. The Office of War Information engaged her as a scriptwriter for documentary films on North American life in 1944. Her book *Faithful Are the Wounds* (1955) considers the events of the McCarthy era. She has also travelled widely, meeting both ▷Virginia Woolf and ▷Elizabeth Bowen, and has worked as a writer-in-residence and lecturer at a number of universities and colleges, including Harvard and Wellesley.

These activities are counterbalanced by her active pursuit of solitude in New Hampshire, as depicted in her journals. Solitude is a key theme which Sarton explores in her work. The poems in *Inner Landscape* (1939) suggest that being alone does not entail loneliness, and Sarton emphasizes that such isolation is necessary for artistic creation. 'Only when she built inward in a fearful isolation / Did any one succeed or learn to fuse emotion / With thought' she writes in 'My Sisters, O My Sisters' about ▷Sappho and ▷Emily Dickinson. As in *The Small Room* (1961), about a small New England college, her fiction shows how female friendships and love affairs can alleviate the loneliness. The poems in *A Private Mythology* (1966) reflect Sarton's inner journeying towards spiritual serenity. Her journals, such as *Journal of Solitude* (1973) and *The Magnificent Spinster* (1985), mix the everyday details of life, cats, gardens, illness, visitors, with musings on art, death, and female creativity, frustrated by the fragmented lives of women caught within 'household chores and family life' and 'with no margin left on any day'. To Sarton, delving into the personal yields the universal.

Other works include: *The Single Hound* (1938), *A Shower of Summer Days* (1952), *Joanna and Ulysses* (1963), *Mrs. Stevens Hears the Mermaids Singing* (1975), *Plant Dreaming Deep* (1968), *Kinds of Love* (1970), *A Grain of Mustard Seed* (1971), *Crucial Conversations* (1975), *The House by the Sea* (1977), *Recovering* (1980), *At Seventy* (1984), *May Sarton: A Self-Portrait* (1988) and *Endgame: Journal of the Seventy-Ninth Year* (1992).
Bib. Evans, Elizabeth, *May Sarton Revisited*.

Sata Ineko (1904)

Japanese novelist. Born in Nagasaki, she changed from one job to another having been forced by poverty to leave primary school. After her first marriage, when she worked as a shopgirl, she and her husband attempted to commit suicide. He was extraordinarily jealous, and there had also been conflict in her family over property. She became acquainted with Nakano Shigeharu and his circle, who were members of Roba, a literary group, while working in a café, after she got divorced and had given birth to a daughter. Following her second marriage to Kubokawa Inejiro, she published *A Factory for Candy* in 1928 and *A Restaurant Called Rakuyo*, which was praised by the esteemed writer Kawabata Yasunari. Sata joined the Union for Japanese Proletarian Literature, and was active as an editor of *Working Women*, a magazine for proletarian women writers. In 1932 she joined the Communist Party. Her wartime days were unhappy, not only because the proletarian movement was being suppressed, but also because her family life was a failure. Her experience at the time is described in detail in *Crimson*. In 1945 she was divorced from Kubokawa and she joined the foundation of Fujin Minshu Club, a women's liberation organization, of which she was president from 1970. She was expelled from the Communist Party in 1951 because she opposed the party's meddling in literature. Her masterpieces are her autobiographical novel *A Girl with Naked Feet*, *My Map of Tokyo*, ▷*A Tree's Shadow* and *Standing Still in Time* which won the Kawabata Yasunari Prize. She received the Asahi Prize in 1984.

Sati/Parvati

A wife of the Hindu god Shiva, the destroyer, who was won to him by his practice of austerities. She embodies many of the characteristics that are cherished in a Hindu wife, and for her supreme act of self-sacrifice in avenging an insult offered to her husband she was rewarded with reincarnation as the lovely Parvati, Shiva's subsequent wife.

In medieval India the concept of wifely self-sacrifice was taken to its extreme with the rise of *sati* (suttee), the self-immolation of Hindu widows on their husband's funeral pyre. *Sati* was outlawed by the British in 1830, although it now seems that they exaggerated the extent of its observance in early 19th-century India. Very occasional cases of widow-burning are still heard of today in parts of rural India, and they may, as in British times, reflect a drastic attempt by conservative groups to hold on to old ways in a rapidly changing society.

Sato Aiko (born 1923)

Japanese novelist and essayist. She was born in Osaka, the daughter of Sato Koroku, a novelist. The poet Sato Hachiro was her brother-in-law. Sato started to write a novel after a divorce left her with two children. *A Mansion in Winter* (1960) was highly praised. *Sunset after Battle* won the Naoki Prize. This work, based on her experience of divorce and remarriage, describes the quarrels between a couple who are in debt because the husband's company has gone bankrupt. In a lighter vein, she produced a series about male egoism. She has also written her father's biography, *A Deep Red Flower – Sato Koroku*.

Sattianathan, Krupabai (1862–94)

Indian fiction writer. Sattianathan was the first woman to study medicine at Madras Medical College, but discontinued her studies because of poor health. She died at the age of thirty-two. Her two autobiographical stories, *Kamala: A Story of a Hindu Life* (1894) and *Saguna: A Story of Native Christian Life* (1895), were first published in *The Journal of Madras Christian College*, and then posthumously in book form. *Saguna* reflects the author's early life in Bombay as the daughter of Christian converts, as does Sattianathan's more explicitly autobiographical *Story of a Conversion*. *Kamala* was inspired by the early death of the author's only child, and was written from her own sick-bed.

Saunders, Margaret Marshall (1861–1947)

Canadian children's writer, especially of animal stories, most notably *Beautiful Joe: the Autobiography of a Dog* (1893). Born in Milton, Nova Scotia, the daughter of a Baptist preacher, her family moved to Halifax in 1867. She spent two years in Edinburgh, Scotland, and France, then returned to Canada and began to write. Saunders' message of kindness to animals permeates her many books, but she was also an activist in favour of social justice for children. The heroine of her adult novel, *The Girl From Vermont: The Story of a Vacation School Teacher* (1910), fights against the exploitation of children. Saunders travelled widely, giving lectures, but died quietly and in poverty.

Saussure, Ferdinand de ▷Difference

Savary, Olga Augusta Maria (born 1933)

Brazilian poet, short story writer, translator and journalist. Daughter of a Russian immigrant who settled in the northern state of Pará, she moved to Rio as a child. The sea, carnival, folklore and urban culture are recurring topics in her poetry. She translated important Spanish American authors, and Japanese poetry has been a constant source of inspiration. She adopted the pen-name Olenka, and writes with a feminine voice, impregnated with hedonism and eroticism, combining descriptions of sensations and pleasures of the natural world – particularly the sea and the sky – with Indian words in tupi-guarani. Her book *Haikais de Olga Savary* (1970) (*Haikus of Olga Savary*) and others have received notable prizes.

Other works: *Espelho provisório* (1970) (*Provisional Mirror*); *Sumidouro* (1977) (*The Drain*); *Altaonda* (1979) (*High Wave*); *Magma* (1982); *Linha d'água* (1987) (*The Waterline*); *Berço esplêndido* (1989) (*Splendorous Cradle*).

Savić-Rebac, Anica (1892–1953)

Serbian scholar and poet. She was a Professor of Classical Philology, and published articles on many European and southern Slavic writers. She is particularly known for her study of the great Montenegrin poet Njegoš, and her translation of his work into English. She wrote on classical philosophy and painting, and made numerous translations from Greek, Latin, German and English. She published a volume of poems in 1929. Her admirers included German writer Thomas Mann (1875–1955) and English novelist ▷Rebecca West (1892–1983)

Savignac, Alida de (Madame de) (1790–1847)

French novelist and educational writer. The author of works which recall those of ▷Stéphanie de Genlis, Savignac was an unmarried woman who nevertheless signed her novels Madame de Savignac because her pious mother thought it more seemly to do so. Her fictional works, which include *La Comtesse de Meley* (1823), *Les Petits Proverbes dramatiques* (1826) (*Little Dramatic Proverbs*), *Les Vacances* (1828) (*The Holidays*), *La Pauvre Cécile* (1829) (*Poor Cécile*) and *La Jeune propriétaire* (1837) (*The Young Proprietor*), were intended to lead young people along the path of virtue and to engender a loathing of vice. What distinguishes her writings from the majority of similar French 19th-century texts is the fact that they were entertaining. The moral message was presented in a lively and attractive fashion, and the material encouraged young readers to use their minds actively and analytically. De Savignac also wrote for women's journals, including the ▷*Journal des Dames* (*Ladies' Journal*), in which she argued that women should receive a genuinely instructive religious education, rather than one which merely advocated virtue and obedience.

▷Feminine/feminist journalism (France)

Savitri

A popular figure in Hindu mythology, who displays unswerving devotion to her husband. She follows him into the realm of the dead and, by outwitting the God of Death, she is able to win back his life and forestall her own widowhood. Her devotion is held out as an example of proper wifely behaviour, but she is equally admired for her mental dexterity.

Savorgnan, Maria Late (15th–16th century)

Italian poet, of whom there exists very little biographical information. It is known that, in 1500–1, she had a passionate affair with the poet Pietro Bembo. This led them to write letters and poetry to each other, and these were collected and published in 1950. She had married into an aristocratic Venetian family and her writings to Bembo were not intended for publication. They express passionate love, intellectual ambition, and reveal a broad literary knowledge. It is especially interesting that she feels herself to be the intellectual equal of Bembo, and that there appears to be a good deal of intellectual jealousy between them. Her poetry forms part of the ▷Petrarchan tradition.

Sawachi Hisae (born 1930)

Japanese non-fiction writer. Born in Tokyo, she worked as deputy editor of *Fujin Koron*. She continues to bring to the forefront little-known protagonists in historical events in works such as *Wives and the Coups d'états Caused by Young Army Officers on 26th February 1936* and *Documents – Midway Sea War. Soldiers' Rebellion at Takenishijiken in 1878* won the Fifth Non-fiction Prize.

Sayers, Dorothy L. (1893–1957)

English detective story writer, dramatist, poet and essayist. She was born in Oxford, educated at Godolphin School, Salisbury, and Somerville College, Oxford, where she gained a first in modern languages. Sayers worked as a teacher and then as a reader for the publisher Basil Blackwell, during which time she produced her first volume of poetry. During her employment with an advertising agency Sayers joined the Detection Club, whose members included G.K. Chesterton (1874–1936), its aim being to improve the style and status of ▷detective fiction. During the late 1920s and 1930s Sayers became the leading figure in detective writing. Her first detective novel, *Whose Body?*, appeared in 1923, and by 1931 the success of her novels provided financial independence.

Sayer's treatment of the aristocratic amateur detective Lord Peter Wimsey, who appears in all but one of her detective novels, draws attention to a sense of social responsibility as his primary motive for involvement. Sayers novels are characteristic in their interest in the mechanisms of murder as much as in the plot's final resolution. The introduction of the semi-autobiographical character Harriet Vane alongside Peter Wimsey in the later novels allows commentary on the traditional centrality of male figures as epitomizing the highly-developed powers of rationality necessary to deducing the murderer's identity.

Sayers's views on the social role of women are discussed in *Are Women Human* (1971), which argues for equal opportunities, but resists the political expediency of claims to difference, including the notion of a feminine aesthetic. Sayers's twelfth and last detective novel was *Busman's Honeymoon* (1937), after which she concentrated on writing religious drama for radio, and broadcasting on numerous topics from detective fiction to theology.

Her writings include: *Clouds of Witness* (1926), *Unnatural Death* (1927), *The Unpleasantness at the Bellona Club* (1928), *Lord Peter Views the Body* (1928), *Five Red Herrings* (1931), *Have His Carcase* (1932), *Murder Must Advertize* (1933), *Hangman's Holiday* (1933), *The Nine Tailors* (1934), ▷*Gaudy Night* (1935), *Unpopular Opinions* (1946) and *The Poetry of Search and the Poetry of Statement* (1963).
▷Mitchell, Gladys

Bib: Brabazon, J., *Dorothy L. Sayers: A Biography*; Brunsdale, M., *Dorothy L. Sayers: Solving the Mystery of Wickedness*; Gaillard, D., *Dorothy L. Sayers*; Kenney, C., *The Remarkable Case of Dorothy L. Sayers*; Lee, G., *Lord Peter Rings the Changes*; Reynolds, B., *The Passionate Intellect: Dorothy L. Sayers's Encounter With Dante*.

Sayers, Peig (1873–1958)
Irish story teller, born in County Kerry, who lived on Great Blasket Island, now uninhabited. Her autobiography, *Peig* (1936), is a remarkable and beautifully told story of island life, and of the pleasures and pains of female experience. *Machtnamh Sean Mhná* (*Reflections of an Old Woman*) was published in 1939, and translated into English in 1962. She is one of the very few women whose work has been accorded authoritative status in modern Irish-language writing.

Scaldic poetry in Iceland
Most of the literature written during the Middle Ages in Iceland is anonymous, but some women are known to have been writing, and some names are preserved, such as Stenunn Refsdóttir, and from around 1000, Thorúnn Jónsdóttir, who wrote a short dancing ballad. Snorris Skáldatal in his *Digterregister* (*Poets Register*) mentions two women, Vilborg Skjald and Steinvór Sighvatsdóttir. Many short ballads seem to have been written by a young woman, Jóreidur i Midjumdal, who lived in the middle of the 12th century.

From the anonymous scaldic poetry it is evident that women in ancient Iceland had a high status compared to other parts of Scandinavia. It seems likely that women participated as writers not only in scaldic poetry but also in the ▷sagas.

Scanlan, Nelle (1882–1968)
New Zealand novelist. Scanlan, like ▷Jane Mander, ▷Rosemary Rees and ▷Jean Devanny, earned her living as a journalist and was the only woman reporter at the Limitation of Arms Conference in Washington (1920). She lived for some years in North America and Europe, and her first two novels are both set in London. But in

1932 she published *Pencarrow*, the opening novel of her famous tetralogy of historical novels set in New Zealand, which many contemporaries saw as the most successful attempt at writing distinctive New Zealand fiction of the time. The Pencarrow novels are a family saga. Most of Scanlan's succeeding novels – sixteen altogether – were ▷romance narratives and were less ambitious than the *Pencarrow* series. Later commentators (Joan Stevens, *The New Zealand Novel*, 1960, and Heather Roberts, *Where Did She Come From?*, 1989) have found Scanlan's work falls too much into the conventions of the romance plot.

Publications: (a selective list): *Primrose Hill* (1931); *The Top Step* (1931); *Pencarrow* (1932); *Tides of Youth* (1933); *Winds of Heaven* (1934); *Kelly Pencarrow* (1939).

Scar, The (1965)
Play by Kenyan writer ▷Rebeka Njau.
▷Essay on East Africa

Scarlet letter
US symbol for adultery. It originated in the 1850 novel by Nathaniel Hawthorne (1804–1864), *The Scarlet Letter*, in which a Puritan community sentences Hester Prynne to wearing a scarlet 'A' as partial, but lifelong, punishment for her sin of adultery. The scarlet letter 'A' and 'scarlet woman' became cultural references for adulterous women and, more generally, for women who were branded by society because their sexuality was outside the bounds of conventional and puritanical morality. It also refers to the double standard of sexual conduct for men and women.

Scarlet Song (1986)
Translation of *Un Chant écarlate* (1981), the second, novel by the Senegalese writer ▷Mariama Bâ, published posthumously. It is an examination of racist, chauvinistic and patriarchal attitudes, through the depiction of a mixed marriage. Mireille, daughter of a French diplomat, marries Ousmane, son of a poor Senegalese family and a Moslem. They marry in Paris and return to Senegal, where gradually the influence of the family, the community and tradition reasserts itself over Ousmane. When he takes a second, Senegalese wife, Mireille breaks down and the novel ends tragically. Bâ has explained that, while marriage between Senegalese women and white men has always been accepted, the position of a son within the family makes conflict inevitable when he marries a white woman. The pain and suffering of both partners are unflinchingly portrayed, without taking sides.

Scenes of Clerical Life (1858)
A series of tales by English novelist ▷George Eliot, first published in *Blackwood's Magazine* and collected as *Scenes of Clerical Life* in 1858. Eliot's earliest works of fiction, the tales are entitled *The Sad Fortunes of the Rev Amos Barton*; *Mr Gilfil's Love Story*, and *Janet's Repentance*.

Sceptred Flute: Songs of India, The (1928)

A collection of poems by the Indian poet
▷Sarojini Naidu. Strongly influenced by Keats
and Wordsworth, Naidu transports romanticism to
an Indian setting, although she sees less of a
moral purpose in her wonderful and mysterious
landscapes than do her European models.

Schaumann, Ruth (1899–1975)

German writer, sculptor and painter, who often
illustrated her own books. Her writing is strongly
influenced by Catholicism, to which she converted
in 1924. She made her literary debut in 1920 with
the collection of Expressionist poems *Die
Kathedrale* (*The Cathedral*). Her later work, which
includes poems, stories, novels and children's
books, tends to revolve around love, marriage and
motherhood. Under Hitler's rule her work was
banned.

Schirmacher, Käthe (1859–1930)

German writer and suffragette. Born in Danzig,
she studied literature in Paris, became a teacher
in Liverpool, and after returning briefly to Danzig,
participated in 1893 in the International Women's
Congress in Chicago. In 1895 she obtained a
doctorate from the University of Zurich, and
began a lively career as an international lecturer,
journalist and champion of women's rights.
However, during World War I she increasingly
modified her views on the role of women to
accommodate the very strict conservative and
nationalistic ideals that prevailed at the time.

Schlegel, Dorothea (1763–1839)

German writer. The daughter of the Berlin
industrialist and philosopher Moses Mendelssohn
(1729–1786), she married the banker Simon Veit
at fifteen, and had two sons. In 1797 she met the
writer Friedrich Schlegel (1772–1829), and
divorced Veit. She became a Christian, and
married Schlegel in 1804. Four years later they
both converted to Catholicism. To support
herself, and in order to free her husband from the
need to earn money, she translated French novels
and transcribed manuscripts from Old German,
which, together with an unfinished novel, *Florentin*
(1801), were published under Friedrich Schlegel's
name. Her numerous letters to her husband, and
to her sister-in-law, ▷Caroline
Schlegel-Schelling, have now been republished.
▷Salon culture (Germany and Austria)

Schlegel-Schelling, Caroline (1763–1809)

German writer and charismatic figure in the early
German romantic movement. The well-educated
daughter of Johann David Michaelis (1717–1791),
Professor of Oriental Studies, she married a
physician in 1784, had three children, and was
widowed four years later. She took an intense
interest in the French Revolution (1789) and in
1793 was briefly put into prison while expecting a
child by a French officer. Rescued by her brother,
she became a protégée of the brothers August
(1767–1845) and Friedrich Schlegel (1772–1829),

and in 1796 married August Schlegel. She wrote
unsigned reviews for their literary magazine,
Athenäum, and worked without acknowledgement
with her husband on a translation of Shakespeare.
After divorcing Schlegel she married the romantic
philosopher Friedrich Schelling (1775–1854).
▷Salon culture (Germany and Austria)

Scholtz, Ingrid ▷Viljoen, Lettie

Schomburg Library of Nineteenth-Century Black Women Writers, The

US reprint series from Oxford University Press
which, for the first time, makes generally available
the 'lost' works of many African-American women
writers – including journals, essays and novels. It
includes works by ▷Phillis Wheatley, ▷Ann
Plato, ▷Frances E. W. Harper, ▷Charlotte L.
Forten Grimké, ▷Harriet Jacobs and ▷Alice
Dunbar Nelson.

Schön, Elizabeth (born 1921)

Venezuelan poet and dramatist. Her full name is
Elizabeth Columbia Schön de Cortina. She
studied literature, philosophy and the history of
music in Caracas, and her first book, *La gruta
venidera* (1955) (*The Future Cavern*), consists of
prose poems with deep inner meaning and
symbolism. Her most famous book of poetry is *El
abuelo, la cesta y el mar* (1965) (*The Grandfather, the
Basket and the Sea*). In later poetic works,
Encendido esparcimiento (1981) (*Scattered Fire*) for
instance, she has played with reality and thought,
logos and emotion, in a pre-Socratic exchange
between the material and the immaterial. She has
cultivated the theatre of the absurd in a country
which did not have many important figures until
the 1960s. Her plays *Intervalo* (1957) (*Interval*)
and (*Melisa y yo*) (*Melisa and Me*) were performed
in Caracas in 1961.

Other works: *En el allá disparado desde ningún
comienzo* (1962) (*In the Mad Place from which there
is no beginning*); *La Aldea* (1967) (*The Village*); *Lo
importante es que nos miramos* (1967) (*The Important
Thing is That We Look at Ourselves*); *La cisterna
insondable* (1971) (*The Bottomless Tank*); *Casi un
país* (1972) (*Almost a Country*); *Es oír la vertiente*
(1973) (*Hearing is the Fountain*); *Al unísono* (1977)
(*In Unison*), and *Incesante aparecer* (1977) (*Incessant
Appearance*).

Schopenhauer, Adele (1797–1849)

German writer. The daughter of ▷Johanna
Schopenhauer, and sister of the philosopher
Arthur Schopenhauer (1788–1860), she grew up
in the lively cultural atmosphere of early 19th-
century Weimar, enjoyed a close friendship with
the Goethe family, and later became a good friend
of ▷Annette von Droste-Hülshoff. Although she
achieved fame primarily for her skill in
ornamental papercutting, she was also a gifted
writer who, besides editing her mother's work,
kept a diary and wrote fairytales, poems and
novels.

Schopenhauer, Johanna Henriette (1766–1838)

German diarist, travel writer, portrait painter and mother of ▷Adele Schopenhauer, and the philosopher Arthur Schopenhauer (1788–1860). When her husband's business collapsed during the Napoleonic Wars and he committed suicide, she earned a living by writing. Her novel, *Gabriele* (1819–1820), is a tale of feminine renunciation, and she also wrote travelogues, such as *Reise durch England und Schottland* (1818) (*Journey Through England and Scotland*). Her memoirs, *Damals in Weimar. Erinnerungen und Briefe* (posthumously published in 1924) (*Those Days in Weimar. Recollections and Letters*) and *Jugendleben und Wanderbilder. Aus Johanna Schopenhauers Nachlaß* (1839) (*Portraits of Youth and Travel. From the Papers of Johanna Schopenhauer*) convey a vivid impression of the cultural life at Weimar in the age of Goethe (1749–1852) and early romanticism.

▷Salon culture (Germany and Austria)

Schoultz, Solveig von (born 1907)

▷Fenno-Swedish poet and prose writer. Solveig von Schoultz was influenced by both her father and mother. Her father was a minister and teacher of religion who set rigorous ethical standards for his large family. Von Schoultz distanced herself from his norms by creating a literary world of tolerance and compassion. From her mother, painter Hanna Frosterous-Segerstråle, she learnt discipline and security, as may be seen from the biography she wrote about her in *Porträtt av Hanna* (1978) (*Portrait of Hanna*).

Solveig von Schoultz is clearly influenced by ▷Karin Boye's poetry, eg in her collections *Min timme* (1940) (*My Hour*) and *Eko av ett rop* (1945) (*The Echo of a Call*). In her later collections she tries a tighter, more experimental form, as in *Nätet* (1956) (*The Net*) and *Sänk ditt ljus* (1963) (*Dim Your Light*). In her prose writing, she deals with everyday life, and is a very fine portrayer of children and young people, eg *De sju dagarna* (1942) (*The Seven Days*) and *Ingenting Ovanligt* (1947) (*Nothing Unusual*).

In her latest works she concentrates on women and feminist understanding, as in the short stories in *Somliga mornar* (1976) (*Some Mornings*). She is a very creative writer, experimenting with literary forms and developing a very individual ▷postmodernism.

Schreiner, Olive (1855–1920)

South African novelist, short-story writer, and political essayist and a central figure in the development of modern, white South African literature. Schreiner was both derided and acclaimed during her lifetime for her pioneering feminist studies, her rejection of Christian convention, and her anti-racist and anti-imperialist stance. Her youth was spent in the Cradock district in the Karoo, first at the London Missionary Society station run by her father, a German Lutheran missionary, then in the house of her brother and his family, housekeeping, and thereafter on various farms in the Karoo, working as a governess. She left for England in 1881, aged 26, with the manuscripts of three novels in her suitcase, only one of which was to be published in her lifetime. This was *The Story of an African Farm* (1883), which brought her immediate success.

During these years Schreiner had begun reading greedily. She said of philosopher Herbert Spencer's (1820–1903) *First Principles* (1862) that it burst on her sixteen-year-old world just as Christianity had burst on the Romans. She also read J.S. Mill's (1806–1873) *Principles of Political Economy* (1848), and widely in history and the natural sciences, as well as in English and German romanticism. In England she formed close friendships with free-thinkers such as Havelock Ellis (1859–1939), Edward Carpenter, Eleanor Marx and Karl Pearson. She was instrumental in setting up the Men and Women's Club, and became a prominent figure in London literary and progressive circles. Returning to South Africa in 1889, she married a man who added her name to his, in accord with her feminism. She had already formed a close friendship with Cecil John Rhodes, which was to be a turbulent one, given her growing criticism of imperialist expansion. Over the years, she developed a sophisticated understanding of political dynamics, and particularly of British settler colonialism, as well as a theory of gender relations that moved well beyond what feminism of the time had to offer.

Her first novel, *Undine* (published posthumously in 1928, but written between 1875 and 1877), presents the life of a young woman growing up in Britain, who then becomes a governess on an isolated Karoo farm and in the Kimberley diamond fields. Clearly autobiographical, it recounts a young woman's desire to break away from the religious and psychological repression of her upbringing. Her second novel, ▷*The Story of an African Farm* (1883), on which her reputation is founded, again portrays a yearning desire for a life other than the one colonial South Africa had to offer, and a bitterness towards its Victorian materialism and spiritual claustrophobia. A powerful, energetic text, *Story* has unfortunately eclipsed the novel she was to spend the rest of her life working on, ▷*From Man to Man* (1926), which has received little critical attention. This massive novel examines two women's lives, split, as in *Story*, between the passionate intellectual and the softer, domestically fulfilled woman. As in her earlier writing, here, too, Schreiner combines naturalistic, symbolist, political and philosophical genres.

During her lifetime Schreiner also published a set of allegories, the highly successful *Dreams* (1890), which reproduced one of her most evocative pieces, 'The Hunter', extracted from *The Story of an African Farm*, and *Dream Life and Real Life* (1893). After her death a third collection was published: *Stories, Dreams and Allegories*

(1923). These philosophical stories and allegories, also anti-Victorian, despite their conventional Victorian form, crystallize Schreiner's deep yearning for universal equality along with individual freedom and spiritual well-being. All Schreiner's writing is based on a holistic philosophy of social evolution, inspired by Spenser as well as by Ralph Waldo Emerson (after whom Waldo in *Story* is named): humanity will progressively evolve to its full potential: it is in this that freedom and truth inhere. Her feminism must be seen in this context: *Woman and Labour* (1911) argues that female parasitism is a symbol of the decay and degeneration of a potentially great civilization. Women's marginalization, and their apparent superfluity in 'public affairs', is a problem not just for women, then, but for the world in general.

She also wrote as a polemicist: a set of newspaper articles on colonial racist and imperialist culture, later collected in *Thoughts on South Africa* (1923); a barely-disguised attack, in the form of allegory, on Cecil John Rhodes (1853–1902), whose Chartered Company colonized Rhodesia, *Trooper Peter Halket of Mashonaland* (1897); and *An English South African's View of the Situation* (1899), which proposed moves to avert the approaching ▷Anglo-Boer war. Schreiner's protectiveness towards Boers gradually faded after the war, her attention turning instead to racism, yet her racial attitudes are often patronizing or worse, marked as they are by then-current trends in social Darwinism. In *From Man to Man*, Rebekah adopts the child of one of the domestic servants, who has been impregnated by Rebekah's husband, in order to bring her up as 'one of the family'. But Rebekah then dismisses the servants, with no thought either to her feelings and claims as a mother, or to her economic needs. Schreiner's identification with Rebekah in this regard is all too apparent in the language of the text: the servant, moreover, is given neither name nor voice.

Schreiner spent the last seven years of her life in England, where she was involved in pacifist political work. She was hounded from one boarding house to the next on account of her German name, separated from her husband, tormented by what she felt was her failure as a writer. She returned to South Africa to die.

There have been various editions of her letters, the most recent being *Letters 1871–99*, edited by Richard Rive (1987).

Other works: *Closer Union* (1909).
Bib: Berkman, Joyce, *The Healing Imagination of Olive Schreiner*; First, Ruth, and Scott, Ann, *Olive Schreiner: A Biography*; Clayton, Cherry (ed.), *Olive Schreiner*; Monsman, Gerald, *Olive Schreiner's Fiction*; Van Wyk Smith, Malvern, and Maclennan, Don (eds). *Olive Schreiner and After*; Vivan, Itala (ed.), *The Flawed Diamond*.

Schriber, Margrit (born 1939)
German-speaking Swiss novelist. Her novels, such as *Aussicht gerahmt* (1976) (*Framed View*),

Kartenhaus (1978) (*House of Cards*), *Vogel Flieg* (1980) (*Bird Flight*) or *Muschelgarten* (1984) (*Shell Garden*), are sensitive investigations of how ordinary women feel to have lost touch with their own selves in the modern world.

Schubert, Helga (born 1940)
East German short story writer. A trained psychologist, she had a first success in 1975 with *Lauter Leben* (*Nothing but Life*), a collection of thirty-one psychological cameos, mainly of women trying to cope with ordinary life in post-war socialist Germany. In the stories of *Das verbotene Zimmer* (1982) (*The Forbidden Room*), the central theme is, once again, the hopes and concerns of a variety of East Germans. The 'forbidden room' of the title is a metaphor, not only for West Berlin and the 'other Germany', but also for the events of 20th-century German history, with which many of the characters still have not come to terms.

Schubin, Ossip (1854–1934)
Pen name of German writer Aloiysia Kirschner. As the carefully brought-up daughter of a Bohemian landowner, she travelled with her mother all over Europe and was introduced to the best literary circles, where she met the authors ▷George Sand and Ivan Turgenev (1818–1883), among many others. Her novellas retain a certain charm and interest because they vividly evoke the ▷salon culture of her time.

Schutting, Jutta (born 1937)
Austrian poet and short story writer. She established herself with two volumes of finely-crafted, intellectual poetry: *In der Sprache der Inseln* (1973) (*In the Language of the Islands*) and *Lichtungen* (1976) (*Clearings*). In her prose she explores a delicate fabric of inner and outer reality, in which fact and fantasy are inextricably interwoven: *Sistiana* (1976), *Der Vater* (1980) (*The Father*), *Wasserbüffel* (1981) (*Water Buffalo*).

Schütz, Helga (born 1937)
East German novelist. Her novels include *Festbeleuchtung* (1973) (*Fairy Lights*), *Jette in Dresden* (1977) and *Julia oder Die Erziehung zum Chorgesang* (1980) (*Julia or Training for Choral Singing*). Each of these books tells the story of a young woman's progress into adulthood within the specific milieu of socialist East Germany. For each character, an important rite of passage is their coming to terms with the recent history of their country – the Third Reich and the post-war division of Germany.

Schuurman (Schurman), Anna Maria van (1607–1678)
Prose writer and poet from the northern Netherlands. The daughter of a nobleman from Antwerp who settled with his family in Utrecht in 1615, she received an excellent education. In an era when the Renaissance adoration of women came into vogue, van Schuurman, with her considerable knowledge of languages and her

artistry, attracted the attention of many people, including Queen Christina of Sweden, and René Descartes (1596–1650). She completed her theology studies in Utrecht, attending lectures in a small room adjacent to the classroom of the male students. Her *Amica dissertatio inter Annam Mariam Schurmanniam et Andr. Rivetum de capacitate ingenii muliebris ad scientias* (1638) (*A Friendly Discourse Between Anna Maria Schurmann and A. Rivetus Concerning the Capacity of Women for Scholarly Pursuits*) is a learned dialogue on the question of whether women are capable of studying the sciences and the arts, and *A Learned Maid*, written in 1641, was translated into English by Clement Barksdale. She devoted herself to Calvinism, and later to Labadism. On her life and theological views she composed in Latin *Eucleria* (1684, Dutch translation *Eucleria of uitkiezing van het beste deel*, 1684) (*Eucleria or Selection of the Best Part*). Apart from poems and letters, she wrote *Paelsteen van den tijt onzes levens* (1639) (*Boundary Stone of Our Lifetime*), and a festive song on the occasion of the inauguration of the University of Utrecht.

Schwaiger, Brigitte (born 1949)
Austrian novelist. After being repeatedly rejected by West German publishers, her first novel, *Wie kommt das Salz ins Meer* (*How does the Salt Get in the Sea*). became an immediate success and was translated into several languages when it appeared in Vienna in 1977. It is the largely autobiographical account of a married woman's struggle for independence, in which traditional middle-class ideas about how women should behave are unmasked as repressive and fascist. Schwaiger's next novel, *Lange Abwesenheit* (1980) (*Prolonged Absence*), is a near-▷psychoanalytical investigation into the author's unresolved relationship with her father. *Schönes Licht* (1990) (*Beautiful Light*) describes a lone woman's desperate search for emotional security.

Schwarz, Sybilla (1621–1638)
German poet. Born during the Thirty Years War (1618–1648), she died at the age of seventeen, but was already the author of a large body of poetic works. Many of her poems revolve around the themes of war, social turmoil and her yearning for the family estate at Fretow, which she was forced to leave. From an early age she wrote poems for family occasions and she was the author of some fine sonnets about friendship, love and death. She often complains about the meanness of people who resent a young woman writing poetry. Her work was published in 1650 in the anthology *Deutsche Poetische Gedichte* (*German Poetic Verses*).

Schwarz-Bart, Simone (born 1938)
This novelist and dramatist of the French Antilles (Caribbean) was born in France, returning with her family to Guadeloupe when she was three. She later studied in France and married the Jewish writer André Schwarz-Bart. Together with her husband, she wrote *Un plat de porc aux bananes vertes* (1967) (*A Dish of Pork With Green Bananas*), which presents the experience of an old woman from Martinique who is ending her life in an institution for the elderly in Paris. Confined with eccentric and sometimes racist people, Mariotte recalls her life in Martinique, especially her grandmother. Some identify Simone's influence in André Schwarz-Bart's recreation of the life of the celebrated maroon (a descendant of fugitive slaves), *La Mulâtresse Solitude* (1972) (*A Woman Named Solitude*, 1988). Best-known for her novel ▷ *The Bridge of Beyond*, Schwarz-Bart has also written ▷ *Between Two Worlds* and a play, ▷ *Ton beau capitaine* (1987) (*Your Fine Captain*). She has successfully created in her work an innovative aesthetic practice, using a creolized language to convey a ▷Creole world-view which incorporates a magical realm that lies beyond empirical reality, and rejoicing in family and island history as a source of nourishment, strength and a sense of permanence and wholeness. Her six-volume *Homage à la Femme Noire* (1989) (*In Praise of Women of Colour*) is a vast celebration of the history and creativity of black women.
▷Identity, Caribbean

Schwarzenbach, Annemarie (1908–1942)
German-speaking Swiss writer. The gifted daughter of a wealthy industrialist family from Zurich, she attracted the attention of many literary figures, Klaus (1906–1949), and Erika Mann (1905–1969), Roger Martin du Gard (1881–1958), André Malraux (1901–1976), and ▷Carson McCullers (1917–1967) among them. She wrote stories, travelogues and novels, but only a few were published, and, in her day, they found no acclaim. A selection of her work is now available in *Eine Frau allein* (1989) (*A Woman Alone*).

Science fiction
▷Mary Shelley's ▷*Frankenstein* (1817) is an early example of science fiction: fiction that uses the concepts or devices of science and technology to make a point about human nature. Or, of course, merely to provide the setting for an adventure story.

For a genre that is overwhelmingly read by men, there are an extraordinary number of good women writers. It is not so surprising that the women who write science fiction novels or short stories tend to pay more attention to character and style than most male sci-fi writers. It is a field that favours 'ideas', or plot gimmicks, above emotional depth or literary values, and many of the most celebrated sci-fi writers, even at its leading edge of the 'New Wave' of the 1960s or 'cyberpunk' in the 1980s, write atrocious dialogue. However, there are female, even feminist writers who have the devices *and* the depth. And they also get the popular acclaim in a genre that is grounded in active fandom. Women writers are well represented among the bestsellers.

'Serious' novelists sometimes wander into sci-fi

(▷Doris Lessing, for example) and popular sci-fi writers sometimes make it to the book reviews (▷Ursula Le Guin has crossed several borders). Sci-fi is only loosely defined by type of plot, and not at all by style or intent. It can be extremely bleak, or end in Utopia. Many sci-fi writers, particularly women, also produce 'sword and sorcery' or magical fantasies, such as Tanith Lee, who also brilliantly reworks fairytales. Although these are distinct genres they are often mistakenly conflated with science fiction.

Short stories are the backbone of serious science fiction, published both in a variety of dedicated magazines and in mixed and single-author anthologies. There are none better than those by 'James Tiptree Jr' (Alice Sheldon) and Ursula Le Guin. Alice Sheldon is particularly interesting for having fooled male critics, who claimed that her stories could only have been written by a man. In fact, she, along with many other women sci-fi writers, uses the genre to make sharp points about women today.

There are anthologies that demonstrate the feminist content in popular sci-fi and the use of sci-fi by feminists. There is a small but dedicated group of feminist readers, publishers and critics in the US and Britain, including the Women's Press science fiction imprint that has reprinted classic novels and encouraged new women writers, and the regular column in *Feminist Bookstore News* by Suzanna Sturgis.

Sci-fi, like any fiction, mostly recycles a limited set of plots. The 'after the apocalypse' plot seems to divide the girls from the boys more than spaceship chases. The best space romps around are by a woman, ▷C.J. Cherryh: though she has written a couple of novels with more profound plots, her raciest is *Downbelow Station*. Space adventures are basically high-tech westerns, but they have been surprisingly egalitarian for many years. Apocalypse novels, on the other hand, aim to say more, and have a nasty tendency towards Hobbesian pessimism and even fascism. Suzy McKee Charnas and Sheri Tepper both make use of and expose the standard assumption that 'men will have to be men' after a nuclear world war, in their rich novels *Walk to the End of the World* and *The Gate to Women's Country*.

Time travel in parallel universes is the plot device to end them all, and the novel to beat them all is ▷Joanna Russ's ▷*The Female Man*. It can be hard to catch if you have never read sci-fi pulp, but it proves that it is worth it. No genre exposes the women we might have been – that is, how we are all created by the social and economic environment in which we live – more effectively.

Other popular women sci-fi writers of note include Mary Gently, Vonda McIntyre, Gwyneth Jones and Octavia Butler. Writers who have made use of the genre include Katharine Burdekin (*Swastika Night*) and ▷Marge Piercy (▷*Woman on the Edge of Time*). There is plenty of academic criticism of science fiction, much of it glorified list-keeping. The magazines, such as *Interzone*, give a more accurate picture of science fiction and

its preoccupations, and these contain a high proportion of women writers.

Italy: Science fiction is still often seen as a marginal genre in literature. Its popularity has militated against its acceptance in academia. It is, in a sense, a variety of ▷*romanzo di consumo*. It has its own conventions, and schemata of possible plots. In the Italian context, it has its roots as far back as 1785 (Bernardo Zamagna, *Navis aerea*), but began to proliferate from the 1950s onwards. Some of its more famous and 'respectable' literary practitioners include Dino Buzzati, Alberto Moravia, Elio Vittorini and Italo Calvino. Women writers have been somewhat slow to adopt the genre, but both ▷Anna Banti and ▷Gilda Musa have produced works of science fiction. Musa is one of the foremost women science fiction writers, and has contributed to, and edited, several collections in Italy. Another prolific producer of science fiction is Anna Rinonapoli.

Scivias (1142–1151) ▷*Know the ways* (1986)

Scotland

In 1930 Glasgow-born novelist and critic Catherine Carswell unleashed the first biography of poet Robert Burns (1759–1796) that cracked the veneer of indulgent myth. Hers was an unsentimental, honest, carefully researched – and rather more realistic – view of the poet's famed drinking and womanizing. The work caused widespread uproar. Mrs Carswell received a bullet through the post from someone who signed himself 'Holy Wullie' and urged her to 'leave the world a better and cleaner place' by putting said bullet to prompt use.

In 1990 the Motherwell-born poet and dramatist ▷Liz Lochhead collaborated with a company called Communicado to create *The Last Burnt Supper*, a piece of music-dance-theatre in which she used the continuing (mostly male) idolatry of Burns as a way of probing unhappy aspects of Scottish national identity, male–female relationships and the whole sorry business of drinking to keep the truth at bay. Fierce, searching and discomfiting stuff – as one has come to expect from this writer. No bullets came Liz Lochhead's way. Times have changed. We are, by force of tabloid and television, more ready to be entertained by exposés of our folk heroes' grubbier moments.

The truly splendid thing, though, is what *hasn't* changed – the provocative, far-reaching and intellectually astute essence of these, and many other, Scottish women writers who seize with sensitive fingers the most profound issues of humanity and sift them into all genres of fiction.

A cursory glance back, to the 19th century and beyond, to the end of the 18th, confirms this vital female undertow in Scottish literature. As the punitive edge wore off English memories of Jacobite insurrection north of the border, Scotland took on a fashionable romantic appeal for the nation's literati and glitterati. Much of what jigged into print was tarted-up tartan fantasy, but there were writers – among them Anne Grant and Elizabeth Hamilton – who drew realistic, shrewdly-observed pictures of the Highland way of life, while poet and dramatist ▷Joanna Baillie won respect for her attempts to restore the dramatic grandeur of true tragedy in plays like *The Family Legend* (about the Argyles). Novelist ▷Susan Ferrier looked more to a combination of humorous satire and moral statement in her sharp appraisals of contemporary society, using – as would later 19th-century writers like ▷Margaret Oliphant and ▷Lucy Walford – the business of matrimony and social aspiration to explore wider issues of principle. Violet Jacob, Sarah Tytler (despite having to write pulp fiction for a living), Mary Brunton and ▷Catherine Sinclair, all produced work that, whatever stylistic label was attached to it then, retains an attractive individuality even now.

Two particular 'tags' adhere to Scottish writing this century: 'kailyard', which slicks over the early decades with connotations of mawkish sentimentality, village worthies and country idylls, and the subsequent 'Scottish Renaissance' (led by poet Hugh MacDiarmid, 1892–1978) which, by the 1930s, had fired several writers to embrace the vernacular.

Most anthologies, indeed most critical assessments of these periods, tend to give the impression that no women of any real merit were writing in Scotland. And with so little of their output still in print, the old unworthy suspicion that women produced 'soft' work of no enduring value persisted.

In the early 1900s the Findlater sisters, Jane and Mary, produced (separately and together) novels and short stories which might have had their roots in the kailyard compost of rural communities and manners, but mostly avoided the slurp of tendentious sentimentality. Rather, they had about them that shrug of irony, that magpie observation which translates the ramshackle nature of insignificant little lives into meaningful words. And four years before Lewis Grassic Gibbon's (1901–1935) celebrated *Sunset Song* (1932) came into print, Nan Shepherd's *The Quarry Wood* (1928) traced, with wry and humane insights, a young woman's journey to an independence beyond the narrow confines of her Aberdeenshire village. Her novels were published, to great critical acclaim, on both sides of the Atlantic. Now – unlike Grassic Gibbon's trilogy – they are largely and unfairly forgotten.

Some Scottish women writers have, however, managed to ride out the tides of literary fashion and are still being read – and producing new work – today. ▷Naomi Mitchison is one, Elspeth Davie (born 1919) another. Born in Edinburgh in 1897, Naomi Mitchison first started writing in the 1920s. Since then she has produced over 70 books, and her creativity has embraced biography, poetry, travellers' tales and fiction. Her fiction often has a historical setting, an approach that – as in her novel about the Celts, *The Conquered*

(1923) – anticipated similarly imaginative reconstructions from later writers such as Neil Gunn and Eric Linklater. Mitchison's lively intellect, her deep hatred of oppression, and her informed zest for people and places as far apart as Orkney and Botswana have won her not just a loyal readership but the respect of fellow writers and leading political figures. She is now very much a *grande dame* of the Scottish literary scene.

The past thirty years have seen Elspeth Davie establishing herself as one of Scotland's finest novelists and short story writers. A quick glance at her work suggests that it is Edinburgh which is her most frequent central character, for she is adept at conjuring up the many faces of the city, from New Town elegance to the squalor and sprawl of modern housing schemes. But this atmospheric description is there as an adjunct to her characters, a vital context for the vulnerabilities that render their ordinary lives so fraught with complexities. Her most effective tales have a deceptive simplicity, a way of shimmering from reality into fantasy, as she explores the disquieting ways in which change overtakes people. She can ambush readers with a sudden sense of intimacy, as if they had become eavesdroppers between the lines.

For women writers, old and new, the 1980s offered something of a turning point. Theatre groups, television producers and publishers began delving after neglected native talents: there was a welcome revival of interest in the work of dramatist Ena Lamont Stewart (whose drama of tenement poverty, *Men Should Weep*, was taken to London in 1948) as well as in the novels of Jessie Kesson and others, who depicted – often from firsthand experience – the harshness and resilient humours of town and country poverty. Suddenly, after decades of near silence, the women's voice was heard again. Not corralled on the level of cosy pot-boiler fictions, not from the distant reaches of another country (▷Muriel Spark is one of the more famous expatriates) but clearly and forcefully demanding to be taken seriously.

Alongside the resurrected were a host of keen new pens. Janice Galloway is one. Her first novel, *The Trick is to Keep Breathing* (1990), and a subsequent collection of short stories, *Blood* (1991), have head-butted critics with their passion, assurance and willingness to experiment with form. She likes to go inside the heads of her characters, find out how memory or skewed perceptions knock folk out of kilter, perhaps even into mental institutions, an event common in many lives now. There are promising first showings too, from A.L. Kennedy (*Night Geometry* and *The Garscadden Trains*), novelist Bess Ross (*Those Other Times*) and poet ▷Jackie Kay, whose collection, *The Adoption Papers*, gives brave and uncloying expression to moments of acute pain, uncertainty and fragile motion. Like the women who, in the early years of the 20th century, brought particular understanding to the daily drudge and aspirations of their times, these writers are in tune with the dilemmas of our age, and have the words and the vision to confront them, and the reader.

▷Douglas, O.; Duffy, Carol Ann; Fell, Alison; Mackay, Shena; McDermid, Val; Storm, Lesley; Sulter, Maud; Tey, Josephine

Scott, Gail

Canadian feminist theorist, essayist and fiction writer. Born in Ottawa, and now living in Montreal, Scott grew up bilingually. She worked as a journalist, writing on Quebec culture and politics. *Spare Parts* (1981) is a collection of five stories tracing a woman's development from puberty to maturity in the 1960s. Her densely textured writing concerns itself with political and personal passage; the novel *Heroine* (1987) is 'desire inscribed in the city'. Her essays, collected in *Spaces Like Stairs* (1989), are semiotically sophisticated explorations of feminism and textuality. She was one of the founding editors of ▷*Tessera*.

▷Mouré, Erin

Bib: Neuman, S. and Kamboureli, S. (eds), ▷*A Mazing Space*; Godard, B., *Border/lines*.

Scott, Mary (Taylor) (1752–1793)

English poet. She lived in the same house as ▷Elizabeth Rowe in Somerset, and who knew ▷Anna Seward. She wrote in favour of women's education. In *The Female Advocate* (designed as a sequel to John Duncombe's *Feminiad*) she praises past and contemporary women writers, saying of ▷Sarah Fielding, "Twas *Fielding's* talent, with ingenious Art, / To trace the secret mazes of the Heart', and of ▷Anne Killigrew 'in thee . . . we find / The Poet's and the Painter's arts combin'd'. In the same text she reserves a special place for ▷Lady Mary Chudleigh, who had the courage to assert that women were naturally equal to men and to 'plead thy hapless injured sex's cause'. She married John Scott in 1788, when her mother died. In the same year she published *The Messiah*, and she also wrote hymns. Her son founded the Manchester *Guardian*.

▷Astell, Mary; Duncombe, Susanna; Williams, Helen Maria

Scott, Mary Edith (1888–1979)

New Zealand novelist. Mary Scott's father died when she was a baby, and she was brought up, with her brother and sister, by her mother and grandparents in Napier, New Zealand. Scott claims of her childhood that she 'ran rather wild'; she certainly experienced more freedom than was conventional for young women. She gained a first class degree in English, and was the first woman to climb the mountain range Remarkables, before she married and went to live on a remote high-country farm in the North Island. Scott wrote occasionally while working on the farm and raising children, but in 1951 she was persuaded to write a novel, and *Breakfast at Six*, an autobiographical fiction, was published in 1952. Before she died in 1979 she published twenty-six novels, plus five detective stories co-written with Joyce West.

Scott's novels are for the most part rural romances, but are distinguished from more mechanical forms of ▷romance narrative by their attention to the realistic detail of farm living, family life, and their ironic treatment of romance stereotype. Immensely popular in their time, Scott's novels are still read as a record of Depression farming.

Publications: (a selective list): *Breakfast at Six* (1952); *Yours to Oblige* (1954); *Pippa in Paradise* (1955); *Families are Fun* (1956); *Dinner Doesn't Matter* (1957); *One of the Family* (1958); *The Unwritten Book* (1957); *Days That Have Been* (autobiography) (1966).

Scott, Rosie

New Zealand fiction writer. Rosie Scott began publishing occasional stories in the 1970s, focused on an itinerant, culturally specific (rock, drugs, sexual freedom) generation in which women were isolated, exploited and disadvantaged. Her novel *Glory Days* (1987) reflects the same environment, but is updated to the 1980s and features a central female character whose unconventionality is an expression of power and resistance to social forces. Scott currently lives and works in Australia, and her most recent collection, *Queen of Love and Other Stories*, was published in 1989.

Scott, Sarah (Robinson) (1732–1795)

English novelist, writer of utopias and historian. She was the sister and correspondent of ▷Elizabeth Montagu, the ▷Bluestocking. She wrote for money after leaving her husband (whom she had married in 1751) and moved with Barbara Montagu to launch a female community at Bath Easton, where they taught poor children. They lived here from 1754 to 1756. Scott wrote six novels, but her well-known *Description of Millenium Hall* (1762) uses this idea of a woman's community. This secular separatist community based around rational virtues provided at least one answer to the unstable social and economic place of the unmarried or – particularly – separated woman. The novel opens with a man whose coach has broken down in Cornwall impressed by the rational yet pleasurable employments of the women. He first sees them engaged in their rational pursuits: 'in the bow [window] sat two ladies reading, with pen, ink and paper on a table before them, at which was a young girl translating out of the French.'

Other publications: *The History of Cornelia* (1750); *A Journey Through Every Stage in LIfe* (1754); *Agreeable Ugliness, or the Triumph of the Graces* (1754); *Sir George Ellison* (1766), and *The Test of Filial Duty* (1772).

Scudéry, Madeleine de (1607–1701)

French writer of epic novels, *nouvelles* (short fiction), letters and occasional verse, and a notable *précieuse* (▷Precious Women). In her youth, she frequented the *Chambre bleue*, the salon of the Marquise de Rambouillet (1588–1665), with her brother, the dramatist and Academician Georges de Scudéry (1601–1667). Madeleine lived with her brother in Paris and Marseille until his marriage to Marie-Madeleine du Moncel de Martinval in 1654, writing a series of *romans-à-clé*, set in exotic locations; the characters, though in disguise, could easily be identified from among their friends and acquaintances. Although mercilessly mocked by the writers Charles Sorel (c 1600–1674), Jacques-Bénigne Bossuet (1627–1704) and others, these novels were of great importance for raising the status of women and fiction.

Ibrahim, ou l'illustre Bassa (1641) contains one of the few theoretical prefaces to be written by a novelist in the 17th century. It seeks to give fiction classical antecedents, by aligning the novel with the epic poem and identifying history as the mainstay of *vraisemblance* (verisimilitude) in the novel. The success of this four-volume novel encouraged Madeleine de Scudéry to use wider canvases for her next two novels, *Artamène, ou le Grand Cyrus* (1649–1653, translated as ▷*Artamenes, or The Grand Cyrus*, 1653–1655), which contained a *mise en abyme* of the Hôtel de Rambouillet and her own *samedis* (Saturday *salons*) at the rue de Beauce in Paris, and *Clélie, histoire romaine* (1654–1660, translated as ▷*Clelia: An excellent new romance*, 1661). Both these novels also appeared under Georges de Scudéry's name, though there is a marked change of tone after their separation at the end of volume 2 of *Clélie*, which is the most 'feminist' of Madeleine de Scudéry's writings and includes the celebrated ▷'*Carte de Tendre*', an allegorical map of love. Known as the 'incomparable ▷Sappho', Madeleine de Scudéry was noted for her intellect and learning even among the most respected scholars of her day, though her lack of Latin and Greek meant that she could not consult the many classical historians on whom she loosely based her fiction in the original. Despite the innumerable anachronisms in her novels, she may be regarded as the 'mother of the historical novel in France'. She also wrote *Les Femmes illustres, ou les Harangues héroïques* (*The Illustrious Women, or The Heroic Speeches*), *Célinte, nouvelle première* (1661), *Mathilde d'Aguilar* (1667) and *Célanire* (1669), which includes *La Promenade de Versailles*.

In 1657, Mademoiselle de Scudéry received a pension from the superintendent of finances, Nicolas Fouquet (1615–1680), to whom she remained a loyal friend. Among her other benefactors were the First Minister, Mazarin (1602–1661), Queen Christina of Sweden (1626–1689) and Louis XIV (1638–1715), though she always had difficulty making ends meet. Madeleine de Scudéry was elected to the Academy of the Ricovrati in 1684 and is said to have been the first woman to have been considered for election to the French Academy. Her ugliness was frequently remarked upon. She admits to having received three proposals of marriage, but, in keeping with the theory of *amitié tendre* (loving friendship) developed in her novels, she refused even to marry the Academician Paul

Pellisson (1624–1693), who was devoted to her. A series of influential selections from the dialogues in her novels was published during the 1680s.

Bib: Tallemant des Réaux, *Historiettes*; Aronson, N., *Mademoiselle de Scudéry*.

Scudéry, Marie-Madeleine du Moncel de Martinval (1627–1711)

French correspondent and co-author of a novel. She helped her husband, the dramatic poet Georges de Scudéry (1601–1667), to write the novel *Almahide, ou l'esclave reine* (1661–1663) (*Almahida, or The Slave Queen*) and is noted for her cultivated correspondence with, among others, the exiled writer Roger de Bussy-Rabutin (1618–1693). The main theme of her letters is the value of friendship. She appears in Somaize's *Dictionnaire des Précieuses* (1659) (*Dictionary of the Precious Women*) under the ▷pseudonym Sarraïde, as '*[l]' une des plus grandes précieuses du royaume*', ('one of the greatest *précieuses* of the realm') (▷Precious Women). The memoir-writer Tallemant des Réaux (1619–1692) portrays her as a romantic woman yearning to work on a novel, and who married late in life under the mistaken illusion that Georges de Scudéry had written the great novels published under his name. Of her relationship with her husband, Tallemant writes: '*leur mariage s'est plustost fait et lié par leurs escrits que par les noeuds ordinaires, car leurs inclinations ne sont venues que de la sympathie de leur style, qui, du moins a précédé leur hymen*' ('their marriage was made in their writings rather than in the normal way, for their mutual inclination was a question of the similarities in their style of writing which came before their wedding'). It was generally felt that her prose was better than his verse, and her letters have recently been reappraised.

▷Scudéry, Madeleine de

Bib: Tallemant des Réaux, *Historiettes*; Mesnard, J., 'Mme de Scudéry', *Actes de Caen* (1980).

Scuola normale femminile (1885) (A Girls' School)

A short story set in a teacher-training school for young women, of the type attended by the Italian author, ▷Matilde Serao. It is narrated in a style which mixes ▷realist and ▷sentimental elements. It draws attention to inadequate teaching and an inadequate curriculum. It is primarily, however, an analysis of passionate adolescent alliances, vividly told. The story also highlights the precarious future of women teachers, their linguistic and geographical isolation when moved far away from home, as was the practice, and their position as easy sexual prey for powerful men in whatever new community they were moved to.

Seacole, Mary (1805–1881)

This Caribbean writer, the daughter of a free black mother and a Scottish soldier father, was born into the mulatto society of ▷Jamaica. Well-educated, she became a businesswoman, a nurse, a doctor, a traveller, an adventurer and a Crimean War heroine. She lived her last years in Britain, and played a crucial role in opening up the medical and nursing professions to women. Known as 'the black Florence Nightingale', she received national recognition for her nursing from Queen Victoria and Lord Palmerston. Her ▷autobiography, ▷*The Wonderful Adventures of Mrs Seacole in Many Lands* was published in 1857. Sadly, Seacole's 19th-century fame was transformed into 20th-century obscurity. As a result of efforts made by black women's organizations to restore Seacole's past recognition, her autobiography was reprinted in 1984.

Her literary skills reveal her as a keen observer of life about her; she gives a remarkable insight into the spirit of early Caribbean women, and adds to our understanding of this era of history. For further information, see Ziggi Alexander and Audrey Dewjee's introduction to the 1984 edition of *The Adventures of Mrs Seacole.*

Seal Press

US publisher. Seal was co-founded by ▷Barbara Wilson and Rachel da Silva in 1976. Located in Seattle, Washington, it initially showcased North-western women poets. In 1979 Seal earned national attention when it reprinted Louise Strong's autobiography, *I Change Worlds.* In 1982 Seal published and marketed Ginny NiCarthy's *Getting Free: A Handbook for Women in Abusive Relationships.* This launched Seal's series of self-help books to empower victims of domestic violence.

In 1984 Seal received a grant from the Norwegian government. It began publishing English translations of Norwegian women's fiction, and this launched Seal's Women in Translation Series which includes works from Egypt, Korea, Japan and the Soviet Union. Seal publishes a variety of voices, including those of sex-trade workers; its only criterion is that a book describes female experience.

Other titles include: *A Vindication of the Rights of Whores* (ed. Gail Peterson, 1989), *Hard-Hatted Women* (ed. Molly Martin, 1988), *Ceremonies of the Heart: Celebrating Lesbian Unions* (ed. Beckey Butler, 1990) and *The Black Women's Health Book.*

Season in Rihata, A (1988)

Translation by Richard Philcox of the novel by the French Antilles writer ▷Maryse Condé, *Une Saison à Rihata* (1981). In this work, Marie-Hélène, the Antillean protagonist, is drawn towards Africa even before she meets her African husband, Zek. Disappointed by the departure of a previous lover for Haiti, Marie-Hélène marries Zek to avoid having to return to Guadeloupe. Viewed with suspicion as a foreigner by Zek's family, Marie-Hélène has an affair with his younger brother, Madou. This illicit union has already been discovered by the family when the novel begins, and Zek has moved his family from the capital city (where Madou soon becomes a minister) to the small town of Rihata. Like Condé's first novel. ▷*Heremakhonon, A Season in Rihata* portrays an Antillean woman's problematic

relation with an Africa which does not correspond to that idealized by some proponents of the ▷*négritude* movement.

Sea Wall, The (1986)

Translation of *Un barrage contre le Pacifique* (1950), fourth novel of French writer ▷Marguerite Duras. It draws on her experience of growing up in a comparatively poor family in Indo-China, and tells the story of Suzanne. Suzanne lives on an infertile plain with her hot-tempered mother and her beloved, though laconic, brother, Joseph, and she dreams of the man who will come to take her to a new life. She is wooed by a rich but unprepossessing and stupid young man, M. Jo, but in the end it is with Joseph and his girlfriend that she leaves, following their mother's death. The novel is critical of the corrupt colonial administration which has contributed to, among other things, the family's poverty and the state of virtual prostitution to which Suzanne is reduced.

Sebbar, Leila (born 1941)

Algerian novelist. Born in Aflou to an Algerian father and a French mother. She left Algeria for Paris at the age of seventeen, and regularly writes in a number of magazines, notably *Les Temps modernes* and *Sans frontières.* She has written a couple of critical essays on the conditions of Algerian women. Her novels include: *Fatima ou les Algériennes au square* (1981) (*Fatima, or the Algerians in the public gardens*), ▷*Shérazade* (1982), *Parle, mon fils, parle à ta mère* (1984) (*Speak, my son, Speak to your Mother*), and *Les Carnets de Shérazade* (1985) (*Shérazade's Notebooks*). Her writing is concerned with the condition of women, notably immigrant Algerian women in France.

Seconde, La (1929) ▷Other One, The (1960)

Second Sex, The (1953)

Translation of *Le Deuxième Sexe* (1949), by French writer ▷Simone de Beauvoir. Possibly the most famous work on women written in the 20th century, de Beauvoir's *The Second Sex* is centrally informed by the author's Existentialist philosophy. Women, in this study, are ▷'the other', the sex defined by men and ▷patriarchy as *not* male, and consequently as less than fully human. De Beauvoir states in the book that 'one is not born a woman; one becomes one', and her study attempts to demonstrate the way in which women internalize negative assumptions about themselves (including their 'naturally' subordinate status).

Although de Beauvoir's book attempts to avoid essentialist ideas about women and men, much of the discussion (particularly about biology) comes very close to the endorsement of 'natural' differences between the sexes. The material on misogyny in myth and literature has been extremely influential (see, for example, ▷Kate Millett's *Sexual Politics*), but recent authors have questioned de Beauvoir's assumption of the male as the norm.

Bib: Walters, Margaret, 'The Rights and Wrongs

of Women: Mary Wollstonecraft, Harriet Martineau, Simone de Beauvoir' in, Oakley A. and Mitchell, J. (eds), *The Rights and Wrongs of Women.*

Secret Garden, The (1911)

Children's novel by Anglo-American writer ▷Frances Hodgson Burnett. This children's 'classic' tells the story of orphaned Mary, who is sent to stay with her reclusive uncle in Yorkshire when her parents die. She is coaxed out of her miserable self-absorption by Dickon, the housemaid's twelve-year-old brother. By teaching Mary about the animals and plants around her, and tending with her a neglected walled garden, Dickon helps restore her to health and happiness.

Mary accidentally discovers the existence of her invalid cousin, Colin, whose presence had been kept secret from her. Colin is disliked and ignored by his father, who cannot bear to see the likeness of his dead wife in the boy. Mary and Dickon interest Colin in nature and the secret garden, and, like Mary, he gains strength and appetite. Colin overcomes his fear of death, and his recovery prompts his father to accept the death of his wife.

The Secret Garden could be described as a pastoral, in that civilization, represented by the higher social classes to which Colin and Mary belong, is seen as unnatural and corrupting. The working classes, like Dickon and his family, are portrayed as existing in a simpler, happier world, closer to life-giving nature. Childhood, too, is allied with nature, in that Mary's and Colin's relinquishing of 'adult' introversion is mirrored by the dead garden's spring blossoming.

The Secret Garden was dramatized on BBC television in the 1970s.

Sedgwick, Catharine Maria (1789–1867)

US popular novelist. Author of *A New-England Tale* (1822) – considered to be the first example of the ▷woman's fiction genre – and of the bestselling ▷*Hope Leslie*, Sedgwick was an innovator, incorporating in her novels many distinctively US elements. She was among the first to use native settings, dialect, characteristic regional types, ▷local color and realistic description. Her plots tend to focus on young women, often orphans, who must make their own way because of neglect and mistreatment. While her heroines often show remarkable independence of action and thought, for most, the ultimate goal and success is happy domestic life. Among the leading novelists of her day, Sedgwick sold well, associated with prestigious literary circles, and became increasingly involved in reform movements and didactic writing, especially for children. Other novels include: *Redwood* (1824), *Clarence* (1830), *The Linwoods* (1835), *Live and Let Live* (1837) and *Married or Single?* (1857), a defence of single life.

Seduzioni, Le (1909) (Seductions)

A collection of Italian poetry by ▷Amalia Guglielminetti. Written in confessional format, these poems provide a portrait of a modern woman who rejects social restrictions and insists on obeying only her own impulses. There are echoes of ▷D'Annunzianesimo here.

Ségalas, Anaïs (1814–1895)

French poet and dramatist. A poet whose work is considered excessively sentimental by many critics, Ségalas's verse was very popular with her contemporaries. She published various collections of poems: *Les Algériennes* (1831) (*Algerian Women*) (which was inspired by the poetry of Victor Hugo; *Oiseaux de passage* (1836) (*Birds of Passage*), and *La Femme* (1848) (*Woman*), which was her most famous work. Despite the title of the latter, Ségalas was no radical feminist. She declared in her preface that she did not intend to exchange her shawl for a revolutionary flag, and that a woman's place was in the home, where she could indulge in 'poetic reveries' and 'élans towards the infinite', while men went about the important but infinitely less spiritual business of running the world. She also wrote short stories, novels and plays, which were performed at the Comédie Française and were well-received.

▷Feminine/feminist journalism (France)

Seghers, Anna (1900–1983)

Pen-name of German novelist, essayist and short-story writer Netty Reiling. She came from a cultured Jewish family, studied art history, and wrote her doctoral thesis on *Aspects of Jews and Jewishness in the Work of Rembrandt*. In 1928 she joined the Communist Party, and in the same year gained public acclaim and a literary prize with her novella, *Der Aufstand der Fischer von St Barbara* (*The Insurrection of the Fishermen of St Barbara*), a story which tells of the spontaneous insurrection of Breton fishermen against their exploitative employers. When Hitler came to power in 1933 her writings were prohibited and she was briefly arrested. She fled to France and lived there amongst other German exiles until the invasion of northern France in 1940, whereupon she made her way to Marseilles, and eventually settled in Mexico.

After World War II she returned to East Germany to play a key role in the cultural development of the new socialist state. By then she had already achieved international fame with her novel *Das siebte Kreuz* (1942) (*The Seventh Cross*), a gripping story about an escape from a concentration camp (first published in English, and made into a successful Hollywood film starring Spencer Tracy), and the novel *Transit* (1944), about the fate of a group of German refugees in southern France. She spent the last thirty years of her life developing a simpler, terser literary style in accordance with the canon of socialist realism that demands all art work 'in the service of socialism'. In all Seghers's writing, women take an essentially subordinate position to a male hero who is seen as the primary agent for bringing about a new socialist order.

Ségou: les murailles de terre (1984) *Segou: la terre en miettes* (1985) ▷*Segu* and *Segu II: The Children of Segu* (1990)

Segu and Segu II: The Children of Segu (1990)

Translation by Linda Coverdale of the two-volume cycle by the French Antilles writer, ▷Maryse Condé, *Ségou: les murailles de terre* (1984) and *Ségou: la terre en miettes* (1985). A vast tableau which covers 60 to 80 years, many different localities, and numerous major historical and fictional characters, and which incorporates a number of major historical events, this has probably been Condé's greatest commercial success. The two novels soon appeared in translation, and were quickly reissued in French in the accessible '*Livre de poche*' ('pocket book') series. The first of the two volumes opens at the beginning of the 18th century when Segu, capital of the Bambara kingdom of Mali, is at the height of its glory. Little by little Segu loses its grandeur as the protagonists of the two novels, descendants of the Bambara noble, Douiska Traoré, decline in power.

Segun, Mabel (born 1930)

Nigerian short story writer, children's author and poet. One of the older generation of Nigeria's women authors, she started writing as a student at the University of Ibadan and has published since the 1950s. She has been a teacher, a broadcaster and a sportswoman, as well as a writer, and is founder and president of the Children's Literature Association of Nigeria, and a senior research fellow at the Institute of African Studies, University of Ibadan. Her anecdoctal collection *Friends, Nigerians, Countrymen* (1977) is a collection of her radio talks. *Conflict and Other Poems* was published in 1989, and she has written several children's books. She has also contributed to the body of autobiographical writing by African women with her story of childhood, ▷*My Father's Daughter* (1965), and *Ping Pong* (1989), an account of her exploits as an international table tennis champion. She was, in fact, the first Nigerian woman to make a name for herself in the sport, which she began playing in 1946, and has consistently given a lead to other Nigerian sportswomen.
▷Children's Literature (West Africa); Journalism (West Africa)
Bib: Otokunefor, H., and Nwodo O., *Nigerian Female Writers: A Critical Perspective.*

Ségur, Comtesse de (1799–1874)

French children's writer. A Russian émigré like ▷Bashkirtseff, Ségur arrived in Paris in 1815, married four years later, and gave birth to eight children, after which – perhaps unsurprisingly – she led the life of a semi-invalid. Once she recovered her health in 1856, she published her *Nouveaux Contes de fées* (*New Fairytales*). This was followed by a long series of tales which were very popular with several generations of children, and

which are contained, together with the three volumes of religious instruction she wrote, in her twenty-volume *Oeuvres complètes* (*Complete Works*). These stories, the most famous of which is undoubtedly *Les Malheurs de Sophie* (*The Misfortunes of Sophie*), are of interest to today's adult readers, if not to today's children, because of the multi-faceted social tableau they offer us. Although she began by depicting only the children of the aristocracy, Ségur introduced characters from other social classes into her novels after 1862 and, while no socialist, portrayed with honesty the difficult existence led by the Parisian working class. Her writings represent a valuable historical testament to the nature of French life during the Second Empire.
Bib: Guérande, P., *Le Petit Monde de la comtesse de Ségur*; de Hédouville, M., *La Comtesse de Ségur et les siens.*

Seidel, Ina (1885–1974)

German poet and novelist. A devout Protestant, she initially wrote lyrical poetry on religious themes, and later composed compassionate verses, prompted by the events of World War I: *Neben der Trommel her* (1915) (*Alongside the Drum*). Her novels became as popular as her poetry, especially during the Third Reich. She achieved her greatest success with *Wunschkind* (1930) (*Wish-child*), a novel set during the Napoleonic Wars, which tells of the relationship between a boy and his mother, a war widow, who senses that her son too will die in battle. Seidel was an enthusiastic supporter of Hitler, yet her novel *Lennacker* (1938) came to be understood as a critique of German fascism. In a sequence of twelve dreams, dreamt by a soldier returning from war, the book tells the story of twelve generations of a Saxon pastor's family. It illustrates the profound changes undergone by German Protestantism. Her last novel, *Michaela* (1959), deals with the guilt of Christian, middle-class Germans who had supported Hitler.

Seifúllina, Lidiia Nikolaevna (1889–1954)

Russian writer. Born and raised in western Siberia in a family of mixed clerical and peasant background, Seifúllina was a teacher before the Revolution. She was one of the few Russian women to begin writing in the hectic years immediately after the 1918–1920 Civil War, and published her early works in *Siberian Fires*, a still extant journal of which she was a founding editor. In the mid-1920s her hospitable home in ▷Moscow became a Soviet salon for writers. Influenced by the experimental prose of contemporaries like Babel' and Pil'niak, Seifúllina wrote her first story, 'Four Chapters: A Novella in Excerpts', in compressed, staccato rhythms; its theme is the evolution of a woman from actress to revolutionary. 'Lawbreakers' (*New Soviet Literature*, 1934) is the story of a street orphan and his rehabilitation in a children's colony. Other stories from the 1920s – 'Humus', ▷'Virineia', 'Birch Ravine' – combine 'ornamental' expressionistic prose, larded with diction reflecting the speech and world view of her characters and a wide-ranging picture of backwoods Siberia in the grip of the Revolution and its aftermath. 'The Old Woman' (*Azure Cities*, 1929) is a graphic tale of alienation between Russian Orthodox parents and their Bolshevik son. Seifúllina's later fiction is an example of the constraints of ▷socialist realism on a distinctive voice.

Sekulić, Isidora (1877–1958)

Serbian writer of stories, a novel, essays, literary and art criticism, as well as pieces of travel writing and translation. Her lyrical, meditative, introspective, refined, analytical, evocative texts may be seen as marking the beginning of modern Serbian prose and a new sensibility. She is one of the most versatile and substantial figures in Serbian literature between the wars.

Kronika palanačkog groblja (1940) (*The Chronicle of a Provincial Graveyard*) observes the destinies of individuals and families, and includes a story of great psychological subtlety, *Gospa Nola*. This is a portrait of a courageous, proud, determined woman with 'masculine energy', and the wisdom to understand the secrets of the human psyche.

Semestr života (1982) (*A Term of Life*)

Novel by Czech writer Jana Červenková (born 1939). It depicts a young woman's disillusion with socialism, Christianity and the male sex. It constitutes one of the strongest criticisms of socialist society to be published within socialist Czechoslovakia. Like the local priest, the one person to whom she acquires a close affinity, the narrator/heroine remains anonymous. After a series of encounters with the police (or military) authorities, the narrator is forced outside the socialist ideal society for women, and decides to get pregnant. She sets off to hitch-hike to an architect she has met, just to have a child by him, because he seems to be as much of an outsider as herself. She is picked up by a lorry in which the workers of the world unite to rape her. Thus the novel ends.

Semiotics

Semiotics and semiology are terms which tend to be used interchangeably for what the Swiss linguist Ferdinand de Saussure called 'a science that studies the life of signs within society' in *Course in General Linguistics* (1915). The objective of semiology, according to Saussure, is 'to investigate the nature of signs and the laws governing them'. A sign is a unit of meaning, originally linguistic, but in later semiotic studies it can also refer to visual or cultural signs. The Italian semiotician and novelist, Umberto Eco, has suggested that, 'Semiotics is, in principle, the study of anything that can be used to lie.' This suggests the purchase of semiotics on the question of how meaning and 'reality' is constructed. It also suggests the usefulness of semiotics for feminist

theories which address the construction of femininity.

▷Difference; Structuralism; Post-structuralism

Sempronia (1st century BC)

A Roman poet and mother of Fulvia (died 40 BC), the wife of the Roman politician Mark Antony (c 83–30 BC). She was attacked for her loose morals, but praised for her skill at the lyre and in writing poetry.

Senior, Olive (born 1943)

Olive Senior

This Caribbean novelist, poet, dramatist and short story writer is described as one of ▷Jamaica's most 'exciting creative talents'. Her writing explores themes of orality rather than literacy. One of ten children in a poor village family, she was adopted by a member of her mother's family, and spent her childhood moving between rural and urban settings. Educated to secondary level, she became Publications Officer at the University of West Indies Institute of Social and Economic Studies, and worked as editor of *Jamaica Journal*. She is currently working as a freelance writer.

Her first collection of short stories, ▷*Summer Lightning*, won the first Commonwealth Writers Prize in 1987. A collection of her poetry, *Talking of Trees*, was published in 1985, and a collection of short stories, *Amral of the Snake Woman and other stories*, in 1989. Other poetry and short stories were published in *Jamaica Journal*, *Savacou*, and ▷Pamela Mordecai and Mervyn Morris, ▷*Jamaica Woman: An Anthology of Poems*. Her other publications include *The Message is Change* (1972), *A–Z of Jamaican Heritage* (1983) and *Working Miracles* (1989). Her plays include *Down the Road Again* (1968).

Señorina de Silva, Doña Isabel (c 1660–1740)

Spanish dramatist. Sister of ▷ Sor Maria do Ceo. Her only extant work is the play *Los celos abren los cielos* (*Jealousy Opens up the Heavens*), which is in manuscript form.

Sensation, Novel of

A genre that emerged in Britain from about 1860, influenced by ▷ Gothic literature and characterized by extravagant, passionate and sometimes horrific events. It is often considered the precursor of the modern thriller. Sensation novels were extremely popular with the reading public and formed a large part of the stock of ▷ circulating libraries. Examples of the genre include ▷ Mary Braddon's ▷ *Lady Audley's Secret* (1862); ▷ Mrs Henry Wood's ▷ *East Lynne* (1861) and ▷ Rhoda Broughton's ▷ *Cometh Up as a Flower* (1867). In *A Literature of Their Own*, ▷ Elaine Showalter argues that sensation novels form a significant part of the tradition of 19th-century women's writing. Novelists such as Mary Braddon subverted the stereotype of the 'blonde angel'; others brought a wide range of suppressed female emotions to the surface of their texts and constructed powerful fantasies of escape and protest.

▷ Corelli, Marie; Gothic

Bib: Hughes, W., *The Maniac in the Cellar: Sensation Novels of the 1860s*.

Sense and Sensibility (1811)

A novel by English author ▷ Jane Austen. The two principal characters, Elinor and Marianne Dashwood, live with their mother and younger sister in comparative poverty, their father having died. The sisters are opposed in temperament: Elinor is practical and self-controlled, Marianne emotional and demonstrative. In the course of the narrative Marianne falls desperately in love with John Willoughby, who betrays her after encouraging her affections. Marianne's misreading of Willoughby's character is symbolic of an epistemological shortcoming: a determination to see experience through the veil of 'sensibility'. When her assessment of Willoughby's personality is questioned so, too, is her view of the world in general, and her mental stability is shaken. Elinor, by contrast, an embodiment of sense, has no such problems. She conceals her distress when she discovers that Edward Ferrers, to whom she is attracted, is already engaged to Lucy Steele. Later, however, Lucy breaks off the engagement and weds Edward's brother, Robert, leaving Elinor and Edward free to marry. Marianne eventually accepts the proposal of an old family friend, Colonel Brandon – a resolution that has been viewed as outrageous. *Sense and Sensibility* is nevertheless one of Austen's most popular novels. An earlier version of the novel, *Elinor and Marianne*, is no longer in existence.

▷ Sentiment and sentimental

Sentiment and sentimental

Sensibility, sentiment and sentimental are terms which belong to 18th-century aesthetics and literature. Sentiment is nevertheless a defining characteristic of much 19th-century British fiction. The Victorian reading public responded to the representation of sympathetic hearts and readily associated virtue with a capacity for copious feeling. There was often a degree of hypocrisy involved, for readers who could weep at the plight of lonely ▷ orphans or destitute children could also condone an economic system that sent seven-year-olds to early deaths in sweatshops. Some writers capitalized on the public's willingness to indulge in sentiment and used it to generate a sympathetic response to a controversial issue. An example of this is ▷ Elizabeth Gaskell's portrayal of the ▷ 'fallen woman' in ▷ *Ruth*. In poetry, the term 'sentimental' is applied to verse preoccupied with the expression of emotion, love and affection. Women poets such as ▷ Felicia Hemans, ▷ Eliza Cook and ▷ Adelaide Procter worked within the conventions of sentimental poetry, yet used them to articulate women's experience in ways which challenged traditional conceptions of gender relations.

▷ Aguilar, Grace; Ewing, Juliana Horatia; Cook, Eliza; Craik, Dinah Mulock; Realism (19th-century Britain)

Seranus ▷ Harrison, Susie Frances

Serao, Matilde (1856–1927)

Italian novelist, short story writer and journalist. Born in Naples, she lived there for most of her life, except for a short sojourn in Rome. She trained as a teacher, and worked in a telegraph office. Both of these experiences provided material for her fiction in ▷ *Scuola normale femminile* (*A Girls' School*) and '*Telegrafi dello stato*' ('State Telegraphs'), respectively. She worked as a journalist throughout her life, running newpapers with her husband, Edoardo Scarfoglio, in both Rome and Naples. When she left her husband, she went on to run her own paper. She was a prolific writer of fiction, covering a range of literary styles. Her ▷ romantic/▷ sentimental novels (such as *Fantasia*, 1883 ▷ *Fantasy*, in English 1890, and *Addio, Amore!*, 1890, ▷ *Farewell, Love!*, 1892 and 1894 in English) are unusual in their negative presentation of the romantic heterosexual relationship, coupled with Serao's positive evaluation of female ties. Her ▷ realist novels, in the manner of *Il paese di cuccagna* (1891) (▷ *The Land of Cockayne*, 1901 in English) and *Mors tua* (1926) (▷ *The Harvest*, 1928 in English), centre particularly on women's experience of poverty and war. In her ▷ Gothic works, for example *La mano tagliata* (1912) (▷ *The Severed Hand*, 1925 in English), she creates strong female characters, through whom she investigates the nature of female identity. She was always concerned to reflect women's position in her writing, and was a selfconscious woman writer,

though she often appeared anti-feminist in her
▷journalism. Of the writers of this period, she
was the most frequently translated into English.

Her other works include: *Cuore infermo* (1881)
(*The Ailing Heart*); *La virtù di Checchina* (1884)
(*Checchina's Virtue*); *Il ventre di Napoli* (1884) (*The
Belly of Naples*); *La conquista di Roma* (1885) (*The
Conquest of Rome*, in English 1902, 1906); *La
donna dall'abito nero* (1892) (*The Woman in the
Black Dress*, in English 1991); *Storia di una monaca
1898* (*A Nun's Story*); *La ballerina* (1899) (*The
Ballet Dancer*, in English 1901); *L'anima semplice:
Suor Giovanna della Croce* (1901) (*A Simple Soul:
Sister John of the Cross*); *Dopo il perdono* (1906)
(*After the Pardon*, in English 1909); *Evviva la vita*
(1909) (*The Desire of Life*, in English 1911); *Ella
non rispose* (1914) (*Souls Divided*, in English 1916).
Bib: Fanning, U., 'Sentimental Subversion:
Representations of Female Friendship in the
Work of Matilde Serao', *Annali d'Italianistica*, 7
(1989), pp. 273–87; Tench, D., 'Gutting the Belly
of Naples: Metaphor, Metonymy and the
Ausculatory Imperative in Serao's City of Pietà',
Annali d'Italianistica, 7 (1989) pp. 287–300.

Serious Proposal to the Ladies, A (1697)
Two-part tract by English writer ▷Mary Astell. It
suggests ways to improve the lot of women in
society. Both parts were published in 1697. Astell
recommended that women retire for varying
periods into all-women communities. Retirement
would, she suggested, 'improve your Charms and
heighten your Value, by suffering you no longer to
be cheap and contemptible'. The social value of
retirement and the autonomy it could give women
were inextricably bound up with the terrible
economic position of women in 17th and 18th
centuries, excluded from the more profitable parts
of the capitalist economy, and always dependent.
However, Astell's own scheme demands that
women have money and the institution would
produce 'Ladies of Quality . . . able to distinguish
themselves from their Inferiors, by the blessings
they communicated and the good they did'.
▷Scott,Sarah.

Sermons Upon the Sonne of Ezechias made after he had bene sicke and afflicted by the hand of God (1560)
▷Translation of French religious reformer John
Calvin's (1509–1604) sermons by English writer
▷Anne Locke. Locke completed her translation
sometime between 1557 and 1559, during her
exile in Geneva. She dedicated it to her fellow
Protestant exile, Catherine Bertie. In the eleven-
page dedicatory ▷preface which she composed,
Locke carried out the *Sermons'* theme of spiritual
affliction as sickness by introducing her own work
of translation as medicine for the soul. Likening
Calvin to an apothecary, she presented herself as
putting the compound 'into an Englishe box'
which she presented to her readers.
▷Protestant Reformation

Seroja Masih di Kolam (1968) (The Lily is still in the Pond)
Novel by Malay writer ▷Khalida Adibah binti
Haji Amin. The heroine, Nur Diana, torn
between two very attractive men, one a successful,
Western-educated bureaucrat, the other a student
activist and amateur actor, finally rejects both
when she discovers they have violated her moral
standards by having had sex with other women.
Although a liberated, modern, educated woman,
she is unable to abandon her traditional values;
but her education means she has at least this
choice of not having to rely on men for self-
fulfilment and happiness. This is a typical example
of Amin's literary attitude – frank in opinion yet
subtle in expression, liberal and yet morally
conservative.

Serrahima, Núria (born 1937)
Spanish writer. Born in Barcelona, Serrahima
worked as a journalist and then began to write
fiction. Her first novel appeared at a time when
few women chose to write in Catalan. *Mala guilla*
(1973) (*A Bad Lot*) is a female *Bildungsroman*
depicting a young girl growing up in the Franco
years (1939–75). *L'olor dels nostres cossos* (1982)
(*The Odour of Our Bodies*) is a collection of three
novellas united by feminist themes. Serrahima's
style is fragmentary, nostalgic and evocative.
▷Catalan women's writing

Serrano, Eugenia (born 1918)
Spanish journalist, short-story writer and novelist.
Her main works are: *Retorno a la tierra* (1945)
(*Return to the Earth*); *Chamberí-Club; Perdimos la
primavera* (1953) (*We Lost Springtime*), and *Pista de
baile* (1963) (*Dance Floor*).

Serreau, Geneviève (1915–1981)
French writer. Co-founder of the *Théâtre de
Babylone* which first staged Beckett's *Waiting for
Godot* in 1953, she championed Adamov, Ionesco,
Beckett and Genet in her best-known work,
Histoire du 'Nouveau théâtre' (1966) (*History of the
'New Theatre'*). Her translations introduced Brecht
to France in the 1950s. She published novels and
short stories, among them *Ricercare* (1973) and
Dix-huit mètres cubes de silence (1976) (*Eighteen
Cubic Metres of Silence*), which attempted to tell the
story of the dispossessed, mostly women, while
rejecting ▷*écriture féminine* (*feminine writing*). She
believed feminine writing represented acceptance
of the male construction of a feminine type. She
remained on the margins of the contemporary
literary scene, and achieved fame only through a
play, *Peines de coeur d'une chatte anglaise* (1977)
(*Emotional Troubles of an English Cat*), which she
adapted from Balzac.

Seton, Elizabeth Ann Bayley (1774–1821)
North American memoirist, diarist and letter-
writer. Born in New York City on 28 August
1774, she became the first North American
Catholic saint and established the Sisters of
Charity, the first North American religious order

of women. The ▷*Memoir, Letters and Journal, of Elizabeth Seton* collects public and private renderings of her spiritual journey from the Episcopal faith to a conversion to Catholicism after the death of her husband. Of particular significance is her voluminous exchange of letters with her friend, Julianna Scott; she finds in 'the midst of my perplexities' that Scott affords her the support and encouragement necessary to her conversion and to the establishment of a religious order for women. She was canonized in 1975.

▷Early North American letters

Setouchi Harumi (born 1922)

Japanese novelist, born in Tokushima prefecture. She was divorced because she fell in love with one of her husband's students and started to write a novel. Although *A Girl Student, Chui Ai Rin* won the Shincho Prize for a Magazine with a Small Circulation, its publication was delayed for some years because her subsequent work, *The Core of a Flower* (1957) was considered pornographic. Five years later *Tamura Toshiko* won the first Tamura Toshiko Prize. *The End of Summer* (1962) describes the sexual desire inherent in both men and women. Her masterpieces such as *Tamura Toshiko* and *Beauty in Resistance* are based on women activists and writers in modern Japan. *From Which Place* is her autobiographical novel. She become a priest in 1973 and is now the chief priest at Tendai temple. She is currently president of Tsuruga Women's College.

Seven Little Australians (1894)

Australian novel for adolescents (and adults) by ▷Ethel Turner. In its subject matter and its impact this novel has been compared to ▷Louisa Alcott's ▷*Little Women*. It concerns the Woolcott family: Captain Woolcott, his second wife Esther, and his seven children ranging from the eldest, Meg, to Esther's baby, 'the General'. The family lives at Misrule, a large house on the Parramatta River. The heroine is undoubtedly Judy, who runs away from school, is hidden by the other children, becomes desperately ill and is forgiven by her father. Her death, after she sustains a broken back while saving 'the General' from a falling tree, has deeply affected generations of Australian youngsters. *Seven Little Australians* has gone through many editions, has been translated into several languages, and made into a successful television series.

▷Children's literature (Australia)

Severed Hand, The (1925)

English translation of *La mano tagliata* (1912), a fully-fledged ▷Gothic novel, by Italian writer ▷Matilde Serao, with an incredibly convoluted plot. A tale of abductions, changed names, dualities and shifting identities. It is, however, above all, an investigation of the mother–daughter bond, which is invested with supernatural properties. Traditional Gothic devices are used in revolutionary ways here to probe issues of female identity.

Severed Head, A (1961)

Novel by English writer ▷Iris Murdoch. A novel which explores Freudian accounts of love, psychic development and surrogate/displaced object choices, its analysis is set within a governing quasi-philosophical framework that assesses these ▷psychoanalytic issues in relation to questions of normality, truth, power and free choice. The novel uses the first-person narrative of Martin Lynch-Gibbon, and looks at a series of triangular relationships involving the narrator, his wife Antonia and a number of closely connected friends and relatives. Central to Murdoch's interrogation of 'truth' are the varied treatments and readings of the Medusa, represented here by the sculpted head of the narrator's wife, Antonia. Murdoch's analysis focuses on male sexuality and desire, and particularly the threat of emasculation. This fear of castration is drawn through the narrator's alignment of the ambivalence of desire with feelings associated with his mother: with 'that particular, painful, guilty, thrilling sense of being both stifled and protected with which a return to my old home always afflicted me'.

▷*Bell, The*

Séverine (1855–1929)

▷Pseudonym of French journalist and novelist Caroline Rémy. Born in Paris, she married at sixteen, and was divorced some years later. In 1881 she was presented to the revolutionary socialist writer Jules Vallès, and began an affair with him. She subsequently wrote for Vallès's paper *Le Cri du peuple* (*The Cry of the People*) and took over its direction after his death in 1885. A keen and lifelong campaigner for the rights of the underprivileged, she used *Le Cri* and the other journals for which she wrote in order to solicit funds for the poor. Although her political stance was rather fluctuating and incoherent – she was by turns a socialist, a communist, a Dreyfusarde and an anti-Dreyfusarde (Alfred Drefus, 1859– 1935, was a French army captain imprisoned for treason in 1894; his case divided French opinion until he was pardoned in 1906) – she was a woman of great generosity and was always a philanthropist. Her writings are contained in the published volumes *Pages Rouges* (1893) (*Red Pages*); *Notes d'une Frondeuse* (1894) (*Notes of a Rebel*); *Pages mystiques* (1895) (*Mystical Pages*); *En Marche* (1896) (*On the Move*) and *Vers la lumière – impressions vécues* (1900) (*Towards the Light – Real-life Impressions*).

▷Le Garrec, Evelyne

Sévigné, Marie de Rabutin-Chantal, Marquise de (1626–1696)

French author of numerous letters. The most celebrated European letter-writer, she was the granddaughter of ▷Jeanne de Chantal, who also wrote an important collection of letters. Orphaned and then widowed at an early age, Madame de Sévigné travelled frequently between the family residences at Livry, Les Rochers and Bourbilly, writing letters to those left behind in Paris. A favourite with all her acquaintances, she wrote her first letters to her cousin, the notorious Roger de Bussy-Rabutin (1618–1693), who called her '*les délices du genre humain*' ('the delight of the human race'). Bussy's witty badinage, veering between flirtation and quarrelsomeness, and his own literary ambitions, were undoubtedly a formative influence on Madame de Sévigné's style, though in his very first letters he notes the love of lively detail for which she would become famous. Bussy's exile to Burgundy for the novel in which he had included a vicious literary portrait of the cousin who had spurned his love, as well as many other members of the court of Louis XIV (1638–1715), made communication by letter imperative, but, though the letters where she scolds him are some of the liveliest in all her correspondence, Madame de Sévigné's interest in him waned.

The vast majority of her letters, almost a thousand in all, are addressed to her daughter, ▷Madame de Grignan, after the latter's marriage and removal to Provence. Many theories have been formulated about the nature of the maternal passion expressed in these letters. Although it has been argued that her love was natural and grounded in reality, it has been contended that her amorous discourse to her daughter was the result of a rhetorical impasse. Her language of love has even been regarded as entirely authentic but indicative of a latent lesbianism. It has further been argued that the daughter served merely as pretext, that writing to Madame de Grignan provided Madame de Sévigné with a way into the text. There has been speculation that, in another time and age, Madame de Sévigné might have tried her hand at other literary genres, such as the novel. In her animated picture of Paris life in the 17th century, she produces the kind of illusion that is usually only found in drama. It is difficult to decide to what extent Madame de Sévigné was consciously developing her talents as a writer. Although she showed parts of her correspondence to her circle of acquaintances, she never sought the wider acclaim that publication might bring, and there is little evidence to suggest that she conceived her letters as a collection. It is clear, however, that, as with her cousin and her daughter: '*Lire vos lettres et vous écrire font la première affaire de ma vie*' ('Reading your letters and writing to you are the most important things in my life'). With the exception of eight letters, all the manuscripts of her letters were burnt with her daughter's after the publication of the first partial editions of letters to her daughter by Bussy and his descendants; the letters were burnt on the orders of Madame de Simiane (1674–1737), Madame de Grignan's daughter, who was concerned for the privacy and good name of her mother and grandmother.
Bib: Sévigné, Madame de, *Correspondance*, ed. R. Duchêne; Jensen, K.A., 'Writer and Mother Love: The Letters of Mme de Sévigné', *French Literary Studies*, XVI (1989).

Seward, Anna (1742–1809)

English poet. Known as 'the Swan of Lichfield', she was born and brought up in the historic village of Eyam in Derbyshire, where her father was rector. In 1754 he became Canon of Lichfield, and Anna looked after him there in his old age. She began to write in her mid-thirties, attending ▷Anne Miller's poetry evenings. Her elegies on David Garrick and Captain Cook brought her to public notice. Her novel *Louisa* was published in 1784, and she continued to publish verse, letters and poems in periodicals, including *The Gentlemans Magazine*. She was very well-known in the 1780s, and a formidable (if ridiculed) figure throughout this and the next decade. Her *Poems* was published in 1810. She knew ▷Helen Maria Williams, the ▷Ladies of Llangollen, and ▷Hester Thrale Piozzi.
▷Scott, Mary
Bib: Lonsdale, R., *Eighteenth Century Women Poets*.

Sewell, Anna (1820–1878)

English novelist, born in Yarmouth. She became a semi-invalid at the age of fourteen and thereafter depended upon horses for mobility. Her single novel is the famous children's classic about the life of a horse, *Black Beauty* (1877). This has remained immensely popular since its publication and has run to numerous editions as well as being filmed for the cinema and adapted for television.
▷Children's literature (19th-century Britain)

Sewell, Elizabeth (1815–1906)

British novelist and polemical writer. She was born in Newport on the Isle of Wight and went to school in Bath until recalled home at the age of fifteen. She began to write partly to help the family finances, publishing her first work, *Amy Herbert*, in 1844. A keen supporter of the ▷Oxford Movement, her novels are deeply religious and moral, yet their focus on women's lives has aroused recent feminist interest. Works include: *Laneton Parsonage* (1846); *Margaret Percival* (1847); *Katherine Ashton* (1854); and *Ursula* (1858). Sewell also wrote devotional works, including *Thoughts for Holy Week* (1857) and *A History of the Early Church* (1861), as well as an *Autobiography* (1907).
Bib: Foster, S., *Victorian Women's Fiction: Marriage, Freedom and the Individual*; ▷Showalter, E., *A Literature of Their Own*.

Sexism

A set of attitudes, statements and practices which assert women's physical and intellectual inferiority, often in the same moment that their sexual attractiveness is celebrated. Feminists working on language, such as ▷Dale Spender, have discovered sexism at work in the asymmetries that characterize couples like master and mistress, governer and governess, bachelor and spinster, where the word for women has negative, belittling connotations, while the word for men implies authority and power.

Sexist representations of women in literature written by men have been exposed by ▷Germaine Greer and ▷Kate Millett, among others.

Sexton, Anne (1928–1974)

US poet. Anne Sexton was born in Newton, Massachusetts, to upper-middle-class parents. After her elopement at the age of nineteen, she trained and worked as a model, and later taught creative writing at Boston University, Colgate and Oberlin. Her education as a writer took place at the Boston Center for Adult Education where, in 1957, Sexton attended a poetry workshop at the same time as ▷Maxine Kumin. Her poetry, which was published in journals such as *Harper's Magazine*, *The New Yorker* and *Saturday Review*, provoked controversy. Sexton's poetry provides an extraordinary testament to the relationship between the psyche and art. Begun as an aid to therapy after her first suicide attempt in 1956 aged twenty-eight, her poetry centres, in the words of a line from 'Consorting with Angels', on the 'gender of things'. The 'gender of things', however, for Sexton is inseparable from an Existential drive toward death that her poetry shares with her contemporaries Theodore Roethke (1908–1963), Robert Lowell (1917–1977) and ▷Sylvia Plath. Thus the poems in *To Bedlam and Part Way Back* (1960), *All My Pretty Ones* (1962), and ▷*Live or Die* (1966) reveal an uncomprising negativity at the heart of women's identity by exploring themes of incest, abortion, drug-addiction and madness. Like Plath, Sexton's explorations of the relation between the body and writing also expose the contradictions of maternity, such as in 'In Celebration of My Uterus' from *Love Songs* (1969). Since her suicide in 1974, the relationships between psyche and art, and mothers and daughters that her work probes, have recently returned in the form of her daughter's controversial release of Sexton's therapist's tape-recordings of their sessions together.

Other works include: ▷*Transformations* (1972), *The Book of Folly* (1972), *The Death Notebooks* (1974), *The Awful Rowing Toward God* (1975), *The Wizard's Tears* (1975), *45 Mercy Street* (1976), *Anne Sexton: A Self Portrait in Letters* (1977) and *Words for Dr Y.* (1978).
Bib: McClatchy, J.D. (ed.), *Anne Sexton: The Artists and Her Critics.*

Seymour, Anne ▷*Mortem Margaritas Valesiae*

Seymour, Frances, Countess of Hertford (1669–1754)

English poet, aristocratic patron and correspondent and editor of ▷Elizabeth Singer Rowe. After her first marriage in 1715 to Algernon Seymour, she moved in court circles, and in 1723 became Lady of the Bedchamber to the Princess of Wales. In 1748 she became the Duchess of Somerset on her marriage to the

Duke of Somerset. Her poems were published in anthologies. She was related to ▷Ann Finch.
Bib: Hull, T. (ed.), *Selected Letters* (1778).

Seymour, Jane ▷*Mortem Margaritas Valesiae*

Seymour, Margaret ▷*Mortem Margaritas Valesiae*

Shaginián, Mariètta Sergeevna (1888–1982)

Poet, prose writer, dramatist, and literary critic. Throughout her long life, Shaginián changed literary directions with such regularity that one senses that she never found a niche, or that writing held her interest only so long as it was an untried area. She began her career as a poet; her first collection (1909) shows her to be an able crafter of short musical lyrics. Becoming close to ▷Zinaida Gíppius and her husband Dmitrii Merezhkovskii and their neo-Christianity, she wrote an analysis and defense of Gíppius's poetry (1912). Her second collection of poems, *Orientalia* (1913), went through six editions and brought her renown. Shaginián's treatment of the theme of the East, which has had a long tradition in Russian poetry and was treated by ▷Lókhvitskaia and ▷Grinévskaia in poems and verse dramas, combines her forerunners' delight in exotic ritual and sensual detail with such specific matters as the four stages of a woman's life (the cycle 'Woman'). Shaginián herself wrote that 'after the sexless and incorporeal treatment of love by the Symbolists, [hers] was a lyric poetry of flesh and blood.'

The restless Shaginián then began writing prose: a pamphlet, *Two Moralities*, a travel book, *Journey to Weimar* (1914), stories, and her first novel, *One's Own Fate* (written 1915, published in full 1923). The pamphlet shows the lingering influence of ▷Gíppius; in it, Shaginián argues at length against biological determinism, particularly as expressed by the pressure on women to bear children for the sake of family continuity. The novel argues against the Freudian approach to the treatment of psychological disorders. In 1918 Shaginián tried yet another genre, a cycle of nine abstract and philosophical verse plays. In 1923, besides *One's Own Fate*, she published two novels: *The Change*, and *Adventures of a Society Lady*, dealing with the Civil War and the problems of adjusting to a new society, for which she was attacked by Trotsky in *Literature and Revolution*. Shaginián developed revolutionary fervour and, throughout the 1920s, did so with imagination. She produced the popular parodic adventure novel ▷*Mess Mend: Yankees in Petrograd*, and its two sequels, stories about the textile industry, and the formally experimental novel *KiK* (1929) (*Sorceress and Communist*). *KiK*, told in various genres including 'documents', poetry, prose, and verse drama, can be seen as an eccentric summation of Shaginián's literary career. This novel too was severely criticized, and she changed course again, becoming a faithful ▷socialist realist, and producing an industrial novel

(*Hydrocentral*, 1931) and four books on Lenin (1938–1970), for which she won the Lenin Prize in 1972. Her last book, the memoir *Man and Time* (1980), includes a section on her former mentor ▷Gíppius.

▷Tsvetáeva, Marina

Bib: Tate, H. (trans.), 'Man and Time' (excerpt), *Soviet Literature* 9 (1980); Kunitz, J. (ed.), 'Three Looms', *Azure Cities: Stories of New Russia*; Cioran, S. (trans.), *Mess Mend: Yankees in Petrograd; Retracing Lenin's Steps* (together with *A Remarkable Year* and *The Blue Notebook*); Terras, V. (ed.), *Handbook of Russian Literature*; Wilson, K. (ed.), *An Encyclopedia of Continental Women Writers*; Kasack, W. (ed.), *Dictionary of Russian Literature Since 1917*.

Shakhovskáia, Zinaida Alekseevna (born 1906)

Russian poet, prose writer, historian, literary critic, and editor. Princess Shakhovskáia was born in Moscow, into an old aristocratic family who emigrated from Russia in 1920, eventually settling in Brussels. When Shakhovskáia went off to Paris to study in the 1920s, she became involved in the *émigré* literary world centred there. She published two volumes of poetry in Russian in 1934–35, and numerous articles, but she felt the urge to write in French, a language she had known since childhood. In the 1930s she wrote in both languages, publishing her works in French under the pen-name Jacques Croise. Between 1949 and 1968 she wrote only in French. Her first novel, *Europe et Valerius*, won a Parisian literary prize. In 1968 she returned to writing in Russian as the editor of the *émigré* weekly journal *Russian Thought*. Since then she has written poetry, prose and criticism (on Vladimir Nabokov, 1899–1977, among others) primarily in Russian. Her memoirs, published in 1975, contain invaluable correspondence from various figures in the *émigré* community. Her editorship of *Russian Thought* ended in 1978, and three years later she and other *emigré* writers founded a new literary journal, *Russian Almanac*, in Paris.

Bib: *The Fall of Eagles: The Precursors of Peter the Great;* 'The Revolution as Seen by a Child,' *Russian Review* (1967); *The Privilege Was Mine: A Russian Princess Returns to the Soviet Union*; Beaujour, E., *Alien Tongues: Bilingual Russian Writers of the 'First' Emigration*; Gibson, A., *Russian Poetry and Criticism in Paris from 1920 to 1940*; Wilson, K. (ed.), *An Encyclopedia of Continental Women Writers* 2.

Shakti

In Hinduism, the feminine energy that empowers a deity and is sometimes embodied as the goddess Shakti, consort of Shiva.

Shange, Ntozake (born 1948)

US dramatist and novelist. Shange was born into an African-American family of professionals in Trenton, New Jersey. At age eight, she moved to St Louis and experienced racial segregation. After several suicide attempts, she graduated from Barnard College in 1970. In 1973 she earned a Master's degree in American Studies at the University of Southern California in Los Angeles.

Shange's dramatic work is known for its innovative mixture of poetry, music and dance. As in ▷*for colored girls who have considered suicide/ when the rainbow is enuf* (1975) and *spell #7* (1971), it celebrates African-American women and their ability to survive, despite physical and emotional abuse from men. Her novella, *Sassafrass, Cypress & Indigo* (1977), focuses on women's alternatives in their relationships with men. A powerful mix of fiction, poetry, songs, letters, journals and recipes, the book applauds female culture, women's bodies and women loving themselves.

Other works include: *Nappy Edges* (1978), *Three Pieces* (1981), *A Daughter's Geography* (1983), *From Okra to Greens: A Different Love Story* (1984), *See No Evil: Prefaces, Essays & Accounts, 1976–1983* (1984) and *Betsy Brown* (1985).

Shapír, Ol'ga Andreevna (1850–1916)

A prolific Russian fiction writer, Shapír defined her life's work as countering what she felt was a prevailing neglect of the 'authentic voice of women's definitions of life'. Her father was an educated Russian peasant, and her mother of mixed German and Swedish ancestry. Shapír grew up on the Gulf of Finland near ▷St Petersburg. Her democratic ideals were shaped as a student in one of the first public secondary schools for women, and during the early years of her happy marriage to a young doctor exiled for political activism. Throughout her lifetime she worked tirelessly for women's emancipation, and copyright protection for writers; she was an ardent pacificist who treated the theme of war as mass murder in her 1904 story 'Repentance'.

Shapír published at least eight novels and over 70 shorter fictional works, and saw two of her plays performed in major theatres. Much of her fiction has a didactic edge, and she was criticized for pretentious style, but her characters are well-etched and her plots carefully developed. Her gloomy novel, *Without Love* (1886), traces the consequences of a woman's choice of duty to her family over emotional fulfilment. Some of her shorter tales are programmatic: in 'Avdot'ia's Daughters' (1898) the cook's two girls, downstairs, rationally plan better lives, while, upstairs, her employers' daughter is lost in books and migraines; in 'The Outcome' (1901) a kept woman coolly announces that she is leaving her lover to become a court reporter. In 1907 relaxation of censorship made it possible to publish the novel *In the Stormy Years*, written in the late 1880s and based on Shapír's experience of the revolutionary ferment of her youth; she considered it her best work.

▷Woman Question (Russia)

Shariat

The complete legal system governing the lives of Moslems. It makes special provisions for women, some of which, such as the maintenance of divorcees, have occasioned controversy in recent years. A married woman should have her own property in the form of *mahr* (also known as dower, or *sadiq*). There is a distinction between prompt *mahr*, paid to the woman by her husband at the time of marriage, and deferred *mahr*, paid to the woman on the dissolution of the marriage by her husband. Islam permits polygamy, and considers marriage to be a contract, without divine sanction, which can be terminated at any time by the husband saying 'Talaq' (I divorce you) three times.

Shaw, Helen (1913–1984)

New Zealand poet and story writer. Shaw began writing by publishing stories for children in a local newspaper, and subsequently became well-known for her short fiction and her poetry. Her fiction is closely associated with the kind of life she led as a child: it focuses on social change and conflict generated by the deterioration and disappearance of generations, a change often imaged in the decay or destruction of an old house. Shaw's poetry is highly abstract and imagistic and became explicitly mystical and spiritual later in her life. Shaw also published critical essays and edited an exchange of letters between ▷Lady Ottoline Morrell and D'Arcy Cresswell.

Publications: *The Orange Tree and Other Stories* (1957); *Out of Dark: Poems* (1968); *The Girl of the Gods* (poems) (1973); *The Word and Flower* (1975); *The Gipsies and Other Stories* (1978); *Ambitions of Clouds* (1981); *Time Told from a Tower* (1985); *Leda's Daughter* (1985).

▷Children's literature, New Zealand

Shchépkina-Kupérnik, Tat'iana L'vovna (1874–1952)

Prose writer, dramatist, translator and memoirist. Shchépkina-Kupérnik was the great-granddaughter of the famous Russian actor Mikhail Shchépkin. In 1886, on the centennial of his birth, she published her first poem. In 1891 she joined the acting troupe of the private Korsh Theatre in Moscow. She said she became an actress because, at the time, women's universities were closed, and the theatre was her family heritage: her aunt, A.P. Shchépkina, acted at the Imperial Theatre, and her mother was a professional musician. Active in the theatrical and literary world, she met the dramatist Anton Chekhov (1860–1904) in 1893, and gave him credit for advising and encouraging her. In 1892 she wrote a one-act vaudeville, *Summer Picture*, successfully staged at the Malyi Theatre. Other dramatic works, primarily one-act plays in verse, ran at various theatres, starring the best actors of the day. *Amor's Revenge* became the basis of a one-act opera by A.S. Taneev. Her long play, *A Happy Woman* (1911), about the mother of a student revolutionary, won the Griboedov Prize.

Shchépkina-Kupérnik's books of poetry include: *From Women's Letters* (1898, second edition 1903), *My Poems* (1901), *Clouds* (1912),

and *Echoes of War* (1915). The poem 'In the Homeland', written in response to the shooting of innocent petitioners on 9 January 1905, was published abroad in ▷*tamizdat*, circulated in Russia as ▷*samizdat*, and became the text of a popular song. She published many collections of short stories. One of them, *This Happened Yesterday*, published in 1907, was confiscated, and the author was called into court for 'insulting the authorities'. Copies were destroyed, but some were salvaged. Her book, *Legends of Love* (1910), retellings of ancient legends, won an honourable mention for the Pushkin Prize.

Although Shchépkina-Kupérnik was capable of writing in a light-hearted vein, as in the story *Sappho* (1894), her prose is mostly tendentious, and her poetry in the civic vein. Her main characters are from different classes: the poor suffer from social injustices, while the upper class is morally corrupt. She cited the influence of Dickens, and Tolstoy's stamp, both in content and narrative technique, is evident. In Shchépkina-Kupérnik's prose of the 1890s there are a number of works that define happiness as devotion to art and emotional closeness between women (see her 1897 novel ▷*Happiness*, which provoked negative criticism for its 'feminism').

After 1917 Shchépkina-Kupérnik became a verse translator of plays by Shakespeare, Goldoni, Calderon, Lope de Vega, Victor Hugo, and others, and also wrote several books of memoirs. In 1944 she received the order of Labour of the Red Banner.

▷Chiuminá, Ol'ga; ▷Superfluous man
Bid: Maegd-Soëp, C., *Chekhov and Women: Women in the Life and Work of Chekhov*; Heim, M. (trans.) and Karlinsky, S. (ed.), *Anton Chekhov's Life and Thought: Selected Letters and Commentary*.

Shearer, Jill

Australian dramatist. Shearer has lived mostly in Queensland and has had at least eleven plays produced, of which *Catherine* (1977), *The Foreman* (1978), and *The Boat* (1978) have been published. She is considered one of Australia's leading modern dramatists. She is currently employed in Brisbane by the Japanese Consul General for Queensland.

▷Dramatists (Australia)

She Came to Stay (1949)

Translation of *L'Invitée* (1943), first novel by French writer ▷Simone de Beauvoir. *She Came to Stay* is the fictionalized account of the relationship between de Beauvoir, philosopher Jean-Paul Sartre (1905–1980), and Olga Kosakievicz. Set in the Parisian intellectual and artistic circles in which de Beauvoir herself lived, the novel is a chilling account of fierce heterosexual jealousy and the competition between two women for one man. The novel was an immediate success when first published, and received acclaim as one of the greatest novels of Existentialism. The themes, particularly of sexual jealousy and sexual licence, were to be continued by de Beauvoir in her later novels.

Shedding (1978)

A German Translation of *Häutungen. Autobiografische Aufzeichnungen, Gedichte, Träume, Analysen* (1975), a German novel by the Swiss feminist writer ▷Verena Stefan. It is an autobiographical narrative about a woman who gradually sheds skin after skin of culturally-acquired womanliness in order to become her true self. As she moves away from a heterosexual relationship towards lesbian love, she also leaves behind alienation and begins to experience the solidarity of an exclusively female community.

The German subtitle of the book translates as *Autobiographical Notes, Poems, Dreams and Analyses*, and the book is conceived as a montage, a kind of diary, comprising short associated texts of all kinds: anecdotes, poems, dreams and analytical passages. Part of the process of shedding skin consists in the heroine's search for a truly feminine idiom which relinquishes all trace of patriarchal influence. The book became an immediate bestseller, and initiated a new wave of radical feminist thinking in Germany.

Shelley, Mary Wollstonecraft (1797–1851)

Mary Shelley

English novelist. The only daughter of feminist ▷Mary Wollstonecraft and rationalist philosopher William Godwin. Her mother died a few days after her birth, leaving Mary to educate herself amongst her father's intellectual circle. In 1812, she met Percy Bysshe Shelley and in 1814 they eloped, travelling through France, Switzerland and Germany and jointly recording their experiences in *History of a Six Weeks Tour* (1817). Thereafter they returned to England and Mary gave birth to a son, William. They spent the summer of 1816 with Byron and Claire Clairmont on Lake Geneva, during which time Mary began to write ▷*Frankenstein* (1818). The same autumn, Shelley's first wife, Harriet, committed suicide and Shelley and Mary immediately married. They stayed in England until 1818, then lived in Italy until Shelley's death in 1822. Mary suffered a nervous breakdown after the death of William in 1819 (she also lost a daughter the previous year) and in 1822 she had a dangerous miscarriage. A short time after Shelley's death Mary returned to England, determined not to re-marry but to support her surviving son, Percy, by working as a professional writer. She continued to write novels, though none is so well-known today as *Frankenstein*. Novels include *Valperga* (1823); ▷*The Last Man* (1826); *Lodore* (1835) and *Falkner* (1837). Shelley also wrote short stories, many of which were published in the annual *The Keepsake*, as well as biographies and the well-received travelogue *Rambles in Germany and Italy* (1844). She attempted a biography of Shelley, which she abandoned, though she edited his poetry, prose and letters. Her life and works have been the subject of much recent feminist criticism.

▷Gothic; ▷Travel writing (19th-century Britain)

Bib: Jones, F.L. (ed.), *Mary Shelley's Journal* and *The Letters of Mary Shelley*; Lyles, W.H., *Mary Shelley: An Annotated Biography*; Poovey, M., *The Proper Lady and the Woman Writer*; Gilbert, S. and Gubar, S., *The Madwoman in the Attic*; Mellor, A.K., *Mary Shelley: Her Life, Her Fiction, Her Monsters*.

Shen Rong (born 1935)

Chinese writer. Shen Rong studied Russian at the Beijing Foreign Languages Institute, and taught in a middle school for a time, but in the 1980s gave up teaching to concentrate on writing. The novella *Everlasting Spring* (1979), explores the dilemma of individuals caught up in the frenzy of the 'cultural revolution' (1966–1976) and portrays the personal tragedy of a dedicated Party woman. The novella ▷*At Middle Age* (1980) won a national prize and was made into a popular film. The story of Lu Wenting – a middle-aged ophthalmologist trying to cope with overwork, underpay, household chores and official harassment – was widely regarded as a protest on behalf of China's intellectuals. Another novella, *Divorce? Why Bother?* (1989), explores the myth of the happy family in China. In *Yang Weiwei and Sartre* (1984) Shen Rong questions the degree of freedom of choice available to women. Concerned with social issues, Shen Rong nevertheless created many memorable images of modern Chinese women in their various predicaments.

Bib: Translation of *At Middle Age* in Lee Yee (ed.), *The New Realism* and Link, Perry (ed.), *Roses and Thorns*.

Sherwood, Martha (1775–1851)

English writer of ▷children's literature, born in Stanford, Worcestershire. She married Captain

Henry Sherwood and they lived in India for eleven years. It was here that Sherwood began to produce her astonishing output of approximately 400 titles, including novels and textbooks. She worked energetically for children's well-being throughout her life, setting up schools and adopting ▷orphans. Her works, which are too fiercely religious and moralistic to be popular today, include *The History of Susan Grey* (1802) and *The History of the Fairchild Family* (1818, 1842, 1847).
Bib: Cutt, M.N., *Mrs Sherwood and Her Books for Children.*

Shérazade (1982)
A novel by the Algerian writer, Leila Sabbar. It is the story of a runaway from a working-class suburb of Paris. Shérazade is a *beur*: she belongs to the second generation of Algerian immigrants in France. In her flight, along with other adolescents, she comes into contact with the world of drugs, prostitution and violence. In *Shérazade* the author gives an account of the adventures of a wildly free, violent and affectionate adolescent in search of identity.

Shibaki Yoshiko (born 1914)
Japanese novelist. She was born the eldest daughter of a dealer in kimono fabrics in Asakusa, in downtown Tokyo. *Fresh Produce Mart*, which appeared soon after her marriage, won the Akutagawa Prize in 1941. This work portrays a heroine working at a vegetable and fruit market, and downtown society is the model for her subsequent works. A series of stories, *Paradise, Suzaki* (1954), describes prostitutes working in bars. *Woman Dealer in Yuba* is based on the life of her grandmother. *River Sumida* (1961) and *The Eighth Building in Marunouchi* (1962) describe downtown scenes and craftsmen. She also portrays the lives of artists – for example, in *Celadon Porcelain.* Her other main works are *Twilight on the River Sumida* (1984), which won the Prize for Japanese Literature, and *Dancing Snow* (1987), which won the Mainichi Prize for Arts. Shibaki is a member of the Japanese Academy of Art.

Shields, Carol (born 1935)
American-Canadian short story writer and novelist, born Carol Warner in Chicago, to a middle-class family. She went to Hanover College, met her Canadian husband at Exeter in England, married in 1957, and moved with him to Vancouver, Toronto and Ottawa. There Shields became interested in Canadian literature and gained an MA for work on ▷Susanna Moodie. Her first novels, *Small Ceremonies* (1976), *The Box Garden* (1977), *Happenstance* (1980) and *A Fairly Conventional Woman* (1982) are realistic tales of marriage and domesticity. Shields breaks through the constraints of narrative convention in her brilliant short story collections, *Various Miracles* (1985) and *The Orange Fish* (1989), which detail startling moments of epiphany. She has also

written poetry, drama, a literary mystery, *Swann* (1987), and a collaborative novel, *A Celibate Season* (1991, with Blanche Howard) about a long-distance marriage. She lives in Winnipeg, Manitoba.
Bib: Special issue of ▷*Room of One's Own*, Vol. 13, No. 1/2.

Shinebourne, Janice (born 1947)
Caribbean novelist and short story writer, born in the Canje area of ▷Guyana where the first 18th-century Dutch plantations were situated. Of Chinese and Indian ancestry, she began to write at an early age while still at school. This youthful writing included school plays, which were performed, and descriptions of the Canje forest, some of which are included in her first novel, *Timepiece* (1986). She attended University in Georgetown, moved to Britain in the early 1970s, completed a BA degree, and taught in colleges in Brixton and Southall. She continues to live in London, and works as a community activist, lecturer and editor.
Timepiece, which won the Guyana Prize in 1987, addresses the conflict between a rural and an urban ▷identity brought about in the consciousness of her female protagonist, Sandra, when she moves from a rural community, with its traditional values, to the city, where she becomes a member of Guyana's educated younger generation. Her second work, *The Last English Plantation*, was published in 1989. Numerous stories and reviews have appeared in international journals and have been broadcast on the BBC World Service. Her work is featured in ▷*Her True True Name*, and she is a contributor to ▷*Caribbean Women Writers.* She was interviewed on the publication of her first novel at the Institute of Contemporary Art in London.

Shingle-short and Other Verses (1908)
Poems by New Zealand writer ▷B.E. Baughan. *Shingle-short and Other Verses* is Baughan's third collection of poems (*Verses*, 1898; *Reuben and Other Poems*, 1903). She published her first collection in London before coming to New Zealand. In her preface, Baughan describes *Shingle-short* as 'New Zealand verse' and comments on her use of Maori words and 'certain current Australasian terms'. As MacD. P. Jackson has pointed out, narrative and dramatic techniques predominate in *Shingle-short* (*The Oxford History of New Zealand Literature in English*, 1990), with long poems unfolding a narrative history of rural New Zealand. Examples are 'Early Days' in which a grandmother nostalgically describes the pioneering life of her family, or 'A Bush Section' in which the problems and issues of colonial life, especially its destruction of the natural environment, are explored. Baughan also retells Maori myths in poems such as 'Maui's Fish'. *Shingle-short and Other Verses* proved Baughan to be one of the most accomplished

colonial poets, and poems from the collection are still anthologized and reprinted.

▷Maori literature

Shiono Nanao (born 1937)

Japanese novelist. Born in Tokyo, she now lives in Florence. Her novels are based on medieval Italian history, and *Renaissance and Women* is her first novel. *The Story of a City Facing the Sea* and *The Story of a City Facing the Sea – Part Two* won the Suntory Prize for the Liberal Arts in 1982 and the Kikuchi Kan Prize in 1983 respectively. *My Friend, Machia Velli and a Collection of His Sayings* also won a Japanese literary award in 1988.

Ship of Fools (1962)

US novel. ▷Katherine Anne Porter's bestseller depicts the tensions among the international passengers aboard a ship. The voyage from Mexico to Germany chronicles the rise of fascism in 1931. The passengers are divided according to nationality and class. Like Hitler, the captain, an absolute ruler, ostracizes Jewish sympathizers from his table. Porter depicts the folly of fascism: it enforces national and racial standards for membership in the human community. The characters' romantic entanglements show that fascism is only one example of humanity's folly. Porter emphasizes the folly of humanity's compulsion to limit human identity and potential.

Ship of Widows, The (1981)

Russian writer ▷I. Grékova's short novel, translated into English in 1985, summarizes the experiences of Russian women during World War II and for twenty years afterwards. The author does this by depicting an 'accidental' family of five women, assigned separate rooms but common kitchen and toilet facilities in a Moscow apartment. The first-person narrator has been psychologically frozen by the bomb that crippled her and destroyed her family. The story's other major protagonists are Anfisa Petrovna, a devoted single mother, and her son, whose perception of the lies and deception underlying Soviet society leads him to make cynical use of the love the emotionally needy women try to give him.

Shippen, Nancy ▷Livingston, Anne Shippen

Shira (1976) (Poetry)

Poetry collection in Hebrew by ▷Yonah Wallach. *Shira* contains poems written between 1963 and 1975, including some from earlier collections – *Devarim* (1966) (*Things*) and *Shney Ganim* (1969) (*Two Gardens*) – as well as previously unpublished work. Wallach's verse is forceful and provocative. Free syntax, unconventional forms and shifting imagery express a rebellious and tormented character. The poems expose and capture the nature of sensual experiences with astonishing, and sometimes disturbing, precision. The poet is torn between the need to exist in the logical world and the desire to live the richness of unprohibited

madness. Wallach's poetry is unique in modern Hebrew writing.

Shirat Rachel (1961) (Rachel's Poetry)

A collection by the Israeli poet ▷Rachel. It includes her books of verse and a selection of her essays. Rachel's poems are personal and lyrical. Through simple structures and imagery, the life of the poet, and the pioneering period in Israeli history in which she lives, unfolds.

Shirim (1963) (Poems)

Collection of poems by Israeli poet ▷Yocheved Bat-Miriam. The poems were written between 1929 and 1948, the year of her son's death in the Israeli War of Independence, when she stopped writing. Bat-Miriam's poetry is a constant challenge to the reader. Tensions and conflicts appear to be at the core of her work. The influence of futurism clashes with her Hasidic background. Astonishing metaphors and unconventional syntax contrast with the conversational rhythm. The poems capture intense emotions, and give a fresh insight into common themes, such as a yearning for childhood innocence, alienation and a fear of death.

Shirley (1849)

A novel by British author ▷Charlotte Brontë. It is set in Yorkshire at the time of the Napoleonic wars and is concerned, like several novels of the 1840s, with labour relations. Robert Gerard Moore is a half-English, half-Belgian mill owner who introduces the latest labour-saving machinery to the workplace, ignoring the protests of his employees. They turn against him and attempt to destroy the mill and to take his life. In an effort to raise funds Robert proposes to the spirited Shirley Keeldar, an heiress. She refuses him and eventually marries Robert's brother, Louis, a tutor in her family. Robert marries Caroline Helstone, his cousin. The novel protests against the limited opportunities available to women, demonstrated particularly in the life of Caroline, confined in her uncle's rectory and prohibited even from working as a ▷governess. In the character of Shirley, Brontë claimed she was drawing a portrait of her sister ▷Emily Brontë, 'had she been placed in health and prosperity'.

Shkápskaia, Mariia Mikhailovna (1891–1952)

Russian poet, journalist and children's writer. Before the 1905 Revolution, Shkápskaia was arrested twice for participating in student demonstrations and illegal groups. She began writing poetry in childhood, and her first published poem, 'On the Death of Tolstoy', appeared in 1910. In the early 1920s, she published six books of poetry, two of which went into second editions.

The title of her first collection of poems, *Mater Dolorosa* (1921), is significant. It summarizes the main theme of her poetry: motherhood in all its aspects – birth, abortion, and death of a child. Shkápskaia acknowledged the influence of

▷Elena Guró, and her feeling of being a universal mother. The traditional love theme is almost totally absent from Shkápskaia's poetry; in 'Ballad' she devalues romantic love. God was her primary masculine addressee, and those poems have a devotional tone. Guró's influence can also be seen in Shkápskaia's blurring of the distinction between the animate and inanimate worlds, and the depiction of the modern industrialized city as a hostile environment. Shkápskaia's imagery, some of it biblical, can be striking and unexpected. She was fond of using a cyclical structure in her poems, in which the end echoes the beginning. Some of her poetry, while maintaining metre and rhyme, was printed as prose paragraphs.

Her poems of female-centred life became unacceptable in the anti-domestic Soviet state. Reviewers criticized her as 'decadent' and self-indulgently 'gynaecological.' In 1925 she turned to the journalism for which she is known today in the USSR. By 1927 she had established herself as a journalist, specializing in the 'sketch.' Republished in the USSR in the 1960s, these works bear little resemblance to her earlier poetry. Her involvement in children's literature was mainly as a reviewer. Her own writings for children are few: a fairytale in 1925, and a book about fascist cruelties during World War II, *It Actually Happened* (1942). A collection of her poetry was published in 1979 in the West.
Bib: Markov, V. and Sparks, M. (eds), *Modern Russian Poetry*; Heldt, B., 'Motherhood in a Cold Climate', *Sexuality and the Body in Russian Culture* and *Terrible Perfection: Women and Russian Literature*.

Short story (Australia)
The 19th century. Short story writing was popular for colonial women as it was one of the few ways in which they could earn extra money, and magazines, including the *Bulletin* (from 1880), encouraged this ladylike pursuit. The quality was, quite understandably, uneven. Although women's stories were usually published in magazines, there have been a number of notable collections, such as *Tales for the Bush* (1845) by ▷Mary Vidal; ▷*The Detective's Album: Recollections of an Australian Police Officer*, (1871) by ▷Mary Fortune ('Waif Wander'), the first Australian woman writer of detective fiction; *Tried as Pure Gold and Other Tales* (1882) and *The Snowdrop's Message and Other Tales* (1888) by Ellen Augusta Chads; *A Sydney Sovereign and Other Tales* (1890) by ▷Jessie Couvreur ('Tasma'); and *At Midnight and Other Stories* (1897) by ▷Ada Cambridge. ▷*From the Verandah: Stories of Love and Landscape by Nineteenth-Century Australian Women* (1987), edited by Fiona Giles, reprints a number of 19th-century women's stories and analyses their variety and excellence, while the introduction to *The Australian Short Story before Lawson* (1986), edited by Cecil Hadgraft, also examines the contribution of 19th-century Australian women to the short story tradition.
The 20th century. The publication of ▷Barbara

Baynton's ▷*Bush Studies* (1902) not only challenged the Australian myths of 'mateship' and the bush, but also initiated a 20th-century tradition of powerful and realistic short stories by women which has proved to be one of the most striking features of Australian literature. Most of the celebrated women fiction writers of this century have written individual stories, or published volumes of them. Significant volumes of short stories published before 1970 have included ▷Katharine Susannah Prichard's *Kiss on the Lips and Other Stories* (1932) and *N'goola and Other Stories* (1959); ▷Henry Handel Richardson's *The End of a Childhood and Other Stories* (1934); ▷Christina Stead's *The Salzburg Tales* (1934); ▷Marjorie Barnard's ▷*The Persimmon Tree and Other Stories*, (1943); ▷Shirley Hazzard's *Cliffs of Fall and Other Stories* (1963); ▷Judith Wright's *The Nature of Love* (1966); Thelma Forshaw's (born 1923) *An Affair of Clowns* (1967) and Lyndall Hadow's (1903–1976) *Full Cycle and Other Stories* (1969).

The 1970s and 1980s, however, have provided a boom in women's short stories, with challenging volumes such as ▷Elizabeth Jolley's *Five Acre Virgin and Other Stories* (1976) and *Woman in a Lampshade* (1983); ▷Thea Astley's ▷*Hunting the Wild Pineapple* (1979); ▷Olga Masters's ▷*The Home Girls*; ▷Beverley Farmer's *Milk: Stories* (1983) and *Home Time: Stories* (1985); Marian Eldridge's (born 1936) *Walking the Dog and Other Stories* (1984); ▷Kate Grenville's *Bearded Ladies: Stories* (1984); ▷Jean Bedford's ▷*Country Girl Again and Other Stories* (1985); ▷Helen Garner's *Postcards from Surfers: Stories* (1985); ▷Jessica Anderson's *Stories from the Warm Zone and Sydney Stories* (1987); ▷Barbara Hanrahan's *Dream People* (1987) and ▷Janette Turner Hospital's *Dislocations* (1987). Taken as a series, these provide a uniquely feminine perspective on Australian experience, whether in the city or the bush.

Showalter, Elaine (born 1941)
North American feminist literary critic and lecturer. She taught English and Women's Studies at Rutgers University, and is now Professor of English at Princeton University. Showalter established herself as a formative feminist influence in the 1970s with the appearance of *A Literature of Their Own: British Women Novelists from Brontë to Lessing* (1977). In addition to ▷Dale Spender, Showalter has made a major contribution to feminist literary history by retrieving women writers marginalized by the male-dominated canon of 'great literature', and establishing a tradition of writing by women. In 'Towards a Feminist Poetics' (1979), she coined the term ▷Gynocritics to denote a ▷woman-centred critical practice that would enable feminists to constitute a record of women's writing and female experience. Gynocritics is distinguished from 'feminist critique', 'which is essentially political and polemical' with affiliations to male theories, such as Marxism. Showalter is

suspicious of 'feminist critique' because of its reliance on theory, which she characterizes as masculine, and because it teaches women to read like men and thereby gloss over the difference of female experience. See Toril Moi for a critique of Showalter's hostility towards theory.

Her other publications include: (ed.), *The New Feminist Criticism* (1986); *The Female Malady: Women, Madness and English Culture 1830–1980* (1987); (ed.), *Speaking of Gender* (1989); (ed.), *These Modern Women: Autobiographical Essays from the Twenties* (1989); and *Sexual Anarchy* (1991), which invents the theory of 'endism' to explain *fin de siècle* social and sexual crises.
▷Canon (literary)
Bib: Moi, T., *Sexual/Textual Politics*.

Shrouded Woman, The (1948)
Translation of *La Amortajada* (1938), a novel by the Chilean author ▷María Luisa Bombal. It might be considered a feminine re-reading of the novel *As I Lay Dying* (1930) by the North American William Faulkner (1897–1962), but without the parody it contains. It is written during the burial of a woman, who retells her life in a fragmented way through flashbacks and in the third person, employing a ▷stream-of-consciousness technique. Other characters carry on a dialogue with the dead woman, thus providing several points of view. Surrealism and the fantastic are joined in the narrative. The narrator recollects her childhood and adolescence in the *hacienda* (farm). Her bourgeois marriage forces a break from the quiet life on the farm, and a move to the rough, urban life of the 'immense, wordless, sad city'. In this novel, as in Bombal's other works, women have a static destiny, while men are part of the dynamic chain of society. The words chosen by the author portray a Surrealist atmosphere, with a sense of indefinite uneasiness and solitude. Bombal aims at impersonalization, so that Ana Maria, the protagonist, could be any woman. Her story is symbolic of the condition of Latin American women in the ▷patriarchal society.

Shu Ting (born 1952)
Chinese poet from Fujian. Shu Ting began to write poetry in 1979 and attracted widespread critical attention. Shu and Gu Cheng (born 1956) are considered representatives of the 'misty' school of poetry which has had a great following since the 1980s (▷Essay on China). Her lyrics, now collected in *The Doublemasted Ship* (1982), are noted for their intensity of feeling and sensitive touch. Shu Ting says she wants to 'rip off masks' and 'explore the path which links human beings to one another'.

Shuttle, Penelope (born 1947)
English poet, novelist and dramatist. Shuttle's first publication was the prize-winning novel *An Excusable Vengeance* (1967). Since 1970 Shuttle has been the companion of the poet Peter Redgrove (born 1932). Together they have written a collection of poetry, *The Hermaphrodite Album* (1973), and *The Wise Wound* (1978), a study of menstruation. Both poets see their writing as a means to interrogate gender. Other volumes of poetry by Shuttle include: *The Orchard Upstairs* (1980), *The Lion from Rio* (1986) and *Adventures with My Horse* (1989), which addresses ovulation and miscarriage. Her novels include *The Mirror of the Giant* (1980).

Sibila, A (1953) (The Sibyl)
Set in a village community in northern Portugal, this early novel by ▷Agustina Bessa-Luís focuses on a well-to-do family, especially on the bond between a matriarchal figure, Quina, who is thought to have prophetic powers, and her granddaughter, Germana. *A Sibila* is told from the point of view of Germana, whose memories of Quina flow back and forth in time. A highly successful novel, it marked the introduction of an Existentialist literature in Portugal. The book comments on a wide variety of topics, including marriage, the relationship between mothers and daughters, religion, and the traditional values of the countryside.
Bib: *Longman Anthology of World Literature by Women*, pp. 647–51.

Sick Woman's Maytime Walk, A (1812)
Russian poet ▷Anna Búnina's bleak 100-line poem (*Russian Literature Triquarterly* 9) is a powerful expression of despair in the face of constant excruciating pain. Feeling herself rejected by God, the narrator finds a pitiful beggar's blessing blasphemous, and the cool beauty of the springtime scene along the ▷St Petersburg embankment powerless to 'quench the fire' within.
Bib: Heldt, B., *Terrible Perfection*.

Si Dao, Ruang (born 1943)
Pen-name of Thai writer Wanna Thappananon, an exponent of the 1970s' leftist, didactic and social realist 'literature for life's sake' movement. Born to a pedlar mother and railway worker father, she failed to complete her education and became instead a domestic help and factory worker. An early literary effort was rejected, but after her marriage in 1973 to the editor and writer Suchat Sawatsi she renewed her efforts and since 1975 has had over 60 short stories published in magazines, plus two collections, *Kaew Yot Diaw* (1984) (*One Drop of Glass*) and *Bat Prachachon* (1984) (*Identity Card*). Several have been translated into English, Japanese, Polish and Chinese. 'Khon Day Ya' ('The Grasscutter') won the 1979 Thailand PEN Award (an English translation appears in the *Thai PEN Anthology*, 1984), while 'Man ma kap kanluaktang' ('It comes With Elections') won the 1979 *Lok Nangsu* (Book World) Prize, and 'Khwam Ngiap Thi Roem Ton' ('The Stillness That Begins') was selected by the Literary Critics Group as the most creative short story of 1979. Among her novels are *Jao Kawao Oey* (1981) (*Oh Mr Kawao*), *Dek Bin Dai* (1984)

(*Kids Can Fly*), and its companion volume, *Son Klin* (*Tuberose*) – named after its heroine – which is about women factory workers. Her literary style and concerns may be gathered from 'The Grasscutter', which without comment depicts chronic poverty, despite long, hard labour, co-existent with get-rich schemes among the poor, involving gambling and cheating. Another typical example of her style is 'Mae Phra Khongka Thaokae Bak Lae Ma' ('Mother of Waters, Thaokae Bak and a Dog'), which originally appeared in *Lalana* (*Woman*) in early November 1977, and in English translation in the anthology *In the Mirror* (1985). A traditional Thai holy festival becomes a sterile activity, corrupted by the monks' implied collusion with a businessman, Thaokae Bak, who, ironically, earns 'merit' for it. At the end of the day, a passing, famished dog, finding no sustenance, defecates on the unlovely debris.

▷ Socialist realism

Sidhwa, Bapsi (born 1938)

Pakistani novelist. She was born in Karachi, brought up in Lahore, and now divides her time between the USA, where she teaches creative writing, and Pakistan. In Pakistan she is an energetic advocate of improved social and legal conditions for women, and supports orphanages and refuges for destitute women. She represented Pakistan at the Asian Women's Conference in 1975.

As a member of the relatively small Parsee (Zoroastrian) community in Pakistan, she is conscious of the problems of insecurity and insularity faced by minority communities everywhere. Her comic novel ▷ *The Crow Eaters* (1978) was written partly in an attempt to explain the Parsees to themselves and to other Pakistanis. It has been translated into Russian. Her novel *The Bride* (1983) is a tribute to another culturally (and also geographically) remote group, the inhabitants of Pakistan's harsh mountainous regions. *Ice-Candy Man* (1988, published in the USA and Canada as *Breaking India*) is unusual for its comic treatment of the trauma of ▷ Partition. Historically precise, it nevertheless explores universal themes of predatory behaviour and exploitation.

Sidney, Margaret ▷ Lothrop, Harriet Mulford Stone

Sidney, Mary ▷ Herbert, Mary Sidney, Countess of Pembroke

Sidneyan Psalms ▷ Psalms of David, The

Sido (1953)

Translation of *Sido* (1929), by French novelist ▷ Colette. Like ▷ *Break of Day*, this semi-autobiographical text celebrates Colette's carefree, rural childhood, and the strength, rooted in her love of nature, and of all living creatures, of her mother, Sido. Here, Colette depicts the past as a garden paradise, marked by intensity of colour and sensation, by the strength of the mother–daughter bond, and by the shared delight in nature.

Siege of Leningrad, The (1987)

Russian writer ▷ Lidiia Gínzburg's description of her experience of the 900-day siege of ▷ Leningrad in World War II is subtitled 'Notes of a Survivor' (*Soviet Women Writing*, 1990). It is a fine example of the mixture of aesthetic and historical elements in documentary writing that she expounded in ▷ *On Psychological Prose*, and was written in three phases: 1942, 1962 and 1983. The narrative intersperses the daily routine of a 'composite and imaginary' male, N., with anecdotes about other people under other initials, first-person memories, and second-person and impersonal passages that draw the reader into the chaotic texture of Leningrad life. Her amusing observations of the difference between the behaviour of men and women in queues offer a few pages of therapeutic relief not unlike that Gínzburg must have derived from using her analytic abilities to pass the time in those queues.

Sierra, Stella

Panamanian 20th-century poet. She considers herself a 'pure' poet, and combines deep mystery with clear images. Her first book of poetry, *Canciones de mar y luna* (1943) (*Songs of the Sea and Moon*), and the most important, *Libre y cautiva* (1947) (*Free and Captive*), give her the same status as the best Latin American women writers. *Cinco poemas* (1949) (*Five Poems*) and *Tamarindos* (*Tamarinds*), a trilogy of sonnets, contain some of her finest poems.

Sigea, Luisa (c 1531–1560)

Spanish scholar. At a young age she knew Latin, Greek and Hebrew. Her father, a teacher, was employed by the Portuguese royal court; she was a student and, later on, a teacher in the household of the ▷ Infanta Dona Maria de Portugal. Her promotion to teacher coincided with the 1546 publication of her long poem in Latin, *Sintra*, about the summer home of the Portuguese royalty. Often referred to as the 'tenth muse' and the 'Minerva of the century', Sigea left the Infanta's household in 1555, and, following her marriage, returned to Spain. She died in childbirth. Unfortunately, with the exception of *Sintra*, little of her work has survived.

▷ Maria de Portugal, The Infanta, Dona; *Infanta Dona Maria de Portugal e as Suas Damas, A*

Sigegyth (8th century)

English correspondent. A single letter (in Latin) from the Anglo-Saxon monk and writer, Aldhelm, survives, addressed to this otherwise unknown recipient. Its existence indicates that there must have been other such letters. Educated women in Anglo-Saxon England were proficient in Latin: Aldhelm wrote treatises on virginity in prose and verse for the nuns of ▷ Barking Abbey.

▷Boniface Correspondence
Bib: Lapidge, Michael and Herren, Michael (eds.), *Aldhelm: The Prose Works*.

Signs: Journal of Women in Culture and Society

One of the first feminist journals to publish theoretical developments in feminist criticism. *Signs* Vol. 7, No. 1, Summer 1981, devoted its pages to ▷French feminist theory, and made many essays available to English-speaking readers for the first time. Begun in North America in 1975 under the editorship of Catharine Stimpson, the journal remains widely influential today.
▷Smith-Rosenberg, Caroll

Sigourney, Lydia Huntley (1791–1865)

US poet, editor and autobiographer. Like so many other US women writers, Huntley Sigourney began writing to support her family. Unlike many other poets, she was successful – publishing in a wide variety of periodicals and selling well in volume collections. Sigourney is in other ways the exception that has been taken as the rule. While many women poets were accused of ▷sentimentality, Sigourney luxuriated in sentimentality and moral piety. Her speciality was poems on the death of children (she lost three of her own); this 'graveyard verse' is parodied in Mark Twain's *Huckleberry Finn* (1884). Among her dozens of books are *Moral Pieces* (1815), *Zinzendorff, and Other Poems* (1835), *The Weeping Willow* (1847), and numerous volumes of nonfiction and works for children. Her autobiography is *Letters of Life* (1866).
▷*Peterson's Magazine*

Silas Marner (1861)

A novel by English author ▷George Eliot. Silas Marner is a weaver who has been driven out of his religious community as a result of a false charge of theft. He loses his religious faith and moves to a midland village, Raveloe, where he re-establishes his trade, but maintains a self-imposed exile from the community. He lives only for money, hoarding his gold until it is stolen from his cottage by Dunstan Cass, son of the local squire. Dunstan then disappears, leaving Silas in despair. A transformation in Silas's life occurs following the mysterious arrival of a young child who finds her way into his cottage. Silas, initially, sees the child as a substitute for his lost wealth, and adopts her. But the relationship soon draws him from his miserly ways and he and the child, whom he calls Eppie, become devoted to one another. It is later revealed that Eppie is the daughter of Dunstan's brother, Godfrey, and Molly Farran, a working-class woman whom Godfrey had married, but refused publicly to acknowledge. Molly and her child had been forced to live in squalor and wretchedness, and Molly eventually dies, abandoned, in a ditch. When Eppie is almost grown up, Godfrey finally acknowledges his paternity, but Eppie refuses to leave the man who has cared for her. She refuses, also, to be seduced by Godfrey's wealth, and remains loyal to the working-class values of her closest friends. In *Silas Marner*, Eliot is critical of the rigid system of patriarchal law and its associated ethics of individualism, and argues for an alternative morality based upon more malleable and socially responsible codes.

Silêncio, O (1981) (The Silence)

In *O Silêncio* the Portuguese novelist ▷Teolinda Gersão focuses on the repressed lives of middle-class women. She attempts to suggest a 'language of silence', thereby articulating a woman's unexpressed desires. Gersão's paradoxical theme leads her to adopt an unusual narrative technique, which blurs the boundaries between characters and between dialogue and narration.
Bib: Sadlier, Darlene J., *The Question of How: Women Writers and New Portuguese Literature*.

Silent Partner, The (1871)

US novel of the New England mills by ▷Elizabeth Stuart Phelps (Ward). Somewhat similar to ▷Rebecca Harding Davis's ▷*Margaret Howth* (1862) in its focus on both the working conditions of industrial workers and the responses of mill-owners, Phelps's novel is notable for its more realistic technique, for its focus on women characters and women's consciousness of themselves as women, and for its early depiction of choice between marriage and career. (The last theme is addressed more fully and directly in later works: Phelps's ▷*Dr Zay* and ▷Sarah Orne Jewett's ▷*A Country Doctor*.) The central characters in *The Silent Partner* are both women – one a mill-worker, the other an owner, the mill's 'silent partner' – who come together in understanding of themselves and of the economic and class imperatives which direct industrial capitalism. Settings contrast the male, industrialized, exploitative mill town with natural surroundings in which the women find themselves, each other, and a more humane world-view.
▷Mill girls

Silko, Leslie Marmon (born 1948)

US novelist and short-story writer. Born in Alberquerque, New Mexico, Silko grew up on the Laguna Pueblo ▷Native American reservation. She graduated from the University of New Mexico in 1969 with top honours, has two sons, and since 1978 has been professor of English at the University of Arizona. Silko identifies herself as an Native American writer, and her work is preoccupied with the difficulties of inhabiting a dispossessed culture and how this culture can be represented in the face of the sentimental stereotypes of Anglo-American literature. Her novel *Ceremony* (1977) uses the Native American concept of reality as mythical narrative to determine its form, telling the story of a dislocated and damaged World War II veteran, Tayo. The disordered and dispossessed world, symbolized by the witchcraft of Emo, and the dualistic and hierarchical perception it induces, is combatted by Tayo with the help of Betonie, keeper of the traditional ceremonies, myths and rituals. Using these, Tayo heals both the land and the community, restoring balance and harmony to his world. Silko has been hailed as one of the most important Native American writers of her time.

Other works include: *Lullaby* (with Frank Chin) (1976), *Laguna Woman*, *Story Teller* (1981), *The Delicacy and Strength of Lace: Letters Between Leslie Marmon Silko and James A. Wright* (ed. Anne Wright) (1986) and *Almanac of the Dead* (1991). **Bib**: Seyersted, Per, *Leslie Marmon Silko*; Velie, Alan R., *Four American Indian Literary Masters*.

'Silly Novels by Lady Novelists' (1856)

An article by English novelist ▷George Eliot, printed in the *Westminster Review*. With scathing ridicule, Eliot attacks the unreality of many women's novels, criticizing their false portrayals of character and sexual relationships, their romantic wish-fulfilment and ludicrous representations of female learning. Eliot argues that the effect of such 'Silly Novels' is to make female aspirations appear risible and to undermine female achievement. '[R]otten and trashy books' depreciate 'the sacredness of the writer's art' and obscure a genuine women's tradition. 'For there is a distinctive women's writing,' Eliot asserts, '"a precious specialty", lying quite apart from masculine aptitude and experience.'

Silva, Clara (1905–1976)

Uruguayan poet and novelist. Her first book, *La cabellera oscura* (1945) (*The Dark Horsewoman*), is Surrealist in style, and *Memoria de nada* (1948) (*Memory of Nothing*) has been described as Existential and egocentric. Silva moved on and in her second phase substitutes free verse for sonnets on human and divine love in *Los delirios* (1954) (*Deliriums*). Her novels either have a religious theme, as in *Las bodas* (1960) (*The Wedding*), or, as in *La sobreviviente* (1951) (*The Survivor*) and *El ama y los perros* (1962) (*The Spirit and the Dogs*), approach the *nouveau roman*. In her novel *Aviso a la población* (1964) (*Advice to the Population*) and the poems of *Guitarra en sombra* (1964) (*Guitar in Shadow*) she searches for the truth of reality.

Other works: *Preludio indiano y otros poemas* (1960) (*Indian Prelude and Other Poems*); *Antología* (1966) (*Anthology*); *Habitación testigo* (1967) (*Witness Room*); *Proibido pasar* (1969) (*No Overtaking*); *Juicio final* (1971) (*Final Judgement*); *La astúcia mística* (1974) (*Mystical Cunning*), and *Los juicios del sueño* (1975) (*Judgements of the Dream*).

Silva, Francisca Júlia da, or Francisca Júlia da Silva Munster ▷Júlia, Francisca

Silva, Luisa del Valle (1902–1962)

Venezuelan poet who was born in Spain. She lived away from groups, schools, tendencies and fads, and adopted a very personal lyrical style, with a sense of classicism matching in expression the most daring forms of contemporary verse.

Her works include: *Ventanas de ensueño* (1930) (*Dream Windows*); *Amo* (1941) (*I Love*); *Humo* (1941) (*Smoke*); *En silencio* (1961) (*In Silence*); *Poesía* (1962); *Sin tiempo y sin espacio* (1963) (*Without Time or Space*), and *Amanecer* (1968) (*To Dawn*).

Silva Vila, Maria Inés (born 1926)

Uruguayan novelist and short story writer. Her first book of short stories, *La mano de nieve* (1951) (*The Hand of Snow*) has been described as poetic, fantastic and supernatural, combining a subtle intuition of life and death, metaphoric and with an open ending. *Felicidad y otras tristezas* (1964) (*Happiness and Other Sadnesses*), which includes some short stories from her previous book, was, according to the critic Arturos Visca, 'one of the most original imaginary worlds in the Uruguayan narratives of the last decades'. *Salto Cancan* (1969) (*Cancan Kick*), her first novel, treats reality and characters of a lower world ironically, mixing the dramatic with the grotesque. She has also written a historical novel *Los rebeldes del 800* (1971) (*The Rebels of the 800*).

Silver Age, The

A term used to designate the period in Russian culture that incorporated various ▷modernist movements (decadence, symbolism, acmeism, futurism). It began as a wave of reaction against ▷realism in literature, utilitarian views of art, posivitist philosophy, and Victorian morality. Nietzsche's propagation of the centrality of art and creativity in human life was of great importance, and other non-Russian influences included Schopenhauer, Wagner, Ibsen, Strindberg, Maeterlinck, the French symbolists, and the Polish writer Przybyszewski. The first Russian journal to make room for modernist literature was *The Northern Herald*, co-edited by Akim Volynskii and ▷Liubov' Gurévich. The period is often dated from 1892, with Dmitri Merezhkovsky's lectures 'On the Reasons for the Decline and on the New Currents in Contemporary Russian Literature', but it can equally be said to have started in 1893 with the appearance of ▷Zinaida Gíppius's iconoclastic poem 'Song'. The end came around 1925 with the growth of a new hierarchy of genres. The term itself arose by analogy to ▷The Golden Age – the great age of Russian poetry in the early 19th century. The Silver Age was perhaps *the* 'Golden Age' for women poets.

The Silver Age was a time of innovation and ferment. Literature of the period often exhibits a duality of mood: on the one hand a *fin de siècle* sense of despair, cynicism and boredom, an apocalyptic sense that an entire way of life is ending; on the other, a sense of excitement, energy and anticipation of the coming of a new age.

Literary life became quite complex, with various modernist groups in poetry, prose, and the theatre competing for dominance. The growth of cities and increasing literacy created conditions for the marketing of a popular literature on a scale never seen before in Russia.

▷Bashkirtseff, Marie; Láppo-Danilévskaia, Nadezhda; Lókhvitskaia, Mirra; Nagródskaia, Evdokiia; Ol'nem; Ratushínskaia, Irina; Pávlova, Karolina; 'Poem Without a Hero'; St Petersburg; Veselítskaia, Lidiia; *Daughter of the People*
Bib: Clowes, E.W., *The Revolution of Moral Consciousness*; Cioran, S.D., *The Apocalyptic Symbolism of Andrej Belyj*; Heim, M.H. (trans.) and Karlinsky, S. (ed.), *Anton Chekhov's Life and Thought*; Bowlt, J.E., *The Silver Age*; Brooks, J., *When Russia Learned to Read*; Donchin, G., *The Influence of French Symbolism on Russian Poetry*; Large, D. and Weber, W., *Wagnerism in Russia*; Poggioli, R., *Poets of Russia*; Pyman, A., *The Life of Aleksandr Blok*; Rabinowitz, S. (ed.), *The Noise of Change*; Richardson, W., *'Zolotoe Runo' and Russian Modernism: 1905–1910*; Rosenthal, B.G., *Dmitri Sergeevich Merezhkovsky and the Silver Age*; Rosenthal, B.G. (ed.), *Nietzsche in Russia*; West, J., *Russian Symbolism*.

'Silver-Fork School, The' ▷Fashionable Novel, The (The Silver Fork School)

Simó, Ana María (born 1943)
Cuban short story writer. She is one of the most outstanding members of an avant-garde group known as '*El Puente*' ('The Bridge'). In her stories there is a constant use of nightmarish fantasies, as in *Las Fábulas (1962) (Fables)*.

Simó, Isabel-Clara (born 1943)
Spanish novelist. Her work is primarily concerned with the oppression of women, workers and the Catalan-speaking people. Her main novels are: *Es quan miro que hi veig clar* (1979) (*It's When I Look that I See Clearly*); *Júlia* (1983); *Bresca* (1985) (*Honeycomb*), and *Idols* (1985).
▷Catalan women's writing

Simons, Beverly (born 1938)
Canadian dramatist, born Beverly Rosen at Flin Flon, Manitoba. She attended McGill University and the University of British Columbia; she now lives in Vancouver, Britich Columbia. Her extensive study of music informs much of the energy of her dramatic dialogue. *Crabdance* (1969), her most famous play, is an abstract and symbolic treatment of an elderly woman. Ritual as a means of maintaining identity and avoiding death is explored in *The Green Lawn Rest Home* (1973); *Preparing/Crusader/Triangle* (1975) is a dramatic trilogy, also about preparing for death. *Leela Means to Play* (1976) is experimental in its reliance on oriental process drama.
Bib: Special issue of *Canadian Theatre Review* (Winter, 1976).

Sinclair, Catherine (1800–1864)
Scottish (▷Scotland) novelist and writer of ▷children's literature. She was born in

Edinburgh and lived there for most of her life, concerning herself with philanthropic work in the city. Her famous novel for children is ▷*Holiday House* (1839), while her adult novels include *Jane Bouverie or, Prosperity and Adversity* (1846, reissued as *Jane Bouverie or, How She Became an Old Maid* in 1855). Most of Sinclair's writings are moralistic and religious, and she published a tract in 1852, *A Letter on the Principles of the Christian Faith*.

Sinclair, Jo (born 1913)
US novelist and short-story writer. Born Ruth Seid, of Russian immigrants, Sinclair grew up in Cleveland, Ohio. She is of the Jewish working class. Unable to afford college, she worked at various tedious jobs and published stories about poverty in *New Masses*, a leftist magazine. In 1946 her novel, *Wasteland*, won a $10,000 Harper Prize. It focuses on a Jew who hates herself.

The Changelings (1955) depicts the friendship between the adolescent Judy, a Jew, and Clara, an African-American. Clara's family move into Judy's Jewish community and are victims of racial intolerance. In Sinclair's analysis, the community scapegoats African-Americans to maintain a stable identity. Its bigotry reflects its own insecurities. The girls' friendship represents the possibility for social reconciliation, and it emphasizes also the importance of female bonding in a male-dominated world.

Sinclair, May (1863–1946)
English novelist, poet, critic and essayist. Born into a shipowning family that went bankrupt, Sinclair lived with her mother from childhood, when her parents separated, until her mother's death in 1901. Sinclair was educated at home, but was placed for one year at Cheltenham Ladies' College and introduced to psychology, philosophy and classical literature. She supported herself consistently by reviews and translations. The success of her novel *The Divine Fire* (1904) created wide public exposure, and led to a promotional tour in the United States. Sinclair is perhaps best-known for her review in 1918 of part of ▷Dorothy Richardson's ▷*Pilgrimage* (1915–1967), in which she appropriated the psychological term ▷stream-of-consciousness to describe Richardson's representational technique.

Yet it is Sinclair's own literary output, as much as this comment, that places her centrally within the ▷modernist movement. Seen as one of the first writers to utilize psychoanalytic material, Sinclair is frequently concerned, as illustrated in *The Three Sisters* (1914), with the psychological struggle of women caught between social/sexual repression and desire. A similar analysis runs through earlier novels, such as *The Judgement of Eve* (1907), *Kitty Tailleur* (1908) and *The Creators* (1910). Sinclair's pamphlet for the Women Writers' Suffrage League, 'Feminism' (1912) and her biography of the ▷Brontës published in the same year, form a link between these novels and the theorization of a 'feminist novel' that underwrites *The Three Sisters*. Sinclair herself utilized the stream-of-consciousness technique in the novels ▷*Mary Olivier: A Life* (1919) and ▷*The Life and Death of Harriet Frean* (1922), although her later novels mark a return to the formal conventions of realism. They include: *The Helpmate* (1907), *The Tree of Heaven* (1917), *The Romantic* (1920), *Anne Severn and the Fieldings* (1922), *The Dark Night* (1924), *Far End* (1926), *The Allinghams* (1927) and *The History of Anthony Waring* (1927).

▷Feminist publishing (Britain); *Mary Olivier: A Life*; Stern, Gladys Berthe
Bib: Boll, T., *Miss May Sinclair: Novelist*; Zegger, H., *May Sinclair*.

Sindoor
The red powder placed by a Hindu groom in the parting of his bride's hair during their marriage ceremony. It is a very distinctive indicator of a Hindu woman's marital status. The colour represents the richness of the wife's married state and, like all forms of colour and decoration in the dress, must be surrendered if she becomes a widow. The *bindi*, a coloured spot worn on the forehead, traditionally conveyed the same information about a woman's marital status.

Single Cell (1986)
Work by Japanese writer Masuda Mizuko (born 1948). Shiiba Mikio, a male graduate student at the Department of Agriculture, is researching the single cell. Both animal and plant cells gather and gel even when they are forced to separate. A cell continues to be isolated when it is perpetually stirred. However, a cell's membrane grows enormously, and eventually suffocates the cell when its protective cover becomes too thick. Ryoko, with whom Shiiba is living, is a woman like a cell. She wants no family, and instead of taking care of him, she is always sleeping. Yet she and he are drawn to each other like cells until she suddenly disappears one day. In this work Masuda, writing entirely from a ▷new woman's perspective, expresses the view that man is as unreliable as woman.

Sing Song, A Nursery Rhyme Book (1872)
A collection of nonsense verse and nursery rhymes by British poet ▷Christina Rossetti. Written for children, the poems explore the imaginative possibilities of language, emphasizing sound, repetition and word play. Notable lyrics include 'Who has seen the wind?' and 'How many seconds in a minute?'. *Sing Song* has been compared to William Blake's *Songs of Innocence and Experience* (1789 and 1794).

▷Children's literature (19th-century Britain)

Sinués y Navarro, Maria del Pilar (1835–1893)
Enormously popular Spanish novelist. She is alleged to be the author of more than a hundred works. Women were her primary and almost exclusive subjects; she wrote about gender roles, marriage, motherhood and domestic life.

Sipolo, Jully (born 1953)
Poet from the Solomon Islands. Sipolo began writing in 1980 after attending the first Solomon Islands Women Writers' Workshop. Her poems tackle gender issues, and parody and challenge the notion of 'civilization'. It has been said of her work that the 'feminist anger is more astringent and uncontrolled' (Subramani, *South Pacific Literature: from myth to fabulation*, 1985). Her only collection is *Civilized Girl* (1981).

Sirisingha, Supa (Luesiri) ▷Botan

Sirota Podhradských (1889) (The Podhradskýs' Orphan)
Novel by ▷Terézia Vansová, the first Slovak novel by a woman. The novel concerns a sensitive, honest, charming young lady, whose father is falsely accused of fraud and arson, becomes bankrupt and dies. After a miserable period in the house of her uncle, she eventually makes a happy marriage, and her father's good name is restored. The character represents Vansová's ideal of a woman, whose fundamental features are goodness and morality. The plot, full of unexpected turns, won many Slovak women readers, and was also praised by critics. Despite its over-sentimentality, the novel is a work of ▷realism whose worth lies mainly in its depiction of character and milieu.

Sister Outsider: Essays and Speeches (1984)
Essays by US writer ▷Audre Lorde which delineate her journey to define herself as an African-American lesbian poet. 'The Master's Tools Will Never Dismantle the Master's House' analyzes how repression is used as a means of social control. 'The Uses of the Erotic, the Erotic as Power' posits that the erotic is the core of self; it is the power of love that arises from the self's deepest non-rational knowledge. 'Poetry Is Not a Luxury' argues for the fusion of ancient and Anglo-American traditions, where the power of feeling is transformed into language; through language ideas arise and then follows action for survival and change. 'Scratching the Surface, some Notes on Barriers to Women and Loving' stresses that difference is a dynamic force which empowers the self and creates dialogues.

Sister To Scheherazade, A (1989)
English translation of *Ombre Sultane* (1987), by Algerian writer ▷Assia Djebar. The second part of Djebar's quartet on Algerian women, using material from the author's life. The first part, *L'Amour, la fantasia*, was translated as ▷*Fantasia: An Algerian Cavalcade* (1989).

Isma, the Scheherazade of the story, decides to act as a matchmaker to her own husband: to find him another wife in order to free herself from his anger and sexual attentions. She thinks of the lives of women she knows: 'The women's wombs bring forth children, their arms are never still, their faces bend low over the fire to stoke the flames under steaming cauldrons . . . As for the man who leaves the house, who comes and goes, who enters to give orders . . . the man, all men – they batten on us, fed every day from our overflowing hands . . . then, as every night approaches, we must submit our weary bodies to them, bodies that yearn for the moment of peace, for the calm lake of prayers.'

Like many older women before her, Isma is replaced by Hajila, a younger co-wife, and can rest and pray in the mosque.

Djebar's 'cinematic' art can be seen in the prevalence of visual imagery and the depiction of scenes against light and darkness. Interiors are always dim or dark, figures are picked against a window or a door, often closed. Exteriors are suffused with sunlight, and the sky shows blue with a distant view of the sea. The camera eye picks out Hajila compulsively roaming 'at liberty through the sunlit spaces of the town', and sees Isma following her and watching over her. Isma rescues her daughter, Meriem, from following the pattern to which she and Hajila have submitted, and takes her away.

Sistren Collective

This community theatre group in Jamaica has been central in drawing international attention to women's theatre in the Caribbean region. Stemming from the idea of popular theatre, a people's theatre drawing on group composition and collective research, Sistren is committed to social change, and has focused its activities on the lives of working-class black Jamaican women. The collective developed out of an experimental theatre project with the Jamaican School of Drama, led by Honor Ford-Smith, one of its directors. For a discussion of women's theatre in the Caribbean and the activities and aims of Sistren see 'Finding a Way to Tell It: Methodology and Commitment in Theatre About Women in Barbados and Jamaica' in ▷ *Out of the Kumbla*. Perhaps Sistren's best-known work is ▷ *Lionheart Gal*.

Sita

One of Hinduism's most popular heroines. She epitomizes the ideal Hindu wife who, in spite of the constant trials that her husband, Rama, forces on her, remains loyal and devoted to him.
▷ *Ramayana*; *Pati vrata dharm*

Sitwell, Edith (1887–1964)

English poet, critic, biographer and novelist. The eldest child of repressive aristocratic parents. The strength and loyalty of the relationship between the Sitwell children is well-documented. Unlike her brothers, Osbert (1892–1969) and Sacheverell (1897–1988), Edith Sitwell was educated at home by governesses, one of whom, Helen Rootham, introduced her to the French symbolist poets, and in particular to the work of Arthur Rimbaud (1854–1891). Publication of *Twentieth-Century Harlequinade* (1916), a compilation of Edith and Osbert Sitwell's poetry, set the tone for the Sitwell's fame, in which artistic merit was heavily imbricated with aristocratic eccentricity. Edith

Sitwell's cultivation of eccentricity is strongly expressed in her much-photographed elaborate style of dress. Her role as editor of the controversial and confrontational journal *Wheels* – committed to the support of formal experimentation in poetry and a vehicle for English ▷ modernist verse – consolidated her notoriety.

Sitwell's first volume of poetry was *The Mother* (1915). With the publication of *Clowns' Houses* (1918), Sitwell had developed a distinctive poetic style, consisting of rhythmic experiments, striking, condensed images, play with 'sense' and 'nonsense', and consistent application of assonance, dissonance and alliterative effects as the dominant experimental devices. *Façade* (1922) is Sitwell's most famous undertaking, a poetic sequence underscored by modern dance rhythms, set to music by William Walton (1902–1983) and performed live by Sitwell in 1923. During the 1930s Sitwell produced a number of critical works, including *Aspects of Modern Poetry* (1934) and a biography, *Alexander Pope* (1930). The end of World War II is frequently seen as marking the second phase in Sitwell's poetic development, with subsequent poems characterized by the use of religious or biblical imagery within a philosophically framed interrogation of war. Sitwell's only novel is *I Live under a Black Sun* (1937), and a compilation of poems by all three Sitwell siblings, *Trio*, was published in 1938. Sitwell's autobiography is *Taken Care Of* (1965).

Selected other writings: *The Wooden Pegasus* (1920), *The Sleeping Beauty* (1924), *Poetry and Criticism* (1925), *Elegy on Dead Fashion* (1926), *Five Poems* (1928), *Poems New and Old* (1940), *Street Songs* (1942), *A Poet's Notebook* (1943), *A Notebook on William Shakespeare* (1948), *The Canticle of the Rose* (1949), *Collected Poems* (1954), *Selected Poems* (1965).
▷ Cunard, Nancy
Bib: Brophy, J., *Edith Sitwell: The Symbolist Order*; Elborn, G., *Edith Sitwell: A Biography*; Joyce, M., *Triad of Genius*; Lehmann, J., *Edith Sitwell*; Lehmann, R., *A Nest of Tigers*; Salter, E., *The Last Years of a Rebel: A Memoir of Edith Sitwell*.

16th-century treatises on women (Italy)

Prose treatises on the equality or superiority of women, written mainly by men, became common in 16th-century Italy. The treatises are, on the whole, abstract works, never works of social analysis. Most of them were concerned only marginally with women, as their main concern was the *effect* of women's superiority on *men*, with women presented as vehicles for inspiration and ennobling of the male. The most famous treatise, with sections for and against the superiority of women, is Baldassare Castiglione's *Il Cortegiano* (1528, translated as *The Courtier*, 1561). There are three famous late contributions by women to this debate, all now available. ▷ Moderata Fonte's ▷ *Il merito delle donne* (*Woman's Worth*) of 1600 reverses the format, with her female characters discussing men; ▷ Lucrezia Marinelli Vacca

attacks misogyny in her *La nobilatà e eccelenze delle donne, et i difetti e mancamenti de gli huomini* (*On the Nobility and Excellence of Woman and the Defects and Failings of Man*) of 1600; Suor Arcangela Tarabotti in her *La tirannia paterna/La semplicità ingannata* (*Paternal Tyranny/Deceived Innocence*) of 1654 speaks out strongly in favour of female self-determination and against the practice of entombing young women in convents against their will.
▷Renaissance

Bib: Fahy, C., 'Early Renaissance Treatises on Women' in *Italian Studies*, 11, 1956, pp. 30–56 (with an extensive appendix); Panizza, L, 'A Guide to Recent Bibliography on Italian Renaissance Writings about and by Women' in *Bulletin of the Society for Italian Studies*, 22, 1989, pp. 3–25.

Skinner, Mollie (1876–1955)

Australian novelist. Skinner was born in Perth and educated in England but returned to Western Australia in 1899. She published *Letters of a VAD* (1918) under the pseudonym of R.E. Leake; *Black Swans* (1925), a romance with a preface by D.H. Lawrence; *Men are We* (1927), a collection of Aboriginal stories; and three other novels. She is most famous for ▷*The Boy in the Bush* (1924), which she wrote in collaboration with D.H. Lawrence.

Skram, Amalie (1846–1905)

Norwegian prose writer. She was born in Bergen, where her father was a businessman who left his family. When she was eighteen, she married a sea-captain and had two sons with him. She left him in 1880 and began to write. In 1882 she had her début with *Madam Höjers Leiefolk* (*Madam Höjer's Tenants*), which had all the ingredients of naturalism. She is considered the first naturalistic writer in Norway. In 1884 she married the Danish writer Erik Skram and lived in Copenhagen; here she wrote *Constance Ring* (1885) and *Lucie* (1888), pessimistic descriptions of women's sexuality and of conventional marriage.

In the autobiographical novels *Professor Hieronimus* and *Paa Sct. Jørgen* (1895) (*At St Joergen's*), she described her depression after having a daughter with Erik Skram when she was in a dilemma between mothering and writing. She criticized the ▷patriarchal mental hospital that forced its female patients into passivity and obedience, but also wrote about the warmth among the patients, and between patients and nurses.

Traditionally the four volumes of *Hellemyrsfolket* (1887–1898) (*The People of Hellemyr*) are considered the classic work of Norwegian naturalism, the story of a family in decay. It contains some very fine descriptions of the relations between children and parents, but today her other novels are more appreciated.

Skram always stated that what she had written was 'true' and that the people she depicted were

'real'. Her social criticism is severe, and though she may seem pessimistic she is not a determinist.

Slater, Frances Charlotte (1892–1947)

South African novelist who published seventeen novels under the pseudonym F. (for Francis) Bancroft. Born on the Slater family farm in the Eastern Cape, she was educated at home and at a local girls' school. She worked first as a teacher and governess for fourteen years, and then as a nurse from 1896 until the end of the Anglo-Boer War (1902). Her fiction writing appears to have started at this point. After living in England for a few years, writing reviews and essays for English magazines, she returned to the Eastern Cape, where she continued her career as a journalist and novelist.

Unfashionable these days (if remembered at all), perhaps partly because of her views on 'the great colour peril' expressed most patently in *Of Like Passions* (1907), and partly because of her racy, popular and now dated style, her books nevertheless engage seriously with contemporary social issues in South Africa: women's suffrage, the Temperance movement, pacifism, problems of loyalty in the conflict between British and Boer. Her novels are particularly interesting for their representation of gender in a specific historical context. *The Veldt Dwellers* (1912) deals with a Boer-British family, its divided loyalties in the Anglo–Boer War (1899–1902), and the parts played by 'manliness' and 'femininity' in the construction of South African patriotism. Bancroft wrote three more novels about this family: *Thane Brandon* (1913), *The Brandons* (1928), and *The Sure Years* (1931). In *The Settler's Eldest Daughter* (1920), which was written for the centenary celebrations of the British 1820 Settlers to the Cape, she examines the problems faced by both Dutch and English settlers.

Her literary remains include an unpublished comedy in four acts, and manuscripts of unpublished short stories, as well as a notebook, extensive correspondence, and manuscripts of published work. These are held at the National English Literary Museum in Grahamstown.

Other novels: *Richard Beverley* (1903), *Her Reuben* (1906), *Time and Chance* (1909), *Dalliance and Strife* (1914), *Money's Worth* (1915), *The Head Man* (1917), *An Armed Protest* (1918), *Great Possessions* (1919), *The Liquor King* (1921), *Love's Bondage* (1929), *Emergency* (1929), and *Green Youth* (1933).

Slave Girl, The (1977)

A novel, by the Nigerian writer ▷Buchi Emecheta, set in the period of early colonialism when village life was relatively undisturbed. Ojebeta, a young village girl, is sold by her brother to a wealthy woman trader in the large market town of Onitsha. The novel portrays both the institution of ▷slavery and the oppression of women within it. Ojebeta's marriage is seen, not as a route to freedom, but as the exchange of one master for another.

Slave narratives (18th and 19th century US)

US literary genre of Afro-American writers, among the earliest unique forms of US literature and the first form to be developed by Afro-Americans. Expressly anti-slavery, directed to national and international audiences, slave narratives in the 19th century became increasingly associated with the abolitionist movement and abolitionist publications. In the pre-Civil War 19th century these personal narratives emphasized slavery's effects on slave and slaveholder alike, calling on prevailing social and moral values to inspire national opposition to slavery. Most women's slave narratives date from the 19th century and expressly address slavery's contradiction to behavioural, maternal, marital, and sexual ideals of 19th-century womanhood. ▷Harriet A. Jacobs's ▷*Incidents in the Life of a Slave Girl* is the best-known woman's slave narrative; Harriet E. Wilson's ▷*Our Nig: or, Sketches from the Life of a Free Black*, often classified as the first Afro-American novel, works from the slave narrative form.

Slavery

England: Slavery grew during the 17th century, and people of colour entered England through the ports, especially Bristol, which was the centre of the slave trade. African slaves were taken to English colonies in the West Indies, where the slaves and the colonized native population might not share a language, so the new forms of English from these regions did not emerge as written discourses until after the 18th century. Writers from ▷Aphra Behn to ▷Hannah More wrote about slavery, and abolitionist activity began towards the end of the 18th century, by which time there was an active oral culture among slaves using song in African and English languages (see Sir Hans Sloane, *A Voyage to the Islands Madera, Barbados, Nieves, S. Christophers and Jamaica*, 1707).
Bib: Pratt, Mary Louise, *Imperial Eyes*:
West Africa: The vast majority of people taken from Africa to the Caribbean, North America and across the Sahara as slaves came from the west coast. Many of their descendants returned to settle, and left their distinctive mark in communities in places like Lagos and Abeokuta. The West African country Liberia was established specifically for returnees from the USA. This wave of immigration had a profound effect on the patterns of class and family status, even of national identity, in the countries concerned. Sierra Leone, Nigeria and Ghana all have families who can trace their ancestry to returned slaves.

It was a sad fact that slavery could not have happened on the scale it did without the collusion of local people, who acted as go-betweens for the slavers. The existence of mulatto families, often with European surnames, is testimony to this. But slavery was also an accepted institution within

many West African societies, as reflected in ▷Ama Ata Aidoo's play ▷*Anowa*, and ▷Buchi Emecheta's novel ▷ *The Slave Girl*.
    ▷Bedford, Simi

Slaves in Algiers; or, A Struggle for Freedom (1794)

The only extant play by North American dramatist and actress ▷Susanna Haswell Rowson. *Slaves in Algiers* was first produced in 1794 by the New Theatre company in Philadelphia. Outspokenly feminist in plot and dialogue, it dramatizes women's power to escape tyranny and control their own lives through the tale of a group of North Americans held hostage in Algiers. While the women reject the submission demanded in this foreign culture, the male characters evoke personas of dominance and control but, in the end, are ineffectual. The following year, the play's concern for women's rights was publicly attacked by the English political writer William Cobbett (1763–1835) in a pamphlet, *A Kick for a Bite*; Rowson responded in the preface to her next work, *Trials of the Human Heart* (1795), by satirizing Cobbett's critical abilities and suggesting he had not actually read her work. *Slaves* is important as a reminder of women's contributions to early North American drama and in broadening our perception of Rowson's feminism.

Slick, Jonathan ▷Stephens, Ann Sophia

Slipperjack, Ruby (born 1952)

Canadian painter and writer. An Ojibway Indian, Slipperjack grew up in northern Ontario on her father's trapline, and graduated from Lakehead University in 1989. The stories she heard as a child made her want to write. Her novel, *Honour the Sun* (1987), is a closely followed account of a young girl's coming of age in an isolated community.
Bib: Lutz, H., *Contemporary Challenges: Conversations with Canadian Native Authors.*

Smart, Elizabeth (1913–1986)

Canadian novelist and poet, born in Ottawa. She attended private school, and at nineteen travelled to England. She returned to Canada and wrote for the *Ottawa Journal*, just before she met and conceived a lifelong and sustained obsession with the poet George Barker, who fathered her four children. She moved to England in 1943, remaining there except for two years (1982–1984) when she held writer-in-residenceships in Canada. She supported herself as a journalist and by writing for advertising agencies, and was for several years literary editor of *Queen* magazine. Her first and most famous novel, ▷*By Grand Central Station I Sat Down and Wept* (1945), is a lyrical and intensely poetic incantation of a love affair. After a long silence, Smart published two volumes of poetry, *A Bonus* (1977) and *Eleven Poems* (1982). *The Assumption of the Rogues and Rascals* (1977), another prose work in the form of a poetic meditation, much concerned with the

dilemmas of the writer, brought her back into the public eye. *In the Meantime* (1984) collects occasional poems and prose pieces. Her journals, *Necessary Secrets* (1986, ed. A. van Wart), and *Early Writings* (1987) are also available.
Bib: Sullivan, R., *By Heart.*

Smedley, Agnes (1892–1950)

US novelist and journalist. Born in poverty in rural Missouri, Smedley dedicated herself to revolutionary causes in the non-Western world. In 1917 she began writing for socialist newspapers. After being imprisoned for associating with the Indian nationalist cause against British colonial rule, she moved to Europe. She spent two years in psychoanalysis after attempting suicide. From 1928 to 1941 Smedley worked as a journalist in China aiding the revolution. She spent the 1940s lecturing about China in the US. However, in the late 1940s Smedley was forced to leave the US as a result of her communist sympathies.

Daughter of Earth (1929) is Smedley's autobiographical novel. Born in poverty, the chief protagonist, Marie, is radicalized by her awareness of women's powerlessness in marriage. Her struggle for a romantic, heterosexual relationship of sexual equality ends in despair. Smedley suggests that the social forces causing Marie's early deprivations have damaged her psyche, irreparably splitting intellect and emotions.

Other works include: *Battle Hymn of China* (1943), *Chinese Destinies: Sketches of Present-Day China* (1933), *China's Red Army Marches* (1934) and *Portraits of Chinese Women in Revolution* (1976).

Smile Please: An Unfinished Autobiography (1979)

This autobiography by the Caribbean writer ▷Jean Rhys was published posthumously. It illuminates much of her fiction, and is particularly important as so much critical assessment of her art tends to take a biographical approach, thus creating what has been called the 'composite' Jean Rhys heroine, who is seen to appear throughout her writing career. The work is not written as a formal autobiography, but comprises sketches and diary entries concerning Rhys's literary life and relationships with men. It is also important in that it reflects the central impact of Rhys's ▷Dominican ▷childhood on her creative imagination. See Carole Angier, *Jean Rhys* (1991).

Smirnóva, Sof'ia Ivanovna (1852–1921)

Russian fiction writer and dramatist. Smirnóva began writing young, and published a number of novels, popular in their time, devoted to the life of the idealists of the 1860s and their struggle to find both love and useful vocations (*A Small Light*, 1871; *Salt of the Earth*, 1872; *The School District Administrator*, 1873; *Strength of Character*, 1876). After her marriage to the actor Nikolai Sazonov in 1877, she saw several plays produced; Chekhov praised her comedy *The Anthill* (1896). The fiction she wrote in the 1890s was more varied in

tone and theme: a comic novella about the life of a disorganized St Petersburg family (*Through Fire and Water*, 1893); a harsh, wrenching story of an orphaned boy's death on the Moscow streets ('The Son of the Soldier's Wife', 1897). In 'A Personal Insult' (1897), set in a factory, and 'Head Over Heels' (1897), which takes place in an urban office, Smirnóva criticizes women's inability to separate the personal and the professional in their working lives.

Smith, Anna Young (1756–?1780)

North American poet. Born on 5 November 1756, she was orphaned at an early age and raised by her aunt, the poet ▷Elizabeth Graeme Fergusson, who supported and encouraged her literary talents. A prolific poet, she addressed conventional poetic themes but did not avoid controversial political and social topics. She published several poems in literary periodicals, including ▷'An Ode of Gratitude' to her aunt for her love and encouragement. She was only in her early twenties when she died from complications during childbirth.

Smith, Barbara ▷Black feminist criticism; Lesbian feminist criticism

Smith, Dodie (Dorothy Gladys) (born 1896)

English dramatist, novelist and writer for children; she also used the ▷pseudonyms C.L. Anthony and Charles Henry Percy. Smith initially worked as an actress and dramatist. The success of her play *Autumn Crocus* (1931) enabled her to write full-time. *Dear Octopus* (1938) was a West-End theatre success and established Smith as a writer. Smith spent World War II in the United States, returning to England in 1950, from which time she has been a prolific writer of novels and children's fiction. Her best-known prose works are the romantic novel *I Capture the Castle* (1948), later a play, and the children's book *The Hundred and One Dalmations* (1956). Her four volumes of autobiography (1974–1985) are entitled *Look Back With . . .*

Smith, Eunice (1757–1823)

North American religious essayist. Born in 1757 in a small western Massachusetts community, she was a devout Baptist whose writings exhort the tenets of that sect. Her most popular publication was her first, ▷*Some Arguments Against Worldly-Mindedness* (1791), in which a dialogue between Mary and Martha is employed to direct women readers' attention to the next world rather than earthly pursuits.

Other works are: *Practical Language Interpreted in a Dialogue Between a Believer and an Unbeliever* (1792), *Some Exercises of a Believing Soul* (1792) and *Some Motives to Engage Those Who Have Professed the Name of the Lord Jesus* (1798).

Smith, Lillian (1897–1966)

US novelist. A transplanted Georgian, Smith was called 'the Negro's White Joan of Arc'. She served as head of the music department at the Methodist Mission School in Huchow from 1922 to 1925. The social upheaval in China stimulated Smith to protest against gender and racial roles in the South. Throughout Smith's career, local and national government agencies harassed her. She observed that people learn racial segregation by segregating minds, hearts and consciences from one another.

As principal of her family's Laurel Falls Camp for Girls from 1925 to 1940, Smith focused on the emotional and psychological integration of the individual, as discussed in *The Girl* (1941). Her novel, ▷ *Strange Fruit* (1944), exposes the 'strange fruit' of Southern racism. *Killers of the Dream* (1949) is an autobiographical account of the South's collective childhood. In 1936 she and Paula Snelling, her lifelong companion, published *Pseudopodia* (later *North Georgia Review* and *South Today*), the only Southern journal to showcase African-American writers.

Other works include: *The Journey* (1954), *Now Is the Time* (1955), *One Hour* (1959), *Memory of a Large Christmas* (1980), *Our Faces, Our Worlds* (1964) and *The Winner Names the Age: A Collection of Writings* (1982).

Smith, Margaret (fl 1660) ▷ Traske, Mary, and Margaret Smith

Smith, Pamela C. (1869–?)

There is little available information on this early Caribbean writer who was a pioneer in documenting ▷ Jamaica's ▷ oral history. Her first publication was 'Two Negro Stories from Jamaica' in the *Journal of American Folk-lore* Vol. IX, No. XXXV October-December 1896. Later she included these stories in a volume of twenty-two narratives, ▷ *Anancy Stories*. She also published *Chim Chim: Folk Stories from Jamaica* (1905).

Smith, Pauline (1882–1959)

South African shory story writer and novelist. Born in Oudtshoorn to British parents who had emigrated to the Cape Colony a few years earlier, she left for school in Britain at the age of twelve, and, because of her father's death, spent the rest of her life away from South Africa, largely in Dorset, making the few return trips her health and pocket would allow. Born out of loss, her writing turns repeatedly to the time and place that spelled home: the Little Karoo and its rural Afrikaans-speaking population, from the last decades of the 19th century into the 20th.

Her first collection of short stories, ▷ *The Little Karoo* (1925; second revised edition 1930; reprinted 1990), confronts the social problems of this poor-white population at a time when the encroaching values of capitalism were beginning to drive a wedge between rich and poor. Although her regional stance is elegiac, and particularly so in her novel, ▷ *The Beadle* (1926), it is also critical: the security offered by the memory of the patriarchal Afrikaner community is offset by patriarchy's processes of subordination – of women, most obviously to her, and also of black South Africans, as she hesitantly recognized. Thus, although *The Beadle* tends to idealization, as if the benevolent patriarchalism of a neo-feudal society could cope with the poverty of the region and the destructive potential of Calvinism, it is haunted by its own repressed questions concerning gender, race and class.

Smith also published *A. B. '. . . a minor marginal note'* (1933), a writer's tribute to British novelist Arnold Bennett (1867–1931), who had introduced her to French and Russian ▷ realism, and encouraged her to write about her South African rather than Scottish heritage. This was followed by a set of children's stories, *Platkops Children* (1935), which she had started writing in her adolescence and revised for publication much later.

That she spent the rest of her life unable to complete her next novel was probably largely due to Bennett's death, for – as a friend who provided constant encouragement – he might have chivvied her out of her increasing self-doubt, her growing despair at European fascism and its implications for a racially-defined South Africa, and even her chronic ill-health, which she sometimes felt was exacerbated by her failure to write. Her literary remains include an unpublished South African journal (1913–14), and a large number of letters, mostly to English writer Frank Swinnerton and South African writer ▷ Sarah Gertrude Millin, as well as other unpublished work.
Bib: Driver, Dorothy (ed.), *Pauline Smith*, and *Pauline Smith and the Crisis of Daughterhood*.

Smith, Sarah ▷ Stretton, Hesba

Smith, Stevie (1902–1971)

English poet and novelist. Born in Hull, Smith lived mainly in north London, working as a secretary to the publishers Newnes and Pearson, and spent most of her adult life caring for an elderly aunt. The frequently cited 'anarchic' characteristic of Smith's poetry and its recurrent theme of sexual anxiety are often read in relation to this domestic context. Suburban life provided the material for much of Smith's writings. During the 1960s renewed interest in her work was encouraged through a successful series of public readings.

Smith's first publication, ▷ *Novel on Yellow Paper* (1936), plays with the generic boundaries of the novel form by inserting a large amount of poetry within the body of the text. Following the publication of her first volume of poetry, *A Good Time Was Had by All* (1937), her subsequent novels, *Over the Frontier* (1938) and *The Holiday* (1949), are more conventional in style, but characterized by intense melancholia. Smith's poetry, typified in the title poem of ▷ *Not Waving But Drowning* (1957), is marked by its tendency towards understatement, and a childlike application of rhyme and rhythm, frequently supplemented by sparse, quasi-comic line drawings. Often the poetry engages in dialogue with Christianity and fairytale themes, and stresses the phonetic aspect of language.

Other works: *Tender Only to One* (1938), *Mother, What Is Man?* (1942), *Harold's Leap* (1950), *Some Are More Human Than Others* (1958), *The Frog Prince and Other Poems* (1966), *Scorpion and Other Poems* (1971), *The Collected Poems of Stevie Smith* (1975) and *'Me Again'* – *The Uncollected Writings of Stevie Smith* (1981).

Bib: Barbera, J., *Stevie: A Biography*, and *Stevie Smith: A Bibliography*; Dick, K., *Ivy and Stevie*; Spalding, A., *Stevie Smith: A Critical Biography*; Whitemore, H., *Stevie: A Play*.

Smither, Elizabeth (born 1941)
New Zealand poet and novelist. Elizabeth Smither began publishing in the mid-1970s and has published collections of poetry as well as some fiction since establishing herself as one of the most productive and visible of New Zealand woman poets. Smither has worked as a librarian, journalist, critic and editor. Her work is highly intertextual, with explicit reference to, and play on, contemporary culture (especially film) as well as historical texts. There is little personal or confessional writing in Smither's work; her poems are usually distanced from emotion or personal experience, and instead she plays wittily with concepts, abstractions, or invents fictions which rewrite history.

Publications: *Here Come the Clouds* (1975); *You're Very Seductive William Carlos Williams* (1978); *The Legend of Marcello Mastroianni's Wife* (1981); ▷*Casanova's Ankles* (1983); *First Blood* (novel) (1983); *Shakespeare Virgins* (1983); *Professor Musgrove's Canary* (1985); *Gorilla/Guerrilla* (1986); *Brother-love, sister-love* (novel) (1986); *A Pattern of Marching* (1989).

Smith-Rosenberg, Caroll
North American feminist historian and lecturer. She is professor of History and Psychiatry at the University of Pennysylvania. Since its resurgence in the 1970s, British and North American feminism has drawn attention to the marginalization of women within traditional history, and has set about producing a new feminist historiography. Smith-Rosenberg was an important figure in the early days of this project. The title of her essay 'The Female World of Love and Ritual: Relations Between Women in Nineteenth-Century America' (1975) indicates the ▷woman-centred nature of her research. The essay appeared in the inaugural issue of the US feminist journal ▷*Signs*, and was tremendously influential, both in helping to shape a political feminist history of changes in class and gender relations and in presenting domesticity and family life as serious areas of historical research. Her other publications include: *Religion and the Rise of the American City* (1971); *Disorderly Conduct: Visions of Gender in Victorian America* (1985), and *The Body Politic* (forthcoming).

Smucker, Barbara (born 1915)
Children's writer, born and educated in Kansas, who worked as a journalist and a teacher until she married a Mennonite minister and professor. In 1969, after living in Chicago and Mississippi, they moved to Waterloo, Ontario, where Smucker worked as a librarian. She has written many award-winning books for children, including *Days of Terror* (1979), *Amish Adventure* (1983) and *Jacob's Little Giant* (1987). *Underground to Canada* (1977), a well-crafted historical novel about black slaves escaping to Canada on the Underground Railway, has been widely translated.

Smyth, Donna (born 1943)
Canadian dramatist and fiction writer, born in Kimberley, British Columbia. Educated at the Universities of Victoria, Toronto and London, she now teaches creative writing and English at Acadia University in Wolfville, Nova Scotia. Her play, *Susanna Moodie* (1976), is a dramatic version combining both ▷Suzanna Moodie's own ▷*Roughing it in the Bush* and ▷Margaret Atwood's ▷*The Journals of Susanna Moodie*. *Giant Anna* (1978–9) is a play based on Anna Swan, a Nova Scotia female giant who worked for P.T. Barnum's circus, who is also the subject of ▷Susan Swan's *The Biggest Modern Woman in the World* (1983). Smyth's novel *Quilt* (1982), uses patchwork as a design for the fiction, bringing three different stories together in communal quilt-making. *Subversive Elements* (1986) is an environmental documentary drama. In 1976, she was one of the founders of ▷*Atlantis: A Woman's Studies Journal*.

Bib: Kulyk Keefer, J., *Under Eastern Eyes*; Smyth, D., in *Gynocritics*.

Snugglepot and Cuddlepie Series , The (1916–1940)
Australian children's book series, written and illustrated by ▷May Gibbs. Gibbs's characters are based upon personifications of Australian wild flowers and bush creatures. The first in the series was *Gumnut Babies* (1916) and the last *The Complete Adventures of Snugglepot and Cuddlepie* (1940).

▷Children's literature (Australia)

Soares, Manuel ▷Lisboa, Irene do Céu Viera

So Big (1924)
US novel. ▷Edna Ferber's Pulitzer Prize-winning book focuses on Selina De Jong, a widow who must support her son. Working unselfishly, she makes the debt-ridden farm prosper. She derives her identity from her work, not from relationships to men. Thus she survives her son's disappointment when he sacrifices principles for material success.

Sobti, Krishna (born 1925)
Indian novelist and short story writer. She was born in the western state of Gujarat, and educated in Delhi, Simla and Lahore. She was an Honorary

Fellow at Punjab University from 1980 to 1982. In 1980 she won both the Sahitya Akademi Award and the Sahitya Shiromani Award. Most of her writing is in Hindi, but several of her works are available in English translation. ▷Blossoms in Darkness (1979) is a translation of Surajmukhi Andhere Ke (1972).

Socialist realism (Russia)

The term came into existence in 1932. Socialist realism was proclaimed the official 'method' of Soviet literature at the First Congress of Soviet Writers in 1934. As a mechanism for social control, centralization, and homogenization, socialist realism required 'a truthful, historically concrete depiction of reality in its revolutionary development'. Moreover, it 'must be combined with the task of the ideological transformation and education of the working men in the spirit of socialism' (Dictionary of Literary Terms, Moscow, 1974). The actual meaning of the term was always imprecise, and therefore open to political manipulation. In practice, socialist realism limited the style of literature to a bland, easily accessible language and to 'positive heroes' working towards a Utopian society, optimistically portrayed as just around the corner.

Socialist realism was particularly detrimental to women writers. These such as ▷Pánova, who did try to write within the canon, were chided for being too 'personal'. Themes that Soviet women writers deal with today, such as 'loneliness, divorce, abortion, illegitimacy, and the delusory nature of sexual equality' (N.N. Shneidman, Soviet Literature in the 1980s) were impermissible. Female characters were often relegated to the function of an obstacle to be overcome by the hero, or else became helpers, stalwart patriots, who served the new state at the cost of personal fulfilment. Original writings like ▷Seifúllina's ▷Virineia (1924) and ▷Shaginián's KiK (1929) were criticized and suppressed. With Stalin's death, the literary scene became less homogeneous, and there was a brief period of experiment and free expression during the ▷thaw. The homogenization of Russian literature, though, truly began disappearing with the introduction of Gorbachev's policy of ▷glásnost'.

▷Berggól'ts, Ol'ga; Going Under; Varlámova, Inna; What Is to Be Done?; Realism
Bib: Brown, E.J., Russian Literature Since the Revolution; Clark, Katerina, The Soviet Novel: History as Ritual; Gasiorowska, Xenia, Women in Soviet Fiction 1917–1964.

Socialist writers (Greece)

Socialist ideas which found their way in Greece at the end of the 19th century were fully embraced by many intellectuals. ▷Galateia Kazantzaki, ▷Elli Alexiou, ▷Lilika Nakou wrote novels dealing mainly with women's unequal relations with men, and women's experiences of an unjust society. Their work does not explicitly proclaim socialism, but indicates the need for change in society by identifying faults.

Society tale

A novella typical of romantic Russian prose of the late 1830s. The plots involve amorous intrigue, often between an idealistic or innocent person and a 'Byronic' cynic, or someone too weak to resist social pressure, to characterize and criticize the mores of wealthy, idle nobility. ▷Rostopchiná, ▷Gan, and ▷Dúrova were among the first women in Russia to write society tales. ▷Zhúkova and ▷Márchenko carried the genre – which made an ideal framework for depictions of the frustration and emptiness of upper-class female life – into the 1850s. Women continued to write society tales sporadically until late in the 19th century. ▷Karolina Pávlova's ▷A Double Life (1848), ▷N. Khvoshchínskaia's ▷In Hope of Better Days (1860), and ▷Veselítskaia's ▷Mimochka trilogy (1883–1893) are satiric deflations of the romantic conventions of the 'society tale'.
▷Rank and Money

Södergran, Edith (1892–1923)

Fenno-Swedish lyric poet. She is considered a revolutionary in ▷Fenno-Swedish literature. She was born in Petrograd, and was a lonely child, closely connected with her mother who was unhappily married. From the age of sixteen until she died, she had tuberculosis, and lived in the shadow of death. After the 1917 Russian Revolution, she was poor and her early death was also due to poverty.

She wrote her first poems in German and German Expressionism was an important inspiration to her. She had her début in Swedish with Dikter (1916) (Poems), the same year as ▷Hagar Olsson, whose poetry resembled hers, and who was the only critic to defend her poems. With Septemberlyran (1918) (September Lyre) modernism and Nietzsche (1844–1900) came into Fenno-Swedish literature, and the visionary line was continued with Rosenaltaret (1919) (The Rose Altar). Her principal work is Framtidens skugga (1920) (The Shadow of Future) an ecstasy of suffering. After this, she stopped writing poems and concentrated on God.

After her death Hagar Olsson published her last poems in Landet som icke är (1925) (The Land Which is Not). Södergran brought about a new epoch in Fenno-Swedish literature and in Scandinavia. Her intense Existentialism, impressive metaphors, and her mystical experiences were of great importance to many Scandinavian women modernists of the following decades.

Sofiia Petrovna (1988)

Novella by Russian writer ▷Lidiia Chukóvskaia written in 1939–1940. Like ▷Anna Akhmátova's long poem, ▷Requiem, this taut novella depicts the Stalin terror of 1937 through the experience of women standing in endless queues in hope of receiving news of arrested loved ones. Sofiia Petrovna cannot reconcile her naïve faith in the justice of Soviet society with the events taking place around her – the harassment and arrest of fellow workers at a publishing firm; the imprisonment and disappearance of her son, a talented and patriotic engineer. The contradictions drive her insane. As Chukóvskaia later noted, 'how can one make sense of deliberately planned chaos?' Like ▷ *Going Under*, *Sofiia Petrovna* was written with no hope of immediate publication, and carefully hidden for many years. It was first scheduled to appear in the Soviet Union in 1963, and was then withdrawn as the ▷thaw cooled toward exposure of past state crimes. With some changes, it was published abroad in English in 1967 as *The Deserted House*; in 1988 Chukóvskaia was finally able to see it into print in Russia, and a new translation based on that edition came out the following year.

Sofola, Zulu (born 1938)

Zulu Sofola

Nigerian dramatist. A prolific writer, Zulu Sofola comes from the Igbo-speaking part of Bendel State in Nigeria. She is head of the Department of Theatre Arts at the University of Ilorin, where she is actively involved in practical theatre production. Her published plays include *Wedlock of the Gods* (1985), *Wizard of Law* (1975), ▷ *King Emene* (1974), *Old Wines are Tasty* (1981), *Fantasies in the Moonlight* (1985), *Song of a Maiden* (1986) and ▷ *The Sweet Trap* (1979).

▷Onwueme, Tess

Bib: James, A., *In Their Own Voices: Interviews with African Women Writers*; Otokunefor, H. and Nwodo, O., *Nigerian Female Writers: A Critical Perspective*.

Sogno d'amore, Un (1905) (A Dream of Love)

Italian novel by ▷Leda Rafanelli, which tells the tale of two women, Anna and Amelia, the latter a romantic, the former politically active. Ironically, it is Anna, the activist, who falls in love. Rafanelli seems to use the character Anna here as a representative of her own experience. Love, for Anna, as for Rafanelli, fuels her rebellion and political activism. The novel is interesting for its interweaving of the romantic and political themes.

Sokhánskaia, Nadezhda Stepanovna (1823–1884)

Russian fiction writer, ethnographer, and publicist. In her remarkable *Autobiography*, written in 1847 and 1848, but only published in 1896, Sokhánskaia discussed the crisis that led to her determination to write, in a society that seemed to have no room for literary women. Returning to a dirt-floored house on the Ukrainian steppes after graduating from a Kharkov boarding school, she had to learn to appreciate the bleak beauty of the steppe, and to accept with religious resignation a future whose only bright spot was her vocation (cf B. Heldt, *Terrible Perfection*). She devoted the rest of her career to writing vivid novellas and stories derived from regional legends and history and, like her pseudonym Kokhanovskaia, from family heritage; she described her mother and aunts as 'living chronicles'. Sokhánskaia's closest affiliation in the radical 1860s was with the conservative Slavophiles, and most of her works were published in their minor journals. Her most conventional novella, in English, *The Rusty Linchpin* (1856; translated 1887), describing a romance between an independent girl and an entrepreneurial estate-owner, is closest to her own life. In her best work, *After-Dinner Guests* (1858), translated into English as *Luboff Archipovna* in 1887, an artless narrator proudly relates to a gentry women the story of her accommodation to a loveless marriage. The gentry woman sees in it the subtext of thwarted love that Liubov', the narrator, has suppressed. Sokhánskaia's tales, interwoven with folklore and told in the distinctive idiom, and reflecting the world view, of their protagonists, entitle her to a place among the great Russian regionalists which she has yet to be granted.

Solaria

An Italian literary magazine of considerable influence, in existence from 1926–1934. Some of the most radical and innovative Italian writers of this period wrote for it and were reviewed in its pages. Women writers were, nonetheless, marginalized in this, as in many other Italian literary journals. ▷Gianna Manzini was a regular contributor.

Soledad ▷Zamudio, Adela

Solidão (1939) (Solitude)

Written by Portuguese writer ▷Irene do Céu
Viera Lisboa and published under the pseudonym
João Falco. Like much of her work, *Solidão*,
subtitled '*Notas do punho de uma mulher*' (*Notes
from a Woman's Fist*), is an unusual book, with
neither a linear plot nor a sense of closure. Part
diary, part literary and social critique, it mixes
information on the author's life and travels with
commentaries on literary form.

Solinas Donghi, Beatrice (born 1923)

Italian novelist and short story writer. She studied
at Genoa University, has contributed several short
stories to Italian literary magazines, and has won
literary awards for her work. Her writing
concentrates on the people of Genoa, their work
in the fields, and at home, their experiences of
life, and the common human emotions of love,
jealousy and greed. The linguistic structures of
her work mirror those of Genoese dialect. *L'estate
della menzogna* (1956) (*The Summer of Lies*), her
first work, is a collection of short stories linked by
common themes and characters. *Natale non mio*
(1961) (*Not My Christmas*), is another collection of
short stories. The title story tells of an ambitious
middle-class family sliding into poverty. Much of
her later work is truly fabulous in tone and in
structure, borrowing its themes and form from
fables.

Her other works include: *L'uomo fedele* (1965)
(*The Faithful Man*); *L'aquilone drago* (1966) (*The
Kite*); *Le fiabe incantate* (1967) (*Enchanted Fables*);
Le voci incrociate (1970) (*Linked Voices*); *Fiabe a
Genova* (1972) (*Fables in Genoa*); *La grande fiaba
intrecciata* (1972) (*The Great Entwined Fable*).

Solitud (1905) (Solitude)

This novel by ▷Caterina Albert is usually
considered to be her masterpiece. It tells the story
of Mila, who accompanies her ineffectual husband
to a remote hermitage where he has taken a
keeper's job. Her husband has a nervous
breakdown and, at the end of the novel, Mila is
left alone but liberated. The novel blends the
naturalist formula (determinism, minute
description of reality) with mythic symbolism.

Solov'ëva, Poliksena Sergeevna (1867–1924)

Russian poet. Solov'ëva was born into an
accomplished family: her father was President of
Moscow University, and her older brother was the
philosopher Vladimir Solov'ëv, who strongly
influenced her. She studied art and voice, and
often illustrated books of her poems with her own
ink drawings. Her first poems, on nature themes,
appeared in 1885. There was a ten-year hiatus
before she moved to ▷St Petersburg, met
▷Zinaida Gíppius, and began to publish again,
this time using the musical term 'Allegro' as a
pseudonym. 'Hoarfrost' (1905) was rated highly
by the poet Aleksandr Blok, who found in it the
conjunction of a mature world view and childlike
simplicity, but Briusov, in contrast thought it
lacked originality. It received the Pushkin Prize in

1908. In 1910 she wrote a play in verse, *The
Marriage of the Sun and Spring*, which was set to
music by Mikhail Kuzmin.

Solov'ëva's poetry is introspective, elegiac and
musical, and tends to have simple metre and
rhyme. Like Gíppius, she used a masculine
persona. Between 1906 and 1913, together with
her companion, the children's writer N.I.
Manaseina, Solov'ëva created a children's
magazine to which the leading writers of the day
contributed. In 1913 she wrote an epistolary novel
in verse, ▷*The Crossroad*, which, like ▷Stólitsa's
▷*Elena Deeva*, dealt with the ▷Woman Question.
Her last collected verse, *Latest Poems*, appeared in
1923.
Bib: Pachmuss, T. (ed.), *Women Writers in Russian
Modernism*.

Some Account of the Fore Part of the Life of Elizabeth Ashbridge (1774)

This autobiographical spiritual narrative follows
▷Elizabeth Ashbridge's decision to leave her
native country of England and to resettle among
the Quakers in Pennsylvania. There she gained
the respect of the leading figures in the Society of
Friends, including John Woolman (1720–1772),
who remarks upon her piety and truth-seeking in
his own autobiography. Her literal journey to the
New World and her subsequent travels act as
metaphors for her spiritual journey and her desire
to work 'in Truth's service'. A beautifully written
autobiography, it remains one of the most
significant contributions to early 18th-century
Quaker literature.
▷Early North American Quaker women's
writings

Some Arguments Against Worldly-Mindedness . . . By Way of a Dialogue or Discourse Between Mary and Martha (1791)

The North American essayist ▷Eunice Smith's
first and most popular religious text uses the
dialogue between two female biblical figures to
exhort her Baptist advocacy of the need to trust
one's worldly problems to Jesus. Stylistically, *Some
Arguments* is typical of this genre of public
exhortations; its woman-centredness had great
appeal, and it was reprinted nine times before the
turn of the century.

Some Old Puritan Love Letters (1618–1638) (1893)

These selected letters cover the correspondence
from 1618 to 1638 of ▷Margaret Tyndal
Winthrop and her husband John, Governor of
Massachusetts Bay Colony. The letters reveal the
deep love between these two important North
American historical figures and are notable for the
details about Margaret's decision to come to the
New World, and her experiences during the years
of the colony's early settlement. The letters were
reprinted in the ▷*Winthrop Papers* (1929), which
also includes other letters by Margaret to her
children and in-laws.

▷Downing, Lucy Winthrop; *Letters of Mrs Lucy Downing*; Early North American letters

Somers, Armonía (born 1918)
Uruguayan short story writer, novelist and critic. She writes about a society and lifestyle in acute spiritual crisis, as did other Uruguayan writers in the 1940s, who belong to the so-called 'generation of the crisis'.

Her works include *El Derrumbamiento* (1953) (*The Fall*); *La calle del viento norte* (1963) (*The Street of the North Wind*); *De miedo en miedo* (1965) (*From Fear to Fear*); *La mujer desnuda* (1967) (*The Naked Woman*); *Todos los cuentos (1953–1967)* (1967) (*Complete Stories 1953–1967*); *Un retrato para Dickens* (1969) (*A Portrait for Dickens*); *Muerte por alacrán* (1978) (*Death by Scorpion*); *Tríptico darwiniano* (1982) (*Darwinian Triptych*); *Solo los elefantes encuentran mandrágora* (1986) (*Only Elephants Find Mandrake*); and *Viaje al corazón del día* (1986) (*Journey to the Heart of the Day*).

Somerville, Edith (1858–1949)
Irish novelist, born in Corfu, and educated at home in Cork. Having studied art in London and Paris, she returned to Ireland, and began an enduring friendship and celebrated literary partnership with her cousin, Violet Ross (▷Martin Ross). They collaborated on humorous stories of life in West Cork which brought them considerable fame, and also on a more serious novel, *The Real Charlotte* (1894), an exploration of class divisions in Ireland. After Violet's death, Edith continued to use the double signature 'Somerville and Ross', and wrote several novels, of which *The Big House at Inver* (1925) is the most interesting. The theme of the ▷'Big House' in Anglo-Irish fiction as a metaphor for the declining Ascendancy class (Anglo-Irish aristocracy) owes much to the Somerville and Ross partnership.

Somerville and Ross ▷Somerville, Edith; Ross, Martin

Sommeil Délivré, Le (1952) (From Sleep Unbound)
Novel by Egyptian/French poet and writer ▷Andrée Chedid. This novel describes the plight of frustrated wife, Samiya, who is trapped in a loveless marriage. In her parents' home she had sensed the hostility of her father, who had wanted a son. She is always guilty of some crime she never committed: the death of her mother, the death of her child. She notes in her journal: 'I hated my reflection in the mirror. I was sure I was something different . . . within me there is another woman young in the depths of her soul, rebelling against this slow death . . . I had wished to find my eyes' reflection in loving eyes . . . but I find nothing but this cold mirror.' In the end she takes the only positive action in her power, even if it ends in her going to prison, and kills her oppressor, her husband.

Song, Cathy (born 1955)
US poet. Song was born and raised on the island of Oahu in Hawaii. After graduating from Wellesley College, she earned a Master's degree in creative writing at Boston University. She teaches creative writing at various universities. She has published two volumes of poetry, *Picture Bride* (1983) and *Frameless Windows, Squares of Light* (1988).

Characterized by its visual quality, her poetry captures a transient moment that evokes memories of childhood or her Asian ancestors. It enables her to identify imaginatively with her ancestors. Poems like 'The White Porch' and 'Lost Sister' assert women's need for a sense of self; this need conflicts with the strictures of their Chinese culture. At the same time, 'Lost Sister', as well as 'Heaven' and 'Chinatown', acknowledge that part of their identity comes from their culture.
▷Asian-American writing

Song of the Lark, The (1915)
North American novel. ▷Willa Cather's semi-autobiographical story focuses on a successful woman artist, Thea Kronborg. Thea is of a Swedish immigrant family in Colorado. As in ▷*O Pioneers!* (1913) and ▷*My Ántonia* (1918), the frontier represents a prehistoric place of feminine strength. It is there that Thea discovers her artistic potential, but while studying music in Chicago, Illinois, she engages in an unsuccessful love affair. She retreats to the Southwest to reflect on her life. There Thea is empowered by a prehistorical woman's art to cultivate her own art. Now a famous opera singer, she reinvents her characters' roles. She mediates the tension between the frontier West and the sophisticated East. Nevertheless Thea's public success excludes a private life of romantic love. The novel emphasizes that woman's social roles and woman's artistry are mutually exclusive.

Song of Youth, The (1964)
Translation of novel by Chinese writer ▷Yang Muo, published in Chinese in 1958. One of the most widely read Chinese novels of the 1960s, this is the story of a young woman's initiation into the path of revolution, reflecting the writer, Yang Muo's, own experience. The heroine, Lin Daojing, offspring of a concubine, has no status in the mandarin family into which she is born. She rebels and leaves home to teach in a village primary school, only to end up cohabiting with a conservative-minded student from Peking University. In the university environment she meets other students and leaves her husband to join the underground movement against the Japanese occupation of north-east China. She falls in love with a student communist leader who dies under torture in prison. The story follows Lin Daojing's career as she leads the precarious existence of a communist agitator, moving from place to place, fleeing arrest, enduring torture in prison, and organizing the peasants. Finally, she falls in love with another leader who is 'both a

worker and an intellectual'. The novel presents different female types: seasoned revolutionaries, helpless victims of poverty and oppression, vain and worldly creatures who marry for money – and Lin Daojing, who achieves maturity by passing through the fire of the revolutionary ordeal.

Sonnets from the Portuguese (1850)
A sequence of forty-four sonnets by Britiish poet ▷Elizabeth Barrett Browning, written during her courtship with Robert Browning in 1845–46. In the course of the *Sonnets* Barrett Browning writes about love from a series of different perspectives, at times positioning her lover as a muse, at other times expressing her willingness to be his inspirational figure. She disrupts the conventions of amatory poetry in her treatment of the lovers' relationship, substituting a fluid and shifting relation for the gendered fixture characteristic of courtly love-poetry. The *Sonnets* were not originally intended for publication, and it was only on Robert Browning's insistence that they were included in Barrett Browning's *Poems* of 1850. Although they attracted little critical attention during the 19th century, they are now considered a major achievement.

Sono Ayako (born 1931)
Japanese novelist. Born in Tokyo, Sono was baptized a Christian when she was seventeen. *The Lower Slope*, published during her student days at the University of the Sacred Heart, was highly praised. She married Miura Shumon, a novelist, in 1953. The following year *The Guests from a Distant Country* was nominated for the Akutagawa Prize, and she was acknowledged as a talented novelist. This work is a cool observation of the behaviour of occupying forces in post-war Japan. Her works cover an enormous range of subjects including social problems and religion, based on her travels abroad. *Rio Grande, An Unsigned Tombstone* and *A Miracle* are about social problems. Her essay *For Whose Sake is Love* (1970) has sold over a million copies. In 1979 the Vatican awarded her the Holy Cross Prize for her work on religious themes, such as *The Dirty Hand of God*. Sono is an active participant on government committees.

Sophia (fl 1739–1741)
English writer. Sophia was the name attached to two out of three essays on the relative merits of the sexes. *Woman not Inferior to Man* (1739) and *Woman's Superior Excellence over Man* (1740) are adaptations of publications by the French ex-Catholic cleric, François Poulain de la Barre, first translated into English in 1677. She wrote, 'surely the *Women* were created by Heaven for some better end than to labour in vain their whole life long.' The whole exchange took the same shape as the French when a reply to the first tract appeared, purporting to be by a man. Sophia refers to her attacker in *Man Superior to Woman* (1740) as 'one of those amphibious things between both, which I think they call a Wit'.

▷Astell, Mary; Chudleigh, Lady Mary
Bib: Ferguson, Moira (ed.), *First Feminists*. Seidel, Michael, *Journal of the History of Ideas* 35, 3 (1974), pp. 499–508.

Soriano Jara, Elena (born 1917)
Controversial Spanish novelist. Soriano Jara published four novels in the 1950s: *Caza menor* (1951) (*Small Game Hunting*), *La playa de los locos* (*Beach of Madmen*), *Espejismos* (*Mirages*) and *Medea 55*. However, only the first of these novels was passed by the censor. The others, which formed a trilogy entitled *Mujer y hombre* (*Man and Woman*) were suppressed, as Soriano Jara's depiction of female eroticism and the portrayal of marriage as 'not-so-happy-ever-after' were considered dangerous. Her work is a testimony to the strict censorship of Franco's regime (1939–75), which policed images of women, banning anything which did not mesh with patriarchal criteria.

Soteriou, Dido (born 1914)
Greek novelist and journalist. She was born in the Aegean town of Smyrna, then in Greece but now in Turkey. Her earliest works tell of the peaceful world of the Asia Minor she knew as a child and how later it was transformed by war, persecution and exile. Her novel *Bloodied Earth* (1962) is the story of the destruction of Smyrna in 1922 and of the exchange of Greek and Turkish populations arranged by the post-war European powers. The whole story unfolds through the experiences of a single character and reveals the shattering of the Hellenistic ideals the Greeks had cherished about Asia Minor. Soteriou was the first woman to write fiction about the event that has most profoundly shaken the Greek people in modern times. *The Dead Are Waiting* (1959), *Commandment* (1976), *Within the Flames* (1978), and *We Are Demolished* (1982) are novels dealing with the political dreams and crises of modern Greece as expressed in the complex lives of the main protagonists.
Bib: Kostas, Myrsiades, *World Literature Today*, 54, No. 1, Winter 1980.

Soueif, Ahdaf (born 1950)
Egyptian/English writer, who went to school in Cairo and London. She obtained her BA in English from Cairo University and her PhD from the University of Lancaster. She has lectured on English literature in the Universities of Cairo and Riyadh. Her first collection of short stories, ▷*Aisha*, was published in London in 1983. She has written reviews and critical essays for *The Times Literary Supplement* and the *London Review of Books*, and a novel in English, ▷*In The Eye of The Sun* (1992).

Sousa, Auta de (1876–1901)
Brazilian poet. Her mother died when she was only three, and her father when she was five, so she was brought up by her grandmother. She caught tuberculosis at fourteen, and because of this was prevented from marrying and died young. She wrote under the pen-names Ida Salúcio and

Hilário das Neves. Her only book of poetry, *Horto* (1900), first called *Dálias* (*Dahlias*) and written between 1893 and 1897, was considered symbolist by some, and late romantic, by others. A mulatto, she never expressed her negro origins in her poetry, although she lived during the abolitionist period. She was a member of '*O Biscoito*', ('Cookie'), a literary group founded in 1894 in Rio Grande do Norte state. She wrote for the local press, often under her pen-names.

Sousa y Melo, Doña Beatriz de (c 1650–1700)
Spanish dramatist. Sousa y Melo was born in Torres-Novas in the mid-17th century. She wrote plays, such as: *La vida de Santa Elena, y invención de la Cruz* (*The Life of Saint Helena, and Discovery of the True Cross*), and *Yerros enmendados, y alma arrepentida* (*Errors Amended and a Repentant Soul*), as well as some religious poetry.

Southern lady
The Southern lady was created in North American literature to perpetuate the supremacy of the white race, elevated onto a pedestal to ensure the purity of white bloodlines. The taboo against miscegenation rendered her inaccessible to black men. Violence against black men became justified as a way to defend Southern womanhood. The Southern lady thus became identified with regional honour and was the repository for traditional Southern values, embodying the ideals of perfection and submission for women. To maintain her sanctity the lady was denied her sexuality, which was displaced onto black women. She became also an image of moral and spiritual power. A concern of Southern women writers now is how their characters struggle with this image of the lady to create their own identities.

South Riding (1936)
Novel by English writer ▷Winifred Holtby, described by the author as 'all about local government and aldermen and county councillors – a romance'. Set in the South Riding of Yorkshire, the novel explores the lives and relationships of a wide array of characters, the most important of whom are Sarah Burton, the newly arrived headmistress of the local girl's school, Mrs Beddows, an elderly alderwoman based on Holtby's own mother, and Robert Carne, the conservative gentleman-farmer with whom the radical Sarah Burton falls in love. Containing faint, and perhaps ironic, echoes of ▷*Jane Eyre*, and strong ones of ▷*Middlemarch*, the novel offers a panoramic view of Yorkshire life. Its concerns are the relationships between individuals, and the effects of public decisions on private lives. Dominant themes in the novel are death and suffering – it was written during the last stages of Holtby's terminal illness – and a passionate advocacy of education for women.
▷Brittain, Vera

Southworth, Mrs E.D.E.N. (1819–1899)
US popular novelist. An extremely prolific and popular novelist, Southworth began writing to support herself and her family after leaving her husband. Many of her novels were first published serially – most under a very lucrative contract with the *New York Ledger*. She wrote more than fifty novels, many in the ▷woman's fiction tradition of heroines who needed to be strong because patriarchial society had left them bereft of support. All her novels questioned convention regarding women; among the most famous and popular was *The Hidden Hand* (1859). Others include: *The Missing Bride* (1855); *The Fatal Marriage* (1869); and *The Maiden Widow* (1870).

Souvenir
US 19th-century miscellaneous periodical compilation of short works of fiction, poetry, essays, etc. The first was *The Atlantic Souvenir*, produced between 1825 and 1832. A form of ▷gift book, souvenir series provided an important source of authors' income before the development of national literary magazines at mid-century.

Souvenirs d'une fille du peuple (1866) (Memories of a Daughter of the People)
An autobiography by ▷Suzanne Voilquin. Dedicated to a beloved niece, Voilquin's memoirs are in fact a lengthy address to the latter, written in a lively, conversational style. Her text is divided into six parts, the first chronicling her poverty-stricken childhood, the second her growing involvement with the ▷Saint-Simonians, the third the protracted journey across France on which she embarked in order to drum up support for the movement, the fourth and fifth her adventures in Egypt after she joined the Saint-Simonian colony Enfantin established there, and the sixth her decision to leave France once more, this time for Russia. What emerges most strongly from Voilquin's autobiography is the intensity of her sense of the determining role played in her (frequently difficult) life by the related factors of class and gender, especially the latter. Since she was subjected to assault and sexual betrayal and was given venereal disease by her husband, it is unsurprising that the vision of sexuality and of male–female relations she offers is a largely pessimistic one.

Although passionately devoted to Prosper Enfantin, the 'father' of the Saint-Simonians, Voilquin makes it evident that Saint-Simonian men, like any others, were prone to exclude or even exploit their female comrades, and she argues forcefully that, if women are to become emancipated, they must ignore male notions of what feminine emancipation means and form their own, separatist groups in order to battle for freedom. As far as she was concerned, access to education, especially in the field of medicine, was the key to the liberation of women. She herself struggled to train as a midwife, despite the financial burden her studies involved, and was consequently able to help women she encountered in Egypt, for whom she felt great sympathy in spite of her distaste for the customs of the East. Voilquin's account of life in Egypt is fascinating, although marred for the modern reader by her very obvious belief in the 'rightness' of French/Saint-Simonian manners and values, and her sense of the 'uncivilized' character of Egyptian culture. Of particular interest is her description of a harem, which she visited in her capacity as midwife.

Souvenirs d'une fille du peuple is a compelling work, less for its literary value than for the insights it offers us into the historical, political and social complexion of early 19th-century France and, above all, for the account it contains of the activities of the Saint-Simonian feminists.

Souza, Adèle de (1761–1836)

Born in Paris and exiled during the Revolution (1789), she published her first novel, *Adèle de Sénange* (1794), in London. This semi-autobiographical work tells the story of a young woman who marries a much older man, and subsequently falls in love with another, despite her good intentions. It was followed by *Émilie et Alphonse* (1800), the tale of an even more unhappy marriage, in which Souza intimates that the young should be able to choose their own destiny instead of following social rules, or the tyrannical dictates of the older generation. She subsequently wrote *Charles et Marie* (1802) and her most famous novel, *Eugène de Rothelin* (1808), which, like its predecessors, represents an attempt to persuade the reader that emotional needs ought not to be ignored. Her novels, which are moralistic in tone but not excessively so, offer a finely drawn account of aristocratic life in early 19th-century France.

▷Krudener, Julie de
Bib: Guy, J., *Femmes de lettres*; Merlant, J., *Le Roman personnel de Rousseau à Fromentin*.

Soveraignty and Goodness of God, The (1682)

Also known by an alternative title, *A True History of the Captivity and Restoration of Mrs Mary Rowlandson*. One of the earliest and certainly the most influential ▷captivity narratives in early North American literature, this text by ▷Mary White Rowlandson became the model for this genre for the next century. Although recalling her period of captivity in Puritan analogies of captivity, humiliation and salvation, she invests her account with realistic details of the slaughter of family and friends, the hardships of her numerous 'removals' and her joy at being returned to her community. Only at one moment in the narrative does she break from the distancing narrative voice that controls the text – when she observes that late at night, alone with her thoughts, she must confront the psychological residuals of her 'afflictions'. *The Soveraignty and Goodness of God* was one of the most popular texts of 17th-century North America and was resurrected again during the American Revolution. It is a classic early North American narrative.

Soviet Writers' Union

Along with the imposition of ▷socialist realism as a sacrosanct guideline for literary works, the formation of the Soviet Writers' Union in 1934 gave the state and the Communist Party a powerful mechanism for control of literature. In a society where all outlets for publication were state-owned, one had to belong to the Union to publish. The advent of ▷*glásnost*' in the mid-1980s ended the monopoly on publishing, but membership in the union continued to offer important privileges – summer colonies, retreats, medical care, access to consumer goods. Women writers have always been in the minority (15 per cent in 1986) in the union, and have rarely occupied posts of power. In 1986 women in larger numbers took part in the organization of the reformist 'April Committee' of the Moscow branch.

▷Akhmadúlina, Izabella; Chukóvskaia, Lidiia; Gánina, Maia
Bib: Garrard, J. and C., *Inside the Soviet Writers' Union*.

Soweto

The name of an urban settlement south-west of Johannesburg, it has also become a byword for a crucial event in South African political and social history: the rebellion of black schoolchildren in June 1976, first in Soweto and then nationally. This movement continued through the 1980s and, arguably, precipitated the negotiations between black and white South Africans in the 1990s. As a historical event it is written into a number of South African novels, ▷*Amandla* and ▷*Burger's Daughter*, most notably. It also figures directly or indirectly in ▷autobiographical writing by black South African women, where it functions as a trope by which mothers know their children as fighters, as adults, and as figures beyond parental control. Such is the theme of Carol Hermer's *The Diary of Maria Tholo* (1980), for instance, whose first words are 'We have Soweto with us', as well as ▷Ellen Kuzwayo's *Call Me Woman* (1985) and ▷Noni Jabavu's preface to the republished ▷*The Ochre People*. Caesarina Kona Makhoere's prison memoir, *No Child's Play: In Prison Under Apartheid* (1988) is written from the perspective of one of the children of Soweto, 1976.

Soweto Stories (1989)

Collection of short stories by South African writer▷Miriam Tlali. Published in South Africa under the title *Footprints in the Quag: Stories and Dialogues from Soweto*, it is the most interesting of her works. Whereas Tlali's two novels present women in a supportive role because – she has said – this is what happens in real life, these stories look more closely at gender. In 'The Point of No Return', the earliest story in the collection, the man is an activist and the woman a patient wife and mother, but in the later stories stereotyping is in one way or another interrogated or disturbed. Moreover, the stories look not only at the subjection of black women by whites, but also at sexist exploitation and abuse within the black community.

The stories also bear an important relation to the African past. In her introduction to the collection, ▷Lauretta Ngcobo says that Tlali is searching for an antidote to the South African present, a prescription from the past to sustain us all until freedom comes. One such antidote may well be provided in her story 'Gone are Those Days', which recalls the structure of some of the stories in the ▷oral tradition, whereby one part of the narrative inverts another. 'Gone are Those Days' includes a dream in which a group of women poison the food at a banquet for white men and their wives. Although this is only a dream, it functions in the story as an inversion of real-life events in such a way as to recall the trickster motif of the oral tradition.

Sow Fall, Aminata (born 1941)
Senagalese novelist. She grew up happily in a large family in the north of Senegal, in which no educational distinction was made between boys and girls. She studied literature and trained as an interpreter in Paris, where she married. For several years she taught in schools in Dakar and Rufisque. In 1979 she joined the Ministry of Culture, and has since personally financed and set up an organization, CAEC (Centre d'Animations et des Echanges Culturelles), which contains a publishing house. She has published four novels, one of which, *La Grève des battu* (1979), is published in English as ▷*The Beggars' Strike*. The others include ▷*L'Appel des arènes* (1982) (*Call of the Ring*) and *Le Revenant* (1976) (*The One Who Came Back*).
Bib: Blair, D.S., *A History of African Literature in French*; Milolo, K., *L'image de la femme chez les romancières de l'Afrique*; Adams Graves, A. and Boyce-Davies, C., *Ngambika: Studies of Women in African Literature*.

Soysal, Sevgi (1936–1976)
Turkish novelist, memoirist and short story writer. She studied in the Universities of Ankara and Göttingen, and worked for Turkish radio and television. She daringly explored the relationships between men and women in Turkish society, and portrayed the character of a sexually unfulfilled wife in her novel *Yurumek* (1970) (*To Walk*). After winning a state prize, the novel was removed from bookshops under a charge of obscenity. She has published three collections of short stories, including *Tante Rosa* (1968) (*Aunt Rosa*), inspired by her life in Germany.

Spark, Muriel (born 1918)
Scottish novelist, poet and critic. Spark was born in Edinburgh, of Jewish-Italian descent, educated at a private school for girls, and converted to Roman Catholicism in 1954. She spent a number of years in Rhodesia (now Zimbabwe), and on her return to Britain in 1944 worked at the Foreign Office on anti-Nazi propoganda. These biographical details inform much of Spark's writings.

In her early writing career Spark concentrated on poetry (gathered in *Collected Poems*, 1967). During the late 1940s she edited the *Poetry Review* and, after leaving that journal, she established the magazine *Forum*. During the 1950s Spark produced a number of articles of literary criticism and biography, including *Child of Light* (1951), a biography of ▷Mary Shelley. After 'The Seraph and the Zambesi' had won Spark the *Observer* short story competition in 1951, her output shifted to prose fiction. Spark's conversion to Roman Catholicism preceded the publication of her first novel, *The Comforters* (1957), a text which develops the twin preoccupations of her writing: her concern with the process of writing fiction, and a textualized dialogue with Catholicism. Catholicism, as both a theme and a backdrop, recurs throughout Spark's fiction, and is foregrounded in novels such as *Memento Mori* (1959) and *The Abbess of Crewe* (1974). Spark's selfconsciousness, introduced in *The Comforters* and taken up in a similarly overt manner in *Loitering with Intent* (1981), interrogates the theological underpinnings of the author's role as both maker and scriptor. Her use of ▷realism, combined with a parable- or fable-like quality as the dominant form, links her work with that of ▷Iris Murdoch. Spark's hallmark of interlacing sharp wit and satire with the bizarre and the sinister is clearly illustrated in her best-known work ▷*The Prime of Miss Jean Brodie* (1961). Spark's short stories are published in two volumes, *Collected Stories 1* (1967) and *The Stories of Muriel Spark* (1985). Her only stage play is *Doctors of Philosophy* (1962), and her radio plays are collected in *Voices at Play* (1961).

Other novels include: *Robinson* (1958), *The Ballad of Peckham Rye* (1960), *The Bachelors* (1960), ▷*The Girls of Slender Means* (1963), *The Mandelbaum Gate* (1965), *The Hothouse by the East River* (1972), *Territorial Rights* (1979). Novellas: *The Public Image* (1968), *The Driver's Seat* (1970) and *Not to Disturb* (1971), and her other poetry in *Sotheby's and Other Poems* (1982).

Ellis, Alice Thomas
Bib: Bold, A., *Muriel Spark: An Odd Capacity for Vision*; Kane, R., *Iris Murdoch, Muriel Spark and John Fowles: Didactic Demons in Modern Fiction*; Little, J., *Comedy and the Woman Writer: Woolf, Spark and Feminism*; Page, N., *Muriel Spark*; Stanford, D., *Muriel Spark: A Biographical and Critical Study*; Whittaker, R., *The Faith and Fiction of Muriel Spark*.

Sparviera, La (1956) (The Hawk)
An autobiographical, but ▷fantastical Italian novel by ▷Gianna Manzini, which makes its author's recurrent cough a character. The protagonist of the text, Giovanni, suffers from this persistent cough from childhood. It is a tyrannical force in his life, and it ultimately leads to his

death. The tale is one of both love and death. Manzini has taken the image of the *sparviera* from Montale: it is an image of predestination, and of death. The violence of life acquires a magical, fantastical force in this novel.

Spaziani, Maria Luisa (born 1924)

Italian poet and journalist. She contributed to numerous Italian newspapers and periodicals from 1940 onwards. She has lived in Milan, Paris and Rome, but from 1963 was a lecturer in German language and literature at the University of Messina. Since 1955, she has written for *Radio-audizioni italiane* (RAI). She is a specialist in Italian, French and German poetry, and in 16th-century French literature. She won the Città di Firenze Prize for her poetry collection *Il gong* (*The Gong*) in 1962. Her academic work includes texts on Ronsard and Prudhomme.

Her other works include: *Primavera a Parigi* (1954) (*Spring in Paris*); *Luna lombarda* (1959) (*Moon in Lombardy*); *Utilità della memoria* (1966) (*The Usefulness of Memory*); *L'occhio del ciclone* (1970) (*The Eye of the Storm*); *Poesia* (1979) (*Poetry*); *Geometria del disordine* (1981) (*The Geometry of Disorder*); *La stella del libero arbitrio* (1986) (*The Star of Free Will*).

Speak Out, Black Sisters (1986)

Translation of *La Parole aux négresses* (1978), a seminal feminist work by the Senegalese writer and social scientist, ▷Awa Thiam. Based on interviews with women in Mali, Senegal, Côte d'Ivoire, Guinea, Ghana and Nigeria, it uncovers the hidden forces which even today distort and inhibit the lives of African women. Prominent among these are the practices of ▷clitoridectomy/infibulation and child marriage. In the second part of the book, the focus shifts to the author's own analysis of the situation of women in those countries considered, culminating in the question, 'What to propose to black women?' The significance of the book lies in the fact that, by providing a channel for the voices of ordinary women, it not only makes their utterances public but gives them the dignity and permanence of print.

Speculum de l'autre femme (1974) ▷*Speculum of the Other Woman* (1985)

Speculum of the Other Woman (1985)

Translation of *Speculum de l'autre femme* (1974), second book by French writer ▷Luce Irigaray. In this published version of her doctoral thesis, she gives a feminist critique of Freud, Plato and others, based on close readings of some of their writings (▷psychoanalysis). Irigaray's work as a whole is informed by her Lacanian training – although she is critical of Lacan – and by her belief that women's sexuality and relation to language are at least dual, if not multiple, and excluded by the dominant masculine forms. They are themselves unified and organized entirely in relation to the phallus. Her approach to the thinkers she discusses is thus to undermine the accepted authority of their writings by asking, but not necessarily answering, questions about what they have to say about women, rather than by setting up an alternative and similarly coherent system on what she regards as the masculine model.

'Speech to the Troops at Tilbury' (1588)

▷Elizabeth I's speech delivered to her English troops assembled in preparation for battle against the Spanish armada. The speech is famous for Elizabeth's particularly keen use of the notion of the king's two bodies. She declared, 'I know I have the body but of a weak and feeble woman; but I have the heart and stomach of a King, and a King of England too.' The speech demonstrates Elizabeth's skillful negotiation of her unusual role as a female monarch.

Speght, Rachel (1597–?)

English poet and polemicist. Her *A Mouzell for Melastomus, the Cynical Bayter of, and foul mouthed Barker against Evah's sex* (1617) was an early rejoinder to Joseph Swetnam's attack on women (see ▷woman controversy). In 1621 she published *Mortalities Memorandum, with a Dreame Prefixed*, noting in the preface that the reception of her earlier work had confirmed the 'apotogeme which doth affirme Censure to be inevitable to a publique act'.

Spence, Catherine Helen (1825–1910)

Australian novelist, non-fiction writer and social reformer. Spence was born in Scotland, emigrated to Adelaide in 1839 with her family, and became a governess at seventeen. She was a pioneer feminist and social reformer, devoting her life to the Unitarian Church, the care of destitute children, the education of girls and the fight for the vote for women. She made lecture tours of the USA and Britain, speaking in favour of women's suffrage, and became Australia's first female political candidate in the Federal Convention elections of 1897. Her first two novels, ▷*Clara Morison: A Tale of South Australia During the Gold Fever* (1854) and *Tender and True: A Colonial Tale* (1856), were published anonymously, but ▷*Mr Hogarth's Will* (1865) and *The Author's Daughter* (1867), both of which were serialized, were published under her own name. These are more than domestic romances; they provide invaluable social and political insights into life in the colonies in the 1850s and 1860s.

Other fiction includes *Gathered In*, serialized in the *Observer*, but unpublished in book form until 1977, and ▷*Handfasted*, a Utopian novel unpublished in her time as it was considered too advanced, but published in 1984. Her non-fiction writing on feminist, social and political themes is considerable, and her *Autobiography* was published in 1910, edited by W.K.Thomas. *Catherine Helen Spence* (1987), edited by Helen Thomson, is a valuable source-book and Susan Magarey's

Unbridling the Tongues of Women (1985) is a modern biography.

▷Feminism (Australia); *Eclipsed: Two Centuries of Australian Women's Fiction*; *On Her Selection*; *Peaceful Army, The*

Spencer, Elizabeth (born 1921)
American-Canadian short story writer and novelist. Born in Carrollton, Mississippi, Spencer attended Belhaven College and Vanderbilt University. She lived and wrote in Mississippi until a Guggenheim Fellowship enabled her to travel to Italy, where she lived for five years. She married in 1956, and moved with her husband to Montreal, Canada, where she is associated with Concordia University. Although primarily a novelist, she is most famous for her short stories. ▷Eudora Welty praises Spencer's 'precise and telling particulars', her 'cool deliberateness' as a writer. *Fire in the Morning* (1948), *This Crooked Way* (1952) and *The Voice at the Back Door* (1956) are all Mississippi novels concerned with the southern world she was raised in. Her novellas, *The Light in the Piazza* (1960), *Knights and Dragons* (1965), and *The Cousins* (1985), are about North Americans in Italy. She is best-known for her acutely drawn short stories, in *The Stories of Elizabeth Spencer* (1981, with a foreword by Eudora Welty) and *Jack of Diamonds and Other Stories* (1988). *The Salt Line* (1984) is her most recent novel.
Bib: Prenshaw, P.W., *Elizabeth Spencer*.

Spender, Dale (born 1943)
Australian literary critic, historian, lecturer and feminist of international standing. Spender was educated at the Universities of Sydney, New South Wales and New England, and worked as a teacher and lecturer before studying for her doctorate in the Philosophy of Language at the University of London. Spender has been Visiting Professor at several North American and Canadian universities, and a Visiting Fellow of the University of London. She was founding editor of *Women's Studies International Forum*, and co-founder of Pandora Press, London.

In the 1980s Spender emerged as a pioneer in feminist explorations of sexism in language. Her main thesis, put forward in *Man Made Language* (1980, 1985), is that language, a supposedly gender-neutral structure, both names and produces male superiority (for example, in the use of a masculine universal pronoun and in words such as chairman and master). Concerned to rescue women from their marginalization by patriarchal structures of language and knowledge, the majority of Spender's later books have as their project the recovery and re-evaluation of women's history and literature. Spender's preoccupation with women's neglected achievements is evident in the titles of her many publications, which include: *Women of Ideas and What Men Have Done to Them* (1982); *Feminist Theorists: Three Centuries of Key Women Thinkers* (1983): *There's Always Been a Women's Movement* (1985); *Mothers of the Novel:*

100 Good Women Novelists before Jane Austen (1986); *Writing a New World: Two Centuries of Australian Women Writers* (1988). Spender has also edited ▷ *The Penguin Anthology of Australian Women's Writing* (1988).
▷Female traditions

Sperani, Bruno (born 1843)
Pseudonym of Italian novelist Beatrice Speraz. She lived for most of her life in Milan, and did some translation and journalistic work for financial reasons, before turning to fiction. ▷*Nell'ingranaggio* (1885) (*Caught in the Wheel*), and ▷*Numeri e sogni* (1887) (*Numbers and Dreams*) are both studies of Milanese society and culture, which are especially concerned with women's position. While Sperani's novels are in some respects ▷sentimental, they are also socially and historically aware. Her later work, *La fabbrica* (1908) (*The Factory*), is an impassioned novel of socialism.

Speranza ▷Wilde, Jane Francesca

Speraz, Beatrice ▷Sperani, Bruno

Spiel, Hilde (1911–1990)
Austrian journalist, translator, critic and novelist. She grew up in Vienna, studied philosophy, and gained her doctorate in 1936. In the same year she married Peter de Mendelssohn and moved to London where she worked as a journalist, occasionally writing cultural essays for *The New Statesman* and *Horizon*. After the war she maintained journalistic links with various German, Austrian and English newspapers, and translated a number of English and North American novels. Her own first novel, *Kati auf der Brücke* (1933) (*Kati on the Bridge*), which is about Viennese newspaper and literary circles in the 1930s, reveals her as a keen observer of manner and milieu. In 1946 she published *Rückkehr nach Wien. Tagebuch 1946* (*Return to Vienna. 1946 Diary*), an autobiographical account of a journalist returning to the ruins of Vienna. Her novel *Lisas Zimmer* (1965) (*Lisa's Room*), first published in English as *The Darkened Room* (1961), describes the fates of a German and an Austrian woman in New York after World War II. Her drama, *Anna und Anna*, a play about the dual existence of a young woman during the war, was a great popular success when it was performed in the Vienna Burgtheater in 1988. Amongst her most interesting work is the fictionalized biography *Fanny von Arnstein oder Die Emanzipation* (1978) (*Fanny von Arnstein or the Emancipation*), about the Jewish Prussian woman who opened one of the first literary salons in Vienna and championed the emancipation of Jews in Austria and Germany at the end of the 18th century.
▷Salon culture (Germany and Austria)

Spinster (1958)
Novel by New Zealand Writer ▷Sylvia Ashton-Warner. Described as one of 'four novels of

marked distinction' (E.H. McCormick, *New Zealand Literature: A Survey*, 1959) that had appeared in 1957–8, *Spinster* describes the life of Anna Vorontosov, who, while she works as a teacher, experiences the most important part of her life as an artist. All Ashton-Warner's novels are about women as artists, and although their lives may involve significant relationships with their work (in Anna Vorontosov's case, with the children in her classroom) and with men, *Spinster* shows that the only place where Anna Vorontosov can escape 'a heavy lid of respectability and tradition' from which eyes peer out like 'the eyes of prisoners in a dungeon' is her house, Selah, where she paints, writes and plays music. The woman as artist is at odds with the more traditional role of mother, and in *Spinster* Anna Vorontosov substitutes mothering her class for bearing her own child. Acclaimed as the 'best novel to come out of New Zealand so far' (*Southland News*, 1958) *Spinster* rewrites the stereotype of the unmarried woman, as well as mounting a critique of the education system and dealing seriously with the role of women as professional teachers.

Spiriti costretti (1963) (*Driven Souls*)

A series of Italian essays by ▷Angela Bianchini. Probably of autobiographical inspiration, they focus on English and North American writers who, in escaping from their native lands, found in other countries a way of freeing themselves from, and writing effectively about, their personal traumas. In some respects, this work provides the reader with a key to Bianchini's own fictional writing.

Spivak, Gayatri Chakravorty (born 1941)

Indian critical theorist, lecturer and translator. After reading for a BA in Calcutta in 1959, Spivak went to Cambridge and then North America. She took her Ph.D. from Cornell in 1967 and has since taught in US universities. She is now Professor of English at the University of Pittsburgh. Although best-known as translator of the French philosopher Jacques Derrida's *Of Grammatology* (1976), her later work addresses the political implications and possibilities of recuperating ▷deconstruction for feminism. In 'Love Me, Love My Ombre, Elle' (*Diacritics*, 1984), Spivak develops Derrida's inscription of the name of woman as a deconstructive figure to show how woman's 'displacement' to the margins of a ▷phallogocentric order simultaneously shores up and deconstructs a ▷binary logic of sexual difference.

Spivak's own displacement to the margins of three cultures has made her a keen critic of cultural politics. She has been quick to tackle white Western feminism for its authoritarian assumption that feminists living in the 'Third World' share the specifically Western-based theoretical concerns of those living in the 'First World'. Her book *In Other Worlds: Essays in Cultural Politics* (1987) urges 'First World'

feminists to consider the political implications of their privileged position, and brings to attention hitherto neglected 'Third World' women writers, such as the Bengali author ▷Mahasweta Devi. Spivak is joint editor with Guha Ranajit of *Selected Subaltern Studies* (1988); Sarah Harasym has edited Spivak's essays in *The Post-Colonial Critic: Interviews, Strategies, Dialogues* (1990).

Spofford, Harriet Elizabeth Prescott (1835–1921)

US short-story writer, poet and novelist. Prescott Spofford came to public attention with a short story in ▷*The Atlantic Monthly*, and went on to publish extensively in a number of prestigious US adult and children's magazines. Her work came to define the standard of the romantic or ▷Gothic magazine tale. Among her story collections are *The Amber Gods, and Other Stories* (1863); *New England Legends* (1871), and *A Scarlet Poppy and Other Stories* (1894).

▷*Frank Leslie's Popular Monthly*

Spondi (1963)

A collection of ten short stories by Greek writer ▷Elli Alexiou. The book is a chronicle of her separation from her sister, ▷Galatea Kazantzaki, who died in a car accident in Athens while Elli was living in Romania. It is a very moving book, recalling the lives of Galateia and the literary people around her.

Sport of My Mad Mother, The (1958)

Play by English dramatist ▷Ann Jellicoe, which established her reputation for ▷*avant-garde* theatre. *The Sport of My Mad Mother* is a play in which 'nothing is put into words that cannot be shown in action.' Focusing on the relationships between a group of teenagers, and set in a back-streets badland of gang fights and conflict, the play is about identity, interaction and modes of expression. It is largely based on myth and ritual, which Jellicoe sees as 'the bodying forth in images and stories of our deepest fears and conflicts'. Verbally articulated musical discordance is frequently substituted for dialogue, thereby foregrounding communication as the key problematic. The emphasis throughout is on theatrical language, and ritual assumes an incantatory mode, playing on the constant repetition of words, phrases, and events between lines and characters. Described by Jellicoe as an anti-intellect play, it diverts sharply from a ▷psychoanalytic analysis of aggressiveness and primal inheritance, attempting to tap the audience's reaction to 'basic stimuli' through rhythm, noise and music.

Spyri, Johanna (1827–1901)

German-speaking Swiss writer of children's fiction. A member of the conservative middle class, she opposed women's emancipation and their admission to universities. Her own literary activity she understood not in terms of self-expression or art, but as a means of educating the young. She wrote over fifty books, mainly about children who, against all the odds, eventually achieve happiness and social esteem. Her story *Heidis Lehr- und Wanderjahre* (1880) (*Heidi's Years of Apprenticeship and Travel*), about an orphaned girl from the Swiss Alps, is, to this day, famous throughout the world.

Square, The (1965)
Translation of *Le Square* (1955), sixth novel by French writer ▷Marguerite Duras. The book consists of a dialogue between a travelling salesman and a maid, who meet by chance in a square. The salesman is dispirited, living from day to day, and dreaming of a faraway city where he was once happy. The maid utterly loathes her job, and is determined to change her life, although she is not quite sure how. Finally, they decide to go dancing together the following Saturday.

Sri Delima ▷Amin, Khalida Adibah binti Haji

Staal-Delaunay, Marguerite-Jeanne Cordier de (1684–1750)
French dramatist, poet and memoir-writer. Daughter of the exiled painter Cordier, she took her mother's name. Educated at the convent of Saint-Saveur in Rouen, she studied metaphysics and geometry. Returning to Paris, she experienced great difficulty in obtaining a place, and eventually became ladies' maid to the Duchesse de Maine at her court at Sceaux, a position she deplored, until her talents as a writer were discovered and she became secretary to the duchess. Later she wrote comedies, verse and songs to amuse the court. When the duchess was implicated in plots against the crown, Delaunay was imprisoned in the Bastille, which she preferred to being in service. Released in 1720, she entered into an arranged marriage with the Baron de Staal. Her memoirs, published five years after her death (re-edited 1970), were compared to the work of the writer La Bruyère. As well as providing incisive satirical portraits of figures at the court, the memoirs evoke her Normandy childhood, her arrival at the Court of Sceaux, and her imprisonment in the Bastille.
▷Deffand, Marquise Du; Lambert, Marquises de
Bib: Buchanan, M., '*Une ombre à la fête de sceaux; Madame de Staal-Delaunay*', *French Review*, 51: 3 (1978); Lescure, M., *Les Femmes philosophes*.

Staël, Germaine Necker de (1766–1817)
French novelist and literary theorist. Educated by her mother ▷Dame Necker, she benefited from attending the latter's literary salon from an early age. She was forced to leave Paris several times, first during the Revolution (1789) and again when exiled by Napoleon, who refused to tolerate her dangerous eloquence (see *Dix années d'exil*, 1829 *Ten years of exile*). During her years of exile, Madame de Staël travelled extensively across Europe, and resided at her home near Geneva, Coppet, where she entertained a cosmopolitan

group of intellectuals. In her early years she wrote plays, short novels and essays, including an assessment of Rousseau and the work *De l'influence des passions sur le bonheur des individus et des nations* (1796) (*The Influence of Passions on the Happiness of Individuals and Nations*), where she argues that philosophical study and religious sentiment are the key resources of the individual and society. In her novels, ▷*Delphine* (1802) (*Delphine*, 1987) and ▷*Corinne ou l'Italie* (1807), (▷*Corinne or Italy*, 1987), she presents exceptionally talented women in conflict with individual men and society. Her major works *De la littérature* (1800) (*A Treatise on Ancient and Modern Literature*, 1803) and the more original *De l'Allemagne* (1810) (▷*On Germany*, 1813) examine the effects of political systems, customs and climate on literature. The latter provided her French audience with their first manifesto of romanticism.

Other works: *Sophie* (1786); *Jane Gray* (1790); *Zulma et trois nouvelles* (1813) (*Zulma and Three Stories*); *Réflexions sur le procès de la reine* (1793) (*Reflections on the Queen's Trial*); *Réflexions sur le suicide* (1813) (*Reflections on Suicide*), and *Considérations sur les principaux événements de la Révolution française* (1818) (*Considerations on the Main Events of the French Revolution*).

English translations of some of her works can be found in: *Corinne or Italy* (1987); *An Extraordinary Woman: Selected Writings* (1987). **Bib:** *Cahiers Staëliens* 1930– ; Balayé, S., 'Le Dossier Staël' in *Romantisme*, No. 20; Balayé, S., *Mme de Staël: Lumières et liberté*; Gutwirth, M., *Madame de Staël, Novelist*; Moers, E., *Literary Women, the Great Writers*; Postgate, H.B., *Mme de Staël*; Peterson, C. L., *The Determined Reader. Gender and Culture in the Novel from Napoleon to Victoria*.

Stafford, Jean (1915–1979)
US novelist and short story writer. Born in California, Stafford earned a Master's degree at the University of Colorado in 1936. In 1940 she married the poet Robert Lowell, and divorced him in 1948. She won a Pulitzer Prize for *Collected Stories* in 1970. Her fiction documents a culture which survives World War II, although it is one which restricts and destroys the individual. Her characters search for their self-survival but often choose the culture's values.

In *Boston Adventure* (1944) Sonia sacrifices her sexuality and innermost self to be integrated into Boston Society, while in *The Catherine Wheel* (1952) Katherine also chooses spiritual death to play a cultural role. In ▷*The Mountain Lion* (1947) Stafford presents the possibility of an alternative choice. She emphasizes that the individual pays dearly for even a small degree of self-knowledge.
Bib: Goodman, Charlotte Margolis, *Jean Stafford: The Savage Heart*.

Stafford, Mary ▷Mayor, Flora M.

Stafford, Mary (fl 1711)
North American letter-writer. Little is known of her early life in England; after her marriage and the birth of two children, poverty drove her and her family to South Carolina in the hopes of economic recovery. In ▷'A Letter . . . by Mary Stafford to a Kinswoman', she first acknowledges the hardship of their condition, but also expresses hope for the future.

Stagel, Elsbeth (c 1300–c 1366)
Swiss nun and chronicler. The daughter of a wealthy butcher in Zurich, she entered the nearby Dominican convent of Töss when still a child. Driven by the notion that the convent should revert to its earlier saintly austerity, she wrote a history of the convent in terms of the mystical lives of several nuns who had lived there a hundred years earlier. Her book, *Das Leben der Schwestern zu Töss* (*The Lives of the Sisters of Töss*) is one of several such accounts written by Dominican nuns and monks in southern Germany and Switzerland in the 14th century.
▷ *Visionsliteratur*

Stampa, Gaspara (c1523–1554)
Italian poet. Born in Padua, she lived for most of her life in Venice where she was a ▷'*cortegiana onesta*'. Her poetry was written in the ▷Petrarchan tradition. Her ▷*Rime d'amore* (1554) (*Love Poems*) were published posthumously by her sister Cassandra. She came from a reasonably wealthy family, and appears to have been taught Latin and some Greek, along with rhetoric and grammar. She was an active member of literary and intellectual Venetian society but, because of her ambiguous social status, she was the subject of some obscene satirical rhymes. She was the only woman of her time to produce so much poetry, and some of her work was published in collections of contemporary poetry. She writes mainly of the nature of love, and stresses its dualistic painful/pleasurable nature. Some of her poems were translated into English in 1881. Most of it is addressed either to Collaltino di Collalto or to Bartolomeo Zen, both of whom she loved passionately in her lifetime.

Stamperius, Hannemieke ▷Meinkema, Hannes

Stanitskii, N. ▷Panáeva, Avdot'ia

Stanley, Margaret ▷Beaufort Stanley, Margaret

Stanley, Mary (1919–1980)
New Zealand poet. Although Mary Stanley's collection *Starveling Year* was published in 1953, her work remained relatively unknown until it appeared in the feminist anthology ▷*Private Gardens* in 1977. Married to the poet Kendrick Smithyman, Stanley was amongst the first in New Zealand to use a domestic environment to examine complex questions of subjectivity and family relationships. Stanley's work was recognized by feminists in the 1970s to have begun exploring, in its characteristically dense and syntactically complex form, feminist questions. Stanley spent much of her life suffering from rheumatoid arthritis which, along with the lack of recognition given to her work, may account for the publication of only one collection.
▷anthologies, New Zealand

Stanton, Elizabeth Cady (1815–1902)
US non-fiction writer and editor, feminist and abolitionist. Among the best-educated of early US women's rights advocates, Cady Stanton helped to organize the first women's rights convention in 1848, produced the *History of Woman's Suffrage* with ▷Susan B. Anthony, and shocked even her fellow suffragists by documenting sexism in religion with *The Woman's Bible* (1895, 1898). Her autobiography, a splendid record, is *Eighty Years and More* (1898).
▷*Una, The*

Stará rodina (1916) (The Old Family) and Synové (1918) (Sons)
Two-part Czech novel by Ana Maria Tilschová (1873–1957). The books describe life in the Prague *haute bourgeoisie* in the first two decades of the 20th century. It has no conventional plot: the numerous characters' lives are dragged along by an oppressive, determinist fate. At the centre of the story is a father and his four sons (the mother is dead). In the first part the father is a cold tyrant, in the second a deposed tyrant. He is a hard-headed recluse and misanthropist, and his lack of affection or spiritual values creates a wall between him and his sons, and between the sons themselves.
The novel depicts the erosion, then total disintegration, of a 'Victorian' morality. The eldest son, the one sensitive member of the family, does manage to find brief happiness in adultery, but that soon ends, and he is eventually killed during World War I. The second son marries into the new, opportunist, dishonourable bourgeoisie. The third is a passive, misogynist weakling, and the fourth a vicious weasel. Tilschová depicts a sick society which is not replaced by a healthy one. The new order is more selfish, ruthless and less industrious. She saw no hope for capitalism.

Star Chernobyl, The (1987)
Novel by *émigré* Russian writer ▷Iuliia Voznesénskaia. *The Star Chernobyl* appeared in Russian, and in English translation, a year after the meltdown of the Chernobyl nuclear plant in the Soviet Ukraine. The disaster is seen through the eyes of estranged sisters – faithful communist Anastasiia in ▷Leningrad and dissident Anna in West Germany – as they combine in a frustrating attempt to trace the family of a third sister, Alena, the wife of a Chernobyl physicist. Each chapter ends with documentation (excerpts from newspaper reports, radio transcripts, and official speeches) of the Soviet cover-up and sluggish response to the crisis.

Stark, Freya (born 1893)

English travel writer and photographer. From the 1930s to the 1970s Stark travelled widely, often alone, through Canada, Persia (now Iran), southern Arabia and Asia Minor. She published numerous accounts of her adventures, including *The Valley of the Assassins* (1934), *The Southern Gates of Arabia* (1938) and *A Winter in Arabia* (1940). *Traveller's Prelude* (1950) is the first volume of her acclaimed autobiographical trilogy. A recognized authority on Arab affairs, Stark was consulted by British Intelligence during World War II. She has also campaigned for women's rights in Europe and in Arab countries. Her other publications include: *Beyond Euphrates* (1951), *The Coast of Incense* (1953) and *Dust in the Lion's Paw* (1961).
▷ Travel writing (19th-century Britain)

Štastie je drina (1989) (*Happiness is Hard Work*)

The third, and worst, novel by contemporary Slovak journalist Gabriela Rothmayerová (born 1951). It concerns a very ordinary woman with vague feminist leanings. The main character is a young, divorced psychologist who tries to get over the permanent stress caused by her work, bringing up a child, and problems in her personal life. Her involuntary freedom forces her to try to win happiness from life, even if it means suppressing her own self. Her deformity is therefore the result of her own error, as well as that of society. Feminism is palpable in Rothmayerová's approach to the male characters, who are either weak or irresponsible. They are unable to understand the 'tender' world of women, who are forced to be strong and cope with life on their own. Rothmayerová's depiction of character and events is superficial and contrived.

Station Life in New Zealand (1870)

Memoirs by New Zealand writer ▷ Lady Barker. Lady Mary Anne Barker came to New Zealand with her husband, Frederick Napier Broome, who tried his hand at sheep farming. *Station Life in New Zealand* is based on letters she wrote to relatives in England about their lives on a high-country station in Canterbury, confronting the difficulties of colonial life. *Station Life* is very much the view of a gentlewoman, and Lady Barker sees New Zealand society and scenery in terms of the England for which she wrote. Nevertheless the continuing popularity of *Station Life* and the record it provides of the experiences and attitudes of the English upper classes in a colonial society has made it a significant, even classic, text in New Zealand literary history.

Stead, Christina (1902–1983)

Australian novelist. Christina Stead was born in Sydney, the daughter of David Stead, an eminent naturalist, socialist and humanitarian. She taught for a time, then travelled extensively before marrying the American William Blake, a Marxist banker. She taught at New York University and

Christina Stead

was a senior writer for MGM before settling in England in 1935, then in Australia in 1974. Stead has always had an international following but gained little recognition in Australia before the mid-1960s. In 1967 she was rejected for the Britannica-Australia award on the grounds that she had ceased to be Australian, but she won the Patrick White Award in 1974. She is now considered to be one of Australia's greatest novelists. Her novels are works of great imaginative power and emotional intensity, and her favourite themes are those of struggle within relationships and the family, and of artistic integrity. ▷ *The Man Who Loved Children* (1940, with an introduction by Randall Jarrell), and ▷ *For Love Alone* (1944), are her most powerful and best-known works. Other fictional works include *The Salzburg Tales* (1934), *Seven Poor Men of Sydney* (1934), *The Beauties and the Furies* (1936), *House of All Nations* (1938), *Letty Fox: Her Luck* (1946), *A Little Tea, A Little Chat* (1948), *The People with the Dogs* (1952), *Cotter's England* (1967), *The Puzzleheaded Girl* (1967), *The Little Hotel* (1973), *Miss Herbert, the Suburban Housewife* (1976), and *I'm Dying Laughing* (published posthumously in 1987).
▷ Autobiography (Australia); Short story (Australia); Feminist literary criticism (Australia); *Gender, Politics and Fiction*

Steele, Danielle

US novelist. Born in New York, Steele was educated in France. She worked in public relations and advertising. She is married, and gave birth to her eighth child in 1986. Her romances focus on women in powerful or glamorous positions, and her heroines have successful careers as well as a domestic side, although often they must choose their priorities. In *Changes*

(1983) a newswoman must decide between her career and her long-distance marriage.

The novels often rely on a formulaic plot centring on romance. But they also emphasize the importance of feminine qualities such as nurturing and caretaking. In *Palomino* (1981) a woman turns her horse ranch into a place for handicapped children. In *Kaleidoscope* a woman survives foster homes, exploitation and rape to reunite her sisters.

Other works include: *Going Home* (1973), *Passion's Promise* (1977), *Now and Forever* (1978), *Season of Passion* (1979), *Summer's End* (1980), *Remembrance* (1981), *To Love Again* (1981), *Crossings* (1982), *Once in a Lifetime* (1982), *A Perfect Stranger* (1982), *Full Circle* (1984), *Secrets* (1985), *Family Album* (1986), *Wanderlust* (1986), *Fine Things* (1987), *Star* (1989), *Daddy* (1989), *Message from Nam* (1990) and *Jewels* (1992).
▷Romance fiction (20th century)

Stefan, Verena (born 1947)
German-speaking Swiss writer. A physiotherapist by profession, she was closely involved with the students' movement in Germany in the 1960s. In 1975 she achieved a phenomenal success with *Häutungen* (1975) (▷*Shedding*, 1978), a novel in which autobiography, critique of ▷patriarchy, poetry, dream-like passages and self-analysis combine to make the most radical of feminist statements. The book ushered in a new era of feminist literature and philosophy in the German-speaking world.

Stein, Gertrude (1874–1946)

Gertrude Stein

US ▷modernist. Born in the US to Jewish-Bavarian parents in 1874, Stein received her education first from the family's brief return to Europe where Stein attended school, and later

from Radcliffe where she studied psychology under William James (1842–1910). James', influence runs throughout her works with its insistence on a 'continuous presence', just as her training in psychology guides her endeavour to describe every possible human type in her epic novel *The Making of the Americans* (1925). It is, however, her life in Paris which provides most of the material for the Stein myth, as it did the motivation for much of her experimental writing. Her and her brother, Leo Stein's, art collection at 27 rue de Fleurus where the work of artists Cézanne (1839–1906), Renoir (1841–1919), Manet (1832–1883), Matisse (1869–1954) and Picasso (1881–1973) lined the walls, is legendary. Cézanne's and Matisse's painting inspired the composition of her early ▷*Three Lives* (1909), whilst Picasso's cubism informs her astonishing prose-poem ▷*Tender Buttons* (1914) as it does her numerous 'portraits' of people and places. As a 'famous' lesbian, Stein's sexuality has been the subject of keen biographical interest. Her early novel, *Q.E.D* (1903) (published posthumously as *Things as They Are*) explores the jealousies and desires between three young women, whilst her well-known, ▷*The Autobiography of Alice B. Toklas* (1932) records her relationship with Alice Toklas. These books, however, compare with Stein's intriguing encoding of lesbian eroticism in poems such as 'Lifting Belly'.

Stein did not become a myth in her own country until the 1930s. Her return to North America gave a platform for Stein's own, curiously neglected, explorations of literary theory collected in *Lectures in America* (1934) and *Narration* (1935). By the time she recorded her experiences as a North American in France during World War II in *Wars I Have Seen* (1942–4) Stein's reputation at home and abroad was finally assured. What she left behind is the demanding task of reading this reputation through her frequently difficult writings, and so beyond, but not behind, her compelling public mask.

Other works include: *Matisse, Picasso and Gertrude Stein* (1909–12); *Useful Knowledge* (1915); *Geography and Plays* (1908); *Lucy Church Amiably* (1927); *Operas and Plays* (1913–30); *The Geographical History of America or the Relation of Human Nature to the Human Mind* (1935); *Everybody's Autobiography* (1936); *Ida, A Novel* (1940); *Selected Writings of Gertrude Stein* (1945); *The Unpublished Writings of Gertrude Stein* (1951–1958), and *Gertrude Stein: Selections* (1980).

Steinem, Gloria (born 1934)
North American feminist writer. She began her career with a series of campaigning articles in North American publications on civil rights issues, and in 1971 became a founding editor of *Ms* magazine. She is now based in New York, and travels extensively raising money for the *Ms* Foundation for Women. Her books include *Outrageous Acts and Everyday Rebellions*, *Marilyn* and *Revolution From Within: A Book of Self Esteem* (1992). In *Revolution From Within* she recounts

how, through returning to her childhood self through techniques such as meditation, she rediscovered the strong person inside her insecure shell. The book aims to inspire other women to similar self-discovery.

Steinwachs, Ginka (born 1942)
German critic and writer. She began her career with a study on André Breton (1896–1966) and French Surrealism, and taught for a time at the University of Vincennes near Paris. Acting on the Surrealist precepts of automatic writing, she published several experimental novels which explore the nature of the creative impulse as a phenomenon in itself. This theme is also central to her innovative play, *George Sand. Eine Frau in Bewegung, die Frau von Stand* (1980) (*George Sand. A Woman in Motion, A Woman of Standing*),

Stella (1905)
The first novel by the romantic Argentinian writer ▷Ema de la Barra de Llanos, published under her pen-name César Duayen. It raised much curiosity and attained immediate fame, partly because it was written by a woman. Soon after its publication, she married Julio Llanos, who many considered must have been the author of her novel, although this was denied. *Stella* is a novel, written in ▷*costumbrismo*, realistic style, but with romantic traits. The plot is centred almost entirely on Argentinian society, and there are numerous descriptions of places: the Jockey Club, the opera, literary evenings and the countryside. They provide a testimony of the times and provide a backdrop to the novel. It has been translated into several languages and published in many editions.

Stephens, Ann Sophia (1810–1886)
US writer of fiction, humour and the first ▷dime novel; editor of ▷*Peterson's Magazine* and *Graham's Magazine*. An extremely prolific and versatile writer, Stephens began with book-length historical fiction on British and US subjects and moved through a range of popular genres, where she was often the first to use a subject or approach. Most notable are her New York books – *High Life in New York* (1843, published under the pseudonym Jonathan Slick, perhaps because its form of humour was associated with male writers) and *Fashion and Famine* (1854) – and ▷*Malaeska: The Indian Wife of the White Hunter* (1860), which introduced the genre of the dime novel.

Stephenson, Clarine
Caribbean novelist and poet, born in ▷Jamaica. Her publications include a novel, *Undine: An Experience* (1911), and poetry, 'The White Man's Prophecy', (Jamaica Times, August 1909).

Step-Mother; a Domestic Tale, from Real Life, The (1799)
Novel by the North American author ▷Helena Wells. As in most late 18th-century North American novels, the assertion of 'from Real Life'

in the title suggests not one correlative life but the lives of women in general. Mortality rates did still lead to numerous instances of stepmothers and stepchildren having to reshape their lives around their new circumstances, and in many such novels the stepmother is depicted as cruel and unloving. In this conservative novel, woman's sphere is depicted as limited solely – and correctly – to the domestic realm; it suggests that the only way for woman to cope with the harshness of her life is to 'think of *man* as a *lord* and *master*' and act accordingly. Like all of Helena Wells's novels, it reveals the realities of woman's life but advocates acquiescence rather than change.

Stern, Daniel ▷Flavigny, Marie de

Stern, Gladys Bertha (1890–1973)
Novelist, born in London to Jewish parents. Her first novel, *Pantomime*, was published in 1914. She is best-known for her five novels about the Rakonowitz family: *Tents of Israel* (1924), re-issued as *The Matriarch* in 1948; *A Deputy Was King* (1926); *Mosaic* (1930); *Shining and Free* (1935), and *The Young Matriarch* (1942). This dynastic saga of a wealthy Jewish family from the late 19th century onwards has been compared to John Galsworthy's *The Forsyte Saga* (1906–1921). Stern's other writings include many novels, short stories, reminiscences and non-fiction works, including works on ▷Jane Austen written with her close friend ▷Sheila Kaye-Smith. Always ambivalent about her Jewish heritage, Stern, Kaye-Smith as has done earlier, converted to Catholicism in 1947. Her reputation as a writer has somewhat faded, but she was much admired by her contemporaries, including ▷May Sinclair and W. Somerset Maugham (1874–1965).

Stern, Karl ▷Daudet, Julia

Stevenson, Anne (born 1933)
US poet and literary critic. Although she was born in England and lived there, Stevenson's parents were North American, and she was educated in New England and Ann Arbor, Michigan. Her poetry attests to this dual existence, moving between poems that investigate US society and history, such as 'Utah', 'Dear Ladies of Cincinnati' and the historical narrative ▷*Correspondences: A Family History in Letters* (1974), and poems such as 'In Middle England', which probes and dignifies the 'desolate neatness' of the undistinguished lives of 'spinster gardens' and 'bungalows'. She has been Compton Fellow in Creative Writing at Dundee University, and helped to found The Poetry Bookshop in Hay on Wye, Wales. She has also held fellowships at Oxford, Reading and Radcliffe College. From 1981 to 1983 Stevenson was Northern Arts Literary Fellow.

She refused the label 'feminist writer' in her essay 'Writing As a Woman', arguing for a 'common consciousness' between men and women writers. However, her most formally exciting work, *Correspondences*, is centrally concerned with the conditions of women's lives, and Stevenson's description of her early self as 'a poet in the plight of ▷Sylvia Plath (married, divorced with small children) who wanted to write poems like ▷Elizabeth Bishop' is still perhaps accurate. Not suprisingly, she has written a critical work on Elizabeth Bishop and a biography of Sylvia Plath, *Bitter Fame: A Life of Sylvia Plath* (1989). Her poetry collections include: *Living in America* (1965), *Reversals* (1969), *Travelling behind Glass* (1974), *Enough of the Green* (1977), *Minute by Minute* (1982), *The Fiction-Makers* (1985), *Winter Time* (1986), *Selected Poems 1956–86* (1986) and *The Other House* (1988).

Stewart, Mary (born 1916)

English novelist. Stewart taught at Durham University for several years, and turned to writing following an ectopic pregnancy. She is a prolific popular writer whose novels are generally love stories played out in exotic settings. Stewart's first publication was *Madam, Will You Talk?* (1955). She has also written a trilogy about Merlin, the magician of Arthurian legend, beginning with *The Crystal Cave* (1970). She has also written several books for children.

Stillborn, The (1984)

A novel by the Nigerian writer, ▷Zaynab Alkali, and the first by a northern, Moslem woman. The story is of three village girls, Li, her elder sister Awa, and her friend Faku, growing up in a village in the Middle Belt of Nigeria, where Christianty and Islam coexist with traditional animist religion. Alkali's purpose is to demonstrate the limited range of choices and fates available to women, and within that, the possibilities for resistance. While Awa remains in the village and follows in the footsteps of her mother, Faku has an unhappy marriage because of her failure to have children, and turns to ▷prostitution. Li, who marries for love, is sorely tested by her husband and leaves him to train as a teacher. In spite of her hard-won autonomy, she is prepared to forgive and accept her husband back after an accident which has made him lame. Alkali skilfully counterpoises her prose narrative with ▷oral elements, and with a shifting chronology using dreams and flashbacks. Through the traditional means of oral abuse, she portrays the power of Li's grandmother; through a riddling song, a woman laments her husband's impotence. A simple story thus acquires depth and significance, and becomes the story of a whole community.

▷Religion, Christianity, Islam and traditional beliefs in West Africa; Infertility/childlessness in West Africa

Stockenström, Wilma (born 1933)

South African Afrikaans poet, novelist, translator and actor. Stockenström was born in Napier, Cape Province. She is most famous for her novel ▷*The Expedition to the Baobab Tree* (1983), translated from *Die Kremetartekspedisie* (1981),

Wilma Stockenström

which seeks a different way of presenting the African landscape than the one offered by expeditions and mapping. Another novel *Uitdraai* (1976) (*Turnoff*) examines the implications of the right of succession for daughters and 'illegitimate' sons born of mixed-race unions.

In her poetry Stockenström searches for a language in which to articulate the African landscape, thus making a significant contribution to Afrikaans literature. Five volumes have appeared: *Vir die Bysiende Leser* (1970) (*For the Near-Sighted Reader*), *Spieël van Water* (1973) (*Mirror of Water*), *Van Vergetelheid en van Glans* (1976) (*Of Oblivion and of Splendour*), *Monsterverse* (1984) (*Monstrous Verses*), and *Die Heengaanrefrein* (1988) (*Refrain of Departure*).

Stockenström is also a distinguished stage and film actor, and has written extensively for the stage. Besides *Dawid die Dik Dom Kat* (1971) (*Dawid the Fat Stupid Cat*), written for children, and some one-act plays in literary magazines, she has published *Trippens se Patatta* (1971) (*Potatoes for Thruppence*), a 'theatre of the absurd' fairytale for adults about a farmer who discovers a giant potato in his garden, and *Die Laaste Middagmaal* (1978) (*The Last Luncheon*), in which a white Afrikaner family has to confront the younger son's relationship with a black woman.

Stockenström has been awarded numerous prizes: the Hertzog prize on two occasions, the South African CNA (Central News Agency) Prize, and the Grinzane Cavour Prize for the Italian translation of *Die Kremetartekspedisie*.

Other novels are: *Eers Linkie dan Johanna* (1979) (*First Linkie then Johanna*); *Kaapse*

Rekwisiete (1987) (*Cape Stage Property*), and *Abjater wat so Lag* (1991) (*The Laughing Abjater*).
Bib: du Plessis, Michael, 'Bodies and Signs: Inscriptions of Femininity in John Coetzee and Wilma Stockenström', *Journal of Literary Studies*, 4, 1 (1988).

Stöcker, Helene (1869–1943)

German essayist. She came from a large Calvinist family in southern Germany, studied German literature, and began to write poems and novellas at an early age. In 1892 she went to live in Berlin, were she became involved with the women's movement. She began to make public speeches and wrote essays on the role of women, and in 1905 became the co-founder of the Association for Sexual Reform and the Protection of Mothers. During World War I she took up a radically pacifist stance. Her essays were first collected in *Die Liebe und die Frauen* (*Love and Women*) of 1906. Her only novel *Liebe* (1922) (*Love*) is a critique of the notion of romantic love.

Stocker-Meynert, Dora von (1870–1947)

Austrian writer. Daughter of the psychiatrist and poet Theodor Meynert (1833–1892). A successful poet and dramatist, she received a prize for her play *Die Blinde* (*The Blind Woman*) in 1907. However, it is her appraisal of her father's work in *Theodor Meynert and seine Zeit* (1930) (*Theodor Meynert and His Time*) which is now considered her most important contribution to Austria's cultural history.

Stockfleth, Maria Katharina (c 1633–1692)

German writer. She was an active member of a flourishing poets' club in Nuremberg during the German baroque period. She wrote a sequel to her husband's novel, *Die Kunst- und Tugendgezierte Macarie* (1673) (*Macarie Adorned by Art and Virtue*), in which their relationship is rendered in idealistic terms. This sequel was recently rediscovered, and is considered far superior to the first part.

Stockley, Cynthia (1872–1936)

Prolific Rhodesian novelist and short story writer, known as 'the lady of the scarlet sunshade' for the colourful and romantic image she cultivated, with the aid of her own autobiographical legend. Born in Bloemfontein, her unhappy childhood was followed by an unhappy first marriage in Rhodesia, experiences which enter her novels *Poppy: The Story of a South African Girl* (1910) and *The Dreamship* (1913, published as *Wanderfoot* in the USA). *Poppy* follows the career of a young woman who undergoes a series of dire misadventures before becoming a celebrated writer and marrying the man of her dreams. In '898 Stockley left for London, where she worked ; a journalist, writer and actress, also travelling to North America and living in Paris.

As regards their interest in heroines whose motivations are often mercenary rather than sentimental, Stockley's novels foreshadow those of

▷Daphne Rooke. In her first novel, *Virginia of the Rhodesians* (1903), the protagonist is a heartless manipulator, and the butt of considerable authorial irony. Although her plots are sometimes convoluted and implausible, veering between the ▷sensational and the ▷sentimental, her work was extremely popular. It was seen as racy and audacious because of its cynicism and relative openness about sexual matters. She also published short stories: *Wild Honey: Stories of South Africa* (1914) and *Blue Aloes: Stories of South Africa* (1918).

Other novels: *The Claw* (1911); *Pink Gods and Blue Demons* (1920); *Ponjola* (1923); *Dalla the Lion Cub* (1924) and *Perilous Women* (1924) (the last two published in one volume under the title of *Perilous Women*, and appearing in the USA as *The Garden of Peril*); *Three Farms* (1925, published in the USA as *The Dice of God* in 1926); *The Leopard in the Bush* (1927); *Tagati* (1930) (*Magic*); *Kraal Baby* (1933); *Perilous Stuff* (1936; made up of three short novels: *The Price of a Rose*, *Show Week*, and *The Suicide Season*).

Stöcklin, Franziska (1894–1931)

German-speaking Swiss poet and painter. The favourite subjects of her poems are dancers, clowns, birds and flowers, which she evokes in the powerful gestural language of Expressionism, sometimes complementing them with her own drawings. In her writing, the sorrow of love, pain and death assumes a mystical dimension, and is experienced as part of a natural world created by God. Her main works are the poetry collections *Gedichte* (1920) (*Poems*) and *Die singende Muschel* (1925) (*The Singing Sea Shell*); the prose poems *Traumwirklichkeit* (1923) (*The Realiity of Dreams*); and the novellas *Liebende: Zwei Novellen* (1923) (*Lovers: Two Novellas*).

Stockton, Annis Boudinot (1736–1801)

North American poet. Born on 1 July 1736 in Darby, Pennsylvania, she published numerous poems in New England and mid-Atlantic states' periodicals. She exchanged poems with other women writers, including ▷Elizabeth Graeme Fergusson, and honoured women and the revolutionary cause in many poems. ▷'To Laura' identifies Fergusson as a 'sister' poet, and ▷'To My Burrissa' acknowledges her admiration for ▷Esther Edwards Burr. Her use of couplets and quatrains reflects the influence of English poets such as Thomas Gray (1716–1771) and Alexander Pope (1688–1744), but her poems are distinguished by their woman-centred themes. Several of her poems are appended to the Reverend Samuel Smith's *Funeral Sermon on the Death of the Hon. Richard Stockton* (1781).

Stojadinović-Srpkinja, Milica (1830–1878)

Serbian poet. Known as the 'Muse of the 1848 Generation' (a year of patriotic revolutions) Stojadinović was the first woman poet of Serbia, and something of a pioneer with her sentimental, exalted patriotic verse. She captured the nationalistic imaginations of her contemporaries and was greatly admired, although her verse is somewhat naïve. She also wrote a cynical diary about the wooded hills of Fruška gora, containing passages of both prose and verse. In her writing she strived for a masculine style which would conceal her female identity.

Stólitsa, Liubov' Nikitishna (1884–1934)

Russian poet and dramatist. Stólitsa grew up in a Moscow merchant household. Her first book of poetry, *Rainia* (1908), displays some of her hallmarks: gathering of poems into cycles, and a folkloric tendency to draw parallels between the human and natural worlds. In 1912 she published *Lada*, a collection of 'songs' in short lines. Stólitsa expanded her range of narratives influenced by folklore in 'Fairytale about the Gentle Princess' (1913) and 'Song of Golden Olona' (1914). The former inverts the traditional roles: the princess sculpts a prince out of snow and, when he disappears, sets out to find him. Stólitsa's third book, *Rus'*, which appeared during World War I, is a celebration of her native land. Her poetry combines a pantheistic adoration of the Russian countryside with primarily ritual aspects of Russian Orthodoxy.

Stólitsa contributed poetry and articles to magazines for women. In the 1914 article 'The New Eve' she depicts the 'woman of the future': 'Of course, she will be free and equal with a man in everything, but she will learn to look at her rights not as a final goal, but as the primary means for achieving her own principles, her own long-lived female hopes, and her own genuinely female strivings.' Starting in 1916, Stólitsa wrote five full-length plays and some dozen mini-dramas, all in verse. *The Blue Carpet* was staged at the Moscow Kamernyi Theatre. Like the novel ▷*Elena Deeva*, the play emphasizes woman's need for choice in matters of love.

Stólitsa and her family emigrated in 1920 and settled in Sofia, Bulgaria. Her poetry appeared in *émigré* journals, and her last book, two long narrative poems, appeared in 1934 in Sofia.

▷Gértsyk, Adelaida; *Nastas'ia Kostër*
Bib: Deutsch, B. and Yarmolinsky, A. (trans.), *Modern Russian Poetry: An Anthology*; Yarmolinsky, A. (ed.), *A Treasury of Russian Verse*.

Stolk, Gloria (1918–1979)

Venezuelan poet, novelist, short story writer, essayist, journalist and critic. She graduated from the Sorbonne in Paris, and studied at Smith College in the United States. She opposed the nativism of the ▷*Viernes* Group of poets, and described cosmopolitan life, social groups, and their language and urban habits, especially in *Amargo el fondo* (1957), a novel which has been translated into English. *Bellas Vegas* (1953) (*Beautiful Plains*) another novel, has been translated into French. In *La casa del viento* (1965) (*The House of The Wind*) she writes about children's recollections and has an evocative feel for nostalgic subjects.

Other works: *Rescate y otros poemas* (1950) (*Ransom and Other Poems*); *El Arpa* (1951) (*The Harp*); *Catorce lecciones de belleza* (1953) (*Fourteen Lessons in Beauty*); *Los miedos* (1955) (*Fears*); *Diamela* (1960); *Cielo insistente* (1960) (*Insistent Sky*); *Cuando la luz se quiebra* (1961) (*When the Light Breaks*); *Angel de piedra* (1962) (*Stone Angel*), and *Manual de buenos modales* (1967) (*Manual of Good Manners*).

Stone, Sarah (fl 1737)

Author of a treatise on midwifery, *A Complete Practice of Midwifery* (1737), with examples of cases. She intervenes on behalf of women in the debate over men and women midwives, and hopes to instruct, particularly, lower-class midwives. She argues that 'the Modesty of our Sex will be in great danger of being lost for want of good Women-Midwives, . . . for it is arrived to that height already that almost any young Man, who hath served his apprenticeship to be a barber surgeon, immediately sets up for a Man-Midwife.'

Stone Angel, The (1964)

Possibly the most celebrated of all Canadian novels, by ▷Margaret Laurence, about a recalcitrant old woman, Hagar Shipley, 'rampant with memory' and full of pride, in the last days of her life. Hagar's 90-year-old present is played against her past, with all its failed relationships and the protagonist's stiff-necked inability to rejoice. The narrative is engaged with a tangible recognition of what it is like to be old; because Hagar is increasingly infirm, her son and his wife, with whom she lives, want to put her in a nursing home, but she, in child-like defiance, runs away to an old fish cannery. There, she has an opportunity to confess her failures and losses before she is shriven and can die, if not peacefully, at least on her own terms. This is an overwhelmingly moving novel, full of allusion and mythology, fierce and yet tender. It is the first in Laurence's 'Manawaka' cycle of novels.

Stonor Letters and Papers (1290–1483)

The collection of documents and letters on domestic, business and administrative matters, from the archives of the Stonor family of Oxfordshire. The languages used are Latin, ▷Anglo-Norman and English, with English predominating by the fifteenth century. There are a number of letters from women, including several from Elisabeth to her husband, Sir William Stonor (1470s). Others are from Jane to her husband, Thomas Stonor, and to her daughter; and from Katherine Arundell to Thomas Stonor. Margery Hampden, Annys Wydeslade, Mary Barantyne, Anne Stonor, and Queen Elizabeth Woodville are also included, as is Alice Stonor's account book for 1432–1433. The documents illustrate the growth of literacy and its use by women, as well as shedding light on other aspects of history, particularly social history.

▷Letters (England, Middle Ages)
Bib: Kingsford, C.L. (ed.), *The Stonor Letters and*

Papers, and *Supplementary Stonor Letters and Papers*.

Storia, La (1977) ▷*History: A Novel*

Storia di Anna Drei (1947) ▷*Story of Anna Drei, The*

Stories of Herself When Young: Autobiographies of Childhood by Australian Women (1990)
This collection, by Joy Hooton, discusses works as varied as those by Miles Franklin, Henry Handel Richardson and Christina Stead, and those of unknown or neglected writers. Its bibliography of the autobiographies of Australian women is particularly helpful.

Storm, Lesley (1898–1975)
Scottish novelist and dramatist. Many of Storm's novels are concerned with issues of sexual morality, and she is particularly interested in transgressive women. Early novels such as *Lady What of Life?* (1927) and *Just As I Am* (1933) address the conflicts and tensions of women's independence, and similar themes orchestrate her plays, most notably *Roar Like a Dove* (1958), which looks at the social emphasis placed on childbearing.

Storni, Alfonsina (1892–1938)
Argentinian poet and dramatist, who wrote under the pen-names Tao-Lao and Alfonsina. She was born in Switzerland to cultured Swiss parents. However, the death of her father in 1900 obliged her to work in a cap factory in Rosario. She then became a teacher, and also published pieces in Rosario magazines, which was unusual in 1910. She had a child, and in 1911 she moved to Buenos Aires, where she taught languages and drama and wrote for the press.

Her first book of poems was *La inquietud del rosal* (1916), (*The Restlessness of the Rose Bush*) and she won prizes for her book *Languidez* (1921) (*Languor*). During her first phase (1916–1921) she dwelt romantically on emotion, subjectivity, spring and the sea, but her expression is more objective in *Ocre* (1925) (*Ochre*), the book most devoted to the sea. In *Mundo de siete pozos* (1934) (*World of Seven Wells*) she made a real break from romanticism, and in 1938 described her poems as anti-sonnets. Alfonsina Storni displays a taste for cynicism, irony and bitterness, as in her most famous poem: '*Hombre pequeñito*', ('Little Man') in which she despises men. She was rebellious against the limitations imposed on women, and used symbols of nature and erotic images in her poetry. Hopelessly ill, she drowned herself in Mar del Plata, after sending her poem '*Quiero dormir*' ('I want to sleep') to *La Nación*.

Other works: *Obra poética completa* (1961) (*Complete Works of Poetry*); *Antología poética* (1956); *El duce daño* (1917) (*Sweet Pain*); *Irremediablemente* (1919) (*Incurably*); *Poemas de amor* (1926) (*Love Poems*); *Mascarilla y trébol* (1938) (*Mask and Trefoil*); *Círculos imantados* (1938) (*Magnetized Circles*), and *El amo del mundo* (1927) (*The Master of the World*).

Story, Gertrude (born 1929)
Short story writer, who was born, and continues to live, in Saskatchewan, Canada. Her fiction reflects her German Lutheran background, and relies on the vernacular of the prairie. Her collections include *The Book of Thirteen* (1981), *The Way to Always Dance* (1983), *It Never Pays to Laugh Too Much* (1984), *The Need of Wanting Always* (1985) and *Black Swan* (1986). *After Sixty: Going Home* (1991) portrays older people searching for their origins. Her work partakes of the enduring quality of folk-tale.

Story of an African Farm, The (1883)
Generally known as South Africa's first novel, it is also the first novel ▷Olive Schreiner published, though the second she wrote. Set in colonial times in the Karoo district of South Africa, it focuses on two young English-speaking girls, Lyndall and Em, who live on the farm under the care of Em's stepmother, Tant Sannie, a Boer woman and widow of the proprietor. Em, who will eventually own the farm, is plain, affectionate, and domestically inclined. Lyndall, her cousin, is beautiful, sharp, and desirous of an intellectually fulfilling life. The novel also focuses on Waldo, son of the German farm manager who is banished from the farm after the arrival of Bonaparte Blenkins, a Dickensian rogue after Tant Sannie's money. Like Lyndall, Waldo yearns for a life other than the cruel and small-minded one on the farm. Waldo finds something of what he wants in his inventions and his art, but Lyndall leaves the farm both to seek her intellectual fortune and to find the kind of freedom denied to women. After giving birth to a child who does not survive, she herself dies before her time, abandoned by her lover, who wanted a more submissive woman, and attended only by a man called Gregory Rose, through whom Schreiner uneasily investigates the fusion of masculine and feminine attributes.

Story of a New Zealand River, The (1920)
Novel by New Zealand writer ▷Jane Mander. As its title suggests, Mander's novel took for its model ▷Olive Schreiner's ▷*The Story of an African Farm*, a novel that one of the characters in *The Story of a New Zealand River* has been reading. It is a realist novel which examines the relationships between women and men both within and outside marriage, and explores the nature of women's lives through the life of the central character, Alice Roland, and her daughter, Asia. Alice, an English gentlewoman, marries Tom Roland, a sawmill boss, and goes with him and her daughter to live in a remote timber settlement on the Kaipara Harbour. The novel deals with the cultural and sexual conflicts of this situation as well as with the difficulties produced by the environment and the characters' dependence on the river as their route of escape.

Alice's daughter becomes a central figure in the latter part of the novel, as she has the courage to do what her mother cannot do: ignore social convention in the interests of personal development. *The Story of a New Zealand River* has remained significant in literary history since its first publication.

Story of Anna Drei, The (1970)

Translation of *Storia di Anna Drei* (1947), a novel by Italian writer ▷Milena Milani, set in Rome. The first-person narrative is transmitted by Elsa, who tells the story of her odd relationship with Anna, apparently a writer. The triangular relationship between Elsa, her lover, Mario, and Anna is constantly shifting. Milani investigates male–female and female–female relationships in this novel. Mario finally kills Anna, but she remains the author of her own destiny, as she has already foreseen this in her writing. The process of narration is a central concern of this work.

Story of Avis, The (1877)

US semi-biographical fiction by ▷Elizabeth Stuart Phelps (Ward). One of Phelps's most feminist and most biographical novels, *The Story of Avis* demonstrated the conflict between traditional marriage and a woman's artistic career. The book attracted much attention in its time because it was generally seen to reflect the story of the author and her mother, ▷Elizabeth Stuart Phelps, women artists in patriarchal families.

Story of Gösta Berling, The (1891)

▷Swedish writer Selma Lagerlöf's first novel, which broke in its form and content with the naturalism of the 1880s in Sweden. Her world was one of celebration, romance and adventures. The novel praises work, discusses how to be both happy and good, and how to combine ethics with beauty, work and art.

The novel is widely translated, and made its author famous. In 1909 she was awarded the Nobel Prize, also a result of ▷*Nils Holgersens underbara resa 1–2* (1906–07) (*The Wonderful Adventures of Nils*, and *The Further Adventures of Nils*). Its saga tone rang a fresh and romantic note in the realist era, taking its influence from the feminine oral tradition.

▷Realism

Story of Zahra, The (1986)

English translation of a novel, originally written in Arabic in 1980 by Lebanese ▷Hanan al-Shaykh. It sounded a completely new voice in Arabic fiction. Zahra, the heroine and chief narrator, is not romantic or even sympathetic. Her story falls in two parts: 'The Scars of Peace' and 'The Torrents of War', both beset by violence. In peace there is the violence of Zahra's father, who uses his leather belt indiscriminately on Zahra and her mother. There is the violence of political parties, represented by the fascist PPS (Popular Syrian Party, advocating a Greater Syria), which Zahra's body-building, weight-lifting uncle joins. Their

attempt at a *coup d'état* is abortive, and Zahra's uncle escapes to West Africa with a forged passport. His is the second voice in the narrative.

Zahra is trapped in a loveless, mechanical sexual relationship, which ends in two abortions and a spell in a mental hospital where she receives electric shock treatment. Her face is scarred with pimples that turn into running sores as she cannot keep her fingernails away from her face. She takes refuge with her uncle in Africa, but there she feels threatened by him. On an impulse she accepts a proposal of marriage from a Lebanese friend of her uncle, but it does not work.

In the second part of the novel, Zahra is back home in Beirut, but the civil war has broken out. The sheer absurdity of the war, the sectarian fighting, the class vengeance, the kidnapping and the looting all seem to settle into an everyday pattern. Zahra is shocked by the senseless destruction all round, and is almost hypnotized into a sexual relationship with a sniper whose lone post is at the top of a deserted building on the other side of town. Strangely enough, this new obsession finally sets her body free of its old numbness. She finds pleasure in the silent embrace of the young man; her pimples are forgotten as her body finds its rhythm. When she finds she is pregnant, the young man unwillingly agrees to marry her, but as she walks away she is hit by three bullets. We leave her lying in the rain wondering if it was *her* sniper.

Storz, Claudia (born 1948)

German-speaking Swiss novelist. Her novel *Jessica mit Konstruktionsfehlern* (1977) (*Jessica with Construction Faults*) is about a young woman suffering from a serious illness, which becomes a metaphor for the alienation she feels as a woman in contemporary society.

Stowe, Harriet Beecher (1811–1896)

US non-fiction and fiction writer, novelist, poet and biographer. Stowe's life and literary career are in many ways both paradigm and pinnacle of 19th-century US women writers. Coming from a family of generations of Puritan clergy, Stowe found her values and inspiration not in Calvinism but in a combination of romanticism (she read Byron, 1788–1824, and Sir Walter Scott, 1771–1832), a religiously inspired commitment to justice, and distinctively US subjects.

Stowe is typical in that she came to literature through writing for magazines. She began publishing when she won a prize contest of the *Western Monthly Magazine* and was soon a regular contributor of stories and essays to a variety of periodicals, including religious weekly newspapers, and a co-author with her sister, ▷Catharine Beecher, of works for children. Her most famous work, ▷*Uncle Tom's Cabin* (1852), grew naturally out of this early literary career. Stowe proposed to the abolitionist *National Era* a series of sketches on the human effects of slavery. These grew to become the serially published novel, which Stowe claimed came to her by divine intervention. *Uncle Tom's Cabin* sold in extraordinary numbers, in the USA and abroad, and galvanized popular sentiment against slavery. Stowe defended its accuracy with *A Key to Uncle Tom's Cabin* (1853) and continued her depiction of slavery in ▷*Dred* (1856).

Stowe's popularity assured her welcome in the national literary magazines, and for some time she was the primary (and occasionally only) woman writer in ▷*The Atlantic Monthly* and the prestigious New England literary clubs. After the anti-slavery novels, Stowe wrote mostly ▷local color stories and novels about her native New England: *The Minister's Wooing* (1859), *The Pearl of Orr's Island* (1862), *Oldtown Folks* (1869), *Sam Lawson's Oldtown Fireside Stories* (1872) and *Poganuc People* (1878).

From 1870, however, her work became more diverse. Her *Lady Byron Vindicated* (1870), which accused the British poet Lord Byron of incest, was first published in the *Atlantic*. Both the magazine and Stowe suffered. The British press, which had been so devoted to Stowe in the 1850s, treated *Lady Byron Vindicated* as calumny and slander. Stowe's vindication of women continued in fiction, with the satirical *Pink and White Tyranny* (1871), *My Wife and I* (1871) and *We and Our Neighbors* (1875). After her retirement to Florida, she published *Palmetto-Leaves* (1873).

Strade di polvere, Le (1987) ▷*Dust Roads of Monferrato, The*

Strange Fruit (1944)
US novel. ▷Lillian Smith's bestseller was considered subversive for its theme of miscegenation. Banned in Boston and by the US Post Office until Eleanor Roosevelt intervened, it focuses on the sexual relationship between a white man, Tracy, and a mulatta, Nonnie. Smith describes it as a fable about a son in search of his mother. Tracy satisfies his incestuous desire for his black surrogate mother through his relationship with Nonnie. Succumbing to social pressure, he also denies this desire; he denigrates his relationship with Nonnie to marry the white ▷Southern lady. Smith emphasizes that the fabric of society is destroyed by society's attitudes to sexuality and racial segregation.

Strauss, Jennifer (born 1933)
Australian poet and literary critic. Strauss was educated at the University of Melbourne before marrying and having three children. She has lived in England, the USA and Germany, and has taught at the universities of New England and Melbourne, and at Monash University since 1964. Her published volumes of poetry are *Children and Other Strangers* (1975), *Winter Driving* (1981), and *Labour Ward* (1988). Individual poems and literary articles have also appeared in many journals and anthologies. Her poems are especially concerned with women's experience and are notable for their wit, irony and sensitivity. Strauss was awarded second prize in the John Shaw Neilson Award of the Fellowship of Australian Writers for 1975, and first prize in the *Westerly* Sesquicentenary Competition for 1979.

Strauß und Torney, Lulu von (1873–1956)
German poet. From an old Friesian and Saxon family, she grew up in a cultured environment, travelled widely as a young girl, and at the age of twenty-five published her first collection of verse, *Balladen und Lieder* (1902) (*Ballads and Songs*). Her best poetry is in ballad form, and she contributed considerably to the revival of this genre, often endowing its stock-in-trade of myth, legend and historical events with a social message.

Strawberry Girl (1945)
US novel that won a Newbery Medal, *Strawberry Girl* is the first in ▷Lois Lenski's regional series. It introduced realism and regional speech into children's literature. Narrated by Birdie Boyer, it chronicles her family's move to Florida's lake section to farm strawberries, and informs children how people live, socially and economically, in this particular region. Lenski shows how a young girl develops character in a grim environment.

Straw Dog, The (1980)
Work by Japanese poet and novelist ▷Tomioka Taeko. Using the Chinese metaphor of a straw dog at a festival, which they throw away when the festival is over, the heroine hunts for one young man after another. The motive behind her a hunt is the desire to have sex with a man. As a result, both the potential relationship and the words exchanged after making love mean nothing to her and, like the straw dog, they are thrown away. Tomioka reverses the conventional relationship between man and woman and shows that women also have carnal desires.

Straw Hats, The (1946)
Novel by Greek writer ▷Margarita Lymberaki. This is a nostalgic book about the life of three young sisters in Athens pursuing different paths in life. Their choices represent women's lives and problems, both within the family and within society at large, realistically. This was the first book written by a woman in 'the adolescent style', a style dealing with the world of young people as they emerge from adolescence into the adult world.

Stream of consciousness
Literary term associated with certain ▷modernist writers. The term originates in the work of North American philosopher William James (1842–1910) to describe the total range of awareness of an individual. The general argument is that in the mind of an individual at a given moment the 'stream of consciousness' is a multiplicity of levels of awareness, representing a constant flow of sensations, thoughts, memories and associations not necessarily organized by the logic of syntax or reason. The emphasis on the disjointed and illogical elements of these thought processes and

on the range of possible impressions, from the preverbal to the fully articulated, had obvious comparisons with modernist experimentation with narrative and narrative organization. The term was first coined as a literary critical term by ▷May Sinclair in her 1918 review of part of ▷Dorothy Richardson's ▷*Pilgrimage* to describe Richardson's narrative technique and representation of subjectivity. ▷Virginia Woolf similarly uses interior monologue to represent stream of consciousness, most notably in ▷*To the Lighthouse* and ▷*The Waves*.

  ▷*Mrs Dalloway*

Street, The (1946)

US novel by ▷Ann Petry which focuses on an African-American woman's struggle to maintain her dignity. It condemns the urban inner-city environment for destroying people's humanity. Lutie Johnson battles against the destructive, deterministic forces of this society, searching for a better life for her son and herself. Initially ambitious, she becomes disillusioned with the American dream of individual success. She learns how her skin colour, gender and social position leave her vulnerable, and she moves to Harlem where her efforts to secure employment remain unrewarded. She becomes the victim of sex and violence. Combating societal forces, Lutie eventually escapes the ghetto, although she loses her son to the street. The novel concludes on an optimistic note with Lutie's hope of salvaging her life.

Street in Bronzeville, A (1945)

US poetry. ▷Gwendolyn Brooks tells stories about everyday lives in this collection describing African-Americans living in a ghetto of Chicago, Illinois, using a range of verse forms including the twelve experimental sonnets of 'Gay Chaps at the Bar'. 'the old marrieds' portrays an older couple who commune in silence, and whose lives and marriage have become routine. The poems also raise social issues: 'The Mother', abortion; 'the ballad of chocolate Mabbie', intra-racial prejudice when a dark-skinned girl is rejected for a light-skinned girl; 'Negro Hero', racial prejudice when an African-American soldier defends democracy against Anglo-American soldiers. The characters in Brooks's poems must contend with their oppression; they desire to share in the American dream of an improved socio-economic life, but they must meet the goals of survival, such as paying the rent. They must settle for lukewarm water in a shower shared by five apartments.

Stretton, Hesba (Sarah) (1832–1911)

English novelist and writer of ▷children's literature. She contributed to Dickens's periodical, *Household Words*, and to *All the Year Round*, and had much work published by the Religious Tract Society. An Evangelical Christian, she wrote a large number of novels with religious messages, which were extremely popular. *Jessica's First Prayer* (1867) made her internationally famous and was translated into several languages. Her works include *Little Meg's Children* (1868); *Alone in London* (1869) and *Pilgrim Street* (1872).

Strong, Eithne (born 1923)

Eithne Strong

Irish poet and fiction writer, born in Limerick. She has worked as a teacher, in the civil service, and in the media, co-ordinated many creative writing workshops, and raised nine children. In 1943, she co-founded the Runa Press, one of the very few outlets for Irish poets at the time. In her forties she took a degree in modern languages at Trinity College, Dublin. She is unusual in that she writes both in Irish and in English. Her novel, *Degrees of Kindred*, appeared in 1979, and a collection of short stories, *Patterns*, in 1981. Her poetry collections in Irish are: *Cirt Oibre* (1980) (*Working Rights*), *Fuil agus Fallaí* (1983) (*Blood and Neglect*), *An Sagart Pinc* (1990) (*The Pink Priest*) (1990), *Aoife Fé Ghlas* and (*Aoife in Chains*). Her collections in English are: *Songs of Living* (1961), *Sarah, in Passing* (1974), *Flesh – the Greatest Sin* (1980), *My Darling Neighbour* (1985) and *Let Live* (1990).

Struck, Karin (born 1947)

German novelist. Her father fled from East Germany with his family when she was still a child, and her adolescence in West Germany was marred by a sense of alienation, guilt and an inability to communicate. These feelings are reflected in her first novel, *Klassenliebe* (1973) (*Lover of Class*), which created a minor sensation. It is written as a fragmented and anarchic autobiography of a woman whose character reflects that of the author herself. While attractive to many feminist radicals, this book was much criticized for being overly self-conscious, as well as for lacking form, focus and narrative distance.

Similar charges have also been levelled against Struck's subsequent novels. *Die Mutter* (1975) (*The Mother*), *Lieben* (1977) (*Loving*), and especially *Glut und Asche* (1985) (*Embers and Ashes*).

Structuralism

A type of textual criticism that analyzes thematic and grammatical structures in language, breaking them up into their component parts, and identifying the role played by each part in generating meaning. In literary texts this sort of analysis would include attention to the separate but related function of imagery, plot, narrative chronology, names, themes, etc. Literary genres are then categorized according to common structural properties rather than content, date or author.

An influential example of this type of criticism applied to literary texts is Vladimir Propp's structural analysis of folklore and fairytale in a book, first published in Russian in 1928, entitled *Morphology of the Folktale* (1968). Two other leading structuralists, Roland Barthes (1915–1980) and Claude Lévi-Strauss (born 1908) have used the methodological tools of structuralism to analyze cultural patterns. In *Mythologies* (1973), Barthes decodes menus and photographs, among other things; and Lévi-Strauss analyzes kinship structures in his influential book *Structural Anthropology* (1963).
Bib: Culler, J., *Structuralist Poetics: Structuralism, Linguistics and the Study of Literature*.

Stuart, Lady Arabella (1576–1615)

English aristocratic correspondent (granddaughter of Bess of Hardwick, of Hardwick Hall). After her secret marriage to William Seymour (1610) she was kept in prison because of her potential claim to the throne. She wrote letters from prison, and pathetically attempts to justify her marriage to James I: 'I most humbly beseech your Majesty . . . to consider in what a miserable state I have been in if I had taken any other course then I did, for my own conscience witnessing before God that I was the wife of him that now I am, I could never have matched with any other man but to have lived all the days of my life as an harlot.' She may have starved herself to death in prison.
Bib: Steen, Sara Jayne, *English Literary Renaissance* No. 18 (1988).

Stuart, Mary ▷ Mary Stuart, Queen of Scots

Stubbes, Katherine Emmes (c 1571–1590)

English devotional writer. The little we know of Stubbes is drawn from her husband's preface to her work. She was the next-to-youngest child of a Dutch mother and an English craftsman who died before she was fifteen. At this age, she married Philip Stubbes, a Puritan pamphleteer and author of *The Anatomy of Abuses*. When she was nineteen, Stubbes gave birth to a son and seemed to recover quickly. Soon afterward, however, she began dying of complications related to the delivery. On her deathbed, she called her neighbours together to make a public ▷confession of faith to them. Her ▷'Most Heavenly Confession' along with 'A Most Wonderful, Conflict betwixt Sathan and her Soule' was published by her husband in *A Christal Glas for Christian Women* (1592), his memorial tribute to her.
▷Confession of faith; Protestant Reformation

Sturm, J.C. (Taranaki) (born 1927)

New Zealand short story writer. Sturm was one of the first Maori writers in English publishing stories in the early 1950s. She was one of a number of writers who published in *Te Ao Hou*, a magazine which encouraged ▷Maori writing, and her story 'For All the Saints' was one of the first stories by a Maori writer to appear in an anthology of New Zealand writing. Sturm's collection *The House of the Talking Cat* was not published until 1985, when it appeared under a feminist publishing imprint. Sturm's stories focus on marriage and the isolation of married women. Some of her stories, such as 'First Native and Pink Pig', are explicitly about racism, but all her fiction implies racism, as her female characters exist on the margins of society, unable to break through an unspecified barrier. Sturm stopped publishing stories after the 1950s, but historically her collection is of extreme importance.

Suárez del Otero, Concha (born 1908)

Spanish novelist. A native of Asturias, Suárez wrote a doctoral thesis for the University of Madrid, where she taught Spanish literature. Her novels include: *Mabel* (1928); *Vulgaridades* (1930) (*Ordinary Things*), and *Satanás no duerme* (1958) (*Satan Never Sleeps*). Her masterpiece is *Me llamo Clara* (1968) (*My Name is Clara*), which is an exercise in metafiction – a novel within a novel. The first part includes a fragment of the manuscript of an autobiographical novel the protagonist is writing.

Suárez Solís, Sara

Contemporary Spanish novelist. Her main novels are: *Camino con retorno* (1980) (*Road with Return*) and *Juegos de verano* (1982) (*Summer Games*). She also writes literary criticism.

Subject

▷Poststructuralism, which claims that meanings are constituted in language, not human beings, distinguishes the subject from the 'individual'. The subject is that which acts and speaks, which takes up a position in language. But because the subject (unlike the ▷humanist concept of the individual) is the effect of meaning (which is always cultural and therefore changing) and not its origin, the subject is split, unfixed, in process. The human being can occupy several subject positions at once, which change over time. Subjectivity does not therefore connote a unified and conscious ego, which would be the source of all thought, speech, action, in the way that 'individual' does. On a poststructuralist understanding of the subject, free individual agency and an autonomous ego are illusory concepts. ▷Psychoanalysis, with its acknowledgement of the existence of the unconscious, also produces a model of the subject which is split and unfixed.

Suffrage

19th-century Britain: The first National Association for Women's Suffrage was formed in Manchester in 1865, and in 1866 a petition of 1500 signatures was presented to J.S. Mill, whose essay 'On the Subjection of Women' had been published that year. Signatories of the petition included ▷Barbara Bodichon, ▷Harriet Martineau and ▷Matilda Betham-Edwards. Mill presented a motion to Parliament to include female suffrage in the 1867 ▷Reform Bill, but he was defeated by 196 votes against 73. Throughout the rest of the 19th century women continued to campaign for the vote. Societies were formed in London, Edinburgh, Birmingham and Bristol in the late 1860s, and the first Women's Suffrage Bill was presented to Parliament by Jacob Bright in 1870. The first reading was carried by 124 votes to 91, but the government then opposed the Bill, and on the second vote it was defeated by 220 to 94. Although hopes were running high when a new Liberal government (led by Disraeli) came to power in 1874, no significant change of policy occurred. In 1880 Gladstone succeeded as Prime Minister, and the first women-only demonstration was held in Manchester's Free Trade Hall. The next major event was the new Parliamentary ▷Reform Bill of 1884 – a crushing defeat for the suffragists since Gladstone made it clear that he was inexorably opposed to the inclusion of women in the Bill. It was defeated by 271 to 135. Among the MPs who voted against the Bill were 104 Liberals who had pledged support.

In 1889 ▷Mrs Humphry Ward led an 'Appeal Against Female Suffrage', stating that 'The political ignorance of women is irreparable and is imposed by nature.' Although Ward had many notable supporters, the tide of public opinion was slowly beginning to turn. Another Women's Suffrage Bill was presented in 1892, and was only defeated by twenty-three votes. In 1897 Millicent Fawcett became President of the new National Union of Women's Suffrage, and the campaign for the vote was boosted after the Boer War, which bridged the end of the 19th and the beginning of the 20th century.

▷Cobbe, Frances Power; Grand, Sarah; Lyall, Edna; Meynell, Alice Thompson; 'New Woman, The'; Ouida; Wolstenholme-Elmy, Elizabeth; 'Woman Question, The'; Yonge, Charlotte

20th-century Britain: A movement which demanded equal rights for women, the right to vote, and the right to stand as candidates in parliamentary elections. The movement began in the late 19th century, and was consolidated around the turn of the century, the first decade marking a shift towards violent action as a means

to secure its aims. Among the leading figures of the movement is Emmeline Pankhurst (1858–1928), who initially campaigned for the Manchester Women's Suffrage Committee before she moved to London in 1905. Her associates included Annie Besant (1847–1933) and the Labour MP Keir Hardie (1856–1915). Emmeline Pankhurst joined the Fabian Society and Independent Labour Party, from which she resigned in 1903 to form the militant Women's Social and Political Union with her daughter, Christabel. The arrest of her daughter Christabel Pankhurst and the Irish trade unionist Annie Kenney during their protest at a Liberal Party meeting in 1905 marked the turning point in the movement's strategies and public profile. Emmeline Pankhurst was first arrested in 1908, and consistently thereafter, while Christabel was forced to escape to France in 1912 following a conspiracy charge. She continued to organize the campaign from France, largely through the magazine *The Suffragette*. Emmeline Pethick-Lawrence, first introduced to the Pankhursts in 1906 by Keir Hardie, was also imprisoned for conspiracy after demonstrations which included window-smashing. Christabel's sister, Sylvia Pankhurst, developed many WSPU branches in the East End of London, and was also imprisoned on numerous occasions. Sylvia's opposition to World War I precipitated a break with her mother, and Sylvia went on to found the socialist-pacifist journal *Worker's Dreadnought*. The suffrage movement ended in 1918 when votes were granted to women at the age of thirty. In 1928 Parliament decreed that women should have equal voting rights with men.

Sugar Heaven (1936)
Australian novel by ▷Jean Devanny. Set in tropical north Queensland, this novel is recognized as one of the earliest and most significant of the socialist realist Australian novels. Its heroine, Dulcie, becomes a political activist as she observes the 1935 strike on the canefields and the contribution of Weil's disease, which is carried by rats, to the terrible working conditions of the cane-cutters.

Sugimoto Sonoko (born 1925)
Japanese historical novelist. Born in Tokyo, she was influenced by the historical novelist, Yoshikawa Eiji. *An Embarkation Filled with Distress*, which describes people engaged in flood control in the 18th century, won the Naoki Prize in 1962. *Takizawa Bakin*, which tells the story of a famous 19th-century novelist, won the Yoshikawa Eiji Prize for Literature. She writes about all historical periods – from ancient to modern – and a pacifist attitude runs through all her work, including the prizewinning *Magnificent Hell*.

Su Hui (4th century AD)
Chinese literary woman of the Eastern Jing (AD 317–420) dynasty. Su Hui, also named Ruolan, was married at sixteen to a general. She was

deserted by her husband for a concubine when he left for another post. In her sorrow, she embroidered palindromic verses on a piece of cloth. The 841 characters could be read forwards, backwards, upwards, downwards, slantwise, reverse, or by every alternate word, a feat unparallelled in Chinese writing, which subsequently gave rise to imitations. However, the content is meagre and artificially controlled by the form.

Sula (1973)
Novel by US writer ▷Toni Morrison. *Sula* tells the story of two African-American women, Sula and Nel. Part one deals with their childhood and their inseparable friendship, and revolves around two deaths, the accidental drowning of Chicken Little, in which both are implicated, and the death by fire of Sula's mother, which she does nothing to stop. In the second part Sula and Nel are driven apart by their acceptance or rejection of community mores. Sula puts her grandmother in a home, and proceeds to sleep with most of the men in Bottom, including Nel's husband, thus outraging family feeling and women's pride. Three years after her return she dies, appeasing the community. Some years later, Nel sees Shadrack, the shell-shocked war veteran who witnessed the death of Chicken Little, and this reminder of her shared past with Sula shocks her into a recognition of her grief at Sula's death.

In this novel Morrison explores the love of women for each other, and the links between the community and the individual. Although Bottom rejects Sula, it needs her to define its own moral values; but even though it is destructive, Sula's energy and defiance is paradoxically more life-affirming than the rigid and sterile morality Bottom espouses. The novel became the focus of Barbara Smith's ground-breaking essay 'Towards a Black Feminist Criticism' in 1977.
▷Black feminist criticism

Sullerot, Evelyne (born 1924)
Eminent French sociologist. Co-founder of the French Family Planning Association and adviser to the United Nations, as well as a member of Paris University, she has written many books on the status of women: *La femme dans le monde moderne* (1970) (▷*Women, Society and Change*, 1971), *Histoire et mythologie de l'amour, huit siècles d'écrits féminins* (1974) (▷*Women in Love: Eight Centuries of Feminie Writing*, 1980), *La Démographie de la France* (1978) (*The Demography of France*) and *L'Age de travailler* (1986) (*A Time for Working*). She also co-ordinates collective enquiries for the Conseil économique et social of the European Community. She is mainly concerned with the impact of women's professional activities outside the home on family structures and demographic trends, and her work thus has relevance for all industrial societies.

Sulpicia (I) (1st century BC–1st century AD)
Poet. She was a member of the cultural circle of the Roman Messalla Corvinus, who was the patron of the poets Ovid (43 BC–AD c 17) and Tibullus (c 55–19 BC). Some suggest she was Messalla's niece. Six elegiac poems survive with the works of Tibullus. Five poems concern her love for the man Cerinthus. She claims she won him through her poetry. Her poems conform to common themes of the genre: complaints about infidelity, love as a disease, the folly of passion. Two poems offer different attitudes towards her birthday: in one she is happy, in the other, sad. Thus some scholars debate their authenticity. However, they are standard examples of the genre in style and theme and were admired by Ezra Pound.
Bib: (text & trans.) Good, G.P., *Catullus*.

Sulpicia (II) (1st century AD)
Poet. No biographical information except that the Roman poet Martial (AD c40–104) records that she wrote not mythology, but of 'honest love, amusements, delights and humour'. There survive 70 lines in hexameter verse of a poem about the expulsion of philosophers from Rome by the Emperor Domitian (1st century AD). The later date probably precludes identification with
▷Sulpicia (I)

Sulter, Maud (born 1960)
Scottish-born black poet and short story writer. Sulter was a Students' Union President as an undergraduate, and has campaigned consistently on civil rights issues. These explicitly political views are expressed in *Through the Break, Women and Personal Struggle* (1986). Sulter's poetry has been strongly supported by ▷Grace Nichols, and Sulter won the Vera Bell Prize with the poem 'As a Blackwoman'. All of Sulter's writing consciously critiques gender and cultural stereotypes, and frequently analyzes sexual desire. Her poetry and prose writings have appeared in a variety of anthologies including *Watchers and Seekers* (ed. R. Cobham and M. Collins, 1987) and the feminist journal *Spare Rib*. Her work as a journalist includes the encouragement of black women writers, and Sulter is on the editorial board of *Feminist Art News*. Other publications include *Echo: Works by Women Artists 1850–1940* (1991) for the Tate Gallery, Liverpool.

Sumii Sue (born 1902)
Japanese novelist. Born in Nara prefecture, she went to Tokyo at eighteen and worked for a publisher. Her first work, *A Conflict*, appeared in 1921. *Women on the Earth* and *Ethics on the Earth* were published in the pre-war period, and deal with agricultural problems. *Dawn and Morning Gloom*, a children's book, won the Mainichi Shuppan Bunka Prize in 1954. The six-volume *A River Without Bridges* (1961–1973), about outcasts, was made into a feature film and became influential. An advocate for equality for the people, she has always been against the imperial system.

Summary History of New England, A (1799)
The North American historian ▷Hannah Adams admitted in her memoirs that 'poverty, not ambition, or vanity' first compelled her to consider the profession of authorship. With her exacting studies of New England history, however, she envisaged her role as author from a new perspective; forgoing the almost requisite woman's 'apology' for addressing the public, Adams believed that her work 'might not only help myself, but benefit the public'. Recognizing that the only extant histories of the region had been dedicated to the early 17th century, and often only to Massachusetts or select colonies, Adams sought to establish a history of the entire region that spanned from the landing of the *Mayflower* in 1621 to the ratification of the federal constitution in 1788. Extraordinary in scope, *A Summary History* was recognized as a major work in the documentation of North American history; it was revised in 1807 and published under the title of *Abridgement of the History of New England for the Use of Young People*.

Summer Lightning (1986)
This collection of ten short stories by the Caribbean writer ▷Olive Senior won the Commonwealth Writers Prize in 1987. These stories (her first collection) are set in rural ▷Jamaica, and recreate with sensitivity and humour a whole range of emotions from the naïve and vulnerable innocence of ▷childhood, as explored in 'Summer Lightning' and 'Do Angels Wear Brassieres?', to the brooding melancholy of the old woman in 'Country of the One Eyed God'. Senior depicts the rural community of Jamaica, in which family life is splintered by the constant barriers of class and colour. Many of the stories were written ten to fifteen years earlier. Senior deals with the authenticity of voice and the question of orality rather than literacy. An extract is included in the anthology ▷*Her True True Name*.

Summer on the Lakes in 1843 (1844)
US travel book by ▷Margaret Fuller. Reflecting Fuller's social analysis that is most evident in her ▷*Woman in the Nineteenth Century, Summer* records Fuller's journey to the city of Chicago and what was then the western frontier of the Great Lakes, and also considers whether western life may provide models for an improved social order.

Summers, Essie (born 1912)
New Zealand novelist. Essie Summers, New Zealand's most prolific ▷romantic novelist, was born in Christchurch soon after her parents' arrival from England. Before she married Bill Flett, a Baptist minister, Summers worked for many years in a drapery shop, and then wrote columns and stories for magazines before her first novel was published by Mills and Boon in 1957. She wrote romances partly for financial reasons. Her narrative model is very much the conventional pattern of courtship difficulties before marriage. Summers herself declared that she deplored 'coarse writing'; her romances stop short of any kind of sexual description, though her plots usually centre on jealousy. A number, though not all, of her works are set in New Zealand.

Publications: (a selective list): *Bachelors Galore* (1958); *The Master of Tawhai* (1959); *The Lark in the Meadow* (1959); *Moon Over the Alps* (1960); *The House of the Shining Tide* (1962); *Meet on My Ground* (1968); *Through All the Years* (1976); *The Essie Summers Story* (autobiography) (1974).

Summers, Merna (born 1933)
Short story writer, born and raised in Alberta, Canada, where she continues to live. Her stories have won numerous awards, including The Katherine Anne Porter Prize for Short Fiction. *The Skating Party* (1974), *Calling Home* (1982) and *North of the Battle* (1988) bring together articulate and skilful moments of recognition.

Summer Will Show (1936)
Novel by English writer ▷Sylvia Townsend Warner. Set in 1848, it tells the story of the aristocratic Sophia Willoughby who, when her children die of smallpox, pursues her estranged husband, Frederick, to Paris. There she meets her husband's mistress, the Jewish actress Minna Lemuel. A relationship develops between the two women, and Sophia commits herself to the revolutionary cause of the Paris Communards. At the heart of the novel is Minna's tale of her Lithuanian childhood and the pogrom, an immensely powerful narrative which bridges the two settings of the novel, conservative rural England and Revolutionary Paris. A complex allegory of political events in the 1930s, the novel also explores the relationship between art and politics, the constraints of woman's position in society, and the liberating effects of love between women.

Sunlight on a Broken Column (1961)
Only novel of Indian-born author ▷Attia Hosain. Set in pre-independence India, it is the sensitively-told story of Laila, the orphaned daughter of a distinguished Muslim family, who is brought up by her aunts in *purdah* (the veil) . It draws extensively on both Hosain's own childhood experiences in the courtly city of Lucknow in northern India, and the impact that the Western, liberal education to which she was exposed had on her relationships with an older, more traditional generation. The novel's style, like the waning feudal culture which it sets out to describe, is complex and ornate.

Suñol, Cèlia (1899–?)
Spanish novelist. She was born in Barcelona and lived most of her life there. Her first novel, *Primera part* (1948) (*Part One*), broke the silence imposed by the Franco regime (1939–75) on things Catalan.

Superfluous man
A Russian literary character type, the disillusioned 'outsider.' His origins can be traced both to Russian historical reality and to the alienated romantic hero, influenced by Schiller and Byron, who appears in the 1820s and 1830s in works by Griboedov, Pushkin and Lermontov. The type is deflated in ▷Elena Gan's *The Ideal* (1837): the heroine, who has worshipped a poet's uplifting work from afar, finds the man himself a cynical seducer. The term comes from a short story by Turgenev, 'The Diary of a Superfluous Man' (1850) and, in the period of Russian realism, the label was applied to the gentry hero who, despite intelligence, moral virtue and good intentions, ended up unfulfilled, inactive, and alienated from society. He was portrayed as a critic of social and political institutions, but as someone who could not translate his insights into meaningful actions. Variations of this character type survived into the 20th century, and appeared in fiction as late as the 1920s.

By the end of the 19th century, women writers (▷Shchépkina-Kupérnik, ▷Avílova, ▷Verbítskaia, and ▷Ol'nem) were creating the female counterpart, the 'superfluous woman.' Shchépkina-Kupérnik even has a story entitled 'From the Diary of a Superfluous Woman' (1903). The heroine characterizes herself as a talented, intelligent, well-to-do woman who finds no outlet for her energies. A number of these 'superfluous' heroines are talented artists who are not content with the traditional roles of wife and mother, but, because they lack willpower or self-discipline, remain unfulfilled.
▷Khvoshchínskaia, Nadezhda; *Mirage*

Su Qing (1917–1969)
Chinese writer. After ten years of marriage, Su Qing was deserted by her husband and left in Shanghai with two small children to support. With no resources, and no higher degree in education, Su took to writing to make a living. The mostly autobiographical *Ten Years of Marriage* (1944) – a young woman's initiation into sexuality and a story of love and betrayal – was a hit, and Su Qing quickly became a bestselling writer in Japanese-occupied Shanghai. A sequel, *Divorce and After* (1947), and short stories and essays followed. Su Qing outraged public opinion by her bluntness about female sexuality and the pervasive sexism in Chinese society. Accused of pornography and reproached for publishing under the Japanese occupation, Su Qing was largely forgotten. She is now being republished in Taiwan as one of the earliest feminist writers of contemporary China.

Sur (1931– present)
One of the foremost literary magazines of Argentina in the 20th century. It was founded by ▷Victoria Ocampo in 1931, and encouraged by the North American novelist and journalist Waldo Frank (1889–1967). The title was suggested to Ocampo by the Spanish writer and philospher José Ortega e Gasset (1883–1955).

Surajmukhi Andhere Ke (1972) ▷*Blossoms in Darkness* (1979)

Surangkhanang, K. (born 1911)
Pen-name of Thai writer Kanha Kiengsiri, who also wrote under the ▷pseudonyms of Rosamalin, Moruedi and Nakhon Suraphan. She was a teacher before she began writing professionally, and became editor of the *Muang Thong* daily newspaper, director of the *Narinat* magazine and owner of the Rosamalin Press.

Once described as 'a conservative writer whose romantic tales about charming princes wedding commoners' daughters are highly popular', she has nevertheless established a serious reputation with two novels, *Ying Khon Chua* (*The Prostitute*), noted for its pioneering ▷social realism and criticism of society's moral hypocrisy, and *Ban Sai Thong* (*Villa of the Golden Sand*). A prolific writer, she has also produced about 300 short stories, one of the best-known of which, 'Malinee' (the name of the heroine), was written when she was still at school. Her works deal mainly with the situation of long-suffering women in a tightly class- and gender-bound society, and the emergence of the kind of educated, free woman described also in the novels of her contemporaries, ▷Sod Dok Mai and ▷Boonlua. *Yai* (▷*The Grandmother*), which is available in English translation, is characteristic of her representation of moral decline in Thai society.

Suraphan, Nakhon ▷Surangkhanang, K.

Surfacing (1972)
▷Margaret Atwood's novel about a nameless narrator who travels, with her lover and two friends, to a remote French-Canadian cabin in search of her missing father. *Surfacing* is a metaphor for male/female, nature/culture, Canadian/American dichotomies, except that the 'other' always turns out to be a reflection of the self. A quest novel about diving below the surface of consciousness to discover the hidden and denied self, the narrator's submersion becomes a recognition of the need for survival, and she can surface again, strong and whole.

Surrealism (Italy)
Inspired by the French surrealist movement of the 1920s and 1930s, which, like ▷futurism, saw itself as a revolutionary genre encompassing politics, philosophy, psychology, literature and art. Sigmund Freud's (▷psychoanalysis) work is more central to the surrealist doctrine than to that of the futurists. Italian women writers whose work bears traces of surrealism include ▷Gianna Manzini with her mix of the fantastical and the baroque, ▷Benedetta – who is primarily a futurist – and, more recently, ▷Anna Maria Ortese.

Survival: a Thematic Guide to Canadian Literature (1972)
▷Margaret Atwood's influential and acerbic reading of the Canadian imagination, premised on

the notion that the key pattern in Canadian writing is that of victimhood. Nature is less than benevolent and idyllic, family and relationships potentially entrapping, and artists stymied in their creation. Surviving in the face of a fate without identity becomes the leitmotif for every Canadian gesture. Although the work garnered a great deal of attention when it appeared, it has since received much drubbing, perhaps because scholars are unwilling to acknowledge Atwood's tongue-in-cheek humour, and only too willing to ascribe paranoia to themselves by reacting to her suggestive text paranoically.

Susan and God (1937)
US play in which ▷Rachel Crothers makes her last statement on the ▷New Woman's evolution. In search of independence and self-fulfilment, Susan Trexel joins a religious movement where she indulges in the opportunities it provides to glorify herself rather than God. When her husband leaves, Susan realizes that her self-gratification will end in loneliness. Crothers warns of the potential for selfishness in the search for independence and self-fulfilment, and emphasizes the need for self-awareness and love.

Susann, Jacqueline (1921–1974)
US novelist. Born in Philadelphia, Pennsylvania, Susann was a Broadway actress. In 1962 she became a bestselling pulp novelist. Her books were considered pornographic. *Valley of the Dolls* (1966) and *The Love Machine* (1969) depict a standard female fantasy: success, glamour, wealth and men. However, the characters take drugs, commit suicide and destroy their lives. Susann criticizes the amoral culture in which these women try to succeed, and suggests that her readers are better off than the characters who are living the fantasy.
    Other works include: *Once Is Not Enough* (1973) and *Dolores* (1976).

Sutcliff, Rosemary (born 1920)
English novelist and children's writer. Sutcliff was born in England, but her early childhood was spent abroad due to her father's postings as a naval officer. Influenced by Kipling, Sutcliff wrote historical novels for adults and children. Her first, *Chronicles of Robin Hood* (1950), was followed by a series of novels for children and adults including: *The Queen Elizabeth Story* (1950); *Simon* (1953); *Sword at Sunset* (1963), about Arthurian Britain, and her autobiography, *Blue Remembered Hills* (1983).

Sutherland, Efua (born 1924)
Ghanaian dramatist. She is author of the plays *Foriwa*, (1967) ▷*Edufa* (1967) and ▷*The Marriage of Anansewa* (1975), and founded the Ghana Drama Studio in 1957. This flourished until 1990, when the building was demolished to make way for a new National Theatre. In recognition of her seminal role in the development of theatre, an exact replica of the Drama Studio was built next

to the Institute of African Studies at the university in Accra.
    Sutherland also started *Okyeame*, a cultural journal, and initiated the Ghana Experimental Theatre Programme. She deliberately turned to the ▷oral tradition of storytelling, as a statement of cultural self-assertion for the newly emerging nation, and this is evident in her own writing. She was very influential in setting up, in 1964, the school of Performing Arts at the University of Ghana, Lagos, where she also worked, and she established the Drama Research Institute in the university's Institute of African Studies. In 1968 she formed the Kuisum Agoromba Players (the name is Akan for 'the right thing to do') to assert the importance of performing in Ghanaian languages and in the community, as opposed to the increasing elitism of the English-language university setting. She has consistently maintained her commitment to creating a vibrant indigenous tradition through her writing and through her other work for children.
Bib: ▷Angelou, M., *All God's Children Need Travelling Shoes*; Brown, L., *Women Writers in Black Africa*; July, R., *An African Voice: The Role of the Humanities in African Independence*; Etherton, E., *The Development of African Drama*.

Sutherland, Margaret (born 1941)
New Zealand novelist. Margaret Sutherland, who has worked as a nurse and a writer, has published many short stories including the much-anthologized 'Codling-Moth', which deals with illicit sexual attraction between two teenage Catholic girls. Sutherland's stories and novels mostly focus on domestic and family environments in which individuals are constrained or repressed, especially sexually, and achieve a partial knowledge of freedom. Sutherland's work is typical of mainstream writing by women in its preoccupation with domestic structures and emotional subjectivity, but avoids romance or sentimentality.
    Publications: *The Fledgling* (novel) (1974); *The Love Contract* (novel) (1976); *Getting Through and Other Stories* (1977).

Suttner, Bertha von (1843–1914)
Austrian novelist, journalist and essayist. She came from an aristocratic family, was well-educated and travelled widely. After the family fortunes declined, she took up work as a governess at the house of Baron von Suttner (1850–1902) in Vienna, and then, briefly, as secretary to Alfred Nobel (1833–1896) in Paris. In 1876 she married the youngest of the von Suttner sons against the wishes of his family, and went with him to Georgia. The couple returned in 1885 to take up residence in the Suttner family home in Lower Austria.
    Bertha von Suttner began her literary career with a number of conventional novels, but achieved world fame in 1889 with her pacifist work *Die Waffen nieder! Eine Lebensgeschichte* (▷*Lay Down Your Arms!*, 1892, 1972), in which

she describes in powerful yet colloquial language the horrors of the battlefield. The book became an immediate bestseller, ran to thirty-seven German editions, and was instrumental in launching the German peace movement. It was translated into many languages, and twice made into a film. She became a co-founder of the German Peace Association, and from 1890 to 1899 she edited a pacifist journal which had the same title as her novel. Often ridiculed by her detractors as the 'Fury of Peace', she nevertheless became a very influential public figure, gave countless lectures throughout Europe and the USA, and in 1905 was awarded the Nobel Prize for Peace.

Sutton, Evelyn Mary (born 1906)
New Zealand children's author. Sutton was born in England and emigrated to New Zealand in 1949. A happy collaboration with her cousin, ▷Lynley Dodd, on a picture book, *My Cat Likes to Hide In Boxes* (1973), which won the New Zealand Library Association's Esther Glen Medal in 1975, thrust her (and Dodd) into the world of children's books. She writes soundly researched and detailed historical adventure stories describing 19th-century pioneer life – farming, gum-digging, gold-mining, and whaling. In 1991 she was the first recipient of an award by the New Zealand Children's Literature Association for her outstanding contribution to children's literature.
   ▷Children's literature, New Zealand

Suze, Henriette de Coligny, Comtesse de la (17th century)
French poet. She was the eldest daughter of the Maréchal de Châtillon. According to the memoir-writer Tallemant des Réaux (1619–1692), she seemed stupid in her childhood, wrote indifferent verses while in Scotland and began to show them round as soon as she married. She later wrote a number of quite popular elegies in the *précieux* style (▷Precious Women). A portrait of the Duchesse de Châtillon under the ▷pseudonym Amarillis was published in the *Recueil de La Suze-Pellisson* (*Collection of La Suze-Pellisson*). Madame de la Suze had many lovers and was the subject of various declarations of love in verse by contemporaries. ▷Madame de Lafayette seems to imply in her correspondence that Madame de la Suze wrote for money. She was appreciated for her use of expressions that were apparently unknown in French before she began to write poetry. Her poetic success seems to have inspired Charles Perrault (1628–1703), Jean de Segrais (1624–1701) and Madame de Villedieu (▷Marie–Catherine Hortense Desjardins).
   Bib: Fukui, Y., *Raffinement précieux dans la poésie française du XVIIe siècle.*

Světlá, Karolina (1830–1899)
Czech novelist. She was the most prolific and, after Božena Němcová, probably the most influential female Czech prose writer of the 19th century. She was a co-founder of Czech poetic

realism. Born into the Prague nobility, she married a melancholic and patriotic schoolmaster, Petr Mužák, who was born in the village Světlá, from which she took her pen-name. She became the mistress of the most influential Czech writer of the period, Jan Neruda (1834–1891), but left him when the gossip among the Prague nobility became too intrusive. In 1871 she founded the first serious Czech women's association, the Women's Work Club. After going blind in 1875 she dictated all her works.
   She began her writing career as a belated romantic patriotic novelist. She wrote short stories, as well as fairytales, and, in the last years of her life, wrote political stories about the year of revolutions, 1848. Best-known among Czech readers is her accomplished tear-jerker, *Kříž u potoka* (1868) (*The Cross by the Brook*), where a young woman does her best to remove a family curse, and to demonstrate that the Czechs' servitude is unnecessary. From a literary point of view, perhaps her most successful work was ▷*Vesnický román* (1869) (*A Village Novel*).

Swamp Angel, The (1954)
Canadian writer ▷Ethel Wilson's novel about a female character, Maggie Lloyd, who simply throws down her apron and walks out of her ill-fitting second marriage. She flees to a fishing camp in central British Columbia, and there is able to regain control over her usurped time. In counterpoint to her story is the story of her friend, Nell Severance, an aged former juggler who keeps herself amused by interfering (fruitfully) with people's lives. The Swamp Angel, a delicate but lethal revolver that Nell Severance used in her juggling act, is passed from Nell to Maggie as an ambivalent symbol of the spirit of survival. A strongly feminist narrative, *The Swamp Angel* and Maggie Lloyd prefigure the many interesting heroines in Canadian literature who follow.

Swan, Susan
Canadian novelist and short story writer. She may be related to Anna Swan, the Nova Scotia giantess who is the subject of her novel *The Biggest Modern Woman in the World* (1983). *The Last of the Golden Girls* (1989) is a sophisticated novel about competition and sexuality.
   ▷Smyth, Donna

Sweet Nosegay, or Pleasant Posye: containing a hundred and ten Philosophical Flowers, A (1573)
Poetry collection by English writer ▷Isabella Whitney. Self-admittedly an imitation of Hugh Plat's *The Flowers of Philosophy* (1572) in particular, Whitney's work belongs generally among the extremely popular collections of poetry, such as George Gascoigne's *A Hundreth Sundry Flowers* (1573). Whitney's collection contains 110 four-line verses of secular moral wisdom composed in the fashion of Seneca's 'Sentences'. Although some of her verses are drawn from Ovid and Virgil, a good number appear to be of her

own composition. The topics covered in her collection include law, friendship and fortune. Of particular interest are the perhaps semi-autobiographical works appended to *A Sweet Nosegay*. These are a collection of thirteen 'Certain familiar Epistles and friendly Letters' written in verse and a feigned 'Wyll and Testament'. Among those addressed by three verse epistles (or ▷letters) are two brothers, two cousins, a married sister, and 'two yonger sisters servinge in London', to whom she proffers advice. The work's concluding piece is a witty leave-taking from London, in which the poet, 'whole in body and in minde / but very weake in Purse: / [Doth] make, and write [her] Testament'. Naming London as her heir, she bestows the city (for example the buildings, the people, butchers, brewers and bakers) upon itself. The poem creates a lively picture of 16th-century London. **Bib:** Beilin, E.V., *Redeeming Eve: Women Writers of the English Renaissance*; Travitsky, B., 'The "Wyll and Testament" of Isabella Whtiney', *English Literary Renaissance*, No. 10 (1980), pp. 76–95.

Sweet Trap, The (1979)

A play by Nigerian dramatist ▷Zulu Sofola. In ridiculing the arrogance and lack of respect for traditional custom displayed by the new breed of Western-educated women, the play comes down heavily on the side of conservatism and the status quo. Set in Ibadan, on the university campus, where the author taught for some time, it parodies the wives of university lecturers, who use their education as a stick with which to beat men. Mrs Ajala represents the strident voice of women's liberation, Mrs Jinadu the sensible, balanced voice of feminine reason. The action of the play concerns Clara Sotuba's birthday party, which is disrupted by the violent intrusion of masqueraders from the Okebadan festival. This is a festival notorious for its intimidation of women, who dare not be seen on the streets of Ibadan while it is taking place. The resolution of the play has Clara seeing the folly of her ways and begging forgiveness from her husband. As a critique of middle-class pretensions, it lays the blame on women's education.

Sweet Whispers, Brother Rush (1982)

US novel for adolescents by ▷Virginia Hamilton which places traditional African-American folklore in a historical and cultural context. Tree and her mentally-retarded brother live with their mother in an impoverished urban neighbourhood. To become an adult Tree must come to terms with her family, particularly her mother. Brother Rush, Tree's mentor, is a ghost who shows her episodes from her family's past, which includes a genetic ancestral disease, child abuse, drug abuse and suicide. Playing out the love/hate relationship between mother and daughter, Tree confronts her mother. Coming to terms with the past opens up possibilities for a future that emphasizes love and nurturing.

Swenson, May (1913–1989)

US poet. Swenson was born in Logan, Utah, and now lives in New York. She has been a journalist, and an editor for the publisher New Directions. Since 1959 she has written full-time. Swenson's work is remarkable for its acuteness of vision, freshness, and minuteness of perception. Starting from the perception of a particular object or natural phenomenon, her poetry typically works to make an equation between external and internal, physical and spiritual, observation and speculation. In *Iconographs* (1970) Swenson used typographical patterns to mirror the subject of the poem, and to give it a spatial as well as temporal dimension. Using wit, riddles and intellectual inventiveness, her poetry is more than description of things (particularly features of landscape), although accuracy and inventiveness in description is important to the work; Swenson approaches human, philosophical and spiritual concerns through such moments of perception, which then become emblems of deeper, more profound speculations.

Other work includes: *Another Animal* (1954), *A Cage of Spines* (1958), *To Mix With Time: New and Selected Poems* (1963), *Poems to Solve* (1966), *Half Sun Half Sleep: New Poems* (1967), *More Poems to Solve* (1971), *The Guess and Spell Coloring Book* (1976), *New and Selected Things Taking Place* (1978) and *In Other Words: New Poems* (1987).

Switha (fl late 8th century)

English abbess. One letter survives from Lull to Switha, rebuking her severely for having allowed her women to go 'into a distant region', 'wandering and disobedient'.
▷Boniface Correspondence

Sykes, Bobbi (born 1943)

Australian poet, non-fiction writer and Aboriginal activist. Sykes left school at fourteen and worked in many jobs before achieving a PhD in Education from Harvard University in 1984. She has lectured overseas on race relations, was first executive secretary of the Aboriginal Embassy on the lawns of Parliament House, Canberra, in 1972, and has worked in Aboriginal legal and medical services. She has published a volume of poetry, *Love Poems and Other Revolutionary Actions* (1979), which deals with the legacy of bitterness which is the result of past treatment of Aborigines (particularly the women) by whites: 'corrugated iron shacks, no water,/ four children from six live births/ and the accumulated pain of two centuries'. Sykes has also published the non-fictional *Black Power in Australia* (1975, with Neville Bonner), *Incentive, Achievement and Community* (1986), and has assisted with *MumShirl: An Autobiography* (1981).
▷Aboriginal women writers in Australia

Sylvia's Lovers (1863)

An ▷historical novel by British writer ▷Elizabeth Gaskell, set in the whaling port of Monkshaven during the Napoleonic wars. The plot revolves around the activities of press-gangs who capture men and force them to work on naval warships. Daniel Robson, Sylvia's father, is hanged after leading an attack on the press-gang's headquarters. Her lover, Charley Kinraid, is seized by the gang, but he sends a note pledging his love and faithfulness via Sylvia's cousin, Philip Hepburn. Philip conceals the message as he loves Sylvia himself, and she later agrees to marry him, believing Charley to be dead. Years later Charley returns, Philip's treachery is revealed, and Sylvia swears lifelong enmity to her husband. The novel explores gender relations through the marriage of Sylvia and Philip and analyzes the interaction of public and private events in its focus on aggression, revenge and rivalry.

Symbolic order
A term associated with the French psychoanalyst Jacques Lacan's (1901–1981) work, where it is used to designate the order of linguistic and cultural difference which succeeds the ▷imaginary and introduces ▷lack into the ▷subject. The symbolic order takes the phallus as the principle signifier, or symbol (of power and sexual difference). The privileging of the phallus – which, despite its inscription as a symbol and not the sexual organ, is difficult to dissociate from the penis – has led feminists to criticize Lacanian ▷psychoanalysis for seeming to define masculinity as the norm, thereby implicitly supporting ▷patriarchy. The symbolic order is crucial in the history of subject, since the human being's acquisition of subjecthood – meaning and of sexual identity – depends upon entry into this order of language and sexual difference.

Symmes, Susanna Livingston (fl 1794–1808)
North American letter-writer. Raised in a comfortable, urban atmosphere, she discovered after her marriage in 1794 to a judge, who was appointed to a frontier settlement in the Miami Purchase, that her spouse's promises of frequent returns to New Jersey were quickly forgotten. Rather than settle for broken promises and an unhappy life, she challenged her husband's decisions. After numerous legal battles, detailed in ▷'The Letters of Susanna Symmes', over her right to distribute her own money as she saw fit, Symmes separated from her husband and resettled in New York, where she found the lifestyle she preferred.

Synové ▷Stará Rodina and Synové

Szabó, Magda (born 1917)
Hungarian novelist and poet. Szabó worked as a teacher and for the ministry of education before becoming a full-time writer in 1959. In the late 1940s she published poetry. Her early novel of manners *Freszkó* (1958) (*Fresco*) describes a family reunion at a funeral. The narrative is condensed into one day's action. The conflicting interests of the characters are portrayed through their inner monologues, giving the novel a dramatic intensity.

Az öz (1959) (*The Fawn*) is again set at a graveside. A famous actress, Esther, addresses her lover, buried the day before. Her life and memories, and her bitter regret at her own duplicitousness, unfold in the monologues of this unlikeable character.

Szabó's best-known work is *Disznótor* (1960) (*Night of the Pig-killing*). Over a day and a half of action, the feuds, class rivalry, religious disputes and financial bickerings of one family are unravelled.

Szumigalski, Anne (born 1922)
Poet. Born Anne Davis in London, England, where she was privately educated, she emigrated to Canada with her husband and family in 1951, and settled in Saskatoon, Saskatchewan. She has worked as a translator, teacher, and editor. Her poetry is engaged with ritual and archetype, although her images emerge from ordinary moments. *Woman Reading in Bath* (1974) was followed by *A Game of Angels* (1980), *Risks* (1983), *Doctrine of Signatures* (1983), *Instar* (1985), *Dogstones: Selected and New Poems* (1986), *Journey* (1988) and *Rapture of the Deep* (1991). *The Word, the Voice, the Text: The Life of a Writer* appeared in 1990.

Szymborska, Wislawa (born 1923)

Wislawa Szymborska

Polish poet. Szymborska was born in Bnin in western Poland. In 1931 she and her family moved to Krakow. During the German occupation of Poland she attended illegal classes. From 1945 to 1948 she studied Polish literature and sociology at the University of Krakow. From 1953 to 1981 she worked on the Krakow literary magazine *Zycie Literackie* as poetry editor and columnist.

Szymborska has published eight volumes of poetry: *Dlagtego zyjemy* (1952), *Pytania zadawanr sobie* (1954), *Wolanie do Yeti* (1957), *Sol* (1962), *Sto pciech* (1967), *Wszelki wypadek* (1972), *Wielka liczba* (1976) and *Ludzie na moscie* (1986) (*People on a Bridge*, 1990).

Taborga de Requena, Lola (born 1890)
Bolivian poet. She studied the Inca culture and customs. Three subjects prevail in Requena's poetry: folklore, the romantic and the mystical. When writing on a mystical theme, she sometimes assumes a tone of Christianized stoicism, full of resignation and gratitude, as in '*Gracias, Señor*', (1948) ('Thank You, Lord'). Her greatest folkloric, historical, lyrical and bucolic work is *Cuadros incásicos* (1952) (*Inca Pictures*), which consists of seven scenes. She received several prizes in literary contests, and her work was published in newspapers.

Other works: *Antología boliviana* (1948) (*Bolivian Anthology*) and *Espigas* (1956) (*Ears of Corn*).

Tadjo, Véronique (born 1955)
Poet, novelist, and children's writer from the Côte d'Ivoire. One of the new generation of African women writers, she has the distinction of writing in both French and English, and both poetry and prose. She has lived in Europe and Africa, and lectures at the University of Côte d'Ivoire in Abidjan. She has published *Latérite* (1984), a volume of poetry, three novels: *À vol d'oiseau* (1986) (*Birdflight*), *La Chanson de la vie* (1990) (*Song of Life*), and *Le royaume aveugle* (1990) (*The Blind Kingdom*), and a children's book in English, *Lord of the Dance* (1988).

▷Children's literature (West Africa)

Tafdrup, Pia (born 1952)
Danish poet and literary theorist. Tafdrup was born near Copenhagen, and her father was a farmer. She received her MA in 1977, and now works as a teacher at a grammar school. She is married and has two sons.

In 1981 she published her first collection of poems *Når der går hul på en engel* (*A Punctured Angel*), in 1982 came *Intetfang* (*Nothing to Catch*) and in 1983 *Den inderste zone* (*The Inner Zone*). She was at once recognized as a leading Danish lyric poet in the movement of ▷new lyric poetry of the 1980s.

Her theme is the relation between a female 'I' and the body, often described in erotic scenes where the body dominates but the 'I' tends to disappear. This gives her an opportunity to reflect upon the relation between language and body and the self. By 1990 she had published six collections of poems, one play and one long poem: *Over vandet går jeg* (1990) (*Over the Water I Walk*).

In 1989 she became a member of the Danish Academy. She has received many prizes and awards, and is widely translated.

Taiwanese women writers
The years under Japanese occupation (1895–1945) did not produce women writers, and little was written by women in Taiwan until the 1960s. Some outstanding contemporary writers include ▷Chen Ruoxi, ▷Li Ang, ▷Nieh Hualing, ▷Yu Lihua, ▷Qiong Yao, ▷San Mao, Guo Lianghui, Pan Renmu, Shi Shuqing and Lung Yingtai. Their work covers a wide spectrum of style and subject matter, from serious writing on social issues and feminist concerns to popular fiction for entertainment. On the whole, they produce a varied representation of life in Taiwan as it is experienced and perceived by women.

Takács, Eva (1779–1845)
Hungarian writer who, with her daughter Teréz Karács, was an early educational reformer.

Takagi Nobuko (born 1946)
Japanese novelist. Born in Yamaguchi prefecture, she worked for a publisher, and began writing novels after her second marriage. Her first work is *An Endless Path* (1980). *A Shining Friend* won the Akutagawa Prize in 1984. It portrays girl students' lives from a new perspective.

Takahashi Takako (born 1932)
Japanese novelist. At university she became interested in Catholicism, and has since delved into the darker side of human nature. *The End of the Sky* won the Tamura Toshiko Prize in 1973, and *Tempter* won the Izumi Kyoka Prize in 1976. Baptized in 1975, she entered a Carmelite convent in Paris in 1986. *Doll Love* describes her confrontation with God.

Takamure Itsue **(1977)**
A biography of Takamure Itsue (1894–1964) by Japanese writers Kano Masanao (born 1931) and Horiba Kiyoko (born 1930). Takamure was the first feminist historian in Japan, as well as a poet and essayist. She criticizes civilization and is against the marriage system. In 1930 she edited the journal *The Women's Liberation Front*, expressing anarchic views. Her research on the matrilineal system implies that the ▷patriarchal system has not been a permanent part of Japanese history, as has been proved by other contemporary women historians. Much of her work appears in the ten-volume *Collection of Essays of Takamure Itsue* (1966–1967).

Takenishi Hiroko (born 1929)
Japanese novelist. Born in Hiroshima, she was atom-bombed while helping the war effort as a student. She worked for several publishers. Her first work, *Two Ways between the Ancient and the Contemporary Times*, won the Tamura Toshiki Prize in 1964. Her profound knowledge of Japanese classical literature is revealed by a number of works including *A Theory on the Tales of Genji*. *Barracks* won the Kawabata Yasunari Prize in 1980.

Tales I Tell My Mother **(1978)**
English short story collection. Subtitled 'A Collection of Feminist Short Stories by ▷Zoë Fairbairns, ▷Sara Maitland, ▷Valerie Miner, ▷Michèle Roberts and ▷Michelene Wandor', the collection arose out of the Feminist Writers Group, a socialist-feminist writing collective formed by these writers. Maitland describes it as 'not an anthology [but] a book, a single entity, an

accumulation of points of view'. The stories were written individually, but were subject to group discussion and criticism; the project was a way of finding a balance between individual authorship and collective work. The stories explore such themes as work, motherhood, lesbianism, marriage, religion and class through the lens of feminist politics, and are grouped into three categories: 'feminist fiction and language', 'feminist fiction and politics', and 'feminist fiction and aesthetics'. Interspersed with the stories are statements from each of the five writers which make explicit their views on the relationship between writing and feminism.

Tales of Hulan River (1988)

Translation of novel by Chinese writer ▷Xiao Hong. Semi-autobiographical reminiscences of a lonely childhood in north China, *Tales of Hulan River* juxtaposes the most colourful descriptions of local customs – village stage performances, exorcist rites, festivals and celebrations – with a blood-curdling account of a ritual killing of a child-bride by her in-laws. The bride was considered a 'demon': 'Whoever heard of a child-bride with no trace of shyness, one who sat up straight as a rod wherever she was, and who walked with a brash, carefree step.' She was the only thing her mother-in-law could touch: 'She could hit the cat, but was afraid it might run away from home. If she hit one of the pigs, it might lose a few pounds of weight, or if she hit one of the chickens, it might stop laying eggs. The only thing she could hit with impunity was the young child-bride.'

In these sketches Xiao Hong manages to convey a sense of an outdated, cruel and barbarous world, her ultimate statement on history and society at a time when China was facing a question of survival in the face of Japanese aggression. The 'woman question' was merged in this larger concern. *Tales of Hulan River*, one of the landmarks in modern Chinese literature, is only now beginning to be recognized as such.

Bib: Goldblatt, Howard and Young, Ellen (trans.), *The Field of Life and Death and Tales of Hulan River*.

Tales of Love (1987)

Translation by Leon Roudiez of French psychoanalyst and cultural theorist ▷Julia Kristeva's *Histoires d'amour* (1983). Kristeva counterpoints her work on the horrors of abjection in ▷*Powers of Horror* with an exploration of love. Taking the ▷psychoanalytic 'transference' between analyst and analysand as a starting point, Kristeva examines amatory codes and discourses in a variety of theological, literary and philosophical texts. Compared to the earlier emphasis on the disruptive charge of the 'semiotic' in ▷*Revolution in Poetic Language*, here the account is of the possibilities of a loving identification which, once found in religious discourse, can now be traced in psychoanalysis and art. What begins in Kristeva's work as a plea

for the recognition of the subversive potential of language, emerges in this book, the most lyrical and personal of these three key texts, as a passionate call for the rejuvenation of our desires through language.

Tal'nikov Family, The (1928)

Russian novella by ▷Avdot'ia Panáeva written in 1848. *The Tal'nikov Family* is a bleak, grotesque depiction of life in what Dostoevsky called an 'accidental' family, here of theatrical performers not unlike the author's own. Her first-person narrative describes with bitter humour the day-to-day existence of a largely undifferentiated litter of children left neglected in the nursery of a cramped ▷St Petersburg apartment, while their parents hold court downstairs and spinster aunts, as confined as the children, squabble in the next room. The work was denied publication by censorship for 'immorality and undermining of parental authority' and appeared only in 1928. It has yet to take its place in Russian literary history as an early example of autobiographical fiction in a totally different vein from the famous novels about privileged boyhood written in the 1850s by Tolstoy (the *Childhood* trilogy) and Ivan Aksakov (*The Childhood of Bagrov's Grandson*).

Tamizdat

The corollary of ▷*samizdat* or self-publishing, *tamizdat* (which literally means 'publishing over there') refers to the fact that, ever since the imposition of official censorship in Russia in the 18th century, Russian writers, despite threats and repression, have chosen to publish politically sensitive works abroad. A flood of Soviet dissident literature appeared in the West during the stagnant years after the ▷thaw of the late 1950s. Some works by women were also published in English translation (eg poems by ▷Akhmátova, ▷Chukóvskaia's novellas of the purges, ▷Evgeniia Gínzburg's memoirs of life in labour camp and exile, and ▷Nadezhda Mandel'shtám's reminiscences). Much of this literature has now been published in the Soviet Union.

▷Shchépkina-Kupérnik, Tat'iana

Tan, Amy (born 1952)

US novelist. Tan was born in Oakland, California, to Chinese immigrant parents. At age fifteen she moved with her widowed mother to Europe, although she later returned to California. In 1987 she visited China for the first time. An ▷Asian-American writer, Tan rescues Chinese-American women from debilitating stereotypes. *The Joy Luck Club* (1989) celebrates basic elements of Chinese life: gambling, eating, ancestral power and community. It explores the tensions between first-generation US daughters and their immigrant mothers, and it focuses on the secrets mothers and daughters keep from each other. In *The Kitchen God's Wife* (1991) the mother tells her secret to her daughter, revealing how male domination and class structures have distorted her. Tan elevates the mother to her rightful place in history.

Tanabe Seiko (born 1928)
Japanese novelist. Born in Osaka, she accepted the Literature Prize for a Citizen of Osaka for *Rainbow*. After *Watching Flowers* (1959), a prize-winning work of *Fujinseikatsu*, a women's magazine, she began to write seriously and at first produced scenarios for radio and television dramas. *Sentimental Journey* won the Akutagawa Prize in 1964. Her works involve the theme of joy and sorrow between men and women (for example *Woman's Sundial* and *The Diary of a Faithful Wife*, written in Osaka dialect), and also the theme of a single life (*A Private Life*). Her other main works are *New Genji Tales*, *Black Hair-Yosano Akiko* (a biography) and *Scenes From My Osaka* (an autobiographical novel).

Tang Min (born 1954)
Chinese writer. From Xiamen in south China, working on the editorial staff of *Xiamen Literature*, Tang Min is known chiefly for her short story 'The Mysterious Miasma of Taimu Shan', a fantasy in which a local official dies and his spirit is believed by the villagers to be transmuted into the body of a cow. The story, however, is based on facts dating from the 1970s, concerning a death and the villagers' superstitious belief. Tang Min was prosecuted and sentenced for libel, but subsequently released. She is also the author of 'Artificially Induced Miscarriage' (1989), about the pains of abortion from a woman's point of view.
Bib: Translation in *In Search of China*, ed. Kellogg, David.

Tao-Lao ▷Storni, Alfonsina

Tarnow, Fanny (1779–1862)
German short story writer. She wrote numerous tales about women's unrequited and unfulfilled love, many of which were published anonymously in women's magazines, and which earned her the epithet of the 'Darling of Women Readers'. Crippled and unmarried, she worked as a governess and teacher, and intermittently lived with friends and her sisters, maintaining friendships with many literary figures, including ▷Amalie Schoppe, ▷Elisabeth von der Recke, Ludwig Tieck (1773–1853) and August von Kotzebue (1761–1819).
▷Bölte, Amely

Tarsouli, Athena (1884–1974)
Greek travel writer. Born in Athens, she studied painting both there and in Paris. Her book *Castles and Cities of Morea* (the south section of the Greek mainland), published in 1934, describes areas of Greece and the local inhabitants with great love and admiration. *Dodecanese* was published the day these islands were reunited with Greece, in 1947, after centuries of foreign rule. *White Islands* (1948) is an anthology of descriptions of the Aegean islands. Her books combine history, mythology and folklore, elements from the distant past which still exist harmoniously with the present. In 1953 she published the useful anthology *Greek Women Poets*.

Taschau, Hannelies (born 1937)
German poet and novelist. She has published several books of poetry, and a novel about two women in Paris, *Die Taube auf dem Dach* (1967) (*The Dove on the Roof*). Her first great success came with *Landfriede* (1978) (*Country Peace*), a novel about a middle-class couple who flee city life in order to seek dignity and peace in the country, only to find themselves facing even greater problems there.

'Tasma' ▷Couvreur, Jessie

Tastu, Amable (1798–1885)
French poet. Born in Metz, Tastu won the friendship and patronage of ▷Adelaïde Dufrénoy after an early piece, '*Le Narcisse*' ('The Narcissus'), was published in the *Mercure de France* (*French Mercury*) in 1816. Her talent was for elegiac poetry, and she published a number of collections of verse, including *Poésies* (1826) (*Poems*), which were praised for their delicacy by the critic Sainte-Beuve, and also the more sophisticated *Poésies nouvelles* (1835) (*New Poems*). She also produced educational works and literary criticism – she wrote, for example, a *Tableau de la littérature italienne* (1843) (*List of Italian Literature*) and a *Tableau de la littérature allemande* (1844) (*List of German Literature*) – and supported her family by working in the book trade after her husband's printing business suffered financial difficulties. After his death, she accompanied her son on diplomatic missions to Cyprus, Baghdad, Belgrade and Alexandria, and only returned to France in 1864 when her sight began to fail.
▷Feminine/feminist journalism (France)

Tate, Ellalice ▷Plaidy, Jean

Tavares, Salette (born 1922)
Portuguese poet. Born in Mozambique, she is best known for her experimental poems, some of which were featured in the *Viso-Poemas* Exposition held in Lisbon in 1965. Tavares also participated in the two phases of the *Poesia Experimental* movement (I, 1964, II, 1966) as well as another vanguard group called *Hidra* (Hydra). Among her principal works are: *Espelho Cego* (1957) (*Blind Mirror*), *Concerto em Mi Maior Para Clarinete e Bateria* (1961) (*Concert in Mi Major for Clarinet and Percussion*) and *Lex Icon* (1971).

Taylor, Ann ▷Taylor, Jane and Ann

Taylor, Elizabeth (1912–1975)
English novelist and short story writer. Taylor's writing subtly and selfconsciously details the 'everyday' lives of English middle-class women, focusing particularly on the social minutiae of

Elizabeth Taylor

village life. Underlying these narratives, however, is the threat of loneliness, despair and mortality. Novels include: *At Mrs Lippincote's* (1945), the best-seller *A Game of Hide and Seek* (1951), *In a Summer Season* (1961) and *Mrs Palfrey at the Claremont* (1971).

Taylor, Jane (1783–1824) and Ann (1782–1866)

English poets, novelists and writers of ▷children's literature. The sisters were born in London and educated by their parents. They contributed verses to *Original Poems for Infant Minds* (1804–1805) which was hugely successful in Britain and North America. Other volumes include *Lime Twigs to Catch Young Birds* (1808) and *Hymns for Infant Minds* (1810). The sisters also wrote individually: Ann published a pastiche entitled *The Wedding Among the Flowers* (1809) and contributed articles to periodicals until she married the Rev. Joseph Gilbert, after which she wrote little. Her most famous poem is 'My Mother', depicting a popular image of woman as an ▷'Angel in the House'. Jane remained unmarried and wrote a moral tale, *Display* (1815), the satirical *Essays in Rhyme* (1816), and many other evangelically inspired essays.
Bib: Stewart, C.D., *The Taylors of Ongar: An Analytical Bio-Bibliography.*

Távola Redonda (1950–1954) (*Round Table*)

A poetry review, *Távola Redonda* was published between January 1950 and July 1954. Functioning as a showcase for new poets, it was associated with the existentialist writings that were typical of Portugal in the 1950s. Among the poets featured

in the journal were ▷Fernanda Botelho and Maria Manuela Couto Viana.

Ta ženská musí být opilá! (1990) (*That Woman Must be Drunk!*)

A collection of verse by Czech poet Svatava Antošová (born 1957). The collection was a culmination for the school of 'Angry Young Women' in Czech literature of the 1980s. It expresses both despair and an optimistic cry for love. The lyrical narrator revolts against helping others (for example, the desperate friend the narrator soothes in lesbian sexual intercourse, or the North American girl naïvely looking for her eastern European roots), against the repulsive arrogance of dissident and Communist Party society, and against the experiences of female friends, whose only goals are to become a clerk or a member of the secret police. She revolts against life as it is, but also against trendy feminism. She longs for love, but doubts it exists. She is suspicious of male domination, but desires it, since anything else sounds like the sort of dangerous Utopianism socialism had offered.

Teasdale, Sara (1884–1933)

US poet. Born in St Louis, Missouri, Teasdale was pampered and sheltered by her parents, and even at age twenty-six, she was dependent on them. Believing that marriage could free her from her family's oppressiveness, she forced herself to marry, but unable to reconcile motherhood with a career, she underwent an abortion. After her divorce, Teasdale suffered a depression and chronic illness that repeatedly plagued her; she eventually committed suicide.

Teasdale was the first person to receive a Pulitzer Prize for poetry. The prize-winning *Love Songs* (1917) established her reputation for feminine love poetry. Her work reflects the conflict between her Victorian upbringing and women's new freedom. *Flame and Shadow* (1920) shows her emotional suffering, the dark side of her public persona. Teasdale's poetry depicts a woman's struggle for identity that yields to despair.

Te Awekotoku, Ngahuia

New Zealand short story writer. Ngahuia Te Awekotoku's fiction reflects her childhood in Ohinemutu, Rotorua. A lesbian, feminist and Maori activist, she lectures in art history at Auckland University and is prominent nationally as an art historian and curator. Her story collection, *Tahuri* (1989), is discontinuous narrative, based partly on her own life, which connects racial and sexual questions to give a double view of female identity in conflict with political and social convention. *Tahuri* raises issues of Maori as well as female disadvantage.
▷Maori literature; Lesbian writing, New Zealand

Tèffi (1872–1952)

Pen-name (taken from Rudyard Kipling) of the prose writer, poet and dramatist Nadezhda Aleksandrovna Buchinskaia, the younger sister of the poet ▷Mirra Lókhvitskaia, who was already famous when Tèffi published her first poem in 1902. As a woman humourist, Tèffi is unique in Russian literature. In 1904 she began writing newspaper *feuilletons* in which she honed the basic traits of her short stories: minimal structure, few characters, a jocular narrative tone, and brief sentences. During the 1905 Revolution and the years following, Tèffi wrote political satire for periodicals. In 1908 she took part in a St Petersburg comic theatre, *The Crooked Mirror*.

In 1910 *Seven Fires*, Tèffi's first poetry collection, appeared, and displayed the influence of symbolism. Collected humorous stories about the absurdities of everyday life came out from 1910 to 1914 and were enthusiastically received. Many of them are built on oppositions: male–female, winners–losers, pragmatists–moralists, serious–jocular, reality–illusion, faithful–unfaithful, Russian–non-Russian, etc. Her 1916 collection *The Lifeless Beast* marks a change of pace, closer to the symbolist prose of writers like Fëdor Sologub. It presents a world in the grip of demonic forces that crush the innocent, especially children. Some of the stories, told with Tèffi's laconic style, eye for detail, and ear for speech, are gripping. Tèffi also wrote one-act plays (▷ *The Woman Question*). A sign of her immense popularity was the marketing of 'Tèffi candy' and 'Tèffi perfume' (E. Haber, 'Nadezhda Tèffi', *Russian Literature Triquarterly* 9).

Tèffi emigrated in 1919 and settled in Paris, where she worked on *émigré* newspapers and published short stories (▷*All About Love*), poetry (*Passiflora*, 1923), a novel (*The Adventure Novel*, 1932), *Memoirs* (1932), and *Plays* (1934). Two of her plays were performed in Paris in 1937 and 1939. In the decade before her death, her productivity dropped because of illness. In the USSR collections of Tèffi's works have been published over the last three decades, and critical articles have now begun to appear. In the West her reputation has suffered from the prejudiced assumption that so popular a writer could not be aesthetically sound or philosophically deep.
Bib: Goldstein, D. (trans.), *All About Love*; Haber, E. (trans.), 'The Dog', *Russian Literature Triquarterly* 9, and 'Time', *The Bitter Air of Exile*; Pachmuss, T. (trans.), *Women Writers in Russian Modernism*, and *A Russian Cultural Revival*; Terras, V. (ed.), *Handbook of Russian Literature*; Kasack, W. (ed.), *Dictionary of Russian Literature Since 1917*.

'Telegrafi dello stato' (1885) ('State Telegraphs')

Italian short story by ▷Matilde Serao, from the collection *Il romanzo della fanciulla* (*The Girl's Story*), autobiographical in inspiration. ▷Realist in tone, this narrative details the harsh nature of the work in the telegraph office at this time. It is a picture of drudgery, long hours and low pay. The inequality of male and female workers is dwelt on by Serao, as she tells of discrepancies in pay and status, of marriage bars and no retirement benefits. The overall narrative is bleak, yet the tone is cheered somewhat by the author's well-observed interactions between the female characters.

Teleki, Blanka (1806–1862)

Hungarian campaigner. Like ▷Eva Takács and her daughter Teréz Karács, Teleki was an early campaigner for women's education.

Telemachus (1769)

The poet ▷Elizabeth Graeme Fergusson's translation of Fénelon's *Telemachus* into English heroic couplets established her at home and abroad as one of North America's most talented literary women. The project took three years of constant endeavour, and Fergusson's own poetic 'Invocation to Wisdom' stands as introduction to the translation. In the 1780s she revised the four-volume work, adding more detailed notes. The revised edition was dedicated to 'my old and faithful friend Eliza Stedman'. Fergusson died before the revised version was printed, and the publication of the project was abandoned.

Teles, Lígia Fagundes (born 1923)

Brazilian short story writer and novelist. A lawyer, for a time she was an attorney general in São Paulo. Her fiction is often centred on women characters, seen from a psychological angle. Her short stories have a hint of Surrealism or ▷magic realism and she excels at a fine, subtle narrative technique.

Her most successful novel, *As Meninas* (1973) (*The Girl in the Photograph*, 1982), is about three adolescents who live in a boarding house during the Brazilian dictatorship (1964–1984). Ana Clara represents the proletarian; Lia, the middle-class revolutionary, and Lorena, the Brazilian false 'aristocracy'. As in ▷Raquel de Queirós's *As três Marias* (1963) (*The Three Marias*), they are unable to communicate. Teles belongs to the ▷postmodernism period, the third phase of ▷modernism in Brazil, alongside ▷Clarice Lispector.

In her latest anthologies of short stories, *Seminário dos ratos* (1977) (*Seminar of the Rats*) and *Mistérios* (1981) (*Mysteries*), she uses ▷magic realism as a way of dealing with the political situation in Brazil during the dictatorship, together with mysterious aspects of the psychology of her characters. She is a member of the Brazilian Academy of Letters. One of her stories and a novel have been made into films, and her work is included in several national and foreign anthologies. She has also won a number of literary prizes.

Other works: *Porões e sobrados* (1938) (*Cellars and Houses*); *Praia viva* (1944) (*Living Beach*); *O cactus vermelho* (1949) (*The Red Cactus*); *Ciranda de pedra* (1954) (*The Marble Dance*, 1956); *Histórias do desencontro* (1958) (*Tale of Misencounters*); *Verão no aquário* (1961); *Histórias escolhidas* (1961); *Os sete pecados capitais* (1964) (*The Seven Capital Sins*); *Jardim selvagem* (1965) (*The Wild Garden*); *Antes do baile verde* (1970) (*Before the Green Dance*); *Filhos pródigos* (1978) (*Prodigal Sons*); *A disciplina do amor* (1980) (*The Discipline of Love*), and *Tigrela e outras histórias* (*Tigrela and other stories*, 1986).

Telesilla ▷Floresta, Nísia

Telesilla (5th century BC)
Poet. Described by Antipater of Thessalonica (2nd century BC) as 'far-famed', she was particularly renowned for the successful encouragement she gave the women of her town of Argos to resist invaders from the enemy state of Sparta (494 BC). She was also a writer of choral poetry. Fragments concern the love of the river god Alpheus for the local nymph Arethusa, and the deities Apollo and Artemis. The deities are all connected with her home town. The Greek travel writer Pausanias (2nd century AD) records a statue of her in Argos. He adds that she was especially famous among women. A metre was named after her, the Telesilleion.
▷Muses

Temblor (1990) (Trembling)
Novel by Spanish writer ▷Rosa Montero, one of the most significant of Spain's New Wave of female novelists. This novel, which is set in an environment recognizable from the world of science fiction, but in which the women have control over the men, is a humorous critique of the patriarchal structures of contemporary Western society.

Tenant of Wildfell Hall, The (1848)
A novel by British writer ▷Anne Brontë, first published under the ▷pseudonym Acton Bell. The tenant of the title is Helen Graham, who has recently moved into the neighbourhood with her son, Arthur. The narrator, Gilbert Markham, falls in love with her, but is puzzled by her relationship with her landlord, Lawrence. Markham ignores the village rumours until he overhears Helen and Lawrence in intimate conversation, after which he assaults Lawrence. Helen reveals the story of her past in a lengthy journal which tells of her unfortunate marriage to Arthur Huntingdon, who, after a short period of happiness with Helen, slipped back into a life of drunkenness and infidelity. It is revealed that Helen has left Arthur to seek refuge with Lawrence, who is in fact her brother. She later returns to Arthur to nurse him through a fatal illness. After his death, Markham and Helen are able to pursue their relationship, and finally agree to marry. The novel was received as a morbid story, especially since it came from a woman's pen. Anne Brontë's comment in the Preface to the 1850 edition highlights the double standards imposed on women writers: 'I am at a loss to conceive how a man should permit himself to write anything that would be really disgraceful to a woman, or why a woman should be censured for writing anything that would be proper and becoming for a man.'

Tencin, Claudine-Alexandrine Guérin de (1685–1749)
French novelist. As the youngest daughter of a family of minor nobility but little fortune, Tencin was forced to enter a convent at sixteen. Having attained the title of canoness, she succeeded in having her vows annulled in 1712. Thereafter she lived in Paris with her brother, the abbé de Tencin, and her sister, Madame de Ferriol. Historians have consistently emphasized Tencin's scandalous reputation, partly acquired for her numerous affairs with fashionable and influential men (including the Regent) but also for the political and financial intrigues in which she was involved. Later, having taken over the salon of the ▷Marquise de Lambert, she presided over a group of *philosophes* and novelists, such as Marivaux and Prévost, as well as diplomats and financiers whom she referred to as the '*bêtes*' ('beasts') of her '*ménagerie*'. Of her own conduct, she is cited as remarking that she aimed 'to defy men on their own territory'. Her novels, *Mémoires du comte de Comminge* (1735) (▷*Memoirs of the Count of Comminge*, 1756); *Le Siège de Calais* (1739) (*The Siege of Calais*, 1740), *Les Malheurs de l'amour* (1747) (*The Misfortunes of Love*) and *Les Anecdotes d'Edouard II* (1776), published anonymously, were attributed to d'Argental and to her nephew, Pont-de-Veyle. They continue the tradition in women's writing of the *galant* historical novel established by Mme de la Fayette and ▷Cathérine Bernard, while introducing new elements, such as sentimentality, which were to flourish in the latter half of the century. Recent editions of her work include *Le Siège de Calais* (1983), and *Comte de Comminge* (1985).
▷de Beaumont, Anne-Louise
Bib: Castries, R., duc de, *La Scandaleuse Mme de Tencin*; Decottignies, J., 'Roman et revendication féminine d'après les Mémoires du comte de Comminge de Mme de Tencin' in *Roman et Lumières au 18ième siècle*; Jones, S., 'Mme de Tencin: an 18th-century Woman Novelist' in *Woman and Society*, 1979.

Ten Days in a Mad House (1887)
US non-fiction exposé by ▷Nellie Bly (pseudonym of Elizabeth Cochrane Seaman). One of the earliest investigative journalists who involved herself in her stories, Bly had herself committed to the insane asylum on Blackwell's Island in order to report conditions there. Originally published in the New York *World* newspaper, the Blackwell's Island stories brought national attention, both to Bly as a writer and to asylum conditions, especially their effect on women.
Bly's style emphasized realistic verisimilitude, making vivid the daily conditions and the large and small horrors of institutions. In this and other investigative reporting, Bly anticipated the

journalistic techniques and reportorial commitment of the decades to follow.

Tender Buttons: Objects, Food, Rooms (1914)

Poetry by US writer ▷Gertrude Stein. Stein's poetry investigates ways of writing about the act of perception itself. For Stein, the problem of poetry is to recreate the thing that is seen without naming it. Exploring this problem, she experimented with various techniques and invented new ways of writing poetry. *Tender Buttons* presents a series of still lives, such as 'A Chair', 'A Box', 'Roastbeef', 'Celery', and 'End of Summer'. Each of these is characterized by unexpected phrases that jar and collide. Stein's poetry disrupts conventional modes of poetry that emphasize linearity, order, hierarchy, reason, coherence and closure.

Tennant, Emma (born 1937)

English novelist. A feminist writer whose novels generally use the techniques of ▷magic realism within a ▷postmodern frame. Tennant's first novel, *The Colour of Rain* (1964), published under the ▷pseudonym Catherine Aydy, was heavily influenced by the writing of her father-in-law, Henry Green. Further novels followed after nearly a decade, including the ▷*The Bad Sister* (1978), the 'fictional childhood memoir' *Wild Nights* (1979), and the autobiographical *Adventures of Robina* (1986). Other novels include: *Woman Beware Woman* (1983), *Black Marina* (1985), *Two Women of London* (1989). During the 1970s Tennant edited the journal *Bananas*, which published early work of ▷Angela Carter, ▷Sara Maitland, J.G. Ballard and ▷Elaine Feinstein, among others. Subsequently she was a director of Next Editions, which first published a translation of the Russian poet Osip Mandelstam's *Journey to Armenia* (1980), Angela Carter's *Black Venus* (1985) and poetry by ▷Liz Lochhead.

Tennant, Kylie (1912–1988)

Australian novelist, historian and children's author. Tennant was educated at the University of Sydney worked as a journalist, in radio, as a barmaid, reviewer and lecturer and lived in many parts of New South Wales. Her social commitment is reflected in fiction which deals with the poor, the powerless, the dispossessed and the society which allows such inequality. Tennant won the S.H. Prior Memorial Prize 1935 for *Tiburon* (1935), the Prior Prize and the Australian Literary Society's Gold Medal in 1941 for *The Battlers* (1941), the Children's Book Award 1960 for *All the Proud Tribesmen* (non-fiction for children, 1959), and was awarded the Order of Australia. She published nine other novels, *Foveaux* (1939), ▷*Ride on Stranger* (1943), *Time Enough Later* (1943), *Lost Haven* (1946), *The Joyful Condemned* (1953), *The Honey Flow* (1956), *Ma Jones and the Little White Cannibals* (1967), *Tell Morning This* (1968) and *Tantavallon* (1983), as well as four plays (three of them for children) and a number of non-fiction and editorial works.
▷Children's literature (Australia); *Peaceful Army, The*

Tenney, Tabitha Gilman (1762–1837)

US satirist. Tenney's principal work, ▷*Female Quixotism: Exhibited in the Romantic Opinions and Extravagant Adventures of Dorcasina Sheldon* (1801), humorously reveals the inadequacy of what was considered proper and sufficient education for women.
▷*Pleasing Instructor, The*

Tenth Muse Lately Sprung up in America, The (1678)

The first volume of poetry published by a North American colonist, ▷Anne Dudley Bradstreet. *The Tenth Muse* is recognized as one of the major works in early North American literature. Although published by her brother-in-law without permission, the collection is an extraordinary presentation of Bradstreet's artistic vision, her literary skills and her interest in challenging women's traditional roles. For many years critical attention was focused upon those poems in the collection ('To My Dear and Loving Husband', 'The Author to Her Book') that suggested an ambiguity in Bradstreet's position on women's capabilities. A fuller knowledge of the collection, however, reveals her determination to present women's lives and national politics in a woman-centred language. Thus, while Bradstreet lauds her mother for being 'a dutiful wife', she presents Old and New England as Mother and Daughter, struggling against inevitable changes in which Old England laments, 'I that no wars so many years have known, / Am now destroyed and slaught'red by mine own.' On the other hand, she presents ▷Queen Elizabeth as a figure of Amazonian strength and declares, 'She hath wiped off th' aspersion of her sex, / That women wisdom lack to play the rex.' In her poetry and meditations, Bradstreet did not hedge against the complexities of being a woman in patriarchal New England; she confronted her doubts and, with honesty and brilliance, committed her intellectual processes to paper.

Teotochi-Albrizzi, Isabella (1760–1836)

Italian writer of memoirs. Born in Corfu of a Greek father and Venetian mother. She married a Venetian at the age of sixteen and moved to Venice. Sixteen years later, this marriage was annulled, and she married another Venetian, a nobleman, and it was this which provided her with material for her literary memoirs. These were published as *Ritratti* (*Portraits*) in 1807, 1808, 1816, 1826 and 1946. They were very popular for their observant, well-written descriptions of such characters as Foscolo, Alfieri and Byron. Teotochi-Albrizzi also produced a study of Canova's work in 1819. She is considered to be one of the most eloquent memorialists of the period.

Teplóva, Nadezhda Sergeevna (1814–1848)

Teplóva was one of the few recognized women poets of the Russian ▷Golden Age. Born into a well-off ▷Moscow merchant family, Nadezhda and her sister, Serafima, who was also a poet, received a fine domestic education and early encouragement of their talents. Her lyrics add a self-flagellating 'feminine' tinge to the common themes of conflict between aspiration and achievement ('A Confession'), love and vocation ('Advice'), hope and disillusion ('Spring'). Occasionally Teplóva finds correlatives for her moods in imagery, comparing poetic inspiration to a lightning storm ('Heights'), and euphoria to flying ('Rebirth'), but overall the effect of her poetry comes from her appealing lyric voice.

Terán, Ana Enriqueta (born (1919)

Venezuelan poet and short story writer. As a diplomat, she lived in Uruguay and Argentina, and her writings often appeared in the press. She belonged to the ▷1945 Generation, and to the experimental ▷*Viernes* Group of poets, along with ▷Enriqueta Arvelo Larriva and ▷Luz Machado. Terán contributed objective, thematic work to the magazine *Viernes* published by these poets. She began by writing simple verses inspired by everyday subjects, and developed to the complex and rather gongoristic style of her book of poems *Al norte de la sangre* (1946) (*To the North of the Flood*).

Other works: *Presencia terrena* (1949) (*Earthly Presence*); *Testimonio* (1954) (*Testimony*); *Cuadernos Cabriales, I* (1949), and *De bosque a bosque* (1970) (*From Wood to Wood*).

Teresa (1886)

A novel by ▷Neera about a wasted life. Teresa, the protagonist, devotes herself to her family, first to her younger siblings and then to her aged parents. When she falls in love, both she and her lover are too weak to take responsibility for their own lives, and so she goes on subordinating her wishes to those of others. Finally, when both parents are dead, her siblings gone, and she is left alone, she hears that her former lover is also alone and ill. For once, and in a sense too late, she throws her reputation to the wind, and goes to be with him. 'I have been paying all of my life for this moment of freedom' she tells her concerned friend. Neera has produced here another tale of female self-sacrifice, and offers her character a bitter crumb of comfort as reward. It could be read as a cautionary tale, but it seems that Neera sees Teresa's destiny as somehow inevitable.

Teresa de Ávila, Santa (1515–1582)

Born Teresa Sánchez de Cepeda y Ahumada, she is the most widely known of all the Spanish mystics, her works are recognised as world classics. Although born in Ávila into a prosperous and respected family, she received little formal education. After becoming a Carmelite nun in 1534, she devoted her life to the reform of the Carmelite Order, and founded her first convent of the discalced Carmelites (a branch which went barefoot) in 1562. Santa Teresa's work encompasses autobiographies, mystical works, a few poems and a large collection of letters. Her most important works are: *Camino de perfección* (1583) (*The Road to Perfection*); ▷*El libro de la vida* (1588) (*The Book of Her Life*); *El Castillo interior o tratado de las Moradas* (1588) (*The Castle Within or Treatise on Spiritual Dwellings*), and *Libro de las fundaciones* (*Book of Foundings*). Santa Teresa's work has recently been re-evaluated in a challenging way by French feminist critics such as Irigaray and Didier.

Teresah (1877–1964)

Pseudonym of Italian novelist and poet Teresa Corinna Ubertis Gray. She lived in Florence and in Rome. In 1902 she entered a short story competition in *La Lettura* magazine, which she won with a tale entitled 'Rigoletto', and this started her on a successful literary career. She was a prolific writer, who concentrated mainly on her female characters and their dilemmas.

Her work includes: *Il campo delle ortiche* (1897) (*The Nettle Field*); *Il libro di Titania* (1909) (*Titania's Book*); *Il cuore e il destino* (1911) (*Heart and Destiny*); *Piccoli eroi della grande guerra* (1915) (*Minor Heroes of the Great War*); *L'ombra sul muro* (1921) (*The Shadow on the Wall*); *Dobbiamo vivere la nostra vita* (1941) (*We Must Live Our Lives*); *Strade mie* (1942) (*My Streets*); *La luna* (1942) (*The Moon*).

Tergit, Gabrielle (1894–1982)

German reporter and novelist. She first established her fame in the 1920s with gripping accounts of court cases in the newspaper, *Berliner Tageblatt* (*Berlin Daily News*), and her ▷realist novel *Käsebier erobert den Kurfürstendamm* (1931) (*Cheese and Beer Conquer the Kurfürstendamm*). Because of her Jewish origins, she had to go into exile when Hitler came to power in 1933. Her memoirs, *Etwas Seltenes überhaupt, Erinnerungen* (1983) (*Something Quite Special, Recollections*) are an important document about the destinies of German Jews during the 20th century.

Terra d'oggi (1959) (Our Land Today)

Italian novel by ▷Lucia Tumiati, written in colloquial language, with occasional snatches of dialect, which tells of a working class Venetian family in the difficult period following the World War II. Against the background of the daily lives and tasks of the family, described in detail, a tragedy takes place when a son is drowned. His death causes great distress, but is also seen as, in some sense, a liberation from the hardships which must still be endured by the rest of the family. The conclusion is religious, advocating faith in God as the only possible hope. Despite the ▷realist elements of the narrative, Tumiati frequently highlights her role as author by commenting on events.

Territoires du féminin avec N. Duras (1977)
(Feminine Territories With N. Duras)
Linguistic study by French psychoanalyst ▷Marcelle Marini. Through her study of ▷Marguerite Duras's practice of writing, Marini seeks to define a feminine language, whose suppression, she says, is the cause of women's alienation. She reads the silence, ambiguity and madness in Duras's work as signs of revolt against the male domination over language, and the production of linguistic meaning as violence against women.

Her interpretation stands in contrast to ▷Michèle Montrelay's reading of Duras's disorienting discourse, in which blanks and syntactic distortions are an admission that women stand outside representation and, for lack of their own words, can only express themselves through inarticulate cries.

Terry, Lucy (c 1730–1821)
North American poet. Born in Africa but kidnapped and sold to a Massachusetts slave-master when she was about five years old, she synthesized her African oral heritage with stories of her new environment and became North America's first African-American poet. Her only extant poem, ▷'Bars Fight', details a Native American raid in the vicinity of her Deerfield home. After marrying a free man and apparently gaining her freedom, she and her family settled in Vermont.
▷Captivity narratives; Wheatley, Phillis

Tesky, Adeline Margaret (c 1850–1924)
Canadian novelist and short story writer, born in Appleton, Ontario, and educated at US art schools. The flavour of her simple, rather moralistic tales is evident from her titles A Little Child Shall Lead Them (1911) and Candlelight Days (1913). The Yellow Pearl: a Story of the East and the West (1911) is about an orphaned Chinese-American girl having to live with her racist aunt and uncle.

Tessera (1984–present)
Canadian feminist journal begun by ▷Daphne Marlatt, ▷Gail Scott, Kathy Mezei and others in order to publish the theoretical and experimental work of Quebec and English-Canadian feminist writers. It offers a forum for dialogue between French and English writers and women interested in feminist literary criticism. It has published special issues on doubleness, translation, narratology, and essentialism. Critic Barbara Godard (Gynocritics) is a member of the editorial collective, and the magazine is now published at York University, Toronto.

Testament of Youth (1933)
First volume of ▷Vera Brittain's autobiography. It covers the years 1900 to 1925, focusing on the years of World War I, when Brittain worked abroad as a Voluntary Aid Detachment nurse. She subsequently wrote (in Testament of Experience, 1957) that the impulse to write the autobiography came from reading the spate of war memoirs published in the 1920s, all of which left her asking 'Didn't women have their war as well? . . . Who will write the epic of the women who went to the war?' Brittain's ambivalent attitude to the war – she thought it futility and barbarity for a 'noble' cause – is apparent throughout the autobiography, although by the time of its writing Brittain was increasingly committed to feminist pacificism.

The second half of Testament of Youth describes her return to Oxford, the start of her intense friendship with fellow undergraduate ▷Winifred Holtby, and their shared life in London before Brittain's marriage. Their friendship provided the standpoint from which Brittain could present her experience as representative of her generation, and use her writing to 'illustrate the influence of world-wide events and movements upon the personal destinies of men and women'.

Tetzner, Gerti (born 1936)
East German writer. She became known in both East and West in 1974 with her novel Karen W., one of the first East German novels to examine critically the role and status of women in a socialist society.

Texidor, Greville (1902–1964)
New Zealand fiction writer. Greville Texidor grew up in Hampstead, knew British painters Augustus John (1878–1961) and Stanley Spencer (1891–1959), worked as a variety dancer and contortionist's assistant, married three times, and ended up in New Zealand. Texidor and her third husband, Werner Droescher, were anarchists who escaped World War II in Europe and arrived in New Zealand in 1940. Befriended by local writers and artists, Texidor began writing, and published stories and a novella in the 1940s. She lived and wrote in New Zealand as an expatriate, and her fiction is concerned with itinerancy, politics, gender relations and subjectivity. She committed suicide in Australia in 1964.

Publications: These Dark Glasses (1949); In Fifteen Minutes You Can Say a Lot, ed. Kendrick Smithyman (1987).

Tey, Josephine (1896–1952)
Scottish dramatist, novelist and crime writer – real name Elizabeth Mackintosh; also used the pseudonym Gordon Daviot. A teacher until her mother's death, when she returned home to manage the house, Tey initially had success writing ▷detective fiction as Gordon Daviot. These novels feature the gentleman detective Alan Grant, who first appeared in The Man in the Queue (1929). As Josephine Tey, she wrote her most famous novel ▷The Daughter of Time (1951), in which Grant 'solves' the mystery of the Princes in

the Tower. Tey also wrote the acclaimed play
Richard of Bordeaux (1933).

Thackeray, Anne ▷Ritchie, Lady

Thaman, Konai Helu (born 1947)
Poet from Tonga. Konai Helu Thaman was born
in Nuku'alofa and educated in Tonga and
Auckland. She has worked as a teacher and
lecturer, and writes in English. She has published
three collections of poetry, and her poems have
appeared in journals internationally. Thaman's
poetry is both feminist and postcolonial, focused
on questions of race, politics and gender.
    Publications: *You, the Choice of My Parents*
(1974); *Langakali* (1981); ▷*Hingano* (1987).

Tham Yew Chin ▷You Jin

Thanet, Octave ▷French, Alice

Thappananon, Wanna ▷Si Dao, Ruang

That Long Silence (1988)
Novel by Indian author ▷Shashi Deshpande.
The novel's protagonist is an Indian woman, the
ironically-named Jaya, which means 'victory'. She
is trapped, not so much by her marriage, but by
her expectations of how a marriage should
function. For years she has been unable to express
herself. All her observations to her husband,
children and outsiders have been determined by
her conviction that she must present a picture of a
happy family. She is so conscious of having forced
herself to meet society's conventions that she
cannot believe it when her husband finally accuses
her of being empty and selfish, of putting no
personality or interest into their marriage. Only
when she begins to accept some of the
responsibility for her own emotional crippling can
she begin to unravel the damage caused by the
years of silence.

Thaw
'Thaw' is the term used for the period after Nikita
Khrushchev's 1956 'secret' speech which
denounced the crimes of the Stalin era. In the
rosy days that followed, writers succeeded in
publishing a number of works written 'for the
drawer' with no hope of seeing them in print. In
the early 1960s the suppression of
▷Chukóvskaia's ▷*Sofiia Petrovna* was an early
sign of the end of the thaw and a partial return to
the norms of ▷socialist realism. The new
repression led to a wave of underground
publication (▷*samizdat*; ▷*tamizdat*).
    ▷Akhmadúlina, Izabella

Thaxter, Celia Laighton (1835–1894)
US poet, prose and children's writer, associated
with her native New Hampshire. Thaxter's
speciality was poetry and prose about the sea.
First published in ▷*The Atlantic Monthly* in 1861
and then in the *Atlantic* as well as almost every
other national literary magazine, Thaxter is

thought to have contributed more poetry to the
Atlantic than any other woman poet.
    Raised in a lighthouse, Thaxter later moved
with her family to a summer resort, which they
ran for a number of years. As the resort became a
summer gathering point on the eastern US
seaboard, Thaxter made contact with a wide range
of US literary figures, from John Greenleaf
Whittier (1807–1892) and Henry David Thoreau
(1817–1862) to *Atlantic* publisher James T. Fields
(1817–1881) and his wife, ▷Annie Adams Fields
who became lifelong friends. Her poetry is
occasionally didactic, but usually descriptive –
focused on nature, landscape and the sea – with
imagery that is notable for not falling into the
prevailing sentimental mode.

Theano (I) (? 4th century BC)
Philosopher. From Metapontum in southern Italy.
Biographical details are very confused, but she
was reputedly the wife of the Greek philosopher
Pythagoras, and the mother of up to four children.
(▷Pythagorean women.) The biographical
dictionary, the *Suda* (10th century AD), records
her works: *About Pythagoras, Concerning Virtue,
Advice for Women, Sayings of the Pythagoreans* and
Concerning Piety. She was also a writer of some
poetry in epic metre on an unknown subject. In
the body of revivalist Pythagorean literature, eight
letters bear her name. They discuss moderation of
jealousy in marriage, toleration of a husband's
infidelity, advice on ▷household management and
child rearing, and advise older women not to try
to recapture their youth by cosmetics. One letter
to another woman philosopher, Rhodope, is
unusual because it does not conform to the
pattern of the 'sermon' adopted in the other
letters. This helps those who argue the question
of its female authorship.
    ▷Philosophers, Ancient Greek and Roman
women

Theano (II) (5th century BC)
Poet. Writer of lyric verse, merely mentioned by
the biographical dictionary, the *Suda* (10th
century AD), and Eustathius. No works survive.

**Theatrum Majorum . . . The Diary of
Dorothy Dudley (1876)**
▷Dorothy Dudley's diary is a record of the initial
battles of the American Revolution during 1775
and 1776; 70 pages of the diary were published as
part of *Theatrum Majorum: The Cambridge of 1776*
for the centennial celebration of Cambridge,
Massachusetts. Dudley was only seventeen when
the battles of Lexington and Concord turned her
home town into 'the seat of war'. With passion
and drama, Dudley recounts the personal
tragedies of war that she witnessed among her
neighbours and friends, and she offers detailed
descriptions of the various leaders who settled
temporarily in the town; these include not only
military leaders but figures such as Martha
Washington (1731–1802), who attended the same
church as Dudley. There is a romantic tone to

much of Dudley's record, yet insights such as the 'grand yet incongruous' nature of war also pervade this remarkably dense text.

Their Eyes Were Watching God (1937)
Novel by US writer ▷Zora Neale Hurston. Hurston's novel focuses on an African-American woman's search for identity. Janie Crawford tells her friend Phoebe about her journey to the horizon and back, allowing Hurston to establish an oral storytelling frame for the novel. The form allows Hurston the flexibility of a narrative voice which mediates between the dialects of the African-American South and a literary voice more commonly associated with ▷modernism. Each of Janie's relationships with men offers a different model of social value for African-Americans. The first is a loveless match engineered by her grandmother, an ex-slave, who fears that Janie's emergent and reckless sensuality will lead to her sexual exploitation. Ironically, financial security and respectablility has to be paid for with the life of drudgery as 'de mule uh de world' which her grandmother feared. Janie's second husband, Joe Starks, represents an energetic, entrepreneurial spirit which establishes him as mayor of the first North American black town. Initially attractive, Stark's values turn out to involve a rejection of African-American culture in favour of a white bourgeois lifestyle. The suppression of women's autonomy and sexuality is intrinsic to this formation of an African-American middle class. Janie's final relationship, with Teacake, entails the rejection of economic security and social status in favour of the fantasy of an equal relationship founded in eroticism. The novel draws on Hurston's folklore research in the US South to construct a specific African-American culture, although this has been seen as controversial. Richard Wright described it as a 'minstrel' novel. However, Hurston's achievement is to construct a viable model of African-American womanhood which avoids the dual traps of sexual predator and asexual propriety.

them (1969)
US novel by ▷Joyce Carol Oates which chronicles the Wendall family's struggle against their lower socio-economic position and shows how capitalism prostitutes women, emphasizing that women have been made dependent on men for their survival. Loretta Wendall and her daughter, Maureen, try to survive by becoming prostitutes. Their attempts at autonomy are punished by patriarchal authority figures. They survive by remaining within the confines of patriarchal law; although they survive socio-economically they lose their self-identity.

Thesen, Sharon (born 1946)
Canadian poet and editor. Born in Tisdale, Saskatchewan, she moved to British Columbia in 1953, and studied English at Simon Fraser University. She edited ▷Phyllis Webb's The Vision Tree: Selected Poems (1982), and The New Long Poem Anthology (1991); she currently lives in Vancouver, and teaches at Capilano College. Poems in Artemis Hates Romance (1980) and Holding the Pose (1983) are about the nature of loss. Confabulations: Poems for Malcolm Lowry (1984) pushes toward Lowry's life and vision. The Beginning of the Long Dash (1987) and The Pangs of Sunday (1990) explore the stretch of imagination and the grammar of discourse.

Théoret, France (born 1942)
French-Canadian teacher and critic, born in Montreal. she attended the Universities of Montreal and Sherbrooke, and studied in Paris (1972–1974). She has been active in the new feminist writing out of Quebec, and collaborated with ▷Nicole Brossard and ▷Marie Claire Blais on La Nef des Sorcières (1976). Her best known works are Nous parlerons comme on écrit (1982), and Homme qui peignait Staline (1991, translated same year). After nineteen years of teaching, she now writes full-time.
Bib: Gould, K., Writing in the Feminine: Feminism and Experimental Writing in Quebec; Scott, G., in ▷A Mazing Space.

Théroigne de Méricourt, Anne-Joseph (died 1817)
Belgian activist during the French Revolution (1789). A farmer's daughter, she was a singer in London before moving to Paris in 1785. She was the co-founder of the Club des Amies de la Loi, and her speech, Discours à la société fraternelle des Minimes (1792) (Speech to the Fraternal Society of Minimes), appears in modern collections of documents relating to women's activities during the Revolution. Attacked and publicly whipped for her support of Brissot, she later became insane, and died in the Salpétrière .

Modern editions of her work can be found in Duhet, P., (ed.), Cahiers de doléances des femmes et autres textes (Register of Women's Grievances and Other Texts); English translations can be found in Levy, Applewhite and Johnson, Women in Revolutionary Paris.
▷French Revolution: pamphlets, registers of grievances, petitions and speeches
Bib: Roudinesco, E., Théroigne de Méricourt, une femme mélancolique sous la Révolution; Kelly, L., Women of the French Revolution.

They Shall Be Chastised (1974)
Novel by Kenyan writer ▷Muthoni Likimani. This describes the clash between Kenyan traditions and the combined forces of missionary religion and colonial education over the issue of circumcision. Likimani reaches the interesting literary resolution that circumcision (in the hands of the old ladies of the village) prepares a girl for life better than education.

Thiam, Awa
Senegalese writer. A social scientist whose interest is in the position of women in West Africa. She has written two books: La Parole aux négresses

(1978) (▷*Speak Out, Black Sisters*), based on personal interviews with women and men in several African countries, and ▷*Continents noirs* (1987) (*Black Continents*), a more distanced, scholarly work of analysis. In the first, she deals with the tenacious practices of ▷clitoridectomy and infibulation and exposes the regressive social customs which keep women from realizing their full potential. In the second, she investigates the ideology of blackness and how it has been used to oppress Africans as a people.

'Thick journals'

Magazines of the type called in Russia 'thick journals' include a mix of fiction, articles, essays and reviews. They originated in the reign of ▷Catherine II and, with circulation in the millions, remain the most important medium of publication for Soviet writers today. Before the 1917 Revolution (and again in the era of ▷*glásnost'*) the journals tended to represent distinct constituencies across the political spectrum, from extreme conservative to radical.

From the 1830s Russian women published in significant numbers in 'thick journals', although in the epoch of realism their tendency to use male ▷pseudonyms partially disguised the extent of their participation. Particularly hospitable to women writers were the Moscow journal *Russian Messenger* (1856–1860), in which ▷Evgenia Tur played an important editorial role, and *Northern Messenger* under the editorship of ▷Liubov' Gurévich (1891–1898).

▷Aníchkova, Anna; Barkóva, Anna; Barýkova, Anna; Dmítrieva, Valentina; Forsh Ol'ga; Gálina, G.A.; Gánina, Maiia; Kirpíshchikova, Anna; Márchenko, Anastasiia; Milítsyna, Elizaveta; Moscow; Nazár'eva, Kapitolina; Ol'nem; Panáeva, Avdotía; Pávlova, Karolina; Petrushévskaia, Liudmila; St Petersburg; Vengérova, Zinaida; *Week Like Any Other, A*

Third Christian School for Girls, The (1934)

Novel by Greek writer ▷Elli Alexiou. It is based on her experience as a teacher in a girls' school, and deals with the life of a naive teacher among the poor and harsh environment of a girls' school deprived of the necessary resources and ideas. The book shocked society by revealing the problems of education and the teachers' struggle to improve conditions in schools.

Thirkell, Angela (1890–1961)

English and Australian novelist who sometimes used the pseudonym Leslie Parker. Thirkell married Australian George Thirkell (her second marriage) and came to Australia in 1920 but returned to England in 1929 following the break-up of her marriage. Of her many popular novels, the most important for Australians is ▷*Trooper to the Southern Cross* (1934).

Thiroux d'Arconville, Marie Geneviève-Charlotte Darlus (?1721–1804)

French essayist, novelist, translator and scientist. Born in Paris, the daughter of a collector of taxes,

Angela Thirkell

she was married at fourteen to a parliamentary advisor. She attended lectures in all branches of the sciences at the Jardin du Roi, including anatomy practicals. She translated Monro's *Traité d'ostéologie* (1759) (*Treatise on Osteology*) from the English, and herself published a *Traité de la putréfaction* (1766) (*Treatise on Putrefaction*). Her work also includes essays on friendship, the passions, and contemporary mores. In addition to her own novels, *L'Amour épouvé par la mort* (1763) (*Love Tested by Death*), *Mémoires de Mlle de Valcourt* (1767), and *Dona Grália d'Araide, comtesse de Meneses* (1770), she published the seven-volume *Mélanges de littérature, de morale et de physique* (1775) (*Melange of Literature, Ethics and Physics*) and several translations including ▷Aphra Behn's *History of Agnès de Castro* and Gay's *Beggar's Opera*. Her *Vie du cardinal d'Ossat* (1771) (*Life of Cardinal d'Ossat*), *Vie de Marie de Medicis* (1974) and *Histoire de François II, roi de France* (1783) (*History of François II, King of France*) also merit her the title of historian.
Bib: Prudhomme, L.M., *Répertoire universal historique et biographique des femmes célèbres*.

'Thirties Generation, The' (Greece)

This term refers to writers whose work appeared for the first time during the 1930s. They were a new generation of young writers, cut off from the traditional literary forms, who sought to present an independent style. Women poets such as ▷Melpo Axioti and ▷Zoe Karelli wrote surrealist poetry, ▷Melissanthi was a a religious poet, ▷Penelope Delta is a popular and much-loved children's writer, ▷Eva Vlami was a novelist of the lost seafaring life of Greece, and ▷Athena Tarsouli was a renowned Greek travel writer. ▷Tatiana Gritsi-Milliex produced many short stories and novels, and ▷Margarita Lymberaki,

▷Dido Soteriou, ▷Galateia Saranti and ▷Alki Zei belong to the group of women who wrote of the years of German occupation, during World War II.

This Bridge Called My Back: Writings by Radical Women of Color (1981)

▷Cherrié Moraga and Gloria Anzaldua edited this collection of writings by radical women of color: ▷Latinas, African-Americans, ▷Native Americans and ▷Asian-Americans. These women break the silence to describe their common experience of oppression and racism. The collection exposes the racism and élitism of the white middle-class feminist movement, and expands the definition of feminism to include women of color. It examines the cultural, class and sexuality differences that divide women of color, marking the emergence of new connections among them. The collection includes the writings of Moraga, ▷Nellie Wong, ▷Mitsuye Yamada and ▷Audre Lorde. Published by ▷Kitchen Table Press, the book won the Before Columbus Foundation American Book Award in 1986.

This Sex Which Is Not One (1985)

Translation of *Ce sexe qui n'en est pas un* (1977), ▷Luce Irigaray's third book comprises a collection of articles, an interview, the transcription of a seminar Irigaray gave where she answered questions from members of the Philosophy Department in the University of Toulouse, and questions asked in other contexts.

As in her *Speculum de l'autre femme* (1974) (▷*Speculum of the Other Woman*, 1985), Irigaray's concern is to elaborate and as far as possible to demonstrate ▷*écriture féminine* or what she calls *parler femme*, 'woman speak', that is the non-unified, non-linear language of multiple meanings which she regards as specific to women. Because she sees femininity as currently suppressed and denied by a culture organized in purely masculine terms, where women are merely 'merchandise' to be exchanged between men, she argues that women need to withdraw from men in order to find out what femininity and *parler femme* might really be. However, since *This Sex Which is Not One*, Irigaray has become interested in analyzing what it is that might support relations between the sexes within what Elizabeth Grosz in *Sexual Subversions: Three French Feminists* (1989) calls an 'ethics of alterity'.

Thomas, Adrienne (1897–1980)

German novelist. She grew up in the bilingual city of Metz (now part of France), and worked as a Red Cross nurse during World War I. Her semi-autobiographical anti-war novel, *Die Katrin wird Soldat* (1930) (*Katrin Becomes a Soldier*), was an immediate popular success in Germany and abroad. When Hitler came to power her work was burnt, and she had to emigrate. All her novels deal with contemporary issues: *Reisen Sie ab, Mademoiselle!* (1944) (*Leave, Mademoiselle!*) takes as its theme the rise of fascism in Germany, while

Ein Fenster zum East River (1945) (*A Window on the East River*) examines the issues of emigration and exile.

Thomas, Audrey Grace (born 1935)

Canadian-based novelist and short story writer, born Audrey Callahan in Binghamton, New York. She studied at Smith College, spent a year at St Andrew's University in Scotland from 1955 to 1956, and after emigrating to Canada in 1959 with her husband, an artist, attended the University of British Columbia, where she gained her MA in 1963. The Thomases lived in Ghana from 1964 to 1966, then in Vancouver, Canada. Although she wrote as a child, marriage and babies left Audrey Thomas little time for her writing, and it was Africa, she says, along with a miscarriage, that made her return to words. 'If One Green Bottle . . .', her first published story, appeared in *The Atlantic Monthly* in 1965. *Ten Green Bottles* (1967) was the first of her many short story collections, which include *Ladies and Escorts* (1977), ▷*Real Mothers* (1981), *Two in the Bush and Other Stories* (1982), *Goodbye Harold, Good Luck* (1986) and *The Wild Blue Yonder* (1990). Thomas's vigorous short stories concern themselves with women in relationship to children, and husbands, lovers; and with women alone, struggling to deal with disappointment and pain, or taking satisfaction in small, meaningful rituals. In her novels, Thomas succeeds in extended and intense ripostes that are stylistically dazzling. Completely in control of language, she is able to evoke the loss of a woman miscarrying in *Mrs Blood* (1970), or a young woman dealing with her own chaos through her summer job in an insane asylum in *Songs My Mother Taught Me* (1973). *Blown Figures* (1974) is a highly experimental novel that uses Africa as dream ground from which to reassemble the fragments of the past. ▷*Latakia* (1979) is a metafiction/travelogue about a failed love affair/*ménage à trois*. *Intertidal Life* (1984) focuses on a woman reflecting on her marital breakup. Although subject matter might suggest that Thomas's work is bleakly concerned with failed relationships, her clear style and sharp ear make her fiction often very funny. She is a vivisector of women's hopes and losses. After her separation and divorce, Thomas taught creative writing at various Canadian universities, and continued her travels abroad. She has won many awards and now lives on Galiano Island in British Columbia.

Bib: Dorscht, S.D., in *Future Indicative*; Howells, C.A., *Private and Fictional Words*; Hutcheon, L., in ▷*A Mazing Space*; Irvine, L., *Sub/Version*; Special issue of ▷*Room of One's Own*, Vol. 10, No. 3/4 (1985–86).

Thomas, Clara (born 1919)

Canadian critic, born Clara McCandless in Strathroy, Ontario. She was educated at the Universities of Western Ontario and Toronto, and has undertaken ground-breaking work on Canadian women writers, particularly ▷Anna

Jameson (*Love and Work Enough: The Life of Anna Jameson*, 1967), ▷Margaret Laurence (*Margaret Laurence*, 1969, and ▷*The Manawaka World of Margaret Laurence*, 1975), and ▷Susanna Moodie and ▷Catherine Parr Traill. She is Professor Emeritus at York University, Toronto.

▷*Canadian Woman Studies*

Thomas, Edith Matilda (1854–1925)

US poet and translator. Thomas's works are distinguished by their careful attention to poetic craft, and refined, traditional form.

She was very popular with magazine editors (often themselves poets) who valued both 'correctness' in poetry, and tractable contributors willing to revise at editors' behest. She was the most frequently published woman poet in the prestigious ▷*Century Illustrated Monthly Magazine*. Quite prolific, Thomas generally offered editors a number of poems at a time, so that the magazine could choose which to publish. Collections of her verse include: *Lyrics and Sonnets* (1887); *The Inverted Torch* (1890); *In Sunshine Land* (1895), and *The Flower from the Ashes* (1915).

Thomas, Elean (born 1947)

Caribbean poet and short story writer. Thomas was born and educated in ▷Jamaica, obtaining a BA at the University of the West Indies. She later became a journalist and publicist, and a member of the Communist Party. Her collection of poetry and short stories, *Word Rhythms from the Life of a Woman* was published in 1986. The collection, which deals with the issues facing women in society, has a useful foreword by Dr Carolyn Cooper, and a critical introduction by Dr Trevor Munroe. It also contains interesting biographical information.

Thorn Birds, The (1977)

Australian novel by ▷Colleen McCullough. This was a spectacular commercial success but had an unenthusiastic reception from the critics because of its sensationalism and stereotyped view of Australian life. It was serialized for television in the USA in 1983.

Thornton, Alice (1626–1707)

English memoirist who seems to have written in the late 1660s and 1670s. There are several different stages and versions of her autobiography, and her recent editors suggest mixed motives for writing, including a defence of her family name against scandal, and justification for her unlucky financial dealings. Thornton's life begins in the 1620s, with family events (usually dire) interspersed with national events. So 1649 reads, 'King Charles beheaded at Whitehall, London, 30th January, 1649. My cousin Julian Norton died at Richmond Green at her father's, 9th April 1649.' Far from her personal circumstances improving, the family fortunes fell. By the time of her husband's death she is both 'afflicted in spirit, low in my estate'. The mixture of her fear of

slander and emotional fervour make the chronicle intense and claustrophobic reading.

▷Fanshawe, Lady Ann; Halkett, Lady Ann; Hutchinson, Lucy

Thorup, Kirsten (born 1942)

Danish lyric poet, prose writer and dramatist, Thorup was born in a small town on the island of Fyn. Her parents were uneducated, but she graduated and began to write.

In 1967 she published her début, a modernist collection of poems *Indeni–Udenfor* (*Inside-Outside*); she also wrote a collection of short stories *Love from Trieste* (1969) and a modernist novel, *Baby* (1973). In 1977 she wrote the ▷realist novel *Lille Jonna* (*Little Jonna*) followed in 1979 by *Den lange sommer* (*The Long Summer*). The novels tell the story of Jonna, from a small town, but in 1982, she had her real breakthrough with another novel about Jonna in two volumes, *Himmel og Helvede* (*Heaven and Hell*). In 1988 it was filmed. The central characters are two other women, an old woman and a young violinist, living in the city of Copenhagen amongst prostitutes and criminals.

In 1989 she continued the stories about Jonna with *Den yderste grænse* (*The Uttermost*). This is even more fantastic in its ▷magic realism. Her social criticism is combined with a psychological insight and the ability to incorporate fantastic elements with realism. Thorup's works show her development from narrow modernist writing to a broad realist and fantastic style which gained a wide audience. She has also written plays for television and radio, has received many prizes and awards, and has been widely translated.

Thoughts on the Education of Daughters (1787)

English writer ▷Mary Wollstonecraft's earlier publication on education. She advocates the education of women both for material reasons – to enable them to obtain such work as is permitted to women, if they have need – and for spiritual and intellectual comfort.

▷*Vindication of the Rights of Women*

Thousand Pieces of Gold (1981)

US novel. Ruthanne Lum McCunn wrote this biographical novel about a 19th-century Chinese-American pioneer woman. Lalu Nathoy spends her childhood in China struggling with poverty. As a child she decides to exercise control over her life, so she unbinds her feet to avoid being sold by her family. She finds satisfaction in working like a man in the fields but, nevertheless, she is shipped to San Francisco, California, and auctioned as a slave. Through her courage and decision-making skills, Lalu earns her freedom and prospers. She needs and loves her Western life, but she feels a nostalgia for things Chinese. McCunn chronicles the contributions and sufferings of Chinese frontier women, restoring Chinese women to their rightful place in US history.

Thrale, Hester Lynch Piozzi ▷Piozzi, Hester (Lynch) Thrale

Three Crabs (1968)
Work by Japanese writer Oba Minako (born 1930), which won the Gunzo Prize for a New Writer and Akutagawa Prize. Yuri, the heroine, is overwhelmed with a feeling that she cannot cope with the sedate social round, so she drives to a recreation ground full of young people. There she enjoys the company of an unknown boy wearing pink shorts, with whom she spends a night at a hotel. She gets nothing from this brief encounter. The story begins with a description of Yuri walking to the bus station on the coast the following morning. The place she returns to is hidden by fog. Through this story Oba expresses the loneliness of housewives, which they themselves do not know how to express.

Three Generations of Women: The Lives of the Discriminated Buraku in East Japan (1974)
The autobiography of a Buraku woman by Japanese writer Kobayashi Hatsue (born 1933). The Buraku woman belongs to the outcast class which was officially abolished in 1871 but descendants of which are still socially discriminated against. Kobayashi Hatsue describes the harsh experiences which the Buraku woman, her grandmother and her mother suffer as a tenant farmer, a Burakumin and head of a household.

Three Girls in Blue (1980)
A major play by Russian writer ▷Liudmila Petrushévskaia, *Three Girls in Blue* (English translation, *Stars in the Morning Sky*) is a wry, pathetic, and yet very funny look at the frustrating life of the Russian urban woman who carries a heavy load of responsibility without ever quite relinquishing rosy dreams of being loved and cared for. Ira, settled for the summer in a cottage with a leaky roof, finds the country far from restful. She must cope with two distant female cousins – the title suggests the parallel to Chekhov's *Three Sisters* – who also have an inherited claim to the cottage, the bickering and spoiled sons of all three women, and a gabby, greedy landlady. When a married neighbour builds her a private lavatory as a token of his regard, she leaves her son with her trouble-making mother in their Moscow apartment to pursue him to the Crimea. In Petrushévskaia's world, Ira's frantic search for fulfilment has no neat resolution.

Three Guineas (1938)
Essay by English writer ▷Virginia Woolf. A socialist, pacifist and feminist polemic, the essay is an argument on the relation between art and propaganda which picks up the main themes of her earlier essay ▷*A Room of One's Own* (1929). Woolf again looks at the enforced development of a 'society of outsiders', which is now considered as a strategic, enabling formation, resistant to dominant social institutions, which can therefore develop its own methods for 'liberty, equality and peace'. Woolf assesses here the notion of woman as the scapegoat of history and argues the necessity for women and other marginalized groups, particularly the working classes, to make a claim for their own history and literature. In its original version, Woolf's critique of nationalism, jingoism and fascism was visually illustrated through the use of photographs depicting a war-torn Spain, juxtaposed with photographs of men in ▷'patriarchal' clothing, the dress of authority and power. This visual element makes an explicit link between fascism and the accepted guise of a patriarchal value system.

Three Lives (1909)
US writer ▷Gertrude Stein's first published book. Even though *Three Lives* has by now an established and deserved reputation as an early ▷modernist experimental classic, the three tightly-observed stories that make up the book also take us beyond the formal and aesthetic aspects of modern literature and into the uncompromising field of literary politics. On a formal level, the three lives that Stein describes here testify to her pioneering disregard for plot and story in favour of an impressionistic and experimental presentation of 'things as they are'. Inspired by by the challenges of impressionism and post-impressionism, artists Cézanne (1839–1906), Picasso (1881–1973) and Matisse (1869–1954) respectively influence and inform 'The Good Anna', 'Melanctha' and 'The Gentle Lena'. More than examples of aesthetic principles, however, Stein's portraits also attempt to represent 'lives' lived at the margins: those of two German immigrant servants ('The Good Anna' and 'The Gentle Lena') and of the rebellious African-American, Melanctha Herbert, Stein's descriptions of the long-suffering Anna and the melancholic Lena, through to Melanctha's jubilatory resistance, confront her readers with a controversial grey area, in which an 'impression' can become but a racial or ethnic stereotype, and formal experimentation a gesture of cultural imperialism.

Three Marias: New Portuguese Letters, The (1975)
Translation of *Novas Cartas Portuguesas* (1972). Published during the Salazar/Caetano regime, the book was banned because of its graphic descriptions of physical love and its critique of government policies. Authored by the ▷'Three Marias' (▷Maria Isabel Barreno, ▷Maria Teresa Horta and ▷Maria Velho da Costa), the book contains letters exchanged among the three writers as well as fictional letters based on the 17th-century Portuguese classic ▷*Lettres Portugaises* (1669). The volume also includes poetry, word games, essays and non-fictional materials, such as excerpts from the Portuguese penal code. The book's rejection of novelistic

conventions is in keeping with the authors' critique of the patriarchal regime.

▷Alcoforado, Mariana; Correia, Natália
Bib: Kauffman, L.S., *Discourses of Desire: Gender, Genre and Epistolary Fictions*; Owen, H. 'The Three Marias: The Case Re-Opened', *ACIS Journal* (Spring 1989); *Longman Anthology of World Literature by Women*, pp. 918–924; Sadlier, Darlene J., *The Question of How: Women Writers and New Portuguese Literature*.

'Three Marias', The

The Three Marias

The name given to ▷Maria Isabel Barreno, ▷Maria Teresa Horta and ▷Maria Velho da Costa, the authors of ▷*Novas Cartas Portuguesas* (1972), who were arrested and put on trial in the early 1970s for having written an 'obscene' book.

Three Miss Kings, The (1891)

Australian novel by ▷Ada Cambridge. This novel, one of Cambridge's best, has a conventional plot in which three orphaned sisters go to Melbourne to make their own way, are rewarded with suitable husbands, and later inherit money. The stereotyped plot is, however, relieved by Cambridge's sardonic view of 'marvellous Melbourne', of the vulgarity of *nouveau riche* pretentions, and of the Great Exhibition of 1880.

Through One Administration (1883)

US novel by ▷Frances Eliza Hodgson Burnett, first serialized in ▷*The Century Illustrated Monthly Magazine*. In a decade when magazine publishing often used a ▷parlour table standard of decency, this novel caused a major flurry by setting its love interest on the affection of a single man for a married woman, while critically viewing the political society of the US capital. While the

Century's editor dealt with criticism of the novel's morality, its political views and realism brought Hodgson Burnett critical respect and some of her first international recognition as a significant adult novelist.

Tibors (early 13th century)

French ▷*trobairitz* of the fourth period. She came from the Grasse region, and is named as the judge of a *partimen* and by another troubadour, Guiraut d'Espanha. As the *vida* makes no mention of a husband, she may well have been unmarried.

Tiempo, Edith L. (born 1919)

Filipino fiction writer, poet, literary critic and teacher. She and her husband, Edilberto K. Tiempo, are closely associated with the Silliman Writers' Workshop, which they co-founded. The Workshop, held annually, has honed the skills of many young Filipino writers in English. Herself a well-known writer, among her works are: *The Tracks of Babylon and Other Poems* (1966), a short story collection, *Abide Joshua and Other Stories* (1964), and two novels: *A Blade of Fern* (1978) and the prize-winning *His Native Coast* (1979), about a Filipino woman who is half-Igorot (an upland tribe of Northern Luzon) and a North American expatriate. Their search is not just for national and cultural identity, but for a meaningful personal identity that cuts across nations and cultures.

Tie Ning (born 1957)

Tie Ning

Chinese writer from Beijing. Tie Ning first impressed the literary world with her short story 'Ah, Fragrant Snow', depicting the vague longings of a little country girl for the great world beyond, symbolized by the railway. Her novella, *The*

Buttonless Red Shirt, about teenage repression, was made into a popular film. *The Rose Door* (1988) is a powerful portrait of an old woman, a remnant of the bourgeoisie, who exploits every crack in the new system to maintain her footing in society. It is also an ingenious study in female relationships wherein the narrator, a little girl, is at once attracted and repulsed by her unscrupulous grandmother.

Tiffany, Consider (1733–1796)
North American poet. A resident of Hartland, Connecticut, in 1767 when several people were struck and killed by lightning, she published a broadside, ▷ *Relation of the Melancholy Death of Six Young Persons* . . ., about the event. It is her only known work.

Tighe, Mary (1772–1810)
Irish poet born in Dublin, the daughter of a Methodist librarian. She married her cousin in 1793, by which time she was writing poetry. In London she studied Latin, and wrote *Psyche, or the Legend of Love* (1805), initially privately printed, and published some four years after she wrote it. She excuses the use of allegory and the story of love and the soul, saying that she has avoided Spenserian archaic language because she knows her poetry will not be worth much study. Nevertheless, she plans, 'To tell of goodly bowers and gardens rare, / Of gentle blandishments and amorous play, / And all the lore of love, in courtly verse essay'. Also published was *Mary, A Series of Reflections During 20 Years* (1811), and she wrote an unpublished autobiographical novel, *Selena*. She suffered from consumption (tuberculosis) when *Psyche* was first published, and retired to Dublin and Wicklow. *Psyche* was published again in 1811, and admired by the poet John Keats (1795–1821). She kept a diary which was destroyed, though a cousin copied extracts.

Ti-Jean L'horizon (1979) ▷ *Between Two Worlds* (1981)

Tikkanen, Märta (born 1935)
▷ Fenno-Swedish lyric poet and prose writer, born in Helsinki. Her father was a professor, and in 1963 she married the writer Henrik Tikkanen (1924–1989), with whom she had five children. She studied literature and languages, and has been a teacher, an editor and head of Helsinki's Swedish Institute for Workers from 1972 to 1981. She is the best, known woman writer in Finland.

Tikkanen's first work was the novel in two volumes *Nu imorron* (1970) (*Now Tomorrow*) and *Ingenmandsland* (1972) (*No Man's Land*). Her principal work is the sequence of poems *Århundradets kärlekssaga* (1978) (*The Love Story of the Century*) and the lyrical novel *Rödluvan* (1986) (*Little Red Riding Hood*). Recently she has had great success with the lyrical novel *Storfangeren* (1990). (*The Great Hunter*). She is one of several Scandinavian women writers who write about their own lives without ever writing

autobiographically. Tikkanen's female characters are bound up within their sexuality, which causes them both to suffer and feel alive. Some reviewers have reacted against this female masochism, others have seen an ambivalent femininity, autonomous in intellect and art, and very dependent on a sexual and emotional life. She has received many prizes and awards and has been widely translated.

Tilghman, Mary (Molly) (fl 1782–1789)
North American letter-writer. A resident of Chestertown, Maryland, she was a member of an upper-class family whose lifestyle, after the American Revolution, invoked wealth and sociability. In letters written to a female cousin (▷ 'Letters of Molly and Hetty Tilghman'), she reveals a young woman's everyday concerns about marriage, childbirth and the responsibilities of raising a family.

Timeless Land, The (1941)
Australian novel by ▷ Eleanor Dark. This is the first volume of Dark's historical trilogy; the succeeding volumes are *Storm of Time* (1948) and *No Barrier* (1953). The trilogy was reprinted as one volume in 1963 and presented as an ABC Television series in 1980. Against the background of the first years of English settlement in Australia (1788), Dark traces the adventures of the Aborigine, Bennilong, the convict woman, Ellen Prentice, her husband, Andrew, and son, Johnny, the landholder, Mannion, who takes Ellen as his housekeeper/mistress after the death of his wife, and influential historical figures such as Governor Phillip. The trilogy ends with the crossing of the Blue Mountains to the west of Sydney in 1913, an event which opened the way to the rich western plains of New South Wales.

Time of Man, The (1926)
US novel. ▷ Elizabeth Madox Roberts modelled her book on the classic epic poem, *The Odyssey*. The heroine, Ellen Chesser, is the wife of a tenant farmer and she combats a rugged physical world for her subsistence. She is unjustly accused of burning barns but she triumphs over her adversities. Ellen relies on her inner strength and learns to trust her intuition. Roberts transforms a male's epic journey into a woman's journey to self-discovery.

Time of the Doves, The (1983) ▷ *Pigeon Girl, The*

Timoxena (2nd century AD)
Philosopher. Wife of the Greek biographer and philosopher Plutarch (AD ?46–c120) of Chaeronea. Plutarch tells us that she wrote a work *On the Love of Adornment* in the form of a letter to another woman, Aristylla. Authorship is not certain because it was possible he wrote the work and circulated it under his wife's name as it was a 'woman's matter'.

Timrava (1867–1951)

Slovak story writer and dramatist. Timrava, whose real name was Božena Slančiková, was one of the leading representatives of the so-called 'Second Wave' of Slovak realism – ▷social realism. She never married, and spent her life far from the main Slovak cultural centres. After unsuccessful attempts at writing verse she turned to fiction.

In her short stories she broke the norm of Slovak woman's literature, removing the folklore element. In her first short story, *Za koho ísť (Whom Should We Marry?)* she attacked the sentimentalization of love-affairs. She was not interested in questions of nation or nobility, but in those of the private life. The influence of money on human relationships was her main theme. One of her best works is the short story *Ťapákovci* (1914) (*The Ťapáks*), in which she contrasts Slovak rural backwardness with the possibility of positive action. In *Skon Pala Ročku* (1921) (*Palo Ročko's Death*) she deals with the decay of relationships caused by poverty. She mocks love and national feeling in *Skúsenosť* (1902) (*Experience*), and political idols in ▷*Hrdinovia* (1918) (*The Heroes*).

Tinayre, Marcelle (1877–1948)

French novelist. Born Marguerite Chasteau in Tulle, she married an artist named Julien Tinayre, published her first two novels (*Vive les vacances*, 1885, *Hurrah for the Holidays*, and *L'Enfant gaulois*, 1887, *The Gallic Child*), ▷pseudonymously, and then began writing under her own name. Love is the major theme of her prose fiction, which includes the novels *La Rancon* (1898) (*The Ransom*), *Hellé* (1899), *La Maison du péché* (1902) (*The House of Sin*), *La Rebelle* (1905) (*The Rebel*) and *L'Ombre de l'amour* (1910) (*The Shadow of Love*). According to the critic Jennifer Waelti-Walters, Tinayre, who exposes her female protagonists to a plethora of sentimental and emotional experiences, is 'the writer of the Belle Epoque who has most comprehensively explored and understood love as a phenomenon'. Her texts, particularly those written during and after the late 1890s, reveal her also to have been a writer committed to the improvement of women's social and sexual lot, which she depicts as rather bleak. A journalist as well as a novelist, she also left a volume of memoirs, *Madeleine au miroir: journal d'une femme* (1913) (*Madeleine at the Mirror: Diary of a Woman*).
Bib: Waelti-Walters, J., *Feminist Novelists of the Belle-Epoque.*

Tin Flute, The (1947)

Translation of *Bonheur d'Occasion* (1945) by French-Canadian novelist ▷Gabrielle Roy. Roy's novel, set in a poor industrial district of Montreal, is about a young woman, Florentine Lacasse, struggling to rise above her limited and squalid life. Florentine is portrayed in relation to her large family. Her desperate need for one man, and the love of another man who marries her, all contribute to a narrative full of despair, and yet, daring to hope.

Tirra Lirra by the River (1978)

Australian novel by ▷Jessica Anderson. This reconstructs, in a retrospective first-person meditation, the life of Nora Porteous, now over seventy. During her review of a failed marriage, expatriation, a brief love affair and abortion, and a subsequent close relationship with women friends, Nora comes to face the rationalizations and self-preserving fictions that such a life, perhaps typical of its time, has necessitated. A constant theme is that of artistic failure, for Nora Porteous obviously has considerable undeveloped artistic talent. As the title suggests, there are constant parallels between Nora and the Lady of Shalott in her lonely tower. *Tirra Lirra by the River* won the prestigious Miles Franklin Award for 1979.

Tlali, Miriam (born 1933)

Miriam Tlali

South African novelist, short story writer and non-fiction writer, who has also written two plays. Born in Doornfontein, Transvaal, she grew up in the black township of Sophiatown (which no longer exists), received her tertiary education at the University of Witwatersrand and the University of Roma, Lesotho, and is now living in Soweto. Her novels are particularly important as one of the earliest representations, at least in English, of South African life by a black woman writer. Tlali's first novel, ▷*Muriel at Metropolitan* (1975), which she completed in 1969, is an ironic record of daily existence in a hire-purchase store. The store acts as a focal point for the vicissitudes of South African urban life, and provides the occasion for social protest at white racism as well as the capitalist exploitation of a black working class. This was followed by ▷*Amandla* (1981), an angrier novel about the ▷Soweto schoolchildren's rebellion and its political aftermath. Both novels were banned under South African censorship regulations, as was one of Tlali's stories in *Staffrider* magazine, 'The Point of No Return'. This story was later reprinted in *Mihloti* (1984), a collection of prose pieces – including journalism, interviews and travelogues – focusing on the lives of black women under apartheid.

Tlali was one of the founders of *Staffrider* magazine, which has been an important forum for black South African writers, and is a member of the board of Skotaville Press, which publishes work by black writers. For a time, before spending a year in Holland in 1984, she worked with a group called 'Women in Writing', which published a weekly column in *City Press*. She also contributes a column called 'Soweto Speaks' to *Staffrider* magazine, which tells the stories of various people on their behalf.

Her most recent and most interesting work is her volume of short stories *Footprints in the Quag: Stories and Dialogues from Soweto* (1989, published under the title ▷*Soweto Stories* in Britain). Some of the stories reveal a shift from the straightforward mimetic ▷realism of her earlier works, not into ▷postmodernism but instead into techniques offered by the ▷oral tradition. Moreover, whereas the earlier writing dealt primarily with racism, here she explores additional forms of subordination.
▷Black Consciousness

To Have and To Hold (1900)
US novel. ▷Mary Johnston's historial romance was the number-one bestseller in 1900. Johnston revises colonial history, chronicling how prospective wives were sent to Jamestown, Virginia, in exchange for tobacco. The story focuses on Lady Jocelyn, the king's ward, who flees to Jamestown to avoid a prearranged marriage. In choosing her own husband, Jocelyn challenges the authority of the Lord, the governor and the king. Johnston presents a woman who determines her own destiny, advocating rebellion against the prescribed hierarchical social order.

Tókareva, Viktoriia Samoilovna (born 1937)
After contemplating other careers (doctor, music teacher, actress), Tókareva became a prizewinning film and television script writer and the author of widely popular short stories. Like ▷Petrushévskaia she takes her subjects from the daily grind of Soviet life, but Petrushévskaia's humour has a bite to it that is missing from Tókareva's more accessible and optimistic prose fables. In an interview (*Soviet Life* 5, 1986) Tókareva, asked how she would define happiness, responded: 'To be really happy is to do work that you like and to have children.' In 'Centre of Gravity' (*Granta* 30) the 'Grand Chain' of people's concern for each other thwarts a woman's attempts to commit suicide. More often, however, Tókareva's stories deal with the failure to connect: in 'Nothing Special' (*Balancing Acts*) Margo accepts love with serene apathy as

something akin to the series of near-fatal accidents she suffers; 'Dry Run' (*Granta* 33) records a conventional woman's aloof fascination with a flamboyant, greedy female friend. Her heroines can also be bound by an anchoring sense of obligation ('Between Heaven and Earth' in *Balancing Acts*, ed. Helena Goscilo; 'Five Figures on a Pedestal', *Soviet Women Writing*).
Bib: *Soviet Literature* 6 (1970), 3 (1975), 3 (1978), and 6 (1986).

To Kill A Mockingbird (1960)
US novel by Harper Lee which won the 1961 Pulitzer Prize and exposes how prejudice perverts justice. Descended from Robert E. Lee, the Southern Civil War general, Lee was born in Monroeville, Alabama, in 1926. In 1949, six months before earning her law degree from the University of Alabama, she went to New York to pursue a literary career. Her novel focuses on the trial of an innocent African-American man found guilty of raping an Anglo-American woman in Alabama in the 1930s. Narrated from the point of view of a six-year-old girl, it emphasizes that children are born with an instinct for justice; they learn prejudice in the socialization process. Lee observes in this, her only novel to date, that Southern culture corrupts children's instinct in preserving the tradition of the past. In 1962 *To Kill a Mockingbird* was made into a film starring Gregory Peck.

'To Laura' (c 1750)
The North American writer ▷Annis Boudinot Stockton's poetic tribute to her 'sister' poet, ▷Elizabeth Graeme Fergusson. The two Pennsylvania poets exchanged poems and supported one another's literary endeavours. Written in rhyming quatrains, it expresses admiration for Fergusson and acknowledges the liberty Stockton feels in sharing her poetry with another woman: 'Permit a sister muse to soar / To heights she never try'd before.' Like many of Stockton's poems, its literary value and themes of sisterhood deserve attention.

To Live the Orange (1979)
French writer ▷Hélène Cixous's own translation of *Vivre l'orange*. This text illustrates the opposition Cixous makes between the *spoken* language, which is analogous to women's relation to the mother, and the *written* language, which is univocal and fixed, in which syntax introduces chronological time. Cixous opts for multiple poetic and narrative levels, investing in the world of myth, and exploring the possibility for words to interrelate through assonance and association of ideas: for example, Oran (her birth-place)/ orange/Iran, even across language barriers, for example, *laranja*. *To Live the Orange* is a hymn to femininity encompassing personal, political, sexual and historical dimensions.

Tolstáia, Tat'iana Mikhailovna (born 1951)
Russian short story writer. Writing runs in
Tolstaia's family: she is the great-granddaughter
of fiction writers Aleksandra Bostrom (1854–
1906) and ▷Anastasiia Krandiévskaia, and
granddaughter of poet ▷Nataliia Krandiévskaia
and the novelist Aleksei Tolstoi. Tolstáia's stories
(published in the USSR in the late 1980s) are
marked by a stylistic complexity, elusive point of
view, wealth of imagery and observed detail, and a
preoccupation with marginal people. Like
▷Petrushévskaia, she has a wicked eye for the
small humiliations of the daily grind, and the
Russian climate and Soviet environment both
form and reflect her characters' lives. Tolstáia is
remarkably good at depicting the inner world of
children ('Loves Me, Loves Me Not', 'Date with a
Bird') and defeated adults who never quite
abandon their dreams ('Fire and Dust', 'Peters').
A collection of her stories which appeared in an
English translation by Antonina Bouis as *On the
Golden Porch* (1989), was hailed in the West as the
first fruit of ▷*glásnost'*.

Tomioka Taeko (born 1937)
Japanese poet and novelist, born in Osaka. Her
first, prizewinning, collection of poems entitled
Return Present was followed by *An Opening Day for
A Story* – a long poem – won the Muro Saisei
Prize in 1961. She divorced her husband, the
wood-block artist Ikeda Masuo, and began to
write a novel in 1971. *The Festival for Plants* won
the Tamura Toshiko Prize in 1973, which was
followed by *Family in Hell*. She pursues a theme
which reverses the established relationship
between the sexes in her works such as *Facing the
Hills They Stand, Waving Ground, A Dress of
Wisteria and Futon of Linen* and ▷*The Straw Dog*.
She has written scripts for films and the theatre
since publishing *A Lover's Suicide – Ten no
Tsunashima*.

Tomorrow and Tomorrow and Tomorrow
(1983)
Australian novel by ▷Marjorie Barnard in
collaboration with ▷Flora Eldershaw. This is an
ambitious anti-Utopian novel, set in the 24th
century, where the protagonist, Knarf, reads his
retrospective novel, set in 20th-century Sydney
during a time of war and pestilence, to his friend,
an archaeologist. Knarf's retrospective deals with
the adventures of Harry Munster, a typical
Australian, during World War III, the destruction
of Sydney and the loss of Australian sovereignty.
The destructive feature of Australian life, in both
centuries, is seen to be apathy. First published in
a heavily censored form in 1947, with an
abbreviated title, *Tomorrow and Tomorrow*, the first
uncensored edition, with the full title, was
published in 1983.

Tomorrow Will Always Come (1965)
A powerful novel by the Caribbean writer ▷Clara
Rosa De Lima, this work depicts 'the poverty, the
corruption and the scheming of some Third

World politicians' in a way that few Caribbean
writers have done before. De Lima examines the
political situation in Brazil before the removal of
the capital city from Rio de Janeiro to Brasilia in
1960, and illustrates the open corruption of the
country's political figures. A central concern is the
use of women as sexual objects, and the poverty
and debasement to which women are subjected.
She depicts sexual desire openly, and suggests
that sexual exploitation is part of the political
process and the culture of poverty.
  Apart from short reviews, little critical attention
has been given to this work.

'To My Burrissa' (1757)
This poem by the North American writer ▷Annis
Boudinot Stockton was composed as a parting
tribute to her friend, ▷Esther Edwards Burr,
after visiting Burr on 11 April 1757. Burr noted
that 'she wrote standing the last thing she did
before she left the house. It was done in about 10.
Minutes or less.' The expedience of its
composition explains some of the unrhymed
quatrains, but it is a testament to Stockton's
poetic abilities and to Burr's qualities as a woman
friend, who, in the opening line, is termed
'Lovliest of Women!'.

**Ton beau capitaine (1987) (Your Fine
Captain)**
This play by the Guadeloupean (French Antilles)
writer, ▷Simone Schwarz-Bart was first
produced by the Centre d'Action Culturelle de
Guadeloupe in 1987. It deals with a Haitian
couple who communicate by 'letters' recorded on
cassette while they are separated. The play is set
in the one-roomed house in Guadeloupe in which
Wilnor, a marginalized migrant labourer from
Haiti, is living. The woman, Marie-Ange, who has
remained in Haiti, is present in her absence
through her voice on the cassette. Incorporating
elements from other traditions – Haitian *vaudou*
(▷voodoo) and the Japanese *Noh* play, for
example – the play not only presents a love
relationship which is shaped and stretched,
threatened and consolidated by the material
pressures of economic reality, but also brings to
the fore the disparity in standards of living and
expectation which drive a man to leave his family
for the lure of prosperity in an island still under
French rule.

Top Girls (1982)
Play by English dramatist ▷Caryl Churchill.
Written in the context of the potential meanings
generated by Margaret Thatcher's role as the first
woman Prime Minister of Britain, Churchill's play
explores the history of female success and
achievement. It opens with a dinner party at which
Marlene is celebrating her appointment as
managing director of an employment agency;
guests include successful and independent women
from history, including Pope Joan, from the 9th-
century and the 19th-century traveller ▷Isabella
Bird Bishop. Churchill uses dialogue to explore

the issue of women's achievement, and to analyze whether success is an individual or a communal goal. The dinner party conservation is a heterogeneous medley of speeches which undercuts any sense of reciprocity of commitment or consensus of ideals. As the play moves into a contemporary scenario, further 'role models' are brought into view, and the play investigates the success of women who have adopted masculine patterns of behaviour. As is typical of Churchill plays, *Top Girls'* analysis of the disjunction between individual achievement and communal responsibility, and whether, for women, this is rooted in the short history of women's active solidarity, is left without resolution or closure.

▷Travel writing (19th-century Britain)

Török, Sophié

Hungarian novelist. Her novel, *Hintz tanársegéd úr* (*Mr Hintz the Professor's Assistant*), describes the pain and misery of wifedom, motherhood, the passing of youthful beauty, and lovesickness. She was married to the poet Babits Mihály (1883–1941).

Torre, Malcolm ▷Mitchell, Gladys

Torres, Xohana (born 1931)

Spanish novelist. Born in Santiago de Compostela, Torres was very involved in the Galician cultural movement. She created the first totally Galician radio programme. Her main literary work is *Adiós, María* (1971), which deals with the problem, endemic in Galicia, of emigration from the deprived, overpopulated areas to the wealthier regions of Spain.

▷Galician women's writing

Torrezão, Guiomar (1844–1898)

Portuguese novelist, dramatist and editor. She spent her childhood in Cape Verde, where her father worked as a customs official. After his death the family moved back to Portugal, and Torrezão took up teaching to help support the family. In 1869 she published her first novel, *Uma Alma de Mulher* (*A Woman's Soul*), which, four years later, was followed by a collection of romantic fiction entitled *Rosas Pálidas* (*Pale Roses*). Among her best-known works is *A Família Albergaria* (1874) (*The Boarding-house Family*), a historical novel beginning in 1824, when royalists and constitutionalists battled for control of the country.

Torrezão also wrote for the theatre, and several of her plays were staged in Portugal and Brazil. But she gained her widest audience with the magazine *Alamanaque das Senhoras* (*Ladies' Almanac*), which she founded in 1871. Ten years later she took on the editorship of another magazine, *Ribaltas e Gambiarras* (*Footlights and Stage Lights*). She was one of the first women in Portugal to make a living as a writer – a fact for which she was both praised and derided. An ardent supporter of women's rights, she wrote eloquently about a number of women's issues, especially about educational reform.

Torriani, Maria Antonietta ▷Colombi, la Marchesa

Tosatti, Barbara Maria (1891–1934)

Italian poet. Born in Modena, She was not particularly well-educated, but appears to have developed a love for poetry through reading other Italian poets, particularly Foscolo and Leopardi. Her own poetry reflects theirs in its melancholic vein. It is also deeply religious, and classically structured (▷poetry). Some of her work was published in *Nuova Antologia* during her lifetime, and a collection came out in 1932, a couple of years before her early death. Her brother edited all of her writings in a posthumous collection, *Canti e preghiere. Liriche, pensieri, lettere* (1939) (*Lyric Poems and Prayers. Poetry, Thoughts, and Letters*).

Tostevin, Lola Lemire (born 1937)

Canadian poet, born Lola Lemire in Timmons, Ontario, she studied in Paris and at the Universities of Alberta and Toronto. Her divided or doubled linguistic (her parents are francophone) is active in *Color of Her Speech* (1982). *Gyno Text* (1983) connects the theorization of woman's body and language (▷*écriture féminine*). *Double Standards* (1985) constructs a refraction, a re-taking of language through writing. *'Sophie* (1988) explores the semiotics of desire; it includes a French section, *'espaces vers'*, Tostevin reintegrating her mother tongue in 'midspeak.'

Bib: Neuman S. and Kamboureli, S. (eds), ▷*A Mazing Space*

To the Lighthouse (1927)

Novel by English writer ▷Virginia Woolf. Written shortly after ▷*Mrs Dalloway* (1925), the novel develops Woolf's ▷stream-of-consciousness technique through its layering of subjective perceptions and rapid transitions between multiple consciousnesses. The novel is composed in three distinct stages, and the final movement picks up the narrative many years after the events described in the first section. This device dramatizes the devastations and disruptions of World War I. Focusing on the holiday home of Mr and Mrs Ramsay, characters loosely modelled on Woolf's parents, the novel explores questions of temporality and 'objective' reality, placing centrally within the narrative a concern with the 'extreme obscurity of human relationships'. Yet, in the comparisons and contrasts made through the central figures of Mrs Ramsay and Lily Briscoe, the novel also ties these issues to a discussion of women's sexuality, creativity and subjectivity, drawing out analyses of masculine and feminine texts, and of the gendering of modes of perception. It is a novel that also engages explicitly with Freudian ▷psychoanalysis, and particularly with Freud's reading of the Oedipal scenario. Not only is the novel seen as one of the exemplary texts of literary ▷modernism, its particular stream-of-consciousness mode has also been treated as the apotheosis of Western ▷realism. *To the Lighthouse* therefore occupies a central place in debates concerning the definitional parameters of literary modernism.

To the Memory of Childhood (1988)
Russian writer ▷Lidiia Chukóvskaia's moral courage and respect for the integrity and power of the written word were formed under the tutelage of her father, the literary scholar, translator and children's poet Kornei Chukóvskii (1882–1969). *To the Memory*, translated into English in 1988, is both loving tribute and pedagogical treatise, entirely focused (to the virtual exclusion of such factors as her mother's role) on the upbringing full of poetry and play which the eccentric and sometimes difficult Chukóvskii managed to give his three children.

'To the Memory of My Late Valuable Friend Susannah Wright' (1981)
Poem by North American author ▷Hannah Griffitts. Written after Wright's death on 1 December 1784 at the age of 88, this poem by Griffitts ('Fidelia') is a memorial to the genius of her lifelong friend and sister poet with whom she had shared her writings and her thoughts. Wright ('Veneria') is lauded for her 'innate powers superior' and for her disdain of the world's 'tinsel and its glare', suggesting that among the circle of Philadelphia women poets who shared their writings the decision not to publish was valued. The style is traditional elegaic form, but the emphasis upon the woman and her writings is notable.

To the Rev. James Davenport on His Departure from Boston (1742)
Poem by North American writer ▷Sarah Parsons Moorhead. As an advocate of the North American evangelical revival known as the Great Awakening, Sarah Parsons Moorhead of Boston, Massachusetts, published this cautionary poem as both an admonishment and a gesture of support to one of the movement's leaders. Moorhead reproves Davenport for his 'naming out' or public criticisms of 'our worthy Ministers'; she suggests that he and the movement would prosper if he were to seek 'Shade' from his public role and reassess the purpose of the Awakening. In a dream sequence, she suggests the gains to be attained if he were to pursue such action. *To the Rev. James Davenport* is a significant contribution to the literature of the Great Awakening, both for its poetic features and for the woman's voice that emerges in what is traditionally deemed a male-dominated religious movement.
　▷'Lines . . . Dedicated to the Rev. Mr Gilbert Tennent'

Touch to My Tongue (1984)
Canadian writer ▷Daphne Marlatt's erotic prose poems express desire for the body of language through the body of skin. 'Musing with Mothertongue', in its essaying, permits the body of language to give birth to the female body: 'putting the living body of language together means putting the world together, the world we live in: an act of composition, an act of birthing, us, uttered and outered there in it.'

Tout compte fait (1972) ▷All Said and Done (1974)

Townsend, Sue (born 1945)
English dramatist and novelist. Townsend's writings are concerned with the effect of Thatcherism on working-class experience, and articulate the concerns and anxieties of multi-cultural urban life in the 1980s. Her first play, *Womberang* (1979), addresses the demise of the 'caring' institutions, and the impoverished state of the British National Health Service. *Bazaar and Rummage* (1982) is a play about agoraphobia, and *Great Celestial Cow* (1984) looks at the effect of cultural displacement on Asian women living in Leicester. Her novel *Rebuilding Coventry* (1990) explores the fantasy life of the protagonist, Coventry, and her liberation from her humdrum existance as a suburban housewife. Townsend is best-known for her two books *The Secret Diary of Adrian Mole Aged 13³/₄* (1982) and its sequel, *The Growing Pains of Adrian Mole* (1984), which provide a teenager's view of life in England under Thatcherism, and which have been dramatized very successfully for television.

Traba, Marta (1930–1983)
Argentinian novelist, art and literary critic who spent most of her life in Colombia. A daughter of Spanish immigrants to Argentina, after her graduation she moved to Colombia, whose nationality she adopted in the year of her death. She travelled widely, spending time in Spanish America, as well as the United States. She studied in Argentina from 1934 to 1946, and graduated in philosophy and history of art at the University of Buenos Aires, earning a scholarship to Chile. She also lived in Italy from 1951 to 1952.
　Latin America was her special focus, and she published in all genres – essays, criticism and novels – and taught art and literature at several Latin American and North American universities.
　In 1954 she moved to Colombia, where she founded *Prisma* magazine and, in 1965, the Museum of Modern Art in Bogotá. She was always an outspoken defender of democracy and human rights, and an opposer of corruption and tyranny in Latin America (see her '*Entrevista atemporal*', 1984, 'Atemporal Interview'), in all her criticism. As a result of her political activism, she was even expelled from Colombia by President Carlos Lleras, following her protest against the presence of the military at the university, on 23 June 1967.

Traba was also a feminist who urged women to speak for themselves. Her first book of poems was *Historia natural de la alegría* (1951) (*Natural History of Happiness*). Her first novel, *Las ceremonias del verano* (1966) (*Summer Ceremonies*), which received the Casa de las Américas Prize of that year, is narrated by a woman who spends her life travelling. Her best-known novel is *Homérica Latina* (1979) (*Homeric Latin*), in which she again combines the idea of a personal odyssey, forced by expatriation, with the fate of Latin America. It was the first novel by a Latin American woman to put forward a personal reaction to the torture of political prisoners and political kidnapping. These are also referred to in *Conversaciqn al sur* (1981) (*Conversation to the South*) and *En cualquier lugar* (1984) (*In Any Place*), the first two novels in a trilogy. This was to be completed by *Veinte ãnos no es nada* (*Twenty Years is Nothing*), but it was left unfinished following her sudden death in an accident. She, her second husband, Angel Rama, and other Spanish American writers who were flying from Paris to attend the First Spanish American Culture Conference in Bogota, were killed when their aeroplane crashed. Several of her novels have been published posthumously.

Other works: *El museo vacio* (1958) (*The Empty Museum*); *Los cuatro monstruos cardinales* (1965) (*The Four Cardinal Monsters*); *Premios de Casa* (1966) (*House Prizes*); *El son se quedó en Cuba* (1966) (*The Sound Stayed in Cuba*); *Los laberintos insolados* (1967) (*Exposed Labyrinths*); *Pasó así* (1968); *La jugada del sexto día* (1969) (*The Sixth Day's Play*); *Dos décadas vulnerables en las artes plásticas latinoamericanas, 1950–1970* (1973) (*Two Vulnerable Decades in the Plastic Arts of Latin America, 1950–1970*); *Siglo XX en las artes plásticas latinoamericanas: una guía* (1982–1983) (*Twentieth-century Plastic Arts in Latin America: A Guide*); *Marta Traba: selección de textos* (1984) (*Marta Traba: Selected Texts*); *De la mañana a la noche* (1986) (*From Morning to Night*), and *Casa sin fin* (1988) (*Endless House*).

Tractarian Movement ▷Oxford Movement (Tractarian Movement)

Tracy, Mona Innes (1892–1959)
New Zealand children's author, journalist. In 1925, in addition to caring for her two small children, she published her first book *Piriki's Princess and other Stories of New Zealand* which contained stories first published in the Christchurch *Sun*. Racy, romantic adventure stories followed which, unusually for children's books of the time, featured strong Maori characters and the issues of mixed marriage, loyalties and race. She wrote stories, serials and poetry for several Australasian magazines, but was best-known through her women's column in *Aussie* magazine. Here she wrote under various pen-names, commenting on the fate of women, women's pastimes, interests and fashions.
▷Children's Literature, New Zealand

Tragedie of Antonie, The (1590)
English writer ▷Mary Sidney Herbert's ▷translation of Robert Garnier's French Senecan play. Part of the Elizabethans' renewed interest in classical models, especially Seneca, *Antonie* conforms to the standard conventions of Renaissance classicism in its adherence to the dramatic unities, its division into five acts, its employment of long and highly rhetorical speeches, and its minimal action. *Antonie* was an important influence on Thomas Kyd's *Cornelia* (1594) and Samuel Daniel's *Cleopatra* (1594) and *Philotas* (1594). Herbert's *Antonie* also exemplifies the activity of Renaissance translation as an art form rather than a purely mechanical exercise. With the exception of most of the speeches by the chorus, Herbert translated Garnier's rhymed alexandrines into blank verse. In doing so, she created a contrast between the three major characters' complicated and evolving dialogue concerning fortune and the chorus's over-simplified ideas.

Tragedie of Mariam, Faire Queene of Jewry, The (1613)
Play by English writer ▷Elizabeth Cary. Written sometime between 1602 and 1604, *Mariam* is the first play originally composed (as opposed to translated) by an Englishwoman to be published. The tragedy opens when false rumours of Herod's death set the fateful actions of various characters into motion. Mariam grieves for the loss of her husband, yet rejoices at his death, for he is also the murderer of her kin; Herod's first wife (whom he abandoned in favor of Mariam) plots to restore her own children as heirs to the kingdom, and Herod's brother makes a forbidden marriage. Upon discovering Herod is alive, his sister, Salome, plots the downfall of her sister-in-law, Mariam, and her own husband. Salome manipulates Herod's already impulsive nature, enflaming his jealousy. He orders the execution of several characters, including his faithful wife. Based on Josephus's *Antiquities*, Cary's play belongs to a tradition of Herod and Mariam plays and is an example of the Renaissance vogue for classical – and Senecan-influenced tragedy. It is characterized by an absence of dramatic action, an adherence to the unities of time and place, and observation of Renaissance notions of decorum.
Bib: Beilin, E.V., *Redeeming Eve: Women Writers of the English Renaissance*; Cotton, N., *Women Playwrights in England, 1363–1750*; Fischer, S.K., 'Elizabeth Cary and Tyrannyk Domestic and Religious' in Hannay, M. (ed.), *Silent But for the Word*; Travitsky, B., 'The *Feme Covert* in Elizabeth Cary's *Mariam*' in Levin C. and Watson, J. (eds.), *Ambiguous Realities: Women in the Middle Ages and Renaissance*; Valency, M., *Tragedies of Herod and Mariamne*.

Tragic Menagerie, The (1907)
This autobiographically-based set of stories from the life of a gentry girl, Vera ('Faith'), growing up in late 19th-century Russia is the finest work of

the author, ▷Lidiia Zinóv'eva-Annibál. The stories owe their success to the fact that she was writing with strong moral passion about a subject, the psychology of children, at which Russian women writers excelled. Despite, or because of, her early death, a nurturing mother forms the moral centre of Vera's life as the child passes from story to story through a series of experiences that foster her growing awareness of injustice in the world. Men are shown in a negative light as generally aggressive, cruel and unjust. Among those who reacted positively to the book were ▷Gíppius, and ▷Tsvetáeva.

Bib: Pachmuss, T. (trans.), *Stories from The Tragic Menagerie, Women Writers in Russian Modernism.*

Traill, Catherine Parr (1802–1899)

Born in London, England to the literary Strickland family, she was a botanist, writer and Canadian pioneer. Her sister ▷Susanna Moodie is known for ▷*Roughing it in the Bush* (1852), and her other sisters, Elizabeth and Agnes wrote *Lives of the Queens of England*. Shortly after Catherine's birth, her father retired and the family moved to Suffolk, which gave the Stricklands an opportunity to enjoy the natural world of Waveney Valley. Their education was informal but pragmatic, and included not only sewing and embroidery but history, English literature and the classics. Their isolation was an impetus to write, and by 1818 Catherine Parr Strickland had published *The Tell Tale: An Original Collection of Moral and Amusing Stories.* The extent of her contribution to periodicals and ladies' magazines of the day is uncertain, but she wrote more than a dozen juvenile and natural history books before her marriage, including one that prefigures her interest in Canada (*The Young Emigrants; or, Pictures of Life in Canada*, 1926). Catherine and her new husband, Thomas Traill, whom she met through Susanna's husband, Dunbar Moodie, emigrated to Upper Canada to take up his military land grant in 1832. There, they lived in various places until after Thomas's death in 1859, when Catherine built a house at Lakefield.

Catherine Traill is essentially considered a Canadian writer because of the many books she wrote about Canada. Her best-known is ▷*The Backwoods of Canada: Being Letters from the Wife of an Emigrant Officer; Illustrative of the Domestic Economy of British America* (1836), which details the Traills's first three years in the bush. Her children's stories and sketches were widely published; *The Female Emigrant's Guide, and Hints on Canadian Housekeeping*, published in 1854, went through several editions as *The Canadian Settler's Guide.* Her pragmatism in the face of hardship and difficulty is evident from her titles; she seemed able to handle every challenge. She wrote many studies of natural history and botany, including *Canadian Wild Flowers* (1868), *Studies of Plant Life in Canada* (1885) and *Pearls and Pebbles; or, Notes of an Old Naturalist* (1895). Late in her life she received considerable public recognition for this writing. She seems, from her writing, an

excellent example of a migrant to the new world; she was interested in its difference, and better able to handle its hardships than her sister, Susanna Moodie. ▷Margaret Laurence makes her an interesting fictional character in her novel, ▷*The Diviners.*

▷Crawford, Isabella Valancy

Bib: Eaton, S., *Lady of the Backwoods*; Fowler, M., *The Embroidered Tent*; Morris, A., *The Gentle Pioneers: Five Nineteenth-Century Canadians.*

Transcendentalism

US 19th-century individualist philosophy. Derived from Kant (1724–1804), transcendentalism was given a distinctive native (and sometimes mystical) focus by a group in Concord, Massachusetts, which included Bronson Alcott (1799–1888), father of ▷Louisa May Alcott; Ralph Waldo Emerson (1803–1882); and Henry David Thoreau (1817–1862). Its most consistent literary expression was in ▷*The Dial*, edited by ▷Margaret Fuller (Ossoli).

Transformations (1972)

Poems by US writer ▷Anne Sexton. The poems in *Tranformations* retell sixteen 'stories from Grimm', reinterpreting them as harshly comic Freudian (▷psychoanalysis) scenarios, with the emphasis placed on female subjects, particularly daughters. Sexton's versions of Snow White, Cinderella, Rumpelstiltskin, the Frog Prince, Rapunzel, Sleeping Beauty, and so on, are narrated by the ironic, North American, disillusioned voice of 'a middle-aged witch: me', well-versed in Freud and cynically aware of the passive and disadvantaged position enforced on the little girl by the myths which define femininity. As she says of Snow White with characteristic knowing irony, 'The virgin is a lovely number . . . rolling her china-blue eyes / open and shut. / Open to say / Good Day Mama / and shut for the thrust / of the unicorn'. Bruno Bettelheim cited these poems to illustrate his psychoanalytically informed re-readings of fairytales in *The Uses of Enchantment* (1978). More recently, feminist critics have admired their sophisticated ironizing of the social construction of women. Alicia Ostriker in her influential essay 'The Thieves of Language: Women Poets and Revisionary Mythmaking' (*Stealing the Language*, 1986) reads Sexton's book as a pioneering work of feminist redefinition, arguing that 'the axis *Transformations* turns on is Necessity (here seen as fixed and damaging psychosocial patterns) versus Freedom.' By contrast, Jan Montefiore has suggested in *Feminism and Poetry*, that the Freudian determinism implicit in the poems' approach may limit the feminist possibilities of their redefinition of myths. Whichever interpretation one sides with, *Transformations* remains among the most powerful, acid and funny of women's rewritings of traditional mythologies.

Transit of Venus, The (1980)

Australian novel by ▷Shirley Hazzard. Two sisters, Caro and Grace, are expatriate Australians engaged on a search for love in a world in which the full ramifications of chance and destiny are explored. The connotations of Venus as both planet in a pre-determined orbit, and as Goddess of Love, its eclipse ('transit'), its connection with the discovery of the new land of Australia, and the extension of this to ships, airships, their vulnerability and the vulnerability of love, make for a complex plot. *The Transit of Venus* won the USA National Book Critics' Award 1980 for the Best Novel of 1980.

Translation (Renaissance England)
During the 16th century the art of translation took on a renewed importance as a result of the rising class of educated ▷humanists and reformers, and the newly imported printing presses. Translations were extremely important to the influx into England of ideas from the contemporary Continent and from classical antiquity. They provided a valuable way of gaining access to the ideas of important works in foreign languages. Humanist educators often required both female and male students to translate texts into English, and then back into the original language. Valued highly during the Renaissance, translation was nevertheless considered 'feminine' enough for women to decently undertake. Most early works by women are translations, primarily religious works. It has been suggested that the act of translation provided women with a way of entering into religious controversies, and several translations by Renaissance Englishwomen were of fair importance to their own time. Among the most influential are ▷Anne Bacon's ▷*An Apologie or answeare in defence of the Churche of England* (1564) and ▷Mary Sidney Herbert's ▷*Psalms of David* (c 1586). Other Renaissance translators include: ▷Mary Basset, ▷Elizabeth Cary, ▷Elizabeth Tudor, ▷Joanna Lumley, ▷Anne Locke, ▷Margaret Roper, ▷Elizabeth Russell, ▷Margaret Beaufort, ▷Margaret Tyler ▷Dorcas Martin, ▷Mary Tudor, ▷Catherine Parr and Katherine Philips.
▷Prefaces; Protestant Reformation

Trapnel, Anna (fl 1650s)
English prophet writing during the Protectorate (1653–1658) of Oliver Cromwell (1599–1658). In a spiritual biography prefacing ▷*The Cry of a Stone* (1654), she writes, 'I am Anna Trapnel, daughter of William Trapnel, Shipwright' – of Poplar in London. *The Cry of a Stone* consists of verse prophecies uttered during a trance and recorded by an amanuensis. In *The Report and Plea* (1654) she records her preaching and prophesy in Cornwall, where she was apprehended on suspicion of being a witch. She tells of her arrest while she was in a prophetic trance: 'They caused my eyelids to be pulled up, for they said I held them fast, because I would deceive the people . . . One of the justices pinched me by the nose, and caused my pillow to be pulled from under my head, and kept pulling me, and calling me, but I heard none of this stir and bustle.' She dramatizes

her interview with the justices and her later imprisonment in Bridewell. Trapnel's prophetic writing is highly politically charged, and (like ▷Mary Cary) she uses the Book of Daniel to talk about political events. In a famous passage she envisions Oliver Cromwell as a bull.
Other publications: *Strange and Wonderful News from White-hall* (1654); *A Legacy For Saints* (1654); *Anna Trapnels Report and Plea* (1654), and *A Voice For the King of Saints* (1656).
▷Wentworth, Anne; Allen, Hannah (Archer)

Traske, Mary, and Margaret Smith (fl 1660)
North American letter-writers. Little is known of their individual lives, but together they provide one of the earliest accounts of the resistance by Quaker women in Massachusetts to persecution by the Puritans. In a ▷'Joint Letter from Mary Traske and Margaret Smith . . . to . . . John Endicott', they admonish the Puritan leaders for their failure to allow dissenters to express their opinions, and they detail at some length the tenets of their faith as further admonishment to the preachings of Calvinism. When the letter was written, they had been incarcerated between eight and ten months in a Boston gaol for speaking freely about their beliefs.
▷Early North American Quaker women's writings

Travel writing (19th-century Britain)
Many 19th-century British women writers travelled abroad and recorded their experiences in published accounts. Some, such as ▷Mary Shelley, ▷Anna Eliza Bray and ▷Frances Power Cobbe were tourists primarily, and travelled mainly within Europe. Others, including ▷Frances Trollope, ▷Anna Jameson, ▷Harriet Martineau and ▷Barbara Bodichon visited North America and wrote about their experiences in the 'New World'. Bodichon also travelled to the Sahara with ▷Matilda Betham-Edwards, who published a record of the trip. Another group of women, including ▷Isabella Bird Bishop and ▷Mary Kingsley were genuine 'explorers'. Bishop journeyed through China, Japan and India; Kingsley in West Africa. In recent years, feminist scholars have begun to examine travel writing in relation to gender and colonialism.
▷Victoria, Queen
Bib: Foster, Shirley, *Across New Worlds: 19th Century Women Travellers and Their Writings.*

Treatise on Ancient and Modern Literature, A (1803)
Translation of *De la littérature* (1800) by French writer ▷Madame de Staël. One of de Staël's major works, exploring the relationship between literature and different social, political, religious and cultural contexts, including variations in climate. In Part One she provides an extensive tableau of literary works and compares the literatures of ancient Greece and Rome, preferring the latter. Part Two analyzes the French Enlightenment, advocating for the future

the study of philosophy, nature, the psychology of passions, and a literature that speaks to the imagination and the heart. She proposes that the criteria of classicism should be rejected in favour of a more personal aesthetic. Arguing that literature has the power to effect social and political change, she denounces the censorship exercised under Napoleon.

Treatise on Domestic Economy, A (1841)
US comprehensive and scientific compendium of household management by ▷Catharine Beecher. The *Treatise* reflected Beecher's valuing of the domestic as emblem and centre of women's separate sphere, as well as her continuous promotion of women's education. Many chapters focus on informed understanding of topics ranging from modern plumbing to physiology. Popular from first publication through a large number of subsequent editions, the *Treatise* made Beecher's fame and fortune. In 1869, Beecher and her sister, ▷Harriet Beecher Stowe, expanded the *Treatise* to *The American Woman's Home*. In 1873, it was revised and retitled *The New Housekeeper's Manual*.
Bib: Beecher, Catharine and Stowe, Harriet Beecher, *The American Woman's Home: Or, Principles of Domestic Science*.

Tree Grows in Brooklyn, A (1943)
US novel. Born of German immigrants, author Betty Smith (1896–1972) concentrates on themes of social mobility and progress. Smith's bestselling semi-autobiography describes urban slum life in the 1900s. Francie Nolan, the young heroine, experiences misery and squalor with humour and pride. Smith juxtaposes scenes of family closeness with scenes of cruelty. Francie is humiliated at school, suffers the consequences of her father's alcoholism, and is almost raped. Typical of Smith's heroines, Francie transcends social, economic and biological forces through her inner strength.
Other works by Betty Smith include: *Tomorrow Will Be Better* (1948), *Maggie-Now* (1958) and *Joy in the Morning* (1963).

Tree's Shadow, A (1970–1972)
Work by Japanese novelist ▷Sata Ineko which won the Noma Prize for Literature. Keiko is a Chinese woman who was atom-bombed. She falls in love with Asada, a painter, who dies of liver cancer caused by the atom bomb. In his last picture there is no colour – only three dead trees drawn in the centre. Keiko shares a sense of deep isolation with Asada and his wife. After Asada's death, she participates in the movement against the atom-bomb, and dies alone, seven years later, at the age of forty-six. Keiko, who tries to find some meaning to her life, can be thought of as standing like a lonely tree.

Trefusis, Violet (1894–1972)
English novelist. The lover of ▷Vita Sackville West, with whom she eloped in 1919, shortly after Trefusis's marriage. The affair was over by 1921, and Trefusis returned to her husband, living in Paris and publishing novels which included *Sortie de Secours* (1929), *Echo* (1931) and *Hunt the Slipper* (1937). Trefusis returned to England during World War II, subsequently publishing her autobiography, *Don't Look Round* (1952). Her fiction takes as its subject the upper classes.

Tremain, Rose (born 1943)
English novelist, historian and dramatist. Tremain is Tutor in Creative Writing at the University of East Anglia. Her first two books, *The Fight for Freedom for Women* (1973), a study of the British and US women's ▷suffrage movements, and a life of Stalin (1975), were published only in the United States. Tremain's first published novel was *Sadler's Birthday* (1976). Her fiction explores the perils of emotional life, looking at the difficulties, but also the support within close relationships. Other novels include: *The Swimming Pool Season* (1985), *Restoration* (1989). Plays include: *Temporary Shelter* (1984), *Mother's Day* (1980) and *Yoga Class* (1984).

Trial of Dedan Kimathi, The (1976)
Play by Kenyan dramatist and academic ▷Micere Githae Mugo co-authored with Kenyan writer Ngugi wa Thiong'o. The play highlights the role of Kenyan women in the nationalist struggle.

Tribuna, La (1883) (The Female Orator)
Novel by Spanish writer ▷Pardo Bazán. It is the first novel written in Spain specifically about the female urban proletariat. The novel is set in a tobacco factory in Galicia; the women are shown to be exploited economically, and sexually, by their male 'masters'.

Trier Mørch, Dea (born 1941)
Danish prose writer, essayist and artist. Trier Mørch grew up in Copenhagen. Her mother was an unmarried architect who had several children. This unusual childhood has been an important theme in her prose, as in *Kastanieallen* (1978) (*Chestnut Avenue*). Because Trier Mørch was dyslexic she was educated as an artist, and worked as a member of the socialist artist's collective 'Røde Mor' ('Red Mother').
By the time she had become a mother of three, she began to write, and illustrated her own books. Her début was the collection of lyrical essays *Sørgmunter realisme* (1968) (*Realism of Joy and Sorrow*), about her education as an artist in eastern Europe. She had her major breakthrough with the novel *Vinterbørn* (1976) (*Winter's Child*, 1986). It takes place in a maternity ward, and follows the pregnancies and deliveries of eighteen women. The novel is simply told, and its clear ▷realism tends to become sentimental. It depicts female solidarity, and is very optimistic about modern technology and hospitals. The strength of Trier Mørch's prose lies in its descriptions of parenthood and childhood, eg *Den indre by* (1980)

(*City*) and *Aftenstjernen* (1982) (*Evening Star*, 1988).

Trifles (1916)

Play by US dramatist ▷Susan Glaspell. Set in rural North America, *Trifles* uses the investigation into the murder of farmer, John Wright, to explore the oppression of women in marriage. While the Sheriff, County Attorney and a neighbouring farmer search for clues 'outside' the house, their wives use a shared experience of marriage and the home to decode the minute signs of disturbance to the domestic order. An untidy kitchen and uneven stitching in a quilt – trifles – indicate to the women that Minnie Wright has killed her husband. A song bird, with its neck wrung, provides both the clue to her motive, and a metaphor for the wife's subjection to physical and emotional abuse. The true criminal is the dead man, not his murderer. The play climaxes in the women's decision to side with Minnie Wright by destroying the clues, and not to preserve a loyalty to their husbands, representative of patriarchal law. The play, also published in short story form as 'Jury of Her Peers', has become an allegory of gender and reading for recent feminist critics.
Bib: Fetterley, Judith, *The Resisting Reader*.

Tri gaštanové kone (1940) (*Three Chestnut Horses*)

Slovak novel by ▷Margita Figuli. It is one of the best examples from the Slovak school of Lyrical Prose. The novel is based on a triangle of intimate relationships between a woman and two men of widely differing values. The ample plot was intended to demonstrate the conflict between aesthetic and moral qualities. The happy ending stresses the triumph of truth, goodness, love, beauty and morality. The fatalism of the characters fits a Christian idea of happiness won through suffering. Figuli has written an apotheosis of woman, and has tried to express the permanency of human feelings. She uses biblical and magical elements, and also elements of folklore and fairytale.

Trilogia (1982) (*A Trilogy*)

A posthumous publication of the three best-known works of ▷Clotilde Marghieri: *Life in a Country House* of 1960, *The Female Boarders of Poggio Gherardo* of 1963 and *The Marked Arm* of 1970. Memory is an important unifying thread through these works. All are given as first-person narratives, more or less autobiographical. Marghieri appears in them as the female protagonist, keen to learn and yet defensive. The narrative is moving, particularly in its description of the mother-daughter relationship, and humorous in its sometimes malicious recreation of famous literary and artistic figures of the period. The collection is interesting for its personalized view of a slice of Italian life.

Trilogy (1973)

Poem sequence by US writer ▷H.D. The three volumes which make up the poem sequence *Trilogy* were written and published in London, England, during World War II. The flexible verse form which modulates between a conversational tone, powerful lyricism and ritual incantation represents the best of H.D.'s mature style. The poem challenges Judaeo-Christian tradition by interweaving Egyptian, classical Greek and gnostic religious myths with biblical stories, providing a critique of religious, cultural and social tradition. Set in the London Blitz, *The Walls Do Not Fall* (1944) constructs authority for the poet, despised by a utilitarian, militaristic society as the purveyor and interpreter of a lost past which will lead to the renewal of civilization. Poets are 'bearers of the secret wisdom' and 'voyagers, discoverers / of the not-known, / the unrecorded;'. *Tribute to the Angels* (1945) uses the vision of a woman within a book, the pages of which are blank, as a vehicle to challenge the patriarchal biblical authority of St John in 'Revelations'. The biblical myth of the apocalypse retains the war motif. The *Flowering of the Rod* (1945) transforms the story of the birth of Christ and the New Testament. Beginning with the crucifixion and ending with the nativity, the third book echoes the entire structure of *Trilogy*, from death to rebirth. *The Flowering of the Rod's* use of anecdote, rumour and personal experience, against the cultural authority of the written word, combines with the centrality H.D. gives to the story of the outcast and fallen woman, Mary Magdalene, to investigate and relocate traditional theology's definitions of woman as mother, virgin and whore. The three sections of *Trilogy* were collected under that title in 1973.

Trinidad and Tobago

This geographical region of the Caribbean is English-speaking. The population of Trinidad comprises 43 per cent of African descent, 40 per cent of Indian descent, and 17 per cent European, Chinese and other. It is the birthplace of ▷Dionne Brand, ▷Rosa Guy, ▷Merle Hodge, ▷Amryl Johnson, Enid Kurton Lewis (born 1940), Marina Maxwell (now known as Marina Omowals, born 1934), Judy Miles (born 1944), ▷Marlene Nourbese Phillip, Shirley Tappan and Marguerite Wyke (born 1928).
  ▷Carnival

Triolet, Elsa (1897–1970)

French novelist, born Elsa Kogan in Russia. She arrived in France in 1928 as the wife of André Triolet, whom she later left for the French poet Louis Aragon. Through him, she was closely involved with the Surrealist movement, sustaining Aragon's creative talent and communist zeal for forty years. He celebrated her in his wartime poetry, *Les Yeux d'Elsa* (1943) (*Elsa's eyes*) and *Le Crève-coeur* (1942) (*Heart break*). Her own works are written in the style of social realism, and adhere to orthodox communist views. *Le Premier accroc coûte deux cents francs* (1945) (*A Fine of Two*

Hundred Francs) won her a literary prize, and it was followed by a cycle of novels: *L'Age du nylon* (1953) (*The Nylon Age*), *Roses à crédit* (1959) (*Roses on Credit*) *Luna Park* (1959) and *L'Ame* (1963) (*The Soul*).

Trip to Parnassus; or, The Judgment of Apollo on Dramatic Authors and Performers: A Poem, A (1788)

A North American dramatist and actress, ▷Susanna Haswell Rowson draws on her own experience in this poem to defend the integrity, morality and talents of dramatists and performers. She was less skilled in poetry than in fiction, and her poem's theme is of greater significance than its quality.

Tristan, Flora (1803–1844)

French political and feminist writer and novelist. The illegitimate daughter of a French mother and a rich Peruvian father, Tristan married her employer, a French lithographer named Chazal, who neglected her except to make her (repeatedly) pregnant, and attempted to kill her in 1838, by which time she had left him. After 1835, Tristan became involved with socialist and feminist groups in Paris, including the group that ran the *Gazette des femmes* (*Women's Gazette*), although she never belonged officially to any established faction. She published some early political pamphlets, and in 1838 wrote her first major work, *Pérégrinations d'une paria* (*Travels of an Outcast*), in which she describes a journey she made to Peru in order to reclaim her paternal inheritance, expresses her horror at the wretched conditions endured by Peruvian women, and argues in favour of feminine emancipation. She subsequently travelled to London to study working-class life in England, and published her influential and highly acclaimed *Promenades dans Londres* (1840) (*London Walks*), which chronicles the squalid existence led by the British urban proletariat, and offers a largely depressing vision of Victorian womanhood. Although impressed by some of the English women she encountered, she was horrified by the 'revolting contrast there is in England between the extreme servitude of women and the intellectual superiority of women authors'.

In 1843 Tristan wrote *L'Union ouvrière* (*Worker's Union*), a colossal theoretical work which is her best-known text, and provides a detailed analysis of the ways in which the working class must organize itself in order to achieve emancipation. For Tristan, effective social change had to involve radical improvements in the status of women – improvements which would enable working-class women to cease to represent an underprivileged sub-stratum, even within the oppressed ranks of the proletariat. She continued to campaign in favour of the Utopian revolution she envisaged, and died in Bordeaux, in the middle of a lengthy lecture tour. The embodiment of French socialist feminism in the 1840s, some of Tristan's most powerful writing is contained in the 1973 edition, *Flora Tristan: vie, oeuvres mêlées*

(*Flora Tristan: Life and Various Works*), presented and annotated by Dominique Desanti. Tristan also left a novel, *Méphis* (1838).

▷Feminine/Feminist journalism (France)
Bib: Balle, J., *Flora Tristan: socialisme et féminisme*; Desanti, D., *Flora Tristan: la femme révolté*; Puech, J., *La Vie et l'oeuvre de Flora Tristan*.

Triumph of Death, The (c 1593)

▷Translation of Petrarch's *Trionfo della Morte* (1470) by English writer ▷Mary Sidney Herbert. The section Herbert translated is divided into two chapters. The first contains a dream vision in which Petrarch meets a group of women who recount the death of his beloved Laura. The second chapter depicts a visionary encounter between the poet and the dead Laura, who finally confesses her love for the poet. Herbert's translation of Petrarch's *Trionfo*, an extremely popular and much-translated work during the Renaissance, remained in manuscript until the 20th century. Her work is especially striking because it retains the complicated *terza rima* (eleven-syllable lines, the last syllable unaccented, following the rhyme scheme aba bcb edc ded etc.) of the original Italian while sustaining a fluent translation into English.
Bib: Waller, G.F. (ed.), *The Triumph of Death and Other Unpublished and Uncollected Poems by Mary Sidney, Countess of Pembroke (1561–1621)*.

Trobairitz

Term referring to early medieval French women poets. The word means 'a woman who composes' and is derived from the Old Provençal word *trobar* meaning 'to invent by finding or discovering'. It was very rare in medieval Occitan, and is only found in one 13th-century romance. It has only recently been naturalized in English to designate the female equivalent of the *troubadour* in early medieval France, but is now widely accepted. The chronology of the *trobairitz*, who number some twenty named poets, is not merely a reflection of the chronology of the troubadours, but can nevertheless be most easily explained in relation to the five periods into which the male poets are usually divided: I (1140–1180); II (1140–1180); III (1180–1220); IV (1220–1260); V (1260–1300). There is no evidence of activity by *trobairitz* during periods I and II, or during the final period. The poetic forms used by the *trobairitz* mirror those used by their male counterparts: the *canso* or song, the *tenso* or alternating verse dialogue, both of which end in a *tornado* or *envoi* (refrain), and the *sirventes*, a song with a non-amorous theme, which may either tell of political passion or be dedicated to the glory of some great figure.

Troll-Borostyani, Irma von (1847–1912)

Austrian writer and feminist who used the pseudonym Veritas Leo Bergen. She wrote political essays, mainly on the rights of women. Her work includes *Die Mission unseres Jahrhunderts. Eine Studie über die Frauenfrage* (1878) (*The Mission of our Century: A Study on the*

Woman Question), *Die Gleichstellung der Geschlechter und die Reform der Jugenderziehung* (1887) (*The Equality of the Sexes and Reform in Education*), *Katechismus der Frauenbewegung* (1903) (*The Catechism of the Women's Movement*), and many more.

Trollope, Frances (1779–1863)

British novelist and ▷travel writer, the mother of novelist Anthony Trollope. She was born Frances Milton at Stapleton, near Bristol, and married Thomas Anthony Trollope in 1809, with whom she had six children. Her husband was continually beginning new careers, and failing at them. He tried his hand at law and farming, then in 1827 moved the family to North America to set up a business. This also failed, as did his next venture into the property market in London. The North American trip, however, stimulated Trollope to write *Domestic Manners of the Americans* (1832), which was a great success in Britain and brought further contracts. *Paris and the Parisians* appeared in 1836, *Vienna and the Austrians* in 1838 and *A Visit to Italy* in 1842. Although Trollope was over fifty when her first work appeared, she went on to publish more than 100 books and was able to support her family after the death of her husband. Although she was politically conservative, her fiction reveals a concern for the poor and oppressed. Works include: *Tremordyn Cliff* (1835); ▷*The Life and Adventures of Jonathan Jefferson Whitlaw* (1836); *The Vicar of Wrexhill* (1837); *Widow Barnaby* (1838); *The Life and Adventures of Michael Armstrong, Factory Boy* (1840); *Jessie Phillips* (1843) and *The Life and Adventures of a Clever Woman* (1854). She settled in Florence in 1843, and shortly before her death received a copy of her son's first novel.
Bib: Heinemann, H., *Life*.

Trooper to the Southern Cross (1934)

Australian novel by ▷Angela Thirkell. *Trooper to the Southern Cross* was first published in 1934 under Thirkell's pseudonym, Leslie Parker, and in 1939 as *What Happened on the Boat*. It is concerned with the experiences of a number of English and Australian passengers aboard a troopship, the *Rudolstadt*, on their way back to Australia immediately after World War I. It is particularly interesting for its depiction of the Australian 'digger'; his anti-authoritarianism, larrikinism and, at the same time, his loyalty to those whom he respects. The novel is based upon Thirkell's experiences on her way out to Australia as a war bride.

Tropisms (1963)

Translation of *Tropismes* (1939 and 1946) by French writer ▷Nathalie Sarraute. The work consists of a series of brief passages evoking subconscious reactions, or 'tropisms', which, according to Sarraute, govern behaviour. This is experimental fiction, showing the contrast between male and female emotional reactions.

Trotter (Cockburn), Catherine (1679–1749)

English dramatist and, after her marriage to the Reverend Patrick Cockburn in 1708, writer of theological works. Until 1707 she was a Roman Catholic. She began publication very young with the epistolary novel *Olinda's Adventures or, the Amours of a Young Lady* (1793), and her verse dramatization of ▷Aphra Behn's story *Agnes de Castro* was acted at Drury Lane in 1695. *The Fatal Friendship* (1698) was her best-liked play. She contributed to ▷*The Nine Muses* (1700). In 'To Mrs Manley' on ▷Delarivier Manley's play *The Royal Mischief* (1696) she wrote 'Th' Attempt was brave, how happy your success, / The Men with Shame our Sex with Pride confess.'

Her other publications include: *The Unhappy Penitent* (1701).
▷Pix, Mary
Bib: Greer, G. *et al.*, *Kissing the Rod*.

'Trotula' (15th century)

English translations. Some of the material in a group of 15th-century English texts concerning women's diseases and childbirth is ascribed to 'Trotula'. It is not known whether the translator or compiler was a woman. Several of the manuscripts urge lettered women to read the texts to women who cannot read, so that women can help and advise one another without showing their diseases to men.
Bib: Rowland, Beryl (ed.), *A Medieval Woman's Guide to Health: The First English Gynecological Handbook*.

Trotzig, Birgitta (born 1929)

Swedish prose writer, and literary and art critic. Trotzig studied literature and art history, and worked as an art critic. From 1954 to 1969 she lived in Paris with her husband, the artist Ulf Trotzig, and their children. In this period, she converted to Catholicism.

She had an early début. When she was twenty-two she published *Ur de älskandes liv* (1951) (*From the Lives of the Lovers*), a novel about young girls and their narcissicism, told in a lyrical voice, which continues in the lyrical prose of *Bilder* (1954) (*Images*). It was *De utsatta* (1957) (*The Exposed*) that established her as a gifted author. These novels, together with *En berättelse från kusten* (1961) (*A Tale from the Coast*), are set in the Middle Ages in Scandinavia, while the following *Sveket* (1966) (*The Betrayal*), *Sjukdomen* (1972) (*The Illness*) and *Dykungens dotter* (1984) (*The Marsh King's Daughter*) are set in more recent times, but with many literary allusions to the old literature of folktales.

Trotzig's works are not easy to read. She writes modern legends of historical times, about religion, life and death, and above all about suffering as a godly experience, because of the absence of God. She use very intense language, and writes in pure lyric prose which combines with her religious sensibility to make her an important writer.

True History of the Captivity and Restoration of Mrs Mary Rowlandson, A
▷*Soveraignty and Goodness of God, The*

True Narrative of the Sufferings of Mary Kinnan, who was Taken Prisoner by the Shawanee Nation of Indians . . ., A (1795)
Published one year after ▷Mary Kinnan regained her freedom, this early North American ▷captivity narrative is one of the last in this centuries-old genre. Although influenced by the sentimental and melodramatic styles of the period, Kinnan's narrative is unique in its sublimation of the restoration process. Perhaps because she was more violently treated than most captives, Kinnan rejected the idea of returning to her native Virginia after she regained her freedom; instead, she describes her resettlement in New Jersey, where she created a new life for herself. Kinnan's narrative is also notable for descriptions of what she deemed 'the humiliating condition' of Shawnee women in their society.

True Story of Ida Johnson, The (1976)
Novel by Canadian writer ▷Sharon Riis. Riis's first novel has attained virtual cult status for its violent and extraordinary refusals. Economically told, it undermines all expectations of truth-telling for women. The 'true' story of the character Ida Johnson is one that she tells to her best friend, Lucy, who is native, other, listener, a version of redeemer in her listening act; but the true story is that there is no truth for these women, only a series of survivals. Both Lucy and Ida reject confinement by a male narrative that has always written them into a victim position, and leave the novel to roam freely together.
Bib: Perreault, J., in ▷*A Mazing Space*.

Trusta, H. ▷Phelps, Elizabeth Stuart

Truth, Sojourner (1797–1883)
US lecturer, preacher, abolitionist, activist for African-American and women's rights – especially those of fugitive and freed slaves. Born in slavery and named Isabella, emancipated at thirty, she named herself Sojourner Truth at the age of forty-six. Sojourner Truth was a gifted and compelling speaker whose personal presence and distinctive speaking style attracted attention both to herself and to the series of religious, abolitionist, human and women's rights movements she advocated. Illiterate herself, Sojourner Truth was known in 19th-century US literature principally through journalists' accounts of her public appearances and through the autobiographical *Narrative of Sojourner Truth* (1850) and ▷Harriet Beecher Stowe's 'Sojourner Truth: The Libyan Sibyl' (1863), published in the ▷*Atlantic Monthly*. While unrecorded at the time, Sojourner Truth's 'Ain't I A Woman?' speech, at the 1851 Akron, Ohio women's rights convention, has come to symbolize the African-American women's reminder that inclusion of their experience is essential to women's rights movements.

Truth Tales (1986)
An anthology of contemporary writing by Indian women, published by India's first feminist publishing house, ▷Kali for Women. All but one of the stories are translated from Indian regional languages. Contributors include ▷Mahasveta Devi, ▷Mrinal Pande, ▷Lakshmi Kannan, ▷Ismat Chughtai and Vishwapriya Iyengar.

Tsébrikova, Mariia Konstantinovna (1835–1917)
Under eleven ▷pseudonyms, as well as her own name, Tsébrikova was a prolific Russian critic, editor and publicist. A Soviet literary historian has described her as one of the radical 'theoreticians of the populist movement' of the 1870s, who found social commitment in literature more important than aesthetic considerations. Well-educated in her gentry home, she wrote about and translated works from German, French, English and North American literature and history. 'Our Grandmothers' (1868) was an early class analysis of the female types in Tolstoy's *War and Peace* (1863–1869), and her overview of Russian women writers (1876) castigates them for narrow themes and lack of professional commitment. Tsébrikova devoted several works to pedagogy, and edited a children's magazine. Although she was an active propagandist for women's rights, she attacked 'ultra-feminism' that favoured communal arrangements for children over a mother's care. In 1889 she printed abroad and circulated in Russia her 'Open Letter to Alexander III', which described the repression and cruelties of his reign, and an article, 'Penal Servitude and Exile'. Long-term exile without trial in punishment for these defiant acts did not keep her from publishing children's works and memoirs.

Tsumura Setsuko (born 1928)
Japanese novelist. Born in Nagano prefecture, she worked for five years before entering junior college. This experience influenced her literary style. *Toys* won the Akutagawa Prize in 1965. *Depressing Years* describes the complex relationship between a woman who wins a prize for a novel before her husband, who is also a novelist.

Tsunoda Fusako (born 1914)
Japanese non-fiction writer, born in Tokyo. She writes about the Japanese living in foreign countries, based on her own experience of living in France for ten years, when she studied at the Sorbonne. *Hilda in East Germany* won the Bungei Shunju Dokusha Prize in 1961, and the following year *The Windy Border* won the Fujin Koron Dokusha Prize. In *Captain Amakasu* she criticizes war.

Tsushima Yuko (born 1947)
Japanese novelist. She was born in Tokyo, the second daughter of Dazai Osamu, a novelist. Her

Tsushima Yoko

first work, *Requiem – For Dog and Adult*, was published in *Mita Bungaku* in 1969. *Carnival* and *The Mothers in the House of Grass* attracted attention, and her literary talent was acknowledged on the publication of *A Shining Room* and *Silent Traders* which won the Kawabata Yasunari Prize. She is against the traditional subservience of Japanese women and describes women living outside ordinary family life, based on her experience as a single mother. When her dearest son died, she was inspired to write *The Light of Night Runs After Me* (1986), which won the Yomiuri Prize for Literature.

Tsvetáeva, Marina Ivanovna (1892–1941)

Poet, prose writer and dramatist. Marina Tsvetáeva is now recognized as one of the greatest Russian poets of the 20th century. Her first book of poems, *Evening Album* (1910), was received sympathetically by ▷Shaginián and other critics. The theme and images of that collection and *The Magic Lantern* (1912) comprise a myth of childhood, and already reflect Tsvetáeva's uncanny ability to fix spontaneity in poetic form. Her dedication of *Evening Album* to the diarist ▷Bashkirtseff, and her own statement that 'My poems are a diary' show the autobiographical basis of her poetry. Although by 1914 Tsvetáeva was the wife of Sergei Efron and the mother of a daughter, Ariadna, she became intimately involved with the poet ▷Sofiia Párnok. The affair resulted in a cycle of poems called 'Girlfriend', in which the sexual identity is muted by Tsvetáeva's general tendency to avoid identifying her lyric voice as female. Like other poets, she responded to World War I by turning to Russian folklore motifs and Russia itself as a theme, in mature poetry that gave the experience universal significance.

After the 1917 Revolution, Tsvetáeva wrote six plays in verse and narrative poems, including *The Tsar's Maiden* (1920). By 1921 she had completed her response to the Civil War, the cycle of poems ▷*The Demesne of the Swans*. In 1922, after her two volumes of poetry entitled *Mileposts* appeared, Tsvetáeva and her family emigrated and settled in Prague and, from 1925, in Paris. In 1923 her collection *Craft* was published in Berlin, and in Prague she wrote two more innovative narrative poems, 'The Poem of the Mountain' and 'The Poem of the End' (both 1924). In Paris she continued writing narrative poetry and two parts of a planned dramatic trilogy, *The Wrath of Aphrodite*, 'Ariadna' (1924) and 'Fedra' (1927). The last collection published in Tsvetáeva's lifetime, *After Russia*, containing the great poems she wrote from 1922 to 1925, came out in 1928.

In emigration Tsvetáeva felt more and more isolated. She, her husband, daughter and son, Georgii, lived in poverty. Their income came almost entirely from her writings, yet, as she wrote to a friend, domestic obligations gobbled up her time. After the lukewarm reception of *After Russia*, she turned more and more to prose – short stories in Russian and French, memoirs and critical articles – largely because it was more profitable. In 1939 Tsvetáeva and her family returned to Russia. After the USSR was invaded in 1941, Tsvetáeva was evacuated to Elabuga, where she committed suicide.

She left behind a great body of work that broke new ground for poets in general and for women poets in particular. While ▷Akhmátova's poetry is marked by restraint, balance and, ultimately, an identity with the Russian people, Tsvetáeva's is marked by extravagance, experimentation, and the defiant voice of an outcast. Like ▷Gíppius, she felt poetically and psychologically confined by the conventional stereotypes of the 'poetess', and her ideal was an androgynous one. Her daring, innovative technique has rarely been matched by poets of either sex.

▷Akhmadúlina, Izabella; Aligér, Margarita; Gértsyk, Adelaida; Moscow; Nastas'ia, Kostër; *Tragic Menagerie, The.*

Bib: Naydan, M. (trans.), *After Russia*; Kimball, R. (trans.), *The Desmesne of the Swans*; King, J. M. (trans.), *Marina Tsvetáeva, a Captive Spirit: Selected Prose*; Feinstein, E. (trans.), *Selected Poems of Marina Tsvetáyeva*; McDuff, D., *Selected Poems: Marina Tsvetáyeva*; Karlinsky, S. and Appel Jr, A. (eds), *The Bitter Air of Exile: Russian Writers in the West, 1922–1972*; Cosman, C. et al. (eds), *The Penguin Book of Women Poets*; Dobson, R. and Campbell, D. (trans.), *Seven Russian Poets*; Murray, M. (ed.), *A House of Good Proportion: Images of Women in Literature*; Karlinsky, S., *Marina Tsvetáeva: The Woman, Her World, and Her Poetry*; Heldt, B., *Terrible Perfection: Women and Russian Literature.*

Tudor, Elizabeth ▷Elizabeth Tudor

Tudor, Mary ▷Mary Tudor

Tueni, Nadia (1935–1983)

Lebanese poet who wrote exclusively in French.
She studied in French schools in ▷Beirut and
Athens, and graduated from St Joseph's College
in Beirut with a degree in law. She published nine
collections of verse in French, for which she was
awarded seven prizes in France and Lebanon.
Her third volume of poetry, *Juin et les Mécreants*
(1968) (*June and the Infidels*) is her poetic
statement on the June War of 1967. She writes of
death and decay in an all-enveloping desert, and:
'Pity for the man of the golden horse . . . that
burns / not by heat but by simple thoughts.'

In 1967 Nadia Tueni became literary editor of
Le Jour, the French supplement of the Beirut daily
newspaper *al-Nahar*. On her death she was
awarded the Gold Medal of Honour for Public
Instruction. Her articles and short stories were
collected after her death in *La Prose Oeuvres
Complètes* (1985) (*The Complete Prose Works*). Her
collections of verse are *Les Textes Blonds* (1963)
(*The Golden Texts*), *L'Age d'Ecume* (1965) (*The Age
of Foam*), *Poèmes pour une Histoire* (1972) (*Poems for
a Story*), *Le Revêur de Terre* (1975) (*The Earth
Dreamer*), *Liban: 20 Poèmes pour un Amour* (1979)
(*Lebanon: 20 Poems for a Lover*), *Archives
Sentimentales d'une Guerre au Liban* (1982)
(*Sentimental Records of a War in Lebanon*) and *La
Terre Arretée* (1984) (*The Firm Earth*).

English translations of extracts from her verse
are published in ▷*Women of the Fertile Crescent:
Modern Poetry by Arab Women* edited by Kamal
Boullata.

Tumiati, Lucia (born 1926)

Italian novelist and children's writer. Born in
Venice, she was involved in the ▷Resistance
movement there. She went to University in
Florence and contributed regularly to Italian
newspapers and magazines. She has written on
the Italian Resistance movement, and on post-war
Italy. ▷*Terra d'oggi* (1959) (*Our Land Today*), is
typical of her accounts of the harshness of life in
Italy during this period. She has written on Carlo
Collodi, creator of Pinocchio, in *Collodi, Verne,
Capuana, Salgari* of 1953. Her work is featured in
Racconti della Resistenza europea (1976) (*Stories of
the Resistance in Europe*).

Her other works include: *Saltafrontiera* (1962)
(*Jump the Border*); *Giungle e savane* (1964) (*Jungles
and Savannahs*); *Una cartella di sogni* (1968) (*A
Page of Dreams*); *Una scuola da bruciare* (1972) (*A
School to Burn*); *Fiabe di libertà* (1980) (*Freedom
Fables*); *Fiabe più belle* (1988) (*More Beautiful
Fables*).

Tuqan, Fadwa (born 1917)

Palestinian poet, born in Nablus on the West
Bank to a middle-class family famous for its soap
products. She grew up in a big family house, an
extension of the family business, where the
multiple despotism of the males of the extended
family fell heavily on her childhood and part of
her youth. In her autobiography she describes the
house's high walls and the stifling atmosphere
created by the ever-watchful eyes of 'them': the
cousins and aunts. At the age of thirteen the thin,
sensitive girl was kept home from school because
of a trifling incident: an adolescent boy who
followed her to and from school had sent her a
jasmine flower. Her brother, Ibrahim Tuqan, a
poet, could not overrule the decree of the family
elders, but undertook to supply her with books
and read with her. She learned thousands of lines
of classical verse by heart. He later took her to
live with him and his wife in Jerusalem where she
met and corresponded with other writers. She was
greatly influenced by the romantic poetry of the
1930s and 1950s, and corresponded with Ali
Mahmud Taha, whose *Lost Sailor* (1934) and
Nights of the Lost Sailor (1940) she greatly
admired.

Fadwa Tuqan lost her brother, Ibrahim, in
1941, when she had to return to the old family
house, that female *qumqum* (the stopped bottle of
▷*The Arabian Nights*) where the females of the
family 'grow old before their time, sitting waiting
against the wall, with no private life of their own'.

Fadwa's father asked her to write 'political'
verse as her brother Ibrahim had done, but she
refused. How could she, a woman behind walls,
take an interest in politics? The disaster of 1948
changed all that. As she herself put it, 'When the
roof fell in over Palestine in 1948, the veil fell off
the face of Arab women; the walls of the harem
were finally broken.' Fadwa Tuqan joined political
as well as literary clubs, and her poetry has
remained involved with politics to this day. She
was not a politically committed poet, however,
which drew a lot of criticism from her younger
brother, a seasoned communist. It was the June
war of 1967 which finally brought her into contact
and into line with the great Palestinian poets of
resistance.

Fadwa Tuqan's early 'sequestration' from
school turned her into a bookworm, as she
describes herself. Her poetry shows a deep
familiarity with the Bible as well as the *Qur'an*,
and she read western European literature in
English or in Arabic translations. Eight volumes of
verse published in Beirut between 1955 and 1974
show the development of her poetry. From the
romantic, inward-looking *Wahdi m'a al-Ayyam*
(1955) (*Alone With the Days*), to the questioning,
meditating *Amam al-Bab al-Mughlaq* (1967) (*Before
the Closed Door*), to deep involvement with the
plight of her people in *al-Layl Wa-al Fursan*
(1969) (*Night and the Horsemen*), *Ala Qimmat al-
Dunya Wahidan* (*Alone, at the Top of the World*,
1973), and *Kabus al-Layl Wa al-Nahar* (1974)
(*Nightmare in Daylight*), it is not only the subject
matter but the technique which is finally liberated.
In her old age, Fadwa Tuqan is one of the leading
▷avant-garde poets in Arabic.

Bib: Boullata, Kamal (ed. and trans.), ▷*Women of
the Fertile Crescent: Modern Poetry by Arab Women*;
Kenny, Olive (trans.), *A Mountain Journey*.

Tur, Evgeniia (1815–1892)

Pseudonym of Elizaveta Vasil'evna Sailhas de
Tournemire, a Russian writer, editor and critic.

Like ▷Zhadóvskaia, her life was marred by love for a tutor whom her noble parents would not permit her to marry. She became a writer from necessity after her French husband's speculations ruined the family. Her fiction, like *A Mistake* and *The Niece*, published between 1849 and 1856, combined love stories based on her own experience of social barriers with an ability to portray male psychology, which pleased commentators like Ivan Turgenev (1818–1883) and dramatist Aleksandr Ostrovsky (1823–1886). Her novel *Three Stages of Life* (1854) was damned by radical critics for its moral of submission to fate. From 1856 to 1860 Tur wrote for the Moscow ▷'thick journal' *Russian Messenger*, which at the time was notably hospitable to women writers. Her critical articles on French and English writers helped to introduce foreign literature to Russia. She founded a short-lived, twice-weekly journal, *Russian Discourse*, in 1861. Her sympathy with Polish nationalists brought her under government surveillance, and in the 1860s she moved abroad and lived in France for a few years for her health. Tur ended her writing career as the author of popular historical novels for young people, including *Princess Dubrovina* (1886) and *Sergei Bor-Ramenskii* (1888). *The Shalonskii Family* (1880) is a chronicle, like Tolstoy's *War and Peace* (1863–1869), set during the Napoleonic Wars.
Bib: Costlow, J., 'Speaking the Sorrow of Women: Turgenev's "Neschastnaia" and Evgeniia Tur's "Antonina"', *Slavic Review* 2 (1991).

Turell, Jane Colman (1708–1735)
North American poet. She was born in Boston, Massachusetts, on 25 February 1708. A precocious child, she rapidly learned the Puritan Calvinism preached by her minister father and the prevailing literary techniques. Blending these forms of knowledge, she began writing poetry at the age of eleven, an endeavour she continued throughout lifelong illness and depression. After her death in Medford, Massachusetts, on 26 March 1735, her husband published a biography of her, ▷*Reliquiae Turellae et Lachrymae Paternal*, which includes selected poems, letters, diary entries and essays by her.
▷Dennie, Abigail Colman; 'Lines from a letter to Her Sister, Jane Colman Turell'

Turner, Ethel (1872–1958)
Australian children's author and novelist. Turner was born in Yorkshire, England and brought to Australia in 1881, where, after attending Sydney Girls' High School, she became editor of the children's column of the *Illustrated Sydney News*. She married Herbert Curlewis (later a New South Wales judge) in 1896. Of her many books for children, and her several books of poetry and non-fiction, her most famous is the classic ▷*Seven Little Australians* (1894).
▷*From the Verandah*; Children's literature (Australia)

Tusquets, Esther (born 1936)
Arguably Spain's most significant contemporary female novelist. Tusquets was born in Barcelona, and writes in Castilian. For many years the director of Editorial Lumen, one of the most adventurous Spanish publishing houses, Tusquets now owns her own publishing house. Her main works are a trilogy of novels which include *El mismo mar de todos los veranos* (1978) (▷ *The Same Sea as Every Summer*), and ▷*El amor es un juego solitario* (1979) (*Love is a Solitary Game*). The final novel of the trilogy, *Varada tras el último naufragio* (1980) (*Beached After the Last Shipwreck*), uses love triangles to explore the problems of role, appearance, sexual identity and authenticity. Among her latest works are: *Siete miradas en un mismo paisaje* (1981) (*Seven Glances at the Same Landscape*), a collection of short stories, and *Para no volver* (1985) (*Never to Return*), a novel about an individual's experience of psychoanalytical treatment. In these she reworks themes, such as homosexual love and the space of the feminine, that were evident in her earlier work.

Tutiyawises (Symbol of Merit)
Novel by Thai writer ▷Boonlua which depicts Thai society after the 1932 coup, and the corruption of the old order. Married to a powerful general, Cha-on is awarded the Tutiyawises Order of Merit, the highest title achievable by a woman, less on her own merits than because of her husband's position. The novel contrasts her current self-serving existence with the personal values and happiness of their past with friends and her young husband.

Tutti i nostri ieri (1952) ▷*All Our Yesterdays*

Tu vipera gentile (1972) (*You, Gentle Viper*)
A collection of three short stories, all historical tales, by Italian writer ▷Maria Bellonci. The first, 'Delitto di Stato' ('State Crime'), is set in Mantua in the 1600s; 'Soccorso a Dorotea' ('Help for Dorothy'), is the story of a young girl caught up in the conflicts between the powerful Sforza and Gonzaga families; 'You, Gentle Viper', the title story, is a tale of intrigue set in Milan between the Middle Ages and the early Renaissance. All are linked by the idea of abuse of power by the powerful, who amorally manipulate individuals for their own purposes. The characters, despite their historical distance, remain credible and interesting. The collection is typical of Bellonci's fictional histories.

Tyler, Anne (born 1941)
US novelist. Born in Minneapolis, Minnesota, Tyler was raised in communes in North Carolina and Maryland. In 1961 she graduated from Duke University, and in 1963 she married. Tyler is the mother of two daughters.
   A Southern writer and Pulitzer Prize-winner, Tyler is concerned with the past impinging on the present, and her novels focus on the tensions between the individual and the family. In *A*

Slipping-Down Life (1970), *Celestial Navigation* (1974), *Earthly Possessions* (1977) and *Dinner at the Homesick Restaurant* (1982), characters are trapped by the past, and they perpetuate the patterns of their lives over which they have little control; they are unable to see their selves or to feel alive. Eccentrics, they try to flee their routines, but inevitably they return. *The Accidental Tourist* (1985) envisions the possibility of a happy accident. Through an accident, the self experiences an epiphany and sees life's possibilities.

Other works include: *If Morning Ever Comes* (1964), *The Tin Can Tree* (1966), *The Clock Winder* (1972), *Searching for Caleb* (1976), *Morgan's Passing* (1980), *Breathing Lessons* (1989) and *Saint Maybe* (1991).

Tyler, Margaret (fl 1578)
English translator. She was one of the first English women to publish a secular work. Most of what we can surmise about her is drawn from her dedicatory ▷preface to her ▷translation, ▷*A Mirrour of Princely Deeds and Knighthood* (1578). She was a member, perhaps a servant, of the household of a family of Catholics named Howard. She dedicates her only extant work to Thomas Howard, whose parents she says she has served. Her employer might have been Thomas Howard, third Duke of Norfolk, executed for his role in the attempt to depose ▷Elizabeth Tudor and replace her with ▷Mary Stuart. It has been suggested that Tyler's real name was Tyrrell, and this would have made her the Catholic sister-in-law of the Howard family. Tyler prefaces *A Mirrour of Princely Deeds and Knighthood* with a justification for choosing a secular subject for translation by a woman: 'And thus much concerning the present story, that it is neither unseemly for a woman to deal in, neither greatly requiring a less staid age than mine is.'
▷Patronage
Bib: Ferguson, M., *First Feminists*; Krontiris, T., 'Breaking Barriers of Genre and Gender: Margaret Tyler's Translation of the Mirrour of Knighthood' in Farrell, K. *et al.* (eds), *Women in the Renaissance*.

Tynan, Katharine (1861–1931)
Irish poet and journalist, born in Dublin, and educated in a Catholic convent school in Drogheda. Immensely prolific and hard-working, she published over 160 volumes of poetry, novels, short stories, articles and memoirs. She was an influential figure in the Irish Revival (the nationalist and cultural movement which flourished in the late 19th century and early 20th century) and introduced Celtic material into her poetry long before the poet and dramatist W.B. Yeats (1865–1939) did. Although she was one of the most highly regarded and popular Irish writers of the period, her work has received no serious critical attention, and even her interesting essays and memoirs are scarcely known today. A selection of her poems, *The Poems of Katharine Tynan*, was reprinted in 1963.

Tyrwhit, Elizabeth ▷*Morning and Evening Praiers*

Über die Verhältnisse (1987) (Beyond Ones's Means)

A novel by the Austrian writer ▷Barbara Frischmuth. As its ambiguous title suggests, the book is an examination of both public and private relationships, and about living beyond one's means. Mela, a single mother, runs a successful restaurant where people come for huge meals. She was once the mistress of her boss, who had unwillingly fathered her child, Mela's daughter, Fro. Mela now has a new young lover and is exceedingly busy with her restaurant, just as Fro runs away to Turkey with her own lover. Although Mela eventually succeeds in bringing Fro home, it is clear that she has lost any true rapport with her daughter.

The novel draws upon the Greek myth of Demeter and its mother–daughter relationship, and Frischmuth succeeds in using this myth to illuminate the issues of social and political power in modern Austria. The complex narrative technique, shifting perspectives and different layers of meaning make this one of the most intriguing novels by a German-speaking woman in the 1980s.

Ugrešić, Dubravka (born 1949)

Dubravka Ugrešić

Croatian novelist and screen writer. Ugrešić was born in 1949, and lives in Zagreb. She has translated and written extensively about Russian literature, and is the author of *Pose For Prose* (1978), *Life Is a Fairy Tale*, and *Fording the Stream of Consciousness*, which, published in English in 1991, combines a highly refined and extensive literary knowledge with wild good humour. A novel-within-a-novel, it is set at an international writers' conference at Zagreb, where murder,

espionage and sexual intrigue are on the hidden agenda. Her stories have been translated into several languages and anthologized in, among others, *The World Comes to Iowa* (1987).

She has also written screenplays for television and film, including a treatment for her own *Steffie Speck in the Jaws of Life* (1981, trans. 1992). The film was awarded the prize for Best Yugoslav Film of 1984.

Uhohho, An Expedition (1983)

Work by Japanese writer Hikari Agata (born 1943). Hikari describes a family in which the parents are divorced, and the children live with their mother. The children and their mother are settled, despite facing loneliness and other difficulties. One of the children, at elementary school, says that their struggle to create a family is like being on an expedition. This work describes the problems of family life and the relationships between men and women and parents and children from the perspective of an emancipated woman.

Ulasi, Adaora Lily

Nigerian novelist. One of the first women journalists in Nigeria, she is the only Nigerian woman to have written detective fiction in English. Her five novels include *Many Thing You No Understand* (1970), ▷*Many Thing Begin for Change* (1971), *The Night Harry Died* (1974), and *The Man from Sagamu* (1973) and *Who is Jonah?* (1978). They are a peculiar amalgam of mystery and suspense, detection, the supernatural, and anti-colonial satire. The writer differentiates her Nigerian characters by making them speak a badly-realized pidgin, which has the effect of turning them into comic stereotypes. However, the Nigerians always get the better of the pompous and self-righteous colonial servants, and the books include passages of description which bring to life an era long gone.

▷Journalism (West Africa)

Bib: Taiwo, O., *Female Novelists of Modern Africa*; Otokunefor, H. and Nwodo, C., *Nigerian Female Writers: A Critical Perspective*.

Ulfelt, Leonora Christine (1621–1698)

Danish prose and memoir-writer. She was a daughter of the Danish King Christian IV and Lady Kirsten Munk, and at the age of fifteen she married Corfitz Ulfelt, who quickly rose to be the Prime Minister of Denmark. She bore ten children.

When the king died and Leonora Christine's half-brother became King of Denmark, the Ulfelt family fell into disgrace. In 1651 they took refuge in Sweden. Later, Ulfelt was sentenced to death in his absence, because of treason. In 1664 he died a natural death, but his wife was caught and imprisoned in the Blue Tower, a prison. Here she began to write. First she wrote an autobiography in French (1673) then she began her famous *Jammers Minde* (1869) (*Memoirs by Leonora Christine, Daughter of Christian IV of Denmark*).

She described her life in prison, and gave a picture of herself as a strong, pious woman with an unusual integrity. She also wrote a biography of outstanding women, *Hæltinders Pryd* (*Ornament of Heroines*), but only the first part of it has survived.

Her prose is very distinct, readable even today, with its brutal realistic images, bitter ironies, and its idealistic personal and human descriptions. She thought that souls were not gendered. The works of Ulfelt are considered the most important writings in 17th-century Denmark.

Ullmann, Regina (1884–1961)

German-speaking Swiss novelist. She lived most of her life with her mother, and together the two women frequented literary circles in Munich and Vienna. She had two illegitimate children, one by the Viennese economist Hanns Dorn, and the other by the psychoanalyist Otto Gross (1877–1920). At one time the protégée of the poet Rilke (1875–1926), she wrote in a rather laboured, neo-romantic idiom. Her stories tend to revolve around minute events in the sparse lives of dispossessed figures, such as neglected children, lonely women and old men. A selection of her work was reprinted in 1978.

Ultraism (*Ultraísmo*)

A ▷modernist or ▷avant-garde movement, originating in Spain, which was introduced to Argentina by the writer Jorge Luís Borges (1899–1986) when he, still very young, returned to Buenos Aires in 1921, having lived in Switzerland during World War I. He founded the magazines *Prisma* and *Proa*, and exposed his new theories in the magazine *Nosotros*. The Argentinian ▷*Martín Fierro* Group of poets was part of this vanguard movement, which spread over the continent.

Ultra-romanticism

Term used to describe a certain tendency towards high melodrama and emotional extremes in the late romantic literature of Portugal. The term is associated with a group of student poets from Coimbra, who, in 1844, founded the review *O Trovador* (*The Troubador*). Lord Byron was an important influence on the movement. One of the most prominent ultra-romantic poets was ▷Maria Browne.

▷Elisa, Henriqueta; Romanticism (Portugal)

Umm Nizar (Salma al-Mala'ika) (1908–1953)

Iraqi poet of the traditional school, educated at home and widely-read in classical Arabic literature and the new romantic poetry of the 1930s. Tutored by her husband, her first poem to be published (in 1936) was an elegy written on the death of the great Iraqi poet Jamil Sidqi al-Zahwi, one of the first champions of women's emancipation in the early decades of the 20th century. Umm Nizar was a mother of seven children at the time, the eldest of whom was ▷Nazik al-Mala'ika, aged thirteen. The proud husband and tutor encouraged Umm Nizar

('mother of Nizar') to recite her verses before their literary friends. She continued to write poetry on conventional topics, nature, social injustice, morals and political and national causes. Her poem 'Baghdad in Captivity' (1941) laments the failure of the national Kilani uprising against the British in 1941. The following year, 'In memory of May 1941' (1942) frankly attacks the ruling government and laments the execution of a number of Kilani's followers. She later wrote three poems on the aborted Baghdad revolution of 1948. A number of her poems deal with the tragedy of Palestine, addressing the Arabs collectively, exhorting them to wake up and unite – or perish. Her verse was collected and published in 1965. Nazik al-Mala'ika called the volume *Song of Glory*, and wrote an introduction describing her mother's life, picturing the Mala'ika household as a hotbed of poetry. Umm Nizar's feminist verse varies, from the lament for the loss of Zahawi, the women's champion, to upbraiding women for allowing themselves to degenerate into slaves in return for fine clothes and precious jewellery.

Una, The (1853–1855)

US periodical. It was established to counter such popular, commercial women's magazines as ▷*Godey's Lady's Book* and ▷*Peterson's Magazine*. Focused on women's rights and women's suffrage, *The Una* published both suffragists, eg ▷Elizabeth Cady Stanton, and their opponents, eg ▷Sarah Josepha Hale.

Una fra tante (1878) (One Among Many)

Italian novel by ▷Emma. Through the story of Barberina, a shepherdess who comes to find work in an impersonal city and ultimately falls into prostitution, Emma attacks the society which allows such things to happen. She is particularly harsh on the bourgeois clients of this impoverished woman. The novel is especially interesting for its movement away from a ▷romantic portrayal of the subject, and the manner in which it anticipates later ▷realist and ▷naturalist treatments of the same theme. The city is presented as a machine which simply swallows its victims. This novel is also interesting for its presentation of female ▷duality: Barberina literally does not recognize herself when she looks in the mirror.

Uncle Piper of Piper's Hill (1889)

Australian novel by ▷Jessie Couvreur ('Tasma'). This was serialized as 'The Pipers of Piper's Hill' in the *Australasian* in 1888, and was published in book form a year later. The plot is conventionally romantic, dealing with a series of love affairs within the Piper and Cavendish families, intricate and interconnected relationships which almost all end in marriage. It is, however, enlivened by its urban setting, by the strength of its characterization (particularly that of the pompous Piper), and by its satiric observation of middle-class life and values in a large and flourishing colonial city.

Uncle Tom's Cabin (1852)

US anti-slavery novel by ▷Harriet Beecher Stowe. Stowe originally conceived and proposed to the editors of the abolitionist periodical *National Era* a series of sketches on the emotional realities of slavery. As public response to the serial swelled, Stowe continued with a number of instalments – incrementally creating what would be her first novel. *Uncle Tom's Cabin* became the popular impetus for the growth of anti-slavery sentiment in the USA and Britain in the decade before the Civil War. (There is a probably apocryphal but often-repeated story that Abraham Lincoln, on meeting Stowe, greeted her as the little lady that started this whole big war.)

Reprinted in scores of unauthorized editions in the USA and abroad, the novel had enormous sales and inspired a range of attacks on both the book and Stowe herself, including ▷Mary Henderson Eastman's answering novel, *Aunt Phillis's Cabin*. Also transformed by other writers into a variety of stage vehicles, the novel and its most memorable characters – Uncle Tom, slavemaster Simon Legree and ▷Little Eva – became the vehicle through which most North Americans came to an emotional understanding of the evils of slavery.

Stowe defended the novel's accuracy with *A Key to Uncle Tom's Cabin* (1853), which listed source documents, and she published a second anti-slavery novel, ▷*Dred*, in 1855. *Uncle Tom's Cabin* is perhaps the most significant novel of the 19th-century USA in terms of its impact on national history, on Stowe's national and international reputation and on the role of women writers in the USA.

▷Grimké, Angelina Emily; Grimké, Sarah Moore
Bib: Bowlby, Rachel, 'Breakfast in America – Uncle Tom's Cultural Histories' in Bhabha, Homi K., *Nation and Narration*, pp. 197–212.

Undset, Sigrid (1882–1949)

Norwegian novelist. Her father was a Norwegian archaeologist and her mother was Danish. She had a happy childhood, but when she was eleven, her beloved father died; she wrote about this, and about her bitterness against her mother, in *Elleve år* (1934) *At Eleven*). She left school at sixteen and worked for ten years in an office. She painted, read, and she wrote historical novels which were rejected until 1907, when she published *Fru Marta Oulie* (*Mrs Marta Oulie*). It was a success, and she travelled to Rome with the money. Here she met the Norwegian painter Anders Svarstad, whom she married. She had three children of her own and her husband's three from an earlier marriage.

In 1911 she published *Jenny*, a bold ▷realist novel. She studied medieval history, and with the historical novel ▷*Kristin Lavransdatter* (1920–1922) she won worldwide fame. Undset's early novels deal with the fates of poor or middle-class women who are spiritually adrift, and who feel trapped by their marriage and family, preventing them from experiencing the full and deep love that seems to be the meaning of their lives, as in *Splinter av troldspeilet* (1917) (*Images in a Mirror*, 1938). For many years, she studied medieval history, and her pessimism in relation to modern times found its counterpart in the Middle Ages and in Kristin Lavransdatter, the woman whose existence revolves around love, sexuality and religion. She wrote another novel of the Middle Ages, a psychological portrait, *Olav Audunssøn* (1925–1934). In 1928 she received the Nobel Prize for literature. In the same year she converted to the Catholic Church, which she saw as a protection against modern materialism. She wrote about this in essays, such as *Katolsk propaganda* (1927) (*Catholic Propaganda*), but also in her later novels, *Gymnadenia* (1929) (*The Wild Orchid*, 1931) and *Den trofaste hustru* (1936) (*The Faithful Wife*, 1937). The women in her later novels long for divine love, and are committed to their family and to God.

During the 1930s she wrote against fascism; her books were prohibited in Germany, and she had to flee Norway in 1940. In her last years she wrote a hagiography of ▷St Catharine of Siena. It was published after her death in 1949.

Un est l'autre, L' (1986) ▷Man/Woman: The One is the Other (1989)

Union Street (1982)

Novel by English writer ▷Pat Barker. Written in Barker's characteristic demotic style, this graphic ▷social realist novel provides seven narratives of urban working-class women's lives. Beginning with the young and rebellious Kelly Brown, who is raped, and ending with the tale of the elderly Alice Bell, the novel gives a panoramic view of women's experiences, frustrations and expectations, exploring also the crucial role of women in coping with economic deprivation.

Uno Chiyo (born 1897)

Japanese novelist. Born in Yamaguchi prefecture, she went to Tokyo to become a writer. *A Powdered Face* won the Prize of Jijishinpo in 1921. She fell in love with one writer after another, including Kitahara Takeo, and a painter, Togo Seiji. *A Confession of Loves* (1935) emotionally relates the narrator's love for a writer. After 1945 she and Kitahara founded the publishing house which issued *Style* magazine. *Ohan* describes the relationship between two women with opposite characters and their mutual male lover. This work won the Noma Prize for Literature in 1957. *A Dollmaker, Tenguya Hisakichi*, *A Cherry of Pale Pink* and *To Stab* portray the world of men and women in her characteristic narrative style. *I Lived Myself*, which was published in the newspaper *Mainichi*, sold a million copies. She accepted the Kikuchi Kan Prize in 1982 and became a member of the Japanese Academy of Arts in 1972.

Unspoken Thoughts (1875)
Poems by Australian writer ▷Ada Cambridge.
Cambridge's poems deal frankly with her opinion
of the inequalities of English society; with sexual
frustration (some critics have discerned lesbian
inclinations); with her views on marriage (seen in
some of the poems as legalized prostitution); and
her religious scepticism. The volume was
published anonymously in 1875 and withdrawn
from circulation almost immediately, probably
because of the controversial nature of the poems.
It was republished, edited by Patricia Barton, in
1988.

Unzer, Johanne Charlotte (1725–1782)
German poet and writer. She was born in Halle
into a wealthy and cultured family, married a
doctor in 1751, and moved to Hamburg. Also in
1751, she published *Grundrißeiner Weltweisheit für
das Frauenzimmer* (*Blueprint of Good Advice for the
Women's Room*), a book of guidance for young
women. Her fame as the 'anacreontic maiden' was
established in the same year, with the publication
of *Scherzgedichte* (*Jesting Poems*), whose cheerful,
idyllic verse responded to the fashion of the time.
The book ran to three editions, and was followed
by *Sittliche und zärtliche Gedichte* (*Virtuous and
Effective Poems*) in 1754. Already, in the preface to
the first collection, Unzer had complained about
the manifold restrictions hampering the woman
poet. In a third collection of poems, *Fortgesetzte
Versuche in sittlichen und zärtlichen Gedichten* (*More
Attempts at Virtuous and Effective Poems*), which
appeared in 1766, long after it had been written,
she speaks in the preface of the great difficulties
she had experienced when trying to remain active
as a poet during pregnancy, childbirth and the
prolonged nursing of two dying children. In 1767
she published a book on the role of women,
*Grundriß einer natürlichen Historie und eigentlichen
Naturlehre für das Frauenzimmer* (*Sketch for a
Natural History and True Study of Nature for the
Women's Room*).

Uomo che parlava solo, L' (1961) (**The Man
Who Spoke Alone**)
Italian novel by ▷Lalla Romano, written in the
form of a diary. It is a narrative of memories, of
the reminiscences of a middle-aged man. He
tries, in the course of his writing, to come to
terms with himself and to understand his past. It
is stylistically interesting, and is constructed in a
manner unlike Romano's other work, although it
covers the same ground.

Up the Junction (1963)
A series of short stories, English writer ▷Nell
Dunn's first publication, and possibly her most
famous work. The stories are linked by characters
and places showing aspects of the lives of
working-class women in Battersea, and are framed
by an enigmatic, middle-class, female narrator,
living and working with them but remaining
anonymous. The raw and economical language of
both *Up the Junction* and its sister work, *Poor Cow*

(1967), and the book's treatment of working-class
subjects in a sympathetic but non-patronizing way,
marked a new approach to ▷realism.

'Uraib (died c 899)
One of the class of ▷*jawari* (concubine or slave-
girl) Arabic poet-singers of the Abbasid age in
Baghdad, she circulated a romance concerning
her origin, which some of her contemporaries
liked to believe. She said that she was really the
daughter of the *wazir* (minister) Ja'far al-Barmaki
(the Barmicide of ▷*The Arabian Nights*) from a
secret marriage with a *sharifa* (a descendent of the
Prophet). At the death of her mother, Ja'far had
put the little girl in the care of a Christian woman.
After the coup against Ja'far and his men, the
woman sold the child to the Master of the Fleet,
who had her trained and educated and set her up
as a professional singer-composer. They noted
that she must excel, being the daughter of Ja'far.
Much of her love poetry is addressed to one man.

Urquhart, Jane (born 1949)
Canadian fiction writer and poet, born in northern
Ontario. Urquhart spent much of her adolescence
in Toronto, later studying art history and English.
Her poetry includes *False Shuffles* (1982), *I am
Walking in the Garden of his Imaginary Palace*
(1982) and *The Little Flowers of Madame de
Montespan* (1983), but it is her fiction that is
extraordinary. *The Whirlpool* (1986) is a historical
tour de force concerning ▷romantic poetry and
19th-century Niagara Falls; *Changing Heaven*
(1990) is a darkly passionate love story that uses
▷Emily Brontë as inspiration.

Urraca (1982)
This novel by Spanish writer ▷Lourdes Ortiz is
one of the literary masterpieces of the 1980s. It
takes its cue from the historical novel, being
ostensibly about Queen Urraca of Castile and
León (1109–1126), but with a feminist dimension.
Ortiz is concerned to bring the history of the
other Urraca to the fore, the one forgotten by
history, rather like ▷Virginia Woolf's idea of a
Judith Shakespeare in ▷*A Room of One's Own*.

Urretavizkaia, Arantza (born 1947)
Spanish writer of prose and poetry. Born in
Donostia (San Sebastián), Urretavizkaia soon
established herself as one of the most significant
Basque writers of the contemporary era. She
contributed to the poetic anthology *Euskal
Literature* (1972) (*Basque Literature*), and won the
City of Irún Prize for her volume of poems
Maitasunaren magalean (1982) (*In the Lap of Love*).
She has also published a novel, *Zerqatik Panpox?*
(1979) (*Why, Little One?*), and a collection of three
stories, *Aspaldian espero zaitudalako, ez nago sekulan
bakarrik* (1983) (*Since I've Waited for You So Long,
I'm Not Alone Any More*). Her work is
characterized by its intimate, tender qualities, and
lyrical sensitivity.
    ▷Basque women's writing

Ursa Major (1870–1871)

Novel by Russian writer ▷Nadezhda Khvoshchínskaia. *Ursa Major*, a panoramic novel set in the pivotal epoch of the Crimean War (1854–1855) played an important part in the continuing social dialogue over the ▷woman question. Unlike Chernyshevsky's heroine in ▷St Petersburg ▷(*What Is to Be Done?*), in the provincial city called N., Khvoshchinskaia's Katerina Bagrianskaia finds no progressive men eager to help her onto the right path in life. She falls in love with a decent liberal named Verkhovskoi, who is in the archetypal female position of having married for money and is too weak to break with his domineering wife. With a scheming brother and a father sinking into religiosity, Katerina has only herself to rely on. Her only constellation to steer by is the example of a woman she never meets, Verkhovskoi's mother who scornfully rejected the help her son bought with his wealthy marriage and made an independent, if humble, life for herself.

'Uthman, I'tidal (born 1942)

Egyptian critic and short story writer. She graduated from the Department of English at Cairo University, and now works as assistant editor of *Fusul*, an important literary quarterly published by the Egyptian Book Organization, which publishes 'modernist' writings from all over the Arab world. I'tidal Uthman is active in promoting the work of younger women and introducing western European feminist criticism among Arabic writers. Drawing attention to the new feminist discourse in Arabic fiction, her studies cut across the whole of the Arab world.

In her short stories, she combines the experience of western European literature with her native 'terms of reference', derived from the *Qur'an*, the Bible and a rich heritage of *Sufi* writings. A collection of her short stories was published as *Jonah and the Sea* (1989). The title story and two others are published in an English translation by Marilyn Booth in ▷*My Grandmother's Cactus* (1991).

Uttley, Alison (1884–1976)

English novelist and writer for children. Uttley was brought up on a remote farm in Derbyshire, which provided the material for *The Country Child* (1931), about growing up in the country. As a teacher in London, she was active in the women's ▷suffrage movement, then moved with her husband to Cheshire in 1911 and began to write. She is best-known for the children's series of books beginning in 1929 with *The Squirrel, the Hare and the Little Grey Rabbit*, which were illustrated by Margaret Temple, and later by Katherine Wigglesworth. Uttley has published nearly 100 books for children, and two adult novels. These include *A Traveller in Time* (1939), which mixes the contemporary with 16th-century history, and the autobiographical *Country Hoard* (1943) and *Ambush of Young Days* (1937). She also kept a diary until 1971, which ran to forty volumes.

Bib: Judd, D., *Alison Uttley: The Life of a Country Child 1884–1976*; Saintsbury, E., *The World of Alison Uttley*.

Uyar, Tomris (born 1941)

Turkish critic and short story writer, graduated from the American College, Istanbul in 1961 and studied journalism at the University of Istanbul. She started her career in writing by translating English literature and became a regular contributor to Turkish periodicals. Her short stories are introspective, depicting the lives of 'little people', and her language poetic. She published five collections of short stories (1971–1979) and a volume of memoirs (1977). She is a recognized critic of contemporary literature.

V

Vaa, Aslaug, (1889–1967)
Norwegian lyric poet and dramatist. She wrote
seven collections of poetry, four plays and around
150 articles and essays. She was born at Rauland,
her father being a farmer. She studied philosophy
and ▷psychoanalysis, and in 1911 married the
philologist and psychoanalyst Ola Raknes, with
whom she had five children. She divorced him in
1938. Because of the children, housekeeping and
undertaking translation work to earn money, her
first works were only published in 1934, a
collection of poems *Nord i leite* (*In the North
Horizon*), and the lyrical play *Steinguden* (*God of
Stone*); but she immediately became an important
voice in Norwegian literature, writing modernist
poetry before ▷modernism arrived in Norway. As
time passed her poems become more searching
and catastrophic; as the unrest and longing grew,
the lyrical form expanded, eg 'Fotefar'
('Footsteps'), 'Skjenkarsveinens Visur' ('The
Innkeeper's Song') and 'Bustader' (1963) ('Living
Quarters'). Mystical as she is, influenced by old
ballads, praising female eroticism, praising the
earth as the giver of all life, she is an early
modernist radical feminist. Her work is not easy
to understand, as she writes a triple dialect of
modernism, ecological feminism and a radical
▷New-Norwegian dialect, *landsmål*.

Vadkerti-Gavorniková, Lydia (born 1932)
Slovak poet. She studied Slovak and Russian at
university, before working as a teacher and
magazine editor. Her first verses appeared only in
the mid-1960s. Vadkerti-Gavorniková partly
followed the 'concrete poetry' trend of the late
1950s and early 1960s, then returned to
subjectivism, sensualism and metaphor. Her
verses are associative and metaphorical, but always
contain a narrative element. Fundamental themes
of her poetry are the home, childhood, family,
work, art, and the relationship between man and
woman.

Her collections of verse include: *Pohromnice*
(1966) (*Candlemas*), *Totožnosť* (1970) (*Identity*),
Kolovrátok (1972) (*Spinning-wheel*), *Kameň a džbán*
(1973) (*The Stone and the Jug*) and *Trvanie* (1979)
(*Permanence*).

Vagabond, The (1954)
Translation of *La Vagabonde* (1911), novel by
French writer ▷Colette. The narrator, Renée
Néré, a music-hall artist, faces a difficult choice
between freedom and the solace of love, and the
narrative consists of her introspection, combined
at the end with letters to her lover. The first-
person narration enables Colette to depict the
details of her heroine's self-confrontation, and
thus to explore the question of female identity; it
is significant that the opening pages present
Renée in front of her mirror, reflecting on
solitude. The novel is remarkable for its
awareness of the particular difficulties which
solitude presents to women, and, although it is
clearly not expressed in these terms, of the
ideological construction of the single 'lady'.

Vaidehi (born 1945)
Indian poet and short story writer. She lives in the
southern Indian state of Karnataka, and writes in
that region's language of Kannada. She has
published three collections of short stories, and
her work has appeared in anthologies compiled
under the auspices of the Kannada Sahitya
Akademi. A short story '*Akku*', translated from the
Kannada, is published in ▷*The Inner Courtyard*.
The title translates literally as 'elder sister', but
what is being particularly stressed is the notion of
kinship.

Vain Gift, A (1842)
▷Elena Gan's unfinished novella *A Vain Gift*
seems to have been planned around the
contrasting fates of two young girls. The first,
completed part was Gan's gloss on the true-life
tale of the prodigy ▷Elizaveta Kúl'man. Instead
of letting her heroine grow up in a relatively
understanding milieu in ▷St Petersburg, Gan
places Aniuta on a remote provincial estate. Like
Kúl'man Aniuta finds a sympathetic German
tutor, but his death leaves her isolated in a world
where even her widowed mother considers her
poetic gifts a form of insanity. She dies of
consumption brought on by despair, and
tumbleweed piles up on the cross over her grave.

Vakalo, Eleni (born 1921)
Greek poet and art critic. She grew up in Athens,
where she studied archaeology at the university.
Later she studied art history at the Sorbonne. She
taught art history at the School of Fine Arts she
and her husband, a stage designer, founded in
Athens in 1958. One of Greece's foremost art
critics, she has written numerous reviews and
articles for newspapers and art journals. Her first
collection of poems, *Themes and Variations*,
appeared in 1945, and her second, *Recollections
from a Nightmarish City*, in 1948. Her writing is
personal and without lyricism, seeking new ways
of expressing ideas, emotions and inner feelings of
alienation. Her poetry is experimental, lacking the
set rhythms of predetermined forms. *The Forest*
(1954), *Description of the Body* (1959) and other
collections are characteristic of her subjective,
automatic, illusionary but never sentimental
writing. She has translated into Greek the poems
of ▷Marianne Moore, whom she finds a kindred
spirit, and also written a number of essays on
modern poetry. Translations of her work have
appeared in English, French and Russian
anthologies.

Vala, Katri (1901–1944)
▷Pseudonym of Finnish lyric poet Karin Alice
Heikel. She is often compared with ▷Edith
Södergran for her intensity, but maybe also
because she too died from tuberculosis and was a
tragic character in Finnish literature. She
introduced free verse into Finland. Her father
died early and Vala grew up very poor. She
became a teacher, and in 1930 she married and
had children. Her early poems are Expressionist,

with stylized magic images, speaking of a pantheïstic religiousness. Her later poetry is political, more radical and formal, speaking in favour of her social reform and against political injustice.

She died in Sweden. In 1945, a volume of her *Collected Poems* was published.

Valedictory and Monitory Writing, A (1681)

▷ Sarah Whipple Goodhue, a North American Puritan, wrote this spiritual autobiography after having a premonition that she would die in childbirth. The text is traditional in form for Puritan death-bed declarations but unique in its insertion of poetic passages and Goodhue's own insistence upon declaring 'something of my mind' about the care of her children. Goodhue's document reveals a generous and loving personality, and through the 19th century it remained a popular record of a devout mother's abiding concern for the welfare of her family.

Valentí, Helena (born 1940)

Spanish novelist Born in Barcelona, Valentí grew up in post-war Spain in the Franco era (1937–75), experiencing the repression typical of that period. Later on she studied in England, and obtained a doctorate from Cambridge University. Her marriage to an Englishman ended in divorce, and she returned to Catalonia in 1974. Her main works are *L'amor adult* (1977) (*Adult Love*), *La solitud d'Anna* (1981) (*Anna's Loneliness*) and *La dona errant* (1986) (*The Errant Female*). All her work is concerned with the problems of womankind.

▷ Catalan women's writing

Valenzuela, Luisa (born 1938)

Argentinian novelist and short story writer. She was a daughter of Luisa Mercedes Levinson, also a writer, which enabled her to meet distinguished literary visitors such as Jorge Luís Borges (1899–1986). She became a journalist at the age of seventeen and worked for the press in Buenos Aires, for *El Mundo* and *La Nación*, and was an editor of *Crisis*. She is well-travelled, and has been widely published in magazines and newspapers throughout Latin America and the United States. Most of her work has been translated into English.

She won a Fulbright scholarship (1969–1970) and a Guggenheim Fellowship (1983) in the United States, and was a visiting writer at the University of Iowa, while working on her second novel, *El gato eficaz* (1972) (*The Efficacious Cat*). A voluntary exile from Argentina since 1979, she has been Director of the New York Institute for the Humanities and Writer-in-Residence at New York University and Columbia University, where she also teaches creative writing. She actively supports Amnesty International and is on America Watch (for Free Expression), the Freedom to Write Committee of Pen International.

She wrote her first short story '*Ciudad ajena*' 'Far City' part of *Los Heréticos* (1967) (*The*

Heretics), when she was eighteen. It was immediately published, and has since been translated and published with her first novel as *Clara: Thirteen Short Stories and a Novel* (1976). The stories in *Los Heréticos* tackle religious dogma and patriarchy, with all its myths, particularly in *El pecado de la manzana* (*The Sin of the Apple*) and *La Profesora* (*The Teacher*).

Valenzuela's first novel, *Hay que sonreir* (1966) (*You Have to Smile*), has a personal viewpoint and is ▷ naturalistic in style. The protagonist, a prostitute, has her throat cut out from her body, which is sometimes interpreted as a symbol for women's oppression. *El gato eficaz* is a novel with a first-person narrator, filled with literary experiment, and the destruction of traditional ideas about genre, ▷ patriarchy, and feminine eroticism. In contrast, *Aqui pasan cosas raras* (1975) (*Strange Things Happen Here: Twenty-six Short Stories and a Novel*, 1979) is a more overtly political work, in which even eroticism is seen in the light of distorted repression. *Cola de largartija* (1983) (*The Lizard's Tail*, 1983), is Valenzuela's most imaginative novel. It deals with political themes written in a more lyrical, metaphoric, and dream-like style, exploiting political figures of Argentina through ironical metaphorical references. Oppression and political tyranny is revealed in its male/female and hierarchical mainfestations through the use of an intricate, even baroque style. Her novel *Como en la guerra* (1977) (*He Who Searches*), developed around the idea of a female narrator travelling in Argentina, reveals glimpses of the frailty of truth. *Donde viven las águilas* (1983) (*Where the Eagles Live*) is a collection of her stories, some of which take place in the plateau of Mexico, with its mythical, magical, ancient civilization; others return to the political themes of previous writings. Valenzuela also wrote *Libro que no muerde* (1980) (*Book That Doesn't Bite*), a series of humorous vignettes on the art of writing, and *Black Novel (With Argentines)* (1992).

Vamvounaki, Maro (born 1948)

Greek novelist. She was born in Hania, Crete, her family moving to Athens while she was still a child. In Athens she studied law. Since 1972 she has lived in Rhodes, where she works as a public notary. She edits a Rhodes literary journal, *The Square*. Vamvounaki says that, for her, writing is a way of clarifying her mind about current issues. Her writing does not seem to have any specific message, and her characters emerge naturally from her own observations. Her characters, she says, seek what is true in life through situations of personal conflict. Her main characters are usually women living on the margins, fighting in their own way to claim their rightful position in society. Her novels include *The Archangel in the Coffee-Shop* (1978), *The Swan and Him* (1979), and *Chronicle of an Adultery*, (1981). Vamvounaki is also a painter. The importance of her writing is acknowledged outside Greece.

van der Mark, Christine (1917–1969)

Canadian novelist. Born in Calgary, she studied at the University of Alberta in Edmonton. Her most important novel, *In Due Season* (1947) is about the hardship of pioneering in the northern Alberta bush. *Hassan* (1960) is set in Pakistan; van der Mark travelled widely with her husband. *Honey in the Rock* (1966) concerns a small religious community in southern Alberta.

van Herk, Aritha (born 1954)

Aritha van Herk

Canadian novelist, critic and editor, born in central Alberta to a Dutch immigrant family. Van Herk studied Canadian literature and creative writing at the University of Alberta in Edmonton. Her first novel, *Judith* (1978), about a secretary who gains her independence by becoming a pig farmer, won the Seal First Novel Award. *The Tent Peg* (1981) uses multiple points of view to show the dynamic tensions between nine men and one woman in a remote geological exploration camp. *No Fixed Address: An Amorous Journey* (1986) is a feminist parody of the picaresque novel. *Places Far From Ellesmere* (1990) calls itself a *geografictione*: it palimpsests autobiographical places to geographically deconstruct Leo Tolstoy's construction of *Anna Karenina* (1875–1877). *In Visible Ink* (1991) crosses the genres of fiction and criticism. Van Herk has edited three collections of western Canadian fiction; she teaches at the University of Calgary. Her work is widely translated.
Bib: Hutcheon, L., *The Canadian Postmodern*.

van Rensselaer, Maria van Cortlandt (1645–1689)

North American letter-writer. Born on 20 July 1645, she was a second-generation Dutch settler whose family held the rights to the colony of Rensselaerswyck in what is now New York State. When her husband Jeremias died in 1674, she became administrator of the colony and sole support of her two children. Her widowhood was scarred by family disputes over control of the

colony. The ▷*Correspondence of Maria van Rensselaer, 1669–1689* reveals a life of hardship as she struggled to support her family and maintain the livelihoods of the other New Netherland colonists.

Vansová, Terézia (1857–1942)

Slovak prose writer and dramatist. From 1898 until 1907 she was the editor of the first Slovak woman's newspaper, *Dennica* (*Morning Star*), and organizer of the woman's movement. After some verse, for example *Moje piesne* (1875) (*My Songs*), she wrote novels by which she sought to bring woman readers to read Slovak rather than German and Hungarian, literature. ▷*Sirota Podhradských* (1889) (*The Podhradskýs' Orphan*) was the first Slovak novel written by a woman. Other novels include *Kliatba* (1927) (*Curse*), and *Sestry* (1930) (*Sisters*). Her complicated stories portray highly sensitive women, and usually end happily. Despite this sentimentality, Vansová is successful in depicting the psychology of her characters and the details of their surroundings. She also wrote a travel book about Prague, and translated Božena Němcová's novel ▷*Babička* (1855) (*Grandmother*) from Czech into Slovak.

'Varlámova, Inna' (born 1922)

Pseudonym of Russian fiction author Klavdia Gustavovna Landau. From 1934 until Stalin's death in 1953 Varlámova, the daughter of a political exile, led a peripatetic existence in the Urals and Siberia. That life, and her travels throughout the Soviet Union afterwards as a journalist, furnishes settings for the stories she has published since the mid-1950s, as well as autobiographical background for her 1975 novel, ▷*A Counterfeit Life*. Her eye for detail, gift for dialect, and sympathetic portrayal of characters of widely differing nationality and background inform stories like 'A Ladle for Pure Water' (*Russian and Polish Women's Fiction*), which is set among the Khant people of Western Siberia. In 'A Threesome' (*Balancing Acts*) a grieving widower finds consolation in returning to the Galician collective farm where his career began – and almost came to an abrupt end; the collective's vigorous director is a nuanced variant of that cliché of ▷socialist realism, the strong Soviet woman.

Varnhagen, Rahel Antonie Friederike (1771–1833)

German writer. She came from a Jewish family and, barely twenty years old and neither beautiful, rich, nor married, opened a salon in a Berlin attic. Her capacity to stimulate interesting discussion, her wit and her vivacity caused many intellectuals to desert the elegant salon of ▷Henriette Herz in her favour. Within five years Rahel's salon had become the focus of Berlin intellectual life and of early romanticism, attracting such literary figures as Hegel (1770–1831), Heinrich Heine (1797–1856), Ludwig Tieck (1773–1853), ▷Bettina von Arnim and many others. She married the author

Karl August Varnhagen von Ense (1785–1858) in 1814. She kept a diary, composed essays, and was, above all, a brilliant and prolific letter-writer, some of her correspondence being published by her husband after her death. Much of her work remains unpublished, but some has been reprinted in recent years. These collections of her writings include *Briefwechsel in vier Bänden* (1979) (*Correspondence in Four Volumes*) and *Jeder Wunsch wird Frivolität genannt. Briefe und Tagebücher* (1983) (*Every Desire Will be Called a Frivolity. Letters and Diaries*).

▷Huch, Ricarda; Salon culture (Germany and Austria)

Vartio, Marja-Liisa (1924–1966)

Finnish lyric poet and prose writer. She was born at Säminge, the daughter of a schoolteacher, studied in Helsinki, and took her MA in 1950. She was married to the writer Paavo Haavikko. In her early work she was an imaginative, even magical writer, as in the poetry collections *Häät* (1952) (*Wedding*) and *Seppele* (1953) (*Wreath*). This lyrical début was related to popular poetry. When she began to write prose she developed an objective style with very sharp analysis. First and foremost she was a portrayer of women, often with an ironic distance. Her principal work is without a doubt the posthumously published *Hänen olivat linnut* (1967) (*His were the Birds*), which has a very balanced structure, but the social novel *Mies kuin mies, tyttö kuin tyttö* (1958) (*A Man Like a Man, a Girl Like a Girl*) and the erotic novel *Kaikki naiset näkevät unia* (1962) (*All Women Dream Dreams*) are also artistically successful, reached a wide audience, and had a great impact on contemporary literature in Finland.

Vasalis, M. (born 1909)

Dutch poet. ▷Pseudonym of Margaretha Droogleever Fortuyn-Leenmans. She studied medicine and anthropology in Leiden, specializing in psychiatry and neurology; initially she was a doctor, and then a children's psychiatrist. Her most important collections are: *Parken en woestijnen* (1940) (*Parks and Deserts*), with the opposing concepts of order and chaos, time and eternity, and restraint and freedom, as a general human problem; *De vogel Phoenix* (1947) (*The Bird Phoenix*), in which the Phoenix symbolizes her child, who died young, as well as poetical inspiration; and *Vergezichten en gezichten* (1954) (*Vistas and Faces*), in which the emphasis is on human imperfection and the impotence of language. Throughout her work, events from reality are placed in the light of eternity, with the poet looking for cohesion in the chaos of reality while trying to restore unity. Vasalis was awarded the 1982 P.C.Hooft Prize for her complete *oeuvre*.

Vasconcelos, Carolina Michaëlis de (1851–1925)

Portuguese university professor and scholar. She was born in Germany and became a Portuguese citizen in 1876, upon her marriage to historian

Joaquim de Vasconcelos. Her extensive scholarship in romance philology earned her a university chair in 1911, the first granted to a woman in Portugal. Among her best-known works is her two-volume critical edition of the ▷*Cancioneiro da Ajuda* (1904), in which she comments on the role of women in the production of early Portuguese verse. Another important study is her ▷*A Infanta Dona Maria de Portugal e as Suas Damas* (1902) (*The Infanta Dona Maria of Portugal and Her Ladies*). A passionate advocate of women's education, she wrote wrote tirelessly on the need for instructional reform, as demonstrated in her study 'O Movimento Feminista em Portugal' (1901) (*The Feminist Movement in Portugal*). Despite the title of this essay, Vasconcelos commented at the time that it was still too early to talk about a feminist movement in Portugal; for such a movement to exist, she argued that more women in the country needed to be educated and economically independent.

▷*Cancioneiros*; Maria de Portugal, The Infanta, Dona; Carvalho, Maria Amália Vaz de

Vaz Ferreira, María Eugenia (1875–1924)

Uruguayan poet, short story writer and dramatist. She belongs to the ▷1900 Generation of ▷*modernismo*, along with Uruguayan writer José Rodó (1872–1917), ▷Delmira Agustini, and her brother, the philosopher Carlos Vaz Ferreira, among others. She wrote Parnassian-romantic verses, and was a ▷regionalist and ▷naturalist. Her main aim was to '*épater les bourgeois*' ('to shake middle-class attitudes'), but later, disdaining fame, she dropped an active social life in Montevideo for seclusion, and near the end of her life suffered a nervous breakdown. As a result, most of her work was published posthumously by her brother. Her first book, *La isla de los cánticos* (1925) (*The Island of Canticles*), and she herself, only became known after 1959.

Vega, Ana Lydia (born 1946)

Puerto Rican short story writer. Vega studied literature at the University of Puerto Rico, and later in Aix-en-Provence, France. She is a professor at the University of Puerto Rico, and founded the journal *Reintegro* (*Repayment*). She has received prizes for several of her short stories. *Encancaranublado y otros cuentos de naufragio* (1983) (*Encancaranublado and Other Shipwreck Stories*) won the 1982 Casa de las Americas Prize. The book is divided into three sections, '*Nubosidad variable*' ('Cloud variable'), '*Probabilidad de lluvia*' ('Probable rain'), and '*Mapa de vientos y tronadas*' ('Map of winds and storms'). The first two each include six short stories, and the last part is a single story. These narratives relate the life, history and culture of the Spanish-speaking Antilles in the Caribbean, especially Havana, San Juan, Jamaica and Port-au-Prince. The plots are treated with humour and in a colloquial style. Her second collection, *Vírgenes y mártires* (1981) (*Virgins and Martyrs*) was written with Carmen Lugo Filippi. She concentrates on female characters, placing them in a social context. The rich rhythm of her language is adapted to a syntax that is typical of the popular speech patterns of her Caribbean settings.

Bib: Marting, D.E. (ed.), *Women Writers of Spanish America.*

Vein of Iron (1935)

US novel by ▷Ellen Glasgow which reaffirms Southern agrarian values from a revisionist point of view; it is Glasgow's response to modern industrialization and urbanization. It focuses on a woman who triumphs over circumstances threatening to overpower her. Ada Fincastle violates her grandmother's values by having an illegitimate child. But she gathers her strength from what she inherited from her grandmother – her grandmother's vein of iron, and her fortitude to conquer life. Returning to her family's house, Ada sees a possibility for a new future. Glasgow suggests that the self can escape the savagery of modern civilization, and that the self learn the legacy of the past. Ada returns to nature and cultivates the land; she learns that the land empowers her.

Velásquez, Lucila (born 1929)

Venezuelan poet and essayist. She has employed different forms and themes in her poetry, from *Poesía, resiste* (1955) (*Poetry, Resist*) to *Claros enigmas* (1973) (*Clear Enigmas*), including political opposition to dictatorship. With the second book, she established herself as a poet full of rhythm and vital experience, and away from the ▷magic realism which was usual in her time.

Other works: *Color de tu recuerdo* (1949) (*The Colour of Your Memory*); *Amada tierra* (1951) (*Beloved Ground*); *Los cantos vivos* (1955); *En un pequeño cielo* (1962) (*In a Little Sky*); *Tarde o temprano* (1964) (*Late or Early*); *A la altura de la aroma* (1966) (*At the Height of the Aroma*); *Indagación del dia* (1969) (*Investigation of the Day*).

Velichkóvskaia, Tamara Antonovna (born 1908)

Emigré Russian poet, prose writer, and literary critic. Velichkóvskaia grew up in Yugoslavia and moved to France in 1942. Encouraged by other *emigrés*, including Ivan Bunin, she began publishing in 1947, although she had been writing poetry since childhood. She has contributed to *emigré* periodicals and anthologies. In 1952 her collection *The White Staff* appeared. Velichkóvskaia is a master of poetic meter and rhyme. In her short lyrics she likes to use extended metaphors, particularly from the world of nature. Her themes include various aspects of love, death, and the difficulty of expressing 'the most important thing.'

Bib: Pachmuss, T. (trans.), *A Russian Cultural Revival: A Critical Anthology of 'Emigre' Literature before 1939.*

Vengérova, Zinaida Afanas'evna (1867–1941)

Literary critic and historian, and translator. Vengérova played a crucial role in introducing European modernism to Russia in the 1890s, analyzed Russian literature for European periodicals, and articulated a strain of Russian feminism that abhorred the word. She was one of the best-educated women of her day. At the university-level Bestuzhev Courses in Petersburg she studied Western European literature under the tutelage of the eminent scholar A.N.Veselovskii. From 1887 to 1891 she attended courses on French and English literary history at the Sorbonne and at several English universities. From 1893 until 1908 Vengérova wrote a monthly column on the latest trends in European literatures for the ▷'thick' journal *The Herald of Europe*. In St Petersburg from the mid-1890s, she established close relations with the modernists grouped around ▷Gurévich's *The Northern Herald* and, later, the supresanio Diaghilev's (1872–1929) *The World of Art*. Her most important essays – among others, on Norwegian dramatist Hennie Ibsen (1828–1906), French poets Paul Verlaine (1844–1896) and Arthur Rimbaud (1854–1891), and English writers William Blake (1757–1827) and John Ruskin (1819–1900) – were published in the three-volume *Literary Characteristics* (1897–1910) and *English Writers of the 19th Century* (1913). In a graceful style, Vengérova sketched the writers' lives and work, emphasizing their talents and interpreting their literary endeavours. She also promoted west European modernists by translating them into Russian. A partial list of authors she translated includes German dramatist Gerhardt Hauptmann (1862–1946), Italian poet Gabriele D'Annunzio (1863–1938) (▷*D'Annunzianesimo*), French writer André Gide (1869–1951), English writer H.G. Wells (1866–1946), and Voinich (*The Gadfly*, 1898). During World War I in England Vengérova gave public lectures on Russian literature and culture and interviews about Russian women. She became familiar with the English imagists – Ezra Pound and Wyndham Lewis in particular – and in 1915 was the first to write about them for the Russian public.

Vengérova also wrote two articles on women, which were shaped by the philosophical and aesthetic stance of Russian modernism. She saw Russian women as the embodiment of moral freedom, spirituality, and aestheticism, in contrast to 'feminists' *per se* who defined freedom in political, legal, and economic terms.

Although she returned to Russia after the 1917 Revolution, Vengérova emigrated permanently in 1921, first to Berlin, then to London. In 1925 she married the poet and literary critic N.M. Minskii. They eventually moved to France and, after his death in 1937, Vengérova lived in New York with her sister, Izabella, a well-known pianist and piano pedagogue.

▷Bashkirtseff, Marie

Bib: 'The Life and Death of Tolstoy', *Fortnightly Review;* 'Variag' (pseudonym), 'The Leader',

Fortnightly Review; Rosenthal, C., 'Zinaida Vengérova: Modernism and Women's Liberation', *Irish Slavonic Studies*; Slonimsky, N., *Perfect Pitch: A Life Story*.

Venn, Anne (died 1658)

English memoirist, daughter of the prosperous merchant John Venn, who (like the father of ▷Celia Fiennes and husband of ▷Lucy Hutchinson) signed the death warrant of Charles I. Her writings, *A Wise Virgin's Lamp Burning* (1658), were published after her death by Thomas Weld and Isaac Knight, and they detail her search for faith.

Ventadorn, Maria de (died after 1225)

French ▷*trobairitz* of the third period. The wife of Elba V, Count of Ventadorn, she debated with Gui d'Ussel on equality between lovers, 'throwing the whole rhetoric of the courtly love game in his face'.
Bib: Ferrante, J.M., 'Notes Toward the study of a Female Rhetoric in the Trobairitz' in Paden, W.D. (ed.), *The Voice of the Trobairitz*.

Ventós i Cullell, Palmira (1862–1917)

Spanish novelist, who wrote under the male pseudonym Felip Palma. Though born in Barcelona, Ventós i Cullell often turns to rural Catalonia as a setting for her creative work. Her most important work is *La caiguda* (1907) (*The Fall*) which depicts the harshness of village life. On her death she left a number of unpublished works which were subsequently collected together as *Asprors de la vida* (1924) (*The Harsh Facts of Life*).
▷Catalan women's writing

Ventre di donna, Un (1919) (*A Woman's Womb*)

Italian novel co-authored by ▷Enif Robert-Angelini, and F.T. Marinetti, the 'father' of ▷futurism. Subtitled 'A Surgical Novel', it is the story of a woman's struggle with abdominal cancer and surgery. It is written in an experimental style: passages supposedly from a diary are interspersed with letters, both real and imaginary, of Marinetti and the actress Eleonora Duse. Robert, for her part, appears to strive to create a new kind of futurist writing for women here, in line with her own wish to move away from inconclusive, romantic fiction. The female character is certainly strong, yet Robert cannot prevent herself from identifying woman with her uterus: 'How disgusting it is to be a suffering womb' the character says. Achievement, too, is confined to the male: 'I think I would have been a good painter, if I had been a man.' The narrative, despite its much-vaunted experimentalism, continues to provide traditional representations of women.

Verbítskaia, Anastasiia Alekseevna (1861–1928)

Prose writer, dramatist, script writer, and autobiographer. In 1887 Verbítskaia made her literary debut with the novella ▷*Discord*, and in 1894 she began publishing fiction on a regular basis. She wrote two plays that were staged at the Malyi Theatre in the 1890s (▷*Mirage*). In stories like 'Happiness' (1904) Verbítskaia advocated women's need for economic independence and 'inspired' work outside the domestic sphere. After 1905 Verbítskaia wrote *Spirit of the Times* (1907) which, like ▷Gíppius's ▷*The Devil's Doll* (1911) and ▷Anastasiia Krandiévskaia's *Secret of Joy* (1916), is a political novel about that period of turmoil. Her works share some of the features of popular fiction – heroes and heroines who are always exquisitely beautiful, clichéd language, and entertaining plots, but she also had a knack for satire. Verbítskaia also wrote a two-volume autobiography, *To My Reader* and *My Reminiscences*. The second volume convincingly traces the process of self-liberation, and depicts a family of strong women.

Verbítskaia reached the height of her popularity with the six-volume novel ▷*The Keys to Happiness* (1909–13), which sold 280,000 copies by 1915 and was made into two films (1913 and 1917), for the second of which she wrote the script. After the 1917 Revolution, Verbítskaia's books were removed from bookstores and libraries because of alleged pornography and anti-Semitism. She supported herself by writing for children under various ▷pseudonyms.
▷*Crossroad, The*; Bashkirtseff, Marie; *Happiness*; ▷Kollontái, Aleksandra
Bib: Pachmuss, T. (trans.), 'Mirage', *Women Writers in Russian Modernism*; Brooks, J., *When Russia Learned to Read: Literacy and Popular Literature, 1861–1917*; Clowes, E.W., *The Revolution of Moral Consciousness: Nietzsche in Russian Literature, 1890–1914*; Wilson, K. (ed.), *An Encyclopedia of Continental Women Writers*.

Verdadeiro Método de Estudar (1746) (*True Method of Study*)

Written by Portuguese scholar and writer Luís António Verney (1713–1792). Born of French parents in Portugal and educated in the Jesuit schools, in 1736 Verney went to Rome to study. Impressed with the progressive educational system there, he wrote the book *Verdadeiro Método de Estudar* (1746) under the pseudonym Barbadinho. This book consists of sixteen 'letters' on educational reform, strongly influenced by the philosophy of John Locke. In it he attacked the antiquated Portuguese system of instruction and proposed massive reforms. So harsh was his criticism that the Portuguese Inquisition confiscated copies of the first edition. A second, revised edition circulated, but was the object of considerable debate. The book is of interest to feminist scholars because of the Appendix to the sixteenth letter, entitled 'Sobre o Estudo das Mulheres' ('On the Study of Women'), in which

Verney denounced women's education in Portugal as 'the very worst'. Verney argues that girls should have an education similar to boys so that, once married, they can instruct their children and be more interesting companions for their husbands. The curriculum he proposes for women includes religion, reading, writing, grammar, history and Latin. He also suggests that girls should receive instruction in more practical areas, such as bookkeeping. 'Sobre o Estudo das Mulheres' is a fascinating commentary which was considered quite progressive in its day.

▷Baroque

Vere, Anne Cecil de (1556–1588)

English poet. The daughter of ▷Mildred Cooke Cecil, Anne Cecil de Vere was one of the few women Latinists of her generation. At the age of fourteen she married Edward de Vere, although she had been considered as a match for Poet Sir Philip Sidney, (1554–1886), ▷Mary Herbert's brother. The marriage turned out to be unhappy, primarily because of de Vere's ill-treatment of his wife, the epitome of which was his denial of paternity to their daughter. In 1584, John Soowthern published *Pandora, the Musyque of the Beautie of his Mistresse Diana*, a sonnet sequence dedicated to Edward de Vere. Among other items included in the work are 'Four Epitaphs made by the Countess of Oxenford, after the death of her younge Sonne, the Lord Bulbecke'. The authorship of the four epitaphs written in sonnet form, however, is not absolutely certain. All four sonnets are in the same rhyme scheme and metre as the rest of Soowthern's sequence, suggesting that if Anne de Vere did not imitate Soowthern's model then he either extensively edited her work, or even wrote the epitaphs himself.

Verismo (Italy)

A late 19th-century literary and theatrical movement, usually translated into English as ▷realism. Italian *verismo* is much influenced by French naturalism, particularly the work of the novelist Emile Zola (1840–1902). Writers in this genre were keen to record the life of the regions, which seemed both threatened and neglected by the newly unified Italian state. ▷Caterina Percoto wrote of Friuli, Giovanni Verga recorded Sicilian life, ▷Matilde Serao that of Naples and ▷Grazia Deledda the Sardinian experience. For many critics, Verga is the supreme practitioner and theorist of Italian realism, but the presence of women writers in this movement is noticeable, as, indeed, is their concern to record in particular detail the experiences of women. Outside the temporal confines of *verismo*, traces of the style linger on in the works of such writers as ▷Laudomia Bonanni, ▷Elsa Morante and ▷Oriana Fallaci.

'Verses on Benjamin Tompson, by his Sister, Anna Hayden' (1927)

Written in remembrance of her brother, the North American poet Benjamin Tompson, this only known poem by ▷Anna Tompson Hayden is undistinguished. It does, however, reflect her awareness of the comparisons made between the siblings: '(Sum yt haue wondred how i could find / Discours with you to pleas your mind)'. Written in the family journal some time before 1715, it was first published in an anthology, *Handkerchiefs for Paul* in 1927.

Vertua Gentile, Anna (1850–1927)

Italian novelist and short story writer. Born in Como, she produced an enormous number of novels, short stories, plays, and moral pamphlets for children and young women. In her lifetime, she was a very popular writer, who selfconsciously addressed herself to her female public. She certainly lectured her readers, but she also represented their problems faithfully in her fiction. Some of her work is comparable to that of ▷Carolina Invernizio. Most of her writing is in a ▷sentimental vein. Her first work, written at the age of eighteen, is typical of much of her later output: *Lettere educative per fanciulle* (*Educational Readings for Young Girls*).

Her work includes: *Come dettava il cuore* (1871) (*As the Heart Dictated*); *Silvana* (1886); *Nora* (1888); *Cuor forte e cuor gentile* (1898) (*A Strong and Gentle Heart*); *La potenza della bonità* (1912) (*The Power of Goodness*); *Voce d'esperienza* (1913) (*The Voice of Experience*); *Castellaccio* (1924) (*The Dreadful Castle*); *Le due cugine* (1930) (*The Two Cousins*).

Very Easy Death, A (1966)

Translation of *Une Mort très Douce* (1966) by French writer ▷Simone de Beauvoir. This is de Beauvoir's short, but moving and eloquent, account of the death of her mother, Françoise de Beauvoir. Madame de Beauvoir had an uneasy relationship with her elder daughter (see the account in de Beauvoir's ▷*Memoirs of a Dutiful Daughter*), most particularly because of Simone's complete renunciation and disavowal of her mother's values and standards, including Catholicism. Yet when her mother died (unexpectedly, and within one month of her final illness) de Beauvoir's grief was deep and lasting. The book is a brilliant, if troubled, account of mother–daughter relations and the strength of irrational ties.

Vesaas, Halldis Moren (born 1907)

Norwegian lyric poet. She was born in Trysil, daughter of the writer Svend Moren. She worked as a secretary, and became a teacher in 1928. In 1934 she married the writer Tarjei Vesaas, had children with him, and lived with him in the Telemark. She has translated a number of plays, edited anthologies, and written essays. She has received several awards and prizes.

In 1929 her first collection of poems *Harpe og dolk* (*Harp and Dagger*) was published, quickly followed by another three. Her early poems are about identity, a woman coming into existence as a gendered subject, pride in being a woman, and a singing woman. Also in her love poems one finds this feeling of a very strong 'I', singing of 'We'.

From her early poetry until the last collection *I ein annan skog* (1955) (*In Another Forest*) she graduated from traditional lyrical poetry to a simple ▷modernism. This did not disturb her many readers. Even if she is not a great innovator of forms or themes, she is outstanding in Norwegian literature.

Veselítskaia, Lidiia Ivanovna (1857–1936)
The works of the talented Russian writer Lidiia Veselítskaia (pseudonym: V. Mikulich) represent the turn from the social concerns of realism to a concentration on individual psychology typical of ▷The Silver Age. In a series of novellas she depicted young women who concentrate their hopes in life on making a happy match that their passive and self-absorbed character debars them from finding. Veselítskaia's quick-paced style and sharp-edged humour made her works instantly popular. Her ▷*Mimochka* trilogy was praised by Tolstoy, and in the 1890s she worked as a translator for his popular publishing enterprise and began grafting unconvincing Tolstoyan morals and characters onto her pessimistic tales. In 'Bird Cherry' (1898) Masha's timidity costs her a man who might have loved her; the man with whom she drifts into marriage is a domestic tyrant, but she accepts her fate with religious resignation. In the story 'In Venice' (1901) Iuliia is subjected to a series of Jamesian revelations of the duplicity of the people she loves; devastated, she becomes a nurse.
▷Gurévich, Liubov'

Veselkóva-Kil'shtét, Mariia Grigor'evna (1861–1931)
Poet, dramatist and novelist. Veselkóva published poetry, began writing plays at the turn of the century, and made an attempt in 1904 to collaborate on an opera, *Undine*, with Sergei Prokof'ev (*Poems and Plays*, 1906; *Poems*, 1908, and *Songs of a Forgotten Estate*, 1911). Her historical novel, ▷*The Kolychevs' Patrimony*, appeared in 1911. Its sequel, *On Native Soil* (1914), is set during the Russo–Japanese War of 1904–5 and the political turmoil of 1905. Veselkóva-Kil'shtét used many of her own poems, published in *Songs of a Forgotten Estate*, as epigraphs for individual chapters of the novels. Both are filled with nostalgia for a bygone period when the gentry lived in harmony with Russian nature and folk on their country estates. During World War I she published both patriotic verse and another collection of poetry, *The Yellowed Pages* (1916). Her career ended with the Bolshevik Revolution in 1917. Her archives in the USSR contain three unpublished novels and poetry.

Vesen'ev', Iv. ▷Khvoshchínskaia, Sof'ia

Vesey, Elizabeth (1715–1791)
English letter-writer and ▷Bluestocking, friend of ▷Elizabeth Montagu, ▷Elizabeth Carter and

▷Hannah More. Famous for her gatherings, which shifted the emphasis from cards to conversation.

Vesnický román (1869) (A Village Novel)
Czech novel by ▷Karolina Světlá. The book is a psychologically analytical *roman à thèse*. It depicts a man, Antoš, formed into a model citizen by three women of conflicting ideologies. First, and last, Antoš is completely under the influence of his strict Roman Catholic mother, Jirovcová. He then comes under the influence of his boss and future wife, the largest landowning farmer in the area. She represents materialism or paganism in the novel. Antoš first loves the wild child of nature, Sylva, representing liberal Protestantism, who eventually goes into a convent to comply with Jirovcová's strict rules. The irony of the novel lies in the fact that, although human suffering and submission to his mother's ideology make Antoš the perfect man, admired by everyone, his submission to moral perfection deprives him of any will to live. Thus, having abided by Jirovcová's ideology, he dies soon after his mother, a broken man.

Vestly, Anne-Cath (Catharina) (born 1920)
Norwegian writer of children's books. She was born in secure circumstances, but her beloved father went bankrupt when she was four, and died when she was eleven. When she was young she wanted to be an actress. She met the artist Johan Vestly, whom she married. He has illustrated all her books.

In the early 1950s she began to make radio broadcasts for children which were later published as children's literature. Her books are about small children such as Ole Alexander, four years old, living in a high-rise flat in the city. It is ▷realistic, anti-authoritarian literature, which has had great impact on modern Norwegian ▷children's literature. She writes about new family patterns, of mothers working outside the home and fathers caring for the children. She has written more than forty books, many of which have been filmed, has been widely translated and has received many awards and prizes.

Vice-Consul, The (1968)
Translation of *Le Vice-consul* (1965), French writer ▷Marguerite Duras's tenth novel. Set in Calcutta, capital of an imaginary India under British rule, it tells a story connected to that of ▷*The Ravishing of Lol V. Stein*. Anne-Marie Stretter is the French ambassador's wife, and has many lovers. The French Vice-Consul in Lahore, who has been removed from his post for shooting at mirrors and lepers, becomes obsessed with her. At a reception held at the ambassador's residence, he is shunned by everyone, except Anne-Marie. She responds to him with calm understanding, but will not let him stay with her. He goes off into the night indecorously screaming her name, after which Anne-Marie goes to her holiday island and drowns herself. Intercut with this story is another,

narrated by a man in Anne-Marie Stretter's entourage. It tells of a beggarwoman for whom Anne-Marie leaves out food. The beggarwoman had been thrown out of home in Laos by her mother when she became pregnant, and subsequently walked all the way to Calcutta, bearing and losing countless children on the way, forgetting all language, and going mad. The novel can be seen as a critique of colonial hypocrisy in the face of human suffering.

Vicens, Antonia (born 1942)

Spanish novelist, born in Santanyi, Majorca. Vicens's work is centred on her home territory (Majorca) but she manages to express universal preoccupations. Her key work is *La festa de tots el morts* (1974) (*All Souls Day*) which, in Kafkaesque style, depicts the relationship between two essentially isolated beings, Coloma and Victor. Her other works are: *39 graus a l'ombre* (1968) (*39 Degrees in the Shade*); *Material de fulletò* (1971) (*Material for a Soap Opera*); *Primera comunió* (1980) (*First Communion*); *La santa* (1980) (*The Saint*); *Quilòmetres de tul per a un petit cadaver* (1982) (*Miles of Tulle for a Little Cadaver*).
▷Catalan women's writing

Vicente, Paula (c 1600–1660)

Spanish dramatist and actress. Paula Vicente was the daughter of Gil Vicente, a famous Golden Age dramatist and poet. She acted in her father's plays, and excelled as a musician. She wrote plays, as well as the guide: *Arte de lengua inglesa y holandesa* (*Art of the English and Dutch Languages*).

Victoria (1786)

First novel by North American author ▷Susanna Haswell Rowson. *Victoria* follows the English tradition of the novel of seduction, and like Rowson's later and better novel in this genre, ▷*Charlotte, a Tale of Truth*, it seeks to temper its melodramatic elements with social realism and the assertion of being rooted in 'real life' events.

Victoria, Queen (1819–1901)

Queen of England from 1837–1901, Victoria came to the throne when she was seventeen, and had the longest reign in British history. She became a monumental symbol for the nation during the 60 years of the greatest power and influence England had known. The British Empire grew and was consolidated during her reign, and Victoria was very much its figurehead. She was also seen as an exemplary wife and mother, having nine children with her husband, Albert, to whom she was devoted. Victoria was well-read; her diaries record her reading the ▷Brontës, ▷Elizabeth Gaskell and ▷George Eliot, as well as many male writers. She especially loved Tennyson, who became her Poet Laureate in 1850. The Queen wrote scores of letters and accumulated over 100 volumes of diaries and journals, selections of which have been published. The only writings published during her lifetime were *Leaves from a Journal of Our Life in the*

Highlands 1848–61 (1868) and *More Leaves* (1883), in which she records her travels in Scotland.
▷Imperialism; Walford, Lucy

Vidal, Mary Theresa (1815–1869)

Australian short story writer and novelist. Vidal was one of the earliest women fiction writers in Australia. She is best-known for her *Tales for the Bush* (1845), containing edifying and instructive stories warning servants, in particular, of the dangers of drink and the desirability of moral rectitude. She published ten other works of fiction, of which two, *The Cabramatta Store* (1850) and *Bengala: Or, Some Time Ago* (1860), deal with specifically Australian experience.
▷Short story (Australia)

Viebig, Clara (1860–1952)

German novelist. One of the most widely-read novelists in Germany at the turn of the century. She was a naturalist writer, who produced vivid portrayals of particular milieux and regions, especially within her native Eifel. Her plots tend to focus on the lives of women struggling with destiny. Amongst her best-known novels are *Das Weiberdorf* (1900) (*The Village of Women*), set in the Eifel, *Die Wacht am Rhein* (1902) (*The Guard on the Rhine*), a tale about the Franco-Prussian War, and *Die vor den Toren* (1910) (*Those Outside the Gates*), which describes the problems of people affected by the urban expansion of Berlin.

Vieillesse, La (1970) ▷*Old Age* (1972)

Vieira, Maruja (born 1922)

Colombian poet and prose writer. Her full name is Maruja Vieira de Vivas, and she has contributed to newspapers. A sensitive and inspired poet, she employs simple, sincere, short verses, and is a plaintive singer of memories. Her poems have a classical tone, but deal with everyday topics, devoid of ▷magic realism. Like many contemporary Colombian poets, she is a humanist, influenced by Surrealism. Her works include *Campanario de lluvia* (1974) (*Rainy Belfry*); *Poesías* (1950) (*Poems*); *Palabras de la ausencia* (1953) (*Words of Absence*); *Ciudad Remanso* (1956) (*Remanso City*); *Clave mínima* (1958) (*Lowest Key*); *Los poemas de enero* (1961) (*January Poems*); and *Mis propias palavras* (*My Own Words*).

Viernes Group of poets

Venezuelan group of poets formed in 1938, who were concerned with the epic dimension of history, the recovery of legends and myths, and the right of minorities to live on their own land. They included ▷Ida Gramcko, ▷Ana Enriqueta Terán, ▷Enriqueta Arvelo Larriva, and ▷Luz Machado, among others. The group published a magazine, also called *Viernes*. The ▷1945 Generation opposed the nativism and free verse favoured by the *Viernes* group.

Viganò, Renata (1900–1976)

Italian poet, novelist, journalist, essayist and short story writer. She was born in Bologna, and lived there for most of her life. Her family were quite comfortably off, but had a financial crisis while Viganò was young, and this resulted in her having to terminate her studies and get a job. She chose to become a nurse, a training which she made use of during the war when she joined a partisan group led by her husband, bringing her baby with her. She began to write at a very early age, as her *Ginestra in fiore* (*Broom in Flower*) of 1913 and *Piccola fiamma* (*Little Flame*) of 1916 indicate. Both were collections of poetry, heavily influenced by her studies of the 'great' Italian poets, such as ▷Carducci. Her best work, however, is generally considered to be ▷*L'Agnese va a morire* (1949) (*Agnes Goes Off to Die*), which arose out of her own experience as a partisan in the ▷Resistance. Agnes is an important character because of her class, and Viganò uses her to show the politicization of the working class; she is also important for her gender, and for her recounting of the Resistance experience from a female point of view. The novel won the Viareggio Prize for 1949. Viganò continued to make women's experience the focal point of her work, with her essays *Mondine* (*Female Rice Workers*) of 1952, and *Donne della Resistenza* (*Women of the Resistance*) of 1955. In her journalism she encouraged women to be socially and politically active. Her later fictional writings, too, like *Una storia di ragazze* (*A Tale of Two Girls*) of 1962, centre on female characters and on their attempts to be independent.

Other works: *Il lume spento* (1933) (*The Extinguished Light*); *Arriva la cicogna* (1954) (*A Visit From the Stork*); *Ho conosciuto Ciro* (1959) (*I Knew Ciro*).

▷Neorealism (Italy)

Vigil, Evangelina

US poet. Vigil is a ▷Latina writer from San Antonio, Texas. Her first book of poetry, *Thirty an' Seen a Lot* (1985), reflects Vigil's search for an authentic self. It portrays the suffering of a Mexican-American woman. The poems attest to the psychological violence Anglo-Americans inflict on Mexican-Americans, and depict the emotional and economic impoverishment of Mexican-Americans. The woman in the poems rejects the Anglo-American world that exploits her; she envisions a new Mexican-American community based on strong personal relationships. Vigil celebrates the customs and traditions of everyday life, emphasizing that they unite individuals and generate a sense of community. In her poems, she grows from an alienated individual to a committed Chicana.

Viidikas, Vicki (born 1948)

Australian poet and prose writer. Her three volumes of poetry are *Condition Red* (1973), *Knabel* (1978) and *Indian Ink* (prose poems, 1984). Other poems have appeared in *Nation Review*, and her only work of fiction is *Wrappings* (1974).

Vik, Bjørg (born 1935)

Norwegian prose writer and dramatist. She was born in Oslo, and trained as a journalist. She made her début in 1963 with the collection of short stories *Søndag ettermiddag* (*Sunday Afternoon*). In 1966 she published *Nødrop fra en myk sofa* (*Emergency Call from a Sofa*) and *Ferie* (*Holidays*), two collections of short stories criticizing convention, and hostility towards sexuality. She wrote many descriptions of sexual intercourse, which gave her a reputation as a soft-porn writer.

In the 1970s she wrote, from a feminist standpoint, *Kvinneakvariet* (1972, *An Aquarium of Women*), but still using sexuality as a method of breaking through to a real, naked contact in every respect, eg the collections of short stories *En håndfull lengsel* (1979) (*Out of Season*) and *Snart er det høst* (1982) (*Soon it will be Autumn*).

Vik has written many stage and radio plays. She writes in a modern style, with the dialogue as the most important trait. She has received many literary awards and prizes, but has been surprisingly little translated.

Vilariño, Idea (born 1920)

Uruguayan poet and essayist, who has also been a teacher and a professor of literature. Her first book of poetry, *La Suplicante* (1945) (*The Supplicant*), uses direct and daring language and a distinctive rhythm. Her poetry is tragic and despairing, dark, sad, and filled with powerful symbols of death or love. Despite the solitude in her poems, Vilariño has become widely known with her book *Poemas de amor* (1957) (*Love Poems*). In 1987, after refusing several prizes, she won the 'Rondô', the City of Montevideo Prize. Her work has appeared in several periodicals, and in the best national anthologies of Latin American poetry. She has become one of the main women's voices representing South America, with an essentially straightforward style.

Other works: *Cielo y cielo* (1947) (*Sky and Sky*); *Paraíso perdido* (1949) (*Lost Paradise*); *Por aire sucio* (1951) (*Through Filthy Air*); *Nocturnos* (1955) (*Nocturnes*); *Pobre mundo* (1966) (*Poor World*); *Treinta poemas* (1967) (*Thirty Poems*); *Poesía* (1970) (*Poetry*); *Segunda antología* (1980) (*Second Anthology*), and *No* (1980) (*No*).

Viljoen, Lettie (born 1948)

Lettie Viljoen (Ingrid Winterbach, or under her married name, Ingrid Gouws), who has also published under the name Ingrid Scholtz, studied art, taught history of art at Stellenbosch university, and now lives in Durban. As a student she corresponded with the Afrikaans writer Etienne Leroux (1922–1990), and this friendship forms the basis of his novel *18–44* (1967). Her first two works, *Klaaglied vir Koos* (1984) (*Lament for Koos*) and *Erf* (1986) (*Plot*), are short novels in which a white woman searches for a significant political role for herself and her young daughter. Deserted by her husband, the woman frees herself from his Marxist ideology to establish contact in her own way with the *lumpenproletariat*. The ending of

Klaaglied vir Koos points to a possible new time outside the patriarchal patterns of history, although it offers no final resolution. An extract from this text has been translated and anthologized in *A Land Apart*, edited by André P. Brink and J.M. Coetzee. In Viljoen's recent novel *Belemmering* (1990) (*Impediment*) the central metaphor is that of mapping new territory. In 1987, in a special issue of *Triquarterly* called *From South Africa*, she published the prose fiction extract 'A Little Cloud Out of the Sea, Like a Man's Hand', which she had translated into English.

Villarino, María de (born 1905)
Argentinian poet, short story writer, dramatist and essayist. Born María de Chivilcoy Villarino, she taught at the University of La Plata, contributed to the national and foreign press, and lectured abroad. Her prose style is careful, and her poetry is classical and precise, influenced by ▷Juana de Asbaje y Ramirez de Santillana. Her short stories and lyrical narratives evoke the past in a clear, seductive style. Her first book of poems was called *Calle apartada* (1930) (*Side Street*). Among others, she won prizes for her sonnets *Tiempo de angustia* (1937) (*Time of Anguish*), her short stories *Pueblo de la niebla* (1943) (*Village of Mist*) and her poems in *La iluminada* (1946) (*The Visionary*).

Other works: *Junco sin sueño* (1935) (*Sleepless Reed*); *Una antigua historia de la niña-niña* (1941) (*An Old Story About the Little Girl*); *Loores de Nuestra Señora de Luján* (1946) (*In Praise of Our Lady of Lujan*); *La rosa no debe morrir* (1950) (*The Rose Mustn't Die*); *Antología poética* (1958) (*Poetry Anthology*); *Los espacios y los símbolos* (1960) (*Spaces and Symbols*); *La dimensión oculta* (1972) (*The Hidden Dimension*); *Memoria de Buenos Aires* (1979) (*Souvenir of Buenos Aires*), and *Los nombres de la vida* (1981) (*The Names of Life*).

Villarta, Angeles (born 1942)
Spanish essayist and novelist. Villarta was born in Belmonte (Asturias), and educated in Switzerland. Her novels include: *Un pleno de amor* (1942) (*A Full Love*); *Por encima de las nieblas* (1943) (*Above the Mists*); *Muchachas que trabajan* (1944) (*Working Girls*); *Ahora que soy estraperlista* (1949) (*Now that I'm a Black Marketeer*), and *Una mujer fea* (1954) (*An Ugly Woman*).

Villedieu, Madame de ▷Desjardins, Marie–Catherine Hortense

Villena, Isabel de (1430–1490)
The most renowned medieval female writer of the Iberian Peninsula. Villena was the illegitimate daughter of the Spanish nobleman and writer, Enric de Villena. She was educated at the Court of Alfonso the Magnanimous, and entered Valencia's Trinity Convent in 1445. She soon became an influential voice both in Valencian society and at the court of the Catholic kings, especially after being elected abbess of Trinity

Madame de Villedieu

Convent for life in 1463. Her major work, ▷*Vita Christi* was published posthumously in 1497.

Villeneuve, Gabrielle-Suzanne Barbot Gallon de (died 1755)
French novelist. Left with only a small income when widowed, she lived in Paris and supported herself by writing, producing twelve volumes of work. She was the original author of the fairytale *La Belle et la bête* (*Beauty and the Beast*) (in *Cabinet des fées*, Vol. XXVI), noted for its Surreal elements. The most successful of her novels was *La Jardinière de Vincennes* (1753) (*The Gardener of Vincennes*). In this text, and the earlier *Le Phénix conjugal* (1733) (*The Phoenix of Marriage*), Villeneuve examines the place of women in society, portraying lower-class women as admirable heroines, showing them at work and praising their modest lifestyle. Her other prose fictions include: *La Jeune américaine* (1740–41) (*The Young American*); *Le Beau-frère supposé* (1752) (*The Presumed brother-in-law*); *Le Juge prévenu* (1754) (*The Biased Judge*); *Anecdotes de la cour d'Alphonse XI* (1755) (*Anecdotes from the Court of Alphonse XI*), and *Mlles de Marsanges* (1757); *Le temps et la patience* (1768) (*Time and patience*). She also wrote the play *Les belles solitaires* (1745) (*Lonely Beauties*), and two collections of tales, *Les Contes de cette année* (1744) (*This Year's Tales*) and *Contes de Mme de Villeneuve* (1765) (*The Tales of Mme de Villeneuve*).

▷Le Prince de Beaumont, Marie Le
Bib: Girou-Swiderski, M., 'Comment peut-on être parvenue?' *Etudes Littéraires*, December.

1979; Remy, P., 'Une version inconnue de *La Belle et la bête*, *R. belge philol.*, XXXV (1957).

Villette (1853)

A novel by British author ▷Charlotte Brontë. Like her earlier novel, ▷*The Professor*, *Villette* is based on the author's experiences in Brussels, where she worked as a teacher. The narrator, Lucy Snowe, loses her family and means of financial support early in the novel, and leaves for Villette (the name Brontë chose for Brussels) to find employment with Mme Beck, initially as a nursery ▷governess and later as a teacher in Mme Beck's school. Lucy's pupils are mostly vain, frivolous and shallow, unlike her in personality, but she succeeds in establishing authority. Much of the novel is devoted to the tempestuous relationship between Lucy and the professor M. Paul Emmanuel, Mme Beck's cousin. Ultimately M. Paul establishes Lucy in a school of her own before leaving on a business trip to the West Indies. The ending is ambiguous, for the reader is left to decide whether he returns to marry Lucy or is drowned on the way back to Belgium. The novel fuses ▷Gothic elements with 19th-century ▷realism, and the narrative strategy is unusual for its time. Recent feminist criticism has focused on the instability of the narrator's discourse and the gaps, ellipses and psychological projections which appear in *Villette*'s exploration of subjectivity.
Bib: Newton, J., 'Villette' in *Feminist Criticism and Social Change*, ed. Newton and Rosenfelt; Jacobus, M., 'The Buried Letter: Romanticism in *Villette*' in *Women Writing and Writing About Women*.

Villinger, Hermine (1849–1917)

German novelist and short story writer. She excelled at stories of village life, such as *Der lange Hilarius* (1885) (*Tall Hilarius*) and *Sommerfrischen* (1887) (*Summer Holidays*). She also wrote literature for young girls, and novels in which she explores the role of women in bourgeois society, and the possibility of their emancipation through self-development and hard work. Among such books are *Mutter und Tochter* (1905) (*Mother and Daughter*) and *Die Dachprinzeß* (1908) (*Princess on the Roof*).

Vindication of the Rights of Woman (1792)

Tract by English writer ▷Mary Wollstonecraft. It follows her *Vindication of the Rights of Man* (1790). She returns to the question of women's education (which she had addressed in ▷*Thoughts on the Education of Daughters*, 1787) to argue that uneducated girls are often 'cruelly left by their parents without any provision, and, of course, are dependent on not only the reason but the bounty of their brothers'. She speaks of such women as 'unable to work, and ashamed to beg'. Thus in Wollstonecraft's polemic, work and the ability to work is increasingly seen as important in terms of a woman's self-definition and survival in the world. This shifts the debate from the terrain of provision to one of rights, but it is coupled with a spiritual and psychological polemic – she wants women to 'acquire strength of mind and body' to combat their situation physically, but also to resist psychologically the categories constructed for them. She asks, 'Why are girls to be told that they resemble angels; but to sink them below women?' In the same work, Wollstonecraft expresses radical views on marriage, including the view that seduction should be regarded as marriage (she was writing after the 1752 Marriage Act made it harder for women to sue for breach of promise) and that 'the man should be legally obliged to maintain the woman and her children, unless adultery, a natural divorcement, abrogated the law.'

Vine, Barbara   ▷Rendell, Ruth

Viramontes, Helena Maria (born 1954)

US short story writer. Of Mexican-American descent, Viramontes was born in Los Angeles, California. She has been the literary editor of *Xisme Arte Magazine*. *The Moths and Other Stories* (1985) depicts the Mexican-American woman's struggles within her own family and community. The stories focus on women's conflicts with male authority figures. Viramontes's female characters fight against the rigid gender roles imposed on them. In 'The Moths' Viramontes shows how the Catholic Church helps to socialize women, while in 'Birthday' a woman has an abortion and radically redefines her relationship to the Church. As in 'Snapshots' and 'The Broken Web', women pay for violating traditional values; they are isolated and lack a sense of identity.

Virgile, Non (1985) ▷*Across the Acheron* (1987)

Virginia (1913)

US novel by ▷Ellen Glasgow which reveals the destructiveness of the idealized ▷Southern lady. Virginia Pendleton is raised and educated to conform to this ideal, but in adhering to this vision she destroys others, turning them into children to make them need her. Virginia also destroys herself. Her training has repressed her intellect and her sexuality, but she dismisses any insights into her aggressive and sexual nature.

Glasgow demonstrates how Southern women adhering to the ideal develop divided selves, seeing themselves outside of history; they avoid seeing the reality of their lives as women. Having sacrificed herself as a Southern lady, Virginia effectively dies upon discovering her husband's adultery.

'Virineia' (1924)

Russian writer ▷Lidiia Seifúllina's most famous story depicts one of the most vital heroines of Soviet literature. Virineia, a woman of independent opinions and loose morals scandalizes a Siberian village until the 1917 Revolution brings her a vocation as helpmate to a Bolshevik activist. The loving and effective adaptation of Virineia staged at the *avant-garde* Vakhtangov theatre in 1925 marked, as one semi-official history put it, 'the point at which all of Soviet theatre turned to contemporary subject matter'.

Virtues of Society: A Tale Founded on Fact, The (1799)

Like all of ▷Sarah Wentworth Apthorp Morton's poetry, this volume reflects her interest in the moral and social development of North American culture. In her earlier poem, ▷'Beacon Hill', she had failed to succeed in reclaiming the mythical aura of the American Revolution; in this poem's romanticized tale, however, she succeeds. Drawing on the moral values of the past, it asserts the appropriateness of those values to contemporary society as well. Blending sentimentalism and historicism, the poem establishes North America's past as a model for the future.

Visionsliteratur

The mystical writings of German nuns and visionaries in the Middle Ages. From the 12th century onwards, mystical texts by women who spent their lives in the seclusion of German convents began to gain wider circulation, attracting attention throughout Europe. While ▷Hrotsvith von Gandersheim in the 10th century and ▷Frau Ava of Melk in the 12th century transcribed legends of the saints, many nuns also began to write about their own personal visions and mystical experiences. A first important example of such writing is *Scivias* (1142–1151) (*Know the Ways*, 1986) by ▷Hildegard von Bingen, whose reputation as a holy woman was to exercise considerable influence. Her texts combine conventional and innovative modes of expression to achieve a 'celestial poetry', and became an inspiration for younger mystics such as ▷Elisabeth von Schönau. A century later, German mystical writing achieved its apogee in the work of ▷Mechthild von Magdeburg's ▷*Das fließende Licht der Gottheit* (1250–1260) (*The Flowing Light of Divinity*). Composed in Swabian dialect in a series of brief paragraphs, the book revolves around the idea of mystical religious love. God is personified as a bridegroom, with whom the soul yearns for a *unio mystica* (mystic union). This notion was further explored by many later writers, such as ▷Mechthild von Hackeborn, ▷Gertrud von Helfta, ▷Christine Ebner, ▷Margarethe Ebner, and ▷Adelheid Langmann. It also informs the many chronicles of the lives of holy sisters at Benedictine and Dominican convents. These chronicles, by such writers as ▷Anna von Munzingen, ▷Katharina von Gebweiler, and ▷Elsbeth Stagel, proliferated in southern Germany and Switzerland in the 14th century.

Vita Christi (1497)

A masterpiece of medieval Spanish devotional literature by ▷Isabel de Villena. Written towards the end of Villena's life, and published posthumously, this work describes the life of Christ, paying special attention to the episodes relating to women. Arguing against the misogyny typical of the times, her work points to woman's fundamental role in the redemption of the human race as well as in Christ's life.

Vitorino, Virgínia (1897–1967)

Portuguese poet and dramatist. She made her literary debut with a book of love sonnets entitled *Namorados* (?1921) (*Lovers*), which saw fourteen editions. Other books of romantic poetry followed, including the sonnets of *Apaixonadamente* (1923) (*Passionately*) and *Renúncia* (1926) (*Renunciation*). She also wrote several plays about the middle class, such as *A Volta* (1930) (*The Return*) and *Manuela* (1934), which one critic classified as 'salon comedies'.

Vivanti, Annie (1868–1942)

Italian poet and novelist. Born in London, she travelled in Switzerland and North America and lived in Italy, before her marriage. She married a North American, and settled in his country for some time, but eventually returned to Italy. She died in Turin. Vivanti had wanted to be an actress, but trained as a teacher of singing and languages. In the end, she followed in the footsteps of her German mother (Anna Lindau), and became a writer. She was romantically involved with Carducci (▷*Carduccianesimo*), who wrote the introduction to her first collection of poems *Lyrica* (*Lyric Poetry*), of 1890. Her writing primarily records the experiences of women during the period in which she lived. The novel ▷*Marion, artista del caffè concerto* (*Marion, A Singer*) of 1891 is, in part, drawn from her own life. In it, she explores the dilemma of the woman artist, a theme which preoccupied her over the years. A different perspective on the same theme is to be found in ▷*The Devourers* (*I divoratori*) of 1910, in which she considers how children destroy the lives of their mothers particularly. *Zingaresca* (1918) (*Gypsy Song*) records her memories of her earlier travels. Her later life was sad, marred by the death of her daughter in an aerial bombardment during the war and her own victimization because of her Jewish faith. She died alone and forgotten.

Her other works include: *Circe* (1912); *L'invasore* (1915) (*The Invader*); *Vae victis!* (1918); *Le bocche inutili* (1920) (*Useless Mouths*); *Naja tripudians* (1920); *Gioia* (1921) (*Joy!*); *Fosca, sorella di Messalina* (1922) (*Fosca, Messalina's Sister*); *Terra di Cleopatra* (1925) (*Cleopatra's Land*); *Perdonate Eglantina* (1926) (*Forgive Eglantine*); *Mea culpa* (1927); *Salvate le nostre anime* (1932) (*Save Our Souls*).

Vivas Briceño, Clara (born 1897)

Venezuelan poet, essayist and biographer. In her first books of poetry she wrote on love topics, with straightforward emotion and lyricism, in the romantic form. In contrast, her *Romancero de Tarma: cantares del llano adentro* (1970) (*The Ballad of Tarma: Poems from the Interior Plain*) describes the Venezuelan plains.

Other works: *La quimera imprevista* (1924) (*The Unexpected Chimera*); *Hostias líricas* (1928) (*Lyrical Punches*); *El romance del abuelo* (1935) (*The Ballad of the Old Man*); *El cántaro vacío* (1939) (*The Empty Jug*); *Gracia plena* (1941) (*Full Grace*); *Plenitud* (1941) (*Abundance*); *A la sombra de nuestros héroes* (1954) (*In The Shadow of Our Heroes*), and *Ala y musgo* (1956) (*Wing and Moss*).

Vivien, Renée (1877–1909)

Anglo-French poet and novelist. Born in London, her real name was Pauline Tarn, but she always wrote in French and lived in Paris for most of her life, part of a circle of women artists which included ▷Colette. The permissive climate of the *belle époque* allowed her to write about lesbian relationships more openly than would have been possible in anglophone culture at this time.

Vivien's lesbian love poetry is stylistically influenced by poets such as Baudelaire and Verlaine, but the content is innovative: it attempts to construct a lesbian cultural identity by reclaiming the traditions of courtly love and by mythologizing ▷Sappho. The poetry celebrates androgyny, virginity and love between women, but Vivien is unable to avoid internalizing homophobia, and terms such as 'perverse' or 'impure' are used in some poems; in general, platonic adoration of an idealized beauty is represented as a higher form of love than either heterosexuality or physical love between women. As her early death induced by drink and starvation might suggest, Vivien is fascinated by death, and there is some association of lesbian love with morbidity.

As well as her poetry, which was collected and published in two volumes in 1923 (*Poèmes*), Vivien produced plays based on the life of Sappho, a novel about her relationship with ▷Natalie Barney – *Une Femme m'apparut* (1904) (*A Woman Appeared to Me*), a life of ▷Anne Boleyn, and translations/elaborations of Sappho.
Bib: Jay, Karla, *The Amazon and the Page: Natalie Clifford Barney and Renée Vivien*; Benstock, Shari, *Women of the Left Bank: Paris, 1900–1940*.

Vivre l'orange (1979) ▷To Live the Orange (1979)

Vlami, Eva (1920–1974)

Greek novelist. She was born in Galaxeidi, the daughter of a sea captain. She studied music. Her book *Galaxeidi* (1947) is the chronicle of the town where she grew up, famous for its sailing ships, rich and powerful until the advent of the steam ship. Her second novel, *The Searock* (1949), is the story of an old captain who does not want to exchange the sails of his ship for a new steam engine. Vlami describes the conflicts of a man faced with the changes of modern times. In 1958 Vlami published an allegorical novel, *The Dreams of Angelika* and in 1963 another novel, *At the Loom of the Moon*, the story of an old woman living in a

small village. Vlami's work describes the seafaring life of Greece, a theme appreciated by all Greeks. She uses a richly creative vernacular language written in a simple and pleasing style. *The Searock* has been translated into Romanian and *At the Loom of the Moon* into German.

Voice of Industry, The

US 19th-century periodical, focused on labour issues. Associated with the Female Labor Reform Association's organizing ▷mill girls, *The Voice* attacked mill-owners' movement from benevolent paternalism to exploitation. In *The Voice of Industry*, Sarah Bagley, a ▷*Lowell Offering* contributor, questioned whether the *Offering*'s focus on mill girls' literary achievements worked against workers' interests. Bagley was especially critical of *Offering* editor ▷Harriet Farley, who promoted workers' intellectual and cultural life (and implied leisure time) to a national audience.

Voices Within the Ark, the Modern Jewish Poets (1980)

An anthology of works by Jewish poets from all over the world. The book is divided into sections according to the original language of the poems, which are presented in English translation. The introductions to each section provide a general historical survey. The Hebrew section presents works by all the major poets since the turn of the century. Women writers included are ▷Yocheved Bat-Miriam, ▷Rachel, Rachel Chalfi, ▷Lea Goldberg, ▷Esther Raab, ▷Dalia Ravikovitch, ▷Yonah Wallach and ▷Zelda.

Voigt-Diederichs, Helene (1875–1961)

German poet and novelist. Her stories are steeped in the atmosphere of the north German landscape, and describe the destinies of women working the land and raising families. Her novel, *Dreiviertel Stund vor Tag* (1905) (*Three-quarters of an Hour Before Dawn*) was acclaimed as the best regional novel of its time.

Voilquin, Suzanne (1801–1877)

19th-century French feminist author. A working-class feminist, Voilquin edited the journal *Tribune des femmes* (*Women's Tribune*) from 1832 to 1834, and was a member of the ▷Saint-Simonian movement. She joined in the expedition to Egypt organized by Enfantin's group, trained in midwifery – which enabled her to gain access to and help the women of the Egyptian harems – and later campaigned in France for better pay and conditions for her fellow midwives. She also exercised her profession in Russia for a time, and is said to have introduced homeopathic medical practices into that country. She used the pages of the *Tribune* in order to give a public account of the breakdown of her marriage, and was the author of a frank and lively autobiographical work, ▷*Souvenirs d'une fille du peuple* (1866) (*Memories of a Daughter of the People*), in which she talks unusually openly – but bleakly – of her sexual experiences. She published ▷Claire Démar's *Ma loi d'avenir* (1834) (*My Law for the Future*) but did not share the latter's radical views on morality.

▷Feminine/feminist journalism (France); Saint-Simonism and Saint-Simonian feminism

Voir dit (Seeing Said) ▷Armentières, Péronnelle d'

Vokins, Joan (died 1690)
English Quaker who travelled to Ireland, North America and the Caribbean, leaving her husband and seven children behind in Berkshire. When she died, the Friends published testimonies to her and her own memoir of God's part in her life in *God's Mighty Power Magnified: as Manifested and Revealed in His Faithfull Handmaid Joan Vokins* (1691). She uses biblical metaphors of travel and transport to describe spiritual states, as in 'I . . . was as a ship without an anchor among merciless waves.' Her only other publication was *A Loving Advertisement* (1671).

▷Evans, Katherine; ▷Quaker women (England)

Voodoo
An ancestral cult of sickness and healing which explains the genesis of illness and misfortune, this is of relevance in Caribbean writing. Although voodoo was never fully practised in ▷Jamaica or in the British West Indies generally, voodoo and ▷*obeah* have certain areas in common, especially those concerned with death, *duppies* (mask wearers) or ▷zombies. Like *obeah*, voodoo is essentially a practice involving magic. Voodoo is associated with Haiti, and originated with the enslaved Africans from Whydah and Dahomey, many of whom were taken to Haiti.

Vorabend (1975) (On the Eve)
A novel by the German-speaking Swiss writer ▷Gertrud Leutenegger. On the surface, the book is about a young woman on an evening stroll through eleven streets of Zurich on the eve of a political demonstration. This privileged moment triggers a lyrical stream of consciousness, in which the heroine embarks on a synchronic, associative investigation into her own life, her experience of love and violence, and the tenuous links she has with public reality. It is one of the more unusual women's novels to have grown out of the revolutionary youth movement of 1968 (with its emphasis on poetry, love and subversive political action), in that it seeks to express the woman's point of view, not so much through content, but rather through an experimental poetic stance.

Vovchók, Marko (1834–1907)
Mariia Aleksandrovna Markovich, author of prose in Ukrainian and Russian under the male pseudonym Marko Vovchók, married the Ukrainian ethnographer and political activist A.V. Markovych in 1851. Fascinated by his research, she learned Ukrainian, and in 1857 published *Ukrainian Folk Tales*. The book won her immediate acclaim from Russian radicals and Ukrainian nationalists, and was translated by Turgenev into Russian. These, and later tales from peasant life written in an impressionistic folk idiom, won her a permanent place in the history of Ukrainian literature. From 1859, when *Tales from Russian Folk Life* appeared, Vovchók also wrote in her native Russian, and from 1863–1876, when publication in Ukrainian was prohibited, her works appeared only in Russian. Her long and eventful life included years abroad (1859–1867) and in ▷St Petersburg, where she worked as an editor and translator with close professional and personal ties to radical circles (1860s–1878). In 1878 a new marriage took her to the provinces; more stories in both Ukrainian and Russian appeared from the 1890s to her death, but in ▷The Silver Age she was seen largely as an honorable relic of earlier ideals.

Although Vovchók wrote stories about urban and gentry life, her most popular works were those which dealt with the hard lot of peasants, especially women. A device she used repeatedly in early works was letting a serf girl narrate a tale about the life of her owners, in which her innate nobility contrasts with their fecklessness and cruelty to her and to one another ('Grusha the Toy', 'Boarding-School Girl' and 'King of Hearts'). 'A Living Soul' (1868) was Vovchók's contribution to the debate over the ▷woman question. The long novella *Notes of a Junior Deacon* (1869–1870) is a merciless satire of clerical life. A collection of her stories appeared in English as *Ukrainian Folk Tales* (1983).

Voyage in the Dark (1934)
This work by the Caribbean writer ▷Jean Rhys is considered to be her most ▷autobiographical. In it she attempts to capture the ambivalence of what it meant to be white and ▷Creole. Rhys first called the novel *Two Tunes*, signifying the double rhythms of the West Indies and England and the divided consciousness of the protagonist as a white colonial subject. The story depicts the life of Anna, who at eighteen has exchanged the warmth and beauty of the West Indian island of her childhood for the cold and grey of England. While working as a chorus girl she has a brief liaison with a kind, unimaginative man. This leads her to abandon the theatre and drift into the *demi-monde* of 1914 London. Through her experience of prostitution, betrayal by men, and the English class system, she comes to understand the harsh reality of being a single woman in a man's world. This account of a woman's journey from innocence to knowledge was way ahead of its time and created a sensation when it was published. Frank, economical and exact, *Voyage in the Dark* is a classic portrait of a woman on her own.

See Teresa F. O'Connor, *Jean Rhys: The West Indian Novels* (1986) for a detailed discussion and critique. For a critical analysis, see Carole Angier, *Jean Rhys Life and Work* (1990) and Carole Ann Howells, *Jean Rhys* (1991).

Voznesénskaia, Iuliia Nikolaevna (born 1940)
Russian prose writer, poet and editor.
Voznesénskaia has been a lifelong rebel against
the enforced conformity of Soviet life. Her fine,
mildly innovative poetry, with its rich sound-
patterning and imagery and combined strains of
religious resignation and outspoken defiance of
the state, was not published in the official press
even during the relatively permissive ▷'thaw'.
Voznesénskaia was active in the Leningrad
Second Culture movement, which gave a forum to
other independent artists. She served time in
labour and prison camps in the mid-1960s and
the late 1970s: it was her participation in a
▷*samizdat* feminist magazine, *Women and Russia*,
that most upset the authoritarian government and,
in 1980, threats against her teenage sons forced
her to emigrate with them to West Germany.
Voznesénskaia remained active in publicizing the
plight of dissidents in the USSR. In the West she
is best known for fictional works that are a semi-
documentary exposé of the defects and
contradictions of Soviet life (▷*The Women's
Decameron*; ▷*The Star Chernobyl*).
  ▷*Counterfeit Life, A*

Vuyk, Beb (Elisabeth) (1905–1991)
Dutch (East Indies) prose writer and journalist.
She grew up in the Netherlands; her father was
part-Indonesian. In 1929 she left for the then
Dutch East Indies to teach. She married an
enterprising planter, an Indo-European like
herself (the position of Indo-Europeans is an
important theme in her work), and the couple
lived in Java and on Buru (in the Moluccas). She
and her family spent the greater part of the war in
Japanese internment, and after Indonesia became
independent they remained in Java, becoming
involved in Indonesia's independence movement
and opting for Indonesian citizenship. For
political reasons they had to leave the country, and
in 1958 Vuyk returned to the Netherlands. She
drew the material for her stories, published from
1930, from her own life and surroundings. Her
style has its roots in the oral tradition (▷Maria
Dermoût), her work leans toward the adventure
genre (her great influences being Rudyard Kipling
and Joseph Conrad). She was partial to
adventurers and pioneers whose lives are filled
with hardship and failed undertakings, and she
conjured up a detailed picture of Dutch East
Indian society (from preparing meals, to the
complex social hierarchy). Apart from many
cookery books and several children's books, Vuyk
wrote the novels *Duizend eilanden* (1937) (*A
Thousand Faces*), *Het laatste huis van de wereld*
(1939) (*The Last House of the World*, 1983, and *Het
hout van Bara* (1947) (*The Wood of Bara*). These
books and her collections of stories have been
included in her collected works, *Verzameld Werk*
(1972). For her work she received several literary
awards.

W

Waard, Elly de (born 1940)

Dutch poet. She studied Dutch for several years in Amsterdam and wrote reviews and articles on poetry in newspapers. Following the death of her partner, the poet Chr. J. van Geel, de Waard began writing poetry, making her début with *Afstand* (1978) (*Distance*). She has outspoken opinions on poetry, and is active in the literary branch of the women's movement, being the driving force behind the *Amazone* festivals of women poets (1985 and 1986), and co-founder of the Anna Bijns Foundation that provides for a biennial award for 'the female voice in literature'. According to de Waard, the Dutch literary ▷canon is a typically male canon, and the figure of ▷Anna Bijns could further the cause of recognizing an alternative, female canon. For the foundation she wrote *Anna Bijns* (1985) on the life and works of Bijns, as well as on a different attitude towards female authors. She also headed the *Nieuwe Wilden* (New Savages), a group of female poets, providing a counter-balance to the *Maximalen* (Maximals), a group of young male poets, who perform frequently all over the country. De Waard also compiled anthologies of their work. She has published the collections *Luwte* (1979) (*Lee*), *Furie* (1981) (*Fury*), *Strofen* (1983) (*Strophes*), *Een wildernis van verbindingen* (1986) (*A Wilderness of Connections*) and *Onvoltooiing* (1988) (*Incompletion*). Themes in de Waard's poetry are the heights and depths of romantic love, the longing for a lover, the (female) body, physical delight, passion and homosexuality.

Waciuma, Charity

Kenyan autobiographer and children's author. Waciuma is the daughter of pioneering parents, both of whom ran away from home to get a Western education, and promoted education for the Kenyan people and recognition for women. Waciuma's own education as a teacher was interrupted during the Mau Mau revolution in Kenya (1952–6). ▷*Daughter of Mumbi* (1969) records her adolescence during the seven-year Emergency period. Waciuma advocates adaptation of traditional cultural values at a time of change and portrays conflicts about medical systems, women's circumcision and polygamy. Her children's writing includes *Mwenu, the Ostrich Girl* (1966), *The Golden Feather* (1966), *Merry-Making* (1972), *Who's Calling* (1973) and *Mweru the Ostrich*. For her juvenile audience Waciuma stresses Kikuyu legends and traditions of storytelling.
Bib: Taiwo, Oladele, *Female Novelists of Modern Africa*; Bruner, Charlotte H. (ed.), *Unwinding Threads, Writing by Women in Africa*; and Neubauer, C.E., *World Literature Written in English*.

Waddington, Miriam (born 1917)

Canadian poet, born Miriam Dworkin in Winnipeg, Manitoba. Her Russian-Jewish parents were political and intellectual, and she was educated in a Yiddish school until Grade Five, when she learned English. Surrounded by Winnipeg's multiple ethnic communities, she developed a powerful sensitivity to language. She studied at the University of Toronto, gaining her BA in 1939, published a number of stories and poems there, and married Patrick Waddington, a journalist. Unable to get satisfactory work, she returned to Toronto University for a Diploma in Social Work (1942), took a Masters degree in Social Work at the University of Pennsylvania (1945), and then became a social services caseworker. Her first book, *Green World* (1945), appeared in the same year that she moved to Montreal, where she wrote, and taught at the School of Social Work at McGill University. *The Second Silence* (1955) and *The Season's Lovers* (1958) describe some of the urban ugliness that she encountered in her job. After separating from her husband in 1960, Waddington moved to Toronto with her sons, and gradually returned to teaching literature at York University, Toronto. This heralded the beginning of a productive period; Waddington's subsequent poetry is observant and understated. *The Glass Trumpet* (1966), *Driving Home: Poems New and Selected* (1972), *The Price of Gold* (1976), *Mister Never* (1978) and *The Visitants* (1981), culminated with her *Collected Poems* (1986). Her later poetry is most effective for its celebration of ageing, and for its abbreviated line and effaced punctuation. She has also published a collection of short stories, and edited *Canadian Jewish Short Stories* (1990).

Waffen nieder! Eine Lebensgeschichte, Die

(1889) ▷*Lay Down Your Arms!* (1892, 1972)

Wägner, Elin Matilda Elisabeth (1882–1949)

Swedish prose writer, journalist and intellectual who fought for pacifism, women's emancipation, and for an improved environment. She was born at Lund, her father a headmaster. Her mother died when she was three, and she lived part of her childhood with her grandparents in Småland. For seven years she went to a girls' school, and later she became a journalist. From 1910 to 1922 she was married to the critic John Landquist.

The style of her novels and books is journalistic. She wrote quickly and radically, and her novels were mostly written as parts of a public debate. Her début was in 1907 with *Från det jordiska muséet* (*From our Earthly Museum*). *Pennskaftet* (1910) (*The Penholder*) was ground breaking with its new insights into eroticism and its fight for woman's suffrage. Wägner was very productive. During World War I, she fought for pacifism, as in *Släkten Jernploogs framgång* (1916) (*The Success of the Family Ironplough*). Her best novel is the lengthy *Åsa-Hanna* (1918) set in the 1880s–1890s; it depicts a strong woman in immoral surroundings.

In the book *Väckarklocka* (1941) (*Alarm Clock*), she tries to bring together her ideas about woman as the saviour of peace and the earth: a 'new-age' book forty years before the concept of 'New Age'. For her biography of ▷Selma Lagerlöf she was rewarded with a seat in the Swedish Academy in 1944. She was an outstanding woman, a ▷new woman in her own time.

Wakosi, Diane (born 1937)

US poet. Wakosi was educated at the University of California, and went on to teach in high school and then in universities and writers' workshops. She is an example of a poet who espouses an expressive autobiographical model of poetry but acknowledges that her poetry constructs the 'I'. 'I feel,' she writes, 'that poetry is the completely personal expression of someone about his feelings and reactions to the world. I think it is *only interesting* in proportion to how interesting the person who writes is.' Yet she also says, 'I write in the first person because I have always wanted to make my life more interesting than it was.'

In addition to her collections of poetry, Wakosi has developed a form of 'poem lecture', such as 'The blue swan, an essay on music and poetry', which mix poetry with prose genres such as letters and personal narrative.

Other works include: *Coins and Coffins* (1962), *The George Washington Poems* (1967) and *Inside the Blood Factory* (1968), collected in *Trilogy* (1974), *The Motorcycle Betrayal Poems* (1971), *Waiting for the King of Spain* (1976), *The Man Who Shook Hands* (1978), *Toward a New Poetry* (1980), *The Lady Who Drove Me to the Airport* (1982), *The Magician's Feastletters* (1982) and *The Complete Greed, Parts 1–13* (1984).

'Waif Wander' ▷Mary Fortune

Walford, Lucy (1845–1915)

Scottish (▷Scotland) novelist, born in Portobello, near Edinburgh. Her first work, *Mr Smith: A Part of His Life*, was published in 1874, and resulted in Walford being presented to ▷Queen Victoria, who had asked to meet the book's author. Walford went on to write more than thirty works, including *Pauline* (1877); *Troublesome Daughters* (1880); *A Pinch of Bubble* (1895); *A Dream's Fulfillment* (1902) and *The Enlightenment of Olivia* (1907). She also published two non-fictional works: *Recollections of a Scottish Novelist* (1910) and *Memoirs of Victorian London* (1912).

Walker, Alice (born 1944)

US novelist, poet, short story-writer, editor and essayist. Throughout her career Walker has tirelessly analyzed the oppressions, contradictions and hidden histories of black African-American women. Born in Eatonton, Georgia into an African-American sharecropper family, Walker was educated at Spelman College and graduated from Sarah Lawrence College. Stories such as those collected in *You Can't Keep a Good Woman Down: Stories* (1981) and poems such as *Revolutionary Petunias* (1973) carefully prise apart sexual and racial taboos, whilst contextualizing black history from its African roots and slavery,

Alice Walker

through to the Civil Rights Movement, in which Walker was active during the late 1960s. Walker's first novel *The Third Life of Grange Copeland* (1970), a family history of the Copelands, enacts the transformation of its central character from violence and self-hatred to a responsibility for his life and actions which becomes the ground for an African-American politics which rejects the traditional role of victim. Central to the novel is an exploration of Grange's violent and abusive behaviour towards women. Between *Grange Copeland* and Walker's Civil Rights novel, ▷*Meridian* (1976), came *In Love and Trouble: Stories of Black Women* (1973) in which Walker developed her now-famous aesthetic metaphor of quilt-making. Walker's best-known novel, ▷*The Color Purple* (1982), dramatically stages the interrelation between racism and the oppression of female sexuality. The book shot onto the bestseller list, assisted by Spielberg's controversial blockbuster film adaptation of Walker's text in 1985, although the film was accused of watering down Walker's racial and sexual politics in favour of a more compromising view of black women. *The Temple of My Familiar* (1989) pursues the theme of an African-American spirituality always near the surface of Walker's writing.

As well as her poetry and prose, Walker's contribution to literary criticism, best represented by ▷*In Search of Our Mothers' Gardens: Womanist Prose* (1983), has been ground-breaking, not only because it has rescued writers such as ▷Zora Neale Hurston from neglect, but also because of the framework it has provided for the development of a black feminist literary criticism. She has edited *I Love Myself When I am Laughing . . .: A Zora Neale Hurston Reader* (1979).

Other works include: *Once: Poems* (1968), *Five Poems* (1972), *Good Night Willie Lee, I'll See You in the Morning* (1979) *Horses Make a Landscape Look More Beautiful* (1985), and *Living By the Word: Selected Writings, 1973–1987* (1988).
Bib: Russell, Sandi, *Render Me My Song: African-American Women Writers From Slavery to the Present.*

Walker, Kath ▷Noonuccal, Oodgeroo

Walker, Margaret (born 1915)

North American poet, novelist and essayist.
Walker was born in Birmingham, Alabama,
graduated from Northwestern University in 1935
and in 1965 was awarded a Doctorate at the
University of Iowa. Since 1949 she has taught at
Jackson State University in Mississipi. Her first
collection of poetry *For My People* (1942) has been
widely influential. Walker uses jazz and blues
rhythms and metres, figures from African-
American folklore, and an evocation of the US
South to explore and condemn the devastating
damage of racism and the strength and survival of
African-Americans. Her prize-winning historical
novel, *Jubilee* (1966), uses the figure of Vyry,
moving from slavery to freedom and searching for
a home and a place of security, to recount the epic
story of African-American history and to celebrate
the richness of African-American culture. *Poems
for a New Day* (1970) explores a later moment in
this history, the Civil Rights Movement. Walker's
work is dedicated to the formation of an authentic
and vital African-American culture.

Other work includes: *Come Down From Yonder
Mountain* (1962), *Ballad of the Free* (1966), *How I
Wrote Jubilee* (1972), *October Journey* (1973), *A
Poetic Equation: Conversations Between Margaret
Walker and Nikki Giovanni* (1974), *The Daemonic
Genius of Richard Wright* (1982), *For Farish Street
Green* (1986), *This is My Century: New and
Collected Poems* (1988) and *How I Wrote Jubilee and
Other Essays on Life and Literature* (1990).

Wallace, Bronwen (1945–1989)

Canadian poet and fiction writer. Wallace was
born and educated in Kingston, Ontario, and at
Queen's University. She worked at various jobs,
including bookstore clerk, and counsellor in a
shelter for abused women and children, as well as
teaching creative writing. Her poetry, *Bread and
Chocolate/Marrying into the Family* (1980, with
▷Mary di Michele); *Signs of the Former Tenant*
(1983); *Common Magic* (1985), and *The Stubborn
Particulars of Grace* (1987) transcends its own
gritty ordinary. *Keep That Candle Burning Bright
and Other Poems* (1991) tributes the
interconnected body of country-and-western
music. Her short story collection, *People You'd
Trust Your Life To* (1990), is a luminous
exploration of storytelling's transcendent space; it
speaks strongly to the authentic voice lost when
she died.
Bib: Special issue of *Open Letter*, 1991.

Wallach, Yonah (1944–1985)

Israeli poet. Wallach, whose first poems were
published in 1963, has made a unique
contribution to Israeli literature. She was
provocative in her life, as in her writing, and the
aggressive tone of her poems is constantly
challenging. The rich imagery is dynamic,
dissolving and reconstructing itself as it follows
the precise movement of emotions and
perceptions. Often the 'self' portrayed in the
poems is confused and tormented, escaping into

madness. The poems express the most intimate
sensual experiences in a powerful and sometimes
shocking way. Wallach is regarded as one of the
most intriguing poets in Israeli literature. Her
works include *Devarim* (1966) *(Things), Shney
Ganim (Two gardens)* (1969) and ▷*Shira* (1976)
(Poetry).
   ▷*New Writing From Israel; Voices Within the Ark*

Wallada bint al-Mustakfi (died c 1091)

An Arab Andalusian princess who had a rich
establishment of her own, where she played
hostess to poets, musicians and politicians. She
was a beautiful, quick-witted woman who wrote to
her lovers in verse. Two statesmen competed for
her favour; one was Ibn Zaidun (1003–1070), an
important poet of the age. Literary histories have
favoured him because of the volume of love poetry
he addressed to her. Apart from satirical
exchanges with her guests, those of Wallada's
poems which have survived are mostly shorter love
poems, explicit in their celebration of fulfilled
love: 'I, your lover, say goodbye to patience when
I say goodbye to you / the secret I left in your
keeping is now open / I bite my lips I did not walk
longer when seeing you off / Brother of the full
moon in light and glory, God bless the time you
shone on us / Now my nights will be long without
you, how often I complained of the shortness of
my nights with you.'

Wallada, who never married, is described in
some literary histories as a libertine, who first set
the model for unveiling and frivolity. Others
protest that she was a chaste woman who did not
fall from grace or commit any sin. It is interesting
to compare her poetry to the earlier poetry of
▷*hara'ir* (free women), among oriental Arabs.

Waller, Lady Anne (died 1662)

English diarist who began her diary in 1649, when
she had already been the widow of Sir Simon
Harcourt for seven years. Her first husband was a
Royalist, her second, Sir William Waller, a
Puritan. She went to prison with him in 1659.

Walsh, María Elena (born 1930)

Argentinian poet. Although she began her career
as a musician and a children's writer, she was
acknowledged as a poet with the publication of
her first book, *Otoño imperdonable* (1947)
(Unforgivable Autumn). It won the City Prize in
1952, and is full of rich lyrics, depth and integrity.
She followed the ▷1945 Generation, which had
exaggerated the esoteric form, filled with ▷magic
realism and metaphysics. *Apenas viaje* (1948)
(Scarcely a Journey) was received by the critics as
the work of a new Rimbaud (1854–1891). *Casi
milagro* (1958) *(Almost a Miracle)*, comprises seven
beautiful sonnets. For the critic Anderson Imbert,
this book confirmed her dazzling poetic capacity
of instantaneous expression. She received a Merit
Degree from the Konex foundation (1982).

Walsh contributes to the newspaper *El Clarín*,
and in 1985 she became an Honorary Citizen of
Buenos Aires. Her compositions for children are

full of poetry. She has recorded children's books, songs and plays, and worked for film and television.

Other works: *Baladas con Ángel* (1951) (*Ballads with Angel*); *Hecho a mano* (1965) (*Handmade*); *Cancionero contra el mal de ojo* (1976) (*Anthology Against Eye Strain*); *A la madre* (1965) (*To The Mother*), and *Los Poemas* (1984) (*Poems*).

Walshe, Dolores (born 1949)

Irish poet, short story writer and dramatist. She was born and educated in Dublin, where she now lives. Her poetry and short stories have been included in numerous anthologies. *In the Dark*, her prize-winning play, was staged by the Manchester Royal Exchange Theatre in 1989, and *A Country in Our Heads* was first performed at the Dublin Theatre Festival, 1991.

Walter, Silja (born 1919)

▷German-speaking Swiss poet, dramatist and nun. She grew up near Zurich one of eight children of a well-known local publisher. A collection of her poems, *Die ersten Gediche* (*The First Poems*), appeared in 1945, four years before she took vows at a nearby Benedictine convent. Musicality of language and serenity of vision characterize her poems, which tend to explore themes of religious and spiritual quests.

Principal pubications: *Der Tanz des Geshorsams oder die Strohmatte. Gedichte* (1970) (*Dance of Obedience or the Straw Mat, Poems*) *Die Feuertaube. Neue Gedichte fur meinen Bruder*) (1985) (*Dove of Fire, New Poems for my Brother*) and *Feuerturm* (1987) (*The Firetower*), a play.

Wander, Maxie (1933–1977)

Austrian writer. Born in Vienna, she grew up to be a rebellious young drop-out who passionately espoused communist ideals, and in 1958 emigrated to East Germany with her husband. In 1977 she published *Guten Morgen, du Schöne. Protokolle nach Tonband* (*Good Morning, Beautiful. Transcripts from Tapes*), a collection of intimate interviews with East German women which broke a number of taboos, and aroused much interest in both Germanies. Her diaries and letters were published posthumously by her husband in *Leben wär' eine prima Alternative* (1980) (*To Stay Alive Would be a Great Alternative*). They offer a moving account of her coming to terms with cancer and early death.

Wandering Girl (1988)

Australian autobiography by Glenyse Ward. An account, written in the vernacular, of Ward's experiences at Wandering Mission, and then later of the humiliation and indignity she suffered as a servant to white farmers in the 1960s. Together with Monica Clare's *Karobran* (1978) and ▷Sally Morgan's ▷*My Place* (1987), it forms part of a new wave of Aboriginal women's literature dealing with issues of white oppression and Aboriginal identity.

▷Aboriginal women writers in Australia

Wandor, Michelene (born 1940)

English dramatist, poet and short story writer of Russian-Jewish parentage. Educated at Newnham College, Cambridge, Wandor has been actively involved in the women's movement from the late 1960s, and her commitment to feminist concerns is expressed throughout her writing. Her plays have often been written directly for women's theatre groups, and include *The Day after Yesterday* (1972), which focuses on the Miss World Contest; *Spilt Milk* (1973), on maternity; and *Aid Thy Neighbour* (1978), on lesbian motherhood. Wandor has been influential in the publication of feminist drama, and her critical studies of women and theatre include *Carry On, Understudies* (1981) and *Look Back in Gender* (1987), which looks at 'sexuality and the family in post-war drama'. Her other writings include: *Upbeat* (1988), a collection of poems and stories; ▷*Arky Types* (1987), a novel co-written with ▷Sara Maitland; *The Wandering Jew* (1987), a translation and adaptation of *Le Juif Errant*, and *Once a Feminist* (1990), interviews with feminists active in the 1960s and 1970s.

▷Maitland, Sara; *Tales I Tell My Mother*; *One Foot on the Mountain*; Kazantzis, Judith

Wang Anyi (born 1954)

Chinese short story writer from Shanghai. Wang worked on the editorial staff of a children's magazine and started to publish in 1976. She writes about the problems of her generation. Her well-known story 'The Rain Patters On' focuses on the frustration of single women in their isolation from social life. 'Destination' describes the desperation of the young generation uprooted from the city during the 'cultural revolution' (1966–1976). Other stories, collected in *Lapse of Time* (1983), reveal the harshness of life for the underprivileged in overcrowded Shanghai. Because of her intimate revelations of life in Shanghai, Wang is sometimes referred to as a writer of 'Shanghai consciousness'. *Baotown* (1986), a novella, is noted for its psychological depths. The *Trilogy of Sexual Love* (1988), in defiance of orthodoxy, explores the area of sexuality. In the short story 'Lao Kang Comes Back', Wang describes in highly controlled language the random destruction of human beings as a result of political campaigns.

Bib: Hung, Eva (trans.), *Love in a Small Town*; Avery, Margaret (trans.), *Baotown*.

Wang Qiang ▷Wang Zhaojun

Wangui, wa Goro

Kenyan poet and translator. Wangui translates Kikuyu into English, French and Italian, and is based in London. She is interested in feminist readings of African literature, in the development of literature in African languages, and has translated James Ngugi's latest novel *Matigari* (1987) into English.

Wang Xiaoying (born 1947)
Chinese writer of children's stories. Originally
from Zhejiang province, Wang now works on the
editorial staff of a children's magazine. She has
published many children's stories, collected in
Gold Fountain and Running Brook Sisters. She is
also author of the novella *River of Stars*, and other
stories based on life in rural areas, where she
spent time after middle school.

Wang Zhaojun (1st century BC)
Chinese poet. Also named Wang Qiang, Wang
Zhaojun was royal concubine to Emperor Yuan of
the Western Han dynasty in the 1st century BC.
She refused to bribe the court painter and thus
was represented unfavourably under his brush. As
the portraits were the only means through which
the emperor picked his favourites, Wang was
totally neglected. In 33 BC Wang, in a mood of
defiance against her fate, volunteered to marry the
chieftain of the Xunnu tribe – the offer of his own
concubines in marriage being the emperor's peace
drive with the barbarians. Wang Zhaojun left with
the barbarian chief and bore him a son. After his
death, she married his son (by another wife) and
successor, according to local custom, and bore
him two daughters. Meanwhile she wrote poetry
to bemoan her fate and to express her longing for
her homeland. Wang Zhaojun and her story have
become part of history and legend. She is sung by
poets, and portrayed in drama, as a patriot and the
cementer of peace between China and the
'barbarians' on its western borders.

Ward, Harriet (1808–c 1860)
South African English novelist. Born in Norfolk,
England, she lived in the Eastern Cape from the
early 1840s, having married a man posted as
commander of the Grahamstown garrison during
the Frontier Wars, and returned to England in
1847. Her experiences are recorded in *Five Years
in Kaffirland* (1848), re-issued in 1851 with the
telling subtitle *The Cape and the Kaffirs: A Diary of
Five Years' Residence in Kaffirland, with a chapter of
advice to emigrants based on the latest official returns
and the most recent information regarding the colony*.
This material is reworked in novelistic form in
Jasper Lyle: A Tale of Kafirland (1851), *Lizzy
Dorian: The Soldier's Wife* (1854) and *Hardy the
Hunter* (1858). Melodramatic, and over-dependent
on the clichés of Victorian ▷sentimental
romance, Ward's fiction nevertheless holds
contemporary interest for its uneasy negotiation of
colonial rule in Africa, although she generally
takes part in the imperialist project with
propagandist fervour. She also wrote *Helen
Charteris* (1848), *Memoirs of Colonel Tidy* (1849),
and *Hester Fleming* (1854), and edited *Past and
Future Emigration, or The Book of the Cape* (1849).

Ward, Mrs Humphry (1851–1920)
English novelist, born Mary Augusta Arnold, the
granddaughter of Dr Arnold and the daughter of
schools inspector Thomas Arnold. She was born
in Tasmania but moved with her family back to

England in 1856, where she was educated in
private boarding schools. In 1872, she married
Thomas Humphry Ward, an Oxford don. She
contributed to the *Dictionary of Christian Biography*
in 1877, and in 1881 moved to London and wrote
for *The Times*, *Pall Mall Gazette* and *Macmillan's
Magazine*, as well as publishing a children's story,
Milly and Olly (1881). Her first novel for adults,
▷*Robert Elsmere* (1888), was instantly successful,
and she wrote twenty-four more novels, including
The History of David Grieve (1892); *Marcella*
(1894); *Sir George Tressady* (1896); *Helbeck of
Bannisdale* (1898); *Lady Rose's Daughter* (1903);
The Marriage of William Ashe (1905); *Diana
Mallory* (1908); *Delia Blanchflower* (1915) and
Cousin Philip (1919). Her novels deal principally
with social and religious themes, often contrasting
tradition and progress. She was a leading
intellectual figure and an active philanthropist, yet
although she campaigned for higher ▷education
for women, she strongly opposed the ▷suffrage
movement. She generated support for an 'Appeal
Against Female Suffrage', published in 1889, and
became the first President of the Anti-Suffrage
League in 1908. Like many Victorians, she
believed that women should set a moral example,
issuing firstly from the home. Ward was also
known to be a severe critic of other women
writers. *A Writer's Recollections*, her autobiography,
was published in 1918.
Bib: Trevelyan, J.P., *The Life of Mrs Humphry
Ward*; Jones, E.H., *Mrs Humphry Ward*; Huw
Jones, E., *Mrs Ward*; Peterson, W.S., *Victorian
Heretic: Mrs Humphry Ward's Robert Elsmere*.

Warder, Ann Head (c 1758–1829)
North American diarist. Born in England, she did
not go to North America until after her marriage
to the Pennsylvanian John Warder. She began
keeping her journal on the journey to North
America in 1786 and maintained it until her death
as an account for her sister Elizabeth who
remained in England. She was an astute observer
of the differences in lifestyles between North
Americans and the English, and she duly
recounted for Elizabeth the 'custom of the
country' in the Quaker society of Philadelphia
where she resided. The ▷*Extracts from the Diary
of Mrs Ann Warder* constitute a well-written
account of woman's perspective on emigrating to
North America and adjusting to her new
environment.
▷Early North American Quaker women's
writings

Warland, Betsy (born 1946)
Poet and editor, born in Iowa. She studied there,
and emigrated to Canada in 1972. Active in the
feminist writing community, she helped to develop
the Toronto Women's Writing Collective, and was
instrumental in the organization of the bilingual
conference for women writers, 'Women and
Words/*Les femmes et les mots*' in 1983. Her poetry
books include *A Gathering Instinct* (1981), *Open is
Broken* (1984), and *serpent write* (1987). *Double*

Negative (1988, with ▷Daphne Marlatt) is a reflective reading of a trip they made to Australia. From its lesbian feminist position, her poetry unties the tongue-tied knots of ▷patriarchal language. She has lived in Vancouver since 1982.

Warmond, Ellen (born 1930)

Dutch poet and prose writer. ▷Pseudonym of P.C van Yperen. She danced for several years with the Rotterdam Ballet Ensemble, but had to abandon her career for health reasons. Until 1983 she was an assistant at the Literary Museum in The Hague. *Proeftuin* (1953) (*Experimental Garden*), a small collection of poems, was her surprising début. While her poetry links up linguistically with the poetry of the '*Vijftigers*', it differs in its content. Dominant themes in Warmond's work are Existential fear, loneliness and alienation. She is attracted to the static way of thought of the East which she had encountered during travels to Nepal. In the poems in *Warmte, een woonplaats* (1961) (*Warmth, a Home*) her scepticism about the possibility offered by love to escape from Existential fear and loneliness is made evident. The themes return in her collections *Vragen stellen aan de stilte* (1984) (*Questioning Silence*), *Vlucht stroken van de taal* (1988) (*Language's Hard Shoulders*) and *Persoonsbewijs voor inwoner* (1991) (*Identity Card for a Citizen*). She received the Anna Bijns Prize for her poetry in 1987. Translations of her poetry are published in *The Shape of Houses: Women's Voices from Holland and Flanders* (1974) and in *Change of Scene: Contemporary Dutch and Flemish poems in English Translation* (1969).

Warm Stone, A ▷'Ashur, Radwa

Warner, Anna Bartlett (1827–1915)

US novelist. Sister of ▷Susan Bogert Warner, with whom she often collaborated. Like many other 19th-century US women writers, Anna Bartlett Warner found a literary career through financial necessity. Both her collaborative and her independent novels reflect the economic imperatives faced by supposedly dependent women. Perhaps the most memorable is *My Brother's Keeper* (1855). She sometimes used the pseudonym Amy Lothrop.

Warner, Marina (born 1946)

English novelist and critic. Concerned with representations of female form and character, Warner has worked out these issues in relation to the Virgin Mary in *Alone of All Her Sex* (1976), *Joan of Arc* (1981), and in the study *Monuments and Maidens: The Allegory of the Female Form* (1985). Her novels deal with similar themes of sexuality, identity and power, and include *The Skating Party* (1982) and *In a Dark Wood* (1977). The autobiographical novel *The Lost Father* (1988) was short-listed for the Booker Prize.

Warner, Susan Bogert (1819–1885)

US popular novelist and children's writer. Pseudonym: Elizabeth Wetherell. Like many other 19th-century US women writers, Warner wrote to support her family, collaborating for some of her later works with her sister ▷Anna Bartlett Warner. Susan Warner's ▷*The Wide, Wide World* (1850) was the first bestselling US novel, and a major influence on later novels by women, especially those associated with the ▷woman's fiction tradition. Strongly religious herself, Warner felt ambiguous about the category 'novel' and called her works 'stories', though they blended strong elements of the novel's realistic technique and character development with religious direction. Warner's works tend to focus on aware, capable young women in financially distressed families. Among her many publications are ▷*Queechy* (1852), another enormously popular novel; *The Old Helmut* (1863); *Daisy* (1868); *Diana* (1877); *My Desire* (1879), and *Nobody* (1882).

Warner, Sylvia Townsend (1893–1978)

Sylvia Townsend Warner

English novelist and poet. Born in London and educated privately, Warner's early interest in music – study under Schoenberg was prevented due to World War I – was followed through in her role as editor of *Tudor Church Music*. Through her friendship with Theodore Powys she met ▷Valentine Ackland, and the two women's joint commitment to the resistance of European fascism forms an important context for Warner's writings. Warner and Ackland remained lovers throughout Warner's life.

Warner's first publication was a collection of poetry, *The Espalier* (1925), which was later followed by the narrative poem ▷*Opus 7* (1931). Although she continued to write poetry, Warner is better known for her prose writings, numerous short stories appearing in the *New Yorker*. Warner's first novel, ▷*Lolly Willowes* (1926), is a supernatural tale that utilizes the frame of a pastoral romance to forge a feminist questioning of gendered values. The character Lolly's insistence on a rural, 'feminine' existence is a politicized theme analogous to Warner's own elected lifestyle. Many biographers have commented on the paradoxical nature of Warner's combining of rural life with public unorthodoxy. *Mr Fortune's Maggot* (1927) juxtaposes the proselytizing zeal of the Christian missionary narrative with the alternative narrative of cross-cultural tolerance. A similar theme of liberation from ideological constraints and awareness of alternative realities is central to ▷*Summer Will Show* (1936) and *After the Death of Don Juan* (1938). As a theme that unifies much of Warner's writing, it also serves to position her work centrally within the women's movement and development of a feminist literary tradition. Warner's short stories have been collected in eight volumes, including *Kingdoms of Elfin* (1977) and *Scenes of Childhood* (1981). Later work includes a biography of T.H. White (1967), and her *Collected Poems* as well as her *Letters* were published in 1982. Other works: *The True Heart* (1929), *A Moral Ending* (1931), *The Salutation* (1932), *More Joy in Heaven* (1939), *The Museum of Cheats* (1947), *The Corner That Held Them* (1948), *Jane Austen* (1951), *The Flint Anchor* (1954), *Winter in the Air* (1955), *The Innocent and the Guilty* (1971), *Selected Poems* (1985).
Bib: Ackland, V., *For Sylvia: An Honest Account*; Harman, C., *Sylvia Townsend Warner: A Biography*; ▷Mulford, W., *This Narrow Place: Sylvia Townsend Warner and Valentine Ackland, Life, Letters, Politics 1930–1951*.

Warren, Caroline Matilda (c 1787–1844)

US novelist and non-fiction writer. Warren's *The Gamesters, or Ruins of Innocence* (1805) is in the tradition of didactic early US novels. Her work for children reflects similar concerns for instruction and religious education.

Warren, Mercy Otis (1728–1814)

North American dramatist, poet and historian. Born in Barnstable, Massachusetts, on 25 September 1728, she was a member of a politically active family that backed the move for independence during the American Revolution. Although she received no formal education, her writings reveal an impressive knowledge of literary, philosophical and political writers of her era. Out of her Patriot convictions, she became North America's major dramatist and historian of the American Revolution. Plays such as ▷*The Group* satirize Tories who market their patriotism for personal profit; even plays that are not set in North America, such as ▷*The Ladies of Castille*, reflect her democratic values and her acknowledgement of women's participation in the processes of independence. Although none of her dramas were published in her lifetime, her work was well-known. Her poetry, collected in ▷*Poems, Dramatic and Miscellaneous*, also addresses political and social issues. Her ▷*History of the Rise, Progress and Termination of the American Revolution* remained the authoritative text on the war for decades after her death. Although nearly forgotten today, she was one of early North America's most prolific and respected political writers. She died on 19 October 1814 at her home in Plymouth, Massachusetts.

Other works include: *The Adulateur: A Tragedy*, (1772), *The Defeat: A Play* (1773), *The Motley Assembly: A Farce* (1779) and an essay, *Observations on the New Constitution* (1788).
▷Murray, Judith Sargent; Adams, Abigail Smith

Waser, Maria (1878–1939)

German-speaking Swiss novelist and critic. She was a prolific writer of both fiction and essays on the subject of art history. To this day her most important work remains the historical novel *Die Geschichte der Anna Waser* (1913) (*The Story of Anna Waser*), a ▷*Bildungsroman* about the 17th-century Zurich painter, Anna Waser. This novel focuses on the difficulties experienced by a woman artist as she struggles to develop her creative talents.

Wasserstein, Wendy (born 1950)

US dramatist. Born in Brooklyn, New York, Wasserstein studied at Yale Drama School. While a student she wrote her first off-Broadway play, *Uncommon Women and Others* (1977) which focuses on a group of women reuniting six years after their college graduation. They are terrified by their new choices in the aftermath of women's liberation; poised for the future, they are also afflicted by it.

Isn't It Romantic (1981) considers the friendship between two women: a Jewish writer and a Protestant business executive. It explores women's conflict between personal independence and romantic fulfilment. *Tender Offers* (1983) describes on a reconciliation between a father and his young daughter. Wasserstein's work is characterized by its satiric humour. *The Heidi Chronicles* (1988) was awarded the Pulitzer Price for Drama in 1989.

Wassmo, Herbjørg (born 1942)

Norwegian lyric poet and prose writer. She was born in Vesterålen, and worked as a teacher. She received the Nordic Council's Award for Literature in 1987.

Wassmo is a very widely-read prose writer in the tradition of psychological ▷realism. She made her début as a lyric poet with *Vingeslag* (1976)

(*Stroke of Wings*), but it was her novels about Tora that won her so many readers. *Huset med den blinde glassveranda* (1981) (*The House with the Blind Glass Veranda*), *Det stumme rummet* (1983) (*The Dumb Room*) and *Hudløs himmel* (1986) (*Raw Heaven*) tell a story of incest and psychosis, depicting the split between body and language as a female and provincial lower-class problem. The novels are at first sight written in a realistic and traditional way, but with a linguistic sensibility that belongs to modernism.

With *Dinas Bok* (1990) (*Dina's Book*) she enters a more modernist and mystical way of writing with great success. She uses a sort of black humour, and the most brutal events, like murder and killing, are lightly described in an understated manner.

Watch Tower, The (1966)

Australian novel by ▷Elizabeth Harrower. A domestic drama concerned with the exercise of cruelty and power within an apparently ordinary domestic situation. The husband, Felix Shaw, is a psychological manipulator who torments his wife and her sister, both of whom are insecure and financially dependent upon him. Issues of power, guilt and collusion are explored with great intuition and sensitivity.

Waterfall, The (1969)

Novel by English writer ▷Margaret Drabble. Its heroine, Jane Gray, is a poet who, abandoned by her husband during her pregnancy, begins an affair with her cousin's husband, James, soon after her child is born. The novel explores the obsessive nature of love and sexuality, women's experiences of childbirth and maternity, and its heroine's isolation and terrifying passivity. Drabble's most experimental work, the novel alternates first- and third-person narration, and provides a 'metafictional' commentary on the truths and falsehoods of storytelling.

Watson, Jean (born 1934)

New Zealand novelist. Watson published her first novel, *Stand in the Rain*, in 1965, which she described as an attempt to write about the woman behind the 'good keen . . . hardcase dinkum-type Kiwi'. Her second novel, *The Balloon Watchers* (1975), is an allegory about a lonely woman who finds tranquillity in watching balloons, a novel in which Watson was influenced, she says, by the 'sociological' fantasies of US writer Richard Brautigan (1935–1984). Watson describes herself as a fantasy writer, though her fictions often imply sharp, if indirect, social commentary. She has received a number of awards for her writing, including the prestigious Scholarship in Letters in 1983.

Publications: *Stand in the Rain* (1965); *The Balloon Watchers* (1975); *The World is an Orange and the Sun* (1978); *Address to a King* (1986).

Watson, Sheila (born 1909)

Canadian fiction writer, teacher and editor, born Sheila Doherty in New Westminster, British Columbia. Her family lived on the grounds of the Provincial Mental Hospital, where her father was Superintendent. Her initial education was in Catholic schools, then she studied English at the University of British Columbia. For ten years Watson taught at school in various communities, most notably the isolated community of Dog Creek, which was to act as the fictional setting for her great novel, ▷*The Double Hook* (1959), perhaps the most purely unconventional and influential novel in Canadian literature. She married noted dramatist and poet Wilfred Watson in 1941; they lived in Toronto, Calgary and Edmonton. Strongly engaged in the sweep of modernism (she recalls her excitement at reading T.S. Eliot's *Four Quartets*, 1935–1942, one by one as they were published), Watson's dissertation (University of Toronto, 1965), under Marshall McLuhan's direction, was on British painter and novelist Percy Wyndham Lewis (1882–1957). In 1961 both Watson and her husband took positions in the Department of English at the University of Alberta in Edmonton. There, for many years, they served as a cultural nexus to the literary community, establishing the periodical *White Pelican*, which published ▷Miriam Mandel's *Lions at Her Face* (1973). All of Watson's work outside of *The Double Hook* appeared in a Special Issue of *Open Letter* (1974–75). *Four Stories* (1979) collects her strangely mythological shorter fiction. *And the Four Animals* (1980) was published as a manuscript edition. There were rumours in 1991 that her unpublished novel, *Deep Hollow Creek*, would soon appear. She lives in Nanaimo, British Columbia.

Bib: Bessai, D. and Jackel, D. (eds), *Figures in a Ground: Canadian Essays on Modern Literature Collected in Honor of Sheila Watson*; Bowering, A., *Figures Cut in a Sacred Ground*.

Waves, The (1931)

Novel by English writer ▷Virginia Woolf. Perhaps Woolf's most sustained experimentation with the ▷stream-of-consciousness technique, *The Waves* is often described as a 'play-poem', given its emphasis on rhythm and dramatic monologue. The novel focuses on six principal characters and describes their experiences from childhood to old age. Character is predicated on inner experience, on memory and symbolism, and Woolf maintains an undifferentiated style of narration through each monologue. Difference is developed through a recognized symbol attachment, while in its linear, developmental trajectory the novel analyzes the notion that individual personality traits are established in early life. Throughout the novel the character of Percival, who died as a result of a riding accident, becomes the central focus of the other characters' fantasies and needs. *The Waves* is a highly complex study of desire and sexuality, and of the production of fantasies about fear, loss and fraternalism.

Way of Reconciliation Touching the True Nature and Substance of the Body and Blood of Christ in the Sacrament (1605)

English writer ▷Elizabeth Russell's ▷translation of John Ponet's French treatise on the sacrament. She dedicated her work as her 'last legacie' to her daughter, Anne Herbert. Russell did not originally intend to publish it, claiming she was forced to do so out of fear that it would be published in a faulty version after her death. She initially translated Ponet's treatise for her own private edification. She lent her work, however, to a friend, who apparently lent it to others. Russell's desire to maintain control over the accuracy of her translation, which had been approved by Ponet himself, motivated her to publish it in spite of her reluctance to make her work public.

Weamys, Anna

English prose writer. Her *A Continuation of Sir Philip Sidney's Arcadia* was published in 1651.
    ▷Wroth, Lady Mary

Weather in the Streets, The (1936)

Novel by English writer ▷Rosamond Lehmann, sequel to *Invitation to the Waltz* (1932). In *Invitation to the Waltz*, the gauche seventeen-year-old Olivia Curtis is invited by Lord and Lady Spencer to a dance at the Big House and meets Rollo, the dashing son of the house. *The Weather in the Streets* takes place ten years later. Olivia, beautiful but still insecure, separated from her husband and living in relative poverty in London, meets the now-married Rollo. They begin a furtive but passionate affair. From the outset, the reader is aware of the emotional danger to which Olivia is made vulnerable. Some time into the affair she becomes pregnant and has an abortion. Rollo's wife, in the meantime, is revealed to be expecting a child. As Olivia is at her most alone, Rollo becomes ever more secured by family life.

The story is told from Olivia's point of view, shifting to first-person narration in the central part of the novel. Lehmann's representation of female consciousness has been compared to writing by ▷Virginia Woolf and ▷Dorothy Richardson, although there are significant differences: for example, Lehmann's extensive use of dialogue. Characterization is of central importance to her writing; she has written that 'characters must make plot or action, never the other way round.' The most striking aspects of the novel are perhaps its frankness about sexuality and its refusal to censure Olivia's actions. It also moves beyond the more limited 'county' class perspectives of the earlier novels (involving containment in large houses and extensive grounds) and into a *déclassé* urban setting in which women are no longer protected from 'the weather in the streets'.
    ▷L-Shaped Room, The

Webb, Beatrice Potter (1858–1943)

English diarist, political writer and social reformer. She was born in Standish, Gloucestershire, and educated at home. She is famous today for her work for social reform; her first publication, *The Co-Operative Movement in Great Britain* appeared in 1891. In 1892 she married Sidney Webb and in 1894 the couple published *A History of Trade Unionism*. Apart from a number of political books Webb also published extracts from her diary as *My Apprenticeship* (1926). This is respected as an honest and well-written account of her life up until marriage; it is also a record of the rapidly changing Britain in which Webb grew up and to whose improvement she devoted her life.
Bib: Muggeridge, K. and Adam, R., *Life*.

Webb, Elizabeth (fl 1781)

North American letter-writer. She was a Quaker minister who travelled from Pennsylvania to England in 1712 to visit friends. While in London, she met Anthony William Boehm, chaplain to Prince George of Denmark. A friendship of mutual respect developed; before Boehm left London, she sent him ▷*A Letter from Elizabeth Webb to Anthony William Boehm*, which is actually a personal spiritual narrative. Boehm shared the letter with friends, who copied it several times for their personal edification. It was not published until 1781, probably from one of the copies.

Webb, Mary (1881–1927)

English novelist. A sufferer from Graves's disease throughout her life, Webb began writing poems and essays during her first period of convalescence. Following the death of her father in 1909, Webb published nothing further until after her marriage to Henry Webb. Her first novel is the semi-autobiographical *The Golden Arrow* (1916), which explores unorthodox religious experience. Her strong pantheism, combined with an interest in the rural working classes, orchestrates the concerns of the novels *Gone to Earth* (1917), *Seven for a Secret* (1922), and the prize-winning ▷*Precious Bane* (1924), novels parodied later by ▷Stella Gibbons. The dialect novel *Armour Wherein He Trusted* (1928) was abandoned, unfinished, shortly before her death.

Webb, Phyllis (born 1927)

Canadian, poet, born in Victoria, British Columbia, in 1927. She studied at the University of British Columbia, and began writing as part of a group that included ▷P.K. Page and ▷Dorothy Livesay. In Montreal, from 1950 to 1956 she was active in the literary scene, and undertook graduate work at McGill University. There, she first published *Trio* (1954, with poets Eli Mandel and Gael Turnbull), then after travelling in Ireland, England and Paris, *Even Your Right Eye* (1956) and *The Sea is Also a Garden* (1962). From 1966 to 1969 Webb was executive producer of *Ideas* for the Canadian Broadcasting Corporation

in Toronto. ▷*Naked Poems* (1965) consolidated her poetic reputation, and was followed by *Selected Poems, 1954–1965* (1971). *Wilson's Bowl* (1980) includes what Webb calls incomplete, failed poems, 'born out of great stuggles of silence'. *The Vision Tree: Selected Poems* (1982, ed. ▷Sharon Thesen) brings together earlier work, and won the Governor General's Award. *Water and Light: Ghazals and Anti Ghazals* (1984) reflects Webb's exploration of unusual forms. *Hanging Fire* appeared in 1990. She is a poet of elegant distinction; her poems are exercises in torment and restraint, passionate calligraphy. *Talking* (1982) selects her essays and talks. She has taught creative writing and acted as writer-in-residence at various Canadian universities. After living in isolation on Salt Spring Island in British Columbia for many years, she now lives in Victoria again.
Bib: Butling, P., in ▷*A Mazing Space*; Special issue of *West Coast Line* (1992).

Webster, Augusta (1837–1894)

English poet, dramatist and essayist, also wrote under the ▷pseudonym Cecil Home. After marrying Thomas Webster at the age of twenty-six, she published her first collection of verse, *Blanche Lisle and Other Poems* (1860). A committed ▷feminist, much of her work focuses on female subjects. ▷*Dramatic Studies* (1866) includes poems about spinsterhood, marriage and motherhood; ▷'A Castaway' (1870) is concerned with prostitution; 'Circe' (1870) is a psychological portrait of the mythological figure; *A Housewife's Opinions* (1878) is a collection of essays on the lives of married women. Webster was at times criticized for her forthrightness and unabashed ▷realism, but she was also favourably compared to ▷Elizabeth Barrett Browning, ▷Christina Rossetti and ▷Jean Ingelow. Her unfinished sonnet sequence, *Mother and Daughter* (1895), was published posthumously, edited by William Michael Rossetti. Dramatic works include *The Auspicious Day* (1872); *Disguises* (1879) and *In a Day* (1882).
▷Drama (19th-century Britain)
Bib: Hickok, K., *Representations of Women: 19th Century British Women's Poetry.*

Webster, Jean (1876–1916)

US novelist. Webster was born and lived in New York, and was educated at Vassar College, graduating in 1901. She was the grand-niece of novelist Mark Twain (1835–1910) (her father was Twain's business partner and publisher). She married in 1915 and died the day after the birth of her daughter. Webster was the close friend of the poet Adelaide Crapsey and modelled the heroine of her 'Patty' stories on her. At Vassar, Webster became interested in orphanages and social welfare, and afterwards served on committees for prison reform and visited Sing Sing prison regularly. Webster's popular novels *Daddy Long-Legs* (1912) and *Dear Enemy* (1915) directly reflect this interest. Using the romance

genre, they tackle issues of inequality in North American society, the failures and problems of the family and the difficulty of independent lives and careers for women at the beginning of the 20th century. The stories of Judy and Sallie are used to explore the effects of institutional care on children, and possibilities for its reform in a way that combines humour, romance and a feminist consciousness.
Other work includes: *When Patty Went to College* (1903), *The Wheat Princess* (1905), *Jerry, Junior* (1907), *The Four Pools Mystery, Much Ado About Peter* (1909), *Just Patty* (1911), *Daddy Long-Legs* (play) (1914) and *Vitriol and Lilacs* (poems) (1943).

Webster, Mary Morison (1894–1980)

South African Scottish novelist and poet, who arrived in South Africa in 1920. She spent the rest of her life in Johannesburg, reviewing books for local newspapers, publishing novels, mainly about Scottish life, and writing poetry. She had three volumes of poetry published by Harold Munro's Poetry Bookshop – *To-morrow* (1922), *The Silver Flute* (1931) and *Alien Guest* (1933) – and three further volumes: *Garland in the Wind* (1938), *Flowers from Four Gardens* (1951), which is a selection from the first four volumes, plus some additional poems, and *A Litter of Leaves* (1977), a later selection. Her poetry is gently lyrical, employing simple, sparse imagery and fairly traditional verse forms. It deals primarily with experiences of sadness, loneliness and insanity, and has strong stylistic and thematic affinities with the work of ▷Christina Rossetti. Her four novels are *Evergreen* (1929), *The Schoolhouse* (1933), *The Slaves of the Lamp; or, The Moon was their Undoing* (1950), and *A Village Scandal* (1965). With her sister, Elizabeth Charlotte Webster, she wrote a prose satire, published under the title *High Altitude: A Frolic* (1949).

Weedon, Chris (born 1952)

British feminist ▷poststructuralist. Lecturer in German at the University of Wales, Cardiff. *Feminist Practice and Poststructuralist Theory* (1987) implicitly argues against ▷Elaine Showalter's resistance to theory, in so far as it makes a case for the feminist appropriation of Jacques Derrida's (born 1930) and ▷Jacques Lacan's (1901–1981) theories of language and ▷psychoanalysis on the grounds that they enable feminists to analyze the construction of gendered meaning in patriarchy, and henceforth to identify possibilities for change.

Weeds (1923)

US novel by ▷Edith Summers Kelley which traces the life of Judith Pippinger from tomboy to wife. As the wife of a tenant tobacco farmer, domestic pressures overwhelm her. Having preferred the masculine sphere of work, Judith rebels against enslavement in the feminine. After a brief affair, Judith reconciles herself to fate, convinced that rebellion is useless. *Weeds* foregrounds the biological, economic and social strictures that farming imposes on women.

Ironically, Kelley's editors originally insisted that the birth scene be cut from the novel.

Week Like Any Other, A (1969)

Novella by Russian writer ▷Natal'ia Baránskaia. When *A Week Like Any Other* was first published in the prestigious Moscow ▷'thick journal' *New World* in 1969, it roused fierce discussion on the semi-taboo subject of the double burden borne by Soviet women. In English translation (1971, 1989), Western women have been struck by its relevance to their lives as well. Pondering over a questionnaire for women that asks about their living conditions and utilization of time, Baránskaia's heroine, Ol'ga, describes in low-keyed, resigned voice the dilemmas she and her female colleagues in a scientific laboratory face in the conscientious effort to juggle multiple responsibilities at home and work.
▷Woman Question (Russia)
Bib: Monks, Pieta (trans.), *A Week Like Any Other*; Kay, Susan, 'A Woman's Work,' *Irish Slavonic Studies* 8.

We Have Always Lived in the Castle (1962)

US novel. ▷Shirley Jackson's bestseller focuses on a sociopathic adolescent girl. Mary Blackwood and her sister Constance represent a dissociated personality: Mary is the vicious self and Constance the passive self. Possessive of her sister, Mary kills those who pose a threat to her. Jackson exposes the savagery hidden beneath the surface of contemporary society. She expresses women's rage at the social environment that renders them dissociated personalities.

Wei Junyi (born 1917)

Chinese writer and literary editor. Wei Junyi joined the leftist student movement in Beijing and later settled in the communist base in Yenan. She worked as a reporter, broadcaster and teacher, and wrote fiction in her spare time. After the founding of the People's Republic (1949), Wei helped launch the national magazine *China Youth*. She later headed the People's Literature Publishing House. Among her writings are short stories, collected in *Frailty* (1983) and *Women* (1980).

Weil, Simone (1909–1943)

French philosophical and political writer. One of France's most important thinkers in the political and philosophical spheres, Weil's writings, mostly collected by others after her death, anticipated many of the ideas of the 1940s and 1950s. At the same time, she was a social activist and the author of mystical letters and essays. Important works of hers include *La Pesanteur et la Grâce* (1947) (▷*Gravity and Grace*, 1952) ▷*L'Enracinement* (1952) (*The Need for Roots*), *Oppression et Liberté* (1955) (▷*Oppression and Liberty*, 1958) and *L'Attente de Dieu*, (1951) (*Waiting for God*).
Bib: Pétrement, Simone, *A Life*; Rees, Richard, *A Sketch for a Portrait*.

Weinzweig, Helen (born 1915)

Born Helen Tenenbaum in Poland, she emigrated to Toronto, Canada at the age of nine. She began writing late in life, and has published two novels, *Passing Ceremony* (1973) and *Basic Black with Pearls* (1980), as well as a collection of stories, *A View From the Roof* (1989), and a play, *My Mother's Luck* (1983).

Weldon, Fay (born 1931)

English novelist, dramatist and critic. Born in Worcestershire, and educated in New Zealand and London, Weldon studied economics and psychology at the University of St Andrews, Scotland. Initially employed as an advertising copywriter, Weldon's first literary output concentrated on plays for radio and television, including the award-winning first episode of the long-running series *Upstairs, Downstairs*. Weldon has also adapted many of her own novels for television, most notably ▷ *The Life and Loves of a She-Devil* (1983). Her first novel, *The Fat Woman's Joke* (1967), brings out Weldon's consistent interest in the biological aspect and reproductive instinct of womanhood, an interest developed further in the temporal scheme of *Puffball* (1980), which utilizes the stages of pregnancy. *The Cloning of Joanna May* (1989) focuses on the contrivances of a male genetic engineer, and alludes strongly to the ▷*Frankenstein* theme in its signalling of male authority and power, Weldon's characteristic tone of ironic understatement provides caustic analyses of sexual politics and the role of women in the highly competitive milieux of contemporary middle-class society.

As a writer whose novels actively question the uses of fiction, Weldon is frequently cited within critical debates on the 'feminist novel'. In exploring friendships between women, as in *Female Friends* (1975), but also rivalries, her writings disturb any notion of a homogeneous or fixed feminist identity. Weldon is also an active campaigner on behalf of writers, and an outspoken critic of exploitative publishers. She has written extensively against acts of censorship, and a pamphlet, *Sacred Cows* (1989), was written in the wake of renewed interest in the issue of the writer's social responsibility. Weldon's other non-fiction writings include *Letters to Alice on First Reading Jane Austen* (1984) and a study of ▷Rebecca West (1985). Her story collections are *Watching Me, Watching You* (1981) and *Polaris* (1985).
Bib: Brandmark, W., *Fay Weldon*; Kenyon, O., *Women Novelists Today*.
▷Austen, Jane

Well, The (1986)

Australian novel by ▷Elizabeth Jolley. It deals with the relationship between Hester Harper, a frustrated, middle-aged eccentric, and a young girl, Katherine, whom she brings home on impulse and with whom she establishes a rich and rewarding relationship. One night, driving along the deserted track to the farm, they run into a mysterious creature and heave its body into the farm's deep well, but its voice returns to lure Katherine away from Hester, closer always to the edge of the well, and to the world of outside experience. *The Well*, a powerful and psychologically rich exploration of sexuality and possessiveness, won a number of literary awards, including the Miles Franklin Award for 1987.

Well of Loneliness, The (1928)

Controversial lesbian novel by English writer ▷Radclyffe Hall. *The Well of Loneliness* was the centre of a famous literary trial immediately after its publication in 1928, on the grounds of its treatment of a lesbian relationship. As a result of the trial it was banned in Britain until 1948, although the US edition continued to have an underground circulation, giving the novel an important subcultural role for lesbians. *The Well of Loneliness* is a mixture of a lesbian ▷*Bildungsroman* and a romance, telling the story of its heroine, Stephen Gordon, a sexual 'invert'. Stephen, an English gentleman in all but gender, heroically gives up her lover, Mary, to a male childhood friend who can offer her respectable heterosexual domestic bliss. The novel's climax is Stephen's recognition of her obligation as a writer to sacrifice her personal fulfilment in order to use her talents to plead for social tolerance for the sexual invert.

The novel is important for its use of the theories of sexologist Havelock Ellis (1859–1939), who wrote a preface to the original edition. Hall attempts to use the theory that homosexuality is innate to promote social tolerance. The masculine Stephen is born with wide shoulders and narrow hips, and grows up to wear men's clothes by contrast with the very feminine objects of her desire. The conservative implications of using heterosexual models for lesbian relationships was already recognized and criticized by ▷Vera Brittain in 1928. Nevertheless the butch–femme model of relationships is still sometimes evident in both fiction and the lives of lesbians to this day. The novel also provides a fascinating picture of the lesbian coterie which surrounded ▷Natalie Barney in Paris in the 1920s.

Wells, Helena (c 1760–c 1809)

North American novelist and essayist. A prolific and successful New England sentimental novelist, she advocated a conservative perspective of woman's sphere. In works such as ▷*The Step-Mother* (1798) and ▷*Constantia Neville; or, The West Indian* (1800), she presented female sacrifice as noble and virtuous, perpetuating patriarchal constructs of women's roles.

Wells (Barnett), Ida Bell (1862–1931)

US non-fiction writer, lecturer, journalist, and activist. The daughter of slaves, Wells Barnett became first an educator and then national spokeswoman, leader and writer to protest injustice against African-Americans in late 19th-century US. A journalist (and part-owner of the Memphis *Free Speech* newspaper), she led national and international protest in the anti-lynching movement of the 1890s. Initially as part of the anti-lynching activism, but continuing on a variety of issues, she helped to organize a significant African-American women's club movement. A dynamic force in women's suffrage and women's rights campaigns, she is also among early public African-American feminists. In addition to newspaper journalism, her 19th-century published works include: *Southern Horrors: Lynch Law in All Its Phases* (1892) and *The Reason Why the Colored American Is Not in the World's Columbian Exposition* (1893). In the late 20th century her writing has appeared in a number of anthologies. Her autobiography, *Crusade for Justice*, was published in 1970.

Welty, Eudora (born 1909)

US short story writer, novelist and essayist. Born in Jackson, Mississippi, Welty graduated from the University of Wisconsin in 1929, and earned a graduate degree in business at Columbia University. In 1931 she returned to Mississippi where she worked as a radio writer and a newspaper social editor, and photographed and interviewed local residents for the Works Progress Administration in the 1930s.

In 1936 Welty launched her literary career with ▷Katherine Anne Porter as her staunch supporter. Welty's fiction focuses on the relationship between the self, and the community, and it celebrates the mystery of the inner life. Stories like 'Death of a Travelling Salesman', 'Keela, the Outcast Indian Maiden', 'The Wide Net', and 'Why I Live at the P.O.' emphasize the inviolable otherness of the self, and celebrate the mystery of human relationships. Welty's novels, ▷*Delta Wedding* (1946), *The Golden Apples* (1949), and ▷*The Optimist's Daughter* (1972), portray women who rebel against their role as the ▷Southern lady. Nevertheless, Welty implies that women's power derives from the traditional domestic sphere. Welty's critical articles and reviews are collected in *The Eye of the Story* (1978).

Other works include: *A Curtain of Green and Other Stories* (1941), *The Robber Bridegroom* (1942), *The Wide Net, and Other Stories* (1943), *The Leaning Tower, and Other Stories* (1944), *The Ponder Heart* (1954), *The Bride of the Innisfallen, and Other Stories* (1955), *The Shoe Bird* (1964), *Loosing Battles* (1970), *One Writer's Beginnings* (1983) and *The Collected Stories of Eudora Welty* (1980).
Bib. Kreyling, Michael, *Eudora Welty's Achievement of Order.*

Wenger, Lisa (1858–1941)

▷German-speaking Swiss writer and painter. Born into an old Bernese family, she was educated in Paris, Florence and Düsseldorf. In the 1880s she founded a school for porcelain painters in Basle. At forty-six she published her first book, *Das blaue Märchenbuch* (1905) (*The Blue Book of Fairytales*), and soon established herself as a writer of lively animal fables. In her most powerful fiction she often explores the demonic power of women, as in the play *Das Zeichen* (1914) (*The Sign*) which is about a mother's curse. Amounst her best novels are *Die Wunderdoktorin* (1909) (*The Miracle Doctor*) and *Der Vogel im Käfig* (1922) (*Bird in a Cage*).

Wen Jieruo (born 1927)

Chinese writer and translator. Wen spent six years in Japan and is one of China's leading experts in Japanese literature. In 1954, she married the prestigious writer and journalist Xiao Qian (based in Britain during the war years). Xiao was deprived of his job when he was labelled 'rightist' in 1957. During the 'cultural revolution' (1966–1976) he was subjected to further humiliations and his house and belongings were confiscated. Wen suffered with her husband and supported him while continuing to work, editing and translating from Japanese literature. She published the *Autobiography of a Hag* (1990) in Taiwan. It is a moving account of shared adversity for a quarter of a century, a study in selfless devotion, a testimony of personal integrity, and a rare and truthful description of how China's various political campaigns were conducted in literary circles. Her translations include *Under the Gallows* (1945), by Julius Fuchik of Czechoslovakia.

Wentscher, Dora (1883–1964)

German writer. An actress, painter and a sculptor living in Berlin, she had her first success with an autobiographical novel about the theatre, *Barbara Velten* (1920). After going into exile in 1933, she wrote anti-military stories and travelogues, and worked for many years on a drama about the late 18th-century German dramatist, Heinrich von Kleist (1777–1811).

Wentworth, Anne (fl 1676)

English Baptist prophet writing during the Restoration, when such sects were persecuted. She records her prophecies and visions in verse and prose, and offers a spiritual justification for having left her husband in *A Vindication of Anne Wentworth* (1677). She seeks to justify her actions against those who are 'representing me as a *proud, passionate, revengeful, discontented* and *mad* woman, and as one that has unduly published things to the prejudice and scandal of my husband, and that have wickedly left him'. Her other publications include: *A True Account* (1676), and *The Revelation of Jesus Christ* (1679).
▷Lead, Jane; Trapnel, Anna

Wen Xiaoyu (born 1938)

Chinese writer. Originally from Zhejiang province, Wen was assigned to teach Chinese literature at the University of Inner Mongolia on graduation from Peking University in 1955. She wrote fiction in her spare time, publishing jointly

with her husband, Wang Zhecheng. *Farewell, Thistles* (1983) is a well-known collection, in which appeared the much-anthologized 'The Darling' and 'The Nest Egg'. Some of her stories use a Mongolian background. She also writes feelingly about poverty-striken intellectuals in their daily struggle to cope with life.
Bib: Translation of 'The Nest Egg' in Link, Perry (ed.), *Roses and Thorns*.

We of the Never-Never (1908)

Australian novel by ▷Jeannie Gunn. A fictionalized account of the life of Jeannie Gunn, as a young bride, on the Elsey cattle station on the Roper River in the 'Never-Never' land south of Darwin. The front gate of Elsey station is 70 kilometres from the homestead, which is 'mostly verandahs and promises', suggesting a building never quite completed, with few inner rooms, and several verandahs for coolness. *We of the Never-Never* has sold over half a million copies. It was made into a very successful film in 1982, and the site of the Elsey homestead is now a national reserve.

Were, Miriam (born 1940)

Kenyan novelist and biographer. Were was born in Lugola Village, Kakamega District, among 'people from many clans' whose 'main common factor was acceptance of the Christian religion'. She was educated at the University of Pennsylvania and studied education at the University of Makerere and medicine at the University of Nairobi, where she now teaches in the department of community health. She was the Kenyan representative to the Nairobi Decade of Women Conference in 1985. She writes in English, having studied Latin, not Swahili, at high school and feels that her Swahili is 'very limited' though she writes to her family in her mother tongue: 'One can say some things better.'
Her four novels explore issues of social conflict, in particular the changing world of women in modern Kenya. *The Boy in Between* (1969) and *The High School Gent* (1969) follow an ambitious boy through the early stages of his education; ▷*The Eighth Wife* (1972) explores conflicts among the Lusui people of western Kenya, arising from the practice of female circumcision and polygamy; ▷*Your Heart Is My Altar* (1980) focuses on cross-cultural marriage and generation differences; *Nurse With a Song* (1978) is a biography of Margaret Owanyoni.
Bib: Gurr, Andrew, and Calder, Angus (eds), *Writers in East Africa*; Schmidt, Nancy, in *WLWE*, 17 (1978); Taiwo, Oladele, *Female Novelists of Modern Africa*.

Werfel, Alma (1879–1962)

Austrian writer and composer. She was the daughter of the landscape painter Jakob Schindler, and wife of the composer Gustav Mahler (1860–1911). After the death of her husband and her two daughters, she married the architect Walter Gropius (1883–1969) and had an affair with the poet Franz Werfel (1890–1945), whom she subsequently married. She is chiefly known for her autobiography, *Mein Leben* (1957) (*My Life*), in which she describes with great candour her adventurous life in the artistic circles of Europe.

Wertenbaker, Timberlake

Timberlake Wertenbaker

English dramatist and translator. The daughter of Anglo-American parents, she grew up in France, and has worked in London, New York and Greece, where her first plays were written and performed. Her plays include *This Is No Place for Tallulah Bankhead* (1978) and *Case to Answer* (1980). *Breaking Through* (1980) and *New Anatomies* (1981) were written for the Women's Theatre Group. *New Anatomies* tells the story of the 19th-century traveller Isabelle Eberhardt; it explores the construction of gender, and one woman's attempt to break through its limitations. *Our Country's Good* (1988) depicts a group of Australian convicts staging a performance of George Farquar's play *The Recruiting Officer* (1706) in 1789, and is based on Thomas Keneally's *The Playmaker* (1987). *Love of the Nightingale* (1988) retells the bloody legend of Philomel and Procte, daughters of King Pandion of Athens. Her other plays include *Abel's Sister* (1984), *The Grace of Mary Traverse* (1985) and *Three Birds Alighting on a Field* (1990). Wertenbaker has also translated plays by Lorca, Marivaux and Anouilh. One of the most radical and original of contemporary dramatists, she has produced powerful reworkings of myth and history.

We Sinful Women: Contemporary Urdu Feminist Poetry (1991)

Selected poems by seven Pakistani women poets, with the Urdu originals alongside English translations by Rukhsana Ahmad. Ahmad suggest that women poets of the 1980s and 1990s are heir to the progressive strain in Urdu poetry, as well as being the current innovators in language and form. She selects poetry with an explicitly political content, including criticism of martial law (introduced in Pakistan by the coup of General Zia al-Haque in 1977) and of the Islamicizing campaign which involved the introduction of ▷*Shariat*; a media campaign enforcing women's seclusion and the wearing of the *chador*, 'the veil and four walls', and legislation attacking women's rights and status. Poets in the collection include ▷Kishwar Naheed, ▷Fahmada Riaz, ▷Zehra Nigah, Sara Shagufta and Saeeda Gazdar.

West, Dorothy (born 1912)

US novelist and journalist. West presents a new dimension of the African-American experience based on her family background. Born in Boston, Massachusetts, West was educated at an exclusive girl's school. Her father was a self-made African-American businessman. West became editor and financial backer of *Challenge*, which promoted young African-American writers.

West's novel, *The Living Is Easy* (1948), introduces a new character to African-American literature, Cleo Judson. Cleo is a determined, controlling woman with some money, whose husband adores her. She likes to exercise power and sees affection as a sign of weakness. This puts a strain on her marriage to an older, self-made businessman. The novel also depicts the attempts of African-American businessmen to survive on their own. West shows that they are isolated from the white society which still controls their destinies.

West, Elizabeth (early 18th century)

Scottish spiritual memoirist and diarist. She wrote, 'I wanted not good education from my mother, and likewise from my aunt who was a godly woman.' Her memoirs, *Memoirs or Spiritual Exercises of Elizabeth West* (1766), record her spiritual struggle – she would retire 'to the fields to pour out my complaint before the lord'. She also registers her increasingly politicized resistance to the orders of England with regard to the Scottish Church.

West, Rebecca (1892–1983)

Novelist and journalist of Scottish-Irish parentage. She was born Cecily Isabel Fairfield in County Kerry, and was educated at George Watson's Ladies College, Edinburgh, and briefly at the Academy of Dramatic Art, from which she emerged to pursue a brief and unsuccessful acting career. When she was twenty she decided to adopt the name of Henrik Ibsen's passionate, self-willed heroine in *Rosmersholm*. West then turned to journalism, having begun contributing magazine

Rebecca West

and newspaper articles while at drama school. Much of her journalism was polemical, and attacked tradition and convention head-on, beginning with an early anti-imperialism piece. West initially joined the staff of the feminist paper *Freewoman*, from which she resigned after four months, and was later a leading writer on the socialist magazine *Clarion*. She also contributed numerous articles to *The Star*, *Daily News* and *New Statesman*, and her journalism was considered to be well-informed and distinctly humourous. West had a ten-year affair with the writer H.G. Wells (1866–1946) (▷Dorothy Richardson), and their son Anthony West was born in 1914. Although West argued throughout this period against the necessity for marriage, she eventually married Henry Maxwell Andrews in 1930, whom she met through ▷Vera Brittain and George Catlin.

West's first full-length critical work, *Henry James*, was published in 1916. It was a mocking attack on a male literary icon, similar to that which characterized the article on H.G. Wells which prompted their initial meeting. Her first novel, *The Return of the Soldier*, followed in 1918, and examines the relationships between three women and a soldier suffering from shell-shock. West claimed that she wrote her novels to find out what she felt, not to display what she knew, and her early fiction was criticized for the apparent dominance of her authorial personality (▷modernism). *The Judge* (1922) explores two generations of the women's ▷suffrage movement. Further novels focusing on women's lives in the early 20th century include *The Fountain Overflows* (1957), an immediate bestseller, and *The Birds Fall*

Down (1966), which explores the Russian Revolution of 1917. The polemical pro-Serbian travel diary *Black Lamb and Grey Falcon: A Journey through Yugoslavia* (1941) was published in two volumes, and a biography, *St Augustine* appeared in 1933. She also wrote *McLuhan and the Future of Literature* (1969).
Bib: Glendinning, V., *Rebecca West*; Orel, H., *The Literary Achievement of Rebecca West*; Ray, G.N., *H.G. Wells and Rebecca West*.

West Indian Poetry (1984)
This volume by Lloyd W. Brown traces the development of West Indian poetry from its origins in 1760 to the present day. It includes references to ▷Louise Bennett, ▷Una Marson, ▷Constance Hollar and ▷Vera Bell.

West Indies Federation (1958–1962)
Established in 1958, the West Indies Federation was a response to the frustration felt in the British West Indies over the slow progress of democracy and the path to independence. Federalism was seen as a vehicle for developing more democratic institutions. The independence movement, however, overtook the desire for federal reform, and the federation was therefore short-lived. When ▷Jamaica withdrew in 1962 the federation fell apart. One lasting legacy of the federation movement is the University of the West Indies which has campuses in ▷Jamaica, ▷Trinidad and ▷Barbados.

▷Phyllis Shand Allfrey won the portfolio of Minister of Labour and Social Affairs in the 1958 elections, and held it until the demise of the federation in 1962. ▷Louise Bennett's poem, 'Capital Site' in ▷*Jamaica Labrish*, is concerned with the problem posed by the choice of location for the federation headquarters. (After much debate they were located in ▷Trinidad.)

Weston, Jessie Edith (1867–1944)
New Zealand novelist. Jessie Weston's novel *Ko Meri* (1890) is one of the earliest to deal with a Maori or part-Maori character, a subject of increasing interest in the 1890s, especially in short fiction. Weston subscribed to the popular and racist belief that the Maori were a dying race and her half-Maori heroine, Mary Balmain, illustrates why, as she proves unable to enter 'civilization' in England and returns to the 'darkness' of her people. Like the work of many of her contemporaries, Weston's novel illustrates the simple oppositions by which colonial imperialism functioned.
▷Maori literature

Wetherald, Agnes Ethelwyn (1857–1940)
Pen-name of Bel Thistlethwaite, Canadian poet and journalist. Born in Rockwood, Ontario, she was educated at a Quaker school in New York, and at Pickering College in Ontario. She wrote variously for the Toronto *Globe*, Toronto *Week*, and the women's magazine *Wives and Daughters*. She published poetry as early as the 1870s, but

her first book, *The House of the Trees and Other Poems*, did not appear until 1895. Other volumes included *Tangled in Stars* (1902), *The Radiant Road* (1904), *The Last Robin: Lyrics and Sonnets* (1907), *Tree-top Mornings* (1921) and *Lyrics and Sonnets* (1931). Her poetry is typical of the Confederation period in its approach to nature, but her sonnets display a sound structural integrity. She also authored a sentimental novel, *An Algonquin Maiden: A Romance of the Early Days of Upper Canada* (1886, with G.M. Adam). She lived in Ontario most of her life.

Wetherell, Elizabeth ▷Warner, Susan Bogert

Wharton, Anne (1659–1685)

English dramatist and poet, niece of John Wilmot, Earl of Rochester. In 1673 she was married to Thomas Wharton, later a Whig politician, who ignored her. Some of her letters to him survive. When Rochester died, she became close to Bishop Gilbert Burnet, who was critical of her poetry. Her tragedy, *Love's Martyr, or Witt Above Crowns* was not acted, but is a political allegory of the Exclusion Crisis (1679–1680). Her poetry circulated during her lifetime, but it only began to appear in print after her death. She paraphrased the letter from Penelope to Ulysses in Ovid's *Heroides*: 'Would Troy were glorious still, so I had you.'

Her other publications include: *Poems by Several Hands* (ed. Nahum Tate 1685); *Idea of Christian Love* (1688); *A Collection of Poems* (1693), and *Whartonia* (1727).
Bib: Greer, G. *et al.*, *Kissing the Rod*.

Wharton, Edith (1862–1937)

Edith Wharton

US novelist, short story writer and poet. she was born Edith Newbold Jones to a wealthy, elite family of 'Old New York', who raised her to be an aristocratic lady, not to pursue intellectual ambitions. However, by the age of sixteen Wharton had already produced a volume of poetry privately published as *Verses* (1878). In 1885 she married and maintained a life of conventional gentility until, following a passionate affair, she was divorced in 1913. Neither her marriage nor the nervous illness from which she suffered for twelve years affected her productivity. She began publishing poetry and stories in major magazines such as *Scribner's*, *Harper's* and the *Century*, and while Wharton is principally known as a 20th-century novelist, her short stories were a significant presence in the major US literary magazines at the turn of the century. She was pursued by magazine editors and was a deft negotiator for her own publishing agenda – including reminding editors that her stories were rare commodities as she turned to writing novels. A first volume collection of her short stories, *The Greater Inclination*, was published in 1899. During this period she also collaborated on *The Great Decoration of Houses* (1897) with the Boston architect Ogden Codman, Jr.

After 1913, Wharton settled in Europe permanently, where she met the novelist Henry James (1843–1916), a major influence on her work, and the art historian Bernard Berenson. A well-respected literary figure, in the 1930s Wharton was elected to both the National Institute of Arts and Letters and the American Academy of Arts and Letters. In 1905 Wharton published ▷*The House of Mirth*, her famous satire on the hypocrisies of the New York aristocracy and its tragic impact on the life of the heroine Lily Bart. In 1921 she won the Pulitzer Prize for ▷*The Age of Innocence* (1920), which also satirizes conventional society. ▷*Ethan Frome* (1911) portrays marriage as a potentially tragic imprisonment, while in novels such as *The House of Mirth* (1905), and ▷*The Custom of the Country* (1913), she analyzes it as an economic transaction. She focuses particularly on the commodification of women, and exposes the hypocrisies that psychologically damage her characters. In addition to her novels and novellas, Wharton wrote travelogues, short stories, ghost tales and her important contribution to aesthetics, *The Writing of Fiction* (1925). Other works include: *The Angel at the Grave* (1901), *Sanctuary* (1903), *The Other Two* (1904), *The Descent of Man and Other Stories* (1904), *Madame de Treyms* (1907), *The Fruit of the Tree* (1907), *Tales of Men and Ghosts* (1910), *The Reef* (1912), *Summer* (1917), *Old New York* (1924), *The Mother's Recompense* (1925), *Here and Beyond* (1926), *A Backward Glance* (1934), *Ghosts* (1937) and *The Buccaneers* (1938).
Bib: Wolff, Cynthia Griffin, *A Feast of Words: The Triumph of Edith Wharton*; Lewis, R.W.B., *Edith Wharton: A Biography*.

What Does a Man Want? (1974)

A series of poetic monologues by Kenyan novelist and poet ▷Muthoni Likimani. In monologues, several women characters express the frustrations of being caught between old and new values. They are depicted as the losers in a relentlessly male world, from the older woman who is rejected after a lifetime spent in helping her husband to succeed to the career woman who regrets having neither husband nor child.

What Is to Be Done? (1989)
Translation of novel by Russian critic Nikolai Chernyshevsky, written in 1863. Chernyshevsky's famous programmatic novel, written while he was awaiting trial on vague charges of sedition, slipped through censorship and was published just as the author was exiled to Siberia for twenty-five years. Chernyshevsky's heroine, Vera Pavlovna, reaches self-fulfilment with the aid of devoted, idealistic men. His prescription for emancipation led some young women (for example, ▷Sofia Kovalévskaia) to escape parental control by contracting fictitious marriages. Others imitated the novel's heroine by setting up communes and sewing co-operatives, none of which were as successful as their fictional model. Literary debate over the novel's revolutionary message was incorporated in a spate of anti-nihilist works including, most notably, Dostoevsky's *The Demons* (1872). However, novels like ▷Nadezhda Khvoshchínskaia's ▷*Ursa Major*, which questioned Chernyshevsky's simplistic solution of the ▷woman question, and ▷Apréleva's *Rufina Kazdoeva*, which cast a cold retrospective look at communal life, have been forgotten. In the 20th century Chernyshevsky's ascetic revolutionary, Rakhmetov, became the model for Jan in ▷Verbítskaia's *The Keys to Happiness*, and innumerable Soviet commissars of ▷socialist realism.

Wheathill, Elizabeth ▷*Handful of Holesome (though Homelie) Hearbes, A*

Wheatley, Nadia (born 1949)
Australian children's novelist. Wheatley was educated at the University of Sydney and Macquarie University. She has won many awards for her writing, including the New South Wales Premier's Award for 1983 for *Five Times Dizzy* (1982), the Australian section of the International Board for Books for Young People 1986 for *Dancing in the Anzac Deli* (1984), and both the Children's Book Award for 1985 and the New South Wales Premier's Prize for 1985 for *The House that was Eureka* (1985).
  ▷Children's literature (Australia)

Wheatley, Phillis (c 1753–1784)
North American poet. Born in Senegal, Africa, kidnapped, and brought to North America in 1760, she was purchased as a slave by Susannah Wheatley, who educated her well but indoctrinated her with her own Christianity. Phillis's innate intelligence is revealed in the rapidity with which she learned and, most notably, in her literary accomplishments. The publication of ▷*Poems on Various Subjects, Religious and Moral* (1773) made her the first published African-American poet. Her poetry was long held to be derivative, but recent analyses have discerned the pre-romantic nature of her poetic vision and the embedded arguments against slavery. She was freed after her mistress's death, and later married, but freedom did not bring success; the novelty of a poet-slave was lost, and she died in poverty on 5 December 1784. Today she is regarded as an oppressed but talented poet whose writings have attained the status of classic works in North American literature.
  ▷Terry, Lucy; Early North American letters

Wheeler, Mercy (fl 1733)
North American essayist. Living in Plainfield, Massachusetts, when she was stricken with a long illness that confined her to bed, she found escape from her confinement by writing an ▷*Address to Young People* in which she cautioned them against worldly ways. The ten-page tract was published in Boston in 1733.

When Rain Clouds Gather (1967)
The first novel written by Southern African writer ▷Bessie Head, and the first novel published in English by a black South African woman. Interested in the ways a community manages to cope with extreme poverty and to get rid of a chief who abuses the power of his position, the novel also looks at the breakdown of the family under the system of migrant labour, suggesting that the development of family feeling in men, and specifically romantic love, might help reinstate family life. The women perform agricultural work, restoring fertility to an overgrazed land and helping relieve the country of poverty. Yet the narrator suggests that, even if a door opened somewhere, they would not be able to grasp their freedom, so accustomed are they to exploitation. One character, Paulina, offers the hint of an exception; the other prominent female character, Maria, is too soft and meditative to break her habits of obedience. Head offers Makhaya as the perfect man: he treats women as his equals. Although the novel is concerned with gender, its primary focus is the celebration of a community which felt like paradise to Head after the horrors of South African life under apartheid.

Whitcher, Frances Miriam Berry (c 1814–1852)
US dialect humorist and satirist. Whitcher's burlesques, monologues and sketches establish her among the earliest women humorists, and as one of the first to develop women comic personae, most notably her Yankee 'Widow Bedott'. Most of her work was originally published in the *Saturday Gazette* or ▷*Godey's Lady's Book*. Collected volumes include *The Widow Bedott Papers* (1856) and *The Widow Spriggins, Mary Elmer, and Other Sketches* (1867). 'Widow Bedott' is sometimes considered a pseudonym.

White, Antonia (1889–1930)

Antonia White

English novelist and translator. She was educated at the Convent of the Sacred Heart, Roehampton, following her parents' and her own conversion to Catholicism. This convent childhood forms the basis of her first novel, ▷*Frost in May* (1933), which she began writing at the age of sixteen. White's early, clandestine attempts at novel-writing led to her being expelled from school, an event which consolidated the ambivalent and complex terms of her relationship with her father and the Catholicism he passionately embraced. Employed initially in teaching and clerical posts, White attended drama school in 1919, and worked as an actress in provincial repertory. During her first marriage, which ended in annulment, she suffered from severe mental disturbances, and was incarcerated in an asylum for nine months. Her second marriage, to H.T. Hopkinson, provided a domestic context which allowed her to complete *Frost in May*, although further bouts of mental illness followed.

Her second novel, *The Lost Traveller*, was not published until 1950, and is a sequel to the first, the protagonist, Nanda Grey, here becoming Clara Batchelor. *The Lost Traveller*, *The Sugar House* (1952) and *Beyond the Glass* (1954) chronicle White's post-school experiences, the last volume exploring Clara's mental breakdown in relation to the complex issues of identity, authority and religious orthodoxy which problematize White's own involvement with Catholicism. White's attitude to religion is dealt with explicitly in *The Hound and the Falcon* (1966), a collection of letters that describe her reconversion to the Catholic faith. White has also translated into English many stories by ▷Colette, ▷Christine

Arnothy and Éveline Mahyère. Her other writings include, *Three in a Room* (1947), *Strangers and Other Stories* (1981) and *Living With Minka and Curdy* (1970).

Bib: Chitty, S. (ed.), *As Once in May: The Early Autobiography of Antonia White*; ▷Showalter, E., *A Literature of Their Own*.

Whitman, Sarah Helen Power (1803–1878)

US poet, essayist, literary critic and journalist. Whitman's first published poem appeared in the ▷*American Ladies' Magazine*, a fitting forum for her early poetry, which was unexceptional and typical of the period. Her most noted poetic work is a sequence of poems on her relationship with the US writer Edgar Allan Poe (1809–1849), to whom she was once engaged. More notable were her strongly written essays (on women's rights, suffrage, etc) and her literary criticism – especially her personal and literary defence of Poe: *Edgar Poe and His Critics* (1860). In US literary history, Whitman is firmly associated with Poe, not only through her own writings but also through Poe's 'To Helen'. During her lifetime her poetry was collected in *Hours of Life, and Other Poems* (1853); a complete edition was published in 1879.

Whitney, Isabella (fl 1567–1573)

English poet. She was one of the earliest English women to write and publish secular literature, and the first English woman to identify herself as a professional writer. She was probably the sister of Geoffrey Whitney, author of *A Choice of Emblemes* (1586). Her first publication was ▷*A Copy of a Letter lately written in Meeter by a Yonge Gentilwoman to Her Unconstant Lover* (?1567), and she later published ▷*A Sweet Nosegay, or Pleasant Posye: contaynyng a hundred and ten Philosophicall Flowers* (1573), in which she addresses the reader, claiming that 'subject unto sickness, that / abroad I could not goe / Had leasure good (though learning lackt) / some study to apply: / To reade such Bookes, whereby I thought / my selfe to edify.' The same volume contains a farewell to London, using in part, the popular form of a last will and testament, in which there is much detail about the business and trade district of the City of London.

▷Collier, Mary; Leapor, Mary; Letters (Renaissance Britain)

Bib: Fehrenbach, R.J. 'Isabella Whitney, Sir Hugh Plat, Geoffrey Whitney, and "Sister Eldershae", *English Language Notes* 21 (1983), pp. 7–11.

Who Do You Think You Are? (1978)

Canadian writer ▷Alice Munro's collection of linked stories (sometimes called a novel, published in Britain and the USA as *The Beggar Maid*) about Rose, who comes from the small town of Hanratty and, surprisingly enough, manages to leave that place and its constraints behind. She enters university, and marries well, but can only return to Hanratty after her marriage dissolves and she is a successful actress, but still wary of the entrapments of home territory.

Who Is She? Images of Woman in Australian Fiction (1983)

Australian collection of critical essays edited and introduced by Shirley Walker. It explores the depiction of the female figure in Australian fiction written by both women and men. Women novelists discussed are ▷Catherine Helen Spence, ▷Rosa Praed, ▷Barbara Baynton, ▷Miles Franklin, ▷Henry Handel Richardson, ▷Katharine Susannah Prichard, ▷Christina Stead, ▷Elizabeth Harrower and ▷Barbara Hanrahan.

Whyte, Violet ▷Winter, John Strange

Wickham, Anna (1884–1947)

English poet, pseudonym of Edith Alice Mary Harper. Born and educated in Australia, she came to London in 1905, where she obtained a scholarship to the Tree's Academy of Acting, and studied singing. After her marriage and the birth of her first child, Wickham developed an interest in social welfare work with working-class mothers, a subject on which she lectured. After the tragic death of her four-year-old son, Wickham spent some time in Paris, where she met the US lesbian writer and literary patron ▷Natalie Barney, with whom she conducted a passionate correspondence between 1926 and 1937.

Her first poems were privately printed in *Songs of John Oland* (1911), but by 1914 Harold Monro of The Poetry Bookshop was publishing her work. *Poetry and Drama* (1914) was followed in 1915 by *The Contemplative Quarry* and *The Man with a Hammer* (1916), *The Little Old House* (1921) and *Richards' Shilling Selections* (1936). During Wickham's lifetime, her work was widely anthologized, attesting to the popularity of her accessible and provocative verse. Her work, with its open treatment of women's sexual passion and the constraints marriage places on women, as well as its polemical satire on English middle-class society, has often been dismissed as 'botched' and insufficiently crafted. However, the combination of her explicit feminist and socialist critical consciousness with an accessible aesthetic make her a significant 20th-century poet. Since her death, by suicide, in 1947 Wickham's work has appeared in *Selected Poems* (1971) and *The Writings of Anna Wickham: Free Woman and Poet* (1984), which includes her autobiographical fragment 'Prelude to a Spring Clean', and occasional prose pieces.

Wicomb, Zoë (born 1948)

South African short story writer, born near Van Rhynsdorp and Vredendal, in a small Griqua settlement in the Western Cape. After attending an Afrikaans-medium school in Cape Town, she graduated first from the University of the Western Cape, and then from Reading University in England. She lived in Britain from 1970 to 1991,

teaching at school and in adult education, and continuing her university career at Strathclyde, Glasgow. She is at present teaching literature and language at the University of the Western Cape. Her work represents a new wave in South African writing.

Her short story collection, *You Can't Get Lost in Cape Town* (1987), is the first fictional account of a Griqua community by one of its own. The Griqua people were frontier pastoralists, deprived of their land by the Dutch settlers. Originally part of the indigenous Khoikhoi people, they became what has been called a 'mixed race', intermarrying with Dutch settlers as well as runaway slaves. Despite the shared language, the shared pastoral tradition, and the physical intermingling between Griqua and Dutch, to be Griqua meant to be classified 'non-white' under South Africa's apartheid laws, and thus to be rendered mute and invisible as political subjects. Wicomb has said that without ▷Black Consciousness, coupled with feminism, she would not have been able to write.

The stories concern Frieda Shenton, although she is sometimes a peripheral character, and not all the stories mention her name. They are arranged chronologically, tracing her upbringing, departure to school, sexual development, university education, her farewell from South Africa, and some return trips from Britain to visit family and friends. Although Wicomb draws extensively on her own experience for the book, it is not autobiographical: the text deliberately flirts with autobiography, yet at the same time contains a number of events and characteristics that loudly proclaim its status as fiction.

Unusually for a South African writer, Wicomb shifts away from a ▷realist tradition. She sets one perspective against another, focusing less on 'reality' than on acts of representation. In 'A Fair Exchange', the narrator places herself as the one who reassembles the fragments of a story whose coherence can only be given in writing. But 'A Trip to the Gifberge' overturns this authority. Speaking to her mother in the voice of authority gained from access to the world of education and politics, Frieda criticizes her for wanting to plant a protea in her garden. The protea, South Africa's 'national symbol', signifies Afrikaner nationalism, in whose name people like the Shentons have lost their claim to the land. But her mother claims the protea as her own in a way it cannot be for the white settlers: 'A bush is a bush; it doesn't become what people think they inject into it. We know who lived in these mountains when the Europeans were still shivering in their own country.'

Wide Sargasso Sea (1966)

This is the best-known work of the Caribbean writer ▷Jean Rhys. Its publication in 1966 resulted in the literal reappearance of the author in the world of letters. Jean Rhys had always been fascinated by the silent Bertha Mason in ▷Charlotte Brontë's ▷*Jane Eyre*, and in this novel she tells the story of Antoinette Cosway (later named Bertha by the unnamed Rochester figure) who, like Bertha in *Jane Eyre*, ends up supposedly 'mad' in the attic of a large English country house. The novel was central in a radical revaluation of the accepted British literary tradition, and uses a number of subversive and elliptical strategies to achieve this purpose. Like the mirrors which are so central to Antoinette's attempts to validate her divided cultural psyche, the novel has many reverberations. It addresses the whole question of the colonial encounter between Britain and the Caribbean through the symbol of 'Thornfield Hall' which was metaphorically built on the spoils of imperialism and Antoinette's sanity. In addition the book looks forward, through its use of modernist and associative techniques, its self-conscious concern with rewriting, and its exploration of the psychological damage caused by the absence of a mother culture, to many works by contemporary Caribbean women writers such as ▷Jamaica Kincaid.

Early critical responses to the book failed to place it within the Caribbean tradition, but in the last fifteen years *Wide Sargasso Sea*'s position as a central Caribbean novel has not been disputed. An enormous amount of critical material is available on this book; a good starting-point would be Jean D'Costa's chapter in ▷*Fifty Caribbean Writers*. See also Teresa F. O'Connor, *Jean Rhys: The West Indian Novels* (1986) and Susheila Nasta (ed.), ▷*Motherlands: Black Women's Writing from Africa, the Caribbean and South Asia*. In the latter, two chapters discuss Rhys as literary mother to the later generation of Caribbean women writers, and illustrate how Rhys's divided cultural heritage and physical exile from the land of her birth have enabled her to reclaim her country through her writing.

Wide, Wide World, The (1851)

US popular novel by ▷Susan Bogert Warner. The first US novel to be a runaway bestseller, it was also the first of three novels – all by women, all in the 1850s – which established women novelists as the cultural and literary centre of mid-century popular US literature. Its two immediate successors were ▷Harriet Beecher Stowe's ▷*Uncle Tom's Cabin* (1852) and ▷Maria Susanna Cummins's ▷*The Lamplighter* (1854).

In the novel, Ellen Montgomery, an adolescent girl who is moved from one relation's home to another, undergoes a psychological journey to moral maturity as she negotiates the conflicts between her own will and position and the expectations of religion and society. A mixture of religious direction with realistic depiction of characters' sense of self, *The Wide, Wide World* is notable for the accuracy of its detail and for its willingness to confront dominance in patriarchal authority.

Wied, Martina (1882–1957)

Austrian poet and novelist. A first collection of her finely-crafted poems, *Bewegung* (*Movement*),

appeared in 1919. Her fiction too is carefully structured, and the main theme of her novels is an Existential sense of uprootedness and homelessness in modern life. These novels include *Das Asyl zum obdachlosen Geist* (1934) (*Hospice for an Itinerant Spirit*), *Das Einhorn* (1948) (*The Unicorn*), an historical novel written in exile in Scotland during World War II, and *Das Krähennest* (1951) (*The Crow's Nest*).

'Wife's Lament, The'

▷Old English poem. One of the Old English ▷'Elegies' of the *Exeter Book* (an English manuscript of c 1000). The details of the situation are unclear, but the female speaker has been separated from her husband by his kinsmen, and she dwells alone beneath an oak tree. The mood is one of desolation, even death.

▷'Wulf and Eadwacer'; 'Creidhe's Lament'; 'Liadain and Cuirthir'
Bib: Hamer, Richard, *A Choice of Anglo-Saxon Verse*.

Wijenaike, Punyakanthi (born 1935)

Sri Lankan novelist and short story writer. She was educated in Sri Lanka, and regularly has short stories and prose pieces published in Sri Lanka's English-language journals and newspapers. Her protagonists are often women trying to find a middle way between the traditional culture of their mother's time and the modern lifestyle which threatens to obliterate all that is familiar and comforting. Her collections of short stories include *The Third Woman* (1963) and *The Rebel* (1979). *A Way of Life* (1987) is a volume of childhood recollections. Her novel *The Waiting Earth* (1966) has been translated into Sinhala. A subsequent one, *Giraya*, about an areca-nut slicer, was published in 1971.

Wild Card (1990)

Australian autobiography by ▷Dorothy Hewett. *Wild Card* details Hewett's turbulent personal life, her failure at university, attempted suicide, disastrous marriage and a more disastrous *de facto* relationship, the death of her first son from leukaemia, and the birth of three more. It is a powerful, intense, and beautifully written account of the difficulties encountered by an ideologically committed artist in Australian society. The first section, which deals with the rich experience of a loved and privileged child on a prosperous property in Western Australia, is particularly moving.

Wilde, Jane Francesca (?1826–96)

Irish writer, born in Wexford, the daughter of an Archdeacon. In 1851, she married a surgeon, Sir William Wilde, and was widowed in 1871. She died in considerable poverty in London in the year her son, Oscar Wilde (1856–1900), was publicly tried and disgraced on grounds of homosexuality. Frequently using the ▷pseudonym Speranza, she contributed regularly to *The Nation*, and published a collection, *Poems*, in 1864. Her writings about folklore and collections of Irish legends include: *Driftwood from Scandinavia* (1884), *Ancient Legends of Ireland* (1887) and *Ancient Cures* (1891). Her other books are *Men, Women and Books* (1891) and *Social Studies* (1893).

Wilder, Laura Ingalls (1867–1957)

US novelist and journalist. Wilder spent her childhood as a pioneer moving throughout the Midwest. However, her family's efforts to settle the frontier were continually thwarted. At fifteen Wilder became a teacher to pay for her blind sister's special schooling. Married in 1885, Wilder eventually settled on a Missouri farm after suffering a series of calamities, and wrote a newspaper column, 'As A Farm Woman Thinks'. In the 1930s, at her daughter's urging, Wilder began writing a series of historical novels for children based on her early life. She wanted children to understand the beginning of white civilization in the US. In 1954 the series, which included ▷*Little House on the Prairie* (1935), earned a special Newbery-Caldecot Award.

Other works include: *Little House in the Big Woods* (1932), *Farm Boy* (1933), *On the Banks of Plum Creek* (1937) and *Little Town on the Prairie* (1941).

Wildermuth, Ottilie (1817–1877)

German writer. A representative of the Biedermeier literary style, her humorous stories about family life in her native Swabia, from *Bilder und Geschichten aus dem schwäbischen Leben* (1852) (*Portraits and Stories of Life in Swabia*) to *Bilder aus einer bürgerlichen Familiengalerie* (1892) (*Portraits from a Middle-class Family Album*), were enormously popular during her lifetime. In all her prolific writing, she extolled Christian values and the moral influence of women.

Wild Geese (1925)

Canadian writer ▷Martha Ostenso's unique novel about a schoolteacher, Lind Archer, who boards with a prairie farm family, the Gares, and who is accessory to Judith Gare's rebellion against her tyrannical father (published in Britain as *The Passionate Flight*). A story of physical hardship juxtaposed with domestic conflict, the subplot of the novel, which has to do with the young schoolteacher's love affair, is far less interesting than the story of Judith, wrestling with her grotesquely domineering partriarch for her birthright. The novel offers a clear delineation between a feminine, almost mystical relationship with the earth, and a masculine urge to possess and exploit the land. *Wild Geese* is important as a realistic rendering of the intensity and loneliness of prairie rural life in the early 1900s.

Wilker, Gertrud (1924–1984)

German-speaking Swiss poet and novelist. Her work addresses a wide range of burning contemporary issues. The story *Flaschenpost* (1977) (*Message in a Bottle*) is a tale about survival after a nuclear explosion, and in *Wolfsschatten* (1966) (*Shadows of Wolves*), *Collages USA* (1968) and *Altläger* (1971) (*Rubbish Dump*), she exposes the dangers of a naïve faith in technological progress and modern consumerism. In *Blick auf meinesgleichen* (1979) (*A Glance at my Peers*), twenty-eight short stories about women combine in a celebration of women's strength and will to survive. Her last novel, *Nachleben* (1980) (*Afterlife*), is a complex retrospective of a woman's life lived within the structures and strictures of modern Swiss society.

Wilkinson, Anne (1910–1961)

Canadian poet, born Anne Gibbons in Toronto, and raised there and in London, Ontario. Wilkinson was a member of the wealthy and powerful Osler family, the subject of her historical mosaic, *Lions in the Way: A Discursive History of the Oslers* (1956). Married in 1932, divorced in 1953, she did not begin to write until after she was thirty. Her first collection, *Counterpoint to Sleep* (1951), was followed by *The Hangman Ties the Holly* (1955), and after her death from cancer, *The Collected Poems of Anne Wilkinson and a Prose Memoir* (1968, ed. A.J.M. Smith). Her poetry is unusually erotic in its physicality, whether she writes to lovers or to her children. She was one of the founding members of *The Tamarack Review*, a Canadian periodical. *Swan and Daphne* (1960) is a fairytale for children. She deserves more critical attention than she has received.
Bib: Armitage, C., *Anne Wilkinson and Her Works*; Barbour, D., in ▷*A Mazing Space*; Lecker, R. in *Studies in Canadian Literature* 3, (1978).

Wilkinson, Eliza Yonge (fl 1779–1782)

North American letter-writer. A resident of Yonge's Island, South Carolina, when Charleston was invaded by the British during the American Revolution, she recounts to a female correspondent her experiences in seeking refuge from the invaders and her growing recognition of the realities of war. A young widow at the time of the invasion, she moved from an attitude of passivity about the war to an ardent belief in the Patriot cause. In ▷*Letters of Eliza Wilkinson*, she details with vivid description the effects of the invasion on her outlying community. The letters conclude with her elation at Cornwallis's surrender.

Wilkinson, Iris ▷Hyde, Robin

Williams, Helen Maria (1762–1827)

English poet, novelist and correspondent. Brought up in Berwick-on-Tweed, she first published the verse romance *Edwin and Eltruda*, and *Peru* (1784) and sonnets in 1786. Her *Poem on the Slave Trade* (1788) was commented on by ▷Mary Scott. After she settled in France she reworked Jean Jacques Rousseau's *Julie: ou, la nouvelle Héloïse* (1761) in *Julia* (1790). Her radical letters from France describing the Revolution were published in 1790. In France she lived with the divorced John

Hurford Stone. She translated the popular bestseller *Paul et Virginie* – the text chosen for its apolitical status in case of raids. She writes, 'no danger could be more imminent than that of living under the very tyranny which I had the perilous honour of having been one of the first to deprecate and to proclaim.' She was lucky enough to get a passport to Switzerland, which resulted in *A Tour in Switzerland* (1798).
Bib: Scheffler, Judith, *The Wordsworth Circle*, No. 19 (1988).

Willumsen, Dorrit (born 1940)

Danish prose writer. Dorrit Willumsen grew up with her mother's parents. Her father, an opera singer, had left the family, and even though her circumstances were secure, she has described this upbringing as an experience of loss and isolation. This theme is the most significant in her writings – children and young women who are alone, unable to love and afraid of being loved. Willumsen's ▷modernism is absurd, fantastic and abrupt. Her earlier works in particular may be read like prose poems. In her later works she writes in a more accessible ▷realist style.

The doll is a central symbol in all her works, the narcissistic self-reflective but dead and stiff sexual neuter that looks like a woman or girl, as in *Modellen Coppelia* (1973) (*The Model Coppelia*), *Neonhaven* (1976) (*The Garden of Neon*) or *Marie. En roman om Marie Tussauds liv* (1983) (*Marie. A Novel of the Life of Marie Tussaud*). Other major works are *Hvis det virkelig var en film* (1978) (*If it really Were a Film*, 1982) and *Suk, hjerte* (1986) (*Sigh, Heart*).

Wilson, Barbara (born 1951)

US novelist. A writer, translator and publisher, Wilson did not learn to read until age seven. In the late 1960s she left college to see the world. She taught herself Spanish, German and Norwegian. She translates works by Scandanavian women writers. In the mid-1970s she worked as an investigative journalist. In 1976 she co-founded ▷Seal Press.

Her lesbian ▷detective novels explore socio-political conflicts. *Murder in the Collective* (1984) raises issues of racism and US imperialism, *Sisters of the Road* (1986) focuses on prostitution, and *The Dog Collar Murders* (1989) satirizes the feminist debate over pornography and lesbian sado-masochism. In this series Wilson's leftist detective, Pam Nilsen, struggles with her sexuality and what it means. *Gaudi Afternoon* (1991) introduces a more sophisticated and worldlywise detective, Reilly, raising issues regarding transsexualism, parenthood and child custody.

Wilson, Ethel (1888–1980)

Canadian novelist and short story writer, born Ethel Bryant in Port Elizabeth, South Africa. After her mother's death in 1890, she returned to England with her father until his death in 1898, when she was sent to live with her maternal grandmother in Vancouver, British Columbia. She attended private school in Vancouver, then boarding school at Trinity Hall, Southport, in England, where she took the junior Cambridge exams. She returned to Vancouver, received a teacher's certificate, and taught until her marriage, to a physician, in 1921. She had always invented stories, and while her husband made house calls, she sat in the car and wrote; but she was surprised when, in 1937, *The New Statesman and Nation* in London accepted and published three of her stories. The publication of her first novel, *Hetty Dorval* (1947), established her reputation; it was followed by the episodic family novel, *The Innocent Traveller* (1949), and two novellas in *The Equations of Love* (1952). Her novel, ▷*The Swamp Angel* (1954), is her most impressive and best-known work. *Love and Salt Water* appeared in 1956; and *Mrs Golightly and Other Stories* in 1961. During her long and happy marriage she travelled widely with her husband, and her fiction's settings range over the world. Her characters are detailed but ambivalent; Wilson often writes about deceptive appearances, and people's unpredictable actions. *Ethel Wilson: Stories, Essays, and Letters* (ed. David Stouck) was published in 1987.
Bib: McAlpine, M., *The Other Side of Silence*; McMullen, L., *The Ethel Wilson Symposium*; Pacey, D., *Ethel Wilson*.

Wilson, Harriet E. ▷*Our Nig*

Wilson, Lady Anne Glenny (1848–1930)

New Zealand novelist and poet. Anne Glenny Wilson was born in Greenvale, Victoria, and educated in Melbourne. She married a sheep farmer in 1874 and came to live in New Zealand. Glenny Wilson published stories and poems in Australian and New Zealand journals during the 1890s and 1900s. She wrote two novels, *Alice Lander, A Sketch* (1893) and *Two Summers* (1900), and published two collections of verse, *Themes and Variations* (1889) and *A Book of Verses* (1917), one of which was used in New Zealand schools for many years. A ▷romance writer, Glenny Wilson used stock situations and language in her writing, but, within the conventions of romance, argued for the independence of women.

Wilton, nun of ▷ Muriel

Winsloe, Christa (1888–1944)

German writer. After a divorce she worked as a sculptor in Berlin, where she had a lesbian affair with the North American reporter Dorothy Thompson (1894–1961). During the Third Reich she lived in exile, helping others who were also outlawed by the German authorities to escape to Switzerland. She was shot by a French criminal just before the end of World War II. Her drama, *Gestern und Heute* (*Yesterday and Today*), first performed in Berlin in 1930, was made into the film *Mädchen in Uniform* (*Girl in Uniform*) of 1931. A novel based on the same story became widely known as *Life Begins* in Britain, and as *Girl Alone* in the USA in 1935. She also wrote film scripts for G.W. Pabst (1885–1967), comedies of manners for the stage, and a number of novels.

Winslow, Anna Green (1759–1779)

North American diarist. Though born in Nova Scotia to Anna Green and Joshua Winslow, she resided in New England for many years and attended a Boston finishing school from 1771 to 1773. During these years, she maintained a diary as a means of informing her parents of her progress. She died of consumption in 1779; she never married. In the ▷*Diary of Anna Green Winslow* (1894), she presents, in often humorous detail, her everyday experiences at school, associations with other young people of her social class, and her responses to the orthodox Calvinist religious training she received at Boston's Old South Church.

Winter, John Strange (1856–1911)

▷Pseudonym of British novelist Henrietta Palmer (she also wrote as Violet Whyte). She was born in York, the daughter of a rector who came from a military family. Winter's writings show the army influence, often describing the lives of wives and children of military heroes. The pseudonym was adopted on the advice of her publishers, who considered that works such as *Cavalry Life* (1881) and *Regimental Legends* (1883) would be more credible if thought to have been written by a man. Winter's most successful work was *Bootle's Baby: A Story of the Scarlet Lancers* (1885), which was serialized in the *Graphic* and adapted for the stage, playing at the Globe theatre in London in 1889. Other works include *He Went for a Soldier* (1890); *A Soldier's Children* (1892), and *A Summer Jaunt* (1899). Winter also founded the *Golden Gates* magazine in 1891, was President of the Writer's Club (1892) and President of the Society of Women Journalists (1901–3).

▷Drama (19th-century Britain)

Winterson, Jeanette (born 1959)

British writer. Born in Lancashire and adopted by Pentecostal Evangelists. She read English at St Catherine's College Oxford. Her first novel ▷*Oranges Are Not the Only Fruit* (1985), which won the Whitbread Prize for a First Novel, uses Winterson as her own fictional character to explore the wilder outposts of religious obsession, love, sex and exile. Adapted by her for television in 1990 the series won international awards including BAFTA Best Drama and the Prix Italia. *The Passion* (1987), which won the John Llewellyn Rhys Prize, and *Sexing the Cherry* (1989), winner of the E.M. Forster Award American Academy of Arts and Letters, both use history as a means of creating an untouched space where the reader is freed from assumptions about narrative, character and linear time. Inside that space Winterson builds extraordinary language-dependent worlds. An experimental writer, Winterson's preoccupation with style never obscures her strong emotional themes of love, loss, ritual and exile. Winterson has also written a comic book,

Boating for Beginners (1985). Her novel *Written on the Body* was published in 1992.

Winter Studies and Summer Rambles in Canada (1838)

▷Anna Jameson's journal to an absent friend, published after she had spent a winter and summer in Upper Canada in 1836–1837. It is the most convincingly authentic of the travel books of that period, capturing the physical configuration of Canada with energy and a keen eye. Her physical explorations of the countryside occur in counterpoint to her inner journey.

Winthrop, Margaret Tyndal (c 1591–1647)

North American letter-writer. Born to the wealthy English estate-owners, Sir John and Lady Anne Tyndal, she was a devout Puritan in 1618 when she married John Winthrop, who later became Governor of Massachusetts Bay Colony. Her correspondence begins several years before her removal to New England in 1631; while it reveals her acceptance of traditional Puritan attitudes towards women's place in society, it also captures her process of determining for herself the correctness of leaving England and the everyday hardships of establishing a colony. Written to family members, her letters (excerpted in ▷*Some Old Puritan Love Letters* and collected in the ▷*Winthrop Papers*) are important contributions to our understanding of the personal as well as historic consequences of the Puritan settlement in the New World, as seen through the eyes of a woman who was at the heart of the social and political life of early Massachusetts. She remained dedicated to the well-being of the colony until her death.

▷Downing, Lucy Winthrop; Early North American letters

Winthrop Papers (1929)

Although this collection is most notable for its inclusion of the extant correspondence of ▷Margaret Tyndal Winthrop (c 1591–1647) and her sister-in-law, ▷Lucy Winthrop Downing (1600/01–1679), who were English Puritan settlers in North America, it also includes epistolary exchanges by several other women, including the daughters and/or stepdaughters of the Winthrop women. Together, these selections give us a unique perspective on the domestic and political aspects of the settlement of the Massachusetts Bay Colony.

▷*Some Old Puritan Love Letters*; *Letters of Mrs Lucy Downing*; Early North American letters

Wiseman, Adele (born 1928)

Canadian novelist, born Adele Waisman in Winnipeg, Manitoba, to Jewish parents who had fled the Ukraine. She was educated at home and in Jewish school. She attended the University of Manitoba, gained her BA in 1949, and became close friends with ▷Margaret Laurence, who introduced the 1978 edition of *Crackpot*. She worked abroad, then returned to Canada, worked as a laboratory technician, and for the Royal

Winnipeg Ballet, until publication of *The Sacrifice* (1956), which won a Governor General's Award; it explores immigrant struggle through a modern Abraham figure. She lived in New York (1957–1960), London (1961–1963), and Montreal (1964–1969), where she lectured at the university. In 1969 she moved to Toronto with her husband and daughter. Her second novel, *Crackpot* (1974), about a hefty, clear-eyed prostitute, is also located in Depression-era Winnipeg. Wiseman's novels explore the conflicts of displacement, race, and class from her particular Jewish outlook; flight and fragmentation are recurrent motifs. *Old Women at Play* (1978) is perhaps Wiseman's best work; it explores her mother's legacy of creativity as seamstress/artist. She has published the autobiographical *Memoirs of a Book Molesting Childhood and Other Essays* (1987), a children's book, *Kenji and the Cricket* (1988), and also written plays.
Bib: Greenstein, M., in *Canadian Writers and Their Works;* Special issue of *Journal of Canadian Fiction*, 31/32 (1981).

Wiseman, Jane (fl 1701)
English dramatist of the generation after ▷Aphra Behn. She wrote *Antiochus the Great, or the Fatal Relapse* (1701), and was a friend of ▷Susanna Centlivre.

Wister, Sarah (Sally) (1761–1804)
North American diarist and poet. She was born into a wealthy Quaker family, was raised in the vicinity of Philadelphia and received an excellent education at the Quakers Girls' School. In ▷*Sally Wister's Journal*, one of the better private journals from the revolutionary era, her education is evident, as is her keen eye for characterizations and her delightful wit. She enjoyed flirting with soldiers stationed at the family's estate and was interested in issues of courtship, but she chose to remain single. As an adult she became very pious, as reflected in her later writings. She died on 21 April 1804. Tributes to her as a 'highly accomplished and valuable lady' appeared in Philadelphia newspapers.

Witchcraft (West Africa)
As in the West, the special powers of wise, older or simply unconventional women have often been associated with sorcery and evil, and such women regarded as witches. This is an especially harsh indictment in societies where the occult is a real presence and magic a lived reality. The fact that many women turn, as a matter of course, to traditional remedies for problems like infertility, or to hold a man's attention, provides ready evidence for accusations of bewitchment, and places additional inhibitions on women. On the other hand, women with special healing powers are respected and accorded high status.

Witt, Henriette de (1829–1908)
French Protestant writer. A prolific author who began her career by translating English texts, she produced a number of works of an educational,

spiritual nature which were aimed primarily at young ladies. These included *Contes d'une mère à ses petits enfants* (*A Mother's Tales to Her Little Children*) (1861); *Petites Méditations Chrétiennes* (1862) (*Brief Christian Meditation*); *Histoire sainte racontée aux enfants* (1863) (*The Bible Story for Children*) and *Scènes historiques et religieuses* (1872) (*Scenes from the Bible and History*). In later years, she sought a wider readership, and wrote some very successful historical and biographical works, most notably *M. Guizot dans sa famille et avec ses amis* (1880) (*M. Guizot with His Family and Friends*), which was a kind of family chronicle, and *Les Chroniqueurs de l'histoire de France* (1882) (*Chroniclers of the History of France*).

Wittig, Monique

Monique Wittig

French writer. The combination of lesbian feminist political commitment and formal and linguistic innovation in her novels, plays and articles has stimulated considerable interest among French and Anglo-American critics. Both in her novels and in articles, such as *On ne naît pas femme* (1980) (*One is not Born a Woman*) and *La Pensée Straight* (1980) (*The Straight Mind*), she provides a critique of the social construction of femininity and of heterosexuality, and, in contrast to many contemporary French theorists, draws attention to the material nature of women's oppression. Her creation of the category 'lesbian' has been criticized as an instance of the very essentialism she is at pains to combat. Wittig's dominant interest in reclaiming and reconstructing ▷patriarchal language, culture and myth, present in all her works, is the main focus of *Brouillon Pour un dictionnaire des amantes*, (1976) (*Lesbian Peoples: Material for a Dictionary*), with S. Zeig. Her novels are *L'Opoponax* (1964) (▷*The Opoponax*, 1966), ▷*Les Guérillères* (1969), *Le Corps lesbien* (1973) (*The Lesbian Body*) and *Virgile, Non* (1985) (▷*Across the Acheron*, 1987).
Bib: Duffy, Jean in Tilby, M.J. (ed.), *Beyond the Nouveau Roman: Essays in the Contemporary French Novel.*

Wives and Daughters (1864–1866)
The last (and unfinished) novel of English writer ▷Elizabeth Gaskell, published serially in the

Cornhill Magazine. It centres on two families, the
Gibsons and the Hamleys, who live in the small
country town of Hollingford. Mr Gibson, a
widower, remarries partly for the sake of his
daughter, Molly, but his new wife, the widowed
Mrs Kirkpatrick, arouses Molly's resentment.
Although outwardly charming, she is shallow and
selfish. Her daughter, Cynthia, who moves into
the Gibson household, is more intelligent and
sincere than her mother, and she and Molly
become friendly. The two young women become
involved with the two sons of Mr Hamley, the
local squire, and Cynthia becomes engaged to the
younger son, Robert, although it is Molly who
feels most for him. The eldest son, Osborne, is
apparently brilliant and seems destined for
success, but he is disowned by his father after the
secret of his marriage to a French nursery maid is
revealed. Osborne dies young, while the seemingly
less talented Robert goes on to academic success
as a scientist. He is cast off by Cynthia and finally
realizes that it is Molly whom he loves. The novel
is generally regarded as Gaskell's best work,
highly successful in its treatment of the
differences between superficiality and depth, and
expertly constructed. Recent feminist critics have
brought out the importance of the theme of
female socialization that runs through the novel.

Gabriele Wohmann

Wobeser, Wilhelmine Karoline (1769–1807)

German novelist. The wife of a retired army
captain, her only book, *Elisa, oder das Weib wie es
sein sollte* (1802) (*Elisa or Woman as She Should
Be*), became one of the most widely-read women's
novels of her time. Clearly influenced by British
novelist Samuel Richardson's *Clarissa* (1747–8), it
is a morbid tale of female self-sacrifice and
suffering. It was subsequently emulated in work
by other, younger women writers, such as
▷Johanna Schopenhauer.

Wohmann, Gabriele (born 1932)

German novelist and short story writer. She grew
up in Darmstadt as the third child of a parson
who opposed the Nazis, studied languages and
philosophy in Frankfurt, and then returned to
Darmstadt, where she married Reiner Wohmann,
a teacher. Since 1956 she has published a steady
stream of stories, novels, radio plays and poems,
establishing herself as a one of West Germany's
best-known authors of post-war fiction.
Essentially a realist writer, she describes the
neuroses of modern West Germans, charting the
banality of their private and public failures in a
terse, often rather pessimistically aggressive idiom.
Among her best work is the novel *Paulinchen war
allein zu Haus* (1974) (*Paulinchen was Home Alone*),
the story of a trendy young couple's abortive
attempt to educate their daughter in a pseudo-
enlightened way. ▷*Ach wie gut, daß niemand weiß*
(1980) (*Oh How Lucky Noone Knows*) is a study of
the slow moral disintegration of a woman
psychotherapist and *Flötenton* (1987) (*Sound of a
Flute*) comments on the powerlessness of the

individual in the face of a castastrophe like the
Chernobyl nuclear disaster.

Wolf, Christa (born 1929)

Christa Wolf

East German writer. Born in Landsberg (now in
Poland), she was old enough to have, in her
formative years, experienced the full impact of
Hitler's fascist ideology, yet young enough to have

enthusiastically espoused the Marxist doctrines of the new East German state in 1949. She studied literature at Jena and Leipzig, compiled anthologies of ▷socialist-realist writing, and, in 1961, published *Moskauer Novelle* (*Moscow Novella*) in the same idiom. However, it was *Der geteilte Himmel* (1963) (*The Divided Heaven*, 1965) which established her as East Germany's foremost woman writer. Set in August 1961, just as the Berlin Wall was being built, the novel is a carefully crafted retrospective analysis of why a young woman chooses not to follow her lover to the West. Investigating German history in order to illuminate the present is also central to the semi-autobiographical novels *Nachdenken über Christa T.* (1968) (*The Quest for Christa T.*, 1982) and *Kindheitsmuster* (1976) (▷*Patterns of Childhood*, 1984). *Kein Ort, Nirgends* (1979) (*No Place on Earth*, 1982, 1983), describes an imagined meeting between the two 19th-century poets Heinrich von Kleist (1777–1811) and ▷Karoline von Günderrode, both victims of a repressive system. In 1982 Wolf had a huge international success with *Kassandra* (1983) (*Cassandra. A Novel and Four Essays*, 1984), a feminist attack on militarism. Her novella, *Störfall* (1987) (*Accidents*), is a meditation on the nuclear disaster at Chernobyl. Always at the mercy of the censors and subject to personal harassment by the state, she published *Was bleibt* (*What Remains*), an analysis of the fear of persecution, just after the collapse of the East German communist government in 1989.

Wolff, Betje (1738–1804)

Poet and prose writer from the northern Netherlands; full name Elizabeth Wolff-Bekker. She grew up in a family of Calvinist merchants, but received a modern education. In 1759 she entered into a 'philosophical' marriage with Adriaan Wolff, a vicar thirty-one years older. Her poetic début, *Bespiegelingen over het genoegen* (1763) (*Reflections on Pleasure*), with which she followed in the footsteps of ▷Lucretia van Merken, consisted of contemplative, moral-philosophical poems. Her later poetry is satirical in character. From 1777, on the death of her husband, she joined ▷Aagje Deken to form a writing partnership. Their joint works include the epistolary novels *Historie van mejuffrouw Sara Burgerhart* (1782) (▷*Sara Burgerhart*) and *Historie van de heer Willem Leevend* (1784–1785), the latter work showing their abhorrence of intolerance, lack of faith and exaggerated sentimentalism. Partly for political reasons, they left for Burgundy in 1788, where they had to make their living from their writings. After returning to The Hague in 1797, their work was much criticized. The most important novel from this period is *Geschrift eener bejaarde vrouw* (1802) (*Document of an Elderly Woman*), a pseudo-autobiography. Their correspondence with each other and with others is of an exceptional quality, as in *Briefwisseling van Betje Wolff en Aagje Deken* (1987) (*Correspondence of Betje Wolff and Aagje Deken*).

Wolff, Victoria (born 1908)

German writer. From her earliest days she has made a living by writing stories, reports and essays for a number of German and, later, Swiss, newspapers. In 1932, she published a novel about ▷George Sand, *Eine Frau wie du und ich* (*A Woman Like You and I*). However, in the following year she was banned from publishing in Germany, and began a long and perilous journey from Switzerland, through France, Spain and Portugal, to the USA, where she finally arrived in 1941. She wrote travelogues, notably the highly successful *Im Tal der Könige* (1945) (*In the Valley of the Kings*) about Egypt and Palestine, countries she had visited for a Swiss newspaper. From 1942 she lived in Beverly Hills, California, working as a script writer, though in later life she returned to the novel form with *Mutter und Tochter* (1964) (*Mother and Daugther*) and *Der Feuersturm* (1977) (*The Fire-storm*).

Wolley (Woolley), Hannah (?1621–?1676)

English writer on household management and ▷conduct, who was a servant and then married a headmaster (and others), and published a sequence of books on cooking, medicine and the household. She writes in *The Cook's Guide* (1664) that she has 'sent forth this book, to testifie to the scandalous world that I do not altogether spend my time idly'.

Her other publications include: *The Ladies Directory* (1661); *The Queen-Like Closet* (1670), and *The Ladies Delight* (1672).

Wollstonecraft, Mary (1759–1797)

Writer on political and social topics, polemicist, writer of fiction, seen by 20th-century critics as a feminist. Her life was unconventional. Her first novel, *Mary, a Fiction* (1788), is related to the early experience of the death of her friend, and she was already keeping the company of Dissenters and radicals, writing her first tract on rights in 1787 – ▷*Thoughts on the Education of Daughters*. Returning from working as a governess in Ireland, Wollstonecraft came to London and worked for a radical publisher, translating and reviewing. During this time she also turned to children's literature, and put together *The Female Reader* (1789). The next year she published her counterblast to Burke on the French Revolution, *A Vindication of the Rights of Men*. She knew London radicals, including Thomas Paine (1737–1809), ▷Anna Laetitia Barbauld, and the anarchist philosopher William Godwin (1756–1836). In 1792, she published one of the most famous texts in the English feminist tradition, ▷*A Vindication of the Rights of Woman*. In the same year she went to Paris and fell for Gilbert Imlay, had a child, and wrote *A Historical and Moral View of the French Revolution* (1794) and *Letters from Scandinavia* (1796). The relationship with Imlay was unhappy, so she returned to England, writing *Maria, or the Wrongs of Woman* (unfinished, but published posthumously in 1798). She began to live with Godwin, and married him in 1797 for the

sake of her child. Her reputation was hotly debated at the time; women like ▷Hannah More saw themselves engaged in a different enterprise. The potential of Wollstonecraft's rationalist polemic remains potentially radical – she wrote: 'From the respect paid to property flow, as from a poisoned fountain, most of the evils and vices which render this world such a dreary scene to the contemplative mind.'
Bib: Tomalin, C., *The Life and Death of Mary Wollstonecraft*.

Wolstenholme-Elmy, Elizabeth (1834–1913)
English essayist and poet, who also wrote under the name of E. Ellis, Ellis Ethelmer, and 'Ignota'. Orphaned as a child and deprived of an adequate ▷education, she became an ardent ▷feminist and vigorous campaigner. She was Honorary Secretary to the Manchester Women's ▷Suffrage Society (1865), Secretary to the Married Women's Property Committee (1867–82), a founding member of the Women's Franchise League (1899) and the founder of the Women's Emancipation Union (1891). She published a long feminist poem, ▷*Woman Free* (1893); two sex education manuals (*The Human Flower*, 1894, and *Baby Buds*, 1895) and many pamphlets, including her last work, *Woman's Franchise: The Need of the Hour* (1907).
Bib: Strachey, R., *The Cause*.

Wolzogen, Friederike Sophie Karoline Auguste von (1763–1847)
German writer. From a cultured family, she was, as a young woman, taken by her mother on an educational journey, during which she met the dramatist and poet Friedrich Schiller (1759–1805), with whom she later fell in love. After an unhappy marriage (and Schiller's marriage to her sister Charlotte), she moved to Swabia and began her literary career by publishing a series of letters from Switzerland in ▷Sophie La Roche's women's magazine, *Pomona*. In 1794 she obtained a divorce and married her cousin Wilhelm von Wolzogen. They moved to Weimar, where their house became an important literary salon and meeting place for many literary figures of the day. Best known for her biography of Schiller, she was also an accomplished writer of fiction; her novel, *Agnes von Lilien*, published anonymously in 1796, was thought by some to have been written by Goethe (1749–1832). Influenced by ▷Sophie La Roche's *Geschichte des Fräuleins von Sternheim* (*The Story of Fräulein von Sternheim*) and Goethe's *Wilhelm Meister* (1771), the work is an interesting early example of a woman's ▷*Bildungsroman*.

Woman, A (1908)
English translation of *Una donna* (1906), a novel by Italian writer ▷Sibilla Aleramo, translated again in 1979. Containing many autobiographical elements, it tells of a woman who is raped, becomes pregnant, and marries the rapist, who is a friend of her family. Her life of entrapment is unbearable, in spite of her love for her son. The notions of 'woman', 'mother' and 'writer' are investigated in this novel in terms of their relationship to each other, and the ideology of motherhood is questioned. Ironically, it is the protagonist's discovery of her own mother's letters, which tell of her unhappiness, that finally pushes her into breaking away from her unhappy marriage and from her son. This woman, unlike the mother whom she had never understood, puts herself first. Her self-affirmation is, nevertheless, a very painful process.

Woman-centred
A literary narrative or critical/historical practice which consciously focuses on women and addresses the distinctiveness of female experience.
   ▷Gilbert, Sandra; Gubar, Susan; Irigaray, Luce; Millett, Kate; Rich, Adrienne; Showalter, Elaine; Smith-Rosenberg, Caroll

Woman controversy (17th-century England)
In 1615 one Joseph Swetnam published a pamphlet entitled the *Arraignment of Lewd, idle, forward and unconstant women* which provoked a sequence of printed responses and defences of women (see also ▷Sarah Fyge's similar response in the 18th century). At least some of these responses seem to have been written by women, and there had been an earlier defence – the possibly pseudonymous ▷*Jane Anger her Protection for Women* (1589). The replies to Swetnam were by Constantia Munda (▷pseudonym), *The Worming of a Mad Dogge* (1617), Esther Sowernam (pseudonym), *Esther hath hang'd Haman* (1617), and ▷Rachel Speght *A Mouzell for Melastomus* (1617). The satires of the 1640s included Mary Tattle-well and Joan Hit-him-home, *The Womans Sharp Revenge* (1640).
Bib: Shepard, Simon (ed.), *The Women's Sharp Revenge: Five Women's Pamphlets From the Renaissance*.

Woman Destroyed, The
Translation of *La Femme rompue* (1968), a volume of three short novels by French writer ▷Simone de Beauvoir. The novels (*The Age of Discretion*, *The Monologue* and *The Woman Destroyed*) are all concerned with the theme of jealousy and emotional loss. Many critics judge the novels to be de Beauvoir's most fluent and engaging work; in the tales of middle-aged women betrayed by their husbands and children she expresses with considerable literary power both the emotional agonies of heterosexual relations and the helplessness of women who have internalized a belief in romance. The theme of the danger of emotional dependence by women on men is found throughout de Beauvoir's work; nowhere is it more powerfully argued than in this trilogy.

Woman Free (1893)
A long poem by English writer ▷Elizabeth Wolstenholme-Elmy, concerned with women's subordination. The poem attacks the 'brainless bondage' to which women are subjected in

marriage, and protests against male sexual aggression, claiming that women must be 'Free from all uninvited touch of man'. The poem also contains many notes which supplement the author's ▷feminist perspective. The author writes: 'Anyone who has looked a little below the surface of women's lives can testify to the general unrest and nervous exhaustion or malaise among them, although each would probably refer her suffering to some cause peculiar to herself and her circumstances, never dreaming that she was the victim of an evil that gnaws at the very heart of society, making almost every woman the heroine of a silent tragedy.'

Woman-identified ▷Case, Sue-Ellen; Rich, Adrienne

Woman in Ancient Times Shines Like the Sun, A (1971)
The four-volume autobiography of Japanese writer Hiratuka Raityo (1886–1971). She published *Seito* (*The Bluestockings*), in 1911, which was not only the first woman's literary journal in Japan, but also a journal of feminist studies. Although it was short-lived (1911–16), its influence was lasting. Hiratuka established the theory of motherhood and women's rights (including abortion), and she continued to campaign for world peace. Much of her work appears in *Selected Collections of Essays of Hiratuka Raityo* (1983–1984) (seven volumes).

Woman in the Nineteenth Century (1845)
Germinal US book on feminism by ▷Margaret Fuller. An outgrowth of her famous ▷*Dial* essay, 'The Great Lawsuit: Man versus Men, Woman versus Women', *Woman* reflects Fuller's Boston 'conversations' (1839–1844). A hybrid of seminars and discussion groups, meeting at the home of educational and social reformer Elizabeth Palmer Peabody (1804–1894), the conversations brought together women's rights advocates, ▷transcendentalists, social reformers and intellectuals of all kinds. The analysis of *Woman* shows Fuller's path-breaking willingness to put women's sexuality and intelligence at the centre of economic and social analysis.

Womanist/womanism
A term associated with black feminism, and defined by feminist critic ▷Alice Walker as the handing down of womanish attributes from mother to daughter. In ▷*In Search of Our Mothers' Gardens* (1983) Walker explains that although womanism describes women's shared emotions, friendship, culture and feminism ('womanist is to feminist as purple is to lavender') it does not necessarily lead to a separatist politics.

Woman of Genius, A (1912)
US novel. ▷Mary Austin's autobiographical work tells the story of Olivia Latimore. Olivia was born with a gift for acting, but to use her gift she must free herself from family obligations. Olivia exemplifies conflicts of a transitional generation of women who pursue careers. To succeed, these women must overcome the sexual and social mores of their time. Olivia refuses to marry the man she passionately loves rather than sacrifice her work. Instead, she marries for companionship a dramatist who shares her work. Through her public achievement Olivia provides an alternative role model to that of her mother. Austin breaks the cultural conspiracy against women telling the truth about their own experiences, and she addresses questions about women's sexuality and its relationship to artistic creativity.

Woman on the Cross (1916)
The novel is the most 'decadent' of the fictional works by the Russian writer ▷Anna Mar. Mar uses a love plot to explore her favourite themes of the closeness of love and hate, agony and ecstasy, heaven and hell. In Mar's earlier works, Catholicism offered salvation, but here the Church is represented by an old priest who actually encourages the heroine to seek punishment from a sadistic tormenter to whom she is fatally attracted. In her descent into agony she rejects the lesbian love of her friend, Christina. The novel is sprinkled with references to modernist literature (Emile Zola, 1840–1902, J.K. Huysmans, 1848–1907, Maurice Maeterlinck 1862–1949) and imperious male conquerors (Napoleon, Julius Caesar), and is an awkward combination of ▷realism and symbolism: Alina's childhood is depicted realistically, but most of the novel verges on symbolism in its abstraction from concrete place or causal explanation.

Woman on the Edge of Time (1976)
US ▷science fiction novel by ▷Marge Piercy. The book moves between a nightmare vision of contemporary North America and a utopian future in which social equality and ecological harmony have been achieved. The two strands of the novel are linked by Connie Ramos, a Chicano woman who is radically dispossessed, separated from her daughter because of one violent outburst, and confined to a mental hospital as a guinea pig for psychiatric experiments. Her 'visits' to the future allow Piercy to explore alternative gender relationships and models of sexuality within a different social structure. In particular, Connie is given the mothering which the reader has earlier learned is at the root of her emotional deprivation. The utopian world shows up the racial, sexual and social inequalities of contemporary US society. However even the utopia is fighting a defensive war, and at one point Piercy depicts another, darker, dystopian future, suggesting to Connie the need to actively fight for a better future.

'Woman Question, The'
From the 1830s onwards Victorian Britain was obsessively concerned with the 'Woman Question', as they themselves called it. The arguments in this debate were complex and multivocal; the issue of woman's role in society

was discussed in newspapers, magazines, and literary, philosophical, educational and medical journals; in Parliament, in church and in the home. No single cultural myth prevailed, and the idea of 'Woman'; her 'mission', her 'sphere' and her 'influence' became a site of struggle where competing ideologies strove for dominance. Some commentators challenged the constraints placed upon middle-class women's lives and argued for greater vocational and educational opportunity; others argued passionately that women and men should operate in separate spheres of existence. Recent critical examination of the 'Woman Question' has explored the interrelationships between the Victorian preoccupation with history, national identity and Empire, and the widespread concern with the status and function of women (see Christina Crosby's *The Ends of History*, 1991). Numerous extracts from contemporary writings on the 'Woman Question' can be found in Helsinger et al. (eds) *The Woman Question: Society and Literature in Britain and America 1837–1883*.

▷Education (19th-century Britain); Feminism (19th-century Britain); 'New Woman, The'; Suffrage (19th-century Britain); *Eliza Cook's Journal*; Stickney Ellis, Sarah; Linton, Eliza Lynn
Russia: In Russia the mid-19th century debate over the status of women was subsumed under the rubric of the 'woman question.' The roots of the debate have been traced to the influence of the French Utopian socialists and ▷George Sand on prominent radical critics like Belinsky and Chernyshevsky (Irina Paperno, *Chernyshevsky and the Age of Realism. A Study in the Semiotics of Behavior*), and Ivan Turgenev's (1818–1883) early novels. Russian women's voices were also raised in protest against ▷patriarchal restrictions and control over their lives. The fiction writer Evgeniia Mikhaelis has been described as having 'discovered the feminist message in the ideas of the Utopians' by the late 1830s, and ▷Maria Zhúkova's works treated the problems of independent-minded but poor young women. The poet ▷Karolina Pávlova and, from the 1850s, fiction writers like ▷Nadezhda Khvoshchínskaia, repeatedly addressed the struggle of women against the limitations of their position in patriarchal society.

Late in the century, gentry and middle-class women sparked a new feminist campaign for women's rights. ▷Ol'ga Shapír devoted her fiction to giving women a voice for their complaints and goals. ▷The Silver Age was rich in women writers who expressed a thirst for self-fulfilment and full acceptance in society. After the 1917 Revolution ▷Aleksandra Kollontái became a prominent propagandist for radical restructuring of relations between the sexes. While women gained full civil rights in the new Soviet Union, they remain handicapped by traditional attitudes and the 'double burden' of work outside and inside the home. The debate about their disabilities surfaced timidly in the late 1960s with works like ▷Baránskaia's ▷*A Week Like Any Other*. The fiction of ▷*glásnost'* has so far remained within conventional bounds in its treatment of women's lives.
▷Vovchók, Marko; *What Is to Be Done?*; *Ursa Major*, *Woman Question, The*

Woman Question, The (1907)
A one-act farce by Russian writer ▷Tèffi, first staged at the ▷St Petersburg Malyi Theatre in 1907. As in much of Tèffi's prose, this play is structured around an opposition – in this case, the typical behaviour of men versus women – and takes aim at an issue of the day – equal rights for women. The young heroine, Katia, is hesitant about marrying her suitor, Andrei. She falls asleep, and in her dream men and women reverse roles and behaviour patterns, and verbal customs are wittily exchanged. Katia concludes from her dream that simply changing roles will not change anything until humanity itself is fundamentally altered. The play ends as she announces her engagement.
▷Woman Question (Russia)

Woman's fiction
US 19th-century popular novel genre. In *Woman's Fiction: A Guide to Novels by and about Women in America, 1820–1870* (1978), Nina Baym named and described this distinctive and enormously popular novel form that she dated from ▷Catharine Maria Sedgwick's *A New-England Tale* (1822). Not totally unlike its predecessors, the shared 'overplot' of woman's fiction focused on a heroine outside the promises and protections of the patriarchal family who overcomes misfortune and adversity by virtue of her own strength and talent. Remarkably for their era, these heroines often succeed by competently taking on professional roles – modelling the acts of their creators, women writers who themselves often overcame adversity and supported themselves and their families by taking on roles as professional authors. What is unique to woman's fiction of the era is that the heroines are rewarded, not with independence, but with marriage and domesticity – albeit a domesticity more fulfilled, more equal, than the traditional wife and mother's role in patriarchal society. Because of these domestic endings, for much of the 20th century critics derided these novels as ▷domestic fiction or as sentimental novels – judgements which hardly could have resulted from a reading of the texts.

Read by women, written by women and centred on women's experiences, woman's fiction dominated the 19th-century US book market.
▷Warner, Susan Bogert; *Wide, Wide World, The*; Wood, Sarah Keating.
Bib: Baym, Nina, *Woman's Fiction: A Guide to Novels by and About Women in America, 1820–1870*.

Woman's Friendship (1853)
A novel by British author ▷Grace Aguilar, concerned with the importance of female bonding. The central character, Florence, becomes friendly

with Lady Ida Villiers, a woman whose social status is considerably higher than her own. Florence is warned by her 'mother' (who turns out to be a foster-parent) that this friendship cannot be mutual because Lady Villiers's class position prohibits it. Later, Florence's true parentage is revealed, and after a period of estrangement from one another Florence and Lady Villiers are re-united in friendship. Aguilar writes at the end of the book that although female bonding is 'in general scorned and scoffed at . . . [it] may be the invisible means of strengthening in virtue'.

Woman's novel ▷Woman's fiction

Woman to Man (1949)
Volume of Australian poems by ▷Judith Wright. The title poem 'Woman to Man' deals with the sexual act from a woman's point of view, and the conception of a child, 'the third who lay in our embrace'. It is one of the most celebrated and frequently anthologized of Australian poems. The remainder of the poems of *Woman to Man* celebrate all aspects of creativity, both physical and aesthetic. 'The Maker', for instance, deals with the creation of a poem, which is seen as an act parallel to that of the creation of the child. Australian natural features, such as the wattle tree and the flame tree, provide the imagery for profound poetic statements concerning the power of love and creativity, and their ability to defeat time and death.

Woman to Woman (1987)
Translation of *Les Parleuses* (1974), a transcription of unscripted interviews of ▷Marguerite Duras by ▷Xavière Gauthier. The interviews cover Duras's work and related topics, establishing the limits of her affinities with the feminist movement.

Woman Travelling on the Earth, A (1982–1983)
Work by Japanese novelist ▷Ohara Tomie. The story is developed through Toshie's exploration of the life of her grandmother, Banba Kame. Kame has lost all her property as a result of taking care of both her husband and her eldest son, and the villagers turn against her when she falls into difficulties. On top of this, she becames almost bedridden following torture after her arrest for *lèse-majesté*. Now disabled, the villagers do not consider her a human being. Nonetheless, Kame feels that the villagers despise her real identity and not her disability. She accepts this calmly. Toshie begins to understand the true nature of her grandmother and then questions her own ten-year relationship with her lover, who has a wife and children.

Woman Warrior: Memoirs of a Girlhood Among Ghosts, The (1976)
US autobiography in which ▷Maxine Hong Kingston blends myth, legend and history. She incorporates these elements to construct her own Chinese-American woman's voice, piecing together her Chinese heritage from the stories her mother tells. In her writing Kingston avenges the victimizations of Chinese women of previous generations. She breaks the silence surrounding 'No Name', an aunt ostracized for giving birth to an illegitimate child, and reports the lesson learned through Moon Orchid, an aunt rejected by her successful Americanized husband. Kingston pays homage to her mother, Brave Orchid, who sacrificed money and position to emigrate to the US. In her Chinese heritage Kingston finds the spiritual strength to become a survivor, and identifies herself with Fa Mu Lan, the legendary woman warrior.

Women and Economics (1898)
US feminist analysis and advocacy of women's independence by ▷Charlotte Perkins Gilman. An internationally read and recognized germinal text of feminist analysis, *Women and Economics* demonstrated the connections between patriarchy and poverty and argued for new, rational conceptions of women's roles in society.

Women and the Bush: Forces of Desire in the Australian Cultural Tradition (1988)
Work by Australian critic Kay Schaffer. It provides a feminist critique of the patriarchal literary and historical tradition in Australia by deconstructing the notion of the bush and of bush society. It is imaginative and innovative in its use of explorer journals, biography, historiography and film, as well as the works of Henry Lawson and ▷Barbara Baynton, to expose the structure of binary oppositions which has traditionally governed Australian value systems and literary representations.

Women and work (18th-century Britain)
Although literary texts often engage only with women confined to the domestic sphere, 18th-century women did work in various industries, and were often very poorly paid. Examples include the cloth industry, (wool, spinning and, latterly, cotton mills), lace-making, and millinery. Other employments included basketwork, mining, fruit and vegetable marketing, baking, trading, washing, in shops and in inns, and as agricultural labourers. Midwifery was a disputed profession. Inevitably, few women who worked in this way made it into print.
▷Cairns, Elizabeth; Cellier, Elizabeth; Leapor, Mary; Little, Janet; Stone, Sarah
Bib: Hill, Bridget, *Eighteenth Century Women: An Anthology*; Landry, Donna, *The Muses of Resistence*.

Women are Different (1986)
A novel by the Nigerian writer ▷Flora Nwapa, in which the focus is on women in contemporary society. The beginning is autobiographical to the extent that it draws on the author's own experience of school in pre-independence Nigeria. Her customary technique of portraying a heroine in the context of a network of friends, family and community is here taken one stage

further, in the creation of a collective heroine. Rose, Agnes and Dora are friends at school who share the values of their Western, missionary education, with its disdain of ▷polygamy and elevation of personal service and romantic love. But in the cut-and-thrust competitiveness of post-independence Nigeria they find that these values are wholly inappropriate. The story traces each of their lives, with their different choices, and concludes that the pragmatic materialism of their daughters' generation serves women better than idealistic self-sacrifice.

Women as They Are, or, The Manners of the Day (1830)

A novel by English writer ▷Catherine Gore, received as belonging to the 'silver-fork' school of ▷fashionable fiction. It brought Gore notable recognition, and provided the model that many of her later works were to follow. Like ▷*Mothers and Daughters* (1831), it centres on fashionable society, describing shopping in chic areas and detailing the latest styles in dresses and accessories. The plot revolves around marriage but is less important than the extraneous detail, which provided a kind of fashion handbook for the wealthy.

'Women in Jamaican Literature 1900–1950' (1990)

This article by Rhonda Cobham, which appeared in ▷*Out of the Kumbla* (pp. 195–222), examines changes in the depiction of the Jamaican woman in literature from the post-emancipation period to the pre-independence era. It includes analysis of the work of ▷Vera Bell, ▷Louise Bennett and ▷Una Marson.

Women in Love: Eight Centuries of Feminine Writing (1980)

Translation of *Histoire et mythologie de l'amour: huit siècles d'écrits féminins* (1974), French sociologist ▷Evelyne Sullerot's thought-provoking discussion of French women's depiction of love and marriage. The texts selected range from courtly love to 20th-century sexuality.

Women of the Fertile Crescent: an Anthology of Modern Poetry by Arab Women (1978)

The first anthology of poetry by Arab women in English, edited with translations by Kamal Boullata. The *Fertile Crescent* of the title is a misnomer, for the volume includes poetry from Egypt and Saudi Arabia, technically not part of the 'Fertile Crescent'. Of the thirteen poets included in the anthology, five wrote their poetry originally in French or English and all the others from ▷Nazik al-Mala'ika to ▷Fadwa Tuqan are in the forefront of the ▷New Movement in modern Arabic poetry. A number of names included are now best known for work in other fields: Mona Sa'udi is a sculptor, Salma al-Khadra' al-Jayyusi is a critic and the Director of PROTA (a project for the translation of Arabic

literature), and Hanan 'Ashrawi is a politician. Their early poetic output shows the ingrained Arab love for poetry; there is no 'closed shop' for poetry in Arabic.

Women's Decameron, The (1986)

Short stories by Russian writer ▷Iuliia Voznesénskaia, first published in Russian in 1985. In this set of bawdy and disturbing tales, Voznesénskaia, like a number of other contemporary Russian women writers, uses the hospital as a microcosm of Soviet society (for example ▷Petrushévskaia's 'The Violin', ▷Varlámova's ▷*A Counterfeit Life*). Ten new mothers, quarantined with skin infections for ten days in a ▷Leningrad maternity ward, amuse each other by telling stories, choosing a new topic each day: love, farcical sex, seduction, bitches, infidelity, rape, money, revenge, good deeds, and happiness. The women have diverse backgrounds, from functionary to tramp, and convictions ranging from rigid conformity to rebellious dissidence, and the experiences they draw on are a catalogue of disasters and humiliations, some specific to Soviet society, and others familiar to women worldwide.

Bib: Goscilo, H., 'Women's Wards and Wardens: The Hospital in Contemporary Russian Women's Fiction', *Canadian Women's Studies*, Winter 1989.

Women's language

A shorthand term suggesting the possibility that women write differently from men. Feminists disagree, however, on the cause of this difference: French feminists like ▷Luce Irigaray and, to a lesser degree, ▷Hélène Cixous have attributed it to women's psycho-sexual difference. British and North American feminists, however, place more emphasis on cultural influences and women's different socialization processes in producing what the title of an essay by ▷Mary Jacobus calls 'The Difference of View' (1979). In *In Search of Our Mothers' Gardens* (1983), ▷Alice Walker, the black feminist critic, fuses psycho-sexual and social factors to produce her theory that women inherit female creativity from their mothers.

▷*Écriture féminine*; Woolf, Virginia

Bib: Cameron, Deborah, *Feminism and Linguistic Theory*.

Women's Liberation Movement

The title which in the West is usually given to the movement for women's rights which emerged in Britain and the US in the 1960s. The aims of women's liberation are several, and changing across cultures. In western Europe, however, and in Britain in particular, the basic request made by women activists of the 1960s and 1970s movement was for an end to women's legal and economic oppression, within and outside the home. Related demands include calls for equal pay; equal job and educational opportunities; free contraception and abortion on demand; childcare facilities for working women; an end to

discrimination against lesbians, and end to rape and violence against women.
Bib: Feminist Anthology Collective (eds), *No Turning Back*.

Women, Society and Change (1971)
Translation of French sociologist ▷Evelyne Sullerot's *La Femme dans le monde moderne* (1970). Sullerot examines the economic and social consequences of women's access to paid employment outside the home, which gave them financial independence. She sees this as the essential condition for women to become equal partners with men on a social and political level.

Women's organizations in colonial North America
The American Revolution served as the impetus for the organization of women into politically active groups. The origins of these groups were rooted in religious meetings in which women gathered and established friendships; eventually they evolved into public activism. As early as 1733 businesswomen in New York City published a protest in the *New York Journal* against biased treatment: 'most of us are Merchants, and as we in some measure contribute to the Support of Government, we ought to be entitled to some of the Sweets of it.' In 1774 a women's organization from Edenton, North Carolina, published an anti-tea declaration, and many of the 'Daughter of Liberty' broadsides were written collectively. The blending of patriotism, economics and sisterhood during these volatile years opened the doors for women's political collectivism.

Women's suffrage ▷Suffrage (19th-century Britain)

Wonderful Adventures of Mrs Seacole in Many Lands, The (1857)
Considered one of the most important personal histories written by a Caribbean-born woman, this ▷autobiography records ▷Mary Seacole's experiences during her travels in North and Central America and Europe, and documents her participation in and service as a nurse to the soldiers of the Crimean War. Her narrative bears witness to the racist attitudes prevailing at the time in England and North and Central America, and provides a view of a black woman who asserts herself in both the colonial and the non-colonial world.
See the introduction by Ziggi Alexander and Audrey Dewjee to the 1984 reprint of this work.

Wong, Jade Snow (born 1919)
US biographer. In *Fifth Chinese Daughter* (1945) Wong transmits Chinese culture to non-Chinese-Americans, and documents her struggle to define herself apart from her family and community.
Wong was born and raised in the Chinatown ghetto of San Francisco, California. As an adolescent, she worked as a servant for Anglo-Americans. Humiliated by her position, she distinguished herself through her skills in cooking Chinese food. Class valedictorian in high school, she attended Mills College. Later she established her own pottery business in Chinatown. Wong succeeds by capitalizing on aspects of her Chinese identity that do not threaten Anglo-Americans and achieves acceptance from Anglo-Americans. Her success renders her a spectator rather than a participant in her own culture.
Other works include: *No Chinese Stranger* (1975).

Wong, Nellie
US poet and essayist. Wong was born in the Year of the Dog and was raised in the Chinatown of Oakland, California. A socialist feminist activist, she is committed to the struggles of her Toisanese forbears. Her commitment to radical social change informs her art. Many poems in *Dreams in Harrison Railroad Park* (1977) feature girls who are coming of age. In 'How a Girl Got Her Chinese Name' the girl risks losing her identity, and in 'Like the Old Woman suggested' the girl discovers her sexuality and becomes aware of her role as a commodity in society. Other poems challenge the stereotypical roles of Wong's race. 'Magazine Poem for Father's Day' reclaims the personal and individual from the stereotypical. 'Picnic' emphasizes the acceptance of heritage to recover the self.

Wong May
Singaporean poet, now emigrated to and living in the USA. Although she began publishing in literary journals in Singapore, all of Wong's volumes (*A Bad Girls' Book of Animals*, 1969; *Reports*, 1972; *Wannsee Gedicte*, 1975 and *Superstitions*, 1978) postdate her departure and have been published and well reviewed in the USA.

Wood, Mrs Henry (Ellen) (1814–1817)
English novelist, who also wrote under the ▷pseudonym Johnny Ludlow. She was born in Worcester, the daughter of a manufacturer. Wood's early short stories appeared in the *New Monthly Magazine* and her first novel, *Danesbury House*, was published in 1860. Her second, ▷*East Lynne* (1861), was hugely successful, selling over 2½ million copies by 1900. The conservatism of this book is also apparent in the rest of Wood's *oeuvre*, with *Mrs Halliburton's Troubles* (1862) and *A Life's Secret* (1867) exhibiting extreme hostility to working-class activism. She was prolific, writing over thirty novels and 300 short stories, as well as editing a periodical, *Argosy*. Most of her works are novels of ▷sensation underscored by a rigid Victorian morality. They include *The Channings* (1862); *The Shadows of Ashlydyat* (1863); *Lady Adelaide's Oath* (1867) and *The Master of Greylands* (1873). Her last work was *Ashley and Other Stories* (1897).
▷Drama (19th-century Britain); Ghost stories (19th-century Britain)

Bib: Hughes, W., *The Maniac in the Cellar: Sensation Novels of the 1860s.*

Wood, Sarah Sayward Barrell Keating (1759–1855)

US novelist. Unlike many other 19th-century US women (eg ▷Sarah Payson Willis Parton) who became writers because of financial exigency when they were widowed, Wood wrote and published as occupation during two periods of widowhood after the death of her husbands.

Her first novels are in the 18th-century British and US tradition: virtuous young women who effect change in their worlds through the power of example. Among her early novels with European settings are *Julia and the Illuminated Baron* (1800); *Dorval, or The Speculator* (1801); and *Amelia; or, The Influence of Virtue* (1802). Wood's novels anticipate the development of US ▷woman's fiction later in the 19th century. While her early work is often classified as Gothic romance, her characters' strength in the face of suffering is typical of fiction by ▷Harriet Beecher Stowe and other ▷local color writers associated with the beginnings of US literary realism. Wood's last published fiction volume, *Tales of the Night* (1827), is set in Maine and is clearly a precursor of local color or regional realism.

'Woodstock Poems, The' (1554–1555)

Two poems composed by ▷Elizabeth Tudor while she was imprisoned during 1554–1555 as a threat to her sister Queen Mary's reign (▷Mary Tudor). One poem, scratched into a window with her diamond, consists of two lines asserting her innocence. The other, derived from the philosopher Boethius (475–524), was written on a shutter. The second poem of ten lines is a vigorous assertion of her confidence in overcoming bad fortune.

'Wooing Group, The' (early 13th century)

An English group of lyrical prayers to Christ and the Virgin Mary, written in rhythmic and alliterative prose, and named from one of the meditations, the 'Wooing of Our Lord'. They express the deep personal devotion which characterized the spirituality of the 12th and early 13th centuries. In the nuptial imagery the speaker employs, the speaker's soul (a noun of feminine gender) is sometimes the bride of the Word. It has been suggested that these expressive meditations may have been written by women.
Bib: Thompson, W. Meredith (ed.), *The Wohunge of Ure Lauerd.*

Woolf, Virginia (1882–1941)

English novelist, essayist and critic. She was born in London, the daughter of Leslie Stephen, literary critic and biographer, and Julia Jackson Duckworth, and was the sister of Vanessa Bell. Following her father's death in 1904, she moved to the house in Bloomsbury which would become central to activities of the ▷Bloomsbury group of intellectuals. Woolf's involvement in this group,

Virginia Woolf by G.C. Beresford

and her marriage in 1912 to the political theorist Leonard Woolf, with whom she established the Hogarth Press in 1917, are seen as central to her literary development. Woolf suffered from a series of acute mental breakdowns following her mother's death in 1895, leading to her suicide in 1941.

Woolf's first two novels, *The Voyage Out* (1915) and *Night and Day* (1919), utilize a conventional, ▷realist framework, but are punctuated by the short story 'The Mark on the Wall' (in *Two Stories*, 1917), which first advanced Woolf's interest in formal experimentation and increasing concern with notions of 'subjective' rather than 'objective' reality. A clear statement of Woolf's innovatory project appears in the essay 'Modern Fiction' (1919), which details her new attitude to the presentation of consciousness and characterization, followed through in her next novel, *Jacob's Room* (1922). The subsequent novels, ▷*Mrs Dalloway* (1925), ▷*To the Lighthouse* (1927) and ▷*The Waves* (1931), maintain Woolf's use of ▷stream-of-consciousness narrative techniques, and preoccupation with questions of temporality, consolidating her position as one of the leading ▷modernist writers.

Woolf's concern with questions of women's subjugation and women and writing are the dominant themes of ▷*A Room of One's Own* (1929), which explores the possibility of an androgynous mind, and ▷*Three Guineas* (1938), her interest in androgyny and the creative process being central also to ▷*Orlando* (1928). A similar preoccupation with the notion of a feminine aesthetic also informs the writings of ▷Dorothy Richardson. Recent interest in Woolf's feminist thematics has teased out similar concerns in other

texts, including the later novel *The Years* (1937), which saw a return to the formal realism of Woolf's earlier work, a trend carried through to her final novel, *Between the Acts* (1941). Woolf's literary criticism appeared in two volumes, *The Common Reader* (1925) and *The Common Reader, Second Series* (1932); her collected essays, together with her letters and diaries, were published posthumously. Other writings: Short stories: *A Haunted House* (1943), *Moments of Being* (1976), *The Complete Shorter Fiction of Virginia Woolf* (1985). Criticism: *The Captain's Death Bed and Other Essays* (1950), *Contemporary Writers* (1965), *Collected Essays* (1966–1967), *Essays* (1987). *Letters* (1975–1980), *The Diary of Virginia Woolf* (1977–1984).
▷Women's language; Bowen, Elizabeth; Cunard, Nancy; Holtby, Winifred; *Hotel du Lac*; Sackville-West, Vita
Bib: Auerbach, E., 'The Brown Stocking' in *Mimesis* (1957); Bell, Q., *Virginia Woolf: A Biography*; Bowlby, R., *Virginia Woolf: Feminist Destinations*; Marcus, J., *New Feminist Essays on Virginia Woolf*, and *Virginia Woolf and the Languages of Patriarchy*; Warner, E., *Virginia Woolf: A Centenary Perspective*.

Woolson, Constance Fenimore (1840–1894)
US short-story writer and novelist. Most of Woolson's work is in the ▷local color tradition, with settings in the Great Lakes region. While she uses many realistic elements in her fiction, there is usually also some element of mystery, Gothic, or focus on bizarre, isolated characters, eg a father who keeps his young daughter in a castle on an otherwise unpopulated island – supporting her by placing false lights to deliberately wreck ships in order to sell the cargo and furnishings that wash ashore.

Critically esteemed in her time, Woolson published extensively in the national literary magazines. Among her most notable books are her local color story collections, *Castle Nowhere* (1875) and *Rodman the Keeper: Southern Sketches* (1880), and novels, *Anne* (1882), *For the Major* (1883), *East Angels* (1886), *Jupiter Lights* (1889) and *Horace Chase* (1894).
▷*Appleton's Journal*

Words to Say It, The (1983)
Translation of *Les Mots pour le dire* (1975), French writer ▷Marie Cardinal's fourth, and most famous, novel. It begins with a description of the narrator's psychosomatic menstrual disorder, and, in a narrative which consists of fragments of experience and memory rather than linear progression, combines the account of a traditional Freudian analysis (▷psychoanalysis) with references to women's oppression. The narrator has no name, and thus her experience seems to represent that of all women, while the confessional tone is clearly designed to appeal to a female readership. The parallels between the novel and Cardinal's own life increase the impression of authenticity, which is typical of the

genre, and the paperback French edition describes the novel as lived experience, a combination of 'a woman's temperament and a writer's talent'. The novel was awarded the Prix Littré in 1976, and has received critical attention. Phil Powrie has used the theories of Chodorow and Klein to provide a psychoanalytical reading of the novel, and particularly of the mother–daughter relationship, which is perhaps the main focus of the narrator's psychoanalysis.
Bib: Powrie, P., in Atack, M. and Powrie, P. (eds), *Contemporary French Fiction by Women*.

Wordsworth, Dorothy (1771–1855)
English writer of diaries and 'recollections'. The younger sister of the romantic poet William Wordsworth (1770–1850). Although her brother copied sections of her nature journal into his own notes and published sections of her texts in his prose output (part of her 'Excursion on the Banks of Ullswater' (1805) was published in his *Guide to the Lakes*), she wrote, 'I should detest the idea of setting myself up as an author.' She began writing in about 1795 when she and her brother shared a house. They eventually (1798) moved to Alfoxden in the Quantocks where she kept a journal of walks, visits and above all the natural world. After they moved to Dove Cottage in Grasmere she continued to keep a journal. Her records of conversations held with local people register the economic pressures generated by war and by the rapid enclosure of land in the Lake District. Often her journal writing takes the form of a reported conversation: for instance, 'At Rydale, a woman of the village, stout and well dressed, begged a half-penny; she had never she said done it before, but these hard times!' As well as diaries she wrote recollections including the memoir *Recollections of a Tour Made in Scotland* (1803). This circulated in manuscript and exists in no less than five manuscript copies. She also wrote a *Journal of a Tour on the Continent* (1820) and wrote up various 'excursions' in the Lakes such as *Excursion Up Scawfell Pike* (1818). She fell ill in 1835 and though she went on writing, the last twenty years of her life were marred by serious illness which affected her both mentally and physically.
Bib: Selincourt, E. de (ed.), *Journals of Dorothy Wordsworth*.

Wörishöffer, Sophie (1838–1890)
German writer. She was an extremely successful writer of adventure stories for young people. Her plots tend to be rather fanciful, though her books are nevertheless full of interesting factual information about peoples and places she never actually visited herself. Amongst her best-known novels are *Robert des Schiffsjungen Fahrten und Abenteuer auf der deutschen Handels- und Kriegsflotte* (1877) (*The Travels and Adventures of Robert the Young Shipmate in the German Merchant Navy and on Battleships*), *Gerettet aus Sibirien* (1885) (*Saved from Siberia*) and *Unter Korsaren* (1889) (*Among Pirates*).

Work: A Story of Experience (1873)
US autobiographical fiction by ▷Louisa May Alcott. An account of the domestic servant jobs Alcott herself undertook, *Work* shows the dark side of the restricted economic roles open to women: mistreatment, exhaustion, isolation and even thoughts of suicide. The Alcott character demonstrates alternative values: self-fulfilment; equality and equality of opportunity for all people; humanity; and a supportive, woman-centred community.

World of Hannah Heaton, The (1988)
Autobiography of North American ▷Hannah Cook Heaton, edited by historian Barbara E. Lacey. In this account of Heaton's autobiography, Lacey excerpts the spiritual meditations of this 18th-century North American woman whose life on a farm in North Haven, Connecticut, is sublimated in her search for spiritual salvation during the Great Awakening of the 1760s and 1770s. Like ▷Sarah Haggar Wheaten Osborn, leader of the evangelical revivals in Newport, Rhode Island, during the same period, she records her life as representative of the movement and the era. Of limited educational background, she records with a commonplace effect her spiritual trials over several decades; her personal exaltations and backslidings reflect the nature of the revival movement in these years.
▷*Nature, Certainty, and Evidence of True Christianity, The*; *Memoirs of the Life of Mrs Sarah Osborn*

Wrath of Dionysus, The, (1910)
Novel by Russian writer ▷Evdokiia Nagródskaia. The heroine, Tat'iana Kuznetsova, a painter, is torn between passionate love for the 'dionysian' Edgar Stark and platonic love for Il'ia Tolchin. Aleksandr Latchinov, a wealthy art lover, helps Tat'iana to resolve her conflict and interprets the world of the novel to the reader. With Edgar, Tat'iana can realize herself in motherhood; with Il'ia, in art. She abandons art. Hence, despite sensational themes like homosexuality, overt female sensuality, sexual role reversals, and deception in personal relations, which disturbed contemporary critics, the novel's message is conservative: happiness for women is ultimately to be found in motherhood. The combination of titillating topics, a fast-paced, tightly designed plot with some surprises, a readily accessible style, and conservative values, made the novel so immensely popular that it went through ten editions from 1910 to 1916. It also indicated the degree to which Nietzsche's influence had spread in ▷Silver Age culture, and can be seen as an ongoing dialogue with Pushkin's novel *Eugene Onegin* (1825–1831) in which the heroine was also named Tat'iana, Tolstoy's *Anna Karenina* (1875–1877), ▷Mariia Krestóvskaia's *The Actress*, and Kuzmin's *Wings*.

Wright, Judith (born 1915)
Australian poet, fiction writer and essayist. Wright was educated by governesses on her family's cattle and sheep station near Armidale, then at the New England Girls' School, Armidale, then at Sydney University. She is a widely published and acclaimed poet, critic, essayist, short story writer and children's author and has received five honorary doctorates from Australian universities for her contribution to Australian literature. Her poetry has attracted many awards, including the Grace Leven Prize for 1949 and 1972, the Encyclopaedia Britannica Prize for 1964, the Robert Frost Memorial Award for 1976 and the ASAN World Prize for Poetry 1984. She is also a dedicated conservationist who was Founding President of the Wildlife Preservation Society of Queensland, and has published widely on conservation issues. She is also one of Australia's best-known social activists who is currently working for the establishment of an Aboriginal treaty. Her volumes of poetry are ▷*The Moving Image* (1946), ▷*Woman to Man* (1949), *The Gateway* (1953), *The Two Fires* (1955), *Birds: Poems* (1960), *Five Senses* (1963), *Selected Poems* (1963), *The Other Half* (1966), *Collected Poems 1942–1970* (1971), *Alive: Poems 1971–1972* (1972), *Fourth Quarter and Other Poems* (1976) *Phantom Dwelling* (1986) and *A Human Pattern: Selected Poems* (1990). A collection, *The Double Tree: Selected Poems 1942–1976* (1978) has been published in the USA, and Wright's poems have been translated into many languages.
Wright has also published books for children, a book of short stories, and many critical, editorial and historical works, as well as numerous articles and several full-length texts on conservation issues. Her two books which deal specifically with Aboriginal issues, *The Cry for the Dead* (1981) and *We Call for a Treaty* (1985), deserve special mention.
▷Aborigine in non-Aboriginal Australian women's writing, The; Short story (Australia); Literary criticism (Australia); *Poetry and Gender*

Wright, L.R. (Laurali) (born 1939)
Canadian novelist and journalist, born Laurali Appleby in Saskatoon. She worked as a journalist and took night classes in creative writing, winning from *The Calgary Herald*, where she worked from 1970 to 1977, a scholarship to the Banff School of Fine Arts. Her mainstream novels, *Neighbours* (1979), *The Favorite* (1982) and *Among Friends* (1984), explore the lives of contemporary women; her psychological mysteries, including *The Suspect* (1985), *Sleep While I Sing* (1986) and *Fall From Grace* (1991), focus on why a crime is committed rather than who committed it. She lives in Vancouver, British Columbia.

Wrightson, Patricia (born 1921)
Australian children's novelist. Wrightson is a prolific and imaginative writer of children's fiction who has won many awards, including the Children's Book of the Year Award for 1956, 1974, 1977 and 1984, inclusion in the honours list for the Hans Christian Andersen Award for four years, and the New South Wales Premier's

Award for ethnic literature 1979. Her publications include *The Crooked Snake* (1955), *The Bunyip Hole* (1957), *The Rocks of Honey* (1960), *The Feather Star* (1962), *Down to Earth* (1965), *I Own the Racecourse* (1968), *An Older Kind of Magic* (1972), *Beneath the Sun* (ed.) (1972), *The Nargun and the Stars* (1973), *Emu Stew* (1976), *The Ice Is Coming* (1977), *The Dark Bright Water* (1978), *Night Outside* (1979), *Behind the Wind* (1981) and *A Little Fear* (1983).
▷Children's literature (Australia)

Wrinkle in Time, A (1962)

US novel. ▷Madeleine L'Engle's adolescent science fiction novel won the 1963 Newbery Medal. It is the first book in her Time trilogy, and focuses on Meg, a social misfit at school, who must rescue her father and her brother, held captive on another planet. Meg battles the evil force, IT, a disembodied brain; as intellect untempered by emotion, IT destroys individuality and creativity. When she realizes her ability to love, Meg overcomes IT.
A Wind in the Door (1973) Meg learns to love her foe to save her brother, and in *A Swiftly Tilting Planet* (1978) her brother undertakes a quest to prevent nuclear war. L'Engle suggests that the universe survives and thrives because of the choices individuals make; to make such choices individuals must know the difference between good and evil.

Writers for film and television (Australia)

The most prominent include ▷Gwen Meredith, who scripted the immensely popular series *The Lawsons* and *Blue Hills* for ABC Radio, and Barbara Vernon, who scripted the *Bellbird* series for ABC Television. Anne Brooksbank has written a number of television and film scripts, has co-written films such as *Newsfront* (1978), and has won numerous awards for best documentary script, best children's script and best original feature film. Other significant writers for radio and television include Marien Dryer (also a successful journalist and dramatist), Catherine Duncan (stage and radio), Lynn Foster (stage, radio and television), ▷Jessica Anderson (radio), ▷Olga Masters (radio), Marjorie McLeod (stage and radio), Jennifer Rankin (stage and radio), Catherine Shepherd (stage and radio) and Barbara Stellmach (has written over twenty plays for theatre, radio and television). Aboriginal writers Maris Hyllus and Sonia Borg scripted the impressive television drama *Women of the Sun*.

Writing a New World: Two Centuries of Australian Women Writers (1988)

Critical work by Australian writer ▷Dale Spender. It provides an overview of women's writing in Australia which counters the view of the country as a cultural desert by analysing the achievements of ▷Barbara Baynton, ▷Dymphna Cusack, ▷Eleanor Dark, ▷Katharine Susannah Prichard, ▷Christina Stead and others.

Wroth, Lady Mary (?1587–?1651)

English writer of prose romance, a fictional genre very fashionable in the 16th and 17th centuries (compare her uncle, Sir Philip Sidney's *Arcadia*, 1590). She also wrote a sonnet sequence in English and a pastoral tragicomedy, *Love's Victorie*. After her husband died in 1614, her cousin, William Herbert became her lover, and she bore him children. She published *The Countess of Montgomerie's Urania* (1621), but withdrew the book after claims that she had drawn figures in it from life.
▷Romance
Bib: Roberts, Josephine, *Tulsa Studies*; Swift, Carolyn Ruth, 'Feminine Identity in Lady Mary Wroth's *Urania*' in Farrell, Kirby *et al.* (ed.) *Women in the Renaissance*.

'Wulf and Eadwacer'

▷Old English poem. This haunting poem is enigmatic, but conveys a powerful sense of the sorrow of separation between the speaker and her lover.
▷'Wife's Lament, The'; Elegies (Old English)

Wuthering Heights (1847)

A novel by British writer ▷Emily Brontë, first published under the ▷pseudonym Ellis Bell. The story is narrated by two characters, Lockwood and Nelly Dean, who recount the tale of Heathcliff and his involvement with the Earnshaw and Linton families. The arrival of the foundling Heathcliff disrupts the lives of Catherine Earnshaw and her brother, Hindley. Catherine and Heathcliff develop an intense bond, but Heathcliff overhears her saying to Nelly Dean that marrying him would degrade her. He then leaves Wuthering Heights, returning three years later, by which time Catherine has married Edgar Linton. In revenge, Heathcliff marries Edgar's sister, Isabella, mistreating her and brutalizing Hindley and his son, Hareton. Catherine dies shortly after giving birth to a daughter, Cathy. After Edgar's death, Cathy is lured to the Heights and subjected to Heathcliff's terrible will. At the end of the novel, Heathcliff dies and Cathy and Hareton are united. *Wuthering Heights* has generated an enormous body of criticism, and has always been recognized as a novel of great power and originality. Recent interpretations have focused on the complex narrative structure, the novel's treatment of temporality, its transgression of conventional sexual and moral codes, and its intense examination of the nature of desire.
▷Orphans; Gothic; Romantic (19th-century Britain)

Wyatt, Rachel (born 1929)

English-Canadian dramatist, born in Bradford, England. She studied nursing in London, emigrating to Canada with her husband and two children in 1957. She has written more than fifty radio dramas for the BBC and the Canadian

Broadcasting Corporation, much reminiscent of the British comic tradition. Her novels, *The String Box* (1970), *The Rosedale Hoax* (1977), *Foreign Bodies* (1982) and *Time in the Air* (1985), often concern characters displaced from their homes.

Wylie, Elinor (1885–1928)

US poet, essayist, short story writer and novelist. Wylie was a public personality whose admirers mythologized her. She was born into a socially and politically prominent family in Somerville, New Jersey, but groomed as a socialite, she was not allowed to further her education. Leaving her son and husband, she eloped with a married man in 1910. Her work focuses on the plight of the woman artist in a hostile world.

The poems in *Nets to Catch the Wind* (1921) emphasize her desire to escape, although the world wounds her sensibilities and restrains her romantic impulses. *Last Poems* (1943) expresses a fear that love destroys women. Her novels, *Jennifer Lorn: A Sedate Extravaganza* (1923) and *The Venetian Glass Nephew* (1925), which both use exotic and historical settings – 18th-century India and Italy respectively – depict a woman's destruction. Her self dies when she marries and becomes a decorative object. As in *Mr Hodge and Mr Hazard* (1928), her last novel, Wylie's work reflects her own disillusionment with the romantic.

Other work includes: *Black Armour* (1923), *The Orphan Angel* (1926), *Trivial Breath* (1928), *Angels and Earthly Creatures: A Sequence of Sonnets* (1928) and *Birthday Sonnet* (1929).

Bib: Farr, Judith, *Life and Art of Elinor Wylie.*

'Wylie and Testament' ▷ *Sweet Nosegay, A*

Wynter, Sylvia (born 1928)

Caribbean novelist, dramatist and essayist, born in Cuba of Jamaican parents. She returned to ▷ Jamaica at the age of two, and was educated there. She won the Jamaica Centenary Scholarship in 1946, and read for a BA at London University (1947–1949). She obtained an MA in 1953, and worked as a writer for radio and television, producing plays for the BBC. She has held posts at the University of the West Indies, Mona, and the Universities of Michigan and California. Her only novel, ▷ *The Hills of Hebron*, deals with politics, religion, race, class, madness, the role of sexuality and the psychic crippling effect on the psyche of physical handicap.

Drama has always been a central interest and she has written the folk musical *Shh . . . It's a Wedding* (1961), *Miracle in Lime Lane* (1962), the historical drama *1865 Ballad for a Rebellion* (1965) and *Maskarade* (1979) for schools.

Wynter has had an important role as critic and essayist – see *Jamaica Journal*, 2, 1968 and *New World Quarterly*, 5, 1975. Critical analysis of Wynter's ideas can be found in the noted Caribbean writer, E.K. Brathwaite's 'The Love Axe/1; Developing a Caribbean Aesthetic', *BIM*, 16 July 1977. See ▷ *Fifty Caribbean Writers* for a full bibliography and critical references.

Xerazade e os Outros: Romance (Tragédia em Forma de) (1964) Scheherazade and the Others: Novel (Tragedy in the Form of)

Written by the Portuguese novelist ▷Fernanda Botelho, *Xerazade* is a ▷modernist and proto-feminist novel. The protagonist, Luísa, is likened to the mythical Scheherazade because of her ability to fascinate and entertain men. Her success is dependent on her beauty as well as on the 'stories' she tells to comply with the society's expectations of her. Published in 1964, eight years before ▷*Novas Cartas Portuguesas*, the book is a subtle critique of the problematic status of middle-class women. It is also an interesting formal experiment, as its subtitle, *Novel (Tragedy in the Form of)* suggests.

▷*Armários Vazios, Os*

Bib: Sadlier, Darlene J., *The Question of How: Women Writers and New Portuguese Literature.*

Xiao Hong (1911–1942)

Chinese novelist and short story writer. Xiao Hong, born Zhang Naiying, left her unhappy home in rural north-east China when she was barely twenty; she cohabited with a budding writer, Xiao Jun, and thus started on her own literary career. Constantly on the move in face of the advancing Japanese army, Xiao Hong completed her first major work, *The Field of Life and Death*, in 1935. It was published under the auspices of China's grand old man of letters, Lu Xun (1880–1936), and was a literary sensation. It is a grim and powerful portrait of the peasants of north-east China with the war in the background. The demeaning position of women is also a prominent theme. In the largely autobiographical ▷*Tales of Hulan River*, Xiao Hong weaves the threads of her own short and unhappy life into a moving indictment of the dehumanizing world in which she found it hard to survive. *Ma Bole* (1941) is a satirical novel in a totally different vein. Some of her short stories, such as 'On the Ox Cart' (1936) and 'Hands' (1936), all based on life in her native north-east, are gems in the genre. She died, aged only thirty-one, alone in Japanese-occupied Hong Kong.

Bib: Goldblatt, Howard and Young, Ellen (trans.), *Tales of Hulan River and The Field of Life and Death*; Goldblatt, Howard (trans.), *Selected Stories of Xiao Hong.*

Xirinacs, Olga (born 1936)

Spanish poet and novelist. Xirinacs was born in Tarragona, and is active in the cultural life of the city. Her main poetry collections are: *Botons de tiges* (1977) (*Grey Stem Buttons*); *Clau de blau* (1978) (*Key to the Blue*); *Llençol de noces* (1979) (*Bridal Sheet*), and *Preparo el te sota palmeres rogues* (1981) (*I Prepare Tea beneath Red Palm Trees*). She has also written novels: *Música de cambra* (1982) (*Chamber Music*); *Interior amb difunts* (1983) (*Interior with Cadavers*), and *Al meu cap una llosa* (1985) (*A Gravestone at My Head*), which uses ▷Virginia Woolf's suicide in Britain in 1941 as a leitmotiv.

▷Catalan women's writing

Xi Xi

Chinese writer. Xi Xi, born Zhang Yan, moved from Shanghai to Hong Kong in 1950 and worked as a teacher. With the publication of *My City* (1979), she became established as a writer of 'Hong Kong consciousness'. *Cross Currents* (1981), *Spring Prospects* (1983), *Beard with a Face* (1986) and other poetry and fiction followed. *The Hunter Who Whistles to Bait a Bear* (1983), a historical novel set in the reign of Emperor Qian Long (1736–1796), juxtaposes the lives of the high and low, and shows the influence of the Latin-American authors Mario Vargas Llosa (born 1936) and Gabriel García Márquez (born 1928). In the short story 'The Cold', a middle-aged woman leaves home to live her own life.

▷Can Xue; Magic realism

Xue Tao (AD 760–832)

Chinese poet of the Tang dynasty (AD 618–907). A native of what is now Sichuan, Xue showed talent at an early age for music and poetry. On her father's death she became a professional singer to support her mother. Renowned in her lifetime for her poetry, she was acknowledged by and associated with the famous poets of the age, in a way that was unusual for a woman at the time. She inscribed her poems on paper she made herself, dyed in vivid colours, and started a vogue called 'Xue Tao stationery'. Xue was also quick at repartee, and some of her *tours de force* have been handed down. It is recorded that she left 500 poems, but only 100 survive.

Xu Naijian (born 1953)

Chinese short story writer. After middle school, Xu spent nine years in the countryside at various odd jobs. Later she studied at a teachers' university in Nanjing and started to write short fiction. She is author of the much-anthologized short story 'Thirty and Unmarried', about the degrading pressures brought to bear on unmarried women. Other well-known stories include 'Poplar and Cypress Pollution', 'Little Smarty and Nimble' and 'Train No 52! Train No 52!'.

Y

Yang Jiang (born 1911)
Chinese writer, translator and scholar. Yang Jiang studied at the prestigious Qinghua University, and went on to further her education in England and France. She began writing satirical comedies in the 1940s while teaching at university in Shanghai. Since the 1950s Yang has worked in Beijing on research in Western literature, particularly in the picaresque tradition, spanning English, French and Spanish works in the genre. Many of her critical essays are collected in *The Slushy Soil of Spring* (1979). Her translations of *Gil Blas* by Le Sage (1956), and Cervantes's *Lazarillo de Tormes* (1951) and *Don Quixote* (1978) into Chinese are acknowledged masterpieces in the art of translation. After the 'cultural revolution' (1966–1976), Yang Jiang resumed creative writing. *A Cadre School Life: Six Chapters* is a semi-autobiographical series of vignettes of her life in the countryside during the 'cultural revolution'. It was widely translated and highly praised for its light touch of humour and controlled irony. *The Bath* (1989) weaves a satirical tale of academia during the 1950s as the newly installed communist leaders struggle with the task of taking over academia while the academics struggle to adapt, each in his or her own way.
Bib: Barmé, Geremie (trans.), *A Cadre School Life: Six Chapters*; Goldblatt, Howard (trans.), *Six Chapters from my Life Down Under*; Diang Chu (trans.), *Six Chapters of Life in a Cadre School*.

Yamada, Mitsuye
US poet, short-story writer and essayist. Born in Japan, Mitsuye grew up in Seattle, Washington. During World War II her family was interned in a concentration camp in Idaho, and her work focuses on this experience. In *Camp Notes and Other Poems* (1976) she struggles to create a new identity as through racial prejudice her identity has been appropriated and her experience misnamed.

Yamada reclaims her experience in 'Desert Storms' by resisting false naming. She learns she cannot escape prejudice by leaving the camp in 'Cincinnati'. Identifying with an African-American man releases her suppressed anger and pain in 'Thirty Years Under'. In *Desert Run: Poems and Stories* (1988) Yamada returns to the place of her internment, and she describes the emotional landscape of a woman who can never take safety for granted.
▷Asian-American writing

Yamada Eimi (born 1959)
Japanese novelist. Born in Tokyo, she was a cartoonist for a while before she was hailed as an outstanding new writer when ▷*Bed Time* was published in 1985. This work claims, through a straightforward description of sexual love between a Japanese woman singer and a black deserter, that lust is a more natural human instinct than spiritual love. *Lovers of Soul Music* won the Naoki

Prize in 1987. Her other main works are *A Harem* and *A Bullied Girl at School*.

Yamamoto, Hisaye (born 1921)
US short story writer and journalist. Yamamoto's parents were Japanese immigrants who settled in Redondo Beach, California. Yamamoto was interned in a Japanese-American concentration camp in Poston, Arizona, during World War II, where she became a journalist for the camp newspaper. She lists her occupation as housewife, although she gained national attention as a writer when anti-Japanese sentiment was rampant. Her fiction, collected in *17 Syllables and Other Stories* (1988), explores three central concerns: the bonding among members of different ethnic groups to cope with racism, the gap between generations of Japanese-Americans reflected in language barriers and disparate cultural values, and the isolation of women immigrants trapped in unhappy marriages. In 1986 she received the Before Columbus Foundation's American Book Award for Lifetime Achievement.
▷Asian-American writing

Yamamoto Michiko (born 1936)
Japanese novelist and poet. Born in Tokyo, she started out as a poet. Her collections of poems include *There is a Snake* and *An Umbrella on Sunday*. *Magic* won the Shincho Prize for a New Writer in 1972 and *Betty-san* won the Akutagawa Prize in the same year. Both novels are based on her experience in Australia, where her husband was transferred. She explores relationships in *Trees of People*.

Yamazaki Tomoko (born 1931)
Japanese non-fiction writer, born in Nagasaki prefecture. *The Eighth House of Japanese Prostitutes in the South Sea Islands*, based on oral history, won the Oya Soichi Prize for Non-Fiction in 1973. She continues to write about the lives of unknown women in history in such works as *The Graves in Sandakan* and *Love and Blood-History of Interchange of Asian Women*.

Yamazaki Toyoko (born 1924)
Japanese novelist, born in Osaka. *A Curtain with a Shop Name*, which portrays the long tradition of powerful Osaka merchants, attracted attention in 1957. Subsequently she published works on the same subject, such as *Hana Noren* which won the Naoki Prize and *Bonchi*. She was recognized as a writer dealing with social problems on the publication of *A Huge White Tower*. It reveals the darker side of a hospital attached to a university. *The Barren Zone* and *Two Fatherlands* criticize Japanese society at the end of the war.

Yamusa, Grace Ake (born 1947)
Nigerian novelist. The career of Yamusa, one of the very few northern Nigerian women to have published, has been entirely centred on her own home area and the needs of its inhabitants. Educated at Wukari Native Authority School and

the Women's Teachers College in Kabba, she was a primary and secondary school principal and vice-principal before going on to gain a degree at the age of thirty-two. She has since been active in the Jukun Language Development Project, for which she wrote her novel *Vokwin* (1983), which she then translated into English as *Clock of Justice*.

Yan, Mari ▷Yáñez, María Flora

Yanaranop, Sukanya ▷Krisan, Asokesin

Yáñez, María Flora (born 1898)
Chilean novelist and short story writer. Born María Flora Yáñez de Echeverria, she adopted the pen-name Mari Yan. Her father was a politician, statesman and the founder of *La Nación*, from Santiago. She studied at the Sorbonne in Paris. Her style is *criollista* (▷*criollismo*), and her narratives describe the beautiful nature of Chile. 'She tended to spiritualize and even to make myths of certain aspects of reality', according to Anderson Imbert. She lectured in Spain, Uruguay and Peru.
   Works: *El abrazo de la tierra* (1933) (*The Embrace of the Earth*); *Mundo en sombra* (1935) (*World in Shade*); *Espejo sin imagen* (1936) (*Mirror Without Image*); *Las Cenizas* (1942) (*The Ashes*); *El Estanque* (1945) (*The Pool*); *Visiones de infancia* (1947) (*Visions of Childhood*); *La Piedra* (1952) (*The Stone*); *Juan Estrella* (1954); *¿Dónde está y el vino?* (1963) (*Where is the Wheat and the Wine?*); *El último faro* (1968) (*The Last Light*), and *El Peldaño* (1974) (*The Step*). She also collected an anthology of Chilean short stories in 1958.

Yang Muo (born 1914)
Chinese novelist. Yang joined the communist underground movement against Japanese invasion during her student years in Beijing. She is best-known for her novel ▷*The Song of Youth* (1958), adapted for film. In the story, Yang drew on her experiences of the underground struggle in both urban and rural areas. It is one of the first novels in the People's Republic in which the intelligentsia, always an object of attack for ideological unorthodoxy, was depicted in a positive light, though still with reservations.

Yardan, Shana (born 1942)
Caribbean poet, born in ▷Guyana. Yardan won second prize and two honourable mentions for her poetry entries in the Guyana National History and Arts Open Competition in 1972. Few biographical details are available for this writer. Her published work includes *This Listening of Eyes* (1976), a cycle of love poems. She was one of the major contributors to *Guyana Drums* (1972), an anthology which includes the work of six women poets. Her work is included in A.J. Seymour (ed.), *New Writing in the Caribbean* (1972) and in R. Weaver and J. Bruchas (eds.), *Aftermath: An Anthology of Poems in English from Africa, Asia and the Caribbean* (1977).
   No critical essays of her work have appeared to date, although mention of her work is made in Jeremy Poynting's article in ▷*Caribbean Women Writers*.

Yates, Frances (1899–1981)
English cultural historian. Yates spent most of her academic career at the Warburg Institute, London, first as a research assistant, then as a lecturer, editor of publications and finally Reader in Renaissance History (1956–1967). Her publications deal with the literature, symbolism and ritual of 16th-century England, France and Italy. These include: *The French Academies of the Sixteenth Century* (1947), *The Art of Memory* (1966), *The Rosicrucian Enlightenment* (1972), *Shakespeare's Last Plays* (1972) and *Occult Philosophy in the Elizabethan Age* (1979). Yates was awarded the OBE in 1972, and made Dame of the British Empire in 1977.

Yearling, The (1938)
North American novel. In ▷Marjorie Rawlings's Pulitzer Prize-winning book, Jody Baxter is forced to kill his pet fawn to protect his family's meagre subsistence. In attaining manhood he accepts the indiscriminate cruelty of the pastoral world, and learns to stand back up every time life's hardships knock him down. *The Yearling* exemplifies Rawling's archetypal vision of the struggle between the human spirit and life.

Yearsley, Ann (1752–1806)
English poet, novelist and dramatist. Originally a milkwoman, she was taught to read and write by her brother. She married John Yearsley in 1774, and in 1784, when her family were living in terrible conditions, she showed her verses to ▷Hannah More, who arranged for the publication by subscription of *Poems on Several Occasions* (1785). However, More kept control of Yearsley's access to the proceeds, and in a later edition she complains of this. More's attitude seems to have been very patronizing – *Poems on Several Occasions* carries a letter from her to Mrs Montagu, in which she discusses Yearsley's 'wild wood notes', and goes out of her way to mention that Yearsley's husband was 'honest and sober'. Eventually, Yearsley rejected More's attempts at intellectual control. She published *Poems on Various Subjects* (1787), including a poem (like More) on the ▷slave trade. Her play, *Earl Goodwin*, was acted and published, she wrote a novel, *The Royal Captives* (1795), and she ran a ▷circulating library. Her final publication was *The Rural Lyre*.
   ▷Collier, Mary; Leapor, Mary; Little, Janet
Bib: Landry, Donna, *The Muses of Resistence*.

Ye Jiayin (born 1924)
Chinese scholar of classical literature. Born in Beijing, Ye later moved to Taiwan, and taught at Taiwan University and various universities in the USA. Now professor of Chinese literature at the University of British Columbia in Canada, she has written many scholarly studies of Chinese poetry

and poetics, and publishes in both Chinese and English.

'Yellow Wallpaper, The' (1892)

US short story by ▷Charlotte Perkins Gilman. A woman's insanity results from domestic oppression and denial of her role as an artist. Confined to an isolated room by her physician husband (a common treatment for women's nervous conditions in the 19th-century USA), she becomes convinced that a woman is trapped behind the room's yellow wallpaper, as all women are entrapped. Since the advent of women's studies, Gilman's story has become one of most widely-read US short stories.

Ye Wenling (born 1942)

Chinese writer, a native of Zhejiang. Ye's own middle-school education was interrupted because her brother had been labelled a 'rightist'. Now a professional writer, she draws on her own varied experiences and the local colour of her province to write about ordinary people. Her works include *Scenes of Life at Changtan Village* and *Glorious Son of the Sun*. 'The Country Girl in the Homespun Blue Apron', with its strong rustic flavour, is typical of her style. *The Fig* (1980) is one of her best-known collections.

Yezierska, Anzia (1885–1970)

US novelist and short story writer. Yezierska was born in a mud hut in Plinsk on the Russian-Polish border. In 1900 her family emigrated to New York, where she worked in a sweatshop and learned English at nightschool. In 1903 she received a scholarship to attend Columbia University. She left her husband and daughter to pursue a career as a writer. Yezierska depicts the Jewish immigrant experience from a woman's point of view.

In Yezierska's autobiographical novel, *Bread Givers* (1925), Sara Smolinsky struggles to achieve her autonomy, determined to overcome poverty by acquiring an education. To pursue the American dream of economic success, Sara must defy her father and her culture. Yezierska condemns patriarchal Jewish attitudes towards women. She cautions that an orthodox, patriarchal and religious culture cannot survive in a land of opportunity.

Other work includes: *Hungry Hearts* (1920), *Salome of the Tenements* (1923), *Children of Loneliness* (1923), *Arrogant Beggar* (1927), *All I could Never Be* (1932) and *Red Ribbon on a White Horse* (1950).
Bib: Shoen, Carol B., *Anzia Yezierska*.

Yonge, Charlotte (1823–1901)

English writer. She was born in Otterbourne, near Winchester, where she remained for the rest of her life, apart from visiting Paris briefly in 1869. In 1838 she came under the influence of John Keble and adopted the religious views associated with the ▷Oxford Movement, which influence all her writing. She was an editor, historian,

biographer and translator as well as a hugely successful novelist. Her most famous novel, ▷*The Heir of Redclyffe* was published in 1853. Other tales of contemporary life include *Heartsease* (1854); *The Daisy Chain* (1856); *The Clever Woman of the Family* (1865) and historical romances for children (*The Prince and the Page*, 1865, and *The Dove in the Eagle's Nest*, 1866). For forty years she edited the girls' magazine, *The Monthly Packet*.

Yonge was highly religious and conservative, opposed to women's ▷suffrage and socialism, and a great defender of traditional Victorian standards and morals. The message of *The Clever Woman of the Family* is that women should not pursue intellectual subjects, but accept their inferiority to men.
Bib: Battiscombe, G., *Charlotte Mary Yonge: An Uneventful Life*; Mare, M. and Percival, A.C., *Victorian Best-Seller: The World of Charlotte M. Yonge*.

Yoruba Girl Dancing (1991)

A first novel by ▷Simi Bedford, a Nigerian educated and resident in England. Though autobiographical, hers is a story common to many upper-class Nigerians of the pre-independence era. It begins with Remi as a small child, growing up in her grandparents' household of thirty people in Lagos, and details the intrigues, loyalties and power struggles within a large extended family. It also captures the niceties of culture, both traditional Yoruba and the Westernized aspirations of the adults. At seven, Remi is sent to boarding school in England, and the narrative embarks on its second phase: the culture shock attendant on finding herself the only black girl in the school, the crude stereotypes with which she had to contend, and school holidays spent with different white families. Finally, she leaves school and is reunited with friends and family in London. It is a fascinating exposé of the effects of cultural alienation on the young girl's attempts to establish an identity, using her weapons of humour, resilience and superior intelligence.

You Jin (born 1950)

Pseudonym of Singaporean Chinese essayist, novelist, short story and travel writer, Tham Yew Chin. She is a Chinese literature graduate of the former Nanyang University and was a secondary school teacher. Her work first appeared in newspapers and magazines in Singapore, Taiwan and Shanghai, and she has now published 39 collections. Immensely popular in China, books of hers published there are inevitable bestsellers. Her five-volume set of stories based on her travels, *Tai Yang Bu Ken Hui Jai Qu* (*The Sun Refuses to Set*), *Lang Man Zhi Lu* (*A Romantic Journey*), *Sha Mo Zhong De Xiao Bai Wu* (*A Little House in the Desert*), *Mi Shi De Yu Ji* (*A Lost Rainy Season*), and *Na Yi Fen Yao Yuan De Qing* (*Distant Love*) has gone into three editions, while a collection of prose, *Ling Long Ren Shen* (*Exquisite Life*) and another collection of travel stories, *Life and Love*, have enjoyed similar success. Such has been the extent of 'You Jin fever' (as it has been described) that her work was published by five Chinese publishers in 1992, and a Shanghai paper has invited her to do a weekly column. A Shanghai critic attributes the popularity of her works to the fact that 'they give readers in China a channel through which they can get to know the world. Her writings also exude wit and humour, as well as warmth and humanity, which are much lacking in the modern world', while a Beijing critic, notes that 'her style of writing is lively and humorous, and she uses analogy well, the content [being] very often inspiring'.

Young, Elizabeth (fl 1558)

English Protestant Reformist. In his *Actes and Monumentes* (1563) John Foxe records nine of the thirteen examinations Young underwent during her arrest for importing Protestant books printed in English. Unlike ▷Anne Askew, Young did not record the account of her imprisonment herself. At the time of her arrest, Young was the mother of three, and, according to her own statement, aged 'forty and upwards'. Her examination reveals her refusal to attend mass, and to accept elements of Catholicism including transubstantiation, purgatory, and the supremacy of the Pope. Her examination also attests to her courage and strength. In spite of repeated threats of burning, she refused to name the printer and translator of the heretical books she imported from Holland. Young was released from prison upon the death of Mary I (▷Mary Tudor), and so escaped the martyr's fate.
▷Confession of faith; Protestant Reformation

Yourcenar, Marguerite (1903–1987)

French writer. Born Marguerite de Crayencour in Brussels of Franco-Belgian parents, she wrote in French but took US citizenship in 1939, sharing her time thereafter between France and the USA, and travelling widely. Her copious output includes novels, plays, poetry, essays and translations from Latin, Greek and English. In 1980 she became the first woman to be elected to the ▷*Académie française*.

She felt she did not write as a woman, but as an author who happened to be a woman, and whose work should be judged on its merit alone. The central figures of her fiction are men torn between society's demands and their passions, rather than women. This caused her to be accused of misogyny by those who feel that women, as writers, should uphold femininity (▷*Coup de Grâce*). She deals with modern issues such as homosexuality and deviance by focusing on key moments of history, such as the end of Roman hegemony in her fictitious *Les Mémoires d'Hadrien*, (1951) (▷*Memoirs of Hadrian*, 1954), or her equally fictitious life of Zenon, the Renaissance man caught in the turmoil of the Reformation in *L'Oeuvre au noir*, (1968) (▷*The Abyss*, 1976). Her essays draw similarly on a vast historical knowledge, from Ancient Greece to contemporary Japan, and include 'Sous bénéfice d'inventaire'

(1962) ('Without Liability to Debts') and 'Mishima ou la vision du vide' (1981) ('Mishima or the Vision of Emptiness'). Her autobiography, *Souvenirs pieux* (1974) (*Pious Memories*), and *Archives du nord* (1977) (*Northern Archives*), provide the same insight into the dramas of 20th-century history, endowing her own experience with universality. Her influence, which is considerable, was not immediately noticed, because she preferred a well-ordered form of narration to the experimental writing of the post-war period.
Bib: Horn, Pierre L., *Marguerite Yourcenar*; Shurr, Georgia, *Marguerite Yourcenar, A Reader's Guide*.

Your Heart Is My Altar (1980)

Novel by Kenyan writer ▷Miriam Were. *Your Heart Is My Altar* takes as its focus cross-cultural marriage and religious rivalry. Were's aim is to suggest hope for the future, and the relationship which develops between two young people towards the end of the novel is designed to show that ethnic hatred need not be passed from parent to child and that tolerance and reconciliation are necessary.

Yuan Jing (born 1914)

Chinese writer. Educated in Beijing, Yuan left home to join the communist-led resistance against the Japanese invasion in the early 1930s and was prominent in the women's movement. She drew on the revolutionary struggle for subject matter and published novels and film scripts. The play *Liu Jiaoer Seeks Justice* is about the new marriage laws first implemented in 1951, outlawing enforced marriages and other feudal practices. The highly popular *Sons and Daughters*, which she co-authored, is a vivid story about the peasant guerrilla war against the Japanese invasion in north China.

Yu Lihua (born 1932)

Chinese writer. Born in Shanghai, Yu Lihua is now settled in the USA. She is a prolific writer of novels and short fiction published in both English and Chinese. She is best-known as a writer of fiction about students from Taiwan studying in the US. She is noted for the satirical *Witness to an Academic Conference* (1972) and for her saga of an old Chinese family, *Sons and Daughters of the Fu Family* (1978). A collection of reportage and short stories, *The Women of New China* (1977), draws on her visits to mainland China.

Yu Luojin (born 1946)

Chinese writer. The child of parents who were persecuted during the 'anti-rightist' campaign of 1957, the sister of a teenaged youth who was executed by firing squad during the 'cultural revolution' for challenging Maoist theories, Yu Luojin began her adult life imprisoned in a labour camp for guilt by association. Her disastrous marriage in the countryside to another uprooted youth, and their subsequent divorce, formed the substance of her first autobiographical work, *A Chinese Winter's Tale* (1980). Many things combined to make Yu Luojin 'notorious' on the Chinese literary scene: the autobiography, with its intimate revelations of marital disharmony and sexual abuse; the circumstances of her second marriage and divorce; the scandal surrounding her relationship with the literary editor of a national newspaper – a man who turned against her when his own position was threatened. Add to that her outspoken views on sexual inequality and it can be seen how Yu Luojin became an easy target for any campaign of the moment. The sequel to her first work, *A Tale of Spring*, was attacked and suppressed, and she finally sought political asylum in Germany.

Bib: May, Rachel and Zhu, Zhiyu (trans.), *A Chinese Winter's Tale*.

Yu Ru

Chinese writer. After a brief stay in Hong Kong, Yu Ru settled in the south of China in the 1950s, where she reports and directs an art section of a newspaper in Guangdong. Her work includes *Faraway Love*, a novella, *Longing for Mangoes*, a collection of reportage and short stories, and *When We Were Young*, a collection of children's stories.

Zagorka (1873–1957)
Pen-name of Maria Jurić, Croatian novelist and dramatist. She wrote popular adventure novels and plays and was also the first Croatian political journalist. She was one of the first women in south-eastern Europe to express feminist ideas. She married, against her will, a wealthy Hungarian, but, forced to choose between social convention and a coveted professional life, she left him after three years of misery, and ran away to join a newspaper. From then on she was a dedicated intellectual. She came in for many misogynist and antiprovincial attacks from contemporary critics, and has, by and large, been under-represented in literary histories. Her work is now being re-evaluated.

Zaïde, histoire espagnole (1669) ▷*Zayde; a Spanish History Written by M. de Segrats* (1678)

Zambrano, María (1904–1991)
Spanish philosopher and essayist. Zambrano was born in Vélez Málaga, and was influenced by Ortega y Gasset during her formative years. After the Spanish Civil War (1936–9), she went into exile, living in various countries including Chile, Mexico, Cuba and France, before returning to Spain in 1985. The main themes of her work are the origins of philosophy, humanity and divinity, and liberty. Her main works are: *Horizontes del liberalismo* (1930) (*The Horizons of Liberalism*); *Filosofía y poesía* (1940) (*Philosophy and Poetry*); *Hacia un saber sobre el alma* (1950) (*Towards a Knowledge of the Soul*); *Persona y democracia* (1959) (*Person and Democracy*), and *La tumba de Antígones* (1967) (*Antigones's Tomb*).

Zami: A New Spelling of My Name (1982)
North American novel. ▷Audre Lorde's 'biomythography' examines the inter-relationship of racism and sexism in African-American women's lives. In her fictionalized memoir, Lorde undertakes to define herself as a African-American woman.

Zami chronicles also her growing recognition that she is a lesbian, providing a history of what it meant to be an African-American lesbian in the 1950s. Lorde celebrates her difference, and emphasizes the erotic in lesbian lovemaking. She sees the source of her difference in her black foremothers in Grenada, and she exposes society's fear of women's independence from men, especially in the African-American community. *Zami* documents the way society impedes lesbian relationships through silence, malice, guilt and violence. Lorde also criticizes the lesbian community for its racism. Nevertheless, she emphasizes the possibilities for change that African-American lesbians engender.

Zamudio, Adela (1854–1928)
Bolivian poet and novelist. At first she used the pen-name Soledad. She never married, and never left Cochabamba. In 1900 she became a primary school teacher.

Beside Rosendo Villalobos, she is the most important national poet in Bolivia. A ▷realist writer, her *costumbrista* (▷*costumbrismo*) scenes mingle authentic and imaginary characters. Her style was melancholy at first, but later became more rational, didactic, critical and philosophical.

Zamudio was a liberal and a Christian. She was popular among poor people, who memorized her poems, as well as with the cultivated classes. Her idea of feminism was one of virtue and heroicism, as witnessed in the poem '*Loca de hierro*' ('Iron madwoman'). She was one of the pioneers of women's rights in Bolivia and South America, and of the Bolivian short story.

Works include: *Ensayos poéticos* (1887) (*Poetic Tests*); *Violeta o la princesa azul* (1890) (*Violeta or the Blue Princess*); *El castillo negro* (1906) (*The Black Castle*); *Intimas* (1913) (*Close Friends*); *Ráfagas* (1914) (*Squalls*); *Peregrinando* (1943) (*Travelling*), and *Cuentos breves* (1943) (*Short Novels*).

Zangrandi, Giovanna (1910–1988)
Italian novelist. She took a degree in chemistry, and taught science for some years. She was actively involved in the ▷Resistance movement, and this provided her with some of the material for her fiction. She writes mainly of country people, and of ex-partisans trying to come to terms with their lives after the war.

Her works include: *Leggende delle Dolomiti* (1950) (*Legends of the Dolomites*); *I Brusaz* (1954) (*The Brusaz Family*); *Orsola nelle stagioni* (1957) (*Ursula in the Different Seasons*); *Il campo rosso* (1959) (*The Red Field*); *Tre signore* (1960) (*Three Ladies*); *I giorni veri, 1943–45* (1963) (*The Real Days, 1943–45*); *Anni con Attila* (1966) (*Years With Attila*); *Il diario di Chiara* (1972) (*Chiara's Diary*).
▷Neorealism (Italy)

Zani, Giselda (1909–1975)
Uruguayan journalist, poet, short story writer and art critic. She worked as a diplomat in Buenos Aires. Her collection of short stories, *Por vínculos sutiles* (1958) (*Tenuous Links*), shows a sense of imagination and mystery. Her work is marked by a conscious effort to disrupt temporality. She also wrote *La costa despierta* (1930) (*The Wide-awake Coast*).

Zäunemann, Sidonia Hedwig (1714–1740)
German poet. She lived most of her life with her family at Ilmenau in Erfurt. Inspired by the example of the German writer ▷Christiana Mariana von Ziegler, she set out, from an early age, to establish herself as a poet and an exceptional woman. In order to write what she considered to be her main work, *Das Bergwerk in Ilmenau* (1737), (*The Mine at Ilmenau*) she went underground to gain firsthand knowledge of the mines in her home town. She was fond of travelling alone on horseback in men's clothing, though it was on one such journey that she fell into a river and died. She wrote a number of humorous social satires, and in her poetry tried to get away from traditional norms, taking her

themes from travel incidents, ordinary daily events, and observations from nature. She achieved high acclaim at the young age of twenty-four when she became Poet Laureate at the new University of Göttingen.

Zayas y Sotomayor, Maria de (1590–1661)

Spanish writer. Born in Madrid, Zayas lived most of her life in Zaragoza. Her major works, which can profitably be seen as a women's *Decameron*, are ▷*Novelas amorosas y exemplares* (1635) (*Exemplary Love Stories*), and *Desengaños amorosos* (1647) (*Disillusionment in Love*). In the foreword to the first collection of stories she scolds the male reader for his surprise that a woman dare write and publish fiction; she goes on to delineate a world in which men and women are at war. Zayas also wrote a play, *La traición en la amistad* (*Treachery in Friendship*), as well as some poetry.

Zayde; a Spanish History Written by M. de Segrats [and the Countess de Lafayette] (1678)

Translation of the French novel *Zaïde, histoire espagnole* (1669), by ▷Marie-Madeleine Pioche de la Vergne, Comtesse de Lafayette. This late example of baroque fiction in the Hispano-Moorish tradition is the longest of the four novels and ▷*nouvelles* (short fiction) attributed to Madame de Lafayette. It is thought, with some justification, to be at least in part the work of Jean Regnald de Segrais (1624–1701), secretary to ▷Mademoiselle de Montpensier. It was originally prefaced by an important treatise on fiction by the Abbé Huet (1630–1721) in honour of the work of ▷Madeleine de Scudéry, underlining the rather old-fashioned narrative construction, following the epic model, and somewhat conventional portrait of love in this novel. The historical background is drawn mainly from the *General History of Spain* by the Spanish Jesuit Mariana (1537–1624) and Marmontel's *Africa*, but with its ambitious princes whose glory threatens to overshadow the king's, duels and internecine conflict, *Zaïde* is also an interesting reflection of the *Frondes* (1648–1653), the brief civil wars which many feared might tear France apart again during the regency of Anne of Austria (1601–1666). Unlike the rest of Madame de Lafayette's fiction, this novel begins in the middle of the action with the chance discovery of the heroine shipwrecked on the beach, and ends happily with the preparations for her wedding to Consalve, though it is also noted for its powerful portrayal of jealous love.

Zeb-un-Nissar (1639–1702)

Indo-Persian mystic (*Sufi*) poet. She was a daughter of Aurangzeb, the last of the great Mughal emperors of India (reigned 1658–1707). She disliked the Islamic orthodoxy of her father, and was imprisoned in the Salimgarh Fort for twenty years because of her hostility to his rule. In her poetry, which has a strong sense of the suffering of the human soul, she tries to bring together elements of Islam, Hinduism and Zoroastrianism. An English translation of some of her work, *The Divan of Zeb-un-Nisa*, was published in 1913. Like ▷Begum Gulbadam and ▷Mirabai, she is an important figure in the history of women's writing in the Indian subcontinent.

Zei, Alki (born 1925)

Greek novelist and children's writer. Born in Athens, she studied Greek literature, drama and music. In 1954 she went to Moscow to study cinema, remaining there until 1964. She had begun writing plays for the puppet theatre when very young. Her first book, *The Tiger in the Shop Window*, published in Greece in 1963, is about the Metaxas dictatorship (1936–1940), and full of autobiographical detail. *Peter's Great Walk* (1971) is a story told through the eyes of children. Her novels, child-centred and free of moralistic teaching, reveal historical realities from a child's point of view. Her novel ▷*Achilles' Fiancée* (1987) follows the story of a woman from the time of the Greek Civil War in 1944 until the dictatorship of the 'Colonels' in 1974. The main female character, marginalized in the service of others, recounts her past life without bitterness or remorse, but rather with warmth and tenderness. Zei's work has been translated into many European languages, and she herself has translated a number of Russian authors into Greek. In the USA she was awarded The Mildred L. Batchelder Award (1973) for the best foreign children's book translated into English. Among her many other successful books for children are *Uncle Plato* and *Hannibal's Shoes*. She has been living in Paris since 1967.

Zeidler, Susanna Elisabeth (around 1686)

German poet. Little is known of her life, but in 1686 she published a collection of poems called *Jungferlicher Zeitvertreiber* (*Pastime for Virgins*). In this anthology, she proclaims, among other things, the right of women to be poets, and argues that what women lack is not talent, but time and opportunity to develop it.

Zelda (1914–1984)

Pseudonym of Israeli poet Zelda Shneurson Mishkowsky, who was born in the Ukraine and emigrated to Palestine in 1926, where she lived in an extremely orthodox Jewish home. She published her first book of verse in 1967, although she had been writing poetry since her adolescence. Zelda's writing is characterized by its simplicity and by a deep, mystic religious faith. The two, often conflicting, poles of religion and secularity seem to merge in her poems. Always there is a prominent mysticism, which is shown as enabling the tormented self to find comfort and beauty.

Her works include: *Pnay* (1967) (*Time*), *Ha'karmel Ha'bilti Niré* (1971) (*The Invisible Carmel*) and *Shirey Zelda* (1985) (*The Poems of Zelda*).

▷*Penguin Book of Hebrew Verse, The; Voices Within the Ark*

Zelinová, Hana (born 1914)
Slovak prose writer and dramatist. Her first work was published in 1933, and her first book appeared in 1941 – a collection of short stories called *Zrkadlový most* (*The Bridge of Mirrors*). Her works include a brief novel, *Diablov čardáš* (1958) (*The Devil's Csardas*), and a trilogy consisting of *Alžbetin dvor* (1971) (*Elisabeth's Court*), *Volanie vetra* (1974) (*The Call of Wind*), and *Kvet hrôzy* (1977) (*The Flower of Fright*).

She was influenced by the Scandinavian ▷saga tradition, as well as by the Slovak 'social' novel. Mostly, her fiction deals with the past and is a romantic, melodramatic portrayal of tragic love, self-sacrifice and hereditary suffering. The publication of the first part of her trilogy *Anjelská zem* (1946) (*Angel's Earth*) provoked a debate about the escapism and harmful idealism of Slovak literature. Despite the negative attitude of critics, Zelinová's work is quite popular among readers. In the 1940s Zelinová wrote three Ibsenesque plays, which were staged in the 1940s. These dealt sentimentally with the problem of the position of women in an urban society.

Zell, Katharina (1497/8–1562)
German Protestant writer during the Reformation. She married the priest Matthias Zell who, in consequence, was excommunicated. All her life she worked for the Reformation, and wrote religious songs, polemics and open letters. In one 170-page letter, *Brief an die ganze Bürgerschaft der Stadt Straßburg* (1557), (*Letter to the Entire Citizenry of the Town of Strasbourg*), she vigorously defends her right to join her husband in his work for the Protestant cause.

Zeller, Eva (born 1923)
German poet and novelist. She took up writing in her forties, after bringing up four children. Her first novel, *Lampenfieber* (1974), (*Stage Fright*) is a deeply-felt and carefully-drawn examination of the problems of being a modern-day parent, while *Hauptfrau* (1977) (*The Head Woman*) takes its place as a fairly standard account of a married woman's psychological awakening. Her best novel to date is the autobiographical *Solange ich denken kann. Roman einer Jugend* (1981) (*As Long as I can Think. Novel of a Childhood*), one of the finest examples of a German author attempting to come to terms with her own and her country's recent past. Besides many short stories, Zeller has also published two collections of poems, *Fliehkraft* (1975) (*The Strength to Flee*) and *Auf dem Wasser gehen* (1979) (*Walking on Water*).

Zetkin, Clara (1857–1933)
German communist and feminist. She trained as a school teacher in Leipzig, joined the German Social Democratic Party in 1881, and a year later married the Russian revolutionary Ossip Zetkin. A socialist above all else, she ran the revolutionary Spartacus Movement with Rosa Luxemburg, and distrusted the bourgeois women's movement, and opposed all collaboration with it, preferring to act as the undisputed leader of German proletarian women. After the war she became one of the founders of the German Communist Party, and represented it in the German parliament until 1932. After the burning of the Reichstag, she emigrated to Russia where she died. She wrote many powerful polemics and Marxist tracts, but her best-known work remains her *Erinnerungen an Lenin* (1929), (*Recollections of Lenin*) which is an account of her long and stormy friendship with Lenin (1870–1924).

Zguriška, Zuska (1900–1984)
Slovak novelist. In the 1920s Zguriška was an actress with the Slovak National Theatre, and then worked for Czechoslovak Radio. In 1944 she studied sociology at Bratislava University. For two years she worked as a script writer for the Czechoslovak State Film Studio near Prague. Zguriška is the author of humorous short stories and novels. Her best-known works include: *Bičianka z Doliny* (1938) (*Bičianka from the Valley*), *Metropola pod slamou* (1949) (*The Metropolis Under the Straw*), *Mestečko na predaj* (1953) (*The Small Town to Be Sold*), and *Zbojnícke chodníčky* (1959) (*The Highwaymen's Paths*). She depicted the decay of relationships in western Slovak small towns and villages. She picked out comic sides of life – the non-problems and pecularities of characters.

Zguriška also wrote a book of memoirs, *Strminou liet* (1972) (*Through the Crevasse of Years*), a historic love novel for young readers, *Husitská nevesta* (1962) (*The Hussite's Bridegroom*) and comedies for amateur theatre. She translated Hašek's *The Good Soldier Švejk* into Slovak.

Zhádovskaia, Iuliia Valerianovna (1824–1883)
Russian poet and fiction writer. Born with one arm missing and the other deformed, as a young woman Zhádovskaia suffered greatly when her autocratic father denied her permission to marry the promising young professor of plebeian background who loved her. Her father did, however, tolerate her interest in literature and permitted her to frequent ▷Moscow and ▷St Petersburg intellectual circles from the 1840s. She made a lasting reputation with poetry expressing naked grief over her lost love. Perceptive critics have noted her rough, colloquial diction and her delicate use of nature's moods as a correlative to her own persistent melancholy and resignation. Several of her lyrics were set to music and became popular romances. Poems depicting the hard life of peasants struck a note of social criticism. In the late 1840s Zhádovskaia turned to prose, writing brief tales in diaries or letters which also rang various changes on the subject of thwarted love. Not until her last major works, the novel ▷*Apart from the Great World* (1857), and the novella *Woman's Story* (1861), were her heroines permitted unambiguously happy endings. The latter has a programmatic set of female characters:

an independent, 'eccentric' young woman who befriends the heroine, Liza; a wealthy girl constricted by social expectations; her idealistic sister who defies society to marry a poor man; and Liza, a poor girl who hopes only to support herself (as a governess) and wins love instead. *Behind the Times* (1861) is a perfunctory novella on the fashionable theme of the transformation of country girl into emancipated woman. In 1862 Zhádovskaia's marriage to the family doctor marked the end of the sad inspiration that had spurred her writing career.

Zhang Ailing (born 1920)

Chinese novelist and short story writer, also known as Eileen Chang. Born in Shanghai, she was educated in Hong Kong and then returned to Shanghai in the early 1940s to begin her literary career, publishing many short stories and novellas, including ▷ *The Golden Cangue* (1943) and *Half a Lifetime's Romance*. In 1952 Zhang left mainland China for Hong Kong and published two novels, *Rice Sprout Song* (1954) and *Naked Earth* (1954), both descriptions of life in the early years of communist rule on mainland China. *The Golden Cangue*, considered 'the greatest novelette in the history of Chinese literature' (C.T. Hsia, *A History of Modern Chinese Fiction*, 1961) is a powerful portrait and psychological study of a woman through unhappy youth to malicious old age.
Bib: (trans.) *Naked Earth*; *Rice Sprout Song*.

Zhang Jie (born 1937)

Zhang Jie

Chinese novelist and short story writer. Born in Beijing, Zhang studied economics at college and worked at the National Bureau of Mechanical Equipment. She started to write after the 'cultural revolution' (1966–1976) and first made a mark with 'Love Must Not Be Forgotten' (1979), one of the earliest works to attack the social, psychological and sexual constraints that bind women. In the novel *Leaden Wings* (1981) Zhang Jie uses her knowledge of the state of industry in China to expose impediments to reform. An array of unhappy marriages provide the human interest as well as exposing the conservative attitudes governing marital and sexual relations. Her major work so far, the novella ▷ *The Ark* (1982), is China's first feminist work of fiction. Through the vicissitudes of three educated women – two divorced, one separated – Zhang Jie makes a passionate denunciation of the overt and covert forms of sexual discrimination in a male-dominated society. Translated into several languages, Zhang Jie is to date one of the few committed feminist writers of China, and is often under attack for her views. Other works include *Emerald* (1984) and *If Nothing Happens, Nothing Will* (1986), a collection of short stories.
Bib: (trans.) *If Nothing Happens, Nothing Will*; *Leaden Wings*; *Love Must Not Be Forgotten*.

Zhang Kangkang (born 1950)

Chinese writer. A native of Zhejiang, Zhang spent nine years in the north-eastern wastelands after middle school. Engaged in a variety of jobs, she observed and learned, and later decided to write about the young people around her, uprooted like herself. The novel *The Boundary Line* (1975) is representative of this period. Zhang later studied at an institute of dramatic art and is now a professional writer. 'The Right to Love' (1979) exposes how young people of the 'wrong' background are stifled, deprived of the right to love, and thus the right to life. 'Summer' (1981), about emotional repression in college, sparked a public debate in the pages of a literary journal. *The Pale Mists of Dawn* (1980), a novella, describes the fortunes of a 'rightist' and his family. The title story in the collection *Aurora Borealis* (1981) idealizes love and deplores the worldliness that clutters the conventional marriage.
Bib: Translation of 'The Wasted Years' in *Seven Contemporary Chinese Women Writers*.

Zhang Xinxin (born 1953)

Chinese writer. One of the generation that grew up during the 'cultural revolution' (1966–1976), Zhang Xinxin joined the army after middle school, and later enrolled at the Central Drama Institute in Beijing. She became famous with her novella *On the Same Horizon*, which describes the breakdown of a marriage through the competing ambitions of the young couple. 'Where Did I Miss You?' exposes the domination of male values as the norm in society and the dilemma this poses for women. *The Dreams of Our Generation* (1986) describes the disillusionment and demoralization of a young woman torn from her roots. Zhang was targeted during the 'anti-spiritual pollution' campaign, which focused on so-called 'perverse' Western influences in literature and theory, for her short story 'Orchid Mania', which draws on absurdist influences to portray mass hysteria. *Chinese Lives* (1986, co-authored with San Ye) is a series of interviews with different segments of the population, which reflects the changes in the attitudes of the 1980s, and also presents candid pictures of Chinese lives through the vicissitudes of revolution and change.

Bib: Jenner, W.F. and Davin, Delia (eds.), *Chinese Lives*; (trans.) *Chinese Profiles.*

Zhao Luorui (born 1912)

Chinese scholar, poet and translator. Zhao has published poetry and prose since the early 1940s. She received her PhD from the University of Chicago in 1949 and returned to teach English and North American literature at Peking University, Beijing. Apart from pursuing teaching and research, Zhao translated T.S. Eliot's *The Waste Land* (1922), Henry Wadsworth Longfellow's *Song of Hiawatha* (1855), Walt Whitman's *Leaves of Grass* (1855), and edited, along with two colleagues, the first *History of European Literature* (1979) in the Chinese language.

Zheng Min (born 1920)

Chinese scholar and poet. Professor of Western literature at Beijing Teachers' University, Zheng Min first studied philosophy in China and later received an MA in literature at the University of Illinois. She has published modernist poetry since the 1930s. Her poems have been collected and republished, with new additions, in *The Nine Leaves* (1980), along with eight other poets sharing modernist influences, currently known as the 'Nine Leaves' school of poetry.

Zhúkova, Mariia Semenovna (1804–1855)

Russian writer of fiction and travel sketches. Zhúkova's works, along with those of ▷Márchenko and ▷Evgeniia Tur, reflect the transition from romanticism to realism in Russian women's writings of the 1840s. The daughter of a government clerk, she grew up in Arzamas (south of Nizhnii-Novgorod) and, most probably, owed her education to the patronage of a noble family with an estate in the area. Some of Zhúkova's early stories, published as *Evenings on the Karpovka* (1837–1838), deal with the position of poor girls in rich provincial households and St Petersburg society. Zhúkova's heroines, unlike those of her contemporary, ▷Elena Gan, accept their limitations and make an independent life for themselves. Other stories are more conventionally romantic: in 'Falling Star' a young man's investigation of the secret of his origins leads to near-incest and shatters him; in 'Black Demon' hypersensitive insight into others' motives destroys a woman's life; in 'The Mistake' the hero is torn between family pride and his love for a sullied woman. Her novella *A Summer Place on the Peterhof Road* (1845) is a clever reversal of the

conventions of romanticism. Zhúkova's lively conversational style and gift for nature description, typical of both her fiction and her travel notes of trips abroad for her health ('Sketches of Southern France and Nice', 1844), made her popular with readers, but the few stories she published in her last ten years, quieter and more resigned in tone, went almost unnoticed by critics.

Zhuo Wenjun (1st century BC)

Literary woman of the Western Han dynasty in the 1st century BC. Widowed when young, she fell in love with one of her father's guests, Sima Xianru, as she watched him unobserved. He sent his messages to her through his singing. The pair came to an understanding and eloped the same night. They lived in poverty until Zhuo Wenjun's father relented and endowed her properly. The couple then lived in style, but Sima Xianru's fancy had flitted to younger women. Zhuo Wenjun wrote the famous *Bai Tou Yin (Song of White Hairs)* in protest against male inconstancy. She has become a legendary figure admired for female assertiveness.

Ziegler, Christiana Mariana von (1695–1760)

German writer. She was born in Leipzig into a well-established family of lawyers which met with disaster in 1706 when her father, accused of treason, was put into prison until his death in 1746. Widowed twice, she returned with her children to her family home and opened a salon, which from 1730 to 1740 became one of the foremost centres of literary and musical activity in Germany. She gained great acclaim as one of the country's most accomplished poets and, encouraged and supported by the critic and poet Gottsched (1700–1766), became the first woman member of his prestigious literary society, the *'Deutsche Gesellschaft'* ('German Society'). A true scholar of the German Enlightenment, she wrote prose and poetry, some of which J.S. Bach (1685–1750) put to music. Works such as her *Vermischte Schriften in gebundener und ungebunder Rede* (1739) (*Miscellaneous Writings in Verse and Prose*) are written in an easy, elegant style, and explore themes of tolerance, liberal values and, in particular, the role and the rights of women. Despite her fame she was often ridiculed, even when, in 1733, she became Poet Laureate of the University of Wittenberg. For generations she remained an important role model for German women writers.

Zinner, Hedda (born 1905)

German writer of political literature. She began her career as an actress, but upon becoming interested in the workers' movement she moved to Berlin and, in 1929, joined the Communist Party. She became a reporter for left-wing journals, and wrote satirical political songs, poems and short stories. When Hitler came to power she moved first to Vienna, and then to Prague where, in 1934, she founded the subversive cabaret *Studio*

1934. In 1935 she emigrated to Moscow, and worked there as a reporter and writer of radio plays. After the war she settled in East Berlin. Her novel *Nur eine Frau* (1954) (*Only a Woman*) traces the story of the revolutionary and early feminist ▷Louise Otto-Peters, and Zinner's own two-volume autobiography, *Ahnen und Erben* (1968) (*Ancestors and Inheritors*) and *Die Schwestern* (1970) (*Sisters*) paints an evocative picture of the problems facing women in early 20th-century Germany.

Zinóv'eva-Annibál, Lidiia Dmitrievna (1866–1907)

Prose writer and dramatist. Best-known in . Russian cultural history as the co-host with her husband, the poet Viacheslav Ivanov, of a literary salon referred to as the 'Tower', Zinóv'eva-Annibál came to writing late in life. Acutely aware of the subordinate position of women in the cultural world, she founded another gathering on Tuesdays to which only women were invited. Ivanov reported his wife's struggle to free herself from his influence. Zinóv'eva-Annibál had only a few years to develop into a mature writer. Her earliest literary effort, an uncompleted novel *Torches* (1903), uses the myth of Dionysus, a subject that Ivanov had written about at length. Zinóv'eva's first important publication, the verse drama, *Rings* (1904), also propagates an idea of Ivanov's: the need to base love on an unselfish and supra-individual basis. The heroine's rings, symbolizing conventional love relations, are tossed away. The play was harshly criticized for artistic shortcomings and an overt sensuality that included incest. Zinóv'eva-Annibál's next work, a novella in diary form, *Thirty-Three Abominations* (1907), attempted to present an ideal world of sensual beauty and aestheticism. Critics treated it as harshly as they had *Rings*. Part of the fault lies in the story's language, which mixes the literal and the abstract in a way that can be unintentionally funny, but the depiction of lesbianism, immodesty, overt sensuality, and anti-male prejudice by a woman writer also fuelled reviewers' wrath. At first forbidden by the censor, the book rapidly went through several editions. The autobiographically-based stories of a girl's childhood and youth collected as ▷*The Tragic Menagerie* (1907) are Zinóv'eva-Annibál's best work, and represent a turn towards psychological realism. She died unexpectedly of scarlet fever. Ivanov supervised the posthumous publication of a collection of her short stories, *No!* (1918), most of which had appeared during the author's lifetime. *Bib:* Cioran, S.D. (trans.), 'Thirty-Three Abominations', *The Silver Age of Russian Culture;* Davidson, P., *The Poetic Imagination of Viacheslav Ivanov.*

Zirimu, Elvania Namukwaya (born 1938)

Ugandan poet and dramatist. Zirimu was educated at Makerere University, where she took a Diploma in Education, and at the University of Leeds, where she read English. She has worked as a teacher and in educational broadcasting in Uganda, as well as spending a.year as Tutorial Fellow in Creative Writing at Makerere. She is married with two children. As a member of the Ngomo Players Zirimu has worked as a producer and actor. Her plays show her concern with the loss of traditional values and the adoption of false European ways. *Keeping up with the Mukasas*, produced at the National Theatre and by the BBC African Theatre and published in David Cook's *Origin East Africa* (1965), is about a family experiencing the conflict between old and new. *When the Hunchback Made Rain* (1975) and *Snoring Strangers* (1975) explore themes of alienation and social division; her radio play ▷*Family Spear*, produced by the BBC African Theatre in 1972 and published in *African Theatre*, edited by Gwyneth Henderson (1973), describes the slow erosion of family ties in a society in which traditionally the father has the right of the first night with his son's new bride. The argument of the play is whether change is desirable or whether it will destroy. *Bib:* Killam, G.D. (ed.), *The Writing of East and Central Africa.*

Zitz, Kathinka (1801–1877)

German writer. After being thrown out by her husband, she lived in penury, trying to support herself with her writing. Under countless pseunonyms she published stories about contemporary German life and society, and later wrote fictional biographies of famous people such as Lord Byron (1788–1824), Goethe (1749–1832), Heinrich Heine (1797–1856) and ▷Rahel Varnhagen.

Ziyadah, May (1886–1941)

Arab poet and essayist. Born in Palestine and educated in Lebanon, she settled in Cairo in 1908, where her father edited a newspaper. She first wrote poetry in French, but turned to Arabic and produced a mass of writing that classes her as the first professional woman writer in Arabic. She is now remembered for her Tuesday salon, which she held in Cairo a few years after settling in the city that became her home. Her visitors were writers, journalists and politicians; all the important names in Arabic literature were regular visitors. She served them as a muse, and a number of them adored her romantically. After reviewing the Lebanese poet Khalil Gibran's (1883–1931) *Broken Wings* in 1912, she started a correspondence with the great ▷*mahjar* (*émigré*) artist, which continued from 1914 to 1931. It was a strange love-relationship at a distance of 7,000 miles. Gibran's letters to May were found after her death, when they were edited and published in Arabic by Salma Haffar-Kusbari and Suhail B. Bushry. The same editors translated them into French under the title *La Voix Ailée* (1982). They were published in English as ▷*Blue Flame* (1987). 'Blue Flame' was Gibran's description of the soul, and could also stand for the 'passion and purity of their love'.

▷al-Taymuriyya, 'Aisha 'Esmat; *Complete Works of May Ziyadah, The*

Zographou, Lili

Greek novelist and essayist. Born in Crete, she first came to notice in 1949 with the publication of a collection of short stories, *Loves*. In her early youth she moved to Athens, living an independent and unconventional life. Her novels, very popular in Greece, have established her as a bold observer of modern life. She admitted in an interview that writing for her was 'torture, but at the same time a beautiful feeling'. Her novels, *Job: Whore* (1979) and *The Woman Lost Riding a Horse* (1981), protest against the stupidity of women and the restrictions imposed upon them by society. Zographou has written essays on the Greek writer Nikos Kazantzakis and on the Greek poet Odysseas Elytis.

Zombies

Of relevance in Caribbean writing, these ▷Haitian beliefs about the dead identify zombies as soulless bodies which are used as slaves. In ▷Jamaica, however, the ▷Kumina cult sometimes uses the term to refer to ancestral spirits. In this context it could refer to a living person who has been possessed by one of the ancestral spirits.

Zong Pu (born 1928)

Chinese writer and scholar. Born Feng Zhongpu, of a prestigious academic family, Zong Pu graduated from the English department of Qinghua University in 1951. As a writer of fiction, Zong Pu first made her mark with the short story 'The Red Beans' (1957), which was attacked for its portrayal of a young woman's private emotions in conflict with revolutionary norms. Other well-known works include 'Melody in Dreams' (1978), about a disillusioned new generation emerging out of the 'cultural revolution' (1966–1976). The novella *The Everlasting Stone* (1980) and 'The Walnut Tree' revolve around the image of women who maintain dignity and integrity under insult and persecution. The short stories 'Who Am I?' (1983), 'A Head in the Marshes' (1985), 'The Shell Dwellers' (1981) and others reflect Kafkaesque influences in the writer's effort to bring out the nightmarish quality of life during the 'cultural revolution'. At present Zong Pu is working on a multi-volume saga, *Ordeal*, centred around a group of Chinese intellectuals from the years of the Japanese occupation to the present. *Heading South*, the first volume, has already been published.
Bib: Translation of short stories in Jenner, W.F. (ed.), *Fragrant Weeds, Seven Contemporary Chinese Women Writers* and *The Serenity of Whiteness*.

Zorlutuna, Halidé Nusret (born 1901)

Turkish poet and novelist, she was the daughter of a political prisoner and later shared his exile in eastern Turkey. Educated in a private girls' school and well-drilled in the classical Arab-Persian tradition, she also wrote in the new style.

Married to an army officer, she moved constantly with him, taught Turkish literature in schools, and participated in movements for the rights of women and children. She published her memoirs in 1973 as *The Novel of an Era*. Her other works include four volumes of poetry (1930–1967), a collection of short stories (1945) and five novels (1921–1974).

Zuccari, Anna Radius ▷Neera

Zu Lin (born 1949)

Chinese writer. Zu Lin's road in life was typical of the generation who had to leave school for the countryside during the 'cultural revolution' (1966–1976) while still in their teens. She now works on the editorial staff of *Shanghai Literature* magazine. Zu Lin excels in writing on the victimization of women. Her first work is a novel, *The Road of Life* (1979), about a young city girl, Tan Juanjuan, rusticating in the country during the cultural revolution. She tries to get into the favour of the local cadre in order to be recommended for university, and is raped by him as a result. When she finally gets the recommendation, she finds herself pregnant, and therefore disqualified for university, so she commits suicide. Another highly praised story is 'Net' (1980), about a rural woman hemmed in on every side by extreme poverty, ignorance and the oppressive rule of the local cadres, until she is driven to madness and death. Zu Lin also writes children's stories.

Zur Mühlen, Hermynia (1883–1951)

Austrian writer and translator. The well-educated daughter of a high-ranking Austrian count, while still young she became interested in socio-political issues, took the side of French novelist Emile Zola (1840–1902) in the Dreyfus Affair, and admired the work of the anarchist philosopher Max Stirner (1806–1856). She joined the Communist Party in 1919 and began to contribute fiction and polemical writings to left-wing journals. Her novella, *Schupomann Karl Müller* (1924), (*Policeman Karl Müller*) caused her to be accused of high treason. In 1935 she wrote a fierce analysis of women's contribution to the development of Nazism, *Unsere Töchter, die Nazinnen* (*Our Daughters, the Nazis*) and, in 1938, went into exile in England. There she began to write novels in English, such as *We Poor Shadows* (1943) and *Came the Stranger* (1946). She translated a large body of socio-critical texts from Russia, France and the USA, and wrote radio plays which were often translated into many languages. Most of all however, it was her 'proletarian fairytales' for children which established her as an important literary and political influence in German-speaking Europe.

Zürn, Unica (1916–1970)

German writer and artist. Born in Berlin, she began her literary career after World War II, with

short stories and radio plays. In 1953 she met the
Surrealist artist Hans Bellmer (1902–1975),
moved with him to Paris, and experimented with
poetry based on anagrams and with automatic
drawing, which she exhibited. *Hexentexte* (1954)
(*The Witches' Texts*) is a dual-media book, blending
the verbal with the visual in typical Surrealist
style. Her last years were marred by mental
illness, and ended in suicide. She is known chiefly
for two posthumously-published works, *Dunkler
Frühling* (1970) (*Dark Spring*) a memoir about
childhood eroticism, and *Der Mann im Jasmin*
(1977) (*The Man in Jasmine*), a gripping account
of her delusions and depressions.

Zuzović, Cvijeta (1552–1648)

Croatian poet. Zuzović was born in Dubrovnik,
and spent her childhood in Italy, where she
received a broad Renaissance education. She
married a nobleman from Florence who came to
Dubrovnik as Florentine consul until 1582, when
he – and she with him – moved back to Italy.
Renowned for her great wisdom and beauty, she
had a formidable reputation as a poet, not only in
Dubrovnik but also throughout Italy, and was
particularly praised for her witty epigrams. None
of her writing has survived. However, her voice
may be heard indirectly in a Neoplatonic dialogue
between herself and a noblewoman, a friend, set
in gardens outside Dubrovnik, in which Zuzović
plays the major part.
Croatian novel by ▷Zagorka. One theme
permeates the whole of this novel: the
unpredictability and irrationality of love. This is
shown as its greatest good and, potentially, its
greatest evil. The theme is developed to good
effect, showing love as merciless in its annihilation
of obstacles and liquidation of opponents. The
narrative is objective, with lively dialogue and
confessional monologues. It stands apart from the
majority of Zagorka's novels, which generally
contain complex plots, action and tension, and are
almost like historical detective stories.

Z vesny života (1895) (*From the Spring of Life*)

Collection by Ludmila Pojavorinská (1872–1951),
the first Slovak female lyric poet. This collection
contains early verses written from the age of
eighteen. It is rather like a lyrical equivalent of a
young girl's diary. The majority of the poems are
inspired by nature. Pojavorinská is attracted by
nature's transformations which, however, lead her

mainly to nostalgia, restlessness and sorrow. Her
love poetry is naïve, sometimes over-sentimental,
and based, not on experience, but on imagination.
Simplicity, sincerity and melodiousness are its
basic qualities.

Zwi, Rose (born 1928)

South African novelist born in Mexico. She lived
much of her life in Johannesburg, before
emigrating to Australia in 1988. In her three
novels to date, she traces the experiences of a
South African Jewish family: *Another Year in Africa*
(1980), which won the Olive Schreiner Prize, *The
Inverted Pyramid* (1981), and *Exiles* (1984).

Another Year in Africa explores the lives of an
immigrant family and members of their close-knit
community with tenderness and acute observation.
Various social forces and divisions act on these
members of the white working class: mobility to
the middle class, Communist Party politics,
emergent fascism and Afrikaner Nationalism, and
the growth of Zionism. These are traced with
historical subtlety. The childhood anxieties and
early development of the girl, Ruth, are closely
portrayed. Ruth's story is taken up in *The Inverted
Pyramid*, her personal development intimately
connected to her experience of the political events
following World War II. In this connection
between the personal and political in South
Africa, Zwi's work is similar to that of ▷Nadine
Gordimer. The title of the novel refers to the
dominant debate in Zionist circles about how best
to rectify the top-heavy class structure of Jewish
society. The novel gives a disturbing vision of the
sexual politics prevailing in the Zionist circles
Ruth frequents.

Zwicky, Fay (born 1933)

Australian poet, short story writer and literary
critic. Zwicky was educated at the University of
Melbourne, has been a senior lecturer at the
University of Western Australia and has lectured
at a number of overseas institutions. She has
contributed literary articles to many prestigious
journals, and has published a collection of them,
*The Lyre in the Pawnshop: Essays on Literature and
Survival 1974–1984* (1985), but is best known for
her poetry which has been published in numerous
journals and magazines, and collected in *Isaac
Babel's Fiddle* (1975) and *Kaddish and Other Poems*
(1982).
▷*Poetry and Gender*

Biographies of main contributors

Koh Tai Ann, Associate Professor of English at the National University of Singapore has published work on South-east Asian and Commonwealth writers. She is currently co-editing a comparative study of the novel in South-east Asia, and an annotated bibliography of the literature in English from Malaysia, Singapore and Brunei.

Catherine Belsey is Professor of English at the University of Wales, Cardiff, where she chairs the Centre for Critical and Cultural Theory. Her books include *Critical Practice, The Subject of Tragedy*, and *John Milton: Language, Gender, Power*. With Jane Moore she is editor of *The Feminist Reader*.

Jennifer Birkett holds the Chair of French Studies at Birmingham University. Her books include *The Sins of the Fathers: Decadence in France and Europe 1870–1914* (1986) and, most recently, *Determined Women: Studies in the Construction of the Female Subject 1900–1990* (1991), co-edited with Elizabeth Harvey.

Jane Bryce studied at St Anne's College, Oxford and Obafemi Anolowo University, Ile-Ife, Nigeria. She teaches at the University of the West Indies, Barbados. Her published work has appeared in *Black Women Writers* (1990, edited by Susheila Nasta), and numerous newspapers and periodicals, including *Marxism Today, Africa Now* and *The Guardian*.

Claire Buck studied English and American literature at the University of Kent at Canterbury. Her publications include *H.D. and Freud: bisexuality and a feminine discourse* (1990) and articles on contemporary feminist theory and 20th-century women's poetry. She is Senior Lecturer in English at the Polytechnic of North London.

Kathryn Burlinson is Lecturer in English at Southampton University, where she teaches 19th- and 20th-century literature, women's writing and feminist theory. She has published articles on Emily Brontë and Elizabeth Barrett Browning, and is currently completing a doctoral thesis on the poetry of Christina Rossetti.

Agnès Cardinal was born and educated in Switzerland, studied in Canada and England and is now Honorary Research Fellow in German at the University of Kent at Canterbury. Her publications include a book on Robert Walser and articles on Swiss literature and East German women writers.

Carol Klimick Cyganowski is an Associate Professor of English, Core Faculty in the American Studies Program, and Director of the Women's Studies Program at DePaul University in Chicago, Illinois. She is the author of *Magazine Editors and Professional Authors in Nineteenth-Century America* (1988).

Risa Domb was born in Israel, and is a Fellow of Girton College, Cambridge. She is the first-ever holder of a Lectureship in Modern Hebrew Literature at the University of Cambridge. She is involved in Jewish education and in the promotion of Hebrew culture. Her published work includes *The Arab in Hebrew Prose*.

Dorothy Driver lectures in the English department at the University of Cape Town, and is South African correspondent for the *Journal of Commonwealth Literature* (London), for which she provides an annual bibliography and survey of South African English literature. She has published various essays on South African writing by women, as well as a book on Pauline Smith.

Ursula Fanning graduated from University College, Dublin and went on to study at the University of Reading. Her doctoral thesis was on Matilde Serao. She has taught at the universities of Sussex and Bath and now lectures at the Department of Italian, University College, Dublin, specializing in 19th- and 20th-century Italian women writers. Her publications include contributions to *The Italianist, Annali d'Italianistica*, and the book *Women and Italy* (1991).

Sharon Harris, Assistant Professor, University of Nebraska-Lincoln, teaches early North American literature and women's studies, specializing in North American women writers to 1900. She is the author of *Rebecca Harding Davis and American Realism* and is currently editing a collection of Judith Sargent Murray's writings, to be published in 1993.

Stephen M. Hart is currently Associate Professor at the University of Kentucky, having graduated with a Ph.D. from Cambridge University in 1985. He has edited two books and is author of *Religión, política y ciencia en la obra de César Vallejo* (1988), *R.J. Sender: Réquiem por un campesino español* (1990), *Spanish, Catalan and Spanish-American Poetry from 'modernismo' to the Spanish Civil War* (1990) and *The Other Scene: Psychoanalytic Readings in Modern Spanish and Latin-American Literature* (1992).

Richard Hawley is both undergraduate and graduate of St John's College, Oxford. His doctoral thesis concerned women in Greek drama, and he co-organizes the Oxford *Women in Antiquity* seminar series. Currently lecturer in Classics at London University, he is also interested in later classical Greek literature.

Noriyo Hayakawa was born in 1941, and studied German philosophy and literature at the University of Keio and Tokyo Metropolitan University. She is currently Lecturer at Iwaki Meisei University, and she has worked as co-editor on several books on women in Japanese history.

Zhu Hong is Professor of 19th-century Anglo-American literature at the Institute of Foreign Literature CASS (Chinese Academy of Social Sciences). She has travelled widely in the West and has published translations of Chinese writing into English, the latest being *The Serenity of Whiteness, Stories by and about Women in Contemporary China*.

Alex Hughes has a Ph.D. from the University of London and currently teaches in the department of French Studies at Birmingham University. Her research interests lie in the field of 19th- and 20th-century French women's writing, gender studies and feminist critical theory.

Maya Jaggi is a London-based critic and journalist who contributes to the *Times Literary Supplement*, *The Guardian* and *New Statesman and Society*, among other publications, and to the BBC World Service. Educated at Oxford University and the London School of Economics, she was formerly editor of the journal *Third World Quarterly*.

Karen Klitgaard was born in 1952, and has an MA in literary history and a Ph.D. in gender, media and culture. She contributed to *Nordic Women's Literary History* (1992), and her work includes research on salons in Denmark and Germany, women's magazines, food, and the writers Karin Michaelis and Christa Wolf. She lives in Aarhus, Denmark.

Joanna Labon is editor of *Storm: New Writing from East and West*, a magazine of literary fiction launched in 1990. She has been a frequent visitor to Eastern Europe since 1983, particularly Hungary. She is foreign literature advisor to Jonathan Cape publishers and consultant on the East European Forum at the Institute of Contemporary Arts.

Vivienne Liley teaches French in London. She has taught a course on Caribbean writing and is currently completing her research on women's writing in French from Guadeloupe.

Luiza Lobo is Associate Professor at the University of Rio de Janeiro. She teaches comparative literature and the theory of literature, and specializes in feminist writers. Her publications include essays, translations, and contributions to Portuguese, North American and Brazilian newspapers and periodicals.

Laura Marcus is a lecturer in English and Humanities at Birkbeck College, University of London. She has written on autobiography, women's writing and literary theory. Her *Autobiographical Theories: the Making of a Literary Genre* is forthcoming, and she is currently working on a study of the role of fiction in post-war feminism.

Mara McFadden earned her Ph.D. at Indiana University. Her work focuses on the literature of the Southern US. She teaches North American literature and film studies at the State University of New York at Brockport.

Maria Moore was born in Greece in 1944. She has studied at the University of Salonica and the University of Kent at Canterbury. Since 1975 she has lived in England, teaching modern Greek language and literature. She has written various articles on Greek themes, including contributions to *The Macmillan Dictionary of Women's Biography* (1982). She is also a professional icon painter.

Fatma Moussa-Mahmoud was born in Cairo and educated in Cairo and London. She has retired as Professor of English and comparative literature, Cairo University. She has published translations of Shakespeare in Arabic and Naguib Mahfouz in English, as well as work on the Arabic novel, the English novel, orientalism, translation theory and practice, and current issues in the Arabic language.

Susheila Nasta is a Research Fellow at the Institute of Commonwealth Studies, University of London, a Senior Lecturer in literary and media studies at the Polytechnic of North London, and is founder editor of *Wasafiri*, a literary review which publishes critical and creative writing from Africa, Asia and the Caribbean.

Akiko Ogata was born in 1945. She is Assistant Professor at Tokyo Jogakukan Junior College, and her publications include three books on women in modern Japanese literature, published in Japan.

Phyllis Pollard is Senior Lecturer in English in the School of Humanities, Humberside Polytechnic. She has taught at the University of Hull and as visiting lecturer in America and Japan. She has written on Katherine Mansfield and Wole Soyinka and has been Africa contributor to the *Year's Work in English Studies*.

Charlotte Rosenthal holds a Ph.D. from Stanford University in Russian literature. She currently teaches at the University of Southern Maine. She has published several articles on the 'Silver Age' and, along with Mary Zirin and Marina Ledkovsky, is preparing a bio-critical guide to Russian women writers.

Gopa Roy was born in Calcutta and was educated in London. She worked on early medieval lives of women saints written in English for her Ph.D. at University College, London. She is currently teaching Old and Middle English at Queen Mary and Westfield College, London.

Darlene J. Sadlier, Professor of Spanish and Portuguese and Adjunct Professor of Women's Studies at Indiana University, is the author of *The Question of How: Women Writers and New Portuguese Literature*, and the editor and translator of *One Hundred Years After Tomorrow: Brazilian Women's Fiction in the 20th Century*.

Ailbhe Smyth is Director of the Women's Education, Research and Resource Centre (WERRC) at University College Dublin and editorial consultant to Attic Press, the Irish Women's publishing house. Her publications include *Women's Rights in Ireland* (1984), *Feminism in Ireland* (as editor) (1988) and *Wildish Things: An Anthology of New Irish Women's Writing* (1989).

Lyn Thomas has a degree in French and German and an MA in film and television studies. She teaches French women's writing, contemporary French popular culture and French language at the Polytechnic of North London. She is currently preparing two articles on Englishness, class and gender in *Inspector Morse*, and has begun research for a Ph.D. on *The Single Person and Popular Television: Viewers and Representations*.

Aritha van Herk was educated at the University of Alberta in Edmonton, and is now Professor of English at the University of Calgary. She teaches Canadian literature, particularly literature by women, and creative writing. She is the author of novels, short stories, and criticism, including *Judith* (1978), *The Tent Peg* (1981), *No Fixed Address* (1986), *Places Far From Ellesmere* (1990), and *In Visible Ink* (1991).

Olga van Marion studied theology and Dutch literature in Leiden. She has worked as a teacher and editor and has lectured at the University of Leiden. She has begun doctoral research on *Heroides* (poetic letters from heroines to their lovers, following Ovid's *Heroides*) in Dutch literature.

Shirley Walker is Director of the Centre for Australian Language and Literature Studies at the University of New England (Armidale, New South Wales, Australia). She has written several books and numerous articles on Australian women writers, and is editor of *Who is She? Images of Women in Australian Fiction*.

Lydia Wevers was born in the Netherlands in 1950 and emigrated to New Zealand as a child. Educated at Victoria University of Wellington and St Anne's College, Oxford, she has taught at Victoria University of Wellington, and the University of New South Wales, specializing in New Zealand and Australian writing and particularly the writing of women. She has edited a number of anthologies and has been a contributor to the *Oxford History of New Zealand Literature in English*.

Sue Wiseman is a lecturer at the University of Kent at Canterbury.

Elizabeth Woodrough is Lecturer in French at the University of Exeter. She has also taught at the University of Bourgogne and the University of Kent. She is currently preparing a study of Molière. Her original research interests lie in 17th-century French comic and serious fiction, and the development of the salon movement.

Mary Zirin, who has a Ph.D. from the University of California, Los Angeles, is an independent researcher-translator based in Altadena, California. Her translation of Nadezhda Durova's journals, *The Cavalry Maiden*, appeared in 1987. With Marina Ledkovsky and Charlotte Rosenthal she is currently compiling a biographical dictionary of 500 modern Russian women writers (1760–1990).

Picture acknowledgements

Angus and Robertson, Publishers – Gwen Harwood; Australian Overseas Information Service – Dymphna Cusack, Dorothy Hewett, Ruth Park, Katharine Susannah Prichard; © Jerry Bauer – Nathalie Sarraute; Bloodaxe Books – Fleur Adcock, Lauris Edmond; The Bodleian Library, Oxford – St Aldehelm presenting his book to the nuns of Barking Abbey (MS Bodl.77, Fol.ii), Christine de Pisan presenting her work to the Duc de Berry (MS Laud Misc 570, Fol.24), Elizabeth I (MS Fr.e.1, Fol.7); Clodagh Boyd/Attic Press – Evelyn Conlon; By permission of the British Library – frontispiece of *The World's Olio* (1671); Tommy Clancy/Attic Press – Eilis Ní Dhuibhne; Ivan Coleman/Serpent's Tail – Alison Fell; Louise Dahl-Wolfe – Carson McCullers; Forest Books – Wislawa Szymborska; Paul Goulding – Eithne Strong; Crispin Hughes/Serpent's Tail – Michele Roberts; Institute for the Translation of Hebrew Literature – Lea Goldberg, Amalia Kahana-Carmon; Roef Kalman – Aritha van Herk; © Joanna Labon – Erzsebet Galgoczi; Longman Group UK Ltd – Miriam Tlali; © Renate von Mangoldt – Ingeborg Bachmann; © John Mastromonaco – Mavis Gallant; Lesley McIntyre – Timberlake Wertenbaker; National English Literary Museum, Grahamstown – Noni Jabavu; by courtesy of the National Portrait Gallery, London – Lady Margaret Beaufort, the Brontë sisters, George Eliot, Lady Jane Grey, Mary I, Catherine Parr, Mary Shelley, Virginia Woolf; Peter Owen Publishers – Natalia Ginzburg, Marga Minco, Monique Wittig; Derek Speirs/Report and Attic Press – Rita Kelly; Ednalva Tavares – Heloísa Maranháo; William Yang – Elizabeth Jolley.

With thanks to: Andre Deutsch Ltd, Australian Bookshop, Faber and Faber Ltd, Great Britain-China Centre, Hellenic Bookshop, Kiwi Fruits Bookshop, Michael Joseph Ltd, Penguin Books Ltd, Quartet Books Ltd, Salmon Publishing, Serpent's Tail, Suhrkamp Verlag, Transworld Publishers Ltd, Virago Press, William Heinemann Ltd, The Women's Press.